Oxford Dictionary of National Biography

IN ASSOCIATION WITH

The British Academy

From the earliest times to the year 2000

Edited by

H. C. G. Matthew

and

Brian Harrison

Volume 39

Morant–Murray

OXFORD

UNIVERSITY PRESS

OXFORD
UNIVERSITY PRESS

Great Clarendon Street, Oxford OX2 6DP

Oxford University Press is a department of the University of Oxford.
It furthers the University's objective of excellence in research, scholarship,
and education by publishing worldwide in

Oxford New York

Auckland Bangkok Buenos Aires Cape Town
Chennai Dar es Salaam Delhi Hong Kong Istanbul Karachi
Kolkata Kuala Lumpur Madrid Melbourne Mexico City Mumbai Nairobi
São Paulo Shanghai Taipei Tokyo Toronto

Oxford is a registered trade mark of Oxford University Press
in the UK and in certain other countries

Published in the United States
by Oxford University Press Inc., New York

© Oxford University Press 2004

Illustrations © individual copyright holders as listed in
'Picture credits', and reproduced with permission

Database right Oxford University Press (maker)

First published 2004

British Library Cataloguing in Publication Data
Data available

Library of Congress Cataloging in Publication Data
Data available: for details see volume 1, p. iv

ISBN 0-19-861389-X (this volume)
ISBN 0-19-861411-X (set of sixty volumes)

Text captured by Alliance Phototypesetters, Pondicherry
Illustrations reproduced and archived by
Alliance Graphics Ltd, UK
Typeset in OUP Swift by Interactive Sciences Limited, Gloucester
Printed in Great Britain on acid-free paper by
Butler and Tanner Ltd,
Frome, Somerset

LIST OF ABBREVIATIONS

1 *General abbreviations*

AB	bachelor of arts
ABC	Australian Broadcasting Corporation
ABC TV	ABC Television
act.	active
A$	Australian dollar
AD	*anno domini*
AFC	Air Force Cross
AIDS	acquired immune deficiency syndrome
AK	Alaska
AL	Alabama
A level	advanced level [examination]
ALS	associate of the Linnean Society
AM	master of arts
AMICE	associate member of the Institution of Civil Engineers
ANZAC	Australian and New Zealand Army Corps
appx *pl.* appxs	appendix(es)
AR	Arkansas
ARA	associate of the Royal Academy
ARCA	associate of the Royal College of Art
ARCM	associate of the Royal College of Music
ARCO	associate of the Royal College of Organists
ARIBA	associate of the Royal Institute of British Architects
ARP	air-raid precautions
ARRC	associate of the Royal Red Cross
ARSA	associate of the Royal Scottish Academy
art.	article / item
ASC	Army Service Corps
Asch	Austrian Schilling
ASDIC	Antisubmarine Detection Investigation Committee
ATS	Auxiliary Territorial Service
ATV	Associated Television
Aug	August
AZ	Arizona
b.	born
BA	bachelor of arts
BA (Admin.)	bachelor of arts (administration)
BAFTA	British Academy of Film and Television Arts
BAO	bachelor of arts in obstetrics
bap.	baptized
BBC	British Broadcasting Corporation / Company
BC	before Christ
BCE	before the common (*or* Christian) era
BCE	bachelor of civil engineering
BCG	bacillus of Calmette and Guérin [inoculation against tuberculosis]
BCh	bachelor of surgery
BChir	bachelor of surgery
BCL	bachelor of civil law

BCnL	bachelor of canon law
BCom	bachelor of commerce
BD	bachelor of divinity
BEd	bachelor of education
BEng	bachelor of engineering
bk *pl.* bks	book(s)
BL	bachelor of law / letters / literature
BLitt	bachelor of letters
BM	bachelor of medicine
BMus	bachelor of music
BP	before present
BP	British Petroleum
Bros.	Brothers
BS	(1) bachelor of science; (2) bachelor of surgery; (3) British standard
BSc	bachelor of science
BSc (Econ.)	bachelor of science (economics)
BSc (Eng.)	bachelor of science (engineering)
bt	baronet
BTh	bachelor of theology
bur.	buried
C.	command [identifier for published parliamentary papers]
c.	*circa*
c.	*capitulum pl. capitula*: chapter(s)
CA	California
Cantab.	Cantabrigiensis
cap.	*capitulum pl. capitula*: chapter(s)
CB	companion of the Bath
CBE	commander of the Order of the British Empire
CBS	Columbia Broadcasting System
cc	cubic centimetres
C$	Canadian dollar
CD	compact disc
Cd	command [identifier for published parliamentary papers]
CE	Common (*or* Christian) Era
cent.	century
cf.	compare
CH	Companion of Honour
chap.	chapter
ChB	bachelor of surgery
CI	Imperial Order of the Crown of India
CIA	Central Intelligence Agency
CID	Criminal Investigation Department
CIE	companion of the Order of the Indian Empire
Cie	Compagnie
CLit	companion of literature
CM	master of surgery
cm	centimetre(s)

Cmd	command [identifier for published parliamentary papers]
CMG	companion of the Order of St Michael and St George
Cmnd	command [identifier for published parliamentary papers]
CO	Colorado
Co.	company
co.	county
col. *pl.* cols.	column(s)
Corp.	corporation
CSE	certificate of secondary education
CSI	companion of the Order of the Star of India
CT	Connecticut
CVO	commander of the Royal Victorian Order
cwt	hundredweight
$	(American) dollar
d.	(1) penny (pence); (2) died
DBE	dame commander of the Order of the British Empire
DCH	diploma in child health
DCh	doctor of surgery
DCL	doctor of civil law
DCnL	doctor of canon law
DCVO	dame commander of the Royal Victorian Order
DD	doctor of divinity
DE	Delaware
Dec	December
dem.	demolished
DEng	doctor of engineering
des.	destroyed
DFC	Distinguished Flying Cross
DipEd	diploma in education
DipPsych	diploma in psychiatry
diss.	dissertation
DL	deputy lieutenant
DLitt	doctor of letters
DLittCelt	doctor of Celtic letters
DM	(1) Deutschmark; (2) doctor of medicine; (3) doctor of musical arts
DMus	doctor of music
DNA	dioxyribonucleic acid
doc.	document
DOL	doctor of oriental learning
DPH	diploma in public health
DPhil	doctor of philosophy
DPM	diploma in psychological medicine
DSC	Distinguished Service Cross
DSc	doctor of science
DSc (Econ.)	doctor of science (economics)
DSc (Eng.)	doctor of science (engineering)
DSM	Distinguished Service Medal
DSO	companion of the Distinguished Service Order
DSocSc	doctor of social science
DTech	doctor of technology
DTh	doctor of theology
DTM	diploma in tropical medicine
DTMH	diploma in tropical medicine and hygiene
DU	doctor of the university
DUniv	doctor of the university
dwt	pennyweight
EC	European Community
ed. *pl.* eds.	edited / edited by / editor(s)
Edin.	Edinburgh

edn	edition
EEC	European Economic Community
EFTA	European Free Trade Association
EICS	East India Company Service
EMI	Electrical and Musical Industries (Ltd)
Eng.	English
enl.	enlarged
ENSA	Entertainments National Service Association
ep. *pl.* epp.	*epistola(e)*
ESP	extra-sensory perception
esp.	especially
esq.	esquire
est.	estimate / estimated
EU	European Union
ex	sold by (*lit.* out of)
excl.	excludes / excluding
exh.	exhibited
exh. cat.	exhibition catalogue
f. *pl.* ff.	following [pages]
FA	Football Association
FACP	fellow of the American College of Physicians
facs.	facsimile
FANY	First Aid Nursing Yeomanry
FBA	fellow of the British Academy
FBI	Federation of British Industries
FCS	fellow of the Chemical Society
Feb	February
FEng	fellow of the Fellowship of Engineering
FFCM	fellow of the Faculty of Community Medicine
FGS	fellow of the Geological Society
fig.	figure
FIMechE	fellow of the Institution of Mechanical Engineers
FL	Florida
fl.	*floruit*
FLS	fellow of the Linnean Society
FM	frequency modulation
fol. *pl.* fols.	folio(s)
Fr	French francs
Fr.	French
FRAeS	fellow of the Royal Aeronautical Society
FRAI	fellow of the Royal Anthropological Institute
FRAM	fellow of the Royal Academy of Music
FRAS	(1) fellow of the Royal Asiatic Society; (2) fellow of the Royal Astronomical Society
FRCM	fellow of the Royal College of Music
FRCO	fellow of the Royal College of Organists
FRCOG	fellow of the Royal College of Obstetricians and Gynaecologists
FRCP(C)	fellow of the Royal College of Physicians of Canada
FRCP (Edin.)	fellow of the Royal College of Physicians of Edinburgh
FRCP (Lond.)	fellow of the Royal College of Physicians of London
FRCPath	fellow of the Royal College of Pathologists
FRCPsych	fellow of the Royal College of Psychiatrists
FRCS	fellow of the Royal College of Surgeons
FRGS	fellow of the Royal Geographical Society
FRIBA	fellow of the Royal Institute of British Architects
FRICS	fellow of the Royal Institute of Chartered Surveyors
FRS	fellow of the Royal Society
FRSA	fellow of the Royal Society of Arts

FRSCM	fellow of the Royal School of Church Music	ISO	companion of the Imperial Service Order
FRSE	fellow of the Royal Society of Edinburgh	It.	Italian
FRSL	fellow of the Royal Society of Literature	ITA	Independent Television Authority
FSA	fellow of the Society of Antiquaries	ITV	Independent Television
ft	foot *pl.* feet	Jan	January
FTCL	fellow of Trinity College of Music, London	JP	justice of the peace
ft-lb per min.	foot-pounds per minute [unit of horsepower]	jun.	junior
FZS	fellow of the Zoological Society	KB	knight of the Order of the Bath
GA	Georgia	KBE	knight commander of the Order of the British Empire
GBE	knight or dame grand cross of the Order of the British Empire	KC	king's counsel
GCB	knight grand cross of the Order of the Bath	kcal	kilocalorie
GCE	general certificate of education	KCB	knight commander of the Order of the Bath
GCH	knight grand cross of the Royal Guelphic Order	KCH	knight commander of the Royal Guelphic Order
GCHQ	government communications headquarters	KCIE	knight commander of the Order of the Indian Empire
GCIE	knight grand commander of the Order of the Indian Empire	KCMG	knight commander of the Order of St Michael and St George
GCMG	knight or dame grand cross of the Order of St Michael and St George	KCSI	knight commander of the Order of the Star of India
GCSE	general certificate of secondary education	KCVO	knight commander of the Royal Victorian Order
GCSI	knight grand commander of the Order of the Star of India	keV	kilo-electron-volt
GCStJ	bailiff or dame grand cross of the order of St John of Jerusalem	KG	knight of the Order of the Garter
		KGB	[Soviet committee of state security]
GCVO	knight or dame grand cross of the Royal Victorian Order	KH	knight of the Royal Guelphic Order
		KLM	Koninklijke Luchtvaart Maatschappij (Royal Dutch Air Lines)
GEC	General Electric Company	km	kilometre(s)
Ger.	German	KP	knight of the Order of St Patrick
GI	government (*or* general) issue	KS	Kansas
GMT	Greenwich mean time	KT	knight of the Order of the Thistle
GP	general practitioner	kt	knight
GPU	[Soviet special police unit]	KY	Kentucky
GSO	general staff officer	£	pound(s) sterling
Heb.	Hebrew	£E	Egyptian pound
HEICS	Honourable East India Company Service	L	lira *pl.* lire
HI	Hawaii	l. *pl.* ll.	line(s)
HIV	human immunodeficiency virus	LA	Lousiana
HK$	Hong Kong dollar	LAA	light anti-aircraft
HM	his / her majesty('s)	LAH	licentiate of the Apothecaries' Hall, Dublin
HMAS	his / her majesty's Australian ship	Lat.	Latin
HMNZS	his / her majesty's New Zealand ship	lb	pound(s), unit of weight
HMS	his / her majesty's ship	LDS	licence in dental surgery
HMSO	His / Her Majesty's Stationery Office	*lit.*	literally
HMV	His Master's Voice	LittB	bachelor of letters
Hon.	Honourable	LittD	doctor of letters
hp	horsepower	LKQCPI	licentiate of the King and Queen's College of Physicians, Ireland
hr	hour(s)		
HRH	his / her royal highness	LLA	lady literate in arts
HTV	Harlech Television	LLB	bachelor of laws
IA	Iowa	LLD	doctor of laws
ibid.	*ibidem*: in the same place	LLM	master of laws
ICI	Imperial Chemical Industries (Ltd)	LM	licentiate in midwifery
ID	Idaho	LP	long-playing record
IL	Illinois	LRAM	licentiate of the Royal Academy of Music
illus.	illustration	LRCP	licentiate of the Royal College of Physicians
illustr.	illustrated	LRCPS (Glasgow)	licentiate of the Royal College of Physicians and Surgeons of Glasgow
IN	Indiana		
in.	inch(es)	LRCS	licentiate of the Royal College of Surgeons
Inc.	Incorporated	LSA	licentiate of the Society of Apothecaries
incl.	includes / including	LSD	lysergic acid diethylamide
IOU	I owe you	LVO	lieutenant of the Royal Victorian Order
IQ	intelligence quotient	M. *pl.* MM.	Monsieur *pl.* Messieurs
Ir£	Irish pound	m	metre(s)
IRA	Irish Republican Army		

m. *pl.* mm.	membrane(s)		ND	North Dakota
MA	(1) Massachusetts; (2) master of arts		n.d.	no date
MAI	master of engineering		NE	Nebraska
MB	bachelor of medicine		*nem. con.*	*nemine contradicente*: unanimously
MBA	master of business administration		new ser.	new series
MBE	member of the Order of the British Empire		NH	New Hampshire
MC	Military Cross		NHS	National Health Service
MCC	Marylebone Cricket Club		NJ	New Jersey
MCh	master of surgery		NKVD	[Soviet people's commissariat for internal affairs]
MChir	master of surgery		NM	New Mexico
MCom	master of commerce		nm	nanometre(s)
MD	(1) doctor of medicine; (2) Maryland		no. *pl.* nos.	number(s)
MDMA	methylenedioxymethamphetamine		Nov	November
ME	Maine		n.p.	no place [of publication]
MEd	master of education		NS	new style
MEng	master of engineering		NV	Nevada
MEP	member of the European parliament		NY	New York
MG	Morris Garages		NZBS	New Zealand Broadcasting Service
MGM	Metro-Goldwyn-Mayer		OBE	officer of the Order of the British Empire
Mgr	Monsignor		obit.	obituary
MI	(1) Michigan; (2) military intelligence		Oct	October
MI1c	[secret intelligence department]		OCTU	officer cadets training unit
MI5	[military intelligence department]		OECD	Organization for Economic Co-operation and Development
MI6	[secret intelligence department]		OEEC	Organization for European Economic Co-operation
MI9	[secret escape service]			
MICE	member of the Institution of Civil Engineers		OFM	order of Friars Minor [Franciscans]
MIEE	member of the Institution of Electrical Engineers		OFMCap	Ordine Frati Minori Cappucini: member of the Capuchin order
min.	minute(s)		OH	Ohio
Mk	mark		OK	Oklahoma
ML	(1) licentiate of medicine; (2) master of laws		O level	ordinary level [examination]
MLitt	master of letters		OM	Order of Merit
Mlle	Mademoiselle		OP	order of Preachers [Dominicans]
mm	millimetre(s)		op. *pl.* opp.	opus *pl.* opera
Mme	Madame		OPEC	Organization of Petroleum Exporting Countries
MN	Minnesota		OR	Oregon
MO	Missouri		orig.	original
MOH	medical officer of health		OS	old style
MP	member of parliament		OSB	Order of St Benedict
m.p.h.	miles per hour		OTC	Officers' Training Corps
MPhil	master of philosophy		OWS	Old Watercolour Society
MRCP	member of the Royal College of Physicians		Oxon.	Oxoniensis
MRCS	member of the Royal College of Surgeons		p. *pl.* pp.	page(s)
MRCVS	member of the Royal College of Veterinary Surgeons		PA	Pennsylvania
MRIA	member of the Royal Irish Academy		p.a.	per annum
MS	(1) master of science; (2) Mississippi		para.	paragraph
MS *pl.* MSS	manuscript(s)		PAYE	pay as you earn
MSc	master of science		pbk *pl.* pbks	paperback(s)
MSc (Econ.)	master of science (economics)		*per.*	[during the] period
MT	Montana		PhD	doctor of philosophy
MusB	bachelor of music		pl.	(1) plate(s); (2) plural
MusBac	bachelor of music		priv. coll.	private collection
MusD	doctor of music		pt *pl.* pts	part(s)
MV	motor vessel		pubd	published
MVO	member of the Royal Victorian Order		PVC	polyvinyl chloride
n. *pl.* nn.	note(s)		q. *pl.* qq.	(1) question(s); (2) quire(s)
NAAFI	Navy, Army, and Air Force Institutes		QC	queen's counsel
NASA	National Aeronautics and Space Administration		R	rand
NATO	North Atlantic Treaty Organization		R.	Rex / Regina
NBC	National Broadcasting Corporation		*r*	recto
NC	North Carolina		*r.*	reigned / ruled
NCO	non-commissioned officer		RA	Royal Academy / Royal Academician

RAC	Royal Automobile Club
RAF	Royal Air Force
RAFVR	Royal Air Force Volunteer Reserve
RAM	[member of the] Royal Academy of Music
RAMC	Royal Army Medical Corps
RCA	Royal College of Art
RCNC	Royal Corps of Naval Constructors
RCOG	Royal College of Obstetricians and Gynaecologists
RDI	royal designer for industry
RE	Royal Engineers
repr. *pl.* reprs.	reprint(s) / reprinted
repro.	reproduced
rev.	revised / revised by / reviser / revision
Revd	Reverend
RHA	Royal Hibernian Academy
RI	(1) Rhode Island; (2) Royal Institute of Painters in Water-Colours
RIBA	Royal Institute of British Architects
RIN	Royal Indian Navy
RM	Reichsmark
RMS	Royal Mail steamer
RN	Royal Navy
RNA	ribonucleic acid
RNAS	Royal Naval Air Service
RNR	Royal Naval Reserve
RNVR	Royal Naval Volunteer Reserve
RO	Record Office
r.p.m.	revolutions per minute
RRS	royal research ship
Rs	rupees
RSA	(1) Royal Scottish Academician; (2) Royal Society of Arts
RSPCA	Royal Society for the Prevention of Cruelty to Animals
Rt Hon.	Right Honourable
Rt Revd	Right Reverend
RUC	Royal Ulster Constabulary
Russ.	Russian
RWS	Royal Watercolour Society
S4C	Sianel Pedwar Cymru
s.	shilling(s)
s.a.	*sub anno*: under the year
SABC	South African Broadcasting Corporation
SAS	Special Air Service
SC	South Carolina
ScD	doctor of science
S$	Singapore dollar
SD	South Dakota
sec.	second(s)
sel.	selected
sen.	senior
Sept	September
ser.	series
SHAPE	supreme headquarters allied powers, Europe
SIDRO	Société Internationale d'Énergie Hydro-Électrique
sig. *pl.* sigs.	signature(s)
sing.	singular
SIS	Secret Intelligence Service
SJ	Society of Jesus

Skr	Swedish krona
Span.	Spanish
SPCK	Society for Promoting Christian Knowledge
SS	(1) Santissimi; (2) Schutzstaffel; (3) steam ship
STB	bachelor of theology
STD	doctor of theology
STM	master of theology
STP	doctor of theology
supp.	supposedly
suppl. *pl.* suppls.	supplement(s)
s.v.	*sub verbo* / *sub voce*: under the word / heading
SY	steam yacht
TA	Territorial Army
TASS	[Soviet news agency]
TB	tuberculosis (*lit.* tubercle bacillus)
TD	(1) *teachtaí dála* (member of the Dáil); (2) territorial decoration
TN	Tennessee
TNT	trinitrotoluene
trans.	translated / translated by / translation / translator
TT	tourist trophy
TUC	Trades Union Congress
TX	Texas
U-boat	*Unterseeboot*: submarine
Ufa	Universum-Film AG
UMIST	University of Manchester Institute of Science and Technology
UN	United Nations
UNESCO	United Nations Educational, Scientific, and Cultural Organization
UNICEF	United Nations International Children's Emergency Fund
unpubd	unpublished
USS	United States ship
UT	Utah
v	verso
v.	versus
VA	Virginia
VAD	Voluntary Aid Detachment
VC	Victoria Cross
VE-day	victory in Europe day
Ven.	Venerable
VJ-day	victory over Japan day
vol. *pl.* vols.	volume(s)
VT	Vermont
WA	Washington [state]
WAAC	Women's Auxiliary Army Corps
WAAF	Women's Auxiliary Air Force
WEA	Workers' Educational Association
WHO	World Health Organization
WI	Wisconsin
WRAF	Women's Royal Air Force
WRNS	Women's Royal Naval Service
WV	West Virginia
WVS	Women's Voluntary Service
WY	Wyoming
¥	yen
YMCA	Young Men's Christian Association
YWCA	Young Women's Christian Association

2 Institution abbreviations

All Souls Oxf.	All Souls College, Oxford
AM Oxf.	Ashmolean Museum, Oxford
Balliol Oxf.	Balliol College, Oxford
BBC WAC	BBC Written Archives Centre, Reading
Beds. & Luton ARS	Bedfordshire and Luton Archives and Record Service, Bedford
Berks. RO	Berkshire Record Office, Reading
BFI	British Film Institute, London
BFI NFTVA	British Film Institute, London, National Film and Television Archive
BGS	British Geological Survey, Keyworth, Nottingham
Birm. CA	Birmingham Central Library, Birmingham City Archives
Birm. CL	Birmingham Central Library
BL	British Library, London
BL NSA	British Library, London, National Sound Archive
BL OIOC	British Library, London, Oriental and India Office Collections
BLPES	London School of Economics and Political Science, British Library of Political and Economic Science
BM	British Museum, London
Bodl. Oxf.	Bodleian Library, Oxford
Bodl. RH	Bodleian Library of Commonwealth and African Studies at Rhodes House, Oxford
Borth. Inst.	Borthwick Institute of Historical Research, University of York
Boston PL	Boston Public Library, Massachusetts
Bristol RO	Bristol Record Office
Bucks. RLSS	Buckinghamshire Records and Local Studies Service, Aylesbury
CAC Cam.	Churchill College, Cambridge, Churchill Archives Centre
Cambs. AS	Cambridgeshire Archive Service
CCC Cam.	Corpus Christi College, Cambridge
CCC Oxf.	Corpus Christi College, Oxford
Ches. & Chester ALSS	Cheshire and Chester Archives and Local Studies Service
Christ Church Oxf.	Christ Church, Oxford
Christies	Christies, London
City Westm. AC	City of Westminster Archives Centre, London
CKS	Centre for Kentish Studies, Maidstone
CLRO	Corporation of London Records Office
Coll. Arms	College of Arms, London
Col. U.	Columbia University, New York
Cornwall RO	Cornwall Record Office, Truro
Courtauld Inst.	Courtauld Institute of Art, London
CUL	Cambridge University Library
Cumbria AS	Cumbria Archive Service
Derbys. RO	Derbyshire Record Office, Matlock
Devon RO	Devon Record Office, Exeter
Dorset RO	Dorset Record Office, Dorchester
Duke U.	Duke University, Durham, North Carolina
Duke U., Perkins L.	Duke University, Durham, North Carolina, William R. Perkins Library
Durham Cath. CL	Durham Cathedral, chapter library
Durham RO	Durham Record Office
DWL	Dr Williams's Library, London
Essex RO	Essex Record Office
E. Sussex RO	East Sussex Record Office, Lewes
Eton	Eton College, Berkshire
FM Cam.	Fitzwilliam Museum, Cambridge
Folger	Folger Shakespeare Library, Washington, DC
Garr. Club	Garrick Club, London
Girton Cam.	Girton College, Cambridge
GL	Guildhall Library, London
Glos. RO	Gloucestershire Record Office, Gloucester
Gon. & Caius Cam.	Gonville and Caius College, Cambridge
Gov. Art Coll.	Government Art Collection
GS Lond.	Geological Society of London
Hants. RO	Hampshire Record Office, Winchester
Harris Man. Oxf.	Harris Manchester College, Oxford
Harvard TC	Harvard Theatre Collection, Harvard University, Cambridge, Massachusetts, Nathan Marsh Pusey Library
Harvard U.	Harvard University, Cambridge, Massachusetts
Harvard U., Houghton L.	Harvard University, Cambridge, Massachusetts, Houghton Library
Herefs. RO	Herefordshire Record Office, Hereford
Herts. ALS	Hertfordshire Archives and Local Studies, Hertford
Hist. Soc. Penn.	Historical Society of Pennsylvania, Philadelphia
HLRO	House of Lords Record Office, London
Hult. Arch.	Hulton Archive, London and New York
Hunt. L.	Huntington Library, San Marino, California
ICL	Imperial College, London
Inst. CE	Institution of Civil Engineers, London
Inst. EE	Institution of Electrical Engineers, London
IWM	Imperial War Museum, London
IWM FVA	Imperial War Museum, London, Film and Video Archive
IWM SA	Imperial War Museum, London, Sound Archive
JRL	John Rylands University Library of Manchester
King's AC Cam.	King's College Archives Centre, Cambridge
King's Cam.	King's College, Cambridge
King's Lond.	King's College, London
King's Lond., Liddell Hart C.	King's College, London, Liddell Hart Centre for Military Archives
Lancs. RO	Lancashire Record Office, Preston
L. Cong.	Library of Congress, Washington, DC
Leics. RO	Leicestershire, Leicester, and Rutland Record Office, Leicester
Lincs. Arch.	Lincolnshire Archives, Lincoln
Linn. Soc.	Linnean Society of London
LMA	London Metropolitan Archives
LPL	Lambeth Palace, London
Lpool RO	Liverpool Record Office and Local Studies Service
LUL	London University Library
Magd. Cam.	Magdalene College, Cambridge
Magd. Oxf.	Magdalen College, Oxford
Man. City Gall.	Manchester City Galleries
Man. CL	Manchester Central Library
Mass. Hist. Soc.	Massachusetts Historical Society, Boston
Merton Oxf.	Merton College, Oxford
MHS Oxf.	Museum of the History of Science, Oxford
Mitchell L., Glas.	Mitchell Library, Glasgow
Mitchell L., NSW	State Library of New South Wales, Sydney, Mitchell Library
Morgan L.	Pierpont Morgan Library, New York
NA Canada	National Archives of Canada, Ottawa
NA Ire.	National Archives of Ireland, Dublin
NAM	National Army Museum, London
NA Scot.	National Archives of Scotland, Edinburgh
News Int. RO	News International Record Office, London
NG Ire.	National Gallery of Ireland, Dublin

NG Scot.	National Gallery of Scotland, Edinburgh
NHM	Natural History Museum, London
NL Aus.	National Library of Australia, Canberra
NL Ire.	National Library of Ireland, Dublin
NL NZ	National Library of New Zealand, Wellington
NL NZ, Turnbull L.	National Library of New Zealand, Wellington, Alexander Turnbull Library
NL Scot.	National Library of Scotland, Edinburgh
NL Wales	National Library of Wales, Aberystwyth
NMG Wales	National Museum and Gallery of Wales, Cardiff
NMM	National Maritime Museum, London
Norfolk RO	Norfolk Record Office, Norwich
Northants. RO	Northamptonshire Record Office, Northampton
Northumbd RO	Northumberland Record Office
Notts. Arch.	Nottinghamshire Archives, Nottingham
NPG	National Portrait Gallery, London
NRA	National Archives, London, Historical Manuscripts Commission, National Register of Archives
Nuffield Oxf.	Nuffield College, Oxford
N. Yorks. CRO	North Yorkshire County Record Office, Northallerton
NYPL	New York Public Library
Oxf. UA	Oxford University Archives
Oxf. U. Mus. NH	Oxford University Museum of Natural History
Oxon. RO	Oxfordshire Record Office, Oxford
Pembroke Cam.	Pembroke College, Cambridge
PRO	National Archives, London, Public Record Office
PRO NIre.	Public Record Office for Northern Ireland, Belfast
Pusey Oxf.	Pusey House, Oxford
RA	Royal Academy of Arts, London
Ransom HRC	Harry Ransom Humanities Research Center, University of Texas, Austin
RAS	Royal Astronomical Society, London
RBG Kew	Royal Botanic Gardens, Kew, London
RCP Lond.	Royal College of Physicians of London
RCS Eng.	Royal College of Surgeons of England, London
RGS	Royal Geographical Society, London
RIBA	Royal Institute of British Architects, London
RIBA BAL	Royal Institute of British Architects, London, British Architectural Library
Royal Arch.	Royal Archives, Windsor Castle, Berkshire [by gracious permission of her majesty the queen]
Royal Irish Acad.	Royal Irish Academy, Dublin
Royal Scot. Acad.	Royal Scottish Academy, Edinburgh
RS	Royal Society, London
RSA	Royal Society of Arts, London
RS Friends, Lond.	Religious Society of Friends, London
St Ant. Oxf.	St Antony's College, Oxford
St John Cam.	St John's College, Cambridge
S. Antiquaries, Lond.	Society of Antiquaries of London
Sci. Mus.	Science Museum, London
Scot. NPG	Scottish National Portrait Gallery, Edinburgh
Scott Polar RI	University of Cambridge, Scott Polar Research Institute
Sheff. Arch.	Sheffield Archives
Shrops. RRC	Shropshire Records and Research Centre, Shrewsbury
SOAS	School of Oriental and African Studies, London
Som. ARS	Somerset Archive and Record Service, Taunton
Staffs. RO	Staffordshire Record Office, Stafford

Suffolk RO	Suffolk Record Office
Surrey HC	Surrey History Centre, Woking
TCD	Trinity College, Dublin
Trinity Cam.	Trinity College, Cambridge
U. Aberdeen	University of Aberdeen
U. Birm.	University of Birmingham
U. Birm. L.	University of Birmingham Library
U. Cal.	University of California
U. Cam.	University of Cambridge
UCL	University College, London
U. Durham	University of Durham
U. Durham L.	University of Durham Library
U. Edin.	University of Edinburgh
U. Edin., New Coll.	University of Edinburgh, New College
U. Edin., New Coll. L.	University of Edinburgh, New College Library
U. Edin. L.	University of Edinburgh Library
U. Glas.	University of Glasgow
U. Glas. L.	University of Glasgow Library
U. Hull	University of Hull
U. Hull, Brynmor Jones L.	University of Hull, Brynmor Jones Library
U. Leeds	University of Leeds
U. Leeds, Brotherton L.	University of Leeds, Brotherton Library
U. Lond.	University of London
U. Lpool	University of Liverpool
U. Lpool L.	University of Liverpool Library
U. Mich.	University of Michigan, Ann Arbor
U. Mich., Clements L.	University of Michigan, Ann Arbor, William L. Clements Library
U. Newcastle	University of Newcastle upon Tyne
U. Newcastle, Robinson L.	University of Newcastle upon Tyne, Robinson Library
U. Nott.	University of Nottingham
U. Nott. L.	University of Nottingham Library
U. Oxf.	University of Oxford
U. Reading	University of Reading
U. Reading L.	University of Reading Library
U. St Andr.	University of St Andrews
U. St Andr. L.	University of St Andrews Library
U. Southampton	University of Southampton
U. Southampton L.	University of Southampton Library
U. Sussex	University of Sussex, Brighton
U. Texas	University of Texas, Austin
U. Wales	University of Wales
U. Warwick Mod. RC	University of Warwick, Coventry, Modern Records Centre
V&A	Victoria and Albert Museum, London
V&A NAL	Victoria and Albert Museum, London, National Art Library
Warks. CRO	Warwickshire County Record Office, Warwick
Wellcome L.	Wellcome Library for the History and Understanding of Medicine, London
Westm. DA	Westminster Diocesan Archives, London
Wilts. & Swindon RO	Wiltshire and Swindon Record Office, Trowbridge
Worcs. RO	Worcestershire Record Office, Worcester
W. Sussex RO	West Sussex Record Office, Chichester
W. Yorks. AS	West Yorkshire Archive Service
Yale U.	Yale University, New Haven, Connecticut
Yale U., Beinecke L.	Yale University, New Haven, Connecticut, Beinecke Rare Book and Manuscript Library
Yale U. CBA	Yale University, New Haven, Connecticut, Yale Center for British Art

3 Bibliographic abbreviations

Adams, *Drama* W. D. Adams, *A dictionary of the drama*, 1: *A–G* (1904); 2: *H–Z* (1956) [vol. 2 microfilm only]

AFM J O'Donovan, ed. and trans., *Annala rioghachta Eireann / Annals of the kingdom of Ireland by the four masters*, 7 vols. (1848–51); 2nd edn (1856); 3rd edn (1990)

Allibone, *Dict.* S. A. Allibone, *A critical dictionary of English literature and British and American authors*, 3 vols. (1859–71); suppl. by J. F. Kirk, 2 vols. (1891)

ANB J. A. Garraty and M. C. Carnes, eds., *American national biography*, 24 vols. (1999)

Anderson, *Scot. nat.* W. Anderson, *The Scottish nation, or, The surnames, families, literature, honours, and biographical history of the people of Scotland*, 3 vols. (1859–63)

Ann. mon. H. R. Luard, ed., *Annales monastici*, 5 vols., Rolls Series, 36 (1864–9)

Ann. Ulster S. Mac Airt and G. Mac Niocaill, eds., *Annals of Ulster (to AD 1131)* (1983)

APC *Acts of the privy council of England*, new ser., 46 vols. (1890–1964)

APS *The acts of the parliaments of Scotland*, 12 vols. in 13 (1814–75)

Arber, *Regs. Stationers* F. Arber, ed., *A transcript of the registers of the Company of Stationers of London, 1554–1640 AD*, 5 vols. (1875–94)

ArchR *Architectural Review*

ASC D. Whitelock, D. C. Douglas, and S. I. Tucker, ed. and trans., *The Anglo-Saxon Chronicle: a revised translation* (1961)

AS chart. P. H. Sawyer, *Anglo-Saxon charters: an annotated list and bibliography*, Royal Historical Society Guides and Handbooks (1968)

AusDB D. Pike and others, eds., *Australian dictionary of biography*, 16 vols. (1966–2002)

Baker, *Serjeants* J. H. Baker, *The order of serjeants at law*, SeldS, suppl. ser., 5 (1984)

Bale, *Cat.* J. Bale, *Scriptorum illustrium Maioris Brytannie, quam nunc Angliam et Scotiam vocant: catalogus*, 2 vols. in 1 (Basel, 1557–9); facs. edn (1971)

Bale, *Index* J. Bale, *Index Britanniae scriptorum*, ed. R. L. Poole and M. Bateson (1902); facs. edn (1990)

BBCS *Bulletin of the Board of Celtic Studies*

BDMBR J. O. Baylen and N. J. Gossman, eds., *Biographical dictionary of modern British radicals*, 3 vols. in 4 (1979–88)

Bede, *Hist. eccl.* *Bede's Ecclesiastical history of the English people*, ed. and trans. B. Colgrave and R. A. B. Mynors, OMT (1969); repr. (1991)

Bénézit, *Dict.* E. Bénézit, *Dictionnaire critique et documentaire des peintres, sculpteurs, dessinateurs et graveurs*, 3 vols. (Paris, 1911–23); new edn, 8 vols. (1948–66), repr. (1966); 3rd edn, rev. and enl., 10 vols. (1976); 4th edn, 14 vols. (1999)

BIHR *Bulletin of the Institute of Historical Research*

Birch, *Seals* W. de Birch, *Catalogue of seals in the department of manuscripts in the British Museum*, 6 vols. (1887–1900)

Bishop Burnet's History *Bishop Burnet's History of his own time*, ed. M. J. Routh, 2nd edn, 6 vols. (1833)

Blackwood *Blackwood's [Edinburgh] Magazine*, 328 vols. (1817–1980)

Blain, Clements & Grundy, *Feminist comp.* V. Blain, P. Clements, and I. Grundy, eds., *The feminist companion to literature in English* (1990)

BL cat. *The British Library general catalogue of printed books* [in 360 vols. with suppls., also CD-ROM and online]

BMJ *British Medical Journal*

Boase & Courtney, *Bibl. Corn.* G. C. Boase and W. P. Courtney, *Bibliotheca Cornubiensis: a catalogue of the writings … of Cornishmen*, 3 vols. (1874–82)

Boase, *Mod. Eng. biog.* F. Boase, *Modern English biography: containing many thousand concise memoirs of persons who have died since the year 1850*, 6 vols. (privately printed, Truro, 1892–1921); repr. (1965)

Boswell, *Life* *Boswell's Life of Johnson: together with Journal of a tour to the Hebrides and Johnson's Diary of a journey into north Wales*, ed. G. B. Hill, enl. edn, rev. L. F. Powell, 6 vols. (1934–50); 2nd edn (1964); repr. (1971)

Brown & Stratton, *Brit. mus.* J. D. Brown and S. S. Stratton, *British musical biography* (1897)

Bryan, *Painters* M. Bryan, *A biographical and critical dictionary of painters and engravers*, 2 vols. (1816); new edn, ed. G. Stanley (1849); new edn, ed. R. E. Graves and W. Armstrong, 2 vols. (1886–9); [4th edn], ed. G. C. Williamson, 5 vols. (1903–5) [various reprs.]

Burke, *Gen. GB* J. Burke, *A genealogical and heraldic history of the commoners of Great Britain and Ireland*, 4 vols. (1833–8); new edn as *A genealogical and heraldic dictionary of the landed gentry of Great Britain and Ireland*, 3 vols. [1843–9] [many later edns]

Burke, *Gen. Ire.* J. B. Burke, *A genealogical and heraldic history of the landed gentry of Ireland* (1899); 2nd edn (1904); 3rd edn (1912); 4th edn (1958); 5th edn as *Burke's Irish family records* (1976)

Burke, *Peerage* J. Burke, *A general [later edns A genealogical] and heraldic dictionary of the peerage and baronetage of the United Kingdom* [later edns *the British empire*] (1829–)

Burney, *Hist. mus.* C. Burney, *A general history of music, from the earliest ages to the present period*, 4 vols. (1776–89)

Burtchaell & Sadleir, *Alum. Dubl.* G. D. Burtchaell and T. U. Sadleir, *Alumni Dublinenses: a register of the students, graduates, and provosts of Trinity College* (1924); [2nd edn], with suppl., in 2 pts (1935)

Calamy rev. A. G. Matthews, *Calamy revised* (1934); repr. (1988)

CCI *Calendar of confirmations and inventories granted and given up in the several commissariots of Scotland* (1876–)

CClR *Calendar of the close rolls preserved in the Public Record Office*, 47 vols. (1892–1963)

CDS J. Bain, ed., *Calendar of documents relating to Scotland*, 4 vols., PRO (1881–8); suppl. vol. 5, ed. G. G. Simpson and J. D. Galbraith [1986]

CEPR letters W. H. Bliss, C. Johnson, and J. Twemlow, eds., *Calendar of entries in the papal registers relating to Great Britain and Ireland: papal letters* (1893–)

CGPLA *Calendars of the grants of probate and letters of administration* [in 4 ser.: *England & Wales, Northern Ireland, Ireland*, and *Éire*]

Chambers, *Scots.* R. Chambers, ed., *A biographical dictionary of eminent Scotsmen*, 4 vols. (1832–5)

Chancery records chancery records pubd by the PRO

Chancery records (RC) chancery records pubd by the Record Commissions

CIPM	*Calendar of inquisitions post mortem*, [20 vols.], PRO (1904–); also *Henry VII*, 3 vols. (1898–1955)
Clarendon, *Hist. rebellion*	E. Hyde, earl of Clarendon, *The history of the rebellion and civil wars in England*, 6 vols. (1888); repr. (1958) and (1992)
Cobbett, *Parl. hist.*	W. Cobbett and J. Wright, eds., *Cobbett's Parliamentary history of England*, 36 vols. (1806–1820)
Colvin, *Archs.*	H. Colvin, *A biographical dictionary of British architects, 1600–1840*, 3rd edn (1995)
Cooper, *Ath. Cantab.*	C. H. Cooper and T. Cooper, *Athenae Cantabrigienses*, 3 vols. (1858–1913); repr. (1967)
CPR	*Calendar of the patent rolls preserved in the Public Record Office* (1891–)
Crockford	*Crockford's Clerical Directory*
CS	Camden Society
CSP	*Calendar of state papers* [in 11 ser.: domestic, Scotland, Scottish series, Ireland, colonial, Commonwealth, foreign, Spain [at Simancas], Rome, Milan, and Venice]
CYS	Canterbury and York Society
DAB	*Dictionary of American biography*, 21 vols. (1928–36), repr. in 11 vols. (1964); 10 suppls. (1944–96)
DBB	D. J. Jeremy, ed., *Dictionary of business biography*, 5 vols. (1984–6)
DCB	G. W. Brown and others, *Dictionary of Canadian biography*, [14 vols.] (1966–)
Debrett's Peerage	*Debrett's Peerage* (1803–) [sometimes *Debrett's Illustrated peerage*]
Desmond, *Botanists*	R. Desmond, *Dictionary of British and Irish botanists and horticulturists* (1977); rev. edn (1994)
Dir. Brit. archs.	A. Felstead, J. Franklin, and L. Pinfield, eds., *Directory of British architects, 1834–1900* (1993); 2nd edn, ed. A. Brodie and others, 2 vols. (2001)
DLB	J. M. Bellamy and J. Saville, eds., *Dictionary of labour biography*, [10 vols.] (1972–)
DLitB	Dictionary of Literary Biography
DNB	*Dictionary of national biography*, 63 vols. (1885–1900), suppl., 3 vols. (1901); repr. in 22 vols. (1908–9); 10 further suppls. (1912–96); *Missing persons* (1993)
DNZB	W. H. Oliver and C. Orange, eds., *The dictionary of New Zealand biography*, 5 vols. (1990–2000)
DSAB	W. J. de Kock and others, eds., *Dictionary of South African biography*, 5 vols. (1968–87)
DSB	C. C. Gillispie and F. L. Holmes, eds., *Dictionary of scientific biography*, 16 vols. (1970–80); repr. in 8 vols. (1981); 2 vol. suppl. (1990)
DSBB	A. Slaven and S. Checkland, eds., *Dictionary of Scottish business biography, 1860–1960*, 2 vols. (1986–90)
DSCHT	N. M. de S. Cameron and others, eds., *Dictionary of Scottish church history and theology* (1993)
Dugdale, *Monasticon*	W. Dugdale, *Monasticon Anglicanum*, 3 vols. (1655–72); 2nd edn, 3 vols. (1661–82); new edn, ed. J. Caley, J. Ellis, and B. Bandinel, 6 vols. in 8 pts (1817–30); repr. (1846) and (1970)

DWB	J. E. Lloyd and others, eds., *Dictionary of Welsh biography down to 1940* (1959) [Eng. trans. of *Y bywgraffiadur Cymreig hyd 1940*, 2nd edn (1954)]
EdinR	*Edinburgh Review, or, Critical Journal*
EETS	Early English Text Society
Emden, *Cam.*	A. B. Emden, *A biographical register of the University of Cambridge to 1500* (1963)
Emden, *Oxf.*	A. B. Emden, *A biographical register of the University of Oxford to AD 1500*, 3 vols. (1957–9); also *A biographical register of the University of Oxford, AD 1501 to 1540* (1974)
EngHR	*English Historical Review*
Engraved Brit. ports.	F. M. O'Donoghue and H. M. Hake, *Catalogue of engraved British portraits preserved in the department of prints and drawings in the British Museum*, 6 vols. (1908–25)
ER	The English Reports, 178 vols. (1900–32)
ESTC	*English short title catalogue, 1475–1800* [CD-ROM and online]
Evelyn, *Diary*	*The diary of John Evelyn*, ed. E. S. De Beer, 6 vols. (1955); repr. (2000)
Farington, *Diary*	*The diary of Joseph Farington*, ed. K. Garlick and others, 17 vols. (1978–98)
Fasti Angl. (Hardy)	J. Le Neve, *Fasti ecclesiae Anglicanae*, ed. T. D. Hardy, 3 vols. (1854)
Fasti Angl., 1066–1300	[J. Le Neve], *Fasti ecclesiae Anglicanae, 1066–1300*, ed. D. E. Greenway and J. S. Barrow, [8 vols.] (1968–)
Fasti Angl., 1300–1541	[J. Le Neve], *Fasti ecclesiae Anglicanae, 1300–1541*, 12 vols. (1962–7)
Fasti Angl., 1541–1857	[J. Le Neve], *Fasti ecclesiae Anglicanae, 1541–1857*, ed. J. M. Horn, D. M. Smith, and D. S. Bailey, [9 vols.] (1969–)
Fasti Scot.	H. Scott, *Fasti ecclesiae Scoticanae*, 3 vols. in 6 (1871); new edn, [11 vols.] (1915–)
FO List	*Foreign Office List*
Fortescue, *Brit. army*	J. W. Fortescue, *A history of the British army*, 13 vols. (1899–1930)
Foss, *Judges*	E. Foss, *The judges of England*, 9 vols. (1848–64); repr. (1966)
Foster, *Alum. Oxon.*	J. Foster, ed., *Alumni Oxonienses: the members of the University of Oxford, 1715–1886*, 4 vols. (1887–8); later edn (1891); also *Alumni Oxonienses … 1500–1714*, 4 vols. (1891–2); 8 vol. repr. (1968) and (2000)
Fuller, *Worthies*	T. Fuller, *The history of the worthies of England*, 4 pts (1662); new edn, 2 vols., ed. J. Nichols (1811); new edn, 3 vols., ed. P. A. Nuttall (1840); repr. (1965)
GEC, *Baronetage*	G. E. Cokayne, *Complete baronetage*, 6 vols. (1900–09); repr. (1983) [microprint]
GEC, *Peerage*	G. E. C. [G. E. Cokayne], *The complete peerage of England, Scotland, Ireland, Great Britain, and the United Kingdom*, 8 vols. (1887–98); new edn, ed. V. Gibbs and others, 14 vols. in 15 (1910–98); microprint repr. (1982) and (1987)
Genest, *Eng. stage*	J. Genest, *Some account of the English stage from the Restoration in 1660 to 1830*, 10 vols. (1832); repr. [New York, 1965]
Gillow, *Lit. biog. hist.*	J. Gillow, *A literary and biographical history or bibliographical dictionary of the English Catholics, from the breach with Rome, in 1534, to the present time*, 5 vols. [1885–1902]; repr. (1961); repr. with preface by C. Gillow (1999)
Gir. Camb. opera	*Giraldi Cambrensis opera*, ed. J. S. Brewer, J. F. Dimock, and G. F. Warner, 8 vols., Rolls Series, 21 (1861–91)
GJ	*Geographical Journal*

Gladstone, *Diaries*	*The Gladstone diaries: with cabinet minutes and prime-ministerial correspondence*, ed. M. R. D. Foot and H. C. G. Matthew, 14 vols. (1968–94)
GM	*Gentleman's Magazine*
Graves, *Artists*	A. Graves, ed., *A dictionary of artists who have exhibited works in the principal London exhibitions of oil paintings from 1760 to 1880* (1884); new edn (1895); 3rd edn (1901); facs. edn (1969); repr. [1970], (1973), and (1984)
Graves, *Brit. Inst.*	A. Graves, *The British Institution, 1806–1867: a complete dictionary of contributors and their work from the foundation of the institution* (1875); facs. edn (1908); repr. (1969)
Graves, *RA exhibitors*	A. Graves, *The Royal Academy of Arts: a complete dictionary of contributors and their work from its foundation in 1769 to 1904*, 8 vols. (1905–6); repr. in 4 vols. (1970) and (1972)
Graves, *Soc. Artists*	A. Graves, *The Society of Artists of Great Britain, 1760–1791, the Free Society of Artists, 1761–1783: a complete dictionary* (1907); facs. edn (1969)
Greaves & Zaller, *BDBR*	R. L. Greaves and R. Zaller, eds., *Biographical dictionary of British radicals in the seventeenth century*, 3 vols. (1982–4)
Grove, *Dict. mus.*	G. Grove, ed., *A dictionary of music and musicians*, 5 vols. (1878–90); 2nd edn, ed. J. A. Fuller Maitland (1904–10); 3rd edn, ed. H. C. Colles (1927); 4th edn with suppl. (1940); 5th edn, ed. E. Blom, 9 vols. (1954); suppl. (1961) [see also *New Grove*]
Hall, *Dramatic ports.*	L. A. Hall, *Catalogue of dramatic portraits in the theatre collection of the Harvard College library*, 4 vols. (1930–34)
Hansard	*Hansard's parliamentary debates*, ser. 1–5 (1803–)
Highfill, Burnim & Langhans, *BDA*	P. H. Highfill, K. A. Burnim, and E. A. Langhans, *A biographical dictionary of actors, actresses, musicians, dancers, managers, and other stage personnel in London, 1660–1800*, 16 vols. (1973–93)
Hist. U. Oxf.	T. H. Aston, ed., *The history of the University of Oxford*, 8 vols. (1984–2000) [1: *The early Oxford schools*, ed. J. I. Catto (1984); 2: *Late medieval Oxford*, ed. J. I. Catto and R. Evans (1992); 3: *The collegiate university*, ed. J. McConica (1986); 4: *Seventeenth-century Oxford*, ed. N. Tyacke (1997); 5: *The eighteenth century*, ed. L. S. Sutherland and L. G. Mitchell (1986); 6–7: *Nineteenth-century Oxford*, ed. M. G. Brock and M. C. Curthoys (1997–2000); 8: *The twentieth century*, ed. B. Harrison (2000)]
HJ	*Historical Journal*
HMC	Historical Manuscripts Commission
Holdsworth, *Eng. law*	W. S. Holdsworth, *A history of English law*, ed. A. L. Goodhart and H. L. Hanbury, 17 vols. (1903–72)
HoP, *Commons*	*The history of parliament: the House of Commons* [*1386–1421*, ed. J. S. Roskell, L. Clark, and C. Rawcliffe, 4 vols. (1992); *1509–1558*, ed. S. T. Bindoff, 3 vols. (1982); *1558–1603*, ed. P. W. Hasler, 3 vols. (1981); *1660–1690*, ed. B. D. Henning, 3 vols. (1983); *1690–1715*, ed. D. W. Hayton, E. Cruickshanks, and S. Handley, 5 vols. (2002); *1715–1754*, ed. R. Sedgwick, 2 vols. (1970); *1754–1790*, ed. L. Namier and J. Brooke, 3 vols. (1964), repr. (1985); *1790–1820*, ed. R. G. Thorne, 5 vols. (1986); in draft (used with permission): *1422–1504, 1604–1629, 1640–1660,* and *1820–1832*]

IGI	*International Genealogical Index*, Church of Jesus Christ of the Latterday Saints
ILN	*Illustrated London News*
IMC	Irish Manuscripts Commission
Irving, *Scots.*	J. Irving, ed., *The book of Scotsmen eminent for achievements in arms and arts, church and state, law, legislation and literature, commerce, science, travel and philanthropy* (1881)
JCS	*Journal of the Chemical Society*
JHC	*Journals of the House of Commons*
JHL	*Journals of the House of Lords*
John of Worcester, *Chron.*	*The chronicle of John of Worcester*, ed. R. R. Darlington and P. McGurk, trans. J. Bray and P. McGurk, 3 vols., OMT (1995–) [vol. 1 forthcoming]
Keeler, *Long Parliament*	M. F. Keeler, *The Long Parliament, 1640–1641: a biographical study of its members* (1954)
Kelly, *Handbk*	*The upper ten thousand: an alphabetical list of all members of noble families*, 3 vols. (1875–7); continued as *Kelly's handbook of the upper ten thousand for 1878* [1879], 2 vols. (1878–9); continued as *Kelly's handbook to the titled, landed and official classes*, 94 vols. (1880–1973)
LondG	*London Gazette*
LP Henry VIII	J. S. Brewer, J. Gairdner, and R. H. Brodie, eds., *Letters and papers, foreign and domestic, of the reign of Henry VIII*, 23 vols. in 38 (1862–1932); repr. (1965)
Mallalieu, *Watercolour artists*	H. L. Mallalieu, *The dictionary of British watercolour artists up to 1820*, 3 vols. (1976–90); vol. 1, 2nd edn (1986)
Memoirs FRS	*Biographical Memoirs of Fellows of the Royal Society*
MGH	Monumenta Germaniae Historica
MT	*Musical Times*
Munk, *Roll*	W. Munk, *The roll of the Royal College of Physicians of London*, 2 vols. (1861); 2nd edn, 3 vols. (1878)
N&Q	*Notes and Queries*
New Grove	S. Sadie, ed., *The new Grove dictionary of music and musicians*, 20 vols. (1980); 2nd edn, 29 vols. (2001) [also online edn; see also Grove, *Dict. mus.*]
Nichols, *Illustrations*	J. Nichols and J. B. Nichols, *Illustrations of the literary history of the eighteenth century*, 8 vols. (1817–58)
Nichols, *Lit. anecdotes*	J. Nichols, *Literary anecdotes of the eighteenth century*, 9 vols. (1812–16); facs. edn (1966)
Obits. FRS	*Obituary Notices of Fellows of the Royal Society*
O'Byrne, *Naval biog. dict.*	W. R. O'Byrne, *A naval biographical dictionary* (1849); repr. (1990); [2nd edn], 2 vols. (1861)
OHS	Oxford Historical Society
Old Westminsters	*The record of Old Westminsters*, 1–2, ed. G. F. R. Barker and A. H. Stenning (1928); suppl. 1, ed. J. B. Whitmore and G. R. Y. Radcliffe [1938]; 3, ed. J. B. Whitmore, G. R. Y. Radcliffe, and D. C. Simpson (1963); suppl. 2, ed. F. E. Pagan (1978); 4, ed. F. E. Pagan and H. E. Pagan (1992)
OMT	Oxford Medieval Texts
Ordericus Vitalis, *Eccl. hist.*	*The ecclesiastical history of Orderic Vitalis*, ed. and trans. M. Chibnall, 6 vols., OMT (1969–80); repr. (1990)
Paris, *Chron.*	*Matthaei Parisiensis, monachi sancti Albani, chronica majora*, ed. H. R. Luard, Rolls Series, 7 vols. (1872–83)
Parl. papers	*Parliamentary papers* (1801–)
PBA	*Proceedings of the British Academy*

Pepys, *Diary*	*The diary of Samuel Pepys*, ed. R. Latham and W. Matthews, 11 vols. (1970–83); repr. (1995) and (2000)	Symeon of Durham, *Opera*	*Symeonis monachi opera omnia*, ed. T. Arnold, 2 vols., Rolls Series, 75 (1882–5); repr. (1965)
Pevsner	N. Pevsner and others, Buildings of England series	Tanner, *Bibl. Brit.-Hib.*	T. Tanner, *Bibliotheca Britannico-Hibernica*, ed. D. Wilkins (1748); repr. (1963)
PICE	*Proceedings of the Institution of Civil Engineers*	Thieme & Becker, *Allgemeines Lexikon*	U. Thieme, F. Becker, and H. Vollmer, eds., *Allgemeines Lexikon der bildenden Künstler von der Antike bis zur Gegenwart*, 37 vols. (Leipzig,
Pipe rolls	*The great roll of the pipe for . . .*, PRSoc. (1884–)		1907–50); repr. (1961–5), (1983), and (1992)
PRO	Public Record Office	Thurloe, *State papers*	*A collection of the state papers of John Thurloe*, ed.
PRS	*Proceedings of the Royal Society of London*		T. Birch, 7 vols. (1742)
PRSoc.	Pipe Roll Society	*TLS*	*Times Literary Supplement*
PTRS	*Philosophical Transactions of the Royal Society*	Tout, *Admin. hist.*	T. F. Tout, *Chapters in the administrative history of mediaeval England: the wardrobe, the chamber,*
QR	*Quarterly Review*		*and the small seals*, 6 vols. (1920–33); repr.
RC	Record Commissions		(1967)
Redgrave, *Artists*	S. Redgrave, *A dictionary of artists of the English school* (1874); rev. edn (1878); repr. (1970)	*TRHS*	*Transactions of the Royal Historical Society*
Reg. Oxf.	C. W. Boase and A. Clark, eds., *Register of the University of Oxford*, 5 vols., OHS, 1, 10–12, 14 (1885–9)	*VCH*	H. A. Doubleday and others, eds., *The Victoria history of the counties of England*, [88 vols.] (1900–)
Reg. PCS	J. H. Burton and others, eds., *The register of the privy council of Scotland*, 1st ser., 14 vols. (1877–98); 2nd ser., 8 vols. (1899–1908); 3rd ser., [16 vols.] (1908–70)	Venn, *Alum. Cant.*	J. Venn and J. A. Venn, *Alumni Cantabrigienses: a biographical list of all known students, graduates, and holders of office at the University of Cambridge, from the earliest times to 1900*, 10 vols. (1922–54); repr. in 2 vols. (1974–8)
Reg. RAN	H. W. C. Davis and others, eds., *Regesta regum Anglo-Normannorum, 1066–1154*, 4 vols. (1913–69)	Vertue, *Note books*	[G. Vertue], *Note books*, ed. K. Esdaile, earl of Ilchester, and H. M. Hake, 6 vols., Walpole Society, 18, 20, 22, 24, 26, 30 (1930–55)
RIBA Journal	*Journal of the Royal Institute of British Architects* [later *RIBA Journal*]	*VF*	*Vanity Fair*
RotP	J. Strachey, ed., *Rotuli parliamentorum ut et petitiones, et placita in parliamento*, 6 vols. (1767–77)	Walford, *County families*	E. Walford, *The county families of the United Kingdom, or, Royal manual of the titled and untitled aristocracy of Great Britain and Ireland* (1860)
RotS	D. Macpherson, J. Caley, and W. Illingworth, eds., *Rotuli Scotiae in Turri Londinensi et in domo capitulari Westmonasteriensi asservati*, 2 vols., RC, 14 (1814–19)	*Walker rev.*	A. G. Matthews, *Walker revised: being a revision of John Walker's Sufferings of the clergy during the grand rebellion, 1642–60* (1948); repr. (1988)
RS	Record(s) Society	Walpole, *Corr.*	*The Yale edition of Horace Walpole's correspondence*, ed. W. S. Lewis, 48 vols. (1937–83)
Rymer, *Foedera*	T. Rymer and R. Sanderson, eds., *Foedera, conventiones, literae et cuiuscunque generis acta publica inter reges Angliae et alios quosvis imperatores, reges, pontifices, principes, vel communitates*, 20 vols. (1704–35); 2nd edn, 20 vols. (1726–35); 3rd edn, 10 vols. (1739–45); facs. edn (1967); new edn, ed. A. Clarke, J. Caley, and F. Holbrooke, 4 vols., RC, 50 (1816–30)	Ward, *Men of the reign*	T. H. Ward, ed., *Men of the reign: a biographical dictionary of eminent persons of British and colonial birth who have died during the reign of Queen Victoria* (1885); repr. (Graz, 1968)
		Waterhouse, *18c painters*	E. Waterhouse, *The dictionary of 18th century painters in oils and crayons* (1981); repr. as *British 18th century painters in oils and crayons* (1991), vol. 2 of *Dictionary of British art*
Sainty, *Judges*	J. Sainty, ed., *The judges of England, 1272–1990*, SeldS, suppl. ser., 10 (1993)	Watt, *Bibl. Brit.*	R. Watt, *Bibliotheca Britannica, or, A general index to British and foreign literature*, 4 vols. (1824) [many reprs.]
Sainty, *King's counsel*	J. Sainty, ed., *A list of English law officers and king's counsel*, SeldS, suppl. ser., 7 (1987)	*Wellesley index*	W. E. Houghton, ed., *The Wellesley index to Victorian periodicals, 1824–1900*, 5 vols. (1966–89); new edn (1999) [CD-ROM]
SCH	Studies in Church History		
Scots peerage	J. B. Paul, ed. *The Scots peerage, founded on Wood's edition of Sir Robert Douglas's Peerage of Scotland, containing an historical and genealogical account of the nobility of that kingdom*, 9 vols. (1904–14)	Wing, *STC*	D. Wing, ed., *Short-title catalogue of . . . English books . . . 1641–1700*, 3 vols. (1945–51); 2nd edn (1972–88); rev. and enl. edn, ed. J. J. Morrison, C. W. Nelson, and M. Seccombe, 4 vols. (1994–8) [see also *STC, 1475–1640*]
SeldS	Selden Society	*Wisden*	*John Wisden's Cricketer's Almanack*
SHR	*Scottish Historical Review*	Wood, *Ath. Oxon.*	A. Wood, *Athenae Oxonienses . . . to which are added the Fasti*, 2 vols. (1691–2); 2nd edn (1721); new edn, 4 vols., ed. P. Bliss (1813–20); repr. (1967) and (1969)
State trials	T. B. Howell and T. J. Howell, eds., *Cobbett's Complete collection of state trials*, 34 vols. (1809–28)	Wood, *Vic. painters*	C. Wood, *Dictionary of Victorian painters* (1971); 2nd edn (1978); 3rd edn as *Victorian painters*, 2 vols. (1995), vol. 4 of *Dictionary of British art*
STC, 1475–1640	A. W. Pollard, G. R. Redgrave, and others, eds., *A short-title catalogue of . . . English books . . . 1475–1640* (1926); 2nd edn, ed. W. A. Jackson, F. S. Ferguson, and K. F. Pantzer, 3 vols. (1976–91) [see also Wing, *STC*]	*WW*	*Who's who* (1849–)
		WWBMP	M. Stenton and S. Lees, eds., *Who's who of British members of parliament*, 4 vols. (1976–81)
STS	Scottish Text Society	*WWW*	*Who was who* (1929–)
SurtS	Surtees Society		

Morant, Geoffrey Miles (1899–1964), anthropologist and statistician, was born in Battersea, London, on 15 July 1899, the third child of Henry Morant, headmaster of an elementary school in Lambeth, and his wife, Maria Elizabeth Miles. He was educated at Battersea secondary school and, after service with the machine-gun corps in the First World War, at University College, London. He obtained a BSc in applied statistics (second-class honours, 1920), an MSc in 1922, and a DSc in 1926. He held board for scientific and industrial research and Crewdson Berington studentships and an 1851 Exhibition from 1920 to 1926. In 1932 he won the Weldon memorial prize. He married, on 31 July 1922, Geraldine Wynne (*b.* 1886/7), who died in childbirth in 1923. The child also died. In 1928 he married Mary Evelyn, daughter of Ernest Hitchcock, caterer; they had one son and one daughter.

Morant was on the staff of the department of applied statistics at University College and was a pupil of Karl Pearson. By the late 1920s Morant was the acknowledged leader of the biometric school of physical anthropologists. Much of his early work appeared in *Biometrika* (of which he was assistant editor). His first paper, 'On random occurrence in space and time when followed by a closed interval' (1921), was soon followed by a number of important contributions to physical anthropology setting new and critical standards. These included 'Tibetan skulls' (1923) and 'Racial history of Egypt' (1925). In 1926 he showed that the so-called Iberian inhabitants of Neolithic Britain were of Nordic not Mediterranean origin. Subsequent work confirmed Morant's views, which were unconventional at that time. Four important studies on Palaeolithic man appeared in the *Annals of Eugenics* (1926–30). In 1935, in collaboration with Pearson, he produced a lavishly illustrated study of the 'Wilkinson' head of Oliver Cromwell. This showed the relic to be the protector's head and shed new light on his death and the disposal of the remains. This work led to the advances in forensic medicine first used in the trial of Dr Buck Ruxton (charged with murdering his wife, Isabella, and their children's nanny).

When Hitler came to power Morant was disturbed by the manner in which his discipline was being perverted for political ends. In an article 'An attempt to estimate the variability of various populations' (1939) in *Zeitschrift für Rassenkunde* he destroyed the foundation of Nazi theories of pure race. This was followed in 1939 by *The Races of Central Europe* (with a preface by J. B. S. Haldane) in which, by using blood groups and anthropometry, he showed that the Germans were racially the most heterogeneous group in Europe. In 1939 the *Biometrika* Trust published a bibliography of Karl Pearson's work prepared by Morant from material given him by Pearson.

At the outbreak of the Second World War Morant joined the Ministry of Information. But by 1942 he was applying his anthropometric methods to help the Medical Research Council's army personnel research committee. The first report (1943), written jointly with Austin Bradford Hill, analysed the heights and weights of 1600 men in the Royal Armoured Corps; later (1945) a more detailed study of 2000 tank personnel gave the information needed to design tanks with the optimal space for the crew. From 1944 Morant worked at the physiological laboratory (the RAF Institute of Aviation Medicine) at the Royal Aircraft Establishment, Farnborough. He prepared many reports for the flying personnel research committee. These covered four main topics: surveys of heights and weights of men and women recruits to the RAF with comparisons with earlier similar surveys; body measurements of aircrew to provide the information needed for improving the fit of services clothing, and for the detailed design of aircraft cockpits, seats, and their controls; statistical analyses of research projects at the establishment, such as the effects of fluoride on dental caries; and experimental studies of decompression and airsickness. Morant worked closely with those making the decisions—the cockpit design teams and the cutters preparing the patterns for the clothing. In this way his work had an important and immediate application.

At the end of the war Morant returned briefly to academic work at University College. This was a period of great disappointment for him. He had expected that the understandings he had had with those in authority before the war would secure him a senior appointment in the department of anthropology or anatomy. But the senior staff had died, others had moved away, and the appointment he had expected had been filled. He therefore returned to the Institute of Aviation Medicine, retiring in 1959.

Morant had an old-world courtesy, a rather diffident manner, and a charming smile which was immediately attractive to the many much younger laboratory members with whom he worked so successfully. He was tall and handsome, with striking dark eyebrows. His modesty prevented many of his colleagues in the services realizing his eminence as an anthropologist. It also perhaps prevented him pushing earlier and harder to ensure his return to academic work at the end of the war. His kindness to many by helping to prepare publications often went unrecorded at his request. He was an eminent anthropologist who made a unique contribution to the needs of the services in the later part of his career. He was appointed OBE in 1952. He died at his home, Southbrook, Brook Street, Bishop's Waltham, Hampshire, on 3 July 1964. He was survived by his second wife.

JOHN C. GILSON, *rev.*

Sources *The Times* (9 June 1964) · *The Times* (13 June 1964) · J. F. Box, *R. A. Fisher: the life of a scientist* (1978) · private information (1981) · personal knowledge (1981) · *CGPLA Eng. & Wales* (1964) · m. cert. [G. M. Morant and Geraldine Wynne]
Wealth at death £6073: probate, 24 Nov 1964, *CGPLA Eng. & Wales*

Morant, Harry Harbord [*called* the Breaker] (1864?–1902), army officer, probably concealed his origins. He seems to have been Edwin Henry Murrant, born on 9 December 1864 at the union workhouse, Bridgwater, Somerset, the posthumous son of Edwin Murrant, master of the workhouse, and his wife, Catherine Riely (or O'Reilly). In 1883 he emigrated to Queensland and within a year married Daisy May O'Dwyer at Charters Towers on 13 March 1884.

Harry Harbord Morant [the Breaker] (1864?–1902), by Gresham Studios, 1900

They soon separated, possibly because of his record of debt and larceny. As Daisy *Bates she became a notable researcher of Aboriginal customs.

Having adopted the surname Morant he led a roving life under that guise in several Australian states. Through his daring horsemanship and reckless feats, which gave rise to his nickname, the Breaker, he became a minor celebrity, but was also known as a brawler and hard drinker. Apparently self-educated he enjoyed good literature and music, and as the Breaker from 1891 contributed rollicking ballads to the Sydney *Bulletin* and other newspapers. In the 1890s he was a crony of A. B. 'Banjo' Paterson, whose sardonic humour he shared. While Morant's verses were often redolent of a bushman's rough life in the outback, he projected himself successfully as a gentleman, the son of Admiral Sir George Digby Morant, a relationship which the admiral and his family later strongly denied.

Responding to an appeal for volunteers to serve in the Second South African War which began in October 1899, Morant enlisted for short service in the 2nd South Australian mounted rifles. He was stocky and, according to an official description in 1902, had grey eyes, a prominent nose, and was 5 feet 6¾ inches in height. An accomplished rider, he was promoted lance-corporal before the contingent sailed for Cape Town in January 1900. Australian horsemen fought on the central front under Major-General J. French and later in the drive through both Boer republics that led to the relief of Kimberley and the occupation of Pretoria on 5 June 1900. Morant was one of French's dispatch riders. At Pretoria he was detailed for a

further short spell as dispatch rider to Bennet Burleigh, war correspondent of the *Daily Telegraph*, but was discharged as time-expired on 31 July 1900. It was probably at Pretoria that he met Lieutenant P. F. Hunt, who was temporarily in the military administration there. Hunt, a former officer in the 13th hussars, had served with French's scouts in the recent British advance. Hunt and Morant returned to England, where Morant seems to have been accepted readily in county and hunting circles. With the prolongation of the Second South African War into a guerrilla struggle, there was a fresh appeal for volunteers, especially riders and marksmen.

The imperial authorities raised several formations of irregulars in South Africa to counter Boer guerrillas, one of which was the bushveldt carbineers (BVC), which was established in February 1901. It attracted veterans, including a strong Australian constituent, and was to serve in a partially occupied region of the northern Transvaal. Morant, described as a 'gentleman', was commissioned lieutenant in the BVC on 1 April 1901 and his friend Hunt transferred to it as a captain soon after. Other commissioned officers closely linked to Morant's future were the Australians Veterinary-Lieutenant P. Handcock and Lieutenant G. Witton.

The BVC was operating in dispersed detachments by May 1901. To the south-east of its base at Pietersburg, Morant led B squadron efficiently and energetically. However A squadron, at remote Fort Edward to the north-east, had a weak commander, and because of indiscipline and rumours of serious offences Hunt replaced him. Morant's squadron moved to Fort Edward too, and the reorganized force, aided by a resourceful but ruthless intelligence officer, Captain Taylor from Rhodesia, sought out the enemy. In a raid on a Boer farm stronghold near Duiwelskloof on 6 August 1901 Hunt—Morant's 'best mate'—was killed, as was Sergeant F. Eland, English by birth, who had been Morant's trusted subordinate in B squadron. Morant was already ill-disposed towards Boer guerrillas, having lost other friends when trains were attacked by them. He was incensed when he learned that Hunt's body had been stripped and mutilated, as he believed by the Boers, although the mutilation might have been performed by local medicine men.

Morant pursued the fleeing Boers, and when one of them, Visser, was taken wounded he was shot on 11 August without having had a proper trial. Morant, now commanding at Fort Edward, was vengeful. Egged on by Captain Taylor he gave short shrift to Boers who surrendered to the BVC, asserting that Lord Kitchener had given verbal orders that Boer prisoners should not be taken. On 23 August eight prisoners were shot, but a passing missionary, the Revd C. A. D. Heese of the Berlin Missionary Society, had spoken to them and was a potentially hostile witness. At Morant's behest, Handcock, a compliant accessory, followed the missionary, whose body was found later. On 7 September three more surrendered Boers were shot. Subsequently Morant undertook a raid into enemy territory which brought in a Boer field-cornet and nine men who, however, were not executed.

By 22 October 1901 Morant, Handcock, and several other BVC officers had been arrested. Among contributing factors the murder of Revd Heese was crucial. The missionary was a British subject born in the Cape Colony, but as he had close German connections the German consul had voiced concern. Also important was a detailed list of allegations of excesses signed by fifteen troopers of the BVC at Pietersburg on 4 October.

A properly constituted court of inquiry was convened at Pietersburg on 16 October. Many depositions were recorded and witnesses mustered. Kitchener's chief legal specialist considered the court's recommendations, and consequently Morant, Handcock, and others appeared before a series of courts martial commencing on 17 January 1902. The proceedings were conducted in accordance with British military law. At short notice an Australian officer, Major J. F. Thomas, was appointed to defend the accused. After lengthy sessions involving more than forty witnesses, Morant was sentenced to death for his part in the shootings of Visser and the groups of eight and three Boers. Handcock and he were acquitted on the charge of Heese's murder. A spokesman of Kitchener denied that any secret orders not to take prisoners had been given. The court's findings were coupled with recommendations for mercy based on Morant's good service, ignorance of military law, and the provocation of the 'maltreatment' of Hunt's body. However, no account was taken of the accused's part in defending Pietersburg against a surprise Boer attack on 23 January 1902. Kitchener confirmed death sentences on Morant and Handcock but commuted that on a third officer, Witton, to life imprisonment. Morant and Handcock were executed by a firing squad at the prison, Pretoria, on 27 February. They were buried in a common grave in the old cemetery there on the same day. Just before execution, Morant wrote some characteristic verses, 'Butchered to Make a Dutchman's Holiday':

And if you'd earn a D.S.O.—
Why every British sinner
Should know the proper way to go
Is: 'Ask the Boer to dinner'

Let's toss a bumper down our throat
Before we pass to Heaven,
And toast: 'The trim-set petticoat
We leave behind in Devon.'
(Semmler, 123)

The executions gave rise to a minor furore in Australia. Witton's account of the trials, published in 1907, reinforced a burgeoning legend in which Morant was portrayed as a victim of a brutal Kitchener and a scapegoat of British imperialism. A considerable literature—some romantic, some fictional—as well as a notable film (*Breaker Morant*, with Edward Woodward), a play, and radio productions, were afterwards devoted to the supposed BVC martyrs. Speculation about Morant's origins entered into the myth-making. His character was complex, and while physical prowess and swagger won him many admirers, it was ultimately dishonesty and gross abuse of authority that were his undoing. On the eve of his execution he wrote to a Pretoria clergyman: 'We shot the Boers who killed and mutilated our friend (The best mate I had on Earth)'. ARTHUR DAVEY

Sources A. Davey, ed., *Breaker Morant and the bushveldt carbineers* (1987) [incl. comprehensive bibliography] · M. Carnegie and F. Shields, *In search of Breaker Morant* (1979) [incl. substantial bibliography] · G. Witton, *Scapegoats of the empire* (1982) · K. Denton, *Closed file* (1983) · C. S. Jarvis, *Half a life* (1943) · F. Renar, *Bushman and buccaneer: Harry Morant, his ventures and verses* (1902) · R. L. Wallace, *The Australians at the Boer War* (1976) · J. M. Gordon, *The chronicle of a gay Gordon* (1921) · F. M. Cutlack, *Breaker Morant: a horseman who made history* (1962) · W. H. Wilde, J. Hooton, and B. Andrews, *The Oxford companion to Australian literature* (1985) · C. Semmler, *The Banjo of the bush: the work, life and times of A. B. Paterson*, 2nd edn (1974); repr. as *The Banjo of the bush: the life and times of A. B. 'Banjo' Paterson* (1987)

Archives National Library of South Africa, Cape Town | National Archives of South Africa, Pretoria, Transvaal archives depot, colonial secretary, Transvaal, vol. 1092 (BVC outrages) · PRO, letter-book, deputy judge advocate-general, 93/41

Likenesses Gresham Studios, photograph, 1900, Australian War Memorial, Canberra [see illus.] · photograph, repro. in Davey, ed., *Breaker Morant*, frontispiece · photograph, repro. in Witton, *Scapegoats of the empire*, 47 · photographs, repro. in Carnegie and Shields, *In search of Breaker Morant*, facing p. 1, and pp. 9, 17, 31, 33, 37, 38, 49, 61 · photographs, repro. in Denton, *Closed file*, 80, 125

Morant, Philip (1700–1770), historian and Church of England clergyman, the third child and second son of Stephen Mouraunt of Jersey and his wife, Mary Filleul, was born at St Saviour's, Jersey, on 6 October 1700. Bilingual from childhood, he was educated at Abingdon grammar school and matriculated from Pembroke College, Oxford, in 1717. He graduated BA in 1721, but took his MA at Cambridge, from Sidney Sussex College, in 1729. He was ordained at St Martin-in-the-Fields in September 1722, and took up a curacy in Essex, at Great Waltham, in the same month. It was the beginning of a long association with the county.

The rector of Waltham was Nicholas Tindal, a fellow of Trinity College, Oxford. Morant visited Waltham in June 1722 and made what was presumably a trial entry in the parish register in his neat and distinctive hand. It seems to have satisfied Tindal, but it was probably Morant's command of French that chiefly recommended him for the curacy. Tindal was then translating a commentary on St Matthew's gospel by two Huguenot divines, and he may already have been planning to translate Paul de Rapin's *Histoire d'Angleterre*, which was published only in 1724. The first part of Tindal's translation appeared in 1725, with an acknowledgement of Morant's assistance. Morant's part was probably considerable, as at that time Tindal made several voyages as a naval chaplain. The work was published in regular instalments until 1731, and Tindal later added a continuation running down to 1727, which he completed in 1745.

Morant's name was now associated with what remained the principal history of England until the completion of David Hume's work in 1761. He also had literary ambitions of his own. In 1724 he dedicated a tract in manuscript, 'Answer to the first part of the discourse of the grounds and reasons of the Christian religion, in a letter to a friend', to the scholarly bishop of London, Edmund Gibson. Gibson thought well of the work and proved a supportive patron.

Morant's first independent published work, a treatise called *The cruelties and persecution of the Romish church displayed, wherein is shown how contrary the persecuting spirit of the church of Rome is to the temper of the Christian religion*, followed in 1728. Its tone is moderate for the time, and its method historical, with some learning in its references to the practices and abuses of papal taxation in the middle ages. The young curate could claim some attention as a divine and as a historian.

Preferment came quite soon, with nomination by Queen Caroline to the English chaplaincy at Amsterdam in 1732. In the meantime Tindal had undertaken a new project, which eventually played a large part in Morant's life. Early in 1732 Tindal acquired, in a transaction witnessed by Morant, the materials which William Holman had compiled to write a history of Essex. The collection was founded on a set of transcripts of public records compiled by Thomas Jekyll (1570–1652). It had been through several hands over the intervening century, and when Holman died in 1730 he left some 400 well-charged parish files. In the event Tindal published only two instalments of a history of Hinckford hundred before his attention was distracted by a dispute over his uncle's estate and, after leaving Essex in 1738, he never returned to the task. In 1739 he sold Holman's papers to Nathaniel Salmon, who published accounts of fourteen of the nineteen hundreds of Essex before his death in 1742.

Morant stayed only two years in Amsterdam. In that time he acquired the Essex rectory of Shellow Bowells, which he resigned on his return to England in 1734 to take up the rectory of Broomfield together with that of Chignall Smealy, where he kept the records in his own hand during his incumbency. For the rest of his career he held two livings simultaneously, and seems always to have given attention to both. His principal preferment came in 1738, with the rectory of St Mary-at-the-Walls, Colchester, in Bishop Gibson's gift. He then resigned Broomfield, and in 1743 resigned Chignall Smealy to take the rectory of Wickham Bishops. He held Wickham until 1745, when Gibson gave him the rectory of Aldham. On 6 February 1738 at his church of St Mary-at-the-Walls, Colchester, he married Anne (d. 1767), daughter of Solomon Stebbing of The Brook, Great Tey, Essex. They had one child, a daughter, Anna Maria.

In the intervening years Morant contributed an appendix to *Caesarea, or, An Account of Jersey* (1734) by Philip Falle, revised Thomas Hearne's *Ductor historicus*, and wrote an account of the Armada campaign to accompany a set of engravings of tapestries in the Palace of Westminster, published by John Pyne in 1739. Between 1740 and 1767 he also contributed 250 lives to the *Biographia Britannica*, signed with a C, for Colchester or *Colcestrensis*. Shortly after his arrival at St Mary's, however, he found a rewarding new theme in the history of the town itself, and by 1745 was ready to discuss his work with Henry Whitridge, the publisher of the *Biographia Britannica*.

The History and Antiquities of Colchester appeared in 1748, the type set by William Bowyer, the leading antiquarian printer of the day. The edition was a small one, of only 200 copies, and its achievement was a matter of anxiety and some disappointment to Morant, whose business sense was not strong. He had probably also excited some local animosity. He had found the books bequeathed to the town by Archbishop Samuel Harsnett neglected, and listed them, with some animadversions. The corporation had been disabled by an action in king's bench in 1742, and its charters were in abeyance. Morant regretted the want of civic spirit, and argued that the charters should be renewed. However, his history was a substantial and meritorious work, even a model of its kind, and though recognition came slowly it included election to the Society of Antiquaries in 1755. By then he had entered into correspondence with Andrew Ducarel, to whom he offered much valuable assistance in his antiquarian researches. Morant also enjoyed the friendship of Charles Gray, the Colchester attorney, antiquary, and MP, who strongly supported and encouraged him, and rehoused the Harsnett Library for the common good. By the time the history was satirized by John Clubbe, in *The History and Antiquities of the Ancient Village of Wheatfield* (1758)—which was fame of a kind, though irksome to its victim—Morant was securely established in Colchester, and had begun work on a history of the county.

When Salmon died, his manuscripts passed first to Anthony Allen and then to John Booth FSA, of Barnard's Inn, who passed them on to Morant in 1750 or 1751. Morant may have thought at first only of completing Salmon's history, but he consulted Bowyer, who advised him robustly to begin again. Whether or not that confirmed his own inclinations, he followed the advice, and began a work that occupied him for more than fifteen years.

The task was not a simple one. The material was abundant, but Morant's prime object was to do what none of his predecessors had done, and complete the work. He naturally wished to put his own impress on it, and he had the example of the history of Colchester before him, but his duty was to publish. In the process he made some painful decisions. He omitted some of Holman's material, and he postponed inscriptions and epitaphs, to which his fellow antiquaries attached great importance, to a separate study, which never appeared. On the other hand he incorporated new material, of which the survey of Moulsham in 1591, since lost, is a striking example. He consequently thought defensively, and was less generous to his predecessors than he might have been. He did not refer at all to Tindal's brief essays, and he referred critically to Salmon's incomplete history. In a sense he was justified, for Salmon, though engaging and lively-minded, was sanguine and fanciful, while Tindal had accomplished very little. Nevertheless the absence of Tindal's name from the list of subscribers is a reminder of a lost friendship.

The History and Antiquities of the County of Essex was published in instalments from 1763 to 1768. The text of volume 2 was completed in 1766, and volume 1, prefaced by a revised edition of the history of Colchester, noting the renewal of the charters in 1763, was celebrated by a new title-page in 1768. The whole work was dedicated to Thomas Barrett-Lennard, third Lord Dacre, as patron and an energetic promoter of the work.

The *History of Essex* is characterized by learning, common sense, and consistency. Morant's great accomplishment was to devise a plan and fulfil it. He could not sustain the scale of the history of Colchester, but he set a pattern against which other county histories could be measured. Some contemporaries and later readers regretted the absence of epitaphs and of heraldic notes, but the *History's* manorial descents were exemplary for their time, and even J. H. Round subsequently built on rather than superseded Morant's work.

His wife's sudden death in 1767 cast a shadow over Morant's pleasure in completing the *History*. In 1765 their daughter had married Thomas *Astle FRS, a lawyer and palaeographer, and Morant resolved to spend some time with the Astles at Battersea Rise. There was a proposal then to publish the earliest records of parliament, and Astle, who had been consulted on the project, suggested that his father-in-law should undertake the work. Between 1768 and his death Morant transcribed and edited, with the aid of John Topham FSA, and to a high standard of accuracy, the parliament rolls from the reign of Edward I to 1436. His copy provided the text of the first four of the six folio volumes which Astle and Topham published in 1783.

After a visit to Aldham in the autumn of 1770 Morant took a chill on the river while returning at night from the Tower to Battersea, and died on 25 November 1770 at Battersea Rise. He was buried at Aldham, beside his wife in the chancel of St Margaret's Church.

Morant's palaeographical and critical skills were notably well suited to his task with the parliament rolls, and his edition crowned his life's work. His contribution to English historical scholarship was a substantial one, in terms both of method and of technical accomplishment, and his two principal works, of which the county history subsumed his pioneering history of Colchester, are a worthy memorial to him.   G. H. MARTIN

Sources G. H. Martin, introduction, in P. Morant, *The history and antiquities of the county of Essex*, 1 (1978), v–xviii · *DNB* · Nichols, *Lit. anecdotes* · N. Briggs, 'Lord Dacre and Morant's *History of Essex*', *Essex Journal*, 2 (1967), 6–12 · Foster, *Alum. Oxon.*
Archives BL, corresp. relating to his proposed history of Essex, Add. MS 34650 · BL, notes and MSS · Bodl. Oxf., notes · Essex RO, Chelmsford, notes and MSS · S. Antiquaries, Lond., notes | BL, corresp. with antiquaries and others, Add. MSS 37216–37222 · BL, letters to Thomas Birch, Add. MS 4314, fols. 192–213 · BL, corresp. with Andrew Ducarel, Add. MSS 37217–37219 · BL, Stowe MSS · Trinity College, Oxford, Ford MSS
Likenesses T. Head, oils (after pencil sketch), Colchester town hall · pencil sketch, Essex RO, Hills–Astle MSS

Morant, Sir Robert Laurie (1863–1920), civil servant, was born at Well Walk, Hampstead, London, on 7 April 1863, the only son of Robert Morant (*d.* 1873), designer of high-class furniture and silk fabrics, of Hampstead, and his wife, Helen, daughter of the Revd Henry Lea Berry, a former headmaster of Mill Hill School. Though his father

Sir Robert Laurie Morant (1863–1920), by George Charles Beresford

died when Morant was ten his family managed to find the money to send him to be educated at Winchester College. When he went up to New College, Oxford, his financial difficulties compelled him to undertake paid tutoring work to enable him to complete his studies. He obtained a third class in classical moderations in 1882, but a first class in theology in 1885. As he decided not to go into the church but into education, the latter qualification was less useful to him than otherwise it would have been, and the undistinguished earlier performance initially excluded him from all but preparatory school teaching. He soon obtained a post at that level at Temple Grove School, East Sheen, Surrey, which he relinquished after a year, departing for Siam in 1886, and soon becoming tutor to the crown prince.

Morant involved himself in the reconstruction of the Siamese educational system, which led him to be called the Big Teacher. He emphasized European, and especially English, educational values, concentrating on the needs of the ruling élite and of secondary education and teacher training. He also engaged in political activity in Siam, believing himself and his country to have a civilizing mission there, and he came to criticize the British legation for not being as active as he wanted in frustrating French imperial designs in Siam. He was seen by some as acting as if he was 'the Uncrowned King of Siam', and his political prominence eventually rendered his position untenable. In 1894 he returned to England where, though he pursued a career in the civil service, he was also to attract public controversy. Florence Nightingale's assessment of Morant as being 'a good genius' was how many came to see him. This was true for Beatrice Webb, who none the less believed him to be 'a strange mortal, not altogether sane' (*Diaries*, 98).

Mrs Webb wrote:

We have known and liked Morant since he appeared as a student in the early days of the London School of Economics—an abnormally tall and loosely knit figure, handsome in feature, shy in manner, and enigmatical in expression. At that time he was a little over thirty and at a loose end, having failed to keep an official position at the court of Siam. (*Diaries*, 97)

On his return Morant took up both residence and a staff appointment at the Toynbee Hall settlement in the East End of London. During a period of poor health he was nursed by Helen Mary Cracknell, daughter of Edwin Cracknell of Wetheringsett Grange, Suffolk; they married in 1896 and had a son and a daughter.

Board of Education From his base at Toynbee Hall, Morant secured an appointment as assistant director of special inquiries and reports in August 1895 in the recently created office of special inquiries and reports at the education department of the privy council. Though the education department did not anyway recruit its equivalent of first-division officials by means of the conventional civil service open competition, the office of special inquiries and reports was even more unusual in that specialized knowledge of foreign systems of education was a requirement. Too old to begin a civil service career otherwise, Morant was fortunate not only that such a tailor-made opportunity occurred, but also that the recently appointed director, Michael Sadler, was prepared to recruit an obviously gifted man, and thus a potential rival, as his deputy. It was a decision that Sadler lived to regret.

The office of special inquiries and reports was later described by Sadler as having been founded on the doctrine that it would 'tell the truth, disclose the strong and weak points of great educational policies, and behave with self restraint but unshakeable honesty in presenting matter to the Department of Education and in its published volumes of reports' (Sadler, 194–5). This definition overstated the independence of the office, given that Sadler had concurred when in 1895 the vice-president of the committee of council on education, Sir John Gorst, had asked that research should be concentrated on areas specified by the Department of Education. Sadler later said that 'Morant had no use for scientific impartiality' (ibid., 195); but, when assistant director of the office, Morant had produced important research studies of the French and Swiss educational systems in 1897 and 1898 respectively.

Morant's involvement with the abortive Education Bill of 1896 seemed to renew his taste for politics, and brought him to the attention of Gorst, whose private secretary he became in November 1899. From this position Morant rose to become the acting permanent secretary of the Board of Education almost exactly three years later and, in April 1903, the substantive holder of that post. 'Morant was a very able, unscrupulous *arriviste* with a lot of educational enthusiasm, great energy, and a tongue that could be honeyed or rasping', Sadler wrote in the 1940s, adding: 'An Italian renaissance type I used to think then, but now I see in him an early arrival of the Fascist mentality' (Sadler, 195). This last observation seems excessive, born of the self-pitying bitterness of bureaucratic politics. It may be, as Sadler observed, that 'ambition, pecuniary and personal' did come to characterize Morant (ibid., 194), but, far

from ruthlessly shouldering aside a much senior colleague, Morant was actually only two years younger than Sadler, and to become a permanent secretary as he did at the age of forty was not without precedent. Indeed, it could even be said to be unremarkable in circumstances in which the existing holder of the post, Sir George Kekewich, was sixty-two years old and openly opposed to government policy. As for Morant then ensuring that Sadler had no alternative to leaving the civil service in 1903, the issue between them, and between Sadler and the president of the board, Lord Londonderry, was whether Sadler could conduct independent educational research with what amounted to academic freedom. When denied this, Sadler, apparently forgetting the arrangement with Gorst eight years before, elected to resign. The main documents in this controversy were published in 1903 in a blue book entitled *Papers Relating to the Resignation of the Director of Special Inquiries and Reports*.

The Education Act of 1902 was politically primarily the work of A. J. Balfour, who became the Conservative prime minister during its passage, although many of the ideas behind the legislation were those of the eventually discarded Gorst. Morant was very important in the role of adviser, ever eager to apply the lessons of the Swiss model to the education system of England and Wales, and in recognition of his work he was made CB in 1902. The Liberal opposition to the legislation of 1902 derived most of its emotional force from the prospect that nonconformists would have to pay local rates which could be used to subsidize Anglican schools. The religious controversy tended to obscure the fact that the act importantly widened the opportunities for secondary education in England and Wales, as well as rationalizing the provision for elementary education. The act also changed the local educational administrative arrangements when it abolished the separate school boards which had been established by the Forster Education Act of 1870, making the counties and county boroughs into the local education authorities. The 1902 legislation was extended to cover London a year later, and opposition to the act elsewhere was eventually overridden.

Morant reorganized the Board of Education into an effective central instrument for the implementation of the act, which was characterized by a balance of power between the centre and the local authorities. The board made its presence felt with a series of regulations issued in bold type in publications with differently coloured covers for each type of institution. Thus, in 1903 Morant and his principal officials issued a green-covered document called *Regulations for the Instruction and Training of Pupil-Teachers*. In 1904 *Elementary School Code* was issued under a dark blue cover, and *Regulations for Secondary Education* was also issued, this time under a pale blue cover. *Regulations for Training Colleges*, issued under a plain white cover, and *Regulations for Evening Schools and Technical Institutes*, under a yellow cover, soon followed. Morant's official biographer was much impressed by the array of colours involved, but what mattered was that for the first time educational objectives were clearly set down. Morant appreciated that there was not much point either in making more formal provision for education or in issuing sets of regulations unless what was being done was evaluated. He therefore gave prominence to rationalizing the arrangements relating to his majesty's inspectorate for schools. Both at the time and subsequently *Regulations for Secondary Education* attracted most controversy for, among other things, assisting arrangements to be shaped by Treasury concerns about financial commitments, and the emphasis on general rather than vocational education proved to be a source of criticism. None the less, overall provision for secondary education increased as a result of the reforms with which Morant was associated.

The advent of a Liberal government in 1905 seemed to threaten the recently established educational system, but it survived. For nearly six years so did the politically contentious Morant, with his being made KCB in 1907 reflecting the respect he had earned from the Liberals for his vigorous style of administration. This was evident in the implementation of the Provision of Meals Act of 1906, which permissive measure led to the introduction of school meals for underprivileged children. The Education (Administration Provisions) Act of 1907 marked the beginning of a system of medical inspection and treatment of schoolchildren. Morant swiftly appointed Dr George Newman as chief medical officer of the board at the head of its medical department. In 1911 Morant established a university department within the board to administer the various grants that the board made for the training of teachers and for advanced science. This was the forerunner of the university grants committee. Morant was also a member of the Haldane royal commission on London University. These links with the universities proved helpful in establishing the broadly based Teachers' Registration Council. Such was Morant's commitment to the work of the Board of Education that he had refused when Lloyd George had offered him the substantially better-paid post of chairman of the Development Commission in 1909; but, two years later, the political controversy surrounding the memorandum circulated by E. G. A. Holmes, chief inspector of elementary schools, criticizing the calibre of local authority inspectors, led to Morant's position at the board being undermined. The greatest of the many achievements of the Morant years at the Board of Education was the expansion of secondary education which, by 1911, had been made available to 60 per cent of former elementary school pupils, at least in part because of the free places regulations of 1907 which Morant had put in place.

National insurance and the Ministry of Health In November 1911 Morant resigned from the Board of Education and accepted an offer from the chancellor of the exchequer to become chairman of the National Insurance Commission for England. He had told Lloyd George that the only reason that he had taken on what the chancellor himself had described as the 'gigantic task' of implementing the National Insurance Act was the opportunity it gave him of working towards the unification of the nation's health services, which had been his ambition ever since Newman and he had issued their first circular on the medical inspection of schoolchildren. The most immediate task was to ensure that the administrative arrangements were in place to ensure that by the set date of 15 July 1912 there was machinery to collect the contributions of 12 million people and their employers. At first Lloyd George supported Treasury objections to more than minimal staffing of the commission, but Morant told him forcefully that the legislation would fail unless he was given a free hand to recruit the people he needed, and the chancellor gave way. Government departments were more eager to get rid of their troublemakers than their most gifted administrators; but, however random the selection, this trawl for talent was the first time that the first division of the civil service had been treated as other than a collection of departmental élites, and among the men who came to work with Morant were future stars of the higher civil service of the order of Warren Fisher, John Anderson, and Arthur Salter. The deadline for establishing the contributions machinery was met on time, but that still left another deadline, that which loomed on 15 January 1913, the date set for the introduction of the general practitioner service. The opposition of the medical profession was overcome, and this deadline was also met. Later in 1913 Morant made use of a provision in the act for the establishment of a fund for promoting medical research and the Medical Research Committee was established, which proved to be the forerunner of the Medical Research Council. Morant was the effective author of the National Insurance Act of 1913, which eliminated various flaws experienced in the working of the earlier legislation.

The coming of the First World War witnessed Morant being generous in releasing staff to other departments, but he was himself in little demand for other work, although he was an important member of the Haldane committee on the machinery of government of 1917–18. When the Ministry of Health was created in June 1919, from a merger of the Local Government Board and the Insurance Commission, Morant became its first permanent secretary, having earlier acted as additional secretary to the former department. Morant set to work with what seemed to be his usual vigour, and soon introduced the reform that led to the registration of nurses and the establishment of the General Nursing Council, and began to devote himself to the subject of housing. However, years of overwork had undermined Morant's constitution, and an attack of pneumonia caused his death at his home, 17 Thurloe Square, London, on 13 March 1920. His wife survived him.

In 1917 Beatrice Webb observed:

> Morant is the one man of genius in the Civil Service, but he excites violent dislike in some men and much suspicion in many men. He is public spirited in his ends but devious in his methods … He certainly does not want social democracy— he is an aristocrat by instinct and conviction … but in spite of his malicious tongue and somewhat tortuous ways, he has

done more to improve English administration than any other man. (*Diaries*, 98)

The passage of time has done nothing to undermine this assessment. GEOFFREY K. FRY

Sources private information (2004) · G. K. Fry, *Statesmen in disguise: the changing role of the administrative class of the British home civil service, 1853–1966* (1969) · B. M. Allen, *Sir Robert Morant: a great public servant* (1934) · *Papers relating to the resignation of the director of special inquiries and reports* (1903) · N. Daglish, *Education policy making in England and Wales: the crucible years, 1895–1911* (1996) · D. N. Chester, 'Robert Morant and Michael Sadler', *Public Administration*, 28 (1950), 109–6 · *Beatrice Webb's diaries, 1912–1924*, ed. M. I. Cole (1952) · V. Markham, 'Robert Morant: some personal reminiscences', *Public Administration*, 28 (1950), 249–62 · M. Sadleir, *Michael Ernest Sadler … 1861–1943: a memoir by his son* (1949) · G. Newman, *The building of a nation's health* (1939) · E. J. R. Eaglesham, *From school board to local authority* (1956) · L. Grier, *Achievement in education: the work of Michael Ernest Sadler, 1885–1935* (1952) · D. K. Wyatt, *The politics of reform in Thailand: education in the reign of King Chulalongkorn* (1969) · N. Brailey, *Two views of Siam on the eve of the Chakri reformation* (1969) · R. Lowe, 'Robert Morant and the secondary school regulations of 1904', *Journal of Educational Administration and History*, 16 (Jan 1984), 37–46 · R. Lowe, 'Personalities and policy: Sadler, Morant and the structure of education in England', *In history and in education: essays presented to Peter Gordon*, ed. R. Aldrich (1996), 98–115 · G. Sutherland, 'Administrators in education after 1870: patronage, professionalism and expertise', *Studies in the growth of nineteenth-century government*, ed. G. Sutherland (1972) · *CGPLA Eng. & Wales* (1920)
Archives BL, corresp. with Arthur James Balfour, Add. MS 49787 · BL, letters to Albert Mansbridge, Add. MSS 65196, 65253 · BLPES, corresp. with Violet Markham · Bodl. Oxf., corresp. with Viscount Addison · Bodl. Oxf., letters to Francis Marvin and Edith Marvin; letters to Sir Michael Sadler and MSS relating to him · HLRO, letters to David Lloyd George · King's AC Cam., letters to Oscar Browning · U. Newcastle, corresp. with Walter Runciman
Likenesses G. C. Beresford, photograph, NPG [*see illus.*] · photograph, NPG
Wealth at death £14,458 14s. 4d.: probate, 20 April 1920, *CGPLA Eng. & Wales*

Moray. For this title name *see* Randolph, Thomas, first earl of Moray (*d.* 1332); Randolph, Thomas, second earl of Moray (*d.* 1332) [*see under* Randolph, Thomas, first earl of Moray (*d.* 1332)]; Randolph, John, third earl of Moray (*d.* 1346); Dunbar, Patrick, eighth earl of Dunbar or of March, and earl of Moray (1285–1369). *See also* Dunbar family, earls of Moray (*per. c.*1370–1430) [Dunbar, John, first earl of Moray (*d.* 1391/2); Dunbar, Thomas, second earl of Moray (*d.* in or before 1422); Dunbar, Thomas, third earl of Moray (*d.* in or after 1425); Dunbar, James, fourth earl of Moray (*d.* 1430)]. *See also* Crichton, James, of that ilk, earl of Moray and second Lord Crichton (*d.* 1454) [*see under* Crichton, William, of that ilk, first Lord Crichton (*d.* 1453)]; Stewart, James, earl of Moray (1500–1544/5); Stewart, James, first earl of Moray (1531/2–1570); Stewart, James, second earl of Moray (1565/6–1592); Stewart, Alexander, fifth earl of Moray (*bap.* 1634, *d.* 1701).

Moray, Gilbert of. *See* Gilbert of Moray (*d.* 1243/1245).

Moray, Sir Robert (1608/9?–1673), army officer and politician, was said to be aged fifty in March 1659; he was the eldest son of Sir Mungo Moray of Craigie, Perthshire, and his wife, a daughter of George Halkett of Pitfirran, Fife. Tradition asserts that he was educated first at the University of St Andrews (where a man of his name matriculated in 1627, though that would of course make him a relatively late arrival), and then in France; references within his own subsequent correspondence, however, make his education at St Andrews unlikely. Near contemporary sources provide fleeting glimpses—often contradictory—of his early career. There is general agreement that by the mid-1630s he was in the French military service as a member of a Scottish regiment, probably the one raised in 1633 by Sir John Hepburn. There is also a consensus that he had developed, though in unknown circumstances, an acquaintance with Cardinal Richelieu, then still the effective leader of Louis XIII's government. In 1639, however, as a well-connected presbyterian of considerable military experience and with strong interests in mathematics, science, and engineering, he returned to Britain to take up the post of general of the ordnance in Scotland.

It has been suggested that during this period Moray acted as Richelieu's agent with the covenanter leadership. The covert purpose of his mission, it is supposed, would have been to stimulate further Scottish resistance to Charles I, the better to nudge the latter towards the defensive alliance with France which was the cardinal's principal diplomatic strategy at this stage of the Thirty Years' War. Yet, other than Patrick Gordon's *Short Abridgement*, no contemporary source supports this over-complicated interpretation of Moray's motives for returning to Scotland. More likely, while obviously well disposed towards France and continuing to garner recruits for the French army, he had stepped into Britain's increasingly dangerous public life out of genuine concern and a sense of duty.

Even though in Britain, however, Moray had secured appointment as lieutenant-colonel in a new French regiment, the Scottish guards, in early June 1642. As late as 10 January 1643 he was still in England, receiving a knighthood from Charles I at Oxford. But his commission meant that his departure for France could not be long delayed. Once there he divided his time between strenuous regimental duties and periods of recreation. In view of his lifelong interest in science, his regular visits to Paris at this time might well have brought him into contact with Gassendi, Pascal, and Descartes, whose intellectual circle was then at the height of its activity in the city.

In late spring 1643 Moray was in the field, serving under the duc d'Enghien at the battle of Rocroy (18 May), where troops from the Spanish Netherlands received a crushing defeat; further active service followed in the successful siege of Thionville (10 August). By the end of the campaigning season, however, the French army, under new leadership and advancing incautiously into Germany, was in disarray. On 24 November 1643 an imperial force fell upon the French at Tüttlingen, scattering them and capturing Moray and several other officers of the Scottish guards. Taken to Ingolstadt in Bavaria, he spent eighteen months in captivity (during which, characteristically, he studied Kircherus's work on magnetism) before, on 28

April 1645, being released, a ransom of £16,500 Scots having been paid on his behalf by John Lindsay, earl of Crawford.

Moray's liberation from his German prison was probably connected with a decision by the Scottish parliament to treat with Mazarin's administration for a Scottish–French alliance aimed at supporting Charles I against the English parliament. Certainly this interpretation fits well with what transpired for Moray spent the latter part of 1645 and much of 1646-7 locked in discussions with the king, trying to build the compromise settlement on which any accommodation between Charles and Scottish presbyterianism would have to rest. Yet the king's mixed motives, and the incompatibility of the two positions (which Moray was inevitably forced to downplay in his conversations, leading to predictable later accusations of double-dealing), continually hampered his attempts to conclude the negotiations.

Moray seems to have spent some of his time in London in 1645-6 mingling with those scientists—notably John Wilkins and Robert Boyle—whose meetings prefigured the later Royal Society; his own keen interest in the study of natural phenomena, fuelled by foreign travel and wide reading and perhaps given further stimulus by his enthusiasm for occult knowledge, must have made their conversation and company an agreeable diversion. In May 1646 he was summoned by the king, who had recently put himself into the hands of the Scottish army, to participate in negotiations. Moray advocated acceptance of the king's terms and by Christmas 1646 was to be found plotting unsuccessfully with his cousin Sir William Murray (Moray) to secure the king's escape from Scottish custody—a sign of his growing impatience with the scheme, though Charles's timidity thwarted the plan. The exasperated Scots simply handed Charles over to the English parliament at Newcastle in January 1647.

Simultaneously with this pivotal role in Anglo-Scottish politics Moray had also resumed his professional commitment to the French crown, becoming colonel of the Scottish guards in late 1645. His chief duty, because he was effectively tied to Britain, was to secure further soldiers for the regiment. Mazarin, however, had cause to be disappointed. First the reluctance of the Scots parliament, and then Moray's own apparent lack of zeal in meeting the agreed targets, limited recruitment as late as June 1648 to just a few hundred. This gave rise at the time to accusations of untrustworthiness on Moray's part which, though almost certainly justified to a degree, need to be set against his substantial salary arrears and the French government's failure to meet his expenses. He persisted with this task through 1649 and into 1650, the French still requiring men, despite the peace of Westphalia, because of the continuing war with Spain. But in June 1650, with Charles II in Scotland to attempt a royal restoration, he quit the French service for the last time, disillusioned at his financial mistreatment and determined to take an active part in defending both the Stuart crown and Scotland's interests against the English republic. It was about this time too that Moray married Sophia (1624–1653), daughter of David Lindsay, first Lord Balcarres, with whom he had no children and whose sudden death just three years later he bore with great stoicism.

Moray was appointed justice-clerk in March 1651, and a lord of session in June, but Charles's shattering defeat at Worcester heralded the conquest of Scotland and its incorporation into the Cromwellian state, and he seems to have performed no judicial functions. Thereafter he was an integral part of Scotland's underground royalist movement, along with Balcarres, Dunfermline, Middleton, Halkett, Mackenzie of Tarbat, and others. He was often in Edinburgh during 1652, working to advance the king's cause. This endeavour, which produced the highland rising led by Glencairn, was, however, undermined by constant disagreement over leadership and tactics. Moray was even accused of plotting the assassination of Charles, and, after the ostentatious discovery early in 1654 of a forged letter, supposedly written by his cousin, he found himself briefly under arrest by the insurgents. By the summer Charles had been persuaded of his innocence and he was released. But the Glencairn rising was predictably disastrous. The royalists' military campaign was a damp squib. May 1655 saw the final capitulation of Scotland's budding counter-revolutionaries to Monck and the republic. Moray, stopping only to make detailed observations of tidal conditions and barnacles as he passed through the Western Isles, followed Middleton to Paris, where Balcarres was also in exile.

Moray passed the next five years on the continent, visiting Bruges, where Charles II was resident (about August 1656), and, from July 1657 until September 1659, living at Maastricht, a congenial base from which to keep in touch with old friends (notably Edward Bruce, second earl of Kincardine, his many letters to whom survive) and swap news and opinions. It seems certain that he passed much of his time in reading, further enhancing his proficiency in Dutch, German, and perhaps Italian, and communicating with his impressive network of international correspondents. Chemistry and music were his chief practical occupations during this period, Rosicrucianism and freemasonry (he had become a member of Edinburgh's lodge as early as 1641) among his other fascinations. Yet politics remained of paramount concern. There is, for example, clear evidence that he was engaged in the preparatory work ahead of Charles's return to London. He and Lady Balcarres procured letters from notable French protestant ministers attesting warmly to the king's zeal for the reformed religion: these were to prove important in convincing wavering British opinion of Charles's suitability as a Christian prince.

More critically still, Moray, whose wide political acceptability remained a great asset, was involved in working out a sustainable religious settlement to underpin the Restoration. In June 1660, with the king safely back in Whitehall, it fell to him to solicit from the French provincial synod at Charenton a declaration in favour of episcopacy, a statement which it was felt would greatly assist in endowing Charles II's proposed system of church government with international respectability. The attempt was unsuccessful but Moray's strenuous endeavours did not go unnoticed or unrewarded. By August 1661 he was back in London. Early in the following year a succession of public offices was bestowed in recognition of his services: lord ordinary of the court of session, privy councillor, lord of exchequer and justice-clerk, all of them Scottish positions and granted without regard to the fact that he proposed to remain resident in England. Indeed, his attachment to London was nowhere more fruitful than in his participation in the formal establishment of the Royal Society: he attended the momentous foundation meeting at Gresham College on 28 November 1660, was chosen to preside at many of the early gatherings (his combination of genuine scientific enthusiasm and impeccable connections proving irresistibly attractive), and oversaw its royal incorporation from Charles II in 1662. Moray also strove energetically to procure funds for the infant society, though his greatest pleasure remained in reporting to his colleagues on the practical experiments and astronomical observations he had personally undertaken.

Amid the murky waters of Restoration Scottish politics, with its treacherous cross-currents of favour and mutual jealousy, and its frequent violent tempests, Moray's role as one of Charles II's advisers was marked by consistent and principled moderation. He disapproved of some of the acts of the Scottish parliament passed in 1661 and associated himself with the Lauderdale faction which opposed Middleton's episcopalian majority and favoured a settlement based on moderate presbyterianism. He argued against the Act Rescissory, disliked the imposition of fines, and resisted English interference (notably by Clarendon) in Scottish religious affairs. Only reluctantly did he acquiesce in the king's desire to send Johnston of Wariston to his death. In 1663 he was involved in securing the dismissal of Middleton.

Between 1664 and 1667, with Rothes in the ascendant, Moray's role in the shaping of policy was less conspicuous, and his work with the Royal Society more prominent. But following the ill-judged phase of repression which provoked the Pentland rising of November 1666, Rothes was eclipsed and Moray was dispatched to Scotland as the harbinger of a new policy of accommodation with the presbyterian conventicles. In September 1667 he promoted a general pardon and indemnity to the rebels. In November he took part in the trial of Sir James Turner, one of Rothes's most unscrupulous operatives. In June 1668, alienated by Lauderdale's growing severity (and, it was rumoured, by the latter's unseemly marriage to the daughter of Moray's cousin Sir William, just six weeks after having been widowed), he returned to London. There, through the last four months of 1670, he served as one of the Scottish representatives engaged in the fruitless discussions at Somerset House on the king's scheme for a parliamentary union of Scotland and England.

This was the final significant episode in a life full of intrigue and activity. On 4 July 1673 Moray was suddenly taken ill at his London home. Though cheered by a visit from his friend Aubrey he died that evening. Lamented by many, and with his passing noted by the admiring pens of Burnet and Evelyn, he was buried two days later, at the king's expense, in Poets' Corner in Westminster Abbey.

DAVID ALLAN

Sources A. Robertson, *The life of Sir Robert Moray: soldier, statesman and man of science, 1608–1673* (1922) · D. Airey, 'Correspondence of Sir Robert Moray with Alexander Bruce, second earl of Kincardin, 1657–1660', *Scottish Review*, 5 (1885), 22–43 · D. Stevenson, 'Masonry, symbolism and ethics in the life of Sir Robert Moray FRS', *Proceedings of the Society of Antiquaries of Scotland*, 114 (1984), 405–31
Archives RS, papers | BL, corresp. with duke of Lauderdale, etc., Add. MSS 23114–23135, 35125 · Buckminster Park, Grantham, corresp. with duke of Lauderdale · NL Scot., Kincardine MSS · NL Scot., corresp. with duke of Lauderdale · NL Scot., papers and corresp. with the first and second marquesses of Tweeddale · NRA, priv. coll., letters to earl of Kincardine · RS, letters to earl of Kincardine [copies] · RS, letters to Henry Oldenburg

Morcar, earl of Northumbria (*fl.* 1065–1087), magnate, was the son of *Ælfgar, earl of Mercia (d. 1062?), and Ælfgifu, possibly the daughter of the Northumbrian thegn Morcar (killed in 1015) who had married into the family of Ælfgifu of Northampton, King Cnut's first wife. Earl Morcar was the younger brother of *Eadwine, earl of Mercia (d. 1071) [see under Ælfgar], and had at least two other brothers, Sigehelm and Burgheard (d. 1061?), as well as a sister, *Edith, who married first *Gruffudd ap Llywelyn, king of Gwynedd (d. 1063), and then Harold Godwineson [see Harold II].

According to the Anglo-Saxon Chronicle, texts C, D, and E, Morcar was elected earl of the Northumbrians in preference to Waltheof, son of Earl Siward of Northumbria (d. 1055), in October 1065 during the revolt against the rule of Earl Tostig Godwineson (1055–65). Morcar's election may have been part of a reaction against the political power of the Godwine family during the 1050s and 1060s and there seems to have been ill feeling between the comital houses of Mercia and Wessex, possibly linked to the circumstances of Earl Ælfgar's exiles in 1055 and 1058. Morcar's appointment has also been seen as an attempt to unite the disparate factions within Northumbria by bringing in a figurehead who was committed neither to the house of Bamburgh nor to the Anglo-Scandinavian party at York. The life of King Edward, a pro-Godwine source, suggested that Morcar was elected in order to give the rebellion against Tostig some semblance of authority. However, if Earl Morcar's grandfather was indeed the Northumbrian thegn Morcar, then a family interest in the region may have lain behind the appointment and Morcar may not have been as passive in the rebellion as the sources suggest. Morcar accompanied the Northumbrians on their march south, gathering support from the men of Nottinghamshire, Derbyshire, and Lincolnshire. At Northampton they were met by Earl Harold who acted as an envoy delivering their request for the recognition of Morcar's appointment to Edward the Confessor. Harold conveyed Edward's assent on 28 October 1065, but this did not prevent the northern army from devastating the area around

Northampton. Little is known about Morcar's government of his earldom although it is likely that he left representatives of the Northumbrian political factions in positions of power at Bamburgh and York, with Earl Osulf ruling the area north of the River Tyne and the Anglo-Scandinavian nobility dominating in Yorkshire.

The exiled earl, Tostig, returned to England from Flanders early in 1066 and began to raid the southern and eastern coasts. In concert with his brother Eadwine, Morcar drove Tostig out of Lindsey and into Scotland where he appears to have joined forces with Harald Hardrada, king of Norway. Tostig and the Norwegians launched an attack upon York in the late summer of 1066 and defeated a combined Mercian–Northumbrian army under Eadwine and Morcar at the battle of Gate Fulford, near York, on 20 September 1066. The battle site was a manor recorded in Domesday Book as held by Earl Morcar in 1066. The brothers escaped the slaughter but do not seem to have participated in the victory of King Harold II over Tostig and the Norwegians at Stamford Bridge on 25 September 1066. It was in the aftermath of the defeat at Gate Fulford that Morcar was replaced by the Yorkshire magnate Mærleswein. This may have led to the disaffection of the brothers, as the chronicle of John of Worcester suggests that Eadwine and Morcar deliberately withdrew their depleted forces from Harold's army, which was defeated by Duke William of Normandy at the battle of Hastings. On hearing of the Norman victory Morcar and his brother sent their widowed sister to Chester and then joined Archbishop Ealdred of York and the citizens of London in the election of Edgar Ætheling as king. It appears that just as support was gathering for Edgar's cause, however, Morcar and his brother decided to withdraw their troops and return home. William of Poitiers states that they submitted to the Conqueror at Barking in January 1067, while the Anglo-Saxon Chronicle and the northern source, the *Historia regum Anglorum*, place this submission at Berkhamsted, possibly in December 1066, before William's coronation. During Lent 1067 Morcar and other English nobles were taken to Normandy to participate in the Conqueror's triumphal procession through the duchy. It may be at this point that Morcar effectively lost even a titular claim to the earldom of Northumbria, as William I seems to have appointed as earl the Yorkshire thegn Copsi, who survived for barely five weeks.

Initially Morcar remained a member of William I's entourage and witnessed as earl at least two of his charters in England, but, according to the twelfth-century chronicler Orderic Vitalis, he and his brother rebelled in 1068, apparently soon after Queen Matilda's coronation on 11 May. Using the lost conclusion to William of Poitiers's *Gesta Guillelmi ducis*, Orderic suggested that Eadwine rebelled because William had failed to honour his promise of his daughter's hand in marriage. Morcar joined his brother in revolt and they enlisted aid from Welsh contingents who had earlier supported their father in his attempts to win back his earldom during the Confessor's reign. After William I's construction of a castle at Warwick, Morcar and Eadwine submitted once again and received the king's pardon, although Orderic doubted William's sincerity in the arrangement. It was probably during the period which followed this reconciliation that Morcar witnessed the Conqueror's charter to Leofric, bishop of Exeter.

Orderic Vitalis, whose opinion is consistently biased in favour of the sons of Ælfgar, possibly due to their reputation in his native Shropshire, describes how, in spring 1071, Morcar and Eadwine were forced to flee William's court. Orderic claimed that the king's mind had been poisoned against the brothers by certain evil counsellors and the *Historia regum Anglorum* noted that they feared imprisonment. Earl Eadwine, probably in company with his brother, attempted to reach Scotland but was murdered by his own men *en route*, leaving Morcar to join Siward Barn, Æthelwine, bishop of Durham, Hereward the Wake, and other rebels at Ely. After William I laid siege to the Isle of Ely, Morcar surrendered and was imprisoned, doubtless because the Conqueror feared that he might foment further rebellion. A note in a thirteenth-century manuscript from Burton Abbey suggests that William I seized Morcar's estates and it seems likely that this would have occurred at his imprisonment in 1071. Morcar's gaoler was Roger de Beaumont (*d.* in or after 1090), whose son, Henry, had been appointed castellan of Warwick, and it was perhaps in the interests of the Beaumont family that Morcar should not be allowed to return to his Mercian homeland. Orderic suggests that the fall of the earls was followed by the redistribution of their lands in favour of French landholders. Morcar appears to have remained in captivity until the Conqueror's death in 1087. William I *in articulo mortis* freed Morcar and other English hostages and Morcar was allowed to accompany William Rufus to England. However, at Winchester the new king committed Morcar to a further term of captivity. Nothing more is heard of Morcar and it seems likely that he died in honourable custody.

Morcar held considerable estates throughout the midland and northern counties with the main concentrations in Yorkshire, Lincolnshire, Shropshire, and Cheshire. Orderic Vitalis described the brothers as 'zealous in the service of God, remarkably handsome, nobly connected with kinsfolk whose power and influence were widespread, and well-loved by the people at large' (Ordericus Vitalis, *Eccl. hist.*, 2.217). There is no record of Morcar marrying or fathering children.   WILLIAM M. AIRD

Sources ASC, s.a. 1065, 1066, 1071 [texts C, D, E] · A. Williams and R. W. H. Erskine, eds., *The Cheshire Domesday* (1989) · A. Williams and R. W. H. Erskine, eds., *The Lincolnshire Domesday* (1992) · A. Williams and R. W. H. Erskine, eds., *The Yorkshire Domesday* (1992) · John of Worcester, *Chron.* · Symeon of Durham, *Opera* · P. H. Sawyer, ed., *Charters of Burton Abbey*, Anglo-Saxon Charters, 2 (1979) · A. J. Robertson, ed. and trans., *Anglo-Saxon charters*, 2nd edn (1956) · Ordericus Vitalis, *Eccl. hist.*, vol. 2 · F. Barlow, ed. and trans., *The life of King Edward who rests at Westminster* (1962) · *Willelmi Malmesbiriensis monachi de gestis regum Anglorum*, ed. W. Stubbs, 2 vols., Rolls Series (1887–9) · *Reg. RAN*, vol. 1

Mordaf Hael [Mordaf ap Serwan] (*fl. c.*550–*c.*575), dynast, was the son of Serwan ap Cedig. He was regarded by later Welsh tradition as one of the three *hael* or 'generous men'.

A late account (*c*.1200) claims that he was one of the three northern rulers who came south to Gwynedd to avenge the killing by Rhun Hir ap Maelgwn of Elidir Mwynfawr during a succession struggle on the death of Maelgwn Gwynedd in 547 or 549. His allies are said to have included Rhydderch Hen of Strathclyde. However, this tradition is late and has little to recommend it historically.

DAVID E. THORNTON

Sources P. C. Bartrum, ed., *Early Welsh genealogical tracts* (1966) · R. Bromwich, ed. and trans., *Trioedd ynys Prydein: the Welsh triads*, 2nd edn (1978)

Mordan, Clara Evelyn (1844–1915), suffragist and benefactor, was born on 28 September 1844 at 2 Barkham Terrace, St George's Road, Southwark, London, the elder of the two daughters of Augustus Mordan (*d.* 1901), manufacturer of mechanical pencils, and his wife, Elizabeth Jane, only daughter of James Thomas Hathaway, merchant, of Southwark and his wife, Mary. Clara Mordan's mother died in 1849. Augustus did not remarry, and it seems probable that Clara and her sister, Ada, were entrusted to the care of governesses, receiving the education traditionally given to girls of that period, mainly art, music, literature, and languages. Ada married, in 1870, Edmund George Johnson, and died in 1876 leaving a son and a daughter.

Clara Mordan was an attractive young woman, as three portraits testify. She was at one time engaged to be married but broke off the engagement partly because of the legal disadvantages incurred by married women. Her lifelong interest in women's suffrage and education may well stem from attending, with her father, a lecture in 1866 in which John Stuart Mill advocated women's suffrage. From the 1880s onwards she was a member of various women's societies, including the London Women's Suffrage Society and the Central Society for Women's Suffrage. Not only did she make generous contributions to the funds of these societies but also donated her time and her administrative talents as a member of their executive committees. In 1906 she turned to a more militant form of suffragism when she joined the Women's Social and Political Union (WSPU), supporting the work of Mrs Pankhurst. She was the first subscriber to the WSPU campaign fund, gave practical help at by-elections, and was a welcome and fluent speaker at suffrage meetings. The 1908 WSPU procession was in part financed by Clara Mordan, who was one of the speakers at the Hyde Park rally. Ill health, in the form of tuberculosis, prevented her from further active participation, but much of her private correspondence up to her death was written on notepaper headed 'Votes for Women'. Her father clearly supported her views and apparently had no objection to her forming her own household and administering her own finances during his lifetime. He died in 1901, leaving an estate, of which she was co-executor, of £117,864.

In 1897, after reading a paper by Annie Rogers, 'The position of women at Oxford and Cambridge', in which the need for endowments and scholarships for women was stressed, Clara Mordan, together with her friend Mary Gray Allen (1846–1925), visited the women's colleges in Oxford and decided that St Hugh's was most in need of financial help. Her first act of generosity was to endow a scholarship in her name, to the value of £40 per annum, the only stipulation being that the holder 'shall not perform or witness any experiment or demonstration on a living animal during her tenure of the scholarship'. The first Mordan scholar, Margaret Mary Crick, was elected in 1898, and Clara Mordan made great efforts to get to know all the holders of her scholarship. It may well have been her influence that caused so many members of St Hugh's, especially the Mordan scholars, to take part in the 1908 WSPU rally. She visited St Hugh's regularly and was remembered very vividly by one of the students, Helena Deneke, whose reminiscences, although written fifty years later, describe 'a queer bird-like little lady [who] might have stepped out of one of Dickens' books, her coal-black hair was worn looped and parted, her garments looked home-made and were old fashioned'. Clara became a close personal friend of the principal, Miss Moberly, sharing her vision of a purpose-built new home for the college. Despite her increasing frailty she wrote regularly to St Hugh's council in support of the proposed new building and, to the end of her life, took great interest in all the details of its construction.

Clara Mordan died on 22 January 1915 at 18 Marine Mansions, Bexhill, Sussex, where she had lived almost exclusively in her final years to derive as much benefit as possible for her ailing lungs from the sea air. Her friend Mary Gray Allen had been her constant companion and support while Clara was bed-ridden and was described by Clara in a personal letter to Miss Moberly, written two months before her death, as 'my dearest friend, who never leaves me'. In her will Clara left to St Hugh's over £10,000, which enabled the college to continue its building despite the economic stringencies imposed by the war. She also made Mary Gray Allen a residuary legatee on condition that she in turn bequeathed this inheritance to St Hugh's. Miss Moberly testified to Miss Gray Allen's support of the college: '[Clara Mordan] has also left us the goodwill of her chief friend, Miss Gray Allen, who has taken her place on the Council … and is prepared to take a continued interest in St Hugh's' (*St Hugh's Club Paper*, 23, Oct 1915). Mary Gray Allen, who had considerable means of her own, died in August 1925 and left to St Hugh's £36,000, the accumulated income from her friend's bequest, a sum which established Clara Mordan's position as the most important female benefactor of women's education of her time.

DEBORAH QUARE

Sources E. E. S. Procter, 'Early history of St Hugh's', 1980, St Hugh's College, Oxford · H. Deneke, 'What I remember', 1934, St Hugh's College, Oxford · letters from C. E. Mordan, St Hugh's College, Oxford · P. Griffin, ed., *St Hugh's: one hundred years of women's education in Oxford* (1986) · b. cert. · d. cert.

Archives St Hugh's College, Oxford

Likenesses H. T. Wells, watercolour, 1858, St Hugh's College, Oxford · H. T. Wells, oils, 1859, St Hugh's College, Oxford · W. Lucas, charcoal and coloured chalk, 1860–1865?, St Hugh's College, Oxford

Wealth at death £47,702 4*s.* 6*d.*: probate, 12 March 1915, *CGPLA Eng. & Wales*

Mordaunt, Anastasia, countess of Peterborough and Monmouth. *See* Robinson, Anastasia (*d.* 1755).

Mordaunt, Charles, third earl of Peterborough and first earl of Monmouth (1658?–1735), army officer and diplomatist, was the eldest of the eleven children of John *Mordaunt, first Viscount Mordaunt of Avalon (1626–1675), royalist conspirator, and Elizabeth (1632/3–1679), daughter and sole heir of the Hon. Thomas Carey (*d.* 1634) and granddaughter of Robert *Carey, first earl of Monmouth.

Charles Mordaunt was probably born in early 1658, as his mother is known to have been pregnant in 1657 and then had a second son in April 1659. Unlike his three younger brothers, who went to Eton, he was educated at Westminster School under its headmaster Richard Busby. In March 1674 he went to Oxford, where he matriculated at Christ Church on 11 April, at the age of sixteen. On his father's death on 5 June 1675 he succeeded to the peerage as the second Viscount Mordaunt of Avalon and Baron Mordaunt of Ryegate, although the bulk of his father's properties reverted to his uncle, Henry *Mordaunt, second earl of Peterborough. The diarist John Evelyn, an intimate friend of his mother, became a trustee for the young Lord Mordaunt and his siblings and was later also a trustee under his mother's will.

Early career Having left Oxford in February 1676, Mordaunt went to France; then in May 1677, perhaps with assistance from his mother's stepbrother Captain Arthur Herbert, later earl of Torrington, he entered the navy as an unpaid volunteer. In 1678, about the age of twenty, he privately married his relative Carey (*c.*1658–1709), maid of honour to Queen Catherine from 1674 to 1680, and daughter of Sir Alexander *Fraizer, first baronet, physician to Charles II. The marriage was kept secret until May 1680, when an observer wrote, 'It is said the marriage between my lord Mordaunt and Mrs. Fraizer will now be speedily consummated, the lady being discovered with child and my lord seeming to own something of a contract' (*Ormonde MSS*, 6.325). Even then it seems it was not until December 1681 that Mordaunt 'brought out as well as owned his lady' (*Rutland MSS*, 2.62). They had two sons, John and Henry *Mordaunt, and a daughter, Henrietta.

On 29 September 1678 Mordaunt joined as a volunteer the 48-gun ship *Bristol*, captained by Anthony Langston, bringing six servants with him. The ship's chaplain, the Revd Henry Teonge, recorded Mordaunt's irritating presence in his diary, noting, on an occasion when he was ill, how Mordaunt presumed to take his place and deliver a sermon. 'I found the zealous lord with our captaine,' Teonge wrote, 'whom I did so handle in a smart and short discourse that he went out of the cabin in a great wrath' (*Diary*, 227). Upon arrival at Cadiz in late November Mordaunt moved into the *Rupert*, commanded by Arthur Herbert. With his mother's death in early April 1679 he inherited Villa Carey, later Peterborough House, at Parson's Green, Fulham, Middlesex, which his grandmother

Charles Mordaunt, third earl of Peterborough and first earl of Monmouth (1658?–1735), by Sir Godfrey Kneller, 1715

Margaret Carey, daughter and heir of Sir Thomas Smith, had bequeathed to his mother.

Mordaunt returned to England in the autumn of 1679. In March 1680 he was wounded in a duel with Lord Cavendish but had recovered by June, when he sailed again for the Mediterranean, this time as a volunteer to serve ashore at Tangier. During the September 1680 siege by the Moors, Mordaunt was a prominent member of a group of young noblemen who were all '(covetous of Honour and ambitiously emulous of Glory) to be partakers of this pleasant (though dangerous) Sport, where they had almost lost their lives' (Ross, 14). Mordaunt's stay at Tangier was brief, but it made an impact. In a conversation about the need to raise professional standards, the diarist and naval clerk Samuel Pepys noted that

> these gentlemen reformados are good for nothing … doing dishonour to the service and themselves by running and keeping ashore, borrowing money of our merchants and running on the score to everybody, as my lord Mordaunt in particular did do, and committing villainies of all sorts and debauching the poor seamen. (Chappell, 120)

Back in England Mordaunt settled in the house at Parson's Green. On 31 December 1680 he took his seat in the House of Lords and became actively engaged in whig politics in association with the earl of Shaftesbury. Mordaunt was one of the sixteen peers who signed the January 1681 petition against parliament meeting at Oxford in March, and then in March protested against the Lords' rejection of the proposal to impeach the informer Edward Fitzharris. In the same month the king directed Sir Leoline Jenkins to persuade Mordaunt to apologize for breaking windows at Prince Philip of Monaco's house on the occasion of a challenge. Five months later, in August 1681, James Hamilton, Lord Arran, wounded Mordaunt in the arm and body during a duel with pistol and sword.

That summer, at his own expense, Mordaunt built at Deptford a 46-gun privateer, *Loyal Mordaunt*. It was unclear what he planned to do with this ship, and when it was ready to sail reports circulated that he might either enter the service of the elector of Brandenburg or sail to the Mediterranean. Fearing the ship might be used to attack Spanish shipping, the Spanish ambassador complained to the king, who, being at that moment on bad terms with Mordaunt, ordered it stopped for more than six weeks. By the end of August Mordaunt was back in favour and on one occasion in early October kept the king up until midnight fruitlessly attempting to reconcile him with the duke of Monmouth. A month later, in November 1681, the king dined on board with him. Mordaunt's departure did not materialize and eventually, in 1683, the navy purchased the ship from him.

Following the murder of the wealthy whig politician Thomas Thynne in February 1682, Mordaunt had to be restrained by a royal writ from crossing the channel to Nieuwport to act as Lord Cavendish's second in a duel with Count Königsmarck, who was widely believed to be behind Thynne's death. Mordaunt continued his association with radical whigs, but his involvement, if any, in the 1683 Rye House plot to assassinate the king is unclear. He was granted a passport to go to Holland in September 1683 and to Flanders in March 1684.

After the accession of James II in 1685 Mordaunt made a speech in the House of Lords supporting Lord Cavendish's motion against a standing army as a danger to civil liberties. Thereafter he actively opposed the king. Visiting the Netherlands in 1686 he was apparently the first English nobleman openly to suggest to William, prince of Orange, that he succeed to the English crown, but, as Bishop Burnet explained, Mordaunt had 'represented the thing [as] so easy, that all this appeared extremely romantical to the prince' (Foxcroft, 287). Mordaunt left England again in August 1687 and later that month a newsletter reported that Mary, princess of Orange, had appointed Lady Mordaunt her groom of the stole and it was expected that Mordaunt would receive a regiment in the Dutch army. By then Mordaunt had already begun to suggest an expedition to William, and in November 1687 plans were laid for him to join Captain Gerard Callenburg, commanding the Dutch naval squadron in the West Indies. The motive for the voyage may have been to discover the strength of loyalty towards James II that might be expected from the English colonies there and from Admiral Sir John Narbrough, whom Mordaunt visited at the site of a Spanish wreck off the coast of Hispaniola.

Revolution and politics, 1688–1704 After his return to Holland, Mordaunt was closely associated with Arthur Herbert and Edward Russell, all three attending William during the invasion. Immediately after the landing at Torbay William ordered Mordaunt to raise a regiment of horse, with which Mordaunt occupied Exeter on 8 November

1688. In advance of the main army Mordaunt raised support for William in Dorset and Wiltshire and by 13 December he was in London. He was among the peers who attended William at Windsor on 17 December, when he was directed by the prince to transcribe a fair copy of their resolution ordering James II to leave Whitehall. Shortly afterwards the earl of Clarendon complained that on one occasion he could not see the prince as 'he was shut up a long time with Lord Mordaunt' (*State Letters of … Clarendon*, 2.130). In January 1689 Mordaunt took a tour of the north to observe the state of the defences and the consolidation of William's power. On his return, Clarendon reported that the earl of Lincoln, 'to confirm the opinion several had of his being half mad, declared that he had come to do what ever my Shrewsbury and Mordaunt would have him' (ibid., 165). Mordaunt was one of the lords who attended the private meeting with William, probably held on the evening of 3 February 1689, when William first announced that he would settle for nothing less than the crown in his own right, with Mary as queen, and preference to Anne as their successor.

William quickly rewarded Mordaunt, making him a privy councillor on 14 February 1689, gentleman of the bedchamber on 1 March, colonel of a regiment of foot on 1 April, lord lieutenant of Northamptonshire, and first commissioner of the Treasury on 9 April. With no prior experience of Treasury affairs, Mordaunt reportedly believed that he 'would understand the business of it as well as Lord Godolphin in a fortnight' (Horwitz, 19). On 28 March a warrant had been prepared to create him earl of Chichester, but when it was passed on 9 April he was instead created earl of Monmouth, a title that had been given to his great-grandfather Robert Carey in 1626 and had become extinct in 1661. During this period Monmouth sought employment for the philosopher John Locke, with whom he had developed a close relationship before the revolution in Holland, using his influence to have him appointed commissioner of appeals.

On 10 May 1689 Monmouth was appointed a commissioner for reforming abuses in the army, and on 9 August water bailiff of the Severn. In March 1690 he was replaced at the Treasury but was granted the manor of Dauntsley, Wiltshire, along with other forfeited lands formerly belonging to the regicide Sir John Danvers, in Gloucestershire, Oxfordshire, Wiltshire, and Yorkshire. When William III left for Ireland on 2 June 1690, Monmouth was among the last-minute additions he made to the council of nine to advise Queen Mary. When Monmouth's uncle, the earl of Torrington, faced the prospect of the French fleet off Beachy Head, Monmouth and others proposed going to the fleet as volunteers and taking command if Torrington should be killed. With the queen's assent, Monmouth set out for Portsmouth on 28 June, but before he could take ship the battle of Beachy Head took place and he returned to London on 2 July.

On Monmouth's return to the council, he continued to raise similarly impetuous plans, which the queen resisted, noting privately, 'Lord Monmouth is mad, and his wife who is madder, governs him. I knew him deeply ingaged in Scotland and not much trusted, yet must know all' (Doebner, 30). Mary sharply rebuked Monmouth in early July for his repeated attempts to discredit the tory earl of Nottingham. Then, as the Treasury's resources grew scarce, Monmouth presented the queen with a scheme that offered a £200,000 loan from his friends in the city, provided that the queen dissolve parliament. Mary refused to accept, unless the money could be raised on other terms. Mary's reservations about Monmouth were based not only on his impetuosity, but also on suspicion of his involvement in a series of secret reports written in lemon juice to a French agent at Antwerp revealing the proceedings of the council of nine. Although they touched only on matters considered in meetings when Monmouth had been present, he successfully denied any participation in the affair.

From January to March 1691 Monmouth was in Holland with the king. After returning to England he went briefly to Ireland in September. In early 1692 he commanded a regiment on Guernsey and Jersey and, during the absence of the governor, Lord Hatton, was in overall command there when the opposing fleets were engaged off Barfleur and La Hogue. In June he was in Flanders with the king and returned to London in mid-July 1692. Despite his support of William, Monmouth could not reconcile himself with the king's tory advisers. In December 1692 in the House of Lords Monmouth was one of the eighteen peers who entered their protests at the defeat of a motion to inquire into the conduct of the war by means of a committee of both houses of parliament. In the following session, on 30 November 1693, he introduced a bill for a triennial parliament which was nearly identical to the one that the king had rejected the previous March. Consequently, in February 1694 the king dismissed him as a gentleman of the bedchamber, gave his regiment to his brother Henry Mordaunt, and no longer summoned him to the privy council. These actions only served to increase Monmouth's support of the opposition. In July 1694, following a Jacobite-motivated disturbance in Northamptonshire, Lord Shrewsbury attempted to assuage the king's suspicions by telling him that, even if Mordaunt had made peace with James II, he preferred loyalty to William. Nevertheless, Monmouth's repeated political opposition to the ministry marked the end of the close personal trust that the king had earlier confided in him and William removed him from his inner circle.

In early 1695 Monmouth was shown favour by the king in an apparent attempt to win him over. He resumed his post as gentleman of the bedchamber in late March 1695 and was subsequently appointed one of the first trustees of Greenwich Hospital, to which he contributed £200, and became a commissioner of appeals for prize cases. Monmouth, however, continued to cause trouble. In April 1695, in connection with a series of parliamentary inquiries into corruption, he moved to censure Lord Normanby for his activities, and lost by only four votes. He angered the king the following year when he indiscreetly let it be known in early 1696 that the king had privately discussed his intention to dissolve parliament on his return from the continent. On the king's departure, Monmouth was not appointed one of the lords justices, as had been expected, and he refused to serve as an Admiralty commissioner when it became clear that he would not replace Russell as first commissioner.

Monmouth strongly supported the attainder of the Jacobite Sir John Fenwick for treason in November 1696, although many had doubts about the procedure. When it emerged that he had encouraged Fenwick and the informer Matthew Smith to incriminate men such as the duke of Shrewsbury and the earl of Marlborough, he was called before the Lords and made a rambling two-hour speech in his own defence, 'as if he designed to make them weary of hearing him again' (James, 164). In the event Fenwick had not followed Monmouth's advice, but the subsequent investigation into the matter condemned Monmouth for having 'a share and part in the contrivance of the papers … and for the undutiful words spoken by him of the king' (ibid., 173). On 16 January 1697 the Lords ordered Monmouth to the Tower, removed from all his places, and his name struck from the privy council list. After a three-month imprisonment, he was released on 30 March 1697.

On the death of Monmouth's uncle on 19 June 1697 he became third earl of Peterborough, styling himself as earl of Peterborough and Monmouth. He retired from public life for some time, coming into public notice momentarily in November 1697, after a French protestant shopkeeper in Soho created a stir, claiming that he had recognized James II's son, the duke of Berwick, in his shop purchasing a hat and stockings, 'dressed in old clothes, and his face very much covered up by his cloak with an old fair peruke on' (*CSP dom.*, *1697*, 165), but the customer proved to have been Peterborough.

Peterborough returned to politics in February 1699, when, in response to the king's speech on the broad political situation in Europe, he supported denunciation of France and voted to authorize the king to enter into a broad alliance. Later that year he was actively involved in working to discredit Shrewsbury and Admiral Edward Russell, now Lord Orford. The secret agent John Macky reported that Peterborough was a co-author, with Dr Charles Davenant, of Matthew Smith's book *Memoir of Secret Service* (1699), recounting information associated with the Fenwick affair. In 1701 Peterborough took a very active role in the motion to impeach Lord Somers, which was managed in the House of Commons by his 21-year-old son John, Lord Mordaunt, MP for Chippenham (1701–8). About this time, Peterborough was described as one who 'affects Popularity and loves to preach in Coffee-Houses, and publick Places; is an open enemy to Revealed Religion; brave in Person; hath a good Estate; does not seem Expensive, yet always in Debt, and very poor. A well shaped thin man, with a very brisk Look' (*Memoirs of the Secret Services*, 66).

Following the death of William III and the accession of Anne in 1702, Peterborough returned to favour at court, having been reconciled with the earl of Marlborough and having gained the support of his wife, the powerful countess of Marlborough. On 15 June 1702 he was returned to one of the places he had lost in 1697 as lord lieutenant of Northamptonshire. By autumn he was actively engaged in planning to command an Anglo-Dutch expedition to protect trade in America and to attack Spanish settlements, and in October 1702 he was appointed governor of Jamaica. Following the failure at Cadiz, the Dutch found themselves unable to supply ships and troops, and Peterborough wrote to John Locke, 'Our American Expedition is fallen as a mushroom rises in the night … I refus'd to goe to the other world loaded with empty titles and deprived of Force' (*Correspondence of John Locke*, 7.740–41).

In January 1703, as these plans fell, Peterborough was actively engaged in the House of Lords as a manager in rejecting the first Occasional Conformity Bill, working closely with Lord Somers, the duke of Devonshire, and Bishop Burnet. In December 1703, at the time of the vote on the second bill, Peterborough told Swift 'that if he had the least suspicion the rejecting of this bill would hurt the Church or do kindness to the Dissenters, he would lose his right hand rather than speak against it' (*Correspondence of Jonathan Swift*, 1.39).

War in Spain, 1705–1707 On 31 March 1705 Peterborough was appointed commander-in-chief of the troops in the fleet. In addition, on 1 May he and Admiral Sir Cloudesley Shovell were appointed 'joint admirals and Chief Commanders of her [Majesty's] fleet, & in case of Death, or in the absence, or inability of either of you, the other of you Admiral & Chief Commander' (PRO, ADM 6/8, fol. 172*v*). With identical commissions, both were authorized and empowered 'to wear the Union Flagg at the Maine Top mast head aboard such ship of her [Majesty's] Fleete, where you shall happen at any time to be' (ibid., fols. 172*v*–173*r*). Although joint commissions were not unprecedented, Peterborough's commission was an exception to the practice since 1660 of restricting such naval appointments to those who had risen by regular service in the fleet.

The fleet of twenty-nine ships of the line sailed from St Helen's on 23 May and reached Lisbon on 11 June. Peterborough's preference for an attack on the French base at Toulon in support of the duke of Savoy was set aside when the allies' candidate for the Spanish throne, Charles III, demanded the fleet sail to Barcelona, where the Catalans might support him. Peterborough landed with the troops without opposition on 12 August, accompanied by Charles and Prince George of Hesse-Darmstadt. Finding the approach to the fortifications difficult and having intelligence that the Spanish outnumbered the allies, Peterborough and others favoured re-embarking the forces and withdrawing, while Shovell strongly dissented. There was considerable debate over the next step, but on the basis of newly received intelligence, Peterborough proposed to Prince George an attack on Montjuich, an unimproved fortification two-thirds of a mile south-west of Barcelona. Prince George and Peterborough joined the attacking forces, which broke through the outer defences on 3 September. When the defending forces made a sally against the attackers, they killed Prince George and forced the attackers back, but Peterborough personally rallied the troops to hold the outer positions. After mortars were brought in, Montjuich surrendered on 6 September.

Now turning their attention to nearby Barcelona, the Anglo-Dutch fleet landed heavy guns and after two weeks of bombardment Barcelona's governor capitulated on 23 September. The following day riots broke out on the streets and, putting himself at great personal risk, Peterborough personally took charge to restore order in the city. With the city fully pacified, Charles III entered Barcelona on 13 October and, for the first time on Spanish soil, was proclaimed king of Spain. When news of this reached London, Peterborough received full credit for the victory.

In England, Peterborough's cousin Mary, the divorced dowager duchess of Norfolk, died on 17 November 1705 and by her death Peterborough became eighth Baron Mordaunt of Turvey, while Drayton House, her seat in Northamptonshire, passed to her second husband, Sir John Germain. Peterborough twice instituted legal proceedings to obtain Drayton and only dropped his suit after Germain's death in 1718, when it passed to his second wife, Lady Elizabeth Germain.

During the winter of 1705 the allied army under Peterborough was distributed in quarters throughout Catalonia at Barcelona, Lérida, Gerona, and Tortosa. As preparations began for the coming campaign season, Peterborough increasingly became involved in quarrels with the various allied commanders and with the court of Charles III. He complained to officials in London particularly about the incompetence and unreliability of Charles's first minister, Prince Anton-Florian of Liechtenstein. They, on the other hand, found Peterborough tactless and overbearing. To solve the disputes with others, Peterborough repeatedly demanded to be made sole commander of the fleet and even vice-admiral of England, an honorary title, which he believed had been promised to him. He complained in November 1705 that unless he received the new titles he would resign, but officials took little notice.

With no appropriate winter base in the Mediterranean for the fleet, Shovell left Peterborough at Barcelona and returned to England, leaving a small squadron at Lisbon under Vice-Admiral Sir John Leake to return to Catalonia in the spring. During the winter Spanish troops in the province of Valencia had defected from the Bourbon Philip V and declared for the Habsburg Charles III. In the face of this the Bourbon government in Madrid acted swiftly to try to recover the province before Charles III and the allied army could consolidate the position in Valencia. Moving quickly, Philip V's forces were able to seize the mountain passes between Valencia and Catalonia before the allies could bar their way. In the process they forced an allied force of thirty English dragoons with 1000 Catalan irregulars and Valencian militia under Colonel John Jones to retire to San Mateo in late December 1705, where they were surrounded.

On 29 December 1705 Charles III appointed Fernando, conde de Cifuentes, as viceroy of Valencia, a man with whom Peterborough repeatedly quarrelled. The following day Charles agreed to allow Peterborough to proceed with about 1500 men to relieve San Mateo and drive the Bourbon forces out of Valencia, a task that Charles III and Cifuentes saw as an easy mission, with bands of partisans ready at hand. Arriving on the scene, Peterborough quickly found that Charles's court had been misinformed. There were no local partisans in sight and Peterborough faced a Bourbon force numbering nearly 7000 men. Quickly assessing the situation, Peterborough divided his force into small units that operated separately from Tortosa, Lérida, and Gerona, and he employed them like guerrilla fighters, using unorthodox methods, ruses, and local spies. Early in January 1706 he sent out couriers to the besieged troops at San Mateo with false documents that suggested a huge reinforcement was on its way. As planned, the enemy captured the messengers and were misled by the false information. The Bourbon commander evacuated his positions and retreated. With a second ruse Peterborough convinced his enemy that he was still in great danger and motivated him to withdraw further, allowing Peterborough's force to get to Albocácer.

At Albocácer, Peterborough received a letter from Charles reporting that three Bourbon armies were about to attack Catalonia. Without positive and direct orders, Peterborough was reluctant to relinquish his independent command for the frustrations he had earlier experienced in Barcelona. Instead, he continued to move south, pursuing the retreating conde de las Torres and his Bourbon forces, taking Nules by bluffing the magistrates into thinking that he had artillery, then Castillón de Plana, both places furnishing horses to mount his troops and to relieve the besieged city of Valencia. In the process he drew troops from Tortosa, that might have been used to support Catalonia, to gather a total force of 3000 regulars and 3500 irregulars, and marched to Murviedro, where Brigadier Daniel Mahoni with 800 Irish dragoons in Bourbon service held the castle and bridge that barred further passage. Without strength for a pitched battle, Peterborough used ruse, bluff, and deceit to inveigle Mahoni, a distant relation on his mother's side, into a meeting and to convince him successfully to retreat from his strategic position. With this obstacle removed, Peterborough and his troops entered Valencia on 4 February 1706, having, in defiance of conventional wisdom, relieved the city with an inferior force that repeatedly avoided battle. From there Peterborough quickly took troops that prevented Bourbon forces from besieging the key positions of Sueca and Alcira, which controlled the supply routes into Valencia.

By early March, Marshal Tessé had moved 20,000 Bourbon troops to besiege Barcelona by land and the French fleet under the comte de Toulouse blockaded it with twenty-eight ships of the line. To save his position Charles III needed both Peterborough's army and the Anglo-Dutch fleet. Peterborough, however, remained reluctant to leave Valencia and thought of a variety of alternatives, suggesting, among other possibilities, that Charles withdraw from Catalonia and form an army to attack from Portugal. Then Peterborough wrote to Admiral Leake, ordering him

to support Valencia with the troops he carried, not Barcelona, where the French fleet were in force. Learning of Peterborough's order, Charles III urgently asked Leake to disregard it and bring his fleet directly to Barcelona. Finally, with great reluctance, Peterborough moved north towards Barcelona with his army, leaving only a small force to hold Valencia. Leake meanwhile obeyed Charles III and sailed for Barcelona, arriving on 8 May off Sitges. There Peterborough embarked some of his men in transports and then boarded Leake's flagship, *Prince George*, unfurling the Union Flag at the main topmast as joint commander-in-chief of the fleet with Shovell, a commission that had been renewed in March 1706. Leake made no protest and he and Peterborough ignored each other. Leake had already dispatched Rear-Admiral Sir George Byng to sail ahead of the main fleet, and on sight of it the French fleet under Toulouse withdrew towards Toulon. While Marshal Tessé continued to bombard the city, Leake landed troops from the fleet. With the departure of the French fleet, Tessé lost his main lines of supply, and the Bourbon army was forced to withdraw on 11 May.

In the aftermath of Leake's relief of Barcelona, Peterborough continued his tense relationship with the court of Charles III. At a general war council in Charles's presence on 18 May the allied commanders decided that they would march on Madrid by way of Valencia. On 29 May Peterborough embarked in Leake's fleet transports and sailed for Valencia, where he arrived on 4 June to prepare for the king's march on Madrid. If Charles was to make good the Habsburg claim, he urgently needed to appear in Madrid, yet Charles repeatedly delayed his march as Peterborough reported needing more supplies and equipment to facilitate it.

Irritation with Peterborough, along with the delays, eventually led the king to make an independent attempt on Madrid through Aragon rather than depend on Peterborough in Valencia. Charles's courtiers, moreover, suggested that Peterborough had been withholding and using English funds intended for Charles. Typically, Peterborough had not accounted for funds received or spent and could not substantiate his denials. Seeing the king tending towards the Aragon route, Peterborough hastened to open the road to Madrid, but when he reported the way open, the king in Zaragoza ignored him. Meanwhile, Lord Galway and an Anglo-Portuguese force had arrived in Madrid from the west, after marching across Portugal. Peterborough took personal offence that Galway addressed his reports to the king and not to him but finally Peterborough and Galway joined forces at Guadalajara on 6 August.

During the month and a half delay the duke of Berwick had been able to reinforce the enemy Bourbon forces. At the same time the allied armies in Portugal and Spain, now brought together for the first time, were paralysed by disputes over who should command. Galway offered Peterborough the supreme command, but his Portuguese colleague, the marquis das Minas, refused to accept him. Peterborough suggested they split into national groups, leaving him to command the Spanish troops. When this and every suggestion for his participation was rejected, Peterborough decided to leave Spain, taking up his earlier orders to assist the duke of Savoy and attempt to arrange a loan in Genoa for Charles III.

Peterborough left on 11 August for Valencia. *En route* he learned that Bourbon forces had plundered the fifty mules and sixteen wagons carrying his personal baggage. Meeting with Leake at Valencia, he decided against an attack on Minorca and sailed instead for Italy, in the 70-gun *Resolution*, commanded by his second son, Captain Henry Mordaunt. He met the duke of Savoy at Turin and Prince Eugene at Pavia to discuss future allied operations against Toulon. After raising a loan of £100,000 at Genoa, at 1 per cent above the normal rate and on the credit of Charles III, the marquis das Minas, and the English Treasury, Peterborough returned to Barcelona on 27 December and went on to Valencia, where he arrived on 10 January 1707. Meeting allied commanders during January and February, he participated in war councils, advising them to remain on the defensive while the fleet, Prince Eugene, and the duke of Savoy undertook the major offensive on Toulon.

Recall and public debate Back in England people had begun to question Peterborough's activities. William Walsh wrote to the poet Alexander Pope expressing a sentiment that Pope adopted as his own, 'it was impossible that a man with so much Wit as he shew'd, cou'd be fit to command an Army, or do any other Business' (*Correspondence of Alexander Pope*, 1.22). A steady stream of complaints reached London from Charles III as well as from Austrian officials. Ministers in London were aware of the lack of skill among Charles III's Austrian courtiers and were reluctant to place all the blame on Peterborough, but they could not continue to ignore the situation. Godolphin summarized the problem for Marlborough when he wrote, 'in a word he is both useless and grieving there, and is preparing to be troublesome, whenever he is called home' (*Marlborough–Godolphin Correspondence*, 2.650). Peterborough's own decision to withdraw from command eased the dilemma in London, and in December 1706 the secretary of state the earl of Sunderland recalled him. This letter apparently went astray and Sunderland repeated the order in January 1707. This instruction reached Peterborough on 22 February 1707, but he did not leave Spain until 13 March, when he took passage for Italy in the *Resolution*. Attacked *en route* by French warships, Peterborough transferred to the *Enterprise* and landed safely at Leghorn.

From there Peterborough took eight months to cross Europe, visiting Turin from the end of May 1707 until 25 June for further discussions with the duke of Savoy and then Vienna for discussions at the imperial court. Having passed through Bohemia and Dresden, he went to Leipzig in early July for discussions with the Swedish chancery, then forced himself into a meeting with King Charles XII on horseback near Altranstädt, in which he suggested that Sweden could act as a war mediator. From there he went to Hanover, where he spent several days in mid-July insisting that a member of the electoral house take up residence in England to ensure the succession. From 29 July

he spent ten days with Marlborough in his camp at Soignes, where Peterborough explained his views at length. Disturbed by reports of these initiatives, officials in London quickly advised foreign governments that Peterborough was not on an official mission. He eventually arrived in London in late August 1707, out of favour with the queen and the government.

Peterborough's delay in returning home allowed events in Spain to justify his actions. The failure of allied commanders to agree on strategy and their rejection of Peterborough's recommendations to remain on the defensive appeared to have led to the allied defeat at Almanza in April 1707. With this in mind Peterborough commissioned his physician John Freind to publish a laudatory account of his actions, *The Conduct of the Earl of Peterborough in Spain* (1707), gaining him a widespread popular following that soon translated into political support from the tories. Only one pamphleteer, Richard Kingston, who had attacked Matthew Smith's pamphlet in 1699, wrote a rebuttal in *Impartial Remarks on Dr. Freind's Account* (1707).

On 19 December 1707 the House of Lords opened debate on the conduct of the war in Spain. With the queen present incognito, tories criticized whigs for not rewarding Peterborough's successes. After the debate an official inquiry opened on 8 January 1708. Charges against Peterborough failed to pass, but no vote of thanks was proposed. The inquiry placed Peterborough in a difficult position. Having failed to keep proper public or private accounts, he could not prove his claim that he had spent large sums of his own money on the war effort or that he had not misspent public funds. The Treasury pursued the matter for more than two years and ordered his property attached until he could prove his innocence of misappropriating funds. On 30 July 1708 Peterborough waited on the queen, for the first time since his return from Spain nearly a year before. While many predicted his disgrace, it was reported that the queen had offered him the governorship of Jamaica, which he refused. He suffered more misfortune when his wife died of quinsy on 13 May 1709 and his two sons, John and Henry, both died of smallpox in 1710.

After the fall of the whig ministry in 1710, the new tory government under Robert Harley quickly moved to use Peterborough against the whigs, capitalizing on his personal and professional antipathy towards Marlborough and Godolphin. In September 1710 it was rumoured that he would be first commissioner of the Admiralty, but in fact he was appointed general of marines on 2 November 1710 and ambassador-extraordinary to Vienna in December. In October Peterborough renewed his acquaintance with the writer Jonathan Swift and the friendship soon became a warm one, Swift describing Peterborough affectionately as 'the ramblingest lying rogue on earth' (Swift, *Journal to Stella*, 102).

On 5 January 1711 the war in Spain was debated in the House of Lords as a committee of the whole, and the generals were examined on their decisions in 1706–7. As a result, Galway, Tyrawly, and Stanhope were censured for advising an offensive campaign in 1707, while Peterborough was praised for having given advice that, if taken, would have averted the disasters that followed. Sir Simon Harcourt, lord privy seal, addressed the thanks of the house to Peterborough, to which he modestly replied, 'No service can deserve such a reward. It is more than a sufficient recompense for any hardships, and to which nothing can give an addition' (Cobbett, *Parl. hist.*, 6, 1702–14, 982). Supporting the government position, Swift wrote in *The Conduct of the Allies* (1711),

> the only General who, by a Course of Conduct and Fortune almost miraculous, had nearly put us into Possession of the Kingdom, was left wholly unsupported, exposed to the Envy of his Rivals, disappointed by the Caprices of a young inexperienced Prince, under the Guidance of a rapacious *German* Ministry, and at last called home in Discontent: By which our Armies, both in Spain and Portugal, were made a sacrifice to avarice, Ill conduct, or Treachery. (*Swift's Political Tracts, 1711–13*, 21)

Subsequently, the Lords ordered the attorney-general to proceed against Richard Kingston for libel against Peterborough in his *Impartial Remarks on Dr. Freind's Account* (1707).

Diplomatic mission, 1711–1714 Peterborough departed for Vienna on 13 January 1711, having agreed with Swift to become 'mighty constant correspondents' (Swift, *Journal to Stella*, 1.152). His diplomatic mission was to attempt to bring about more cordial relations between the emperor and the duke of Savoy. He was in Vienna from 28 February until about 23 April 1711, and Turin from late April to 8 May. While there he received the news that Emperor Joseph I had died. This provided the opportunity for him to revive his idea to improve the allied position in Spain by persuading the duke of Savoy to become the allies' new candidate for the Spanish throne. While the duke thought this idea fanciful, Peterborough's further suggestions that Savoy acquire Sicily as a block to Habsburg ambitions and that the prince of Piedmont marry a Habsburg both foreshadowed post-war diplomacy. On his return to Vienna in June he received notice from London censuring him for exceeding his instructions. He immediately returned to England, scattering straggling servants and baggage along the route in his haste. He arrived in late June, and was graciously received by the queen and immediately appointed ambassador-extraordinary to the imperial diet. From 17 September to mid-December 1711 he resided at Frankfurt and Augsburg. While he was away from England, Peterborough authorized his friends to make occasional use of his home and garden at Parson's Green. On a visit in November 1711 Swift wrote, 'It is the finest garden I have ever seen about this town; an abundance of hot walls for grapes, where they are in great plenty, and ripening fast' (ibid., 1.349).

Given further diplomatic credentials, throughout 1712 Peterborough shuttled between Venice and Turin, also visiting Genoa, before returning to England on 9 January 1713. During his absence, on 19 November 1712, he had been appointed to succeed Lord Rivers as colonel of the Royal regiment of horse guards. Swift, who saw him on the day after his return, commented,

> He left Engld with a Bruise by his Coach overturning, that made him spitt Blood, and was so ill, we expected every Post to hear of his Death: but he outrode it, or outdrank it, or something: and is come home lustyer than ever, he is at least 60 & has more Spirits than any young fellow I know in Engld,

and added, 'I love the hangdog dearly' (Swift, *Journal to Stella*, 2.600). Soon Peterborough became a regular diner with the Saturday Club, whose members included Lord Bolingbroke and Swift.

Made a knight of the Garter on 4 August 1713, in November Peterborough was appointed ambassador-extraordinary to the duke of Savoy, now king of Sicily, and to the other Italian states. He took with him as his chaplain George Berkeley, later bishop of Cloyne, whom Swift had introduced to him. He arrived in Paris on 29 November 1713, where he discussed the plight of the Catalans. He left Paris on 14 December, and passed through Lyons, Toulon, and Genoa before going incognito to Palermo, Sicily, where he remained in February and March to present the queen's compliments to the new king. While there, in March 1714, he was appointed governor of Minorca, but before he could reach his new post the queen died and the new ministry immediately recalled him. On his return journey he stopped in Paris and had an interview with Louis XIV at Marly on 6 August 1714.

Final years, 1715–1735 With his diplomatic and military career at an end, Peterborough returned to London and was instructed not to appear at court. Nevertheless, he attended the House of Lords frequently until 1731, where he had a reputation as a witty speaker. On 13 May 1715 the duke of Argyll replaced him as colonel of the Horse Guards. In 1717 he made a private visit to Italy and was mistakenly arrested and detained for a month in Bologna on suspicion of being involved with a conspiracy to kill the Pretender, then living in Urbino. In 1719 he returned again to Italy on a private visit to the duke of Parma. He was in France in 1720. On 24 May 1722 he was appointed general of all the marine forces.

From 1722 stories began to circulate about Peterborough's relationship with the singer Anastasia *Robinson (d. 1755), the daughter of the portrait painter Thomas Robinson, whom he had seen that year in the role of Griselda in Buononcini's opera. Peterborough secretly married her. The exact date of the marriage is not known, but in August 1723 Peterborough made a brief visit to the continent, and temporarily settled her, along with her stepmother, in a house at Fulham near his own at Parson's Green. The marriage is believed to be the first between a peer and an actress, singer, or dancer. Sometime later he rented for her a cottage and property named Bevis Mount overlooking the River Itchen at Padwell, Southampton.

From about 1723 Peterborough became an intimate friend of the poet Alexander Pope, who often came to lodge with him at his London residence in Bolton Street and at Parson's Green. He too shared Peterborough's love of gardening and described him at the centre of five friends: 'He, whose Lightning pierc'd the *Iberian* Lines, /

now forms my Quincunx, and now ranks my Vines' (*Imitations of Horace*, 2.2.29–30). Peterborough also began a correspondence with Henrietta Howard, the mistress of the prince of Wales, later George II, whom Peterborough himself addressed in verse: 'I said in my Heart, between Sleeping and Waking, / Thou wild Thing, that always art Leaping or Aching' (*British Journal*, 67, 28 Dec 1723, 3). Later Peterborough and Lord Bathurst were involved in designing her garden at Marble Hill.

About 1726 Swift addressed a poem 'to the Earl of P-b-w', which concluded 'Heroick Actions early bred in, / Ne'er to be match't in Modern reading, / But by his Name-sake Charles of Sweden' (*Poems of Jonathan Swift*, 2.396–8). For three months in the spring of 1728, and perhaps at other times between 1726 and 1728, Peterborough was Voltaire's host at Parson's Green. During Peterborough's final years, however, he lived at Bevis Mount. In poor health from 1729 onwards, he became seriously ill in January 1733 and had to return temporarily to London from Bevis Mount. On 6 March 1734 Peterborough cancelled Mrs Robinson's lease on Bevis Mount and purchased it, making an agreement with the owner, Queen's College, Oxford, to exchange it for his estate Wakes at Clifton Reynes, Buckinghamshire. He purchased additional land adjoining Bevis Mount, and furnished the garden with 'Statues, Vases, Marble Stone and other Ornaments' that made it, in Pope's words, 'beautiful beyond imagination' (will, PRO, PROB 11/674, fol. 122v.; *Correspondence of Alexander Pope*, 3.426). Later, in the summer of 1734, Peterborough and Pope sailed around the Isle of Wight, stopping at various places to explore the island.

By the spring of 1735 Peterborough's death seemed imminent, and his doctor advised him to have an operation for the stone. Just before the operation Peterborough invited friends to the lodgings of his niece's husband, Stephen Poyntz, at St James's Palace and there publicly introduced Anastasia Robinson as the countess of Peterborough for the first time. Shortly afterwards a public marriage was performed in Bath, where Peterborough's operation took place. Immediately after the operation Peterborough went by coach to Southampton, where in September his friend Alexander Pope went to Bevis Mount 'to take last leave of [him], at his setting sail for Lisbon: No Body can be more wasted, no soul can be more alive' (*Correspondence of Alexander Pope*, 3.508–9).

Initially intending to sail in his yacht for the south coast of France, but apparently with no firm objective in mind, Peterborough reached Lisbon and died shortly after his arrival there 'of a Flux, by eating grapes' (*GM*, 681) on 21 October 1735. On his deathbed he asked that the watch given to him by the duke of Savoy and carried with him on all his travels be given to his friend Alexander Pope. Peterborough was buried in the Mordaunt family vault under the church chancel at Turvey, Bedfordshire, on 21 November 1735. His grandson and namesake succeeded to all his titles. Peterborough left his lands in joint trust to several family members, particularly instructing them to preserve Bevis Mount, with its cottage and garden, as an heirloom. They survived for some time, but the cottage was

eventually pulled down and the land became built-up sections of Southampton called Bevois Mount and Bevois Town.

For both contemporaries and historians, Peterborough's activities have seemed more fable than history. The traditional accounts of Peterborough's military adventures in the 1706 campaign were influenced by the excessive claims made for him by John Freind's account of 1707 and by an elderly soldier, Captain George Carleton, who may have consulted Freind's work in writing *The Memoirs of an English Officer* (1728). In politics Peterborough was a consistent whig for over forty years but in the 1690s his ambitions for high office put him at odds with the whig leadership, who appear to have had doubts about his capabilities, and eventually he turned to the tories. Irritating and inscrutable to some, a romantic hero to others, Peterborough became a notable figure in English political, military, naval, diplomatic, literary, and gardening history. JOHN B. HATTENDORF

Sources warrants and commissions, PRO, ADM 6/8 · *The Marlborough–Godolphin correspondence*, ed. H. L. Snyder, 3 vols. (1975) · *Letters illustrative of the reign of William III from 1696 to 1708 addressed to the duke of Shrewsbury by James Vernon*, ed. G. P. R. James, 3 vols. (1841) · *CSP dom., 1679–84; 1689–98; 1700–02* · *CSP col.*, vol. 12 · *The state letters of Henry, earl of Clarendon*, 2 vols. (1763) · *Correspondentie van Willem III en van Hans Willem Bentinck*, ed. N. Japikse, 5 vols. (The Hague, 1927–37), vol. 2/1 · *Correspondence of John Locke*, ed. E. S. de Beer, 8 vols. (1982) · J. Ross, *Tangers rescue, or, A relation of the late memorable passages at Tanger* (1681) · *Private diarie of Elizabeth Viscountess Mordaunt* [1658–78] (1856) · E. Chappell, *The Tangier papers of Samuel Pepys*, Navy RS, 73 (1935) · *Calendar of the manuscripts of the marquess of Ormonde*, new ser., 8 vols., HMC, 36 (1902–20), vol. 6 · GEC, *Peerage* · *Letter from the earl of Peterborough to General Stanhope in Spain* (1834) · *GM*, 1st ser., 5 (1735) · *The correspondence of Alexander Pope*, ed. G. Sherburn, 5 vols. (1956) · J. Swift, *Journal to Stella*, ed. H. Williams, 2 vols. (1948) · *Poems of Jonathan Swift*, ed. H. Williams (1958) · *The correspondence of Jonathan Swift*, ed. H. Williams, 5 vols. (1963–5) · W. Coxe, *Memoirs of John, duke of Marlborough*, 2nd edn, 3 vols. (1818–19) · *The letters and dispatches of John Churchill, duke of Marlborough*, ed. G. Murray, 5 vols. (1845) · *A supplement to Burnet's History of my own time*, ed. H. C. Foxcroft (1902) · R. Doebner, ed., *Memoirs of Mary, queen of England* (1886) · *Calendar of the Stuart papers belonging to his majesty the king, preserved at Windsor Castle*, 7 vols., HMC, 56 (1902–23), vol. 5 · *The manuscripts of his grace the duke of Rutland*, 4 vols., HMC, 24 (1888–1905), vol. 2 · H. T. Dickinson, 'The earl of Peterborough and the capture of Barcelona', *History Today*, 14 (1964) · H. T. Dickinson, 'The earl of Peterborough's campaign in Valencia, 1706', *Journal of Army Historical Research*, 45 (1967), 35–52 · H. T. Dickinson, 'The recall of Lord Peterborough', *Journal of Army Historical Research*, 47 (1969), 175–87 · G. M. Trevelyan, 'Peterborough and Barcelona, 1705', *Cambridge Historical Journal*, 3 (1929–31), 253–9 · C. B. Chase, *The young Voltaire* (1926) · *The prose works of Jonathan Swift, 6: Political tracts, 1711–1713*, ed. H. Davis (1951) · *Memoirs of the secret services of John Macky*, ed. A. R. (1733) · H. Horwitz, *Parliament, policy and politics in the reign of William III* (1977) · *The diary of Henry Teonge*, ed. G. E. Manwaring (1927) · A. D. Francis, *The First Peninsular War, 1702–1713* (1975) · *Report on the manuscripts of the marquis of Downshire*, 6 vols. in 7, HMC, 75 (1924–95), vol. 1

Archives BL, corresp. and papers, Lansdowne MS 488 · BL, papers relating to arrest in Rome, Add. MSS 20292, 20312 · NRA Scotland, priv. coll., family corresp. | BL, letters to Lord Godolphin, Add. MS 39757 · BL, letters to duke of Marlborough, Add. MS 61169 · BL, corresp. with Lady Suffolk, Add. MS 22625 · Bodl. Oxf., corresp. with John Locke · CAC Cam., corresp. with Thomas Erle · CKS, letters to Alexander Stanhope, U1590/O34 · CKS, corresp. with James

Stanhope and private papers, U1590/O136–145 · W. Sussex RO, letters to marquess of Huntly

Likenesses G. Kneller, oils, c.1689–1697, Ranger's House, London · P. van Gunst, mezzotint, 1705 (after G. Kneller), BM, NPG · J. Simon, mezzotint, 1705 (after G. Kneller), BM, NPG · P. Angelis, group portrait, oils, c.1713 (*Queen Anne and knights of the Garter*), NPG · G. Kneller, oils, 1715, NPG [*see illus.*] · G. Kneller, oils, Gov. Art Coll. · J. Simon, mezzotint (after M. Dahl), BM, NPG · oils, Burley House, Northamptonshire

Mordaunt, Henry, second earl of Peterborough (*bap.* 1623, *d.* 1697), nobleman, was baptized at St Ann Blackfriars, London, on 18 October 1623, the son and heir of **John Mordaunt**, first earl of Peterborough (*bap.* 1599, *d.* 1643), and his wife, Elizabeth Howard (1603–1671), daughter of William, Lord Howard of Effingham; Henry was the brother of John *Mordaunt, first Viscount Mordaunt of Avalon (1626–1675). John Mordaunt, first earl of Peterborough, was baptized on 18 January 1599 at Lowick, Northamptonshire. Margaret Compton (*d.* c.1645) was his mother. The Mordaunt family had been prominent Northamptonshire Roman Catholics, and John Mordaunt's father, Henry, fourth Lord Mordaunt (c.1568–1609), was implicated in the Gunpowder Plot. As a result, in 1610 James I handed his son John (then fifth Lord Mordaunt) as a ward to Archbishop Abbott to ensure that he received a protestant education. Educated at Oxford, he enjoyed success at court, becoming a knight of the Bath in 1616, and he accompanied the king on his Scottish progress in 1617. Known in Northamptonshire as an ally of the first duke of Buckingham, he was prominent in local affairs, raising loans for the crown, and serving as a deputy lieutenant and as forester of part of Rockingham Forest. He had married Elizabeth Howard by 7 April 1621. In March 1628 he was raised to the earldom of Peterborough. Peterborough's relations with Charles I were complicated, however; after Buckingham's death he seems to have lost some favour at court, though he continued to serve loyally in the lieutenancy and on the bench, and was appointed lord lieutenant of Northamptonshire in 1640. He was fined £5000 for encroaching on Rockingham Forest, and resisted calls to contribute to the king's service in the bishops' wars. He refused to pay ship money and in January 1642 protested the Lords' defeat of the House of Commons' demand for control of the militia. Though suspicious of his religious background, parliament confirmed him as lord lieutenant of Northamptonshire in 1642 and gave him command of a regiment of foot as well as its army's artillery train. However, his military career was brief, for, already in ill health, he died of consumption on 19 June 1643; he was buried five days later at Turvey. His son Henry, second earl of Peterborough, said of him that 'he was not born for the advancement of his house', and criticized him for 'a humour he had, which was averse to constraint, and indulgent to all his passions' (Halstead, 404).

Henry Mordaunt succeeded to his father's title only two months after abandoning the captaincy of his father's horse troop in parliament's army for a command under the king. Educated at Eton College (1635–8) and in France,

where his tutor, Thomas Raymond, described him as a 'noble and hopefull … cavalier' (GEC, *Peerage*, 10.497), his defection to the royalist cause earned him command of a regiment of horse. He was seriously wounded at the first battle of Newbury in September 1643, but retained his command, serving at Cropredy and Lostwithiel (both 1644). He submitted to parliament after the battle of Naseby in 1645, and compounded for his estate, but a 1647 interview with the captive Charles I inspired him to join the earl of Holland's ill-fated uprising in July 1648. Peterborough escaped capture, but was ultimately forced to compound a second time. During the 1650s he lived quietly in the country, attempting to pay his debts.

Peterborough's reward after the Restoration was the governorship of Tangier, a prize of dubious value. Appointed on 16 September 1661, he took possession of the city in January 1662. While there he struggled against hostile Berbers and, he claimed, disloyal subordinates. He was recalled in December 1662 and compensated with a £1000 pension—which, however, was rarely paid. Commenting on the earl's recall, Pepys wrote 'though it is said [it] is done with kindness, yet all the world may see it is done otherwise' (Pepys, 3.283).

Although in 1667 Pepys commented that the earl's wife complained 'how they are forced to live beyond their estate and do get nothing by his [Peterborough's] being a courtier' (Pepys, 8.459–60), Peterborough's growing friendship with James, duke of York, offered brighter prospects. Probably thanks to James's patronage, in 1665 he served as a volunteer aboard the second rate *Unicorn* in the Second Anglo-Dutch War, and in 1678 he commanded a troop in York's regiment of horse. In 1666 he became lord lieutenant of Northamptonshire, a post he held until 1688; under James II he was colonel of the 2nd dragoon guards. Though his military experience undoubtedly endeared him to James, it was his service as a courtier and political ally that cemented their relationship. As early as 1663 he announced that 'old notions of mixed governments' were obsolete, and he advocated an expansion of the crown's authority (P. Seaward, *The Cavalier Parliament and the Reconstruction of the Old Regime*, 1989, 23). His connection with the duke became closer still in 1673 when Charles II appointed him ambassador-extraordinary, charged with arranging James's second marriage. Princess Mary of Modena, though not the duke's first choice, emerged as the successful candidate, and Peterborough stood as James's proxy in the royal wedding, which took place on 30 September 1673. He escorted the duchess back to England, where he took his seat as a privy councillor in 1674. Peterborough's close association with James resulted in accusations that he played a role in the Popish Plot. He was dropped from the council in 1679, and he and his wife took shelter in Brussels. He was back in England by 1680, and he worked passionately against moves to secure the exclusion of James from the succession in the House of Lords and as a lord lieutenant. He played a role in the uncovering of the Rye House plot in 1683, and was restored to the council in February 1683.

Peterborough carried the sceptre at James II's coronation and the king awarded him the Garter in June 1685. He was also appointed groom of the stole and first gentleman of the bedchamber and in 1686 he became Queen Mary's high steward and chief bailiff. In March 1687 he converted to Catholicism. A reliable supporter of James's policies, he assisted in the king's purges of the bench and lieutenancy, and added the lieutenancy of Rutland to his other places in January 1688. He was a witness at the birth of the prince of Wales in June 1688, and at the revolution he fell with his mentor. His home in Northamptonshire, Drayton, was sacked by a mob, and in December he was captured at Ramsgate attempting to flee the kingdom.

Imprisoned in the Tower from December 1688 to October 1690, Peterborough was impeached by the Commons in October 1689, though the proceedings were dropped. Although he rejoined the established church in 1692 he remained a Jacobite; in March 1692 he showed John Evelyn a portrait of the prince of Wales 'newly brought out of France' (Evelyn, 4.92), and in April he asked permission of the secretary of state to visit the exiled king. Past seventy, he was held under house arrest from February to March 1696 suspected of involvement in the assassination plot against William III. An illness occasioned by 'too liberal feeding on oysters' nearly killed him in September 1696, and thereafter his health declined. He died on 19 June 1697 and was buried ten days later in the parish church at Turvey, Bedfordshire. His wife, Lady Penelope O'Brien (b. c.1622), daughter of the fifth earl of Thomond, whom he married in 1644, survived him and died in 1702. They had two daughters: one, Elizabeth, never married, and a second, Mary (later Mary *Howard), became duchess of Norfolk, and was divorced from her husband in 1700. No less passionate a man than his father had been, Peterborough 'used his wife ill, … taking his pleasures elsewhere', but in his later years, after his many reverses, he was described as behaving himself 'humbly and sadly' (Fitzherbert MSS, 268; Rutland MSS, 2.127). With his chaplain, Richard Rands, he compiled a collection of Succinct Genealogies (1685), published under the pseudonym Robert Halstead. At his death his title passed to his nephew, Charles Mordaunt, third earl of Peterborough.   VICTOR STATER

Sources GEC, Peerage · R. Halstead [H. Mordaunt, second earl of Peterborough], Succinct genealogies of the noble and ancient houses (1685) · Pepys, Diary · Evelyn, Diary · P. R. Newman, The old service: royalist regimental colonels and the civil war, 1642–1646 (1993) · E. Cope, The life of a public man: Edward, first Baron Montagu of Boughton, 1562–1644 (1981) · The manuscripts of Sir William Fitzherbert … and others, HMC, 32 (1893) · Calendar of the manuscripts of the marquess of Ormonde, new ser., 8 vols., HMC, 36 (1902–20) · The manuscripts of his grace the duke of Rutland, 4 vols., HMC, 24 (1888–1905) · The manuscripts of S. H. Le Fleming, HMC, 25 (1890) · The manuscripts of the House of Lords, 4 vols., HMC, 17 (1887–94), vols. 2–3 · Report on the manuscripts of Allan George Finch, 5 vols., HMC, 71 (1913–2003) · C. Russell, The fall of the British monarchies, 1637–1642 (1991)
Archives BL, Egerton MS 2538 | BL, Governership of Tangier MSS

Mordaunt, Henry (1681?–1710), naval officer, was the second son of Charles *Mordaunt, third earl of Peterborough (1658?–1735), soldier and statesman, and Carey Fraizer (c.1658–1709). On 9 April 1703 he became captain of the Mary Galley; subsequently he commanded the Pendennis and Medway. In 1705 he was returned to parliament for Malmesbury; at this time he was said to be 'a very pretty gentleman, sober and well bred' (Ormonde MSS, new ser., 8.191). In 1706 he was captain of the Resolution (70 guns) in the Mediterranean.

On 13 March 1707, with the frigates Enterprise and Milford in company, Mordaunt sailed from Barcelona for Genoa, carrying as passengers his father and an ambassador from the titular king of Spain to the duke of Savoy. On 19 March he fell in with a French squadron of six ships of the line, newly out of Toulon, which came up fast with the English. The earl and the ambassador went on board the Enterprise, which, with the Milford, made her escape. By daybreak on 20 March the enemy's ships were well up with and engaged the Resolution, which defended herself stoutly. In the afternoon, when she was much shattered, Mordaunt ran her ashore near Ventimiglia. The French then sent in their boats to burn her, but these were beaten off.

During the night an 80-gun ship succeeded in getting within range, and as the Resolution was by this time full of water, and her magazine waterlogged, it was decided to set her on fire and abandon her. This was done during the morning of 21 March; her men were all landed, and by eleven o'clock the ship was burnt to the waterline. Mordaunt was severely wounded in the thigh, and obliged to return to England, which he did overland, through France, on a passport readily given on his father's request. On 25 November 1709 he was tried by court martial for the loss of his ship, and acquitted, the court resolving that he had behaved with 'great courage and conduct'.

Mordaunt died, unmarried, of smallpox on 24 February 1710 at Bath, at a time when he was intending to return to sea, having just recovered from the wound received on the Resolution. He was buried at Turvey, Bedfordshire on 1 March.   J. K. LAUGHTON, rev. J. D. DAVIES

Sources HoP, Commons, 1690–1715 [draft] · Calendar of the manuscripts of the marquess of Ormonde, new ser., 8 vols., HMC, 36 (1902–20), vol. 8, p. 191 · W. L. Clowes, The Royal Navy: a history from the earliest times to the present, 7 vols. (1897–1903); repr. (1996–7), vol. 2, pp. 515–16 · NMM, Sergison MSS, SER/136 · J. Charnock, ed., Biographia navalis, 3 (1795), 274–7 · parish register (burials), 1710, Turvey, Bedfordshire
Likenesses G. Kneller, oils; in possession of F. Milner in 1894

Mordaunt, Sir John (d. 1504), lawyer and administrator, was the son of William Mordaunt (d. 1481) of Turvey and his wife, Margaret (d. after 1481), daughter of John Peeke of Cople. Both his parents came from Bedfordshire, where the Mordaunts had been long established. No independent evidence survives to support the family tradition that John Mordaunt was an officer of Richard Neville, earl of Warwick, and in 1471 was wounded fighting for the earl at Barnet, and he is first reliably recorded only in 1483, as a JP and then as a commissioner to assess a subsidy, on both occasions in Bedfordshire. Legal practice was his first source of advancement and wealth, and he became a member of the Middle Temple. But he was also summoned by Richard III to serve against the Scots in 1484, and fought for Henry VII at Stoke in 1487.

As his fighting at Stoke shows, Mordaunt made the transition from York to Tudor without difficulty, and advanced rapidly under the new regime. In 1486 he was appointed to an important commission investigating concealed lands and royal rights in Bedfordshire. He had been MP for an unidentified constituency in the parliament of 1485–6. In 1487 not only was he again returned (and again, his constituency is unidentified), but he was also elected speaker of the Commons. That a substantial grant of taxation was made perhaps owed something to skilful management by Mordaunt, who afterwards received (as was customary) a grant of £100 from the king. MP for Grantham in 1491–2, he sat for Bedfordshire in 1495. In the same year he became both a serjeant-at-law and a king's serjeant. His appearances as a pleader are reported with some frequency in the year-books, which show him acting for the crown in some important lawsuits, for instance *Stonor's case* (1495–6), concerned with the king's rights of wardship. Regularly a JP for Bedfordshire, during the 1490s he became a justice of assize and gaol delivery, and consequently also a JP, for several other counties, principally in the south and south-west.

From the early 1490s Mordaunt was also increasingly involved in government, perhaps thanks to the patronage of Sir Reynold Bray. He was appointed to hear cases in the court of requests, was concerned with the administration of the duchy of Cornwall, and became a member of the king's council 'learned in the law' when that came into being c.1500. Several times recorded as investigating charges of riotous behaviour, he sat in Star Chamber, and was among the king's councillors summoned to parliament in 1497 and 1504. On 23 February 1501 he was granted an annuity of £100 during good behaviour. Although he served the crown above all as a lawyer, Mordaunt is also often recorded as involved in the implementation of Henry VII's policy of using financial instruments to control his subjects, by receiving bonds and recognizances on the king's behalf. Moreover he became a councillor to the king's mother, Lady Margaret Beaufort, and attorney to Prince Arthur, and was retained by such magnates as the duke of Buckingham and the earl of Surrey. About 1499 he was made chief justice at Chester. On 18 February 1503 he was knighted, and on 6 April 1504 he was appointed high steward of Cambridge University. Shortly afterwards, on 24 June, Mordaunt was nominated to succeed Bray as chancellor of the duchy of Lancaster, with an annual salary of 200 marks.

Mordaunt's rise to great place would go no further, for what was probably a sudden sickness struck him down. He made his will on 5 September 1504, and died six days later, most likely at Turvey. To his inherited estates in Bedfordshire he had added property in Dorset and Somerset by his marriage, before November 1484, to Edith, coheir of Sir Nicholas Latymer. In the years that followed he also acquired estates not only in the home counties and south-

east, but also in Northamptonshire and even in Northumberland. Shortly before his death he could afford to pay the king £1600 for the wardship of the heiress Jane Sayntmaur. His will records bequests to two sons and a daughter, and also the endowment of a chantry at Turvey, one of whose chaplains was to be qualified to teach grammar free of charge to all children coming there. However, the will also provided that should the chantry not be established within ten years, the endowment was to go to Mordaunt's heirs, as apparently happened. Mordaunt is nevertheless still commemorated by his effigy on his tomb in Turvey church, representing him in full armour. His wife survived him, and may afterwards have married a member of the Carew family. His eldest son, another John *Mordaunt, would become first Lord Mordaunt.

HENRY SUMMERSON

Sources Chancery records · R. Halstead [H. Mordaunt, second earl of Peterborough], *Succinct genealogies of the noble and ancient houses* (1685) · CIPM, Henry VII, 3, no. 875 · Baker, *Serjeants* · R. Somerville, *History of the duchy of Lancaster, 1265–1603* (1953) · E. W. Ives, *The common lawyers of pre-Reformation England* (1983) · J. S. Roskell, *The Commons and their speakers in English parliaments, 1376–1523* (1965) · *The Anglica historia of Polydore Vergil*, AD 1485–1537, ed. and trans. D. Hay, CS, 3rd ser., 74 (1950) · I. S. Leadam, ed., *Select cases in the court of requests*, AD 1497–1569, SeldS, 12 (1898) · C. G. Bayne and W. H. Dunham, eds., *Select cases in the council of Henry VII*, SeldS, 75 (1958) · J. C. Wedgwood and A. D. Holt, *History of parliament*, 1: *Biographies of the members of the Commons house, 1439–1509* (1936), 607–8 · C. Rawcliffe, *The Staffords, earls of Stafford and dukes of Buckingham, 1394–1521*, Cambridge Studies in Medieval Life and Thought, 3rd ser., 11 (1978), 202 · M. Condon, 'An anachronism with intent? Henry VII's council ordinance of 1491/2', *Kings and nobles in the later middle ages*, ed. R. A. Griffiths and J. Sherborne (1986), 228–53
Likenesses alabaster tomb effigy, All Saints' Church, Turvey, Bedfordshire

Mordaunt, John, first Baron Mordaunt (c.1480×85–1562), landowner and administrator, was the eldest son of Sir John *Mordaunt (d. 1504) and his wife, Edith Latymer. He was born in Bedfordshire, probably at the family seat of Turvey. His father's service to Henry VII gave him the entrée to court, and to the household of Prince Arthur, whose approximate contemporary he must have been. Between March and September 1499 he married Elizabeth, daughter and coheir of Sir Henry Vere of Great Addington, Northamptonshire, and his wife, Isabella (née Tresham). Mordaunt was made knight of the Bath when the future Henry VIII was created prince of Wales on 18 February 1503. On 3 July that year he was admitted to the Middle Temple, his father's inn, of which he was subsequently elected bencher.

Mordaunt succeeded to his father's estates in September 1504. On 1 November 1509 he was pricked sheriff for Bedfordshire and Buckinghamshire, and on 28 February 1513 he was granted arms. From the latter year he was increasingly employed in local government; he was also, in 1514, licensed to remain covered in the king's presence (probably because of some ailment). He attended many of the great public occasions of Henry VIII's reign, though never as more than one of the supporting cast. He was at the Field of Cloth of Gold in 1520, and was with the king at his meetings with Charles V later that year at Gravelines and in 1522 at Canterbury. By February 1526 he was of the king's council. In the same year he was appointed joint surveyor of woods in all crown lands. Following Wolsey's fall in 1529 he was among those who investigated the cardinal's possessions. In 1532 he was created (it is assumed by writ of summons) Baron Mordaunt of Turvey, taking his seat in the House of Lords on 4 May.

Mordaunt was one of two peers resident in Bedfordshire, where his chief interests lay. For a while he continued to travel further afield. In October 1532 he went with the king to France. He attended Queen Anne at her coronation in May 1533; he would have done likewise for Queen Jane, but instead bore a banner at her funeral. At the treason trial of Lord Dacre of Gilsland in 1534 Mordaunt, as junior peer, was the first to pronounce his (not guilty) verdict. He participated in several other state trials. When the north rose in 1536 he was seemingly too old for personal service, and was merely ordered to provide troops. In 1538 he came under suspicion after making his Lent confession to John Forest, a London Observant Franciscan soon afterwards executed. Mordaunt explained that the contact involved no discussion of public controversy. From 1538 he was regularly a commissioner of oyer and terminer on the East Anglian circuit. In 1539, following a fall, he was licensed to be absent from parliament; he was present there during 1540, but never again. Also in 1540 he attended in Star Chamber, though he was not a member of the newly defined privy council. In May 1546 he was a tax assessor for his county.

Mordaunt continued active as JP and on other commissions in the reigns of Edward VI and Mary I. At the start of Edward's reign he was again excused parliamentary attendance; the one record of his presence is probably a clerical error. In 1551 he was named to a commission inquiring into grain prices. His first duty on Mary's accession was to give a Bedford woman a ducking for speaking ill of the queen. In 1557 he was a commissioner for assessing the forced loan. Lord Mordaunt and his eldest son, Sir John *Mordaunt, had co-operated in building up the family estates, but relations between them soured when Sir John attempted to compel his own son, Lewis, to marry his stepsister (whom he had, it seems, compromised). Lord Mordaunt took his grandson's side and sought to make him his direct heir. This feud was more or less composed by the time Mordaunt made his will on 1 August 1560. He died at Turvey on 18 August 1562 and was buried in the church there on 16 September following. He provided £60 for the erection of an alabaster monument to himself and his wife, who had predeceased him. Mordaunt's eldest son succeeded as second baron. His second son Edmund was MP for Bedford in three Marian parliaments. His other children were William, George, Edith, Margaret, Etheldreda (a nun of Barking, perhaps later married to John Broun), and Winifred.

Mordaunt has been instanced as typical of the backwoods peer who 'retained the mentality of a country gentleman' but on whom the crown could rely for performance of all manner of public duties (Graves, 38–9). Mordaunt himself had entertained larger aspirations. In 1528 he offered the king £100 and Wolsey 500 marks (towards the building of Cardinal College, Oxford) to secure the under-treasurership of England. In this and all other suits for office he was unsuccessful. In April 1539 he told Cromwell the king 'never gave me nothyng' (PRO, SP 1/150, fol. 191; new fol. 171). This was not quite true, since Mordaunt had acquired much property by crown grant; he had also been a keen collector of monastic land, and in late 1535 he and his eldest son allegedly browbeat the nuns of Harrold, Bedfordshire, in attempting to annex property of the house. But the Mordaunts were unsympathetic to further religious reform, which may have contributed to the first baron's failure to achieve the place he coveted in central government.

C. S. KNIGHTON

Sources F. A. Blaydes, ed., *The visitations of Bedfordshire, annis Domini 1566, 1582, and 1634*, Harleian Society, 19 (1884), 40–2 · R. Halstead [H. Mordaunt, second earl of Peterborough], *Succinct genealogies of the noble and ancient houses* (1685), 525–603 · BL, Harley MS 6767, fols. 18v–21 (pp. 30–33); Cotton MS Cleopatra E.iv, fols. 161–161v; MS Titus B.i, fols. 326–326v · GEC, *Peerage*, 9.193–5, appx B, p. 18 [see also pp. 195–6, 2nd baron] · LP *Henry VIII*, 4/2.4452; 4/3, appx 67–8; 9.1005; 11.844; 13/1.880; 14/1.845 · State papers general series, Henry VIII, PRO, SP 1/150, fol. 191 · CPR, 1547–8, 75, 76, 80, 85, 87; 1549–51, 51; 1550–53, 140–41, 311; 1553, 351, 356; 1553–4, 17 (*bis*), 20, 22, 29, 343; 1554–5, 107; 1555–7, 375; 1557–8, 401, 428 · APC, 1552–4, 332; 1554–6, 66, 144; 1556–8, 320 · CSP dom., 1547–1580, 81, 85, 295 · M. A. R. Graves, *The House of Lords in the parliaments of Edward VI and Mary I* (1981), 38–9, 68, 84, 243 n.69 · H. Miller, *Henry VIII and the English nobility* (1986), 24–5, 45, 54–5, 66, 96–8, 125, 151, 157, 179, 203, 244 · J. A. Guy, 'Privy council: revolution or evolution?', *Revolution reassessed*, ed. C. Coleman and D. Starkey (1986), 81 · Y. Nicholls, ed., *Court of augmentations accounts for Bedfordshire*, 1, Bedfordshire Historical RS, 63 (1984), 70, 97, 107, 203, 209; 2, Bedfordshire Historical RS, 64 (1985), 94 · W. Jerdan, ed., *Rutland papers: original documents illustrative of the courts and times of Henry VII and Henry VIII*, CS, 21 (1842), 33, n. b · *The diary of Henry Machyn, citizen and merchant-taylor of London, from AD 1550 to AD 1563*, ed. J. G. Nichols, CS, 42 (1848), 292 · H. A. C. Sturgess, ed., *Register of admissions to the Honourable Society of the Middle Temple, from the fifteenth century to the year 1944*, 1 (1949), 5, n.1 · N. M. Fuidge, 'Mordaunt, Edmund', 'John Mordaunt', HoP, *Commons, 1509–58*, 2.614; 614–16 [Edmund, 2nd son, and John, 1st son; 2nd Baron Mordaunt] · will, PRO, PROB 11/45, sig. 22 · S. B. Chrimes, *Henry VII* (1972), 150, n. 3

Likenesses T. Kirby, alabaster effigy, c.1560, All Saints' Church, Turvey, Bedfordshire

Wealth at death land in Bedfordshire: will, PRO, PROB 11/45, fols. 151–153v; Nicholls, ed., *Court of augmentations*

Mordaunt, John, second Baron Mordaunt (1508–1571), landowner and administrator, was the eldest son of John *Mordaunt, first Baron Mordaunt (c.1480x85–1562), and his wife, Elizabeth Vere. He married, before 24 February 1526, Ela, daughter of John FitzLewis (son and heir of Sir Richard FitzLewis of West Horndon, Essex) and Alice, daughter and coheir of John Harleston. He was made knight of the Bath on 31 May 1533, the eve of Anne Boleyn's coronation. This launch of his public career involved expense unwelcome to his father, but led to a succession of appointments. In 1534 he was a collector of the Bedfordshire subsidy, and in January 1535 he was appointed a commissioner for the spiritual tenth in the county. Despite Catholic sympathies father and son co-operated in the suppression of their local monasteries. During his father's lifetime Sir John lived mostly at the

John Mordaunt, second Baron Mordaunt (1508–1571), by unknown artist, 1564

Essex property which he had acquired by marriage. After being nominated sheriff for Bedfordshire and Buckinghamshire (1537) and for Essex and Hertfordshire (1538 and 1539), he was pricked for the latter shrievalty in November 1540. His wife died on 2 June 1543, having had four sons and six daughters. At this time Sir John acquired the bailiffship of the duchy of Cornwall manor of Newport Pound, Essex; meanwhile he was building up his own landholdings. He supplied men for the 1543 expedition to Flanders, and to the rearguard of the army which went to France in the following year; he does not appear to have served in person with either force. In 1544–5 he first sat on the Essex bench. By licence of 3 December 1545 he married as his second wife Joan, widow of Robert Wilford, merchant tailor (who had died on 18 or 19 September that year). She was the daughter of Sir Richard Fermor of Easton Neston, Northamptonshire, and was sometime maid of honour to Princess Mary. There were no children of the marriage. Mordaunt had no enthusiasm for the religious policy of Henry VIII's last years and of Edward VI's reign, and his public duties were slight. In December 1550 he was a taxation commissioner for Bedfordshire, and in 1552 he was given the stewardship of the duchy of Lancaster manor of Olney, Bedfordshire.

The accession of Mary in 1553 brought Mordaunt the place in government which had eluded his father. He was among those who joined the queen's array at Kenninghall (between 9 and 12 July) as she prepared to claim her crown. Mordaunt was admitted to the privy council, one of several on whom this honour was rather abruptly conferred. He was clearly not part of the core group of Mary's East Anglian affinity: the Suffolk chronicler Wingfield refers to him with others as 'ex longioribus locis' ('from further

away'; Wingfield, *Vita Mariae*, 206, 255). His wife's attachment to the queen doubtless assisted his elevation. His first duty (23 July) was to escort the marquess of Northampton to the Tower. He then joined the queen at Richmond (22 August), and for the next three years was fairly regular in attending the council, but he never belonged to the inner group of policy makers. In October 1553 he sat as MP for Bedfordshire, as he did in the parliaments of 1554 and 1555. He was appointed to the commissions of sewers and oyer and terminer for Essex, as well as continuing as JP for the county. In February 1554, following Wyatt's rebellion, he also sat with the justices of oyer and terminer for Middlesex at Old Bailey, and with those for Sussex at Southwark. Also in 1554 he was made constable of Hertford Castle and (29 June) received with his father and Lord Bray a substantial grant of property in Bedfordshire.

On 8 February 1557 Mordaunt was named to the heresy commission. Between 18 May and 14 December that year he attended no council meetings, and his appearance on 15 December was his last. He was, however, busy during that summer in supervising the Essex musters, and in January 1558 he helped to assemble men from the county for the aborted expedition in defence of Calais. On Elizabeth's accession he ceased to be a councillor, and seems also to have lost his other crown offices. In April 1561 he was briefly imprisoned in the Tower for hearing mass. He attended the parliament of 1563 and served as commissioner for musters for Essex again that year. He is last recorded on the county bench in 1564. In 1571 at the time of the Ridolfi plot he was considered a potential friend by the duke of Norfolk and his associates, but there is no evidence that Mordaunt was then or ever engaged in conspiracy.

Mordaunt's relationship with his father had been amicable until the time of his second marriage. A dispute then arose because his son and heir, Lewis, compromised his stepsister, and the girl's mother insisted on a marriage. Sir John sought to debar Lewis from succeeding to the Fitz-Lewis lands in Essex, but Lord Mordaunt was persuaded to take Lewis into his custody and to disinherit Sir John from the main Mordaunt estate in Bedfordshire. Concord was largely restored before the old Lord Mordaunt died on 18 August 1562, though the second baron still attempted to impede his son's full enjoyment of the Essex inheritance. Mordaunt was too ill to attend the parliament summoned for April 1571: he made his will on 16 April and died at Turvey some time before 19 October. He was buried in Turvey church, and left £250 for the erection of his monument there. His widow married Sir Thomas Kempe (d. 1591) and died in 1592.

C. S. KNIGHTON

Sources GEC, *Peerage*, new edn, 9.195–6 · HoP, *Commons, 1509–58*, 2.614–16 · R. Halstead [H. Mordaunt, second earl of Peterborough], *Succinct genealogies of the noble and ancient houses* (1685), 401–2, 599–603, 605–7 · *LP Henry VIII*, 6, no. 562(i), p. 246; 7, nos. 884, 1496; 8, no. 149(54); 9, no. 1005; 12/2, no. 1150(18); 13/2, no. 967(26); 14/2, no. 619(38); 16, no. 305(80); 18, no. 832, p. 468; 19, no. 273 (150), 276; 20, no. 623(vi), p. 322 · *CPR, 1553*, 352; *1553–4*, 19, 27, 36, 343; *1554–5*, 94, 107; *1555–7*, 125, 281–2, 405 · *CSP dom.*, rev. edn, *1547–53*, 15, 48, 88, 119; rev. edn, *1553–8* 83; *1547–80*, 225; *addenda, 1547–65*, 510 · *CSP Rome, 1558–71*, 68 [incorrectly called 'Sir Thomas'], 265, 400, 412 ·

APC, 1552–4, 302, 327, 374, 398; 1556–8, 160, 162, 237; 1558–70, 242 · D. MacCulloch, 'The *Vita Mariae Angliae Reginae* of Robert Wingfield of Brantham', *Camden miscellany*, XXVIII, CS, 4th ser., 29 (1984), 181–301 · D. E. Hoak, 'Two revolutions in Tudor government: the formation and organization of Mary I's privy council', *Revolution reassessed: revisions in the history of Tudor government and administration*, ed. C. Coleman and D. Starkey (1986), 100 and n. 39, 114 **Likenesses** portrait, 1564, Brasenose College, Oxford [*see illus.*] · J. Fittler and J. Skelton, engraving, 1816, BL, Add. MS 32352, fol. 277 · effigy on marble monument?, Turvey church, Bedfordshire **Wealth at death** £400 to daughter Ursula, £133 6s. 8d. to granddaughter Anne Actem, £250 for building aisle in Turvey church and tomb there; no other large bequests: will, quoted in [Halstead], *Succinct genealogies*, 600–03

Mordaunt, John, first earl of Peterborough (*bap.* 1599, *d.* 1643). *See under* Mordaunt, Henry, second earl of Peterborough (*bap.* 1623, *d.* 1697).

Mordaunt, John, first Viscount Mordaunt of Avalon (1626–1675), royalist conspirator, was born on 18 June and baptized on 20 June 1626 at Lowick, Northamptonshire, the second son of John *Mordaunt, fifth Baron Mordaunt and later first earl of Peterborough (*bap.* 1599, *d.* 1643) [*see under* Mordaunt, Henry], and his wife, Elizabeth (1603–1671), daughter of William, first Baron Howard of Effingham. He was educated privately in France and Italy and it is unclear when he returned from the continent. However, he was in England by July 1648 when he joined his elder brother Henry *Mordaunt, second earl of Peterborough, in a royalist uprising. John raised 200 horsemen for the king, but the rising failed and he, along with his brother, fled into exile, staying for a time at The Hague.

Mordaunt had returned to England by 1652, when a challenge to a duel from Brian Cockayne ended in a brief stay in the Tower. He was on the fringes of royalist conspiracy throughout the early and mid-1650s; in 1654 Sir Edward Hyde wrote to him, accepting his offer of service. But he did not play an important role until after his marriage, on 7 May 1657, to Elizabeth (1632/3–1679), daughter of Thomas Carey, second son of Robert, earl of Monmouth. That year he promised 400–500 men for Charles II, and in 1658 he plotted with the marquess of Ormond, in England on a secret visit. A royalist turncoat, John Stapley, betrayed Mordaunt and he was arrested on 1 April 1658. Closely questioned by Cromwell himself he was released and rearrested on 15 April, charged with treason. Mordaunt's trial, before a special commission of forty, began on 1 June, and he avoided the block by a mixture of judicious bribery and blind luck. After first refusing to accept the court's jurisdiction he finally pleaded not guilty. A key witness, one Morley, escaped—possibly through Elizabeth Mordaunt's means—and one of the judges, Colonel Thomas Pride, who was expected to favour a conviction, was taken ill and did not vote. There were nineteen votes for acquittal and nineteen for conviction; the president of the court, John Lisle, spared Mordaunt with his casting vote.

Released shortly afterwards Mordaunt immediately returned to his work for the king. His career as a royalist plotter was difficult: though he had the support and trust of the king, Ormond, and Hyde, many royalists disliked

John Mordaunt, first Viscount Mordaunt of Avalon (1626–1675), by William Faithorne the elder (after Adriaen Hanneman, 1648)

and resented him. Through his mother, a devout presbyterian, he had connections with discontented peers and gentlemen, once parliamentarians, who now favoured a restoration. The exiled court hoped that he could forge an alliance between presbyterians and royalists. Older royalists, particularly members of the devoted, if ineffectual, Sealed Knot, refused to co-operate with Mordaunt, who did not make matters any easier by his headstrong impatience. Hyde expected Mordaunt to be the acknowledged leader of the royalist cause in England and in March 1659 Charles named Mordaunt, along with several members of the Knot, to a 'Great Trust and Commission' whose charge was to effect a restoration. The members of the Knot refused to act, and by July 1659 the commission was a largely presbyterian body, dominated by Mordaunt. A mark of the king's favour came in March 1659, when he signed a warrant for Mordaunt's viscountcy as Viscount Mordaunt of Avalon. Despite this, however, bitter divisions among the royalists continued.

About June 1659 Mordaunt returned from a trip to Brussels prepared to lead a new rising. The confused political situation after Richard Cromwell's fall in April offered new hope for the royalist cause. But continuing bickering among royalists and the efficiency of the government's intelligence doomed Mordaunt's plans. Originally planned for July, the uprising was delayed several times, and on 28 July the council of state ordered his arrest, though he was not taken. The Sealed Knot once again refused to lend any assistance, and when Mordaunt finally appeared for the king near Barnstead Down in Surrey in early August only thirty men turned up. He and his followers narrowly avoided capture, and Mordaunt hid in London until he could make his escape to France. He landed at Calais on 7 September 1659.

By the time Mordaunt arrived in France the only serious royalist uprising, led by Sir George Booth in Cheshire, had been put down. This left the erstwhile royalist general kicking his heels in Calais, assigning blame for the disaster to others, though his own poor planning undoubtedly played a role in the defeat. In the following weeks Mordaunt nursed hopes of a falling out between parliament and the army. When General Lambert expelled the Rump on 13 October 1659 Mordaunt prepared his return to England, and was in London by 22 October. Indefatigable as ever he worked to advance the king's fortunes, plotting a French invasion and yet another uprising. But during these months Mordaunt's credit was on the wane at court. Perceived as a creature of Hyde's, his attempt to distance himself from Sir Edward did him no good with any faction. Sir John Grenville, a kinsman of General George Monck, overshadowed Mordaunt during the winter of 1659–60. The viscount's effectiveness was further reduced as his relations with the presbyterians frayed over their insistence upon a conditional restoration.

Despite these setbacks Mordaunt remained among the most active and well-known royalist conspirators. He was again in France in November 1659, consulting with the king and arguing fruitlessly for a French invasion. He was still in France when the Rump was restored on 26 December, but he had returned to London by 13 January 1660, still pleading for French intervention and warning the court against trusting Monck. Mordaunt remained in the dark about Grenville's negotiations with the general; his days of leadership were now over, and he became a spectator more than an actor in the events leading up to the Restoration. In March he failed in his desire to obtain a vacant secretaryship of state, a sign of his waning influence. The post went to William Morice, a client of Monck's. Mordaunt was among the thousands who welcomed Charles II to Dover on 25 May, and Charles knighted him there, along with his rival, the general.

Although Mordaunt devoted a dozen years to the king's cause—he was certainly among the most active, if not the most successful, of royalist conspirators—his rewards were comparatively modest. Charles named him lord lieutenant of Surrey and gave him command of a regiment of horse. The king also appointed him governor of Windsor Castle and ranger of the forest there, and gave him the keepership of the Great Park of Windsor. He did at least obtain a partial share of the Newcastle coal farm, which must have provided a steady income. His lack of success at the Restoration court must in some part be due to his personality: he was clearly difficult to deal with at times. In 1664 he served as a volunteer in the Royal Navy, provoking Samuel Pepys to complain bitterly about 'gentlemen reformadoes' who were 'good for nothing while they serve but to impoverish their captains and enslave them … as my Lord Mordaunt in particular did do' (*Tangier Papers*, 120). Pepys even disliked Mordaunt's literary efforts, writing about some of the viscount's poetry, 'But lord they are but sorry things, only, a lord made them' (Pepys, *Diary*, 5.352).

Clarendon believed that his friend was unjustly treated, but when Mordaunt was attacked in the parliamentary session of 1666 many hoped to see him punished. William Taylor, surveyor of Windsor Castle, complained to the Commons that in 1661 Mordaunt had turned him out of his lodgings, imprisoned him, and attempted to rape his daughter. The truth of the most sensational charge was questionable, but it is clear that Taylor had provoked Mordaunt to act precipitately by standing for the Commons from New Windsor against the governor's wishes. Parliament duly impeached Mordaunt on 18 December 1666. He responded to the charges in January 1667 in a written answer, but the Lords never heard witnesses in the case. The king prorogued the session in February, and pardoned Mordaunt in July, before proceedings resumed. The case was briefly a *cause célèbre*; Pepys's friend Captain Cocke claimed that people were so incensed about Mordaunt's escape that a new civil war threatened. An attempt to revive the charges in the next session fizzled out, but by summer 1667 rumours circulated that Mordaunt would lose his offices. In fact he retained his Windsor offices until September 1668, when he did resign, keeping only his lieutenancy of Surrey. The fall of his friend and protector, Clarendon, probably played a part in his retirement; he never took any significant part in politics afterwards. In 1668 Mordaunt joined his wife in Montpellier, France, where she had gone for her health, and which was also Clarendon's home in exile. The Mordaunts remained in France until 1669, when they returned to their house at Parson's Green, Middlesex. Mordaunt died of a fever at Parson's Green on 5 June 1675 and was buried in All Saints' Church, Fulham, on the 14th. He left eleven children; the eldest was Charles *Mordaunt, third earl of Peterborough, the famous general of the War of the Spanish Succession. VICTOR STATER

Sources *The letter-book of John, Viscount Mordaunt, 1658–1660*, ed. M. Coate, CS, 3rd ser., 69 (1945) · GEC, *Peerage* · Clarendon, *Hist. rebellion* · *The life of Edward, earl of Clarendon … written by himself*, new edn, 3 vols. (1827) · *Calendar of the Clarendon state papers preserved in the Bodleian Library*, ed. O. Ogle and others, 5 vols. (1869–1970) · D. Underdown, *Royalist conspiracy in England, 1649–1660* (1960) · Evelyn, *Diary* · Pepys, *Diary* · *The Tangier papers of Samuel Pepys*, ed. E. Chappell, Navy RS, 73 (1935) · *Tenth report*, HMC (1885); repr. (1906), 188–216 · DNB · *Northamptonshire*, Pevsner (1961)

Archives Berks. RO, letters to Sir Nicholas Carew · Bodl. Oxf., Clarendon papers

Likenesses W. Faithorne the elder, line engraving, *c*.1661, BM, NPG · J. Bushnell, statue on marble funeral monument, *c*.1676, All Saints' Church, Fulham, London · line engraving, pubd 1796 (after unknown artist), BM, NPG · W. Faithorne the elder, engraving (after A. Hanneman, 1648), BM [*see illus.*]

Mordaunt, Sir John (1696/7–1780), army officer, was the eldest son of Lieutenant-General Harry Mordaunt (1663–1720), MP and treasurer of the ordnance, a brother of Charles Mordaunt, third earl of Peterborough, and his first wife, Margaret (1674–1706), illegitimate daughter of Sir Thomas Spencer, third baronet, of Yarnton, Oxfordshire. He entered the army in 1721, and became captain in the 3rd dragoons in 1726 and captain and lieutenant-colonel in the 3rd foot guards in 1731.

About this time Mordaunt also began a parliamentary career, as MP for Pontefract from February 1730 to 1734, in the interest of John Monckton, first Viscount Galway. He later (from 1735) represented Whitchurch, Hampshire, in the gift of John Wallop, Viscount Lymington, and from 1741 Cockermouth, where he acted as political guardian for a succession of young heirs to the Lawson family, into which his sister had married. A staunch whig, Mordaunt was a strong supporter of Robert Walpole, and was especially active during army debates. By June 1744 he had risen to the rank of colonel of the 18th foot, and was sent to Flanders as part of the British force assembled to meet the French invasion of the Netherlands. The allied army, commanded by William Augustus, duke of Cumberland, suffered defeat at Fontenoy in May 1745. Having been recalled in November and promoted brigadier-general, Mordaunt was sent against the Jacobite rising in Scotland. At Falkirk, Mordaunt rallied the scattered battalions and corps after the defeat of the government forces.

During the decisive battle of Culloden in April 1746 Mordaunt commanded the reserve. After the battle he was detached with 900 volunteers to pursue the fleeing rebels. For these actions Cumberland later presented him with Charles Edward Stuart's coach, on condition that he drove to London with it: 'That I will, sir,' he replied, 'and drive on till it stops at the Cocoa Tree'—a well-known tory haunt (Walpole, *Corr.*, 9.35).

The following year (1747) Mordaunt was appointed major-general and colonel of the 12th dragoons, and he distinguished himself at the battle of Laffeldt in July. In 1749 he was made colonel of the 4th Irish horse, and moved later that year to the 10th dragoons. Following the end of the war Mordaunt was appointed KB, and he became one of the inspecting generals. In 1752 he was appointed governor of Sheerness. In peacetime Mordaunt revealed his relaxed nature—James Wolfe, then a lieutenant-colonel and in love with Mordaunt's niece Elizabeth Lawson, described a stay at Mordaunt's home, Freefolk, near Whitchurch, in July 1754: 'Sir J. Mordaunt's civility, good breeding and good humour make his house easy and pleasant to his guests' (Willson, 237).

The outbreak of the Seven Years' War in January 1756 immediately brought intelligence of a plan for an invasion of England, and with it the chain of events which would lead to the expedition against Rochefort which would define Mordaunt's lasting reputation. A number of army camps were set up in southern England to meet the threat, with Mordaunt commanding the camp at Blandford. In this situation, and with the war in North America going badly, it was felt that Great Britain needed to deliver a powerful counterstroke to regain the initiative. In the earliest phase of the war the prime minister, Thomas Pelham-Holles, duke of Newcastle, had proposed a diversionary raid, mentioning a number of possible objectives including Minorca, Corsica, St Domingo, Luxembourg, or the French coast itself. In November 1756, following the formation of the ministry of William Cavendish, fourth duke of Devonshire, with William Pitt as secretary of state for the southern department, the cabinet wished to support Cumberland's campaign in Germany without engaging additional British troops in the field. Sir John Ligonier, lieutenant-general of the ordnance and most senior army officer after Cumberland, had earlier in the year received a report from Lieutenant Robert Clerk, an engineer, which drew attention to the meagre defences of the naval base at Rochefort. On a visit in 1754 he had judged that the French town had inadequate fortifications, only an incomplete rampart about 25 feet high with a dry ditch protecting the town. The idea of a diversionary attack on Rochefort was supported by Pitt, who took the lead in arranging the flotilla. An additional factor which further favoured the choice of Rochefort was Ligonier's belief that there were a number of disaffected Huguenots in the area.

By the summer of 1757 a cabinet committee attended by Ligonier had accepted Clerk's report. Mordaunt was personally selected by George II to command the expedition, supported by Henry Seymour Conway and Edward Cornwallis. Both Mordaunt and Conway doubted whether the attack on Rochefort could succeed, and their fears were shared by the naval commanders Admiral Sir Edward Hawke and Vice-Admiral Sir Charles Knowles. Ligonier endeavoured to overcome Mordaunt's doubts, acknowledging that where 'neither the country nor the number of troops you are to act against is known with any precision a good deal must be left to fortune' (Whitworth, 221). However, he was confident that there were only 10,000 or fewer defending the western coast of France, and that the expedition was unlikely to be overwhelmed. Mordaunt and Conway remained unhappy—a 'tip and run' strategy held no appeal for contemporary army officers who preferred the set-piece tactics in progress in Germany—but with the political will behind the scheme they, Hawke, and Knowles eventually accepted the plan.

Pitt's instructions stated that the force was to take Rochefort if practical, and that it might venture to attack other French ports on its return. It was required to return by the end of September. Following the news of the defeat of Cumberland at Hastenbeck on 26 July, and the deployment of forty French battalions in Flanders, a French invasion was viewed as a real threat. After numerous delays the force, which consisted of thirty-one warships, forty-nine transports, and ten battalions of soldiers, sailed from the Isle of Wight on 6 September, and reached the Basque Roads on the 21st. The fleet was at first becalmed, but two days later captured the Île d'Aix, which guarded the mouth of the River Charente on which Rochefort lay. The two services were generally in agreement about where to land along the Bay of Chatelaillon, but a factor unconsidered in London now arose: shallow water would prevent the troop transports and naval vessels from approaching within a mile and a half of the shore. Mordaunt called a council of war on board the *Neptune* on 25 September. The meeting, which lasted all day, included a further report from Clerk, now a lieutenant-colonel, which suggested that Rochefort's defences could have been improved since 1754. Neutral ships also reported French preparations for British attack. The assembled senior officers of both services declared unanimously that an assault on Rochefort was 'neither advisable nor practical' (*London Magazine*, 651–2). Time was running out for the expedition as the equinox was expected to bring a prevailing westerly wind, which could generally delay or impede the fleet's movements. After two more days' reconnaissance and offers from General Conway to attempt a feint towards the Île de Ré or lead a real assault against the Île d'Oleron or Fort Fouras, Mordaunt summoned another council of war on the *Ramillies* on 28 September. This meeting unanimously decided to make a night attack on the forts at the mouth of the Charente. Mordaunt placed himself in the first embarkation. At the last moment naval officers called off the operation, as a strong wind from the shore threatened to hamper the longboats and prolong the embarkation. The tensions inherent in a divided command surfaced on the following day, when Hawke declared in a written note his intention of immediately sailing for England in default of any further military plans. A meeting of the land officers could only concur. The fleet set sail on 1 October and began arriving in Portsmouth on the 6th—with no new incursions upon the French coast.

The news of the failure of the expedition was received with fury by Pitt. The common council of the City of London demanded an inquiry. The cost of the expedition had been upwards of a million pounds. Mordaunt found he was in disgrace at court and also pressed for a formal hearing. George II instituted a board of three senior army officers: Charles Spencer, third duke of Marlborough; Lord George Sackville; and John Waldegrave. Witnesses included Mordaunt, Conway, and the expedition's quartermaster-general, James Wolfe. However, the board's report found 'It does not appear to us that there were then, or at any time afterwards either a Body of Troops or Batteries on the Shore sufficient to have prevented the attempting a Descent' (*Report of the General Officers*, 60). The board added that it rejected the notion that Rochefort's defences could have been so improved to have prevented any assault.

The findings of the general officers inevitably entailed a court martial. Mordaunt's trial took place from 14 to 20 December 1757. He remained confident of acquittal. His initial instructions had left much to his discretion. The charge of disobedience was unsustainable and he was unanimously acquitted. George II reluctantly confirmed the verdict. Nevertheless, the following July he struck the names of Mordaunt, Conway, and Cornwallis from the staff. Mordaunt also lost his post as governor of Sheerness.

Mordaunt remained in the army, but after Rochefort never again held a senior command in the field. He retired from the Commons in 1768. He became a full general in 1770 and was governor of Berwick from 1778 until his death. He died at Bevis Mount (his home from the mid-1750s), near Southampton, on 23 October 1780, aged eighty-three. He never married. He was buried on 28 October 1780 at St Mary's, Southampton. At the time of his death he was second general in the army list.

CLIVE TOWSE

Sources J. S. Corbett, *England in the Seven Years' War: a study in combined strategy*, 2 vols. (1907) · H. Walpole, *Memoirs of King George II*, ed. J. Brooke, 3 vols. (1985) · [C. S. Marlborough and others], *The report of the general officers, appointed … to inquire into the causes of failure of the late expedition to the coasts of France* (1758) · *Proceedings of the general court martial* (1758) · A. Collins, *The peerage of England*, ed. B. Longmate, 5th edn, 8 vols. (1779) · W. K. Hackmann, 'The British raid on Rochefort, 1757', *Mariner's Mirror*, 64 (1978), 163–75 · R. Middleton, *The bells of victory: the Pitt–Newcastle ministry and the conduct of the Seven Years' War, 1757–1762* (1985) · R. Whitworth, *Field Marshal Lord Ligonier: a story of the British army, 1702–1770* (1958) · R. R. Sedgwick, 'Mordaunt, John', HoP, *Commons, 1715–54* · *The life and letters of James Wolfe*, ed. H. B. Willson (1909) · Walpole, *Corr.* · L. B. Namier, 'Mordaunt, Sir John', HoP, *Commons, 1754–90* · *GM*, 1st ser., 50 (1780), 495 · *London Magazine*, 26 (1757), 651–3 · W. A. Shaw, *The knights of England*, 1 (1906), 169 · parish register, Southampton, St Mary's, 28 Oct 1780 [burial]
Archives BL, letters to Sir Thomas Robinson, Add. MSS 23827–23829
Likenesses B. Dandridge, oils, 1735, Althorp, Northamptonshire

Mordell, Louis Joel (1888–1972), mathematician, was born on 28 January 1888 in Philadelphia, Pennsylvania, the third in the family of eight children (four sons and four daughters) of the Hebrew scholar Phineas Mordell (1861–1934) and his wife, Annie, *née* Feller (1865–1938), who were both recent immigrants from Lithuania. When at the age of fourteen he entered the Central High School of Philadelphia he was already fascinated by mathematics and had read widely. In 1906 he scraped together the single fare to Cambridge to compete in the scholarship examination. Top of the list, he was awarded a scholarship at St John's College. In 1909 he sat part one of the mathematical tripos and was third wrangler. The following year he was put in the middle of the three divisions of the first class in part two.

Mordell's reading had already attracted him to the theory of numbers, which in its various aspects was to become his life's work. There was little interest in the subject at that time in England, and he regarded himself as self-taught, but his investigations won him a Smith's prize.

In 1913 Mordell left Cambridge for a lectureship at Birkbeck College, London, where he remained, apart from two years as a statistician at the Ministry of Munitions, until 1920. On 24 May 1916 Mordell married Mabel Elizabeth (1895/6–1971), the only daughter of Rosa and Joseph Cambridge, a small farmer in the town of the same name. They had a son and a daughter. His years at Birkbeck were productive, his main interest being in modular functions and their application to number theory.

From 1920 to 1922 Mordell was lecturer at the Manchester College of Technology. This period saw his most important single discovery, his 'finite basis theorem'. This states that the rational points on a non-singular plane cubic can all be obtained from a finite number of them by a definite process, confirming the earlier conjecture of

Poincaré. It seems likely that Mordell failed to realize the full significance of his work: in any case he had no part in later developments. In 1922 he moved to the University of Manchester where, after a year as reader, he was appointed to the Fielden chair of pure mathematics, which he occupied until 1945. He was now a leading figure in the mathematical world and was elected FRS in 1924. He took British nationality on 10 December 1929.

Mordell was an enlightened head of department and very concerned with the quality of the teaching. He built up an extremely strong school of mathematics, particularly in the 1930s when almost every young mathematician of note seems to have passed through the department. He was very active in assisting refugee mathematicians from Germany or Italy. A topic which occupied him at this time was the estimation of the number of points on algebraic varieties over finite fields; in the early 1940s he became interested in the geometry of numbers and initiated a period of great advance by himself and others.

In 1945 Mordell succeeded G. H. Hardy in the Sadleirian chair in Cambridge and was elected to a fellowship of St John's. He rapidly built up a powerful research school. After his retirement in 1953 he retained his fellowship and his house in Cambridge, though he travelled extensively. His enthusiasm for the theory of numbers never left him: he was working and publishing right to the end. He was a problem solver of great ingenuity and it gave him particular pleasure to obtain or extend by elementary means results that had first been found by sophisticated ones. He had the gift of imparting his enthusiasm and was in great demand as a lecturer. He enjoyed travelling. He was awarded the Sylvester medal of the Royal Society in 1949. He was president of the London Mathematical Society (1943–5) and received both its De Morgan medal (1941) and its senior Berwick prize (1946). He was a foreign member of the academies of Norway, Uppsala, and Bologna and an honorary doctor of the universities of Glasgow (1956), Mount Allison (1959), and Waterloo (1970).

Mordell, who had enjoyed robust health throughout his life, died from a brain haemorrhage at Addenbrooke's Hospital, Cambridge, on 12 March 1972.

J. W. S. CASSELS, *rev.*

Sources J. W. S Cassels, *Memoirs FRS*, 19 (1973), 493–520 • L. J. Mordell, 'Reminiscences of an octogenarian mathematician', *American Mathematical Monthly*, 78 (1971), 952–61 • L. J. Mordell, *Reflections of a mathematician* (Montreal, 1959) • J. W. S. Cassels, *Bulletin of the London Mathematical Society*, 6 (1974), 69–96 • H. Davenport, 'L. J. Mordell', *Acta Arithmetica*, 9 (1964), 3–12 • 'Phineas Mordell', *Universal Jewish encyclopedia* (1971) • *ILN* (19 June 1909) • personal knowledge (1986) • m. cert. • d. cert.

Archives St John Cam., papers • Trinity Cam., corresp. with Harold Davenport

Likenesses photograph, repro. in Cassels, *Bulletin* • portrait, repro. in *Strand Magazine* (Jan 1950)

Wealth at death £143,881: probate, 26 May 1972, *CGPLA Eng. & Wales*

Morden, Sir John, baronet (*bap.* 1623, *d.* 1708), founder of Morden College, Blackheath, son of George Morden (*d.* 1624), stocking seller and freeman of the Goldsmiths' Company, and Martha Harris (*d.* 1623), was baptized at St

Sir John Morden, baronet (*bap.* 1623, *d.* 1708), by unknown artist, *c.*1690

Bride's, Fleet Street, London, on 13 August 1623. He served an apprenticeship to William Soame (1582–1671), Levant Company assistant, from 1643 to 1650. Throughout the 1650s Morden was resident at the British factory at Aleppo in the Ottoman empire. While there he was briefly one of the Levant Company's treasurers and in 1659 was declared a freeman of that company. On 2 June 1662 he married Susan Brand (*bap.* 1638, *d.* 1721), a member of a prosperous Suffolk family engaged in merchant activities in London. After his return from Aleppo he bought property, his most considerable purchase being the manor of Wricklemarsh in the parish of Charlton in 1669. He also continued and expanded his mercantile activities, serving on the Levant Company board (as an assistant and treasurer) and becoming an East India Company committee man. Successful as a merchant, he was made a baronet by James II three months before the king's flight in 1688, and under the new regime was, the next year, appointed a commissioner of excise (serving until 1691). Subsequently he was appointed commissioner for the million lottery in 1694. In 1695 he was declared the winner of a seat in parliament for Colchester. The election was closely fought however, and after a challenge his seat was awarded to an opponent the next year on the basis of voting irregularities.

Childless, Morden perpetuated his family name when in 1695 he established Morden College at Blackheath for the reception of

> poor, honest, sober and discreet Merchants … such as have lost their estates by accidents, dangers, and perils of the seas, or by any other accidents, ways, or means, in their honest endeavours to get their living by way of merchandising. (Richardson, 1)

The pensioners were to be at least fifty years old, bachelors or widowers, and members of the established church; and they had to adhere to strict regulations. The first admission took place on 24 June 1700. The college, built according to a design attributed to Sir Christopher Wren, is a brick structure forming a quadrangle, with stone coigns and cornices, surrounded by piazzas. Over the front are statues of Morden and his wife, in the hall their portraits. An interesting and popular foundation myth developed at the college subsequently (recorded in the nineteenth century by a college treasurer). The myth: on leaving Aleppo Morden sent all his merchandize to London aboard three ships. Arriving in London on another vessel he waited for ten years, giving up hope and taking odd jobs, before news came that his three ships had finally arrived, richly laden. It was then that he made the decision to establish his college for decayed merchants so that others ruined in trade would not suffer as he had.

Morden died at Morden College, Blackheath, parish of Charlton, Kent, on 6 September 1708, and was buried on 20 September in the chapel of his foundation. Morden College is important as a unique institution that illustrates the chronic instability of contemporary mercantile and City ventures. Trade and speculation could and did go spectacularly wrong, the well-to-do gentle encountering financial disaster and poverty. Morden College protected and separated the mercantile impoverished—the shame-faced poor—from the perceived dishonour of the parochial poor law and its working poor recipients. In establishing an estate and his college in what was then the countryside Morden illustrated the trend towards fusing mercantile wealth and landed status. Morden College has since grown significantly in wealth and property, and in its provision for the gentle less fortunate.

GEOFFREY L. HUDSON

Sources parish register, St Bride's, Fleet Street, GL, MS 6536, 6538 · parish register, St Dunstan-in-the-East, GL, MS 7857 · Aleppo factory letter and minute books, PRO, state papers, 110/11, 54–5 · Levant Company court books, PRO, state papers, 105/112, 151, 153–4 · W. A. Shaw, ed., Calendar of treasury books, 9–11, PRO (1931–5) · JHC, 11 (1693–7) · [S. Lee], A collection of the names of the merchants living in and about the City of London (1677); repr. as The little London directory of 1677 (1863) · will of George Morden, PRO, PROB 11/144/78 · P. Joyce, Patronage and poverty in merchant society: the history of Morden College (1982) · H. Lansdell, Princess Aelfrida's charity, pt 3 (1912) · [H. S. Richardson (?)], Rough notes towards a memoir of Sir J. Morden, bart., founder of Morden College (1867) · S. Anderson, 'Sir John Morden's early career as a Levant merchant', Morden College, muniment room · DNB

Archives BL, case as to election for Colchester, upon the petition of the inhabitants complaining that R. Cook had the majority, 816.M4.46 · Morden College, Blackheath, Kent, administration MSS incl. register, and minute book

Likenesses portrait, c.1690, Morden College, Blackheath, London [see illus.] · effigy or statue, c.1717, Morden College, Blackheath, London · attrib. P. Lely, print, Morden College, Blackheath, London

Wealth at death approx. £34,000: Morden College, muniment room, account book 1705–07

Morden, Robert (d. 1703), maker of maps and globes, is first documented in 1668 having the foundations for a new building staked out on Cornhill after the great fire of London. His family background remains untraced, but, as a fellow freeman of the Weavers' Company, he had almost certainly been an apprentice of Joseph Moxon, printer and globe maker, a Yorkshireman. His earliest imprint records an address on 'New Cheapside' in 1669 but by 1671 he was installed at the Atlas on Cornhill (an address earlier used by Moxon), where he remained throughout his career. By 1670, when their first child was baptized, he had married; his wife's name was Mary. Four sons and three daughters were baptized between 1670 and 1682 at St Christopher-le-Stocks (where Morden served as churchwarden), four of whom, together with a nameless child, presumably stillborn, were buried by 1684.

Morden speaks of himself, in his Geography Rectified, or, A Description of the World (1680), as having 'lain latent under the horizon of unknown obscurity, and irresistible poverty', although towards the end of his life the scale of his activities in making and selling all kinds of maps, charts, and globes appears to indicate some degree of commercial success. His trading career is amply chronicled in his frequent advertisements in the London Gazette. It was one characterized by ad hoc partnerships, evidently to provide joint funding for expensive and time-consuming projects, with colleagues such as William Berry (apprenticed to Moxon in 1656) and Philip Lea (apprenticed to Morden in 1675). An inventory drawn up after Lea's death in 1700 reveals that Lea, Morden, and Berry all had shares in 'two size of globe plates'; an incomplete set of printed gores from one of these delicately worked sets of plates survives (BL, Maps *920.(69)). Morden's best-known maps are those of the English counties produced for Edmund Gibson's edition of Camden's Britannia (1695). Based on improved sources and further corrected by local enquiry, they remained standard maps for fifty years and helped establish a more settled orthography of English place names. Smaller versions of these maps appeared in Morden's own The New Description and State of England (1701).

Less well known but even more impressive are Morden's larger, separately published maps, the poor survival rate of which has hindered his reputation. At his best, this innovative cartographer achieved a relative accuracy, polish, and decorative finish quite the equal of his foreign contemporaries. His output included large-scale maps of London (in one of which he had half shares with Lea), a fine wall map of Essex, important early maps of the American colonies, and improved maps of many parts of Europe, reflecting and often providing a gloss on the political concerns of the day. His magnificent thirteen-sheet map of the world, This New Map of the Earth and Water (1699), engraved by Herman Moll, is remarkable in its ambition.

Morden also dealt in mathematical instruments and wrote explanatory treatises, publishing An Introduction to Astronomy, Geography, Navigation, and other Mathematical Sciences in 1702. He published his friend Robert Anderson's works on gunnery and rocketry and was present (with Thomas Tompion) when Anderson made his observations of falling bodies from Cripplegate steeple in 1686. Among his other acquaintances were William Leybourne and

Robert Hooke, whose diary records meetings with Morden and Berry at Man's Coffee House. Evidence of Morden's private life and character derives largely from his own writings. He wrote well, with a capacity for muscular yet often moving imagery. If occasionally liable to disparage his rivals, 'great pretenders to geography', the overriding impression is none the less one of intelligent endeavour, unaffected humility, and manifest piety. *Geography Rectified* ends with a powerful plea for the humane treatment of the indigenous peoples of the colonies and an attack on slavery.

Morden's wife, Mary, was buried at St Christopher-le-Stocks on 23 July 1690. Morden himself was buried on 25 August 1703 alongside his wife and children in the north aisle of the church. Administration of his estate was granted to his son Edward (*b.* 1682).

LAURENCE WORMS

Sources S. Tyacke, *London map-sellers, 1660–1720* (1978) · BL cat. · parish register, St Christopher-le-Stocks, GL · E. G. R. Taylor, *The mathematical practitioners of Tudor and Stuart England* (1954) · P. Mills and J. Oliver, *The survey of building sites in the City of London after the great fire of 1666* (1967) · *The diary of Robert Hooke … 1672–1680*, ed. H. W. Robinson and W. Adams (1935) · L. Rostenberg, *English publishers in the graphic arts, 1599–1700* (1963) · R. A. Skelton, *County atlases of the British Isles, 1579–1830: a bibliography* (1970) · J. B. Harley, 'Introduction', *The county maps from William Camden's Britannia 1693 by Robert Morden: a facsimile* (1972) · R. W. Shirley, *The mapping of the world: early printed world maps, 1472–1700* (1983) · J. Howgego, *Printed maps of London, circa 1553–1850*, 2nd edn (1978)
Archives BL
Wealth at death see administration, Sept 1703, PRO, PROB 6/79, fol. 144

Mordington. For this title name *see* Douglas, George, fourth Lord Mordington (*d.* 1741).

More [Morus], **Alexander** (1616–1670), Reformed church minister and writer, was born on 25 September 1616 at Castres, Languedoc, France. His father was a Scottish clergyman and principal of the protestant college at Castres, and his mother was French, but neither of their names is known. Brought up entirely in France and speaking French with a native fluency but a provincial accent, he began his education at the college at Castres. In 1634 he went to study theology at the University of Geneva, where in 1639, at the age of only twenty-three, he was elected professor of Greek over the head of Stephen le Clerc. In October 1641 he was ordained, but even at this stage his Calvinist orthodoxy was questioned: he was thought to be influenced by the Arminianism disseminated from Saumur. In January 1642 he was made professor of theology at Geneva, a controversial appointment. In 1648 he published his oration *Calvinus*, a eulogy and defence of Calvin, but accusations of Arminianism and of unchastity persisted, and he resigned from the university in the same year.

More's reputation as a scholar and preacher was now so high that he had offers of posts in London and Lyons, as well as in the Netherlands, where the exiled queen of Bohemia is said to have sought his services. His friend Salmatius (the French scholar de Saumaise) obtained for

Alexander More (1616–1670), by Crispijn de Passe the elder

More the post of pastor at Middelburg, where he was soon elected professor of theology.

In 1652 More became involved in a breach of promise case brought by Elisabeth Guerret, a servant in the Salmatius household in Leiden where he had been a frequent guest. She named More as her seducer, under promise of marriage, and as the father of her child. More made a testimonial from Middelburg on 10 July 1652 denying that there had been any promise of marriage. He had many influential friends and patrons, including David Blondel, Godofroid Hotton, and Henri Charles de Tremouille, prince of Tarente (grandson of William the Silent), who tried to arrange an out-of-court settlement. The synod of Utrecht neither barred More from preaching nor exonerated him, but in 1653 he was banned from preaching in Leiden. Madame Salmatius is known to have sided with her former employee in the case.

In 1653 More edited and contributed an unsigned preface to the anonymous royalist publication *Regii sanguinis clamor ad coelum*. The English Commonwealth government, finding itself attacked in strong terms, instructed its Latin secretary, John Milton, to reply. Milton's *A Second Defence of the English People* (1654) took More as one of its principal targets, making full use of the recent Guerret scandal. More's friendship with Salmatius, another antagonist of Milton, increased suspicion that he was the author of the tract. Milton, whose blindness had been cruelly mocked by the royalists, used every technique of polemic and ridicule to hit back, punning on the Greek meaning of 'morus' (a fool) to belittle More's scholarship, and on the Latin meaning (a mulberry bush) to indulge in bawdy innuendo. Guerret had been known in the Salmatius household as Bontia, and Milton changed this to 'Pontia' for the sake of word-play. In 1654 More published his *Fides publica contra calumnias Joannis Miltoni*, and added to it a *Supplementum* defending himself against Milton. Cunningly, More exploited certain inaccuracies in Milton's account, denying that he had been banned from preaching by the Amsterdam magistracy (implying a denial that he had been banned anywhere, which was untrue). In the following year Milton replied in his *Defence of Himself Against Alexander More*.

In 1655 More visited Italy and fell dangerously ill at Florence, but was treated by a doctor who introduced him on his recovery to the grand duke of Tuscany. On returning to the Netherlands he found that the Guerret scandal lingered on, and eventually in 1659 he had to resign his professorship. The protestant church of Charenton, near Paris, had invited him in 1657 to become its pastor, and after being lengthily investigated he was allowed to take up this post in 1659. In 1664 More was again examined for Arminian heresies by synods of Loudon and Berri: his powerful friends, such as the duchesse de La Tremouille, exerted influence on his behalf. He died, still unmarried, at Charenton on 28 September 1670 and was buried there.

While an early nineteenth-century biography of More refuted Milton's depiction of him, modern scholarship rejects this view: as one historian has written, 'Milton had things essentially right about More's actions and character' (Sellin, 248). The lack of a reprimand from the synod of Utrecht in 1653 was the result of 'clever political and legal maneuvering' (ibid., 246). Some contemporaries also found More superficial. According to the historian and alleged Catholic spy Chevreau: 'Morus has a great deal of learning and genius, but little religion or judgement. He is unpolished, ambitious, restless, fickle, bold, presumptuous and irresolute. He understands Latin, Greek, Hebrew and Arabic, but knows not human life' (Bayle 566).

JULIA GASPER

Sources J. Milton, 'A second defence of the English people', trans. H. North, *Complete prose works of John Milton*, ed. D. M. Wolfe, 4 (1966), 538–686 • J. Milton, 'John Milton Englishman his defence of himself against Alexander More', trans. P. W. Blackford, *Complete prose works of John Milton*, ed. D. M. Wolfe, 4 (1966), 687–825 • P. R. Sellin, 'Alexander Morus before the synod of Utrecht', *Huntington Library Quarterly*, 58 (1996), 239–48 • A. Bruce, *A critical account of the life, character and discourses of Mr. Alexander Morus* (1813) • P. Bayle, *Dictionnaire historique et critique*, 10 (Paris, 1820), 555–66 • *DNB*
Likenesses C. de Passe the elder, line engraving, BM, NPG [*see illus.*] • L. Visscher, line engraving (after W. Vaillant), BM, NPG • oils, St John Cam.

More, Alexander Goodman (1830–1895), naturalist, was born on 5 September 1830 in London, the first of three children of Alexander More (d. 1886). He was a delicate child and when, in 1834, his younger brother, George, died of scarlatina, the family moved to Renens, Switzerland. More was educated by a nursery-governess until he was nine, when he went to live with a tutor. When almost

eleven he was sent to Mr Bailey's School in Clifton where he remained for two years, and in February 1842 he entered Rugby School. He was a good scholar and, although always sickly, a keen athlete. By this time his parents and sister, Frances (Fanny) Margaret, had settled at Bembridge, Isle of Wight. More entered Trinity College, Cambridge, in October 1851 to study the classics, but bouts of illness disrupted his studies and he left in February 1855 without graduating. While at Cambridge he became friendly with the botanists Charles C. Babington (1808–1895) and the Revd William W. Newbould (1819–1886), and with the ornithologists F. D. Goodman and Edward Newton.

For the next twelve years More occupied himself studying natural history and visiting Ireland, especially co. Galway where his friends the Shawe-Taylors lived. Sometimes his sister, also a keen naturalist, accompanied him. He observed plants, birds, and insects. It is clear from More's numerous publications and correspondence that he was an all-round naturalist, interested in both plants and animals. He corresponded with a number of other naturalists, including Charles Darwin (1809–1882).

More displayed a strong bias towards the study of distribution patterns. His major ornithological work, *On the Distribution of Birds in Great Britain during the Nesting Season* (1865), reported the results of a survey for which he employed the same scheme of districts that Hewett C. Watson (1804–1881) had defined for recording plant distribution. More had also used the same scheme in an earlier paper, 'On the geographical distribution of butterflies in Great Britain', which he wrote in collaboration with Thomas Boyd. *Contributions towards a Cybele Hibernica, being outlines of the geographical distribution of plants in Ireland*, published in 1866, was compiled by More in collaboration with David Moore (1808–1879), director of the Royal Dublin Society's Botanic Gardens, Glasnevin. They also read a paper on the climate, flora, and crops of Ireland at the International Horticultural Exhibition and Botanical Congress, London, in May 1866. These botanical works contained one of the first maps to show plant distribution patterns by means of isopleths and points.

In January 1867 More was appointed assistant naturalist in the Royal Dublin Society's Natural History Museum; the museum was transferred to government control in 1877. Following the death of Dr Alexander Carte in 1881 More was promoted to curator, but ill health obliged him to retire in July 1887. He never married. After their mother's death in 1888 he and his sister made their home in Dublin. More continued to write about a wide variety of topics and was working on a second edition of *Cybele Hibernica* when he died at his home, 74 Leinster Road, Rathmines, co. Dublin, on 22 March 1895. He was buried at Mount Jerome cemetery, Dublin.

More (known simply as A. G. More) was a member of the Botanical Society of Edinburgh, the British Ornithological Union, and the Royal Irish Academy, and was elected to fellowships in the Linnean Society of London, and the Royal Society of Edinburgh. After his death Nathaniel

Colgan (1851–1919) and Reginald Scully (1858–1935) completed the second edition of *Contribution towards a Cybele Hibernica* (1898). On its title-page was the byline 'founded on the papers of the late Alexander Goodman More'; the omission of any reference to David Moore caused embarrassment to Fanny More, and she apologized to his son, Frederick Moore. David Moore had previously honoured his colleague by naming *Isoetes morei*; this large quillwort from Lough Bray, co. Wicklow, is now considered to be a form of *Isoetes lacustris*. E. CHARLES NELSON

Sources C. B. Moffat, ed., *Life and letters of Alexander Goodman More* (1898) • E. C. Nelson, 'Mapping plant distribution patterns: two pioneering examples from Ireland published in the 1860s', *Archives of Natural History*, 20 (1993), 391–403 • E. C. Nelson and E. M. McCracken, *The brightest jewel: a history of the National Botanic Gardens, Glasnevin, Dublin* (1987) • C. E. O'Riordan, *The Natural History Museum, Dublin* (1983) • *CGPLA Ire.* (1895)
Archives Linn. Soc., annotated catalogues • National Botanic Gardens, Glasnevin, Dublin, herbarium • Royal Irish Acad., corresp. and papers | Ulster Museum, Belfast, letters to Samuel Stewart
Likenesses oils, National Botanic Gardens, Glasnevin, Dublin • photograph, repro. in Moffat, ed., *Life and letters*
Wealth at death £1086 13s. 9d.: probate, 7 May 1895, *CGPLA Ire.*

More [*née* Harpur; *other married name* Middleton], **Alice, Lady More** (*b.* in or after **1474**, *d.* in or before **1551**), second wife of Sir Thomas More, was born, probably at Epping, Essex, to Elizabeth (*d.* in or after 1510), coheir of Sir Peter Ardern of Markhall, Essex, and her second husband, Sir Richard Harpur (*d.* 1492). After her father's death her mother married Sir Andrew Dymoke (*d.* 1508). Before 1492 Alice married John Middleton, a London mercer, who named her co-executor of his will in 1509 and left his fortune to her and their daughters, Alice (*c.*1501–1563) and Helen (*d. c.*1510).

In 1511, about a month after his first wife's death, Alice married Thomas *More (1478–1535) and moved to his London home. He forwarded her thanks to Erasmus in 1516 for his wish that she have a long life, for it would enable her, she joked, to plague her husband all the longer. On a tomb at Chelsea, where they moved in 1525, Thomas lauded both wives as 'beloved' (Norrington, 56).

As his career advanced, More frequently left Alice alone to supervise the household; his only extant letter to her concerns their barn that burned down in 1529. Around the end of 1534, although she did not understand the reasons for his imprisonment, she petitioned the government for his relief. After his execution the crown voided the trust he had belatedly established for her but granted her an annuity of £20 in 1537. She became entangled in lawsuits, one of them initiated by William *Roper, her stepson-in-law, who depicted her as an interfering busybody in his account of Thomas's life. Writers have disparaged her role as a martyr's wife, even identifying her as the hook-beaked harpy mentioned in a letter of October 1511 from Ammonio, Henry VIII's Latin secretary, to Erasmus; Holbein's portrait contradicts this claim. She died on or before 25 April 1551 and was probably buried at Chelsea. Her daughter Alice had three children with Thomas

Elrington and nine with her second husband, Sir Giles Alington. Through the Alington line Alice was an ancestor of Elizabeth II. RETHA M. WARNICKE

Sources DNB • R. Norrington, *In the shadow of a saint: Lady Alice More* (1983) • R. Warnicke, 'The harpy in More's household: was it Lady Alice?', *Moreana*, 22 (1985), 5–13 • W. Roper, 'The life of Sir Thomas More', *Two early Tudor lives*, ed. R. Sylvester and D. Harding (1962) • *Opus epistolarum Des. Erasmi Roterodami*, ed. P. S. Allen and others, 12 vols. (1906–58)
Archives BL, Arundel MSS 152, 300
Likenesses H. Holbein, sketch, 1526 (More household), Basel Museum • R. Lockey, oils, 1593 (More household), Cockthorpe Park, Ducklington, near Whitby • brasses on tomb, Bodl. Oxf.; repro. in *Gough's Maps*, 1798 • oils (after sketch by H. Holbein, 1526), Nostral Priory • oils (after sketch by H. Holbein, 1526), repro. in Norrington, *In the shadow of a saint*

More, Christina (*fl.* 1412–1414). *See under* Lollard women (*act. c.*1390–*c.*1520).

More, Sir Christopher (*b.* in or before **1483**, *d.* **1549**), landowner and administrator, was the son of John More, a London fishmonger active in the 1480s and his wife, Elizabeth, and the grandson of a Thomas More recorded at Norton, Derbyshire, earlier in the fifteenth century. Such particulars are owing to the remarkable collection of Loseley papers (now kept at the Surrey History Centre, Woking), one of the largest to survive for an early modern English gentry family. By 1504 Christopher More had married Margaret, daughter of Walter Mugge of Guildford, with whom he had five sons and seven daughters. In the following year he was recorded as a clerk in the exchequer, where he rose to become king's remembrancer in 1542. In 1505, for £23 6s. 8d., he bought the office of alnager of Surrey and Sussex, and in 1508 he purchased one half of Loseley Manor, 2 miles outside Guildford, acquiring the other half later and obtaining licence to empark 200 acres in 1530. By 1545 Loseley and surrounding lands were valued at £66 8s. 4d. per annum. He also acquired property elsewhere in Surrey and Sussex.

Christopher More owed his success to powerful patrons, who included Henry VIII, to financial and legal expertise, and to his good relations with local magnates, which enabled him to avoid the factional battles that plagued Henrician Surrey. He was admitted to the Inner Temple in 1513, and in the same year became under-steward of Witley and Worplesdon. He subsequently became verderer of Windsor Forest in 1519; surveyor of lands for Margaret Pole, countess of Salisbury, in 1521; master of game at Merrow and West Clandon in 1540; and steward of West Horsley in 1547. He also performed services for Viscount Lisle and the earl of Rutland. He served on Surrey subsidy commissions from 1515 and became a JP about 1521, showing that he enjoyed Cardinal Wolsey's favour.

On the evidence of his will, which though drawn up in 1549 bequeathed his soul to God, the Virgin, and the holy company of heaven, Christopher More was conservative in religion. Nevertheless he acquiesced in Henry's break with Rome and co-operated with Thomas Cromwell. He was sheriff of Surrey and Sussex in 1532–3 and 1539–40 and commissioner for tenths of spiritualities in 1535. In 1539 he was Cromwell's choice as knight of the shire and arranged the return of a Cromwellian burgess in Gatton (More may have been a burgess earlier). In November 1539 he was appointed to the guard of honour prepared for Anne of Cleves, and was instructed to attend with six servants, riding in a coat of black velvet and with a gold chain about his neck. Between August 1540 and February 1541 he was knighted. Sir Christopher enforced religious policy, dealing with the 'naughty curate' of Witley in 1544 and dissolving chantries in 1546 and 1548. Perhaps a burgess in 1542 and 1544 he was again knight of the shire in Edward VI's first parliament in 1547. More was a commissioner for gaol delivery in 1530–31, of oyer and terminer in 1538 and 1544–5, and of musters in 1544 and 1548, and during the 1549 insurrections the protector, Somerset, called upon him to raise troops. He died on 16 August 1549 and was buried in the Loseley chapel in St Nicholas's, Guildford, survived by his second wife, Constance (daughter of Richard Sackville and widow of William Heneage), whom he had married by 1535. She died in 1554.

Sir William More (1520–1600), landowner and administrator, the only survivor among his father's sons, was born on 30 January 1520. There is no evidence of formal schooling. Before 12 June 1545 he married Mabel, daughter of Mark Digneley of the Isle of Wight; she had died by 1551, when he married Margaret, daughter of Ralph Daniel of Norfolk; they had a son and two daughters. A burgess for an unknown constituency in 1539 and for Reigate in 1547, William More began appearing on subsidy commissions in 1547 and muster commissions in 1548 and became alnager in 1549. Though not on any extant commission of the peace before 1555 he probably became a JP upon his father's death, when Henry Polsted wrote to Sir William Cecil urging his appointment. The duke of Northumberland appointed him to arbitrate a Star Chamber case in 1552 and to be a commissioner for church goods in 1553; the marquess of Northampton, lord lieutenant of Surrey, made him provost marshal in 1552.

More shared his protestantism with Sir Thomas Carwarden, an influential figure at court, where he was master of the revels, and also in Surrey, as lord of the manor of Bletchingley from 1547. The two men became close friends—More was later Carwarden's executor—and together they headed an evangelical grouping in the county. Unlike Cawarden, however, More was not involved in either Northumberland's attempt to enthrone Lady Jane Grey in 1553 or Sir Thomas Wyatt's rebellion in 1554. But he did support protestantism in Mary's first parliament of October 1553, and perhaps as a result was absent from the February 1554 commission of the peace and the April 1554 parliament. However, he was a burgess for Guildford in the November parliament that year and a JP again in 1555. He opposed Marian religious policy in the 1555 parliament, was hauled before the council for 'lewd words' in 1556, and was reprimanded for his remissness in investigating conventicles in 1557. Nevertheless the council gave him important responsibilities in Mary's final months.

William More flourished under Elizabeth. He was sheriff of Surrey and Sussex in 1558–9 and 1579–80, and sat in every Elizabethan parliament: for Grantham (Lincolnshire) in 1559, for Guildford in 1572, 1589, and 1597, and as knight of the shire for Surrey in 1563, 1571, 1584, 1586, and 1593. Though he generally co-operated with the powerful Howards of Effingham, in 1559 he refused to accept their candidate in preference to Cawarden (who was returned), and was no more co-operative in 1584 when they asked him to stand aside himself. Vice-admiral of Sussex from 1559 and deputy lieutenant for Surrey and Sussex from 1569, he played a major role in levying troops and securing the south-east against invasion during the Anglo-Spanish war which began in 1585. Verderer of Windsor Forest by 1561 he became constable of Farnham Castle in 1565, treasurer of the lottery for Surrey in 1567, commissioner for ecclesiastical causes in 1572, collector of the loan in 1589, chamberlain of the exchequer in 1591, master of swans for Surrey in 1593, and deputy *custos rotulorum* in 1594. He also served on several commissions of oyer and terminer. More was active in enforcing the Elizabethan religious settlement, dealing with sectaries like the Family of Love (1560–61, 1580), and recusants, though he maintained a long friendship with the Catholic loyalist Anthony Browne, Viscount Montague. From 1570 he had intermittent custody of Montague's son-in-law Henry Wriothesley, second earl of Southampton.

A wealthy man, between 1562 and 1568 More spent £1661 on the building of Loseley House, using stone from Waverley Abbey provided by Montague. Its north wing survives, along with a good deal of its sixteenth-century panelling and paintwork, and has been described as 'The best house of its date in the county' (Pevsner, 353). The restraint of its somewhat conservative exterior is offset by some of the internal details, notably a spectacular fireplace in the drawing room. Its owner several times received Queen Elizabeth at Loseley, probably in 1567, certainly in 1569, 1576 (when he was knighted on 14 May), 1583, and 1591. He enjoyed the friendship of notables like William Cecil, Lord Burghley; Edward Clinton, earl of Lincoln; Robert Dudley, earl of Leicester; and Sir Francis Walsingham; and also of Robert Horne, bishop of Winchester, who on one occasion asked More to provide him with a dentist. Indeed, some passing quarrels notwithstanding (for instance with the earl of Arundel in 1562), Sir William seems to have been generally liked and respected. In spite of their religious differences he was regarded as a friend by his involuntary guest the earl of Southampton, and by the retired Marian archbishop of York, Nicholas Heath, while in 1597 Tobie Matthew, bishop of Durham, praised More's religious fervour and conscientious care for justice:

> which doth argue that he that beganne the good work in you, doth and will continewe it to the daie of Christ, as it becometh me to judge of you, because I have you, as the apostle saieth, in my heart, being companions together of grace through the Gospell. (*Seventh Report*, HMC, 657)

It is a tribute to More's integrity that he should have been often employed as an arbitrator in disputes.

Sir William More died on 20 July 1600 and was buried in

the family chapel in St Nicholas's Church, Guildford. He left extensive lands in Surrey, Sussex, and Kent, and also an estate in Blackfriars, London. In January 1596 he sold part of the latter to James Burbage, who converted his purchase into a theatre, later the winter house of the King's Men. More's daughter Elizabeth was one of the queen's ladies, and married successively Richard Polsted of Albury, the queen's Latin secretary John Wolley, and the lord chancellor, Thomas Egerton, while her sister Anne married Sir George Mainwaring of Ightfield, Shropshire. His heir was his son George *More (1553–1632), who followed his father into parliament and was similarly active in local government, while also becoming chancellor of the Order of the Garter and lieutenant of the Tower of London.   WILLIAM B. ROBISON

Sources Loseley MSS, Folger · Surrey HC, Loseley papers · HoP, *Commons, 1509–58*, 2.616–17, 624–6 · HoP, *Commons, 1558–1603*, 3.81–3, 86–9 · W. B. Robison, 'The justices of the peace of Surrey in national and county politics, 1483–1570', PhD diss., Louisiana State University, 1983 · W. B. Robison, 'The national and local significance of Wyatt's rebellion in Surrey', *HJ*, 30 (1987), 769–90 · R. Munden, 'George More, 1553–1632: county governor, man-of-business and central government office holder', *Surrey Archaeological Collections*, 83 (1996), 97–124 · *VCH Surrey* · *VCH Sussex* · J. E. Neale, *The Elizabethan House of Commons* (1949) · 'Sir George More', *DNB* · J. T. Cliffe, *The puritan gentry: the great puritan families of early Stuart England* (1984) · *Surrey*, Pevsner (1971) · *Seventh report*, HMC, 6 (1879) [More-Molyneux (Loseley MSS)] · A. J. Kempe, *The Loseley manuscripts* (1836) · will, PRO, PROB 11/33/9 [Sir Christopher More] · will, PRO, PROB 11/96/70 [Sir William More] · will, PRO, PROB 11/37/F4 [Constance More]
Archives Folger, estate surveys and other papers, account book, personal papers, library catalogue · Surrey HC, deeds, estate papers, family papers, incl. some household papers | E. Sussex RO, lieutenancy papers
Likenesses portrait (William More), Loseley House, Surrey · portrait (George More), Loseley House, Surrey · portrait (Robert More), Loseley House, Surrey · portrait (Poynings More), Loseley House, Surrey
Wealth at death Loseley Manor and immediately surrounding lands valued at £66 8s. 4d. p.a. in 1545

More, (Christopher) Cresacre (1572–1649), biographer, was born on 3 July 1572 at Barnborough, Yorkshire, the youngest of the thirteen children of Thomas More (1531–1606), gentleman and landowner, and his wife, Maria Scrope (1534–1607), daughter of John Scrope, second son of Henry, sixth Lord Scrope of Bolton; Sir Thomas *More (1478–1535) was his great-grandfather. Although he was baptized Cresacrus, after his paternal grandmother's maiden name, legal documents give his first names as Christopher Cresacre. In 1584 he was sent to the Jesuit school at Eu in northern France, transferring in 1586 to the English College at Rheims. Four years later, in 1590, he received the tonsure and minor orders, and by 1593 was studying theology in the English College at Douai, but he was recalled by his family to England when his eldest brother died. Some time between 1603 and 1605 he married Elizabeth Gage, daughter of Thomas Gage and Elizabeth, daughter of Sir Thomas Guldeford. On his father's death in 1606 he inherited not only the family's estates in

Yorkshire and Hertfordshire, but also the financial penalties which accompanied its Roman Catholic recusancy. Before his wife died in 1610, they lived at Low Leyton, Essex, and had three children—Helen *More (1606–1633) and Bridget, who both became Benedictine nuns, and Thomas, who was dissuaded from the priesthood to marry Mary, daughter of Sir Basil *Brooke. After 1617 More lived at Gobions in the parish of North Mimms, Hertfordshire.

More's *The Life and Death of Sir Thomas Moore* was written between about 1616 and 1620 and published undated at Douai between about 1626 and 1631. Formerly it was attributed to Cresacre's older brother Thomas, a secular priest, who died in Rome in 1625, making Cresacre his heir. The issue of authorship arises from discrepancies between the 'Epistle Dedicatory' and the 'Preface to the reader' in the first edition. The 'Epistle' clearly ascribes the authorship to Thomas, referring to him in the third person and as deceased. The 'Preface' just as clearly refers to the author as the youngest of thirteen children, as baptized on the anniversary of Sir Thomas More's death, as a parent, and as the only one of his brothers not to be in a religious estate. Conceivably Cresacre revised a biography first written by his brother but there is no acknowledgement of this possibility in the 'Preface'. It is likely that the 'Epistle' was added at a late stage, quite probably, in view of More's vulnerable position as a recusant, in an attempt to obscure his responsibility for the work. The dedication of the *Life* to Queen Henrietta Maria, whose marriage negotiations Thomas furthered, could also have rendered the illusion of double authorship desirable.

More's biography of his great-grandfather is largely derivative, drawn mainly from the lives of William Roper and of Thomas Stapleton, but also using materials from Nicholas Harpsfield's life and from Edward Hall and John Stow's historical accounts. His chief accomplishment is to present a fully rounded portrait of his ancestor, in which he deftly combines the personal emphasis of Roper's biography, with its cameos of wit and family life, and the internationalist emphasis of Stapleton's, which depicts Sir Thomas the European humanist, man of letters, statesman, and martyr for the universal Catholic church. From a literary point of view his achievement is considerable. Two other works once ascribed to More, *Meditations and Devout Discourses upon the Blessed Sacrament* and *A Myrhine Posie*, have now been identified as the work of Matthew Kellison.

More, who appears to have spent much time in London, settled all his Hertfordshire lands on his son in 1629. He was living on a leasehold farm at Chilstone, in Madley, near Hereford, when he died on 26 March 1649.

JUDITH H. ANDERSON

Sources M. A. Anderegg, 'The tradition of early More biography', *Essential articles for the study of Thomas More*, ed. R. S. Sylvester and G. P. Marc'hadour (1977), 3–25 · C. More, *The life and death of Sir Thomas Moore* [n.d., 1630?] · C. More, *The life of Sir Thomas More*, ed. J. Hunter (1828), ix–lxiv · A. F. Allison and D. M. Rogers, eds., *The contemporary printed literature of the English Counter-Reformation between 1558 and 1640*, 2 (1994) · Gillow, *Lit. biog. hist.* · D. Shanahan, 'The family of St. Thomas More in Essex, 1581–1640', *Essex Recusant*, 1 (1959), 62–74; 2 (1960), 76–85; 3 (1961), 71–81; 4 (1962), 55–64, 103–

6; 5 (1963), 49–57 • P. R. P. Knell, 'The descendants of St. Thomas More in Hertfordshire: 1617–1693', *Essex Recusant*, 6 (1964), 1–12 • *STC, 1475–1640* • H. Collins, *The life of Dame Gertrude More, order of S. Benedict* (1880?)

Likenesses R. Lockey, group portrait, oils, *c*.1595–1600 (after H. Holbein (partly)), NPG

More, Edward (1479–1541), headmaster, was born at Havant, Hampshire. Nothing is known of his parents except that his father was a tenant of Winchester College in Winchester itself. This enabled More to be elected a scholar of the college in 1492. He proceeded to New College, Oxford, in 1496 and subsequently took the degrees of BA and MA. He was ordained deacon on 15 March 1511.

In 1508 More returned to Winchester College as headmaster. In this capacity he was remembered chiefly as a disciplinarian, at least according to Christopher Johnson (himself headmaster in 1560–71), who wrote 'Qui legit hic Morum, qui non et sensit eundem, Gaudeat, ac secum molliter esse putet' ('He who reads More here, and has not felt him, let him rejoice, and think himself well off'; Willes). As a teacher More seems to have followed the methods of the pedagogue William Horman, his own headmaster at Winchester, who bequeathed him books in 1534 on condition that More arranged for the publication of a new edition of Horman's *Vulgaria*.

In 1517 More resigned from his headmastership—an onerous post with only one assistant—and concentrated on his clerical career. In 1518 he supplicated for the degree of BTh at Oxford. From 1514 he had been vicar of Heston, Middlesex, and in 1521 he became vicar of Isleworth, Middlesex; both livings were in the gift of Winchester College. In 1521 he also became rector of Cranford, Middlesex. To his fellow Wykehamist Robert Sherborne, bishop of Chichester, More seems to have owed his further appointments as canon and prebendary of Chichester (from 1521), archdeacon of Lewes, Sussex (from 1527), and vicar of Bexhill, Sussex (from 1529). In 1527 More was also made vicar of Gillingham, Dorset, by the patronage of his school contemporary William Fleshmonger. He retained most of these preferments until his death.

In 1526, in the middle of his career as a pluralist, More was elected warden of Winchester College. He was therefore in a prominent and exposed position when the dramatic changes of the Henrician reformation came about in the 1530s. Although he and the fellows of the college were entirely conservative in belief, More's policy was outwardly conformist. He made a formal protest against Archbishop Cranmer's visitation of the college in June 1535 but this was probably only on the grounds that the bishop of Winchester ought to be the college's visitor. When Cromwell, as vicegerent in spirituals, visited in person in September 1535, More did not repeat his protest. Inwardly, however, the college remained a stronghold of the old religion, a tradition notably upheld by John White, appointed headmaster by More in 1535 and who succeeded him as warden in 1542. More died (unmarried) late in 1541 and was buried in the choir of Winchester College chapel.   R. D. H. CUSTANCE

Sources Emden, *Oxf.*, vol. 2 • R. Willes, *Poemata* (1573) • 'Liber Albus', Winchester College archives, fol. 181 • J. Hutchins, *The history and antiquities of the county of Dorset*, 2 (1774) • P. McGrath, 'Winchester College and the old religion in the sixteenth century', *Winchester College: sixth-centenary essays*, ed. R. Custance (1982), 229–80 • *DNB*

More, Edward (*c*.1537–1620), poet, was the third son of Anne Cresacre (1511?–1577), and John More (1510–1547), the only son of Sir Thomas *More. He married Mary, whose maiden name is unknown. More's poem in ragged fourteeners, *A lytle and bryefe treatyse called the Defence of Women, and especially of Englyshe women, made agaynst 'The Schole House'* [an anti-feminist poem by Edward Gosynhyll with which it was bound], was printed in London by John Kynge in 1560, licensed in 1557–8 and 1563. The dedication to Sir Philip Hoby is dated 20 July 1557, from Hambleden, Buckinghamshire, the seat of John Scrope, whose daughter married Edward's eldest brother Thomas. More describes himself at the time as twenty years old. Wood states that he wrote 'several little things' besides (2.249–52).

Part of a long-standing, stylized formal controversy about women, More's poem has a textbook quality; it makes the obligatory defence of Eve, rehearses familiar exempla such as Susanna, Judith, and Lucretia, and employs standard tropes: misogynists' ingratitude toward their mothers, and defenders of women as chivalric champions. More's distinguished family background helps situate works of this genre in the educated classes rather than as products of popular culture, as its later anthologizing in Utterson's *Select Pieces of Early Popular Poetry* (1817) might suggest. Thomas More's emphasis on educating his daughters may help explain his grandson's choice to write in defence of women. More was buried at Barnborough, Yorkshire, on 2 May 1620.

LINDA WOODBRIDGE

Sources Wood, *Ath. Oxon.*, new edn • C. More, *The life of Sir Thomas More, knight, lord high chancellor of England under King Henry the Eighth and his majesty's ambassador to the courts of France and Germany*, ed. J. L. Kennedy (1941) • T. E. Bridgett, 'Sir Thomas More's book of hours', *N&Q*, 8th ser., 2 (1892), 121–2 • *DNB* • E. E. Reynolds, *The field is won: the life and death of Saint Thomas More* (1968) • H. C. Adams, *Wykehamica: a history of Winchester College and commoners, from the foundation to the present day* (1878) • T. F. Kirby, *Winchester scholars: a list of the wardens, fellows, and scholars of … Winchester College* (1888) • E. V. Utterson, ed., *Select pieces of early popular poetry* (1817)

More, Elizabeth (*d*. 1807). *See under* More, Thomas (1722–1795).

More, Sir George (1553–1632), soldier and administrator, was born on 28 November 1553 at Loseley, Surrey, the only son of Sir William *More (1520–1600), landowner, of Loseley, and his second wife, Margaret, daughter and heir of Ralph Daniel of Swaffham, Norfolk. He was admitted to Corpus Christi College, Oxford, in the summer of 1570, and was placed by his father under the personal supervision of the president, William Cole. He left the college without taking a degree, and entered the Inner Temple in 1574. In 1604 he donated to the Bodleian Library some manuscripts and £40 for the purchase of books. More was

Sir George More (1553–1632), by unknown artist, 1608

given an honorary MA on James I's visit to Oxford on 30 August 1605.

More received his political tutelage under Robert Dudley, earl of Leicester, whose service he had entered by 1579 after a brief stay at the Inner Temple. According to Leicester, he was 'as much to my own liking and contention every way as my heart can wish … he is dear to me for his own sake' (Kempe, xiii). More married Ann (d. 1590), daughter and coheir of Sir Adrian Poynings of Wherwell, Hampshire, and his wife, Mary, before 1581. They had four sons and five daughters. The eldest, Sir Robert More (1581–1626), was an MP and gentleman pensioner to James and Charles I. He predeceased his father, who was succeeded by his second son, Poynings More (d. 1649). Sir George More's third daughter, Ann (1584–1617), secretly married John *Donne in December 1601.

More was elected MP for Guildford, Surrey, in 1584, and sat there again in 1586, 1589, 1593, 1604, and 1624. He was elected a knight of the shire for Surrey in 1597, 1601, 1614, 1621, 1625, and 1626. He owed his electoral success to his father, a leading gentleman esteemed by Elizabeth I, and his sister Elizabeth (1552–1600), who married prominent government officials—successively Sir John Wolley and Sir Thomas Egerton. More was a frequent speaker in the late Elizabethan parliaments, sat on most of the important committees in the House of Commons, and excelled as a committee man. He spoke openly against Catholics, and strongly for the privileges of the house and the reform of purveyance and of the exchequer. In the parliament of 1601 he advocated the suppression of ale houses and drunkenness, strong laws against horse theft and against the plurality of ecclesiastical benefices, and a bill for mandatory monthly church attendance. He was a JP for Surrey from about 1582 and much concerned with local matters.

Knighted probably on 28 February 1598, More was appointed sheriff of Surrey and Sussex from 1597 to 1598. About this time he obtained the wardship of Edward Herbert (1582?–1648), afterwards first Lord Herbert of Cherbury, after paying £800 to his guardian, Sir Francis Newport. He also served as deputy for his father's local offices because of Sir William's infirmities in his final years. More succeeded to the Loseley estate on his father's death in July 1600. He was appointed to his father's position of chamberlain of receipt in the exchequer in early 1601, and received a grant of the lordship and hundred of Godalming, Surrey, on 3 November 1601. These offices were rewarded as the result of his father's lavish entertainment of the queen four times in the later years of her reign. Sir George More also dedicated to her his religious tract, *A Demonstration of God in his Workes* (1597), just to curry more favour.

James continued the royal favours by visiting More at Loseley in August 1603 and 1606. More was appointed treasurer and receiver-general to Henry, prince of Wales, soon after the accession, a position he held until the latter's death in November 1612. On 9 July 1611 he was made chancellor of the Order of the Garter. In the next year he sought the mastership of the court of wards but was unsuccessful. His lavish spending, and the new east wing, gallery, and chapel at Loseley, suggest that he prospered during the years 1603 to 1612 and beyond. A man on the rise, More was noted by John Chamberlain in November 1612 as one who 'hath not wanted the voice of a great prelat: who hath many irons in the fire' (*Letters of John Chamberlain*, 1.385). By 1613 his subsidy assessment was among the highest in the country.

More was appointed lieutenant of the Tower of London in October 1615 at the request of Lord Ellesmere (Egerton), lord chancellor, to keep close watch over Robert and Frances Carr, earl and countess of Somerset, over the poisoning of Sir Thomas Overbury in 1613. The king used More to communicate his mixed feelings to Somerset; the earl and countess used him to transmit their own twisted stories. More eventually persuaded Somerset to accept a trial by assuring him that it was only a matter of form. When Somerset protested before going to trial in May 1616, James directed More to induce him to submit; if he still refused, he was to be forced. The king afterwards rewarded More with a gift of £1000, half of which was actually taken by John Murray, later first earl of Annandale. In January 1617 More, 'wearie of that troublesome and dangerous office', was trying to sell it, and did so in March to Sir Allen Apsley for £2500 (*Letters of John Chamberlain*, 2.58).

Retiring to Loseley, in August, More entertained Charles, prince of Wales. In 1621 he was granted a lease of crown lands worth £601 per annum in lieu of his pension as chancellor of the Order of the Garter, and in 1629 received a grant of £1200 for the surrender of the office.

James is said to have neglected him after 1616, and there are many unanswered memorials of his to the king. More distinguished himself, however, in the parliament of 1621 in arguing the case for compromise. He stated that grievances and supply must go together like twins in order for the Commons to maintain their privileges. In 1624 he took a pro-war stance against Spain, and moved the resolution for it. Considered infirm and weak, he nevertheless continued to serve on numerous parliamentary committees. In August 1625 he opposed as unconstitutional John Whistler's proposal to consult the House of Lords on the question of supply. But he supported many of Charles I's early policies, as shown by the remark in March 1626 that he had 'lately shown leanings to the court' (Forster, 1.315). In 1625 he was one of the collectors of loans in Surrey.

More died intestate at Loseley on 16 October 1632, and was buried in the chapel there. Lacking the perquisites of high office after 1617, he continued his lavish spending and this, together with the growing debts of his grandson and heir Poynings, meant that More's wealth was in decline by his death. A creditor conducted an inventory of his property. More has been regarded as a major factor in Donne's disgrace, dismissal as Egerton's secretary, and brief imprisonment for secretly marrying Ann More without his permission. More felt Donne's actions were deceitful and unchristian. However, he relented somewhat and gave his son-in-law a quarterly allowance until Christmas 1621, by which time Donne's wealth and reputation were restored. Donne then gave More financial assistance. When Ann Donne died in childbirth on 15 August 1617, Donne asked More for his critical comments on his *memento mori* to her. Considered impulsive, emotional, and energetic, More none the less maintained a balanced approach to life that enabled him to participate fully in the affairs of people and of state. His standing at court was enhanced by his staunch protestantism.

LOUIS A. KNAFLA

Sources Wood, *Ath. Oxon.*, 1st edn, 2.354 • Foster, *Alum. Oxon.* • HoP, *Commons, 1558–1603*, 3.80–83, 86–9 • A. J. Kempe, ed., *The Loseley manuscripts* (1836) • administration, PRO, PROB 6/14B, fol. 147 • J. Spedding, *An account of the life and times of Francis Bacon*, 2 vols. (1880), vol. 2, pp. 103–5, 131 • J. Nichols, ed., *The progresses and public processions of Queen Elizabeth*, 3 vols. (1821), vol. 2, p. 7; vol. 3, p. 81 • J. Nichols, *The progresses, processions, and magnificent festivities of King James I, his royal consort, family and court*, 4 vols. (1828), vol. 1, pp. 250–51, 556; vol. 2, p. 374; vol. 3, p. 119 • *CSP dom., 1601–31* • APC, 1580–81, 1601, 1621–3 • *Calendar of the manuscripts of the most hon. the marquis of Salisbury*, 24 vols., HMC, 9 (1883–1976), vols. 4, 11 [1590–94, 1601] • S. D'Ewes, *The journals of all the parliaments during the reign of Queen Elizabeth* (1682) • H. Townshend, *Historical collections, or, An exact account of the proceedings of the four last parliaments of Queen Elizabeth of famous memory* (1680) • *Seventh report*, HMC, 6 (1879) • S. R. Gardiner, *History of England from the accession of James I to the outbreak of the civil war, 1603–1642*, 10 vols. (1883–4), vol. 2, pp. 351, 353; vol. 4, pp. 66, 120 • E. Gosse, *The life and letters of John Donne, dean of St Paul's*, 2 vols. (1899) • T. Birch, ed., *The life of Henry, prince of Wales* (1760), 228 • *The letters of John Chamberlain*, ed. N. E. McClure, 2 vols. (1939), vol. 1, pp. 357, 374, 377, 385, 392, 619; vol. 2, pp. 13, 49–50, 58 • B. White, *Cast of ravens: the strange case of Sir Thomas Overbury* (1965), 136, 144–53, 172–5, 183, 193, 239 • A. Somerset, *Unnatural murder: poison at the court of James I* (1997), 300, 313–26, 345, 357 • R. Zaller, *The parliament of 1621: a study in constitutional conflict* (1971), 38, 47, 105, 109, 125, 163–8, 174 • R. E. Ruigh, *The parliament of 1624: politics and foreign policy* (1971), 205 • A. Weldon, *The court and character of King James, written and taken by Sir A. W.*, 2 vols. (1650), vol. 2, p. 233 • J. Forster, *Sir John Eliot: a biography*, 2 vols. (1864), vol. 1, p. 277, 311, 315

Archives Surrey HC, papers | Berks. RO, Reading, letters to Sir Nicholas Carew of Beddington • Folger, Loseley manuscripts collection, corresp. and papers

Likenesses oils, 1608, Loseley Park, Surrey [*see illus.*]

More, Hannah (1745–1833), writer and philanthropist, was born on 2 February 1745 at Fishponds, in the parish of Stapleton, a couple of miles north of Bristol, the fourth of the five daughters of Jacob More (1700–1783), schoolmaster, and Mary, the daughter of John Grace, a farmer at nearby Stoke. Her father was born at Thorpe Hall, Harleston, Norfolk, and educated at Norwich grammar school, where he excelled in classics. Despite the powerful influence of his mother's Presbyterian piety and principles Jacob More adopted the high-church Anglicanism of his father's side of the family, and was destined for a career in the church when his prospects were dashed by losing a lawsuit with a cousin over an inheritance. After working for the excise in Bristol his friendship with Norbonne Berkeley, later Lord Bottetourt, led to his appointment as master of the free school at Fishponds, where he settled, married, and brought up his family.

Hannah and her sisters Hannah More grew up in a loving, intellectual, and predominately female environment. A precocious child and the acknowledged genius of the family, she displayed a quick-witted cleverness and passion for learning which were nurtured not only by her scholarly father, who taught her Latin and mathematics, but also by her mother and sisters. Hannah and her four sisters, Mary (1738–1813), Elizabeth (Betty; 1740–1816), Sarah (Sally; 1743–1819), and her beloved younger sister, Martha (Patty; 1747–1819), were educated so as to earn a living for themselves, and ran a boarding-school for girls. To this end Mary was sent to a French school in Bristol and each week shared her lessons with her younger sisters, so that Hannah gained an early fluency in the language. Entranced by the stories of John Dryden told by her nurse, who had lived in the poet's household, Hannah, according to family tradition, started scribbling down stories and verses almost as soon as she could write, and read them aloud to entertain Patty. At twelve she became a pupil, together with Sarah and Martha, at the girls' boarding-school that her father set up at 6 Trinity Street in Bristol for Mary and Elizabeth More to run; her parents also moved to Bristol and opened a school for boys up the road, at Stony Hill. In addition to taking lessons in French, Italian, and Spanish from visiting masters, Hannah made good progress in her Latin under James Newton, of Bristol Baptist Academy, but her mathematical studies were halted when her father feared that her proficiency would mark her out as a female pedant. By her late teens she was teaching at the school, which in 1767 moved to a purpose-built house in Park Street; there it remained until her sisters retired in 1789. The success of the More sisters' school ensured that the women became highly respected figures

Hannah More (1745–1833), by John Opie, 1786

in Bristol society, and Hannah's developing literary talents attracted the attention of family friends and future patrons, such as their neighbour the Revd James Stonhouse, Ann Lovell Gwatkin (whose daughter was at the school), Josiah Tucker, dean of Gloucester, and Elizabeth Somerset, fifth duchess of Beaufort. Her most valuable emotional mainstay was her sisters' love and friendship, sustained by constant correspondence while they were apart, and throughout their lives she benefited from their guidance, encouragement, and praise.

In her late teens Hannah More composed her first significant work, a pastoral verse drama for schoolgirls entitled *The Search after Happiness*, published in Bristol in 1762, in which she expresses her views on women's education and role in society. Speeches from archetypal female characters such as the fashionable Euphelia, the bookish Cleora, and the lazy Laurinda describe the various unhappinesses arising from a mistaken education, and it is left to the wise Urania to counsel her sex to cultivate the domestic virtues and to be 'Fearful of Fame, unwilling to be known' (H. More, *The Search after Happiness*, 1773, 1.277). The play was performed at the Mores' school and, once republished in London in 1773, was eagerly bought by the public; over 10,000 copies had been sold by the mid-1780s and a twelfth edition appeared in 1800. More's desire to provide suitably moral material for her pupils to act led her to write five short dramas based on Old Testament stories, later published as *Sacred Dramas* (1782). Keen to improve her knowledge of the stage, she frequented the King Street theatre in Bath, often accompanied by her pupils, and by 1774 had freely translated, from the Italian,

Metastasio's play *Attilio Regolo*, the heroic tragedy of the Roman general Marcus Attilius Regulus.

In 1767 More accepted a proposal of marriage from William Turner, of Belmont House, Wraxall, whom she knew through young cousins of his who were pupils at the sisters' school. She exchanged her teaching duties for preparation for her future as the wife of a wealthy country gentleman; she advised Turner on landscaping the gardens at Belmont, now part of the Tyntesfield estates (National Trust). However, Turner, who was twenty years her senior, proved a nervous and uncertain fiancé and postponed their wedding three times; on the first occasion he allegedly jilted her at the altar. Patient and forgiving, More, after listening to her concerned family and friends, finally broke off their engagement in 1773, apparently triggering a nervous breakdown. Little is known of the relationship of More and Turner, and less of their feelings for each other, but this was almost certainly More's only serious romantic attachment. Soon afterwards she resolved never to marry, and refused several subsequent proposals, including one from the poet John Langhorne. Turner sought to make amends for his inconstancy by offering her an annuity to enable her to pursue a literary career. Having at first declined she was at length persuaded to accept a smaller annuity of £200 through a trust set up by her friend Stonhouse. By overcoming her scruples she gained both financial security and independence.

Bluestocking and dramatist In the winter of 1773–4 More, together with Sarah and Martha, made the first of thirty-five consecutive annual visits to London. An initial recommendation of her literary talents from Stonhouse and Ann Lovell Gwatkin ensured that within the space of ten days she had met David and Eva Garrick, Elizabeth Montagu, and Joshua Reynolds, who in turn introduced her to Dr Johnson and Edmund Burke. Back in Bristol she contributed to Burke's successful campaign to be elected MP for the city in September 1774 by ghosting some of his letters to the local press and writing verses singing his praises. Her second visit to London, early in 1775, secured her place in literary circles when she was invited to her first bluestocking party, at Elizabeth Montagu's house in Hill Street. When Johnson asked her opinion on a recent play More overcame her diffidence in front of so many 'luminaries' by characteristically reasoning 'it a less evil to dissent from the opinion of a fellow creature, than to tell a falsity', and 'ventured to give her sentiments'; Johnson agreed with her and, her critical credentials established, she never looked back (W. Roberts, 1.52–3). She quickly forged lifelong friendships not only with Montagu and Johnson but also with Frances Boscawen, Elizabeth Carter, Hester Chapone, and Elizabeth Vesey. She enthusiastically joined in the endless mutual flattery indulged in by members of the bluestocking circle; she and Johnson competed to see who could 'pepper the highest' (ibid., 1.54), yet on another occasion he mockingly reprimanded her, 'Consider with yourself what your flattery is worth, before you bestow it so freely' (J. Boswell, *Life of Johnson*, ed. P. Rogers, 1980, 1328). As a second-generation bluestocking More was the ideal chronicler of their talents in her poem *The Bas Bleu, or, Conversation* (1784), written in 1782, in which she hailed virtuous conversation as:

The noblest commerce of mankind,
Whose precious merchandise is MIND!
(ll.250–51)

More's reputation for lionizing the London literati might be regarded as shameless sycophancy were it not for the fact that she was busy making a name for herself. She had earned Johnson's good opinion of her literary merit when she showed him two ballads, *Sir Eldred of the Bower* and *The Bleeding Rock*, published by Cadell in 1776. Her passion for drama was nurtured by Garrick, her favourite actor and increasingly her close friend and mentor, who put on her first play, *The Inflexible Captive* (a reworking of her Metastasio translation), at the Theatre Royal in Bath in April 1775. The encouraging audience notwithstanding, she resisted Garrick's suggestion to transfer the play to the London stage and instead began writing a new play, *Percy*. This was a tragic tale, set in the borders in the twelfth century, of two lovers whose happiness was doomed by the feud between the Douglas and Northumberland families. Despite its static nature and stilted dialogue *Percy* met with a rapturous reception at Covent Garden in December 1777. After attending the first and second nights More wrote home all of a flutter at its success, even with the critics. In keeping with her conviction that the theatre could have a powerful moral influence what pleased her most was the audience's reaction: 'One tear is worth a thousand hands [applause], and I had the satisfaction to see even the men shed them in abundance' (W. Roberts, 1.125). She made nearly £600 from the rights (the first edition of nearly 4000 sold out within weeks) and, to her barely concealed delight, her authorship of the season's hit became an open secret. Her celebrity was marked by requests for her to sit for her portrait from Daniel Gardiner (1778), Frances Reynolds (1780), and John Opie (1786; commissioned by Elizabeth Montagu), and she was depicted as Melpomene, the tragic muse, in Richard Samuel's *The Nine Living Muses of Great Britain* (NPG), which was exhibited in 1779. Reynolds considered her the embodiment of all the muses and fondly christened her Nine, a nickname that was taken up by Garrick. To add to her honours she was in 1782 elected a fellow of the Académie des Arts, Sciences et Belles Lettres in Rouen.

More confirmed her bluestocking credentials by seeking to promote a fellow woman writer, Anna Yearsley, nicknamed the Bristol Milkwoman. On hearing that Yearsley, a destitute labourer's wife with a young family, was a talented poet More expertly exploited her literary and aristocratic connections to canvass subscriptions for a volume of her verses. Published in 1785, Yearsley's *Poems, on Several Occasions* generated profits of about £600 that More and Elizabeth Montagu placed in a trust to protect Yearsley's earnings from her allegedly feckless husband. More's good intentions were coloured by her paternalist attitudes towards the lower classes, and she expressed her hope that 'all these honours will not turn her head, and indispose her for her humble occupations' (W. Roberts,

1.332). Her pride wounded, Yearsley demanded access to her earnings and acrimoniously accused More and Montagu of stealing her money. The trust was rapidly wound up and, unlike Montagu, who was incensed by Yearsley's 'open and notorious ingratitude' (ibid., 1.387), More refused to trade insults or to respond to Yearsley's increasingly public accusations. The controversy added to More's disillusionment with the literary world. Ever since Garrick's death in January 1779 she had lost her appetite for the glittering London scene, and this was compounded by the theatrical failure in the summer of her third and final play, *The Fatal Falsehood*, which played for only a few nights. Furthermore she was embarrassed by Hannah Cowley's public accusation that she had plagiarized Cowley's tragedy *Albina*, a charge that she categorically refuted in the *St James' Chronicle*. Although a second edition of *The Fatal Falsehood* appeared in 1780, her publisher Thomas Cadell advised More that she was 'too good a Christian for an author' (W. Roberts, 1.172).

Writing for women The experience that More had gained as a teacher at her sisters' school provided the material for *Essays on Various Subjects, Principally Designed for Young Ladies*, published anonymously in 1777. The eight essays dealt with many of the favourite topics of moralists—such as dissipation, conversation, sentimental connections, education, and religion—and also addressed a subject close to More's bluestocking heart: 'Miscellaneous thoughts on wit'. In the introduction she counselled her sex to succeed as women rather than to aspire as men, and throughout the essays she upheld sexual difference, both in terms of natural abilities and of social roles. In declaring that women excelled in tasks that did not demand a strong intellect she argued against her own literary pursuits, for she wrote that women:

may cultivate the roles of imagination, and the valuable fruits of morals and criticism; but the steeps of Parnassus few, comparatively, have attempted to scale with success … The lofty Epic, the pointed Satire, and the more daring and successful flights of the Tragic Muse, seem reserved for the bold adventurers of the other sex. (pp. 6–7)

Convinced of the reciprocal relationship between female education and conduct, she called for greater attention to be paid to the intellectual, sentimental, and religious education of girls, and described female conduct as 'one of the principal hinges on which the great machine of human society turns' (p. 19).

By the time when More wrote her definitive work on women's education, twenty-two years later, she was a household name. As a consequence of her celebrity as a woman writer copies of her *Strictures on the Modern System of Female Education* (2 vols., 1799) rushed off the shelves; seven editions were printed in the first year alone. In her review of her contemporary attitudes towards female education she criticized both Jean-Jacques Rousseau's doctrine of sensibility, which turned women into creatures of mere sentiment, and Mary Wollstonecraft's belief in female rights, which encouraged women to adopt an aggressive independence; she proposed that women should be educated neither as Circassians nor as Amazons but as Christians. At the heart of her educational ideas lay the evangelical conviction that children were tainted with mankind's original sin and so should be considered 'as beings who bring into the world a corrupt nature and evil dispositions, which it should be great end of education to rectify' (vol. 1, p. 57). Notwithstanding the apparent pessimism of such beliefs she rejoiced at the situation of her sex in the Britain of the 1790s and called on her fellow women to take advantage, as she had, of these blessings.

The logical progression of More's view that women's education and conduct determined the moral state of a nation was that the education of a female monarch, who was the ultimate moral exemplar, was the most important concern to a moralist. She therefore addressed Princess Charlotte, who was second in line to the throne, in her third work on female education, *Hints towards Forming the Character of a Young Princess* (2 vols., 1805). Despairing of the immoral conduct of the prince of Wales and fearful of a return of George III's incapacitating illness, More, in common with her fellow evangelicals, viewed the young princess as the saviour of the nation. She outlined a curriculum suitable for a future monarch that was rich in classical and English history, Christian theology, and the nature of royal duties. This highly specific conduct book was not her final word of advice to her sex, for her only novel, *Coelebs in Search of a Wife* (1809), succeeds more as a treatise on female manners and education than as a work of fiction. *Coelebs* is essentially a parable about marriage that More specifically wrote for 'the subscribers to the circulating library' as an alternative to the romantic novels usually on offer at 'that mart of mischief' (W. Roberts, 3.322). Charles, a young bachelor (hence the title, *Coelebs*) of independent fortune, meets countless young women who prove themselves to be unsuitable as his wife and, after much guidance from his late father's friend Mr Stanley, an evangelical, about the qualities and character of the ideal wife, he meets and marries the personification of female virtue, Lucilla Stanley, the eldest daughter of his mentor. Despite poor reviews *Coelebs* was More's most successful work to date and sold 'ten large impressions in the first six months' (ibid.), ample compensation, as she commented, for the adverse critical reception.

'Saint Hannah' Throughout her life More steadfastly adhered to the orthodox trinitarian doctrines and episcopalian structure of the Church of England, yet in the 1780s her faith was both energized and transformed by evangelicalism. Accustomed to the Christian observance of her family circle in Bristol and of her favourite friends in London, she viewed with increasing dismay the irreligion of the fashionable world. On an early visit to London she was reprimanded by one of her oldest Christian mentors, Stonhouse, for dining out on a Sunday, and thereafter she consciously tried to avoid social situations that compromised her faith. Furthermore she sought out new acquaintances who shared her religious outlook and who became close friends and correspondents, such as the philanthropical Countess Spencer, the educational author Sarah Trimmer, and John Newton, rector of St Mary Woolnoth. Newton's *Cardiphonia, or, The Utterance of*

the Heart (1780) had deeply impressed her—'it is full of vital, experimental religion' (W. Roberts, 1.189)—and he became perhaps her most important spiritual counsellor. Together with her influential backers in the Anglican hierarchy, namely Robert Lowth, Josiah Tucker, George Horne, and Beilby Porteus, these friends urged her to use her talents and connections to further two evangelically inspired campaigns: abolition of slavery and reformation of manners. Although she spent less time in London and more at her retreat at Cowslip Green, Somerset, where she had built a cottage in 1784, the next decade saw her acquire a national reputation.

In 1776 More had met Charles and Margaret Middleton, whose home at Teston, Kent, became the headquarters of the parliamentary campaign to abolish the slave trade in the late 1780s. More's correspondence documents how she and her fellow abolitionists canvassed MPs by letter and in person. At one dinner party in April 1789 she was showing the company Thomas Clarkson's cross-section of a slave ship when she was interrupted by the arrival of John Tarleton, a leading Liverpool slave trader and opponent of the bill to regulate the trade; fearing a row, she 'popped the book out of sight, snapped the string of my eloquence, and was mute at once' (W. Roberts, 2.152). Newton's eye-witness accounts of the inhumanities of the west African slave trade doubtless inspired her poetical contribution to the campaign, *Slavery*, which she wrote in great haste in January 1788 to maximize publicity for William Wilberforce's bill. In the poem she declared that the nation was shamed and compromised by its participation in the slave trade and challenged her countrymen and -women to abandon such hypocrisy:

Shall Britain, where the soul of Freedom reigns
Forge chains for others she herself disdains?
(ll. 251–2)

Wilberforce, whom she met in autumn 1787, became a firm friend and a valued correspondent. More continued to champion the cause throughout the long struggle to secure parliamentary abolition of both the trade and slavery itself; she subscribed to the African Institution, which replaced the Society for the Abolition of the Slave Trade in 1807, and in the later 1820s she was nominated to the committee of the Female Anti-Slavery Society at Clifton in Bristol.

More's disenchantment with the prevailing manners and morals of London society motivated her repeated attempts to reform the behaviour and beliefs of the fashionable and aristocratic world. The respect and reputation in élite circles that she had earned in the 1770s could be exploited to good effect. This was well understood by John Wesley, who remarked: 'Tell her to live in the world; there is the sphere of her usefulness' (Jones, *Hannah More*, 103), for unlike the clergy she could guarantee a favourable hearing in the drawing-rooms of the upper classes. She endeavoured to set an example in her personal conduct by keeping the sabbath, avoiding card parties, and introducing religious topics and sentiments into general conversation. In addition she followed Bishop Horne's advice to write 'for the benefit of *the great and the gay*' (W. Roberts,

2.37), and in 1788 published anonymously *Thoughts on the Importance of the Manners of the Great to General Society*. It proved phenomenally popular: the second edition sold out in six days, the third in four hours, and an eighth edition appeared in 1790. In admonishing the upper classes More made clear her belief in a hierarchical and deferential society and argued that a reformation of manners could be achieved only if the leaders of society reformed themselves. She renewed her mission to the great in *An Estimate of the Religion of the Fashionable World* (1790), which went to a fifth edition. Despite their success, symbolized by their favourable reception at court, these two works were unpalatable reading in some quarters; Hester Thrale reported that the effigy of the killjoy More was burnt by pupils at Westminster School. Newton's assurance to her in September 1791 that 'your sex and your character afford you a peculiar protection' (ibid., 272) proved to be only half true: by taking full advantage of the moral authority accorded to her sex More was criticized for her unfeminine behaviour in speaking out so publicly. Depressed and demoralized by the political situation at home and abroad in the 1790s, she became less convinced that her exhortations to the great were having any effect. In 1795 she wrote to a friend, 'I think I have done with the aristocracy', and concentrated instead on her duties to 'her poor barbarians' (ibid., 455).

Philanthropist More's 'poor barbarians' were the parishioners of several parishes in the Mendips in Somerset, for whom she was attempting to provide educational and religious succour. In August 1789 Wilberforce stayed with her at Cowslip Green, and on visiting the nearby village of Cheddar he and More were appalled to find 'incredible multitudes of poor, plunged in an excess of vice, poverty, and ignorance beyond what one would suppose possible in a civilized and Christian country' (W. Roberts, 2.178). Encouraged by Wilberforce, More and her sisters resolved on a plan to alleviate their ignorance and hardship by setting up schools where the children of the poor would be taught to read. Following the pattern set by the charity schools of Robert Raikes and Sarah Trimmer, Hannah and Martha More rented a house at Cheddar and engaged teachers to instruct the children in reading the Bible and the catechism. More was adamant that the poor should not be taught writing, as it would encourage them to be dissatisfied with their lowly situation; over twenty years later she strongly criticized the National Society for teaching their school pupils the three Rs.

The school at Cheddar quickly attracted 300 pupils, and the sisters proceeded to set up a second school, at Shipham; within a decade they were running twelve schools scattered across the Mendips. In keeping with their objective 'to train up the lower classes to habits of industry and virtue' the sisters also started evening classes for adults, weekday classes for girls to learn how to sew, knit, and spin, and a number of women's friendly societies, where the virtues of cleanliness, decency, and Christian behaviour were inculcated. From 1791 annual picnics were organized for the schools and societies, rewards for good conduct were handed out, and incentives of gingerbread or 1*d*. were offered to the children for regular attendance at church. From May to December, Hannah and Martha More visited and inspected the schools in turn each Sunday, but the work of maintaining them occupied most of their energies during the week. More's four sisters retired from the boarding-school at Christmas 1789, handing over the business to Selina Mills, the future wife of Zachary Macaulay, and thereafter divided their time between Cowslip Green and Bath, where they had bought a house in Great Pulteney Street; all five sisters moved into a large house, Barley Wood, at Wrington, Somerset, in 1801.

More received warm praise for her energetic philanthropy from her evangelical friends, and even Horace Walpole paid tribute to his friend's extraordinary achievements. At the same time as he teased her for her 'cruelty of making the poor spend so much time in reading books, and depriving them of their pleasures on Sundays' he wrote:

> How I admire the activity of your zeal and perseverance! Should a new church ever be built, I hope in a side chapel there will be an altar dedicated to Saint Hannah, Virgin and Martyr; and that your pen, worn to the bone, will be enclosed in a golden *reliquaire*, and preserved on the shrine.
> (Walpole, *Corr.*, 31.398)

In setting up her charity schools More encountered considerable hostility from local farmers and landowners, who feared that schooling would make their labourers 'lazy and useless' (W. Roberts, 2.207); she had to draw on all her canvassing skills to persuade them to support the venture. The most public opposition, however, came from several of the local clergy, who suspected, quite correctly, that her philanthropy called into question their pastoral care; by contrast the local bishop, Dr Charles Moss, gave her steadfast support throughout. She was shocked to discover the extent of clerical absenteeism: there was no resident curate in any of the thirteen neighbouring parishes, and in Cheddar one clergyman 'rode over, three miles from Wells, to preach once a Sunday, but no weekly duty was done, or sick persons visited; and children were often buried without any formal funeral service' (ibid., 2.301). Determined not to ignore 'so wide-spread an evil' on her doorstep, she introduced sermons often 'of the most awakening sort' and scriptural readings into the schools and evening classes, which attracted accusations of Methodism (ibid., 2.213, 303). Whereas some locals signalled their dislike of her methodistical measures by breaking a few windows in the schools, local clergymen vented their disapproval in a full-blown religious controversy of national significance: the Blagdon controversy of 1800–03. In 1800 Thomas Bere, curate of Blagdon, published a stinging attack on More's school at Blagdon, accusing the schoolmaster of holding Methodist meetings in the evenings, encouraging extempore prayer, and undermining the authority of the ordained clergy. High-church clerics such as Charles Daubeny seized the opportunity to denounce More for fostering schism, Methodism, and Jacobinism at her schools, and two local clergymen—

Edward Spencer of Wells, and William Shaw, rector of Chelvey (using the pseudonym of the Revd Sir Archibald Macsarcasm)—wrote scurrilous attacks on the 'She-Bishop'. Angry at the accusation that she was endangering the Church of England and anxious to clear herself, More wrote a long self-justificatory letter in 1802 to the new bishop of Bath and Wells, Dr Richard Beadon, who came to her defence. However, mauled by the abuse and suffering worsening health, she backed down and closed Blagdon School, primarily in order to protect the reputation of her other schools. 'Battered, hacked, scalped, tomahawked' (Jones, *Hannah More*, 185), she may have won a moral victory over the Blagdon affair but her character, charitable works, and faith were vilified on a scale perhaps unprecedented for a woman; as she wrote to Beadon, 'my conduct' has been attacked 'with a wantonness of cruelty which, in civilized places, few persons, especially of my sex, have been called to suffer' (W. Roberts, 3.123).

'Bishop in petticoats' Hannah More's role as moral guardian of the nation became increasingly politicized as a consequence of the French Revolution. Horrified as much by the atheism as by the political radicalism of the revolutionaries, she denounced their attack on revealed religion in her *Remarks on the speech of M. Dupont, made in the National Convention of France, on the subjects of religion and public education* (1793), having waited in vain 'for our bishops and clergy to take some notice of them' (W. Roberts, 3.360). Tellingly Bishop Porteus insisted that she add her name to the publication in order to maximize its public impact; three editions appeared that year. Porteus also encouraged her to write the tracts for which she is best-known. To counter the revolutionary politics circulating in cheap editions of Tom Paine's *Rights of Man* she 'scribbled' *Village politics: addressed to all the mechanics, journeymen, and day labourers, in Great Britain* (1792) by 'Will Chip, a country carpenter', in which Paine's political ideals are ridiculed in a dialogue between a blacksmith and a mason. She was hesitant about writing such an overtly political work, yet the threat of revolution and war impelled her to write dozens of similarly loyalist, moral, and Christian tales specifically for the lower classes that were published anonymously as Cheap Repository Tracts (1795–8). A total of 114 tracts, including some by Sarah and Martha More, were sold for ½d. or 1d. every month from 1795 to 1798, funded by subscriptions, and distributed by booksellers and pedlars across the country; Hannah wrote forty-nine tracts and masterminded the whole operation. Sales were enormous: within four months 700,000 had been sold, within a year over 2 million. They were mainly bought by the middling and upper classes to distribute to the poor but they also found a ready market in the United States, and Bishop Porteus sent large quantities to Sierra Leone and the West Indies. Though their influence on their intended audience cannot be measured the Cheap Repository Tracts certainly 'established themselves as the safe reading' (Jones, *Hannah More*, 145) of the poor and paved the way for the work of the Religious Tract Society, founded in 1799.

During the final years of the Napoleonic wars More published three works that showed a more reflective side to her religious writing. *Practical Piety, or, The Influence of the Religion of the Heart on the Conduct of the Life* (1811; 12th edn, 1821) and *Christian Morals* (2 vols., 1813) pleaded the cause of a Christian life to the middle and upper classes, a familiar message but one that still appealed to the public, for both books were repeatedly reprinted. The death of her eldest sister, Mary, on 18 April 1813, led More to seek spiritual consolation by immersing herself in scripture; she indulged herself by writing the biographical *Essay on the Character and Practical Writings of St Paul* (1815), which she believed would be her last work. She predicted that her attempt at such a major biblical subject would be considered presumptuous and anticipated criticism from 'two classes of enemies, the very high Calvinists, and what is called the very high Church party' (W. Roberts, 3.430). Since the 1780s More's theological views had been those of the evangelical party, as demonstrated by her involvement with the Clapham Sect, a group of Anglican evangelicals centred on Battersea Rise, the Clapham home of the banker Henry Thornton, yet she continued to deplore the religious factions that divided both the Church of England and the Christian church in general. Despite her hostility towards Calvinists and Methodists, however, her reading and acquaintance were far from confined to the established church, and her evangelical piety aligned her with dissent as much as with Anglicanism.

More willingly re-entered the realm of public controversy in 1817, once again to do battle with home-grown political and religious radicalism. The economic hardships suffered by the poor in the years following the peace of 1815 had stimulated a new appetite for radical literature, typified by the 'twopenny trash' of William Cobbett's *Political Register*. More was urged by her evangelical friends in government to contribute to *The Anti-Cobbett, or, The Weekly Patriotic Register* in 1817, to recast her old tracts (*Village Politics* was reprinted as *Village Disputants*), and to compose new ones, including *The Loyal Subject's Political Creed*, thereby earning Cobbett's derisive nickname of the 'old bishop in petticoats'. In her final didactic work, *Moral Sketches of Prevailing Opinions and Manners, Foreign and Domestic* (1819), she was at her most conservative and patriotic in championing the politics, religion, and manners of Britain in contrast with those of France, and indeed with the rest of Europe.

Final years, death, and reputation The last twenty years of More's life were dominated by ill health and loss. She nursed her beloved sisters through successive illnesses and provided unstinting spiritual comfort as they approached their deaths. Left alone at Barley Wood following Martha's death, on 14 September 1819, she succumbed to a series of serious illnesses through the following decade. During her phases of good health she was rarely without company, for her friends and fans flocked to visit and entertain her to such an extent that she had to insist on limiting their visits to certain days in the week. Friends were the chief pleasure of her life since she found herself deeply out of sympathy with the politics and literature of the time. She had recognized that she had become more reactionary in her old age as early as 1820, when she wrote, 'These turbulent times make one sad. I am sick of that liberty which I used so to prize' (W. Roberts, 4.160). Marianne Thornton recalled how More humorously named her two cats Passive Obedience and Non-resistance, and More proved a determined opponent of both Catholic emancipation and parliamentary reform. Plagued by her unmanageable servants and confined to her room by growing infirmity, she was persuaded to leave Barley Wood in 1828 and move to Clifton, where she could be cared for by her friends, and where she died, aged eighty-eight, on 7 September 1833. Her mind wandered in the weeks before her death, yet she continued to profess her absolute trust in Christ, her redeemer; she spoke for the last time, calling out 'JOY!', on the day before she died. On 13 September she was buried next to her sisters in the graveyard of All Saints' at Wrington. She left about £30,000, most of which she bequeathed to charities and religious societies. In his funeral sermon her curate and subsequent biographer Henry Thompson quoted from *Coelebs* to describe her guiding principle in life: 'If it be absurd to expect perfection, it is not unreasonable to expect *consistency*' (H. Thompson, *The Christian an Example*, 1833, 7).

The life and works of Hannah More were praised in countless obituaries and lauded at length in William Roberts's *Memoirs of the Life and Correspondence of Mrs Hannah More* (4 vols., 1834). Roberts's pompous and reverential tone led W. H. Prescott to comment that 'Hannah More has been done to death by her friend Roberts' (Jones, *Hannah More*, 229). A string of nineteenth-century biographies, including one by the high-churchwoman Charlotte M. Yonge, kept her name alive, but her high reputation was gradually worn away by accusations of vanity, worldliness, and religious hypocrisy. Furthermore her archconservative and paternalist views on education, the poor, and women's role in society quickly dated as the political tide turned against her, and have ensured that she remained an unfashionable subject of study for much of the twentieth century. The literary merit of her prose and verse works has been dismissed, even by her most thorough biographer to date, M. G. Jones, who described their 'literary value' as 'negligible' (Jones, *Hannah More*, x), and Norma Clarke has rightly commented that Anna Yearsley's poetry has been more studied in recent years than More's own. However, historical re-evaluation in the 1990s of her political and religious writings has demonstrated that More 'cannot be seen as merely the reactionary antithesis of Mary Wollstonecraft' (Stott, 'Patriotism and providence', 39), and, long taken for granted, she is being recognized as a unique public figure in late Georgian Britain.

More's overt display of her evangelical faith has led to her being characterized as smug and self-righteous, yet, as her spiritual diary reveals, she was acutely conscious of her unworthiness before God. She was ever thankful for her conversion and reacted with a shudder to the death of the irreligious John Wilkes:

> awful event! talents how abused! Lord, who hath made *me* to differ; but for thy grace, I might have blasphemed thee like him. In early youth I read Hume, Voltaire, Rousseau &c. I am a monument of mercy, not to have made a shipwreck of my faith. (W. Roberts, 3.56)

Quite disingenuously she often commented that she took little account of public opinion; in 1795 she wrote, 'I have not myself any vain curiosity to know what people at large think of me; but if there is any one over whom their good opinion may give me useful influence, I think it of importance' (ibid., 2.454). In fact she was shrewdly aware of the power that she had acquired through her phenomenally popular works, even though she perpetually referred to herself as a weak instrument of God. 'Usefulness'—the justification of all her writing and her philanthropy—allowed her to break the boundaries of gender and class and to assume a moral, religious, and political authority that was unprecedented for a middle-class woman of the period. The same motivation to further the work of the Lord made her one of the most prolific British woman writers before the Victorian age, for her collected works run to eleven volumes. It also drove her to broadcast her views to the country when asked by her publisher to write a tribute to the late George III, even though she was struck down by illness. On her sickbed she secretly 'began to scribble', despite 'a high fever, with my pulse above a hundred, without having formed one idea', and by the following day had sent fourteen pages to Cadell. 'I got well scolded, but I loved the king, and was carried through by a sort of affectionate impulse; so it stands as a preface to the seventh edition of her *Moral Sketches*' (ibid., 4.154). Such devotion to her public duty as a Christian writer, mixed with a due sense of her own importance, characterized the life and mission of Hannah More.   S. J. SKEDD

Sources W. Roberts, *Memoirs of the life and correspondence of Hannah More*, 3rd edn, 4 vols. (1835) · M. G. Jones, *Hannah More* (1952) · A. Stott, *Hannah More: the first Victorian* (2003) · H. Thompson, *Life of Hannah More with notices of her sisters* (1838) · *Mendip annals, or, A narrative of the charitable labours of Hannah and Martha More in their neighbourhood*, ed. A. Roberts (1859) · *Letters of Hannah More to Zachary Macaulay*, ed. A. Roberts (1860) · Walpole, *Corr.*, vol. 31 · G. H. Spinney, 'Cheap repository tracts: Hazard and Marshall edition', *The Library*, ser. 4, 20 (1939), 295–340 · A. Stott, 'Patriotism and providence: the politics of Hannah More', in K. Gleadle and S. Richardson, *Women in British politics, 1760–1860: the power of the petticoat* (2000), 39–55 · A. Stott, 'Hannah More and the Blagdon controversy, 1799–1802', *Journal of Ecclesiastical History*, 51 (2000), 319–46 · S. Skedd, 'The education of women in Hanoverian Britain, c.1760–1820', DPhil diss., U. Oxf., 1997 · M. A. Hopkins, *Hannah More and her circle* (1947) · S. Pederson, 'Hannah More meets Simple Simon: tracts, chapbooks and popular culture in late eighteenth-century England', *Journal of British Studies*, 25 (1986), 84–113 · S. Harcstark Myers, *The bluestocking circle: women, friendship, and the life of the mind in eighteenth-century England* (1990) · N. Clarke, *Dr Johnson's women* (2000) · R. Hole, introduction, in *Selected writings of Hannah More*, ed. R. Hole (1996) · M. G. Jones, *The charity school movement* (1964) · E. Kowaleski-Wallace, *Their fathers' daughters: Hannah More, Maria Edgeworth, and patriarchal complicity* (1991) · C. Midgley, *Women against slavery: the British campaigns, 1780–1870* (1992) · will, PRO, PROB 11/1822, fols. 366r–369v

Archives BL, letters and papers, Add. MS 42511 · Bodl. Oxf., letters · Boston PL, corresp. and papers · Bristol Reference Library, letters · Bristol RO, letters and literary MSS · Duke U., Perkins L., papers · Hist. Soc. Penn., papers · Hunt. L., letters · Knox College, Galesburg, Illinois, Seymour Library, papers · Yale U., Beinecke L., letters and literary MSS | BL, letters to C. Hoare, RP 140 [copies] ·

BL, letters to Frances Reynolds, RP 186 [copies] · BL, corresp., mainly with Lady Olivia Sparrow, Egerton MS 1965 · Bodl. Oxf., letters to Dr Carrick · Bodl. Oxf., letters to Charles Ogilvie · Bodl. Oxf., corresp. with William Wilberforce · Christ Church Oxf., archives, letters to Cadell and Davies · CKS, letters to the bishop of Lincoln · CUL, corresp. with Thornton family · CUL, letters to Marianne Thornton · Hunt. L., letters to Zachary Macaulay · Hunt. L., letters to Elizabeth Montagu · NRA, priv. coll., corresp. with Maria, duchess of Gloucester, and Princess Sophia of Gloucester · NRA, priv. coll., corresp. with Felicia Horne · St Deiniol's Library, Hawarden, Flintshire, letters to Anne Gladstone · V&A NAL, letters to David Garrick

Likenesses R. Samuel, group portrait, oils, exh. 1779 (*The nine living muses of Great Britain*), NPG · J. Opie, portrait, 1786, Girton Cam. [*see illus.*] · E. Scriven, stipple, pubd 1814 (after J. Slater), BM, NPG · H. W. Pickersgill, oils, 1822, NPG · A. Edouart, silhouette, 1827, NPG · A. Edouart, silhouette, 1831, Scot. NPG · J. Godby, stipple (after E. Bird), BM, NPG; repro. in *Contemporary portraits* (1809) · J. Heath, stipple and line engraving (after J. Opie), BM; repro. in *The works of Horatio Walpole*, 5 vols. (1798) · J. Jackson, pencil drawing, BM · H. Raeburn, oils (of More?), Louvre, Paris · F. Reynolds, oils, Bristol City Museum and Art Gallery

Wealth at death approx. £30,000

More, Helen [*name in religion* Gertrude] (**1606–1633**), Benedictine nun, was born on 25 March 1606 in Low Leyton, Essex, the daughter of Cresacre *More (1572–1649) and Elizabeth Gage (*d*. *c*.1611), and great-great-granddaughter of Thomas More. Her mother died young, her father taking over her education. Benet Jones OSB urged the family to consider her for a monastic vocation. The English Benedictine congregation had been refounded in 1619 and sought to start a house of nuns in exile from England to support the monks' hazardous work on the English mission through their prayer. Helen was seventeen and had misgivings, but left England with two More cousins and four other young Englishwomen to travel to Douai, where they were joined by Catherine Gascoigne. In 1623 they founded Our Lady of Comfort at Cambrai, the house which later became Stanbrook Abbey. Helen was clothed on 31 December 1623 and professed her vows on 1 January 1625, taking the name of Gertrude from the mystic Gertrude of Helfta.

Contemporary prayer practices were Ignatian. Gertrude More found these troubling. She also rebelled against the contemplative practices of medieval mystics, many of them women, taught to the nuns by Augustine Baker OSB from 1624 to 1633. Trained as a lawyer, he had converted to Catholicism and worked among the manuscripts owned by Sir Robert Cotton. Baker encouraged forms of prayer drawn from the Desert Fathers, Benedict, and the later mystics, and he encouraged the English nuns to copy out and themselves write contemplative books. 'Good books', he said to the nuns, 'are a necessary good to your soul'. He taught the nuns above all to heed their call from God, to live their vocation. At first the restless and doubting Gertrude More adamantly opposed these practices, while Catherine Gascoigne quietly adopted them. Finally Gertrude confronted Augustine Baker, who commented, 'What she needed was to be brought into a simplicity of soul which is the immediate disposition to union with God, and that can be done only by the Divine working with the soul's co-operation, aided by Divine grace'. He

had her live her 'way of love', laying down scruples and becoming internally obedient. She expressed it as 'Consider your call, That's all in all.' Concerning her past scruples she laughingly quoted her ancestor, Thomas More, 'The urchin wench goes whining up and down as if nothing she did or could do did please [God].'

Gertrude More's writings, discovered after her early death in 1633, included the 'Confessio amantis' (published at Paris in 1658 by Serenus Cressy OSB), based on Augustine's *Confessions* interwoven into the divine office, the 'Fragments', and the 'Apology', the last defending Baker's teachings, which describes the quieting effect of prayer in loving God and humbling herself, and in which she appreciates his non-authoritarian approach, that God is the authority, not the confessor or director. In 1629 Catherine Gascoigne became second abbess, Gertrude being considered too young for the post, though founder; she acted instead as cellarer and overseer of the lay sisters. In this year her younger sister Bridget More also joined the community, as did Catherine's sister Margaret Gascoigne. The chaplain Francis Hull opposed Augustine Baker's teachings and caused turmoil in the community in 1633. Gertrude encouraged the sisters but herself fell ill with smallpox in the midst of the row, which saw both Hull and Baker recalled to Douai. She died serenely at Cambrai in the presence of her cousin Ann More on 17 August 1633, and was buried there. She was twenty-seven years old. Augustine Baker OSB wrote *The Inner Life of Dame Gertrude More*, demonstrating his teaching on prayer, and edited her writings.   JULIA BOLTON HOLLOWAY

Sources J. McCann and H. Connolly, eds., *Memorials of Father Augustine Baker and other documents relating to the English Benedictines*, Catholic RS, 33 (1933) · A. Baker, *Sancta Sophia, or, Directions for the prayer of contemplation, &c. extracted out of more than XL. treatises written by the late Ven. Father F. Augustin Baker, a monke of the English congregation of the order of St Benedict: and methodically digested by the R. F. Serenus Cressy of the same order & congregation and printed at the charges of his convent of S. Gregories in Doway*, 2 vols. (1657) · 'Cambrai: Dame Catherine Gascoigne, 1600–1676', Benedictines of Stanbrook, *In a great tradition: tribute to Dame Laurentia McLachlan, abbess of Stanbrook* (1956), 3–29 · J. McCann, ed., *The cloud of unknowing and other treatises by an English mystic of the fourteenth century, with a commentary by Father Augustine Baker, O.S.B.* (1924) · J. Hall, 'Dame Gertrude More (1606–1633): the living tradition', *Medieval women monastics: wisdom's wellsprings*, ed. M. Schmitt and L. Kulzer (1996) · D. Latz, 'Glow-worm light': writings of seventeenth century English recusant women from original manuscripts (1989) · A. More, *The building of divine love*, ed. D. Latz (1992) · G. More, *The holy practices of a devine lover, or, The sainctly ideot's devotions*, ed. A. Baker (1657) · *The inner life of Dame Gertrude More*, ed. A. Baker and B. Weld-Blundell (1910) · *The spiritual exercises of the most vertuous and religious D. Gertrude More*, ed. A. Baker (1658) · *The writings of Dame Gertrude More*, ed. A. Baker and B. Weld-Blundell (1910) · J. Gillow, ed., 'Records of the abbey of Our Lady of Consolation at Cambrai, 1620–1793', *Miscellanea, VIII*, Catholic RS, 13 (1913), 1–85, esp. 77–8 · F. Sandeman, 'Dame Gertrude More', *Benedict's disciples*, ed. D. H. Farmer (1980), 263–81 · H. W. Owen and L. Bell, 'The Upholland anthology: an Augustine Baker manuscript', *Downside Review*, 107 (1989), 274–92 · P. Salvin and S. Cressy, *The life of Father Augustine Baker*, ed. D. J. McCann (1933) · P. Spearitt, 'The survival of medieval spirituality among the exiled black monks', *American Benedictine Review*, 25 (1974), 187–309 · records of the community of Our Lady of Comfort, Cambrai, Archives du Nord, Lille · M. Norman, 'Dame Gertrude More and the English mystical tradition', *Recusant History*, 13 (1975–6), 196–211

Archives Ampleforth Abbey, MSS · Archives du Nord, Lille, MSS · Bibliothèque Mazarin, Paris, MSS · Downside Abbey, near Bath, MSS · Mediathèque Municipale, Cambrai, MSS · St Mary's Abbey, Colwich, MSS · Stanbrook Abbey, MSS
Likenesses R. Lochon, line engraving, BM; repro. in Baker, ed., *Spiritual exercises* · engraving, repro. in Baker, ed., *Spiritual exercises*, frontispiece

More [Moore], **Henry** (*c*.1587–1661), Jesuit, was the son of Edward More (*d.* 1605) of Haddon Bampton, Oxfordshire (not Edward More of Barnborough as asserted by his biographers), and Mary More (*b.* 1553), great-granddaughter of Sir Thomas More and daughter of Thomas More and Maria Scrope, of Leyton, Essex. Born in Leyton about 1587 More studied at the English Jesuit college in St Omer from 1597 until 1603 before transferring to the English College in Valladolid in the spring of 1603. For reasons of health he returned to the Spanish Netherlands in June of 1607 and completed his course of philosophy in Douai. On 19 November 1607 he entered the English Jesuit noviciate in Louvain. Aside from at least one year at the English College in St Omer, More completed his studies in Louvain and was ordained in 1614. In 1614 and 1615 he worked as assistant to John Gerard, the novice master, first in Louvain and then in Liège. From 1617 until spring 1622 More served in different positions at St Omer. He was in London by 12 May when he pronounced his final vows.

Throughout the 1620s More worked in London, presumably using the Jesuit noviciate as his base. On 15 March 1628 pursuivants, acting on suspicions of neighbours, raided the house in Clerkenwell owned by and rented from George Talbot, earl of Shrewsbury. More was one of seven Jesuits captured and he probably remained in prison until December 1633. From his release until his appointment as provincial on 11 August 1635 he served in the College of the Holy Apostles (East Anglia) as chaplain to Robert, Lord Petre, the college's founder. Thomas Grene, Catholic rural dean of Essex, complained that More was 'a good getter of monyes' (Knell, 74). Under his direction the province was financially strong. Numbering more than 350 men, nearly 200 of whom worked in England and Wales, the English province was thriving. Because of royal disapproval of his successor Edward Knott (*vere* Matthew Wilson), More acted as vice-provincial in England from 1639 until 1642. Apparently he was again imprisoned at some unspecified date and was freed in December 1640. After a year as tertian master in Ghent he returned to London in 1644 as rector of the house of probation of St Ignatius and again as vice-provincial.

In 1647 Catholic leaders and army leaders discussed the possibility of rescinding all penal laws if Catholics would accept certain conditions including a prohibition to write, teach, preach, and publish on 'three propositions' regarding papal deposing power. As senior Jesuit in England, More approved the agreement. On 15 January 1648 Pope Innocent X condemned the propositions. In the aftermath More was recalled from England more or less in disgrace. His exile did not last long: on 27 July 1649 he was appointed rector of the English College in St Omer. He returned to the College of the Holy Apostles in 1652 and served as admonitor, spiritual prefect, and confessor to Jesuits, and probably as chaplain to the Petre family. Recalled to Liège in 1656 to work on a proposed history of the English province he was again appointed rector of St Omer on 7 April 1657 in order to reverse the college's financial deterioration. He completed his second term in 1660. In 1661 he was moved to the noviciate in Watten and, despite his advanced age and ill health, he still served as a consultor to the provincial.

More translated Jesuit spiritual literature into English. His *Vita et doctrina Christi domini*, published at Antwerp in 1649, with an English translation published in Ghent in 1656, juxtaposed scenes from the gospels with suggestions for prayer and meditation. Despite lack of enthusiasm from the Jesuit censors, who recommended publication be postponed, his important *Historia provinciae Anglicanae Societatis Iesu* was published at St Omer in 1660. According to a later editor More 'was honest, devoted, painstaking, with a careful eye for detail' (Edwards, *Elizabethan Jesuits*, 9). He died, apparently of apoplexy, at Watten on 8 December 1661, and was buried at St Omer.

His brother, **Thomas More** (*c*.1586–1623), was born in Cambridge. He entered the Jesuits in Louvain on 30 July 1610, having been ordained in Rome in 1609. He served in England for four years 'chiefly employed in assisting the poorer class of Catholics; never using a horse, but making his circuits on foot' (Foley, 5.703). He was arrested and sent into exile about 1621. He died in Ghent on 2 January 1623 as he was completing his Jesuit formation.

THOMAS M. McCOOG

Sources T. M. McCoog, *English and Welsh Jesuits, 1555–1650*, 2 vols., Catholic RS, 74–5 (1994–5) · T. M. McCoog, ed., *Monumenta Angliae*, 1–2 (1992) · D. Shanahan, 'The family of St. Thomas More in Essex: 1581–1640', *Essex Recusant*, 1 (1959), 62–74; 2 (1960), 44–5 · P. R. Knell, 'The relation of Thomas Greene for Essex—1635', *Essex Recusant*, 8 (1966), 72–6 · E. Henson, ed., *The registers of the English College at Valladolid, 1589–1862*, Catholic RS, 30 (1930) · G. Holt, *St Omers and Bruges colleges, 1593–1773: a biographical dictionary*, Catholic RS, 69 (1979) · E. H. Burton and T. L. Williams, eds., *The Douay College diaries, third, fourth and fifth, 1598–1654*, 1, Catholic RS, 10 (1911) · F. Edwards, 'Henry More, S.I., administrator and historian, 1586–1661', *Archivum Historicum Societatis Iesu*, 41 (1972), 233–81 · H. Foley, ed., *Records of the English province of the Society of Jesus*, 7 vols. in 8 (1875–83) · T. H. Clancy, 'The Jesuits and the Independents: 1647', *Archivum Historicum Societatis Iesu*, 40 (1971), 67–90 · A. Kenny, ed., *The responsa scholarum of the English College, Rome*, 1, Catholic RS, 54 (1962) · *The Elizabethan Jesuits: Historia missionis Anglicanae Societatis Jesu (1660) of Henry More*, ed. and trans. F. Edwards (1981)
Archives Archivum Romanum Societatis Iesu, Rome · Stonyhurst College, Lancashire

More, Henry (1614–1687), philosopher, poet, and theologian, was born in Grantham, Lincolnshire, on 12 October 1614, the youngest of the seven sons of Alexander More, sometime alderman and mayor (1617) of Grantham, and his wife, Anne (*née* Lacy). He attended Grantham grammar school until his uncle, Gabriel More, took charge of his education and sent him to Eton College in 1628. In 1631 he was entered under Robert Gell at Christ's College, Cambridge, where his uncle was a fellow and where his brothers Richard and Alexander, who both matriculated

Henrici Mori Cantabrigiensis S. S. T. D. Effigies. Æ. 61.
Salomon Prov. c. 4. v. 23.
Præ omni Custodia Serva cor tuum quia ex ipso sunt Vitarum Egressus.
M. Antoninus Med. lib. 10.
O Chara Anima quando una eris et nuda et Simplex.
S. Paulus. 1. ad. Cor c. 16.
OMNIA VESTRA FIANT IN CHARITATE.

Henry More (1614–1687), by William Faithorne the elder, pubd 1675

in 1615, and Gabriel, who matriculated in 1627, had studied before him. While at Cambridge, More probably came to know Gell's friend the biblical scholar Joseph Mede, who was also a fellow of Christ's. He graduated BA in 1636 and MA 1639 and was elected fellow of Christ's College in place of Gell in 1641. In the same year he was ordained, and his uncle, Gabriel More, presented him with the benefice of Ingoldsby near Grantham. He survived the earl of Manchester's purge of Cambridge dons in 1644 by taking the covenant (though he later denied this). He remained a fellow of Christ's College for the rest of his life, declining preferment.

More was in his day regarded as one of the leading philosophers of his time. He was the most prolific of the group of philosophical divines known now as the Cambridge Platonists. He was also a theologian of tolerant stamp who was regarded as a founder of the broad-church movement nicknamed latitudinarianism. His religious convictions were formed in reaction to the strict Calvinism of his upbringing. In the autobiographical preface to his *Opera omnia* he records his horror when still a boy at school at the Calvinist doctrine of predestination. His philosophical preference for Platonism was formed later, after a period of intense study while still an undergraduate, which nearly resulted in a sceptical crisis.

More's first writings were philosophical poems, composed in 1639 and 1640. The first of these, *Psychodia Platonica*, was published in 1642, and then again in a collection with the others in 1647. These poems not only established More as a Platonist, but also showed his interest in the new science of Galileo and Copernicus and in the new philosophy of Descartes. More was one of the first Englishmen to show an interest in Cartesianism. In 1648, at the behest of Samuel Hartlib, he entered into correspondence with Descartes. More at this time admired Cartesian physics as being able to account for the phenomena of nature better than any other philosophy. He was, however, unsuccessful in persuading Descartes to accept modifications that would support the kind of metaphysics of spirit to which More subscribed. Although More recommended that Cartesianism be taught as part of the curriculum of English universities, he subsequently revised his initial view of Cartesianism on theological grounds.

Between 1647 and 1650 More made the acquaintance of John Finch (1626–1682), then a student at Christ's College. Finch and his companion Thomas Baines were to remain lifelong friends of More. About 1650, probably at the behest of her brother, More agreed to give Finch's sister Anne Conway instruction in philosophy. The result was a friendship and intellectual companionship that lasted until Lady Conway died in 1679. Through Lady Conway and her brother he enjoyed the patronage of the influential Conway and Finch families. Nevertheless, More refused attempts of Lord Conway, who was also patron of Jeremy Taylor, to persuade him to accept a bishopric in Ireland or to appoint him prebend of Worcester.

In 1650–51, under the pseudonym Alazonomastix Philalethes, More entered into a controversy with the alchemist Thomas Vaughan, who wrote under the name of Eugenius Philalethes. He was probably motivated by a desire to distance his own philosophical Platonism from the mystical Paracelsianism of Vaughan. More later dismissed this as a light-hearted episode. At all events the lampooning name-calling style of this polemic was not one that More ever employed again.

In 1653 More published *An Antidote Against Atheisme*, dedicated to Lady Conway. This was the first of his serious apologetic works, and shows clearly the philosophical turn of his theology, and his opposition to the materialist philosophy of Thomas Hobbes. In it More sought to use arguments for the existence of God that would be acceptable to any rational person—that is, arguments based on the nature of the human mind and the evidence of the phenomena of nature. *An Antidote* was followed in 1655 by *Conjectura cabbalistica*, written at the behest of Lady Conway and dedicated to Ralph Cudworth. In this work More presented an atomist natural philosophy in conjunction with a Platonist metaphysics as the core elements of what he believed to be the original and true philosophical system compatible with biblical teaching and 'hidden' in the book of Genesis. His *Enthusiasmus triumphatus* (1656) analyses the phenomenon of pretension to divine inspiration, which More dubbed 'enthusiasm' and explained as a physiological disorder.

In 1659 More published *The Immortality of the Soul*, which takes up the apologetic themes of *An Antidote* and sets out more fully his philosophy of spirit. As in *An Antidote* he sought to demonstrate the existence of incorporeal substance by adopting a mode of rational demonstration that, he believed, any rational materialist would be bound to accept. The book is founded on the premise that the existence of spirits is logically connected to the existence of God. As he put it, 'That saying is no less true in Politicks, *No Bishop No King* than this in metaphysics, *No spirit no God*' (*An Antidote*, 3.16.17). To demonstrate the immortality of the soul he mounted a combination of types of demonstration: deduction from self-evident axioms, sense perception, and natural phenomena. In *The Immortality* he first proposed his theory of the 'spirit of nature' to explain causal agency in the natural world.

After the death of Cromwell, More was engaged with writing the fullest statement of his theological latitudinarianism, his *An Explanation of the Grand Mystery of Godliness*, which was published in 1660. This was, in many ways, a propaedeutic to the restoration of the Church of England; in it he proposed a minimum set of essential doctrines as a conciliatory means of restoring a national church. More's theological tolerance and the heterodox character of some of his personal beliefs (notably his revival of the Origenist doctrine of the pre-existence of the soul) made him a target for some of the more rigid Anglicans, in spite of the fact that he wholeheartedly embraced the restored church. Chief among his opponents were Joseph Beaumont and Herbert Thorndike, in response to whose attacks More published *The Apology of Henry More* (1664), which constitutes a careful statement of his understanding of the role and importance of reason in divinity. More's Platonism and Origenism were also attacked by Samuel Parker, future bishop of Oxford, although Parker did not actually name More when doing so.

In 1662 More published a collected edition of his philosophical writings, *A Collection of Several Philosophical Writings*, which included appendices and scholia on the constituent works where he develops and defends his ideas, as well as *Epistola H. Mori ad V. C.*, which contains a more cautious appraisal of Descartes. In 1664 he was elected fellow of the Royal Society. Shortly afterwards he published two works aimed at a more popular audience: his manual of ethics, *Enchiridion ethicum* (1667), and *Divine Dialogues* (1668). The latter is an accessible recension of his philosophico-theological position in dialogue form and issued under the pseudonym Franciscus Evistor Palaeopolitanus. More's plans to publish his ethical manual brought him into conflict with his friend Ralph Cudworth, who had been appointed master of Christ's College in 1654. The dispute appears to have done no lasting damage to their friendship, but it is the most likely explanation of why Cudworth never published his treatise on ethics.

More consolidated his reputation as a leading philosophical mind of seventeenth-century England with his *Enchiridion metaphysicum* (1671). In this work he radically revises his earlier enthusiasm for Cartesianism in favour of his own theory that the operative causal agent in the natural world is an incorporeal spirit that he calls the 'Spirit of Nature' or 'Principium Hylarchicum'. In the course of this treatise he restates his theory of infinite space adumbrated in earlier writings. The *Enchiridion metaphysicum* was the occasion of controversy, however, on account of More's attempt to use the findings of Robert Boyle's *New Experiments Physico-Mechanical* to underwrite his concept of the 'Spirit of Nature'. The result was censure by Robert Boyle in *Tracts … Containing New Experiments Touching the Relation betwixt Flame and Fire* (1672). More's *Enchiridion metaphysicum* was also attacked by Sir Matthew Hale, who criticized his 'spirit of nature' hypothesis in *Difficiles nugae* (1675).

In the 1670s More faced further intellectual challenges, first of all in his encounter with Jewish culture, in the form of cabbalistic writings mediated to him by Francis Mercury van Helmont, friend of the German cabbalist scholar Christian Knorr von Rosenroth. At that time Knorr was engaged in preparing a Latin translation of cabbalist writings, which he published as *Kabbala denudata* (1677–84). More entered into correspondence with Knorr, and contributions by More are included in the first volume of Knorr's *Kabbala denudata*. More's study of cabbala was an interest he shared with Lady Conway, who occasioned a further challenge for More by persuading him to join her dialogue with the leading Quakers (Robert Barclay, George Keith, William Penn, and others). For More this dialogue entailed, in many ways, a resuscitation of his arguments against sectarian extremists that he had undertaken in the 1650s. For Lady Conway it resulted in her conversion to Quakerism. It was during this period that More read the philosophy of Spinoza, which he attacked as materialistic and atheistic.

In the 1680s, after the death of Lady Conway, More was increasingly occupied with theological issues that had earlier concerned him in his *Synopsis propheticon* (1664). Between 1681 and 1682 he was involved in a controversy with the nonconformist leader Richard Baxter about the immortality of the soul and interpretations of the apocalypse. More took over the mantle of Joseph Mede, his learned forebear at Christ's, and published a number of works on the interpretation of biblical prophecy, including *Apocalypsis apocalypseos*, *Exposition of … Daniel*, and *Paralipomena prophetica*.

More's studies of prophecy and cabbala and his belief in witchcraft make him a puzzling figure for later ages where such interests are perceived as incompatible with philosophical rationalism. Yet More was well read in contemporary philosophy and a fellow of the Royal Society. It should, of course, be remembered that his apparently extraneous interests were shared by many of his time, including other fellows of the Royal Society: Joseph Glanvill and Isaac Newton are outstanding examples. In 1681 More edited Joseph Glanvill's *Sadducismus triumphatus*, a compilation of data intended to demonstrate the reality of supernatural phenomena. In 1680 he records discussing the book of Revelation with the young Isaac Newton.

Within the Church of England, More's theological tolerance was his most important legacy among such figures as Simon Patrick, Edward Fowler, and John Tillotson—all prominent latitudinarians. His philosophical legacy is most evident in the younger thinkers he inspired, among them George Rust, Anne Conway, John Norris, and John Ray. His concept of infinite space has been identified as an important precursor to Newton's. During his lifetime his work was widely read: according to his publisher, Richard Chiswell, his publications 'ruled all the booksellers in London'. Interest in his works continued long after his death; there was a spate of republication in the early eighteenth century. His later admirers included John Wesley, who included some of his sermons in his Christian Library. His reputation abroad was assured by the Latin translation of his works and by his three-volume *Opera omnia*, financed by a legacy from John Cockshute and published in 1675–9, through which he came to the notice of the French prelate and scholar Pierre Daniel Huet and of G. W. Leibniz.

More never married. His circle of loyal friends and admirers included, besides Sir John Finch and Anne Conway, Henry Hallywell, John Sharp (future archbishop of York), Edmund Elys, William Outram, John Davies, and his biographer, Richard Ward. His humanity and generosity towards his friends is testified in his loyal support for Anne Conway through the tribulations and isolation of illness. In 1666 he came to the rescue of John Worthington, who faced destitution after failing to secure a permanent living after his ejection from Cambridge after the Restoration. More bestowed on him his living at Grantham in 1666. More was a man of deep piety, ascetic in his habits. For relaxation he played the lute. He was tall in stature, with hazel eyes. Ward describes him as serene, rather than melancholic, his studious disposition suffused with a joyous piety and tempered with good humour. In his younger days, More is reputed to have been known as 'the Angel of Christ's'. He died on 1 September 1687 after a short illness, and was buried in Christ's College chapel.

SARAH HUTTON

Sources H. More, 'Praefatio generalissima', *Opera omnia*, 2 (1679) · *The Conway letters: the correspondence of Anne, Viscountess Conway, Henry More, and their friends, 1642–1684*, ed. M. H. Nicolson, rev. edn, ed. S. Hutton (1992) · R. Ward, *The life of the learned and pious Dr. Henry More*, ed. S. Hutton and others (2000) · J. Peile, *Biographical register of Christ's College, 1505–1905, and of the earlier foundation, God's House, 1448–1505*, ed. [J. A. Venn], 2 vols. (1910–13) · R. Crocker, 'Henry More, a biographical essay', *Henry More, 1614–1687: tercentenary studies*, ed. S. Hutton (1990) · Venn, *Alum. Cant.* · R. Hall, *Henry More: magic religion and experiment* (1990) · C. Webster, 'Henry More and Descartes, some new sources', *British Journal for the History of Science*, 4 (1968–9), 359–77 · J. Peile, *Christ's College* (1900) · W. Sterry, ed., *The Eton College register, 1441–1698* (1943)
Archives Christ's College, Cambridge, letters | BL, corresp. with Anne Conway, Add. MSS 23, 216 · BL, letters to Lord Conway

and Lady Conway, Add. MS 23216 · BL, letters to John Pell, Add. MS 4279, fol. 156 · BL, letters to John Sharp, Add. MS 4276, fol. 41 · Bodl. Oxf., letters to William Sancroft and Simon Patrick · DWL, letters to Richard Baxter · Hunt. L., letters to Sir George Rawdon · U. Nott., letters to Francis Finch · University of Amsterdam, corresp. with Philip van Limborch · University of Sheffield, letters to Samuel Hartlib
Likenesses W. Faithorne, engraving, repro. in Nicolson and Hutton, eds., *Conway letters* · W. Faithorne the elder, line engraving, BM, NPG; repro. in H. More, *Henrici Mori Cantabrigiensis opera theologica* (1675) [*see illus.*] · P. Lely, oils, RS · D. Loggan, engraving, repro. in M. H. Nicolson, ed., *The Conway letters* · D. Loggan, line engraving, BM, NPG; repro. in H. More, *Henrici Mori Cantabrigiensis Opera Omnia*, 2 vols. (1679)
Wealth at death £200 to 'mend' niece's marriage portion; £2 10s. to bedmakers at Christ's; living; books; instruments; rings; pictures; no mention of debts or provision for paying them: will, PRO, PROB 11/388/127, repr. in *The Conway letters*, ed. Nicolson, 481

More, Jacob [*known as* More of Rome] (1740–1793), landscape painter, was probably born in Edinburgh, the son of William More (*d.* in or before 1764), a merchant. He was first apprenticed to a goldsmith and then, from 1764, to the Norie family of house-painters; he also worked with Alexander Runciman (1736–1785), who became More's master on Norie's death in 1766. In the 1760s he produced numerous sketches of the Scottish lowlands (examples in the National Gallery of Scotland, Edinburgh) and in 1769 he designed and executed stage sets at the Theatre Royal, Edinburgh, for the first productions after the legalizing of the theatre in Scotland. More's Edinburgh period culminated in a series of oil paintings of the Falls of Clyde, three of which are in public collections: *Corra linn* (National Gallery of Scotland, Edinburgh), *Stonebyres linn* (Tate collection), and *Bonnington Linn* (Fitzwilliam Museum, Cambridge). These paintings are regarded as the first serious artistic interpretations of the Scottish landscape, depictions by previous artists having been essentially topographical in character. More exhibited a set of them in London in 1771, establishing his name and gaining the personal encouragement of Sir Joshua Reynolds. He stayed in London for a couple of years, studying under Richard Wilson and working as a scene-painter.

By 1773 More was in Rome, where he quickly established his reputation as the leading landscape painter of the thriving colony of British artists. He produced increasingly large Italianate landscapes with an acknowledged debt to Richard Wilson and Claude Lorrain: a typical example is *Tiber Estuary* (1784; St Catharine's College, Cambridge). He excelled in depicting atmospheric effects in glowing colours. The vast, brilliantly lit skies that dominate his compositions demonstrate clearly his theatrical training (such as *Morning* and *Evening*, a pair, 1785; Glasgow Museums), as do the dramatic waterfalls and volcanic eruptions (for example, *Mount Vesuvius in Eruption: the Last Days of Pompeii*, 1780; National Gallery of Scotland, Edinburgh).

More travelled widely in Italy on sketching trips and his numerous *plein-air* sketches reveal a light, rapid touch; his finished watercolours are competent but pedestrian (examples in National Gallery of Scotland, Edinburgh, and Yale Center for British Art, New Haven, Connecticut).

Jacob More (1740–1793), self-portrait, 1783

In the 1770s and 1780s More worked with the Scottish painter Allan Ramsay, preparing illustrations for Ramsay's projected treatise on Horace's Sabine Villa. He was commissioned by Prince Borghese to contribute a painting to the refurbished gallery in the Villa Borghese, Rome, followed by a further commission in 1785 to design and lay out a garden in the grounds of the villa, in the 'English picturesque' style, much of which has survived.

More's success and status were recognized in 1781 with his election to the Accademia di San Luca, Rome, followed by the invitation to present his *Self-Portrait* to the Uffizi Gallery, Florence, in 1784 (still *in situ*), the scale of which caused some jealousy among other artists in Rome. Sir Joshua Reynolds referred to More as the 'best painter of air since Claude' (BL, Cumberland MSS, III fol. 128) and Goethe bestowed praises on his work on visiting his studio in 1787 (Goethe, 356–7). His work commanded high prices and he enjoyed a full order book—in 1785 he had a two-year waiting list of orders, mainly from British patrons—but he chose to work increasingly as an agent and dealer. With an independence (sometimes described as an aloofness) from the various artistic factions in Rome, plus a cool business head, he dealt patiently with his capricious principal patron, Frederick Augustus Hervey, fourth earl of Bristol, for whom he produced at least twenty paintings. More's letter-book (1786–7; Edinburgh University Library) contains details of transactions with Bristol and other patrons, including illustrated advice on the techniques of landscape painting for Sir George Beaumont.

More, who never married, exhibited regularly in London in the 1770s and 1780s. He was preparing to return to Britain when he died suddenly in Rome on 1 October 1793. He was buried at Rome in the protestant cemetery on 6 October; his executors were Thomas Jenkins, Sir James Wright, and his fellow Edinburgh artist Richard Cooper. His *Panorama of Rome*, commissioned by Prince Augustus Frederick, duke of Sussex (1773–1843), the sixth son of George III, was erected at Buckingham House, London, soon afterwards. The artist's nephew Jacob More, a jeweller in Covent Garden, London, who inherited much of his property, visited Italy the following year. He cleared up his uncle's affairs, ordered a headstone for his grave, and brought back to London some of his paintings, which were sold at Christies on 26 February 1796.

More's importance lies chiefly in his early achievements as the first major painter of his native landscape, paving the way for more prolific artists such as Alexander Naysmith. The highly polished and theatrical style of his later work was hugely popular in its day and obscured his earlier achievements, a fact acknowledged by his own contemporaries. He became unfashionable in the nineteenth century, and only after the 1960s was his importance once again established.   PATRICIA R. ANDREW

Sources P. R. Andrew, 'Jacob More, 1740–1793', PhD diss., U. Edin., 1981 · P. R. Andrew, 'Jacob More: biography and a checklist of works', *Walpole Society*, 55 (1989–90), 105–96 · P. R. Andrew, 'Rival portraiture: Jacob More, the Roman academician', *Apollo*, 130 (1989), 304–7 · P. R. Andrew, 'Jacob More and the earl-bishop of Derry', *Apollo*, 124 (1986), 88–94 · P. R. Andrew, 'Jacob More's Falls of Clyde paintings', *Burlington Magazine*, 129 (1987), 84–8 · P. R. Andrew, 'An English garden in Rome', *Country Life*, 169 (1981), 1136–8 · J. Ingamells, ed., *A dictionary of British and Irish travellers in Italy, 1701–1800* (1997) · J. Holloway, 'Jacob More, 1740–1793', in National Gallery of Scotland, *Scottish masters*, 4 (1987) · B. Ford, 'The earl-bishop: an eccentric and capricious patron of the arts', *Apollo*, 99 (1974), 426–34 · I. G. Brown, J. D. Hunt, B. D. Frischer, and P. R. Andrew, *Allan Ramsay and the search for Horace's villa* (1999) · J. Cririe, *Scottish scenery* (1803) · Farington, *Diary* · J. W. Goethe, *Italian journey, 1786–1788*, trans. W. H. Auden and E. Mayer (1962) · A. P. Oppé, ed., 'Memoirs of Thomas Jones, Penkerrig, Radnorshire', *Walpole Society*, 32 (1946–8) [whole issue] · *Descriptive catalogue of a choice assemblage of original pictures, selected … by George Walker* (1807) [sale catalogue, Christies] · *GM*, 1st ser., 63 (1793) · *European Magazine and London Review*, 24 (1793), 407 · *Scots Magazine*, 55 (1793), 619 · *Public Advertiser* (14 Dec 1793)

Archives U. Edin., letter-book, corresp., and notes by George Laing | BL, Cumberland MSS

Likenesses J. More, self-portrait, oils, 1783, Uffizi Gallery, Florence [*see illus.*] · C. Lasinio, coloured mezzotint (after J. More), BM · engraving (after J. More), Scot. NPG

Wealth at death a considerable sum, incl. annuities and personal items to sister, niece, and nephew; annuity to servant in Rome; books, studio drawings, and studies to servant's family: will and inventory, Archivio di Stato, Rome; Holloway, 'Jacob More'

More, Sir John (*c.*1451–1530), judge, was the son and heir of William More (*d.* 1467), citizen and baker of London, and of Joanna, daughter and heir of John Joye, citizen and brewer of London, and granddaughter and heir of John Leycester of London, a clerk in chancery. More did not follow in the family business but entered the law, a profession that offered better prospects, although the links of his great-grandfather with chancery may also have been a

Iudge More S' Tho: Mores Father.

Sir John More (*c.*1451–1530), by Hans Holbein the younger, 1526–8

factor. He can be identified either with the John More who secured entry to Lincoln's Inn in 1470 after serving first as its domestic steward, or the More admitted directly in 1475. He supported himself by acting as a clerk in king's bench, but he went through the full *cursus honorum* at Lincoln's Inn, serving as the autumn reader in 1490, and from time to time thereafter as governor of the society; he gave his second and more prestigious reading in Lent 1495. In keeping with the tradition that London looked after its own, More was retained by the city, but very little else is known about his practice. He provided in his will for prayers for Edward IV's soul, but what this indicates is not known.

On 24 April 1474 More married Agnes (*d.* 1499?), the daughter of a London alderman, Thomas Graunger. After her death he married three widows in succession: the widow of a John Marchall; Joan, the widow of Thomas Bowes, citizen and mercer of London; and Alice, the daughter of John More (no relation), sister of Christopher More of Loseley in Surrey and widow of John Clerk. Like the others, this last union was rooted in London, since Alice's father had been a citizen and fishmonger. The lawyer's London home was in the parish of St Lawrence Jewry, but he also inherited the manor of Gobions in Hertfordshire from his mother. He bought other land in the county, and his position was recognized in 1488 when he became a JP.

John More was called to be a serjeant-at-law in 1503. The ceremonies were graced by the king's presence, but More was never retained by the crown and was the last of the call of 1503 to reach the bench, only becoming a justice of the common pleas in 1518. In 1520 he was moved to the less lucrative king's bench, perhaps receiving his knighthood in compensation, and he remained there until his death. A legal career that promoted John More to the bench at the age of sixty-seven hardly appears brilliant, and scholars have usually assumed that he owed this late advancement to his eldest son, Thomas *More. This is not necessarily the case. John More may not have been the most prominent lawyer of the day, but many of the serjeants of the call of 1503 were victims of 'career-block' when the generation before them proved unusually long-lived. More certainly progressed to the coif in normal time, and from 1513 served as justice of assize on the plum home circuit. On the other hand, there is a story that his career suffered a set-back when he fell foul of Henry VII. The king did come down heavily on legal misbehaviour, or what he chose to consider misbehaviour, and serjeants in pursuit of their clients' and their own interests did sometimes sail close to the wind. However, the elaboration that More was imprisoned in revenge for the heroic opposition of his MP son to royal demands for taxation can probably be dismissed as retrospective embellishment by a family keen to promote a 'saint'.

John More died on 5 November 1530. Among his children (all from his first marriage) to live to maturity were: Joanna (*b.* 11 March 1475), who married Richard Staverton, a Londoner whom Sir John sponsored at Lincoln's Inn; Thomas (*b.* 7 Feb 1478), the future lord chancellor; John (*b.* 6 June 1480), whom Erasmus noted working as Thomas's secretary; and Elizabeth (*b.* 22 Sept 1482), who married the author and printer John Rastell of the Middle Temple, and whose son William edited Thomas More's works, wrote a biography of his uncle, and became in 1558 justice of the queen's bench. Two daughters appear to have died in infancy.

Writers on Thomas More frequently criticize his father for using financial pressure to compel Thomas to study the law instead of the classics. On the contrary, by the values of the time John More was very indulgent. Thomas's entry to Lincoln's Inn was deferred to allow two years' social training in the household of Cardinal Morton, followed by a period at Oxford, and even then it was a further four years before his father became insistent. John was certainly not a philistine. As well as the law books he collected and compiled, he had works of literature, and his will provided for one scholarship at Oxford and one at Cambridge. Thomas might, in the epitaph he composed for himself, describe his father as 'civil, pleasant, innocent, gentle, merciful, just and uncorrupted' (*Workes of Sir Thomas More*, 1421), but John More's real personality emerges from the realistic, sceptical, misogynist anecdotes about him which his son remembered—clearly there was a considerable similarity between the two. It is also probable that John shared Thomas's interest in worlds overseas; he helped to finance the abortive expedition of his son-in-law John Rastell to the New World.

A chalk drawing of John More by Hans Holbein the

younger is in the Royal Collection and he figures in Holbein's *The More Family*, of which the original design is in the Kunstmuseum at Basel and a copy by Rowland Lockey at Nostell Priory.   E. W. IVES

Sources E. W. Ives, *The common lawyers of pre-Reformation England* (1983) · M. Hastings, 'The ancestry of Sir Thomas More', *Essential articles for the study of Thomas More*, ed. R. S. Sylvester and G. P. Marc'hadour (1977), 92–103 · Sainty, *Judges* · Baker, *Serjeants* · *The notebook of Sir John Port*, ed. J. H. Baker, SeldS, 102 (1986) · *The reports of Sir John Spelman*, ed. J. H. Baker, 2 vols., SeldS, 93–4 (1977–8) · HoP, *Commons* · R. W. Chambers, *Thomas More* (1935); repr. (1938) · J. A. Guy, *The public career of Sir Thomas More* (1980) · R. Marius, *Thomas More: a biography* (1984); repr. (1985) · will, PRO, PROB 11/23, fol. 185
Archives Trinity Cam., MS O.2.21
Likenesses H. Holbein the younger, chalk and watercolour wash, 1526–8, Royal Collection [*see illus.*] · H. Holbein the younger, group portrait, pen-and-ink, 1527–8 (*Thomas More, his father and his household*), Kunstmuseum, Basel, Switzerland · R. Lockey, group portrait, oils, c.1595–1600 (after H. Holbein the younger), NPG
Wealth at death see will, PRO, PROB 11/23, fol. 185

More, John [*called* the Apostle of Norwich] (c.1542–1592), Church of England clergyman, was born at Betham, Westmorland. He matriculated as a pensioner at Christ's College, Cambridge, in 1560, probably aged about eighteen, was soon elected a scholar, and graduated BA in 1563. He was ordained deacon in London on 15 February 1568 and made a fellow of Christ's during that year. At Cambridge he was influenced by Thomas Cartwright, in whose support he and other divines petitioned Sir William Cecil in 1570. He resigned his fellowship, probably on marriage, in 1572 and was collated by Bishop John Parkhurst to the living of Aldborough, Norfolk. With his wife, Elizabeth, whose maiden name is lost, he had two daughters, Elizabeth and Sara, both still minors when he made his will on 20 November 1591.

In 1573 More became the senior of the two preachers at St Andrew the Apostle, the principal puritan civic church in Norwich, where the 'Saint Andrewes Birds' were so called for their early morning habits of psalm singing, prayer, and hearing sermons. He remained until his death as 'pastour' there, refusing all other preferment. He or his colleague preached daily, and up to four times every Sunday, and made an enormous impact, not just in the city but throughout much of Norfolk, in keeping with his conviction, as set out in the catechism which he wrote with Edward Dering (*A Bryefe and Necessarie Catechisme*, 1577), that 'Without this preaching of the word, wee can never have fayth'. Only three of his numerous sermons survive, but they show him following a line characteristic of Elizabethan puritanism, 'declaring first how we may be saved in the day of judgement and so come to life everlasting: secondly, how we ought to live according to God's will during our life'. And to this end he urged the need for preachers, begging his hearers at a quarter sessions:

> so many of you as have any voyces in place and parliament where these things may be reformed, consecrate your tongues to the Lord in the behalfe of your poore brethren, that ignorant and blind guides … be remooved, and true preachers placed in their roomes. (Collinson, *Godly People*, 296–7)

More's theological position was such as to bring him into trouble with the church hierarchy. He first alarmed Bishop Parkhurst by attacking a sermon given in the cathedral by the turncoat master of Peterhouse and dean of Ely Andrew Perne, causing 'some jare here amongst men' (*Letter Book of John Parkhurst*, 208). Parkhurst reported to Archbishop Parker of the city preachers that:

> I do fynd them tractable, … saving that one Mr More, a lerned man … sticketh at the wering of the surples [in case] he shold be offensive to some. I have told him it were better to offend a fewe private persons then to offend God and disobey his prince. I have not knowen that he hath spoken against her Majesty's book [of Injunctions] at any tyme, neither can I finde any manner of stubberness in him, and surely he is godly and lerned, and hath done much good in this cittye. (ibid., 216)

More was not forced to wear the surplice.

When Edmund Freake succeeded Parkhurst as bishop, everything changed and ceremonies were imposed. On 25 September 1576 More and other puritan clergy from around Norwich presented the council with their humble supplication against them, and More was shortly afterwards suspended by Freake. More used this time to help puritan patrons to appoint godly preachers to vacant livings in their gift. On 21 August 1578, however, during a royal progress in East Anglia, the privy council forced Freake to accept an application by More and his friends, in which they 'humbly crave favour to be restored to their preaching, upon submission to all those articles which concern the confession of the true Christian faith and doctrine of the sacraments, according to the words of the statute' (Brook, 1.450). Such was More's pre-eminence that, though a joint submission, this was called 'Mr More's conformitie'. It is not clear how long More remained under episcopal censure, but more trouble flared up two years later. After the publication of Whitgift's three articles in 1584, More and over sixty other Norfolk ministers presented the archbishop with their reasons for refusing to subscribe.

Widely learned in Greek and Hebrew, More was described as 'seemly in his movements, modest in dress, sparing in food and wine, sober in company, companionable in sobriety' (Holland, 210). It was later reported of him that he 'gave the best reason that could be given for wearing the biggest and largest beard of any Englishman of his time; namely "That no act of his life might be unworthy of the gravity of his appearance"' (Brook, 1.451). Despite his ostensibly humble position, for twenty years he unofficially supervised church affairs throughout much of Norfolk, earning more respect than the bishops of the period—in Patrick Collinson's words, 'Without doubt More performed in Norfolk what protestants took to be the whole office of a godly bishop' (Collinson, *Elizabethan Puritan Movement*, 186–7). It is highly probable that More was the 'godly learned man' whom the playwright and pamphleteer Robert Greene heard preach in St Andrew's about 1585, when he 'did beate downe sinne in such pithie and perswasive manner, that I began to call unto mind the daunger of my soule' (*Life and Complete Works*, 12.175–6).

More died shortly before 16 January 1592, when he was buried in St Andrew's churchyard. In his will, drawn up on the previous 20 November, he set forth 'the faithe that I dye in by gods grace. I utterly renounce alle heresy and doctrine of popery, especially that of meritts, purgatory & flyinge to Saynts &c'. He left £50 apiece to his daughters, and 40s. to his niece Ellen, who was then living in his house. She was the daughter of his brother Miles, who attended his deathbed. More bequeathed to his wife the moiety of the manor of Hethel which the corporation of Norwich had leased to him; he also made her his residuary legatee and sole executor. On 3 October 1592 Elizabeth More married Dr Nicholas Bownd, from 1585 parson of Norton near Bury St Edmunds. Bownd became More's literary executor and eventually succeeded him at St Andrew's from 1611 until his death in December 1613. Elizabeth Bownd probably died during 1610, a year for which the register at Norton has no entries.

More left much for Bownd to edit and publish, for he had studied maps and chronology as well as theology. His *A table from the beginning of the world to this day, wherein is declared in what yeere of the world everything was done, both in the scriptures mentioned and also in prophane matters* appeared at Cambridge in 1593. In the dedication, Bownd expressed his concern that 'the paucitie of Hebrue and Greeke characters in this land' and 'the great cost and charges of Printing Maps' might prevent his completing his editorial work. *John More his Three Sermons* appeared with Bownd's own *Treatise of a Contented Minde* the following year. The last work was *A lively anatomy of death, wherein you may see from whence it came, what it is by nature, and what by Christ, &c.* (London, 1596). His catechism, though written jointly with Edward Dering, was in Norfolk known as 'Mr More's catechism', appropriately, since it was largely his work. Thomas Fuller records that he made an excellent map of the land of Palestine.   J. M. BLATCHLY

Sources P. Collinson, *Godly people: essays on English protestantism and puritanism* (1983) · P. Collinson, *The religion of protestants* (1982) · P. Collinson, *The Elizabethan puritan movement* (1967); repr. (1982) · *The letter book of John Parkhurst, bishop of Norwich*, ed. R. A. Houlbrooke, Norfolk RS, 43 (1974–5) · H. H. [H. Holland], *Herōologia Anglica* (Arnhem, 1620) · R. Greene, *The repentance of Robert Greene* (1592) · J. Peile, *Biographical register of Christ's College, 1505–1905, and of the earlier foundation, God's House, 1448–1505*, ed. [J. A. Venn], 1 (1910) · T. Fuller, *The history of the University of Cambridge from the conquest to the year 1634*, ed. M. Prickett and T. Wright (1840) · Venn, *Alum. Cant.*, 1/3.205 · will, Norfolk RO, NCC 371 Andrewes 1591 · B. Brook, *The lives of the puritans*, 3 vols. (1813), vol. 1 · *The life and complete works of Robert Greene*, ed. A. B. Grosart, 12 (1881–3)

Likenesses C. Ammon, line engraving, 1652, BM, NPG · Passe, line engraving, repro. in H. Holland, *Herōologia Anglica* (1620) · oils, Christ's College, Cambridge

Wealth at death daughters left £50 each; other bequests totalling £6: will, Norfolk RO, Norwich, NCC 371 Andrewes 1591, 20 Nov, proved 4 Feb 1592

More, Kenneth Gilbert (1914–1982), actor, was born on 20 September 1914 at Raeden, Vicarage Way, Gerrards Cross, Buckinghamshire, the only son and second child of Charles Gilbert More (1886/7–1931/2), a pilot in the Royal Naval Air Service, and his wife, Edith Winifred Watkins, the daughter of a Cardiff solicitor. Distantly related, so he

Kenneth Gilbert More (1914–1982), by Charles Trigg, 1956 [as Douglas Bader in *Reach for the Sky*]

always believed, to Henry VIII's chancellor Sir Thomas More, Kenneth More grew up in the reasonable security of the home counties after the First World War until his father was struck by the double blow of ill health and financial collapse in the late 1920s. Charles More found work temporarily in the Far East, and More and his sister were sent to boarding-school in Jersey, near the headquarters of the Jersey Eastern Railway, of which his father was general manager.

Charles More died at forty-five, just after his son, then seventeen, had taken up an apprenticeship in his office. Shortly afterwards, More applied to join the RAF, but was rejected on the grounds of his lack of educational qualifications. Instead he set off for Canada, fully intending to become a fur-trapper, but he had no immigration papers and was sharply returned to London. After several anxious weeks without work he became an assistant stage manager at the Windmill, the Soho 'nudes' theatre run by an old friend of his father's, Vivian Van Damm. Once there he eagerly volunteered to replace an indisposed comedian's stooge, and his career at last began in earnest. Seasons in repertory theatres around the country followed, notably at Newcastle and Wolverhampton, where he stayed until the outbreak of the Second World War. Throughout the war he served in the Royal Navy as a lieutenant. In 1946 he returned to acting and played in the first drama to be televised by the BBC after the war, *Silence of the Sea*.

More began to be cast in small parts in the West End theatre, but his career did not really take off, despite a well-reviewed performance in Noël Coward's post-war *Peace in our Time*. However, in 1952 he made a great impact when chosen to play the feckless RAF pilot Freddie, having an affair with a judge's wife, in Terence Rattigan's *The Deep Blue Sea*. He appeared in it first on stage with Peggy Ashcroft, and a few years later in a less successful film version with Vivien Leigh. On stage, he also gave a brilliant performance in J. M. Barrie's *The Admirable Crichton*.

More came of the first post-war screen generation of J. Arthur Rank, which included John Gregson, Donald Sinden, Jack Hawkins, Dirk Bogarde, and Richard Attenborough. Uniquely, however, More was able to play both romantic heroes and charming cads, so his screen career went from strength to strength throughout the late 1950s and early 1960s. An early success was *Genevieve* (1953), in which he and his rival John Gregson, accompanied by Kay Kendall and Dinah Sheridan, raced classic old cars to Brighton. In the following year, along with Dirk Bogarde and Donald Sinden, he played a medical student in the popular film *Doctor in the House* (1954). But it was his role as Douglas Bader in *Reach for the Sky* (1956), portraying a pilot who was determined to fly despite losing both legs, which proved to be the climax of his film career.

More was married three times, first, on 26 April 1940, to the actress (Mary) Beryl Johnstone (1914/15–1969); they had a daughter, but were subsequently divorced. A second marriage, to Mabel Edith Barkby, *née* Porter (*b*. 1913/14), known as Billie, took place on 18 August 1952; they also had a daughter. In the mid-1960s More left his second wife, who was much loved in the movie circles in which they moved, for the young actress Angela Douglas (Angela Josephine McDonagh; *b*. 1940); the subsequent divorce was bitter, and it cut More off from most of his friends and family for many years at a time when his public and private life were at their lowest ebb. His third marriage, to Angela, which took place on 16 March 1968, was eventually very happy.

During the mid-1960s More quarrelled bitterly with John Davis, the head of the Rank Organisation, and was denied a long-promised role in *The Guns of Navarone* (1961). During the same period a new type of cinema had evolved which had little or no place for the type of stiff-upper-lip English heroes More usually played. Nevertheless, he was the gentleman crook in *The Greengage Summer*, and a welfare worker in *Some People* (about the duke of Edinburgh's award scheme). In *The Comedy Man* (1963), the last film in which he took a leading role, he played an ageing actor trying to sustain a faltering career. He returned periodically to the theatre, notably in 1964 as the superman-butler in a musical version of J. M. Barrie's *The Admirable Crichton*, and in the long-running comedy *The Secretary Bird*, by William Douglas-Home. More also appeared in an acclaimed revival of Terence Rattigan's *The Winslow Boy*, as the defence counsel; and, rather less happily, as a Labour Party MP in Alan Bennett's *Getting On*. He was offered the part of Claudius in the opening *Hamlet* of the National Theatre, but his nerve failed him, and he did not take up the role. By the later 1960s, in any case, television had taken his career in a different direction. As Jolyon, in the BBC television adaptation of John Galsworthy's *The Forsyte Saga* in 1967, 'More carried off the ageing, from a young to

an old man, with great skill' (*The Times*). The television series brought him a new and lasting popularity. Tragically, however, Kenneth More then began to suffer from Parkinson's disease. After four long years of illness faithfully tended by Angela Douglas, it ended his life prematurely. He died on 12 July 1982 at 27 Rumbold Road, Fulham, London.

More was unique in his ability to play heroes as well as bounders, and his performance in the second *Titanic* movie, *A Night to Remember* (1958), is one of the greatest ever given in a British film. For fifteen years he was hardly ever out of film studios in the UK and on location, and, though he never achieved Hollywood success, he was almost the last of the purely 'local' stars, preceding the more internationally renowned Roger Moore, Sean Connery, and Michael Caine. More wrote two autobiographical volumes: *Happy Go Lucky* (1959) and *More or Less* (1978). A book of reminiscences, *Kindly Leave the Stage*, appeared in 1965.

In a curious, sometimes jocular, sometimes sheepish way, More stood for something very English on screen; after his death at sixty-seven, his wife Angela set up a charity in his name to help other sufferers from Parkinson's disease. She later married the film director Bill Bryden, and published a touching memoir of her life as Mrs Kenneth More entitled *Swings and Roundabouts* (1985).

SHERIDAN MORLEY

Sources K. More, *Happy go lucky* (1959) · K. More, *More or less* (1978) · *WWW* · *The Times* (14 July 1982) · A. Douglas, *Swings and roundabouts: an autobiography* (1985) · *CGPLA Eng. & Wales* (1982) · b. cert. · m. certs. · d. cert.

Archives FILM BFI NFTVA, news footage · BFI NFTVA, performance footage | SOUND BL NSA, 'Kenneth More: a memoir', NP6472R TR2 · BL NSA, documentary recordings · BL NSA, performance recordings

Likenesses C. Trigg, photograph, 1956, NPG [*see illus.*] · photographs, Hult. Arch.

Wealth at death £186,918: probate, 8 Dec 1982, *CGPLA Eng. & Wales*

More, Margaret. *See* Roper, Margaret (1505–1544).

More, Mary (*d. c.*1713), writer and artist, is of unknown origin. Information about her adult life can be derived from the lives of her two children from her first marriage, Elizabeth and Richard Waller, and from the preface to her manuscript essay, 'The woman's right'. On 17 April 1680 Elizabeth Waller married Alexander Pitfield in St Leonard, Shoreditch, giving her age as seventeen and listing 'Mary More, residing in the parish of Saint Andrew's Undershaft, Bishopsgate', as her mother.

In the 1680s and 1690s, the More, Waller, and Pitfield households were residing close together. Richard Waller was the secretary of the Royal Society of London in nearby Gresham College from 1687 to 1709 and Alexander Pitfield its treasurer from 1700 to 1728. References in Waller's and Pitfield's correspondence reveal that Mary More was linked through them to other members of the Royal Society, including the scientist Robert Hooke (whose diary records discussing dreams with Mrs More), Sir Hans Sloane, and William Derham.

More's initial claim to attention lay in her work as a portrait painter. Only one of her portraits is still known to exist, heavily retouched by restorers: a copy of a Holbein portrait of Thomas Cromwell, which she presented to the Bodleian Library in 1674 as being a portrait of Sir Thomas More. More's connection with Oxford was through Robert Whitehall, tutor of John Wilmot, earl of Rochester, who delivered the painting and also printed a heavy-handed commendatory verse to her. More (and another anonymous poet who wrote verses in reply) perceived the poem as insulting not only to More, but also to women in general. This exchange of verses may have laid the ground for their essays debating the equality of the sexes, 'The woman's right' and 'The woman's right proved false', preserved in a manuscript miscellany along with Whitehall's occasional verse (BL, Harley MS 3198).

The full title of More's essay provides an accurate overview of its contents and position: 'The woman's right or her power in a greater equality to her husband proved than is allowed or practised in England from misunderstanding some scriptures, and false rendring others from ye originall, plainly shewing an equality in man & woman before ye fall, & not much difference after. The equality of their souls is also proved in that women have done whatever is of value that men have done, what hath been done may be done'. In the preface dedicated to her daughter, More observes that it may seem odd for her to embark on such a topic, 'having never had any Reason as to my self to complain of the least Ill Cariage of my Husbands to me'. Foreshadowing the arguments of early feminists such as Mary Astell, More asserts that in her society in general she has observed 'the sad consequences & events that have fallen on men and their Wives, through this mistake of mens pretending a Power over their Wives, that neither God nor nature doe allow'. More concludes that 'it is the want of learning, & the same education in women that men have, which makes them loose their right' and since men have always dominated parliament and made English law, women have been unjustly denied control of property and access to education.

The date of More's death is unknown, but it was after Richard Waller drew up his will leaving his property in Gloucestershire to his wife Anna only after his mother's death (PRO, PROB 11/546/104) but before his own death in 1715, when his wife, not Mary More, proved the will.

MARGARET J. M. EZELL

Sources M. J. M. Ezell, *The patriarch's wife: literary evidence and the history of the family* (1987) · BL, Harley MS 3198 · RS, W. 3.70, D. 1.60 · *The diary of Robert Hooke … 1672–1680*, ed. H. W. Robinson and W. Adams (1935) · H. Walpole, *Anecdotes of painting in England … collected by the late George Vertue, and now digested and published*, 3 (1763), 135–6 · will, May 1715, PRO, PROB 11/546, sig. 104 · E. C. Clayton, *English female artists*, 1 (1876), 38–9 · J. L. Chester and J. Foster, eds., *London marriage licences, 1521–1869* (1887), 1065

Archives RS | BL, Harley MSS · U. Nott., Portland MSS

More, Richard (*c*.1575–1643), religious writer and politician, was the son of Robert More (*d*. 1604) and his wife, Susan, a member of the Davenport family of Weston in Arden, Warwickshire. In 1583 his father acquired the manor of Linley in the parish of More in southern Shropshire, a property of some 3000 acres plus numerous gardens and orchards. Older accounts took the Mores to be direct local descendants of the Norman de la More family. At most, however, Robert may have been returning to a region with some ancestral connections. His cousin Jasper (1547–1613) held about 1000 acres around Larden by Wenlock Edge.

Richard did not attend university but was later known as a man of pious learning who reputedly had been able to read Old Testament Hebrew by the age of ten. On 22 May 1592, when he was about seventeen, he married Sara Harris (1570–1644), daughter of a substantial Shrewsbury draper. The marriage probably reinforced the local credibility of the Mores and eased the Harris family onto the controversial cusp of gentility: Sara's brother Paul was later knighted and became sheriff of Shropshire. In 1604 Richard succeeded officially to the Linley estates, which now included the lands of the village of More itself, purchased by him in 1602; to this he subsequently added property adjacent to the Harley lands in Herefordshire. In 1610 he sat as MP for Bishops Castle. In 1613 he succeeded to the Larden estates of his cousin Jasper, whose direct heir had been killed in a duel, and in 1619 he was sheriff of the county. Active also in trade, he became a member of the corporation of Bishops Castle in 1632 and a bailiff there in 1637.

A seemingly stern and formidable man, More was involved in two major scandals before the outbreak of civil war: the first luridly domestic, the second presciently public. Encouraged or undeterred by the age discrepancy in his own arranged marriage, he arranged that his eldest son Samuel *More (1594?–1662) should marry in 1611 his Larden cousin Katherine (*b*. 1586), thus ensuring the consolidation of estates and avoiding an extra-familial dowry. However, the bride may already have been engaged in an affair with a local villager, and this continued openly for several years. After a difficult separation, in 1620 Richard and Samuel had the 'spurious broode' of four children born during the marriage dispatched for America on the *Mayflower* (Harris, 44/2, pt 3, 109–13).

In 1633 a young local farmer, Enoch ap Evan, spectacularly decapitated members of his family. Following sentence, his hanged body was feloniously removed from the gibbet and buried. More and Sir Robert Howard as investigating justices took no action on discovering that ap Evan's sisters had been responsible. This clemency might have ended the matter but for ap Evan's eccentric religious views. Peter Studley, a Shrewsbury clergyman, argued in *The looking-glasse of schism* (1635) that his persistent refusal to kneel in church was a sign of puritanism, the murders were a consequence of puritanism, and the judicial leniency was proof of puritan conspiracy. In *A True Relation*, More denied the odious charges, explaining ap Evan's insistently erect demeanour in church as fear of uneven spiritual nourishment should he kneel. His murderous behaviour was attributed to acute, recurring melancholy. The work was possibly written with the ameliorating aid of George Lawson (1598–1678), who was living locally even before being given the rectory of More by Richard in 1637. Permission to print, however, was refused until parliament's order in 1641.

To the delight of his friend and fellow puritan Brilliana, Lady Harley, More was elected in the spring of 1640 as MP for Bishops Castle. He was re-elected that autumn to the Long Parliament. There is no record of his speaking, but he was busy on committees concerning scandalous ministers and sequestrations, and was said to have given plate to the embattled cause. Parliament ordered the publication of his translation of Joseph Mede's eschatological treatise *Clavis apocalyptica* (1623), which appeared in 1643 under the title *The key of Revelation*, with a preface by William Twisse, prolocutor of the Westminster assembly. Some time in the autumn of 1643, while his son Samuel was first besieged at Brampton Bryan with Lady Harley and then engaged in looking after the Harley estates following her death, More too died. His funeral sermon, preached by Humphrey Hardwick, a 'neighbour' and chaplain to the parliamentarian commander the earl of Essex, extolled him as 'a true Mecenas, a real Patriot', who had been a friend on the bench to 'the cause of piety and Professors … in our parts', and praised his skill in languages, 'his much zeal for Religion', and 'his great love to zealous, able Ministers, a good people in the worst times'. Published as *The saints gain by death* (1644), it was dedicated by More's nephew Matthew Clarke to Sir Robert Harley, More's 'bosom friend' (Hardwick, dedication and 23). Thomas Froysell, the Shropshire minister who later preached Harley's funeral sermon, described More and Harley as pillars of godliness in the area.

Of More's seven children all but two, Grace (1599–1623) and Susanah (1610–1626), survived him. His younger sons James, Robert, and Thomas and daughter Ann were all separately provided for. His widow, Sara, died in 1644 and was buried on 10 November (Cockell, 23).

CONAL CONDREN

Sources Sir Jasper More family papers relating to the seventeenth century, Shrops. RRC, 1037 • will, PRO, PROB 11/199, fols. 466v–467v • E. M. Cockell, ed., *The register of More, Shropshire, 1569–1812* (1900) • *DNB* • D. F. Harris, 'The More Children of the Mayflower, their Shropshire origins and the reasons they were sent away with the Mayflower community', *Mayflower Descendant*, 43/2 (1993), pt 1, 124–32; 44/1 (1994), pt 2, 11–20; 44/2 (1994), pt 3, 109–18 • C. Condren, *George Lawson's 'Politica' and the English revolution* (1989) • H. T. Weyman, 'The members of parliament for Bishops Castle', *Transactions of the Shropshire Archaeological and Natural History Society*, 2nd ser., 10 (1878–1900), 33–67 • H. Hardwick, *The saints gain by death* (1644) • P. Studley, *The looking-glasse of schisme*, 2nd edn (1635) • J. Eales, *Puritans and roundheads: the Harleys of Brampton Bryan and the outbreak of the English civil war* (1990) • D. Brunton and D. H. Pennington, *Members of the Long Parliament* (1954)

More, Richard (bap. 1627, d. 1698), politician and lawyer, was baptized on 18 October 1627, the eldest son of Samuel *More (1594?–1662), of Linley, and his second wife, Elizabeth, née Worsley (d. 1655). At the outbreak of the civil wars, like his father and his grandfather, also Richard *More, he committed himself to the parliamentarian cause. At seventeen he was commissioned as a lieutenant in Lord St John's regiment. He was admitted to Gray's Inn

in 1646 and became a serjeant of the inn. He was a commissioner for compounding from 1646 and for the advance of money in 1648. Most of his time was probably spent in and around London, where he became well connected in parliamentarian circles. In 1641 Sir Isaac Penington, lord mayor of London, parliamentarian financier, and later regicide, had married his eldest daughter, Abigail, to Samuel More's cousin and close friend, Justice John Corbet (1609–1670) of Auson, Shropshire (Weyman, 48–9). Some time later Richard married a second Penington daughter, Bridgett (d. 1700/01). There were no children and the couple were estranged. Samuel and Richard More became disenchanted with the Commonwealth. The father was excluded from Cromwell's last parliament as a potential threat to the protector; the son raised troops to support the restoration of the monarchy.

In 1662 Richard succeeded to the More and Larden estates on the death of his father. These seem to have been in some financial disrepair, due in part to the costs of Samuel More's divorce in 1620, the need to provide for a large family, and the commitment to parliament. For some years Richard's life was quiet and parsimonious, not having, he claimed £100 a year to spend on himself (letter, c.1665, 'More family papers', 4134). During the Restoration, however, he nevertheless incurred a number of debts, most substantially to his kinswoman Anne Corbet (whom he owed £2000) and most awkwardly to his youngest brother, Robert (1635–1719), who, Richard thought, threatened the whole estate by wanting to sue for the debt's recovery (ibid.). In 1679 he was returning officer for Bishop's Castle in the election, but resisted the pressures of another old family friend, Sir Robert Harley, to stand himself. Two years later, however, he entered parliament as member for Bishop's Castle. Everything suggests he would have been an exclusionist, and prior to his election he had defended himself against the accusation of being both a presbyterian and a republican. Not surprisingly he was removed as a commissioner for peace in 1687, but was reinstated in the following year, a beneficiary of James II's policy of trying to buy off potential enemies. It may be significant that in his notebook Richard copied out Sexby's *Killing No Murder* and Halifax's *The Character of a Trimmer* ('More family papers'). The former was a spirited justification for tyrannicide, written with Oliver Cromwell in mind; the latter an urbane defence of strategic political oscillation. At the revolution of 1688 he summoned Shrewsbury to surrender to William of Orange. He was probably responsible for the republication of George Lawson's *Politica sacra et civilis* in 1689. This ambitious and subtle treatise of 1660 on sovereignty had initially fallen on largely deaf ears, but after its republication and marginal emendation, it became a significant text in and around the allegiance debates.

More was active in the Convention Parliament of 1689. He sat on twenty-nine committees, including those concerning the reversal of attainders, restoration of corporations, and the inspection of the accounts of the previous Treasury solicitors; he was named as a member of the committee for the general oath of allegiance. Just prior to this late re-entry into national politics he had restored the Shropshire church of Shelve (probably generating the debt to Anne Corbet) and after the dispersal of the Lawson Library in 1680 Richard donated a remarkable teaching library to the church of More, which he valued at over £100. A book list drawn up just before his death indicates extensive and wide-ranging holdings. Predictably, he was a signatory to the Commons' association of 1696, formed to protect and voice its loyalty to William III in fear of Jacobite conspiracies.

More was buried at More on 7 July 1698. He left two adult illegitimate children by his mistress, Dorcas Owen: Richard, killed in battle in 1709, and Thomas, who died in 1731. His will made provision for both sons against the possible predations of his brother and his 'now wife', but made no mention of their mother. She had been an independent woman of modest background from the vicinity of More who, like Richard, had been involved in legal disputes from an early age ('More family papers') and whom More kept on the Larden estates; she was buried at Shipton as Dorcas More in 1712. The Larden and More estates passed to Richard's estranged brother Robert, by now a London merchant, possibly a skinner. In 1719 the estates would pass to a child of Robert's old age with his second wife, Sarah, daughter of John Walcot, of Walcot, Shropshire. **Robert More** (1703–1780) was born in May 1703. He matriculated from Queens' College, Cambridge, in 1723 and graduated BA in 1725 and MA in 1728. He travelled widely, especially in Spain, and sustained strong botanical interests. He was a friend of Benjamin Keene and of Carl Linnaeus. He was a fellow of the Royal Society (1729), MP for Bishop's Castle (1727–41) and for Shrewsbury (1754–61), of which he was also mayor in 1737. More married first, in 1750, Ellen, daughter of Thomas Wilson of Denbighshire, and second, on 8 February 1768, Catherine, daughter of Thomas More, of Millichope, Shropshire. He was, as Horace Walpole called him, a whig of 'primitive stamp' and he proudly proclaimed his family's passionate commitment to liberty (HoP, *Commons, 1790–1820*, 164). He rebuilt Linley Hall in Palladian style, was renowned locally for his wit, and may have been responsible for introducing the larch to England. He died at Linley on 5 January 1780; his will, proved on 23 February that year, suggests he died childless.   CONAL CONDREN

Sources Sir Jasper More family papers relating to the seventeenth century, Shrops. RRC, 1037 · Richard More, will, 1698 · HoP, *Commons, 1660–90* · *The registers of More, Shropshire, 1569–1812*, Parish Register Society, 34 · C. Condren, 'More Parish Library, Salop', *Library History*, 7, 5 (1987) · HoP, *Commons, 1754–90* · *DNB* · H. T. Weyman, 'The members of parliament for Bishop's Castle', *Transactions of the Shropshire Archaeological and Natural History Society*, 2nd ser., 10 (1898), 33–68 · 'Defence of Richard More against the Rev. Mr Billingsley's charges', *c*.1681, priv. coll. · A. Browning, *Thomas Osborne, earl of Danby and duke of Leeds, 1632–1712*, 3 vols. (1944–51) · J. B. Lawson, 'More, Robert', HoP, *Commons, 1715–54* · Venn, *Alum. Cant.* · will, PRO, PROB 11/1061, fols. 384r–385v [Robert More]
Wealth at death estate of 3000–4000 acres but considerable debts: 'Sir Jasper More family papers relating to the seventeenth century', Shrops. RRC

More, Robert (1671–1727), writing master, was the son of a writing master, also named Robert More (*fl.* 1675–1699), who was based in King Street, Westminster, London. As no other references to his training have come to light, it is probable that he studied penmanship under his father. By 1696 he had established a boarding-school at the Golden Pen in Castle Street, Leicester Fields, where students were taught 'writing in all the hands … Arithmetick, Vulgar and Decimal, Merchants Accots. and short hand' (Heal, 76); in the same advertisement More also offered his services as a tutor to more genteel students who preferred to learn penmanship in their own homes. Judging from his several publications, More had considerable skill in penmanship as well as a reasonable level of commercial acumen. During his career he published a number of engraved copybooks, some in several editions, and the appearance of each seems to have coincided with key events in his career as a schoolmaster. This was the case with his *The Writing Master's Assistant* (1696), which, though dutifully dedicated to his father, was evidently intended to raise his profile as an independent penman at the moment when he had just opened his writing school in Castle Street. We can assume that this copybook (costing 18*d*.) sold well, for in 1704—the year that he took over Colonel John Ayres's writing school in St Paul's Churchyard—More published a second edition of it. While still comprising the same octavo plates of penmanship, fashionably 'adorned with [a] variety of pencilled flourishes' (Massey, 2.105), this new edition was extended by a preface written by Ayres, who extolled More's virtues as a precocious and 'ingenious penman'.

For the following three years More was happy to remain at the writing school at St Paul's Churchyard. But in 1708 he began a more peripatetic phase, during which his academy—still named the Golden Pen—was located first at Brownlow Street, then in 1709 at Howard Street, near the Strand, and finally, in 1710, at Castle Street, Charing Cross. This last was an eventful year for More, and it is characteristic that his next publication, *A New Striking Copy Book*, a series of decorative capital letters in the English, French, and Italian styles, was published in this year. Although he had unsuccessfully applied for the prestigious post of writing master at Christ's Hospital, which was awarded to George Shelley, it was also in 1710 that he was involved in a 'pen-combat' (D'Israeli, 190) with John Jarman, another rival writing master. The contest involved both men writing out the same text, which was then judged to see whose was better; More won by a hair's breadth when it was found that his opponent had missed out a single dot on an 'i'.

One of More's last publications was *The First Invention of Writing* (1716), a short essay on the history of writing followed by seven plates of calligraphy. This essay, first published as a preface to Shelley's *Second Part of Natural Writing* (1714), led William Massey to conclude that More 'had more grammatical and historical learning, than most of our writing masters' (Massey, 2.104). The fact that More dedicated this copybook to Shelley suggests the friendship and respect between these two men, even though

Shelley had previously beaten More to the post at Christ's Hospital. Little is known of More's personal life except that he was married and had a daughter named Elizabeth, whose own capacity for penmanship is manifested in her designs for several of the pages in *The Writing Master's Assistant*. Massey records the year of More's death as 1727, and suggests that it occurred while he was either travelling to, or returning from, the north of England, where he was visiting friends.   LUCY PELTZ

Sources miscellaneous pieces concerning writing masters, V&A NAL, box 3, res X · A. Heal, *The English writing-masters and their copybooks, 1570–1800* (1931) · I. D'Israeli, *Curiosities of literature*, 14th edn, 3 vols. (1849) · W. Massey, *The origin and progress of letters: an essay in two parts* (1763) · *A biographical history of England, from the revolution to the end of George I's reign: being a continuation of the Rev. J. Granger's work*, ed. M. Noble, 3 vols. (1806) · *Engraved Brit. ports.* · *The Tatler* (8–11 July 1710)
Likenesses G. Bickham, group portrait, engraving, repro. in *A poem on writing* [n.d.] · W. Sherwin, line engraving, BM; repro. in R. More, *General penman* (1725)

More, Robert (1703–1780). *See under* More, Richard (*bap.* 1627, *d.* 1698).

More, Samuel (1594?–1662), parliamentarian army officer, was the eldest son of Richard *More (*c.*1575–1643) of Linley in the parish of More, Shropshire, and his wife, Sara Harris (1570–1644) of Shrewsbury. He was admitted to Shrewsbury School in 1609. Like his father, Samuel did not attend university and was subject to an early arranged marriage to an older woman. On 4 February 1611 Samuel married his cousin Katherine More (*b.* 1586) from the family's Larden estates by Wenlock Edge. She later claimed a prior contract with Jacob Blakeway, a modest tenant of the Mores of Larden, and so the marriage may have been as much to bring her into line as to avoid paying a weighty dowry out of the family. Katherine proved distinctly uncompliant, conducting an open affair with Blakeway and, in 1616, she applied unsuccessfully to the Hereford consistory court for jactitation, a suit which, by charging More with falsely claiming a marriage between them, amounted to seeking an annulment.

Samuel immediately proceeded against Blakeway, who after much costly legal wrangling was ultimately condemned for trespass and adultery. Facing either imprisonment or a £400 fine, he ran away. Samuel then sought a separation which, though it would not allow remarriage while Katherine lived, would gain him control over the children of the marriage—Ellen, Jasper, Richard, and Mary—whom he deemed illegitimate. Katherine fought the matter with all the More resources at her command but the separation was finalized in July 1620. Within weeks her children were on the *Mayflower*. Samuel, his father, and their adviser Edward La Zouche, Lord Zouche, had been singularly expeditious in purifying the family. The children were embarked as enforced adventurers but only young Richard survived to take advantage of his status. Katherine then seems to have been bought off; and presumably, despite later rumours to the contrary, she died before June 1625, for it was then that Samuel remarried.

More had been a secretary to Lord Zouche certainly from about 1620, and his second wife was Elizabeth Worsley (*d.* 1655), kinswoman to the second wife of his patron, the marriage possibly taking place in Lord Zouche's chapel at Odiham, Hampshire. The couple went to live on the Linley estates by More and Bishop's Castle. Four children are recorded as baptized at More, though the family was certainly larger: Richard *More (18 October 1627); Thomas (5 October 1628), who became a physician; Elizabeth (14 September 1634); and Robert (25 February 1635), who became a merchant and eventually inherited the estates. The tight baptismal chronology between Elizabeth and Robert suggests that the Mores had been residing elsewhere and that Elizabeth was presented to her home parish unusually late. More's wife was buried on 17 November 1655.

At the outbreak of the civil wars More, like his father, involved himself deeply in the parliamentarian cause. He was with Brilliana, Lady Harley, in the early stages of her defence of Brampton Bryan, Herefordshire. On leaving her he spent March 1643 imprisoned at Hereford before parliament briefly took the city. At the end of the year More commanded Hopton Castle. The region bristled with contested fortifications and Hopton, owned by the reputedly 'rabid' republican Robert Wallop (Auden, 'Clun', 293), lay between the More and Harley estates. Samuel held it with a tenacity reminiscent of his first marital engagements. With only thirty-one men he survived for over a month, inflicting heavy losses on royalist forces of up to 500 (ibid., 306, 310). This resilience was doubly remarkable given Hopton's uncommanding position at the bottom of a deep valley. The castle was defended after a breach and was surrendered unconditionally only when it became apparent that it had been mined and would be blown to the hilltops around it. With the exception of More the garrison was executed. He languished briefly in Ludlow and was then put on parole at Upton Cresset, Shropshire, until exchanged for its owner, Edward Cresset, in May 1645 (ibid., 310). More's moving account of the siege to his wife is now illegible but has been reprinted (ibid., 305–8; Blakeway, 217–20). Once more into the fray, his forte as a defender of bastions was clearly recognized. He had the sad task of recommending the surrender of Brampton Bryan after its second siege early in 1644 (ibid., 310–11) and he became commander of Montgomery Castle and governor of Montgomery (on 26 September 1645). As the tide of war turned he became governor of both his earlier lodgings, Ludlow (December 1645) and Hereford (17 June 1647). He ended the wars as the major commander of the region.

During the interregnum More was active in Shropshire politics and ecclesiastical reform, first as member of the sixth Salopian classis, then as a commissioner or 'trier' appointed under the 1654 ordinance for ejecting 'scandalous ... ministers and schoolmasters' (Auden: 'Ecclesiastical History', 269, 284). Such flexibility was typical of the region and gave considerable stability in local government. In 1656 he was elected to parliament for Shropshire, but he was one of many excluded by the council of state as a potential danger to Cromwell. Republican plots were feared but the grounds and extent of More's hostility to the protector are unclear. Samuel and his family remained on good terms with his cousin Justice John Corbet (1609–1670), a regicide and commissioner to secure the protector. Yet the handwritten copy of Edward Sexby's *Killing No Murder*, belonging to Richard More, his eldest son from his second marriage, survives in the More papers. More was re-elected to parliament in 1659. At the Restoration he was reappointed governor of Ludlow and he lived his last two years with a raised drawbridge and low profile. Despite the extent of the More estates he was by now nursing considerable debt, the legacy of adamantine commitment to parliament, contumacy in divorce, and indulgence towards his daughters. Lands were sold to dower two and a late debt of £1000 was accrued for the marriage of his favourite, Anne, to John, later Justice Turton. Samuel More died at Linley Hall and was buried at More on 7 May 1662. A fine portrait of him survives at Linley Hall showing a supercilious and suspicious face with a lugubrious jowl and a neck moderately laced.

CONAL CONDREN

Sources Sir Jasper More family papers relating to the seventeenth century, Shrops. RRC, 1037, 4134 · A. M. Auden, 'Clun and its neighbourhood in the first civil war', *Transactions of the Shropshire Archaeological and Natural History Society*, vol. 8, 3rd ser. (1901–10), 287–336 · A. M. Auden, 'The ecclesiastical history of Shropshire during the civil war, Commonwealth and Restoration', *Transactions of the Shropshire Archaeological and Natural History Society*, vol. 7, 3rd ser. (1901–10), 241–307 · J. Blakeway, *The sheriffs of Shropshire* (1831) · *CSP dom.*, vols. 116, 119 · D. F. Harris, 'The More children of the *Mayflower*, their Shropshire origins and the reasons why they were sent away with the *Mayflower* community', *The Mayflower Descendant*, 43/2 (1993), pt 1, 124–32; 44/1 (1994), pt 2, 11–20; 44/2 (1994), pt 3, 109–118 · *Letters of the Lady Brilliana Harley*, ed. T. T. Lewis, CS, 58 (1854) · E. Cruickshanks, 'More, Richard', HoP, *Commons, 1660–90* · *DNB* · E. M. Cockell, ed., *The register of More, Shropshire, 1569–1812* (1900)

Likenesses P. Lely?, portrait, *c*.1650, priv. coll.

Wealth at death many debts but estate intact: documents (creditors) in 'Sir Jasper More papers', Shrops. RRC

More, Sir Thomas [St Thomas More] (**1478–1535**), lord chancellor, humanist, and martyr, was born, most scholars agree, between two and three in the morning of 6 February 1478 (alternative dates are 7 February, 1477 or 1478) in Milk Street, Cheapside, London, the eldest of three sons and second of seven children of Sir John *More (*c*.1451–1530) and his first wife, Agnes Graunger (*d*. 1499?). More's mother was the daughter of Thomas Graunger, a tallow chandler, citizen and later sheriff of London. More's father, John, the son of William More (*d*. 1467), a wealthy baker, was a barrister who was later knighted and served as a judge of the king's bench.

More's parents came from wealthy families with a history of service to their guilds, the city, and the crown. As More says in his epitaph on the tomb he had made for himself in the church in Chelsea, he was born not of noble, but of honest stock. His family moved in London's governing class with one foot in trade and the other in the law. John More had inherited property in Hertfordshire, the manor of Gobions in the parish of North Mimms, and his four marriages only increased his wealth. Under Edward

Sir Thomas More (1478–1535), by Hans Holbein the younger, 1527

IV he was given permission to bear a coat of arms, and he developed close relationships with members of Edward IV's and later Henry VII's councils. Particularly strong was his connection to Bishop John Morton, who would later play an important role in the life of his son Thomas. Having studied at Lincoln's Inn, John More rose steadily to become serjeant-at-law in 1503, judge of the common pleas in 1518, and finally judge of king's bench in 1520. At a time when occupations frequently followed family lines—both of More's sisters married lawyers—John More clearly intended his eldest son to capitalize on the strong professional connections he had cultivated in his own career.

Education and legal training Sir John arranged for Thomas to study Latin at St Anthony's School in nearby Threadneedle Street, London's finest grammar school and one which, according to the Tudor chronicler John Stow, 'commonly presented the best scholars' in citywide schoolboy competitions held on the feast of St Bartholomew (Ackroyd, 23). This early training in Ciceronian rhetoric would prepare More for a career before the bar as well as in the service of the city.

More left St Anthony's about 1489 at the age of twelve and entered the Lambeth Palace household of Archbishop Morton, then lord chancellor of England. Morton's household was a school in itself. In addition to formal lessons, the palace offered a level of cultural exposure that rivalled even the court, and some of More's love of drama can be traced to Lambeth and its chaplain, the playwright Henry Medwall. There More's wit and intelligence so impressed the archbishop that he was invited to attend Morton personally. More's son-in-law and early biographer, William Roper, records that More often stepped in among the actors at Christmas revels and gave impromptu performances, which prompted Morton to say of him to his noble guests 'This child here wayting at the table, whosoever shall live to see it, will prove a mervailous man' (Roper, 5). This remark, remembered and passed on either by Morton or by one of his guests, is the first example of the impact More's extraordinary personality made on his contemporaries. It would later be amplified by Erasmus's long pen-portrait of More in his early forties, sent to the German nobleman Ulrich von Hutten, and three near contemporary biographies written shortly after More's execution. As an adult, More remembered Morton well and praised him for his statesmanship during the difficult years between the death of Edward IV and the accession of Henry VII. He admired Morton's expert legal mind, which was able to cut to the heart of an issue despite a welter of conflicting and competing legal authorities. This archbishop and lord chancellor, More said, 'had gotten by great experience, the very mother and mistress of wisdom, a deep insight in politic worldly drifts' (*Works*, 2.91). It was the sort of insight for which More himself became known when he occupied the office of lord chancellor in equally difficult times.

Recognizing More's potential, Morton placed him at Canterbury College, Oxford, probably in the autumn of 1492. He was a secular scholar, one of Morton's protégés in this Benedictine college, and would have followed the ordinary curriculum of the liberal arts, or trivium, for the duration of his two years at university: grammar, rhetoric, and logic. He later used his rhetorical skills to denounce what he saw as an inappropriate emphasis on Aristotle and the scholastic preoccupation with logical structure and petty questions, calling it 'stultissima solertia' (*Works*, 15.36). After two years at Oxford, More returned to London where 'He was then for the study of the lawe of the Realme put to an Inne of Chauncery called Newe Inne, where for his tyme he very well prospered' (Roper, 5). Erasmus states that More was urged to study the law by his father. After two years at New Inn, More was formally admitted on 12 February 1496 to Lincoln's Inn, where he remained until he was called to the bar five or six years later.

The decade from the time More left Oxford about 1494 until the time he married was one of intense intellectual, spiritual, and cultural ferment and clearly set the stage for the remainder of his life. It was during this time that he was brought into direct contact with the wider world of European learning through men such as Desiderius Erasmus, John Colet, Thomas Linacre, William Grocyn, and William Lily. During these years he also became intimately acquainted with the austere devotions of the Carthusians and the lay piety they promoted. He wrote verse, translated spiritual works, lectured on St Augustine as well as on English law, studied Greek, and competed with Erasmus in translations and imitations of Lucian. At the end of this period he married and settled into the life of a London lawyer. Scholars have argued about the supposed familial breach caused by More's parallel pursuits of the law, classical studies, and monastic seclusion. In 1519 Erasmus wrote for More and all his friends to read that More's father threatened to disinherit him if he did not follow a legal career in the inns. This may be only Erasmian pique over losing More to fields where Erasmus was a stranger. More's association with the Carthusians, and a casual remark made to Erasmus in a letter in which More daydreams about being a Franciscan, continue to fuel speculation that he had once discerned in himself a vocation to the priesthood. His training in the common law and his marriages suggest otherwise.

In 1499, while still at Lincoln's Inn, Thomas More met Erasmus, then on his first visit to England in the company of William Blount, Lord Mountjoy, one of his pupils. Just how they met is not clear—although it was certainly through the agency of Mountjoy. An apocryphal story has it that More and Erasmus, as yet unknown to one another, found themselves seated together at dinner at the lord mayor's table, and were so impressed with each other's wit that they exclaimed 'You must be More or no one' and 'You must be Erasmus or the Devil' (Chambers, 70). What is certain about their meeting is that during the summer of 1499, while Erasmus was staying in Greenwich with Mountjoy, he met More in the company of More's friend from Lincoln's Inn, Edward Arnold. Mountjoy had been selected by the king as a companion for his younger son, Henry, and the four of them—More, Erasmus, Arnold, and Mountjoy—walked over to visit the royal palace where they met the prince. Clearly More, known and trusted by Mountjoy, already moved easily in high circles. Within two months, Erasmus (then at Oxford) and More had established a warm correspondence which would last for the remainder of More's life.

Spiritual training More cultivated other friendships during the years he spent at Lincoln's Inn. Erasmus describes him as being among a group of men, all prominent scholars who, unlike More, had travelled to Italy and were interested in applying Greek language and classical culture towards revitalizing theology. Towards the end of this period More wrote a letter to John Colet, the future dean of St Paul's, whom More chose as his spiritual director. In it he describes the priest William Grocyn as 'vitae meae magistro'; his Greek teacher Thomas Linacre, a physician, as 'studiorum praeceptor'; and his fellow Greek student William Lily as 'charissimo rerum mearum socio' (*Correspondence*, 9). In keeping with his belief that theological works, especially those of the church fathers, should be made as widely accessible as possible, More lectured on Augustine's *City of God* in Grocyn's church of St Lawrence Jewry. He drew inspiration from Colet's rigorous piety and Grocyn's pioneering example of combining classical scholarship with Christian education. Both men influenced More's efforts to acquire the training in language and discipline necessary to lead, as a professional and a layman, the sort of Christian life formerly available only to the most dedicated priests or in the cloister.

More's interests at this point in his career suggest that

he envisaged the sort of life described by an earlier English spiritual writer, Walter Hilton (*d.* 1396), in his advice to a lay enquirer published under the title *The Mixed Life*. Hilton's works, along with other classics of English spirituality, became an avenue for More to explore as he complemented his academic training with his spiritual exercises of a quite different nature. At some time about 1500 More began a close association with the London Carthusians, although it is not clear whether he lived 'nere the Charterhouse, frequenting daily their spirituall exercises without any vowe' or actually 'in the Charter house of London, religiously lyving there, without vowe, about iiii yeares' (Ackroyd, 93). It is clear that, whatever the case, More was then lecturing on English law in Furnivall's Inn. His legal career was well in hand, and his desire for training in other areas continued to develop. More's interest in practical piety, seen in its most eloquent and laudable form among the English Carthusians, would have been a logical complement to his theological studies of Augustine, his Greek lessons, and his interests in classical virtue. The Carthusians had long established a reputation as a clearing-house for devotional works, both popular and mystical. The London house with which More was connected owned and copied works such as *The Cloud of Unknowing*, Hilton's *Scale of Perfection*, and à Kempis's *The Imitation of Christ*, to quote three titles More himself recommended in 1532 to his own readers. Such works had a profound effect on More: references to them crop up throughout his writings, and their spirit clearly conditioned his own practical approach to Christian living. Under their guidance, More would embrace both the world of learned piety and the duties and joys of a married professional.

Marriage and early career In January 1505 More married Jane (*c.*1489–1511), the daughter of Sir John Colt of Netherhall in the parish of Roydon in Essex, not far from the Mores' Hertfordshire estate of North Mimms. Although no record of their marriage survives, it was presumably celebrated in Roydon church where the Colt family had its tombs. An anecdote passed on by Roper, who may have heard it from More himself, tells of More's preference for a younger Colt daughter, but:

> when he considered that it wold be both great greif and some shame also to the eldest to see her yonger sister in mariage preferred before her, he then of a certayne pity framed his fancy towardes her, and soon after maryed her. (Roper, 6)

The Mores settled into the Old Barge, Bucklersbury, in the parish of St Stephen Walbrook. Their first daughter, Margaret (1505–1544) [*see* Roper, Margaret], was born later that year, followed by two more daughters, Elizabeth (1506) and Cicely (1507), and a son, John (1509–1547). Shortly after More's move to Bucklersbury he was visited by Erasmus, and the two, now both fluent in Greek, began translations of Lucian, whom More praised for his wit as much as his dialogic mode of moral teaching.

More's balanced approach to Christian living combined an interest in classical texts (notably Greek satirists) with more recent and clearly more devotional authors. In harmony with the Carthusian practice of disseminating spiritual texts, More translated and published the life of a contemporary Italian nobleman, Pico della Mirandolla, and a selection of his letters and verse (*c.*1510). In the dedicatory letter to a nun, More stressed the practical benefits of the works: there are none more profitable

> neithir to thachyvynge of temperaunce in prosperitie
> nor to the purchasynge of patience in adversite
> nor to the dispising of worldly vanite
> nor to the desiring of hevinly felicite.
> (*Works*, 1.52)

More's desire for temperance, patience, humility, and hope, here expressed at the outset of his career, is repeated frequently during the next thirty years until it reaches its final and most eloquent formulation in the prayer he penned in the margins of a book of hours while awaiting execution in the Tower.

More's household held a magnetic attraction for Erasmus, who visited again in August 1509 at the urging of Mountjoy as well as of Archbishop Warham of Canterbury. Henry VIII's accession that year promised to make England the centre of learning: 'Heaven smiles, earth rejoices; all is milk and honey and nectar', wrote Mountjoy to Erasmus, 'You are about to approach a prince who can say, "Take then these riches, and be first of bards"' (*Collected Works*, 2.147–8). When Erasmus arrived, he lodged with More, whom he found charming, affable, and above all busy. He had served in the House of Commons in 1504, perhaps as member for Gatton (which his father had represented in 1492), and his career had been steadily advancing. He was granted membership of the powerful Mercers' guild in 1509, and was already playing a noticeable role in public affairs. He was appointed justice of the peace for Middlesex in 1509, and at the year's end represented Westminster in Henry VIII's first parliament. His public activities increased rapidly: in addition to serving on the commissions of the peace, More was appointed one of two under-sheriffs for the city of London in 1510, and became autumn reader at Lincoln's Inn for the following year. Under More's presiding inspiration, while waiting in Bucklersbury for his books to arrive before taking up a position at Cambridge, Erasmus wrote *Moriae encomium—The Praise of Folly*.

In the summer of 1511 More's wife, Jane, died, and within a month he married Alice [*see* More, Alice (*b.* in or after 1474, *d.* in or before 1551)], the widow of John Middleton, a wealthy London merchant. She brought a daughter, Alice (*c.*1501–1563), later the wife of Sir Giles Alington, into the More household. More later wrote that he could not tell which was dearer to him, the wife who bore their children or the wife who raised them, although privately he intimated that his second wife was less intellectually capable than his first. He continued his rapid rise, both in the eyes of his fellow Londoners and in the wider world of letters: he sat again in parliament in 1512 to debate the pope's call to arms in the Holy League against France, and served the mercers in their negotiations with the merchant of the staple. While reader in Lincoln's Inn (1514) he was elected into membership of Doctors' Commons.

In all this More found time to write humanistic works like his unfinished Latin and English histories of Richard III (*c*.1513–1518). In his epigrams of a similar date he frequently explored the problems of tyranny, and, despite the laudatory verses on the accession of Henry VIII, he reveals a profound unease with the corruption often associated with kingship. The reign of Richard III had already been roughly received by the Tudor apologists Polydore Vergil and John Rous, and More borrowed freely from their accounts when creating his own. Yet More's treatment is characteristically more complex and ironic. He blurs the sharply defined moral categories on which Vergil relied, and, although More depicts Richard as an ambitious usurper, he acknowledges that the saintly Edward IV was himself far from guiltless when consolidating his political power. More's *History of Richard III* may have originated in an exploration of tyranny, but it ends by exposing both the instability of any understanding of the past and the ironic consequences of attempts to predict the future based on that understanding. Given this rather bleak inversion of the humanists' optimism that history can teach specific moral lessons, one astute commentator concludes that after More's exploration of Richard's reign, 'it is therefore not at all surprising that the next major work he should have written was his meditation on *The Four Last Things*' (Fox, *Politics and Literature*, 126).

More's expanding legal expertise in dealing with issues of international trade, and in particular his learned handling of a notorious case involving a ship carrying papal alum seized illegally by the duke of Suffolk, brought him to the king's or Wolsey's attention. It is impossible to date precisely when More entered royal service, and to know whether it was Henry or Wolsey who recruited him. But it is certain that in May 1515 More received the first of his many commissions to represent England's interests in negotiations on the continent. Along with Cuthbert Tunstall and others, he went to Bruges to treat with the Flemish in a commercial treaty on a trip destined to bring him worldwide fame.

Utopia The most enduring feature of More's embassy to Bruges in 1515 took place not at the negotiating table but in Antwerp, where he had gone during a lull in the proceedings. There he met Erasmus's friend Peter Giles, Antwerp town clerk. In the course of his visit he conceived the nucleus of *Utopia*. By the time he returned to England in the autumn he had drafted the second part of this quintessential humanist dialogue and after adding an introductory framing narrative, the so-called 'Dialogue of Counsel', he let the work be published (1516). Written in Latin for a European audience, *Utopia* is More's most popular legacy, a prism through which he is still seen.

The work reveals its origin in More's imminent entry into orbit around the king's court. Despite Erasmus's complaint that More was reluctantly dragged into Henry VIII's service, much evidence suggests that, when More joined the king's council in 1518, he did so because his training and inclinations had prepared him for exactly that. Upon his return from the embassy to Bruges, More was said to be haunting Westminster, where he was the first to greet Archbishop Wolsey, then lord chancellor. By 1517, shortly before More was sworn into the council, several of his fellow humanists—not to mention his father—were already members. More was no longer content with the academic contests he had earlier pursued with Erasmus. His negotiating ability and his abiding interest in the relationship of virtue to politics, visible in his English and Latin histories of Richard III and his various Latin poems, propelled him into the practical arena of public policy. The very fact that he had written two extensive works for an English audience argues that More had, by the time he joined the king's council, decided to direct his attention not only to the world of international scholarship but also to the more local world of English politics and piety. It was a decision he honoured for the rest of his life. More's Latin-reading compatriots who could appreciate *Utopia*'s dense ironies and the specifically English setting of its opening section were precisely those who would direct England's future in one way or another, and More's thinly veiled advice to them discloses one of his major motivating factors: More wrote *Utopia* as much to reform as to entertain. The same is true for several other major Latin works of the period, including his open letters to an English monk (1520) and to Oxford University (1518), which offer practical solutions to academic and theological controversies.

From the moment of its publication, *Utopia* was a sensation and rapidly went through a number of editions. Set as a dialogue in Antwerp between a tantalizingly fictionalized More and a voyager recently returned from newly discovered lands, the work exposes the heart of More's concerns about English and European society and parades the cautious optimism of the humanists regarding the possibilities of political and spiritual change. Charged with delightful and disturbing ironies, *Utopia* is the most elaborate and appealing demonstration that at the time of its publication there existed in Europe a powerful and closely knit community of scholars whose agenda strongly advocated the uses of literature in the service of reform.

Utopia's dense layering of dialogues—between Morus and the traveller Hythloday, and Hythloday and Archbishop Morton in book 1, and between More and Giles in the introductory epistle—kept it slippery, and guaranteed that it would have nearly as many interpretations as readers. Although the mixture of utopian and dystopian elements in the work generates profound ambivalence and paradoxes which make it difficult precisely to discern its author's intent, More's humanist contemporaries could easily catch linguistic cues that illuminated the satire—'Utopia' is Greek for 'nowhere', and the island's main features are named for their antitheses. They could also delight in the elaborate efforts at presenting the work as a bona fide traveller's account mirroring the many such works then pouring off the presses. If his less educated countrymen failed to catch the ruse, like the cleric Rowland Philipps, 'a devout man and a theologian by profession' (*Works*, 4.43) who asked to be sent to evangelize the island, it only underscored More's point that to be educated, and particularly a theologian, one should know Greek as well as Latin.

Utopia broadly satirizes European society for its shortsighted love of gain, its lack of true Christian piety and charity, and its unreasonableness. But the island society the traveller describes is itself not entirely admirable, and More clearly did not intend to limit attention to his fantastic nation. The traveller only introduced Utopia during an argument concerning the institution of private property that itself arose in a discussion of the possibility of enlightened reform in contemporary Europe.

It was this last topic that preoccupied More and his humanist contemporaries. Citing examples of current English injustices in the criminal code, the first part of *Utopia*, the 'Dialogue of Counsel', not only indicts the institutionalized injustices of a moribund legal system, but also proposes the conditions for their remedy through the agency of Cardinal Morton, then lord chancellor. More depicted Morton as flexible, humane, industrious, and, above all, sensitive to the wisdom offered by experience and willing to listen to unconventional but sound advice. In short, Morton's behaviour is held up as an example of enlightened leadership. But Morton's example was ironically lost on the traveller, who concluded that European society was itself beyond remedy, because justice will always take second place to political expediency: 'there is no room for philosophy with rulers' (*Works*, 4.99). In what has become the *locus classicus* of humanist political philosophy, Morus counters that what was needed was for virtuous courtiers to adopt a more nuanced and indirect approach when attempting to steer policy. Admitting that rulers care little for academic philosophy, Morus suggests:

> there is another philosophy, more practical for statesmen, which knows its stage, adapts itself to the play in hand, and performs its role neatly and appropriately ... If you cannot pluck up wrongheaded opinions by the root, if you cannot cure according to your heart's desire vices of long standing, yet you must not on that account desert the commonwealth. You must not abandon the ship in a storm because you cannot control the winds. (ibid.)

And the process of 'adapt[ing] ... to the play in hand' required skills that the humanists particularly favoured: the ability to discern the path of virtue and to persuade others to adopt it.

This position, espoused by a thinly fictionalized More on the eve of his entry into the world of court politics, exposes the situation facing More and his humanist colleagues who likewise were entering public service. Knowing the preponderance of overwhelming and uncontrollable 'vices of longstanding' present in the service of princes, the humanist was bound to seek out subtle strategies to deflect, overcome, or neutralize them. The assertion that this is always necessary but only sometimes successful suggests that More saw clearly the dangers of shipwreck awaiting those whose virtue obliges them to

remain steadfast. In his *History of Richard III*, More had described eloquently the dangers to the individual and the state when those to whom the commonwealth had been entrusted lack the courage to resist the evils of a misruled and misruling prince. Here, as he entered the troubled waters of national politics, he reasserted optimistically the need for virtuous men to remain true to their convictions. Underneath its dazzling word play and satiric genius, *Utopia* charts the course More navigated until it became no longer possible for him to 'adapt ... to the play in hand' and he was forced to choose between virtue and political expedience.

Defence of humanism The optimism implicit in More's position is notable on the eve of the Reformation. The year that closed with the publication of *Utopia* had opened with two works from Erasmus: his *Novum instrumentum*, a new Latin translation of the New Testament intended as the key to a revitalized theology characterized by a return to the Bible and patristic scholarship, and his highly popular *Institutio principis Christiani*, which detailed a programme of political reform. Erasmus's earlier satire of clerical ignorance, the *Praise of Folly*, begun at More's house in Bucklersbury in 1509, stung theologians at Louvain to respond, and the ensuing controversy drew More into the first of his many public epistolary defences of Erasmus's writings. Although he did not set the terms of the debate, the controversy gave More an opportunity to spell out, more clearly if less playfully, the religious reforms he had dangled before the readers of his *Utopia*.

One of the most vociferous of the Louvain theologians to criticize Erasmus's satire was Martin van Dorp, and in answering Dorp's objections More laid bare his views on the shortcomings of certain scholastic preoccupations. Intended for a professional readership, More's condensed argument against the 'supersophistical trifling' of the scholastics (*Works*, 15.27) in his *Letter to Dorp* is narrowly academic. At the heart of the humanists' pedagogical agenda was the relationship between Christian wisdom and secular learning, and their views rested on a profound shift in the accepted notion of human psychology. Contemporary clerical education, More argued, focused primarily on the intellect trained in a technique of argumentation known as dialectic, without developing other mental and emotional faculties. In essence, scholastics had corrupted the curriculum by stripping rhetorical studies of an ethical or persuasive dimension (which reduced it to mere grammar) and elevating dialectic to the level of a philosophical discipline. The general effect, More said to Dorp, of this focus on dialectic was that too much time was wasted on ridiculous sophisms and inconsequential logical games in pursuit of philosophical exactitude while the real work of theology—bringing souls to Christ—lay undone. And in addition to debasing the field of theology, scholastic dialectic invaded other fields with its methods and terminology, smothering and impoverishing them without furnishing any new insights. To redress this imbalance and restore a more holistic approach, More proposed that educators shift the emphasis away from an obsessive preoccupation with dialectic to those disciplines—rhetoric, for example—that train the student in the role of language's ability to address the will as well as the intellect.

To satirize contemporary preoccupation with logical quibbles was far easier than to convince Dorp, and others, that the humanist pursuit of eloquence was not mere word play divorced from everyday life, and that it prepared one well for theological study. More showed that, contrary to scholastic claims, dialectic itself, while seemingly concerned with reason alone, was not founded on a priori principles but instead originated from the same rules governing grammar and syntax as other forms of human communication. Consequently More argued that mere grammatical techniques must not claim to occupy a privileged place in the preparation for theological study—in fact, quite the opposite, since the sterile and artificial nature of dialectical training removed its adherents from practical involvement with the issues at hand. After More restored dialectic to its place within the context of the trivium, he championed Erasmus as an example of the consummate man of letters whose philological skill was better able to renew the Christian cultural tradition than the dogmatic pronouncements of the casuists and scholastics.

Conscious of the need to relate his views on training in the pagan classics to a Christian context, More argued that study of the liberal arts, including Latin and Greek, 'prepares the soul for virtue' (*Works*, 15.139) by providing a laboratory for human psychology, a training ground for rhetoric, and, finally, expertise in biblical languages without which the study of scripture shrinks to a discussion of commentaries. More carefully integrated the liberal arts into the entire theological edifice as its foundation and framework, and implicitly but forcefully rejected the separation between secular and sacred disciplines. Using patristic models of exegesis as his primary example—both Latin and Greek—he argued that the church fathers have a privileged place in the transmission of the living gospel of faith. His views on what he called positive theology united this rediscovery of the fathers with Erasmus's emphasis on philological expertise and practical results—much to the consternation of the disputatious theologians who were more interested in logical subtleties than scriptural truth. Two of the most striking features of More's approach to the fathers, seen here for the first time but later echoed in his defence of Christian unity, was the sense that as a group their authority transcended the individual authority of any single theologian among them, and that together they represented as well as guaranteed the essential unity of the church. Positioned between the apostolic age and all later times, the fathers were examples for More of what living the gospel entailed. They embodied Christian principles not found in any subsequent age, and stood as theologians *par excellence*, in stark contrast to the theologians Erasmus had skewered in his *Praise of Folly*.

More's forceful and eloquent letter proved effective. When Dorp dropped his criticisms of Erasmus and later adopted Erasmus's views on the need for sound philological education, he credited More with leading him to this conclusion. Even more telling was Dorp's use of More's own arguments in his later discussions about Pauline letters. After Dorp there were others, and from 1515 until 1520 More campaigned actively in theological controversies as a supporter of Erasmian reform. His letters, whether circulated in manuscript or published in his lifetime—notably to Oxford University in 1518 and to Edward Lee (the future archbishop of York) and John Batmanson in 1519–20—repeat the argument set out in his controversy with Dorp. But by 1520 the grounds had shifted, and the dispute concerning the revitalization of theology along humanist lines had been eclipsed by a challenge aimed at the sacramental core of the church.

More and his household More's engaging personality, his wit, and his brilliant conversation were frequent subjects of remark among his friends. Through Erasmus's letters, where he is depicted as the model humanist, a man of letters, whose deep and sincere piety are salted with a lively wit, More's character became famous. In July 1519 Erasmus offered a lengthy portrait of More, then in his early forties, to Ulrich von Hutten. The letter was printed in October, and increased More's fame throughout Europe. Calling him England's only genius and a man born and framed for friendship, Erasmus described More's appearance:

> He is not tall, without being noticeably short … his complexion tends to be warm rather than pale … [with] eyes rather greyish-blue, with a kind of fleck in them, the sort that usually indicates a gifted intelligence … His expression shows the sort of man he is, always friendly and cheerful, with something of the air of one who smiles easily, and … disposed to be merry rather than serious or solemn, but without a hint of the fool or the buffoon. (*Collected Works*, 7.17)

His indifference to fine food, his fondness of beef, eggs, and fruit, his preference for small beer or water rather than wine, and his carelessness about his dress were traits that supported Erasmus's assessment that More eschewed vanity and display. More was, in effect, the model Christian layman. Erasmus's praises were echoed by other contemporaries: in a treatise on Latin translation published in 1521, Richard Whittington described More as 'a man of an aungels wyt & syngler lernyng' and Englished Erasmus's earlier praise into the most famous epithet of all—More is 'A man for all seasons' (R. Whittington, *Vulgaria*, ed. B. White, 1932, 64).

More's household was a model of humanistic interests. The famous Holbein group sketch of his family at home in Chelsea, where they had moved by early 1526, reveals musical instruments, a relatively large number of books, and a monkey. He built a study behind the great house for his books, and his garden—itself a significant landmark—contained a small menagerie. He educated his first wife in music as well as in literature, but his second wife, already a mature woman when they married, proved less tractable in both. His household was known for its piety and erudition, 'a school for the knowledge and practice of the Christian faith' as Erasmus noted (Stapleton, 91), and

More's interest in educating his daughters as well as their brother was as laudable as it was rare. Women and men, he wrote to his children's tutor, are 'equally suited for those studies by which reason is cultivated and becomes fruitful like a ploughed land on which the seed of good lessons has been sown' (*Selected Letters*, 122). He specifically instructed the tutor to see that his daughters were educated in the fathers, particularly Jerome and Augustine. Lessons and devotions marked the daily routine of the house, and More's gentle care is reflected in his correspondence with his children.

Distant enough from Westminster to offer relief from the distractions of the city, More's manor in Chelsea was a Renaissance masterpiece, and encapsulated everything about the man his contemporaries found so attractive: piety, erudition, industry, and hospitality. He built a chapel for his private devotions and penance. His garden offered mulberry trees, orchards of fruits, and a variety of shrubs and herbs. And suitors, guests, the poor and needy, detained heretics, even the king himself all walked through his doors. Unable to accommodate the growing influx of the needy, More built a separate house for the poor and instructed his daughter Margaret to oversee its operation. He clearly expected to enjoy the fruits of his labours for years there on the banks of the Thames, reforming the unresponsive English legal system, carrying on his campaign against English heretics, watching his family grow and prosper. But it was not to be. At its core, More's position as lord chancellor was compromised from the start because he could not support the king in the very thing most pressing. Hoping that his service in other fields, including the extirpation of heresy, would suffice, and that the king's infatuation with Anne Boleyn might resolve itself, More was led by his optimism into a struggle he could have foreseen.

Royal councillor After More's admission to the king's council in 1518 his career was steered largely by Wolsey's hand. Wolsey had concentrated the largest group of councillors around himself at Westminster; from the beginning More's most important role was not there but among the smaller group of councillors whom Wolsey trusted to remain in attendance on the king. Beginning in 1518, Wolsey used More equally with Richard Pace, the official secretary, and as time went on he increasingly relied on More as a conduit to the king. Pace was sent abroad to Rome in 1521 and his replacement, Richard Sampson, was relegated to Spain the following year, so More assumed the position of sole royal secretary until 1526 and several times afterwards—largely because during these years of political upheaval Wolsey felt he could trust no one else. Despite acting as an intermediary between the lord chancellor and the king, More was among the most active participants in council meetings and dealt with the full range of conciliar activity. In addition to managing the king's correspondence, he by 1520 was entrusted by Wolsey with the king's signet, and he embellished the royal train when Henry met François I at the Field of Cloth of Gold, and the emperor Charles V shortly afterwards.

In addition to his duties as *ad hoc* royal secretary, More

held a number of official positions because of his legal training. Having resigned his post as under-sheriff of London in 1518, he sat on the bench hearing 'poor men's suits' as master of requests. In 1521 he was knighted and made under-treasurer of the exchequer, and in 1525 he succeeded Sir Richard Wingfield as chancellor of the duchy of Lancaster. Throughout these years he was, as he complained, almost constantly in attendance upon the king. Roper reports that because More:

> was of a pleasaunte disposition, it pleased the kinge and Queene, after the Councell had supte, at the time of their supper, for their pleasure, comonly to call for him to be merry with them. Whom when he perceaved so much in his talke to delight, that he could not once in a moneth gett leave to goe home to his wife and children (whos company he moste desired) and to be absent from the courte two dayes together … he, much mysliking this restraint of his libertie, began thereupon somewhat to dissemble his nature, and so litle and litle from his former accustomed myrthe to disuse himself, that he was of them frome thenceforthe at suche seasons no more so ordinarily sent for.   (Roper, 11–12)

In *Utopia* More had argued that councillors must practise a philosophy which 'knows its stage, adapts itself to the play in hand, and performs its role neatly and appropriately' (*Works*, 4.99). But if it had something essentially dramatic about it, politics was no mere play. More knew that royal service exposed him to evils far greater than temporary separation from his family, and as he rose in favour with both the king and Wolsey he increased his exposure to those risks. His *History of Richard III* had charted much of the territory he was now traversing, and in it More turned again and again to a darker image of the play he was engaged in: politics 'bee Kynges games, as it were stage playes, and for the more part plaied upon scafoldes. In which pore men be but the lokers on' (ibid., 2.81). More knew the risks when he stepped onto the stage. And in 1521, with Henry VIII's execution of the duke of Buckingham, echoes of a similar execution under Richard III were clearly audible. More was intimately acquainted with the entire Buckingham affair: his father had been on the commission that indicted the duke and had himself received profits from some of the duke's confiscated lands.

About this time More began writing a massive spiritual work, in English, on a very traditional theme: the four last things. Long considered a watershed between More's Latin humanistic works and his English theological polemics, this treatise on death, judgment, heaven, and hell adapted a medieval genre to a contemporary English context. Significantly, it is the first extended work More undertook in English, and his style hearkens back to the great English writer Walter Hilton, whose works he had read in London's Charterhouse. In Hilton can be seen all the elements of More's later writings—his reliance on merry tales, his liveliness and humour, his optimism that sin can be successfully rejected, and his reliance on the concrete 'homely example' (*Works*, 1.149). More's gift as a natural raconteur lay in blending formal rhetorical devices with the earthiness of daily life—something he doubtless gleaned from his years in London's Guildhall, hearing litigants in the sheriff's court; and here he presented for the first time the lively English style for which he became famous. Part scriptural exposition and part exhortation, *The Four Last Things* opens a window into More's mind at a time when his interest in the practical piety of the *Life of Pico* seems to belong to the distant past. Whether More conceived of the work as a tonic to bolster his courage in the face of Buckingham's execution (significantly More compared worldly events to a stage play here as well) or more broadly as an addition to his earlier forays into English devotional literature, *The Four Last Things* was abandoned shortly after it was begun. Despite his prolific output in the following years, he would not again achieve its meditative depth until his masterly Tower works written during his incarceration. Instead of producing devotional works, and initially at the invitation and defence of his king, More entered the theological controversies already raging on the continent and began writing polemics.

Early polemics Henry VIII had written an anti-Lutheran tract in 1521 (with help from More and Fisher) that earned him the papal title *Fidei defensor*. Luther's vituperous rejoinder (1522) was so scurrilous that Henry could not decorously reply. More stepped in to dirty his hands in the king's defence with his *Responsio ad Lutherum* (1523). Using a method which served him in later polemics, he adopted a thin disguise and engaged in an often *ad hominem* attack while rebutting Luther's argument in painstaking detail. At issue was the reformer's doctrine of *sola scriptura*, which denied the validity of Catholic tradition, written and unwritten, and undermined the sacramental system of the church. More's defence relied on the Catholic teaching that the Holy Spirit preserved and guided the church both through scripture and through tradition, and that, as a visible institution containing all Christians, the church operated by Spirit-guided consensus, not individual persuasion. The emphasis on the essential unity of the church, on the 'common corps of Christendom' against the divisive tendencies of individual or minority conviction, was to be a hallmark of More's ecclesiology, and one to which he would appeal at his trial a decade later.

More's increasing activity on behalf of Catholic orthodoxy kept pace with his growing reputation as statesman and diplomat. In 1523 the king summoned parliament to finance war with France, and More was elected speaker of the House of Commons where his skill as a mediator bridged an impasse between the house and Wolsey over grants and taxation. His success in placating a hostile Commons so pleased Wolsey that he asked the king to grant More an additional £100, money More used towards the building of his great house at Chelsea. Following his election as speaker, More was made high steward of Oxford University (1524), where he used his influence to recruit the Spanish humanist Juan Luis Vives for the university. Vives, whom More met a few years earlier in Bruges in the train of Charles V, had written on such topics as the education of women, Augustine's *City of God*, and the proper conduct of public officials—all topics in which More himself was deeply interested. In an ironic letter to Erasmus, More confided wistfully that in Vives he saw a man whose scholarship made him feel ashamed of his own lack of industry. More's extraordinary workload as a councillor, judge, and head of household left him little time for scholarly pursuits.

The rise of English heresy Although war with France was over by the summer of 1525, a new front was already opening: heresy. In September, inspired by Luther's German Bible, William Tyndale began printing his English New Testament in Cologne, and, although his printing was interrupted, he completed the edition in Worms within the year. Lutheranism surfaced in England in a sermon delivered by Robert Barnes at Cambridge on Christmas eve. Only the month before More had been named high steward of Cambridge, joining Bishop Fisher as chancellor. Cambridge became a seedbed of protestant beliefs, and a centre, along with London, for the distribution of protestant books. The suppression and refutation of these books and those who wrote them became the focus of More's activities for the rest of his career.

In December 1525 More organized and led the first of two raids on the London house of the Hanseatic merchants. Under the pretext of searching for further evidence against the merchants (one of whom had recently been arrested for clipping coin), More's real goal was to enforce the bishop of London's ban on Lutheran works. His raid turned up no books, but did lead to the indictment of several merchants with heterodox beliefs who confessed to having seen forbidden works. In a ceremony at St Paul's the following month, four German merchants were forced to abjure their heresies on pain of death, along with Barnes, whose Christmas sermon had proved so inflammatory. More's role in the struggle against Lutheranism was set, and he would play it until he found himself a prisoner of conscience in the Tower in 1534. By late 1526 Tyndale's translation of the New Testament began arriving in shipments from abroad—Barnes imprudently sold a copy to a group of Lollards following his recantation—and London's Bishop Tunstall, a close friend and frequent companion of More, issued a second warning about the danger of the Lutheran heresy. The recent violent upheavals in Germany were attributed to the breakdown of traditional obedience and discipline brought about by Luther's defiance of church authority, and both state and church authorities in England were determined to prevent what they saw as certain antinomianism should Luther's ideas take hold in England. More's faith in the sanctity of the institutional church, and his dedication to the law of the land, meant that his career was at a crucial juncture: he would, in effect, use his official position in the government to defend the church's traditional teaching. It was an unusual position for a layman. In his *Apology* (1533), More equated heresy with treason, saying that the heretic 'bycometh a false traytour to god' (*Works*, 9.136), and tied both to the misalignment of the will brought about by disordered appetite. What made heresy worse than ordinary felony in More's eyes was that its effect, the corruption of the soul, was eternal. In order to prevent this doubly treasonous disintegration in England, More accepted Tunstall's commission in March 1528 to read heretical works and refute them in English. Within fifteen months, More produced his masterly *Dialogue Concerning Heresies* (1529).

More's polemical activity, public as it was, concealed the fact that he had removed himself from another momentous struggle at court over the king's growing alienation from Queen Katherine and his open dalliance with Anne Boleyn. Unable to support the king in his attempts to break his marriage, More left that issue to Wolsey and the canon lawyers, and occupied himself with the legal matters associated with the duchy of Lancaster and with fighting the spread of heresy. After Wolsey's fall in 1529, More was in a position to combine the duties of lord chancellor with those of his campaign against heresy, all the while steering clear of the dangers involved in the king's marital difficulties. Soon, however, those difficulties would border, if not invade, More's defence of the church.

Lord chancellor At some point before the summer of 1529, More told his son-in-law William Roper that there were three things which, should they be established, would cause him to be content to have himself 'put in a Sack and here presently cast into the Thames'. The first was that 'where the moste parte of Christen princes be at mortall warre, they were all at an universall peace', a peace soon established at the treaty of Cambrai (signed in August 1529) where More and Bishop Tunstall represented England. More's two remaining desires proved more elusive:

> that wheare the Church of Christe is at this presente sore afflicted with many errors and heresees, it were setled in perfecte uniformity of religion. The third, that where the kings matter of his mariage is nowe come in question, it were to the glory of god and quietnes of all partes brought to a good conclusion.

Regarding this final point Roper adds that More 'judged that otherwise it wold be a disturbance to a great parte of Christendome' (Roper, 24–5). The story of More's career as lord chancellor and Catholic apologist is, in effect, dominated by these two desires.

When Wolsey failed to settle the 'king's matter' and was stripped of his office, More was chosen to replace him. Roper records that when the duke of Norfolk, speaking for the king, publicly congratulated More on this singular mark of the king's great favour, More mused philosophically that, while he was grateful for the king's good favour, he felt 'unmeete for that roome, wherein, considering howe wise and honourable a prelate had lately before taken so greate a fall, he had … thereof no cause to rejoice' (Roper, 40). Whether Roper inserted these words into More's mouth—there were witnesses, Roper says—they echo cautionary sentiments found in many of More's writings. Having worked closely with Wolsey for more than a decade, More knew better than most the mercurial nature of power in Henry's court, and had presciently remarked on it earlier when Roper had complimented him on earning the king's exceptional favour. 'I thancke our lord, sonne', More said,

> I find his grace my very good lord indeed; and I beleeave he dothe as singulerly favour me as any subjecte within this

realme. Howbeit, sonne Roper, I may tell thee I have no cawse to be prowd thereof, for if my head could winne him a castle in Fraunce … it should not faile to goe. (ibid., 21)

Within days of his swearing in as lord chancellor More wrote to Erasmus that, having set his heart on a 'life of retirement', he was unexpectedly 'tossed into a mass of vital business' and was now busy 'adjusting … to circumstances'. He added, cryptically, that the post 'involves the interests of Christendom' (*Selected Letters*, 172). By this time More had already published two English polemics against domestic heresy, and would doubtless have anticipated others; it may be that waging a campaign against English heretics was the 'life of retirement' for which he had planned. His elevation to the post of lord chancellor gave him greater scope for his efforts, if less time—in his opening speech to the so-called Reformation Parliament a few days later he talked about reforming 'certain errors and abuses' in both the temporal and spiritual laws.

More's position against heresy was widely known and supported by the king, but the problem with his new office lay elsewhere. After the pope decided to hear Queen Katherine's appeal to Rome, the real test for loyalty was support for the king's divorce and, as More made plain, he could not help in this. He did not give his reasons openly to the king, but it seems clear from his later statements that he accepted the legitimacy of the king's marriage to Katherine, and disapproved of any attempts to impugn the papal dispensation that allowed it in the first place. The king assured More that if he 'could not therein with his consciens serve him, he was content taccept his service otherwise' (Roper, 50). There is no indication that when he accepted the position as lord chancellor More foresaw the later connection between the formation of the Church of England and the king's Great Matter. Rather, More's work in the conciliar courts and his interest in legal reform led him to see the office of lord chancellor as an opportunity to update and improve England's laws—both secular and spiritual—and the justice they upheld. Although he was not the first lay chancellor, nor the first one trained in common law, in a 'magisterial' performance More 'ensured a smooth transition from the age of clerical to that of common-law chancellors' (Guy, *Public Career*, 93).

Legal reforms More's legal reforms followed a pattern largely set by Wolsey. They streamlined outdated practices in the common-law system and opened up access to equity courts. More presided over the two equity courts of Star Chamber and chancery which Wolsey had used in his attempts to make English justice more effective. But he also had tools Wolsey lacked: expertise in common law and a fearless integrity based on his conviction that judges should act according to their judicial consciences. More's equity courts saw those cases—in growing numbers—which the common-law courts had proved themselves deficient in resolving. In a famous meeting in Star Chamber, More confronted common-law judges with a list of cases in which he had recently issued injunctions removing them into his own jurisdiction despite the complaints this had caused:

when he had broken with them what complaintes he had heard of his Injunctions, and moreover shewed them bothe the number and causes of every one of them, in order, so plainely that, uppon full debating of thos matters, they were all inforced to confes that they, in like case, could have done no other wise themselfes.   (Roper, 44–5)

But More was not content to let the matter rest there—he informed the judges that it fell to them most particularly to reform the deficiencies of the law 'by their owne discretions' (Roper, 45). Having the jury determine cases according to a strict interpretation of the law absolved the judge of the burden of handing down just but difficult judgments in those areas where the law had not kept pace with changes in English society. Speaking privately to Roper of this failure of nerve on the bench, More said that judges 'see that they may by the verdicte of the Jurye cast of all quarrells from them selves uppon them, which they accompte their chief defens' (ibid.). More's invitation to them to join him in reforming the law and its application relied not on the creation of new judicial processes but rather on the use of conscience as well as precedent when handing down their decisions. And he set them an example with a personal impartiality that challenged a judicial system bloated on favouritism and privilege. When More's own son-in-law Giles Heron presumed upon his leniency in a chancery suit, More bound him over to an appearance in Star Chamber or face imprisonment. Roper recounts that, when a litigant with a case pending before More offered him an elegant gilt cup as a new year's gift, More accepted the cup, and with characteristic irony returned a more valuable but less artistic cup to the donor—defusing a charge of bribery and perhaps teaching the litigant a lesson.

As England grew more litigious, final judgment could be elusive as obstructive litigants pursued cases through various competing courts for years. More favoured stiff penalties for contempt of decrees. In addition to the customary use of penal recognizances to enforce judgments in Star Chamber and chancery, he also used liens on goods and property, writs of assistance directed to sheriffs, and automatic gaol terms for those who failed to comply. He was the first lord chancellor to punish contempts in chancery cases by a summary Star Chamber judgment.

More as parishioner In 1529 More was at the height of his career, yet was characteristically concerned about his local community and his church. When a fire in his barns destroyed not only his grain but that of his neighbours, he instructed his wife:

> to make good ensearch what my poor neighbors have lost and bid them take no thought therefor, for and I shouyld not leave myself a spoon there shall no poor neighbor of mine bear loss by any chance happened in my house.   (*Selected Letters*, 171)

He also proved solicitous to find his farmers 'other masters' before discharging them. Despite his high position, More took an active part in his parish church of Chelsea where he provoked Norfolk's rebuke by singing in the choir wearing a surplice. When told that the king would be displeased to see his lord chancellor in such a lowly position, More replied 'It cannot be displeasing to my lord the King that I pay homage to my King's Lord' (Stapleton, 64).

More's interest in his parish went well beyond participating in the liturgy. He transferred his first wife's remains to his family chapel in Chelsea church, and there wrote his epitaph on a tomb he was destined not to occupy. In 1530 the ordinary patrons allowed him to present the next priest to the rectory of Chelsea and More chose John Larke. Having grown up with priests such as John Colet and William Grocyn as examples, More had high standards. He expected higher conduct of priests than he did of laymen, saying that 'as for vyce, I hold yt myche more dampnable in a spyrytuall person then in a temporall man' (*Works*, 9.48), although there is no evidence he exercised any undue severity towards those in orders when they came before him as litigants. It may be assumed that Larke impressed More as pastor, although there is no precise information on his qualities. More had known Larke for years, and had presented him in 1526 to the rectory of Woodford in Essex. Although Larke was sworn to the oath that More refused, he left London in 1540 (and was cited for his unlicensed absence from his cure) and retreated to the Roper family estate in Kent. On 7 March 1544 he was executed at Tyburn, along with the Roper family chaplain John Ireland, for his resistance to Archbishop Cranmer.

More and the English Reformation Although More's belief in the validity of the king's marriage did not permit him to join with other councillors in supporting the royal manoeuvres for a divorce, he could none the less assist the Defender of the Faith by honouring Tunstall's commission to refute heretical books in English. In 1529, shortly before he became lord chancellor, More published his brilliant *Dialogue* (now called the *Dialogue Concerning Heresies*), the wittiest and most forceful polemic to emerge from the English Reformation. In it a nameless 'messenger' engages in dialogue at Chelsea with a slightly fictionalized version of More himself. The dialogue's narrative frame is indicative of the tensions under which More wrote: the messenger is a young, university-trained Englishman sent to the author by a friend who is concerned about the young man's Lutheran leanings. Distrustful of the way in which weighty matters became distorted even under the best of circumstances, More's work took the form of a written report back to his friend detailing the conversations he had with the young messenger. Although More protested repeatedly that he had no cause to mistrust the messenger's honesty or wit, he decided to write down their dialogue so that:

> if it happed that his messenger had for any sinyster favour borne toward the wrong side purposely mangled the mater, his maister shold not only know the treuth, but also have occasion the better to beware of his messenger, which elles might hap to hurte while he were mystaken for good. (*Works*, 6.22)

The implications were clear—in More's London, written transcripts were more trustworthy than oral reports delivered by those whose religious orthodoxy, like that of the messenger and countless other young scholars, was shaky or unproved.

Their discussions were lively and discursive—More's famous wit is here coupled with an interlocutor who is, according to the friend who sent him, 'more then meanlye lerned, with one thing added where with ye be wont well to be content, a very mery wit'. Nor is the young man reticent. If More relished conversation, here he found one with whom he could converse at length, for the messenger was 'of nature nothing tonge tayed' (*Works*, 6.25). A lengthy dialogue of four conversations with a fortnight interval in the middle, between an older councillor and a younger scholar concerning the religious matters then being debated, provided More with ample opportunity for what would prove to be his most successful excursion into the genre of the polemical dialogue. None of his other polemical works achieve the *Dialogue*'s relaxed charm, or have its potential to persuade.

The work confronts the Lutheran teachings of William Tyndale, and it is More's purpose to show the essential identity between the two writers. Having castigated Luther in 1523 as both licentious and heretical, More in his *Dialogue* painted Tyndale in much the same colours. But by the time he wrote against Tyndale in 1529 the heresy he combated had grown enormously in popularity and gravity, reflected in a growing apocalyptic strain in his thought. He linked Luther and Tyndale as 'forwalkers' of the antichrist, whose appearance 'whyche so helpe me god I very greatly fere is now very nere at hande' (*Works*, 8.479, 6.434–5). More sensed that the European Catholic hegemony he so assiduously promoted was coming to an end. 'I pray god', he said to his son-in-law:

> that some of us, as highe as we seeme to sitt upon the mountaynes treading heretiks under our feete like antes, live not in the day that we gladly wold wishe to be at a league and composition with them, to let them have their churches quietly to them selfes, so that they wold be contente to let us have ours quietly to our selves. (Roper, 35)

Most of this early polemic, written before More's rise to the chancellorship had imposed tighter restrictions on what he could say about the rapidly deteriorating religious situation in England, is a defence of current Catholic practice against the criticisms of what More perceived to be a growing anti-clericalism in England and abroad. More rejected the protestant reliance on scripture alone as the sole vehicle of revelation, a view of the clergy that would reduce priests to mere vehicles of the Word rather than its guardians and interpreters. Because scripture 'far excedeth in many placys the capacyte and perceyvyng of man', it was the duty of the clergy to adapt its message to the needs and abilities of the people (*Works*, 6.335–7). And the church itself, as a body of believers in possession of an authoritative tradition of interpretation, was guaranteed inerrancy in its interpretation and transmission. Pressed by reformers who saw the Catholic reliance on tradition—and in particular the claims to inerrancy in interpretation—as elaborate attempts to justify the clergy's illegitimate authority over lay Christians, More summoned an unbroken line of saints and martyrs stretching back to gospel times whose consensus confirmed Catholic orthodoxy and, implicitly and explicitly, condemned Tyndale and his tribe as innovators. His own criticisms of ignorant, hypocritical, and ineffective priests notwithstanding, More argued that the clergy occupied a privileged place in Christian society not only as dispensers of sacramental grace but as bearers of correct scriptural teaching. Because they stood as successors to the apostles, they were officers of a very visible, if flawed, church—a church that had been promised inerrancy by God.

In the course of his *Dialogue* More took up many clerical issues which had long been notorious: pluralism, non-residence, avarice, licentiousness. While he stuck to the traditional defence of immoral or ignorant priests as dispensers of sacramental grace, he offered his readers a tantalizing if oblique remedy for England's overwhelming number of inadequate priests. When the messenger suggested that bishops exercise tighter control over the selection and training of priests by waiting until 'romes & lyvynges' fell vacant before ordaining men, More mused 'Surely … for ought I se sodeynly that wolde not be moche amysse' (*Works*, 6.302).

While reformers were bent on achieving a Christianity purged of medieval accretions and stripped of idolatrous sacramentals, More pleaded cogently for the traditional understanding of affective piety: statues, rites and rituals, shrines, practices such as pilgrimages, and works of self-sacrifice. Keeping his own penitential practices hidden—his hair shirt and other mortifications—More urged similar works on his readers in imitation of Christ, who instituted for his followers ascetic practices to nurture a spirit of self-denial. The pain of these works was real, he argued, and their value lay in turning attention towards their promise of heaven. Christ asked for obedience, 'not any delyverynge from the lawes of the chyrch or from any good temporall lawes eyther in to a lewde lyberte of slouthfull rest. For that were not an easy yoke but a pullyng of the hed out of the yoke' (*Works*, 6.106). Few statements as clearly indicate More's trust in the value of ascetic practices, however mild. From his earliest writings up to his meditations written in the Tower, More's belief was that 'God sent men hither to wake and work' (ibid., 11.33). Exercises in self-denial inured Christians against the deadening effects of a life where comfort and ease formed the only horizons. By rejecting longstanding church practices, More believed Tyndale and other reformers were running the grave risk of forsaking a heavenly example for a little earthly ease.

Opposition to the royal divorce Although several councillors, notably Thomas, Lord Darcy, and the duke of Suffolk, called for drastic overhaul of the church following Wolsey's fall, few could have anticipated that parliament, when it met in November 1529, would address issues of clerical reform. But parliament's first order of business when it opened was to turn its attention to the clergy, and the list of grievances the Commons presented to the king for redress included many of the issues More had defended against Tyndale in his *Dialogue*. Bishop Fisher led a futile resistance to these bills, and openly suggested they sprang from heretical motives inspired by German protestants. More shared this view, arguing later in his *Apology* that it was not for the laity to reform the spiritualty despite the clergy's reluctance to reform itself. When parliament took upon itself the task of regulating the church, More was pushed further to the edge as government policy now seemed bent on claiming the one area in which he was free to operate.

Early in 1530 Henry VIII's divorce case had been summoned to Rome, and the concord between the emperor and pope made it unlikely that a judgment favourable to the king would be forthcoming. With most of the king's councillors working to break the deadlock, More was deliberately excluded from council meetings, although he did retain the king's support for his continued attacks on heresy. Changes in the council stripped More of whatever other support he had. Bishop Tunstall was translated north to Durham and replaced on the council by Anne Boleyn's father, Thomas, earl of Wiltshire and Ormond, and by John Stokesley in the see of London. An inner ring of councillors was gathered around Norfolk, its main purpose to solve the king's Great Matter. Like Fisher and Tunstall, More was not among the group of councillors who signed Henry VIII's letter to Clement VII presenting the divorce as a purely national issue. Thomas Cranmer had suggested that the king take unilateral action, and by late 1530 the king's denial that he was subject to the pope polarized the debate and in effect sealed More's fate.

Henry's caesaro-papism, fostered by Cranmer and Cromwell, effectively prohibited More from exercising his influence except according to his brief to fight heresy. Now that the crown was enlarging its jurisdiction, the danger for More lay in assuming that the traditional teaching on church authority and ecclesiastical immunity from secular control still held. While the king groped for a plan of action, parliament went into recess for the entire year, and More renewed his assault on protestantism.

More's orthodoxy, coupled with his exclusion from the inner circle of councillors concerned with the divorce proceedings, meant that he increasingly allied himself with churchmen and bent all his talents to help them eradicate heresy. In 1530 he oversaw two proclamations proscribing a number of heterodox publications, including vernacular scriptures, and prohibiting the importation of any foreign imprints of English works. Offenders in breach of royal proclamations were to appear in Star Chamber rather than before an ecclesiastical court, and almost immediately More imprisoned a number of men for owning banned books. Collaborating closely with Bishop Stokesley of London, More engineered the arrest of several noted colporteurs and the execution of three heretics, and publicly approved of the execution of others. The vigour with which More pursued heretics through the courts was mirrored by the relentlessness with which he fought them, or those he felt abetted them, in his polemics. The times demanded strictness, he repeatedly argued, because the stakes were so high. No other aspect of More's

life has engendered greater controversy than his persecution of heretics. Critics argue that as one of Europe's leading intellectuals, and one with particularly strong humanist leanings, More should have rejected capital punishment of heretics. His supporters point out that he was a product of his times, and that those men he most admired (including Bishop Fisher, also martyred by Henry VIII) lamented but accepted as necessary the practice of executing heretics.

Parliament remained adjourned throughout 1530 while the *praemunire* proceedings began against several churchmen for violating the prerogatives of the crown. When it reconvened in 1531 the king confirmed his intent to separate from Roman jurisdiction by rejecting papal authority in England and styling himself supreme head of the church in England. The move was a crushing defeat for the Aragonese group, who had opposed the divorce from the beginning, made worse for More because he had to deliver to both houses of parliament selected opinions in favour of the divorce which Cranmer had begun collecting the year before. An unwilling tool of a policy he could neither openly oppose nor work to prevent, More asked Norfolk to facilitate his resignation on grounds of ill health, but for obscure reasons he did not resign. He continued to work for the queen's cause so assiduously that the emperor sent him a letter of thanks in March 1531, which More declined to receive. Ever cautious of his precarious position, More began to avoid the imperial ambassador on the grounds that:

> he ought to abstain from everything which might provoke suspicion; and if there were no other reason, such a visitation [by the ambassador] might deprive him of the liberty which he had always used in speaking boldly in those matters which concerned … the Queen. (*LP Henry VIII*, 5.171)

Hopeful that he could at least salvage something of the church's independence, More discreetly cultivated a group of MPs for the parliamentary session in early 1532, led by Sir George Throckmorton. When the Commons submitted a list of grievances against the clergy in March 1532, inviting the king to use his new prerogative as supreme head of the church to regulate certain issues touching on ecclesiastical authority, More led the direct if futile opposition to Henry's policy. Hours after the clergy yielded their long-standing independence on 16 May 1532 More again confronted the king, this time to resign the chancellorship in an act of public defiance.

Second defence against Tyndale If More's resignation signalled his withdrawal from the world of official politics, it did not remove him from the struggle with the crown on behalf of a church that he now saw threatened from every side. More's campaign, waged as a private citizen, against what he knew to be government policy was dangerous and severed his once-friendly relationship with the king. In the next twenty months he published five major controversial works against protestant doctrine and its connections to the more local English political threat to the church. In 1532 came the first part of his massive *Confutation of Tyndale's 'Answer'*—refuting point by point elements of Tyndale's scriptural translations and the *sola* *scriptura* basis for an institutional church. Tyndale, and Luther before him, had denied various beliefs and practices such as purgatory and the veneration of saints on the basis of insufficient scriptural attestation. To refute them, More worked his way through the fundamentals, arguing forcefully for the authority of the church as the bearer and interpreter of scripture itself—a far more comprehensive view of the community of the faithful than Tyndale was prepared to allow, and one which challenged the emerging political redrawing of the church–state relationship. In 1533, when the second part of More's *Confutation* appeared, the English crown, despite its forays into many areas of church jurisdiction, had not yet made significant moves to challenge church dogma or to abolish sacraments. But elsewhere in Europe things were different. After the reformers' failure to unite in 1530 at Augsburg, the various protestant camps had settled in uneasy co-existence under the protection of reforming princes. Each had abrogated established practices and reformed dogma in different ways, and representatives of these churches set out on vigorous evangelization campaigns aimed at converting England. Parliament's first moves against the church's independence threatened the entire Catholic sacramental system and More, fully aware of the changes already taking place on the continent, took every opportunity to plead against secular control of the church's ancient and sacred role as guardian and vehicle of revelation.

In his first work against Tyndale, More had championed the visible and institutional church, presided over by the pope but stretching back through history to the first gatherings around Jesus. The *consensus fidelium*, facilitated by the reliable transmission of the patristic tradition and guided by the Spirit, shaped and perpetuated the church and accounted for its unity and independence from secular control. After parliament began to reform ecclesiastical practices, the question of jurisdiction was complicated by threats against particular sacraments voiced not only by Tyndale, but by a host of other reformers whose pamphlets were filtering into England, urging the secular authorities to regulate doctrine. The second part of More's *Confutation* dealt most explicitly with the nature of the church as the sacred community through which the indelible primitive revelation achieves new expression. Rejecting the reformers' view that the development of doctrine since apostolic times represented novel accretions and should be rejected as un-scriptural, More argued that such developments were rather 'the appropriation in consciousness by the community of the significance of primitive revelation' (Gogan, 233).

If the nature of the church consumed most of the *Confutation*, the nature of the eucharist claimed More's attention in his shortest polemical work, his *Letter Against Frith*, completed in December 1532 but not printed until a year later. John Frith's Zwinglian denial of the real presence, expressed in a short treatise which More read in manuscript, rejected both the Catholic notion of transubstantiation and the Lutheran doctrine of 'consubstantiation' and represented the most serious threat to the sacrament

of the altar then present in England. Frith's rejection of papal supremacy had prompted the king to intervene when he was arrested in 1531 and he was released with a warning, but after a period of exile Frith returned to England and was rearrested in October 1532. More's somewhat attenuated *Letter* takes into account the interest Henry had in enlisting Frith to his cause, and Frith's youth led More earnestly to urge him to recant.

More's defence of the eucharist rested on the centuries-old tradition of the church, commonly held and commonly transmitted, and he lost no time in pointing out that even among reformers, whose lack of visible unity was a sure sign of an empty if not fraudulent theology, Frith's sacramentarianism was discredited. Referring to a letter that Robert Barnes, the former friar with Lutheran leanings who had already fallen foul of the authorities, had written to him disclaiming any association with Frith's views, More wrote:

> It well contenteth me that frere Barnes beynge a man of more age, and more rype dyscressyon … & in these thynges better lerned than thys yonge man is abhorreth thys yonge mannes heresy in this poynt, as well as he lyketh hym in many other. (*Works*, 7.256)

More circulated his response to Frith privately because, as he said, 'I wolde wysshe that the comon people sholde of suche heresyes never here so myche as the name' (ibid., 9.123), and because Frith's own work had not been printed. So far, England was free from the sacramentarian heresy, but More perceived also that Henry's interest in Frith might cool if he knew the extent of Frith's heterodoxy. As it was, Frith went to the stake in July 1533 for his beliefs.

Final manoeuvres Although More had retired from public affairs, his involvement with Frith indicated that he had not abandoned his efforts at influencing government policy. Denied a voice in parliament and council, he sought other means of making his views known. In May 1533 Cranmer, having declared null the king's first marriage, declared valid the second—and secret—marriage, to Anne. Sensing disaster, More remarked ominously to Roper, 'God geeve grace … that thes matters within a while be not confirmed with othes' (Roper, 57). He pointedly refused to attend her coronation, and to the bishops who urged his attendance he related a parable whose application he summed up for them:

> Your lordshippes have in the matter of the matrimony hitherto kepte your selves pure virgines, yeat take good head, my lordes, that you keepe your virginity still. For some there be that by procuringe your lordshippes first at the coronacion to be present, and next to preach for the setting forth of it, and finally to write bookes to all the world in defens thereof, are desirous to deffloure you; and when they have defloured you, then will they not faile soone after to devoure you. Nowe my lordes … it lieth not in my power but that they may devoure me; but god being my good lord, I will provide that they shall never deffloure me. (ibid., 59)

More's pointed opposition made him a marked man, and his final campaign to deflect the oncoming reforms drew him into a dangerous confrontation with a very learned common lawyer whom he knew to be openly writing for Cromwell and the king: Christopher St German. The task of persuading the English public to accept the Reformation statutes fell in part to St German, whose writings urging secular control of ecclesiastical practices, published anonymously, engaged More throughout 1533. In two works, the *Apology* and *The Debellation of Salem and Bizance*, More defended the church's independent legal system and its procedures, particularly with regard to heresy laws. Careful to preserve the fiction that his unnamed opponent was a renegade cleric like Tyndale, More decried the apparent tolerance with which the English greeted the recent changes and derided St German's tactic of exploiting supposed animosity between the clergy and laity for the purpose of reducing the church and its ministers to a state of subservience. He had to be careful to avoid defending the papal primacy, since that could be construed as treasonable (as he himself pointed out to Cromwell in March 1534). If More could claim victory in his unmasking of Frith, here against St German he clearly failed. In 1534 parliament established secular control over the English church's heresy laws.

More's final foray into religious controversy was his *Answer to a Poisoned Book*, also written in the hectic year of 1533 (but dated 1534). As in his work against Frith the previous year, More defended the Catholic understanding of the real presence in the eucharist, but, unlike the earlier controversy which had been aired among a limited readership, this one was waged in print.

Personal troubles In January 1534 parliament convened for its sixth session since November 1529, and in the following February the king insisted that More be included in a bill of attainder for conspiring with Elizabeth Barton, the so-called Nun of Kent who had uttered dire prophecies against the king's new marriage. So great was the king's animosity against his former lord chancellor that he even believed More was the chief 'deviser' of Barton's utterances (Guy, *More*, 169). More requested a formal hearing before the Lords, but in the end the king insisted that he be deposed before a commission of four councillors: Cromwell, Norfolk, Cranmer, and Audley. Although Roper's account of the matter effaces any mention of the bill and instead recounts More's pleasure at finding himself able to resist this naked attempt at coercion, the commissioners had been able to persuade the king to drop More's name from the bill on the very probable grounds that his inclusion threatened the bill's passage. When that news reached More, he said to his daughter 'In faith, Megge … *quod differtur non aufertur*' ('what is set aside is not put away'; Roper, 71). Other royal opponents were not so lucky. Bishop Fisher was fined £300 (a year's income from his diocese), and another defendant was sent to the Tower. Barton herself, and five of her associates, including two Franciscan priests, were executed.

Once executions for political opposition had begun, More fully expected that his continued resistance would prove his end. He expressed his relief at remaining steadfast in the face of pressure despite his overwhelming fear of a traitor's death. He saw his courage in apocalyptic

terms, and told his son-in-law he had 'geven the divell a fowle fall … and had gone so farre as without greate shame [he] could never goe back agayne' (Roper, 69). He was still officially a king's councillor, and very much in the public eye—recruiting him would greatly aid the king's cause and make the recent executions for treasons more palatable. Although More was denied the hearing before the House of Lords that he had requested, his steadfast resistance was now a matter of public record, and there is an inescapable sense that he engineered his open defiance as an example not only to others but also to support his own weakness.

As efforts continued to bend his will, More's ironic playfulness seems to have blossomed. Roper records many characteristic remarks that seem scripted from the earlier days of his *Richard III* when he combined political with theatrical metaphors, flavoured now perhaps by his self-consciousness as an example of resistance to religious persecution. Warned by Norfolk that the wrath of the king meant death, More replied 'Is that all, my Lord? Then in good faith is there no more differens betweene your grace and me, but that I shall dye today and yow tomorrowe' (Roper, 72). Despite his courage, More did not court martyrdom, but grew increasingly circumspect. In his eloquent letters of March 1534 to Cromwell defending his connections with Elizabeth Barton and his inability to support the king's divorce, More reminded Cromwell that, when he was made lord chancellor, the king, despite More's opposition to the divorce, had advised him to 'fyrst loke unto God and after God unto hym' (*Correspondence*, 495). Excused from participating in the divorce proceedings, More claimed that 'it shold well appere that I never have had agaynst his Gracis mariage eny maner demeanure, wherby his Highnes myght have eny maner cause or occasion of displeasure toward me' nor would he ever 'murmure at it, nor dispute upon it, nor neuer did nor will' (ibid., 497). Coming at the end of a vigorous print campaign against the government's recent actions restricting the ancient liberties of the church, and from a man who not only refused to attend the coronation of England's queen but organized parliamentary opposition to the mechanisms that placed her on the throne, these words protesting innocence and inaction seem at best to be forward-looking promises of future inaction rather than descriptions of past behaviour. In short, More promised Cromwell that he would remain silent for, as they both knew, under English law silence implied consent.

Trial and imprisonment But silence was impossible when oaths were administered. More was asked to swear to the Act of Succession on 12 April 1534, which he refused to do because of the oath's preamble rejecting papal jurisdiction. Having made up his mind to adhere to his conscience in this case rather than to his oath of obedience to the king, More refused to elaborate on his reasons, saying that if he 'should open and disclose the causes why, I shoulde therwith but further exasperate his Highnes, which I wolde in no wise do' (*Correspondence*, 504–5). As a result, More was imprisoned in the Tower on 17 April. The king accused him of 'obstinacy' (*Selected Letters*, 250), a charge that hints at a malicious refusal to obey. Whether the king had in mind More's lengthy campaign, now over, against St German and others in addition to his refusal to swear the oath tendered him is impossible to say, but it is likely. More had worked assiduously to undermine official policy, and the king knew it. Seeking refuge in silence could only be construed as further opposition.

During his imprisonment More finished a series of short treatises on the eucharist which had occupied him at the time of his arrest, and composed two further works which have since been seen as masterpieces: *The Sadness of Christ* and the *Dialogue of Comfort*. Despite their differences—*The Sadness of Christ* is a Latin meditation on Christ's agony in Gethsemane, while the English *Dialogue of Comfort* extols the spiritual benefits of tribulation—both works centre on the remembrance of Christ's passion as an aid during persecution.

Composed under intense emotional and spiritual pressure, the *Dialogue of Comfort* achieves a level of lively serenity unmatched in Tudor prose, and some commentators feel it is More's greatest work. Ostensibly set in Hungary after the Turkish invasion in 1526, the *Dialogue* is both a cogent commentary on human suffering in general and on More's particular struggle to prepare himself for his death. As one prominent scholar noted, it is 'an ultimate spiritual testament' (Martz, 64), applicable as easily to More's treatment at the hands of Henry VIII as it is to any human sufferer. *The Sadness of Christ*, altogether a different sort of work, reflects on the gospel accounts of Christ's own fear as he conforms his will to God's. Unfinished, the work has survived in More's own hand, and reveals his shaping of the treatise to reflect acutely on his own situation—that of the fearful martyr comforted by Christ's example. In addition to these works, More also wrote from the Tower several short meditative prayers on his spiritual struggles, and over a dozen closely worded letters to his family and friends from this period survive that convey his determination to obey his conscience while remaining silent on his reasons for doing so.

More's steadfast refusal to bend to the king's demands and the scandal of his imprisonment proved embarrassing to the government and a dangerous example to others. Various councillors, including Cromwell, made repeated attempts to cow him into submission. In one instance, after the trial and condemnation of a small group of Carthusian monks who had denied the king's new title, Cromwell made a visit to More, saying that 'as the Kyngis Hyghnesse wolde be gracyous to them that he founde comfortable, so his Grace wolde folow the course of hys laws toward such as he shall fynde obstynate', and—in a clear reference to the monks even then awaiting execution—that More's 'demeanour in that matter was of a thyng that of likelyhode made now other men so styffe therin as they be'. This account, contained in a letter from More to his daughter Margaret, hinted at his weariness after fourteen months in prison:

> I am ... the Kyngis trew faythfull subiect and daily bedesman and pray for hys Hyghnesse and all hys and all the realme. I do nobody harme, I say none harme, I thynk none harme,

but wysh everye bodye good. And yf thys be not ynough to kepe a man alyve in good fayth I long not to lyve.
> (*Correspondence*, 553)

More's trial took place on 1 July 1535, and its outcome was never in doubt despite the dubious grounds for his indictment. Although he was originally imprisoned for refusing to swear to the succession, in November 1534 parliament had passed the Act of Supremacy which gave the king the title of supreme head of the church in England, and More was put on trial for denying the king's new style. The witness in the government's case was Richard Rich, the solicitor-general, who claimed More had rejected the king's title in his presence on 12 June 1535. On Rich's testimony More was found guilty, although several of More's judges, notably the attorney-general, Sir Christopher Hales, were ready to convict him for his very silence which, Hales felt, was 'a sure token and demonstration of a corrupt and perverse nature, maligning and repyning against the statute' (Harpsfield, 185).

When the jury had returned the expected verdict, More was at last able to discharge his conscience. After denouncing Rich's perjury, he delivered a forceful and well-reasoned repudiation of temporal control over the church. The concept of royal supremacy, More said, was 'directly repugnant to the lawes of God and his holye Churche' (Harpsfield, 193), and England's separation from the universal church fractured the body of Christ. In support of this common corps of Christendom against the narrow, national views of England's bishops, More appealed to the unified teachings of all bishops which stretched over time and across national boundaries, and told his judges:

> For of the aforesaide holy Bisshopps I have, for every Bisshopp of yours, above one hundred; And for one Councell or Parliament of yours (God knoweth what maner of one), I have all the councels made these thousande yeres. And for this one kingdome, I have all other christian Realmes.
> (ibid., 196)

Sentenced to a traitor's death, More was executed at the Tower on 6 July 1535, his sentence being commuted to beheading out of deference to his former office. On the scaffold his wit flashed once more—to the officer who assisted him, More said 'I pray you, master Leiuetenaunte, see me salf uppe, and for my cominge downe let me shifte for myself' (Roper, 103). There were few witnesses. Margaret Clement, More's adopted daughter, was the only member of his household to watch the execution. Although accounts of More's death could not be published in England during Henry VIII's lifetime, a French account began circulating in London within weeks. It is generally assumed that More's body was buried in or around St Peter ad Vincula at the Tower of London. His head was entrusted to Margaret Roper and it was presumably buried with her in Chelsea church in 1544. When her husband William died and was buried in January 1578, Margaret's body and More's head were transferred to the Roper vault in St Dunstan's, Canterbury.

Aftermath News of More's execution shocked Europe. The emperor Charles V remonstrated with Sir Thomas Elyot, the English ambassador to the imperial court, saying that he 'wold rather have lost the best city of our dominions then have lost such a worthy counsellour' (Roper, 104). Tributes to More as a martyr were quickly forthcoming on the continent, where Tudor efforts to suppress outrage were ineffectual. Writing in Mainz in 1550, Maurice Chauncy included accounts of More and Fisher in his often-reprinted history of martyrs, as did the Italian Niccolo Circignani in 1584. At home even More's detractors admitted that the widespread popularity of his example would inspire future generations. Writing in 1563 the protestant martyrologist and apologist John Foxe predicted More's canonization. Tudor biographies of More by William Roper, Nicholas Harpsfield, and the enigmatic Ro.Ba. enjoyed widespread if underground circulation, and all but Roper's remained unpublished until the twentieth century. More's writings were suppressed until the reign of Mary, when William Rastell oversaw the publication of his complete English works (1557); but parts of his *History of Richard III* were incorporated, with attribution, in Hall's *Chronicle* in 1548, and an English translation of *Utopia* by Ralph Robinson appeared in 1551. It was not until well into Elizabeth's reign that his *Dialogue of Comfort* was reprinted, and not until the middle of the seventeenth century that any of his works, in either English or Latin, were printed in England. On the continent things were different: various individual works and letters were printed from time to time, *Utopia* was constantly reissued, and More's Latin works were published in Basel (1563), Louvain (1565), and Frankfurt (1689). Thomas Stapleton published a biography in Douai in 1588, based on his interviews with survivors of the More household and their descendants in exile, and Cresacre More published an account in Douai in 1631. The seminal biography of More by his son-in-law William Roper, containing many eyewitness accounts of More's life, was published in 'Paris' (a false imprint used by the Jesuits at St Omer, in Artois) in 1626.

More's reputation as a writer, in both Latin and English, had been long established by the time of his death, and his fame continued to grow. The later Elizabethans, removed by generations from the early Henrician struggles, were particularly appreciative of More's wit, and ranked him with Chaucer and Plato. Ben Jonson praised More's eloquence, and Michael Drayton referred to him as 'that ornament of England' (Drayton, 76). When Samuel Johnson sought examples of English eloquence for his dictionary in 1755 he turned to More's prose style, although by then his works were considered rare. Popular interest in More was kept alive mainly by his *Utopia* until T. E. Bridgett's biography in 1891 following More's beatification by Pope Leo XIII in 1886. He was canonized in 1935 by Pope Pius XI, the same year as R. W. Chambers's masterly biography framed More's life and martyrdom as a drama of human freedom under tyranny. Following the success of the brilliant play by Robert Bolt, *A Man for All Seasons* (1960), and the highly popular film adaptation under Fred Zinnemann's direction in 1966, More became well known on both sides of the Atlantic. Although sporadic attempts

had been made to offer More's writings to a broader public, it was not until 1958, twenty years after it dedicated a chapel to More, that Yale University founded the More project, which brought critical editions of all his works to an international readership. One of the consequences of this expanded interest in More was a renewed scrutiny of his unyielding activities against heretics and the legalistic, if not politically opportunistic strategies he employed in the defence of his principles. Because of this, his reputation is now as controversial as at any time since his death. Significantly, More's career as a politician led Pope John Paul II to pronounce him the patron saint of politicians on 5 November 2000. His involvement in many fields—literature, politics, education, religion—and his prolific output have ensured that interest in More has increased rapidly among scholars of all aspects of early modern Europe, and his engaging personality and the drama of his death have won for him a devoted following worldwide.   SEYMOUR BAKER HOUSE

Sources St Thomas More, *The Yale edition of the complete works of St Thomas More*, 15 vols. (1963–97) · *The correspondence of Sir Thomas More*, ed. E. Rogers (1947) · *St Thomas More: selected letters*, ed. E. Rogers (1961) · W. Roper, *The lyfe of Sir Thomas Moore, knighte*, ed. E. Vaughan Hitchcock, EETS (1935) · T. Stapleton, *The life and illustrious martyrdom of Sir Thomas More*, ed. E. E. Reynolds, trans. P. Hallett (1984) · N. Harpsfield, *The life and death of Sr Thomas Moore, knight*, ed. E. V. Hitchcock, EETS, original ser., 186 (1932) · G. Marc'hadour, *L'universe de Thomas More: chronologie critique de More, Erasmus, et leur époque (1477–1536)* (Paris, 1963) · R. W. Chambers, *Thomas More* (1935) · E. E. Reynolds, *The trial of St Thomas More* (1964) · E. E. Reynolds, *The field is won: the life and death of Saint Thomas More* (1968) · J. Guy, *The public career of Sir Thomas More* (1980) · J. Guy, *Thomas More* (2000) · B. Gogan, *The common corps of Christendom: ecclesiological themes in the writing of Sir Thomas More* (1982) · D. Baker-Smith, *More's 'Utopia'* (1991) · A. Fox, *Thomas More: history and providence* (1982) · A. Fox, *Politics and literature in the reigns of Henry VII and Henry VIII* (1989) · E. McCutcheon, *My dear Peter: the 'ars poetica' and hermeneutics for More's 'Utopia'* (Angers, 1983) · L. Martz, *Thomas More: the search for the inner man* (1990) · J. Boswell, *Sir Thomas More in the English Renaissance* (1994) · R. W. Gibson, *Sir Thomas More: a preliminary bibliography of his works and of Moreana to the year 1750* (1961) · A. Geritz, *Thomas More: an annotated bibliography of criticism, 1935–1997* (1998) · *LP Henry VIII* · R. Sylvester, ed., *St Thomas More: action and contemplation* (1972) · S. House, 'Sir Thomas More and holy orders: More's views of the English clergy both secular and regular', PhD diss., U. St Andr., 1987 · P. Ackroyd, *The life of Thomas More* (1997) · *Opus epistolarum Des. Erasmi Roterodami*, ed. P. S. Allen and others, 12 vols. (1906–58) · *Collected works of Erasmus*, ed. W. K. Ferguson and others, [86 vols.] (1974–) · J. B. Trapp and H. Schulte Herbrüggen, 'The King's Good Servant': Sir Thomas More, 1477/8–1535 (1977) [exhibition catalogue, NPG, 25 Nov 1977 – 12 March 1978] · M. Drayton, *Englands heroicall epistles* (1597)

Archives BL, MSS Arundel 43, 152, 249 · BL, Cotton MSS, Caligula B, D, E · BL, Cotton MSS, Cleopatra E · BL, Cotton MSS, Galba B · BL, Cotton MSS, Titus B, D · BL, Cotton MSS, Vespasian F · BL, MSS Harley 902, 6989 · BL, MS Royal 17 D XIV · BL, MS Sloane 1825 · Bodl. Oxf., Corpus Christi College D · Bodl. Oxf., Ballard 72 · Bodl. Oxf., Balliol 354 · Bodl. Oxf., Bod. 431 · Deventer Library, Deventer, letters to Erasmus, Deventer MS 91 · PRO, State Papers, Henry VIII · Royal College and Seminary of Corpus Christi, Valencia, holograph of *De Tristitia Christi*

Likenesses H. Holbein the younger, coloured chalks, 1526–7, Royal Collection · H. Holbein the younger, oils, 1527, Frick Collection, New York [*see illus.*] · H. Holbein the younger, group portrait, pen and ink, *c.*1527–1528 (*Thomas More, his father and his household*), Oeffentliche Kunstsammlung Basel · R. Lockey, group portrait, oils, c.1590–1599 (More and his household), Nostell Priory, Yorkshire · R. Lockey, group portrait, oils, c.1595–1600 (after *Sir Thomas More and his descendants* by H. Holbein), NPG · C. Bevis, bronze statue, 1969, Chelsea · H. Holbein the younger, oils, second version, NPG · medals, BM · portrait (after H. Holbein the younger), NPG

Wealth at death estates forfeited to crown upon attainder

More, Thomas (c.1586–1623). *See under* More, Henry (c.1587–1661).

More, Thomas (d. 1685), author, was the son of John More of Paynes Farm, Taynton, near Burford, Oxfordshire. More claimed the name 'Thomas de Eschallers De la More' and descent from 'the Eschallers of Whaddon, near Royston, Cambridgeshire', providing a pedigree on the title-page of his *The English Catholike Christian* (1649). This appears to be accurate for several generations of the Scaler family, which gave its name to a manor of Whaddon. A certificate from Merton College, Oxford, printed by More in 1649, states that he was admitted 'twenty years ago' and stayed for five years. More is officially listed as matriculating on 22 June 1632, so it seems he had entered originally as a child servitor; a pledge by his father to pay chamber costs at St Alban Hall, dated 22 March 1633 or 1634, may indicate the date of his leaving Merton. However, it seems that he did not take a degree.

On leaving Oxford, More lived in London and studied law. Admitted to Gray's Inn as a student on 23 June 1637, he was called to the bar on 20 May 1642. At the inn, More had many contests with 'papists, Arminians, self knowing, conceited men and others popishly affected in the society wherein I live', and sought to defend 'the honour, the wisdom and justice of the proceedings of the High Court of Parliament', but his opponents labelled him 'a time-server, a puritan, a Brownist, an ignoramus, if not a separatist, a schismatic, a heretic, and one that had the spirit of giddiness' (More, *English Catholike Christian*, 35–6). More joined the parliamentary army, and tells us he suffered nine weeks' imprisonment in Oxford Castle. He served from 10 January to 4 December 1643 as a cornet of the life guard of General Thomas Fairfax, earl of Essex, then, until 2 July 1644, as lieutenant to Captain Richard Aylworth's troop in Edward Massey's regiment of horse, serving afterwards in a reformado cavalry regiment, before returning on 28 October 1644 to the life guard, where he remained until 5 May 1645. More gives this information in a pamphlet of 1649, printed in an effort to secure the several hundred pounds still due for his long tour of duty.

According to Anthony Wood, More was 'naturally or hereditarily crazed' and had 'an high conceit of his own wit and good parts'; Wood considered that his mental powers were not improved by frequent recourse to drink, and that as a result of this unpromising combination he failed in both the army and the law (Wood, *Ath. Oxon.*, 4.179). Was Wood right about More's sanity? The preface to *The English Catholike Christian*, signed from 'my quarters at Spaldwick in Huntingdonshire, 22 Feb 1646', is certainly very eccentric, but most of More's literary output is quite reasonable. The passages written in 1641 record his opposition to episcopacy: 'the High Commission, with the whole regiment of its subsidiary offices; likewise deaneries, and chapters with their dependencies, are all contrary to God's word' (More, *English Catholike Christian*, 7). There is a complaint against 'sluggish drones in our universities, I mean those masters and fellows of colleges who misemploy their wealth' (ibid., 11); there are thoughts about law and the prerogative—though 'the King can do no wrong', nevertheless 'the King's prerogative, we know, is bounded with the rules of God's word, and impaled within the limits of the laws of the realm' (ibid., 18); and there is an attack on unlearned and unscrupulous physicians who 'haunt markets and publick meetings and so become juglers of mens purses' (ibid., 27). It may be that his protracted struggle to win payment of his arrears made Thomas bitter and obsessive. During the war he lost his brother William in the west, 'died a prisoner by the barbarous usage of Sir Richard Grenville, 1643', and his father, 'vilely intreated by ... desperate cavaliers that constantly quartered at his house, in the grief whereof he died 1645'. In 1649 he urged 'the elect brethren this day ... to pray for the eternal salvation of his brother Francis More, a distracted poor distressed citizen of London inhabiting in the Hospital of Bethlem' (More, *True Old News*, sig. A2). Perhaps this illness affected his own mental state, or perhaps it was through association with his brother that More 'lived always after under the character of mad-man' (Wood, *Ath. Oxon.*, 4.179).

More had signed *True Old News* on 15 June from 'my study in Coney Court of Grayes Inn'. We know nothing certainly about his later activities. Remarkably, of a man he diagnosed as both conceited and insane, Wood wrote that More was, when sober, 'of moderate and excellent discourse'; Dr Robert Skinner, successively bishop of Oxford and Worcester, was so taken in by this enigmatic figure as to ordain him, but later, hearing of More's unsavoury character, regretted his decision (Wood does not tell us if More remained in orders). Even if we accept that this has some basis in truth, it is likely that, once Skinner learned of More's lack of a degree and his long background in the parliamentarian army, he would have found in them ample reason for regret. It seems that, here as elsewhere, Wood may have been indulging his spite against a character he disliked, and who, as he dismissively recorded, 'had one of his ribs broken, in his mad fits, by a fall down stairs at Burford, died of it about Michaelmas' in 1685 (Wood, *Ath. Oxon.*, 4.180). We do not know how much of this is true, though More must have been aged about sixty-five at the time of this fall. He was buried at Taynton, Oxfordshire.   STEPHEN WRIGHT

Sources T. More, *The English Catholike Christian* (1649) [E556/21] · T. More, *True old news, as it may appear by several papers and certificates* (1649) · Wood, *Ath. Oxon.*, new edn, vol. 4 · Foster, *Alum. Oxon.* · J. Foster, ed., *Admissions to Gray's Inn* (1889) · R. J. Fletcher, ed., *The pension book of Gray's Inn*, 1 (1901), 348

More, Thomas (1722–1795), Jesuit, was born on 19 September 1722, the eldest of the six children of Thomas More (1692?–1739) and his wife, Catherine (d. 1767), daughter of

Peter Giffard of Black Ladies and Chillington, Staffordshire. The Mores lived at Barnborough Hall in the West Riding of Yorkshire. Two sons, Thomas and Christopher (1729–1781), became Jesuits; Basil died young. Of the three daughters, Catherine died unmarried, Elizabeth [*see below*] joined the Austin canonesses at Bruges, and Bridget married twice and had descendants, but Thomas was the last descendant in the direct male line of Sir Thomas More (1478–1535), lord chancellor of England.

Thomas More's early education was at the English College, St Omer, in France. In 1741 he went to the Scots College at Douai for further studies; the entry in the college diary reads 'ultimus haeres in linea directa Thomae More Cancellarii' ('the last heir in the direct line of Chancellor Thomas More'; *Records of the Scots Colleges*, 83). In 1752 he entered the noviciate of the English Jesuits at Watten in France. He studied at Liège College from 1754 until his ordination as priest about 1760. In 1763 he went to England and lived in London in Gloucester Street, and later in Little Ormonde Street, Queen Square, for many years. Apart from pastoral work, his duty was to care for the financial affairs of the English Jesuits and the funds needed for their work. A special problem was that created by the loans made by the English Jesuits and some of their friends to the French Jesuit Antoine La Valette, who traded in the produce—coffee and sugar—of the lands in the mission of Martinique in the West Indies. He went bankrupt in 1756. In addition to the financial losses, the English Jesuits lost the English College, St Omer, and Watten when the *parlement* of Paris brought about the destruction of the society in France in 1762.

In 1769 Thomas More was appointed provincial superior of the English Jesuits. His duty was to govern the 140 Jesuits in England and Wales, as well as those in the English houses on the continent and in the mission in the colony of Maryland in America. These were the years when hostility to the Jesuits at the Bourbon courts of France, Spain, and Naples was bringing pressure on the pope to suppress the Jesuits throughout the world. When the Brief of Suppression was published in August 1773 More ceased to be provincial superior, and the Jesuits in England and Wales became the subjects of the four vicars apostolic.

From the suppression until the restoration of the society by Pius VII in 1814 the English Jesuits preserved their own organization and consulted together in congresses, appointing officials to manage their affairs. Much respected by all, Thomas More reluctantly allowed himself to be persuaded to act with another as administrator of their affairs, a post he held from 1776 to 1784. He was in Bath in 1787, where he baptized his great-nephew Richard Fitzgerald, and in 1793 retired there, where his widowed sister, Bridget Dalton, lived. He died in Bath on 20 May 1795. His burial was in the old St Joseph's Catholic chapel in Trenchard Street, Bristol, where a tablet was erected in his memory. He left the bulk of his estate to his sister Bridget, but other family members, including his other sister, Prioress Mary Augustina More, received legacies too.

More's Jesuit contemporaries thought highly of him.

One of them, Joseph Reeves, secretary of the congress of 1776, wrote

> Some proposals to that effect [calling the congress] had long been expected from Mr Thomas More to whom all looked up with respect and whom all considered as the head of our … brethren, but … the humble and unassuming Mr More declined taking the lead until the exigencies of our disorganized state compelled him to come forward. (Restoration papers, fol. 9*v*)

More could be said to have lacked decision at a time of unprecedented crisis; but alternatively his conduct shows an example of calm when it was necessary to adapt to a changing world.

More's sister **Elizabeth More** [*name in religion* Mary Augustina] (*d.* 1807) joined the English Austin (Augustinian) canonesses at Bruges about 1752, taking the name Mary Augustina, and succeeded Olivia Darell as prioress in 1766. She offered bed and board to Jesuits expelled from the great and little colleges at Bruges following the suppression of the society in 1773, and sheltered or arranged lodgings for the members of other orders whose houses in the Austrian Netherlands were suppressed by Joseph II in the 1780s. At the onset of the Revolutionary War she began negotiations to find a refuge for the canonesses in England, and on 15 June 1794 left Bruges with the majority of the canonesses for London, arriving on 12 July. From there they moved to Hengrave Hall, Suffolk—a house belonging to a Catholic minor nobleman, Sir Thomas Gage, bt. While there, Elizabeth More relaxed the usual rules of enclosure to allow the protestant inhabitants to see the nuns in chapel; they earned money by embroidery, and received a licence to keep a school. This openness did much to help reduce protestant apprehensions. Following the treaty of Amiens, the community voted on 27 March 1802 to return to Bruges. The *Bury Gazette* paid tribute to 'the courtesy shown to their visitors by the sequestered females and their amiable patroness, Mrs. More' (Durrant, 395). Elizabeth returned to the Bruges convent in November 1802 and remained there for the rest of her life. She died there on 23 March 1807, and was buried at the convent. She left a vertebra of her ancestor Sir Thomas More to the convent; she also owned Sir Thomas's rosary ring.

GEOFFREY HOLT

Sources G. Holt, 'Haeres … Thomae More Cancellari; Fr Thomas More, 1722–95', *Recusant History*, 24 (1998), 76–88 • H. Foley, ed., *Records of the English province of the Society of Jesus*, 7 vols. in 8 (1875–83), vol. 5, pp. 702–4; vol. 7, pp. 520–21 • G. Holt, *The English Jesuits in the age of reason* (1993), 154–9 • G. Holt, *William Strickland and the suppressed Jesuits* (1988), 110–11 • P. J. Anderson, ed., *Records of the Scots colleges at Douai, Rome, Madrid, Valladolid and Ratisbon*, New Spalding Club, 30 (1906), 83 • G. Holt, *The English Jesuits, 1650–1829: a biographical dictionary*, Catholic RS, 70 (1984), 169–70 • Gillow, *Lit. biog. hist.*, 5.94 • G. Holt, *St Omers and Bruges colleges, 1593–1773: a biographical dictionary*, Catholic RS, 69 (1979), 184 • J. Kirk, *Biographies of English Catholics in the eighteenth century*, ed. J. H. Pollen and E. Burton (1909), 169 • J. C. H. Aveling, *Catholic recusancy in the city of York, 1558–1791*, Catholic RS, monograph ser., 2 (1970), 389 • E. H. Burton, *The life and times of Bishop Challoner, 1691–1781*, 2 vols. (1909), vol. 2, pp. 162–70 • *The manuscripts of the earl of Westmorland*, HMC, 13 (1885); repr. (1906), 191 • Restoration papers, Jesuit British Province Archives,

London · J. A. Williams, ed., *Post-Reformation Catholicism in Bath*, 2 vols., Catholic RS, 65–6 (1975–6), vol. 1, p. 73; vol. 2, p. 40 · C. Durrant, *A link between Flemish mystics and English martyrs* (1925) · M. J. Mason, 'Nun of the Jerningham letters. Elizabeth Jerningham (1727–1807) and Frances Henrietta Jerningham (1745–1824), Augustinian canonesses at Bruges', *Recusant History*, 22 (1994–5), 350–69

Archives Archives of the British Province of the Society of Jesus, London, letters · Archives of the British Province of the Society of Jesus, London, papers · Archives of the British Province of the Society of Jesus, London, Restoration papers | Archives of the British Province of the Society of Jesus, London, College of St Augustine papers · Archives of the British Province of the Society of Jesus, London, English Province corresp. · Archives of the British Province of the Society of Jesus, London, Galloway letters · Archives of the British Province of the Society of Jesus, London, letters of bishops and cardinals · Lancs. RO, Thomas West papers, corresp. with Thomas West

Wealth at death approx. £2000 in legacies: will, 2 June 1794, *Westmorland manuscripts*

More [Moore], **Sir Thomas Laurence de la** (*fl.* 1327–1358), landowner and supposed chronicler, was the son of John Laurence de la More and a kinsman (*nepos*), possibly nephew, of Archbishop John *Stratford (*c.*1275–1348). Thomas's wife was called Isabel, a name also borne by Stratford's mother. The family came from Oxfordshire and in 1331 John granted a messuage in Little Haddon within Bampton parish to Thomas, his wife, and the heirs of Thomas. Nothing is known of Thomas's earlier life, and his principal importance derives from the fact that he was the eyewitness of an incident in Geoffrey Baker's *Chronicon*, and was for centuries assumed to be the author of a brief chronicle given the title *Vita et mors Edwardi secundi, Gallice conscripta a generosissimo milite Thoma de la Moore, et in Latinum reducta ab alio quodam eius synchrono* ('The life and death of Edward II, written in French by the most noble knight Thomas de la Moore, and rendered into Latin by another his contemporary'). First printed in 1603 by Camden in his *Anglica, Normannica, Hibernica, …*, it was re-edited for the Rolls Series by William Stubbs (1883) in the second volume of *Chronicles of the Reigns of Edward I and Edward II*. This chronicle, with its graphic details of Edward II's sufferings following his capture, was long regarded as a Latin translation of a French work by de la More, from which the *Chronicon* of Geoffrey Baker of Swinbrook, extending from 1303 to 1356, was thought to have been derived. Stubbs demonstrated that the *Vita et mors* is merely abstracted from Baker's *Chronicon*, though he deemed it possible that de la More's lost original might one day be recovered. E. M. Thompson rejected the notion of any such original. Its existence had been inferred from the passage in Baker where, in speaking of the deputation that went to Kenilworth in January 1327 to receive the king's abdication, he added effusively:

> You, noble knight, Sir Thomas de la More, with your wisdom and distinguished presence, being in attendance on the bishop of Winchester, were an ornament to the company; I am but the interpreter, as it were, of what you saw and wrote down in French. (Gransden, 38–9)

Thompson's interpretation is that Baker was merely acknowledging his indebtedness to de la More's account of a scene in which the latter played a subordinate part.

The putative author of his protégé's work was said by Camden in his preface to have belonged to a Gloucestershire family, and to have served Edward I, who knighted him. But William Stubbs showed that Baker's patron, who as a young man was in Bishop Stratford's entourage in 1327, can in fact be safely identified as one of the de la Mores from Northmoor in southern Oxfordshire, a few miles south-west of Oxford and some seven south-east of Swinbrook. As late as the mid-seventeenth century a Thomas de la More held land at Pagan's Court close to Swinbrook.

Thanks to John Stratford's influence, in November 1327 Thomas de la More was exempted for life from being put on assizes or appointed sheriff against his will, and two years later this relative, as bishop of Winchester, appointed him, as his 'dear and well-loved nephew', constable of Taunton Castle. He could also be the man named on a commission of 1336 following a petition by the abbess of Godstow. De la More sat as knight of the shire for Oxford in the parliaments of February and July 1338 and in the first two parliaments of 1340, when he served on the great committee appointed in the second session to sit from day to day until the business was finished and the petitions turned into statute. He was re-elected in 1343 and 1351. It was at his instance, Baker relates, that he wrote his shorter chronicle or *Chroniculum*, finished in 1347, and in his larger *Chronicon*, besides the passage already quoted, he once addresses him as *miles reverende*. It is likely, therefore, that de la More was still alive when Baker wrote the final lines of the *Chronicon* in 1358, and perhaps even in 1370 when a Thomas atte More was a witness in a proof of age at Bampton, Oxfordshire.

The *Vita et mors* exists in at least three Elizabethan transcripts: BL, Cotton MS Vitellius E.v, folios 261–70 (mutilated), perhaps copied by Samuel Daniel (d. 1619) and said to be from a transcript by Laurence Nowell; BL, Harley MS 310, folios 92–102; London, Inner Temple, Petyt MS 47, folios 303–14, formerly belonging to John Foxe the martyrologist. Its use by Holinshed and by Stow ensured that it became widely known.   ROY MARTIN HAINES

Sources BL, Cotton MS Vitellius E.v · BL, Harley MS 310 · Inner Temple Library, London, Petyt MS 47 · J. Stratford, bishop's register, Hants. RO, Winchester diocesan records, fol. 183v · W. Camden, ed., *Anglica, Normannica, Hibernica … * (1603) · W. Stubbs, ed., *Chronicles of the reigns of Edward I and Edward II*, 2 vols., Rolls Series, 76 (1882–3) · *Chronicon Galfridi le Baker de Swynebroke*, ed. E. M. Thompson (1889) · *RotP*, 2.531 · *Chancery records* · W. Stubbs, *The constitutional history of England in its origin and development*, 2 (1875), 2.383–4 · W. R. Williams, *The parliamentary history of the county of Oxford* (privately printed, Brecknock, 1899) · R. M. Haines, *Archbishop John Stratford: political revolutionary and champion of the liberties of the English church*, Pontifical Institute of Medieval Studies: Texts and Studies, 76 (1986) · R. M. Haines, *The church and politics in fourteenth-century England: the career of Adam Orleton, c. 1275–1345*, Cambridge Studies in Medieval Life and Thought, 3rd ser., 10 (1978) · A. Gransden, *Historical writing in England*, 2 (1982)

Archives BL, Cotton MS Vitellius E.v, fols. 261–270; Harley MS 310, fols. 92–102 · Inner Temple, London, Petyt MS 47

More [Peers], **William** (1471/2–1552), prior of Worcester, was the son of Richard and Ann Peers of the manor of le More in Lindridge parish, near Tenbury, Worcestershire. He took the name of his birthplace as his name in religion when in 1488, aged sixteen, he was admitted a Benedictine monk in Worcester Cathedral priory. There is no evidence that he went to university (the More of Worcester who studied at Oxford in the late fifteenth century was almost certainly Thomas More), but nevertheless from 1495 he held a series of obedientiary positions in the monastery, successively as fourth prior, cellarer, kitchener, and subprior. Finally on 9 October 1518 he was elected prior.

More played small part in national affairs, though in 1519 he attended the special chapter of the black monks summoned by Cardinal Wolsey to discuss measures for the reform of their order and in 1526 he entertained Princess Mary and the countess of Salisbury at Worcester for some weeks. His involvement in his priory was likewise restricted, as his extant journal, recording his day-by-day expenses and receipts, amply documents. From no later than 1524 he was normally resident on his manors of Battenhall, Crowle, and Grimley for at least two-thirds of the year. More was a careful manager of these properties and spent much money on building and repairs. He also made regular visits to London, principally for shopping; on one of these excursions he bought himself a very expensive mitre and pastoral staff, on another a gravestone. Leading what was essentially the life of a wealthy country squire, he became a JP, was generous with hospitality, travelled with a retinue of up to twenty-five men, and maintained a fool. All the year round he laid out small sums on plays and other entertainments; in June 1519, for instance, he gave 'rewards to Robin Whod and hys men for getheryng to tewksbury bruge' (Knowles, 116). He showed a kindly side to his personality in the gifts he made to his relatives and servants, while appropriately to his religious calling he gave plate and vestments to Worcestershire churches and money to the friars of Worcester. In 1527 he himself became a Franciscan tertiary.

Prior More's concern for the welfare of his own manors does not appear to have extended to that of his cathedral priory, where his prolonged absences allowed divisions and discontent to arise; indeed he exacerbated these when about 1528 he dismissed the cellarer in favour of a nominee of his own, thereby helping to create two parties among the monks. On 17 August 1534 all the inmates of the convent took the oath of supremacy, but any impression of unity this may have given was misleading. In the injunctions which Archbishop Cranmer issued in February 1535, following his metropolitical visitation of the diocese of Worcester in the previous summer, More was ordered to provide for a resident grammar teacher to offer basic education to the monks, to ensure that enough food was served, to provide attendants for the infirmary, and to avoid encouraging overmuch criticism of the monks by lay servants. Most striking of all was the simple injunction that he should 'show more kindness' to those under him. Acrimony persisted, however, and the royal visitation of July 1535 produced further charges by monks against the prior and one another, including allegations of treasonable words. Thomas Cromwell became involved, and More was taken into custody, probably in Gloucester Abbey. The accusations could not be sustained, and by 11 February 1536 he was back in Worcester, where his return immediately triggered further disputes. Hugh Latimer, bishop of Worcester, had already advised Cromwell against allowing More to resume his office, observing caustically that 'it were pity to trouble him in his age with a charge he was not able to discharge in his youth' (*LP Henry VIII*, vol. 10, no. 56). The minister clearly agreed with the bishop, and by 7 March More had resigned as prior. Generous provision was made for his retirement: the manor of Crowle for his residence, a quarterly pension, payment of his debts, and the right to take his personal possessions with him. He died at Alveston, near Stratford upon Avon, in September 1552 and was buried in the parish church there on the 16th. The effigy under which he had hoped to be buried was placed in Worcester Cathedral.

More shared the interest in classical and theological learning common to many of his monastic contemporaries and collected a large personal library of mostly printed books. Among the surviving volumes are two which bear his inscription, a commentary on Aristotle and the *De universalibus* of Duns Scotus. But it is the shortcomings of his rule which provide the most enduring memory left by this penultimate representative of the great tradition of priors of Worcester, during whose years in office 'the soul of Worcester Cathedral priory … departed before the body was removed' (Greatrex, 761).

ANTHONY MARETT-CROSBY

Sources E. S. Fagan, ed., *Journal of Prior William More*, Worcestershire Historical Society, 32 (1913–14) · J. Noake, *The monastery and cathedral of Worcester* (1866) · J. Greatrex, *Biographical register of the English cathedral priories of the province of Canterbury* (1997), 848–50 · D. Knowles [M. C. Knowles], *The religious orders in England*, another edn, 3 (1979) · G. R. Elton, *Policy and police: the enforcement of the Reformation in the age of Thomas Cromwell* (1972) · *LP Henry VIII*, vols. 7–10

Likenesses effigy, Worcester Cathedral

More, William (d. 1540/41), abbot of Walden and bishopsuffragan of Colchester, is recorded as the brother of John More of Whaddon, Cambridgeshire, esquire. He also had at least three sisters. He was educated at Cambridge, where he proceeded BCnL in 1531–2, having studied canon law for nine years previously. By 2 October 1534 he was a master in chancery, and also rector of Bradwell-juxta-Mare, Essex, and of Barnardiston, Norfolk; on 3 January 1535 he was collated to the prebend of Sutton in Marisco in Lincoln Cathedral. There is no record of his taking orders, and he is next recorded, on 13 August 1536, in a secular context, as steward to Lord Chancellor Audley. He had ecclesiastical ambitions, however, for with Audley's support he was then endeavouring to obtain promotion as suffragan bishop of Colchester within the diocese of London. His suit was successful, he was appointed on 26 September and consecrated by Archbishop Cranmer at the London Blackfriars on 20 October. On 10 August 1537, still styled only clerk, he was dispensed to hold the Benedictine abbey of Walden, and on 29 September following he was presented to the vicarage of Saffron Walden.

More's abbacy at Walden may have been intended to further the designs of his patron Audley, to whom the monastery and its lands were granted on 14 May 1538, less than two months after their surrender to the crown on 22 March. Audley subsequently obtained for More the archdeaconry of Leicester, probably in lieu of the pension of £200 which the chancellor had originally proposed that More should receive. He was formally collated on 24 September 1539. More remained suffragan and archdeacon until his death, and in his will, drawn up on 19 April 1540, he showed himself fully conscious of his ecclesiastical status. If the clergyman who buried him was 'a bisshop as I am', he was to receive a crozier, two rochets and a scarlet gown, as well as 20s., but 'any other seculler preest' was to have only a cap, gown, tippet, and 7s. 6d. Five hundred poor people were to have 1d. each, 'whiche I have in a boxe redy for the same purpose'. There were also bequests to his church, to relations and servants, and to 'the yomanry of my lorde chaunclers howse' (PRO, PROB 11/29, fol. 96r–v). His executor and residuary legatee was his steward John Cottun, but on 11 February 1541 administration was granted to John More, in the mistaken belief that William had died intestate. As a result the will was not proved until 15 November 1542.

MARY BATESON, *rev.* ANDREW A. CHIBI

Sources Venn, *Alum. Cant.*, 1/3.208 · J. E. Oxley, *The Reformation in Essex to the death of Mary* (1965) · Rymer, *Foedera*, 1st edn · R. Newcourt, *An ecclesiastical parochial history of the diocese of London*, 2 vols. (1708–10) · Wood, *Ath. Oxon.*, new edn, 2.754–5 · Cooper, *Ath. Cantab.*, 1.77 · will, PRO, PROB 11/29, fol. 96r–v · D. S. Chambers, *Faculty office registers, 1534–1549* (1966) · W. G. Searle, ed., *Grace book Γ* (1908) · *Fasti Angl., 1541–1857*, [Lincoln] · LP Henry VIII, vols. 11–15

More, Sir William (1520–1600). *See under* More, Sir Christopher (*b.* in or before 1483, *d.* 1549).

Morecambe, Eric [*real name* John Eric Bartholomew] (1926–1984), actor and comedian, was born in Morecambe, Lancashire, on 14 May 1926, the only child of George Bartholomew, a manual worker for the Morecambe and Heysham corporation, and his wife, Sarah (Sadie) Elizabeth Robinson. Educated at Euston Road elementary school, he was prompted by his mother to leave school at thirteen and embark on the professional stage as a child act.

In 1940, as a result of winning one of the many juvenile talent contests then in vogue, Eric Bartholomew earned a place in a touring 'discovery' show, *Youth Takes a Bow*, presented by Bryan Michie under the emergent impresario Jack Hylton. Coincidentally, Ernest Wiseman [*see* Wise, Ernie] was a fellow juvenile already engaged on the show. In 1941 Sadie Bartholomew inspired the pair to form a double act (at the Empire Theatre, Liverpool), but it was some years before they adjusted their roles with Eric predominantly as the comedian. The war intervened and Eric was drafted as a 'Bevin boy' in the mines; he was discharged unfit eleven months later. Upon Ernie's release

Eric Morecambe (1926–1984), by Arnold Newman, 1978 [left, with Ernie Wise]

from the merchant navy the couple resumed their partnership in 1947 in *Lord George Sanger's Variety Circus*. Over the next five years, now billed as Morecambe (the name taken from Bartholomew's birthplace) and Wise, they gradually broke into radio and television. In 1952 Morecambe married a dancer, Joan Dorothy, daughter of Harold Bartlett, a captain in the Royal Army Medical Corps. They had a son and a daughter of their own and they later adopted another son.

The critics' response to the first Morecambe and Wise television series, *Running Wild* (BBC, 1954), indicated that they had not yet discovered a winning combination. Soul-searching and experimentation filled their subsequent summer seasons and pantomimes. In 1958 they undertook a six-month variety tour of Australia. Upon their return, their act was purged of its brashness and relied more on subtlety.

Morecambe and Wise became regular guests on television variety shows, being at their most effective on Val Parnell's *Sunday Night at the London Palladium*. They felt at home on the ATV commercial network. By this time Morecambe's burgeoning genius as a comedian was making a mark. The first period of the long-running *The Morecambe and Wise Show* ran uninterruptedly on ATV between 1961 and 1968 and undoubtedly established them as national favourites. Their writers, Sid Green and Dick Hills, stimulated by Morecambe's limitless range, were inexhaustibly inventive. The first of many distinguished awards came in 1963 when Morecambe and Wise were chosen by the Guild of Television Producers and Directors as top television light entertainment personalities of the year.

In 1968 Eric Morecambe suffered a major heart attack, but he recovered sufficiently to continue the outstanding run of *The Morecambe and Wise Show*, which had now moved to the BBC and was aided by its more opulent budgets and the new scriptwriter, Eddie Braben. Meanwhile the pair had appeared many times on the *Ed Sullivan Show* in New York, and in several royal command performances. At Windsor they were favourites at royal family Christmas parties. Their three films for the Rank Organization—*The Intelligence Men* (1964), *That Riviera Touch* (1965), and *The Magnificent Two* (1966)—made noble attempts to translate their comedy on to the large screen. In 1979 Morecambe had to undergo open-heart surgery. During his convalescing periods he turned author: *Mr Lonely*, a novel, was published in 1981. Then followed two children's books—*The Reluctant Vampire* (1982) and *The Vampire's Revenge* (1983), which were subsequently translated into several languages. *Eric Morecambe on Fishing* (his main hobby) was published posthumously.

Morecambe was a director of Luton Town Football Club from 1969, retiring in 1975 to become a vice-president. He served as president of the Lord's Taverners between 1976 and 1979. He actively supported the Variety Club's charities, the Stars Organization for Spastics, the Sport Aid Foundation, and (among others) the British Heart Foundation. In 1976 he was appointed OBE and in the same year became a freeman of the City of London. Lancaster University conferred upon him an honorary degree of DLitt in 1977.

Morecambe's eyebrows arched over the upper rims of his spectacles like twin circumflexes of bewilderment and surprise; his chirpy head movements, like a sparrow's, showed him as always on the qui vive, while his baggy underlids hinted at the world-weariness and sadness of the clown. Apart from various running jokes, among them 'What d'you think of the show so far?' (audience: 'Rubbish!'), Morecambe did not cultivate catch-phrases for the sake of them, although some of his stock comments—'There's no answer to that!', 'My buddy Ern with the short fat hairy legs', 'What do I think of it? Not a lot'— and his habit in moments of endearment towards Wise of clapping both hands on his partner's cheeks will evoke memories of his style.

Morecambe and Wise, like Laurel and Hardy and Hope and Crosby, gave the double act a new dimension, moulding the archetypal 'straight man and comic' into a more complex but totally believable human relationship, and shared their art of being able to involve mass audiences in an enormous sense of fun. Morecambe possessed a needle-sharp awareness of the comic potential in any situation, and a comedic flexibility which enabled him, more even than past masters such as Robb Wilton and Jimmy James, to rebound off any number of characters on stage and so widen the comedy impact. No comedian can achieve greatness, however, unless he embodies those endearing human weaknesses which are the essence of laughter. This Morecambe did in his classic roles with Wise, as the one whose unquenchable exuberance often caused embarrassment, whose performance never quite matched his self-proclaimed ability, and whose sharp wit was used to cover up his ignorance or as a Parthian shot to rescue his self-esteem. Later in life he became more the nation's humorist, with prestigious people queuing up to be the buttress of his quips. Whatever the role, Eric Morecambe shared the talent of, for example, Will Fyfe and Gracie Fields, to inspire as much love and affection as

laughter. By the time of his death he was a national institution. He died from a heart attack on 28 May 1984 in Cheltenham General Hospital, to which he had been taken after performing at the Roses Theatre, Tewkesbury. He was survived by his wife.   DICK HILLS, *rev.*

Sources E. Morecambe and E. Wise, *Eric and Ernie* (1973) · G. Morecambe, *Funny man* (1982) · personal knowledge (1990) · private information (1990) · *The Times* (29 May 1984) · *CGPLA Eng. & Wales* (1985) · J. Waterman, 'Double vision', *The Listener* (16 March 1978) **Archives** FILM BFI NFTVA, *Omnibus*, BBC1, 23 Dec 1998 · BFI NFTVA, *Parkinson*, BBC1, 3 Sept 1999 · BFI NFTVA, performance footage |SOUND BL NSA, 'interview', 1976, B7643/02 · BL NSA, documentary recordings · BL NSA, performance recordings **Likenesses** A. Newman, bromide print, 1978 (with Ernie Wise), NPG [*see illus.*] **Wealth at death** £517,205: probate, 15 Jan 1985, *CGPLA Eng. & Wales*

Morehead, Charles (1807–1882), physician, was born in Edinburgh on 8 February 1807, the second son of Robert Morehead, rector of Easington in the North Riding of Yorkshire, and Margaret, daughter of the Revd Dr Charles Wilson, professor of church history at the University of St Andrews. His brother, William Ambrose *Morehead, rose to the highest position in the Madras civil service. Charles attended the Royal High School, Edinburgh, and after taking a short course of lectures in Glasgow he went on to study medicine at Edinburgh University.

Morehead was an earnest student, and at Edinburgh his zeal for clinical medicine attracted the attention of Professor William Pulteney Alison, whose clinical clerk he became. After gaining his MD at Edinburgh in 1828 he continued his medical studies in Paris under Pierre Louis. In 1829 he entered the Bombay medical service, and served on the personal staff of Sir Robert Grant, governor of Bombay. After Grant's death in 1838 Morehead was appointed to the European and native general hospitals of Bombay. He was a supporter of medical education for Indians, and on the establishment of the board of native education in 1840 he was appointed secretary, a post he held for five years.

In 1844 he married Harriet Anne, daughter of the Venerable George Barnes, first archdeacon of Bombay and founder of the Bombay Education Society.

Owing to Morehead's efforts the Grant Medical College was built at Bombay in 1845 as a memorial to Grant. Here Indians were educated for independent medical practice. Morehead was appointed the first principal of the Grant College, and was its first professor of the principles and practice of medicine. He was also the first physician of the Jamsetjee Jeejeebhoy Hospital, founded in Bombay in 1843 by the philanthropist Sir Jamsetjee Jeejeebhoy and the government. It was here that the students of the college received their clinical instruction. Morehead held these positions until 1859, when he returned to Europe. On 6 September 1861 he was appointed honorary surgeon to her majesty. He retired from service in June 1862.

Morehead founded the Medical and Physical Society of Bombay, and served as president from 1837 to 1859. He also organized the Grant College Medical Society, which served to unify former students of the college. As an author Morehead was known for his works discussing medical practice and disease of Europeans in India. Based on years of clinical experience his *Researches on the Diseases of India*, first published in 1856, passed through two editions and was considered by contemporaries to be a standard authority. He was a fellow of the Royal College of Physicians (1860), a fellow of the Edinburgh Royal Society (1866), and in recognition of his services to Indian education he was created a companion in the Order of the Indian Empire in 1881. Morehead died at Wilton Castle, Redcar, Yorkshire, the home of his brother-in-law Sir Charles Lowther, on 24 August 1882.

A. J. ARBUTHNOT, rev. CLAIRE E. J. HERRICK

Sources *Edinburgh Medical Journal*, 28 (1882–3), 379–82 · *The Lancet* (16 Sept 1882), 468 · *BMJ* (23 Sept 1882), 601 · H. A. Haines, *Memorial of the life and work of Charles Morehead* (1884) · *The Times* (28 Aug 1882) · A. Boyle and F. Bennet, eds., *The Royal Society of Edinburgh: 100 medical fellows elected 1841–1882* (1983), vol. 4 of *Scotland's cultural heritage* (1981–4) · *CGPLA Eng. & Wales* (1882) · *IGI*
Likenesses R. J. Lane, lithograph (after photograph by H. Watkins), Wellcome L. · drawing, repro. in Haines, *Memorial*
Wealth at death £9315 17s. 9d.: confirmation, 10 Oct 1882, *CCI*

Morehead [Moorhead], **William** (1637–1692), Church of England clergyman, was born at Lombard Street, London, the son of William Morehead, and a nephew of General *Monck. Morehead entered Winchester College at the age of eleven and proceeded to New College, Oxford, where he graduated BA on 3 May 1660 and MA on 14 January 1663. In 1657 he had entered Gray's Inn. Having been elected a fellow of New College in 1668, he resigned in 1672.

Morehead wrote a poetic tract on Monck's departure from Scotland for England in 1660. The title-page runs: *Lachrymae sive valedictio Scotiae sub discessum clarissimi, &c. gubernatoris domini Georgii Monachi in Angliam revocati, authore Gulielmo Moorhead Nov. Coll. Oxon. soc: The tears and valediction of Scotland upon the departing of her governor the Lord-General Monck*. The verse is in both Latin and English, the two renderings appearing on opposite pages. There may be a pun on 'monarchy' in 'Monachi'. Engraved portraits of both Charles II and of Monck are inserted, the latter being the work of Richard Gaywood.

Morehead is also credited with an anonymous translation, published posthumously, of a famous treatise of Giordano Bruno. Bruno's work, first published in 1584, bears the title *Spaccio de la bestia trienfante*. It has Paris as its place of publication, but was most likely printed in London. The English version bore the title *Spaccio de la bestia trienfante, or, The expulsion of the triumphant beast, translated from the Italian*. It was published on the continent in 1707 and at London in 1713. The deist John Toland was allegedly instrumental in its publication, and the translation has been attributed to him. According, however, to the testimony of the well-known bookseller Samuel Paterson, the work was translated by a William Morehead, but this Morehead, on Paterson's account, lived far into the eighteenth century, more than fifty years after the death of Monck's nephew.

Morehead was presented to the college living of Bucknell, Oxfordshire, by the warden and fellows of New College (14 July 1670), and also held the living of Whitfield in Northamptonshire, to which he was presented by Sir Thomas Spencer of Yarnton, Oxfordshire, lord of the manor. He chiefly resided there, employing a curate at Bucknell, which prompted complaints from parishioners and a petition to the bishop in 1680 or 1681 for a resident minister. The petition seems to have produced some effect on Morehead, who died at Bucknell on 18 February 1692, and was buried there.

CHARLOTTE FELL-SMITH, rev. WILLY MALEY

Sources Foster, *Alum. Oxon.* · *DNB* · Wood, *Ath. Oxon.*, new edn · T. F. Kirby, *Winchester scholars: a list of the wardens, fellows, and scholars of … Winchester College* (1888)

Morehead, William Ambrose (1805–1863), East India Company servant, was born on 17 October 1805, in the parish of St Cuthbert, Midlothian, the eldest son of Robert Morehead DD, rector of Easington, Yorkshire, and his wife, Margaret, *née* Wilson. Charles *Morehead (1807–1882), of the Bombay medical service and honorary surgeon to Queen Victoria, was a younger brother. William was educated privately at Ashburnham House, Blackheath, under Mr Wigan, and, from 1822 to 1824, at the East India College at Haileybury. He arrived at Madras on 16 October 1825. In March 1828 he was appointed assistant to the principal collector of North Arcot and later the same year became registrar of the district court of Chingleput. On 12 January 1830, at Chingleput, he married Catherine Magrath, with whom he had two daughters and a son. In January 1836 he was appointed assistant judge at Chingleput.

Morehead returned to England for three years from the end of 1836, but otherwise remained at Chingleput until 1846, becoming civil and sessions judge on 15 August 1843. In September 1846 he was appointed officiating puisne judge of the *sadr adalat*, the highest of the East India Company's courts, in which position he was confirmed on 23 March 1847. In 1850 he was one of two Indian judicial officers sent, at the request of the Colonial Office, to Ceylon to conduct an inquiry into Lord Torrington's suppression of the uprising of 1848. Morehead and his colleague avoided overt personal criticism of Torrington, a whig appointee with no previous experience of colonial administration, but were sufficiently critical of his administration in general to force his recall.

In December 1855 Morehead was appointed provisional member of the Madras legislative council. He took twelve months' leave in 1856–7 because of poor health, after which, on 29 October 1857, he assumed his seat as the third member in council and became chief judge of the *sadr adalat*. Under the invigorating governorship of Sir Charles Trevelyan (1859–60) Morehead served on the four-man commission to formulate principles of judicial reform for Madras. On the question of financial reform, Morehead, like Trevelyan, opposed the range of income and professional taxes by which the government of India hoped to recoup the costs of the recent uprising and he wrote a trenchant minute lamenting the impolicy of imposing novel taxes on India so soon after the upheavals of 1857. Nevertheless, when Trevelyan published his council's minutes as a way of alerting the home authorities to the local opposition to Calcutta's proposals, Morehead distanced himself from Trevelyan and declared that had he known of his intentions he would have withdrawn his own contributions from the council table.

In May 1860, upon Trevelyan's recall for indiscipline, Morehead served for a month as acting governor pending the arrival of Sir Henry Ward. When Ward died later the same year, Morehead again acted as governor for the six months prior to Sir William Denison's arrival in early 1862. During this period it fell to him to introduce the licence tax which had sparked so much opposition, and to effect heavy reductions in the standing army.

Morehead's term on the Madras council expired in 1862. Lord Canning, impressed by his loyalty, had offered him a seat on the central legislative council, but Morehead declined it on the grounds of his failing health and, with his wife, finally left India in October 1862. He was given an unusually warm send-off by the Indian and European leaders of Madras's population, who, still smouldering over the recall of Trevelyan and the 'tyranny' of the government of India, had regarded Morehead as one of their own and much preferred him as governor to Denison. The Morehead law scholarship at Presidency College was established by public subscription in his honour. For the two years before his retirement Morehead had served as vice-chancellor of Madras University. He was also a vice-president of the Madras Literary Society, vice-patron of the local agriculture and horticultural society, and a member of the financial board of the Free Church of Scotland and presbytery of Madras.

Morehead died at his residence at 12 Oxford Terrace, Edinburgh, on 1 December 1863, survived by his wife. He was buried in the Dean cemetery in Edinburgh, where in 1866 a number of his friends erected an imposing cross of Peterhead granite in his memory.   KATHERINE PRIOR

Sources W. Thomas, *The Asylum Press Almanac, 1862* (1861) • *Madras Times* (6 Oct 1862), 946 • *Madras Times* (7 Oct 1862), 950 • B. S. Baliga, *Studies in Madras administration*, 1 (1960) • J. J. Paul, *The legal profession in colonial south India* (1991) • ecclesiastical records, BL OIOC • BL OIOC, Haileybury MSS • *The Times* (3 Dec 1863), 1 • C. F. Brackenbury, *Madras district gazetteers: Cuddapah* (1915) • C. E. Buckland, *Dictionary of Indian biography* (1906) • *DNB* • *The Scotsman* (9 Jan 1866)

Likenesses portrait, 1862?; formerly at Madras Banqueting Hall, 1894

Wealth at death £14,144 16s. 3d.: probate, 15 Jan 1864, NA Scot., SC70/1/119, 260–7

Morel, Edmund Dene [*formerly* Georges Edmond Pierre Achille Morel de Ville] (1873–1924), campaigner on international issues and journalist, was born in avenue d'Eylau, Paris, on 10 July 1873, the only child of Edmond Morel de Ville (*c.*1848–1877), a middle-ranking French civil servant of good family, and his wife, Emmeline de Horne, an Englishwoman of Quaker ancestry from East Anglia. His father died when he was four and Morel was raised by his mother, who quarrelled with her French relatives, changed her name to Deville, and taught English and music so as to be able to send him to be educated at Madras

House, Eastbourne, and Bedford modern school, until her failing health forced his return to Paris at the age of fifteen to obtain paid employment in a bank. In 1891, however, the offer of a clerkship in the Liverpool office of Elder Dempster, a shipping firm which traded with the Congo Free State, enabled Morel and his mother to return to England.

In 1896, the year he was naturalized, Morel married (on 26 August) Mary Florence Yonge Richardson, daughter of John William Richardson, a Liverpool printer. They had four sons and one daughter. To help support his family he began writing articles calling for the defence of free trade in west Africa against the protectionism of the encroaching French and the special privileges of the Royal Niger Company. Though initially little more than special pleading for Liverpool shipping interests, his journalism taught him radical attitudes, most notably a hatred of the Foreign Office, for according so low a priority to west Africa, and a sympathy for African culture, which was reinforced by meeting the traveller Mary Kingsley in 1899.

By 1900 Morel's radicalism had prevailed over his loyalty to his employer. In that year he began campaigning against the brutal system of forced labour employed by Leopold II, king of the Belgians, as absolute personal ruler of the Congo Free State, even though this forced him to leave Elder Dempster, where he had become head of the Congo department. In 1903 he launched a paper, *West African Mail* (later the *African Mail*), as a vehicle for his campaign, and in 1904 also founded the Congo Reform Association with Roger Casement. These made his name—which by now was E. D. Morel—but also revealed his bellicosity (he favoured sending a gunboat to the Congo), capacity for self-deception (he forgot his own previous defence of the Leopoldian system), and vanity (he resented sharing the limelight even with activists of longer standing). His Congo campaign achieved its preliminary aim in 1908 when the free state was handed over to Belgium, and thereafter had some success in pressing the latter to adopt specific reforms, despite the reluctance of the British and French governments to antagonize Belgium, on whose friendship their European policies depended.

Within a month of the testimonial luncheon of 29 May 1911 which concluded his Congo activities, the Agadir crisis gave Morel a new cause that enabled him to develop his opposition to British and French policy. In 1912 he published an impressively researched study, *Morocco in Diplomacy*, and became Liberal candidate for Birkenhead. Sympathetic to Germany, hostile to the entente with France, and unmoved by Belgium's plight, he campaigned for neutrality in 1914 and, as soon as this effort failed, launched the Union of Democratic Control (UDC), which opposed annexationist war aims and later also called for a negotiated peace.

Morel's secretaryship of the UDC, which he held until his death, cost him his Liberal candidacy and led to six months' imprisonment for a technical breach of the Defence of the Realm Act. It also brought him, via the Independent Labour Party, which he joined in April 1918, into the Labour Party, whose international thinking was considerably shaped by the UDC's criticisms of the treaty of Versailles (and French attempts to enforce it) and even the League of Nations. But, although winning a famous victory over Winston Churchill to become Labour MP for Dundee in November 1922, he was passed over for the foreign secretaryship of the first Labour government fourteen months later. This disappointment was all the more galling for the fact that the prime minister and eight other cabinet ministers had been his colleagues in the UDC; and, unmollified by nomination for the Nobel peace prize, Morel became almost as bitter a critic of the Ramsay MacDonald government as of its predecessors. His health never recovered after his imprisonment, and he died at Aller Farm, North Bovey, Devon, from a heart attack on 12 November 1924, shortly after retaining his seat in the general election. He was survived by his wife. His funeral was held at St Martin-in-the-Fields, London, on 25 November.   MARTIN CEADEL, rev.

Sources C. Cline, E. D. Morel, 1873–1924: the strategies of protest (1980) · F. S. Cocks, E. D. Morel: the man and his work (1920) · The Times (14 Nov 1924) · WW (1908–24) · M. Swartz, The Union of Democratic Control in British politics during the First World War (1971) · m. cert. · CGPLA Eng. & Wales (1925)
Archives BLPES, London, corresp. and papers | BL, corresp. with C. W. Dilke, Add. MS 43897 · BLPES, corresp. with the independent labour party · Bodl. Oxf., letters to Arthur Ponsonby · Bodl. RH, corresp. with F. E. Colenso · Bodl. RH, corresp. with John Holt · Bodl. RH, corresp. with Sir Matthew Nathan · HLRO, corresp. with John St Loe Strachey · McMaster University, Hamilton, Ontario, Bertrand Russell archives, corresp. with Bertrand Russell · Nuffield Oxf., corresp. with Lord Emmott · U. Birm. L., corresp. with W. A. Cadbury · U. Hull, Union of Democratic Control MSS · U. Newcastle, Robinson L., corresp. with Walter Runciman · U. Newcastle, Robinson L., corresp. with C. P. Trevelyan
Likenesses photograph, repro. in Cline, E. D. Morel, jacket · photographs, repro. in Cocks, E. D. Morel
Wealth at death £5358 0s. 4d.: probate, 4 March 1925, CGPLA Eng. & Wales

Morell, John (1775–1840), Unitarian minister and schoolmaster, was born on 16 May 1775 at Maldon, Essex, the second of the four children of Stephen Morell (1727–1815) and his wife, Mary, née King (1739–1810). His great-grandfather Daniel Morell (b. 1666) was a Huguenot from the Champagne area of France who fled to Ireland, and whose son married into the Conte family of similar descent.

The Morells had close connections with the Independent church at Maldon, and all three sons became ministers of Independent churches. Following removal to London, John and his elder brother Stephen (1773–1852) were sent to Rothwell, Northamptonshire, to prepare for the ministry, and later to the grammar school at Hitchin, where the family then resided. Entry to Homerton College followed, the brothers being Trotman grantees in 1792 and 1793 respectively. Their younger brother Thomas (1781–1840) followed in 1799, having received a grounding in classics from his brothers.

Morell started his ministry in Independency at Foulmire, Cambridgeshire, then at Blandford, Dorset. In 1796 he took the pulpit formerly occupied by Thomas Belsham

at Daventry, where he may have come in contact with Unitarian thinking. For health reasons he moved to a Presbyterian pulpit at Enfield, Middlesex, about 1798. The failure of his voice and his altered religious opinions led to his resignation in 1802.

Morell successively kept schools in Exeter, Nottingham, and in various places around London until 1816. He married Elizabeth (1779–1852), daughter of Revd John Reynell and his wife, Mary, of Thorverton, Devon, on 5 August 1812; they had two daughters and a son. In 1814 he was awarded a doctor of laws degree, probably from a German university, 'procured for him by his friends, entirely without his knowledge' (Christian Reformer, May 1840). By this time he was firmly in the Unitarian fold, and during 1816 and 1817 was classical and mathematical tutor at Hackney Academy, run by Revd Robert Aspland for intending ministers of Unitarian congregations. From at least 1815 he wrote regularly for Unitarian journals.

In January 1818 Morell moved to Brighton, Sussex, where he ran a successful school, as well as becoming Unitarian minister at Cavendish Street Chapel. It was decided to erect a new Unitarian church in New Road on land purchased from the prince regent, and Morell was appointed as first minister. He was charged with the design, which he believed should be classical in style. Opened in 1820, it was based in outline on the Temple of Theseus. Admired by many as elegant, the church was dismissed by the Royal Brighton Guide of 1827 'as built after the manner of a heathen temple'. Its Doric portico was a striking addition to the centre of Brighton.

Morell's importance lies in the influence he had over his pupils at his school at Hove. These included Isambard Kingdom Brunel, Professor Thomas Solly, Henry Solly, and Henry Acton. The last two were Unitarian ministers, and there were several other men whom Morell influenced to take a similar path by his fine mind, classical learning, and liberal sentiments. Henry Solly writes at length about his time at Morell's school and what was taught: 'The good Dr … had a very kindly heart, large sympathies, and in general a pleasant genial manner' (Solly, 1.93).

Apart from John, the numerous other Morells who became ministers of religion remained Independent (later Congregationalist). His brother Stephen ministered at Little Baddow, Essex, for over fifty years and was succeeded by his son. Another died at the start of a ministerial career, while the youngest, John Daniel *Morell, left the ministry to become the first inspector of schools. Thomas Morell was a leading theological writer and tutor, who at the time of his death in February 1840 was president of Coward College; his only son died at the start of a ministerial career.

John Morell retired from the Unitarian ministry at Brighton in 1827, passing his school at Hove to his successor in that pulpit, J. P. Malleson. Morell then travelled with his family in Germany, Switzerland, and Italy for the next few years, returning to settle in Bath in 1836, where he died on 11 April 1840. He was buried on 19 April in Lyncombe cemetery near Bath.   ALAN RUSTON

Sources J. R. W., *Christian Reformer, or, Unitarian Magazine and Review*, 7 (1840), 348–50 [incl. list of Morell's published works] · H. Solly, *'These eighty years', or, The story of an unfinished life*, 2 vols. (1893), vol. 1, pp. 86–125 · H. Acton and J. R. Wreford, *Sermon and sketch of life of Rev. Dr J. Morell* (1840) · R. M. Theobald, *Memorials of J. D. Morell* (1891) · *Christian Reformer, or, Unitarian Magazine and Review*, new ser., 8 (1852), 195–6 · *Congregational Year Book* (1853), 216–17 · J. Rowland, *The story of Brighton Unitarian Church* (1972), 6–7 · T. Coleman, *Memorials of independent churches of Northamptonshire* (1853), 207 · I. Brunel, *Life of I. K. Brunel* (1870), 3–5 · H. McLachlan, *The Unitarian movement in the religious life of England: its contribution to thought and learning, 1700–1900* (1934), 87, 102, 129–30, 179
Archives Harris Man. Oxf., Wood MSS
Wealth at death see will, PRO, PROB 11/1929; PRO, death duty registers, IR 26/1554

Morell, John Daniel (1816–1891), philosopher and inspector of schools, born at home at Little Baddow manse, Little Baddow, near Chelmsford, Essex, on 18 June 1816, was the ninth child of Stephen Morell and Jemima Robinson, his wife. The family was of French origin, and settled in England on the revocation of the edict of Nantes. The father was a Congregationalist minister in Little Baddow from 1799 to 1852. The ministerial calling was widely followed in the family, and Morell himself said he chose it as his own 'destination even from a child'. At seventeen, therefore, after attending his father's school in Little Baddow, he was entered as a probationer at Homerton College for the education of dissenting ministers (1834–8) under Dr Pye Smith. He travelled far outside the ordinary class-work, and Greek and Latin, French and German, were added to the study of theology.

The theological course over, Morell's health was so impaired that he decided to qualify as a teacher, in case pastoral work should be found beyond his strength. From Homerton he accordingly went to Glasgow University, where he gained first prizes for logic and moral philosophy. He graduated BA with honours in 1840, and proceeded MA in 1841. After leaving Glasgow, he went, in the summer of 1841, to the University of Bonn, where he studied theology and philosophy under Fichte, whose influence he felt all his life.

After returning to Britain, Morell began his ministry as an independent at Gosport in August 1842, and in October of the same year was fully 'ordained'. His creed was hardly of the type usually associated with the nonconformity of a place like Gosport, and his ministry there closed in 1845. The congregation there was used to orthodox evangelism and labelled Morell's opinions 'rationalism and neology'. Although he did not associate himself with any sect, his views were close to those of Coleridge, later given fuller expression by Richard Whately, Thomas Arnold, F. D. Maurice, and R. Chenevix-Trench.

In 1843 Morell married Elizabeth Morell Wreford (1810?–1881), a cousin by marriage. They had no children. In 1846 he published his *Historical and Critical View of the Speculative Philosophy of Europe in the Nineteenth Century*. Although the book came from a young and unknown author, it reached a second edition in the year after its appearance. It broadened the outlook of English philosophy by introducing its readers to German idealist thought. Like other works by Morell, it is marked by an easy and unadorned style which gives it clarity and accessibility. Not the least of its praises was H. L. Mansel's confession, years after its appearance, that this was the book which 'more than any other gave me a taste for philosophical study'. Thomas Chalmers was so impressed that he tried to secure for Morell the chair of moral philosophy at Edinburgh. Laurence Oliphant took it as a guide in his researches (M. O. W. Oliphant, *Memoir of the Life of Laurence Oliphant*, (7th edn, 1891), 1.217); while Lord Lansdowne, then president of the privy council, who wanted a nonconformist as inspector of schools, offered the post to Morell on reading his book.

After some hesitation Morell accepted the office, which he held from 1848 until 1876. His responsibility was for dissenting schools throughout north-east England. As an inspector, Morell was thorough, conscientious, and searching, kindly and sympathetic to children and teachers.

But the new duties did not halt Morell's literary work. Four lectures on 'The philosophical tendencies of the age', delivered in Edinburgh and Glasgow, were followed by a careful and suggestive inquiry into *The Philosophy of Religion* (1849), which was keenly discussed, especially in Scotland. Profiting by his close acquaintance with elementary school life, Morell published in 1852 the first of his works dealing with English grammar, *The Analysis of Sentences*. Then came, in 1855, *The Essentials of English Grammar and Analysis* and the *Handbook of Logic*, while *The Grammar of the English Language* appeared in 1857. Few educational works of that period had a larger circulation, and he mainly devoted his leisure thenceforth to their compilation; but the issue of his *Philosophical Fragments* in 1878 showed that Morell's regard for philosophic inquiry was not diminished. For some years he edited the *School Magazine*, to which he contributed some verses of more than respectable merit. In 1881 his health began to break. He suffered from a progressive dementia, and died at his home, Clevelands, Fitzjohns Avenue, Hampstead, on 1 April 1891.

Morell's own position in metaphysical philosophy was that of an eclectic, with a decided leaning to idealism. His theological position showed the same independence. From the creed of Homerton he passed into a broader faith, which allowed him to worship for some years with protestant nonconformists, then with Anglican churchmen, and finally with Unitarians.

Besides the books already mentioned, Morell published several other texts on English grammar, works on psychology, religion, the English education system, and employment in the civil service. He translated works by I. H. Fichte, G. Bosco, and Hausrath.

A. R. BUCKLAND, *rev.* C. A. CREFFIELD

Sources R. M. Theobald, *Memorials of John Daniel Morell* (1891)
Likenesses A. Roffe, steel plate engraving, 1852 (after portrait by Heisenbach?), repro. in Theobald, *Memorials* · R. T. & Co., wood-engraving, NPG; repro. in *ILN* (4 April 1891) · photograph, repro. in Theobald, *Memorials*
Wealth at death £40,590 19s. 11d.: probate, 8 May 1891, *CGPLA Eng. & Wales*

Morell, Thomas (1703–1784), classical scholar and librettist, was born on 18 March 1703 at Eton, Buckinghamshire, the eldest child of the two sons and two daughters of Thomas Morell (*d.* in or after 1720), saddler, and his wife, Eleanor Tipping (*d.* 1738/9). As a widow Morell's mother maintained herself as a boarding-house keeper or 'dame' for Eton College, where Morell was enrolled as a foundation scholar in 1715. In 1722 he matriculated at King's College, Cambridge, where he became a fellow in 1725. He was ordained deacon on 19 September 1725 and graduated BA in 1726, leaving Cambridge for 'a curacy and small sinecure' at Kelvedon, Essex (CUL, Add. MS 4251.979). His poems (Yale MS) show him in Lincolnshire in 1729. Subsequently he graduated MA (Cambridge) in 1730, MA (Oxford) in 1733, and DD (Cambridge) in 1743. About 1730 he was appointed sub-curate of the chapel of St Anne, Kew Green, where he served unofficially as curate from 1733 to 1745, being dismissed when he asked the non-resident vicar for an increase in his stipend. At Kew, Queen Caroline commissioned him to prepare a commentary on Locke for her grotto (published in 1794 as *Notes and Annotations on Locke on the Human Understanding*) but, as throughout his life, his hopes of preferment were frustrated, and he was mortified when she appointed as her preacher the 'thresher poet' Stephen Duck, whose verse he had praised. On 25 March 1737 Morell became rector of Buckland, Hertfordshire, a King's College living which he held, from 1741 *in absentia*, until his death. On 20 October 1737 he was elected a fellow of the Society of Antiquaries. Early biographies describe him as curate of Twickenham but there is no evidence of his appointment or activity as such.

On 6 April 1738 at Kew, Morell married Anne Barker (*d.* 1785), one of the daughters of Henry Barker, of The Grove, Chiswick. Affectionate testimonies of his devotion to her give warmth to the Yale manuscript of his occasional verses, copied out for her in 1779. They had no children. From *c.*1750 (probably earlier) until their deaths they lived at Turnham Green. In 1768 Morell was elected FRS and became a salaried secretary of the Society of Antiquaries at £20 per annum, responsible for publications and foreign correspondence, a post he held until his death. From 1776 to 1782 he was chaplain to the Portsmouth garrison on a yearly stipend of £121 13s. 4d. Early biographies mention that he regularly preached the Fairchild botanical sermon at St Leonard, Shoreditch. Evidently in some demand as a visiting preacher, he was heard at the Temple Church in 1769 by James Boswell, who was 'much pleased' with his 'simple faith' and recommendation of 'plain, rational, calm piety' (J. Boswell, *Private Papers*, ed. G. Scott and F. A. Pottle, 1930, 8.89). Morell never prospered materially—according to William Cole, because he kept low company, especially with musicians, and was irremediably improvident. His friends, who valued his good humour and entertaining anecdotes, included James Thomson, to whom he addressed Spenserian stanzas urging him to finish *The Castle of Indolence*; David Garrick, who raised subscriptions for his *Prometheus*; and William Hogarth, whom he helped with the final draft of his *Analysis of Beauty*.

Thomas Morell (1703–1784), by James Basire, pubd 1762 (after William Hogarth)

Morell supplemented his income with a variety of publications. He was a lifelong natural versifier, practising diverse styles and moods and engaging with political issues. Initially he wrote in support of the patriot opposition party, with some deft verses praising Pulteney in the *Gentleman's Magazine* and a poem to Frederick, prince of Wales (in the Yale MS), to whom he also dedicated his edition of modern versions of parts of *The Canterbury Tales* (1737); but he had better returns from William, duke of Cumberland, whose suppression of the Jacobite rising of 1745 he celebrated in his first libretto for Handel, *Judas Maccabaeus* (1747). He subsequently wrote the librettos for Handel's *Alexander Balus* (1748), *Theodora* (1750), and *Jephtha* (1752), and the new text required for *The Triumph of Time and Truth* (1757). Handel bequeathed him £200. He recorded that he began writing for Handel in response to a request from the composer backed by the prince of Wales; but this account (CUL, Add. MS 4251.979), written late in life, is not wholly reliable. For J. C. Smith he confected oratorio librettos to existing music by Handel: *Nabal* (1764), *Tobit* (1764?), and *Gideon* (1769). His religious verses (*Poems on Divine Subjects*, 1732; *The Christian's Epinikion*, 1743; *Hope*, 1745) contributed to the contemporary defence of orthodox Christianity against freethinking and shed interesting light on his librettos. The versification in his hand of a letter by Pope suggests that he had contact with the literary circle of Lord Burlington, whose Chiswick House backed onto his in-laws' property.

In his lifetime Morell was chiefly known, and widely esteemed, as a classical scholar. He produced editions (some his own, some revisions of others') of plays by Aeschylus (*Prometheus Bound*, 1767, with translation), Sophocles (*Philoctetes*, 1757), and Euripides (*Hecuba, Orestes, Phoenissae, Alcestis*, 1748; translation of *Hecuba*, 1749); he translated Seneca's epistles with an extensive commentary (begun by 1753, published 1786), produced a thesaurus of Greek prosody (1762) which remained in use into the nineteenth century, and revised Hederich's Greek lexicon (1766) for 200 guineas, and Ainsworth's Latin dictionary (1773) for £218 8s. Several of his classics texts and his retelling of the gospels, *Sacred Annals* (1776), were produced for Eton, where he was—unjustly, according to contemporaries—denied his hope of a fellowship. He was widely read in contemporary as well as classical literature; his natural style was whimsical and discursive, and he worked best within disciplined forms. A letter to Robert Cory Sumner on Sophocles' versification proves his sensitivity to metrical variation and other details of aural effect. He was reputedly a good organist, and James Basire's engraving of his portrait by Hogarth (published as a frontispiece to his Greek thesaurus), which captures his raffish liveliness, depicts an organ as background. His manuscripts in the British Library include a commonplace book (Add. MS 28846) and uncompleted projects. The list of publications in Nichols includes several works that cannot now be traced.

Morell died in Turnham Green on 19 February 1784 and was buried at Chiswick parish church on 27 February 1784, having asked to be interred next to Hogarth. He left very little property, but his library, of which some handsome items survive in the British Library, was sufficiently valuable to be auctioned by Leigh and Sotheby in 1785 after the death of Mrs Morell on 19 November 1785.

RUTH SMITH

Sources R. Smith, 'Thomas Morell and his letter about Handel', *Journal of the Royal Musical Association*, 127 (2002), 191–225 · parish registers, Eton, Bucks. RLSS · parish register, Chiswick, Chiswick Library, local studies collection · parish register, Chiswick church, Chiswick · note books, Chiswick Library, local studies collection · parish registers, Buckland, Herts. ALS · G. E. Cassidy, *The chapel of St Anne, Kew Green, 1710–1769*, Richmond Historical Society Paper, 2 (1985) · T. Harwood, *Alumni Etonenses, or, A catalogue of the provosts and fellows of Eton College and King's College, Cambridge, from the foundation in 1443 to the year 1797* (1797), 302–4 · Nichols, *Lit. anecdotes*, vols. 1, 3–6, 8–9 · council books, minute books, S. Antiquaries, Lond. · R. G. King, 'John Christopher Smith's pasticcio oratorios', *Music and Letters*, 79 (1998), 190–218 · S. Parks, 'The Osborn collection: a 4th biennial report', *Yale University Library Gazette*, 50 (1975–6), 182 · W. Hogarth, *The analysis of beauty*, ed. R. Paulson (1997) · *The curatial battel for Q. Chappel: address to the Reverend Parsons, D---k and M---l* (1746) · *The letters of David Garrick*, ed. D. M. Little and G. M. Kahrl, 2 (1963), 897–900 · will, PRO, PROB 11/1114 · R. A. Austen-Leigh, ed., *The Eton College register, 1698–1752* (1927) · Venn, *Alum. Cant.*, 1/3 · R. Smith, *Handel's oratorios and eighteenth-century thought* (1995) · R. Smith, 'Handel's English librettists', *The Cambridge companion to Handel*, ed. D. Burrows (1997), 92–108 · R. Paulson, *Art and politics* (1993), vol. 3 of *Hogarth: James Thomson (1700–1748): letters and documents*, ed. A. D. McKillop (1958), 135–6 · W. Draper, *Chiswick* (1923); repr. with additions (1973) · M. Noble, 'The lives of the fellows of the Society of Antiquarians in London', 1818, S. Antiquaries,

Lond. · R. S. Cobbett, *Memorials of Twickenham* (1872), 125–6 · *DNB* · *Army List* (1776–82)
Archives BL, Add. MS 5151, fol. 249 · BL, Add. MS 6402, fol. 142 · BL, commonplace book, Add. MS 28846 · BL, papers, Burney MSS 401, 404, 522–523 · BL, printed works with his MS notes and additions · CUL, Add. MS 4251.979 · S. Antiquaries, Lond., notes relating to ancient customs and tenures · Yale U., Beinecke L., commonplace book | Bibliothèque Nationale, Paris, Rés. VS 1378–1380 · BL, Add. MS 27992
Likenesses P. Sandby, etching, 1753, repro. in R. Paulson, *Hogarth: his art, life and times* (1971) · P. Sandby, etching, 1753–4, repro. in R. Paulson, *Hogarth: his art, life and times* (1971) · J. Basire, line engraving, 1762 (after W. Hogarth), BM, NPG; repro. in Morell, *Thesaurus* (1762) [*see illus.*] · W. Hogarth, drawing, 1762, repro. in R. Paulson, *Hogarth: his art, life and times* (1971), vol. 2; priv. coll.
Wealth at death £120 in bequests; widow was chief beneficiary; debts: will, PRO, PROB 11/1114, sig. 151 · house valued at £20 p.a.: Chiswick rate books · library, incl. at least one valuable edition: Nichols, *Lit. anecdotes*; *N&Q*, 1st ser., 5.604

Moreman, John (*c*.1490–1554), Roman Catholic priest, was born at South Hole, Hartland, Devon, about 1490, to unknown parents. He graduated BA at Oxford on 29 January 1509, and on 29 June 1510 was admitted fellow of Exeter College, being preferred for his 'more eminent learning and accomplishments' (Prince, 600) to the candidate of Bishop Oldham. He incepted MA on 10 October 1512, and subsequently proceeded BD (1527) and DD (1530). He had been ordained subdeacon on 23 December 1514 and priest on 24 March 1515. In November 1522 he vacated his fellowship on becoming principal of Hart Hall, where he remained until 1528. On 11 June that year he preached before the university. He was still at Oxford in 1531 when he was noted as 'well learned' and a likely divinity lecturer (*LP Henry VIII*, 5, no. 6). On 14 July 1516 he had been instituted to the vicarage of Midsomer Norton, Somerset, on the presentation of Merton Priory; he resigned by 18 October 1528. He was also rector of Instow, Devon (instituted on 16 August 1522, vacated by March 1536), and of Holy Trinity, Exeter (instituted on 25 August 1528, vacated by January 1530).

However, it was as vicar of Meheniot, Cornwall, to which he was instituted on 21 February 1529 on the presentation of Exeter College, and which he retained until death, that Moreman was best known. The Exeter historian John Hooker was tutored to university entrance in Moreman's vicarage; there is no evidence of his keeping a formal school as some have supposed. Despite his predominant conservatism, Moreman was praised by the protestant Hooker for introducing the teaching of the Lord's prayer, the creed, and the commandments in English to the parishioners. Hooker also said he was 'of a very honest and good nature, loving to all men, and hurtful to none' (Rose-Troup, 108). On 1 March 1532 Moreman received a prebend in the college of Glasney, Cornwall. In January 1534 he was delated to Cromwell as an enemy of the king's cause. He was also noted as a particular supporter of Queen Catherine. Nevertheless, on 7 March 1535 he accompanied his bishop, John Veysey, in renouncing papal jurisdiction at a ceremony in St German's Priory. Veysey appointed him to a stall in his cathedral (where the traditionalist chapter was already at odds with its reforming dean, Simon Heynes) on 19 June 1544. Moreman resigned his Glasney prebend before accepting that of Exeter, holding the latter until death. He was further beneficed with the vicarage of Colebrooke, Devon, from 25 October 1546 until death.

Soon after Edward VI's accession Moreman was arrested for subversive preaching, at the instance of William May, dean of St Paul's, and other commissioners. He must first have been committed to the Fleet, where his goods and his offending sermon remained on 22 October 1549, though by then Moreman himself was in the Tower. The west country rebels of that summer had called for his release and that of his colleague in the Exeter chapter, Richard Crispyn, demanding that they be given additional benefices to sustain their Catholic preaching ministry. This naturally ensured their continued detention. Cranmer, who examined Moreman personally, dismissed the two clerics as 'wilful, crafty and full of dissimulation' (Cox, 184). In May 1552 the privy council thoughtfully directed the dean and chapter of Exeter to pay Moreman and Crispyn their prebendal dividends to provide their diets and fees in the Tower. Moreman was greeted there by Mary at her accession, and promptly released. In October 1553 he defended Catholic teaching on transubstantiation in convocation. He was back at Exeter during the security scare of early 1554. On 22 May 1554 the queen made Moreman, by now her chaplain, a canon of Westminster, where he appeared only once in chapter. He was designated dean of Exeter but died, by 20 August 1554, before the appointment was confirmed. He bequeathed a copy of Froben's edition of Augustine to the rector of Exeter College, Oxford, on condition of its being made available to fellows studying theology. Thanks chiefly to Hooker's encomium, Moreman is remembered as 'the most distinguished parish priest of his time in Cornwall' (Rowse, 152).

C. S. KNIGHTON

Sources Emden, Oxf., 4.400 · LP Henry VIII, 5, no. 6; 7, no. 101; 8, no. 311 · CSP dom., 1547–53, no. 418; 1553–8, no. 38 · APC, 1552–4, 63 · CPR, 1554–5, 203 · J. Prince, Danmonii orientales illustres, or, The worthies of Devon, 2nd edn (1810), 600–02 · F. Rose-Troup, The western rebellion of 1549 (1913), 107–9 · BL, Harleian MS 5827, fols. 45v–46v · N. Orme, Education in the west of England, 1066–1548 (1976), 102 · Miscellaneous writings and letters of Thomas Cranmer, ed. J. E. Cox, Parker Society, [18] (1846), 183–4 · A. L. Rowse, Tudor Cornwall: portrait of a society (1957), 151–2, 233 · C. W. Boase, ed., Registrum Collegii Exoniensis, new edn, OHS, 27 (1894), 52–3 · C. S. Knighton, ed., Acts of the dean and chapter of Westminster, 1 (1997), 86 · J. Youings, 'The south-western rebellion of 1549', Southern History, 1 (1979), 99–122, esp. 115 · The acts and monuments of John Foxe, new edn, ed. G. Townsend, 6 (1846), 397–8, 404 · will, PRO, PROB 11/37, sig. 10

Wealth at death see will, PRO, PROB 11/37, sig. 10

Mores, Edward Rowe (1730–1778), antiquary and historian of printing, was born on 13 January 1730 in Tunstall, Kent, the son of the Revd Edward Mores (d. 1740), rector of Tunstall, and Sarah Windsor, of London. He was a descendant of two lord mayors of London, Sir Thomas Rowe (1568) and his son Sir Henry Rowe (1607).

In 1740, the year of his father's death, Mores entered Merchant Taylors' School, London; he matriculated from

Edward Rowe Mores (1730–1778), by J. Mynde (after Richard van Bleeck)

Queen's College, Oxford, as a gentleman commoner in June 1746. He received his BA in 1750 and proceeded MA in 1753. At Oxford, Mores developed an interest in English antiquities that continued throughout his life. He published his first work, *Nomina et insignia gentilitia nobilium equitumque sub Edoardo primo rege militantium*, at Oxford in 1749 at the age of nineteen. During this time he helped to update an edition of Mario de Calasio's *Concordantiae sacrorum bibliorum Hebraicorum* (1621), which was published in 1747, and completed a Latin translation of Dionysius of Halicarnassus as *De antiquis oratoribus*, which was published after his death, in 1781. At Oxford he had made over thirty engravings of architectural elements of the university, all of which were subsequently torn down by the end of the eighteenth century. In 1751 he assisted John Bilstone in the preparation of a satirical subscription announcement for a history of the Mallardians, a society of All Souls, to which he contributed engravings of two grotesque busts on the college's walls and an image of a cat said to have starved to death in their library.

Mores spent several years at work on the Queen's College archives in the 1750s, arranging the records, studying the history of the college, and amassing a collection of works on the college and the university for a proposed history. This, along with several other scholarly projects of his later life, was never completed.

In 1752 Mores was elected a fellow of the Society of Antiquaries. In the following year he was elected a member of the society's council, and served several additional council terms during the next decade. He also served on several of the society's committees, including one charged with reviewing members' works for possible publication. He was interested in Roman and Anglo-Saxon coins that were periodically unearthed and corresponded with other fellows of the society about their discovery and authenticity. Mores saw through to publication in 1754 a reproduction of the Bodleian Library's Anglo-Saxon Genesis manuscript by Caedmon, under the title *Figurae quaedam antiquae ex Caedmonis monachi paraphraseos in Genesin exemplari pervetusto*.

After proceeding MA, Mores travelled on the continent and returned to England where he resided in London at the College of Arms and studied there with the intention of becoming a member. He was introduced into the college by his brother-in-law John Warburton, an antiquary and herald. He moved to Low Leyton, Essex, where he had inherited property from his father, in 1759. There he designed and built the somewhat fanciful Etlow House, which he said was reminiscent of buildings he had seen in France.

In 1757 Mores had circulated a query to gather sources on a history of Berkshire, which he printed himself at Leyton in 1759. Though some progress was made on this project, it was not completed. The manuscript was purchased from his estate by Richard Gough and published in 1783 as *Collections toward a Parochial History of Berkshire*. Other unpublished works printed after his death include 'The history and antiquities of Tunstall in Kent', as part of the first volume of John Nichols's *Bibliotheca Topographica Britannica* (1780), and *De Aelfric, Dorobernensi archiepiscopo, commentarius* (1789).

In 1754–5 Mores spent several months assisting the antiquary Andrew Ducarel in preparing and writing a history of Croydon for the archbishop of Canterbury. In the course of their work they arranged the registers of the archbishops at Lambeth Palace, and Mores prepared a summary of the first volume of the registers. Mores felt slighted at the meagre credit he received from Ducarel after the final manuscript of the history was prepared; he was incorrectly listed as co-author of only one chapter, rather than the entire work. Mores took his revenge by having printed an early work of Ducarel, *De registris Lamenthanis dissertatiuncula* (1756), which clearly showed Ducarel's ignorance of Latin, and to which he added a final note of his own to clarify that any errors should not be blamed upon the printer, but were in fact the author's own.

Mores was elected overseer of Leyton church in 1769 and served as churchwarden in 1774–5. He was listed as one of the governors of Bridewell and Bethlem hospitals in 1765. While he was at Low Leyton, some of his eccentricities became more pronounced. He took to wearing academic garb, which he told acquaintances was the dress of a Dominican friar. He alluded to having been made a doctor of divinity in France, though no proof has ever been evinced. When asked about religion, he professed to be of 'the Religion of Erasmus' (Nichols, *Lit. anecdotes*, 5.395).

In 1753 Mores married Susannah (1730–1767), daughter of Richard Bridgman, a prominent Whitechapel grocer. Richard Bridgman was Mores's stepfather, having married his mother Sarah after his father's death. Susannah died on 8 January 1767, and was buried in the churchyard at Walthamstow. She and Mores had two children: a daughter, Sarah, who married in 1774 John Davis, a house decorator from Walthamstow, but did not outlive her father, and a son, Edward Rowe (d. 1846), who married a Miss Spence in 1779. Mores believed strongly in the superiority of Latin, and spoke exclusively in Latin to his children. There is a story that a guest at his house was amazed to see Mores correct his two-year-old daughter in Latin at the dinner table; she understood his request and quickly made the correction. His children were sent abroad for their education, his daughter to the convent of St Joseph in Rouen, where she later converted to Roman Catholicism, and his son to Holland. At the death of his wife Mores is said to have composed a Latin mass for her entitled *Ordinale quotidianum* and printed it himself with the false date of 1685. No copy or manuscript of this work has survived.

Mores had a lifelong interest in the history of printing in England. In 1772 he purchased from the estate of the prominent type-founder John Jones a large collection of matrices, punches, and type said to date back to Wynkyn de Worde, the second printer in England. Using his collection as a starting point, he prepared and printed himself *A Dissertation upon English Typographical Founders and Founderies* in 1778. It was printed in eighty copies, none of which was sold or distributed before his death later that year. The work was intended to have included extensive type specimen sheets, which were not printed. The literary historian and publisher John Nichols purchased all the copies in the following year at the sale of Mores's library, added an appendix of his own, and distributed the work.

The *Dissertation* was the first study of English typefounders; it remains an essential text on its subject, one which cannot be overlooked in any research into early English typography. The work's influence was immediately limited because of its small press run and a number of eccentricities of Mores's that appeared in the printing. He believed in emulating manuscript tradition and only capitalized the first word of every paragraph, not that of every sentence. He also made unusual abbreviations and insisted upon Latinizing names, thus making the work even more difficult to read. In its treatment of the very earliest English printers and type-founders the work falls short, comprising little more than a description of their presses and types, but as a whole its importance and influence were widespread and significant.

Mores was a founding member and director of the Society for Equitable Assurances. He may have been brought into the project by his father-in-law Richard Bridgman, also a founding member, because of his membership of the Society of Antiquaries, which had recently been given its own charter. Efforts to secure a charter for the Equitable Society failed, but a deed of settlement was drawn up for it in 1762. At this time Mores was made one of fifteen directors for life, with a payment of £100 per annum. He published a number of pamphlets describing society practices, as well as a history of the society (1765). Two years later this work had reached its seventh edition. Mores later fell out with some members, and he resigned his directorship in 1768.

Mores died at Etlow House, Low Leyton, Essex, on 28 November 1778 of a 'mortification', or gangrene, of the leg. During his final illness he refused to see a doctor or nurse. He is buried with his wife in Walthamstow churchyard. After his death, his collection of books and manuscripts was sold at an auction in August 1779 that lasted two weeks and comprised over 3000 lots. His collection of type, printing, and type-founding equipment was sold in a separate auction later that same year. His manuscripts and correspondence are housed in the British Library and the Bodleian Library.   JEFFREY MAKALA

Sources H. Carter and C. Ricks, introduction, in E. R. Mores, *A dissertation upon English typographical founders and founderies*, ed. H. Carter and C. Ricks, new edn (1961) · D. B. Updike, introduction, in E. R. Mores, *A dissertation upon English typographical founders and founderies*, ed. D. B. Updike, new edn (1924) · R. Gough, 'Memoirs of the author', in E. R. Mores, *A dissertation upon English typographical founders and founderies*, ed. D. B. Updike, new edn (1924) · Nichols, *Lit. anecdotes*, 5.389–405 · S. Paterson, *Bibliotheca Moresiana: a catalogue of the library of Edward Rowe Mores* (1779) · *GM*, 1st ser., 53 (1783), 848 · J. Nichols, ed., *Bibliotheca topographica Britannica*, 1 (1780) · *DNB*
Archives BL, antiquarian notes and papers, Stowe MSS 123, 782–784, 872, 1051 · BL, collections, Add. MSS 5526, 5528, 5532, 6408, 6110–6112, 6114 · Bodl. Oxf., collections · S. Antiquaries, Lond., notebook of drafts for his *Nomina et insignia gentilitia* | Bodl. Oxf., Berkshire collections · Queen's College, Oxford, MS calendar of Queen's College muniments
Likenesses J. Mynde, line engraving (after R. van Bleeck), BM, NPG [*see illus.*]

Moresby, Sir Fairfax (1786/7–1877), naval officer, the son of Fairfax Moresby of Stow House, Lichfield, Staffordshire, and his wife, the daughter of Robert Rotton of Driffield, Derbyshire, was born at Calcutta in 1786 or 1787. He entered the navy in December 1799, on the *London*, with Captain John Child Purvis, whom he followed in 1801 to the *Royal George*. In March 1802 he joined the *Alarm*, with Captain William Parker (1781–1866), and in November went with him to the *Amazon*, in which he served in the Mediterranean and in the chase of the French fleet to the West Indies. In December 1805 he was appointed to the *Puissant* at Portsmouth, and on 10 April 1806 he was promoted lieutenant of the *Ville de Paris*. A few months later he was appointed to the *Kent*, in which, and afterwards in the *Repulse*, he was frequently on boat service in the Mediterranean. After some weeks in acting command of the *Eclair* and *Acorn* he was promoted commander of the brig *Wizard* (18 April 1811), and was sent to the Aegean to suppress the pirates who, along with the French privateers fitted out in Turkey, were then very active. He captured several, and for his services was presented by the merchants of Malta with a sword. Towards the end of 1812 the *Wizard* was sent to England with dispatches, but after returning to the Mediterranean was through the summer of 1813 attached to the squadron in the Adriatic, under the command of Rear-Admiral Thomas Fremantle. On several occasions, especially at the siege of Trieste in October, Moresby's services were highly commended. With the other captains of the squadron he was awarded, on 23 May 1814, the cross of the order of Maria Theresa. He was advanced to post rank on 7 June 1814, and was nominated a CB on 4 June 1815.

Moresby married at Malta on 6 August 1814 Eliza Louisa, the youngest daughter of John Williams of Bakewell, Derbyshire, and the granddaughter of General Archer, lieutenant-governor of Portsmouth. They had two daughters and three sons, of whom the eldest son, Fairfax, a commander in the navy, was lost in the brig *Sappho*, which

sank with all hands in Bass's Strait early in 1858. Their second son was John *Moresby. In April 1819 Moresby was appointed to the frigate *Menai*, bound for the Cape of Good Hope station. In 1820 he surveyed Algoa Bay and its neighbourhood, arranged the landing of 2000 settlers, and organized the colony. In 1821 he was senior officer at Mauritius, with orders to suppress the slave trade. He captured or destroyed several slaving vessels, prosecuted the owners, and concluded a treaty with the imam of Muscat restricting the scope of local slave trading and conferring on English warships the right of searching and seizing local vessels. At the request of Wilberforce he was kept out an additional year, until June 1823. The *Menai* was paid off in September. Moresby's African service had broken his health. From 1837 to 1840 he commanded the *Pembroke* in the Mediterranean, and from 1845 to 1848 the *Canopus* on the home station, where he demonstrated great skill in the sailing trials. On 20 December 1849 he was promoted rear-admiral, and from 1850 to 1853 he was commander-in-chief in the Pacific, during which time he recommended the development of a naval base at Esquimault on the west coast of Canada. In 1854 he was made a DCL of Oxford. He was nominated vice-admiral on 12 November 1856, admiral on 12 April 1862, GCB on 28 March 1865, and admiral of the fleet on 21 January 1870. He died at Bronwylfa, near Exmouth, Devon, on 21 January 1877.

J. K. LAUGHTON, *rev.* ANDREW LAMBERT

Sources J. Moresby, *Two admirals* (1913) · B. M. Gough, *The Royal Navy and the north-west coast of North America, 1810–1914* (1971) · R. Howell, *The Royal Navy and the slave trade* (1987) · O'Byrne, *Naval biog. dict.* · *Dod's Peerage* (1858) · Walford, *County families* (1860) · Boase, *Mod. Eng. biog.*
Archives BL, letters to Sir Charles Napier, etc., Add. MSS 40042–40043 · Bodl. Oxf., letters to Sir Henry Wentworth Acland · Devon RO, letters to Sir Thomas Dyke Acland
Likenesses E. A. Gifford, oils, 1870, NMM · portrait, repro. in Moresby, *Two admirals*
Wealth at death under £14,000: probate, 8 Feb 1877, *CGPLA Eng. & Wales*

Moresby, John (1830–1922), naval officer and explorer, was born at Allerton, Somerset, on 15 March 1830, the second son of Admiral of the Fleet Sir Fairfax *Moresby (1786/7–1877) and his wife, Eliza Louisa, the youngest daughter of John Williams, of Bakewell, Derbyshire. He was educated at a private school until the age of twelve, when he joined the Royal Navy in the *Caledonia*, then the port flagship at Devonport. In 1845 he sailed as a midshipman in the frigate *America* for the Pacific via Cape Horn. The *America* returned to England the following year, and Moresby next served with the Channel Fleet. He was in the paddle frigate *Odin* at Palermo during the 1848 rising. In 1849 he joined the *Excellent* for gunnery instruction, and was then appointed gunnery mate of the frigate *Amphitrite*. In 1850 he sailed for the west coast of South America. Shortly afterwards he was transferred to the frigate *Thetis* as gunnery lieutenant, and in 1853 commanded a punitive expedition against the natives of Vancouver Island. After returning home on promotion, Moresby joined the paddle sloop *Driver* as first lieutenant in 1854, on the eve of war with Russia. For two summers he was on reconnaissance

John Moresby (1830–1922), by Debenham

work in the Baltic, and participated in the taking of the Bomarsund forts and the abortive attack on Riga.

On the conclusion of peace with Russia, Moresby was appointed flag lieutenant to the admiral in command of the Irish station and was given leave to accompany his father to Austria when Sir Fairfax Moresby represented the British navy at the centenary of the order of Maria Theresa.

In 1858 Moresby became commander. The following year he married Jane Willis (d. 1876), the eldest daughter of Philip Scott JP, of Queenstown (later Cobh), Ireland; they had one son and four daughters. In 1861 he was appointed to command the gun vessel Snake on the China station, where he took part in the suppression of the Taiping uprising and saw action at Shanghai. The Snake was later engaged in suppressing piracy on the coasts of southern China and in safeguarding the rights of British ships trading in opium. In the sloop Argus, of which he took command in 1863, Moresby went to Japan and took part in the international attack on the Shimonoseki forts in 1864 and in the subsequent naval demonstration in Japanese waters.

In 1865 Moresby was promoted captain and went on half pay until 1871, when he was given command of the paddle sloop Basilisk for service on the Australian station. The Basilisk was not a surveying vessel and carried no officers specially trained for such work, but the opportunities for exploration in her cruising area led Moresby to apply for a small outfit of surveying instruments. Between 1872 and 1874, except for two cruises to New Zealand and among the south sea islands respectively, the ship was in Torres Strait and along the coasts of New Guinea. Although primarily concerned with the suppression of the kidnapping of native labour, she carried out a series of important explorations, charting much coastline hitherto very imperfectly known.

In the last year of Moresby's work the hydrographer sent him a surveying officer, but otherwise he received scant encouragement until, at the end of her commission, the Basilisk was ordered to return home round to the north of New Guinea in order that the survey work might be continued. The south-east coast of New Guinea was then scarcely known. (The work of Luis Vaes de Torres in 1606 at the eastern end of the island was revealed only in 1878 by the discovery of his map in Madrid.) Moresby surveyed, on the south coast, Hall Sound and Redscar Bay, and discovered Port Moresby, Fairfax harbour (which he named after his father), and Discovery Bay, as well as charting their approaches and various islets and reefs in Torres Strait. By Hilda and Ethel rivers he tried to penetrate the unknown interior. He next surveyed at the east end Hayter, Basilisk, and Moresby islands and China and Fortescue Strait, and took possession of the islands in the name of Queen Victoria (1873). Of the eastern part of the north coast nothing was known at the time except a few vague landfalls of J. A. B. d'Entrecasteaux in 1793. Moresby charted the whole coast westward to Astrolabe Bay as well as the islands of the d'Entrecasteaux group—Normanby, Ferguson, and Goodenough. In all, his surveys covered 1200 miles of unknown coastline and about a hundred islands.

Moresby returned home at the end of 1874 to find that, while geographers realized the value of his work, the hydrographer had become strangely indifferent and the government of the day had no anxiety to establish a British claim to eastern New Guinea. It was not until 1884 that the hand of the government was forced by the action of Queensland, and a British protectorate, with its capital at Port Moresby, was proclaimed in the south-east of the island. The greater part of Moresby's discoveries eventually fell into German hands, but on 17 September 1914 Kaiser Wilhelm Land, as the territory had been called, surrendered to an Australian force; it was administered by Australia from 1920 until it gained independence as a part of Papua-New Guinea in 1975.

After a short spell in charge of the coastguards between Cromer and St Abb's Head, Moresby was senior naval officer in charge of the Bermuda Dockyard from 1878 to 1881; there he effected many improvements. In 1881 he became rear-admiral and was appointed assessor to the Board of Trade. He retired in 1888 with the rank of vice-admiral and became admiral on the retired list in 1893. In 1909 he published an autobiography, Two Admirals, which included an account of his father's career. In recognition of his discoveries in New Guinea he enjoyed the distinction of having his name bestowed on a destroyer built in 1916. He died at 9 Lindon Grove, Alverstoke, Hampshire, on 12 July 1922.

R. N. RUDMOSE BROWN, rev. R. O. MORRIS

Sources J. Moresby, *Two admirals* (1909) · *The Times* (13 July 1922) · A. Day, *The admiralty hydrographic service, 1795–1919* (1967) · *GJ*, 60 (1922)
Archives CAC Cam., corresp. with Lord Fisher
Likenesses Debenham, photograph, NPG [*see illus.*] · photograph, repro. in Moresby, *Two admirals*, 264
Wealth at death £8265 13s. 4d.: probate, 18 Aug 1922, *CGPLA Eng. & Wales*

Moret, Hubert (*fl.* **1531–1536**), goldsmith and jeweller, was thought to be a Paris merchant but was mentioned in French royal papers as a Lyons jeweller. From December 1532 to June 1533 he supplied François I with pearls, rubies, emeralds, and other jewels, as well as goldsmiths' work, such as rings, bangles, and gold caskets (Laborde, 2.222–58). He also was in the habit of visiting London with jewels and plate. Henry VIII occasionally purchased jewels from him for a considerable amount; in 1531 he received £56 9s. 4d., and in 1536 £282 6s. 8d. for jewels bought by the king.

Moret was a friend of Hans Holbein and is said to have carried out in goldsmith's work many of Holbein's designs. His portrait was formerly supposed to have been painted by Holbein, but the portrait in question (picture and drawing at Dresden) actually represents Charles de Solier, seigneur de Morette, an ambassador in the French service, who flourished in 1534.

WILLIAM CARR, *rev.* M. BIMBENET-PRIVAT

Sources L. de Laborde, *Les comptes des bâtiments du roi (1528–1571)*, 2 vols. (Paris, 1880) · *APC* · *LP Henry VIII*, 5.757 · BM, Add. MS 20030

Moreton, Edward (*c.*1599–1675). *See under* Moreton, William (1640/41–1715).

Moreton, Henry George Francis, second earl of Ducie (1802–1853), agriculturist and cattle breeder, was born on 8 May 1802 in Conduit Street, London, the eldest son in the family of three sons and five daughters of Thomas Reynolds Moreton, fourth Baron Ducie of Tortworth and first earl of Ducie (1775–1840), and his wife, Lady Frances Herbert, only daughter of Henry, first earl of Carnarvon. Ducie was educated at Eton College. In 1826 he married Lady Elizabeth Dutton, elder daughter of John Dutton, second Baron Sherborne, of Sherborne, Gloucestershire. They had eleven sons and four daughters. From 1830 to 1835 he was MP for East Gloucestershire. He succeeded his father as the second earl of Ducie in June 1840.

Ducie moved the address at the opening of parliament in January 1841, but apart from two other occasions he does not appear to have spoken again in the house. On the formation of Lord John Russell's first administration Ducie was appointed a lord-in-waiting to the queen (on 24 July 1846), a post which he resigned in November 1847. He served on the Charity Commission which was appointed on 18 September 1849. Ducie was a strong advocate of free trade, and the speech which he delivered in favour of the repeal of the corn laws at the Hall of Commerce, London, on 29 May 1843, attracted considerable attention.

Ducie was best-known, however, as a breeder of shorthorns and as one of the leading agriculturists of the day. He was master of the Vale of White Horse hounds from 1830 to 1842, when he gave up hunting and turned to the promotion of agriculture. He used modern methods on his Whitfield Example Farm, and improved his estates and cottages. He was president of the Royal Agricultural Society in 1851–2. During the last seven years of his life he was a prominent member of the Evangelical Alliance. The sale of his famous collection of shorthorns in August 1853 brought in over £9000. The 'Ducie cultivator', the invention of which is generally ascribed to him, appears to have been invented by the managers of his ironworks at Uley, Gloucestershire.

Ducie died on 2 June 1853 at Tortworth Court, Gloucestershire, and was buried in Tortworth church. His wife survived him, dying on 15 March 1865.

G. F. R. BARKER, *rev.* ANNE PIMLOTT BAKER

Sources *Sporting Review*, 30 (1853), 140–41 · *GM*, 2nd ser., 40 (1853), 87 · Burke, *Peerage* · *WWBMP* · *The Times* (4 June 1853) · *Gloucester Journal* (4 June 1853) · *Journal of the Royal Agricultural Society of England*, 2 (1841), 42 · *Journal of the Royal Agricultural Society of England*, 3 (1842), 122
Likenesses S. Bellin, group portrait, mixed engraving, pubd 1850 (*Meeting of the council of the Anti-Corn Law League*), BM, NPG · H. P. Briggs, portrait, repro. in *Sporting Review*, 28 (1852), 64–6

Moreton, William (1640/41–1715), Church of Ireland bishop of Meath, was born in Chester, the eldest son of **Edward Moreton** (*c.*1599–1675), Church of England clergyman. Edward Moreton was the son of William Moreton of Moreton and his wife, Jane, daughter of Thomas Lancaster of Raynhill, Lancashire. He was educated at Eton College and, from 1619, at King's College, Cambridge, and was incorporated MA at Oxford in 1626, and DD in 1636. He was appointed vicar of Grinton, Yorkshire, in 1634; rector of Tattenhall, Cheshire, chaplain to Sir Thomas Coventry, lord keeper, and prebendary of Chester, all in 1637; and vicar of Sefton, Lancashire, in 1639. It appears that his property was sequestrated in 1645, and that he was nominated by Lord Byron a commissioner to superintend the capitulation of Chester to the parliamentary forces in January 1646. Restored to his benefices at the Restoration, he died at Chester on 28 February 1675, and was buried in Sefton church, where a Latin inscription commemorates his equanimity under misfortune.

William Moreton matriculated from Christ Church, Oxford, aged nineteen, on 5 December 1660 and graduated BA on 19 February 1664, MA on 21 March 1667, and BD on 3 November 1674. In 1669 he became rector of Churchill, Worcestershire, and was also for some time chaplain to Aubrey Vere, earl of Oxford. He went to Ireland in 1677 as chaplain to James, duke of Ormond, then beginning his third period as lord lieutenant of Ireland. He was created DD of Oxford by special decree on 12 December 1677 and appointed dean of Christ Church, Dublin, on 22 December.

Moreton was appointed bishop of Kildare on 14 January 1682, through the influence of Ormond and against the wishes of archbishops Michael Boyle of Armagh and Francis Marsh of Dublin, the former in particular being deeply hostile to him. He was consecrated on 19 February. Owing to the poverty of the diocese he was allowed to retain the deanery of Christ Church, along with the preceptory of Tully. He later petitioned persistently, both before and after the revolution, for the implementation of a clause in the Act of Settlement which would have augmented the revenues of the see, said not to exceed £175 per annum, with forfeited lands worth a further £700 per year. In 1704 he joined with the chapter of Christ Church in rejecting the claim of William King, newly installed as archbishop of Dublin, to rights of visitation. The case was continued after Moreton's transfer to Meath in 1705, and was finally resolved, in the archbishop's favour, only in 1724.

In May 1687 Moreton wrote to Ormond lamenting the state of the church in Ireland and describing how he and others had petitioned the lord deputy, Tyrconnell, and his council over the Roman Catholic clergy's prohibition of the payment of tithes. He is generally listed as one of those who subsequently fled from Tyrconnell's rule. However, when James Bonnell, on 28 January 1689, reported Moreton's recent departure to England he added that it was supposed this was to seek preferment from the new regime, since he had considerable friends (Strype correspondence, 1, fol. 82*v*). Back in Ireland by November 1691, Moreton preached an important sermon defending the treaty of Limerick against the criticisms of Bishop Dopping of Meath. This led the Irish lords justices, Sir Charles Porter and Baron Coningsby, to renew earlier recommendations that he be added to the privy council as 'a discreet person and fit to moderate that spirit of revenge which they find in the English against the Irish' (Nottingham to Sydney, 24 July 1691, *Finch MSS*, 3.176). Later, during 1693–4, Porter lobbied strenuously to have Moreton appointed to the vacant archbishopric of Dublin, while his whig rival Sir Henry Capel dismissed the bishop as 'a rank Jacobite' (Capel to Shrewsbury, 12 April [1694], *Buccleuch MSS*, 2.62).

As bishop of Kildare, Moreton ordained Jonathan Swift deacon on 25 October 1694 and priest on 13 January 1695. In the reign of Anne he was a prominent member of the tory and high-church majority among the Irish bishops. When an act of parliament in 1702 gave him control of the Huguenot settlement at Portarlington he used his power to remove the pastor and replace him with a minister who would conform to the Church of Ireland's liturgy. He was probably the 'Bishop M.' who in 1691 advocated paying pensions to four Roman Catholic bishops, while banishing all regulars. In 1709 he was one of the eight archbishops and bishops who voted against a new Popery Bill.

Moreton was translated to Meath on 18 September 1705. In 1682 he had married Mary Atkins (*b. c.*1656), daughter of Sir Richard Atkins, bt, in London. A son by this marriage, Richard Moreton (*c.*1685–1736), was prebendary of Connor in 1731–6. William Moreton later married Mary, *née* Harman, widow of Sir Arthur Jones. His second son by this marriage was Sir William Moreton (1696?–1763), who graduated from Trinity College, Dublin, in 1714, was called to the English bar in 1722, and subsequently served as recorder of London (1753–63) and MP for Brackley (1755–

61) in the British parliament. Bishop Moreton died at Dublin on 21 November 1715 and was buried three days later in Christ Church there.

G. LE G. NORGATE, *rev.* S. J. CONNOLLY

Sources Wood, *Ath. Oxon.*, new edn · *CSP dom.*, 1682–5; 1700–02 · W. Sterry, ed., *The Eton College register, 1441–1698* (1943) · *Report on the manuscripts of Allan George Finch*, 5 vols., HMC, 71 (1913–2003), vol. 3 · *The manuscripts of his grace the duke of Buccleuch and Queensberry … preserved at Drumlanrig Castle*, 2 vols., HMC, 44 (1897–1903), vol. 1 · *Calendar of the manuscripts of the marquess of Ormonde*, new ser., 8 vols., HMC, 36 (1902–20), vols. 6–8 · T. W. Moody and others, eds., *A new history of Ireland*, 9: *Maps, genealogies, lists* (1984) · C. E. J. Caldicott, H. Gough, and J.-P. Pittion, eds., *The Huguenots and Ireland: anatomy of an emigration* (1987) · L. B. Namier, 'Moreton, Sir William', HoP, *Commons, 1754–90* · W. Troost, 'William III and the treaty of Limerick, 1691–1697', Doctor in de Lettern diss., University of Leiden, 1983 · Strype correspondence, CUL, Baumgartner MSS · NA Ire., Wyche MSS · Venn, *Alum. Cant.* · H. Cotton, *Fasti ecclesiae Hibernicae*, 6 vols. (1845–78)

Archives BL, letters to John Ellis, Add. MSS 28875–28892, 28927 · BL, corresp. mainly with his uncle, Add. MS 33937 · JRL, corresp. with William King · NA Ire., Wyche MSS, incl. letters to Sir Cyril Wyche

Likenesses M. Dahl, oils, Christ Church Oxf.

Morfill, William Richard (1834–1909), Slavonic languages scholar and university teacher, was born on 17 November 1834 at Maidstone, Kent, the second of the three children of William Morfill (1807–*c.*1870), a professional musician, and his wife, Elizabeth (*fl.* 1816–1836), *née* Couchman. The Morfills are thought to have been of Huguenot origin, but William was baptized into the Church of England, together with his sister and younger brother, at All Saints' Church, Maidstone, on 26 October 1838. He was educated at Maidstone grammar school and (from 1848) at Tonbridge School. On 28 May 1853, with a scholarship from his school, he entered Corpus Christi College, Oxford, as a commoner, but migrated on 5 December of that year to Oriel College on election to an open classical scholarship there. In Michaelmas term 1855 he was placed in the first class in classical moderations, but during finals (*literae humaniores*) in 1857 he was taken seriously ill, had to retire from the examination, and was awarded only a pass degree. This seemed to be the end of his aspirations for an academic career, but he stayed on in Oxford, supporting himself by giving private tuition from his rooms in Oriel Street. On 6 September 1860, in the parish church of St Martin, Welton, Northamptonshire, he was married to Charlotte Maria (*d.* 1881), the daughter of Thomas Lee of Welton, a grazier. They had no children. By 1863 he was living with his wife at 4 Clarendon Villas, Park Town, Oxford, and from 1865 to 1869 he was a lecturer in philosophy and modern history at Charsley's Hall (one of the Oxford private halls).

A precocious interest in exotic languages and the gift of a Russian grammar from one of his teachers at Tonbridge led Morfill to apply himself seriously to the study of Russian. His first published translations from that language date from 1860, and in 1870 he made the first of many visits to Russia. He also learned other Slavonic languages and travelled to the countries where they were spoken; his first visit to Prague took place in 1871. He soon acquired

William Richard Morfill (1834–1909), by Sir William
Rothenstein, 1893

a reputation as an expert in Slavonic languages, a subject
which until 1870 was not represented at any British university. On 8 June that year he was appointed by the University of Oxford to give the first series of lectures in
accordance with the provisions of the newly endowed
Ilchester Foundation for the encouragement of the study
of Slavonic languages. He still had no permanent appointment, but he was engaged to give further Ilchester lectures in 1873 and 1883. The substance of some of these lectures was published in his *Dawn of European Literature: Slavonic Literature* (1883).

His wife's early death in 1881 was a blow from which
Morfill never fully recovered, but he sought solace in his
work. About this time regular gatherings of his friends
began to take place on Sunday afternoons at his house in
Clarendon Villas for learned and literary conversation.
The 1880s saw the appearance of Morfill's grammars of
Polish (1884), Serbian (1887), and Russian (1889), though
his command of languages extended beyond the Slavonic
field. He also turned his attention to Georgian and, following a visit to Georgia in 1888, he wrote a well-informed article on Georgian literature for *The Academy* (21 July 1888).
Official recognition came late. It was only in December
1889 that the university appointed him reader in Russian
and the other Slavonic languages, and it was not until
1900, when he was sixty-six years old, that he was promoted to professor. He had meanwhile added to his publications a history of Russia (1890), a history of Poland
(1893), and grammars of Bulgarian (1897) and Czech (1899).
From 1890 he was a corresponding member of the
Královská Česká Společnost nauk ('Royal Czech Society of

Sciences') and, from 1905, of the Česká akademie císaře
Františka Josefa pro Vědy, slovesnost a Umění ('Francis
Joseph Czech Academy for Sciences, Literature, and Arts').
He was elected a fellow of the British Academy in 1903 and
in July 1908 he was awarded an honorary doctorate by the
Charles University, Prague.

Believing that the account of the Slavs fed to the British
public was tainted by German prejudice, Morfill saw himself as an enlightener, but, though he claimed that his
own work was without bias, he had a distinctly Russian
view of Slavonic brotherhood. In 1904 Russian became a
full degree subject at Oxford. The university's approval of
the languages he had cultivated while they lay outside the
curriculum is Morfill's most enduring achievement. He
had a genial personality and was renowned for the charm
of his conversation. Even while he was an undergraduate
'the epigrammatic vigour of his sentences' (Murray, 369)
was noted. He was good-looking but had a squint, which
he endeavoured to hide, when drawn or photographed, by
appearing in profile. Before he reached his sixtieth birthday he was bald on top and had grown a full beard to
replace the whiskers he had worn as a young man. He died
of old age and a weak heart at 4 Clarendon Villas, Park
Town, on 9 November 1909. The first part of the funeral
service was held at the church of St Philip and St James,
Oxford, and he was buried in the same grave as his wife in
St Sepulchre's cemetery, Walton Street, Oxford, on 13
November.   GERALD STONE

Sources J. A. H. Murray, 'William Richard Morfill, 1834–1909',
PBA, [4] (1909–10), 368–74 · J. S. G. Simmons, 'Slavonic studies at
Oxford, 1844–1909', *Oxford Slavonic Papers*, new ser., 13 (1980), 1–27 ·
J. D. Naughton, 'Morfill and the Czechs', *Oxford Slavonic Papers*, new
ser., 17 (1984), 62–76 · private information (2004) · *DNB* · V. E.
Mourek, *Almanach České Akademie Císaře Františka Josefa pro Vědy,
Slovesnost a Umění*, 20 (1910), 120–25 · C. Firth, *Modern languages at
Oxford, 1724–1929* (1929) · R. Filipović, *Englesko-hrvatske književne veze*
(Zagreb, 1972) · *The Times* (12 Nov 1909) · *The Times* (15 Nov 1909) ·
C. L. Shadwell, *Registrum Orielense*, 2 (1902) · *Dutton, Allen, & Co.'s dir-
ectory and gazetteer of the counties of Oxon., Berks. and Bucks.* (1863) · m.
cert. · d. cert.

Archives Institute of Russian Literature (Pushkinskii dom), St
Petersburg, corresp. · Literární archiv Památníku národního
písemnictví na Strahově, Prague, corresp.

Likenesses J. Guggenheim, photograph, *c.*1854, priv. coll. ·
J. Guggenheim, photograph, *c.*1864, priv. coll. · V. Unie, photo-
graph, 1891, repro. in Mourek, *Almanach*, following p. 120 ·
W. Rothenstein, lithograph, 1893, NPG [*see illus.*] · group portraits,
photographs, 1899–1906 (of Oriel Senior Common Room reunion),
Oriel College, Oxford · photograph, British Academy, London

Wealth at death £10,054 16*s.* 4*d.*: resworn probate, 23 Dec 1909,
CGPLA Eng. & Wales

Morgan ab Athrwys (*d. c.*665/710), king of Glywysing, was
son of Athrwys ap Meurig. He ruled the kingdom of
Glywysing, probably incorporating a large part of south-
east Wales, during the second half of the seventh century.
Though he had long been identified with the Morgan who
died in 665, more recent analysis of the charters in the
Book of Llandaff (from which most of the information
about him derives) would suggest he ruled from about 670
until about 710. He has also been regarded as the eponym
of the later kingdom of Morgannwg, though this honour
should probably go to his descendant *Morgan Hen ab

Owain. Morgan's land grants recorded in the Book of Llandaff are scattered throughout south-east Wales, identifying the extent of his landholding and possibly also that of his royal authority. It appears that there were a number of other kings and sub-kings in this region at that time (including Morgan's brother Ithel), but Morgan was probably the predominant ruler. He seems to have succeeded his father Athrwys ap Meurig (*c.*670), though his grandfather Meurig ap Tewdrig was still active after this point. One incident in the Book of Landaff describes Morgan slaying his uncle Ffriog ap Meurig, possibly about 675, and then (allegedly) submitting to Euddogwy, bishop of Llandaff. That the two kinsmen had previously sworn oaths to keep the peace between them indicates that relations had not always been amicable. Ffriog is not entitled king, though their rivalry may have been dynastic in origin. Morgan's wife may have been one Ricceneth, and his sons were called Ithel and Gwyddnerth. On his death, whether in 665 or about 710, Morgan was succeeded by Ithel from whom the later kings of Morgannwg claimed descent.

DAVID E. THORNTON

Sources J. Williams ab Ithel, ed., *Annales Cambriae*, Rolls Series, 20 (1860) • P. C. Bartrum, ed., *Early Welsh genealogical tracts* (1966) • J. G. Evans and J. Rhys, eds., *The text of the Book of Llan Dâv reproduced from the Gwysaney manuscript* (1893) • W. Davies, *An early Welsh microcosm: studies in the Llandaff charters* (1978)
Wealth at death extensive landholding

Morgan ap Caradog (*d. c.*1208). *See under* Iestyn ap Gwrgant (*fl. c.*1081–*c.*1120).

Morgan ap Hywel (*d.* 1248). *See under* Iorwerth ab Owain (*d.* 1175x84).

Morgan ap Maredudd (*fl.* 1270–1316), rebel, was the son of Maredudd ap Gruffudd (*c.*1234–1270) of Machen, Gwent, and Maud, daughter of Cadwallon and a descendant of the native Welsh dynasty of Gwynllwg; his uprising in 1294–5 was part of widespread Welsh resentment against Edward I and certain marcher lords. In 1270 his family was deprived of its estates by Gilbert de Clare, earl of Gloucester, and lord of Glamorgan, and Morgan's attempt to recover them in 1278 failed; in 1283 he supported the rebellion of Dafydd ap Gruffudd, prince of north Wales. Morgan rose in October 1294 against Earl Gilbert; the Welsh of the Glamorgan uplands were also alienated by Edward I's taxation in 1292 and 1293 and his demand for soldiers for Gascony in 1294. Several strongholds were captured, but Abergavenny was relieved by the earl of Hereford (February 1295). By November Edward I had assembled a force of about 4000 at Cardiff and a counter-attack in April 1295 restored Gloucester's control there. When Edward I approached, Morgan submitted, claiming his followers had risen against Gloucester, not the king; Edward received their homage on 7 June 'against the earl's will' (*Ann. mon.*, 4.526). Morgan became an esquire of Edward's household and his agent in south Wales in 1297, and after Earl Gilbert's death in 1295 he was granted some of his father's lands. But he was dispossessed, *c.*1307, by the new earl, who conceded him a small property. Nevertheless Morgan stayed loyal, even when Llywelyn Bren rebelled in 1316. R. A. GRIFFITHS

Sources G. Williams, ed., *Glamorgan county history*, 3: *The middle ages*, ed. T. B. Pugh (1971) • M. Altschul, *A baronial family in medieval England: the Clares, 1217–1314* (1965) • *Ann. mon.*, vols. 3–4 • E. B. Fryde, ed., *Book of prests of the king's wardrobe for 1294–5* (1962) • J. C. Davies, ed., *The Welsh assize roll, 1277–1284* (1940) • J. G. Edwards, *Calendar of ancient correspondence concerning Wales* (1935) • *Chancery records* • PRO • P. C. Bartrum, ed., *Welsh genealogies, AD 300–1400*, 8 vols. (1974), vol. 4, p. 779

Morgan ap Morgan (*d.* 1241). *See under* Iestyn ap Gwrgant (*fl. c.*1081–*c.*1120).

Morgan Gam. *See* Morgan ap Morgan (*d.* 1241) *under* Iestyn ap Gwrgant (*fl. c.*1081–*c.*1120).

Morgan Hen [Morgan Mawr] (*d.* **974**), king of Morgannwg, was the son of Owain ap Hywel ap Rhys of south-east Wales. Morgan was the dominant king in that part of Wales from about 930 until his death in 974. He is variously known as Hen ('the Old') or Mawr ('the Great'), and has been regarded as the eponym of the kingdom of Morgannwg, though his ancestor *Morgan ab Athrwys has also been suggested as a candidate. The exact date of Morgan's accession to the kingship is not known. His father, Owain ap Hywel, was still alive in 926 if he was the Owain, king of Gwent, who submitted to the English ruler Æthelstan, possibly at Hereford, in that year. Morgan had probably become king at least by 931 when he witnessed a charter of Æthelstan. However, he seems to have shared power with his brothers Gruffudd and Cadwgon, who are entitled kings in the Book of Llandaff *c.*925 and *c.*935 respectively. Gruffudd was slain in 935 by the men of Ceredigion (then probably under the authority of Hywel Dda ap Cadell) and Cadwgon met his death at English hands in 949. After this point Morgan was probably dominant.

Along with the contemporary Welsh rulers Hywel Dda and Idwal Foel of Gwynedd, Morgan was a regular visitor to England, where he witnessed royal charters of Æthelstan and later Eadred and Eadwig. Such witnessing was probably a practical recognition of Anglo-Saxon supremacy rather than a deliberately pro-English policy on the part of these Welsh kings. In 931 Morgan witnessed a charter at Worthy (now in Hampshire), though he was not among the Welsh at Luton in the same year. He also witnessed Æthelstan's charters at 'Middleton' in 932, Winchester and Nottingham in 934, and Dorchester twice in 935. He witnessed a charter of Eadred at Kingston in 946 and 'Chetwode' and Bourton in 949; but the charter of Eadwig for 956 is possibly spurious. Less is known of Morgan's relations with other Welsh kings. For example, the episode in the Book of Llandaff, according to which Hywel Dda contested Morgan's hold of the regions Ystrad Yw and Ewias, seems to be a late composition, since the two kings are then said to have gone to the English court of Edgar to settle the dispute (which was resolved in Morgan's favour): the reigns of Hywel Dda and Edgar do not coincide so this exact sequence of events is impossible. However, in 960 Hywel's son Owain, king of Deheubarth, raided Gorfynydd in Morgannwg; and it is also possible that the raid by his son Einion on Gower in 970 was directed against Morgan if he temporarily held this region at that time. Morgan is conspicuous by his absence from the lists of Welsh kings who are said to have submitted to Edgar at Chester after his 'coronation' at Bath in 973 and rowed him along the Dee. It is possible that after a reign spanning over forty years Morgan, in agreement with his cognomen, was a little too old to engage in these naval activities; indeed, he died a year later in 974. The kingship possibly passed to his son Idwallon, who died in 975, and thence to another son Owain, ancestor of the later rulers of Morgannwg. His other sons were called Cadell and Cynfyn; his wife may have been Lleucu ferch Enflew.

DAVID E. THORNTON

Sources J. Williams ab Ithel, ed., *Annales Cambriae*, Rolls Series, 20 (1860) • T. Jones, ed. and trans., *Brenhinedd y Saesson, or, The kings of the Saxons* (1971) [another version of *Brut y tywysogyon*] • T. Jones, ed. and trans., *Brut y tywysogyon, or, The chronicle of the princes: Peniarth MS 20* (1952) • T. Jones, ed. and trans., *Brut y tywysogyon, or, The chronicle of the princes: Red Book of Hergest* (1955) • P. C. Bartrum, ed., *Early Welsh genealogical tracts* (1966) • J. G. Evans and J. Rhys, eds., *The text of the Book of Llan Dâv reproduced from the Gwysaney manuscript* (1893) • *AS chart.*, S 407, 413, 417, 425, 434–5, 520, 544, 550, 566, 633 • J. E. Lloyd, *A history of Wales from the earliest times to the Edwardian conquest*, 3rd edn, 2 vols. (1939); repr. (1988) • W. Davies, *An early Welsh microcosm: studies in the Llandaff charters* (1978) • H. R. Loyn, 'Wales and England in the tenth century: the context of the Athelstan charters', *Welsh History Review / Cylchgrawn Hanes Cymru*, 10 (1980–81), 283–301

Morgan of Caerleon. *See* Morgan ap Hywel (*d.* 1248) *under* Iorwerth ab Owain (*d.* 1175x84).

Morgan, Abel (1673–1722), Baptist minister, was born at Allt Goch, Llanwenog, Cardiganshire. He was one of three sons of Morgan ap Rhydderch (*b. c.*1642), deacon and later minister of the Rhydwilym Baptist Church. Abel was born into a family already known for its dedication to secular and religious literature. His uncle, Siôn Rhydderch, poet and printer, compiled the first English–Welsh dictionary and translated a number of religious works into Welsh. A great-grandfather, Dafydd ap Grufydd, was also a writer of note.

Morgan was preaching by the age of eighteen, and by the time he was twenty-three he was chosen pastor of the Blaenau Gwent church at Llanwenarth, near Abergavenny. Four years later he was ordained as minister. From 1700 he remained at Blaenau Gwent until 1711, when he accepted an earlier invitation from his brother, Enoch, and other Baptists in North America to take over the mother church near Philadelphia, Pennsylvania. His success in Blaenau Gwent may be judged from the fact that four years after his departure his church numbered 1000 members. He bade farewell to his flock at a meeting held on 23 August; on 28 September he took ship at Bristol. The voyage was a long and stormy one, and in the course of it he lost his wife, Priscilla Powell (*d.* 1711), and son. Their daughter survived and Morgan subsequently married

Martha Burrows; they had no children. Following her death he married Judith Gooding, *née* Griffith; they had four children.

Shortly after his arrival in Philadelphia, Morgan wrote to his former church in Wales describing the city of Philadelphia, where 'the poorest are doing as well as those who possess twenty pounds a year in Wales' (Jones, 305–6). Concerning the prospects for Baptist churches in North America, he noted that eight more churches were planned in Pennsylvania and New Jersey in the coming year. He was responsible for centralizing and systematizing the Baptist churches under an association centred in Philadelphia. He also imposed his version of the 'century of confession' upon the member churches. Included in his translation were articles on singing of psalms and laying on of hands. He also helped to form the Hopewell Baptist Church in New Jersey, from which the first academy for ministers emerged. It was the germ from which grew Brown University in Rhode Island. At his death Morgan left a sizeable library, which is now housed at Rutgers University.

Morgan is best known as the compiler of the first concordance of the Welsh Bible. This he left in manuscript at his death. It was not published until 1730, when Enoch Morgan and some other friends caused it to be printed at Philadelphia. The printers were Samuel Keimer and Dafydd Harry, both well known from the *Autobiography of Benjamin Franklin*. Morgan's concordance was the basis of the one published in 1773 by Peter Williams.

Abel died in Philadelphia on 16 December 1722 and his remains were originally buried at the back of the Philadelphia church in Lagrange Place. His remains were subsequently removed to Mount Moriah cemetery in Philadelphia and interred in a communal plot for ministers of the church. A monument marks the spot. His original tombstone, complete with a daffodil, is housed in the First Baptist Church in 17th Street in Philadelphia. One of his sons, also named Abel Morgan, followed in his father's footsteps and became a noted preacher during the Great Awakening and the American War of Independence.

MARY K. GEITER

Sources Rhydwilym Baptist church register, NL Wales, Minor deposit 127A, pp. 26, 28, 29 • Llanwenarth churchbook, NL Wales, Deposit MS 410B • H. G. Jones, *Pennsylvania Magazine of History and Biography*, 6 (1882), 300–10 • T. Rees, *History of protestant nonconformity in Wales*, 2nd edn (1883), 300, 301 • M. Edwards, *Materials towards a history of the American Baptists*, 1: *Materials towards a history of the Baptists in Pennsylvania* (1770) • W. Cathcart, ed., *Dictionary of Baptists* (1883) • J. Stillwell, *Historical and genealogical miscellany: data relating to the settlement and settlers of New York and New Jersey*, new edn, 2 (1970), 274 • *DNB* • *DAB* • *IGI*

Morgan, Alice Mary. *See* Havers, Alice Mary (1850–1890).

Morgan, Sir Anthony (*d.* 1665). *See under* Morgan, Sir Anthony (1621–1668).

Morgan, Sir Anthony (1621–1668), politician and army officer, was the son of Anthony Morgan DD, an Oxford don and rector of Cottesbrook, Northamptonshire. He may have been intended for a clerical career and from the age of fifteen attended Magdalen Hall, Oxford, where he was appointed a demy of the university in 1640 and graduated BA on 6 July 1641. With the outbreak of civil war, Morgan abandoned his studies and served with the royalist forces in south Wales led by the earl of Worcester. In the spring of 1645, however, he joined Sir Trevor Williams in making overtures to parliament, offering to betray the king's forces in Monmouthshire and Glamorgan in return for commands in the parliamentarian army. Morgan and Williams fulfilled their side of the bargain, and the two counties had duly come under parliament's control by the end of 1645. But it was not until 1646 that Morgan's lands were freed from sequestration, and he had to wait until 1647 before he was commissioned in the New Model Army, and then only as captain in Henry Ireton's regiment of horse. His patron at this time was Sir Thomas Fairfax, who had secured him this command and in 1648 intervened with parliament to indemnify him for his former activities as a royalist. Morgan repaid Fairfax's trust by his loyalty to the army commanders, refusing to become involved in the radicalism which marked Ireton's regiment in the next few years. In 1649 he played a part in putting down the Leveller mutiny, and was promoted to the rank of major as a result.

Morgan went with his regiment to Ireland in July 1649, and became a trusted supporter of Ireton and (after Ireton's death in 1650) Charles Fleetwood, who were successive lords deputy of Ireland in the early 1650s. As a result, in April 1652 he was granted special permission to hold 'any office of trust' under the Commonwealth, despite his earlier delinquency (*JHC*, 7, 1651–9, 169), and went on to serve on civilian commissions, including the high court of justice in Dublin and the commission to settle Ulster. He was also involved in the early stages of the land settlement in Ireland, and himself received lands in co. Kildare. Such employments brought him into close contact with the Irish protestant community, and his election as MP for Kildare and Wicklow in 1654, as partner to the Old Protestant William Meredith, occurred as part of a successful local challenge to the army and the administration in Dublin. The departure of Fleetwood and arrival of Henry Cromwell as acting governor of Ireland in 1655 accelerated Morgan's move away from the army interest. By the summer of 1656 Henry Cromwell counted Morgan as one of his most trusted subordinates and sent him to London to defend his policies before the English council. Morgan was knighted by the protector in July 1656. He was again elected for Kildare and Wicklow in the 1656–8 parliament, and was one of the most important managers of Irish legislation in the house, especially in such matters as the bill of attainder and the Irish assessments. He also played a part in the kingship debates and sent regular accounts of proceedings to Henry Cromwell in Dublin, including news that the protector had refused the crown. A measure of Morgan's attachment to the Cromwellian interest can be seen in the elections for the 1659 parliament, when he was put forward as a candidate for Cambridge University (through the efforts of Henry's father-in-law, Sir Francis Russell) as well as for counties Meath and Louth in Ireland.

In this parliament, Morgan again worked as the spokesman of the Irish administration, and defended Henry Cromwell from being implicated in the corruption charges brought against Dr William Petty.

This close association with Henry Cromwell made Morgan particularly vulnerable when the protectorate collapsed in May 1659. He lost his regiment in the summer and was forced to retire to his house in Abbey Street, Dublin. At the Restoration he immediately threw in his lot with Charles II, much to the disgust of his wife, Elizabeth (*d.* in or after 1668), who was a committed republican, and the two became estranged. Morgan's last shift of allegiance was aided by friends in high places, including Viscount Conway, George Rawdon, and Lord Broghill (created earl of Orrery in 1660). It was probably Orrery who recommended Morgan for another knighthood, awarded in November 1660, and as MP for Taghmon in co. Wexford in 1661 Morgan acted as intermediary between Orrery and his rival, the duke of Ormond, in an attempt to unite the protestant interest. In 1663 Morgan moved to London, where he became involved in the scientific endeavours of Orrery's brother, Robert Boyle. He helped to found the Royal Society, drafting its charter in 1663 and serving on its council in 1663 and 1666–7. Samuel Pepys, meeting Morgan at Lord Brouncker's house in May 1668, thought him 'a very wise man' (Pepys, 9.104). In his will, written in September of that year, Morgan left his wife only 5 *s.*, while leaving all his lands in England, Wales, and Ireland, with his personal property, to his sister, Elizabeth Moore. He died leaving no surviving children late in 1668.

Morgan should not be confused with his namesake **Sir Anthony Morgan** (*d.* 1665), royalist army officer, son of Sir William Morgan, of Tredegar, Monmouthshire, and Bridget, daughter and heir of Anthony Morgan of Heyford, Northamptonshire. A Roman Catholic, he was knighted by Charles I on 21 October 1642, two days before the battle of Edgehill, and commanded a royalist regiment from June 1643. On the death of his half-brother Colonel Thomas Morgan at the battle of Newbury, he inherited the family estates in Northamptonshire, Monmouthshire, Warwickshire, and Westmorland. He went abroad at the end of the first civil war, but returned in 1648 and tried to compound for his lands, despite being branded a 'papist delinquent'. He died in St Giles-in-the-Fields, London, in June 1665, leaving an only daughter, Mary, by his marriage to Elizabeth (Fromond?). A further **Anthony Morgan** (*b.* 1627), royalist army officer, of Marshfield, Monmouthshire, served with the earl of Worcester in the civil war, possibly as a colonel, and as a result had his lands sequestered and sold by parliament in 1652.

PATRICK LITTLE

Sources 'Morgan, Sir Anthony', HoP, *Commons, 1690–1715* [draft] · Thurloe, *State papers* · R. Dunlop, ed., *Ireland under the Commonwealth*, 2 vols. (1913) · PRO, SP 28/61–88 · *Manuscripts of the earl of Egmont: diary of Viscount Percival, afterwards first earl of Egmont*, 3 vols., HMC, 63 (1920–23) · W. Petty, *The history of the survey of Ireland: commonly called the down survey, AD 1655–6*, ed. T. A. Larcom (1851) · *JHC*, 4 (1644–6) · *JHC*, 7 (1651–9) · *Diary of Thomas Burton*, ed. J. T. Rutt, 4 vols. (1828) · BL, Lansdowne MSS 821–823 · Pepys, *Diary* · PRO, PROB 11/328, fols. 236–7 · *DNB*

Morgan, Anthony (*b.* 1627). *See under* Morgan, Sir Anthony (1621–1668).

Morgan, Augustus De (1806–1871), mathematician and historian, fifth child of Colonel John De Morgan (1772–1816) of the Indian army, was born on 27 June 1806 at Madura in the far south of India. His mother, Elizabeth (1776–1856), was the daughter of John Dodson of the custom house, and granddaughter of James Dodson. Seven months after De Morgan's birth his family sailed for England with their five children, settling at Worcester. The youngest son, Campbell Greig De *Morgan, born in 1811, made his career in medicine.

De Morgan was educated privately and sent to various schools, one of his teachers being J. Fenner, a Unitarian minister and an uncle of H. Crabb Robinson. He pricked out equations on a pew at St Michael's Church, Bristol, some of which remained after his death, instead of listening to the sermon. In February 1823 he entered Trinity College, Cambridge, where he soon showed his mathematical ability. He made many friends at college, including his teachers William Whewell and George Peacock. He belonged to a musical society called the Camus (Cambridge Amateur Musical Union Society), and was a skilful flautist. In 1827 he graduated as fourth wrangler, though far superior in mathematical ability to any man in his year. He was disappointed by the result, which was due to his discursive reading. He always disliked competitive examinations as tending to give the advantage to the docile over the original students, and because they encouraged 'cramming'.

De Morgan's career was now affected by religious issues. His parents had inculcated their strict religious principles into him from a very early age; but even at school he had revolted from the doctrines held by his mother, and at Cambridge he became heterodox. He was throughout life a strong theist and preferred the Unitarian to other creeds, but he never definitely joined any church, calling himself a 'Christian unattached'. His scruples prevented him from proceeding to the MA degree or becoming a candidate for a fellowship. After some thoughts of medicine he resolved to go to the bar, and entered Lincoln's Inn.

Professor of mathematics At this time London University was established, without adherence to any religious institution. De Morgan found law unpalatable, and, though the youngest applicant, he was unanimously elected on 23 February 1828 the first professor of mathematics on the strength of very high testimonials from Peacock, G. B. Airy, and other Cambridge authorities. He gave his introductory lecture, 'On the study of mathematics', on 5 November 1828. However, difficulties soon arose in the working of the new institution: the council claimed the right of dismissing a professor without assigning reasons, and so dismissed the professor of anatomy. De Morgan immediately resigned his post in a letter dated 24 July 1831.

In October 1836 his successor, G. J. P. White, was accidentally drowned, whereupon De Morgan offered himself as a temporary substitute. He was then invited to resume the

Augustus De Morgan (1806–1871), by John Jabez Edwin Mayall

chair and, as the regulations had by then been so altered as to give the necessary independence to professors, he accepted the invitation. He was reappointed and served as professor for the next thirty years. At that time King's College, London, was being formed as an institution under the Church of England, London University became University College, and the two colleges merged as the University of London, an examining body which conferred degrees.

De Morgan revealed a power of clear exposition, often though not always combined with learning and original genius, a quaint sense of humour, and a thorough contempt for sham knowledge and low aims in study. He did much work with his students beyond regular lecture times, and occasionally took private pupils. His income as professor never reached £500, and in later years declined, seldom exceeding £300.

In the autumn of 1831 De Morgan moved to 5 Upper Gower Street, where he was a neighbour of William Frend, mathematician and political reformer. He married Frend's daughter, Sophia Elizabeth (1809–1892) on 3 August 1837, and settled in 69 Gower Street. Of his seven children, William Frend De *Morgan (1839–1917), was to make a distinguished career as a ceramicist and novelist, while George Campbell De Morgan [*see below*] showed great promise in mathematics before his early death. Augustus De Morgan was so much absorbed in various kinds of work that he had little leisure for domestic recreation. His lectures permitted him at first to return home at midday, but this practice had to be abandoned on his move to 7 Camden Street, Camden Town, in 1844. After 1840 he gave up the practice of taking a holiday with his family in the country. An inveterate Londoner, he loved the town, and had a humorous detestation of trees, fields, and birds. He could not even bear Blackheath, calling the heath 'desolation', although he liked the steamboats.

Membership of societies From the first De Morgan was a most energetic worker in other London institutions. Elected in May 1828 a fellow of the Astronomical Society, he was placed on its council in 1830. He was secretary from 1831 to 1838 and from 1848 to 1854, and at other periods held office as vice-president. He took a keen interest in its proceedings, edited its publications, and made many intimate friends at its meetings. By contrast, he never became a fellow of the Royal Society, and held that it was too much open to social influences to be thoroughly efficient as a working institution. He did, however, become a member of the Society for the Diffusion of Useful Knowledge (SDUK), founded by Lord Brougham and others in 1826. It published some of his early writings, and he contributed a great number of articles to its other publications: the *Penny Cyclopaedia*, for which he wrote about 850 of the articles, the *Quarterly Journal of Education*, and the unfortunately short-lived *Biographical Dictionary*. He also published with the society an *Elements of Algebra* (1835), and, especially, a massive and high-level *Treatise on the Differential and Integral Calculus*, which appeared in instalments between 1836 and 1842. He became a member of the committee in 1843. (The society was dissolved in 1846.)

For many years De Morgan promoted the adoption of a decimal coinage. He gave evidence before commissions, and was on the council of the Decimal Association formed in 1854. A commission finally decided against the measure in 1859 and the agitation dropped.

Development of logic De Morgan read and wrote much despite losing an eye in childhood. In a brilliant remark made in a book review in 1868 he commented that mathematics and logic constituted the 'two eyes of exact science', but that each was trying to put out the other one, 'believing that it can see better with one eye than with two' (*The Athenaeum*, 2, 1868, 71–3). This point surrounded much of his research work, for his mathematical speciality was algebra, and his contributions to logic drew upon certain algebraic principles.

As an undergraduate De Morgan fell under the influence of Peacock and Whewell; from them he studied the distinction, then widely discussed in Britain, between form and matter in common algebra. Form related to the general conception of an algebra, like his 'double algebra' where the elements could be combined in two different ways (like + and × in ordinary arithmetic); his work here helped W. R. Hamilton to develop his quaternion algebra in 1843. Matter arose in particular cases such as the 'real' existence of negative numbers.

In 1836, De Morgan wrote for the *Encyclopaedia metropolitana* the first comprehensive survey of functional equations, a fairly new algebra which had been brought into English mathematics in the 1810s by John Herschel and especially Charles Babbage. The task was to find mathematical functions which obeyed some given particular property. His work was to relate to the last of his four main contributions to logic, which he had begun to study at this time and most of which appeared in a suite of five papers, 'On the syllogism', published between 1846 and 1862, and in his book *Formal Logic* (1847).

First, De Morgan published in 1831 a book, *On the Study and Difficulties of Mathematics*, followed in 1839 by a booklet, *First Notions of Logic (Preparatory to the Study of Geometry)*, in which he tried to discern the logical manoeuvres involved in Euclid's logic. The status of the parallel postulate in geometry concerns the axiomatization of the theory, which is a different question.

De Morgan was then, in the 1840s, involved in a priority dispute initiated by the Scottish philosopher Sir William Hamilton over the 'quantification of the predicate', in which propositions such as 'all Xs are some Ys' were added to syllogistic logic. They greatly expanded the range of valid and invalid modes. A pair of laws now named after him arose in this context in 1853, in his third paper: 'The contrary of an aggregate [the complement of the union of two classes] is the compound [intersection] of the contraries of the [two] aggregants; the contrary of a compound is the aggregate of the contraries of the components'. However, he did not realize their full importance for logic.

De Morgan's third contribution was his examination of various aspects of his expanded syllogistic logic. These included 'numerically definite' ones such as 'Each of the 50 Xs is one or other of the 70 Ys'. He also studied algebra-like properties of the copula such as transitivity, and stressed its various roles, such as predication distinct from identity. He noted analogies with algebra, such as logical inference with algebraic elimination. He devised ingenious semiotic notations using dots and brackets to represent propositions—for example, for predicates X and Y: 'X).(Y' for 'No X is Y', and 'X(.)Y' for 'Y sometimes not in X'. (His handling of classes of objects satisfying predicates was of the part-whole kind, then the usual way of treating collections of things.) These notations also provided concise ways of representing valid modes.

De Morgan's fourth paper, *On the Logic of Relations*, published in 1860, contained arguably his most substantial innovation in logic. He outlined many of the basic properties of a logic of two-place relations, such as 'brother of' or 'greater than', and operations such as composition and inversion (if possible) upon them. He deployed algebraic notations to signify many of his notions and findings. From a structural point of view this work showed close kinship with his study of functional equations; several principal properties, for example, the existence of inverse(s), are common to both.

Most of De Morgan's work in logic can be characterized as conservative (though valuable) extensions of syllogistic logic—less radical than the efforts of his friend George Boole in 1847. But he was well aware of the limitations of syllogism, not only the absence of relations but also non-syllogistic inferences such as 'man is animal, therefore the head of a man is the head of an animal'.

On the more informal side of logic, De Morgan produced *A Budget of Paradoxes*, which was based on many short articles in *The Athenaeum*. The book was published in 1872 shortly after his death, under the editorship of his widow. He assembled many newspaper reports, short articles, poems, and much other material, commenting with logical acumen and wit.

In 1837 De Morgan wrote another article for the *Encyclopaedia metropolitana*, on probability theory. He considered probabilistic inference, that is, the transmission of probability values from premises to consequences. In *An Essay on Probabilities* of the following year he emphasized the importance of the subject in life contingencies, which gave his book a good reception in the assurance industry. Indeed, during 1831–6 when he was absent from the university, he often worked as an actuary; he also contributed to the *Insurance Record*.

Other writing De Morgan also wrote extensively on the history of mathematics and astronomy, including a long series of articles in the journal *Companion to the Almanac* and many of the SDUK pieces in the *Quarterly Journal of Education* and the *Penny Cyclopaedia*. His two most substantial topics were an annotated bibliography of books in arithmetic, information which he gathered together in *Arithmetical Books* (1847), and articles in which he exposed for the first time the dishonest way in which Isaac Newton had argued within the Royal Society in the early eighteenth century that G. W. Leibniz had plagiarized him in the invention of the calculus. Until the First World War, De Morgan's historical work was well remembered; in particular, it was cited in many articles in the *Dictionary of National Biography*. He was a prolific correspondent, often adorning his letters with well-drawn caricatures and sketches. He had a love of puns, and of ingenious puzzles and paradoxes. A year before his death an annuity of £100 was obtained from the government, and accepted with some reluctance.

Among other activities De Morgan collaborated with his wife on pioneering studies of psychical mediumship. As 'C. D.' she published *From Matter to Spirit* in 1863, to which her husband, 'A. B.', contributed an excellent preface.

In 1866 the chair of mental philosophy and logic at University College became vacant. A discussion arose as to the principle of religious neutrality avowedly adopted by the college when refusing to appoint as professor of philosophy James Martineau, who, as a Unitarian minister, was pledged to maintain the creed of a particular sect. De Morgan, on the other hand, held that any consideration of a candidate's ecclesiastical position or religious creed was inconsistent with the principle, so again resigned his office, in a letter dated 10 November 1866. Though no personal bitterness was produced, De Morgan had felt the blow so keenly that it injured his health. Some of his old students begged him to allow his portrait to be painted for the library of 'our old college'. But he objected on principle to testimonials, and is alleged to have replied that 'our old college no longer exists'.

De Morgan died on 18 March 1871 at his home, 6 Merton Road, Hampstead, and was buried in Kensal Green cemetery. His library consisted at the end of his life of about three thousand volumes. He was a genuine book-hunter,

though his means compelled him to limit himself to occasional treasures from bookstalls. He made many amusing marginal and learned annotations, and turned his bibliographical researches to a good account in his historical writings. His library was bought after his death by Lord Overstone and presented to the University of London, where it became part of the University Library at its foundation.

De Morgan's son **George Campbell De Morgan** (1841–1867) was born on 16 August 1841 at Gower Street. He was educated at University College School, 1856–7, then under his father at University College, 1857–60, graduating MA in 1863 with the award of a gold medal. He was appointed mathematics master at the school in 1866; at the time of his death he was vice-principal of University Hall. As well as producing some promising mathematical work, he was one of the founders in 1865 of the London Mathematical Society (and his father was the first president). He died on 14 October 1867 at Ventnor, Isle of Wight.

LESLIE STEPHEN, *rev.* I. GRATTAN-GUINNESS

Sources S. E. De Morgan, *Memoirs of Augustus De Morgan* (1882) · M. Panteki, 'Relationships between algebra, logic and differential equations in England, 1800–1860', PhD diss., Middlesex University (CNAA), 1992 · A. Rice, 'Augustus De Morgan and the development of university mathematics in London in the nineteenth century', PhD diss., Middlesex University, 1997 · A. Rice, 'Inspiration or desperation? Augustus De Morgan's appointment to the chair of mathematics at London University in 1828', *British Journal for the History of Science*, 30 (1997), 257–74 · A. Rice, 'Mathematics in the metropolis: a survey of Victorian London', *Historia Mathematica*, 23 (1996), 376–417 · A. Rice, R. J. Wilson, and J. H. Gardner, 'From student club to national society: the founding of the London Mathematical Society in 1865', *Historia Mathematica*, 22 (1995), 402–11 · A. Rice, 'Augustus De Morgan: historian', *History of Science*, 34 (1996), 201–40 · P. Heath, ed., *On the syllogism, and other logical writings* (1966) · A. De Morgan, *A budget of paradoxes* (1872) · d. cert. · b. cert. [G. C. De Morgan] · d. cert. [G. C. De Morgan]

Archives American Philosophical Society, Philadelphia, letters · Bodl. Oxf., corresp.; family corresp. · LUL, corresp. and papers · RAS, corresp. and papers; letters to RAS · Royal Observatory Library, Edinburgh, catalogue of mathematical books · UCL, corresp. and papers · UCL, letters to Society for the Diffusion of Useful Knowledge | BL, corresp. with Charles Babbage, Add. MSS 37185–37200, *passim* · Bodl. Oxf., corresp. with Lady Byron · CUL, corresp. with Sir George Airy · CUL, letters to William Hepworth Dixon · CUL, letters to Lord Kelvin · NL Scot., letters to Alexander Campbell Fraser · RS, corresp. with Sir John Herschel · RS, letters to Sir John Lubbock · TCD, letters to Sir William Hamilton · Trinity Cam., letters to William Whewell · U. Edin. L., special collections division, letters to James Halliwell-Phillips · UCL, corresp. with George Boole · UCL, corresp. with Lord Brougham · UCL, letters to F. Hendriks

Likenesses T. Woolner, marble bust, after 1876, U. Lond. · A. De Morgan, self-portrait, pen-and-ink drawing, RAS · Maull & Polyblank, carte-de-visite, NPG · J. J. E. Mayall, photograph, NPG [*see illus.*] · carte-de-visite, NPG · wood-engraving, NPG; repro. in *ILN* (22 April 1854)

Wealth at death under £7000: probate, 29 April 1871, *CGPLA Eng. & Wales*

Morgan, Campbell Greig De (1811–1876), surgeon, was born at Clovelly, near Bideford, Devon, the youngest of the three sons of Colonel John De Morgan (1772–1816) of the Indian army, and his wife Elizabeth (1776–1856), the daughter of John Dodson and granddaughter of James

Dodson. Augustus De *Morgan, the mathematician, was his elder brother. He was educated at University College, London, and afterwards at the Middlesex Hospital. In 1835 he became a member of the Royal College of Surgeons and in 1841 he was lecturer on forensic medicine at the Middlesex Hospital. In 1842 he became assistant surgeon there and he held the chair of anatomy in 1845. He became a fellow of the Royal College of Surgeons in 1843 and then full surgeon at the Middlesex on the retirement of Mr Tuson in 1854.

With John Tomes, De Morgan contributed a paper to the Royal Society on the development of bone, which gained him election as FRS and which was printed in the *Philosophical Transactions* for 1852. He wrote the article 'Erysipelas' in Holmes's *System of Surgery* (1860) and in 1865 he joined the Pathological Society and began contributing papers to its *Transactions*. In 1872 he published a work entitled *Origin of Cancer*, following a series of papers on that subject published in *The Lancet* in 1871. This was a subject which he had studied during thirty-four years in the special cancer wards of the Middlesex Hospital.

De Morgan continued his teaching career, lecturing on anatomy, physiology, and forensic medicine, and on the retirement of Mr Shaw he became sole lecturer on surgery at the Middlesex. He worked as a consulting surgeon to the London Fever Hospital and to the East Grinstead Dispensary, and he was also a surgeon at the Institution for Invalid Gentlewomen.

In addition to his professional attainments De Morgan was said to be an accomplished musician and a gifted caricaturist. He was described as a man who, under a somewhat cold manner, had great kindness and warmth of heart, and his contemporaries knew him as a modest and generous man of deep religious convictions. His last act was one of devoted attention to his old friend J. G. Lough, the sculptor; after sitting up with him through the night, he returned home to 29 Seymour Street, Portman Square, London, in the cold of an early morning and caught a fatal chill. He died at home on 12 April 1876 and was buried in Kensal Green cemetery, on 18 April. His wife (formerly Miss Hobson) had died in 1856.

JAMES DIXON, rev. KAYE BAGSHAW

Sources E. M. Rosser, 'Campbell de Morgan and his spots', *Annals of the Royal College of Surgeons of England*, 65 (1983), 266–9 · *BMJ* (22 April 1876), 523–4 · *The Lancet* (22 April 1876), 621 · V. G. Plarr, *Plarr's Lives of the fellows of the Royal College of Surgeons of England*, rev. D'A. Power, 2 vols. (1930)
Archives W. Sussex RO, letters to duke of Richmond
Likenesses J. G. Layh, marble bust, c.1875, Middlesex Hospital, London · G. R. Black, lithograph, 1876; formerly at RCS Eng.
Wealth at death under £4000: probate, 20 May 1876, *CGPLA Eng. & Wales*

Morgan, Sir Charles (1575/6–1643), army officer, was a younger son of Edward Morgan (1530–1585) of Pen-carn, Monmouthshire, and his wife, Frances Leigh, of London. His uncle, Thomas *Morgan, 'the Warrior' (d. 1595), had served long in the Dutch struggle for independence, being among the first English and Welsh volunteers to join the cause in 1572, and Charles followed him into a military career. He seems to have served first in the Netherlands,

and through his marriage to Elizabeth or Eliza (d. in or before 1634), the daughter of the Flemish nobleman Philip Marnix of St Aldegonde (d. 1598), he was linked to the family of a man who as propagandist and secretary to William the Silent had helped make the uprising. During the expedition to Cadiz in 1596 Morgan served as a captain in Sir John Wingfield's infantry regiment (of which his elder brother Matthew was lieutenant-colonel). On 4 April 1597 he was ordered to take four infantry companies to Guernsey and Jersey. Upon his return to the Netherlands he served under Sir Francis Vere at the battle of Nieuwpoort on 2 July 1600 and in the long defence of Ostend from July 1601. During the siege he went to England and was knighted by James I at Whitehall on 23 July 1603, but he returned to Ostend and was there when the town surrendered on 20 September 1604.

Morgan came home to the Welsh marches, and served as JP in Monmouthshire and possibly Herefordshire. Following the outbreak of 'popish' disturbances in Herefordshire and south Wales, Morgan's role, notwithstanding his protestant martial career, seems to have come under suspicion. The rioting had occurred, the bishop of Hereford reported, in part because

> sundry of the justices are unworthy of their places, for that their mothers, wives, brethren or allies and whole families are totally recusants ... as Sir Charles Morgan, whose mother, uncle, brother, whole allies and tenants are that way infected. (*Salisbury MSS*, 17.235)

Within a few days Morgan was sent to the Fleet prison for having neglected his duty by coming to London 'in a time of such disorder' (ibid., 17.254). His imprisonment was brief, as he was evidently soon back in the marches pursuing priests. However, while there is no certain knowledge of there being more than one knight named Charles Morgan at this time, it is possible that the suspect and the priest-hunter were two different men. This would explain the anomaly that the bishop's letter which voiced his suspicions about Sir Charles Morgan also carried the signature of Sir Charles Morgan. By August 1607 Morgan was back in the Netherlands again, with Edward Vere successfully defending Cassant against the Spanish. During the twelve-year truce (1609–21) between Spain and the Netherlands, Morgan carried letters between the English ambassadors in The Hague and the Netherlands. With the ending of the truce Morgan's services as a soldier in the Dutch cause were once again called upon. He commanded the English troops at the unsuccessful siege of Bergen-op-Zoom in 1622, and in 1624 he was assigned the defence of the 's-Hertogenbosch gate when Breda was besieged, a position in which he served until the town fell the following year. That July, with the English ambassador Sir Dudley Carleton, he received Elizabeth of Bohemia and her party in Amsterdam. At the siege of Groenlo he lost his skilful lieutenant-colonel, Sir John Prowde.

Following the defeat of Christian IV of Denmark at the battle of Lutter in August 1626 by the imperialist forces under Marshal Tilly, the English privy council appointed Morgan the senior officer of the expedition sent to aid the king's uncle. The force was initially made up of four regiments, 2472 men, who had been sent to fight for the Dutch in 1624. Reinforcements brought Morgan's force to 5013 men, which rapidly shrank to 2472 in February 1627, had risen to 4913 men by June but dropped over the next eleven months to 1630 men. In April 1627 he had built a sconce on the Weser, above Bremen, to prevent Tilly from drawing supplies from the city. Later in the month, reinforced by Mackay's foot, a German regiment, and several hundred horse, he established his camp 10 miles southeast of the city. In June he formed a camp at the confluence of the rivers Weser and Aller. On 5 July 1627 he was noted as commanding the garrison of Bremen. From there on 23 July Morgan wrote that his men were so mutinous from lack of pay that they would probably not even fight to defend themselves against an enemy attack. On 5 August Edward Clarke arrived with bills of exchange worth a month's pay for Morgan's regiment, but they proved useless and Sir Charles borrowed 3000 rixdaler on his own credit to pay the soldiers. The 1400 recruits accompanying Clarke proved equally disappointing. Sir Charles found that the 223 ill and underclothed men meant for his regiment were as desertion-prone as the entire force. On 7 September he wrote to Secretary Carleton concerning the poor quality of his troops, 'What service can the king expect or draw from these unwilling men?' (*CSP dom.*, 1627–8, 389). Following the margrave of Baden's defeat at Heiligenhaufen on 14 September Morgan successfully brought his command to the east bank of the Elbe. In the winter of 1627–8 he commanded 2000 English and Scots in the defence of Christian IV's fortress at Stade.

The English government continued to ignore his financial needs. With the assistance of Sir Robert Anstruther, the ambassador to Denmark, he raised enough money to buy supplies and stockings for his men. On 25 January 1628 he wrote to Conway, 'I will not yet abandon myself, nor this place as long with cat and dog (the present diet) we shall be able to feed an arm to that strength that it may lift a sword: for this is my resolution' (PRO, SP 75/9, fol. 30). On 27 February he burnt the enemies' siege quarters outside Stade. He reported to the English government that he could only hold the town and river if he received additional money. On 18 March he wrote to the duke of Buckingham complaining about the lack of money and the dwindling quantity of supplies, stating that 'he and his troops seem to be forgotten of all the world' (*CSP dom.*, 1628–9, 25). On 25 April he surrendered the fortress to Tilly on the condition that the garrison marched out with the honours of war. He had the 1000 sick survivors sent to Christian's fortress at Glückstadt, and brought 1400 English and 230 Scots to the Netherlands. In June he returned with them to England. The government ordered him to muster these survivors and to sail back to the king of Denmark with them. In July he had an audience with Charles I in Southwick, near Plymouth, where he unhesitatingly told the king that unless the soldiers had their pay, food, and clothing they could not be expected to do their duty. With just 1200 English soldiers he arrived at Glückstadt on

31 October, but owing to disagreements with the town's governor the men landed only on 1 December. On 10 April 1629 he led a Dutch and Scottish force from Glückstadt to the islands off Jutland's west coast, where more Dutch and Scottish troops, as well as four English companies, joined him. He landed on the Jutland peninsula with 4700 men and after 22 May liberated its west coast from the imperialists.

Morgan returned to the Dutch service, though the Danish experience was to haunt him for several years as he went in fear of arrest by creditors who had supplied his men during the Stade campaign. In 1629 he was a colonel of foot when twenty-six English gentlemen volunteers joined him during the campaign against 's-Hertogenbosch and Maastricht. His regiment, eleven companies strong, served with forty-six English companies in the latter campaign. He suffered a period of captivity when he was captured by a Dunkirk privateer in February 1631 as he was voyaging between England and the Netherlands. His wife Elizabeth died in or before May 1634, and was buried at Delft Old Church. In late August 1637 he was with the prince of Orange's army besieging Breda. Later he became governor of Bergen-op-Zoom, and it was from there, on 7 March 1643, that he issued a pass for a subordinate to recruit troops in England for his regiment. He died shortly afterwards and was buried in Bergen-op-Zoom, aged sixty-seven.

Morgan's daughter and heir Anne (d. 1688) was born in the Netherlands. She married first Sir Lewis Morgan (d. 1635) of Rhiwperra, Monmouthshire, and second Walter *Strickland (1598?–1671), parliament's ambassador to the United Provinces from 1642 to 1651, and a prominent ally of Cromwell in the 1650s. She herself played a part as an intermediary in Anglo-Dutch relations in the early 1650s. She was naturalized by parliamentary ordinance on 18 February 1651. Her third marriage was to John Milborne of Wonaston, Monmouthshire, and she died at Chelsea in 1688.

William Crosse praised Morgan in his poem *Belgiaes Troubles and Triumphs* in 1625. Morgan's steadfast service for the protestant states makes him an exemplar of those British gentry who took up the profession of arms not only as a means of employment, but also as an ideological statement against the Habsburg forces of the militant Counter-Reformation. His failure to return to England in 1638–9 to serve Charles I against the Scots may have arisen not merely from his age, but also from his disappointments as a commander for that monarch in the previous decade.

EDWARD M. FURGOL

Sources DWB · A. H. Dodd, *Studies in Stuart Wales* (1952) · C. R. Markham, *The fighting Veres* (1888) · E. A. Beller, 'The military expedition of Sir Charles Morgan to Germany, 1629–9', *EngHR*, 43 (1928), 528–39 · *CSP dom.*, 1603–37 · G. Parker, *The Thirty Years' War* (1984) · P. D. Lockhart, *Denmark in the Thirty Years' War* (1996) · M. A. E. Green, *Elizabeth electress palatine and queen of Bohemia*, rev. edn (1909) · *Calendar of the manuscripts of the most hon. the marquis of Salisbury*, 24 vols., HMC, 9 (1883–1976), vols. 6, 11, 16–17 · *Report on the manuscripts of Lord De L'Isle and Dudley*, 2, HMC, 77 (1933) · *Fifth report*, HMC, 4 (1876)

Morgan [*formerly* Gould], **Sir Charles**, first baronet (1726–1806), judge, was born on 25 April 1726, elder son of King Gould (*d.* 1756) and Elizabeth Shaw, of Besthorpe, Norfolk. He was educated at Westminster School (he was a scholar in 1739) and Christ Church, Oxford (BA, 1747; MA, 1750; DCL, 1773); he was called to the bar at Lincoln's Inn in 1750.

In 1754 Gould became a KC and also succeeded his father as deputy judge advocate. In February 1758 he married Jane (*d.* 1797), elder daughter of the judge advocate-general, Thomas Morgan of Tredegar, Monmouthshire. They had three sons and two daughters. In 1769 he succeeded Morgan in that office, the Tredegar family discreetly changing from opposition to government in parliament at this time in order to ensure his appointment. He discharged the duties of this office, which brought him into close contact with the king, in such a manner as to win the high opinion of George III. Among the favours bestowed on him were a knighthood on 5 May 1779, the post of chancellor of Salisbury Cathedral in 1772 and that of chamberlain of the Brecon, Radnor, and Glamorgan legal circuit on 7 September 1779. He sat in parliament for Brecon borough (1778–87) and Brecknockshire (1787–1806), both constituencies controlled by the Tredegar family. He was generally a member of the court party in the Commons, but deserted over the Regency crisis of 1788–9. His few speeches concerned the business of his office.

On 27 June 1792 Gould's personal situation was transformed when he succeeded his brother-in-law John Morgan in the entire Tredegar inheritance which, by 1806, yielded a rental income of £11,000. He was given a baronetcy on 15 November, and next day took the surname of Morgan. Sir Charles Morgan was a member of the board of agriculture from 1793 until his death, and was sworn of the privy council on 2 September 1802. From 1774 he was also president of the Equitable Assurance Society. He retained the post of judge advocate-general until 1806, when he was eighty, and there is evidence that he was no longer able to cope with a workload rendered heavier by the French wars.

Morgan died on 7 December 1806 at Tredegar, and was succeeded in his title and estates by his eldest son, **Sir Charles Morgan**, second baronet (1760–1846), who was also educated at Westminster School. He served in the army, becoming an ensign in the 2nd foot guards in 1777. He served in the war in America, and was taken prisoner at York Town. In 1792, shortly after his father's inheritance, he also changed his name to Morgan and retired from the army. He sat in parliament for Brecon borough (1787–96) and Monmouthshire (1796–1831). By 1820 industrial development had increased the value of the Tredegar estates to £40,000 a year; but he nevertheless did a great deal to advance agriculture in Brecknockshire and Monmouth. He was married to Mary Magdalen, daughter of Captain George Stoney RN. Their eldest son, Charles Morgan Robinson Morgan, was created Baron Tredegar in 1859; a younger son was Charles Octavius Swinnerton *Morgan, an antiquary.

FRANCIS WATT, *rev.* PETER D. G. THOMAS

Sources HoP, *Commons, 1790–1820* · HoP, *Commons, 1754–90* · W. R. Williams, *The history of the great sessions in Wales, 1542–1830* (privately printed, Brecon, 1899) · P. D. G. Thomas, *Politics in eighteenth century Wales* (1997) · GEC, *Baronetage* · *Old Westminsters* · Foster, *Alum. Oxon.* · W. P. Baildon, ed., *The records of the Honorable Society of Lincoln's Inn: the black books*, 3 (1899), 346
Archives NL Wales, Tredegar Park MSS | BL, letters to Lord Grenville, Add. MS 58974 · BL, corresp. with first earl of Liverpool, Add. MSS 38217–38230, 38308–38309, 38447, *passim* · NL Scot., corresp. with Lord Charles Hay · U. Mich., Clements L., corresp. with Thomas Gage
Wealth at death under £11,000—income of estates: HoP, *Commons*

Morgan, Sir Charles, second baronet (1760–1846). *See under* Morgan, Sir Charles, first baronet (1726–1806).

Morgan, Charles Langbridge (1894–1958), novelist and journalist, was born on 22 January 1894 at Warreston, Rodway Road, Bromley, Kent, the youngest of four children of Sir Charles Langbridge Morgan (1855–1940), civil engineer, and Mary (*d.* 1906/7), daughter of William Watkins. Both Charles and Mary Morgan spent their youth in Australia, but later returned to England, where Charles Morgan senior had a distinguished career, becoming president of the Institution of Civil Engineers in 1923–4. The young Charles Morgan entered the Royal Navy in 1907 and received his education at Osborne and Dartmouth, where he was cadet captain, and served as midshipman in the Atlantic Fleet and on the China station. Morgan experienced the ill treatment then common in the Royal Navy while serving in the *Good Hope*, but found encouragement for his literary aspirations in his immediate superior in the *Monmouth*, Commander Christopher Arnold-Forster, great-grandson of Thomas Arnold, headmaster of Rugby, and lifelong friend.

With the support of his father, Morgan resigned from the navy to follow a literary career, and was to have gone up to Brasenose College, Oxford, in 1914, but on the outbreak of war, he rejoined the Royal Navy and was involved in the Antwerp expedition with the naval brigade of the Royal Naval Volunteer Reserve. After the fall of Antwerp, Morgan crossed into the Netherlands, where he remained interned until 1917. After a period of imprisonment Morgan was given parole and lived on the Rosendaal estate belonging to the De Pallandt family in Guelderland. It was among this family that he was introduced to the French language and culture which would become a lifelong influence. During this period Morgan had the opportunity to begin his apprenticeship as a novelist with a first novel, *The Gunroom* (1919), recounting his experiences as a young midshipman in the pre-war Royal Navy.

In 1919 Morgan was able to take his place at Oxford where he read history at Brasenose (1919–21), and became president of the Oxford University dramatic society. Through the good offices of A. B. Walkley, francophile drama critic of *The Times*, Morgan joined the editorial staff of the paper, and on Walkley's death in 1926 he took over as principal theatre critic until 1939. Journalism was to provide the financial security he needed to begin writing novels.

On 6 June 1923 Morgan married fellow novelist Hilda

Charles Langbridge Morgan (1894–1958), by Augustus John, 1944

Campbell *Vaughan (1892–1985), daughter of Hugh Vaughan Vaughan of Builth, Brecknockshire, and Morgan's letters to her reveal how important she was in helping him to develop as a writer. Their two London homes were first at More's Garden in Chelsea and then from 1933 16 Campden Hill Square. They had two children, Elizabeth Shirley born in 1924, who married the seventh marquess of Anglesey in 1948, and Roger, born in 1926.

In 1925 Morgan published another apprentice work, *My Name is Legion*, but in 1929 he had greater success with *Portrait in a Mirror*, which won the Femina Vie Heureuse prize (1930). This was followed in 1932 by *The Fountain*, which drew on his wartime experience in the Netherlands and proved very popular in both England and America, winning the Hawthornden prize (1933). Another ambitious novel, *Sparkenbroke*, appeared in 1936, and *The Voyage* (1940), set in France in the late nineteenth century, came out just at the beginning of the Second World War and was awarded the James Tait Black memorial prize. In 1935 he published an essay, *Epitaph on George Moore*, in place of the biography of the novelist that Moore had wished him to write, and in 1938 his play *The Flashing Stream* was produced in London.

During the Second World War, Morgan worked for naval intelligence and made a lecture tour of the United States for the Institute of International Education. He still found time to write: he brought out a short novel, *The Empty Room*, in 1941 and in 1942 he began a series of weekly articles for the *Times Literary Supplement* under the title 'Menander's mirror', republished in two volumes as *Reflections in a Mirror* (1944–6). His love of France and its culture led him to become involved with the Free French in London, and a *Spectator* article translated as *Du génie français* was published by Éditions de Minuit in 1943. He also wrote an *Ode to France* (1942) which was read in September 1944 at the reopening of the Comédie Française in Paris.

After the war Morgan returned to novel writing and produced an allegorical fable of good and evil, *The Judge's Story* (1947), and a tale of the resistance, *The River Line* (1949), which was turned into a play in 1952. A dark note, caused by his fears concerning the power of modern science, entered into his book of essays *Liberties of the Mind* (1951) and into his last play, *The Burning Glass* (1953). A long novel dealing with a similar theme was never completed and his two final novels, *A Breeze of Morning* (1951) and *Challenge to Venus* (1957), returned to lighter subjects.

During his career Morgan received honorary degrees from Scottish and French universities and was made an officer of the French Légion d'honneur (1936). He took great satisfaction in 1949 when the Institut de France made him one of its members. From 1953 to 1956 he held the presidency of International PEN.

Although Morgan never sought a wide audience for his novels, they did achieve some degree of popularity during the 1930s, with *The Fountain* reaching a printing of 144,000. He claimed the seventeenth-century Neoplatonist Henry Vaughan and the Romantic poets as his literary antecedents, although his contemporaries compared him more with Walter Pater and George Moore. After the Second World War his abstract, almost allegorical stories and careful attention to style failed to reach wide audiences when social realism and satire proved more popular. His work was never taken seriously among literary critics in Britain, but in France his novels aroused some academic interest. Marius-François Guyard explained this by the French discovering in the novels their own idea of England, and pointed out that critics as varied as Paul Valéry and François Mauriac took notice of Morgan's work (Guyard, 77–9). Morgan died on 6 February 1958 at his home, 16 Campden Hill Square, Kensington, London.

TANIS HINCHCLIFFE

Sources DNB · *Selected letters of Charles Morgan*, ed. E. Lewis (1967) · *The new Cambridge bibliography of English literature*, [2nd edn], 4, ed. I. R. Willison (1972) · M.-F. Guyard, 'Morgan en France', *Revue de Littérature Comparée*, 23 (1949), 71–9 · J. Vallette, 'Hommage à Morgan', *Mercure de France*, 332 (April 1958), 723–5 · [S. Norman], 'The fountain stops', TLS (1 Jan 1960), 8 · H. C. Duffin, *The novels and plays of Charles Morgan* (1959) · *WWW* · b. cert. · m. cert. · d. cert.

Archives News Int. RO, papers · Shrewsbury School, Shropshire, letters | BL, corresp. with Society of Authors, Add. MS 56758 · JRL, letters to Richard Church · Royal Society of Literature, London, letters to the Royal Society of Literature · U. Birm. L., corresp. with Francis Brett Young; letters to Jessica Brett Young · U. Glas. L., letters to D. S. MacColl · U. Reading L., letters to Herberth Herlitschka and Marlys Herlitschka

Likenesses H. Coster, photographs, 1934–55, NPG · A. John, chalk drawing, 1944, NPG [*see illus.*] · W. Stoneman, photographs,

1948, NPG · R. Morgan, photograph, 1950–59, NPG · M. Gerson, photograph, 1954, NPG · photographs, priv. coll.

Wealth at death £104,984 6s. 9d.: probate, 2 July 1958, *CGPLA Eng. & Wales*

Morgan, Charles Octavius Swinnerton (1803–1888), antiquary, was born on 15 September 1803, probably at Tredegar Park, Newport, Monmouthshire, the fourth son of Sir Charles *Morgan, second baronet (1760–1846), of Tredegar Park, army officer and MP [*see under* Morgan, Sir Charles, first baronet], and Mary Magdalen, daughter of Captain George Stoney RN. Charles Morgan Robinson Morgan, Baron Tredegar (1794–1890), was his elder brother. Educated at Westminster School and Christ Church, Oxford, where he matriculated in 1822, he graduated BA in 1825 and MA in 1832. He was elected FSA in 1830 (proving to be an active member from 1848 onwards and several times a vice-president of the society), and FRS in 1832. From 1840 to 1874 he was the Conservative member of parliament for the county of Monmouth, of which he was a JP and deputy lieutenant. A knowledgeable practising archaeologist, he read numerous papers before the Caerleon Antiquarian Association, of which he was president, and many (some jointly authored with Thomas Wakeman) were subsequently printed between 1850 and 1866 and in 1882 and 1885. In 1849 he exhibited a collection of ancient watches at the Society of Antiquaries, which was followed by a paper entitled 'Observations on the history and progress of the art of watchmaking from the earliest period to modern times'. Subsequently he wrote other papers on astrolabes and episcopal rings, which were published in *Archaeologia* (33, 34, 36). Another major interest was church plate: in the *Archaeological Journal* he published his 'Observations on the early communion plate used in the Church of England, with illustrations of the chalice and paten of Christchurch'. Other papers on these and antiquarian or local history topics were published in the *Archaeological Journal*, *Archaeologia Cambrensis*, and the *Journal of the Royal Archaeological Institution*. In 1872 he published a valuable account of the monuments in the church at Abergavenny.

Morgan died, unmarried, on 5 August 1888 at his home, The Friars, Newport, and was interred in the family vault at Basaleg churchyard, Monmouthshire. He bequeathed his collection of clocks, astronomical instruments, and papal rings to the British Museum. His working manuscripts, transcripts of extents and charters, pedigrees, notes and drafts of articles, sketches, and translations of Welsh poetry, together with his scholarly, scientific, and political correspondence are in the National Library of Wales.　　　　　J. A. JENKINS, *rev.* BRYNLEY F. ROBERTS

Sources *Proceedings of the Society of Antiquaries of London*, 2nd ser., 12 (1887–9), 384–6 · G. T. Clark, *Limbus patrum Morganiae et Glamorganiae* (1886), 311–13 · NL Wales, J. Davies papers · E. Poole, *Old Welsh chips* (1888), 248–51 · *CGPLA Eng. & Wales* (1888)

Archives NL Wales, antiquarian, political, and other corresp. and papers · S. Antiquaries, Lond., travel journals, notebook, and Monmouthshire historical collections

Wealth at death £68,545 7s. 8d.: probate, 14 Nov 1888, *CGPLA Eng. & Wales*

Morgan, Conwy Lloyd (1852–1936), comparative psychologist and philosopher, was born in London on 6 February 1852, the second son of James Arthur Morgan, solicitor, and his wife, Mary Anderson. He received his early education at Brenchley, Kent, and at the Royal Grammar School, Guildford, his parents having moved to Weybridge a few years after his birth. The focus at the latter school was mainly on classics, with some mathematics but no science. Lloyd Morgan was, however, early attracted to scientific studies, and his father had concerns in several mining companies. Consequently, at the age of seventeen, he entered the School of Mines in London, where he was duke of Cornwall scholar, with the intention of becoming a mining engineer. Although he excelled in his studies, achieving both the Murchison and the de la Beche medals, he became increasingly interested in the pursuit of pure science. On obtaining his diploma as associate in mining and metallurgy, he accepted a post as private tutor to a wealthy Chicago family which gave him the opportunity of extensive travel in North and South America. On his return he resumed his scientific studies at the Royal College of Science, where he worked, among other teachers, under T. H. Huxley, whose influence upon him was profound.

During this later period as a student Lloyd Morgan acted as an assayer for a mining company in Cornwall. In addition he was a lecturer at Weybridge School and, later, visiting master at Chatham School, Ramsgate. But his first regular professional post was in South Africa at the Diocesan College at Rondebosch, where he was appointed in 1878 to teach not only the physical sciences in general, but also English literature and, for a time, constitutional history. On 12 June of the same year he married Emily Charlotte Maddock (*b.* 1850/51), daughter of the Revd Henry William Maddock, vicar of All Saints, St John's Wood, London. They had two sons, the elder of whom predeceased Lloyd Morgan.

In 1884 Lloyd Morgan returned to England to succeed W. J. Sollas in the chair of geology and zoology at University College, Bristol, where he was destined to pass the rest of his professional career. Three years later he was elected principal of the college, a post which in the early days of the university colleges was regarded as compatible with the continued tenure of a chair. But as the college developed the administrative work grew with it, and when in 1910 the university charter was granted Lloyd Morgan accepted the vice-chancellorship of the new university only in order to give it a start. After a tenure of about three months he resigned and resumed the work of his chair, by then renamed the chair of psychology and ethics, from which he retired in 1919. He lived on in Clifton until 1926, and even on one or two occasions returned to the university to give temporary assistance in the department of philosophy, as it had by then become.

As principal Lloyd Morgan's impressive appearance, his upright and kindly personality, and his intellectual eminence commanded universal respect and liking, particularly among those most closely associated with him, but he had little taste for administration and was not particularly well equipped to handle some of the more assertive academic politicians of the time. On the other hand there can be no reservations about the value of his services to learning. A self-proclaimed sufferer from 'cacoethes scribendi', he was an exceptionally prolific author. Between 1876 and 1934, only one year (1918) passed without a publication from Lloyd Morgan. Following his *Water and its Teachings* (1882) and *Facts around Us* (1884) with approximately a dozen papers on Palaeozoic rocks of the Bristol area, his main interest in the early days of his tenure of the chair at Bristol was on the side of geology. But that soon gave place to what for many years occupied the centre of his attention, the study of animal and comparative psychology. As literary executor to George J. Romanes, Lloyd Morgan assumed the reputation of one of the foremost researchers in the field of mental evolution. Indeed, it would not be too much to say that, in the English-speaking world at any rate, he was one of the chief founders of the scientific study of animal psychology. He was among the first to apply systematically the methods of experiment to the subject. The results of his investigations appeared in a long series of publications of which the most important are *Animal Life and Intelligence* (1890–91), *Habit and Instinct* (1896), *Animal Behaviour* (1900), and *Instinct and Experience* (1912).

Lloyd Morgan is perhaps best known for his statement about assessing the relative roles of instinct, intelligence, and reason in the experimental study of animal behaviour. First presented at the International Congress of Experimental Psychology, held in London in 1892, and subsequently published in his *An Introduction to Comparative Psychology* (1894), this later became known as Lloyd Morgan's canon. Stating that in no case is 'an animal activity to be interpreted as the outcome of the exercise of a higher psychical faculty, if it can be fairly interpreted as the outcome of one which stands lower on the psychological scale', the canon was designed to bring scientific rigour and evolutionary continuity to the anthropomorphic psychological approach to animals. Arguably its misinterpretation had a profound impact on the development of behaviourism.

With J. M. Baldwin, H. F. Osborn, and E. B. Poulton, Lloyd Morgan arrived independently at the theory of organic selection, or the Baldwin effect, in the early 1890s. This theory explained apparently Lamarckian evolution in neo-Darwinian terms. According to this theory an organism exposed to a new environment might initially survive through adaptation borne of learned habits. Among these successful organisms spontaneously generated hereditary adaptations that are identical to the previously learned habits might arise. Although generated through the random action of natural selection, successful behavioural attributes may, therefore, appear to be the result of use inheritance.

Influenced by the writings of George Berkeley from an early age Lloyd Morgan grappled with the problem of mind–body dualism. His proposed solution was shaped by his combined interests in metaphysics and experimental evolutionary psychology. Committed to a monism of 'mind stuff' throughout most of his active career in comparative psychology, Lloyd Morgan accorded mentality a positive role in evolution. In his later years, however, his interest turned more exclusively to the metaphysical underpinnings of his monism. In this field he developed and gave his own interpretation to the idea of the emergence of novelty which was being discussed by Samuel Alexander and others at that period. His most important works in this field of investigation are his two courses of Gifford lectures delivered at St Andrews University in 1922 and 1923 and published as *Emergent Evolution* (1923) and *Life, Mind and Spirit* (1926). Although he rejected religious orthodoxy he detected a divine plan at work in emergent evolution, which denied materialist reductionism in evolutionary explanations of the natural world. In short, evolution generated novel products that could not be explained strictly on the basis of component elements or causes. Undoubtedly his explications of emergent evolution contributed to his election as president of the Aristotelian Society in 1926.

Lloyd Morgan's pre-eminence in his chosen field was rewarded with numerous honours. He was elected FRS in 1899, being the first fellow to be elected for psychological work, and he was elected first president of the psychological section of the British Association for the Advancement of Science in 1921. He received honorary degrees from the University of Aberdeen (1903), the University of Wisconsin, Madison (1904), and Bristol University (1910). On two occasions (1895/6, 1904), he was selected to deliver a course of Lowell lectures at Harvard.

Throughout his life Lloyd Morgan seemed intent on being the living embodiment of his emergent monism. In *Mind at the Crossways* (1929) he argued that art and science represented emergent attitudes towards beauty and truth respectively. Both the contemplative and the emotional constituted the emergent level. Determined to balance his science with art, Lloyd Morgan was an integral part of the various facets of Bristol community life: he was president of the Bristol Cambrian Society; vice-president of the British Empire Shakespeare Society; member of the committee controlling Leigh Woods; and president of the Clifton High School for Girls. He was also an active participant in university extension work in Bristol and the surrounding region. Contemporaries remembered him as 'tall and spare of figure, with humorous eyes' (*The Times*, 9 March 1936, 8a). 'In the town he was a familiar and respected figure, who could be seen every day cycling to work, to golf, or to Church, with no overcoat in any weather, and his long beard resting on the handlebars, or blowing wildly over his shoulder' (Grindley, 1). In 1926 Lloyd Morgan finally retired to Hastings, where he died at his home, 23 Elphinstone Road, on 6 March 1936. He was buried at the borough cemetery, Hastings.

G. C. FIELD, *rev.* J. F. M. CLARK

Sources *The Times* (9 March 1936), 8 • *Nature* (8 March 1936), 521–2 • *Western Daily Press and Bristol Mirror* (6 March 1936) • *Bristol Evening Post* (7 March 1936) • *Hastings Observer* (14 March 1936) • G. H. Leonard, *The influence and life of Dr Lloyd Morgan: some memories of old*

University College [privately printed by G. H. Leonard as a memorial booklet. First appeared in *Western Daily Press Bristol* (17/3/1936)] · E. Clarke, 'Morgan, Conwy Lloyd', *DSB* · J. H. Parsons, *Obits. FRS*, 2 (1936–8) · C. L. Morgan, 'Autobiography', *A history of psychology in autobiography*, ed. C. Murchison, 2 (1932), 237–64 · C. G. G. [C. G. Grindley], 'Obituary notice: Professor C. Lloyd Morgan 1852–1936', *British Journal of Psychology*, 27 (1936), 1–3 · A. Costall, 'How Lloyd Morgan's canon backfired', *Journal of the History of the Behavioral Sciences*, 29 (1993), 113–24 · A. Costall, 'Lloyd Morgan and the rise and fall of "Animal Psychology"', *Society and Animals*, 6 (1998), 13–29 · A. Costall, J. F. M. Clark, and R. H. Wozniak, 'Conwy Lloyd Morgan (1852–1936): an introduction to his work and a bibliography of his writings', *Teorie & Modelli*, new ser., 2 (1997), 65–92 · *WWW* · R. H. Wozniak, 'Conwy Lloyd Morgan, mental evolution, and the *Introduction to comparative psychology*', in C. L. Morgan, *Introduction to comparative psychology* (1993), vii–xix · R. Boakes, *From Darwin to behaviourism: psychology and the minds of animals* (1984) · R. J. Richards, *Darwin and the emergence of evolutionary theories of mind and behavior* (1987) · G. Radick, 'Morgan's canon, Garner's phonograph, and the evolutionary origins of language and reason', *British Journal for the History of Science*, 33 (2000), 3–23 · G. G. Simpson, 'The Baldwin effect', *Evolution*, 7 (1953), 110–17 · R. Smith, *The Fontana history of the human sciences* (1997) · A. Beckermann, H. Flohr, and J. Kim, eds., *Emergence or reduction? Essays on the prospects of nonreductive physicalism* (1992) · m. cert. · d. cert.

Archives University of Bristol Library, corresp. and papers | BL, Alfred Russel Wallace papers · JRL, letters to Samuel Alexander · Oxf. U. Mus. NH, letters to Sir E. B. Poulton, together with notes on evolution

Likenesses photograph, 1900, repro. in Richards, *Darwin*, 386 · J. Duthoit, pencil sketch, 1911, University of Bristol, C. Lloyd Morgan papers, MS scrapbook, 128/555 · R. A. Bell, oils, *c.*1920, University of Bristol · W. Stoneman, photograph, 1921, NPG · Elliott & Fry, photograph, repro. in C. G. G., 'Obituary notice', facing p. 1 · group portrait, photograph (with family and servants), repro. in Boakes, *From Darwin to behaviorism*, 34 · photograph, repro. in Parsons, *Obits. FRS*, facing p. 25

Morgan, Daniel (1735?–1802), revolutionary army officer in America, was born, according to family tradition, to Welsh parents, who lived in New Jersey. Details of his family background and life before appearing on the Virginia frontier about 1753 are unclear. As a teenager he is thought to have run away following an argument with his father.

Except for his years in public service, Morgan spent his life after 1753 in the Shenandoah valley, in Frederick county, Virginia. He was a part of the great human tide of German, Scottish-Irish, and English immigrants who were lured by available land southward from the middle colonies over the Great Wagon Road that ran from Pennsylvania to the Carolinas. During the French and Indian War he was a teamster with the ill-fated Braddock expedition of 1755, and later in the conflict helped patrol the backcountry against enemy attacks as a member of the Virginia rangers. Poor and only semi-literate, Morgan was known as something of a rowdy and heavy drinker before he settled down about 1761 with Abigail Curry (*d.* in or after 1802), the daughter of a relatively prosperous Frederick county farmer. They did not formally marry until about ten years later; two daughters were born to them. Morgan achieved considerable success as a wagoner and farmer, growing tobacco and hemp. After renting land for some years, he purchased a 255 acre tract from his wife's

Daniel Morgan (1735?–1802), by Charles Willson Peale, 1794

uncle, Samuel Blackburn, and also acquired ten slaves. In 1774 he headed a militia company that fought in Dunmore's War against the Shawnee.

The following year, after the outbreak of the American War of Independence, the continental congress appointed Morgan commander of a company of backcountry riflemen. These were the type of frontier soldiers with whom he was associated during his later military career. Morgan first gained notoriety by marching his men to General George Washington's camp outside Cambridge, Massachusetts, 600 miles in only 21 days, and giving exhibitions of their shooting with the so-called long rifle, a weapon used on the frontier because of its range and accuracy. In the autumn of 1775 Morgan marched through the Maine wilderness with Benedict Arnold's small army that failed in its attack on the fortress of Quebec, though Morgan himself fought heroically before being captured. The following year, after being exchanged and released, Morgan received a colonel's commission and appointment as head of a hand-picked regiment of frontier riflemen. After using Morgan's riflemen for reconnaissance and for harassing the enemy in New Jersey, Washington dispatched this regiment to upstate New York, where it joined the American northern army under General Horatio Gates. Gates, who was contesting British General John Burgoyne's southward march down the Lake Champlain–Hudson River trough, employed Morgan's woods-wise men in the two so-called battles of Saratoga, fought on 19 September and 7 October 1777. Morgan initiated both contests in the rugged, wooded area known as Bemis Heights, and earned the respect of Burgoyne, who acknowledged the riflemen's role in bringing about his surrender on 17 October.

Morgan's career had its ups and downs during the next three years. He and like-minded officers were suspicious that a plot existed in congress and the army to remove Washington as commander-in-chief after he suffered defeats in Pennsylvania in 1777, though it is doubtful that any organized movement of that kind existed. Morgan was also disappointed that some of his best rifle companies had been detached for service in the west. He resented the fact that congress failed to promote him to brigadier-general. When he tried to resign from the army, congress persuaded him to take a furlough until a more prestigious assignment could be found for him.

Morgan's great opportunity for military fame came in the southern theatre of the war. In 1780 he agreed to raise another force of frontier light infantry to fight in the Carolinas, and he received promotion to brigadier-general. But General Cornwallis destroyed most of the American southern army at Camden, South Carolina (16 August 1780), just before Morgan arrived. General Nathanael Greene succeeded the disgraced General Gates as head of the southern department. With Morgan's help the southern forces were revived and reorganized. Greene divided his army, sending Morgan with one wing into western South Carolina to harass Cornwallis, while Greene himself moved eastward so that the American forces sat on each side of the British army. When Cornwallis sent Lieutenant-Colonel Banastre Tarleton's legion to destroy Morgan, the American general all but wiped out Tarleton's contingent at the Cowpens. Morgan deployed his regulars and militiamen superbly so as to gain the maximum benefit from his mixed command. Morgan's men were rested and well positioned in a series of lines, whereas Tarleton's legionnaires were badly fatigued and thrown forward without a battle plan. After the forty-minute engagement, Tarleton escaped with only a handful of what had been a force of over a thousand men. Morgan's victory, which included capturing over 800 men, has been called the tactical masterpiece of the war.

Cowpens was Morgan's final military achievement. In poor health he reunited his command with Greene's in North Carolina, and then retired to his home in Virginia. He returned to the field briefly during the Yorktown campaign later in 1781 and afterwards helped supervise British prisoners held in Winchester, Virginia. Having returned to farming, Morgan also operated a grist mill. In the 1790s he returned to public life, commanding the militia units that garrisoned Pittsburgh following the end of the whiskey rebellion in 1794. From 1797 to 1799 he sat in the US house of representatives as a member of the Federalist Party. He heatedly opposed the Republican Party of Thomas Jefferson, which he believed was subverting the constitution. Crippling arthritis led to Morgan's retiring from congress and moving to Winchester, where he could receive better medical attention. He died there on 6 July 1802, and was buried in the local Presbyterian cemetery.

A soldier in two colonial wars, in the American War of Independence, and afterwards in the Virginia militia as a major-general, Morgan with good reason considered himself an expert on guerrilla or partisan warfare, his experience initially gained as a frontier Indian fighter. Tall and muscular, he was noted for his informality and colourful language—he was the 'Old Wagoner' to his soldiers. He excelled in commanding men of his own backcountry origins, who were skilled in Indian conflicts and the use of the rifle. No strategist, he was a battlefield tactician, the best in the American army with the possible exception of Benedict Arnold. Morgan's advance through the ranks from modest beginnings would have been impossible in a European army of that age. He symbolized the decline of deference and the emergence of a democratic spirit in revolutionary America. DON HIGGINBOTHAM

Sources D. Higginbotham, *Daniel Morgan* (1961) • L. Babits, *A devil of a whipping: the battle of Cowpens* (1998) • J. Graham, *Life of General Daniel Morgan* (1856) • D. Higginbotham, 'Daniel Morgan: guerrilla fighter', *George Washington's generals*, ed. G. Billias (1964), 291–316 • N. Callahan, *Daniel Morgan* (1961) • W. Hill, Morgan biographical notes, Virginia Historical Society, Ludwell-Lee MSS
Archives NYPL, T. B. Myers collection
Likenesses C. W. Peale, portrait, 1794, Independence National Historical Park, Philadelphia [*see illus.*]

Morgan, Daniel [Dan] (*c.*1830–1865), bushranger, alias John Smith, Sydney Bill, Dan Owen, and otherwise Down-the-River Jack or Bill the Native, is believed to have been born about 1830 at Campbelltown, New South Wales. Nothing definitive is known of his parentage, childhood, or schooling, but as a youth he reputedly worked on sheep and cattle stations as a stockboy, and was later a notorious horse thief. In 1854 he was sentenced, as John Smith, to twelve years' hard labour for robbing a hawker near Castlemaine. He was released on a ticket-of-leave in 1860, and in July of that year, after failing to report to police, was declared illegally at large. In 1863 a series of highway robberies was attributed to him, and on 5 January 1864 a reward of £500 was offered for his apprehension by the government of New South Wales. In June 1864 he shot and killed John McLean and wounded two others at Round Hill station, and a few days later murdered police sergeant David Maginnity near Coppabella. The reward offered for his capture was now increased to £1000. In September 1864 he shot police sergeant Thomas Smyth, and his raids continued with robberies at Yarribee station, Wagga Wagga, and Kyamba Gap and the shooting of a Chinese man at Kyamba.

The last weeks of his life were typical of Morgan's proceedings. During March–April 1865 he crossed from New South Wales into Victoria, stealing horses and robbing or threatening people wherever he ventured. He visited Evans's Whitfield station and fired the haystack, then headed for the Melbourne Road, where he committed a series of highway robberies, arriving at Peechelba station on Saturday 8 April. He held the McPherson family and workers hostage at gunpoint at Peechelba and spent the evening with them, inviting them to sit down with him to tea, requesting Miss McPherson to play the piano to him, and talking freely of his activities. A maidservant managed to evade his vigilance, and gave the alarm to a neighbour; the house was soon surrounded by civilians and a few police, who waited for the morning, when Morgan came out of the house driving his hosts before him with a revolver. One Wendlan (or Quinlan), to whom the duty had been assigned, shot him in the back at sixty paces from behind cover. Morgan survived about six hours, and died on 9 April without making any confession. One Colt revolver, a bag of bullets, and other personal effects were found upon him at death. The coroner's jury returned a verdict of justifiable homicide, adding a rider in praise of the conduct of all concerned. Morgan's head was cut off and sent to Melbourne; his headless body was buried at the Wangaratta cemetery on 14 April 1865.

Morgan was one of the most violent of the Australian bushrangers. A contemporary account described his 'villainously low forehead with no development' and his peculiarly long nose; he was said to be 5 feet 10 inches high, and of spare build, so emaciated when captured as not to weigh more than 9 stone. Rolf Boldrewood's novel *Robbery under Arms* (1888) is said to be based in part on Morgan's activities.   C. A. HARRIS, *rev.* ROBERT HALDANE

Sources M. Carnegie, *Morgan the bold bushranger* (1975) · E. F. Penzig, *Morgan the murderer* (1989)
Likenesses photograph, *c*.1865, Victoria Police Historical Unit Archives, Melbourne, Australia

Morgan, David Thomas (*c*.1695–1746), Jacobite campaigner, was the only son of Thomas Morgan of Pen-y-graig House, Glamorgan, and his wife, Dorothy, daughter of David Mathew of Llandaff Court. His father, an under-sheriff of Glamorgan in 1682, was a distant connection of the influential Morgan of Tredegar family, while his mother was the first cousin of Admiral Thomas Mathews. This was a powerful whig connection, but Morgan followed a quite different political path. He was educated at the Middle Temple (admitted 1711, called 1721), and practised at Westminster Hall and probably also on his home Brecon circuit of south-east Wales. He married a London woman (identity unknown), through whom he acquired property in Shoreditch. They had one daughter, Mary. Although he inherited Pen-y-graig House, in the then rural parish of Merthyr Tudful, he spent most of his time in London, albeit not in assiduous pursuit of his profession. 'As to my capacity as one bred to the law, I confess that I never pretended to much knowledge that way', he said at his treason trial. Morgan claimed then to have served in two military campaigns on behalf of the crown, and he was certainly a man of many parts. A devout Anglican, he set out his faith in a book, *The Christian Test*. He also sufficiently dabbled in verse for Horace Walpole to call him 'a poetical lawyer' at his execution (Walpole, *Corr.*, 19.287). But his chief diversion was politics. He wrote a pamphlet attacking Sir Robert Walpole for corruption, and in the 1740s was a member of an opposition organization, the Independent Electors of Westminster, before he took part in the Jacobite rising of 1745.

Together with Monmouthshire squire William Vaughan of Courtfield, Morgan joined the army of Charles Edward

Stuart at Preston. As Squire Morgan he busied himself in Manchester, recruiting and requisitioning arms. He was offered but declined command of the 'Manchester regiment', and was co-opted onto the prince's council as an expert on England, his legal status earning him the nickname 'the Pretender's Counsellor' (Walpole, *Corr.*, 19.287). He argued that Wales should be the target destination both from Manchester and after the retreat from Derby, where he strongly advocated a bold march on London. Reputedly declaring, 'I had rather be *hanged* than go to Scotland to *starve*', he deserted the Jacobite army in Staffordshire on 7 December, and was at once arrested at Stone and put in Stafford gaol. There on 9 December he asked for pardon, denying that he had been a rebel, and took the same line at his trial in London from 18 to 22 July 1746. A succession of witnesses, including his own servant John Barry, there described how he had paraded at Preston with a white cockade and sword, and how on the march to Manchester and Derby he often rode alongside the Pretender. Morgan's defence was that he had been taken prisoner by the rebels while visiting friends in Cheshire, and had escaped at the first opportunity. This was so unconvincing that the jury found him guilty of high treason without leaving the courtroom. Morgan was sentenced to be hanged, drawn, beheaded, and quartered. The execution took place on 30 July 1746, when he was about fifty-one, and his head was stuck up at Temple Bar. His last request was for coffee 'very good and strong'. Posthumous blackening of his character is reflected in this observation from Howell's *State Trials* (18.389):

> He was a person of a very mean look, and seldom kept company with any gentleman of his neighbourhood; and if it had not been for his estate, he might have starved, for he was so very lofty, and of so bad a temper, that nobody but such as were beholden to him cared to employ him.

PETER D. G. THOMAS

Sources *State trials*, 18.371–89 · W. Llewellin, 'David Morgan: the Welsh Jacobite', *Transactions of the Liverpool Welsh National Society*, 10 (1894–5), 75–108 · F. J. McLynn, *The Jacobite army in England, 1745: the final campaign* (1983) · *DWB* · Walpole, *Corr.*, 19.287
Wealth at death his estate was either not confiscated, or it was later restored, since it was subsequently held by his daughter: Llewellin, 'David Morgan'

Morgan, Edward Delmar (1840–1909), linguist and traveller, born at Stratford, Essex, on 19 April 1840, was the only son of Edward John Morgan, an officer in the Madras artillery and later a member of the English factory or merchants' company in St Petersburg, and his wife, Mary Anne Parland. Educated at Eton College (1854–7), he showed a talent for languages from an early age. After leaving school he lived with his parents in St Petersburg, and learnt Russian.

In 1872 Morgan travelled first in Asia, making a journey in Persia with Sir John Underwood Bateman-Champain, a director of the Indo-European Telegraph Company. Morgan subsequently visited Kulja and the neighbouring parts of central Asia. In 1876 he translated from the Russian the central Asian explorer Colonel Nikolay Przhevalsky's *Mongolia, the Tangut Country and the Solitudes* of *Northern Tibet* (2 vols., 1876, with an introduction and notes by Henry Yule). Przhevalsky was one of the most successful Russian explorers in central Asia and winner of the Royal Geographical Society's founder's medal for his exploits. Morgan's translation made accessible his discoveries to an English audience keenly interested in, and deeply suspicious of, Russian activity in central Asia. With Sir Thomas Douglas Forsyth, Morgan translated the same author's *From Kulja across the Tien Shan (Tianshan) to Lobnor* (1879). Morgan made later expeditions to Ukraine, being familiar with its language and literature; to the lower part of the Congo (1883), which gave him a keen interest in the affairs of the Free State; to east Africa; and to the Baku oil region of Caucasia.

Morgan, who was a fellow of the Royal Geographical Society for forty years and served on its council, contributed much to its *Journal*. He was also honorary secretary of the Hakluyt Society (1886–92), and collaborated with C. H. Coote in editing for it (1886) the *Early Voyages and Travels to Russia and Persia, by Anthony Jenkinson and other Englishmen*. He was honorary treasurer for the Ninth International Congress of Orientalists (1892), in London, under Max Müller's presidency, and edited its transactions (1893). He, with two other fellows, successfully persuaded the Royal Geographical Society to organize the Sixth International Geographical Congress in 1895.

Morgan married on 25 September 1873 Bertha Jardine, daughter of Richard Thomas and his wife, Louisa de Visme. They had four sons and three daughters; the eldest son, Edward Louis Delmar Morgan, lieutenant RN, died in 1900. Morgan died at 15 Roland Gardens, South Kensington, London, on 18 May 1909, and was buried at Copthorne, Sussex, his main home in his later years.

O. J. R. HOWARTH, rev. ELIZABETH BAIGENT

Sources *GJ*, 34 (1909), 94 · private information (1912) · *CGPLA Eng. & Wales* (1909) · *The Eton register*, 2 (privately printed, Eton, 1905) · H. R. Mill, *The record of the Royal Geographical Society, 1830–1930* (1930)
Wealth at death £87,810 17s. 7d.: resworn probate, 3 July 1909, *CGPLA Eng. & Wales*

Morgan, Eluned (1870–1938), Welsh-language author, was born on 20 March 1870, on board the ship *Myfanwy* in the Bay of Biscay during a voyage to Patagonia. She was the daughter of Lewis Jones (1836–1904), a printer and editor and one of the founders of the Welsh settlement established in 1865 in the Chubut valley, Argentina, where the town of Trelew is named after him, and his wife, Ellen Griffith (1840–1930). She was given the surname Morgan because she was born at sea (Welsh *môr ganwyd*). She received her elementary education at Glan Tywi, a Welsh school run by T. G. Prichard in Patagonia, before being sent to Dr Williams's boarding-school in Dolgellau, where she led fellow pupils to demand greater respect for the Welsh language within the school. After returning to Patagonia, she ran a boarding-school for girls at Trelew for two years. She began to enter prose items at the colony's eisteddfod, and for a while she edited and typeset the colony's newspaper *Y Dravod* ('The discussion'). After her

return to Wales in 1896 she began submitting articles to the journal *Cymru*, encouraged by the editor, O. M. Edwards, whom she admired greatly. She strove hard to establish a Welsh intermediate school at Gaiman on her return to Patagonia and toured the Andes in 1898, a journey which led to further articles for *Cymru* which appeared in 1899 and 1900.

Encouraged to write and guided by her colleague Ifano Jones, Eluned was employed at the Cardiff Free Library during a period in Wales from 1903 to 1909, and it was during this visit that she was influenced by the 1904–5 religious revival. Her last visit to Wales was from 1912 to 1918, when she was again based in Cardiff. She spent the remaining twenty years of her life at her home in Gaiman.

Eluned wrote four creative works: *Dringo'r Andes* ('Climbing the Andes') (1904), *Gwymon y môr* ('Ocean seaweed') (1909), *Ar dir a môr* ('On land and sea') (1913), and *Plant yr haul* ('Children of the sun') (1915). She also adapted an English book on domestic and family life by Esther Emment, *Traethodau ar drevnusrwydd teuluaidd* ('Essays on family orderliness'), which was published in the colony in 1892. *Dringo'r Andes* describes her adventure on horseback to the foothills of the Andes, leaving behind civilization and opting for the loneliness of mountains and forests. Her most successful work is undoubtedly *Gwymon y môr. Ar dir a môr* is the most uneven and undiscerning, while *Plant yr haul* is a retelling of an English book recounting the history of the Inca dynasty in Peru.

Influences of the romantic awakening which flourished in Wales between 1902 and 1918 pervade Morgan's work, especially the heroic poetry and ideals found in the works of T. Gwynn Jones. She was, however, a true romantic, living and experiencing the incidents which she chronicled, for example being voluntarily strapped to a ship's mast in order to gain first-hand experience of the ferocity of an Atlantic storm.

Two volumes of Eluned's correspondence have been published. The first, *Gyfaill hoff* ('Dear friend') (1972), contains her correspondence with William George, brother of David Lloyd George. The second, *Tyred drosodd* ('Come Over') (1977), publishes her correspondence with the Revd W. Nantlais Williams, which contains a recurring appeal that he and other Welsh ministers should visit the colony to preach the gospel. It was at the end of Nantlais Williams's preaching tour of Patagonia, on 29 December 1938, that Eluned Morgan died, at home at Plas-y-graig, Gaiman, and he postponed his return in order to assist at her funeral. She was buried at Gaiman cemetery on the following day.

Eluned Morgan is certainly the most important prose writer to have lived in the Welsh colony. A leader in the religious life of the colony, she was a key figure at Bethel Congregational Church, Gaiman, and an ardent Sunday school teacher both there and at Cardiff during her stay in Wales. The Welsh colony's life and ideals permeate her writing and the spirit of the early settlers is ever present. Often called 'Plentyn yr haul' ('child of the sun'), she has won a unique place in Welsh literature with her intermingling of traditional Welshness and South American adventure. 　　　　　　　　　　　　　　DAFYDD IFANS

Sources R. Bryn Williams, *Eluned Morgan: bywgraffiad a detholiad* (1948) · W. R. P. George, *Gyfaill hoff* (1972) · D. Ifans, *Tyred drosodd* (1977) · R. Bryn Williams, *Rhyddiaith y Wladfa* (1949) · D. Ifans, 'Synaidau crefyddol Eluned Morgan', *Y Traethodydd*, 28 (1973), 274–85 · G. Roberts and M. E. Roberts, *Byw ym Mhatagonia* (1993), 106–15 · Nantlais [W. Williams], *O gopa Bryn Nebo* (1967), 102–25 · J. E. Lloyd, R. T. Jenkins, and W. L. Davies, eds., *Y bywgraffiadur Cymreig hyd 1940* (1953), 605 · M. Stephens, ed., *Cydymaith i lenyddiaeth Cymru*, rev. edn (1997), 511 · S. Lewis, *Ysgrifau dydd Mercher* (1945), 84–92 · M. Jones and G. Jones, eds., *Dewiniaid difyr* (1983), 134–5 · J. Aaron, 'Eluned Morgan a'r angen am wreiddiau', *Efrydiau Athronyddol*, 61 (1998), 86–103 · C. Lloyd-Morgan and K. Hughes, *Dringo'r Andes a Gwymon y môr* (2001)
Archives Museo Histórico Regional, Gaiman, Chubut, Argentina, family papers · NL Wales, corresp. · priv. coll., papers |SOUND BBC, Llandaff, Cardiff, CF5 2YQ, Marion Griffith Williams (producer), Welsh Home Service (1965), programme rel. to Morgan
Likenesses photographs, repro. in *Los galeses en Chubut—fotografías* (1987) · photographs, repro. in *Gwymon y môr* (1909) · photographs, repro. in Bryn Williams, *Eluned Morgan* · photographs, NL Wales · photographs, priv. coll.
Wealth at death Argentinian estate

Morgan, (Mary) Evelyn De [*née* Mary Evelyn Pickering] (1855–1919), painter, was born on 30 August 1855 at 6 Grosvenor Street, London, the first of the four children of Percival Andre Pickering (1811–1877), QC, and his wife, Anna Maria Wilhelmina (1824–1901), daughter of John Spencer-Stanhope and his wife, Elizabeth. Evelyn displayed a talent for drawing at an early age and, despite a certain amount of disapproval from her parents, declared a serious intent to become a professional artist. Her maternal uncle, the painter John Roddam Spencer-Stanhope, encouraged her to develop her artistic skills and introduced her to Italian Renaissance painting which was to be a significant influence on her work. In 1873 she enrolled at the Slade School of Fine Art in London, where she was among the first generation of women artists to attend. She soon became a distinguished scholar, winning several prizes for drawing and painting, and was later awarded the prestigious Slade scholarship. However, Pickering was keen to learn more and between 1875 and 1877 she made several trips to Italy to study Renaissance painting at first hand. As a young woman, she showed remarkable ambition and independence, as well as an extraordinary commitment to her art. On her return to London she was invited to exhibit at the Grosvenor Gallery, where she chose to show her first major painting, *Ariadne in Naxos* (1877; De Morgan Foundation, London), a simple yet powerful composition depicting a distraught Ariadne abandoned on the beach. On 5 March 1887 she married the potter William Frend De *Morgan (1839–1917), who, along with his friend and business associate William Morris, became a prominent figure in the decorative arts movement. The De Morgans settled at The Vale in Chelsea, where they lived until 1910, although they often spent the winter in Florence due to William's bad health.

While financial gain was considered less important to the De Morgans than artistic pursuits, any income that was generated from the sale of Evelyn's paintings was used to help finance her husband's pottery business. Her exhibitions attracted a great deal of critical appraisal, so much so that the late Victorian painter G. F. Watts reportedly proclaimed her to be 'the first woman artist of the day—if not of all time' (Stirling, 193). The subjects of her oil paintings draw on a rich variety of sources including mythology, literature, the Bible, and war, and represent an attempt by the artist to 'explore both cosmic mysteries and contemporary issues through myth and symbol by developing an aesthetic that was personally authentic' (Gordon, 34). During the 1890s De Morgan painted several canvases featuring solitary full-length female figures in the landscape. The influence of her travels in Italy and her interest in Botticelli is particularly striking in the painting *Flora* (1894; De Morgan Foundation, London), generally considered to be her masterpiece. Her attention to detail, in particular her observation of nature, creates an exquisite and delicate background to the serene goddess of fruitfulness. Her acquaintance with the later generation of Pre-Raphaelite artists, and the symbolist painter Edward Burne-Jones whose work she admired, helped to raise her profile in the Victorian art world. Indeed, such was Burne-Jones's stylistic influence that De Morgan's *Aurora triumphans* (1886; Russell-Cotes Art Gallery and Museum, Bournemouth) was for a time wrongly attributed to Burne-Jones due to the forged inscription 'EBJ'. The influence of the Pre-Raphaelites can be seen in later works such as *Queen Eleanor and Fair Rosamund* (De Morgan Foundation, London) with its vivid colours and medieval theme. The use of narrative details, for example, literary references, emblems, and symbols, which are typical of the Pre-Raphaelite style, creates an image of intense drama. The preparatory drawings for this painting, like so many of her figurative studies, highlight De Morgan's meticulous and highly accomplished technical skills.

In 1906 De Morgan held a solo exhibition at the Bruton Gallery in London, and a year later showed twenty-five works at Wolverhampton Art Gallery. The horrors of the Second South African War and the First World War had a profound effect on De Morgan who was a staunch pacifist. She painted over fifteen war paintings including *The Red Cross* (exh. 1916; De Morgan Foundation, London) which shows the figure of Christ surrounded by angels, floating above a field of white memorial crosses. She died of nephritis at her home, 127 Old Church Street, London, on 2 May 1919 and was buried in Brookwood cemetery on 8 May.

After her death, De Morgan's sister, Anna Maria Wilhelmina Pickering (1865–1965), later Mrs Stirling, published *William De Morgan and his Wife* (1922), a lively, if somewhat unreliable, account. The De Morgan Foundation at Old Battersea House, London, was formally established in 1968 and houses Mrs Stirling's extensive collection of De Morgan's painting and drawings, although many works were destroyed in a fire in 1991. In the 1990s several exhibitions of De Morgan's paintings, drawings, and sculpture helped to bring her work to a wider audience. In addition, feminist art historians have reappraised De Morgan's work in the context of her female contemporaries and not simply in relation to the male artists associated with the Pre-Raphaelite movement. Her enduring reputation as an artist of extraordinary imagination and ambition was anticipated in an obituary written in 1920: 'it is safe to prophesy that Evelyn De Morgan's works will be eagerly sought after as some of the Old Masters are today' (McAllister, 29).   RACHEL S. GEAR

Sources C. Gordon, ed., *Evelyn De Morgan: oil paintings* (1996) · J. Marsh and P. G. Nunn, *Pre-Raphaelite women artists* (1998) · *The De Morgan Foundation at Old Battersea House*, 2nd rev. edn (1993) · A. M. W. Stirling, *William De Morgan and his wife* (1922) · J. Marsh and P. G. Nunn, *Women artists and the Pre-Raphaelite movement* (1989) · P. Dunford, *A biographical dictionary of women artists in Europe and America since 1850* (1990) · J. Marsh, *Pre-Raphaelite women: images of femininity in Pre-Raphaelite art* (1987) · I. McAllister, 'In memoriam: Evelyn de Morgan', *The Studio*, 79 (1920), 28–31 · J. Christian, ed., *The last Romantics: the Romantic tradition in British art* (1989) [exhibition catalogue, Barbican Art Gallery, London, 9 Feb – 9 April 1989] · D. Cherry, *Painting women: Victorian women artists* (1993) · P. G. Nunn, *Victorian women artists* (1987)

Archives Courtauld Inst., Witt Library

Likenesses photograph, Courtauld Inst.; repro. in Marsh and Nunn, *Women artists*

Wealth at death £18,518 6s. 2d.: probate, 23 June 1919, CGPLA Eng. & Wales

Morgan, Frederick Charles (1878–1978), antiquary and book collector, was born on 29 June 1878 at 11 High Street, Stratford upon Avon, the sixth of nine children of John Morgan (1830–1908), bookseller and printer, and his second wife, Mary Kibler (1846–1929). After attending Stratford grammar school until the age of thirteen, he assisted his father in running a circulating library. In 1902 John Morgan printed *The Campden Wonder* and *An Account of the Battle of Stratford-upon-Avon*, both edited by his son, but in the following year he closed his business. F. C. Morgan obtained a part-time post at the Shakespeare Memorial Library and subsequently at the Stratford Public Library. During these years his delight in antiquarianism began to develop with cycling expeditions into the Cotswolds. He became an ardent admirer of William Morris, collected illustrations of Morris's craftsmanship, and visited Kelmscott; he later claimed that Morris's *Earthly Paradise* (1870) exactly fitted his political ideas.

In 1910 Morgan was appointed librarian at the new public library in Malvern where, in 1911, he organized the first exhibition of children's books, many of which came from his own collection, which eventually contained over a thousand examples dating from the early eighteenth century. In 1954 this was given to the Baillieu Library at Melbourne University. The catalogue for the exhibition was revised and republished in 1976. On 29 August 1914 Morgan married Emma (1877–1967), daughter of Richard Jones, of Radbrook, near Clifford Chambers, Warwickshire; their only daughter, Penelope, was born in 1916. While at Malvern, Morgan made contact with several eminent local botanists and geologists and met the Herefordshire antiquary Alfred Watkins. During the First World War he served with the Royal Garrison Artillery.

Morgan was appointed librarian and curator of the art gallery and museum at Hereford in 1925 and thus began his connection with the cathedral city with which his

reputation is inextricably linked. For the next half-century he dominated antiquarian pursuits in his adopted county and revealed through his many publications the rich vein of documentary sources and archaeological artefacts which lay uncatalogued and unexplored in the institutions of the county town and the countryside which surrounded it. Through his wide contacts he built up an outstanding reference library but he was also proud of his achievements as curator: he established an important collection of English topographical paintings and, with the help of his wife, a famous collection of English costumes. He found an outlet for his researches in the *Transactions* of the Woolhope Naturalists' Field Club, the Herefordshire archaeological society, and during his life he held all the executive offices of the club, including president in 1937 and 1951. Morgan pioneered an interest in vernacular architecture, and published several articles illustrated with his own photographs; he was especially depressed by the spate of demolitions of timber buildings after the Second World War, fighting hard to convince the authorities of their worth.

Long before the age of record offices, Morgan was actively seeking archive material, preserving it and making it publicly available at the Hereford Reference Library. Many documents were carefully transcribed and printed in the Woolhope *Transactions*. While fire-watching on the roof of the library during the Second World War he began the major task of cataloguing and transcribing the muniments of the city of Hereford. The result after thirteen years was a ten-volume calendar of the city records from *c.*1500 to 1700.

In 1945 Morgan retired but now embarked upon a catalogue of the printed books of the famous library of Hereford Cathedral, together with the 30,000 items in its archive. He was assisted here by his daughter, Penelope. He remained honorary librarian until his death in Hereford on 16 July 1978. He was buried in Hereford Cathedral on 20 July. F. C. Morgan produced 165 books, pamphlets, and articles which were listed in a catalogue published by his friends to mark his 100th birthday. He received many honours: fellow of the Library Association (1910), FSA (1938), an honorary MA from Birmingham University (1952), and chief steward of the city of Hereford (1975). His important photographic collection was shared by the cathedral and city libraries in Hereford, and the National Monuments Record. In honour of its most famous member the Woolhope Club inaugurated an annual F. C. Morgan lecture.

DAVID WHITEHEAD

Sources *Transactions of the Woolhope Naturalists' Field Club*, 44 (1982–4), 9–11 · P. Morgan, *Library History*, 4 (1978), 137–40 [contains a select bibliography] · F. C. Morgan, *Trivial reminiscences*, 2 vols. (1968–9) · F. C. Morgan, *Stratford upon Avon: a 19th century library and my reading from 4 to 20 years* (1977) · P. Morgan, ed., *A list of writings by F. C. Morgan* (1978) · *Transactions of the Woolhope Naturalists' Field Club*, [28]–41 (1935–74) · F. C. Morgan, *Address when appointed chief steward of the city of Hereford* (1975) · *Friends of Hereford Cathedral Newsletter* (1979)

Archives Hereford Cathedral Library · Hereford City Library · Herefs. RO | English Heritage, Swindon, National Monuments Record, photographic negatives and slides · Hereford Cathedral

Library, photographic negatives and slides · Hereford City Library, photographic negatives and slides

Likenesses photograph, 1965 (with his daughter, Miss P. E. Morgan), repro. in *Woolhope Naturalists' Field Club, general index, 1955 to 1987*, frontispiece

Wealth at death £25,610: probate, 2 Oct 1978, *CGPLA Eng. & Wales*

Morgan, Sir Frederick Edgworth (1894–1967), army officer, was born in Paddock Wood, near Tonbridge, Kent, on 5 February 1894, the eldest son in a family of nine children of Frederick Beverley Morgan (*d.* 1934), a timber importer and merchant from a line of timber merchants, of Mascalls, Paddock Wood, and West Pallant House, Chichester, and his wife, Clara Elizabeth, daughter of Edgworth Horrocks, squire of Paddock Wood, Kent. Morgan was educated at Hurstleigh private school, Tunbridge Wells (1902–7), Clifton College (1907–11)—where he was a successful cricketer and cadet commander of the Officers' Training Corps—and the Royal Military Academy, Woolwich (1912–13), before being commissioned second lieutenant, Royal Field Artillery, on 17 July 1913. He returned from India with the Lahore divisional artillery in 1914 and served in France and Belgium throughout the war, taking part in most of the major battles and being twice mentioned in dispatches and promoted captain in 1916. Early in the war he was blown up and suffered severe shell-shock, but he returned later to serve on the staff of the Canadian Corps. On 15 August 1917 he married Marjorie Cecile, daughter of Colonel Thomas du Bédat Whaite, of the Army Medical Service; they had a son and two daughters.

From 1919 to early 1935 Morgan served with his regiment in India (major 1932, brevet lieutenant-colonel 1934), where he did much pigsticking and was a keen cricketer. He attended the Staff College, Quetta, in 1927–8, and held staff appointments in India and at the War Office (general staff officer, grade 2 (GSO 2), Royal Artillery, India, 1931–4; GSO 2, War Office, 1936–8). He later described his term at Whitehall as a nightmare as there was so little sense of urgency to prepare for the impending war.

Promoted colonel in 1938 and temporary brigadier in 1939, Morgan was for a short period GSO 1 to the 3rd division (1938–9); but he was then given command of the support group of the 1st armoured division, with which he went to France in 1940. During the retreat of the British expeditionary force he took part in the fighting south of the Somme, and escaped from Brest. Between 1940 and 1943 he held appointments at home culminating in the command of 1st corps (1942–3), and in 1942 he was promoted acting lieutenant general. In March 1943 he was appointed COSSAC (chief of staff to the supreme allied commander [designate]). He was faced with the gigantic task of planning the invasion of north-west Europe and a follow-up attack into the heart of Germany with an eventual force of 100 divisions, and also a deception scheme (Cockade) to keep the Germans alert for landings in 1943. He set up his headquarters at Norfolk House in St James's

Square where he assembled an Anglo-American staff of all three services. Although a number of studies for a landing on the coast of Normandy had already been made, Morgan and his team faced enormous difficulties. The chief of the Imperial General Staff, Sir Alan Brooke, after outlining the problem is alleged to have remarked 'Well, there it is. It won't work, but you must bloody well make it.' If in the end Morgan failed to provide a plan which satisfied the eventual executants, they could not have managed without it. He devoted himself tirelessly to the task, working seven days a week and sleeping beside his desk. The happy relations he fostered in his inter-allied staff was a remarkable achievement in view of the misunderstandings and differences of opinion sometimes prevalent between the allies on a higher level.

The inadequacies of COSSAC's planning in 1943 and early 1944 were principally due to two factors: the absence of a supreme commander and the shortage of means then available. Despite the representations made by Churchill and the British chiefs of staff at the Quebec conference in August 1943, it was not until after the appointment of General Eisenhower and his deputy commanders at the end of 1943 that the Americans fully grasped the size of the problem and began to make provision for it. The planners' most acute difficulty was undoubtedly the lack of a sufficient number of landing-craft (the Pacific theatre and to some extent the Mediterranean then enjoyed a higher priority), but there were many other serious deficiencies, including ships and aircraft for lifting airborne troops. When Churchill showed General Montgomery a draft of COSSAC's plan at Marrakesh at the end of December 1943, the latter submitted a trenchant memorandum arguing that in its present form it was impracticable. In particular Montgomery pointed out that the allocation of only three infantry divisions for the initial landing would entail far too narrow a front: 'By D + 12 a total of 16 divisions have been landed on the same beaches as were used for the initial landings. This would lead to the most appalling confusion on the beaches, and the smooth development of the land battle would be made extremely difficult—if not impossible.' Montgomery significantly extended the scope of the landings and also strengthened the command structure; his plan called for an attack by two armies side by side, British Second Army on the left with three divisions in line, and US First Army on the right with two divisions. Montgomery himself held the executive command of Twenty-First Army group, under Eisenhower's supreme direction, until after the break-out was achieved.

Nevertheless the great expansion of the forces available for Overlord and the consequent modifications of the plan in the first five months of 1944 should not obscure the fact that COSSAC and his staff had laid the essential foundations for the greatest amphibious operation ever undertaken. Among the many novel features of Morgan's plan perhaps the most remarkable and successful was the provision for large-scale maintenance from artificial harbours (Mulberries). Montgomery later wrote that Morgan 'did a good job … and produced an outline plan for OVER-LORD which served as a basis for future planning' (Montgomery, 219). Eisenhower later wrote that Morgan made D-day possible.

When, early in 1944, Morgan was relieved on the arrival of the British and American commanders with their own chiefs of staff, he was appointed deputy chief of staff at Eisenhower's headquarters (SHAEF). His advice to the supreme commander frequently conflicted with the views of Montgomery, who later wrote of Morgan in his *Memoirs* that 'He considered Eisenhower was a god; since I had discarded many of his plans, he placed me at the other end of the celestial ladder' (Montgomery, 256).

In September 1945 Morgan took on probably the most difficult and ultimately most unhappy assignment of his career as chief of operations in Germany to the United Nations Relief and Rehabilitation Administration (UNRRA). During the next year he applied his qualities of drive, intelligence, and sympathy to the desperate problems presented by at least a million displaced persons. Although remarkably successful in some aspects of his work, he soon became disillusioned with UNRRA, which he believed was being exploited by sinister organizations. In January 1946 he created a furore by asserting at a press conference that a secret organization existed to further a mass movement of Jews out of Europe. Although his suspicion was possibly well founded, critics held that he should not have made a public statement while officially concerned with provision for numerous Jewish refugees. Six months later he was dismissed after alleging that UNRRA organizations were being used as a cover for Soviet agents who were fomenting trouble among displaced persons. This episode is related in full and strikes an uncharacteristically bitter note in Morgan's autobiography.

Freddie Morgan was a tall, cheerful soldier with a fresh complexion and blue eyes. Behind a somewhat untidy appearance and a droll sense of humour he concealed one of the sharpest minds of his generation in the army. His charm and courtesy were invaluable assets in a senior staff officer, yet he also had a strong personality and great courage in voicing unpopular views. Throughout his career he displayed ability and competence well above the average.

In 1946 Morgan retired from the army with the honorary rank of lieutenant-general. In 1951 he succeeded Lord Portal of Hungerford as controller of atomic energy, and witnessed Britain's first atomic tests at the Monte Bello Islands in October 1952; and in 1954–6 he was controller of atomic weapons under the Atomic Energy Authority. He published his account of the work of the COSSAC team, *Overture to Overlord* (1950), and his autobiography *Peace and War, a Soldier's Life* (1961).

He was appointed CB in 1943 and promoted KCB in 1944, and received US and French honours. He was a colonel-commandant, Royal Artillery, from 1948 to 1958. Morgan died at Mount Vernon Hospital, Northwood, Middlesex, on 19 March 1967.   BRIAN BOND, *rev.*

Sources *The Times* (21 March 1967) • private information (1980) • F. E. Morgan, *Overture to Overlord* (1950) • F. E. Morgan, *Peace and war, a soldier's life* (1961) • *WWW* • Burke, *Peerage* (1959) • B. L. Montgomery, *The memoirs of field-marshal the Viscount Montgomery of Alamein* (1958) • B. Bond, *British military policy between the two world wars* (1980) • J. Keegan, *Six armies in Normandy: from D-Day to the liberation of Paris, June 6th–August 25th, 1944* (1982) • *CGPLA Eng. & Wales* (1967)
Archives IWM, papers as chief of operations, United Nations relief and rehabilitation administration, Germany • King's Lond., Liddell Hart C., corresp. with Sir B. H. Liddell Hart | FILM IWM FVA, actuality footage • IWM FVA, news footage
Wealth at death £12,433: probate, 26 June 1967, *CGPLA Eng. & Wales*

Morgan, George Cadogan (1754–1798), dissenting minister and scientist, was born at Bridgend in the county of Glamorgan. His father, William Morgan (1708–1772), was a surgeon and apothecary, practising at Bridgend; his mother, Sarah (1726–1803), was the daughter of Rice and Catherine Price of Tyn-ton, Llangeinor, and sister to Dr Richard *Price (1723–1791). William *Morgan (1750–1833), who became actuary to the Society for Equitable Assurances, was his elder brother.

Morgan was educated at Cowbridge grammar school, where he acquired some reputation as a classical scholar and became head of school. He matriculated at Jesus College, Oxford, on 10 October 1771. His intention was to prepare for a career in the church but his stay at Oxford was cut short during the summer term of 1772, possibly because the sudden death of his father left his mother unable to support a son at Oxford, and also because a change in his religious beliefs in an unorthodox direction precluded a career in the Church of England.

On his uncle's advice, Morgan moved to the dissenting Hoxton Academy, where he turned his attention to mathematics and the physical sciences. On leaving the academy in December 1776 he accepted a call to preach at the Octagon Chapel at Norwich. His appointment at the age of twenty-two to a post once held by the celebrated Dr John Taylor is a striking testimony to his growing reputation as a scholar. At Norwich he developed his scientific interests and submitted a paper entitled 'Observations on the light of bodies in a state of combustion', which was published in the Royal Society's *Philosophical Transactions* (75, 1785, 211ff.).

In 1783 Morgan married Anne (Nancy), daughter of William Hurry, a wealthy merchant and a prominent dissenter at Great Yarmouth. In 1785 he left the Octagon at Norwich to become a minister at Great Yarmouth, but his stay there was not long. Richard Price had been morning preacher at the Gravel Pit meeting-place at Hackney, Middlesex, since 1770, and both morning and afternoon since 1783. By the autumn of 1786 he found these duties onerous, and to help him the congregation invited Morgan to become his uncle's assistant. Morgan settled at Hackney with his family and pupils in March 1787, and preached his first sermon to the afternoon congregation on 1 April 1787. In the previous year the dissenters had established an academy at Hackney, known as New College, and Price had accepted an invitation to be one of the first tutors. But at this period of his life his health was not robust; he soon found teaching too taxing and was much relieved when the college allowed Morgan to give lectures in his place. It was at Hackney that Morgan delivered the lectures that he later published under the title *Lectures in Electricity* (2 vols., 1794). He also published 'Directions for the use of a scientific table in the collection and application of knowledge' (*Monthly Magazine*, 39, 1798; repr. 1826).

In July 1789 Morgan with three friends went on a continental tour. They arrived in Paris on the 9th and were in the capital when the Bastille fell. Morgan stayed up all night to communicate news of the event to his uncle in London. He warmly approved of what he saw happening in France and openly shared the enthusiasm for the implementation of revolutionary principles. His letter to Price was published in *The Gazetteer*: no copy seems to have survived, but extracts were used by the anonymous author of a pamphlet, *A Look to the Last Century*, to attack the dissenters, and, for the same purpose, by Edmund Burke in his *Reflections on the Revolution in France*.

Price died on 19 April 1791 and it might have been expected that Morgan would have succeeded him as pastor. Why he did not do so is unclear, but soon afterwards he left Hackney and set up a school at Southgate in Middlesex, where he enjoyed considerable success. George Cayley, a future pioneer in aviation, was one of his pupils.

In 1792 Morgan published anonymously a pamphlet, *An address to the Jacobine and other patriotic societies: urging the establishment of a republican form of government*. This essay is a bitter and vehement attack upon all monarchical and aristocratic forms of government, a plea for the abolition of hereditary privileges, and a defence of republicanism and the absolute sovereignty of the people. The ideas expressed in this pamphlet are much more radical than those espoused by his uncle, and much more radical than those he himself expressed in a speech delivered at Norwich eight years earlier. On that occasion Morgan limited himself to advocating parliamentary reforms that would make the Commons a more effective representative of the people. In his later years his ideas showed the influence of Thomas Paine, whom he entertained at a republican party at New College.

Morgan died on 17 November 1798. It is said that he inhaled some poison while conducting a chemical experiment, which caused a pulmonary infection that led to his death. Unfinished projects included a book on chemistry, a history of the American War of Independence, and a biography of Richard Price. This last, *Memoirs of the Life of the Rev. Richard Price*, was completed by his brother William and published in 1815.   D. O. Thomas

Sources DNB · W. Morgan, *Memoirs of the life of the Rev. Richard Price* (1815) · C. E. Williams, *A Welsh family from the beginning of the 18th century*, 2nd edn (1893) · D. O. Thomas, 'George Cadogan Morgan', *The Price–Priestley Newsletter*, 3 (1979), 53–70 · *The correspondence of Richard Price*, ed. W. B. Peach and D. O. Thomas, 3 (1994), 106 · 'Richard Price's journal for the period 25 March 1787 to 6 February 1791', ed. D. O. Thomas, *National Library of Wales Journal*, 21 (1979–80), 366–413 [deciphered by B. Thomas] · D. O. Thomas, 'Edmund Burke and the reverend dissenting gentlemen', *N&Q*, 227 (1982), 202–4 · D. A. Rees, 'George Cadogan Morgan at Oxford', *Enlightenment and Dissent*, 1 (1982), 89
Likenesses Opie, portrait

Morgan, George Campbell De (1841–1867). *See under* Morgan, Augustus De (1806–1871).

Morgan, George Campbell (1863–1945), Congregational minister, was born on 9 December 1863 at 12 Cutwell Street, Tetbury, Gloucestershire, the second child of George Morgan (1828–1907), unattached minister, and his wife, Elizabeth Fawn Brittan (d. 1911). His father was a Baptist minister before working as an independent preacher. Soon after Morgan's birth the family moved to Roath in south Wales and began attending a Wesleyan Methodist church. At first Morgan was educated at home, but after a family move to Cheltenham he attended Gratton House School in the town. He preached his first sermon in Monmouth Methodist Chapel in 1876, at the age of thirteen.

After an adolescent crisis of faith, Morgan had to abandon plans for a university education in order to earn his own living. A year in a teaching post in the Wesleyan School for Boys in Birmingham was followed in 1883 by three years in a similar post in the Jewish Collegiate School for Boys. Here his interest in Hebrew and the Old Testament was stimulated, and the principal, Lawrence Levy, became a personal friend. His interest in preaching was unabated, and while acting as one of the team of helpers on the occasion of the visit of Dwight L. Moody and Ira D. Sankey to Birmingham in 1883 he became convinced of a vocation to preach. When he was made redundant because of the imminent closure of the collegiate school, he applied to the Wesleyan Methodist church as a candidate for ministry, but was rejected. This did not dim his resolve, and he continued with mission preaching in Hull, following the work of the evangelist Gypsy Smith.

Three months after his rejection Morgan married his cousin, Annie (always known as Nancy) Morgan, on 20 August 1888. He soon received a call to minister to the Congregational church in Stone, Staffordshire, where he began a two-year ministry on 18 August 1889. He was ordained on 22 September and the following day received into the Congregational Union as an accredited minister.

There followed three further ministries in England, at Rugeley (1891–3), Westminster Road, Birmingham (1893–7), and New Court, Tollington Park, north London (1897–1901). During these years Morgan began the systematic Bible lectures which formed an essential part of his ministry, and began his regular visits to the United States. He made a deep impression on D. L. Moody and on many others when he participated in the Northfield summer conference. After Moody's death in 1899 his son, Will Moody, invited Morgan to carry forward the work of the Northfield extension programme. He left London in 1901 and travelled all over the United States engaged in this work for the next three years. Chicago Theological Seminary conferred the degree of DD on him in 1902.

Under repeated pressure to return to his homeland Morgan accepted a call to Westminster Chapel, in central London, in 1904. Despite an initially small congregation in a large building, this proved to be the scene of his greatest work during two outstanding ministries (1904–17 and 1933–43). Here he became known as one of the world's finest expository preachers. A tall, lean, striking figure in the pulpit, with a strong, well-modulated voice, he attracted congregations of more than 1500 to his regular Friday evening Bible lectures. He did not engage in theological controversy, but throughout his life concentrated on the detailed study and exposition of the Bible. His great work was preaching, whether in London at the weekends, elsewhere during the week, or at the annual Mundesley Bible conferences in Norfolk. A staff of assistants carried on the regular activities of the church. For three years, from 1911 until 1914, he also made time to combine his London weekend ministry with the training of future Congregational ministers as president of Cheshunt College, Cambridge (where he was the inspiration behind a new building programme).

Morgan resigned from Westminster Chapel in 1917 and, after short spells of lecturing at the YMCA's Mildmay College and a brief ministry at Highbury Quadrant Church, he returned to the United States in 1919, and remained until 1932. At first he had an itinerant ministry based in Indianapolis and then in Athens, Georgia; there followed work at the Biblical Institute in Los Angeles, ministry at Tabernacle Presbyterian Church, Philadelphia, and teaching at Gordon College, Boston.

In 1933 Morgan began his second ministry at Westminster Chapel (at first in collaboration with Hubert Simpson, later with Martyn Lloyd-Jones). His expository preaching continued unabated until his health began to give way in 1943, leading to his resignation. He died at home, 345 St Ermins, Westminster, on 16 May 1945, and was cremated three days later at Golders Green. A memorial service was held in Westminster Chapel on 28 May. He and his wife had four sons (all of whom followed their father into ordained ministry) and three daughters (one of whom died in childhood). Morgan published more than forty books, most of them based on his biblical expositions, which had a wide circulation in the English-speaking world.   ELAINE KAYE

Sources J. Morgan, *A man of his word* (1951) · J. Harries, *G. Campbell Morgan: the man and his ministry* (1930) · H. Murray, *Campbell Morgan: Bible teacher* (1938) · H. Davies, *Varieties of English preaching, 1900–1960* (1963), 198–205 · *Christian World* (24 May 1945) · *Congregational Year Book* (1946), 447 · M. J. Drake, 'G. Campbell Morgan: preacher and teacher', BD diss., U. Wales, 1997 · D. M. Wagner, *The expository method of G. Campbell Morgan* (1957) · *Westminster Record*, 19/7 (July 1945) [memorial number for G. Campbell Morgan] · *The Times* (18 May 1945) · *CGPLA Eng. & Wales* (1945)
Archives Westm. DA · Westminster College, Cambridge, Cheshunt Foundation
Likenesses F. O. Salisbury, oils, Westminster College, Cambridge, Cheshunt Foundation
Wealth at death £3340 4s. 5d.: probate, 12 Oct 1945, *CGPLA Eng. & Wales*

Morgan, Sir George Osborne, first baronet (1826–1897), lawyer and politician, was the eldest son of Morgan Morgan (1796–1870), for thirty-one years vicar of Conwy, Caernarvonshire. His mother, Fanny, was the daughter of John

Sir George Osborne Morgan, first baronet (1826–1897), by Lock & Whitfield, pubd 1883

Nonnen of Liseberg, Göteborg, who was descended from the Huguenot family of De Lorent. His younger brother was John Edward Morgan, professor of medicine at Owens College, Manchester (*d.* 4 September 1892), and his youngest brother, the Revd Henry Arthur Morgan DD, became master of Jesus College, Cambridge. George Osborne Morgan, who derived his name of Osborne from the marriage in 1764 of Egbert Nonnen, his great-grandfather, with Anne Osborne of Burnage, Cheshire, was born at Göteborg in Sweden on 8 May 1826, during the temporary occupancy by his father of the post of chaplain there. At the age of fifteen, after spending some time at the Friars' School, Bangor, he entered Shrewsbury School under B. H. Kennedy, who said of him that he had never known a boy 'with such a store of undigested information' (*DNB*).

Kennedy's reservations notwithstanding, Morgan went on to a glittering undergraduate career. Although his father had intended him for Cambridge and the church, Morgan preferred Oxford and matriculated from Balliol College on 30 November 1843. He then returned to Shrewsbury, and while still a schoolboy performed the extraordinary feat of obtaining the Craven scholarship at Oxford (16 March 1844), before going back again to school. In the following autumn he stood for a scholarship at Balliol and was awarded an exhibition, after which he went into residence. In 1846 he was *proxime accessit* for the Ireland scholarship, and in the same year he won the Newdigate prize for English verse, on the subject of 'Settlers in Australia'. In 1847 he moved as a scholar to Worcester College, where he obtained a first class in *literae humaniores* that year, and graduated BA in 1848. He won the chancellor's English essay prize in 1850 for *The Ancients and Moderns in Regard to the Administration of Justice*, and was elected Stowell civil law fellow of University College. He won the Eldon law scholarship in 1851. During his short residence as civil law fellow at University College he took private pupils, among them A. W. Peel, M. E. Grant Duff, and J. W. Chitty. His most intimate friends at this period, which was marked by vehement religious controversies, were the opponents of Tractarianism, such as A. P. Stanley, W. Y. Sellar, and A. H. Clough. He figures in Clough's poem 'The Bothie' as Lindsay.

In 1851 Morgan left Oxford and—after declining a post at Kneller Hall, a teacher training college in Twickenham—threw himself into a legal career that immediately brought him considerable success. He entered Lincoln's Inn, having been admitted a student there on 6 June 1850, and was called to the bar on 6 June 1853. He practised as an equity draftsman and conveyancer, and among his pupils were W. W. Byrne, C. P. Ilbert, and Robert Herbert. In 1858 he published *Chancery Acts and Orders, being a Collection of Statutes and General Orders Recently Passed*, which, with slight variations in the titles, ran through six editions: the second was published in 1860, and the last in 1885. He also became one of the four joint editors of the *New Report*, which reported equity cases between 1862 and 1865. In 1856 he had married Emily Circe, daughter of Leopold Reiss of Eccles.

With his legal career thus established, Morgan began to develop that deep interest in politics upon which his future fame was to rest. After leaving Oxford, he contributed political articles to the *Morning Chronicle*, and after the staff of that newspaper founded the *Saturday Review* he wrote very occasionally for the new periodical. In 1861 he published a sympathetic lecture on the Italian revolution of 1860, *The Italian revolution of 1860: A lecture delivered at the working men's college, Manchester, Feb 1 1861*. The largest influence on his political outlook, however, seems to have been his knowledge of Wales. He was one among a group of London Welshmen actively committed to the idea of establishing a university in the principality, and was also a keen proponent of disestablishment—the severance of ties between the Church of England and the state: he held meetings on the subject in his chambers at Lincoln's Inn. This policy, which was heavily supported by nonconformists such as the great radical leader Edward Miall, of whom Morgan was a close friend, was instrumental in persuading the radicals of the Caernarvonshire boroughs (in 1857) and of the Denbighshire boroughs (in 1867), to invite Morgan to stand for parliament in their constituencies. On both occasions he withdrew in order not to split the Liberal vote; in 1868, however, he made a dramatic entry to parliament. His eleventh-hour candidature for the two-member seat of Denbighshire wrong-footed one of the sitting MPs, Colonel Robert Biddulph, an Adullamite who had voted against Gladstone's proposals for parliamentary reform, and propelled Morgan into parliament as partner to the great tory landowner Sir Watkin Williams Wynn.

Once in parliament, Morgan quickly demonstrated why his return had been greeted with such enthusiasm by the radical wing of the Welsh Liberal Party. He supported several causes of interest to nonconformists in general, notably the abolition of university tests and Sir Wilfrid Lawson's permissive Prohibitory Liquor Bill; more significantly, he took it upon himself to introduce two bills relating to issues particularly relevant to Welsh nonconformists. In 1870 he sought to settle the issue of burials, by introducing a bill which would permit the use of any Christian service in a parish churchyard; the measure did not become law until 1880, after Morgan had introduced it for ten consecutive sessions. Alongside this, in 1870, he introduced a Places of Worship (Sites) Bill, which would have allowed religious groups the right to purchase land compulsorily for the erection of schools or places of worship. The matter was thought particularly relevant to Wales, where the Anglican landowners were said to deny grants of land to local nonconformists for these purposes. W. E. Forster borrowed the compulsory purchase clauses for his 1870 Elementary Act; Morgan's original bill reached the statute book, heavily amended, in 1873. In a more secular vein, Morgan also backed Henry Richard in his campaign against the Conservative landowners in Wales who had allegedly threatened tenants in 1868 with eviction if they voted for Liberal candidates, and spoke out against the appointment of English-speaking judges to Welsh circuits in 1871.

Yet there was more to Morgan's politics than his Welsh radicalism. As his speech on Welsh judges indicated, his professional background played an important role in directing his political activities. In 1869 he had been appointed a queen's counsel, and was elected a bencher of Lincoln's Inn in the Michaelmas term following. In 1870 he was one of those to whom Gladstone turned for advice on filling the vacant chair in civil law at Oxford (Morgan to Gladstone, 8 April 1870, BL, Add. MS 44426). In 1871 and 1872 he seconded Sir Roundell Palmer's resolutions in favour of creating a general school of law; this led the inns of court to institute examinations before calling students of law to the bar. On all topics directly associated with law, such as bills to reconstitute the courts of judicature (1873 and 1875), he frequently had the ear of the house. He also became a keen advocate of land law reform. In 1878 he chaired a Commons select committee on land titles and transfer, and drafted its report, dated 24 June 1879. He also contributed an article upon the subject to the *Fortnightly Review* for December 1879, and in 1880 reprinted it as a pamphlet under the title *Land Law Reform in England*.

By 1880 Morgan's political stock had risen so high that, when Gladstone was returned to power, he joined the ministry as judge-advocate-general. The job, 'no sinecure' as he informed an influential supporter, obliged him to retire from the bar, and he was also nominated a privy councillor (Morgan to T. Gee, 3 May 1880, NL Wales, MS 8307D, fol. 201). In 1881 he provided for the abolition of flogging in the army in the annual Army Discipline Bill, and carried it in spite of a strong opposition. In 1882 he had sole charge of the Married Women's Property Bill, a measure bristling with legal difficulties, which required exceptionally skilful handling when passing through the House of Commons. As befitted his Welsh radical credentials, he was a strong supporter of both the Welsh Sunday Closing Act (1881) and of intermediate and higher education in the principality. In 1884 he supported Stuart Rendel's motion that the Aberystwyth College should receive the same recognition and financial support as the colleges at Bangor and Cardiff. He was also a keen proponent of women's education, and helped to found a women's hostel at Bangor College; an Osborne Morgan exhibition was established at the University College of North Wales (which Bangor College became) after his death to commemorate his services.

The redistribution of constituencies in 1885 pitched Morgan directly against the mighty interest of the Wynn family of Wynstay in the new, one-member constituency of East Denbighshire. Morgan's victory, which amazed even his own supporters, denied the Wynns representation of the county for the first time in 182 years. Gladstone offered Morgan the office of judge-advocate-general again, but the East Denbighshire MP feared his seat would not be secure in the contest which his acceptance of such a post would have entailed (Morgan to Gladstone, 4 Feb 1886, BL, Add. MS 44494, fols. 149–52). He accepted instead the post of under-secretary for the colonies: 'to serve under you in any capacity', he told Gladstone, 'is in itself, a privilege' (Morgan to Gladstone, 29 April 1886, BL, Add. MS 44463, fol. 279). His new chief, Lord Granville, sat in the House of Lords, so the work of representing the department in the Commons fell upon Morgan. His tenure of office was marked by exceptional activity. The distress which he experienced at hearing of the sufferings endured by Welsh settlers in Patagonia, as well as by emigrants to Canada, led to his foundation of the emigration inquiry office.

The government lasted for only six months, but Morgan found the pressure of work immense. This, combined with a strenuous electoral contest in July 1886, when he held his East Denbighshire seat by a mere twenty-eight votes from Wynn, brought on a severe illness from which he never fully recovered. Nevertheless, Morgan remained committed to the Liberal cause and to his parliamentary career. He retained his seat in 1892 with a considerably enhanced majority, and from 1888 to 1895 was alternately chairman of the standing committees on law and trade. On Welsh matters he continued to take a leading part, and accepted the leadership of the Welsh party in the Commons, although he had earlier opposed the formation of such a group. Despite his continued involvement in the daily life of parliament, he had felt unequal to resuming office when offered the chance by Gladstone after the election in 1892 and accepted instead his leader's offer of a baronetcy.

Morgan's last public appearance, a week before his death, was at an eisteddfod at Chirk, at which he delivered a speech on the effects of music upon character. He died on 25 August 1897 at his home—Moreton Hall, Chirk, Denbighshire—and was buried in the churchyard of Llandysilio-yn-Iâl, near Llangollen. He was survived by his wife, Emily. Their marriage seems to have been happy and to have focused on Morgan's political career. As he told a supporter in 1873, when rumours of an opposition were circulating ahead of the imminent general election:

> My wife & I although by no means rich, have lived carefully & having no children have been enabled to put by a fund for a rainy day … neither my wife nor I are in the least disheartened [at rumours of a likely contest] & rather like the idea of a fight.   (Morgan to Thomas Gee, 17 March 1873, NL Wales, 8307D)

Morgan was characteristic of the moderate Welsh Liberalism of his time. His ambition to develop Welsh education was part of a larger ambition: to endow Wales with the qualifications to stand by the side of her 'predominant partner', England, as a nation with a character and aims of its own. His enthusiasm for a Welsh university, disestablishment, and Irish home rule was thus tempered by hostility to the establishment of an antagonistic Welsh party in the Commons on Irish lines. Beyond the world of politics, Morgan was considered an excellent raconteur and a brilliant conversationalist. In addition, he retained the interest in writing that had distinguished him at Oxford. Like many of Kennedy's pupils at Shrewsbury, Morgan wrote elegant Greek verse and in the year of his death (1897) published, with a dedication to Gladstone, a translation into English hexameter verse of Virgil's *Eclogues*; the work, perhaps a sign of Clough's influence on Morgan, was very well received. He also contributed various articles on contemporary topics to the *Contemporary*, *Fortnightly*, and *Nineteenth Century* reviews.

MATTHEW CRAGOE

Sources DNB · J. B. Edwards, 'Sir George Osborne Morgan, MP (1826–97): nineteenth century mould breaker', *Transactions of the Denbighshire Historical Society*, 46 (1997), 91–108 · M. Cragoe, 'George Osborne Morgan, Henry Richard, and the politics of religion in Wales, 1868–74', *Parliamentary History*, 19 (2000), 118–30 · D. Wiggins, 'The Burial Act of 1880, the Liberation Society and George Osborne Morgan', *Parliamentary History*, 15 (1996), 173–89 · G. O. Morgan, 'Dwy flynedd ar hurgain yn nhy y cyffredin', *Y Traethodydd*, 46 (1891), 176–83 · G. O. Morgan, 'The Victorian era: what has it done for Wales?', *Young Wales* (Aug 1897)
Archives BL, corresp. with W. E. Gladstone, Add. MSS 44424–44789 · Bodl. Oxf., corresp. with Sir William Harcourt · NL Wales, Gee MSS
Likenesses Lock & Whitfield, woodburytype photograph, pubd 1883, NPG [*see illus.*] · Spy [L. Ward], caricature, chromolithograph, NPG; repro. in VF (17 May 1879)
Wealth at death £11,490 0s. 4d.: probate, 28 Oct 1897, CGPLA Eng. & Wales

Morgan, Sir Gilbert Thomas (1870–1940), chemist, was born at Essendon, Hertfordshire, on 20 October 1870, the son of Thomas Morgan, a butler, and his wife, Marie Louise Corday, a ladies' maid of French–Swiss nationality. After education at the local school he attended the Central Foundation School, Cowper Street, London, and in 1886 enrolled at Finsbury Technical College as a certified student. Influenced by S. P. Thompson, John Perry, and Raphael Meldola, by the time he left three years later he had prepared a series of new derivatives of benzeneazo-β-naphthol and assisted in the extraction of ceria from cerite. The widely differing natures of his early ventures in research were afterwards to have a far-reaching effect, since he never specialized in any one branch of chemistry, but was at home in its organic, inorganic, and physical branches.

Morgan left Finsbury in 1889 and was employed as assistant chemist for five years in the firm of Read Holliday & Co., dye manufacturers, at Huddersfield (later British Dyes, Ltd). In 1894 he decided to give up his industrial career and resume his scientific education; he was awarded a royal scholarship and became a mature student at the Royal College of Science. He soon began assisting Professor W. A. Tilden with various research projects, and graduated BSc with first-class honours in 1896. He then became successively demonstrator, lecturer, and assistant professor at the Royal College.

In 1912 Morgan married Kathleen Nembhard (d. 1944), daughter of George Desborough. They had no children. In the same year he was appointed professor of chemistry at the Royal College of Science in Dublin; in 1916 he returned to Finsbury as professor in succession to Meldola, and in 1919 he was elected Mason professor of chemistry at Birmingham University. Six years later he crowned his career as the first director of the Chemical Research Laboratory which at the instance of Sir Richard Threlfall had been set up at Teddington. In 1937 he retired, but not into inactivity, for he had become chairman of the research fund committee of the Institute of Brewing, and entered actively into a new and large field of research.

Morgan's experimental work had an important impact in two areas: chemical reactions under high pressures and synthetic resins. The first of these arose from his use of the autoclave at Huddersfield, where he produced the dyestuff titan como blue which enjoyed a brief period of high popularity. The second also made its appearance towards the end of his period as a commercial chemist, for he made an observation which in other hands assumed unusual importance. By the condensation of phenol with formaldehyde he obtained a clear amber resin, possessing unexpected physical properties but useless as a source of dyes; the experiment was therefore laid aside and forgotten, until in 1906 the first of the Baekeland patents for the manufacture of synthetic plastics showed how narrowly Morgan had missed a fortune.

Research into colours and the improvement of autoclaves together with co-ordinated compounds were Morgan's chief areas of study at Dublin and Birmingham; it was Morgan who introduced the term 'chelate', which became widely used for rings containing co-ordinated links (bidentate ligands). At Finsbury during the First World War he devoted his time to investigations carried out for the Chemical Warfare Committee. He constructed autoclaves out of military and naval shell, and used them in making organic arsenicals and antimonials that could be applicable to chemical warfare and also in the preparation of colour intermediates. His former experiences as a colour chemist were of great importance, since materials previously imported from Germany now had to be made

in Britain, and Morgan helped to reconstruct the industry.

When Morgan took up his post at Teddington his university research topics, together with the examination of low-temperature tars, became its basic studies. Later he directed investigations into a wide range of microbiological problems, including those relating to chemotherapy, water pollution, and the chemical constituents of woodsmoke.

Morgan's publications were regarded as authoritative in their day, and included *Achievements of the British Chemical Industry in the Last Twenty-Five Years* (1939), *British Chemical Industry: its Rise and Development* (1938), *Inorganic Chemistry: a Survey of Modern Development* (1936), and *Organic Compounds of Arsenic and Antimony* (1918). He also contributed alone or in collaboration over 350 original scientific papers, always being careful to acknowledge the work of others, and from 1903 to 1906 he was editor of the *Journal of the Chemical Society*.

Many honours were bestowed upon Morgan: he was appointed OBE in 1920 and knighted in 1936; he was elected a fellow of the Royal Society in 1915, and he received honorary degrees from the universities of Dublin, St Andrews, and Birmingham. In 1921 he was awarded the gold medal of the Dyers' Company; in 1931 he was president of the Society of Chemical Industry, which in 1939 awarded him its medal, and in 1933 he was president of the Chemical Society.

Morgan possessed an extraordinarily retentive memory and his love of work was matched by his energy, thoroughness, and efficiency. He died of uraemia at the Royal Hospital, Richmond, Surrey, on 1 February 1940, and was cremated at Golders Green crematorium on 6 February. As a legacy to his interest and competence in all branches of chemistry, he left a bequest to the Chemical Society to fund the Corday–Morgan medal and prize, and established the Corday–Morgan memorial fund, which was to be used 'to assist in the unification of the chemical profession'.   J. C. IRVINE, *rev.* K. D. WATSON

Sources J. C. Irvine, *Obits. FRS*, 3 (1939–41), 355–62 · G. T. Morgan, 'Personal reminiscences of chemical research', *Chemistry and Industry* (15 July 1939), 665–73 · *JCS* (1941), 689–97 · *Chemistry and Industry* (10 Feb 1940), 97–8 · *The Times* (2 Feb 1940), 11f · *The Times* (6 Feb 1940), 9e · *The Times* (8 Feb 1940), 11b · *Nature*, 145 (1940), 252–3 · W. Wardlaw and H. D. K. Drew, 'Gilbert Thomas Morgan, 1870–1940', *British chemists*, ed. A. Findlay and W. H. Mills (1947), 316–52
Archives ICL, papers relating to training of chemists
Likenesses photograph, repro. in Irvine, *Obits. FRS*, facing p. 355 · photograph, repro. in *JCS*, 689 · portrait, repro. in *Journal of the Institute of Brewing* (April 1940)
Wealth at death £29,285 17s. 8d.: probate, 30 April 1940, *CGPLA Eng. & Wales*

Morgan, Griffith [*known as* Guto Nyth-brân] (1700–1737), long-distance runner, was a celebrated athlete of phenomenal speed and stamina. Guto is the Welsh diminutive of Griffith, and Nyth-brân ('crow's nest') was the name of the farm where he lived, in the parish of Llanwynno, in the Glamorgan hills between Porth and Mountain Ash. Nothing is known of his upbringing beyond the fact that his parents moved to Nyth-brân Farm from his birthplace in neighbouring Llwyncelyn when he was little more than a year old.

Foot-racing and pedestrian contests, like prize-fighting and wrestling matches, were regular features of pre-industrial sporting life; arranged locally by publicans or local shopkeepers in the absence of more professional promoters, they were invariably an outlet for gambling and the expression of parochial pride. Little celebrated in his own day, Guto's remarkable feats were revived for posterity by the Revd William Thomas (Glanffrwd; 1843–1890), whose history of the parish of Llanwynno appeared in 1888 at a time of emerging Welsh national consciousness. Guto, it appears, was a fleet-footed, multi-terrain specialist who could round up sheep without the help of a dog, chase hares until they were reduced to exhaustion, and outrun horses. His mother once sent him on an errand to Aberdâr, more than 3 miles away, and was amazed to find he had completed the 7 mile round trip before the kettle had boiled. Only a cynic would query the capacity of the kettle or the intensity of the flames which heated it.

Capable of covering 50 yards in four seconds and 10 miles in forty-five minutes, this Welsh Olympian attracted backers whose wagers were taken by the formidable Siân o'r Siop ('Jane of the shop'), a local admirer who became Guto's lover as well as his manager. Having seen off numerous opponents from near and far, in 1737 Guto, despite not having run competitively for four years, accepted the challenge of an Englishman, Prince, to a 12 mile race from Newport to Bedwas church, near Caerphilly, for a large money prize. Siân wagered a thousand sovereigns, and the life savings of every resident in the parish of Llanwynno were said to have been placed on Guto. The race took place on 6 September, and after adopting his usual malodorous pre-match practice of sleeping in warm manure, as much to deter any opponent from getting too close to him as to loosen his limbs—which according to Glanffrwd were 'like whipcord and as flexible as whalebones' (Glanffrwd, 92)—Guto felt confident enough during the race to chat with spectators along the route, thereby enabling Prince to open up a large gap. Guto eventually overhauled him, ran alongside for a short while dispensing advice and then, with fine but foolhardy bravado, sprinted up the steep mile-long gradient to the church to win in the astounding time of fifty-three minutes. An ecstatic Siân collected two full aprons of winnings and thumped the back of her triumphant but exhausted champion, who promptly fell dead at her feet.

Guto was buried in St Gwynno's churchyard, Llanwynno, on 18 September 1737. His original gravestone still lies under the south wall of the churchyard, while another was erected in 1866, bearing two verses in Welsh, one of them by Glanffrwd, whose subsequent history of the parish did most to revive the reputation of this remarkable athlete.   GARETH WILLIAMS

Sources Glanffrwd [W. Thomas], *History of Llanwynno*, ed. H. Lewis, trans. J. E. Evans (1950) · B. Baldwin, *Mountain Ash remembered* (1984) · T. M. Rees, *Notable Welshmen* (1908) · gravestone, St Gwynno's Church, Llanwynno, Glamorgan, Wales · parish register, St Gwynno's Church, Llanwynno, NL Wales [burial], 18 Sep 1737

Morgan, Hector Davies (1785–1850), Church of England clergyman, was the only son of Hector Davies of London (*d.* 6 March 1785, aged twenty-seven) and Sophia, daughter of John *Blackstone, first cousin of Sir William Blackstone. Hector's grandfather, the Revd David Davies, master of the free school of St Mary Overy, Southwark, took the name and arms of Morgan on his second marriage, to Christiana, one of the four nieces and heirs of John Morgan of Cardigan. Upon her death in 1800 Hector succeeded to the name. He matriculated from Trinity College, Oxford, on 24 February 1803, and proceeded BA in 1806 and MA in 1815.

About September 1809 Morgan was presented by Lewis Majendie to the donative curacy of Castle Hedingham in Essex, where he remained for thirty-seven years. On 7 October 1817, under the new statute of 57 George III c. 130, one of the earliest savings banks in Essex was opened by Morgan's exertions at Castle Hedingham for the Hinckford hundred. He was acting secretary until 28 November 1833, and while serving in this capacity published *The Expedience and Method of Providing Assurance for the Poor* (1830) and an address, *The Beneficial Operation of Banks for Savings* (1834), with a brief memoir of Lewis Majendie. About the same time Morgan became chaplain to George, second Baron Kenyon.

Morgan was appointed Bampton lecturer in 1819, and was collated by the bishop of St David's, on 7 August 1820, to the small prebend of Trallong, in the collegiate church of Brecon. He resigned the cure of Castle Hedingham in July or August 1846, and moved to Cardigan, where his second son, Thomas, was living. Morgan, who was married but whose wife's name is unknown, died there on 23 December 1850.

Two essays by Morgan—*A survey of the platform of the Christian church exhibited in the scriptures* (1816) and *The doctrine of regeneration as identified with baptism and distinct from renovation, investigated, in an essay on baptism* (1817)—each won a prize of £50 from the Society for Promoting Christian Knowledge and Church Union in the diocese of St David's, established on 10 October 1804 by Thomas Burgess, bishop of St David's. But his principal work was *The Doctrine and Law of Marriage, Adultery, and Divorce* (2 vols., 1826), which shows accurate and extensive reading and legal knowledge.

Morgan's eldest son, John Blackstone Morgan (*d.* 1832), was curate of Garsington, Oxfordshire. A third son, **James Davies Morgan** (1811–1846), was an architect who unsuccessfully submitted designs for the Palace of Westminster in 1835 and for the Ashmolean Museum, Oxford, in 1839. He lived principally at Hedingham, Essex, and designed St John's Church, Cornish Hall End, Essex. There were also two daughters.

CHARLOTTE FELL-SMITH, *rev.* H. C. G. MATTHEW

Sources Foster, *Alum. Oxon.* · *GM*, 1st ser., 97/2 (1827), 224 · *GM*, 2nd ser., 35 (1851), 562 · J. Foster, ed., *Index ecclesiasticus, or, Alphabetical*

lists of all ecclesiastical dignitaries in England and Wales since the Reforma-
tion (1890) · *Collectanea Topographica et Genealogica*, 5 (1838), 402 ·
Colvin, *Archs.*

Morgan, Henry (d. 1559), bishop of St David's, was born in
Dewisland, Pembrokeshire, and educated at Oxford University. He received the degree of BCL in 1522 and supplicated for, but may not have received, the degree of BCnL in
1523. He then received the degree of DCL in 1525. Morgan
served as principal of St Edward's Hall, Oxford, between
1527 and 4 July 1528. He was also the moderator for students who performed exercises for their degrees in civil
law at Oxford for several years, probably in the late 1520s
and early 1530s.

Beginning in May 1528 and continuing until March 1552
Morgan was the recipient of a number of clerical preferments. In 1528 he became rector of Uplyme, Devon; in
1530 he was collated to the rectory of Walwyn's Castle,
Pembrokeshire; in the following year he was admitted to
the rectory of Wood Eaton, Oxfordshire; in 1532 he
received the prebend of Sanctae Crucis or Spaldwick, Lincoln; four years later he was given the vicarage of West
Alvington, Devon, and the prebend of St Margaret, Leicester; in 1537 he became rector of Mells, Somerset, and by
that same year he was chaplain to Henry VIII. In 1542 Morgan was admitted to the third stall of Bristol; two years
later he became chancellor of the diocese of Llandaff and
vicar-general of the diocese of Exeter; in 1547 he was collated to the prebend of the collegiate church of Crantock,
Cornwall; in 1548 he was made prebendary of Exeter; in
1549 he was instituted to the rectory of Mawgan, Cornwall; a year later he became rector of St Columb Major,
Cornwall; and in 1552 he was given the prebend of Hampton, Hereford. He may also have been the Henry Morgan
who served as proctor of the clergy for the diocese of Llandaff in 1529, and also, or alternatively, the Henry Morgan
cited in the *valor ecclesiasticus* who held the prebend of St
Cross, Llandaff, and the rectory of Arley, Warwickshire, by
1535.

Although little is known about Morgan's religious
beliefs before 1554, it would be logical to assume from the
preferments he received that he accepted—or at least did
not openly resist—the religious changes of the 1530s,
1540s, and early 1550s. However, he was serving as Mary I's
chaplain when he was chosen to replace the deprived Robert Ferrar as bishop of St David's. He was thus elected on
26 March 1554, consecrated on 1 April of the same year,
and received the temporalities on 23 April. Once installed,
Morgan faithfully carried out the Marian religious directives. Between April 1554 and March 1555 (the height of the
deprivations of the married clergy), there is only one
known deprivation recorded in Henry Morgan's register,
but there are eighty-eight vacancies brought about *de iure*.
If these vacancies were caused by deprivations—and
there is every reason to believe that they were—then St
David's would have had one deprivation for approximately every four benefices. As Glanmor Williams has
shown, although the exact cause of only one of these
vacancies is known, the majority were probably brought

about because the incumbents were married. As for burn-
ings for heresy, two martyrs—Robert Ferrar, the former
bishop of the diocese, and William Nichol—were executed in St David's during Morgan's episcopate, though it
is not known if Morgan had any hand in Nichol's condemnation. Outside his own diocese Morgan was present at
the condemnations of Thomas Tomkins and John Rough,
but Edmund Bonner was the bishop who passed sentence
against these two martyrs.

Approximately seven months after Elizabeth I came to
the throne, Morgan was deprived of his bishopric for
refusing to accept religious change. However, perhaps
because he did not preach against the changes, or perhaps
because the queen favoured him, Morgan was permitted
to retire quietly to Wolvercote, Oxfordshire, where he
lived among friends until his death there on 23 December
1559. His body was then interred in the church at Wolvercote. His will was dated December 1559 and proved on 24
January 1560. He bequeathed £4 a year for five years to two
MAs of Oxford 'to pray for my frynds soules', including
that of Edward Penant, parson of Stanlake.

ANGELO J. LOUISA

Sources Emden, *Oxf.*, 4.401 · Wood, *Ath. Oxon.*, new edn, 2.788–
90 · Wood, *Ath. Oxon.: Fasti* (1815), 57, 59, 67 · registers, diocese of St
David's, NL Wales, SD/BR/2 [Henry Morgan, Thomas Young, and
Richard Davies] · G. Williams, 'The second volume of St David's
register, 1554–64', *BBCS*, 14 (1950–52), 125–38 · *The acts and monuments of John Foxe*, ed. S. R. Cattley, 8 vols. (1837–41), vol. 6, p. 721;
vol. 7, pp. 23–5; vol. 8, pp. 447, 462, 629, 636, 694 · *Reg. Oxf.*, 1.124 ·
LP Henry VIII, 4/3, no. 6047; 12/2, no. 1008(8); 14/1, no. 1065(4); 17, no.
443(9) · *CPR, 1553–4*, 8, 112; *1554–5*, 199 · *Fasti Angl.* (Hardy), 1.229,
301, 505; 2.169, 201 · Foster, *Alum. Oxon.* · J. Caley and J. Hunter, eds.,
Valor ecclesiasticus temp. Henrici VIII, 6 vols., RC (1810–34), vol. 2, pp.
172, 302; vol. 3, p. 80; vol. 4, p. 348 · *Fasti Angl., 1300–1541*, [Lincoln],
79, 102 · *Fasti Angl., 1300–1541*, [Welsh dioceses], 29
Archives NL Wales, diocese of St David's, Registers of Henry Morgan, Thomas Young, and Richard Davies, SD/BR/2
Wealth at death see Wood, *Ath. Oxon.*, 2.790; Yardley, *Menevia
Sacra*, 95–6

Morgan, Sir Henry (c.1635–1688), privateer and colonial
governor, was the eldest son of Robert Morgan of Llan-
rhymny, Glamorgan.

Early years in the Caribbean, c.1658–1667 Nothing certain is
known about Morgan's education, although he later
claimed that it was limited, and that having left school
young, he was 'much more used to the pike than the book'
(*CSP col.*, 9, no. 1304). It has been suggested that Morgan
was taken to the Caribbean as an indentured servant, or as
a soldier in the army that conquered Jamaica, but there is
no evidence in the surviving records to substantiate either
claim. According to Richard Browne, surgeon on Morgan's
flagship in 1670, the admiral had gone to the West Indies
about 1658, shortly after the English captured Jamaica
from the Spaniards in 1655, and as a 'private gentleman' in
his early twenties, had 'by his valour raised himself to a
position of fame and fortune' (ibid., 1669–75, no. 293).

Many young men were drawn to the Caribbean in pursuit of riches. Sugar offered high returns but required a
large capital investment, and those with limited
resources, such as Morgan, looked in other directions. The
Spanish empire had long offered rich pickings through

Sir Henry Morgan (c.1635–1688), by unknown engraver, pubd 1684

trade and plunder, and Jamaica, in the heart of the Caribbean, provided a good base for both activities. Privateering flourished during the Anglo-Spanish War, and continued after it ended in 1660, using the widely accepted pretext that there was 'no peace beyond the line'. This argued that, as the Spaniards treated any foreigners they found in American waters as pirates, English retaliation was justified, and in any event it was generally believed that only force would persuade the Spaniards to open their colonial ports to foreigners. Charles II effectively endorsed this policy when he dispatched Thomas Windsor, Lord Windsor, to establish civil government in Jamaica with instructions that allowed him to proclaim war after a peremptory effort to establish trade with the Spanish colonies. Windsor could then set up an Admiralty court to issue commissions and manage the 1500 or so privateers based at the island. Crown and Admiralty collusion in plunder were encouraged by their respective rights to a tenth and a fifteenth share of prize taken at sea.

Morgan first appears in the historical record in August 1665 when he entered Port Royal with captains John Morris and Jacob Fackman after a plundering expedition in Central America lasting twenty-two months. Both Fackman and Morris had commissions from Windsor's Admiralty court but there is no record of papers given to Henry Morgan. Perhaps he assumed command during the long expedition, owing to the death or desertion of another officer. During the raids he became familiar with Central American territory and the local Indians. He also developed a lasting disdain for Spanish defences. 'Every action gives new encouragement to attempt the Spaniard finding them in all places very weak and very wealthy' and he judged that '2000 men, some say 500, might easily conquer all this territory' (examinations of Capt. John Morris, Capt. Fackman, and Capt. Henry Morgan, PRO, CO 1/20, fol. 38).

During Morgan's adventure in Central America a new governor, Thomas Modyford, had arrived in Jamaica with strict instructions to end privateering and promote peaceful trade. However, Modyford soon realized that this would be difficult, if not impossible, as the island's 4000 or so residents had planted a mere 3000 acres and their prosperity rested heavily on the privateering business. Furthermore, as the island had no permanent defence force the privateers provided valuable security. Modyford decided to tread carefully and, after an initial proclamation against privateering, the trade carried on in stealth. Morgan and his colleagues were not rebuked for their depredations on the grounds that they had left port with lawful commissions (although they had long expired and did not authorize actions on land). It was already evident that Modyford would prove an enthusiastic patron of the privateers and the home authorities continued to turn a reassuringly blind eye.

Morgan's activities are not documented during the two years after his return although he was certainly based in Port Royal and his marriage to Mary Elizabeth (d. 1696), daughter of the island's deputy governor, Edward Morgan, placed him in influential circles, although it did little for his fortune, as the colonel was reported to be poor. Mary's older sister, Anna Petronella, married the merchant and planter Robert Bindloss (a former ship's surgeon) and member of the council of Jamaica from 1664, who remained a close friend and business associate of Morgan throughout his life. A third Morgan sister also settled in Jamaica after marrying the planter Henry Archbould. Henry and Mary did not have children but they were surrounded by numerous nephews and nieces.

After the outbreak of war with the Dutch in 1665 Modyford was able to issue commissions against them but Jamaica's privateers showed little interest in this new enemy. An attack launched against Curaçao, the most important Dutch base in the Caribbean, foundered on the death of its leader, Morgan's father-in-law, Edward Morgan, at Statia. Meanwhile most privateers continued to pick on their traditional prey and, in February 1666, the governor and council decided to put a legal gloss on what was happening in practice and declared war on the Spaniard, compiling a list of grievances as justification. Late in 1667, shortly after an Anglo-Spanish peace treaty was signed in Europe, Modyford appointed Henry Morgan as admiral of the privateers with orders to gain information about Spanish designs on Jamaica. Morgan had clearly gained a reputation for courage and competence in action, and in the next four years this was proved well deserved as he led a series of spectacular raids against the Spanish empire.

The sack of Portobello Morgan's commission authorized action at sea alone. However, he knew that if he provided information about intended Spanish aggression any attack on land could be portrayed as a preventive strike and would not be punished. Apart from the likelihood of greater plunder the tenths and fifteenths of sea prize given to the crown and Admiralty were not levied on land actions. Morgan took great care to secure the documentary evidence needed to justify such profitable enterprise.

In January 1668 Morgan and a group of French privateers conducted a successful raid far into the interior of Cuba, sacking Puerto de Principe. The plunder was small but it was easy to frighten prisoners into providing information about intended Spanish hostility which could be used to justify this and further action. After dividing the plunder Morgan suggested an attack on Portobello, a reputedly rich and well fortified town on the Caribbean coast of the isthmus of Panama which served as the terminus of the Spanish fleets that collected Peruvian silver. The audacity of Morgan's proposal was reflected in the French captains' refusal to join the enterprise believing it 'too full of danger and difficulty' (Morgan's relation, 7 Sept 1668, PRO, CO 1/23, fol. 101). But Morgan pressed on with 500 men of various nationalities, knowing that the town was more vulnerable than commonly supposed, especially when there was no treasure fleet present. The two forts guarding the entrance to the harbour were in disrepair and the garrison was below strength, as well as short of food and arms.

In contrast to the demoralized Spanish troops the privateers who swarmed the Caribbean were reported to be 'very happy, well paid and … [living] in amity with each other. The prizes that they make are shared with much brotherhood and friendship' (Earle, 66). As was customary in all privateering ventures Morgan signed articles of association with his twelve captains and twenty-six other representatives of the men before embarking on the enterprise in 1668. The agreements were designed to maintain discipline and ensure a fair division of the expected plunder with agreed premiums for rank and bravery, and compensation for loss of a limb or an eye. Morgan had the respect of his men and morale was good. Their trust was shown to be well placed as Morgan carried off a successful surprise attack on Portobello in July, with loss of only eighteen men and thirty-two wounded, displaying the clever cunning and expert timing which marked his brilliance as a military commander.

Morgan's forces occupied the town for thirty-one days, gathering plunder from within the walls and the citizens who had fled into the surrounding country. Stories differ about the men's behaviour, and no firsthand reports describe the extremes of drunkenness and debauchery narrated by Exquemelin in his *History of the Bucaniers*, but torture was almost certainly used to extract information about the whereabouts of hidden riches. The acting president of Panama attempted to relieve the city without success and agreed to a ransom of 100,000 pesos (£25,000) for its safe return. After receiving the treasure Morgan sent polite thanks to the president with a typically insolent sting in the tail. He hoped that he would have the pleasure of meeting the president face to face in Panama. Morgan enjoyed playing the gallant gentleman and he later claimed that several ladies of 'great quality' were offered liberty to go to the president's camp, but they chose to stay, 'saying they were now prisoners to a person of quality, who was more tender of their honours than they doubted to find in the president's camp among his rude Panama soldiers' and at the surrender of the town they were full of thanks (Morgan's relation, PRO, CO 1/23, fol. 103). Given that the citizens had been stripped of valuables and forced to borrow funds to pay the large ransom the thanks must have been through gritted teeth.

The capture of Portobello was the most profitable of Morgan's exploits. The total plunder was reported to be worth between £70,000 and £100,000, substantially more than the total value of Jamaica's annual agricultural output at this time, and almost half the value of Barbados's sugar exports. Each man received a basic share of about £120, five or six times the annual wage of a seventeenth-century seaman. Not surprisingly the fleet was given a warm welcome on its return to Jamaica. James Modyford, the governor's brother, remarked that the glut of prize goods allowed anyone with cash to 'double nay treble [their] money without any hazard' (Sir James Modyford to Sir Andrew King, 4 Nov 1668, Westminster Abbey muniments, 11921).

The Spanish ambassador in London expressed horror as Morgan's prize goods were brought into the Thames. His complaints were received with polite attention and an indication that the privateers' action was viewed as regrettable, but easy to understand, in the light of Spanish acts of hostility in America. One Spanish report claimed that James, duke of York (the future James II), the lord high admiral, wrote to Morgan asking why he had not retained Portobello. A diplomatic hard line reflected general support for imperial expansion and greed for cheaply won Spanish plunder. Morgan was widely viewed as a national hero and neither he nor Modyford were rebuked for their actions.

Royal interest, especially on the part of the duke of York, led to the dispatch of a naval frigate, the *Oxford*, to join the privateers, as well as at least one smaller ship, the *Lilly*, but with disappointing results. In December 1668 they joined Morgan and his men at Isla Vaca, off the south coast of Hispaniola, a usual assembly point, and began to make ambitious plans to attack another major city. However, the *Oxford* was destroyed in a mysterious explosion. A council of war was underway on the ship at the time but Morgan, and the captains sitting on his side of the table, miraculously survived, although about 200 others died. After this loss of flagship and forces Morgan scaled down his plans and turned his attention eastwards.

The admiral led a fleet of eight ships and 500 men to Maracaibo, situated in a large inland lagoon on the north coast of what is now Venezuela, which was prosperous cattle and cocoa producing territory. After a successful assault, and a month of looting, Morgan prepared to leave the lake and found that the armada de Barlovento, a Spanish defence squadron, was awaiting him outside and had garrisoned the castle at the entrance. With characteristic cunning and audacity Morgan managed to extract his men and booty from this seemingly impossible situation using fireships and decoys, and destroying the remains of the Spanish squadron in the process. The fleet returned to Jamaica for another spending spree with plunder worth £30,000.

The sack of Panama Again the marauders went unrebuked by the home authorities but in summer 1669 there were new hopes of a treaty with Spain offering trade concessions in America. Furthermore, the death of George Monck, duke of Albemarle, a kinsman of Modyford's, deprived the governor of valuable protection at court. The secretary of state, the earl of Arlington, sent orders to cease hostilities, which Modyford received in May 1670 and, on 24 June, peace with the Spaniards was publicly proclaimed by beat of drum. Nevertheless residents reported that the privateers continued to come in and out of Port Royal. In fact, even the pretence of peace was short-lived as the queen regent of Spain had responded to the tide of depredations by dispatching orders to her governors allowing the issue of letters of marque. Tension mounted, and after a series of Spanish attacks on Jamaican trade and territory Modyford called the council and revealed that, in his orders, the king had given permission to deal with extraordinary circumstances in an extraordinary way. War with the Spaniards was renewed, and on 1 August 1670, ten days after the signing of the treaty of Madrid which promised peace and friendship between Spain and England in America, Modyford gave Morgan a commission to

> put to sea for the security of the coasts of this island and of our merchants ships and other vessels trading to and about the same … to do and perform all manner of exploits, which may tend to the preservation and quiet of this island. (Morgan's commission and instructions, BL, Add. MS 11268, fols. 68–72)

Morgan spent over three weeks assembling a force of eleven ships and 600 men in Port Royal and sailed to the rendezvous point at Isla Vaca to wait for further recruits. Parties were dispatched to Hispaniola and the Main to obtain victuals and Spanish prisoners who would provide information to excuse aggression. News of these activities reached Europe but, despite the recent treaty with Spain, the English authorities took no action apart from sending a letter that reached Modyford in November and instructed the governor to keep the privateers in whatever state they were in on its receipt and forbear hostilities on land. By December, Morgan had gathered a multinational force of more than 2000 men in thirty-eight ships, ranging from the *Satisfaction* of 120 tons to the tiny *Prosperous* of 10 tons, totalling 1585 tons (List of ships under command of Admiral Morgan, PRO, CO 1/138, fol. 105). It was the largest army of privateers ever seen in the Caribbean and a mark of Morgan's renown.

On 12 December 1670 Morgan held a council of war which concluded articles of association among the thirty-seven captains, issued commissions to those without, and agreed to attack Panama City as likely 'to put the greater curb on the insolence of the enemy … the president thereof having granted several commissions against the English to the great annoyance of the island of Jamaica and our merchants', realizing Morgan's promise to the acting president in 1668 (BL, Add. MS 11268, fol. 75). The plan was designed to humiliate Spain and provide massive plunder as the town, located on the Pacific coast at the narrowest point of the isthmus of Central America, had immense wealth and strategic significance as the depot for Peruvian silver which was then taken the 70 miles across to Portobello for shipment to Europe.

Joseph Bradley took an advance party of about 480 men to seize the castle guarding the Caribbean entrance to the River Chagres which ran 50 miles into the isthmus. After two days of bitter fighting and heavy losses, including Bradley's death, the castle was taken. Meanwhile, Morgan seized Providence Island and gathered some guides and arrived with the main fleet a few days later, losing the *Satisfaction* and four other ships at the mouth of the river. After a week spent repairing the castle, which he left in charge of 300 men, Morgan set out up the river towards Panama with about 1400 men and a few Indian guides in seven small ships and thirty-six boats.

The president of Panama had been warned of an attack and had stationed defence forces at points along the river but as the large army of privateers approached the small groups of Spanish troops fled. The dense tropical forest proved harder to deal with, and the river proved more difficult to navigate than Morgan, who was in new territory, had anticipated. After three days the privateers decided to abandon most of the canoes and stores and continued on foot, cutting a path through the tangled, wild woods. This decision almost caused the army's undoing as, despite the luxuriant vegetation, they did not find food and they marched four days without a meal. Despite the difficulties Morgan managed to maintain discipline and when the privateers reached the plains around Panama they fell upon the grazing cattle and indulged in a great feast of roast meat which revived their strength and spirits.

Panama City had no walls, relying on the thickly forested isthmus for protection, and the president had dispatched his small garrison to defend Chagres Castle and river. The president did rally about a thousand men but almost all were totally inexperienced and badly armed. Their main hope was that they could use a herd of bulls to drive back the privateers but the animals merely added to the chaos when, on 28 January 1671, the two forces met on the plain. The Spaniards were routed, losing 400 or 500 men against fifteen privateer losses. In capturing 'the famous and ancient city of Panama … the greatest mart for silver and gold in the whole world' Morgan and his men had triumphed where many, including Sir Francis Drake, had failed (Morgan's relation, BL, Add. MS 11268, fol. 78).

The president had ordered that in the event of defeat the town should be burnt and residents later claimed that this action caused losses valued at 12–18 million pesos (£4–6.5 million). Furthermore the citizens had time to escape with valuable property before Morgan took possession of the city. The privateers were hugely disappointed with their plunder. The army spent a month searching the offshore islands and surrounding country for runaway citizens. Spanish reports suggest that the privateers were unusually brutal in torturing captives to obtain information about hidden property and many died in the process. Disappointment seems to have sharpened the customary cruelty although it was Edward Collier, the vice-admiral, rather than Morgan, who was most blamed for the 'diverse barbarous acts' (Lynch to Arlington, 17 Dec 1671, BL, Add. MS 11410, fol. 446). At the end of February the privateers set out across the isthmus with a train of 175 mules laden with silver plate, coins, and 500 or 600 prisoners who were later ransomed at 120 pesos (£30) per head.

On returning to the mouth of the Chagres, Morgan sent to Portobello to demand a ransom for the castle. The citizens refused, having barely recovered from paying to release their town in 1668, and the privateers burnt the fortress to the ground. The privateers then divided their loot, which amounted to a disappointing £30,000 (less than half the prize at Portobello), yielding each of the 2000 or so men about £20 which they viewed as small reward for the months of hardship and risk. Morgan blamed the evacuation and destruction of Panama for the disappointment but many suspected that the admiral had embezzled part of the prize and suspicions were heightened when he was cast away at Old Harbour in Jamaica, 'designedly as it is said to have the better opportunity to carry the plate on shore' before sailing on to Port Royal (Lynch to Arlington, BL, Add. MS 11410, fol. 378). Even the surgeon, Browne, a great admirer of Morgan, reported that he 'cheated the soldier of a very vast sum' (Browne to Williamson, 21 Aug 1671, PRO, CO 1/27, fol. 69). Furthermore, the wreck of boats on the outward voyage meant that there were too few ships to carry all the privateers home and a number were left behind at Chagres to make their way as best they could.

Morgan arrived back in Port Royal in mid-April. On 10 June his report was read in council and he was thanked for the execution of his commission. The island grandees were pleased with Morgan's victory although there were reported to be grumblings among the privateers, victuallers, and tradesmen of Port Royal, who were disappointed with the prize. Many debts remained unpaid (Lynch to Arlington, 27 June 1671, BL, Add. MS 11410, fol. 377).

Imprisonment and office, 1671–1675 Despite the treaty of Madrid neither the king nor his ministers had made any attempt to curb Jamaica's predators other than the ambiguous letter of the previous autumn. But if the treaty was to have any meaning, and lead to the desired trade concessions, above all the opening of the market for slaves, it was now necessary to take action and the king appointed a new governor, Sir Thomas Lynch, who had been involved in the conquest of Jamaica and had left after Modyford's arrival. He was dispatched to the island with strict instructions to end privateering, promote peaceful trade with the Spaniards, and send Modyford home under arrest.

Lynch arrived in Jamaica on 1 July 1671 and was greeted with full honours by Modyford and Morgan. The new governor immediately issued a proclamation against privateering but offered full pardon to those operating under existing commissions. It was accepted that the privateers had been acting perfectly legally and no action would be taken against them and Henry Morgan was not excepted. Lynch was nervous of public reactions to the arrest of Modyford and delayed a few weeks before sending him home. Meanwhile news of Morgan's most recent exploits caused great rage in Madrid and the English, still anxious for trade concessions, decided to offer a further sop to Spanish sensibilities by ordering Morgan's arrest. Again Lynch was nervous:

> he is here taken for an honest stout man and people whisper his case is to be hard, because he undertook that fatal command by Sir Thomas Modyford's desire and at return had his services approved and thanked by the council on record and what is more was not excepted in the King's most gracious Act of indemnity. (Lynch to Williamson, 29 March 1672, BL, Add. MS 11410, fol. 446)

Despite a loud chorus of supportive words and offers of security from fellow islanders Morgan was sent home on the *Welcome* in April 1672, and imprisoned with Modyford in the Tower of London, where he lived at his own expense. His friends claimed that the charge bore heavily on him as 'his estate was but mean' (Lynch to Arlington, 3 April 1672, BL, MS 11410, fol. 552). Despite his large prize money in the previous years he does not yet seem to have settled a plantation in Jamaica as he does not appear in a survey of landowners taken in 1670 and, according to Lynch, 'in England he has neither friends nor money' (ibid., fols. 552–4).

Morgan's disgrace was short-lived and he was released from the Tower by 1674 without being tried for any offence. The admiral's heroic reputation was reflected in John Evelyn's report of dining with him at Lord Berkeley's in October. The diarist listened with admiration to the story of 'that gallant exploit from Nombre de Dios to Panama' and Morgan's boasts that with 10,000 men he could easily conquer all the Spanish Indies (*The Diary of John Evelyn*, ed. G. de la Bédoyère, 1995, 202). The king displayed his own approval when he gave the privateer a warm reception at court and, in March 1674, despite Spanish dismay, Morgan was appointed lieutenant-governor of Jamaica, to serve under John Vaughan, Lord Vaughan. Morgan was knighted in November and set sail for the Caribbean in January 1675.

The new lieutenant-governor was warmly welcomed in Jamaica and the assembly voted him a salary of £600 per annum 'for good service to the country' (*CSP col.*, 9, no. 537). Morgan was appointed to the council in July and became a judge in the Admiralty court. In Port Royal, where Morgan took up residence in the king's house, he later became *custos rotulorum* (the chief justice of the peace) and captain of the militia. Having secured a powerful position Morgan exploited it to raise the substantial funds needed to build up plantations in the interior (it was usually reckoned that it cost £4000 to set up a sugar plantation). At the same time he was able to maintain a large household in Port Royal (containing eleven white residents and fourteen black slaves in the census of 1680), and finance his notoriously 'generous humour' (Carlisle to Jenkins, 18 April 1681, *CSP col.*, 11, no. 85), which found expression in lavish hospitality and heavy drinking and gaming in the taverns.

Unsurprisingly privateering played an important part in Morgan's business affairs although he now took a passive role. The lieutenant-governor took care to reach Jamaica before Vaughan so that he could arrange his affairs to suit himself, and ordered his ship's captain to put in to Isla Vaca, the privateers' rendezvous point, on the outward journey. The ship was wrecked in the shallow waters but Morgan realized his probable aim of renewing old contacts when the passengers were rescued by Thomas Rogers, an English privateer now sailing under a French commission issued at Tortuga. Despite the treaty of Madrid and Lynch's enthusiasm for promoting peaceful trade with the Spaniards, the profits and protection offered by plunder continued to tempt many Jamaicans.

Lieutenant-governor, 1675–1682 On arrival in Jamaica Morgan dispatched letters to prominent privateers assuring them that they would be welcome in Port Royal; invested in privateers' ships; corresponded with du Casse, the French governor of Tortuga, who issued letters of marque; and colluded with his brother-in-law, Robert Bindloss, in obtaining a deputation from du Casse to collect the tenths of prizes brought into Port Royal by French commissioned captains. Du Casse provided the marauders with a legal veneer for their activities and Port Royal merchants fitted the ships and fenced the loot, with Morgan's support as long as he received his dues. Vaughan condemned these activities but admitted that Morgan and Bindloss 'would not be persuaded but what they did was lawful' (Vaughan to Coventry, 2 Aug 1676, *CSP col.*, 9, no. 1006). Morgan shared the widely held view that 'there is a great deal of difference between a privateer and a buccaneer, or freebooter', and provided men had a commission almost any action, other than attacking English trade, was excused (Barham's history of Jamaica, BL, Add. MS 12422, p. 80). The retired privateer was fastidious about his own reputation. When two English translations of Exquemelin under the title *History of the Bucaniers* appeared in 1684 describing him as a buccaneer he prosecuted both publishers for libel. In his affidavit he stated that he had 'against evil deeds, piracies and robberies the greatest abhorrence and distrust' and 'for the kind of men called buccaneers he always had and still has hatred'. The suits were settled by consent and the publishers printed apologies prefaced to new editions (Cundall, 70).

Vaughan took an intense dislike to Morgan and, as he had been given strict instructions to end privateering, he used evidence of Morgan's involvement in the business to try to discredit him and exclude him from office. The king stood by Morgan and, despite the weight of evidence against the lieutenant-governor, action was limited to a series of rebukes from the secretary of state, Henry Coventry. Peace with Spain plainly rested on shallow foundations. Vaughan was recalled in 1678 leaving Morgan in charge of the island for three months until July when Charles Howard, first earl of Carlisle, arrived to take over as governor. Carlisle and Morgan acted in close collaboration, and in these years, and Morgan's second period as acting governor between 1680 and 1682, Morgan was best able to profit from the patronage and perquisites of office.

Friends, including Morgan's brother-in-law Robert Bindloss (who had been turned out by Lynch), were appointed to the council and Bindloss also replaced Samuel Long as chief justice. Other enemies were turned out and friends put in key positions, such as Thomas Martyn who was appointed receiver-general and oversaw the collection of port duties, which were reported to be extortionate and shared with Morgan. When Francis Mingham attempted to avoid payment in December 1678 his ship was seized and condemned for evasion of the Navigation Acts (on account of carrying French brandy). This began a long series of legal embroilments (involving the captain in imprisonment and payment of very substantial security) culminating in a hearing before the lords of trade and plantations who found in Mingham's favour. John Bindloss, Robert's brother and Morgan's agent in London, obtained life patents for fourteen or fifteen minor offices and, after protests were made to the lords of trade about pluralism and absenteeism, he divided them between himself and Charles Morgan, Henry's brother-in-law, who went out to the island in 1682 as captain of Port Royal Castle.

During this period the 1200 privateers operating in the Caribbean conducted a number of spectacular raids on Spanish territory and brought a large part of the prize into Jamaica without fear of molestation provided they paid the heavy duties levied by Morgan's officers at Port Royal. Apart from the financial temptations of plunder the strong threat of war with the French in the late 1670s increased reluctance to alienate the privateers as the island's only other protection was the militia and two companies of a hundred foot soldiers apiece, brought to the island by Carlisle in 1678 and commanded by the governor and Morgan.

Morgan made a valuable contribution to island security. He kept his Port Royal militia and foot company in good training and used his contacts among seamen to obtain intelligence. The threat of war with the French allowed him to introduce martial law in 1678 and 1680 and secure the resources needed to improve the fortifications at Port Royal by levying financial contributions and requisitioning slave labour to build three new forts. He also increased the number of guns mounted at the forts from sixty in 1675 to over a hundred by 1680. By 1682 Port Royal was the best fortified town in English America.

Meanwhile Morgan's enemies became increasingly anxious to recover control of government, especially as there were signs that the Spanish market for slaves was opening up in promising ways and Morgan's anti-Spanish attitudes were regarded as unhelpful. Carlisle had been instructed to introduce a bill granting a permanent revenue which the assembly resisted, fearing that it would place too much power in the hands of the governor and the king, and when Samuel Long, the speaker, returned home to argue their case he was accompanied by William Beeston, who had raised funds to finance a campaign to secure the reappointment of Lynch as governor. Carlisle hurriedly decided to follow him home to protect his reputation.

When Morgan was left in charge he took steps to protect his reputation without much change in policy. He expressed abhorrence for 'pirates' in his letters home, but also stressed the 'unkindness' of the Spaniards to English traders; the impossibility of controlling the predators without substantial naval support; and his uncertainty about the legal position of those with foreign commissions (Morgan to lords of trade and plantations, 27 Jan 1681, PRO, CO 138/3, fols. 470–71). In fact predators continued to be welcome in Jamaica as revealed in November 1681 when, despite the presence of a major Spanish slave trader in port, Morgan allowed four frigates with commissions from 'the duke of Brandenburgh' (presumably the elector of Brandenburg) to enter and sell two Spanish prizes. Not surprisingly the Spanish captain was nervous about their presence and 'pained by the apprehension that they would intercept him'. Morgan acknowledged that 'they would certainly have done so (the temptation being so high) had I not very pressingly interposed for his protection; which they so generously granted to the great satisfaction of the Spaniard' (ibid., fols. 468–9).

Morgan's arrogant disregard for authority became more muted as it became plain that his enemies at home were gaining ground with a 'malicious confederacy' accusing him and Carlisle of 'countenancing pirates' (Morgan to Jenkins, 9 April 1681, PRO, CO 138/3, fols. 480–81). The distance which had allowed him freedom from scrutiny was now bemoaned, for 'the remoteness of the place gives so much opportunity to the hand of malice that the greatest innocence cannot be protected without much care and watchfulness' (Henry Morgan to Jenkins, 13 June 1681, *CSP col.*, 11, no. 138). Morgan arrested a number of men who were, even in his book, pirates: men who operated without commissions or seized English ships. But he had little heart for punishing even such outright scoundrels, and when they were sentenced to death Morgan sought reprieves. After orders to proceed with execution Morgan could not disguise his distaste 'for I abhor bloodshed and I am greatly dissatisfied that in my short government I have been so often compelled to punish criminals with death' (Morgan to Jenkins, 8 March 1682, *CSP col.*, 11, no. 431). The lieutenant-governor also sought credit by obtaining the Permanent Revenue Bill desired by the home authorities but spoilt the achievement by allowing the assembly to tack on other acts, including a law imposing a tax on exported slaves, plainly aimed at the widely unpopular Spanish slave trade. Above all Morgan relied on the friendship long shown by the king and the duke of York to shelter him from criticism and sent them presents and smooth words (Bindloss to Carlisle, 28 Nov 1682, BL, Sloane MS 2724, fol. 207).

John Bindloss and Charles Morgan represented Sir Henry's interests before the committee of trade and plantations in London but his enemies gained strength as the whiggish private slave traders associated with Beeston were joined by the tory Royal African Company, which also hoped to gain from making Jamaica a base for the Spanish slave trade. Morgan's salary was stopped in 1680; the foot companies were disbanded and attendant payments stopped in 1681; his commission as lieutenant-governor was revoked on 27 July 1681, and his 'profest enemy' Lynch was appointed governor (Martyn to Carlisle, 29 June 1681, BL, Sloane MS 2724). At the same time Morgan had to support the considerable expense of government, an especial burden when the assembly was sitting and he was expected to keep open house, leaving him with hard feelings.

Island politics, 1682–1688 Lynch arrived to take up the post of governor on 14 May 1682, and immediately read the revocation of Morgan's commission as lieutenant-governor, but allowed him to remain on the council. Lynch was determined to secure the revenue bill required by the king and wished to maintain as much unity as possible. However, once the bill was passed Lynch rapidly discarded Morgan, condemning his ingratitude and incivility, above all his wearing of new and light coloured clothes on news of the death of Lady Lynch (a kinswoman of Morgan).

The main clash of interests continued to arise over the Spanish slave trade. Lynch used all his power to promote this very lucrative commerce by contracts with the asiento agents, who had licences to supply Spanish colonial markets. However, the governor also used his position to ensure that the trade was monopolized by himself and a few friends, including Hender Molesworth, the Royal African Company's factor. Their business aroused widespread hostility in Jamaica as, although a few profited, it damaged small traders and raised the price of slaves within the island. Henry Morgan, Bindloss, and their associates spoke for these interests and led a vigorous opposition to the Spanish trade, using the Navigation Acts to justify seizure of ships involved, and lobbying for a tax on exported slaves. They also attacked Lynch and his followers for supporting religious dissent and disloyalty to the duke of York, the Catholic heir to the throne, forming a club called the Loyal Club. The governor complained that 'people began to think it looked as if he [Morgan] designed to be head of the tories and therefore I must be head of the whigs' (Lynch to Jenkins, March 1684, *CSP col.*, 11, no. 1573).

In October 1683 a disturbance at Port Royal involving Morgan's brother-in-law, Charles, gave Lynch a pretext for action. Lynch charged Sir Henry with 'disorder, passions and miscarriages at Port Royal on various occasions and for countenancing sundry men in disloyalty to the governor' (minutes of council of Jamaica, 12 Oct 1683, *CSP col.*, 11, no. 1302). He persuaded the assembly to support him in suspending both the Morgans, Bindloss, and other associates such as the lawyer Roger Elletson from all offices and employments. After this purge Lynch claimed that the 'drunken, silly, party of Sir Henry Morgan's was rendered harmless' (Lynch to lords of trade and plantations, 2 Nov 1683, *CSP col.*, 11, no. 1348). Lynch further consolidated his position by obtaining a lieutenant-governor's commission for Hender Molesworth and ended Sir Henry's hope of taking over in event of accident. When Lynch died in 1684, and Molesworth assumed charge of the island, little changed. Although deprived of real power Morgan continued to do all he could to obstruct the Spanish slave trade, campaigning vigorously to secure Roger Elletson and other friends places in the assembly 'in order to disturb the proceedings' (Molesworth to Sunderland, 28 April 1686, *CSP col.*, 12, no. 643).

In December 1687 Christopher Monck, second duke of Albemarle, who was involved in a major wreck salvage project in the Caribbean, arrived to take over the government of Jamaica and immediately aligned himself with Morgan and the anti-Spanish privateering interest. Shared political sympathies and common financial interests were combined with a mutual liking for heavy drinking, gaming, and keeping late hours. Albemarle requested that Morgan should be readmitted to the council and he was formally reinstated on 8 August but was unable to attend the meeting, 'being extraordinaryly ill' (PRO, CO 140/4, fol. 177). Morgan had suffered repeated bouts of extreme sickness since the 1670s, and judging from remarks made by the duke's physician, Hans Sloane, was suffering from liver problems related to his excessive drinking. Sloane described him as 'lean, sallow coloured, his eyes a little yellowish, and belly a little jutting out or prominent' (BL, Sloane MS 3964). Morgan died on 25 August 1688. On the following day the retired privateer was given something resembling a state funeral in St Catherine's Church. The captain of the *Assistance* reported:

> he was brought over from Passage Fort to the King's House at Port Royal and from there to the Palisadoes and there buried. All ships fired an equal number of guns. We fired 22 and after we and the *Drake* all the merchant men fired. (Ship's log of HMS *Assistance*, Institute of Jamaica, Kingston, MST 288)

Morgan had used his years in office to build up one of the most substantial fortunes in Jamaica, owning three plantations, 122 black slaves, seven Indians, and eleven white servants. His inventoried personal wealth amounted to £5263 1s. 3d. His personal property included a library of 123 bound books and a parcel of sermons, plays, and pamphlets. Perhaps less surprising was the collection of twenty-seven guns, miscellaneous pistols, and swords. By his will the bulk of his estate was left to his wife, who lived until 1696, and on her death to his nephew Charles, second son of Robert Bindloss, on condition that he took the surname Morgan. Morgan bequeathed lands in St Georges to Bindloss's eldest son (again requiring a change of name) and land in St Mary's to his friend Roger Elletson. He made a further small bequest to Thomas Ballard and left £100 to the parish of St Mary where he had his main plantation.   NUALA ZAHEDIEH

Sources *CSP col.*, vols. 1, 5, 7, 9–12 · Colonial papers, America and the West Indies (general series), 1660–88, PRO, CO 1/14–65 · Jamaica, entry books, 1661–90, PRO, CO 138/1–6 · Jamaica, sessional papers: council, 1661–72, PRO, C 140/1 · miscellaneous papers relating to West Indies, BL, Add. MS 11268 · papers relating to West Indies, 1654–82, BL, Add. MS 11410 · journal kept by Colonel W. H. Beeston, BL, Add. MS 12430, fols. 41–79 · Coventry papers, IV, BL, Add. MS 25120 · papers of the earl of Carlisle relating to Jamaica, BL, Sloane MS 2724 · E. Long, 'Jamaica genealogies', BL, Add. MS 27968 · inventory, Jamaica Archives, Spanish Town, 1B/11/3, vol. 3, fols. 259–67 · will, BL, Add. MS 27968, fol. 14 · P. Earle, *The sack of Panama* (1981) · A. P. Thornton, 'The Modyfords and Morgan', *Jamaican Historical Review*, 2 (1952), 36–60 · A. P. Thornton, *West India policy under the Restoration* (1956) · F. Cundall, *The governors of Jamaica in the seventeenth century* (1936) · E. A. Cruikshank, *The life of Sir Henry Morgan* (1935) · W. A. Roberts, *Sir Henry Morgan, buccaneer and governor* (1933) · A. O. Exquemelin, *The history of the bucaniers* (1684) · M. Pawson and D. Buisseret, *Port Royal, Jamaica* (1975) · V. Barbour, 'Privateers and pirates of the West Indies', *American Historical Review*, 16 (1911), 529–66

Likenesses line engraving, pubd 1684, BM, NPG [*see illus.*]

Wealth at death £5263 1s. 3d.—excl. plantations and other lands and properties: inventory, 19 Feb 1689, Jamaica Archives, 1B/11/3, vol. 3, fols. 259–67

Morgan, Hugh (*c.*1530–1613), botanist and apothecary, was the elder son of John Morgan of Great Bardfield, Essex, and his wife, Joan, daughter of Richard Copcott of Buckinghamshire. Hugh's brother John was to succeed to the family estates. Hugh was apprenticed to a London grocer, William Chick, from August 1543 (as he must then have been no older than twenty-four, Morgan's presumed age at death of 103 is impossible). He was made free of the Grocers' Company, as was appropriate for an apothecary, and in 1552 of the city of London, which suggests that he was then about twenty-two. Ever wary of encroachments upon its monopoly, the College of Physicians censured Morgan in 1556 for dealing in medicines, and in 1559 for selling pills without having a doctor's permission.

The property Morgan held in Gutter Lane, St Vedast's parish (as in 1557), of Robert Whetstone was probably his home. He married Lucy, one of the two daughters, and coheir, of Nicholas Sibell of Farningham and Eynsford, Kent. Although he was assessed for subsidy in St Vedast's parish in 1564 (on £60), 1582 (£150), and 1589 (£200), the parish registers mention only Samuel (buried 1575) and Lucy (married 1587) as possible kinsfolk.

William Turner gave Morgan some roots of hedge hyssop, *Gratiola officinalis*, brought from Brabant. Morgan's garden, near Coleman Street, contained a nettle tree, *Celtis australis*; and he introduced shrubby althea, *Hibiscus syriacus*; corn marigold, *Chrysanthemum segetum*; 'Cicercula altera an Phaseolus Diosc.' (possibly chickpea, *Cicer arietinum*); and, in 1569, purple clematis, *C. viticella*, into English horticulture. In 1578 he gave some eastern gladiolus, *G. communis*, to William Mount, who planted it in his own garden at East Malling, Kent. Morgan's collection included oak mistletoe, *Viscum album*, from Essex, some aloe wood, from an *Aquilaria* (1581), and maize, *Zea mays*. Morgan collaborated with several leading botanists: John Gerard styled him 'a curious conserver of rare simples' (Raven, 117), and Lobel's *Adversaria* mentions Morgan more than twenty times. By receiving specimens of tropical plants from sea captains and foreign merchants he became an authority on them: a genus of Australian plants in the Scrophulariaceae, one of the figworts, was named *Morgania* after him.

As a grocer Morgan also traded in expensive spices, and his name appears in a list of the 'wisest and best merchants in London' (BL, Lansdowne MS 683, fol. 63, undated). He was a warden of the Grocers' Company (1574), and appointed apothecary-in-ordinary to the queen on 15 July 1583. When elected master warden of the Grocers his letter requesting to be excused was read out on 19 July 1584. However, asked to spare whatever time his royal duties allowed, his took office next day.

In a pamphlet of 1585 Morgan inveighed against imports of defective theriacle (a popular remedy for poisoning), whereas his own compound was claimed to be better than that of Constantinople and Venice. His father's arms—Morgan quartering Copcott—were confirmed to him in 1588.

Latterly Morgan lived in Battersea, Surrey, where he had a Judas tree, *Cercis siliquastrum*, in his garden. Hoping to evade payment of a special London tax, he claimed to have given up his London shop, but his deception was detected in 1592. Morgan's will styles him apothecary extraordinary to James I, hence following supersession—as yeoman apothecary—by George Shiers, his former apprentice. Morgan's wife, Lucy, was buried in St Mary's Church, Battersea, on 3 May 1606, and Hugh, dying on 13 September 1613, was interred there on 15 September. By his will, made on 25 April 1608, Morgan's adopted daughter, Elizabeth Fleming, was to be maintained for life. He left small bequests to his 'cosins', including a cleric, John Morgan (his late brother's illegitimate son), and Captain Robert Morgan, his executor; to Colthurst and Hyde, relatives of his sister-in-law's successive husbands; and to the poor people of the parishes of Great Bardfield, Little Hallingbury, Farningham, and Battersea. Probate was granted on 25 September 1613. Hugh's nephew Robert placed a monumental brass (not now extant) in Battersea church, referring to his uncle's professional skill, religious strength, and kindliness, the favour he had enjoyed from Elizabeth I, and his—supposed—age of 103 years.

JOHN BENNELL

Sources J. J. Howard and G. J. Armytage, eds., *The visitation of London in the year 1568*, Harleian Society, 1 (1869), 95 · R. T. Gunther, *Early British botanists and their gardens* (1922), 237–8, 258, 346, 354, 366 · C. E. Raven, *English naturalists from Neckam to Ray: a study of the making of the modern world* (1947), 115–17, 242 · C. Welch, ed., *Register of freemen of the city of London* (1908), 24 · PRO, PROB 11/122, fols. 149– · G. S. Fry, ed., *Abstracts of inquisitions post mortem relating to the City of London*, 1: *1485–1561*, British RS, 15 (1896), 166 · W. A. Littledale, ed., *The registers of St Vedast, Foster Lane, and of St Michael le Quern, London*, 2, Harleian Society, register section, 30 (1903), 7, 131, 6, 128 · R. G. Lang, ed., *Two Tudor subsidy assessment rolls for the city of London, 1541 and 1581*, London RS, 29 (1993), 225 · parish register, Battersea, St Mary, 1559–1812, LMA [microfilm], X.055/1 [marriage, burial] · Desmond, *Botanists*, 450 · R. Cooke, *Visitation of London, 1568*, ed. H. Stanford London and S. W. Rawlins, [new edn], 2 vols. in one, Harleian Society, 109–10 (1963), 158 · PRO, E 179/145/219 [lay subsidy roll, 1563–4] · L. G. Matthews, *The royal apothecaries* (1967) · A. C. Wootton, *Chronicles of pharmacy*, 2 (1910), 44 · W. Le Hardy, ed., Grocers' Company, calendar to the court minute books, 1556–1692, c.1930, GL, vols. 1, pts 1–3; 2, pts 1–3; index vols. 1–2 · W. W. Grantham, *List of the wardens of the Grocers' Company from 1345 to 1907* (1907), 21 · BL, Lansdowne MS 683, fol. 63

Morgan, James (1799–1873), minister of the Presbyterian Church in Ireland, was the son of Thomas Morgan, a linen merchant, of Cookstown, co. Tyrone, and Maria Collins of the same town. He was born there on 15 June 1799. After attending several local schools he entered Glasgow University in November 1814 to prepare for the ministry, but after one session there studied at the Royal Belfast Academical Institution. In February 1820 he was ordained by the presbytery of Dublin as minister of the Presbyterian congregation of Carlow, a very small charge, which, however, increased considerably under his care. He married, on 28 February 1823, Charlotte, daughter of John Gayer of Derriaghy House, Lisburn, co. Antrim. Gayer had been one of the clerks of the Irish parliament at the time of the Union. James and Charlotte had three sons and three daughters. Their son Thomas was the compiler of his father's autobiography published posthumously in 1874. In 1824 Morgan accepted a call from Lisburn to be colleague to the Revd Andrew Craig, and for four years worked there, opening a Sunday school and beginning a Sunday evening service.

In 1827 a new church was opened in Fisherwick Place, Belfast, and Morgan became its first minister in November 1828. The congregation soon became one of the most active in Belfast. Morgan also became prominently associated with many of the benevolent and philanthropic schemes in the town. In 1829 he joined in the foundation of the Ulster Temperance Society. He was also particularly active in promoting church extension in Belfast, using informal but effective measures to bypass ecclesiastical bureaucracy. In 1840, when the general assembly's foreign mission was established, he was appointed its honorary secretary, and continued to hold this position until his death. In 1842 he helped to found the Belfast town mission, and became one of its honorary secretaries. He was appointed moderator of the general assembly in 1846, and in the following year received the degree of DD from the University of Glasgow. He took a leading part in the establishment of the assembly's college in Belfast (now Union Theological College), which was opened in 1853. Morgan published a considerable number of works, besides sermons and tracts. These include: *The Lord's Supper* (1849), *Rome and the Gospel* (1853), *The Hidden Life* (1856), and an *Exposition of the First Epistle of John* (1865). He was also for a time joint editor of the *Orthodox Presbyterian* and was one of Belfast's most important and influential Presbyterian ministers. He died in Belfast on 5 August 1873, and was buried in the city cemetery.

THOMAS HAMILTON, *rev.* DAVID HUDDLESTON

Sources T. Morgan, ed., *The life and times of the Rev. James Morgan* (1874) · J. S. Reid, *History of congregations of the Presbyterian church in Ireland*, ed. W. D. Killen (1886) · Fisherwick Presbyterian Church, *Our past years, 1823–1973* (1973) · D. Hempton & M. Hill, *Evangelical protestantism in Ulster society, 1740–1890* (1992)

Likenesses woodcut, repro. in Morgan, ed., *Life and times of the Rev. James Morgan*

Morgan, James Davies (1811–1846). *See under* Morgan, Hector Davies (1785–1850).

Morgan, Jane Macnaughton Egerton. *See* Brownlow, Jane Macnaughton Egerton (1854/5–1928).

Morgan, John [*called* John Young] (*d.* 1504), bishop of St David's and administrator, was a brother of Trahaearn ap Morgan of Kidwelly, lawyer, and a son of Morgan ap Jenkin ap Philip. His maternal grandmother was Margaret St John (*née* Beauchamp), also grandmother to Henry VII. Morgan was called 'Young' to distinguish him from another brother called John; it should be noted that he was not related to Richard III's attorney-general, Morgan Kidwelly. He was educated at Oxford, and graduated BCnL by 1450, being still such in 1471. He later became DCnL and was incorporated at Cambridge on 20 December 1500. He practised as a proctor in the chancellor's court in 1450 and 1453, and again in 1468 and 1469. He was admitted rector of Great Parndon, Essex, as an acolyte, on 12 February 1453, and became rector of Cornwell, Oxfordshire, in 1471.

The absence of Morgan's name from the records between 1471 and 1485 has led to the suggestion that he may have been in exile with Henry Tudor 'and in his employment as chaplain or clerk, or perhaps both' (Pollard 157). But an old, if not altogether reliable, biography of Sir Rhys ap Thomas maintains that Morgan was active in Wales before 1485 and that he won Rhys over to Henry's cause.

Morgan's rapid promotion following the battle of Bosworth suggests that he was one of Henry's trusted supporters as well as being second cousin to him. On 9 October 1485 he became clerk of the parliament; in November he appeared as a receiver of petitions, later became a master in chancery, and in 1494–5 heard cases in the court of requests. He received many ecclesiastical preferments in England and Wales between 1485 and 1494.

Morgan was papally provided to the diocese of St David's on 3 August 1496, and consecrated in November 1496, when he gave up his other preferments and secular offices. During his episcopate, for part of which his register has survived, he increased the number of cathedral choristers, and appropriated the churches of Llanwnnen, Silian, and Llan-y-cefn for their support. He probably erected the episcopal throne in the choir of his cathedral. He died in Carmarthen Priory between 24 April and 19 May 1504. In his will (PRO, PROB 11/14, sig. 8), dated 24 April and proved 19 May 1504, he directed that a chapel be raised over his grave. No such chapel was built, but his table-top tomb, complete with effigy, lies, sadly mutilated, under the south-east arch of the nave of St David's Cathedral, near the pulpit.   **GLANMOR WILLIAMS**

Sources A. F. Pollard, 'Fifteenth-century clerks of parliament', *BIHR*, 15 (1937–8), 137–61, esp. 156–8 · P. C. Bartrum, ed., *Welsh genealogies, AD 1400–1500*, 18 vols. (1983) · W. O. Pughe, ed., *The Cambrian register*, 3 vols. (1796–1818) · R. F. Isaacson, ed. and trans., *The episcopal registers of the diocese of St David's, 1397–1518*, 2 vols. in 3, Honourable Society of Cymmrodorion, Cymmrodorion Record Series (1917–20) · *Heraldic visitations of Wales and part of the marches … by Lewys Dwnn*, ed. S. R. Meyrick, 2 vols. (1846) · Emden, *Oxf.* · H. T.

Evans, *Wales and the Wars of the Roses* (1915) · R. A. Griffiths, *Sir Rhys ap Thomas and his family: a study in the Wars of the Roses and early Tudor politics* (1993) · G. Williams, *The Welsh church from conquest to Reformation*, rev. edn (1976) · E. Yardley, *Menevia sacra*, ed. F. Green (1927) · will, PRO, PROB 11/14, sig. 8
Archives NL Wales, St David's diocesan registers, SD/BR/1 · NL Wales, Peniarth MS 131 [fol. 251]
Likenesses tomb effigy, St David's Cathedral, Pembrokeshire, Wales; mutilated
Wealth at death see will, PRO, PROB 11/14, sig. 8

Morgan, John [*known as* John Morgan Matchin] (1688–1733/4), Church of England clergyman and Welsh scholar, was born on 7 February 1688 at Llangelynnin, Merioneth, north Wales, younger son of Edward Morgan (*fl.* 1651–1700), curate of Llangelynnin, and his wife, Margreta (*fl. c.*1660–1700). From 1704 to 1708 he studied with his elder brother, Edward (*d.* 1749)—also to become a cleric and man of letters, at Jesus College, Oxford, where he is thought to have come under the influence of the renowned Welsh antiquary Edward Lhuyd. Having been ordained in 1709, he became curate of Llandegfan, Anglesey (1709–10), and of Llanfyllin, Montgomeryshire (1710–13). In 1713 Morgan left his native Wales to become curate in the village of Matching, Essex, where he served as vicar from 1728 until his death. He was commonly known as John Morgan Matchin, and there is no evidence that he married.

Morgan's interest in Welsh literature and scholarship, which he shared with a number of other Oxford-educated Welshmen of the time, is reflected in a collection of proverbs and colloquialisms and in a verse collection including some of his early work (NL Wales, Llanstephan MSS 20 and 15). He is thought to be the author of the translations from Tertullian and Cyprian, *Llythyr Tertulian at 'Scapula* (1716). He is best known, however, for his short prose work, *Myfyrdodau bucheddol ar y pedwar peth diweddaf* ('Devout musings on the four last things'), which appeared in eight editions between 1714 and 1830. Although partly based on an earlier translation from English, *Cadwyn euraidd o bedair modrwy* (1706), its clarity of expression and classically influenced economy of style set it apart from other devotional and didactic writing of the period. In three letters addressed to his Oxford contemporary Moses Williams (BL, Add. MS 14934, fols. 175–7), as well as discussing literary and antiquarian matters Morgan voiced his concern for the educational and spiritual well-being of his fellow countrymen, denouncing the folly of the English-only education policy of the Society for Promoting Christian Knowledge, 'the consequence [of which] at last will be barbarism, which necessarily introduces ignorance and irreligion'. These letters eventually came into the hands of the Morrisian circle of writers and antiquarians, making John Morgan a link between Edward Lhuyd and the cultural revival of mid-eighteenth-century Wales. He died at Matching on 28 February 1734 (or possibly 1733) and was buried on 2 March in the chancel of the parish church.   **HUW M. EDWARDS**

Sources A. D. Carr, 'John Morgan, Matching, 1688–1733', *Journal of the Merioneth Historical and Record Society*, 5 (1965–8), 127–32 · S. Lewis, 'John Morgan', *Y Llenor*, 1 (1922), 11–17; repr. in *Meistri'r*

Canrifoedd, ed. R. G. Gruffydd (1973), 225–31 · W. Davies, 'Morganiaid Llangelynin Meirion', *Yr Haul* (1939), 93–8, 151–6, 216–18, 254–6, 274–6 · W. L. Davies, 'John Morgan, Matchin, and John Morgan, Aberconway', *Journal of the Welsh Bibliographical Society*, 5 (1937–42), 110–13 · S. Lewis, *A school of Welsh Augustans* (1924) · J. Davies, *Bywyd a gwaith Moses Williams* (1937) · G. H. Jenkins, *Literature, religion and society in Wales, 1660–1730* (1978) · C. Ashton, *Hanes llenyddiaeth Gymreig o 1651 o. C. hyd 1850* [1893] · 'Extracts from old wills relating to Wales', *Archaeologia Cambrensis*, 4th ser., 13 (1882), 118–26 · J. E. Lloyd, R. T. Jenkins, and W. L. Davies, eds., *Y bywgraffiadur Cymreig hyd 1940* (1953) · Foster, *Alum. Oxon.* · NL Wales, Llanstephan MSS 20 and 15 · will, Essex RO, D/ABW90/30

Archives NL Wales, notebook, Llanstephan MS 15 | BL, letters to Moses Williams, Add. MS 14934, fols. 175–77·3

Wealth at death books to brother; most of remaining personal possessions to clerk and clerk's wife: will, Essex RO, D/ABW90/30; Carr, 'John Morgan'; 'Extracts from old wills'

Morgan, John (*bap.* 1739, *d.* 1805). *See under* Morgan, Robert (*bap.* 1708, *d.* 1778).

Morgan, John Hartman (1876–1955), lawyer, was born on 20 March 1876, the son of the Revd David Morgan, Congregationalist minister of Ystradfellte, Glamorgan, and his wife, Julia, daughter of Felix Wethli, of Zürich. From Caterham School he went with a scholarship to the University College of South Wales where he obtained his London MA in 1896, and with another scholarship to Balliol College, Oxford, where in 1900 he was placed in the second class of the honour school of modern history. He made his mark at the Oxford Union, and developed a strong interest in diplomatic history. When he left Oxford he joined the Inner Temple, and began to read for the bar (to which he was called in 1915), and joined in 1901 the literary staff of the *Daily Chronicle* (where he stayed until 1903). But at the same time he continued his postgraduate studies at the London School of Economics under W. A. S. Hewins. He gained a research studentship with which he studied for a time at the University of Berlin. Shortly after his return to England he became a leader writer for the *Manchester Guardian* (1904–5). In addition, he had political ambitions, standing unsuccessfully in 1910 as a Liberal candidate for the Edgbaston division of Birmingham in January and West Edinburgh in December. In 1905 he married Clara Maud (*d.* 1967), daughter of Henry Anthony Hertz; she was an actress known under the name Margaret Halstan. The marriage did not last.

At the outbreak of war in 1914, Morgan volunteered for combatant service, but his special qualifications were responsible for his appointment to the adjutant-general's staff as Home Office representative with the British expeditionary force, to inquire into the conduct of the Germans in the field. His report was published by the parliamentary recruiting committee. In 1919 he attended the peace conference as assistant adjutant-general, and was later sent to Cologne to report on the British occupation of the Rhineland, becoming British military representative on the prisoners of war commission. Later still, he was for some years in Germany as a member of the subcommission on disarmament of the Inter-Allied Control Commission for Germany, finally retiring from the army in 1923 with the rank of brigadier-general. Morgan was convinced from the outset of his work with the control commission that Germany had no intention of disarming, and after his return he attempted by letters and articles to show that Germany was preparing for another war. But his efforts evoked little response, until, at the conclusion of the Second World War, his book, *Assize of Arms* (1945), gathered together the record of his experiences into a formidable indictment.

In 1916 Morgan appeared as counsel for the defence in the trial of Sir Roger Casement and it was at Morgan's suggestion that, on appeal, it was strenuously argued on Casement's behalf that seeking to seduce troops from their allegiance while prisoners of war in Germany was not within the Statute of Treason of 1351. Morgan had given some lectures on constitutional law as early as 1908, and in 1915 had been appointed professor of constitutional law at University College, London. During his absence, Dr Thomas Baty deputized for him, but in 1923 Morgan returned to active teaching and until his retirement in 1941 his lectures, with their forceful expression of clear-cut opinions upon constitutional developments, never failed to attract large audiences. In addition, from 1926 to 1936 he was reader in constitutional law to the inns of court. He took silk in 1926 and his authority in the field of constitutional law was recognized by his appointment, first to advise the Indian chamber of princes on constitutional changes in India from 1934 to 1937, then to advise Western Australia at the hearing before parliament of the secession petition of that state in 1935.

To the end of his life Morgan remained actively opposed to German rearmament, and he appeared in person at Nuremberg at the trial of the major war criminals, most of whom he had himself interrogated, and his last official duty was to act as legal adviser to the American war crimes commission from 1947 to 1949.

Morgan wrote freely, and with the same force which he displayed in court and in lecturing, and he enjoyed controversy. Among his principal publications were *The House of Lords and the Constitution* (1910); a translation entitled *The German War Book* (1915); *War, its Conduct and Legal Results* (with T. Baty, 1915); *Leaves from a Field Note-Book* (1916); *Gentlemen at Arms* (1918); *The Present State of Germany* (1924); *Viscount Morley, an Appreciation* (1924); *Remedies Against the Crown* (1925); *The Great Assize* (1948); and many contributions to legal and other periodicals. Morgan died at 46 Wood Street, Wootton Bassett, Wiltshire, on 8 April 1955.

G. W. KEETON, *rev.*

Sources personal knowledge (1971) · *CGPLA Eng. & Wales* (1955) · *WWW* · H. O. Mackey, *The life and times of Roger Casement* (1954) · H. M. Hyde, *Trial of Sir Roger Casement* (1960) · *The Times* (21 April 1955)

Archives BL, corresp. with Society of Authors, Add. MS 56758 · Bodl. Oxf., letters to Lady Milner · JRL, Guardian archives, corresp. with the *Manchester Guardian* · King's Lond., Liddell Hart C., corresp. with Sir B. H. Liddell Hart · NL Scot., letters to Lord Haldane

Wealth at death £4474 4s. 9d.: probate, 7 July 1955, *CGPLA Eng. & Wales*

Morgan, John Minter (1782–1854), educationist and socialist, was baptized in Westminster on 1 October 1782, the eldest son of John Morgan (1741–1807), a stationer, and his wife, Dorothy. His education is obscure; however, brought up among the radical guild traditions of Stationers' Hall, he was intellectually influenced by Thomas More's reissued *Utopia* and Charles Hill's critique of civilization (1805). His communitarian vision of 'practical Christianity' was inspired by the achievements of the suppressed Jesuit–Guarani communities in Paraguay. At the age of twenty-five in 1807, he inherited a City fortune, including a seat on the stock exchange, the Ludgate Hill wholesale stationery family business, and a Suffolk manor. Inspired by Robert Owen's *New Views* (1812–13) and businesslike evidence to Archbishop Sutton (1816), Morgan devoted his entire life, most of his writings, and much of his wealth to championing the co-operative cause.

Morgan's London salon (at Blackfriars and then Piccadilly) remained an intellectual centre of communitarian endeavour and co-operative experiment for more than thirty years: it sustained close but difficult working alliances between Christian co-operators and the secular-minded disciples of Robert Owen from 1819 until 1838, and eventually drew in the new generation of Christian socialists, such as John Ludlow and Thomas Hughes. An anti-Malthusian Anglican, Morgan increasingly articulated co-operative ideology with the unorthodox moral theology of F. D. Maurice, offering in 1833 to endow a professorship in education and co-operative studies at King's College, London. Among numerous articles, pamphlets, and books, *The Revolt of the Bees* (1826), aimed at an artisan readership, and *Hampden in the Nineteenth Century* (1834)—a co-operative sequel to Robert Southey's *Colloquies* directed towards thoughtful gentry—were widely acclaimed.

Morgan powerfully defended Owen's social plans, promoting publicly the co-operative conscience of the British and Foreign Philanthropic Society (1822–3) and subscribing to various domestic schemes, including the Orbiston community (1825–7). A founder member of the London Co-operative Society (1824), he enlisted the intellectual gifts of the social economist William Thompson (an agnostic) and Connop Thirlwall (a future bishop), subsidized William Lovett's store employment, and financed the influential *Co-Operative Magazine*. He persuaded the Jewish financiers Sir Isaac Lyon Goldsmid and Nathan Rothschild to support communitarian ventures, including the 1828 Texas scheme adventured by Owen, but failed to raise £250,000 from stock exchange members for the 1832 Home Colony plan. However, in the latter year, together with Philip O. Skene and Byron's widow, Lady Byron, he persuaded the Co-operative Congress to dissociate officially the burgeoning retail-producer co-operative movement from Owen's controversial quasi-theological beliefs and precipitous large-scale 'incipient community' ambitions.

Morgan's greatest services lay in diplomacy rather than organization. In 1840, at the peak of the parliamentary condemnation of socialist Owenites as 'infidels', he protected the contentious Owenite Harmony Hall settlement in Hampshire by nationally expanding his 1830 appeal, originally directed to the bishop of London. In 1841 he launched a nationwide campaign to promote a scheme for communitarian 'self-supporting villages' under the sponsorship of the Church of England, enlisting Lord Melbourne's nephew W. F. Cowper, a lifelong co-operator, as his parliamentary ally, and welcoming as a vice-president Bishop Henry Philpotts, previously the most vociferous opponent of Robert Owen. Lord John Manners (Disraeli's associate) and Richard Monckton Milnes became enthusiastic Morganites by 1846. Ever optimistic, Morgan received a favourable interview from the cautious Pius IX, in 1847, when seeking Vatican approval for similar Catholic-led communities in Italy and famine-stricken Ireland. Dropped after failing to raise £50,000 for a pilot venture in 1850, the domestic scheme was later modified and taken up by General William Booth of the Salvation Army.

A campaigner for universal free education and professional teacher training, Morgan had been defrauded of £3000 by an Anglican clergyman appointed to head his experimental Hanwell School. He was also a Pestalozzian educationist, and promoted Alcott School and the Concordium (1841–8), a commune of 'sacred socialists' close to his Ham Common home, converting the buildings into an orphanage in 1849. His final communitarian manifesto, *The Triumph, or, The Coming Age of Christianity*, appeared in 1851.

Morgan's eclectic impact has been much underestimated in the intellectual history of both Christian socialism and Zionist communitarianism. Acknowledging the Essenes, Morgan directly influenced the *vrai Christianisme* doctrines of the French Icarian socialist Étienne Cabet. Like Martin Buber, he shared the conviction that experimental economic communities involving religious principles would ultimately prove capable of producing a morally higher form of communal life than economic individualism. His propaganda displays, paintings, and models were renowned. At the time of his death, at his home, 12 Stratton Street, Piccadilly, London, on 26 December 1854, Morgan possessed reputedly the finest collection (contemporary and antiquarian) of books and writings upon co-operation and utopian community subjects in the world. He was buried in St Andrew's Church, Ham, Surrey, on 3 January 1855. JOHN G. CORINA

Sources National Co-operative Archive, Rochdale, Robert Owen MSS · W. H. G. Armytage, 'John Minter Morgan, 1782–1854', *Journal of Education*, 86 (1954), 550–52 · W. H. G. Armytage, 'John Minter Morgan's schemes, 1841–1845', *International Review of Social History*, 3 (1958), 26–42 · J. F. C. Harrison, *Robert Owen and the Owenites in Britain and America: the quest for the new moral world* (1969) · J. Saville, 'Morgan, John Minter', *DLB*, vol. 1 · S. T. Hall, *Biographical sketches of remarkable people* (1881) · Ward, *Men of the reign* · *ILN* (24 Aug 1850), 177–81 · *GM*, 2nd ser., 44 (1855), 430–31
Archives Co-operative Union, Holyoake House, Manchester, Robert Owen MSS
Wealth at death £12,000 left in trust for sister and her children: Saville, 'Morgan'

Morgan, John Pierpont (1837–1913). *See under* Morgan, Junius Spencer (1813–1890).

Morgan, Joseph (*fl.* 1707–1739), historian, was born in the late seventeenth century but little is known about his life.

He was the author of numerous books and treatises, the first of which was probably *The Phoenix* (2 vols., 1707–8) which was revived in 1721 as *A Collection of Choice, Scarce and Valuable Tracts*. These were the forerunners of his most significant work, the monthly pamphlet, *Phoenix Britannicus: a Miscellaneous Collection of Scarce and Curious Tracts*. The first number appeared in January 1732 and ran for six successive months before lack of subscribers led to its discontinuation. Among Morgan's other publications were *The History of Algiers* (2 vols., 1728–9), which was translated into Dutch in 1733, and *Mahometism Fully Explained* (1723) and a sequel, *Mahometism Explained* (1725). These were in part based on Muhammad Rabadan's manuscript of 1603. Morgan also translated several historical works from French into English, including Rapin de Thoyras's *The History of England* (1732) and De la Motte's *Voyage to Algiers and Tunis in 1720* (1735). To both he added extensive notes and appendices. His last definite publication was *The Lives and Memorable Actions of many Illustrious Persons of the Eastern Nations* (1739) which was based on the manuscripts of George Sale and other orientalists. The British Library catalogue credits Morgan with the authorship of *A Complete History of the Piratical States of Barbary* (1750) but there is some doubt as to whether he was still alive at this time.

GORDON GOODWIN, *rev.* M. J. MERCER

Sources H. Sirr, 'Joseph Morgan of *Phoenix Britannicus*', *TLS* (15 Dec 1932), 963 · Allibone, *Dict.* · Watt, *Bibl. Brit.*

Morgan, Junius Spencer (1813–1890), merchant banker, was born on 14 April 1813 in West Springfield, Connecticut, USA, the third child and only son of Joseph Morgan (1780–1847), farmer, merchant, dealer in real estate, and a founder of the Aetna Insurance Company, and his wife, Sarah Spencer. He was educated in Connecticut at the American Literary, Scientific, and Military Academy in Middletown (1826–7), and then at a private academy at East Windsor (1827–9). At the age of sixteen it was clear that he would follow his father into business, and rather than send him to university, his father apprenticed him for five years to Alfred Welles of Boston, a merchant and banker, to learn the practical details of running a business. He was then briefly a partner with Welles, and was subsequently a partner in 1834–5 in Morgan, Ketchum & Co., a private bank at 40 Wall Street, New York. In 1835 Morgan married Juliet (*b.* 1816), daughter of the Revd John Pierpont, the pastor of Boston's Hollis Street Unitarian Church; they had two sons and three daughters. After returning in 1836 to his home town of Hartford, Connecticut, Morgan became a partner in the wholesale dry-goods house of Howe, Mather & Co.

Upon the death of his father in 1847 Morgan came into a sizeable fortune. In February 1850 he became the senior partner of his firm, now called Mather, Morgan & Co., and in May 1850 he left on his first business trip to Europe, intending to meet some of London's leading bankers and to investigate business prospects. In the autumn of 1850 he went into partnership with James M. Beebe, the founder and owner of one of the largest wholesale dry-goods houses in the country; on 1 January 1851 the firm became J. M. Beebe, Morgan & Co.

It was on a business trip to London in 1853 that Morgan met George Peabody (1795–1869), as a result of which he gave up the partnership with Beebe and moved to London as Peabody's partner. Peabody was a merchant and banker, the head of the most important American house in the City of London, George Peabody & Co. He was fifty-eight, over-worked and ill, and had been looking for a partner for some time. Morgan was to provide £40,000 of the firm's capital of £450,000, in exchange for which he would receive (or be liable for) 28 per cent of the profits or losses.

In 1864 Peabody retired, and the bank changed its name to J. S. Morgan & Co. Morgan's intention was to make the firm a merchant bank of the first rank, and over the next quarter of a century he did just that. Prudence was displayed in the basic business of a merchant bank—the financing of foreign trade—but daring was shown when Morgan organized a loan of $50 million to the French government in 1870 during the Franco-Prussian War, against the threats of Bismarck, chancellor of Prussia. Profits from the loan helped to raise the bank's capital by £1.5 million and the episode was perhaps the most important event in Junius's career. It also placed J. S. Morgan in the front rank of issuing houses: leading merchant banks had to arrange lending to governments, and over the rest of the century Morgans negotiated finance for an increasing number of governments, from Scandinavia to Latin America. Nevertheless, the major interests of the bank lay in the United States, and this was to remain the case during Junius Morgan's lifetime. He died on 8 April 1890 as a result of being thrown out of his carriage in the village of Eze, near Monte Carlo. His body was taken back to Hartford, where he was buried at Cedar Hill cemetery on 6 May. He left an estate estimated at $12.4 million gross (excluding artworks). His wife predeceased him by some years.

Junius Morgan's eldest son, **John Pierpont Morgan** (1837–1913), investment banker, was born on 17 April 1837, in the house of his grandfather Joseph Morgan, on Asylum Street, Hartford, Connecticut. He was educated at the Cheshire School, at the Pavilion family school, and at the Hartford public high school, where his record was undistinguished; at the Institution Sillig, Vevey, near Geneva, Switzerland, where he did well and also consolidated his French and German; and then at the University of Göttingen. By then he was eager to start work, and in August 1857 he became a non-salaried clerk in the New York bank Duncan, Sherman & Co. In 1864 one of the partners, Charles Dabney, joined Pierpont Morgan in the new firm of Dabney, Morgan & Co., which acted in New York as the representative firm of Morgans of London. In 1871 Morgan became a partner in the firm Drexel, Morgan & Co., which had houses in Philadelphia and Paris in addition to New York. In 1893 the name was changed to J. P. Morgan & Co., and this firm together with the London house was to constitute the house of Morgan.

Pierpont Morgan was married twice, first to Amelia,

daughter of Jonathan Sturges, in October 1861; already seriously ill with tuberculosis, she died four months later. His second wife, whom he married in May 1865, was Frances Louisa (*b.* 1845), the daughter of Charles Tracy, a prominent Wall Street lawyer. They had one son, John Pierpont Morgan Jr. (1867–1943), known as Jack, and three daughters. Jack Morgan was a partner in the family firm from 1898, when he was resident in London, until long after he returned to New York, where he worked with his father and ultimately succeeded him as head of the house of Morgan.

Pierpont Morgan's reputation in the USA rested upon his prowess as the financier and reorganizer of various railways, and as the supreme corporate banker. In the UK he succeeded his father in 1890 as the head of J. S. Morgan & Co., which in 1910 became Morgan, Grenfell & Co.; by the 1920s it was probably the premier merchant bank in London. During Junius Morgan's lifetime, London was the major international capital market, but during the lifetime of his son, the pendulum gradually swung towards New York; the relative importance of the London and New York banks mirrored this change.

Pierpont Morgan bestrode the American investment banking world like a Titan: to his admirers he was straight, dependable, and powerful, but to others he represented the threat of monopoly capital and manipulative power. In Britain his impact was frequently great. In 1900, when for the first time since the eighteenth century the British government turned abroad to raise funds for war, they turned to the house of Morgan to issue loans in New York for the Second South African War. In 1904 Morgan caused a political crisis by his attempts to do for Atlantic shipping what he had already done for steel in the USA— namely, to put together by merger and acquisition a firm which would dominate its sector (as he had done with the United States Steel Company). Morgan believed that competition was wasteful and that co-operation was more logical; but the British government viewed his attempts to establish a 'shipping trust', made up of American and British shipping lines but run by Americans, as a threat to the national interest, particularly during wartime. The International Mercantile Marine merger went through, though with substantial concessions by Morgan to the British government, but Pierpont Morgan's relations with the British political élite never recovered fully.

The house of Morgan was built up by the intelligence, personalities and wills of the two Morgans, who shared an absolute integrity and devotion to first-class banking which inspired the trust of their banking and corporate colleagues. Junius Morgan was quieter and led a more private life than did Pierpont, who like his father lived well, but not quite as unostentatiously: he was almost as famous for his yacht *Corsair*—his personal pennant was a white crescent and a star on a red background—and his fabulous art and manuscript collection as he was for his banking prowess. He was also known for his mistresses. These included a number of actresses and society beauties. At one time he and Edward VII both had a relationship with the actress Maxine Elliott. Junius and Pierpont Morgan were intense Anglophiles, and when Pierpont died on 31 March 1913 at the Grand Hotel, in Rome, Italy, two of his four houses were in Britain: Dover House, Roehampton, which was given to the British government for a hospital during the First World War, and 13 Prince's Gate, London. He was buried near his father at Cedar Hill cemetery, Hartford, USA, on 14 April 1913. His wife survived him. He left an estate of $68.3 million, excluding artworks, which were estimated as worth another $50 million.

The two Morgans, father and son, together played an increasingly important role in British financial life. Their London firm came to have great historical importance after their deaths: Pierpont Morgan's son Jack led J. P. Morgan & Co. to act for the British government and the US government during the First World War, both as the financial agent for Britain and as the American purchasing agent. Furthermore, the house of Morgan took the lead in the private reconstruction of Europe during the 1920s, when Morgan Grenfell acted as the chief banker in London for the loans leading to the re-establishment of the currencies of Germany, Belgium, and Italy.

KATHLEEN BURK

Sources GL, Morgan Grenfell MSS · K. Burk, *Morgan Grenfell, 1838–1988: the biography of a merchant bank* (1989) · V. P. Carosso, *The Morgans: private international bankers, 1854–1913* (1987) · Essex Institute Library, Salem, Massachusetts, USA, G. Peabody MSS · *Who was who in America*, 2 (1943) · *WWW* · *Money trust investigation: investigation of financial and monetary conditions in the United States*, US House subcommittee of the committee on banking and currency, 62nd congress, 3rd session, 3 vols. (1913) [House resolution nos. 429, 504]
Archives GL, Morgan Grenfell MSS · Morgan L., Morgan Grenfell MSS
Likenesses photograph, 1881, Morgan L. · photograph, 1889 (John Pierpont Morgan), Morgan L. · E. Steichen, photograph, 1903 (John Pierpont Morgan) · oils, Morgan Grenfell Group, 23 Great Winchester Street, London · photograph (John Pierpont Morgan), Bettmann archives
Wealth at death £1,842,348 3s. 1d.: resworn probate, April 1891, *CGPLA Eng. & Wales* (1890) · $12.4m in USA excluding art works · £1,179,831 15s. od.—John Pierpont Morgan: probate, 11 Oct 1913, *CGPLA Eng. & Wales* · $68.3m in USA—John Pierpont Morgan · $50m in USA works of art—John Pierpont Morgan

Morgan, Macnamara (*c.*1720–1762), playwright, born in Dublin, was the second son of Charles Morgan of Kilcolgan, co. Galway, Ireland, and was called to the bar at the Middle Temple on 20 June 1744. He practised law at Dublin, but from the 1750s also tried his hand as a playwright, encouraged by his friend the actor Spranger Barry.

Morgan wrote a tragedy, *Philoclea*, based on part of Sidney's *Arcadia*, which ran at Covent Garden for nine nights in January 1754. It was published in London that same year, but did not earn critical esteem. Morgan's lighthearted and bawdy adaptation of Shakespeare's *The Winter's Tale*, entitled *Florizel and Perdita, or, The Sheepshearing*, was first performed in Dublin. On 25 March 1754 it was staged at Covent Garden, starring Barry, and it had some success, being produced more than once. Possibly the songs, by Thomas Arne, contributed to its popularity. It was one of hundreds of adaptations of Shakespeare which were staged throughout the century, and, in keeping with the taste of the times, it omitted the statue scene. In fact, it entirely omitted Leontes and Hermione, making the statue scene superfluous, and communicating the story of the first three acts through analepsis, an approach often favoured in this period in order to bring old stories closer to the classical unities. The adaptation was published in London in the same year and reprinted in Dublin in 1767.

Morgan was the author of two satirical poems, *The Causicade* (1743) and *The Processionade* (1746), both of which are attacks on the appointment of William Murray, later earl of Mansfield, to the post of solicitor-general in November 1742. A poem sometimes wrongly attributed to Morgan, *The Pasquinade*, was actually written by William Kenrick LLD. Morgan died in 1762.   JULIA GASPER

Sources A. Vicars, ed., *Index to the prerogative wills of Ireland* (1897) [gives date of death] · H. A. C. Sturgess, ed., *Register of admissions to the Honourable Society of the Middle Temple, from the fifteenth century to the year 1944*, 3 vols. (1949) · H. Boylan, *A dictionary of Irish biography*, 3rd edn (1998) · G. Lester, 'Retelling the tale', www.amrep.org/past/ winter/winter1.html

Morgan, Mary Augusta De (1850–1907). *See under* Morgan, William Frend De (1839–1917).

Morgan, Matthew (1652–1703), translator and poet, was born in the parish of St Nicholas in Bristol, where his father, Edward Morgan (d. 1669), was alderman and mayor. He was educated by Walter Rainstrop until 1667 when he entered St John's College, Oxford, under the tuition of John Rainstrop, Walter's son. Morgan graduated BA on 18 May 1671, MA on 9 July 1674, and BCL and DCL on 7 July 1685. In 1684 he contributed to a translation of Plutarch's *Morals* by several hands. This volume was the focus of some controversy. In the epistle dedicatory addressed to the archbishop of Canterbury, Morgan expressed the unorthodox hope that philosophers such as Plutarch might enjoy the same state of bliss as Christians in the afterlife. And in the preface a reference to 'Ashmole's rarities' and the 'insect-cabal' who cared for them displeased Robert Plot, who carried his complaint to John Lloyd, the vice-chancellor (*Ath. Oxon.*, 711). Morgan was threatened with expulsion, but he disowned his work, the responsibility for which was assumed by John Gellibrand, the bookseller.

Besides his work on Plutarch, Morgan contributed the life of Atticus to a translation of Cornelius Nepos rendered as *Lives of Illustrious Men* (1684) and the life of Augustus to a translation of Suetonius (1688). He also wrote a number of occasional poems including *An Elegy on … Robert Boyle* (1692) and *A Poem upon the Late Victory over the French at Sea* (1692). In the epistle dedicatory to this latter work Morgan voices strongly anti-Catholic sentiments:

> I should think myself very prophane, nay almost blasphemous, if I should call it a Religion, it is rather a Complication of all the Villanies that were ever acted under the Sun, colour'd over with that Name.

Thomas Hearne mentions Morgan in his *Remarks and Collections*. After listing his translations Hearne concludes 'He also writ a Poem upon the Death of Mr Boyce, & several other Poems which are of no great Note' (*Remarks*, 2.60). This is not an unfair assessment of Morgan's verse. Typically clumsy is this couplet from *A Poem upon the Late Victory over the French at Sea*:

> For the French Sun hath in the Ocean set
> Out of those Depths he never up shall get.
> (p. 2)

In 1688 Morgan was presented to the vicarage of Congresbury, Somerset, but forfeited it owing to his failure to read the articles within the stipulated time. He was vicar of Weare in Somerset from 1693 until his death, probably in Weare, in 1703.   SARAH ANNES BROWN

Sources Wood, *Ath. Oxon.*, new edn, 4.711 · Foster, *Alum. Oxon.* · *Remarks and collections of Thomas Hearne*, ed. C. E. Doble and others, 2, OHS, 7 (1886), 60 · *BL cat.* · Wood, *Ath. Oxon.: Fasti* (1815) · *DNB* · A. B. Beavan, *Bristol lists, municipal and miscellaneous* (1899)

Morgan, Sir Morien Bedford (1912–1978), aeronautical engineer, was born on 20 December 1912 at Caroline Street, Bridgend, Glamorgan, the elder son (there were no surviving daughters) of John Bedford Morgan (1883–1961), draper, and his wife, Edith Mary Thomas (1884–1960), teacher. He was educated at Bridgend elementary school; Magdalen College School, Oxford; Aberdâr Boys' County School; Canton secondary school, Cardiff; and finally Rutlish School, Merton, London. His family was very musical and he became a skilled pianist and organist as well as having a good tenor voice.

Morgan entered St Catharine's College, Cambridge, in 1931 and obtained a second class in part one of the mathematical tripos (1932) and a first class in the mechanical sciences tripos (1934) in which he specialized in aeronautics and was awarded the prestigious John Bernard Seely prize. During both his last two vacations he had spent some time at Vickers Aviation and was keen to make a career in aeronautics, but jobs were scarce and he spent an unhappy nine months as an apprentice with Mather and Platt Ltd in Manchester before being recruited in 1935 as a junior scientific officer at the Royal Aircraft Establishment (RAE), Farnborough. There he met, and on 19 April 1941 married, Sylvia Axford (b. 1919), a civil servant, the daughter of George Frederick Axford, instrument maker, of Farnborough. They had three daughters.

Morgan spent his first thirteen years at RAE doing research with Aero Flight (a division of the establishment concerned with all the flying qualities of an aircraft), leaving as its head in 1948 to become head of the new guided weapons department, where he remained until 1953. In 1954 he became deputy director (A) of the establishment, in charge of its aircraft, as distinct from its equipment half. In 1959 he was moved from RAE to spend one year as scientific adviser to the Air Ministry, followed by nine years in the Ministry of Aviation headquarters, first as deputy controller of aircraft (research and development) until 1963, then as controller of aircraft until 1966, when he became controller of guided weapons and electronics, before his final government posting as director RAE from 1969 to 1972.

By 1939 rearmament prior to war meant that there were more than a dozen major aircraft firms each designing and building one or more prototype aircraft. Before these were off the drawing board others would be started, and twelve months could see an aircraft through from first concept to first flight. The man to whom each firm took its aerodynamic problems was Morgan, and his unique blend of knowledge, research experience, scientific judgement, energy, and enthusiasm often led to successful solutions being quickly found. In addition, his infectious good humour inspired the whole of Aero Flight, and created a talented team. In his Cambridge days Morgan learnt much from B. Melvill Jones and W. S. Farren, and at Farnborough he worked closely with S. B. Gates. At Aero Flight he was particularly concerned with aircraft control and stability, and especially with making these as congenial as possible for the pilot, thus improving both safety and handling characteristics. Moreover, he felt strongly that practical experience was important, and held a pilot's A licence himself from 1944. Many if not all of Britain's wartime aircraft were improved in their fighting qualities by application of Morgan's ideas and suggestions.

After leaving Aero Flight, Morgan contributed greatly to the growth of Britain's guided weapons industry, but the years from 1948 to 1959 will probably be chiefly remembered for two undertakings while he was deputy director. The first of these was the public inquiry into the Comet accidents, in which he directed the scientific investigation that demonstrated in the astonishingly short time of three months that metal fatigue of the pressure cabin was to blame. The second was the programme of research he directed into the feasibility of a supersonic civil aircraft, which culminated in Concorde. Once again he welded together a talented team and the remarkable technical success of Concorde owes much to him, whatever view is taken of its commercial significance.

During Morgan's time in higher management at headquarters many far-reaching decisions were taken, including a few much publicized cancellations of aircraft projects, sometimes against his advice. He showed much humanity and understanding in persuading so many diverse groups of people to work together, and also great courage in refusing to be browbeaten into taking decisions that were against his better judgement.

In 1972 Morgan became master of Downing College, Cambridge, where his enthusiasm and good humour together with his Welsh charm, eloquence, and love of music made sure that he was well received. He got on well with both young and old, and was happy to chat (or to have a serious argument) with anyone; he was completely unaffected and had a knack of getting to know and understand all kinds of people. At home he enjoyed a happy and relaxed family life until the day of his death.

Morgan was appointed CB in 1958 and knighted in 1969. He was president of the Royal Aeronautical Society in 1967–8 and was awarded the society's silver medal in 1957, the gold medal in 1971, and an honorary fellowship in 1976. He was elected to an honorary fellowship at St Catharine's College, Cambridge, in 1972, became a fellow of the Royal Society in 1972, and was a founder fellow of the Fellowship of Engineering in 1976. He was also awarded honorary doctorates at Cranfield and Southampton in 1976. He was a governor of the College of Aeronautics and later (1971) a council member of the Cranfield Institute of Technology. In 1973 he became a member of the Airworthiness Requirements Board and chairman of its research committee, and in 1975 he was appointed chairman of the Air Traffic Control Board and a member of the Post Office Board. His chief publications were his lectures to the Royal Aeronautical Society, published in its journal, and various reports and memoranda for the Aeronautical Research Council. He died suddenly at the master's lodge, Downing College, Cambridge, on 4 April 1978. His remains were cremated on 11 April and his ashes buried in St Benet's churchyard, Cambridge.   E. G. BROADBENT

Sources E. G. Broadbent, *Memoirs FRS*, 26 (1980), 371–410 · *The Times* (6 April 1978) · private information (2004) [Lady Morgan, widow]

Likenesses photograph, 1972, Hult. Arch. · photograph, repro. in *Memoirs FRS*, facing p. 371

Wealth at death £9957: probate, 11 May 1978, *CGPLA Eng. & Wales*

Morgan, Philip [Philip ap Morgan] (*d.* 1435), diplomat and bishop of Worcester and of Ely, was a Welshman from Llandaff diocese, but held his earliest preferments in St David's diocese, from before July 1390. He had a sister, Tanylwyst, and nephews Lewis Morgan and John Water. He was DCL of Oxford by 28 May 1397 and DCnL by 1404. Licensed to farm his rectory of Aberedw, Radnorshire, for ten years on 16 May 1401, he was still at Oxford, arbitrating a dispute, in February 1404, and representing the university in the town court in March 1406.

Morgan entered the service of Archbishop Thomas Arundel of Canterbury, probably by 20 November 1407, and occurs as his auditor of causes many times between 10 February 1410 and 29 November 1413. He was a proctor in parliament in November 1411 for Christ Church, Canterbury, and the bishop of Norwich. He had occasional commissions from the crown in 1409 and 1412 to hear ransom suits and appeals from the court of admiralty. Morgan was present at Blackfriars, London, when the heretic Sir John Oldcastle appeared before Arundel for a second time on 25 September 1413. On 16 December he gained exemption from the royal order to all Welsh people to return home. On 12 February 1414 he was named as an executor by Archbishop Arundel, who left him a book, and he was present at the election of Archbishop Henry Chichele on 14 March.

Hereafter, whether by coincidence or through some unrevealed lack of empathy, Morgan left the service of the archbishopric for that of the crown. On 22 May 1414 he was asked to investigate alleged violations of safe conducts by English subjects. From 26 June to 4 October 1414 he was on an embassy to discuss with the duke of Burgundy a proposed marriage for Henry V, and on 5 December was appointed to the crucial, if ultimately futile, peace embassy to France, also to prorogue truces with France on 13 April and 5 June 1415. Between the periods 19 August – 19 December 1415 and 12 March – 3 May 1416 he was engaged again in talks with Burgundy, and between 3

July and 21 October 1416 on peace talks with the visiting Emperor Sigismund and with France. On 2 December 1416, and again on 25 February 1417, he was appointed to treat with various trading partners on the continent.

His service now took Morgan with Henry V into the war in Normandy. On 6 November 1417 he received the usual licence to hear confessions and grant absolutions in the king's army while abroad, and in January and February 1418 he was helping with musters at Bayeux and elsewhere, routine work to which he returned on occasion over the next eighteen months. Appointed chancellor of Normandy on 8 April 1418, he was empowered on 10 November to treat with the dauphin at Alençon, on 5 July 1419 with the French crown, with a papal envoy on 16 October, with the French around Paris for a truce on 20 November, for a general truce on 26 December, and for the release of Arthur, duke of Brittany, on 12 July 1420.

Morgan had enjoyed only modest ecclesiastical preferment from the archbishopric and crown, until he became the (entirely absentee) archdeacon of Norfolk by royal grant on 18 February 1418. He was now elected bishop of Worcester on 24 April 1419, papally provided on 19 June, had the temporalities on 18 October, and was consecrated at Rouen on 3 December. His episcopal register records him at 'Campaine' on 21 May 1420, and in Paris on 1 October and 9 November. However, he had returned to London by 24 February 1421, and was appointed to investigate the condition of St Bartholomew's Hospital, Gloucester, on 3 April 1421. From 31 July to 10 October he is found exploring his new diocese, from 11 November to 17 December in London, and from 26 December to 14 May 1422 visiting monasteries in his diocese. He preached in convocation against the heretic William Taylor, whom he held in prison, on 27 May 1421, and attended his trial in convocation on 11 February 1423 (although not thereafter).

It is curious that Morgan (like Henry Ware) should have withdrawn so suddenly from the king's service in France. There is no sign of any disfavour. He was appointed to the regency council in England after Henry V's death, and proved a regular attender until his own death, yet managing almost all the time to retain personal and resident supervision of his successive dioceses. He was appointed on 22 February 1423 to represent the crown at the Council of Pavia–Siena, but did not go. From 6 July 1423 he was a member of the several delegations that negotiated the liberation of James I of Scotland. On 25 January 1424 his election as archbishop of York was given the assent of the regency council, whose candidate he was. However, Martin V, at that time surly about the English government's stance towards papal finance and patronage, translated Richard Flemming of Lincoln, who had been a good friend to him at Siena. There was an impasse over this and other appointments, until John Kemp of London was promoted as a face-saving compromise on 25 July 1425. Morgan, however, was translated thereafter as part of the settlement to Ely on 27 February 1426, in the face of both the chapter's election of its own prior, Peter Ely, and the crown's original nomination of William Alnwick, who was given Norwich instead. There was much faction on the council at this time, which the pope only partly understood, and a good deal of shuffling of candidates for episcopacy and enhancement. Morgan, however, seems to have been a respected neutral in this, his claims to a senior bishopric being generally agreed. On 7 March 1426 he was an arbitrator between Bishop Henry Beaufort and the protector, Humphrey of Gloucester, in parliament.

Morgan continued to attend the council through various shifts of power, and between 17 April and 11 November 1430 accompanied Henry VI to France for his coronation. Although Morgan had not been enthroned at Ely until 23 February 1427, thereafter he commuted energetically between there and Westminster, although on 21 December 1433—perhaps for political reasons—he said he would attend the council only whenever other duties permitted. He enjoys the rare distinction of praise from the curmudgeonly Oxford commentator Thomas Gascoigne, who applauds his stand against unlicensed pluralism and other clerical abuses. On 15 November 1428 Morgan was on the committee of convocation to discuss the defence of orthodoxy. In 1430 a commission set up by Martin V declared that the University of Cambridge was exempt from Morgan's authority, and that he could not have an oath of obedience from the chancellor-elect; Morgan failed to have this decision reversed by Eugenius IV.

Morgan never retired from public life and, although formal records can flatter, he appears to have established a deservedly notable reputation both in his dioceses and in affairs of the realm. He only drew up his will on 21 October 1435 when very sick, and perhaps for that reason made a very simple one; he singled out Abergwili collegiate and parish churches in St David's diocese for bequests. He died at Bishop's Hatfield, Hertfordshire, just four days later, and was buried, as he requested, in the London Charterhouse, to the last a man of a sensitivity that the official records of his sort of career cannot show but which, unusually, they do hint at. R. G. DAVIES

Sources Emden, *Oxf.*, 2.1312–13 · R. G. Davies, 'The episcopate in England and Wales, 1375–1443', PhD diss., University of Manchester, 1974, 3.cc–cciv · E. F. Jacob, ed., *The register of Henry Chichele, archbishop of Canterbury, 1414–1443*, 2, CYS, 42 (1937), 530–32 · episcopal register, Worcs. RO, b716.093 — BA 2648/5 (iii) · Ely episcopal register, 1426–35, CUL

Archives CUL, Ely episcopal register · Worcs. RO, episcopal register

Morgan, Sir Richard (d. 1556), judge, was the second son of Philip ap Morgan Watkin of Llanfair Cilgoed, Monmouthshire. He was admitted to Lincoln's Inn in 1524, and is mentioned as counsel in the duchy chamber as early as 1528, the year before his call to the bar. He can hardly have been forty years old when he gave his first reading, in the autumn of 1542, on the action of replevin, when he somewhat unusually took two statutes (of 1285 and 1529) as his text. A mere four years later, in June 1546, he was called by Henry VIII to the degree of serjeant-at-law, though the creation was delayed until February 1547 by the demise of the crown. His patrons at the ceremony were Stephen Gardiner, bishop of Winchester, and Lord Mordaunt. He gave his second reading, as serjeant-elect, on the Statute of

Marlborough, c. 12. By this time he was recorder of Gloucester, and from 1545 to 1553 he served as member of parliament for that borough. He had also married Mary, daughter of Sir Robert Bailey, with whom he had three sons and three daughters.

A Roman Catholic in religion, Morgan was committed to the Fleet prison in 1551 for hearing mass in Princess Mary's chapel, but was discharged by the privy council with a caution a few weeks later. On the death of Edward VI, Morgan joined Mary and her adherents at Kenninghall Castle, Norfolk, and was rewarded for his loyalty with membership of the privy council (on 16 August 1553), the chief justiceship of the common pleas (on 23 August), and a knighthood (on 2 October). He was active in the proceedings against the rebels, and took part in the trial and condemnation of Lady Jane Grey in November. However, he was to enjoy his new station for less than a year, for he lost his mind the following May. Although he is said to have been stricken while sitting at the Guildhall, London, it was found by an inquisition taken at the Guildhall that Morgan became a lunatic on 8 May 1554 in the parish of St Magnus the Martyr, Bridge ward, where he had a London residence. He was replaced as chief justice on 8 October. According to Foxe and Holinshed, he had been driven mad by remorse at the fate of Lady Jane Grey, though this may well have been another invention. He probably died in May 1556, and was buried on 2 June in the church of St Magnus the Martyr. The family home at Skenfrith, Monmouthshire, passed to his eldest son, Sir Thomas.

J. H. BAKER

Sources HoP, Commons, 1509–58, 2.629–30 · W. P. Baildon, ed., The records of the Honorable Society of Lincoln's Inn: the black books, 1 (1897) · Baker, Serjeants, 169, 434, 527 · Sainty, Judges, 48 · D. MacCulloch, 'The Vita Mariae Angliae Reginae of Robert Wingfield of Brantham', Camden miscellany, XXVIII, CS, 4th ser., 29 (1984), 181–301 · G. S. Fry, ed., Abstracts of inquisitiones post mortem relating to the City of London, 1: 1485–1561, British RS, 15 (1896), 143–4 · University of Illinois, Urbana-Champaign, MS 27 · PRO, DL 5/5, fol. 363v · printed yearbook 7 Hen. IV etc., note on fly-leaf, Lincoln's Inn, London · T. D. Fosbrooke, Gloucester (1819), 421 · J. Stow, A survey of the cities of London and Westminster and the borough of Southwark, new edn, ed. J. Strype, 1/2 (1720), 175
Archives University of Illinois, Urbana-Champaign, volume of legal notes

Morgan, Richard Cope (1827–1908), journal editor and publisher, was born on 13 May 1827 at Abergavenny, Monmouthshire, the son of James Hiley Morgan, a nonconformist printer and philanthropist, and his wife, Emily Williamson, the daughter of the Revd Richard Cope (1776–1856). Educated at the Old Priory School, Monk Street, Morgan began working, at fourteen, in his father's printing shop. About 1844 his pious mother died of tuberculosis, aged forty, as did his only sister, Christiana, three years later. At twenty-one Morgan moved to London and then to Bath, where he was foreman-printer for Binns and Goodwin. About this time, a Bristol Methodist minister's preaching led to his evangelical conversion. On 22 June 1850 he married Lydia Margaret Taylor (1819/20–1895), the daughter of a Bristol merchant, but almost immediately returned to Abergavenny because of ill health. On resuming his work in Bath in 1851 he was associated for a time with the Brethren movement. As a publisher's assistant in Paternoster Row, London, from 1855, he adopted rather wider evangelical loyalties, and in 1859, with another Christian Welshman, Samuel Chase, he established the publishing firm Morgan and Chase. One year before Chase's death in 1870, they were joined by a Glasgow merchant, Robert Scott, and soon the firm became Morgan and Scott. The magazine The Revival (first published in 1859 and renamed The Christian in 1870) rapidly became, under Morgan's guidance, an unofficial mouthpiece of that distinctive variety of non-denominational evangelicalism which flourished in the years following 1859, typified by such men as Brownlow North (1810–1875) and Henry Varley (1835–1912). His enthusiastic editorials treated the campaigns of the American evangelist D. L. Moody as a natural extension of the earlier revival, and Moody's first sermon in England, in 1867, was delivered in the Wood Green 'Gospel Hall', of which Morgan was the acknowledged though unpaid pastor while he lived in north London.

From the outset of his London career Morgan supported the YMCA and likewise the Evangelical Alliance, championing the cause of persecuted Christians whether in Spain, Russia, or Armenia, but rigorously opposing anything he deemed to be unorthodox, from Roman Catholicism to Christian Science. It has been suggested that he attended one of the many Holiness meetings in America in 1869 (Bebbington, 161), and certainly Morgan was an early supporter of the Keswick Convention, though he rejected its later perfectionist aberrations, avoiding both extremism and personalized controversy. He actively encouraged temperance work and foreign missions, especially in north Africa and China, and defended Josephine Butler's campaign against the Contagious Diseases Acts. Predeceased by four of his five sons, the second of whom, Cope, aged seventeen, was drowned in 1870, he moved in 1879 to Bournemouth because of his wife's ill health, though he continued to work in London. His wife died in 1895 and he moved back to north London, spending more time travelling abroad. On 7 October 1897 he married a younger Polish woman, Wilhelmina Marsyjanna Phillipina Daneske Mazur (b. 1866/7). At the age of eighty-one he suffered a stroke and died on 29 October 1908 at his home, Northfield, Crescent Road, Crouch End. He was buried on 2 November in the Great Northern London cemetery, Southgate, Middlesex.

TIMOTHY C. F. STUNT

Sources G. E. Morgan, 'A veteran in revival': R. C. Morgan, his life and times (1909) · P. G. Scott, 'Richard Cope Morgan, religious periodicals and the Pontifex factor', Victorian Periodicals Newsletter, 5/2 (1972), 1–14 · D. W. Bebbington, Evangelicalism in modern Britain: a history from the 1730s to the 1980s (1989), 116, 161–2, 173 · m. certs. · CGPLA Eng. & Wales (1908)
Likenesses four photographs, repro. in Morgan, 'A veteran in revival'
Wealth at death £30,092 4s. 6d.: probate, 1 Dec 1908, CGPLA Eng. & Wales

Morgan, Robert (1608–1673), bishop of Bangor, was born at Bronfraith in the parish of Llandysilio in Montgomeryshire, the third son of Richard Morgan (*d. c.*1630), who had been MP for Montgomery (1592–3) and deputy sheriff of the county in 1600, and his wife, Margaret (*d.* in or after 1630), daughter of Thomas Lloyd of Gwernybuarth and widow of Charles Powell of Llandysul. He received his education at Bronfraith and was instructed by the father of Simon Lloyd, the archdeacon of Merioneth. On 6 July 1624 he entered Jesus College, Cambridge; he graduated BA in 1628 and proceeded MA in 1631, having been ordained by the bishop of Peterborough in December 1629.

Upon the election of David Dolben to the bishopric of Bangor, Morgan was appointed as his chaplain, and on 16 September 1632 he was nominated by Dolben to the vicarage of Llanwnnog in Montgomeryshire. He subsequently became the rector of Llangynhafal and Dyffryn Clwyd. In 1633, after Dolben's death, he returned to Cambridge and on 25 June 1634 it was recorded that 'at his own request and for his own benefit' (*DNB*) he transferred to St John's College. It is, therefore, presumed that he had returned to his former college during 1633–4. A certificate granted to him by Richard Sterne, master of Jesus College, referred to Morgan's 'manye yeares' civill and studious life there' (Mayor, 18), and in 1638 he attained the degree of BD.

In 1637, after the appointment of William Roberts to the bishopric of Bangor, Morgan returned to Wales as Roberts's chaplain and in the same year was appointed vicar of Llanfair in the deanery of Dyffryn Clwyd. The following year he was appointed as rector of Efenechdyd and on 1 July 1642 he became, after the resignation of David Lloyd, a prebendary of Chester. It is noted, however, that he did not retain or recover the position at the Restoration. This point is nevertheless disputed in John Walker's *Sufferings of the Clergy*.

After he resigned his position at Llangynhafal, Morgan was, on 16 July 1642, appointed to Trefdraeth in Anglesey. During this year it was recorded that he resigned his position at Llanfair. On 19 November 1642 he was inducted at Llanddyfnan in Anglesey—a living worth only £38 per annum. Using £300 of his own money he purchased from the Bulkeleys of Baron Hill the unexpired term of a 99-year lease of the tithes of Llanddyfnan parish. During the upheaval of the civil war years his title to the living of this parish was unchallenged. This contrasted with his removal from other ecclesiastical positions during the same period. On 14 July 1648 he drafted the loyal declaration from Anglesey with 'high-swelling words and bitter language' (Phillips, 2.399–400).

During the Commonwealth period Morgan lived mainly at Henblas in Llangristiolus in Anglesey. There is evidence that on 2 December 1656 he gave a funeral sermon for Owen Holland of Berw whereby he castigated the 'new and phantastick revelations' of the puritan preachers (NL Wales, MS 3069). Yet most of his sermons were 'mostly prosaic save for those which called for a keener awareness of the state of the soul and the overwhelming necessity of regeneration' (Jenkins, *Literature*, 22). In 1657, on the death of Robert White, he was nominated to the prebend of Penmynydd in the diocese of Bangor. He was, however, not installed until after the Restoration and relinquished the post before April 1661. Morgan was married by this date to Anne, the daughter and heir of William Lloyd, the rector of Llaneilian, Anglesey. They had several children: Richard, who died young; Owen (*d.* 1679), a student at Jesus College, Cambridge, and Gray's Inn, who later attended Sir Leoline Jenkins at the treaty of Nijmegen; William (*b.* 1664), who graduated with an LLB from Jesus College, Oxford, in 1685 and later became the chancellor of the diocese of Bangor; and Robert (*b.* 1665), who graduated DD from Christ Church, Oxford, and subsequently became a canon of Hereford in 1702 and rector of Ross, Herefordshire. Robert and Anne also had four daughters: Margaret, who married Edward Wyn; Anna, who married Thomas Lloyd of Cefn, the registrar of St Asaph; Elizabeth, who married Humphrey Humphreys, the dean of St Asaph; and Katherine, who remained unmarried and was buried with her father.

Following the Restoration, Morgan recovered his living of Trefdraeth. On 24 August 1660 he was appointed archdeacon of Merioneth and during the same month he became the comportioner of Llandinam. In 1666 he received a DD from Cambridge. On 8 June 1666, after the death of Robert Price, he was elected bishop of Bangor and on 1 July was consecrated at Lambeth Palace. During the period July 1660 to 23 October 1666 Morgan held the archdeaconry of Merioneth *in commendam* before he was succeeded by John Lloyd. This was in spite of his petition on 21 June 1666 to continue to hold the position *in commendam*. It was furthermore his successor who achieved the unification of the archdeaconry and bishopric of the county.

For many years Morgan was engaged in litigation against Thomas Jones (1622?–1682) over the living of Llandyrnog parish. This was normally held by the bishops of Bangor *in commendam* as a result of its convenient location. In 1669 Jones sought to bring the issue of the living to the court of arches and brought a charge against the bishop and two others. Morgan did not, however, court trouble and did not seek the persecution of conventiclers in his diocese. He also ignored the appeals of Michael Roberts for help to regain his fellowship at Jesus College, Oxford. Similarly he did not assist his 'cousin' Sir Richard Wynn of Gwydir by making preferential appointments. During his lifetime Morgan produced several works worthy of publication, but refused to allow them to be published. It has also been suggested that he caused 'considerable restorations in Bangor Cathedral, and gave an excellent organ' (*DNB*). He preached both in English and Welsh, and his exertions in the pulpit may have contributed to his death in Bangor on 1 September 1673. He was buried on 6 September in Bangor Cathedral in the tomb of Bishop Robinson, on the south side of the altar. According to Bishop Humphrey, his son-in-law, Morgan was 'a man of great prudence in business, good learning, and eloquence' (Wood, *Ath. Oxon.*, 2.890). A modern evaluation has similarly suggested that Morgan and his predecessor, William

Roberts, were 'zealous churchmen who reasserted epis-copal authority and recruited able incumbents' (Jenkins, *Foundations*, 177).   W. A. SHAW, *rev.* RICHARD C. ALLEN

Sources DWB · Foster, *Alum. Oxon.* · R. Williams, *Enwogion Cymru: a biographical dictionary of eminent Welshmen* (1852), 340–41 · Wood, *Ath. Oxon.*, 1st edn, 1.441; 2.890 · T. Richards, *A history of the puritan movement in Wales* (1920), 32, 283–4 · T. Richards, *Religious develop-ments in Wales, 1654–1662* (1923), 148–9, 274, 362, 370, 428, 510 n. 1 · T. Richards, *Wales under the indulgence, 1672–1675* (1928), 28, 129, 130, 138 · T. Richards, *Wales under the penal code, 1662–1687* (1925), 23, 39, 61, 137, 151, 159 · T. Jones, *Elymas the sorcerer, or, A memorial towards the discovery of this Popish Plot* (1682), 25–31 · A. H. Dodd, 'Morgan, Richard', HoP, *Commons, 1558–1603* · J. Walker, *An attempt towards recovering an account of the numbers and sufferings of the clergy of the Church of England*, pt 2 (1714), 11 · G. H. Jenkins, *Literature, religion and society in Wales, 1660–1730* (1978), 22 · G. H. Jenkins, *Protestant dissen-ters in Wales* (1992), 47 · G. H. Jenkins, *The foundations of modern Wales, 1642–1780* (1987); pbk edn (1993), 177 · P. Jenkins, 'The Anglican church and the unity of Britain: the Welsh experience, 1560–1714', *Conquest and union: fashioning a British state*, ed. S. G. Ellis and S. Barber (1995), 115–38 · J. E. B. Mayor, ed., *Admissions to the College of St John the Evangelist in the University of Cambridge*, 1: *Jan 1629/30 – July 1665* (1882), 18 · J. R. Phillips, *Memoirs of the civil war in Wales and the marches, 1642–1649*, 2 (1874), 399–400
Archives Bodl. Oxf., Bishop Kennett's collections, Lansdowne MS 986, fol. 168 · Bodl. Oxf., Tanner MS xliii, fol. 68 · Bodl. Oxf., Tanner MS cxlvi, fol. 70 · LPL, Lambeth Palace MS 639, fol. 140 · LPL, Lam-beth Palace MS 902, fol. 52 · NL Wales, funeral sermon of Owen Holland by Dr Robert Morgan of Llanddyfnan, Mostyn MS 229 [par-ticularly fols. 1, 8, 27, 29] · NL Wales, MS 3069 · U. Wales, Bangor, Henblas MSS 9A; 10A

Morgan, Robert (*bap.* **1708**, *d.* **1778**), ironmaster, was born at Kidwelly, Carmarthenshire, and baptized there on 20 July 1708, the second son of Christopher Morgan, a coal factor of Kidwelly, and Sage Howell. On 29 November 1736 he married, in Llangyndeyrn, Frances Hughes (1703–1773), the daughter of Arnold Bowen, the mayor of Carmarthen in 1722, and widow of Lewis Hughes, attorney and town clerk of Carmarthen, with whom she had four children. There were a further six children of her marriage to Mor-gan, the first two of whom suffered some form of mental handicap. It was the second son, **John Morgan** (*bap.* 1739, *d.* 1805), baptized on 18 December 1739 at Llangyndeyrn, who took charge of the business after the death of his father.

In the late seventeenth and early eighteenth centuries there was a perceptible extension of the iron industry into west Wales, attracted by excellent supplies of water and charcoal. One prominent figure was an English ironmas-ter, Peter Chettle (1681–1729), who owned a furnace at Pont-henri and two forges at Kidwelly and Whitland, which were sold to Lewis Hughes in 1729. Presumably these fell to Morgan when he married Hughes's widow in 1736. At all events the first distinctive contribution of Rob-ert Morgan to the industry in this area was to bring together under common ownership a number of iron establishments: in this respect he was a consolidator rather than a pioneer. But this is to underrate his contribu-tion both in organizing production and in seeking new markets. On the production side he built up a fully integ-rated enterprise from manufacturing pig iron to rolling tin plate, and to do so he bought iron ore from Lancashire

and Cumberland, and tin from Cornwall. In marketing it was his restless activity which turned to producing guns during the Seven Years' War and, more abidingly, sought outlets for the newer business of tin-plate manufacture. By the late 1750s Morgan was the sole, or major, owner of a blast furnace at Carmarthen, two air furnaces, four forges—at Whitland, Kidwelly, Cwmdwyfran, and Black-pool (Pembrokeshire)—and a tin-plate works at Kidwelly. His blast furnaces at Carmarthen produced pig iron, which was converted into bars at the forges and then, from 1758, rolled and tinned at Kidwelly lower works, where Morgan was a partner. By the time this partnership was dissolved in 1761 he had built a new tinworks at Car-marthen.

For a time, during the Seven Years' War, Morgan consid-erably modified the production pattern to take advantage of the high profits made possible by the wartime demand for ordnance, although the difficulties of finding—and keeping—a reliable gun-founder made it a precarious ven-ture. For a few years from mid-1757 guns and shot were cast for the Board of Ordnance, and guns were also sup-plied for merchant ships at Bristol and Liverpool. But by the late 1750s tin plate had become the stable core of the business. The scale of his activities was substantial: Car-marthen was unusual for the time in having two mills, built at a cost of £3300; Morgan operated a fully integrated enterprise; there were agents in Bristol, Liverpool, and London; and he told his representative at the twice yearly meeting of ironmasters at Bristol that, because of the size of the works, 'you are Entitled to the First or second Vote' (National Library of Wales, Morgan letter book, 22 Jan 1761).

Morgan accumulated a substantial landed estate rich in woodlands for charcoal making, and about 1760 built a Georgian residence, Furnace House, in St Peter's Street, Carmarthen, complete with iron rails made in his own works. Frances Morgan died in 1773, and Morgan's own death occurred on 30 April 1778 at Furnace House (not in 1777 as generally given). He was buried in St Peter's churchyard in Carmarthen. After his death the manage-ment of the business passed to his second son, John Mor-gan. This met the wishes of Robert Morgan, who stated in his will that he was 'desirous of having the business of the iron trade carried on properly' and that 'my son John seems to take a delight in the iron trade' (will, quoted in Green, 225). Under John Morgan, who was sheriff for Car-marthenshire in 1782, the works continued to flourish: he was one of a small group of tin-plate manufacturers recorded as meeting in London 'to settle prices, weights and sizes' (Minchinton, 17); and in 1800 the firm main-tained three sloops to transport raw materials and fin-ished output. However, in the latter year he leased the undertaking to a partnership including his nephew, also John Morgan. John Morgan sen. remained unmarried and died on 23 March 1805. From 1800 the enterprise was said to have declined through mismanagement, and the fam-ily connection was much reduced after the death of John Morgan jun. in 1808, although the Carmarthen works were not finally closed until 1900. Gradual decline was in any event unavoidable for a firm rooted in charcoal iron, even though some coke bars were brought from Monmouthshire from 1800 on: but Robert and John Morgan were undoubtedly pre-eminent among those who laid a tradition which made west Wales the dominant region for tin-plate production for nearly two centuries.

JOHN WILLIAMS

Sources L. J. Williams, 'A Carmarthenshire ironmaster and the Seven Years War', *Business History*, 2 (1959–60), 32–43 · F. Green, 'Carmarthen tinworks and its founder', *Transactions of the Historical Society of West Wales*, 5 (1915), 245–70 · parish register (burial) St Peter's, Carmarthen, Dyfed RO · L. J. Williams, 'The Welsh tinplate trade in the mid-18th century', *Economic History Review*, 2nd ser., 13 (1960–61), 440–49 · M. Evans, 'The pioneers of the Carmarthenshire iron industry', *Carmarthenshire Historian*, 4 (1967), 23–40 · T. James, 'Carmarthen tinplate works, 1800–21', *Carmarthenshire Antiquary*, 12 (1976), 31–48 · N. D. Ludlow, 'The first Kidwelly tinplate works', *Sir Gaer: studies in Carmarthenshire history*, ed. H. James (1991), 79–100 · W. Morris, 'Kidwelly tinplate works: 18th century leases', *Carmarthen Antiquary*, 5 (1964–9), 21–4 · W. Rees, *Industry before the industrial revolution*, 1 (1968) · W. E. Minchinton, *The British tinplate industry: a history* (1957) · E. H. Brook, *Chronology of the tin-plate works of Great Britain* (1944) · W. Spurrell, *Carmarthen and its neighbourhood*, 2nd edn (1879)

Archives NL Wales, letter-book | Dyfed RO, Carmarthen, Yelverton MSS

Likenesses A. Kauffman, miniature set in gold bracelet (John Morgan), repro. in Green, 'Carmarthen tinworks and its founder', 255

Wealth at death approx. £15,000–£20,000; bequests of over £8000: Green, 'Carmarthen tinworks', 254; will, 11 April 1777

Morgan [*née* Owenson], **Sydney**, Lady Morgan (*bap.* **1783**, *d.* **1859**), novelist and socialite, was baptized in Dublin in 1783, the elder child of Robert *Owenson (1744–1812), an actor of Irish origin noted for his comic roles, and Jane Hill (*d.* 1789), the protestant daughter of a Shrewsbury tradesman. Named after her paternal grandmother, Sydney was born in Dublin on 25 December of a year she later claimed to be 1785. Though probably born in or about 1778, she was so elusive about her age that even her death certificate could state only 'about 80 years'. As an adult she was extremely short, scarcely above 4 feet (a height which gave credence to her claims of being younger than she was), and she also had a slight deformation to the spine and face, one eye being larger than the other. Her whole life was a bravura performance in which she triumphed over these deficiencies through determination, wit, and sustained creativity.

Although Robert Owenson (whose father's name had been the more purely Irish MacOwen) had been brought up in London, he returned to Ireland in 1776 and chose to remain there, playing various roles in Dublin, Drumcondrath, and Sligo. Until she died in 1789, Jane Owenson educated her daughters, Sydney and Olivia, at home (60 Dame Street, Dublin). An early influence was the schoolboy prodigy Thomas Dermody (1775–1802), rescued from poverty by Robert Owenson (whose only son died in infancy), and hired by him to teach reading and writing to his daughters, though Dermody was scarcely older than they. Some of his early poems were addressed to the Owenson girls. After Jane Owenson's death, Robert sent Sydney and Olivia to private schools. Sydney spent three years at a

Sydney Morgan, Lady Morgan (*bap.* 1783, *d.* 1859), by René Théodore Berthon

Huguenot academy in Clontarf and then attended a finishing school in Earl Street, Dublin, before moving with her father to Sligo.

In 1798, following a downward turn in her father's fortunes, Sydney left home to seek employment as a governess in Dublin. She was hired in that capacity by the Featherstone(haugh)s of Bracklin Castle, co. Westmeath, and soon blossomed into an avid reader, a witty conversationalist, and an unabashed performer of songs and dances. Inspired in part by such feminine predecessors as Anna Seward and Helen Maria Williams, she began to write poetry. Her first volume of verse, conventionally imitative and uniformly self-centred, was published early in 1801 as *Poems*.

In April 1801 Sydney left the Featherstones to join her father at Coleraine in Ulster. She then obtained another position as governess with the Crawford family of Fort William, co. Tipperary, who were unusually inclusive and encouraging. Her long elegy on the death of Tom Dermody in 1802 recalled their relationship in detail ('He taught my timid muse t'expand her wing') and was published in *Walker's Hibernian Magazine*, together with a sonnet of his about her.

Owenson's first novel, *St. Clair*, appeared in Dublin late in 1802 and in London (with a different subtitle) the next year. Written in epistolary form, it is a short idyll of romantic passion, like Goethe's *Werther* and Rousseau's *Nouvelle Héloïse*, but set in Sligo. The female protagonist, called (like her real-life sister) Olivia, is based on Owenson herself, as all of her future heroines would be. After praising Irish music in *St. Clair*, Owenson published separately her versions of two old Irish songs, 'Ned of the Hill' and 'Castle Hyde'.

Owenson's second novel, set in sixteenth-century France, began with an idealized portrait of Thomas Moore (who had performed for the Featherstones and Sydney) and was originally called *The Minstrel* but emerged in published form, much abridged, as *The Novice of St. Dominick* (1805). Filled with rhetoric, adventures, and footnotes, it anticipated the historical novels of Scott. The novel's heroine, Imogen, is again self-referential but more complex than the Olivia of *St. Clair*. Owenson's third and most famous novel (though not her best) was *The Wild Irish Girl* (1806), a heavily footnoted nationalistic tract that she had researched assiduously. Led by his daughter Glorvina (yet again a figure based on Owenson herself), its male protagonist learns gradually to shed his typically English prejudices against all things Irish. The religious strife so crippling to Ireland is deplored. Like her author, Glorvina is 'fairy-like' in stature, well read, and a proficient dancer, singer, and harpist. Once the novel appeared, Owenson herself became known as Glorvina, a major Irish author, and a lion of Dublin society.

The lengthy praise accorded Irish music in *The Wild Irish Girl* had been anticipated by Owenson's own recoveries of it, notably her *Twelve Original Hibernian Melodies* (1805). In 1807 she published a comic opera, her only work of that kind, chimerically entitled *The First Attempt, or, The Whim of a Moment*. The chief comic role, that of a facetious Irish servant, was played by her father; it succeeded admirably, and was his last stage appearance. *The First Attempt* was followed by a volume of rather weak poems, *The Lay of an Irish Harp* (1807) and, in non-fictional prose, *Patriotic Sketches of Ireland* (1807), which included some trenchant social criticism.

Having exhausted her Irish vein for a time (a further novel set in Sligo was laid aside), Owenson turned to the broader themes of women's rights and freedom. William Gell the antiquary suggested that she write about the cause of liberty in Greece and recommended several books for her to consult. But a reading of Germaine de Staël's novel *Corinne* (1807), set in Italy, convinced Owenson to write the novelized tract that *Ida of Athens* became. In her preface to it, she described *Woman, or, Ida of Athens* (1809) as an attempt to delineate perfected feminine character in its natural state and Greece as the perfect setting for doing so—although the final scenes (with Ida suddenly enriched) take place in London. In addition to its feminist concerns, the book includes long philosophical discussions on such Romantic topics as education, civil and religious freedom, and the moral influence of natural beauty.

Owenson's next novel was dedicated to Lady Abercorn, third wife of the first marquess, who had persuaded Sydney to join her as a lady companion at Baron's Court, in Campbell, co. Tyrone (and later at Bentley Priory, Stanmore, Middlesex). Her singing, dancing, and harp-playing continued to be popular. *The Missionary* (1811), with an unsigned portrait of Owenson by Sir Thomas Lawrence as its fashionable frontispiece, is set in India and reflects two religious conflicts: that between the Franciscans and the Dominicans, and that between Christianity and Hinduism. Surpassing both conflicts is the supremacy of love, especially as embodied in Owenson's greatest heroine, the Hindu priestess Luxima, who dies to save her Franciscan missionary lover from the inquisition of the Dominicans.

On 12 January 1812 at Baron's Court, Owenson married the Abercorns' family physician, Sir Thomas Charles *Morgan (*c.*1780–1843), who had been knighted only shortly before, largely at Lady Abercorn's request. Handsome, short, witty, well educated, and musical, he seemed to the Abercorns an ideal match for Sydney, even if a few years younger. She was thereafter Lady Morgan and published her later books under that name. They maintained a residence at 35 Kildare Street, Dublin, from 1812 to 1837.

Lady Morgan did not write another novel until 1814, when *O'Donnel* appeared. No less popular than her earlier ones, and better work, it was realistic, lively, and satiric, with minimally disguised portraits of Lady Abercorn and other offended friends, as well as the usual semi-autobiographical heroine. *O'Donnel* condemned the injustice of British laws penalizing Roman Catholics. Lady Morgan returned to this same theme and conflict—vapid, insolent English pitted against noble, dispossessed Irish—once again in her last Hibernian novel, *The O'Briens and the O'Flahertys* (1826), which displays the influence of Sir Walter Scott and the Gothic romances of Ann Radcliffe.

Lady Morgan also wrote three further novels, *Florence Macarthy* (1818), a serious examination of contemporary Ireland; *The Princess* (1834), begun as a travel book, and set in newly independent Belgium; and, in 1859, *Luxima the Prophetess*, a revised version of *The Missionary* intended to accommodate the recent Sepoy mutiny.

Woman and her Master (1840, but written earlier), a non-fictional attempt at historical scholarship, was a more explicit affirmation of the same concern with women's rights that had infused her novel about Ida; its title is ironic because Lady Morgan argues that women have always been the real leaders of civilization. Of an announced four volumes, only two were published (Old Testament and classical examples), the remainder having to be relinquished because of eye strain. It was her last major literary project.

From 1814 onwards Lady Morgan regarded herself as a perceptive observer of the contemporary scene. Still a devotee of Madame de Staël, she wrote two books about France, which, after the peace of 1815, was again open to English tourists. Her much-noticed visit in 1816 led to many invitations and a two-volume *France* (1817). Revolutionary turmoil and a further visit then prompted *France in 1829–30* (1830), also two volumes, with two two-volume Italian studies in between, *Italy* (1821, appendices by her husband) and *The Life and Times of Salvator Rosa* (1824, a fictionalized biography). Of lesser importance were her essay entitled *Absenteeism* (1825); *The Book of the Boudoir*

(1829), a miscellany; *The Book without a Name* (1841), a collection of previously published essays; *Letter to Cardinal Wiseman* (1851), disputing the authenticity of St Peter's chair; and *An Odd Volume* (1859), composed of autobiographical extracts. Nearly all were forthright, argumentative, and controversial.

Throughout her writing career, Lady Morgan was unusual among women authors for the amount of malicious criticism which she attracted and to which she replied. She was, for example, the presumed author of a spirited reply to John Wilson Croker's anonymous attack, 'Present state of the Irish stage', called 'A few reflections' (both 1804). Croker then became her nemesis for life and pilloried her later productions at every opportunity, beginning retrospectively with *St. Clair*. William Gifford, possibly with Croker's collaboration, rubbished *Woman* in the first issue of the *Quarterly Review* (February 1809). Anticipating his own interest in Greece, Byron mentioned the novel whimsically in a note to *Childe Harold*. But he commented favourably on *The Missionary* in letters, as did Moore and especially Shelley (on whom it was a major influence). In 1814 Byron dismissed *O'Donnel* as 'feminine trash' but Scott read the novel more than once, thinking it 'incomparably superior to *The Wild Irish Girl*—having nature and reality for its foundation' (*The Letters of Sir Walter Scott*, ed. H. J. C. Grierson and others, 12 vols., 1932–7, 3.465). Mary Russell Mitford and Maria Edgeworth also spoke highly of *O'Donnel*. *France* proved to be controversial in both countries, enraging English tories and even attracting a book-length attempt at refutation by William Playfair. In her preface to *France*, Lady Morgan had replied explicitly to the *Quarterly*'s foul review of *Woman*, so in April 1817 Croker and Gifford responded with further savagery, against which Byron protested to John Murray. Lady Morgan then satirized Croker as the suitably detestable Crawley in her novel *Florence Macarthy*. She also responded to critics in a separately published *Letter to the Reviewers of Italy* (1821). That same year Byron praised *Italy* to Moore as 'fearless and excellent'; by then the book and its author were banned in Italy, the Papal States, and Germany. Later on, *Blackwood's Magazine* and *Literary Gazette* also published diatribes against her. In response to *Woman and her Master* in 1840, however, the *Quarterly* partially recanted.

In 1837 the Morgans moved from Kildare Street, Dublin, to 11 William Street, Lowndes Square, London, and thereafter devoted themselves to society. That same year Lady Morgan was granted a civil-list pension of £300 per year 'in acknowledgement of the services rendered by her in the world of letters', the first such pension ever given to a woman. She wrote occasionally for *The Athenaeum* in 1837 and 1838. Outliving her husband, Lady Morgan died on 13 April 1859 at 11 William Street and was buried in Brompton cemetery, where a tomb by Westmacott was placed over her grave. She left an estate of almost £16,000 to her nieces and bequeathed her papers to W. Hepworth Dixon, later to be her first biographer (1862). The Morgans had no children.　　　　　　　　　　　　　　　　　　DENNIS R. DEAN

Sources L. Stevenson, *The wild Irish girl: the life of Sydney Owenson, Lady Morgan* (1936); repr. (New York, 1969) · W. J. Fitzpatrick, *Lady Morgan: her career, literary and personal, with a glimpse of her friends, and a word to her calumniators* (1860) · *Lady Morgan's memoirs: autobiography, diaries, and correspondence*, ed. W. H. Dixon, 2 vols. (1862) · *DNB* · D. R. Dean, introduction, in S. Owenson, *The missionary* (1981) · d. cert.

Archives Bodl. Oxf., letters · Hunt. L., letters · NL Ire., diaries and commonplace books; letters · University of Iowa, Iowa City, papers · Yale U., Beinecke L., MSS | Herts. ALS, letters to Lord Lytton · Leics. RO, letters to Lady Braye and Lady Beauchamp · Maryland Historical Society, Baltimore, letters, mostly to Mrs Patterson [copies] · NL Ire., letters, mostly to Mrs Patterson [copies] · Trinity Cam., letters to Milner Gibson

Likenesses J. Godby, stipple, pubd 1811 (after drawing by T. Lawrence), NG Ire. · T. Levant, portrait, 1811, probably NPG · R. T. Berthon, oils, 1818, NPG · H. Meyer, stipple, pubd 1818, NPG · H. H. Meyer, stipple, pubd 1818 (after C. T. Wageman), NG Ire. · A. Schaffer, portrait, 1819, repro. in Stevenson, *Wild Irish girl* · S. Lover, miniature, 1824, repro. in Stevenson, *Wild Irish girl*, 246 · H. Meyer, stipple, pubd 1824 (after W. Behnes), NG Ire. · R. Cooper, stipple, 1825 (after S. Lover), BM, NPG · R. Cooper, stipple, pubd 1825 (after drawing by S. Lover), NG Ire. · D. D'Angers, medallion, 1829, repro. in Stevenson, *Wild Irish girl* (1936), 274–5 · R. Lefèvre, portrait, 1829, repro. in Stevenson, *Wild Irish girl*, 272 · D. D'Angers, marble bust, c.1830, Bethnal Green Museum, London · C. Martin, pencil drawing, 1844, BM · J. H. Lynch, lithograph, pubd 1855 (after S. Gambardella), NPG · W. Behnes, pen-and-ink drawing, NPG · R. T. Berthon, oils, NG Ire. [*see illus.*] · Bortolius, model of head, repro. in Stevenson, *Wild Irish girl*, 216 · D. D'Angers, bronze medallion, Musée des Beaux Arts, Angers, France · D. D'Angers, plaster bust, Musée des Beaux Arts, Angers, France · T. Lawrence, drawing, Wellington Museum, Apsley House, London · D. Maclise, lithograph, NPG; repro. in *Fraser's Magazine* (1835)

Wealth at death under £16,000: probate, 15 July 1859, *CGPLA Eng. & Wales*

Morgan, Sylvanus (1620–1693), arms painter and author, was born in London in March 1620. Having completed his apprenticeship to John Aleyn (or Allyn), warden of the Painter–Stainers' Company, he became a freeman of the company on 8 April 1644. In 1642 he had written 'A treatise of honor and honorable men', which remained in manuscript. His first printed work, in 1648, was a poem entitled *London, King Charles his Augusta, or, City Royal of the Founders*, which was followed in 1652 by *Horologiographia optica, Dialling Universal and Particular*.

Morgan's best-known work, *The Sphere of Gentry, Deduced from the Principles of Nature: an Historical and Genealogical Work of Arms and Blazon, in Four Books*, was published in 1661–3. Since it was written and partly printed during the Commonwealth, hurried revisions were made to meet the new circumstances of the Restoration; perfect copies are rare. The title-page includes a portrait of Morgan etched by Gaywood. The book was criticized as pedantic by contemporaries, among them the antiquary and Garter king of arms Sir William Dugdale. Some alleged that it was really the work of Edward Waterhouse, the author of *A Discourse and Defence of Arms and Armory* (1660). From its inclusion of substantial information on the Waterhouse family, it is evident that Waterhouse assisted in its compilation. Some perceived merit in parts of the work, but the general view has been critical. M. A. Lower wrote of Morgan's 'antediluvian heraldry' (*The Curiosities of Heraldry*, 1845, 4); the journalist and heraldist Oswald Barron deplored 'the needless complexities [he] introduced into heraldic terminology and practice' (Wagner, *Heralds of*

England, 542), and Wagner himself referred to Morgan's 'wild extravagance' (*Pedigree and Progress*, 1975, 37). Owing to the time and effort expended on this work, Morgan says he neglected his trade as an arms painter and suffered much illness, his house being burnt down. In 1666 Morgan published a supplement, entitled *Armilogia, sive ars chromocritica: the Language of Arms by the Colours and Metals*.

Morgan was a leading member of the Painter–Stainers' Company and was involved in attempts to settle disputes between the company and the College of Arms. On becoming master in 1676 he presented the Painter–Stainers with a portrait of the antiquary and historian William Camden, a former benefactor of the company. This portrait (Painter–Stainers' Hall, London) was worked up from an engraving by R. Gaywood for *The Sphere of Gentry*; the original portrait from which the engraving was taken was destroyed in the great fire of London in 1666. Morgan, who lived near the Royal Exchange in London, died on 27 March 1693, and was buried in the church of St Bartholomew by the Exchange. He was survived by his second wife, Sarah, and a daughter from each of his two marriages; Alice, his first wife, was buried on 8 April 1677, and a son of that marriage predeceased him. The writer on heraldry John Gibbon, a friend, described Morgan as 'a witty man, full of fancy, very agreeable company, [who] lived credibly'. He was, he wrote, 'the prince of armes-painters' (*GM*, 1st ser., 66, 1796, 367). Morgan left a large collection of manuscripts, which came by marriage to Josiah Jones, heraldic painter and painter to Drury Lane Theatre, by whom they were sold by auction in 1759. In the Cambridge University Library there is a manuscript catalogue of books and manuscripts owned by Morgan which relate to heraldry (Dd VI78). Other manuscripts are in the British Library and the Bodleian Library, Oxford.

L. H. CUST, *rev.* COLIN LEE

Sources *GM*, 1st ser., 66 (1796), 366–7 · T. Moule, *Bibliotheca heraldica Magnae Britanniae* (privately printed, London, 1822), 165–8, 176–8 · J. H. Parker Oxspring, 'The Painter–Stainers and their dispute with the heralds', 3 vols., 1966, GL, 49, 155, 300 · will, 2 Feb 1692, GL, MS 9171/45, fols. 108v–109v · parish register, St Bartholomew by the Exchange, 8 April 1677, GL [burial] · A. Wagner, *Heralds of England: a history of the office and College of Arms* (1967) · A. R. Wagner, *Pedigree and progress: essays in the genealogical interpretation of history* (1975) · R. Strong, *Tudor and Jacobean portraits in the National Portrait Gallery* (1969), vol. 1, p. 37 · R. Hyde, *The A–Z of Restoration London* (1992), 27 · court minutes of Painter–Stainers' Company, 1623–49, GL, MS 5667-1, 186 · *IGI* · S. E. Brydges, *Censura literaria*, 10 vols. (1805–9), vol. 2, p. 236

Archives BL, collection of pedigrees, Stowe MSS 599, 639 · BL, occasional additions to an earlier visitation of Yorkshire, Add. MS 18011 · Bodl. Oxf., notes, papers, and pedigrees made and collected by him · CUL, catalogue of books and MSS relating to heraldry in his possession and genealogical notes on various families, Dd VI78

Likenesses R. Gaywood, etching (aged forty-one), BM, NPG; repro. in S. Morgan, *The sphere of gentry* (1661–3), frontispiece

Wealth at death will mentions separate deed of settlement for house; left furnishings to immediate family; large manuscript collection: will, 2 Feb 1692, GL, MS 9171/45, fols. 108v–109v

Morgan, Sir Thomas (d. 1595), soldier, was the third son of William Morgan, a landed gentleman of St George's, Glamorgan, and Pen-carn, Monmouthshire, and his second wife, Ann, daughter of Robert Fortescue of Wood, Devon. Like many other younger sons of gentry origin, Thomas devoted his career entirely to military service and related matters, and he became known as the Warrior. By 1572 he had gained enough experience, perhaps elsewhere in the British Isles or in France, to distinguish him among the English contingents who joined the Dutch revolt against Spain. The capture of Brill by the Sea Beggars on 1 April of that year, rapidly followed by the revolt of Flushing, drew the first of them to the Netherlands, with Morgan commanding a company, 300 strong, to which the British army's 3rd regiment of foot, known as the Buffs, would later trace its origins. At Flushing, where his men contributed vigorously to the town's defence and behaved in less predatory fashion than other foreign forces, Morgan declined an offer of the governorship. However, he rapidly acquired the rank of colonel, after engagements in Zeeland which involved much hand-to-hand fighting and mistaken tactics, owing not least to his own and his fellow commanders' ignorance of the local terrain. Difficulties arose also over the pay of his troops and in his relations with certain of the Netherlands leaders, problems that were to bedevil the remainder of his career.

In January 1574 Morgan returned to England, and was promptly dispatched with some 400 men to Ireland. There, he was sent to assist the president of Munster, his fellow Welshman Sir John Perrot, in monitoring the activities of the earl of Desmond, recently released from imprisonment in London upon conditions that, once home, Desmond seemed reluctant to fulfil. Wounded near Cork, Morgan returned again to England in January 1575. An interlude followed of some three years, possibly spent in Wales, until in 1578 he volunteered afresh for the Netherlands, this time under John Norris's command, and linked to his offer of service a proposal to supply arms and armour to the troops. In August he was at Rijmenant in Malines, where the rebels and their allies defeated Spain's forces led by Don John of Austria and the duke of Parma. In 1581 he assisted in the defence of Ghent, hotbed of radical Calvinism, and in the relief of the northern fortress town of Steenwijk, which Parma captured in the following year. Having again visited England for reinforcements in 1584, Morgan participated in the defence of Antwerp, most notably in recapturing the Kouwensteyn Dyke, key to the plan of the lately assassinated William of Orange to shield the city by flooding the land between it and the Scheldt. But Antwerp fell in August 1585, three days before England was formally committed by the treaty of Nonsuch to the rebels' support.

Having quarrelled repeatedly with Norris, Morgan expected the arrival of the earl of Leicester—who had no time for Norris—as governor-general to bring him enhanced recognition as well as improved conditions for his men. Recognition came in the shape of a series of important commands, beginning with the governorship of Flushing and culminating with that of Bergen op Zoom. But, as he unceasingly complained, his troops continued desperately to lack pay and supplies. Responsibility for these was shuffled between the English government and competing Netherlands authorities with results which, meagre as they were, corrupt suppliers contrived to diminish still further. Yet Morgan remained Leicester's man despite the earl's manifest failure in the Netherlands, and even after his return to England. He himself was there in the spring of 1587, to receive a knighthood from the queen and letters reaffirming his own appointment to Bergen op Zoom which Leicester's replacement, Lord Willoughby d'Eresby, claimed to have no power to confirm. In August 1588 he was there again, this time accompanied by 800 men to assist, belatedly, in the defence against the Spanish Armada. But in September he was hastening back to Bergen op Zoom, armed at last with the Netherlands council of state's confirmation of his governorship, and arrived just in time to repel a major Spanish offensive upon the town.

For the last few years of his active career Morgan remained in charge at Bergen op Zoom, while the rebel provinces shook off their subservience to England and slowly gained the initiative against Spain. There was no direct successor to Willoughby, who withdrew in 1589. Sir Francis Vere became commander-in-chief of the English forces whose commanders had increasingly to defer to the authority of the states general. Nevertheless, the experienced Morgan not infrequently resisted that authority on the strength of his own assessments of military priorities. In any case, no simplification of the chain of command seemed capable of solving the endemic problems of pay and supply. In March 1592 Morgan and eight other leading captains petitioned the privy council for 'an abstracte of a complainte exhibited in the highe courte of parliament' concerning the abuses of merchant suppliers to the Netherlands (PRO, SP 12/244/149). Subsequently Morgan petitioned on his own account, claiming to have been underpaid for several years, to have guaranteed sums in fact owed by Norris, and so to be seriously and unjustly in debt. Prospects of recovery did not improve when in April 1593 the council of state deprived him of his governorship, despite Queen Elizabeth's prompt and personal intervention on his behalf.

Back in Wales, Morgan was sent in October 1595 to garrison and fortify Pembroke Castle against an anticipated Spanish invasion. He died between 22 and 26 December, the same month as his old companion-in-arms, Sir Roger Williams. His contemporaries rated him highly for valour and military expertise: thus, the men he led into Ireland were, according to Williams, 'the first troupes that taught our Nation to like the Musket' (*Works of Sir Roger Williams*, 148). He himself considered his service undervalued in official circles, a view reiterated after his death by his widow, Anna (*d.* 1634), daughter of John de Merode, baron of Julich, whom he had married in 1589. By her account sums amounting to £4200 were due to her late husband under warrants issued long before by Leicester and Willoughby. Yet neither Morgan's legacies of personal effects, including gilt armour, to some of the leading courtiers and soldiers of his day, nor the substantial landed properties which he left in south Wales, indicate his to have been the estate of an impoverished soldier. His two sons having predeceased him, those lands passed to Anne, the elder of his two daughters; while his widow in due course married Justin of Nassau, a natural son of William of Orange whose cause Morgan had so strenuously served.

HOWELL A. LLOYD

Sources G. T. Clark, *Limbus patrum Morganiae et Glamorganiae* (1886) · *The works of Sir Roger Williams*, ed. J. X. Evans (1972) · G. B. Morgan, *Historical and genealogical memoirs of the Morgan family*, 2 vols. (1891–5) · *CSP for.*, 1547–95 · PRO, SP 84/36–46 · BL, Cotton MSS, Galba, Nero, Titus · BL, Egerton MS 1943 · *CSP dom.* · PRO, SP 12/244; 12/250 · H. Sydney and others, *Letters and memorials of state*, ed. A. Collins, 1 (1746) · *The manuscripts of Sir William Fitzherbert ... and others*, HMC, 32 (1893) · *Correspondentie van Robert Dudley graaf van Leycester en andere documenten betreffende zijn gouvernement-generaal in de Nederlanden, 1585–1588*, ed. H. Brugmans, 2 (Utrecht, 1931) · *DNB*
Wealth at death see will, summarized in Clark, *Limbus patrum*

Morgan, Thomas (*b.* 1543, *d.* in or after 1611), Roman Catholic conspirator, came from south Wales and is believed to have been the son of John Morgan of Basaleg (*d.* 1568), a scion of the Tredegar house. He had two brothers, Rowland, a seminary priest who later converted to the Church of England, and Henry, who in 1585 was employed as a customs officer at Cardiff. At an unknown date he married Jane Lewis; they had at least two sons. Although he claimed to have been born of 'honourable and Catholic parents', Thomas began his career as a scrivener in the service of William Alley, bishop of Exeter, before progressing to become secretary to Thomas Young, archbishop of York. After Young's death in 1568, Morgan joined the household of the earl of Shrewsbury, where he came to know the captive Mary, queen of Scots. According to his own account, Morgan made himself useful to her by passing on information which he was able to glean from Shrewsbury, warning her when her rooms were likely to be searched, helping to conceal any incriminating papers, and acting as postman for her private letters.

Morgan's activities started to come to light in the aftermath of the Ridolfi plot early in 1572, and it was Queen Elizabeth herself, 'calling to remembrance his fond busy head, always seeking to deal in other men's matters', who prompted Shrewsbury to make further enquiries (*CSP Scot.*, 4.138). As a result Morgan was sent up to London to the privy council, arrested and committed to the Tower, where he remained for about ten months. No record survives of any interrogation or indictment and he was released, again according to his own account, under a bond of £10,000 not to leave the country or meddle in the queen of Scots's affairs. But in 1574 the matter of Mary's illicit correspondence was once more under investigation and once again Morgan's name came up. In February 1575 Francis Walsingham recommended that he should be arrested. This time, though, he was able to escape to France. A year later Sir Amias Paulet, then ambassador in Paris, reported that an Italian agent, Masino Delbene, had told him that Morgan 'now being in this Towne, is not ignorant of the bottom of all the latter conspiracies betwene the Queene of Scots and her confederats', and was offering to have him kidnapped, on condition only that he 'should not be touched in his lyfe' (Morris, xxv).

The plan came to nothing, but in January 1577 Morgan himself wrote to Lord Burghley protesting his innocence of any crime other than leaving the country without licence, which he had only done for fear of hard usage and imprisonment, and bemoaning the fact that he was thus constrained to live 'with a heavy heart in a foreign land' (Hicks, 96). However, he appears to have been back in England early in 1579. Later that year he visited Rome, becoming involved in the quarrel between the English and Welsh students at the English College, which subsequently developed into the long-running and bitter feud between the secular missionary priests and those belonging to religious orders, especially the Jesuits.

By 1580 Morgan was back in Paris, where he struck up a close friendship with Charles Paget, another member of the expatriate Catholic community. He had also kept in touch with the queen of Scots, who had been sending him money and trying to find him a job, but it was not until May 1581 that she began to give him a regular pension and asked James Beaton, archbishop of Glasgow, her ambassador in France, to employ him as a cipher clerk. This was a position of considerable influence and from now on Morgan became a key figure in the various plots against Elizabeth, controlling as he did virtually all Mary's secret correspondence with foreign powers—he is said to have constructed no fewer than forty cipher alphabets. He was certainly heavily involved with Francis Throckmorton and in autumn 1583 had an interesting conversation with his disreputable fellow countryman William Parry, urging him, so Parry subsequently confessed, to undertake 'some notable Service for God and the Catholick Church'. When Parry said he was prepared to kill the greatest subject in England, Morgan had replied 'why not the Queen herself?' (Holinshed's Chronicles, 4.567–8). After Parry's trial and execution in February 1585, Queen Elizabeth demanded Morgan's extradition. Instead the king of France had him arrested and consigned to the Bastille, an incarceration which does not seem in any way to have hindered him from communicating with the outside world.

The queen of Scots had now been transferred to the custody of Amias Paulet, who had finally succeeded in cutting her off from all unsupervised contact with friends abroad. Then, in October 1585, Morgan received a visit from Gilbert Gifford, one of William Allen's former students, now on his way over to England. Apparently unsuspicious, Morgan pressed him into service as a courier and gave him a letter of introduction to Mary, recommending him in the warmest terms as a well-disposed and trustworthy Catholic gentleman who had 'offered to do all the friendly Offices he may do' (Murdin, 454). This letter was in fact the first to reach her by way of the route set up and controlled by Paulet and Francis Walsingham. During that winter Morgan was busy helping to organize the conspiracy of Anthony Babington and his various associates and in May 1586 advised Mary 'to write three or four lines of your owne Hande to the said Babington, declaring your good Conceit of him, and the Confidence you repose in him' (ibid., 513).

Morgan was finally released from the Bastille in August 1587, some six months after the queen of Scots's execution. In 1588 he made his way to Flanders in order, so he said, to serve the king of Spain, but in January 1590 he was arrested by order of the duke of Parma and tried on suspicion of being an English spy. The result was inconclusive, but Morgan stayed in prison for another two years and was banished from the Low Countries on his release. Whether he had been acting as a double agent remains a matter of speculation. There was certainly some circumstantial evidence against him, and a report by Walsingham's agent Giordano Bruno, who visited him in 1586, indicates that he had helped to betray the Babington plot and was prepared to reveal 'many things' if Elizabeth would get him out of the Bastille (Bossy, 246). Many of his fellow exiles distrusted him, and the queen of Scots was warned more than once that he was 'of all men most suspected to hinder many good attempts enterprised on your Majesty's behalf' (CSP Scot., 7.590). Mary, however, continued to believe in him. Morgan's hostility towards Cardinal Allen and the Jesuits had won him some powerful enemies eager to discredit him. Said to be of 'a most restless and factious disposition' (Foley, 6.14) he was an inveterate intriguer and, like many of his contemporaries in that shadow world of spy and counter-spy, no doubt his first loyalty would always have been to himself.

After leaving Flanders, Morgan travelled to Italy and Spain, and was in Madrid at the time of Allen's death in 1594, when he began to urge the promotion to the cardinalate of his friend and protector Owen Lewis, bishop of Cassano. This led to his expulsion and he went back to Paris, where he became involved in a plot with Henri IV's mistress. He seems to have returned briefly to England in the early 1600s and in August 1605 there is mention of a legacy of 2000 French livres 'left by the late Queen of Scots to Thomas Morgan her faithful servant' (CSP dom., 1603–10, 454). The place of his death is not known, but a letter was addressed to him in Rome in 1611 when he was last known to be alive.

ALISON PLOWDEN

Sources L. Hicks, *An Elizabethan problem: some aspects of the careers of two exile-adventurers* (1964) · W. L. Williams, 'Welsh Catholics on the continent', *Transactions of the Honourable Society of Cymmrodorion* (1901–2), 46–144, esp. 124–7 · *CSP Scot.*, 1571–4; 1584–5 · *A collection of state papers … left by William Cecill, Lord Burghley*, ed. W. Murdin, 2 (1759) · H. Foley, ed., *Records of the English province of the Society of Jesus*, 6 (1880) · 'The memoirs of Father Robert Persons', ed. J. H. Pollen, *Miscellanea, II*, Catholic RS, 2 (1906), 12–218, esp. 48–185 · *CSP Spain, 1568–79* · *The letter-books of Sir Amias Poulet*, ed. J. Morris (1874) · J. H. Pollen, *Mary queen of Scots and the Babington plot*, Scottish History Society, 3rd ser., 3 (1922) · J. Bossy, *Giordano Bruno and the embassy affair* (1991) · *Holinshed's chronicles of England, Scotland and Ireland*, ed. H. Ellis, 6 vols. (1807–8)

Morgan, Sir Thomas, first baronet (1604–1679), army officer, was born on 10 December 1604, probably at Llangattock Lingoed, Monmouthshire, the eldest of the four children of Lewis Morgan, landowner. Aged sixteen, a monoglot Welsh speaker, he joined Sir Horace Vere's protestant volunteer expedition to the Netherlands, where, his diminutive height prompting his commander to liken him to a racoon, he took umbrage and sought service in Germany under Bernard of Saxe-Weimar and, later, the

French. There are few records of his campaigns, but he married on 10 September 1632 an unknown first wife, who seems to have died childless in January 1644. By 1642 he was a captain in Dutch service, where he had fought alongside George Monck and Charles Fairfax; in September he was back in England.

Morgan was a captain of dragoons in Yorkshire under Lord Fairfax by March 1643, and, after the defeat at Adwalton Moor in June, Morgan's troops held up the royalist advance *en route* for Hull. After contributing to the parliamentarian victory at Nantwich on 25 January 1644 Morgan was promoted major and was the chief engineer at the siege of Lathom House the following March. In May he retired, probably through ill health (he was ever a martyr to gout), to Yorkshire, where he married in August his second wife, Delariviere Cholmondeley (*d.* in or before 1683), daughter of John Cholmondeley of Braham Hall, Spofforth, near Knaresborough.

Morgan was made a colonel in February 1645, and, probably on Lord Fairfax's recommendation, was appointed on 18 June governor of Gloucester, in succession to the high-handed Edward Massey, with the task of restoring morale and discipline among unruly soldiers whose just demands for pay arrears he had no means of satisfying. Despite parliament's victory at Naseby, Gloucester was isolated amid royalist garrisons at Worcester, Bristol, Monmouth, Chepstow, Raglan, and Hereford, and needed a governor of the utmost vigilance. Although at first unable to counter Rupert's *chevauchées* from Bristol, and desperately short of cavalry, Morgan gradually won the respect of the citizens of Gloucester and of his metropolitan masters. He captured Berkeley Castle on 25 September 1645 and, alongside Sir Trevor Williams, Chepstow (10 October) and Monmouth (25 October).

In conjunction with John Birch, Morgan led the surprise capture of Hereford on 18 December. In March 1646 he was allotted the task of shadowing Sir Jacob Astley's royalist force as it moved south to join Charles I, and he was in command, alongside Birch and Sir William Brereton, when Astley was defeated at Stow on the Wold on 21 March. By now (25 April) commander of all parliament's forces in Gloucestershire, Herefordshire, and Monmouthshire, Morgan failed to capture Worcester, but he took Hartlebury Castle on 16 May and then began a three-month siege of Raglan Castle, which surrendered on 19 August once Sir Thomas Fairfax arrived to stiffen the assault. Morgan arranged the conditions of surrender. Although granted £500 for faithful service in January 1647, Morgan then seems to have fallen out of favour as his troops became mutinous over disbandment, pay arrears, and possible dispatch to service in Ireland; he was superseded as governor of Gloucester in January 1648 by Sir William Constable. Despite a recommendation from Lord Fairfax, Morgan failed to secure an Irish command in October, and he retired to his wife's property in Yorkshire until 1651.

For six years from mid-1651 Morgan was Monck's faithful adjutant in Scotland. He was at the sack of Dundee on 1 September 1651 and captured Dunnottar Castle on 26 May 1652, though the royal regalia stored there slipped through his hands. Activity then moved to the highlands, and Morgan was put in command of all forces north of the Tay, based on Inverness. He found great difficulty in engaging Middleton's elusive royalist troops, but finally defeated him at Dalnaspidal, near Loch Garry, on 19 July 1654. By September he had settled Caithness to Monck's satisfaction, and he was appointed major-general in February 1655.

In April 1657 Morgan was sent to aid the French in Flanders, as second-in-command to Sir John Reynolds, who was often ill or in England, having recently married a young wife. Morgan, who thought the French commander, Marshal Turenne, dilatory, was slightly wounded at the siege of St Venant in August, but he captured Mardyke the following month. On Reynolds's death in December Morgan's failure to deal adequately with Anglo-French antagonisms probably lost him the overall command to Sir William Lockhart, the English ambassador in Paris, who was thought to have the diplomatic skills lacking in the stubborn, choleric Welshman. Morgan, who was not the man to forget an injury, fancied or real, bore a lasting grudge against Lockhart and at times did his utmost to thwart his plans. He effectively led the English contingent's major contribution to the victorious battle of the Dunes (4–14 June 1658), and after the capture of Dunkirk on 25 June continued to serve under Turenne, helping to capture Bergues, Furnes, Nieuport, Gravelines, Oudenarde, and Ypres (June–August), at the last of which he was again slightly wounded. Morgan's *Narrative* of the campaign, dictated in 1675 (and published in 1699) is a highly coloured exercise in nationalistic braggadocio, but the facts he relates are confirmed by other evidence, and years later his exploits before Dunkirk were extolled by Matthew Prior to his tutor in Paris. Possibly its most important value is in its depiction of a Cromwellian soldier: his pre-battle cheerfulness, eagerness to fight, and merciless ferocity in action.

Knighted by Richard Cromwell on 25 November 1658, Morgan hoped for a speedy return to his Scottish command, where Monck needed him to restore discipline among his discontented troops. As Morgan moved north in October 1659, a letter to him from Monck was intercepted by Robert Lilburne at York. To Lilburne and Lambert, whose expulsion of the Rump Parliament was disliked by Monck, Morgan simulated disgust at Monck's behaviour, promised to induce him to disarm, and seems to have suggested that, in the event of Monck's obduracy, he would try to alienate his soldiery from their commander. But once in Edinburgh, on 8 November, Morgan, bringing him a letter of support from Lord Fairfax, threw in his lot with Monck, who confided in him his intention to restore the monarchy. 'By his brisk energy, [Morgan] transformed the indifferent into active partisans and the sullen into obedient troops' (Lewis, 219), especially reorganizing Monck's cavalry. He accompanied Monck into England in January 1660, but at York he was sent back to Scotland to take command of the forces left there, and in Edinburgh he lived with his wife in Holyroodhouse in some pomp. At the celebration of the king's Restoration on 19 June, Morgan himself let off the huge cannon, Mons Meg. His services in Scotland were rewarded by a baronetcy on 1 February 1661.

Morgan left Scotland on 20 May 1662 for Portugal, where, in the aftermath of Charles II's Portuguese marriage, English troops were sent, under Inchiquin, to bolster the national struggle against Spain, with Morgan commanding the infantry. But Alfonso VI looked on the English as intruders, tried to incorporate them into the Portuguese forces, failed to pay them, and housed them in hovels. Morgan formally protested to Charles II at their treatment in November and himself returned to England the following month. He spent the years 1662–5 building up a landed estate in Herefordshire, centred on Chanstone Court, near Vowchurch, and Kinnersley Castle.

On 20 December 1665, at Monck's suggestion, Morgan was made governor of Jersey, with the task of ordering its military defence against a putative French assault from St Malo (which was in fact abandoned soon after his arrival). Although his imperious behaviour had increased with age, his vigilance and care endeared him to the local inhabitants, even if, as an autocratic man of action who failed to see the need for endless debates on comparatively trivial matters, he found the discussions of the states insufferably tedious, and their obstructiveness at times depressing. Morgan repaired the island's forts, especially Elizabeth Castle in St Helier, reorganized and armed the local militia, fitted out ships against the French and Dutch privateers who disrupted the island's trade, pandered to the states' little vanities, and undertook in 1671 to pay for the construction of a pier at St Aubin, in return for a share of the enhanced customs duties its erection would produce. He even advanced original ideas to combat increasing poverty on the island—urging the inhabitants to settle in Ireland, New England, and New Jersey, and the states to introduce a modified primogeniture in land inheritance instead of the prevailing gavelkind.

Increasingly wracked by gout, Morgan spent long periods of the 1670s in England; but he failed to engineer his retirement, and died at Elizabeth Castle in St Helier on 13 April 1679. His entrails were buried in St Helier parish church on 16 May, his body in St Martin-in-the-Fields, London, on 1 June. In addition to Chenstone and Kinnersley in Herefordshire, Morgan had inherited land in Monmouthshire and bought Henbury Park, Tutbury, Staffordshire (1650) and Braham Hall, near Knaresborough, his second wife's home, a few years before his death. Of his ten children, four sons and a daughter survived him. His eldest son, John (c.1650–1693), became governor of Chester (1689) and MP for New Radnor (1681) and for Herefordshire (1685, 1689, and 1690–93). The baronetcy became extinct in 1767.

Undersized, pipe-smoking, and with a distinctive high-pitched voice, Morgan—though almost illiterate and signing his name with difficulty—was one of the most efficient officers thrown up by the civil war. Although no innovator in methods of attack or strategic planning, he was a master of drills and siege warfare. Popular with his men, whose welfare was always his especial concern, he had an explosive temper and susceptibility to flattery, but even these were considered lovable traits. He was surprisingly dogged and tenacious for such an impatient man, and, as Monck's valued lieutenant, his supreme self-confidence and contempt for danger were an inspiration. He was as chivalrous in victory as he was stubborn in defeat. At bottom a loyal and obedient professional soldier, he had no pronounced political or religious views, accepting changes of government with calm indifference.   BASIL MORGAN

Sources D. G. Lewis, 'Sir Thomas Morgan bart, 1604–1679', MA diss., U. Wales, 1930 · *DNB* · *DWB*, 652–3 · GEC, *Baronetage*, vol. 3 · M. Ashley, *General Monck* (1977) · A. C. Saunders, *Jersey in the 17th century* (1931) · G. R. Balleine, *A history of the island of Jersey* (1950) · HoP, *Commons, 1660–90*, 3.97–8 · *Aubrey's Brief lives*, ed. O. L. Dick (1949); repr. (1962), 284 · R. Hutton, *The royalist war effort, 1642–1646*, pbk edn (1984) · A. Clark, *The story of Monmouthshire*, 1 (1962) · J. D. Griffith Davies, *Honest George Monck* (1936) · C. H. Firth, *Cromwell's army*, 3rd edn (1921); repr. (1962) · J. Childs, *The army of Charles II* (1976) · C. J. O. Evans, *Monmouthshire* (1954)

Archives NAM, corresp. and papers · NL Scot., corresp. relating to Scottish regalia · S. Antiquaries, Lond., account of travel in France and Flanders | BL, letters as governor of Jersey to Lord Hatton, Add. MSS 28552–29557

Likenesses G. Smeeton, engraving, pubd 1814 (after drawing by unknown artist), NPG · C. W. Bampfylde, wash drawing (after Sir A. Vandyke), AM Oxf. · E. Gulston, etching (after wash drawing by C. W. Bampfylde), BM, NPG

Wealth at death left land in four counties (Yorkshire, Staffordshire, Herefordshire, and Monmouthshire); land and money to all four sons; £6000 to daughter; manor house of Chanstone in Vowchurch, Herefordshire, and Kinnersley Castle, Herefordshire, to his eldest son: will, Lewis, 'Sir Thomas Morgan', 316

Morgan, Thomas (d. 1743), theological and medical writer, was of Welsh origin and is said to have been 'a poor lad in a farmer's house' (*Protestant Dissenter's Magazine*, 258) near Bridgwater, Somerset. Of his parents nothing is known. In his youth he showed enough promise for a dissenting minister, John Moore (1642?–1717), to give him a free education, the cost of his living being provided by his friends. He was made Independent minister at Bruton in Somerset but was ordained by the Presbyterian minister John Bowden at Frome in 1716 and was subsequently minister of a congregation at Marlborough, Wiltshire. He married Mary, eldest daughter of Nathaniel Merriman, a prominent dissenter of Marlborough.

Although orthodox at the time of his ordination Morgan was dismissed from the ministry soon after 1720 on account of his views. These had been made public in a pamphlet controversy relating to the Salters' Hall conference in 1719, at which dissenters had debated the need for subscription to articles of faith by their ministry. The contours of the controversy can be traced in *A collection of tracts, relating to the right of private judgement, the sufficiency of scripture, and the terms of church-communion; upon Christian principles: occasion'd by the late Trinitarian controversy* (1726), a compilation of Morgan's writings from the years 1717 to 1724. Advocacy of the anti-subscription position and expression of doubts regarding the Athanasian view of the Trinity in these writings show the seeds of Morgan's subsequent development from 'Protestant Dissenter', as he described himself in a 1720 pamphlet, to self-professed 'Christian Deist'.

Following the loss of his livelihood Morgan took to the study of medicine, although where and when he acquired his degree is unknown; he describes himself as MD on the title-pages of his books in 1726 and afterwards. What he gained from his medical studies may be gauged from his *Philosophical Principles of Medicine* (1725; 2nd edn, 1730), an intriguing attempt to apply the principles of the mechanical philosophy to medicine. A further work on this theme, *The Mechanical Practice of Physic*, appeared in 1735, followed by a defence addressed to the physician George Cheyne, *A Letter to Dr. Cheyne in Defence of the Mechanical Practice* (1738). In philosophical matters Morgan was much puzzled by the problem of free will, and in *A Letter to Mr T. Chubb Occasioned by his … Vindication of Human Nature* (1727) he defended the corruption of human nature against the more optimistic assessment of the deist Thomas Chubb. A year later he again wrote against Chubb, in *A Defence of Natural and Revealed Religion* (1728), this time in support of the views of the Quaker apologist Robert Barclay.

Despite his opposition to certain of Chubb's views Morgan himself was destined to be labelled a fellow deist. This reputation was due largely to the work for which he is best known, *The Moral Philosopher*, published anonymously in 1737 (2nd edn, 1738), which took the form of 'a dialogue between Philalethes, a Christian Deist, and Theophanus, a Christian Jew'. A second volume, by Philalethes, in answer to John Leland and John Chapman, appeared in 1739, and a third, against Leland and Moses Lowman, in 1740. In this work Morgan suggested that the relative merits of competing religions should be determined by moral criteria. He also highlighted the diverse nature of early Christianity; as Leland put it, 'He pretends that the Apostles preached different gospels, and that the New Testament is a jumble of inconsistent religions' (Leland, 131). With the appearance of what is sometimes referred to as a fourth volume in the series, *Physico-Theology* (1741), Morgan generated further controversy by casting doubt upon the moral probity of the Old Testament patriarchs. As a consequence of this work he became embroiled in an acrimonious dispute with the dissenting minister Samuel Chandler, whose father, ironically, had preached at Morgan's ordination. His last works, *Vindication of the Moral Philosopher* (1741) and *The History of Joseph Considered* (1744), are responses to Chandler.

While commonly regarded as just another deist Morgan's originality lay in his application of the tools of historical criticism to scripture and to the history of religions. In the various controversies in which he was engaged he showed a keen intelligence and an enviable ability to turn the arguments of his opponents against them. He died 'with true Christian resignation' (*GM*) on 14 January 1743. He was survived by his wife and an only son.   PETER HARRISON

Sources DNB · *Protestant Dissenter's Magazine*, 1 (1794) · R. Williams, *Enwogion Cymru: a biographical dictionary of eminent Welshmen* (1852) · GM, 1st ser., 13 (1743), 51 · *Monthly Repository*, 13 (1818), 735 · J. Leland, *A view of the principal deistical writers*, 3rd edn, 1 (1757) · P. Harrison, *'Religion' and the religions in the English Enlightenment* (1990) · L. Stephen, *History of English thought in the eighteenth century*, 3rd edn, 1 (1902) · H. Chandler, *A sermon preach'd at the ordination of Mr. Thomas Morgan … with Mr. Morgan's confession of faith … and the exhortation … by the Reverend Mr. John Bowden*, 2nd edn (1717)

Morgan, Sir Thomas Charles [*pseud.* µ] (*c*.1780–1843), philosopher and writer, was the eldest son of John Morgan of Charlotte Street, Bloomsbury, London. He was educated at Eton College, the Charterhouse, and Peterhouse, Cambridge, where he graduated MB in 1804 and proceeded MD in 1809.

Morgan practised at first as a surgeon in Charlotte Street, and on 13 April 1805 married a daughter of William Hammond of Queen Square, Bloomsbury, and the stock exchange. She died in 1809, leaving one child, a daughter. Morgan was a friend and admirer of Edward Jenner, the discoverer of vaccination, and published in 1808 *An expostulatory letter to Dr. Moseley on his review of the report of the London College of Physicians*. On 30 September 1809 he was admitted a candidate, and on 1 October 1810 a fellow of the College of Physicians.

As his physician, Morgan attended the first marquess of Abercorn to Ireland, and through the marquess's interest was knighted by the lord lieutenant, Charles Lennox, fourth duke of Richmond, in Dublin on 17 September 1811. At Abercorn's seat, Baron's Court, co. Tyrone, Morgan met, and on 12 January 1812 married, a protégée of the marchioness, Sydney Owenson (*bap.* 1783, *d.* 1859) [see Morgan, Sydney] then rising into repute as a popular author. After the marriage Morgan obtained the post of physician to the Marshalsea, Dublin, a sinecure that he retained until its abolition in 1834. He took a house in Dublin, at 35 Kildare Street, with the view of establishing a practice. Between 1815 and 1824, however, most of his time was spent abroad with Lady Morgan to whose works *France* (1818) and *Italy* (1821) he contributed appendices on law, medicine, industry, finance, political opinion, and literary disputes.

In 1818 Morgan published *Sketches of the Philosophy of Life*, and in 1822 *Sketches of the Philosophy of Morals*, in which he attempted to popularize the ideas of Bichat, Cabanis, and Destutt de Tracy. The former work, a medical treatise, was unsparingly attacked for its materialism by the Revd Thomas Rennell, and Morgan's professional reputation was so seriously damaged that he retired from practice. The latter book fell almost stillborn from the press. Both works were, however, welcomed on the continent and translated into French under the supervision of de Tracy. *Sketches of the Philosophy of Morals* was published in a new edition in 1916 under the title *The Moral Philosophy of Free Thought*. In it Morgan argues for a moral code founded upon the observation of human conduct, rather than on abstract reasoning, and endorses a species of utilitarianism.

Morgan was a strenuous advocate of Catholic emancipation and other liberal measures, and on the return of the whigs to power was placed on the commission of inquiry into the state of Irish fisheries (1835). He took an active part in the investigation, and compiled a 'Historical sketch of the British and Irish fisheries', for the appendix to the first report (*Parl. papers*, 1837, 22). In 1824 the Morgans returned to their home at 35 Kildare Street, Dublin, where their evening receptions became famous. In 1837 they moved to William Street, Lowndes Square, London, where Morgan died on 28 August 1843. Morgan contributed over 150 slight essays to the *New Monthly Magazine* from its inception under the editorship of Thomas Campbell until 1843. He also wrote for *The Metropolitan* and other periodicals. Those in the *New Monthly* are distinguished by the signature μ. The best of these trifles are collected in the *Book without a Name* (2 vols., 1841), to which Lady Morgan also contributed.

Morgan was an extremely minute philosopher, or rather *philosophe*. His mental calibre is evinced by an anecdote recorded by Crabb Robinson. Robinson quoted Kant's well-known apophthegm, 'there are two things which excite my admiration—the moral law within me and starry heavens above me', upon which Morgan exclaimed contemptuously 'German sentiment, and nothing else', adding, 'The starry heavens, philosophically considered, are no more objects of admiration than a basin of water' (*Diary, Reminiscences, and Correspondence*, 1.408).

J. M. RIGG, *rev.* C. A. CREFFIELD

Sources Munk, *Roll* · *GM*, 2nd ser., 20 (1843), 436 · *Lady Morgan's memoirs: autobiography, diaries, and correspondence*, ed. W. H. Dixon, 2 vols. (1862) · L. Stevenson, *The wild Irish girl: the life of Sydney Owenson, Lady Morgan* (1936) · *The Athenaeum* (2 Sept 1843), 794 · *Diary, reminiscences, and correspondence of Henry Crabb Robinson*, ed. T. Sadler, 3rd edn, 2 vols. (1872) · Venn, *Alum. Cant.* · *Wellesley index* · W. J. Fitzpatrick, *Lady Morgan: her career, literary and personal, with a glimpse of her friends, and a word to her calumniators* (1860)
Likenesses J. Clarke, lithograph, pubd 1841, BM, NPG

Morgan [Morgan Wolff], **Walter** (*b. c.*1550, *d.* in or after 1604), soldier and map maker, probably originated from Monmouthshire, where a Morgan Wollph is recorded as the earl of Pembroke's tenant in 1583. His parentage and education are unknown. He supplied some autobiographical details in a letter to Walsingham of 19 June 1587: his childhood ambition was to be a soldier; after serving on the protestant side in France he joined William I of Orange in the Low Countries, *inter alia* acting as his cartographer. This could refer to William's campaign in 1568.

Service in France qualified Walter for joining the levy raised by his relative Thomas Morgan in London in the spring of 1572 in aid of the rebellious provinces. Sir Roger Williams, a volunteer in the expeditionary force, praised Captain Morgan's valour at Middelburg and Goes, where he was wounded. In December 1572 Morgan was one of the officers on whose behalf the high court of admiralty issued warrants to ensure payment of arrears to them and their soldiers. He possibly took part in the famous capture of Brill, the first of the exploits described in the account of the campaign he sent to Burghley early in 1574. This manuscript, now in All Souls College, Oxford, has eighteen coloured maps of battles and sieges, based partly on personal experience and partly on existing illustrated broadsides, though opinions differ on which these were. The dedicatory letter envisages a continuation which was never added. Authors before Barber, ignorant of Morgan's full name, assume that he died during his next stay in the Netherlands, for which he is said to have levied troops in 1574. One report alleges that the Spanish tried to subvert him. If true, Morgan would undoubtedly have rejected such proposals.

Among references pointing to Morgan are strong recommendations to William Davison in Brussels of 'Captain Morgan' by Edward Horsey in Windsor (*CSP for.*, 11 Nov 1577), and to Walsingham of his 'cousin Morgan Woollphe' by Thomas Morgan, of 'my friend and kinsman Capt. Morgan' by John Herbert, and of 'Captain Morgan Wolfe' by Lord Willoughby (*CSP for.*, 12 June 1587, 17 Nov 1587, and 13 Dec 1587). As 'Morgan' he may have been captured and ransomed in 1588 (Churchyard, sig. D1), and, as 'Capitaine Wolf', played a prominent part in the capture of Geertruidenberg in 1593, described in d'Aubigné's *Histoire universelle* (identified without source by the modern editor as 'Christophle', but more likely from the context to be Walter Morgan).

There are firmer proofs of Morgan's survival. His letters to Walsingham of 9 May and 19 June 1587 attest his presence in Flanders, as do two maps dated 1588 now in the British Library (BL, Cotton MSS Aug. I.ii.107 and 115). The map of Bergen op Zoom is signed 'wallter morgan wooullphe Proffesor of Arms'; that of Flushing is unsigned, but its handwriting and style declare Morgan's authorship. The text in the cartouches also has much in common with his letters to Walsingham, remarking on both personal and military matters. Any other extant manuscript maps by Morgan will be unsigned and still unrecognized. A large printed map of 1604 of the siege of Ostend proves him to have been alive then, so far the latest known date. The map, which shows the town in April 1604 and has two insets depicting it in July and August, is signed 'WOLFF.INVENT.FLOR.BALT.SCULP ET IMPRE^s' (that is, Walter Morgan Wolff designed it and Florens Balthasarsz van Berckenrode, cartographer to Prince Maurice of Orange and the states general of the United Provinces, engraved and printed it). It may have been made at Maurice's request. It has been reproduced from a broadside (Hollstein, 2.9), and from its inclusion at the end of part 1 in *Belägerung der Statt Ostende* (Simoni, 60–61).

The quality of Walter Morgan's work as a map maker has been disputed. Oman accuses him of inaccuracy in the All Souls manuscript drawings, though their artistic merit is generally acknowledged. However, Morgan never intended technical correctness in them, as he explains in the dedication of his book. Groenveld stresses their place in the visual sources for Dutch history, which makes them important also for English military history. The manuscript maps in the British Library are well drawn and their lettering is of high quality. Their military value would have been immediate. The printed map of Ostend presents detailed historical information. Moreover, like other maps of the time, it makes a political as well as a factual statement, extolling English and Dutch defiance of Spanish aggression, linking it to the whole body of contemporary literature on this event. ANNA E. C. SIMONI

Sources D. Caldecott-Baird, *The expedition in Holland, 1572–1574: the revolt of the Netherlands: the early struggle for independence, from the manuscript of Walter Morgan* (1976) • *CSP for.*, esp. 1577–8; 1587 • A. E. C. Simoni, 'Walter Morgan Wolff: an Elizabethan soldier and his maps', *Quaerendo*, 26 (1996), 58–76 • C. Oman, 'On Walter Morgan's sketches presented to Lord Burghley', *Archaeological Journal*, 87 (1931), 1–17 • T. S. Jansma, 'Een Engels kroniekje over de eerste jaren van de Opstand (1572–1574)', *Bijdragen en mededelingen betreffende de geschiedenis der Nederlanden*, 93 (1978), 450–82 • S. Groenveld, 'Het Engels kroniekje van Walter Morgan en een onbekende reeks historieprenten', *Bijdragen en mededelingen betreffende de geschiedenis der Nederlanden*, 98 (1983), 19–74 • P. Barber, 'England II: monarchs, ministers and maps, 1550–1625', *Monarchs, ministers and maps: the emergence of cartography as a tool of government in early modern Europe*, ed. D. Buisseret (1992), 57–98, esp. 75–6 • R. Williams, *The actions of the Low Countries*, ed. D. W. Davies (1943) • F. A. d'Aubigné, *L'histoire universelle*, ed. A. de Ruble, 10 vols. (1886–1909), vol. 8 • *Belägerung der Statt Ostende* (1604–5) • T. Churchyard, *A plaine or moste true report of a daungerous service … by English men, Scottes men, Wallons and other worthy soldiours, for the takyng of Macklin* (1580) • D. J. B. Trim, 'Fighting "Jacob's wars": the employment of English and Welsh mercenaries in the European wars of religion; France and the Netherlands, 1562–1610', PhD diss., U. Lond., 2002 • F. W. H. Hollstein, *Dutch and Flemish etchings, engravings and woodcuts, c.1450–1700*, 1 (1949) • BL, Add. MS 26156
Archives All Souls Oxf. • BL, Cotton MSS Aug.I.ii.107; 115

Morgan, Sir William (1541–1583), soldier, was probably born at Pen-coed Castle, Monmouthshire, where his great-grandfather had settled from nearby Langston Court, the family's ancestral home. He was the eldest son of Sir Thomas Morgan (d. 1565), a landed gentleman and soldier, and his wife, Cecilia, daughter of Sir George Herbert of Swansea. Knighted for military service like his father and grandfather before him, Sir Thomas was by the time of his death an influential local figure (though perhaps not as influential as they), and had added considerably to his landed estate. William, his heir, soon embarked upon a military career. In 1572, following the Dutch Sea Beggars' momentous capture of Brill in April, England's ambassador in Paris, Sir Francis Walsingham, helped him to join the army led by Louis of Nassau from France towards the Netherlands. Morgan distinguished himself in action at Valenciennes, and especially at Mons for refusing to surrender to the Spaniards on terms dictated by their general, Alva.

Morgan returned to England early in 1573 to participate, with several companies from his Netherlands campaign, in the colonizing venture to eastern Ulster organized by his 'cousin' Walter, first Devereux earl of Essex. The venture proved disastrous. Inadequately resourced, it degenerated into acts of reprisal against Irish occupants of the lands at issue. The terms and conditions that the earl had agreed with the queen were ruinous to him. Other private investors were insufficient and unreliable. This was not so with Morgan whom Essex adjudged 'wise, honest and valiant', promoting him to the rank of marshal and recommending him for a knighthood. The queen dubbed him accordingly, at Bristol in August 1574; but by then the recipient had paid a heavy price for engaging in military,

and especially Irish, affairs. Having served, as Essex noted, 'to his own great charge and travail' (PRO, SP 63/46, fol. 13), he had soon to sell several of his Welsh manors, including Langston, to pay his debts. His marriage to Elizabeth Judde, daughter of the prosperous London alderman Sir Andrew *Judde, founder of Tonbridge School, probably dates from this time.

Appointment as vice-admiral of south Wales brought Morgan opportunities to restore his fortunes, and not only through his rightful share of wrecks and salvage within his jurisdiction. Vice-admirals were expected to combat piracy, a sufficiently irksome problem around the kingdom's western coasts. While he left the duties of the office largely to deputies who included his own kinsmen, suspicions arose that they and he connived with the very predators they ought to have suppressed. In Morgan's case the admiralty judges found such allegations unproven; yet they served to alert the privy council to his activities. In 1577 the council investigated reports that he was preparing in Wales a secret naval, expedition. In 1578 a further investigation followed an official report that the London watch had discovered Morgan, in company with Sir Warham St Leger, grandson of a former Irish lord deputy, in clandestine conversation with the French ambassador at a place that agents of the imprisoned queen of Scots were known to frequent. Nothing came of either inquiry, but Morgan's tenure of the vice-admiralty was not renewed after 1578.

Meanwhile Morgan's financial circumstances worsened, for reasons reminiscent of the royal 'bargain' that Essex had struck in 1573. It was Morgan's failure to settle a sizeable debt to the queen that led to the crown's seizing nearly all his remaining property in 1579. Ireland seemed again to offer prospects at least of employment, and perhaps of relief. Following the outbreak of the Desmond rebellion in the summer and autumn of that year, the English garrison in Munster was augmented. Morgan obtained command of a force of cavalry and foot, to be recruited largely in Wales and then shipped to Cork, where St Leger was now provost-marshal. While the appointment involved him in significant initial expenditure, it brought him the constableship of Dungarvan Castle, eastwards along the coast from Cork, beyond Youghal where he was made governor as well. His resourcefulness and reliability again won him his fellow officers' applause; yet sixteenth-century Ireland in a condition of active unrest was no place for a soldier to make money. Despite operating successfully inland from his Youghal base, Morgan was soon driven to beg Lord Treasurer Burghley for a grant that might yield him profit. None was forthcoming, though in due course the suppliant was repaid some of his earlier outlay.

Problems of supply, in a context of revolt and countermeasures which spread desolation and impoverishment on all sides, accelerated Morgan's disillusionment. By February 1581 he was appealing to his old supporter Walsingham for leave to return home. Almost another year went by before he obtained his discharge. Even then financial difficulties pursued him. Having cleared £300 by selling his governorship of Dungarvan, he was alleged by the vice-treasurer for Ireland to have obtained improperly sums in excess of that amount, from government sources. Thus embarrassed, Sir William died in the autumn of 1583, his wife apparently having predeceased him. As there were no surviving children of the marriage, his gravely depleted estate was inherited by the infant daughter of his late brother, Henry.

Highly regarded by the members of the military fraternity with whom he served, Morgan may fairly be seen as a victim of the ethos, prevalent among large sections of the gentry and the peerage, upon which the Elizabethan regime relied for the conduct of its Irish and other wars. Lacking a standing army, the regime could not meet from crown revenues and taxation the cost of military, naval or colonizing ventures. Much of the cost had therefore to be met through the willingness of military adventurers to spend their substance and even their lives accordingly, to the point of mortgaging their own fortunes to the crown for the purpose. That they did so in hope of material reward scarcely detracts from their commitment. And that the ethos survived their regular disappointments contributed critically to the survival of the regime itself.

HOWELL A. LLOYD

Sources A. C. Miller, 'Sir William Morgan of Pencoed: "a man much to be accounted of"', *Welsh History Review / Cylchgrawn Hanes Cymru*, 9 (1978–9), 1–31 · *CSP Ire.*, 1574–85 · State papers, Ireland, PRO, SP 63/40–88 · W. B. Devereux, *Lives and letters of the Devereux, earls of Essex … 1540–1646*, 2 vols. (1853) · *DNB* · O. Morgan and T. Wakeman, *Notices of Pencoyd Castle and Langstone* (1864) · G. T. Clark, *Limbus patrum Morganiae et Glamorganiae* (1886) · W. R. B. Robinson, 'Sir William Morgan of Pencoed (*d.* 1542) and the Morgans of Tredegar and Machen in Henry VIII's reign', *National Library of Wales Journal*, 27 (1992), 405–29 · PRO, SP 12/124/12 · H. A. Lloyd, 'The Essex inheritance', *Welsh History Review / Cylchgrawn Hanes Cymru*, 7 (1974–5), 13–39 · H. Sydney and others, *Letters and memorials of state*, ed. A. Collins, 2 vols. (1746) · C. G. Cruickshank, *Elizabeth's army*, 2nd edn (1966)

Archives PRO

Morgan, William (1544/5–1604), bishop of St Asaph and biblical translator, was born between 19 December 1544 and 14 April 1545, but most probably early in 1545, in 'y Tyddyn Mawr ym mlaen Wybrnant', that is Tŷ-mawr Wybrnant, in the parish of Penmachno, Caernarvonshire, the second son of John Morgan and Lowri Williams. Both his parents were gently born, the father claiming descent from Nefydd Hardd, the mother from Marchudd. John Morgan was a subtenant of the Wynn family of Gwydir near Llanrwst; his home, which has been restored by the National Trust, is that of a relatively prosperous yeoman farmer.

Education The Wynns of Gwydir kept a family chaplain who also taught the sons of the family and, it seems, selected pupils from the locality. It was in this way that William Morgan acquired a grammar school education, although he may have later (about 1564) gone to Westminster School to achieve a final polish before proceeding to university. Probably because the Wynn family had connections with St John's College, Cambridge, Morgan joined that college, and matriculated early in 1565, first as a sub-sizar and later as a proper sizar. He graduated BA in 1568, MA in 1571, BTh in 1578, and DTh in 1583; on the last occasion he disputed with Peter Baro, the Lady Margaret professor of divinity. His Cambridge education provided him not only with a general mastery of the liberal arts but also with a thorough knowledge of the original languages of the Bible: his Hebrew tutors probably included two able Frenchmen, Antoine Chevalier and Philip Bignon. Morgan's theological position as a Calvinist episcopalian was also clearly in evidence during his college career: he refused to discard his surplice during the puritan demonstrations at St John's College in late 1565, and some four years later he was satirized by Stephen Valenger in his poem 'The Cuckolds' Calendar', almost certainly as a member of the anti-puritan faction led by John Whitgift. Morgan's appointment as a university preacher in 1575 may be thought to confirm his position as a spokesman of the ecclesiastical establishment.

Progress in the church William Morgan's career in the Welsh church began, at least formally, long before he completed his studies at Cambridge. He was admitted to deacon's orders by the bishop of Ely on 15 April 1568 and to priest's orders on 18 December 1568. Fairly soon after graduating MA, Morgan was in 1572 preferred by Richard Davies, bishop of St David's, to the vicarage of Llanbadarn Fawr in Cardiganshire, but it is unlikely that he spent much time there. In 1575 the recently installed bishop of St Asaph, William Hughes, a fellow Cantabrigian, took Morgan under his wing and preferred him to the vicarage of Welshpool in Montgomeryshire and the sinecure rectory of Denbigh. In 1578, with the completion of his degree of BTh, he was ready for pastoral responsibility, becoming on 1 October vicar of Llanrhaeadr-ym-Mochnant (with Llanarmon Mynydd Mawr), a parish straddling the border between Montgomeryshire and Denbighshire. At the same time he relinquished Welshpool but retained Denbigh. The rectory of Llanfyllin and the sinecure rectory of Pennant Melangell, both in Montgomeryshire, were added to him in 1579 and 1588 respectively. The four benefices together brought him a comfortable annual income of rather more than £100; his appointment as a bishop's chaplain on 9 March 1582 would have added to his prestige rather than his income.

William Morgan's time at Llanrhaeadr was turbulent. He seems to have married Katherine ferch George (*d.* 1605/6), formerly Katherine Davies and the widow of Oliver Thomas, his predecessor in the vicarage, about 1579, but no children were born to them. Morgan's own marriage, and the match he arranged between a scion of the house of Gwydir and a local heiress, gave great offence to a powerful neighbouring gentleman, Evan Meredith, of Lloran-uchaf in Llansilin. Litigation followed, and the whole affair culminated in a near riot at Llanrhaeadr on 21 April 1591, which led to action and counteraction in Star Chamber. Morgan for a time felt constrained to carry a pistol under his cassock in church. Peace was restored only through the good offices of Sir John Wynn.

Throughout this difficult time, Morgan appears to have carried out his work as a parish priest assiduously, with the help of his curate Lewis Hughes and two young amanuenses, John Davies of Llanferres in Denbighshire and Jasper Gryffyth of Guilsfield in Montgomeryshire. He preached regularly, oversaw the morals of his flock, and dispensed what hospitality he could. The professional poets who journeyed to Llanrhaeadr to sing his praises—Rhys Cain (two poems), Siôn Tudur, Owain Gwynedd, Ieuan Tew, and Siôn Mawddwy—portray him and his wife as models of generosity, and it is perhaps unwise to conclude too hastily that this was merely a matter of convention. Morgan's main contribution during his years at Llanrhaeadr was his translation of the Bible into Welsh.

Bishop of Llandaff In 1595 Morgan was appointed bishop of Llandaff, then the poorest see in England and Wales, being valued at £155 in the *valor ecclesiasticus* of 1535. Within a week of his consecration at Croydon on 20 July 1595, Morgan applied for the temporal income of his see to be restored to him from the date of his predecessor's translation to Exeter (11 March 1595); he was also allowed four years for the payment of his first-fruits. Morgan had already resigned the rectory of Llanfyllin in 1592, and he now vacated the vicarage of Llanrhaeadr and the sinecure rectories of Denbigh and Pennant as well. He and his family, which included John Davies and (for a time) Jasper Gryffyth, lived without ostentation in the episcopal palace of Matharn near Chepstow in Monmouthshire. Morgan proved himself a diligent and effective bishop. He attended fairly regularly the meetings of the cathedral chapter, insisting in his first meeting that the obligation of members of the chapter to preach regularly be strictly fulfilled. In his appointments to benefices, in spite of the preponderance of lay impropriations, he appears to have striven to improve the quality of the clergy, and in particular to ensure that as many as possible of them were able to preach: in 1602 the diocese had a total of fifty preachers. Jasper Gryffyth was made rector of Langston, near Newport, in late 1595, but migrated to Ruthin in 1599; John Davies, on the other hand, remained in the episcopal household, perhaps acting as the bishop's secretary. One notable appointment by Morgan was that of Edward James, later translator of the homilies into Welsh. Evan Morgan, the son of Morgan's eldest brother and a graduate of Oxford, although vicar of Llanrhaeadr since March 1597, was a canon of Llandaff by 1598 and precentor by 1600; he disappears from the chapter records after June 1602.

One significant act of the chapter was to restrict the term of leases of church property to no more than twenty-one years. The most pressing problem facing Morgan, however, was that of Roman Catholic recusancy, for which the diocese was notorious: six weeks after his departure it was reported that there was 'a great backsliding in religion in these parts' (*Salisbury MSS*, 460), and in 1603 the diocese returned 381 convicted recusants, which represented a higher proportion of recusants to communicants than in any other diocese except Chester. The three professional poets whose poems for Morgan and his wife were declaimed at Matharn—Huw Machno, Siôn Mawddwy, and Lewys Dwnn—seemed blissfully unaware

of this problem, concentrating rather on the couple's generosity to poets and suppliants, on their high lineage, and on Morgan's virtues as a father in God. They were aware, however, of his secular obligations as a justice of the peace (in Monmouthshire only), as a member of the council in the marches, and as one of the lords spiritual, although there is no evidence that he fulfilled any of these obligations with outstanding distinction.

Bishop of St Asaph Following the death of Bishop Hughes of St Asaph on 18 or 19 November 1600 Morgan's translation there was confirmed on 17 September 1601. The see was worth £188 but, like his predecessor, he was allowed to hold the archdeaconry of St Asaph *in commendam*, which added a further £75 to his income. Because the bishop's palace at St Asaph was dilapidated, as was the cathedral itself (Morgan did much to repair both), Morgan and his family lived in the archdeacon's house in Dyserth, some 3 miles distant from St Asaph. As at Llandaff, Morgan early evinced his determination to ensure that his diocese was relatively well supplied with preaching clergy, as the fragmentary chapter acts show: it was an uphill struggle, since the diocesan tally of forty-five preachers in 1592 had fallen to forty-one by 1602. John Davies was collated to the rectory of Mallwyd in Merioneth, where he became in due course the finest Welsh scholar of the Renaissance. Morgan's desire to safeguard the property of the church was evidenced in more dramatic fashion in St Asaph than in Llandaff. Soon after his translation he clashed with a powerful local gentleman, David Holland of Teyrdan in Llanelian-yn-Rhos, regarding the tithes of the parish of Abergele, a tenth of which formed a substantial part of the episcopal income, and Sir John Wynn of Gwydir had again to intervene to restore calm. Within a year Morgan had clashed with Wynn himself regarding the tithes of Llanrwst, which Wynn wished to lease for a term of three lives, an arrangement at which Morgan demurred because it would lessen the ability of the church to support and reward preachers. It is this clash that accounts for the unfavourable notice of Morgan in Wynn's *History of the Gwydir Family*. Morgan's motives were certainly mixed, but that they included a genuine determination to guard the church against depredation can scarcely be denied.

Another of Morgan's preoccupations at St Asaph was recusancy, for which St Winifred's Well in the parish of Holywell provided a focus: in 1602 he presented 65 recusants from Denbighshire at the court of great sessions, but the following year there were still 250 of them in the diocese as a whole. Morgan's appearance in court is a reminder of his continued secular functions: as a justice of the peace in the three north-eastern counties of Wales, as a member of the council in the marches, and, of course, as a member of the House of Lords, which sat twice during his tenure of the see. Unfortunately, by the second session (19 March – 7 July 1604), Morgan was already ailing and his attendance was intermittent. Although he apparently attended a chapter meeting on 6 September, he died in the early hours of 10 September 1604 at the bishop's palace at St Asaph, and was buried the following day in his cathedral church: a stone bearing the letters 'W. M.' may once have marked the place of his burial, but no effigy (or portrait) has been preserved. Five professional poets—Owain Gwynedd, Morus Berwyn, Rhys Cain, Huw Machno (three poems), and Simwnt Fychan—attended him and his wife at St Asaph, but of these only Huw Machno composed an elegy for him. He apparently died in debt to the crown, probably because his clergy were in arrears with their taxes, and his goods were valued at £110 1s. 2d. No will by him has been traced. His widow seems to have returned to her family in Oswestry after her husband's death, and she was buried there on 7 January 1606.

Translating the Bible Morgan has been called 'the single most important figure in the history of the Reformation in Wales' (Williams, *Wales and the Reformation*, 342), because it was he who brought to completion the translation of the Bible into Welsh. The Book of Common Prayer, including the psalter, and the New Testament had been translated in 1567, but the task was left unfinished. It is unlikely that Morgan began his task as a translator before his installation as vicar of Llanrhaeadr in 1579, although his devotion to the Bible was already apparent in his selection of Romans 1: 16 as the verse to quote during his ordination as deacon in 1568, a verse that he repeated on the title-page of his New Testament of 1588; it is fitting that the only book dedicated to him, Gabriel Powel's *Prodromus* (1602), is a meditation on the first chapter of Romans. He himself states that he would have abandoned his task after publishing no more than his version of the Pentateuch had not John Whitgift, by then archbishop of Canterbury, persuaded him to continue and lent him his support and aid. Other supporters rallied round him: his own bishop and the bishop of Bangor, Hugh Bellott, lent him books and examined and approved his work, while his friends Edmwnd Prys, Richard Vaughan, and David Powel, vicar of Ruabon (1570–98), gave him help which he described as 'not to be despised'.

Morgan's copy of the first volume of Daniel Bomberg's Hebrew Bible printed at Venice in 1524–5 has survived (NL Wales, 13181B), but at some point it was superseded as an aid by the great Antwerp polyglot Bible of 1572 which contained not only a Hebrew text but also a literal Latin translation by Sanctes Pagninus as well as texts of the Septuagint, the Vulgate, and the Greek and Syriac New testaments, with Latin translations where appropriate. Other scholarly aids that Morgan used from time to time included (in order of importance) the Latin versions of John Immanuel Tremellius (1579), Robert Estienne (1557), and Sebastian Münster (1525), the English Geneva Bible (1560), Bishops' Bible (1568), and Great Bible (1539), and, for the New Testament, Theodore Beza's Greek text and Latin translation of 1582; Beza's French translation of the Apocrypha (1551) also proved helpful. Morgan's biblical scholarship was therefore thoroughly up to date, but he used it with rare discrimination, sometimes preferring his own rendering of the original Hebrew or Greek to any other.

Thus equipped, and with the help of his two young amanuenses, Morgan was able by late 1587 to produce a new translation of the Old Testament (except the Psalms) and Apocrypha, and a revision of the translation by Salesbury and his colleagues of the Psalms and New Testament. He brought to his task not only biblical scholarship of a high order but also a thorough knowledge of the Welsh literary tradition, including both Middle Welsh prose and the work of the professional poets. That he had an academic interest in the language is strongly suggested by his intention—unfortunately unfulfilled—to produce a Welsh dictionary. The way he handled the language, however, was more than a matter of mere knowledge: he had an instinctive feeling for the aptness of a word in its context, for the shape of a sentence, for the architecture of a passage; and he clearly had a developed awareness of verbal music. Most important of all, he had a sure sense of what was linguistically acceptable to his fellow countrymen. Morgan replaced Salesbury's unfortunate miscellany of linguistic characteristics with a calm uniformity based on the common practice of his own day, particularly that of the professional poets, although a limited number of spoken forms was admitted. In his original translation of the rest of the Old Testament and the Apocrypha, Morgan applied the same principles: humanistic flourishes were eschewed in favour of contemporaneity and lucidity, although old terms and new coinages were admitted as necessary; and in the matter of orthography Morgan clearly aimed at consistency throughout, based on the practice of the poets, although he occasionally admits dialect forms and shows himself to be not entirely unsusceptible to the attractions of *copia*. Two further features of Morgan's Welsh may reflect his humanistic proclivities: his almost exclusive choice of what is known as the abnormal sentence, which corresponds well with the rules of Latin grammar, as the means of making a positive statement; and also his treatment of the demonstratives *yr hwn* and suchlike as true relatives, comparable to Latin *qui, quae, quod*.

Morgan's Bible was undoubtedly a great literary and linguistic triumph: as the traditional custodians of the Welsh literary language, the professional poets, went into steep decline, Morgan provided the language with a body of authoritative, regular, and eloquent prose, reflecting faithfully the genres of the original texts—narrative, law, wisdom literature, poetry, hortatory letters, apocalypse—and thus expanding significantly the scope of the written language, and at the same time establishing its claim to be regarded as a learned language in the eyes of contemporary humanists. This explains why not only the professional poets (and the occasional amateur) but also such Welsh humanists as George Owen, John Davies of Brecon (Siôn Dafydd Rhys), Maurice Kyffin, and Huw Lewis welcomed the new translation unreservedly, in poignant contrast to the silence or disapproval which, with one or two exceptions, greeted Salesbury's version. Lord Burghley welcomed it for a different reason, in that it provided a bulwark against Roman Catholicism.

Morgan's Bible was a year in the printing, ostensibly by the deputies of Christopher Barker, the queen's printer, but in fact by some master printer who has yet to be identified. Morgan spent the year in London correcting the proofs and lodging with Gabriel Goodman at Westminster Abbey, having declined John Whitgift's invitation to stay with him at Lambeth Palace, because that would involve twice-daily crossings of the Thames. It has been authoritatively suggested that Whitgift was particularly anxious to see the Welsh Bible published in order to counter the puritan John Penry's accusations that the episcopal hierarchy was uncaring of the souls of his fellow countrymen. Goodman was able to help Morgan with some of the minutiae of the translation, of which he thought highly. On 22 September 1588 the privy council heard that the Welsh Bible was printed and ordered its dissemination to the parishes at the price of £1 a copy, the incumbent to pay one half and the parishioners the other; each parish was also ordered to buy two copies of the psalter, which had been printed separately. The Bible is a squat folio of 1116 pages and contains a fine Latin dedication by Morgan to the queen (later translated by Gladstone, BL, Add. MS 44447, fol. 233), in which he argues passionately against those who opposed the licensing of his translation (who may originally have included his own diocesan), maintaining that the unity of a kingdom depended more on uniformity of religion than uniformity of language.

While in London, Morgan appears to have printed a Welsh funeral sermon for Sir Evan Lloyd of Bodidris, who had died in the capital on the way home from fighting in the Low Countries and who apparently had some connection with Llanrhaeadr; it is a matter of much regret that no copy has survived. An elegant Latin epigram dating from the same period and commending Maurice Kyffin's English translation of Terence's *Andria* is, however, extant. Following Morgan's removal to Llandaff, he and John Davies (and possibly Jasper Gryffyth) set about revising Salesbury's Book of Common Prayer, at the same time undertaking a revision of the 1588 New Testament, as promised in a list of errata attached to some copies of the 1588 Bible. The Book of Common Prayer appeared in 1599 and was a crucial step forward in establishing the definitive form of the book (which appeared in 1621, following the definitive Bible of 1620): the diction and orthography of the liturgical parts were modernized and regularized, and the scriptural passages carefully revised in the light of the Bishops' Bible and Beza's Latin New Testament of 1582. The revision of the New Testament was ready for publication by the London-Welsh stationer Thomas Salisbury by 1603 but, with the rest of Salisbury's stock, was lost in the great plague of that year: much of the substance of the revision has, however, been preserved in the Book of Common Prayer of 1599, Morgan's final bequest to his fellow countrymen.　　　　　R. GERAINT GRUFFYDD

Sources I. Thomas, ed. and trans., *Y Testament Newydd Cymraeg, 1551–1620* (1976) · I. Thomas, *Yr Hen Destament Cymraeg* (1988) · G. Williams, 'Bishop William Morgan and the first Welsh Bible', *The Welsh and their religion* (1991), 173–229 · G. Williams, 'William Morgan's Bible and the Cambridge connection', *Welsh History Review / Cylchgrawn Hanes Cymru*, 14 (1988–9), 363–79 · G. Gruffydd, 'Y Beibl a droes i'w bobl draw' (1988) · R. G. Gruffydd, *William Morgan: dyneiddiwr* (1989) · R. G. Gruffydd, ed., *Y gair ar waith* (1988) · A. O. Evans, 'Edmund Prys: archdeacon of Merioneth', *Transactions of the Honourable Society of Cymmrodorion* (1922–3), 112–68 · C. Davies, 'Dysg ddyneiddiol cyfiethwyr y Beibl', *Llên Cymru*, 16 (1989–91), 7–22 · G. A. Williams, 'William Morgan ac Edmwnd Prys yng Nghaergrawnt', *BBCS*, 29 (1980–82), 296–300 · W. P. Griffith, *Learning, law and religion: higher education and Welsh society, c.1540–1640* (1996) · I. ab O. Edwards, 'William Morgan's quarrel with his parishioners at Llanrhaeadr ym Mochnant', *BBCS*, 3 (1926–7), 298–339 · N. M. W. Powell, 'Dr William Morgan and his parishioners at Llanrhaeadr ym Mochnant', *Transactions of the Caernarvonshire Historical Society*, 49 (1988), 87–115 · G. Williams, *Wales and the Reformation* (1997) · J. G. Jones, 'Bishop William Morgan's dispute with John Wynn of Gwydir in 1603–4', *Journal of the Historical Society of the Church in Wales*, 22 (1972), 49–78 · G. M. Griffiths, 'Glimpses of Denbighshire in the records of the court of great sessions', *Transactions of the Denbighshire Historical Society*, 22 (1973), 93–120 · D. Ll. Morgan, *William Morgan a'i Feibl: William Morgan and his Bible* (1989) · *Calendar of the manuscripts of the most hon. the marquis of Salisbury*, 11, HMC, 9 (1906) · Gladstone, *Diaries* · J. Berlatsky, 'The Elizabethan episcopate: patterns of life and expenditure', *Princes and paupers in the English church, 1500–1850*, ed. R. O'Day and F. Heal (1981), 117, 125 · P. C. Bartrum, ed., *Welsh genealogies, AD 1400–1500*, 18 vols. (1983) · J. Wynn, *The history of the Gwydir family and memoirs*, ed. J. G. Jones (1990), 63 · Venn, *Alum. Cant.* · D. R. Thomas, ed., *Y cwtta cyfarwydd* (1883), 240

Wealth at death £110 1s. 2d.: will, Berlatsky, 'The Elizabethan episcopate'

Morgan, William (1623–1689), Jesuit, was born in February or March 1623 at Cilcain, Flintshire, the second son of Henry Morgan and his first wife, Winefrid, or Gwen. His parents were from the minor gentry and he was brought up as a protestant. He was sent to Westminster School in 1638 and then in 1640 went on to Trinity College, Cambridge. Here he studied philosophy for two years, with, as he put it, little profit. At the outbreak of the civil war he was ejected from university by the earl of Manchester and joined the king's army. He was captured at the battle of Naseby in 1645 and imprisoned in the bishop of Winchester's palace in London, but after six weeks was granted permission by parliament to go abroad. He served for a year and a half as a sergeant in Colonel Cobbe's regiment in the Spanish army in the Low Countries. Here he was converted to Catholicism, and, having abandoned soldiering, went to the English Jesuit establishments at Ghent and Liège, where, as he reports himself, he spent most of his time transcribing books.

On 1 August 1648 Morgan departed for Rome and enrolled in the English College to train as a priest. He was admitted to the Society of Jesus on 30 September 1651, and passed the rest of the decade in Rome working at both the English and Greek colleges engaged variously as professor of philosophy, minister, and prefect of studies. He was ordained priest about 1657.

In 1661 Morgan moved back to Liège and taught there until 1670 when he was sent on the mission to his native north Wales. He held the position of superior of the residence of St Winefrid, and in 1675 became chaplain to Lord Powis at Powis Castle. He was named by Titus Oates in 1678 as one of the popish plotters and a search was made for him in the London house of Powis, but he was not found. He managed to escape abroad in February 1679, where he published a pamphlet, *A Letter from Amsterdam to a Friend in Paris*, defending his colleagues from the calumnies of Oates.

In 1679 Morgan was named as assistant to the new Jesuit provincial, John Warner. The plot had virtually destroyed the Jesuit mission in England, leading to the imprisonment, flight, or execution of most of the fathers, and a breakdown of the intricate administrative structures for which the order was renowned. Warner, himself in exile, sent Morgan back to England in October 1680 to report on the state of Jesuit affairs there, but as soon as he arrived in England he was arrested. This clearly placed him in danger, but the great excitement of the Popish Plot had passed and although he was imprisoned he was released in 1683. He returned to Rome, where he held the position of rector of the English College until 1686. He was in the Netherlands in 1687, and then in 1689 he was made provincial of the English Jesuit mission. Within a few weeks of his appointment, on 28 September 1689, he died at St Omer. THOMPSON COOPER, *rev.* PETER HOLMES

Sources H. Foley, ed., *Records of the English province of the Society of Jesus*, 6 (1880), 373–4 · H. Foley, ed., *Records of the English province of the Society of Jesus*, 7/1 (1882), 523–4 · G. Oliver, *Collections towards illustrating the biographies of the Scotch, English and Irish members of the Society of Jesus*, 2nd edn (1845) · W. Kelly, ed., *Liber ruber venerabilis collegii Anglorum de urbe*, 2, Catholic RS, 40 (1943), 42 · A. Kenny, ed., *The responsa scholarum of the English College, Rome*, 2, Catholic RS, 55 (1963), 510–11 · Venn, *Alum. Cant.* · J. Welch, *A list of scholars of St Peter's College, Westminster* (1788), 36 · T. P. Ellis, *The Catholic martyrs of Wales, 1535–1680* (1933), 131 · J. Warner, *The history of English persecution of Catholics and the presbyterian plot*, ed. T. A. Birrell, trans. J. Bligh, 2, Catholic RS, 48 (1953), 1.243 · G. Holt, *The English Jesuits, 1650–1829: a biographical dictionary*, Catholic RS, 70 (1984) · *DWB* · *Old Westminsters*, 2.665

Morgan, William (1750–1833), actuary, was born on 26 May 1750 at Bridgend, Glamorgan, the third of the eight children of William Morgan (1708–1772), physician of Bridgend, and his wife, Sarah, *née* Price (1726–1803), sister of the well-known radical and writer Richard Price (1723–1791). George Cadogan *Morgan was his only brother. Aged eighteen Morgan went to London to study medicine, as his father wished, initially staying with his uncle, Dr Price, in Newington Green. Owing to his father's limited means, he found work as an apothecary's assistant at Limehouse docks. He entered St Thomas's Hospital as one of the pupils and dressers on 28 May 1770. Towards the end of 1771 he returned home to assist his father. However, his youth and his deformity—he had a club-foot—apparently made him objectionable in the eyes of some of his Bridgend patients. On his father's death in 1772, he relinquished the family practice to his brother-in-law and returned to London.

Through the influence of Dr Price, Morgan became in February 1774 an assistant actuary, and in February 1775 chief actuary to the Equitable Assurance Society, a post which he held until his resignation in 1830. Equitable

William Morgan (1750–1833), by Charles Turner, pubd 1830 (after Sir Thomas Lawrence, 1818)

Assurance was founded in 1762 as a mutual partnership. In 1768 its actuary, John Edwards, turned to Price for help in calculating survivorship and endowment tables. It is said that when Edwards fell ill in 1773 Price asked Morgan whether he knew mathematics; Morgan replied that he did not, but that he could learn. As actuary one of Morgan's first tasks was to estimate the liabilities on the 922 policies then in force. This work, completed in 1776, represented the world's first valuation of a life-assurance business. Over the next half-century Morgan's work provided the basis for the growth of Equitable Assurance into the largest and most solid of British life offices. By 1829 Equitable had over 8800 policies and £12.4 million assured.

Morgan ranks high among the pioneers of scientific life assurance in England. The phenomenal success of the Equitable Society in the midst of so many contemporary failures was mainly due to his careful administration and sound actuarial advice. The details which he published from time to time as to the mortality experience of that society furnished data for the amendment of the Northampton tables, and the construction of others by various actuaries, such as Joshua Milne, actuary to the Sun Life Assurance Society. The first instalment of Morgan's statistics was published in his *Doctrine of Annuities and Assurances on Lives and Survivorships Stated and Explained* (1779), with a preface by Dr Price. From 1786 onwards he delivered to the court of governors a series of addresses reviewing the policy of the society. Nine of the most important of these addresses were published, along with the *Deed of Settlement of the Equitable Society*, in one volume in 1833. On the basis of Morgan's statements new tables of mortality were constructed, most notably by Griffith Davies and by T. Gompertz in 1825, and by Charles Babbage in 1826. Morgan also published a table of his own in *A View of the Rise and Progress of the Equitable Society* (1828), revised by his son Arthur, and reissued in 1834.

In 1783 Morgan sent a paper, 'Probability of survivorship', to the *Philosophical Transactions*, and was awarded the gold medal of the Royal Society, being admitted a fellow in 1790. Other papers, which appeared in *Philosophical Transactions* for 1791, 1794, and 1799, were embodied in the second edition of his *Doctrine of Annuities* (1821). He served twice on the council of the Royal Society, in 1798–1800 and 1810–12. Influenced by his uncle's friend Joseph Priestley (1733–1804), he also conducted scientific experiments on electricity and combustion. He was consulted by several new assurance companies over actuarial appointments, prepared annuity tables for the National Debt Office in 1808, and advised parliamentary committees on the poor laws in 1817–18 and friendly societies in 1827. He was also much consulted on questions relating to ecclesiastical property. Morgan was a Unitarian of a presbyterian type, like his uncle, Dr Price, whose views on finance and politics he also inherited. He vigorously denounced the accumulation of the national debt. In the 1790s he edited Price's writings on public finance, and published a series of his own pamphlets attacking the financing of Pitt's war against France. He also edited Price's *Observations on Reversionary Payments* (5th edn, 1792), the *Works of Dr Price* (with a biography, 1816), and a collection of Price's sermons.

During his first seven years with Equitable, Morgan lived at the company's offices at Chatham Place, near Blackfriars Bridge. The house was threatened during the Gordon riots of June 1780. In 1781 Morgan married Susannah, daughter of John Woodhouse, a London merchant. Susannah inherited a small estate at Portway, Staffordshire. Morgan and his wife had six children. His eldest son, William, appointed assistant actuary to the Equitable in 1817, died of a chest infection in 1819, aged twenty-eight. Morgan's youngest son, Arthur, took over his brother's post, and succeeded his father as actuary in 1830.

Early in his marriage Morgan took a 99-year lease of land at Stamford Hill, and built a spacious house there, with gardens and paddocks. The house became a centre of family, social, and political life. Morgan's brother, George Cadogan Morgan, who lived at nearby Southgate, was a regular visitor, as were the members of the circle of radicals associated with Richard Price; John Horne Tooke, Sir Francis Burdett, and Tom Paine were among those who joined the lively gatherings at Stamford Hill on Sunday evenings, when the shutters were drawn and songs such as 'The trumpet of liberty' would be sung. In 1794, when Horne Tooke and others were indicted for treason, Morgan escaped with a warning from the authorities. Samuel Rogers, who regularly dined at Morgan's, described him as 'a strong silent man but very emphatic in his language' (Ogborn, 196). Others remarked that he was a good conversationalist with a mordant wit, and a smile which could turn to a sneer if provoked. Morgan died from influenza at Stamford Hill on 4 May 1833, and was buried at Hornsey on 11 May. He left life policies worth £7495. His wife predeceased him.   D. L. THOMAS, *rev.* ROBIN PEARSON

Sources M. E. Ogborn, *Equitable assurances … the Equitable Life Assurance Society, 1762–1962* (1962) · C. E. Williams, *A Welsh family from the beginning of the 18th century*, 2nd edn (1893) · C. Walford, *The insurance cyclopaedia*, 2–3 (1873–4) · *The Times* (15 May 1833) · *GM*, 1st ser., 103/1 (1833), 569–70 · W. P. Elderton, 'William Morgan, FRS, 1750–1833', *Journal of the Institute of Actuaries*, 64 (1933), 364–5 · *Index of parish registers* · *DWB* · *DNB*
Archives Equitable Life, London, notebooks | BL, letters to Babbage, Add. MSS 37182, 37184
Likenesses T. Lawrence, oils, 1818, Equitable Life Assurance Society · C. Turner, mezzotint, pubd 1830 (after T. Lawrence, 1818), BM, NPG [*see illus.*]
Wealth at death £7495 in life policies: Ogborn, *Equitable assurances*

Morgan, Sir William (1829–1883), merchant and politician in Australia, the son of George Morgan, farmer, and his wife, Sarah, *née* Horne, was born on 12 September 1829 at Wilshamstead, near Bedford. In 1848 he emigrated with two brothers and a sister, and arrived in South Australia in February 1849. He took the first work he was offered, but after a short experience of bush life became an assistant in the Adelaide grocery store of Messrs Boord Brothers. In 1851, he went with his brother Thomas to the Bendigo gold diggings in Victoria, and, succeeding better than most, returned to Adelaide, rejoined the Boords, and purchased and extended their business until, under the name of Morgan & Co., it became one of the leading mercantile houses in the colony. On 8 July 1854 he married Harriett, daughter of Thomas Matthews, of Hurd's Hill, Coromandel valley, in the Adelaide hills. In 1865 he was one of the founders of the Bank of Adelaide and in 1867 he was the first member 'in trade' to be elected to the Adelaide Club.

That August, Morgan was also elected to the legislative council as a free-trader. Although not a minister, he was chosen in 1871 to be one of the South Australian delegates to the abortive intercolonial conference on reciprocal intercolonial trade agreements, and during the 1870s he had two short stints of office in the many short-lived South Australian ministries, when he was most noted for his advocacy of railway extension and free trade. However, his business interests, which then included the Balade copper, silver, and nickel mines in New Caledonia, at times made him anxious to retire from political life.

In September 1878 Morgan became premier in a more stable administration, whose chief measures included the extension of sewerage in Adelaide (ten years before any other Australian city), a slight liberalization of the legislative council, and the building of the first parts of the University of Adelaide, the public library, and the national gallery. Morgan supported federation and attended another inconclusive intercolonial conference on the subject in 1880–81. He resigned in June 1881 to attend to his financial affairs, and in 1883 he went to England to recruit his health. On his arrival he was created KCMG, in May, having declined a baronetcy. He died on 2 November, at Brighton, survived by his wife and five of his nine children. He was buried beside his parents at Wilshamstead.

Morgan displayed much administrative capacity; he was far-sighted, energetic, shrewd, honest, genial, and loyal. Contemporaries referred to him as the Cobden of South Australia.   A. G. L. SHAW

Sources *AusDB* · P. A. Howell, 'Constitutional and political development, 1857–1890', *The Flinders history of South Australia*, ed. D. Jaensch, 2: *Political history* (1986), 95–177 · J. Quick and R. R. Garran, *The annotated constitution of the Australian commonwealth* (1901) · G. D. Combe, *Responsible government in South Australia* (1957) · *South Australian Register* (10 Nov 1883) · *South Australian Advertizer* (10 Nov 1883) · *The Australasian* (10 Nov 1883)

Morgan, William Frend De (1839–1917), potter and novelist, was born on 16 November 1839 at 69 Gower Street, London, the second child of Augustus De *Morgan (1806–1871) and Sophia Frend (1809–1902). His father was the first professor of pure mathematics at University College, London, a man of severe integrity who resigned on two occasions when he believed the college had transgressed its founding principle of religious toleration. His mother was active in the anti-slavery movement, the reform of prisons and workhouses, the founding of Bedford College for Women, and the suffrage movement. The atmosphere of the De Morgan household, at first in Bloomsbury and then in Primrose Hill, was a mixture of intellect, high-mindedness, word play—the professor of pure mathematics had a terrible weakness for puns—and mortality, for the family suffered from tuberculosis. William inherited the intellect and the word play in good measure: his simple nature delighted in intellectual and verbal fantasy. But the high-mindedness seems to have passed him by; he greeted life with innocent, quizzical humour. Mercifully, the tuberculosis also passed him by. Though never strong, he outlived his six brothers and sisters, four of whom did not reach the age of forty.

Education De Morgan was educated at University College School, London, and at the college itself, and then entered the Royal Academy Schools in 1859, hoping to become a painter. With his great domed forehead (inherited from his father) and his wavering, high-pitched voice which ended every sentence with a drawl, he was a strange and humorous figure among the students. He left the schools in 1862, doubting that he would make a painter. Not much is known of his activities in the 1860s, except that he met William Morris and Edward Burne-Jones, who became perhaps his closest friends, and that, probably encouraged by Morris, he began to design tiles and stained glass. Towards the end of the decade he was working at 40 Fitzroy Square, where he had a kiln in his studio. In 1872 he burnt the roof of the house off, and had to leave.

Mary De Morgan De Morgan's father had died in 1871, and *c.*1872 De Morgan went to live at 8 Great Cheyne Row, Chelsea, with his mother and his youngest sister, **Mary Augusta De Morgan** (1850–1907), children's writer. The Burne-Jones, Morris, and De Morgan households were all now in west London, and there was much coming and going between them. Mary De Morgan, a small, abrupt but lovable figure, told fairy stories to the Morris and Burne-Jones children, which were then successfully published. Her first book of children's stories, *On a Pincushion* (1877),

William Frend De Morgan (1839–1917), by Evelyn De Morgan, 1909

was illustrated by her brother, who, typically, invented a special method for reproducing his drawings. Mary De Morgan died in Egypt in 1907.

William built a pottery kiln in the garden of the house in Great Cheyne Row, but it was soon too small, and about 1873 he rented Orange House, almost next door, and started a pottery there. It is on the products of this pottery, which he carried on at various sites for over thirty years, that his reputation mainly rests today.

Potter De Morgan's work at Orange House was devoted almost exclusively to decorating tiles and different kinds of pots—dishes, bowls, and vases. At first he bought ready-made tiles and pots to work on, and later the pottery made its own. But De Morgan was always much less interested in the shape and structure of pots than in their glazes, from a scientific as much as an artistic point of view. Some wares were decorated with enamel underglaze colours, others with the sheen of lustre, in emulation of the Renaissance technique which De Morgan was partly responsible for reintroducing in Britain. The pottery was small, and devoted almost entirely to his own designs; he was essentially a painter who had turned to the decorative arts, as did others in the 1870s. In this sense it stood alongside Morris & Co. as one of the first workshops of the arts and crafts movement in Britain. As it happens, both workshops were short of space by the end of the decade, so Morris and De Morgan searched together for new premises. In 1881 Morris moved his works to Merton Abbey in south London; in 1882 De Morgan built his kilns near by.

The appeal of De Morgan's pottery lies in his glazes,

which are richer and softer than those of his contemporaries; in his skill with colour—his one-time partner Halsey Ricardo wrote of 'the pools of colour into which one can dive and scarce plumb the full depth' (Hamilton, 69); in his happy reinterpretation of Islamic pottery of the fifteenth and sixteenth centuries; and in his decorative handling of birds, animals, and fish, some from nature, others from the comic bestiary of his own imagination—one never knew there could be so many varieties of amiable dragon. Lewis Carroll admired his tiles, and had them installed in Christ Church, Oxford.

De Morgan appeared before the public as an artist, a decorator of pots and tiles. But the public did not see him at the pottery, absorbed in its technicalities, working at the chemistry of his glazes, overseeing the tense and unpredictable business of firing lustre wares. His friends and associates saw him, rightly, as an inventor and a scientist. And though he had little to do with the pottery industry in Stoke-on-Trent or elsewhere, his workshop was, in a quite untheoretical way, a real combination of art and science.

On 5 March 1887 De Morgan married Evelyn Pickering (1855–1919) [see Morgan, (Mary) Evelyn De]. Talented, humorous, and forthright, she had established herself as a successful painter despite, it seems, the opposition of her wealthy family. He was forty-eight, she was thirty-two. She painted sumptuous figure subjects with lofty themes in a late Pre-Raphaelite manner—all that her whimsical husband's pots and tiles were not. But they made an excellent couple. As a small sign of their mutual eccentricity, they were married quietly, went to the railway station, and caught the first train that happened to be available; it took them to the Isle of Wight. On their return they settled into 1 The Vale, King's Road, Chelsea, next door to James McNeill Whistler. It was a childless marriage, but successful; they laughed at each other a lot, and she strengthened his resolve.

The daily journey to Merton Abbey taxed De Morgan's health, and in 1889 he moved the pottery to purpose-built premises nearer home, off Townmead Road in Fulham. These were financed partly by Evelyn and partly by the architect Halsey Ricardo, with whom he formed a partnership in 1888. The Fulham phase of De Morgan's work lasted longer than any other and saw its crowning achievements, especially in lustre wares of great technical and aesthetic sophistication. But the benefit of the move was partly lost in 1892, when doctors advised that he should spend the winters outside Britain. From 1892 the De Morgans wintered in Florence. It was difficult to run the pottery from a distance and De Morgan's long absences were felt by the staff; in his busy, boffinish way, he had always been its moving spirit. His letters from Florence refer to financial losses. There was a temporary closure in 1903; around 1904 he had to stop designing because of neuritis in his thumb; and the company was finally wound up in 1907, though several of De Morgan's employees continued under their own names. He was in his mid-sixties, and had perhaps reached his natural term for such work. Commentators nod sagely over his lack of business sense, and quote him as saying 'It is not well organised, it

is very ill De Morganised in fact!' (Hamilton, 48). But that was self-deprecation. De Morganization had worked well enough for more than thirty years.

Novelist Just as the pottery was closing down, De Morgan became a best-selling novelist. This man in his sixties, who had hardly written anything and not read much, who had been absorbed all his life in the wordless conventions of the decorative arts, was now full of words. In 1901 he had begun to write a story, and then put it by. He was about to throw it away with other papers when Evelyn looked at it and encouraged him to go on. By 1904 there was a manuscript of 500,000 words. It was published in July 1906 as *Joseph Vance: an Ill-Written Autobiography* and became a best-seller. The inconsequence of the whole affair delighted De Morgan, and he continued to be puzzled by his own success. Sometimes he reflected on how the money he earned as an author might have allowed him to continue as a potter.

Joseph Vance was followed by *Alice-for-Short* (1907), *Somehow Good* (1908), *It can Never Happen Again* (1909), and *An Affair of Dishonour* (1909), which was set, exceptionally, in the seventeenth century. Then came *A Likely Story* (1911) and *Ghost Meets Ghost* (1914). His two last novels, *The Old Madhouse* (1917) and *The Old Man's Youth* (1921), were completed by Evelyn and published after his death. All were published in London by Heinemann, and all but one by Henry Holt in New York. The typical De Morgan novel is long, crowded with characters, rambling in construction, and set in mid- or late Victorian London. De Morgan's cockneys, who are often rescued from poverty or the dangers of drink by a benign member of the middle class, are memorable, and he was proud to acknowledge Dickens as his model. Although they appeared around 1910, these novels were a throwback to an earlier style of storytelling. But to see them as neo-Dickensian is to notice their externals and to overlook the gentle, puzzled inwardness with which he reflected on life. He was more open to complexity than Dickens, less indignant at the evils of society. Dotheboys Hall in *Nicholas Nickleby* was a fierce and successful attack on the 'Yorkshire schools' system. De Morgan's young hero Joseph Vance experienced the violence and stupidity of the English public school system, but he also excused it to those he loved. He behaved 'more puerorum', as De Morgan put it, 'as boys do' (W. De Morgan, *Joseph Vance*, 1906, 145).

De Morgan left it up to his characters to develop the story, and he read each week's writing over to his wife, thus populating their homes. He found it easier to write in Florence, and their flat in the via Lungo il Mugnone, which had been full of Evelyn's high themes and William's comic frogs and startled deer, became full of Evelyn's high themes and William's cockney scamps. But by 1914 Florence had become melancholy to them through the deaths of friends, and they went back to London for good. In 1910 they had moved from The Vale to 127 Church Street, Chelsea, where they lived for the rest of their lives. De Morgan, now seventy-five, was still writing, though constantly disturbed by fierce anti-German feelings. He was a familiar figure in the streets of Chelsea during the war, carrying the shopping home, taking his evening walk on the Embankment, white-haired, a little bent, but brisk and frank. He died at his home on 15 January 1917 and was buried in Brookwood cemetery, Surrey, five days later. Evelyn died on 2 May 1919 and is buried with him. The draped classical figures of Grief and Joy on their tombstone, which she designed, recall her more than him.

Reputation An image like the wheel of fortune is needed to give shape to William De Morgan's life and reputation. (Evelyn would have given such an image its full solemnity; William, perhaps feeling its power more, would have drawn it as a joke.) It had operated in his own life, taking him up to fame as a potter, down to financial failure, up again to fame as a novelist and down to death. And it went on turning. His friends thought that, because the British like literature more than art, his novels would survive better than his tiles and pots, and there was some interest in the novels between the wars. But gradually they lost their readership and reputation. *Joseph Vance* was last republished in 1954; since the late 1950s all of De Morgan's novels have been out of print. The pots and tiles started from a position of low esteem: in 1939 an official guide to the tile collections in the Victoria and Albert Museum referred to their 'dank period flavour' (Catleugh, 76–7). But since the mid-twentieth century their reputation has risen with the tide of interest in Victorian decorative art. In 1968 the De Morgan Foundation was set up to preserve the paintings of Evelyn and the pottery of William De Morgan collected by her sister Anna Maria Stirling at Old Battersea House in south London. Today De Morgan's pots and tiles are eagerly studied and collected (examples are in the Victoria and Albert Museum, London; Birmingham Museums and Art Gallery; the De Morgan Foundation; and the William Morris Gallery, London), while his novels are unregarded. It has been so for about forty years. It almost seems as if the wheel has stopped.   ALAN CRAWFORD

Sources A. M. W. Stirling, *William De Morgan and his wife* (1922) · M. Hamilton, *Rare spirit: a life of William De Morgan, 1839–1917* (1997) · W. Gaunt and M. D. E. Clayton-Stamm, *William De Morgan* (1971) · C. Gordon, ed., *Evelyn De Morgan: oil paintings* (1996) · W. De Morgan, 'Lustre ware', *Journal of the Society of Arts*, 40 (1891–2), 756–67 · J. Catleugh, *William De Morgan tiles* (1983) · M. Greenwood, *The designs of William De Morgan: a catalogue* (1989) · M. Morris, *Burlington Magazine*, 31 (1917), 77–83, 91–7 · J. Cartwright, 'William De Morgan: a reminiscence', *Cornhill Magazine*, [3rd] ser., 42 (1917), 461–71 · D. Laird, 'William De Morgan', *Late-Victorian and Edwardian British novelists: first series*, ed. G. M. Johnson, DLitB, 153 (1995), 68–75 · R. L. Green, introduction, *The necklace of Princess Fiorimonde and other stories: being the complete fairy tales of Mary De Morgan* (1963), 7–13 · d. cert. · *CGPLA Eng. & Wales* (1917)

Archives BL, papers relating to his report on possible manufacture of pottery in Egypt, Egerton MS 3293 · De Morgan Foundation, London, MSS, diaries, corresp., and photographs · LUL, corresp. and papers · U. Cal., Berkeley, corresp. · Yale U., Beinecke L., corresp. and papers | Birmingham Museums and Art Gallery, Alan Green bequest, incl. working drawings, sketchbook, and Halsey Ricardo's MS, 'William De Morgan as I knew him' · RIBA, Halsey Ricardo's out-letter book · V&A NAL, papers relating to William De Morgan & Co., and corresp. · Yale U., corresp. with Lionel Phelps

Likenesses E. De Morgan, oils, 1893, De Morgan Foundation, London · Montabone, cabinet photograph, *c*.1898, NPG · A. L. Coburn, photograph, 1908, NPG · A. L. Coburn, photogravure, 1908, NPG · J. K. Lawson, pencil drawing, 1908, NPG · E. De Morgan, oils, 1909 (after photograph), De Morgan Foundation, London, NPG [*see illus.*] · group portrait, oils, 1914, De Morgan Foundation, London · J. Russell & Sons, photograph, NPG

Wealth at death £3953 16*s*. 0*d*.: probate, 24 March 1917, *CGPLA Eng. & Wales*

Morgann, Maurice (1725–1802), colonial administrator and literary scholar, was born in Blaenbylan, Pembrokeshire. He directed the executors of his estate to destroy all his personal papers, and nothing is now known of his family or education. Politically he became associated with the Welsh tories led by Sir John Phillips, bt, and was a longstanding family friend to Phillips's kinsman John Symmons, the member for Cardigan Boroughs (1746–61). Morgann's first published work, *An Inquiry Regarding the Nature and End of a National Militia* (1757), clearly reflected tory opposition to a standing army, increased taxation, and a large national debt. His political connections probably led to his appointment in June 1758 as a weigher and teller at the Royal Mint, a lucrative sinecure he kept until his death. His friends' support of Lord Bute may have led to his introduction to William Petty, second earl of Shelburne, whom Morgann served for over twenty years as a private secretary.

When Shelburne served as president of the Board of Trade, from April to September 1763, Morgann acted as an official adviser. His influence on policy remains unclear, but he was hardly the anti-American imperialist some historians, such as Franklin B. Wickwire, have suggested. Morgann strongly objected to the American Stamp Act of 1765, as well as to other measures implemented by George Grenville, and he advised Shelburne that the colonists would rightly object to taxation without representation. With Shelburne's return to office as the southern secretary of state in July 1766, Morgann became one of his four under-secretaries. In charge of the department's American business, he was rewarded by the colonial sinecure of secretary to New Jersey and helped shape many of Shelburne's policies, especially regarding westward colonial expansion. A voice for toleration regarding the Catholic Canadian population, he was appointed the privy council's agent to Quebec in August 1767. Visiting the province, he collated information in the preparation of a new Canadian bill and returned to London in January 1770. He was later consulted regarding the Quebec Act of 1774. In opposition Morgann reflected Shelburne's increasing interest in humanitarian and political reform; he also opposed the American war. Believing that slavery was against natural law, he published in 1772 *Remarks upon the Slave Trade*, a work predicting a future fearful and cruel racial war in the colonies.

In 1777 Morgann published his best-known work, *An Essay on the Dramatic Character of Sir John Falstaff*. He never reissued the work in his own lifetime, but editions did appear in 1820 and 1825, and it greatly influenced literary criticism of *1 Henry IV* well into the twentieth century. Central to Morgann's interpretation of the play was the character of Falstaff, and he took issue with Dr Johnson as to whether the knight was a fat, drunken coward or a figure worthy of admiration. In a close analysis of Shakespeare's technique as a dramatist, Morgann argued that Shakespeare's intent was to gain sympathy from the audience for Falstaff at the expense of the virtuous young king and, in doing so, reverse or question accepted moral values. Consequently, in Morgann's essay, Falstaff becomes something of a witty, good-natured Don Quixote figure who displays true courage.

Morgann used humour in attacking a bill sponsored by the bishop of Llandaff, who supported the American War, regarding the growing number of cases of adultery. In *A Letter to my Lords the Bishops, on Occasion of the Present Bill for Preventing Adultery* (1779), Morgann suggested that the notion of preventing adulterers from remarrying as a means of lessening debauchery was a mistake; their lordships did not, he argued, understand sin. Forcing adulterers to remarry would have the desired result of lessening the crime, and he used the occasion to attack a corrupt parliament which believed that new penal laws were the answer to social ills.

When Shelburne returned to power in March 1782, he mistakenly believed that the colonies and Britain could be reunited through a commonwealth of interest. Consequently he dispatched Morgann to New York on a secret mission to renew old bonds of affection. Disappointed at the refusal of congress even to receive him, Morgann wrote to Shelburne in June 1782, recommending the acceptance of American independence. Until he returned to London in July 1783, he acted as General Carleton's private secretary. His last official duty was as secretary to the embassy which formally ratified the peace treaty between Britain and the United States in September 1783. For this service he was appointed to a lucrative sinecure as a commissioner of the Hackney coach office.

Living in retirement in Knightsbridge, Morgann was remembered by his own private secretary, William Cooke, as a cheerful man always engaged in some interesting research. Horrified at the violence which accompanied the outbreak of the French Revolution, he often wrote to the *Public Advertiser* as A. B. on developments in France. Following the outbreak of war between Britain and revolutionary France in 1793, he published *Considerations on the Present Internal and External Condition of France* (1794), which attacked French radicalism and called for the United States, which he greatly praised, to return to her true natural interest, an alliance with Britain. Morgann died of causes unknown at his home on 28 March 1802. His obituary in the *Gentleman's Magazine* noted that he had been a man well known for his distinguished and extensive knowledge.　　　　　　　　　　　　RORY T. CORNISH

Sources W. Cooke, *The pleasures of conversation: a poem*, 2nd edn (1822) · W. A. Gill, *Morgann's 'Essay on the dramatic character of Sir John Falstaff'* (1912) · P. Lawson, *The imperial challenge: Quebec and Britain in the age of the American revolution* (1989) · J. Norris, *Shelburne and reform* (1963) · C. Symmons, *The life of John Milton* (1810) · F. B. Wickwire, *British subministers and colonial America, 1763–1783* (1966) · *GM*, 1st ser., 72 (1802), 470–71 · *Report on American manuscripts in the Royal Institution of Great Britain*, 4 vols., HMC, 59 (1904–9) [Morgann's correspondence from NYC]
Archives PRO, corresp., PRO 30/55 | U. Mich., Shelburne Papers

Mori, Francis (1820–1873). *See under* Mori, Nicolas (1796/7–1839).

Mori, Nicolas (1796/7–1839), violinist, was born on 24 January 1796 or 1797 in London, the son of an Italian wig maker in the New Road. He received his first instruction from François Hippolyte Barthélémon on a miniature violin at the age of three, and at a concert for his benefit given at the King's Theatre on 14 March 1805, under the patronage of the duke and duchess of York and the dukes of Sussex and Cambridge, he played a concerto by his teacher known as the 'Emperor'. In 1808 the child prodigy took part in the concerts promoted by Mr Heaviside, a surgeon, and became a pupil of Giovanni Battista Viotti, then in exile in London. He remained under Viotti's tuition until 1814, and under his auspices took part in the first concert of the Philharmonic Society in 1813. The following year, while still in the Philharmonic orchestra, he acted as one of the society's directors and was a soloist at the second concert. In 1816 he was appointed as one of the orchestra's leaders, subsequently playing at ninety-two of the society's concerts. He also led the King's Theatre orchestra under Michael Costa until 1839.

In 1819 Mori married Elizabeth Lavenu, the widow of the music publisher Lewis Lavenu, and carried on the business at 28 New Bond Street, London, in conjunction with his stepson, Louis Henry Lavenu. The firm operated as Mori and Lavenu from about 1828 to 1839, and it was in this capacity that Mori published annually for a few years (in collaboration with W. Ball) the *Musical Gem*. In addition he issued the English editions of works by Mendelssohn, including (in 1837) his violin concerto in D minor. Mori was also respected as a teacher, and from 1819 to 1826 taught Joseph Dando, who was later to become a prominent leader and chamber musician. In 1823, following the establishment of the Royal Academy of Music, he became a member of the first board of professors, and among his pupils there were Oury, Patey, Richards, Musgrove, and his own younger son, Nicholas. As one of the principal orchestral leaders of London concerts and provincial festivals he appeared in September and October 1824 at the Wakefield and Newcastle festivals, and on 13 September 1825, in conjunction with Franz Cramer, Christoph Gottfried Kiesewetter, and John Loder, at the York festival. It was here that he challenged comparison with Kiesewetter by playing Joseph Mayseder's concerto no. 3 in D, which Kiesewetter had chosen as his *pièce de résistance*. A contemporary critic remarked: 'The two artists are not comparable together. Mr. Mori excels in tone and vigour, Mr. Kiesewetter in delicacy and feeling.' In 1826 Mori led the band at the Covent Garden oratorios, and from 1827 to 1834 was leader of the Covent Garden opera orchestra. After becoming a member of the orchestra of the Concerts of Ancient Music in 1831, which were then based at the Hanover Square Rooms in London, Mori restricted his public appearances mainly to his own benefit concerts.

These were generally held in May and attracted a great deal of attention. For example, the concert given on 25 May 1832 at the concert room in the King's Theatre included performances by Mendelssohn and Domenico Dragonetti, and Mendelssohn appeared the following year (17 May) in a performance with Ignaz Moscheles. Other important figures, such as Paolo Spagnoletti and Cramer, were often engaged to lead the large forces of the orchestra. At his concerts in 1835 and 1836 Mori is said to have raised more than £800. In 1836 he instituted a series of chamber music concerts, in continuation of, and in competition with, those conducted by Henry Blagrove.

While Mori composed a number of works for the violin, he earned his reputation as a violinist, and as such was acknowledged in *The Harmonicon* as 'one of the finest violin-players in Europe' and in the *Quarterly Musical Magazine* as a 'champion of England upon his instrument'. The same publication goes on to discuss how he produced a 'firm, full, and impressive' tone and played with a 'bold, free, and commanding' bow arm, complemented by precision and neatness and a remarkable command over technical difficulties. It is suggested, however, that the force, fire, and 'manly confidence' of his playing meant that a certain degree of refinement and expressive subtlety was lacking. This view is supported by Dubourg in 1852, who provides perhaps the most detailed evaluation of Mori, both as an artist and a person. He portrays him as having had an irritable and brusque manner, which was perhaps attributable to the medical condition that eventually caused his death, and of being too eager in the pursuit of 'pecuniary advantage'. Apparently an eccentric, he announced his own memorial concert shortly before his death, using the legend 'Memento mori' at the head of the programmes. He died in London on 14 June 1839 from a ruptured aneurysm.

Both Mori's sons were musicians, and the eldest, **Francis [Frank] Mori** (1820–1873), became a well-known composer and conductor in London. He was born in the capital on 21 March 1820 and studied with Henry Forbes and Sterndale Bennett and also with Pierre-Joseph-Guillaume Zimmermann in Paris in 1836. He directed the London Orchestra in 1854 and composed numerous ballads in addition to a cantata, *Fridolin*, performed at the Worcester festival in 1851; an operetta, *The River Sprite* (to a libretto by George Linley), produced at Covent Garden on 9 February 1865; and a series of vocal exercises (c.1870). He died at Chamant, near Senlis, France, on 2 August 1873. The younger son, Nicholas Mori (1822–c.1890), was also a composer, while the elder Mori's sister was reputed to have been a successful contralto.

EDWARD HERON-ALLEN, *rev.* DAVID J. GOLBY

Sources G. Dubourg, *The violin*, 4th edn (1852), 285–9 · 'Messrs Mori, Spohr, and Kiesewetter', *Quarterly Musical Magazine and Review*, 3 (1821), 323–7 · review, *The Harmonicon*, 9 (1831), 154 [benefit concert for Mr Cipriani Potter, 10 May 1831, Opera Concert Room] · review, *The Harmonicon*, 10 (1832), 154 [benefit concert for Mr Mori, 25 May 1832, Concert Room, King's Theatre] · review, *The Harmonicon*, 11 (1833), 156–7 [benefit concert for Mr J. B. Cramer, 14 June 1833, Opera Concert Room] · E. W. Duffin, *Particulars of the illness and death of the late Mr Mori the violinist* (1839) · C. Humphries

and W. C. Smith, *Music publishing in the British Isles, from the beginning until the middle of the nineteenth century: a dictionary of engravers, printers, publishers, and music sellers*, 2nd edn (1970), 238 · W. J. Thoms, sonnet, *Musical World* (12 Aug 1836), 144 · T. J. Bhills, sonnet, *Musical World* (9 Sept 1836), 207 · F.-J. Fétis, *Biographie universelle des musiciens, et bibliographie générale de la musique*, 2nd edn, 6 (Paris, 1864), 199 · K. Horner, 'Mori (1)', *New Grove* · F. M. Palmer, *Domenico Dragonetti in England (1794–1846): the career of a double bass virtuoso* (1997)
Likenesses stipple (aged eight), BM
Wealth at death under £3000—Frank Mori: will, 1873

Moriarty, David (1814–1877), Roman Catholic bishop of Kerry, was the son of David Moriarty (d. 1827), a farmer, and Bridget, *née* Stokes. He was born at Derryvrin, in the Catholic parish of Lixnaw, co. Kerry, on 18 August 1814 and baptized at a local Catholic church on 21 August. He was educated at home by private tutors, at Boulogne, France, in the Institution Haffreingue, and at St Patrick's College, Maynooth, co. Kildare (1831–9). In 1839 he was appointed vice-rector of the Irish College, Paris, and professor of sacred scripture. In 1844 he joined the staff of All Hallows College, Drumcondra, Dublin, and in 1846 he became president of the college. He was appointed coadjutor-bishop of Kerry in 1854, and succeeded to the see on the death of Bishop Cornelius Egan on 24 July 1856. He was a friend and confidant of John Henry Newman. He was often called upon to preach on important church occasions. Some of his sermons, pastorals, and allocutions were later edited and published. An admirer of the Young Irelanders, he opposed the Fenians and also opposed the home-rule movement. At the First Vatican Council he argued that it was inopportune to define papal infallibility, but he accepted it when it was defined. He died at Killarney, co. Kerry, on 1 October 1877 and was buried at St Mary's Cathedral, Killarney, on 4 October.

THOMPSON COOPER, *rev.* KIERAN O'SHEA

Sources K. O'Shea, 'David Moriarty, 1814–77: the making of a bishop', *Kerry Archaeological and Historical Society Journal*, 3 (1970), 84–98 · K. O'Shea, 'David Moriarty, 1814–77: reforming a diocese', *Kerry Archaeological and Historical Society Journal*, 4 (1971), 107–26 · K. O'Shea, 'David Moriarty, 1814–77: politics', *Kerry Archaeological and Historical Society Journal*, 5 (1972), 86–102 · K. O'Shea, 'David Moriarty, 1814–77: ecclesiastical affairs', *Kerry Archaeological and Historical Society Journal*, 6 (1973), 131–42 · P. J. Corish, *Maynooth College, 1795–1995* (1995) · *The Tablet* (6 Oct 1877) · parish register (baptism), Lixnaw, Kerry, 21 Aug 1871 · *Tralee Chronicle* (5 Oct 1877) · CGPLA Ire. (1877)
Archives Birmingham Oratory, letters to J. H. Newman · Limerick University Library, letters to Lord Dunraven · NL Ire., corresp. with Lord Emly
Likenesses F. D'Alessandri, carte-de-visite, NPG · photograph, St Brendan's College, Killarney, co. Kerry
Wealth at death under £2000: probate, 14 Dec 1877, CGPLA Ire.

Moriarty, Denis Ignatius. *See* Daunt, William Joseph O'Neill (1807–1894).

Moriarty, Henry Augustus (1815–1906), naval officer, the second son of Commander James Moriarty RN, and his wife, Catherine Webb, was born on 19 May 1815 in the signal tower on Valentia Island, co. Cork, Ireland. He was educated by the Revd J. Neave at Portsmouth, and entered the navy on 18 December 1829 on board the frigate *North Star*. In 1837 he was promoted second master and appointed to the flagship *Caledonia* in the Mediterranean, and during the war on the coast of Syria in 1840 served on board the *Ganges* (84 guns). He was promoted master in June 1844, and in 1848, while master of the flagship *Penelope* on the west coast of Africa, commanded a paddle-box boat in an expedition to destroy the slave barracoons on the River Gallinas. In the Crimean War he was master of the *Duke of Wellington*, the flagship of Sir Charles Napier, in the Baltic; he was mentioned in dispatches for surveying work done under fire, and was employed under Captain Bartholomew J. Sulivan in placing the mortar vessels preparatory to the bombardment of Sveaborg on 9 August 1855.

In 1857 and in 1858 Moriarty was appointed to navigate the battleship *Agamemnon*, lent by the Admiralty to lay the first Atlantic telegraph cable. In June 1863 he was promoted staff commander, and in August was appointed to the flagship *Marlborough* (121 guns) in the Mediterranean.

In 1865 and 1866 Moriarty navigated the *Great Eastern* when she was employed in laying the second and third transatlantic cables, and, when the cable broke in mid-ocean in 1865, he fixed the position so accurately as to ensure the subsequent recovery of the broken end. In 1866 he was created CB for this success, and received a valuable testimonial from his brother officers. In December 1867 he was promoted staff captain and was appointed to Portsmouth Dockyard as assistant master attendant; in November 1869 he became master attendant and queen's harbour master. He held this post until 3 December 1874, when he was placed on the retired list with the rank of captain.

After his retirement Moriarty was occasionally employed as nautical assessor to the judicial committee of the privy council, and frequently as nautical expert before parliamentary committees, including those on Barry docks, the Tay Bridge, the Forth Bridge, and Tower Bridge. His chief publications were four volumes of sailing directions (1887–93) compiled for the Admiralty, and the articles on seamanship and navigation in the *Encyclopaedia Britannica* (9th edn).

Moriarty married first, on 30 July 1852, Lavinia Charlotte (*d.* September 1874), the daughter of William Page Foster; they had two sons and two daughters. His second wife, whom he married in 1875, was Harriet Elizabeth, the daughter of Robert Avent of St Budeaux, Devon, who died childless in March 1892. Moriarty died at his home, 35 Manor Park, Lee, Kent, on 18 August 1906, and was buried in the cemetery there.

L. G. C. LAUGHTON, rev. ROGER MORRISS

Sources *The Times* (20 Aug 1906) · private information (1912) · *WWW* · A. D. Lambert, *The Crimean War: British grand strategy, 1853–56* (1990) · W. E. F. Ward, *The Royal Navy and the slavers* (1969) · D. R. Headrick, *The tentacles of progress: technology transfer in the age of imperialism, 1850–1940* (1988)
Likenesses engraving (after photograph by Mayall), NPG; repro. in *ILN* (12 Jan 1867)
Wealth at death £1681 1*s.*: probate, 27 Oct 1906, *CGPLA Eng. & Wales*

Morice, Humphrey (*c.*1638–1689). *See under* Morice, Sir William (1602–1676).

Morice, Humphry (*bap.* **1679**, *d.* **1731**), merchant and fraudster, was baptized at All Saints, Stamford, Lincolnshire, in June 1679, the son of Humphry *Morice (*c.*1638–1689) [*see under* Morice, Sir William], a London merchant, and Alice, daughter of Sir Thomas Trollope, first baronet, of Casewick, Lincolnshire. His mother died when Humphry was a boy and he was reared with his younger first cousin Nicholas Morice, who succeeded as second baronet in 1690. When approximately eighteen, Morice took over his father's business and during the next three decades conducted a far-flung trade with Holland, Africa, the West Indies, and British North America. In 1704 he married Judith (*bap.* 1685?, *d.* 1720), daughter of a London merchant, Thomas Sandes, with whom he had five daughters, including Judith (*c.*1710–1743), who became the wife of the politician Sir George Lee (1700?–1758). Following his first wife's death in 1720, on 2 June 1722 at St Paul's, Covent Garden, he married Catherine (*d.* 1743), widow of William Hale, and daughter of Peter Paggen of the Manor House, Wandsworth, Surrey. The couple had two sons, Humphry [*see* Morice, Humphry (1723–1785)] and Nicholas (*bap.* 14 Oct 1724, *d.* Nov 1748).

By the early eighteenth century Morice had become deeply involved in the African trade. Between 1702 and 1712 he consigned cargoes to Africa of sworn value of £5720. He also insured cargoes and held shares in ships. This was a period in which the Royal African Company was in decline, from which many private London merchants benefited during the first three decades of the century. For many years Morice actively resisted the company's struggle to regain its monopoly. When in 1708 the Board of Trade undertook a massive inquiry concerning the African trade, Morice and others offered a series of criticisms of the company. They argued that although the company's trade relied on the ships of individual merchants, for it had only two or three of its own, its forts offered these ships no protection against pirates. They argued that the company was unable to provide sufficient slaves to meet demand, and that it treated African rulers badly and sometimes joined with one prince to depose others, thereby threatening trading interests. Summoned before the Board of Trade in 1712, Morice and the leading slave trader Richard Harris offered a fresh settlement of the African trade. They asked parliament to incorporate a regulated company changed annually to export goods to the value of £100,000. The separate traders in the new company would supply the Spanish colonies as agreed in the *asiento*, give parliament security for executing the arrangement, and assurance that they would provide enough goods to pay trading expenses in Africa. A bill to free the African trade passed the Commons but failed in the Lords.

Morice was by this time looking for a seat in the Commons. His cousin Sir Nicholas Morice, a tory, had interests in the Cornish parliamentary boroughs of Launceston and Newport, and although his request for a seat at the 1710 election could not be met, he entered the Commons as member for Newport on 7 September 1713, where he remained until 1722. Morice's parliamentary career was marked by close friendship with Sir Robert Walpole. In 1716 Morice voted for the whig-inspired Septennial Bill. Walpole wrote to Morice on 7 April 1717, 'I am to goe a little into ye country to see a horse or two, and I shall be glad of your company and judgement' (Walpole to Morice, 7 April 1717, Morice papers, Bank of England). In 1719 Morice joined Walpole to vote against the repeal of the Occasional Conformity and Schism Acts. In December 1720 Walpole appealed to Morice, thrice influential as MP, London merchant, and (from 1716 to 1725) a director of the Bank of England:

> The question of the forces comes on this morning, and I am certainly informed the Tories are resolved to give a direct opposition. Pray go to the Bank and speak to all our friends there, and send to all our Members that live in the city to beg they will be in the House before one o'clock. (Walpole to Morice, 14 Dec 1720, Morice papers, Bank of England)

His closeness to Walpole conflicted with the toryism of Sir Nicholas Morice, and in 1722 he was returned by the administration as member for Grampound.

All the while Morice was flourishing in the African trade. In 1726 he owned seven ships employed in the trade. His ships were capable of carrying 2500 slaves, or 9.4 per cent of London's slave transport capacity. In a group of forty-nine shipowners, most of whom owned a single ship, Morice stood foremost. His conduct of his slaving business was distinctive. From his office in Mincing Lane he dispatched a large volume of detailed correspondence. Many of his vessels were very large; the *Katherine* could carry 550 slaves. Some ships were constant traders, making periodic voyages to Africa. Continuity in pursuing his business was strengthened by the extended service of the captains in his employ.

Morice's African-bound cargoes mainly were English, but often included Dutch wares. In 1730 the Board of Trade wanted to know why British ships were carrying foreign goods to Africa. Summoned to appear on 18 March, Morice responded that his ships loaded only gunpowder and spirits in Holland, which British policies had made cheaper. The board asked whether it was true that the Dutch in Africa seized British vessels because they carried Dutch goods. Morice denied this, but did not disclose that he may have had special favour from the Dutch. William Smith in *A New Voyage to Guinea* (1744) remarked, 'I had heard that all the *Dutch* chiefs, at the Outports, were ordered to supply no *English* Ship whatsoever with either Wood or Water, except the Ships belonging to a certain worthy and eminent Merchant of *London*' (Smith, 118). A footnote gives the name Mr Humphrey Morrice.

Without doubt Morice cultivated commercial relations with the Dutch, looking to merchants in Holland for cargoes and Dutch traders in Africa for gold. The House of Lords heard at an inquiry after his death that he 'carried on a very extensive Trade to the Coast of Africa ... and also to Holland' (BL, Add. MS 36153, fol. 76). In his instructions to one of his captains, William Snelgrave, about to embark in 1729 on a voyage to Africa in the *Katherine*, Morice wrote:

> I would have you touch at the Mine [Elmina, a Dutch fort] and deliver my Letters to the Dutch gentlemen there, and ... Possibly you will be able to sell part of your Cargo at the Mine for Gold, which I would have no endeavors on your part be wanting to accomplish. (Morice to Snelgrave, 22 Sept 1729, Morice papers, Bank of England)

Morice was familiar with African conditions and gave minute orders to his ship captains. Take care, he told one, not to be imposed on in dealing with the Africans at Whydah, where they seem to increase their duties. Another was told to sell his entire cargo to the governor of the Royal African Company's Gambia fort, who had been left without supplies. At Commenda, he instructed, a large canoe should be bought to go down the coast, but at 'Jacqueen you must discharge your canoe men, because they would not be allowed to work there' (ibid.). To slave in the Gambia River, he advised, the Royal African Company should be avoided, and his captains were to go upstream where slaves, gold, ivory, and beeswax could be bought cheaply. Their worst goods were to be sold first. His trading pattern also entailed maintaining several ships simultaneously in Africa. The practice earned him several advantages, expediting transaction of business. His ship captains could exchange goods and information, all the while selling cargoes for gold rather than slaves whenever possible. He conducted his trade with marked efficiency, desiring to shorten turnaround time and thus increase profits. John Atkins remarked that 'The late Mr. *Humphry Morice* was the greatest private Trader this way, and unless Providence had fixed a Curse upon it, he must have gained exceedingly' (Atkins, 158–9).

Morice's mercantile traits included trust in his captains and concern for his human cargo. To one captain he wrote that he left management of the ship's cargo and investment entirely to him. Half a century before parliament required slave ships to carry surgeons, Morice installed a surgeon on each ship. 'Be careful of and kind to your Negroes', he adjured a departing commander (letter, 22 Sept 1729, Morice papers, Bank of England). His losses on the notorious middle passage were, in consequence, minimal, about one half the average in his time.

A critical episode in the government's role in the slave trade occurred in February 1726, when the Royal African Company, deeply distressed by competition from the separate traders, memorialized the Board of Trade for relief. The board began an extended inquiry into whether trade should be conducted by a company or laid entirely open, and the status of the forts and settlements on the coast of Africa. Morice among others argued on behalf of the separate traders. He testified that 'the Plantation trade is now the most considerable branch of the trade in this kingdom'. London had eighty-seven ships in the African trade, Bristol sixty-three, and Liverpool twenty-one. He apprehended that by excluding the separate traders the trade 'would soon become of little consequence'. The African trade 'occasioned a great exportation of our own manufactures'. The company had not annually exported to the plantations more than 5400 slaves, whereas the separate traders during the present year had 'made a disposition for furnishing of fifty thousand negroes'. As to the African forts, the greatest trade was conducted at places distant from them, and company forts had frequently fired at separate traders' ships. In short, the company forts and settlements were of little consequence. 'One single man of war could destroy them all' (*Journal of the Commissioners for Trade*, 1723–8, 249–50).

Morice was able to marshal witnesses to support his case, including Mr Newport, 'a considerable trader to Barbadoes, and Mr Knight of Jamaica' (*Journal of the Commissioners for Trade*, 1723–8, 258), as well as his own captain, Snelgrave, all of whom testified to the weakness or self-interest of the company, and the success of the independent traders. Morice and his allies convinced the Board of Trade to decide against the company.

In his final years Morice continued to influence British slave trade policy. He joined in the City of London petition protesting against the Virginia legislature's duty on imported slaves. Acting for the traders to Jamaica he successfully urged the duke of Newcastle, secretary of state, to release upwards of 100 ships detained by the governor of Jamaica, intended by the traders for defence against the Spanish. With other London merchants trading to the plantations he urged passage of the Credit Act of 1731, removing colonial obstruction of debts. The Jamaica assembly appropriated money for the use of Morice in his role as an advocate of the Molasses Act of 1733 to protect the British West Indies from competition of the foreign West Indies.

Morice was a successful merchant and respected authority on the African and West Indian trade whose financial standing seemed to be as sound as his political alliance with Walpole. His appointments as deputy governor of the Bank of England from 1725 to 1727, and governor from 1727 to 1729, expressed his position as a pillar of the British mercantile economy. He died unexpectedly on 16 November 1731 and was buried at St Peter-le-Poer, London. He had long been troubled by gout, but gossip held 'Tis supposed he took poyson' (BL, Add. MS 21500, fol. 62). The Bank of England soon discovered that its former governor, reputedly rich and renowned for his 'great fairness and integrity' (Acres, 1.154), had defrauded the bank by more than £29,000. Many of his bills of exchange 'which on the Face thereof appear'd to be foreign Bills, and drawn at different Places beyond the Seas, were not real but fictitious Bills, and feigned Names set thereto, by the Order of the said Humphry Morice' (*DNB*) to convince his business partners of his credit. He was also found to have abused funds of which he was a trustee. Litigation delayed settlement. His widow, still resisting restitution, died of a carriage accident in 1743. Not until forty-three years after Morice's demise was a final settlement reached. Despite Morice's great wealth in ships, land, and bank stock, his estate proved insufficient to satisfy his creditors.

Though he died disgraced, Morice had figured importantly in Britain's African and North American trade. As a merchant of much magnitude, expert witness, and frequent petitioner to the Board of Trade, parliamentary supporter of Walpole, exporter of European goods, importer of gold, and transporter of enslaved Africans to America, he held a place of great and enduring influence in England's commercial and political life.

JAMES A. RAWLEY

Sources J. A. Rawley, 'Humphry Morice: foremost London slave merchant of his time', *De la traite à l'esclavage* [Nantes 1985], ed. S. Daget, 1 (1988), 269–81 · *N&Q*, 192 (1947), 178–80 · *Journal of the Commissioners for Trade and Plantations, 1704–1782*, 14 vols. (1920–38) · *CSP col.*, vols. 1, 5, 7, 9–45 · J. Atkins, *A voyage to Guinea, Brazil, and the West Indies* (1735) · W. M. Acres, *The Bank of England, 1694–1900*, 2 vols. (1931) · W. Smith, *A new voyage to Guinea* (1744) · Bank of England, London, Morice papers · account book of the *Judith*, 1728–9, Col. U. · corresp. with board of trade, PRO, CO 388/11 · C. Kynaston, letter to T. Carte, 1731, BL, Add. MS 21500, fol. 62 · Bank of England, note of suit, BL, Add. MS 36153, fols. 68, 84–8 · E. Cruickshanks, 'Morice, Humphry', HoP, *Commons, 1715–54* · *DNB* · *IGI*
Archives Bank of England, London, prints, private papers · BL, corresp. and papers, Add. MS 48590, fols. 21–34b · Chiswick Library, London, local studies department, letters | BL, covenant of marriage, 1722, Add. MS 33579, fol. 63 · BL, petitions to Queen Anne, Add. MSS 61510, fols. 152–153b; 61620, fols. 202b–203 · PRO, corresp. with board of trade, CO 388/11
Likenesses G. Kneller, oils, Bank of England Museum, London
Wealth at death bankrupt: Acres, *Bank of England*, vol. 1, p. 154

Morice, Humphry (1723–1785), politician and art collector, was baptized on 20 May 1723 at St Dunstan-in-the-East, London, the elder son of Humphry *Morice (*bap.* 1679, *d.* 1731), governor of the Bank of England, and his second wife, Catherine (*d.* 1743), daughter of Peter Paggen, and widow of William Hale. Nothing is known of his education, and after his father's death and disgrace he may have lived in financially straitened circumstances.

On the death of his second cousin, Sir William Morice, third baronet (1707?–1750), Morice inherited a picture collection acquired from Owen Swiny, including most of the series of twenty-four tomb paintings Swiny had commissioned from Venetian and Bolognese artists commemorating heroes of recent British history. Extending the collection became one of his principal activities. He also inherited from Sir William the estate of Werrington in Devon and the patronage of the nearby parliamentary boroughs of Launceston and Newport. Sir William had been a tory, but Morice sought office and placed his boroughs at the disposal of Henry Pelham's government, despite an offer from the duke of Bedford, his rival for control of the boroughs, that Morice should join with him in opposition. Bedford's ire may have prompted his agent Richard Rigby to dismiss Morice as 'Little Morice' who was 'as peevishly well tired at an election as he is at a whist table when he loses a rubber' (Namier). At the election of 1754 Morice returned himself and Sir George *Lee, who was married to his half-sister Judith, for Launceston, and Lee's brother Colonel John Lee and Edward Bacon, a connection of the Walpoles, for Newport, after a contest with Bedford's nominees. Morice requested a place on the board of green cloth from the prime minister, Thomas Pelham-Holles, duke of Newcastle, but Newcastle would not commit himself.

Morice's request was recalled when Newcastle was trying to form an administration without William Pitt in

April 1757, and on 5 May, Morice kissed hands on his appointment as a clerk-comptroller of the board of green cloth; a fortnight later he was re-elected for Launceston without opposition. Following the death of Sir George Lee in winter 1758, Morice tried to play off Newcastle's interest in retaining the other Launceston seat with his own wish to reach an accommodation with Bedford, and instead of accepting Newcastle's candidate, Edward Simpson, proposed John Tylney, second Earl Tylney, a relative of Bedford. He seems to have had second thoughts, as he then wrote to Newcastle saying that he had found Tylney unpalatable to the Launceston electorate, and replaced him with Peter Burrell. At the by-election on 30 December 1758, Sir John St Aubyn, fourth baronet, nephew of Sir William Morice, won by fifteen votes to fourteen, and Burrell was only seated on petition on 21 February 1759.

Later in 1759 Morice received letters from four conspirators who threatened that unless he acceded to their financial demands they would accuse him of sodomy. When one, Peter Parry, turned informer, Morice was able to have two others, Samuel Scrimshaw and James Ross, tried and sentenced to three years' imprisonment in Newgate, but the fourth blackmailer, Richardson, evaded arrest. Although Morice was cleared, his health suffered from the stress of the case, and he decided to travel abroad, asking leave from Newcastle on 7 June 1760. He had already been recommended to Horace Mann in Florence by Horace Walpole, who described him as 'a friend of Mr [John] Chute' (Walpole, *Corr.*, 21.389); Mann declared, when Morice arrived in Florence in October, that Mann would 'take to him violently' (ibid., 21.442). He took a house at Naples, and was still there when George II died. Despite protests from his friends, he was replaced on the board of green cloth. On his return to London for the autumn sitting of parliament he sided with John Stuart, third earl of Bute, rather than with Newcastle, but he returned to Italy in 1762.

Morice used his stay in Italy to enlarge the art collection he had inherited from Sir William Morice. In 1762, for example, he bought *Venus and Cupid* (also known as *Diana and Cupid*) from Pompeo Batoni, and in that year sat for what was Batoni's only portrait of a sitter in a reclining pose. He again returned to London for the parliamentary session, and in December was appointed comptroller of the household by Bute. Bute immediately regretted the appointment, but was unable to persuade Morice to exchange offices with Lord Charles Spencer, who had the less prestigious sinecure of surveyor of gardens and outranger of Windsor Forest. Morice was sworn of the privy council on 10 January 1763. In April 1763, when George Grenville's administration was formed, he gave up the comptrollership for the post of lord warden of the stannaries. Morice remained a supporter of government, transferring his loyalties from Grenville to Rockingham in 1765, and to the Chatham administration in 1766. He continued to sit for Launceston in the 1768–74 parliament, but returned to Naples in winter 1768–9, and spent time in Rome. Only two of his votes are recorded for the 1768–74 parliament, and in both cases (the committal of Brass

Crosby to the Tower of London on 27 March 1771, and the Royal Marriages Bill, March 1772) he voted with North's government. He seems to have maintained his political interest in Cornwall, as he was chosen recorder of Launceston on 4 February 1771, and was sworn the following December. At the election of 1774 there was a struggle against his influence, and in 1775 he sold the Werrington estate to Hugh Percy, first duke of Northumberland, and with it his electoral influence in Launceston and Newport, for a price estimated at about £100,000. He remained member for Launceston for the duration of the 1774–80 parliament, but showed little interest in the Commons, which he was reported as hating. He spent the early months of 1780 in Italy and retired from parliament that year. Following his return to Britain he was asked by Cavaliere Giulio Mozzi, residual legatee of Horace Walpole's sister-in-law Margaret, countess of Orford, to take up his case against the countess's son, George, third earl of Orford, who claimed several thousand pounds of the estate. Walpole doubted that Morice was well enough to represent Mozzi; in October 1781 he was in Bath being treated for gout by Dr John Turton, and when Walpole dined with Morice in July 1782, he reported 'He has totally lost the use of his legs and feet' (Walpole, *Corr.*, 25.298). On 24 July 1782 he made his will, and in that month abandoned Mozzi's case and left for Italy for the last time. He resigned his recordership at Launceston, and on 20 November 1783 the Fox–North coalition ousted him from the lord wardenship of the stannaries.

Morice spent the last years of his life at a villa near Naples. His main concern was his estate. At Nice in October 1782, he executed a codicil to his will giving to his trustees £600 yearly from the estates he still possessed in Devon and Cornwall, 'to pay for the maintenance of the horses and dogs I leave behind me, and for the expense of servants to look after them' (will, PRO, PROB 11/1139, sig. 106, fol. 30). Morice never married. He left the bulk of his estate to Mrs Levina Luther, stepdaughter of his friend and fellow art collector Richard Bull. This included Grove House, Chiswick, which he had bought in 1772 from the estate of Lady Frances Elliot, daughter of the last Nassau d'Auverquerque earl of Grantham. According to George Colman the younger, 'all the stray animals which happened to follow him to London he sent down to this villa … The honours shown by Mr Morrice to his beasts of burthen were only inferior to those which Caligula lavished on his charger' (Colman, 280). He explained in a codicil to his will that he did not want to give annuities to his animals in case the subsequent ridicule would embarrass his friends, but would instruct his trustees by letter. In 1783 Walpole wrote to the countess of Upper Ossory that, whether Morice was better in health or worse, he was always in good spirits. But Morice was steadily preparing for death, and in a second codicil to his will, executed at Naples on 14 March 1784, he requested that he be buried at Naples in a lead coffin, and that a surgeon take out his heart 'to ascertain my being really dead' (will, PRO, PROB 11/1139, sig. 106, fol. 31). He died at Naples on 18 October 1785, and was presumably buried there. He had earlier wished to be buried in the Paggen family vault at the French protestant burial-ground on Wandsworth Hill. His house in Chiswick was apparently the residence of his favourite horse for another twenty-five years. His art collection was sold to John Ashburnham, second earl of Ashburnham, who dispersed most of it, retaining works by Salvator Rosa, Nicolas Poussin, and Mola.

A. F. ROBBINS, *rev.* MATTHEW KILBURN

Sources Walpole, *Corr.* · L. B. Namier, 'Morice, Humphrey', HoP, *Commons, 1754–90* · E. Cruickshanks, 'Morice, Humphrey', HoP, *Commons, 1715–54* · J. Ingamells, ed., *A dictionary of British and Irish travellers in Italy, 1701–1800* (1997), 678–9 · J. Turner, ed., *The dictionary of art*, online edn, 18 March 2002 · *Annual Register* (1759), 99–100 · D. Lysons, *The environs of London*, 2nd edn, 2 vols. in 4 (1811), 2/1.126–7 · H. Walpole, 'Horace Walpole's journals of visits to country seats', *Walpole Society*, 16 (1927–8), 9–80 · 'Grove House', www.old-father-thames.co.uk/sector04/1004html/jd084021.html, 11 Feb 2002 · corresp. with duke of Newcastle, BL, Add. MSS 32856, fols. 17, 459; 32860, fols. 142, 199; 32870, fol. 457; 32871, fol. 23; 32876, fol. 108; 32879, fol. 348; 32886, fols. 397, 505, 539; 32887, fols. 99, 197, 408; 32905, fol. 250; 32907, fol. 70; 32914, fol. 37; 32920, fols. 57, 62, 308, 315, 362; 32930, fols. 70, 72; 32935, fol. 133; 33067, fol. 161 · *European Magazine*, 8 (1785), 395 · *GM*, 1st ser., 55 (1785), 919 · *Pocket Magazine*, 13 (1795), 171 · will, PRO, PROB 11/1139, sig. 106 · J. Redington and R. A. Roberts, eds., *Calendar of home office papers of the reign of George III*, 1: 1760–1765, PRO (1878) · JHC, 29 (1761–4), 646 · Boase & Courtney, *Bibl. Corn.* · W. H. Smyth, *Ædes Hartwellianæ* (1851), 114 · W. H. Smyth, *Ædes Hartwellianæ: addenda* (1864), 137 · G. Colman, *Random records* (1830) · T. Faulkner, *The history and antiquities of Brentford, Ealing and Chiswick* (1845), 484–5 · R. Peter and O. B. Peter, *The histories of Launceston and Dunheved* (1885), 406 · A. F. Robbins, *Launceston, past and present* (1888), 259–76 · N&Q, 2nd ser., 9 (1860), 486 · *The Western Antiquary*, 8 (1888), 20, 53, 75, 146; 9 (1889), 61, 85, 111; 11 (1891), 6–9 · J. T. Squire, *Mount Nod, a burial ground of the Huguenots at Wandsworth* (1887) · W. P. Courtney, *The parliamentary representation of Cornwall* (1889) · IGI

Archives Northumbd RO, Newcastle upon Tyne, corresp. | BL, corresp. with duke of Newcastle, etc., Add. MSS 32856–33067 · Chiswick Library, Local Studies department, corresp.

Likenesses P. Batoni, oils, 1762, priv. coll.; copy, 1762, priv. coll. · P. Batoni, oils, 1762?, Wadsworth Athenaeum, Hartford, Connecticut

Wealth at death see will, PRO, PROB 11/1139, sig. 106

Morice, James (1539–1597), lawyer, was the eldest son of William *Morice (d. 1554) of Chipping Ongar, Essex, courtier and MP [*see under* Morice, Ralph], and his wife, Anne Isaac of Kent, who was related to Sir Thomas Wyatt and Sir Thomas Wroth. Little is known of his early life or education before he entered the Middle Temple in 1558, but his paternal uncle Ralph Morice was the long-time secretary of Thomas Cranmer, and his father was at one point imprisoned by Henry VIII for his protestant sympathies. James married Elizabeth, daughter of George Medley of Tilty Abbey, Essex, some time before 1560; they had four sons and three daughters. He was probably chosen MP for Wareham, Dorset, in 1563, but he was active mainly in London and Essex, where he had inherited his father's house at Chipping Ongar. He became an Essex JP in 1573, was town clerk of Colchester by 1578, and a member of the Essex quorum in 1586. He was on the commission for piracy in 1577, and on that for musters in 1583.

In 1578 Morice was raised to the bench and appointed autumn reader at the Temple, an obligation he met by delivering a series of lectures on the royal prerogative. Taking a short saving clause of the Statute of Westminster I as his text, he argued that 'a Lawfull Prynce by Justice, and not pleasure, rules and governes the People commytted to his Charge' (BL, Add. MS 36081, fol. 230). Monarchy established by law and the 'prudent Rules and Precepts of Reason agreaed upon and made in the Covenant of the Comon wealth' was the best form of government because it prevented the absolute authority of one person from turning into 'hatefull Tirany, and Insolent oppression' (ibid., fol. 231). At the same time Morice's precocious treatment of English kings' 'imperial prerogatives' (BL, Egerton MS 3376, fol. 45v) over the church traced the royal exercise of ecclesiastical patronage back to the pre-conquest era. Despite numerous attempts by the churchmen to undermine the prerogative, godly kings had often acted in concert with parliament to make laws that overthrew 'unlawful intrusions' and usurpations. Furthermore, by focusing on the long history of the common-law writ of prohibition, Morice demonstrated that the jurisdiction of the church courts had always been determined by the 'ancient Customes' (ibid., fol. 58v) and usages of the realm, as interpreted by the common-law judges.

Although Morice's treatment of the ecclesiastical jurisdiction contains nearly all of the arguments employed by the common lawyers in subsequent quarrels with the churchmen, the reading appears not to have been considered overly controversial at the time. William Cecil asked for a copy of the lectures, and thanks to his influence Morice was appointed to the post of attorney in the court of wards in 1579, the same year in which he gave a speech welcoming Queen Elizabeth to Colchester. Enjoying the support of Sir Francis Walsingham, he became MP for Colchester in 1584 and continued as its member in the parliaments of 1586, 1589, and 1593, serving on many committees (sixteen in 1584 alone). In 1586 he became recorder of Maldon, and he was one of sixteen lawyers asked by the privy council in 1588 to prepare bills on judicial reform and to consider the revision of existing statutes.

Morice was also involved in defending laymen and clerics brought before high commission and other church courts for breaches of ecclesiastical discipline. *A Briefe Treatise of Oathes*, which he published in Middelburg in 1590 or 1591, attacked the ecclesiastical courts' use of the oath *ex officio*, which obliged defendants to swear (on pain of imprisonment) to answer questions put to them before any formal charges had been brought. Claiming that it smacked of the Spanish Inquisition, Morice argued that tendering the oath was contrary to canon law as well as the common law of England, and that it was a 'wrong and injury to the freedom and liberty of the subiectes' (Morice, *Briefe Treatise*, 57). In all likelihood he worked with Robert Beale on the defence of Thomas Cartwright and other presbyterian ministers, and in July 1591, probably at the instigation of Burghley, he agreed to handle the appeal of Robert Caudry of South Luffenham, Rutland, who had been deprived of his living by high commission for allegedly speaking against the Book of Common Prayer. Although he accurately predicted that Caudry would have little chance of success in the courts, Morice took the case because he thought it unconscionable for a lawyer to refuse to help those 'wronged' (BL, Lansdowne MS 68, fol. 125). Furthermore, on 27 February 1593 he introduced two bills into the House of Commons that aimed to outlaw oaths, inquisitions, and subscriptions and to abolish imprisonment as a sanction against refusing them. Claiming that the practices of the church courts were contrary to Magna Carta, his long speech sparked a heated debate. On the following day Morice was examined by privy councillors, who committed him to the custody of Sir John Fortescue at his London house, where he remained until 16 April.

Morice evidently enjoyed the support of the earl of Essex, who suggested later in 1593 that he be made attorney-general, as well as that of his kinswoman Lady Elizabeth Russell, who praised his learning and piety to Robert Cecil. But his advancement was now thwarted by the queen, who recognized his abilities but could not forgive him the indiscretion of speaking against her in parliament, according to Burghley. Nevertheless, he continued to campaign against the oath *ex officio*. By 1594 he had completed a much enlarged manuscript treatise on the subject that was framed as an answer to Richard Cosin's *An Apologie for Sundrie Proceedings by Jurisdiction Ecclesiasticall* (1591), which contained an attack on Morice's earlier pamphlet. Although he lent this second work to Archbishop Whitgift at the latter's request, Morice was frustrated that he could not make him see that the oath *ex officio* was significantly different from oaths employed in lay courts such as chancery or Star Chamber. Writing to Burghley in 1596, Morice complained that while Cosin had been allowed to take his case before the public in print, he was unable to put his 'without some blot or blemish' (BL, Lansdowne MS 82, fol. 150) on himself. Although he was in June of that year appointed treasurer of the Middle Temple, he was unsuccessful in seeking further public employment, telling Burghley that while he had not been 'idle or prodigal' (ibid., fol. 148), he had not over the years been able to add much to the inheritance left him by his father. He died on 2 February 1597, leaving £200 that had passed through his hands as treasurer of the Temple unaccounted for. His will expressed the hope that his children would be 'profitable members of Christ's church and good subjects in the commonwealth'. To his eldest son, John, he bequeathed his 'books of the laws of England' as well as 'Latin, Greek and French books' (HoP, *Commons, 1558–1603*, 3.100).   CHRISTOPHER W. BROOKS

Sources DNB · HoP, *Commons, 1509–58*, 2.631–3 · HoP, *Commons, 1558–1603*, 3.98–100 · C. T. Martin, ed., *Minutes of parliament of the Middle Temple*, 4 vols. (1904–5) · BL, Lansdowne MS 68 [papers relating to *Caudry's case*], fols. 104, 106, 108, 117, 123, 125, 127, 129 · Morice to Burghley, 1596, BL, Lansdowne MS 82, fols. 148–50 · BL, Egerton MS 3376 [reading of 1578] · BL, Add. MS 36081 [incomplete version of Morice's reading on the royal prerogative] · 'A remembrance of certaine matters concerning the clergie and their jurisdiction, by James Morice [a zealot] and member of parliament', CUL, MS Mm. 1.51, fols. 105–34 · J. Morice, 'A just and necessarie

defence of a briefe treatise made ageinst generall oathes', 1594, LPL, MS 234 · J. Morice, *A briefe treatise of oathes exacted by ordinaries and ecclesiasticall judges* (Middelburg, 1590?) · R. Cosin, *An apologie for sundrie proceedings by jurisdiction ecclesiasticall* (1593)

Morice [Morys], **Sir John** (*d.* 1362), justiciar of Ireland, is probably to be identified with the Bedfordshire knight of that name who represented the county in parliament and was frequently a commissioner of array, of oyer and terminer, and of the peace. He enjoyed a long public career which, because of his association with John Darcy of Knaith (*d.* 1347), lay mostly in Ireland, where Darcy was often justiciar between 1324 and 1344. Between 1309–10 and 1324 Morice and Darcy served in the retinue of Aymer de Valence, earl of Pembroke and lord of Wexford, of whose heirs Morice and his wife, Agnes, held lands at Everton Mosbury, Bedfordshire. Morice may have had a second wife, Margaret, though the identification of the John Morice in this marriage is uncertain. In 1341 his son, John (who may have predeceased him), was seneschal of Wexford, an office that his father had earlier held. In 1324 Morice was said to be going to Ireland in Darcy's company. He undoubtedly did so in 1329, when he was appointed escheator, a position he held until 1336. He visited England on several occasions during that period; in 1331 he was returning to Ireland in the company of William de Burgh, earl of Ulster, of whom he held lands at Steeple Claydon, Buckinghamshire, and one of whose executors he became. The escheatorship was an important office, which involved taking distant lordships into the king's hand, as Morice did in 1333 after the murder of Earl William. In 1330 he had lost horses, harness, armour, clothing, bedding, silver bullion, and a psalter in an attack by the Irish as he journeyed from Connacht to Tipperary in the course of his duties.

In 1341 Morice acted as one of the judges inquiring into ministerial oppressions in Oxfordshire, Berkshire, and Buckinghamshire. He was removed in order to go to Ireland as deputy to Darcy. His rule proved controversial. Edward III's wrath at the failure of his ministers to raise resources for the French war extended to Ireland, where he denounced locally born officials and authorized the revocation of grants made since 1307. Morice was unable to carry this ill-judged policy through. In 1342 protests from the settler community reached the king; they included a complaint (possibly directed at Morice) about rule by men who lacked experience of war. Edward withdrew the measures. Unlike other members of the government Morice continued in office; his eventual removal in July 1344 was to make room for the new administration of Ralph Ufford. Early in 1346 he was sent to Ireland again, probably to raise troops for France. Since the king knew that Ufford was mortally ill, he was also given authority to assume the justiciarship if necessary. Following Ufford's death he served as justiciar between 16 May and 28 June, after which he held the chancellorship until December. He helped to handle the aftermath of Ufford's forfeiture of the earls of Kildare and Desmond, arranging the first steps in Kildare's rehabilitation. This took him to England and Calais during the winter of 1346–7. He does not appear to have returned to Ireland after 1347, though he continued to appoint attorneys to look after his interests there until May 1362. He had died by the following August.   ROBIN FRAME

Sources Chancery records · PRO · VCH Bedfordshire · R. Frame, *English lordship in Ireland, 1318–1361* (1982) · A. J. Otway-Ruthven, *A history of medieval Ireland* (1968) · G. O. Sayles, ed., *Documents on the affairs of Ireland before the king's council*, IMC (1979) · H. G. Richardson and G. O. Sayles, *The administration of Ireland, 1172–1377* (1963) · *Inquisitions and assessments relating to feudal aids*, 6 vols., PRO (1899–1921) · J. R. S. Phillips, *Aymer de Valence, earl of Pembroke, 1307–1324: baronial politics in the reign of Edward II* (1972)
Likenesses G. V. Du Noyer, portrait (after Charter roll, 1860–69), Royal Society of Antiquaries of Ireland, Dublin, Du Noyer's sketchbooks · portrait, Waterford municipal archives, Charter roll of the city of Waterford; repro. in A. Cosgrove, ed., *Medieval Ireland, 1169–1534* (1987), pl. 26b

Morice, Ralph (*fl.* 1522–1570), principal secretary to Thomas Cranmer, was a younger son of James Morice (*d.* 1557) of Roydon, Essex, clerk of works to Lady Margaret Beaufort, and his wife, the daughter and heir of a man named Buckbeard. James's eldest son, **William Morice** (*c.*1500–1554), was a gentleman usher first to the scholar and diplomat Richard Pace (probably by 1525), and then to the royal household (by 1533). He was also joint receiver-general with his father, both in the court of general surveyors (1530–47) and for possessions recovered by the court of common pleas (from 1536). A fervent evangelical, he, along with his brother Ralph, Edward Isaac, and Hugh Latimer, visited James Bainham on 29 April 1532 in the Newgate prison the day before he was burnt as a relapsed heretic. A year later Latimer was corresponding with one of the Morice brothers about his troubles in Bristol. By 1539 William had married Isaac's sister Anne. The following year he was made JP for Essex, where on 20 May 1542 he began a long-term lease of Chipping Ongar. His forthright manner and protestant sympathies, and also (it is said) his lease, made him enemies, notably Sir Richard Rich, who was himself engaged in building up an estate in Essex. On 15 May 1546 the privy council sent for William Morice over his involvement with Edward Crome, an evangelical preacher recently charged with heresy. By 16 July he was under house arrest with Sir Richard Southwell and he was not released until the new reign. Subsequently an MP three times (1547 and March and October 1553), Morice obtained a private act for uniting his parish of Ongar with Rich's Greenstead (2 and 3 Edward VI, no. 55). Rich received the advowson, Morice Ongar's church building and yard. Shortly after his death on 17 January 1554 parliament repealed the parish union, charging Morice with unworthy motives.

Ralph (Raphe) Morice was listed at Christ's College, Cambridge, in 1522, graduated BA in 1523, and proceeded MA in 1526. On the recommendation of George Boleyn, Viscount Rochford, he was appointed Cranmer's secretary to help with the king's divorce, probably in 1531. When Cranmer became archbishop in 1533 Morice assisted his reformist programme for the realm by toilsomely writing 'no small Volumes' (Strype, appx, no. 103). His surviving secretarial work includes a copybook of Cranmer's letters

(BL, Harley MS 6148), copies of Cranmer's politically sensitive correspondence for Thomas Cromwell (PRO, SP 6/2, fols. 86–91), Morice's own draft for a royal letter abolishing ceremonies (PRO, SP 1/213, fols. 146–7) and fair copies of an initial draft against the council summoned to Mantua by the pope in 1537 (LPL, MS 1107, fol. 163), the text on holy orders for the *Bishops' Book* (BL, Cotton MS Cleopatra E. V. fols. 48–50r), and portions of Cranmer's two schemes to revise the daily offices (BL, Royal MS 7.B.IV, fols. 48–150r).

On 18 June 1537 Morice was made joint bailiff with his father for some crown lands in Hertfordshire and Somerset. Later that year Cranmer arranged for him to have the lease of Ospringe, Kent, from St John's College, Cambridge, but the king intervened on behalf of another. Two years later Morice petitioned the king and Cromwell for the modest lease of Bigging in Hichin, being content now with a 'deformed Lia, leaving faire Rachell' for the more deserving (SP 1/113, fol. 208v). On 29 June 1540 he had to answer to the privy council for gossiping about the king's marriage to Anne of Cleves.

Eventually Morice received the lease on the parsonage of Chartham, Kent, and secured the evangelical Richard Turner as his curate. In 1543 Kentish JPs who were conservative in religion attacked his preaching as a part of the 'prebendaries plot' against Cranmer, citing Turner to the king as an example of the archbishop's protection of heretics. Working closely with court evangelicals Sir Anthony Denny and Dr William Butts, Morice orchestrated a 'counter-plot'. His timely interventions were instrumental in saving both Turner and Cranmer.

On 2 March 1543 Cranmer made Morice a grant in reversion after the death of Richard Watkins of the office of scribe of the court of arches; this was approved by the Canterbury chapter on 22 November 1550. Then on 1 October 1543 Cranmer made Morice warden for life, with his own house, of the archbishop's palace at Bekesbourne, a grant approved by the Canterbury chapter on 25 November 1545. It was as a gentleman of Bekesbourne that Morice stood bond with James Terry of Chartham for John Styll's lease of Stone, Isle of Oxney, on 10 February 1546.

In 1547 Cranmer made Morice a registrar for the ecclesiastical commissioners appointed to visit the dioceses of Rochester, Canterbury, Chichester, and Winchester. On 4 October 1550 he also gave Morice a 21-year lease of Enbroke, Kent. Under Mary, Morice's home was raided three times in two years, as a result of which he lost many Cranmer papers and finally had to flee. He was captured and gaoled, but eventually he was able to 'brake prison frome the Justices' (BL, Harley MS 416, fol. 183r). By November 1557 he was able to act as executor of his father's will, which granted him a close and a house called Fosters in Roydon.

Under Elizabeth, Morice rendered valuable assistance to protestant historiography. He first wrote to John Day, the future publisher of Foxe's *Actes and Monuments*, on 10 January 1566, and subsequently supplied Foxe with stories about Cranmer and Canterbury School, the martyrdom in 1532 of Thomas Dusgate, Hugh Latimer's conversion, the wit of the evangelical Thomas Lawney, and Latimer's visit to the imprisoned James Bainham. Foxe also included information from Morice in his accounts of Henry VIII, Laurence Barber of Oxford, Thomas Cromwell, Thomas Thirlby, Richard Turner, and, from a manuscript evidently first prepared for Archbishop Matthew Parker (Corpus Christi College, Cambridge, MS 128), Thomas Cranmer.

Morice twice addressed petitions to Elizabeth. About 1565 he asked her for the pension of John Wilbore, the recently deceased former abbot of St Augustine's, Canterbury, citing both his own needs and those of his four daughters 'left by their mother marriageable' (Strype, appx, no. 103). When a new leaseholder disputed his Roydon inheritance, probably in 1567, Morice asked the queen to confirm his rights. It would appear both suits were answered in some form, for in January and February 1571 Margaret, Mary, and Anne Morice were all married in the parish church of Bekesbourne, and a map of about 1597 still showed Morice land in Roydon. Alyce Morrys, buried on 25 February 1562, may have been Ralph's wife. At least between 1537 and 1543 Morice also had a son and namesake, Ralph. Foxe reported Morice as still alive in 1570, and it is not known when he died.

ASHLEY NULL

Sources D. MacCulloch, *Thomas Cranmer: a life* (1996) · HoP, *Commons, 1509–58*, 2.631–3 · M. Buxton, 'Chipping Ongar and the Morices', *Aspects of the history of Ongar*, ed. M. Leach (1999), 34–49 · J. Strype, *Memorials of the most reverend father in God, Thomas Cranmer* (1694), 68, 90, 123–6, 274–5, 424–8, appx no. 103 · J. G. Nichols, ed., *Narratives of the days of the Reformation*, CS, old ser., 77 (1859), 43–6, 234–78 · *LP Henry VIII*, 6, nos. 1600–01; 7, no. 90; 11, nos. 1479–80; 12/2, nos. 191 (28), 796 (5); 17, no. 283 (48, 59); addenda 1/1, 108 · J. Foxe, *Ecclesiasticall history, conteynyng the actes and monumentes of martyrs* (1570), 1134–5, 1168–72, 1180–84, 1355–60, 1382, 1425–7, 1477–8, 1903, 1910–12, 2032–72 · R. Morice, letters to Cromwell, PRO, state papers Henry VIII, general ser., SP 1/113, fols. 206–8 · R. Morice, letter to John Day, BL, Harley MS 416, fols. 183–184r · R. Morice, petition to Queen Elizabeth for Roydon properties, BL, Lansd. MS 108, fols. 14–15 · Canterbury Cathedral, dean and chapter, Canterbury Archives, Register U, fols. 125v–126v, 135v–136v, 226v · Canterbury Cathedral, dean and chapter, Canterbury Archives, Bond 138 · Bekesbourne parish registers, Canterbury Archives · *CPR, 1566–9*, nos. 398, 564 · M. Bateson, ed., *Grace book B*, 2 (1905), 105, 130 · *APC, 1542–7*, 417, 490 · will, PRO, PROB 11/37, fol. 19 [W. Morice] · will, PRO, PROB 11/39, fol. 367r [J. Morice] · researcher for Lord Herbert of Chirbury, notes on gossip about Anne of Cleves, Bodl. Oxf., MS Jesus 74, fol. 299 · map of Roydon, c.1597, Bodl. Oxf., MS Essex Roll 9 · *Miscellaneous writings and letters of Thomas Cranmer*, ed. J. E. Cox, Parker Society, [18] (1846), 259 · M. K. Jones and M. G. Underwood, *The king's mother: Lady Margaret Beaufort, countess of Richmond and Derby* (1992) · G. Bray, ed., *Tudor church reform: the Henrician canons of 1535 and the Reformatio legum ecclesiasticarum*, Church of England Record Society, 8 (2000), 749 · VCH *Essex*, vol. 8 · *DNB* · Cooper, *Ath. Cantab.*, 1.293–4 · Venn, *Alum. Cant.*, 1/3.215 · inventory, PRO, PROB 2/255 [William Morice]
Archives BL, Harley MS 6148 · BL, Lansdowne MS 108, fols. 14–15 · BL, Royal MS 7.b.IV, fols. 48–150r · CCC Cam., MS 128, pp. 405–40 · LPL, MS 1107, fol. 163 | BL, Foxe's papers, Harley MSS 416, fols. 183–184r; 419, fols. 115, 125; 422, fols. 84–8, 90 · BL, Cotton MSS Cleopatra E. V., fols. 48–50r · PRO, SP 1/113, fols. 206–8 · PRO, SP 1/213, fols. 146–7 · PRO, SP 6/2, fols. 86–91
Wealth at death retained property in Roydon; requested crown pension in 1565: Strype, *Memorials of … Cranmer*, appx no. 103 · William Morice: will, PRO, PROB 11/37, fol. 19; inventory, PRO, PROB 2/255

Morice, William (c.1500–1554). *See under* Morice, Ralph (*fl.* 1522–1570).

Morice, Sir William (1602–1676), politician, was born on 6 November 1602 in St Martin's parish, Exeter, the first son of Dr Evan Morice (d. 1605), chancellor of the diocese of Exeter, and his wife, Mary (d. 1647), daughter of John Castell of Ashbury, Devon. In 1611 his mother married again, her second husband being Sir Nicholas Prideaux of Soulden, Cornwall. In 1619 Morice went to Exeter College, Oxford, whose warden was a Prideaux (the later moderate bishop of Worcester). His tutor was the respected scholar Nathaniel Carpenter. After graduating BA in 1622, Morice returned to Devon. About 1627 he married Elizabeth (d. 1663), daughter of Humphrey Prideaux of Soulden and granddaughter of his stepfather, Sir Nicholas. They had four sons and four daughters.

Living in Putford, north Devon, Morice was entrusted by friends and relatives with estate matters: Sir Bevil Grenville, a close friend, settled land on him and others in trust in a will of 1639; and a distant kinsman, George Monck, later commander of the Commonwealth's army, committed the care of his own estate to Morice during his absences from England in the 1640s. By 1640 Morice was a Devon justice. In 1642 he was appointed a royal commissioner of array, although there is no evidence that he served as such, nor that he did anything to assist the royal cause in Devon during the civil war, although after Bevil Grenville was killed in 1643 his trusteeship of the estate on behalf of Grenville's son, Sir John, provoked for a while in 1649–50 the interest and suspicion of the committee for the advance of money.

That interest may have been linked to the beginnings of Morice's active involvement in politics. His return to the Long Parliament as a recruiter MP on 15 August 1648 came as presbyterians and the peace party made their last attempts to secure negotiations with the king, although there is no evidence that he sat in the Commons before or after Pride's Purge, when he was among those formally excluded. Morice continued to serve in the commission of the peace in Devon, despite his exclusion, and was returned again for Devon in Barebone's Parliament in July 1653. From about the mid-1650s, however, Morice was probably more concerned with fighting the spread of Independency in Devon and the growth of those congregations which excluded from communion those deemed not worthy of it—'the new way … of gathering Churches, and making a kind of monopoly of the sacrament' (Morice, 1). His manuscript tract against the practice provoked some ministers in Devon, and particularly Henry Saunders, the rector of Holworthy (in his *Anti-Diatribe* of 1655), to respond. Morice claimed to be reluctant to engage in public controversy—he was 'one of those plants that most love and best thrive in the shadow … and like coral am more verdant under water, but am red with blushing when I came up above it' (ibid., preface)—but he was moved to polish and publish his own vastly learned work as *Coena quasi koinē* in 1657; a further edition was planned in 1658, although not issued until 1660.

The controversy was perhaps why, though again elected to parliament for Devon for the 1656 parliament, Morice was one of those prevented from taking his seat by the council of state, and among the signatories to the remonstrance against its action published in September. Cromwell's death seems to have encouraged Morice to take a larger role in political resistance to the protectorate. In the elections of 1658–9 he was returned for Newport, Cornwall, together with Sir John Grenville; taking his seat, he contributed lengthy and learned speeches to the campaign of various factions to wreck the attempts of Richard Cromwell's government to obtain a constitutional settlement. After the collapse of the protectorate Morice was said to have been involved in the plans for a presbyterian–royalist rising in July, at about the same time as the Rump appointed him a commissioner for the militia in Devon. The following year, in January 1660, his kinsman General George Monck contacted him as he marched south from Scotland, requesting a meeting in London.

Morice seems to have arrived in London at, or soon after, the time of the readmission of the secluded members of the Long Parliament on 21 February. Lodging with the general at St James's, he was Monck's 'Elbow-Counsellor and a State Blind' (Price, 119) and his agent in parliament. Monck valued him for his 'great Abilities in History and other Learning, which the General admired in his youth' (Gumble, 268). That admiration was said to be sufficient for Monck to make Morice, implausibly, governor of Plymouth in early March so that he could help the general to persuade senior officers against remonstrating against the actions of parliament—although, as Thomas Skinner wrote, 'being a Gentleman that had spent his Time in the Silence of his Books and Studies, it render'd him uneasy in the company of such rude and clamorous conventions' (Skinner, 280), and Monck's brother-in-law, Thomas Clarges, did most of the talking. Morice was no doubt also intended to appeal to the presbyterian faction. But Morice's principal value for Monck was as an intermediary with Sir John Grenville, and therefore an indirect and deniable channel to the royal court.

Monck was not ready to make direct contact with Grenville until after the dissolution of the Long Parliament on 17 March. When their meeting finally took place, about two days later, it was set up by Morice; a further meeting, at which Monck indicated what he believed the king would need to offer in order to achieve a restoration, took place in Morice's own chamber. After Grenville took the message to the king, providing the court with a clear indication of the likelihood of restoration, Charles II wrote both to Monck and to Morice on 6 April 1660 NS, and during April agreed to Monck's proposal, relayed again by Sir John Grenville, that Morice be appointed secretary of state (in the process embittering one old royalist, Sir Richard Fanshawe, who had confidently expected the post for himself). After the assembly of the Convention Parliament (for which Morice was elected at both Newport and Plymouth) the presentation of the king's letter to both houses was delayed because Morice's election return had not yet been received. But on 1 May Morice spoke to recommend to the Commons the king's restoration. He went with Monck to greet the king at Dover, and was knighted on the day Charles landed, 27 May 1660.

For eight years after the Restoration Morice held the post of secretary of state. In a court dominated by those with royalist backgrounds and much greater experience in politics and administration, Morice was an outsider. Regarded by many as owing his post solely to Monck's patronage, his promotion was seen as an odd one for a man with so little facility in modern languages—'he gave the king often occasion to laugh at his unskilful pronunciation of many words' (*Life of … Clarendon*, 1.632). After the replacement of his fellow secretary, Sir Edward Nicholas, by Sir Henry Bennet in 1662 Morice seems to have felt threatened by Bennet's attempts to dominate the administration (and when Bennet sought to have his own under-secretary elected for Dartmouth in 1667, Morice successfully promoted his own candidate, Walter Yonge, instead). A number of Anglican royalists plainly suspected him as one of the pro-presbyterian Trojan horses within the government, and undoubtedly he took a role in protecting those he regarded as worthy ministers from their efforts to force them into conformity. But the earl of Clarendon, lord chancellor and the king's principal minister, regarded Morice as 'having behaved himself very honestly and diligently in the king's service, and had a good reputation in the house of Commons, and did the business of his office without reproach' (ibid.).

In the political débâcle following the defeat by the Dutch in 1667 and the dismissal and impeachment of Clarendon, Morice (though he was sent by the king to demand the seals from the chancellor) took Clarendon's part; but he found the aftermath so unpleasant that he was reported as being keen to resign as early as October 1667. It was almost another year before he actually did so, in September 1668, having passed the secretaryship on to Sir John Trevor for a large fee. He retired to his estate in Werrington in Devon, where his large collection of books 'was the principal divertisement and most sensible pleasure he took during the last years of his life' (Wood, *Ath. Oxon.*, 3.1090), and was regarded as having escaped from a vicious court with his integrity intact. He died on 12 December 1676 at Werrington, where he was buried.

Morice's third son, **Humphrey Morice** (*c*.1638–1689), administrator and merchant, succeeded to the post of auditor of the exchequer by 8 August 1667, having held the reversion since March 1664, and later became a merchant, trading with Hamburg. On 8 January 1670 he married Alice, daughter of Sir Thomas Trollope, first baronet, of Stamford, Lincolnshire. He was buried on 29 December 1689 at Werrington.　　　　　　　PAUL SEAWARD

Sources M. W. Helms, J. S. Crossette, and B. D. Henning, 'Morice, Sir William', HoP, *Commons, 1660–90* · M. Coate, 'William Morice and the restoration of Charles II', *EngHR*, 33 (1918), 367–77 · W. Morice, *Coena quasi koinē* (1657) · J. Price, *The mystery and method of his majesty's happy restauration* (1680) · R. Bell, ed., *Memorials of the civil war … forming the concluding volumes of the Fairfax correspondence*, 2 (1849), 140–44 · T. Gumble, *The life of General Monck, duke of Albemarle* (1671) · *Diary of Thomas Burton*, ed. J. T. Rutt, 4 vols. (1828) ·

Thurloe, *State papers*, vol. 1 · *The Clarke Papers*, ed. C. H. Firth, 4, CS, new ser., 62 (1901) · J. L. Vivian, ed., *The visitations of the county of Devon, comprising the herald's visitations of 1531, 1564, and 1620* (privately printed, Exeter, [1895]) · *CSP dom.* · Wood, *Ath. Oxon.*, new edn · C. W. Boase, *An alphabetical register of the commoners of Exeter College, Oxford* (1894) · T. Skinner, *Life of General Monck* (1723) · *The life of Edward, earl of Clarendon … written by himself*, 2 vols. (1857) · M. A. E. Green, ed., *Calendar of the proceedings of the committee for compounding … 1643–1660*, 5 vols., PRO (1889–92) · W. M. Acres, 'The Morice family of Werrington', *N&Q*, 192 (1947), 178–80
Archives BL, letters to G. Downing, Add. MSS 22919–22920 · BL, letter-book of Sir W. Vane, Add. MS 16272 · Cornwall RO, letters to Edmund Prideaux · Leics. RO, corresp. with earl of Winchilsea
Likenesses oils, after 1660, Exeter College, Oxford · attrib. J. Huysmans, oils, *c.*1666, Antony, Cornwall · J. Houbraken, line engraving, 1747, BM, NPG; repro. in T. Birch, *The heads and characters of illustrious persons*, vol. 2 (1751), (pl.) · oils, Antony, Cornwall

Morice, William (1733–1819), Church of England clergyman, was born on 28 January 1733, the second son of William Morice, high bailiff of Westminster from 1719 to 1731, of Delahay Street, Kensington, and his second wife, Anne (1705–1743), daughter of Captain John Philpot of Rotherhithe. He matriculated at Hertford College, Oxford, on 8 December 1750, graduating BA in 1754 and MA in 1757. Ordained deacon on 16 May 1756 and priest on 6 March 1757, he served as curate at St Peter-le-Poer, London. On 2 September 1762 he married Hannah Voyce (1737–1789), with whom he had seven children.

Richard Terrick, bishop of London, collated Morice in September 1767 to Wennington, Essex, and Frederick Cornwallis, archbishop of Canterbury, presented him to All Hallows, Bread Street, and St John the Evangelist, in September 1771. He began assisting Dr Daniel Burton, secretary of the Society for the Propagation of the Gospel (SPG), in 1768, and was himself elected secretary in 1778. Salters' Hall Company elected him lecturer in St Dunstan-in-the-East, Fleet Street, in December 1768. After being commissioned chaplain in the 103rd regiment of foot in June 1769, he was appointed chaplain-in-ordinary to the king in 1772. Archbishop Cornwallis conferred a DD degree on him in 1781.

Morice's career was notable for its dedication and efficiency. He served sixteen years as a curate, forty-five as rector of Wennington, forty-eight at All Hallows and St John the Evangelist, and fifty-one years in service to the SPG. He regularly conducted two Sunday services at All Hallows and for twenty years he delivered the Thursday evening lecture. A notice of the bishop's visitation received on 9 March 1790 was answered the next day. His tenure with the SPG is noted for consistent attendance and diligence in his duties, for example in managing all books and papers and waiting upon the archbishop of Canterbury (president of the society) and the bishop of London, in whose overseas diocese missionaries served. Morice prepared and published annual reports with sermon for distribution to all members. Copies of his correspondence fill seven volumes. In addition to official minutes, he kept a private account of the society from 1751 to 1819.

Major events during Morice's years with the SPG were the American War of Independence and the challenge to provide missionaries for Canada. The SPG charter of 1701 limited their service to British possessions. By 1781 the society knew it had to discontinue work in the independent states but it offered continued employment to those who repaired to the king's dominions. It was Morice's responsibility to inform the missionaries of this and help to arrange new assignments. In 1778 the SPG had ninety-four missionaries registered in the independent states but by 1785 there were none. Canada and its neighbouring provinces had twenty-two missionaries in 1785. That same year parliament directed that Canada should be divided into parishes, and provided the society with a grant. The consecration on 12 August 1787 of Charles Inglis, a loyalist missionary from New York and the first colonial bishop, assigned to Nova Scotia, initiated a new era in the society's work. Inglis's consecration fulfilled the SPG's desire for local supervision of their missionaries and Morice's co-operation with Inglis provided seventy-nine appointees to Canada and neighbouring provinces by 1818.

Morice was described as 'firm' and 'friendly'. His greeting was 'your affectionate brother and humble servant'. His resignation in 1814 was withdrawn at the request of Archbishop Charles Manners-Sutton. The qualities that characterized his SPG service were evident in his family relations. His journal reveals affection and encouragement towards his children. Two of his sons, William and Henry, followed his clerical example. A third son, Burton, a barrister, became secretary to the lord chamberlain. His desire was to be buried beside his daughter Charlotte (*d.* 6 May 1775) and wife, Hannah, beneath the communion table in All Hallows, Bread Street. He died at his home, 53 Gower Street, London, on 7 January 1819. Archbishop Charles Manners-Sutton described him as 'their Venerable Secretary … zealous and faithful … upwards of 50 years' (*SPG Minutes*, 32, 1819–20, 22).

FREDERICK V. MILLS, SR.

Sources G. Hennessy, *Novum repertorium ecclesiasticum parochiale Londinense, or, London diocesan clergy succession from the earliest time to the year 1898* (1898) · Foster, *Alum. Oxon.* · vestry records, All Hallows, Bread Street, GL · Bodl. RH, United Society for the Propagation of the Gospel, MSS ser. X · memoranda and journals, 1775–1817, Herts. ALS [2 vols.] · archbishops' and bishops' of London visitation records, LPL · royal household index, 1660–1837, Royal Arch. · H. P. Thompson, *Into all lands* (1951) · J. Pratt, *Propaganda: being an abstract of the designs and proceedings of the Incorporated Society for the Propagation of the Gospel in Foreign Parts* (1819)
Archives Herts. ALS, memoranda and journals | Bodl. RH, Society for the Propagation of the Gospel MSS · GL, vestry records, All Hallows
Likenesses A. Cardon, engraving (after drawing by H. Edridge), USPG, Partnership House, 157 Waterloo Road, London
Wealth at death bequeathed £1600 to relatives; real and personal estate divided into equal parts: will, PRO, PROB 11/1613 ff., sig. 79

Morier, David (1701/2–1770), painter, was born at Bern, Switzerland. Nothing is known of his early career before 1743 when he was introduced to William Augustus, duke of Cumberland, by Sir Everard Fawkener, possibly in Germany where the duke was on campaign. His first notable painting was an equestrian portrait of George II (Royal Collection), with a view of the battle of Dettingen (27 June

1743) beyond, which was later engraved by Francis Simon Ravenet and published by the artist.

Morier is principally known for small military equestrian portraits with battles or reviews in the background, including many of the duke of Cumberland and several of George II, and also for depictions of soldiers, detailing their uniform (principally in the Royal Collection and at Wilton House, Wiltshire). In 1746 his commemoration of the duke's victory against the Jacobites, *The Battle of Culloden* (Royal Collection), was criticized by Colonel William Windham for representing troops drawn up in the line of battle, giving 'little idea of the victory' (G. Thomas, earl of Albemarle, *Fifty Years of my Life*, 2 vols., 1876, 1.108). To achieve accuracy in another painting, *An Incident in the Rebellion of 1745* (Royal Collection), captured clansmen were reputedly brought from Southwark gaol to pose.

In 1747 Morier accompanied his patron to the Low Countries, painting *Royal Artillery in the Netherlands* and a series of sixty pictures of the allied troops under the duke's command (all Royal Collection). In 1751 the first British uniform regulations were issued by royal warrant and Morier, made 'Limner' to the duke with a salary of £100, embarked on further series, including the light dragoon regiments raised in 1759 and 1760. When the duke of Cumberland died in 1765, his second home, Cranbourn Lodge, Berkshire, housed 106 of these paintings and only works by Morier hung in the picture gallery.

Morier's work is of varying quality and he may have had collaborators: Henry Angelo, whose father he had portrayed (*Domenico Angiolo Malevolti Tremamondo*; Wilton House, Wiltshire), stated that Richard Brompton frequently 'put the figures on [Morier's] horses' (*Reminiscences of Henry Angelo*, 2 vols., 1904, 1.24). A founder member of the Society of Artists, Morier exhibited at its first show in 1760, and then in 1762, 1765, and 1768. In the mid-1760s he undertook an important commission for the earl of Pembroke, which included eight paintings of the 15th light dragoons. He also produced several 'small paintings' for George III for 10 guineas apiece, but after June 1767 royal patronage ceased. Falling into financial difficulties, on 23 June 1768 he was arrested for debt. Although released on bail, he surrendered himself to the Fleet prison on 10 November 1768. The following April he was released on a bond of £4 14s. 6d. and was formally discharged as insolvent on 8 July 1769. He died at Clerkenwell, London, in early January 1770 and was buried on 8 January at St James's, Clerkenwell Green, at the expense of the Society of Artists.　　JENNY SPENCER-SMITH

Sources A. E. H. Miller and N. P. Dawnay, *Military drawings and paintings in the collection of her majesty the queen*, 2 vols. (1966–70) · O. Millar, *The later Georgian pictures in the collection of her majesty the queen*, 2 vols. (1969) · O. Millar, *The Tudor, Stuart and early Georgian pictures in the collection of her majesty the queen*, 2 vols. (1963) · Royal Arch., RA CP/42/105; RA CP/71/80; RA CP/71/85; RA CP, vol. 1; RA GEO/17117; RA GEO/17127; RA GEO/17131; RA GEO/17145; RA GEO/17181 · Sidney, sixteenth earl of Pembroke, *A catalogue of the paintings and drawings in the collection at Wilton House, Salisbury, Wiltshire* (1968) · Redgrave, *Artists* · Graves, *Soc. Artists* · *Journal of the Society for Army Historical Research* · *Engraved Brit. ports.* · PRO, prison commitment order, PRIS 2/18 · PRO, Fleet prison commitment book, PRIS 10/21 · register, St James's Church, Clerkenwell Green, London, LMA [microfilm] [burial, March 1742–March 1770]
Likenesses P. Sandby, watercolour, c.1747, Royal Collection

Morier, David Richard (1784–1877), diplomatist, was born on 8 January 1784 at Smyrna, the third of the seven surviving children of Isaac *Morier (1750–1817) and his wife, (Elizabeth) Clara, née Van Lennep (1760–1834). The family moved to England in 1787 and he was educated privately in London and at Harrow School (1796–8), where he was a contemporary of George Hamilton-Gordon, later fourth earl of Aberdeen, with whom he formed a lifelong friendship.

In February 1804 Morier accompanied, as secretary, his eldest brother, John Philip *Morier, on his appointment as consul-general for the Morea, Albania, and the adjacent territories of the Ottoman empire, with the task of countering French influence in the area and winning the support of Ali Pasha of Yanina. He was sent home with dispatches in July 1806, and in June 1807 left again for Turkey in the suite of Sir Arthur Paget on his (unsuccessful) mission to re-establish diplomatic relations, which had been broken off at the beginning of the year. In September he was sent on his own to negotiate with Mehmet Ali, pasha of Egypt, for the release of the British prisoners captured at Rosetta, but when he arrived he found that General Alexander Fraser had already done this. In accordance with his instructions he then went to Malta to await further orders. From here, in August 1808, he joined Robert Adair on his mission to Turkey and played a part in the negotiations that resulted in the treaty of the Dardanelles of 5 January 1809.

Apart from a nine-month detachment during 1809 and 1810 as temporary replacement for his brother James Justinian *Morier as secretary to Sir Harford Jones (later Jones-Brydges) in Persia, Morier remained engaged in the business of the embassy at Constantinople until 1812, first under Adair and then under his successor as chargé d'affaires, Stratford Canning, with whom he established a close friendship. Despite the efforts of Adair and others on his behalf, Morier was never given the formal appointment of secretary of embassy, and in July 1812 he left for England with Canning.

In August 1813 Morier was attached to Lord Aberdeen's mission to allied headquarters in Europe—Aberdeen considered him 'a treasure' (Aberdeen to Castlereagh, 29 Oct 1813, BL, Add. MS 43075)—and subsequently to Lord Castlereagh's private office during the negotiations that led to the signing of the first treaty of Paris in May 1814, and then at the Congress of Vienna. He returned with Castlereagh to England in February 1815 and accompanied him to Paris after Waterloo for the work of drafting the second treaty of Paris. On 18 August 1815 he married Anna (1793–1855), daughter of Robert Burnett Jones, a former attorney-general of Barbados.

In September 1815 Morier took up the post of consul-general for France, to which he had been appointed in November 1814, being also made a commissioner for the settlement of the claims of British subjects upon the French government. His post in Paris was abolished in

April 1832 and on 5 June he was appointed minister-plenipotentiary to the Swiss confederation, a post he held until, following disagreement with Palmerston over the policy to be adopted towards the confederation, he was forced into retirement on 19 June 1847 at the age of sixty-three.

Morier was a tall, good-looking man of warm sympathies and transparent simplicity of character. He was a fine linguist, at home in French, Italian, German, and demotic as well as classical Greek. He had a wide circle of friends in several countries, retaining into his later years his youthful characteristic of seeing the best in everyone with whom he came in contact. He was a naturally devout man whose deep sense of religion led him to publish two pamphlets, entitled *What has Religion to do with Politics?* (1848) and *The Basis of Morality* (1869). At the age of seventy-three he published his one novel, *Photo, the Suliote: a Tale of Modern Greece* (1857), in which 'imperfect sketch' or 'fragment', as he called it, he attempted to paint a picture of Greek and Albanian life in the first quarter of the nineteenth century. The materials for the story, beyond his personal recollections, were supplied by a Greek physician with whom Morier was compelled to spend a period of quarantine at Corfu in December 1804.

Morier and his wife, Anna, had four daughters, two of whom died young, and a son, Robert Burnet David *Morier. Morier died on 13 July 1877 of 'pleuritis' at his home, 45 Montagu Square in London, aged ninety-three but in full possession of his natural vivacity—a model, as Dean Stanley said, of the 'piety and virtue of the antique mould' (*The Times*, 16 July 1877).

STANLEY LANE-POOLE, rev. HENRY MCKENZIE JOHNSTON

Sources Morier MSS, Balliol Oxf. · Foreign Office MSS, PRO · *The Times* (16 July 1877) · d. cert.
Archives Balliol Oxf. | All Souls Oxf., Vaughan MSS · BL, Add. 43151, 43183 · PRO, Granville MSS · U. Southampton L., Broadlands MSS
Likenesses D. E. Arnold, portrait, repro. in R. Wemyss, *Memoirs of the Rt Hon. Sir Robert Morier*, ed. V. Wemyss, 1 (1911), facing p. 292 · F. C. Lewis, stipple (after Slater), BM, NPG; repro. in *Members of Grillion's Club from 1811 to 1863*, Grillion's Club, 1 (privately printed, 1864)
Wealth at death under £18,000 in England: probate, 6 Aug 1877, *CGPLA Eng. & Wales*

Morier, Isaac (1750–1817), merchant and diplomatist, was born at Vevey, in Switzerland, on 11 August 1750, the son of François Isaac Augustin Morier (1715–1764), a master carpenter, and Jeanne Barby. He was descended from a Huguenot family which, on the revocation of the edict of Nantes, had migrated to Château d'Oex. His great-grandfather Abraham moved to Vevey and there, as a master shoemaker, had been awarded the hereditary honour of *bourgeoisie*. Isaac's father sent him as a youth to work with an uncle who had set up business in London. Later he went to Smyrna to join the merchant house of another uncle, Samuel, who put him under British protection, by which means he subsequently gained British naturalization. On this uncle's death he was taken into the merchant house of David Van Lennep (1712–1797), president of the Dutch Levant Company, before setting up in business on his own as a member of the English Levant Company. On 18 February 1778 he married (Elizabeth) Clara (1760–1834), eldest daughter of David Van Lennep and his wife, Anne Marie Leystar (1734–1784). His wife's sister Cornelia married the Hon. William Waldegrave, younger son of the third Earl Waldegrave, a naval officer who rose to be admiral and was created Baron Radstock in 1800; and another sister, Annette, married Jean-Frédéric, comte de Chabannes la Palice, a cousin of Talleyrand. The Moriers had eleven children, three daughters and eight sons, four of whom died in infancy. John Philip *Morier, James Justinian *Morier, and David Richard *Morier were born in Smyrna and William *Morier was born in England.

In 1787 Morier took his family to England where they became close friends of their Waldegrave cousins. William Waldegrave commissioned a portrait of Clara, a beautiful woman, by George Romney and helped Morier's sons to make distinguished careers. He played a part in settling Morier's debts when his business collapsed in 1803, and in getting him appointed by the Levant Company as consul-general in Constantinople in 1804. The Turks, who had not been consulted, at first refused to allow Morier to perform any consular functions. When Charles Arbuthnot arrived as ambassador in the following year he also objected to an arrangement (over which he too had not been consulted) whereby Morier would in effect exercise consular functions outside the ambassador's control. Being a kindly man, who recognized Morier's need of the income, Arbuthnot arranged for him to be concurrently his Britannic majesty's consul-general, responsible to him except for purely Levant Company business, an arrangement reluctantly accepted by the Turks. Morier also obtained from the East India Company the post of their representative in Turkey, which further improved his financial position. He had to leave Turkey with Arbuthnot when diplomatic relations were broken off in 1807. He went to Malta, where he remained with other members of the Levant Company from Smyrna, who had also had to leave, until he could return to Turkey after relations were restored in 1809.

Morier was a man of deep religious faith but he also had a sense of fun and was fond of music. He was an amateur cello player, and became a popular and well-respected figure in Constantinople. But Morier was modest and insisted on living very simply, always hoping that he could save enough money to bring his wife and daughters out to join him, or to be able to retire with them to a property he had bought in Switzerland. Neither ambition was realized. He died in Constantinople on 17 August 1817, six days after his sixty-seventh birthday, almost certainly from cancer of the stomach, and with no member of his family near him. He was buried in Constantinople; his wife died in London on 17 March 1834, aged seventy-four.

HENRY MCKENZIE JOHNSTON

Sources Balliol Oxf., Morier MSS · PRO, Foreign Office papers · *DNB*
Archives Balliol Oxf., corresp. and MSS, incl. journal | Herefs. RO, corresp. with Sir Harford Jones

Morier, James Justinian (1782–1849), diplomatist and novelist, was born in Smyrna on 15 August 1782, the second of the seven surviving children born to Isaac *Morier (1750–1817), consul-general of the Levant Company at Constantinople, and his wife, (Elizabeth) Clara (1760–1834), daughter of David Van Lennep, the Dutch consul-general and president of the Dutch Levant Company. His brothers were David Richard *Morier, John Philip *Morier, and William *Morier. His father was of Huguenot descent and James's first language was French. The family came to England in 1787, and James was educated at schools in Andover and then Wimbledon. He began to learn the Levant trade in his father's business, working from about 1796 to 1799 in the London office, and from 1799 to 1806 in the Smyrna office. In 1806, visiting his father in Constantinople where the latter was consul-general, he met Harford Jones. As his secretary he accompanied Jones to Persia when Jones was appointed special envoy to the shah to negotiate a treaty designed to protect India from attack by Russia or France. They left England in 1807 and arrived in Tehran in 1809. Jones concluded a preliminary treaty with the shah, by which he declared invalid all previous treaties with European powers and pledged the country, in return for British help, to resist all attempts by European armies to pass through it *en route* for India. Morier was sent to England with Mirza Abul Hasan to finalize the treaty, which proved difficult in the face of differences between the British government and the East India Company over responsibility for policy in the Persian Gulf. They left Tehran on 7 May, travelling overland to Constantinople and thence by ship to Smyrna and London.

After nearly a year in London as aide to Abul Hasan, Morier was appointed secretary to Sir Gore Ouseley on his mission to Persia to obtain Persian ratification of the treaty and to try to arrange peace between the Persians and the Russians who had invaded Persia's northern provinces. They sailed in July 1810, reaching Tehran in November 1811. Morier was deputed to negotiate with the Russians for an armistice in 1813 and was interim minister when poor health compelled Ouseley to return home in 1814. Shortly afterwards Henry Ellis arrived to complete the negotiations. This being achieved by November 1814, Morier recommended that he be replaced by a chargé d'affaires. His recommendation was accepted and he left Persia in October 1816 with few regrets.

Morier reached London in 1817 and retired with a pension. On 17 June 1820 he married Harriet (1788/9–1858), daughter of William Fulke Greville. He came out of retirement in 1819–20 to act as aide to Abul Hasan when the latter was in London, and in 1824–6 to go to Mexico to negotiate a treaty, and only finally ended his diplomatic career after 1826.

In retirement Morier pursued the writing career which was far more to his taste than diplomacy and on which he had already made a start. His two travel books, *A Journey through Persia, Armenia and Asia Minor* (1812) and *A Second Journey* (1818), both met with critical acclaim and were welcomed by a public which knew little of these areas. His

James Justinian Morier (1782–1849), by Samuel William Reynolds junior, pubd 1850 (after Sir William Boxall)

major work, the novel *Adventures of Hajji Baba of Isphahan* (1824), at once achieved popularity and critical acclaim for its humorous and perceptive portrayal of Persian life and its easy style. It was followed by three other novels based on his Persian experiences and a variety of other novels, many of which were popular successes, although not of the same calibre as his first novel.

Morier lived initially in London, where in 1824 he was a founder member of the Athenaeum, and was a noted society figure, collector, and amateur artist. Fond of food, he was always overweight. His religious beliefs were deeply held, and he was greatly attached to his family. His wife's poor health led them to travel on the continent from 1829 to 1831 and then retire to Brighton. Morier died suddenly on 19 March 1849 in Brighton of 'cerebral congestion'. He was survived by his wife and their only son, Greville (1822–1870). There is still considerable literary interest in *Hajji Baba*, and in Morier's memorable evocation of Persian life and character, in Europe, America, and the Middle East.

STANLEY LANE-POOLE, *rev.* ELIZABETH BAIGENT

Sources private information (1894) · private information (2004) [Henry McKenzie Johnston] · J. B. Kelly, *Britain and the Persian Gulf, 1795–1880* (1968) · G. A. Tavassuli, *La société iranienne et le monde oriental vus à travers l'oeuvre d'un écrivain anglais James Morier et d'un écrivain français Pierre Loti* (1966) · K. M. Goad, *Hajji Baba of Isphahan* (1956)
Archives Balliol Oxf., corresp. and papers, incl. cash book and sketchbooks · BL, journals, Add. MSS 33839–33844 · priv. coll. | BL, business transactions with Richard Bentley, Add. MSS 46612–46613, 46649–46650 · BL, official corresp. with Fath' Ali Shah, Add. MS 19529 · BL, Prinsep MSS · BL OIOC, corresp. with Sir Henry Willock, etc., MSS Eur. D 488, 527 · Herefs. RO, Brydges MSS · Herefs. RO, corresp. with Sir Harford Jones

Likenesses S. W. Reynolds junior, mezzotint, pubd 1850 (after W. Boxall), NPG [*see illus.*] · D. Maclise, lithograph, BM; repro. in *Fraser's Magazine* (1833) · portrait, repro. in W. Bates, *The Maclise portrait-gallery of illustrious literary characters* (1883)

Wealth at death £14,000: private information (2004) [Henry McKenzie Johnston]

Morier, John Philip (1776–1853), diplomatist, was the eldest of the four surviving sons of Isaac *Morier (1750–1817), of Huguenot origins, and his wife, (Elizabeth) Clara (1760–1834), daughter of David Van Lennep, Dutch consul at Smyrna. All four sons entered the diplomatic service. Morier was born at Smyrna on 9 November 1776. His father worked for the Turkey Company and was later British consul in Constantinople. Morier was attached to the embassy at Constantinople on 5 April 1799, where he acted as private secretary to the ambassador, the seventh earl of Elgin, best known for his acquisition of the Elgin marbles. Morier was dispatched to Egypt on 22 December 1799 on special service of observation, to accompany the grand vizier in the Turkish expedition against General Kléber, whom Napoleon had left to hold the country. Morier joined the Turkish army at al-Arish, on the Egyptian frontier, on 31 January 1800, and remained with it until July. He published an admirable account of the campaign, under the title *Memoir of a Campaign with the Ottoman Army in Egypt from February to July 1800* (1801). According to the *Nouvelle biographie* he was taken prisoner by the French, but in spite of his position as the representative of a hostile power, and his secret mission to co-operate diplomatically with the Turks with a view to the expulsion of the French from Egypt, he was set at liberty, with a warning that should he again be found in Egypt he would meet the fate of a spy. No authority, however, is adduced for this story, which is unsupported by any public or private evidence.

In December 1803 Morier was appointed consul-general in Albania, where the policy of Ali Pasha of Yanina, the most powerful of the semi-independent vassals of the Porte, was for many years an especial concern of both English and French diplomacy. In April 1810 he was promoted to secretary of legation at Washington, DC, and in October 1811 he was gazetted a commissioner in Latin America. On his return to England he became for a while acting undersecretary of state for foreign affairs in August 1815. In the following year, on 5 February, he was appointed envoy-extraordinary to the court of Saxony at Dresden, which post he held until his retirement, on pension, on 5 January 1825.

On 3 December 1814 Morier married Horatia Maria Frances, eldest daughter of Lord Hugh *Seymour, youngest son of the first marquess of Hertford; they had seven daughters, one of whom, Horatia, married the fourteenth duke of Somerset. Morier died in London on 20 August 1853 and his wife died six days later. His nephew was the diplomatist Sir Robert *Morier.

STANLEY LANE-POOLE, rev. H. C. G. MATTHEW

Sources *FO List* (1854) · *Annual Register* (1853) · R. Wemyss, *Memoirs and letters of the Right Hon. Sir Robert Morier*, 2 vols. (1911) · [J. C. F. Hoefer], ed., *Nouvelle biographie générale*, 46 vols. (1852–66)

Archives Balliol Oxf., corresp. and papers incl. sketchbook · NRA, priv. coll.

Morier, Sir Robert Burnet David (1826–1893), diplomatist, was born on 31 March 1826, at Paris, the fourth child and only son of David Richard *Morier (1784–1877) and his wife, Anna (c.1790–1855), née Jones. He was educated privately in Switzerland, by tutors in England, and at Balliol College, Oxford (1845–9). At Oxford he began a lifelong intimacy with Benjamin Jowett, and enjoyed friendships with A. H. Clough, J. A. Froude, F. Max Müller, F. T. Palgrave, and A. P. Stanley. From this time dated his lifelong appetite for 'burning the midnight oil with intelligent, well-informed boon companions' (*The Times*, 17 Nov 1893). More unfortunately, he acquired a copious, declamatory, slangy prose style reminiscent of Carlyle.

Although Morier was intensely patriotic, he hated chauvinism and English insularity. Shortly after leaving Oxford he founded the Cosmopolitan Club, which originally met bi-weekly in his rooms at 49 New Bond Street; when the brilliant conversation there attracted hosts of the intelligentsia, the club migrated to the spacious studio of G. F. Watts. In 1851 Morier was appointed as a clerk in the privy council office, but he resigned in 1852 to enter the diplomatic service. He became an unpaid attaché at Vienna in 1853.

Diplomacy in Germany Baron Stockmar, whom Morier adulated, arranged with the prince consort for Morier's appointment as paid attaché at Berlin (February 1858) after the marriage of the princess royal to Crown Prince Frederick of Prussia. Morier accompanied Henry Elliot on a special mission to King Francis II in Naples (1859) and was assistant private secretary to Lord John Russell during Queen Victoria's visit (1860) to Ernst II, duke of Saxe-Coburg and Gotha. These appointments brought him the favour of both Russell and the royal family. He also began a long confidential correspondence with Mary, marchioness of Salisbury (afterwards countess of Derby), in which he aired opinions intended to reach beyond Hatfield House into the cabinet. On 26 September 1861, Morier married Alice (d. 1903), second daughter of General Jonathan *Peel. In early days she was a great help in his work, copying dispatches and taking dictation, and she continued to support and influence his career. They had a son and daughter. Morier was promoted second secretary in 1862 and nominated in 1865 as secretary of the Athens legation (an appointment he held only briefly).

Morier's expertise in German-speaking countries was fortified by appointments as British commissioner at Vienna for the arrangement of the tariff in 1865 (and again in 1867) and for carrying out the treaty of commerce (1866). He thus developed an unmatched expertise in formulating the economic elements that increasingly underlay nineteenth-century diplomacy. There followed a succession of appointments to minor German courts. In 1866 he was appointed as chargé d'affaires in the grand duchy of Hesse and by Rhine. At Darmstadt he joined a group, including the duke of Saxe-Coburg and Gotha and the

Sir Robert Burnet David Morier (1826–1893), by Walery, pubd 1889

grand dukes of Weimar and Baden, which favoured German federation under Prussian hegemony but opposed Prussian domination. Most members of the group eventually attracted the malevolence of Bismarck. In 1871 Morier was transferred to Stuttgart in the kingdom of Württemberg, and in 1872 he became chargé d'affaires at the Munich legation to King Ludwig II of Bavaria.

Although Morier chafed at the pettiness of German provincial life, he cultivated intellectuals (notably Döllinger in Munich), befriended liberals, and meddled in local politics. A man of gigantic, gouty physique, he was impulsive, argumentative, and even rude. He was eager for demanding work, but too excitable and self-centred for consummate diplomacy. Tension seemed to stimulate his faculties. Germans liked his camaraderie and boisterous jokes, appreciated his earnest outlook, and recognized his desire for friendship between the German and British nations. He was trusted by Crown Princess Frederick and her husband, at whose instigation Queen Victoria unsuccessfully urged Morier's transfer to Berlin as chargé d'affaires in 1867. Morier's allegiance to the princess drew the implacable enmity of Bismarck, with whom he became locked in a lifelong battle. His masterful analyses of German political and constitutional changes were uncomfortable for the Iron Chancellor. He was one of the chief authorities on the Schleswig-Holstein question, though his advice was disregarded. In 1872 he was one of the earliest to divine the secret agenda in Bismarck's policy towards the

Vatican. In 1875 his part in alerting Europe to Germany's possible mobilization against France further drew Bismarck's ire.

Morier was a founder member of the Cobden Club (reconstituted from the Political Economy Club in 1866) and contributed to *Cobden Club Essays* on the agrarian legislation of Prussia (1870) and on local government in Germany (1875). The latter 'brilliant' essay 'might almost be described as philosophical flippancy' noted one reviewer, to whom its 'epigrams' were reminiscent of 'a peroration of Mr. Disraeli's' (*The Athenaeum*, 13 March 1875, 352–3). Morier's imperialism led to a rupture with the Cobdenites in the late 1870s. He published an anonymous pamphlet, *The Dano-German Conflict and Lord Russell's Despatch* (1863) and a study of 'Reconstruction in Germany' (*North British Review*, 51, 1869). Morier, who deplored 'the odious revival of theological passion which is the disgrace of our age' (*Macmillan's Magazine*, 31, 263), offended Manning with his anonymous five-part analysis of 'Prussia and the Vatican' in *Macmillan's Magazine* (September 1874–January 1875). In the aftermath of this controversy, Morier fell into 'a profound state of moral prostration and discouragement' (Morier to Gladstone, 29 March 1875, BL, Add. MS 44446, fol. 349).

Minister in Portugal and Spain Morier's promotion to the Berlin embassy was impossible in Bismarck's lifetime. For many years Morier yearned to succeed his beloved friend Odo Russell as British representative in Rome. Having specialized in Germany for twenty-three years, he was finally given a chance of wider experience by his appointment as minister-plenipotentiary to King Luis I of Portugal in March 1876. His rattling ardour and forceful ambition were ill-adapted to the life of an envoy in a small European capital. Morier on his own initiative proposed a general settlement of all outstanding colonial questions with Portugal, but reactions in London to his exuberant conception left him feeling snubbed and isolated. He complained in May 1880 that 'the inconceivable buck jumping of the C[olonial] O[ffice] and its systematic throwing of sticks into my wheels apparently out of mere cussedness has driven me well nigh wild' (BL, Add. MS 43883, fol. 178). In the event, the modest plan embodied in the Anglo-Portuguese treaty of 1884 (signed after Morier had left Lisbon) was never ratified, owing to German opposition. Otherwise, Morier renewed British assurances of support for Portuguese independence, negotiated the Goa treaty of 1878 concerning railways and trade in India, and secured better facilities for British trade in Portuguese East Africa. Morier was a formidable antagonist who browbeat the Portuguese; he interrupted their unfortunate foreign minister expatiating on the illustrious virtues of Portuguese national character with characteristic brutality: 'Monsieur, si j'avais eu le malheur d'être né Portugais, je me serais suicidé entre les mamelles de ma nourrice' ('If I had had the misfortune to be born Portuguese, I would have killed myself between the breasts of my wet-nurse'; *The Times*, 17 Nov 1893). His partisan friendships in Lisbon aroused 'a bitter hatred such as only these southern Yahoos are capable of' (Morier to Dilke, 31 Dec

1880, BL, Add. MS 43883, fol. 179). He not only challenged his instructions from London and obtruded his opinions in dispatches, but also publicized his long-running grudge against the permanent under-secretary, Lord Tenterden, as an inhuman bureaucrat. Yet there was self-doubt and hesitation beneath the bluster. He wrote from Lisbon:

> I am painfully conscious of being a bore and of the horror with which my despatches are greeted by the Office. But I should be infinitely less of a bore if I was not systematically Boycotted and if I was now & then told what I should do & what I should abstain from doing. It is this *trappiste* silence in which the F.O. wraps itself & the consequent sense of groping in the dark which forces me to write everything which I consider necessary to the F.O. to judge of every side of the question. If I knew exactly what side they cared about & what was required of me I should stick to that.   (Morier to Dilke, 19 April 1881, BL, Add. MS 43883, fol. 220)

Lord Granville, who considered Morier 'much the cleverest' man in the diplomatic corps, 'but with a temper, self-conceit and huffiness beyond belief' (Ramm, *Political Correspondence*, 1.160; 2.227), appointed him in June 1881 as minister at Madrid. Although he was more discreet there than in Lisbon, his self-dramatization and hustling proved incorrigible in the Anglo-Spanish commercial treaty negotiations. His enthusiastic but pompous opening of an interminable speech on commercial treaties to the lord mayor's banquet at the Mansion House was disastrous: 'A subdued groan ran through the spacious hall, and before Sir Robert had spoken for five minutes a general hum of conversation marked the indifference of the company and disconcerted the unfortunate orator' (Rivers Wilson, 240).

Ambassador to Russia When, despite his personal shortcomings, Morier was, perhaps surprisingly, nominated to the embassy at St Petersburg in December 1884, there was much apprehension. 'We shall be lucky if he does not get us into a scrape with the Russians', judged E. W. Hamilton, Gladstone's secretary. 'He is clever; but garrulous and fussy beyond measure. I can hardly conceive a man less fitted to conduct delicate negotiations with a Foreign Power; and his diffuse tirades will be a heavy tax on the patience of any Secretary of State' (*Diary*, 2.775). Hamilton also judged 'there was a good deal of the snob about the man' (BL, Add. MS 48661, fol. 130, 17 Nov 1893). Yet once accredited to a great power and freed from the harassing technical minutiae of commercial treaties, Morier reached his apogee.

In 1882 Morier had rejoiced at

> the splendid success of our Egyptian campaign, morally, politically, and militarily. For an imperialist liberal like myself whose entire professional career is conterminous with the period marked by the loss of prestige consequent on the Crimean war suddenly to find himself reinvested with that all powerful instrument *for good*, and to know that this restoration has been effected under a *Liberal* Govt, is sometimes almost more than I believe can be true.   (Morier to Dilke, 1 Nov 1882, BL, Add. MS 43883, fol. 288)

His promotion to St Petersburg enabled him to exploit this opportunity. He set himself to reverse the Russophobia that had dominated British foreign policy for nearly half a century, and strove for an entente that would have constituted a diplomatic master-stroke. He believed that Britain should accommodate Russia in the Balkans so as to avoid disturbance by Russian designs in Asia. This policy he pursued with audacity, vision, and steadfastness. Although he was at times bamboozled by the Russians and clumsy in judging the reactions of his colleagues, his objectives were finally achieved in 1905–7 after the Russo-Japanese War.

Morier's earliest priority was the conciliation of Russia over Egypt. The first great test of his personal policy came in 1885 with the divergence of British and Russian interests after the union of Bulgaria with Eastern Roumelia breached the treaty of Berlin. Morier's handling of the matter was adept, although his relations with the new foreign secretary, Lord Rosebery, became so strained that his recall was contemplated. He prevented recriminations after Rosebery protested in July 1886 at Russia breaking the Berlin treaty by rescinding the status of Batumi as a free port. When Queen Victoria, who repeatedly denounced Morier as a Russophile at this time, urged Rosebery's successor as foreign secretary, Lord Iddesleigh, that Morier should be transferred to a colonial governorship, he replied, 'But which of your Majesty's Colonies is your Majesty prepared to lose?' (Rennell, 1.92–3). Although Morier mitigated the difficulties arising from Anglo-Russian rivalry for Persian concessions in 1888–90, Central Asian frontier questions were for him supreme in Anglo-Russian relations. His most important success was in adjusting tensions over the Russo-Afghan frontier. He skilfully handled the Pamir incident of 1891, in which two British officers were expelled by the Russians from territory claimed by Britain for Afghanistan.

Morier maintained his German connections, and continued to work against Bismarck. A great stir was raised when Morier was accused, first privately in a letter of May 1888 to the prince of Wales, and then publicly in December in the *Kölnische Zeitung*, of having forewarned Marshal Bazaine of Prussian forces crossing the Moselle in 1870. This charge of betrayal, which was inspired by Bismarck, was furiously denied by Morier, who briefly in 1889 became an international celebrity. Morier lost his relish for political issues after the Bazaine calumnies; he diverted his formidable energies into encouraging British investment in Siberia as a way of breaking Russian tariff protectionism. In 1889–91 he acted as company promoter in London, syndicate organizer in Siberia, and concession hunter in St Petersburg. In 1891 Morier (whose physical powers were failing) requested transfer to the Rome embassy, but Tsar Alexander III besought him to remain; reluctantly, knowing the risks to his survival, Morier consented. This act of patriotic duty foreshortened his life.

In 1890, Morier's only son, Victor, 'clumsily' shot himself for love of 'a married Russian woman of high degree' (Leveson-Gower, 105), and was sent home from St Petersburg; it was a heavy blow when he died in 1892, while serving on the Anglo-Portuguese delimitation commission in Africa. The Moriers' only daughter, Victoria, married Rosslyn Wemyss. Morier received the following honours: CB (1866), KCB (1882), PC (1885), GCMG (1886), and GCB (1887).

He was honorary DCL of Oxford University (1889) and LLD of Edinburgh.

Morier died of gout, internal disorders, and influenza, on 16 November 1893, at the Hotel National, Montreux, Switzerland, and was buried on 21 November at Northwood churchyard. He thought of himself as having spent his life beating against closed doors. 'His interminable monologue wearies everybody, and though he has much to say, and is really worth hearing, he is so long in saying it, and so apt to mix egotistical comments with remarks on public affairs, that he becomes a bore', wrote Lord Derby after Morier had stayed as his guest in 1887. 'Nothing less than his remarkable industry, energy, and acquired knowledge, would have given him diplomatic distinction in spite of his absolute want of tact … I am never sorry when he goes away: nor as far as I have seen, is anyone' (*Later Derby Diaries*, 123–4).   RICHARD DAVENPORT-HINES

Sources *The Times* (17 Nov 1893), 10a • *ILN* (25 Nov 1893) • R. Wemyss, *Memoirs and letters of the Right Hon. Sir Robert Morier*, 2 vols. (1911) • A. Ramm, *Sir Robert Morier: envoy and ambassador in the age of imperialism, 1876–1893* (1973) • *Disraeli, Derby and the conservative party: journals and memoirs of Edward Henry, Lord Stanley, 1849–1869*, ed. J. R. Vincent (1978) • *The diaries of E. H. Stanley, 15th earl of Derby, 1869–1878*, CS, 5th series, 4 (1994) • *The later Derby diaries … selected passages*, ed. J. Vincent (privately printed, Bristol, 1981), 123–4 • *The political correspondence of Mr Gladstone and Lord Granville, 1876–1886*, ed. A. Ramm, 2 vols. (1962) • F. B. M. Hallyday, 'Bismarck, Herbert and the Morier affair', *Central European History*, 1 (1968), 56–79 • C. R. Wilson, *Chapters from my official life*, ed. E. MacAlister (1916) • G. G. Leveson-Gower, *Years of content, 1858–1886* (1940) • *The diary of Sir Edward Walter Hamilton, 1880–1885*, ed. D. W. R. Bahlman, 2 vols. (1972) • J. Rennell, *Social and diplomatic memoirs*, 1 (1922) • H. Sutherland Edwards, *Sir William White* (1902)
Archives Balliol Oxf., corresp., diaries and papers; corresp. and papers incl. commonplace books, journals, and sketchbook | Balliol Oxf., corresp. with Benjamin Jowett • BL, corresp. with Sir Charles Dilke, Add. MS 43883 • BL, corresp. with W. E. Gladstone, Add. MSS 44320–44785, *passim* • BL, Iddesleigh MSS • BL, letters to Sir Austen Layard, Add. MSS 38993–39120, *passim* • BL OIOC, Ava MSS; Dufferin MSS • Bodl. Oxf., Russell MSS, letters to Lord Clarendon • Hatfield House, Hertfordshire, Salisbury MSS • Lpool RO, corresp. with Lord Derby • NRA, priv. coll., corresp. with Robert Loyd-Lindsay • PRO, Granville MSS • PRO, corresp. with Lord John Russell, PRO 30/22 • PRO, corresp. with Odo Russell, FO 918 • PRO, letters to Sir William White, FO 364/1–11 • SOAS, letters to Sir William MacKinnon
Likenesses Richmond, drawings, 1838–59, repro. in Wemyss, ed., *Memoirs*, frontispiece, facing p. 102 • oils, 1860–1869?, repro. in Wemyss, ed., *Memoirs*, 350 • Walery, photograph, pubd 1889, NPG [*see illus.*] • F. von Lenbach, oils, Balliol Oxf.; repro. in Ramm, *Sir Robert Morier*, frontispiece • R. T., wood-engraving, NPG; repro. in *ILN* (19 Jan 1889)
Wealth at death £7897 0s. 4d.: probate, 2 Dec 1893, CGPLA Eng. & Wales

Morier, William (1790–1864), naval officer, the fourth son of Isaac *Morier (1750–1817), consul-general of the Levant Company at Constantinople, and his wife, (Elizabeth) Clara, née Van Lennep (1760–1834), was born at Smyrna, Turkey, on 25 September 1790. David Richard *Morier, James Justinian *Morier, and John Philip *Morier were his brothers. He spent two years at Harrow School, entered the navy in November 1803 as first-class volunteer on board the *Illustrious* (74 guns), and became midshipman on the *Ambuscade*, seeing much service in the Mediterranean.

From 1807 to 1810 he was employed on the Mediterranean and Lisbon stations, during which time he became acting lieutenant of the *Zealous* (74 guns) and took part in the defence of Cadiz. In 1811, aboard HMS *Thames* (32 guns) under Captain Charles Napier, he took part in the capture of the island of Ponza and displayed characteristic zeal in the destruction of ten armed feluccas on the beach near Cetraro and other boat engagements on the Calabrian coast. In the Anglo-American War (1812–14) he was at the bombardment of Stonington in 1813, and on 13 June 1815 he was promoted commander. In 1828 he commanded successively the sloops *Harrier* and *Childers* (each 18 guns) on the North Sea station. After his promotion to post captain on 18 January 1830 he immediately retired. In 1841 he married Frances (Fanny) Lee, the daughter of D. Bevan of Belmont, Hertfordshire. He attained the rank of retired rear-admiral on 9 July 1855 and vice-admiral on 16 June 1862. He died at his home, Brunswick House, Eastbourne, Sussex, on 29 July 1864, survived by his wife.

STANLEY LANE-POOLE, *rev.* ANDREW LAMBERT

Sources D. Syrett and R. L. DiNardo, *The commissioned sea officers of the Royal Navy, 1660–1815*, rev. edn, Occasional Publications of the Navy RS, 1 (1994) • H. N. Williams, *Life of Sir C. Napier* (1917) • *GM*, 3rd ser., 17 (1864), 395 • O'Byrne, *Naval biog. dict.* • *Navy List* • private information (c.1894) • CGPLA Eng. & Wales (1864)
Archives Balliol Oxf., corresp.
Wealth at death under £3000: probate, 9 Sept 1864, CGPLA Eng. & Wales

Morin [*née* Barnard], **Nea Everilda** (1905–1986), rock climber and mountaineer, was born at Headley rectory, Headley, Surrey, on 21 May 1905, the second of three children, and only daughter of Percy Mordaunt Barnard (1868–1941), a lapsed clergyman who was the rector of Headley from 1898 until 1905, when he became an antiquarian bookseller. Her mother, Alice Mary Taunton (1872–1951), sold artwork within her husband's business, and then worked as an independent dealer. Nea was principally educated at home at Tunbridge Wells, where her father had established his bookshop. Her father's membership of the Alpine Club and his encouragement of the children's climbing activities at Wellington Rocks, Tunbridge Wells, made her passage into the sport an easy and acceptable one. Family holidays in the Tyrol, at Diablerets, Switzerland, and her first guided season, aged sixteen, revealed her natural ability. She financed an independent holiday to the Dauphiné Alps in 1925 by working in her father's bookshop. The season of 1926 yielded a list of guided, classic alpine climbs, which secured her membership of the Ladies' Alpine Club. During this trip she became associated with members of the prestigious Groupe de Haute Montagne from France. They were at the forefront of a movement committed to tackling difficult ascents in the Alps without guides. Invited to climb with them, success was early achieved when in 1927 Nea was one of the party which made the first guideless ascent of the Aiguille de Roc. Thereafter, the experience she accrued and shared as a member of the group in Britain, France, and the Alps, rendered her a valuable link between British and continental schools of climbing.

Nea Everilda Morin (1905–1986), self-portrait, 1933 [centre, with Micheline Morin (left) and Alice Damesme (right) at the Aigle hut after a traverse of the Meije]

After marrying, on 9 June 1928, Jean Ferdinand Joseph Morin (1897–1943), a company director and one of the leading lights of the Groupe de Haute Montagne, Nea lived in Paris. Her husband was the son of Michel Morin, a rear-admiral in the French navy. They undertook much weekend climbing at nearby Fontainebleau, but the economic climate of the 1930s and the birth of their children Denise (1931) and Ian (1935) served to curtail regular trips to the Alps. These restrictions did not prevent Nea from becoming a leading exponent of the *cordée féminine*, the practice of making guideless alpine ascents on an all-female climbing rope. Early successes with Alice Damesme and Micheline Morin (Nea's sister-in-law) included a first feminine traverse of the Meije in 1933 and an ascent of the three summits of the Aiguille de Blaitière in 1934. The menfolk associated with these female climbers understood the risks attached to guideless ascents, and only reluctantly agreed to their climbing at such unprecedented high standards. They did, however, defer to their exceptional talent, as demonstrated by Nea's first feminine lead of the traverse of the Aiguilles Mummery and Ravanel with Maurice Damesme in 1938. For Nea, until the end of the 1950s, there were to be several more remarkable guideless ascents, *en cordée féminine* and on mixed ropes.

In north Wales during the Second World War, Nea Morin climbed some of the hardest routes of the day. In 1941 she became one of the few women to pioneer a route bearing her own name on Clogwyn Y Grochan (she had already pioneered the Rocher de Nea in France). After the death of Jean, serving as a colonel in the Free French forces, in 1943 (the military transport plane in which he was travelling went down in the sea near Gibraltar), Nea accepted the presidency of the Ladies' Alpine Club. Resident again in her native Tunbridge Wells, in 1947 she joined the Pinnacle Club and was destined to become one of its most committed members. During the 1950s, *en cordée féminine* with her daughter Denise, Nea enjoyed innumerable successes

in the Alps. They also climbed together at every grade of difficulty on British rock and became a renowned climbing partnership.

A highly successful climber over a period of four decades, and still active thereafter in Britain and the Alps, Nea Morin was remembered as a supremely modest individual. She was an exceptionally gifted all-round climber who selflessly extended her enthusiasm for the mountains to others: 'She wanted to make better climbers of those she led and instructed, and gave them time and energy that could have gone to building up her own reputation' (Adam Smith, 292). Her several works of translation included the best-seller *Annapurna*, by Maurice Herzog (1952, in collaboration with Janet Adam Smith), and her autobiography, *A Woman's Reach* (1968), became a classic of mountaineering literature. While recounting the progress of her own career, it highlights the talent of her contemporaries and incorporates a comprehensive record of feminine achievement in the mountains, a record to which she contributed so much and through her own example determined to elevate and encourage. She died at St George's Nursing Home, Westminster, London, on 12 July 1986, and was cremated at Mortlake crematorium four days later. CAROL A. OSBORNE

Sources N. Morin, *A woman's reach: mountaineering memoirs* (1968) · J. Adam Smith, *Alpine Journal*, 92 (1987), 290–92 · private information (2004) · B. Burkett and B. Peascod, 'Nea Morin: a family affair', *Women climbing: 200 years of achievement* (1989), 58–68 · C. Williams, *Women on the rope: the feminine share in mountain adventure* (1973) · N. Morin, climbing list, 1925–38, 1950–58, Alpine Club Library, London, Ladies' Alpine Club, G25 · N. Morin, application form, 1925, Alpine Club Library, London, Ladies' Alpine Club, G25 · b. cert. · m. cert. · d. cert. · *CGPLA Eng. & Wales* (1987)
Likenesses N. Morin, group photograph, 1933, Alpine Club, London [*see illus.*]
Wealth at death £230,974: probate, 7 Jan 1987, *CGPLA Eng. & Wales*

Morins, Richard de [*called* Ricardus Anglicus] (**early 1160s–1242**), canon lawyer and historian, is recorded in some canonistic sources as Ricardus Anglicus, and was properly identified only in the course of the twentieth century. Hitherto he had been identified, on the basis of meagre circumstantial evidence, with various other individuals, including the theologian Ricardus Anglicus (*fl.* early 13th cent.), Richard Poore, the bishop of Salisbury and Durham (*d.* 1237), and Richard de Lacy, official of the bishop of Winchester and civil lawyer during the late thirteenth century. Such misapprehensions were effectively demolished by a positive identification in Trinity College, Dublin, MS 275 (fol. 183), which states that Richard de Morins was the author of a work (*Summa brevis*) hitherto ascribed to the Bolognese law professor Ricardus Anglicus, and by the notice in the *Gesta abbatum monasterii sancti Albani* that Prior Richard had taught law in Bologna and elsewhere.

Probably born in Lincolnshire during the early 1160s, Morins first appears in Paris during the late 1180s as an associate of those canonists whom Kuttner and Rathbone called the Anglo-Norman school. There he taught and penned his earliest work, the *Summa questionum*, a compilation of questions on canonistic doctrine formally posed and solved by Morins on Fridays during a regular course of classes. The zenith of his academic career occurred, however, during the next decade, when he established his reputation as one of the leading teachers of canon law—and the first English one—in the schools of Bologna; towards the end of the 1190s he was a regent master there. All of Morins's other extant canonistic writings were written during this period. He produced a *Summa de ordine judiciario*, a popular procedural treatise of Romano-canonical legal practice which remains the only one of his works edited and printed in modern times. Two more works concentrated on Gratian's *Decretum* (*c*.1140), the *Summa brevis*, an introductory treatise, and the *Distinctiones decretorum*, a systematic presentation of legal distinctions drawn from Gratian's book. His *Argumenta* or *Notabilia decretorum* is no longer extant. Three further works focused more strictly on the *ius novum*, the new pope-made decretal law recently collected by Bernardo da Pavia in the *Breviarium extravagantium* or *Compilatio prima*. Morins's *Apparatus decretalium* was one of the earliest glosses on Bernardo's compilation, and was utilized by the canonist Tancred in his ordinary gloss. As a result some of Morins's own observations passed into Bernardo da Parma's ordinary gloss on the *Liber Extra*. In his *Brocarda* or *Generalia* Morins collected commonplaces from the decretals in the *Breviarium*; each general statement provoked the adducing of citations pro and contra, a juxtaposition of dialectical opposites intended to produce a harmonious solution. And in his *Casus decretalium* Morins provided an individual summary of most of the decretals collected in Bernardo's *Breviarium*; perhaps this work represented his own lecture notes or was intended as an aid for students.

For reasons now unknown Morins left Bologna, perhaps as early as 1198, to return to his native land; none of his canonistic works refers to any of Innocent III's decretals. Suggestions that he became at this time a member of the entourage of Archbishop Hubert Walter or a law teacher in Oxford remain speculation. At some point during this period, however, he entered religious life in the priory of Augustinian canons at Merton in Surrey; his presence in that convent is attested in 1202 by the same notice in the Dunstable annals which announces his election as prior of Dunstable in Bedfordshire (Lincoln diocese). Still only in diaconal orders, Morins assumed his new responsibilities in the late summer of that year and served in this post until his death. He was ordained a priest on 21 September and celebrated his first mass eight days later on Michaelmas.

Morins's new career as an administrator, man of affairs, and historian is well documented by a wide range of sources: the Dunstable annals and other monastic chronicles, his priory's cartulary, rescripts, and letters associated with litigation in courts Christian, and the various records associated with the workings of common-law courts. In 1203 he served King John as ambassador to Pope Innocent III and accompanied the papal legate Giovanni da Crema back to England. In 1206, 1223, 1228, and 1236 he served as visitor to religious houses, within the diocese of Lincoln as well as elsewhere. After the end of the interdict in 1212 Morins was one of the inquisitors into damages and losses suffered by the English church in that diocese. He saw duty as a crusade preacher in Huntingdonshire, Bedfordshire, and Hertfordshire during 1212, served as papal commissary in 1218 and 1240–41, acted as an arbiter in 1222 in a dispute between the bishop of London and the abbots and monks of Westminster, and was a counsellor in 1235 to the monks of St Albans regarding the election of a new abbot. There are more than forty attested instances of his service to the papacy as judge-delegate or sub-delegate presiding over various cases in English ecclesiastical courts, and he also occasionally appeared as a litigant or proctor. Morins also appeared very frequently as litigant before the king's justices to defend or promote the rights, revenues, and properties of his priory. As lord of the town of Dunstable he became involved during the 1220s in protracted disputes with the burgesses concerning seigneurial jurisdiction and revenue. He attended the Fourth Lateran Council at the end of 1215, and took the opportunity on his return journey to halt in Paris and enjoy a year-long sabbatical dedicated to the study of theology.

In 1210 Morins initiated the compilation of the Dunstable annals. This historical work, derivative regarding events from the creation until 1202, is considered today to be quite useful in its account of the four decades following. After Morins's death on 9 April 1242 the chronicle was continued until 1297. Before 1202 the annals consist of a straightforward crib from two works by Ralph de Diceto (*Abbreviationes chronicorum* and *Imagines historiarum*), with a few snippets from the histories of Florence of Worcester and Martinus Polonus. The entry for AD 1 notes that 1210 years have elapsed until the eighth year of Morins's priorate. The final borrowing from Diceto in the entry for 1201 is followed immediately by the account of how Morins became prior of Dunstable. Research by C. R. Cheney argues persuasively that he was personally responsible for only a portion of the entries for this period, while loosely supervising a fellow canon or canons in the composition of other portions of the annals. His tenure of office coincided with John's troubled reign, civil war, the long minority of Henry III, and that king's first decade and a half of true rule. The annals for that period report not only events of local and conventual interest (especially the priory's finances and property concerns), but also news of national importance.   ROBERT C. FIGUEIRA

Sources *Ann. mon.* · *Curia regis rolls preserved in the Public Record Office* (1922–) · R. de Morins, *Magistri Ricardi Anglici ordo judiciarius*, ed. C. Witte (1853) · *Gesta abbatum monasterii Sancti Albani, a Thoma Walsingham*, ed. H. T. Riley, 3 vols., pt 4 of *Chronica monasterii S. Albani*, Rolls Series, 28 (1867–9), vol. 1 · S. Kuttner and E. Rathbone, 'Anglo-Norman canonists of the twelfth century', *Traditio*, 7 (1949–51), 279–358 · C. R. Cheney, 'The making of the Dunstable annals, AD 33 to 1242', *Medieval texts and studies* (1973), 209–30 · G. H. Fowler, ed., *A digest of the charters preserved in the cartulary of the priory* *of Dunstable*, Bedfordshire Historical RS, 10 (1926) • R. C. Figueira, 'Ricardus de Mores and his *Casus decretalium*: the birth of a canonistic genre', *Proceedings of the Eighth international congress of medieval canon law* [San Diego, CA 1988], ed. S. Chodorow (1992), 169–87 • R. C. Figueira, 'Ricardus de Mores at common law: the second career of an Anglo-Norman canonist', *Regensburg, Bayern und Europa: Festschrift für Kurt Reindel*, ed. P. Segl and L. Kolmer (Regensburg, 1995), 281–99 • J. E. Sayers, *Papal judges delegate in the province of Canterbury, 1198–1254* (1971)

Archives TCD, MS 275, fol. 183 | Österreichische Nationalbibliothek, Vienna, MS 2194 • Biblioteca Apostolica Vaticana, Vatican City, MSS Vatican lat. 2691, Vatican pal. 652, Vatican pal. 696, Chis. E. VII 218 • Biblioteca Nazionale Marciana, Venice, MS VIII 22 • Bibliothèque Municipale, Douai, MS 644 • Bibliothèque Municipale, Laon, MS 385 • Bibliothèque Municipale, St Omer, MS 476 • BL, Cotton MS Tiberius A.x [LPL, MS 335] • Bodl. Oxf., Summary Cat. 3475 • City Library, Rheims, MS 692 • Staatsbibliothek, Munich, MSS 3879, 6352, 16083 • Staatsbibliothek, Bamberg, MS Can. 20 • Staatsbibliothek, Berlin, MS lat. fol. 306 • Stadtbibliothek, Nuremberg, MS Cent. V. 95 • Trier City Library, MS 978 • University Library, Würzburg, MS Mp. Th. 122 • University Library, Wrocław, MS II F. 44 chart. an. 1457 • University Library, Halle, MSS Ye 52, Ye 80 • University Library, Leipzig, MS Haen. 18 • Worcester Cathedral, F. 122

Morison, Sir Alexander (1779–1866), alienist, was born on 1 May 1779 at Anchorfield, near Edinburgh, and was educated at the high school and university of Edinburgh, where he graduated MD on 12 September 1799. His graduation thesis was 'De hydrocephalo phrenitico', and he continued throughout life to take special interest in cerebral and mental diseases. He became a licentiate of the Royal College of Physicians of Edinburgh in 1800, a fellow in 1801, and president in 1827. He practised in Edinburgh for a time, but became a licentiate of the Royal College of Physicians, London, in 1808, and became a fellow in 1841. He was made inspecting physician of lunatic asylums in Surrey in 1810, and in 1835 physician to the Bethlem Hospital and later to several other asylums. Unable to find an institution in Edinburgh willing to let him have teaching facilities he nevertheless organized his own course of lectures. In 1816 he was appointed physician-in-ordinary to Princess Charlotte of Wales, and later to her husband, Prince Leopold, and in 1838 he was knighted. His publications included *Outlines of Lectures on Mental Diseases* (1826), *Cases of Mental Disease, with Practical Observations on the Medical Treatment* (1828), and *The Physiognomy of Mental Diseases* (1840). These works are notable for a large series of interesting portrait drawings of the insane, among which is a striking one of Jonathan Martin, the man who set fire to York Minster. Morison was twice married. He died at Balerno Hill House, Currie, near Edinburgh, on 14 March 1866 and was buried at Currie. Morison endowed a prize and lectureship to the College of Physicians of Edinburgh with funds realized by the sale of his property at Larchgrove, which he left to the college.

NORMAN MOORE, *rev.* HUGH SERIES

Sources Munk, *Roll* • *Edinburgh Medical Journal*, 11 (1865–6), 962 • H. Smailes, *Method in madness, 5 December 1980 – 31 January 1981* (1980) [exhibition leaflet for Richard Dadd's portrait of Morison] • W. S. Craig, *History of the Royal College of Physicians of Edinburgh* (1976), 491–2 • *London and Provincial Medical Directory* (1860)

Sir Alexander Morison (1779–1866), by Richard Dadd, 1852

Archives RCP Lond., reports and notes on cases of insanity, essay on insanity • Royal College of Physicians of Edinburgh, diaries, corresp.

Likenesses M. Gauci, lithograph, pubd 1830 (after J. Irvine), BM • R. Dadd, oils, 1852, Scot. NPG [*see illus.*] • P. Westcott, portrait, Royal College of Physicians of Edinburgh

Wealth at death £5573 2s. 5d.: confirmation, 5 July 1866, NA Scot., SC 70/1/130/655–62

Morison, Douglas (1814–1847), watercolour painter and lithographer, was born at Tottenham, in Middlesex, on 22 August 1814, the son of Richard Morison, a doctor, of Datchet, near Windsor. He was a pupil and friend of the sporting artist Frederick Tayler. Morison was elected a member of the New Society of Painters in Water Colours in 1836; he exhibited eight Scottish landscapes there in 1837, but resigned in 1838. Between 1836 and 1841 he exhibited six paintings at the Royal Academy. In 1844 he was elected an associate of the Society of Painters in Water Colours; the fifteen paintings he exhibited there included several views of Furness Abbey, Lancashire.

Morison was also a lithographer, publishing *Views of Haddon Hall* (1842). Prince Albert commissioned *Views of the Ducal Palaces and Hunting Seats of Saxe Coburg and Gotha* (1846), which was based on drawings he had made during visits to Coburg and Gotha in 1841 and 1842. This led to a commission for Morison to paint views of Prince Albert's sitting-room at Windsor, and a series of interiors of Buckingham Palace, produced in 1843–4.

Morison died on 12 February 1847 at his home in Datchet, Buckinghamshire. His death was attributed to exhaustion following a day's deerstalking with Frederick Tayler in Scotland.

L. H. CUST, *rev.* ANNE PIMLOTT BAKER

Sources D. Millar, *The Victorian watercolours and drawings in the collection of her majesty the queen*, 2 vols. (1995) • J. L. Roget, *A history of the 'Old Water-Colour' Society*, 2 vols. (1891) • Mallalieu, *Watercolour artists*, vols. 1–2 • *The Royal Watercolour Society: the first fifty years, 1805–1855* (1992) • Graves, *RA exhibitors* • Wood, *Vic. painters*, 3rd edn • private information (1894) [Mrs D. Kemp and F. J. Furnivall]

Morison, George (1757–1845). *See under* Morison, James, of Elsick (1708–1786).

Morison, James, of Elsick (1708–1786), provost of Aberdeen, was the fifth son of James Morison (1665–1748), merchant and lord provost of Aberdeen (1730–31) and Anna Low (1672–1713). Nothing is known of Morison's childhood and early adult years. In 1740 he married Isobell Dyce (d. 1781), eldest daughter of James Dyce, merchant of Disblair, Aberdeenshire; they had five sons and eleven daughters.

Morison was elected provost of Aberdeen in 1744 and held office at the outbreak of the Jacobite rising in the autumn of 1745. His attempts to defend the city were prevented by a ruling from Sir John Cope, who ordered that arms be sent to Edinburgh. In late September, elections for a new provost were halted by the arrival of John Hamilton, chamberlain to the duke of Gordon, representing the Young Pretender. With no new provost having been elected, Morison was summoned to appear before Hamilton. After hesitation and threats he and two other magistrates were taken as prisoners to hear the proclamation of James VIII and III (James Francis Edward Stuart) at the town cross. Morison declined to drink James's health, and the wine was poured down his breast. His defiance earned him the praise of Lord President Forbes.

Morison died on 5 January 1786, five years after his wife's death on 23 January 1781. He was buried at St Nicholas's Church, Aberdeen. Only two of his sons survived him, and the estate passed to the elder, **Thomas Morison** (d. 1824), an army surgeon. He was best-known for publicizing the medicinal springs at Strathpeffer, Ross-shire.

The younger son, **George Morison** (1757–1845), Church of Scotland minister, was educated at Marischal College, Aberdeen, where he graduated MA on 14 February 1776. In January 1782 he was licensed as a probationer of the Church of Scotland, and in the following year was ordained minister of Oyne, Aberdeenshire. From here he moved to Banchory-Devenick in 1785, where he remained for sixty-one years. On 26 June 1786 he married Margaret Jeffray (1757?–1837), daughter of Gilbert Jeffray of Kingswell; they had no children. He received a doctorate of divinity from Aberdeen in 1824, and in the same year succeeded to the family's estate of Elsick and Disblair.

A generous man, Morison's benefactions to his parish were large. The most important was the suspension bridge across the River Dee, built at a cost of £1400 and for many years the means of communication between the north and south portions of the parish. The years after his wife's death on 11 June 1837 were taken up in part by work on two studies, *A Brief Outline of the Church of Scotland* and *State of the Church of Scotland in 1830 and 1840 Contrasted* (both 1840). He died, 'Father of the Church of Scotland', on 13 July 1845.

ROBERT MACPHERSON, *rev.* ROBERT CLYDE

Sources A. M. Munro, *Memorials to the aldermen, provosts, and lord provosts of Aberdeen, 1272–1895* (1896) · *Fasti Scot.*, new edn
Likenesses photograph (after portrait), Town House, Aberdeen

Morison, James (1762–1809), publisher and writer on theology, was born at Perth on 13 December 1762, the son of Robert *Morison (1722–1791), a bookseller and postmaster there, and his wife, Margaret Russel (1720–1800). He too became a bookseller, first at Leith and later at Perth. He was also a papermaker and publisher, and was appointed printer to St Andrews University. On 13 December 1778 he married Margaret, a daughter of Thomas Mitchel, writer, of Perth; she died in 1789 and he married Grace Lindsay (d. 1845) on 20 December 1790.

In religion Morison was a member of the Glasite church. In 1799 he and most of the members of the Perth and Arbroath Glasite churches separated from the rest of the movement on the subject of Christian assurance, but he remained a Glasite. He published an account of the reasons for the split in 1799. He was a frequent preacher with considerable gifts of exposition and linguistic ability, publishing several hymns and elegies. In 1806 he published a *New Theological Dictionary*, and *An Introductory Key to the First Four Books of Moses* appeared posthumously in 1810. He died at Perth on 20 February 1809. From each marriage he left a large family, some of whom followed him in trade and religion.

DEREK B. MURRAY

Sources *GM*, 1st ser., 79 (1809), 379–80 · D. C. Smith, *The historians of Perth* (1906)
Archives priv. coll.

Morison, James (1770–1840), pill manufacturer, was born on 3 March 1770 at Bognie, Aberdeenshire, the youngest of four sons (there were no daughters) of Alexander Morison, laird of Bognie, and his wife, Katherine, daughter of John Duff of Culbin, Morayshire, and great-granddaughter of James Sharp, the murdered archbishop of St Andrews. He studied at Marischal College, Aberdeen, in 1783–4, and prepared for a commercial career at Hanau, Germany.

Morison then travelled extensively in Europe; later he became a dealer in wines and spirits in the West Indies. Some time before 1810, he married Anne Victoire, daughter of Baron de Lamarre of Remiremont, Lorraine. They had three sons and two daughters. For a decade he lived in Bordeaux, having lost the fortune he had earlier made. Returning to Aberdeen, he began to experiment with pill-making in the dispensing room of a druggist friend.

According to his own account, Morison had suffered excruciatingly from ill health from 1786 until 1820, brought on by costiveness during residential education. He consulted no fewer than fifty medical men, including John Hunter; all the cures recommended by them proved useless. His condition became so piteous that his life was despaired of. Morison came to believe that bad humours had spread from his digestive tract throughout his body, and that the only certain cure was an all-vegetable remedy capable of purifying the blood and hence his entire system.

Many questions about Morison's illness have never been answered. Why did half a lifetime elapse before he discovered such a simple and permanent cure, and how did he manage to undertake so much travel, win a spouse, and father robust children in such a dismal state of health? Was he an all too plausible and unscrupulous quack, or a genuine victim of chronic hypochondria?

In 1825, Morison began to market his Universal Vegetable Pills in England. Three years later, in partnership

James Morison (1770–1840), by unknown engraver, 1828 (after George Clint?)

with Thomas Moat, a merchant from Devon, he erected in what later became the Euston Road, London, a grandiose building which proclaimed itself the British College of Health. There he made two brands of pill, no. 2 being a strong purgative. Their composition, mainly of aloes and gamboge, was nothing new, and although he had two steam engines for manufacturing, the pills were very uneven in size and inadequately mixed. Yet the pills' defects were more than offset by Morison's vigorous promotion of his product. He was striving to offer not merely a commodity but also a vision of well-being, which his College of Health—an Exeter branch being opened in 1835—advanced with gusto. This was the Hygeian system, according to which every ill sprang from impurities in the blood; hence purging by means of vegetable agents was the only way towards recovery. Moreover, the stomach and bowels could never be purged too much. Morison publicized his message through press advertising, which cost thousands of pounds annually, through a monthly *Hygeian Journal*, and through a veritable shower of pamphlets.

Morison soon built up a network of agents in Britain, who sought orders and supplied local retailers. Since he would have nothing to do with chemists or druggists, his pills sold through outlets ranging from grocers and stationers to circulating libraries. Sales in France and elsewhere in Europe were also lucrative. In the early 1830s Moat's son travelled to the United States to open up the market there; he appointed agents for all the states then incorporated in the Union. American rivals soon began to counterfeit the pills, but were restrained by a landmark court case in 1834 in New York. Morison's declared tax

expenditure on patent medicine stamps suggests that his home turnover rose from an annual average of £24,000 in 1825–9 to £34,000 in 1830–31. It then jumped to £65,000 annually in 1832–3, which means that, if the discount (of about one-third) given to retailers is allowed for, British consumers were spending almost £100,000 on his pills in each of these two years.

Meanwhile, Morison's detestation of doctors was being reciprocated with interest. Thomas Wakley, founder and editor of *The Lancet*, maintained a tenacious campaign against secret medicines, and against Morison in particular. From the early 1830s onwards, Morison's advice to take his pills in very large doses precipitated a sequence of sudden deaths and harsh observations by coroners. When some of his agents were convicted of manslaughter, he cheerfully paid their fines, and to one who was jailed he gave a piece of silver plate. By 1834 it was becoming too hazardous for Morison to remain in Britain, and he decamped to Paris. He was accompanied by his second wife, Clarinda Sharmer, daughter of Captain Cotter RN, and by his only surviving son from that marriage, James Augustus Cotter *Morison.

Predictably, Morison's pills suffered a sharp fall in sales, to an average of no more than £26,000 a year between 1834 and 1839. Morison died at his home, 3 rue des Pyramides, Paris, on 3 May 1840, and was buried in Kensal Green cemetery, Middlesex. He was survived by his wife. His estate in Britain was initially valued at £9000, then written up to £25,000, but in 1845 reduced to £8816. His notoriety inspired dozens of satirical cartoons, and also the ironic remarks of Thomas Carlyle, who in *Past and Present* (1843) observed that Morison's simple message of restoring the sick to health could profitably be extended to curing the ills of society. The College of Health was swept away when the Euston Road was widened in 1928; moribund for many years, the firm itself quietly expired in the following decade. T. A. B. CORLEY

Sources W. H. Helfand, 'James Morison and his pills', *Transactions of British Society for the History of Pharmacy*, 1 (1970–77), 101–35 · J. Morison, *Morisoniana*, 3rd edn (1831) · *Biographical sketch of Mr Morison the Hygeist* (1873) · Burke, *Gen. GB* · *GM*, 2nd ser., 14 (1840), 437–8 · *Medical Circular* (5 Jan 1853), 8–10 · *Medical Circular* (12 Jan 1853), 25–7 · *Report of a trial in the superior court of the state of New York wherein James Morison and Thomas Moat were plaintiffs, and Moses Jaques and Jonathan B. Marsh, defendants* (1834) · 'Chancery and bankruptcy: Morison v. Moat', *Law Journal Reports*, new ser., 20/1 (1851), 513–29 · *The Lancet* (1833–40) · will, PRO, PROB 11/1931/516 [8 Jan 1836]

Likenesses Castle, stipple, 1828 (after G. Clint), Wellcome L. · line engraving, 1828 (after G. Clint?), NPG [*see illus.*] · G. Cruickshank, etching, 1833, Wellcome L. · H. Berthoud, coloured aquatint, Wellcome L. · portrait, repro. in R. Porter, *Quacks* (2000) · woodcut, BM

Wealth at death £9000: 4 July 1840, PRO, death duty registers, IR 26/1555, 474 · £25,000: 11 Oct 1840, PRO, death duty registers, IR 26/1555, 474 · £8816: Sept 1845, PRO, death duty registers, IR 26/1555, 474

Morison, James (1816–1893), United Secession minister and a founder of the Evangelical Union, was born at the Secession manse at Bathgate, Linlithgowshire, on 14 February 1816, one of three children of Robert Morison (1782–

1855), a minister in the Secession church, and his wife, Jessie Rollo. His mother died when he was only five years of age but not before she expressed the wish that James should become a minister. Educated at Bathgate parish school, Morison entered Edinburgh University in 1830, where he attracted the special interest of James Pillans and John Wilson (who wrote under the pseudonym of Christopher North). In 1834 he commenced his attendance at the theological hall of the United Secession church. He was later recalled as 'a tall, somewhat eccentric youth, … stalking the bridges or Prince's street, with a white hat put awry on his head, and some half dozen volumes under his arm' (Smith, 305). Though troubled with ill health, and at one stage threatened with blindness, Morison distinguished himself as a divinity student, and his professor, John Brown, favoured him with the key to his extensive library. Morison was licensed by the Secession Presbytery of Edinburgh on 7 May 1839.

Morison was initially placed at the disposal of the presbytery of Elgin for the purposes of itinerant preaching in the north of Scotland. Influenced by his reading of Charles Finney's *Lectures on Revivals of Religion* and by the prevailing climate of religious fervour, Morison developed his extemporaneous preaching style at Cabrach in Banffshire and at the other stations to which he was sent. In response to the numerous enquiries he received, Morison prepared a pamphlet, *The Question, 'What must I do to be saved?' Answered*, which was published under the *nom de plume* Philanthropos in 1840. This articulated Morison's view that the atonement had been for all men, not just for the elect. This inevitably placed him on a collision course with the Calvinist orthodoxy of his church. Morison was called to Clerk's Lane Church, Kilmarnock, but on the day of his ordination, 1 October 1840, he first had to undergo an inquisition by the presbytery. Any satisfaction which they received was short-lived, as Morison issued a new pamphlet, *The Nature of the Atonement*, in January 1841, an offence compounded by the re-publication of his earlier work. The presbytery brought charges of errors in doctrine and disingenuous conduct against him in March 1841 and Morison was suspended, pending the meeting of the synod in June. Morison took advantage of this interval to marry Margaret Dick (*d*. 1875), who had Bathgate connections but was then residing in London. The couple were married in Shoreditch parish church before returning to Scotland. There were three children from the marriage.

On 11 June Morison's appeal to the synod was dismissed and his suspension confirmed on a motion of Dr Heugh's, John Brown dissenting from the verdict. This effectively marked the end of formal proceedings in his case, for although a committee was meant to confer with Morison, the latter had already decided to secede, accompanied by a majority of his congregation, which had augmented considerably since his appointment. They were able to retain their building. Morison's departure was merely the beginning of a period of turbulence in the church he left behind in what became known as the atonement controversy. His father was suspended in 1842 and a further two suspended

ministers, Alexander Rutherford of Falkirk and John Guthrie of Kendal, later joined the Morisons in Kilmarnock to establish the Evangelical Union on 16 May 1843, an event somewhat overshadowed by the Disruption in the Church of Scotland two days later. A theological academy was established under Morison, its student numbers augmented by an influx of Congregationalists expelled from their academy for heresy. It had not been intended to establish a new denomination, merely a society for the promotion of evangelical work, but the practical effect was to create a church which in its organization hovered between Presbyterianism and Congregationalism, and whose most distinctive feature was its championing of total abstinence before it became a popular cause in other churches.

In 1851 Morison was called to a Glasgow church to which he was inducted on 5 October. The congregation was smaller than in Kilmarnock, but offered the inducement of a more influential setting. An attack of pleurisy the following year was indicative of further health problems to come. The new church built for him in North Dundas Street opened in February 1853, but in 1855 poor health required him to take an extended break from his duties, which he spent on the continent and in the Holy Land. An operation on his throat proved a failure and his preaching was impaired thereafter. In 1858 he took on a colleague at North Dundas Street.

Following the move to Glasgow, Morison was more inclined to exert his influence through the printed word. In 1854 he launched a quarterly magazine, the *Evangelical Repository*, which ran for fifteen years. He had already renewed his assault on Calvinism with *An Exposition of the Ninth Chapter of Paul's Epistle to the Romans* (1849), which he followed with *A Critical Exposition of the Third Chapter of Paul's Epistle to the Romans* (1866). This was, in turn, followed by two popular commentaries on the gospels of *Matthew* (1870) and *Mark* (1873), which were part of an intended examination of the New Testament curtailed by ill health. Morison's reputation was recognized by the award of the degree of DD by Adrian College, Michigan, in 1862. In 1882 the same honour was bestowed by Glasgow University.

Increasing infirmity began to tell on Morison and in 1876 he resigned his professorship at the theological academy, while accepting the position of principal. He married, secondly, Margaret Aughton, who survived him, at Preston on 4 September 1877. Morison resigned from his pastorate in January 1884, while remaining as honorary pastor. He was still able to work on publications such as *St Paul's Teaching on Sanctification* (1886). A gesture of reconciliation was made in 1893 when Morison received an illuminated address signed by 1946 ministers and laymen of the United Presbyterian church, earlier attempts formally to reverse the sentence of 1841 having come to nothing.

At the end of his life Morison presented a slight, venerable, white-haired and full-bearded figure. In his career he challenged the prevailing Calvinism of the protestant churches in Scotland, while resisting the over-speculative approach which had been the undoing of Edward Irving with whom, in his early career, he had invited comparison. It was widely acknowledged that the views that had brought Morison before the church courts fifty years before now represented the mainstream of Christian thought in Scotland. Morison died on 13 November 1893 at his residence, Florentine Bank, Hillhead, Glasgow. He was buried on 16 November in the Glasgow necropolis, where a granite obelisk was later erected.

LIONEL ALEXANDER RITCHIE

Sources W. Adamson, *The life of the Rev James Morison DD* (1898) · O. Smeaton, *Principal James Morison: the man and his work* (1901) · *Ministerial jubilee of the Rev Principal Morison DD* (1889) · *The Scotsman* (14 Nov 1893) · *Glasgow Herald* (14 Nov 1893) · *Christian Leader* (16 Nov 1893) · *Christian Leader* (23 Nov 1893) · R. Small, *History of the congregations of the United Presbyterian church from 1733 to 1900*, 2 (1904), 288–91 · J. Smith, *Our Scottish clergy*, 2nd ser. (1849), 302–6 · private information (1894) · *DSCHT* · D. M. Lewis, ed., *The Blackwell dictionary of evangelical biography, 1730–1860*, 2 vols. (1995) · *DNB*
Archives Mitchell L., Glas., student's notebook
Likenesses photograph (in old age), repro. in Smeaton, *Principal James Morison* · six portraits (at various ages), repro. in Adamson, *Life*
Wealth at death £3860 14s. 11d.: confirmation, 21 April 1894, *CCI*

Morison, James Augustus Cotter (1832–1888), author, was born in London on 20 April 1832, the only surviving child of James *Morison (1770–1840) and his second wife, Clarinda Sharmer Cotter, known as Clara, only daughter of Captain Cotter. Morison's father lived in Paris from 1834 until his death, where he had many distinguished friends. His son thus learnt French in his infancy, and afterwards gained a broad knowledge of French history, life, and literature. After his father's death in 1840 he lived with his mother near London and was educated at the Highgate grammar school. After travelling in Germany, in March 1850 he entered Lincoln College, Oxford. He was popular in university society, a 'good oar', fencer, and rider, and a wide reader, although not according to the regular course. His university career was interrupted by visits to his mother, whose health was failing. He graduated BA and MA in 1859, and left Oxford, having acquired many friends, especially Mark Pattison, Thomas Fowler (then fellow of Lincoln, later president of Corpus), and John Morley.

Morison was a student of Lincoln's Inn in 1857 but was, apparently, never called to the bar. His father, the inventor and manufacturer of Morison's pills, had left him with considerable independent means and he soon began to write for periodicals, and became one of the best known of the staff of the *Saturday Review* while John Douglas Cook was editor. In 1861 he married Frances Virtue (d. 1878), the daughter of George *Virtue (1794–1868), the publisher [see under Virtue, James Sprent]. In 1863 he published his interesting *Life of St Bernard*, a book which was praised by Mark Pattison, Matthew Arnold, and Cardinal Henry Manning. It showed great historical knowledge, and a keen interest in the medieval church. He afterwards contemplated a study of French history during the reign of Louis XIV, which occupied him intermittently during the rest of his life, but remained incomplete at his death.

Morison's wife died in 1878, and he moved to 10 Montague Place, in order to be near to the British Museum, and afterwards to Fitzjohn's Avenue, Hampstead. He was elected a member of the Athenaeum and was a very active member of the London Library committee. He was a member of the Positivist Society, served on the positivist committee of seven, occasionally lectured at Newton Hall, and left a legacy of £500 to the society. A few years before his death, symptoms of a fatal disease showed themselves, and he was forced to abandon the completion of his French history. In 1887 he published his *Service of Man, an Essay towards the Religion of the Future*. Although he regarded this as his best work, and contemplated a second part, to be called 'A guide to conduct', his positivist friends were alarmed by the book's central argument that the concept of moral responsibility was a fallacy, as man was born, not made, virtuous. His other works were numerous articles in the chief periodicals, a pamphlet on *Irish Grievances* in 1868, *Mme de Maintenon, an étude* in 1885, and excellent monographs on Gibbon (1878) and Macaulay (1882) in John Morley's Men of Letters series.

Morison was very widely read, but the multiplicity of interests (from which contemporary politics alone were excluded) prevented his producing any substantial work. A lively companion, he had a wide and affectionate circle of friends; he was a sympathetic reviewer, who was eager to meet the authors of the works he admired. His closest friends were drawn from positivist circles, and included Frederic Harrison and Vernon Lushington, but he also cultivated literary lions such as George Meredith, who dedicated a volume of poems to him. Towards the end of his life, he neglected his positivist friends for literary and drinking companions, whom he entertained at his home and on board his yacht (travelling and yachting were his main recreations). The 'boozy skipper', as Harrison dubbed him, died at home, Clairvaux, 30 Fitzjohn's Avenue, Hampstead, on 26 February 1888. He left three children: a son, Theodore *Morison, principal of the college of Aligarh, India, from 1899–1905 and member of the Council of India from 1906; and two daughters, Helen Cotter, and Margaret.

LESLIE STEPHEN, *rev.* NILANJANA BANERJI

Sources *The Times* (28 Feb 1888) · M. S. Vogeler, *Frederic Harrison: the vocations of a positivist* (1984) · Foster, *Alum. Oxon.* · private information (1894) · personal knowledge (1894) · probate · *CGPLA Eng. & Wales* (1888)
Archives U. Leeds, Brotherton L., letters to Sir Edmund Gosse
Wealth at death £7153 1s. 8d.: probate, 13 April 1888, *CGPLA Eng. & Wales*

Morison, John (1750–1798), hymn writer, was born at Cairnie, Aberdeenshire, in June 1750. Educated at King's College, Aberdeen, he spent some years as a private tutor, first at Dunnet, Caithness, and afterwards at Banniskirk. He graduated MA in 1771, was schoolmaster at Thurso about 1773, and subsequently went to Edinburgh University for further study. In September 1780 he was appointed minister of Canisbay, Caithness, the most northerly church on the mainland.

From 1771 to 1775 Morison contributed verses, under the

signature Musaeus, to Ruddiman's *Edinburgh Weekly Magazine*, but these are of no particular merit. Morison's claim to remembrance rests on his contributions to the final edition of the *Scottish Paraphrases* (1781). When the collection was in preparation he submitted twenty-four pieces to the committee, of which he was himself a member; only seven were accepted, and some of these were slightly altered, probably by his friend John Logan. Most of the seven became household words in the Presbyterian churches, and one or two are freely used as hymns by other denominations. The thirty-fifth, ''Twas on that night when doom'd to know', has long been the Scottish communion hymn, but it appears to be founded partly on Watts's ''Twas on that dark, that doleful night', and partly on a Latin hymn by Andreas Ellinger. In 1787 Morison published an English version of books 2 and 4 of the *Aeneid*. He wrote the account of the parish of Canisbay for Sinclair's *Statistical Account*, and collected the topographical history of Caithness for Chalmers's *Caledonia*. A translation of Herodian's *History* from the Greek remained in manuscript. He was an accomplished classical scholar and an able preacher. In 1792 he received the degree of DD from Edinburgh University. He died, after many years' seclusion, at Canisbay, on 12 June 1798.

J. C. HADDEN, *rev.* S. R. J. BAUDRY

Sources *Fasti Scot.*, 3.359 · J. T. Calder, *Sketch of the civil and traditional history of Caithness* (1861) · D. J. Maclagan, *The Scottish paraphrases: being the translations and paraphrases … of sacred scripture* (1889) · J. Julian, ed., *A dictionary of hymnology* (1892) · R. Burns, *Memoir of the Rev. Stevenson Macgill* (1842) · H. Bonar, notes, *Free Church hymnal*, ed. J. Bonar (1880) [printed for private circulation] · *Free Church Magazine* (May 1847) · *Life and Work* (Jan 1888) · 'Private papers put forth by authority during the reign of Queen Elizabeth', Parker Society, 405 · parish register, Cairnie

Morison, John (1791–1859), Congregational minister, was born on 8 July 1791 at Millseat of Craigston, in the parish of King Edward, Aberdeenshire, the elder of the two sons of John Morison (*d.* 1833), later an elder of the Independent church at Banff. He was apprenticed to a watchmaker at Banff, but was released from his apprenticeship in 1811 in order to enter Hoxton Academy to train for the ministry.

Morison was ordained on 17 February 1815, and became pastor of a congregation at Union Chapel, Sloane Street, Chelsea. In 1815 he married Elizabeth, daughter of James Murray of Banff. Most of their seven children died young. At the end of 1816 Trevor Chapel, Brompton, was opened, and he was minister there for more than forty years. From about 1827 to 1857 he was editor of the *Evangelical Magazine*, and the University of Glasgow conferred upon him the degree of DD in 1830.

Morison's many publications included *Counsels to a Newly-Wedded Pair, or, Friendly Suggestions to Husbands and Wives* (1830), *An Exposition of the Book of Psalms, Explanatory, Critical and Devotional* (1832), *Family Prayers for every Morning and Evening throughout the Year* (1837), *A Commentary on the Acts of the Apostles, in the Catechetical Form* (1839), *The fathers and founders of the London Missionary Society, with a brief sketch of Methodism and historical notices of several protestant missions from 1556 to 1839* (1840), and *The protestant Reformation in all*

countries, including sketches of the state and prospects of the reformed churches (1843). Morison died at his home, 27 Montpelier Square, Westminster, on 13 June 1859, after several years of illness, and was buried in Abney Park cemetery, Stoke Newington, a week later. His wife survived him.   THOMPSON COOPER, *rev.* ANNE PIMLOTT BAKER

Sources A. T. [A. Tidman], 'Memoir of the Rev. John Morison', *Evangelical Magazine and Missionary Chronicle*, [3rd ser.], 1 (1859), 607–20 · *Congregational Year Book* (1860), 200–03 · W. M. Statham, *The voice of the dead: a sermon, on the occasion of the death of J. Morison* (1859) · J. Darling, *Cyclopaedia bibliographica: a library manual of theological and general literature*, 2 vols. (1854–9) · *CGPLA Eng. & Wales* (1859)
Archives DWL, letters
Likenesses J. Blood, stipple, 1818, BM, NPG · J. Thomson, stipple, 1828 (after Wilson), BM, NPG · Cochran, engraving · J. Whitehead, mezzotint (after H. Room), NPG
Wealth at death under £450: probate, 6 July 1859, *CGPLA Eng. & Wales*

Morison, Sir Richard (*c.*1510–1556), humanist and diplomat, was the second son of Thomas Morison of Sandon, Hertfordshire, and his wife, a daughter of Thomas Merry of Hatfield, Hertfordshire. His father was probably originally from Chardwell, Yorkshire, but it remains possible that the Chardwell and Sandon Morisons are unrelated. His family was of modest means. Morison's connection with Cardinal Thomas Wolsey, archbishop of York, as well as the traces of northern dialect which have been detected in his writings, suggest, perhaps, Yorkshire origins.

Early years and education, 1518–1536 Morison was admitted as a petty canon of Wolsey's Oxford foundation, Cardinal College, probably in 1526. He supplicated for admission to the BA on 19 January 1528, was admitted on 5 November, and determined in Lent 1529. Wolsey granted Morison a pension for life of 54s. 4d., and their friendship was recalled by the latter years after the cardinal's death.

On 30 December 1533 Morison wrote a patronage-seeking letter to Thomas Cranmer, archbishop of Canterbury, from Venice in which he claimed that he had left Wolsey's service to go to Cambridge, out of admiration for Hugh Latimer, and that while there he had several times met Cranmer, in the company of William Gonnell. The stay in Cambridge probably took place in 1528 and / or 1529 and was evidently followed by a return to Oxford before Morison embarked, in 1532, on a four-year stay in Italy at the University of Padua, where he studied law and acted briefly as *consiliarius* of the English 'natio' in August 1534; he was deprived of his position after accusations by some French students that he had participated in a plot to block the election of a French rector. But his studies in this period do not seem to have focused principally on law. From his contemporary correspondence as well as his writings of the later 1530s it is clear that he undertook an intensive and eclectic course of reading, which included patristic writings, Aristotelian philosophy, the works of the Greek dramatists (which he read with the English student George Lily), such humanist standards as Cicero, and such modern Italian writers as Marc Antonio Sabellico and, more significantly, Niccolò Machiavelli, of whose works he became one of the earliest English advocates and a lifelong admirer. He was particularly interested in political history, added fluency in Italian to his Latin and Greek, and was a lively observer of the contemporary Italian world. It is probably also in the cosmopolitan environment of the Veneto that he first became converted to the Lutheran ideas which he may earlier have encountered in Oxford or Cambridge and which dominate his later thought; the 1533 letter to Cranmer is the earliest extant expression from him of evangelical sentiment.

Morison first went to Padua as the client and servant of Wolsey's illegitimate son Thomas Winter, who was also there from 1532. Funds from this source seem to have dried up by about 1534, the year of Winter's departure. Suffering poverty in the following year, Morison asked Thomas Starkey, formerly at Padua and by then a servant of Thomas Cromwell in England, to arrange with Winter for Morison's pension from Wolsey to be sold. In the meantime he pawned his books and was helped materially by other Englishmen in Padua and Venice, among them Michael Throckmorton, Henry Cole, John Friar, and Henry VIII's cousin Reginald Pole, in whose home he stayed for some time. Many of his letters from this period complain bitterly of his poverty, which was partly why he decided to follow Starkey's example and try to enter Cromwell's service. This attempt was successful, and Morison went on to write Cromwell news reports and intelligence from Italy. He advised Cromwell on how to respond to Italian reactions to the executions of Sir Thomas More and John Fisher, bishop of Rochester, and sent him his English translation of the German Lutherans' answer to Pier Paolo Vergerio, who had been sent as papal diplomat to sound them out about a general council of the church in 1535. At the same time he continued to plead for help: 'He who has saved all England from papal tyranny has promised to free Morison from the tyranny of poverty' (BL, Cotton MS, Nero B vi, fol. 135r).

Cromwell's servant and propagandist, 1536–1540 Cromwell eventually summoned Morison home in May 1536 and made him a member of his household. Morison was not simply following in Starkey's footsteps but to some extent stepping into his shoes, Starkey having been somewhat disgraced by mid-1536 because of his continued association with Pole, whose defiant opposition to the king was by then known. Morison, on the other hand, had not been as close to Pole and rapidly distanced himself from the latter and his circle. Nevertheless, in one of his earliest tasks for Cromwell—to write a précis of Pole's De unitate, which is entitled 'Abbreviations of a certain evill willyed man or wryt agenst the kynges doinges'—he considerably toned down the extent of Pole's challenge to Henry VIII. Notwithstanding this, vitriolic denunciation of 'Mr Traitor Pole' would become one of the keynotes of his writings; their contrasting responses to Machiavelli are one of the indices of the attitudes which, among other things, separated them. Between 1536 and 1540 Morison worked in Cromwell's secretariat, and sat on the commission of 1537

which drafted Henry's response to the papal call for a general council of the church at Mantua in May 1537.

Morison is best known, however, as 'the man who wielded far and away the best propagandist pen in Henrician England' (Elton, 199). His propaganda output in the 1530s was significant. It reveals the application of humanist learning to the advocacy of a highly authoritarian model of kingship, and it shows the government harnessing the printing press to further its policies on an altogether new level; all of his propaganda writings were published by the royal printer Thomas Berthelet. His only book printed in Latin was the first he wrote, the *Apomaxis calumniarum* (1537 or 1538), which was dedicated to Cromwell. The *Apomaxis* is a comprehensive defence of Henry's schism and supremacy and an attack on the papacy, all drawing on scriptural and patristic sources. It was written in response to *De matrimonio serenissimi regis angliae Henrici Octavi* by the Catholic polemicist Johannes Dobnek (Cochlaeus). Dobnek would reply in turn to Morison with his *Scopa in araneas Ricardi Morison Angli*. Morison followed the *Apomaxis*, in the autumn of 1536, with the hurriedly written *Lamentation in whiche is Shewed what Ruyne and Destruction Cometh of Seditious Rebellyon*, addressed to the Lincolnshire rebels—it appears that by the time it was printed the rebellion had died out—and its effective sequel, the longer *Remedy for Sedition*, addressed to the members of the Pilgrimage of Grace. In these Morison first put forward his case for obedience to the king which was to become a major theme of his writings. The works are also noteworthy for his introduction of the quasi-humanist idea that virtue was synonymous with nobility (in answer to the rebels' complaint that the king had appointed low-born counsellors), combined, nevertheless, with a commitment to social hierarchy; the *Remedy* contains interesting observations on the country's social problems and the main means of resolving them: education in the gospel.

In 1537 Morison's little-known work *A comfortable consolation wherin the people may se, howe far greatter cause, they have to be glad for the joyful byrth of Prince Edwarde* was published and about two years later he wrote the verses on Hans Holbein's portrait of Edward, prince of Wales. *The epistle sent to the cardinals and prelates that were chosen and appointed by the byshop of Rome* appeared in March 1538. This was Morison's translation of a public letter by the Strasbourg humanist and reformer Johann Sturm, in which Sturm insisted that the only path to reconciliation with the protestants was the extirpation of superstition. Morison would later develop a friendship with him. *An Invective agenste the Great and Detestable Vice, Treason* was published in 1539. Directed against the Exeter conspiracy, it scurrilously condemns the 'archetraytour' Pole. Later in the same year Morison's *Exhortation to Styrre up All Englishemen to the Defence of their Country* was published as a result of the government's preparations for war. And the same programme prompted his translation of the *Stratagemata* by the ancient Roman governor of Britain, Frontinus, entitled *The Stratagemes, Sleyghtes, and Policies of Warre*, also printed in 1539.

It is impossible to measure the contemporary impact of

these works and the extent to which the government directed their contents. Morison's writings are witty, forceful, and colourful, and reveal inventiveness and a considerable breadth of learning. Despite the erudition, however, the works are intensely polemical and quite populist, having been written in accessible language. They testify, in contrast to the propaganda of the early 1530s, to the government's belief that the opinions of relatively ordinary people could and should be manipulated by persuasion during the political and religious changes of the period. In addition, there is some evidence of the diffusion of these works on the continent. Morison saw the break with Rome as a delivery to be compared with the Israelite exodus from Egypt, and he justified the royal supremacy and exhorted obedience to the king on the model of divinely ordained Old Testament kingship. A number of his unpublished writings are characterized by the same biblicism and evangelism, commitments which he shared with Cromwell and which no doubt underscored their relationship. For example, extant in Morison's hand are a treatise on the seven sacraments, which became part of the *Bishops' Book* printed in September 1537; a collection of extracts from the Old Testament dated October 1537; the draft of a sermon on Proverbs; and a translation of, and brief commentary on, Luther's sermon on Psalm 127, derived from the 1534 edition of Luther's works and written probably in the later 1530s (it was clearly intended for publication).

Most important among Morison's unpublished religious writings is a treatise on faith and justification, which later came into the hands of the martyrologist John Foxe. Influenced heavily by Luther's *On the Freedom of a Christian Man* of 1520, the treatise represents the culmination of Morison's religious thought, dealing with the most pressing theological issues of the day and at the same time fusing them with the notion of divine right monarchy. The work is saturated with protestant ideas on freedom, justification, and obedience. Also unpublished but reflecting rather his commitment to the practical application of humanist learning is *A Perswasion to the King that the Laws of the Realme Shulde be in Latin*, together with an example of how this might be achieved, a Latin codification of English land law entitled *Liber dominorum et tenentium*. A pragmatic approach to humanist studies also emerges from Morison's *Introduction to Wisdome*, an English translation of Juan Luis Vives's Latin original. The first of several editions was printed in 1540 and was dedicated to Cromwell's son Gregory.

The king's servant, 1540–1556 During the late 1530s and 1540s Morison accumulated a range of benefices, lands, and offices. Between 1537 and 1539 he was prebendary of Yetminster Secunda in Salisbury, Wiltshire, a position which he took over from Pole. In 1539 he was appointed master of St James's Hospital in Northallerton, Yorkshire, and provost of St Wulfstan's Hospital in Worcester. He was granted them at their dissolution in May 1540 and obtained in addition the library and other portions of the house of the white friars in Fleet Street, London. In 1545 he was granted the manor of Cassiobury, Hertfordshire, a

former monastic property, and began to build a house there, which was left unfinished at his death. At about the same time he undertook a number of land acquisitions designed to provide for his illegitimate children, two sons and a daughter. His mistress Lucy (d. 1552), daughter of Thomas Peckham, had married George Harper. Morison married Bridget (1525/6–1601), eldest daughter of John Hussey, Baron Hussey, of Sleaford, Lincolnshire, and his second wife, Anne, in 1546. They had one son, Charles (1549–1599), and three daughters, Jane, Elizabeth, and Mary. From 1545 to 1550 he was collector of the little custom and subsidy in the port of London.

Morison's most important offices, however, were gentleman of the privy chamber, MP, and ambassador. The first two appointments (both 1539), reflect Cromwell's attempts to shore up his position against mounting political enmity by placing his own men in influential offices. Morison was possibly reluctant—and certainly surprised—to be made a gentleman of the privy chamber, perhaps sensing the dangers that accompanied close access to the king. It does not appear that he retained this office for long. As an MP he drafted, and presumably delivered, a speech to parliament in 1540 on the importance of granting the king a new subsidy for naval defence and coastal fortifications. The bill was approved by May. His career survived Cromwell's fall. He was a special ambassador to Denmark between 23 December 1546 and March 1547 with a daily stipend of 26s. 8d., serving as Henry's delegate in Holstein for the peace conference held there by the duke of Holstein and Christian III, king of Denmark. He also visited several Hanse towns on this mission.

Morison enjoyed even more favour from the government of Edward VI, including a pension of £20. In 1547 he was a JP for Middlesex and MP for Wareham, Dorset, probably on the recommendation of Sir William Paget, chancellor of the duchy of Lancaster, to Edward Seymour, duke of Somerset and lord protector, and the privy council. In May 1549 he was appointed as one of the commissioners to visit St George's Chapel, Windsor, Winchester College, and the University of Oxford, where he judged positively the controversial teachings on the eucharist of the Italian exile Pietro Martire Vermigli. This was the prelude to the second major phase of his career, as resident ambassador to Charles V, primarily based in Germany. His salary was a generous £1000 per annum and the celebrated scholar Roger Ascham was appointed as his secretary. Before his departure in October 1550 he was made a privy councillor, although he never attended a meeting, and knighted (27 July). He drew up a will on 22 September. He left the statutory third of his inheritance to the crown during the minority of his heir, requesting that the wardship might go to Catherine Brandon, dowager duchess of Suffolk. Morison left Cassiobury and all his property in London to his wife for life, with any remaining unmoveables to go to his heir and to his illegitimate children. He appointed his wife and his close friend John Hales as executors and Suffolk as overseer.

Morison's first year as ambassador was not a success and

he was briefly recalled in 1551. He offended Charles by 'preaching' to him his own religious views. In the autumn of 1551 he encountered difficulties with Charles over the privy council's refusal to permit Princess Mary liberty of conscience in England; Morison wrote an account of the case. Indeed, as ambassador he gained a reputation in imperial circles as a notorious heretic. At the end of 1551 Morison's London house was the site of one of two conferences on the eucharist attended by prominent political figures and divines. He returned to Germany and remained in post until September 1553. His movements and concerns, during a period in which Charles's peripatetic habits were accentuated by the exigencies of war with German protestant states, can be reconstructed from his letters to Sir William Cecil, principal secretary, and to the privy council, and from Ascham's many extant letters. He found that his stipend was insufficient and it was frequently paid in arrears. In early 1552 Morison's party, which included his wife, was based at Augsburg, but from then on they followed Charles to Hall in the Tyrol, Innsbruck, Speyer, and Brussels. The flippancy and prolixity of his dispatches were complained of at this time, and his achievements as ambassador were questioned. Nevertheless he emerges most sympathetically from Ascham's letters. According to Ascham, he was genial and kindhearted, as well as wise, insightful, and humane on matters of public policy. His nickname was Merry Morison (*LP Henry VIII*, 12 pt 1, no. 430). Most of all, they shared a passion for humanistic scholarship, reading ancient Greek authors together, often on a daily basis. These included Herodotus, Isocrates, and Demosthenes. Morison also transmitted his admiration for Machiavelli to Ascham, whose 'Discourse on the affairs of Germany', a product of his experiences there with the ambassador, is influenced heavily by that author; Morison read the works of Machiavelli and of the Sienese reformer Bernardino Ochino to his household.

Following the accession of Mary I in July 1553 Morison joined the English protestant exiles on the continent. Together with his family and other prominent exiles such as Sir John Cheke and Sir Anthony Cooke, he stayed for the most part in Strasbourg, studying under Vermigli and corresponding with Heinrich Bullinger and John Calvin. With Cooke and Edwin Sandys, he successfully petitioned the city council for temporary residence in September 1555, but he died there on 20 March 1556. In a codicil added to his will on 15 March and witnessed by Cheke and Sir Thomas Wroth, Morison gave his wife all his moveable goods unconditionally. She returned to England on the accession of Elizabeth I and remarried.

JONATHAN WOOLFSON

Sources D. S. Berkovitz, *Humanist scholarship and public order* (1984) • L. Nicod, 'The political thought of Richard Morison: a study in the use of ancient and medieval sources in Renaissance England', PhD diss., U. Lond., 1998 • C. R. Bonini, 'Lutheran influences in the early English Reformation: Richard Morison re-examined', *Archiv für Reformationsgeschichte*, 64 (1973) • G. W. G. Zeeveld, *Foundations of Tudor policy* (1948) • G. R. Elton, *Policy and police: the enforcement of the Reformation in the age of Thomas Cromwell* (1972) • J. M. Woolfson, *Padua and the Tudors* (1998) • *Letters of Roger Ascham*, ed. and trans. M. Hatch and A. Vos (1984) • Emden, *Oxf.* • *LP Henry VIII* • *CSP for.*, 1547–53 • *APC*, 1547–52 • C. H. Garrett, *The Marian exiles: a study in the origins of Elizabethan puritanism* (1938) • Cooper, *Ath. Cantab.* • HoP, *Commons, 1509–58* • will, PRO, PROB 11/39, sig. 28

Archives BL, account of dispute with emperor on granting liberty of conscience to Princess Mary, Harley MS 353, fols. 130–38 • BL, collection of extracts from Old Testament, Royal MS 7 C xvi, fols. 212–40 • BL, draft of parliamentary speech, Cotton MS Titus B.i, fols. 109–16 • BL, king's response to call for a council of the church at Mantua, Cotton MS Cleopatra E.vi, fols. 322–4 • BL, treatise on faith and justification, Harley MS 423, fols. 12–33 • BL, treatises on law, Royal MSS 18 A i, 11 A xvi • BL, various letters, Cotton MS Nero B.vi, *passim* • PRO, draft of sermon on Proverbs, SP 1/123, fols. 168–9 • PRO, treatise on seven sacraments, SP 6/8, fols. 137–50 | BL, Cotton MSS, letters and dispatches • PRO, state papers

Wealth at death see will, PRO, PROB 11/39, sig. 28

Morison, Robert (1620–1683), botanist, was born at Aberdeen, the son of John Morison and his wife, Anna Gray. The family was native to Aberdeen, and Morison himself entered Marischal College there in 1635. He graduated as MA in 1638 and stayed on to teach in the university. As a student he cultivated his abilities in mathematics and learned Hebrew, at the insistence of his parents, who intended him for the ministry, but his principal interest was already in botany, particularly the flowers of his own country. His career was interrupted by the civil war, in which he fought on the royalist side. He was wounded in the head at the battle of the Bridge of Dee in 1644. Once his life was out of danger, he fled to France, settling first in Paris, where he served as tutor to the son of a councillor named Bizet. He studied anatomy, botany, and zoology, and in 1648 took the degree of MD at Angers. The royal botanist, Vespasian Robin, recommended him for service as a physician in the household of Gaston, duc d'Orléans, Louis XIV's uncle, and between 1650 and 1660 he worked in the duke's fine garden at Blois. He was encouraged to develop his ideas about the classification of plants and travelled extensively in search of new species in Burgundy, the Lyonnais, Languedoc, and Brittany. Morison later referred to the incorporation of 360 new plants into the garden at Blois, many of them thanks to his efforts. He may also have assisted Abel Brunyer and Nicolas Marchant in the preparation of the catalogue of the garden, published at Paris in 1653 and revised in 1655. Shortly before Gaston's death in February 1660, Morison was presented to the duke's nephew, Charles II; the same year, despite the rival interest in his skills of Louis XIV's minister Nicolas Fouquet, Morison accepted an invitation from the newly restored king of England. He arrived in London in August 1660.

Charles II gave Morison the title of royal physician and professor of botany, with a notional stipend of £200 per annum. Morison seems to have lived in London throughout the 1660s and to have continued his work on the classification of plants, building on the publications of Andrea Cesalpino and of Caspar and John Bauhin. The first published fruit of his activity was the *Hortus regius Blesensis*, which was advertised in May 1669. This work was based on the catalogue of the garden at Blois, augmented by Morison's additions, which included the description of 260

Robert Morison (1620–1683), by Robert White, pubd 1680 (after William Sonmans or Sunman)

the following autumn, but was sometimes hindered from his intention of lecturing each spring and autumn thereafter by the demands created by the publication of his works. In 1675 he was a candidate for the Sedleian chair of natural philosophy. His lack of success on that occasion owed more to the electors' sense of the breadth of natural philosophy than to any doubts about Morison's ability as a herbalist. It seems probable that Morison had been taken to Oxford primarily to advance the reputation of the university press through the publication of a grand herbal, organized according to his new principles of taxonomy. In 1672 he issued a specimen of this work from the Oxford press, *Plantarum umbelliferarum distributio nova*. This was dedicated to the duke of Ormond, the university's chancellor, and embellished with twelve plates, three of which were engraved at the expense of delegates of the press, the remainder being supported by prominent members of the university. Morison's system for classifying plants was displayed here for the first time, successfully isolating umbelliferous plants from others with similar forms of inflorescence. Following Cesalpino, whose work he had read, Morison argued that plants should primarily be distinguished by the single, key principle of differences in fruit and seed characteristics. He deployed vegetative characteristics for subsidiary taxonomic purposes only and argued that this method reflected the simplicity of the divine ordering of creation, as manifested in the book of nature. Properly observed, plants would reveal the secrets of their taxonomy and their beneficial uses, which had been known to providentially inspired botanists such as King Solomon. Morison would later suggest that the division of plants according to fruit and seed could be found in the words of Genesis 1: 11–12.

In 1674 the Oxford press published Paolo Boccone's *Icones et descriptiones rariorum plantarum Siciliae, Melitae, Galliae, et Italiae*, edited by Morison from a manuscript sent to him by Charles Hatton, whom he had met in Paris during the 1650s. Morison's edition, dedicated to Hatton, demonstrated that his method of classification could be extended to ferns and other plants which had traditionally been thought to be without flowers or seed. In December 1679 Morison abortively offered to dedicate a much more substantial publication to Hatton. This was the first of three projected volumes of a new universal herbal that Morison had advertised to subscribers at the time of the publication of *Plantarum umbelliferarum*. Between 1669 and 1672 he had worked on the first 108 plates for the herbal, but the cost of employing suitable engravers led him to seek subscriptions of £5 for each plate. Despite attracting interest from several noblemen and many members of the Royal Society and the College of Physicians, the subscription failed to generate sufficient funds and between 1677 and 1680 Morison was forced to take out three loans of £200 each from the Oxford press, using the completed plates as security. *Plantarum historiae universalis Oxoniensis pars secunda, seu, Herbarum distributio nova* was eventually published in 1680, with 126 plates, many of them drawn or engraved by Dutch craftsmen resident in London as well

plants for the first time. Although arranged according to an orthodox system, the catalogue was supplemented by Morison's critical animadversions on the taxonomic work of the Bauhins and a dialogue which outlined his view of the shortcomings of contemporary botanical classification. This dialogue was prefaced by a letter to John Fell, vice-chancellor of the University of Oxford and an active delegate of the newly revived university press which Morison admired. Here Morison referred to the antiquity and perfection of plants, which, he thought, survived in exactly the form in which they had been made by God on the third day of the creation.

On 16 December 1669 Morison was elected professor of botany at the University of Oxford and on the following day he was incorporated as doctor of medicine from University College, where he had the strong support of a senior fellow, Obadiah Walker, also a delegate of the university press. He gave his first lecture on 2 September 1670 and transferred three days later to the physic garden, where he lectured at a table covered with plant specimens. Morison gave further lectures in such surroundings three times a week for five weeks, attracting a considerable audience. He repeated the lectures in May 1673 and in as by the university's engraver, Michael Burghers. It consisted of five sections, giving the first part of Morison's descriptions of herbs, in his opinion the earliest plants created by God.

For many years Morison's salary had been in arrears and by January 1682 his efforts to repay his debts to the university had reduced him to a state of near penury, but he continued to work on his herbal. On 9 November 1683, while crossing the Strand during a visit to London in connection with the work, he was struck on the chest by the pole of a coach and badly injured. He was carried to his house in Green Street, Leicester Fields, where he died the next day, 10 November. He was buried in St Martin-in-the-Fields.

Following his death Morison's papers passed via Obadiah Walker to Jacob Bobart the younger, the keeper of the Oxford Physic Garden. Morison had left in draft a further four sections of his descriptions of herbs, which Bobart augmented with his own descriptions (translated into Latin by Mr Dale of Queen's College) to complete the full fifteen sections that Morison had planned for his account of herbs. With the financial support of the Oxford press to help meet the cost of engraving and correcting the 165 plates, *Plantarum historiae universalis Oxoniensis pars tertia* was finally published in 1699. The work included a life of Morison by Archibald Pitcairne, who had given the oration at his funeral. The university's support for Morison's work was reckoned by one estimate to amount to over £2000, yet the press found it as difficult to sell the herbal as its author had done. Morison's widow, of whom nothing is known but who was described by Thomas Tanner on 28 April 1699 as 'that sharp Gentlewoman' (Bodl. Oxf., MS Ballard 4, fol. 36), proved a tough negotiator in subsequent attempts to recoup the university's losses and many volumes remained unsold in 1713, when a final agreement was reached between the press and Gideon Murray, her representative.

The first volume of Morison's history of plants, projected to include descriptions of trees, was never published, and claims that some of his contemporaries had seen it in manuscript appear to be based on misunderstandings. A plan to augment Morison's descriptions of plants with their names in oriental languages, supplied by Thomas Hyde, also foundered. In publishing Morison's work Bobart seems to have carried out his intentions quite closely, as he did when he assembled a herbarium of 5000 plants to illustrate Morison's system. Nevertheless the history of plants failed to follow Morison's own taxonomy exactly, and was largely eclipsed by the writings of John Ray. Ray's criticisms of Morison's shortcomings as a writer of Latin seem valid, despite Wood's remark that 'though a master in speaking and writing Latin, yet [Morison] hath no command of the English, as being much spoyled by his Scottish tone' (Clark, 49–50). Morison's system was adopted by Paul Ammann and Paul Hermann, but generally found few followers. This situation perhaps reflected the relative isolation in which Morison had worked in his own lifetime: he seems, for example, never to have become a fellow of either the Royal Society or the Royal College of Physicians. He was frequently criticized for

ingratitude to earlier writers, yet both Tournefort and Linnaeus looked back on him with justification as the principal pioneer of taxonomy in botany. Richard Gray, who accused Ray of plagiarizing him, recorded that Morison was 'communicative of his knowledge, a true friend, an honest countreyman, true to his religion whom neither the faire promises of the papists nor the threatenings of others could prevail upon to alter or change' (BL, Sloane MS 3198, fol. 29r).   SCOTT MANDELBROTE

Sources [A. Pitcairne], 'Vita Roberti Morisoni', in R. Morison, *Plantarum historiae universalis Oxoniensis pars tertia*, ed. J. Bobart (1699) · Richard Gray MSS, BL, Sloane MS 3198, fols. 17–29 · Oxf. UA, SEP/Z/28 · S. H. Vines and G. C. Druce, *An account of the Morisonian herbarium in the possession of the University of Oxford* (1914) · Wood, *Ath. Oxon.: Fasti* (1820), 314–15 · *The life and times of Anthony Wood*, ed. A. Clark, 3, OHS, 26 (1894), 49–50 · U. Oxf., department of plant sciences, MSS Sherard 26–28, 34–35, 731 · Bodl. Oxf., MS Ballard 4, fol. 36 · Bodl. Oxf., MS Tanner 36, fol. 216 · BL, Add. MS 29557, fols. 299–300 · BL, Add. MS 29558, fol. 533 · *Further correspondence of John Ray*, ed. R. W. T. Gunther, Ray Society, 114 (1928) · R. Pulteney, *Historical and biographical sketches of the progress of botany in England*, 1 (1790), 298–312
Archives Oxf. UA, MSS relating to publication of work, SEP/Z/28 | U. Oxf., department of plant sciences, Sherard MSS, botanical MSS
Likenesses R. White, engraving, pubd 1680 (after W. Sonmans or Sunman), BM, NPG [*see illus.*] · W. Sonmans, oils, Botanic Gardens, Oxford
Wealth at death probably not substantial: complained of having spent estate in Jan 1682: Bodl. Oxf., MS Tanner 36, fol. 216

Morison, Robert (1722–1791), bookseller and publisher, was born in Perth, the son of Francis Morison (*d.* in or before 1741) and Elizabeth Mitchell. His father was a freeman glazier and bookbinder in Perth from 1706 onwards, and deacon of the Wright Calling there. Robert was educated at the Perth grammar school before learning his trade at the property his father owned and occupied in the High Street. His father died before Robert was admitted as glazier, stationer, or bookbinder (31 December 1741).

Morison became Perth's postmaster about 1745, and his printed *Regulations of the Post Office* carries advertisements of his stock, including Bibles, children's books, stationery, and proprietary medicines, as well as offering bookbinding and window glazing. He married Margaret Russel (1720–1800) and the couple had at least two children, James *Morison (1762–1809) and Robert Morison (1764–1853). The extent of Morison's business is indicated by the fact that he trained eleven local boys, in addition to his two sons, as booksellers between 1751 and 1790. He carried a wide range of Edinburgh and London magazines and began a commercial circulating library in 1752. His publishing activities began in 1772. George Johnston had introduced a printing office to Perth in 1770, printing for himself and Morison. Perth's first periodical, the *Perth Magazine of Knowledge and Pleasure* (1772–3), was published by the two men together. On Johnston's departure in 1774, the Morisons acquired the press.

With the aid of his sons, Morison expanded his father's modest business into the Morison Press. From 1776 they not only printed the typical ephemeral output of a small town press, meeting the needs of local businessmen, authors, and the Glasite church, to which the Morisons were adherents, but also cultivated a nationwide Scottish readership by issuing a stream of literary publications featuring Scottish names such as Gawin Douglas, William Dunbar, Blind Harry, John Ramsay and Ossian. They also issued editions of popular English writers such as Oliver Goldsmith and Captain James Cook. In 1782 the publishers were Morison and his son James. By 1785, the younger Robert Morison, who had trained as a printer, appeared in the imprint: 'Printed by R. Morison, Junior, for R. Morison and Son, Booksellers in Perth'—a formula that survived until 1798, despite the elder Robert's death (in Perth) in 1791.

In its heyday, the Morison Press was the most significant publishing and bookselling enterprise in Scotland outside Edinburgh and Glasgow. Financial difficulties in the 1790s owed much to James's involvement in large-scale publishing schemes such as the *Encyclopaedia Perthensis*, which overcommitted a press otherwise known for its 'unpretentious little volumes pleasantly printed in readable type' (Carnie, *Publishing in Perth*, 22). The Morison Press continued to be an important bookselling and publishing enterprise for the Perth area until the 1880s. At this final stage of its development the business was continued by a third generation, the sons of James and grandsons of Robert Morison.   ROBERT HAY CARNIE

Sources R. H. Carnie, *Publishing in Perth to 1807* (1960) · D. C. Smith, *The historians of Perth* (1906) · J. Minto, 'A notable publishing house: the Morisons of Perth', *The Library*, new ser., 1 (1900), 254–63 · R. H. Carnie, 'Scholar-printers of the Scottish Enlightenment', *Aberdeen and the Enlightenment*, ed. J. Carter (1987), 298–308 · R. H. Carnie, 'Perth booksellers and bookbinders in the records of the Wright Calling', *The Bibliotheck*, 1 (1958), 24–39 · A. R. Urquhart, 'Literature in Perth, with a bibliography', *Auld Perth*, ed. A. R. Urquhart (1906), 118–91 · U. Durham, Forbes MSS [partial transcripts] · Wrights Hall, Perth, Perth Wright Calling MSS
Archives U. Durham, Forbes MSS · Wrights Hall, Perth, Perth Wright Calling MSS

Morison, Rosa (1841–1912), educationist, was born on 5 June 1841 in The Broadway, Hammersmith, Middlesex, the fifth daughter of William Morison, a baker, and his wife, Catherine Agutter. She was educated at a private school in Greenwich, and at Queen's College, Harley Street. In 1866 she was appointed tutor in German, Italian, and Latin at Queen's. A few years later she found an ally in her desire to revitalize and develop the college when Eleanor Grove was appointed first as assistant secretary and then as Lady Resident. She and Eleanor Grove shared a love of German as well as an enthusiasm for the higher education of women, and they became lifelong friends. Frustrated by the refusal of the college council to deal with patent inefficiencies and slackness and to take advantage of the new opportunities open to women through London University, they both resigned in 1881 and went to Germany for some months.

When the two friends heard of the opening of the first hall of residence for women studying at University College and the London School of Medicine for Women, they offered their services free for the first year. Within twelve months Eleanor Grove had been appointed principal of the new College Hall, and Rosa Morison vice-principal. In 1883 the University College council decided to appoint Rosa Morison to the new post of lady superintendent of women students, which she combined with the honorary vice-principalship of College Hall for the remainder of her life. Her responsibilities within the college required great tact and delicate judgement, qualities she revealed in good measure; she gained the confidence of both staff and students, and was known and respected well beyond the walls of University College.

Rosa Morison was an active supporter of women's suffrage, and of women's participation in local government. Just before her death, she was furthering a scheme for the rebuilding of College Hall. She died suddenly, in the college, on 8 February 1912 of chronic bronchitis and heart failure. The large gathering, including most of the college professors and representatives of many other organizations, at her funeral in St Pancras Church on 12 February indicated the respect in which she was held. She was buried at Hammersmith cemetery. Her legacy to the college was used to endow a Rosa Morison scholarship in the faculty of arts.   ELAINE KAYE

Sources *University College London (UCL) Magazine*, March 1912, UCL, Archives · miscellaneous letters and papers, UCL, Archives · H. H. Bellot, *University College, London, 1826–1926* (1929) · A. M. Copping, *The story of College Hall* (1974) · E. Kaye, *A history of Queen's College, London, 1848–1972* (1972) · UCL annual report, 1884, UCL, Archives · UCL annual report, 1912–13, UCL, Archives · Queen's College London, Council minutes, Queen's College, London · *The Times* (20 Feb 1912) · b. cert. · d. cert. · *CGPLA Eng. & Wales* (1912) · *The Times* (10 Feb 1912) · *The Times* (13 Feb 1912)
Archives UCL
Likenesses portrait, UCL; repro. in *UCL Magazine*, facing p. 289
Wealth at death £39,414 9s. 10d.: probate, 27 March 1912, *CGPLA Eng. & Wales*

Morison, Stanley Arthur (1889–1967), typographer, was born at Kent Villa, Tavistock Road, Wanstead, Essex, on 6 May 1889, the only son and second of the three children of Arthur Andrew Morison (1856–1932) and his wife, Alice Louisa (1863–1951), daughter of Charles Cole, clerk, of Hackney, London. His father, an unsuccessful and intemperate commercial traveller, deserted the family when Morison was fourteen, causing him to leave Owen's School, Islington, in 1903 and to find paid work. After a phase of sharing his mother's agnosticism, he was received into the Roman Catholic church in December 1908. Unhappy as a clerk with the London City Mission (1905–12), he spent his spare time in museums and public libraries. The *Times* printing supplement of 10 September 1912 concentrated his mind on the study of letter-forms, printed and written, and early in the following year he was fortunate in securing a post as assistant in the office of *The Imprint*, a new monthly periodical devoted to design in printing. When *The Imprint* seemed likely to fail in the following year, the editor recommended Morison to Wilfrid Meynell, husband of Alice Meynell and managing director of Burns and Oates, Roman Catholic publishers, who took

Stanley Arthur Morison (1889–1967), by Sir William Rothenstein, 1924

him on his staff. Morison afterwards felt deeply grateful to the Meynell family for their help and encouragement.

In 1916 Morison made known his conscientious objection to war service. His appeal against conscription on religious and moral grounds was dismissed, and on 7 May 1916 he was arrested. Eventually he accepted alternative employment, and by the time the war ended he was engaged in farm work. Meanwhile, on 18 March 1916 he had married Mabel Williamson (1872–1961), a school-teacher. Not until many years later did Morison learn that she was not seven but seventeen years older than himself. Morison never spoke of his marriage: late in 1926 he made a settlement on his wife and they separated. He had formed a close relationship, undoubtedly amorous but as certainly chaste, with the American historian of typography and publicist Mrs Beatrice Lamberton Warde. They remained attached until he died.

After the war Wilfrid and his son, Francis Meynell, found Morison temporary employment until, in June 1921, he went as typographer to the Cloister Press near Manchester. The press was liquidated in July 1922 and Morison was never again employed full-time. At various

times he acted as freelance consultant to several publishers including Benn, Gollancz, Cape, and Heinemann, but his position as Britain's greatest authority on letter-design was won by his career with the Lanston Monotype Corporation, for which he acted as typographical adviser from 1922 until 1954. A dozen typefaces made to his specifications, some rendering old designs, others drawn by living artists including Eric Gill and Berthold Wolpe, became those most commonly used for printing in Great Britain and to a large extent abroad.

Morison's writings, over two hundred books, articles, collections of specimens, reviews, and prefaces, strongly affected the taste and enlarged the knowledge of experts and amateurs concerned with book production. A succession of learned essays in the annual *The Fleuron* (1923–30), founded in conjunction with Oliver Simon, discovered much that was of value in the history of type and its relation to the work of scribes and writing masters. The final one, 'First principles of typography', was frequently reprinted, and was translated into six languages during Morison's lifetime. On weekly visits to Cambridge, where from 1925 he was part-time typographical adviser to the university press, he was the perfect collaborator for its printer, Walter Lewis, until 1945 and for his successor, Brooke Crutchley, until 1959.

Morison's great service to *The Times* over thirty years made him known to a wider public, though in this, and in most of his work for other organizations, he believed that the authority of joint responsibility depended on anonymity. His appointment as typographical adviser was the result of his caustic comments on the paper's drab and old-fashioned look made in 1929. His views, reported to the manager, led eventually to his being asked to submit proposals. Through 1930 and 1931 he advocated typographical changes, including the abandonment of the ornamental gothic for the title. As a consequence a new typeface was cut, and when *The Times* first appeared in Times New Roman on 3 October 1932 almost all correspondents found it a relief to their eyes. Morison's position at *The Times* developed into something much more than adviser on printing. He edited and largely wrote the four-volume *History of 'The Times'* (1935–52) and was for two years, 1945–7, editor of the *Times Literary Supplement*. He was consulted about organization and appointments of personnel, and even for a time about editorial policy. He retired from *The Times* in 1960.

Morison's researches in newspaper history, first presented at length in his Sandars lectures, published as *The English Newspaper*, at Cambridge in 1932, led to a fascination with the power of the press. He relished the friendship of Lord Beaverbrook, who entertained him in the years 1948–63 to holidays in the Bahamas and on the Riviera.

Morison's involvement with the *Encyclopaedia Britannica* began in 1949, when he met the publisher William Benton; in 1961 he was added to the editorial board. In this connection he made periodic visits to Chicago (the city that came nearest to rivalling London in his affections: he disliked country living) and enjoyed Mediterranean cruises in Senator Benton's yacht.

Morison far excelled other typographers of his day in point of erudition; and his choice of type-designs, prompted by a fastidious mind and a sensitive eye, was enduring. His capacity for gaining the confidence of managements and commanding the skill of technicians made him a leader in his profession. Consequently, his influence on book printing was powerful, and he exerted it in favour of an austere and traditional style, with an improved repertory of type. As a scholar he was quick to grasp essentials but could be inaccurate in details. In his ambitiously conceived Lyell lectures at Oxford in 1957 (published in 1972 as *Politics and script: aspects of authority and freedom in the development of Graeco-Latin script*, edited by Nicolas Barker) he drew especially on almost thirty years' advice and friendship of the palaeographer E. A. Lowe. His work on the history of the Fell types at Oxford University Press, a project with a similarly long history, relied in its last stages principally on Harry Carter. These two works preoccupied him in the last years of his life, and offer a summation of his scholarly interests.

Cambridge University honoured Morison with the degree of LittD in 1950, and he held honorary doctorates also from Birmingham and Marquette (Wisconsin). He was elected FBA in 1954 and appointed royal designer for industry in 1960; but he declined three offers of knighthood, one shortly after playing a pivotal part in the acquisition by the British Museum of the Codex Sinaiticus in 1934.

Morison was of spare build; wore spectacles (steel-rimmed) from his youth up, the lenses thickening as he aged. Dressed invariably in a black suit with a white shirt and black tie, outdoors with a rather small black hat, he struck strangers as looking like a Jesuit. He was vigorous and did not spare himself; in middle life he travelled a great deal in search of information. His talk was pugnacious in a humorous way. Victorian in morals, on other subjects he would differ without bitterness, although he had no doubts about his own opinions. In politics he was radical; he spoke contemptuously of the Roman curia, resented monarchy, and thought capitalism was wrong but invincible. Communist friends dissuaded him in 1921 from applying for membership of their party. Apart from the breviary, which he always carried, he read only for information, increasingly about liturgy and ecclesiology; in music he eventually cared only for plainchant. His fine collection of books was presented by Sir Allen Lane to Cambridge University Library, where it is kept in the Morison Room.

Given handsome parting presents from *The Times* and the Monotype Corporation, and a generous subsidy from Senator Benton, Morison lived his declining years in comfort in a double suite of rooms at 2 Whitehall Court, Westminster, and indulged a discriminating taste in food and wines. He visited Chicago in 1966, but by May 1967 he had taken to a wheelchair because of spinal weakness, and he could hardly see. He died of heart failure at home, on 11

October 1967. Following a requiem mass in Westminster Cathedral he was buried at Paddington new cemetery, Mill Hill, on 18 October.

H. G. CARTER, rev. DAVID MCKITTERICK

Sources N. Barker, *Stanley Morison* (1972) · A. Appleton, *The writings of Stanley Morison: a handlist* (1976) · S. H. Steinberg, 'Stanley Morison, 1889–1967', *PBA*, 53 (1967), 449–68
Archives CUL, MSS · News Int. RO, papers | Bodl. Oxf., corresp. with Robert Bridges · Bodl. Oxf., letters to O. G. S. Crawford · HLRO, corresp. with Lord Beaverbrook · King's Cam., letters to Sir George Barnes · U. Birm., corresp. with Lord Avon
Likenesses W. Rothenstein, charcoal drawing, 1924, CUL [*see illus.*] · R. Lutyens, lithograph, *c.*1961–1962, NPG · R. Lutyens, reproduction of drawing, ferro-gelatine, 1962, repro. in *The old Burgundians* (privately printed, 1962) · R. Lutyens, oils, Times Newspapers, London · R. Lutyens, wash drawing, Garr. Club · photographs, CUL
Wealth at death £20,238: probate, 29 April 1968, *CGPLA Eng. & Wales*

Morison, Sir Theodore (1863–1936), educationist and writer, was born in Malta on 9 May 1863, the only son of the author James Augustus Cotter *Morison (1832–1888) and his wife, Frances Adelaide (d. 1878), daughter of George *Virtue, the publisher [*see under* Virtue, James Sprent]. Educated at Westminster School (1876–82), he was Westminster scholar at Trinity College, Cambridge (1882–5), where he took a second class in the classical tripos.

Morison went to India in 1886 as tutor to the young maharajas of Chhaturpur and Charkhari. In 1889 he was appointed professor of English at the Muhammadan Anglo-Oriental College at Aligarh, founded by Sir Saiyid Ahmad Khan to provide a western education for Muslims within the context of Islamic culture and religion. He succeeded Theodore Beck as principal of the college in 1899, the year in which he published *Imperial Rule in India*. He regarded Khan as 'the most remarkable man [he] had ever met' but himself played an important part in making the Aligarh college a success. During his principalship student numbers almost doubled, discipline improved through the introduction of a proctorial system, and the finances recovered. Known as Soldier Morison on account of his fondness for riding and shooting, he mixed freely with the students and maintained good relations between the Indian managers of the college and their European staff of teachers, though his wife, Margaret (d. 1931), daughter of Arthur *Cohen, whom he married in 1895, was regarded by the students as rather aloof. Gertrude Bell, who visited them in January 1903, found Morison 'an enchanting person' and his wife 'a bit of a prig, but I got to like her' (Bell MSS). Morison encouraged extra-curricular activities, particularly physical exercise, though he maintained his predecessor's policy of discouraging students' involvement in politics. He was a leading supporter of the movement to raise the Aligarh college to the status of a residential, denominational university for Indian Muslims, and at the Muhammadan Educational Conference at Lahore in December 1898 he moved a resolution in favour of creating a Muslim university. Although the movement was delayed by the decision in 1904 of Curzon, the viceroy, to halt the creation of further universities, the college finally achieved university status in 1920.

In 1905 Morison returned to England for family reasons, published his *The Industrial Organisation of an Indian Province* in 1906, and was exceptionally appointed to the Council of India that year by his old friend John (later Viscount) Morley, the secretary of state. He held the position until 1916, and was appointed KCIE in 1910 and KCSI in 1917. His unrelenting advocacy of Muslim claims to representation in government matters led Morley in 1909 to understand the pressures which had led Oliver Cromwell to 'send his counsellors packing' (J. Morley, *Recollections*, 2 vols., 1917, 2.315). In 1911 Morison produced a third book, *The Economic Transition in India*, and in 1913 Lord Crewe appointed him to the royal commission on the Indian public services under the chairmanship of Lord Islington. In 1915, however, he excused himself and despite his age went on active service, becoming attached to the east African expeditionary force at the request of General Smuts and to the Belgian forces in May 1917, in which year he later became senior political officer in charge of the southern area of German East Africa. When the army's educational department was established in 1918 he was put in charge of one of its sub-departments.

After demobilization Morison became principal of Armstrong College, Newcastle upon Tyne, in 1919; from 1924 to 1926 he was vice-chancellor of Durham University. He carried the main burden of reorganizing the college, which had such serious financial difficulties that its closure was contemplated in 1921, although it had then more than half the full-time students of the University of Durham. His exceptional energy and enthusiasm brought about not only the college's survival, but also the creation of among other things a new library and a mining department in his time. His last annual report characteristically referred to the possibilities of development, to further co-operation between the scientific departments and local industries, to the establishment of a department of social science, and to closer association with the local Society of Antiquaries to further Roman studies. His last official act was to press upon the council of the university the need for a hall of residence for male students. He retired a year early on medical advice in 1929, and went to live at Weybridge. His close friend and successor as principal of Armstrong College, the former Indian civil servant Sir William Marris, later paid tribute to his kindness and generosity, though an obituarist in *The Times* remarked that he 'had no use for extremists and freaks, and did not hesitate to let them know it' (15 Feb 1936).

Morison's only daughter died in 1928 and his wife in 1931, leaving him with just a son, but he was not one to give way to sorrow or to be inactive for long. In 1933 he became director of the British Institute in Paris, appropriately, for he had spent part of his youth there and had a special affection for the French and for French literature. He was made an officer of the Légion d'honneur and of the Belgian order of Leopold, and in 1920 he received the honorary degree of DCL from Durham. He worked hard in

Paris but his health was failing; he died at his home there, 4 Cité Vaneau, on 14 February 1936 and was cremated in Paris.   G. R. BATHO

Sources *The Times* (15 Feb 1936) • *The Times* (21 Feb 1936) • *The Northerner* (Nov 1929) [Journal of Armstrong College] • *The Northerner* (March 1936) [Journal of Armstrong College] • *Durham University Journal*, 22 (1921–2) • *Durham University Journal*, 24 (1924) • *Durham University Journal*, 26 (1929) • U. Newcastle, Morison MSS • U. Newcastle, Robinson L., Bell MSS • C. E. Whiting, *The University of Durham, 1832–1932* (1932) • S. K. Bhatnagar, *History of the M.A.O. College Aligarh* (1969) • K. A. Nizami, *1920–1945* (1995), vol. 1 of *History of the Aligarh Muslim University* • S. Y. Shah, *Higher education and politics in colonial India: a study of Aligarh Muslim University* (1996) • CGPLA Eng. & Wales (1936)

Archives U. Newcastle, MSS | BL OIOC, notes to Lord Morley • CUL, corresp. with Lord Hardinge

Likenesses J. Russell & Sons, photograph, c.1915, NPG • H. Knight, oils, 1925, U. Newcastle • T. B. Garvie, oils, 1930, U. Newcastle • photograph, repro. in *The Northerner* (March 1936), facing p. 63

Wealth at death £32,369 4s.: probate, 7 May 1936, CGPLA Eng. & Wales

Morison, Thomas (d. 1603), physician and diplomat, is thought to have come from Aberdeen, but nothing is known of his early life, and his styling himself *Aberdonanus* may imply only that he was educated at Aberdeen University. He also studied in France at Montpellier, where in 1582 he was tutored by the chancellor of the university, and possibly first met Anthony Bacon. Morison corresponded frequently with Bacon, though only a few letters survive; the earliest of these, from 1592, describes how Alessandro Farnese, duke of Parma, had died in agony as a result of poison.

Morison's powers of persuasion stood him in good stead with Bacon, who brought him to the notice of Elizabeth I's favourite Robert Devereux, second earl of Essex. In the early 1590s the English court was often preoccupied both with the claim of the Scottish king, James VI, to succeed Elizabeth, and with the danger to protestant England as well as Scotland from the links of the Roman Catholic nobility in Scotland with Spain. Morison was hired to negotiate in the queen's name with the Catholic sixth earl of Huntly. Robert Bowes, the English ambassador to Scotland, told Essex in July 1593 that Morison was in great credit with Huntly, and believed that his correspondent could 'procure large overtures' to the queen on behalf of the dissident Scottish earls (Birch, 121). During August, Anthony Bacon rewarded Morison with the sum of £30. Morison was also highly regarded by Anthony's brother, the philosopher Francis Bacon, another member of Essex's circle, who in September 1593 wrote of Morison's 'serviceable diligence and fidelity' (ibid.); Essex rewarded him with a further 100 crowns.

Morison's letters were ciphered, often in French, and used code words; for instance James VI was *le chevalier*. There survive fragmentary instructions, probably conveyed to Morison from Essex in December 1593, which required information on James's progress in the reformed religion; his favour or disfavour with his nobles; possible intrigues with Spain and the papacy; and how the princes of Germany and France were perceived at the Scottish court. In March 1594 Morison was again paid 100 crowns, Essex writing with approval that they would have yet more cause to use him.

The opportunity to do so came later that month when Morison informed Anthony Bacon how the king had assured him that Huntly and the ninth earl of Erroll would be passing through England to go to Spain or Rome. In a later letter he also told of a Jesuit named John Morton, who upon examination had revealed that on the continent James was regarded as a Catholic 'ipso facto' (Birch, 224–5). Such disclosures have been described as a brief 'intelligence coup for Essex' (Hammer, 166), but Elizabeth had become more cautious by early 1594, when it was clear that Huntly and his allies were not going to make any kind of deal; Morison's importance dwindled as a result.

During these years Morison also published two books, both dedicated to James VI. His *Liber novus de metallorum causis et transubstantione*, printed at Frankfurt in 1593, comprises a learned attack on alchemy, based on classical, scholastic, and contemporary writings, and also on personal experience—Morison tells of a monstrous birth he had delivered in Norfolk, a 'many-footed creature, black, agile, in length shorter than a lizard' (*Liber novus*, 82). His second book, *Papatus, seu, De pravatae religionis origo et incrementum*, appeared in Edinburgh in 1594. In it Morison draws on nearly 200 sources, as varied as Lucretius, the Koran, and the *Malleus maleficarum*, and presents Roman Catholic practices in alphabetical order with a commentary to show how they had dangerous pagan origins. A fascinating exercise in early ethnography, this book too draws on Morison's own recollections, for instance concerning the treatment of newborn babies in Scotland, welcomed into the world with a ritual in which the swaddled infant was passed over a flame while a charm was recited three times.

Morison's own religious position is unclear. It is likely that he was a protestant when he studied at Montpellier in the early 1580s, since that town was a centre for the reformed religion in southern France. But his reference to the Jesuit John Morton as his old schoolfellow suggests at least a period of Catholic observance, which in turn could explain the detailed knowledge of Roman rites and practices apparent in his *Papatus*. A subsequent crisis of confidence with Catholicism may thus have led him to denounce the papacy with the added zeal of a convert. In a letter of July 1595 Roger Aston even told Robert Bowes that 'Your doctor, Mr Morison, has become a minister' (*CSP Scot.*, 642), but there is no evidence that he received a benefice, and in the end he seems to have remained a medical practitioner. In 1603 Francis Bacon wrote to Morison asking him to 'further good opinion of me' with the king, believing that the old doctor's skill at 'feeling pulses' made him still the ideal person for such a task (*Works of Francis Bacon*, 3.66), and when Morison's will was registered in Edinburgh, on 12 July 1603, it was as that of a doctor of medicine.

A man of considerable learning, whose writings demonstrate the kind of originality that was admired by contemporaries such as the Bacons, in his time Morison was primarily valued for the competence and integrity which made him the trusted and respected servant of rival monarchs, able to serve Essex and Queen Elizabeth as an intelligencer without compromising his position at the Scottish court. SARAH CLAYTON

Sources T. Birch, *Memoirs of the reign of Queen Elizabeth*, 2 vols. (1754) · P. E. J. Hammer, *The polarisation of Elizabethan politics: the political career of Robert Devereux, 2nd earl of Essex, 1585–1597* (1999) · *CSP Scot., 1593–5* · DNB · *The works of Francis Bacon*, ed. J. Spedding, R. L. Ellis, and D. D. Heath, 14 vols. (1857–74) · Tanner, *Bibl. Brit.-Hib.* · J. Bruce, *Lives of the eminent men of Aberdeen* (1841) · F. J. Grant, ed., *The commissariot record of Edinburgh: register of testaments*, 2, Scottish RS, old ser., 2 (1898)
Archives LPL, papers of Anthony Bacon, letters, MSS 647–662

Morison, Thomas (d. 1824). *See under* Morison, James, of Elsick (1708–1786).

Morison, William Maxwell (d. 1821), advocate, was the eldest son of James Morison, factor to William Maxwell of Nithsdale. He was admitted advocate on 20 July 1784, and was from 1787 to 1789 sheriff-substitute for Clackmannan. On 27 April 1786, in Alloa, Clackmannanshire, he married Sibella Stephen (c.1765–1840), daughter of James Stephen, merchant, and Sibella Milner. They had one daughter, also Sibella, who may have died young.

Morison is remembered for the monumental dictionary of decisions of the court of session which still goes by his name. The need for such a collection, setting out systematically the decisions of Scotland's highest civil court from the beginning, had long been recognized. However, with the exception of the *Dictionary of Decisions* by Henry Home, Lord Kames, first published in 1741, and continued by Alexander Fraser Tytler, Lord Woodhouselee, in 1797, little had been achieved. Even the more limited objective of collecting the contemporary decisions of the court of session had proved difficult, despite the steady support of the Faculty of Advocates throughout the eighteenth century. In 1800 Morison advertised his intention of publishing 'a complete and uniform edition' of the decisions of the court of session since its institution, following the general method of Lord Kames, and using both published and manuscript sources. He sought subscribers, the venture being at his own risk. The first volume appeared in 1801, with thirty-seven others following in rapid succession, the titles running alphabetically from 'Abbey of Holyroodhouse' to 'Wrongous imprisonment'. In the standard edition of 1811 the original thirty-eight volumes are bound as nineteen, containing 17,074 pages, excluding the appendix, and covering cases from 1540 until 1808.

The history of the various aids and additions to the dictionary is complicated. Morison produced a 'synopsis' or digest of the collected decisions from 1804 on. This eventually ran to two volumes, commonly numbered 20 and 21. He also produced an appendix (appendix I) of additional cases as he went along. These are usually bound with the original. More confusingly, Morison edited another two-volume 'synopsis', containing cases from 1808 to 1812 and 1812 to 1816 respectively, these volumes sometimes being bound as numbers 23 and 24. He also edited the *Decisions of the Court of Session* from the year 1733 to the year 1754, originally collected by Patrick Grant, Lord Elchies. These appeared in two volumes in 1813 as 'branch I' of 'appendix II' of his *Dictionary*. In practice, these are rarely bound with the *Dictionary*. A further projected 'branch II' of appendix II did not appear. In addition to all these, Morison edited the fifth edition (1812) of the classic *Institute of the Law of Scotland* by John Erskine of Carnock.

The value of the *Dictionary* was enhanced by the publication of W. Tait's *Index to the Decisions of the Court of Session* (1823), M. P. Brown's *Supplement to the Dictionary of Decisions* (5 vols., 1826) and Brown's *General Synopsis of the Decisions of the Court of Session* (4 vols., 1829). Tait's *Index* also contains an invaluable survey of the history of law reporting in Scotland, including a detailed and critical analysis of Morison's achievement. Despite his criticisms, however, Tait acknowledged that 'Mr Morison's courage and perseverance are entitled to the highest praise. By the publication of his Dictionary he certainly rendered an essential service to the profession, which might have in vain been looked for from another' (Tait, 515). Nearly two hundred years later, Morison's work has still not been replaced or supplanted.

Morison's Dictionary, as it is universally known, is still cited on occasion in court. Thus, the leading case of *Steel's Tr. v. Bradley Homes* (1972), on error in contract, looked back to *Sword v. Sinclair* (1771), while *Morgan Guaranty v. Lothian Regional Council* (1995), on unjustified enrichment, looked back to *Stirling v. Earl of Lauderdale* (1733)—and, indeed, beyond to the original session papers. Quite apart from its significance as a formal source of law, *Morison's Dictionary* is an important, although as yet underused source for Scottish social history. William Maxwell Morison died at Portobello, Edinburgh, on 30 June 1821. He was survived by his wife, who died on 26 December 1840.

W. D. H. SELLAR

Sources F. J. Grant, ed., *The Faculty of Advocates in Scotland, 1532–1943*, Scottish RS, 145 (1944) · W. Tait, *Index to the decisions of the court of session* (1823) · J. S. Leadbetter, 'The printed law reports, 1540–1935', *Sources and literature of Scots law*, ed. H. McKechnie (1936), 42–58 · W. M. Morison, *Advertisement* (20 Dec 1800), reprinted in *Morison's dictionary* · *Edinburgh Magazine* (Aug 1821) · parish register, Alloa, Clackmannan, NA Scot., OPR, 22 April 1786 [banns and marriages]

Morland, Egbert Coleby (1874–1955), physician and writer on medicine, was born in Croydon on 3 September 1874, the seventh of the fourteen children of Charles Coleby Morland JP (1839–1908), an umbrella maker, and his wife, Jane, *née* Fryer (1843–1923). Of a Quaker family Morland was sent in 1889 to Bootham School, the Friends' institution at York, where he distinguished himself in science, languages, and mathematics. He enrolled at Owens College, Manchester, and gained a London BSc degree in zoology (first-class honours); he was then old enough to study medicine at St Bartholomew's Hospital, London, whence he graduated in 1898 with the gold medal in physiology.

In his working life Morland suffered two serious reverses. At first he seemed destined for a career in London medicine, but the usual succession of junior hospital appointments was interrupted after three years when he developed tuberculosis. Recovering after lengthy treatment in Switzerland under the devoted eye of his fiancée, Mary Windsor Latchmore (1873–1948), he decided to remain in that country and become a specialist in tuberculosis. He married Mary in 1903 and returned to student life, and received an MD degree (Bern) in 1907. The Morlands then moved to the isolated mountain resort of Arosa, Switzerland, where he built up a sizeable practice, mainly of British patients. They adopted the first of their three children in 1912. Then, two years later, came the second blow: the beginning of the First World War caused Morland's British clientele to melt away, and in 1915 he returned to England, pausing for a few months to assist the Friends' war victims' relief committee on the Marne. While in Arosa he had made several contributions to *The Lancet*; so, once in London, he called on the editorial office. The editor, Squire Sprigge, was short-handed and invited him to stay and help.

The editor of a general medical journal, it might be thought, should be a good communicator with a broad vision of medicine and a strong commitment to scientific truth. Whatever his character in 1915, Morland diverged increasingly from this model as his *Lancet* years went by. Though skilful in stripping the work of others to its essentials, his own conversation and writing displayed an enigmatic quality that continually perplexed his acquaintances. His reasoning was characterized by alarming leaps—the knight's move in thought. His most lucid pronouncements were to be found on postcards and on the edge of office documents. Colleagues were sometimes dismayed by his habit of adding creative touches to the work of others—especially when coupled with the dictum, 'Better be wrong than dull' (*The Lancet*, 1955, 974–6). Morland always needed someone on hand to say, 'think again'. Abjuring anything in the nature of an editorial mission or policy, he was himself a mass of contradictions—a pacifist who favoured conscription; an idealist deeply tinged with cynicism; and a man of high intelligence who was often content to indulge in wishful thinking. These characteristics were apt to frighten and exasperate people who did not know him well, and some who did. A fellow Quaker confessed that he seldom knew whether Morland's words were intended in jest or in earnest (Braithwaite, 475–6).

Before and after taking the chair as editor Morland's work depended inseparably on the efforts of others. Under Sprigge his oblique way of thinking was catalytic:

> At the central table sat Sir Squire, small, urbane, aquiline, in black coat and striped trousers; a cultivated man of his world; beloved but irascible. Behind a vast mahogany desk was Morland, tall, solemn, gaunt, with noble brow, in a grey tweed morning coat like a coachman's; surer of his worth than his welcome; overworked and often maddening. (*The Lancet*, 1955, 974–6)

For all the friction between them, Morland and Sprigge made a good partnership, the latter preserving continuity and good sense while Morland gave the journal life. But by the time Morland took the chair his eccentricities, coupled with a sharpening tongue, were less of an asset.

Closer to Old Testament prophet than to commander, he inspired fear as well as affection, and loyal assistants were needed to preserve continuity and balance. They were hard-pressed. Morland's editorship, if ever there had been a right time for it, had come too late.

The Morlands spent much of their later years in Wooldale, Yorkshire, where they lived at Pellcroft, beside the ancient Friends' meeting-house. Mary died in 1948, and Egbert Morland died at Nunthorpe Nursing Home, York, on 26 April 1955. In the annals of medical editing, what was his special contribution? In the years of his editorship his personal enthusiasms are reflected in a notable emphasis on maternal and child health and the new subject of social medicine. But his best work was done earlier. For the editors who followed, his most lasting bequest was a tradition of good writing and gentle wit. The editor of *Nature* remarked, 'Having found *The Lancet* humane, he left it human' (*The Lancet*, 1944, 633–4). ROBIN FOX

Sources *The Lancet* (7–14 May 1955), 974–6, 1030–31 · *BMJ* (7 May 1955), 1159–61 · *The Lancet* (11 Nov 1944), 633–4 · A. A. Braithwaite, 'Egbert Morland', *The Friend* (6 May 1955), 475–6 · d. cert. · 'Dictionary of Quaker biography', RS Friends, Lond. [card index]

Likenesses photograph, The Lancet, 42 Bedford Square, London

Morland, George (1763–1804), landscape and genre painter, was born on 26 June 1763 at the Haymarket, London, the eldest of the six children of Henry Robert *Morland (1716x19–1797), painter, engraver, and art dealer, and his wife, Jenny or Jane Lacam (*fl.* 1740–1780), an amateur artist and daughter of a French jeweller. His paternal grandfather, George Henry *Morland (*d.* 1789) [*see under* Morland, Henry Robert], was also a painter. His claim to a baronetcy, through a descendancy from the seventeenth-century scientist Sir Samuel Morland, seems to be erroneous.

Childhood and apprenticeship, 1763–1784 Morland's father had been wealthy and owned a house at 47 Leicester Fields, London, which he sold to Joshua Reynolds in 1760. However, he had been made bankrupt in 1762, shortly before the birth of his son. The fall in the family fortunes may have spurred him to encourage George's artistic talents at an early age, in the hope of financial gain, and he was keen to display his son's precocious talent. The young artist reputedly began drawing as early as three, and at the age of ten, in 1773, exhibited 'sketches by Master George Morland' at the Royal Academy. His childhood seems to have been highly disciplined and he was isolated from companions of his own age. His father carefully cultivated his abilities as a draughtsman and supervised him copying casts and old-master drawings long before his apprentice years commenced. His strict upbringing and enforced study in early childhood may account for his wayward and rebellious character in later life.

At the age of fourteen Morland's official seven-year apprenticeship with his father began. As in his early years, Henry Morland tutored him with close scrutiny and encouraged him in studying anatomy and in copying the work of earlier masters, particularly seventeenth-century Dutch landscapes and genre scenes. Some of his copies after such works seem to have been appropriated by the

George Morland (1763–1804), self-portrait, *c*.1795

father as forgeries. Other works copied during his apprenticeship, such as shipwreck subjects by Claude-Joseph Vernet (1714–1789) and landscape and fancy pictures by Thomas Gainsborough (1727–1788), also had an important impact on his later work. His ardent study was carried out entirely at home while he worked in his father's studio as an assistant and restorer. He was not permitted to study at the Royal Academy Schools, perhaps from parental concern for his moral welfare or from his father's disregard for the validity of an academic training. Throughout his apprentice years he exhibited works at the Society of Artists, the Royal Academy, and the Free Society of Artists and began to build up a reputation in artistic circles in London. Towards the end of his apprenticeship he was reportedly offered the opportunity to work in the studio of George Romney (1734–1802), but declined, desiring an end to his strict training. Nevertheless, the industrious work ethic, instilled in him by his father during these years, remained with him throughout his career: he was extremely prolific, despite his undisciplined lifestyle.

Early career, 1784–1790 In 1784, when his apprenticeship expired, Morland set up on his own account and moved out of the family home. Once freed from parental constraints, his life of extravagance, hard drinking, and association with low-life characters commenced. At first he was exploited by an unscrupulous picture dealer in Covent Garden, for whom he produced 'galanteries' of an immodest nature. In 1785 a Mrs Hill from Margate employed him to paint portraits there. With her he travelled to France in October 1785, the only continental trip of his career. However, his attempts at portraiture clearly did not suit him and he returned to London, where he began to work for print dealers, among them the print publisher and engraver John Raphael Smith, who may well have encouraged the young Morland in his dissolute habits.

In 1786 Morland lodged in Kensal Green with the engraver William Ward (1766–1826), whom he had probably met through J. R. Smith. Morland's fruitful partnership with Ward and Smith was to continue for most of his career. On 22 September 1786 he married Ward's sister Anne (Nancy; c.1765–1804) at St Paul's, Hammersmith, while William Ward married Morland's sister Maria shortly afterwards, on 19 October. The two couples shared a household together for a few months in High Street, Marylebone. The Morlands then took lodgings in Great Portland Street and afterwards moved to Camden Town, beginning a largely nomadic life, continually changing addresses in or around London, primarily for the purpose of escaping his creditors. In 1787 the Morlands had a stillborn son, but no further children.

Between 1786 and 1790 Morland established his reputation as a painter of moralizing and domestic genre subjects. His earliest known dated work, *Valentine's Day* (1786–7; V&A) was part of a series, the Progress of Love, produced in collaboration with Francis Wheatley (1747–1801), whose success as a painter of sentimental genre no doubt influenced Morland. Many of Morland's early pictures of this type were elegant portraits of attractive young ladies, such as *The Squire's Door* (c.1789; Yale U. CBA). They were primarily intended for the popular print market and were thus frequently designed as pairs or in series. The subjects were usually of a didactic, moralizing nature, portraying contrasting virtues and vices, as in *The Fruits of Early Industry and Economy* (1789; Philadelphia Museum of Art) and *The Effects of Youthful Extravagance and Idleness* (1789). The subject matter and moral tone of many of these works were closely modelled on those by William Hogarth (1697–1764) of fifty or so years earlier but they were also in tune with contemporary notions of sensibility and were thus more refined and actively appealing to the emotions than were Hogarth's. The strong narrative content lent itself, in particular, to paintings in series, such as the four canvases of *The Recruit, or, Deserter* (1788–9; no. 1, priv. coll., no. 4, Holburne Museum of Art, Bath), which recount the tale of a soldier's desertion and final reprieve.

Morland's most popular series was *Laetitia, or, A Harlot's Progress* (1786), engraved in 1789 (ex Sothebys, London, 8 November 1995, lot 115). The six scenes narrate the story of an innocent young country girl's seduction, fall into vice, and ultimate repentance. The series was clearly modelled on Hogarth's own *Harlot's Progress* of 1732, although the story of *Laetitia* (unlike that of Hogarth's 'heroine') has a happy ending with her return to the bosom of her family. Of a similar sentimental appeal were Morland's childhood and juvenile scenes and those reflecting late eighteenth-century interest in motherhood and family

life, such as *A Visit to the Boarding School* (1788; Wallace Collection, London). There was a growing popularity in the 1780s for such pictures, following on from the success of the childhood genre subjects of William Redmore Bigg (1755–1828). Morland's scenes of playful or mischievous children, such as *Blind Man's Buff* (1788; Detroit Institute of Arts), were particularly popular as engravings. Most of Morland's themes up to 1790 were those that were fashionable at the time and reflected the sensibility, refined tastes, and manners of society of the period, as in *A Tea Garden* (1789; Tate collection), and his similar English *fêtes galantes*. In stark contrast to such works was the pair of paintings on the slave trade that he exhibited at the Society of Artists in 1790, *African Hospitality* (1788–9) and *The Slave Trade* (1788–9; ex Sothebys, London, 16 November 1983, lot 79), which are probably the first oils on the subject by any artist and coincided with the period when the abolitionist movement was at its peak.

Height of career, 1790–c.1794 In 1790 Morland seems to have made a conscious decision to change his subject matter from domestic and moralizing genre scenes, with a strong narrative content, to rustic genre subjects, notable for their conspicuous lack of incident. Humble life in the country became the hallmark of his paintings and was to remain his sole theme. The shift in subject matter may have been made because Morland sensed that the commercial appeal of elegant and refined domestic genre scenes had drawn to a close and a new fashion for the picturesque had dawned. Such rustic subjects were also refreshing antidotes to 'grand-style' academic paintings, esteemed by the art establishment but less popular with middle-class patrons.

Although not as abruptly as he changed subject matter, Morland also modified his style in accordance with his new subjects at about this time. The highly finished, linear, and at times rococo flourish of his earlier work gave way to an altogether more robust style that was richer in texture and colouring and more painterly in its handling.

About 1790 Morland moved to the rural village of Paddington and took up residence in a house opposite the White Lion inn, used by drovers *en route* for the city. There he found his ideal subjects in the country folk and their animals around the picturesque inn. It was this period, from 1790 until about 1794, which though unsettled was more stable than that which followed, and was the height of Morland's career. During this short time he produced his most important and original pictures. His output was prodigious and he had a reputation for painting rapidly without sacrificing quality. He continued to exhibit occasionally at public institutions, such as the Royal Academy, between 1791 and 1794, but this seems to have been prompted more by a desire to be in the public eye than necessitated by a need to sell, for many works had already been sold in advance to his agents or dealers. While at Paddington he painted *Inside of a Stable*, exhibited to huge critical acclaim at the Royal Academy in 1791 (Tate collection) and generally considered to be his most important work. Its originality lies not so much in its utterly simplistic subject and composition but in the fact that it was produced on a massive scale, one that was unprecedented for a landscape or genre scene.

Morland's work from 1790 to about 1794 was lively and fresh, although he often relied on repetitive themes, using stock characters, animals, and settings. His most enduring subjects were of farmyards, cottage scenes, stables, and country alehouses, of which *Morning: Higglers Preparing for Market* (1791; Tate collection), *Horses in a Stable* (1791; V&A) and *The Bell Inn* (1790; Metropolitan Museum of Art, New York) are typical examples. He painted few pure landscapes, although in many scenes of open countryside the figures are almost incidental. A consistently popular theme was that of Gypsies, such as *Gypsy Encampment* (1790; Detroit Institute of Arts), a subject that was clearly borrowed from Gainsborough. From about 1790 until the end of his career Morland visited the Isle of Wight on several occasions; this proved the inspiration for numerous coastal scenes of fishermen, smugglers, and shipwrecks, including *Coast Scene with Smugglers* (1790; Philadelphia Museum of Art).

Morland was an avid draughtsman as well as painter. Most of his drawings date from the early 1790s and were compositions in their own right, rather than preparatory works for paintings. Many were later etched and published in a series of seventeen 'sketchbooks' by John Harris (1792–9).

The figures that populate most of Morland's rural genre compositions consist of passive groups of rustics, as in *Morning, or, The Benevolent Sportsman* (1792; FM Cam.). They have an apparent authenticity not usually found in paintings by his contemporaries, no doubt a result of Morland's direct observation of such low-life characters, with whom he consorted. Morland's rustic genre paintings epitomize the picturesque, a movement which was at its height in Britain in the 1790s as an aesthetic theory that was applied to both landscape and genre scenes. Morland's fascination with tumbledown cottages or benign Gypsies would have appealed to the prevailing taste for picturesque landscape.

In most of Morland's paintings the influence of earlier masters is evident, despite his own protestations that he did not study the works of others. In his choice of low-life subjects and picturesque landscapes he was clearly indebted to Dutch painters of the seventeenth century, many of whose works he had copied in his youth. The influence of more recent British painters, particularly Gainsborough and Philippe-Jacques de Loutherbourg (1740–1812), can be traced both in his choice of subject matter and in his colouring and handling. His originality lay in his successful fusion of a variety of artistic sources but above all in his unique observation of the agricultural poor, which avoided overt sentimentality without resorting to coarse realism. To his middle-class buyers they were reassuring images of a contented and industrious rural class. His achievement in his best work of the early 1790s was to offer the viewer a relatively unaffected representation of rural life and yet to do so in conformity with the standards of taste of the period that would have found ugliness offensive. His pictures can thus be described as having a 'picturesque propriety' that sets them apart from his contemporary landscape and genre painters.

The details of Morland's movements during the early 1790s are uncertain and he seems to have continued his hunted life, shifting abode frequently. While he was at Paddington his mounting debts did not prevent him from leading an extravagant lifestyle, relying on his credit and future sales. He stayed only a year or two there before fleeing about 1792 to Enderby in Leicestershire, but he returned to London to live in Charlotte Street once a letter of licence to repay his principal creditors was agreed upon. Such letters, periodically renewed with the aid of Morland's solicitor Mr Wedd, but rarely honoured, became the pattern for the rest of his life. Despite his unconventional lifestyle as a professional artist, he managed to take on two pupils during this period, David Brown and Thomas Hand, both of whom made copies after their master, adding to the confusion surrounding the authenticity of Morland's works.

The marketing of Morland's work Morland's practice as an artist is important in that he was one of the first painters to break away from the traditional arrangements between artists and patrons. He produced his own designs, not relying on commissions, and sold directly to dealers, print publishers, or 'agents'—who were friends or pupils (such as David Brown) who acted as middlemen. Although this practice would have suited his recalcitrant, independent nature and preserved his artistic freedom, it was clearly to his financial detriment, for he had no head for business and was easily exploited. Moreover, his aversion to polite society meant that he missed out on important commissions; he reputedly refused a commission from the prince of Wales in 1789 for works for Carlton House. Despite his enormous output—probably in the region of 1000 paintings—his life of poverty and debt is evidence that the pictures were usually sold for little, or traded against debts.

Most of the pictures sold to dealers or print publishers, such as J. R. Smith, were engraved and Morland's contemporary reputation relied almost solely on prints after his work: William Ward alone engraved nearly seventy plates after Morland. Over 250 engravings, mostly in stipple or mezzotint, were published in his lifetime, often in large editions, and distributed in Britain and on the continent—indicative of his enormous popularity. Many of the subjects were prettified and made more sentimental in order to increase their popular appeal. Some of the publishers, including Smith in Covent Garden, held exhibitions of his work, which were especially important in so far as the method of selling his paintings meant that Morland himself had little need to exhibit his work at public institutions.

Last years, *c*.1794–1804 The last decade of Morland's career was one of decline, as drink, debt, and poor health took their toll on him, and his powers as a painter diminished rapidly. He remained prolific in order to try to sustain himself financially, but most of his paintings of this period were carelessly executed parodies of his own earlier style and lacked vitality and originality. One of the few works of interest is *The Artist in his Studio with his Man Gibbs* (1801; Castle Museum, Nottingham), a self-portrait, which expressively documents his bleak state at that time. Morland's notorious behaviour and eccentric dress seem to have fascinated his contemporaries and no doubt contributed to his fame. Once it was apparent his health was in decline, buyers were increasingly eager to obtain pictures by him, in case they were his last.

In April 1799 Morland fled to Cowes, on the Isle of Wight, to avoid his London creditors but returned to the city in November, when he was arrested for debt and committed for two years to the king's bench prison. He was allowed to live under the 'rules', in lodgings on the Lambeth Road, St George's Fields, while working to pay off his bills. In 1802 he was released under the Insolvency Act, but by this time his health was ruined. On 19 October 1804 he was arrested again for a publican's score and taken to a spunging house (a bailiff's lodging-house), in Eyre Street Hill, Cold Bath Fields. There he died on 29 October 1804, reportedly from a brain fever. He was buried with his wife, who died four days later on 2 November, at St James's Chapel, on the Hampstead Road, London.

Morland's reputation Morland's reputation in his own lifetime was high and based primarily on the large number of prints after his works. The appeal of his rustic scenes to collectors was satirized in 1807 in a print by the caricaturist James Gillray (*Connoisseurs Examining a Collection of George Morland's*; impression, BM), where the admirers of his paintings of fat pigs and bucolic life are shown to be ordinary coarse-bred men, rather than the largely aristocratic élite which made up the cognoscenti of the period.

Following Morland's death four biographies appeared in quick succession, including those by Collins and Dawe, but these tended to focus on his extraordinary lifestyle and character, rather than attempting to analyse or contextualize his work. The portrait of the artist as a moral degenerate yet artistic genius was perpetuated throughout the nineteenth and twentieth centuries in several biographies or articles, largely made up of anecdotal (and probably apocryphal) information recounting his drunken escapades, eccentric dress, and dissipated behaviour. The disapprobation regarding his alcohol consumption, apparent in these accounts, appears to be based as much on Morland's habit of carousing with low-life characters in public houses as on the actual amount he drank, although a list of Morland's 'bub' for one day shows that this could be considerable (Dawe, 77).

The fact that very few attempts have been made to study Morland's artistic development or achievements is somewhat understandable, for his dissolute and chaotic life has left a problematic legacy. Without any written records or account books by him and with very little information regarding his places of residence, professional contacts, or other documentation, only his paintings, or engravings after them, remain. Yet the extent of his *œuvre* is also unclear. There is a wide variety in the quality of his work (perhaps the result of producing pictures quickly in order to settle debts or due to illness in his last years), making authentication difficult, a problem which is compounded by the volume of mostly poor-quality copies or pastiches of his paintings, both contemporary and nineteenth-century.

These difficulties have led to a long period of neglect of Morland and his work. Aside from a few centenary publications about 1907, virtually nothing of note was published on the artist throughout the twentieth century and only two exhibitions of his paintings were held after 1950 (Arts Council, 1954, and Reading Museum and Art Gallery, 1975).

However, Morland's importance as an artist began to be reassessed somewhat in the last decade or two of the twentieth century, such as in John Barrell's analysis of Morland in *The Dark Side of the Landscape*, where the author attempts to dispel the view of the artist's work as unduly sentimental. While Morland's present-day reputation remains coloured by the earlier portrayals of him and public familiarity with his work still relies largely on engravings or poor-quality copies, he is now regarded as an interesting minor master, much of whose work was innovative at the time in both subject matter and style and who can now be seen as a recognizable influence on both John Constable and David Wilkie.   DIANE PERKINS

Sources G. Dawe, *The life of George Morland* (1807) · W. Collins, *Memoirs of a painter: … a biographical sketch of … the late Mr. George Morland* (1805) [vol. 2 of *Memoirs of a picture*, 3 vols.] · D. Winter, 'George Morland', PhD diss., Stanford University, 1977 · D. Thomas, *George Morland: an exhibition of paintings and drawings* (1954) [exhibition catalogue, Arts Council of Great Britain, London] · R. Dorment, *British painting in the Philadelphia Museum of Art: from the 17th through the 19th century* (1986), 228–45 · J. Barrell, *The dark side of the landscape: the rural poor in English painting, 1730–1840* (1980), 89–129 · *DNB* · J. T. H. Baily, 'George Morland', *The Connoisseur*, extra number, 1 (1906) · R. Richardson, *George Morland's pictures: their present possessors, with details of the collections* (1897) · W. Gilbey and E. D. Cuming, *George Morland: his life and works* (1907) · *The England of George Morland*, Shipley Art Gallery, Gateshead (1948) [exhibition catalogue] · *George Morland, 1763–1804: paintings, drawings and engravings*, Reading Museum and Art Gallery (1975?) [exhibition catalogue] · E. G. D'Oench, 'Copper into gold': prints by John Raphael Smith, 1751–1812 (1999) · F. W. Blagdon, *Authentic memoirs of the late George Morland* (1806) · J. Hassell, *Memoirs of the life of Morland* (1806)

Likenesses H. R. Morland, oils, c.1779–1780, Yale U. CBA · T. Rowlandson, watercolour drawings, c.1785, BM · Mackenzie, engraving, 1792 (after drawing by S. Jones), BM · G. Morland, self-portrait, chalk drawing, c.1795, NPG [*see illus.*] · G. Morland, self-portrait, oils, 1801 (with Gibbs), Nottingham Castle Museum · T. Gauguin, chalk manner print, pubd 1804 (after G. Morland), BM, NPG · S. Jones, pencil and chalk drawing, 1805, NPG · J. R. Smith, mezzotint, pubd 1805, BM, NPG · W. Ward, mezzotint, pubd 1805 (after R. Muller), BM, NPG · G. Morland, self-portrait, oils, NPG · pen-and-ink drawing, NPG

Wealth at death nil: Dawe; Collins; etc.

Morland, George Henry (d. 1789). *See under* Morland, Henry Robert (1716×19–1797).

Morland, Sir Henry (1837–1891), naval officer and official in the Indian service, born on 9 April 1837, was the third son of John Morland, barrister, descendant of the Morlands of Capplethwaite and Killington Halls, Westmorland, and his wife, Elizabeth, daughter of James Thompson, of Grayrigg Hall, Westmorland. He was educated at Heversham and Bromsgrove schools, and also privately by Dr Webster, mathematical master at Christ's Hospital.

Morland entered the Indian navy in June 1852, being appointed to the *Akbar* on 5 June, and in September joined the steamer *Queen* as a midshipman. Between 1853 and 1856 he served on the north-east coast of Africa. He was present at the engagement with the Arabs at Shugra in 1853, and was in charge of the barque *Norma*, by which an Arab bugla which broke the Berbera blockade was captured in 1855. He next served on the Arabian coast, commanding a schooner at the reoccupation of Perim on 12 January 1857, and a division of boats at the bombardment of Jiddah in July 1858. On 21 November 1857 he became mate of the *Dalhousie*, and in November 1858 was fourth lieutenant on the *Assaye*. In October 1859, as the first lieutenant of the *Clive*, he took part in the naval operations on the coast of Kathiawar, Bombay presidency, by which the Wagheer rising was put down. His last active service was with the *Semiramis*, January 1863, in the expedition by which the murderers of the officers of HMS *Penguin* were punished. On 30 April 1863, when the order abolishing the Indian navy came into operation, he was placed on the retired list, with the rank of honorary lieutenant, and received a pension of £150. In 1863 he was transferred to the Indian marine (captain, 1877) and in spring 1864 commanded the *Dalhousie* when laying the marine cable of the Indo-European telegraph. Later that year he accompanied the convoy of the mission to Abyssinia, and was detained for some months at Massawa. In 1865 he became transport officer at Bombay, as well as dock master and signal officer; and in the following year superintendent of floating batteries, a pair of modern coast service ironclads. These were the most powerful warships in the region for the next twenty years. In 1866 he was in command of the party which rescued the *Dalhousie* when stranded on the Malabar coast on the sunken wreck of the *Di Vernon*.

Morland superintended the equipment and dispatch of the fleet of transports of the Abyssinian expedition in 1867, when, besides 27,000 men and 2000 horses, 45 elephants, 6000 bullocks, and 3000 mules and ponies were shipped. Morland was transport officer at Bombay until 1879, and in 1873 became conservator of the port, president of the board of marine examiners, and registrar of shipping. From April 1875 he also acted for a few months as secretary to the Bombay port trust.

Morland married in 1870 Alice Mary, second daughter of A. W. Critchley, of Manchester; she died in 1871, leaving a daughter. In 1875 he married Fanny Helen Hannah, second daughter of Jeronimo Carandini, twelfth marchese di Sarzano, with whom he had five children, of whom two died before him; she survived him. Morland was highly esteemed in India and was a most efficient administrator. He was also an enthusiastic freemason. In 1870, having served in several minor offices, he was appointed by the grand lodge of Scotland provincial grandmaster for western India, including Ceylon, and in 1874 grandmaster of all Scottish freemasonry in the Indian empire, including Aden. The foundation of the Muslim lodge, Islam, was almost entirely due to his influence. He was for some years secretary of the Bombay Geographical Society, to which in 1875 he read a paper on Abyssinia, and was also a fellow of Bombay University and of the Astronomical Society, and an associate of the Indian College of Engineers.

In 1872 Morland went to Madras as a member of the commission to inquire into the recent wrecks, and he organized the commissariat and transport of the Second Anglo-Afghan War. Meanwhile he also began to take an active part in municipal affairs at Bombay. In 1868 he had been appointed JP, and became a member of the corporation. In 1877 he was appointed a member of the town council. On 23 June 1886 he was elected chairman of the corporation, and was re-elected on 5 April 1887. He was chairman of the committee which drew up the Bombay 1887 jubilee address, which he took to England and presented to the queen at Windsor on 30 June, when he was knighted. He died at his residence in Rampart Row, Bombay, on 28 July 1891. He was buried in Bombay with military honours.

G. Le G. Norgate, *rev.* Andrew Lambert

Sources *Bombay Gazette* (5 July 1887) · *Bombay Gazette* (31 July 1891) · *Bombay Gazette* (7 Aug 1891) · *Times of India: Overland Summary* (31 July 1891) · *Times of India: Overland Summary* (7 Aug 1891) · *The Times* (4 Aug 1891) · Burke, *Peerage* (1889) · C. R. Low, *History of the Indian navy, 1613–1863*, 2 (1877) · D. Bates, *The Abyssinian difficulty: the Emperor Theodorus and the Magdala campaign, 1867–68* (1979) · F. Myatt, *The march to Magdala* (1970) · Boase, *Mod. Eng. biog.* · C. E. Buckland, *Dictionary of Indian biography* (1906)
Wealth at death £7683 7s. 7d.: administration with will, 16 Feb 1892, *CGPLA Eng. & Wales*

Morland, Henry Robert (1716x19–1797), painter and engraver, the son and pupil of the genre painter **George Henry Morland** (d. 1789) of St James's Square, London, was born on 6 October 1716 or in 1718 or 1719. Although his existence was doubted by Martin Davies (p. 101), an entry for George Henry Morland is included in Ellis Waterhouse's *British 18th Century Painters in Oils and Crayons* (p. 247). Joseph Farington recorded on 15 June 1795 that Morland was seventy-six years old (Farington, *Diary*, 2.353). Morland worked in oil and crayons, and between 1760 and 1792 exhibited 123 works at the Society of Artists, the Free Society of Artists, and the Royal Academy. He also engraved in mezzotint, cleaned, restored, and dealt in pictures, and sold artists' materials, including crayons of his own manufacture. His painting *A Lady in a Masquerate Habit*, exhibited in 1769, became popular as an engraving entitled *The Fair Nun Unmask'd* which 'depicts a "nun" who has discarded her habit (except for a veil) but still toys with a mask' (Egerton, 169). In spite of all these means of livelihood and marriage in London at St James's, Westminster, on 20 June 1757 to Jane Lacam, the daughter of a Huguenot jeweller, he was financially unsuccessful. He sold his house at 47 Leicester Fields to Sir Joshua Reynolds in 1760, and accepted charity from the Society of Artists and the

Royal Academy. He was declared bankrupt in January 1762.

Morland painted a portrait of George III, which was engraved by Houston, and a portrait of Garrick as Richard III (Garrick Club, London). He often repeated and re-exhibited his domestic 'candlelight' scenes which were reproduced by engravers such as Philip Dawe. These included firstly in 1764 *A Ballad Singer* (version, Tate collection), *Girl Opening Oysters* (exh. Free Society, 1769, and Society of Artists, 1783; Glasgow Art Gallery and Museum), and *Laundry Maid Ironing* (exh. Free Society, 1768; Tate collection). His work in restoration gave him access to collections of paintings belonging to art connoisseurs such as Mr Angerstein, Lord Scarsdale, Mr Child, and Lord Grosvenor, and it is likely that the seventeenth-century Dutch paintings that he would have seen as a result influenced his own work.

Morland frequently moved house and died in Stephen Street, Rathbone Place, London, on 30 November 1797. He was buried at St Anne's, Westminster, on 6 December 1797. He was the father of the genre painter George *Morland (1763–1804) and the brother of Maria Morland, also an artist, who exhibited at the Royal Academy in 1785 and 1786.   W. C. MONKHOUSE, *rev.* KATE RETFORD

Sources H. Belsey, 'Morland, Henry Robert', *The dictionary of art*, ed. J. Turner (1996) • Redgrave, *Artists* • C. Farthing, 'George Morland's father: a neglected painter', *The Connoisseur*, 114 (1944), 101–4 • Bryan, *Painters* (1903–5), 3.371 • Graves, *Soc. Artists*, 175–6 • Graves, *RA exhibitors*, 5 (1906), 295 • W. Gilbey and E. D. Cuming, *George Morland: his life and works* (1907), 3–10 • B. Stewart and M. Cutten, *The dictionary of portrait painters in Britain up to 1920* (1997) • Waterhouse, *18c painters*, 247–8 • M. Davies, *The British school* (1956), 101–2 • W. T. Whitley, *Artists and their friends in England, 1700–1799*, 2 (1928), 263–4 • Graves, *Artists* • IGI • J. Egerton, *The British school* (1998)

Likenesses G. Morland, pencil drawing, NPG • pencil and watercolour drawing, BM

Morland, Sir Samuel, first baronet (1625–1695), natural philosopher and diplomat, was born in Sulhampstead-Banister, Berkshire, the son of the Revd Thomas Morland (*b.* 1574/5), the rector, who came from Westmorland; he had two brothers, Thomas and Martin. From 1638 he was educated at Winchester College, and in May 1644, aged nineteen, he entered Magdalene College, Cambridge, where he graduated BA in 1648 and proceeded MA in 1652. Elected a fellow of the college, he remained there until 1653. Among others he tutored the young Samuel Pepys, who wrote of him that he was 'looked upon … [by] all men as a knave' (Pepys, *Diary*, 1.141).

Career, 1653–1660 In his youth Morland was greatly interested in mathematics and languages and at Magdalene he hesitated to take holy orders. Instead, after a recommendation by Walter Strickland in 1653, he gained a place in the ambassadorial family of Bulstrode Whitelocke. The embassy left England in November that year for the court of Queen Kristina of Sweden. While Morland's part in its deliberations was negligible, he did complete an Anglo-French grammar and engage in debate with some Latin scholars there. When the treaty with Sweden was finally

Sir Samuel Morland, first baronet (1625–1695), by Pierre Lombart, pubd 1658 (after Sir Peter Lely)

concluded in April 1654 Morland returned home. Whitelocke noted that Morland was a 'very Civil Man and an excellent Scholar; modest and respectful; perfect in the Latin tongue' (*Diary of Bulstrode Whitelocke*, 2.205). In his last work Morland noted how in his youth and early days 'I rather chose to gratify my own roving Fancy, and satisfy my Vain Curiosity' (Morland, 38); these attributes John Thurloe now sought to use for the new protectorate.

In May 1655 Morland was sent to the duke of Savoy as a commissioner-extraordinary and formed part of the Cromwellian regime's attempt to resolve the problem of the persecution of the protestant Vaudois in Piedmont. Having visited the Savoy court at Rivoli, Morland moved to Geneva as a resident and there acted under Dr John Pell, ambassador to Switzerland. Although Morland negotiated with the Savoy court he also succeeded in gathering material for a book on the Waldensian churches. In addition he learned both Dutch and Italian and distributed large amounts of Cromwell's money to the protestant poor of Piedmont. By December 1655 he had returned to England. A report on his proceedings was submitted to the House of Commons in January 1657 and Morland also prepared his history for publication. Heavily illustrated with melodramatic prints of the agony of the Vaudois, the publication of *The History of the Evangelical Churches of the Valleys of Piedmont* (1658) was officially sanctioned and partly paid for by the government. It also carried Morland's effusive dedication to Oliver Cromwell. After the Restoration, Morland was said to have tried to withdraw this from all of the copies of his work that he could find, but at the time he was keen to cultivate any connection with Cromwell, mainly because other posts came his way as a consequence. It was claimed that he had been close to the affairs of state; he was made a clerk to his highness signet (30 June 1656) and although he asked for the clerk of the pells in the exchequer, he failed to obtain the latter post.

Morland was notorious for being unable to manage his income and he always tended towards extravagant tastes and a lifestyle of wine, expensive homes, and good show. His talents, however, appealed to Thurloe and the latter began to employ him as part of the intelligence team engaged in opening and copying letters in the Post Office. In the reign of William III, Morland was to write a theoretical manuscript entitled 'A brief discourse concerning the nature & reason of intelligence' illustrating his experience of this shady side of government life. He was to put this knowledge to even better use under the republican and Restoration regimes. By 1657 he was flourishing and living in some state in a house near Bow with some £1000 per annum. In August that year Morland married his first wife, Susanne, daughter of Daniel de Milleville, baron de Boissy, a Huguenot from Normandy; they had three children—Samuel (1663–1716), Susannah (b. 1666), and Anne (d. 1670). Lorenzo Magalotti noted that Susanne eventually 'acquired a great power over her husband' and was partly responsible for turning him to the royalist cause (*Lorenzo Magalotti*, 60).

As was characteristic of most of his career, Morland's loyalty was dubious and being placed in Thurloe's office he was well aware of the secret dealings of that office to thwart the designs of the royalist party. There seems little doubt that in this period Morland began to play a double game and took to providing intelligence to the exiled Charles II. He was aware of several of the Cromwellian regime's intelligence activities to 'trepan' royalists such as Dr Hewitt and he is alleged to have betrayed Thurloe's double agent Sir Richard Willis to the king and Sir Edward Hyde. Morland was to declare that he had even saved Charles II from the effects of one scheme to take his life. It was the latter, he said, which finally turned his loyalty from the republic to the exiled monarchy. Indeed it was also claimed that on one occasion he had overheard both Cromwell and Thurloe discussing secret affairs and pretended to be asleep at his desk. When the lord protector saw Morland, Thurloe only just managed to dissuade Cromwell from using a poniard on him in case he had overheard their plans. Whatever the truth of this, and the other unlikely tales Morland later related about the lord protector, the death of Cromwell in September 1658 and the disarray that followed led to his dismissal alongside his master, John Thurloe, in April 1659.

Career and family life, 1660–1685 Morland was to remain in the country out of the way for much of the crisis that followed, although he was keen to stress his value to Charles II in supplying information. Although Thurloe was reappointed in 1660 Morland apparently thought it safe enough now openly to choose the other side and on 16 May 1660 he crossed over to Breda to wait upon the exiled Charles Stuart. Charles, as a reward for his services, knighted Morland on 20 May and treated him generously, even making Morland a promise of a Garter, or so Morland and his wife thought. On 18 July that year Morland was made a baronet, of Sulhampstead-Banister, and a gentleman of the privy chamber, but he was not a popular man at court, and his expenses at the coronation were to prove costly. As with his fellow turncoat Sir George Downing, Morland was considered an untrustworthy 'knave' by many and in a petition to the king in July 1660 he complained of being pointed 'at … as a perfidious fellow that betrayed his own masters, and will have spy's reward' (Pepys, *Diary*, 1.141; *CSP dom.*, *1660–61*, 336). Nevertheless a pension of some £500 out of the Post Office was granted to him. Unfortunately Morland was then informed that the duke of York was soon to have the Post Office revenues settled upon him and being once more in debt and fearful that his pension would be lost, in alarm he sold out to Sir Arthur Slingsby for a lump sum. Most of the money had been frittered away by 1663, spent on a 'ground and farme in the country … and God knows what' according to Pepys (Pepys, *Diary*, 4.274–5). Indeed, in the next year Morland was 'believed to be a beggar' (ibid., 5.330).

In 1668 Susanne Morland died, possibly in childbirth after suffering a long-standing bout of 'dropsy'. On 26 October 1670 Morland married, at Westminster Abbey, Carola (1651–1674), daughter of Sir Roger Harsnett, sergeant-at-arms to the House of Lords. Lady Morland had a daughter, Thynne (b. and d. 1671), and a son, Edward (1674–1675), before her death in October 1674. Morland's third marriage, on 16 November 1676 in Westminster Abbey, was to Ann Feilding (1660–1680), daughter of George and Mary Feilding of Solihull. Her brother was Beau Feilding, and gossip said that Morland married her for her looks rather than any fortune. The marriage was a short one, for she died on 20 February 1680. There were no children. Morland's rumoured fourth marriage, in 1680, was to the daughter of one Frost, a lawyer at Westminster, but little is known of her other than that she died of smallpox at some point in 1681.

Meanwhile, Morland attained some further public offices. He was a commissioner of appeals in excise (1668–70) and a commissioner of excise (1670–79), and he was even recommended as a possible member of parliament by Monmouth at one stage; however, he was not elected. Instead, disappointed at his lack of advancement at court and constantly living in fear of either financial feast or famine, Morland undertook mathematical and scientific experiments and 'found [that they] pleased the King's Fancy' (Dickinson, 117).

Scientific experimentation Morland's scientific experimentation had already attracted some notice. Samuel Hartlib mentions some of Morland's early experiments in the nature of flight in the 1650s. His first practical investigations, however, linked the world of mathematics and science with a calculating machine based upon the previous work of Blaise Pascal, who in turn had based his work upon the Scottish mathematician John Napier's 'bones'. Morland published a book on the subject, *The Description and Use of Two Arithmetick Instruments* (1673), and several versions of the pocket calculator created by Morland still exist. One, made in brass, was 4 inches by 3 inches and bore the inscription 'Samuel Morland Inventor 1666'. This was not strictly true, for a description of a similar machine created by Pascal and mentioned to Samuel Hartlib in 1648 remained very close to Morland's final design. In the event examples of the calculator were presented to his patron Charles II in 1662 and Morland, who was ever keen to acquire new patrons, also made a presentation copy of one of his machines to the grand duke of Tuscany upon the latter's visit to England in 1667. Morland recommended to his readers Humphery Adamson, who could manufacture further copies of the machines in the Tower of London. The principles of the machine paralleled that of Napier's original, except that the rods now became wheels. According to the inventor the machine was a 'New and most useful Instrument for Addition and Subtraction of Pounds, Shillings, Pence and Farthings; Without charging the Memory, disturbing the Mind or exposing the Operator to any uncertainty; Which no Method hitherto published can justly pretend to' (*Two Arithmetick Instruments*). Various versions were made of the machine, and these would, technically, allow the purchaser to work out his or her arithmetic. Having said this, Pepys thought them very pretty but not very useful, while Morland's rival, Robert Hooke, simply condemned the machine as 'very silly' (Pepys, *Diary*, 9.116–17; Hooke, 25). Indeed the devices look not only cumbersome but rather too complicated for their own good. Other mathematical inventions followed: a trigonometrical calculating machine, which was advertised in the *London Gazette* in August 1666 and which was designed to solve problems in plain trigonometry; a *Perpetual Almanack and Several Useful Tables* (1673), which became a standard work and was frequently republished, and the *Doctrine of Interest both Simple and Compound* (1679). In the latter the author seems to have used his own machine for the calculations.

An additional activity to Morland's mathematical quest lay in his writings upon cryptography. *A New Method of Cryptography* (1666) was one outcome of his work for the government with ciphers. More furtive work for the Restoration regime took place in the opening of letters in the Post Office. Under John Thurloe this practice had become almost a fine art. Morland and Isaac Dorislaus were employed by Cromwell's secretary to rifle the post at night and thus uncover treasonable words and any conspiracies. Morland later turned his practical mind towards inventions that could assist in the opening and copying of letters. Machines were built which could dextrously open letters, quickly copy the correspondence, and counterfeit handwriting, seals, and wafers. The copying machine appeared to involve an offset process by pressing damp tissue paper on the ink. At the Restoration Morland placed these ideas before Charles II and Lord Arlington and, as they proved successful, they swiftly ousted the previously crude systems and were incorporated in the new regime's

intelligence-gathering activities. Most of the machines were destroyed in the great fire of London in 1666. Morland persisted, however, and in 1688 he offered versions of the designs to the Venetian ambassador, but the revolution scotched this plan. The designs subsequently fell into the hands of John Wildman and in 1689 Morland offered to create similar machines for the new regime of William III. Although Wildman took up this offer and encouraged Morland to the extent that the latter hired some sixty workmen in 1690 to prepare the engines, he was thwarted once more as the new king proved, surprisingly enough, unresponsive and the idea was eventually dropped.

In the 1670s Morland established a private printing press for King Charles II. He also made additions to ships' capstans, invented a portable stove for use in confined spaces, and attempted improvements to the barometers of his day. By this stage he had also begun to experiment in acoustics and sound. His other work in this period included a translation of a French treatise of fortifications, published as *The Count of Pagan's Method of Delineating All Manner of Fortifications* (1672), and a plan to open up the River Ouse in Norfolk, during which Morland stayed with Arlington at Euston Hall to view the project in 1670. Nothing came of this although Morland did assist Arlington in the design of the gardens at Euston; in particular he created a 'small cascade of the Canale' there that was contrived by a new device that not only allowed fountains of water to run, but also served to grind the estate's grain (Evelyn, *Diary*, 2.591).

Early work on a speaking trumpet, said to be Morland's own invention, culminated in the 1670s with his experiments in St James's Park before Charles II and a number of courtiers. With the king's encouragement various types of trumpet were manufactured and used, the three largest being sent off to Deal Castle for trials there. The navy was also given orders for their use at sea. It was claimed that voices could be heard at a distance of over a mile, although Morland was also to claim that he could have perfected the trumpet to 'the distance of eight, nine or ten miles', but was discouraged (Morland, 27). A natural self-publicist, Morland advertised a work on the matter entitled *Tuba Stentor-Phonica, an instrument of excellent use, as well at sea, as at land, invented and variously experimented in … 1670* (1671). The trumpets attracted lively debate, were marketed by Simon Beal in Suffolk Street, and were frequently mentioned in the literature of the day, Samuel Butler's work *Hudibras* being a case in point. Various other acoustic machines followed. The Otacousticon, a listening device, was again tried out in St James's Park on a 'still evening' and according to Morland it 'brought into it (as I thought) innumerable Sounds of Coach and Cart-wheels and humane Voices, in, and throughout all the Streets … but those sounds being often confused, and those that were nearer, drowning those which were more remote' (ibid., 27–8). Pepys tried out a version of this instrument in April 1668 and was impressed at what he heard. In a number of ways the device was forerunner of similar listening devices used in the First World War. It may have had other uses, for in 1668 Morland was involved in covert work for the French ambassador by assisting in the trepanning of the French dissident Roux de Marcilly.

One of Morland's main talents in these years was for the construction of mechanical engines for the supply or removal of water for domestic or industrial purposes. Hydrostatics and hydraulics became his forte and in 1675 he took a lease upon Vauxhall House in Kennington on the site of the ordnance factory established by Charles I, most probably because of his need to be close to the workshops there. His subsequent improvements to the house included a table in the dining-room with its own fountain, and a moveable kitchen. His first attempts at a gunpowder engine (designed to use the explosive power of gunpowder to propel water in an early form of the internal combustion engine) were unsuccessful. In 1661 a royal warrant gave him a grant for the sole use of the idea during fourteen years and further experiments on this idea were subsequently undertaken by Denis Papin and Christiaan Huygens under the auspices of the Royal Society of France in 1674. A number of other experiments on hydrostatic equipment followed throughout Morland's career. He mostly based his 'inventions' on previous work, but he does have some claim to originality. In September 1670 mechanical pumps devised by him were shown before Charles II and the latter, always amused by Morland's creations, was impressed enough to order further trials at Chatham Dockyard. He gave Morland £350 for this purpose. These trials were to drag on until 1676. Morland made several attempts to protect his inventions through parliament, but these failed. In spite of his claim to have spent some twenty years and thousands of pounds on experimentation he was forced to be content with a patent for his 'plunger-pump'; the novel features in this instrument were the gland and stuffing box, with which James Watt was later, wrongly, credited as having invented.

In 1675 Morland went into a partnership with Isaac Thompson in Great Russell Street to produce various Morland pumps commercially for domestic use, or in mines, wells, ships, and drainage schemes, for extinguishing fires, and for a multitude of other uses. The shop had advertised prices and costing for various pumps between £5 and £63. In the 1680s Morland undertook his major waterworks at Windsor Castle, their ultimate aim being to bring the water supply to any desired point in the buildings there. The king, queen, prince of Orange, and many foreign dignitaries observed the Windsor Castle trials in July 1681. Morland managed to pump water by himself with the strength of eight men:

> in a continuous stream, at the rate of above sixty Barrels an hour from the Engine below the Parkpale, up to the top of the Castle, and thence into the Air above sixty Foot high, to the great admiration of Their Majesties and all the Beholders … who unanimously concluded that this was the boldest and most extraordinary Experiment that had ever been performed by Water in any part of the World. (*London Gazette*, 18–21 July 1681)

As a reward Morland was awarded the title of 'Master of Mechanicks' on 14 August 1681 by the king. Ever vain, Morland also paid for a gold medal set with diamonds that he wore as a badge of office.

In December 1681 the master of mechanics left for France to construct more works at the palace of Versailles. Morland was involved in the construction of the so-called 'machine of Marly' designed to bring water from the Seine into Versailles. His designs were simpler and more functional and after lengthy negotiations he finally carried out his trials under the stern gaze of Louis XIV in 1682 at a model plant constructed on a considerable scale at the Château de Maison near St Germain. Unfortunately Morland lost out to the more tried and trusted methods advocated by his rivals. As a record of his schemes however he published *Élévation des eaux par toute sorte de machines reduite à la mesure, au poids, à la balance par le moyen d'un nouveau piston & corps de pompe d'un nouveau mouvement cyclo-elliptique … avec huit problèmes de mécanique … pour le bien public, par le Chevalier Morland* (Paris, 1685). In this he gave an account of his work in France and of his experiments over the previous thirty years. He also proposed using steam pressure to raise water. Although no description is given of the engine proposed by Morland he did experiment on the subject, and in this also he prefigured Watt. At one stage he also apparently seriously considered adapting this method to drive ships at sea.

Last years After his experiments, however, Morland was stranded in France, short of money, and forced to beg for supply from the English ambassador. His pensions and other emoluments had been stopped on his leaving England, on the ground that he would presumably receive money from the French for his work. By 1684 he was languishing in a state of some poverty and blamed the French minister Louvois for his lack of funds. In debt for both the work in France and that carried out at Windsor, at one point he noted that if King Charles could not supply him with work or funds then he would be forced to seek his fortune either in the mines in the north of England or in the service of the grand duke of Tuscany. However, relief eventually arrived in the shape of a sum of money from Louis XIV who had heard of his distress. Morland saw his latest work through the press before returning to England.

The upkeep of Vauxhall House ultimately proved too much for Morland in his later years and he was forced to remove to Hammersmith in 1684. In addition the death of Charles II in 1685 left him without a real patron. While James II renewed his pension, it was only after Lord Treasurer Rochester had taken out some of the money to pay the workmen for their work on the Windsor Castle engines. Some suggested improvements to gun carriages led to further trials in 1686 but little came of these schemes. Short of funds and 'almost distracted for want of Moneys, my privat Creditors tormenting mee from morning to night and some of them threatening mee with a prison' on 1 February 1687, at Knightsbridge Chapel, Morland married once more (*Letters and the Second Diary*, 175–6). He was under the impression he was marrying an heiress, worth £500 per annum in land and with £4000 in ready money; unfortunately he was deceived and the affair ended in acrimony and disappointment. In fact Mary Aylif, the 'gilded bait' as he called her, was the penniless daughter of a coach-maker (Dickinson, 118). Although he was unaware of her bad reputation—her adultery, an illegitimate child, and moreover that she was 'not worth a shilling'—these parts of her life were soon revealed (*Letters and the Second Diary*, 176). After various attempts to buy her off, Morland obtained a divorce for her adultery on 16 July that year. She subsequently remarried, but the disaster left Morland ill.

None the less in 1690, under the new Williamite regime, there was the possibility of more work at Hampton Court. Unfortunately blindness, or as he noted 'Silence and Shades of Night', struck Morland in his last years and in the final decade of his life he turned for consolation to religion (Morland, 9). His work from these years reveals a somewhat morbid humour. In it Morland reviewed his career as an engineer from a spiritual point of view and even compared his own engineering work—unfavourably, but only just—to that of the great 'spiritual Engineer' God (ibid., 31). He also warned eager 'young Mechanick[s]' of his day from seeking after perpetual motion, the philosopher's stone, and the ideas of Thomas Hobbes (ibid., 64). In October 1695 John Evelyn paid a visit to the seventy-year-old Morland in the company of Thomas Tenison, archbishop of Canterbury. Evelyn found Morland 'a very Mortified sight & person', but he was still proud enough to show off his inventions (Evelyn, *Diary*, 5.221). Morland also claimed to have buried his secular music books to rid himself of vanity, although he still played psalms and religious hymns on the theorbo. One of his last acts was an uncharacteristically generous one for the invariably prodigal inventor: he paid for a pump and a drinking fountain for the use of the inhabitants of Hammersmith; it was erected on 8 July 1695.

Morland died in Hammersmith on 26 December 1695, having been ill for some time, and was buried on 9 January 1696 in Hammersmith churchyard in a vault for which he had paid in his lifetime. It seems likely that Morland had once more fallen into problems with a woman for in his will, dated 25 December, on which he was only able to make his mark, he left his estate to Mrs Zenobia Hough of the parish of St James, Westminster, and disinherited Samuel, his only surviving son from his first marriage. The younger Samuel Morland had been educated at Westminster School and Magdalene College and in 1679 he was in the Middle Temple and became a lawyer. Father and son do not appear to have been on good terms. He succeeded his father as second baronet but died without children in 1716.

Reputation Morland's character was typical of his times. Magalotti noted that his 'talent for politics [was] not wonderful' and Morland's was a shifting personality, often selfish and frequently extravagant, particularly over wine, on which he was something of a connoisseur (*Lorenzo Magalotti*, 62). The Italian also described his temperament as more than a 'little melancholy and … queer', but Morland's personal life was relatively happy until his fifth marriage, when both his greed and credulity were illuminated (ibid.). Conversely, Morland himself claimed never to have 'frequented either tavern, or kept in pension women of pleasure', but his money all too often went to pay workmen 'for Engins and chargeable experiments to please and divert his Majesty' (Dickinson, 118). Frequently impoverished as a result, the financial crises in his life were a result of his taste for show and splendour, as well as his investment in his own inventions.

In his politics Morland was both shifty and untrustworthy, a traitor to Cromwellian government and a turncoat in 1660. In the Restoration period he was a placehunter and careerist. While in this he was no worse than many of his contemporaries, his personality does seem to have attracted the particular abhorrence of his fellows. His talent for innovation, however, is not to be underestimated. In his inventions Morland's work ranged over a wide field, from mechanical water-pumps for domestic and industrial use, to a mechanical glister machine for giving himself enemas while in bed, to the speaking trumpet, and a proto-steam engine. Although his inventions were rarely perfected and he lived off the work of others, and was a skilled self-publicist, ultimately his eminence was rather more as an engineer than as an original thinker.

ALAN MARSHALL

Sources S. Morland, *The urim of conscience* (1695) · H. W. Dickinson, *Sir Samuel Morland, diplomat and inventor, 1625–1695* (1970) · Pepys, *Diary* · *Lorenzo Magalotti at the court of Charles II: his Relazione d'Inghilterra of 1668*, ed. and trans. W. E. K. Middleton (1980) · *The diary of Bulstrode Whitelocke, 1605–1675*, ed. R. Spalding, British Academy, Records of Social and Economic History, new ser., 13 (1990) · *CSP dom.*, 1660–85 · *The diary of Robert Hooke … 1672–1680*, ed. H. W. Robinson and W. Adams (1935); repr. (1968) · *Letters and the second diary of Samuel Pepys*, ed. R. G. Howarth (1932) · Foster, *Alum. Oxon.* · GEC, *Peerage* · will, PRO, PROB 11/429, fol. 240v
Archives BL, tract relating to the discovery of the steam engine, Harley MS 5771 · LPL, corresp. and papers | BL, corresp. with John Pell, Add. MSS 4279, 4393, 4417, *passim* · BL, letters to John Thurloe, Add. MS 4365 · BL, Add. MS 47133, fols. 8–13
Likenesses W. Hollar, etching, 1650 (after Conzal), BM · G. Bower, silver medal, BM · S. Cooper, miniature, V&A · P. Lombart, engraving (after P. Lely), AM Oxf., BM, NPG; repro. in S. Morland, *History of the evangelical churches of the valley of Piedmont* (1658) [*see illus.*] · J. Roettier, silver medal, BM · line engraving, BM, NPG; repro. in S. Morland, *The description and use of two arithmetick instruments* (1673), frontispiece
Wealth at death all goods and chattels left to Mrs Zenobia Hough: will, PRO, PROB 11/429, fol. 240v

Morland, Sir Thomas Lethbridge Napier (1865–1925), army officer, was born on 9 August 1865 at Montreal, Canada, the eldest son of Thomas Morland, a manufacturing engineer, who, after emigrating to Canada as a young man, played an important part in the construction of the Canadian Pacific Railway, and his wife, Helen Elizabeth, daughter of General Henry Servante. On losing both his parents when still a child, Morland was brought to England to be educated, and sent to Charterhouse School (1878–83) and the Royal Military College, Sandhurst (1883–4). He was gazetted into the King's Royal Rifle Corps in August 1884. While still a subaltern he attended the Staff College, Camberley (1890–92). On 18 February 1890 he married Mabel Elinor Rowena (*d.* 1901), daughter of

Admiral Henry Craven St John; they had two daughters. After being promoted captain in April 1893 Morland was appointed aide-de-camp to General Sir A. J. Lyon Fremantle, commander-in-chief in Malta, in February 1895.

Being of an adventurous disposition, and a good horseman, Morland desired more active employment. This he found in Nigeria. In February 1898 he joined the West African frontier force in time to take part in the operations which were then in progress in the River Niger valley and hinterland. This was the first of six minor campaigns in those regions in which he participated with credit. Morland was rewarded with a brevet majority in July 1899 and given command of the 1st battalion West African frontier force with the temporary rank of lieutenant-colonel. Early in 1900 he commanded the little column engaged in the Kaduna expedition in Northern Nigeria; later in the same year he took part in the Asante operations, after which he obtained the brevet of lieutenant-colonel. In 1901 he conducted the operations against the emir of Yola, during which he was slightly wounded, and subsequently he received the DSO (1902). In the latter year he was given the command of the small Bornu expedition. Finally, in 1903, he was engaged in the campaign against the rulers of Kano and Sokoto. In the following March (1904) he was created CB. After a spell of leave Morland was promoted colonel in September 1905 and returned to Africa as inspector-general of the West African frontier force with the temporary rank of brigadier-general. He was engaged in no more fighting, and returned home in 1909.

Morland remained unemployed until June 1910 when he became general officer commanding (GOC), 2nd infantry brigade, at Aldershot. He held this command for three years, winning the good opinion of Sir Douglas Haig, who later described him as 'one of our best brigadiers' (Blake, 155). Morland spent the last year of peace on half pay owing to ill health, an occupational hazard of service in west Africa. Nevertheless after the outbreak of the First World War he was appointed (August 1914) to the command of the 47th (2nd London) division of the Territorial Force; soon afterwards he was transferred to the command of the newly created 14th division of the New Armies, and two months after that he was transferred to the vacant command of the 5th division. After arriving in Flanders on 18 October he led part of his new command at La Bassée during the first battle of Ypres. In July 1915 he was promoted GOC, 10th corps, with the temporary rank of lieutenant-general, and was created KCB; 10th corps was then in process of formation, and so did not participate in any important engagement until it was allotted to the Fourth Army before the opening of the battle of the Somme (1 July 1916).

Morland's performance on the Somme won him some notoriety, especially during the first day when he insisted on positioning himself on an observation platform in a tree 2 miles from his headquarters. He saw nothing to cheer him from this vantage point; the 10th corps's attack against the Thiepval heights on 1 July was a complete failure and follow-up attacks were equally barren. General Sir Hubert Gough, then GOC, Reserve Army, expressed a lack of confidence in Morland to Haig on 23 July and at the end of the month the 10th corps was withdrawn to the Fourth Army reserve. On 17 August, however, Morland took over temporary command of the 14th corps. During his three-week stay the corps eventually managed to capture Guillemont and Ginchy after several reverses. Morland returned to the 10th corps on 10 September.

The 10th corps was transferred to the Second Army at Ypres in October 1916 and the following year participated in two of General Plumer's greatest successes. At Messines (7 June 1917) the corps captured Hill 60 and Mount Sorrel, weakening the German position east of Ypres. At the Menin Road ridge (20 September) it spearheaded the attack on the important tactical position of Gheluvelt, clearing the wooded area which had held up the British advance for two months. Later attacks across the Menin Road failed to repeat this success. Morland was knighted (KCMG) at the end of the year.

During the winter of 1917–18 Morland and his staff were withdrawn into reserve, and 10th corps remained there throughout the German spring offensive (March–April 1918). On 12 April Morland was transferred to the command of the 13th corps in the First Army reserve. He spent the summer cautiously advancing across the Lys plain. In September, 13th corps was transferred again, this time to the Fourth Army for the attack on the Hindenburg line; 13th corps' assault, on 5 October, was a great success, capturing a large section of the Hindenburg defences known as the Beaurevoir line. Morland pursued the retreating Germans, advancing 11 miles in four days. On 5 November 13th corps crossed the Sambre. In the last few days of the war it advanced 18 miles in six days, entering Belgium shortly before the armistice.

Morland was promoted substantive lieutenant-general in January 1919. But he was then struck down by the pandemic influenza and never really recovered good health. In March 1919 he returned to the command of his former troops, the reconstituted 10th corps, in the army of occupation at Cologne. A year later he succeeded Sir William Robertson as commander-in-chief of that army, and became temporary general. In March 1922 he returned home in order to assume the chief command at Aldershot in succession to Lord Cavan, and in November of that year he was promoted full general. Owing, however, to his impaired health he vacated his appointment at the end of February 1923. He never obtained further employment, and died rather suddenly at Villeneuve, Montreux, Switzerland, on 21 May 1925; he was buried in the English cemetery at Villeneuve. He had been appointed colonel of the Suffolk regiment in 1919, and an aide-de-camp general to George V in 1922.

Morland's record as a corps commander was patchy. In many ways it reflects that of the British expeditionary force as a whole. In 1916 he experienced more failures than successes, but in 1917, especially under Plumer, he performed well in limited set-piece operations. During the final advance, in the autumn of 1918, he also did well. He made no reputation as an innovative tactician and left little impression on the men he commanded. Morland was in appearance and manner an old-fashioned English officer and gentleman, calm, courteous, unselfish, and loyal. Towards the end of the war his health—weakened by service in west Africa—began to fail and he developed indolent habits which concerned his staff.

J. M. BOURNE

Sources DNB · J. E. Edmonds, ed., *Military operations, France and Belgium, 1916*, 1, History of the Great War (1932) · J. E. Edmonds, ed., *Military operations, France and Belgium, 1917*, 2, History of the Great War (1948) · *The private papers of Douglas Haig, 1914–1919*, ed. R. Blake (1952) · *The Times* (25 May 1925) · R. Prior and T. Wilson, *Passchendaele, the untold story* (1996) · T. Travers, *How the war was won: command and technology in the British army on the western front, 1917–1918* (1992) · *CGPLA Eng. & Wales* (1925) · private information (2004) [A. Simpson, J. Lee, A. Rawson]
Archives IWM | IWM, corresp. with Sir Henry Wilson
Likenesses F. Dodd, charcoal and watercolour drawing, IWM · photograph, repro. in A. H. Hussey and D. S. Inman, *The fifth division in the Great War* (1921), 70 · portrait, repro. in *The Times history of the war*, 22 vols. (1914–21), vol. 9, p. 490
Wealth at death £10,078 4s. 4d.: administration with will, 1 Aug 1925, *CGPLA Eng. & Wales*

Morley. For this title name *see* individual entries under Morley; *see also* Parker, Henry, tenth Baron Morley (1480/81–1556); Parker, Henry, eleventh Baron Morley (1531/2–1577); Parker, William, thirteenth Baron Morley and fifth or first Baron Monteagle (1574/5–1622); Parker, John, first earl of Morley (1772–1840); Parker, Edmund, second earl of Morley (1810–1864) [*see under* Parker, John, first earl of Morley (1772–1840)]; Parker, Albert Edmund, third earl of Morley (1843–1905).

Morley, Agnes Headlam- (1902–1986), historian, was born on 10 December 1902 in Cambridge, probably at home at 1 Benet Place. She was the second and youngest child of Sir James Wycliffe Headlam (1863–1929), diplomatic historian [*see* Morley, Sir James Wycliffe Headlam-], and his wife, Elizabeth Henrietta Ernestina Charlotte (Else), *née* Sonntag (1866–1950), a musician and composer who had been born in Lüneburg into an artistic family and had moved to Dresden as a child. Agnes grew up in Wimbledon, and from 1915 to 1921 attended Wimbledon high school, where she did well scholastically and in hockey, swimming, and other activities. In the pre-war years her mother was an articulate and active supporter of women's suffrage. The First World War created special challenges for the family: while her father was working for the political intelligence department of the Foreign Office and was opposed to a negotiated peace with Germany, her mother (according to Agnes's later account)

> turned in love and loyalty to her own country. She made no secret of it … We children did not take it too tragically. My mother assumed that we would wish Britain to win the war, but we were brought up not to deny our German ancestry. It was an open battle. Unlike so many children of mixed marriages we had no secret sense of shame in being half-German. ('Introduction' to J. Headlam-Morley, *A Memoir of the Paris Peace Conference, 1919*, 1972, xix)

Agnes's whole career was to be concerned with Anglo-German relations, in which her family was so deeply involved.

In 1921 Headlam-Morley went to Somerville College, Oxford, to read modern history; she gained a second class in her final examinations in 1924. She then embarked on graduate research. Her thesis, for which she was awarded the degree of BLitt in 1926, was published in 1928 as *The New Democratic Constitutions of Europe*—her first and only single-author non-fiction book. A comparative examination of Germany, Czechoslovakia, Poland, Finland, Yugoslavia, and the Baltic states, it noted the rapid reaction against a belief in the absolute value of democracy and concluded that the failures of democracy were due less to the system itself than to the method by which it had been applied.

In 1930 Headlam-Morley's appointment to an assistant tutorship in politics at St Hugh's College, Oxford, was complicated by her withdrawal and subsequent reinstatement of her application, and her frequent failure to answer letters. Finally she deferred taking up the post so that she could act as research worker and election helper for her cousin Cuthbert Morley *Headlam MP, to whom she was very attached. All this was a reflection of the conflicting personal and professional interests that were to both hamper and help her work as a teacher in the school of philosophy, politics, and economics (PPE) at Oxford. In the four decades of her fellowship at St Hugh's, from 1932 to 1970, her teaching was enlivened by her firsthand knowledge of the politics and international relations of her own time. A former colleague has given a vivid picture of her 'stimulating, astonishing, admonishing, teaching and informing her pupils in between whiles of carrying on her own varied private life' (Trickett, 28–30).

During the Second World War, with many colleagues absent, Headlam-Morley took on heavy examining duties; and she was also a member of the Social Reconstruction Survey committee, under the chairmanship of G. D. H. Cole, which in its chequered and controversial existence failed to make a significant mark on wartime efforts at post-war planning. Her record of publication was thin. Before her appointment to St Hugh's, she and her brother Kenneth had helped to edit a collection of her late father's memoranda, *Studies in Diplomatic History* (1930). Not until forty-two years later, and two years after her retirement from Oxford, was there another academic book on international relations, and again it was a co-edited edition of her father's work: *A Memoir of the Paris Peace Conference, 1919* (1972). There were also a few essays, including a short one on Gustav Stresemann published in *The History Makers*, edited by Sir John Wheeler-Bennett and Lord Longford (1973). She left a large quantity of unpublished and disorganized notes on these and related topics.

Preoccupation with her family was a pervasive feature of Headlam-Morley's published work and public life. She accompanied her uncle Arthur Cayley Headlam (who had baptized her as a child and was now bishop of Gloucester) on a mission to Berlin in 1938 at a time of concern for the sufferings of Christians in Germany: he was later considered to have failed to take the dangers of national socialism sufficiently seriously. She said nothing of this episode when she wrote a biographical essay about her uncle in her introduction to his posthumous book *The*

Fourth Gospel as History (1948). Her essay does, however, reveal her sadness at the division of European Christendom into different states, churches, and sects, and it identifies strikingly with the bishop's role in the ecumenical movement and his belief in a 'higher loyalty to the Universal Church'. It helps to explain her decision to be received into the Roman Catholic church, also in 1948.

In the same year, with the support of J. W. Wheeler-Bennett, Headlam-Morley was appointed to the Montague Burton professorship of international relations at Oxford, established in 1930, and one of the very few such posts in the UK. She was the first woman to be elected to a full professorship at Oxford (though Ida Mann, the reader in ophthalmology, had a few years earlier been accorded the title of professor). She was to hold the international relations chair for longer than any other incumbent before or since, up to the end of the twentieth century. Many graduate students whose work she supervised remained friends for life. However, at a time when international relations was developing as an academic subject in other British and American universities, she stuck to a restricted vision of it as recent European diplomatic history. A PPE bibliography she co-authored, published in 1949, listed under 'General works on international relations' not a single book on any subject other than inter-war history. She was resistant to syllabus changes, and had no talent for administration or academic entrepreneurship. It was only in 1971, a year after her retirement, that the first taught graduate degree at Oxford in the subject, the BPhil (later renamed the MPhil) in international relations, was belatedly introduced.

Headlam-Morley's lectures, while not as popular or famous as those of her contemporary A. J. P. Taylor, conveyed a sense of the dilemmas faced by statesmen in the inter-war years, and showed an understanding of Anglo-French policies of appeasement as well as of their failure. She saw Nazism as a baffling aberration from, not a culmination of, German history.

Headlam-Morley had interests in many fields other than the academic. An outstanding hostess, her dinner party guests at her rooms at St Hugh's spanned a broad range. She was a Conservative in politics, and had been adopted as prospective Conservative parliamentary candidate for Barnard Castle (co. Durham) in 1936: the anticipated election was not called, and she did not in the end contest the seat. She was an enthusiast for Luther, despite his protestantism, and for Brecht, despite his communism. Like her mother, to whom she had remained very close, she loved music. In 1960 she published a sensitive novella, *Last Days: June 1944 to January 1945*, based on the sad experiences of a German friend in Berlin towards the end of the war. She was a member of the Longford committee investigating pornography, which issued its report in 1972. She was especially warm towards children, to whom she would relate long adventure stories. Her health was not robust: she had bouts of tuberculosis in the 1930s and 1950s. She died, unmarried, in St Anthony's Hospital, Cheam, Surrey, from bronchopneumonia on 21 February 1986. After cremation her ashes were buried in her parents' grave at St Mary's Church, Whorlton, Barnard Castle. To the end she still lived in the family house at 29 St Mary's Road, Wimbledon, in which she had grown up.

ADAM ROBERTS

Sources R. Trickett, 'Agnes Headlam Morley', *St Hugh's College Chronicle*, 50 (1986–7) [text of address at memorial service] · *WWW*, 1981–90 · CAC Cam., James Headlam-Morley MSS · private information (2004) · marriage certificate, LMA [parents'] · *Oxford University Calendar* · register, Somerville College, Oxford · Wimbledon high school archives · *The Times* (24 March 1986) · R. C. D. Jasper, *Arthur Cayley Headlam: life and letters of a bishop* (1960), 290–99 · N. Chester, *Economics, politics, and social studies in Oxford, 1900–85* (1986)
Archives priv. coll. · priv. coll., notes of lectures · University of Coleraine, Northern Ireland, papers | CAC Cam., James Headlam-Morley MSS
Likenesses R. Lutyens, portrait, St Hugh's College, Oxford · photograph (in school hockey team), Wimbledon high school, London · photograph (after R. Lutyens), priv. coll. · photographs, priv. coll.
Wealth at death £11,128: probate, 13 May 1986, *CGPLA Eng. & Wales*

Morley, Christopher Love (*b.* 1645/6), physician, may, from his name, have been related to Christopher Love (1618–1651), the Presbyterian minister. He entered Leiden University as a medical student on 18 February 1676, claiming to be thirty years of age, and graduated MD in 1679. According to a short Latin account of Morley in the preface to his *Collectanea chymica Leydensia* (1684) he travelled widely, and apparently practised medicine before going to the Netherlands. At Leiden he attended the medical practice of H. Schacht and C. Drelincourt, with the anatomical lectures of the latter, and also studied chemistry with C. L. Maëts and others. Morley was accustomed to take copious notes of lectures and cases, which ultimately extended, it is said, to more than forty quarto volumes. Thirty-six of these survive, and are now in the British Library (Sloane MSS 1256–1258, 1259–1280, 1282–1294, 1297–1299). They are dated 1677 to 1679, and not only show Morley's diligence as a student, but give an interesting picture of the state of medical education in Leiden at the time.

On his return to England, Morley published a little volume, *De morbo epidemico* (1679), on an epidemic fever then prevalent in England, the Netherlands, and elsewhere, which he dedicated to the Royal College of Physicians. It contains an account of his personal experience of the disease, and a letter from Professor Schacht of Leiden on the same subject, together with remarks on the state of medical practice in England and the Netherlands. This probably led to his election as an honorary fellow of the College of Physicians on 30 September 1680 (since, not being an English graduate, he was not eligible to become an ordinary fellow). He did not immediately settle in London, for in 1683 he went on a voyage to the Indies, but in 1684 he was practising in London.

In the new charter granted to the college in 1686 by James II, Morley was named as an actual fellow, and was admitted in the following year. This suggests that he was a supporter of James II, and probably a Roman Catholic. In 1700 his name was withdrawn, at his own request, from the college list, 'because he could not act, as not having taken the oaths required by the Government' (Munk, *Roll*). His subsequent career cannot be traced.

Morley was evidently a man of wide knowledge in medicine and other sciences, but he did nothing in later life to fulfil his early promise. His *Collectanea chemica Leydensia* was based on material extracted from the notebooks referred to above. It consists of a large number of chemical and pharmaceutical receipts taken from the lectures of three professors of chemistry at Leiden—C. L. Maëts, C. Marggraff, and J. le Mort. It was translated into German (Jena, 1696), and appeared in a second Latin edition (Antwerp, 1702). The date of Morley's death is unknown.

J. F. PAYNE, *rev.* PATRICK WALLIS

Sources Munk, *Roll* · R. W. Innes Smith, *English-speaking students of medicine at the University of Leyden* (1932) · C. L. Morley, *Collectanea chymica Leydensia* (1684)
Archives BL, Sloane MSS, case books, notebooks, commonplace book, catalogues of plants, and corresp.

Morley, Daniel of (*d.* in or after **1210**), philosophical writer, was a native of Norfolk, where he held the hereditary rectory of Flitcham, near Holkham, and was later succeeded in it by John of Morley, probably his son; he also had a son called Geoffrey. He appears to have been a man of means, since although he was among the debtors to a Jewish moneylender of Castle Rising in the mid-1180s, he was able to pay 40 marks for a settlement over land at Hillington, Norfolk, in 1190, and incurred a debt of 200 marks for disseisin, also in Norfolk, in 1210. The debt was never paid, and it is likely that Morley died around that time. It has been suggested that he served as a royal justice, presumably on the strength of an identification with the Master Daniel who acted in that capacity in Sussex, Hampshire, and Wiltshire in 1190, but this seems improbable. His closest association was not with the crown, but with John of Oxford, bishop of Norwich between 1175 and 1200, who arbitrated in a dispute between Morley and Wymondham Priory in the 1180s and subsequently instituted Daniel as parson of North Wootton at the priory's presentation. It was to Bishop John that Morley addressed his only surviving work, the *Philosophia*.

Explaining the genesis of his treatise, Morley recounts that he went to Paris to seek out masters, but found them to be nothing but ignoramuses expounding Roman law. Hearing that the 'doctrina Arabum' which 'consisted almost entirely of the quadrivial arts' flourished in Toledo, he hurried there, in order to attend the lectures of the 'wisest philosophers in the world' (Morley, 212). The only such philosopher he mentions in the course of his *Philosophia* is Gerardo da Cremona, the leading translator of scientific texts from Arabic into Latin in Toledo, whose death in 1187 provides a *terminus ante quem* for Daniel's work, since he implies that Gerardo is still alive. When Daniel returned to England, 'with a pile of books', he was disappointed to find that the English schools were now as devoted to the study of Roman law as the French ones had been. But the bishop of Norwich asked him to speak about the wonderful things and the *disciplinae* of Toledo, and the *Philosophia* was the result.

This work is divided into two books, on the sublunary and superlunary world respectively (hence the title found in one of the manuscripts: 'liber de naturis inferiorum et superiorum') and dealing with man, the creation of the world, matter, the elements, the nature of the stars, and the usefulness of astrology. In spite of Morley's repeated reference to Gerardo da Cremona, and his reporting of a conversation between himself and Gerardo on the subject of astrology, the sources of the *Philosophia* are not the translations of Gerardo. Rather they are, first, original works by, and an Arabic–Latin translation of, Adelard of Bath, with which Daniel shows a greater familiarity than any other scholar, and on which he models the form and even the phraseology of his own work; second, other Arabic–Latin translations of the first half of the twelfth century, including Hermann of Carinthia's translation of the *Great Introduction to Astrology* of Abu Ma'shar of Balkh, Juan de Sevilla's translation of al-Farghani's *Rudiments of Astronomy*, and the anonymous *De ortu scientiarum*; and third, Aristotle's *On Generation and Corruption* in a Greek–Latin version and the anonymous *De caelo et mundo* later attributed to Avicenna, which in turn quoted Aristotle's *Physics*, *On the Heavens*, and *On Sense and Sensibilia*. These last two works were known to Morley's English contemporaries Alexander Neckham and Alfred of Shareshill, and exist together in a late-twelfth-century manuscript (Bodl. Oxf., MS Selden supra 24), but whether Daniel was responsible for introducing them to England along with other translations is, as yet, unclear.

Morley's *Philosophia* belongs to the genre of comprehensive works on natural science written in a literary manner, which was popular in the first half of the twelfth century, such as Adelard of Bath's *Quaestiones naturales* and William de Conches's *Dragmaticon*. His work differs from these in that it includes among its sources new translations of works on natural science from Greek and Arabic by, or at least thought to be by, Aristotle, but it does not yet have the air of university texts of the early thirteenth century which relied more exclusively on these translations.

CHARLES BURNETT

Sources T. Silverstein, 'Daniel of Morley, English cosmologist and student of Arabic science', *Mediaeval Studies*, 10 (1948), 179–96 · C. Burnett, 'The institutional context of Arabic-Latin translations of the middle ages: a reassessment of the "School of Toledo"', *Vocabulary of teaching and research between middle ages and Renaissance* [London 1994], ed. O. Weijers (Turnhout, Belgium, 1995), 214–35 [on Morley's debt to Adelard of Bath] · C. Burnett, *The introduction of Arabic learning into England* (1997), 61–9 · B. Lawn, *The Salernitan questions* (1963), 58–63 · J. C. Russell, 'Hereford and Arabic science in England, *c.*1175–1200', *Isis*, 18 (1932–3), 14–25 · R. W. Southern, *Robert Grosseteste: the growth of an English mind in medieval Europe*, 2nd edn (1992), 88–90 · Daniel of Morley, 'Philosophia', ed. G. Maurach, *Mittellateinisches Jahrbuch*, 14 (1979), 204–55 · Pipe rolls, 31 Henry II; 2 Richard I; 12 John · C. Harper-Bill, ed., *Norwich, 1070–1214*, English Episcopal Acta, 6 (1990), nos. 315, 317 · D. M. Stenton, ed., *Pleas before the king or his justices, 1198–1212*, 3, SeldS, 83 (1967), lxxxii

Morley, Ebenezer Cobb (1831–1924), lawyer, sportsman, and sports administrator, was born at Hull, Yorkshire, on 16 August 1831, the son of Ebenezer Morley and his wife, Hannah Cobb, who had been married at St Mary's, Kingston upon Hull, five years earlier. Morley was baptized at an independent chapel in the same place on 11 September

1831. No details of his education have been discovered. As the first secretary of the first organized football body, the Football Association of England (FA), Morley may be described as the 'father' of the world's most popular game. He initiated the series of London meetings at which, on his proposal, the FA was formed in 1863. He also drafted the FA's first set of laws for a game which, hitherto, had been a violent thing of the streets and fields or a collective exercise, with many confusing variations, of the public schools. Morley and the FA gave the game shape and direction which led, a decade later, to the birth of tournament and international football.

From 1858 Morley lived in Barnes, Surrey, and, having qualified in law four years earlier, he practised as a solicitor at various addresses in London, including 10 King's Bench Walk and 53 Gresham House, Old Broad Street, until 1921. He was always ready to give free legal advice to the poor and he also supported working men's clubs. He was a justice of the peace and he represented Barnes on Surrey county council between 1903 and 1919, attending meetings of the music and dancing houses, racecourses and explosives licensing committee, and various education committees. He was also a conservator of Barnes Common.

Morley was often referred to as 'the grand old sportsman of Barnes', and sport, in several forms, was his abiding interest. He was an accomplished oarsman and, in 1864, rowed in the London Rowing Club's eight for the Grand Challenge Cup at Henley. He was secretary of the London Rowing Club for many years and also founder and secretary (1862–80) of the Barnes and Mortlake regatta. He also helped to organize a big annual athletics meeting on the day of the university boat race. He kept a pack (twelve couples) of foot beagles, and for nearly fifty years he hunted with the Surrey union foxhounds and, for twenty years, the Devon and Somerset staghounds. He also built and equipped a small gymnasium—near his Thames-side home, 26 The Terrace, Barnes, Surrey—which was used by footballers and oarsmen.

Football, however, was the sport on which Morley made his biggest mark. He played the game on Barnes Common before he formed the Barnes football club in 1862, which was based at the Limes Field at Mortlake. There were regular disputes about the way the game was played: Should the ball be handled as well as kicked? Should 'hacking' an opponent be permitted? Morley, a natural and willing organizer, wrote to *Bell's Life* suggesting that football have set rules in the way that cricket had. This led to the meeting of representatives of a dozen London and suburban clubs at the Freemasons' Tavern, Great Queen Street, London, on 26 October 1863, at which the FA was formed. Morley was a clever and effective player himself and he scored the first goal in the first representative match (London versus Sheffield, 31 March 1866).

Morley himself drafted the FA's first set of playing laws, but several meetings were held before there was agreement, and 'hacking' was forbidden. The FA's early influence was confined largely to the London area, but its motives and ambitions were honourably based and its authority grew steadily. Morley's strong handwriting can be seen in the first minute book which is still in the possession of the FA. Morley was secretary of the FA for three years (1863–6), and as its second president (1867–74) he was the first man to present the FA cup in 1872. He was a principal guest at the FA's golden jubilee dinner in 1913. His wife, Frances (*b.* 1837/8), had died on 15 August 1911, and Morley himself died of pneumonia at his Barnes home on 20 November 1924—eighteen months after the opening of Wembley stadium—at the age of ninety-three. He was buried in Barnes old cemetery five days later.

BRYON BUTLER

Sources council reports, Surrey county RO · *Richmond and Twickenham Times* (Nov 1924) · *Richmond Herald* (22 Nov 1924) · *Barnes and Mortlake History Society Newsletter*, 63 (Dec 1977), 11 · private information (2004) [Law Society] · *Kelly's directory of Surrey* (1909); (1913) · G. Green, *The history of the Football Association* (1953) · W. Pickford, *A few recollections of sport* (1938) · *Bell's Life* (March 1863) · *Bell's Life* (March 1864) · *The Times* (24 Nov 1924) · IGI · d. cert. · d. cert. [Frances Morley]
Wealth at death £48,994 10s. 9d.: probate, 3 Feb 1925, CGPLA Eng. & Wales

Morley, Edith Julia (1875–1964), literary scholar and suffragette, was born on 13 September 1875 at 25 Craven Hill Gardens, London, the fourth of six children of Alexander Morley (*d.* 1915), surgeon-dentist, and his wife, Leah Reyser (1840–1926). Born into a Jewish, professional household and spoiled as the only daughter, Morley professed to hate being a girl because of the extreme restrictions of Victorian convention on her personal freedom. Unusually, both parents united in their desire for her to have as full an education as her brothers. Her mother was a great ally, allowing her unrestricted access to their extensive library from an early age.

Proximity to home for ease of chaperonage was a criterion for the choice of Edith Morley's English education, with five years, from 1880, at a local kindergarten, followed by four years at Doreck College in Kensington. From 1889 she attended a finishing school in Hanover, the principal being a friend of her mother's, where she became fluent in German and French. On her return in 1892, the question of continuing her education in the year before she 'came out' led to her studying at King's College women's department, University of London, in Kensington—again, her mother's choice. From 1894 the new principal, Lilian Faithfull, a Somerville scholar, developed the women's department and nurtured Morley, with fellow student and friend Caroline Spurgeon, to read for the Oxford honour school of English language and literature. Two of the first three students of the department to study a degree course, they were both placed in the first class of the English honour school at Oxford in 1899.

Attending lectures at University College, London, during the last two years of her course, Morley gained inspiration from the teaching of Professor W. P. Ker. A bar on women matriculating at King's when she began her studies denied her a degree when she took her London final examinations in June 1899. She was offered and accepted the associateship of King's College, the only letters after her name despite seven years of arduous study. Subsequently, King's College for Women honoured her with a fellowship of the college, and in 1926 she was granted an Oxford honorary MA degree.

Morley overcame her parents' reservations about her career and, remaining single, taught at King's women's department with a class in Germanic philology. She was to remain there, teaching English literature, until the department was subsumed into the main college in 1914. In 1902 she had also accepted a post as an assistant lecturer in English, with some German teaching, at Reading College. Her enthusiastic commitment to working with the newly established Workers' Educational Association was a reflection of her social and political concerns.

After working as a lecturer in English language and literature from 1903 to 1907 at Reading, Morley experienced the prejudice faced by women which she had always struggled against. In summer 1907 the college prepared for university status by awarding professorships to all heads of departments, except Edith Morley. Refusing to accept such overt discrimination, she tendered her resignation, which was refused. As a feminist, she then began a battle for her rights, which she saw herself fighting for all professional women. In October 1908 she was awarded her professorship, becoming the first woman professor at a British university or university college. Nevertheless, the university succeeded in diminishing her achievement by awarding her a chair in English language, when literature was her main discipline. With literature given to a male professor, her chair ceased with her retirement. She was also denied a male assistant; the authorities recorded that no male academic could be expected to work under a woman.

The experience of the college parliament at King's encouraged Morley's interest in politics, and at Reading her concern for the suffrage issue led to her becoming a suffragette, joining the Women's Social and Political Union. With characteristic modesty she underplayed her contribution, but, nevertheless, had her goods seized and sold at auction for refusal to pay her rates as part of the tax resistance campaign. She also participated in the 'No votes, no census' campaign of 2 April 1911 (spending the night walking with Dr Elizabeth Garrett Anderson), marched in London demonstrations, and was asked by Mrs Pankhurst to use her title to sign a letter to *The Times*, to aid publication.

In 1908, deserting her family's adherence to the Conservative Party and becoming a socialist, Morley joined the Fabian Society. In 1911 she began work on *Women Workers in Seven Professions* (1914). During this, and as a member of the Fabian executive, she worked with such pioneer women as Mrs Pember Reeves, Letitia Fairfield, and Susan Lawrence. Her dedication to active citizenship was demonstrated in her work with organizations such as the British Federation of University Women, of which she was an original member of the London association, formed in 1909. She also undertook work at St Helen's Settlement in Stratford-at-Bow. In the 1930s she helped to establish the Reading branch of the Townswomen's Guilds, which educated women in their rights and responsibilities as citizens. A member of the Howard League for Penal Reform, she found her duties as a magistrate, which she took up in 1934, 'of absorbing interest', and was later chair of the Reading probation committee.

During the First World War, Morley worked for the National Council of Women's Voluntary Patrols, the forerunner to women police, gave talks for the Ministry of Food, and assisted Belgian refugees. But it was her work for refugees during the Second World War which gained her an OBE in 1950. In 1938 she had set up the Reading Refugee Committee, and her empathetic understanding of the refugees' horrific experiences led her to condemn the ignorance and prejudice demonstrated by presidents of refugee tribunals and to decry the conditions of internment camps. Sir Arthur Racker said of her that she 'fought not only with courage but sometimes aggression and always with passionate sincerity for Human Rights and freedom' (*Reading Standard*, 24 Jan 1964).

The focus of Morley's research and publications is best shown in her editing of the three-volume *Henry Crabb Robinson on Books and their Writers* (1938). However, *Women Workers in Seven Professions*, which she edited for the studies committee of the Fabian women's group, is still referenced by historians. Part of a six-year investigation into women's economic position, many of the contributors were, like Morley, former suffrage campaigners. Examining the major professions open to women, such as teaching, the civil service, medicine, and acting, Morley concluded optimistically that status and recognition were gradually being accorded to professional women who had chosen freedom above parasitism and dependence.

Despite the professional affronts inflicted on Morley by the male establishment, the University of Reading recognized her contribution to the corporate life of the college and her teaching excellence. Her great interest in promoting the success of her female students reflected her passionate belief that young women should enjoy the intellectual, social, and professional freedoms for which she had fought throughout her life. As a result of the physical restraints of her own Victorian childhood, she relished the freedom which sport and outdoor pursuits, such as hockey, cycling, and rowing, provided. Edith Morley died at her home, 96 Kendrick Road, Reading, on 18 January 1964, after a long and crippling illness, which colleagues and friends remarked that she had endured with her customary fortitude. She was cremated at a private service at Reading crematorium on 22 January.   CHERYL LAW

Sources E. J. Morley, 'Looking before and after: reminiscences of a working life', U. Reading, E. J. Morley MSS • *The Times* (21 Jan 1964) • *Reading Standard* (24 Jan 1964) • *Reading Mercury* (25 Jan 1964) • *University of Reading Calendar* (1902–3) • *University of Reading Calendar* (1908–9) • *CGPLA Eng. & Wales* (1964)
Archives U. Reading, reminiscences, incl. unpublished autobiography and corresp. relating to battle for professorship
Likenesses photograph, c.1893, U. Reading, E. J. Morley MSS • photograph (in later years), U. Reading, E. J. Morley MSS

Wealth at death £41,544: probate, 17 April 1964, *CGPLA Eng. & Wales*

Morley, Eric Douglas (1918–2000), impresario, was born at 13 Macklin Street, London, on 26 September 1918, the son of William Joseph Morley, hotel chef, and Bertha Emily, *née* Menzies.

Inclined to hyperbole, Morley claimed that his father had been at Oxford and spoke nine languages. What is more certain is that his father died when the boy was two, and his mother then married a sergeant-major. Both of them had died of tuberculosis before he was twelve. He had been educated in St Martin-in-the-Fields and at Whitstable grammar school, but after his parents' death was sent by the London county council to the Royal Naval training ship *HMS Exmouth*, where he showed an early flair for business by splitting bars of toffee into forty squares and selling them on credit to fellow trainees. At fourteen he switched to the Royal Fusiliers as a bandboy, continuing to play the French horn for relaxation for the rest of his life. He claimed to have been promoted from private to sergeant in six weeks. In Norway after the war he took over when the sports and entertainments officer was ill.

Demobbed in 1946 as Captain Morley RASC (motor boats), he remembered himself as an acting major and joined Mecca, the dance hall and entertainments group then run by Carl Heimann and Alan Fairley, who paid him £15 a week to take charge of publicity. He proved to be an inspired choice. In 1949, with the co-operation of the BBC, he began the ballroom dancing competition *Come Dancing*, which became the world's longest-running television series; and when he heard that an international beauty contest for the Festival of Britain (1951) was being mooted as a relief from the austerity of post-war Britain, he saw himself as the ideal man to handle the publicity, a view which was widely shared. He was soon in charge of the whole operation. It was initially a one-off event, but when the Americans launched a 'Miss Universe' competition in 1952, Morley persuaded Mecca to make 'Miss World' an annual event, which was held every November in the Royal Albert Hall, and televised from 1959. Morley managed the event, presented the pageant, and acted as agent for the winners. His book, *Miss World Story*, was published in 1967. On 13 August 1960 he married fashion model Julia Evelyn Pritchard (*b.* 1939/40); they had four sons and adopted a daughter who died in 1985.

Morley's rise through various positions at Mecca was steady. In 1969 he became managing director and also a director of Grand Metropolitan Hotels, a company which took over Mecca the following year, when Morley became joint chairman and managing director of Mecca. In the following year he was made sole chairman and managing director, which better suited his autocratic style.

Morley stood, unsuccessfully, as a Conservative candidate for parliament at Dulwich in 1974 and in 1979; he was a Thatcherite, and in 1979 slashed the former Labour minister Sam Silkin's majority to 122.

The Miss World contest had its share of problems. The pageant at the Royal Albert Hall in 1970, compèred by Bob Hope, was disrupted by flour-bomb-wielding feminists, in

Eric Douglas Morley (1918–2000), by Stephen Markeson

one of the first demonstrations by the British women's liberation movement. Marjorie Wallace, the Miss World of 1974, was adjudged to have spent too much time enjoying herself with the footballer George Best and the singer Tom Jones rather than attending to her Miss World duties, and was stripped of her title. In 1980 it turned out that the German winner had starred in pornographic films and was the partner of the man who had produced them. There was more bad publicity when Morley was revealed to have had a ten-year affair with a younger woman, not a contestant. He explained that he made it a rigid principle not to mix work with pleasure. His formidable wife, Julia, worked closely with him in organizing the contest and took over the day-to-day running in the 1970s.

Despite increasing criticism by feminist groups, who saw beauty contests as injurious to the dignity of women, and by critics, who tended to see the contests as merely tacky, the Miss World contest was broadcast by the BBC until 1979, after which Thames Television transmitted it from 1980 to 1988. By this time, however, audiences in Britain had fallen from the 1968 peak of 27.5 million to 12.5 million and no other terrestrial broadcaster was willing to face the growing opposition until the newly established Channel 5 took it up in 1999. In 1997, now as chairman of Miss World Ltd, having long parted company from Mecca, Morley claimed that the pageant had an audience of over 2.5 billion in 155 countries. The attempts made to suggest that contestants were judged not only on beauty but also on deeper matters—in 1989 contestants were told to wear cosmetics made without cruelty to animals and asked questions about the ozone layer—were not convincing to everyone, despite Julia Morley's coining of the new slogan, 'Beauty with a Purpose'.

Eric Morley had other ventures, including introducing

commercial bingo to Britain in 1961, entering betting and gaming, and, in a misplaced attempt to placate his feminist critics, introducing the Mr World contest in 1996. He also helped raise millions for charity as, from 1977, the first British president for fifty years of Variety Clubs International. But his stocky frame, pugnacious face, and swept-back coal-black hair will be most associated with the Miss World contest, seen by millions of people worldwide through link-ups—an audience that comfortably viewed the objectors as humourless prudes. He died on 9 November 2000 in London, survived by his wife and sons.

DENNIS BARKER

Sources personal knowledge (2004) · *Daily Telegraph* (10 Nov 2000) · *The Times* (10 Nov 2000) · D. Barker, *The Guardian* (10 Nov 2000) · A. Hayward, *The Independent* (10 Nov 2000) · b. cert. · m. cert.

Likenesses photograph, 1965, Hult. Arch. · group photograph, 1975, Hult. Arch. · S. Markeson, photograph, News International Syndication, London [*see illus.*]

Morley, George (1598?–1684), bishop of Winchester, was born in Cheapside, London, probably on 27 February 1598, and was baptized at St Matthew's, Friday Street, on 5 March, the eldest son of Francis Morley (*d. c.*1604) and his wife, Sarah Denham (*d. c.*1610). His parents were of gentle stock—his mother's brother was the judge Sir John Denham—but Francis Morley sank into debt and by the age of thirteen George was an orphan. Nevertheless he was admitted king's scholar at Westminster School in 1611 and entered Christ Church, Oxford, in 1615. At Christ Church, Morley's tutor was John Wall; having matriculated on 17 December 1618, he graduated BA two days later and proceeded MA in June 1621.

Early career and social circle Most of what is known of Morley's career in the Oxford of the 1620s and 1630s stems from his portrait in the memoirs of his friend Edward Hyde, later earl of Clarendon, and from the biography by Anthony Wood in his *Athenae Oxonienses*. Hyde judged Morley a man 'of eminent parts in all polite learning, of great wit, readiness and subtlety in disputation, and of remarkable temper and prudence in conversation' (Hyde, *Life*, 1.46). Morley moved in the same college and university circles as Gilbert Sheldon, Henry Hammond, Robert Payne, Robert Sanderson, William Chillingworth, and Lucius Cary, Viscount Falkland. The poet Edmund Waller was a distant relation of Morley's and it is possible that he obtained the young clergyman's initial introduction to Falkland's circle. Clarendon's portrait of the conversation and meetings at Falkland's house at Great Tew evokes a liberal and cultivated milieu in which the witty Morley was at home. One famous piece of repartee has been persistently attributed to Morley: when asked what the Arminians held, he replied that they held all the best bishoprics and deaneries in England. There is no evidence of his relationship with the Arminian Archbishop Laud, but his Calvinist theological views, his worldliness, and his wide circle of friends, including Arthur Goodwin and John Hampden, left him slightly outside the Laudian élite of Charles I's church. Wood states that he was chaplain to Robert Dormer, earl of Carnarvon, until he was forty-

George Morley (1598?–1684), by Sir Peter Lely, *c.*1660–62

three, which would be about 1640 or 1641, when he was presented to the sinecure rectory of Hartfield in Sussex. Edward Hyde may well have been promoting his cause because in 1641 Morley was appointed a royal chaplain and made a canon of Christ Church. He also exchanged his sinecure with Dr Richard Stewart for the rectory of Mildenhall in Wiltshire.

Royalist in England and in exile, 1642–1660 As the political crisis of the early 1640s worsened Morley's royalism came to the fore. When he preached before the Commons in 1642 the house did not make the customary request for the sermon's publication. Although appointed to the Westminster assembly of divines he never attended. Morley was almost certainly in Oxford during the civil war. In 1645 he was a royalist delegate to the Uxbridge peace negotiations. He attended Charles I as chaplain at Newmarket in the summer of 1647. In the same year he served on the committee appointed by the University of Oxford to resist the parliamentary visitation and was charged with selecting legal counsel to represent the heads of houses. When deprived of his canonry he resisted. Wood claimed that he refused an offer to retain his place if he abstained from opposition to the visitors and that he suffered a short period of imprisonment. He was finally ejected in the spring of 1648 and he remarked in a letter to Bulstrode Whitelocke that 'seeing I could not keep it with a good conscience, I thank God it doth not trouble me at all' (Whitelocke, 2.149–50). Wood stated that Morley took part in the Newport negotiations in the autumn of 1648. In March 1649 he attended his friend Arthur Capel, Lord

Capel, after his condemnation for royalist plotting and accompanied him to the foot of the scaffold. Then, says Wood, he quit the country resolved never to return until king and church were restored. Morley later claimed that he took all he had—a total of £130—with him. The House of Lords had already given him a pass to go abroad dated 25 January 1648.

Morley went to the court of Charles II at St Germain and then moved among the royalist exile community for several months. In November 1649 he was officiating in Sir Richard Browne's chapel in Paris. He followed Charles II to Breda and preached before him on the eve of his departure for Scotland. He then served as chaplain to Lady Ormond at Caen before arriving at Sir Edward Hyde's household in Antwerp in November 1650. He travelled so incessantly that some of the details of his movements may have become confused. He was based at The Hague, but also spent three or four years in Hyde's house at Antwerp and that is the address on most of his letters of 1652 and 1653 written under the pseudonym Jasper Gower to friends in England like Gilbert Sheldon. He moved around this corner of northern Europe tending to the spiritual needs of various royalists, especially ladies like Frances, Lady Hyde, Elizabeth, Lady Thynne, and Elizabeth, queen of Bohemia, and he followed Charles's court—to Düsseldorf, for example, in October 1654. He made the acquaintance of leading scholars such as Rivetus, Heinsius, and Salmasius, and he tangled with Roman Catholic priests. On paying a visit to the Jesuits' college in Brussels on 23 June 1650 Morley and Dr Creighton were drawn into a debate with Father Darcy about the merits of their respective churches. Morley was later adamant that while in exile he remained faithful to the Church of England, constantly used its prayer book, and did not attend reformed services.

As the protectorate regime began to collapse in the late 1650s, Morley became one of the most important conduits of information between the exiles and their Anglican royalist sympathizers in England. According to Richard Baxter, for instance, in 1659 the royalist gentry of Worcestershire were being told by Henry Hammond on Morley's authority that a moderate religious settlement with only the most vestigial form of episcopacy was acceptable to the king. In April 1660 Morley was sent to England by Hyde so that he, Barwick 'and other discreet men of the clergy should enter into conversation and have frequent conference with those of the presbyterian party' (Barwick, 525). Morley was to reassure them, to rebut claims that Charles II was a Roman Catholic, and even to tempt them with the prospect of preferment. He was also to allay 'the too much Heat and Distemper' of some of our friends. He reported back that his discussions with Edward Reynolds, Edmund Calamy, and the earl of Manchester had gone well, not least because they perceived him as 'somewhat more moderate than others of our clergy'. On the central issue of whether ordinations received during the 1650s from presbyterian classes rather than bishops were to be valid, Morley proposed 'two expedients': either the question could be simply ignored or there could be a 'hypothetical re-ordination by Bishops' which would regard the first orders not as 'nullities but only irregular and uncertain' (Hyde, *State papers*, 3.727, 738). It is not unfair to say that Morley's powers of persuasion were one of the keys to reconciling the leaders of the presbyterian party to the restoration of the monarchy and some form of national church.

Restoration triumph and the see of Worcester, 1660–1662 In the first years of the Restoration, Morley was everywhere. He was in Oxford, and there he regained his canonry at Christ Church. Long promised the deanery, and greeted by a cavalcade of over eighty horsemen and cheering crowds, he was installed in that office on 26 July 1660. He was also to be found at court exercising his characteristic diplomacy. In October 1660 he was required to interview Anne Hyde, duchess of York, about the legitimacy of her new-born son. Along with Humphrey Henchman, Morley represented the episcopalian interest at the Worcester House discussions which fleshed out the plan for a comprehensive church settlement. He wrote enthusiastically to friends in Scotland about the broad church which was emerging. On 28 October he was consecrated as the bishop of Worcester alongside four other new bishops, Sheldon, Sanderson, Henchman, and George Griffith. Morley was also dean of the Chapel Royal and preached at Charles II's coronation on 23 April 1661, when he remarked that Charles had been marked out by heaven and providence and that one good prince could do more than many preachers for the public reformation of church and state. It was published as *A Sermon Preached at the Coronation* the same year.

In the following May Morley was the prime manager for the episcopalian party at the Savoy conference. Here he began to shed the conciliatory guise which had served him so well in previous negotiations with the presbyterians. This also marked a deterioration in his relationship with their spokesman, Richard Baxter. Baxter, upon whose testimony historians depend so heavily for the details of religious negotiations in this period, developed a personal animosity towards Morley. This had its roots in Morley's refusal to license Baxter to preach in the diocese of Worcester. Baxter had served in the Worcestershire parish of Kidderminster in the 1650s but lost the living when its previous incumbent was restored in 1661. What Baxter resented was Morley's part in preventing him from maintaining any relationship with his previous flock: not only was he barred from any kind of preaching in the diocese, but Bishop Morley himself preached in the parish 'a long Invective against them [the parishioners], and me, as Presbyterians' (*Reliquiae Baxterianae*, 2.376). Baxter responded by publishing an attack on Morley and he replied with *The bishop of Worcester's letter to a friend in vindication of himself from Mr Baxter's calumny* (January 1662) which dwelt upon Baxter's disruptive part in the Savoy conference and upon the dangerous opinions contained in his *Holy Commonwealth* (1659). Morley had arrived in his diocese in September 1661, when he was 'solemnly brought into Worcester by my Lord Windsor, Lord Lieutenant of the County, and most of the gentry and all the clergy' and the militia and trained bands (Bosher, 234).

Bishop of Winchester and the imposition of uniformity, 1662–1667 In May 1662, however, Morley was translated to the wealthy see of Winchester. He was in his diocese as the Act of Uniformity came into force. His first visitation began at Winchester with 'all the considerable men of the county' on 26 August and lasted until 27 September. His own account described how he confirmed 300 in Romsey, 600 in Southampton, and 'neere a 1000 of all sorts, and amongst them all the Gentry male and female young and old' of the Isle of Wight. In his charge at each place Morley 'did … invite those that had not or would not subscribe to come and speak with me, professing that if they would yet conforme, they should find me as ready to receive and encourage them, as any other of the clergy that had never offended in that kind' (Bodl. Oxf., MS Clarendon 73, fols. 216–17). Morley estimated that only twelve clergy in the whole diocese would refuse to conform and he wanted to 'give them some time' (ibid.), but eventually nearly fifty ministers were ejected. His letters to Clarendon encouraged the chancellor to resist all attempts to dilute the Act of Uniformity and while recognizing that some of the metropolitan presbyterian leadership might have a claim to some indulgence on the strength of their role in the Restoration, Morley was adamant that there could be no compromise with the dissident ministers of the shires.

Morley was soon back in the capital. On Christmas day 1662 he preached at Whitehall. Pepys thought it a poor sermon, 'but long and reprehending the mistaken jollity of the court … perticularized concerning their excess in playes and gameing'—yet he was dismayed to hear the bishop laughed at for his pains (Pepys, 3.292–3). Although generous and charitable Morley had a serious frame of mind and austere personal habits. He rose at 5 a.m. every day, eschewed a fire on winter mornings, and ate only once a day. He had many responsibilities beyond his diocese. He was appointed a governor of the Charterhouse in May 1663. As bishop of Winchester he was *ex officio* prelate to the Order of the Garter and visitor to five Oxford colleges. In 1664 he visited all five colleges and took corrective action at only one, Corpus Christi. Politically Morley remained close both to Clarendon and to Archbishop Sheldon and the church party who promoted punitive legislation against the nonconformists. During the debate on the Five Mile Act at the Oxford session of parliament in October 1665 Morley spoke passionately against the nonconformists and the religious and political dangers posed by conventicles. The bill, he claimed, 'doth but send them where they shall doe noe hurt to themselves nor others'. He was particularly suspicious of their refusal to renounce the solemn league and covenant: 'here they sticke. They will not say they will renounce the last Warr, and they will forestall another' (Robbins, 223–4). He returned to the subject in a sermon, published in 1683 as *A Sermon Preached before the King at White-Hall … Novemb 5 1667*, when he proclaimed it 'the peculiar Glory of the Church of England' that she had declared 'without Iffs or

Ands, or any other clause, or words of exception or reservation' that it was unlawful for subjects to take up arms against the sovereign (pp. 36–7).

Morley's position could not but be damaged by the fall of Lord Chancellor Clarendon in 1667. After the impeachment was drawn up against Clarendon, Morley and Bishop Herbert Croft visited the disgraced minister to explain that the king wished him to leave the country. But soon Morley himself, like other Clarendonians such as Bishop Dolben of Rochester, was out of favour; in February 1668 Morley lost his position as dean of the Chapel Royal and withdrew from court.

Scholar and patron Morley was more than a court prelate, however. He was a significant intellectual and theological figure. His substantial library, which was catalogued in 1672 and 1682 and eventually bequeathed to Winchester Cathedral, was rich in titles relating to philosophy and science, including works by Thomas Hobbes, Descartes, Pascal, the Jansenists, and the Cambridge Platonists. Morley advised the exiled Clarendon over the composition of his *Brief View*, a reply to *Leviathan*, which was completed by 1673 and published at Oxford in 1676. Morley's patronage was extensive and eclectic. He is alleged to have helped Henry Stubbe to a medical position in Jamaica; he asked Adam Littleton to complete Bishop John Earle's translation of Richard Hooker's *Ecclesiastical Polity* into Latin; and, most famously, he supported Izaak Walton. In dedicating the 1670 edition of his *Lives* to Morley, Walton referred to 'the advantage of forty years friendship' with him. They knew each other in pre-civil war Oxford, and at the Restoration Morley was in a position to help his old friend, who served briefly as his steward at Worcester in 1661–2 and thereafter spent the rest of his life as a member of Morley's household. Walton's *Life of Robert Sanderson* (1678) was shaped by his relations with Morley as much as by his admiration for Bishop Sanderson; indeed, about 1638 Morley had introduced Walton and Sanderson, possibly at Great Tew. Many strands of Morley's life and thought can be traced back to those Oxford intellectual circles of the 1630s. The other abiding influence in his life was his Calvinism. Wood noted that 'he was a great Calvinist, and esteemed one of the main patrons of those of that persuasion' (Wood, *Ath. Oxon.*, 4.154). This is evident in his role as dedicatee, if not sponsor, of the publications by Thomas Tully and other Oxford theologians designed to refute the Arminian teachings of George Bull in the early 1670s. Both Calvinism and 1630s Oxford explain his long-lasting relationship with Thomas Barlow, Calvinist provost of the Queen's College and from 1675 bishop of Lincoln: the two men swapped papers and books throughout their long lives.

Calvinist bishop in the 1670s The early 1670s were a disheartening time for Morley and his Anglican brethren. The conversion to Catholicism and early death of Morley's former pupil Anne Hyde, duchess of York, were disquieting. The 1672 declaration of indulgence and French alliance were a blow. Remarking at the time to Sheldon on his own loyalty to the doctrine, discipline, and government of the Church of England, Morley remarked 'but perhaps I be the worse lookd upon at Court because I am soe'. Despite rumours he was neither 'a Popish Bishop' nor 'a Presbyterian Man' (Bodl. Oxf., MS Tanner 43, fols. 32–3). As he told the earl of Anglesey in July 1672, he was for the incorporation, not comprehension, of the presbyterians within the Church of England: 'I am very confident that there are no Presbyterians in the world (the Scotch only excepted) that would not conform to all that is required by our Church, as especially in such a juncture of time as this is' (Bodl. Oxf., MS Carte 69, fol. 447). After the cancellation of the indulgence in 1673 the Commons considered ways to improve the position of moderate dissenters, but Morley told Sheldon that while he could accept concessions to divide 'the Presbyterians from the rest of the Sectaries … yet I never would have consented nor ever will consent to that w[hich] they call a Comprehension' (Bodl. Oxf., MS Tanner 42, fol. 7). Such statements are significant because of Morley's continuing involvement in negotiations to win over presbyterians and moderate dissenters. In December 1673 Morley, along with Osborne and Orrery, asked Richard Baxter to prepare a scheme for comprehension. And in February 1674 Morley intervened when a proposal was made in the Commons to lift most of the oaths and subscriptions required of dissenters; Morley forced this bill's withdrawal and promoted another in the Lords which eleven other bishops opposed. He encouraged and then scuppered another round of negotiations with dissenters in the following winter. As Richard Baxter is reported to have remarked when told that Morley was involved, 'then it will come to nothing if he, that is the B[isho]p of Winchester, be concerned in it' (DWL, Morrice Entring Book P, fol. 359).

Morley was no unreflective conservative. He was always ready to consider reform of the church. As parliament assembled in January 1674, for example, he had Francis Turner write to William Sancroft for proposals for 'restoring our discipline and maintaining our doctrine. The canons of [16]40 against the Socinians are desird to be reinforct, and many Expedients are in the minds of our Governors to the reformacion of Abuses.' Altruism was not Morley's only motive: 'that good old Lord is very full of Church-affaires to do som[e]w[ha]t, if it be possible for the removing of the unsupportable clamor of the people against the Bishops' (Bodl. Oxf., MS Tanner 42, fol. 75). When the earl of Danby initiated the court's new policy of pandering to the 'church and cavalier' interest in October 1674, his first step was to visit Bishop Morley at Farnham Castle. He told Morley that the king wished the bishops to meet and propose 'some things that might unite and best pacify the minds of people' for the next meeting of parliament (Bodl. Oxf., MS Carte 72, fol. 229). Morley played an important role in the meetings of the bishops over that winter which produced a plan of general moral and religious reform, aimed equally at profanity, popery, and nonconformity. He subsequently made a bold defence of Danby's proposed test oath in parliament in 1675, and is alleged to have claimed that before Calvin's time there were no Christian churches that lacked bishops.

Last years and legacy Little came of all these initiatives, and meanwhile Morley, like other leaders of the church, was ageing; but he kept a watchful eye on developments. He was delighted by the protestant marriage of Princess Mary and William of Orange in 1677 and hoped that popular sentiment and parliamentary pressure would restrain pro-French and pro-Catholic tendencies at court. He backed Bishop Henry Compton of London as a suitable successor to Archbishop Sheldon and also thought highly of Bishop Seth Ward of Salisbury as a potential primate. Morley himself was now blind in one eye, but piously hoped for more such afflictions since they were spiritually beneficial. The political prospects for the Church of England continued to deteriorate. In February 1679 Charles sent Morley and Sancroft to the duke of York in a forlorn attempt to reclaim him for the Church of England from popery. At the same time, noted Morley, the bishops were regarded with 'an Evill Eye' by the people (Bodl. Oxf., MS Tanner 38, fol. 20). In 1679 Morley withdrew from court. In July he described himself as old and ailing while sending Sancroft what he foretold would be his last gift of venison from Hampshire. He had left the 'encumbrance and noise of all Secular Affairs' to live in the country at Farnham Castle and prepare 'for a quiet and comfortable Exit out of this … World'—a statement which would have been more convincing if it had not been made in the *Several Treatises, Written upon Several Occasions*, also known as *The Vindication*, that he published in 1683 to rebut allegations recently renewed by that other long-lived controversialist, Richard Baxter (*The Bishop of Winchester's Vindication*, 1683, sig. a3). In 1681 Morley published a defence of his dealings with Anne, duchess of York, to counter allegations that he had undermined her protestantism. Even in semi-retirement he continued to write letters and recommend protégés and to worry over the dangers faced by the Church of England. In the summer of 1684 Morley ordered John Foster, curate of a Hampshire chapelry, to desist from daily prayer and weekly celebration of the sacrament until he had received a ruling from the archbishop for fear that 'it may grow to a schisme in the orthodoxe and conformable party of the church' (Bodl. Oxf., MS Tanner 32, fols. 80, 106). On 29 October 1684 Morley died, unmarried, at Farnham Castle; he was buried in Winchester Cathedral.

Morley was a generous benefactor: he spent £4000 purchasing Winchester House in Chelsea as an episcopal residence, £8000 on remodelling Farnham Castle, and he rebuilt Wolvesey House. He gave generously to Christ Church and Pembroke College, Oxford, to Chelsea Hospital, and to the 'college' for widows of clergy at Winchester Cathedral. His reputation suffered thanks to his dealings with the nonconformists. His name was still mud among moderate dissenters and a warning against trusting the Anglicans in James II's reign. 'It is well remembered that Dr Morley gave as fair words and made as many promises' to presbyterian leaders in 1660, remarked Roger Morrice in October 1687, 'and yet he tooke vengiance upon them when he had power, and turned them all out, and was also false to them in all his negotiations with them' (DWL, Morrice Entring Book Q, fol. 176).

But his contribution to the Church of England cannot be denied. He was a tireless figure and offered the church leadership for several decades, perhaps most significantly at the Restoration and again in the mid-1670s when Sheldon's energy seemed to flag. He was a staunch Calvinist and yet an unwavering defender of the episcopacy and liturgy of the Church of England.   JOHN SPURR

Sources BL, Add. MS 17017; Harley MS 6942 · Bodl. Oxf., MSS Tanner; MSS Clarendon 71, 72, 73; MS Carte 69; MS Tanner 40, fols. 74, 102 · R. Morrice, 'Ent'ring book', DWL, Morrice MS P–Q [vols. 1–2] · D. Novarr, *The making of Walton's 'Lives'* (Ithaca, NY, 1958) · R. S. Bosher, *The making of the Restoration settlement: the influence of the Laudians, 1649–1662* (1951); rev. edn (1957) · J. Spurr, 'The Church of England, comprehension and the Toleration Act of 1689', *EngHR*, 104 (1989), 927–46 · C. Robbins, 'The Oxford session of the Long Parliament of Charles II, 9–31 October, 1665', *BIHR*, 21 (1948), 214–24 · J. C. Hayward, 'New directions in studies of the Falkland circle', *The Seventeenth Century*, 2 (1987) · *Calendar of the correspondence of Richard Baxter*, ed. N. H. Keeble and G. F. Nuttall, 2 vols. (1991) · *Walker rev.* · *Hist. U. Oxf.* 4: *17th-cent. Oxf.* · Wood, *Ath. Oxon.*, new edn, 4.149–58 · Wood, *Ath. Oxon.: Fasti*, new edn · Foster, *Alum. Oxon.* · W. Kennett, *A register and chronicle ecclesiastical and civil* (1728) · *Fasti Angl.* (Hardy) · Evelyn, *Diary* · Pepys, *Diary* · B. Whitelocke, *Memorials of English affairs*, new edn, 4 vols. (1853) · R. Scrope and T. Monkhouse, eds., *State papers collected by Edward, earl of Clarendon*, 3 vols. (1767–86) · E. Hyde, earl of Clarendon, *Life* (1843) · E. Hyde, earl of Clarendon, *The history of the rebellion and civil wars in England*, new edn (1843) · P. Barwick, *The life of Dr John Barwick* (1724) · *Reliquiae Baxterianae, or, Mr Richard Baxter's narrative of the most memorable passages of his life and times*, ed. M. Sylvester, 1 vol. in 3 pts (1696) · G. B. Tatham, *The puritans in power* (1913) · *Burnet's History of my own time*, ed. O. Airy, new edn, 2 vols. (1897–1900) · I. M. Green, *The re-establishment of the Church of England, 1660–1663* (1978) · *The poetical works of Edmund Waller*, 2 vols. (1777), vol. 1, pp. viii–ix · R. Ollard, *Clarendon and his friends* (1987) · A. M. Coleby, *Central government and the localities: Hampshire, 1649–1689* (1987) · IGI

Archives Bodl. Oxf., letters and MSS · New College, Oxford, letters · Portsmouth Museums and Records Service, accounts of repairs to episcopal properties, donations to charities, and letter to earl of Clarendon | BL, corresp. with H. P. De Cressey, Add. MS 21630 · NRA, priv. coll., letters to Sir Charles Cottrell · Worcs. RO, corresp. with Lady Pakington

Likenesses P. Lely, oils, *c.*1660–1662, Christ Church Oxf. [*see illus.*] · studio of P. Lely, oils, *c.*1662, NPG · S. Cooper, 1667, Walters Art Gallery, Baltimore · P. Lely, oils, second version, Rousham House, Oxfordshire · E. Luttrell?, chalk drawing (after Lely?), NPG; repro. in Ollard, *Clarendon* · portrait, Farnham Castle, Surrey · portrait, Oriel College, Oxford · portrait, Pembroke College, Oxford · portrait, Charterhouse

Morley, Harbert [Herbert] (*bap.* **1616**, *d.* **1667**), politician and parliamentarian army officer, was baptized on 2 April 1616, the eldest son of Robert Morley (*c.*1577–1632) of Glynde in Sussex, and his wife, Susan (*d.* 1667), daughter of Thomas Hodgson of Framfield in the same county. His family was prominent during the late sixteenth and early seventeenth centuries, both in local administration, and 'godly' circles, and Morley received a puritan education at Southover School, Emmanuel College, Cambridge (1632), and the Inner Temple (1634), as well as under the guidance of his guardian, Sir Thomas Pelham.

Morley was first elected to parliament in a by-election at Lewes in the Short Parliament (1640), and he was then elected to the Long Parliament, where he soon emerged as an advocate of 'further reformation' of the church, and in

taking action against prominent courtiers. He was prominent enough to be involved in plans to draft parliament's demands to the king, and to be named to the 'recess' committee in September 1641. In the wake of news of the uprising in Ireland, Morley participated in measures to deal with the rebels and with Catholics in general, and in organizing the military response and the relief of Ireland's protestants. As tension rose in late 1641 Morley was involved in considering the controversial business of providing a guard for parliament, and he was subsequently nominated to investigate the attempt to arrest the five members in January 1642. During the following spring he was also appointed to committees regarding the demand for parliamentary control over the militia, and to consider the numerous messages between king and parliament during the 'paper war'.

Although county affairs clearly occupied a larger amount of his time in the early summer of 1642, Morley was active at Westminster in pressing for vigorous pursuit of the war effort after the outbreak of the civil war, and by the end of the year he had been commissioned colonel of a troop of harquebusiers. He remained in the army until the creation of the New Model in 1645, and during this period his activity at Westminster was dominated by practical matters relating to the local war effort and to Sussex affairs. His military exploits at Chichester, Winchester, Southampton, and Arundel, and at the prolonged siege at Basing House in 1644, earned him a reputation for valour, while his activity in the county, as the most powerful member of the county committee, led to his being singled out by royalists, as 'the crooked rebel of Sussex' (*Mercurius Rusticus*, 1685, 161), and as one of the 'principle sticklers in the county' (*Mercurius Aulicus*, 27, 2–8 July 1643, 352). His prominence in the region probably explains his inclusion on a list, compiled for Charles I in June 1644, of those who were to be indicted for treason.

By the summer of 1643 Morley was clearly aligned at Westminster with radical members of the Commons such as Henry Marten and Cornelius Holland, and was prepared to resist John Pym and his allies on certain measures, and to display his suspicions regarding the loyalty of parliamentarian grandees such as the earl of Northumberland. Morley gradually became more involved in matters of military strategy, and was involved in plans for the self-denying ordinance, and the creation of the New Model Army in late 1644. With the reorganization of the parliamentarian army, and the surrendering of his own commission, Morley devoted his efforts to civilian activity in support of the cause, both at Westminster and in the county, where he developed a considerable power base built around friends and kinsmen, both inside and outside parliament.

After the end of the first civil war Morley emerged as a prominent political and religious Independent, concerned with religious reform, control of the London militia, opposition to the Scots, and securing the person of the king. He joined those Independents who fled to the army after the 'forcing of the Houses' (26 July 1647), signed their declaration of protest, and returned to parliament only under the army's protection in early August. Thereafter he sought to distance himself from both those 'royal Independents' who supported a negotiated settlement with the king, and the radical army faction whose rise posed a threat to civilian government. In the debates over the move to make 'no further addresses' to Charles I (3 January 1648), Morley was reported to have been one of the 'four principal firemen' who made speeches against the king (*Mercurius Pragmaticus*, 17, 4–11 Jan 1648, sig. Rv) and in April 1648 he sided with those radicals who refused to commit themselves to maintaining the monarchical constitution. After assisting the defence of Sussex during the second civil war, Morley continued to resist plans for a negotiated settlement with the king.

Morley played a less prominent part in parliamentary business in the second half of 1648. He may have been partly distracted by personal matters, as on 27 October he married Mary (d. 1656), daughter of Sir John Trevor of Trefalun in Denbighshire. They had several children. But he was also perhaps alienated by both the growing threat from the army and the renewal of peace negotiations. Nevertheless he remained in the Commons after Pride's Purge in December, and was an obvious choice to be a commissioner for the trial of Charles I. However, he attended only three of their meetings in the painted chamber (12, 15, and 18 January), stayed away from the sessions of the trial itself, and declined to sign the death warrant. He continued to sit in the Rump, however, though he may have supported the retention of the House of Lords, and though his appearances were relatively rare for much of the year. Nevertheless he was elected to the council of state in February 1650, took the engagement, and was awarded lodgings in Somerset House. His most important allies during this period appear to have been leading civilian republicans such as Henry Marten, Thomas Chaloner, Luke Robinson, and Lord Grey of Groby, and his influence was enhanced by his ability to muster his own caucus of Sussex members. After being removed from the council of state in February 1651 Morley once again withdrew from a prominent place at Westminster, but he remained faithful to the Rump, and late in the year resisted Cromwell's plans to set a deadline by which parliament should be dissolved, and he was not only returned to the council on a wave of republican enthusiasm after the battle of Worcester, but was able to retain his place in elections held in November 1652. Although less prominent during the last weeks of the Rump, Morley was present at the dissolution on 19 April 1653, a move which he almost certainly opposed.

Thereafter Morley consistently opposed Cromwell, and withdrew from political affairs until the elections for the first protectorate parliament in 1654, when he was returned for both Rye and as a knight of the shire. He opted to sit for Sussex, and played a prominent part in issues relating to the settlement of the government, as a firm opponent of the protectorate. After the dissolution in January 1655 rumours emerged that Morley was involved in republican plots, but he was prepared to accommodate

the new regime, and to serve in a local administrative capacity. When he returned to prominence during the elections for the 1656 parliament, however, William Goffe, the major-general responsible for, among other counties, Sussex, reported that Morley 'ruled the roost by help of the disaffected party, much to the grief of the honest party', adding that 'it was their design to have no soldier, decimator or any man that hath salary' (Thurloe, *State papers*, 5.341). Returned as a knight of the shire, Morley was barred from sitting, though he subsequently denied any part in the declaration of the excluded members, and announced his intention to 'live quietly at my own house' (ibid., 5.456, 490–91). Nevertheless he took his seat when readmitted to the Commons in early 1658, and was subsequently approached to participate in royalist plots in 1658, though both Morley and Charles II refused to work with each other. Morley sat for Sussex in the 1659 parliament, and played a part in the protracted debates in the Commons, by which the republicans sought to wreck proceedings. He returned to real prominence, however, upon the reassembly of the Rump in early May 1659, both as a member of the council of state, and a commissioned officer. Tensions soon emerged between Morley and the military, however, and his appointment as a commissioner for the army may have helped precipitate the decision to end the Rump's sittings (13 October), despite the attempt by Morley's regiment to guard the palace of Westminster.

Contemporary royalists evidently felt that Morley was now inclined towards supporting Charles II, and Viscount Mordaunt and John Evelyn both regarded him as the best hope of orchestrating a restoration in late 1659. In public Morley worked with a cabal which sought to restore the Rump, and which helped to secure Portsmouth in early December, but less obvious were his ongoing talks with royalists, and the possibility of a strategic alliance with Monck in Scotland. Morley's triumphant entry to London following the return of the Rump in December 1659 was followed by his nomination to the council of state, and his appointment as lieutenant of the Tower on 7 January 1660. Morley was disabled from sitting on the council by his refusal to take the oath adjuring the house of Stuart, but though he developed an alliance with Monck, Morley doubted the general's intentions, and evidently declined to make a stance for the king on his own. Nevertheless his relations with other republicans became strained and he was involved in discussing future constitutional arrangements, and in meetings which led to the readmission to the Commons of the secluded members in February 1660. Thereafter, as a member of the council, Morley was involved in planning forthcoming elections for the Convention Parliament, to which he himself secured election for Rye.

Morley's former radicalism, and his hesitancy in supporting Charles II, meant that he only secured a pardon with some difficulty upon the Restoration, and he received little royal favour thereafter. He was largely inactive in politics for the remainder of his life, though he offered shelter to religious nonconformists at Glynde. He retained his seat at Rye in 1661, and represented the town until his death, on 29 September 1667. One son had died before him; a daughter, Anne, and two sons, Robert and William, both of whom represented Sussex constituencies during the reign of Charles II, survived him.

J. T. PEACEY

Sources J. T. Peacey, 'Morley, Harbert', HoP, *Commons, 1690–1715* [draft] • *JHC*, 2–8 (1640–67) • *CSP dom.*, 1640–60 • C. H. Firth and R. S. Rait, eds., *Acts and ordinances of the interregnum, 1642–1660*, 3 vols. (1911) • Evelyn, *Diary* • B. Worden, *The Rump Parliament, 1648–1653* (1974) • Thurloe, *State papers* • *Diary of Thomas Burton*, ed. J. T. Rutt, 4 vols. (1828) • *The memoirs of Edmund Ludlow*, ed. C. H. Firth, 2 vols. (1894) • E. S. De Beer, 'Evelyn and Colonel Harbert Morley in 1659 and 1660', *Sussex Archaeological Collections*, 77 (1937), 177–83 • *The letter-book of John, Viscount Mordaunt, 1658–1660*, ed. M. Coate, CS, 3rd ser., 69 (1945) • J. G. Muddiman, *The trial of King Charles the First* (1928) • A. Fletcher, *A county community in peace and war: Sussex, 1600–1660* (1975)
Archives E. Sussex RO, Rye MSS

Morley, Henry (1822–1894), apothecary, journalist, and university teacher, was born at 100 Hatton Garden, London, on 15 September 1822, the younger of the two sons of Henry Morley (1793–1877), a member of the Society of Apothecaries, and his wife, Anne Jane Hicks (*d.* 1824). Morley attended private boarding-schools, where flogging was common, before being sent, aged ten, to the Moravian school at Neuwied, on the Rhine, in 1833. He later recalled these two years as the happiest of his life, discussing them in a *Household Words* article entitled 'Brother Mieth and his brothers' (*HW*, 9, 27 May 1854, 344–9), and acting as editor of the *Old Neuwieder* from 1886 until his death.

In 1835, Morley returned to a preparatory school in Stockwell, where he developed the propensity to scribble, producing poetry, plays, and a twice-weekly school newspaper. In 1838 he began medical studies at King's College, London, and, in 1841, founded the short-lived *King's College Magazine*. Graduating in 1843, he worked as a physician's assistant in Somerset, then established a partnership with another doctor in Madeley, Shropshire, but was ruined when his partner proved dishonest. Refusing to declare himself bankrupt, Morley spent the ensuing six years repaying his debts.

Determined on a new career, Morley decided to establish a school along the lines of the Moravian school. By January 1849 he was living in Manchester, where he met the Revd William Gaskell and his wife, Elizabeth Gaskell. Her cousin, Charles Holland, sought a good education for his children while keeping them at home, and Morley was employed as their tutor. By April 1849 Morley was settled at 2 Marine Terrace in Liscard, with a mixed school, girls outnumbering boys, teaching a range of ages. Two three-hour sessions were broken up by eight minutes of recreation, when pupils and teacher would run and tumble on the sands in front of the house. He refused to administer corporal punishment in any form. How revolutionary Morley's approach to teaching was, is apparent in his article 'School-keeping', published in *Household Words*, in which he wrote: 'it is only when his teaching gives great pleasure to himself that it can give any pleasure whatever to his pupils' (vol. 8, 21 Jan 1854, 499–504).

Henry Morley (1822–1894), by W. & D. Downey, pubd 1892

Meanwhile, in 1847, Morley had published two 'Tracts upon health for cottage circulation', based on his medical experiences in Somerset and, as a result, he was invited to write for the newly formed *Journal of Public Health*. His involvement in the measures taken to combat the cholera epidemic in October 1848 became the basis for two articles in 1849, at a time when over 13,000 Londoners died of cholera. The articles were noticed in *The Times* and *The Examiner*, to whose editor, John Forster, Morley wrote on 26 March 1850, offering to contribute without fee (his first leader appeared on 30 March). Soon afterwards, Morley was invited by Charles Dickens to write on sanitary matters in *Household Words*, which he did on a once weekly basis until June 1851, when Dickens offered Morley 5 guineas a week to join the staff and, although this was less than the £300 a year provided by his school, he accepted the offer. The Hollands even moved to London with him, so that he could continue teaching their children.

Morley was the only university-educated man on the staff of *Household Words*, from 1851 to 1859, and then on Dickens's second journal, *All The Year Round*, from 1859 to 1865. Morley preferred his weekly political reports, book and dramatic reviews for *The Examiner* (the latter republished in 1974) for which he received 1 guinea a week, and later served as editor from 1861 to 1867. Although Morley referred to much of his writing for *Household Words* as 'quizzical slip-slop' (quoted in Lohrli, 371), he contributed over 300 items—more than any other writer—including a controversial series of articles on factory accidents which aroused the anger of the National Association of Factory Occupiers, and provoked an impassioned response from Harriet Martineau, in a pamphlet entitled *The Factory Controversy: a Warning Against Meddling Legislation* (1855). Morley's articles included 'Ground in the mill' (*HW*, 9, 22 April 1854, 224–7), a graphic rendering of individual cases of workers (many of them children) unprotected by sufficient safety measures, and so mutilated or killed when caught up in the factories' machinery. At the same time, he also worked with Sir John Robinson on the Unitarian journal, *The Inquirer*, from 1855 to 1858, and contributed to *Fraser's*, the *Athenaeum*, the *Quarterly Review*, the *Edinburgh Review*, and other periodicals.

Once he had cleared his debts, Morley was free to marry his fiancée of nine years, Mary Anne (*d.* 1892), the daughter of Joseph Sayer, a Unitarian draper of Newport, Isle of Wight. Mary Anne's mother had initially opposed the match, in 1848 burning all of Morley's letters to her daughter. She eventually relented, however, and the couple were married on 15 April 1852; they had three daughters and two sons, and settled at 4 Upper Park Road, in Hampstead, London.

With the help of John Forster (Morley's first son was named Forster), Morley secured a commission of 100 guineas from the publisher Chapman to write the biography of Bernard Palissy, entitled *Palissy the Potter* (1852). Other biographies followed, but Morley found his true métier when invited to teach a course of evening lectures on English literature at King's College, London, in October 1857, for which he received 21 guineas. One of his earliest students was H. R. Fox Bourne, who later assumed the management of *The Examiner* for a few years. Fox Bourne remembered Morley as a chatty, witty, and humorous lecturer who often spoke *extempore*.

Morley soon became involved in the university extension movement and travelled widely for the service during the next twenty years. He also lectured on behalf of the Ladies' Educational Association, which sought university entrance for women. He became acquainted with John Churton Collins, providing him with written recommendations for various academic posts. When David Masson resigned as professor of English language and literature at University College, London, Morley submitted the first volume of his *English Writers* (1864) as his application. He became professor in December 1865 and welcomed women students, enthusiastically supporting London University's decision of 1878 to award degrees to women. A year later, in 1879, he was awarded an honorary LLD degree by the University of Edinburgh.

In abandoning daily journalism, Morley lost £700 a year and, as the professorship was unendowed, he had to rely on fees paid by his students, whose numbers increased from 52 in 1865, to 109 in 1888. He augmented his income lecturing to philosophical and debating societies, throughout the country, each of which yielded a fee of 15 guineas. He also served as principal of University Hall, a hall of residence, from 1882 until he retired in 1889, to devote more time to writing and editing, and settled in the Isle of Wight. He became a liveryman of the Society of Apothecaries in 1871 and, after retirement, served as junior, then senior, warden at Apothecaries' Hall from 1892 until his death.

Morley died on 14 May 1894 at Palissy, his home at Carisbrooke, on the Isle of Wight, and was buried in the Carisbrooke cemetery on the 17th. At the time of his death he had completed ten volumes of *English Writers* (out of a proposed series of twenty), and edited some 300 volumes of English and foreign classics, which constituted Morley's Universal Library, Cassell's National Library, and other series. As the *Dictionary of National Biography* entry recorded: 'It is as a populariser of literature that he did his countrymen the highest service'. Morley also bequeathed 8000 volumes from his library to the Hampstead Central Library, when it was established on 10 November 1897.

FRED HUNTER

Sources H. S. Solly, *The life of Henry Morley* (1898) · H. Morley, *The journal of a London playgoer, 1851–1866*, 2nd edn (1891); repr. (1974) · A. Lohrli, ed., *Household Words: a weekly journal conducted by Charles Dickens* (1973) · UCL · *Wellesley index* · H. Morley, *Early papers and some memories* (1891) · *Directions '97: a guide to services and amenities in the Camden area* (*Camden New Journal*, 1997), 4 [about Morley's library] · *The letters of Charles Dickens*, ed. M. House, G. Storey, and others, 6–10 (1988) · b. cert. · m. cert. · d. cert. · J. Sutherland, 'Journalism, scholarship, and the University College London English department', *Grub Street and the Ivory Tower: literary journalism and literary scholarship from Fielding to the internet*, ed. J. Treglown and B. Bennett (1998), 61–70

Archives BL, letters to Royal Literary Fund, Loan 96 · Dickens Fellowship Library, Doughty Street, London, letters · Hunt. L., letters · King's Lond., archives, letters · Princeton University Library, Morris L. Parrish collection of Victorian novelists, *Household Words* Office Book · UCL, letters | UCL, letters to W. J. Hiscoke · UCL, letters to G. C. Robertson

Likenesses W. & D. Downey, woodburytype, NPG; repro. in W. Downey and D. Downey, *The cabinet portrait gallery*, 3 (1892) [*see illus.*] · I. R. Morley, oils, Apothecaries' Hall, London

Wealth at death £3364 8s. 7d.: probate, 23 June 1894, *CGPLA Eng. & Wales*

Morley [*married names* Coates, Jacob], **Iris Vivienne** (1910–1953), novelist and writer on ballet, was born on 10 May 1910 in Carshalton, Surrey, the elder daughter (there were no sons) of Lieutenant-Colonel Lyddon Charteris Morley CBE (1877–1954), of the Hampshire regiment, and his wife, Gladys Vivienne Nassau Braddell. Being an army officer's daughter, Iris Morley attended a succession of schools, including the Royal School at Bath and Mannamead School, Plymouth. She studied, briefly, at the Royal Academy of Dramatic Art. On 10 January 1929, at the age of eighteen, she married Ronald Gordon Coates (*b.* 1898/9), a lieutenant in the Devonshire regiment. She was divorced in 1934, and on 2 August of the same year she married Alaric Jacob (*b.* 1908/9), the son of Lieutenant-Colonel Harold Fenton Jacob, of the Indian army. Her second husband was a journalist in whose *Scenes from a Bourgeois Life* (1949) she appears as Miranda Ireton; there was one daughter of the marriage.

Iris Morley's ancestors included George Morley, the bishop of Winchester under Charles II, and William Henry Zuylestein, first earl of Rochford. Her three novels set in late seventeenth-century England, with James Scott, duke of Monmouth, and William III as central characters—*Cry Treason* (1940), *We Stood for Freedom* (1941), and *The Mighty Years* (1943)—were widely acclaimed as being among the best historical novels of their time. Her posthumously published study of their factual background, *A Thousand Lives: the English Revolutionary Movement, 1660–1685* (1954), showed her to be an able popularizer of history. She also produced, with Paul Hogarth RA, a guide to Hampton Court Palace, near which she lived, in 1951. Of her other novels, *Nothing but Propaganda* (1946) and *Not without Fantasy* (1947), set in wartime Britain and Russia, were perhaps the most interesting. She also wrote *The Proud Paladin* (1936) and *Rack* (1952).

Iris Morley had gone to Moscow in 1943 as correspondent for *The Observer* and the *Yorkshire Post*, and from this experience wrote *Soviet Ballet* (1945), which helped to introduce contemporary Russian dancing to the British public. It was followed in 1949 by *The Rose and the Star* (with Phyllis Manchester), a comparison between Russian and British ballet. Thanks to her political views, the communist *Daily Worker* enjoyed for several years the services of a perceptive ballet critic.

Iris Morley was a woman of delicate beauty and also (despite lifelong migraine) of gracious charm. She died from cancer in Trimmers Hospital, Farnham, Surrey, on 27 July 1953.   BRIAN PEARCE, *rev.*

Sources   *The Times* (28 July 1953) · *The Times* (7 Aug 1953) · personal knowledge (1993) · private information (1993) · m. certs. · *WWW* · d. cert.

Wealth at death   £4125 19s. 9d.: probate, 5 Nov 1953, *CGPLA Eng. & Wales*

Morley, Sir James Wycliffe Headlam- (1863–1929), historian, was born at Whorlton, near Barnard Castle, co. Durham, on 24 December 1863, the second son of the Revd Arthur William Headlam (1826–1909), the vicar of Whorlton, and his wife, Agnes Sarah (d. 1871), the daughter of James Favell, of Normanton, Yorkshire. He was the nephew of Thomas Emerson Headlam, judge-advocate-general, and cousin of Walter George Headlam, scholar and poet. His elder brother, Arthur Cayley *Headlam, became bishop of Gloucester in 1923. James Headlam assumed by royal licence in 1918 the additional surname (and arms) of Morley, on inheriting the property of the last member of the West Riding family from which he was descended through the wife of his paternal grandfather.

Headlam was educated at Eton College, where he was a king's scholar, and in 1883 he entered King's College, Cambridge, where he achieved a double first in the classical tripos (1885, 1887); he went on to hold a fellowship at King's from 1890 to 1896. His fellowship dissertation, 'Election by lot at Athens', won the prince consort's prize in 1890. He went on to study in Germany, first at Göttingen and then at the University of Berlin under Heinrich Treitschke and Hans Delbrück. While in Germany he met Elizabeth Henrietta Ernestina Charlotte Sonntag (Else) (1866–1950), whom he married on 6 April 1893. The youngest child of August Sonntag, a medical doctor from Lüneburg then resident at Dresden, she was a musician, having been a

pupil of Liszt. After her marriage she concentrated on composition, her works including two operas, and songs and works for piano and for orchestra. Before the First World War she was active in the women's suffrage movement. They had a son and a daughter, the latter, Agnes Headlam-*Morley, eventually becoming the first woman to hold a chair at Oxford.

From 1894 to 1900 Headlam was professor of Greek and ancient history at Queen's College, London. He also served as an honorary assistant commissioner to the royal commission on secondary education chaired by James Bryce, 1894–5. In 1902 he joined the Board of Education, and became a permanent staff inspector of secondary schools in 1904. He retained a strong interest in educational issues even after he moved into areas of foreign policy, and insisted on serving on the prime minister's committee on modern languages even during the First World War. His work on education led him to an interest in German reforms, and this in turn led to his writing the well-received book *Bismarck and the German Empire* (1899). This was the beginning of a growing focus on contemporary affairs. Together with W. Alison Phillips and A. W. Holland, he produced *A Short History of Germany and her Colonies* (1914).

At the beginning of the First World War, Headlam was invited to join the new propaganda department being established at Wellington House by Sir Claud Schuster, the secretary of the new body. Headlam's first assignment was to produce an account of the crisis that led to the outbreak of war, published as *The History of the Twelve Days* (1915), based on a scrupulous examination of all documents then available. During the war he also contributed to several periodicals, among them the *Round Table*, the *New Europe*, the *Daily Chronicle*, and the *Atlantic Monthly*. His articles in the *Westminster Gazette* were reproduced as *The German Chancellor and the Outbreak of War* (1917), and some of his articles in the *Nineteenth Century* and the *Westminster Gazette* were published as *The Issue* (1917). While at Wellington House he also produced many pamphlets, including *Belgium and Greece* (1917), *Dead Land of Europe* (1917), *The Starvation of Germany* (1917), and *The Truth about England* (1915). In 1917 he became assistant director of the department of information's intelligence bureau, under Lord Edward Gleichen. In 1918 he moved to the Foreign Office to become assistant director of the newly created political intelligence department (PID), serving under William George Tyrrell. The department consisted mainly of talented young scholars who became involved in British preparations for the post-war peace conference. During the preparatory phase Headlam oversaw their work while he dealt with issues relating to Germany.

Headlam-Morley (as he had now become) participated in the Paris peace conference of 1919. His most notable service during this period was to act as an interlocutor between the Foreign Office staff and the prime minister's secretariat. The prime minister, Lloyd George, had developed a deep suspicion of the career members of the Foreign Office, but Headlam-Morley was able to establish good relations with a key member of the secretariat,

Philip Kerr, which in turn allowed important advice to reach the prime minister without interference. This became one of the critical links between the prime minister's office and the Foreign Office, and did much to ensure the efficacy of British policy.

Headlam-Morley was also active in the day-to-day work of the conference through serving on a number of official and *ad hoc* committees (Belgium and Denmark, Danzig, Saar, Alsace-Lorraine, minorities, eastern frontier of Germany, new states). He further played an important advisory role in several sensitive instances. On Belgian affairs he was a powerful advocate of a Belgian annexation of Luxembourg, in part to assure the western European balance of power by preventing it from falling to France. He was the key actor in the solution to the issue of the Saar which allowed France control of its coalfields for a term, while placing its administration under the League of Nations. He was likewise influential in the Polish settlement where he overcame an initial plan for a much larger Poland that would have included a substantial German minority. He later claimed that the one part of the treaty for which he could take credit was the solution to the Danzig issue that made this strategically important and largely German port a free city under the League of Nations, rather than allowing it to Poland. The basic tenet of Headlam-Morley's advice, if the object was to avoid future conflict, was to try to achieve borders as closely in accord with ethnicity as possible, regardless of geographic or economic factors. Where this was not feasible he promoted the use of minority protection treaties. He robustly defended the territorial settlement after 1919, but always thought the financial and reparations clauses open to revision.

Headlam-Morley stayed on at Paris until the signing of the peace treaty with Austria in August 1919. Despite his efforts to have the PID made a permanent part of the Foreign Office's establishment it was wound up in 1920. His services, however, were retained, and he was appointed to the specially created post of historical adviser to the Foreign Office. As a result he now entered into a new and final phase of his career, as a prolific writer on current affairs and history. He frequently contributed leaders to *The Times*, and during the 1920s he published a vast quantity of articles and book reviews, as well as internal Foreign Office memoranda which are themselves exquisite historical essays. He intended to produce a history of the Paris peace conference, and though it was never completed as a single work it can be reassembled from the twenty-one chapters that appeared in the Foreign Office's confidential print series. When G. P. Gooch and H. W. V. Temperley were commissioned to produce British Documents on the Origins of the War they found that Headlam-Morley had done much work on the subject, and they arranged for his work to appear in volume 11 of the series as *The Outbreak of War: Foreign Office Documents, June 28th – August 4th, 1914* (1926). He also contributed significant portions to the six-volume *History of the Peace Conference of Paris* edited by H. W. V. Temperley. Headlam-Morley assisted Winston

Churchill with writing his history of the war, *The Great Crisis*—in particular, the section on the peace settlement. Because of his official position almost all of his articles, reviews, and leaders were published anonymously. A selection of his work was published posthumously in 1930 as *Studies in Diplomatic History*.

Headlam-Morley was much involved with promoting a better understanding of international affairs and was a founder of what became the Royal Institute of International Affairs (Chatham House). He chaired its research committee and was influential in recruiting his former PID colleague Arnold Toynbee, in the wake of the latter's disastrous appointment to the Koraes chair at King's College, London, to become the editor of the institute's *Annual Survey*.

Headlam-Morley retired in December 1928 and was knighted in June 1929. Described as 'tall, clean-shaven, with a keen and pale intellectual face' (*DNB*), he was a modest individual of great intellectual capacity and charm. He combined academic abilities in ancient history, educational practice, and contemporary international affairs, and was in addition a keen amateur geologist. He died on 6 September 1929 at 9 Grosvenor Hill, Wimbledon, Surrey, and was buried at Whorlton, co. Durham.

ERIK GOLDSTEIN

Sources DNB · J. Headlam-Morley, *A memoir of the Paris peace conference*, ed. A. Headlam-Morley and others (1972) · E. H. Carr, *From Napoleon to Stalin and other essays* (1980) · A. Toynbee, *Acquaintances* (1967) · H. Seton-Watson and C. Seton-Watson, *The making of a new Europe: R. W. Seton-Watson and the last years of Austria-Hungary* (1981) · G. Martel, 'The prehistory of appeasement: Headlam-Morley, the peace settlement and revisionism', *Diplomacy and Statecraft*, 9/3 (1999), 242–65 · A. Sharp, 'James Headlam-Morley: creating international history', *Diplomacy and Statecraft*, 9/3 (1999), 266–83 · S. Marks, *Innocent abroad: Belgium at the Paris peace conference of 1919* (1981) · CAC Cam., Leeper MSS · Foreign Office papers, PRO · private information (2004) [Agnes Headlam-Morley, daughter] · Burke, *Gen. GB* (1937) [Headlam of Cruck Meole House] · *CGPLA Eng. & Wales* (1929) · m. cert. · d. cert. [Elizabeth Sonntag]

Archives CAC Cam., corresp. and papers · University of Ulster, Magee campus, near Derry, corresp. relating to Paris peace conference | King's Cam., letters to Oscar Browning · NA Scot., corresp. with Philip Kerr

Likenesses E. Walker, photogravure, Royal Institute of International Affairs, Chatham House, London

Wealth at death £6471 13s. 6d.: resworn probate, 1929, *CGPLA Eng. & Wales*

Morley, John (1656–1732), land agent, was born on 8 February 1656, in Halstead, Essex. He started work as a butcher, but became one of the leading land jobbers, or land agents, in the country. He reputedly killed a pig every year in Halstead market, and received a groat for the job. When he applied for a grant of arms in 1722, he used the figure of a butcher holding a pole-axe, bend-wise, for his crest. He became a business agent for the Harleys, and in 1713 he negotiated the marriage between Edward Harley, later second earl of Oxford, and Lady Henrietta Holles, only daughter and heir of the fourth duke of Newcastle. He received a two and half per cent commission on the dowry: £10,000.

Morley was always known as 'Merchant Morley', and

John Morley (1656–1732), by John Simon (after Sir Godfrey Kneller, 1716)

Jonathan Swift had a low opinion of him. Writing to John Barber on 8 August 1738, Swift wrote: 'I remember a rascally butcher, one Morley, a great land jobber and knave, who was his lordship's manager, and has been the principal cause of my lord's wrong conduct' (*Correspondence*, 118). A vivacious sketch of Morley's character forms the staple of Matthew Prior's ballad 'Down Hall' (1723), and Morley was probably the jobber named the 'hearty Morley' in John Gay's 'Welcome' (Gay, 254–60). He was a friend of Pope, to whom he occasionally sent presents of oysters and eringo roots, and when he was seriously ill during 1725–6, Pope sent him a sympathetic letter.

About 1700 Morley bought the property of Munchensies, in Halstead, and filled it with treasures, including an ancient Greek altar from Smyrna. He rebuilt the house in 1713. As patron of Gestingthorpe in Essex, he increased the living by adding £200. Morley married Elizabeth, daughter of Matthew Baker, and they had at least one child, a son. His grandson was the medical writer John *Morley (d. 1776/7).

Morley died at Munchensies on 20 January 1732. He was buried beneath an altar tomb in Halstead church, with the arms of the Butchers' Company blazoned above.

THOMAS SECCOMBE, *rev.* ANNE PIMLOTT BAKER

Sources *A biographical history of England, from the revolution to the end of George I's reign: being a continuation of the Rev. J. Granger's work*, ed. M. Noble, 3 (1806), 261–4 • W. J. Evans, *Old and New Halstead* (1886), 22 • *VCH Essex*, 372 • P. Morant, *The history and antiquities of the county of Essex*, 2 (1768), 257 • *The works of Alexander Pope*, ed. W. Elwin and W. J. Courthope, 10 vols. (1871–89), vol. 10, pp. 247–9 • *Miscellaneous works of his late excellency Matthew Prior*, ed. A. Drift, 1 (1740), 306–8 •

'Down Hall: a ballad', in *Selected poems of Matthew Prior*, ed. A. Dobson (1889), 93–105 • *Southey's common-place book*, ed. J. W. Warter, 4 (1851), 618 • private information (1894) • J. Gay, 'Mr Popes welcome from Greece: a copy of verses wrote by Mr Gay upon Mr Popes having finisht his translation of Homers Ilias', in *John Gay: poetry and prose*, ed. V. A. Dearing and C. E. Beckwith, 1 (1974), 254–60 • *The correspondence of Jonathan Swift*, ed. H. Williams, 5 (1965), 118

Archives BL, corresp., loan 29 | BL, corresp. with Lord Oxford • Essex RO, letters to W. Holman

Likenesses G. Vertue, line engraving, 1726 (after J. Richardson), BM, NPG • G. Kneller, portrait • J. Simon, mezzotint (after G. Kneller, 1716), BM, NPG [*see illus.*]

Morley, John (*d.* 1776/7), medical writer, the son of John Morley, was grandson and eventual heir of John *Morley (1656–1732), land agent, of Halstead, Essex. Morley acquired a method of treating scrofula and other similar diseases, and published it as *An Essay on the Nature and Cure of Scrophulous Disorders* (1767). The principal cure, it appears, was a preparation of vervain root. The work was still in print in 1800, when a thirty-second edition was published. Morley is also said to have given advice to all who sought it, without asking a fee.

Morley died in either December 1776 or January 1777, and was buried with his grandfather in Halstead church. With his wife, Elizabeth, who survived him, he had three sons, John Jacob, Hildebrand, and Allington, and a daughter, Dorothy, married to Bridges Harvey. To his eldest son he bequeathed as an heirloom the coronation cup and cover of George I.

GORDON GOODWIN, *rev.* MICHAEL BEVAN

Sources will, PRO, PROB 11/1027, sig. 30 • *GM*, 1st ser., 47 (1777), 47 • *BL cat.* • *DNB*

Wealth at death messuage and house of Munchensies, in parish of Halstead: will, PRO, PROB 11/1027, sig. 30

Morley, John, Viscount Morley of Blackburn (1838–1923), politician and writer, was born on 24 December 1838 in Blackburn, Lancashire, the second of the four children of Jonathan Morley (*d.* 1862), surgeon, and Priscilla Mary Donkin (*d.* 1870). Jonathan was the son of a manufacturer of woollen cards and cotton who lived at Mytholmroyd in the Calder valley, Yorkshire. Morley's mother came from a North Shields shipowning family. Both were Wesleyans. They met in North Shields where Jonathan was apprenticed as a medical student.

Education: early journalistic career in London John Morley was educated at the Queen Elizabeth Grammar School in Blackburn and at Hoole's Academy. He appears to have been a very bookish student who learned to commit large sections of scripture to memory. In later life Morley liked to learn by heart poems and classical texts. In 1852 his father sent him to University College School, London. From February 1855 to December 1856 he attended Cheltenham College where he did well as a scholar.

Morley won an open scholarship to Lincoln College, Oxford, in 1856 and was assigned rooms once occupied by John Wesley. Morley later expressed contempt for the rector and most of the fellows, apart from Mark Pattison. He

John Morley, Viscount Morley of Blackburn (1838–1923), by W. & D. Downey

occasionally spoke at the Oxford Union. But he seems to have made little impact at Oxford and it made little impact on him. In 1896, when he was awarded the degree of DCL by Oxford University, he described himself as 'one whose opinions, whether in politics or deeper things than politics, Oxford does not favour' (Morley, 2.102). He later (1903) became an honorary fellow of All Souls.

Morley's father, now an Anglican communicant, wanted him to enter holy orders. But at Oxford, Morley lost his faith and a serious quarrel developed. His allowance was cut off and he had to leave Oxford in 1859 with only a pass degree. That this was a traumatic experience is shown by numerous echoes of it when as biographer he examined similar crises in the lives of others. He became friendly with contemporaries such as Leslie Stephen and Frederic Harrison who had undergone a similar experience, and concluded that an inevitable aspect of 'an epoch of transition in the very foundations of belief and conduct' was that the opinions of fathers and sons should diverge in this traumatic way (Hamer, 2). He remained to the end of his life a freethinker and something of a stoic with a particular attraction to the philosophical stance of Marcus Aurelius.

Morley's parents went to live at Lytham, where his father died in 1862 and his mother in 1870. Morley was particularly close to his sister Grace, two years younger than himself. He often wrote to her, and she gave him constant encouragement. One of his two brothers, William, died in India, leaving a son, Guy, whom Morley adopted in 1877.

Morley's move to London in 1860 marked the beginning of the critical phase in his intellectual development. Being not at all well off, he took lodgings first at a lawyers' inn in Holborn, where he saw something of London poverty, then in King's Bench Walk at the Temple. He found employment teaching and tutoring, and undertook a range of miscellaneous literary and journalistic work. His first editorial responsibility was on the short-lived *Literary Gazette* (1858–62); Morley was the fourth of five editors, probably in 1861. He may also have worked on *The Leader*, which expired at about this time. In 1863 he joined the staff of the *Saturday Review*, for which he was required to write anonymously—a practice which he strongly opposed thereafter. His *Saturday Review* 'middles' were published in *Modern Characteristics* (1865) and *Studies in Conduct* (1867), the latter of which he withdrew from sale shortly after it was published. He later ignored these works in reviewing his literary achievements. Although he read for the bar and was called (Lincoln's Inn, 1873), economic circumstances left him with no real alternative to a career in journalism. He later described his stillborn legal career as 'my long enduring regret' (Morley, 1.32). In 1893 he was elected a bencher of Lincoln's Inn, where he often dined.

During this period Morley widened his circle of acquaintances and secured an entrée into London's literary world. A new friend who made a particular impact was the novelist George Meredith. In 1867, with the aim of gaining 'freedom from journalistic urgencies' (Hirst, 1.59) by finding alternative sources of income, he became a reader for the publishing house Macmillans. He later described Alexander Macmillan as his earliest and greatest benefactor. One of his tasks was to report on some early writings by Thomas Hardy; his adverse comments have long been held against him, although he did acknowledge Hardy's potential. A significant part of his work in the 1870s consisted of literary criticism. This has a wider range and a good deal more sympathy with the avantgarde than an often cited puritanical review of Swinburne might indicate.

Morley visited the United States in 1867. An intended book on the 'dominant social ideas' of that country was never completed. The visit was important for its effect on his views about the Irish question, particularly because of what he discovered about the depth of feeling concerning British rule in Ireland among Irish immigrants. After his return, on 28 May 1868, he gave an address at Blackburn on 'Ireland's rights and England's duties' which marked a significant development in his interest in issues which dominated much of his political career.

Marriage and personal life; editorship of the *Fortnightly Review* There has long been considerable mystery about Morley's marriage with Rose Mary Ayling (1840–1923). Some uncertainties may never be cleared up, given the shortage of documentary information on some crucial aspects and Morley's own reticence on the subject. They lived together, it seems, for a period, possibly from 1867, before marrying on 28 May 1870. Lord Rosebery later referred to Morley as unsuitable for the foreign secretary-ship because he had anticipated the ceremony of mar-riage. Hirst described Rose as 'slim, but not tall, with flaxen hair and light blue eyes, a good walker and after-wards an ardent cyclist, fond of the country, of trees and plants and birds'. He also says that she 'never cared much for politics, books, or society; seldom visited, or dined out' (Hirst, 1.60), which meant that there was a large part of her husband's life that she did not share. Rose already had two children of uncertain paternity. In November 1907 one of them, John, was sentenced to ten years' penal servi-tude in Scotland. He had forged Morley's signature on let-ters which sought money in return for promises of polit-ical influence. At a time when he believed himself to be held in high general regard, this came as a grievous blow to Morley. He wanted to retire from public life but was per-suaded not to by Asquith. In 1870 Morley moved to Surrey, always his favourite county, where he liked to walk on the heaths. He rented a series of houses. In 1873 Mrs Morley fell ill and the doctors recommended that they move to Tunbridge Wells. Continuing concern about her health led to a move to Brighton in 1875. Although he missed Surrey greatly and was not very fond of the sea, Morley came to like Brighton. In 1879, finding it too far from his work, he moved to Wimbledon, to a large house called Berkeley Lodge, near Putney Heath. From the later 1880s he lived at Elm Park Gardens, South Kensington. In later years he lived at a house called Flowermead in Wimble-don, where he died.

In 1867 Morley was appointed to succeed G. H. Lewes as editor of the *Fortnightly Review* (founded in 1865 and by this time a monthly). He also edited the *Morning Star* from June 1869 until its final issue on 13 October. By 1872 he had increased the circulation of the *Fortnightly* from 1400 to 2500. It became a leading journal of opinion, carrying a wide range of essays on topics of current interest. Morley wrote about one-eighth (some 200) of the articles which appeared during his editorship. One of the best-known stories about his spell as editor is that he allowed the word 'god' to be printed without a capital. The secret of his suc-cess lay in his ability to develop the *Fortnightly* as a partici-pant in and reflection of the major currents of thought in an age of exceptional intellectual ferment. If possible, every controversial contribution received its response from someone with an alternative and thoughtful point of view. He insisted that all articles should be signed so that there should not appear to be any '*auto-Fortnightly*' or 'uni-versal essence and absolute *idea* of *Fortnightly*'.

Morley was initially very optimistic about political pro-spects after 1867. He hoped to see an alliance of 'brains and numbers' (Hamer, 71) and looked forward to a new 'party' 'out of doors', working on public opinion and ultimately replacing the Liberals as the 'party of progress' (Hamer, 103). He saw his role as preparing ideas and pol-icies for the time when the masses awakened to a realiza-tion of their new political power. He placed particular weight on the development of a relationship between practical politicians and intellectuals such as himself.

Such a partnership was essential to steer the nation through the perils of the new democratic era.

Positivism and John Stuart Mill; personal characteristics At this time Morley was closely associated with the positiv-ists, the English disciples of the French sociologist Auguste Comte. The appeal of this self-confident group, who claimed to have found the key to understanding the evolution of human society as well as a substitute for reli-gious faith, was strong. Morley's interest in positivism was a double search: for a new faith relevant to the modern age which would replace outworn Christian shibboleths but also for a faith whose adoption would give less pain to adherents of the old faith—such as parents—than straight adoption of a freethinking or agnostic position. Positivism provided a view of order in history and, while being strongly evolutionary in structure, was consider-ably more moral than Darwinism, about which Morley showed much less enthusiasm.

John Stuart Mill's *On Liberty* (1859) profoundly affected Morley. Impressed by an essay which Morley wrote for the *Saturday Review* in 1865, Mill wrote asking to make his acquaintance, and subsequently introduced Morley to an alternative circle of non- or anti-positivist intellectuals. A close friendship developed. Mill saw in the young journal-ist a disciple who would propagate the Millite creed very effectively. Mill, who had been interested in Comtism but had rejected it as a system, influenced Morley away from a doctrinaire positivist position. Morley came to prefer 'the critical, individualist, scheme of things, wh[ich] my prot-estant upbringing and the influence of Mill have made congenial to me' (letter to Richard Congreve, 8 January 1874, BL, Add MS 46241, fols. 61–2; Hamer, 28). To the posi-tivists' great disappointment, Morley moved the *Fort-nightly* in a Millite direction, developing it as a forum for 'the unbiased expression of many and various minds'.

Writing did not come particularly easily to Morley, but, when it did, it was invariably highly polished. He was well known for the neatness of his manuscripts. He hated untidiness and liked to write with a clean shirt and a clean desk. His style was at first somewhat overwrought, but he became a powerful stylist, capable of writing prose of great force and lucidity. He was a master—in both conver-sation and writing—of appropriate allusion to an immense range of literature. He was not a particularly effective parliamentary debater, his style being at its best when there had been time for polishing. Nor did he enjoy addressing large audiences out of doors, though he could be very effective on the public platform, especially when well prepared.

Contemporaries found Morley a fascinating companion and conversationalist. Although customarily gracious and urbane ('exquisitely polite', according to J. A. Spender; (Spender, 116), he was well known for his prickliness and sensitivity about imagined slights. He was capable of great friendship but as a friend could be very demanding. Many of his friendships were punctuated by episodes of strain and divergence which, however, were usually amic-ably settled. Lord Samuel thus described him at the age of sixty: 'a man of slight build, not tall; with keen twinkling eyes; the nose strong, the chin somewhat receding; he had a voice that was clear and friendly, his manner was kindly and gentle' (Robertson Scott, 46).

Two trades: literature and politics; into parliament Morley was interested in a political career from an early stage. Although highly talented as a writer and very successful as biographer, critic, and essayist, he was constantly beset by a craving for a life of action. He once remarked that the 'bane' of his life had been a continual conflict between the claims of literature and of politics. When he came to write his *Recollections* he feared that his career would seem to lack coherence, disorganized as it had been by the oscillation of interest between his 'two trades—letters and politics' (Hamer, 59). He was ambitious but lacked the political skills needed to fulfil his ambitions. His fondness for intrigue sometimes got the better of him, as in the succession crisis of 1894 when he tried to execute devious plans with an excess of calculation. He tried to avoid having to settle definitively for one career or the other. Literary work continued throughout his time in politics. The result was that he had careers of almost equal distinction in both spheres running in parallel over almost half a century.

Morley stood unsuccessfully for parliament at a by-election at Blackburn in 1869 and for Mill's old constituency, Westminster, in 1880. Shortly after the general election of 1880 he failed to get the Liberal nomination for the Nottingham by-election. His financial position and his reputation as a freethinker were obstacles to winning a seat.

Morley's essays and other miscellaneous pieces were published in two series of *Critical Miscellanies* (1871 and 1877). In 1867 he published *Edmund Burke: an Historical Study*. He later (1879) wrote a study of *Burke* for his English Men of Letters series. He greatly admired Burke, especially for rejecting the idea of basing politics on abstract doctrine. French topics engaged much of his attention in the 1870s. Morley wrote a series of studies, varying from short essays to full-scale biographies, of French intellectuals of the eighteenth century: Voltaire, Rousseau, Diderot, Vauvernargues, Holbach, Turgot, Condorcet. He prided himself on being prepared to study and take seriously individuals such as de Maistre and Rousseau who had political outlooks and personal traits very different from his own. The major works were *Voltaire* (1872), *Rousseau* (1873), and *Diderot and the Encyclopaedists* (1878). Although Morley's work appeared rather miscellaneous in focus, a systematic purpose eventually emerged. He intended that his writings should culminate in a history of the French Revolution. The general theme was a 'survey of the intellectual preparation of the French Revolution' (Hamer, 39). The only study of the revolution itself which he published was an essay on Robespierre in 1876. In it is plainly evident an intention to study how the French proceeded to 'translate the word' of the *philosophes* into 'social action'. When Morley was ill in 1877 Joseph Chamberlain advised him to abandon thoughts of a parliamentary career and lent him money to help him write the history. He did not complete it, turning his attention instead to the

biography of Richard Cobden, published in 1881. This important work (dedicated to John Bright) set a new benchmark for documentation and analysis in political biography, and provided a vital exposition of the character of Cobdenite radicalism: the issue-by-issue approach to reform politics which Morley—at least initially—sought to emulate. The book also sold very well, especially in the north of England, where Cobden was most widely revered. Morley studied de Maistre as well as Voltaire, Burke as well as Rousseau, and manifestly had little sympathy for the French revolutionaries. He was sometimes accused of being too sympathetic to French atheism and communism because of his strong interest in French literature and political thought. Yet he distrusted the French and was strongly Germanophile—even though he frequently visited France and seldom visited Germany or wrote about German culture. Positivism, despite the influence of Mill, was an obvious influence, and Morley owed much to discussions with the French positivist Pierre Lafitte.

Morley's radicalism was characteristic of an era when radicalism was associated particularly with views on the role of the church in national life. Strongly anti-clerical, he supported disestablishing the Church of England. He was drawn into political controversy by the nonconformist reaction to the Education Act (1870). Although a freethinker himself, he sought to identify himself with nonconformity. When attending a conference of a nonconformist pressure group, the National Education League, in 1873, he met Joseph Chamberlain, the radical mayor of Birmingham (1873–6). Sensing his great potential as a radical leader, Morley cultivated him, working to establish a partnership between this man of action and himself as the supplier of ideas. A close personal friendship developed. Morley saw the relationship as complementary, each compensating for qualities lacking in the other. Chamberlain was impressed by Morley's knowledge and learning, while Morley gained vicarious satisfaction from Chamberlain's political advancement, especially after he entered parliament in 1876. In 1873 Morley invited Chamberlain to launch a new political movement with a manifesto in the *Fortnightly*. He himself assisted the cause by a series of articles on the education issue. These were published as *The Struggle for National Education* (1873). But he soon turned away from 'national education', regarding it as too narrow; he had no interest in enlarging it into a campaign for more general educational reform. He turned to disestablishment as a rallying cause for Liberals concerned to destroy the regime of 'privilege'. He assisted the Liberation Society to prepare a scheme of disendowment. By 1876 he was losing his enthusiasm for this issue, seeing it as too narrowly nonconformist to secure the support of working men and 'secular Liberals'.

Morley's health gave concern at various times in the 1870s. The basic problem appeared to be overwork and stress. His financial situation threatened to limit his ability to fulfil his political ambitions. His attempts to enter the house in 1868–9 left him financially drained and bitter at the advantage that wealth conferred in politics. In 1873 he referred to himself as 'a poor man who lives up to his income' (Hamer, 123). As editor of the *Fortnightly* he earned about £800 per annum, adding some £500 more through royalties and other employment. Chapman paid him £500 for *Rousseau*. His finances were also strained by his frequent moves. He was very careful about money matters, a habit which he learned in his early years in London. For instance, he ensured that he had good life insurance cover. As editor of the *Pall Mall Gazette* he earned £2000 a year; he left a personal estate of nearly £60,000.

One of Morley's most influential books was *On Compromise* (1874), a study in political ethics and one of his few pieces of extended non-biographical writing. Through it he transmitted into later nineteenth-century liberalism some of the key Millite messages. It was wrong, he insisted, to see error as having a social utility. Adherence to error involves hypocrisy and damages prospects of social progress. He believed in rule by an educated, progressive élite and devoted himself in *On Compromise* to advising those who aspired to form that élite on how to conduct themselves in public life, explaining, for example, when it was justifiable to compromise one's principles. He preached the duty of the 'well-instructed' to involve themselves in political life. This aspect of the book made a strong impression on younger Liberals in the 1880s and 1890s.

Morley edited the *Pall Mall Gazette* from 1880 to 1883. This marked a further step towards direct involvement in practical politics, as it was a form of journalism that required responses to events as they arose. Numerous able young journalists worked for him, including W. T. Stead, E. T. Cook, and Alfred Milner. Morley entrusted a good deal to Stead as assistant editor, especially when he was researching and writing the *Life of Cobden*. In Stead's opinion, Morley, because he lacked interest in most of the matters that concerned the general reader, was not suited to the life of a journalist. He 'had no eye for news, and he was totally devoid of the journalistic instinct. To him a newspaper was simply a pulpit from which he could preach' (F. Whyte, *The Life of W. T. Stead*, 1925, 7.79). Morley retired from editing the *Fortnightly* in October 1882, lamenting the absence of system in political thinking and acknowledging the deficiencies in remedying this state of affairs of a journal committed to 'open-sidedness'. In order to have an income to support his political career, he edited *Macmillan's Magazine* from May 1883 until summer 1885.

The Newcastle Liberals had been interested in Morley as a candidate for some time. The problem was the need to discover the right sort of relationship to establish with Joseph Cowen, the maverick independent radical member who had a substantial local following. Morley was anxious not to stand directly against Cowen. This problem was avoided when a by-election became necessary in 1883 following the death of the second member for Newcastle. But Morley soon found Cowen an impossible colleague. Morley had in effect become the 'caucus' candidate and member, his position being contrasted by Ostrogorski and other critics of the caucus system with the independent anti-caucus position of Cowen. Morley accepted the necessity of party politics and the caucus, reminding himself that Mill had been a good party man in the house. He tried to reconcile the two spheres of his life, telling Chamberlain that 'it is exactly because I hope to become a thoroughly useful political writer that I lean to parliament' (Hamer, 126) and by analysing in his book on Burke how Burke had made a very similar career move and locked away 'the fragments of [a] History' on which he had been engaged (ibid.). Not being a local man and maintaining his residence and journalistic interests in London, Morley became dependent on the Newcastle Liberal machine and its leader, Robert Spence Watson, for his hold on the seat. In 1885, when he had a 'safe seat free of expense pressed upon me' at Leeds, he said that 'I feel bound to stick to my friends on the Tyne, as long as they stick to me' (Hirst, 2.223).

Meanwhile Morley's alliance with Chamberlain was coming under increasing strain. From 1880 Chamberlain was a member of the Gladstone cabinet whose Irish and imperial policies Morley criticized. Because of their close relationship Chamberlain was suspected of using Morley to advance his own causes. Morley gained notoriety when W. E. Forster resigned the Irish secretaryship in 1882 after a sustained campaign against his policies in the *Pall Mall*. In 1883–4 Morley was prominent in the campaign for parliamentary reform and advocated 'mending or ending' the House of Lords.

Gladstone's 'main prop': home rule and the social question Morley reacted unenthusiastically to Chamberlain's 'unauthorised programme' (1885), partly because of antagonism to programmes and partly through concern at Chamberlain's use of the rhetoric of 'natural rights' in relation to land reform, an issue which concerned property rights. To Morley such talk was dangerously close to French Jacobinism. This was not ground on to which he wished to see English radicalism venturing. He came to see Chamberlain as having allowed dangerous 'socialist doctrine' to seep through into radical policy. Chamberlain, for his part, found Morley 'dreadfully timid' (Hamer, 157). Although he contributed a chapter on religious equality to the *Radical Programme* of 1885, Morley became increasingly detached from the development of radical strategy. He did not approve of Chamberlain's plan for refusing to join any Liberal government which did not adopt the programme.

By 1885 Morley was convinced that home rule was the only answer to the Irish crisis. He decided that it must be given principal place among policies because no other reforms could be attended to until the obstructive presence of the Irish question—and in particular of the Irish nationalist members of parliament—was removed. After the 1885 election, which left the Parnellites holding the balance of power, he opposed leaving the Conservatives in office. He decided to support Gladstone's leadership, seeing him as the indispensable leader to guide the country through this crisis, while Gladstone came to regard Morley as 'about the best stay I have', and 'a main prop to me' (Hamer, 181). He was one of the few prominent Liberals to declare approval of Gladstone's alleged intentions with regard to Irish policy. He offered to write editorials for the *Daily News* 'turning' it in the direction of support for Gladstone if the latter would tell him what was in his mind. According to Morley, Gladstone did so, and he had already written three of the editorials and had embarked on the fourth when Gladstone invited him to call and on 31 January 1886 offered him the post of Irish secretary. This was interpreted as a signal of Gladstone's intention to proceed with the preparation of a Home Rule Bill. Morley's acceptance effectively ended his alliance with Chamberlain, though the latter also joined the government, resigning two months later.

Morley was one of the principal architects in 1886 of the Home Rule Bill. He stood out from other Liberals as largely untrammelled by earlier statements on the Irish question which could be used to allege an opportunistic reversal of position to win Irish support. Leading Conservatives acknowledged that he was a 'Home-Ruler by conviction' (Hamer, 210). He thus held a unique position in the leadership of the party now that it was committed to home rule. But Morley was always aware that his position was fragile, dependent as it was on the continuation of that commitment and especially on the maintenance of Gladstone's leadership. Some thought he harmed his prospects for future leadership by concentrating so exclusively on Ireland.

Morley saw great advantage for the Liberal Party in being preoccupied with the Irish question. Although reduced in size and out of power, it was now much more disciplined and focused. He was one of the most hostile of the Liberal leaders to the compromises that would have been required for Liberal reunion, as discussed with Chamberlain at the round table conference early in 1887. He saw home rule as an 'unselfish', moral issue untainted by distinctions of class, and tried to use it to redevelop a distinction between traditional Liberalism and reactionary toryism, as manifested in Balfour's coercionist regime in the late 1880s. Thus he placed home rule in the tradition of the great reforms that Liberals had promoted in the past. He strongly favoured excluding the Irish members from the British parliament once Ireland had its own parliament.

Morley was never comfortable with social and economic questions, and, though he also knew that they ought not to be evaded, welcomed the opportunity which the Irish preoccupation afforded for going slow in this area of policy. But he took more interest in social problems than did many of his political contemporaries: it seems that the memories of the poverty he had seen when he first came to London in 1860 never left him. He had long believed that Liberals needed to rethink the role of the state with regard to social questions. It was an issue to which he kept returning without being able to define clear principles to guide safe action in this area. He came under increasing pressure from radicals and socialists in Newcastle to define where he stood on social and labour questions. They were less and less ready to accept the Irish

'obstruction' as an excuse for non-commitment. Local government and temperance reform attracted his attention. In December 1888 he outlined at Clerkenwell a programme which he thought appropriate to the social problems of London. He became associated with a group of younger Liberals, of whom R. B. Haldane, H. H. Asquith, and Edward Grey were the most prominent, who sought to prevent 'dangerous' radicals such as Henry Labouchere from filling what they perceived as a vacuum in domestic policy. They had admired Morley's *On Compromise* and looked to him now to be a guide to right political conduct in these challenging circumstances. In November 1889 he gave an important speech at the Eighty Club on Liberalism and social reform. Morley did his best to help these young men gain political promotion. Later he and they fell out when their policies moved towards 'Liberal Imperialism' which was completely against Morley's Cobdenite and 'Little England' principles.

The issue which most seriously damaged Morley's efforts to bring Liberalism into the social area was the proposal, which he opposed, legally to enforce a maximum working day of eight hours. This proved to be a major turning point for Morley's reputation and career. As the issues on which his reputation as a radical had been made faded, notably those associated with the role of the church, and as social questions came to the fore, he began to be regarded as a conservative, even reactionary, influence in the Liberal Party. He saw the 'eight hours' issue as a test case and his stand as one of principle against 'socialism'. His outspokenness concentrated on himself the enmity of socialists who sought an issue that might cause working men to rebel against the Liberal Party. In the general election of 1892 Morley came second in the two-member constituency of Newcastle, behind the tory candidate for whom the socialists had urged working men to vote. When he faced the voters again, following appointment as a minister, a strong rally to him by Irish voters enabled him to win comfortably. Afterwards he abandoned any serious effort to come to terms with the 'new Liberalism' and adhered to a fairly strict Cobdenism in social and economic policy.

Morley's literary work did not altogether cease. He edited the Twelve English Statesmen series for Macmillan and contributed *Walpole* (1889). In 1891 a collection of his miscellaneous writings appeared as *Studies in Literature*. A biography of Oliver Cromwell was published in 1900.

Ireland and the succession crisis; Gladstone's biographer The Parnell divorce crisis of 1890–91 was a severe blow, but Morley remained resolutely in favour of home rule. He gave lukewarm support to the attempt to widen the Liberals' appeal via the Newcastle programme of 1891. He was again chief secretary for Ireland from 1892 to 1895, first in Gladstone's government and then from March 1894 under Rosebery. He frequently visited Ireland to witness conditions at first hand. His particular role since 1886 had been to maintain contact with the Irish party and act as a go-between in negotiations. Following the Parnellite split of 1891 he had to hold the ring between contesting nationalist factions. This was difficult for one who believed that the Irish should be administering their own affairs. The requirement that he administer the law and even on occasions sanction action against unrest resulted in strained relations with the Irish nationalists. He tried to give Irish administration a home rule flavour, and reduced the predominance of protestants in local administration from a ratio of 3 or 4 to 1 to one of approximately 2 to 1.

Morley played a key role in the determination of who would succeed Gladstone as prime minister in 1894. He threw his weight behind Rosebery against Harcourt, with whom he had had substantial disagreements over the home rule policy. Morley feared Harcourt's 'opportunism' whereas Rosebery appealed as someone who could be relied on to keep the Liberal Party 'on the high level of principle on which Mr. Gladstone has always spoken for it' (Morley, 1.313). Morley was very interested in securing either the exchequer or the Foreign Office, and his moves were made partly with these posts in view. He had come to believe that, if Rosebery were premier, the foreign secretary would have to be in the Commons, and was very indignant when Rosebery gave the post to Lord Kimberley. He bitterly accepted continuation in what he called the Irish 'back-kitchen' (Hamer, 297).

Morley lost his Newcastle seat at the general election of 1895, but was returned at a by-election for Montrose Burghs in 1896. His defeat was largely attributable to the Labour campaign against him and the desertion of hitherto staunch Irish voters. His relationship with his constituents at Montrose Burghs was very detached: he attributed his election to 'the zeal of the local leaders and … the aid of Scottish members who came to speak on my behalf' (Morley, 2.47). His role in politics now seemed rather peripheral and he contemplated retirement. In 1899 he told F. W. Hirst that, although Ireland remained the one subject that really interested him, 'I shall be dead before it comes up again'. Two years later he even complained (to Campbell-Bannerman) of having 'wasted ten years on Ireland' (Hamer, 320). On 14 December 1898, when Harcourt resigned the Liberal leadership in the Commons, he and Morley exchanged letters in which Morley appeared to indicate that he no longer wished to be considered part of the front bench. He confirmed this in a speech six weeks later.

At Gladstone's suggestion Morley had set about compiling a history of the Irish question between 1885 and 1895. Although never published, this contributed substantially to his *Life of Gladstone*, which was commissioned by the family and published in 1903. The family gave him £10,000 for it and an additional £3000–£4000 later. Although it absorbed most of his energies during these years, he claimed that it was not an alternative to political activity. Indeed, he said in 1898: 'I really do not know that I can perform a better service to the party' (Hamer, 325). The Gladstone biography, based on extensive use of Gladstone's papers, was widely acclaimed. Morley believed that biography should be a 'means of edification' (ibid., 43), and he disliked those which provided too much detail about the personal lives and foibles of great personalities. The *Life of Gladstone* fitted that mould, and established Morley as the custodian of the Gladstonian legacy and conscience. This made him indispensable as a member of the next Liberal government.

Since the mid-1890s Morley had been a severe critic of imperial adventures. He played a significant although intermittent part in the 'pro-Boer' campaign against the Second South African War. The high point was a speech at Manchester on 15 September 1899 when he effectively reiterated the message that the war was 'wrong'. But other anti-war radicals were disillusioned by his inability to take the lead and commit himself to a substantial course of action.

Morley was rather at a loss about what to do after the Gladstone biography. He collected material towards a life of Cavour to complete a trilogy of studies of great nineteenth-century Liberal statesmen, 'brushed up my Italian, and was soon diligently at work' (Morley, 2.135). As late as October 1905 he was threatening to announce his 'final' exit from politics because 'I have another calling that I do better and like better' (Hamer, 337). Yet two months later he accepted appointment as secretary of state for India in the Campbell-Bannerman government, becoming the first 'humble man of letters', he proudly claimed, to have been made a secretary of state since Addison.

Secretary of state for India; last years Even so Morley would have preferred to be appointed chancellor of the exchequer. At first he was inclined to regard the India Office as another 'back-kitchen'. But gradually he became absorbed in Indian issues and developed confidence in handling them. In Indian policy he found numerous testing grounds for Liberal principles. He was extremely anxious to maintain continuity and consistency between his past and present practice as a Liberal. The past loomed large in the judgements and expectations of colleagues, critics, and in those of his many admirers in India, who referred to their hopes of the Morley of *On Compromise*. Sir Edward Grey believed that one of the government's greatest assets for warding off criticism from the left of its Indian policies was the fact that India was in the charge of someone with so 'unimpeachable' a record who was known to regard 'the Jingo' as 'the devil incarnate' (Hamer, 346). Morley was very sensitive to criticisms that he was betraying the principles of a lifetime and went to considerable lengths to prove that he was not. But it was Ireland over again. The law had to be enforced and he was bound to approve actions which were unacceptable to opponents of British rule in India. When rioting occurred in the Punjab and Bengal in 1907, Morley invoked a regulation of 1818 to have the ringleaders arrested and deported.

Morley had much less sympathy for the Indian than for the Irish demand for home rule. The Indian Councils Act (1909) enlarged the provincial councils in India and doubled Indian membership on them. It allowed the members to debate budgetary matters. Official majorities were done away with on the provincial councils, although not on the Indian council. The crucial question was whether a native member should be appointed to the viceroy's council. On 10 March 1909 Morley proposed P. S. Sinha as the legal member of the council, and cabinet approved without dissent. To check Conservative criticism, he saw that Lord Minto, the viceroy, an appointee of the Balfour tory government, received much of the credit for what became known as the Morley–Minto reforms. His view was that that the British were in India 'to implant … those ideas of justice, law, humanity, which are the foundations of our own civilisation' (Koss, 128). His strategy was to encourage 'moderate' Indian nationalists and detach them from the extremists. It was a strategy several steps back from the one he had adopted in regard to Ireland. He had no long-term goals and did not believe that self-government would come in his own lifetime. He did not see himself as preparing the way for Indian self-rule; nor did he see what he was doing as staving off that development, though he doubted whether British rule would last. One of his main concerns was to achieve a practical reform—something which had eluded him in the case of Ireland and which mattered a great deal to someone so sensitive to accusations of being 'literary' and unpractical.

Morley himself knew little about India, which he never visited, and manifested little sustained interest in Indian history and culture. His main concerns were with the health of British parliamentary government faced with the responsibility of the government of a vast and turbulent empire consisting of hundreds of millions of people who had no wish to be governed by a foreign power. He lectured Minto on the basics of the British parliamentary system and the limits of its readiness to tolerate arbitrary government in India. The problem, he knew, lay in influencing Indian government at such a distance. He insisted on the primacy of the British parliament and refused to allow unfettered discretion to the viceroy and the men on the spot. In practice he found it very difficult to enforce this principle.

Morley was a very trying colleague, constantly threatening to resign. Campbell-Bannerman referred to him as 'that old-maidish Priscilla' (Hamer, 57). Yet he still wanted to be involved in political business, and the leaders of the government were anxious to retain him. As a symbol of the 'old' Liberalism he had a role to play in retaining the party's traditional supporters at a time of major new initiatives in social and fiscal policy. But he showed little interest in or sympathy for the social policies of Churchill and Lloyd George. His health and energies were declining and it was as much as he could do to keep abreast of the vast and complex issues associated with the Indian portfolio. In December 1906, much to his chagrin, he found himself at the head of a list of ministerial non-attenders for Commons divisions.

On 2 May 1908 Morley was created Viscount Morley of Blackburn. He was the first peer to refuse a coat of arms. According to the earl of Midleton, he seldom attended the House of Lords, other than when Indian matters were under discussion. In November 1910 he offered his resignation as secretary of state for India, pleading tiredness,

the need for a new secretary to work with Minto's replacement as viceroy, and his desire for a last chance at 'literary self-collection' (Morley, 2.343). To his surprise Asquith at last accepted one of his resignations. But Asquith retained him in cabinet in the undemanding position of lord president of the council. He returned to the India Office from March to May 1911 when his successor, Lord Crewe, fell ill. Before leaving office, he had successfully resisted the selection of Lord Kitchener as Minto's successor as viceroy.

In the Parliament Bill crisis of 1911 Morley read out to the peers the statement that should they veto the bill the king would create as many new peers as were needed to ensure its passage. A marginal player when the home rule issue reappeared on the government's agenda, he strongly opposed excluding Ulster from a home rule Ireland. On the other hand, he was very nervous about the prospect that Ulster would have to be coerced into such a settlement. During the uprising on the Curragh in 1914 Morley was the only cabinet minister to see and approve the paragraphs that the secretary of state for war, Seely, added to the memorandum assuring officers from Ulster that they would not be required to participate in its coercion.

Morley resigned from cabinet on the outbreak of the First World War in August 1914. He wrote a *Memorandum on Resignation*, describing the events of July–August 1914, but it was not published until 1928—after his death. Longstanding pro-German sympathies and antipathy to Russia and 'Slav aspirations' reasserted themselves: he feared that the defeat of Germany would lead to Russian pre-eminence in Europe. He opposed entry into the war and did not even find a *casus belli* in German aggression against Belgium. The prospect of being a member of a war cabinet he found abhorrent.

In 1917 Morley published two volumes of *Recollections*. These consist mainly of extracts from his diaries and letters, which are now of particular value, as some of the original material has since disappeared. But it is a rather miscellaneous assortment of items with disappointingly little sustained reflection. Parts of it—for example the 'Easter digression' on Lucretius—read like a collection of unpublished papers taken from a drawer where they had been left. He wanted no biography written of him. In his will he ordered that his papers be destroyed, and it seems that his nephew Guy largely kept his wish with the notable exception of his diaries. The *Recollections* have very little to say about his early life. Fortunately, F. W. Hirst found a source about which Morley had apparently forgotten: his letters to his sister Grace. She was beginning to burn them—not because of any instruction from Morley, but because of the personal character of some of them—when Hirst intervened and persuaded her to let him use them for his *Early Life and Letters*.

Morley was appointed to the Order of Merit in 1902. A supporter of university extension and a promoter of English literature as a degree subject, he was, from 1908, chancellor of the University of Manchester, to which he left his enormous library, now housed at Ashburne Hall. In 1921 he made a last appearance in the House of Lords, to speak of the 'ugly failure' of the renewed coercion in Ireland and to declare that only through ending this resort to force could Britain again have 'a good conscience' (Hamer, 375).

John Morley died at Flowermead, his home in Princes Road, Wimbledon, on 23 September 1923. He was cremated at Golders Green and his ashes were interred at Putney Vale cemetery on 29 September. His wife died a few weeks later on 28 November. They were childless, and the viscountcy became extinct.

Morley had long since become deeply alienated from the world around him. His reputation as the last of the great nineteenth-century Liberals was secure, despite a comparatively slender record of practical political achievement—partly attributable to his having spent many of his prime years in opposition—but the twentieth-century decline of the Liberal Party pushed Morley, together with many Liberal intellectuals, somewhat into the shade. In 1944, regretting this development, Hayek thought it 'scarcely an exaggeration to say that the more typically English a writer on political or social problems then appeared to the world, the more is he to-day forgotten in his own country'; among the forgotten he instanced Morley with Dicey, Henry Sidgwick, and Lord Acton as 'to the present generation largely obsolete Victorians' (Hayek, 136). The aspects of Morley's life and work which attracted most twentieth-century attention were his notable editorship of the *Fortnightly Review*, his friendships with and influence on so many of the leading Liberal political personalities of the era from 1870 to 1914, and the ways in which his Cobdenite and Gladstonian Liberal principles responded to the challenges of that era in Irish, Indian, and domestic social policy.　　David Hamer

Sources D. A. Hamer, *John Morley: liberal intellectual in politics* (1968) · J. Morley, *Recollections*, 2 vols. (1917) · F. W. Hirst, *Early life and letters of John Morley*, 2 vols. (1927) · J. W. Robertson Scott, *The life and death of a newspaper* (1952) · J. W. Bicknell and C. L. Cline, 'Who was Lady Morley', *Victorian Newsletter* (autumn 1973), 28–31 · D. J. DeLaura, ed., *Victorian prose: a guide to research* (1973) · E. Alexander, *John Morley* (1972) · C. Kent, *Brains and numbers: elitism, Comtism, and democracy in mid-Victorian England* (1978) · S. A. Wolpert, *Morley and India, 1906–1910* (1967) · S. E. Koss, *John Morley at the India office, 1905–1910* (1969) · J. H. Morgan, *John, Viscount Morley: an appreciation and some reminiscences* (1924) · *Private diaries of the Rt. Hon. Sir Algernon West, G.C.B.*, ed. H. G. Hutchinson (1922) · J. A. Spender, *New lamps and ancient lights* (1940) · F. A. von Hayek, *The road to serfdom* (1944) · DNB

Archives BL, papers relating to *Life of Gladstone*, Add. MS 56453 · BL OIOC, corresp. and papers relating to India, MS Eur. D 573 · BL OIOC, papers relating to India, MS Eur. D 717 · Bodl. Oxf., diaries · Bodl. Oxf., corresp. and papers · NL Wales, letters · St Deiniol's Library, Hawarden, Flintshire, corresp. and papers relating to *Life of Gladstone* · W. Sussex RO, notes, etc., relating to his *Life of Cobden* | BL, corresp. with Arthur James Balfour, Add. MS 49778, *passim* · BL, corresp. with J. E. Burns, Add. MS 46283 · BL, corresp. with Sir Henry Campbell-Bannerman, Add. MS 41223 · BL, letters to Richard Congreve, Add. MS 54241 · BL, letters to G. L. Craik, Add. MS 61894 · BL, corresp. with Sir Charles Dilke, Add. MS 43895 · BL, letters to T. H. S. Escott, Add. MS 58787 · BL, corresp. with Lord Gladstone, Add. MS 45988 · BL, letters to Catherine Gladstone, Add. MS 46226 · BL, letters to Mary Gladstone, Add. MS 46240 · BL, corresp. with W. E. Gladstone, Add. MSS 44255–44257 · BL, letters to Sir Edward Walter Hamilton, Add. MS 48618 · BL, corresp. with Lord Kilbracken, Add. MS 44902 · BL, corresp. with Macmillans, Add. MSS 55055–55057, 61894 · BL, corresp. with Lord Ripon, Add. MS 43541 · BL, corresp. with E. R. Russell, Add. MS 62993 · BL, corresp. with J. A. Spender, Add. MS 46391–46392 · BL OIOC, corresp. with Lord Ampthill, MSS Eur. E 233 · BL OIOC, corresp. with Sir G. Fleetwood Wilson, MS Eur. E 224 · BL OIOC, letters to Arthur Godley, MS Eur. F 102 · BL OIOC, letters to Sir Mountstuart Grant-Duff, MS Eur. F 234 · BL OIOC, letters to Sir Alfred Lyall, MS Eur. F 132 · BL OIOC, letters to Sir Richmond Ritchie, MS Eur. C 342 · BL OIOC, corresp. with Sir James Dunlop Smith, MS Eur. D 686 · BLPES, letters to A. G. Gardiner · BLPES, corresp. with Frederic Harrison · Bodl. Oxf., corresp. with Herbert Asquith · Bodl. Oxf., letters to Richard and George Bentley · Bodl. Oxf., letters to Lady Edward Cecil · Bodl. Oxf., letters to Geoffrey Dawson · Bodl. Oxf., letters to H. A. L. Fisher · Bodl. Oxf., corresp. with Sir William Harcourt · Bodl. Oxf., corresp. with Lord Kimberley · Bodl. Oxf., letters to Gilbert Murray · Bodl. Oxf., corresp. with Lord Ponsonby · CAC Cam., letters to Ashton Wentworth Dilke · CAC Cam., letters to W. T. Stead · Co-operative Union, Holyoake House, Manchester, corresp. with George Holyoake · CUL, letters to Lord Acton · CUL, corresp. with Lord Hardinge · CUL, corresp. with Henry Jackson · Glos. RO, letters to E. J. C. Morton · Herts. ALS, letters to Robert Lytton · HLRO, corresp. with Herbert Samuel · HLRO, corresp. with J. St L. Strachey · HLRO, letters to R. Spence Watson · Hove Central Library, Sussex, letters to Lord Wolseley and Lady Wolseley, NRA 10471 Wolseley · ICL, archives, letters to Thomas Huxley · JRL, corresp. with C. P. Scott · King's AC Cam., letters to Oscar Browning · London Library, letters to W. D. Christie · Lpool RO, letters to Sir Edward Evans · LUL, letters to Austin Dobson · LUL, letters to Herbert Spencer · NAM, letters to Lord Roberts · NL Ire., letters to Alice Stopford Green · NL Ire., letters to John Redmond · NL Scot., corresp. with Lord Haldane · NL Scot., letters to Lord Kimberley · NL Scot., corresp. with Lord Minto · NL Scot., corresp. mainly with Lord Rosebery · NL Wales, letters to T. E. Ellis · NL Wales, corresp. with Lord Rendel · NL Wales, letters to A. J. Williams · NRA, priv. coll., letters to Lord Aberdeen · NRA, priv. coll., corresp. with Sir John Ewart · Plunkett Foundation, Long Hanborough, Oxfordshire, corresp. with Sir Horace Plunkett · PRO, corresp. with Lord Midleton, PRO 30/67 · Queen Mary College, London, letters to Lady Lyttelton · Royal Literary Fund, London, letters written to the Royal Literary Fund as a sponsor · Som. ARS, letters to William Arthur Duckworth · St Deiniol's Library, Hawarden, Flintshire, letters to W. E. Gladstone and H. N. Gladstone · TCD, corresp. with John Dillon · TCD, letters to Edward Dowden · Trinity Cam., letters to Lord Houghton · Trinity Cam., letters to F. W. H. Myers · Trinity Cam., letters to Henry Sidgwick · U. Birm. L., corresp. with Joseph Chamberlain · U. Birm. L., letters to R. W. Dale · U. Leeds, Brotherton L., letters to Sir Edmund Gosse · U. Leeds, Brotherton L., letters to Clement Shorter · U. Leeds, Brotherton L., letters to A. C. Swinburne · U. Newcastle, Robinson L., corresp. with Walter Runciman · U. Reading L., letters to G. W. Palmer · UCL, letters to G. C. Robertson · UCL, letters to James Sully · University of Sheffield Library, letters to A. J. Mundella · W. Sussex RO, letters to W. S. Blunt · W. Sussex RO, letters to F. A. Maxse

Likenesses J. Collier, oils, Lincoln College, Oxford · Downey, photograph, Madras Times picture library; repro. in Koss, *John Morley* · W. & D. Downey, photograph, BL OIOC [*see illus.*]

Wealth at death £59,765 19s. 9d.: probate, 16 Nov 1923, *CGPLA Eng. & Wales*

Morley, Muriel Elizabeth (1899–1993), speech therapist, was born on 20 February 1899 at The Wells, Skircoat, Halifax, Yorkshire, the eldest daughter of Samuel Edwin Morley, a boiler composition manufacturer, and his wife, Helen Ann Monk, *née* Fletcher. Morley was educated at Halifax and Monkseaton high schools, then read physics and biology at Armstrong College, a division of the University of Durham located in Newcastle upon Tyne. She graduated in 1920 with a BSc and a certificate of education. She taught physics at the Church high school in Newcastle for ten years and then took a teaching post in India. While in India she contracted dysentery and, on her return to England, was advised that she was no longer strong enough for work in the classroom.

Thus forced into a change of career, after a period working as a secretary, in 1932 Morley responded to an advertisement placed by William Wardell, a Newcastle plastic surgeon. Wardell had developed a new type of pharyngoplasty for children with cleft palate and wanted an 'educated woman' (*The Times*) to assess the children's speech before and after surgery in order to determine the effectiveness of the operation. Morley, who had not even heard of the profession of speech therapy before applying for the post, was appointed and immediately immersed herself in her new job, reading everything available on the subject of cleft palate and also learning photography as a useful adjunct to her work. The work interested her immensely and she became a leading authority of international repute in this field. After some five years, patients with disorders of speech other than cleft palate were referred to her and she realized that she needed to further her knowledge. Unable to afford the part-time speech therapy training that was available in London, she devised her own scheme. This included working with speech therapy colleagues in hospital and school clinics in Liverpool and London. Her efforts were rewarded when she gained the diploma of the British Society of Speech Therapists in 1938.

Now qualified, Morley was, in 1939, appointed as a speech therapist at the Royal Victoria Infirmary in Newcastle. Initially she worked for just two sessions a week at the rate of 1 guinea per session and spent her spare time preparing a thesis on cleft palate. Her thesis, later the basis for her book *Cleft Palate and Speech*, was passed in April 1939 and she gained membership of the British Society of Speech Therapists; its members were admitted to the College of Speech Therapists, founded in 1945. The book gave thorough descriptions of the anatomy of cleft palate, surgery, associated speech problems, and practical suggestions for treatment. Published in 1945, it became a standard work in this field.

It was during the early 1940s that people became increasingly aware of speech therapy and the profession gained more recognition. By 1945 Morley had set up Newcastle's hospital speech therapy service and was working full-time as a therapist in three hospitals, treating people with a variety of speech and language disorders, including former servicemen suffering from dysphasia as a result of head injuries sustained during the Second World War. Morley's practice grew apace and she was obliged to involve parents in their children's treatment in order to enable her to treat her ever-burgeoning caseload. She soon recognized the benefits of this, however, and became an exponent of parental involvement in speech therapy.

Between 1950 and 1953 Morley's department researched into the normal and abnormal development of speech in a group of over 1000 children as part of the Newcastle family survey. In 1957 she published part of this study together with examples of her work in multidisciplinary clinics as *The Development and Disorders of Speech in Childhood*. This work was regarded as a landmark in speech pathology in the USA and it was on the basis of this book that she was awarded the degree of DSc by the University of Durham in 1958.

Morley made the first of many visits to the USA in 1951, finding that the standard of clinical work was below that of the UK but that academically the training was more extensive. In the hope that a university degree course might 'convince those concerned of the true status of the profession' (Morley, 3), she eventually persuaded the university in Newcastle, still then part of the University of Durham, to investigate the possibility of setting up such a degree. Her idea was finally realized in 1959 and Morley delayed her retirement, due at this time, in order to establish the course. She was appointed lecturer in speech and speech pathology in the departments of child health and education. Morley eventually retired in 1963 from what was by then the University of Newcastle upon Tyne.

Morley's contribution to the speech therapy profession was considerable. In addition to her pioneering clinical work, her professional philosophy that language and speech must be taught in universities and that studies of speech pathology must always be based on sound knowledge of normal behaviours, was innovative at the time. She strove to convince people within the profession of the need for research into the origins and treatment of speech disorders and those outside it of the importance of speech therapy. Morley joined the ultimately successful campaign against registration under the Bill for Professions Supplementary to Medicine because she was convinced that the profession, in order to survive, must exist as a discipline completely separate from general medicine. She also wrote numerous articles concerning speech disorders and their treatment.

As a member of the College of Speech Therapists, Morley served many terms on the council as a fellow's representative and served as its third president from 1971 to 1973. In retirement she edited the college journal from 1967 to 1973, effecting significant changes and encouraging international distribution and contributions for the first time. She forged strong links with the speech therapy professions in Australia, New Zealand, and the USA, where she travelled widely as a visiting professor. She was involved in achieving reciprocal recognition of speech therapy qualifications with the USA and was made an honorary member of the American Cleft Palate Association and honorary fellow of the Australian College of Speech Therapists.

Morley was appointed OBE in 1980 in acknowledgement of her pioneering work in research and education in speech therapy. Donald Court, professor of child health at Newcastle and her former colleague, described Morley in 1984 as a 'remarkable woman' who was 'fuelled and directed by her unwavering belief in the value of her subject and an unyielding commitment to its practice at the highest level' (*The Times*).

For the last thirty years of her life, Morley lived in Northumberland, a place she loved. The photography that she originally learned as part of her cleft palate work remained a lifelong hobby; she also enjoyed painting with oils, baking, making carpets and tapestry kneelers, gardening, sewing, and knitting. Muriel Morley never married but was devoted to her family. She died of bronchopneumonia on 15 September 1993 at Greenfields, Powburn, Alnwick, Northumberland.

JANE H. SCHOFIELD

Sources M. Morley, 'Profile', *Bulletin of the College of Speech Therapists* (April 1983), 2–5 · *A history of the college, 1945–1995* (Royal College of Speech and Language Therapists) · *The Times* (20 Sept 1993) · *The Guardian* (5 Oct 1993) · *Daily Telegraph* (4 Oct 1993)
Likenesses photograph, repro. in *A history of the College*, 37
Wealth at death £394,332: probate, 19 Jan 1994, *CGPLA Eng. & Wales*

Morley, Robert, second Lord Morley (*b*. in or before **1295**, *d*. **1360**), administrator and soldier, was the son and heir of William Morley, first Lord Morley (*d. c*.1302), of Morley and Roydon, Norfolk, and his first wife, Isabel, sister and heir of Robert Mohaut, Lord Mohaut (*d*. 1329). He was born in or shortly before 1295, as his mother was dead by October of that year. He married, first, in or before 1316, Hawise, sister and heir of John Marshal, Lord Marshal of Hingham, Norfolk (*d*. 1316) and daughter of William Marshal, Lord Marshal (*d*. 1314), who had been Morley's guardian. This marriage brought Morley estates in Norfolk, Essex, Hertford, and elsewhere, together with the claim to the hereditary marshalship of Ireland, of which he was given possession in July 1324, by which date he had been knighted. Morley married, second, by September 1334, Joan (*d*. 1358), who was perhaps the daughter of Sir Peter Tyes.

Morley's career in war and administration was long, varied, and distinguished. It is not known when he first bore arms, but in the summer of 1315 he served in Scotland, in the retinue of his uncle, Robert, Lord Mohaut; and he returned there, under the same captain, in the autumn of 1316. He was first summoned to parliament on 20 November 1317, with regular summonses for forty years thereafter, the last on 15 December 1357. Morley sided with Edward II against Thomas of Lancaster. In February 1322 he was ordered to recruit as many men as possible and bring them to muster at Coventry. During the summer following the battle of Boroughbridge (16–17 March 1322), Morley took part in Edward II's disastrous expedition to Scotland. On 26 October 1326 he was a member of the council of prelates, barons, and knights at Bristol that declared Prince Edward 'keeper of the realm', and on 13 January 1327 he was a party to the Guildhall oath to support Queen Isabella and Prince Edward. During the following summer he took part in the dispiriting Weardale campaign, which ended inconclusively at Stanhope Park. On 2 November 1327 he was appointed to a peace commission in Norfolk and Suffolk, and thereafter, when not on campaign, he was employed in Norfolk and neighbouring

counties on commissions of oyer and terminer and in various other administrative capacities with great regularity. On 16 June 1331 he staged a tournament at Stepney, probably to celebrate Prince Edward's first birthday, and with twenty-four others he defended himself against all comers.

Morley fought at the battle of Halidon Hill on 19 July 1333 and served in Scotland during the winter of 1334–5. In June 1335 he quitclaimed the Mohaut inheritance, to which he was blood heir, to Queen Isabella, in exchange for the manor of Framsden, Suffolk. In mid-August 1335, intent on a journey to Santiago de Compostela, he appointed attorneys for a year, although it is not clear that he completed this pilgrimage. In May 1336 he was appointed keeper of the maritime land in Norfolk, a commission that was renewed in June 1337 and March 1338. However, from November 1336 until August 1337 he was actually serving with a retinue in the garrison of Perth. On 6 July 1338 he was appointed justice in Norfolk with peacekeeping and defence responsibilities. Consequently he did not accompany Edward III to France later the same month; but on 18 February 1339 he was appointed admiral of the northern fleet. Morley quickly showed himself to be an energetic naval commander. During the summer of 1339, having repulsed a French maritime attack on the Cinque Ports, he successfully raided the Normandy coast. This was followed by a leading role in the battle of Sluys on 24 June 1340. Although, according to the chronicler Robert Avesbury, counselling against the venture, Morley nevertheless played a distinguished part in the battle, leading the English attack on the French fleet in the Zwin estuary, his role being celebrated by the contemporary patriotic poet, Laurence Minot. Morley continued to serve as admiral of the northern fleet until December 1342 and it was in that capacity that he accompanied the earl of Northampton's expedition to Brittany in August 1342.

At the Smithfield tournament of June 1343, perhaps the colourful climax of a long tourneying career, Morley competed dressed as the pope, accompanied by twelve cardinals. In June 1345 he secured a letter of protection for service in France in the retinue of Hugh Despenser; and in July 1346 he accompanied Edward III to Normandy, and fought at the battle of Crécy and the siege of Calais. During the siege Morley played an active role in the blockade, while successfully defending his right to bear the arms argent, a lion rampant sable, crowned and armed or, against a challenge from Sir Nicholas Burnell before the court of chivalry. Having once again been appointed admiral of the northern fleet in July 1350, Morley fought in the battle of 'les Espagnols sur Mer', off Winchelsea, on 29 August 1350. In May 1351 he was again appointed keeper of the maritime land of Norfolk and in June 1354 became a justice in the same county to keep the Ordnance and Statute of Labourers. In March 1355 Morley was reappointed admiral of the northern fleet and in August of the same year he became constable of the Tower of London, posts that he continued to hold until his death. Serving with a retinue of sixty men-at-arms and archers, Morley died early in 1360, during the French campaign begun by Edward III late in the previous year, thus bringing to an end a career in arms that had lasted forty-five years. It had clearly earned him the high esteem of Edward III, perhaps especially as a naval commander; and there is a story, told by a number of witnesses in the court of chivalry, that the king personally intervened in his suit with Nicholas Burnell to ensure to him the right to the arms he claimed, on account of the prowess he had displayed while bearing them. Morley left, from his first marriage, a son, William (1319–1379), who became third Lord Morley; and from the second, a son Henry (b. c.1344), who may have died in the same year as his father. ANDREW AYTON

Sources GEC, *Peerage* · various chancery and exchequer classes; esp. important are the records of the *Lovel v. Morley* case before the court of chivalry, PRO, C 47/6/1; PRO 30/26/69 · *Chancery records* · *CIPM*, vol. 10 · *Calendar of inquisitions miscellaneous (chancery)*, 7 vols., PRO (1916–68), vols. 2–3 · *RotS*, vol. 1 · *Inquisitions and assessments relating to feudal aids*, 6 vols., PRO (1899–1921) · P. Chaplais, ed., *Treaty rolls preserved in the Public Record Office*, 1 (1955) · BL, Cotton MSS, Nero C. VIII, fol. 250r · Rymer, *Foedera*, new edn · F. Palgrave, ed., *The parliamentary writs and writs of military summons*, 2 vols. in 4 (1827–34) · *The poems of Laurence Minot, 1333–1352*, ed. T. B. James and J. Simons (1989) · G. Wrottesley, *Crécy and Calais* (1897); repr. (1898) · F. Blomefield and C. Parkin, *An essay towards a topographical history of the county of Norfolk*, [2nd edn], 11 vols. (1805–10) · A. H. Thomas and P. E. Jones, eds., *Calendar of plea and memoranda rolls preserved among the archives of the corporation of the City of London at the Guildhall*, 1 (1926) · *Knighton's chronicle, 1337–1396*, ed. and trans. G. H. Martin, OMT (1995) [Lat. orig., *Chronica de eventibus Angliae a tempore regis Edgari usque mortem regis Ricardi Secundi*, with parallel Eng. text] · *Adae Murimuth continuatio chronicarum. Robertus de Avesbury de gestis mirabilibus regis Edwardi tertii*, ed. E. M. Thompson, Rolls Series, 93 (1889) · W. Stubbs, ed., 'Annales Paulini', *Chronicles of the reigns of Edward I and Edward II*, 1, Rolls Series, 76 (1882), 253–370 · *CIPM*, 10, no. 634

Archives PRO, ancient correspondence, SC 1
Wealth at death manorial holdings: *CIPM*, 10, no. 634

Morley, Robert Adolph Wilton (1908–1992), actor and playwright, was born on 26 May 1908 in Semley, Wiltshire, the son of Major Robert Wilton Morley, retired, of the 4th dragoon guards and his wife, Gertrude Emily Fass. He was educated at several preparatory schools—his parents' lives being somewhat itinerant—and at Wellington College (1921–4), which he detested. He was by nature an individualist, unathletic, and opposed to formal teaching. At Folkestone, aged thirteen, he saw Bernard Shaw's *The Doctor's Dilemma* and was immediately determined to be an actor: his love of Shaw and hatred of public schools probably activated his lifelong socialism.

After leaving Wellington and studying in Germany, France, and Italy, his father favouring a diplomatic career, Morley chose to study for the stage at the Royal Academy of Dramatic Art. His first professional theatre engagement was at the Hippodrome, Margate, on 28 May 1928 after which he spent several years touring and in repertory theatres. Working with the fading and forgetful Shakespearian actor Frank Benson, Morley learned some invaluable lessons: how to improvise, how not to believe in the sanctity of any text, the joy of being surrounded by eccentrics (S. Morley, 38). With another humorous heavyweight, Peter Bull, he essayed repertory at Perranporth, Cornwall. After almost deciding to give up the stage he

Robert Adolph Wilton Morley (1908–1992), by unknown photographer

was chosen to play Oscar Wilde at the Gate Theatre in London (September 1936). He made a considerable success in the role, displaying both wit and pathos.

He had another flamboyant role as Alexandre Dumas in *The Great Romancer* (May 1937) and was soon established as a leading actor, repeating his success as Oscar Wilde in New York (October 1938). On 23 February 1940 he married Joan North Buckmaster (b. 1910), the eldest child of the actress Dame Gladys *Cooper and her first husband, Herbert John Buckmaster; they had two sons and a daughter. As the outrageous Sheridan Whiteside in *The Man who Came to Dinner* (Savoy, 1941) he had a tremendous success; the play ran in London and on tour until 1943. In July 1945 he played the prince regent in *The First Gentleman*, which ran for over a year. After this came his greatest all-round success *Edward, my Son* (1947) which he co-wrote with Noel Langley—starring as a ruthless but amusing media mogul: it subsequently played in New York, Australia, and New Zealand (1948–1950).

Morley then discovered a new comic writer suited to his talents: the Frenchman André Roussin, whose *The Little Hut* (1950), adapted by Nancy Mitford, achieved another long run. In 1954 Morley himself adapted and starred in Roussin's *Hippo Dancing* and in 1958 he repeated the formula with *Hook, Line and Sinker*. Before this last he had appeared in the musical *Fanny* (1956). Although unable to sing or dance he gave a performance of rare emotional depth. Later successes included Peter Ustinov's *Halfway up the Tree* (1967), considerably rewritten by Morley, and *How the Other Half Loves* (1970) by the young Alan Ayckbourn. The new school of playwright was not used to *monstres sacrés* with a cavalier attitude to the text, and when he told Ayckbourn 'I've left a trail of richer but sadder authors behind me' (*The Times*, 4 June 1992), he was right on both counts. *A Ghost on Tiptoe* (1974) did well enough but by then boulevard comedy was on its way out. Morley, despite his progressive views, was uneasy with contemporary drama and, when asked by Peter Hall to play Falstaff, declined, never having enjoyed Shakespeare. Life continued with some brilliant journalism, solo performances, and lucrative commercials: at length he found two more plays to match his talents. The first was *Banana Ridge* (Savoy, 1976), an uproarious Ben Travers revival, the second Alan Bennett's *The Old Country* (Australian tour, 1980). Morley played a Philbyesque spy in exile; his son, the critic Sheridan Morley, extolled 'a truly breathtaking performance' in this his father's last stage appearance (S. Morley, 208).

Morley's film career was prolific almost to the end. Following his first New York appearance he went to Hollywood to play Louis XVI in *Marie Antoinette* (1938). Back in England he was an outstanding Undershaft in *Major Barbara* (1941). Always the lead in stage plays, in films he was content to play supporting parts, enlivening scores of routine pictures by his zestful personality. Among his best screen roles were the gross Almayer in *Outcast of the Islands* (1951), Katharine Hepburn's brother in *The African Queen* (1952), Gilbert in *Gilbert and Sullivan* (1953), a comically evil mobster in *Beat the Devil* (1953), a heart-rending if overmature reprise of *Oscar Wilde* (1960), a gentleman crook in *Topkapi* (1965), and a fastidious critic in *Theatre of Blood* (1973).

Morley's own plays included *Short Story* (1935) starring Marie Tempest, *Goodness how Sad* (1937), written for the Perranporth company, and the domestic tragedy *Edward, my Son*. None of them has been revived—nor indeed have many of the plays in which he starred and which he cheerfully rewrote. The lack of his own presence in them leaves a void hard to fill.

Robert Morley was unique. 'Your father always seemed to be having so much fun in the theatre' said a slightly puzzled Peggy Ashcroft (S. Morley, 86). That sentence encapsulates the secret of his success. Although his outsize form and features—equally adept at expressing pompous petulance, astonishment, and hearty *joie de vivre*—are happily preserved on film, his true place was on the stage creating enormous fun for himself and his audiences: a heavyweight with a charmingly light voice and the lightest of comic touches. Like a hotelier, each night he catered for a different clientele. To suit it he would unabashedly readjust his performance, sometimes disconcerting his fellow players but never short-changing his public. On stage and off, the perfect entertainer, he was the last light comedian in the Edwardian Hawtrey and Du Maurier tradition. For all his television 'personality' chat-show appearances he was, like his predecessors, a thoroughly accomplished actor.

In 1957 Morley was appointed CBE. In 1966 he wrote (with Sewell Stokes) *Robert Morley, Responsible Gentleman*, and he subsequently brought out a number of journalistic anthologies. For a time he was in management with Robin Fox. Morley's was a happy life: he was an enthusiastic gourmet, traveller, and gambler whose faults—childlike egotism and obstinacy—were far outweighed by his virtues: huge generosity, love of life, devotion to family and friends. He died, following a stroke, at Dunedin Hospital, Bath Road, Reading, on 3 June 1992: many of his friends commented that he would have been annoyed to have missed the Derby, which was run later that day.

JONATHAN CECIL

Sources *The Times* (4 June 1992) · *Daily Telegraph* (4 June 1992) · *The Guardian* (4 June 1992) · *The Guardian* (6 June 1992) · *The Independent* (4 June 1992) · R. Morley, *Robert Morley: responsible gentleman* (1966) · S. Morley, *Robert my father* (1993) · *WWW, 1991–5* · personal knowledge (2004) · private information (2004) · b. cert. · m. cert. · d. cert.

Likenesses photograph, repro. in *The Times* · photograph, repro. in *Daily Telegraph* · photograph, repro. in *The Guardian* (4 June 1992) · photograph, repro. in *The Independent* · photographs, Kobal Collection, London [*see illus.*]

Morley, Samuel (1809–1886), businessman, politician, and philanthropist, born in Well Street, Hackney, on 15 October 1809, was the youngest child of John Morley of Sneinton, Nottingham, and his wife, Sarah, daughter of Richard Poulton of Maidenhead. The Morley family manufactured hosiery in Nottingham, and John had moved to London about 1796 to set up a branch of that business at 18 Wood Street. It traded under various names, becoming I. and R. Morley in 1820.

Early business career and marriage Samuel entered the London branch of the family firm at the age of sixteen, having been educated at dissenting boarding-schools at Melbourn in Cambridgeshire and at Southampton. His training was in the counting-house, from which he acquired a general oversight of the business. Methodical, painstaking, and neat, he contributed much to the relentless growth of the business by his financial and management skills. His father retired in 1840 and his brother, with whom he had then run the London branch, in 1855; in 1860, when his cousin died, he became responsible for the Nottingham branch too, though he relied heavily on a manager. Between 1848 and 1850 a five-storey warehouse block was built in Wood Street in order to meet demand for the increasing volume and range of hosiery goods which the firm produced. Sales, just over £100,000 in 1830, exceeded £500,000 in 1848, £1 million in 1859, and £2 million in 1871. After initial resistance, the business adjusted well to the factory system; its first factory was built in 1866 and there were seven by the mid-1880s, though in 1900 there were still more domestic workers on the payroll than factory hands. By the 1850s, Morley was recognized as one of the most significant entrepreneurs in the country—and as one of the most dependable, steady, and honourable. A year after his father's retirement, Morley married, on 19 May 1841, Rebekah Maria, daughter of Samuel Hope of Liverpool, a Congregationalist banker. They had five sons and three daughters.

Religion and philanthropy Morley's father was a leading Hackney Congregationalist, a philanthropist and a supporter of radical political causes, and Samuel followed in

Samuel Morley (1809–1886), by Lock & Whitfield, pubd 1882

his footsteps. For him, there was an intimate relationship between these diverse fields. He believed unquestioningly in the truths of evangelical dissent in which he had been reared. As an adult, he had neither the time nor the inclination for extensive reading in science or theology. His favourite preachers were those, such as Thomas Binney of the King's Weigh House Chapel in the City, who conveyed the orthodoxies of Congregationalism with fervour, simplicity, and robustness. Morley believed that the future of England depended on the vigour with which the protestant religion was propagated and the resulting 'purity and harmony of society'. He maintained that every man had a right to be brought into contact with the Bible and to interpret it in his own way. His concern to strengthen the arm of evangelical dissent prompted some of his most important charitable efforts. From 1858 he was treasurer of the Home Missionary Society and attended most of its district conferences, urging the need for local evangelization. He spent £14,400 on new dissenting chapels between 1864 and 1870 alone; he gave £6000 to the erection of the Congregationalist Memorial Hall in Farringdon Street, London, and contributed to the building expenses of at least eleven Congregational training colleges in England and Wales.

Morley was led into politics by his anxiety to secure dissenters' freedom to preach their ideals, and to release England from the complacency of the church establishment and the traditional governing classes. From the 1840s he was one of the few manufacturers willing to adopt a radical political stance. Equating freedom of international commerce with the beneficial development of God-given resources, he took part in the Anti-Corn Law League's

campaign for the Liberal candidate at the City of London by-election in 1843. In the same year he began his association with the education issue, serving as treasurer of the Congregational fund established to fight against the Conservative government's scheme for factory schools. In 1847 he became chairman of the dissenters' parliamentary committee, formed to oppose the extension of state intervention in elementary education proposed by the Liberal government of Lord John Russell. For Morley, this policy smacked of a return to the principle of state control of religion, thus degrading 'God's appointed instrumentality for the regeneration of the world into a mere system of police'. Electors were urged to abstain rather than vote for Liberals who would not pledge their opposition to the government scheme, and supporters were encouraged to buy freeholds and thus county voting rights. Morley pursued similar tactics from March 1855 as chairman of the electoral committee of the Liberation Society, the dissenting body advocating church disestablishment and the abolition of church rates; he became a freeholder in Hertfordshire himself.

Politics, administrative reform, and disestablishment It was not a big step for this efficient, hard-headed, well-endowed dissenting lobbyist, frustrated with the state of parliamentary politics, to become chairman of the Administrative Reform Association (ARA), the organization founded in May 1855 to capitalize on the public dissatisfaction at the political and military management of the Crimean War. As he made clear in his speeches at the meetings of 5 May, 13 June, and 27 June, Morley's interest was not in the conduct of the war—about the morality of which he had misgivings—so much as in the opportunity that it gave to encourage principles of 'efficiency and honesty' in government. Morley urged government not by businessmen, but on the principles followed in well-run businesses—that meritorious individuals should exercise responsibility and demonstrate accountability and integrity, and that patronage, nepotism, and factionalism should find no place. But he also considered that the real fault lay 'with the people themselves' for surrendering their own responsibility to choose honest and independent MPs. He envisaged the ARA, like his other pressure groups, as a teaching organization operating in the constituencies, rather than as a mass movement in itself. However, the issues on which the 1857 election were fought were unpropitious for the ARA, and it fell from view.

In the 1860s, Morley maintained interest in dissenting causes—especially church rates and voluntary education—and regained hopes of influencing the political climate in favour of reform. He became a major proprietor of the *Daily News* and reduced its price from 3*d*. to 1*d*. in 1868; he was instrumental in making it a more popular advocate of Liberal principles. At the general election in November 1868 he became MP for Bristol, and sat until 1885. He had been urged to seek a seat in parliament in 1857 by Richard Cobden, who appreciated the weight that Morley's wealth, integrity, and influence would add to radical causes. Morley was reluctant, partly because of his great workload but perhaps also because of a residual suspicion of the purity of the political process. That suspicion was amply borne out at his first election, at Nottingham in 1865. He was victorious after a bitter contest, but in 1866 was unseated on grounds of colourable employment by his agents. Morley, who did not lack in self-esteem, was bitter at the imputation cast on his integrity and refused to be associated with such a corrupt constituency again. He was also defeated at a by-election for Bristol in April 1868, partly because of the opposition of temperance zealots.

As an MP Morley upheld the principles of disinterestedness and public service which he had previously advocated, but also indicated that his political interests were not those of a sectarian dissenter. 'Our foe', he once said, was not other sects but 'the evil nature in each one, in you and in me.' He resigned from the executive committee of the Liberation Society in December 1868, after telling a Bristol clergyman that he did not support a campaign for the disestablishment and disendowment of the Church of England. From then on he consistently worked with evangelical Anglicans in joint campaigns to spread public morality and the protestant message against the twin threats of atheism and Romanism. He collaborated with Shaftesbury (to whom he had given an interest-free loan of £12,500 in the mid-1860s) and stepped up his support for interdenominational charitable endeavours (he had served on the executive committee of the YMCA since its foundation in 1844). He spoke out against the growth of ritualism in the church and voted for the Public Worship Regulation Act of 1874. He gave money to Bristol Cathedral and to the school and vicarage of his local parish, at Leigh, near Tonbridge, where he was patron of the living from 1870. Most controversially, Morley renounced his long-standing commitment to voluntary education around the time of the 1867 Reform Act. He now advocated a partnership between the state and the churches in order to spread the principles of the Bible, with the parents' right to withdraw children from that Bible teaching safeguarded in legislation. He advocated nondenominational religious teaching in the board schools set up by the 1870 Education Act, and opposed the secularist group of radical nonconformists. He was instrumental in defending religious teaching on the London school board, on which he served between 1870 and 1876. However, he sought compromise with radical dissenters by proposing various restrictions on the funding of denominational schools, most importantly the repeal of the controversial section 25 of the 1870 act.

Trade unions and Liberalism This emphasis on education and religion must have been related to Morley's anxiety to improve the morals and skills of the working classes, who seemed equally critical for the future of Britain as voters and as hands in the new, disciplined factory regime. Morley was a paternalist employer: his factories were kept clean, light, and well-ventilated; he paid high wages and dispensed with the truck system; he gave good pensions, at a cost of over £2000 a year; he installed reading-rooms and parlours at the Wood Street warehouse. To him, these policies made economic sense as well as being a social and moral duty. In I. and R. Morley's dominant and established position, trade unions seemed a beneficial force; by disciplining the workforce they smoothed workplace relations and made wage negotiations easier, while their pressure for good wages helped to benefit employer and workers alike by preventing unscrupulous small firms from undercutting prices when trading conditions were good. Morley held that capital and labour had common interests and that the co-operation attained in his factories should be encouraged nationally through the agency of the Liberal Party. He was a firm friend of respectable working-class politicians. Aware of the importance of providing pressure groups with adequate funding, he was a donor to both the middle-class National Reform Union, advocating household suffrage and the ballot, and the Reform League, which urged manhood suffrage. Without his support, the latter could not have appeared so strong a force during the reform crisis of 1866–7. Morley also acted as treasurer of a special Reform League fund to mobilize working-class effort on behalf of sympathetic candidates at the 1868 election, on condition that they did not stand against official Liberals. He himself gave £1900 to this fund. Morley supported the trade union legislation of 1871–5, advocated the nine-hour day, urged the establishment of boards of conciliation to settle disputes, and was one of three MPs on the consulting committee of the Agricultural Labourers' Union founded in 1872.

Morley remained loyal to Gladstone's brand of Liberalism. He pressed for retrenchment, bankruptcy law reform, and the defence of free trade (in the 1880s, he pumped fresh life into the Financial Reform Association in reaction to increases in continental tariffs). But public morality concerned him most in his later career. Abandoning his earlier belief that temperance could effectively be promoted by voluntary efforts, he became an advocate of the local veto. He was himself now a total abstainer and a strong supporter of the Blue Ribbon movement. He was an active Sabbatarian, was involved in the campaign to repeal the Contagious Diseases Acts from 1875, and, having been appalled by the newspaper exposure of organized prostitution on the streets of London, put his weight behind the 1885 Criminal Law Amendment Act, arguing that the legislature must not sanction sin. In the 1880s he was one of very few Liberals who voted against the admission of Charles Bradlaugh to the House of Commons, regarding him as a missionary of atheism among the working classes. He advised electors in Bradlaugh's Northampton seat to vote Conservative as an 'act of allegiance to God and to public morality'. He strongly backed the Bulgarian agitation of 1876. Though in 1878 he had publicly opposed the idea of Irish home rule, he followed Gladstone when the latter declared for it in 1886.

Death and character Morley, who disapproved of the House of Lords, declined a peerage from Gladstone in June 1885. He was in ill health through the early part of 1886, and never recovered from a severe attack of pneumonia in the summer. He died on 5 September at his London house, 34 Grosvenor Street, Mayfair; his wife survived him. He was buried at Abney Park cemetery, Stoke Newington. Deputations from ninety-seven associations and institutions with which he was connected attended his burial, reflecting the immensity of his charitable giving, estimated at £20,000–£30,000 a year. He left a great fortune, and a 1400 acre estate at Hall Place, Leigh, which he bought in 1870 in place of the 70 acres of Craven Lodge, Stamford Hill, where he had lived since 1854.

Firm, frank, and somewhat severe in manner, Morley disliked laziness, time-wasting, and hesitancy and was impatient and irritable on encountering them. He did not know self-indulgence. He entertained little, rarely read a book through, played no sport, and disapproved of gaming and dancing; he had no hobbies except singing with his family (he did not care for classical music). A friend, Arthur Mursell, said that he was 'not a man of humour', at least outside the patriarchal circle. Imperious and austere, he embodied rectitude. Immensely shrewd and diligent in business, he devoted what was left of his time to serving his religion, in politics and philanthropy, and died a Victorian hero. JONATHAN PARRY

Sources E. Hodder, *The life of Samuel Morley* (1887) · S. D. Chapman, 'Morley, Samuel', *DBB* · C. Binfield, *George Williams and the YMCA: a study in Victorian social attitudes* (1973) · O. Anderson, 'The Administrative Reform Association, 1855–1857', *Pressure from without in early Victorian England*, ed. P. Hollis (1974), 262–88 · G. R. Searle, *Entrepreneurial politics in mid-Victorian Britain* (1993) · D. A. Hamer, *The politics of electoral pressure* (1977) · R. Harrison, *Before the socialists: studies in labour and politics, 1861–1881* (1965) · F. M. Leventhal, *Respectable radical: George Howell and Victorian working class politics* (1971)
Archives DWL, letters and papers · NRA, family papers | Bishopsgate Institute, London, letters to George Howell · BL, letters to W. E. Gladstone, Add. MSS 44398–44787, *passim* · UCL, corresp. with Sir Edwin Chadwick
Likenesses H. T. Wells, oils, exh. RA 1874, Congregational Memorial Hall, London · Lock & Whitfield, woodburytype photograph, pubd 1882, NPG [*see illus.*] · J. H. Thomas, plaster statuette, *c.*1885, NPG · Elliott & Fry, cartes-de-visite, NPG · Elliott & Fry, photographs, NPG · F. Gutekunst, photograph, NPG · London Stereoscopic Co., carte-de-visite, NPG · PET, caricature, chromolithograph, NPG; repro. in *Monetary Gazette* (28 July 1877) · R. Taylor, wood-engraving, NPG; repro. in *ILN* (18 Feb 1871) · J. H. Thomas, statue, Bristol · J. H. Thomas, statue, Nottingham · caricature, chromolithograph, NPG; repro. in *VF* (15 June 1872) · chromolithograph, NPG
Wealth at death £467,474 7*s.* 3*d.*: probate, 20 Nov 1886, *CGPLA Eng. & Wales*

Morley, Thomas (*b.* 1556/7, *d.* in or after 1602), composer, was probably born in Norwich. His father was Francis Morley, a beer brewer of Norwich or, possibly, a verger of the cathedral. The sole evidence for his date of birth is a note at the conclusion of the second contratenor part of a motet by Morley preserved in the Bodleian Library, Oxford, *Domine, non est exaltatum cor meum*, which reads: 'Thomas Morley aetatis suae 19 ano Domini 1576'. Morley was first mentioned in connection with the music of Norwich Cathedral when, on 16 September 1574, he was granted the reversion of the position of master and instructor of the choristers on the death of Edmund Inglott. He received a salary as master of the choristers from 25 March 1583 to 24 June 1587. Moreover, the account roll

for 1583–4 shows Morley in receipt of 10*s.* from the cathedral, an extra payment made to him towards the costs he incurred in a dispute with John Amery, one of the lay clerks. The latest documentary reference to Morley at Norwich dates from 25 May 1587, when an entry in the chapter minute book, 1, recorded the lease of a cathedral house which was 'late in the tenure of Thomas Morley'. The vacation of his residence virtually coincided with the cessation of his salary as master of the choristers.

As a boy Morley may have been a chorister at Norwich Cathedral; he was certainly listed as a chorister of St Paul's Cathedral in July 1574. This appointment explains how the young Morley could have been in London to study with William Byrd, a gentleman of the Chapel Royal since 1572. On 6 July 1588 he graduated BMus in the University of Oxford. The following year he was living in London, for on 14 February 1589 the registers of St Giles Cripplegate recorded the burial of 'Thomas, son of Thomas Morley organist'. This church was approximately 1/3 mile from St Paul's, where probably Morley was now vicar-choral and organist.

Two pieces of historical evidence associate Morley with St Paul's in 1591. First there is the description of the entertainment provided for Queen Elizabeth by the earl of Hertford at Elvetham House on 20 September:

> after supper was ended, her Majesty graciously admitted unto her presence a notable consort of six musicians, which the Earl of Hertford had provided to entertain her majesty withal. ... Their music so highly pleased her, that in grace and favour thereof, she gave a new name unto one of their Pavans, made long since by Master Thomas Morley then Organist of St Paul's Church. (Nichols, 119)

Second there is the letter written in the Low Countries by Charles Paget to 'Mons. Giles Martin, Frenchman, London', dated 3 October 1591:

> There is one Morley that plays on the organ[s] in Paul's that was with me in my house. He seemed here to be a good Catholic and was reconciled, but not withstanding suspecting his behaviour I intercepted letters that Mr. Nowell wrote to him whereby I discovered enough to have hanged him. Nevertheless he showing with tears great repentance, and asking on his knees forgiveness, I was content to let him go. I hear since his coming thither he has played the promoter and apprehends Catholics. (*CSP dom.*, vol. 240, no. 19)

Thomas Phellippes, secretary to Sir Francis Walsingham, suggested a reply to this letter: 'It is true that Morley the singing man employs himself in that kind of service ... and has brought diverse into danger' (ibid., no. 53). This correspondence has prompted the view that Morley entertained Roman Catholic sympathies despite his appointments in the established church, and the texts of some of his Latin motets appear to endorse his Catholicism. However, his inner faith may never be for certain known. The Paget correspondence implies that Morley was a spy; it was not uncommon for musicians in Elizabethan England to be employed as agents, and Sir Francis Walsingham controlled a considerable network of spies.

Paget's letter refers to Morley as organist at St Paul's, but the reply speaks of him as a singer, indicating that he was employed as both singer (vicar-choral) and organist, in the manner often observed at the cathedral in this period. Thus he could have worked at St Paul's after leaving Norwich in 1587 until 1592.

On 24 July 1592 Morley was admitted to membership of the Chapel Royal, almost certainly as a counter-tenor. On 18 November the old cheque book of the chapel recorded that he was 'sworn ... from the Epistler's place to the Gospeller's place and wages ... in the vestry at Hampton Court' (the 'Epistler' was the singer who intoned the epistle, the 'Gospeller' the gospel, at the service of holy communion). This rapid promotion suggests that Morley had some advantage of talent or promise over his colleagues. His election as a gentleman of the Chapel Royal was a mark of distinction and an achievement which brought a good stipend, generous vacations, and considerable free time. Above all it offered an immediate entrée into court circles and thus an opportunity to gain influential patronage, such as permission to use a well-respected name for the dedication of a forthcoming publication. The dedicatees of Morley's published works included, for instance, Mary, countess of Pembroke, Sir Robert Cecil, Lady Periam, Sir George Carey, Sir Stephen Some (lord mayor of the city of London), Sir Gervase Clifton, and Lord Howard of Effingham. Both Carey and Howard, at different times, held the post of lord chamberlain to the Queen's household.

During the last quarter of the sixteenth century music printing in England was controlled by two monopolies granted by the monarch. The earlier of these, historically, was restricted to psalms; the later patent encompassed all other music and music paper, and was bestowed on Byrd and Tallis jointly in 1575. The patent holders were really publishers who engaged the services of professional printers. After Tallis died in 1585 the printing monopoly remained with Byrd, who in 1593 authorized the first set of madrigalian works by an English composer, Morley's *Canzonets or Little Short Songs to Three Voyces*. Morley followed this with his *Madrigalls to Foure Voyces* in 1594. The year 1595 saw the publication of two more madrigalian collections by Morley, *The First Booke of Balletts to Five Voyces* and *The First Booke of Canzonets to Two Voyces*, which included nine pieces for two unspecified instruments, each with an Italian title. Both of these volumes appeared simultaneously in two versions, one in English and the other in Italian, the latter probably intended for sale abroad. The *Canzonets to Two Voyces* was inscribed to Lady Periam and the dedication contained the only reference Morley ever made to his wife, Susan: he implied that she had previously worked for Lady Periam, a great patron of learning and probably the wife of Sir William Periam, lord chief baron of the exchequer under Elizabeth I.

Between 1596 and 1600 the registers of St Helen, Bishopsgate, London, recorded the baptism of three children of Thomas Morley and his wife: Frances (who died aged three), Christopher, and Anne. As well as Morley, the parish's residents included Byrd, Bull, Farnaby, and, occasionally, Wilbye. Shakespeare too lived in the parish; and

for a time at least he and Morley were there simultaneously, as they were both assessed for the same amount of tax in the assessment rolls of 1598. It is possible, though not proven, that the playwright and musician collaborated, for the song 'O mistress mine' (*Twelfth Night*) appeared as an instrumental piece in Morley's *Consort Lessons* (1599), but with only the three title words cited and with no composer named. Additionally, the song 'It was a lover and his lass' (*As You Like It*) was the sixth song in Morley's *First Booke of Ayres* (1600).

In January 1596 Byrd's printing licence expired, and between 1596 and early 1598, when there was no licence holder to whom fees were due, a large number of musical publications were issued, including madrigalian works by Farnaby, Kirbye, Weelkes, and Wilbye, Dowland's *Firste Booke of Songes or Ayres of Foure Partes* (1597), and three more volumes by Morley. These were his own *Canzonets or Little Short Aers to Five and Sixe Voices* (1597), *Canzonets or Little Short Songs to Foure Voices: Celected out of the Best and Approved Italian Authors* (1597), an anthology of Italian canzonets edited by Morley, and his great work of scholarship, *A Plaine and Easie Introduction to Practicall Musicke* (1597), dedicated to William Byrd. Another Italian collection edited by Morley, *Madrigals to Five Voyces: Celected out of the Best Approved Italian Authors*, appeared in 1598. On 28 September that year Morley himself was awarded for twenty-one years the printing monopoly formerly enjoyed by Byrd. In 1599 he published his *First Booke of Consort Lessons, Made by Divers Exquisite Authors, for Six Instruments to Play Together*, a collection of pieces by various (unnamed) composers scored for treble lute, pandora, cittern, bass viol, flute, and treble viol which Morley edited and in many instances presumably arranged. The contents ranged from popular tunes to marches, dance movements, and madrigals. As Morley explained in the dedication, he envisaged the *Consort Lessons* as apt music for the 'excellent and expert musicians' maintained by the city of London, known as the city waits.

Morley published his *Firste Book of Ayres or Little Short Songs, to Sing and Play to the Lute, with the Base Viole* in 1600. The following year he issued what has become his most famous work, *Madrigales: the Triumphes of Oriana to 5 and 6 Voices: Composed by Divers Several Authors*. This was an anthology of twenty-five madrigals by twenty-three English composers, including Morley, who, like Ellis Gibbons, contributed two madrigals. Morley compiled and edited the collection, which was published in honour either of the aged Elizabeth I or of Anne of Denmark.

The old cheque book of the Chapel Royal contains the final record of Morley: on 7 October 1602 George Woodson from Windsor replaced him in the choir, and it is likely that Morley had died in office shortly before Woodson's appointment or resigned through ill health. The case for 1602 being the year of Morley's death is strengthened by references he had made to his poor health in the preceding five or so years, in the *Plaine and Easie Introduction* (1597) and in the address 'to the reader' in his *Ayres* (1600).

Morley created the English madrigal out of the long-established Italian madrigal tradition. Many of his texts owed a debt to Italian sources, but from them he fashioned an English madrigal verse ideally suited to the kind of music he wished to write. His first two madrigalian publications of 1593 and 1594 were musically more original than his later ones, for in the publications of 1595, the *Balletts* and the *Canzonets to Two Voyces*, he became much more evidently Italianate by basing his music specifically on that of Italian composers, particularly Gastoldi and Anerio. In 1597 he capitulated even further to Italian conventions in his five- and six-voice *Canzonets* and followed these by two anthologies of Italian madrigalian music. The move towards Italy closed with his plan for the *Triumphes of Oriana*, probably conceived initially in 1597–8, the idea for which had Italian precedents. For unknown reasons he then abandoned Italianism and turned to more English genres, editing and arranging instrumental music and writing lute songs to mainly high-quality poetry rather than the contrived verse of his madrigals.

Morley is most famous for establishing the English madrigal by his own publications, which inspired many English composers to write madrigalian works, and for his outstanding scholarship in the *Plaine and Easie Introduction to Practicall Musicke* (1597), which has retained its importance as a musical textbook. Additionally, he wrote pieces for viol consort and keyboard (preserved in the Fitzwilliam virginal book and Will Forster's Virginal Book). However, as a composer of sacred music he was of the very best, both in his pioneer achievements in verse services and verse anthems for church use, such as 'Out of the deep', and in his Latin motets, such as *Eheu sustulerunt dominum meum*.   MICHAEL W. FOSTER

Sources E. H. Fellowes, ed., *The English madrigal school*, 36 vols. in 19 pts (1913–24), vols. 1–4, 32 · E. Fellowes, ed., *The English lute songs*, rev. edn, rev. T. Dart, 1st ser., 16, ed. T. Morley (1969) · *First book of consort lessons*, ed. S. Beck (1959) · H. W. Shaw, 'Thomas Morley of Norwich', *MT*, 106 (1965), 669–73 · H. W. Shaw, *The succession of organists of the Chapel Royal and the cathedrals of England and Wales from c.1538* (1991) · F. Harrison, 'Thomas Morley's biography', *Music and Letters*, 42 (1961), 97–8 · D. Brown, 'Thomas Morley and the Catholics: some speculations', *Monthly Musical Record*, 89 (1959), 53–61 · E. F. Rimbault, ed., *The old cheque-book, or book of remembrance, of the Chapel Royal, from 1561 to 1744*, CS, new ser., 3 (1872), 5, 6, 34 · P. Brett, 'Morley, Thomas', *New Grove* · D. W. Krummel, *English music printing, 1553–1700* (1975) · J. Kerman, *The Elizabethan madrigal: a comparative study* (1962) · J. Nichols, *The progresses and public processions of Queen Elizabeth*, new edn, 3 (1823), 3.119 · W. B. Bannerman, ed., *The registers of St Helen's, Bishopsgate, London*, Harleian Society, register section, 31 (1904), 7, 262, 268

Morley, William Hook (1815–1860), orientalist and lawyer, born at St Michael's Place, Brompton, London, the second son of George Morley of the Inner Temple, distinguished himself in 1838 by discovering a missing manuscript of Rashidudin, *Jámi Al Tawaríkh*. He entered the Middle Temple on 12 January 1838, was called to the bar in 1840 and in 1846, and in 1849–50 published a valuable digest of cases decided in the supreme courts of India (2 vols., 1852).

Morley was a trustee of the Royal Asiatic Society of Great Britain and Ireland, and during the last year of his life also librarian; he published a *Catalogue of the Historical Manuscripts in the Arabic and Persian Languages* in the possession of the society (1854). In 1856 he published a description of a planispheric astrolabe constructed for Shah Sultan Husain Safavi. He also edited in 1848, for the Society for the Publication of Oriental Texts, Mir Khwand's *History of the Atabeks of Syria and Persia*.

Morley died at his home, 35 Brompton Square, London, on 21 May 1860.   HENRY BEVERIDGE, *rev.* PARVIN LOLOI

Sources *Journal of the Royal Asiatic Society of Great Britain and Ireland*, 18 (1861), v–vi · Numismatic Society, 'Annual report', May 1861 · *Proceedings of the Numismatic Society* (21 June 1860) · *Numismatic Chronicle*, 20 (1857–8), 34 · Boase, *Mod. Eng. biog.* · J. Hutchinson, ed., *A catalogue of notable Middle Templars: with brief biographical notices* (1902) · Allibone, *Dict.* · C. E. Buckland, *Dictionary of Indian biography* (1906) · d. cert.
Archives BL OIOC, MSS and oriental collections, MSS Eur. C 46–49, D 271–278, E 115
Wealth at death under £2000: probate, 5 June 1860, *CGPLA Eng. & Wales*

Mornington. For this title name *see* Wesley, Richard, first baron of Mornington (1690–1758); Wesley, Garrett, first earl of Mornington (1735–1781); Pole, William Wellesley-, third earl of Mornington (1763–1845); Wellesley, William Pole-Tylney-Long-, fourth earl of Mornington (1788–1857) [*see under* Pole, William Wellesley-, third earl of Mornington (1763–1845)].

Moro, Peter Meinhard (1911–1998), architect, was born on 27 May 1911 in Heidelberg, Germany, the only son of the two children of Professor Ernst Moro (1874–1951) and his wife, Margareta Hönigswald. His father was from Ljubljana, Yugoslavia, and his mother from Vienna, Austria. His father became a German national on being granted the chair of paediatrics at Heidelberg University, where he noted the characteristic startle reflex in babies, now universally called the Moro reflex. Peter Moro was baptized as a Roman Catholic on 12 September 1911 and was later confirmed by Eugenio Pacelli, the future Pope Pius XII.

Educated in Heidelberg, Moro spent the obligatory six months' preparation for architecture school in the building trade, as a bricklayer and carpenter. In 1929 he attended first-year architecture at Technische Hochschule, Stuttgart, before moving in 1930 to the Technische Hochschule, Berlin Charlottenburg, under Heinrich Tessenow and Hans Poelzig. In 1934, during the advent of the Nazis to power, Moro was forced to leave his place at the university upon the discovery, unknown to him until then, that his maternal grandmother was Jewish. Deciding that he could not live under the oppressive regime, he moved to Zürich, Switzerland, and qualified as an architect in July 1936 after completing his studies at the Eidgenössich Technische Hochschule under Otto Salvisberg.

Not wishing to return to live in Germany, Moro went to Britain in 1936 and became an architectural assistant in the office of Tecton, the architectural firm founded by Berthold Lubetkin that was pioneering the emerging modern movement style in Britain. In his unpublished autobiography Moro said that 'it was Lubetkin who first opened my eyes to the real meaning of architecture, an art based on reason'. In 1938 Moro worked on his first solo job, given to him by the former Bauhaus master Laszlo Moholy-Nagy, to design the entrance screen to the 1938 MARS (Modern Architectural Research) Group exhibition held at the Burlington Galleries, London, and opened by Le Corbusier. He then gained his first large-scale commission, Harbour Meadow, a large country house near Birdham, Sussex, which he did in partnership with his friend Richard (later Baron) Llewelyn-Davies. Although uncompromisingly modern in style, the house was innovational in its plan and materials, elements which humanized the design and became the trademarks of Moro's reputation. On 2 March 1940 Moro married Anne Margaret Theodosia (1918–2001), daughter of William Charles Arcedeckne Vanneck, sixth Baron Huntingfield. They had three daughters: Frances (*b.* 1945), Alice (*b.* 1948), and Dinah (*b.* 1960). They were divorced in 1984.

In 1941 Moro was held for six months in internment camps, a period which held bitter memories for him. Upon his release he was appointed as an architectural tutor at the Regent Street Polytechnic, London, where he taught for seven years, influencing many architects who became prominent after the war.

In 1947, the year he became a British subject, Moro began to collaborate with the industrial and furniture designer Robin Day on a series of exhibition designs. In the following year Sir Leslie Martin chose Moro as his associate architect on the Royal Festival Hall, South Bank, London, which opened in 1951. Moro was responsible largely for the interior architecture, with its open and flowing spaces, sound-protected auditorium, and beautiful materials—all characteristics that mark this concert hall as one of the finest examples of British public architecture.

On the strength of the Royal Festival Hall, in 1952 Moro set up Peter Moro & Partners (later the Peter Moro Partnership, dissolved in 1984), a practice specializing in theatre design (the firm built eight in total) and, to a smaller extent, in public housing and schools. The Playhouse Theatre, Nottingham, completed in 1964, was notable for its elegant design and the cylindrical auditorium, which brings the audience close to the stage. In the same year Moro replaced the gallery and amphitheatre of the Royal Opera House, Covent Garden, London, which gave him the reputation for being a modernist who could work with the traditional. Thus came his commission for alterations and additions to the historic Theatre Royal, Bristol, completed in 1971. His other distinguished theatres included the Gulbenkian Centre, Theatre, and Television Studio, Hull University (1969), the Riverside Theatre, University of Ulster, Northern Ireland (1975), and the Theatre Royal, Plymouth (1982). He was appointed CBE in 1977. He was a member of the council, Royal Institute of British Architects (1967–73), a member of the Arts Council's housing and arts committee (1975–8), and governor of Ravensbourne College of Art and Design (1976–87).

Reinforced by his own socialist commitments, Moro understood the importance of domesticity in the design of his public housing schemes, which he undertook mainly for the London borough of Southwark. His own house, 20 Blackheath Park, London, built in 1957, is considered an architectural gem. It is an open-planned, split-level brick and wooden box, which in its manipulation of space, and use of detailing and materials well illustrates Moro's style of design, which was, he explained 'an attempt to breathe life into the banality of functionalism' (Emanuel). Moro died at home of a stroke on 10 October 1998; his body was cremated on 21 October and the ashes scattered under an ash tree at 20 Blackheath Park.

NEIL BINGHAM

Sources P. Moro, 'A sense of proportion: memoirs of an architect', 1990, RIBA BAL, MSS collection [unpublished manuscript] · P. Moro, 'Harbour Meadow, Birdham, Sussex', *Twentieth century architecture*, 2 (1996), 8–14 · N. Bingham, 'A home with a human spirit: 20 Blackheath Park', *Country Life*, 194 (4 May 2000), 118–21 · M. Emanuel, ed., *Contemporary architects*, 3rd edn (1994), 672–4 · b. cert. · m. cert. · d. cert.

Archives RIBA BAL, lectures, notes, cuttings, brochures, and designs; memoirs

Morow [Morvo], **John** (*fl. c.*1430), master mason, was of French origin, but came to work in Scotland. Practically all that is known of his life is derived from an inscribed panel he inserted in the south aisle of the Cistercian abbey of Melrose, which records that he was born in Paris, and had been in charge of masonwork at St Andrews, Glasgow, Paisley, Nithsdale (this may refer to Lincluden), and Galloway (possibly Whithorn). His contribution to Melrose is probably identifiable in a number of windows inserted into the presbytery, the south transept, and the first of the chapels along the south nave flank. It thus fits between the start of rebuilding the abbey church after its destruction by Richard II of England in 1385 and the completion of the south transept and continuation of work into the nave by Abbot Andrew Hunter (who was in office from 1444 to some date between about 1465 and 1471).

Morow's work at some of the other churches listed on the panel may be identified through the use of an identical tracery type in the east bays of the north nave aisle at Paisley Abbey and in the choir of Lincluden collegiate church. The former can be approximately dated as being between operations supported by Robert II in 1389 and Abbot John Lithgow's selection of his burial place (apparently in the vicinity of the north porch) in 1434. Lincluden was founded about 1389, but much of the building is of the period between 1406, when correspondence with the pope refers to it as unfinished, and about 1451, when Princess Margaret, countess of Douglas and duchess of Touraine, whose tomb is a prominent feature of the choir, died. The tracery in these buildings is marked by a sensitive balance of restrained flowing forms with 'spherical' figures, which has few parallels in Scotland, but is reflected in several French buildings. The mouldings associated with the windows at Melrose, Paisley, and Lincluden are also closely similar to one another.

A further pointer to Morow's contribution may be the use of corbels with crouching biblical figures holding a scroll. This motif, common in continental Europe, is found in Scotland only at Melrose and Lincluden, and in two displaced fragments which are thought to come from the demolished south-western tower at Glasgow Cathedral; they are thus all at churches included on Morow's list. Of the other churches listed at Melrose, it might be argued there is some degree of French inspiration in the fragmentary remains of the nave of St Andrew Cathedral as rebuilt after the fire of 1378, when the bishop was Walter Trail (d. 1401), a graduate of Paris and Orléans. This is best seen in the stilted-arched west windows and in the way the sub-bases of the arcade piers are elongated towards the main space, presumably to support full-height wall shafts on this side. However, there is nothing that could be associated specifically with Morow from what is known of his work elsewhere, and it may be that any French-inspired elements at St Andrews were the contribution of his colleagues.

Morow's work represents a highly significant contribution to Scottish architectural thought at a time when there was a resurgence of ecclesiastical building activity after the long wars with England, and English influences were being increasingly rejected in favour of a synthesis in which continental European inspiration played an important part.　　　　RICHARD FAWCETT

Sources R. Fawcett, *Scottish architecture from the accession of the Stewarts to the reformation, 1371–1560* (1994) · *Inventory of Roxburghshire … fourteenth report*, 2 vols., Royal Commission on the Ancient and Historical Monuments of Scotland (1956) · J. A. Smith, 'Notes on Melrose Abbey, especially in reference to inscriptions on the wall of the south transept', *Proceedings of the Society of Antiquaries of Scotland*, 2 (1854–7), 166–75, 295 · R. Monteith, *An theater of mortality, or, A further collection of funeral-inscriptions over Scotland*, 2 (1713) · P. M. Chalmers, *A Scots medieval architect* (1895) · G. G. Coulton, *Scottish abbeys and social life* (1933)

Morpeth. For this title name *see* Howard, Charles James Stanley, Viscount Morpeth and tenth earl of Carlisle (1867–1912) [*see under* Howard, George James, ninth earl of Carlisle (1843–1911)].

Morphett, Sir John (1809–1892), landowner and politician in Australia, was born in Holborn, London, on 4 May 1809, the son of Nathaniel Morphett (1778–1848) and his wife, Mary Gliddon (d. 1849), of Cummins, Ide, Devon. His father was a London solicitor, from a Kentish family; his mother's family was associated with a coterie which included Leigh Hunt, Shelley, Lamb, Keats, and Byron. After being educated in private schools for a mercantile career, at the age of sixteen Morphett entered a London commercial house, and when he was twenty-one he joined the counting house of Harris & Co. in Alexandria, Egypt. He was American consul for twelve months.

Morphett returned to London in 1834 and, with his younger brother George and other members of his family, became interested in the campaign for a new colony in southern Australia along principles advocated by E. G. Wakefield and the 'Adelphi party' with whom he cultivated his business interests. By 1835 he was already one of the most vocal advocates of the new colony, advertising his services in the *Globe and Traveller*. When the South Australian Act was passed in 1834 Morphett issued a four-page circular, *Reasons for the purchase of land in South Australia by persons resident in Britain; with a view to the removal of labourers and the profitable employment of capital.*

Morphett sailed in the pioneer voyage of the *Cygnet*, which arrived at Kangaroo Island on 11 September 1836. He was a practical colonist who played his part in reconnoitring the colony, influencing settlement, and government. He was in the party that discovered the freshwater River Torrens in November, and reported favourably on the mainland after two visits, declaring it more suitable than Kangaroo Island for settlement; he was also involved in the discovery of the site of Port Adelaide. His reports were published as letters in England and he was influential in the vital decision to site Adelaide in February 1837. He was heavily involved in the moves to unseat governor John Hindmarsh, especially through the pages of the *Southern Australian* newspaper, in which he held an interest. In 1839 he participated in six special surveys, selecting land on behalf of English friends and clients and the secondary towns associations. He established himself as a general merchant and was influential in the layout of Adelaide and in establishing regular government in the colony.

On 15 August 1838 Morphett married Elizabeth (1815–1905), the eldest daughter of Sir John Hurtle Fisher. Earlier that year he had journeyed to Rapid Bay and the Fleurieu peninsula and reported to government on the capabilities of the district, and on 26 March he was appointed as a member of the committee for the protection of the Aborigines. He founded the Literary Association and the Mechanics' Institute. He promoted the South Australian Joint Stock Association Company. He was a prominent public figure, the source of the best advice, and an energetic proponent of the development of the colony. He prospered in the first Adelaide boom and sold his main business before the collapse of 1841.

Morphett's earlier experience of the Mediterranean gave authority to his views on sheep and cattle management. He was treasurer of Adelaide's municipal corporation from 1840, a founder of the Agricultural Society of South Australia in 1844, a supporter of St Peter's College (founded 1847), and the Society for the Propagation of the Gospel, and, in the economic sphere, a director of the South Australian Banking Company from 1845 and a member of the local committee of an English company for a proposed railway to Port Adelaide in 1846. In 1838 he was a trustee of the short-lived South Australian Club. In addition he was a member of the (also short-lived) Statistical Society, president of the South Australian Subscription Library in 1846, and a member of the South Australian Book Club. As a freemason, he helped to propagate the fraternity in the colony.

On 5 December 1840 Morphett became treasurer to the corporation of Adelaide, and the following April he was made a justice of the peace. In June he was nominated to the colony's first legislative council, where he strongly supported state aid to religion and was involved in the lengthy debates about mining royalties. He visited England in 1847 to oppose both Lord Grey's idea of federation and local proposals for vote by ballot. Later he pressed for the reform of the council, of which he was speaker from 1851 to 1855. In 1857 he was elected to the new council in the first election held under responsible government—of which he had been the first advocate. He was chief secretary for nine months in 1860–61, but he disliked party politics and, though he accepted the presidency of the council from 1865 to 1873, he did not then seek to renew his membership of it.

As well as business and politics, Morphett was much interested in sport and culture and was a patron and enthusiast of the turf from its start in the colony. He was active in the foundation of the famous Adelaide Club, but generally his life gradually became more secluded; however, he continued to serve as a company director, especially on the board of the Bank of South Australia, and was knighted on 16 February 1870.

Morphett died of pneumonia at his home, Cummins House, Morphettville, on 7 November 1892, survived by his wife, six sons, and four daughters. He was buried in the West Terrace cemetery, Adelaide, on 8 November. A popular and charitable man, he was a much respected citizen who may be regarded as one of the true founders of South Australia, and whose name was much remembered in the names of local streets and districts.   ERIC RICHARDS

Sources Adelaide Observer (12 Nov 1892) · G. C. Morphett, ed., The life and letters of Sir John Morphett (1936) · AusDB · A. Young, 'Thornton Leigh Hunt (1810–73) and the colonization of South Australia', Proceedings of the Royal Geographical Society of Australasia, South Australian Branch, 59 (1957–8), 71–7 · South Australian Register (8 Nov 1892) · J. Blacket, History of South Australia (1911)
Likenesses S. Laurence, crayon drawing, priv. coll. · photograph, repro. in Morphett, ed., Life and letters, frontispiece · photograph, repro. in Adelaide Observer, 33 · woodcut, NPG

Morrah, Dermot Michael Macgregor (1896–1974), journalist and herald, was born in Ryde, Isle of Wight, on 26 April 1896, the eldest in the family of two sons and two daughters of Herbert Arthur Morrah (1870–1939), a novelist and poet whose career reached its peak early with his election to the presidency of the Oxford Union, and his wife, Alice Elise, daughter of Major Cortlandt Alexander Macgregor, of the Royal Engineers, who was of mixed Scottish and Polish descent. Morrah sometimes claimed, though not entirely seriously since historical evidence was lacking, descent from the Dermot MacMurrough of Leinster who invited Strongbow to Ireland. His second forename, Michael, was given to him not at his baptism but at his reception into the Roman Catholic church. At Winchester College, which awarded him an exhibition in classics, he was almost equally distinguished as a classicist and mathematician, and it was as a mathematical scholar that he entered New College, Oxford. He played against Cambridge in the Oxford chess team. In 1915, to his disappointment, he obtained only second-class honours in mathematical moderations and promptly joined the Royal Engineers, where his mathematical learning could be put to practical use.

In 1916–18 Morrah served in Palestine and Egypt, being wounded at Gaza, but one of his commanding officers is said to have described him, with exasperated affection, as

the 'most unsoldierly soldier I've ever known'. On demobilization he returned to New College, deserted mathematics for history, and in 1921 after two years' study obtained first-class honours in modern history. In the same year he was elected to a prize fellowship at All Souls College which was to play an important role in his life. In the immediately succeeding years, however, there occurred two events of even greater importance to him: his reception in 1922 into the Roman Catholic church, and in 1923 his marriage to Gertrude Ruth (1899–1990), daughter of Wilmott Houselander, a bank manager. They had two daughters. His wife, who also read history at Oxford (as a member of the Society of Oxford Home Students), subsequently had a distinguished career as a magistrate, being for twenty years (1945–64) a chairman of the metropolitan juvenile courts.

At All Souls, Morrah's fellowship expired after seven years, as then invariably happened in the case of married non-academic fellows, but he remained a permanent member of common room and was invited to all college gaudies, which are held three times a year. At these feasts Morrah was the most regular of attenders, and he became the omniscient collector and recorder of college customs and conventions, however recondite or trivial. In the 1920s the fellows included two groups who were to be of particular importance to him. One consisted of two editors of The Times, G. E. Buckle (by then a quondam fellow) and G. Geoffrey Dawson, and the other included Lionel Curtis, R. H. Brand, L. C. M. S. Amery, and, as a frequent visitor though not as a fellow, Philip Kerr, later marquess of Lothian. All of these had been members of 'Milner's kindergarten' and had been associated with Baron Milner in his work in South Africa after the Second South African War. Kerr for some years edited Round Table, a journal which reflected the group's political philosophy and which, despite its small circulation, exercised considerable influence. This editorship was a post which Morrah himself was to fill some years later.

In 1922 Morrah entered the civil service and until 1928 worked in the mines department, an occupation which was to him profoundly boring. When G. E. Buckle, who was then at work on the great history of The Times, invited him to become his assistant, Morrah accepted without hesitation. At the suggestion of Dawson, who had earmarked him as a future Times leader writer, he joined the Daily Mail, in effect to serve an apprenticeship in journalism; in 1931 this period of training came to an end and he became in 1932 a full member of The Times staff, which he remained for twenty-nine years.

During this period Morrah began to publish. In his Daily Mail days there was an entertaining jeu d'esprit, If it had Happened Yesterday (1931), a retelling of various important events in English history in the style of popular journalism, and shortly afterwards The Mummy Case (1932), a detective story with an Oxford setting; in collaboration with G. Campbell Dixon he wrote a play, Caesar's Friend (1933), about the events of the first Good Friday, which ran for only a week in the West End. He also wrote a nativity play for children, *Chorus angelorum*, originally for the convent where his two daughters were at school but rejected by the nuns as too frivolous. It was eventually performed successfully in London with music specially written for it by Sir H. Walford Davies. More importantly, Morrah embarked after the Second World War on a series of studies of the royal family, which included books on Elizabeth II both before and after her accession and on Charles, prince of Wales. Respectful but unsycophantic, lively but serious, based on a Bagehotian view of the monarchy's role in modern constitutional politics, these were widely admired and earned for him in 1953 not the knighthood which some had expected—at the time the convention still prevailed at *The Times* that members of its staff did not accept honours—but something which gave him infinitely more pleasure: the position of Arundel herald-extraordinary, which was specially revived for him. It enabled him to take part in the coronation ceremony, in full heraldic splendour.

In 1961 Morrah retired from *The Times* at the age of sixty-five and was invited to join the *Daily Telegraph* as a leader writer. He continued to edit *Round Table*, a task which he first took up in 1944, and continued to make occasional contributions to journals as various as *West Indian Cultural Circular*, *Farmers' Weekly*, and the *Policewoman's Gazette*. A prominent member of the Commonwealth Press Union, he sat as a member of its council and from 1956 to 1971 was chairman of its press freedom committee. Wine was among his chief outside interests (he was a member of the Saintsbury Club), and between 1959 and 1963 he was chairman of the Wine Society and for two years (1964–6) chairman of the Circle of Wine Writers.

In 1972, at a requiem mass at Westminster Cathedral for his friend Charles Curran, Morrah suffered a severe stroke and from then until his death in the Westminster Hospital, London, on 30 September 1974, he never fully recovered his faculties.

Dermot Morrah possessed a very individual and richly flavoured personality. In 1938, at the Oxford encaenia garden party, one of his vocal cords was suddenly paralysed and afterwards he always spoke in a hoarse, penetrating croak as distinctive as his herald's tabard. A polymath traditionalist, he was deeply attached to the Roman Catholic church, the Tridentine mass, the constitution, common law, all ritual both sacred and secular, heraldry, the medieval concepts of feudalism and status, such pleasures as wine, chess, and the ancient card game of ombre (which he firmly pronounced 'umber'). Driven neither by worldly ambition nor by the desire for wealth, he pursued a varied life at a pace not unduly hurried. In later years his appearance—erect, of medium height and build, with luxuriant grey hair and moustache, alert, friendly eyes, quick movements—recalled that of an elderly but active and distinguished bird. In heraldic plumage he was particularly impressive. Until his stroke his conversation was lively, wide-ranging, informative, but never boring. Unsurprisingly, he had a wide and very varied circle of friends.　　　　　　　　　　Charles Monteith, *rev.*

Sources　private information (1986) · personal knowledge (1986) · *The Times* (1 Oct 1974) · *The Times* (12 Oct 1974)
Archives　Bodl. Oxf., corresp. with L. G. Curtis; Round Table corresp.

Morrell family (*per. c.*1790–1965), brewers, came to prominence with **Mark Morrell** (1771–1843) and **James Morrell** (*bap.* 1773, *d.* 1855), who established a long-lasting brewing business. They were the second and third sons in the family of three sons and two daughters of Mark Morrell (1737–1787), a miller, and his wife, Phyllis Greenwood (*d.* 1780). Their father had taken over the subtenancy of the mills at Wallingford, Berkshire, from his own father, Jeremiah (*d.* 1766). A part-time brewer, Mark Morrell senior could not compete seriously with the Wells family, the dominant brewers in Wallingford.

The younger Mark Morrell was born in March 1771 at Wallingford and baptized at St Peter's Church, Wallingford, on 24 April 1771. He was educated at a private academy in Reading and at the age of fifteen, in the year before his father died, was apprenticed to a London brewer, William Tunnard of Southwark. James Morrell was born in Wallingford and baptized at St Peter's, on 14 September 1773, and served an unhappy apprenticeship, in his home town, probably to a maltster, before briefly setting up a business there on his own account. After the death of their father in 1787, the family milling business was inherited by their elder brother, Charles.

In 1797 Mark and James Morrell together moved to Oxford, where their uncle James Morrell (1739–1807) was a solicitor and one of the most influential men in the city. With loans of capital from him (which they repaid out of income during the course of the next ten years), they went into partnership with the brewer Edward Tawney, a bachelor in his early sixties, who owned a brewing business in the suburb of St Thomas's. The intention was that they would buy out Tawney, and he handed over the brewery to them in 1798. After Tawney's death in 1800, the trustees of his estate signed over to them the lease of the brewery premises from the ground landlord, Christ Church, with the freeholds of a malthouse and nine tied public houses in Oxford and the surrounding country.

Under the ownership of the Morrell brothers, the brewery greatly expanded its output and tied estate. In common with many other brewers in early nineteenth-century England, they benefited from the national recession of the 1790s and the post-war slump which followed Waterloo: such businesses gained trade at the expense of small-scale brewing victuallers and other individuals and independent institutions. By the time James—who outlived Mark—transferred his share in the brewery to his son in 1851, the number of public houses attached to the brewery had increased to a sizeable tied estate of about seventy-five houses, of which two-thirds were freehold. Much of the brewery premises, including Edward Tawney's former malthouse in Tidmarsh Lane, Oxford, was rebuilt, and two steam engines were installed to power machinery in the brewhouse.

On 17 December 1807 James Morrell the brewer married Jane Wharton (1789/90–1814), the seventeen-year-old great-niece of Edward Tawney; they had two sons and one surviving daughter. In keeping with the frequent practice of brewers to invest their substantial earnings in banking, James entered in 1808 into a partnership with his cousin Robert Morrell (d. 1849), an Oxford solicitor, and Richard Cox, a former mercer and experienced banker, and Cox's son. All the partners utilized the bank's funds; but the Coxes borrowed so flagrantly that the Morrells expelled them from the partnership in 1831, acquiring most of Richard Cox's assets, including various landed properties near Oxford and a share in a coalmine in the Forest of Dean.

Mark Morrell never married. He died, of bronchitis, aged seventy-two, on 20 March 1843 at 1 Fisher Row, Oxford (a riverside house occupied by three generations of the family between 1800 and 1856). He was buried close to the brewery, at St Thomas's Church. Mark Morrell's main recreation was hunting, and for the last two decades of his life he leased Bradley Farm, Cumnor, from Merton College, as a country residence. He died a wealthy man, with investments worth over £113,000, in addition to his share in the brewery and its various properties. Both he and his cousin Robert, whose death in 1849 brought to an end the banking partnership, left their main estate to James Morrell.

The surviving founding partner of Morrells brewery lived for six more years. James Morrell died at his house on Headington Hill, St Clement's, Oxford, on 10 November 1855, and was buried at St Clement's Church on 15 November 1855. The main beneficiary of his brother and cousin, he died a wealthy man. His only surviving son was also a **James Morrell** (1810–1863), who was born at 1 Fisher Row, Oxford, in March 1810.

Educated at Eton College, James Morrell junior inherited an extensive patrimony, and became a JP and master of the old Berkshire hunt (1848–1858). He married Alicia Harriet Everett (1821/2–1864), daughter of a former high sheriff, the late Revd William Everett, in November 1851, and had one child, Emily Alicia [see below]. In 1856, the year after his father's death, he employed the fashionable London architect John Thomas to build Headington Hill Hall as an extension to his father's former small country house on the hill just east of Oxford. He also employed W. H. Baxter, the superintendent of the university botanic garden, to plant the grounds with exotic trees and shrubs. At the brewery he appointed a manager, who took responsibility for most administrative decisions and also oversaw the running of the brewery and the family home farm at Blackbird Leys, part of an extensive freehold landed estate which James and his father had acquired piecemeal to the south and east of Oxford.

The younger James was a portly figure, fond of lavish entertainment, and with many friends in county society. His early death at his home on 12 September 1863 came at the end of five years' worsening disease of the lungs following a fall while out hunting. On 10 February 1864 his widow, Alicia, also died, and the orphan heir, Emily, was entrusted to the care of an aunt, while the brewery and the family's landed estates were administered for the next

half-century by trustees. In the late nineteenth century the trustees presided over continuing expansion at the brewery, which, by the end of the century, with an estimated working capital of £760,000, was high in the second rank of richest British breweries. Tied public houses doubled in number between the 1850s and 1900, and in 1878 the trustees bought the freeholds of the brewery premises and adjoining properties from Christ Church, allowing them to expand beyond the original cramped site.

One of the trustees originally appointed in James's will was his friend, solicitor, and second cousin Frederick Joseph Morrell (1811–1883), a grandson of the James Morrell (1739–1807) who had founded the law firm of Morrell in Oxford and had acquired the freehold of his business premises at 1 St Giles'. Frederick Morrell was solicitor to the University of Oxford and, with the brewery manager as co-trustee, he effectively administered the brewery and the family's estates during the eleven and a half years between James's death and the appointment of new trustees a year after Emily's marriage. His son Frederick Parker Morrell (1837–1908), the last of the line of Oxford solicitors, was a close and supportive friend of George Herbert Morrell (1845–1906), Emily Morrell's third cousin and later her husband. Neither of the younger Frederick's sons, Hugh or Philip Morrell (d. 1943), kept up the family's connection with the law firm; and, while Philip and his wife, Lady Ottoline *Morrell, constituted a notable presence on the Oxford social scene through their tenancy of Garsington Manor both during and after the First World War, Philip Morrell's pacifism alone would have ensured that they remained remote from their more conventional brewery cousins.

Emily Alicia Morrell (1854–1938), born on 4 January 1854, at 20 St Giles', Oxford, became the richest heiress in Oxfordshire. A ward in chancery, she led a sheltered life until the age of twenty, when she married George Herbert Morrell. The latter was a demonstrator in physiology at Oxford's university museum, and courted Emily in the face of stern opposition from two of the trustees of her estate. G. H. Morrell later served as high sheriff of Oxfordshire in 1885 and was MP for Mid-Oxfordshire in 1891–2 and 1895–1906. The couple had two sons, and lived at Headington Hill Hall in some state: the house and grounds were used for large parties and lawn meets and provided the venue for some of the earliest outings of the Morrell brewery employees. Emily's husband died on 30 September 1906, at Bad Nauheim, in Germany, but she lived on for over thirty years. Her own death occurred at Streatley House, Streatley, Berkshire, on 14 September 1938.

James Herbert [Jimmy] **Morrell** (1882–1965), George Herbert's and Emily's elder son, was born on 9 July 1882 at Headington Hill Hall, and was educated at Eton College and Magdalen College, Oxford, where he rowed in the college eight and studied physics, graduating with a third-class degree in 1904. In 1913 he married Julia Denton, daughter of Sir George Denton, a former governor of the Gambia; they had two sons and two daughters. Like his father and grandfather before him, Jimmy Morrell strongly supported the Oxford (University and City) volunteer rifle corps, the university branch of which became the Officers' Training Corps (OTC) shortly before the outbreak of the First World War; he served as adjutant to the Oxford OTC during the war. Having attended meetings of the brewery trustees in an unofficial capacity since at least 1914, he became acting manager of the brewery in 1926, and continued in that capacity, drawing a salary from the trustees, until the trusts were broken in 1943. He then converted the private firm to a limited company, Morrells Brewery Ltd, with himself as chairman, and with a board initially composed of himself and two former trustees. He was highly regarded as a county councillor, served as high sheriff of Oxfordshire, and until the mid-1930s combined his brewery duties with a position as university demonstrator in physics.

During the inter-war years, as colleges ceased to brew their own beer and a large proportion of Oxford undergraduates spent part of their free time drinking beer, Morrells Brewery began 'to identify and target a specifically university element among its customers' (Allen, 116). The university rowing club eight was first supplied with free pre-boat race beer in 1938: they received College ale, which at 1073° had the highest gravity of all Morrells beers. After the wartime period of austerity, when only 'dark' and 'light' beers were produced, a wide range of distinctive traditional ales, including College, Graduate, and Varsity, were reintroduced. These were sold through a smaller number of refurbished tied houses, mainly within a 30 mile radius of Oxford. The brewery's ordinary beer became lighter, in order to suit changing tastes, and it also began to produce lager under licence.

Jimmy Morrell fought off many takeover bids and worked to preserve the integrity of his small, independent brewery, by then the only one still brewing in Oxford. He died of complications following a hip replacement, at the Nuffield Orthopaedic Centre, Oxford, on 17 July 1965. His eldest son, Colonel Herbert William (Bill) James Morrell (b. 1915), succeeded him, first as managing director, then as chairman of Morrells Brewery Ltd until 1986. In the 1990s competition from larger breweries led to the company being put up for sale. Purchased by Michael Cannon's Morrells of Oxford Ltd, the Oxford brewery was closed in 1998 and relocated to Dorchester.

BRIGID ALLEN

Sources B. Allen, *Morrells of Oxford: the family and their brewery, 1743–1993* (1994) · *The late James Morrell esq* (1863) · H. S[topes], *Brewery companies* (1895) · *Oxford Times* (23 July 1965) · F. Tarrant, 'Guardian of Morrells', *Oxford Times* (15 July 1994) [interview with Margaret Morrell] · T. R. Gourvish and R. G. Wilson, *The British brewing industry, 1830–1980* (1994) · M. Seymour, *Ottoline Morrell: life on a grand scale* (1992) · d. cert. [James Morrell (1773–1855)] · d. cert. [James Herbert Morrell] · d. cert. [Mark Morrell] · d. cert. [Emily Alicia Morrell] · d. cert. [James Morrell (1810–1863)] · b. cert. [Emily Alicia Morrell] · *CGPLA Eng. & Wales* (1863) [James Morrell (1810–1863)] · *CGPLA Eng. & Wales* (1966) [James Herbert Morrell] · *CGPLA Eng. & Wales* (1939) [Emily Alicia Morrell] · *CGPLA Eng. & Wales* (1906) [George Herbert Morrell]
Archives Oxon. RO, title deeds, family and estate papers
Likenesses portrait (James Morrell), priv. coll.

Wealth at death investments over £113,000, plus share in brewery and its various properties—Mark Morrell · under £100,000—James Morrell: probate, 16 Nov 1863, *CGPLA Eng. & Wales* · £42,577 19s. 5d.—Emily Alicia Morrell: probate, 10 June 1939, *CGPLA Eng. & Wales* · £196,254—James Herbert Morrell: probate, 4 Feb 1966, *CGPLA Eng. & Wales*

Morrell, Derek Holtby (1921–1969), civil servant, was born at 41 Mostyn Avenue, Wembley, Middlesex, on 10 August 1921, the son of Donald Morrell (d. c.1973), an architect with the Ministry of Works, and his wife, Dorothy Gladys Dawe (d. 1946). He attended Park Lane primary school, Wembley, and Harrow County School for Boys, with an exchange at the Lycée Malherbe in Caen, where he developed a deep love of France. In 1939 he entered Keble College, Oxford, where he read history, graduating with a second in 1942. From 1942 to 1947 he served in the armed forces (Royal Electrical and Mechanical Engineers (REME), reaching the rank of captain). He learned Cantonese at the School of Oriental and African Studies, London, in 1945 before serving as assistant to the secretary of Chinese affairs in Singapore. On leaving the army in 1947, he became a civil servant. He married on 20 June 1953 Margaret Evelyn Dean (b. 1926), a musician, the daughter of Albert John Dean. They had a son and a daughter.

Morrell served in the Ministry of Education from 1947 to 1966, including over three years (1956–9) as principal private secretary to successive ministers of education. His main postings concerned school building, as principal in 1949–54 and assistant secretary in 1960–62 in the architects and buildings (A & B) branch, and curriculum matters, as assistant secretary 1962–6 in the schools branch. He was founding joint secretary of the Schools Council, 1964–6.

Morrell was one of the talented civil servants responsible for the remarkable success of the post-war school building programme, which enabled the aims of the 1944 Education Act to be met. School building was one of the few direct levers of central government influence on education, and the key to the success of the policy was the creation of an effective partnership of administrators, educationists, and architects which established standards of provision combining economy with effective design and attention to educational need. Morrell's contribution was original, and reflected the principle of co-operation which was his lifelong aim.

By the time Morrell moved to the schools branch of the Ministry of Education in 1962, central government interest in curriculum matters, jealously guarded as the preserve of the local education authorities and teachers—the 'secret garden', as the minister, David Eccles, described it—was growing in response to social and economic change, and because of the need to create an effective new certificate of secondary education examination. Morrell was responsible for the creation and leadership, within the ministry, of the multi-disciplinary curriculum study group, which was designed to enable the ministry to play a more active role in curriculum development. However, it aroused suspicions within the teaching profession and local authorities of undue central control. In its place Morrell drew up proposals for an independent body, comprising representatives of the Department of Education and Science (as the ministry became in 1963), local education authorities, and the teaching profession. This was established in 1964 following the Lockwood committee as the Schools Council for the Curriculum and Examinations, with Morrell as joint secretary from 1964 to 1966. The Schools Council sponsored influential curriculum projects and promoted a wider debate over curriculum policy. Morrell, with his passionate belief in the education of the whole person and respect for the professional freedom and creativity of the teacher, left a deep impression on those he encountered in the educational world. After his death the council established a development fund for teachers in his memory.

In 1966 Morrell was transferred to the Home Office on promotion to under-secretary in charge of the children's department (an example of the new blood the home secretary, Roy Jenkins, was anxious to bring to the Home Office). The main task was to take forward the new Labour government's policy on children in trouble. A 1965 white paper had envisaged the replacement of juvenile courts by family councils and had provoked bitter opposition, especially from the magistracy. Morrell, with his key colleague, Joan Cooper, the chief inspector, led a children's department team in developing new proposals, set out in a white paper, *Children in Trouble*, in 1968. The white paper proposed retention of juvenile courts but envisaged giving local authorities responsibility for determining the treatment children needed. Approved schools would be replaced by local authority community homes. A lasting innovation was the proposal for 'intermediate treatment' as an alternative to residential treatment; intermediate treatment (between home and residential care) covered a range of community-based services which a child attended on a daily basis, often with short periods of residential 'outward bound' activity attached. The white paper had a better reception and passed into law as the Children and Young Persons Act of 1969. Morrell died before the act was implemented and the change of government in 1970 led to a decade of controversy. Nevertheless he had left a deep impression on the children's world and the act was an important milestone in the development of children's policy, in particular in taking account of the background and upbringing of the child, and the need for appropriate supportive, educational, and therapeutic responses.

Morrell's encounter with delinquency, deprivation, and social work response prompted, characteristically, much soul-searching (worked out in private writings which he shared with close colleagues). The draft white paper contained the seeds of an initiative to tackle family breakdown on a wider basis. This coincided with the work of the Seebohm committee, whose 1968 report (*Parl. papers*, 1967–8, 32, Cmnd 3703) led to the creation of local authority social service departments (with which Morrell was quite intimately involved). The initiative was held over until after the Seebohm report was published and took the form of the community development programme, an initiative for co-ordinated action research projects in twelve deprived areas. Endorsed by ministers, the idea owed most to Morrell personally. He intended it as an experiment aimed at tackling social deprivation by combining better service provision with self-help and community participation, monitored by research teams. He died before the community development programmes were established and, deprived of his leadership and marooned in the Home Office following the transfer of the children's department to the Department of Health and Social Security, they had a troubled history. But they marked a key stage in the establishment of community development and Morrell's personal commitment was remembered by all who were exposed to it.

Morrell believed deeply in the need to base social policy on proper objective inquiry, supported by a development stage during which all concerned could contribute. His concept of development groups, in which the views of professionals counted for as much as those of administrators, was central to the process. In addition, Morrell brought a deep personal, moral, and religious commitment and an openness of approach unusual in a civil servant. Many found his practical idealism and personal commitment an inspiring contrast to the dispassionate approach prevailing in the civil service of the 1960s. Others, from Richard Crossman downwards, were put off by his language, which some saw as a mixture of religiosity and sociological jargon. Some in government considered such personal commitment incompatible with the need for objectivity in policy analysis which they saw as the proper role of the administrative civil servant.

Morrell expressed his philosophy of public service, at a time when the Fulton report advocated a vision of a more specialist professional civil service, in a notable address to the First Division Association (FDA) of senior civil servants. While accepting the notion of professionalism, he rejected what he regarded as the myth of total objectivity in issues of social policy. He called passionately for the recognition of the creative moral individual. His statement of the ethos of the civil service left such an impression that it was, by members' request, republished by the FDA (*FDA News*, October 1989).

A tall figure, with little interest in socializing for its own sake, Morrell was intense, charismatic to many, off-putting to some. His way of working was unusually personal (especially for the 1960s), seeking to mobilize support for his initiatives in ways some thought inappropriate for a civil servant. He was committed to work as the expression of personal belief. This was founded on a lifelong, intensely personal, Christian belief, shared with a like-minded group and ultimately leading to deathbed reception into the Roman Catholic church. He died in the Royal Free Hospital annexe in Islington, London, on 10 December 1969, of post-operative complications following abdominal surgery, and was buried at the church of the English Martyrs, Reading. A memorial service was celebrated in Westminster Cathedral by Cardinal Heenan.

Both the intensity of his personality and the importance of his initiatives left an unusually lasting impact for a civil servant in a career cut short at the age of forty-eight.

RICHARD FRIES

Sources The Times (13 Dec 1969) · Times Educational Supplement (19 Dec 1969) · The Friend (9 Jan 1970) · Approved School Gazette (Jan 1970) · private information (2004) [son; Margaret Morrell, wife] · b. cert. · m. cert. · d. cert. · B. St G. Drennan, The Keble College centenary register, 1870–1970 (1970) · S. Maclure, Educational development and school building: aspects of public policy, 1945–73 (1984) · M. Plaskow, ed., The life and death of the Schools Council (1985) · D. Dean, 'The rise and demise of the curriculum study group', Contemporary British History, 2/1 (spring 1997) · J. Tomlinson, The Schools Council: a chairman's salute and envoi (1987) · D. H. Thorpe and others, Out of care: the community support of juvenile offenders (1980) · J. Higgins and others, Government and urban policy (1983) · R. H. S. Crossman, The diaries of a cabinet minister, 3 (1977) · D. Thomas, The making of community work (1983) · R. Lees and M. Mayo, Community action for change (1984) · A. Ioannou, 'Public sector entrepreneurship: policy and process innovations in the UK', PhD diss., London School of Economics
Likenesses photograph, priv. coll.
Wealth at death £36,675: probate, 7 April 1970, CGPLA Eng. & Wales

Morrell, Emily Alicia (1854–1938). See under Morrell family (per. c.1790–1965).

Morrell, Hugh (fl. 1601–c.1664), merchant, was probably a native of Exeter, where in 1601 he was bailiff. In 1608 he complained to Salisbury, the lord treasurer (then high steward of Exeter), that officials at the port of Topsham were levying excessive charges on merchants bringing corn into the country. His family had long aimed to improve cloth manufacture in England (as well as the production of coal, alum, and other metals), and about 1623 Morrell proposed to James I a scheme for the improvement of commerce, probably by the establishment in each town of a corporation to regulate the woollen industry. To this end he secured a patent for Hertfordshire (1624) and for Devon (1626) and later promoted a similar scheme in Worcester.

Some time before this Morrell was established at Rouen in partnership with Charles Snelling, a London merchant. In 1627 their goods, valued at £7600, were confiscated by the French in reprisal for goods seized by English ships. Ruined, and fearing for his life, Morrell was obliged to escape from France, and in June 1627 he petitioned the crown for redress, either from the profits of the sale of the French prizes or through reduction of customs duties in his favour. Later it was proposed to reimburse him from an additional duty on sea coals exported from Newcastle, but by 1641 nothing had been done, probably because of opposition by the farmers of the coal duties.

In 1630–31 there were several petitions from Morrell's fertile mind to the crown and privy council concerning remedies for the decay of trade and consequent loss of customs duties, the export of west country corn to dearth-stricken Ireland, and the secret export of gold from England to France, where it fetched a higher price. In 1633, representing Exeter merchants trading with France, Morrell complained about the banning of their cloth at Morlaix, Rouen, Caen, and Paris, contrary to Anglo-French peace terms, and demanded the transfer of their trade to

Le Havre and the appointment of an English consul. Morrell was chosen, together with Spicer, their governor, to represent the merchants at a conference with their London counterparts, which drew up articles of agreement between them.

Meanwhile Morrell had not abandoned his scheme to reorganize the cloth trade. A committee of merchants recommended it to parliament in 1638. Morrell was one of thirty commissioners appointed to examine the state of the woollen industry and was one of the fifteen who signed its report in 1640. This advocated a ban on the export of wool, the cutting out of middlemen (to reduce the price of wool and yarn), negotiations with the Netherlands to reduce the tax on English cloth, and a general tightening up of the machinery that enforced standards. Unfortunately the civil war was at hand, and there is no proof the report was even considered by the privy council. Morrell brought up the matter again in 1647 and suggested the appointment of a commission of merchants or council of trade to consider the establishment of a bank like the Bank of Amsterdam, removal of most of the duties on manufactures and the customs on imported wool, and the setting up of a merchants' court.

In 1650 Morrell was employed by parliament in commercial negotiations with France, but he seems to have exceeded his authority, since in December he was ordered to cease meddling in affairs of state. His services, however, continued to be used, and he lived in Paris until the Restoration. In 1653 he sought English protection for some French merchants who had bought an island in America and in return promised to pay English customs duties on the goods they transported. He also wrote to Cromwell about the importance of an Anglo-Dutch peace. As late as 1660 he had a petition on the woollen industry referred to the committee for trade: it emphasized the benefits of a corporation in each town to regulate manufactures and keep the poor at work, so preventing rebellions and improving customs revenue by £100,000 per annum. In December 1660 Morrell forwarded to Secretary Nicholas a request from English merchants at Rouen for the re-establishment of a French company and a merchant court. If these were granted, they promised to set up a brass statue of Charles II at the Royal Exchange, to rival that of Henri IV in Paris. Morrell probably died about 1664.

BASIL MORGAN

Sources CSP dom., 1623–62 · Thurloe, State papers · Third report, HMC, 2 (1872) · Fourth report, HMC, 3 (1874) · Eleventh report, HMC (1887) · Report on records of the city of Exeter, HMC, 73 (1916) · G. D. Ramsay, 'The report of the royal commission on the clothing industry, 1640', EngHR, 57 (1942), 482–93 · DNB

Morrell, James (1773–1855). See under Morrell family (per. c.1790–1965).

Morrell, James (1810–1863). See under Morrell family (per. c.1790–1965).

Morrell, James Herbert (1882–1965). See under Morrell family (per. c.1790–1965).

Morrell, Mark (1771–1843). See under Morrell family (per. c.1790–1965).

Morrell [*née* Cavendish-Bentinck], **Lady Ottoline Violet Anne** (1873–1938), literary hostess, was born at 5 Portman Square, London, on 16 June 1873, the youngest child and only daughter of Lieutenant-General Arthur Cavendish-Bentinck (1819–1877) and his second wife, Augusta Mary Elizabeth Browne (1834–1893). Her mother was the younger daughter of Catherine de Montmorency and Henry Montague Browne, dean of Lismore. In 1879 Ottoline's brother Arthur inherited the title and estates of their wealthy and somewhat mysterious relative the fifth duke of Portland. Mrs Bentinck was created Baroness Bolsover in 1880, while her own children, Henry, William, Charles, and Ottoline, were given the titles and precedence of the children of a duke.

Early life Following this change of circumstances, the family moved from East Court, a pleasant manor house in Berkshire, to the few habitable rooms of Welbeck Abbey, a more handsome but forbidding edifice in north Nottinghamshire. Spread below it and connected to the house by a labyrinth of tunnels under the park was the subterranean kingdom created by their reclusive relative, who had stored his possessions away and allowed the house to become derelict.

Ottoline was educated at home by a kind and highly religious governess. Her romantic love of history was stimulated by helping her mother to unpack the Welbeck treasures; these included a magnificent set of Gobelin tapestries and paintings which were stacked, without frames, three deep around the walls of the empty staterooms when they arrived. Here, as she looked at portraits of courtiers 'with pearls in their ears and long trailing lovelocks of golden hair hanging over their collars, and of ladies whom they loved, with very low-cut dresses, showing pearly breasts, and embroidered skirts and exquisite shoes' (*Ottoline: the Early Memoirs*, 76), Ottoline's enduring love affair with the costumes of the past began. She took inspiration both from her eccentric Stuart ancestor Margaret, duchess of Newcastle, and from the Venetian red and sea-green colouring which she saw in the deserted rooms of Bolsover Castle, a ruined keep which formed part of her half-brother's vast inheritance. The duchess of Newcastle offered her an image of courage, individuality, culture, and simplicity to which she would aspire; Bolsover, 'my darling castle', was both the home she longed to inhabit and a mirror for her own proud reclusiveness. 'High, tall, fair and proud it stood' (Seymour, 35), she wrote in retrospect, but the gift was never made and the castle remained uninhabited.

Baroness Bolsover left Welbeck as a querulous and dependent invalid shortly after her son's marriage in 1889. Ottoline accompanied her, to Chertsey and then to stay with relatives at the Villa Capponi in Italy, before nursing her mother through the final months of illness that ended in her death in 1893. Forced to return to Welbeck at the age of nineteen, she felt herself to be an outsider. The young duchess mocked her attempts to benefit the estate workers by organizing carving classes and offering religious instruction, but Welbeck's new librarian, Arthur Strong, and his wife, the classicist Eugenie Sellers,

Lady Ottoline Violet Anne Morrell (1873–1938), by Augustus John, 1919

became her welcome allies. The more worldly affection of William Maclagan, archbishop of York, marked the beginning of a series of troubled relationships with men who were intrigued by Ottoline's unusual beauty (she was almost 6 feet tall, with red-gold hair and turquoise eyes) and by her ardent desire to do good. Other important friendships at this time were with Mother Julian, the aristocratic head of a Cornish sisterhood which Ottoline often visited, and with the author George Macdonald.

In 1896 Ottoline returned to Italy with a chaperone and a distant cousin, with whom she went to St Andrews the following year to study logic for two terms. An invitation from Axel Munthe, the Swedish-born doctor and writer, on her return to London resulted in a visit to his home in Capri with her cousin Hilda Douglas Pennant. The relationship with Munthe was intense but short-lived. Back in England in 1899, Ottoline began studying political economy and Roman history as an out-student at Somerville College, Oxford, probably on the advice of her new admirer, the married Herbert Asquith.

Marriage to Philip Morrell The *Morrell family, connected to both the law and brewing, owned a fine collection of Italian paintings at Black Hall, their family home in Oxford. Ottoline visited the house to inspect the pictures and returned, dazzling in black satin and pearls, to dine. Philip Morrell (*d*. 1943), a young solicitor with dreams of being an architect or a Liberal politician, was rapidly enamoured. Encouraged by his socially ambitious mother, he proposed to a woman they wrongly assumed to be an heiress (Ottoline's mother had cut her out of her will). They were married in February 1902, and settled at 39 Grosvenor Road by the Embankment in a house which Ottoline began brightening with the rich but subtle colours she loved. In 1903 she vigorously supported Philip Morrell's campaign for a Liberal seat in Oxfordshire and they rented Little House in the village of Clifton Hampden in order to give him a local address. Ottoline is credited with having restored and designed the garden of that house. Philip Morrell's first illegitimate child, a daughter, was born in 1904.

Philip Morrell won his Oxfordshire seat in 1906, in which year the Morrells moved across London to 44 Bedford Square, the handsome Bloomsbury house which became famous for its owner's bohemian gatherings. There, on 18 May 1906, Ottoline gave birth to twins, a sickly girl and a healthy boy. The boy, named Hugh after Philip's dead brother who had committed suicide in 1897, died within a few days; the girl, who survived, was named Julian in memory of her mother's old friend in Cornwall. Hospitalized shortly after the death of her baby son, Ottoline was told that an operation had ended any chance of her having further children. The child was buried at Clifton Hampden and was in due course (in 1908) joined by his grandfather Frederick Parker Morrell. Ottoline continued to visit the graveyard until her own death, when Julian took on the task of tending her twin brother's grave.

In 1907 the Morrells rented a second home, Peppard Cottage, not far from her childhood home in Berkshire. This was the period during which Ottoline began to be portrayed by a wide variety of painters, from James Pryde to Augustus John, Henry Lamb, and Roger Fry. Some became her lovers; few were able to resist her combination of innocence, aristocracy, and the singularity of a true eccentric. Her style, as they admiringly noted, was all her own, as original and confident as her sense of colour. She created it, on a shoestring budget, by paying her friendly dressmaker Miss Brenton ('Brenty') to copy costumes from masterpieces which she saw in galleries (Velázquez was a striking inspiration) and to make use of velvets and brocades in startling colours. Encouraged by Miss Brenton, she became increasingly bold. Her high-heeled shoes, often scarlet, had 'elevators' in the soles; her velvet hats were sometimes the size of a small cartwheel. This was the arresting and easily mocked figure who, in 1907, began holding weekly parties at Bedford Square for the artists and writers she met and whom she hoped to help by offering introductions to rich patrons. Henry James was among those who feared that her generosity would be abused. He was right.

Ottoline's efforts were often successful. She assisted the careers of Mark Gertler, Jacob Epstein, the Spencer brothers, and Henry Lamb among many others. She was, however, easily ridiculed. Her shyness made it difficult for strangers to discover her sense of humour (she loved going to music halls and singing ditties), and she could appear overbearing and intense. Her religious faith, in an age of atheism, was mocked and distrusted. Virginia Woolf, Vanessa Bell, and Lytton Strachey seldom resisted the temptation to jeer behind her back; Duncan Grant, Maynard Keynes, Augustus John, and the Spencers were among her defenders. In 1909 Roger Fry invited her to join the newly formed Contemporary Art Society, designed to help young artists and to make their work accessible to provincial galleries. Ottoline bought paintings for the new society and provided her cousin, Lord Howard de Walden, as its first president, while her art-loving brother Lord Henry Bentinck became its chairman. In 1910 she became an enthusiastic supporter of the notorious 'Manet and the post-impressionists' exhibition.

Bertrand *Russell (1872–1970), Ottoline's lover and lifelong friend, became aware of her while helping Philip Morrell's political campaign in 1909. In 1911, disenchanted by his first wife, Alys Pearsall Smith, Russell turned to Ottoline and was, for a time, inspired by her, although he could not sympathize with her Christian beliefs. Their relationship was fought over and celebrated in a remarkable correspondence, often amounting to four letters a day. Ottoline's sexual coldness and Russell's possessiveness caused difficulties which prompted suicide threats on both sides; Philip Morrell, engaged in his own busy extramarital love life, was able to take a fairly detached view of the situation.

Garsington Ottoline's relationship with Russell had already begun to wane in 1915, when she and Philip moved to their most celebrated home, Garsington Manor in Oxfordshire. The house and the making of its colourful Italianate garden became Ottoline's recreation, while Philip Morrell used his considerable architectural skill to improve the layout of the lower floors of the house and to embellish the exterior with a loggia. Here, as the Morrells provided a refuge for conscientious objectors during the war years, the low, dark rooms were decorated by visitors, though always to Ottoline's taste. The conversations and daily life of Garsington were recorded, sometimes with the malice of unease (Lytton Strachey, Dora Carrington, Clive and Vanessa Bell), sometimes with amusement (Aldous Huxley), and occasionally, with a lyricism which suggests that the house came to represent the passing of a lost world of elegance and civilization which would not easily be recovered (Juliette Baillot, D. H. Lawrence, Siegfried Sassoon). Garsington and its hostess featured in the work of contemporary novelists, with Bertrand Russell often in a leading role. Huxley and Lawrence were among those who drew on Ottoline's unconventional country court for their fictions. Her manner, her beliefs, and her appearance were exhibited and parodied, a form of betrayal which hurt her less than the revelation (the truth being exposed to her by Mark Gertler) that she was despised and disliked by many of the people to whom she had given her support. 'I am known as a dangerous and designing woman, immoral and unclean' (Seymour, 397), she wrote in her private journal (January 1918) after this distressing conversation.

Affection mattered to Ottoline too much for her own happiness. (One of her many doctors, a Dr Combe, told Bertrand Russell in confidence in 1912 that her *nervosité* was the only illness he had no hope of curing.) Constantly betrayed by her husband and let down by Russell, she found unexpected comfort in a late relationship with Lionel Gomme, a young bisexual stonemason who died, tragically, of a brain haemorrhage in 1922.

In 1927 Ottoline began writing the memoirs which were published, following some manipulative editing by her husband and, to a lesser extent, by her literary executor, Robert Gathorne-Hardy, after her death. Financial difficulties led to the sale of Garsington in 1928. Ottoline's last ten years were spent with Philip at a modest London home, 10 Gower Street, which survives as part of London University. There, while she became increasingly deaf and troubled by illness, she continued to entertain a remarkable circle of people including W. B. Yeats, T. S. Eliot, and the Huxley brothers. Dame Ethel Smyth was a new friend, but many of those who had mocked her in the past, like Virginia Woolf, returned now to honour Ottoline's courage in adversity. Philip's peculiarities and his philandering had become common knowledge; Ottoline herself still hungered for relationships of spiritual affinity. Charlotte Mew, Dilys Powell, and Elizabeth Bowen were among the many intelligent younger women she sought out in the hope, sometimes rewarded, of forming a substantial friendship. A whole generation of young men became the willing and occasionally disrespectful court to this intense, demanding, and unpredictable old lady. Reconciled with D. H. Lawrence shortly before his death, she was touched to be told that there was none other like her: 'there is only one Ottoline' (Seymour, 362). Frieda Lawrence also came to Gower Street for a reconciliation before leaving for New Mexico.

Significance   T. S. Eliot, her regular companion to the music-halls which they both enjoyed, helped Virginia Woolf to draft a memorial tablet after Ottoline's death in 1938. Hinting at her rejection by Philip, its last lines honoured

> A brave spirit, unbroken
> Delighting in beauty and goodness
> And the love of her friends.
> (Seymour, 361)

Eliot's own gratitude was partly inspired by Ottoline's unfailing consideration for his wife, Vivien, at a time when her troubled mental state had cut her off from many of their friends.

Ottoline's flaws remain more immediately apparent than her virtues. She was a demanding and oppressive mother, she could be tyrannical in her desire to control the lives of her friends, and she was reckless in her gossip about other people's private opinions. Her craving for affection could seem discomforting. Her clothes, acknowledged now as pioneering in their imaginative presentation, often provoked mockery and even disgust. One young visitor to Garsington never forgot the horror of seeing her hostess's skirts, a mass of net under which flies swarmed and pressed, as Ottoline stooped to embrace her.

Yet Ottoline Morrell's merits were outstanding. Courageous in her friendships, in her readiness to stand by her beliefs and to support work in which she had faith, she was a trailblazer in fashion, the bohemian ancestor of all that is most adventurous in modern design. As a friend, she was matchless. Henry Yorke (the novelist Henry Green) spoke for many when he wrote to Philip after her death that she had been someone who did good:

> to literally hundreds of young men like myself who were not worth her little finger, but she took trouble over them and they went out into the world very different from what they would have been if they had not known her.   (Seymour, 556)

This was Ottoline's greatest gift, the ability to inspire and encourage, to create the idea of an achievable good. 'It is very difficult to think of anyone who meant so much to me' (ibid., 518) wrote T. S. Eliot. Aldous Huxley remembered that she had given him a 'complete mental reorientation' (ibid., 12); Lord David Cecil romantically hailed 'a princess of the Renaissance risen to shame our drab age' (ibid.). Duncan Grant honoured her singular moral and physical courage (ibid.). Augustus John paid tribute to her 'most noble and generous soul … there is no one to be compared to her' (ibid.).

Laid low by a mysterious illness, Ottoline Morrell received treatment at Sherwood Park, a clinic in Tunbridge Wells run by Dr A. J. Cameron. She died there on 21 April 1938 after being injected with Prontosil, an untested new drug about which there were serious misgivings in the medical world. Cameron, a doctor who freely encouraged the drug's injection at his clinic, had committed suicide on 19 April, possibly after realizing the irresponsibility of his actions. His records were subsequently destroyed. His former patient was buried with her Bentinck relatives on the Welbeck estate. A memorial service was held at St Martin-in-the-Fields on 26 April. Her obituary in *The Times* was written by Virginia Woolf.

Philip Morrell died five years later, in 1943. Their daughter, Julian, who had married Victor Goodman in 1928, returned to her earlier love, Igor Vinogradoff, after her mother's death. She had two sons and a daughter from her first marriage. She met her illegitimate half-brothers for the first time at the funeral for Philip Morrell.

MIRANDA SEYMOUR

Sources   M. Seymour, *Ottoline Morrell: life on the grand scale* (1992); rev. edn (1998) · unpublished journals of Lady Ottoline Morrell, priv. coll., Goodman papers · *Ottoline: the early memoirs of Lady Ottoline Morrell*, ed. R. Gathorne–Hardy (1963) · *Ottoline at Garsington: memoirs of Lady Ottoline Morrell, 1915–1918*, ed. R. Gathorne-Hardy (1974) · *DNB* · Burke, *Peerage* (2000) · *CGPLA Eng. & Wales* (1938) · b. cert. · d. cert.

Archives   McMaster University, Hamilton, Ontario, papers · priv. coll., papers · Ransom HRC, corresp. | BL, letters to S. S. Koteliansky, Add. MS 48971 · Internationaal Instituut voor Sociale Geschiedenis, Amsterdam, corresp. with Dora Russell · King's AC Cam., letters to John Hayward · King's AC Cam., letters to John Maynard Keynes · King's Cam., letters to W. J. H. Sprott · LUL, letters to T. S. Moore · NL Scot., letters to March Cost · Stanford University, corresp. with D. H. Lawrence and Frieda Lawrence · U. Sussex, letters to Virginia Woolf | SOUND BL NSA, 'Ottoline: a portrait of Lady Ottoline Morrell', 1973, P 938R TR1

Likenesses   C. Morton, platinum prints, c.1904–1911, NPG · J. Pryde, oils, 1905 · C. Conden, portrait, 1906 · N. Lytton, oils, 1906, priv. coll. · H. Lamb, crayon drawing, c.1911–1913, priv. coll. · H. Lamb, pencil drawing, c.1912, NPG · S. Bussy, oils, 1913, NPG · D. Grant, oils, 1913, NPG · D. Grant, oils, c.1913–1914, Leicestershire Museums and Art Galleries, Leicester · A. John, oils, 1919, NPG [see illus.] · S. Bussy, portrait, c.1920, NPG · C. Beaton, photograph, NPG · A. John, chalk and wash drawing, Man. City Gall. · photographs, NPG

Wealth at death £1832 17s. 8d.: probate, 20 July 1938, CGPLA Eng. & Wales

Morrell, William (*fl.* 1611–1625), poet, matriculated as a sizar at Magdalene College, Cambridge, at Easter 1611, where he graduated BA in 1614–15. He was ordained deacon at Peterborough on 23 May 1619 and priest on 24 May. In 1623 he joined the company that was sent out to Massachusetts by the Plymouth council under the command of Captain Robert Gorges, son of Sir Ferdinando Gorges. He bore a commission from the ecclesiastical court to exercise superintendence over the churches that were, or might be, established in the colony. The attempt by this company to form a settlement at Wessagussett was unsuccessful. After Gorges's departure Morrell remained a year at Plymouth, out of curiosity to learn something of the country, but made no use of his commission nor even mentioned it until just before he sailed for England. His interests seem to have been primarily scientific and anthropological, and he evidently spent much of his time studying local flora and fauna alongside the traditions and rituals of the Native Americans.

Morrell recorded the results of his observations in some elegant Latin hexameters, which he translated into English heroic verse couplets, published under the title of *New-England, or, A briefe enarration of the eyre, earth, water, fish, and fowles of that country, with a description of the natures, orders, habits and religion of the natives; in Latine and English verse* (1625). The English version is preceded by an address to the 'Understanding Reader', a dedication to the lords, knights, and gentlemen, whom he considered the 'Adventurers for New England', and a poetic epistle to the king. The poem itself opens with a description of the glories of New England, which is seen as a garden paradise. Plants and animals are listed through the varying seasons and even the fish in the sea are detailed in their size and variety. Most of the work, however, is concerned with the ways of the indigenous peoples, who are described with a mixture of fear, respect, and awe. The mission was to convert them to Christian ways, and Morrell felt the need to inform all those who would travel to New England for such a venture. In a postscript he announced his intention of publishing another book on the locality, but this did not materialize. The work was reprinted in 1762 in the collections of the Massachusetts Historical Society (1st ser., vol. 1, 1762) and a facsimile of the edition of 1625 was printed in 1895.

GORDON GOODWIN, *rev.* JOANNA MOODY

Sources lion.chadwyck.co.uk [Literature Online (LION)], June 1999 · F. W. Bateson, *The Cambridge bibliography of English literature*, 1 (1940), 795, 893 · Watt, *Bibl. Brit.*, 2.685 · W. T. Lowndes, *The bibliographer's manual of English literature*, ed. H. G. Bohn, [new edn], 2

(1864), 1617 · STC, 1475–1640, no. 18169 · Venn, *Alum. Cant.* · *Collections of the Massachusetts Historical Society*, 1 (1792), 125–39

Archives BL, MSS

Morren, Nathaniel (1798–1847), Church of Scotland minister, was born in Aberdeen on 3 February 1798, the son of George Morren. By the time he was seven both his parents were dead and he was brought up in the home of his maternal grandmother. He was educated at Aberdeen grammar school and at the city's Marischal College, where he graduated MA in 1814. He became a tutor at Fort George before going to work at Caen, in France, in 1815. In 1818 he returned to Aberdeen to study divinity at the university. He was licensed by the presbytery of Aberdeen in October 1822 and appointed minister of Blackhall Street Chapel, Greenock, in June 1823. On 26 April 1825 Morren married Mary Shand, the second daughter of Alexander Shand, advocate, of Aberdeen.

In his ministry Morren combined intense scholarship with an equal devotion to the pastoral care of his congregation. As well as articles and translations he published the authoritative *Annals of the General Assembly of the Church of Scotland from … 1739 to … 1766* (1838–40). However, as the non-intrusion controversy reached its height, he turned his pen from scholarship to church politics. An evangelical himself, he none the less came to believe that the church should abandon the Veto Act. His views brought him into conflict with another Greenock minister and prominent non-intrusionist, Patrick Macfarlan. By temperament he may have been ill-suited to such activity: the memoir attached to his posthumously published *Sermons* (1848) describes him as being sensitive to the point of irritability and inclined to boil over in the heat of debate. The Disruption of 1843 did, however, give him the opportunity to advance, at last, to the dignity of a full parochial ministry. He was translated to First Charge, Brechin, in September, to a position left vacant by James McCosh's adherence to the Free Church. He did not long enjoy his new situation, suffering serious illness in April 1846 from which he never really recovered. He died on 28 March 1847.   LIONEL ALEXANDER RITCHIE

Sources N. Morren, *Sermons … to which is prefixed a memoir of the author* (1848) · *Fasti Scot.*

Morres, Hervey Montmorency (1767–1839), Irish nationalist, was born on 8 March 1767 at Rathailean Castle, Nenagh, co. Tipperary, the eldest son of Matthew Montmorency Morres (1726–1795) and Margaret, second daughter of Francis Magan of Emo, co. Westmeath. Aged fifteen he travelled to continental Europe with his father's relation General Count Edward Dalton, who served with the Austrian army. He joined the Austrian army and was assigned to Field-Marshal Lacy's regiment. On 4 October 1782 he joined Liégeois regiment of Vierzet as gentleman-cadet. During 1784 he served in Flanders. In 1786 he served in Richard d'Alton's regiment as an ensign, returning as sub-lieutenant to Lacy's regiment in 1787. 1790 saw him in Kavanagh's regiment of cuirassiers but later that same year he again returned to Lacy's regiment where he was promoted to the position of lieutenant of grenadiers. He saw much active service, most notably against the Turks in 1788 and in Silesia in 1790, serving under Field-Marshal Loudon, where he participated in the siege of Thionville. In 1792 he fought against the French as a volunteer in Prince Hohenlohe's army. He was also involved in the blockade of Landau and fought at Soultz in Alsace where he was slightly wounded on 24 December 1793. During 1793, as lieutenant of grenadiers, he fought in the army of the Rhine under Marshal Wurmser and the following year was aide-de-camp to Prince Charles of Fürstenberg. Having attained the rank of captain he left the Austrian service in 1795.

In 1795 Morres married Louise de Helmstadt (1771/2–1798) at Heidelberg and later that year returned to Ireland. They lived at Knockalton in co. Tipperary, where the eldest of their four children, Louise, was born on 20 September 1795; she became a maid of honour to Queen Caroline of Bavaria. Upon learning of the likelihood of a French expedition to Ireland in 1796 Morres accepted a commission as aide-de-camp to General Dundas. Disgust at the measures adopted by the government led him to join the Society of United Irishmen in November 1796. In May 1797 he became a county representative for Tipperary and was chosen as colonel of the regiment of Nenagh infantry. In February 1798 he became involved with the general military committee of the United Irishmen and shortly after was appointed adjutant-general of Munster. Following the arrest of many of the leaders of the United Irishmen on 12 March 1798 he became a member of the new executive. He avoided an attempt made to arrest him on 28 April and concentrated his efforts on organizing the capture of strategic positions around west Dublin, but plans were thrown into disarray by the capture of his good friend and United Irish leader, Lord Edward Fitzgerald, on 19 May. On 4 June he escaped from Dublin and hid in co. Westmeath until 22 August when news of the landing of General Humbert's expedition at Killala, reached him. By his own, exaggerated, account he then organized upwards of 7000 men to provide assistance to Humbert's troops; the numbers involved were probably no more than 2000. Following the defeat of Humbert's troops at Ballinamuck, Morres escaped to Dublin and from there travelled through Britain and on to continental Europe, finally arriving at Hamburg on 7 October 1798.

In Hamburg, Morres stayed with Lady Pamela Fitzgerald, the widow of Edward. From her residence he wrote to the French resident, Marragon, requesting permission to enter France. Having been included in the Rebel Fugitives Act (where he was named as Harvey Morris) he felt it was unsafe to remain in Hamburg. And so it proved. Following information received from Samuel Turner, a spy from Newry, co. Down, his correspondence with Marragon along with a memorial he had written to Breuix were intercepted by the British and on 24 November 1798 he was arrested, by the orders of Sir James Crawford, the British agent, at the American Arms. Arrested with Morres were other United Irishmen, Napper Tandy, Corbet, and Blackwell. These arrests did not go unnoticed; it was claimed that they were contrary to the law of nations, and

the French directory claimed Morres and Napper Tandy as their own. In a decree issued on 9 October 1799 the French directory severed all diplomatic relations with Hamburg and relations were restored only following a public apology and the payment of 4.5 million francs. Morres and the other men were extradited to Britain on 28 September 1799 but the prosecution against Tandy and Morres collapsed on a point of law: it was successfully argued that the arrests had been premature. In December 1801 Morres was released, on bail, from Kilmainham gaol. He went first to Paris but returned to Dublin shortly after, where he married Helen, the widow of Dr John Esmonde, a United Irishman who had been hanged as a traitor in 1798. Morres's first wife had died aged twenty-six on 24 November 1798, the day of her husband's arrest. Morres and his second wife had three sons, Hervé, Geffroy, and Mathieu, who all became officers in the Austrian army.

At the invitation of General Clarke, duke of Feltre and minister of war, Morres joined the French army in 1812 and was promoted to adjutant-commandant. In 1814 he served on the staff of General Augereau at Lyons. Despite many requests he never became a member of the Légion d'honneur but was made a knight of Saint-Louis in June 1817. Miles Byrne met him in Paris in March 1812. Following the abdication of Napoleon he offered to serve Britain but both Wellington and Castlereagh were unwilling to accept him. On 3 November 1816 he received letters of nationalization from the French government. With the restoration of the French monarch he was anxious to associate himself with the noble family of Montmorency in France. To prove his case he spent time compiling a genealogical memoir but the evidence he provided was ignored by the French Montmorencys. In addition to his interest in genealogy he published several books on Irish topography in the 1810s and 1820s. Upon his retirement he received the half pay of a staff colonel until his death. He died at St Germain-en-Laye on 9 May 1839.   GILLIAN O'BRIEN

Sources *Memoirs and correspondence of Viscount Castlereagh, second marquess of Londonderry*, ed. C. Vane, marquess of Londonderry, 12 vols. (1848–53) · F. W. Van Brock, 'Morres memorial', ed. H. Murtagh, *The Irish Sword: Journal of the Military History Society of Ireland*, 15 (1982–3), 36–44 · R. Hayes, *Biographical dictionary of Irishmen in France* (1949) · H. H. Morres, *Les Montmorency de France et les Montmorency d'Irlande* (1828) · R. R. Madden, *The United Irishmen: their lives and times* (1860), vol. 1 · W. J. Fitzpatrick, *Secret service under Pitt* (1892) · *Memoirs of Miles Byrne*, ed. F. Byrne, 3 (1863) · *DNB*

Morres, Hervey Redmond, second Viscount Mountmorres (1741/2–1797), politician, was the eldest son of Hervey Morres, first Viscount Mountmorres of Castle Morres in co. Kilkenny (d. 1766), MP for Irishtown (1734–56) and mayor of Kilkenny (1752–3), for whom the viscountcy was created in 1763. His mother was the viscount's first wife, Lady Letitia Ponsonby (d. 1754), daughter of Brabazon Ponsonby, first earl of Bessborough. He was educated at Christ Church, Oxford, from where he graduated MA on 3 July 1766, and DCL on 8 July 1773. On the death of his father in April 1766 Morres succeeded to a very small, encumbered estate, but by his prudent and even parsimonious manner of life he succeeded before his death in creating a fortune of £5000 a year, and was able to make a liberal allowance to the two children of his father's second wife. He resided for some time in Dublin, where he fought a duel in which he was shot but not badly wounded, although he stayed in bed for a month as he enjoyed receiving sympathetic visitors.

Mountmorres took a profound interest in all questions affecting the privileges of the Irish House of Lords, and was noted for his Irish patriotism, on one occasion in 1785 attending the house in the uniform of the Irish Volunteers. On another occasion he caused some amusement by publishing in the Dublin newspapers a speech on the appellant jurisdiction of the Lords which he intended to deliver, but the debate never took place. He spoke frequently in the house, generally adopting a position opposed to the administration, but on the regency question in 1788 he dissented from the view generally taken in Ireland, and argued strongly in support of the course pursued by William Pitt and the English parliament.

Mountmorres resided often in London and contested an election for the seat of Westminster in 1774, which he lost because he was too closely associated with John Wilkes. He became a fellow of the Royal Society on 12 December 1793, and inherited a family baronetcy on the death of a distant cousin in 1795 or 1796.

Mountmorres was a prolific political writer and published numerous works, chiefly on Irish politics and economics, but also on European politics and Irish history. He was an advocate of emancipation for Irish Catholics, and wrote on this topic as well. He was planning to produce a new translation of Herodotus's *Histories* at the time of his death. He was greatly distressed by the news that reached him of the disturbed state of Ireland in 1797 and this may have been the cause of his shooting himself at his London lodgings in York Street, St James's Square, on 17 or 18 August of that year; he was fifty-five. The coroner's verdict was one of temporary lunacy and witnesses at the inquest testified that he had been depressed about Irish affairs for some days before his death. He was buried on 22 August 1797 at St James's Chapel, Tottenham Court Road, London, and, never having married, was succeeded in the titles by his half-brother, Francis Hervey Morres, though his estates were left to his full sisters.

ROBERT DUNLOP, rev. ALEXANDER DU TOIT

Sources GEC, *Peerage* · GEC, *Baronetage* · H. M. Morres, *Les Montmorency de France et les Montmorency d'Irlande* (1828) · *GM*, 1st ser., 67 (1797), 717–18, 743–44, 885 · *Walker's Hibernian Magazine* (July–Dec 1797), 306–10 · J. Barrington, *Personal sketches and recollections of his own times*, [another edn] (1876?) · *The Times* (1876)
Archives BL, Hardwicke MSS
Wealth at death estate valued at £5000 p.a.: GEC, *Peerage*; *GM*

Morrice, Bezaleel (*bap.* 1678, *d.* 1749), writer and sea captain, the third son of William (*d.* 1701) and Jane Morrice (*fl.* 1672–1703), was baptized on 8 May 1678 at St Dunstan and All Saints, Stepney. He received a classical education, probably in England, but it is not known where. His father was the East India Company factor at Fort St George, Madras, when Bezaleel, aged fourteen, was appointed writer (that is, clerk or assistant factor) on 10 March 1693

and went out to Madras. William died in 1701, soon after which Bezaleel briefly returned to England, where his *The Muse's Treat*, a collection of love lyrics and imitations of Ovid, with a pastoral 'To the Sacred Memory of William III', was published in 1702.

Morrice returned to India as factor at Fort St David (Negapatam, south of Madras), where it was wrongly rumoured that he had died in 1705. However, it seems that he went to sea. Both his elder brothers were seafarers. Salman Morrice (1672–1749) was a Royal Navy captain by 1697 and eventually rose to the rank of vice-admiral. William Morrice the younger (*b.* 1670) was captain of an East Indiaman when, in 1701, he was captured by Arabs and carried to Muscat. Bezaleel too became captain of an East Indiaman. His *Voyage from the East-Indies* (1716), sold by Arabella Morrice, bookseller, possibly a relation, describes perhaps his last voyage.

In 1712 Morrice was in England long enough to publish two volumes of verse and prose. It seems that he was permanently ashore from 1715. Between that year and 1742 he published and republished a series of satirical verse epistles attacking Thomas Tickell, Leonard Welsted, Richard Blackmore, and especially and repeatedly Pope's translation of Homer, so, unsurprisingly, he is among the targets of Pope's *Dunciad*. In *Dissectio mentis humanae* (1730) Morrice satirized 'modern critics, stage and epic poets, translators, drolls, etc.'. His large outpouring of non-satirical verse and prose includes love lyrics, pastorals, translations from Latin and Greek, allegories, descriptive verse, and old-fashioned 'character' writing. The largest collection is *A Miscellany in Verse and Prose* by Captain Morrice (1739), but he constantly reworked his poems and prefaces, reissuing them 'with alterations, additions, and embellishments'. His version of the Venus and Adonis story was recycled with particularly irritating frequency. Morrice was a regular contributor of verse to *Mist's Journal* and contributed to Eustace Budgell's *The Bee*. Towards the end of his life he lived in or near Battersea. He died on 9 June 1749. The name of his wife is not known; she died in 1790. They had no children.

JAMES SAMBROOK

Sources East India Company, minutes of the court of directors, BL OIOC, B/39:13; 40:17–8, 174, 178; 43:281, 354, 369; 44:116; 46:44 · D. F. Foxon, ed., *English verse, 1701–1750: a catalogue of separately printed poems with notes on contemporary collected editions*, 2 vols. (1975) · W. C. Morice, *A collection of Morice and Morrice biographies* (1923) · parish register transcript, St Dunstan and All Saints, Stepney · *London Magazine*, 10 (1741), 154 · *London Magazine*, 18 (1749), 288 · Captain Morrice [B. Morrice], *A miscellany in verse and prose* (1739) · A. Pope, *The Dunciad*, ed. J. Sutherland (1943), vol. 5 of *The Twickenham edition of the poems of Alexander Pope*, ed. J. Butt (1939–69); 3rd edn [in 1 vol.] (1963); repr. (1965), 449 · E. Hood, 'Fly leaves xxxiv', *GM*, 1st ser., 97/1 (1827), 29

Morrice, Roger (1628/9–1702), diarist and historian, was probably the son of a yeoman farmer of the parish of Leek in the north Staffordshire moorlands. He was registered as 'plebeian' when he matriculated from Magdalen Hall, Oxford, on 22 February 1651, and as a sizar when he migrated to St Catharine's College, Cambridge, in 1654. He graduated BA in 1656 and proceeded MA in 1659. He was vicar of Duffield, Derbyshire, from 11 September 1658 until 24 August 1662, when he was ejected under the Act of Uniformity. For some part of the next three decades he was chaplain in London to Denzil, first Baron Holles of Ifield (whose will he witnessed in 1670 and funeral he attended in 1680), and to the eminent lawyer Sir John Maynard. Both were parliamentarian veterans of puritan persuasion. Morrice became well off, presumably by the largesse of his patrons, and spent generously on the education of young men for the dissenting ministry.

Morrice occasionally surfaces in contemporary comment as a chronicler and collector of manuscripts. He helped Edmund Calamy list the ejectees of 1662, and he supplied manuscripts to John Strype. Under the will of Richard Baxter, Morrice was responsible, with Matthew Sylvester, for distributing Baxter's library and publishing posthumous works. (Among recipients of books was the young John Toland, later a deist firebrand.) Morrice followed Baxter's 'middle way', both in the theological retreat from Calvinist orthodoxy and in pursuit of the ecclesiastical ideal of accommodation with Anglicanism through 'comprehension', which entailed a modified episcopacy and leniency over rubrics. In 1676 he signed a Baxterian manifesto against antinomianism.

Morrice's importance is twofold. He left a journal of his own times and a large manuscript collection on puritan history, housed in Dr Williams's Library, London. The first is indispensable to historians of later Stuart England, the second to those of Elizabethan puritanism. The 'Ent'ring book' is an account, about a million words long, of public affairs from March 1677 until April 1691. It is so detailed, and its appearance so like a newsletter, that its author must have been, in effect, a full-time journalist, perhaps supplying newsletters to a group of presbyterian-whig politicians. This circle included the Maynards, Hampdens, Harleys, Foleys, Hobarts, Howes, Pagets, and Swinfens. (The few extant letters by Morrice show him serving the Pagets as an election agent.) In the 'Ent'ring book' Morrice emerges as self-effacing, astonishingly well informed, diplomatic, and an astute political barometer. He is a valuable source for high politics, religious history, state trials, the flow of news and information, and much else besides, such as public festivals and entertainments, duelling, and the theatre. Morrice was especially concerned with the fate of nonconformity, when persecuted, when wooed by James II, and when grudgingly tolerated in 1689; and, more broadly, with the fate of English protestantism in the face of the Counter-Reformation. He acted as go-between in Anglican–dissenter negotiations, particularly on the eve of the revolution of 1688. He appears never to have been arrested, though in the autumn of 1683, when the government rounded up large numbers of suspects in the wake of the Rye House plot, he was glad of an offer to stand bail from Sir John Baber (the court's go-between with the dissenters) and the whig MP William Harbord. In February 1689, in the aftermath of the revolution, he records that he walked in Westminster Hall 'with true liberty' and 'without fear' for the first time since 1662 (Morrice MS Q, p. 458).

Morrice hoped to write the history of puritanism. He drafted an outline in the 1690s but his hope was not fulfilled and the job was done by Daniel Neal in the *History of the Puritans* (1732). The documents he provided for Strype helped counter-balance the reliance upon official sources in Strype's histories of Elizabethan archbishops. Morrice's materials today serve the study of the earliest presbyterians, particularly John Field, whose campaigns for a purer teaching ministry are recorded in his *Register*, Morrice's luckiest find. Field was often in trouble for nonconformity, yet spurned the excesses of the sectaries. Morrice continued that tradition: in the 'Ent'ring book' he deplored the opposing zealots, the 'hierarchists' and 'fanatics', while applauding the 'sober churchmen' and 'old Puritans'. Morrice was a last voice of old puritanism, before permanent denominational separation became unavoidable after 1689.

Morrice fell seriously ill in the late 1690s and, probably in 1698, retired to Leek, living most probably with his nephew Isaac, whose home was licensed for presbyterian worship in 1699. He died unmarried, aged seventy-three, at Hoxton, Middlesex, on 17 January 1702, and was buried in Bunhill Fields. His elaborate will reveals his friendships. His pallbearers were senior presbyterian ministers, including Vincent Alsop, John Howe, Daniel Williams, Edmund Calamy, and Matthew Sylvester. He was also close to the latitudinarian clergy of the established church: Bishop Edward Fowler, Bishop Richard Kidder, and Bishop John Moore. He appointed as his principal executor the puritan-whig MP Edward Harley. In all, his will names 180 people, from the speaker of the House of Commons, Robert Harley, to a wheelwright's wife in Stepney. Morrice's papers include a library list of some 1250 items. The only surviving memorial to him is a charity board in Meerbrook Chapel near Leek. MARK GOLDIE

Sources DWL, Morrice MSS · *Roger Morrice's 'Entring book'*, ed. M. Goldie and others, 5 vols. [forthcoming] · *Calamy rev.* · will, PRO, PROB 11/463 · A. Peel, ed., *The seconde parte of a register*, 2 vols. (1915)
Archives DWL, 'Ent'ring book'
Wealth at death est. over £1500 in bequests: will, PRO, PROB 11/463

Morrice, Thomas (1659/60–1748), nonjuring Church of England clergyman, was possibly the Thomas Morris who graduated BA from King's College, Cambridge, in 1683 and MA in 1688. In the latter year he was a minor canon of Worcester and vicar of Claines, Worcestershire. Having refused to take the oath of supremacy in 1689, he was deprived of his ecclesiastical preferments, and reduced to live on the generosity of affluent Jacobites. This did not prevent him from undertaking acts of charity, as a result of which he was, according to the *London Evening-Post*, 'so well esteemed … that he was never disturb'd … in the most suspicious Times … always protected by those who were Enemies to his politics'. As a member of the chapter at Worcester, he belonged to a strong group of later nonjurors, including Bishop Thomas and Dean Hickes. Described by Hearne as a widower without children (1730), he died in Worcester on 15 June 1748, aged eighty-eight, and was buried at the west end of the north aisle of the cloisters of Worcester Cathedral under a flat grave-stone, on which was inscribed, at his request, the word, 'Miserimus', without name, date, or comment. This inscription was nearly obliterated in 1829, but was soon after renewed with the more correct spelling, 'Miserrimus'. This monument excited the imagination of several early nineteenth-century writers, including Wordsworth (1828), inspiring at least three sonnets and one novel, F. M. Reynolds's *Miserrimus: a Tale* (1832), none of which was grounded in Morrice's life. The *Gentleman's Magazine* described Reynolds's work as 'a posthumous libel on an innocent and helpless person whose story is widely different from that here inflicted on his memory; … a sufferer for conscience' sake … in consequence of political changes' (*GM*, 245).

A. F. POLLARD, rev. EIRWEN E. C. NICHOLSON

Sources London Evening-Post (20–22 Sept 1748) • J. H. Overton, *The nonjurors: their lives, principles, and writings* (1902) • *Remarks and collections of Thomas Hearne*, ed. C. E. Doble and others, 10, OHS, 67 (1915), 324 • Venn, *Alum. Cant.* • *VCH Worcestershire*, 2.82 • *GM*, 1st ser., 103/1 (1833), 245

Morris. *See also* Maurice, Morice, Morrice.

Morris, Benjamin Stephen (1910–1990), educationist, was born on 25 May 1910 in Long Street, Sherborne, Dorset, the only child of Benjamin Stephen Morris (1869–1910), a Baptist minister, and his wife, Annie McNicholl Duncan, of the island of Bute. On the sudden death of his father in June 1910, his mother moved back to her family in Bute, where Ben Morris later attended Rothesay Academy. In 1929 he went to Glasgow University, and he graduated BSc in chemistry in 1933. He then trained as a teacher at Jordanhill College, Glasgow, but returned to the University of Glasgow to study education, graduating with first-class honours in 1937. The combination of the skills of the analytic scientist with the insights of the humanist characterized all his later work.

Ben Morris taught in primary and secondary schools in Glasgow in the late 1930s. On 2 July 1938 he married Adeline Margaret (*b*. 1910), a dietician, daughter of Thomas Fleming Lamont, a company secretary; they had three children. In 1939 Morris returned to Jordanhill Training College to lecture in psychology, logic, and ethics for a year before going to the University of Glasgow to lecture in education alongside his admired mentor William Boyd. In 1941 he was attached to the Ministry of Food, and a year later to the army, where he worked on improving officer selection. Hitherto officers had been selected by a tribunal-like interview lasting perhaps twenty minutes before three serving officers. Morris was part of the team recommending instead the institution of War Office officer selection boards consisting of several officers with regimental experience plus psychologists and psychiatrists who over three days would organize relevant activities and administer tests to assess candidates' personality and potential. He was made senior psychologist and awarded the honorary rank of lieutenant-colonel.

Between 1945 and 1946 Morris and some of his wartime colleagues formed themselves into a multidisciplinary body dedicated to the solution of peacetime problems involving social psychology. They used the Tavistock Clinic as their base, and in 1947 became an independent organization called the Tavistock Institute of Human Relations—which outlived Morris himself. Ben Morris was one of its founders and chaired its management committee from 1947 to 1949. Most of the institute's activities involved fieldwork, being concerned with community education, and involving such problems as mediating between a village community and a planning authority or the civil resettlement of returning prisoners of war. Simultaneously Morris was a student at the Institute of Psychoanalysis.

In 1950 Morris was appointed to succeed Sir Peter Innes as director of the prestigious National Foundation for Educational Research in England and Wales, founded in connection with the University of London Institute of Education in 1943 and an independent national body since 1947. His immediate tasks were to formulate a clearly articulated education policy, to improve the testing for secondary selection, and to persuade local education authorities to provide the necessary funding, all of which took Morris into the heart of educational politics and administration. In 1956 he was appointed to a chair at the University of Bristol's Institute of Education. He saw one of his main tasks as being to raise the status and self-esteem both of state school teachers (perhaps especially women) and of the teacher training colleges. To that end he collaborated very closely with the eleven such colleges in his area, in the teeth of opposition from Whitehall and some university senates. It was largely owing to the perseverance of Morris and like-minded associates on the University Council for the Education of Teachers (UCET) that the period of teacher training was extended from two years to three and the bachelor of education degree was instituted, both of which made teaching into a fully graduate profession in Britain.

Morris was not only an outstandingly shrewd and successful negotiator whose reputation penetrated even UNESCO; he was also an exceptionally warm and vital teacher. He believed that learning flourishes best in group situations and acknowledged that he himself had learned this from his own first tutor, William Boyd, who had allegedly coped with a student–staff ratio of 500 to one. Morris was a superb seminar leader, in which he felt greatly helped by his own study of the foundations of psychodynamic theory and the work of W. R. Bion at the Institute of Psychoanalysis.

During the exhilarating period of the late 1960s Morris's influence spread to experienced teachers whom he supervised at Bristol for their masters' and doctoral research. His own thinking and research had been published as occasional journal articles and these were revised and collected during his visiting professorship in education at Harvard in 1970 as *Objectives and Perspectives in Education* (1972). That book revealed his consistent emphasis on the supreme importance of personal relations in all education, a view he backed both by empirical evidence and by philosophical argument. 'For me, education is an adventure in human mutuality in which persons in relation (to use Macmurray's phrase)—in our own case younger and older persons—together set out to discover what it means to be human' (Morris, 51). Martin Buber, whom Ben Morris often quoted alongside John Macmurray, spoke of the child's need and capacity to trust the teacher: 'Trust, trust in the world, because this human being exists—that is the most inward achievement of the relation in education' (M. Buber, *Between Man and Man*, 1947, 125). Morris was not even shy of quoting Christ's 'I am come that ye might have life, and that ye might have it more abundantly', adding, 'This statement would appear to express precisely our purpose as educators' (Morris, 256). That idealistic, humanist emphasis, which he shared with such contemporary educationists as James Britton, Harry Rée, Francis Cammaerts, and Connie and Harold Rosen, was Morris's major contribution to the post-war British education system.

Morris, who never lost his Bute accent, retired in 1975 to that 'living in the country' which he listed as his sole recreation in *Who's Who* for 1981. He died, survived by his wife, on 8 June 1990 in the Friarage Hospital, Northallerton, Yorkshire.   DEREK OLDFIELD

Sources WWW · *The Times* (30 June 1990) · *The Guardian* (30 June 1990) · B. Morris, *Objectives and perspectives in education* (1972) · D. Oldfield, 'The true educational experience', *Universities Quarterly*, 29/1 · W. R. Niblett, *How and why do we learn?* (1965) · A. Yates, *The first twenty-five years* (1972) [National Foundation for Educational Research in England and Wales] · *Baptist handbook* (1911), 493–4 [Regent's Park College, University of Oxford] · private information (2004) [Carol Rooley, daughter] · b. cert. · m. cert. · d. cert.
Archives U. Sussex, Gorer papers, letters to Geoffrey Gorer

Morris, Sir **Cedric Lockwood**, ninth baronet (1889–1982), painter and plantsman, was born in Sketty, Swansea, on 11 December 1889, the only son and eldest of the three children of George Lockwood Morris (*d.* 1947), ironfounder and later eighth baronet, and his wife, Wilhelmina Elizabeth, daughter of Thomas Cory of Swansea. He was educated at Charterhouse School, Surrey. Although living chiefly in England, he was proud to be Welsh, admiring the Welsh character and abhorring the English class system. He worked to foster Welsh self-confidence in the arts.

After failing his examinations to enter the army, Morris sailed to Canada and worked on a farm. On his return he entered the Royal College of Music, London, to study singing, but later turned to art, and in April 1914 he enrolled in the Académie Delacluse in Paris. On the outbreak of the First World War he returned to England, but his health prevented him from fighting. Instead, as a civilian, he joined the remounts, training horses to be sent to the front. When the remounts were taken over by the army in 1916, he was discharged.

Morris lived in the Cornish art centre of Newlyn between 1917 and 1920. In 1918 he met the painter Arthur Lett-Haines (1894–1978), and despite other liaisons the two lived together for sixty years until Lett-Haines's death. Difficult but fundamental, theirs was a partnership of complementaries. Morris was quiet, humorous, impractical, country-loving, and determined to concentrate on his art (with its key activity of human observation) and on the world of plants and animals. Lett-Haines was complex and sophisticated, a natural organizer, and dedicated to expanding recognition of Morris's art. The two lived in Paris (1921–6), London (1926–9), and Higham, Suffolk (1929–40), travelling extensively and always the centre of a lively circle in the arts. Morris's first one-man exhibition, closed by the fascists, was in Rome in 1922. He was elected to the Seven and Five Society in 1926, having been proposed by Winifred Nicholson and seconded by Ben Nicholson, and he was close to Frances Hodgkins and Christopher Wood.

Morris was one of the finest twentieth-century British painters of flowers and garden produce. His wide engagement with the natural world was reflected equally in his remarkable paintings of birds (shown in their habitats, yet often seen almost as personalities), of animals, and of British and foreign landscapes. No less distinguished was his achievement as a portrait painter, his approach extending from the satirical to the deeply affectionate. Unblinkingly observed, his portraits seem close at times to the spirit of the German Neue Sachlichkeit. Although he attended *académies libres* in Paris (1914 and from 1920), he was self-taught. In all periods his work was strikingly fresh in conception and observation, the motif being conveyed very directly and with formal economy. The main subject was usually juxtaposed boldly with its background, imagery ranging from the startlingly forceful to the extremely delicate. His use of colour was original and his paint texture distinctive at once in its richness, simplicity, and tactility.

In 1937 Morris and Lett-Haines founded the East Anglian School of Painting and Drawing in Dedham, Essex, with Morris as principal. In 1940 the school was moved to Benton End, Hadleigh, Suffolk, where the two men lived until their deaths. Students included Lucian Freud and Maggi Hambling. Inspiring and unconventional, the teaching aimed to develop a student's own free yet serious self-realization. It was enhanced both by fusion of the school with the teachers' personal circle and by the remarkable resource of Morris's last and finest garden. A lifelong plantsman, who established rare species collected overseas, he won national acclaim as a breeder of irises.

Morris empathized with the underdog. A strong sense of right and wrong inspired paintings satirizing puritan hypocrisy and the destruction of wildlife. During and after the depression years he taught in an educational settlement at Dowlais, near Merthyr Tudful. Well known and successful as an artist between the wars, he sank from fashionable consciousness after 1940, though a major and admired figure in the art community of East Anglia. Deteriorating eyesight compelled him to give up painting in 1975, but he lived to see the beginning of a major revival of his reputation. He died in Ipswich on 8 February 1982. A retrospective exhibition of his work was held at the Tate Gallery, London, in 1984.   RICHARD MORPHET, *rev.*

Sources R. Morphet, *Cedric Morris* (1984) [exhibition catalogue, Tate Gallery, London, 28 March – 13 May 1984] · personal knowledge (1993) · *CGPLA Eng. & Wales* (1982) · B. Tufnell, *Cedric Morris and Lett Haines: teaching art and life* [exhibition catalogue, Norwich Castle Museum and Art Gallery, Oct 2002 – Jan 2003, and NMG Wales, Jan–April 2003] · G. Reynolds and D. Grace, eds., *Benton End remembered: Cedric Morris, Arthur Lett-Haines, and the East Anglian School of Painting and Drawing* (2002)

Archives Tate collection, letters [photocopies]

Likenesses J. Norris Wood, photograph, 1975, repro. in R. Morphet, *Sir Cedric Morris* [Tate Gallery exhibition leaflet, 28 March 1984 – 13 May 1984]

Wealth at death £117,048: probate, 31 Aug 1982, *CGPLA Eng. & Wales*

Morris, Charles (1745–1838), army officer and songwriter, was born probably near Cork, the fourth son of Captain Thomas Morris (*d. c.*1752), author of the song 'Kitty Crowder', and his wife, Mary (1709?–1804). The family was originally Welsh. After his father's death, Charles was educated by his mother near Carlisle, perhaps at the small property of Bell Bridge where his grandfather and father had resided before him. At sixteen he became enamoured with a local beauty, Molly Dacre (afterwards Lady Clarke), and forever claimed inspiration from this undeclared love; he wrote a touching poem on it in old age.

In 1764 Morris procured an ensigncy in his brother Thomas's battalion of the 17th foot, the regiment of their father and grandfather (who had commanded it and been wounded in the French wars under Marlborough). He served in America, and was promoted captain, but on returning to Ireland exchanged first to the Royal Irish Dragoons and then—being disinclined to live anywhere but in London—to his majesty's Life Guards. With this came a taste for fashionable pursuits beyond his modest means. He courted society ladies such as the singer Elizabeth Ann Linley (afterwards Mrs R. B. Sheridan), in despair of winning whom he took to drink. Following a successful foray at Bath, however, he married at Marylebone on 8 February 1773 Anne Hussey Delaval (1737–1812), estranged wife and by then widow of Sir William Stanhope, second son of Philip, earl of Chesterfield.

Morris was greatly prized as a witty, bacchanalian performer at the London tavern and elsewhere. Among his numerous songs, set to popular tunes of the day, were shamelessly bawdy ones such as 'The Virgin Minister' and 'Jenny Sutton' (in praise of a late army whore), but also more urbane efforts, such as 'The Town and the Country' and 'The Tear that Bedews Sensibility's Shrine'. Mingling as he did with whigs, Morris turned his pen to political songs at the time of the Fox–North coalition of 1783 and the emergence as prime minister of the young William Pitt. The anti-tory satire of 'Billy's too Young to Drive Us' and 'Billy Pitt and the Farmer' was enjoyed even by those who disparaged the balladist's philosophy. Meanwhile, his 'Pat-Riot: a Revolutionary Song' was a hilarious attack on Irish zealotry. Above all, he produced drinking songs, such as 'The Toper's Apology', beloved of Tom Moore, and 'Ad poculum', which won him the gold cup of the Harmonic Society. First gathered in 1786 as *A Collection of Songs by the Inimitable Captain Morris*, his lyrics were augmented

and republished many times, with titles like *The Festival of Anacreon* and *Songs, Political and Convivial*.

On 14 February 1785 Morris had been elected to the Sublime Society of Beef Steaks, an exclusive group of twenty-four men who dined on Saturdays at Covent Garden Theatre, washing down their meat with arrack punch. His first function was to concoct this drink, but he quickly became the society's laureate. The introduction as a 'steak' of the prince of Wales proved a boon to Charles, bringing him frequent invitations to Carlton House and subsequently an annuity of £200, and his intimacy with Charles Howard, eleventh duke of Norfolk, for long president of the society, led to junketings at Norfolk House and a life interest in Brockham Lodge, a beautiful if modest retreat near Dorking. Here Morris spent the summers with his second wife and their daughter.

Morris was habitually cheerful and courteous, and also surprisingly steady for one whose verse was so shocking. He did give way to gloom for a time, as his political associates either died or (as he believed) cut him for sticking to his principles; the bitterness is movingly expressed in 'An Old Whig Poet to his Old Buff Waistcoat'. But he continued his regular attendance at the Beef Steak Society, undeterred by weather or competing engagements, and although he officially took leave of the steaks in 1831, they awarded him a silver bowl for his ninetieth birthday in 1835.

At the urging of more temperate friends, Morris collected his less racy poems, ones which 'might be read by a modest female without a blush', but even here, while fiercely repudiating the abuse of wine, he made no apology for celebrating it. These so-called *Lyra urbanica* appeared only posthumously, however. After a short internal inflammation, Charles Morris died of 'natural decay' at Betchworth on 11 July 1838 and was buried in St Michael's churchyard there.

Thomas Morris (*bap.* 1732, *d.* 1818?), army officer, songwriter, and translator, was Charles Morris's eldest brother. Born perhaps near London, but baptized at Carlisle on 22 April 1732 and first brought up there, he entered Winchester College in 1741 and displayed a gift for poetry and the classics. After a period of tuition at London in mathematics, French, dancing, and fencing, in 1748 he joined the 17th foot at Kinsale. In fulfilment of a promise to his late father, he took leave of absence in 1753 and spent a year in Paris. Here he polished his French by attending theatres assiduously, and wrote dramatic criticism; to his love of Shakespeare was added a passion for French tragedy.

In 1757 Morris embarked for America, where he participated in the siege of Havana and the descent on Martinique, was promoted captain, and became commandant of Niagara. He conceived a high regard for the character and values of the Native Americans, despite being captured and nearly killed by them while on a difficult mission (recorded in his diary for 1764). He also managed to climb unscathed beneath the Niagara Falls. In 1767 he returned to England and, while recruiting at Bridgwater, met a merchant's daughter, a Miss Chubb; they married there in 1769, and had six children.

On retiring from the army, Morris devoted himself to writing. His first *Collection of Songs* (1786) was followed by another, *The Busy Bee* (1790), and by *Miscellanies, in Prose and Verse* (1791), which included some of his extensive translations from Juvenal and a discourse on acting. Although his version of Racine's *Phèdre* remained unpublished, he pursued his interest in theatre with an epilogue to *The Ton, or, Follies of Fashion* by Eglantine, Lady Wallace (1788), and by playing the lead in *Richard III* at the Haymarket in 1791–2. This last production was in support of the Royal Literary Fund, of which Morris was an original member; he also gave recitations for it, and in 1792 published a study of the life and work of its founder, the Revd David Williams.

Morris's libertarian philosophy is seen in his poem *Quashy, or, The Coal-Black Maid* (1796), a noble if sentimental attack upon the slave trade. But he became increasingly despondent about the betrayal of the principles of the French Revolution, and pined for the beauty of the American wastes. He withdrew from public life, first to Hampstead and then to a cottage and nursery garden at Paddington. Here he spent many happy years, constantly rereading the *Odyssey* and the *Iliad*, and, with the help of his friend George Dyer, correlating Pope's translations with the Homeric originals. Thomas Morris probably died at London on 10 February 1818, leaving his family well cared for.   PATRICK WADDINGTON

Sources *Public characters of 1806* (1806), 322–51 · J. Timbs, *Clubs and club life in London: with anecdotes of its famous coffee houses, hostelries, and taverns, from the seventeenth century to the present time* (1872) · J. Timbs, *Anecdote lives of the later wits and humorists: Canning, Captain Morris, Curran, Coleridge, etc.*, 2 vols. (1874), 69–75 · W. Hone, *The Every-day Book and Table Book*, 2 (1833), col. 221 · R. Dexter, *Captain Charles Morris, the bard of the Sublime Society of the Beef Steaks* (1923) · D. Williams, *Claims of literature: the origins, motives, objects and transactions of the Society* [i.e. the Royal Literary Fund]… (1802), 169, 171, 181, 192 · *The correspondence of George, prince of Wales, 1770–1812*, ed. A. Aspinall, 5: *1804–1806* (1968) · *N&Q*, 2nd ser., 2 (1856), 412 · *N&Q*, 4th ser., 1 (1868), 244 · *N&Q*, 6th ser., 2 (1880), 369 · *The journal of Thomas Moore*, ed. W. S. Dowden, 6 vols. (1983–91) · G. W. Thornbury, *Two centuries of song* (1867), 123–6 · J. Timbs, *A century of anecdote, from 1760 to 1860* (1887), 280–82 · J. Timbs, *Curiosities of London* (1855) · *GM*, 2nd ser., 10 (1838), 453 · *The letters of Thomas Moore*, ed. W. S. Dowden, 2 vols. (1964) · F. Locker-Lampson, *Lyra elegantiarum: a collection of some of the best social and occasional verse by deceased English authors*, revised and enlarged edition (1891) · D. J. O'Donoghue, *The poets of Ireland: a biographical dictionary with bibliographical particulars*, 1 vol. in 3 pts (1892–3) · G. Croly, 'Lyrics [by Charles Morris]', *Blackwood*, 49 (1841), 47–55 · *Irish Quarterly Review*, 3 (March 1853), 140–44 · *Irish Quarterly Review*, 3 (Sept 1853), 649–53 · review of *Lyra urbanica*, *Monthly Review*, 152 (1839), 25ff. · *Life and letters of Sir Gilbert Elliot, first earl of Minto, from 1751 to 1806*, ed. countess of Minto [E. E. E. Elliot-Murray-Kynynmound], 3 vols. (1874) · *The diary of the Right Hon. W*[*illiam*] *W*[*indham*]*, 1784–1810*, ed. Mrs H. Baring (1866), 47

Likenesses print, 1790 (Thomas Morris), BM · T. Hodgetts, mezzotint, pubd 1808 (after A. J. Oliver), BM · J. Lonsdale, oils, NPG · Van Assen, portrait (Thomas Morris), repro. in T. Morris, *The busy bee* (1790) · portrait, repro. in *The festival of Anacreon*, 1 (1783) · portrait, repro. in C. Morris, *A complete collection of songs, by Captain Morris*, 8th edn (1788); 12th edn (1790) · portrait, repro. in C. Morris, *The songs by Captain Morris, complete*, 13th edn (1793) · portrait, repro. in C. Morris, *A collection of political and other songs*, 15th edn (1798) · portrait, repro. in *Hilaria, the festive board* (privately printed, London, 1798) · portrait, repro. in *Songs, political and convivial*, 24th edn (1802) · portrait, repro. in *Capt. Morris's songs. A very capital collection of bacchanalian, amatory, and double entendre songs, etc.* (1840?) · portrait, repro. in *Lyra urbanica, or, The social effusions of the celebrated Captain Charles Morris*, 2 vols. (1840) · stipple, BM; repro. in T. Morris, *The busy bee* (1790)

Morris, Charles Richard, Baron Morris of Grasmere (1898–1990), university teacher and administrator, was born on 25 January 1898 in Sutton Valence, Kent, the elder child and elder son (the younger was Sir Philip Robert *Morris, educationist) of Meshach Charles Morris, inspector of schools, and his wife, Jane, daughter of James Brasier, of St Cross, Winchester, Hampshire. He was educated at Tonbridge School and at Trinity College, Oxford, where he obtained a first class in *literae humaniores* (1921). He then became a fellow and tutor in philosophy at Balliol College, Oxford, and held these posts until 1943.

Morris's natural inclination towards an educational career was fostered by his parents and augmented by the general ethos of Balliol under the inspiring mastership of A. D. Lindsay. The horror of the First World War turned that inclination into an absolute commitment to education as the great liberating force beneficial to individuals and society alike. Morris gave this expression in many ways, including by financially supporting his younger sibling's education and by espousing movements to enlarge access to education at all levels at home and abroad.

The first dozen years at Balliol were 'paradise'. Morris had able and responsive pupils who admired him for his mastery of the subject and respected him for his remarkable insight into their nature and capability. He wrote three, largely expository, books. The first, *A History of Political Ideas* (1924), was written with his wife, Mary. She was the daughter of Ernest De *Selincourt, professor of English, and his wife, Ethel, *née* Shawcross. They had a long, mutually supportive marriage, based on shared values; the marriage produced a son and a daughter. Her brother introduced him to the Lake District, for which he developed a lasting affection. The other books were *Locke, Berkeley, Hume* (1931) and *Idealistic Logic* (1933).

The comfortable life of the archetypal Oxford don was challenged in the early 1930s by the vast social tragedy of the depression and the evident threat to democracy posed by the European dictators, especially Adolf Hitler. The Morrises responded privately by assisting refugees and publicly by Morris's becoming an Oxford city councillor (1939–41) and campaigning against the election of a Conservative member in the Oxford parliamentary by-election of 1938, because he deemed inadequate and unacceptable the Conservative government's responses to the dictators' threat to democracy and to evident social injustice in Britain. In this period Morris joined with J. S. Fulton to write *In Defence of Democracy* (1935).

In 1939 Morris became a wartime civil servant in the ministries of Supply (until 1942) and Production (1942–3), experiencing at first hand the workings of a command economy and negotiating with counterparts in the USA for the supply of essential war materials. After this he did not return to Oxford but took up the post of headmaster of King Edward's School, Birmingham, to which he had been appointed in 1941. He stayed until 1948, when he became vice-chancellor of the University of Leeds. This brought him and his wife closer to the Lake District, where in 1943 she had inherited a house, gloriously situated above Grasmere, which was to become their real home for the next forty-seven years.

Morris was ideally suited to this vice-chancellorship, for which it seemed all his previous experience had been a preparation. Though he was short of stature, his bright eyes and lively intelligence commanded the affection and respect of colleagues and students. He led the university through post-war austerity and produced a development plan to ensure that Leeds was well placed to take early advantage of the resources which accompanied the government's acceptance of the report of the committee on higher education chaired by Baron Robbins (1961–4). He also foresaw that internal structures of universities must change. He was an influential figure in the Committee of Vice-Chancellors and Principals, was its chairman from 1951 to 1955, and was much in demand for service on public bodies in the United Kingdom as diverse as the royal commission on local government in Greater London (1957), the Schools' Broadcasting Council (1954–64), and the advisory committee for the wool textile industry (1952). He made a major contribution to the development of universities overseas through his membership of the Inter-University Council for Higher Education Overseas (1957–64) and of the committee of inquiry into Australian universities (1957), whose definitive report was accepted. Some of these activities continued in retirement, when he also helped the newer universities of Bradford and Lancaster.

Morris was one of Britain's outstanding university administrators and was universally admired for his combination of practicality and total commitment to education. He was knighted in 1953, appointed KCMG in 1963, and made a life peer in 1967. He received eight honorary doctorates. He died, as he would have wished, at Grasmere, on 30 May 1990, two years after his wife's death. There is a portrait of him in the University of Leeds by Robert Buhler.   FRED DAINTON, *rev.*

Sources *The Independent* (6 June 1990) · *The Independent* (14 June 1990) · *The Independent* (23 June 1990) · *The Times* (6 June 1990) · personal knowledge (1996) · private information (1996) · *CGPLA Eng. & Wales* (1990)
Likenesses R. Buhler, portrait, U. Leeds
Wealth at death £135,496: probate, 25 July 1990, *CGPLA Eng. & Wales*

Morris, Sir Christopher (*d.* 1545), soldier and military administrator, was married to Elizabeth, but nothing else is known of his family or background, and there is no evidence of surviving children. His promotion within the office of ordnance—effectively from bottom to top—is unique in the sixteenth century. It is likely he had some relevant experience before he was appointed a gunner in the Tower of London in 1513 at 12*d.* a day, since within the year he was master gunner on the king's great galley and was taking part in the testing of pieces of ordnance 'called the xii sisters' (*LP Henry VIII*, vol. 1, pt 2, no. 3614). Furthermore, in November 1515, as quartermaster gunner, he was granted the unusual privilege of passing to and from Tournai on the king's warrant. The governor was told to give him help and pay his wage, now 18*d.* a day. It is possible he was already acting as the government's ears in matters of artillery. However, there is no doubt that he was highly regarded. He was appointed master gunner in 1527 with oversight of gunnery training and the task of surveying all ordnance, old or new. He became master of the ordnance in 1536 and was knighted three years later. Political and administrative convenience moved him sideways into the new office of lieutenant of the ordnance, with his salary nearly doubled, when Thomas Seymour took over the mastership in 1544.

The growing importance of the cannon and handgun on land and the heavily gunned man-of-war at sea during the reign of Henry VIII was to transform the administration that supplied them. The crown used the office of ordnance to encourage, produce, and oversee the developing weaponry at home. Morris fitted into the scheme of things perfectly. His particular expertise was artillery, especially its deployment and manning. Thomas Cromwell and garrison commanders valued him. Morris actively supported home-produced ordnance, writing in 1536 to Lord Lisle, 'as you love the two young men', Robert and John Owen, to support the demonstration of their 'fair double cannon' before the king, 'for I have bid them make 12 new pieces' (*LP Henry VIII*, vol. 10, no. 756). As master gunner he showed a clear preference for English trainees: 'I had rather have one Englishman, as he is, than five strangers, for gunner's work' (*LP Henry VIII*, vol. 7, no. 1131). He was clearly committed to a national sufficiency in gunnery. Promotion to the mastership of the ordnance brought with it the responsibility for office finance at a time when the multiplicity of particular payments was being replaced by larger sums, advanced ahead of expenditure.

For some twenty years as a senior ordnance officer, Morris's brief included a wide range of government commissions. It was a period of bravura foreign expeditions, tempered by the fear of retaliatory invasion. As a younger man he saw active service. Older and more senior, he became an administrator, though he was to be fatally wounded at Boulogne while directing the artillery. Morris was expeditionary master gunner on the earl of Surrey's invasion of Picardy in 1522, playing a key role at Morlaix, and was a lieutenant on the duke of Suffolk's French campaign the following year. In 1536 he was recalled from his duties of inspection at Calais to co-ordinate the issue of weapons and supplies during the Pilgrimage of Grace. Three years later, under the threat of foreign invasion, he organized the London musters at Stepney with between 20,000 and 25,000 men in three 'battles', drew up a comprehensive book of the king's ordnance within his dominions, and inspected the fortifications at Wark, Berwick, Newcastle, and Guînes. The following year he completed the national military stocktake with a 'book of rates', establishing the manning levels at castles and forts.

Other of Morris's commissions might well have had

military significance. The investigation into the Llantrisant mines in 1531 and the expedition to Denmark in 1535 (another was aborted) sought raw materials and skilled men, though Henry was careful to deny the latter. Morris's rising professional career was mirrored in his other responsibilities: investigating Portuguese claims of theft from a vessel grounded on the Isle of Thanet in 1525, acting as diplomatic courier between Wolsey and Edward Lee at Valladolid in 1527, and 'to lie outside the walls [of Dover] and give immediate notice of fair weather' for the arrival of Anne of Cleves in 1539 (*LP Henry VIII*, vol. 14, pt 2, no. 677). He prospered, though official thanks came late. He was a citizen of some standing in Cornhill, London, by 1523, and a shipowner by 1531. Nine years later he obtained the site of St Mary Graces with several tenements near the Tower and the manors of Gravesend and Parrocke in Kent with other property attached. The Lisles stayed with him on their visits to London, and the families exchanged gifts and medicinal remedies. There was some criticism, although remarkably little in so successful a career. The abiding impression is of valued competence.

In 1544 Hertford requested Morris's urgent posting to aid his invasion of Scotland. Morris organized the supply and transport of equipment, though his ordnance proved unable to take Edinburgh Castle. Within two months he had reshipped the great ordnance to Boulogne, where he was given responsibility for distributing the artillery and organizing the pioneers, and then 'to take the quarter between the castle and the green bulwark' by mining, breach, and assault (*LP Henry VIII*, vol. 19, pt 1, no. 1003). It is likely that it was there Morris was wounded by a handgun in the evening of 3 September having 'demeaned himself very valiantly before and killed all the master gunners of Bulloin' (ibid., pt 2, no. 424). He made his will the following January and was dead by May 1545. In his will he had asked to be buried in St Peter Cornhill.

ROGER ASHLEY

Sources *LP Henry VIII* · H. M. Colvin and others, eds., *The history of the king's works*, 4 (1982), vol. 4 · C. G. Cruikshank, *The English occupation of Tournai, 1513–1519* (1971) · R. Ashley, 'The organization and administration of the Tudor office of ordnance', BLitt diss., U. Oxf., 1973 · will, PRO, PROB 11/32, sig. 38 · *DNB*

Morris, Claver (*bap.* 1659, *d.* 1727), physician, was baptized on 1 May 1659 at Bishops Caundle in Dorset, the youngest of four known children (and second son) born to William Morris, rector of Manston, and his wife, Hannah (1632?–1724). Morris matriculated at New Inn Hall, Oxford, in March 1676, and received degrees including the BA (1679), MA (1682), MB (1685), and MD (1691). In 1683 he became an extra licentiate of the Royal College of Physicians. Morris was not a widely known figure in his own day: he neither published nor participated in any but local politics. He would have been remembered only by his family and friends had he not kept detailed accounts between 1684 and 1726, and diaries for March 1709 to March 1710, and June 1718 to August 1726. These manuscripts provide a unique glimpse into the life of a successful provincial professional man in late Stuart and early Hanoverian England.

Beginning in the 1680s, Morris practised medicine in Wells, serving as that city's only physician (although not its only medical practitioner) for many years. He apparently was an iatrochemist, developing remedies in his home laboratory which he dispensed directly to patients or distributed through a local apothecary's shop. Morris's therapeutic approach was conventional for the period, involving generous prescription of emetics, laxatives, enemas, sweating, and blood-letting. He performed no surgery, but referred surgical cases either to Mr Lucas of Wells or to surgeons in London or Bristol. He maintained good professional relationships with other physicians in the region, occasionally consulting on their cases or inviting them to serve as consultants on his own.

Morris's practice included patients ranging from regional gentry families to the poor of Wells, whom he charged on a sliding scale depending on their means. He visited patients in their own homes, sometimes at distances of 25 miles from Wells, travelling on horseback. At the height of his career in 1719, when he was about sixty years old, Morris was paid more than £300 by the 258 patients who sought 'my advice and prescriptions in physick'. Between 1712 and 1723 his annual earnings from this source averaged approximately £250.

In addition to developing a substantial medical practice, Morris was a social and financial success. Indeed, he exemplifies one route to upward social mobility for talented, impecunious, young men of his era. Morris married well—three times. His first wife, Grace, *née* Green, of London, whom he married on 13 October 1685, brought him two valuable London properties and £400 in cash. She died in January 1689. In 1696 Morris married the widow Elizabeth Jeans, daughter of Edward Dawe of Ditcheat, near Castle Cary. She brought him property at West Pennard. Having borne him his beloved daughter Betty in 1697, Elizabeth died in 1699. In 1703 Morris married Molly Bragge, who came with a portion of £3000. In 1709 she gave birth to his only surviving son, William. Molly died in 1725.

Morris became a wealthy man. He invested in property and lent money at interest. He augmented his property by requesting enclosure (carried out in 1722) of Baltonsbury Northwood and Glastonbury Common Moor. In 1723 his income from investments was nearly £400, which, combined with his medical earnings, yielded approximately £600. Morris enjoyed the lifestyle this income afforded. Between 1699 and 1702 he had a grand house built in Wells at a cost of £807. He spent freely on household goods, clothing, horses, and entertainment. He set a lavish and hospitable table and, at 5 feet 6 inches tall and 15 stone in weight, apparently enjoyed its bounty.

Morris was well regarded in Wells. He held several local offices, serving from 1706 as commissioner for the land tax, and from 1709 as commissioner for sewers. In 1717 he became a member of the Company of Mercers and was made a burgess of the city of Wells. In 1724 he served as a district commissioner charged with collecting a special tax levied on Roman Catholics.

Like many educated people of his time, Morris was

interested in natural philosophy, particularly chemistry. He regularly purchased books on this topic and ordered chemical ingredients for the experiments he conducted in his laboratory, where he also developed recipes for remedies and cosmetics, and constructed mechanical devices.

In addition to his other activities, Morris was an enthusiastic and expert musician. He sang, played several instruments, and was an active member of a music club that met weekly for many years. He also attended public concerts and musical gatherings in private homes. He purchased and performed pieces by a wide range of contemporary composers. He also owned a number of instruments and experimented with innovations in their construction and tuning.

Claver Morris died, aged sixty-seven, on 19 March 1727, of an illness which he diagnosed as 'a consumption & a growing phthisis' (probably tuberculosis). He was buried in Wells Cathedral, where a tablet was erected to his memory. His epitaph describes him as he would have wished to be remembered: the royalist and tory son of a clergyman 'who had suffered greatly in the King's cause in the Civil War'; an accomplished musician; a natural philosopher, who understood chemistry, anatomy, herbs, and mathematics; a physician who invented remedies effective against 'grievous diseases'; and a charitable, well-respected citizen.   Lucinda McCray Beier

Sources C. Morris, diaries and accounts, 1684–97, Som. ARS, AHZ − 1–3 · C. Morris, diaries and accounts, 1709–26, Som. ARS, 1–3 G/1332 · E. Hobhouse, ed., *The diary of a west country physician, AD 1684–1726* (1934), vol. 1 · G. Holmes, *Augustan England* (1982) · H. J. Cook, *The decline of the old medical regime in Stuart London* (1986) · R. French and A. Wear, eds., *The medical revolution of the seventeenth century* (1989) · Foster, *Alum. Oxon.*

Archives Som. ARS, diary [photocopy] · Som. ARS, account book [microfiche]

Morris, Corbyn (1710–1779), customs administrator and economist, is a figure about whose origins and early life nothing is known. He was probably the son of Edmund Morris and his wife, Margaret, and baptized at Bishop's Castle, Shropshire, on 19 August 1710. He first attracted notice by the publication in 1741 of *A Letter from a Bystander to a Member of Parliament*, in which he discussed the financing of a large standing army by crown and people since the Restoration. The pamphlet was an unashamed defence of Sir Robert Walpole. In it Morris argued that the power of the crown depended upon economic factors; after an elaborate discussion of the relative resources of the crown and the people, he concluded that 'our tendency at present, unless it be rightly moderated, lies much stronger to democracy than to absolute monarchy' (C. Morris, *A Letter from a Bystander*, 2nd edn, 1743, 58). His estimates of national income were based on the mercantilist theory that 'the whole annual income at any period is greater or less according to the quantity of coin then circulating in the kingdom' (ibid., 107). This pamphlet drew a response attributed to William Pulteney and another from the Oxford historian Thomas Carte, both of which were published in 1742. Morris replied to his critics with *A*

Letter to the Rev. Mr. Thomas Carte … by a Gentleman of Cambridge (1743). The controversy terminated with the publication by Carte of *A Full and Clear Vindication of the Full Answer* (1743).

Morris's identification with the Walpole regime was extended with the publication in 1744 of his *Essay towards Fixing the True Standards of Wit, Humour, Raillery, Satire and Ridicule*, which contained a 34-page dedication to Walpole eulogizing his career in language which even by contemporary standards might be termed extravagant. Years later David Hume quoted Morris in a letter to Gilbert Elliot when he wrote that 'I am become much of my friend Corbyn Morrice's Mind, who says, that he writes all his books for the sake of the Dedications' (*Letters*, 12 March 1763). Morris included a fulsome dedication to Henry Pelham in *An Essay towards Illustrating the Science of Insurance* (1747), and in the second edition of that work published in 1758 he addressed the duke of Newcastle.

Morris's dedications can be said to have made his career. His *Letter from a Bystander* had been prescient in predicting vulnerability to foreign-supported incursions in Scotland drawing upon Jacobite support. Once the uprising of 1745 had been suppressed, Morris immediately submitted to Newcastle (8 May 1746) several proposals for the regulation of the highlands. He suggested the registration of all lands and deeds at London and Stirling, and the reversion to the crown of lands not so registered. Entail was to be abolished and landowners were to be vested with absolute property in the land. He pressed for the division of the land among the children on the death of a landowner, and argued that the payment of rent should be governed by a written agreement between landlord and tenant. Morris proposed not only the settlement of all forfeited lands with new tenants, but also the universal abolition of highland dress. He pointed out that, unless they were dispersed, the power of the old highland families would be increased by the encouragement of trade and manufactures.

In 1751 Morris was appointed by Pelham secretary of the customs and salt duty in Scotland. His salary was £500 per annum. He was sent to Scotland to inquire into the state of the customs and the practices of smugglers. He sent a steady stream of letters to Pelham and the duke of Newcastle relating to his activities. In 1757 he listed his achievements as having regulated the method of weighing tobacco, thus augmenting the customs, and having suppressed the importation, under the Spanish duty, of French wines into Scotland, 'which had long been complained of by the English merchants'. He also claimed that during the first five years of his secretaryship more money had been remitted from the customs in Scotland to the receiver-general in England than in all the preceding years since the union. As a result of his experience he submitted to Newcastle in 1752 and 1758 several suggestions for the better regulation of the customs and salt duties.

Morris continued to publish on economic matters in London after his appointment to Scotland in order to further his ultimately successful goal of obtaining a government post in London. In 1753 he prepared a bill for a general registry of the population of Great Britain, involving the collection of birth and death statistics. He explained the advantages of a census to the duke of Newcastle, under whose 'immediate direction' the bill was introduced into the House of Lords.

Elected FRS on 19 May 1757, Morris was admitted to the society a week later. On 15 September 1758 he married a Mrs Wright. Reflecting on his years in Scotland, Morris wrote to Newcastle in 1758:

> my view, having been, to make the Secretary's office in Scotland a nursery for young English Gentlemen, who might be transplanted from thence, according to their Merits, and become faithfull officers of the Revenue in that country, where the English are now allmost weeded out.   (BL, Add. MS 32878, fol. 96)

In 1759 Morris reminded the government:

> In obedience to Mr. Pelham's commands, I applied myself to the study of the public Revenue,—It was his Pleasure to send me to Scotland for the Detection of Smuggling, where he honour'd me frequently with his own correspondence; and assur'd me that I should soon be called back from thence to obey his commands here [London], under his own Eye.   (BL, Add. MS 32900, fol. 431)

His appointment to a place on the English board of customs in 1763 recognized his claim, but with the retirement of his last patron, Newcastle, from government any channel for direct influence of government policy on his part ceased. Morris died on 24 December 1779, and was buried at Wimbledon, Surrey, on 1 January 1780.

An ingenious and well-connected writer on economic matters, Morris was one of a number of Englishmen who obtained preferment in Scotland following the Jacobite rising of 1745–6 through the patronage of Henry Pelham and his brother the duke of Newcastle. Whether his efforts to improve the collection of customs revenue in Scotland were as successful as he claimed in his letters to the duke of Newcastle remains to be proven.

ALEXANDER MURDOCH

Sources *The letters of David Hume*, ed. J. Y. T. Greig, 1 (1932), 380 · BL, Newcastle MSS, Add MSS 32731, 32860, 32864, 32866, 32872, 32877, 32878, 32900, 33049 · NL Scot., MSS 5025, 5078, 16676, 16679, 16688, 16693 · J. Oswald, *Memorials of the public life and character of the Rt. Hon. James Oswald of Dunniker* (1825) · DNB · IGI
Archives BL, letters mainly to duke of Newcastle, Add. MSS 32705–32968 · BL, letters to Charles Yorke, Add. MSS 35634–35639, *passim* · U. Nott. L., corresp. with Henry Pelham

Morris, Edward (*bap.* 1633, *d.* 1689), drover and Welsh-language poet, was born at Perthillwydion, Cerrigydrudion, Denbighshire, and baptized on 30 July 1633, the elder son of Morris ap Hugh (*bap.* 1601) and his wife, Lowri (*d.* 1669/70); in addition to a younger boy there were five sisters. Nothing is known of his education, and the presumption of a classical education, based on the extensive classical references in his poetry, overlooks the fact that translations were available in English printed sources. He would have been fluent in English since he earned his living as a drover, bringing cattle from the Welsh uplands to fairs at Barnet and Smithfield.

How Morris acquired his bardic knowledge is a matter of conjecture, since he acknowledged no specific professional bard as his teacher, although he refers to two patrons, one of whom owned a book from which he learnt, while the other is referred to as *hen athro* ('old teacher'). By the time Morris was learning his craft the old rigorous bardic codes had slackened, and he may well have acquired his knowledge in an unorthodox manner. But no matter how he came by it, he became one of the greatest practitioners of strict-metre poetry, displaying all the traditional flourishes and observing its restrictions such as *cymeriad* (starting every line in a poem with the same letter or even the same word), in addition to the use of *cynghanedd* in each line. His willingness to experiment and technical mastery made it easy for him to embrace the *canu rhydd* ('free-metre poetry') which was gaining in popularity in the post-Restoration period. Some of the newer metres could be sung to tunes which had English names, and he may well have heard these on his travels, especially in London, where there was a renaissance in drama and popular music after the reopening of the theatres in 1660.

Morris combined the seasonal work of the drover with the traditional bardic round of *clera*, visiting the gentry houses of north Wales at Christmas, Easter, and Whitsun in the manner of the professional poets, singing the praises of patrons and mourning the dead, in return for payment and hospitality. His favourite house was Gloddaith, Caernarvonshire, home of Thomas Mostyn, heir to the baronetcy of Mostyn, himself a scholar and collector of books and manuscripts; one of Morris's most intricate poems is in praise of the library at Gloddaith. In Morris's eyes not least of the virtues of Mostyn was the honourable status he accorded the Welsh language. In several poems Morris lamented the general decline in honour and respect for the language as the gentry became ever more Anglicized and abandoned their Welsh estates for London. A patron such as William Lloyd, bishop of St Asaph, merited special praise for learning the language and encouraging the use of it in his diocese.

Morris is better known for his poems in the free metres, often called carols; he wrote Christmas carols which were not limited to the story of the nativity, but told the story of man's redemption from the fall to Calvary. His faith inspired him to write carols for other festivals as well, and his staunch Anglicanism is obvious throughout. Religious affiliation was bound up with royalism, and although careful not to criticize Cromwell's regime overtly, his joy at the restoration of Charles II was expressed in a poem which made clear that this was not merely a political restoration, but the reassertion of the natural order which had been overturned by the execution of Charles I. God's approbation was revealed by the largely peaceful and bloodless course of the Restoration.

Morris's most charming pieces are his love poems, such as those where he sends Summer as a messenger to his lady love; Summer, personified as a generous youth scattering flowers and other gifts of nature, extols the virtues of this season for lovers. His *Carol Ciwpid*, in which the poet converses with Cupid, uses many of the well-known attributes of the classical figure but also refers to more recondite stories. Another facet of the free-metre poetry is the mixture of high literary tone, for example, the use of the subjunctive mood and the evocation of the vocabulary of the fourteenth- and fifteenth-century love poetry, together with the demotic, speech-based language which used dialect endings for words and an increasing number of crude English borrowings.

Morris's knowledge of English was put to good use near the end of his life, when asked by Mrs Margaret Vychan of Llwydiarth, Montgomeryshire, to translate J. Rawlet's *Christian Monitor* for her. She paid for its publication and it appeared in 1689 under the title *Y rhybuddiwr Christnogawl*. The Welsh version was very popular and was reprinted in 1699, 1706, and twice more at the turn of the next century. Examples of Morris's handwriting survive, notably in NL Wales, Peniarth MS 200, which contains several poems in his hand, with the date 1670 on page 26.

Edward Morris married, about 1670, Sarah Davies of Llaethwryd, the daughter of a local yeoman and one of Morris's patrons. They had six children. He died in Essex in November 1689 during one of his droving trips and was buried there, in Braintree, or Brentwood, or at Fryerning church near Ingatstone. Attempts to find his burial place have been unsuccessful, since the restoration and extension of all these churches destroyed any memorial which might have been erected. His wife survived him. He was mourned by Huw Morys, Siôn Dafydd Laes (twice), and several other poets.   NESTA LLOYD

Sources G. Thomas, 'Changes in the tradition of Welsh poetry in north Wales in the seventeenth century', DPhil diss., U. Oxf., 1966, 264–311 · G. Jones, 'Bywyd a Gwaith Edward Morris, Perthi Llwydion, 1633–89', MA diss., U. Wales, 1941 · N. Lloyd, 'Late free-metre poetry', *A guide to Welsh literature*, ed. R. G. Gruffydd, 3: *c.1530–1700* (1997), 100–27 · index of Welsh manuscript poetry, NL Wales [computerized]

Morris, Edward Patrick, first Baron Morris (1859–1935), politician in Newfoundland, was born at St John's on 8 May 1859, the third son of Edward Morris, originally of Waterford, Ireland, and his wife, Catherine Fitzgerald. His father was a cooper and later keeper of the St John's poorhouse. Morris received as good an education as the colony could offer, at St Bonaventure's College. He taught at Oderin, Placentia Bay, from 1874 to 1878, and then spent a year at the high school attached to the University of Ottawa. On his return he studied law, and was called to the bar in 1885. He started a law firm with his brother soon afterwards.

In 1885 Morris was also elected to the house of assembly as an independent member for the largely working-class and Roman Catholic district of St John's West. He promoted himself as a champion of working people, and adopted the then novel tactic of door-to-door canvassing. He proved to be a consummate local politician, and became enormously popular among his constituents. Re-elected nine times, he represented the district to the end of his political career in 1917. He became so influential

Edward Patrick Morris, first Baron Morris (1859–1935), by Sir James Guthrie

in the town of St John's as a whole that by 1890 some newspapers were referring to him as 'Boss Morris'.

In the assembly Morris championed social legislation such as workmen's compensation and safety standards on fishing vessels. He also supported electoral and local government reform, particularly in St John's. In 1889 he joined the Liberal Party, led by Sir William Whiteway, who appointed him to the cabinet (without portfolio) after his election victory that year. Morris's appointment recognized his influence in St John's and bolstered Roman Catholic representation in the government. He deputized for Whiteway in the attorney-general's office and handled a significant number of law bills, besides steering important legislation dealing with higher education. He was not closely involved in the major controversies with which the government had to deal, however, and did not achieve real prominence until the late 1890s, in which decade he also edited the *Newfoundland Law Reports*.

In December 1894 the two local banks suspended payment, creating financial chaos and a real possibility of colonial bankruptcy. Morris was a member of a delegation, led by Robert Bond, which went to Ottawa in 1895 to discuss confederation. The draft terms were ungenerous, depended on British financial aid (which was refused), and, had they been accepted, would almost certainly have pitted Morris against his constituency, since most Newfoundland Roman Catholics were committed anti-confederates. In the end the colony survived by floating a loan.

In 1898 Morris dramatically broke away from the Liberal

Party, then in opposition and led by Bond, over the tory government's decision to transfer the operation and ownership of the colony's railway and telegraph systems, as well as other franchises and much land, to Robert G. Reid of Montreal (who had built most of the railway). Morris, who was close to the Reid family, thought the deal promised economic development at little risk to the colony, while Bond considered it an immoral sell-out. As it also envisaged a considerable number of jobs in St John's West, Morris and a small number of supporters voted in favour of the deal, and sat thereafter as independent Liberals. In 1901 Morris married Isobel Langrishe (d. 1934), the daughter of the Revd William Le Gallais and the widow of James P. Fox.

By early 1900 the tory government was on the verge of collapse. Morris saw that if the fiercely anti-contract Bond became premier, the Reid deal and its supporters might well be sent into oblivion. Morris therefore astutely joined Bond in defeating the government, thereby safeguarding his political future, and enabling him to salvage the essence of the Reid contract. He joined the cabinet, becoming minister of justice in 1902, and pressured Bond into modifying rather than repealing the contract. He was knighted in 1904.

Morris remained in the Bond government until 1907, when he suddenly resigned his portfolio and from the party. It was the first step in a carefully planned strategy. Bond had made himself unpopular with the imperial government by his anti-American fisheries policy, with the Canadian government by raising the question of American fishing rights at all, and with the Reid family by continued hostility to their ambitions. Since the tory party was weak, Morris was seen as the only politician who could challenge Bond's dominance. With substantial financial backing from the Reids, and winks and nods from other influential allies, he launched the People's Party in 1908. The election that autumn resulted in a tie. Bond mishandled the crisis, giving Morris (who had the sympathetic ear of the governor) the opportunity to form a government in March 1909. He was speedily granted a dissolution and confirmed in office with a comfortable majority.

The record of the Morris government was mixed. It was relatively free-spending, it launched into an overly expensive and arguably unwise programme of building branch railways, and there is evidence that some of its members were involved in speculation in timber lands. Against this must be set the competent handling of the arbitration at the Hague tribunal on American fishing rights under the 1818 convention (Morris appeared for the colony), the introduction of old-age pensions, and needed investment in education and agricultural development. Aided by a buoyant economy and a disorganized opposition, the government was re-elected in 1913, but by this time it was under sustained criticism from the Fishermen's Protective Union, which had elected eight members to the assembly. Morris's attempts to respond to some Union demands upset his mercantile and Roman Catholic supporters, and for the first time cracks in the party began to appear. They were temporarily papered over, however, by the outbreak of war.

The government's unusual method of handling the colony's war effort was in part the result of energetic intervention by the governor, Sir Walter Davidson. Without convening the legislature, the government expanded the local Royal Naval Reserve and created a 500 man regiment. Morris and Davidson organized the Newfoundland Patriotic Association, a politically neutral body involving both citizens and politicians, to supervise the war effort. This unique arrangement lasted until 1917. Morris represented the colony in the imperial war cabinet (1916–17) and attended the imperial war conference in 1917. By this time his government was becoming unpopular, mainly because it seemed incapable of curbing profiteering and controlling inflation. The regiment had suffered heavy losses, and conscription seemed a real and much-resented possibility. Morris proposed a coalition government, making it clear that he would postpone the election scheduled for the autumn of 1917. The resultant National Government, nominally headed by Morris, took office in July. A legislative session soon afterwards wound up the Patriotic Association, which had outlived its usefulness, created a department of militia, and increased direct taxation.

Morris had agreed, before the formation of the National Government, that he would resign as prime minister before the end of the year if appointed Newfoundland's high commissioner in London, but on the recommendation of Davidson, who was ending his term as governor, he received a peerage for his services to the war effort (1 January 1918). It was a rare honour for any colonial politician, and the only case in Newfoundland's history. Morris moved to London and spent the rest of his life in England, and, though he returned to Newfoundland infrequently, championed the colony's interests whenever possible. He held a number of directorships, and served as vice-chairman of the Imperial Mineral Resources Bureau. He was also on the governing bodies of the Royal Empire Society, Imperial College, Cardinal Vaughan's School, and the Hospital for Diseases of the Skin. He died of bronchopneumonia at his home, 4 Onslow Square, London, on 24 October 1935, and was succeeded as second baron by his only child, Michael William Morris.

Eloquent, witty, and politically shrewd, Morris climbed the greasy pole without difficulty and remained at or near the top for some thirty years. Though a man of real abilities, he never became a truly dominant figure, relying on alliances with, for example, Robert Reid and Governor Davidson, who did much to influence his policies. He was a survivor and compromiser rather than a visionary, but his premiership nevertheless made a permanent mark on Newfoundland's history, largely as a result of his controversial (and expensive) handling of the war effort.

JAMES K. HILLER

Sources J. K. Hiller, 'A history of Newfoundland, 1874–1901', PhD diss., U. Cam., 1971 · M. Baker, 'The government of St. John's, Newfoundland, 1800–1921', PhD diss., University of Western Ontario, 1981 · P. R. O'Brien, The Newfoundland Patriotic Association: the administration of the war effort, 1914–1918, MA diss., Memorial

University, 1983 • I. D. H. McDonald, 'To each his own': William Coaker and the Fishermen's Protective Union in Newfoundland politics, 1908–1925 (1987) • S. J. R. Noel, Politics in Newfoundland (1971) • J. K. Hiller, 'The political career of Robert Bond', Twentieth-century Newfoundland: explorations, ed. J. K. Hiller and P. Neary (1994), 11–45 • The Times (25 Oct 1935) • J. P. Greene, 'Edward Patrick Morris, 1886–1900', student paper, Memorial University, 1974
Archives BL, corresp. with Lord Northcliffe, Add. MS 62165 • PRO, CO 194
Likenesses J. Guthrie, oils, Scot. NPG [see illus.]
Wealth at death £24,119 12s. 7d.: probate, 4 Jan 1936, CGPLA Eng. & Wales

Morris, (Alfred) Edwin (1894–1971), archbishop of Wales, was born at Lye, near Stourbridge, Worcestershire, on 8 May 1894, the eldest of four sons (a daughter died in infancy) of Alfred Morris, jeweller, of 42 Stourbridge Road, and his wife, Maria Beatrice Lickert. His first school was at Stambermill, Worcestershire, and he later went to St David's College School, Lampeter.

In the First World War Morris joined the Royal Army Medical Corps, returning to St David's College, Lampeter, in 1919 with a senior scholarship. He took his initial degree (BA) there in 1922, and gained a first class (BA) in theology at the University of Oxford in 1924. He won the junior Septuagint prize at Oxford in 1923, and the junior Greek Testament prize in 1924. After appointment to the chair of Hebrew and theology at Lampeter in 1924, he was made deacon that year, and priested the following year, both ordinations taking place at St David's Cathedral. In 1925 Morris married Emily Louisa (d. 1968), daughter of William Charles Davis, gardener at Prestcot House, Stourbridge. They had four sons and a daughter.

Morris was an examining chaplain to the bishop of Bangor (1925–8), and the bishop of Llandaff (1931–4). From 1931 to 1945 he was Lloyd Williams fellow of St David's College, Lampeter, taking his Lampeter BD degree in 1932. In 1945 he was elected to the bishopric of Monmouth on the death of A. E. Monahan. There appeared in quick succession his The Church in Wales and Nonconformity (1949), The Problem of Life and Death (1950), and The Catholicity of the Book of Common Prayer (1952). He became a DD (Lambeth) in 1950 and an honorary DD of the University of Wales in 1971. In 1957, on the death of Archbishop John Morgan of Llandaff, he was elected to the archbishopric of Wales, though remaining bishop of Monmouth with his residence at Newport, Monmouthshire. In 1958 he became an honorary fellow of St John's College, Oxford. After his retirement he commented wryly: 'I was the first Englishman to become archbishop of Wales and probably I shall also be the last'.

Morris was a controversial figure and rather enjoyed being such. There were controversies during his time at Lampeter, where he clashed with others on the staff there. One colleague insinuated that Morris, an Englishman by birth, was learning Welsh with a view to promotion in the Church in Wales. When he began to learn Welsh in 1924 he was put off by those who should have encouraged him. One ardent Welshman commented that he supposed that Morris was aiming to become a Welsh bishop. This wounded him so deeply that he resolved that he would never lend any colour to such an innuendo and at once dropped his attempt to learn Welsh. Perhaps he was oversensitive, but the thought of being suspected of scheming to use the Welsh language to aid an ambition which seemed to him to be wrong in itself was most distasteful to him.

Later in his life Bishop W. Glyn H. Simon of Llandaff was critical of the electoral college of the Church in Wales for electing Morris as the fifth archbishop of Wales. Simon regarded Morris as an Englishman through and through and, at a time when the Welsh language movement was gaining strength, not prepared to bow to the 'winds of change', a phrase whose inventor was half English and half Celtic.

Nevertheless Simon acknowledged that Morris was a good theologian who argued his proposals and statements from firm theological bases. As one who felt tempted to pay little attention to the piles of documents that reached the episcopal desks, Simon acknowledged that he could rely on Morris for a well-balanced and theologically informed summary of these.

Other controversies in which Morris became involved were the papal utterances about the choice between mother and unborn child where it was a case of saving one or the other. He always saw to it that the press received advance copy of what he intended to say at his diocesan conference, or at the governing body of the Church in Wales, or wherever else he chose to make his platform. One such occasion caused much publicity, for Morris had been invited to preach in Westminster Abbey on the Sunday before the coronation of Elizabeth II. His exposition of the so-called 'protestant oath' in the coronation service provoked a battle of words that raged for many weeks, first in the columns of The Times, then in the Spectator, with the result that the Dixie professor of ecclesiastical history at Cambridge entered the arena with some considerable force and achieved a superiority which Morris refused to acknowledge.

Morris has been described as probably the last archbishop who spurned the typewriter and wrote his own letters in longhand. He was a considerable correspondent, taking infinite pains in answering those who sought his advice on a variety of subjects.

Among his recreations were gardening, painting (in oils), swimming, and writing letters to newspapers. Morris retired in 1967 to Llanfair Clydogau, near Lampeter, retaining his holiday bungalow at St David's. He died at Hafdir, Lampeter, on 19 October 1971.

C. WITTON-DAVIES, rev.

Sources O. W. Jones, Glyn Simon: his life and opinions (1981) • J. S. Peart-Binns, The life and letters of Alfred Edwin Morris, archbishop of Wales (1983) • The Times (20 Oct 1971) • personal knowledge (1986) • private information (1986) • CGPLA Eng. & Wales (1971)
Likenesses W. Bird, photograph, 1962, NPG • C. Jones, portrait, Bishopstow, Newport • portrait, U. Wales, Lampeter
Wealth at death £5269: probate, 21 Dec 1971, CGPLA Eng. & Wales

Morris, Ernest (1889–1962), bell-ringer and author, was born at 60 Pasture Lane, Leicester, on 28 July 1889, the son of Josiah Morris, himself a well-known ringer, and his wife, Louisa, née Johnson. Ernest Morris had only elementary education, as his father, a shoemaker by profession, was unable to send him to high school; thus he was largely self-educated. At the age of fourteen he left school and went to work in a leather warehouse. After service during the First World War, partly abroad, eventually in 1937 he succeeded his father as verger of St Margaret's Church, Leicester. In 1957 their combined service in this post was fifty years. He retired the following year, on 1 March.

Ernest Morris is known both for the number of his recorded performances in change-ringing and for his writings about it. He learned to ring at Leicester in 1900 and, while he made good progress, he did not ring a peal (in the technical sense of 5000 or more changes) until 1906 (Grandsire Triples at Grimsby), and rang his fiftieth peal in 1911. However, it was after his war service that his ringing career really took off. It was interrupted by the Second World War, and it was in 1947 that he rang his thousandth peal, the fifteenth person to achieve this total. His father rang in both his first and thousandth peals. Along the way he rang in a number of record lengths. Among these were 12,896 Cambridge Surprise Major (Stoney Stanton, 28 April 1923) and 12,663 Stedman Cinques (Christ Church, Oxford, 26 August 1946, the first post-war long peal). With increased opportunity his tally of peals grew rapidly, and he rang his two thousandth peal at Loughborough Bell Foundry campanile on 27 February 1961, the first person to achieve this total. The final number of peals that he rang was 2076, of which 336 were at the Bell Foundry campanile. Criticism of the number of peals that he rang on the lower numbers of bells (489 of doubles and minor) overlooks the fact that he was only too willing to help younger ringers to achieve their first peal.

Morris's first book was a small work on St Margaret's Church, Leicester, published in 1912. However, his reputation was made with his *History and Art of Change Ringing*, published in 1931. Essentially this consists of a compendium of information that had appeared in the pages of *Church Bells*, *Bell News*, *Ringing World*, and other printed works. The material was organized in topics, but was selected uncritically and with appendices, and ran to 673 pages. A great success at the time, it is still a very useful source of reference, but certain of his conclusions must be used with caution. As well as writing a number of articles on a variety of topics for publication in the *Ringing World* and elsewhere, Morris published four other books. *Legends o' the Bells* (1935) was another compendium, this time of legendary material, while *Bells of All Nations* (1951) dealt with the subject on a very general basis. *Towers and Bells of Britain* (1955) was a summary in book form of a series of articles that had appeared in the *Ringing World* during the war years and was to a large extent based on his own experiences. A collector of small bells, his final work, *Tintinnabula* (1959), dealt with the small bells of the world. It is said that these general books were well received in the United States.

Morris died suddenly at Leicester Royal Infirmary on 28 April 1962 having apparently progressed well after an emergency operation. He was survived by his wife, Beatrice. His remains were cremated after a funeral service at St Margaret's, Leicester, on 1 May. His death was marked with extended coverage in the *Ringing World*.

JOHN C. EISEL

Sources *Ringing World* (1938), 313 · *Ringing World* (1962), 282, 298 · *Ringing World* (1911–98) · *Bell News and Ringers' Record*, 1–34 (Feb 1881–25 Dec 1915) · b. cert. · d. cert.
Archives Leics. RO, collection relating to history of bell-ringing
Wealth at death £876 13s. 0d.: probate, 16 May 1962, CGPLA Eng. & Wales

Morris, Francis Orpen (1810–1893), Church of England clergyman and naturalist, was born on 25 March 1810 near the Cove of Cork, the eldest son of Admiral Henry Gage Morris RN (d. 1852), then serving on the Irish station, and his wife, Rebecca Newenham Millerd, youngest daughter of the Revd Francis Orpen, vicar of Kilgarvan, co. Kerry. His formal schooling began when his family moved to Worcester in 1824. Morris became a pupil at Bromsgrove School, Worcestershire, where he began his collection of birds and insects, and formed friendships that would last throughout his life. He left Bromsgrove School in 1828 to study for two years under a private tutor, J. M. Butt, vicar of East Garston, Berkshire, and despite suffering scarlet fever, ague, jaundice, and inflammation of the lungs during this period, he matriculated at Worcester College, Oxford, on 17 June 1829. While reading for honours classics, Morris continued to pursue his interest in natural history. At the request of the keeper, J. L. Duncan, he arranged the Ashmolean Museum's collection of insects, and his membership of the Ashmolean Society undoubtedly dated from the same period.

Morris graduated in 1833 and entered the church. Ordained deacon on 3 August 1834, he briefly held the curacies of Hanging Heaton, near Dewsbury, Yorkshire, and Taxal, Cheshire, before moving to Doncaster, where he was ordained priest and became assistant curate of Armthorpe and Christ Church in October 1835. He married, on 1 January 1835, Anne (d. 1877), second daughter of Charles Sanders of Bromsgrove. In 1837 he took charge of the parish of Ordsall, near East Retford, Nottinghamshire, where he almost lost his life from smallpox at the age of twenty-eight. About May 1842 he became curate in charge of Crambe, a small parish between York and Malton, where he remained until 22 November 1844 when Archbishop Vernon Harcourt presented him to the living of Nafferton in the East Riding of Yorkshire. Morris's nine years at Nafferton were marred by the death in 1847 of Emily, the eldest of his six daughters and three sons. With a parish population of 1400, and a net living of approximately £40, Nafferton presented Morris with relatively trying circumstances. Consequently, in 1854, he embraced the offer of Nunburnholme, East Riding, a smaller parish (240 persons) that provided a considerably greater living, and where he remained thereafter.

A man of seemingly boundless energy, Morris engaged in numerous parish and literary pursuits. His son described him as:

Of medium height, and of spare, wiry, and upright form, he looked like one who could do a good day's march without fatigue. To many he appeared to have not a little of the strict officer about him. … Still, beneath a somewhat reserved manner … there was ever beating the kindest of hearts. (M. C. F. Morris, 113–14)

He established a parish school and occasionally sat on the magistrate's bench at the Pocklington petty sessions. As he had done in Nafferton, in 1873 he oversaw the restoration of the parish church. Four years later, however, he suffered a tragic loss when a cart accidentally backed over his wife, who died from the ensuing injuries on 18 April 1877. Undoubtedly Morris's *Handbook of Hymns for the Sick Bedside* (1877) was a product of this experience.

Morris was a prodigious author of tracts and leaflets. Committed to the belief that his writing should provide moral and religious guidance, he often compiled excerpts from other authors to support his cause, as in his *Words of Wesley on Constant Communion* (1869), *The Darwin Craze* (1880), and *Experiments on Living Animals* (1890). Morris was equally prolific in his countless letters and contributions to newspapers and periodicals spanning more than fifty years. While they addressed subjects as diverse as railway fares, the Nonconformist Burial Bill, and Post Office grievances, the majority dealt with evolution, church defence, the sparrow, and close time for birds. He succeeded his brother, Beverley Morris, as editor of *The Naturalist* from 1856 to 1860, and when the *Animal World* first appeared in 1869 he contributed 'British birds' to the inaugural issue; he was a regular contributor to each of the monthly issues for the next three years. His letters to *The Times* on bird protectionism became so numerous that he republished them as a small book in 1880.

Of all his publications, Morris was perhaps best known for his voluminous, illustrated books on natural history. His collaboration with the Driffield woodblock colour printer Benjamin Fawcett in the production of *Bible Natural History* (1849–50) was followed by the successful six-volume *History of British Birds*, initially issued in monthly parts over seven and a half years, beginning in June 1850, *A Natural History of the Nests and Eggs of British Birds* (1853–6), *A History of British Butterflies* (1853), and *County Seats of the Noblemen and Gentlemen of Great Britain and Ireland* (1866–80). When Fawcett declined further collaboration, Morris produced *A Natural History of British Moths* (1859–70). In all his work on natural history he espoused the belief that his studies 'infallibly lead from the works of nature up to the God of Nature' (F. O. Morris, viii). Combined with his tory, high-church leanings, Morris's natural theology clashed with Darwinian theories of evolution. He first proclaimed his vehement opposition in his paper, 'On the difficulties of Darwinism', which he read at the 1868 meeting of the British Association for the Advancement of Science. He also supported the causes of bird protectionism and antivivisectionism—in a rare absence from his parish he travelled to London to give evidence before the select committee on wild birds protection on 26 June 1873. He was instrumental in establishing the Plumage League in 1885, and he was one of the earliest members of the Selbourne

League, which was created in December of the same year. In 1888 the government acknowledged his work as a naturalist with the award of a civil-list pension of £100 per annum.

Throughout most of his adult life Morris enjoyed a robust constitution, but a painful attack of eczema in 1886 weakened him; by 1892 he required permanent help with his clerical work, and in January the following year an attack of bronchitis left him bedridden. After fourteen days in this state he died, at the rectory, Nunburnholme, on 10 February 1893. His funeral was held five days later, when he was buried near the south wall of the Nunburnholme parish church. J. F. M. CLARK

Sources *The Entomologist*, 26 (1893) · *Natural Science*, 2 (1893) · *The Ibis*, 6th ser., 5 (1893) · *Nature*, 47 (1892–3) · *The Times* (13 Feb 1893) · *Nature Notes*, 5 (Jan 1894) · *Good Words*, 34 (Sept 1893) · M. C. F. Morris, *Francis Orpen Morris: a memoir* (1897) · B. Dyson, 'Ornithological observations', *Paragon Review* [Hull], 5 (1996) · 'Select committee on … the Wild Fowl Protection Act', *Parl. papers* (1873), 13.647, no. 338 · F. O. Morris, *A history of British butterflies* (1864) · d. cert.
Archives U. Hull, Brynmor Jones L., corresp. and papers, DX/21, DP/180 | BL, Gladstone MSS · Oxf. U. Mus. NH, Hope Library, letters to J. C. Dale · U. Hull, Brynmor Jones L., papers regarding Association for the Protection of Sea Birds
Likenesses Gowland of York, photograph, repro. in Morris, *Francis Orpen Morris*, frontispiece · Swan Electric Engraving Co., photogravure, NPG · lithograph, U. Hull, Brynmor Jones L., DP/180 · photographs, U. Hull, Brynmor Jones L., DX/21
Wealth at death £557 3s. 9d.: probate, 22 June 1893, CGPLA Eng. & Wales

Morris, Gouverneur (1752–1816), revolutionary politician and diplomatist in the United States of America, was born on 31 January 1752 at Morrisania, Westchester county, New York, son of Lewis Morris jun. (d. 1762), New York landlord and politician, and his second wife, Sarah Gouverneur (d. 1786). His father was of Welsh descent and his mother belonged to a French Huguenot family that migrated to New York after the revocation of the edict of Nantes.

The Morris family ranked among New York's landed gentry. Their estate (in what is now the Bronx) enjoyed formal manorial status, though it was small by comparison with other New York manors. The Morrises were extremely well connected within their own province, in other colonies, and in England. Gouverneur Morris's grandfather and father were judges and assemblymen. His uncle Robert Hunter *Morris, became lieutenant-governor of Pennsylvania and royal governor of New Jersey. His half-brother Staats Long *Morris entered the regular army and went to England, where he rose to lieutenant-general, married a dowager duchess, and won a seat in parliament. Gouverneur Morris's own mother was a committed loyalist during the war.

Young Gouverneur received his early education in the Huguenot school at New Rochelle, acquiring the fluent French that served him very well later in life, and then at the Academy of Philadelphia. He earned his BA at King's College in 1768, which meant that he had the chance to observe closely New York's tumultuous resistance to the Stamp Act (1765), the Townshend taxes, and the New York Restraining Act (both 1767). That may have stimulated his

Gouverneur Morris (1752–1816), by Thomas Sully, 1808

lifelong mistrust of street politics. He trained for the bar in the office of William Smith jun., future loyalist chief justice and foremost attorney in the province. He began practising law when he was nineteen.

Morris recorded his earliest political position in 1774, as he observed a popular meeting to elect a revolutionary committee. He saw 'the mob' who were beginning 'to think and to reason' as 'poor reptiles' enjoying their 'vernal morning'. 'Ere noon', he predicted, 'they will bite'. By contrast Morris considered 'reunion with the parent state' to be 'the interest of all men' (Sparks, 1.23–6). Yet he did not become a loyalist. Instead he joined a group of young upper-class New Yorkers, most of them fellow King's graduates, who moved slowly toward independence and sought to limit its social consequences. To a large extent they succeeded, taking advantage of unfolding events and creating a state government with institutional protection for private property and a strong governorship to check popular desires. But despite his conservatism on class relations among white New Yorkers, Morris was deeply radical on the subject of black slavery, seeking its abolition as part of New York's revolutionary settlement.

Morris represented New York in the continental congress at Philadelphia in 1778 and 1779, where he drafted a number of major state papers and closely observed the effects of runaway inflation. He stayed in Pennsylvania after leaving congress, practising law, writing a major series of essays on the problem of American finance, and working with the revolution's financier Robert Morris (no relation) to stabilize the American economy.

Morris's adopted state made him a delegate to the constitutional convention in 1787, which gave him the chance to take a major role in the creation of the American republic. He still distrusted the 'mob' and his ideal government would have had a life presidency and a senate whose appointed members would amount to life peers. That government would virtually obliterate the power of the separate states. On slavery Morris remained radical. His stance against counting slaves for the purpose of apportioning the house of representatives and against the slave trade nearly split the convention. As a member of the convention's committee of style Morris had the largest role in the final wording of the constitution. Its memorable preamble ('We the People of the United States of America … do ordain and establish this Constitution') was the product of his facile pen.

Morris went to France on private business in 1788 and stayed in Europe for the next decade, serving from 1792 to 1794 as American minister. His undoubtedly brilliant personality, his *bon vivant* style, and his complete command of the French language served him very well. Appalled by what he saw as the French Revolution developed, he advised French conservatives including Louis XVI and the marquis de Lafayette, sheltered possible terror victims, and established good relations with other diplomats who shared his perspective. Unlike all other envoys he stayed in Paris throughout the terror, and the diary he kept is a major historical source for the period. Though formally recalled in 1794, he stayed in Europe for another four years, acting in part as an informal adviser to the British Foreign Office.

Despite Morris's opposition to slavery his French experience confirmed his hostility to popular politics so strongly that he favoured putting down the great uprising in San Domingo. When he returned to America and took up residence at Morrisania, the conservative Federalist Party controlled both the national government and New York, and the state legislature sent him to the United States senate in 1800. He served until 1802 and then left formal politics, although he opposed most policies of the Jefferson and Madison administrations, especially in regard to foreign affairs. He endorsed the abortive secession movement of New Englanders in 1814, in protest against the Anglo-American War of 1812–14. On 25 December 1809, after many amorous adventures, he married the Virginian Anne Cary Randolph (b. 1774), showing complete contempt for rumours that she had been the mistress of her brother-in-law. They had one son. Morris died at Morrisania on 6 November 1816 of infection caused by an attempted self-remedy for a urinary blockage. His wife survived him.   EDWARD COUNTRYMAN

Sources M. M. Mintz, *Gouverneur Morris and the American revolution* (Norman, OK, 1970) · M. Swiggett, *The extraordinary Mr Morris* (1952) · T. Roosevelt, *Gouverneur Morris* (New York, 1908) · J. Sparks, *The life of Gouverneur Morris* (1832) · M. Knobloch, 'The French Revolution as seen through the eyes of Gouverneur Morris', *Bulletin of Bibliography*, 50/1 (1993), 55–73 [annotated bibliography] · M. Mintz, 'Morris, Gouverneur', *ANB*
Archives Col. U. · L. Cong.
Likenesses E. Quenedy, physionotrace, 1789, repro. in A. C. Morris, ed., *Diary and letters of Gouverneur Morris* (1888) · T. Sully, oils, 1808, Atwater Kent Museum of Philadelphia [*see illus.*] · J. Sharples, pastel, 1810, Frick Art Reference Library, New York · G.-L. Chrétien, engraving (after E. Quenedy) · B. L. Prévost, engraving (after P. E. Du Simitière, 1779), NYPL, Emmet Collection

Morris, Sir Harold Spencer (1876–1967), barrister and industrial arbitrator, was born at 21 Compton Terrace, Highbury, London, on 21 December 1876, the second son of Sir Malcolm Alexander Morris FRCS (Edin.) (1849–1924)

and his wife, Fanny Cox of Dorchester-on-Thames. Malcolm Morris had a distinguished career as a consulting surgeon and as a specialist in skin diseases, practising from 8 Harley Street, London, where he moved with his family in September 1887 from their former home at 63 Montagu Square.

Harold Morris was educated at Westminster School, Clifton College, and from 1894 at Magdalen College, Oxford, where he read law, graduating in 1897 with a fourth-class degree. Having joined the Inner Temple he was called to the bar on 26 January 1899. Among those called the same night there were three others who, like him, later became benchers; in 1949 on the fiftieth anniversary of their call to the bar (as indeed on some later anniversaries) the four dined together in hall in company with and to the delight of their fellow benchers. The other three were John Simon, who to his other high offices added that of lord chancellor from 1940 to 1945, Rayner Goddard, who was appointed lord chief justice of England in 1946, and the Hon. Victor Alexander Russell, a popular and respected practitioner in the Probate, Divorce, and Admiralty Division.

Morris practised at the common-law bar and was a member of the south-eastern circuit. For anyone who had been building up a practice in the years after 1899, and especially for someone with a young family, the outbreak of war in 1914 threatened grievous professional upset. In 1904 Morris had married Olga, the daughter of Emil Teichman, of Chislehurst. It was a happy marriage. They had four daughters and one son, Malcolm John Morris, who followed his father into the legal profession. Malcolm Morris was called to the bar by the Inner Temple in 1937, became QC in 1959 and a bencher (in his father's lifetime) in 1965; he held various recorderships and then became a judge at the central criminal court where he sat until his untimely death in 1972.

Anxious to serve in the war, Morris was commissioned in the Coldstream Guards on 2 June 1916. In June 1918 he was transferred to the Royal Flying Corps as deputy assistant adjutant-general; he was appointed a court-martial officer with the rank of major, was mentioned in dispatches, and in 1919 was appointed MBE. After demobilization in February 1919, Morris returned to the bar where he successfully re-established himself and took silk in 1921. As an advocate he was competent; as a speaker either in court or on social occasions he was pleasing, lively, and interesting. He possessed a natural buoyancy and gaiety and courtesy; he had good looks. The combination of all these qualities seemed to augur for him a legal career of promise which could lead to a thriving practice with prospects of elevation to the High Court bench. He was appointed recorder of Folkestone in 1921 and held the post until 1926. In November 1922 he entered parliament as National Liberal member for East Bristol but in the general election of the following year he lost the seat.

In 1925 Morris was asked to chair a court of investigation to consider a dispute in the woollen industry. His success in that capacity doubtless led to his being invited (as he was in 1925) to succeed Sir William Warrender MacKenzie as chairman of the railways national wages board and to his being appointed in the following year (1926) to succeed Sir William as president of the industrial court—a position which he continued to hold until 1945. He was knighted in 1927.

In the period before Morris accepted these positions his health was for a time not good. In such situations a secure position freed from the stresses and strains of life at the bar holds attractions, and Morris was probably so influenced. Though his appointment as president of the industrial court was to a position of great national importance and prestige, it meant that after only four or five years in silk Morris would have to abandon any prospects of building up a large practice and of being appointed to the High Court bench.

Wise and impartial, Morris had the qualities which fitted him to be an admirable president of the industrial court. Assuredly his tenure of the presidency during years of economic difficulties and anxieties gave satisfaction and inspired confidence. For a short time (from 1930 to 1935), he added to his work by chairing the coal wages board after the passing of the Coal Mines Act of 1930.

Even after retiring in 1945 he continued to render public service: very acceptably, he sat judicially from time to time at Middlesex quarter sessions, at the central criminal court, and in other courts.

Morris's happy appreciation and understanding of life at the bar inspired him to write in 1930 an entertaining book, *The Barrister*. Years later, in 1960, came an autobiographical volume of much interest, *Back View*. He died at his home, 21 Lichfield Road, Kew, Surrey, on 11 November 1967.   MORRIS OF BORTH-Y-GEST, *rev.*

Sources H. Morris, *Back view* (1960) · *The Times* (13 Nov 1967) · personal knowledge (1981) · *CGPLA Eng. & Wales* (1968)
Likenesses W. Russell, portrait, priv. coll.
Wealth at death £39,207: probate, 6 Feb 1968, *CGPLA Eng. & Wales*

Morris, Henry (1889–1961), educational administrator, was born on 13 November 1889 at 131 Poulton Road, Southport, Lancashire, the fourth son and seventh of the eight children of William Morris, journeyman plumber, and his wife, Mary Ellen Mullin (*d*. 1901/2). His mother was Irish, a Roman Catholic until her marriage, and perhaps an influence on his early inclination to a career in the church, though she died when he was twelve. Morris left school at the age of fourteen to work as an office boy on the *Southport Visiter*, and from 1906 to 1910 continued his education through adult classes at the Harris Institute, Preston. At the age of twenty-one he began to train for the priesthood at St David's College, Lampeter, and after obtaining a second class in theology moderations, he entered Exeter College, Oxford, in 1912. In military service from 1914, he was commissioned in the Royal Army Service Corps and served in France and in Italy. He completed his undergraduate studies at King's College, Cambridge, from 1919 to 1920, in which year he gained an upper second in moral sciences.

Henry Morris (1889–1961), by unknown photographer, c.1938 [left, with two students]

Morris made his mark in the inter-war period of educational reorganization, when so much was hoped for and so little realized in the reform of state schooling. Beginning as assistant education secretary in Kent under the careful tutelage of E. Salter Davies in 1920–21, he soon moved to Cambridgeshire and in 1922 succeeded to the post of county education secretary there. His rapid and politically astute achievement of an agreed religious syllabus for the county schools, the first of its kind in England, was a prelude to his inspirational and energetic campaign for village colleges. These entailed the consolidation of county and denominational schools in order to provide a panacea for the widely recognized 'rural problem'. The village college was to provide a focus for educational, cultural, and social activity in increasingly depopulated and economically deprived agricultural areas. Morris's achievement in founding four such colleges in Cambridgeshire by 1939 was the result of determined pursuit of the requisite funding, and resolute handling of the resistance which he encountered. The first village college opened at Sawston in 1930. Village colleges aimed to provide not only juvenile and adult education, but also the social and cultural activities Morris saw as necessary for a healthy and progressive rural community. At Oxford he had been deeply influenced by Hastings Rashdall's exposition of the medieval university in its integral relationship with society, but he had been inspired too by the fine architecture of the ancient university town, and he believed passionately in the educational importance of an aesthetic environment, epitomized in the distinguished design which he secured from Walter Gropius for Impington Village College, opened in 1939. R. A. Butler, wartime minister of education, made frequent acknowledgement of Morris's achievement, and in the 1942 birthday honours Morris was made CBE. Cambridgeshire's village colleges provided the model for many developments in community education after the Second World War, for example in Leicestershire, Derbyshire, and Devon.

Morris continued as director of education for nine years after the war, and by this period he had acquired a national reputation, resulting in advisory work for the Colonial Office on provision of further education in west Africa. From 1947 he was seconded part-time by the Ministry of Town and Country Planning to advise on social and cultural provision for the new towns, an extension of his life's work in the context of a highly significant policy developed by the post-war Labour government. One notable achievement in this connection was the establishment of the Digswell community of artists and craftsmen near Welwyn Garden City, a project intended as part of a greater aim of bringing artists into contact with town planners, architects, manufacturers, and the local public. Trustees such as Herbert Read and Gordon Russell demonstrate the level of support which Morris received. He put a great deal of personal commitment and energy into this project, and despite many difficulties it was formally opened in 1959.

Morris's educational innovations sprang from a set of ideals based on his interest in religion, education, science, and the arts. Religion in its widest and deepest sense meant much to him, though his early attachment to the church was severed by war experience and by the teachings of scientific humanism. But above all it was his intense love of beauty in various forms—music, art, poetry, and especially architecture—which underlay his professional and personal life. Dorothy Bimrose, his personal secretary for many years, recalled that 'he had no beliefs, no formal religion, yet his passionate belief in beauty and graciousness and in the possibility of full and complete living, was his religion' (Rée, Lupton, and others, 13). Friends felt privileged to share his practical gospel of enhancing life by regenerating the culture as a whole, and this gospel was realized through his firm belief in local government and through his pragmatism.

Nan Youngman, art adviser in Cambridgeshire from 1944, described Morris as

> tall, with a long pale face and wild blue eyes. His hair was mousy, sparse and straight—there was always one long wisp hanging out at the back. He had a beautiful voice, and, as many testify, he was unpredictable in his moods, but never dull. (Rée, Lupton, and others, 32)

His unpredictability embraced a social ambivalence; he despised pomposity but could be snobbish, and embarrassment about his own humble origins is evident from the testimony of former colleagues and from misleading entries in Oxford and Cambridge college registers. He could be by turns generous and close-fisted. He was difficult to work with, demanding and intolerant, and a master of the premeditated insult. Yet Morris inspired loyalty among close friends who admired his infectious and vituperative vivacity and who recorded his antipathy to prejudice and hypocrisy, his deep sense of the humane, and compassion for human suffering. He was hospitable to artistic and intellectual company in the elegance of three successive homes which he occupied throughout his years in Cambridge; both there and on European travel with friends he indulged his aesthetic and culinary tastes. His homosexuality was generally concealed from acquaintances in his lifetime, but more intimate friends later described his sexual passions and frustrations, and his long-standing friendship with Charles Fenn has been well documented by Rée. Nan Youngman observed that although a homosexual he was almost never unfriendly to women; Jack Pritchard recalled his love of happy families with children and his sadness that he would never marry and have a family himself.

In 1960 Morris officiated at the opening of Comberton Village College in spite of his declining health, and at the end of that year he was persuaded to retire from the ministry of town and country planning. Physical and mental deterioration compounded his characteristically eccentric behaviour, but he continued to receive support from friends and former colleagues. Dementia, pneumonia, and Parkinson's disease combined to cause his death on 10 December 1961 at Hill End Hospital, St Albans, where he had spent his last months. A simple cremation ceremony at Golders Green crematorium on 14 December was attended by Henry Moore and J. B. Priestley, among many old friends. Published tributes and commemorations following his death, and later marking the centenary of his birth, reflected the inspiration and the affection felt by many who had been influenced by his work.

PETER CUNNINGHAM

Sources H. Rée, *Educator extraordinary: the life and achievement of Henry Morris, 1889–1961* (1973) · H. Rée, ed., *The Henry Morris collection* (1984) · W. van der Eyken and B. Turner, *Adventures in education* (1969), 145–81 · H. Rée and K. Foreman, 'A genius in the education office: the vision and achievements of Henry Morris', *RSA Journal*, 138 (1989–90), 458–68 · J. Pritchard, *View from a long chair: the memoirs of Jack Pritchard* (1984), 44–51 · *Recalling Henry Morris, 1889–1961: a celebration of this remarkable educator through the personal memories of his friends* [n.d., 1990?] · *The Times* (12 Dec 1961) · N. Fisher, 'Henry Morris', *Education* (29 Oct 1954) · H. Dent, *The countryman's college* (1943) · D. J. Farnell, 'Henry Morris, an architect of education', thesis, Cambridge Institute of Education, 1968 · 'A typewriter for Henry Morris: education committee tributes', *Cambridge Independent Press and Chronicle* (24 Dec 1954), 17 · *Cambridge Daily News* (12 Dec 1961), 13 · A. B. How, *Register of Exeter College, Oxford, 1891–1921* (1928) · J. J. Withers, *A register of admissions to King's College, Cambridge, 1797–1925* (1929) · b. cert. · d. cert.
Archives University of East Anglia Library, corresp. and MS PP/22
Likenesses photograph, c.1938, University of East Anglia Library [*see illus.*] · photograph, repro. in van der Eyken and Turner, *Adventures*, pl. 19 · photographs, repro. in Rée, *Educator extraordinary*, pl. 1, 2, 3, 7 · photographs, repro. in Pritchard, *View from a long chair*, pl. 9, 12
Wealth at death £4134 0s. 10d.: administration, 15 Feb 1962, CGPLA Eng. & Wales

Morris, Ivan Ira Esme (1925–1976), Japanologist, was born on 29 November 1925 at 45 Cromwell Road, London, the son of Ira Victor Morris and Edit Dagmar Emilia (*née* Toll). His father, an American, was a member of a well-to-do family related to the Guggenheims; his mother the daughter of a Swedish general. His father was a journalist and both parents were successful novelists. Morris's childhood language was Swedish, and when he first attended school in Britain he was taunted because of his Swedish accent. His elementary and secondary schooling were in Britain (at some point he attended Gordonstoun School), and he struck everyone who met him as being English, but he had American as well as British citizenship, and during the Second World War studied at the Japanese language

school of the United States navy. After the war, in 1946, he obtained his bachelor's degree at Harvard University.

Morris subsequently returned to Britain and continued his study of Japanese at the School of Oriental and African Languages of the University of London. While writing his thesis on *The Tale of Genji* (he received the degree of PhD in 1951) he became acquainted with Arthur Waley. He would later acknowledge his indebtedness to Waley, his teacher and model, by editing *Madly Singing in the Mountains* (1970), a collection of remembrances of Waley written by friends. In the elegance of the English prose into which he rendered the Japanese classics, Morris was Waley's only successor.

Morris entered the Foreign Office as senior research assistant after receiving his doctorate, then went on to Japan with a grant from the Royal Institute of International Affairs. His *Nationalism and the Right Wing in Japan* (1960) reflects his early interest in Japanese politics. He and his students also translated *Thought and Behaviour in Modern Japanese Politics* (1963), a collection of essays by the political scientist Masao Maruyama. His name, however, is most frequently associated with the works of Japanese literature, both classical and modern, that he translated and discussed. Perhaps his most beautiful translations are *The Pillow Book of Sei Shōnagon* (1961) and the diary he called *As I Crossed a Bridge of Dreams* (1971), both works by court ladies of the eleventh century. His English was that of a virtuoso; the translation, into an idiom reminiscent of Defoe, of the seventeenth-century novelist Saikaku's *The Life of an Amorous Woman* (1963) is nothing short of dazzling. It was typical of his scholarship that he verified each word in his translation to be sure it was used in the eighteenth century. Although he intended his books for non-specialists and was at pains to make his writings not only scholarly but a delight to read, no Western scholar of Japanese literature has given more attention to small details; there is a whole volume of footnotes accompanying *The Pillow Book*. He loved research into minutiae, and could make the smallest item of information of interest by his witty presentation; but his original works, such as *The World of the Shining Prince* (1964), a study of the Japanese aristocracy in the eleventh century, and *The Nobility of Failure* (1975), were conceived on a grand scale. The latter work uses examples chosen from as far back as ancient Japanese legend and as recently as the kamikaze attacks of the Second World War to illustrate Morris's belief that the typical Japanese hero is a man who, having known glory, finally suffers defeat. Of his translations of modern Japanese literature, the best-known is *The Temple of the Golden Pavilion* (1959) by Yukio Mishima.

In 1960 Morris joined the department of east Asian languages and cultures at Columbia University, New York, where he taught Japanese literature and history and served as chairman of the department from 1966 to 1969. Apart from his teaching and scholarship, he wrote theatrical criticism, compiled puzzle books, and was an enthusiastic chess player. He was the founder of the United States section of Amnesty International and spent innumerable hours on behalf of prisoners of conscience. He was president of the American affiliate at the time of his death. His three marriages (the second to Ayako Ogawa, the third to Nobuko Uenishi) all ended in divorce. He died in Bologna of a heart attack on 19 July 1976, and was buried at Nesle, near Rozay-en-Brie, Seine et Marne, France, where he had a home. D. KEENE

Sources personal knowledge (2004) · *The Times* (26 July 1976) · *The Times* (9 Aug 1976) · *New York Times* (21 July 1976) · b. cert. · H. Cortazzi, ed., *Britain and Japan: biographical portraits*, 4 (2002)

Morris, Sir James Nicoll (1763?–1830), naval officer, probably born in 1763, was the son of Captain John Morris RN, who, in command of the *Bristol*, was mortally wounded in the unsuccessful attack on Sullivan's Island on 28 June 1776 and died on 2 July. James is said to have entered the navy under the immediate command of his father, but by 1778 he was in the *Prince of Wales*, the flagship of Rear-Admiral Samuel Barrington, in the West Indies, and in her was present at the battles of St Lucia and Grenada. He was promoted lieutenant on 14 April 1780, and served on board the *Namur* in the action off Dominica on 12 April 1782. He was again with Barrington in the *Royal George* during the Spanish armament in 1790, and by his interest was promoted commander on 21 September. In 1791 he was appointed to the sloop *Pluto* on the Newfoundland station, where, on 25 July 1793, he captured the French sloop *Lutine*. On 7 October 1793 he was posted to the frigate *Boston* (32 guns), which he took to England and commanded for the next four years in the channel and the Bay of Biscay and on the Spanish coast, cruising successfully against merchant ships and privateers. Towards the end of 1797 Morris was moved into the frigate *Lively* (32 guns), which was lost on Rota Point, near Cadiz, in the early part of 1798. The following year he was appointed to the *Phaëton* (38 guns), in which in the autumn he carried Lord Elgin to Constantinople. In May 1800 the *Phaëton* was with the fleet off Genoa, and being detached to co-operate with the Austrians, inflicted severe loss on the retreating French at Loano and Alassio. In October she was off Malaga, and on the 28th her boats, under the command of Mr Beaufort, her first lieutenant, captured and brought off a heavily armed polacca, which, with a French privateer schooner, was lying under the protection of a five-gun battery. During 1801 the *Phaëton* continued active on the coast of Spain, and in the winter returned to England.

On 25 October 1802 Morris married Margaretta Sarah, the second daughter of Thomas Somers Cocks, a banker (1737–1796), and the niece of Charles Somers Cocks, first Lord Somers. On the renewal of the war he was appointed to the *Leopard* (50 guns), but was shortly afterwards moved into the *Colossus*, a new 74 gun ship, which, after some eighteen months off Brest under Admiral Cornwallis, was, in October 1805, with Nelson off Cadiz, and on the 21st took part in the battle of Trafalgar. She was the sixth ship in the lee line, following Collingwood, and sustained greater damage and heavier loss of men than any other ship in the fleet. Morris himself was severely wounded in the thigh but, the bleeding being stopped by a tourniquet, remained on deck until the close of the action. For the

next three years he continued in command of the *Colossus*, on the home station or in the Mediterranean, and in 1810 he commanded the *Formidable* (98 guns). On 1 August 1811 he was promoted rear-admiral, and in 1812, at the special request of Sir James Saumarez, was appointed third in command in the Baltic. On 2 January 1815 he was made a KCB, and on 12 August 1819 he became vice-admiral. He died at his house at Marlow, Buckinghamshire, on 15 April 1830. J. K. LAUGHTON, rev. ROGER MORRISS

Sources J. Marshall, *Royal naval biography*, 4 vols. (1823–35) [with 4 suppls.] · *GM*, 1st ser., 100/1 (1830), 467 · pay books of HMS *Bristol*, PRO · W. James, *The naval history of Great Britain, from the declaration of war by France in 1793, to the accession of George IV*, [4th edn], 6 vols. (1847) · *The dispatches and letters of Vice-Admiral Lord Viscount Nelson*, ed. N. H. Nicolas, 7 vols. (1844–6) · J. Ralfe, *The naval biography of Great Britain*, 1 (1828) · A. B. Rodger, *The war of the second coalition: 1798–1801, a strategic commentary* (1964) · R. Muir, *Britain and the defeat of Napoleon, 1807–1815* (1996)

Morris [*née* Burden], **Jane** (1839–1914), embroiderer and artist's model, was born in Oxford on 19 October 1839, the daughter of Robert Burden (d. 1865), a stablehand in Oxford, and his wife, Ann Maizey (d. 1871). Little is known of her childhood, but it was clearly one of poverty and deprivation.

In October 1857 Jane Burden and her sister, Elizabeth, were seen by Dante Gabriel *Rossetti (1828–1882) and Edward Burne-Jones at a performance of the Drury Lane Theatre Company in Oxford. The two men were painting murals based on Arthurian tales for the Oxford Union together with a group of artists who included William *Morris (1834–1896). Struck by Jane's beauty, Rossetti and Burne-Jones sought her to model for them. Jane initially sat mainly to Rossetti, who needed a model for Queen Guinevere for the murals. After this, Jane sat to Morris, who had begun an easel painting, *La belle Iseult* (Tate collection). During this period Morris fell in love with Jane and they were engaged. Although the details are not known, it seems clear that Jane was privately educated before her marriage. Her keen intelligence allowed her essentially to re-create herself. She read widely, became proficient in French and later Italian, and was an accomplished pianist. Her manners and speech became refined to such an extent that contemporaries referred to her manner as 'regal' or 'queenly'. Jane Burden married William Morris on 26 April 1859 at St Michael's Church, Oxford.

The Morrises moved to Red House in Bexleyheath, Kent, in 1860. Their two children, Jenny and May Morris [see Morris, Mary], were born in 1861 and 1862 respectively. Creating furnishings for Red House led to the founding of Morris, Marshall, Faulkner & Co. Morris had begun experimenting with embroidery before he met Jane, and soon after their marriage he began working with her to refine embroidery techniques. They studied old pieces of embroidery and recovered knowledge of some stitches by unpicking these old fragments. Jane was apparently already an accomplished needlewoman, and her embroidery shows remarkable technical skill. For Red House, Jane completed panels with repeating floral designs. A

Jane Morris [Burden] (1839–1914), by unknown photographer, 1865

number of these designs were worked on blue wool serge which she found in a London shop. This was significant, as wool became the preferred background for the firm's embroideries. Jane also contributed to a series of panels depicting great women with her sister, also an accomplished embroiderer. During the creation of these panels, Jane later recalled, 'we were making experiments in silk and gold wools afterwards to bloom into altar cloths etc.' (BL, Add. MS 45341). In 1865 the Morrises began living over the firm's premises at Queen Square, Bloomsbury, and Jane was in charge of a group of women who did needlework for the firm, producing a variety of ecclesiastical and domestic embroideries. Jane continued to embroider at least until 1910 for friends and, while her husband was still alive, important clients of the firm. Both William Morris and Philip Webb created designs for Jane's embroidery. She embroidered screens, drapery, and other items. In the late 1880s and early 1890s she exhibited her work at the Arts and Crafts Exhibition Society. One of her most notable embroideries was the coverlet for William Morris's bed which she worked with her friend Mary De Morgan (now at Kelmscott Manor). The design is based on antique flower patterns and is signed 'Si je puis Jane Morris'.

In the late 1860s Jane Morris began a romantic liaison with Rossetti which lasted until 1876. This corresponded with a period during which Jane was the model for some of Rossetti's most famous paintings, including *Venus Astarte* (Manchester City Galleries), *Proserpine* (Tate collection), *La pia de Tolomei* (Spencer Art Gallery, University of Kansas), and *The Day Dream* (V&A). Her striking appearance

provided inspiration to Rossetti for over twenty years. Henry James described her after their first meeting:

> such a wife! Je n'en reviens pas—she haunts me still … an apparition of fearful and wonderful intensity … Imagine a tall lean woman in a long dress of some dead purple stuff … with a mass of crisp black hair heaped into great wavy projections on each of her temples, a thin pale face, a pair of strange sad, deep dark Swinburnish eyes … in fine Complete. (Henry James to Alice James, 10 March 1869, *Letters of Henry James*, 1, 1974)

It is clear from Jane's correspondence with Rossetti that she was a participant in his creative work: she frequently created costumes for his paintings, often of her own design.

In addition to her embroidery, Jane Morris produced a number of books. These are elaborately decorated and bound in vellum, velvet, or leather. They were apparently intended as gifts, and their texts are generally handwritten English and French verse, with illuminated capitals or other decoration. The bookbinder Thomas James Cobden-Sanderson first learned his craft at Jane's suggestion.

Jane Morris was actively involved in many of her husband's endeavours. In addition to her contributions to the firm, which continued until his death, she worked for the Society for the Protection of Ancient Buildings, the 1882 Icelandic Famine Relief Committee, and later the Kelmscott Press. She did not however share his political views. Despite her husband's commitment to socialism, Jane maintained an allegiance to the Liberal Party, although her sympathies leaned towards the party's radical wing. She also ardently supported Irish home rule, a view which she shared with her close friends Rosalind Howard, countess of Carlisle, and Jane Cobden.

In 1883 Jane Morris met the poet and political activist Wilfrid Scawen *Blunt (1840–1922) and by 1887 at the latest the couple had become lovers. Jane designed the cover for Blunt's volume of poetry *In vinculis*, published in 1889. It was also probably through Jane that Blunt came to have his poetry published by the Kelmscott Press.

After her husband's death in 1896 Jane Morris worked with Sydney Cockerell in the winding-up of operations of the Kelmscott Press. In 1904 she modelled for the queen in Evelyn De Morgan's painting *The Hour Glass* (Evelyn De Morgan Foundation, London). Jane made a substantial contribution to May Morris's edition *The Collected Works of William Morris*. She assisted her daughter with dating and identifying manuscripts as well as providing her with material for use in the introductions, including reminiscences of Morris; she also reviewed drafts of all the introductions to the volumes, corrected errors, and offered suggestions for improvements. She died on 26 January 1914 at 5 Brock Street, Bath, and was buried at St George's Church, Kelmscott, Oxfordshire.   FRANK C. SHARP

Sources J. Marsh, *Jane and May Morris* (1986) · *Dante Gabriel Rossetti and Jane Morris: their correspondence*, ed. J. Bryson (1976) · L. Parry, *William Morris textiles* (1983) · A. R. Dufty, *William Morris embroideries* (1985) · *CGPLA Eng. & Wales* (1914)

Archives BL, corresp. and papers, Add. MSS 45298, 45328, 45341, 45346, 45348–45349, 45351–45353 | BL, corresp. with Sir Sydney Cockerell, Add. MS 52738 · BL, William Morris papers, Add. MSS

45341, 45346, 45349 · FM Cam., letters to W. S. Blunt · Hammersmith and Fulham Archives and Local History Centre, London, letters to Sir Sydney Cockerell · W. Sussex RO, Jane Cobden papers
Likenesses D. G. Rossetti, watercolour drawing, 1856, Tate collection · D. G. Rossetti, pen-and-ink drawing, 1857, Birmingham Museums and Art Gallery · W. Morris, oils, 1858 (*Queen Guinevere*), Tate collection · D. G. Rossetti, oils, 1858–64, Llandaff Cathedral · D. G. Rossetti, oils, 1859 (*The salutation of Beatrice*), National Gallery of Canada, Ottawa · photograph, 1865, St Bride Institute, London, St Bride Printing Library [*see illus.*] · D. G. Rossetti, oils, 1866–8 (*Mrs Morris in a blue dress*), Kelmscott Manor, Oxfordshire · D. G. Rossetti, watercolour drawing, 1867, Cecil Higgins Art Gallery, Bedford · D. G. Rossetti, pencil drawing, c.1868, Harvard U., Fogg Art Museum · D. G. Rossetti, oils, 1868–80 (*La pia de' Tolomei*), University of Kansas, Museum of Art · D. G. Rossetti, chalk, 1869, Man. City Gall. · D. G. Rossetti, chalk, 1870, Man. City Gall. · D. G. Rossetti, chalk drawing, 1870, Brooklyn Museum, New York · D. G. Rossetti, oils, 1870 (*Mariana*), Aberdeen Art Gallery · D. G. Rossetti, pencil drawing, 1870, National Gallery of Canada, Ottawa · D. G. Rossetti, oils, 1871 (*Water willow*), Wilmington Society of Fine Arts, Delaware · D. G. Rossetti, pastel drawing, 1871, AM Oxf. · D. G. Rossetti, oils, 1877 (*Astarte Syrica*), Man. City Gall. · D. G. Rossetti, crayons, 1879, Harvard U., Fogg Art Museum · D. G. Rossetti, oils, 1879 (*La donna della finestra*), Harvard U., Fogg Art Museum · D. G. Rossetti, oils, 1880 (*The day dream*), V&A · D. G. Rossetti, oils, 1880–81 (*The salutation of Beatrice*), Toledo Museum of Art, Ohio · C. Gere, pencil and body colour drawing, c.1900, BM · P. Lombardi, photographs, NPG · W. Morris, drawing (as Iseult), William Morris Gallery, Walthamstow · W. Morris, pencil, pen, and ink drawing, BM · H. F. Phillips, photographs, NPG · D. G. Rossetti, drawings, Kelmscott Manor, Oxfordshire · D. G. Rossetti, drawings, NG Ire. · D. G. Rossetti, drawings, FM Cam. · D. G. Rossetti, drawings, Harvard U. · D. G. Rossetti, drawings, Galleria Nazionale d'Arte Moderna, Rome · D. G. Rossetti, drawings, Museum of Fine Arts, Boston · D. G. Rossetti, drawings, BM · D. G. Rossetti, drawings, William Morris Gallery, Walthamstow · D. G. Rossetti, drawings, University of Manchester · D. G. Rossetti, drawings, Walker Art Gallery, Liverpool · D. G. Rossetti, drawings, Birmingham Museums and Art Gallery · D. G. Rossetti, drawings, Cincinnati Art Museum · D. G. Rossetti, drawings, Art Gallery of South Australia, Adelaide · D. G. Rossetti, drawings, Wightwick Manor, Wolverhampton · D. G. Rossetti, pen-and-ink caricatures, BM · D. G. Rossetti and F. M. Brown, oils, Wightwick Manor, Wolverhampton · E. Walker, photograph (in old age), NPG · photographs, NPG · photographs, V&A · photographs, William Morris Gallery · photographs, Kelmscott Manor, Oxfordshire
Wealth at death £9560 5s. 2d.: resworn probate, 20 April 1914, CGPLA Eng. & Wales

Morris, John (d. 1658), antiquary and book collector, was born in London, the son of Peter *Morris (d. 1588), a mechanical engineer in the service of Sir Christopher Hatton, and Anne Boteler (d. 1617), great-aunt of Sir Oliver Boteler, who, as a widow, remarried in 1590, becoming the wife of George Digby of Barnes, Surrey. Morris inherited the London watermills, built near London Bridge in 1580 by his father. Little is known of his early life and education. He may have been to the inns of court or to Cambridge; he was surely conversant with Latin, Greek, Hebrew, and the Romance languages. In 1608 he visited Leiden, in the Netherlands, and he made the grand tour in 1610–11, visiting Paris, Madrid, and a number of towns in Italy, while in 1617 he was in Lisbon. Morris married his stepfather's daughter Mary Digby (d. 1627), and they had three children. In 1628 he married Lettice Fitzgerald, second daughter of Thomas Fitzgerald (d. 1619) of Walton-on-Thames,

Surrey, and Frances, eldest daughter of Sir Thomas Randolph, Queen Elizabeth's postmaster-general, and sister of George *Fitzgerald, sixteenth earl of Kildare (*bap.* 1612, d. 1660). He settled in Isleworth, Middlesex, where he owned a house with a 2 acre garden on North Street, but he also had a house in London near London Bridge, where he resided during the civil war. In a 'List of the principal inhabitants of London' (1640) he is ranked among the second group of richest citizens.

Morris's interests were mainly scholarly. He was an avid book collector with a keen interest in heraldry, geography, botany, history, and religion. In his will he called his library 'the cheife pleasure and imployment of my life' (Bekkers, 224). His friends included the botanists John Parkinson (Morris contributed liminary poems for the latter's *Theatrum botanicum* [1640]) and the Tradescants, father and son, royal gardeners. His interest in Anglo-Saxon antiquities, aroused by his 'worthy freind and old acquaintance' (ibid.) Johannes De Laet, brought him into contact with Sir Henry and Sir John Spelman, Sir Simonds D'Ewes, and William Somner. However, he was an unproductive scholar: apart from the poems, he published nothing. His completed biography, 'dull and laborious' (Birrell, xiv), of Sir John Hawkwood, the fourteenth-century *condottier*, remains in manuscript, as do three commonplace books. An 'orthodox Protestant, anti-Laudian, a moderate Puritan and a moderate Parliamentarian' (Bekkers, xiii), he was acquainted with John Milton and abhorred Charles I's execution. From his correspondence with De Laet he emerges as a melancholic preoccupied with his health; the royal physician Theodore de Mayerne counted him among his patients.

Morris died in the summer of 1658 at Isleworth. His will was proved on 23 July. In 1660 and 1661 his widow sold a major part of his book collection to the Royal Library at St James's; the British Library still held 1300 items at the end of the twentieth century. She died in 1668 or 1669.

ROLF H. BREMMER JUN.

Sources *Correspondence of John Morris with Johannes De Laet (1634–1649)*, ed. J. A. F. Bekkers (1970) · T. A. Birrell, *The library of John Morris: the reconstruction of a seventeenth-century collection* (1976) · F. Clifford, *A history of private bill legislation* (1887), 2.52–4 · *Analytical index, to the series of records known as Remembrancia, preserved among the archives of the City of London*, Corporation of London, ed. [W. H. Overall and H. C. Overall] (1878), 550–53 · R. Sisly, *The London water supply* (1899), 5–6 · Venn, *Alum. Cant.* · J. Foster, *The register of admissions to Gray's Inn, 1521–1889, together with the register of marriages in Gray's Inn chapel, 1695–1754* (privately printed, London, 1889) · J. B. Whitmore and A. W. Hughes Clarke, eds., *London visitation pedigrees, 1664*, Harleian Society, 92 (1940), s.v. 'Morris' · J. L. Chester and J. Foster, eds., *London marriage licences, 1521–1869* (1887), 402 · J. L. Chester and G. J. Armytage, eds., *Allegations for marriage licences issued by the bishop of London*, 1, Harleian Society, 25 (1887), 187 · G. W. Wallard, *Registers of the parish of Barnes, Surrey*, MS, Society of Genealogists, London
Archives BL, commonplace books · Bodl. Oxf. | BL, book collection · Utrecht University, corresp.
Likenesses A. Hanneman, portrait, before 1640 (with his eldest son)
Wealth at death considerable: *CSP dom.*, 1640, 170; PRO, SP 16/453, p. 233, item 75; will, PRO, PROB 11/277, sig. 298; printed in Bekkers, ed., *Correspondence*, 223–5

Morris, John (*c.*1615–1649), army officer, was the eldest son of Matthias Morris of Esthagh, South Elmshall, near Pontefract, Yorkshire, and was brought up in the household of Thomas Wentworth, the future earl of Strafford. Following Wentworth's appointment as lord deputy of Ireland in 1631, Morris was commissioned ensign in his personal regiment of foot at the early age of sixteen and later lieutenant of his guard, earning the warm approval of the lord deputy, who predicted that he would outshine many more experienced officers. In Ireland, Morris later became a captain in Sir Henry Tichborne's regiment and, on 2 June 1642, major in that of Sir Francis Willoughby. While badly wounded during the storming of Ross Castle, he turned apparent defeat into victory by rallying the English soldiers then in flight before Preston's Irish insurgents. After returning to England to serve in the royal army in the civil war, he became the object of royalist opprobrium for changing sides following parliament's capture of Liverpool on 1 November 1644. In his speech from the scaffold on 23 August 1649 he vigorously contested the widely held belief that he personally had been responsible for the betrayal of Liverpool. Initially he prospered from his defection. According to Clarendon, who came to admire his daring and panache, Morris, 'by the coolness of his courage and the pleasantness of his humour, made himself not only very acceptable, but was preferred to the command of a colonel … being a stout and bold undertaker in attempts of the greatest danger' (Clarendon, *Hist. rebellion*, 4.396–7). But the following year saw the foundation of the New Model Army, whose military saints resented the ridicule to which Morris mercilessly subjected them and were appalled by what Clarendon describes as 'his life of great license' (ibid., 397). Clarendon also emphasizes Morris's increasing remorse about his defection and consciousness that he could atone for it only by an act spectacular enough 'to wipe off that blemish by a service that would redeem him' (ibid.).

That Morris, who had virtually retired to his estate at Esthagh, was nevertheless able to conceal his change of heart is suggested by his friendship with his neighbour Colonel Robert Overton, the governor of Pontefract Castle. Clarendon writes that Overton 'loved him above all men, and delighted so much in his company that he got him to be with him sometimes a week and more at a time in the castle, where they always lay together in one bed' (Clarendon, *Hist. rebellion*, 4.397). If Morris had intended to exploit his intimacy with Overton to weaken the castle's defences, his plan was frustrated when Overton became governor of Hull in November 1647. This necessitated a change of strategy since Overton's successor at Pontefract, Colonel Cotterell, was as yet not in thrall to Morris's charms, as Overton had been.

Morris now sought to suborn some members of the garrison to assist local cavaliers in scaling the walls. On 18 May 1648 this enterprise failed because one of Morris's internal contacts was hopelessly drunk at the time. The new governor, still apparently unsuspicious of Morris—who had gone some way towards winning his trust by exhibiting concern for the castle's defences—now insisted that those of the garrison who had lodged in the town must sleep in the castle. Morris exploited this situation with characteristic ingenuity and daring, gaining admittance for some of his followers on 1 June on the pretext of bringing in beds for the increased number of soldiers sleeping in the castle, which was captured with astonishing ease. The only casualty was the governor, who was wounded in bed while resisting arrest. Morris and his men were joined by other royalists from the locality and further afield. On 17 June he appointed a council of war with himself as president. Sir John Digby was made governor but Morris remained the controlling influence. The threat from an augmented besieging force under Colonel Rainsborough was countered on 29 October by a daring sally from Pontefract orchestrated by Morris but carried out by others. If Clarendon is to be believed, the object was to seize Rainsborough at Doncaster in order to exchange him for the captured royalist general Sir Marmaduke Langdale, but Rainsborough was killed while resisting capture. On 9 November Cromwell, who had now taken over the siege, summoned the insurgents to surrender, but ten days later he had to inform Speaker Lenthall that the castle could perhaps hold out for another year. In fact it held out until the following March. The then commander of the besieging force, Major-General Lambert, clearly felt the need to offer excuses for what some in parliament would regard as over-lenient surrender articles, stressing the fact that the garrison was probably capable of holding out for another two months.

Morris had earlier offered to surrender, but on absurdly unrealistic terms. Lambert's terms, which were accepted on 19 March 1649, excepted six persons, one of whom was Morris, from the benefits of the otherwise generous surrender articles, while allowing them six days' grace in which to attempt to fight their way out. Morris was one of those who succeeded in doing so, and to Lambert's disgust parliament disregarded his own generous assurance that no attempt would be made to recapture anyone who escaped to a distance of more than 5 miles from the castle. In fact Morris and a cornet named Blackborne were captured some ten days later in the Furness district of Lancashire and imprisoned in Lancaster Castle. Despite repeated orders from the council of state from 10 April onwards for them to be conveyed to Yorkshire to stand trial, they were still in Lancaster as late as 24 July, the day after the council of state decided that they should be tried at York assizes and not by a council of war, a decision which was unavailingly contested by Morris at their trial at York on 16 August. Defiant to the last, he also took objection to the personnel of the jury; to being denied the services of counsel and a copy of his indictment; and to being put in irons, 'not only a disgrace to me but in general to all soldiers which doth more trouble me than the loss of my life' (*State trials*, 4.1266). His last words to the court as he was carried off in irons after the death sentence was pronounced were 'God blesse King Charles the 2d and defend those that have fought for him' (Leeds City RO, Bacon

Frank MSS, BF7, p. 86). Astonishingly both he and Black-borne managed to escape from York Castle, but Black-borne broke a leg in the process and Morris refused to abandon him. Following their recapture, they were executed on 23 August 1649, Morris making a spirited defence of his actions in his speech from the scaffold. At his own request he was buried at Wentworth, Yorkshire, near the grave of his former patron, the earl of Strafford.

Morris had married Margery Dawson (1627?–1665), daughter of the bishop of Clonfert and Kilmacduag, who bore two sons and a daughter. His second son, born in Pontefract Castle and appropriately named Castilian, was in 1672 rewarded for his late father's services by a lease of 6000 acres of land in Knaresborough Forest at a rent of £4 per acre. In 1684, at the instance of Lord Chief Justice Jeffreys, he became town clerk of Leeds.

ROBERT ASHTON

Sources Leeds City Record Office, Bacon Frank MS BF3, 80–89, 148–55; BF7, 1–8, 86; BF13, 146, 155 · Clarendon, *Hist. rebellion*, 4.395–407 · *State trials*, 4.1249–70 · PRO, state papers domestic, SP 23/14/201; 23/101/671; 23/237/234 · *CSP dom.*, 1649–50; 1672–5 · R. Holmes, *The sieges of Pontefract Castle* (1887) · *Oliver Cromwell's letters and speeches*, ed. T. Carlyle, 1 (1857), 330–33 · 'A full relation of the killing of Colonell Rainsborough, Capt. Layton and others', Oct 1648, BL, MS E470/4 · *JHC*, 6 (1648–51), 60, 174 · Bodl. Oxf., MS Tanner 57, fol. 365 · *Bloody newes from the army*, 1648, BL, MS E470/5 · P. R. Newman, *Royalist officers in England and Wales, 1642–1660: a biographical dictionary* (1981), 265 · R. Ashton, *Counter-revolution: the second civil war and its origins, 1646–8* (1994), 261–2, 405–6 · examination of John Morris, PRO, A 551 44/3 box 2

Archives BL, corresp., Add. MS 36996 | Leeds City RO, Bacon Frank MSS

Likenesses J. Stow, line engraving, BM, NPG

Morris, John (1810–1886), geologist, was born on 19 February 1810 at Homerton, London, the son of John Morris, a timber merchant in the City of London. He was educated at private schools at Clifton, in Berkshire, and at Parsons Green, Fulham. For some years from 1830 he was apprenticed to an aunt, who had a pharmaceutical chemist's shop at Kensington, and became its dispenser and manager. However, he became interested in geology and other branches of science, and about 1865 relinquished his links with the pharmaceutical business. Along with other London geologists, he had become a member of the London Clay Club. His published papers soon attracted notice, and critical evaluation following publication of his *Catalogue of British Fossils* in 1845 enhanced his reputation. Woodward regarded it as 'the first really important critical list of British fossils' (Woodward, *History of the Geological Society*, 159) and considered that the 8359 species listed in the enlarged second edition (1854) made it the most useful reference.

In 1853 and 1854, Morris accompanied Roderick Murchison (1792–1871) on his geological tours of Europe. At Murchison's instigation, Morris was appointed professor of geology at University College, London, in 1854, an office he retained until 1877. On his retirement he was appointed emeritus professor in acknowledgement of his services.

Morris wrote numerous scientific papers and notes, mainly on geological subjects; the Palaeontographical Monograph on Great Oolite mollusca (1850–53), written in collaboration with John Lycett, was one of his more significant publications. He was elected a fellow of the Geological Society in 1845, served on its council in 1848–9, 1853–7, 1859–67, and 1876–83, was presented with a testimonial in 1870 in appreciation of his services to geology, and received the balance of the Wollaston Fund in 1842, 1843, 1850, and 1852. He was the first recipient of the Lyell medal in 1876 and was given the balance of the Lyell Fund the same year. Morris held various lectureships and examiner positions and was twice president of the Geologists' Association (1868–70; 1877–8). He was a freeman of the Wheelwrights' Company and a freeman and liveryman of the Turners' Company. In 1878 he was awarded an honorary MA degree from Cambridge University.

As a practical geologist, Morris enjoyed fieldwork and is mentioned as a regular companion by his contemporaries on their research forays (Prestwich). However, he was equally happy when bad weather forced him to continue with his library researches. In later life, when ordered to exercise outside, he would be found tracing earthworms, or molehills in the garden. This enthusiasm, together with his remarkable power of lucid exposition and a memory of extraordinary retentiveness, made him a born teacher. Although fond of conversation Morris had to be induced to address an audience other than his own classes of students, on account of his modesty. Bonney stated that 'he was able, even at the shortest notice, to express his ideas simply but clearly, clothing a train of thought with unusual felicity' (Bonney, 45). Other geologists considered him a walking encyclopaedia and praised his critical acumen, but his indecision and dislike of the labour of composition is reflected in his relatively small number of papers and their need for further research. He undoubtedly had considerable influence on the progress of geology through his various publications, but, more especially, through his readiness to impart knowledge and help others. Topley in his obituary maintained that it was this power to induce others to devote themselves to geological work that was one of the greatest services that John Morris rendered to English geology.

Following a lengthy illness, Morris died on 7 January 1886 at his home, 22 Bolton Road, St John's Wood, London, and was buried at Kensal Green. Although nothing is known of a wife, he was survived by at least one daughter, Georgiana, whose married name was Sanger.

R. J. CLEEVELY

Sources [H. Woodward], 'Eminent living geologists: no. 3, Professor John Morris', *Geological Magazine*, new ser., 2nd decade, 5 (1878), 481–7 · T. G. Bonney, *Quarterly Journal of the Geological Society*, 42 (1886), 44–7 · W. Topley, 'The life and work of Professor John Morris', *Proceedings of the Geologists' Association*, 9 (1887), 386–410 · *Nature*, 33 (1885–6), 248 · H. Woodward, *Geological Magazine*, new ser., 3rd decade, 3 (1886), 93, 95–6 · H. B. Woodward, *The history of the Geological Society of London* (1907) · G. A. Prestwich, *Life and letters of Sir Joseph Prestwich* (1899), 228–9 · *CGPLA Eng. & Wales* (1886)

Archives GS Lond., annotated catalogues · Institute of Geological Sciences, Keyworth, Nottinghamshire · National Museum of Victoria, Melbourne · NHM | Wellcome L., letters to Henry Lee

Likenesses R. and J. W. Breakley, photocard, GS Lond. • C. E. Corke, photograph, repro. in Prestwich, *Life and letters*, facing p. 38 • Maull & Co., photograph, GS Lond. • drawings, repro. in Woodward, 'Eminent living geologists', facing p. 481 • group portrait, photograph (*A conference on flint implements*), NHM, Palaeontology Library

Wealth at death £12,841 9s. 9d.: probate, 8 Feb 1886, *CGPLA Eng. & Wales*

Morris, John (1823–1905), lawyer and businessman, was born on 12 December 1823 at South Molton, Devon, the third of four children of George Morris, a wool-stapler, and his wife, Elizabeth Hutchings. He had one brother, William Morris, later a promoter of tramways, and two sisters. Educated privately, he then served for three years (1838–41) as a clerk in the offices of Gilberd Pearse, a local solicitor, before moving to the London office of William Ashurst. After completing his articles, Morris joined Ashurst as a partner in 1854. In the same year Morris married Sarah Taylor; they had six children.

In 1862, following the appointment of William Ashurst to the post of solicitor to the General Post Office, Morris became senior partner. By this time the most important clients of Ashurst and Morris were the merchant bankers James Morrison and his son Charles Morrison, and it was this connection that was to lead to the transformation of the firm John Morris now managed. Soon to be styled Ashurst, Morris, Crisp, the business became one of the first British law firms to specialize in corporate business.

As a solicitor, Morris played a part in numerous company liquidations, rescues, and reconstructions, especially of railway and urban utility companies. The Grand Trunk Railway Company of Canada retained him to work, along with Sir Edward Watkin, on the measures that led to the Grand Trunk Arrangement Act of 1863. Morris was also involved in the affairs of a number of other ailing North American railways, including the Great Eastern Railway in Canada and, in the United States, the Erie, the Wabash, and the Baltimore and Ohio. But it was as a company director, an organizer of long-term investment syndicates, and a provider of management services that Morris was to be best-known during the later years of his career.

Following his clients the Morrisons into Latin America, Morris became solicitor in 1881 to the River Plate Trust Loan and Agency Company Ltd, a company founded to salvage the failed Mercantile Bank of the River Plate, in which Charles Morrison had invested heavily. Morris became a director of the River Plate Trust in 1883 and chairman the following year, a position he was to occupy for more than twenty years. The Trust company was to be one of the most profitable of British investments in Argentina, yielding an annual average return of 16.5 per cent to its ordinary shareholders between 1881 and 1905. Moreover, it provided the managerial and financial core of a group of more than a dozen London-registered Anglo-South American railway, utility, land, and financial companies with a combined capital of about £7 million, most of whom were also clients of Ashurst, Morris, Crisp.

Notoriously shy, and well known as someone who conducted business through lieutenants, Morrison appears to have withdrawn from daily engagement with these Latin American businesses by the 1880s, preferring the roles of rentier and collector. He continued to hold about £0.5 million in shares of Anglo-South American companies in the 1890s, but it was Morris, whose own River Plate investments amounted to £100,000, who maintained meticulously detailed correspondence with local managers of the half-dozen companies with which he was closely associated. Morris also constructed, sometimes with, and sometimes independently of, Morrison, but almost always working closely with the stockbroker Sir William Cuthbert Quilter, numerous investment syndicates including those responsible for the famous railway bridge over the Firth of Forth, Scotland, the introduction of telephones to London, the construction of the first underground railway in the City (the District line), and the waterworks of Saratov and Beirut. By 1895, the corporate clients of Ashurst, Morris, Crisp numbered close to 150, divided more or less equally between Britain, the Americas, and the rest of the world. The legal business arising from these multifarious connections yielded profits of £117,851 to Ashurst, Morris, Crisp in 1891 on a fee income of over £600,000.

Morris had a long and wide-ranging business career. Heavily involved in railways and public utilities, he also organized a syndicate to buy the Liberal newspaper the *Daily News* in 1868. However, he seldom went to the City of London after 1898, preferring to spend his summers in the south of France and the remainder of the year at Abbot's Cliff House, near Folkestone. He died at his London town house, 34 Hyde Park Square, on 22 March 1905. He fainted while in his bath, and his death was due to asphyxia from drowning. He was buried at Highgate cemetery.

CHARLES JONES

Sources C. A. Jones, 'Great capitalists and the direction of British overseas investment in the late nineteenth century: the case of Argentina', *Business History*, 22 (1980), 152–69 • *Report of the proceedings at the golden wedding presentations … on Mr. Morris's eighty-first birthday, 12th December 1904* (privately printed, London, 1904) • R. B. Morris, *The Morris family of South Molton, Devon* (privately printed, Guildford, 1908) • *Mr Morris' 80th birthday celebrations: … with a brief record of the life of William Henry Ashurst* (1904) • W. Redpath, *History in the making: one hundred and fifty years in the progress of a famous firm, c.1971, Ashurst, Morris, Crisp, London* • C. A. Jones, 'Morris, John', *DBB* • *CGPLA Eng. & Wales* (1905) • L. Dennett, *Slaughter and May: a century in the City* (1989) • d. cert.

Archives Ashurst, Morris, Crisp, London

Likenesses portrait, Ashurst, Morris, Crisp, London; repro. in Jones, 'Morris, John'

Wealth at death £392,402: probate, 2 May 1905, *CGPLA Eng. & Wales*

Morris, John (1826–1893), Jesuit and ecclesiastical historian, was born at Ootacamund, in the Nilgiri hills, southern India, on 4 July 1826. He was the eldest of the fifteen children of John Carnac *Morris (1798–1858) and Rosanna Curtis (1803–1894), second daughter of Peter Cherry of the East India Company. He was sent to England in 1829 and attended Dr Pinckney's school in East Sheen from 1834. In 1838 he was sent to Harrow School, but in September 1839 he returned to India with a tutor. In February 1842 he was sent back to England with a new tutor, the Revd John Challis Street, with whom he lived until his mother returned to England in 1845.

By this time Morris had become the pupil of the Revd Henry Alford, vicar of Wymeswold, and had come to share his tutor's sympathies with the Oxford Movement. In October 1845 he was admitted to Trinity College, Cambridge, where, as a member of the Ecclesiological Society, he met F. A. Paley. Correspondence with Ambrose Phillipps De Lisle, whom he had previously visited with Alford, influenced his conversion to Roman Catholicism; he was received into the Catholic church on 20 May 1846 at Northampton by William Wareing, vicar apostolic of the eastern district. Paley was subsequently attacked in *The Times* over Morris's conversion.

In the autumn of 1846 Morris entered the English College at Rome, where he was ordained priest on 13 May 1847. In spring 1851 he took over the mission at Great Marlow, and also began to study history. In 1853 he was appointed vice-rector of the English College at Rome, but he returned to England in 1856 to take charge of the mission of St Thomas of Canterbury at Fulham. In 1858 Bishop Amherst made him secretary, diocesan archivist, notary, and ceremonialist at Northampton, and in the following year appointed him to the church of Northampton. He became private secretary to Nicholas Wiseman in 1861, an office which he held for the first two years of Henry Manning's episcopate. He also became canon penitentiary at Westminster, and was appointed to a committee for the improvement of the conditions of the Catholic poor in state institutions.

In 1866 Morris decided to enter the Society of Jesus, and began his noviciate at Manresa House, Roehampton, on 28 February 1867. In March 1868 he was sent to Tronchiennes in Belgium, and in September moved to Louvain to read theology at the Catholic university. In Belgium he made Bollandist friends, who later helped him with archival research. After passing his examinations he returned to England in autumn 1869. In 1871 he was appointed socius to Father Robert Whitty, the superior at Manresa, and in 1872 he was sent to Oxford. In September 1873 he was appointed professor of ecclesiastical history and canon law at the Jesuit college of St Beuno in north Wales. Free time was spent at the Public Record Office and in other archives, pursuing his historical research. In September 1877 he was appointed first rector of St Ignatius' College in Malta, but the climate proved unbearable; in 1878 he returned to St Beuno's where he became vice-rector and master of novices and where, from 1880 to 1886, he was rector.

Morris's works of ecclesiastical history were inspired by his deep devotion to English heroes of the Catholic faith. His earliest publication was *The Life and Martyrdom of Saint Thomas Becket* (1859), a work of hagiography, but one which, in the words of David Knowles, 'remains the best life of its kind' (D. Knowles, *Thomas Becket*, 1970, 176). Although Morris retained an interest in his original subject, publishing in 1888 *The Relics of Saint Thomas of Canterbury*, his later works dealt with other eminent English

Catholics. While in Rome in 1853–6 Morris had assisted Wiseman in petitioning for Bede to be recognized as a doctor of the church. He also acted as postulator for the cause of the English martyrs. Extensive research in the Belgian and York archives led to the publication of his most significant work, *The Troubles of our Catholic Forefathers, Related by Themselves* (1872–7), in three ponderous volumes and much less readable than the biography of Becket. The cause of the English martyrs met with some success: in December 1886, 255 of them were admitted as venerable, and 53 were beatified. He also published other works relating to sixteenth- and seventeenth-century Catholic history, including *Sir Amias Poulet's Letter-Books* (1874), in which he exposed the inaccuracies of J. A. Froude's account of Mary queen of Scots. He was also a contributor to *The Month*, the *Dublin Review*, and *The Tablet*.

On 10 January 1889 Morris was elected fellow of the Society of Antiquaries. In 1890 he became the head of a staff of writers at the Jesuit house at Farm Street, London. In May 1892 he was asked by the archbishop of Westminster to write a biography of Wiseman. He retired to Wimbledon in 1893, and had written a few chapters of the life, when he died suddenly while preaching at the Sacred Heart Church at Wimbledon on 22 October 1893. He was buried in the Catholic part of Wimbledon cemetery.

Morris was one of a circle of late nineteenth-century Catholic historians who devoted themselves to correcting protestant historical inaccuracies and misconceptions, and to documenting the English recusant experience. His research was painstaking, but 'his passion for facts and figures and details outweighed every other consideration' (Pollen, 219), sometimes rendering his prose little more than a link between extensive quotations from documents. He was a strong-willed and forceful individual: a contemporary described him as 'a very intense military spirit … a soldier by nature' with a 'certain sternness of exterior' which made him look severe (Clarke, 8–9, 11–12).

ROSEMARY MITCHELL

Sources J. H. Pollen, *The life and letters of Father John Morris* (1896) · R. F. Clarke, *Father John Morris* (1894) · *The Speaker*, 8 (28 Oct 1893), 462 · *The Tablet* (28 Oct 1893), 685–6 · *The Tablet* (4 Nov 1893), 727–8 · DNB

Archives Archives of the British Province of the Society of Jesus, London, corresp. and papers · Westm. DA, letters relating to biography of Wiseman

Likenesses photograph, repro. in Clarke, *Father John Morris*, frontispiece · two photographs, repro. in Pollen, *Life and letters*

Morris, John Brande (1812–1880), Roman Catholic convert and devotional writer, was born at Brentford, Middlesex, on 4 September 1812. He was the elder son of the Revd John Morris, sometime Michel fellow of the Queen's College, Oxford, and his wife, Anna F. Brande, sister of the chemist William Thomas Brande (1788–1866). His brother was Thomas Edward Morris (1814–1885), a committed Tractarian and vicar of Carleton, Yorkshire, from 1854 until his death. After being educated by his father at home, Morris matriculated at Balliol College, Oxford, on 17 December 1830 and graduated BA on 20 November 1834 with a second class in classics. On 30 June 1837, having proceeded MA, he was elected a fellow of Exeter College,

Oxford. There he lectured in Hebrew and Syriac, and devoted himself to patristic theology. Eccentric in appearance and manner, he combined multifarious erudition with extreme credulity. An ardent Tractarian, he often embarrassed the more moderate of his party by *outré* pronouncements from the pulpit or in the pages of the *British Critic*. While deputizing for J. H. Newman in the university church of St Mary's, Oxford, during autumn 1839 he provoked the vice-chancellor by a sermon on angels which extolled the virtues of fasting and anathematized those who rejected the Roman Catholic doctrine of the mass. In 1843 Morris published an *Essay towards the Conversion of Learned and Philosophical Hindus*, for which he obtained a prize of £200 offered by the bishop of Calcutta. It was learned, but ineffective, not being read by Hindus. In 1842 he published a mystical poem, *Nature a Parable*, and for the Library of the Fathers translated St John Chrysostom's *Homilies on Romans* (1841) and, from the Syriac, *Select Homilies of St Ephrem* (1846). Morris's advocacy of fasting and startling views on celibacy, expounded in a letter to F. W. Faber of 20 October 1840 (*Letters and Diaries of John Henry Newman*, 7.420–21), earned him the nickname of Simon Stylites. No surprise was felt when he followed Newman into the Church of Rome on 16 January 1846. He resigned his Oxford fellowship eight days later.

On leaving Oxford, Morris joined Newman at Maryvale, Birmingham, but he had scant aptitude for community life and departed after only four months. He was ordained priest at St Mary's College, Oscott, in 1849. His theological work, *Jesus the Son of Mary*, published in 1851, disconcerted Newman by its reference to Mary as the 'mother of Jehovah' but Newman recommended him, unsuccessfully, for a post in the Catholic University of Dublin, describing him to Archbishop Cullen as a man of versatile genius but little judgement (*Letters and Diaries of John Henry Newman*, 14.267). He was appointed canon of Plymouth Cathedral by Bishop Errington in December 1853, but was too restless to settle anywhere for long. After three years in the household of the convert Edmund Bastard of Kitley, Devon, he moved on in 1855 to Aldenham Hall, Shropshire, as chaplain to Sir John Acton, whom he offended with his racy language. Morris, who never unpacked his books, eventually left in 1861. In 1868 he was briefly chaplain to Coventry Patmore at Heron's Ghyll, Sussex. By 1871 he was reduced to such poverty that his friend the Oratorian J. D. Dalgairns had to organize a fund for his relief, to which Newman contributed. He spent the last twelve years of his life as chaplain to a community of nursing nuns, the Sœurs de Miséricorde, at Queen Caroline Street, Hammersmith, where he died on 9 April 1880. He was buried at Mortlake Catholic cemetery. Morris's closest and lifelong friend, F. W. Faber, in one of many letters (preserved at the London Oratory) chaffed him affectionately as having 'a screw loose' (Mathew, 72). G. MARTIN MURPHY

Sources *The letters and diaries of John Henry Newman*, ed. C. S. Dessain and others, [31 vols.] (1961–), vols. 6–25 · D. Mathew, *Lord Acton and his times* (1968), 65–72 · T. Mozley, *Reminiscences, chiefly of Oriel College and the Oxford Movement*, 2 (1882), 10–12, 229 · M. Pattison, *Memoirs*, another edn (1969), 184, 222 · *The Times* (12 April 1880) · *The Tablet* (17 April 1880) · I. Ker, *John Henry Newman: a biography* (1990), 186, 271 · R. Hill, *Lord Acton* (2000), 55–6

Archives Brompton Oratory, letters | CUL, letters to Lord Acton · CUL, letters to Sir Peter Le Page Renouf

Morris, John Carnac (1798–1858), Indologist, was born on 16 October 1798, the second son of John Morris of the Bombay civil service, who was subsequently a director of the East India Company. Morris entered the Royal Navy as a midshipman in 1813 and saw active service during the last two years of the French war. On the conclusion of the war in 1814 his father sent the following laconic note to his captain, George Sartorius: 'Your trade is up for the next half-century. Send my son John home by the next coach'.

In 1815 Morris enrolled in the East India College at Haileybury, Hertfordshire, and afterwards entered the Madras civil service, reaching India in 1818. Five of his brothers obtained similar employment under the East India Company. Morris distinguished himself in language study at Fort St George College, Madras, earning prizes in Telugu and Urdu. In 1819, after only ten months of study, he became eligible to leave the college and received his first appointment during the following year. He initially served at several provincial locations in the Madras presidency. In 1823 a stroke paralysed his legs. Thereafter, most of his time was spent at Madras in the secretariat, but his energy was not impaired and his industry remained exceptional.

On 4 February 1823 Morris married Rosanna Curtis (1803–1894), second daughter of Peter Cherry of the East India Company's Madras civil service; they had several sons, including John *Morris (1826–1893), Jesuit and ecclesiastical historian, and Henry Morris (1829–1912) of the Madras civil service, biographer and historian.

Morris was appointed Telugu translator to the government in India from 1832, and became civil auditor in 1839. Among his most successful services in Madras was the establishment in 1834 of the Madras government bank, of which he was the first secretary and treasurer, and from 1835 superintendent. The bank was subsequently transferred by the government to private hands.

Morris devoted his leisure to the study of Urdu, and became very proficient in it; but Telugu was his primary language of interest. He was compiler of a textbook which was widely used for several decades, *Telugu selections, with translations and grammatical analyses: to which is added a glossary of revenue terms used in the Northern Circars* (1823; new and enlarged edn, 1855). He was author of an *English–Telugu Dictionary* (1835–9), based on Johnson's *English Dictionary*. It was the first undertaking of its kind and remained an important text for some time. However, C. P. Brown's *English–Telugu Dictionary* (1852) proved to be more comprehensive and became a more standard work. From 1834 Morris was also editor of the *Madras Journal of Literature and Science* for several years. While on leave in England between 1829 and 1831 he was elected a fellow of the Royal Society. He was very popular in Madras society, and was an enthusiastic freemason there and in England. He left India in July 1846.

Morris settled in Mansfield Street, Portland Place, London, in 1848 and spent much of his time in commercial enterprises. Although he failed in his persistent efforts to become, as his father had been, a director of the East India Company, he successfully established a company to run steamers between Milford Haven and Australia by way of Panama. This company lasted only a few years. He then promoted and was managing director of the London and Eastern Banking Company and became its chairman in 1855. However, the bank was involved in rash speculations, and in 1858 it was wound up. Morris placed all his resources at the disposal of the official liquidator and retired to Jersey, where he died at St Mark's Crescent, St Helier, on 2 August 1858. He was buried at St Helier.

[ANON.], *rev.* PETER L. SCHMITTHENNER

Sources private information (1894) · C. C. Prinsep, *Record of services of the Honourable East India Company's civil servants in the Madras presidency from 1741 to 1858* (1885) · *Madras Athenaeum* (30 June 1846) · *Madras Athenaeum* (9 July 1846) · *Madras Spectator* (29 June 1846) · *Madras Spectator* (2 July 1846) · P. Schmitthenner, *Telugu resurgence: C. P. Brown and cultural consolidation in nineteenth-century south India* (2001)
Wealth at death under £5000: probate, 1858, *CGPLA Eng. & Wales*

Morris, John Humphrey Carlile (1910–1984), jurist, was born on 18 February 1910 at Rosewall, Calonna Road, The Common, Wimbledon, Surrey, the elder son and eldest of three children of Humphrey William Morris, a solicitor in the firm of H. C. Morris, Woolsey, Morris, and Kennedy (founded by his father), and his wife, Jessie Muriel Vercoe. Educated at St Peter's, Seaford, and Charterhouse, he was awarded a Holford history scholarship to Christ Church, Oxford. He obtained first classes in jurisprudence (1931) and in the BCL (1932), and was elected Eldon law scholar (1933). He was elected Lord Justice Holker senior scholar of Gray's Inn and was called to the bar in 1934, spending the next two years in practice. In 1936 he was elected a fellow of Magdalen College, Oxford. He married (Mercy) Jane (*b.* 1917/18), daughter of Stanley Asher Kinch, a retired civil servant, at St Luke's, Chelsea, on 21 June 1939; they had no children. In 1940 he joined the Royal Naval Volunteer Reserve, serving in the Faeroe Islands, and in Ayrshire to assist with the preparations for the Normandy invasion. Released from naval service in 1945 as lieutenant-commander, he returned to Oxford.

Morris's career as an academic lawyer was centred in Oxford: fellow of Magdalen College from 1936 to 1977; All Souls lecturer in private international law from 1939 to 1951; and reader in the conflict of laws from 1951 to 1977. The one period of absence was 1950–51, spent as a visiting professor at Harvard. He declined all similar invitations until his retirement. In Magdalen, with A. Rupert N. Cross, he transformed the study of law. He was an exacting tutor; but he inspired great affection and loyalty in his pupils, several of whom reached high office in the law and elsewhere. He was proud of their success and reciprocated their affection. His impact as a teacher was not restricted to Magdalen. In his university teaching of the conflict of laws, he had a major influence on generations of legal

John Humphrey Carlile Morris (1910–1984), by William Dring, 1968

scholars, expounding with extraordinary clarity some of the most complex aspects of that subject.

Morris was a big man, physically and intellectually, and few who attended his seminars can forget the sense of expectation (and trepidation) as he swept into the room, gown billowing, attaché case in hand. It would have surprised those graduate students to know that Morris was often as concerned after the seminar as they had been before it, anxious as to whether all the issues had been properly explored. Morris was a scholar of great intellectual power and breadth of knowledge which impressed all who knew him; few realized that he could be confronted with real doubts on legal matters. When, however, principle demanded a resolute approach, he would be vigorous in its defence, crossing swords with many colleagues at one time or another, though usually quick to make up any differences.

Morris was author of or contributor to twenty-seven different volumes of legal works, extending over four major fields, and the whole gamut of types of publication. His monograph *The Rule Against Perpetuities* (1956; 2nd edn, 1962, with W. Barton Leach) is a model of clarity and precision; he was the editor of three editions (1939–54) of *Theobald on the Law of Wills*, and general editor of the twenty-second edition of *Chitty on Contracts* (1961). It is, however, as a profound influence on the conflict of laws that his scholarship best stands the test of time. The list of publications is impressive: *Cases on Private International Law* (1939–68), *Cases and Materials on Private International Law* (with P. M. North, 1984); and three editions of his students' textbook, *The Conflict of Laws* (1971–84). However, his outstanding work was as general editor of five editions (1949–80) of A. V. Dicey and Morris, *The Conflict of Laws*. This became probably the most influential English practitioners' work in any area of law, which was due in the main to the incisiveness, subtlety, and elegance of Morris's legal writing.

Although in the years since Morris's death the focus of the conflict of laws has moved from issues of choice of law to those concerned with jurisdiction and recognition of foreign judgments, the influence of his writing has remained profound. His influence on the development of the law was also to be found in his relations with judges and practitioners, by whom his advice was sought. It was sought more formally by the Law Reform Committee and the Law Commission on whose work on perpetuities and the conflict of laws he had a significant impact.

Morris's scholarly distinction achieved wide public recognition. He was awarded a DCL at Oxford in 1949; was elected an associate member of the Institute of International Law (1954), associate member of the American Academy of Arts and Sciences (1960), honorary fellow of Magdalen College (1977), fellow of the British Academy (1966), and honorary bencher of Gray's Inn (1980); and was appointed QC in 1981. He spent 1978–9 in Cambridge as Arthur Goodhart visiting professor of legal science and fellow of Gonville and Caius College. In 1964 he had declined the Vinerian chair of English law at Oxford, a chair held at All Souls, a college for which he had no affection.

An ardent sailor for most of his life, Morris cruised extensively in north European waters, and the accounts of his cruises, elegantly written as ever, are to be found in the *Journal* of the Royal Cruising Club. In *Thank you, Wodehouse*, a set of essays published in 1981, Morris applied both his analytical and stylistic skills to produce a self-parody which informs as it entertains. Who else would have tackled the problem of determining 'The domicile of Agnes Flack'? Of his further work on Dorothy L. Sayers only some of the essays were published.

In retirement Morris lived at Sparepenny Cottage, Front Street, Orford, Suffolk. He died of heart failure on 29 September 1984 at the Ipswich Surgical Home Association, in Ipswich, and was cremated on 4 October.

PETER NORTH

Sources G. H. Treitel, 'In memoriam: on J. H. C. Morris', *Magdalen College Record* (1985), 34–41 · P. North, 'John Humphrey Carlile Morris', *PBA*, 74 (1988), 443–81 · *The Times* (2 Oct 1984) · A. V. Dicey and J. H. C. Morris, *The conflict of laws*, 11th edn (1987), xxi–xxiii · K. R. Simmonds, ed., *Contemporary problems in the conflict of laws* (1978), 1–2 · private information (2004) · personal knowledge (2004) · *CGPLA Eng. & Wales* (1985) · b. cert. · m. cert. · d. cert. · WWW
Likenesses W. Dring, pastel, 1968, Magd. Oxf. [*see illus.*] · P. Laib, portrait, 1968?, Magd. Oxf.
Wealth at death £175,990: probate, 27 March 1985, *CGPLA Eng. & Wales*

Morris, John Webster (1763–1836), Particular Baptist minister and author, was born in 1763. He was baptized at the Baptist church at Worsted, Norfolk, in 1784. A printer by trade, he successfully combined that occupation with his ministry. In 1785 he accepted the pastorate of the Baptist church at Clipston, Northamptonshire, and filled the post for eighteen years. While at Clipston he became acquainted with the Baptist ministers Andrew Fuller, Robert Hall, and William Carey. He was a prominent figure in the Northamptonshire Baptist Association, serving as moderator in 1798. He was author of the association's circular letter in 1794, 1801, and 1805.

Morris joined the committee of the Baptist Missionary Society in March 1793, and for some years acted as Andrew Fuller's assistant in the society's secretarial duties. Under Fuller's superintendence he edited and printed the first three volumes of the *Periodical Accounts of the Baptist Missionary Society* (1800–06). From 1801 to 1807 he was proprietor and editor of the *Theological and Biblical Magazine*. Despite a distinguished ministry at Clipston, Morris left in 1803 to become minister at the Baptist chapel in Dunstable. There also he continued his business as a printer, setting up in type the works of Fuller, Hall, and others. In 1806, with a fellow minister, Thomas Blundell, he advocated the claims of the Baptist Missionary Society in Ireland. In 1809 Morris left Dunstable and he devoted the remainder of his life to writing, editorial work, and occasional preaching.

Morris was best known for his *Memoirs of the Life and Writing of Andrew Fuller* (1816). Following the publication of a second edition in 1826 he issued a companion volume, *Miscellaneous Pieces on Various Subjects, being the Last Remains of the Rev. Andrew Fuller* (1826). His work on Fuller was well received in evangelical circles. He edited an abridgement of William Gurnall's *The Christian in Complete Armour* and *The Complete Works of Robert Hall* (both 1828). In 1833 he published his *Recollections of the Rev. Robert Hall*. Most of these works were printed by his son, Joseph M. Morris, at Bungay, Suffolk.

Morris spent much time before his death in editing a new edition of Joseph Sutcliffe's *Commentary on the Holy Scriptures*, which was published posthumously in 1838–9. Morris, who was married, died suddenly at Ditchingham, near Bungay, where he had lived for some years, on 19 January 1836.   WILLIAM PERKINS, *rev.* L. E. LAUER

Sources E. C. Starr, ed., *A Baptist bibliography*, 16 (1971), 155–7 · D. M. Lewis, ed., *The Blackwell dictionary of evangelical biography, 1730–1860*, 2 vols. (1995) · E. A. Payne and A. R. Allan, *Clipston Baptist Church: the record of one hundred and fifty years' witness* (1932) · T. S. H. Elwyn, *The Northamptonshire Baptist Association* (1964) · *Baptist Magazine*, 28 (1836), 76 · *New Baptist Magazine*, 2/17 (April 1826), 142–4 [review of *The domestic preacher*] · *New Baptist Magazine*, 2/20 (July 1826), 273–4 [review of *A brief descriptive history of Holland*] · *New Baptist Magazine*, 2/23 (Oct 1826), 389–97 [review of *Memoirs of the life and writings of the Rev. Andrew Fuller*] · *New Baptist Magazine*, 2/26 (supplement) (1826), 502–4 [review of *Miscellaneous pieces on various religious subjects*] · *Baptist Union Annual Proceedings* (1836), 20

Morris, John William, Baron Morris of Borth-y-Gest (1896–1979), judge, was born at 189 Faulkner Street, Liverpool, on 11 September 1896, the only son and younger child of Daniel Morris (1852–1946), a bank manager in that city, and his wife, Ellen (*d.* 1946), daughter of John Edwards, of Liverpool. He was educated at the Liverpool Institute, which he left in 1914 to join the Royal Welch Fusiliers at the outbreak of war. He saw service in France, reaching the rank of captain, and was awarded the MC. On demobilization he went to Trinity Hall, Cambridge—that breeding ground of eminent lawyers—of which he subsequently (1951) became an honorary fellow. In 1919 he was elected president of the Cambridge Union. He gained second classes in parts one (1919) and two (1920) of the law tripos and gained his LLB degree in 1920. In the same year he was awarded a Joseph Hodges Choate fellowship at Harvard University, where he remained for a year.

In 1921 Morris was called to the bar at the Inner Temple, of which he became a bencher in 1943 and treasurer in 1967. A Liverpool man, he localized there and naturally joined the northern circuit, quickly acquiring a large junior practice. In 1923 and 1924 he unsuccessfully contested the Ilford division in the liberal interest. On taking silk in 1935 he moved to London and in a short time became an established and busy leader. In 1945 he was appointed a judge of the King's Bench Division and in 1951 he became a lord justice of appeal. From 1960 to 1975 he sat as a lord of appeal-in-ordinary, having assumed on elevation in 1960 the title of Baron Morris of Borth-y-Gest, the charming seaside village near Porthmadog which he had loved from childhood. Although not obliged to do so, he retired from his judicial appointment in 1975, and he was created CH in the same year. He had been appointed CBE and knighted in 1945 and admitted to the privy council in 1951.

Morris was a tall, handsome man possessed of great charm, a prodigious worker, and a golden-voiced orator. His chief personal characteristics were unfailing courtesy, instinctive kindness, devotion to duty, and unsparing readiness to serve the public interest. His life was by no means restricted to the law, for he was called on to preside over many wide-ranging committees, of which probably the most important was the Home Office committee on jury service (1963–4). He was a deeply impressive speaker on formal occasions and a delightful one at social events.

Throughout his long tenure of judicial office, Morris was the soul of consideration to all who appeared before him. Some would say that at times he was over-patient and could with advantage have speeded the hearing of a case. But in his determination to ensure that a just conclusion was arrived at, he saw to it that every point raised was carefully and, indeed, exhaustively examined. Above all, he was vigilant in protecting the freedom of the individual when threatened by the executive, and he exhibited judicial valour consistently and in full measure.

Morris's judgments were most learned, admirably lucid, and of high literary quality. These virtues were recognized by the conferment on him of honorary doctorates in law by the universities of Wales (1946), British Columbia (1952), Liverpool (1966), and Cambridge (1967). He was an honorary member of both the Canadian and the American bar associations, and a member of the Pilgrims' Society, of the University Grants Committee (1955–69), and of the Charing Cross Hospital council of management (1941–8, chairman of the board of governors, 1948–68).

Probably owing to his Liverpool upbringing, Morris was not fully fluent in Welsh. He was nevertheless devoted to Wales and he served her splendidly. While in practice at the bar he was honorary standing counsel to the University of Wales from 1938 to 1945, and he was its pro-chancellor from 1956 to 1974. A member of the Gorsedd of Bards, he regularly robed and processed at the annual royal national eisteddfod, he was a vice-president and life member of the Honourable Society of Cymmrodorion, and he presided over the London Welsh Association (1951–3). For over a quarter of a century he sat as chairman of Caernarvonshire quarter sessions. When in London he worshipped regularly at the Welsh Congregational chapel in King's Cross. After retirement from judicial office he took particular interest in Welsh political affairs, and during the 1977 parliamentary debates over the ill-fated Wales Bill he spoke most eloquently in favour of devolution. Morris never married, and he died on 9 June 1979 at Porthmadog.   EDMUND-DAVIES, rev.

Sources personal knowledge (1986) · *Daily Telegraph* (12 June 1979) · *The Times* (16 Nov 1979) · Burke, *Peerage* (1967)
Archives Caernarfon area RO, family corresp. · HLRO, papers · NL Wales, corresp. and MSS | NL Wales, letters to Thomas Iorwerth Ellis
Wealth at death £760,412: probate, 8 Aug 1979, *CGPLA Eng. & Wales*

Morris, Lewis (1613?–1691), merchant and colonist in America, details of whose parentage and birthplace are uncertain, has traditionally been identified as Lewis (*b*. 1601), eldest son of William Morris of Tintern Manor, Monmouthshire, Wales. This has been disputed, however, on the basis that no record of him exists prior to his term of indenture to the Providence Island Company about 1629 (Smith, 4 n.1).

While working for the Providence Island Company, Morris learned navigation. In 1635 he was navigator of the *Swallow*, commanded by Captain Sam Axe in privateering expeditions against Spain. He settled in Barbados and married Anne, widow of Thomas Barton, in January 1638. In 1639, while *en route* to examine a silver ore deposit in the Bay of Darien, Morris and his shipmates were captured by Barbary corsairs and were imprisoned for six months in Algiers. From 1642 to 1645 he sailed with the privateer William Jackson, during which time he was promoted from the rank of master to captain. Jackson had Morris imprisoned for debt following an argument over the division of plunder in 1645, but the case against him was discharged. Morris returned to Barbados, where he mustered with Colonel James Drax's militia against the royalist party uprising led by Humphrey Walrond. He was one among twenty Independent leaders who were named to be disarmed and brought to trial in May 1650, whereupon he escaped to England.

Morris fought for the Commonwealth cause under command of Sir George Ayscue, and was commended for his 'courage and gallantry' in leading a successful military landing in the Isles of Scilly in May 1651 (*Mercurius Politicus*). Some months later he accompanied Ayscue's expedition to Barbados, where he led two successful night-time raids, for which Oliver Cromwell promoted him to the rank of colonel.

By the mid-1650s Lewis was a prominent planter–merchant in Barbados. He was elected to the Barbadian assembly in 1655, and was appointed to the governing council in 1657. During this period he became one of the island's leading Quakers. In December 1656 he had invited the Quaker missionary Henry Fell to his home and soon joined the growing religious movement. He entertained George Fox, who visited Barbados in 1671 on his American travels. Between 1660 and 1678 he was heavily fined for refusing to support the militia and the Church of England establishment. Nevertheless, he was still a member of the Barbadian council in 1667, and was recognized as 'an honest man though a Quaker' (*CSP col.*, 5.1283). In June 1668 he was kidnapped by the French, who accused him of privateering. Morris protested his innocence as a Quaker, although within days of his capture one of his ships took a French prize at St Lucia.

Seeking to expand his business interests into the American mainland, Morris sent his younger brother Richard to New York in 1664 to manage a branch of their sugar trade enterprise. Shortly before his French captivity in 1668 he and his brother purchased a 500 acre estate in the Bronx area of New York, which they named Morrisania. Morris continued to acquire large tracts of land in the 1670s in New York, Oyster Bay, and New Jersey. He retained his 400 acre Barbadian plantation until 1679, evidently commuting between his Barbadian and New York residences until 1673. The Morris brothers appeared often in the New York court to defend their mercantile interests. In 1672 Richard Morris and his wife died, leaving an infant son named Lewis *Morris (1671–1746). In 1673 the Dutch seized New York and confiscated Morris's estate, at which time Morris left Barbados and took up residence in New Jersey. His petitions to become the child's ward and to regain his property were denied by the colonial Dutch governor. However, in 1674 he won his petition to become his nephew's guardian, when New York came under the governorship of Sir Edmund Andros, a one-time royalist adversary of Morris's but by the 1670s a friend. Morris also regained his estate and acquired an additional 1420 acres.

Morris's entrepreneurial and political interests continued to flourish. In December 1675 he purchased a half-interest in bog iron property in Monmouth county, New Jersey. On 5 May 1676 the Tinton Iron Works began production. From 1683 to 1686 he served simultaneously on the New York governing board and the East New Jersey council. He was also a member of the chief court of sessions and the presiding officer in the New Jersey court of common right. During these years his wife, Anne, died and Morris remarried; his second wife's name is recorded only as Mary. He died at Morrisania, New York, on 14 February 1691, followed one week later by his second wife; he was buried at Morrisania. A controversy over the inheritance of his estate was resolved in favour of his nephew and ward Lewis Morris, who became governor of New Jersey in 1738.　　　　　　　　BARBARA RITTER DAILEY

Sources S. S. Smith, *Lewis Morris: Anglo-American statesman, ca. 1613–1691* (New Jersey, 1983) • *CSP col.*, vols. 1, 5, 7, 10–12, 14 • G. P. Putnam, ed., *The papers of Lewis Morris, governor of the province of New Jersey, from 1738 to 1746*, Collections of the New Jersey Historical Society (1852), 1–5, 323–6 • R. Bolton, *History of the county of Westchester*, 2 (New York, 1848), 280–305 • *The journal of George Fox*, ed. J. L. Nickalls, rev. edn (Philadelphia, 1985), 596–7, 600–01, 626 • J. C. Brandow, *Genealogies of Barbados families* (Baltimore, 1983), 417–18 • J. Bradney, *A history of Monmouthshire*, pt 1, 4 (1929), 38–9 • V. T. Harlow, 'The voyages of Captain William Jackson, 1642–5', *Camden miscellany, XIII*, CS, 3rd ser., 34 (1924), 13–14 • K. O. Kupperman, *Providence Island: the other puritan colony* (1993), 96–101, 156–7, 282–3, 346–7, 350–51 • *Caribbeana*, 5/2 (April 1917), 84 • RS Friends, Lond., Swarthmore papers • Swarthmore College, MSS 67, 108 [microfilm copy] • *Mercurius Politicus* (1651), 789, 794 • J. Besse, *A collection of the sufferings of the people called Quakers*, 2 (1753) • *The papers of William Penn*, ed. M. M. Dunn, R. S. Dunn, and others, 5 vols. (1981–7), vol. 2, pp. 256–9, 339–42, 469–71; vol. 3, pp. 129–30 • J. Riker, *Harlem: its origin and early annals* (New York, 1881), 262, 316–17, 397, 401, 412–15, 429–41 • J. R. Brodhead, *History of the state of New York*, 2 (New York, 1871), 227–8, 368–9, 571 • E. R. Sheridan, *Lewis Morris, 1671–1746: a study in early American politics* (Syracuse, NY, 1981), 1–17

Archives New York Historical Society, MSS | Barbados Public Library, Bridgetown, minutes of the Council of Barbados • Friends Religious Society, New York, Flushing monthly meeting minutes, vol. 1 • Monmouth County Historical Association, Freehold, New Jersey, Tinton Iron Works manuscript collection • NYPL, New York colonial manuscripts • PRO, colonial records • RS Friends, Lond., Swarthmore papers • Rutgers University, New Jersey, Morris papers

Wealth at death inventory 'exhibited February 17, 1691' (new ser. 1692), fol. 4071/1/16, personal property: repr. in Bolton, *History*, vol. 2, p. 300 • owned thousands of acres of land in New York and New Jersey

Morris, Lewis (1671–1746), politician in America, was born on 15 October 1671 at New York city, the only child of Richard Morris (1616–1672), a merchant from Monmouthshire, and Sarah Pole (c.1649–1672) of Barbados. Following the deaths of his parents his uncle Lewis Morris (1601–1691) relocated to New York from Barbados to raise him at Morrisania Manor in Westchester county.

As a young man, Morris rebelled against his uncle's Quaker faith and in 1688 embraced the Church of England; in 1701 he became the first American member of its missionary arm, the Society for the Propagation of the Gospel in Foreign Parts, which attempted to reclaim dissenters into the Anglican communion. At home he received a classical education from tutors, and later amassed 3000 books, a collection ranking among British America's half dozen largest private libraries. At the age of nineteen he inherited an estate of 6200 acres in East Jersey, 3420 acres in New York, the largest ironworks in the mid-Atlantic colonies, two mills, and sixty-six slaves, whose possession made him the largest slave owner north of Maryland. Soon afterwards, on 3 November 1691, he married Isabella Graham (1673–1752), daughter of the speaker of New York's assembly; they had fifteen children, of whom eleven, including the jurist Robert Hunter *Morris, reached maturity.

In 1692 Morris gained appointment to both the governor's council and the highest court in the proprietary colony of East Jersey. A combative personality, driving ambition, and 6 foot stature earned Morris the nickname Goliath by 1701. He thereafter ranked foremost among the handful of landed grandees who dominated the governments of New Jersey and New York. He waged his earliest

Lewis Morris (1671–1746), by John Watson, *c*.1726

political battle against East Jersey governor Jeremiah Basse, who threatened the title of large land grants claimed by himself and his political allies. He sparked such a groundswell of indignation through his inflammatory 'Redd-hott letters' (Purvis, 14)—which castigated Basse for misgovernment and corruption—that he was arrested for sedition. After a mob demolished the gaol holding Morris on 13 May 1699, Basse found himself forced to listen while the erstwhile prisoner defiantly celebrated his freedom by firing off guns on a ship anchored safely offshore from the governor's Perth Amboy residence.

Morris played a critical role in Basse's removal from office by East Jersey's British proprietors just as they decided to cede their colony to the crown. While attending negotiations at London between the proprietors and the Board of Trade during 1701–2 he decisively influenced the settlement that created the crown colony of New Jersey. His efforts secured the landed gentry's political ascendancy by requiring high property qualifications for voters and assemblymen.

Morris returned to New Jersey after the negotiations as senior member of its governor's council. Governor Edward Hyde, Viscount Cornbury, allied with Morris's political enemies and solicited bribes and appointed hirelings who abused the public trust. Morris denounced Cornbury in the council until he was dismissed in 1705; he then fought Cornbury as an elected assemblyman until 1708, when Cornbury was recalled by the crown in disgrace.

Morris's influence was raised to its apogee by Robert Hunter, joint governor of New Jersey and New York. He had relocated to Morrisania Manor by 1710, when he won

election to New York's assembly; he then served as legislative manager for royal governors until 1725. Hunter appointed him to New Jersey's supreme court in 1711 and named him New York's chief justice in 1715.

William Cosby, an avaricious and arrogant Irishman, provoked Morris's final campaign to unseat a governor. In 1733 Cosby dismissed Morris as New York's chief justice after he had overruled Cosby's attempt to sue a political adversary for a large sum of money without impanelling a jury. Morris won a seat in the assembly to rally the opposition but was outvoted by Cosby's partisans; he then went to London, where he lobbied incessantly during 1734–5 for Cosby's recall. Morris failed to have Cosby removed because the governor's wife enjoyed close connections to several privy councillors, but Cosby obligingly died of tuberculosis in 1736.

Sir Charles Wager, a privy councillor, befriended Morris during his London sojourn and helped to persuade Sir Robert Walpole to separate the governorship of New Jersey from that of New York and to appoint Morris to the former, in January 1738. Morris's pugnacious personality ill served him as chief executive. Even after the legislature named a county in his honour he provoked a succession of rancorous disputes with the assembly, especially by vetoing bills to issue paper money. The government was in stalemate from 1744 to 1746, when the assembly refused to pay Morris's salary.

Morris died on 21 May 1746 at his home, Kingsbury Plantation, in Hunterdon county, New Jersey; he was buried six days later at Morrisania Manor. Having brought down two venal governors and waged unrelenting war upon a third he ended his life embittered by defeat and political isolation. Despite phenomenal economic success—his wealth increased from £16,800 in 1691 to well over £100,000 by 1746—Morris's instinctive aversion to compromise left him discredited in a province that had once esteemed him a hero.   Thomas L. Purvis

Sources E. R. Sheridan, *Lewis Morris, 1671–1746: a study in early American politics* (1981) · *The papers of Lewis Morris, 1698–1746*, ed. E. R. Sheridan, 3 vols. (1991–3) · J. E. Stillwell, 'Morris of Monmouth county', *Historical and genealogical miscellany*, 4 (1916), 14–70 · T. L. Purvis, *Proprietors, patronage, and paper money: legislative politics in New Jersey, 1703–1776* (1986) · IGI

Archives L. Cong., corresp. and papers · New Jersey Historical Society, Newark, corresp. and papers · New York Historical Society, papers · Rutgers University, New Brunswick, New Jersey, family papers | L. Cong., Morris–Popham papers · New Jersey Historical Society, Newark, New Jersey MSS · New York Historical Society, James Alexander papers · New York Historical Society, Rutherfurd collection

Likenesses J. Watson, oils, *c*.1726, Brooklyn Museum, New York [see illus.]

Wealth at death total estate at least £100,000 (his 10,000 improved acres probably worth at least £50,000); also owned ironworks and mills; had money lent at interest; also slave force worth up to £10,000; many tracts held for land speculation; plus plate and much other valuable personal property

Morris, Lewis (1701–1765), land surveyor and author, was born on 27 February 1701 in the parish of Llanfihangel Tre'r-beirdd, on the island of Anglesey, the first of the five children of Morris Prichard (1674–1763), cooper, tenant

Lewis Morris (1701–1765), by unknown artist

farmer, and small merchant, and Marged Morris (1671–1752). About Michaelmas 1707 he moved with his parents and two brothers (Richard *Morris and William *Morris) to Pentre-eiriannell, a farm of 187 acres bordering on Traeth Dulas in the neighbouring parish of Penrhosllugwy, where his only sister, Elin, and another brother, John, were born. Lewis, a precocious boy, was taught to read and write by his father, attended a rustic school at Penrhosllugwy, and may have attended Beaumaris grammar school between the ages of ten and twelve; for the remainder of his life, Lewis was self-taught. His early interest in Welsh poetry was probably inspired by his parents, and since his brother Richard, at the age of thirteen years and nine months, began recording the poetry which he learned from his parents and others, it is likely that Lewis did likewise.

Surveyor and hydrographer in Anglesey Shortly after settling at Pentre-eiriannell, Morris Prichard acquired a small sloop and began trading coastwise as far as Liverpool and Caernarfon, employing his eldest son, Lewis, not only as a clerk but also as one of the two persons required to sail the sloop. These early years spent in sailing had a great influence on Lewis's future career.

By the time he was twenty-two years old Lewis Morris had attracted the attention of Owen Meyrick (1682–1760) of Bodorgan in Anglesey, an eminent landowner, who engaged him to make a survey of the Bodorgan estate in over thirty parishes in Anglesey, a project which was to keep him occupied for three and a half years, from September 1723 until the beginning of 1727, and which had already led him, in May 1723, to London; in all he visited this city nine times. The making of this vast survey led

Morris to almost every corner of Anglesey, and orally and by observation he amassed a great deal of knowledge relating to every aspect of the history of the island, its antiquities, geology, natural history, and traditions. His surveying work was carefully supervised by his patron. Both his field notebook and the complete survey contained in two folio volumes have survived, supreme unpublished treasures. The whole exercise was to be an excellent preparation for Morris's hydrographic work, and its successful completion secured for him the continued favour of Owen Meyrick.

After completing the survey Morris reverted to the task of assisting his father. Even so his services as a land surveyor were called upon occasionally in Anglesey and elsewhere in north Wales. He may have contemplated spending the remainder of his life in this capacity, but soon realized that he could not gain a livelihood solely as a land surveyor. On 29 February 1729 he married Elisabeth Griffith (*bap.* 1713, *d.* 1733), an heir to about 250 acres, mostly in the two neighbouring parishes of Holyhead and Rhoscolyn in Anglesey; she had lost her father when she was about nine months old. From this marriage were born Lewis (1729–1730), Marged (1731–1761), Elin (1732–1823), and William (*b.* 26 February 1733, died in infancy). Elisabeth was buried on 21 June 1733 at Rhoscolyn church, leaving Morris a widower with two infant daughters.

On 9 July 1729, shortly after his marriage, Morris was appointed surveyor, waiter, and searcher at Holyhead at a salary of £20 per annum and the searcher's fees. Regarding this post as that of a customs officer, Morris informs us: 'Mr. [Owen] Meyrick is the person that got me the place.' He occupied the post for the following thirteen years, during which time he also secured other minor posts—water-bailiff, deputy to the vice-admiral of north Wales, collector of the Skerry lights, and salt officer. In March 1737 his brother William was also appointed a customs officer at Holyhead. Following the death of his wife, Morris placed his daughters in the care of nurses, and thus freed himself in order to pursue his varied interests. He was always on the lookout for a more remunerative post.

Before 1 October 1736 Morris had entertained the idea of making a 'Hydrographical description of the coast' of Wales under the auspices of the commissioners of the customs. True to his nature, he renewed his application to the authorities and in the spring of 1737 he was in London meeting the civil servants at the board of customs, the Treasury, and the Admiralty, and conveying to them his plan for making a survey of the coast from Whitehaven in Cumberland to Haverfordwest in Pembrokeshire. In this venture, as before, Morris had the backing of Owen Meyrick. The secretary of the Admiralty, Josiah Burkett, decreed that the Admiralty would allow him 10s. per day for the intended survey, provided the board of customs would make available one of their 'cruizers', a vital facility which was refused. Despite this disappointment Morris eventually secured a promise of 5s. per day and was ordered on 21 June 1737 to return to Wales to proceed with the survey. Unwilling to relinquish his post as customs officer Morris submitted frequent applications to the board of customs to be released temporarily from his duties, something which caused animosity and complications. However, the presence of his brother William at Holyhead was a great help in the face of many predicaments. Beginning the survey in Anglesey and continuing in Caernarvonshire, Morris was, by 5 April 1738, able to submit some of his charts to the Admiralty, and by 1744 he had completed a survey of the west coast of Wales as far as Tenby. In the meantime he had visited London twice between November 1741 and 14 February 1742, and between February 1743 and 8 June 1743, persistently seeking payment for work done, reviving flagging interest, and requesting a boat; he did eventually succeed in securing a suitable boat in order to carry out his hydrographical survey. The completed survey, one of Morris's major achievements, is now in the hydrographic office, Taunton, and contained in two volumes: 'Cambrian coasting pilot, the first part, 1737 and 1738' (comprising eleven charts), and 'the second part', 1741–4 (comprising eighteen charts, but not including the chart for Milford Haven which Morris withdrew, intending to publish it privately). Morris utilized some of these charts in his *Plans of Harbours* (1748) and *A Chart of the Coast of Wales* (1748), both dedicated to the lords of the Admiralty; both publications led him to London between April and December 1748, where they were published. One cannot but admire the tenacity and perseverance of Lewis in completing the survey, in the face of innumerable difficulties. Not only had he learned a great deal through trial and error but he had also made many new friends and contacts.

Poetic and scholarly career in Anglesey As a customs officer at Holyhead, Morris had enjoyed plenty of leisure time, much of which was devoted to composing poetry and study. He had benefited greatly in his youth from being brought up on a background of lively culture which included poetry and music. His first attempts at composing Welsh poetry seem to have been connected with the celebration of Candlemas (2 February) when he was about fifteen years old, and were recorded by Richard, his younger brother; they display a flair for rhyme. By the age of twenty-one he had mastered the intricacies of composing poetry in strict metre. Even though he destroyed many of his early compositions there remain, for the period up to 1742, over 200 *englynion*, at least 20 *cywyddau*, 3 *awdlau*, and over 400 verses in free metre which include 14 poems in English. He soon surpassed most of his contemporaries in poetic skill and became their acknowledged tutor. He continued in this capacity throughout his life and was instrumental in raising the standard of Welsh poetry, in correctness and in dignity. Both Evan Evans (1731–1788) and Goronwy Owen (1723–1769) were his pupils in the art of composing elegant poetry in strict metre.

From early boyhood Morris was particularly attracted by four-line verses in rhyming couplets, which he heard orally from his parents and others. Many of these verses crystallized a certain general topic and conveyed an enduring truth. He began to compose a flood of verses on this measure, sometimes single verses but more often a series of verses on one topic and connected with an oft-repeated word or name or phrase, thus giving unity. Some of these poems are simple in their presentation, but display much wit and craftsmanship.

Cardiganshire: mining ventures and second marriage Early in 1742 Morris left Anglesey (returning only once, in 1747, to cast his vote in a parliamentary election) and settled in Cardiganshire, where he had, by August of that year, become greatly interested in lead mining in the northern part of the county and could not resist becoming a mining adventurer, hoping to make his fortune. By 9 January 1743 he had secured a lease on land which contained ore, and in a letter dated 17 December 1743, to his friend William Vaughan, MP for Merioneth, he refers to 'our Cwmsymlog Mine', which was 8 miles east of Aberystwyth. This venture failed, but undeterred Morris transferred his interest to other mines. Unfortunately there is insufficient evidence to reconstruct in detail Morris's mining ventures. However, in 1756, he was the lessee of four mines and in 1744 went to Shropshire 'to set going a Copper mine &c.'

After being a widower for over sixteen years, on 20 October 1749 Morris married Anne Lloyd (d. 1785), an only child and heir to a small estate called Penbryn a few miles south of Galltfadog, a farm which he had acquired in 1746. From this second marriage were born Lewis (1750–1779), John (1751–1763), Jane (b. 1753, died in infancy), Elisabeth (1754–1833), Richard (b. 1755, died in infancy), Jane (b. 1756), William (1758–1808), Mary (b. 1760), and Prys (1761–1796/7).

For almost three years, between the end of January 1751 and December 1753, Morris served as estate agent to Henry, earl of Lincoln (1720–1794); the estate was in Montgomeryshire. Apart from his private mining ventures Morris, because of his undoubted expertise in mining, was employed in various capacities directly by the crown. On 2 August 1744 a warrant was issued by order of Thomas Walker, surveyor-general of his majesty's land revenues, authorizing him to prepare 'a correct survey and plan' of the crown manor of Cwmwd Perfedd (in Cardiganshire). In his search for encroachments on the unenclosed lands which were claimed by the crown, Morris found himself in dispute with some of the local landowners. In 1746 William Corbett, steward of the crown manors in Cardiganshire, whom Morris had met two years earlier at Penrhyn (near Bangor, in Caernarvonshire), appointed him his deputy. His duty henceforth was to enforce the rights of the crown as lord of these manors, especially its right to the common land of the manor. His investigations into the crown manors of Creuddyn and Mefenydd (to the south of Cwmwd Perfedd) are extant.

Since William Corbett had also obtained a lease of all mines within the wastes (unenclosed lands) of the manor of Cwmwd Perfedd, Morris was both a servant of the crown and a servant of the private interests of the steward. In 1751 deposits of lead ore were found at Esgairmwyn in the manor of Mefenydd (near Ysbyty Ystwyth). Morris, acting as deputy steward, let the mine to the poor miners who had discovered the ore and their partners for a year from 1 July. A few months later Morris himself entered into the partnership for the remainder of the term. At the end of the term, on 15 July 1752, he was appointed by the Treasury agent and superintendent of this mine, and any others that he should discover on the wastes and common of the crown manors. The local gentry claimed that the mine at Esgair-mwyn was not on the common of the manor and therefore did not rightly belong to the crown. On 23 February 1753 two magistrates, together with the sheriff and an armed mob, invaded the mine to possess it and took Morris prisoner to Cardigan gaol; but he was quickly released on bail and returned home. Then commenced lengthy and worrying court proceedings, and the sending of troops to protect the mine after Morris returned from London in September of the same year, after spending five months in the capital. The following year, on about 26 April, he returned to London, this time in the company of many witnesses, in order to establish in court the right of the crown to Esgair-mwyn. After a brief hearing on 24 May the case was decided in favour of the crown and Morris returned home in triumph.

But on 21 January 1755 he set out for London again, this time to defend himself in a dispute arising from his accounts as agent and superintendent of the king's mines; he remained in the city for about eleven months. The following year he set out on his last visit to the capital, arriving on 22 March 1756 and remaining for almost two years. He was dismissed in 1756 not only from his post as agent and superintendent but also from the post of collector of the customs at Aberdyfi, a post which he had filled since 25 February 1752. The dispute about the accounts was finally settled and the mine itself was leased from the crown by the earl of Powis in 1757. Because of the stress and harassment incurred in serving the crown Morris probably regarded his dismissal as a relief. The several visits to London had made inroads into the money which he had struggled to save.

Later poetic and scholarly career Morris's poetic output was slightly less prolific during his time in Cardiganshire and it appears that he did not compose any poetry during the last three years of his life. Of the seventy poems which belong to this period, some are single verses and others lengthy poems, about half in free metre and half in strict metre; they include one long English bawdy song which he composed to entertain his friend William Vaughan, whom he had first met in June 1737. Much of Morris's poetry displays great ingenuity. He was allowed to select a number of his poems (and prose work) for publication in *Diddanwch teuluaidd* (1763).

Among Morris's many visions was the collecting of material for the publication of two volumes: 'A natural history of Anglesey' and 'Celtic remains'. With the first volume in view he did, during the years spent in Anglesey, garner a wealth of knowledge and drew the project to the attention of various influential friends who included William Vaughan in 1740 and Dr Edward Wynn in 1743. In a letter to the latter he expressed his hope for 'Encouragement from the Gentlemen of the Island'. He also drew up some 'Heads of enquiries' to be printed and distributed in the parishes of Anglesey. The work was to contain a map of the island as well as illustrations. Because of the lack of financial backing and his departure from Anglesey in 1742 this vision did not come to fruition.

The same fate happened to 'Celtic remains', a work of broader scholarly scope which survives in manuscript, the basis of which was the names of rivers, mountains, places, and people in Wales, collected either orally or from printed publications, but mostly from reading manuscripts and documents and ancient inscriptions which Morris saw and copied. In 1757 he doubted whether he would ever finish 'a Critical, Historical, Etymological, Chronological & Geographical Dictionary of Celtic & British names of Men & places'. The fruit of his labour was eventually published in part, long after his death, in 1878, under the editorship of Daniel Silvan Evans.

A third venture of Morris's which gradually foundered was the setting up of a printing press in Anglesey in order to print some of the literary treasures of Wales. By the end of 1730 he had secured the backing of two members of the Anglesey gentry, Robert Owen of Penrhos and William Bulkeley of Brynddu, and had also secured the service of John Rhydderch, a printer of Shrewsbury. Proposals were printed, dated 26 March 1732, 'For erecting by Subscription, a Printing Pres, at *Lannerch-y-medd*'. Unfortunately, the printer decided to leave Anglesey. Morris then removed the press to Holyhead and printed on it *Tlysau yr Hen Oesoedd* (1735), which was intended as the first issue of a quarterly literary magazine to introduce the readers to the literature of Wales. He provided all the material for this first issue, which was also the last. There is evidence that he entertained the idea of printing various Welsh books on his press. However, the whole venture had to be abandoned when in 1737 he began work as a hydrographer. Yet another vision which did not come to fruition was the revision and republication of Dr John Davies's *Dictionary*, which had been printed in 1632.

Morris delighted in writing prose in Welsh and sometimes in English, taking his patterns from many sources including the Welsh literature of the middle ages, as well as contemporary and earlier English prose writers. From 1733 until he left Anglesey nine years later Morris entertained a select group of literary men in Anglesey—including poets, clerics, and a doctor—with witty and sarcastic prose, he himself being by far the main contributor. This circle widened in 1737 with the admission of William Vaughan. Over thirty pieces of Morris's prose have survived, the majority of which remain unpublished. The literary circle disappeared in 1742, although it continued in vestigial form for a few years in the correspondence between Morris and William Vaughan. A selection of Morris's prose was printed in *Diddanwch teuluaidd* (1763).

The sound basis of Morris's scholarship was the fine content of his library, his interest in the old Welsh manuscripts, and his correspondence with other scholars. He began copying Welsh poetry from manuscripts at an early age, and by purchase or gift he collected a corpus of at least fifty manuscripts himself and saw and borrowed many more. He soon became thoroughly acquainted with the whole span of the Welsh poetic tradition. Even during his visits to London he would enquire for manuscripts.

Some of the manuscripts which he handled contained medieval historical tracts and Welsh prose works. He endeavoured by letter to correct any fallacies entertained by other scholars relating to the literature and the history of Wales, and was highly regarded as an authority on these matters.

Comparatively few of Morris's early letters have survived. Of those which have, most have been published, those between him and his brothers as well as those between him and other various correspondents. The letters confirm Morris's great appetite for learning as well as portraying his character. He was constantly troubled with cough and asthma, and his obesity was a hindrance to his health. After early manhood he turned his back on organized religion and mocked Howel Harris, the Methodist, and his followers. He was always persistent in his aims and avoided politics lest he gain the displeasure of his influential friends. Although accused of being miserly with his money, he was intent on securing the future of his children.

Final years and death In the spring of 1757, while her husband was in London, Anne Morris and her children moved from Galltfadog to Penbryn, near Goginan, where her husband joined her in January 1758. Morris spent the remainder of his life there, rearing his children, farming, and gardening, pursuing his many interests, engaging in further lawsuits, and dreaming of the fortune that the lead mines in northern Cardiganshire would certainly yield him some day. His health gradually deteriorated and he made his last will on 24 June 1761. He died on 11 April 1765 and was interred in Llanbadarn Fawr church. He was survived by his wife, who on 27 May 1772 married William Jones, a widower of Gwynfryn near Tre Taliesin in the parish of Llangynfelyn in north Cardiganshire. Anne Morris died in 1785. A great-grandson of hers and Lewis Morris was the poet and educationist Sir Lewis Morris.

DAFYDD WYN WILIAM

Sources *The letters of Lewis, Richard, William and John Morris of Anglesey*, ed. J. H. Davies, 2 vols. (1907–9) · *Additional letters of the Morrises of Anglesey, 1735–1786*, ed. H. Owen, 1 (1947) · *Additional letters of the Morrises of Anglesey, 1735–1786*, ed. H. Owen, 2 (1949) · E. G. Jones, 'More Morris letters', *National Library of Wales Journal*, 6 (1949–50), 191–2 · E. G. Jones, 'Llythgran Lewis Morris at William Vaughan, Corsygedol', *Llên Cymru*, 10 (1968–9), 3–58 · *Tlysau'r Hen Oesoedd*, 3 (1998), 2 · *Tlysau'r Hen Oesoedd*, 5 (1999), 9–15 · H. Owen, *The life and work of Lewis Morris (Llewelyn Ddu o Fôn), 1701–1765* (1951) · T. Jones, *Y llew a'i Deulu* (1982) · D. W. Wiliam, *Wiliam Morris, 1705–63* (1995) · D. W. Wiliam, *Lewis Morris, 1700/1–63* (1997) · D. W. Wiliam, *Richard Morris, 1702/3–79* (1999) · D. Bick and P. W. Davies, *Lewis Morris and the Cardiganshire mines* (1994) · A. R. Jones, 'A critical study of the literary works of Lewis Morris, 1701–1765', DPhil diss., U. Oxf., 1997 · parish register, Llanfihangel Tre'r-beirdd

Archives BL, corresp., collections, and papers, Add. MSS 14866–15059, *passim* · BL, several printed works with copious MS notes added by him · Bodl. Oxf., letters relating to Geoffrey of Monmouth and Welsh antiquities · hydrographic office, Taunton · NL Wales, corresp., and papers · NL Wales, collection of Welsh poetry and business papers · priv. coll. · U. Wales, Bangor | U. Wales, Bangor, letters to William Vaughan

Likenesses oils, NMG Wales [*see illus.*]

Wealth at death £66 19s.—list of goods: will, repr. in Owen, *Life and work*, xcviii–xcix

Morris, Sir Lewis (1833–1907), poet and educationist, was born on 23 January 1833 in Spilman Street, Carmarthen, the second of the five sons of Lewis Edward William Morris (*d.* 1872), a prosperous solicitor, and Sophia, the daughter of John Hughes, shipowner and merchant of the same town who had made a fortune as a drysalter. His great-grandfather was Lewis Morris (1701–1765) of Anglesey, a celebrated antiquary and, in 1751, one of the founders of the Honourable Society of Cymmrodorion. Despite his distinguished ancestry, a fervent 'British/Welsh' patriotism typical of his time, and a gift for languages, Morris had very little knowledge of Welsh, for social class and a wholly English education had insulated him from the richly Welsh-speaking culture of Carmarthen town and county.

Lewis Morris was educated at the Queen Elizabeth Grammar School, Carmarthen (1841–7), at Cowbridge School (1847–50), and at Sherborne (1850–51). He graduated from Jesus College, Oxford, in 1856, and was the first student in thirty years to gain first-class honours in both classical moderations and Greats; two years later he was awarded the chancellor's prize for an English essay entitled 'The greatness and decline of Venice'. Morris was admitted to Lincoln's Inn on 21 November 1856 and called to the bar on 18 November 1861, practising mainly as an equity draftsman and conveyancing counsel in London until 1880. The work, although financially rewarding, was not demanding and, for Morris, it had the advantage of allowing him time to write.

In 1868, according to early accounts of Morris's life, he married Florence Julia Pollard (1847–1927), the 21-year-old widow of Franklyn C. Pollard of New York, but no record of the marriage has been found. It seems, rather, that during the late 1860s, while living in Hampstead, he employed Florence as a housekeeper and that, shortly afterwards, they began living together as man and wife. By 1873 they had three children, but managed to conceal their liaison from the world, not announcing their marriage until 1902. Apart from the possibility of parental disapproval, it is not known why the relationship was kept a secret for so long, but Morris may have felt that Florence's Roman Catholicism would have prejudiced his chances of a political career. It almost certainly cost him the poet laureateship, as a result of Queen Victoria's disapproval on learning that he had a common-law wife and three children. Shortly after the appointment of Alfred Austin as poet laureate in January 1896, Morris (according to one of his descendants) married Florence Pollard and 'went to considerable pains to legitimise his children—which was successfully achieved'.

Almost from the outset Morris enjoyed immense popularity as a poet and became a well-known figure in London literary circles and in Wales. Although his first book of lyrical verse, *Songs of Two Worlds* (three series, 1872, 1874, 1875; new edn in one vol., 1878), was published anonymously, with the appearance of *The Epic of Hades* in 1877 won immediate and widespread fame. Written, he claimed, while he was commuting to work on the London Underground, this long poem in blank verse describes a

Sir Lewis Morris (1833–1907), by W. & D. Downey, pubd 1890

visit to the classical underworld in a series of episodes in which characters such as Tantalus, Orpheus, and Aphrodite tell their tales and the author adds comment of a moralistic nature. The book lacks vitality, its effect amounting to little more than a vague sense of moral uplift, but it ran to twenty editions (more than 50,000 copies) during the poet's lifetime and is now generally considered to be his finest work.

Morris earned his vogue as a poet by his ability to express simple truths in lucid language and traditional metre. He dispensed a cheerful optimism about this world and the next which appealed, in particular, to the morality of middle-class Victorian England. In the anonymously published *Gwen* (1879), which owes something to Tennyson's 'Maud', he traced the course of a secret marriage in a rural setting and extolled the landscape of his native county. The first book of his to appear under his own name was *Songs Unsung* (1883). By the year of its publication the Morris ménage was settled at Penbryn (formerly Mount Pleasant), a small mansion which the poet inherited from his father, and renamed after his illustrious forebear's old home, above the village of Pen-sarn, in the parish of Llangunnor, about a mile from Carmarthen. There he was to spend the rest of his life in comfortable circumstances and enjoying a patriarchal relationship with local people. He was, by all accounts, a tall, handsome, bearded, powerfully built man with little trace of a Welsh accent; he dressed in Welsh tweeds and had a

reserved, courteous, rather patrician manner which reflected what was thought to be his shy character. Some of his critics thought him a volatile man, lacking stability and patience, especially in his professional dealings, and tending to see intrigue where none existed.

It was only in his fifties that Morris began to take an interest in the language, literature, and history of Wales. His volume *Songs of Britain* (1887) contains some patriotic odes such as that on the jubilee of Queen Victoria and three long poems based on Welsh legends. But for the most part he went on writing poems on classical themes, many of which are vapid outpourings remarkable more for their length and fluency than for any literary quality. His last poem of any note, *A Vision of Saints* (1890), which he intended to be the Christian counterpart of the pagan *Epic of Hades*, consists of a series of nineteen monologues by people such as Elizabeth Fry and Father Damien whom he had selected for their 'saintly' qualities. His other books were *Songs without Notes* (1894), *Idylls and Lyrics* (1896), *Harvest Time* (1901), and *The Life and Death of Leo the Armenian: a Tragedy in Five Acts*. A volume of his *Selected Poems* appeared in 1905, and the last edition of his *Collected Poems* (comprising some 840 double-columned pages) in the year of his death. A selection of his prose writings, mainly essays and speeches, in which he discussed his ideals as a poet, answered some of his severest critics, and expressed his progressive views of society, appeared under the title *The New Rambler* in 1905.

Many of the articles in *The New Rambler* deal with education and other aspects of the cultural life of Wales, which became—albeit somewhat belatedly—the second great passion to which Morris devoted his energies. In 1878, encouraged by Hugh Owen, he had been appointed joint honorary secretary of the recently established University College of Wales, Aberystwyth. He threw himself into all aspects of the college's work, drafting various appeals and constitutions on its behalf, and serving as its joint treasurer from 1889 to 1896, and thereafter, until his death, as one of its two vice-presidents. He was a dedicated member of a committee appointed in 1880 to look into the state of intermediate and secondary education in Wales, which recommended the establishment of two new university colleges at Cardiff and Bangor and the passing of the vital Intermediate Education (Wales) Act of 1889. He was particularly interested in the higher education of women, whom he believed to have a moral sensibility superior to that of men. After the establishment of the federal University of Wales in 1893 he became its junior deputy chancellor (1901–3). He was a prominent member of the Honourable Society of Cymmrodorion and served as chairman of the council of the National Eisteddfod Association after that body had been reformed by Sir Hugh Owen in 1880.

Morris was knighted in 1895 and received the honorary degree of DLitt from the University of Wales in the year before his death. Political success eluded him, however. He was a Gladstonian Liberal in favour of home rule and the disestablishment of the Church in Wales, but he suffered from a shyness often mistaken for hauteur and was never a popular public speaker. He stood as Liberal candidate in the Pembroke Boroughs in 1886 but lost the candidature at Carmarthen in 1892 when another Liberal was appointed as the official candidate. Although he failed to achieve his ambition to enter parliament, Morris remained an active Liberal and was a member of the political committee of the Reform Club and, for several years, its vice-chairman.

Morris died at Penbryn on 12 November 1907 and was buried in the family grave in the hilltop churchyard at Llangunnor four days later. His widow died on new year's eve 1927; in her obituary no personal detail was given. During his lifetime the literary reputation of Sir Lewis Morris was second only to that of Alfred, Lord Tennyson, but soon after his death it went into rapid decline. George Saintsbury in *The Cambridge History of English Literature* (1916) wrote: 'He had, sometimes, a faculty—which in a satirist, would have been admirable—of writing things which looked like poetry till one began to think of them a little.' Although Morris had several virtues both as man and poet, from the obloquy of this harsh judgment posterity has so far resolutely declined to rescue him.

MEIC STEPHENS

Sources D. Phillips, *Sir Lewis Morris* (1981) • M. Stephens, ed., *The Oxford companion to the literature of Wales* (1986) • *DNB* • L. Morris, *The new rambler* (1905) • d. cert.
Archives NL Wales, corresp., journal and papers | BL, letters to W. E. Gladstone, Add. MSS 44390–44516 • NL Scot., corresp. incl. with Lord Rosebery • NL Wales, letters to T. C. Edwards
Likenesses J. M. Griffith, finished by P. R. Montford, plaster bust, 1897–1900, NMG Wales • C. Morris, portrait, 1906; formerly at Penbryn, 1912 • W. & D. Downey, woodburytype photograph, NPG; repro. in W. Downey and D. Downey, *The cabinet portrait gallery* (1890) [*see illus.*] • H. Foulger, finished by B. A. Lewis, oils, U. Wales, Aberystwyth • W. G. John, plaster bust, U. Wales, Aberystwyth
Wealth at death £13,416 10s.: probate, 20 Dec 1907, *CGPLA Eng. & Wales*

Morris, (John) Marcus Harston (1915–1989), magazine editor and publisher, was born on 25 April 1915 in Preston, Lancashire, the second child and eldest of three sons, the youngest of whom died in childhood, of the Revd Walter Edmund Harston Morris and his wife, Edith Nield. In 1918 his parents moved to Southport. He was educated at Dean Close School in Cheltenham and at Brasenose College, Oxford, where he obtained a second class in *literae humaniores* in 1937. He then moved to Wycliffe Hall and gained a second in theology in 1939. A curate from 1939 to 1940 at St Bartholomew's, Roby, he was ordained priest in 1940 and went to Great Yarmouth (1940–41). He was a chaplain in the Royal Air Force Volunteer Reserve from 1941 to 1943 and rector of Weeley thereafter. In 1945 he became vicar of St James's, Birkdale in Southport, where his talents as a Christian publicist were shown in a unique magazine, *Anvil*, which circulated far beyond the parish.

In 1948 Morris engaged a young artist, Frank *Hampson, to work first on *Anvil* and by 1949 on a new project, a strip cartoon magazine for boys. Morris saw clearly that boys were buying horror comics, produced for American servicemen of limited intelligence, because they wanted action stories in strip cartoon form, and not because they wanted pictures of savage sexual assaults on busty women. Hampson turned out to be a great strip cartoon artist, devising his own stories and characters and inventing spaceships and futuristic gadgets. He devised a cartoon about Dan Dare, space pilot, and he and Morris sent the dummy of a new paper, *Eagle*, to publishers. In October 1949 the dummy was bought by Hulton Press, which employed Morris and Hampson.

After unprecedented publicity, the first issue of *Eagle* went on sale on 14 April 1950 and was an immediate success. It was printed on good paper in four-colour rotogravure, on presses built by Eric Bemrose of Liverpool. The stories boys wanted, and features they did not know they wanted until they had them, such as adventures of Christian heroes (these last proved fifth in popularity), were told in strip cartoon form. The depiction of historical scenes and clothing had to be accurate and the science in Dan Dare, space pilot of the future, must be beyond criticism: Hampson could invent what did not yet exist, provided there was no reason why it should not, but Dan must never do anything impossible, such as travelling at more than the speed of light.

The Morris family moved to Epsom in 1950 and Hampson's team was given a studio in the house. Although many girls read *Eagle*, the majority wanted their own paper; *Girl* appeared in November 1951, to be followed in January 1953 by *Robin* (to teach smaller children to read), and in March 1954 *Swift* bridged the gap to the papers for older readers. The popularity of these magazines was not weakened by the fact that parents and teachers approved of them. They gave rise to annuals, the Eagle Club, and other expressions of belonging, including carol services, which filled St Paul's and other cathedrals. Morris dressed as a parson only for these events. His brilliance as an editor was recognized when Edward Hulton made him managing editor of *Housewife* in 1954, a post he held until 1959, and included him as a member of the Hulton Press management committee.

Morris left at the end of 1959 to join the National Magazine Company (a subsidiary of the Hearst Corporation of America) as editorial director in 1960. From 1964 until 1982 he was managing director and editor-in-chief. In the 1960s the company published eleven magazines, including *Good Housekeeping*, *She*, *Vanity Fair*, and *Connoisseur*. In the 1970s Morris bought *Queen* and amalgamated it with *Harper's*, and launched *Cosmopolitan* in Britain. In association with Condé Nast he formed COMAG, perhaps the biggest media distribution company in the country. He became deputy chairman of the National Magazine Company in 1979 (the chairman had to be American). He increased the circulation of his company's magazines at a time when other magazines were struggling or going out of business. He retired in 1984. From 1952 to 1983 he was honorary chaplain of St Bride's, Fleet Street.

Morris's nine years at Hulton Press were exceeded in responsibility and success by his twenty-five years at the National Magazine Company, and yet it was for his creation of *Eagle* and *Girl* and for his powerful influence for good on a whole generation that he is remembered and revered. He was appointed OBE in 1983.

Morris was tall, thin, and fair, and looked like a sardonic Leslie Howard. In 1941 he married Jessica, one of two actress daughters of John Hamlet Dunning, a representative for Clark's shoes. They had a son, who died in a car accident in 1968, and three daughters. Morris, who lived latterly at the Mill House, Midford, Bath, died on 16 March 1989 at the King Edward VII Hospital for Officers, London. His memorial service filled St Bride's in Fleet Street to overflowing.   CHAD VARAH, *rev.*

Sources C. Varah, *Before I die again* (1992) · private information (1996) · personal knowledge (1996) · *CGPLA Eng. & Wales* (1989)
Wealth at death £296,257: probate, 16 June 1989, *CGPLA Eng. & Wales*

Morris, Margaret Eleanor (1891–1980), teacher of dance, was born on 10 March 1891 at 28 Collingham Place, Kensington, London, the daughter of an artist, William Bright Morris (1844–1896), and his wife, Emily Victoria Maundrell. Her parents took her to live in Boulogne when she was a few weeks old, so she grew up both bilingual and Francophile. In 1900 she joined the Ben Greet Shakespeare Company. Child parts in Drury Lane melodramas followed, and between tours she studied classical ballet techniques with John d'Auban, the ballet master at Drury Lane Theatre. In 1907 she joined Frank Benson's Shakespearian company as *ingénue* principal dancer and understudy to Lady Benson.

From the age of twelve Morris started to rebel against the limitations of classical ballet, in particular its insistence on the formal positions of the spine. In 1909 she met Isadora Duncan's brother, Raymond, who was lecturing in London on the dance and music of ancient Greece. He emphasized the significance of the six Greek positions (copied from Greek vases) with their accentuated opposition of arms and legs which used every muscle in the body to achieve body control and balance. She began to evolve a freer, more expressive style of dancing, where her emphasis was on the 'natural' rather than the formal. In ballets which she composed, tutus and ballet shoes were never seen. She and her dancers tended to wear flowing clothes and little or no make-up; they danced in bare feet, and trained out of doors wherever possible.

Using her new concepts, in 1910 Morris composed *Dance of the Furies*, and trained a troupe of children to play the furies for Marie Brema's production of Gluck's *Orpheus* at the Savoy Theatre, for which she also designed the costumes and the decor. Her work met with great critical success, and her career as a choreographer was launched. She was a startlingly beautiful woman who always attracted men's attention. In 1910 she had a brief but intense love affair with the writer John *Galsworthy (1867–1933). He broke off the relationship because of the pain it caused his wife; after his death Morris wrote a highly censored version in *My Galsworthy Story* (1967). With his financial support she founded a school of dancing in St Martin's Lane, London, to train children in her methods, and she formed her first touring company, Margaret Morris and her Dancing Children. Galsworthy's influence seems to have

Margaret Eleanor Morris (1891–1980), by Fred Daniels, 1922

switched her career path from that of a potential leading dancer herself towards a career devoted primarily to teaching.

Margaret Morris not only trained dancers for the theatre but, over her long career, she translated, modified, and refined her avant-garde ideas on dance into creative exercise systems for extremely diverse groups of people. She adapted her techniques of breathing, posture, and movement so that they could be used to teach very young children, physically and mentally handicapped children, prenatal and post-natal women, and to aid post-operative recuperation. In 1922 she started the first 'educational school' in England to combine normal educational subjects with professional training in dancing and acting. She became increasingly interested in the health-giving and remedial applications of her work. From 1925 she gave lecture-demonstrations to doctors and midwives and physiotherapists. In 1928 she published *The Notation of Movement*, which detailed the system she had been evolving and teaching since 1913, and which was publicized in the *Margaret Morris Movement Magazine*. In 1930 she passed the Chartered Society of Massage and Medical Gymnastics examination with distinction.

The teachers whom Morris had trained in her system of 'Margaret Morris movement' (MMM) started to be appointed residents at schools for disabled children. In 1935, in an attempt to influence the education authorities and to obtain wider recognition as a training college, she set up a non-profit making company in her London headquarters, in Cromwell Road. By 1937 MMM was officially endorsed as relevant to the 'health of the nation' when she was invited to become a founder member of the government's

National Advisory Council for Physical Training and Recreation. The fifth marquess of Cholmondeley who, as chair of the Basic Physical Training Association, was concerned that the level of physical fitness in Britain was less than that of other nations, was impressed by Morris's creation of special exercises for each sport. He wrote an introduction to her book *Basic Physical Training* (1937). Male MMM teachers ran courses at Loughborough College, which had set up a department of physical education in 1931, offering a three-year course to men wishing to become games teachers. Arguably Morris's influence on mainstream education was at its height just before the outbreak of the Second World War.

It would be impossible to give a full picture of Margaret Morris without speaking of her productive partnership with the Scottish painter and sculptor John Duncan *Fergusson (1874–1961) [*see under* Scottish colourists], whom she first met in Paris in 1913. As both travelled widely in pursuit of their work they could not always live together, though they were always in vital communication. Their dynamic relationship is recorded in what she called her 'biased' biography, *The Art of J. D. Fergusson* (1974). When the First World War started Fergusson joined her in London, where they started the Margaret Morris Club in Chelsea to replicate the Parisian café life they both adored. It became a meeting place for writers, artists, and musicians; members included Augustus John, Jacob Epstein, Katherine Mansfield, Ezra Pound, and Charles Rennie Mackintosh. In 1917 they ran a summer school in Devon, where she was dance director and he art director, and they continued to run summer schools together in Devon and in the south of France annually. Morris was Fergusson's model and his muse, while she was inevitably influenced by his delight in form and colour and his interest in Indian and Cambodian sculpture. As well as becoming an accomplished artist in her own right she increasingly incorporated modernist ideas into her dance teaching. In her choreography she created overall designs of movement, expression, and colour.

In 1939, when Morris had to close down her seven MMM training centres, she and Fergusson settled in Glasgow, where they set up clubs as they had in London during the First World War. These were the New Art Club and the Celtic Ballet Club. After the war she choreographed and produced ballets and toured with her new company to the USA in 1954 and Russia, Austria, and Czechoslovakia in 1958. In 1960 she launched a Scottish National Ballet which opened at the Festival Theatre, Pitlochry, and afterwards toured leading theatres in Britain. When Fergusson died in 1961 she closed down her Glasgow school but remained active in Glasgow, at the age of eighty-one training dancers for a production of *Hair*. During the last years of her life she concentrated on the establishment of MMM training centres nationally and internationally. From 1976 MMM received a Sports Council annual grant in recognition that its teachers continued to bring dance exercise to both children and adults across a wide social, age, and ability range. In the late 1970s it was established in Canada, Switzerland, France, Germany, and Japan. Morris died at the Western Infirmary, Glasgow, on 29 February 1980. Many of the avant-garde ideas which she put forward in the 1920s and 1930s have become part of the vocabulary of modern dance. PAM HIRSCH

Sources *The Times* (3 March 1980) • M. Morris, *My life in movement* (1969) • M. Morris, *My Galsworthy story* (1967) • *Fergusson at Stirling: an illustrated catalogue* (1991) [with an introduction by Guy Peploe; exhibition catalogue, University of Stirling] • M. Morris, *The art of J. D. Fergusson* (1974) • b. cert. • d. cert.
Archives Fergusson Gallery, Perth • International Association of MMM, Garelochhead, Helensburgh • University of Stirling | FILM BFI NFTVA, performance footage | SOUND BBC WAC
Likenesses J. D. Fergusson, pencil drawing, c.1916, Scot. NPG • F. Daniels, two photographs, 1922–7, NPG [*see illus.*] • photograph, c.1935, Fergusson Gallery, Perth • F. Daniels, photographs, repro. in M. Morris, *Margaret Morris dancing* (1925) • J. D. Fergusson, charcoal drawing, Scot. NPG • J. D. Fergusson, sculpture, repro. in Morris, *The art of J. D. Fergusson*, 208

Morris, Mary [May] (1862–1938), designer and craftswoman, was born on 25 March 1862 at Red House, Upton, Bexleyheath, Kent, the younger daughter of William *Morris (1834–1896), poet, designer, and political activist, and his wife, Jane *Morris (1839–1914), daughter of Robert Burden, stablehand, of Oxford. From 1865 to 1872 the family lived in Queen Square, Bloomsbury, where her father's company, later known as Morris & Co., had its office and workshop. From infancy May and her elder sister Jane Alice (Jenny) were in close contact with artists' families, including those of Edward Burne-Jones, whose children were her playmates, D. G. Rossetti, and Ford Madox Brown, all original partners in Morris & Co. According to her own *Who's Who* entry, she received 'ordinary schooling at Notting Hill high school; artistic education from her father', and from 1871 summer holidays were spent at Kelmscott, Oxfordshire, in a Cotswold manor house that became a major source of inspiration. Imbibing practical skills from her mother and maternal aunt Elizabeth, both expert embroiderers, as well as the literary and artistic interests of her father, from 1880 to 1883 May studied textile arts at the South Kensington School of Design. From 1885 she managed Morris & Co.'s embroidery section where until her father's death in 1896 she supervised orders, made designs, and executed commissions, first in the family home in Upper Mall, Hammersmith (where two sisters of the poet W. B. Yeats were employed), and later at her own house nearby. Also in demand as a craftswoman (see for example the episcopal gloves executed for Charles Ricketts now in the Victoria and Albert Museum, London) and as a private teacher, from 1888 she established her position through the Arts and Crafts Exhibition Society, the organized arm of the movement to revive the fine crafts, based on traditional techniques and materials with individual design and handwork. According to textile historian Linda Parry, May Morris became a leading exponent of the revivalist needlecrafts, one of the most significant manifestations of the British Arts and Crafts movement. She exhibited embroidery, including a fine cover for a copy of *Love is Enough* by her father, bound by T. J. Cobden-Sanderson (1889; Delaware Art Museum), and

Mary [May] **Morris** (1862–1938), by unknown photographer

also jewellery, and contributed essays to the society's catalogues (1889 and 1890). Other publications include *Decorative Needlework* (1893), a practical guide for beginners; 'Coptic textiles' in *Architectural Review* (1899); and three articles on opus anglicanum in the *Burlington Magazine* (1905). She also designed wallpapers for Morris & Co., lettering, and bookbindings. In 1905 she held a joint exhibition with her childhood friend, the bookbinder Katharine Adams Webb. From 1897 to 1910 she taught at the Central School of Arts and Crafts under W. R. Lethaby, and occasionally at Birmingham School of Art, as well as lecturing widely on embroidery, costume, and pattern designing. She exhibited at the Universal Exhibition in Ghent (1913) and the Exposition d'Arts Décoratifs in Paris (1914). As women were excluded from the professional craft association the Art Workers' Guild, in 1907 May Morris founded the Women's Guild of Arts, remaining president until 1935. She also served on the committee of the Society for the Protection of Ancient Buildings.

As a young woman May Morris followed her father politically, joining the Socialist League alongside figures like Eleanor Marx and Edward Aveling, with whom she shared a passion for the new drama, acting with them in a private production of Henrik Ibsen's controversial *A Doll's House* in 1886, as well as the celebrated Socialist League burlesque *The Tables Turned, or, Nupkins Awakened* (1887), written by her father. May herself wrote 'Lady Griselda's Dream', a dramatic dialogue (*Longman's Magazine*, June 1898), and *White Lies*, a one-act play (privately printed in 1903). But promotion of her father's life and work effectively formed her second career: in 1906 she began the demanding task of editing *The Collected Works of William Morris* (24 vols., 1910–15) in which the introductions to each volume build a cumulative, personal memoir of the man she later (in two

supplementary volumes) described as 'artist, writer, socialist'. In 1909–10 she lectured on her father's legacy in the eastern United States and Canada. Following a romantic attachment to the writer George Bernard Shaw, in 1890 she married Henry Halliday Sparling, the son of an Essex agriculturalist and a fellow member of the Socialist League, from whom she was divorced in 1898 or 1899; there were no children and May resumed the name Morris. In 1910 she was briefly smitten by the American lawyer and art patron John Quinn. After her mother's death in 1914, she spent much time at Kelmscott Manor, where during the First World War she helped to establish the local Women's Institute, and where she built two cottages in her mother's memory and, in 1934, a village hall to mark the centenary of her father's birth; the architect for both projects was Ernest Gimson, and the opening of the hall was attended by the prime minister, Ramsay MacDonald. During her last decade, spent in rural retirement with her companion Mary Lobb, May Morris was active in schemes to improve village life and culture. She died at Kelmscott on 16 October 1938, following influenza, and was buried with her parents in Kelmscott village church. Devotion to her father's ideals, coupled with a personally retiring manner (despite firmly expressed views) and her choice of a craft form deemed essentially feminine and lowly led to May Morris's own career being wholly overshadowed; only since 1980 have her own achievements been researched and revalued. Examples of her work are in the William Morris Gallery, and the Victoria and Albert Museum, London (embroidery, jewellery, and sketchbooks), the Ashmolean Museum, Oxford (designs and pounced patterns), and the Crafts Study Centre, Surrey Institute of Art and Design, University College, Farnham. Kelmscott Manor, which she initially bequeathed to Oxford University (it later reverted to the residuary legatee, the Society of Antiquaries), contains examples of May Morris's work and some of her personal possessions; it is open to the public in summer.   JAN MARSH

Sources H. F. Sloan, *May Morris, 1862–1938* (1989) [exhibition catalogue, William Morris Gallery, London, 10 Jan – 11 March 1989] · J. Marsh, *Jane and May Morris* (1986) · L. Parry, *Textiles of the arts and crafts movement* (1988) · L. Parry, 'May Morris, embroidery, and Kelmscott', *William Morris: art and Kelmscott*, ed. L. Parry, Society of Antiquaries of London Occasional Papers, new ser., 18 (1996), 57–68 · J. Londraville, *On poetry, painting, and politics: the letters of May Morris and John Quinn* (1997) · M. Tidcombe, *Women bookbinders, 1880–1920* (1996) · Central Television, *May Morris and the art of embroidery* (1988) · *The collected works of William Morris*, ed. M. Morris, 24 vols. (1910–15) · M. Morris, ed., *William Morris: artist, writer, socialist*, 2 vols. (1936) · A. Callen, *Angel in the studio: women in the arts and crafts movement, 1870–1914* (1979) · E. Leary, 'William Morris and May Morris', *Embroidery*, 32/2 (1981), 47–9 · registrar of births · J. Marsh, 'May Morris: ubiquitous, invisible arts and craftswoman', *Women artists and the decorative arts, 1880–1935: the gender of ornament*, ed. B. Elliott and J. Helland (2002)

Archives BL, corresp. and MSS, incl. notes relating to father's works, Add. MSS 45298–45337, 45346–45348; Add. Charter 71267 · Hunt. L., corresp. · S. Antiquaries, Lond., corresp. and papers · William Morris Gallery, London, corresp. and MSS | BL, corresp. with Sir Sydney Cockerell, Add. MS 52740 · BL, letters to George Bernard Shaw, Add. MS 50541 · Internationaal Instituut voor Sociale

Geschiedenis, Amsterdam, corresp. with Andreas Scheu · S. Antiquaries, Lond., corresp. with N. L. MacMinn · U. Lpool L., letters to John Bruce Glasier and Katharine Bruce Glasier · V&A NAL, archives relating to Morris & Co., daybook, embroidery orders **Likenesses** D. G. Rossetti, chalk drawing, 1871, Kelmscott Manor, Oxfordshire · E. Burne-Jones, group portrait, oils, 1880 (*The golden stairs*), Tate collection · W. Rothenstein, pencil, 1897 (*May Morris*), NPG · M. A. Sloane, watercolour drawing, c.1910–1911 (*May Morris correcting galley proofs of the Collected works of William Morris*), William Morris Gallery, London · E. Burne-Jones, pencil drawing, V&A · F. Hollyer, five photographs, NPG · cartes-de-visite, NPG · photograph, NPG [*see illus.*] · photographs, William Morris Gallery, London

Morris, Matthew Robinson-, second Baron Rokeby (1713–1800), politician, was born Matthew Robinson on 6 April 1713, the eldest of the six sons of Matthew Robinson (1694–1778), landowner, of Edgely and West Layton, Yorkshire, and Elizabeth (d. 1746), daughter of Robert Drake of Cambridge. His sisters were Elizabeth *Montagu and Sarah *Scott and his brothers were Thomas *Robinson (d. 1747), Morris Robinson (1715/16–1777), a solicitor in chancery in Ireland, John Robinson, a fellow of Trinity Hall, Cambridge, William Robinson (1726–1803), and Charles Robinson (1733–1807), MP for Canterbury from 1780 to 1790. His parents inherited substantial estates, on his father's side at Rokeby from Matthew *Robinson (*bap.* 1628, d. 1694), and on his mother's side at Monk's Horton, near Hythe in Kent, from Morris Drake *Morris (1695–c.1733). Matthew Robinson was educated at Westminster School (1723–9) and was admitted to Lincoln's Inn (1730), and to Trinity Hall, Cambridge (1731). He graduated LLB in 1734 and became a fellow of his college in the same year.

In 1746, on inheriting, through his mother, the Morris property at Monk's Horton, Robinson took the additional name of Morris. He was elected MP for Canterbury on 1 July 1747 and was re-elected in 1754, apparently without incurring any election expenses; he relinquished his seat in 1761. Politically he was 'an old and true whig', but he acted independently of successive ministries. He published between 1774 and 1777 four pamphlets against the American policy of Lord North, and in 1797 an *Address to the County of Kent*, advocating the dismissal of Pitt. His political independence was matched by his singular appearance and eccentric habits. He was distinguished by his patriarchal beard and his fondness for sea bathing, which he believed would cure an intestinal disorder. On the death of his cousin Richard *Robinson, first Baron Rokeby, he succeeded to the Irish title on 10 October 1794. Unmarried, he died at his seat of Mountmorris on 30 November 1800, and was buried at Monk's Horton on 8 December. He was succeeded as third Baron Rokeby by his nephew, **Morris Robinson-Morris** (1757–1829), politician and pamphleteer, the son of his brother Morris Robinson and Jane, daughter of John Greenland of Lovelace, Kent. Admitted to Trinity Hall, Cambridge, in 1775 he matriculated in 1777 and was also admitted to Lincoln's Inn in 1775. He was elected MP for Boroughbridge in the duke of Newcastle's interest in 1790. Initially a biddable government supporter, from 1714 onwards he displayed some of his

uncle's characteristic independence and frequently voted with the opposition. His persistent opposition cost him his seat in 1796 when the ministry refused to back his re-election. He published an anonymous attack on government financial policy in his 1811 pamphlet, *Essay on Bank Tokens, Bullion*, and may have written the tragedy of *The Fall of Mortimer* (1806). He never married but fathered an illegitimate son, who died in August 1811. He died at Thoralby, near Leyburn, Yorkshire, on 10 May 1829, and was succeeded by his brother, Matthew Montagu (formerly Robinson), who had been adopted by his aunt, Elizabeth Montagu. G. LE G. NORGATE, *rev.* S. J. SKEDD

Sources M. M. Drummond, 'Robinson Morris, Matthew', HoP, *Commons, 1754–90* · W. Stokes and R. G. Thorne, 'Robinson, Morris', HoP, *Commons, 1790–1820* · GEC, *Peerage* · *A biographical peerage of Ireland* (1817) · *GM*, 1st ser., 70 (1800), 1219–20 · *GM*, 1st ser., 81/2 (1811), 291 · E. Hasted, *The history and topographical survey of the county of Kent*, 2nd edn, 8 (1799), 34, 55–8 · S. E. Brydges, *A brief character of Matthew, Lord Rokeby* (1817) · *Public characters of 1798–1799*, 4th edn (1803), 554–66 · Allibone, *Dict.*
Archives Hunt. L., letters to Elizabeth Montagu
Likenesses J. Chapman, stipple, pubd 1801, BM, NPG

Morris, Michael, first Baron Killanin (1827–1901), judge, was born at Spiddal, co. Galway, Ireland, on 14 November 1827, the eldest son of Martin Morris JP (1784–1862) and Julia Blake, the daughter of Dr Charles Blake of Galway. His father was the first Catholic since 1690 to hold the office of high sheriff of Galway. His mother died of cholera in 1837, and his younger brother, George (1833–1912), grew up to be high sheriff of Galway (1860–61), MP for Galway City (1867–8 and 1874–80), and a member of the Irish Local Government Board (1880–98), and was knighted in 1898. Morris was educated at Erasmus Smith School in Galway, and at Trinity College, Dublin, where he matriculated as an exhibitioner on 2 July 1842. As a Roman Catholic he was disqualified from competing for a scholarship, but in 1846 or 1847 he graduated as first senior moderator in ethics and logic and won a gold medal. As well as working hard as an undergraduate, he developed a passion for tennis.

Morris entered as a student of Lincoln's Inn, London, on 3 May 1847. After a year's foreign travel he was called to the Irish bar, in Trinity term 1849, and joined the Connaught circuit. He rose quickly in his profession and, like his father, became high sheriff of Galway (1849–50). From 1857 to 1865 he held the post of recorder of Galway, and in February 1863 he took silk. On 18 September 1860 he married Anna Hughes (d. 17 Oct 1906); they had four sons and six daughters.

Such was Morris's popularity in Galway that although he identified himself with no political party and gave no electioneering address he was returned as MP for Galway in July 1865 with 90 per cent of the vote. Once in the House of Commons he sat with the Conservative Party since, though he was scornful of party ideologies, he was mistrustful of any further widening of the franchise and was opposed to home rule for Ireland, being firmly unionist in his sympathies. In July 1866 he was appointed solicitor-

Michael Morris, first Baron Killanin (1827–1901), by Henry
Tanworth Wells, 1895

general for Ireland by Lord Derby, being the first Roman
Catholic to hold that office under a Conservative administration. He was re-elected unopposed by his constituents.
In November 1866 he was promoted to the attorney-
generalship; also in 1866 he was sworn of the Irish privy
council, where his knowledge of local politics helped him
to undertake useful judicial work.

In 1867 Morris was raised to the Irish bench as puisne
judge of the court of common pleas, being succeeded in
Galway by his brother George. He became chief of his
court in 1876, and lord chief justice of Ireland in 1887. He
was said to have managed juries with an appealing bonhomie and, even at the height of the emotive land league
agitation (1880–83), to have been measured and just in his
judgments.

Morris was created a baronet on 14 September 1885, and
on 25 November 1889 he was promoted to the judicial
committee of the English privy council; he received a life
peerage on 5 December 1889 as Baron Morris of Spiddal.
Although his new duties forced him to move to London,
his permanent residence and interests remained in Ireland. As appellate judge of the privy council his good
humour again helped him to retain his popularity. He
often dissented from the majority of the committee, but
held his own in argument with his colleagues. His best-
known judgment was that delivered in *McLeod* v. *St Aubyn*
(1899), a case dealing with contempt of court. Although
both an Irishman and a Catholic, Morris was well liked in
English society and he integrated easily. He became a
member of Grillion's Club, and in 1890 he received the

unprecedented honour of being elected a bencher of Lincoln's Inn, though he had never been called to the English
bar.

Morris took a keen interest in the topical question of
Irish education. From 1868 to 1870 he was a member of the
royal commission on Irish primary education; in 1868 he
became a commissioner of national education, and later
he was chairman of the board. On the foundation of the
Royal University in 1880 he was appointed a senator, and
in 1899 he was elected vice-chancellor. He was a visitor of
Trinity College, Dublin, and in 1887 received the honorary
degree of LLD from his old university.

Morris retired from the privy council in 1900, when he
accepted the hereditary barony of Killanin in the peerage
of the United Kingdom; he became known as Lord Morris
and Killanin. He died at Spiddal on 8 September 1901. His
wife, two sons, and five daughters survived him, and he
was succeeded in the barony of Killanin by his eldest son,
Martin Henry Fitzpatrick, who had been elected as a Conservative MP for Galway in 1900 despite the opposition of
'home rulers' and with his father's considerable help.

Morris's judicial decisions were of a kind which often
warmed the public, being concerned with the spirit rather
than the letter of the law, scorning precedent and being
without pretence to legal erudition. His popularity with
middle-class Irish opinion, and with his loyal Galway ten-
antry, was unrivalled. Although implacably opposed to
the nationalist dream of an independent Ireland, his ability to make jests in Irish, and to be immune from the
charge of racism or anti-Catholic feeling, helped to make
his position more palatable and to keep him from being
hated personally. Even during attempted Fenian insurrections and the Land League movement, he never received a
threatening letter, and he used to joke that Ireland's
troubles could be blamed on a wet climate and a lack of
coal. He also agreed with the nationalists that financial
relations between Ireland and England were unjust,
speaking up for Ireland in the House of Lords on 23 March
1894. He detested developments which laid further financial burdens on Irish tenants, and he could be caustic on
the subject of English ineptitude in the governing of Ireland. It was he who came up with the neat epigram,
quoted by Randolph Churchill in the debate on home rule
of 17 April 1893, that Ireland was 'a quick-witted nation …
being governed against its will by a stupid people' (Lucy,
108). G. S. WOODS, *rev.* SINÉAD AGNEW

Sources Burke, *Peerage* (1980) · F. E. Ball, *The judges in Ireland, 1221–
1921*, 2 (1926), 301, 306, 310, 314, 316, 328–30, 366–7 · *Men and women
of the time* (1899), 774 · *Men of the time* (1875), 741 · Burtchaell & Sadleir, *Alum. Dubl.*, 2nd edn · J. S. Crone, *A concise dictionary of Irish biography*, rev. edn (1937), 160 · *Annual Register* (1901), 139 · A. T. C. Pratt,
ed., *People of the period: being a collection of the biographies of upwards of
six thousand living celebrities*, 2 (1897), 189 · *Law Magazine*, 5th ser., 27
(1901–2), 63–81 · *The Times* (9 Sept 1901), 5 · H. W. Lucy, *A diary of the
home rule parliament, 1892–1895* (1896)
Archives HLRO, Gibson MSS, letters to Lord Ashbourne
Likenesses H. Tanworth Wells, drawing, 1895 (reproduction),
NPG [*see illus.*] · Spy [L. Ward], caricature, chromolithograph, NPG;
repro. in *VF* (14 Sept 1893) · Spy [L. Ward], pencil and watercolour

caricature, NG Ire. • Messrs Walton & Co., engraving (after photographs), Shaftesbury Avenue, London • photograph, King's Inns, Dublin

Wealth at death   £43,314 1s. 4d. (in England): Irish probate sealed in England, 30 Nov 1901, *CGPLA Eng. & Wales* • £127,766 9s. 7d.: probate, 21 Nov 1901, *CGPLA Ire.*

Morris, Morris Drake (1695–*c*.1733), biographer, was born in Cambridge, and baptized Morris Drake on 2 November 1695 at St Michael's Church there, the son of Robert Drake, barrister and recorder of Cambridge. His mother was Sarah (*d*. 1731), daughter of Thomas Morris, a London merchant of Mount Morris in Horton, Kent. Following Drake's father's death his mother married Conyers Middleton in 1710. After schooling at Dr Tooke's academy in Bishop's Stortford, Drake was admitted to Trinity College, Cambridge, on 8 June 1714, aged eighteen; he did not take a degree. Between 1715 and 1716 Morris compiled a two-volume *Lives of Famous Men Educated in the University of Cambridge*, illustrated with engraved portraits, which he presented to Lord Oxford. On the death of his grandfather Thomas Morris in 1717 he assumed the additional surname of Morris as the condition of succeeding to Mount Morris. He died about 1733, without an heir, at Coveney in the Isle of Ely, where he possessed property, and he was buried at Horton; his death was accelerated by intemperance. The estate of Mount Morris passed to his sister Elizabeth Drake, wife of Matthew Robinson of West Layton, Yorkshire, and mother of Elizabeth Montagu. In 1749 Conyers Middleton presented Morris's rough drafts to the Cambridge antiquary William Cole. Cole indexed this material and included it in his manuscripts presented to the British Museum.

GORDON GOODWIN, *rev.* PHILIP CARTER

Sources Venn, *Alum. Cant.* • S. E. Brydges, *Restitution, or, Titles, extracts, and characters of old books in English literature*, 4 vols. (1814–16) • E. Hasted, *The history and topographical survey of the county of Kent*, 4 vols. (1778–99)

Morris, Morris Robinson-, third Baron Rokeby (1757–1829). *See under* Morris, Matthew Robinson-, second Baron Rokeby (1713–1800).

Morris, Mowbray (1819–1874), newspaper executive, was born in Jamaica, the third son of John Ball Morris, merchant. The family moved to England in Mowbray's youth. He matriculated at Trinity College, Cambridge, in 1835, but did not proceed to a degree. He was admitted to the Inner Temple in 1838 and practised briefly as a barrister in Jamaica (1842–4). In 1847 he became manager of *The Times*, a post which he held for twenty-six years.

Morris was John Walter III's first and perhaps most successful appointment to *The Times*. It is not known how they met. As manager, Morris was J. T. Delane's partner and, explicitly, John Walter's deputy. On him fell the day-to-day duty of ensuring the newspaper's efficiency and profitability as a business concern, although the strategic decisions, such as pricing and technological innovation, were taken (after consulting the manager) by the chief proprietor alone. Morris was also, in effect, foreign editor, with the job of hiring and supervising all the foreign and special correspondents: 'Morris found the brains', it was

Mowbray Morris (1819–1874), by George Richmond, 1858

said at the time, 'and Delane used them' (Dasent, 2.313). It was for Morris to ensure the flow of full, accurate, and early foreign news. He seems also to have been largely responsible for the literary and dramatic reviewers, and, being a regular first-nighter, sometimes wrote theatre reviews himself.

Morris's many-sidedness was characteristic of *The Times's* direction during Delane's editorship. If Morris had his finger in many pies, so did his principal associates, Delane, Walter, and George Dasent: it was Delane who sent William Howard Russell to cover the Crimean War. *The Times* was then a family concern: Morrises, Delanes, and Dasents married each other (on 6 November 1858 Morris married Emily, the editor's sister, as his second wife, and his sister married Delane's brother), and lived near each other (and John Walter) at Ascot; Delane and Morris also hunted together. Morris was often a leading influence in shaping the policy of *The Times*, but his most conspicuous achievement in that area was unfortunate: his obstinate prejudice against the North in the American Civil War was largely responsible for his paper's gross misrepresentation of that great crisis. As a white West Indian native, a conservative, and an anti-democrat, Morris sympathized too eagerly with the South, and so did at least two of the reporters he sent to cover the war.

Nevertheless Morris was a highly successful foreign editor, scrutinizing his correspondents' work meticulously, guiding them in brilliant letters, and dismissing them when necessary with prompt ruthlessness. He was also successful as manager, meeting such business challenges as the invention of the electric telegraph and the abolition of the 'taxes on knowledge', although the rise of the provincial press and of a cheap metropolitan press brought changes to which he and John Walter were reluctant to adapt: they believed, because they wanted to believe, that a comparatively expensive but comprehensive paper of record would always enjoy sufficient support to be comfortably profitable; yet in Morris's last years the circulation of *The Times* tended to stagnate, or even decline.

Morris described his job as 'an engrossing occupation' (*History of The Times*, 276), but it did not save his private life from disorder. Extremely handsome, he was horsewhipped in 1854 by an enraged husband. His personal finances were chaotic. He was distressed in every sense by the gambling addiction of the son of his first marriage to Kate (d. 1857) (there were also a son and a daughter from his second marriage). Morris's health began to fail in 1869; he resigned from *The Times* in April 1873, and died at Painswick, Gloucestershire, on 27 April 1874 of epilepsy and general paralysis (caused by tertiary syphilis).

HUGH BROGAN

Sources [S. Morison and others], *The history of The Times*, 2 (1939) · News Int. RO, *The Times* archive · m. cert. · d. cert. · Venn, *Alum. Cant.* · A. I. Dasent, *Life of John Thadeus Delane*, 2 vols. (1908)
Archives News Int. RO, papers
Likenesses G. Richmond, oils, 1858, News International Syndication, London [*see illus.*]

Morris, Peter (d. 1588), mechanical engineer, was first recorded in 1575, when he was said to be of Dutch origin and a servant of Sir Christopher Hatton, captain of the queen's guard. In that year Morris petitioned for a patent for his 'hydraulic engines', or water-pumps. On 24 January 1578 he was granted a licence for twenty-one years to build and operate this machinery, and he negotiated with the lord mayor and corporation of London to erect such engines at London Bridge, to supply the city with water. At this time he was the only foreigner named by the Plumbers' Company as following that trade. The authorities were slow in granting him a piece of ground at Oystergate on which to erect his machinery, and Morris wrote to complain that not only had he laid out £200 on piling and stones for foundations, but the delay was also preventing him attending to his own business. On 30 May 1581 the city fathers granted him a 500 year lease of the first arch of London Bridge, but within two years the scheme was so successful that another lease was granted for his use of the second arch. Bernard Randolph (d. 1583), common serjeant, in an act of charity made money available through the Fishmongers' Company to pay for the new engines, which had commenced work by Christmas eve 1582. At the same period river water was conducted to houses in the highest part of Norwich, but it is not known if Morris, as the patent holder, was in any way involved.

The force pumps which Morris claimed to have invented, which were operated by undershot waterwheels set in the bridge arches, had been unknown since classical times; only the less effective suction pumps had been built thereafter in Europe. Morris's system distributed Thames water by conduit to houses in the upper part of the city as far as Gracechurch Street. In Leadenhall Street it fed a water standard with four spouts which ran at every tide. Morris, who lived near the bridgehead, died in 1588, and was buried in his parish church of St Magnus the Martyr on 5 August, leaving a wife, Anne Boteler (d. 1617), great-aunt of Sir Oliver Boteler, and at least two sons, Thomas and John *Morris. In 1590 Anne remarried to George Digby of Barnes, Surrey.

After the water-wheels and machinery were damaged in the great fire, Thomas Morris was empowered to rebuild his 'waterhouse', and it continued in family hands until 1701, when it was sold. In 1828 workmen excavating for the new London Bridge found the remains of pumps in use at the time of the fire, including two cast-iron cylinders, 4 feet long by about 6 inches diameter, with feed and delivery pipes of brass neatly brazed on, valves seated in separate chambers, and charred remains of oak piston rods.

ANITA McCONNELL

Sources E. W. Hulme and R. Jenkins, 'London bridge waterworks', *The Antiquary* (1895), 243–6, 261–4 · J. Bate, *The mysteries of nature and art*, 2nd edn (1635) · W. Matthews, *Hydraulia* (1835), 26–30 · *CSP dom.*, 1547–80, 512 · *Remembrancia*, 1.28, 1.45, 1.102, 1.449 · 'Remains of ancient waterworks discovered at London Bridge', *Mechanic's Magazine*, 9 (1828), 155–6 · probate of will in archdeaconry court, GL, MS 9050/2, fol. 10v (1588) · parish register, St Magnus the Martyr, London, 5 Aug 1588 [burial] · R. E. G. Kirk and E. F. Kirk, eds., *Returns of aliens dwelling in the city and suburbs of London, from the reign of Henry VIII to that of James I*, Huguenot Society of London, 10/2 (1902), 309

Morris, Philip Richard (1836–1902), genre and marine painter, was born in Devonport, Devon, on 4 December 1836, the son of John Simmons Morris, an iron-founder, and his wife, Anne Saunders. His father took him to London in 1850 to train for the family business, but, fascinated by plates he saw in periodicals, Morris became more and more interested in art. With the encouragement of Holman Hunt, who intervened on his behalf with his father, he began to study art, first drawing in the evenings at the British Museum, and then, in 1855, in the Royal Academy Schools. He did well there, winning silver medals for drawing, painting, and portraiture. In 1858 he was awarded the gold medal and a travelling studentship for *The Good Samaritan*; he used this to visit Italy and France, where he stayed until 1864. It was also in 1858 that he submitted two paintings to the Royal Academy exhibition, and, with only a few breaks, he exhibited there until 1901; he also exhibited regularly at the Society of British Artists and, between 1877 and 1888, at the Grosvenor Gallery.

Of Morris's early paintings the best known are his seashore subjects, for example, *Voices from the Sea* (1860), based on verses by Tennyson, *Drift Wreck from the Armada* (1867), and *The Sailor's Wedding* (1876). He painted several allegorical scenes of country life, such as *The Mowers* (1875), *The Reaper and the Flowers* (exh. Grosvenor Gallery 1877), *Death and the Woodman* (1879), and *Garland Day, Dorsetshire Coast* (1893). Under the influence of Hunt, Morris painted a number of religious subjects, most notably *Golgotha, or, Where they Crucified him* (1862; Sunderland Museum) and *The Summit of Calvary* (1871), engraved by Paul Jonnard. But the most popular of his works was *Sons of the Brave* (1880), which showed the orphaned boys of soldiers of the Chelsea Hospital, emerging into the street as a musical band, a painting noted by a contemporary critic as full of character and ability. His later career was dominated by portraiture, and his sitters included Daniel Adamson, the chairman of the Manchester ship canal (1884), Colonel Edis (1889), and Sir Robert Rawlinson KCB (1892).

Morris was elected an associate of the Royal Academy in 1877, but gradually his powers as an artist were seen even by sympathetic contemporaries to be on the wane, and he began to suffer from ill health. In 1900 he resigned his associateship. He died on 22 April 1902 at his home, 92 Clifton Hill, Maida Vale, London, and was buried at Kensal Green cemetery. He was married to a widow, Mrs Sargeantson, the daughter of J. Evans of Llangollen, and had two sons and three daughters. Paintings by Morris are in the collections of Blackburn Art Gallery, Leeds City Art Gallery, the Walker Art Gallery, Liverpool, Manchester City Galleries, and Sunderland Museum.

P. G. KONODY, rev. DAVID CAST

Sources J. Dafforne, 'Philip Richard Morris', *Art Journal*, 34 (1872), 161–3 · 'A word on behalf of Philip Richard Morris, A.R.A.', *Magazine of Art* (1902), 423–5 · Graves, *RA exhibitors*, 5.301–2 · C. Newall, *The Grosvenor Gallery exhibitors* (1995), 107

Likenesses P. R. Morris, self-portrait, oils, Aberdeen Art Gallery · R. W. Robinson, photograph, NPG; repro. in *Members and associates of the Royal Academy of Arts* (1891) · wood-engraving, NPG; repro. in *ILN* (14 July 1877)

Morris, Sir Philip Robert (1901–1979), educationist, was born on 6 July 1901, the younger son of Meshach Charles Morris, HM inspector of schools, of Sutton Valence, Kent, and his wife, Jane, daughter of James Brasier, of St Cross, Winchester, Hampshire. He was educated at Tonbridge School, St Peter's School, York, and Trinity College, Oxford, where he obtained a second class in philosophy, politics, and economics in 1923. He then gained a teacher's diploma at London University (1924) and became a lecturer in history and classics at Westminster Training College (1923–5). In 1926 he married Florence Redvers Davis, daughter of Walford Davis Green, barrister; they had two sons and two daughters.

Morris's career fell into three main parts: service in local government administration; war service as the head of army education; and in higher education, as vice-chancellor of Bristol University (1946–66). The record overall shows him to have been one of the two or three ablest administrators of his time in English education.

Morris graduated at a critical time for English education, which faced new responsibilities under the 1918 Education Act of H. A. L. Fisher. Morris joined the Kent education authority and was soon picked out by Salter Davies, a remarkable director of education under whom Kent education was forging ahead. Both before and after 1938, the year in which he succeeded Salter Davies as director, Morris was especially concerned with the new relationship that was called for between administrators, teachers, and governing bodies of all the schools of the county, whether grammar schools or village schools. He was given

Sir Philip Robert Morris (1901–1979), by Elliott & Fry, 1956

credit for somehow managing to build this personal relationship between the director, the teachers, and the laymen. His was a new style and he thought it the style of the future.

In the second phase, Morris was appointed to a newly created post as director-general of army education (1944–6). His single-minded aim was to build a bridge between the experiences of war and the return of the servicemen to peacetime occupations: and the measure of his success was the confidence he won for the programme from soldiers and civilians alike. Whether, as some have thought, it affected the politics of the time, the essential achievement was undoubtedly an educational one.

The third stage began in 1946 when Morris was appointed vice-chancellor of Bristol, undoubtedly because the university felt the need for first-rate administration in the post-war years. Although some doubted the wisdom of a transplant to a university from the world of local government, Morris quickly showed that he combined in himself the necessary ingredients: administrative skills, familiarity with the world of affairs, and sympathy with the special aspirations of academic workers. As in Kent, his personal influence on individuals under his authority was strongly felt. One who worked closely with him wrote:

> He asked a lot from those under him … and encouraged everyone to give more than they thought they had to give; they were rewarded by the satisfaction of having contributed to the whole. Above all, he communicated to individuals his confidence in them.

He took pride in the distinction of the university's scholarship; building on it, he consolidated the support of the great manufacturing and mercantile interests that had been the mark of Bristol through centuries of enterprise, as well as that of the elected governments of the city and the region.

Morris's contribution to the well-being of the universities was not confined to Bristol; it was most widely evident during his chairmanship (1955–8) of the vice-chancellors' committee. He succeeded his brother, Charles Richard *Morris, who was then vice-chancellor of Leeds, in that office, and the six years of their tenure wrote a notable chapter in the history of the growth of collaboration between universities during the critical post-war decade of the 1950s. Among other things, Morris clearly foresaw that the universities would have to submit to a degree of social audit and accountability, and that they would be wise to see that they themselves should be the main architects of the new structures. He pointed to methods and practices where his experience of public affairs suggested that changes were needed; in particular, he ensured the establishment of the Universities Central Council on Admissions; and he played a decisive part in the discussions with the Treasury which resulted in a radical provision of supplementary pensions for university teachers from public funds. To the end of his career he believed that by active discussion and negotiation in all matters affecting the universities and government the essential interests of the universities could be made secure.

Beyond these major elements in his career, Morris contributed with seemingly tireless effectiveness to the work of many public bodies and causes. Three need special mention, because they illustrate the range of his interest and the issues he regarded as of primary importance. He served on the committee on the supply and training of teachers (1942–4), chaired by Sir Arnold McNair, and on the committee on higher education (1961–4), chaired by Lord Robbins—two committees which laid down the pattern for teachers' colleges and for universities in Great Britain for ensuing years. Both reports gave inspiration for a period of lively development.

Morris was long a member (latterly as chairman) of the Secondary Schools Examination Council. Here he revealed his stance on a major social and educational issue of his time. Morris believed that the grammar schools were on their way to success in their task of providing centres of excellence in the state system to match the best of the private schools. But he felt a deep concern for the 70 per cent or so of boys and girls outside the range of these schools. He would have no part with those who saw only a downward adjustment of the grammar schools as appropriate for this great majority of young people. On the contrary, he took the view that a fundamental re-thinking was needed to provide positively the education that suited their needs.

Many individuals and groups turned to Morris for help because of his exceptional skill in administration and also because they recognized a characteristic he brought from his parental home. Both his parents had been committed teachers in village schools. Thus the family background was one in which teaching as a vocation was of the very essence. To the end of his life there was a natural rapport between him and those who in a great variety of forms shared such a commitment; in the medical, nursing, and other social services; in the BBC (as governor from 1952 to 1960 and vice-chairman from 1954 to 1960); in the fine arts and the Bristol Old Vic Trust, of which he was chairman from 1946 to 1971.

Morris was a man who stood out in his time for his skill in getting things done. He believed that almost anything could be done by good administration. And his personal mark was to use his administrative skills to release the abilities and enthusiasms of others.

Morris was appointed CBE in 1941, knighted in 1946, and created KCMG in 1960. He had honorary degrees from many universities and was FRSA (1961) and honorary FRCS (1966). He died at his home, the vicarage, Bryncoedifor, Rhyd-y-main, near Dolgellau, Merioneth, on 21 November 1979.   JOHN FULTON, rev.

Sources Kent Education Authority · War Office · Bristol University · personal knowledge (1986) · private information (1986) · *The Times* (24 Nov 1979) · *Daily Telegraph* (6 Dec 1979) · *Daily Telegraph* (7 Dec 1979) · *WWW* · CGPLA Eng. & Wales (1980)
Archives University of Bristol, speeches and pamphlets
Likenesses Elliott & Fry, photograph, 1956, NPG [see illus.]
Wealth at death £93,183: probate, 5 March 1980, CGPLA Eng. & Wales

Morris, Reginald Owen (1886–1948), composer and musicologist, was born on 3 March 1886 at 3 Grosvenor Terrace, St Giles, York, the son of Reginald Frank Morris, army officer, and his wife, Georgiana Susan Sherard.

Morris was educated at Harrow School, New College, Oxford, and the Royal College of Music, where he was later appointed to the teaching staff. Before the First World War he began to attract attention as a music journalist, and he contributed a memoir of George Butterworth to *George Butterworth, 1885–1916* (1918). In 1920 Oxford University Press invited him to write the introduction and notes for their new edition of *Lorna Doone*, and his article on Hubert Parry appeared in *Music and Letters*. In the following year that journal printed his essay on Maurice Ravel, and in 1922 his first composition, *Fantasy*, a string quartet, was published under the Carnegie scheme. In that year Oxford University Press issued his *Contrapuntal Technique in the Sixteenth Century*, which secured his reputation as a musicologist. The book was praised for its use of deductive reasoning, its balanced scholarship, and its literary style. More important, it broke new ground by distinguishing between national schools and by arguing that the study of counterpoint should be based on the techniques of individual composers rather than on arbitrary trends.

After *Contrapuntal Technique in the Sixteenth Century*, Oxford University Press published Morris's *Foundations of Practical Harmony and Counterpoint* in 1925. With these books he began to attract international attention, and in

1926 he was appointed head of the department of theory at the Curtis Institute, Philadelphia. But his tenure was short, and he rejoined the staff of the Royal College of Music in 1928. Though occupied principally with his duties as professor of harmony, counterpoint, and composition, he returned briefly to composing. Between 1929 and 1933 he arranged two groups of English folksongs; set texts by Sir Walter Scott, Thomas Campion, and Robert Bridges; composed *Corinna's Maying* for chorus and orchestra; and wrote a series of instrumental works that included a symphony and a violin concerto. While his arrangements and song settings were only moderately popular, his works for orchestra commanded greater respect: in November 1930 Adrian Boult and Arthur Bliss conducted a concert devoted to his instrumental music, and on 1 January 1934 his symphony in D was performed at the Queen's Hall. But by the early 1930s he had lost interest in composing, and he refused to discuss his music in later life.

Having rejected composition, Morris began to concentrate on writing and teaching, and as an author his body of work expanded rapidly: published in 1931 were *Preparatory Exercises in Score-Reading* (with Howard Ferguson), *Figured Harmony at the Keyboard*, and 'An introduction to music', in *An Outline of Modern Knowledge* (ed. W. Rose); in 1935 *The Structure of Music* was released; in 1937 he gained his DMus by examination; in 1944 *Introduction to Counterpoint* was issued; and in 1946 *The Oxford Harmony: Volume 1* became available. Never given to oversimplification, his books were designed to educate rather than to entertain; they were for the professional or the aspiring professional, and not for the layman. He was concerned that theory and execution should be complementary, and this belief dominated his activities as a teacher. In the classroom he argued that technical ability should be matched by a clear understanding of music history and style; that formalist ideas should be avoided; that students should expand their knowledge through experience; and that strict counterpoint should not be taught, as it was based on a false premise. He had the ability to explain clearly when teaching, often drawing upon parallels when clarifying an obscure point. But he was a hard taskmaster and he expected his students to work diligently; he had little sympathy for those who lacked dedication.

Morris's complex personality often puzzled those in his circle: he was pernickety about food, but was knowledgeable about wines; he could be austere, but often displayed a good sense of humour; he disliked ostentation and ebullience, but was often relaxed about life; and he could be aloof, yet was passionate about cats, cricket, and crossword puzzles. Professionally, he was also a paradox: composers like Ralph Vaughan Williams, Gerald Finzi, and Edmund Rubbra spoke highly of his works but performers generally ignored them. W. H. Mellers, writing in *Musical Opinion*, probably assessed Morris best:

> [He] is a teacher who writes music rather than a composer who teaches, and perhaps because of rather than in spite of our respect for him as a teacher we tend to lose sight of the

fact that he is, if a small composer, a real one.   (*Musical Opinion*, July 1941, 437–8)

Morris died at 2 Addison Gardens, Kensington, London, on 15 December 1948.   RAYMOND HOLDEN

Sources H. K. Andrews, *RCM Magazine*, 45/2 (1949), 56–7 · G. Finzi, *RCM Magazine*, 45/2 (1949), 54–6 · 'Morris, Reginald Owen', *Grove, Dict. mus.* (1927); (1954) · W. H. Mellers, 'The music of R. O. Morris', *Musical Opinion*, 65 (1941–2), 437–8 · H. C. Colles and H. Ferguson, 'Morris, Reginald Owen', *New Grove* [see also *New Grove*, 2nd edn] · *New Grove*, 2nd edn · M. Roberts, 'R. O. Morris, 1886–1948: a tribute', *Music in Education*, 13/146, 147 (May–June 1949) · E. Rubbra, 'R. O. Morris: an appreciation', *Music and Letters*, 30/2 (1949), 107–8 · *Baker's biographical dictionary of musicians*, rev. N. Slonimsky, 8th edn (1992) · R. Vaughan Williams, *RCM Magazine*, 45/2 (1949), 54 · CGPLA Eng. & Wales (1949) · b. cert. · d. cert.

Wealth at death £21,196 13s. 5d.: probate, 1949, CGPLA Eng. & Wales (1949)

Morris, Richard (1703–1779), clerk and promoter of the Welsh language, was born on 2 February 1703 in Fferam in the parish of Llanfihangel Tre'r-beirdd in Anglesey, the second son of Morris Prichard (1674–1763), cooper, tenant farmer, and small merchant, and Marged Morris (1671–1752). His elder brother was the poet Lewis *Morris (1701–1765), and a younger, the antiquary William *Morris (1705–1763). About Michaelmas 1707 the family moved to the Pentre-eiriannell in the neighbouring parish of Penrhosllugwy. Richard Morris was taught to read and write by his father and attended a local rustic school. At the age of thirteen he began recording in a book the Welsh folk poetry which he heard from his parents and others and continued with this task for a year and a half. During these years he probably assisted his father with his carpentry and became immersed in the local culture, which included poetry and music.

On the first day of August 1722, after serving as a clerk at Beaumaris for four years, Morris went to London where he remained for the rest of his life. There he worked in turn as a labourer, a teacher of navigation in Stepney, a clerk, and in 1732 as a corn merchant. About March 1735 he was imprisoned in the king's bench prison following his action in becoming surety for a debtor who subsequently fled, but he was released after a year's imprisonment. Following another two years of hardship he secured work as a clerk and on 28 March 1748 was appointed a clerk in the Navy Office where he remained until his retirement on 30 March 1775; he was sometimes able to supplement his income by serving as a private agent. He was married three times: first to Margaret (d. 1750) in 1737; second to Betty (c.1733–1772) in 1753; and finally to Mary, widow of John Major, in 1775. Of the many children born from the first two marriages only four survived infancy and early childhood.

During his early years in London, Morris delighted in composing poetry, mostly in Welsh, but stopped abruptly in 1740 and devoted himself to encouraging Welsh poets and scholars. He was editor of two impressions of the Welsh Bible and Book of Common Prayer in 1746 and 1752 as well as editor of several other Welsh publications, and in September 1751 was instrumental in founding the Honourable Society of Cymmrodorion, a society with both cultural and philanthropical aims. Morris became its first president, and served in that post with great diligence until his death. In his editorial work he insisted on upholding the best standards of orthography. It was he who kept so many of his brother Lewis's letters as well as securing their manuscripts which in 1841 were deposited in the British Museum. Although burdened with ill health he was an integral part of the Welsh classical revival of the eighteenth century and Lewis's description of him who 'loves his country to excess' (Davies, 2.27) was true.

Morris died in 1779 in the Tower of London, probably in Royal Mint Street where he had resided since 1763, and was buried on 29 December 1779 in St George-in-the-East.

DAFYDD WYN WILIAM

Sources D. W. Wiliam, *Cofiant Richard Morris, 1702/3–79* (1999) · *The letters of Lewis, Richard, William and John Morris of Anglesey*, ed. J. H. Davies, 2 vols. (1907–9) · *DNB* · BL, Add. MS 14992, fol. 756 · parish register, Anglesey, Llanfihangel Tre'r-beirdd parish church [baptism], 7/2/1703
Archives BL, poems, notes, extracts, corresp., and papers, Add. MSS 14866–15037, *passim* · BL, printed works with MS additions made by him · BL, Add. MSS 14866–14961
Wealth at death see will, 7 Nov 1773, University of Bangor archives department, MS no. 10477; Wiliam, *Cofiant*

Morris, Richard (1833–1894), scholar of early English and philologist, was born at Bermondsey, London, on 8 September 1833, the son of David Morris, a Welsh hatter. He trained as an elementary schoolmaster at St John's College, Battersea, Surrey, though his education was largely self-acquired. On 16 March 1856 he married Hannah (*d.* in or after 1894), the daughter of John Ary, a coachman.

Morris displayed his scholarly interests as early as 1857 by publishing a little book, *The Etymology of Local Names*. He was one of the first to join as an active member the Chaucer, Early English Text, and Philological societies founded by his lifelong friend F. J. Furnivall. In 1869 he was appointed Winchester lecturer on English language and literature in King's College School. In 1871 he was ordained, and served for two years as curate of Christ Church, Camberwell. In 1870 he was awarded the LLD degree by Archbishop Tait, and the University of Oxford conferred upon him the honorary degree of MA on 28 May 1874. That year he became president of the Philological Society. From 1875 to 1888 he was headmaster of the Royal Masonic Institution for Boys at Wood Green, and afterwards for a short time master of the old grammar school of Dedham in Essex.

None of Morris's colleagues surpassed him in his devotion to editing the oldest remains of English literature from the original manuscript sources, on the same scientific principles as adopted by classical scholars. Between 1862 and 1880 he brought out no fewer than twelve volumes for the Early English Text Society, of which may be specially mentioned three series of *Old English Homilies* (from 1868) and two of *Early English Alliterative Poems* (1864). In 1866 he edited Chaucer for the Aldine Poets (2nd edn,

1891). This was the first edition to be based upon manuscripts since that of Thomas Tyrwhitt, and it remained the standard one until it was superseded by W. W. Skeat's edition (1894–7). In 1869 Morris edited Spenser for Macmillan's Globe edition, again using manuscripts as well as the original editions. He also published at the Clarendon Press, Oxford, *Specimens of Early English* (1867), which was augmented in subsequent editions by Skeat (1872–94).

Morris's long experience as a schoolmaster induced him to undertake a series of educational works, designed to place the teaching of English upon a sound basis. The first of these was *Historical Outlines of English Accidence* (1872), which, after passing through some twenty editions, was thoroughly revised by Henry Bradley and L. Kellner (1895) after Morris's death. In 1874 he published *Elementary Lessons in Historical English Grammar* and in 1875 an *English Grammar* primer. These were widely used in the late nineteenth century.

Turning from this profitable type of publication Morris devoted the remainder of his life to a specialized branch of philology—the study of Pali, the sacred language of Buddhism. The stimulus came from his intimacy with Rhys Davids, the founder of the Pali Text Society, for which he edited, between 1882 and 1888, four texts, more than any previous contributor. But he did not confine himself to editing. His familiarity with the development of early English caused him to take a special interest in the corresponding position of Pali, as standing midway between the ancient Sanskrit and the modern vernaculars, and as branching out into various dialects known as Prakrits. These relations of Pali he expounded in a series of letters to *The Academy*, which are valuable not only for their lexicographical facts, but also as illustrating the historical growth of the languages of India. His last work was a paper on this subject, read before the International Congress of Orientalists in London in September 1892 and printed in the *Transactions*.

For the last two years of his life Morris was prostrated by an incurable and distressing illness, which he bore with characteristic courage, preserving his cheerfulness and his love of a good story to the last. He retired to the railway-side hamlet of Harold Wood in Essex. He died on 12 May 1894 at his home, Rothesay Villa, of a rodent ulcer, leaving his widow, Hannah, and three daughters. He was buried on 17 May at Hornchurch, Essex. In 1893 Gladstone had conferred upon him a pension of £150 on the civil list, and on 2 June 1896 new pensions of £25 each were created in favour of his daughters. Most of his valuable philological library was acquired by the bookseller David Nutt.

J. S. COTTON, *rev.* JOHN D. HAIGH

Sources personal knowledge (1901) · private information (1901) · Boase, *Mod. Eng. biog.*, 2.985–6 · *Men of the time* (1875) · Allibone, *Dict.* · J. Green, *Chasing the sun: dictionary-makers and the dictionaries they made* (1996), 307 · W. Benzie, *Dr F. J. Furnivall: Victorian scholar adventurer* (1983) · m. cert. · d. cert. · *CGPLA Eng. & Wales* (1894)
Likenesses P. N., wood-engraving, NPG; repro. in *ILN* (26 May 1894)
Wealth at death £615 19s. 4d.: probate, 13 June 1894, *CGPLA Eng. & Wales*

Morris, Robert (*bap.* 1701?, *d.* 1768), industrialist, was born to Robert Morris of Bishop's Castle and Cleobury Mortimer, Shropshire, whose family was said to be of north Welsh stock, and Mary, the daughter of Richard Tristram of More Hall, Worcestershire. He was probably the Robert, son of Robert and Mary Morris, baptized at the parish church, Clunbury, on 22 June 1701. Little is known of his early years before he moved to south Wales, but he was married on 9 September 1725 at St John's Church in Swansea to Margaret (*d.* 1786), the daughter and heir of David Jenkins of Machynlleth, Montgomeryshire, and his wife, Bridget Parry. Through her mother she was related to some of the leading families of Cardiganshire, and as a descendant of Owain Gwynedd she belonged to one of the so-called fifteen tribes of north Wales, a fact of which the family was suitably proud.

Robert Morris had been drawn to the Swansea area about 1724 by the copper-smelting works (known as the Landore works) that had been operated at Llangyfelach from 1717 by Dr John Lane of Bristol. Lane became bankrupt in November 1726 and Morris took over the works as receiver until he eventually secured sufficient capital from, among others, Richard Lockwood, Edward Gibbon (a relation of the historian), and Robert Corker, to buy the works in 1727. He himself became a partner in 1728, so forming the company of Lockwood, Morris & Co. which would play a large part in the history of Swansea over the next century and more. Morris was the most active partner, and his success lay in his realization that whereas copper ore could be easily imported from Cornwall, it was the availability of a local, and therefore inexpensive, supply of good coal that was vital for the operation. This awareness soon gave rise to a dispute with Thomas Popkins of Fforest, a local mine owner who failed to keep to his part of the covenant in the original lease to supply coal. Morris was able to gain advantage over Popkins and other competitors by winning the support of Gabriel Powell, the duke of Beaufort's steward in Gower, in the competition for leases. He was soon mining his own coal, and by 1735 he was the biggest exporter out of the port of Swansea. His long and profitable direct involvement in the town of Swansea was evident by 1733, when he was granted a lease near the River Tawe to build a dock for coal ships, and over the following years his efforts at improving facilities at the port included bringing in better horses to haul coal and an attempt to improve postal facilities. In 1748 the works at Llangyfelach ceased to operate and were moved further up the valley to Fforest.

The tensions between Morris and his rivals did not cease after the early years of the enterprise, however, but led to a series of mineral property disputes through the 1730s, 1740s, and 1750s which saw the Popkins of Fforest and the Prices of Penlle'r-gaer line up against Morris and Powell and the party of the dukes of Beaufort. Like Henry Somerset, third duke, and Charles Noel Somerset, fourth duke, Robert Morris was a high tory, and possibly a nonjuror. In this he conformed with most of the entrepreneurs who had a share in the industrial boom which Swansea experienced in the years 1720–70. His interests in the lead mines of Cardiganshire, an area in which his wife had family ties, also brought him into contact with like-minded families such as the Powells of Nanteos. This probably aided the process by which he became largely accepted into the gentry circles of Glamorgan, becoming a justice of the peace by the 1760s and acting as high sheriff of the county in 1763. The building of the mansion of Clasemont in Llangyfelach, with which the family's name was later linked, and the innovative workers' residences known as Morris Castle have been attributed to Robert Morris, but it seems likely that they were built by his son John Morris soon after his father's death. It was through this son that Robert's surname was given to the industrial suburb of Morriston on the outskirts of Swansea.

Robert himself probably lived at the house of Tredegar in Llangyfelach, and was the owner of other small estates in the Swansea valley as well as a town house in High Street, Swansea. He and his wife had twelve children who were baptized at St Mary's Church, Swansea, but six of them died in childhood. Of the survivors, four girls, Bridget (*b.* 1729), Margaret (*b.* 1731), Mary (*b.* 1736), and Jane (*b.* 1739) were followed by two boys, Robert *Morris (1743–1793), and John (1745–1819). Robert, best-known for his political radicalism, played only a small role in the development of his family's business, although it was he who, in 1774, compiled the manuscript 'A history of the copper concern' that is such a vital source for the early years of the business. It was the younger brother John (knighted in 1806) who took care of the business after their father's death. Robert Morris died between January and April 1768 at his London home in Mortimer Street, Cavendish Square, and was buried at St John's Church, Swansea. After his death, his son John spoke affectionately of his father that 'His amiable manner, his Countenance, his deportment, Language and voice, in fact every word and every action announced the good man, as well as the accomplished Englishman of his day' (Ross, 40).

Robert Morris is remembered as one of the foremost industrial pioneers in south Wales. He has been characterized both as an unusually successful example of a native Welsh entrepreneur and as a typical example of how the large profits from Welsh mineral resources went into English hands. His importance in the development of Swansea and its hinterland is not open to doubt, however, and the industrial dynasty which he founded played a foremost role in the development of the town at a time when it was arguably the most important in Wales.

DYLAN FOSTER EVANS

Sources Burke, *Peerage* (1999) [Morris, Bt] • R. Morris, 'A history of the copper concern', 1774, University College, Swansea, Morris MSS • J. Martin, 'Private enterprise versus manorial rights: mineral property disputes in eighteenth-century Glamorgan', *Welsh History Review / Cylchgrawn Hanes Cymru*, 9 (1978–9), 155–75 • J. E. Ross, *Letters from Swansea* (1969) • P. Jenkins, 'Tory industrialism and town politics: Swansea in the eighteenth century', *HJ*, 28 (1985), 103–23 • J. Childs, 'The growth of the Morris estate in the parish of Llangyfelach, 1740–1850', *Gower*, 42 (1991), 50–69 • W. H. Jones, *History of the port of Swansea* (1922) • W. J. Lewis, *Lead mining in Wales* (1967) • G. Williams, ed., *Swansea: an illustrated history* (1990) • *IGI* • *GM*, 1st ser., 38 (1768), 198

Archives U. Wales, Swansea, extracts from his letter-books
Wealth at death £5710; plus businesses and land: will, repr. in
Ross, *Letters from Swansea*, 41–3

Morris, Robert (1703–1754), writer on architecture, was
born in February 1703 at Twickenham, the son of Thomas
Morris, a joiner. Nothing else is known about his early life.
In 1728 he published his first theoretical treatise, *An Essay
in Defence of Ancient Architecture*. Modern baroque buildings
(including examples encountered in Twickenham, where
he was still living) were contrasted unfavourably with
those based on ancient models, especially as these had
been interpreted by the Italian Renaissance architect
Andrea Palladio. Morris mentions three living architects—Lord Burlington, Henry Herbert, tenth earl of Pembroke, and Sir Andrew Fountaine—as evidence that his
contemporaries were not entirely 'lost in a Circle of Follies' ('Dedication', p. xiii), but there is no evidence of personal contact with them, and his appreciation of buildings by Christopher Wren and James Gibbs distinguishes
him from these more strictly partisan practitioners of the
Palladian revival.

Morris's next and most important work was a two-
volume series of *Lectures on Architecture* (1734–6), consisting
of fourteen lectures dated from 22 October 1730 to 13 January 1735 and supposedly read to an otherwise untraced
'Society established for the Improvement of Arts and Sciences'. In this work Morris insisted that the site of a building should determine its design—that, for example, 'a
Champaign open Country, requires a noble and plain
Building, which is always best supplied by the Dorick
Order, or something analogous to its Simplicity' (vol. 1, pp.
67–8). He later developed this essentially pictorial view of
architecture and landscape in two further works, both
published anonymously: *An Essay on Harmony. As it Relates
Chiefly to Situation and Building* (1739) and *The Art of Architecture, a Poem. In Imitation of Horace's 'Art of Poetry'* (1742). In
the *Lectures* Morris also identified seven ideal geometric
proportions for any building and its parts, beginning with
the cube. He claimed that these proportions, comparable
to the seven notes in an octave, could 'produce all the different buildings in the universe' (vol. 1, p. 94). Such a
modular system of building, and the grid planning that it
might seem to prefigure, are perhaps Morris's most interesting contributions to British architectural theory. It is,
however, unlikely that his work was widely read by his
contemporaries: a second edition of volume 1 of the *Lectures* did not appear until 1759, and then only to accompany unsold copies of volume 2.

Morris also published two architectural pattern books:
Rural Architecture (1750) and *The Architectural Remembrancer*
(1751). The regular Palladianism of most of his designs
make them unremarkable except as demonstrations of
his belief in 'the purity and simplicity of the art of designing' (*Rural Architecture*, title-page). In 1755, a year after Morris's death, both works were republished by the book and
print publisher Robert Sayer, but retitled *Select Architecture*
and *Architecture Improved* respectively. Further issues of
these titles in 1757 coincided with Sayer's addition of a few
left-over designs in Morris's hand produced for *The Modern*

Builder's Assistant, by William Halfpenny, John Halfpenny,
and Thomas Lightoler.

There is no evidence that Morris ever travelled outside
Britain or invested in a second language; his opinions
were principally derived from better-known authors such
as the third earl of Shaftesbury, Joseph Addison, and perhaps Francis Hutcheson, combined with English translations of books by Palladio, Roland Fréart, and the Dutch
scholar Lambert Ten Kate. Alexander Pope was his poetical touchstone. Until recently Morris's reputation suffered by a misattribution of some of his anonymous
works to John Gwynn. His writings are now seen to form
the most substantial and coherent contemporary commentary on British architecture in the first half of the
eighteenth century.

Described in his will as a surveyor, Robert Morris's professional career included managing building work for Sir
Michael Newton at Culverthorpe Hall, Lincolnshire, in the
early 1730s, a valuation for the City of London of a model
of George Dance's Mansion House design in 1740, a survey
of brickwork for the banker George Middleton at Twickenham in 1743, and measuring plasterer's work at Sir William Beauchamp Proctor's house in Bruton Street, London, in 1753 or 1754. He was also paid to supply unex-
ecuted designs for the Octagon Chapel in Norwich (1753–
4). He may have made designs for the south front of Culverthorpe, but features of the finished building can be
more reliably attributed to his kinsman Roger Morris.

Morris was also the anonymous author of several minor
literary excursions, mainly poetical, including *An Enquiry
into Virtue* (1740), *Yes, they are* (1740), *Have at you All* (1740),
and *Rupert to Maria: an Heroic Epistle* (1748). He may have
been the author of a political play, *Fatal Necessity, or, Liberty
Regain'd* (Dublin, 1742), and he wrote two pamphlets for
his professional colleagues: *The Qualifications and Duty of a
Surveyor* (1752) and a *Second Letter* on the same subject
(1752). In 1740 he was living in Hyde Park Street, near Grosvenor Square, London, where he remained until at least
1751. According to an eighteenth-century inscription on
the title-page of a copy of his *Essay*, he died on 12 November 1754 (RIBA BAL, 3.1183). In his will, which described
him as 'of St. George's, Hanover Square, Surveyor', he left
his books and drawings to be sold for the benefit of his
children—Thomas, Mary, James, and Hannah—and an
auction of his possessions was reported in the *Public Advertiser* of 8 April 1755.   GERALD BEASLEY

Sources Colvin, *Archs.* · E. Harris and N. Savage, *British architec-
tural books and writers, 1556–1785* (1990) · N. Savage and others, eds.,
*Early printed books, 1478–1840: catalogue of the British Architectural Lib-
rary early imprints collection*, [5 vols.] (1994–) · D. Cruickshank, 'An
English reason: theories behind the formation of a rational architecture, 1712–1750', *ArchR*, 173 (1983), 49–58 · D. Leatherbarrow,
'Architecture and situation: a study of the architectural writings of
Robert Morris', *Journal of the Society of Architectural Historians*, 44
(1985), 48–59

Morris, Robert (1735–1806), financier and revolutionary
politician in America, was born on 20 January 1735 in Liverpool to Robert Morris (1711–1750) and Elizabeth Mur-
phet. Nothing further is known of his mother, and Morris

Robert Morris (1735–1806), by Charles Willson Peale, c.1782

was probably raised by his grandmother. Before 1740 his father left nail-making in Liverpool to become agent for Liverpool tobacco merchants at Oxford, Maryland. Robert joined him there in 1748, and was soon sent to Philadelphia to be educated and apprenticed. Robert pleased his master, merchant Charles Willing, so well that he became a partner in 1754. In 1757 Morris together with Willing's son Thomas began a long and very successful mercantile partnership. Morris managed the business by the time of independence. He later claimed that he had owned more ships than any other American merchant. On 2 March 1769 he married Mary White (1749–1827), daughter of a wealthy Maryland landholder residing in Philadelphia. They had seven children.

Although English-born, Anglican, and having commercial ties to Britain, Morris was a fervent whig who differed little from the most extreme advocates of resistance to Britain. He began his political career in 1765, when he headed a committee of leading citizens to press Pennsylvania stamp distributor John Hughes to refuse that appointment. He served on Philadelphia's or Pennsylvania's committees of resistance during the 1760s and in 1774–6. In 1770, after the North ministry's partial repeal of the Townshend duties, Morris resigned from the Philadelphia non-importation committee, but he did not publicly oppose the boycott. After hostilities commenced at Lexington and Concord he pledged to support the rebel side. The Pennsylvania assembly elected him to the second continental congress in November 1775. He served on congress's major committees. He thought independence premature, and abstained from voting on the resolution

on it on 2 July 1776. Yet he signed the Declaration of Independence in August 1776.

When congress retreated to Baltimore, Morris remained in charge in Philadelphia to save ships from capture, prepare defences, and forward supplies and money to George Washington. He raised $50,000 on his own credit to pay a promised bounty to Washington's troops. Morris's opponents in the Pennsylvania legislature, who favoured the radical state constitution, re-elected him to congress in February 1777, showing non-partisan appreciation for his important service. When John Hancock resigned the congress presidency in October 1777 the members asked Morris to replace him. He declined for business reasons, and in November asked the Pennsylvania council of safety for a leave of absence from congress to attend to his private affairs. The state legislature re-elected him to congress in December and granted his request. He returned to congress to sign the articles of confederation in July 1778, denoting Pennsylvania's ratification. At the end of his 1778 congress term he was ineligible for re-election. He returned to the Pennsylvania legislature for 1778–9 as a partisan opponent of the constitution, but did not succeed in getting it revoked.

Morris as manager of his mercantile firm continued public and private trading, and began privateering, while he was in congress. He became more active in expanding his trading relationships and more prosperous; by 1781 his peers ranked him as the leading merchant in the United States. Richard Henry Lee and some others in congress charged he had misappropriated public funds, designated for supplies, to his own use. He did mix public and private business in his accounting, and in his warehouse and ships. Through loose or inaccurate accounting he may have benefited personally. He also in 1779 incurred the wrath of Philadelphians who believed he sold dry goods above the set price and exported flour in time of great scarcity. Probably these accusations cost Morris his legislature seat and re-election to congress in 1779. Morris and other opponents of Pennsylvania's constitutionalist legal and monetary policies, which had created great controversy, regained their seats in the legislature in 1780 and brought more stability to Pennsylvania's chaotic monetary system. Morris thought this effort so crucial that he delayed taking up the post of superintendent of finance for congress until he completed his legislative agenda in July 1781.

As superintendent, Morris initiated and planned important innovations that were designed to improve the financial and monetary circumstances of the impoverished, powerless confederation government. In September 1781 he got congress to charter the Bank of North America, which would make loans to congress and issue notes. In 1782–3 he also emitted 'Morris's notes', backed by the public credit and his own. The 1783 issue was to pay the army when it was furloughed. Morris's notes were not as well accepted as banknotes, and passed at a discount in markets distant from Philadelphia, but they were an important medium of exchange. Morris signed notes on his credit totalling over $1 million, which he redeemed with timely loans from France and the Netherlands. In July 1782 Morris announced a comprehensive plan for setting the finances of the confederation aright. He advocated domestic and foreign borrowing that would be supported by federal land, poll, and excise taxes both to pay the interest on the debt and to maintain a sinking fund. The plan, Morris noted, would benefit particularly the mercantile community, but also commercial farmers. Morris did not advocate reducing state power generally or increasing upper-class influence in government, only compelling the states to pay their apportionments. Others saw a threat to states' rights. His plan foundered when the impost proposal of 1781 was rejected by Rhode Island and Virginia, and when congress would attempt only another impost that Morris thought inadequate.

In January 1783 Morris suddenly announced his resignation as superintendent, believing that only such a dramatic gesture would get congress and the states to take meaningful action. He also apparently acquiesced in a drastic measure known as the Newburgh conspiracy. He knew that Gouverneur Morris and Alexander Hamilton hoped to use the army as a pressure group to get the state legislatures to grant permanent funding to congress. Robert Morris and his friends ignored the fundamental republican principle of keeping the army out of politics; Washington's address to his officers upheld it.

Morris continued his political activity in the Pennsylvania assembly in 1785–6, arguing against annulling the charter of the Bank of North America and vigorously defending the sanctity of charters once issued. He represented Pennsylvania at the Annapolis convention in 1786 and at the Philadelphia convention in 1787. Uncharacteristically, he did not enter into debate about the particular terms of the proposed constitution. Morris claimed that he refrained because he was no lawyer; he also likely thought that proposals for extending federal power might be better received coming from others. He was undoubtedly satisfied that the new government had the power to tax, to incur debt, and perhaps to charter corporations, and that state paper-money and state abrogation of contracts were prohibited.

Washington invited Morris to be secretary of the treasury, but he declined and recommended Alexander Hamilton. Already in September 1788 the Pennsylvania legislature had elected him senator, and he previously had more success in making policy as a legislator than he had as superintendent of finance. The senate relied on him for advice on commerce, borrowing, raising revenue, and settling accounts. In 1794 he refused re-election because his business interests, particularly land speculation, demanded his time. In these he overextended himself and was sent to debtors' prison in 1798. The Federal Bankruptcy Act of 1800, perhaps passed with Morris's plight in mind, effected his release in 1801. His wife's annuity supported both of them until his death in Philadelphia on 8 May 1806. He was buried at Christ Church, Philadelphia.

BENJAMIN H. NEWCOMB

Sources C. L. Ver Steeg, 'Morris, Robert', *ANB* · E. P. Oberholtzer, *Robert Morris: patriot and financier* (1903) · C. L. Ver Steeg, *Robert Morris: revolutionary financier; with an analysis of his earlier career* (1954) · *The papers of Robert Morris, 1781–1784*, ed. E. J. Ferguson and others, 9 vols. (1973–99) · E. J. Ferguson, *The power of the purse: a history of American public finance, 1776–90* (1961) · J. N. Rakove, *The beginnings of national politics: an interpretive history of the continental congress* (1979) · R. L. Brunhouse, *The counter-revolution in Pennsylvania, 1776–1790* (1942) · R. A. Ryerson, *The revolution is now begun: the radical committees of Philadelphia* (1978) · G. D. Rappaport, *Stability and change in revolutionary Pennsylvania: banking, politics, and social structure* (1996) · B. A. Chernow, *Robert Morris: land speculator, 1790–1801* (1978)
Archives Hist. Soc. Penn. · Hunt. L. · L. Cong. · National Archives and Records Administration, Washington, DC · NYPL · Pennsylvania State Archives, Harrisburg
Likenesses C. W. Peale, oils, *c*.1782, Independence National Historical Park, Philadelphia · C. W. Peale, oils, *c*.1782, New Orleans Museum of Art, Louisiana [*see illus.*]
Wealth at death bankrupt: Ver Steeg, 'Morris, Robert', *ANB*

Morris, Robert (1743–1793), radical, was born in Swansea on 4 August 1743, the elder surviving son, of two sons and four daughters, out of twelve children born to Robert Morris (*d.* 1768), copper industrialist of Swansea, and his wife, Margaret, *née* Jenkins (*d.* 1786), of Machynlleth. Educated at Charterhouse and Oriel College, Oxford (1760–64), Morris enrolled in 1763 at Lincoln's Inn and was called to the bar in 1767. He assisted in the successful defence of Lord Baltimore in a notorious rape case of 1768, but was diverted from his legal career into politics by the Middlesex election episode of 1768–9 concerning John Wilkes, and on 25 February 1769 was elected secretary of the new Society of Supporters of the Bill of Rights. Morris was the public face of the society, since all its notices appeared over his name until he resigned eighteen months later, pleading overwork, and he was known in the press as 'Bill of Rights Morris'. It was Morris, Wilkes, and journalist John Almon who in 1771 concocted the scheme of deploying against parliamentary privilege the chartered rights of the City of London in order to provide a refuge there for printers reporting parliamentary debates. Morris played an active part in the plot, which secured that press freedom, contacting various printers and acting as their learned counsel with the advice that the House of Commons had no legal right to order their arrest. The City of London acknowledged his role by giving him a general retainer and bestowing on him the freedom of the City in April 1771.

Then occurred an escapade that ended both Morris's legal career and his political aspirations. On the death of Lord Baltimore in 1771 Morris was appointed a guardian of his illegitimate children, but in May 1772 eloped to the continent with one of them, twelve-year-old Fanny (Frances Mary) Harford (1759–1832), twice illegally marrying her—at Ypres on 21 May and at Ahrensburgh on 3 January 1773. Fanny soon decided to end the relationship, and returned to Britain in January 1774, Morris following in April. For a decade he fought to prevent annulment of the marriage, which was pronounced void on 21 May 1784. Morris, meanwhile, debarred from his profession, lived off his wits, gambling with loaded dice and suspected even of being a highwayman. In 1785 he turned over a new leaf, returning to south Wales on marrying a farmer's daughter, Sarah Prichard (*d.* 1789), on 28 June 1785 and inheriting the family estate of Tredegar Fawr, near Swansea, on his mother's death in 1786. Now a small squire, Morris participated in a Glamorgan by-election of 1789, writing several pamphlets to support a candidate successfully challenging the local oligarchy.

Respectability beckoned, but on the sudden death of his wife in 1789 Morris again threw discretion to the winds. In 1790 he obtained permission from the East India Company to practise law in Bengal, but found on his arrival that the judges there, aware of his unsavoury past, refused to allow him to do so. Morris then visited numerous gaols in Bengal, informing many prisoners that they were being illegally detained and should break out. He died of a liver complaint, and was buried in India on 29 November 1793. 'I do love bustle, variety and disturbance to my very soul', Morris wrote in his diary for 12 May 1774, and that may serve as his epitaph (*Radical Adventurer*, 172). His lively and erratic career contrasts with that of his younger brother John, who so well managed the family copper business that Morriston developed as a company town, and he obtained a knighthood in 1806.   PETER D. G. THOMAS

Sources P. D. G. Thomas, '"Bill of Rights Morris", a Welsh Wilkite radical and rogue: Robert Morris (1743–1793)', *Hanoverian Britain and Empire: essays in memory of Philip Lawson*, ed. S. Taylor, R. Connors, and C. Jones (1998), 267–87 · *Radical adventurer: the diaries of Robert Morris, 1772–1774*, ed. J. E. Ross (1971) · P. D. G. Thomas, *John Wilkes: a friend to liberty* (1996) · W. Jones, 'Robert Morris, the Swansea friend of John Wilkes', *Glamorgan Historian*, 11 (1975), 128–36 · *Memoirs of William Hickey*, ed. A. Spencer, 4 vols. (1913–25) · N. C. Davies, 'The Bill of Rights Society and the origins of radicalism in Britain', MA diss., U. Wales, 1986
Archives U. Wales, Swansea, journal | BL, corresp. with John Wilkes, Add. MSS 30865–30896
Likenesses caricature, 1787, repro. in *Radical adventurer*, 22
Wealth at death see will, described in *Radical adventurer*, 42–3

Morris, Robert Hunter (*c*.1714–1764), jurist and colonial governor, was born at Morrisania Manor, Westchester county, New York, to Lewis *Morris (1671–1746), politician, and Isabella Graham (1673–1752). He obtained a classical education at home from tutors. In 1735 and 1736 he lived in London, where he broadened his cultural horizons and met many of Whitehall's leading figures. Although raised in the Church of England, he enthusiastically embraced deism. Morris inherited Tinton Manor, an estate of 6000 acres with an ironworks, in Monmouth county, New Jersey. He never married, but in his will he acknowledged two illegitimate children, a daughter, Mary, whose mother was Elizabeth Stogdale, and a son, Robert, who in 1777 became the third generation of his family to sit on New Jersey's supreme court (as chief justice), whose mother is unknown.

Morris attained high public office in his mid-twenties, not by virtue of his considerable erudition and talents but through unabashed nepotism. Within months of assuming New Jersey's governorship in 1738, his father named him to the colony's royal council (the legislature's upper house) and appointed him chief justice in 1739 despite his lack of any judicial experience. The younger Morris nevertheless acquitted himself well on the bench, and was later eulogized for having 'reduced the pleadings to precision and method' (Smith, 439). As a councillor he dominated the upper house of the legislature, where he acted as his father's cat's-paw to block legislation sought by the assembly. After his father provoked a succession of rancorous disputes with the lower house, in particular by repeatedly obstructing bills to issue paper money, government became deadlocked. The assembly halved the salaries of both Morrises in 1744, and then left them completely unpaid until the new governor, Jonathan Belcher, arrived in 1747.

Violence meanwhile had ensued from lawsuits by the East Jersey Board of Proprietors (to which Morris belonged) to dispossess innumerable landowners occupying 330,000 acres, as crowds forcibly blocked evictions, assaulted proprietary tenants, and staged gaolbreakings. The proprietors' influence upon the colony's supreme court proved highly inflammatory, especially after allegations surfaced in 1745 that Chief Justice Morris relied on perjured testimony to overturn a verdict against another proprietor sitting on his court in a case involving 17,500 acres. Morris orchestrated the council's demands for draconian measures (including bills of attainder) to quell the unrest and for payment of all salary arrearages due to his father and himself; when the assembly and governor baulked, he stymied government by mobilizing the upper house to forestall appropriating the new governor's salary and to obstruct important legislation.

In 1749 Morris went to London and pilloried his political adversaries' reputations at Whitehall with such venom as could only spew from 'a young man full of malice', as Belcher derided him (Nadelhaft, 50). Morris could not persuade the Board of Trade to suppress the land disorders with British regulars or to recall Belcher, but he convinced it to disallow several bills eagerly sought by the assembly. He furthermore preserved the proprietors' majority on the council by inducing the board to disqualify two of Belcher's nominees and substitute his own supporters in 1751.

Morris sailed to America in 1754 as Pennsylvania's chief executive (deputy governor), who represented the proprietary interest of the Penns. He met his match in its Quaker-dominated assembly, whose popularity with the voters left him too politically isolated to influence legislation. After twenty-two inglorious months in office, he resigned, and resumed his chief justiceship, whose commission the crown had neglected to rescind when he became governor. Again in London in 1757, he unsuccessfully lobbied to increase the East Jersey Board of Proprietors' landholdings by adjusting New Jersey's boundary at New York's expense. He left England in 1759 to thwart the Board of Trade's attempt to have an English placeman supersede him as chief justice, and triumphed over Whitehall in 1760 when New Jersey's supreme court sustained his own claim to that post.

On 27 January 1764, at a ball in Shrewsbury, New Jersey, Morris capped an evening of raucous merrymaking by dancing down six couples who challenged him and his partner to jigs—and suddenly dropped dead. He was buried at his home, Tinton Manor, Monmouth county. Samuel Smith, his fellow councillor, characterized him as a man whose 'easy address, smooth flow of words', and sophisticated demeanour belied a 'formidable enemy', who was 'sometimes whimsical, always opinionated, and mostly inflexible' (Smith, 439).   THOMAS L. PURVIS

Sources J. E. Stillwell, 'Morris of Monmouth county', *Historical and genealogical miscellany*, 4 (1916), 14–70, esp. 25–37, 44 • S. Smith, *The history of the colony of Nova-Caesaria, or New Jersey* (1765) • J. J. Nadelhaft, 'Politics and the judicial tenure fight in colonial New Jersey', *William and Mary Quarterly*, 28 (1971), 46–63 • T. L. Purvis, *Proprietors, patronage, and paper money: legislative politics in New Jersey, 1703–1776* (1986) • E. R. Sheridan, 'Morris, Robert Hunter', *ANB* • E. R. Sheridan, *Lewis Morris, 1671–1746: a study in early American politics* (1981)
Archives New Jersey Historical Society, Newark • Rutgers University, New Brunswick, New Jersey, family MSS | New Jersey Historical Society, Newark, New Jersey MSS • New Jersey Historical Society, Newark, F. J. Paris MSS • New York Historical Society, J. Alexander MSS
Likenesses oils, *c*.1750, Frick Art and Historical Center, Pittsburgh, Pennsylvania
Wealth at death £6115 12*s*. 3*d*. in personal property; approx. £20,000 in real estate: inventory, 24 July 1764, Newark, New Jersey Historical Society, Stevens family MSS

Morris [Morys], **Roger** (1551/2?–1597×1600), antiquary and recusant, was perhaps the Roger Morris of Flintshire at Hart Hall, Oxford, aged nineteen in 1571. His later home was at Coedytalwrn, parish of Llanfair Dyffryn Clwyd, Denbighshire.

Morris is hardly known except through his manuscripts, written in a notably neat and unostentatious hand, a hand which would be nameless had not two contemporaries, John Jones and Thomas Evans, left notes identifying it as that of Roger Morris. His early hand is seen in parts of the National Library of Wales, Peniarth MS 169 and Cwrtmawr MS 530, written before 1582: by that date he had adopted the dotted Welsh orthography of Gruffudd Robert, which he adhered to for the rest of his life. Early interests were Welsh grammar, including bardic grammar and the bardic musical tradition; later ones included history, hagiography, narrative (he was an early transcriber of the *Mabinogion*), Welsh law, and medicine. He had access to good manuscripts, among them the Black Book of Carmarthen and the White Book of Rhydderch, and to others now lost; he was generally a careful noter of sources. His manuscripts link him to scholars and antiquaries both protestant and Catholic, including William Salesbury, Thomas Wiliems, Richard Langford, and Simwnt Fychan, and probably Gruffudd Robert. Some texts in his manuscripts appear to be of his own composition. These include a treatise on British history (in Peniarth MS 168, dated 1589–90), tracts on grammar (in BL, Add. MS 15046, written after 1591), and additions to William Salesbury's herbal (in NL Wales, MS 4581, dated 1597). Ten manuscripts written by him survive: NL Wales, MSS 1553, 3032, 3043, and 4581, Llanstephan MSS 9 and 34, Peniarth MSS 168 and 169, and Cwrtmawr MS 530; and BL, Add. MS 15046.

Morris's Roman Catholic inclinations are evident in some of his manuscripts (an invocation of St Winifred in Llanstephan MS 34, his collection of *vitae*, a favourite recusant text, in NL Wales, MS 1553). In 1594, as Roger Morris, 'gentleman', of Llanfair Dyffryn Clwyd, he was bound in £100 to receive holy communion.

Morris's last dated manuscript is from 1597. He was probably dead by 1600. In 1600 one Robert ap Huw (the famous harper, as seems likely, at that time a youth) was indicted in Denbighshire for theft, of papers among other things. Robert ap Huw in his examination refers to papers and Welsh books which he had from Edward ap John of Coedytalwrn: questions arise about the occupancy of Coedytalwrn by that year and the dispersal of Roger Morris's manuscripts. Several of Morris's manuscripts were by 1607 in the possession of Thomas Evans of Hendreforfudd. The contents of many of his manuscripts, including some which do not survive, are preserved in copies made by John Jones of Gellilyfdy in the years 1604–12; the contents of other lost manuscripts are preserved in copies by Thomas Wiliems, John Davies of Mallwyd, and William Jones of Llangadfan.   DANIEL HUWS

Sources *DWB* • R. I. D. Jones, 'Astudiaeth Feirniadol o Peniarth 168B (tt. 41a–126b)', MA diss., U. Wales, 1954 • N. Lloyd, 'A history of Welsh scholarship in the first half of the seventeenth century, with special reference to the writings of John Jones, Gellilyfdy', DPhil diss., U. Oxf., 1970 • N. Watcyn-Powel, 'Robert ap Huw: a wanton minstrel of Anglesey', *Welsh Music History / Hanes Cerddoriaeth Cymru* [Robert ap Huw issue, ed. S. Harper], 3 (1999), 5–29 • great sessions records, NL Wales, 4/11/4/13–15, 19–20 • G. J. Williams, *Gramadegau'r Penceirddiaid* (1934) • I. Edgar, *Llysieulyfr Salesbury* (1997)
Archives NL Wales, collection of Welsh anecdotes, proverbs, poems, etc.

Morris, Roger (1695–1749), architect, was born in London on 19 April 1695, the eldest son in the family of two daughters and five sons of Owen Morris and his wife, Rebecca. Little is known of his early life except that his background was in the building trades—he was described in 1724 as a bricklayer, and later as a carpenter—but by the mid-1720s he had established two connections which gave him a place among the innermost circles of English Palladianism. One was with the architect Colen Campbell, to whom he acted as assistant for a time. He was certainly performing this service in 1729, towards the end of Campbell's life, drawing out designs for works at Studley Royal, Yorkshire, and he appears to have done so previously.

The other connection was with Henry Herbert, later ninth earl of Pembroke. Morris was to become Herbert's architectural collaborator, in effect succeeding Campbell in this role. The contact presumably originated at Pembroke House, the building of which appears to have constituted Lord Herbert's architectural apprenticeship. The collaboration was then inaugurated at Marble Hill, Twickenham (1724–9), which was the first of the buildings credited to Lord Herbert, and it was continued at most, if not all, of his subsequent works—including among others the White Lodge, Richmond Park (1727–8), for King George II, and the Palladian Bridge at his own seat of Wilton House, Wiltshire (1736–7). Morris's role appears to have been both that of a clerk of works, responsible to a greater or lesser degree for the erection of the buildings, and that of an architectural amanuensis employed to make 'drawings and explanations of his lordship's directions' (M. P. G. Draper and W. A. Eden, *Marble Hill House*, 1971, 6); but to what extent he was involved in the actual process of design is not certain. At any rate Herbert clearly had a high regard for his services, for in 1734 he presented him with a large silver cup as a token of his appreciation.

From this position Morris was soon able both to develop a practice of his own and to secure the fruits of public office: as early as 1727 he was referred to in print as 'the noted architect Mr. Morris' (E. Laurence, *The Duty of a Steward to his Lord*, 1727, 50), and in 1731–2 he made a visit to Italy. His private practice was never very large but it was highly prestigious. His principal patrons were the family of the dukes of Argyll, his commissions from them including Combe Bank, Kent (*c.*1725)—his first major independent work—Whitton Place, Twickenham (*c.*1732–9; dem.), and his largest undertaking, Inveraray Castle, Argyll (begun 1745); and this was a contact which appears to have originated at Marble Hill. In addition he developed an association with Richard Boyle, third earl of Burlington: it was under the direction of Burlington and Herbert that he remodelled Castle Hill, Devon (1729–40); and Kirby Hall, Yorkshire (begun 1747), was their joint design. Meanwhile, in the Office of Works he was in 1727 appropriately appointed to the new post of clerk of the works at the White Lodge, doubtless through the influence of Herbert; in 1734 he was made master carpenter to the Board of Ordnance, a lucrative preferment which he undoubtedly owed to John Campbell, second duke of Argyll, who was then master-general of the ordnance; and at the time of his death he held the position of surveyor to the mint. A final aspect of his career was his extensive involvement in speculative building development in London, in Argyll Street (1736) and New Palace Yard (1740–42), an activity which evidently made a significant contribution to his prosperity.

The sum of the projects with which Morris was involved represents a major contribution to more than one strand of eighteenth-century architecture. Of his collaborative works with Herbert, Marble Hill and the White Lodge are classic examples of the first-generation Anglo-Palladian villa, of which the former in particular was to be a highly influential model among later designers; while the bridge at Wilton is one of the most perfect and most memorably inventive of all Anglo-Palladian images, and was to be faithfully copied on four occasions—at Stowe (by 1742), Prior Park, Bath (1756), Hagley (by 1764), and Amesbury (1777). His own Palladian compositions show a number of idiosyncrasies of detail, the only significant one being a frequent use of the pyramidal roof form derived, *inter alia*, from Palladio's Villa Emo and already repeated at Pembroke Lodge and Marble Hill; but other elements are more noteworthy. At Whitton Place he appears to have been one of the first Palladian architects to employ the three-sided bay-window motif; his stable block at Althorp, Northamptonshire (1732–3), with its portico derived from Inigo Jones's St Paul's Church, Covent Garden, is exceptional

for the time in its exploitation of the bold simplicity of the Tuscan order; and a similarly austere, proto-neo-classical manner characterizes certain other works which may be attributable to him, notably the church at Mereworth, Kent (1744–6). Also remarkable are his two houses in the Gothic style. Clearwell Castle, Gloucestershire (*c.*1728), is a unique building, with no affinity either to the contemporary medievalizing modes of Sir John Vanbrugh and Nicholas Hawksmoor or to the subsequent rococo Gothic of William Kent; while Inveraray Castle, by contrast, was to be another immensely influential creation, standing at the head of a whole series of castle-style houses throughout the eighteenth century.

Morris had as a 'kinsman' the architectural writer Robert *Morris (1703–1754), who in the dedication to his *Lectures on Architecture* (1734) acknowledged the 'erudition' he had received in Roger's service. He was married twice. His first wife, Mary, daughter of Sir Peter Jackson of London, a merchant trading with Turkey, died in 1729; his second, Elizabeth (*d.* 1744), whom he married in 1731, was the daughter of Sir Philip Jackson of Richmond, Surrey. With his first wife he had two children who survived infancy, both of them sons, and with his second wife he had a son and four daughters. The eldest son, James, succeeded his father as master carpenter to the ordnance and lived the life of a country gentleman in Surrey, serving as high sheriff of the county in 1764. The second son was the soldier and American loyalist Colonel Roger *Morris (1727–1794). Morris died in London on 31 January 1749 and was buried at St George's, Hanover Square.

ROSEMARY MITCHELL

Sources *The Builder*, 33 (1875) · Colvin, *Archs.* · [W. Papworth], ed., *The dictionary of architecture*, 11 vols. (1853–92) · G. L. M. Goodfellow, 'Colen Campbell's last years', *Burlington Magazine*, 111 (1969), 85–91 · J. Lees-Milne, *Earls of creation* (1962) · H. Walpole, *Anecdotes of painting in England: with some account of the principal artists*, ed. R. N. Wornum, new edn, 3 (1849) · P. Leach, 'The Thompson mausoleum at Little Ouseburn and its architect', *Georgian Group Journal*, 8 (1998) · S. Parissien, 'The careers of Roger and Robert Morris', DPhil diss., U. Oxf., 1989
Archives Yale U. CBA | NL Scot., MS 17878

Morris, Roger (1727–1794), army officer and landowner, was born in Yorkshire on 28 January 1727, the second son of Roger *Morris (1695–1749), an architect of Netherby, in the North Riding of Yorkshire, and Mary (*d.* 1729), the daughter of Sir Peter Jackson, a London merchant with Turkish trading connections. On 13 September 1745 was appointed captain in Francis Ligonier's 48th regiment of foot, and served at Falkirk and Culloden, and in Flanders. Morris went to America with his regiment in 1755, and was aide-de-camp to Major-General Edward Braddock in the ill-fated expedition against Fort Duquesne (9 July 1755), where he was wounded. On 16 February 1758 he purchased a major's commission in the 35th regiment of foot and took part in the siege of Louisbourg. In the same year he married Mary (Polly) Philipse (1729/30–1825), the daughter of Frederick Philipse, second lord of Philipsborough Manor, a substantial landowner: they had four children. His union with Mary, whom George Washington had previously hoped to marry, brought Morris considerable wealth by way of his father-in-law's landholdings. In September 1759 he served with General James Wolfe at Quebec, and was involved in its subsequent defence at the battle of Sillery in April 1760. In the following month he was made lieutenant-colonel of the 47th regiment of foot. During the final years of his military career Morris served as aide-de-camp to generals Thomas Gage and Jeffrey Amherst, Lord Amherst, and commanded a detachment at the successful siege of Montreal (8 September 1760).

On 15 June 1764 Morris sold his commission and moved to a house on the corner of Whitehall and Stone Street, New York, and in the following year the family purchased a homestead, Mount Morris (later known as Jumel Mansion) in upper Manhattan Island. From 1764 Morris served on the royal council for the colony of New York. In May 1775 he travelled to England and returned to New York in December 1777, whereupon, after some equivocation, he chose to support the loyalist cause during the American War of Independence. He resumed his position on the council under the tory military administration of James Robertson, and on 1 January 1779 became, until the war's conclusion, inspector of the claims of refugees.

In October 1777 the Morrises' estates were confiscated by the New York state legislature's act of attainder. In July 1784 the commissioners of sequestration and commissioners of forfeiture sold Mount Morris for £2250; by this date the family had moved to England. Morris died at York on 13 September 1794, and is thought to have been buried at the city's St Saviour's Gate Church. He was survived by his wife, the inspiration for the heroine of James Fenimore Cooper's novel *The Spy* (1831); she died, also in York, in 1825 aged ninety-five. Their elder son, Amherst (d. 1802), entered the Royal Navy, and was first lieutenant of the frigate *Nymphe* in her famous action with the French frigate *La Cléopâtre*. His brother Henry Gage Morris, the father of the naturalist Francis Orpen Morris, became a rear-admiral in the Royal Navy; he died at Beverley on 24 November 1851. Claims by the Morris family to gain compensation for the loss of their American estates met with only partial success: the British government awarded them just over £12,000 in response to their claim for £68,384. It was judged that Morris's children held reversionary interests to the property; these were sold after Morris's death and subsequently resold to the state of New York for $500,000.   PHILIP CARTER

Sources H. M. Ward, 'Morris, Roger', *ANB* · W. H. Shelton, *The Jumel mansion* (Boston, MA, 1916)

Morris, Staats Long (1728–1800), army officer, was born in New York on 27 August 1728, a younger son of Lewis Morris (d. 1762) of Morrisiana, New York, a judge of admiralty court and prominent landowner in the colony, and his wife, Tryntie (or Catherine) Staats. His grandfather was Lewis *Morris (1671–1746). Despite attending Yale College from 1743 to 1746, Morris determined on a military career and obtained a free commission (death vacancy) as a lieutenant in Captain John Rutherford's New York independent company on 23 July 1748, purchased the captain-lieutenancy of the governor's New York independent

company on 1 November 1751, and then became a captain in William Shirley's regular 55th foot on 12 February 1755.

In December of that year Shirley sent Morris to England with dispatches and he exchanged as a captain into the 36th foot with effect from 31 May 1756, thus avoiding the destruction of the 55th when it surrendered to the French at Fort Oswego. Equally fortunately, in the meantime he had married Catherine *Gordon, dowager duchess of Gordon (1718–1779), on 25 March 1756. It was felt in some quarters that the duchess had married beneath herself, but according to the *English Chronicle* in 1781 Morris

> conducted himself in this new exaltation with so much moderation, affability and friendship, that the family soon forgot the degradation the Duchess had been guilty of by such a connexion, and received her spouse into their perfect favour and esteem. (Haden-Guest, 168)

His marriage also brought with it the political influence to obtain letters of service for the raising of his own 89th highlanders, also known as the Gordon Highlanders, of which he was commissioned lieutenant-colonel commandant on 13 October 1759. Once complete the regiment was ordered to India but, although it served at the capture of Pondicherry in 1761, Morris himself apparently did not leave England until April 1762. Nevertheless by 21 January 1763 he was in command of British troops in Bombay and given a local commission as brigadier in the East Indies on 7 July 1763, before returning home in December and going on to half-pay when his regiment was disbanded early in 1765. On 25 May 1772 he was promoted colonel by brevet and during the American War of Independence was successively promoted to major-general on 29 August 1777 and lieutenant-general on 20 November 1782. However, apart from commanding a brigade in the Coxheath camp in 1778–9, he saw no active service during this period, probably because his elder brother Lewis was one of the signatories of the American Declaration of Independence and he was consequently reputed to be averse to service in America. His half-brother, Gouverneur *Morris (1752–1816), was also a prominent revolutionary. Instead, with the support of his stepson Alexander *Gordon, fourth duke of Gordon, he was returned to parliament in 1774 for the Elgin burghs and there consistently voted with the administration. This did not go unnoticed and after Lord North testified to 'Colonel Morris's most constant, uniform, zealous and disinterested support of Government ever since he has been in the House of Commons' (*Correspondence*, ed. Fortescue, 3.411) he was made colonel of the 61st foot on 14 May 1778.

After the death of his wife on 16 December 1779, and his second marriage on 23 December 1780 to Jean (Jane) Urquhart (1748–1801), of Craigston, Morris's relationship with the duke of Gordon deteriorated sharply. Without the Gordons' influence he lost his seat in the 1784 election and the next ten years were virtually spent in retirement. He and his wife divided most of their time between London and France, where they were in the habit of wintering at Avignon and Spa. In 1793, however, he was given an active appointment on the staff, as second-in-command of the western district, with particular responsibility for Dorset and Cornwall. He held this post until promoted to general on 3 May 1796. At this point he was again retired, but was appointed governor of Quebec on 15 December 1797. The recommendation of Morris for the post by Frederick, duke of York, was hardly enthusiastic, for he wrote to the king:

> The only officers of any length of service who have applied for Governments are Generals Morris, St. John and Lieutenant General Dalrymple. As I am not aware of any distinguishing feature of military merit amongst these three, your Majesty may possibly prefer the oldest and poorest of them, which is General Morris, and promote him to the Government of Quebec. (*Later Correspondence of George III*, 2.646)

The post was however a sinecure and Morris died at his home, Berrymead Lodge, Acton, Middlesex, on 2 April 1800. While his career was by no means distinguished it clearly demonstrated that being born an American was no impediment to attaining high rank in the British army. He is also said to be the only American buried in Westminster Abbey, where he was interred in the north aisle of the nave on 7 April 1800. STUART REID

Sources E. Haden-Guest, 'Morris, Staats Long', HoP, *Commons, 1754–90* · M. M. Boatner, *Cassell's biographical dictionary of the American War of Independence, 1763–1783* (1973) · J. M. Bulloch, *Territorial soldiering in the north-east of Scotland during 1759–1814* (1914) · PRO, W03, W025, W031, W064 · *Army List* · *The correspondence of King George the Third from 1760 to December 1783*, ed. J. Fortescue, 6 vols. (1927–8) · *The later correspondence of George III*, ed. A. Aspinall, 5 vols. (1962–70) · burial register, Westminster Abbey
Archives BL, military letter-book, Add. MS 5939
Likenesses J. Wollaston, oils, *c.*1748–1752, New Orleans Museum of Art; repro. in *Antiques* (Nov 1977)
Wealth at death see will, PRO, PROB 11/1340, sig. 296

Morris, Thomas. *See* Morrice, Thomas (1659/60–1748).

Morris, Thomas (*bap.* 1732, *d.* 1818?). *See under* Morris, Charles (1745–1838).

Morris, Thomas (*b. c.*1750, *d.* in or after 1811), engraver, the son of Samuel Morris, a hatter of Southwark, London, was born about 1750 or a little earlier. On 2 May 1764 he was apprenticed for seven years to the line engraver William Woollett, and in 1766 and 1767 he exhibited engravings with the Free Society of Artists, giving Woollett's house in Long's Court, St Martin's Lane, as his address. These landscapes, after George Smith of Chichester and Richard Wilson, were published by Thomas Bradford and, together with another after Aelbert Cuyp, exhibited in 1768, they launched Morris's career as a line engraver specializing in landscape and architecture. Morris had also begun to engrave architecture while still an apprentice, when he produced plates for James Paine's *Plans, Elevations and Sections, of Noblemen and Gentlemen's Houses* (1767) and one for Matthew Brettingham's *Plans, Elevations and Sections, of Holkham in Norfolk, the Seat of the Late Earl of Leicester* (1761, but Morris's plate was probably added later to a growing compilation); he engraved a further six plates for the second edition of 1773. He produced one plate for *The Works in Architecture of Robert and James Adam Esquires* (1773–9) and in 1775 and 1776 exhibited engravings of architecture and

ornament with the Society of Artists. As a landscape engraver Morris became the favourite interpreter of the animal painter Sawrey Gilpin and his pupil and son-in-law George Garrard. For them he produced a number of his most distinguished publications, including *The Happy Meeting* (1780), *Hawking* (1780), and *Foxhunting* (1783), after Gilpin, and *Mares and Foals* (a pair, 1793). Other notable engravings include *A View of Ludgate Hill* and *A View of the Monument*, after William Marlow (1795), and views of the ranger's house in Greenwich Park and of Sir Gregory Turner's Blackheath villa for the set of six after George Robertson, these being the only plates that Morris produced for Boydell. He etched a few of his own designs, among them London stable scenes published by George Townly Stubbs (1795) and a pair of views on the Avon near Bristol (1802). His last known plate was *Wobourn Sheepshearing* (1811), after Garrard. F. M. O'DONOGHUE, *rev.* TIMOTHY CLAYTON

Sources Graves, *Soc. Artists* · E. Harris and N. Savage, *British architectural books and writers, 1556–1785* (1990) · Goldsmith's Company, Binding Book VIII, p. 25 · *Public Advertiser* (29 July 1766) · *Neue Bibliothek der schönen Wissenschaften und der freyen Künste*, 26 (1781), 362 · *Neue Bibliothek der schönen Wissenschaften und der freyen Künste*, 30 (1785), 149 · D. Snelgrove, *British sporting and animal prints, 1658–1874* (1981) · private information (2004)

Morris, Thomas [Tom; *called* Old Tom Morris] (1821–1908), golfer, second son of John Morris, a postman in St Andrews, Fife, who later became a caddie, and Jean Bruce, who came from Anstruther, was born in North Street, St Andrews, on 16 June 1821. After a sound elementary education at Madras College in the town he was expected to train as a general carpenter but was apprenticed instead to a St Andrews golf club maker, Allan Robertson, for whom he worked for nine years, the last four as a journeyman. Like most boys in his situation he also caddied and played golf intermittently and his involvement in the sport became more serious as he began to partner Robertson in local exhibition matches. These often attracted considerable prize and betting money from local gamblers, the most notable example being a stake of £400 placed on them to defeat a similar pair.

The partnership ended in 1851 following Morris's marriage to a coachman's daughter, Nancy Bayne, with whom he had two sons and a daughter. He moved to Prestwick, Ayrshire, where he combined keeping the new golf links with making clubs and balls and playing exhibition matches for cash prizes. It is said that after he defeated Robertson in one such match in 1853 the latter refused to play him again because Morris had forsaken the old feather balls for the new 'gutties', stuffed with gutta-percha and offering a longer range. Morris's subsequent adversary was Willie Park of Musselburgh, whose flair and strength were matched by Morris's careful and unflustered skills. Over the next twenty years the two men dominated matches in Scotland, each winning as often as the other and together doing a great deal to popularize the game at home and among English holiday visitors.

From its institution in 1860 until 1896 Morris played the open championship every time it was staged. He won four strength and skill into old age provided another reason for golf's growing popularity, as a life-extending activity for middle-aged businessmen.

Morris's longevity was tragically not matched by that of his eldest son, **Thomas** [Tom] **Morris** [*called* Young Tom Morris] (1851–1875). Born at St Andrews on 20 April 1851, Young Tom together with his younger brother, J. O. F. Morris (*d.* 1906), followed his father into the clubmaking business and into competitions. By the time he reached twenty Young Tom was an outstanding player. In 1868 he won the open and he went on to win the next three titles as well, becoming outright winner of the championship belt. He was clearly expected to be the greatest golfer of late Victorian Britain, with a style far more graceful than his father's and a capacity for consistent record scores; Old Tom claimed that his son was the one opponent he could not match. However, the younger man's ebullient career ended unexpectedly on Christmas day 1875, when he was found dead in his bed, following a lung haemorrhage, at his home, 6 Pilmour Links, St Andrews. He was buried in St Andrews Cathedral churchyard. Less than four months earlier, on 4 September 1875, his wife had died, together with their baby, in childbirth. The sense of loss throughout the game was considerable and members of some sixty golfing societies subscribed to buy a three-quarters life-size memorial, executed by John Rhind and placed in St Andrews Cathedral cemetery, which shows him playing.

Despite his son's death, Old Tom continued to play, and recovered some form in the later 1870s, when he won professional matches both in England and in Scotland. Although he was eventually given a handicap, to reflect the slow decline brought about by age, he still stayed among the leaders until he reached his seventies. At the age of seventy-two he won the annual St Andrews competition held between his own employees and those of his commercial rival, the club maker Robert Forgan; despite his handicap of five, he finished well ahead of the younger men.

By this time Morris was almost as much a tourist attraction in St Andrews as the old course itself, and he clearly enjoyed this and the deference shown by both visitors and fellow townsmen. The members of the Royal and Ancient commissioned a portrait of him from Sir George Reid in 1903 and he retired from their paid employment the following year, although he continued to occupy an emeritus position. Old Tom died after a fall on the stairs of the New Golf Club in St Andrews on 24 May 1908.

With Morris's death golf's first era of great expansion ended. A club and tournament professional and a successful businessman, Old Tom epitomized the uncertain social position of an outstanding 'artisan' player who depended on amateurs for patronage and employment. He offered a model for many ambitious young Scotsmen who staffed the links of England and North America, usually with far less prestige. He became golf's greatest icon, and was represented subsequently in photographs, paintings, cigarette cards, Staffordshire ware pottery, and hundreds of different souvenirs. His death symbolized the

Thomas Morris [Old Tom Morris] (**1821–1908**), by Sir George Reid, 1903

times: in 1861, 1862, 1864, and 1866. In 1863 he was persuaded to return to St Andrews, as greenkeeper to the Royal and Ancient Golf Club, a job which he combined with running a flourishing manufacturing and retail business. His presence at the Royal and Ancient did much to extend the game; he provided advice on developing new links, supplied the implements of play, and, above all, became the epitome of the canny Scottish golfer. He was a key figure in the series of booms which transformed golf from 'Scottish croquet' into a game played internationally. His personal style helped to ensure the continuation of Scottish moral hegemony through all the changes. Just as the club which employed him eventually became the official arbiter of golfing etiquette, so Morris's advice was frequently and urgently sought on many issues. By the 1890s he was regarded widely as 'the veritable Nestor' of the game, a wise peacemaker in many disputes.

Although he owed much of his initial fame to playing in wagered matches, Morris held strong religious beliefs, deeply rooted in Scottish Presbyterianism. He took his turn as an elder in St Andrews parish church, served briefly on the general assembly of the Church of Scotland, and opposed Sunday play (on the grounds that the links needed a rest as much as did the players and staff). A sturdy, black-bearded figure—in his later years gradually whitening (*DNB*)—he enjoyed robust good health, swam daily in the sea, and was an enthusiast for fresh air. His apparent end of an age of supposed innocence for a game that he had done so much to popularize and which in the course of his career had become far more sophisticated.

J. R. LOWERSON

Sources W. W. Tulloch, *The life of Tom Morris* (1907) • H. G. Hutchinson, *Golf* (1893) • G. Cousins, *Golf in Britain* (1975) • T. Barrett, *The complete golf chronicle* (1994) • J. Lowerson, 'Golf and the making of myths', *Scottish sport in the making of the nation*, ed. G. Jarvie and A. Walker (1994) • DNB • Boase, *Mod. Eng. biog.* [Thomas Morris the younger]
Likenesses G. Reid, oils, 1903, Royal and Ancient Golf Club, St Andrews [see illus.] • Rodgers?, photograph (Thomas Morris the younger), repro. in Tulloch, *Life of Tom Morris*, 154 • memorial (Thomas Morris the younger), St Andrews Cathedral cemetery • photograph (Thomas Morris the younger), repro. in *British Sports and Sportsmen*, 2 (1908), 291
Wealth at death £300 8s.: confirmation, 9 Oct 1908, CCI

Morris, Thomas (1851–1875). *See under* Morris, Thomas (1821–1908).

Morris, William (1705–1763), antiquary and botanist, was born on 1 May 1705 at Fferam in the parish of Llanfihangel Tre'r-beirdd, Anglesey, the third of five children of Morris Prichard (1674–1763), cooper, tenant farmer, and small merchant, and Marged Morris (1671–1752). Both parents were of Anglesey gentry stock. In 1707 William moved with his parents and three brothers to Pentre-eiriannell, a farm in the neighbouring parish of Penrhosllugwy, overlooking the Dulas estuary.

William was taught to read by his father and for a short time attended a school near the parish church. As well as helping his father on the farm it is more than likely that he also assisted him in running a sloop which traded on the coast of north Wales and as far as Liverpool. This activity eventually led him, in 1726, to that port, where, for the following ten years, he was employed by a Welsh merchant, Owen Prichard, a native of Anglesey, who through his marriage with Philipia Wright in 1718 had become stepfather to Fortunatus Wright (1712–1757), the famous privateer.

In March 1737 Morris was appointed deputy comptroller of the customs and also comptroller of the coal duties at Holyhead, where his elder brother, Lewis *Morris, had been customs officer since 1729. William was to hold this post, with its short hours and long periods of inactivity, for the remainder of his life. On 5 February 1745 he married Jane (1719–1750), daughter of Robert Hughes of Holyhead, the owner of a small estate in the parish of Llanfigel, Anglesey, which was subsequently inherited by William's son, Robert. Two other children were born of this marriage: William (died an infant in December 1748) and Jane. Morris's wife died and was buried on 2 May 1750; he did not remarry.

From early childhood Morris had been immersed in the folk culture of Anglesey, where poetry and music were still transmitted orally. Little is known of his literary pursuits while he was at Liverpool, but from there he began to correspond with his brother Richard *Morris, who had settled in London in 1722, and with his brother Lewis in Anglesey, a correspondence which continued for the remainder of their lives. A substantial number of these letters has survived, and show how varied the Morrises' interests were.

While settled at Holyhead, William Morris's various interests became evident. He derived great pleasure from gardening and not only secured seeds and plants from various contacts in London but also from seamen, who at his request brought them from foreign lands. This led him to a serious study of botany. With the help of specialist books on the subject he began forming a catalogue of plants with their Latin, Welsh, and English names, and his search for specimens took him to Snowdonia and as far as Flintshire. Morris's life as a naturalist was in part inspired by his relationship with the young Thomas Pennant (1726–1798), the famous naturalist, whom he assisted unsparingly. Not surprisingly Morris was the only subscriber from north Wales to Pennant's *British Zoology* (1766), which began to appear in parts before Morris's death. He formed his own collection of fossils, shells, birds, minerals, and such like, and through Pennant became acquainted with other botanists and naturalists in England, Ireland, and on the continent. This meant that when he discovered a unique fish, *Leptocephalus*, near Holyhead, not only was this recorded by L. T. Gronovius of Leiden in his *Zoophylacium*, but also it was named after Morris 'in memory of our worthy friend' (Pennant, 139).

Morris was also a staunch and reliable supporter of his brother Richard's literary and scholarly pursuits in London. This brother edited the Welsh versions of the Bible and Book of Common Prayer in 1746 and 1752, and secured the help of William and others to read the proofs. Richard Morris was secretary of the Cymmrodorion Society, established in 1751 and based in London, and his brother William participated fully in its activities, becoming a corresponding member.

Through the guidance and influence of his elder brother, Lewis, William Morris mastered the whole span of the Welsh bardic tradition. He formed his own collections of poetry and notably acquired a seventeenth-century manuscript which contained the poetry of the Welsh princes (BL, Add. MS 14869). The collection ranged from the works of the fourteenth-century poet Dafydd ap Gwilym to that of his own eighteenth-century contemporaries. Morris's antiquarian interests extended from Celtic saints and Welsh proverbs to Welsh traditional music.

Although William Morris lacked the academic ability of his brother Lewis, the mainspring of the great Welsh literary revival of the first half of the eighteenth century, William, through his genial support and varied and general interests, was an integral part of that revival; and through his untiring correspondence he was an inspiration to the other members of the Morris literary and scholarly circle. He was nevertheless also fond of people and strove to help the needy. He died on 28 December 1763 at Holyhead and was buried the following day, probably with his infant son and wife in the churchyard at Holyhead.

DAFYDD WYN WILIAM

Sources D. W. Wiliam, *Wiliam Morris (1705–63)* (1995) • T. Pennant, *British zoology*, 4th edn, 4 vols. (1776–7), vol. 3, p. 139 • J. H. Davies,

The Morris letters (1907) · parish register (baptism) of Llanfihangel Tre'r-beirdd, Anglesey County RO

Archives BL, collections of poems, notes, and corresp. with his brothers and others, Add. MSS 14867–15037 · NL Wales, letters to Thomas Pennant incl. description of fish found in Irish Sea

Morris, William (1834–1896), designer, author, and visionary socialist, was born at Elm House, Walthamstow, on 24 March 1834, eldest surviving son and fourth of the ten children of William Morris (1797–1847), financier in the City of London, and his wife, Emma (1805–1894), daughter of Joseph Shelton, a teacher of music in Worcester, and granddaughter of John Shelton, proctor of the consistory court of the diocese of Worcester. William Morris's paternal ancestors were Welsh; his grandfather was the first of this family to drop the Welsh 'ap' ('son of') from his surname, and moved to Worcester from the upper Severn valley late in the eighteenth century.

Childhood and Marlborough, 1834–1852 With the growing success of William Morris senior's dealings as a partner in the discount house of Sanderson & Co., which included speculation in copper mines in Devon, Morris was brought up in what he later referred to as 'the ordinary bourgeois style of comfort' (MacCarthy, 1). Rapidly the family accumulated wealth, and in 1840 moved to Woodford Hall in Essex, an imposing Georgian mansion on the edge of Epping Forest. William was a delicate child, cosseted by his mother and his older sisters Emma and Henrietta. He was a precocious reader, claiming to have started on the works of Sir Walter Scott at the age of four and to have completed the entire *œuvre* by the time he was seven. Already he was highly receptive to medievalism and romance.

From Woodford Hall, Morris would set out on his pony, sometimes dressed in a miniature suit of armour given to him by his parents, to explore the countryside and riverbank, seeking out small remote churches, early examples of the purist English architecture Morris was to champion all through his adult life. His visual memory was peculiarly retentive. From those first expeditions into the Essex countryside Morris's observations of birds, trees, and flowers began accumulating and he used them like a library to provide the sources for his later work in pattern design.

From the age of nine Morris attended a small local school, the Misses Arundale's Academy for Young Gentlemen. He quickly learned to write, but was always to regard spelling as superfluous. In 1848 he was sent to Marlborough College, then a new school, badly organized and prone to violence. A serious school riot broke out in 1851. Morris was unhappy, isolated, and claimed later to have learned next to nothing at Marlborough 'because next to nothing was taught' (P. Henderson, *William Morris, his Life, Work and Friends*, 1967, 7). His profound dislike of a system of tuition rooted in the classics, based on learning by rote, underlies his later educational theories, influential on the 'new schools' of the 1880s. Morris argued that children should acquire practical skills as well as intellectual knowledge, and that education should be lifelong.

At Marlborough, Morris made his own escape routes,

William Morris (1834–1896), by George Frederic Watts, 1870

reading antiquarian history in the new Adderley Library and exploring Savernake Forest and the prehistoric landscapes of Avebury and Silbury Hill. He was already developing the manual skills that were to become almost an addiction, weaving strings attached to his classroom desk to make fishing nets and traps for birds. He was also discovering his talents as a storyteller, transfixing his schoolfellows with rambling Gothic stories and establishing the persona of the oddball or outcast that clung to him in later life. Morris, having been brought up in what he called 'rich establishment puritanism' (MacCarthy, 11), veered towards the high church while he was at Marlborough, then a distinctly Anglo-Catholic school. The bishop of Salisbury confirmed him in Marlborough College chapel in March 1849.

In 1847 William Morris senior had died suddenly, leaving the family finances in turmoil. His widow moved to a smaller although still substantial home, Water House in Walthamstow (later the William Morris Gallery). Morris's emotional equilibrium was further threatened by the marriage of his eldest sister, Emma, on whom he had been especially dependent. The year 1852 was spent partly at home and partly as a pupil with the Revd Frederick Guy, a young high-church clergyman and an assistant master at the Forest School in Walthamstow. In June 1852 he took Oxford matriculation and he entered Exeter College in January 1853. Although he later became strongly anticlerical Morris was at this stage intended for the church.

Oxford: early poetry, architecture, and crafts, 1853–1856 William Morris as a boy was in some respects mature for his years, widely read, with an enormous store of arcane knowledge. But he lacked direction and was prey to moodiness. At Oxford he began to orientate himself. For the first time he found friends who shared his interests. His closest Oxford companion was Ned Jones (later Sir Edward Burne-Jones), who was also at Exeter and also, at that time, a fervent Anglo-Catholic planning to take holy orders. They were to be lifelong friends and artistic collaborators.

Through Burne-Jones, Morris was introduced into the Set, a remarkable group of young men, most of whom had been at school with Burne-Jones in Birmingham. The Set consisted of William Fulford; Charles Faulkner, the Oxford mathematician; R. W. Dixon, later Canon Dixon, the Pre-Raphaelite poet; and Cormell Price, who founded the United Services Colleges and who is immortalized as the unconventional headmaster in the novel *Stalky & Co.* by his former pupil Rudyard Kipling. Such self-contained male groupings, with their robust humour and their private language of camaraderie, were always to be important to Morris, a socially awkward man who longed to be gregarious. His friends christened Morris Topsy, after the little slave girl in Harriet Beecher Stowe's *Uncle Tom's Cabin*, because of his uncontrollably curly hair.

The Set were literary men, worshippers of Tennyson. They read, recited, wrote. There is a well-known legend, which Morris himself helped to disseminate, that at Oxford he discovered almost overnight his fluency in composition, and that 'The Willow and the Red Cliff' was the first poem he ever wrote. In fact it seems probable he started writing earlier, perhaps even at Marlborough. But at Oxford, Morris began to write with a new obsessiveness. He later destroyed many of the poems of this period, but the surviving lyrics, though obviously influenced by Keats and by Elizabeth Barrett Browning, show that Morris was already finding his own poetic voice.

At the same time Morris's youthful inwardness was being challenged. His Oxford friends came from a midlands industrial environment, and their awareness of social problems was more highly developed than Morris's own. He now had his indoctrination into reformist politics, reading the polemical novels of Charles Kingsley and attuning himself to Ruskin and Carlyle. Ruskin's writings on art and workmanship struck him as a 'sort of revelation' (MacCarthy, 69). He later described the impact of Ruskin's chapter in *The Stones of Venice* (1853) entitled 'On the nature of Gothic architecture': 'To some of us when we first read it … it seemed to point out a new road on which the world should travel' (MacCarthy, 69). In the summer vacation of 1855 Morris, Fulford, and Burne-Jones made a journey around the great Gothic cathedrals of northern France, and from then on he defended the Gothic as the only morally viable architectural style.

In the course of those travels Morris and Burne-Jones came to a joint decision. They would not, after all, be entering the church. Instead Morris would train as an architect and Burne-Jones as a painter. They were dismayed by the condition of England, its social complacency, and its visual squalor. They had recently discovered

Sir Thomas Malory's *Morte d'Arthur*. Full of Arthurian fervour they embarked on what they called a campaign 'against the age' (MacKail, 1.63).

Morris reluctantly returned to Exeter to take his pass degree before articling himself, on 25 January 1856, to G. E. Street, one of the leading English Gothicist architects, then diocesan architect for Oxford. In Street's office he made the second of his intimate and lifelong male friendships, with Street's senior clerk, the architect Philip Speakman Webb. Although Morris never practised as an architect, his two years in Street's office were crucial in terms of the experience he gained in techniques and materials as well as in his growing awareness of the psychological importance of buildings as orientation points within society, repositories of history, and keepers of the soul.

William Morris's personal practical involvement in handmaking was his radical departure. Ruskin had first explored the social dangers of separating intellectual and manual activity, arguing that class divisions were exacerbated by the traditional definitions of work for gentlemen and work for artisans. Ruskin himself was not a maker. It was Morris, in the next generation, who developed these perceptions in his own exuberant creative terms. His principle was to be that no work should be carried out in his workshops before he had mastered the technique of it himself.

While still in Street's office, Morris had begun to experiment with stone carving, clay modelling, wood carving, and the first of his illuminated manuscripts. In Oxford he had an embroidery frame made to an old design, and found a retired French dyer to dye worsteds for him. From a smith with a forge near Oxford Castle he ordered a mail surcoat and a bassinet (an Arthurian type of helmet), which closed on him when he first tried it on and trapped him. Burne-Jones described him 'embedded with iron, dancing with rage and roaring inside' (MacCarthy, 133).

Morris's notorious nervous irritability was probably a facet of an epileptic tendency inherited from his mother. Although his friends joked about his 'rages', contemporary descriptions suggest that Morris suffered from a serious medical condition, marked by fits in which he would lose consciousness temporarily. Later, when his daughter Jenny developed epilepsy in her mid-teens, this was a bitter grief, since Morris felt himself to blame.

Pre-Raphaelite London and *The Defence of Guinevere*, 1856–1858

In late summer 1856 Street's office moved to London and Morris moved with it, joining Burne-Jones who had preceded him to the place they came to call, in mingled despair and affection, 'the Great Wen' (MacCarthy, XV). They took temporary rooms at 1 Upper Gordon Street, Bloomsbury, then moved to 17 Red Lion Square. Here Morris commissioned the robust timber furniture described by Dante Gabriel Rossetti, who assisted Morris and Burne-Jones in painting it, as 'intensely mediaeval … tables and chairs like incubi and succubi' (ibid., 118). Red Lion Square was the first of a long sequence of Victorian interiors that Morris imbued with his highly personal decorative style. In his serious attentiveness to domestic detail, and in particular his sensitivity to the colour, sheen, and tactility of textiles, Morris can be seen as entering what, in his class and culture, was the traditional female domain. He was later to become an accomplished cook.

In London, Morris was absorbed into Pre-Raphaelite circles. Dante Gabriel Rossetti, one of the founders of the Pre-Raphaelite brothers and already established as a painter and a poet, was influential on the two less sophisticated young men. He persuaded William Morris he too ought to be a painter. At the end of 1856 Morris left Street's office. He had already started taking life classes. Although he was never to feel confident in drawing from life, he was always insistent that drawing skills were the basis of design.

Simultaneously Morris continued with his writing. Through 1856 his main outlet was the short-lived but intellectually ambitious publication he financed, the *Oxford and Cambridge Magazine*. The chief contributors were former members of the Oxford Set, later reconstituted as the Brotherhood. For the twelve issues Morris provided at least five poems; eight prose tales, including 'The Story of the Unknown Church' and 'The Hollow Land'; reviews of Alfred Rethel's engravings and Robert Browning's *Men and Women*; and an article on Amiens Cathedral which suggests themes developed more fully in his mature lectures on the politics of art.

In London the next year Morris wrote the majority of the thirty poems included in *The Defence of Guinevere, and Other Poems* published in 1858 by Bell and Daldy (again at Morris's expense). The volume was badly received, by critics who found Morris's subject matter wayward and his language jarring. It suffered from association with the notorious Pre-Raphaelite paintings of that time. But these small, spare, violent poems have always had admirers, from Gerard Manley Hopkins to the imagists.

One of the most lastingly persuasive of William Morris's tenets was that of the inherent joy in labour. He argued that without dignified, creative human occupation people became disconnected from life. In summer 1857, in the decoration of the newly built Oxford Union, Morris had his first experience of the 'working holiday'. Rossetti had negotiated the commission for the decoration of the walls of the debating hall. Morris decorated the ceiling and was responsible for one of the ten bays, on which he painted in tempera the tragic triangle of Sir Tristram, Sir Palomydes, and La Belle Iseult. Among his fellow artists were Burne-Jones, Spencer Stanhope, Arthur Hughes, and Val Prinsep. The atmosphere of unrelenting male badinage, with loud popping of soda water corks, caused the episode to enter history as 'the jovial campaign' (MacCarthy, 129).

Marriage, Red House, and 'the Firm', 1859–1865　In the winter of 1857 Morris met, and fell in love with, Jane Burden (*d.* 1914) [*see* Morris, Jane], daughter of an Oxford stableman. Janey, then eighteen, dark, and exotic, soon to be the ideal of a Pre-Raphaelite 'stunner', was spotted at the theatre by Rossetti and Burne-Jones. Originally she modelled for Rossetti. Morris then used her as his model for *La Belle Iseult*,

the painting now in the Tate collection, his only surviving work in oils. His family were not, apparently, present at the marriage, held on 26 April 1859 in St Michael's parish church in Oxford. The honeymoon was spent in Bruges.

Philip Webb designed Red House, in close collaboration with Morris, for his marriage. This famous red-brick building, at Upton, near Bexleyheath, in Kent, was a creative reworking of the architectural style of the thirteenth century, with a steep red-tiled roof and a well in the courtyard. During construction Morris and his bride lived temporarily at Aberley Lodge, close to the site, and they moved into Red House in June 1860. The house lay along the ancient pilgrims' route to Canterbury and Morris cast himself in the role of genial Chaucerian host. His artist friends, including Edward Burne-Jones (now married to Georgiana Macdonald), came to assist with decorations in another working holiday that gave the impetus for the foundation of the decorating company eventually known as Morris & Co.

Red House was the first tangible expression of the reductionist principles for which Morris became famous: 'Have nothing in your houses that you do not know to be useful or believe to be beautiful' (MacCarthy, 185). In its time Red House was seen as startling in its fluidity of planning and its brilliant clashing colour. This quasi-medieval building was to become the paradigm of all arts and crafts houses and a potent influence on twentieth-century modernist architecture.

William Morris's decorating company—originally Morris, Marshall, Faulkner & Co.—was founded in 1861. Unofficially, it was referred to as the Firm. From this time on, Morris's energies as a designer were focused on the 'lesser' or domestic arts, and their gradual rise in status in Europe and America through the nineteenth century was largely due to his proselytizing fervour.

The Firm, as originally constituted, was an artistic brotherhood with seven partners. Besides Morris himself, Peter Paul Marshall, and Charles Faulkner, the partners were Dante Gabriel Rossetti, Edward Burne-Jones, Philip Webb, and the Pre-Raphaelite painter Ford Madox Brown. At a period of widespread ritualist revival, work for new and restored churches was the basis of their early success.

The Firm first exhibited at the International Exhibition at South Kensington in 1862, winning two gold medals and a special jury mention for the colour and design of its stained glass. The Firm's catalogues offered painted furniture, mural decoration, metalware and glass, embroidery and hangings, jewellery, and hand-painted tiles. Some of these products were made in the Firm's workshops, some were subcontracted. The first of William Morris's wallpapers, always to be one of the Firm's staples, were produced by the Islington firm of Jeffrey & Co. from 1862. The Firm's original workshops were at 8 Red Lion Square, with a retail shop attached, reflecting Morris's faith in the face-to-face transaction (though he was shy of dealing with customers himself). By 1865 the exhaustion of daily commuting and his own financial problems, caused by decrease in value of his family shares, forced Morris to sell Red House.

The building remained in sympathetic private ownership until its acquisition by the National Trust (for £2 million) in January 2003. Morris moved his home and workshop to 26 Queen Square, Bloomsbury, now living literally above the shop.

The Earthly Paradise and Iceland, 1865–1871 Since *The Defence of Guinevere* Morris had written little, partly out of depression at its critical reception, mainly because he was preoccupied with decorating Red House and establishing the Firm. But, as Burne-Jones noted, Morris's life went on in cycles, one immense enthusiasm taking over from another, and in the mid-1860s Morris entered a vigorous new poetic phase which established him as one of the most popular poets of his period, regarded as being on a par with Browning, Tennyson, and Swinburne. In 1877 he was offered nomination to the Oxford professorship of poetry. In 1892 he was sounded out discreetly as to whether, if offered the poet laureateship (left vacant by Tennyson's death), he was likely to accept it. Both honours Morris rejected scornfully.

The poem that made Morris famous, *The Earthly Paradise* (1866–70), is a large, highly coloured, hugely energetic sequence of narrative poems, a Victorian reworking of Chaucer's *Canterbury Tales*. It was originally envisaged as an illustrated poem with woodcuts by Burne-Jones published in a folio volume. Morris's friends, whose loyalties were tested by his late-night readings of his work in progress, referred to it as 'the big story book'. A foretaste, in the form of *The Life and Death of Jason*, a 13,000-line poem too long to be included in the major enterprise, was published on its own in 1867. This time the reviews were unanimously good. Critics judged that in comparison Tennyson sounded orotund. Morris seemed to have invented 'an entirely new fashion of telling a story in verse' (MacCarthy, 204).

The first volume of *The Earthly Paradise* was published in 1868, and the final two volumes in 1870. The framework is the story of a band of late fourteenth-century Norsemen, fleeing the black death, setting sail in search of the reputed earthly paradise 'Where none grow old'. Failing to find it, they arrive at 'a nameless city in a nameless sea' where they are welcomed by the elders of the city. The twenty-four tales, exchanged by the wanderers and their hosts, draw on a variety of sources: classical, Norse, medieval, and the Icelandic literature which was beginning to fascinate Morris at this time. Intertwined with the tales is a more personal poetic narrative, in which Morris hints at the stresses in his own emotional life.

The first years of his marriage were apparently contented. At Red House, Janey gave birth to two daughters: Jane Alice (Jenny) in 1861 and Mary (May) *Morris in 1862. But soon after the family removal to Queen Square, Janey began showing signs of a debilitating illness, possibly gynaecological in origin. In 1869 Morris accompanied her to the German spa town of Bad Ems. All her life she remained a semi-invalid. She appears in memoirs and cartoons of the period as the archetypal Victorian *femme souffrante*, supine on a couch. Janey nevertheless acquired two famous lovers, Dante Gabriel Rossetti, painter and poet, her husband's brother artworker and partner in the Firm, and later, after Rossetti's death in 1882, the aristocratic Victorian philanderer, orientalist, and maverick politician Wilfrid Scawen Blunt.

Morris responded with stoic generosity. It was part of his then radical morality to believe that we are not one another's keepers. Grieving for the loss of love he threw himself more avidly into the manual disciplines of craftwork. He returned with new intentness to illumination and calligraphy, reviving techniques that had been neglected since the fifteenth-century development of printing. The first of his manuscripts was *A Book of Verse*, written out in 1870 for Georgiana Burne-Jones, to whom he was now increasingly attached. Morris's ornate, labour-intensive manuscripts culminate in his magnificent *Aeneid* on vellum, begun in 1874.

Simultaneously Morris was immersed in the Icelandic. This was another aspect of his fortitude. He identified himself with the heroes of the nationalistic sagas of the tenth and thirteenth centuries, studying the language and beginning his long sequence of translations in collaboration with the Icelandic scholar Eiríkr Magnússon. Morris travelled very little outside Britain. His two voyages to Iceland, in 1871 and 1873, must rank with his undergraduate tour of the Gothic cathedrals of France as the most influential journeys of his life.

Morris's route in 1871 took him from Reykjavík around the saga sites of the western coast. He travelled by Icelandic pony, accompanied by Magnússon and his old Oxford friend Charles Faulkner. Edward Burne-Jones drew a delicious series of cartoons of his rotund friend Morris in the land of raw fish. On his second, and more arduous, journey Morris traversed the desolate, rocky interior of Iceland to Akureyri, on the northern coast. Iceland's wild volcanic landscape, lit with lurid sunsets, recurs frequently in Morris's later poetry and fiction. Morris was moved to find evidence of art and literature enduring in social conditions of such abject poverty.

Iceland braced Morris. He returned from his journeys in a new mood for experiment, exploring themes of possession and dispossession in a not wholly convincing quasi-medieval alliterative verse drama *Love is Enough*, published in 1873. In 1875 Morris and Magnússon completed their translation, entitled *Three Northern Love Stories*, from the Icelandic. *Sigurd the Volsung and the Fall of the Niblungs*, Morris's own version of the Icelandic epic, his longest and most ambitious poem, was published in 1876. This four-book narrative in resounding rhyming couplets is constructed with the confidence of one of the great Victorian feats of engineering. *Sigurd* was Morris's own favourite of all his works.

Kelmscott and Merton Abbey: Morris's mature design, 1872–1882 In 1871, just before he left for Iceland, Morris had discovered Kelmscott Manor, near Lechlade on the borders of Gloucestershire and Oxfordshire. He took the house in joint tenancy with Dante Gabriel Rossetti, in effect establishing an unconventional rural *ménage à trois*.

Morris was never to live at Kelmscott permanently. His main family home was still in London. From 1872 to 1882 the Morrises lived at Horrington House, Turnham Green, then moved to Kelmscott House in Hammersmith. But Kelmscott Manor was the building that affected him most deeply. The mainly sixteenth-century gabled grey stone manor on the edge of the village was from then on William Morris's architectural ideal. Indeed he claimed to have seen the building in a dream before he located it in real life. To Morris, Kelmscott stood for Englishness, and permanence, and unpretentious excellence of craftsmanship. It appeared as the frontispiece to the Kelmscott Press edition of Morris's utopian novel *News from Nowhere* in 1893.

From his natural surroundings at Kelmscott, Morris drew direct inspiration for many of his wallpaper and textile designs of the 1870s and early 1880s. This was his most fecund period of pattern design. 'Strawberry thief' was taken from an incident in the Kelmscott garden, in which thrushes stole the fruit from underneath the strawberry nets. The best known of all Morris's patterns, 'Willow', derives from the leaves of the trees that edged the river where Morris used to fish for gudgeon and perch.

In March 1875, after much acrimonious argument, the Firm was reconstituted under William Morris's sole ownership. From this time the company was officially Morris & Co. Morris's family finances had not recovered, he earned little from his writing, and he was almost entirely dependent on his income from the Firm. The company had never lacked prestigious clients: it had received commissions from the South Kensington Museum (for the green dining-room) and, in its early years, even from St James's Palace. But the Firm had been under-capitalized and managerially disorganized. It now entered a new period of consolidation. Morris & Co. was both creating the style of the time and accruing profits from it as the aesthetic movement of the 1870s and 1880s got under way.

Morris's perfectionist standards made it difficult for him to rely on subcontractors. His aim was now to bring as many manufacturing processes as possible under his own control. First he tackled dyeing, developing his own vegetable dyes as an alternative to the alkaline dyes in general commercial use. He was determined to revive indigo dyeing, and in 1875 spent several weeks in Leek carrying out experiments at Thomas Wardle's Hencroft works, disconcerting his friends by returning to London with his arms dyed blue.

Morris next threw himself into the revival of handweaving, setting up a loom in his own bedroom at Hammersmith, rising at dawn to take advantage of the natural light. By 1881, when Morris & Co. moved out of Queen Square to much larger working premises at Merton Abbey in south London, they were independent in dyeing and block printing, and rug and carpet making, and were at the early stages of developing high-warp tapestry, which had for many years been Morris's 'bright dream' (MacCarthy, 401).

Concurrently Morris & Co.'s retailing activities were expanding. A shop was opened at 264 (later 449) Oxford Street in 1877 and a branch at 35 John Dalton Street, Manchester, in 1883. Morris perceived the bitter irony of his easy success with the discriminating middle classes while his aims of bringing art to the working people had so far failed. On a professional visit to one of his most faithful clients, the northern ironmaster Sir Isaac Lowthian Bell, Morris could be heard storming through the rooms of Rounton Grange. When Bell asked for explanation Morris turned on him 'like a wild animal', exclaiming 'It is only that I spend my life ministering to the swinish luxury of the rich' (MacCarthy, 210).

From the mid-1870s Morris's growing despair at Britain's class divisiveness, and the almost universal apathy to art, had been propelling him into public action. In 1876 he became treasurer of the Eastern Question Association, a Liberal pressure group formed to prevent Disraeli's alliance with the Turks in the Russo-Turkish War. The following year Morris founded the Society for the Protection of Ancient Buildings (known as SPAB or Anti-Scrape), the earliest conservation society, and gave the first of many hundreds of lectures in which, with characteristic common sense and passion, he related the aesthetic standards in any given country to its prevailing social conditions. The first collection of these lectures was published in 1882 as *Hopes and Fears for Art*.

Revolutionary London, 1883–1890 On 13 January 1883, three years after Morris & Co. had been commissioned to decorate the throne room at St James's Palace, Morris joined the Democratic Federation, a new revolutionary socialist party led by the Marxist Henry Mayers Hyndman. This was a decisive move out of his class, entailing rifts with many friends, professional opprobrium, and absence from many of the places and activities that Morris depended on and loved. His involvement in the socialist cause depleted his income and damaged his never robust health. At the age of almost fifty, at a time when the Firm was prospering and Morris's literary reputation was secure, it was an act of almost insane courage, and he wrote of it in terms of a homecoming, a final recognition of inevitable destiny. His 'conversion' (MacCarthy, 462), as he called it, came as an all-suffusing joy.

Morris taught himself socialism with the doggedness with which he acquired a handicraft. He read Marx's *Das Kapital*, in French, and studied Marx's theories of work and wages, admitting that he found them hard going. He was deeply affected by Sergey Stepniak's *Underground Russia*, and in taking upon himself the task of 'spreading discontent among all classes' (MacCarthy, 470) Morris saw himself as part of an international struggle for freedom from oppression. There was perhaps a strain of masochism in his insistence in sharing in all the mundane detail of the Democratic Federation's propaganda work, from 'street preaching' (MacCarthy, 474) in all weathers to writing and selling *Justice*, the federation's newsheet. In November 1883 Morris spoke in Oxford, in the hall of University College, with John Ruskin in the chair. His inflammatory speech, 'Art and democracy', was reported widely. It had the effect of a final declaration. Tennyson asked to see a copy of *Justice* and owned himself appalled.

In 1884 *A Summary of the Principles of Socialism*, written jointly by Morris and Hyndman, was published. But by now a serious rift had taken place in the Democratic Federation between the parliamentarians and more purist anti-parliamentarian socialists. Morris, who saw parliamentary government as essentially corrupt, emerged as the inevitable (though unwilling) leader of the breakaway group. The Socialist League was formally inaugurated on 30 December 1884. The manifesto was written by Morris and his fellow seceder E. Belfort Bax, and put forward a lucid and attractive argument for 'a change in the basis of Society—a change which would destroy the distinctions of classes and nationalities' (W. Morris, *Socialist League Manifesto*, 1885, 1). Morris, a man so rooted in the practicalities of designing and making, also had the imaginative range to envisage a new kind of society, a total overthrow of the status quo. The manifesto was signed by the twenty-two members of the league's provisional council, including Edward Aveling and his lover, Karl Marx's daughter, Eleanor Marx.

The Socialist League was relatively small, but Morris's personal charisma gave it a political importance far beyond its size. In 1885, at the end of the first year, membership stood at about 230. There were by then ten branches, most in southern England, with a London headquarters at 113 Farringdon Street. Over the next few years the league's membership expanded into the northern manufacturing cities. Its presence in Glasgow was particularly strong. Hammersmith was the most high profile of the branches. Its meetings were held in the coach house adjoining Kelmscott House, Morris's own home, where speakers and favoured guests would be entertained to dinner by Morris and his daughter May, who acted as his lieutenant in the league. The list of Hammersmith speakers is eclectic, including almost every important socialist thinker of the period: Graham Wallas, Annie Besant, John Burns, Sydney Olivier, Sidney and Beatrice Webb, Sergey Stepniak, and Peter Kropotkin. Morris's links with the Russian anarchists in exile were important and affectionate. The most regular guest speaker was Bernard Shaw who, in *Morris as I Knew him* (1936), gives a vivid account of Hammersmith politics and his own 'mystic betrothal' (MacCarthy, 523) to May Morris.

In September 1885, after a wave of socialist arrests at Dod Street in Limehouse, Morris appeared before the magistrate at Thames police court charged with assaulting a policeman and breaking his helmet. To the question, 'What are you?', Morris replied, 'I am an artist, and a literary man, pretty well known, I think, throughout Europe' (MacCarthy, 527). He was immediately set free. A cartoon of the period shows Morris holding up a banner inscribed 'The earthly paradox' while a helmeted policeman blacks his boots. The paradox was all too clear to Morris, the capitalist owner of a decorating firm who was also a leader of the British revolutionaries. His letters of the period reveal his doubts and anguish. But Morris could never contemplate half measures. He was working for total social transformation. Abandoning his own 'special work' as a designer–manufacturer or resorting to palliatives such as profit sharing would, in his view, have been a worthless compromise.

Morris was at the centre of political protest in Britain in 1886 and 1887, years of exceptional public unrest exacerbated by a long trade depression and the effects of unemployment. As a prominent public figure he came under police surveillance and, on 18 July 1886, was issued with a summons for obstruction in Bell Street, Marylebone. Morris was fined 1s. plus costs. He drove himself hard, travelling the country, preaching insurrection in working men's clubs. He took part in at least 105 public protest meetings in 1887 alone. On Easter Monday of that year Morris addressed a crowd of 6000 striking miners and their families at Horton in Northumberland. On 13 November 1887, later known as 'bloody Sunday', Morris was marching in one of the protesters' processions broken up by the police as it was advancing towards Trafalgar Street. When, in the aftermath of bloody Sunday, a young radical law writer was knocked down by a police horse in Northumberland Avenue and subsequently died, Morris wrote 'A Death Song' for him and spoke at his funeral, ending by crying out 'Let us *feel* he is our brother!' (MacCarthy, 573).

In these socialist years his writing became more populist. William Morris, so bashful in expressing his personal emotions, articulated the aspirations of the emerging British working class. His *Chants for Socialists* (1885) continued to be sung well into the twentieth century. The *Socialist Diary*, kept by Morris for a few months in 1887, details his encounters with the underclass with a rage and accuracy prophetic of George Orwell's. True to form, Morris was the chief contributor, as well as financier and editor, of the Socialist League newspaper, *The Commonweal*. His editorials and reportage—urgent, angry, rough and ready—show what a proficient journalist he was. For his working-class readers he wrote *The Pilgrims of Hope*, a long narrative poem, ostensibly a love story of the Paris commune but also an account of Morris's own political rebirth. The most highly regarded of William Morris's prose writings—*A Dream of John Ball* (1888) and his utopian novel *News from Nowhere* (1890)—first appeared as serials in *The Commonweal*. At this period he wrote several satiric playlets, in one of which, *The Tables Turned, or, Nupkins Awakened* (1887), Morris took the part of the archbishop of Canterbury at a Socialist League benefit performance. He entertained himself on his socialist travels by translating Homer's *Odyssey*, published in two volumes in 1887. He also translated Virgil's *Aeneid* (1876), much of it accomplished while travelling on the London Underground, and, less successfully, the Anglo-Saxon epic *Beowulf* (1895).

By 1888, the year in which Morris's second volume of political essays, *Signs of Change*, was published, dissensions had developed in the Socialist League. The Bloomsbury branch, including Edward Aveling and Eleanor Marx, seceded on the parliamentarian issue, leaving Morris vulnerable to the increasingly extremist anarchist members of the league. Morris had accepted that a national revolution was unlikely to be achieved without violence, but was opposed to undirected violence that would undermine socialism's credibility.

Morris was gradually edged out of the league and removed from the editorship of *The Commonweal*. In 1890 the Hammersmith branch severed its connections, becoming the Hammersmith Socialist Society. Ironically, as his own political base dwindled, Morris's international standing had never been so high. As an English delegate to the International Socialist Working Men's Congress in Paris in 1889 he gave one of the key speeches. His socialist colleague Edward Carpenter described him on the platform, in his navy blue pilot shirt, 'hacking and hewing the stubborn English phrases out—his tangled grey mane tossing, his features reddening with the effort! But the effect was remarkable' (MacCarthy, 581).

Late prose romances and the Kelmscott Press, 1890–1896 In the last years of his life Morris entered a new creative phase. Far from abandoning his interest in politics he began appearing on the socialist inter-party platforms and was active in forming the Joint Committee of Socialist Bodies in 1893. His richness of experience gave new authority to his lectures of this period. His originality as a political thinker always stemmed from his belief in the supremacy of art.

Morris invented a new genre of fiction writing with his series of magic–realist romances, set in imaginary historic landscapes. The first of these, *The House of the Wolfings* (1884), combined verse with prose. Morris reverted to prose only for *The Roots of the Mountains* (1890), *The Wood beyond the World* (1894), *Child Christopher* (1895), and *The Well at the World's End* (1896). His final two romances, *The Water of the Wondrous Isles* (1897) and *The Story of the Sundering Flood* (1898), were published after his death. It appears that this sequence of highly coloured, supremely visual narratives of love, quest, and battle answered a deep need in him. 'I must have a story to write now as long as I live' (*Collected Letters*, 3.115), he wrote to his wife in 1889.

In the 1890s Morris was able to return to a fuller involvement with the Firm at its Merton Abbey factory, which by this time employed around a hundred men, women, and boys. Many of the projects set in motion thirty years before were now reaching their culminating phase. Morris & Co. stained glass achieved its height of technical perfection in Edward Burne-Jones's series of windows for St Philip's Cathedral, Birmingham. Morris & Co. interiors reached its apotheosis at Standen in Surrey (now a National Trust property) and at Stanmore Hall. The six huge tapestry panels commissioned for Stanmore, narrating the quest of the San Graal, are a *tour de force* of craftsmanship, and emphasize the quality of story-telling that was, for Morris, an essential component of democratic art.

Having at first viewed them with suspicion, Morris gradually began to play an active role in the arts and crafts societies that had developed as a direct result of his own championing of craftsmanship. In 1888 Morris's work was included in the first exhibition of the Arts and Crafts Exhibition Society in London, where he gave a lecture on tapestry weaving. Morris seated at his loom demonstrating weaving to a reverential public is the subject of another of Burne-Jones's delicately malevolent cartoons.

In 1891 Morris became president of the Arts and Crafts Exhibition Society and in 1892 master of the Art Workers' Guild. Although acutely aware of the threat to society inherent in mechanization, Morris was by no means opposed to industry *per se*, seeing the potential of technical advances for freeing the operative from repetitive and deadening hand processes. He was involved in the first moves towards industrial design, attending the first conferences of the National Association for the Advancement of Art and its Application to Industry in Liverpool in 1888 and in Edinburgh in 1889.

In 1891 Morris embarked on his last great opus in practical designing, setting up the Kelmscott Press at 16 Upper Mall in Hammersmith. As he explained it, the essence of his undertaking was 'to produce books which it would be a pleasure to look upon as pieces of printing and arrangement of type' (MacCarthy, 609). He designed three Kelmscott typefaces—Golden, Troy, and Chaucer—besides numerous ornamental letters and borders. Morris supervised all the details of production and evolved his own idiosyncratic list, explaining that the books he wanted to print were those he most loved to read and own. Besides Morris's own works, beginning with a volume of his shorter poems, *Poems by the Way* (1891), the press specialized in reprints of medieval texts and English classics. The monumental Kelmscott *Chaucer*, with engravings from Burne-Jones and a binding by Douglas Cockerell, was completed just before Morris's death.

By early 1896 Morris was visibly failing. With his heightened nervous energy and tendency to gout, he had never been as robust as he appeared. The exertions of the socialist activist years had taken their toll. Diabetes was diagnosed. Morris endured long weeks of exile in Folkestone followed by a dismal cruise around the fjords of Norway in the cruise ship SS *Garonne*. He had by then developed lung trouble that proved to be tubercular, and congestion of the lung set in. His reduced energy was an immense ordeal to Morris, but he kept his curiosity and fondness for things as well as people. He still collected books and manuscripts with his former avidity, acquiring a magnificent twelfth-century English bestiary and buying a thirteenth-century illuminated psalter from Lord Aldenham in the weeks before he died. Morris retained a strange aura of innocence. A friend observed that in old age he looked like an ancient child.

Morris died at Kelmscott House in Hammersmith on 3 October 1896. Three days later his body was transported by train from Paddington to Lechlade. The coffin was then transferred into a traditional farmers' wagon, painted yellow and red and festooned with vine leaves, for the final few miles' journey to Kelmscott church, where Morris was buried on a stormy day. Philip Webb later designed his tomb.

Reputation and legacy At the time of his death Morris's reputation stood highest as a poet, but his more enduring influence has been that of a social critic of peculiar insight and a designer of great sweetness and enormous versatility.

Morris's visionary novel *News from Nowhere* became one

of the essential early twentieth-century socialist texts, translated into numerous languages and widely distributed in Russia in pre-revolutionary years. In Britain his political influence ran through from R. H. Tawney and G. D. H. Cole to Clement Attlee and the founders of the post-war welfare state. The full extent of Morris's revolutionary activism was played down by his executor and former secretary, Sir Sydney Cockerell, and by his first biographer, J. W. Mackail, son-in-law of Sir Edward Burne-Jones, but emerged with the publication of E. P. Thompson's *William Morris: Romantic to Revolutionary* (1955). From the 1970s onwards Morris's protectiveness of the environment led him to be recognized as a founding father of green politics.

Morris's tangible legacy is in his works of art. In spite of attempts by such modernist critics as Sir Nikolaus Pevsner to claim Morris as a modernist, he had come to be defined by the end of the twentieth century as a conservative radical designer. Morris's wallpapers and textiles, still in quantity production a hundred years after his death, make him arguably the most successful industrial designer ever known. Morris & Co. stained glass appears in retrospect as one of the wonders of Victorian church art. The Kelmscott Press generated the private press movement, important in its influence on twentieth-century European and American typography and book design.

William Morris's belief in the centrality of buildings profoundly influenced twentieth-century architectural theory and practice. His disciples W. R. Lethaby, C. F. A. Voysey, Ernest Gimson, and Edward Prior were the chief protagonists of what came to be known as English 'free style'. Morris's views on truth to materials and 'right-making' became a fundamental tenet of the arts and crafts movement. His vision of the self-sufficient rural group of craft workers, an ideal Morris himself never fully put into practice, was pursued by such English entrepreneur craftsmen as C. R. Ashbee and Eric Gill. Under the influence of Morris, craft communities proliferated in the early years of the twentieth century, especially in Scandinavia and the United States.

In his grand and sympathetic view of human potential Morris was both of his own Victorian age and far beyond it. E. P. Thompson described him correctly as 'a man whom history will never overtake' (E. P. Thompson, 730).

FIONA MACCARTHY

Sources *The collected works of William Morris*, ed. M. Morris, 24 vols. (1910–15) • F. MacCarthy, *William Morris: a life for our time* (1994) • *The collected letters of William Morris*, ed. N. Kelvin, 4 vols. (1984–96) • J. W. MacKail, *The life of William Morris*, 2 vols. (1899) • *Introductions to the collected works of William Morris*, ed. M. Morris, 2 vols. (1973) • M. Morris, ed., *William Morris: artist, writer, socialist*, 2 vols. (1936) • E. P. Thompson, *William Morris: romantic to revolutionary* (1955) • A. Vallance, *The life and work of William Morris* (1897) • R. Watkinson, *William Morris as designer* (1967) • P. Thompson, *The work of William Morris* (1967) • C. Harvey and J. Press, *William Morris: design and enterprise in Victorian Britain* (1991) • G. Burne-Jones, *Memorials of Edward Burne-Jones*, 2 vols. (1904) • J. Marsh, *Jane and May Morris* (1986) • S. Cockerell, diaries, BL, Add. MSS 52623–52624

Archives BL, corresp., literary MSS, and papers, Add. MSS 37497–37498, 45298–45353, 45407–45412, 45891–45894; M/1009; Ashley MSS A230, 4902; RP1355, 3957; Egerton MS 2866 • BLPES, letters relating to the Social Democratic Federation • Cheltenham City Art Gallery and Museum, Emery Walker Library • FM Cam., literary MSS, incl. 'The earthly paradise', travel journals, and papers • Getty Research Institute for the History of Art and the Humanities, California, letters • Hammersmith and Fulham Archives and Local History Centre, London, letters and papers relating to Morris & Co.; letters and printed material relating to him; papers of trustees and executors of William Morris • Hunt. L., letters and literary MSS • Internationaal Instituut voor Sociale Geschiedenis, Amsterdam, letters and MSS • Kelmscott House, Hammersmith • Kelmscott Manor, Oxfordshire • NRA, corresp. and papers • Ransom HRC, papers • S. Antiquaries, Lond., calligraphic fragments and notebook incl. corresp. of Mary Morris • S. Antiquaries, Lond., literary MSS and papers • S. Antiquaries, Lond., papers relating to Society for the Protection of Ancient Buildings • Society for the Protection of Ancient Buildings, London, letters • V&A NAL, corresp. and literary MSS • V&A NAL, notebook, partly written by him, of technical notes relating to printing and dyeing techniques used by Morris & Co. • William Morris Gallery, London, corresp., designs, drawings, and other MSS | BL, letters to Philip Burne-Jones, Add. MS 52708 • BL, letters to Joseph Lane, Add. MS 46345 • BL, letters to George Bernard Shaw, Add. MS 50541 • Bodl. Oxf., letters, postcards, and notes to Leightons • Bodl. Oxf., letters to Dante Gabriel Rossetti • Bodl. Oxf., letters to Messrs Whittingham and Messrs Leighton • Castle Howard, North Yorkshire, letters to ninth earl of Carlisle • FM Cam., Blunt MSS • FM Cam., Burne-Jones MSS • FM Cam., Lytton MSS • Harvard U., Houghton L., letters to Robert Thomson • Internationaal Instituut voor Sociale Geschiedenis, Amsterdam, corresp. with Andreas Scheu • L. Cong., corresp. of Morris & Co. with James McNeill Whistler • priv. coll., Walpole MSS • Staffs. RO, letters to Sir Thomas Wardle [copies] • V&A NAL, letters to Wilfrid Scawen Blunt • V&A NAL, Philip Webb archive, corresp. with Cockerell and Warington Taylor

Likenesses W. Morris, self-portraits, pencil, *c*.1855, V&A • D. G. Rossetti, pencil study, 1856, Birmingham Museums and Art Gallery • D. G. Rossetti, group portrait, oils, 1858–64 (*The seed of David*), Llandaff Cathedral • E. Burne-Jones, caricatures, *c*.1860 (copies), William Morris Gallery, Walthamstow • D. G. Rossetti, caricatures, 1860–69, BM • E. Burne-Jones, group portrait, oils, 1861 (*The adoration of the magi*), Tate collection • C. F. Murray, oils, *c*.1870, William Morris Gallery, Walthamstow • G. F. Watts, oils, 1870, NPG [see *illus.*] • Elliott & Fry, photograph, 1877, William Morris Gallery, Walthamstow • W. B. Richmond, oils, exh. 1882, NPG • Elliott & Fry, photograph, 1886–9, Hammersmith and Fulham Archive • F. Hollyer, double portrait, photograph, 1890 (with Edward Burne-Jones), William Morris Gallery, Walthamstow • E. Walker, photographs, *c*.1890, NPG, V&A • C. Fairfax-Murray, two drawings, 1896, Tate collection • A. Walker, sculpture, 1909, V&A • M. Beerbohm, pencil and watercolour drawing, 1916, Tate collection • E. Burne-Jones, caricatures, BM • E. Burne-Jones, caricatures, Harvard U., Fogg Art Museum • W. Crane, caricature, William Morris Gallery, Walthamstow • G. Howard, double portrait, drawing (with Thomas Carlyle), Carlisle Art Gallery • D. G. Rossetti, caricatures, Birmingham Museums and Art Gallery • D. G. Rossetti, caricatures, William Morris Gallery, Walthamstow • watercolour drawing, NPG

Wealth at death £54,117 11s. 7d.: resworn probate, March 1897, CGPLA Eng. & Wales (1896)

Morris, William O'Connor (1824–1904), judge and historian, was born in Kilkenny city, Ireland, on 26 November 1824, the son of Benjamin Morris (*d.* 1846), sometime rector of Rincurran in the diocese of Cork and Cloyne, and Elizabeth, youngest daughter and coheir of Maurice Nugent O'Connor of Gartnamona, near Tullamore, King's county. Morris was educated at a private school at Epsom (1837–41) and under the rector of Laugharne in south Wales (1841–3). On 15 June 1843 he matriculated at Oriel

College, Oxford, and in 1844 he was elected a scholar. He left university for a year and a half because of financial difficulties at home during the height of the great famine (1846–7), but resumed his studies in 1847 and graduated BA in 1848. His father had died in 1846.

Despite early thoughts of a military career, Morris entered the King's Inns, Dublin, as a law student in 1851. On 30 April 1852 he was admitted a student of Lincoln's Inn, London, and was called to the Irish bar in early spring 1854. He chose the home circuit and by 1862 had been elected a professor of common and criminal law at King's Inns. The following year he was appointed a commissioner to investigate the rights of owners of fixed nets for salmon in Ireland. However, owing to a difference of opinion with Robert Peel, then chief secretary, he was compelled to resign. Meanwhile, on 16 March 1858, Morris married Georgina Lindsay (d. 1910), and he established himself at Blackrock, co. Dublin, having also inherited, through his advantageous marriage, the property of Gartnamona. They had five daughters and one son.

Morris began to contribute articles on historical, legal, social, and political subjects to the *Edinburgh Review*, whose editor, Henry Reeve, had become a friend. He also reviewed books, mainly on his favourite subject, military history, for *The Times*. As a landlord Morris paid close attention to the conditions of land tenure in Ireland, and he was asked by John Thadeus Delane, the editor of *The Times*, to contribute a special series of articles on the land question, which had been made topical by Gladstone's determination to engage with Irish problems. Morris's letters to *The Times*, which advocated the legal recognition of tenant right in Ulster, attracted attention, and the Land Act of 1870, though not entirely to his satisfaction, drew upon many of his ideas.

In 1869–70 Morris served on a commission to inquire into the corrupt practices surrounding the election of freemen of the city of Dublin, and in 1872 he was appointed county court judge for the county of Louth. Six years later he was transferred to co. Kerry. Morris found co. Kerry much less agreeable than Louth, since he was utterly opposed to the home rule movement there, which was accompanied by rural violence. He disapproved of the Land Act of 1881, which he administered, and never lost an opportunity of denouncing it. He reduced rents by 15 to 20 per cent on well-managed estates and by 30 to 40 per cent on badly managed ones, but he refused to submit to local opinion. In 1880 he moved with his family from Dublin to Gartnamona, and was, at his own request, transferred in 1886 to the county judgeship of the united counties of Sligo and Roscommon. His position there was easier, but his attitude towards recent Irish legislation and his unsympathetic treatment of the de Freyne tenants in 1901 led to his being bitterly criticized.

Morris then buried himself in his writing, publishing historical works which served as a welcome distraction, such as *Hannibal … and the Crisis of the Struggle between Carthage and Rome* (1890), *Napoleon … and the Military Supremacy of Revolutionary France* (1890), and *Moltke: a Biographical and Critical Study* (1893). He examined the Irish past in works

such as *Ireland from 1494 to 1868* (1894), *Ireland from '98 to '98* (1898), and *Present Irish questions* (1901); and he published his autobiography, *Memories and Thoughts of a Life*, in 1895. Morris died at Gartnamona on 3 August 1904, and was survived by his wife.

ROBERT DUNLOP, rev. SINÉAD AGNEW

Sources Burke, *Gen. Ire.* · W. O'C. Morris, *Memories and thoughts of a life* (1895) · J. S. Crone, *A concise dictionary of Irish biography*, rev. edn (1937), 160 · Foster, *Alum. Oxon.* · W. P. Baildon, ed., *The records of the Honorable Society of Lincoln's Inn: admissions*, 2 (1896), 256 · Allibone, *Dict.* · *The Times* (4 Aug 1904)
Archives NL Scot., corresp. with Blackwoods
Likenesses Chancellor & Son, photograph, repro. in Morris, *Memories*, flyleaf · Farringdon, photogravure (after photograph by Chancellor & Son), NPG
Wealth at death £554 18s. 3d.: probate, 4 Oct 1904, CGPLA Ire.

Morris, William Richard, Viscount Nuffield (1877–1963), motor manufacturer and benefactor, was born on 10 October 1877 in the parish of St John, Worcester, the eldest son of Frederick Morris (1849–1916) from Witney and his wife, Emily Ann (d. 1934), daughter of Richard Pether, of Wood Farm, Headington, Oxford. He was one of seven children, but only two sisters survived into adulthood. Both parents came from Oxfordshire farming stock, which Morris later traced back to the thirteenth century. When Morris was born his father worked for a draper, but in 1880 moved to his wife's farm in Headington to become bailiff. Morris was brought up there, and attended the Cowley village school until the age of fifteen. His father was forced to retire from farming because of asthma and in 1893 Morris was apprenticed for a short time to a cycle maker in St Giles', Oxford.

First enterprises From this modest, though not impoverished, background Morris rose to become the most famous industrialist of his age. His first enterprise began at the age of sixteen, when he left his apprenticeship and set up a small cycle-repair business in his parents' house at 16 James Street, Oxford, with £4 of capital. He began to assemble his own bicycles made from parts ordered from the flourishing midlands cycle industry, and his custom-built machines developed a reputation in Oxford for reliability and good value. In 1901 he set up as a cycle maker at 48 High Street, Oxford, and in 1902 bought stables in Holywell Street to manufacture motor cycles. The following year he entered into a partnership with a wealthy undergraduate whose spendthrift ways brought bankruptcy to the Oxford Automobile and Cycle Agency, of which Morris was works manager. A small bank loan allowed him to restart in business, but his primary interest was now in motor cars. He sold the cycle business and in 1909 set up the Morris Garage, where he sold, hired, and repaired cars. Sales quadrupled in four years and by 1913 Morris was a successful and respected Oxford businessman.

Morris was an energetic and ambitious young man who made the most of the opportunities offered by the booming midlands industrial area and the dawning age of mass consumption. He had no formal training except for an

William Richard Morris, Viscount Nuffield (1877–1963), by Walter Stoneman, 1934

evening class in engineering at the Oxford schools of technology, which he attended only twice. He disliked working for others, or depending on loans. His financial prudence and rigid individualism were bitter lessons learned from his bankruptcy, and he carried them on into later life. Most accounts show a personable but rather distant character, noted for his drive and competitiveness. He became a champion cyclist in the 1890s, winning more than a hundred events in and around Oxfordshire. Cycling introduced him to his future wife, Elizabeth Maud (Lilian) Anstey (c.1884–1959), daughter of William Jones Anstey, an Oxford farrier. She worked in a department store and shared Morris's obsession with cycle touring. They married on 9 April 1904. The couple were childless, to Morris's profound regret. Elizabeth always remained in the background and their relationship was regarded by others as not particularly happy. The surviving photographs show a handsome couple. Morris was good-looking, of medium height and athletic physique, with dark hair smoothed back from his forehead. Although his hair turned silver by the 1930s his appearance changed remarkably little over the course of a very long life.

Car manufacturer In 1912 Morris took the predictable step of moving from the sale and hire of cars to actual manufacture. He adopted what had been until then a predominantly American practice, by buying in components from other suppliers which he assembled into a car of his own design and specification. This reduced the initial capital costs very considerably, and allowed him to buy supplies from the most competitive contractor in order to keep the costs low. His early experience with motor cars also convinced him of the importance of reliability. The car he designed in 1911–12, which became the Morris Oxford, was aimed at a broad popular market where price and easy maintenance were priorities. Delays in producing the engine forced Morris to sell his car from blueprints at the 1912 Motor Show. He sold 400, and the first was produced in April 1913. That year he produced 1300 cars, putting him at once among the top British car makers. In 1912 he founded W. R. M. Motors Ltd with himself as the sole ordinary shareholder, and £4000 borrowed from the earl of Macclesfield in the form of preference shares. Morris had met the latter in 1905, when the undergraduate was involved in a collision while at the wheel of a car hired from Morris. A motoring enthusiast, Macclesfield was prepared to support Morris in his manufacturing of cars.

Morris's business career was again the victim of circumstance when war broke out in 1914. Car production collapsed during the war, but Morris had already begun to prepare for large-scale production. In 1914 he rented a disused military training college at Temple Cowley on the outskirts of Oxford. There he began to plan production of a second car, the Morris Cowley, to be manufactured from American components, which were cheap and reliable. Instead Morris found himself producing an assortment of military products, which made the company little profit (though Morris was rewarded by being made OBE in 1917) but provided further experience in mass production at the state's expense. In 1919 he began car production in earnest, but could produce only 387 cars that year. The British Ford company dominated the market. By 1923 Morris produced more than 20,000 cars a year at an exceptionally low price. He achieved this by forcing his suppliers to cut their prices and risk large-volume output. The economies of scale thus achieved allowed Morris to undercut almost all his competitors. His cars also developed a reputation for reliability, ease of maintenance, and innovation. Morris kept a careful eye on American practice, which led to the widespread introduction of hire-purchase schemes in the 1920s, aggressive advertising, and a system of Morris dealerships across the country. Morris exploited the growing car culture of the inter-war years more effectively than his rivals, including Ford, whose fortunes in Britain went into decline in the mid-1920s.

Morris soon developed a circle of subsidiary businesses which were almost wholly dependent on supplying Morris cars. In 1923 he took over ownership of his engine, body, and radiator suppliers, and Morris Engines was founded in May of that year. In 1926 he took over his main carburettor supplier. This expansion called for a regular reorganization of the business. In July 1919 Morris had set up Morris Motors Ltd, with £29,000 of preference shares and £75,000 of ordinary stock, all of which he owned. In 1926 he floated shares in Morris Motors (1926) Ltd. He kept control of the ordinary shares, now valued at £2 million, and floated £3 million of preference shares which were oversubscribed. Over the 1920s capital in the company expanded at over £500,000 per year, much of the new capital coming from re-invested profits.

Management style From the late 1920s, when Morris supplied a third of all cars made in Britain, the fortunes of the company went into a slow decline. The launch of the successful Morris 8 and Morris 10 range in the 1930s kept Morris in the lead, but the competing pack closed in and other businesses imitated him successfully. Morris came to rely on the initiative of others in the organization, most notably the engineer Leonard Lord, who succeeded in reversing the decline in the early 1930s by modernizing factory practice (including the building of Europe's largest integrated car plant) and rationalizing the corporation as far as Morris would allow. His resignation in 1936, following Morris's refusal to give him a share of the profits, left the business in a difficult position, unable to rationalize effectively because of the insistence of its founder that he should keep general strategy in his own hands, and hostage to Morris's increasingly old-fashioned view of what would sell. Like Henry Ford in America, Morris exercised a damaging authoritarianism over his enterprise at a time when up-to-date production and sales required the move to more modern systems of management and control. Product development stagnated, and the successful post-war Morris Minor was only introduced into mass production against Morris's initial wishes. In 1951, disillusioned by the new era of state controls and the difficulties of holding his rambling industrial empire together, Morris merged the business with Austin to form the British Motor Corporation. He was its first president until he retired in 1954, and continued to interest himself in the affairs of the business until his death in 1963.

Morris's routine involvement in the affairs of the company ended in the 1920s after the successful launching of volume car production. From 1927 he began a long series of annual cruises to Australia, which left him absent even from general policy-making for months at a time. His subordinates, whose views were recorded in the 1950s by Morris's official biographers, Philip Andrews and Elizabeth Brunner, have left a generally unkind picture of their leader. Morris had strong views, which he expected others to respect and interpret. He disliked committee meetings, and instead discussed issues face-to-face with particular individuals. Collective decisions were seldom made by the directors unless they were confident that Morris endorsed them; on occasion Morris could go behind the backs of his directors and authorize policy on his own. One manager recalled that 'Cowley politics' were 'too fierce for words' (Church, 'Deconstructing Nuffield', 571). Morris did not like yes-men, but he disliked being crossed or ignored. His chairmanship of the Morris company was, as a result, arbitrary and often ill-informed. His was a familiar experience of the small-time entrepreneur who found himself in the space of a decade or so riding the wave of a remarkable consumer boom, forced to cope with the administration of an organization and workforce for which he had little experience. For all his faults Morris did retain values which were commercially sensible. He insisted on low price combined with quality; he believed that after-sales service was a vital key to high sales; and he did not over-commit the business financially. The merger of 1951, which Morris's managers resisted, was on the surface a realistic decision which might, under different circumstances and leadership, have produced a successful post-war volume car industry.

Public life In the 1920s Morris became a figure of national importance, enjoying publicity and honours. In 1929 he was given a baronetcy, in 1934 a barony, and in 1938 he became Viscount Nuffield, of Nuffield in the county of Oxford, where he had settled with his wife in 1925. He was showered with academic honours, including five honorary LLD degrees, and honorary fellowships at four Oxford colleges, St Peter's, Pembroke, Worcester, and Nuffield, the college he founded in 1949. He became a fellow of the Royal Society in 1939, a fellow of the Royal College of Surgeons in 1948 (following extensive medical benefactions), and was made a Companion of Honour in 1958. For all these honours, Morris remained a man of simple tastes and pleasures. He liked golf and excelled at deck games on his many cruises. His habits were modest. He drove a small Wolseley car and kept his small office at the Cowley works for his entire business life.

Morris's brief forays into public affairs ended unhappily. He was persuaded by Oswald Mosley during the slump to put up £50,000 to help found his 'New Party' in 1930, in the mistaken belief that Mosley favoured some of his ideas on involving businessmen in government to secure economic stability and rational action. Once Mosley began to demonstrate his more fascist aims Morris abandoned support, and any idea of businessmen's rule. In 1935 began a sharp dispute with the government over re-armament plans which ended with the exclusion of Morris from the so-called 'shadow factory' scheme.

After 1945 Morris undertook a long and unsuccessful assault on the new Labour government's economic controls. His political instincts were profoundly conservative. He disliked socialism and delayed the introduction of trade unions at Cowley for as long as he could. As late as 1956 Morris Motors was only twenty-five per cent unionized: like Henry Ford, Morris believed that the loyalty of the workforce could be bought with high wages. He was an individualist of a classic Victorian kind and distrusted the mass culture and economic collectivism to which his product and business had in part contributed.

Benefactions Morris's greatest public achievements lay in philanthropy. He began to make educational and medical donations in the 1920s, and as his personal fortune grew he became aware of the contribution he could make to relieve suffering in a pre-welfare state. In 1936 he floated much of his ordinary stock in order to release funds that he could use for benefaction. In total he donated £30 million, two-thirds of it for educational and medical purposes. He was instrumental in establishing a network of provident societies which formed the basis of the British United Provident Association (BUPA), founded in 1947. He established a medical school in Oxford with a donation of £2 million in 1936. In 1937 he granted land and an initial

£900,000 for the founding of an Oxford college. He wanted a college of engineering, which would link the world of industry and the university, but instead the Oxford authorities wanted a college to provide social studies. Morris reluctantly agreed, but he took very little interest in the new college and refused to favour the university again. His later donations went to hospitals, and in 1939 to the Nuffield Trust for the Forces of the Crown, which helped to provide welfare facilities for the military. In 1943 he agreed to set up the Nuffield Foundation with a capital of approximately £10 million. Its purpose was to provide medical and social relief, but from the 1950s it also provided educational grants.

Morris took a lively personal interest in his medical benefactions. 'The progress of medical science and the conditions under which medical practice is carried on have long been … among my main interests', he wrote to the vice-chancellor of Oxford in 1936 (Andrews and Brunner, 288), and his endowments were especially important at the Radcliffe Infirmary in Oxford (which successfully resisted the addition of Nuffield to its title) and at Guy's Hospital in London, where a statue was erected in his honour. He retained a lively and informed interest in medical science and was responsible for the initial supply of iron lungs to British hospitals when still in an experimental stage. Morris himself was a lifelong hypochondriac, constantly anxious about his health despite his early robustness. In fact he remained in good health for a man who chain-smoked until four years before his death, when he was forced to give up. His obsession with health perhaps owed something to his father's frail condition and the death of five siblings at a young age.

Morris did finally decline physically after the death of his wife in 1959. Following surgery in 1963 he died on 22 August at his Oxfordshire home, Nuffield Place, Nuffield. His ashes were buried in Nuffield parish church, though Morris himself had taken almost no interest in religion throughout his life. The bulk of his remaining estate, valued at over £3 million, was given to Nuffield College.

R. J. OVERY

Sources P. W. Andrews and E. Brunner, *The life of Lord Nuffield* (1955) · M. Adeney, *Nuffield: a biography* (1993) · R. J. Overy, *William Morris, Viscount Nuffield* (1976) · F. H. Ellis, 'The author of Wing C6727: Daniel Coxe, FRS, or Thomas Coxe, FRS', *Notes and Records of the Royal Society*, 18 (1963), 36–8 · R. Church, 'Deconstructing Nuffield: the evolution of managerial culture in the British motor industry', *Economic History Review*, 2nd ser., 49 (1996), 561–83 · R. Church, *The rise and decline of the British motor industry* (1994) · R. Jackson, *The Nuffield story* (1964) · J. Foreman-Peck, S. Bowden, and A. McKinlay, *The British motor industry* (1995) · S. Tolliday and J. Zeitlin, eds., *The automobile industry and its workers: between Fordism and flexibility* (1986) · *CGPLA Eng. & Wales* (1963) · GEC, *Peerage*

Archives Nuffield Oxf., corresp. and papers · Oxford Central Library | BLPES, LSE archives, Andrews and Brunner MSS · CAC Cam., corresp. with Lord Weir · Nuffield Oxf., corresp. with Lord Cherwell; Chester MSS · U. Oxf., MSS | FILM BFI NFTVA, documentary footage | SOUND BBC WAC, oral history interviews

Likenesses B. Patridge, chalk and pencil drawing, 1927, NPG · A. Cope, oils, 1929, Nuffield Oxf. · H. Coster, photograph, 1930–39, NPG · W. Stoneman, photograph, 1934, NPG [*see illus.*] · B. Enes, oils, *c.*1937, Guy's Hospital, London · P. A. de Laszlo, oils, *c.*1937, St Peter's College, Oxford · M. Lambert, bronze statue, *c.*1948, Guy's Hospital, London · J. Wheatley, oils, 1949 (after photograph), RCS Eng. · O. Birley, oils, before 1952, Nuffield Foundation, London · Mme Lejeune, bronze bust, Nuffield Oxf. · F. Lion, pencil drawing, Nuffield Foundation, London · two photographs, NPG

Wealth at death £3,252,764 2s.: probate, 26 Sept 1963, *CGPLA Eng. & Wales*

Morrison, Agnes Brysson Inglis [Nancy; *pseud.* Christine Strathern] (1903–1986), writer, was born on 24 December 1903 at Merchiston, Scotstounhill, Renfrew, near Glasgow, the fifth of six children of Arthur Mackie Morrison, engineer, son of a Glasgow baillie, and his wife, Agnes Brysson Morrison CBE, *née* Inglis, who invented and organized flag days during the First World War. She was educated at the Park School for Girls, Glasgow, and briefly at Harvington College, London, and came from a family of writers: five out of the six Morrison children went on to have a career in some way connected to literature. Morrison herself began writing as a child and describes herself rising 'early in the morning to do it in secret', claiming 'as far back as I can remember I have had the wish, or urge, to write. It goes right back to my nursery days' (NL Scot., MS 27354, fol. 36).

Morrison's first novel, *Breakers*, notable for containing one of the earliest fictional depictions of the highland clearances, was published by John Murray in 1930, and she went on to publish nine more, as well as biographies of Mary queen of Scots, Henry VIII, the Brontës, and Thomas and Jane Carlyle. Between the years 1942 and 1959 she also published twenty-eight romantic novels under the pseudonym Christine Strathern. A lifelong and committed member of the Church of Scotland, many of Morrison's novels are set in manses or reflect church life, and some of her non-fiction, such as *The Keeper of Time: Stories of the Disciples* (1953) and *They Need No Candle: the Men who Built the Scottish Kirk* (1957), has a more overt Christian content.

During her own life Morrison's fiction met with much acclaim, being commended for its 'painting of Scottish scene and character' and its blending of 'literary delicacy and terse, ironic realism' (NL Scot., MS 27373, fol. 27). *The Gowk Storm* was a Book Society choice when it was first published in 1933 and was later adapted for radio, stage, and film, and *The Winnowing Years* (1949) won the first Frederick Niven award. Her fiction also gained praise from her contemporaries, including Edwin and Willa Muir. Morrison's work was highly regarded in the United States where her last novel, *Thea* (1962), was published and where her biography of Mary queen of Scots received a Literary Guild award in 1961. Literary interest in Morrison's work began to revive in the late twentieth century, particularly in relation to her treatment of women.

Nancy Brysson Morrison never married and was an extremely private person, but it is clear that her family was of lifelong importance to her. For much of her life she lived with her sister Mary, first of all in Glasgow, and then from the sixties in Edinburgh. Later, she moved to Hampstead, London, to be near her brother Tom. This importance is reflected in literary correspondence, much of which, in particular from her eldest sister Peggy (who published romantic novels under the name March Cost), involves detailed commentary on drafts of her work along with suggestions and encouragement. 'Another advantage of all being writers', writes Morrison, 'is that we can discuss ideas, themes, and situations amongst ourselves' (NL Scot., MS 27354, fol. 41).

As a young woman Morrison enjoyed riding and walking, and, throughout her life, travel. She visited Italy and Switzerland in the thirties, and Sweden in 1946. She was also an active member of PEN, believing firmly in its principles of free speech and taking a strong interest in its debates after the Second World War.

After her death, Nancy Brysson Morrison's literary papers were deposited in the National Library of Scotland, and they show that in her working practices Morrison was both disciplined and methodical. Notebooks give evidence of meticulous research, along with ideas for themes, settings, and even words and phrases jotted down over a number of years. 'My brothers and sisters can write anywhere, in a room with other people talking,' writes Morrison, 'but neither my sister Peggy nor I am like that. We have to have peace and quiet. That is why I have a small office in town, with no telephone, where I work and keep business hours' (NL Scot., MS 27354, fols. 38–9). Nancy Brysson Morrison died of cancer in St Mary's Hospital, Paddington, London, on 27 February 1986. Her ashes were taken north to be buried in her sister Mary's grave in Ballater, Deeside.   ALISON LUMSDEN

Sources NL Scot., MSS 27287-27373 · private information (2004) · E. Morgan, introduction, in N. B. Morrison, *The gowk storm* (1989), vii–xii · D. Gifford and D. McMillan, eds., *A history of Scottish women's writing* (1997) [incl. bibliography, 594–5] · M. Palmer McCulloch, 'Poetic narrative in Nancy Brysson Morrison's *The gowk storm*', *Scottish women's fiction, 1920s to 1960s: journeys into being*, ed. C. Anderson and A. Christianson (2000) · b. cert. · *The Times* (27 March 1986)
Archives NL Scot., corresp., notebooks and MSS, MSS 27287-27373
Wealth at death £13,347.13: confirmation, 7 Oct 1986, *CCI*

Morrison, Alfred (1821–1897), autograph and art collector, was born on 28 April 1821, the second son in the family of seven sons and four daughters of James *Morrison (1789–1857) and his wife, Mary Anne (*d.* 1887), daughter of Joseph Todd. Their father's lucrative City of London drapery business of Morrison, Dillon & Co. and his large landed properties assured his children of substantial fortunes. Morrison was educated at Edinburgh University (1836–9), and spent a year at Trinity College, Cambridge, in 1839–40. He joined the family firm and travelled on business in North America in 1841–3 and 1845. He twice stood for parliament, attempting Wallingford in the 1847 election, but neither business nor politics was to be his main concern. He inherited the Fonthill estate near Hindon, Wiltshire, with its house based on the remaining portions of Alderman William Beckford's Fonthill *splendens*, acquired by James Morrison in the 1830s, and was high sheriff of his county in 1857. At Fonthill, and from 1865 at his London home at 16 Carlton House Terrace, Morrison showed himself a discriminating collector of *objets d'art* displayed in opulent surroundings. He commissioned craftsmen of many countries, specialists in cameo-cutting, metal-inlaying, and glass-enamelling. He was a notable patron of Plácido Zuloaga of Eibar, the leading damascene artist. Between 1860 and 1878 Morrison formed a large collection of engraved portraits, many of which were described in a privately printed catalogue (of which 100 copies were published in 1868) by M. Holloway.

From about 1865 until his death Morrison assembled what the Historical Manuscripts Commission described as 'the most remarkable gathering of historical autographs ever formed by a single private collector in Great Britain' (*Ninth Report*, HMC, 2.406–93). He searched for the finest specimens, using as his agent A. W. Thibaudeau of Green Street, Leicester Square, and his collection was remarkable in the number of letters it contained both from and to prominent persons. Major individual items—of which the last letter of Mary, queen of Scots, now in the National Library of Scotland, is an important example—were complemented by groups such as 111 letters from Admiral Lord Nelson to Lady Hamilton, with her replies, and the papers of Sir Richard Bulstrode. A six-volume folio *Catalogue*, compiled initially under Thibaudeau's direction, was privately printed in an edition of 200 copies between 1883 and 1892: it is notable for its facsimiles of especially important items. A second series, in smaller format, followed, with three volumes on the general collection, A–D (1893–6), two on the Hamilton and Nelson papers (1893–4), one on the Blessington papers (1895), and a first volume (1897), covering the years 1667 to 1675, devoted to the Bulstrode papers.

Morrison married, on 12 April 1866, Mabel (1847–1933), daughter of the Revd Robert Seymour Chermside, rector of Wilton, Wiltshire. They had two sons: Hugh (1868–1931), who inherited Fonthill House from his father, and also estates on Islay, Argyll, from his uncle, and James Archibald (1873–1934), who inherited Basildon Park, Berkshire, from his uncle. They also had three daughters, one of whom died in infancy. Morrison died at Fonthill on 22 December 1897. His widow, a striking and spirited personality who shared many of her husband's collecting interests, died in 1933.

Morrison's collection of gems, arranged by Castellani, was sold at Christies in 1898, and his prints were dispersed in a number of Sotheby and Christie sales between 1897 and 1908. The autograph collections, made up of 204 portfolios, sixty-eight 'special' groups, and three series, were sold at auction by Sothebys between 1917 and 1919. In 1927 Morrison's portrait engravings were sold at auctions in London and Leipzig, but not before items of special rarity or in particularly fine condition had been selected for the British Museum: 543 Dutch and Flemish portraits were the gift of Morrison's widow and the remainder was purchased anonymously for the museum on favourable terms by Samuel Courtauld. Many specimens from Morrison's collection of damascene work found their way into the Nasser D. Khalili collection and were exhibited at the Victoria and Albert Museum, London, in 1997.

ALAN BELL

Sources R. Gatty, *Portrait of a merchant prince: James Morrison, 1789-1857* (privately printed, Northallerton, Yorks., [1977]) · A. N. L.

Munby, *The cult of the autograph letter in England* (1962) · *DNB* · Burke, *Gen. GB* (1965) · E. Olivier, *Four Victorian ladies of Wiltshire* (1945) · *Ninth report*, 2, HMC, 8 (1884)

Archives NRA, priv. coll., MSS | BL, autograph collections, Add. MSS 39672–39673, 39757, 39779–39793, 39839–39842
Likenesses H. J. Brooks, group portrait, oils (*Private view of the Old Masters Exhibition, Royal Academy, 1888*), NPG
Wealth at death £869,174 12s. 6d.: probate, 5 April 1898, *CGPLA Eng. & Wales*

Morrison, Arthur George (1863–1945), writer and novelist, was born at 14 John Street, Poplar, in the East End of London, on 1 November 1863, one of the three children of George Richard Morrison (d. 1871), an engine fitter in the docks, and his wife, Jane, *née* Cooper. These details about his birth conflict with the biographical details that Morrison himself later supplied—he maintained that he had been born in Kent, the son of a 'professional man', and had been educated at private schools. These details are only the first of the false trails that Morrison laid for future scholars, in a largely successful attempt to conceal the extent of his working-class origins from his contemporaries.

Little is known about Morrison's childhood or education, but he probably spent most of his adolescence in the East End; in 1879 he worked as an office boy at the architect's department of the London school board, where he earned 7s. a week. A year later his mother took over a haberdasher's shop in Grundy Street, and it was at about this time that Morrison began submitting comic verse to the magazine *Cycling*. He became involved in boxing and cycling, and contributed to various cycling journals. His first serious journalism, however, was published in *The Globe* in 1885. A year later, at twenty-three, he was working as a clerk to the Beaumont Trustees, a charitable trust that administered the People's Palace, in Mile End, in the East End of London. The People's Palace was designed as an educational and cultural centre for the community, and consisted of the Queen's Hall, a library, a swimming bath, a gymnasium, and a winter garden as well as schools. Lectures and exhibitions were held at the palace, in addition to concerts and recitals. Morrison became sub-editor of the house paper, the *Palace Journal*, and reprinted in it pieces that he had already published as Cockney Corners in *The People*. It was Morrison's work with the People's Palace that later allowed him to describe his previous employment as 'the secretary of an old Charity Trust' or a 'civil servant', 'both of which terms are half-truths calculated to add social respectability to the post he actually held' (Keating, 'Biographical study', 11). And yet this post was also useful in defending the realism of Morrison's depiction of the East End in his novels, as it meant that he could disguise his personal and autobiographical connections to the slums; he could subsume them by references to his professional connection.

Morrison left the People's Palace at the end of September 1890, and joined the editorial staff of the evening *Globe*. He also freelanced, and in 1891 published his first book, *The Shadows around Us*, a collection of supernatural tales originally printed in *The People*. More significantly, however, in October 1891 he contributed a story called 'A

Arthur George Morrison (1863–1945), by Frederic G. Hodsoll, 1902

Street' to *Macmillan's*. Its conciseness and distinct lack of sentimentality in its portrayal of the East End were praised, and its positive reception encouraged Morrison over the next year to submit fourteen tales in a similar vein to his friend W. E. Henley, editor of the *National Observer*. On 22 August 1892 Morrison married Eliza Adelaide (Elizabeth) Thatcher (1864/5–1956) at Forest Gate; they lived at Chingford, and then at Salcombe House, Loughton, Essex. In 1893 they had a son, Guy (d. 1921). A year later Morrison collected and reprinted the East End tales, and published them as *Tales of Mean Streets* (1894), dedicated to Henley, their first publisher. While the volume was a success, running into several editions, and prompting a great deal of discussion about new developments in English realism, many of the reviews focused on the violence of one tale in particular, 'Lizerunt', and there was a backlash. The book was removed from Clerkenwell Library by local authorities, and W. H. Smith temporarily refused to supply it to circulating libraries.

Although angry at the negative characterization of the collection based on only one of its tales, Morrison went on to write next the novel for which he is most famous: *A Child of the Jago* (1896), the violence of which led to similar critical charges. Not content to base his work solely on his own experience of the East End, Morrison did a significant amount of research in the parish of the Revd A. Osborne Jay, vicar of Holy Trinity, Shoreditch, and author of *Life in Darkest London* (1891) and *The Social Problem: its Possible Solution* (1893). Jay had written to Morrison after reading *Tales of Mean Streets*, praising it but pointing out that monotony and attempted respectability were certainly not features of his own parish, which demonstrated problems more akin to those of the alcoholism, domestic violence, and crime portrayed in 'Lizerunt'. The impact of his visit to Jay's parish led Morrison to a determination to write a novel in which 'I should tell the story of a boy who, but for his environment, would have become a good citizen' (Keating, 'Biographical study', 23). The novel is a powerful evocation of life in an east London slum, with extreme violence, crime, riots, and an absolute sense of the impossibility of escape for its inhabitants. The novel is indebted to *Oliver Twist*, and yet represents a darker vision of themes and characters presented in that novel—Dicky Perrott, the 'child of the Jago', is not rescued by providence or by the discovery of providentially rich relatives; he instead is a 'Jago rat', unredeemed and dying at the end of the book, with his last breath adhering to the Jago code, and refusing to 'nark' on the boy who has killed him. In this vision of the slum, death represents the only ''nother way out—better' for this anti-Oliver of the late nineteenth century (Morrison, *A Child of the Jago*, ed. Miles, 173).

The book came in for a great deal of criticism, much of it focusing on the naturalistic handling of violence and slum life. *A Child of the Jago* became a document in the debate over the nature and merits of late Victorian realism, and one of the most vehement criticisms was found in H. D. Traill's article in the *Fortnightly Review* (67, 1897, 63–73), in which he both doubted the veracity of Morrison's observations and took issue with his method of presentation. Morrison felt it necessary to answer the charges of such an eminent critic personally, and his reply was to form the preface to the third edition of *A Child of the Jago*, in which Morrison maintained the right of the author to present scenes of ugliness and, indeed, stated that such a right was also a duty: 'If the community have left horrible places and horrible lives before his eyes, then the fault is the community's; and to picture these places and these lives becomes not merely his privilege, but his duty' (Morrison, *A Child of the Jago*, ed. Miles, 5).

Morrison went on to write another novel set in the East End, *To London Town* (1899), but this had neither the critical nor the popular success of his previous two East End fictions. He also produced a detective novel, *The Dorrington Deed-Box* (1897), which complemented his earlier works of detective fiction written in the Conan Doyle vein, which had featured a detective called Martin Hewitt who 'shrewdly solved many crimes in a manner that would have done credit to the Great Detective himself' (*Martin Hewitt: Investigator*, new edn, 1971, dust-jacket). A historical novel, *Cunning Murrell* (1900), dealing with witchcraft in mid-nineteenth-century Essex, was skilfully written, and *The Hole in the Wall* (1902), another East End novel, but this time set in the 1860s and 1870s, represents some of his finest writing. Four more collections of stories followed: *The Red Triangle* (1903), *The Green Eye of Goona* (1904), *Divers Vanities* (1905), and *Green Ginger* (1909).

By 1913 Morrison had retired from writing fiction and journalism, and settled down in a house at High Beach, Essex, to devote time to his amateur passion: collecting and studying Chinese and Japanese works of art. He had

begun his collection as early as 1890, and in 1902 published a series of articles on the subject in the *Monthly Review*. The culmination of his work in this area was his two-volume *The Painters of Japan* (1911), largely illustrated from his own collection. Two years later Sir Watkin Gwynne purchased the bulk of his Chinese and Japanese prints, and presented them to the British Museum, where they were the subject of a catalogue and placed on public exhibition in 1914.

During the First World War, Morrison's son, Guy, served in the army, and Morrison himself served in the Essex special constabulary; in this capacity he had the distinction of phoning in the news of the first Zeppelin raid on London. After the war the Morrisons moved to Cavendish Square, London, where in 1921 Guy died of malaria that he had contracted while on active duty. Almost as little is known of Morrison's later life as is known of his early life. In 1924 he was made a member of the Royal Society of Literature, and in 1930 he moved to High Barn, Amersham Road, Chalfont St Peter, Buckinghamshire, where he lived quietly until his death fifteen years later. He was a freemason and a member of the Japanese Art Association. Arthur Morrison died at High Barn on 4 December 1945, a wealthy but little-known figure. After his death his wife, acting on his instructions, sold his library and burnt all his papers apart from the manuscript of *A Child of the Jago*, which he had presented to the Bethnal Green Library in 1936. A collection of 140 Japanese paintings and woodcuts and a collection of tea ceremony porcelain was bequeathed to the British Museum.

At the time of his death Morrison had slipped into relative literary obscurity: as J. Bell wrote, Morrison 'was one of those contemporary bestsellers who could be found on every Edwardian bookshelf, but who vanished in the Great War and were unknown to the new and changed generation which followed' (Miles, xxvi). V. S. Pritchett, however, wrote an enthusiastic article, 'An East End novelist', in the *New Statesman* in 1944 which inspired a slight revival of interest in his work, and *A Child of the Jago* has attracted a great deal of late twentieth- and early twenty-first-century critical and popular attention, as its uncompromising view of late nineteenth-century slum life continues to strike a chord. An opera by Shirley Thompson, based on the novel, was staged at the Royal Festival Hall, London, in 1997.　　　　M. CLARE LOUGHLIN-CHOW

Sources P. J. Keating, 'Biographical study', in A. Morrison, *A child of the Jago* (1896); P. J. Keating, ed., new edn (1969) • P. Miles, introduction and notes, in A. Morrison, *A child of the Jago* (1896); P. Miles, ed., new edn (1996) • b. cert. • m. cert. • d. cert. • P. J. Keating, *The working classes in Victorian fiction* (1971) • P. J. Keating, *The haunted study* (1989) • R. Calder, 'Arthur Morrison: a commentary with an annotated bibliography of writings about him', *English Literature in Transition, 1880–1920*, 28 (1985), 276–97 • J. Rennie, 'A life in books', www.towerhamlets.gov.uk/templates/news/detail.cfm?newsid=369, 11 March 2002

Archives Royal Society of Literature, London, letters to Royal Society of Literature

Likenesses F. G. Hodsoll, photograph, 1902, NPG [*see illus.*]

Wealth at death £45,645 19*s.* 8*d.*: probate, 1946, *CGPLA Eng. & Wales*

Morrison, Charles. *See* C. M. (*fl.* 1753).

Morrison, Charles (1817–1909), merchant banker, was born in London on 20 September 1817, the eldest of seven sons and four daughters of James *Morrison (1789–1857), then a humble shopman but later to become a self-made wholesale textile warehouseman, merchant banker, and MP, who made himself one of the very wealthiest men in Britain, leaving perhaps £5 million at his death, as well as over 100,000 acres of land. Charles Morrison's mother, Mary Anne Todd (*d.* 1887), was the daughter of the proprietor of Todd & Co., the textile warehouse at Fore Street in the City of London, of which James Morrison became manager after his marriage and which he then developed into perhaps the largest business of its kind in Britain. Charles Morrison was educated at private schools in London and Geneva until the age of fifteen, and spent three years each at the University of Edinburgh, and at Trinity College, Cambridge. Although he won several prizes at Edinburgh, through ill health he was forced to leave Cambridge without taking a degree.

In 1841 Charles Morrison and his younger brother Alfred *Morrison joined their father in a new firm, Morrison, Sons & Co., located at 62 Moorgate Street, which took over the financial and merchant banking interests their father had been developing. While Charles Morrison remained a partner in the Fore Street textile warehouse until it became a limited company in 1864, it was chiefly as a financier and merchant banker that he spent the remainder of his long life.

Morrison, Sons & Co. chiefly expanded into two types of investment: lending money on the security of mortgages to British aristocrats (among them the duke of Buckingham and Chandos, who became a spectacular bankrupt), and investments in foreign railroads, especially in France and the United States. Charles Morrison travelled extensively throughout the United States in the early 1840s, and his surviving letters and diaries offer a vivid description of America in a time of great economic and demographic expansion. Although Morrison, Sons & Co. was heavily hit by the liquidation of the Bank of the United States in 1841, it prospered thereafter. James Morrison owned £800,000 in American securities at his death in 1857.

In the 1850s Morrison, Sons & Co. appears to have been wound up, and, enriched by a generous inheritance from his father, Charles Morrison spent the next sixty years as an independent merchant banker, though he also sat on the boards of several companies, and served as chairman of the Hounslow and Metropolitan Railway Company and of the North British and Mercantile Insurance Company. Morrison increasingly specialized in South American securities, becoming prominent, in particular, in the River Plate Trust, which built many of the railways and utilities in Argentina from the 1870s onwards. He continued as well with mortgage, railway, and utility investments in Britain, and for many years made a speciality of purchasing good securities at what an obituarist described as 'absurdly low prices' during times of economic disturbance, frequently selling when their prices

rose. It is believed that he kept a large sum in gold as a reserve against a time of serious financial trouble. Although no miser, he lived a bachelor existence with some frugality, and habitually saved most of his vast income. By these means, continued over many decades, Morrison greatly increased even his father's princely wealth, and was certainly among the half-dozen wealthiest men in Britain when he died. Although Morrison was well-known to the financial *cognoscenti*—a 300-word obituary appeared in *The Times* when he died—he was virtually unknown to the general public and is a classic instance of a virtually unknown man who, quietly and behind the scenes, exercised perhaps greater economic influence than many household names. At his death Morrison left the extraordinary sum of £10,936,666, considerably more than the value of any estate ever left previously by a British businessman. Despite his near total obscurity, Morrison was probably the wealthiest financier in Britain, far richer than any individual member of the renowned Baring and Rothschild families. Charles Morrison and his family also remained totally unknown to economic historians until the 1970s, when they were rediscovered as remarkable leviathans of wealth.

Apart from his business interests, Charles Morrison was also a landowner on a grand scale, inheriting the entire island of Islay in Argyllshire from his father, who had purchased it in 1849. In 1883 Charles Morrison owned 75,732 acres with an annual rental income of £31,434. Apart from Islay's 67,000 acres in Argyllshire, Morrison owned the 7000-acre Basildon Park estate in Berkshire, and smaller holdings in Essex, Oxford, and Suffolk. The five Morrison brothers, who are recorded in John Bateman's *Great Landowners* (1883 edn), owned 106,915 acres, yielding £53,740 in landed income, more than that of most dukes. Although Charles Morrison occasionally visited Islay, he spent most of his time at Basildon Park. At Islay, however, he maintained a steamer service at an annual loss of £6000 in order to benefit his tenants, who had no other way of getting their stock to market.

Throughout his life Morrison was shy and retiring, and suffered from cystitis. He took little or no direct part in public life, although he served as deputy lieutenant for Argyllshire and Berkshire. In 1854 he published an *Essay on Labour and Capital* in which he advised workers to marry late, produce fewer children, and thus raise their living standards; he also praised the cautious, intelligent businessman as superior to the speculator. At his Basildon home he maintained a valuable painting collection, which included works by Leonardo, Rembrandt, Rubens, Turner, and Watteau. He was an Anglican, and a supporter of the Liberal Party throughout the nineteenth century.

Charles Morrison died at Basildon Park on 25 May 1909. He was unmarried, and his enormous estate was divided among his many relatives, with his nephew Hugh Morrison (1868–1931) (later a Conservative MP) inheriting the Islay estate and a larger share of his vast personal fortune than anyone else. W. D. RUBINSTEIN

Sources C. A. Jones, 'Morrison, Charles', *DBB* · R. Gatty, *Portrait of a merchant prince: James Morrison, 1789–1857* (privately printed,

Northallerton, Yorks., [1977]) · *The Times* (26 May 1909) · *The Times* (27 May 1909) · *The Times* (5 June 1909) · W. D. Rubinstein, *Men of property: the very wealthy in Britain since the industrial revolution* (1981) · J. Bateman, *The great landowners of Great Britain and Ireland*, 4th edn (1883) · Burke, *Gen. GB*
Archives priv. coll., family papers | GL, papers of Morrison, Cryder & Co.
Wealth at death £10,936,666: resworn probate, 7 June 1909, *CGPLA Eng. & Wales*

Morrison [*née* Cooper; *other married name* Sutton], **Frances** (1807–1898), socialist writer, was born at Petworth, Sussex, in January 1807. Her mother was an unmarried farmgirl (with the surname of Cooper) who shortly after Frances's birth married John Bromley, a groom and possibly Frances's father. The Bromleys moved to Pershore, Worcestershire, but Frances remained in the care of her maternal grandmother until her adolescence, when she joined her mother and stepfather. A spirited and very attractive girl of strong will and a highly romantic imagination, for a time she attended a boarding-school in Bury St Edmunds, Suffolk, which gave her some training in 'accomplishments'; altogether a daunting addition to a poor family. She felt a misfit, and unhappy, until in 1822 at the age of sixteen she met and fell in love with the journeyman house-painter James *Morrison (1802–1835). The young couple moved to Newcastle upon Tyne, James's native city, where they lived in a common-law union. After four or five years Frances became pregnant and they married—a common order of events in the early nineteenth-century working class.

For the rest of the 1820s Frances Morrison was kept busy with child rearing (she had at least five children, of whom four survived), housekeeping, and running a small newspaper shop in Birmingham, where the family moved in 1828. She also began, with the encouragement of her husband, to educate herself in radical ideas—particularly those of Robert Owen. 'Long 'ere I began to think, my reason warred with the absurd forms of society,' she later wrote to Owen, 'but from an ill-cultivated and wrong direction given to my mind, I could never get a solid idea until the perusal of your Essays' (Sever, 13). In 1833 James Morrison, also a radical thinker and trade union activist, became editor of *The Pioneer*, a newspaper committed to Owenite principles and the creation of a 'general union of all trades' to serve as the basis of a workers' democracy. Frances Morrison wrote articles for *The Pioneer* under the pseudonym 'a Bondswoman', while she and James initiated a 'Woman's page' (possibly the first in any English periodical) and co-authored a series of editorials which dealt with issues affecting women, ranging from the inequities of the marriage law to the demand for equal pay for equal work. 'A woman's wage is not reckoned at an average more than two-thirds of a male,' one of these editorials ran:

> and we believe in reality it seldom amounts to more than a third (and wives have no wages at all). Yet, is not the produce of female labour as useful? … The industrious female is well entitled to the same amount of remuneration as the industrious male. (*The Pioneer*, 12 April 1834)

Owenite socialism had a strong current of women's rights running through it, so to discover such views in an Owenite paper is not surprising, though the Morrisons were unusual in making such clear links between the economic demands of Owenite unionism and the case for female equality. Other Owenites, including Owen himself, placed much more emphasis on educational and marital reform, and these were the issues on which Frances Morrison later lectured when, after James's premature death from a fall in 1835, she became a paid publicist for the socialist cause. Immediately after James's death a fund was set up within the Owenite movement to assist Frances Morrison and her daughters, and with this she purchased a small shop at 6 St Paul Street, Finsbury, London. But apparently the business proved unsuccessful since in the late 1830s she moved to Salford where she served as official 'hostess' in the Owenite Social Institution and then became a stipendiary lecturer, travelling on a northern speaking circuit. 'We have had a glorious day today', a Huddersfield socialist reported in a letter to the movement newspaper, *New Moral World*:

> Mrs Morrison lectured in the afternoon on the rights of women, and … in the evening on the marriage question. On both occasions the institution was densely crowded, and from 200 to 300 most respectable females attended each lecture … some hundreds must have returned, disappointed, being unable to obtain admittance. (*New Moral World*, Nov 1838)

What Frances Morrison actually said on this occasion is not recorded, but it was probably similar to arguments made in a lecture she had delivered two months earlier, published under the laborious title, *The influence of the present marriage system upon the character and interests of females contrasted with that proposed by Robert Owen, esq., a lecture delivered in the Social Institution … Manchester*. The Owenites were notorious for their liberal views on marriage, with Owen himself having outraged conventional opinion in 1835 with a series of lectures denouncing marriage and the nuclear family. Only a few Owenites (and very few female Owenites) held Owen's extreme libertarian views (and he himself later repudiated them), but most were committed to the replacement of the existing marital system with one based on communality and sexual equality. Frances Morrison's lecture, in which she argued that only the Owenite system of co-operative communities could provide the conditions for happy marriages, was typical. In the 'old immoral world' of nineteenth-century Britain, she noted, women's economic dependence on men often forced them into unions which were cruelly oppressive— a vision which clearly appealed to many of the poor women drawn to the Owenite ranks:

> But in community, money will not be known, neither will the want of it be dreaded, for all that can minister to the comforts of life will be had in abundance. There will be no marrying for convenience merely (a very cold word), but real affection inspired by real and known worth on both sides. (Morrison, 10)

Morrison's stint as a lecturer was short-lived. Soon she apprenticed her oldest daughter to the tape-weaving trade and, with Owen's help, found a teaching post in Hulme.

She then effectively disappeared from the Owenite scene, though in the mid-1840s a woman claiming to be her began delivering anti-socialist lectures in Manchester and elsewhere, saying she had recanted on her earlier beliefs. Her husband's biographer, however, claims that Frances Morrison maintained her Owenite views until her death, so this episode remains unexplained (certainly false recantations from impostors did occur). In the 1850s Frances Morrison married her second husband, a London pastry-cook named Robert Sutton, with whom she had another daughter. Three of her children had by then emigrated to Australia. Her husband having predeceased her, she spent her final years with her eldest married daughter. She died on 29 August 1898 at 11 Station Road, Dovercourt, Harwich, Essex. BARBARA TAYLOR

Sources J. Sever, 'James Morrison of the Pioneer', 1963, BL · B. Taylor, *Eve and the new Jerusalem: socialism and feminism in the nineteenth century* (1983) · *The Pioneer* (1833–4) · *New Moral World* (1838–41) · F. Morrison, *The influence of the present marriage system* (1838) · d. cert.

Morrison, George (1703/4?–1799), military engineer and army officer, entered the train of artillery as a gunner on 1 October 1722, and was quartered at Edinburgh Castle until 1729. He distinguished himself in suppressing the Jacobite rising of 1745, and was sent to the Royal Military Academy at Woolwich as a cadet gunner. After he had been instructed in the theory of a profession of which he had already learned the practice he was sent to Flanders with the temporary rank of engineer-extraordinary from 3 February 1747, and served under Captain Heath, chief engineer of the duke of Cumberland's army. He was present at the battles of Roucoux and Val (July) and at the siege of Bergen op Zoom (12 July – 16 September). With the assistance of Engineer Hall he made a survey of the River Merk and of the adjoining country from Breda to Stoutersgut.

Following the peace treaty of Aix-la-Chapelle, on 2 April 1748 Morrison was appointed to the permanent list as sub-engineer, and on his return home he was sent to Scotland and employed in surveying the highlands and constructing roads on a plan laid down by Marshal George Wade. Under Morrison's superintendence part of the trunk road from Stirling to Fort William was made, and also the road through the wilds of Glenbeg and Glenshee to Dalbriggan. Part of the road between Blairgowrie and Braemar was made by a detachment of George Keppel, Viscount Bury's regiment under Morrison's orders.

In April 1750 Morrison was sent to Northallerton in Yorkshire. Possessed of personal attractions and accomplishments, and having earned the good opinion of the duke of Cumberland, he was about this time brought to the notice of George II; and in 1751 he joined the household of the young prince of Wales, later George III. He was promoted engineer-extraordinary on 1 January 1753. During the 1750s he married; his wife's name was Mary, and their eldest child, Henrietta Jane (d. 1849), was baptized at St Anne's, Soho, on 2 December 1757. The Morrisons had five other children. In May 1757 the officers of the corps were granted military rank and Morrison was made a captain-lieutenant.

On 25 April 1758 Morrison was appointed to the expedition assembled in the Isle of Wight for a descent on the French coast. He took part under Charles Spencer, third duke of Marlborough, in the landing in June in Cancale Bay, near St Malo, and the destruction of St Servan and Solidore. The troops were thence conveyed to Le Havre and to Cherbourg, and returned home again. Morrison embarked under General Bligh at Portsmouth on 23 July and sailed on 1 August for Cherbourg. Forts Tourlaville, Galet, Hommet, Esqueurdreville, St Anines, and Querqueville, with the basin, built at considerable expense, were all destroyed. Bligh sailed for England on 15 August. On 31 August, Morrison again sailed with General Bligh with troops for St Malo; he took part in the action of 9 September and in the battle of St Cas on 11 September. At the termination of these expeditions Morrison returned to court. He was promoted full captain and engineer in ordinary on 3 March 1759.

On 22 February 1761 Morrison was promoted lieutenant-colonel in the army and appointed deputy quartermaster-general on the headquarters staff. After the death of General Bland in June 1763 he was appointed quartermaster-general to the forces, and was in frequent attendance on George III. He was appointed equerry to the king's brother Edward, duke of York, and travelled with him in 1764. He accompanied the duke when he left England on 7 July 1767, attended him assiduously during his illness at Monaco, and was present at his death in September of that year. Morrison was ill himself, and it was said that it was only with much difficulty that the dying prince could be prevailed on to accept his services. Morrison accompanied the duke of York's remains to England, and attended their interment on the night of 3 November in Westminster Abbey.

In 1769 Morrison was a member of a committee appointed to consider the defences of Gibraltar. He was promoted colonel in the army on 22 December 1772 and sub-director and major in the corps of Royal Engineers on 2 February 1775; and he was made a major-general on 29 August 1777. In 1779 he was appointed colonel of the 75th regiment, and in 1781 he attended Jeffrey, first Baron Amherst, the commander-in-chief, on an inspection of the east coast defences on the outbreak of the war with the Netherlands. On 29 May 1782 he was transferred from the colonelcy of the 75th foot to that of the 17th regiment, and on 20 November he was promoted lieutenant-general. On 8 August 1792 he was transferred from the colonelcy of the 17th foot to that of the 4th King's Own regiment of foot. But little more is recorded of the ancient quartermaster-general except the changes of his residence. He was living at Sion Hill near Barnet in 1792, and at Fairy Hall near Eltham on 3 May 1796, when he was promoted general. Morrison died at his house in Seymour Street, London, on 26 November 1799, at about the age of ninety-five. He was the oldest staff officer in the service.

Many of Morrison's military maps and plans are in the British Library or the Public Record Office. His eldest daughter, Henrietta Jane, married George Arnold, gentleman to the privy council. She also lived to an old age, dying on 17 September 1849, aged ninety-two.

R. H. VETCH, rev. JONATHAN SPAIN

Sources N&Q, 3rd ser., 1 (1862), 372, 420, 474 · W. Porter, *History of the corps of royal engineers*, 2 vols. (1889) · R. Cannon, ed., *Historical record of the seventeenth, or the Leicestershire regiment of foot* (1848) · *GM*, 1st ser., 33 (1763) · *GM*, 1st ser., 62 (1792) · *GM*, 1st ser., 69 (1799) · *Annual Register* (1799), 176

Morrison, George Ernest (1862–1920), journalist and traveller, was born on 4 February 1862 at Geelong, Newtown, Victoria, Australia, the second child and eldest son of the five sons and two daughters of George Morrison (1830–1898), founder and principal of Geelong College, a boys' private school, and his wife, Rebecca Greenwood, from Yorkshire. Morrison went from his father's school to Melbourne University in 1879 to study medicine but failed a crucial professional examination in 1882. By this time, however, he had acquired a reputation for making long-distance walking tours and for selling his accounts of them to the newspapers. He broadened his journalistic scope in 1882 when he signed on as an able seaman and went from Port Mackay to the south sea islands to study the slave traffic in Kanaka islanders, and from 1882 to 1883 when he crossed Australia north to south in the footsteps of Burke and Wills, selling stories to the newspapers about each exploit. His report on slave trafficking proved very controversial.

In June 1883 a newspaper financed an expedition to New Guinea, from which Morrison returned with severe spear wounds. In March 1884 he resumed his medical studies at Edinburgh University (his father was a Scot) and graduated MB, CM from there in 1887. After a rather aimless period in the USA and the West Indies he returned to Australia in 1891 to become resident surgeon at Ballarat Hospital. He stayed there for two years until his urge to move on took him to Hong Kong, and then, in 1894, on a journey on foot and by horse across China from Shanghai to Rangoon.

In February 1895 Morrison returned to London to seek a publisher for *An Australian in China* (1895), an account of his latest journey which met great acclaim, and to graduate MD of Edinburgh with a thesis on malformations. On the strength of his book C. F. Moberly Bell, manager of *The Times*, offered him work as a secret correspondent in Asia. His cogent reports on French influence in Siam won him appointment in 1897 as resident correspondent of *The Times* in Peking (Beijing). During his twenty years as Far Eastern correspondent of *The Times* he visited every province of China, though he never reached Tibet. He proved an intelligent and courageous reporter, at a time when Western interest in China was increasing. During the Boxer uprising in 1900 he was seriously wounded while rescuing another man and was thought to have been killed. His obituary, published in *The Times* on 17 July, described him as 'devoted, ... fearless, and ... able ... [the source of] the earliest and most accurate intelligence concerning events in which the interests of this country have been so largely involved'.

Morrison survived to be, during the next ten years, a determined exponent of events impinging upon British interests in the Far East, particularly in respect of German and Russian activity there. He vigorously supported the Japanese in the Russo-Japanese war of 1904–5 and represented *The Times* at the Portsmouth peace conference in 1905 at the end of that war. In 1910 he made the last of his great journeys across China, travelling from Honan (Henan) in central China to Russian Turkestan, a distance of 3750 miles, in 174 days.

On 26 August 1912 at Croydon, Surrey, Morrison married his secretary, Jennie Wark (d. 1923), daughter of Robert Robin. They had three sons. His marriage brought him personal happiness, but his new role as adviser to the president of the new Chinese republic, Yuan Shih K'ai, proved unsatisfactory. He complained of being kept in the dark and his role in the preparation of China's submissions to the 1919 Versailles conference could not prevent the subordination of China's interests to Japan's; but by this time Morrison was ill with chronic pancreatitis. He died, while on leave in England, at Devoran Esplanade, Sidmouth, Devon, on 30 May 1920. He was buried in Sidmouth cemetery.

'Chinese Morrison' or 'Morrison of Peking', as he was known, was one of the greatest newspaper correspondents of his age. The Morrison lectures, founded in his memory in 1932, are held each year at the Australian National University, Canberra.　　　H. F. OXBURY, rev.

Sources *The Times* (31 May 1920) · C. Pearl, *Morrison of Peking* (1967) · T. S. Gregory, 'Morrison, George Ernest', *AusDB*, vol. 10 · B. R. Keith, 'Morrison, George', *AusDB*, vol. 5 · [S. Morison and others], *The history of The Times*, 3 (1947) · *WWW* · *CGPLA Eng. & Wales* (1920)
Archives King's Lond., papers relating to Jesuit missionaries · Mitchell L., NSW, corresp. and papers · News Int. RO, papers | BL OIOC, corresp. with Frederick Bailey, MSS Eur. F 157 · U. Newcastle, Robinson L., letters to Gertrude Bell
Wealth at death £27,545 5s. 8d.: probate, 1920, *CGPLA Eng. & Wales*

Morrison, Herbert Stanley, Baron Morrison of Lambeth (1888–1965), politician, was born at 240 Ferndale Road, Brixton, London, on 3 January 1888. His father, Henry Morrison (1849/50–1917), was a police constable of Conservative politics and with a liking for alcohol; his mother, Priscilla Caroline Lyon (1848/9–1907), daughter of an East End carpet fitter, had been in domestic service. With six children surviving infancy, conditions were hard, but Morrison's father was a member of the uniformed working class. This meant both status and regular earnings. The family appears to have had no significant religious affiliation; Morrison's upbringing was largely secular.

Organizing Labour in London In one respect Morrison's childhood was distinctively difficult. An eye infection immediately after birth destroyed the sight in his right eye. During his schooldays, first at the Stockwell Road board school and from eleven at St Andrew's Church of England School, he was often marginal to children's pursuits. On leaving school he entered the world made famous in H. G. Wells's portrayal of Mr Kipps; he worked as a shop assistant in south London and then in Pimlico. Hours

Herbert Stanley Morrison, Baron Morrison of Lambeth (1888–1965), by Bassano, 1940

were long; at the Pimlico shop he 'lived in'. In 1908 he moved to Whitbread's brewery as a switchboard operator. This post brought him into the National Union of Clerks, his only direct experience of trade union activity. These jobs offered minimal long-term prospects; from 1912, when he took a post as a circulation traveller for the new Labour newspaper, the *Daily Citizen*, his career lay within the labour movement.

Morrison's political formation was based on a dedication to self-education. Apparently on the advice of a phrenologist, he read extensively in history and economics, and gradually became a socialist. In October 1906 he joined the Brixton branch of the Independent Labour Party; however the ILP was relatively weak in London and he soon shifted to the formally Marxist Social Democratic Federation (Social Democratic Party from 1908). His wide reading now included not just radical economists and historians, and progressive fiction, but English translations of Marx, Engels, and Kautsky. His commitment to socialism produced rows with his tory father; he finally left home and lived in a succession of south London bedsitters. His appearance was shabby; his meals were irregular. Taken in hand by concerned comrades, his clothes became smarter. He ceased in public to be Bert Morrison and became Herbert. An effective outdoor speaker, he became increasingly interested in political organization and in specific achievements rather than symbolic protests.

These priorities led Morrison back to the Independent

Labour Party, which was allied with the trade unions in the Labour Party. In contrast the Social Democrats, relatively strong in London, and more pragmatic than some stereotypes suggest, stood alone. By 1910 he was clearly committed to a gradualist vision of economic and social transformation; his journalism in the ILP newspaper *Labour Leader* proclaimed a socialist solution to the contemporary debate over national efficiency. His hopes for socialist transformation placed significant weight on the reform of local government; his first municipal candidacy, at Vauxhall in 1912, ended in defeat but his campaign was notable for the quality of the publicity material.

This failure must be placed in the broader context of pre-1914 London Labour politics. Trade unionism was relatively weak and the continuing strength of the Social Democrats militated against the construction of a socialist–trade union alliance. Only in May 1914 did the diverse socialist and trade union elements combine to form the London Labour Party. The initial secretary, Fred Knee, died within months, and on 27 April 1915 Morrison by one vote was elected his successor. At twenty-seven he had secured his first significant base.

The post not only solved an immediate problem—the *Daily Citizen* had folded the previous month—it also gave Morrison a congenial and creative task for the remainder of a war that he opposed. His response to the outbreak of hostilities was one of political opposition to what he characterized as a capitalist and imperialist conflict. In 1916 he received his call-up papers; his disability would have been sufficient for exemption but he opposed the call-up on socialist grounds. Characteristically he rejected an absolutist position and accepted alternative work of national benefit. He became a rather incompetent gardener at Letchworth Garden City where a politically sympathetic employer gave him scope to carry out his work for the London Labour Party.

Morrison's task was formidable. Labour successes in the capital before 1914 had been fragmented; the war threatened to be a divisive issue. His concentration on organizational improvements and on domestic topics produced little reward in the 1918 general election, but in the municipal contests of 1919 Labour achieved a sensational breakthrough. Before 1914 Labour had only forty-eight councillors in London; in 1919 the party won over 550 seats. It controlled twelve of the twenty-eight London boroughs. The reasons for this breakthrough were complex, and some of the ground was lost three years later; but Labour had become a credible force in London, and Morrison took much of the credit.

Morrison now lived in Hackney, one of the twelve boroughs captured by Labour, and in 1920 became mayor. This appointment came despite his not being a member of the council. In office he was predictably efficient, and for a mayor took an unusually active role in making policy. Two characteristics of this early experience of political leadership proved enduring. His relationship with council officers involved frank debate followed by a firm decision. On a broader canvas he responded to the challenge of unemployment by insisting that action must be constitutional.

This position contrasted with the contemporary and illegal response of George Lansbury and the Poplar councillors, which he saw as conducive to chaos. The gaoled Poplar councillors gained sympathy within the labour movement. But as post-war radicalism diminished, Morrison's municipal strategy became dominant within the party.

From 1922 Labour lost control of Hackney. Morrison's political priorities shifted above all to the London county council (LCC). His power base remained the London Labour Party, which during the 1920s became a formidable political machine. In 1922 Morrison entered the LCC as a councillor for Woolwich. The borough had been a precocious Labour stronghold; it had an impressively large local party and a Labour newspaper, and from the late 1920s the Royal Arsenal Co-operative Society was uniquely affiliated to the national Labour Party. Woolwich offered for Morrison a model of Labour organization—extensive, efficient, and concerned not just with conventional political issues, but also with a variety of cultural activities. He moved to nearby Eltham; this suburb was Morrison's home for the rest of his life. For him Labour's appeal should not be restricted to established working-class communities: it must include the 'useful people' of the suburbs who would respond to a reasoned programme of reform. Within the LCC Morrison became chief whip in 1923 and then leader of the Labour group in 1925. Vigorous advocacy in debate was combined characteristically with more efficient group organization.

Although Morrison was identified inevitably with London politics, he also emerged on the national scene as a significant figure in the 1920s. First elected to the Labour Party's national executive committee (NEC) in 1920, he remained a very active member, with three brief intervals, for over three decades. In the early years he was prominent in the tortuous discussions over the complex relationship between the Labour Party and the Communist Party. An early advocate of a hard line towards the communists, he ensured that local Labour parties in London with communist involvement were reorganized. At party conferences he established himself as an effective debater combining a firm defence of the party leadership with thoughtful and accessible presentations of issues. Labour Party chairman in 1928–9, he presided in 1929 over the party conference, a celebration of electoral victory that nevertheless contained harbingers of future disillusion. Morrison's conduct of the proceedings was assessed critically by an astute observer. Walter Citrine, the general secretary of the TUC, noted 'his peculiar insistence upon his own correctness of ruling. He was not only confident, but rubbed it into the Conference that he was right' (BLPES, Citrine papers, pt 1 7/8).

Morrison's first period as a member of parliament was as a backbencher during the first Labour government. Elected for South Hackney in a three-cornered contest in December 1923, he initially found the Commons less congenial than local government. His first speech was unpersuasively partisan; his subsequent interventions were stronger, reflecting his increasing grasp of parliamentary procedure, and his concentration on London issues. This led him to oppose the government's London Traffic Bill, which he attacked as the adoption of a Conservative proposal that would give regulatory powers to central government, not least for road passenger transport. In the election of October 1924 Morrison was defeated in a straight fight with a Liberal, but in May 1929 divided opposition helped to give him a comfortable victory in South Hackney.

Minister of transport, 1929–1931 Despite his limited parliamentary experience Morrison went straight into the second Labour government as minister of transport. One observer wondered whether there was not 'a great future in the Party for the self-sacrificing, simple, honest and retiring devotion of Herbert Morrison' (Wertheimer, 188). In many respects his record over the government's troubled career enhanced his reputation, culminating in his promotion to the cabinet in March 1931. His ministerial performance in his department and in the Commons was recognized widely as a high point in an increasingly demoralized government. The skills polished in municipal administration and debate were appreciated more widely. Morrison's success owed something to the relative distance of his departmental concerns from the immediate impact of the depression. He could reform areas of transport policy without confronting immediately the constraints of Treasury orthodoxy.

Morrison's first bill responded to the extensive growth of road traffic by modernizing the law. Although it included controversial elements, most notably the abolition of the speed limit for cars, it did not divide MPs on partisan lines. The passage of this complex legislation raised Morrison's profile; he then turned to a favourite topic, the reform of London transport. He began by killing off inherited proposals for a private combine; gradually, through ministerial discussions and bargaining with interest groups, an alternative emerged—a public corporation responsible for most passenger traffic undertakings within the London area. Some elements would come from private ownership, others (the tramways) from municipal authorities.

Morrison's persistent advocacy within the government brought the bill to the Commons in March 1931. His case combined both a partisan appeal—this was practical socialism—and an attempt to gain cross-party support through emphasizing the economic merits of the proposals. For Morrison well-thought-out schemes could be both socialist and consensual. But his expectations for the bill were not realized. The collapse of the second Labour government in August 1931 meant an end to the bill. Yet by 1933 the London Passenger Transport Board was formed following legislation by the National Government.

Morrison's record at the Ministry of Transport earned widespread approval but helped to secure him the enmity of one increasingly powerful Labour figure. Ernest Bevin, the Transport Workers' leader, was a 'good hater' with a suspicion of many career politicians, especially of those whose links with the trade unions were sparse. After the general strike of 1926, Bevin became a dominant figure on the general council of the Trades Union Congress and within the Labour Party—a man whose support was worth courting. His suspicion of Morrison might have begun with the latter's revolt in 1924 on the London Transport Bill; this legislation had had the support of Bevin's union. Certainly there was considerable friction during the second Labour government. When Morrison's modernization of the road traffic law included powers to limit lorry drivers' hours, Bevin objected on the ground that this was a matter for trade union negotiators. More basically Bevin attacked Morrison's proposals for the composition of the London Passenger Transport Board. For Morrison ability should be the sole criterion; for Bevin trade unionists should be involved preferably as board members or at least in the consultations over membership. The exchanges on the principle carried on beyond the demise of the Labour government; they raised serious issues about the purpose and structure of publicly owned industry.

This breach affected the remainder of Morrison's career. Widespread approval of Morrison's ministerial record was also eroded by rumours about his behaviour in the crisis of August 1931. During cabinet discussions over expenditure cuts gradual and often ambiguous opposition developed among some ministers to cuts in much social provision and especially in unemployment benefit. Morrison took no part in this opposition; he was loyal to MacDonald and voted with the majority in favour of a 10 per cent reduction in unemployment benefit. That much is clear, as is Morrison's subsequent decision, along with five others from this majority, to go into opposition with the Labour Party. The uncertainty concerns how far Morrison was attracted by a post in the newly formed National Government. Reasons might have included admiration for MacDonald, a concern to safeguard his London transport reforms, and an expectation that the new government's life would be short. Contemporary press speculation and contradictory accounts by some contemporaries suggest some uncertainty—among others and, not least, within himself—about his likely choice. The calling of an election meant the exorcism of residual doubts; it also produced Morrison's defeat in South Hackney.

The 1931 crisis effectively terminated the leadership of the Labour Party's first generation; the initiative passed to those born largely in the 1880s who had established their political reputations after 1918. Among this group Morrison had established himself as a ministerial success; but like many of his peers he no longer had a parliamentary base. However, the small size of the post-1931 parliamentary party meant that influence within the party's NEC acquired an unusual significance. Along with another ambitious ex-minister, Hugh Dalton, Morrison played a critical role in the party's post-1931 policy making. He was a leading figure on the NEC's policy sub-committee, and especially in the study group on the reorganization of industry. Within this body he championed the public corporation as the preferred approach to nationalization, a method that he defended effectively in his 1933 book *Socialisation and Transport*. Such advocacy reopened the

argument with some trade unions, most notably Bevin's Transport Workers, and there were serious but inconclusive debates at the party conferences of 1932 and 1933. However, the lack of a formal victory for Morrison proved irrelevant; after 1945 the public corporation was the form of public ownership chosen by the Attlee government.

More broadly Morrison's contribution to policy making helped to provide the party with a coherent programme of specific economic and social measures that could be represented as the first practical steps towards the replacement of capitalism by a socialist commonwealth. This combination of the practical and visionary had shaped the politics of Morrison and many colleagues since before 1914. The synthesis, aided by Morrison's presentational skills, made him a dominant figure at the party conferences of the 1930s. He defended specific policies and their gradualist rationale against the criticism of those who wished to draw more radical lessons from the débâcle of 1931. As the challenge of fascism deepened, he insisted that the independence of the Labour Party offered the best defence; he thoroughly opposed proposals for a popular front with the communists and an increasingly ecumenical spectrum of progressives.

Leader of the London county council, 1934–1940 Yet despite his national prominence Morrison's greatest achievement in the 1930s was in London. Labour's electoral recovery after 1931 was uneven. In the general election of 1935 the party gained significantly in the popular vote, but fared disappointingly in terms of seats. In contrast, under Morrison's leadership Labour took control of the LCC in March 1934. The result was unexpected; Morrison was greeted as the architect. Beatrice Webb paid tribute to his talents—'a long pull and a hard pull lasting twenty years'—the final victory doing endless credit to his doggedness, skill and masterfulness' (*Diary*, 14 March 1935).

Morrison's strategy as leader of the LCC majority was to demonstrate Labour's capacity to govern both in implementing a coherent programme of reform and modernization, and in meeting high standards of efficiency and procedural propriety. Success could remove doubts about the party that were the perceived legacy of 1931. A competent team delivered distinctive policies combined with financial prudence. Schools were built; a significant start was made on the clearance of East End slums and on their replacement by modern LCC estates. The green belt was introduced to check the city's unplanned expansion. The provision of public assistance was humanized. A symbolic and successful battle with central government over the replacement of Waterloo Bridge allowed Morrison to portray the LCC as decisive and forward-looking. The popularity of these policies was demonstrated when the LCC elections were held in 1937. Turnout increased and although the opposition Municipal Reformers improved their vote, so did Labour, maintaining its share of the poll and gaining six more seats. This outcome testified to Morrison's skills in policy and administration, party organization and publicity. The Labour Party had other inter-war municipal achievements, but London's size and symbolism gave Morrison's record a unique prominence.

In contrast Morrison's parliamentary standing following his success at South Hackney in the 1935 election was ambiguous. In part this reflected his absence from the 1931 parliament. Under George Lansbury's leadership Clement Attlee, far less prominent than Morrison before 1931, had become deputy leader; Arthur Greenwood, whose status in 1929–31 had been similar to Morrison's, had returned to parliament after winning a by-election in April 1932. Following Lansbury's deposition from the leadership prior to the 1935 election, Attlee had served as temporary leader, and both he and Greenwood were candidates for the permanent post following the election. Morrison also stood. He had the support of influential MPs and advocates from both right and left who praised his drive and openness to discussion. They felt that he was interested in ideas. Yet in the first ballot he secured only forty-four votes to Attlee's fifty-eight and Greenwood's thirty-three. In the second round Morrison's vote increased by only four and Attlee's grew to eighty-eight.

No doubt Attlee benefited from the loyalty of those who had appreciated his virtues in the difficult parliament of 1931. Morrison's parliamentary experience was comparatively slight, and it was widely believed that his priority would remain the LCC—a concern that Morrison did nothing to dispel by an ambiguous comment at the decisive meeting of the Parliamentary Labour Party (PLP). Indeed Morrison was regarded by some as too narrowly a London politician in style and interests. Above all there was a bloc of trade union opinion in the PLP and beyond that distrusted Morrison as devious and potentially disloyal, a man who stood outside the relaxed alcohol-lubricated camaraderie that prevailed within a section of the PLP. The leadership election of 1935 was the first sign of a bloc within the party that would resist Morrison's attempts to achieve the leadership. Whatever his achievements, this rejection coloured the rest of his career; his initial response was to refuse nomination as deputy chairman of the PLP. For the remainder of the decade Morrison placed the LCC as his first priority.

As international crises increasingly dominated political debate, Morrison's national contribution became less distinctive. He travelled widely in the 1930s, but unlike his views on many domestic questions his line on international issues tended to reiterate conventional party themes. He favoured collective security through the League of Nations; with the dismemberment of Czechoslovakia in late 1938 he had to rethink the feasibility of this position. On the narrower question of whether the PLP should continue to oppose the National Government's defence estimates Morrison's reluctance to abandon his position put him at odds with his enemy Bevin and his previously supportive senior colleague, Dalton.

Morrison's significant contribution to wartime politics began in May 1940. He intervened in the crucial parliamentary debate on the failure of the Norwegian expedition, widening the indictment to a general criticism of the government's policy on the war. His criticism included a statement that the Labour Party would divide the house. The resulting vote, with Conservative rebels joining Labour or abstaining, meant the end of the Chamberlain government and the formation of the Churchill coalition. In all probability Morrison took the initiative in this parliamentary strategy within the PLP leadership; however, in the subsequent negotiations to construct a coalition Morrison was a peripheral figure.

The wartime coalition: supply and the Home Office Labour's entry into the coalition meant Morrison's return to government office and his effective farewell to the LCC; initially he was minister of supply. His time there was brief and assessments of his performance vary. As an organizer of his department and as a publicist he was predictably effective; but interdepartmental wrangles undermined attempts to organize raw materials and labour. One sympathetic observer felt that Morrison lacked the required sensitivity towards economic questions. His earlier achievements had not involved the need for a sophisticated appreciation of economic complexities and arguably this appointment did not capitalize on his strengths.

At the beginning of October 1940, in the context of the blitz and the feared social disintegration of British cities, Morrison was appointed home secretary. He held the post until the end of the coalition in May 1945, and entered the war cabinet in November 1942. This department was ideal for him. His relatively weak areas were irrelevant; the skills, techniques, and flair evident at the LCC were transferred effectively to a more extensive brief. He responded to the blitz with administrative flair and with a sensitive grasp of popular feelings. His visits to devastated cities, his responsiveness to local needs, and his characteristically careful discussions with officials produced new policies for civil defence and a radical reorganization of fire services, with control passing from local authorities to the Home Office.

Inevitably Morrison had to resolve conflicting pressures over civil liberties questions. In general he was a force for liberalism against Churchill's sporadic demands for more control of the press, though he banned the communist *Daily Worker* and the politically similar *The Week* in January 1941. The ban on the *Daily Worker* remained until August 1942, more than a year after the German invasion of the Soviet Union. The most significant challenge on a civil liberties issue came, however, because of Morrison's allegedly excessive liberalism. In November 1943 he released from detention, on medical grounds, the leader of the British Union of Fascists, Sir Oswald Mosley. Protests came not just from communists and the Labour left, but also from the Labour Party's NEC and the TUC general council. Morrison won the vote in the Commons, but there was abundant evidence of dissatisfaction within the PLP.

This controversy exemplified a persistent problem for senior Labour figures within the coalition. Their commitment to winning the war entailed a loyalty to their Conservative colleagues; but this was combined no doubt with awareness that their individual performances, not least that of Morrison, were strengthening belief in the competence of Labour. Yet they also had to contend with a PLP and a party in the country that feared loss of party identity through involvement in the coalition. This danger seemed the more serious since there was abundant evidence that popular sentiment was moving to the left. Frequently Morrison acted as a conciliator, arguing against those who claimed that Labour ministers were neglecting to exploit their indispensability to win progressive measures from the coalition. His most praised intervention, in February 1943, ironically failed to prevent a widespread PLP revolt against the discouraging coalition response to the Beveridge proposals on social security.

Morrison's credibility as a ministerial troubleshooter was enhanced by his continuing commitment to party activities. He remained an assiduous attender at the NEC and its sub-committees and demonstrated eagerness to discuss the content of post-war reconstruction. Once again there appeared a central theme in Morrison's politics: the hope of a consensual basis for incremental progress towards socialism. That advance would involve significant elements of public ownership.

This combination of ministerial success and principled and persuasive partisanship suggested that Morrison's claims to the Labour Party leadership were strengthening. However, the party conference of 1943 underlined for Morrison the limits to his support. The party treasurership had become vacant. This was a post elected by the whole of the party conference; significant trade union support was therefore essential. Morrison stood and was opposed by Arthur Greenwood, now widely recognized as in significant decline. A third candidate, William Glenvil Hall, had the benefit of the Miners' substantial vote, but little else. The unions were divided; Bevin's Transport Workers predictably provided the nucleus of Greenwood's support. Greenwood, the genial 'has-been', defeated the consummate politician on a minority vote.

Nevertheless Morrison's role in the preparations for a post-war election was indispensable. He chaired both the campaign and policy committees and produced the initial draft of what became the election manifesto, *Let us Face the Future*. His belief that Labour must appeal to progressive and useful people of all classes was expressed in his decision to leave South Hackney and move his candidacy to suburban East Lewisham. This seat had never been won by Labour; it was close to Morrison's home at Eltham and typified perhaps a social milieu in which Morrison felt particularly comfortable. His switch and his underlying expectations were justified by a majority of over 15,000 at the general election of 1945.

The Attlee government: lord president and deputy prime minister The election of the first majority Labour government brought an immediate attempt by Morrison to supplant Attlee. He argued for a leadership election by the new PLP, citing constitutional reforms made in the aftermath of the 1931 split. Given Labour's victory under a leader who had held the post for almost a decade, the ploy was doomed to fail. Indeed, whenever the party leadership was his concern, Morrison's political touch seemed to desert him; such manoeuvres served only to deepen the image of him as a conspirator among those who distrusted him. One of Attlee's qualities as a leader, was a

magnanimity that allowed him to reward talent whatever the personal issues. Morrison emerged from the post-election allocation of offices with the lord presidency of the council (28 July 1945), a supremo on the home front. He was also deputy prime minister and presided over the cabinet whenever Attlee was absent.

Morrison played a pivotal role in implementing the government's extensive domestic programme. He co-ordinated the passage of contentious bills through the Commons; as leader of the house he also had good relations with a Conservative opposition that recovered from the shock of defeat and resolved to contest government legislation vigorously. Respect for Commons procedures was combined with a desire to fulfil heavy legislative commitments; at the start of the new parliament the Labour majority endorsed Morrison's proposal that the government should take over all private members' time.

The skills demonstrated by Morrison were those central to his success on the LCC and now transferred to a national reform programme. Similarly Morrison spent much time responding to the concerns of a PLP which contained many new members, much idealism, and a significant number who positioned themselves on the Labour left. A liaison committee, with Morrison as the leading figure, facilitated communication between ministers and backbenchers. The government's large majority posed the problem of tasks for potentially bored backbenchers; Morrison responded with the introduction of policy groups, an experiment whose success varied with the topic and relevant ministers' support or lack of enthusiasm. Above all Morrison instituted a relatively liberal disciplinary regime with sanctions reserved for the most serious offences. Morrison's style, a broader ethos of loyalty, and the government's record combined to produce a more harmonious and generally more tolerant PLP than that of 1929–31.

One further initial responsibility posed more problems for Morrison. Charged with the co-ordination of economic planning, and armed with planning machinery inherited from the war, most observers felt that—as at the Ministry of Supply—he lacked a subtle appreciation of economic factors. Attlee, at a nadir in the government's fortunes, claimed that Morrison read out 'briefs in Cabinet without really understanding them' (*Political Diary of Hugh Dalton*, 413, mid-Sept 1947). A sympathetic civil servant felt that his mastery of economic detail and of the broader arguments was solid but that a deeper feel for the subject was lacking. Moreover the planning machinery was complex and fragmented, and defied Morrison's attempts at rationalization.

The year 1947 was critical for the government. A harsh winter and coal shortages led to industrial dislocation; the convertibility of sterling against the dollar introduced in mid-July precipitated a financial crisis and the rapid suspension of convertibility. From January to June serious illness removed Morrison from decision making; the summer economic crisis, which raised fears of another 1931, produced conspiratorial conversations among senior ministers. Cripps, Morrison, and Dalton felt that Attlee was indecisive and should be replaced, although predictably they differed as to the appropriate replacement. Bevin, preferred by Cripps, was not prepared to replace Attlee, and was anathema to Morrison. The latter naturally felt that he was the best replacement. Attlee's response demonstrated the skill that had maintained his position for so long. Cripps was strongly critical of Morrison's grasp of economic issues. Attlee successfully offered Cripps a new and senior post in charge of economic planning. Morrison found his responsibilities curtailed, admittedly to those areas where he was most effective. Once again when the party leadership was under discussion—this time among a very small circle of senior ministers—Morrison was not viewed as the obvious successor.

More congenially Morrison had charge of the government's nationalization programme. Predictably these years witnessed the triumph of the public corporation. The nationalization of public utilities was uncontentious within the Labour Party. Some viewed each individual measure as economically justifiable on its own merits; others emphasized their collective contribution to the realization of a socialist commonwealth. In contrast the iron and steel industry was a controversial candidate; Morrison was dubious about its merits, and in 1946 several within the cabinet wished to defer nationalization. The cabinet returned to the issue concurrently with the 1947 economic crisis; Morrison favoured a compromise—public supervision of the industry but not full-scale public ownership. The deal had been negotiated by Morrison in conjunction with the industry and had the support of the steelworkers' trade union. Cabinet arguments resulted in the defeat of Morrison's scheme and led eventually to a long-running parliamentary struggle over a nationalization bill. On this issue Morrison found himself opposed by senior cabinet colleagues and out of step with dominant sentiments within the PLP. For many a firm line on iron and steel demonstrated a continuing commitment to socialist transformation.

Morrison took particular pride in the legislative achievements of the 1945 parliament; his political skills were utilized to their best advantage. He loved the negotiations between ministers over priorities and the give and take of the bargaining with the opposition. Meticulous attention to detail cohabited with a broader vision. At one level this emphasized efficiency. Morrison insisted that the government's implementation of his programme showed that 'Parliament could be a workshop as well as discharging its necessary functions as a talk-shop' (H.S. Morrison, *Government and Parliament*, 2nd edn, 1959, p. 244). Moreover Labour's election manifesto of 1945 had proclaimed the party's commitment to a socialist commonwealth. In the aftermath of the 1931 collapse some on the Labour left had asked, 'Can socialism come by constitutional means?' For Morrison the record of the first majority Labour government provided a conclusive answer.

The fidelity with which Labour had carried out its domestic agenda required the party to develop a new programme for the forthcoming election. Morrison's positions in government and party ensured that he played a central role. The challenge was not just that the programme which he and others had developed in the 1930s had been largely achieved; it was that the link between those measures and the advance to socialism had become tenuous. Full employment and a much more extensive welfare system appeared to meet many of the labour movement's central ambitions; but Britain in the late 1940s was clearly not socialist. The party could choose to rest largely content with these achievements, or to promote measures intended as the next stage of the transition to socialism.

Morrison's response was at one level a compromise, but it also became characterized as the slogan of the Labour right: a second term must be one of 'consolidation'. Further nationalization measures should be at best limited; instead, the emphasis should be on improving the existing public sector. 'Consolidation' was an appropriate priority for someone concerned with administrative efficiency; Morrison also believed that his approach could help to retain the relatively broad social base of Labour's 1945 victory. His approach became a benchmark of a lengthy left–right dispute over public ownership. Yet the term 'consolidation' did not imply abandonment of any commitment to socialist transformation, and it remains unclear how far Morrison ever relinquished the basic objective of replacing capitalism by socialism through an accumulation of specific reforms. What is apparent is that by the late 1940s he was in significant respects an increasingly conservative figure, who had been in senior ministerial positions for a demanding decade, and had seen many of his political objectives achieved. The balance of radicalism and consensus that had characterized his politics from the 1920s had tilted away from radicalism.

The Labour Party fought the general election of 1950 on a compromise platform that included a few candidates for public ownership. Morrison was returned comfortably in his redistributed seat, renamed South Lewisham, but Labour lost considerable support in south-eastern England while maintaining its strength in the older industrial areas. Morrison's concern about Labour's electoral base was thus confirmed, although the loss of such support probably owed far more to the government's austerity policies than to any unhappiness with proposals for more public ownership. Predictably, however, Morrison, who remained as lord president of the council in Attlee's government, continued through election post-mortems to insist on the need for 'consolidation'. Doubts and divisions about the future direction of Labour policy became focused narrowly on the issue of public ownership.

Whatever the doubts about future policy, Morrison's touch within the Commons and the PLP enabled him to cope effectively with the reduction of Labour's majority to six. The physical decline of other leading ministers increased his eminence; however, a third leadership generation was beginning to emerge as Hugh Gaitskell became chancellor of the exchequer in succession to

Cripps in October 1950. Morrison ruled himself out as an alternative chancellor—'I listen to Stafford explaining those figures, and I just know I could not do it' (Donoughue and Jones, 466). Yet Gaitskell's only budget in April 1951 precipitated the most divisive crisis of the Attlee government: Aneurin Bevan, Harold Wilson, and John Freeman resigned from the government specifically over National Health Service charges and rearmament expenditure, but in Bevan's case at least also over the government's alleged departure from socialist rectitude. Bevan's explosive exit was directed not just against Gaitskell's budget, but in effect against Morrison's emphasis on 'consolidation'; it scarred the Labour Party for over a decade. Attlee was ill and Morrison chaired the critical cabinet meetings without securing a compromise. There was little evidence of those managerial skills that had marked his successes on the LCC and in the Commons. Some felt that his own political sympathy for Gaitskell prevented him from seriously seeking a settlement. Yet there seemed little desire for compromise by the principal protagonists. The political cohesion that Morrison had nourished since 1945 was disintegrating.

Foreign secretary, 1951; deputy leader of the opposition, 1951–1959 The government's crises were compounded by international pressures. With the resignation of Ernest Bevin in March 1951, Morrison became foreign secretary (12 March 1951), attracted perhaps by the status of the post, but it took him into a field remote from his expertise and skills. Once again a concern with his credibility as potential leader might have been decisive. Yet his seven months at the Foreign Office damaged his reputation. Critics blended reasoned assessments of Morrison's capabilities with snobbish references to Morrison's style, pronunciation of foreign place names, and lack of 'background'. As with economics, Morrison's touch often seemed unsure. International developments could not be moulded into his favoured rational structures. Characterizations of him as parochial seemed vindicated when he spent more time on the Festival of Britain on London's south bank than on his departmental affairs. These involved serious challenges particularly in Iran, where Dr Mossadeq nationalized British oil interests and Morrison raised the prospect of military action. This one-time opponent of capitalist war was now characterized by a cabinet colleague as 'rather a fire eater' (*Diary of Hugh Gaitskell*, 11 May 1951). His interventionist views were not endorsed by most of his cabinet colleagues; the limits of Britain's claim to great power status were already evident.

Along with senior cabinet colleagues Morrison had evinced a blend of scepticism and hostility towards the first moves for European co-operation. His concerns were fed in part by domestic political considerations. Confronted by the Schuman Plan for a European Coal and Steel Community in May 1950, his alleged response was that 'the Durham miners won't wear it' (Donoughue and Jones, 481). His pride in British political institutions also fuelled his distaste for any proposal that hinted at supranational erosion of parliamentary sovereignty. As foreign secretary his position mellowed—at least on defence,

where cold war pressures forced west European co-operation.

The narrowness of Labour's electoral defeat in October 1951 suggested the feasibility of an early return to office. However, the party was riven by factionalism resulting from the Bevanite resignations and the associated and often confused debates about policy and strategy. Morrison remained deputy leader; he still hoped to succeed Attlee, and played a vigorous role in factional battles. Once away from international affairs, his speeches inside and outside parliament regained much of their quality. Yet gradually his position within the party was undermined. In October 1952 a shift to the left among party activists was demonstrated when a Bevanite slate made an advance in the elections to the constituency party section of the NEC. The victims were senior figures, Hugh Dalton and Morrison, who lost their places.

Morrison was then taken up as their political champion by some trade union leaders who wished to block the Bevanite left and found Attlee lacking in determination and firmness. The consequence of this support was damaging for Morrison. His trade union backers wished to organize his return to the NEC. The only option for this strategy was the party treasurership occupied by the increasingly ineffective and ailing Arthur Greenwood, an incumbency that had begun with his defeat of Morrison in 1943. The attempt to remove Greenwood produced significant sympathy for him. Morrison could be portrayed as the insensitive instrument of authoritarian trade union leaders; on the eve of the party conference in 1953 he withdrew his candidacy. An amendment to the party constitution brought him onto the NEC as deputy leader. Some right-wing trade union leaders began to shift their backing from Morrison to Gaitskell. The former's hesitancy and withdrawal had fed doubts about his willingness to deal firmly with the left. Gaitskell showed no such inhibitions.

Morrison remained for many the most credible successor to Attlee, but a gradual erosion of his support became terminal in the second half of 1955. A second election defeat eroded hopes of a quick return to office. The issue of Morrison's age became more salient as the party began slowly to consider a more thorough reassessment of its policies. It seemed that Attlee, born in 1883, would be better followed by Gaitskell, born in 1907, rather than by Morrison. The latter's parliamentary performances also deteriorated, reinforcing the claim that he was a declining force. Arguably Attlee remained leader until he felt that Morrison's prospects had been destroyed. If so then his judgement was sound. The contest for his successor in December 1955 signalled the end of Morrison's hopes. Long-standing supporters of Morrison shifted to Gaitskell, and Bevan had the backing of the left. The first ballot was decisive—Gaitskell 157, Bevan 70, Morrison 40. Arguably the election of Gaitskell indicated more than the arrival of a new leadership generation. Whereas Morrison in all probability retained a basic belief that cumulative reforms would transform capitalism into socialism, Gaitskell and his closest supporters understood socialism as the more thorough realization of appropriate values. Yet Gaitskell's subsequent difficulties showed that many within the party, not least on the right, remained attached to older expectations. But Morrison's involvement in subsequent controversies was minimal. A quest for the leadership over two decades had ended in humiliation. Morrison resigned the deputy leadership and moved to the back benches. His interventions were few, and he retired from the Commons in 1959.

Despite his earlier opposition to the unreformed House of Lords, Morrison took one of the recently introduced life peerages and went to the upper house as Baron Morrison of Lambeth (November 1959). He was an active peer, and from 1960 served as president of the British Board of Film Censors. His last political battle was in opposition to the Conservative government's plan to replace the LCC with a greater London council. He died in Queen Mary's Hospital, Sidcup, Kent, on 6 March 1965. He was cremated at Eltham on 11 March and the ashes were spread on the Thames at County Hall. The London county council which had been the arena for some of his greatest achievements disappeared less than a month later.

A life dedicated to politics Morrison was a massive asset to the Labour Party. Pugnacious and reasonable, indulging in knockabout partisanship and seeking broad agreement on specific reforms, he was a commanding presence in parliament and Labour Party institutions for over thirty years. As a minister he had major successes at transport and the Home Office and as lord president of the council. His periods at supply, in charge of post-war economic planning, and above all the Foreign Office were less successful. His ministerial talents were limited, but within their range they were outstanding. As a party organizer his skills were widely acknowledged; while intolerant of communists and their sympathizers, he was not a crude authoritarian. His managerial style combined bonhomie, discussion, the calculated use of threats, and the effective interpretation of party rules. Above all his record in London politics greatly enhanced Labour's administrative credibility and brought significant benefits to the people. His style was characterized often as that of the archetypal Cockney—self-confident, humorous, a deflator of pretence. The portrait owed as much to social considerations as to geography. Morrison was thoroughly incorruptible. His tastes were essentially those of the south London lower middle class among whom he lived. Political concerns relegated all else to the sidelines. Suits bought from the Royal Arsenal Co-operative Society were worn not for style, but for their pockets which provided a home for the papers that Morrison's politicking inevitably attracted. His quiff, spectacles, and taste in bow ties provided the raw material for countless political cartoons.

Beyond the achievements and the homespun image lay complexities. Morrison's later career was damaged not least for himself by his failure to secure the party leadership. Perhaps he lacked the toughness needed to grasp opportunities. Certainly his failures suggested that his support within the party was limited. This was not just the visceral contempt of Bevin. Arguably he suffered from his

distinctive route to the party's ruling group. Many of his contemporaries had risen through the trade unions; others were from the middle class, with the educational background that Morrison lacked. He was almost unique within his generation of leaders in having a working-class background and a social mobility provided solely by the party. It probably did not help that his closest counterpart in this respect in the preceding generation was Ramsay MacDonald. Such distinctiveness could lead to the criticism that he was simply a party boss, a fixer with no wider interests. This was unfair. Although his years of extensive reading predated the First World War, he remained interested in ideas. In particular his time at the Ministry of Transport and his long-standing involvement in party policy making demonstrated his concern not just with the detail of reforms, but with a broader vision of social change. As a result he gained respect from intellectuals such as Harold Laski who disagreed with him on specific policies.

Morrison's life was dedicated thoroughly to politics. This could appear dubious to many colleagues and fed unreasonable claims that Morrison lacked depth. The preoccupation indicated tensions in his personality. The marginal youth had sought comradeship in the socialist movement. His marriage on 15 March 1919 to Margaret Kent (1896–1953), a secretary and daughter of a railway clerk, was not a success. Morrison spent little time with his wife and their daughter. His wife did not share his political enthusiasms; his private world withered. Following her death in July 1953, he married Edith Meadowcroft (*b.* c.1908) of Rochdale. This marriage on 6 January 1955 to a businesswoman of Conservative politics appeared much more successful; but by then his career was in decline.

The complexities within Morrison's politics and personality are evident in his published writings. *Socialisation and Transport*, published in 1933, is a lucid and knowledgeable analysis involving a reasoned defence of the public corporation. This was Morrison the sagacious yet creative reformer. Perhaps significantly the subtitle is 'the organisation of socialised industries with particular reference to the London Passenger Transport Bill'. Twenty-one years later Morrison published *Government and Parliament*. This was the product of his visits to Nuffield College, Oxford. His drafts were revised by the warden of Nuffield, D. N. Chester. The result was an accessible and authoritative book on British government which was widely read. The subtitle, 'a survey from the inside', was not a harbinger of sensational disclosures nor heterodox views. Instead Morrison celebrated British exceptionalism in a resolutely empiricist style. 'The fact that the House of Lords has many irrational features is not in itself fatal in British eyes, for we have a considerable capacity for making the irrational work' (H.S. Morrison, *Government and Parliament*, 2nd edn, 1959, 194). This was Morrison the seeker after consensus, whose radicalism was giving way to conservatism.

The book can be located within a very specific context. Morrison and his Labour Party contemporaries had never shown much interest in constitutional reform; for them economic and social questions provided the real business of politics. Moreover the record of the Attlee government suggested that existing institutions could be used effectively by a reforming administration. In the early 1950s few raised questions about the failings of British government. Within a decade the mood would be very different.

Finally in 1960 Morrison published his *Autobiography*, the product of an unsatisfactory relationship with a ghost writer, F. G. Kay. The book was marked by the legacy of Morrison's failure to become party leader. His family were largely, and in the case of his first wife and daughter wholly, invisible. On critical moments in his career the text was laconic and misleading. This was the insecure Morrison behind the public style and the achievements.

Morrison should be located in historical context. As with other socialists of Labour's second generation, his ideas were largely formed at a time when Britain's great power status seemed assured, but problems of modernization were increasingly evident. For him, as for many contemporaries, socialist solutions implemented through British institutions seemed feasible and desirable. Morrison justified his agenda with the belief that the resulting society would be more efficient and fairer; yet it would retain the best of past practices. The reforms would strengthen an ethic of public service and could be characterized as early steps in a socialist transformation. Morrison's achievements in office, especially at the London county council, and in government from 1945 to 1950, marked the apotheosis of this strategy.

DAVID HOWELL

Sources B. Donoughue and G. W. Jones, *Herbert Morrison: portrait of a politician* (1973), new edn (2001) [foreword by Peter Mandelson] · D. Marquand, 'Herbert Morrison: the socialist as consolidator', *The progressive dilemma* (1991) · K. O. Morgan, 'Herbert Morrison', *Labour people* (1987) · DNB · H. Morrison, *Looking ahead: wartime speeches* (1943) · Lord Morrison of Lambeth, *Herbert Morrison: an autobiography* (1960) · *The backbench diaries of Richard Crossman*, ed. J. Morgan (1981) · *The political diary of Hugh Dalton, 1918–1940, 1945–1960*, ed. B. Pimlott (1986) · *The Second World War diary of Hugh Dalton, 1940–1945*, ed. B. Pimlott (1986) · *Labour and the wartime coalition: from the diaries of James Chuter Ede, 1941–1945*, ed. K. Jefferys (1987) · *The diary of Hugh Gaitskell, 1945–1956*, ed. P. M. Williams (1983) · *Patrick Gordon Walker: political diaries, 1932–1971*, ed. R. Pearce (1991) · *The diary of Beatrice Webb*, ed. N. MacKenzie and J. MacKenzie, 4 vols. (1982–5), vol. 4 · D. Acheson, *Present at the creation: my years in the state department* (New York, 1969) · K. Harris, *Attlee* (1982) · A. Bullock, *The life and times of Ernest Bevin*, 3 vols. (1960–83) · P. Clarke, *The Cripps version: the life of Sir Stafford Cripps* (2002) · H. Dalton, *Call back yesterday* (1953) · H. Dalton, *The fateful years: memoirs, 1931–1945* (1957) · H. Dalton, *High tide and after: memoirs, 1945–1960* (1962) · B. Pimlott, *Hugh Dalton* (1985) · P. M. Williams, *Hugh Gaitskell: a political biography* (1979) · R. Skidelsky, *Oswald Mosley* (1975) · F. Brockway, *Bermondsey story: the life of Alfred Salter* (1946) · P. Addison, *The road to 1945: British politics and the Second World War* (1975) · S. Brooke, *Labour's war: the labour party during the Second World War* (1992) · P. Hennessy, *Never again: Britain, 1945–1951* (1992) · L. Hunter, *The road to Britain Pier* (1959) · K. O. Morgan, *Labour in power, 1945–51* (1984) · B. Pimlott, *Labour and the left in the 1930s* (1977) · E. Shaw, *Discipline and discord in the Labour Party: the politics of managerial control in the Labour Party, 1951–87* (1988) · P. Thompson, *Socialists, liberals and labour: the struggle for London, 1885–1914* (1967) · A. Thorpe, *The British general election of 1931* (1991) · P. E. Wertheimer, *Portrait of the Labour Party* (1929) · P. Williamson, *National crisis and national government: British politics, the economy and empire, 1926–1932*

(1992) · S. V. Bracher, *Herald book of Labour members: supplement* (1924) [dated 1924 but with 1923 on title-page]

Archives BLPES, biographical papers · Nuffield Oxf., corresp. and papers · PRO, Foreign Office papers | Bodl. Oxf., corresp. with Clement Attlee · Bodl. Oxf., corresp. with R. R. Stokes · Durham RO, corresp. with Lord Londonderry · HLRO, corresp. with Lord Beaverbrook · HLRO, letters to Lord Samuel · JRL, letters to the *Manchester Guardian* · Labour History Archive and Study Centre, Manchester, corresp. with Morgan Phillips · NL Wales, corresp. with Huw T. Edwards · PRO, corresp. with Sir Henry Dale · Welwyn Garden City Central Library, corresp. with Frederic Osborn | FILM BFI NFTVA, documentary footage · BFI NFTVA, news footage · BFI NFTVA, party political footage · BFI NFTVA, propaganda film footage (ministry of health) · IWM FVA, actuality footage · IWM FVA, home footage · IWM FVA, news footage | SOUND IWM SA, oral history interview · IWM SA, recorded speech

Likenesses Bassano, photographer, 1940, NPG [*see illus.*] · W. Stoneman, photograph, 1941, NPG · Y. Karsh, bromide print, 1943, NPG · H. Coster, photographs, 1953, NPG · Y. Karsh, sepia-toned bromide print, 1954, NPG · W. Bird, photograph, 1961, NPG · J. Pannett, chalk drawing, 1961, NPG · D. Low, chalk caricature, NPG; pencil study sketch, NPG · B. Partridge, pen-and-ink caricature, NPG; repro. in *Punch* (30 Jan 1935) · F. Topolski, NPG · photographs, Labour History Archive and Study Centre, Manchester · photographs, Hult. Arch.

Wealth at death £28,600: probate, 5 Aug 1965, CGPLA Eng. & Wales

Morrison, James (1789–1857), merchant, politician, and art collector, was born at Middle Wallop, Hampshire, the second son of Joseph Morrison, innkeeper, and his wife, Sarah Barnard, of Shapwick in Somerset. One brother and two sisters reached maturity. Orphaned at the age of fourteen, he pursued an obscure career until his employment as shopman by Todd & Co., wholesale haberdashers of Fore Street, London, in March 1809. On 1 August 1814 John Todd took Morrison into partnership; just five days later he gave his daughter, Mary Anne (1795/6–1887), in marriage to his new partner.

The business grew rapidly, turnover rising from £64,449 in 1813 to £650,570 four years later. By 1826 Morrison was senior partner, with a personal fortune already estimated at £150,000. The firm, now trading as Morrison, Dillon & Co., had acquired an international network of trading connections. Large profits came from buying goods direct from distressed or bankrupt manufacturers for rapid sale at low profit margins, as well as from importing lamb and kidskins and finished gloves from southern Europe, cutting out middlemen and paying scant regard to customs regulations.

By the 1820s Morrison's increasing wealth was enabling him to help the radical friends and causes of his youth. Robert Southey met him at Keswick in 1823, on his way to see Robert Owen with a view to investing £5000 in New Lanark. The next year Morrison and Francis Place discussed the distribution of simple tracts on political economy to industrial workers. Though he did not join Joseph Hume and John Bowring on the London Greek Committee, Morrison contributed; he also helped Bowring to arrange loans for the newly independent state. And throughout these years, he read extensively, compensating for the brevity of his formal education.

Morrison's wealth permitted him to enter parliament in

1830 as member for St Ives, Cornwall. By voting for the 1832 Reform Bill, he helped reduce his constituency from two members to one. Prudently he sought election elsewhere and was returned as member for Ipswich in December 1832. Out of parliament after the dissolution of 1837, in March 1840 Morrison stood successfully for the Inverness burghs, which he continued to represent until 1847. Once in parliament, Morrison was soon elected to Brooks; he was also on the founding committee of the Reform Club. Resolutely Church of England in spite of his free-thinking friends, Morrison represented himself as an 'independent reformer'. This did not stop him from seconding the address at the invitation of Lord Althorpe in January 1834 as a leading radical ally of the whig administration. The same year, he was elected to the Political Economy Club, a better indication of the tendency of his parliamentary career. Indeed for the most part Morrison confined himself to matters of commercial and industrial policy, making his mark chiefly as a persistent advocate of state regulation of the railways between 1836 and 1847.

To avoid any conflict of interest, Morrison declined to invest to any extent in British railway companies. This, together with his radical convictions, may account for his decision to seek fresh investment opportunities in the United States of America. Together with an American merchant, John Cryder, Morrison began trading as Morrison, Cryder & Co. on 1 January 1836, reportedly committing £1 million to the new firm, which quickly developed a large Anglo-American merchant banking business on lines similar to that of Baring Brothers, and was jokingly referred to in the City as 'over-Baring'. The new firm was preserved by a Bank of England loan in the crisis of March 1837, and its successor, Morrison, Sons & Co., in which James was joined only by his two eldest sons, Charles *Morrison (1817–1909) and Alfred *Morrison (1821–1897), pursued a more conservative policy from its inception in January 1841. This marked in effect his transformation from merchant banker to investment banker. A third son, Walter *Morrison, businessman and politician, is separately noticed.

In addition to a town house in Harley Street, Morrison bought several extensive country estates of which the most notable were Fonthill in Wiltshire, Basildon Park in Berkshire, and Islay. These he furnished richly, establishing a notable collection of Italian and Dutch old masters and contemporary English paintings. Probably the richest commoner of the nineteenth century, he died at Basildon Park on 30 October 1857, leaving property worth between £4 and £6 million in addition to more than 100,000 acres of land. He was survived by his wife. CHARLES JONES

Sources R. Gatty, *Portrait of a merchant prince: James Morrison, 1789–1857* (privately printed, Northallerton, Yorks., [1977]) · J. Morrison, *Observations … of the defects of the English system of railway legislation* (1846) · J. Morrison, *The influence of English railway legislation on trade and industry* (1848) · W. D. Rubinstein, *Elites and the wealthy in modern British history* (1987) · R. W. Hidy, *The house of Baring in American trade and finance: English merchant bankers at work, 1763–1861* (1949) · *Names of members … rules of the club, and list of questions discussed*, Political Economy Club of London, 3 vols. (1860–81) · *Autobiographical recollections of Sir John Bowring*, ed. L. B. Bowring (1877) · *DNB*

Archives NRA, priv. coll. | GL, Morrison Cryder records · UCL, corresp. with Sir Edwin Chadwick

Likenesses F. Chantrey, plaster bust, *c.*1842, AM Oxf. · F. Chantrey, pencil drawing, NPG · H. W. Pickersgill, oils, repro. in Gatty, *Portrait of a merchant prince* · portraits, repro. in Gatty, *Portrait of a merchant prince*

Wealth at death £4,000,000–£6,000,000—US securities and lands: Gatty, *Portrait of a merchant prince*

Morrison, James (1802–1835), journalist and trade unionist, was born in Newcastle upon Tyne to working-class parents, probably of Scottish descent. A house-painter by trade, he first came into public life in Birmingham in his mid-twenties. In 1822 he began to live with the sixteen-year-old Frances Cooper [see Morrison, Frances (1807–1898)]. They married about 1827, and had at least five children. Frances became a socialist writer and publicist for the cause.

By 1828 Morrison was an enthusiastic follower of Robert Owen, to whom he wrote: 'I shall look to you as a father, and try to become a faithful son' (Saville, 127). Radical activity in general and Owenism in particular were much in evidence in Birmingham in the early 1830s, especially among the trade unions of the building and related trades. In 1832 Morrison began his career as a radical journalist by initiating a weekly newspaper for the Builders' Union, *The Pioneer*. In December 1833 there began a lock-out of silk weavers in Derby by employers seeking to destroy their union, which was to prove a catalyst for Morrison and the trade union movement. Unions came together across trades to assist the locked-out weavers and provide them with financial support.

From these activities there emerged in London in the course of February 1834 the Grand National Consolidated Trades Union (GNCTU), the most ambitious of British attempts at general unionism. Morrison became a member of its executive and *The Pioneer* moved from Birmingham to become its newspaper, circulation of which at its peak may have reached 30,000 copies. The GNCTU had its moment on 21 April 1834, when Owen headed a march of 30,000 in protest at the sentencing of the Tolpuddle Martyrs, but its career was short-lived. Its fortunes were tied to those of a major strike of London's tailors, which began in April 1834. The failure of this strike largely ended the progress of the GNCTU, and its demise was brought about by organizational problems and financial irregularities, which included the absconding by the executive member James Hall with its funds to Australia.

Morrison had already resigned from the executive in March 1834, for reasons which are unclear, but which probably reflected his increasing separation from Owen. Along with James E. Smith, the editor of the official Owenite paper *The Crisis*, he had come to propagate a view of the separate and conflicting interests of labour and capital. In short, against the class-collaborationist views of Owen, Morrison and Smith emphasized class conflict and advocated militant trade unionism. The historian of British socialism Max Beer described Morrison as 'the originator of the syndicalist conception of class-antagonism on the part of the working classes' (Beer, 328). In May 1834 Morrison refused Owen's demand that he hand over the editorship of *The Pioneer* and struggled to produce it up to its final issue on 5 July 1834.

Little is known of Morrison's later activities. He seems to have been involved with other (unsuccessful) radical journals until October 1834 but from then nothing is known, except that he died, physically exhausted and penniless, in Manchester Infirmary on 21 August 1835, at the age of thirty-three. Nothing seems to have been recorded of his appearance and little of his life, except for the period of intense activity between 1832 and 1834. Morrison left no major published work, but his writings in *The Pioneer* add up to a significant contribution to the history of socialist thought and of the labour movement in Britain. JOHN RULE

Sources J. Saville, 'J. E. Smith and the Owenite movement, 1833–1834', *Robert Owen, prophet of the poor: essays in honour of the two hundredth anniversary of his birth*, ed. S. Pollard and J. Salt (1971) · W. H. Oliver, 'The Consolidated Trades' Union of 1834', *Economic History Review*, 2nd ser., 17 (1964–5), 77–95 · M. Beer, *A history of British socialism*, 1 (1953), 328–47 · G. D. H. Cole, *Attempts at general union: a study of British trade union history, 1818–1834* (1953) · *The Pioneer* (1833–4)

Morrison, James Horne (1872–1947), Church of Scotland minister and author, was born on 2 September 1872 in Aberdeen, the youngest of the four sons and one daughter of William Morrison (1835–1912), head gardener at the Aberdeen Mental Asylum, and his wife, Jane (1832–1925), a domestic servant, daughter of John Horne and his wife, Jane, both of Forgue, Aberdeenshire. When his father became head gardener to the dowager duchess of Gordon at Huntly Lodge, Aberdeenshire, James Morrison attended the local Gordon Schools (c.1878–1888) and was dux of his upper school. In 1888, at the age of sixteen, he entered the University of Aberdeen, from which in 1892 he received his MA degree with honours in classics and philosophy, in the process taking prizes in mathematics and physics. Later that year he entered New College, Edinburgh, to prepare for the ministry of the Free Church of Scotland, and in his first year won prizes in Hebrew and natural science.

Following his second year at Edinburgh, Morrison offered himself as a student missionary in the Canadian North West Territories. He was sent to the district known as Assiniboia in April 1894, where for twelve months he laboured among mostly Scottish settlers in the area of Buffalo Lake, north of Moose Jaw. He arrived in North America at the height of agrarian unrest caused by a combination of commercial depression and crop failure during a devastating summer. Only his fine equipoise enabled Morrison to overcome the drought and heat of that summer and the bitter cold of the subsequent winter. All this he described in a compelling personal journal, a rare firsthand account of prairie life during the period, containing evocative accounts of settlers' lives. He also revealed high descriptive powers in portrayals of natural phenomena.

Morrison returned to Scotland in April 1895 and that autumn commenced his third year of theological study. Elected president of the New College missionary society

during his fourth year, he graduated in March 1897. He served as an assistant minister, first at the South Free Church, Aberdeen, until 1899, and then at St Leonard's United Free Church, Perth, to 1901. In July 1901 he was ordained and was inducted as minister of the United Free Church of Falkland, Fife. On 3 September he married Lizzie Jane Milne (1874–1962); the union produced three sons and two daughters.

From March to September 1914 Morrison travelled in central Africa as one of the delegates to foreign missions of the United Free Church general assembly, having published in 1913 *On the Trail of the Pioneers: a Sketch of the Missions of the United Free Church of Scotland*. He published a booklet, *Forty Years in Darkest Africa: the Life of Dr Laws of Livingstonia*, in 1917 and two years later his second book, *Streams in the Desert: a Picture of Life in Livingstonia*. In 1917 he was inducted as minister of Newhills United Free Church, Bucksburn, Aberdeenshire. For several months during 1918 and 1919 he served with the YMCA in France, lecturing to British troops. During the 1920s he published three further books on overseas missions: *Missionary Heroes of Africa* (1922), *William Carey: Cobbler and Pioneer* (1924), and *The Scottish Churches' Work Abroad* (1927), and he contributed fifty-seven sermons and two general introductions to the *Speaker's Bible*.

The early 1930s saw the publication in the *Expository Times* of several articles on Christianity and science. This led to Morrison's invitation to deliver the Cunningham lectures at New College, University of Edinburgh, in 1936, a penetrating analysis of the relationship of, and the boundaries between, science and Christian faith. These were published later that year as *Christian Faith and the Science of To-Day*. In 1937 he produced a booklet for the Church of Scotland, *God and the Atom*, and in the same year received the degree of doctor of divinity from the University of Aberdeen. Morrison remained at Bucksburn until his retirement in 1942, when he moved to Edinburgh. He died there of heart failure on 2 January 1947, and was buried in the city's Morningside cemetery.

BOYD STANLEY SCHLENTHER

Sources *The diary of James Horne Morrison, (1894–1895), a Scots missionary in Canada*, ed. B. S. Schlenther (1995) · B. S. Schlenther, 'James Horne Morrison: a New College student in the Canadian wilderness, 1894–1895', *Records of the Scottish Church History Society*, 21 (1981–3), 263–74 · *The College Calendar for the Free Church of Scotland* (1893–4) · *The College Calendar for the Free Church of Scotland* (1894–5) · *The College Calendar for the Free Church of Scotland* (1896–7) · *The College Calendar for the Free Church of Scotland* (1897–8) · *Proceedings and Debates of the General Assembly of the Free Church of Scotland* (1894) · *Proceedings and Debates of the General Assembly of the Free Church of Scotland* (1895) · *DSCHT* · J. A. Lamb, ed., *The fasti of the United Free Church of Scotland, 1900–1929* (1956) · private information (2004) [family] **Likenesses** photographs, priv. coll.

Morrison, John Robert (1814–1843), interpreter and colonial official, was born on 17 April 1814 in Macao, the third of eight children of the Revd Dr Robert *Morrison (1782–1834), missionary and Sinologue, of Morpeth and Newcastle, and the third child of his first wife, Mary Morton (1791–1821), eldest daughter of John Morton, surgeon-in-chief of the Royal Irish Artillery, of Dublin, and his wife,

Rebecca. On 21 January 1815 Mary Morrison, who was chronically ill, returned to England with John and his elder sister, Mary Rebecca, his elder brother James having died at birth. In 1820 all three returned to Macao, but on the death of their mother John went once again to England, in 1822. There he studied first at the academy of the Revd John Clunie at Manchester, and then at Mill Hill grammar school in Holloway, London. In 1824 his father returned to the UK for two years, and during that time John apparently began studying Chinese under his father's tutelage. John joined his father in the anniversary meeting of the British and Foreign Bible Society in 1824 when Robert Morrison presented a copy of the Chinese Bible to the society. One person present at the meeting wrote:

> Beside him stood his youthful son, brought forward, as it were, like another Hannibal, not indeed to stand pledged against his country's foe, but to be consecrated, on the altar of the Bible Society, against those of his Redeemer, and to share with his father in the honour of extending his everlasting kingdom. (Morrison, *Memoirs*, 2.269–70)

In October 1826 John Morrison returned to Macao with his father, his sister, and his father's second wife, Elizabeth (Eliza) Armstrong. By November 1826 he was in Canton (Guangzhou) with his father, and he began to study Chinese, a lifelong study which brought him prominence. He went to Malacca in early 1827, to the Anglo-Chinese College established by his father and the Revd Dr William Milne. There he continued his study of Chinese, in addition to other subjects, taught some of the local students, and began to learn the printing craft. According to observers, he had 'great maturity of mind' which in his boyhood 'almost amounted to precocity; so that it was remarked that he had the body of a child, and the mind of a man' (Brown, 11). At his father's urging, in 1829 he began work on a 'Chinese Gazetteer'. This work was eventually to result in his first published book, *The Anglo-Chinese Kalendar and Register, for the Year of the Christian Era 1832*, which was published in Macao in 1832 by the East India Company Press.

In June 1830 Morrison returned to Macao and Canton, where he continued to study Chinese. Although he was still only sixteen years old, the British 'country traders' in Canton hired him as their translator. However, this work was interrupted in 1832 when he served as interpreter for the American trade mission, under Edmund Roberts's leadership, to Cochin-China and Siam. He returned from the voyage in June 1833 and would spend the remainder of his life in Macao and China; as he wrote to his sister later that month: 'In China I hope to spend the greater part of my life, and in China I hope to end my days' (Hobson and Morrison MS 5834, no. 53).

Morrison was described by a contemporary as 'small in person, with a youthful appearance, coupled with a great maturity of mind, and [he] possessed rare accuracy of knowledge on a greater variety of subjects than come within the range of ordinary minds' (Dean, 349). With a 'well ordered mind', he was able to work quickly amid confusion, and although 'he abhorred deceit and falsehood' and spoke truthfully and even bluntly at times, the American missionary Samuel Wells Williams described him as 'a man whom it was impossible to know without loving' (Williams, 103).

While continuing his normal translation duties, in 1834 Morrison assisted his father in Lord Napier's negotiations with the Chinese. When Robert Morrison died in August 1834 most of his responsibilities fell to his son, who was appointed to take his father's place as Chinese secretary and interpreter to the British superintendent of trade.

From the end of the Napier mission in 1834 until 1839 Morrison spent his time mainly at Canton continuing his study of Chinese language, literature, law, and customs, thereby preparing himself for the prominent role he was to fill in the future. He also helped to establish, and was recording secretary for, the Morrison Education Society (named in honour of his father), the Society for the Diffusion of Useful Knowledge, and the Medical Missionary Society. During these years he also continued writing and printing. By 1832 he had published *Some account of charms, talismans, and felicitous appendages, worn about the person, or hung up in houses, &c. used by the Chinese*, and in 1834 he published his best-known work, *A Chinese Commercial Guide* (printed at the Albion Press, which he and his father had established). He wrote frequently (and without payment) for the *Chinese Repository* (published by E. C. Bridgman) and for Charles Gutzlaff's *Chinese Magazine* (*Dongxi Yang Kao*). He also began working with Bridgman, Gutzlaff, Walter Medhurst, S. W. Williams, Ira Tracy, and Edwin Stevens on a revision of his father's Chinese Bible and was considering a new edition of his father's dictionary.

Morrison's literary and philanthropic pursuits were interrupted in 1839 at the commencement of the difficulties between the British and the Chinese which led to the First Opium War. From that year until his death in 1843 he carried on his duties for the superintendent of trade; however, he was also the chief interpreter (and at times negotiator) in the conflict between the two countries, which culminated in the treaty of Nanking (Nanjing) in 1842 and the supplementary treaty of 1843. During the course of the negotiations the Chinese felt that through Morrison's ability, 'when there was business one could discuss it' (Swisher, 155); nevertheless, they also issued a proclamation in February 1841 offering a reward for his capture or head, according to some sources 50,000 'dollars' or 30,000 'dollars' respectively.

The first governor of Hong Kong, Sir Henry Pottinger (who was also British plenipotentiary from 1842), came to rely heavily on Morrison. On 21 August 1843 he appointed the 29-year-old to the first legislative and executive councils of Hong Kong, as well as to the positions of Chinese secretary, acting colonial secretary, and JP. Pottinger also stipulated that should he himself be absent from Hong Kong, ill, or otherwise indisposed, Morrison should take over as 'head of Affairs'. Unfortunately, eight days later, on 29 August 1843, Morrison died, unmarried, in Macao as a result of 'Hong Kong fever', probably brought on, at least in part, by overwork. In his official announcement Pottinger referred to Morrison's death as a 'positive national calamity' (Hobson and Morrison MS 5831, no. 6). He later wrote to Lord Stanley that Morrison's death was 'an event which has overwhelmed all classes not only of Her Majesty's Subjects, but all other Foreigners, as well as the Natives of this part of China, with inexpressible and lasting sorrow'. He also asserted that Morrison was 'a faithful, devoted, and invaluable Servant whose loss it is impossible to replace' (PRO, Pottinger MSS, CO 129/2, page 304). In the negotiations which followed in later months, the loss of Morrison's linguistic abilities and his understanding of Chinese culture was keenly felt.

Morrison was buried in Macao on 30 August 1843, next to his mother and father in the protestant cemetery which had been established at the time of his mother's death. The young man who had accomplished so much and who had risen to a position of prominence had his grave marked with a stone which said simply 'John Robert Morrison'. J. BARTON STARR

Sources Wellcome L., Hobson and Morrison MSS · SOAS, Archives of the Council for World Mission (incorporating the London Missionary Society), home and general, South China, and Ultra Ganges · S. R. Brown, *The memory of the righteous: a sermon, preached on the occasion of the death of the Hon. John Robert Morrison* (1844) · E. Morrison, *Memoirs of the life and labours of Robert Morrison*, 2 vols. (1839) · F. W. Williams, *The life and letters of Samuel Wells Williams* (1889) · N. P. Hodges, ed., *The voyage of the Peacock: a journal of Benajah Ticknor, naval surgeon* (1991) · E. J. G. Bridgman, ed., *The pioneer of American missions in China: the life and labors of Elijah Coleman Bridgman* (1864) · W. Dean, *The China mission; embracing a history of the various missions of all denominations among the Chinese* (1859) · W. D. Bernard and W. H. Hall, *The Nemesis in China*, 3rd edn (1847) · Ssŭ-Yü Têng, *Chang Hsi and the treaty of Nanking, 1842* (1944) · J. K. Fairbank, *Trade and diplomacy on the China coast: the opening of the treaty ports, 1842–1854*, 2 vols. (1953); repr. in 1 vol. (Cambridge, MA, 1969) · E. Swisher, *China's management of the American barbarians: a study of Sino-American relations, 1841–1861, with documents* (1953) · F. Leung Chung Yan, 'A bilingual "Barbarian"—a study of John Robert Morrison (1814–1843) as the translator and interpreter for the British plenipotentiaries in China between 1839 and 1843', MPhil diss., Hong Kong Baptist University, 2001

Archives PRO, corresp. at Macao, FO 705 · Wellcome L., letters and papers, MSS 5829–5831 | SOAS, Council for World Mission archives

Likenesses G. Chinnery, double portrait, oils (with his secretary), Jardine House, Hong Kong

Wealth at death left most of estate to sister and step-mother. 'Chinese & other coins and curiosities' left to Alexander Anderson of Canton; Chinese books left to 'London University College'; 'English and other European books' left to the Morrison Education Society (after Elijah Coleman Bridgman selected 'such as he deemed suitable as presents to the several members of my family, and to my immediate friends in China'); 'Celestial & Terrestrial Globes & other Scientific Instruments' left to Bridgman: will, Wellcome L., MS 5831, no. 10

Morrison, John Sinclair (1913–2000), classical scholar and college head, was born on 15 June 1913 at Walstead Grange, Lindfield, Sussex, the grandson of William Morrison of New York, USA, who settled at Stagbury, Chipstead, Surrey, and the son of Sinclair Morrison, a company director, and his wife, Maria Elsie, the daughter of William Lamaison of Salmons, Kenley, Surrey. He was educated at

John Sinclair Morrison (1913–2000), by Elliott & Fry, 1950

Charterhouse School, where he became head of school, and at Trinity College, Cambridge, where he arrived as a classical scholar in 1932 and graduated in 1935 with a first in both parts of the classics tripos.

Morrison was elected a fellow of Trinity in 1937, and in the same year took up an assistant lectureship at the University of Manchester, which he held until 1939. Back at Trinity, he served as editor of the *Cambridge Review* in 1939–40, and his early research was on ancient philosophy, an interest which he maintained throughout his career. This interest also introduced him to the world of ancient oared ships as a result of trying to understand a simile in a passage of the tenth book of Plato's *Republic*. He became intrigued by the construction of triremes and concluded that, contrary to the ideas prevailing at the time, these warships were rowed with oars on three levels. When these conclusions were published in the *Mariner's Mirror* for 1941, they were greeted with scepticism, and the then doyen of ancient maritime studies, W. W. Tarn, advised him to confine himself to philosophy.

In 1940 Morrison volunteered for war service in the Royal Navy as an ordinary seaman, but in the following year was attached to the British Council in the Middle East, serving in Cairo and Zaqaziq in Egypt, and Baghdad in Iraq. There, in 1942, he met and married Elizabeth Helen (Betty; 1909–2003), the daughter of S. W. Sulman of Bexhill, Sussex, who was at the time governess to the seven-year-old Feisal II, the last king of Iraq; they later had three sons and two daughters. From 1942 until the end of the war Morrison served as British Council representative in Palestine and Transjordan, based in Jerusalem.

On his return to England in 1945 Morrison resigned his fellowship at Trinity to become professor of Greek and head of classics at the University of Durham, but in 1950 he returned once more to Trinity, now as senior tutor. His administrative and diplomatic skills in this post led to his being invited in 1960 to become senior tutor and vice-master of the newly created Churchill College, Cambridge (of which he subsequently became an honorary fellow). At both colleges he showed a firm commitment to improving school and university education. He was also active in attempting to reform admissions procedures to widen access to Cambridge, and was involved both in setting up the Universities Central Council on Admissions (UCCA) and in ensuring, despite internal opposition, that both Cambridge and Oxford universities joined.

In 1965 Morrison was invited to be the first president of a new Cambridge college for graduate students only, both male and female, to be known as University College. Here, he did away with a high table and separate common room for the dons, and created a strong sense of community between teachers and students. He was also exceptionally successful as a fund-raiser and oversaw a huge expansion of the college, which was renamed Wolfson College in 1973 and incorporated as a full college of the university in 1976. Nor did he neglect his scholarship and research. From 1968 to 1975 he was joint editor of *Classical Review*, and in 1968, shunning Tarn's advice, he wrote *Greek Oared Ships, 900–322 BC* with Roddi Williams. This was followed up by a number of papers on triremes in learned journals and by *Long Ships and Round Ships* (1980). In 1975 his theories sparked a record-length correspondence in *The Times* (6 September to 4 October).

Morrison retired in 1980, after fourteen years as president of Wolfson College, but continued research on triremes from his home at Granhams in Great Shelford, near Cambridge. In 1981 he enlisted the aid of a naval architect, John Coates, who found that, when the principles of naval architecture were applied to the ancient data, they determined the design of the classical trireme within very tight parameters. In 1984 they set up the Trireme Trust, with Morrison as chairman, aiming to build an experimental ship. He eventually persuaded the Greek government to fund the construction of the Hellenic Navy trireme *Olympias*, which was launched in June 1987. Meanwhile, Morrison and Coates had published in detail the evidence and the multi-disciplinary argumentation behind the reconstruction in *The Athenian Trireme* (1986). The magnitude of the achievement was recognized immediately, and Morrison was made an honorary fellow of the British Academy in 1988 and was both awarded the Caird medal of the National Maritime Museum and created CBE in 1991.

Despite hostility from many nautical archaeologists who disapproved of making a reconstruction without physical remains, *Olympias* proved an outstandingly successful experiment, and the design is now accepted by most scholars as likely to be valid in its essentials. Morrison applied what was learned from *Olympias* to the problems of reconstructing the later Hellenistic and Roman polyremes in *Greek and Roman Oared Warships, 399 to 30 BC* (1996), and a second edition of *The Athenian Trireme*, incorporating a chapter on the conclusions from the sea trials, was published only a few months before his death, in Addenbrooke's Hospital, Cambridge, on 25 October 2000. His wife survived him.

Morrison had an open-mindedness which allowed him equally to understand the need for modernization at Cambridge and to embrace a radical new approach to the trireme question. This was coupled with a personal warmth and enthusiasm and a willingness to devote himself, which enabled him to persuade others that he was right and that they too should devote their money or labours. He both helped to shape the modern University of Cambridge and made tangible a significant aspect of the ancient world.

BORIS RANKOV

Sources WW (2001) · *The Times* (27 Oct 2000) · *Churchill Review*, 38 (2001), 95–7 · *The Independent* (25 Nov 2000) · *The Guardian* (31 Oct 2000) · personal knowledge (2004) · private information (2004) · b. cert. · d. cert.
Archives priv. coll., papers | FILM Henley River and Rowing Museum, Henley-on-Thames, video clip footage · 'The Trireme Quest', BBC Norwich, 1987
Likenesses Elliott & Fry, photograph, 1950, NPG [see illus.] · photograph, repro. in *The Times*

Morrison, John William, second Viscount Dunrossil (1926–2000), diplomatist, was born on 22 May 1926 at 4 Crown Office Row, Temple, London, the eldest of the four sons of William Shepherd (Shakes) *Morrison, first Viscount Dunrossil (1893–1961), Conservative politician, speaker of the House of Commons from 1951 to 1959, and governor-general of Australia from 1960 to 1961, and his wife, (Catherine) Allison (d. 1983), daughter of William Swan, minister of South Leith parish. He was educated at Fettes College, Edinburgh, then served in the RAF as a pilot from 1945 to 1948, rising to the rank of flight lieutenant. From 1948 to 1950 he took a war-shortened course at Oriel College, Oxford, where he read history and became president of the university Conservative Association. On 3 July 1951 he married Mavis Dawn Spencer-Payne, daughter of Arthur Llewellyn Spencer-Payne, dental surgeon, of Somerset West, South Africa. They had three sons and one daughter.

In 1951 Morrison joined the Commonwealth relations service (subsequently amalgamated into the diplomatic service). His first post was as assistant private secretary to the secretary of state for Commonwealth relations, Lord Swinton, from 1952 to 1954. In the latter year he was posted to Canberra as second secretary. After returning to the Commonwealth Relations Office in 1956, he was promoted first secretary in 1957 and then posted to Dacca (East Pakistan) in 1958. He was to spend almost his entire diplomatic career in, or dealing with, Commonwealth countries.

In 1961 Morrison inherited his father's title, and in the

same year was posted to South Africa, still as first secretary. While there he was present as an official observer in the courtroom when Nelson Mandela was sentenced to his twenty-seven-year prison sentence, and Dunrossil—recognizing that Mandela was likely to become an even more significant figure in the future—arranged a supply of history and law books to help him expand his knowledge while incarcerated on Robben Island. With this help and other intervention by Dunrossil, Mandela was able to study for a London University law degree. But while earning the gratitude of Mandela (whom he never met), Dunrossil attracted by these actions unfavourable attention from the South African security forces who at times had him shadowed. He returned to London in 1964 and, after four years in the Foreign Office, was attached to the International Maritime Consultative Organization for a further two years in London. His first marriage having been dissolved in 1969, he married the same year Diana Mary Cunliffe Vise, daughter of C. M. Vise. With his second wife he had two further daughters.

Dunrossil's next overseas posting was again a Commonwealth one, as counsellor and head of chancery in Ottawa, from 1970 to 1974. While there he helped negotiate the release of a colleague, James Cross, who had been kidnapped by the FLQ (Quebec liberation front). Ottawa was followed by three years as counsellor in Brussels (1975–8) before he was appointed high commissioner in Fiji and simultaneously (though not resident there) to Nauru and Tuvalu. He was appointed CMG in 1981. From the Pacific he was moved in 1982 to the Caribbean, where his next post, as high commissioner to Barbados, also involved similar responsibilities for Antigua, Barbuda, Dominica, Grenada, St Vincent, and the Grenadines.

Dunrossil had spent little more than a year getting to know this wide-ranging parish when a crisis in Bermuda precipitated another move. The previous governor of Bermuda had left following allegations of irregularities and a breakdown in his relations with local ministers. With relations between Government House and the local administration having reached an awkward juncture, the British government was looking for someone of notably genial temperament and social standing to mend the fences: Dunrossil fitted this requirement admirably, and spent five happy and successful years as governor and commander-in-chief of Bermuda.

On retirement, in 1988, Dunrossil took on several directorships, including the vice-chairmanship of the Bank of Bermuda (Luxembourg), and the chairmanship of Bison Books Ltd, and assumed his seat on the cross-benches of the House of Lords, playing an active part on various select committees. He was disappointed not to be elected one of the hereditary peers to remain in the upper house following the Labour government's reforms in 1999. However his greatest interest and pleasure in retirement was his life at his family home, Dunrossil House, on North Uist in the Outer Hebrides. There he became a JP and in 1993 was appointed lord lieutenant of the Western Isles, a post which he still held at the time of his death on holiday in Lanzarote on 22 March 2000. His second wife and six children survived him, and the title passed to his eldest son, Andrew William Reginald Morrison (b. 1953).

Dunrossil was never among the most heavyweight intellects of the diplomatic service, nor did he seek out particularly challenging appointments. But he brought qualities of integrity, good sense, and relaxed good humour to a wide range of service within the Commonwealth and in the western highlands of Scotland, where he consolidated the affection in which his more celebrated father had been held. JOHN URE

Sources *The Times* (27 March 2000) · *Daily Telegraph* (25 March 2000) · *The Guardian* (31 March 2000) · *The Guardian* (4 April 2000) · WWW · Burke, *Peerage* · *FO List* · personal knowledge (2004) · b. cert.

Morrison, Sir (William) Murray (1873–1948), metallurgist and electrical engineer, was born on 7 October 1873 at Birchwood, Lower Drummond, Inverness, the younger child of William Morrison (b. 1841/4), wood merchant and shipowner, and his wife, Marjory, daughter of Charles Innes, solicitor. Educated at Inverness College in 1889 he went to Edinburgh University to study natural philosophy; in 1892–3 he attended the West of Scotland Technical College, Glasgow. He trained at various engineering works in Glasgow, and then began a career in the aluminium industry.

British Aluminium was established in May 1894 to extract the metal by using electricity generated at the Falls of Foyers, Inverness-shire, through the new Hall–Herrault process, and, at twenty, Morrison, whose maternal grandfather was associated with the company, joined it as its first engineer. Lord Kelvin, later joint technical adviser to British Aluminium with Morrison, who became a personal friend, designed some of the equipment. The process was imperfectly understood, but Morrison improved it by trial and error. On 15 June 1896 Foyers opened, and within a year it was producing one tenth of the world's aluminium. When it closed in 1967 much of the original equipment was still in use, a testimony to the conception and execution of the scheme.

After 1904 Morrison worked on Kinlochleven, six times bigger than Foyers, which involved building a village, a huge reservoir, a power plant, and a smelter. The complex opened in 1908, in a remote Scottish glen, and in that year Morrison became general manager and sole technical adviser. On 13 June 1913 he married, in London (where the company had its headquarters), Marie Vera Markel (b. 1887/8), the daughter of Dr K. E. Markel, a chemist. The Morrisons, who had one daughter, lived in London, in Kent, and later in Norfolk, though Murray remained dedicated to things Scottish: he was a collector, a skating and curling enthusiast, and a member of the Clan Moriston Society.

After 1924 Morrison worked on the great Lochaber scheme. This involved the then longest tunnel of its kind in the world, under the foot of Ben Nevis, which was inaugurated by his wife. The scheme was opened in December 1929, expanded by 1938, and completed in 1943, and involved Canadian troops. Morrison became managing director of British Aluminium in 1927 and deputy chairman in 1934. He was largely responsible for technically innovative, socially ambitious, and, at times, controversial projects, for solving scientific problems and negotiating with the powerful interests affected, and for drafting the acts of parliament which transformed the landscape and economy of the highlands.

Morrison became associated with production in Norway in 1907 when British Aluminium established reduction facilities at Stangfjord and Kristiansand. In recognition of this he was created commander of the order of St Olav in 1933. He was acknowledged as a leading authority in other countries, and at home he gave valuable evidence to government committees investigating hydro-electric power. He was associated with the construction of factories for the production of alumina at Burntisland, Fife, in 1918, which was convenient for the company's operations in both Scotland and Norway, and at Newport, Monmouthshire, in 1938; he also helped to establish a state-of-the-art rolling mill, essential to the war effort, at Falkirk in 1944. He was knighted in 1943.

Morrison had charm, foresight, judgement, and energy. He was essentially a practical man whose expertise spanned several disciplines: he was a founder member of the Institute of Metals, a council member of the Institution of Electrical Engineers, a member of the Institution of Civil Engineers, a vice-president of the Faraday Society, a fellow of the Institute of Physics, and an early advocate of the National Physical Laboratory. When the Institute of Metals honoured him in 1942 with its platinum medal he first paid tribute to his collaborators. Morrison retired in 1947. He died of cancer at his home, 29 Bramham Gardens, Kensington, London, on 21 May 1948, and was cremated. His wife survived him.

Through his outstanding scientific and managerial abilities Sir Murray Morrison established the industrial use of hydro-electric power in the highlands and significantly developed economical ways of extracting aluminium, previously a rare metal. According to an obituary, not only was he responsible for the creation of a new Scottish industry, but 'The ramifications of that enterprise spread through half the world' (*Chemical Age*, 5 June 1948).

LOUIS STOTT

Sources W. M. Morrison, 'Aluminium and highland water power', *Journal of the Institute of Metals*, 65 (1939), 17–36 · *Aluminium in the Highlands, 1894–1955*, British Aluminium, 1955?, U. Glas., Archives and Business Records Centre · *Journal of the Institute of Metals*, 74 (1948), 790–92 · *Journal of the Institution of Electrical Engineers*, 95/1 (1948), 413–14 · *Inverness Courier* (25 May 1948) · *Chemical Age*, 58 (1948), 791 · 'Minutes of the annual general meeting', *Journal of the Institute of Metals*, 68 (1942), xxvii · W. M. Morrison, 'Aluminium: notes on its production, properties and use', *Journal of the Institution of Electrical Engineers*, 31 (1901–2), 400–19 · P. L. Payne, *The hydro* (1988) · P. MacGill, *Children of the dead end* (1914) · *New York Times* (24 May 1948), 19 · L. Stott, 'That first rush of protest', *The Herald (Weekender)* [Glasgow] (29 June 1996), 33 · b. cert. · m. cert. · d. cert. · *IGI*
Archives U. Glas., Archives and Business Records Centre, 'British Aluminium' (British Alcan), photographs; details of a British Aluminium film about work in the highlands; etc.
Likenesses portrait, 1935, U. Glas., Archives and Business Records Centre, 'British Aluminium' (British Alcan), UGD 347 [UGD 347/21/53/407] · portrait, U. Glas., Archives and Business Records Centre, 'British Aluminium' (British Alcan), UGD 347 [UGD 347/21/53/409] · portrait, repro. in *Chemical Age*

Morrison, Sir Richard (1767–1849), architect, was the son of John Morrison (*fl. c.*1740–1785) of Midleton, co. Cork, an architect whose career failed to live up to his high social and professional ambitions. He invited the earl of Shannon and the future earl bishop of Derry to stand as his son's godparents. A career in the church was intended for Morrison but abandoned owing to the declining state of his father's affairs. Instead he was enrolled in 1786 in the Dublin Society's School of Architectural Drawing, where he soon won the first-class medal for elevations and plans and studied under Henry Aaron Baker. Although Morrison's own son John claimed his father was a pupil of James Gandon (who later employed Baker), there is no independent evidence of this. He married in 1790 Eliza Ould (*d.* 1854), daughter of the Revd William Ould, rector of Philipstown, and granddaughter of Sir Fielding Ould, former master of the Dublin Lying-in Hospital. They had four sons. He set up in practice in Clonmel, co. Tipperary, where he enjoyed the patronage of his father's old client Archbishop Agar, for whom he designed the tower and spire of Cashel Cathedral (1791). In 1793, by which time he had moved to Dublin, he published and dedicated to Agar a volume of designs for domestic buildings (more remarkable for their planning than for their elevations).

In Dublin, Morrison was somewhat in the shadow of Francis Johnston, against whom he competed unsuccessfully for St George's Church (1800) and the conversion of the parliament house to the Bank of Ireland (1802). In 1805, however, Johnston joined the board of works, relinquishing most of his private practice. This gave Morrison the opportunity to expand his own practice in the provinces, particularly in the design of country houses and public buildings, though he made little impact on metropolitan architecture. Notwithstanding this success, in 1822, when Johnston was (incorrectly) rumoured to be contemplating retirement, Morrison canvassed for his job. Morrison's assistants included John B. Keane and John Bowden, both of whom later entered private practice, and the draughtsman Owen Fahy.

Morrison's principal works in Dublin were Sir Patrick Dun's Hospital (1803) and, at Trinity College, the Botany Bay quadrangle (1813) and the Anatomy House (1823; dem.). His provincial public buildings included the court houses at Clonmel (before 1801), Wexford (1803; dem.), Naas (before 1807), and Galway (1812), and the county gaols at Tralee (1812), Enniskillen (1812; dem.), and Roscommon (*c.*1814; dem.). For domestic work Morrison was adept at a variety of styles, with a good eye for detail and craftsmanship. His classical villas included Castlegar, co. Galway (1801), Bearforest, co. Cork (1807), and Kilpeacon, co. Limerick (attributed). Among his surviving Gothic works are Shanganagh Castle, co. Dublin (*c.*1803), and Castle Howard, co. Wicklow (*c.*1911); Moydrum Castle, co. Westmeath (*c.*1812), has been demolished, while Thomastown Castle, co. Tipperary (1812), and Castle Freke, co. Cork (*c.*1812; des.

1910), are both ruinous. He also altered a number of country houses including Lyons (1802) and Carton (c.1815), both in co. Kildare. In addition to this corpus of work, Morrison collaborated from time to time with his son and pupil **William Vitruvius Morrison** (1794–1838), architect, who was born on 22 April 1794 at Clonmel, co. Tipperary, and later ran an architectural practice independently of his father.

While enjoying great intellectual and creative powers, William Morrison had a rather retiring manner in contrast to his father's assertive and sometimes argumentative personality. None the less, their collaborative ventures demonstrate a successful aesthetic symbiosis. Country houses on which the Morrisons worked jointly included Borris, co. Carlow (c.1813), Shelton Abbey (c.1819) and Kilruddery (1820) in co. Wicklow, Ballyfin, Queen's county (1822), Fota, co. Cork (c.1825), Rossmore Park, co. Monaghan (c.1824; dem.), and the reconstruction of Baronscourt, co. Tyrone (1835). William Morrison's independent commissions in the classical style included the court houses at Carlow and Tralee (both 1828) and the reconstruction of Oak Park, co. Carlow (1832). In 1821 he made an extensive tour on the continent, visiting Rome, Paestum, and Paris. While passing through England on his return, he made a study of Tudor architecture which he later used to good effect in such manorial designs as Hollybrooke, co. Wicklow (c.1831), and Clontarf Castle, co. Dublin (1836). In an effort to find relief from increasing bouts of depression arising from an old medical condition, William Morrison visited France in 1836 but returned to Ireland in mid-1837 after a mental seizure. He rallied, but suffered paralysis a year later and died, unmarried, at his father's villa, Walcot, near Bray, co. Wicklow, on 16 October 1838. He was buried in Dublin's Mount Jerome cemetery. The Royal Irish Academy, of which he was a member, has a marble bust of him, carved by Terence Farrell.

Towards the end of his career Richard Morrison was involved in establishing the Institute of the Architects of Ireland, the inaugural meeting of which took place in his town house at 10 Upper Gloucester Street, Dublin, on 1 October 1839. He was elected vice-president (effective head) and in this capacity was knighted in January 1841 by the lord lieutenant, Viscount Ebrington. He was also elected a member of the Royal Irish Academy and a fellow of the Royal Institute of British Architects. Although Morrison remained in office for a decade, his vice-presidency was a chequered one. George Papworth resigned after a row in 1841, and by 1844 support had dwindled, leaving the institute virtually moribund; a revival took place only after his death, which occurred at his home, Walcot, on 31 October 1849. Morrison, his wife, and four sons were all buried beneath a tomb of William Morrison's design in Mount Jerome cemetery.   FREDERICK O'DWYER

Sources Irish Architectural Archive, *The architecture of Richard Morrison (1767–1849) and William Vitruvius Morrison (1794–1838)* (1989) · J. Morrison, 'The life of the late William Vitruvius Morrison of Dublin, architect', *Quarterly Papers on Architecture*, 1 (1843–1844?), 1–8 · [W. Papworth], ed., *The dictionary of architecture*, 11 vols. (1853–92) · J. Turpin, *A school of art in Dublin since the eighteenth century: a history of the National College of Art and Design* (1995) ·

F. O'Dwyer, 'The foundation and early years of the RIAI', *150 years of architecture in Ireland*, ed. J. Graby (1989), 9–21 · *The Builder*, 7 (1849), 557 · *DNB*
Archives NA Ire., state and private MSS
Likenesses T. Farrell, marble bust (William Vitruvius Morrison), Royal Irish Acad. · J. E. Jones, bust · photograph (after oil painting), Royal Institute of the Architects of Ireland, Dublin
Wealth at death extensive property interests: will, NA Ire.; Irish Architectural Archive, *Morrison*, 11

Morrison, Richard James [*pseud.* Zadkiel] (1795–1874), astrologer and inventor, was born on 15 June 1795, the son of Richard Caleb Morrison, a gentleman pensioner under George III. His grandfather, Richard Morrison, was a captain in the service of the East India Company. He entered the Royal Navy in 1806 as a first-class volunteer on the cruiser *Spartan*, and saw much service in the Adriatic. He left the *Spartan* in December 1810 and later served as master's mate in the *Elizabeth* and the *Myrtle*. He was commissioned as a lieutenant on 3 March 1815. His last appointment was to the coastguard at Ardmore, co. Waterford, in April 1827. Morrison married three times. On 23 August 1827 he married Sarah Mary Paul (1809/10–1849), daughter of Sir Joshua Paul bt, of Waterford; they had nine children. After her death from scarlet fever on 14 January 1849 he married, on 22 May the following year, Mary Stokes, daughter of George Stokes, clerk. It is not known when or why this marriage ended. On 5 December 1855 he married his third wife, Louisa Smith, daughter of Thomas Smith of Austrey, Warwickshire. His second and third wives were both minors at the time of their marriage. His third wife survived him.

For leading a rescue of the wrecked sloop *Mermaid* in February 1828 Morrison was awarded a silver lifesaving medal from the Royal National Lifeboat Institution. He resigned from the coastguard in October 1829, owing to ill health induced by the exposure suffered during the rescue. He spent some years in Cheltenham before establishing himself in the metropolis about 1840. He lived initially in Dulwich and Brixton, before moving to the West End of London some time before 1855. In later life he lived at Hyde End, Surbiton, and at Kingston upon Thames.

Morrison was chiefly remarkable as the most famous astrologer of Victorian times. His pseudonym Zadkiel became synonymous with the subject. His fascination with the stars dated from 1820 when he witnessed an eclipse from Strawberry Hill in London. He trained under a London astrologer called Dixon, and was associated for a time with Robert Cross Smith (Raphael) before setting up as his competitor with the publication of *Herald of Astrology* in 1830. He produced *Zadkiel's Almanac*, as the *Herald* became by 1836, yearly until the end of his life, when the publication was continued by a successor under the same name. The almanac, which sold up to seventy thousand copies a year, extolled astrology as a respectable and Christian science, and campaigned against the legal penalties attached to the practice.

Much of Morrison's effort to advance astrology centred on meteorology. From the commencement of his *Almanack*, he promoted a theory of planetary influences on the weather and challenged the government ventures into forecasting in the 1860s. He also designed and attempted to market an instrument for measuring atmospheric electricity in 1837. He joined the first Meteorological Society of London in 1837 and served on its council from 1840 to 1843. A decade later he was president of a new version of the society, though he did not become involved in the third and surviving meteorological society, the British (later Royal) Meteorological Society of 1850. In 1860, however, he helped to found the short-lived Astro-Meteorological Society in London.

Morrison experimented with several unsuccessful journals (*The Horoscope*, 1841; *The True Philosopher*, 1845; *Zadkiel's Magazine*, 1849; *Voice of the Stars*, 1862), and produced works on astrology (*Grammar of Astrology*, 1833; *Handbook of Astrology*, 1861–3), all of which were published under his pseudonym. As Lieutenant Morrison he floated an unsuccessful weather almanac (1837) and wrote works outlining a geocentric astronomy, including *The Solar System as it is and Not as it is Represented* (1857) and *New Principia* (1868). Typical, though late, examples of anti-Newtonian literature, they, unlike his *Almanack*, do not seem to have circulated widely.

Morrison also published books and pamphlets on his various inventions and projects. Perhaps the most notable of the latter was an elaborate plan mounted in 1852 and 1853 for a giant telescope of 29 inches diameter to be built near the Crystal Palace in Sydenham, both as a public attraction and as a school for astronomy. It was never built. He made his living chiefly from his *Almanack*. The moment of his greatest notoriety occurred in 1863, when he sued Admiral Sir Edward Belcher for libel. Belcher accused him of deliberate fraud in connection with displays of a crystal ball in London society that had taken place a decade earlier. However, the trial on 29 June 1863 successfully established Morrison's sincerity, while simultaneously exposing him and some of his clients to considerable ridicule. Morrison died of heart disease at his home, Sunnyside, Knights Park, Kingston upon Thames, Surrey, on 5 February 1874. KATHARINE ANDERSON

Sources C. Cooke, *Curiosities of occult literature* (1863) · *Zadkiel's almanac and herald of astrology for 1846* · P. Curry, *A confusion of prophets: Victorian and Edwardian astrology* (1992) · E. Howe, *Urania's children* (1967) · *The Times* (11 May 1874) · *The Athenaeum* (9 May 1874), 630 · *The Athenaeum* (23 May 1874), 701 · *The Athenaeum* (16 May 1874), 666 · J. M. Walker, 'Pen portraits of presidents', *Weather*, 49 (1994), 71–2 · *The Times* (30 June 1863) · *The Times* (1 July 1863) · T. Moody, *A complete refutation of astrology* (1838) · Royal National Lifesaving Institution, *Annual Report, 1828* · DNB · d. cert. · m. cert., 22 May 1850 · m. cert., 5 Dec 1855 · *CGPLA Eng. & Wales* (1874)

Archives Meteorological Office, Bracknell, Berkshire, Meteorological Society of London MSS

Likenesses engraving, 1870, repro. in *Zadkiel's Almanack … for 1871*

Wealth at death under £1,500: probate, 13 Feb 1874, *CGPLA Eng. & Wales*

Morrison, Robert (1782–1834), missionary and Chinese scholar, youngest son among the eight children of James Morrison, manufacturer of lasts and boot-trees, and Hannah, *née* Nicholson (*d.* 1802), was born on 5 January 1782 at Buller's Green, Morpeth, in Northumberland. In 1785 his parents moved to Groat Market, Newcastle. He was

Robert Morrison (1782–1834), by John R. Wildman, in or before 1824

apprenticed to his father's trade but his pious upbringing led him to join the Presbyterian church in 1798. Three years later, having decided to enter the ministry, he began the study of Latin, Greek, and Hebrew. In 1802 his mother died, and a sentimental barrier to leaving home was removed.

Morrison next entered the nonconformist Hoxton Academy, in London, on 7 January 1803, and developed a practical interest in missionary work. He applied to join the London Missionary Society (LMS) on 27 May 1804, and was quickly accepted. In September 1804, it was decided that he should go to China, to learn Chinese, and to translate the scriptures. He was sent to David Bogue's missionary academy in Gosport, and in August 1805 he returned to London to study medicine at St Bartholomew's Hospital and astronomy at Greenwich. Jesuit missionaries had successfully entered the service of the Qing court because the Manchu emperors found such skills useful. Morrison studied Chinese with a Cantonese teacher, Yong Samtak, and, becoming familiar with the written language, he transcribed a Chinese manuscript at the British Museum and copied a manuscript Latin–Chinese dictionary lent him by the Royal Society. On 8 January 1807 he was ordained, and on 31 January he sailed from Gravesend for Canton (Guangzhou) via the USA, as the East India Company was opposed to the introduction of protestant missionaries into China.

Morrison arrived in Canton on 7 September 1807. There he faced opposition from both the East India Company and the Portuguese authorities in Macau (Macao), and he therefore chose to live clandestinely with American merchants. Despite these problems he built up a strong friendship with the writer Sir George Thomas Staunton, then in Canton. Initially Morrison adopted Chinese dress and lifestyle, but this, coupled with a ferocious regime of study and writing, put great strains on his health and spirits, as did the secrecy he laboured under. All this while he compiled his Chinese dictionary and grammar, and worked on translations of the scriptures. Fearfully lonely, he married Mary Morton (1791–1821) on 20 February 1809; on the same day he was appointed translator to the East India Company. Mary's health suffered in China and on 21 January 1815 she left for Britain with their two children, Rebecca (*b.* 1812) and John Robert *Morrison.

Morrison's job was onerous, but it secured his residence in Canton, and his Chinese swiftly improved. His critics claimed that he adopted the self-indulgent life of a company official but there is no evidence for this. The East India Company also developed an interest in his dictionary and in 1814 shipped out a press and a mechanic, P. P. Thoms; the volumes were published in Macau between 1815 and 1823. In 1815 the company published his *Grammar of the Chinese Language*. The fact that he had printed and published Chinese translations of the New Testament and other tracts came to the notice of the company's directors in 1815 and they ordered his dismissal, a proposal successfully resisted by Staunton. From 13 July 1816 to 1 January 1817, Morrison at last travelled in the Chinese interior as interpreter on Lord Amherst's abortive mission to Peking (Beijing), an account of which he published in 1819. The thrust of Morrison's work was as much institutional as scholarly, but the hostility of the East India Company still meant that any expansion of his efforts had to be undertaken elsewhere.

In July 1813 a colleague had at last been provided for him when William *Milne (1785–1822) arrived in Macau. In 1814 the two men formulated plans for the pioneering Anglo-Chinese College at Malacca, and it opened in 1818, for the 'reciprocal cultivation of Chinese and European literature' and the training of Chinese, Malay, and European missionaries. On 25 November 1819 Morrison wrote to the LMS that he and Milne had completed their translation of the Bible (it was published in 1823), the task he had been assigned in 1807. Mary returned in August 1820 but she died, pregnant, on 10 June 1821. In 1824, sick, tired, and worn out, Morrison returned to Britain, bringing his substantial Chinese library, which later became the core of the collection at the School of Oriental and African Studies in London. In November 1824 he married Eliza Armstrong (1795–1874). In Britain he tried to raise funds for the Anglo-Chinese College, but he was also involved in the establishment of a language institution in Bartlett's Buildings, London, where, in 1825, he taught the first classes in Chinese to be held in Britain.

On 1 May 1826 Morrison returned to Canton with his family. Although he had a new contract with the East India Company, his position was more difficult. The atmosphere in Canton and Macau had changed. The company's staff were more hostile and few of Morrison's old friends remained. Relations between the British and the Chinese were deteriorating over the vexatious issue of opium smuggling, and the smugglers themselves greatly opposed the missionary presence. In 1833 the Portuguese authorities in Macau ordered the closing down of his press. The contrast with 1807 was marked also by the more happy facts that, as he wrote in his journal in December 1832, among the foreign community 'Chinese scholars, missionary students, English presses, and Chinese scriptures, with public worship of God, have all grown up since that period' (Morrison, 2.465). Eliza, owing to ill health, left Canton for home in December 1832 and took their five children with her. In the following year the company's charter was terminated, and its monopoly ended in 1834. Lord Napier arrived in Macau on 15 July 1834 and appointed Morrison his Chinese secretary the following day. But Morrison had been ill, and he died in Canton shortly afterwards, on 1 August 1834. He was buried in Macau.

Morrison was a voluminous writer both in Chinese and in English. His *magnum opus* was his dictionary but he is also remembered for his grammars and guides, and for his numerous contributions to the *Canton Register*, which he effectively edited from 1828 to 1830. Stout in figure and rather short, he was also patient and determined. His work in Canton had secured no more than a dozen converts, but his genius lay elsewhere. His reputation stands today first as a protestant pioneer, both physically and methodologically—he proved that it was possible for Europeans to publish works in Chinese in China itself; and second as a scholarly facilitator of cultural exchange between Europe and China. As the report of the East India Company's select committee in Canton stated in 1827, Robert Morrison was considered the chief person who opened to his countrymen the road to the knowledge of the language of China.

R. K. DOUGLAS, rev. ROBERT BICKERS

Sources E. Morrison, *Memoirs of the life and labours of Robert Morrison*, 2 vols. (1839) · L. Ride, *Robert Morrison: the scholar and the man* (1957) · B. Harrison, *Waiting for China: the Anglo-Chinese college at Malacca, 1818–1843, and early nineteenth-century missions* (1979) · S. R. Stifler, 'The language students of the East India Company's Canton factory', *Journal of the North China Branch of the Royal Asiatic Society*, 69 (1938), 46–82 · H. B. Morse, *The chronicles of the East India Company trading to China, 1635–1834*, 3–4 (1926) · L. Ride, 'Robert Morrison and Alexander Wylie', *Memorials of protestant missionaries to the Chinese* (1867) · candidates' papers and letters, SOAS, Archives of the Council for World Mission (incorporating the London Missionary Society), South China and Ultra Ganges files
Archives DWL, letters and papers · SOAS, Archives of the Council for World Mission, journals, letters, and papers · Wellcome L., memoir of his wife | BL OIOC, East India Co. MSS · Wellcome L., family corresp. incl. letters to his son John Robert Morrison
Likenesses J. R. Wildman, oils, in or before 1824, NPG [*see illus.*] · G. Chinnery, double portrait, *c.*1826–1833 (with Eliza Morrison), priv. coll. · T. Blood, stipple, pubd 1827 (after J. Wildman), BM, NPG · G. Chinnery, oils, 1828 · C. Turner, mezzotint, pubd 1830 (after G. Chinnery), BM, NPG · attrib. G. Chinnery, oils, NPG · W. Nicholson, pencil and watercolour drawing, Scot. NPG · J. Wildman, drawing, Hong Kong Museum of Art; repro. in P. Conner, *George Chinnery, 1774–1852: artist of India and the China coast* (1993), 236–7

Morrison, Roderick [An Clàrsair Dall, the Blind Harper] (1656?–1713/14), Scottish Gaelic poet and harpist, was the eldest son of John Morison (*b. c.*1630), tacksman of Bragar in the island of Lewis, and descended from the Morison breves, or hereditary judges, who were latterly located in Ness, Lewis. He is said to have fallen ill with smallpox while at school in Inverness, and lost his sight. Instead of following a clerical career, like a younger brother, he seems to have cultivated playing musical instruments, and is said to have spent some time in Ireland developing his skill as a harpist. From internal evidence in one of his poems he spent some time roving with a band of musicians and entertainers, before meeting Iain Breac, a chief of the MacLeod clan at Dunvegan, Skye, in Edinburgh, probably in 1681. By 1683 Morrison was established in Dunvegan, holding a farm in tack from the chief, and acting as harpist and apparently as poet in some situations. William Matheson, in his introduction to the edition of Morrison's poems, argues that he was not employed as a professional musician or poet, but rather enjoyed patronage as a fellow-gentleman who had highly developed artistic skills. Morrison had two younger brothers who were clergymen, one (Angus) the author of some entertaining verses. Roderick Morrison was married to Catherine Stewart, from Lochaber. The close relationship between Morrison and Iain Breac seems to have broken down after some years, and Morrison was given the tenancy of a farm in Glenelg, on the mainland opposite southern Skye, where he felt remote and estranged. This move may have taken place as early as 1688, the year of the Jacobite rising, and may be connected with Morrison's Jacobite sympathies. He came to have closer ties after this with John MacLeod of Talisker (also in Skye).

Only seven poems survive with unambiguous ascriptions to An Clàrsair Dall. Some of these are still sung, and there are published transcriptions of the song airs in eighteenth- and nineteenth-century sources, but the evidence of tunes for the harp composed by Morrison is scanty and inconclusive (Matheson, 169ff.). Two of the poems are about Iain Breac, one praising him in conventional eulogistic language but with personal and emotional commitment also, and the other a moving elegy on his death in 1693. Iain Breac was buried in Rodel, Isle of Harris, and Morrison is thought to have been at the funeral. In a stanza from this elegy he records Iain Breac's role as a patron of poets and musicians:

> Wrapped in the linen shroud did I leave the strength of the weak, the journey's end of men of song, as also the wealth of men of ancient lore, and the treasury of learned poets—your death has set them in disarray; and since you went into the coffin I am no object of envy.　('Creach na Ciadaoin', 'Wednesday's bereavement', Matheson's translation)

Probably the best-known of Morrison's poems is addressed to Iain Breac's son Roderick, who succeeded him as chief. This poem creates as a main character the Echo of past generosity and greatness, who still resounds in Dunvegan but who has been replaced by a quite different image, that of the young fashionable spendthrift who spends most of his time in the south and who cares little for his family's native traditions. This gives an early and detailed picture both of the traditional, idealized concept of the clan chief and artistic patron, and of the de-Gaelicized chief: over the next two centuries the latter was to become the norm. One aspect of this revolution is detailed in the following stanza:

> He comes out of the shop with the latest fashion from France, and the fine clothes worn on his person yesterday with no little satisfaction are tossed into a corner—'The style is unmodish, not worth a plack. On the security of a townland or two, take the pen and sign a bond'. ('Oran do Mhac Leòid Dhùn Bheagain', 'A song to MacLeod of Dunvegan')

This attitude was later to contribute to the clearing of clansmen and to the sale of estates to incomers. An Clàrsair Dall is a percipient observer of such trends. The poet died in 1713 or 1714. His work has been carefully and judiciously edited by William Matheson.

DERICK S. THOMSON

Sources W. Matheson, ed., *The blind harper / An clarsair dall*, Scottish Gaelic Texts Society, 12 (1970) · D. S. Thomson, *An introduction to Gaelic poetry*, 2nd edn (1990) **Archives** U. Glas., Fernaig MS; McLagan MSS

Morrison, Sophia (1859–1917), cultural fieldworker in the Isle of Man and campaigner for the Manx language, was born on 24 May 1859 at Peel, Isle of Man, the third of nine children of Charles Morrison (1824–1880), merchant and ship owner, and Louisa Crellin (1830–1901). Her father was a well-respected figure who owned a fleet of fishing boats operating from the western fishing port of Peel. His relative wealth provided sufficient means to fund training for the professions of doctor and chemist for two of her brothers. From a background where education was keenly encouraged Morrison developed an interest in languages, particularly those of the Romance and Goidelic Celtic groups. As well as Manx Gaelic she was fluent in French and possessed a working knowledge of Italian, Spanish, and Irish and Scottish Gaelic. Diary entries reveal that she was already well read in European literature as a teenager.

Despite being brought up in an English-speaking household Morrison became a fluent speaker of Manx Gaelic. She taught the language at evening classes in Peel, and in 1899 was among the founder members of Yn Cheshaght Ghailckagh (YnCG; the Manx Language Society), of which she was appointed honorary secretary in 1901. She was editor and proprietor of the society's journal, *Mannin*, which appeared between 1913 and 1917, in nine volumes.

Morrison was in constant contact with Manx antiquarians, including A. W. Moore (1853–1909), J. J. Kneen (1873–1938), and W. H. Gill (1839–1922), and held the post of vice-president of the Isle of Man Natural History and Antiquarian Society in 1912. She contributed an article on A. W. Moore to the *Dictionary of National Biography* and to the *Celtic Review*. Influenced greatly by figures of the previous generation such as the poet T. E. Brown and the music collector Dr John Clague she was committed to collecting and promoting all aspects of Manx culture. Furthermore she acted as a facilitator, securing the publication of pioneering teaching aids such as Goodwin's *First Lessons in Manx* (1901). As a member of YnCG she was frequently part of the Manx delegation to the pan-Celtic movement, and her attitude was firmly that of the pan-Celticist rather than the narrowly nationalist. Her work as secretary to YnCG also brought her into regular contact with leading Celticists such as professors John Rhŷs (Oxford), Quiggin (Cambridge), and Watson (Edinburgh), as well as with Douglas Hyde (Dublin).

Morrison's collection of folklore was greatly influenced by her friendship with the German folklorist Charles Roeder (1848–1911), who was based in Manchester; together with Roeder she published *Manx Proverbs and Sayings* (1905). She bridged the worlds of informant and collector, and of educator and educated. She was widely accepted as the island's authority on Manx fairy lore, having published research in *Folk Lore*, for example. She contributed the Manx sections in *Fairy Faith in Celtic Countries* by Evans-Wentz (1911), and her own publication *Manx Fairy Tales* appeared in 1911, with subsequent editions in 1929 and 1991.

In addition to her work for Manx Gaelic, Morrison was an important figure in developing 'Anglo-Manx' dialect writing, working extensively with the local theatrical company the Peel Players, who performed on the island and in Liverpool. She staged many plays by Christopher Shimmin and Josephine Kermode (Cushag). Joseph Wright's *English Dialect Dictionary*, for which she was an invited reader, proved invaluable in preparing *A Vocabulary of the Anglo-Manx Dialect* (1924). The *Vocabulary* was instigated by A. W. Moore and completed by Morrison with the aid of her relative the linguist Edmund Goodwin (1844–1924). It represents a series of snapshots of the Manx English linguistic situation of the late nineteenth century in particular, and draws on literary and oral sources.

Morrison, who did not marry and lived with her parents until their decease, suffered in later life from neuralgic headaches and severe problems with her eyes, and underwent several operations. She died, of cancer, on 14 January 1917 at her home, 15 Athol Street, Peel. Her funeral, in Peel on 17 January, was well attended, her coffin being carried by members of the Peel Players. She was buried in Peel cemetery. 'No heavier blow has ever befallen the cause of Manx nationality' (Caine, 499).

It is only Morrison's extreme sense of modesty that has concealed her contribution to the Manx revival. During a period of cultural and linguistic activity on the Isle of Man she was instrumental in introducing Manx Gaelic teaching in schools, and pioneered phonograph recordings of Manx Gaelic and Manx English speech and music. The all-encompassing nature of her contribution to Manx culture means that Sophia Morrison was the very locus for Manx revivalist, antiquarian, and folklore circles at the turn of the twentieth century. BREESHA MADDRELL

Sources Archive of Manx National Heritage, Douglas, Isle of Man, Sophia Morrison papers [uncatalogued] • P. W. Caine, 'In memoriam', *Mannin*, 9 (May 1917) • W. Cubbon, *Island heritage* (1952), 339–43 • M. Douglas, *This is Ellan Vannin* [n.d.], 129–31 • B. Maddrell, 'Contextualising *A vocabulary of the Anglo-Manx dialect*: developing Manx identities', PhD diss., U. Lpool, 2001 • *Isle of Man Weekly Times* • *Isle of Man Examiner* • *Peel City Guardian* • *Ramsey Courier* (16–20 Jan 1917) • *Mona's Herald* • d. cert. • census returns, 1881, 1901
Archives Archive of Manx National Heritage, Douglas, Isle of Man, MSS
Likenesses photograph, repro. in Douglas, *This is Ellan Vannin* • photograph, repro. in Cubbon, *Island heritage*

Morrison, Thomas (d. 1839?), surgeon, matriculated at the University of Edinburgh for the sessions of 1783–4 and 1784–5. He did not graduate, however, and may have continued his medical studies in London. He practised as a surgeon accoucheur in Dublin from the early 1790s, though there is no conclusive proof that he ever received a formal qualification. The available evidence suggests that Morrison had no official connection with any of the Dublin hospitals or with the city's medical charities.

An account of two of Morrison's early Dublin cases, dating from May 1794 and March 1795, appeared in Andrew Duncan senior and Andrew Duncan junior's *Annals of Medicine … 1797* (1798, 2.240–45, 246–9). These were titled 'The history of a case of venereal ulcer, effectually cured by the topical use of an arsenical corrosive application' and 'The history of an inveterate case of tinea capitis, successfully treated by an application of an adhesive paste'.

Morrison's name appeared in an unbroken sequence in the Dublin directories from 1794. Its disappearance in 1839 suggests that he died in that year. The *Dictionary of National Biography* appears to have confused him with Thomas Morrison (d. 1835?), a London medical practitioner, who was listed in 1825 as living in Vale Grove, Chelsea, and whose works included *Reflections upon Armed Associations in an Appeal to the Inhabitants of Chelsea* (1798) and *An Examination into the Principles of what is Commonly called the Brunonian System* (1806). LAURENCE M. GEARY

Sources U. Edin. • RCS Eng. • *Dublin directory* (1794–1839)

Morrison, Walter (1836–1921), businessman, politician, and benefactor, was born in London on 21 May 1836, the fifth son of James *Morrison (1789–1857), of the firm of Morrison, Dillon, & Co., and his wife, Mary (d. 1887), daughter of John Todd, of the same firm. Walter Morrison inherited a share, which grew considerably during his own lifetime, of his father's vast fortune made in wholesale textiles, drapery, and haberdashery during the Napoleonic wars and later expanded through merchant banking and judicious investment in North America. He was educated at Eton College and at Balliol College, Oxford, where, like two of his brothers, he became a redoubtable oar, and gained a first-class degree. The mental and physical vigour shown in his youth was maintained throughout a long life.

Morrison left Oxford in 1858, made a 'grand tour', which included Egypt, Palestine, and the United States, and entered the House of Commons in 1861 as Liberal member for Plymouth. He held that seat until the Liberal débâcle of 1874, stood unsuccessfully for the City of London in 1880, parted from Gladstone over his Irish programme, and twice subsequently (1886–92 and 1895–1900) represented, as a Liberal Unionist, the Skipton division of Yorkshire, in which his home was situated. He finally retired from candidature in 1900 after a broken career in parliament extending over nearly forty years. It was a career, however, which was neither conspicuous nor, in all probability, congenial.

A man of strong convictions and great independence, but neither an orator nor an ambitious politician, Morrison was never at any period an enthusiastic party man. In his early Liberal days his interests were largely centred on the co-operative movement for improving working-class dwellings. In the years following his break with Gladstone all his energies and resources were thrown into opposing home rule for Ireland.

Morrison's intermittent absorption in politics did not keep him from a careful stewardship both of his private fortune and of the various business interests from which it arose. In particular he joined in 1874 the board of the Central Argentine Railway, in which his family possessed a large stake, became its chairman in 1887, and soon afterwards paid a protracted visit to South America which resulted in an elaborate report and the eventual absorption of the Buenos Aires and Rosario line. To the end of his life his portfolio included an unusually large holding in this company. The British Aluminium Company, in which his brother Charles was the largest investor, also stood out from the pack, as did a politically inspired investment in the Sligo, Leitrim, and Northern Counties Railway. These exceptional holdings had a nominal value of £149,000, £112,287, and £93,489 respectively. He was also director of a number of local concerns and chairman of the Craven Bank, travelling constantly between London and Yorkshire in discharge of these duties. His wealth grew partly by inheritance from a childless brother and sister who died before him, and partly through the simplicity of his personal tastes. At his death, his stocks and shares amounted to a nominal £3.5 million in several hundred companies located mainly in Britain (54 per cent) and Latin America (16 per cent).

Despite all his miscellaneous interests, a remarkably large part of Morrison's time was spent at Malham Tarn, the wild moorland estate in Craven which had been acquired for him when he came of age, from the Listers of Gisburn. Here he indulged his love of walking, of folklore, and of local leadership. Always something of an aloof and self-centred figure, he played host at Malham to a number of eminent Victorians, including Henry Fawcett, John Ruskin, Charles Darwin, John Stuart Mill, Sir William Harcourt, and especially Charles Kingsley. As his guests, they witnessed numerous innocent eccentricities. These included a refusal to imbibe the wines of imperial France (he instead placed republican chianti on his dining table); the substitution of blue crockery for yellow following his break with Gladstone; and a smoking room papered with 6 inch Ordnance Survey sheets of the surrounding countryside to prevent the servants from tidying them away. It was at Malham Cove, below the house, that Kingsley had the idea of *The Water Babies*, and Walter Morrison was his 'Squire'.

At Malham, away from the glare of publicity, Morrison planned his benefactions. He played a considerable part in the development of the northern universities—a single anonymous gift of £10,000 to the new school of agriculture at Leeds was revealed almost by accident after his death. For Giggleswick School, where he was chairman of the governors for many years, he built and furnished down to the smallest detail, in celebration of Queen Victoria's diamond jubilee, that remarkable 'chapel with a dome' which was the expression both of his lifelong interest in oriental architecture and of his personal predilections in English history. The pews, of wood from the Argentine province of Tucuman, bore witness to a major source of his wealth. The windows of the clerestory display his judgement of English history and politics, placing Arnold, Livingstone, and Gordon alongside such older figures as Wykeham, Columba, and King Alfred. He supported Lord Roberts's campaign for national service; for some years he made an annual contribution of £10,000 to King Edward's Hospital Fund, and contributed to innumerable relief funds during both the South African and the European wars. He was a founder of the Palestine Exploration Fund, a society dedicated, in the words of the archbishop of York, to the rescue of Palestinian history 'from darkness and oblivion', and regarded himself in that connection as the 'discoverer' of Kitchener. His gift of £15,000 funded the Hittite excavations at Carchemish undertaken by the British Museum, and underpinned the short-lived Society of Biblical Archaeology.

Towards the end of his life Oxford University became the special object of Morrison's benefactions. Fired perhaps by his experience at Giggleswick, he offered to rebuild the new chapel at Balliol College on the lines of the old, which he greatly preferred; on the rejection of this somewhat startling proposal, he gave £30,000 to the university to support a readership in Egyptology, a professorial pension fund, and the study of agriculture. Finally, in 1920, he endowed the Bodleian Library with a single payment of £50,000, which placed him among its chief benefactors. The honorary degree of DCL, which was conferred upon him in the following year, was the only public recognition which he received, or indeed would have valued. He died at Sidmouth, Devon, on 18 December 1921, and was buried at Kirkby Malham. Morrison left an estate with a gross value of £2 million, the greater part of which passed to his nephew, James Archibald Morrison.

GEOFFREY DAWSON, rev. CHARLES JONES

Sources G. Dawson, 'Walter Morrison', *National Review*, 78 (1921–2) · R. Gatty, *Portrait of a merchant prince: James Morrison, 1789–1857* (privately printed, Northallerton, Yorks., [1977]) · W. R. Mitchell, *Walter Morrison: a millionaire at Malham Tarn* (1990) · *Giggleswick School: notes on the history of the school and an account of the new chapel* (1901) · Royal Commission on Historic Monuments, London, Palestine Exploration Fund archives · priv. coll., Morrison MSS · d. cert.

Archives priv. coll. · Royal Commission on Historic Monuments, London, Palestine Exploration Fund archives | Bishopsgate Institute, London, letters to George Howell · Richmond Local Studies Library, London, Sladen MSS

Likenesses photographs, repro. in Mitchell, *Walter Morrison* · portrait, Royal Commission on Historic Monuments, Palestine Exploration Fund

Wealth at death £2,000,000: probate, 30 Jan 1922, *CGPLA Eng. & Wales*

Morrison, William Douglas (1852–1943), criminologist and prison chaplain, was born at Kirriemuir, Forfarshire, on 15 May 1852, the son of Robert Southmuir Morrison, a merchant, and Ann Donald-William. Educated at nearby Trinity College, Glenalmond, he was ordained deacon in 1877 and priest in 1878 by the bishop of Ripon. From 1877 to 1883 he was a curate: first at Sandal Magna, then at St John's, Wakefield. He was appointed assistant chaplain at Wakefield prison in 1883, moving in 1887 to Wandsworth prison. Marrying this practical experience with voracious reading, he turned himself into one of the foremost authorities on crime and prisons in the country.

In 1889 Morrison published *The Jews under the Roman Empire*. This was followed by a spate of criminological works. His books *Crime and its Causes* (1891) and *Juvenile Offenders* (1896) were widely read. Morrison was attracted by the Italian positivist school, particularly by its renunciation of repressive punishment and by the principle that sentences needed to be individualized according to the characteristics of offenders. But he was never a true convert. He accepted that criminals were a 'degenerate class' produced by the 'anomalous biological and social conditions' of urban life, but rejected the pessimistic view that criminality was innate and associated with distinctive physiological or mental characteristics, believing rather that the 'prison look' was 'prison made'. Furthermore, he came to appreciate the injustices to which indeterminate sentences could lead. Morrison edited the first criminological series to be published in England, including translations of Enrico Ferri's *Criminal Sociology* (1895) and Cesare Lombroso and William Ferrero's *The Female Offender* (1895), and published at least fourteen articles in a wide range of learned and more popular periodicals. In 1898 the University of St Andrews conferred on him an honorary LLD.

Although undoubtedly learned, Morrison was more a controversialist than a social scientist and was accused, sometimes justifiably, of drawing inferences to suit his argument. A tall, distinguished looking man of great determination, he was a Christian socialist and progressive Liberal. A member of the Reform Club, he was also active in Henry Salt's Humanitarian League. In January 1894 the *Daily Chronicle* published a series of damning articles on the prison system, 'Our dark places'. The articles were almost certainly written by the assistant editor Henry Massingham, but Morrison undoubtedly provided much of the fuel. In April 1894 he savagely attacked Sir Edmund Du Cane's stewardship of the prison system in the *Fortnightly Review*. His article, 'Are our prisons a failure?', claimed that the system created recidivism by its inhumane insistence on relentless discipline, uniformly applied. Contrary to some accounts, Du Cane did not sack him. A departmental committee on prisons (chaired by Herbert Gladstone) was set up to which Morrison gave extensive critical evidence. When its progressive report was published in 1895 both R. B. Haldane, a member of the committee, and Massingham in the *Daily Chronicle* paid tribute to Morrison for being 'the real instrument' of the

changes and as one of 'the great prison reformers'. Yet, disappointed at the slow progress of reform, he continued to be a thorn in the flesh of the administration. He was regarded as 'a dangerous man' not only by Du Cane but also by his more progressive successor, Sir Evelyn Ruggles-Brise. Morrison drew attention to the plight of Oscar Wilde, and played a part in getting him transferred from Wandsworth to better conditions at Reading gaol.

In 1898 Morrison left the prison service. Over the next ten years he was a member of staff first of the *Daily Chronicle* and then of *The Nation*. He edited four religious works but still continued to write on criminological themes, publishing his last article in the *Sociological Review* in 1908. In that year he obtained the crown living of St Marylebone, a post which he held until 1941. He was knocked down by a motorcycle on 13 December 1943, and died the same day at St Mary's Hospital, Paddington East, London, aged ninety-one, his criminological fame forgotten by his obituarists. He was survived by his wife, Alice, *née* Butler, and by their son and their daughter, who was the wife of Sir Albert Dykes Spicer, second baronet.

ROGER HOOD

Sources L. Radzinowicz and R. Hood, *A history of English criminal law and its administration from 1750*, 5: *The emergence of penal policy in Victorian and Edwardian England* (1986) • *The Times* (15 Dec 1943) • *Marylebone Record* (17 Dec 1943) • S. McConville, *English local prisons, 1860–1900: next only to death* (1995) • G. D. Robin, 'William Douglas Morrison, 1852–1943', *Pioneers in criminology*, ed. H. Mannheim, 2nd edn (1972) • A. F. Havighurst, *Radical journalist: H. W. Massingham* (1974) • G. Hendrick, *Henry Salt: humanitarian reformer and man of letters* (1977) • b. cert.

Wealth at death £26,401 16s. 3d.: probate, 6 April 1944, *CGPLA Eng. & Wales*

Morrison, William Shepherd, first Viscount Dunrossil (1893–1961), speaker of the House of Commons and governor-general of Australia, was born at Torinturk, Argyll, on 10 August 1893, the sixth son of John Morrison (b. 1842), who had been a diamond prospector in South Africa before settling as a farmer at Torinturk, and his wife, Marion, daughter of Ronald McVicar, of North Uist. He was educated at George Watson's College, Edinburgh, and in 1912 entered Edinburgh University, where he obtained his MA in 1920. His studies were interrupted by distinguished service in France in the First World War: he reached the rank of captain in the Royal Field Artillery, was wounded, and was awarded the Military Cross. He married on 22 April 1924 Katherine Allison (d. 1983), daughter of the Revd William Swan, minister of South Leith parish. She was herself an Edinburgh graduate and was then reading for the bar; she was called by the Inner Temple in 1926. They had four sons, the eldest being John William *Morrison, the diplomat.

Morrison, like others of the trenches generation, sought public life in order to repay some of the comradeship experienced in wartime, and determined on the law as the prelude to politics. He was called to the bar at the Inner Temple in 1923 on the advice of two established Scottish Conservatives, Sir Robert Horne and the duchess of Atholl. In spite of these connections, he did not have an easy start and was defeated candidate in 1923 and 1924 in the difficult Western Isles. Though a man proud of his Scottish birth, accent, and skill in Gaelic, he had to go south to Cirencester and Tewkesbury to find a winnable seat. He was elected there in 1929 but then easily held it for thirty years.

Morrison had acquired the nickname Shakespeare, or more often Shakes (Bernard Shaw's abbreviation of Shakespeare's name), because he had not only a deep love of Shakespeare's verse, from which he could quote extensively, but something of the playwright's way with words too. His speaking skills and striking appearance, a shock of early white hair overhanging black eyebrows and deep-set eyes, ensured that he quickly acquired the attention of the house, and the broad admiration for him on the Conservative side led to his election as only the second chairman of the 1922 committee in 1932 in a contested election against the committee's founder. Sir Gervase Rentoul had of late been dividing members by his high-handed attitude and now bitterly remarked that Morrison won 'partly because he was regarded as a neutral, having hardly ever attended a meeting of the Committee, or taken any part in its struggles or activities' (Goodhart, 60). The '1922' was in 1932 only a shadow of what it later became, but this was an early achievement, and his four years as chairman were an important phase in the committee's development. He was not 'an energetic innovator' but he 'guided the Committee with distinction through a difficult period of transition' (ibid., 74).

Alongside politics, Morrison continued his legal career, which had begun as secretary to Thomas Inskip, the solicitor-general, taking silk in 1934 and becoming recorder of Walsall in 1935. In November 1935 his political career took off and then accelerated quickly, with appointment as financial secretary to the Treasury. In the following October he reached the cabinet as minister of agriculture and fisheries, and was sworn of the privy council in 1936. Unfortunately he was not successful either in dealing with the intractable agricultural depression, or in raising the morale of the farming community. As the European situation deteriorated he attracted criticism for refusing to prepare agriculture for war, arguing that to do so would injure the industry further, and unnecessarily so since war was not in his view inevitable. In much of this he was typical of the government in which he served, and paid the same penalty as others when war came and found them unready in 1939. On wider issues, Morrison was critical of appeasement, but ineffectively so, and his decision not to resign over Munich, if indeed he ever seriously considered it, weakened his influence further. Neville Chamberlain considered him one of the 'weaker brethren' in his team, and demoted him in January 1939 to the non-departmental duchy of Lancaster. This was combined for a few early months of wartime with the new Ministry of Food, but in April 1940 he moved to the non-cabinet post of postmaster-general, a backwater in wartime, and when Churchill became premier a month later he left Morrison there, though even the Chamberlainite chief whip Margesson wanted him sacked altogether as a manifest failure.

Morrison's final ministerial post came when made first minister of town and country planning in February 1943, with a brief to implement the Uthwatt report. He piloted through parliament the Town and Country Planning Act (1943), a milestone in legislation for building control, but though he had had little to do with its gestation he was caught in the crossfire between Labour MPs who wanted more intervention and Conservatives who wanted none at all, at least during a party truce. He sadly confessed to Hugh Dalton in November 1943 that he was 'having rows all round just now' (War Diary, 663). When Churchill briefly formed a caretaker government with a full quota of Conservative ministers in May 1945, he left Morrison at the Ministry of Town and Country Planning and offered him no cabinet seat, and he carried on until Labour swept into office two months later. It was remarkable how rapidly Morrison's ministerial career waxed and waned. 'Chips' Channon, a friend of Morrison but an astute taker of political temperatures, noted in January 1943 that though 'once the hope of enlightened Tory England', he was 'now an amiable white-headed boy taken seriously by nobody'. By March 1945 Morrison was 'a ghost of his former self. He has lost all but the vaguest vestiges of power' (Chips, ed. James, 349, 389).

In the Conservative opposition after 1945, Morrison occasionally attended shadow cabinets, but took no active part in the work of the opposition. When not away pursuing his legal career he was more often seen sleeping in the library than speaking in the chamber. Through an intervention by Churchill, however, he suddenly re-emerged into the limelight in October 1951 when persuaded to stand for the vacant speakership. For the first time since 1895 the speaker's election was contested and went to a vote, for many Labour MPs were not happy to support a former minister with no experience of chairing the house. Morrison was elected on a mainly party vote, but rapidly established his authority, and was unanimously re-elected speaker in 1955. He used his rich voice, wit, and Scottish accent to considerable effect, jollying the house along with the frequent plea that 'We must get on', but exhibiting exemplary firmness. This was certainly the case during the Suez debates of 1956, when he had frequently to urge restraint on hot-headed MPs and on one occasion was obliged to adjourn the house altogether so that tempers could cool. He was generally thought to have done this difficult job very well indeed.

Physically he looked the part to perfection, with his towering figure and finely modelled countenance, so fitly framed in the wig. No man wore the habiliments of his office with such elegance. The Speaker's procession, with Morrison's presence to grace it, was a rewarding sight … His patience was wellnigh inexhaustible, and his courtesy, even with bores, was exquisite … To points of order and procedural conundrums he brought a lambent clarity, and his judgements usually commanded acceptance. But in such matters he was always meticulous in acting as one who essentially was the servant of the House. (The Times, 3 Feb 1961)

Morrison's health was, however, undermined during

the long hours and continuous strain of eight years as speaker, and in February 1959 he announced that he would not seek re-election to the house. He last presided over the Commons on 19 September, and was granted at the house's request a viscountcy (November 1959), the speaker's usual title in retirement, and a pension. This latter was soon the subject of controversy when it transpired in November that though leaving through ill health he had almost at once accepted, on the invitation of his friend Robert Menzies, the arduous post of governor-general of Australia, with a salary of £10,000. He arrived in Australia early in 1960, and whole-heartedly threw himself into the post, visiting every state capital within the first few months and embarking on an active social round to introduce himself to ordinary Australians. His health was not up to the exertion, though. He was ordered to rest in September and died suddenly of pulmonary embolism at Government House, Canberra, on 3 February 1961. His eldest son, John William (b. 1926), succeeded him as Viscount Dunrossil, and Morrison was buried four days later at St John the Baptist Anglican Church, Canberra, with a state funeral and military honours.   JOHN RAMSDEN

Sources *The Times* (3 Feb 1961) · *The Times* (4 Feb 1961) · *The Times* (6 Feb 1961) · *The Times* (8 Feb 1961) · *WWW, 1961–70* · 'Chips': the diaries of Sir Henry Channon, ed. R. R. James (1967) · *The Second World War diary of Hugh Dalton, 1940–1945*, ed. B. Pimlott (1986) · N. Smart, *The national government, 1931–40* (1999) · M. Cowling, *The impact of Hitler: British politics and British policy, 1933–1940* (1975) · P. Goodhart, *The 1922: the story of the 1922 committee* (1973) · S. Ball, 'The 1922 committee: the formative years, 1922–1945', *Parliamentary History*, 9 (1990), 129–57 · K. Jeffreys, *The Churchill coalition and wartime politics* (1991) · b. cert. · Burke, *Peerage* (2000) · *AusDB*
Archives Welwyn Garden City Central Library, Hertfordshire, corresp. with F. Osborn | FILM BFI NFTVA, news footage
Likenesses O. Birley, oils, Arundel · E. O. Fearnley-Whittingstall, oils, Palace of Westminster, London
Wealth at death £5973 10s. 7d.: administration with will, 24 April 1961, *CGPLA Eng. & Wales*

Morrison, William Vitruvius (1794–1838). *See under* Morrison, Sir Richard (1767–1849).

Morrissey, Richard Edwin [Dick] (1940–2000), jazz musician, was born at The Gables, a nursing home in Bonehurst Road, Horley, Surrey, on 9 May 1940, the eldest son of Dennis Richard Lawrence Morrissey (d. 1975), a bank clerk, and his wife, Edwina Joan Walker (d. 1995), a teacher. The family was Roman Catholic. Morrissey had a younger brother, Christopher, and a sister, Elizabeth, the youngest child. The family lived for a while in Billericay, Essex, and then at 28 Manor Park Road, Sutton, Surrey, where Morrissey attended Sutton High School for Boys. It was at this school that Morrissey learned to play a variety of instruments including the bugle, accordion, piccolo, and violin, but he eventually settled on the clarinet, modelling his style on the playing of the great pre-war New Orleans clarinettist Johnny Dodds and his follower, the Scottish clarinettist Sandy Brown. While still at school he played the clarinet with other boys in a New Orleans-style band, the Original Climax Jazz Band.

On leaving school Morrissey became an apprentice jeweller, and from the age of seventeen worked with the

trumpeter Gus Galbraith's septet. About this time the alto saxophonist Pete King played to him the records of Charlie Parker, the American alto saxophonist and founder of the bebop jazz idiom. Parker's playing was a revelation to him, and changed his musical direction. He bought a tenor saxophone, and early in 1960 began working regularly as a semi-professional with a quartet after work. His influences in this period were Stan Getz and Sonny Rollins, but he was also impressed by the British saxophonist Tubby Hayes. Such was Morrissey's success that by August 1960, when he was only twenty, he was appearing with his own quartet at the Marquee Club in Soho. Later that year he led his own band at the Flamingo Club, also in London. Soon he was earning more as a saxophonist than as a jeweller's apprentice, and, realizing that the difficulties of getting to work on time after a late session were likely to lead to his dismissal, he gave up his day job and turned fully professional. He then left for India to play a nine-month residency (1960–61) at the Trincas restaurant in Calcutta, with a quartet led by the double bass player Ashley Kozac and featuring the pianist Harry South. On his return in 1961 he made his first recordings as a leader for the Fontana label, issued as *It's Morrissey, Man!* (1961). He continued to work with his own quartet, working with musicians like the pianist Michael Garrick, Harry South of the Calcutta quartet, and the leading British drummer Phil Seaman. He played often at Ronnie Scott's club in Soho in this period. In 1966 he made an album with the American blues singer Jimmy Witherspoon. He also played with the Harry South Big Band, and in 1967 with the Freddy Mack Sound. Now a fully established and sought-after musician, he accompanied many visiting American musicians, including the trombonist J. J. Johnson early in 1969. But musical tastes were changing radically in the aftermath of the Beatles and work was becoming more difficult to find for 'straight' jazz musicians.

As early as 1968 Morrissey had begun to experiment with a new jazz-rock band, which now became the group If. This was co-led by the guitarist Terry Smith. Morrissey and Smith moved to Sweden and made the country their base for the group's international activities, which included many tours of the United States, continuing until the early 1970s. If disbanded in 1974, although Morrissey and Smith still worked together from time to time in 1976 and 1977. Morrissey continued to live in Sweden for a year, then in 1975 returned to London, where he worked with the organist Mike Carr's trio during the summer. Then he teamed up with the Glasgow-born electric guitarist Jim Mullen to form a new group, Morrissey-Mullen, in 1976, before leaving for America to join a Scottish soul and funk group, the Average White Band. Working in the United States for eight months, he also played with the American jazz flautist Herbie Mann, and with his own group. On his return to Britain he resumed working and recording with Jim Mullen until 1985. An important recording from this period is *Cape Wrath* (1979). He also recorded the first digital single ever issued by EMI, *Love Don't Live Here Anymore* (1979). Another recording was *After Dark* (1983). This proved Morrissey's status as one of the leading European tenor saxophonists, with a big-toned 'straight from the heart' style and a lightning facility in complex improvisation. From 1986 he led his own quartet, but he also played with John Burch's quintet in 1987. *Happy Hour* (1988) was another notable recording. He continued with his own group in the late 1980s and early 1990s, but appeared with other groups and toured Germany with the drummer Pete York's band. An outstanding recording was *Good Times and the Blues* (1993), which featured both Mike Carr and Jim Mullen.

For some time Morrissey lived in Portugal; apart from his jazz activities, he worked as a session musician for many pop and rock recordings, including tracks with Peter Gabriel and Roy Harper, and with Paul McCartney on *The Long and Winding Road*. He also played and composed for film soundtracks, in particular contributing the love theme to Ridley Scott's film *Bladerunner*. But ill health from the mid-1990s restricted his activities, and he eventually had to use a wheelchair. In the words of his long-standing co-leader Jim Mullen he was 'An easy-going guy with no axes to grind. Big, bearded, and dark-haired, he had something of the "absent-minded Professor" about him, but he took a workmanlike, "sleeves rolled-up" approach to his saxophone playing and life.' His last public appearance was at a reunion session of the Morrissey-Mullen band at the Astor Theatre in Deal on 26 August 2000, when he played with his usual drive and swing. Morrissey died from cancer in the Applecroft Nursing Home, Sanctuary Close, River, Dover, on 8 November 2000, and was buried in Deal cemetery. He left three children, Phillip, Yohanna, and Jasper, and a stepson, Patrick; his marriage, to a Swede named Birgitta, had ended in divorce.

A. J. H. LATHAM

Sources J. Chilton, *Who's who of British jazz* (1998) · B. Kernfeld, ed., *The new Grove dictionary of jazz* (1994) · *The Independent* (9 Nov 2000) · *The Scotsman* (13 Nov 2000) · *The Guardian* (9 Nov 2000) · *The Times* (9 Nov 2000) · *Daily Telegraph* (9 Nov 2000) · www.jimmullenjazz.com, accessed c. 4 Jan 2002 · b. cert. · d. cert. · private information (2004) [Christopher Morrissey, brother]
Wealth at death gross under £210,000: probate, *CGPLA Eng. & Wales* · net under £70,000: probate, *CGPLA Eng. & Wales*

Morritt, John Bacon Sawrey (1771–1843), traveller and classical scholar, was born on 27 October 1771 at Cawood, Yorkshire, the eldest of three sons and a daughter of John Sawrey Morritt, who died at Rokeby Park, Yorkshire, on 3 August 1791, and his wife, Ann (d. 1809), daughter of Henry Peirse of Bedale, MP for Northallerton. Morritt was educated at Manchester grammar school, and, after an interlude in Paris in 1789, went up to St John's College, Cambridge, where he graduated BA in 1794 and MA in 1798. From 1794 to 1796, accompanied by his tutor, Robert Stockdale, he travelled through Austria, Hungary, Turkey, Greece, and Italy. In the course of these travels, after some weeks in Constantinople, where they were joined by the Revd James Dalloway, they crossed to the Asian side in order to investigate the ancient sites celebrated in the *Iliad*. The exact location of Homer's Troy was still a matter of controversy and Morritt gave his preference to Burnabashi, a site now discarded in favour of Hissarlik.

His exploration of this region earned him the nickname 'Troy' Morritt, and enabled him subsequently to defend Homer against the claims of Jacob Bryant that the city of Troy had never existed; the two men contested this matter in print for some years. Morritt toured extensively through Greece, and was one of the earliest travellers in that region.

Morritt inherited a large fortune, including the estate of Rokeby, which his father had purchased in 1769 from Thomas Robinson. The so-called *Rokeby Venus*, a seventeenth-century painting of the toilet of Venus by Diego Velázquez, now in the National Gallery, London, was formerly in his possession. Morritt passed the remainder of his life, with the exception of a single visit to France, in Britain. While at university he had joined the Lancashire militia, and in 1803 he served with the Teesdale Volunteers. On 19 November 1803 Morritt married Katharine Stanley, daughter of the Revd Thomas Stanley, rector of Winwick in Lancashire. The marriage took place at the London house of her brother, Thomas Stanley MP, Morritt's former militia colonel. Morritt held office as high sheriff of Yorkshire in 1806, and sat as a JP for north Yorkshire. He was MP for Beverley, 1799–1802, Northallerton, 1814–18, and Shaftesbury, 1818–20. In parliament he maintained an independent stance, though generally well disposed to government. In 1815 he spoke for the landed interest on the Corn Bill; on other occasions he voted with the minority.

Morritt's travels endowed him with a lifelong taste for the arts and he had a wide knowledge of painting and sculpture. Elected to the Society of Dilettanti in 1799, he became one of its leading and most popular spirits, and edited some of the society's publications. Sir Martin Archer Shee's fine portrait of him, painted for the society in 1832, shows Morritt in the robes of the arch-master of the society. Having been in Athens in 1795, Morritt was a consistent supporter of Lord Elgin in the controversy over the Parthenon marbles, and gave evidence on his behalf to the parliamentary inquiry of 1818. He was also a founder member of the Travellers' Club in 1819.

From about 1808 until his death in 1831, Sir Walter Scott was a close friend of Morritt and his wife. They visited each other regularly and kept up a warm correspondence; Scott dedicated his poem 'Rokeby' to Morritt and confided to him the secret of the authorship of *Waverley*. Morritt cultivated a broad circle of erudite friends, which included men as diverse as Henry Lascelles, second earl of Harewood, Sir William Gell, William Stewart Rose, Richard Payne Knight, William Wilberforce, Sir Humphry Davy, Sir Roderick Murchison, and Robert Southey.

Katharine, Morritt's wife, died in 1815. Morritt himself died, after a lingering illness, on 12 July 1843, at Rokeby Park, and was buried by his wife's side in a vault under Rokeby church, where a marble tablet, surmounted by a bust of him, was placed in their memory. There were no children of the marriage.

An obituarist described Morritt as a man of high principle and sterling honour, one who regarded his large fortune as an important trust committed for a time to his keeping for the benefit of others, yet liberal, charitable, and benevolent with his resources. Scott commended his mixture of sound good sense and high literary cultivation, and hailed him as a man possessed of a sweet, kind temper; Wilberforce described him as full of anecdote, and Sir William Fraser mentioned him as a brilliant raconteur.

ANITA MCCONNELL

Sources GM, 2nd ser., 20 (1843), 547–8 · J. B. S. Morritt, *The letters of John B. S. Morritt of Rokeby … in the years 1794–96*, 2nd edn (1985) [with introduction by P. J. Hogarth] · L. Cust and S. Colvin, eds., *History of the Society of Dilettanti* (1898) · *The Times* (15 July 1843) · HoP, *Commons*

Archives Durham RO, letters and family legal papers | BL, Murchison MSS · BL, Rose MSS · Bodl. Oxf., corresp. with Louisa Stuart [copies] · NL Scot., letters to Lord Muncaster · NL Scot., notebook, corresp. with Sir Walter Scott and Lockhart

Likenesses M. A. Shee, oils, 1832, Society of Dilettanti, Brooks's Club, London · marble bust, Rokeby church, Yorkshire

Wealth at death under £25,000: Bank of England, London, registered will abstracts

Mors, Roderyck [Roderigo]. *See* Brinklow, Henry (d. 1545/6).

Morse, Sir Arthur (1892–1967), banker, was born on 25 April 1892 in Bohercrowe, co. Tipperary, Ireland, one of the seven children of Digby Scott Morse, a cashier with the Bank of Ireland, and Lizzie Jane Holmes. Educated at Foyle College, Londonderry, Arthur Morse joined the London office of the Hongkong and Shanghai Banking Corporation in 1912.

Morse's early career was unexceptional. He went to the East with the Hongkong Bank in 1915 and served routinely in Hong Kong, Tientsin (Tianjin), and Shanghai, returning in 1929 to the Hong Kong head office. Morse married Margery May (1893/4–1966), probably in 1923 or 1924; they had no children. From 1929 to 1940 Morse served under the irascible Sir Vandaleur Grayburn, who detected his potential. Indeed, Morse underwent an extraordinary physical and personality metamorphosis; early photographs show a slim, even emaciated figure, but, by the end of the 1930s, he had become a larger man in every sense. 'Latterly he used to roar like a bull', his hearty laugh marking 'the Arthur Morse we all knew so well' (King, *Hongkong Bank*, 4.36).

Grayburn determined that any further promotion for Morse in the East was unlikely and in 1940 sent him to London as a supernumerary manager. However, within months one manager died and the second retired. In consequence, just thirty-seven days before Pearl Harbor, Morse became manager and, *ex officio*, chairman of the bank's London consultative committee. Before Hong Kong surrendered on 25 December 1941, the bank had secured promise of an order in council making London the head office and the consultative committee the effective board of directors. Authorized to act on this promise, Morse was now in virtually total control.

Despite the loss of the East, the Hongkong Bank was in a surprisingly sound position. Morse was able to build on the bank's sterling reserves, even while meeting the extraordinary expenses of wartime. He had been treasurer of the University of Hong Kong, and he cared for escaped bank and Hong Kong University staff and for families with members in internment; he reconstituted the books with smuggled documents and kept contact with Free China through the establishment of the Chongqing office. For his management of the Far Eastern Relief Fund and related problems he was created a CBE in 1944.

As for the future, Morse acted on his conviction, not universally shared, that the Hongkong Bank's head office would return to a British Hong Kong. He promised that any rational request for finance for Hong Kong would be forthcoming; he guaranteed funds for heavy equipment, on occasion committing a company whose senior officials were interned. Such decisions placed the colony at the head of the queue during post-war shortages. Although impatient with officialdom, Morse put £5 million at the disposal of the Hong Kong planning unit without government guarantee. Japan surrendered unexpectedly; consequently destruction was not as disastrous as anticipated, and Morse rushed his officers east to finance the reconstruction, while he himself remained in London; there were war-created problems to resolve, including the reception and rehabilitation of interned staff.

Morse returned to Hong Kong in 1946 and served on the colony's executive council. He was the leader in some twenty-two organizations covering a broad range of economic, sporting, and charitable affairs. Morse exuded confidence and was a 'presence'; but he was also shrewd and secretive. He had the instincts of an accountant, the inspiration of a statesman. Tough negotiations relative to legislation designed to regularize his bank's 'duress note issue', that is, banknotes issued during the Japanese occupation without appropriate backing, for example, led the Treasury's Norman Young to insist the governor be 'peremptorily' ordered to 'tell [Morse] where he got off' (King, *Hongkong Bank*, 4.240). In the event, cooler counsels prevailed. As a senior colleague noted, 'Morse knew little about technical banking, but banking is both an art and a science, and in the former he excelled' (ibid., 37).

Morse's knighthood in 1949 was interim recognition. His decisive actions had re-established his bank as the colony's *de facto* central bank and, through loans to established customers and innovative accounts and other payment devices, had facilitated the restoration of Hong Kong as a trading entrepôt. Confidence would be restored following the conclusion of China's civil war, and by the end of 1952 the bank's total assets of HK $3.5 million were approximately three times the total at the end of 1940. In 1953 Morse retired triumphantly from the East.

In London, Morse became, as had a predecessor, Sir Thomas Jackson (1841–1915), 'permanent' chairman of a reorganized consultative committee. He maintained a correspondence with Sir Michael Turner, the new chief executive in Hong Kong, and was a key negotiator in the 1959–60 acquisitions of the Mercantile Bank (of India) and of the British Bank of the Middle East, on whose boards he subsequently served until 1965. He was chairman of Bowmakers, 1954–62, and in 1958 served as president of the Finance Houses Association. Concurrently, as the unsalaried chairman of the British Travel and Holiday

Association, 1954–60, Morse made two promotional tours of North America. Not only did he prove a successful advocate of Britain as a tourist destination, he was also active in encouraging the very necessary improvement of tourist facilities. He was created KBE in 1961.

With the change of the Hongkong Bank's chief executive in 1962 and the death in 1966 of his wife, who was acknowledged to have been a major supportive influence in his life, Morse's active career faded. He retired to his garden flat at 26 St James's Place, overlooking Green Park, London. Morse died there on 13 May 1967.

As chief executive and chairman of the Hongkong Bank from 1941 to 1953, Morse was one of the two principal architects (with the governor, Sir Alexander Grantham) of Hong Kong's post-war recovery. After his return to London in 1953 he was instrumental in effecting the rationalization of British overseas banking and the promotion of British tourism.   FRANK H. H. KING

Sources F. H. H. King and others, *The history of the Hongkong and Shanghai Banking Corporation*, 4 vols. (1987–91) · F. H. H. King, ed., *Eastern banking: essays in the history of the Hongkong and Shanghai Banking Corporation* (1983) · G. Jones, *The history of the British Bank of the Middle East*, 2: *Banking and oil* (1987) · *The Times* (15 May 1967), 12b · *The Times* (18 May 1967), 12g · *The Times* (8 June 1967), 12d · personalities files, HSBC Group Archives, London, Midland Bank archives · b. cert., Ireland · d. cert. · d. cert. [M. M. Morse]
Archives HSBC Group Archives, London, Midland Bank archives, Hongkong Bank [especially 'personalities' files and oral history transcripts incl. (i) T. J. J. Fenwick, (ii) Sir Michael W. Turner, and (iii) Lady Turner] · HSBC Group Archives, London, Midland Bank archives, R. P. Moodie, 'Autobiography' (TS)
Likenesses photographs, 1953 (with Lady Margery), HSBC Group Archives, London, Midland Bank archives, Hong Kong Bank Group archives, PHST 42 · photographs, 1955 (British Travel Association album), HSBC Group Archives, London, Midland Bank archives, Hong Kong Bank Group archives, S16.7c · photographs, 1959 (British Travel Association album), HSBC Group Archives, London, Midland Bank archives, Hong Kong Bank Group archives · S. Elwes, portrait, Hong Kong Bank, Hong Kong · photographs, HSBC Group Archives, London, Midland Bank archives, Hong Kong Bank Group archives, PHST 42.9
Wealth at death £321,610: probate, 19 July 1967, *CGPLA Eng. & Wales*

Morse, Henry (1595–1645), Jesuit, who used the aliases Claxton, Ward, and Sheppard to conceal his identity, was born in his mother's house at Broome in Suffolk, the sixth of nine sons of Robert Morse (*d.* 1612), a minor landowner of Tivetshall St Mary, Norfolk, and his wife, Margaret Collinson. His family had Catholic sympathies, but Morse was brought up to conform to the Anglican religion. He attended Corpus Christi College, Cambridge, and then studied law at Barnard's Inn in London.

In 1614, having undergone a conversion, he went into exile and enrolled as a student at the English College, Douai. After a few months he returned to England on family business, but was arrested as soon as he landed, and imprisoned as a Catholic for the next four years in the New prison, Southwark. Released in 1618 he returned to Douai and was then sent to the English College, Rome. He returned to England in 1624, now ordained, to work there as a missionary priest. He spent eighteen months in London and then Newcastle, before being arrested again in 1626 when leaving the country by ship, bound for the English Jesuit noviciate at Watten. He was imprisoned in York Castle until 1630, when he was released, and with other Catholic prisoners was sent into exile. He worked for three years in the Southern Netherlands, first at Watten, where he also ministered to English soldiers in the Spanish army billeted in the area, and then at the English Jesuit establishment at Liège.

In 1633 he returned to London, working in the parish of St Giles-in-the-Fields. He became well known for his courageous pastoral work there during the outbreak of the plague in 1636; regardless of his own personal safety he ministered to both Catholics and protestants. With the secular priest John Southworth he made an appeal to the Catholics outside London for alms to relieve the suffering of those quarantined in the stricken capital. He contracted the disease himself in the course of his work, but recovered. His efforts were obstructed by pursuivants and by an anti-Catholic excitement which the plague and the growing political tensions of the time provoked. He was eventually arrested late in 1636, the priest searchers having been tipped off by a nurse. He was put on trial in 1637 as a Catholic priest, but although convicted he was saved by the intercession of Charles I's Catholic wife, Henrietta Maria, and was eventually released on the grounds of ill health.

Morse worked in London and the south-west of England until he was arrested yet again on 17 June 1640 and brought before Archbishop Laud and the court of high commission. Six years later, at Laud's own trial, one of the charges against the archbishop was that he had released Morse, but Laud said that it was due to Lady Cornwallis, who had 'stood by and made herself merry to hear me chid' by Henrietta Maria, whom she had told of the arrest of the Jesuit, and who had then interceded again on his behalf (Caraman, 140–41). In 1641 Morse took himself into exile as London became more dangerous. He served as a chaplain to Henry Gage's English regiment, which was fighting for Spain in the Netherlands. In early 1643 he crossed back to England and resumed his work as a priest in the north-eastern counties of England. Late in 1644 he was arrested by the parliamentary forces who had recently captured Newcastle, and was sent to London. This time there was no French queen to protect him, and he was sentenced to death, the conviction he had received eight years earlier being revived. He was executed at Tyburn on 22 January 1645.

William Morse (1591–1649), Jesuit, was an elder brother of Henry, and preceded him abroad, arriving at Douai in 1611. He was ordained in 1617 and returned to England as a missionary priest the following year. He became a Jesuit and had a much less eventful life than Henry, working in several parts of the country until he died in Norfolk on 1 January 1649.   PETER HOLMES

Sources DNB · P. Caraman, *Henry Morse* (1957) · H. Foley, ed., *Records of the English province of the Society of Jesus*, 1 (1877), 566–611 · H. Foley, ed., *Records of the English province of the Society of Jesus*, 6 (1880), 288–9 · H. Foley, ed., *Records of the English province of the Society of Jesus*, 7/1 (1882), 527–8 · G. Anstruther, *The seminary priests*, 2

(1975) · T. M. McCoog, ed., *Monumenta Angliae*, 1–2 (1992) · R. Challoner, *Memoirs of missionary priests*, ed. J. H. Pollen, rev. edn (1924), 467ff. · [J. Keynes and T. Stapleton], *Florus Anglo-Bavaricus* (Liège, 1685); facs. edn with new introduction by T. A. Birrell (1970), 82–4 · C. Dodd [H. Tootell], *The church history of England, from the year 1500, to the year 1688*, 3 (1742), 120 · Venn, *Alum. Cant.* · C. Talbot, ed., *Miscellanea: recusant records*, Catholic RS, 53 (1961), 407 · E. H. Burton and T. L. Williams, eds., *The Douay College diaries, third, fourth and fifth, 1598–1654*, 1, Catholic RS, 10 (1911), 122–4, 129, 132–3, 144, 181, 367, 370 · W. Kelly, ed., *Liber ruber venerabilis collegii Anglorum de urbe*, 1, Catholic RS, 37 (1940), 189–90 · G. Oliver, *Collections towards illustrating the biographies of the Scotch, English and Irish members of the Society of Jesus*, 2nd edn (1845) · H. Morse and J. Southworth, *To the Catholics of England* (1636)

Archives BL, portion of journal, Add. MS 21203 | Archivio Vaticano, Vatican City, Nunziatura d'Inghilterra, portion of journal, 4/54–6

Likenesses line engraving, c.1645, NPG · engraving (after unknown artist), repro. in H. Foley, *Records of English province*, 7 vols. (1877–83), vols. 1, 7

Morse, Hosea Ballou (1855–1934), customs official and historian of China, was born on 18 July 1855 in South Brookfield, Queens county, Nova Scotia, the first of the four children of Albert David Morse (1832–1900) and his wife, *née* Mercey Dexter Park (c.1830–c.1900). A fifth-generation Nova Scotian, whose earlier ancestors had emigrated from England to Massachusetts Bay in 1635, Hosea lived in South Brookfield and then in Halifax, before moving with his parents to Medford, Massachusetts, near Boston, in 1865.

As a young boy Morse had an active imagination, but he reportedly 'preferred books to play'. His father, a struggling but determined shoe merchant, decided to send him to the prestigious Boston Latin school, which he attended from 1866 to 1870; Hosea excelled in his studies, particularly foreign languages. In 1869 both he and his father became naturalized United States citizens. The next year Hosea entered Harvard College, graduating with highest honours in 1874. At that time he accepted an offer from an influential Harvard alumnus to join the Chinese Imperial Maritime Customs Service under its renowned inspector-general Robert Hart.

From a lowly clerk during the mid-1870s, when he began learning Chinese with the assistance of a Chinese tutor, who worked with him each day for an hour before breakfast, Morse gradually rose in the ranks to become a full commissioner in 1898 and statistical secretary in the early 1900s. During this period he served in nearly a dozen places, from the vibrant metropolitan centres of Peking (Beijing), Tientsin (Tianjin), and Shanghai to such lonely backwater ports as Kiungchow (Qiongshan), Pakhoi (Beihai), and Lungchow (Longzhou). He married Annie (Nan) Josephine Welsford (1853–1940) on 8 February 1881.

Like many other customs personnel in late nineteenth-century China, Morse undertook a number of non-customs assignments with Hart's encouragement. For example, he distributed relief during the great famine of 1876–8, taught English in the Peking Interpreters' College during 1878–9, served as a Chinese-language interpreter in Peking, Tientsin, and London from 1879 to 1882, superintended the exchange of prisoners after the Sino-French

War of 1884–5, and advised the China Merchants' Steam Navigation Company from 1885 to 1887.

During the Sino-Japanese War of 1894–5 Morse became deeply involved in delicate diplomatic negotiations, and in 1899 he handled the sensitive and dangerous opening of the port of Yochow (Yeuzhou) in Hunan province. After an offer from President William Howard Taft to become the United States minister to China (which Morse refused on grounds of poor health) and official retirement in 1909, he continued to assist the Chinese government. In 1920, for instance, he travelled to Brussels as an adviser to the Chinese delegation to the Economics and Financial Conference of the League of Nations, for which he received the order of the Excellent Crop.

Morse enjoyed a distinguished career as a historian following his departure from China in 1907. In the early stages of the First World War (1915)—and after nearly a decade of residence in England—he applied to become a British citizen again, moved by Great Britain's heroic war effort. In 1924 he received an honorary doctor of laws degree from Harvard University. Among Morse's most famous and influential works on China were *The Trade and Administration of the Chinese Empire* (1908), *The International Relations of the Chinese Empire* (3 vols., 1910–18), and *The Chronicles of the East India Company Trading to China, 1635–1834* (5 vols., 1926–9). He also wrote a fascinating historical novel based on the military exploits of Frederick Townsend Ward and Charles G. Gordon during the Taiping uprising (1850–64), entitled *In the Days of the Taipings* (1927).

On 13 February 1934 Morse died of pneumonia at his home, Arden, Grange Road, Camberley, Surrey, where he had lived since 1914. His remains were cremated and buried at Brookwood on 16 February. His devoted wife, Nan, died six years later. Although childless, they cared for the two children of Hosea's brother, Albert Morse (*b.* 1864), after the death of Albert's wife in 1893.

RICHARD J. SMITH

Sources J. K. Fairbank, M. H. Coolidge, and R. J. Smith, *H. B. Morse: customs commissioner and historian of China* (1995) · *Robert Hart and China's early modernization: his journals, 1863–1866*, ed. R. J. Smith, J. K. Fairbank, and K. F. Bruner (1991) · m. cert. · *CGPLA Eng. & Wales* (1934) · *The Times* (20 Feb 1934)

Archives Harvard U., Houghton L. · priv. coll. · RBG Kew, notes relating to Chinese plants | Case Western Reserve University, Cleveland, Ohio, Twing collection · Public Archives of Nova Scotia, Halifax, Unitarian-Universalist Church of Halifax records

Wealth at death £20,160 2s. 9d.: probate, 11 April 1934, *CGPLA Eng. & Wales*

Morse, Robert (1741/2–1818), military engineer, was the second son of Thomas Morse, the rector of Lamyatt, Somerset. He entered the Royal Military Academy, Woolwich, on 1 February 1756, and while still a cadet received a commission as an ensign in the 12th foot on 24 September 1757. Appointed a practitioner engineer on 8 February 1758 he took part in the three raids mounted in that year against the north-west coast of France; during the disembarkation at Cherbourg in August he was slightly wounded. He then sailed with General Hopson's expedition to the Caribbean, and was present at the capture of

Guadeloupe in May 1759. Having been promoted lieutenant and sub-engineer on 10 September 1759, on his return to England he was employed on the coast defences of Sussex.

In 1761 Morse served in the expedition against Belle Île, off the coast of Brittany, under General Studholme Hodgson. A landing was made in April and a siege mounted against the citadel of Palais; it surrendered on 7 June. Morse helped to repair the fortifications before returning home. He served in Germany during the campaign of 1762, as an engineer and assistant quartermaster-general, and acted as aide-de-camp to the British commander, the marquess of Granby. In 1763, at the close of the war, he was part of the delegation that negotiated the passage of British troops through the territory of the Dutch republic. He was promoted captain-lieutenant and engineer-extraordinary on 6 May 1763.

Through the good offices of Colonel George Morrison, quartermaster-general of the forces, Morse was appointed, on his return to England, assistant quartermaster-general at headquarters; he was simultaneously engineer for the Medway division (until 1766) and afterwards (until 1769) for Tilbury. In 1773 he was appointed commanding royal engineer of the West Indian islands of Dominica, St Vincent, Grenada, and Tobago. He was promoted captain and engineer-in-ordinary on 30 October 1775. He returned to England in 1779, and after working on the coastal defences of Sussex he was posted to Plymouth and Falmouth.

In June 1782 Morse sailed with Sir Guy Carleton to New York. He was promoted lieutenant-colonel on 1 January 1783. In July 1783, with British evacuation of New York imminent, Carleton sent Morse to report on the defences of Nova Scotia, instructing him to look for sites for magazines and to examine communication links with Canada. Although he was called upon while there to remedy the local garrison's shortage of barrack accommodation and stores, his report, 'A general description of the province of Nova Scotia', was completed in 1784; by then he was styled chief engineer in America. A seven-week cruise round Fundy Bay and its inlets served as the basis of his comments on the territory's harbours and rivers. He also described the inhabitants, warned of the potential for boundary disputes with America on the St Croix River, and urged the upgrading of fortifications at Halifax and Annapolis Royal.

Following his return to England, Morse married, on 20 April 1785, Sophia (1749/50–1818), daughter of Peter Stephen Godin of Southgate, Middlesex; they had a daughter, Harriet. Between 1785 and 1790 Morse was a member of the select Tower committee of engineers, and was made colonel on 6 June 1788. He was promoted major-general on 20 December 1793, while commanding royal engineer at Gibraltar (1790–95), and lieutenant-general on 26 June 1799. When the office of inspector-general of fortifications was created in April 1802 Morse was its first incumbent, and was made colonel-commandant of Royal Engineers at the same time. He remained inspector-

general until 1811, overseeing the construction of considerable defensive works in Sussex and Kent against the threat of French invasion. Though Morse has been accused by one historian of compiling a report 'of quite astonishing fatuity' on the subject of Martello towers in 1804 (Glover, 115–17) the charge is ill-founded; he was well versed in the use of round towers for coastal defence, having inspected them on Guernsey as early as 1787.

Morse was promoted general on 25 April 1808, before his retirement from the service, on grounds of ill health, on 22 July 1811. He died, aged seventy-six, at his home in Devonshire Place, Westminster, on 28 January 1818, seventeen days after his wife, and was buried on 10 February in St Marylebone Church.   ALASTAIR W. MASSIE

Sources Royal Engineers Library, Chatham, Conolly papers · R. Morse, 'A general description of the province of Nova Scotia', 1784, BL, King's MSS 208–209 · S. G. P. Ward, 'Defence works in Britain, 1803–1805', *Journal of the Society for Army Historical Research*, 27 (1949), 18–37 · R. Glover, *Britain at bay* (1973) · *Report on American manuscripts in the Royal Institution of Great Britain*, 4 vols., HMC, 59 (1904–9), vols. 3–4 · *DCB*, vol. 5 · W. Porter, *History of the corps of royal engineers*, 2 vols. (1889) · S. Sutcliffe, *Martello towers* (1972) · *GM*, 1st ser., 55 (1785), 323; 88/1 (1818), 91, 377 · parish register, St Marylebone, 10 Feb 1818, City Westm. AC, [burial] · R. F. Edwards, ed., *Roll of officers of the corps of royal engineers from 1660 to 1898* (1898)
Archives BL, 'A general description of the province of Nova Scotia', King's MSS 208–209 · PRO, corresp., PRO 30/55

Morse, William (1591–1649). *See under* Morse, Henry (1595–1645).

Morshead, Edmund Doidge Anderson (1849–1912), schoolmaster and translator, was born on 4 February 1849 at Salcombe Regis, Devon, the third of the four sons of the Revd John Philip Anderson Morshead (1810–1881) of Salcombe Regis and his wife, Alethea, *née* Yonge. He was the grandson of Colonel John Anderson (d. 1831), who married a Miss Morshead of Plymouth in 1800 and added her surname to his own in 1805. In 1861 Edmund was sent to Winchester College, his father's former school, as were his brothers. He soon gained a reputation for his wit and his remarkable capacity to memorize poetry. Proceeding on a scholarship to New College, Oxford, in 1867, he went on to gain firsts in moderations (1869) and in *literae humaniores* (1871). In 1874 he was made a fellow of the college, but by that time had been appointed to the staff at Winchester College, where, apart from a period in Oxford in 1874–5, he spent the rest of his career. On 1 August 1878 he married Mary Fearon, whose brother W. A. Fearon was Morshead's colleague and, from 1884 to 1901, headmaster of Winchester.

Morshead's career was in many ways typical of the learned schoolmasters of the later nineteenth century, before the professionalization of academic life drove a wedge between school and university teaching. He produced several translations of Aeschylus and Sophocles, edited selections from Schiller and Byron, and published occasional verse compositions. His main claim to fame, however, rests on what was written about him. In 1880 his pupils Charles Locock and Francis Montagu produced a 'pronouncing dictionary' of his speech mannerisms

('Morsheadic', soon changed to 'Mushri'). This was first circulated in manuscript and later 'jellygraphed'; printed editions appeared in Oxford (1880, 1888) and London (1901). The *Mushri–English Pronouncing Dictionary* was a spoof, yet it included a detailed, and apparently accurate, account of Morshead's strange phraseology and pronunciation. The most sustained jest of its kind, it is also perhaps unique in being an idiolectal dictionary.

Several influences combined to provoke the dictionary's appearance. The idiosyncrasy it celebrated was already manifested by Winchester Notions, the most venerable and complex of all school slangs. Awareness of individual differences was also heightened in Winchester in 1880 by the successful campaign to have a Liberal candidate elected to parliament. Feelings ran high in the school, where most of the staff were Conservative supporters; Morshead belonged to a small group of Liberals. The form and style of the dictionary owe much to the comparative philology then popular; it is probably significant that it appeared soon after James Murray's appeal in April 1879 for lexicographical information for the *New English Dictionary*.

Morshead's individuality was reinforced in the classroom by his mobile countenance, which his pupils watched for signs of impending jokes; a feature caught by two surviving photographs. Morshead was, however, not just an eccentric; the sparse evidence for his educational thinking suggests that he was a civilized and liberal man, free from many of the prejudices of his time and class. Speaking at the inauguration of the Birmingham branch of the Classical Association in 1906, he described its extreme attackers and defenders as impatient Philistines in the first case, and bigoted Pharisees in the second. Morshead was a keen walker and fisherman, both in his native Devon and abroad. In 1903 deteriorating eyesight forced him to retire, and he moved to Southwark—a somewhat surprising decision that evidenced a commitment to charitable work; he gave lectures at the working men's college and also served as manager of local elementary schools. He died at his home, 29 Trinity Square, Southwark, on 24 October 1912, survived by his wife.

CHRISTOPHER STRAY

Sources C. Stray, ed., *The Mushri–English pronouncing dictionary: a chapter in 19th-century public school lexicography*, 7th edn (1901); repr. (1996) · An Old Wykehamist [W. H. B. Bird], 'Doidge', *Cornhill Magazine*, [3rd] ser., 49 (1920), 459–68 · H. J. Hardy, ed., *Winchester College, 1867–1920: a register*, 2nd edn (1923), 17 · J. A. P. E. [J. Edgcumbe], 'The Doidge', *The Wykehamist*, 714 (28 May 1929), 121–3
Likenesses C. K. Aitchison, two photographs, c.1894–1898, Winchester College, Wiccamica archives
Wealth at death £4039 6s. 5d.: probate, 11 Nov 1912, CGPLA Eng. & Wales

Morshead, Henry Anderson (c.1774–1831), army officer, was the son of Colonel Henry Anderson of Fox Hall, co. Limerick. He entered the Royal Military Academy, Woolwich, on 29 May 1790, and became a second lieutenant, Royal Artillery, on 18 September 1792. He served in the duke of York's Flanders campaign in 1793–4, being present at the action of Famars (23 May 1793), the sieges of Valenciennes (June–July), and Dunkirk (August–September), and the battle of Hondschoote (8 September). He gained the respect of his superiors, and as a result was transferred, at his own request, to the Royal Engineers on 1 January 1794. He took part in the siege of Landrecies in April 1794, the battle of Tournai on 23 May, and the siege of Nijmegen in November.

After his return to England, Morshead was sent to Plymouth in June 1795. He was promoted first lieutenant on 19 November 1796. The following May he sailed with two companies of Royal Military Artificers to St Domingo in the West Indies. On the island's evacuation in 1798 he was attached to the staff of his close friend, Sir Thomas Maitland. When he returned to England in November 1798 Morshead was employed in the Thames division, and stationed at Gravesend. He was promoted captain-lieutenant on 18 April 1801, and was sent to Portsmouth and then Plymouth. He was promoted captain on 1 March 1805, and in the same year he received royal licence to add the surname Morshead to that of Anderson. In 1800 he had married Elizabeth, the only daughter of P. Morshead, esquire, of Widey Court, Plymouth, Devon. They had eleven children.

In July 1807 Morshead was sent to Dublin; three months later he was appointed commanding royal engineer of the expedition, under Brigadier-General Beresford, which sailed from Cork and captured Madeira in February 1808. On his return from Madeira to England in November 1812 he was posted to the Plymouth division. He was promoted lieutenant-colonel on 21 July 1813, and again sent to Dublin. He was next appointed commanding royal engineer for Scotland (March 1814), and in July 1815 was transferred in order to serve as commanding royal engineer of the western district in Plymouth. In this post he carried out important work for the ordnance and naval services in consultation with the duke of Wellington and Lord Melville. On 29 July 1825 Morshead was promoted colonel.

In 1829 Morshead was appointed commanding royal engineer for Malta. He died at Valletta on 11 November 1831, while acting as governor. He was honoured with a public funeral, and was buried in the old saluting battery overlooking Valletta's grand harbour. Not surprisingly for someone with an engaging personality, Morshead was fond of society and was a good conversationalist. His writing is notable for its clarity.

R. H. VETCH, *rev.* S. KINROSS

Sources Royal Engineers' Records, Chatham · PRO, War Office and Board of Ordnance Records · *United Service Journal*, 1 (1832), 142–3 · A. B. Rodger, *The war of the second coalition: 1798–1801, a strategic commentary* (1964) · R. Muir, *Britain and the defeat of Napoleon, 1807–1815* (1996)
Likenesses bust, c.1832, Royal Engineers' Office, Valletta, Malta

Morshead, Sir Leslie James (1889–1959), army officer, was born on 18 September 1889 at Ballarat, Victoria, Australia, the fourth son and fifth child of William Morshead, a miner, and his wife, Mary Eliza Rennison. He was educated at Mount Pleasant state school, Ballarat, and the teachers' training college, Melbourne. He taught at the

Armidale School, New South Wales, and when war broke out in 1914 was a master at the Melbourne Church of England grammar school. Having been commissioned in the 2nd battalion, 1st Australian Imperial Force, in September 1914, he landed at Anzac Cove, Gallipoli, on 25 April 1915, the first day of the Gallipoli landings, as a captain and second-in-command of a company. He was promoted major in June 1915 but in October he contracted enteric fever and was invalided to Australia. On recovery he was promoted lieutenant-colonel and given command of the new 33rd battalion (part of Major-General John Monash's 3rd division), which he trained in Australia and England and took to France in September 1916. He commanded it until the conclusion of hostilities, leading it with rare distinction at Armentières, Messines, Passchendaele, Villers-Bretonneux, and along the Somme in the 1918 final offensives. By the end of the war he had been wounded twice, mentioned in dispatches, and received the DSO (1917), CMG (1919), and Légion d'honneur.

After demobilization Morshead tried sheep farming near Merriwa, New South Wales, but soon joined the staff of the Orient Steam Navigation Company; in 1948 he became its general manager in Australia. In 1921 Morshead married Myrtle, daughter of William Woodside, of Melbourne; they had one daughter.

Between the wars Morshead combined success in business with continued interest in the citizen military forces. From 1920 to 1931 he commanded citizen force battalions, and in 1933 he was promoted colonel and given command of an infantry brigade. When war broke out in 1939 he was selected to command 18th brigade, one of the first formations raised for overseas service with the 2nd Australian Imperial Force (AIF). In February 1941 he was promoted major-general and given command of the new 9th Australian division.

Incomplete, ill-equipped, and only partly trained, Morshead's division was sent to Cyrenaica, Libya, in March 1941 to relieve the more experienced 6th division withdrawn for Greece. When the British forces in Cyrenaica were driven back in April 1941 into Tobruk (which had been captured by the Australian 6th division in January 1941) by the sudden onslaught of the Afrika Korps, Morshead became the fortress commander (from 14 April). His resolute leadership quickly welded his motley collection of Australian, British and other troops into an effective fighting force which vigorously fought off Rommel's attempts to capture Tobruk.

The division was relieved in October 1941 and was recuperating in Syria when the remainder of the AIF was transferred from the Middle East to the Pacific early in 1942. Morshead was promoted lieutenant-general and became general officer commanding (GOC) the AIF in the Middle East. He led his division with distinction at the battles of El Alamein (July and October–November 1942), and then took it to the south-west Pacific area. After a short period in command of New Guinea force (GOC 1943) he commanded the 1st Australian corps (1944) and directed the complicated amphibious operations which resulted in the

recapture of Borneo (1945). He was mentioned in dispatches and made CBE (1941), KBE (1942,) and KCB (1942), and was awarded foreign honours.

Morshead was one of the finest products of the Australian citizen force system of military service. Slight of build, he had a mild facial expression which masked a strong personality, the impact of which, even on first acquaintance, was quickly felt. He was unsparing and outspoken in criticism, yet also quick to commend and praise. Nicknamed 'Ming the Merciless' by his troops, he became just 'Ming' as they learned to appreciate the quality of his leadership, particularly his talents as a battle commander.

After the war Morshead returned to business pursuits and occupied important positions in Australian commerce and industry: general manager in Australia of the Orient Line and a director of the Bank of New South Wales, Mutual Life and Citizens Assurance Company, Trustees Executors and Agency Company, and the Australian National Airways and Commonwealth Aircraft Corporation. In 1957 the Menzies government appointed Morshead chairman of a high-level committee (the Morshead committee) on the defence departments. It reported in December 1957 and February 1958 and its recommendations included amalgamation of the three service departments with the department of defence. However, most of the recommendations were shelved. Morshead died in Sydney on 26 September 1959.

E. G. KEOGH, *rev.* ROGER T. STEARN

Sources Australian War Memorial Records · G. Long, ed., *Australia in the war of 1939–45*, 7 vols., ser. 1 (Army) (1952–63) · private information (1971) · personal knowledge (1971) · *WWW* · Burke, *Peerage* (1959) · P. Dennis and others, *The Oxford companion to Australian military history* (1995) · J. Gooch, ed., *Decisive campaigns of the Second World War* (1990)

Archives FILM IWM FVA, actuality footage

Likenesses I. Hele, portrait, Australian War Memorial, Canberra, Australia

Morshead, **Sir Owen Frederick** (1893–1977), librarian, was born on 28 September 1893 at Camplehaye, Tavistock, Devon, the youngest of the seven children of Reginald M. Morshead (1848–1914), banker, and his wife, Ella Mary (1852–1920), daughter of Henry Grace Wilson Sperling and his wife, Mary Maitland Wilson. He was educated at Marlborough College (1907–11), before entering the Royal Military Academy, Woolwich (1911–13). In 1913 he went to Magdalene College, Cambridge, but his education there was interrupted by the outbreak of war. Throughout the First World War he served in the Royal Engineers, was awarded the DSO, the MC, the French Légion d'honneur, and the Italian *croce di guerra*, and was mentioned in dispatches five times, ending the war with the brevet rank of major. He returned to Cambridge, becoming a fellow of Magdalene College in 1920. The following year he became Pepys librarian, which position he relinquished in 1926, when he published *Everybody's Pepys*. From 1922 to 1926 he was secretary to the Cambridge University appointments board. On 29 December 1926 he married Francisca de la Escosura (Paquita) Hagemeyer (*b.* 1905), the daughter of

American parents living in Florence. They were to have two daughters and a son.

Also in 1926 Morshead was appointed librarian at the Royal Library, Windsor Castle. He owed the position to the patronage of the prince of Wales, who had served with him during the war, and the dukes of York and Kent, who knew him at Magdalene; his military record weighed heavily in his favour with the king. His first work at Windsor was with the outstanding collection of old master drawings. He enlisted the assistance of Kenneth Clark, whose two-volume *Catalogue Raisonné* (1935) of the 600 drawings by Leonardo da Vinci in the library was the first in a very distinguished series organized by Morshead. By his retirement in 1958, fourteen volumes had been published. Morshead also enabled the public to see selections of the drawings for the first time, by having three display units placed in the state entrance of the castle in 1937.

In June 1930 Morshead also became deputy keeper of the Royal Archives, and oversaw the use of the archives for the production of a number of important royal biographies (including Harold Nicolson on George V, John Wheeler-Bennett on George VI, and Philip Magnus on Edward VII) and editions of historical royal correspondence (including Arthur Aspinall's editions of the papers of George III and George IV, and Roger Fulford's editions of Queen Victoria's letters to her eldest daughter). He arranged for the indexing of the large collection of papers of the exiled Stuarts, and acquired for the archives the military papers of George, duke of Cambridge (1819–1904). In 1932 he instituted an extensive card index of royal employees from 1660 to 1837. In the library he added a number of important volumes to the collection, and took a particular interest in books from private presses. For the Roxburghe Club (to which he was elected in 1931) he had printed *Some Variants in Wordsworth's Text, in the Volumes of 1836–7 in the King's Library* (1949).

An excellent communicator rather than an academic, Morshead produced many elegantly written lectures, articles, books, and broadcasts on royal history, Windsor Castle, and the Royal Library. These included a history of the castle (1951), the official castle guidebook (1948), and the monographs *George IV and Royal Lodge* (1965) and *Royalist Prisoners in Windsor Castle in the Civil War* (1958). He contributed lives of George V and Lord Stamfordham to the *Dictionary of National Biography*. His twenty-nine broadcasts, mostly for the BBC overseas service, also covered a wide spectrum of subjects, and his skill with the written and spoken word made him a valued source of advice on royal speeches.

Morshead's relationship with the royal family was dominated by his long friendship with Queen Mary. From 1926 until her death in 1953 she sought his views, advice, and help with her avid collecting of *objets d'art* and particularly of miniatures. In 1948 he was 'sorry to leave Sandringham and the dear Queen Mary, indeed more like a beloved aunt' (Morshead, diary, 21 Aug 1948). Morshead's active role in the Home Guard in the Second World War brought him into close contact with George VI and Queen Elizabeth, whom he helped with her collections. In 1944 the

queen wrote to him 'You are such a charmingly "accessible" librarian … we are most thankful that we have in you an informed and interesting expert and thank God a lover of beauty and all that means' (11 June 1944, Royal Archives). He shared George VI's interest in orders of chivalry and medals, and helped the king with the design of the George Cross and medal in 1940.

Morshead gave a great deal of time to the local community, in Windsor and beyond, and was a much respected member of many educational, arts, and medical committees. After the war his work in health administration increased greatly—he was appointed a member of the North-West Metropolitan Regional Hospital Board from 1947 and of the Central Health Services Council of the Ministry of Health in 1948. For over twenty years he served on the selection board for the colonial service, and on the British Council's fine arts committee; he was the sovereign's representative on the Royal Mint advisory committee from 1951. He also maintained close contacts with the leaders of the country's literary, artistic, social, political, and academic worlds through his membership of the Roxburghe Club (from 1931), the Society of Dilettanti (from 1945), and The Club (from 1942). A devout Christian and regular worshipper at St George's Chapel and Windsor parish church, Morshead was above all a happy man with a sunny personality. His old friend Albert Baillie, dean of Windsor, wrote to him 'You have a rare power of winning the affection of the people among whom you live' (26 Oct 1944, Royal Archives).

After thirty-two years in the royal household Morshead retired in 1958 and became emeritus librarian. He also became an honorary fellow of Magdalene College. He was appointed MVO (1933), CVO (1937), KCVO (1944), KCB (1953), and GCVO (1958). He moved to Sturminster Newton in Dorset, where he soon became founder chairman of the Dorset Historic Churches Trust, an interest which kept him absorbed until his death at his home, Lindens, Sturminster Newton, on 1 June 1977. His remains were cremated.   OLIVER EVERETT

Sources O. Morshead, diaries, 1926–58, Royal Arch. • Royal Arch. • private information (2004) [subject's widow and daughters] • *WWW*

Archives IWM, diary and papers relating to his service on the western front and in Italy • Royal Arch.

Likenesses S. Warburton, miniature, 1930, priv. coll. • Elliott & Fry, photograph, 1947, NPG • D. Nemon, clay bust, 1953 • D. Nemon, drawing, 1953 • W. Bird, photograph, 1958, NPG • G. Kelly, oils, 1963, priv. coll.

Wealth at death £15,933: probate, 15 Sept 1977, *CGPLA Eng. & Wales*

Morson, Thomas (1825–1908), pharmaceutical manufacturer, born in London, was the son of **Thomas Newborn Robert Morson** (1800–1874), pharmaceutical manufacturer, born in Stratford-le-Bow, London, who served his apprenticeship with an apothecary in the Fleet Market before studying alkaloid chemistry in Paris. When the elder Morson returned to London in 1821 he established himself as a retail pharmacist in Southampton Row, Bloomsbury, and soon acquired a leading position in the import and supply of quinine and morphia. By 1837 demand for his range of products—which included perfumes and dyes as well as pharmaceuticals and their ingredients—was growing, and, like other pharmacists, he found that the back of the shop was inadequate for manufacturing; he set up a separate factory in Hornsey Road. In 1869 the factory was moved further out of London, to the Summerfields works, Ponder's End, in Middlesex. The elder Morson was a founder member of the Chemical and Pharmaceutical societies; he was a member of the Pharmaceutical Society's council, serving as vice-president and president. He died at his house, 38 Queen Square, Bloomsbury, on 3 March 1874.

Thomas Morson was educated at University College School and then studied pharmacy in France before joining his father's business. In 1857 he married the daughter of a Boulogne pharmacist, whose family name was Dagomet. There were two sons of the marriage, Thomas Pierre and Albert Robert. When his father died in 1874, Morson took over the running of the business. He employed the chemist Robert Taubman to run the laboratory the Morsons had by then established, and from 1891 until his death in 1905 Taubman was also a partner in the business.

The Morsons enjoyed a high reputation and a number of leading medical scientists, including Joseph Lister (1827–1912), consulted the firm. This led to the development and marketing of Lister's cyanide and other named products, but, despite its standing, the Morson business and laboratory, like others in Britain at that time, did not engage in speculative research and development leading to innovation of the kind that was taking place in the industry in Germany in the 1890s and the first decade of the twentieth century. The pharmacy in Southampton Row was closed in 1900 and new offices and warehouses were opened in Elm Street, Gray's Inn Road.

Morson was essentially a private rather than a public person, with artistic interests and friends, and he built up a collection of contemporary paintings. Like his father his interest in science reached beyond pharmacy and he was a member of the Geological and Zoological societies. He died at his home, 30 Elsworthy Road, Primrose Hill, London, on 5 February 1908.

The business was inherited by his sons who converted it in 1915 into a private limited company. It was later acquired by the American pharmaceutical company, Mercke, Sharp, and Dohme. JUDY SLINN

Sources J. Liebenau, 'Morson, Sir Thomas', *DBB* • Boase, *Mod. Eng. biog.* • *Chemist and Druggist* (8 Feb 1908) • *Chemist and Druggist* (28 March 1908) • *Pharmaceutical Journal and Transactions*, 3rd ser., 4 (1873–4), 726–7 • d. cert. • d. cert. [Thomas Newborn Robert Morson]
Archives Wellcome L., family and business papers | Royal College of Surgeons, Edinburgh, corresp. with Joseph Lister
Likenesses photograph, Pharmaceutical Society, London
Wealth at death £4947 1s. 2d.: probate, 20 March 1908, *CGPLA Eng. & Wales* • under £12,000—Thomas Newborn Robert Morson: resworn probate, Oct 1875, *CGPLA Eng. & Wales* (1874)

Morson, Thomas Newborn Robert (1800–1874). *See under* Morson, Thomas (1825–1908).

Morstede, Thomas (*d.* 1450), surgeon, was the son of Thomas and Alianora Morsted of Betchworth, Surrey. He is first recorded, as Thomas Morstede, 'leech', in a London deed of 1401. He had been apprenticed to the London surgeon Thomas Dayron (*d.* 1407), who bequeathed him two books of surgery and physic. By 1410 'Thomas Morstede, surgeon', had entered Henry IV's service, receiving an annuity of £40, and for the next twelve years he was on active royal service. In 1411 he occurs as king's surgeon; in 1412 Henry V appointed him searcher of vessels in the port of London, an office previously held by the royal surgeon John Bradmore. Morstede's appointment was reconfirmed in 1438.

In April 1415 Morstede and William Bradwardine, described as the king's surgeons, contracted to serve the king abroad for a year, each bringing a team of surgeons. They served on the Agincourt campaign from 8 July to 24 November 1415 and in June 1416 contracted to supply surgeons and makers of surgical instruments for the next campaign, which departed for France in July 1417. Morstede, who was acquiring property in London in February 1417, probably served in this campaign as well and returned with the king to England in February 1421, for he is next recorded in London in March 1421 when he obtained the wardship of an orphan. He probably went back to France with the king in June 1421 and remained there until Henry V's death (31 August 1422); he next appears in December 1422, when his annuity of 1410 was reconfirmed.

Morstede then returned to London, where by May 1423 he had joined with the eminent physicians Gilbert Kymer, John Sumbreshede, and Thomas Southwell, and with the surgeon John Harwe, to found a conjoint College of Physicians and Surgeons. The college had collapsed by November 1424, but Morstede's personal fortunes flourished. He is named as a master of the mystery of surgeons of London in 1423, 1424, 1428, and 1431. By 1424 he had adopted the style of 'esquire' and in 1426 he was the first witness to the will of the king's uncle Thomas Beaufort, duke of Exeter. In the London lay subsidy of 1436 Morstede's income from lands and annuities in London, Essex, Surrey, Middlesex, and Lincolnshire was valued at £154, the second highest assessment. In 1437 Morstede and John Beford (later one of Morstede's legatees) were engaged in property transactions in London with John Redenhale.

Some of Morstede's wealth probably came through marriage. His first wife, Juliana (mentioned September 1420), had died by 1431, when he married his second wife, Elizabeth. She was the childless widow of William Fitz-Harry or FitzHenry (*d.* 1431), a wealthy Londoner for whom Morstede had served as executor, and was the daughter and coheir of John Michell (*d.* 1445) and his wife, Margaret (daughter and coheir of Hamelin de Matham; *d.* 1452). Michell, a wealthy London grocer and stockfishmonger, had served as alderman (1414–44), sheriff (1413–15), mayor (1424–5, 1436–7), mayor of the staple of Westminster (1425–30), and member of parliament (1411–35). Despite his wealth, Morstede remained an active surgeon until his death in the parish of St Olave Jewry, London, in 1450. His will of that year (dated 20 April; proved 8 June) forgives a debt of 10 marks owed by a former apprentice, Edmund Burcetre, 'for his apprenticeship', and leaves extensive bequests, including 'my English book bound with two *latitudinibus*' and 'all my instruments of surgery', to his current apprentice, Robert Bryttende or Briggend (Beck, *The Cutting Edge*).

In an earlier will (dated 19 March 1445) Morstede had included bequests for the souls of his parents; his will of 1450 added bequests for the souls of his (unnamed) brothers and sisters (one brother, John Morested, had died in 1421 while serving abroad with the duke of Clarence). Neither will mentions children, living or dead. A London fishmonger named Thomas Morstede (sheriff 1436–7) may have been a relation. Morstede's widow, Elizabeth, later married (by July 1452) John Wode, under-treasurer of London, exchequer clerk, and member of parliament (speaker 1483); she died childless in 1464. In addition to Morstede's lavish pious bequests, he built a chapel in the north aisle of his parish church of St Olave Jewry, where he was buried.

Talbot and Beck's attribution to Morstede of a surgical treatise written in English in 1446 (BL, Harley MS 1736) has been questioned by Lang.   MARTHA CARLIN

Sources R. T. Beck, *The cutting edge: early history of the surgeons of London* (1974) · C. H. Talbot and E. A. Hammond, *The medical practitioners in medieval England: a biographical register* (1965) · S. J. Lang, 'John Bradmore and his book *Philomena*', *Social History of Medicine*, 5 (1992), 121–8 · S. L. Thrupp, *The merchant class of medieval London, 1300–1500* (1948), 356, 383 · Rymer, *Foedera*, 3rd edn, 4/2.117, 123, 166 · C. Allmand, *Henry V* (1992), 214 · J. S. Roskell, *Parliament and politics in late medieval England*, 3 vols. (1981–3), vol. 3, pp. 383–4 · J. S. Roskell, *The Commons in the parliament of 1422* [1954], vi, 203–4 · J. Stow, *A survay of London*, rev. edn (1603); repr. with introduction by C. L. Kingsford as *A survey of London*, 2 vols. (1908), vol. 2, pp. 262, 281–2 · R. R. James, 'The will of Thomas Morstede: surgeon to Henry the Fifth', *The Lancet* (30 Dec 1933), 1513–14 · F. Getz, 'Medical practitioners in medieval England', *Social History of Medicine*, 3 (1990), 245–83, esp. 278–9 · D'A. Power and J. F. South, eds., *Memorials of the craft of surgery in England* (1886) · C. H. Talbot, *Medicine in medieval England* (1967) · A. H. Thomas and P. E. Jones, eds., *Calendar of plea and memoranda rolls preserved among the archives of the corporation of the City of London at the Guildhall*, 4 (1943) · P. E. Jones, ed., *Calendar of plea and memoranda rolls preserved among the archives of the corporation of the City of London at the Guildhall*, 5: *1437–1457* (1954) · R. R. Sharpe, ed., *Calendar of letter-books preserved in the archives of the corporation of the City of London*, [12 vols.] (1899–1912), vol. K · Chancery records · London, Goldsmiths' Company, register of deeds and wills, 1. fols. 191r–191v · CLRO, husting roll, 148 (39) · BL, Harley Charter 55, B.37 · CLRO, husting roll 170 (8); repr. in R. R. Sharpe, ed., *Calendar of wills proved and enrolled in the court of husting, London, AD 1258 – AD 1480*, 2 (1890), 492
Archives BL, Harley MS 1736
Wealth at death very wealthy: Beck, *The cutting edge*

Mort, Thomas Sutcliffe (1816–1878), entrepreneur in Australia, was born at Bolton, Lancashire, on 23 December 1816, the fourth of six children and the second son of Jonathan Mort (*d.* 1834) and his wife, Mary, *née* Sutcliffe. After his father's death the family was in financial difficulty and Thomas was obliged to take a job as a clerk with H. and

Thomas Sutcliffe Mort (1816–1878), by unknown photographer

S. Henry of Manchester. On 19 September 1837 he sailed from Liverpool, and arrived in Sydney, Australia, on 25 February 1838. His two younger brothers, Henry (1818–1900) and James (*d.* 1879), followed him to Australia. In 1838 Thomas entered the firm of Aspinall, Browne & Co., the Sydney correspondents of H. and S. Henry. He worked for them and their successors for five years as clerk and salesman, gaining considerable knowledge of local business. On 27 October 1841 he married his first wife, Theresa Shepheard (*d.* 1869), daughter of Deputy Commissioner-General James Laidley. They lived happily together for twenty-eight years and had six sons and two daughters. Mort was closely attached to his family and some of his sons and brothers were involved in his business ventures.

In September 1843, after the failure of his employers' firm, Mort began his career as an entrepreneur and speculator. He set up as an auctioneer, combining general sales with specialist wool sales. The latter became particularly successful, being well-managed occasions where specialists could meet, buy and sell, finance their purchases, and consign goods for shipping. From the wool auctions he expanded into the warehousing and shipping of wool, and into pastoral land deals. He also began to speculate in other areas, chiefly the exploitation and transport of natural resources and produce. He promoted steam navigation and particularly railways, and the production of sugar, silk, and cotton. He also speculated in gold and land, and dabbled in finance. From 1854 he developed and operated Mort's Dock at Waterview Bay, Belmain, Sydney. From 1856 he developed land at Bodalla, originally Boat

Alley, near the mouth of the Tuross River, which eventually amounted to 38,000 acres, as a rural settlement for the supply of dairy goods to large towns, particularly Sydney. He also sent a consignment of salt meat to England in a venture which foreshadowed his later experiments with the transport of frozen meat. In 1846 he bought land at Darling Point, moving from the cottage at Double Bay which he and his family had occupied in the early 1840s. Mort was a keen gardener and he created the fine estate of Greenoaks on his new land, decorating the house with his collections, including *objets* from Alton Towers, Staffordshire. However, a riding accident in 1855 exacerbated long-standing ill health and hypochondria, and Mort spent the years 1857 to 1859 in England, too seriously ill to play a significant part in his business activities. A further blow came in 1869 when his wife died.

Mort recovered, and went on to continue and expand his various enterprises. He promoted coal and copper exploitation, and marine and railway engineering. From 1866 he began experiments with E. D. Nicholle to find a way of freezing meat, seeing in the new technology a way of expanding and commercializing pastoral agriculture and associated processing in New South Wales and beyond. This venture was both an end in itself and an effort to protect and consolidate his investments in pastoral farming, heavy engineering, and transport infrastructure. However, although he guided to fruition the transport of frozen and chilled food within New South Wales, he did not live to see frozen meat being shipped internationally as, much to his disappointment, public embarrassment, and personal financial cost, mechanical failures with the refrigeration machinery could not be overcome. He had, however, laid the foundations for successful shipment, which was achieved in 1879, just eighteen months after his death. From 1872 he converted Bodalla into a centralized business, amalgamating farms, substituting labourers for tenants, and building food processing plants. He spent much time there, particularly after his second marriage, at St Mark's Church, Darling Point, on 30 January 1874 to Marianne Elizabeth Macauley (*b*. 1841), with whom he had two sons.

Mort died at Bodalla on 9 May 1878 from pleuropneumonia, and was buried there. He was survived by five sons and two daughters from his first marriage and by his second wife and their children. £600,000 was distributed from his estate to them and to other beneficiaries. His death occasioned eulogistic obituaries.

Mort was undoubtedly a man of energy and enterprise, determination and family loyalty. However, his reputation as an able businessman has been tempered since his death. A. Barnard (*Visions and Profits*, 1961) admits him to have been a man of vision, but suggests that, while in his youth this was combined with a keen business sense, in his later years Mort became an erratic manager, and many of his more substantial ventures either lost money (as with the frozen meat scheme) or made less than might have been expected because of overcapitalization (as with Bodalla and Mort's Dock). He took investment decisions not purely on business grounds, but to realize his long-term vision for the colony. This impressed contemporaries, who saw his pioneering schemes as beneficial to the colony, but his fortune was probably diminished as a result.   ELIZABETH BAIGENT

Sources A. Barnard, *Visions and profits* (1961) · *AusDB* · *Sydney Mail* (25 May 1878)
Likenesses Birch, bust; formerly in possession of William Mort, 1894 · P. Connolly, statue, Macquarie Place, Sydney · lithograph, repro. in *Sydney Mail* · photograph, State Library of New South Wales [*see illus.*]
Wealth at death £600,000 distributed to beneficiaries; plus further £200,000: Barnard, *Visions*, 212

Mortain. For this title name *see* Robert, count of Mortain (*d.* 1095).

Mortain, Robert of. *See* Robert, count of Mortain (*d.* 1095).

Morten, Thomas (1836–1866), illustrator and painter, was born on 27 March 1836 at Uxbridge, Middlesex, the son of Thomas Morten (*d.* 1861), a builder, and his wife, Ann. His earliest studies in art were at Leigh's Central Practical School of Art, but he also attended the Royal Academy Schools and Langham's. In 1855 he began exhibiting at the Royal Academy, and in 1858–9 he also showed works at the Portland Gallery. In 1858 he was elected to the Hogarth Club, but he proved unpopular with several of the Pre-Raphaelite members, notably Dante Gabriel Rossetti, and was swiftly removed from the membership. In contrast, however, he was accepted by the so-called Paris Gang, which included Whistler, George Du Maurier, and Edward Poynter. On 23 August 1862 Morten married Henrietta, the daughter of Edward Heaton; they lived in Mornington Place, near Regent's Park.

Morten was one of a large number of illustrators of the 1860s who worked in black and white, and his work should be considered alongside that of George Pinwell, Matthew Lawless, and John Millais. He made a considerable number of designs for periodicals; some of the most important of these appear in *Good Words* (1861–3), *London Society* (1862–9), *Once a Week* (1861–6), and *The Quiver* (1865–6). As a book illustrator Morten was much less prolific. His most sustained, although now controversial, publication was *Gulliver's Travels* (1865), the only significant project which he undertook single-handed. Discussion of this book is problematic, as a later commentator has correctly pointed out that in it Morten plagiarized an edition published the previous year and illustrated by John Gordon Thompson. Notwithstanding such unacknowledged borrowings, Morten's treatment of the text so enlarges that of his workaday predecessor that his own version is an undeniable triumph. His fine line and disconcerting whimsy are memorable, and this is one of few such illustrated volumes of the period to merit a modern reprint. Morten also borrowed without permission elements from the work of other artists, and on occasion his monogram can be confused with that of Millais. Such questions over the originality of his vision ensure that, as an artist, Morten is difficult to judge.

In August 1865 Morten entered the Savage Club, and the following year he exhibited at both the Society of British

Artists and the Royal Academy. On 23 September 1866, prompted by debt and possibly also by his epilepsy, he hanged himself at 18 Langham Street, Portland Place. His obituarist in the *Art Journal*—after regretting his premature death—praised his exhibit at the Royal Academy of that year, *Pleading for the Prisoner*, commenting that it 'indicated that his eye for colour was as correct as his appreciation of the truth of line'. Arthur Boyd Houghton, a friend and executor of Morten's will, superintended a fund to support Morten's widow, and *The Savage Club Papers* (1867) were published for her benefit. The Victoria and Albert Museum, London, holds some of Morten's drawings, while his wood-engravings can be found in collections at the British Museum.   PAUL GOLDMAN

Sources A. Life, 'That unfortunate young man Morten', *Bulletin of the John Rylands University Library*, 55 (1972–3), 369–402 · *Art Journal*, 28 (1866), 364 · R. K. Engen, *Dictionary of Victorian wood engravers* (1985) · P. Goldman, *Victorian illustration* (1996) · F. Reid, *Illustrators of the eighteen sixties* (1928) · *The Athenaeum* (29 Dec 1866), 876
Wealth at death money raised for widow: Life, 'That unfortunate young man'; Engen, *Dictionary*

Mortensen, Stanley Harding (1921–1991), footballer, was born at 23 Lord Nelson Street, South Shields, on 26 May 1921, the second son of Christopher Hardwick Mortensen, butcher, and his wife, Sarah Ellen, *née* Baker. His Scandinavian surname, the cause of many journalistic misprints, was inherited from his Norwegian grandfather, a sailor based in South Shields. Educated at St Mary's School, Tyne Dock, he was selected for the school football team when only nine years old and for South Shields schoolboys at the age of thirteen. After leaving school at fourteen he worked in a timber yard for three years before joining Blackpool United Football Club as an inside-right in 1938, after impressing club scouts in a junior match. The club considered releasing him because of his lack of pace, but diligent training eventually made him one of the fastest forwards in the English game. In 1941 he joined the RAF as a wireless operator–gunner; he subsequently survived an aircrash near Lossiemouth which killed two members of the crew and saw a third lose a leg. Although he received serious head injuries, he soon resumed his football career, and played for at least eleven clubs in various wartime competitions. He regarded this period as an important part of his football education and made sufficient progress to be selected first for the RAF and then for the England squad against Wales in 1943. In the somewhat relaxed atmosphere of wartime football he played for the Welsh side when cover could not be found for an injured player. He made his first appearance for the 'correct' team against Wales the following year. On 2 November 1943 he married Jean Galloway (*b.* 1920/21), clerk, and daughter of William Galloway, plasterer. They had met on Mortensen's first day as a Blackpool footballer.

When the Football League programme resumed in 1946, Mortensen was an automatic choice in the Blackpool side, either at inside-right or centre-forward. His acceleration, ability to shoot fiercely from awkward angles, and general quick-wittedness, soon made him one of the most effective goal-scorers in the English game. Between 1946 and

Stanley Harding Mortensen (1921–1991), by Mike Lawn, 1947

1955 he scored 197 goals for his club in 325 league games and a further 25 in 29 FA cup games: he scored in every round (including the final) in 1947–8. He finished on the losing side in 1948 and again in 1951, but in 1953, against Bolton Wanderers, he became the first player to score a hat-trick in a Wembley FA cup final. The game was error-strewn and turned on injuries to Bolton players, but it provided a dramatic climax as Blackpool came from 3–1 down with only ten minutes remaining to win 4–3. The game is invariably termed the 'Matthews final' in honour of Stanley Matthews, who played a major role in wearing down a tired Bolton side but, as Matthews always acknowledged, Mortensen's goals were the crucial ingredient. Although the football world was delighted with his achievement, until his final goal was scored the television commentator continued to describe his first as an 'own goal', since his shot had taken a decisive deflection off a Bolton player. Mortensen also enjoyed a prolific goal-scoring record at international level, particularly in his early games: he scored four times on his full international début in a 10–0 defeat of Portugal in 1947, and completed a hat-trick against Sweden later in the year. Overall, he scored twenty-three times in twenty-five England appearances between 1947 and 1953.

Mortensen left Blackpool in October 1955 for Hull City, then joined Southport for the 1956–7 season. Between 1957 and 1962 he played non-league football with Bath and then Lancaster City, before finally retiring in 1962 to run a betting shop and a sports outfitter's in Blackpool, where he also served as a Conservative councillor. He returned to football in February 1967 as manager of Blackpool, but despite only narrowly failing to secure the team promotion to the first division in the following year, and proving himself popular with supporters, he was sacked in April 1969. He returned to his business interests but, by the early 1980s, increasingly poor health forced him into a less than financially secure retirement. Morty remained a respected local figure, however, not least because of his considerable work for local charities, and he was rewarded with the freedom of Blackpool in March 1990.

Mortensen died at the Victoria Hospital, Blackpool, following a heart attack, on 22 May 1991. His well-attended funeral was held at St John's parish church, Blackpool, and he was cremated at Carleton crematorium, on 29 May. He was survived by his wife. Although not a significant figure in the sense of having made a distinctive contribution to the game's evolution or to the nature of the football profession, Mortensen was undoubtedly one of the best players of his generation, much liked and respected by his fellow players, and a major attraction at grounds throughout the country in the ten years after the Second World War.   DAVE RUSSELL

Sources S. Mortensen, *Football is my game* (1949) · *The Times* (24 May 1991) · *The Independent* (23 May 1991) · B. Hugman, *Football league players records* (1992) · R. Calley, *Blackpool: a complete record, 1887–1992* (1992) · *West Lancashire Evening Gazette* (31 March 1990) · *Evening Gazette* [Blackpool] (30 May 1991) · b. cert. · m. cert. · d. cert. **Archives** Blackpool Central Library, collection of press cuttings **Likenesses** M. Lawn, photograph, 1947, Hult. Arch. [*see illus.*] · photographs, 1948–54, Hult. Arch. · photograph, repro. in *The Independent* · photograph, repro. in *The Times* · photographs, repro. in Mortensen, *Football is my game* **Wealth at death** under £115,000: probate, 24 June 1991, *CGPLA Eng. & Wales*

Mortimer, Cromwell (*c.*1693–1752), physician and antiquary, born in Essex, was the second of the four sons (there were two daughters) of John *Mortimer (1656?–1736), writer on agriculture and merchant, and his third wife, Elizabeth, daughter of Samuel Sanders of Derbyshire. He was educated under Boerhaave at Leiden University, where he was admitted in the medical division in 1719 and graduated MD in 1724. He became a licentiate of the College of Physicians, London, in 1725, and a fellow in 1729. He was created MD at Cambridge in 1728.

Mortimer practised at first in Hanover Square, London, but moved in 1729, at the request of Sir Hans Sloane, to Bloomsbury Square, where he had the benefit of Sloane's collections and conversation, and assisted until 1740 in prescribing for his patients. For ten years Mortimer was also physician of a London infirmary. In 1744, when resident in Dartmouth Street, Westminster, he issued a circular describing the system of payment for his services. This involved offering medicines free of charge when he was called in for a consultation, and the treatment of certain classes of patients for an annual fixed fee of about a guinea. This did not make him popular with his professional colleagues and some apothecaries refused to attend patients when Mortimer was called in. A satirical print of him, designed by Hogarth and engraved by Rigou, with several lines from Pope appended to it, was published

about 1745. In that year he published his *Address to the publick, containing narratives of the effects of certain chemical remedies in most diseases*.

Mortimer was elected FSA in 1734 and FRS in 1728, and, mainly through the interest of Sloane, he was acting secretary to the Royal Society from 1730 until his death. He edited volumes 36–46 of the society's *Philosophical Transactions*. He also produced a number of works on medical, antiquarian, and other subjects. From 1737 he was a member and correspondent of the Gentlemen's Society at Spalding, and he was also a corresponding member of the Royal Academy of Sciences at Paris. It is said that about 1738 'his vanity prompted him to write the history of the learned societies of Great Britain and Ireland, to have been prefixed to a volume of the *Philosophical Transactions*', whereupon Maurice Johnson furnished him both with a history of the Spalding Society and with much other information about the Society of Antiquaries, but these materials were never used, prompting a long complaint from Dr Johnson (Nichols, 6.23).

Mortimer was also absorbed in new schemes. In 1747 he proposed to establish in the College of Arms a registry for dissenters, and articles of agreement, approved by all parties, were drawn up. It was opened in 1748, but did not succeed, through a misunderstanding between the ministers and the deputies of the congregations. About 1750 Mortimer promoted the scheme for the incorporation of the Society of Antiquaries, and he was one of the first members of its council. On the death of his elder brother, Mortimer inherited the family estate of Toppingo Hall, Hatfield Peverel, Essex. He and his wife, Mary, had one son. Mortimer died at Toppingo Hall on 7 January 1752, and was buried on 13 January; a monument was erected to his memory.   W. P. COURTNEY, rev. MICHAEL BEVAN

Sources *GM*, 1st ser., 22 (1752), 44 · *GM*, 1st ser., 47 (1777), 266 · *GM*, 1st ser., 50 (1780), 17, 510 · Nichols, *Lit. anecdotes*, 6.2–3, 99, 144–5; 9.615; 7.27, 423–6, 433 · Munk, *Roll* · *The family memoirs of the Rev. William Stukeley*, ed. W. C. Lukis, 3 vols., SurtS, 73, 76, 80 (1882–7), vol. 1, pp. 233–4; vol. 2, pp. 10–11, 320; vol. 3, pp. 6–7, 468 · P. Morant, *The history and antiquities of the county of Essex*, 2 (1768), 133 · M. Noble, *A history of the College of Arms* (1804) · T. Thomson, *History of the Royal Society from its institution to the end of the eighteenth century* (1812) **Archives** Leics. RO, corresp. and papers · RS, corresp. **Likenesses** Rigou, line engraving (after W. Hogarth), BM, Wellcome L.

Mortimer, Edmund (III), third earl of March and earl of Ulster (1352–1381), magnate, was the son of Roger (VI) *Mortimer, second earl of March (1328–1360), and his wife, Philippa, daughter of William Montagu, first earl of Salisbury (*d.* 1344). Edmund was born at Llangoed in Llyswen, Brecknockshire, on 1 February 1352, and his father died when he was a child, on 26 February 1360. A substantial portion of the very extensive Mortimer estates had been granted to trustees, who were permitted by the crown to retain them during Edmund's minority, while the lordship of Denbigh, which was held of the prince of Wales, remained in trustees' hands even though the trust had not formally been completed. Mortimer's mother, Philippa, who outlived her son, had dower. These liberal arrangements allowed the greater part of the inheritance to be saved from the king's control. The remaining lands, which fell into the king's hands, were administered by the former earl's steward, John Gour, and in 1364 leased to the countess of March for a rent of 1000 marks. Edmund Mortimer was a ward of William *Wykeham, bishop of Winchester (d. 1404), and Richard *Fitzalan, earl of Arundel (d. 1376). In 1358 he had been betrothed to Philippa, daughter and heir of Edward III's son *Lionel of Antwerp, duke of Clarence; Lionel died in 1368, the year of their marriage, and Mortimer and his wife thus became heirs to very considerable estates, second only to those of the duke of Lancaster, and including the original Mortimer lands in the Welsh march (in Monmouth, Brecknockshire, Radnorshire, Shropshire, Herefordshire, and Montgomeryshire), the lordship of Denbigh, the Clare estates in East Anglia, Ulster, and other lands in Ireland. In January 1373 the acquisition of his father's estate completed Mortimer's inheritance, but he had already become active in military affairs. In 1369 he went on an expedition to France. In January 1371 he was summoned to parliament as earl of March; his final title was earl of March and Ulster, and he was also marshal.

In 1372 March contracted to take part in another expedition to France with the substantial retinue of 19 knights, 60 esquires, and 120 archers. This expedition was a failure and was broken off, the earl incurring some loss of money. He was also involved in an abortive expedition to Brittany in 1375. This was intended to back up the duke of Brittany in his hostility to the French crown, and crossed to Brittany in April 1375. But, as a result of a truce agreed by negotiators at Bruges in May, the English force was compelled to leave the duchy and return home in July. Financial losses were not made good by the crown until 1377. As a military commander in the 1370s March was not badly treated by the crown, in comparison with normal standards of payment, but he was certainly short of money and, in 1375, was in debt both to the bishop of London and to Lord Latimer. The Brittany enterprise had also been the second humiliating failure within four years with which March had been associated, and this must have been one of the main reasons for his hostility to the court party dominated by the duke of Lancaster, William Latimer (d. 1381), and Alice Perrers (d. 1400/01) in the Good Parliament of 1376. Another may have been his close connection with William Wykeham, who had also come under attack from Lancaster. That the earl of March was firmly allied with the critics of the court in the Commons is made fairly clear by the facts that the man chosen as speaker, Sir Peter de la Mare, was his steward and retainer, that he was one of the group of magnates asked by de la Mare to negotiate with the Commons early in the parliament, that he was a member of the continual council set up to control the court at the end of May 1376, and that he attended the celebratory feast held by the Commons at the end of the session. The death of Edward, the Black Prince, Edward III's eldest son, during the Good Parliament, meant that, as the husband of Lionel's daughter, the earl of March became a conceivable claimant to the throne. This consideration does not seem to have played an important part in the life of this earl, but it was, of course, important for his great-grandson, Richard, duke of York (d. 1460), in the following century.

The end of the Good Parliament was followed by a very rapid political reversal in the autumn of 1376, marked by the imprisonment of Sir Peter de la Mare and by the earl's resignation of his office of marshal. The death of Edward III and accession of his young grandson Richard II in June 1377 undermined the position of the court party, and renewed the earl of March's importance. De la Mare was once again speaker in the parliament of October 1377. Having been prominent at the coronation, bearing the second sword and spurs, March became a member of the minority council. In 1378 he acted in several roles connected with Anglo-Scottish relations, dealing with the truce, inspecting the fortifications of the border castles, and eventually, in February 1379, being sent on an embassy to Scotland.

The last stage of the earl's life was initiated by his appointment on 22 October 1379 as lieutenant of Ireland. This must have been a post with mixed implications. The appointment may have been stimulated by the duke of Lancaster's wish to see March out of England, and therefore not a rival. The Irish problem, made no better by the recent expedition of Sir William Windsor (d. 1384), could be seen as a poisoned chalice, the English interest being hard pressed by the native revival. On the other hand, as the greatest Irish landowner, March was extremely suitable for the position. His status as landowner in Ireland had led the other English settlers to request that he should be sent as lieutenant as early as 1373. That proposal had been abandoned, no doubt because March preferred to campaign in France, and as a result the control of Ireland had been entrusted to Windsor, with disastrous consequences. By 1379 a new effort was needed, following unsuccessful English efforts to confront the native population. March probably thought that, in the circumstances of a minority dominated by Lancaster, he had little hope of success in France, and was therefore willing to go west instead. He was given fairly full control of Irish revenues, and promised additional money from England. March was in Ireland from May 1380, and operated with moderate success. He established control of part of his own earldom of Ulster, and part of Connacht. The chroniclers report that the prospects were generally hopeful. But on 27 December 1381, having been taken ill in Munster, he died at Cork. He had been in Ireland too short a time for the results of his policy to be really clear.

March's wife had predeceased him, dying in 1378. He was buried at Wigmore Abbey, the traditional ecclesiastical focus of Mortimer devotion in Herefordshire. His will and gifts recorded elsewhere suggest a substantial devotion to the abbey church, which was partly reconstructed in his lifetime and at his expense. After his death there was a long minority until his son and heir, Roger (VII) *Mortimer (1374–1398), succeeded in 1393. March's mother lived until January 1382, holding a third of the inheritance in dower. Most of the old Mortimer lands had been granted in 1374 to a group of trustees who regranted them to the earl for a nominal rent in 1380. After his death they were held by his executors. The Clare estate, the dower lands, and some other properties were in 1382 committed by the crown to three keepers, two of whom were the earl's executors. They were granted to the heir and three other magnates in 1383. The inheritance was therefore passed on intact, without being seriously affected by escheat to the crown. The earl had a brother, Sir Thomas Mortimer, who was retained by him with an annuity and who survived him. Apart from his heir, Roger, the fourth earl, he had a son Sir Edmund (IV) *Mortimer, born on 9 November 1376, who was later captured by Owain Glyn Dŵr and died at Harlech Castle in 1408/9. He had two daughters, Elizabeth, born 12 February 1371, who married first Henry Percy (Hotspur; d. 1403), and then Sir Thomas Camoys, and Philippa, born 21 November 1375, who married first John Hastings, earl of Pembroke, second Richard (III) Fitzalan, earl of Arundel (d. 1397), and third Sir Thomas Poynings; she died on 25 September 1400.

GEORGE HOLMES

Sources GEC, *Peerage*, new edn · G. A. Holmes, *The estates of the higher nobility in fourteenth-century England* (1957) · G. Holmes, *The Good Parliament* (1975) · *Chancery records* · RotP · H. G. Richardson and G. O. Sayles, *The Irish parliament in the middle ages*, 2nd edn (1964) · W. M. Ormrod, 'Edward III and his family', *Journal of British Studies*, 26 (1987), 398–422
Archives PRO, E159 · PRO, E368 · PRO, E101 | BL, Egerton rolls

Mortimer, Sir Edmund (IV) (1376–1408/9), landowner and rebel, was the youngest child of Edmund (III) *Mortimer, third earl of March (1352–1381), and his wife, Philippa (b. 1355, d. before 1381), the daughter of Lionel, duke of Clarence, and heiress of Ulster. He was born at Ludlow on Monday, 9 November 1376. Portents were later said to have attended his birth. His father died when he was only five years old, but left him well provided for, bequeathing him and the heirs of his body land of the yearly value of 300 marks and various silver plates and dishes and a magnificent bed. He was also very handsomely endowed by his eldest brother, Roger (VII) *Mortimer, fourth earl of March, who gave the manor of Gussage in Dorset and annuities totalling 240 marks to him and his heirs tail. Relations between the two brothers were exceptionally close: Edmund served as Earl Roger's lieutenant in Ireland in 1397 and was executor of his will. On the death of Earl Roger, on 15 August 1398, Edmund became, by reason of the minority of his nephew, Edmund (V) *Mortimer, the most prominent representative of the family interests in the Welsh marches. He also held considerable lands in the border counties and in Wales (including the lordship of Narberth and the Mortimer share of the lordship of St Clears) in respect of family endowments. When Henry of Lancaster passed through the marches on his way to his final triumph over Richard II in north Wales, Mortimer at once adhered to his rising fortunes, and on 2 August 1399 went with the bishop of Hereford to make his submission to Henry at Hereford.

Mortimer resided on his estates, and when the revolt of Owain Glyn Dŵr broke out was closely associated with his brother-in-law, Henry *Percy, the famous Hotspur, in the measures taken for putting down the Welsh rebel. In June 1402 Glyn Dŵr led a raid deep into the Mortimer lordships in eastern central Wales. He took up a position on a hill called Bryn-glas, between Pilleth and Knighton, not very far from Ludlow. Mortimer was at the time at 'his own town' of Ludlow, and at once raised the men of Herefordshire and marched against Glyn Dŵr. His Welsh tenants of Maelienydd obeyed his summons and joined his forces, but on 22 June they were heavily defeated by Glyn Dŵr. Some of Mortimer's Welsh supporters were alleged to have defected to Glyn Dŵr's side and his own loyalty to the English cause was later regarded as suspect. Several prominent Herefordshire knights were killed on the field, and among those taken prisoner were Thomas Clanvow and Mortimer. Stories of atrocities committed by Welsh women on the bodies of Englishmen killed at the battle were soon circulating widely.

Glyn Dŵr took Mortimer captive to the 'mountains and caves of Snowdon', but he treated him not only kindly but considerately, hoping to get political profit from his prisoner, and there is evidence that Mortimer was used as an intermediary in unsuccessful English negotiations with Glyn Dŵr. Mortimer's friends, especially the Percys (Edmund's sister, Elizabeth, was Hotspur's wife), busied themselves about procuring his ransom. But sinister rumours were abroad that Mortimer had himself sought the captivity into which he had fallen, and Henry now forbade the Percys to seek for their kinsman's liberation. By early October 1402 the king had concluded that Mortimer had defected to Glyn Dŵr's cause: he began to confiscate his estates (granting several of them to the king's sons) and seized his plate and jewels. Mortimer may have believed that the king did not want him released; he may also have decided that an alliance with Glyn Dŵr offered the best prospect of realizing the Mortimer claim to the English throne. Be that as it may, on about 30 November he married Glyn Dŵr's daughter, Catherine, with great pomp and solemnity. Early in December he was back in Maelienydd as the ally of Glyn Dŵr and on 13 December he issued a circular to Sir John Greyndour, Hywel Fychan, and 'all the gentles and commons of Radnor and Presteigne', in which he declared that he had joined Glyn Dŵr in his efforts either to restore the crown to King Richard, should the king prove still to be alive, or, should Richard be dead, to confer the throne on his honoured nephew Edmund (V) Mortimer, 'who is the right heir to the said crown' and to secure Glyn Dŵr's 'right in Wales'. Most of the Mortimer lands in Wales, so he claimed, had already come under his control.

The alliance of 1402 between Glyn Dŵr and Edmund Mortimer was joined by a third party when the Percys rose in revolt in June 1403. The alliance received a major setback when Hotspur was killed at the battle of Shrewsbury (21 July 1403); but it survived and found expression in the tripartite indenture, normally ascribed to February 1405. In the threefold division of the kingdom which this proposed, Mortimer (his nephew's claims now put on one side) was to have most of the south of England, though an engagement in which he resigned to Glyn Dŵr the area west of the River Severn, in which his family was supreme, clearly bore the marks of coercion. The tripartite indenture plainly stands in close connection with the attempted abduction of Edmund (V) Mortimer in the same month and Northumberland's second rising in May 1405. But the failure of the general English attacks on Henry gradually reduced Glyn Dŵr's revolt to its original character of a native Welsh rising against the English. Mortimer therefore gradually sank into the background. As his father-in-law's cause began to lose ground, Mortimer himself was reduced to great distress. He was finally besieged in Harlech Castle by the now victorious English, and perished miserably during the siege which ended in February 1409. His prowess had clearly entered folk memory, since Adam of Usk records that his adventures were commemorated in songs at feasts.

With Glyn Dŵr's daughter, Mortimer had one son, named Lionel (doubtless so called after his great-grandfather, Lionel of Clarence), and three daughters. She, with her family, was already in the hands of Henry V in June 1413, perhaps since the capture of Harlech, being kept in custody within the city of London. But before the end of the same year Lady Mortimer and her daughters were dead. They were buried at the expense of £1 within the church of St Swithin, London.

T. F. TOUT, rev. R. R. DAVIES

Sources Chronicon Adae de Usk, ed. and trans. E. M. Thompson, 2nd edn (1904) · 'Annales Ricardi secundi et Henrici quarti, regum Angliae', Johannis de Trokelowe et Henrici de Blaneforde ... chronica et annales, ed. H. T. Riley, pt 3 of Chronica monasterii S. Albani, Rolls Series, 28 (1866), 155–420 · G. B. Stow, ed., Historia vitae et regni Ricardi Secundi (1977) · H. Ellis, ed., Original letters illustrative of English history, 2nd ser., 1 (1827) · Dugdale, Monasticon, new edn, vol. 6 · Chancery records · J. A. Giles, ed., Incerti scriptoris chronicon Angliae de regnis trium regum Lancastrensium (1848) · F. Devon, ed. and trans., Issues of the exchequer: being payments made out of his majesty's revenue, from King Henry III to King Henry VI inclusive, RC (1837) · J. E. Lloyd, Owen Glendower (1931) · R. R. Davies, The revolt of Owain Glyn Dŵr (1995) **Archives** NL Wales, Slebech collection

Mortimer, Edmund (V), fifth earl of March and seventh earl of Ulster (1391–1425), magnate and potential claimant to the English throne, was the last earl of March of the family of Mortimer of Wigmore; his descent from Edward III blighted his career and threatened the usurping Lancastrian dynasty after 1399. According to a contemporary family history (Chicago University Library, MS 224), he was born on 6 November 1391 in the New Forest, the elder son of Roger (VII) *Mortimer, fourth earl of March (1374–1398), and Eleanor (d. 1405), daughter and coheir of Thomas *Holland, earl of Kent. After his father's death Edmund and the Mortimer estates in England, Wales, and Ireland were at Richard II's disposal; Edmund's mother's dower third was valued at £1242 a year.

Following Richard II's deposition by Henry Bolingbroke in October 1399 rebels periodically publicized Mortimer's claim. Though plausible, this was weakened by descent through a female—his father's mother, Philippa, daughter of Lionel of Clarence, Edward III's second surviving son—and by Edmund's youth; nevertheless, Henry IV

placed this potential rival under strict supervision. Mortimer's estates were transferred, at first, to the Percys (1399–1401), while Edmund and his younger brother Roger (d. c.1413) lived as royal wards, mostly at Windsor. When Henry IV campaigned in Wales in 1402, as a precaution the boys were transferred temporarily to Berkhamsted Castle, in the care of the Lancastrian knight Hugh Waterton. The wisdom of this was demonstrated when the boys' uncle, Sir Edmund (IV) *Mortimer (d. 1408/9), who had been captured by Owain Glyn Dŵr in June 1402, went over to the Welsh rebels, announcing that his nephew Edmund was Richard II's rightful heir. The name of Mortimer struck a chord in Wales, not simply as that of the greatest of marcher families, but also because the earls of March descended from Llywelyn ab Iorwerth (d. 1240), prince of Gwynedd. In the following year the Percys also rebelled ostensibly in Mortimer's interest; the earl of Northumberland's heir, Henry *Percy (Hotspur), was married to Edmund's aunt. In May 1405 the Scrope revolt in Yorkshire publicized the Mortimer claim once again. In February of that year a daring attempt had been made to abduct the two boys from Windsor Castle and convey them to Wales, probably to join Glyn Dŵr and Sir Edmund Mortimer, who were allegedly negotiating a tripartite alliance with the earl of Northumberland whereby Sir Edmund (perhaps on behalf of his nephew) would receive the southern part of the English realm. Constance, Lady Despenser, was responsible for the abduction, encouraged by her brother Edward, duke of York, who was briefly arrested. While making for Cardiff the party was apprehended near Cheltenham, Lady Despenser was arrested, and the boys returned to Windsor. More secure custody was recommended by the council, and in February 1406 they were put in the charge of another of Henry IV's retainers, Sir John Pelham, at Pevensey Castle.

Mortimer's estates experienced difficulties in these years: the earl of Orkney attacked Ulster c.1401, and although Glyn Dŵr's forces may have spared the lordship of Denbigh while it was in Hotspur's custody, c.1401–2, other of Mortimer's Welsh estates were devastated from 1403, thereby contributing to his later financial problems. As he grew older (and Henry IV felt less threatened), Edmund's future merited special consideration. On 24 February 1408 his marriage was granted to Queen Joan, on condition that he could marry only with the king's assent and the council's advice. A year later, he and his brother were placed in the care of their cousin, Prince Henry; the younger Mortimer may have died soon after the prince became king in 1413. Their sisters, Anne and Eleanor, in the care of their mother who in 1400 married Edward Charlton, Lord Powys, fared less well after Countess Eleanor died in 1405, for they were shortly described as destitute and needed £100 per annum for themselves and their servants.

The death of Henry IV may have prompted renewed murmurings about Edmund Mortimer's claim. Nevertheless, Henry V released him from custody and knighted him on the eve of his coronation (9 April); in parliament in June he was declared of age and allowed to inherit his estates. Yet suspicions remained, and on 18 November 1413 Mortimer concluded a recognizance for 10,000 marks with the king to ensure his loyalty. Moreover, his privy purse expenses for 1413/14 show the 23-year-old earl still in the king's company. His gift to the king about 1414, from one bachelor to another, of a Welsh boy (aged nine) and girl (aged seven) and the child they produced—'an event which caused widespread amazement' (*Chronicle of Adam of Usk*, 245)—may have seemed like misplaced irony. Mortimer may already have identified his own intended bride, for in February 1415 he secured a dispensation from Pope John XXIII to enable him to marry 'a fit woman related to him in the third degree of kindred or affinity' because he 'desires to have children, but being related to divers magnates cannot find a wife suitable to his rank whom he can marry without papal dispensation' (*CEPR letters*, 6.456). This woman was Anne (*d.* 1432), daughter of Edmund, earl of Stafford, and herself descended from *Edward III. Henry understandably disapproved and imposed on Mortimer the large fine of 10,000 marks, which became a significant element in Henry's war finances.

Mortimer was involved in preparations for the invasion of France, and on 24 July 1415 he witnessed the king's will at Southampton. But already the 'Southampton plot' was laid, notably by Edmund's brother-in-law, Richard, earl of Cambridge, with the aim of taking Edmund to Wales to proclaim him king. At Portchester on 31 July Mortimer, who rarely took the initiative in the movements in his name, surprised the conspirators by revealing all to the king. Henry accepted his protestations of loyalty and placed him on the commission (5 August) that tried and condemned his erstwhile accomplices; on 7 August he was granted a pardon.

Bound to the king and deeply in debt, Mortimer participated in Henry V's Normandy campaigns, usually in the king's company. In August 1415 he led 59 men-at-arms and 160 archers across the channel, but during the siege of Harfleur he was invalided home suffering from dysentery. In 1416 he joined Bedford to relieve Harfleur; in 1417, as well as taking a larger retinue (100 lances and 300 archers) to France, he had charge of a fleet to patrol the seas. As the king's lieutenant in Normandy (June 1418) he was responsible for the Cotentin, Domfront, and Caen, and he joined the king for the taking of Rouen; but he received no significant war profits. When Henry and Queen Catherine travelled to England in February 1421, Edmund Mortimer accompanied them and bore the queen's sceptre at her coronation. He returned to France with Henry V in June, and was at the siege of Meaux when the king fell mortally ill.

After Henry V's funeral at Westminster, Mortimer was appointed one of the new king's councillors in November 1422. It may be that the accession of the nine-year-old Henry VI threw into sharper relief the activities of Mortimer's likely kinsman, Sir John Mortimer, a suspected traitor who was executed in 1424 for plotting a rising in Wales to make Edmund king. Certainly, in 1424 Henry VI's uncle, Humphrey, duke of Gloucester, expressed unease at the size of Edmund Mortimer's retinue—larger than Henry V

had allowed—and this may explain why Mortimer was appointed the king's lieutenant in Ireland in March 1423, though a visit to his ravaged estates there (they included the lordships of Trim and Connacht) was long overdue. Ships were commissioned for his journey in 1423–4, and Mortimer was paid most of his first year's stipend, but not until the autumn of 1424 did he set sail. On 18 January 1425, at his castle of Trim, he died of plague. His body was conveyed to England for burial in the Augustinian friary at Clare, Suffolk, which his ancestors had patronized. Mortimer had no children of his own and his heir was Richard, duke of York (1411–1460), the son of Mortimer's sister Anne and Richard, earl of Cambridge, whose own descent from Edward III's fourth son fortified York's regal connection. During York's minority, the dukes of Gloucester and Exeter enjoyed most of the Mortimer estates, with dower provision made (after some difficulty) for the earl's widow Anne, who shortly married (by 1427) John Holland, earl of Huntingdon. She died in September 1432. The family chronicle describes Edmund Mortimer as 'severe in his morals, composed in his acts, circumspect in his talk, and wise and cautious during the days of his adversity'. He earned the epithet the Good because of his kindness, and he was noted for his devotion to God, his discretion, and generosity (Dugdale, *Monasticon* 6.355, from Chicago University Library, MS 224). This is likely to be a sympathetic gloss on the character of a rudderless noble whose lineage placed him at the mercy of others.   R. A. GRIFFITHS

Sources esp. CIPM C139/19 no. 4; exchequer lord treasurer's remembrancer, issue rolls E 403 · *Chancery records* · GEC, *Peerage*, 8.450–53 · N. H. Nicolas, ed., *Proceedings and ordinances of the privy council of England*, 7 vols., RC, 26 (1834–7) · *CEPR letters*, vol. 6 · Dugdale, *Monasticon*, new edn, vol. 6 · *The chronicle of Adam Usk, 1377–1421*, ed. and trans. C. Given-Wilson, OMT (1997) [incl. Chicago University Library MS 224] · J. H. Wylie, *History of England under Henry the Fourth*, 4 vols. (1884–98), vol. 2 · G. A. Holmes, *The estates of the higher nobility in fourteenth century England* (1957) · C. L Kingsford, *English historical literature in the fifteenth century* (1913) [incl. *Brut* chronicle, 303–6] · C. M. Woolgar, ed., *Household accounts from medieval England*, 2 vols., 2.592–603 · *RotP*, vol. 4 · E. Powell, 'The strange death of Sir John Mortimer: politics and the law of treason in Lancastrian England', *Rulers and ruled in late medieval England*, ed. R. E. Archer and S. Walker (1995), 83–97 · J. Gairdner, ed., *The historical collections of a citizen of London in the fifteenth century*, CS, new ser., 17 (1876)
Wealth at death approx. £3700: CIPM C139/19 no. 4

Mortimer, Elizabeth. *See* Ritchie, Elizabeth (1754–1835).

Mortimer [*née* Bevan], **Favell Lee** (1802–1878), educational writer, was born on 14 July 1802 at Russell Square, London, second daughter of David Bevan (1774–1846), a banker, and his wife, Favell Bourke (1780–1841), daughter of Robert Cooper Lee. Educated at home, she was a 'delicate and fractious' child (Meyer, 2), early addicted to reading 'books of all kinds, especially poetry' (ibid., 12). An evangelical governess and an Independent minister, George Collison, strongly influenced the Bevan household, but Favell Bevan herself did not undergo a conversion experience until May 1827. Turning aside from her busy London social life, she began visiting and teaching the poor on her father's estate at Belmont, near Barnet. She heard the leading evangelical preachers of the day (including Henry Irving and Baptist Noel), and cultivated a circle of pious female friends.

Through her brother Robert Cooper Lee *Bevan, Favell Bevan became acquainted with the young Henry Edward Manning, who was then debating his future career. Believing him to be 'in bondage to the law' (Meyer, 43) she endeavoured to convert him to evangelicalism. On Favell Bevan's part, at least, the relationship was more than a friendship, and in 1832 she ended a correspondence with Manning at her mother's request. For the rest of his life Manning held that he owed her a great debt, apparently regarding her as his 'spiritual mother', although her desire to convert him seems to have been frustrated. Her comments on his character were, however, perceptive: while admiring his talents, independence of mind, and candour (not a quality always associated with Manning), she identified 'pride of virtue' as the predominating aspect of his personality (Meyer, 35–6).

Favell Bevan continued her good works, establishing a school at Fosbury House, her father's Wiltshire estate. In 1836 she published her first book, *The peep of day, or, A series of the earliest religious instruction the infant mind is capable of receiving*, a reading book which grew from her own teaching efforts. Convinced that simplified biblical narratives were the best means of teaching Christian doctrines (and, indeed, practically anything else) to children, she followed it with similar manuals, including *Line upon Line* (1837) and *More about Jesus* (1839). None, however, achieved the popularity of *The Peep of Day*, which passed through numerous English editions and was published by the Religious Tract Society in thirty-seven different dialects and languages. The pietistic tone of *The Peep of Day* is decidedly unappealing to the modern reader, who may well find her later publications less trying. These included geography books, such as *Near Home, or, The Countries of Europe Described* (1849), and reading books, such as *Reading without Tears* (1857). This practical and well-arranged little work showed her energetic interest in devising original ways to teach reading to young children: in her own schools she used large cards, rather than hornbook alphabets, in what may have been an early version of flashcards.

In 1836 Favell Bevan went on a tour of northern England and Scotland with her brother, Barclay, during which she met and stayed with several evangelical Anglican families, including that of the Revd Carus Wilson, one of whose daughters Barclay married. Wilson later married Favell Bevan herself, on 29 April 1841, to the Revd Thomas Mortimer of Gray's Inn proprietary chapel; family sources hint at an elopement and pass unflattering comments on Mortimer's apparently excessive girth. A widower with two daughters, he had served as a relief preacher at Robert Bevan's newly built church at Belmont. The couple lived first at Finchley, and later in Camden Town, before moving in 1847 to Mornington Road, London.

In 1847 Manning wrote to request the return of his letters; Favell Mortimer asked him to reciprocate, but allowed him to keep her letters when he expressed a wish

to do so. They met in June 1847, when the stern, unbending hope of the rising Catholics rebuked his former mentor for insufficient seriousness, while acknowledging his spiritual debt to her.

In November 1850 Thomas Mortimer died at Broseley, in Shropshire; his widow lived there for four years after his death, before moving to Hendon. Her main consolation in widowhood was her 'adopted' son, Lethbridge Charles Moore (1823–1894), a young soldier who subsequently became a priest under her influence and patronage. When he became vicar of Sheringham in Norfolk in 1862, Favell Mortimer accompanied him and his family to his new parish. She spent the rest of her life in Norfolk, living at Runton, mainly in The Rivulet which she purchased, looking after six orphans and continuing to write. She died on 22 August 1878 at The Rivulet and was buried in the churchyard at Sheringham.   ROSEMARY MITCHELL

Sources L. C. Meyer, *The author of the 'Peep of day', being the life story of Mrs Mortimer* [1901] · *Family Friend*, new ser., 9 (1878), 183 · *The Times* (20 Jan 1892) · E. S. Purcell, *Life of Cardinal Manning*, 1 (1896), 62–6 · R. Gray, *Cardinal Manning: a biography* (1985), 31–5 · H. Carpenter and M. Prichard, *The Oxford companion to children's literature*, pbk edn (1999), 361–2, 399 · Burke, *Gen. GB* · Allibone, *Dict.* · A. N. Gamble, *A history of the Bevan family* [1924] · C. A. O'Gorman, 'A history of Henry Manning's religious opinions, 1808–1832', *Recusant History*, 21 (1992–3), 152–66, esp. 159–61

Likenesses woodcut, 1878, BM · C. H. Jeens, engraving (after pencil sketch by G. Richmond, *c*.1840–1850), repro. in Meyer, *Author of The peep of day*, frontispiece · wood-engraving, repro. in *The family friend*, 184

Wealth at death under £25,000: probate, 29 Oct 1878, *CGPLA Eng. & Wales*

Mortimer, George Ferris Whidborne (1805–1871), headmaster, was born on 22 July 1805 at Bishopsteignton in Devon, the eldest son of William Mortimer, a country gentleman there. He was educated at Exeter grammar school and at Balliol College, Oxford, where he matriculated in 1823 and obtained an exhibition. In the same year he migrated to Queen's College, where he secured a Michel exhibition, and was placed in the first class of the final classical school, graduating BA in 1826. He was for a while a private tutor. He proceeded MA in 1829 and DD in 1841, having been ordained on 24 February 1829. In 1830 he married Jane (*d*. 1901), daughter of Alexander Gordon of Bishopsteignton.

Mortimer was successively headmaster of Newcastle grammar school (from 1828) and of the Western Proprietary School at Brompton, London (from 1833). In 1840 he was appointed to the headship of the City of London School in succession to John Allen Giles. The school was opened in 1837, but its prosperity had been injured by the action of the first headmaster, who was a poor disciplinarian. Mortimer's administrative ability and genial manner transformed its fortunes. He treated with conspicuous honesty and fairness the large proportion of boys at the school who were not members of the Church of England. In 1861 he had the unique distinction of seeing two of his scholars respectively senior wrangler and senior classic at Cambridge. Charles Kingsley read privately with him for ordination. In 1864 Mortimer was nominated to an honorary prebendal stall in St Paul's Cathedral, and for many years was evening lecturer at St Matthew's, Friday Street. At Michaelmas 1865 he resigned his headmastership, and for the next few years interested himself actively in the Society of Schoolmasters and other educational institutions. He died on 7 September 1871, at Rose Hill, Hampton Wick, Middlesex, and was buried in Hampton churchyard. He had a large family; four sons were Cambridge graduates. Besides two sermons, Mortimer published while at Newcastle a pamphlet entitled *The Immediate Abolition of Slavery Compatible with the Safety and Prosperity of the Colonies* (1833). J. H. LUPTON, *rev.* M. C. CURTHOYS

Sources Boase, *Mod. Eng. biog.* · Ward, *Men of the reign* · Foster, *Alum. Oxon.* · private information (1894) · personal knowledge (1894)

Likenesses C. Bacon, bust, exh. RA 1866, City of London School

Wealth at death under £70,000: probate, 5 Oct 1871, *CGPLA Eng. & Wales*

Mortimer, Harry (1902–1992), cornet and trumpet player and brass band conductor, was born on 10 April 1902 in Hebden Bridge, Yorkshire, the eldest of the three sons of Fred Mortimer (1879–1953), at that time a cloth maker in a woollen mill, and his wife, Sarah, *née* Midgeley, who had been a 'mender' in a woollen mill before her marriage. Both his father and his grandfather, after whom he was named, were much respected brass band players and conductors. Mortimer received his early education at Stubbings School, Hebden Bridge, and then (following the family's move to Luton in 1910, when Fred Mortimer became the conductor of the Luton Red Cross Band) at Old Bedford Road Boys' School, Luton. Fred Mortimer and his three sons, Harry, Alex, and Rex, became the most influential brass band musicians of their generation, but it was Harry who gained the greatest celebrity and made the strongest mark on broader aspects of British musical life.

As a child Mortimer demonstrated a precocious talent as a cornet player. He played in his first national brass band championship at the age of eleven, by which time he was already being featured as a soloist. At fourteen he was conducting his father's band, and at seventeen he made the first of his many solo recordings. He left school in 1915 and undertook no further education, except for private studies with the band trainer and composer William Rimmer. His first paid employment was as an office boy for the Great Northern Railway, but after a short time he went to a similar post at Vauxhall Motors. These jobs allowed him to perform with amateur brass bands and professional orchestras such as the Luton Palace Orchestra. Apart from two years with the Mansfield colliery band, he remained at Luton until 1925, when he moved to Sandbach to become principal cornet of the Foden's Motor Works Band, which his brother Alex was then conducting. On 20 June 1927 he married Annie Bullock, *née* Blissett (1904/5–c.1984), drapery assistant, of Elworth, Cheshire, daughter of Jack Blissett. There were two daughters of the marriage, Brenda and Margaret.

In 1927, at the invitation of Sir Hamilton Harty, Mortimer became third trumpeter of the Hallé Orchestra. In 1930, after a year as principal trumpeter of the Liverpool Philharmonic Orchestra, he returned to be principal trumpeter of the Hallé. He went to the BBC Northern Orchestra in 1935, where he remained until the outbreak of the Second World War; he then returned to Foden's Motor Works to supervise the production of tanks. From 1936 to 1940 he was also professor of trumpet at the Royal Manchester College of Music.

In 1942, at the suggestion of Sir Arthur Bliss, Mortimer joined the BBC as adviser on brass and military bands, and he remained there until his retirement in 1964. His time with the BBC was significant for the brass band movement. He was well respected in the corporation, and proved himself to be a good advocate and administrator. Under his charge, brass and military bands became a ubiquitous and popular feature of the BBC's programming.

Harry Mortimer (1902–1992), by unknown photographer

He increased the weekly allocation of hours to band broadcasting fourfold during his term of office. His first marriage having ended in separation in 1942 and divorce in 1951, in the latter year Mortimer married (Hilda) Margaret Bailey (1917–1999), a personal assistant at the BBC, originally from Yorkshire. They had one son, Martin.

Throughout his career as a professional trumpeter and administrator, Mortimer retained strong links with the amateur brass band movement, both as a player and as a conductor, and it was with this movement that he was always most popularly associated. He conducted all of the major brass bands, and was the most successful conductor in the national and open championships during the 1940s and 1950s, conducting the winning band on no fewer than eighteen occasions. In the early 1950s he formed two virtuoso bands, Men of Brass and the All Star Band. The former was a seventy-five-strong massed band, made up of the three finest bands of the time; the latter was a select group of the finest players. Throughout this period and beyond retirement, Mortimer continued as an energetic and innovative administrator of brass band contests and other events. He was appointed OBE in 1950 and CBE in 1984. He received an honorary fellowship from the Royal Northern College of Music in 1987 and an honorary doctorate from Salford University in 1988.

Mortimer had a distinguished career as a trumpeter, but it was as a cornet player and brass band personality that he achieved greater significance. He was an authoritative player, with brilliant technical virtuosity and a distinctive gift for fluent and highly expressive lyricism. His technique always revealed his brass band origins; indeed, his playing (and eventually his conducting) did much to define the brass band idiom in the twentieth century. His greatest achievement was that he became the first and perhaps the only figure to exploit the British brass band idiom in the wider arena of mainstream musical life, and in so doing he invested it with a special dignity. There is considerable cause to regard him as the most celebrated British brass band player of all time. His musicianship was natural and instinctive, rather than measured and cultivated. He was a brilliant communicator, with a compulsive and contagious enthusiasm for music in general and brass bands in particular. The success of his many projects owed much to his personal charisma, but he was a musician and administrator of considerable depth. He had a warm, often mischievous sense of humour, and an ability to address people from all branches of society successfully with a single and natural voice.

Within the band world Mortimer was sometimes referred to as HM. He published some compositions under the pen-name Harry Morton, but he had no aspirations as a composer. His autobiography, *Harry Mortimer on Brass* (1981), was co-authored by Alan Lynton. Mortimer died suddenly of heart failure at his home, 50 Ladbroke Grove, London, on 23 January 1992. He was survived by his second wife, the two daughters of his first marriage, and the son of his second. He left his body to medical research. His remains were returned for cremation in Streatham Vale on 25 January 1995; his ashes were then scattered in the private gardens behind his home, where a tree was planted and a memorial plaque unveiled in his memory.

TREVOR HERBERT

Sources H. Mortimer, *Harry Mortimer on brass* (1981) · *The Times* (27 Jan 1992) · *The Independent* (27 Jan 1992) · C. Bainbridge, *Brass triumphant* (1980) · private information (2004) [Mrs Margaret Mortimer; Martin Mortimer] · m. cert.
Archives SOUND BL NSA, *Talking about music*, 151, 1LD0200074 S1 BD2 · BL NSA, documentary recordings · BL NSA, performance recordings
Likenesses photograph, News International Syndication, London [*see illus.*] · photograph, repro. in *The Independent* · photographs, repro. in Mortimer, *Harry Mortimer on brass*
Wealth at death £305,419: probate, 1993, *CGPLA Eng. & Wales*

Mortimer, Hugh (I) de (d. c.1148x50). *See under* Mortimer, Hugh (II) de (d. 1181?).

Mortimer, Hugh (II) de (d. 1181?), magnate, was the second son of **Hugh (I) de Mortimer** (d. c.1148x50) and an unknown wife, and not, as the foundation narratives of Wigmore Abbey have it, of the Domesday tenant-in-chief Ralph (I) de *Mortimer (*fl.* c.1080–1104), who was the younger Hugh's grandfather. The two Hughs are not always easily distinguishable in the sources, but it seems clear that the elder Hugh was involved in local Herefordshire feuds arising from the contest between Stephen and Matilda. That he was on the whole a supporter of Stephen may be deduced from that king's exception of Mortimer's lands in Herefordshire from the grant of that shire to Robert, earl of Leicester, probably made in 1144. He was also involved, and with some success, in episodes in the long struggle between the marcher lords and the Welsh for the cantrefs of Maelienydd and Elfael in Powys. The clearest accounts of his activities there are to be found in the Peniarth MS 20 and Red Book of Hergest versions of the Welsh *Brut*. In 1144 Hugh fitz Ranulf—identifiable with Hugh (I) de Mortimer—repaired the castle of Cymaron in Maelienydd, and a second time subjugated that cantref; meanwhile Colunway (Colwyn) Castle in Elfael was rebuilt a second time, and Elfael was a second time subjected to the 'French', probably the men of Philip de Briouze. Hugh (I) thus inaugurated another period of Mortimer possession of Maelienydd. Further entries in the *Brut* reveal the attendant brutalities: in 1145 Hugh (I) de Mortimer seized and imprisoned Rhys ap Hywel of Brycheiniog, and in 1148 had Rhys blinded; in 1146 he killed Meurig ap Madog ab Idnerth, another of the princes of the Welsh middle march. However, although Meurig's death is also attributed to Hugh (I) de Mortimer by *Brenhinedd y Saesson*, according to other sources he was killed by the treachery of his own men.

The elder Hugh de Mortimer probably died in the period 1148–50. Information in the Wigmore chronicle has allowed a depiction of this Hugh as 'a swashbuckling, choleric man given over to pleasures and amusements, an evil-tempered and wilful lord, a quarrelsome neighbour, and a lusty warrior' (Davies, 83). Details in the romance of *Fouke le Fitz Waryn*, concerning the long feud between

Hugh and Josce de Dinan of Ludlow, bear out this summary. Hugh was succeeded by his elder son, Roger, who was dead by 1153. It was therefore Hugh (II) de Mortimer who faced the emergency of 1154. (The descent given here is approved by L. C. Loyd and consistent with the description of the first Ralf as *abbavus* of the second (Dugdale, *Monasticon*, 6.349).)

Early in 1153 the new lord had secured from Duke Henry, the future Henry II, an exception of his fee from the shire of Stafford when the latter was granted to Ranulf (II), earl of Chester, by the so-called 'treaty of Devizes' (*Reg. RAN*, 3.180). Yet despite this special treatment, Hugh (II) de Mortimer was within two years a rebel in arms against the new king, and a major opponent of Henry II's attempt to restore royal authority. The first Ralph de Mortimer, according to an early fourteenth-century statement, had been seneschal of the Montgomery earls of Shropshire, and in that capacity keeper of their castle at Bridgnorth (in fact built by the third and last earl). This stronghold fell into royal hands on the forfeiture of the Montgomery family in 1102; Ralph's descendant Hugh (II) de Mortimer took advantage of the anarchy of Stephen's reign to resume its custody, and refused to surrender the castle when so bidden by Henry II. In or before 1148, moreover, Hugh (II) de Mortimer had also secured custody of a castle belonging to the bishop of Hereford. As well as the king's castle of Bridgnorth, Mortimer also held his own castles of Cleobury (Cleobury Mortimer) and Wigmore against the new king.

Hugh (II) de Mortimer's rising was one of several against the new king at this time, largely prompted by Henry's demand for the return of alienated royal lands and castles. But resistance was unco-ordinated: there was no co-operation, for instance, between Mortimer and his neighbour Earl Roger of Hereford. It was at Easter 1155, according to the Battle Abbey chronicle, that Mortimer, 'estimating the king to be a mere boy and indignant at his activity' (Searle, 159–61), fortified Bridgnorth and refused to submit to royal orders. The king promptly placed Bridgnorth, Cleobury, and Wigmore under siege, surrounding Bridgnorth Castle with a rampart and ditch, so that Mortimer could not leave it. With no choice but to surrender, therefore, on 7 July he made his peace with the king, at an impressive assembly of lay and ecclesiastical magnates. He was treated lightly, for whereas the earldom of Hereford was allowed to lapse when Earl Roger died, also in 1155, Hugh de Mortimer soon recovered Bridgnorth and Wigmore (Cleobury had been destroyed), and retained the privileged status of a tenant-in-chief. The fact that King Henry was himself frequently active in Wales may subsequently have had a constraining effect on Mortimer's activities there. In any event, after 1155 he seems to have turned his attention to the affairs of Wigmore, and especially of its abbey.

The overall trustworthiness of the foundation narrative of Wigmore Abbey is uncertain, but some of its statements about members of the Mortimer family are demonstrably correct, and it can be accepted that the origin, endowment, and construction of the abbey originated in the deathbed wish of the first Ralph, and that action thereon was taken by Ralph's son Hugh (I), who (reasonably enough in view of his youth) was put in the care of Oliver de Merlimond. Merlimond later appears as steward, probably to Hugh the elder, and first took action on Ralph's dying wish by establishing a house of Augustinian canons, affiliated to St Victor in Paris, at Shobdon. According to the Anglo-Norman chronicle of Wigmore, Hugh de Mortimer promised to give Chelmarsh to Shobdon, but having fallen out with Merlimond, fell out with the canons as well, and not only failed to give them Chelmarsh, but deprived them of Shobdon vill too.

The value of the chronicle at this point is somewhat diminished by its failure to distinguish clearly between the two Hughs. It is consequently uncertain whether it was the father or the son who transferred the canons to Aymestrey, a few miles north-west of Leominster. But it was probably the younger Hugh who, afraid that his enemies might exploit a monastery at Aymestrey to his own disadvantage, by using it as a fortress, persuaded the canons to move again, to Wigmore. There he established them at a nearby place called 'Bethun', where they erected small wooden buildings with his help. Nevertheless they were to move again twice more, first back to Shobdon, and finally to a site just north of Wigmore. The foundation ceremony there took place in 1172. Mortimer laid the first stone of the church, and pledged to pay 10 marks towards the cost of the building, but later completed it at his own expense. He gave the canons the manor of Caynham in Shropshire, together with its church, and a number of other churches, chapels, lands, and rents in Herefordshire and Shropshire. In 1179 he had the church dedicated by Bishop Robert Foliot of Hereford, and not only confirmed all his previous gifts, but also gave a chalice and cup for the reserved sacrament, both of gold, and two silver-gilt candlesticks.

Hugh (II) de Mortimer died at Cleobury in 1180–81; the foundation narrative errs in placing his death in 1185, but may be correct in attributing the event to 26 February, since his anniversary was later commemorated in Lent. He had bequeathed his body to Wigmore Abbey, and it was taken there for burial. In his earlier days he had been described by Robert de Torigni as a man of extreme arrogance and presumption, while William of Newburgh regarded him as notable for pride and wrath. But to the canons of Wigmore he had died 'at a ripe old age and full of good works' (Dickinson and Ricketts, 437). With his wife, Matilda, widow of Philip de Belmeis and daughter of William le Meschin of Egremont, he is said to have had four sons, Hugh, Roger, Ralph, and William. Hugh, the eldest, predeceased his father, who was therefore succeeded as lord of Wigmore by **Roger (II) de Mortimer** (*d.* 1214).

To the Wigmore chronicler Roger (II) de Mortimer was 'as befitted his years, gay, full of youth and inconstant of heart, and especially somewhat headstrong' (Dickinson and Ricketts, 439). He had served Henry II faithfully during the rebellion of the king's sons in 1173–4, but at the time of his father's death he was in King Henry's prison, because in 1179 his men had killed Cadwallon ap Madog, the ruler of Maelienydd, when the latter was returning from court with a royal safe conduct. He may not have been released until 1182. Roger's conflicts with the Welsh would persist throughout his life, as he struggled to establish his rule over the middle march of Wales. In 1195 he brought Maelienydd under his control, rebuilding the castle at Cymaron. A grant to the abbey of Cwm-hir in Powys in 1199, commemorating 'our men who died in the conquest of Maelienydd' (Davies, 85), points to casualties as well as achievement (in 1196 his forces were among those heavily defeated at Radnor by the Lord Rhys of Deheubarth), but in 1202 he could be described as supreme in central Wales.

Roger de Mortimer also became involved in English affairs. In 1191 he was accused by William de Longchamp, the justiciar, of having entered into an unexplained conspiracy with the Welsh against the king, and was forced to abjure the realm, though his exile was much shorter than the three years reported by Richard of Devizes. It is possible that he had become a supporter of Count John, Richard I's brother. But if this was so, he soon transferred his allegiance back to the king, for it was with royal support that he attacked Maelienydd in 1195. However, he later served in Normandy under John as king, and in 1205 was captured when trying to occupy Dieppe, subsequently paying a ransom of 1000 marks. Roger de Mortimer remained loyal to John for the rest of his life. With his wife, Isabella de Ferrers, he had at least two sons and one daughter. Being overcome by ill health, he transferred his lands to his son, and by 19 August 1214 he was dead. He was buried at Wigmore Abbey. He had at first been on bad terms with the canons, and tried to revoke grants made to them by his father, until the solemnity with which they commemorated Hugh's anniversary reconciled him to them.

Roger's eldest son and heir, **Hugh (III) de Mortimer** (d. 1227), followed his father in remaining loyal to John, whose burial in Worcester Cathedral he attended in October 1216. Equally loyal to the young Henry III, in February 1222 he took part in the siege of Bytham Castle, held against the government by the rebellious count of Aumale, and in 1225 he witnessed the reissue of Magna Carta. But he was principally occupied on the Welsh march, where about 1215 his father's conquests in Maelienydd had been reversed by *Llywelyn ab Iorwerth; when Hugh (III) died, on 10 November 1227, Maelienydd was still in Welsh hands, and he had also been unable to establish his right to two manors, which he had nominally acquired by exchange, but which were in fact under Llywelyn's control. Hugh (III) was buried at Wigmore Abbey. There were no children of his marriage to Annora de Briouze, and he was succeeded by his younger brother, **Ralph (II) de Mortimer** (d. 1246). Ralph, too, was continually engaged on the Welsh marches. At first he stood on the defensive, unable to make much impression on Llywelyn's power. No doubt it was for this reason that in 1230 he married Gwladus Ddu (d. 1251), daughter of Llywelyn and widow of Reginald de Briouze. It was only after the death of his father-in-law in 1240 that Mortimer was able to take the

military initiative again, with attacks upon the Welsh. In the summer of 1241 there was war in Maelienydd, and this time the Mortimers prevailed, ending Welsh control of the lordship of Gwrtheyrnion. Ralph (II) died on 6 August 1246 and was buried at Wigmore Abbey, where he was remembered as 'a warlike and energetic man' (Dugdale, *Monasticon*, 6, pt 1, 350). His heir was Roger (III) de *Mortimer (1231–1282), the son of his marriage to Gwladus. It is a measure of Ralph's ultimate success in extending and consolidating the Mortimer lordship, that Roger should have paid 2000 marks to have his family's lands until his coming of age.   J. F. A. MASON

Sources T. Jones, ed. and trans., *Brut y tywysogyon, or, The chronicle of the princes: Peniarth MS 20* (1952) · T. Jones, ed. and trans., *Brut y tywysogyon, or, The chronicle of the princes: Red Book of Hergest* (1955) · T. Jones, ed. and trans., *Brenhinedd y Saesson, or, The kings of the Saxons* (1971) [another version of *Brut y tywysogyon*] · J. Williams ab Ithel, ed., *Annales Cambriae*, Rolls Series, 20 (1860) · Dugdale, *Monasticon*, new edn, 6/1.344–50 · GEC, *Peerage*, new edn, 9.266–76 · R. W. Eyton, *Antiquities of Shropshire*, 12 vols. (1854–60), 4.194–205 · R. R. Davies, *Conquest, coexistence and change: Wales, 1063–1415*, History of Wales, 2 (1987); repr. as *The age of conquest: Wales, 1063–1415* (1991) · *Reg. RAN*, vol. 3 · E. Searle, ed., *The chronicle of Battle Abbey*, OMT (1980) · R. Howlett, ed., *Chronicles of the reigns of Stephen, Henry II, and Richard I*, 1, Rolls Series, 82 (1884) · *Chronicon Richardi Divisensis / The Chronicle of Richard of Devizes*, ed. J. T. Appleby (1963) · R. Howlett, ed., *Chronicles of the reigns of Stephen, Henry II, and Richard I*, 4, Rolls Series, 82 (1889) · J. C. Dickinson and P. T. Ricketts, eds., 'The Anglo-Norman chronicle of Wigmore Abbey', *Transactions of the Woolhope Naturalists' Field Club*, 39 (1967–9), 413–46 · *Letters and charters of Gilbert Foliot*, ed. A. Morey and others (1967) · J. B. Smith, 'The middle march in the thirteenth century', *BBCS*, 24 (1970–72), 77–93 · C. Hopkinson, 'The Mortimers of Wigmore, 1086–1214', *TWNFC*, 46 (1989), 177–93 · *Chancery records* · E. J. Hathaway, ed., *Fouke le Fitz Waryn*, Anglo-Norman Text Society, 26–8 (1975–6) · J. J. Crump, 'The Mortimer family and the making of the march', *Thirteenth century England*, ed. M. Prestwich, R. H. Britnell, and R. Frame, 6 (1997), 117–26 · *Archaeological survey of Wigmore sites* [forthcoming] · G. Zarnecki, 'The priory church of Shobdon and its founder', *Studies in medieval art and architecture presented to Peter Lasko*, ed. D. Buckton and T. A. Heslop (1994), 211–20 · private information (2004) [B. Wright]

Mortimer, Hugh (III) de (d. 1227). See under Mortimer, Hugh (II) de (d. 1181?).

Mortimer, John (1656?–1736), writer on agriculture, was born in London, the only son and heir of Mark Mortimer, of the old Somerset family of that name, and his wife, Abigail Walmesly, of Blackmore, Essex. He received a commercial education, and became a prosperous merchant on Tower Hill. On his retirement he bought, in November 1693, the estate of Filiols, Essex, to put into practice his ideas on agricultural improvement, his paternal estate having been damaged by flooding; he subsequently changed the name of his estate to Toppingo Hall. He greatly improved it; a number of fine cedar trees planted by him on the estate were still thriving in 1829.

Mortimer married three times. His first wife, Dorothy, born at Hursley, near Winchester, on 1 August 1660, was the ninth child of Richard *Cromwell, and it is supposed that the former protector's return to England in 1680 was prompted by a desire to be present at the wedding; she died in childbirth on 14 May 1681, within a year of the marriage. He next married Sarah, daughter of Sir John Tippets, surveyor of the navy, with whom he had a son and a daughter. His third wife was Elizabeth, daughter of Samuel Sanders of Derbyshire; they had four sons and two daughters, of whom the second son was Cromwell *Mortimer (c.1693–1752), a physician active in the Royal Society and other learned bodies.

Mortimer's claim to remembrance is based on his work entitled *The Whole Art of Husbandry, in the Way of Managing and Improving of Land* (1707), which forms a landmark in English agricultural literature, and largely influenced husbandry in the nineteenth century. Compiled from earlier books and from the practice of husbandry as he observed it, it dealt with the usual branches of agriculture, and also fish ponds, orchards, the culture of silkworms, and the making of cider. The work was dedicated to the Royal Society, of which Mortimer had been admitted a member in December 1705. A straightforward and well-arranged treatise, if somewhat inaccurate factually and in the spelling of varietal names, the book was very popular; there appeared five more editions between 1708 and 1716, one in Dublin in 1721, a Swedish translation in 1727, and a revised edition by Thomas Mortimer, his grandson, in 1761. Mortimer also published some moralistic pamphlets. He died in 1736.

THOMAS SECCOMBE, *rev.* ANITA MCCONNELL

Sources R. P. Brotherston, 'John Mortimer and the art of husbandry', *Gardeners' Chronicle*, 3rd ser., 46 (1909), 257–8 · P. Morant, *The history and antiquities of the county of Essex*, 2 (1768), 133 · T. Wright, *The history and topography of the county of Essex*, 2 (1836), 743 · will, PRO, PROB 11/677, sig. 134

Mortimer, John Hamilton (1740–1779), painter and etcher, was born on 17 September 1740 in Eastbourne, Sussex, the fifth and youngest child of Thomas Mortimer (1697–1774), a mill owner and customs officer, and his wife, Catherine, *née* Smith (d. 1746). Little is known of Mortimer's childhood. According to Joseph Farington's diary entry for 9 September 1797 he was at school at Lewes, Sussex (Farington, *Diary*, 3.893). He may have received some instruction in painting from a paternal uncle, Roger Mortimer (1700–1769), an itinerant artist. In 1756 or 1757 Mortimer's father paid £100 for him to be placed in London for three years in the studio of the portrait painter Thomas Hudson (1701–1779). Finding Hudson's studio regime unsympathetic, Mortimer was by March 1759 working under Robert Edge Pine (1730–1788), a history painter and portraitist of republican views who later moved to America. Although Mortimer did not stay with Pine for long he was influenced by his painting style, his subject matter, and probably his radical political views. As important as the influence of Pine, if not more so, was the opportunity for drawing and contact with other students and artists in London which Mortimer found in the duke of Richmond's sculpture gallery, the St Martin's Lane Academy, and Shipley's drawing academy. Mortimer won prizes (1759–1762) offered by the Society for the Encouragement of Arts, Manufactures, and Commerce, for drawings done in the duke of Richmond's

John Hamilton Mortimer (1740–1779), self-portrait, c.1775–8 [*Self-Portrait in Character*]

sculpture gallery and the St Martin's Lane Academy. Mortimer met the painter Joseph Wright of Derby (1734–1797), with whom he became friends, in Hudson's studio, and in Shipley's drawing school he probably met two of his closest artist friends, Thomas Jones (1742–1803) and James Gandon (1742–1823).

In 1759 the Society for the Encouragement of Arts, Manufactures, and Commerce began to offer premiums for English (and later British) history painting. Mortimer won second prize in 1763 and in 1764 he won the first prize for *St Paul Preaching to the Ancient Britons* (Guildhall, High Wycombe, Buckinghamshire). This success established his reputation as a history painter. Increasingly from the 1760s artists in Britain came to treat subjects from national history, particularly from the Saxon up to the Tudor period. Mortimer began to develop this and other subject matter which in its content and treatment looks forward to Romanticism. At the same time, more conventionally, he painted portraits and particularly group portraits, in the style of John Zoffany and Francis Wheatley.

Mortimer exhibited at the Society of Artists every year from 1762 until 1777. Unlike many of the older established artists he did not transfer to the Royal Academy on its foundation in 1768, but remained loyal to the Society of Artists along with more radical artists such as Joseph Wright of Derby. He was active in setting up the society's academy of drawing and painting in Maiden Lane, Covent Garden, in 1769, having become a director of the society in 1768. He was made vice-president in 1770 and was president in 1774–5.

Mortimer collaborated on works with other artists during the 1760s and early 1770s, no doubt largely as a result of friendships formed in the drawing academies and the Society of Artists. He painted figures in landscapes by Thomas Jones before the latter's departure for Italy in 1776, and he worked with Richard Paton, introducing some figures into Paton's views of the royal dockyards, 1770–71 (Royal Collection). He painted a large decorative ceiling for the saloon of Brocket Hall, Hertfordshire (c.1770–73), in which he was assisted by Francis Wheatley and James Durno. Mortimer even painted figures in Richard Wilson's *Meleager* and *Atalanta* (Tate collection) but this was most likely done, c.1770, at the request of the print publisher, Robert Sayer, who owned the pictures, and without the agreement of Wilson.

Mortimer was a lively and reckless companion. Early biographers mention his athletic physique and love of sports, as well as extravagance in dress. Though self-portraits do not actively confirm this (for example the *Self-Portrait with Father and Brother*, mid-1760s; Yale U. CBA), Thomas Jones described adventurous trips (1769–71) made by boat around the south-east coast with Mortimer taking a leading part and including artist companions such as Joseph Farington and James Gandon (Oppé, 15.24). It seems that Mortimer's high spirits degenerated into dissipation and folly. Edward Dayes claimed that in a bout of drinking Mortimer ate a wineglass, 'of which act of folly he never recovered' (*Works*, 340).

In the early 1770s Mortimer turned to more disturbing subject matter, such as scenes of witchcraft, monsters, and, in particular, banditti or bandit scenes, which came to be considered his speciality. Influenced by the etchings of the seventeenth-century artist Salvator Rosa, Mortimer's banditti subjects, often in narrative series, were frequently drawn and etched, either by himself or by engravers such as Robert Blyth, the drawings being exhibited as finished works at the Society of Artists (1772, 1773). In 1774 and 1775 he exhibited two painted series with banditti, *The Progress of Vice* (two out of four known; priv. coll.) and *The Progress of Virtue* (four paintings; Tate collection). Mortimer also produced illustrations to literature, and had great success with his twelve Shakespearian heads, finished drawings exhibited at the Society of Artists in 1775 and etched and published by himself in two parts in 1775 and 1776. Mortimer's delicate but taut draughtsmanship, with fine lines and hatched shading, echoed in the etchings, was derived partly from Guercino and Salvator Rosa.

On 11 February 1775 Mortimer married Jane Hurrell (1738–1824), fifth child of William and Elizabeth Hurrell of Foxton, Cambridgeshire, whom he had known since at least the mid-1760s. While Mortimer had lived at various addresses in Covent Garden in London since his student days, Jane Hurrell lived nearby at 33 Norfolk Street. Early biographers say that she brought a calming influence to bear, steering him away from a dissipated and extravagant life. Soon after marriage they moved to a house in Aylesbury, Buckinghamshire, provided by a patron, Dr Benjamin Bates. Mortimer returned to portraiture, painting some of the local families, which enabled him to improve his poor financial state. He also continued to paint and

draw historical subjects, such as *King John Delivering Magna Charta to the Barons* (1776; duke of Rutland collection, Belvoir Castle, Leicestershire), and literary illustrations, for example *Sir Artegal the Knight of Justice, with Talus the Iron Man*, from Spenser's *Faerie Queene* (1778; Tate collection). In addition he illustrated a number of books, producing many frontispieces for John Bell's *The Poets of Great Britain, Complete from Chaucer to Churchill*, 109 vols. (1779–88). His range of subject matter, strenuous treatment, and search for depicting extremes of passion link his work to that of artists such as Henry Fuseli and James Barry. Unlike those two artists, he never travelled to Italy, but found his sources in predominantly seventeenth-century Italian art from engravings and paintings which could be seen in England.

Mortimer exhibited at the Royal Academy for the first time in 1778 and was elected an associate of the Royal Academy in the same year. In the following year, at the age of thirty-eight, he was quickly and fatally 'seized with a violent fever' (*Monthly Magazine*, 25) and died at his home, 33 Norfolk Street, Covent Garden, on 4 February 1779. It was said that early dissipation had damaged his health and that this had not been offset by a steadier life after marriage. He was buried, according to a memorial tablet in High Wycombe church, Buckinghamshire, at Little Missenden church, Buckinghamshire; his remains were moved to High Wycombe church in 1780.

JOHN SUNDERLAND

Sources J. Sunderland, 'John Hamilton Mortimer: his life and works', *Walpole Society*, 52 (1986) [whole issue] · *John Hamilton Mortimer, ARA, 1740–1779*, Towner Art Gallery (1968) [exhibition catalogue, 1968] · G. Benthall, 'John Hamilton Mortimer, ARA: drawings and engraved works with a revised account of his life', typescript MS, c.1950, V&A · Libra, *Monthly Magazine*, 1 (1796), 22–5 · A. Cunningham, *The lives of the most eminent British painters, sculptors, and architects*, 5 (1832), 186–203 · E. Edwards, *Anecdotes of painters* (1808); facs. edn (1970), 60–65 · A. P. Oppé, ed., 'Memoirs of Thomas Jones, Penkerrig, Radnorshire', *Walpole Society*, 32 (1946–8) [whole issue] · Farington, *Diary*, 3.893 · J. Sunderland, 'John Hamilton Mortimer and Salvator Rosa', *Burlington Magazine*, 112 (1970), 520–31 · J. N. Sunderland, 'Mortimer, Pine and some political aspects of English history painting', *Burlington Magazine*, 116 (1974), 317–26 · W. T. Whitley, *Artists and their friends in England, 1700–1799*, 2 vols. (1928) · *The works of the late Edward Dayes*, ed. E. W. Brayley (privately printed, London, 1805) · *Morning Chronicle* (27 April 1788) · baptismal register, Eastbourne parish church · registers, St Paul's Church, Covent Garden, London

Likenesses J. H. Mortimer, self-portrait, oils, in or after 1763–1767, Yale U. CBA · J. H. Mortimer, self-portrait, oils, c.1765, Royal Academy of Arts, London; version, NPG · J. H. Mortimer, self-portrait, oils, c.1775–1778, Towner Art Gallery, Eastbourne [*see illus.*] · R. Blyth, engraving, 1782 (after Mortimer), V&A · A. Van Assen, etching, pubd 1810 (after J. H. Mortimer), BM, NPG, V&A · J. Gillray, sketch (for *Connoisseurs examining a collection of George Morland's*), V&A · by or after J. H. Mortimer, pen-and-ink drawing, V&A · J. H. Mortimer, self-portrait, NPG · R. Wilson, portrait, RA

Wealth at death c.1777 earned £900 from portraits: *Monthly Magazine*, 24

Mortimer, John Robert (1825–1911), archaeologist and geologist, was born on 15 June 1825 in Fimber, a wold village in the East Riding of Yorkshire. He was the eldest of three children of James Mortimer, a farmer, and his wife, Hannah, daughter of John Welburn, a farmer of Fimber. He was educated at the village school in Fridaythorpe. He started a business as a corn merchant in Fimber, and moved in 1869 to Driffield, where he remained for the rest of his life. Here he built up a trade in seeds, corn, manure, and fertilizer, with a malt kiln in Driffield and a brewery and kilns in Malton. On 7 August 1869 he married Matilda (d. 1905), daughter of the Revd Thomas Mitchell, vicar of Sancton and Holme on the Wolds. They had six children.

Mortimer's scientific interests were kindled by visits to the Great Exhibition of 1851 and to the private collection formed by Edward Tindall of Bridlington. At first he collected chalk fossils and flint implements from the Yorkshire wolds, encouraging farm workers to bring him specimens and offering prizes to those who brought in the largest quantity. So well known did he become that flint implements soon became known as 'mortimers' in his locality. With increased competition for an ever-decreasing supply of choice finds, Mortimer turned in his spare time to the excavation of the Bronze Age burial-mounds of the southern wolds, judging that by 1863 some twenty-five per cent had already been destroyed. By the end of his life, and with the occasional help of his younger brother Robert, he had opened over 300 round barrows, and two long barrows; sometimes in company with Canon William Greenwell (1820–1918) and Thomas Boynton, he excavated over seventy burials in the Iron Age 'Danes' graves' cemetery near Driffield, as well as a number of Anglo-Saxon interments. In addition he mapped the linear earthworks which crossed the wolds. The bulk of this work was published in his major work, *Forty Years' Researches in British and Saxon Burial Mounds of East Yorkshire* (1905). In this he mapped the positions of the fifteen groups of barrows he had examined, and included plans of each group, together with a plan of each barrow indicating the positions of the interments, their postures, and other details. Mortimer's ability to record detail in the field is well shown by his excavation of barrow 23 of the Calais wold group, which contained concentric circles of stake-holes. By taking plaster casts he was able to demonstrate that some had contained pointed, and the others blunted, stakes. What was lacking, however, was an awareness of detailed stratigraphy which often makes the use of the information recorded problematic. All the finds (about a thousand) were illustrated from beautiful drawings by his youngest daughter, Agnes, then between thirteen and nineteen years old.

Mortimer moved his collection, which had begun life in a showcase in his office at Fimber, to a purpose-built museum at Lockwood Street, Driffield, in 1878. This was equipped not only with display galleries but also with two large workshops. He was very keen for his collection to stay in the locality and had been shocked to see other collections leave the area. Accordingly, he offered his collection at half its value to the East Riding county council. Like most public bodies of the time, the council was not yet ready to take on this role, but through the generosity of

Colonel G. H. Clarke, the collection in its entirety was finally accepted and moved in 1914 to Hull, where, despite damage during the Second World War, the bulk survives.

Though he was self-taught, Mortimer's fieldwork compares well with that of his more famous contemporary Canon William Greenwell, and his recording is in many ways superior. Unlike Greenwell, however, he confined his interests very much to the locality in which he lived, publishing over forty articles on items of antiquity and the geology of the wolds. Mortimer's collection, along with those made by Greenwell, Thomas Bateman, and Richard Colt Hoare, were to provide the foundations on which later work on British prehistory was built.

Mortimer died on 19 August 1911 at his home in Driffield. He was survived by five of his children.

L. V. GRINSELL, rev. I. H. LONGWORTH

Sources J. R. Mortimer, *Forty years' researches in British and Saxon burial mounds of east Yorkshire* (1905) · G. W. Lamplugh, 'In memoriam: John Robert Mortimer (1825–1911)', *Proceedings of the Yorkshire Geological Society*, new ser., 17 (1909–11), 258–60 · G. W. Lamplugh, 'John Robert Mortimer', *Geological Magazine*, decade 5/8 (1911), 479–80 · T. Sheppard, 'Prominent Yorkshire workers, V: John Robert Mortimer', *The Naturalist* (May 1911), 186–91 · T. Sheppard, *A descriptive catalogue of the specimens in the Mortimer Museum of Archaeology and Geology* (1900) · T. Sheppard, *Catalogue of the Mortimer collection of prehistoric remains from east Yorkshire barrows* (1929) · I. M. Stead, *The Arras culture* (1979) · J. D. Hicks, ed., *A Victorian boyhood on the wolds: the recollections of J. R. Mortimer* (1978) · B. M. Marsden, *The early barrow-diggers* (1974) · T. Sheppard, 'Two east Yorkshire antiquaries', *Transactions of the East Riding Antiquarian Society*, 18 (1912), 53–5 · m. cert.
Archives Hull Museum
Likenesses Brown, photograph, repro. in Sheppard, 'Prominent Yorkshire workers', pl. xiii
Wealth at death £4627 19s. 2d.: probate, 21 Nov 1911, CGPLA Eng. & Wales

Mortimer [née Fletcher; *other married name* Dimont], **Penelope Ruth** (1918–1999), novelist, was born on 19 September 1918 at Shincliffe, Highfield Park, Rhyl, Denbighshire, the daughter of Arthur Forbes Gerald Fletcher (1880–1956), a Church of England clergyman, and his wife, Amy Caroline, née Maggs (1876–1973). Arthur Fletcher lost his faith early in his career, but continued to serve as a vicar. From an early age Penelope Fletcher wanted to become a writer. Because of her father's work, she was educated at many different schools: Croydon High School; New School, Streatham; Blencathra, Rhyl; Garden School, Lane End, near High Wycombe; St Elphin's School for Daughters of the Clergy; and the Central Educational Bureau for Women, Russell Square, London. She studied to become a journalist at University College, London, before marrying Charles Francis Dimont (1913–1993), himself a journalist, on 6 November 1937. They had two children. Under her married name, Penelope Dimont, she published her first novel, *Johanna*, in 1947, which, as she recalled in her autobiography, 'died at birth' having received virtually no attention in the press (Mortimer, *About Time Too*, 46). But she wrote for the *New Yorker* and was an agony aunt, under the pen-name Ann Temple, for the *Daily Mail*.

Penelope Ruth Mortimer (1918–1999), by David Bennett, 1994

In 1949 Penelope and Charles were divorced. Men were attracted to her throughout her life, and she to men. Her relationship with the scientist Kenneth Harrison produced a daughter, Julia (b. 1945), and she had another daughter, Deborah (b. 1948), with the novelist and playwright Randall Swingler (1909–1967). On 27 August 1949, the day her divorce was made absolute, she married the writer and barrister John Clifford Mortimer (b. 1923), five years her junior. They had two children, Jeremy and Sally. The Mortimers were a fashionable and radical London couple. John had a number of not particularly successful novels under his belt but he was beginning to make a splash with one-act plays of a slightly surreal quality. Penelope was noticeable for her smouldering, dark good looks and her penchant for wearing blue jeans and exotic black leather jackets, a cigarette dangling *de rigueur* from her lips.

Mortimer's second novel, *A Villa in Summer* (1954), was followed by *The Bright Prison* (1956) and the travel book *With Love and Lizards* (1957), co-authored with her husband. The magnificent *Daddy's Gone a-Hunting*, which confronted marital angst, was published in 1958. Her luminous, incisive short stories written for the *New Yorker* were collected as *Saturday Lunch with the Brownings* in 1960.

Mortimer was at the height of her reputation as a novelist in the 1960s and was the toast of the town. She was not regarded particularly as a feminist, yet her nine published novels (others were unfinished and unpublished) all took up the cudgels on behalf of women, most notably *The Pumpkin Eater* (1962). Her fifth novel, it tells, with a commendable spareness of prose, the story of the emotional

disintegration of a mother with numerous children, and of her husband's increasing estrangement. The autobiographies of novelists are more likely to be found in their fiction than in their published memoirs, and so it is with Mortimer. Dedicated 'to John', *The Pumpkin Eater* when published led to speculation about its autobiographical content. Edna O'Brien, equally in demand at the time, wrote, 'Almost every woman I can think of will want to read this book.' Mortimer was fond of a remark by Raymond Chandler: 'Scarcely nothing in literature is worth a damn except what is written between the lines.' Thus, for the screenplay of the Jack Clayton film of the novel (1964), starring Anne Bancroft and Peter Finch, Harold Pinter was the ideal interpreter. In this period, Mortimer was giving her opinions everywhere. She reviewed novels for the *Sunday Times*, succeeded Penelope Gilliatt as film critic of *The Observer*, and taught creative writing courses at various universities in the United States.

By the 1970s her novels had become bleaker. While domestic, they echoed the increasing aridity, sterility, and hostility of a world beyond the hearth. *The Home* (1971) is about a woman who, after twenty years of increasingly unfulfilled marriage, finds herself alone with her adult children. By the book's end, she is on her own, left to face up to whatever remains of her life. The reader is bleakly left to wonder if this is what the business of living, if not loving, is all about. Tensions and jealousies between Penelope and John Mortimer led to their divorce in 1972. She never fully recovered from the split, and as John became one of the most popular and successful writers in England, her reputation began to decline. Nevertheless, she regarded *Long Distance* (1974) as the most important achievement of her art. The *New Yorker* printed the entire novel, the first time they had done this since J. D. Salinger's *Raise High the Roof Beam, Carpenter* in 1955. Her memoir, *About Time* (1979), a severe look at her life up to her twenty-first birthday, won the Whitbread prize. There was one more published novel, *The Handyman* (1983).

In the mid-1980s Penelope's publisher, Macmillan, rather bizarrely commissioned her to write a biography of the queen mother. The editors were appalled when the manuscript was delivered, as the writer, no reader of royal biographies, had recorded her majesty's life as if she were any other famous person and concluded by questioning its point. The book, *Queen Elizabeth: a Life of the Queen Mother*, eventually published by Viking in 1986, was the most radical biography of a royal since Lytton Strachey. A revised edition, subtitled *An Alternative Portrait of her Life and Times*, was brought out in 1995.

The second volume of Penelope Mortimer's autobiography, *About Time Too, 1940–1978* (1993), sold so indifferently that her publishers declined to bring out the third instalment, 'Closing time'. In her later years Mortimer spent much of her time in the village of Chastleton, Oxfordshire, where she took great joy in cultivating and writing about her garden; she regarded it as her most satisfying achievement. She remained remarkably good-looking, a little like a sparrowhawk, sharp, elegant, and thin. She died of cancer at the Pembridge palliative care centre, St Charles Hospital, Kensington, on 19 October 1999.　　　　　　　　　　　　　　　　　GILES GORDON

Sources P. Mortimer, *About time, 1918–1939* (1979) · P. Mortimer, *About time too, 1940–1978* (1993) · private information (2004) · *The Guardian* (22 Oct 1999) · *The Times* (22 Oct 1999) · *The Independent* (23 Oct 1999)
Archives NRA, corresp. and literary papers
Likenesses D. Bennett, photograph, 1994, NPG [*see illus.*]
Wealth at death £355,831, gross; £275,296 net: probate, 28 Jan 2000, *CGPLA Eng. & Wales*

Mortimer, Ralph (I) de (*fl. c.*1080–1104), magnate, was the son of Roger (I) de *Mortimer (*fl.* 1054–*c.*1080), lord of St Victor-en-Caux in Normandy. His mother, Hawise, inherited land in the county of Amiens and he may have been named from her lord, Ralph, count of Amiens and the Vexin. In Normandy Ralph succeeded his father *c.*1080. William I probably gave him extensive lands in England during his father's lifetime, as there is no evidence that the latter was ever an English landowner.

By 1086 Ralph was in the second rank of the Anglo-Norman baronage. His possessions in England, like those of many others, had been accumulated in stages. The earliest major component was the Hampshire estate of the English thegn Cypping of Worthy, whose chief manor of Headbourne Worthy on the outskirts of Winchester became Mortimer's capital in southern England even though it was held only on a lease of three lives (Ralph's being the third) from the Old Minster at Winchester. His other lands in Wessex included Earl Harold's large Wiltshire manor of Hullavington. The next acquisitions were perhaps manors in Lincolnshire and Yorkshire which had belonged before the Conquest to Eadgifu, Orm, and Copsi. The large estate in the Welsh borders came to him no earlier than 1075. It centred on Wigmore Castle in Herefordshire, built by Earl William fitz Osbern (*d.* 1071), which his son Roger, earl of Hereford, forfeited for rebellion in 1075; and it included several manors which belonged to Queen Edith until her death (also in 1075). Others had belonged to the rebel Englishman Eadric the Wild, whose non-border manors of Amport, Hampshire, Osbaston and Weston, Leicestershire, and Stretton Baskerville, Warwickshire, were also given to Mortimer. Ralph was also a tenant in Shropshire of Roger, earl of Shrewsbury. Although much later in the middle ages he was remembered as the earl's steward there is no contemporary evidence that he served the earl or owed his position in the borders to him: he did not witness the earl's charters, or make gifts to his favoured abbeys, or hold land from him anywhere but Shropshire.

Ralph's English lands, in 1086, extended to twelve counties and touched Southampton Water, the Bristol Channel, and the Humber, but he had concentrated what he controlled directly into three areas: a dispersed but valuable estate in central Wessex (mainly Hampshire but extending into Berkshire and Wiltshire), some manors in Yorkshire and Lincolnshire, and the district around Wigmore on the Shropshire–Herefordshire border. The lands around Wigmore were less than half the estate in 1086,

and there is no evidence that Ralph fought the Welsh with any success, but the border manors proved to be the foundation of his family's considerable importance in English history until the fourteenth century.

Ralph had about eighteen knightly tenants in England in 1086, among whom Odilard and Richard de Barre were pre-eminent. He gave both of them manors divided between the Welsh border and richer, more settled counties. The latter originated not far from the Mortimer heartland in Normandy, but it is striking how many of Ralph's other tenants were not his own men from the Norman patrimony but rather his kinsmen or his new neighbours in England. That circumstance may illustrate the difficulties Ralph had in finding tenants in England while his father was still active in Normandy.

Ralph was conventionally pious in the manner of the great Anglo-Norman lords, though he did not spend much of his landed resources in endowing the church. In Normandy his father had founded an abbey at St Victor-en-Caux; Ralph gave it a single small manor in Hampshire and confirmed his mother's gift of land in the diocese of Amiens. In England he singled out Wigmore parish church for his patronage, an indication of the importance he attached to his marcher stronghold. He had begun giving it land in a small way by 1086, but Wigmore's own later traditions were that Ralph endowed it as a college of three prebends in 1100 and that the bishop of Hereford dedicated the church in 1105. Later in the twelfth century it became an Augustinian priory. Ralph gave his consent to his men's donations to the abbey of Jumièges and Worcester Cathedral priory.

Ralph was not especially prominent in English politics under William I, but he attested royal charters when his kinsman William (I) de Warenne had the king confirm his foundation of Lewes Priory, and once in the company of the leading barons of Hampshire and Wiltshire. On William I's death he threw in his lot with Robert Curthose, and was with him in Normandy at the end of March 1088, planning the invasion of England which followed. Later in the year he himself returned to England in rebellion against William II, in common with the other most prominent marcher lords. With Roger de Lacy, Bernard de Neufmarché, and Earl Roger of Shrewsbury's barons he led an army from the Welsh marches into Worcestershire, ravaging the countryside. They attacked Worcester but were beaten off by Bishop Wulfstan, and the rebellion collapsed. Ralph may then have withdrawn to Normandy. In 1090 William II was able to buy his support for a time but later in the decade he was back in Duke Robert's camp and a party to several charters issued by the duke or his supporters. A further and final reconciliation with William II should probably be dated after Duke Robert left Normandy on the first crusade in 1096. By 1104 Mortimer was among the great Anglo-Norman barons who had sided with Henry I against the duke. There is no later reference to him and the date of his death is unknown.

Ralph was married twice; first to Millicent, and then (by 1088) to Mabel. He was succeeded in both England and Normandy by his eldest son, Hugh (I) de *Mortimer [see *under* Mortimer, Hugh (II) de]. A younger son William, perhaps illegitimate, was set up as a landowner in the borders, and a daughter Hawise made a good marriage to William I's nephew Stephen, count of Aumale, with whom Ralph acted in concert in the politics of the 1090s and 1100s. C. P. LEWIS

Sources GEC, *Peerage* · A. Farley, ed., *Domesday Book*, 2 vols. (1783) · Ordericus Vitalis, *Eccl. hist.*, 4.178–81, 6.56–7 · *Florentii Wigorniensis monachi chronicon ex chronicis*, ed. B. Thorpe, 2, EHS, 10 (1849), 24–5 · J. C. Dickinson and P. T. Ricketts, eds., 'The Anglo-Norman chronicle of Wigmore Abbey', *Transactions of the Woolhope Naturalists' Field Club*, 39 (1967–9), 413–46 · *Reg. RAN*, vol. 1 · C. H. Haskins, *Norman institutions* (1918), 290–92 · W. H. Hale, ed., *Registrum, sive, Liber irrotularius et consuetudinaris prioratus Beatae Mariae Wigorniensis*, CS, 91 (1865), 206

Mortimer, Ralph (II) de (*d.* 1246). *See under* Mortimer, Hugh (II) de (*d.* 1181?).

Mortimer, (Charles) Raymond Bell (1895–1980), writer on literature and art critic, was born at 62 Albert Gate Mansions, Knightsbridge, London, on 25 April 1895, the only child of Charles Edward Mortimer, a prosperous parliamentary solicitor of Devon stock, and his wife, (Marion) Josephine Cantrell. His mother dying young, Mortimer was brought up in Redhill, Surrey, by an aunt and uncle, and by two educated Swiss girls, who taught him French. Although the household, he reported, was neither intellectual nor aesthetic, he 'relished pleasant old pictures, furniture and, above all, quite a lot of books' (Mortimer, ix). He later gave a self-effacing glimpse of this phase in a sketch contributed to a collection of childhood reminiscences edited by Alan Pryce-Jones (*Little Innocents*, 1932). He was also often taken for holidays to France, where the foundations of a lifelong affinity were laid.

Mortimer was sent away at nine to 'an over-large, harsh preparatory school' at Eastbourne, moving in 1909 as a minor scholar to Malvern College, which he was later to describe as 'one of the most philistine and brutal public schools of the period' (Mortimer, ix). He went to Balliol College, Oxford, to study history in 1913, but in 1915, medically rejected for active service, he worked at a hospital for French soldiers in the south of France. In 1918, again medically rejected, he returned to England as a cipher clerk in the Foreign Office. After the war he did not return to Oxford, but was given a 'war BA'. He also briefly joined the Roman Catholic church; this voyage of spiritual exploration proved fruitless, his subsequent interest in religion being confined to a lively relish for the intellectual and personal oddities of Anglican bishops.

In 1922, in collaboration with Hamish Miles (J. E. Miles, a Balliol friend), Mortimer published a light-hearted and insubstantial novel, *The Oxford Circus*. A Jamesian pastiche, 'The Lion's Den', achieved inclusion in *The Best British Short Stories of 1924*. During this period Mortimer lived in London, but continued to travel frequently on the continent, and by 1923 was a holiday companion of George Rylands and Maynard Keynes in Dorset, where he met the Woolfs. In 1924 Mortimer moved from Chelsea to Gordon Place, completing his induction into the New Bloomsbury group.

(**Charles) Raymond Bell Mortimer** (1895–1980), by Sir Cecil Beaton, 1942

Self-proclaimedly both hedonistic and highbrow, Mortimer embodied a curious mixture of intimidating intellectual rigour and mischievous frivolity. Reading, looking at pictures, and party-going were, with the help of a private income, diversified by swimming, skating, skiing, and later bridge and croquet, which he played with stern intensity. In 1924 he embarked on an intimate affair with Harold Nicolson, the diplomatist and author, whom he had first met at the Foreign Office. He continued to travel, and in Paris almost established a second home, rapidly becoming friendly with such leaders of contemporary art and letters as Jean Cocteau, Tristan Tzara, and Louis Aragon.

In 1927, at the instigation of Virginia Woolf, Mortimer joined the *New Statesman*, an organ whose politics were at best precariously congenial to his own 'old-fashioned liberalism' (Hyams, 168). His lively and provocative style won him a readership in *Vogue* and *The Nation*, and he also took over from T. S. Eliot the 'London Letter', which appeared for some years in *The Dial*, an influential New York periodical. It was, however, ultimately in the *New Statesman*, under the gratefully acknowledged tutelage of Desmond MacCarthy, that he made his mark as an outstanding critic and reviewer of the arts, imparting to its pages something of what V. S. Pritchett termed the 'Bloomsbury spirit' (Hyams, 165).

Mortimer's interest in the visual arts was marked in 1929 by the publication of *The New Interior Decoration* in association with Dorothy Todd. In 1932 he published *The*

French Pictures: a Letter to Harriet in the Hogarth Letters series: a genial exposition of how to look at pictures; and in 1944 he published an introduction to Édouard Manet's *Un bar aux Folies-Bergère* and a small monograph on Duncan Grant (the artist who had painted murals in Mortimer's Bloomsbury flat). He was for some years a member of the Royal Fine Arts Commission and contributed forewords to several photographic collections, including Bill Brandt's *The English at Home* (1936), and Martin Hürlimann's *Europe* (1957).

Mortimer became literary editor of the *New Statesman* in 1935, retaining the post until 1947, with an interlude in 1940–41, when he went to the Ministry of Information, playing a large part in liaison with the BBC and the setting up of the Free French Service. His contributions to his own *New Statesman* pages, under the heading 'Books in General', fully established his reputation. His editorship of the 'back half' of the weekly in no way reflected the political pressures of the front half—the editor, Kingsley Martin, treated Mortimer with unwonted respect—but greatly enhanced the already high standing of its arts and book reviews. He was assiduous, like Desmond MacCarthy before him, in supervising his contributors and their use of English, and even more so in searching out and encouraging new talent. In 1948, however, he went to the *Sunday Times* as second string to his former mentor, MacCarthy, whom he succeeded as chief reviewer after the latter's death in 1952, and was soon joined by another MacCarthy-trained critic, Cyril Connolly. He continued to write for the paper until his death.

Mortimer's qualities as a critic are fully displayed in two collections, *Channel Packet* (1942) and *Try Anything Once* (1976). These seventy or so selected pieces reflect little of his interest in painting, except in occasional cross-reference, and a third of them are not specifically concerned with literature, being mostly travel sketches. Nevertheless, the best writing in the books is to be found in his response to literature. Unrelentingly hostile to and derisive of an academicism which placed evaluation before delight, he yet saw the art of reading as requiring a pleasurable concentration of the faculties. His own concentration on nineteenth-century England and France may be seen as a limitation; and at times his connoisseurship could assume a certain patrician air, but at its best it was illuminated by a vigorous lyricism of phrase and shot through with ironic humour. It is significant that, although Proust and Gide ranked high for him, he considered Balzac 'the greatest of novelists' (H. de Balzac, *Lost Illusions* 1951, 7)—and it is no wonder that he was instrumental in introducing the works of Simenon to Britain. His cultural Francophilia was further evidenced in his foreword to a revised edition of Ralph Dutton's *The Land of France* (1968).

Mortimer greatly valued the London Library, and was for many years a most effective member of its committee, where he was much appreciated. In 1955 he was appointed CBE and an officer of the French Légion d'honneur. In 1977 he was awarded the prize of the Académie Française.

Unmarried, Mortimer lived with Geddes Hyslop, the architect, in the Bloomsbury flat, and after 1952 in a handsome house at 5 Canonbury Place, Islington, London; in Dorset he enjoyed a delightful country house, Long Crichel House, Wimborne, with his fellow critics Edward Sackville-West, fifth Baron Sackville, and Desmond Shawe-Taylor. Portraits were painted by Derek Hill and Edward Le Bas, the latter notably characteristic, showing him, as relaxed as he ever was, on the sofa in the dining-room of the Bloomsbury flat, his much-loved pictures (which included works by Picasso and Matisse) lining the wall behind him. Mortimer died on 9 January 1980 at his home in Canonbury, Islington.

J. W. Lambert, *rev.* P. J. Connell

Sources R. Mortimer, *Try anything once* (1976) · private information (1986) · personal knowledge (1986) · *The Times* (10 Jan 1980) · *The Times* (18 Jan 1980) · *Sunday Times* (13 Jan 1980) · V. Trefusis, *Don't look round* (1952) · E. Hyams, *New Statesman* (1963) · A. Palmer and V. Palmer, *Who's who in Bloomsbury* (1987) · J. Lees-Milne, *Harold Nicolson* (1980) · K. Martin, *Father figures* (1966) · F. Partridge, *Memories* (1981) · F. Partridge, *A pacifist's war* (1978) · A. Pryce-Jones, ed., *Little innocents* (1932) · H. de Balzac, *Lost illusions* (1951)

Archives Princeton University Library, New Jersey, notebooks and corresp. | Bodl. Oxf., letters to members of the Lewis family · Bodl. Oxf., corresp. with J. W. Lambert incl. some of Lambert's papers relating to Mortimer · Harvard University, near Florence, Italy, Center for Italian Renaissance Studies, letters to Bernard Berenson · King's AC Cam., letters to Clive Bell; letters and postcards to G. H. W. Rylands · Tate collection, corresp. with Lord Clark · Trinity Cam., postcards to Clive Bell · U. Sussex, corresp. with Virginia Woolf

Likenesses P. Hamann, plaster mask, 1930, NPG · C. Beaton, photograph, 1942, NPG [*see illus.*] · E. Le Bas, oils, *c.*1946, NPG · D. Hill, portrait

Wealth at death £106,855: probate, 18 Feb 1980, *CGPLA Eng. & Wales*

Mortimer, Robert Cecil (1902–1976), bishop of Exeter, was born at Bishopston, Bristol, on 6 December 1902, the youngest but one in the family of three sons and three daughters of Edward Mortimer, vicar of the parish of Bishopston, and his wife, Ellen Merrick. In 1916 he won an entrance scholarship to St Edward's School, Oxford, an Anglo-Catholic foundation where the worship of the chapel was a major influence in determining Mortimer's religious outlook throughout his life. Here he also acquired his lifelong interest in a wide variety of sporting activities.

In 1921 Mortimer entered Keble College, Oxford, as a classical exhibitioner. His moral tutor was K. E. Kirk, later bishop of Oxford, who became a close personal friend and later directed his interests to the study of moral theology. He gained firsts in classical honour moderations (1923) and *literae humaniores* (1925). In 1925 he proceeded to Wells Theological College, and in 1926 he was ordained deacon to a title at the important parish of St Mary Redcliffe, Bristol.

A turning-point in Mortimer's life came with his appointment as lecturer in theology at Christ Church, Oxford, in 1929, and as a student the next year. He devoted himself to the specialist study of canon law, an area hitherto somewhat neglected in Anglican scholarship, and was made university lecturer in this subject in 1935. His researches bore fruit in his first important book, *The Origins of Private Penance in the Western Church* (1939). In the same year he became a member of the archbishops' commission for the complete revision of the canon law of the Church of England. This work was to occupy him for some thirty years, but perhaps his most important contribution was to the commission's report of 1947, which owed much to his scholarship and literary skill.

In 1933 Mortimer had married Mary Hope, daughter of James Ronald Walker, a barrister, of Kensington. They had two sons and two daughters. Mortimer's reputation in Oxford continued to grow and it was no surprise when in 1944 he was appointed regius professor of moral and pastoral theology in succession to Leonard Hodgson. The year 1947 saw the publication of his best-known work, *The Elements of Moral Theology*, as a result of which he was awarded the degree of DD. He had been elected proctor in convocation for Oxford University in 1943, beginning a membership of convocation and church assembly which continued until 1973, and in 1948 his eminence as a canonist received singular recognition when he was appointed chancellor of the diocese of Blackburn.

By this time Mortimer was clearly marked out for high preferment and in 1949 he was appointed to the see of Exeter. The diocese was still suffering from the effects of the war and his first years were occupied with the work of reconstruction. He made no spectacular innovations, for his temperament was essentially conservative and pragmatic, and he never allowed himself to be overwhelmed by administration. Rather, he devoted himself to the steady improvement of church life and worship and to laying a foundation for future growth. Tall, handsome, and dignified, he was an impressive figure, although he could sometimes appear remote: he had little small talk, tended to find ordinary parochial occasions something of a bore, and was at his best in a small group of like-minded friends. But his diocese respected his intellectual gifts and soon came to be aware of his deep pastoral concern, especially for the clergy and their families, whom he knew well. His learning was worn lightly and he could appear indolent—his letters of two or three lines, in reply to correspondence, were renowned—but he was a hard worker who never neglected essential business. He was an excellent, and very succinct, preacher and his addresses to his diocesan conference and his monthly contributions to the *Exeter Diocesan Leaflet* were models of clear, yet profound, exposition of complicated issues affecting church and state. The affection in which he was held found expression in the celebrations, which deeply moved him, of the twenty-first anniversary of his episcopate in 1970.

Mortimer's episcopal responsibilities prevented him from writing the major scholarly contributions which many hoped for, but he found time to publish during his period at Exeter a number of short popular books in his particular field: *Christian Ethics* (1950), *The Duties of a Churchman* (1951), and *Western Canon Law* (1953). Much of his most significant thinking went anonymously into a series of important reports of convocation and church assembly commissions, of which he was a member or chairman. As time went by he became one of the elder statesmen of the church and, as one of the few members of the bench with an academic background, his speeches in debate were impressive and influential. Although he was always recognized as a leader of the Anglo-Catholic wing of the church, his views grew increasingly independent of any narrow party line: he was, for example, a strong supporter both of the Church of South India and of the Anglican–Methodist unity scheme.

In 1955 Mortimer was introduced into the House of Lords and was soon recognized as one of the church's leading spokesmen on moral and social questions: probably no other bishop made more expert contributions in these areas during his seventeen years in the upper house. He was a member of a number of government committees on the treatment of prisoners and other offenders, but perhaps his most significant achievement was in connection with the reform of the divorce laws. He was the chairman of the archbishop of Canterbury's group that in 1966 produced the report *Putting Asunder*, which became the basis of the Divorce Reform Bill of 1969. It was largely Mortimer who negotiated with the Law Commission the compromise which made marital breakdown a sole ground for divorce, as proposed by *Putting Asunder*, but without its further proposal for a preceding inquiry into the state of the marriage. Although he felt bound to support the bill in parliament, the eventual outcome was little to Mortimer's liking since he feared it would open the door to divorce by consent. He always insisted that the reform was concerned with secular law and society and he remained resolutely opposed to any suggestion that divorced parties should be allowed to remarry in church.

As he neared the age of seventy, Mortimer found the strain of a large diocese, involving a great deal of travelling, increasingly tiring and his health seems to have begun to deteriorate. He announced his resignation in 1973 and retired with his wife to Newton Reigny, near Penrith, in Cumberland. There he lived quietly until his sudden death at his home, the Old Rectory, on 11 September 1976. He was cremated at Carlisle on 17 September and on 22 September there was a requiem mass in Exeter Cathedral, after which the casket containing his ashes was laid to rest in St Gabriel's Chapel in the cathedral. He was an honorary fellow of Keble (1951) and an honorary student of Christ Church (1968).   J. R. PORTER, *rev.*

Sources B. G. Skinner, *Robert Exon* (1979) · *The Times* (13 Sept 1976) · private information (1986) [Canon F. G. Rice] · personal knowledge (2004) · CGPLA Eng. & Wales (1976)
Archives LPL, corresp. with Edward Palmer and memoranda
Likenesses oils, bishop's palace, Exeter · photographs, repro. in Skinner, *Robert Exon*
Wealth at death £49,434: probate, 20 Dec 1976, CGPLA Eng. & Wales

Mortimer, Roger (I) de (*fl.* 1054–*c*.1080), magnate, may never have set foot in England but was the progenitor of the Mortimer family whose importance in English history lasted until the male line died out in the early fifteenth century. His parentage is not certain, and different theories have been put forward to account for the evidence, in particular a charter attestation by a 'Roger, son of Ralph de Warenne', and the statements of the earliest genealogist of the family, Robert de Torigny, in the early twelfth century. Most plausibly Roger was the son of Ralph (I) de Warenne and his wife, Béatrice, who is shown to have been a niece of Duke Richard of Normandy by the later statement of Archbishop Anselm that the Warennes and the dukes then shared an ancestor four generations back on one side and six on the other. That parentage would make Roger (I) de Mortimer a second cousin once removed of Duke William, the conqueror of England. In any case he was certainly related in some way to the ducal house.

Probably it was Duke William who gave the young Roger custody of the castle of Mortemer on the Norman frontier towards Amiens, the castle from which he and his descendants took their family name. He had extensive lands in the Pays de Caux and forged alliances with the local aristocracy, taking as his wife Hawise, who inherited land in the diocese of Amiens, and swearing homage to a neighbouring count, Ralph de Crépy, count of Valois.

In 1054 King Henry I of France invaded Normandy. One of his allies was Count Ralph, who was in the French army which made for Mortemer. Duke William sent a force commanded by Roger de Mortimer and Robert, count of Eu, which fought and won a pitched battle against the French in the vicinity of Roger's castle. Count Ralph was taken prisoner. Roger behaved with propriety towards his lord the count: he took Ralph into the castle, protected him there for three days, then escorted him to safety. But he thereby prejudiced the interests of his other lord, the duke. William was furious and banished him, confiscating all his estates. When the duke calmed down and took Roger back into his friendship, he restored everything except Mortemer, which he gave instead to Roger's kinsman William (I) de *Warenne.

Roger de Mortimer afterwards made his chief residence at St Victor-en-Caux, where he and Hawise evidently established a priory which in 1074 was made into an abbey with the permission of the archbishop of Rouen. Although wealthy and well connected, Roger was apparently excluded by the duke from any further participation at the centre of power, since he did not witness any ducal charters before 1066. The family did participate in and profit from the conquest of England, though it was probably through Roger's son Ralph (I) de *Mortimer rather than through Roger himself. Roger's only other known public act was between 1078 and 1080, when he witnessed the royal charter which confirmed William (I) de Warenne's foundation of Lewes as a Cluniac priory; his approval might have been sought in Normandy rather than in England. Roger's date of death is unknown; it need not have been before 1086, when his son was in possession of the lands that had been acquired in England.

C. P. LEWIS

Sources GEC, *Peerage*, new edn, 9.266–7 · Ordericus Vitalis, *Eccl. hist.*, 4.86–9 · D. Bates, ed., *Regesta regum Anglo-Normannorum: the Acta of William I, 1066–1087* (1998), nos. 101, 245 · K. S. B. Keats-Rohan, 'Aspects of Robert of Torigny's genealogies revisited', *Nottingham Medieval Studies*, 37 (1993), 21–7, at 21–3 · D. C. Douglas, *William the Conqueror: the Norman impact upon England* (1964), 67–70 · M. Fauroux, ed., *Recueil des actes des ducs de Normandie de 911 à 1066* (Caen, 1961), no. 136

Mortimer, Roger (II) de (d. 1214). *See under* Mortimer, Hugh (II) de (d. 1181?).

Mortimer, Roger (III) de, lord of Wigmore (1231–1282), magnate, was the first son of Ralph (II) *Mortimer (d. 1246), lord of Wigmore [*see under* Mortimer, Hugh (II) de] and his wife, Gwladys Ddu (d. 1251), the daughter of *Llywelyn ab Iorwerth and widow of Reginald de Briouze.

Early history and marriage Roger Mortimer is said to have been born at the family's castle of Cymaron in the Welsh march, and in 1242 he was already in service on the march where he fortified a castle in Maelienydd. At the time of Mortimer's birth his family had already been engaged in a struggle for dominance in the middle march with the native rulers of Maelienydd and Gwrtheyrnion for over a century. The marriage of Ralph Mortimer and Gwladys, probably in June 1230, made the family one of the most influential in the march. Ralph Mortimer died on 6 August 1246, and his estate was in the king's hand until his son made a fine of 2000 marks to compensate the crown for its remaining rights of wardship. On 26 February 1247 Mortimer received livery of his lands. Later the same year, though still a minor, he married Maud (or Matilda) de Briouze (d. 1300/01), eldest daughter and coheir of William (V) de Briouze (d. 1230) and Eva Marshal, daughter of William (I) *Marshal, earl of Pembroke. William de Briouze had been executed by Llywelyn ab Iorwerth in 1230 for his illicit relationship with Llywelyn's wife, Joan, and his estate divided among his three daughters. When the last of the sons of William (II) Marshal died without heirs in December 1245, the great Marshal patrimony also passed to Eva de Briouze and her Marshal sisters. His marriage to Maud thus greatly augmented Mortimer's holdings in the march, and he acquired Radnor, portions of Brecon, and a share in the holdings of the earls Marshal which included lands in Ireland. The marriage propelled the Mortimer family into the first rank of the English baronage, and the extinction of the Marshal and Briouze lines drastically altered the political character of the Welsh march. Maud's inheritance proved problematic as well however, and the royal government's sloth and inefficiency in distributing these estates was probably one reason for Mortimer's early support of the baronial reform movement. Mortimer's share of his wife's estate was not finally determined until February 1259, but the settlement continued to be controversial into the next decade. Similarly contentious was Mortimer's loss to the crown earlier in the decade of the Gloucestershire manors of Lechlade and Longborough and their grant to Richard of Cornwall. Mortimer's attempts to recover them continued for several years and likewise helped to direct his political decisions.

In the march of Wales and England, 1253–1260 Personal grievances apart, the primary reason for Mortimer's prominent involvement in the reform movement was the steady erosion of his position in Wales under military pressure from Llywelyn ap Gruffudd. After the death of Llywelyn ab Iorwerth in 1240 the Mortimers were able to re-establish their lordship over the Welsh cantrefs of Gwrtheyrnion and Maelienydd which they had held sporadically for a century or more. But after Llywelyn ap Gruffudd gained control of Gwynedd in 1255 that lordship was challenged once again. At the Whitsuntide court of 1253 at Winchester, Mortimer was knighted by Henry III. In August he went with the king to Gascony where he served until the following year. Upon his return he found that Llywelyn was threatening to recover all the lands his grandfather had held at his death. In 1256 Llywelyn deprived Mortimer of Gwrtheyrnion without provoking the slightest response from the king's government. On 18 January 1257 Mortimer received letters of protection while engaged in the king's service in Wales. Later that year the king promised him 200 marks in gold to assist him in resisting the growing power of Llywelyn, but by the following year 100 marks of this sum was still owing. On 11 June 1259 Mortimer was among those commissioned to treat with Llywelyn, and on the 25th he joined in concluding a truce that was to last for a year from 1 August. But on 10 January 1260 Llywelyn took the cantref of Builth from Mortimer who was holding it as Prince Edward's representative, and on 17 July Llywelyn's men took the castle itself and destroyed it. The loss of this strategic castle was a great blow to Mortimer's reputation. He had been in London at the time of the attack, pursuing his claim to Lechlade and Longborough, and although Henry and Edward issued a writ absolving him of any blame, the affair led to an estrangement between Mortimer and Edward who then supported Simon de Montfort.

At first a strong supporter of reform Mortimer attended the parliament at Oxford of June 1258 where he was one of the twelve chosen by the barons to serve with the twelve chosen by the king. He served on the council of fifteen, and was among those appointed to negotiate an aid for the king. On 18 October he attested the king's proclamation upholding the provisions of Oxford. In July 1259 Mortimer was present at the confirmation of the treaty with France, and in October the provisions of Westminster directed that Mortimer and Philip Basset be in attendance on the justiciar. In May of 1260, however, Mortimer was granted custody of Hereford Castle by a council already beginning to fragment. Concern for the deteriorating situation on the march brought him into the camp of Richard de Clare, earl of Gloucester, and Edward's alliance with Simon de Montfort and his reluctance to forgive Mortimer for the loss of Builth began to drive a wedge between Mortimer and the baronial cause. The king at this time also began actively to woo certain members of the baronial party. On 3 August Mortimer was granted 60 marks at the exchequer in lieu of a fee that Henry promised to provide him out of his wards or escheats. Later that year Mortimer received various other gifts out of the king's resources, and in December Mortimer and four others, now described as *de familia regis*, were granted Christmas robes.

When the king blamed the barons in the spring of 1261 for what he called his disherison in Wales, the barons replied that the castle of Builth had been Edward's anyway, and laid the blame for its loss on Mortimer alone. Thus abandoned by the barons, Mortimer was already a supporter of the crown when on 7 December the king formally pardoned him for his participation in the barons' movement. Though his loyalties remained unsettled for some time, from this point he was an increasingly fervent supporter of the king's cause.

English politics and warfare in Wales, 1260–1265 In the summer of 1260, however, Mortimer's most pressing concerns were in the march. It looked then as though a serious effort might be made to block Llywelyn's advances. In August Mortimer was entrusted with letters from the archbishop of Canterbury to the bishops of Bangor and St Asaph excommunicating Llywelyn and placing his lands under interdict. At the same time Mortimer was summoned along with Gloucester to join the king's army against Llywelyn. Llywelyn had everything to gain, however, by biding his time, and to Mortimer's disappointment war was averted by a two-year truce concluded on 22 August. Mortimer apparently did not wait for the expiry of the truce however, and in June 1262 Llywelyn was seeking redress from the king for Mortimer's violation of its terms. In November the same year the men of Maelienydd took matters into their own hands. They transferred their loyalties to Llywelyn and took the castles of Knucklas, Bleddfa, and Cefnllys. Mortimer and his retinue were allowed to depart unharmed after the fall of Cefnllys, giving rise to rumours of treachery, and the bishop of Hereford reported to the king that the whole march was in confusion. On 9 February 1263 Mortimer and the other marchers were granted letters of protection to midsummer or for as long as the Welsh war should last. In March John de Grey reported that more men in the southern and middle march had gone over to Llywelyn, and though he and Mortimer beat the 'woods and glens' (Edwards 17–19) they were unable to force a decisive confrontation. In November the marchers' letters of protection were renewed, and in December Mortimer was appointed *custos pacis* of the counties of Shropshire and Staffordshire.

By this time the Welsh cause was increasingly associated with that of the barons, and Mortimer's position in the march was correspondingly more difficult. His relations with Montfort had been strained since Henry granted several manors in the march to the latter in 1259. In late June 1263, in circumstances which remain obscure, Mortimer joined Montfort in the defence of the Channel ports, but their rapprochement did not last, and by October Mortimer was back in the king's camp. In mid-December relations between the two men deteriorated further when, perhaps as a stratagem to prevent Montfort attending the impending meeting at Amiens, the king gave three of the earl's manors in Hereford to Mortimer. These manors Mortimer promptly devastated, ransoming the earl's bailiff of Dilwyn for 200 marks. In January 1264 Mortimer was among those who agreed to the arbitration of Louis IX, and his dispute with the earl of Leicester was clearly laid out in the barons' complaints. Montfort refused to accept the mise of Amiens, however, and sent his sons Henry and Simon to attack Mortimer in the march. Mortimer's *caput* at Wigmore was taken, along with the castles of Roger Clifford and Thomas Corbet. Edward, returning from France too late to save Wigmore, re-established his lifelong friendship with Mortimer by turning over to him the castles of Huntingdon and Hay taken from Humphrey (V) de Bohun.

Mortimer played a leading role in the siege of Northampton in April 1264 and he and his marchers took a great number of captives there. Montfort's counter-stroke at Lewes the following month resulted in the capture of nearly all the royalist army save Mortimer and his marchers. Lest Llywelyn completely overrun England, the marchers were allowed to return to their lands in arms on the condition that Edward and Henry of Almain remain as hostages. On 7 July Mortimer and the others were summoned to deliver the prisoners taken at Northampton as required by the mise of Lewes. But the marchers disclaimed knowledge of the agreement and sent only messengers instead. Accordingly they were summoned again on 24 August, and, although Mortimer gave his son William as hostage for his good behaviour, the marchers continued to refuse throughout the rest of the summer either to give up their prisoners or come to Montfort's council at Oxford in the autumn. Finally an army was assembled to compel them. Early that winter Montfort, now openly colluding with Llywelyn, fell upon the march. Taking the castles of Hereford and Hay, and putting Mortimer's lordships to the torch, Montfort drove all the way to Montgomery forcing the marchers to seek terms. On 12 December at Worcester it was agreed that Mortimer and the other leading marchers should go to Ireland for a year and a day. The marchers repeatedly managed to defer their departure however, buying time for defectors like John Giffard and Gilbert de Clare to swell their ranks while Montfort's government began to crumble around him. Hoping to stem the tide, Montfort marched on Gloucester taking Edward with him, still a hostage. On 28 May Mortimer engineered his friend Edward's escape from his keepers at Hereford, taking him first to Wigmore and then to Ludlow where he joined forces with Gilbert de Clare and reignited the civil war that culminated at the battle of Evesham. Mortimer commanded one of the three divisions of the royalist force on 4 August 1265 when Simon de Montfort was finally slain—according to a chronicle account in College of Arms MS 3/23B, first published in 2000, he himself struck the blow which killed his adversary. The marchers dismembered the earl's body on the battlefield and sent his head as a grisly gift to Mortimer's wife at Wigmore.

Growing prominence, 1265–1274 In the aftermath of the war Mortimer was equally savage in pursuit of gain at the expense of the king's erstwhile enemies. He was at the September parliament at Winchester where he is described by Rishanger as being greedy for spoils (Rishanger, *Chronicle*, 49). Nor was he disappointed, for he was richly rewarded with the lands of the king's enemies, including the entire county and honour of Oxford forfeited by Robert de Vere. He served as sheriff of Hereford from Easter 1266 to Michaelmas 1267, and on 4 May 1266 he was appointed with Edmund the king's son to repress the king's enemies. Shortly thereafter, on 15 May, he suffered a terrible defeat at the hands of the Welsh in Brecon, barely escaping with his life. In June Mortimer commanded one of the three divisions of the king's army at the siege of Kenilworth, and after the dictum of Kenilworth was established, Mortimer quarrelled violently with Gilbert de Clare, insisting on the harshest possible interpretation of the terms by which the disinherited should recover their lands. Gloucester's more moderate view prevailed, however, and Mortimer had to accept a fine from Robert de Vere for the restoration of his honour of Oxford. This fine was accompanied by a marriage agreement concerning de Vere's son and Mortimer's daughter Margaret. In November 1266 Mortimer received a charter withdrawing his manor of Cleobury from all suits to either county or hundred courts, in effect making it an autonomous marcher liberty.

The war in Wales was brought to a close on 25 September 1267 with the treaty of Montgomery, which was nothing less than a triumph for Llywelyn. After a decade of war with the Welsh, Mortimer's status in the march was no better than when he began. Llywelyn was granted nearly all he had won including Maelienydd if he could prove his right to it. The only concession to Mortimer was that, until Llywelyn could show such proofs, Mortimer should be allowed to build a castle there. Although he had lost ground in Wales, Mortimer's support of the king and his friendship with the king's son had made him a great power in England. When Edward went on crusade in August 1270, Mortimer was one of those chosen as trustee for his children and estates. When Henry III died in 1272, these trustees, especially Mortimer, Philip Basset, and Robert Burnell, were virtual regents until Edward's return in August 1274.

If the realm was well governed during Edward's absence it was because of the diligent efforts of these regents. Mortimer was active in quelling a rising in the north just after the old king's death. He responded swiftly and effectively to reports of Reynold de Grey's rapacity as justiciar of Chester. Indeed Mortimer seemed bent on repairing the damage done by the barons' wars. He mended fences with his recent enemy, Gilbert de Clare, and went with him in 1272 or 1273 along the rivers of the south issuing instructions for the repair of bridges. Close co-operation between Gloucester and the regents served good government, but it also served the private interests of both Clare and Mortimer who wished to undermine the strong position in the march occupied by Llywelyn ap Gruffudd after the treaty of Montgomery. Unreconciled to their losses under the treaty, marcher lords like Mortimer kept up their pressure on Llywelyn, who complained in 1273 or 1274 that Mortimer was fortifying his castle of Cefnllys in violation of the agreement of 1267. In response to this harassment in the march, Llywelyn refused in 1273 to offer his fealty to the new king. He also ceased payment on the fine imposed by the treaty, pushing relations between England and Wales towards their final breakdown.

Final years and death, 1274–1282 In the closing years of his life Mortimer played a prominent role in Edward I's conquest of Wales, and was finally able to reverse the encroachments of his kinsman Llywelyn upon his lordships there. In November 1276 Mortimer was appointed one of the guarantors of Llywelyn's safe conduct in coming to the king to do homage. Llywelyn did not come however, and Mortimer and the other magnates decided that the king should again take arms against him. Three days later Edward named Mortimer captain of Shropshire, Staffordshire, and Herefordshire. Mortimer and the earl of Lincoln led one of the three armies sent into Wales where they restored Gruffudd ap Gwenwynwyn to his territories and recovered Cedewain, Ceri, Gwrtheyrnion, and Builth for the king. In 1277 they besieged Llywelyn's great castle of Dolforwyn and took it in a fortnight. Llywelyn soon sought terms, and the treaty of Conwy was concluded on 9 November. In 1279, for his service in this war, Edward awarded Mortimer the lordships of Ceri and Cedewain and Dolforwyn Castle, and made him keeper of all of west Wales. Curiously, in spite of all the blood between them, Mortimer and his old enemy Llywelyn struck an agreement in 1281, swearing to aid each other in peace and war.

Mortimer had already retired in 1279, celebrating the occasion at Kenilworth with a great tournament which he called a 'round table'. His military career was not quite over however, as his commission as captain was renewed in March of 1282 for Edward's final Welsh campaign. That summer Mortimer fell ill and sought confirmation of his will from Archbishop Pecham. On 26 October 1282 Roger Mortimer died at Kingsland, Herefordshire, and was buried at the family's priory of Wigmore. The next day Edward granted a singular favour, ensuring that the execution of his will would not be impeded on account of his debts at the exchequer. This is perhaps why there was never a complete *inquisition post mortem* for Mortimer's lands. The only such inquisition was for lands held in right of his wife. Edward's sorrow at the death of his longstanding friend is plain in the letter he wrote to Mortimer's son, Roger Mortimer of Chirk. That friendship is memorialized in Mortimer's epitaph as well, along with the observation that 'all Wales feared his power' (Dugdale, *Monasticon*, 6.355). Mortimer was a ruthless and determined man, jealous of the privileges that his family had acquired in the march, eager to define them further and to secure more. His marriage to Maud de Briouze made him one of the wealthiest men in England; his military service against Llywelyn ap Gruffudd and his friendship with Edward I made him indispensable in the conquest of Wales; and his service to the royal government gave him influence and power far beyond the essentially local importance enjoyed by his predecessors in the Welsh march. With Roger the Mortimer family had achieved comital rank in all but title. Building on this foundation

his successors attained the appropriate title as well: the earls of March.

Roger Mortimer and Maud de Briouze had at least four sons. Ralph (III), the eldest, was called to the parliament of 1271 along with his father; he succeeded his uncle Hugh Mortimer of Chelmarsh as sheriff of Shropshire and Staffordshire while his father was co-regent, and died childless before 10 August 1274. Edmund (I), the second son, had been destined for the church, but succeeded his father as baron of Wigmore. It was he who was responsible for the death of Llywelyn ap Gruffudd only a few months after that of his father. Edmund married Margaret Fiennes, a kinswoman of Eleanor of Castile, and was the father of Roger (V) *Mortimer, first earl of March. The third son, Roger (IV) *Mortimer of Chirk, married Lucy Wafre, and died in the Tower of London on 3 August 1326. William, who was hostage for his father in 1264, married Hawise, daughter and heir of Robert de Mucegros, and died without children before June 1297. Roger and Maud had at least two daughters: Margaret, who married Robert de Vere, sixth earl of Oxford; and Isabel, who married John (III) Fitzalan and was the mother of Richard (I) *Fitzalan, earl of Arundel. J. J. CRUMP

Sources Chancery records · *Ann. mon.* · R. F. Treharne and I. J. Sanders, eds., *Documents of the baronial movement of reform and rebellion, 1258–1267* (1973) · J. R. Maddicott, *Simon de Montfort* (1994) · R. F. Treharne, *The baronial plan of reform, 1258–1263* (1932) · J. E. Lloyd, *A history of Wales from the earliest times to the Edwardian conquest*, 3rd edn, 2 vols. (1939); repr. (1988) · F. M. Powicke, *King Henry III and the Lord Edward: the community of the realm in the thirteenth century*, 2 vols. (1947) · [W. Rishanger], *The chronicle of William de Rishanger, of the barons' wars*, ed. J. O. Halliwell, CS, 15 (1840) · T. Jones, ed. and trans., *Brut y tywysogyon, or, The chronicle of the princes: Red Book of Hergest* (1955) · R. W. Eyton, *Antiquities of Shropshire*, 12 vols. (1854–60) · H. R. Luard, ed., *Flores historiarum*, 3 vols., Rolls Series, 95 (1890) · J. G. Edwards, *Calendar of ancient correspondence concerning Wales* (1935) · Dugdale, *Monasticon*, new edn · BL, Cotton MS Nero A.iv, fol. 43v · *CIPM*, 4, no. 41 · D. A. Carpenter, 'A noble in politics: Roger Mortimer in the period of baronial reform and rebellion, 1258–1265', *Nobles and nobility in medieval Europe*, ed. A. Duggan (2000), 183–203 · O. De Laborderie, J. R. Maddicott, and D. A. Carpenter, 'The last hours of Simon de Montfort: a new account', *EngHR*, 115 (2000), 378–412 · private information (2004) [Dr Susan Stewart]

Mortimer, Roger (IV), first Lord Mortimer of Chirk (c.1256–1326), baron, was the third son of Roger (III) de *Mortimer (1231–1282), lord of Wigmore, and his wife, Maud (or Matilda) de Briouze (d. 1300/01), and the uncle of Roger (V) *Mortimer (d. 1330), eighth lord of Wigmore and first earl of March. Edmund (I) de Mortimer, his surviving elder brother, the seventh lord of Wigmore, was born in or before 1255, and it is probable that Roger was born not much later than 1256.

Early career Unlike Edmund, who had been destined for the church, Roger Mortimer was knighted in his father's lifetime. In 1281 he received licence to hunt the fox and hare throughout Shropshire and Staffordshire, provided that he took none of the king's great game (chiefly stags). On 31 October 1282, following his father's death, Edward I wrote to Mortimer urging him to attend to his duties in combating the Welsh uprising under the orders of Roger

Lestrange (d. 1311), who had succeeded to the senior Mortimer's command in the march of Wales. The king expressed the hope that he would recover in the son something of what he had lost by the father's death, and conveyed that he might thus be the more strongly bound to Mortimer in the future. Mortimer had in fact already secured the first of the major grants of forfeited lands of Welsh princes to be made to English magnates. By a charter of 2 June the lands of one of the heirs of Gruffudd ap Madog (d. 1269) of Powys Fadog, Llywelyn ap Gruffudd ap Madog, who had risen in rebellion upon the outbreak of hostilities, were granted to Mortimer. The lands of Nanheudwy, Cynllaith, and Mochnant Is Rhaeadr came to form the lordship of Chirk, and its lord became known as Mortimer of Chirk. He built at Chirk a large and formidable castle.

Lands and liaisons Mortimer's brother Edmund was given livery of his inheritance on 24 November 1282 after a delay which may suggest that he did not enjoy the favour evidently extended to his younger brother. The lands, which included the lordships of Maelienydd and Gwrtheyrnion, were retained in the king's hands and his officers were concerned for the fidelity of the Welsh communities in the absence of a lord. The uncertain loyalties of the Mortimer tenants may, however, have lent credence to a ruse by which Edmund, anxious perhaps to curry the king's favour, was able to draw Prince Llywelyn ap Gruffudd to the march in the neighbourhood of the Mortimer lands. Llywelyn was killed in combat near Builth on 11 December 1282, and Roger Mortimer was among the commanders of forces deployed in the area. Those killed in the engagement included Llywelyn ap Gruffudd ap Madog, whose estates had already been granted to Roger.

At the same time Mortimer was accused by Archbishop Pecham, who was then making a visitation of the vacant diocese of Hereford, of adultery with Margaret, wife of Roger of Radnor, and other women. He aggravated his offence by putting into prison a chaplain who had reproved him for his sins. Pecham, fearing that on his leaving the district Mortimer might get off scot-free, empowered the bishop of Llandaff to act for him and impose canonical penance.

By his marriage with Lucy Wafre, daughter and heir of Robert Wafre, Mortimer secured the lordships of Pencelli and Tir Ralph in the honour of Brecon. He held them as a tenant of Humphrey (VI) de Bohun, earl of Hereford (d. 1298), against whom, from 1279 onwards, he brought a series of actions *coram rege* claiming that Bohun had failed to do him justice in his court of Brecon. In 1310 Mortimer secured a grant for life of the lordship of Blaenllyfni, formerly held by Reginald Fitzpeter, which he received in fee six years later. He also possessed the lordship of Narberth and a third of St Clears, lands that were partly of the inheritance of his mother.

Military service, 1287–1306 Upon the rebellion of Rhys ap Maredudd of Ystrad Tywi (d. 1292) in the summer of 1287 Mortimer was among the marchers required to provide soldiers from their lands and commanded to remain in their lordships. The Roger Mortimer engaged in the conflict in west Wales during the campaign, and captured when Rhys took Newcastle Emlyn in November, was another person of that name who held lands in the commotes of Is Coed and Genau'r-glyn in Cardiganshire. When rebellion again occurred in Wales in 1294 Mortimer was taking part in the expedition to Gascony and, on the recapture of Bourg and Blaye, was made joint governor of those towns. He was again in Gascony three years later. In 1298 he served on a commission of array to raise Welsh foot soldiers for Scotland, and served in the campaigns against the Scots in 1300 and 1301. He was among those present at the siege of Caerlaverock in 1300, and he and William of Leybourne were appointed as guides and guardians of Prince Edward. Mortimer was first summoned to parliament as a baron in 1299, and at Lincoln in 1301 he was among those who subscribed to a letter of the barons, prepared for dispatch to Pope Boniface VIII, asserting the rights of the king of England over Scotland. He was in Scotland in 1303 and again in 1306, when he was among several barons who incurred the king's displeasure for leaving the army without permission and whose lands were for a time seized on that account.

Service under Edward II, 1307–1320 Following the accession of Edward II, Mortimer was restored to favour and, though the lordship of Blaenllyfni was subject to resumption under the ordinances of 1311, he was not permanently disadvantaged. On 15 February 1308 he took up the office of justice of north Wales and fifteen days later the same office in south Wales. After a break from 19 February 1314 to 23 November 1316 in north Wales, and from 3 April to 30 October 1317 in south Wales, he was appointed to the offices for life and held them until 1322. In June 1309 he was ordered to take possession of the lands of Gruffudd de la Pole (also known as Gruffudd ab Owain), the recently deceased heir to Owen de la Pole's lordship of Powys. In the ensuing dispute in which another Gruffudd de la Pole, Owen's brother, challenging the succession of John Charlton and Hawise de la Pole, laid siege to Welshpool Castle, Mortimer was ordered to raise the siege and was employed in efforts to achieve a solution. In 1316, along with Humphrey (VII) de Bohun, earl of Hereford (c.1276–1322), and his nephew, Roger (V) Mortimer of Wigmore, he was engaged in putting down the rebellion of Llywelyn Bren (d. 1318) in Glamorgan. They received Llywelyn's surrender, and the Mortimers were with Bohun when, evidently concerned at the fate that might befall the rebel if the influence of Hugh Despenser the younger were to prevail, he urged the king not to make any harsh decision until the earl had the opportunity to speak to him. As justice over the whole extent of the principality of Wales, Mortimer exercised great power and aroused considerable animosity among leading members of the Welsh community for the severity of his rule. He incurred particularly the wrath of *Gruffudd Llwyd, the crown's leading servant among the men of north Wales, who probably held Mortimer responsible for his prolonged imprisonment in 1316–17. His Welsh adversaries were to seize the opportunity to wreak their retribution in 1322.

Rebellion, imprisonment, and death The Mortimers, who had themselves negotiated with William de Briouze (d. 1326) for the purchase of the lordship of Gower, were among the marchers incensed by Hugh Despenser's action in persuading the king to take the lordship into his hands in December 1320 on the pretext that John Mowbray, Briouze's son-in-law, had taken possession without royal licence. Regarded as a breach of the custom of the march, the decision was one instance of the Despensers' presumptuousness, greed, and control over the king's will which made the Mortimers prominent participants in a baronial alliance against them. Roger Mortimer of Chirk and his nephew were among the marchers who joined Humphrey (VII) de Bohun upon an invasion of Glamorgan in May 1321 and who, formally pardoned, forced Despenser's exile from the kingdom three months later. They were present at a gathering at Sherburn in Elmet in June 1321 when Thomas, earl of Lancaster, and the marchers affirmed their alliance for the further prosecution of the Despensers. At the end of the year the marchers were forced to hurry from another meeting with the earl at Doncaster to meet the king's forces moving westwards to the march. By the beginning of 1322 Edward II advanced to the Severn, first at Worcester and then at Shrewsbury, where he achieved a crossing on 14 January. The Mortimers' resistance was broken by the advance from the principality of north Wales of forces brought to the king's aid by Gruffudd Llwyd. He was able to take a number of marcher strongholds, including Chirk. Mortimer surrendered on 22 January, and, along with his nephew, was imprisoned in the Tower of London. The process against them charged them with treason. Mortimer of Chirk was spared his life but his lands were forfeited. In April 1322 Edward summoned twenty-four men from north Wales and the same number from south Wales to the York parliament where petitions were presented enumerating the injuries inflicted by Mortimer of Chirk upon the king's tenants in his Welsh lands. Roger Mortimer of Wigmore escaped in 1323, but his uncle remained imprisoned in the Tower and died there, after years of severe captivity, on 3 August 1326. The Wigmore chronicle states that he was buried with his ancestors at the priory of Wigmore, by Adam Orleton, bishop of Hereford, on 14 September.

Fate of the Mortimer estate, 1322–1359 Roger (III) Mortimer and Lucy, who died in 1324, had a son named Roger, who succeeded to the inheritance of his maternal grandfather in Pencelli and Tir Ralph and at Tedstone Wafer in Herefordshire. Chirk and the other lands were taken by Roger (V) Mortimer of Wigmore (d. 1330). When the latter's estates were forfeited in 1330, Roger, the heir of Roger (IV) of Chirk, and then his son John, each made efforts to recover the estate but to no avail. Chirk was granted to Richard (II) Fitzalan, earl of Arundel, in 1332. The younger Roger, who married Joan de Turberville, left as his heir his son John, who in 1359, from among the lands once held by

his grandfather, quitclaimed Blaenllyfni, Narberth, and St Clears to the earl of March and Chirk to the earl of Arundel. The baronial estate that had been created by the initiative of Roger (III) Mortimer and royal favour in the late thirteenth century had thereby ceased to exist.

LLINOS SMITH

Sources PRO · *Chancery records* · Dugdale, *Monasticon*, new edn · GEC, *Peerage* · R. R. Davies, *Lordship and society in the march of Wales, 1282–1400* (1978) · J. R. Maddicott, *Thomas of Lancaster, 1307–1322: a study in the reign of Edward II* (1970) · J. B. Smith, 'Edward II and the allegiance of Wales', *Welsh History Review / Cylchgrawn Hanes Cymru*, 8 (1976–7), 139–71 · J. C. Davies, *The baronial opposition to Edward II* (1918) · G. Williams, ed., *Glamorgan county history*, 3: *The middle ages*, ed. T. B. Pugh (1971) · L. B. Smith, 'The death of Llywelyn ap Gruffydd: the narratives reconsidered', *Welsh History Review / Cylchgrawn Hanes Cymru*, 11 (1982–3), 200–13 · R. A. Griffiths and R. S. Thomas, *The principality of Wales in the later middle ages: the structure and personnel of government*, 1: *South Wales, 1277–1536* (1972) · R. W. Eyton, *Antiquities of Shropshire*, 12 vols. (1854–60) · [Walter of Exeter?], *The siege of Carlaverock … with a translation, a history of the castle and memoirs of the personages commemorated by the poet*, ed. and trans. N. H. Nicolas (1828)

Mortimer, Roger (V), first earl of March (1287–1330), regent, soldier, and magnate, was the son and heir of Edmund (I) de Mortimer, lord of Wigmore, and his wife, Margaret de Fiennes.

Early years and territorial power Roger Mortimer was born in April or May 1287. On the death of his father in July 1304 his wardship was granted to Piers *Gaveston, the favourite of Edward, prince of Wales. He was given livery of his lands in April 1306 while still under age and on 22 May 1306 was knighted by Edward I, along with Edward, prince of Wales, Edmund Fitzalan, earl of Arundel, and a large crowd of bachelors. He was first summoned to parliament as Roger Mortimer of Wigmore in February 1307. The Wigmore Priory chronicle reports that Mortimer gave Gaveston 2500 marks to recover his lands before the end of his minority and for the right to choose his own marriage partner. In fact he had already been betrothed on 20 September 1301, during his father's lifetime, to Joan (1286–1356), the only daughter of Peter (d. 1292) and Joan de Geneville. It was a singularly important marriage for the Mortimer family. Two of the daughters of Peter and Joan de Geneville became nuns at the priory of Acornbury, Herefordshire, leaving their sister Joan as sole heir to the large Geneville inheritance currently held by her grandfather, Geoffrey de Geneville.

Roger Mortimer was already a powerful landowner in respect of his paternal inheritance. His family had been lords of Wigmore in western Herefordshire since the days of William I and had pushed thence deep into central Wales. But it was from the late thirteenth century—partly through marriage links to the Marshal and Briouze families and especially through the munificence of Edward I—that the Mortimers graduated to be among the most prominent of English baronial families. By 1304 the Mortimers, in addition to the family headquarters at Wigmore and manors in Herefordshire, Shropshire, Gloucestershire, and Worcestershire, also held seven important marcher lordships, mainly in the uplands of central Wales

(Maelienydd, Gwrtheyrnion, Cwmwd Deuddwr, Radnor, Ceri, and Cedewain), but with outliers in south-west Wales (Narberth and a third share of St Clears). They also owned properties in southern England and, from the Briouze–Marshal connection, in Ireland (especially Dunamase in co. Leix). It is true that more than half of these Mortimer lands were in the hands of Roger's mother, Margaret, and since she outlived him (dying in February 1334) he never enjoyed the whole of his paternal inheritance.

However, Mortimer's misfortune in this respect was more than counterbalanced by the Geneville inheritance which came under his control through his wife. These estates greatly consolidated Roger Mortimer's territorial power in western England and the march of Wales. They included half of Ludlow—which soon became a favourite Mortimer residence—a group of manors in Shropshire, and the marcher lordship of Ewyas Lacy. But it was in Ireland that the Geneville estates transformed Roger Mortimer's power and standing. They included the castle of Trim and a share of the great Lacy liberty of Meath. These Irish lands—worth at least £300 p.a.—were formally transferred to Roger Mortimer and Joan, his wife, in December 1307 by Joan's grandfather, Geoffrey de Geneville, who retired into the house of the Dominicans in Trim.

Career in Ireland, 1308–1320 Much of Mortimer's career during the next twelve years was to be spent in Ireland where he was now one of the premier English landowners. He and his wife first crossed to Ireland in October 1308 and returned there twice in the next two years. He was soon securing privileges for his estates there—such as a seven-year grant of murage and pavage (licences to levy tolls for walls and paving) for his town of Trim and, most valuable of all, in July 1310 the restoration of full liberty rights (including chancery and exchequer) in the lordship of Trim. But power in Ireland also brought with it challenges and responsibilities, as Mortimer was to discover from 1315. Edward Bruce, brother of Robert I of Scotland, landed at Larne on 25 May 1315. In early December 1315 Roger Mortimer's forces were defeated by Bruce (partly, according to the Dublin annals, because of the desertion of some of Mortimer's troops) and Mortimer fled to Dublin. He spent most of 1316 in England and Wales. On 23 November 1316 he was appointed justiciar of Ireland with the responsibility of defeating Edward Bruce, quelling the risings of the native Irish, and sorting out the quarrels and bitter recriminations among the English communities in Ireland. Crossing from Haverfordwest with a large army he arrived at Youghal on 7 April 1317. During the next twelve months he dealt vigorously and effectively with a whole host of problems in Ireland: he secured the release of Richard de Burgh, earl of Ulster, who had been imprisoned in Dublin for suspected complicity with Edward Bruce, in May 1317; he defeated and eventually exiled the Lacy family of Rathwire, who were claimants to the Irish lands of Mortimer's wife and who had likewise allegedly collaborated with Bruce; he held a parliament outside Dublin in June; he led forays against the Irish in the Wicklow Mountains; and generally reimposed the

government's authority in the south and south-west of Ireland. When Mortimer was recalled to England on 5 May 1318, Edward Bruce's forces were still entrenched in north-east Ireland, but in October of that year Edward himself was killed and his forces crushed at the battle of Faughart.

Roger Mortimer's record in Ireland in 1317–18 was one of which he could be proud. It is no wonder that he was reappointed justiciar there in March 1319, taking up his office in June of that year. He was also entrusted with the custody of the royal castles of Roscommon, Randown, and Athlone. During his second period in office Mortimer seems to have pursued a policy of reconciliation towards the Irish, and was given power to receive into English law all Irishmen who wished to come to it. In May 1320 he held a parliament at Dublin, issued statutes regarding order and administrative efficiency, and initiated a review to see which items of English legislation should be appropriately applied to Ireland. When he departed for England in September 1320 the citizens of Dublin, not normally noted for paying compliments, commended his efforts 'in saving and keeping the peace' (Gilbert, 392). As he became increasingly involved in English politics in 1321 he did not forget his Irish interests. At Wigmore on 11 February 1321 he concluded a marriage agreement whereby he granted to one of his sons, Roger, all his Irish lands on the occasion of Roger junior's marriage to Joan, daughter of Sir Edmund Butler, who paid £1000 for the marriage.

Career in England and Wales to 1321 Up to 1318 Roger Mortimer's career in England was by no means exceptional or particularly noteworthy. He was given a ceremonial role in Edward II's coronation in 1308 and was present at the great gathering of earls, barons, and knights at Dunstable for a tournament in late March–early April 1309. He was naturally called upon to raise troops from Wales for service in Scotland and went to Gascony on the king's behalf in 1313. Returning from Ireland in late 1315, he was soon involved in repressing the revolt of Llywelyn Bren in Glamorgan in February–March 1316. The fact that Llywelyn was executed by the younger Despenser two years later may well have served to inflame Mortimer's growing dislike of Despenser, especially as one of the other leaders of the Welsh revolt, Llywelyn ap Madog ap Hywel, was pardoned specifically at Mortimer's request. Later, in July 1316, Roger Mortimer was one of those who helped to suppress a revolt in Bristol.

There was nothing as yet to suggest that Mortimer was involved in the tensions of English politics. He did, it is true, support the king's chamberlain, John Charlton, in his bid to secure the lordship of Powys; and given the political alignments of the period, this could be seen as identifying him with the king's supporters. But local rather than national political considerations probably shaped his decision. Roger Mortimer's primary concern in these years was to arrange for the future of his estates and of his growing family. In May 1315 he had provided 100 librates of rent for his son John. In May 1316 he made a contract whereby his eldest son and heir, Edmund, was to be married to Elizabeth, daughter of Bartholomew Badlesmere.

Badlesmere paid 2000 marks for the marriage and in return Roger endowed his son and daughter-in-law with the Mortimer manors in Somerset and Buckinghamshire and the reversion of lands in the western shires of England and the march of Wales, and granted five Mortimer manors to Elizabeth for life and a reversionary interest in 200 marks of rent. It was a marriage link with portentous consequences for the future.

The rewards of service which Mortimer picked up were modest: the grant of Cwmwd Deuddwr in the Welsh uplands in August 1309; the constableship of Builth Castle in February 1310; and the marriage of the heir of Nicholas Audley (specifically for his service in Ireland) in December 1316. His circle of followers was also as yet largely drawn from the Mortimer estates—families such as the Harleys and Hakluyts and individuals such as Hugh Trumpington, who was later appointed constable of Kildare Castle at Mortimer's request and was killed defending his lord in 1330.

It was with his return from Ireland in May 1318 that Roger Mortimer began to occupy a much more prominent role in English politics. His own record in Ireland may have stood him in good stead; so doubtless did the marriage link with Bartholomew Badlesmere (promoted to be steward of the household in October 1318); and so did the fact that he was regarded as a political neutral in the venomous politics of the period. His growing stature and acceptability were demonstrated by the fact that he was a member of the delegation which conducted negotiations between Edward II and Thomas of Lancaster in July 1318, culminating eventually in the treaty of Leake on 9 August 1318. Mortimer was a member of the standing council of sixteen appointed under the terms of the treaty and he served as such until spring 1319. He was also placed on the commission appointed to reform the royal household. Mortimer's personal fortune as well as his public standing was also rising rapidly. On 20 July 1318 he was granted a handsome share worth 1600 marks in the marriage of the heir to the earldom of Warwick—a clear indication of his status. Marriage links further enhanced his power in the west: in 1319 one of his daughters married the son and heir of Maurice, Lord Berkeley, and another daughter married John Charlton, likewise son and heir of the lord of Powys.

When Roger Mortimer returned from Ireland in September 1320 he found that the political situation had altered yet again in England. The Despensers, father and son, were now monopolizing the king's ear and using every opportunity to feed their insatiable greed for land and power in the most ruthless fashion. Roger Mortimer, like all the barons of the Welsh march, had a particular reason for fear. It was to the southern march of Wales that the younger Despenser's ambitions were especially directed. Personal venom was added to territorial greed, for a well-informed chronicle suggests that the younger Despenser was anxious that the Mortimers should now pay the price for his grandfather's death at the battle of Evesham (1265) at the hands of Roger Mortimer (*d*. 1282). The immediate trigger for the confrontation between the

Mortimers—both Roger and his uncle and namesake, Roger (IV) *Mortimer of Chirk—and the Despensers lay in the dispute over the lordship of Gower. The Mortimers were only one of several marcher families who believed that they had paid a deposit on the succession to the lordship on the death of its indigent lord, William (VII) de Briouze. Edward II, however, was intent that the younger Despenser should add Gower to his vast territorial empire in the march, and on a legal technicality he ordered the seizure of the lordship in November 1320. It was an action which drove Mortimer, and most of the other marcher lords, into open defiance.

An opponent of the king, and a prisoner in the Tower By early 1321 the rift that had now opened between Edward II and the lords of the southern march over Despenser's ambitions, especially regarding Gower, was irreparable. The earl of Hereford, Hugh Audley, Roger Damory, and Roger Clifford were prominent opponents of Despenser; but the two Mortimers were particularly singled out by contemporaries as fomenters of the quarrel. In February 1321 Roger Mortimer was formally replaced as justiciar of Ireland. By now the marcher dissidents were holding discussions with the earl of Lancaster, and by late March–April 1321 repeated royal commands were issued to the marcher lords (including Roger Mortimer) to keep the peace and not to devastate Despenser's lands. But such commands and prohibitions were in vain. Roger Mortimer took a prominent part in the five-day rampage through the Despenser lordships in south Wales from 4 to 9 May 1321. He was involved in the taking of Cardiff Castle on 9 May, and led its constable as prisoner to his own castle at Wigmore; he also seized the earl of Arundel's castle at Clun and took the homage of the tenants of the lordship.

Mortimer was now, along with other marchers, firmly allied to the king's opponents. He was present at the assembly convoked by the earl of Lancaster at Sherburn in Elmet on 28 June 1321, with the purpose, at least in part, of forging closer bonds between the earl and the marchers and preparing the ground for drafting an indictment against the Despensers. Mortimer and the other marchers then moved towards London. He was supported by troops 'all clothed in green, with their right sleeves yellow' (Dugdale, *Monasticon*, 6, pt 1, 352), and took up his lodging at the hospitallers' house at Clerkenwell. On 14 August the king in effect capitulated and the Despensers were exiled. Roger Mortimer was one of those pardoned for acting against them between 1 March and 19 August 1321.

The victory proved to be a very short-lived one. The refusal of Bartholomew Badlesmere (the father-in-law of Roger Mortimer's heir) to admit Queen Isabella to Leeds Castle in Kent on 13 October provided Edward II with a pretext to resume hostilities and annul proceedings against the Despensers. Roger Mortimer with his uncle and the earl of Hereford collected a large force to go to the rescue of Leeds Castle: but they got no further than Kingston. Mortimer and his allies were driven back into Lancaster's arms and attended the meeting he had convened at Doncaster on 29 November. The king now went on the offensive, leading a force westwards to challenge the marchers. His forces reached Worcester on 31 December. The marchers, who had already captured Gloucester, seized Bridgnorth. But they were quickly outmanoeuvred by the king who reached Shrewsbury on 14 January 1322 and crossed to the west bank of the River Severn. On 23 January Roger Mortimer and his uncle surrendered to the king at Shrewsbury. Contemporary accounts provide different reasons for their sudden capitulation from what seemed to be a position of strength. Some ascribed it to the mediation of the earls of Richmond and Arundel; others to the duplicitous promises of the earls of Pembroke, Surrey, and Norfolk; yet others mention shortage of cash. But the most likely reason is that given in the *Vita Edwardi secundi*: the failure of the earl of Lancaster to come to their aid on the appointed day. Both Roger Mortimer and his uncle were dispatched to the Tower of London, contrary (according to one report) to a promise made earlier to them by the king. In July 1322—following the defeat of Lancaster and his allies at Boroughbridge on 22 March 1322—they were tried and condemned to death; but on 22 July their sentence was commuted to one of perpetual imprisonment.

Roger Mortimer and his uncle were kept in close and uncomfortable custody in the Tower. On 1 August 1323 (the feast of St Peter in Chains), with the connivance of Gerard de Alspaye, who had custody of him, and after the guards (and Stephen Seagrave, the constable) had been drugged, Roger Mortimer escaped. He crossed the Thames in a boat which awaited him, rode to Dover, and, in spite of strenuous efforts to recapture him, succeeded in crossing to France. He was welcomed in Paris by Charles IV, then at war with Edward II over Guyenne. *Isabella of France, Edward II's wife, came to Paris in April 1325 and on 12 September she was joined by her son, the young Prince Edward, dispatched to do homage on his father's behalf by Edward II. During the next few months a close liaison blossomed between Queen Isabella and Mortimer; by 1326 it was known in England that they were lovers. Mortimer's hold on Isabella was now so strong that Walter Stapledon, bishop of Exeter and former treasurer of England, who had accompanied the young Prince Edward to Paris, felt that he had no alternative but to flee back to England, if only for his own safety.

By 1326 there was no doubt that Mortimer and Isabella had decided on a scheme to invade England. They moved from Paris to the Low Countries, arranged the betrothal of Prince Edward to Philippa of Hainault, and gathered the troops and the money for the invasion. Mortimer and John of Hainault led the forces which crossed to England, landing at Orwell on 24 September 1326. They had judged the moment and the mood of the country well. They found ready support from many quarters united in their hatred for the Despensers. Within weeks the cause of Edward II had collapsed completely, and the king himself was captured at Llantrisant in the lordship of Glamorgan on 16 November. Mortimer and Isabella were triumphant.

Mortimer's years of domination, 1326–1330 For almost exactly four years Roger Mortimer was, with Queen Isabella, the dominant figure in England. He and his allies set about liquidating the supporters of the old regime at once, Roger Mortimer himself (though still only a baron) taking a prominent personal role in the process. He was present at Bristol when the elder Despenser was executed on 27 October 1326; it was by his command that the earl of Arundel met the same fate at Hereford on 17 November; and it was there likewise that the younger Despenser was sentenced to death by Mortimer and the earls of Lancaster and Kent. There was a certain appropriateness that it was in the west, close to Mortimer's centre of power, that the new regime was asserting itself. Roger Mortimer spent Christmas with Queen Isabella and her son at Wallingford.

The parliament that was summoned to effect the deposition of Edward II met on 7 January 1327. Mortimer curried favour with the Londoners by visiting the city on 13 January and confirming its liberties, to be followed in March by the grant of a new charter. He was naturally prominent at the coronation of the young Edward III on 1 February, and it was on that occasion that three of his sons (Edmund, Geoffrey, and Roger) were knighted. His hold on the royal family was made more complete by the transfer of the unfortunate Edward II from the custody of the earl of Lancaster in April 1327 to that of Mortimer's son-in-law Thomas Berkeley at Berkeley Castle. The particulars of Edward's fate, and Mortimer's role in it, remain shrouded in mystery.

Roger Mortimer held no official position in the governance of England in the next few years. He was not a member of the council established to direct the government during the minority of Edward III; but some of his closest associates, notably Bishop Adam Orleton and Sir Oliver Ingham, served on it. The crucial key to Mortimer's power lay in the position he held in the royal court and in the affections of the queen. He was regularly referred to as 'the king's kinsman', and was treated in effect as a member of the royal family, receiving his livery as part of the family. He spent long periods in personal attendance on the king and was to be awarded 500 marks per annum in May 1330 'in consideration of his continual stay with the king'. His influence was such that contemporaries came to charge him with usurping royal power and accused him of preventing the king from speaking to anyone except with his permission and of bypassing the council of fourteen set up to govern the kingdom.

Some of these charges no doubt were made with the advantage of hindsight; but it is clear that by autumn 1328 there was growing restiveness among the higher aristocracy about the personality and behaviour of Mortimer. Dissatisfaction also centred on the record of the government itself. In particular the Scottish raids into northern England and Ireland in 1327 showed the vulnerability of the kingdom; and the 'shameful peace' which the English were eventually forced to conclude with the Scots at Edinburgh and Northampton (March and May 1328) was regarded as particularly Mortimer's responsibility. The terms—including the recognition of Scottish independence and the title of Robert I as king of Scots—were so demeaning that rumours were rife that Isabella and Mortimer had made a pact with the Scots while they were in exile in France.

Humiliation at the hands of the French and the Scots damaged Roger Mortimer's reputation; but it was his own overweening power and greed which doubtless prompted the emergence of domestic opposition to him. Henry, earl of Lancaster, who was in effect head of the standing council of regency, felt that his influence was being increasingly ignored. He had been deprived of the custody of Edward II in April 1327 and during the next eighteen months or so—as his followers and kinsmen were eased out of key posts—he became steadily disillusioned and his followers increasingly unmanageable. Lancaster registered his protest at the Mortimer regime by refusing to attend the parliament convened at Salisbury on 16 October 1328. It was a parliament overawed by Mortimer's supporters and the occasion for conferring the novel title of earl of March on Roger Mortimer. Lancaster tried to whip up opinion against Mortimer in London and drew up a formidable list of accusations against him. But on this occasion Mortimer completely outmanoeuvred Lancaster, persuaded his allies (especially the earls of Kent and Norfolk) to desert him, raided his lands, and seized Leicester. By mid-January 1329, with many of his followers deserting him, Lancaster had no option but to make a humiliating surrender: enormous fines were imposed on him and some of his followers; some of his closest dependants (including Thomas Wake, his son-in-law, and Henry Beaumont) were forced to flee the country and saw their estates confiscated.

Mortimer's position was now even more unassailable. When Edmund, earl of Kent, the brother of the late Edward II, was duped into a plot based on the assumption that his brother was alive, Mortimer seized the opportunity to remove another possible threat to his position. On 19 March 1330 the earl of Kent was executed, some of his confiscated lands being given to one of Roger Mortimer's younger sons. In fact the judicial murder of Kent served only to heighten tensions and to compound the sense of hatred and fear that was now welling up against Mortimer. He took measures to secure his personal safety, making arrangements in May 1330 for some of his leading followers such as Maurice Berkeley and Simon Bereford to provide a specified number of men of arms to be continuously present at court, in effect to act as personal bodyguards for Mortimer and Queen Isabella.

Mortimer's personal aggrandizement Mortimer's regime was based on fear; it was also based on what almost all contemporaries agreed was his insatiable greed and his determination to put himself into the premier rank of the English aristocracy in landed wealth, status, and display. He proved more than a match for the younger Despenser in his anxiety to turn his political power to his own personal and family advantage. His territorial ambitions were concentrated in the two areas in which Mortimer power was already remarkable—Wales and Ireland. In Wales he stepped into the shoes of the opponents whom he had

liquidated in the coup of 1326. He secured the great lordship of Denbigh (15 December 1326) on the forfeiture of the elder Despenser; the lordships of Oswestry and Clun and the Fitzalan estates in Shropshire from the estates of the earl of Arundel (13 September 1327); and custody of the vast lordship of Glamorgan (12 June 1327) from the younger Despenser's widow. He also obtained the reversion of the crown lordships of Montgomery and Builth (2 September 1329) from Queen Isabella and was later granted the lordship of Montgomery in fee (April 1330). Most brazen act of all, he appropriated the marcher estates (Chirkland, Blaenllyfni, Narberth, and a share of St Clears) of his uncle and namesake, Roger Mortimer of Chirk, who had died in the Tower in 1326, even though the elder Roger had a legitimate son of full age. The custody and also (or perhaps alternatively) the marriage of James Audley (lordships of Cemais and Cantref Bychan), Laurence Hastings (lordships of Pembroke, Abergavenny, and Cilgerran), and of the heir to the earldom of Warwick (lordship of Elfael) gave him control of more marcher lordships. If to this is added the official positions he held—justiciar of the principality of Wales (22 February 1327, converted into a life grant 8 June 1328), justiciar of the bishoprics of Llandaff and St David's; chief keeper of the peace in Worcestershire, Herefordshire, and Staffordshire (8 June 1327), and custodian of Bristol (16 August 1330)—it can be seen that he had accumulated unparalleled territorial and official power in Wales and the far west of England.

The other area in which Roger Mortimer used his special power at court to enhance his own territorial standing was Ireland. He was one of Ireland's leading lords in respect of his wife's inheritance. He knew the country well from his earlier visits there and his two spells as justiciar. Once he had concluded a peace with Scotland (May 1328) he was free to devote more of his attention to Irish affairs. He worked hard and effectively to repair some of the deep divisions in the ranks of the English aristocracy in Ireland. It was as part of that process that in October 1328 James Butler was created earl of Ormond and later given Tipperary as a liberty. Similarly in August 1329 Maurice Fitzthomas Fitzgerald was promoted to be earl of Desmond and granted the liberty of Kerry. Both men would henceforth be beholden to Roger Mortimer. But Mortimer also looked after his own interests in Ireland, especially during 1330. He reserved for himself the custody of the lands of the earldom of Kildare and the marriage of the heir and in June 1330 he secured for himself royal jurisdiction throughout Meath and Louth to add to the privileged status he already enjoyed on his wife's lands in Trim. His acquisitiveness seemed to know no bounds. On top of all that he had already acquired, he was granted in May 1330 a further annual pension of 500 marks a year from royal estates in Wales. It was little wonder that a contemporary chronicler accused him of 'appropriating to himself royal power in many things and the treasure of the king also' (*Chronicon Henrici Knighton*, 1.447).

But Mortimer was attracted not only by land and wealth

but also by the trappings of power. As one chronicler commented: 'Roger Mortimer persisted in his displays of magnificence' (*Chronica monasterii de Melsa*, 2.359). He held round tables at Bedford in 1328 and another at Wigmore which lasted for several days and at which he distributed large presents to various earls and barons. Most magnificent of all was the great tournament he arranged at Hereford in June 1328 at which the young Edward III and his mother were the principal guests. It was on this occasion that he gave two of his daughters in marriage—Beatrice to Edward, the son of the earl of Norfolk and the king's cousin, and Agnes to Laurence Hastings, the heir to the earldom of Pembroke. Both marriages indicated Mortimer's anxiety to bind his family into the premier comital families of his day. This was an appropriate prelude to his own elevation to the rank of earl at the Salisbury parliament in October 1328. Contemporaries were astonished at the novelty of the title he gave himself, that of earl of March, not least because it was the first comital title not linked to a named English county. But the new title correctly identified the territorial basis of Roger Mortimer's power, and any anomaly in the title was soon rectified by granting him £10 a year from the issues of Shropshire and Staffordshire (just as other earls received a similar fee from the shire whose name they bore in their title).

Downfall, execution, and reputation The grandiose title that Mortimer gave himself and his flaunting of his power certainly offended contemporaries. According to one chronicler no one dared to address him other than by his title as earl of March; his retinue was larger than that of the king; and his arrogance was visibly displayed by walking side by side with the king, sometimes indeed going ahead of the king and even allowing the king to rise to him. Such outrageous breaches of etiquette were manifestations of the overweening power that Mortimer exercised and of the insensitive way he flaunted it. If to such behaviour were added his boundless acquisitiveness, the sense of outrage at his liaison with Queen Isabella, and the way in which he used his armed bands of followers, including unruly crowds of Welshmen, to overawe his opponents, it was not surprising that rumours circulated that he intended to usurp the kingship itself.

Tension built up against him in particular after the execution of the earl of Kent on a trumped-up charge in March 1330. None of the English magnates could now feel safe; but after the abysmal failure of the rising of Henry, earl of Lancaster, in 1328–9, and given the way Mortimer had entrenched his power, success could only attend a plot in which the young king (now aged seventeen) was himself personally involved.

Edward III was more than a willing party to such a plot. He was abetted by a group of close friends—notably Richard Bury, keeper of the privy seal, William Montagu (future earl of Salisbury), Robert Ufford (future earl of Suffolk), John Molyns, Edmund de Bohun, and John Neville of Hornby. When Mortimer summoned a parliament to meet at Nottingham in October 1330—most of the parliaments during Mortimer's years of domination met away

from Westminster—the conspirators seized the opportunity to put their plan into action, especially when the constable revealed a secret underground passage into the castle. On the night of 19 October, Montagu and his fellow conspirators entered the castle where they were joined by the king. In spite of some doughty resistance by Mortimer and his bodyguard, Mortimer was arrested. He and his close associates, Sir Oliver Ingham and Sir Simon Bereford, were taken under close escort to the Tower of London. Meanwhile the king issued a proclamation that he had taken the government into his own hands.

Mortimer was brought before the parliament, which had been prorogued from Nottingham to Westminster, on 26 November. Fourteen charges were preferred against him. He was accused, *inter alia*, of accroaching royal power and the government of the realm, moving Edward II from Kenilworth to Berkeley, granting lands and rewards to himself and his family, appropriating crown money and jewels and the 20,000 marks that the Scots had paid for the peace of 1328, riding against the earl of Lancaster, knowingly misleading the earl of Kent and securing his execution, sowing discord between Edward II and Isabella, and encompassing the death of those close to Edward III. The sentence was a foregone conclusion. Indeed Mortimer was given no opportunity to answer the charges; he was declared guilty by the peers on the basis of the common notoriety of his crimes. He was executed as a common criminal at Tyburn on 29 November 1330 and his body was left on the gallows for two days and nights, before being interred at Coventry at the house of the Franciscans, who proved very reluctant to hand it over to his widow to be reinterred in the family priory at Wigmore. His widow, Joan, died in 1356, and his eldest son and heir, Edmund, in 1331.

Roger Mortimer found few friends among contemporary chroniclers; modern historians have been equally harsh in their condemnation. Only the chronicler of the family's own foundation at Wigmore found it in him to call him 'a large-hearted and vigorous man', and he was remarkably economical with the truth in his account of Roger's career (Dugdale, *Monasticon*, 6, pt 1, 351). Perhaps his greatest achievements lay in Ireland: there, after initial defeat, he laid the ground for the defeat of Edward Bruce; he showed considerable imagination in his attempts to bring more of the native Irish within the ambit of English law; and his actions in 1328–9 showed that (as might be expected) he had a better grasp of the quarrelsome world of Anglo-Irish politics than the vast majority of English political leaders. Even the treaty with Scotland in 1328 which brought Mortimer such opprobrium can be regarded as an imaginative attempt—even if it was made under duress—to recognize the reality of Scottish independence and to bring a period of prolonged and costly warfare to an end. On the other hand, the contemporary view of Roger Mortimer and of his uncle in Wales was that of avaricious, ruthless men who ruled 'by extortion'. Indeed the Welsh in 1322 threatened to leave their lands if the Mortimers were pardoned and restored to their former position in Wales.

Had Roger Mortimer ruled under a strong and competent king, he would doubtless have been regarded as an effective soldier and as a baron who pursued his career, especially in Wales and Ireland, to the maximum advantage of himself and his family. It was the unusual circumstances of Edward II's reign, especially after 1318, and the exceptional power Mortimer wielded in the court after 1326 through his liaison with Queen Isabella that brought him to prominence and notoriety. From 1326 onwards he showed himself as self-seeking, acquisitive, and vain to a quite exceptional degree. His extravagant and unrestrained abuse of his position in these years—and the shameless way in which he expropriated his uncle's family—showed that he was, ultimately, a man without political principle or political judgement. His overweening ambition seemed to have destroyed a family with an unbroken record of 250 years as leading English barons.

R. R. DAVIES

Sources Chancery records · Rolls of parliament · J. T. Gilbert, ed., *Chartularies of St Mary's Abbey, Dublin: with the register of its house at Dunbrody and annals of Ireland*, 2 vols., Rolls Series, 80 (1884–6) · 'The Wigmore chronicle', Dugdale, *Monasticon*, 6/1, esp. 351 · N. Denholm-Young, ed. and trans., *Vita Edwardi secundi* (1957) · *Ann. mon.* · *Chronicon Henrici Knighton, vel Cnitthon, monachi Leycestrensis*, ed. J. R. Lumby, 2 vols., Rolls Series, 92 (1889–95) · *Chronicon Galfridi le Baker de Swynebroke*, ed. E. M. Thompson (1889) · W. Stubbs, ed., *Chronicles of the reigns of Edward I and Edward II*, 2 vols., Rolls Series, 76 (1882–3) · J. G. Edwards, *Calendar of ancient correspondence concerning Wales* (1935) · C. M. Woolgar, ed., *Household accounts from medieval England*, 1, British Academy, Records of Social and Economic History, new ser., 17 (1992), 173–7 · J. T. Gilbert, ed., *Historic and municipal documents of Ireland, AD 1172–1320, from the archives of the city of Dublin*, Rolls Series, 53 (1870) · *Chronica monasterii de Melsa, a fundatione usque ad annum 1396, auctore Thoma de Burton*, ed. E. A. Bond, 3 vols., Rolls Series, 43 (1866–8) · G. A. Holmes, *The estates of the higher nobility in fourteenth-century England* (1957) · R. Frame, *English lordship in Ireland, 1318–1361* (1982) · R. R. Davies, *Lordship and society in the march of Wales, 1282–1400* (1978) · Tout, *Admin. hist.*, vol. 3 · J. C. Davies, *The baronial opposition to Edward II* (1918) · J. R. Maddicott, *Thomas of Lancaster, 1307–1322: a study in the reign of Edward II* (1970) · J. R. S. Phillips, *Aymer de Valence, earl of Pembroke, 1307–1324: baronial politics in the reign of Edward II* (1972) · N. Fryde, *The tyranny and fall of Edward II, 1321–1326* (1979) · GEC, *Peerage* · G. A. Holmes, 'The rebellion of the earl of Lancaster, 1328–9', BIHR, 28 (1955), 84–9 · E. L. G. Stones, 'The date of Roger Mortimer's escape from the Tower of London', EngHR, 65 (1951), 97–8 · CIPM, 3, no. 43; 4, no. 235 · W. Rees, ed., *Calendar of ancient petitions relating to Wales* (1975), 89, no. 3027

Archives BL, inventory of his confiscated goods at Wigmore, 1322, Add. MS 60584 · Hereford Cathedral Library, papers relating to his rising against Edward II | BL, charters in the Black Book of Wigmore, Harley MS 1240 · BL, Egerton roll 8723–8724 · BL, list of charters, Add. MS 6041 · PRO, ministers' accounts, some estate accounts, SC6 [incl. 1206/1]

Mortimer, Roger (VI), second earl of March (1328–1360), magnate, was the son of Edmund (II) Mortimer (d. 1331) and his wife, Elizabeth Badlesmere. He was born at Ludlow, his grandmother's home, on 11 November 1328. The execution of his notorious grandfather, Roger (V) *Mortimer, first earl of March, on 29 November 1330, followed by the death of his own father, Edmund, in December 1331, threatened the whole future of the Mortimer family and its landed inheritance. It was the major achievement of Roger (VI) during his short life to remove

that threat and to recover the inheritance in its virtual integrity.

Some early close connections with favoured members of the English aristocracy doubtless helped Mortimer's cause. In 1335 his mother took as her second husband William de Bohun, future earl of Northampton and one of Edward III's close companions; another of the king's close friends, William Montagu, future earl of Salisbury, bought Roger's marriage in 1336 for 1000 marks; while yet a third leading nobleman, Richard (II) Fitzalan, earl of Arundel, secured custody of some of the Mortimer estates. The first clear sign that Mortimer fortunes were beginning to recover came in 1341 when, at the request of his stepfather, William de Bohun, Roger was allowed to take control of Radnor and associated lordships for a yearly rent of £280; he recovered the family seat at Wigmore in July 1342 and further estates on the Welsh marches in March 1344.

But it was Mortimer's own military prowess which established his credentials as a man worthy to be re-endowed with the vast territorial empire which his grandfather had so ruthlessly assembled in the years 1326–30. Mortimer distinguished himself as early as September 1344 (when he was only fifteen) in a great tournament at Hereford, in which the earls of Arundel, Pembroke, Suffolk, and Warwick also took part; but it was Edward III's wars in France which provided him with the opportunity to carve a military reputation for himself. He crossed to France in 1346; was knighted at La Hogue by the Black Prince on 12 July; fought alongside Edward III at Crécy on 26 August; and 'for his laudable service' was given livery of all his lands in Herefordshire and the Welsh marches on 6 September. He had thereby set the pattern for the rest of his short career: that of military service to the king and the recovery of the family estates and dignity.

In 1348 Mortimer was summoned to parliament as Roger Mortimer of Wigmore, and his standing was confirmed by his appearance as a founding member of the Order of the Garter. In 1352 he raised Welshmen from his estates to serve the king and was with the Black Prince at Calais; he saw service both in France and against the Scots in 1355. Mortimer was a key figure in Edward III's great invasion of France in 1359–60: he raised forces from his lordships in Wales; personally headed a force of 600 men-at-arms and 1000 archers; was made constable by Edward III who, according to Froissart, greatly loved him; led a preliminary raid from Boulogne to Étaples ahead of the main expeditionary force, and then headed one of the three parallel columns which marched through eastern France to the siege of Rheims (4 December 1359–11 January 1360).

In the meantime, with the full support of the king, Mortimer had recovered almost the whole of his grandfather's estates. In April 1354 the judgment on his grandfather was annulled in parliament and Mortimer's claim to the title of earl of March and to all his grandfather's estates established. In a series of remarkably high-handed decisions over the next few months, Edward III dismissed any counter-claims by those who had held the Mortimer estates in the meantime. Only Richard (II) Fitzalan, earl of Arundel, was able to salvage his claims from this quasi-judicial restoration of Mortimer fortunes. He struck a bargain with Roger Mortimer—including a marriage alliance between their offspring, which in the event was not activated—and this left him in control of the great lordship of Chirk (to which, in fact, the Mortimers of Wigmore had no valid claim, since it was part of the inheritance of the Mortimers of Chirk and Tedstone Wafer). But the bargain struck with Arundel only serves to highlight how comprehensive was the rehabilitation of the Mortimer family, a rehabilitation which cost other families—notably Montagu, Berkeley, and Talbot—dearly.

Earl Roger—for he had now assumed his grandfather's title as earl of March as well as his estates—received other tokens of royal favour, including the posts of keeper of Clarendon forest, Dover, and the Cinque Ports, with handsome fees for life. He was a frequent witness of royal charters from 1354 and appears as a member of the king's council. His own territorial position was further enhanced when he succeeded to a share of the Geneville inheritance (including Ludlow, which henceforth became a favourite Mortimer residence) on the death of his paternal grandmother, Joan Geneville, in 1356, while the Mortimer position in the Welsh borders was enhanced by a grant of the hundred of Munslow to him in fee in September 1358.

Mortimer married before 1352 Philippa, daughter of William Montagu, first earl of Salisbury, with whom he had one son, Edmund (III) *Mortimer, later third earl of March (d. 1381). In 1359, before his departure for France, he transferred the title to a considerable part of his estates to a group of friends and councillors. He died, much to Edward III's distress, during the French expedition at Rouvray near Avalon on 26 February 1360. His body was eventually brought back to England and interred in the family abbey of Wigmore. His widow died on 5 January 1382. The characterization of him in the Mortimer family's chronicle (of Wigmore Priory) as 'stout and strenuous in war, provident in counsel, and praiseworthy in his morals' seems more or less consistent with what is known of him from surviving historical evidence.

R. R. DAVIES

Sources Chancery records · Liber niger de Wigmore, BL, Harleian MS 1240 · 'The Wigmore chronicle', Dugdale, Monasticon, 6/1, esp. 352–3 · Adae Murimuth continuatio chronicarum. Robertus de Avesbury de gestis mirabilibus regis Edwardi tertii, ed. E. M. Thompson, Rolls Series, 93 (1889) · Chronicon Galfridi le Baker de Swynebroke, ed. E. M. Thompson (1889) · G. A. Holmes, The estates of the higher nobility in fourteenth-century England (1957) · R. R. Davies, Lordship and society in the march of Wales, 1282–1400 (1978) · K. Fowler, The king's lieutenant: Henry of Grosmont, first duke of Lancaster, 1310–1361 (1969) · Œuvres de Froissart, ed. K. de Lettenhove, 17 (Brussels, 1872), 386–7 · CIPM, 9, no. 247; 10, no. 640 · F. S. Haydon, ed., Eulogium historiarum sive temporis, 3 vols., Rolls Series, 9 (1858), vol. 3, p. 312

Archives BL, Harley MS 1240 · BL, Thoresby Park collection, Egerton charters and rolls · PRO, ministers' accounts, SC6

Mortimer, Roger (VII), **fourth earl of March and sixth earl of Ulster** (1374–1398), magnate and soldier, was the eldest son and second child of Edmund (III) *Mortimer, third earl of March (d. 1381), and his wife, Philippa of Clarence (d. 1376), granddaughter of Edward III and daughter of *Lionel of Antwerp. He was born at Usk on 11 April 1374. He inherited from his father the huge Mortimer complex of estates in Wales and the borderlands, and the lordship of Trim and half of Meath in Ireland; while through his mother he was heir to major estates (formerly of the Clare family) in eastern and southern England and south-east Wales, and also to the earldom of Ulster and lordship of Connacht in Ireland.

The question of who should have the guardianship and marriage of such an important heir as Roger (VII) Mortimer, and the wardship of his estates, became issues of political moment in the years 1382–4. The estates (other than those in the hands of Earl Edmund's executors) were divided initially between a number of minor grantees; but such a policy offended many of the leading magnates, who insisted that their interests and those of the young Mortimer heir were being overlooked. Richard II eventually relented, and on 16 December 1383 the Mortimer estates in England and Wales were granted en bloc for an annual rent of £4000 to the young Mortimer himself, the earls of Arundel, Northumberland, and Warwick, and John, Lord Neville. Almost simultaneously the guardianship of Mortimer himself was bestowed on Richard (III) Fitzalan, earl of Arundel; but it, along with his marriage, was subsequently transferred in August 1384, at the instance of Richard II's mother, to Thomas Holland, earl of Kent and the king's half-brother, for £4000. By about 1388 Roger Mortimer had married Holland's daughter, Eleanor.

The extent of the Mortimer estates, and the fact that so many of them were concentrated in large blocks in Wales and the borderlands and were now controlled by a consortium headed by the earls of Arundel and Warwick, gave them a strategic importance in the struggle between Richard II and the lords appellant in 1387–8. Furthermore, so long as Richard II remained without an heir of his body, Roger (VII) Mortimer, as lineal descendant of Edward III's second surviving son, Lionel of Antwerp, could lay a claim to be next in line to the royal succession. Although the story that Richard publicly proclaimed Mortimer as heir presumptive to the throne in parliament in October 1385 is without foundation, it is clear—especially from the account in the Westminster chronicle, which is all the more significant for being composed well before 1399—that his claim in this respect was being openly discussed.

During Mortimer's prolonged minority the Mortimer estates were run by a council headed by his uncle Sir Thomas Mortimer and Walter Brugge as chief financial officer. The family chronicler claimed that so effective had they been that they had accumulated a surplus of over £26,000 for the young earl. The young Mortimer was dubbed a knight by the king on 23 April 1390; but when Richard II tried to give him possession of his family estates before he was of full age he met with opposition from the consortium which had controlled them since 1383. In March 1393, however, the king took Earl Roger's homage and gave him livery of his Irish estates. His English and Welsh estates were granted to him in February 1394, and at that juncture Richard II retained him to stay with him for life.

Roger Mortimer now began on his short public career. He went on a progress around his Welsh estates in 1393, and in February and March 1394 served on an embassy to the Scottish border. But Ireland was to be the main theatre of his activity. His father, Edmund, was serving as the king's lieutenant in Ireland at his death, and the same office was, briefly and incongruously, bestowed on the seven-year-old Roger in January 1382. He was reappointed to the post just over ten years later in July 1392, but was not able to take up the position for another two years. He resumed his Irish ambitions in earnest in the summer of 1394 when he accompanied Richard II on his first expedition to Ireland, attended by a large force assembled at Conwy and Chester. Mortimer had a huge personal stake in the outcome of the expedition, nothing less than the recovery of his family's control in Meath, Ulster, and Connacht. The native Irish leaders in Meath and Ulster came in to make their submissions to the king in 1394–5; but the relative claims of the Ó Neill family and Roger Mortimer to power in Ulster remained unresolved and the temporary accommodations that were reached soon collapsed. On 28 April 1395 Richard II appointed Mortimer lieutenant in Ulster, Connacht, and Meath, and the earl spent much of the next three years in Ireland. He remained the royal lieutenant there until his death, his appointment being renewed for three years in April 1397; but his authority in the lordship was circumscribed by the power conferred on the king's favourite, William Scrope, as justiciar of Leinster, Munster, and Leith.

Mortimer's Irish preoccupations and relative youth meant that his role in English political life in the 1390s was limited. He had close relations with his brother Edmund (IV), whom he endowed generously with lands and annuities; with the Percy family—Henry Percy (Hotspur) was married to his elder sister; and with the earl of Arundel, who had married Mortimer's younger sister and for whose good behaviour towards the king Mortimer became a guarantor in August 1394. His own wealth and lineage meant that, sooner or later, he would be caught up in the political turmoil of Richard II's last years. In parliament in September 1397 one of Richard's confidants, John Montagu, earl of Salisbury, was given permission to begin a legal action to try to recover the lordship of Denbigh from the Mortimers. Earl Roger and his advisers successfully fought off the challenge, and pre-empted a further challenge by persuading Thomas Despenser, newly created earl of Gloucester, to quitclaim any rights he might have in the Mortimer lordships of Denbigh, Usk, and Caerleon.

Mortimer's sense of insecurity was doubtless greatly compounded by the order sent to him on 4 September 1397 to arrest Sir Thomas Mortimer, his father's illegitimate brother and close companion and the man who had headed the Mortimer council during Earl Roger's minority. Sir Thomas was now declared to be a hunted man for his part in the campaign of the lords appellant in 1386–7. Earl Roger seems to have made little attempt to arrest him, thereby arousing the king's suspicions. On 15 October 1397 Mortimer was specially summoned to attend the parliamentary session convoked at Shrewsbury for January 1398. According to Adam Usk (himself a protégé of the Mortimer family) and to the Wigmore family chronicler, the young earl was rapturously received on his return from Ireland by a vast crowd of supporters, wearing hoods in his colours of red and green. He swore on the cross of Canterbury to observe the ordinances agreed in parliament in the previous September and acted with great circumspection in the fraught political atmosphere in England.

Adam Usk claims that Richard II was now bent on Mortimer's downfall, and that, when Earl Roger returned to Ireland, his brother-in-law, Thomas Holland, duke of Surrey, was dispatched there to take him. What is undoubtedly true is that on 27 July 1398 it was announced that Mortimer's term as lieutenant for Ireland (which had been renewed for three years fifteen months earlier) was to be terminated on 1 September and that he was to be replaced by the duke of Surrey. In the event death anticipated the royal command by one week. On 20 July 1398 Earl Roger was killed in a skirmish with the Irish at Kellinstown, near Carlow. According to the family chronicle he was dressed in Irish clothes at the time and was not recognized by those who killed him. His badly mutilated body was eventually brought back to the family abbey at Wigmore for burial.

Roger Mortimer cut a dashing figure during his short life. He was remembered for his fine and handsome appearance, his ready wit and affability, his liberality with gifts and banquets, his skill in tournaments, and his conspicuous, if rash, bravery. His moral conduct did not please the chroniclers; but none doubted his popularity. He was the subject of a panegyric ode by the Welsh poet, Iolo Goch. He left two sons (the eldest of whom, Edmund (V) *Mortimer, eventually succeeded him as fifth earl of March), and two daughters. His widow married Edward Charlton of Powys and died in October 1405.

R. R. DAVIES

Sources Chancery records · Chronicon Adae de Usk, ed. and trans. E. M. Thompson, 2nd edn (1904) · 'The Wigmore chronicle', Dugdale, Monasticon, 6/1, esp. 354–5 · L. C. Hector and B. F. Harvey, eds. and trans., The Westminster chronicle, 1381–1394, OMT (1982) · E. Curtis, ed., Richard II in Ireland, 1394–1395, and submissions of the Irish chiefs (1927) · G. A. Holmes, The estates of the higher nobility in fourteenth-century England (1957) · R. R. Davies, Lordship and society in the march of Wales, 1284–1400 (1978) · A. J. Otway-Ruthven, A history of medieval Ireland (1968) · A. Tuck, Richard II and the English nobility (1973) · D. Johnston, 'Richard II and the submission of Gaelic Ireland', Irish Historical Studies, 22 (1980–81), 1–20

Archives BL, Egerton collection, Thoresby Park MSS · PRO, ministers' accounts

Wealth at death £3400—in England and Wales: PRO SC 11/23; Davies, Lordship and society, 188

Mortimer, Thomas (1730–1810), writer on trade and finance, was born on 9 December 1730 in Carey Street, Lincoln's Inn Fields, London, the only son of Thomas Mortimer (1706–1741), principal secretary to Sir Joseph Jekyll, master of the rolls, and grandson of John Mortimer (1656?–1736), author of *The Whole Art of Husbandry* (1707). He was from an old Somerset family. His mother died in 1744, and John Baker of Spitalfields became his guardian. He was educated at Harrow School, under the Revd Dr Cox, and then at a private academy in the north of England, but he was largely self-taught.

In 1750 Mortimer published *An Oration on the much Lamented Death of H. R. H. Frederick, Prince of Wales*. Encouraged by its success, he taught himself French and Italian, and in 1751 he published *Life and Exploits of Pyrrhus*, translated from the French of J. Gautier. He married twice, the first time when he was very young, and had a large family, including two sons who served in the navy.

In November 1762 Mortimer went to Ostend as English vice-consul for the Austrian Netherlands, on the recommendation of John Montagu, fourth earl of Sandwich, secretary of state. He was promised the consulship by two secretaries of state, Lord Sandwich and the marquess of Rockingham, and he was strongly recommended by Sir James Porter and his successor, Sir William Gordon, English ministers at Brussels, but as a result of an intrigue perpetrated by Robert Wood, under-secretary to Lord Weymouth, he was removed from office in 1768. The excuse was that he had been too friendly with John Wilkes, and too hostile towards Jesuits and Jacobites. He returned to England and in 1770 published a pamphlet, *The Remarkable Case of Thomas Mortimer, Esq.*, addressed to Lord Weymouth, protesting against his treatment.

Mortimer spent the rest of his life teaching and writing. His largest work was *The British Plutarch* (6 vols., 1762) containing lives of famous British people from the sixteenth to eighteenth centuries, but otherwise he wrote mainly on economics. His publications included *Every Man his Own Broker, or, A Guide to Exchange Alley* (1761), based on his own experience of losing a lot of money on the stock exchange in 1756; *The Universal Director* (1763); *A New and Complete Dictionary of Trade and Commerce* (1766); *The Elements of Commerce, Politics, and Finance* (1772), based on a series of lectures he had given in London; *Student's Pocket Dictionary* (1777); and *A Grammar Illustrating the Principles and Practice of Trade and Commerce*, published after his death in 1810. He published revised editions of his grandfather's *Whole Art of Husbandry* in 1761, and of Wyndham Beawes's *Lex mercatoria rediviva* in 1783, and a translation from the French of Jacques Necker, *Treatise on the Administration of the Finances of France* (1785).

Mortimer died on 31 March 1810 at Clarendon Square, Somers Town, London. His son George published *Observations and remarks made during a voyage to the islands of Tenerife, Amsterdam … in the brig 'Mercury', commanded by J. H. Cox, esq* (1791).

CHRISTABEL OSBORNE, *rev.* ANNE PIMLOTT BAKER

Sources *European Magazine and London Review*, 35 (1799), 219–22 · *The remarkable case of Thomas Mortimer esq.* (1770) · J. R. McCulloch, *The literature of political economy: a classified catalogue* (1845) · *N&Q*, 5th ser., 1 (1874), 268, 315–16 · private information, 1894

Likenesses W. Beechey, portrait, repro. in *European Magazine and London Review*, facing p. 219 · W. Ridley, stipple (after W. Beechey), BM, NPG; repro. in *European Magazine and London Review*

Mortimer, William Egerton (1878–1940), lawyer, was born on 9 August 1878 in Ash, Shropshire, the son of Christian Mortimer (*d.* 1916), vicar of Ash and later canon residentiary of Lichfield Cathedral, and his wife, Lucy Sarah Hannah Scholfield. Canon Mortimer was one of the seventeen children of George Ferris Whidborne Mortimer, headmaster of the City of London School between 1840 and 1865. Mortimer was educated at Shrewsbury School before reading Greats at Christ Church, Oxford, where he held the Careswell and Boulter exhibitions, was president of the boat club, and took a second in jurisprudence in 1901.

In October 1904 Mortimer was admitted a solicitor; he then practised alone at 21 Cannon Street for eight years. During this time it seems that he made the acquaintance of William May, partner of and co-founder in 1889, with William Slaughter, of the City firm known then and ever since as Slaughter and May. Mortimer's name is entered as a member of various shooting parties, from 1908 on, in the gamebook of Pitt Hall Farm, an estate near Basingstoke belonging to William May. Mortimer was also, like May, a keen yachtsman, although no record survives of whether these shared sporting interests played any part in securing for Mortimer an invitation, which he accepted, to join Slaughter and May as a partner. In 1912 Mortimer left Cannon Street and became one of the five partners at 18 Austin Friars.

When war broke out in 1914 Mortimer was thirty-six and too old for active military service. He spent most of the war at Austin Friars, although in 1917 he was seconded to the Air Ministry for a time. Sir William Slaughter, the firm's senior partner since 1889, died in 1917 and many of his clients and directorships were passed on to William May. Mortimer, who already shared some of the firm's significant commercial clients, particularly banks, in the City with May, took on more of these in the 1920s. The merchant banks Schroders, Barings, and Rothschilds were all clients of the firm and more specifically of Mortimer in the 1920s. When Sir Frank Crisp of Ashurst Morris Crisp died in 1919, Morgan Grenfell, formerly his client, moved to Slaughter and May. By the mid-1920s Mortimer's reputation was sufficient to warrant an invitation to sit on the committee chaired by Wilfrid Arthur Greene, appointed in 1925 to review the body of company law and consider what, if any, amendments were required. In the event the committee, after lengthy sittings, recommended only some slight changes.

From the late 1920s until 1940 Mortimer was, according to the firm's historian, its driving force, although he did not become senior partner until 1933. In these years, as his own reputation and that of the firm grew in the City, the firm acquired 'the stamp of Mortimer's complex and forceful personality' (Dennett, 158). From 1924 he was a member of the council of the Law Society, but otherwise he did not seek influence in wider public spheres. He was well known among British and foreign bankers, particularly after his involvement, representing British interests, in the creation of the foreign creditors' standstill committee, set up after the collapse of the Credit Anstalt in 1931.

City law firms were at this time—and most remained so until the 1960s—hierarchical and conservative in character, formal in dress and manners. In the office, Mortimer—known as Mortie, although whether any dared to address him as such is doubtful—was autocratic and demanding, a stickler for accuracy as far as work and behaviour were concerned. A bachelor himself at this time, he dedicated his considerable energies and abilities to Slaughter and May and tended to expect the same of his partners and staff. He could also, however, as articled clerks and members of staff found, be unobtrusively kind and generous.

By the late 1930s Slaughter and May, with nine partners, was a large firm in City terms and with a reputation for excellence that Mortimer had done much to sustain and enhance after the deaths of the founders. On 7 or 8 August 1938 Mortimer married Cicely Eleanor, widow of Major-General Neville-White and daughter of William Melville Pigot, rural dean of Ipswich. Two years later, while sheltering from an air raid, he suffered a heart attack. A few days later, on 3 December 1940, he died of bronchitis at his home at 95 Eaton Square, London; his wife survived him.

JUDY SLINN

Sources J. Slinn, 'Mortimer, William Egerton', *DBB* · L. Dennett, *Slaughter and May: a century in the City* (1989) · *The Times* (8 Aug 1938) · *The Times* (10 Dec 1940) · *Law Lists* (1904–13) · *WWW* · R. Palin, *Rothschild relish* (1970)
Archives Slaughter and May archives, London
Likenesses photograph, priv. coll.
Wealth at death £66,617 15s. 1d.: probate, 8 May 1941, *CGPLA Eng. & Wales*

Mortlock, John (*bap.* 1755, *d.* 1816), banker and mayor of Cambridge, was born at Cambridge and baptized at St Edward's Church there on 17 October 1755, the only son of John Mortlock (*d.* 1775), a prosperous woollen draper and his wife, Sarah, *née* Davy (*d.* 1800). He is often referred to as John Mortlock III to distinguish him from his father and grandfather. On 3 October 1776 he married Elizabeth Mary Harrison (1756/7–1817), daughter of Stephen Harrison, a wealthy Presbyterian grocer, and they had ten children.

Mortlock became the first banker to the town and university of Cambridge and achieved rapid success and popularity, for his business was conducted 'liberally and cheerfully' (Gunning, 1855, 1.128) and answered a real need. He entered politics in 1780 as a would-be reformer and supporter of the fourth duke of Rutland, and was rewarded with the receivership of the Cambridgeshire land tax, which he relinquished on his unopposed election as MP for Cambridge in April 1784. His parliamentary career was brief and inglorious; he narrowly avoided censure in 1786 for tampering with a list of commissioners of the land tax, and was equivocal in his allegiance to the administration, causing Rutland to write to Pitt in September 1786: 'Personally he weighs not a feather; but he

has decided influence in the town of Cambridge, which I am apprehensive he will throw into the hands of the duke of Bedford' (*VCH Cambridgeshire*, 74).

For part of 1788 Mortlock was mayor, member of parliament, and recorder of the borough, but he resigned the last two of these positions in favour of Rutland nominees, and afterwards continued to enjoy the patronage of the family and of government ministers, while managing Cambridge with its small electorate of freemen as a pocket borough in the Pittite interest. His recompense was a lucrative office as receiver-general in the Post Office, and other preferments for his sons. His power depended on his mastery of the town corporation into which he had bought his way in 1778, becoming alderman in 1782. His election as mayor in 1785 was followed by alterations in the manner of appointment; he held office thirteen times in the following thirty years, turn and turn about with his sons and protégés. Besides his wealth he employed legal tactics ruthlessly and altered by-laws at will to transform an oligarchy into a dictatorship. His use of corporation funds and leases as well as charitable trusts was self-serving. During the danger of the French wars he was strongly conservative and did little to prevent the persecution of his former allies, the dissenters of Cambridge, although he was usually an able magistrate and checked food riots in 1795. He died at his town house in Cambridge, after a short illness, on 7 May 1816, a landed gentleman, owner of Abington Lodge and a substantial fortune possibly worth £120,000. He was buried at St Edward's, Cambridge.

Mortlock's reputation suffered greatly when Liberal and municipal reformers of the 1830s delved into events of the previous fifty years. The learned town clerk of Cambridge, Charles Henry Cooper, blamed him for most of the corruption in local affairs, remarking that, had he wished, Mortlock could have made his own footman MP for Cambridge. He became the villain of modern studies by Helen Cam and Sir Lewis Namier. His rule, however, 'although despotic was not inefficient' (Gray, 54), and he was probably no worse a grafter than others of his time. His probity as a banker was not undermined and attempts to bankrupt him for political ends always failed. Henry Gunning, that staunch and argumentative whig, who differed markedly in politics, none the less maintained a long and cordial friendship with him. '"Without *influence*," he would say, "which you call *corruption*, men will not be induced to support government though they generally approve of its measures"' (Gunning, 1855, 1.127).

JOHN D. PICKLES

Sources H. M. Cam, 'John Mortlock III, master of the town of Cambridge', *Proceedings of the Cambridge Antiquarian Society*, 40 (1939–40), 1–12 · HoP, *Commons* · H. Gunning, *Reminiscences of the university, town, and county of Cambridge, from the year 1780*, 2nd edn, 1 (1855), 124–9, 294–5; 2 (1855), 5–6, 65 · J. M. Gray, *Biographical notes on the mayors of Cambridge* (1922), 52–6 · *VCH Cambridgeshire and the Isle of Ely*, vol. 3, esp. 21–4, 66–8, 73–6 · H. M. Cam, 'Quo warranto proceedings at Cambridge, 1780–90', *Cambridge Historical Journal*, 8 (1944–6), 145–65 · parish register, Cambridge, St Edward's, Cambs. AS [baptism], 17 Oct 1755 · memorial inscription, Cambridge, Great St Mary's · parish register, Cambridge, Great St Mary,

Cambs. AS [marriage], 13 Oct 1776 · memorial inscription, Cambridge, St Edward's
Archives Belvoir Castle, Leicestershire, Rutland MSS · BL, Cole MSS · PRO, Chatham MSS
Likenesses J. Downman, oils, *c*.1779, repro. in *The Connoisseur*, 61 (1921), 199
Wealth at death £120,000: HoP, *Commons* · under £30,000: PRO

Morton. For this title name *see* individual entries under Morton; *see also* Douglas, James, first earl of Morton (*d*. 1493); Douglas, James, fourth earl of Morton (*c*.1516–1581); Douglas, William, sixth earl of Morton (*c*.1540–1606); Maxwell, John, earl of Morton (1553–1593); Douglas, Archibald, eighth earl of Angus and fifth earl of Morton (*c*.1555–1588); Leslie, Agnes, countess of Morton (*d*. in or after 1606); Douglas, William, seventh earl of Morton (1582–1648); Douglas, James, fourteenth earl of Morton (1702–1768).

Morton, (Richard) Alan (1899–1977), biochemist, was born on 22 September 1899 in Garston, Liverpool, the younger child and only son of John Morton, an engine driver, and his wife, Ann Humphreys, maidservant, of Nant Gwynant, Caernarvonshire. He was baptized Richard Alun (though he was known in later life as Alan) at the Welsh Calvinistic Methodist chapel in Chapel Road, a church of which he remained a staunch member all his life (he later undertook various offices in the chapel community). At the age of ten he won a junior city scholarship as well as a prize for the best handwriting in all Liverpool schools. After leaving Oulton School he worked briefly for a consultant chemist before entering the army. He spent only nine months as a soldier during which time he contracted Spanish influenza and became seriously ill. Nevertheless he entered the University of Liverpool in 1919, graduating with first-class honours in chemistry in 1922. He then studied under Professor E. C. C. Baly, a pioneer in the application of spectroscopy to chemical problems, and in 1924 he was appointed special lecturer in spectroscopy. In 1926 he married Myfanwy Heulwen, a childhood friend from the Welsh chapel in Garston, and daughter of Elizabeth and Hugh Roberts. They had one daughter, Gillian (whose married name was Lewis), later a fellow at St Anne's College, Oxford.

Absorption spectroscopy now became the core of Morton's research, and for his remarkable work correlating spectra with structure he was awarded the Meldola medal in 1930 by the Institute of Chemistry. In that year he also spent a sabbatical at Ohio State University as visiting professor.

Morton's interest in applying spectroscopic methods to biological problems was aroused mainly by the American Selig Hecht (a postdoctoral fellow in the Liverpool laboratories when Morton was working towards his PhD), and by Ian Heilbron. With Heilbron, who was professor of organic chemistry at Liverpool, he found an impurity in the cholesterol isolated from cod liver oil which showed absorption bands in the ultraviolet region of the spectrum; this was the compound that was converted by a photochemical reaction into vitamin D. He thereby helped to elucidate a crucial step in the process whereby vitamin D could be made cheaply in large amounts. Morton expanded his work on the fat-soluble vitamins, studying the spectroscopic labels of vitamin A to develop an analytical procedure that was used throughout the world for many years, and discovering a second form of the vitamin, A2. In partnership with Dr J. A. Lovern of Aberdeen he discovered (in 1937) that the liver oil industry was throwing as much vitamin A back into the sea as it was retaining. Although trawlers were collecting halibut and cod livers, Morton showed that fish intestines (as well as the pyloric caeca) were rich sources of vitamin A. Though Morton took out a patent and passed it on to the Medical Research Council, which was funding his research, nothing materialized.

The secretary of the Medical Research Council, Sir Edward Mellanby, held Morton in high regard and during the Second World War asked him to join a team to determine the vitamin A needs of a group of conscientious objectors based at Sheffield. The resulting report, *Vitamin A Requirements of Human Adults*, was of great significance. During the war Morton also worked on the biochemistry of vision. George Wald had found the light absorbing portion of rhodopsin (the pigment of low intensity vision) to be a substance which he named retinene. From its spectrum Morton deduced it to be the aldehyde of vitamin A, a deduction he proved through synthesis. Retinal (as it is now known) is the light receptor in all visual pigment and an essential intermediate in the perception of light by all members of the animal kingdom. In addition to his wartime research into biochemical fields, Morton (with J. Proudman and T. P. Hilditch) also spent a great deal of time in the often dangerous investigation of fire outbreaks caused by the German bombing of Merseyside.

In 1944 Morton was appointed to the Johnston chair of biochemistry, an appointment aided by the strong advocacy of Sir Jack Drummond, who had co-operated with him in research into nutrition. Over the next twenty-two years Morton built up a talented research team and welcomed generations of students. (He and his wife were particularly hospitable to his many foreign research students.) He persuaded the university to erect new buildings for his department, while his pastoral care for students was immortalized in a new hostel at the Carnatic site called Morton House (opened in 1971). His own research continued; it culminated in his discovery of the dolichols, *cis*-polyprenols, and the classification of tocopherol chemistry, as well as outstanding work on ubiquinone (a component of the respiratory chain involved in the harnessing of energy by cells), and the polyprenols (involved as carriers of sugar molecules in the biosynthesis of many glycoproteins). Morton did a great deal of work on the fat-soluble vitamins, and extended his interest to other lipid compounds. When the Biochemical Society funded the Morton lectureship in his memory it was to be on lipid biochemistry, for that was the field in which his later reputation lay.

Morton served on a large number of scientific, professional, and government committees, notably as chairman of the food additives and contaminants committee. He was twice a member of the council of the Royal Society, and served as chairman of its publication board. He was chairman of the Biochemical Society, and an editor of the *Biochemical Journal* and the *British Journal of Nutrition*. In his retirement Morton travelled as visiting professor to the University of Malta in 1969 and was examiner in 1970, 1972, and 1974; he produced *The Biochemical Society: its History and Activities, 1911–1969*, completing fourteen articles, a small number of the total of 282 that he was involved in (many of them with other scientists) between 1923 and 1978. His own books include *Radiation in Chemistry* (1928), *Absorption Spectra of Vitamins, Hormones and Co-Enzymes* (1942), which broke fresh ground, and the two-volume (a total of 873 pages) *Biochemical Spectroscopy*, which he completed with a Leverhulme Trust grant and published in 1975. Elected FRS in 1950, he received honorary degrees from the University of Coimbra in Portugal (1964), University of Wales (1966), and Trinity College, Dublin (1967), and was elected an honorary member of the Biochemical Society and of the American Institute of Nutrition, a high professional distinction.

Morton loved his Welsh associations and for years he spent some of his leisure time in Llansannan near the Hiraethog Mountain, where he sketched, and read Welsh sermons. He died, as a result of a coronary attack, at his home, 39 Greenhill Road, Allerton, Liverpool, on 21 January 1977, having returned only recently from an international symposium in India. His remains were cremated at Springwood crematorium, Liverpool. He was survived by his wife and daughter. D. BEN REES

Sources *The Times* (26 Jan 1977) · G. A. J. Pitt, 'Alan Morton, 1899–1977', *Chemistry in Britain*, 15 (1979), 85 · *Nature*, 266 (1977), 394 · J. Glover and others, *Memoirs FRS*, 24 (1978), 409–42 · *DNB* · private information (2004) · personal knowledge (2004)
Archives U. Lpool, MSS
Likenesses S. Reed, portrait, U. Lpool, Life Science Building
Wealth at death £52,397: probate, 2 May 1977, *CGPLA Eng. & Wales*

Morton, Alan Lauder (1893–1971), footballer, was born at Skaterigg Farm, Jordanhill, Renfrewshire, on 24 April 1893, the youngest of five sons of William Storey Morton, colliery manager, and his wife, Mary Scott. His father did not like the idea of his sons playing professional football instead of pursuing a career. Morton did both. He signed for the famous Glasgow amateur team, Queen's Park, in 1913, to join his elder brother Bob, and, while playing for the amateurs, studied to become a mining engineer.

Morton was already an outstanding footballing talent when he was signed by Rangers' new manager, William (Bill) Struth, as a professional in June 1920; in 1920 he won two international caps for Scotland against Wales and Ireland and was deprived only by injury of a cap against England. Coming from the amateur team, Morton was able to arrange his own financial terms with Rangers and, although his salary was never disclosed, it has been said to have been as much as £4000 a year, an immense sum for the time. Whatever the exact amount, it was undoubtedly

the highest of any player in a decade in which Scottish football talent was thick on the ground. Moreover, he continued to work as a mining engineer; as the only Rangers player allowed to play part time, he avoided the daily routine of other professional players and trained only twice a week, on Tuesdays and Wednesdays.

Known as the Wee Blue Devil after his performance against England in 1928, Morton shared with his fellow professional footballer of the 1920s Patsy Gallacher a slight build (5 ft 4½ in., 9 stone 7lb) and an extraordinary ability to dominate much larger opponents; but there the comparison ends. Morton came from a different social class and joined a different team; he came from a solidly middle-class family and played for Glasgow Rangers, Scotland's premier establishment club.

The Scottish talent of this time was displayed at its best in the famous 5–1 victory over England by the Wembley Wizards in 1928, a game in which Morton stood out in a diminutive forward line whose skilful attacking game has never been equalled; in Scotland he was supreme, matched only by Patsy Gallacher, but he was never tempted to follow such other talents as Hughie Gallacher and Alex James to England: Morton was too much a Rangers man.

In the inter-war years Rangers dominated Scottish football, and it was in this time that their practice of not playing Catholic footballers became an unwritten policy. Under directors staunchly unionist in politics, royalist in sympathies, and active in freemasonry, Rangers stood in sharp contrast to their Old Firm rivals, the Irish-Catholic Glasgow Celtic. Morton appears to have been in complete sympathy with the ethos of the club and this, as well as his middle-class social credentials, allowed him to go straight from being a player to a position on the board of directors of Rangers after playing six games of the 1932–3 season. In 1933 he enjoyed the rare honour of being the only player invited by the Scottish Football Association to take part in its diamond jubilee dinner.

Morton was Struth's first signing, and the two were instrumental in defining the Rangers' image in this period. In addition to an employment policy that was, like that of all major protestant firms in Scotland at this time, effectively anti-Catholic, Struth and Morton emphasized the social superiority of the protestant Scot in the way they dressed. This amounted almost to a fetish in the case of Struth; and Morton was known as the Wee Society Man for his dapper dress—the business suit, the bowler hat, the leather gloves, and the rolled-up umbrella, characteristic of an insurance society collector.

It was as a footballer, however, that Morton made his name, and this came from dedicated practice to hone his natural talent. In much the same way as young Donald Bradman practised with a golf ball and a cricket stump against a water tank, the young Morton practised chipping a ball through the delivery hole in the family coal cellar. On errands for his parents he was never without a ball as he dribbled it with one foot against the wall on the way to the shops, and dribbled with the other foot on the way back. The result was his remarkable confidence with both feet. He made his name as an outside left, and in addition to his uncanny ball control and dribbling, he perfected a cross that seemed to hang in the air and puzzled opposing defences—probably more taken in by his reputation than the actual flight of the ball, although he did practise the then unfamiliar skills of imparting spin to the ball.

Morton won an unprecedented thirty-one caps for Scotland. His career with Queen's Park was mainly during the years of the First World War, when he played in 247 competitive games. Between 1920 and his retirement in 1933 he played in 498 games for Rangers, won nine league championships and two Scottish cup medals. He was never as much as cautioned by the referee, and remained remarkably free from injury—when he missed the 1926 international against England it became known as the one 'where Alan Morton did not play'—and Scotland lost.

Morton remained on the Rangers' board until shortly before his death, at his home, Marchmont, Victoria Place, Airdrie, on 14 December 1971. In the 1959 general election his sister was put forward to oppose Labour in one of its safest seats, Coatbridge and Airdrie, and such was the power of the Morton name that she lost by only 759 votes. Morton never married.   BILL MURRAY

Sources J. Allan, *The story of Rangers: fifty years in football, 1873–1923* (1923) · J. Allan, *Eleven great years: the Rangers, 1923–1934* (1934) · I. Sharpe, *40 years in football* (1952) · R. Ferrier and R. McElroy, *Rangers: the complete record* (1996) · b. cert. · d. cert.

Wealth at death £76,267.27: confirmation, 18 Feb 1972, CCI

Morton, Alastair James Fagan (1910–1963), textile manufacturer and abstract painter, was born on 12 February 1910 at Home Acres, Brampton Road, Carlisle (now Cumbria College of Art and Design), the elder son and fifth of the six children of Sir James *Morton (1867–1943) and Beatrice Emily Fagan (1871–1958). Both his father and grandfather Alexander Morton (1844–1923) were textile manufacturers.

Morton was educated at St George's School, Harpenden, but his attendance was dogged by illness, which permanently impaired his heart. In 1929–30 he studied mathematics at Edinburgh University before going to Balliol College, Oxford, where he spent a year. On 17 September 1931 he married Flavia Birrell (1910–2001), whom he had met at school. They had three children: Alec (*b.* 1932); Joslyn (*b.* 1934), a sculptor who married the artist Joe Tilson in 1956; and Rachel (*b.* 1938).

Morton joined Morton Sundour Fabrics Ltd, an offshoot of the family firm of Alexander Morton & Co., in 1931. In 1932 he moved to Edinburgh Weavers, a research unit established by his father in 1928 to pioneer fabric design in keeping with contemporary architecture and interior decoration. Morton emerged as a designer of considerable talent, and was appointed the unit's artistic director. Edinburgh Weavers became the most innovative textile producers in Britain, as Morton commissioned leading artists and designers to design fabrics of outstanding originality and quality. Perhaps the high point of its pre-war production was the range of 'constructivist fabrics' of 1937, featuring designs by, among others, Ben Nicholson, Barbara Hepworth, and Ashley Havinden.

Morton began painting in 1936, and is best-known for his abstract work in the modernist style. He was one of a small group of artists in pre-war Britain who championed the new movement, and showed in exhibitions such as 'Living Art in England' at the London Gallery, London (1939), 'Abstract Paintings by Nine British Artists' at the Lefevre Gallery, London (1939), and 'England Today', a touring exhibition shown in Melbourne and Sydney in 1940. His work was shown alongside that of artists who included Piet Mondrian, Naum Gabo, Barbara Hepworth, and Henry Moore. After the war he began to create exquisitely rendered botanical drawings (examples of which are in the Whitworth Art Gallery, Manchester). His commitment to modernist architecture was shown in 1936, when he commissioned Brackenfell, near Brampton, Carlisle, a house designed by Leslie Martin and Sadie Speight into which he moved with his family in 1937.

Delicate health prevented Morton from fighting in the war, and he worked as a photographer for the National Buildings Record before studying handweaving and spinning with Ethel Mairet in Sussex during the winter of 1943–4. In 1945 he and Flavia divorced, and in July he married (Mary Isabella) Cherry Lawson (1907–1998). They moved to the Lake District, where they lived until Morton's death and where he set up a handweaving studio to produce striking ranges of fabrics and rugs. They had one child, Alison (*b.* 1946), a handweaver and designer. Between 1947 and 1954 Morton designed a popular and critically acclaimed series of dress prints for Horrockses Fashions Ltd, of Preston, while restrictions after the war led him to experiment with ramie fibre, as well as cowhair and wool. In 1946 he launched his 'unit prints', a system of screen prints that could be mixed and matched at will.

Morton became increasingly concerned with teaching design, and during the 1940s regularly wrote articles and lectured on the subject to bodies such as the Design and Industries Association and the Cotton Board, who commissioned him to enquire into the state of textile design in 1944. He also became assessor for textiles for the four central Scottish art schools. He led a renaissance at Edinburgh Weavers between 1955 and 1963 as a new generation of artists including William Scott, Victor Vasarely, and Marino Marini designed fabrics for him and allowed their images to be used for production. At the same time his professional responsibilities grew, culminating in his appointment as chief executive director of Morton Sundour Fabrics Ltd in 1962. He was elected a fellow of the Society of Industrial Artists in 1947, was made an honorary designer of the Royal College of Art in 1954, and became a royal designer for industry and a member of the Council of Industrial Design in 1960. In 1961 Edinburgh Weavers received the royal warrant of appointment, with Morton as warrant-holder. His hobbies included hill farming (in particular the breeding of Belted Galloways), photography, natural history, and music. He died of heart failure at his home—Hollows, Dockray, near Penrith—on 30 June 1963, and was cremated at Carlisle crematorium on 3 July.

Morton was a pioneer of modernism in Britain. His innovative textile designing and weaving, his enlightened commissioning of other artists, his practical knowledge of textile manufacture and willingness to experiment, and his work as a painter have secured him a permanent place in the history of twentieth-century design. Edinburgh Weavers changed the face of the European textile industry, while Morton's achievements as a painter have been recognized more recently in various exhibitions, including those at the Scottish National Gallery of Modern Art, Edinburgh, and Abbot Hall Art Gallery, Kendal. His work, both as a painter and as a textile designer and weaver, is represented in many public collections, most importantly those in the Victoria and Albert Museum, London; the Whitworth Art Gallery, Manchester; the Abbot Hall Art Gallery, Kendal; and the Craft Study Centre at the Surrey Institute of Art and Design.

ALICE DEWEY

Sources J. Morton, *Three generations in a family textile firm* (1971) · Morton of Darvel muniments, NA Scot., GD326 · R. Calvocoressi, *Alastair Morton and Edinburgh Weavers: abstract art and textile design, 1935–46* (1978) [exhibition catalogue, NG Scot., 29 April – 29 May 1978] · private information (2004)
Archives NA Scot., Morton of Darvel muniments, GD 326 | Scottish National Gallery of Modern Art, Edinburgh, Ashley Havinden archive, GMA.A39 · Tate collection, Cecil Collins archive, TGA 923 · Tate collection, Ben Nicholson archive, TGA 8717 · University of Brighton, Design Council archive · V&A, James Morton archive, AAD/1978/4; AAD/1991/3 · V&A NAL, Cotton Board and Design Industries Association material
Likenesses R. Sivell, oils, 1929, priv. coll. · photograph, 1937, priv. coll. · C. Harrison, oils, 1963, priv. coll.
Wealth at death £19,905 19s.: probate, 11 Dec 1963, *CGPLA Eng. & Wales*

Morton, Sir Albertus (1584?–1625), diplomat, was the youngest of three sons of George Morton (*d. c.*1613), of East Stour, near Chilham, Kent, and Mary, daughter of Robert Honeywood of Charing, Kent. His father was half-brother to the renowned diplomat, philosopher, and conversationalist Sir Henry *Wotton, who sponsored Albertus Morton's education and career. A brother, Sir Robert Morton, was a captain in the English garrison at Flushing; Robert's second son was named Albertus in honour of his uncle, and is often mistaken for him. Morton attended Eton College from 1596 and was admitted to King's College, Cambridge, in 1602; the following year he was elected a scholar by royal nomination. In 1604 he accompanied Wotton on his first embassy to Venice, and was presented to the doge. He is said to have taken the degrees of BA and MA at Cambridge during these years, but the dating is confused. On a trip to England in 1609 he carried letters of introduction to Prince Henry and lord treasurer Salisbury, though the main purpose of the trip was to present the king with the crest of the conspirator earl of Gowrie, which Wotton had stumbled upon in a Venetian church. Two years later he returned to England with Wotton via Paris, and in November 1611 was reported to be back at Cambridge while his benefactor looked for other employment. He again interrupted his academic life, to accompany Wotton to Turin in 1612.

Wotton clearly had high expectations for his nephew, frustrated by Morton's tendency to accident and consequent frail health. In the spring of 1613 when his appointment as English agent to Savoy was expected he suffered a serious head injury when the carriage in which he was riding near Charing Cross collided with a beer cart. He snagged his hose on the boot of the carriage as he climbed out of it and the waistband gave way throwing him violently to the ground. Unconscious for several hours, he could not talk when he regained consciousness. While he recovered Wotton lobbied to have him sworn an extraordinary clerk of the privy council, or at least to secure him a reversion to the next vacancy. In August he was reported well enough to depart for Savoy, though he still experienced numbness in one hand; indeed he seems never to have fully recovered. Detained in England for lack of money he finally left to take up his post in May 1614 but was back home to be sworn as an extraordinary clerk of the privy council in December 1614. He returned to Savoy via Paris in the company of Savoy's ambassador to London in the new year. In the spring of 1615 he was allowed to return to England 'because of an old bruse which he gotte with a fall out of a coache' (*Downshire MSS*, 5.187). At the time his rival Sir Dudley Carleton described him as so melancholy he could hardly speak without dissolving into tears.

In 1616 Morton accepted the dual post of English agent to the princes of the protestant union and secretary to King James's daughter Elizabeth, electress palatine, again obtained for him by Wotton. He was granted a pension of £200 per annum as the electress's secretary and knighted by the king at Hampton Court with a group of his fellow privy council clerks in September 1617. He reached the palatine court at Heidelberg late in December. Three months later he represented the prince of Wales as godfather to the electress's son, Charles Louis, reportedly spending 100 ecus on clothing suitable for the occasion. Elizabeth called him 'my honest Morton' and held him in high esteem throughout his life (*Letters of Elizabeth of Bohemia*, ed. L. M. Baker, 1953, 58). By the summer his health had failed yet again, and in July he travelled to Spa seeking recovery. In September he was back in England at Bury St Edmunds under the care of a famous Italian physician and had improved enough to be back at court by the end of the year; it was reported that 'He eates and sleepes well, and grows fatter and lookes cheerefully' (*Downshire MSS*, 6.598). When Sir George Calvert replaced the disgraced Sir Thomas Lake as secretary of state, Morton was advanced to Calvert's council clerkship in ordinary in February 1619. His diplomatic career was laid aside in the next two years or so as he served in the clerks' ordinary rotation, performing clerical duties at the council table, broken only by a trip to see the palatines crowned in Bohemia.

With the escalation of the Thirty Years' War in 1620, Morton was called back to the diplomatic service, delivering £30,000 which had been collected in England for the war effort of the princes of the protestant union. He was soon back in England with his career under a cloud, though the reasons are unclear. He evidently decided to leave government service, attempting to obtain the position of provost of King's College, Cambridge, late in 1622. Frustrated by the incumbent's refusal to vacate the position, but apparently back in favour, he received the promises of the king, the prince of Wales, and the duke of Buckingham that he was meant for better things. His career path remained bumpy, however. Allegedly impatient with James's pro-Spanish policy, he resigned his council clerkship in a huff in 1623. He still hoped to succeed his uncle at Venice and was discussed as a possible candidate for a post as master of requests as part of Wotton's deal to become provost of Eton, or as a replacement for Sir Francis Cottington as secretary to the prince of Wales. In April 1624 it was rumoured that he would be offered the post of ambassador in Paris, but that he planned to refuse the offer. The news writer John Chamberlain commented that 'though he be a sufficient gentleman I shold as much marvaile at his refusall as at the offer' (*CSP dom.*, 1623–5, 551–2). The offer was genuine and Morton accepted. In August he hung around London viewing the runaway theatrical hit, the political satire *A Game at Chess*, while his patent was in preparation.

At this time Morton finally proposed marriage to Elizabeth Apsley, daughter of Sir Edward Apsley of Kent, whom he had met years before at the court of Elizabeth of Bohemia where she served as a maid of honour. The prospective bride travelled to England in November 1624 and, while on his way to meet her at Gravesend, Morton suffered a serious fall from his horse. Although some feared he might not recover, his typical resilience prevailed and on 13 January 1625 he and Elizabeth were married at Eton. His career prospects also seemed to be looking up, undoubtedly due to the more secure patronage of the duke of Buckingham. Before he could take up his post in Paris he was being talked of as successor to Calvert, who had recently resigned from the secretaryship. Morton agreed to pay £3000 for the office and on 9 February at Newmarket took the oath of office and received his seals of authority. The king was said to have spoken favourably on the occasion of Wotton 'who had bred him up to service' (*CSP dom.*, 1625–7, 472).

In the parliamentary elections of the spring of 1625 Morton, as was expected of crown officers, stood for election, in Kent and at Cambridge University. The county election in Kent was hotly contested and he was reported to have 'made an oration or speech none of the wisest' (*Letters of John Chamberlain*, 2.615). Morton had court support, including that of the earl of Montgomery, and although Chamberlain alleged that he lost by a margin of 3 to 1 in Kent, he was returned for the county as well as for the university seat, having apparently spent £200–£300 in the effort. His parliamentary career was almost immediately overtaken when he accompanied Buckingham to France to assist with negotiations late in May 1625. He returned to England with a delegation from Buckingham to discourage the king from going in person to claim his French bride, and within a fortnight was dispatched to replace Carleton

as ambassador at The Hague. He shuttled back and forth across the channel in the summer months of 1625 and joined the royal court at Southampton on 24 August.

Morton returned to England so ill with a fever that he did not stop to see his wife, nor did he report the results of his negotiation to the king. He was believed to have a tertian ague and kept to his chamber for several days. The court physicians reported that he was in no danger of death and his wife was invited to court to see him. On the way she met a messenger with the news that her husband had died about 7 p.m. on Tuesday 7 September. His illness was probably considered contagious as his body was buried immediately at Southampton, on 8 September. He died intestate and childless. Elizabeth Morton was treated generously by the king, who granted her Morton's pension of £500 per annum for life and paid her the money owed Morton for his services to the crown. Suitors were soon vying both for her husband's office and her hand in marriage, apparently seeing the two as a package deal. She frustrated her suitors, however, by dying within a few months of her husband. Both were eulogized in poems by Sir Henry Wotton. S. A. BARON

Sources *The life and letters of Sir Henry Wotton*, ed. L. P. Smith, 2 vols. (1907) · *CSP dom.* · *The letters of John Chamberlain*, ed. N. E. McClure, 2 vols. (1939) · PRO, state papers domestic, James I, SP14 · PRO, state papers domestic, Charles I, SP16 · *Report on the manuscripts of the marquis of Downshire*, 6 vols. in 7, HMC, 75 (1924–95), vols. 5–6 · *GM*, 1st ser., 68 (1798) · Wood, *Ath. Oxon.*, new edn · J. Nichols, *The progresses, processions, and magnificent festivities of King James I, his royal consort, family and court*, 4 vols. (1828) · C. Oman, *Elizabeth of Bohemia* (1938) · F. M. G. Evans, *The principal secretary of state: a survey of the office from 1558 to 1680* (1923) · BL, Trumbull MSS · *Calendar of Wynn papers*, National Library of Wales (1926)

Morton, Andrew (1802–1845), portrait painter, born at Newcastle upon Tyne on 25 July 1802, was the son of Joseph Morton, master mariner in Newcastle, and was an elder brother of Thomas *Morton (1813–1849), the surgeon. He went to London and studied at the Royal Academy Schools, gaining a silver medal in 1821, the first year he exhibited there. From 1821 to 1845 he exhibited at the Royal Academy, the British Institution, and the Society of British Artists in Suffolk Street. He confined himself entirely to portraits, painting in the style of Sir Thomas Lawrence. He had a large practice and many distinguished society sitters, including William IV, the duke of Wellington, Sir James Cockburn, Marianna, Lady Cockburn, and Marianna Augusta, Lady Hamilton. The National Portrait Gallery, London, and the Scottish National Portrait Gallery, Edinburgh, among other galleries, hold works by him. Morton died of inflammation of the lungs on 1 August 1845 in London.

L. H. CUST, rev. EMILY M. WEEKS

Sources Redgrave, *Artists* · Graves, *Artists* · Wood, *Vic. painters*, 3rd edn · B. Stewart and M. Cutten, *The dictionary of portrait painters in Britain up to 1920* (1997)

Morton, Charles (*bap.* 1627, *d.* 1698), nonconformist minister and tutor, was born at Pendavy, Cornwall, and baptized at Egloshayle in the same county on 18 February 1627, the son of Nicholas Morton (*d.* 1640), clergyman, and Frances, daughter of Thomas Kestell of Pendavy. His mother died a few years after his birth; his father, who was educated at Emmanuel College, Cambridge, and was thought by Edmund Calamy to have been a nonconformist, had just left the rectory of St Ive, Cornwall, to become chaplain and preacher at St Saviour's, Southwark. After his father's death in 1640 Charles lived with his mother's family in Pendavy. He entered Queens' College, Cambridge, on 19 June 1646 but moved to New Inn Hall at Oxford in 1648 as part of an influx of Cambridge men into the older university after it was purged of royalists by the parliamentary visitors. On 7 September 1649 he was admitted to Wadham College, Oxford, graduating BA on 6 November of that year and proceeding MA on 24 June 1652. Under its warden, John Wilkins, Wadham was a centre for the study of the new science. Among Morton's fellow students was Samuel Lee, with whom Morton was also later to be acquainted at Newington Green and in New England.

In February 1653 Morton left Oxford to become vicar of Takeley in Essex, but later moved to Blisland, near Pendavy in Cornwall. By 1654 he had married his wife, Joan (*d.* 1693), as a daughter, Alice, was baptized at Blisland in that year. Morton was admitted as rector of Blisland on 11 July 1655 and remained there until ejected at the Restoration in 1660. Thereafter he settled nearby on a property of his own at St Ive and preached to a small group until moving to London in 1666 in order to take care of his affairs there, having sustained considerable loss as a consequence of the great fire of that year. There Morton entered the wider world of London dissent. In 1672 he had a house in the neighbourhood of Kennington, where he was licensed, as a presbyterian, to preach under the declaration of indulgence; his house at St Ive was also licensed as a meeting place.

Morton's fame came from his work as an educator of protestant dissenters excluded by the universities. He may have first accepted pupils, at Kennington but by 1675 he was conducting an academy at Newington Green on the outskirts of London. Before Morton was forced to close it in 1685, it was probably the most impressive of the dissenting academies, enrolling as many as fifty pupils at a time. Many educated there entered the dissenting ministry. Besides the usual religious and classical curriculum there was instruction in history, geography, mathematics, natural science, politics, and modern languages, and a laboratory equipped with air pumps, thermometers, and various mathematical instruments. There was a bowling green for recreation. Instruction was in English, and Daniel Defoe, who was educated there, thought that the pupils gained a greater mastery of English than at any other contemporary school. Samuel Wesley, another pupil, described Morton as universal in his learning. As a teacher Morton was skilled in making difficult subjects understandable and drew up summaries of knowledge for the use of his pupils who copied them. Some survived in manuscript, including 'Ethicks', his modification of traditional Aristotelian ethics, and 'Compendium physicae', a summary, with diagrams, of scientific knowledge, which grafted Copernican astronomy, Cartesianism, and some of the investigations of the Royal Society onto an Aristotelian trunk. The latter was used at Harvard as late as 1728.

Morton's manuscript 'Eutaxia', no longer extant, set forth an ideal politics, and was considered republican by Samuel Wesley, who later decried his fellow students at Newington Green as opponents of episcopacy and monarchy, though acknowledging that Morton rebuked their disloyalty. But Morton must have been under suspicion, for harassment forced him to abandon his academy. He was charged with violation of the generally ignored Stamford oath, taken by recipients of the MA at the two universities, which forbade graduates from teaching elsewhere. Morton was excommunicated and arrested, and though he defended himself in the bishop's court, arguing that his academy gave no degrees, he none the less found it expedient to leave for New England.

Morton arrived in Boston with his wife and a daughter, Mary, in June 1686, responding to an invitation to be pastor of the first church in Charlestown, Massachusetts, but also with the understanding that it was likely that he would be offered the presidency of Harvard College. His arrival was widely hailed; the diarist Samuel Sewall often heard him preach and considered it memorable to have dined with him. But the royal governor, Sir Edmund Andros, also arrived in Boston in 1686, jeopardizing Massachusetts institutions, and it would have been impolitic then to give Morton the presidency of Harvard, though later he was named to its corporation and in 1697 became its vice-president, a largely honorific post. He was installed as pastor at Charlestown on 5 November 1686. However he instructed a few private pupils until advised against doing so by the Harvard authorities; he occasionally lectured at Harvard.

Two of Morton's ecclesiastical practices startled New England: he insisted on being merely installed at Charlestown rather than ordained by the laying-on of hands (to the chagrin of Cotton Mather) as he had already been ordained to the ministry (though there is no record of it); and he performed marriages, hitherto purely a civil activity, for his parishioners. Both of these practices became increasingly common thereafter. Morton also led in the founding of a Cambridge Ministerial Association; he had been prominent in such an association while at Blisland. His views on ordination and associations represented somewhat presbyterian modifications of the 'congregational way'. He strongly identified with the colony's traditions, however, when in a 1687 sermon he criticized the revocation of the colony's charter; as a consequence the governor's council brought him to trial in the superior court for sedition, but the jury acquitted him. In 1692 he joined in signing an advice to the judges in the Salem witchcraft trials, cautioning against the admission of spectral evidence. In 1693 his *The Spirit of Man* was published in Boston; his most significant publication, it was a learned psychological treatise that discussed the relation of temperament to morality, developing a typology of temperaments and analysing the effect of grace upon persons of different dispositions. It recommended a 'cheerful' Christianity.

Morton's wife died in 1693; her family and the precise date of their marriage are unknown. Not long afterwards Morton's health began to fail. The Charlestown church tried unsuccessfully to provide him with an assistant. In June 1697 Morton confided to Sewall that he thought his death was near. In January 1698 he took to bed, dying on 11 April 1698, and was buried at Charlestown on 14 April. He left £50 to Harvard College.

Morton published relatively little, and was known for citing the adage 'a big book is a big evil'. His significance was as a teacher who through his compendia and instruction disseminated new ideas in philosophy and natural science in both England and New England. Although his own contributions to science were negligible (his recommendation of the use of sea sand for fertilizer was printed in the *Philosophical Transactions of the Royal Society* for April 1676; his speculation that migrating birds flew to the moon was published posthumously in London in 1703), he recognized the importance of observation and measurement and of such new instruments as the telescope and microscope, and was a proponent of experimental method. Morton thought that the study of nature displayed the power and wisdom of God. His writings suggest a moderate Calvinism, a strong moralizing tendency, and a warm-hearted, practical piety rather than a concern with theological orthodoxy.

DEWEY D. WALLACE, JUN.

Sources S. E. Morison, 'Charles Morton', in *Charles Morton's Compendium physicae* (1940), vii–xxix · F. L. Harris, 'Charles Morton: minister, academy master and emigrant (1627–1698)', *Journal of the Royal Institution of Cornwall*, new ser., 4 (1961–4), 362–52 · E. Calamy, ed., *An abridgement of Mr. Baxter's history of his life and times, with an account of the ministers, &c., who were ejected after the Restauration of King Charles II*, 2nd edn, 2 vols. (1713), vol. 2, pp. 144–6 · E. Calamy, *A continuation of the account of the ministers … who were ejected and silenced after the Restoration in 1660*, 2 vols. (1727), vol. 1, pp. 177–211 · *Calamy rev.* · E. J. McManus, 'Morton, Charles', *ANB* · N. Fiering, *Moral philosophy at seventeenth century Harvard* (1981), 207–38 · F. A. Turk, 'Charles Morton: his place in the historical development of British science in the seventeenth century', *Journal of the Royal Institution of Cornwall*, new ser., 4 (1961–4), 353–63 · J. W. Ashley Smith, *The birth of modern education: the contribution of the dissenting academies, 1660–1800* (1954), 56–61 · T. Hornberger, 'The compendium physicae', in *Charles Morton's Compendium physicae* (1940), xxxi–xl · *The diary of Samuel Sewall, 1674–1729: newly edited from the manuscript at the Massachusetts Historical Society*, ed. M. H. Thomas, 2 vols. (1973) · *DNB* · *CSP col.*, vol. 13 · R. Frothingham, *The history of Charlestown, Massachusetts* (1843), 193–6 · J. F. Hunnewell, *Records of the first church in Charlestown, Massachusetts, 1632–1789* (1880) · L. Tyerman, *The life and times of the Rev. Samuel Wesley* (1886), 66–75

Wealth at death £50 bequeathed to Harvard University; plus property in Cornwall and Charlestown left to two nephews and a niece: Morison, 'Charles Morton'

Morton, Charles (1716–1799), physician and librarian, was born in Westmorland. Nothing is known of his parents or his early life. He entered the medical school at Leiden University, the Netherlands, on 18 September 1736. After initial training Morton returned to Westmorland, where he practised at Kendal. In 1744 he married Mary Berkeley (d.

1768), with whom he was to have his only child, Elizabeth. His thesis, *De tussi convulsiva*, was published in 1748 (2nd edn), and he graduated as a doctor of medicine on 30 August of that year. He was admitted to the Royal College of Physicians the following month. By April 1750 he had transferred to London and had been elected consultant physician at the Middlesex Hospital. He held this post for four years, at which point he was appointed physician to the Foundling Hospital. He was admitted a licentiate of the Royal College of Physicians (1 April 1751) and elected a fellow of the Royal Society (16 January 1752).

At the establishment of the British Museum in 1756 Morton accepted an appointment as one of three underlibrarians. His salary was small, although an apartment at the museum was provided free of charge. Initially he was responsible for most manuscripts (although not the Sloane collection), the Edwards books, coins, and medals. However, the need for a more logical arrangement was identified and in 1758 the department of manuscripts was created, with Morton at its head. While in charge of manuscripts he was elected a fellow of the Society of Antiquaries (24 November 1757) and served as secretary to the Royal Society (1759–74). He also became a fellow of the Imperatorskaya Akademiya Nauk at St Petersburg and was admitted to both the Königliche Gesellschaft der Wissenschaften at Göttingen and the Deutsche Akademie der Naturforscher Leopoldina. Scholars, including Sir John Hawkins and probably also Dr Samuel Johnson, were often permitted to consult manuscripts in his office or private apartments. Work progressed on cataloguing the principal collections, and in 1762 he wrote an introduction to *A Catalogue of the Harleian Collection of Manuscripts* (2 vols., 1759–63). Work had also began on an edition of the Domesday Book. Originally the text for this was to be engraved, but when Morton was appointed to the project about 1768, he proposed the use of metal types. Eventually he was to receive £500 'for doing little or nothing', and nearly £200 more for types that were 'of no use' (Nichols, *Lit. anecdotes*, 3.263). Abraham Farley, who successfully went on to publish the facsimile in 1783, stated that 'he was for a little time sadly mortified by Dr Morton having been appointed his associate in the revision of the press' (ibid., 3.266). Morton himself published a revised edition of Edward Bernard's table of alphabets entitled *Tabulam hanc à se restauratam* (1759), an edition of *Whitelockes Notes uppon the Kings Writt for Choosing Members of Parlement* (2 vols., 1766), and an edition of the *Journal of the Swedish Ambassy, in the Years 1653 and 1654* (2 vols., 1772). He published two articles in the *Philosophical Transactions of the Royal Society* (1769 and 1777), the former of which, concerning a possible relationship between Chinese ideographs and Egyptian hieroglyphs, was republished as an extract in 1770. By this time his scholarly interests appear to have been focusing increasingly on literature, philosophy, and oriental languages. This period also saw the death of his first wife, Mary, in 1768 and his marriage to Lady Mary Savile, *née* Pratt (c.1706–1791), in 1772. She was the daughter of John Pratt, the deputy vice-treasurer of Ireland, and his wife, Honoretta Brooker, had previously been married to Sir George Savile, seventh baronet (*bap.* 1678, *d.* 1743), and was the mother of Sir George *Savile, eighth baronet (1726–1784). She provided a house in Heath Road, Twickenham, Middlesex, which was to become Morton's summer residence.

In 1776 Morton succeeded Matthew Maty as principal librarian, a post which he was to hold until his death. He appears to have been neither hard-working nor innovative. Miller states that he 'was a man of sedentary habits, extremely idle, disposed to let things run on from day to day' (Miller, 83–4). He increasingly suffered from gout, which caused him to take extended absences from the museum. During the Gordon riots of 1780, part of the York regiment was stationed at the British Museum. Morton, however, decided to remain in Twickenham, and even failed to appear when George III visited Bloomsbury to inspect the troops. The museum trustees demanded an explanation, and in February 1781 Morton replied that he had been absent owing to ill health. He was subsequently directed not to live away from the museum without their leave. Lady Mary died on 10 February 1791 and two months later, in April, Morton married Elizabeth Pratt (*b.* 1755/6) of Cabra Castle, co. Cavan. His third wife was a close relative of his second and, as pointed out in *The Times* of 29 April 1791, was just thirty-five years of age to Morton's near eighty years. Morton died on 10 February 1799 at his apartments in the British Museum. He was buried in the cemetery in Back Lane, off London Road, Twickenham, on 18 February 1799. His third wife survived him.

ADRIAN S. EDWARDS

Sources A. Esdaile, *The British Museum Library: a short history and survey* (1946) · E. Miller, *That noble cabinet: a history of the British Museum* (1973) · P. R. Harris, *A history of the British Museum Library, 1753–1973* (1998) · Munk, *Roll* · A. Chalmers, ed., *The general biographical dictionary*, new edn, 32 vols. (1812–17) · A. E. Gunther, *The founders of science at the British Museum, 1753–1900* (1980) · R. S. Cobbett, *Memorials of Twickenham* (1872) · E. Peacock, *Index to English speaking students who have graduated at Leyden University* (1883) · Nichols, *Lit. anecdotes* · *GM*, 1st ser., 69 (1799), 173, 250 · J. Evans, *A history of the Society of Antiquaries* (1956) · T. Thomson, *History of the Royal Society from its institution to the end of the eighteenth century* (1812) · *The Times* (19 Feb 1791) · *The Times* (28–9 April 1791) · *The Times* (13 Feb 1799) · *The record of the Royal Society of London*, 3rd edn (1912) · *A catalogue of the library of the late Chas. Morton* (1800) [sale catalogue, Sothebys, 10 March 1800] · *IGI* · parish register (burials), Twickenham, 6 Oct 1768

Archives BL, official diary, Add. MS 54871 · BL, official diary, Add. MS 45872 | BL, letters to Thomas Birch and others, official diaries, etc.

Wealth at death left house, cottages, and fields at Twickenham, Middlesex; estates in Ireland; British and Irish currency; main beneficiaries were wife, daughter, her husband and children: will

Charles Morton (1819–1904), by Elliott & Fry, pubd 1904

Morton, Charles (1819–1904), music-hall and theatre manager, was born in Hackney, Middlesex, on 15 August 1819. Little is known of his early life, but he was established as a publican by about 1840. In 1849 he acquired the Canterbury Arms in Upper Marsh, Lambeth, where he boosted custom by organizing concerts. In May 1852 he opened a custom-built concert hall on the skittle alley, to which admission was gained by a 6*d.* refreshment ticket, redeemable for drinks. The venture proved sufficiently popular for an improved hall to be opened in December 1854, at a reputed cost of £40,000.

It was, above all, this early phase of Morton's career that eventually earned him the title 'Father of the Halls'. Most modern students of music-hall history agree that this claim was in many ways undeserved. Morton's reputation owed much to his longevity and his popularity with certain key figures in the worlds of entertainment and journalism, and these factors combined to marginalize the achievements of others. Although his decision to build a 'music-hall' that was physically separate from the public house was unusual, many publicans, in the provinces as well as London, were developing concert halls from the 1840s and 1850s and utilizing several of the practices once commonly seen as peculiar to the Canterbury. Nevertheless, Morton was a significant figure in the growth of the industry, above all as a skilled publicist at an important moment in its development. Particularly in the 1870s, he also made a substantial contribution to the development of musical theatre and light opera in London.

Arguably Morton's most distinctive contribution to the nascent industry can be seen in his attempt to develop a refined style of entertainment that helped to earn much needed respectability and publicity. More forcefully and effectively than most of his contemporaries, he stole the clothes of those potential enemies who sought to reform popular recreation by placing great emphasis on the moral and educational tone of certain elements of the Canterbury's programme. He employed a choir which performed operatic selections, glees, and madrigals; indeed, Gounod's *Faust*, or at least extracts from it, was given for the first time in Britain at the Canterbury in 1859. A small art gallery was established in an annexe in 1856, along with a small reading-room. In 1855 and 1856 Morton produced theatrical entertainments at the hall, although the fact that he did so without the necessary licence brought him into conflict with the local magistracy. Even then, the subsequent publicity helped to boost the hall's success even further. Morton thus foreshadowed much of the philosophy that underpinned the growth of the so-called variety industry from the late nineteenth century.

The music-hall industry had begun its colonization of London's West End in 1857 with the opening of Weston's

Music Hall, and Morton followed this trend by opening the Oxford Music Hall in Oxford Street in March 1861. Significantly, the hall opened with a concert featuring Charles Santley, a leading young bass-baritone in the fields of oratorio and opera, and the operatic soprano Euphrosyne Parepa. Rather more typical fare followed this skilfully designed publicity stunt, with most leading music-hall performers of the period appearing at the Oxford. In the late 1860s the hall was strongly associated with the Great Vance, a leading comic singer. The Oxford burnt down in February 1868, an event which was to sever Morton's connection with the industry for some time. From 1868 to 1870 he was proprietor of the North Woolwich Gardens, which featured a combination of concerts, acrobatic entertainments, and ballet, but, partly as a result of poor weather, the venture failed. In 1870 he took over as part proprietor of the Philharmonic in Islington, where he began a new phase of his career as a promoter of light opera and musical theatre. His greatest success came with the production of Offenbach's *Geneviève de Brabant*, starring Emily Soldene, which opened in November 1871. A dispute with his business partner at the Philharmonic led to Morton's leaving the theatre in 1873 to spend the next four years in a number of short-term ventures, including a tour of the United States with the Soldene Opera Bouffe Company, one of the earliest light opera companies to tour America. The venture lost £8000, and Morton spent the rest of his career in managerial positions as a result of his lack of capital. For most of the period between 1877 and 1890 Morton managed the Alhambra, first as a theatre and light opera house, later as a variety theatre. He was forcibly retired by the directors in 1890, and it was in a poem read at his farewell benefit concert that the journalist Clement Scott awarded him the sobriquet 'Father of the Halls'. In 1891 Morton became manager of the Tivoli Music Hall, and he completed his career at the Palace. He retired on account of ill health in August 1904, and died at his home, 11 Oval Road, Regent's Park, on 18 October 1904.

Morton's private life is decidedly obscure. He was, at least in his old age, almost teetotal, a non-smoker, and a vegetarian. He was married twice—his first wife died in the 1840s—and his death left his second wife, Kate, in *The Era*'s words, 'very inadequately provided for'. A benefit concert was held for her in November 1904. Morton also left at least one daughter, Olive Meads, who was present at his death.   DAVE RUSSELL

Sources W. H. Morton and H. C. Newton, *Sixty years stage service: being a record of the life of Charles Morton, 'the Father of the Halls'* (1905) · *The Era* (13 Jan 1894) · *The Era* (22 Oct 1904) · H. Scott, *The early doors: origins of the music hall* (1946); repr. (1977), 220–25 · P. Bailey, ed., *Music hall: the business of pleasure* (1986) · CGPLA Eng. & Wales (1904) · d. cert.

Likenesses Elliott & Fry, photograph, pubd 1904 [*see illus.*] · portrait, repro. in *The Era* (22 Oct 1904) · print, Harvard TC

Wealth at death £2078 13s.: probate, 22 Nov 1904, CGPLA Eng. & Wales

Morton, Sir **Desmond John Falkiner** (1891–1971), army

officer and intelligence officer, was born on 13 November 1891 at 9 Hyde Park Gate, London, the only son of Colonel

Sir Desmond John Falkiner Morton (1891–1971), by Howard Coster, 1944

Charles Falkiner Morton (*d.* 1929), Royal Dragoons, and his wife, Edith Harriet, daughter of John Towlerton Leather of Middleton Hall, Bedford, Northumberland. Educated at Eton College and the Royal Military Academy, Woolwich, he joined the Royal Horse and Royal Field Artillery in 1911 and served throughout the First World War. While he was commanding a forward battery at Arras a bullet lodged in his heart, but with characteristic resilience he survived to be awarded the MC and become an aide-de-camp to Field Marshal Douglas Haig. The appointment profoundly affected his future career. He had to conduct round the front line the minister of munitions, Winston Churchill, who formed what in his memoirs he called a great regard and friendship for this brilliant and gallant officer. In 1919 the influence of Churchill, Lloyd George, and Sir Eyre Crowe drew Morton into the Foreign Office as an intelligence officer.

Morton's work was at its peak in the thirties. From 1929 to September 1939 he was head of the committee of imperial defence's industrial intelligence centre, concentrating for his masters on the rearmament of Germany but also using his private sources to keep Churchill, then in the political wilderness, fully briefed. He did so—it has been claimed—by a unique authority granted to him by Ramsay MacDonald and endorsed by Stanley Baldwin and Neville Chamberlain, though according to Churchill's official biographer, Martin Gilbert, no evidence has been found for any of these assertions. In any case the relationship was eased by the fact that Morton lived only a mile from Churchill's home at Chartwell, where, apart from regular meetings to share his secret information, he assisted Churchill in his literary work—notably during the composition of *The World Crisis* (5 vols., 1923–31). In 1947 Churchill wrote to Morton: 'When I read all these letters and papers you wrote for me and think of our prolonged conversations I feel how very great is my debt to you, and I know that no other thought ever crossed your mind but that of the public interest.' The private papers of Sir Maurice Hankey, the pivot of the cabinet and the committee of imperial defence, also disclose an intimate collaboration with Morton during this decade.

On the outbreak of war Morton was made a principal assistant secretary, Ministry of Economic Warfare, but when Churchill became prime minister in May 1940 he placed Morton in his private office as his personal assistant. Here, for a time, Morton's position was central and strong. Initially he was the filter through which Churchill received the Ultra intelligence obtained at Bletchley Park from breaking the German Enigma cipher, and he was active in liaison with the foreign governments in exile. Morton played an enthusiastic early role in the formation of the Special Operations Executive and in plans for aid to the French resistance, in particular. But as the war ran on Churchill depended increasingly on the chiefs of staff and their highly integrated network of subsidiary committees, while the voluminous flow of Ultra and other intelligence required a systematic handling. Inevitably, therefore, Morton's role was reduced. In contemporary documents and in photographs of the major wartime conferences his name and his face often appear, but as an *éminence grise* his authority waned.

Morton was appointed CMG in 1937, CB in 1941, and KCB in 1945. In addition he was awarded the Croix de Guerre *avec palmes*, the officership of the Légion d'honneur, and the knight's grand cross of Orange Nassau. In 1949 he served on the economic survey mission, Middle East, and from 1950 to 1953 he was seconded to the Ministry of Civil Aviation.

In spite of an ebullient style Morton was a man of inner sensitivities, and obsessive about preserving his anonymity in respect of secret matters. Before the First World War he became a Roman Catholic, and he relished theological discussion. His post-war home at Kew, though small, was distinctively elegant. After his retirement in 1953 he committed himself wholeheartedly to the governorship of the Hammersmith group of hospitals. Yet the extensive correspondence between Morton and the military commentator R. W. Thompson (which was published posthumously) reveals him as a man diminished by disappointment. His criticisms of Churchill, though sometimes just, at other times have almost a vengeful character. The letters are an unhappy footnote to the story of one who had done the state much service.

Morton died at Hammersmith Postgraduate Hospital, London, on 31 July 1971. He was unmarried.

RONALD LEWIN, *rev.*

Sources M. Gilbert, *Winston S. Churchill*, 5: *1922–1939* (1976) • R. W. Thompson, *Churchill and Morton* (1976) • J. Colville, *The Churchillians* (1981) • R. Lewin, *ULTRA goes to war: the secret story* (1978) • private information (1986) • *WWW*, *1971–80* • Burke, *Peerage* (1967) • Burke, *Gen. GB* (1937) • *The Eton register*, 7 (privately printed, Eton, 1922) • *The Times* (2 Aug 1971) • W. K. Wark, *The ultimate enemy: British intelligence and Nazi Germany, 1933–1939* (1986) • b. cert. • *CGPLA Eng. & Wales* (1971)

Archives PRO, papers, PRE M7 | King's Lond., Liddell Hart C., corresp. with R. W. Thompson • King's Lond., Liddell Hart C., corresp. with Sir B. H. Liddell Hart • Nuffield Oxf., corresp. with Lord Cherwell

Likenesses H. Coster, photograph, 1944, NPG [*see illus.*]

Wealth at death £114,025: probate, 22 Sept 1971, *CGPLA Eng. & Wales*

Morton, (Henry) Digby (1906/7–1983), couturier, was born in Ireland. His death certificate states his date of birth as 27 November 1907; this is contradicted, however, by records in the archives of the Dublin Metropolitan School of Art, which place his birth as one year earlier, at an unspecified date in 1906. The academic registers of that institution for 1919–20 also provide the only available information about Digby Morton's parents; at that time they lived at 20 Belgrave Square, Rathmines, which was a well-to-do residential area on the south side of Dublin. Only one sibling, a sister, is recorded in the available sources. Information about Morton's marriage and the subsequent birth of his offspring is also extremely limited. However, it is known that he married a journalist named Phyllis, and that they had a granddaughter, Susan Caroline Bishop. As Elizabeth Crum notes, Morton 'was a gregarious man who "rejoiced in his Irishness"' (McCrum, 26). More nuanced representations of his personality are offered in four photographic portraits by Francis Goodman (NPG), in which his facial expression ranges from charming and almost cheekily suave London couturier to thoughtful and melancholic Irish expatriate.

Morton attended the Dublin Metropolitan School of Art as an evening student from 1919 to 1923. The archival records of the college do not indicate the classes that he attended or what, if any, qualifications he attained; however, several sources state that he was a student of art and architecture. After studying in Dublin he attended the Polytechnic Art School, London.

Morton began his London-based fashion career in 1928 as the first designer at the British couture house of Lachasse, which was a newly formed sportswear offshoot of Gray and Paulette Ltd. This firm's clientele consisted of 'mostly the rich racing set', for whom Morton created innovative and exquisite tailoring, as Hardy Amies noted in 1984:

> Morton's philosophy was to transform the suit from the strict *tailleur*, or the ordinary country tweed fit only for the moors, into an intricately cut and carefully designed garment, so fashionable that it could be worn with confidence at the Ritz. Such clothes have become so much a part of the fashion picture … during more than the last fifty years that it is hard to realise how much they owe to Morton's original ideas. (Amies, 21)

Encouraged by this success, Morton left Lachasse in 1933 and opened his own couture house in Palace Gate, London, introducing a ready-to-wear collection in 1939. His

(Henry) **Digby Morton** (1906/7–1983), by Francis Goodman

work retained a focus on the tailored tweed suit, although he also designed other day wear and evening wear and was noted as one of the first fashion designers to use Aran knitwear. One of Morton's suits was famously featured in the Cecil Beaton 'Fashion is Indestructible' *Vogue* shoot of September 1941. Morton was also a founder member of the Incorporated Society of London Fashion Designers, which was set up in 1942. This group was asked by the wartime Board of Trade to create a series of designs based on the regulations of the resource-saving utility scheme. A WVS uniform designed by Digby Morton and made by John Barran & Sons in 1942 is in the Museum of London. From 1953 to 1957 Morton worked for American manufacturers, while continuing to run a successful couture house until it closed in 1957. In 1958 he became design director of Reldan–Digby Morton, where he worked until he retired, in 1973.

Morton died in the Middlesex Hospital, Westminster, on 5 December 1983, when his address was recorded as 199 Richmond Road, Twickenham, Middlesex. A collection of garments and accessories designed by him, mostly in the 1940s and 1950s, is in the Victoria and Albert Museum, London; further small collections are held by the Museum of Costume, Bath, and Manchester City Art Galleries (Platt Hall).   FIONA ANDERSON

Sources Dublin Metropolitan School of Art, payment registers, 1919–20, 1921–2, 1922–3, National Irish Visual Arts Library · E. McCrum, *Fabric & form: Irish fashion since 1950* (1996) · H. Amies, *Still here: an autobiography* (1984) · V. Mendes and A. de la Haye, *20th century fashion* (1999) · A. de la Haye, ed., *The cutting edge: 50 years of British fashion, 1947–1997* (1997) [exhibition catalogue, V&A, March 1997] · L. Watson, *Vogue twentieth century fashion: 100 years of style by decade and designer* (1999) · G. O'Hara, *The encyclopedia of fashion* (1989) · J. Mulvagh, *Vogue history of twentieth century fashion* (1988) · G. Howell, *In Vogue: sixty years of celebrities and fashion from British Vogue* (1978) · C. McDowell, *McDowell's directory of twentieth century fashion* (1984) · d. cert.
Likenesses F. Goodman, four photographs, NPG [*see illus.*]

Morton, Fergus Dunlop, Baron Morton of Henryton (1887–1973), judge, was born at Wilmore, Kelvinside, Glasgow, on 17 October 1887, the youngest of the four children (three boys and a girl) of George Morton (1849–1927), of Troon, Ayrshire, a Glasgow stockbroker, and his wife, Janet (d. 1938), daughter of William Wilson, of Richmond House, Dowanhill, Glasgow. His father, who came of long-established Ayrshire farming stock, left school at thirteen to become a stockbroker's clerk, rose to be chairman of his own firm of stockbrokers, and amassed a considerable fortune. Morton entered Kelvinside Academy in 1897; and in 1906 he won an open exhibition in classics to St John's College, Cambridge. He narrowly missed a first class in part one of the classical tripos in 1909 (taking the examination in bed on account of an attack of influenza), but in 1910 obtained the first place in the first class of part two of the law tripos.

After spending a year in a solicitor's office, Morton was called to the English bar by the Inner Temple in December 1912. In 1914 he also joined Lincoln's Inn. He was a pupil first of A. L. Ellis, a distinguished conveyancer, and then of Dighton Pollock, who enjoyed a large junior practice at the Chancery bar. On 17 December 1914 Morton married Margaret Greenlees (1893–1986), elder daughter of James Begg, a grain merchant.

Morton's legal career was interrupted by military service in the Highland light infantry during the First World War. He saw active service in German East Africa, attained the rank of captain (1915), and was awarded the Military Cross. His two brothers were killed in the war. In September 1919 he returned to the bar. His practice soon grew rapidly, and when he took silk in 1929 he was one of the busiest Chancery juniors. His advocacy was consistently careful, constructive, concise, and cogent.

Morton was knighted and appointed High Court judge (Chancery Division) in 1938. In 1944 he was promoted to the Court of Appeal and sworn of the privy council. In 1947 he became a life peer as Baron Morton of Henryton, and a lord of appeal in ordinary, a position which he held until his retirement in 1959.

As a first-instance judge, Morton dealt courteously and efficiently with the business then typical of the Chancery Division. Who, for example, was entitled to the income arising under a protective trust when the life tenant's interest was sequestrated? Could trustees properly exercise a power to advance capital when the trust instrument stipulated that the consent of a person who had become an enemy alien be first obtained? In the Court of Appeal his judgments evidence a cautious and conservative approach to issues of legal policy: Morton spoke out strongly against extending the legal definition of charity, for example. In the House of Lords he was for many years somewhat reticent, delivering substantive opinions only comparatively rarely. He did give a number of important opinions about the validity of charitable gifts; but perhaps his most significant contribution to the development of the law was indirect. In *Chapman* v. *Chapman* (1954) the Lords held that the Chancery court had no inherent jurisdiction to approve rearrangements of beneficial interests under settlements in order to secure benefits (often by minimizing the then crippling burden of taxes) and that the recognized power of the court to sanction compromises could not extend to cases in which the 'dispute' had been created only by the ingenuity of Chancery counsel. The lord chancellor immediately referred the decision to the Law Reform Committee, which advised that the only satisfactory solution would be to give the court the unrestricted power to sanction beneficial variations which it had in fact freely exercised for some years; the Variation of Trusts Act of 1958 was the outcome. The younger generation of Chancery judges and practitioners dealing with the large number of applications under the 1958 act did not seem to share Morton's concern that judicially sanctioned tax avoidance could involve an 'undignified game of chess between the Chancery Division and the legislature'.

Morton's skills were highly regarded in the Lord Chancellor's Office, and in 1950 he was appointed chairman of the committee on the law of intestate succession. The main problem was that the existing scheme of entitlement, established in 1925, meant that widows often had to be turned out of the family home. But to increase the widow's entitlement might operate unfairly in the increasingly common case where the deceased had been married more than once, especially if the second marriage occurred late in life. The committee's solution was to recommend a substantial increase for the widow, while extending to intestacy the discretionary powers of the court to order 'reasonable financial provision' for dependants.

Morton's brisk chairmanship enhanced his reputation, and made him appear well qualified to chair the royal commission on marriage and divorce established in 1951 in response to strong parliamentary and other pressure for reform. But the outcome was a disappointment. The commission was hopelessly divided on the question whether the law should allow divorce founded on the fact that the marriage had irretrievably broken down. The commission's failure to establish relevant demographic facts about the incidence of marital breakdown made its report an easy target for savagely hostile criticism, focusing in part on the commission's supposedly legalistic approach. Yet in retrospect the commission's numerous recommendations for detailed reform, based on close and meticulous analysis, not only led to useful legislation but kept the issue of broader reform before parliament and the public and perhaps thereby fostered a climate of opinion favourable to the changes eventually made by the Divorce Reform Act of 1969.

In 1939 Morton was appointed deputy chairman of the contraband committee at the Ministry of Economic Warfare and from 1941 to 1946 he was chairman of the blacklist committee at that ministry. From 1949 to 1953 he was chairman of the Council of Legal Education.

Morton was tall, slim, and lithe in appearance; his expression was mild but lively, and he possessed a ready and impish sense of humour which won him general friendship and affection. As might be expected of one who never set foot outside his native Scotland before he first went to Cambridge and who continued throughout his life to pay regular visits to Scotland, his conversation and his advocacy were graced by a gentle and melodious Scottish accent. He was an enthusiastic and skilled golf player and a keen spectator of other ball games.

Morton received honorary degrees of LLD from the universities of Cambridge (1951), Glasgow (1951), St Andrews (1956), and Sydney (1957). He became an honorary fellow of St John's College, Cambridge (1940), and was deputy high steward of Cambridge University. From 1932 he was an elder at St Columba's Church, Pont Street, London. In 1953 he received the unusual honour of election as an honorary member of the Faculty of Advocates, which had thitherto been conferred only on reigning sovereigns. In the same year he served as treasurer of Lincoln's Inn, of which he had been elected a bencher in 1932. He received the grand cross of the order of Orange Nassau (Netherlands) and the US medal of freedom (with silver palms). He died after a fall on 18 July 1973 at his country house, Grey Thatch, Winter Hill, Cookham, Berkshire, and was buried at Putney Vale cemetery. His wife survived him, as also did their only child, a daughter who was herself called to the bar by Lincoln's Inn in 1979.

DENYS B. BUCKLEY, rev. S. M. CRETNEY

Sources personal knowledge (1986) · *WWW* · archives, Lincoln's Inn, London · *Law Reports* (1938–60) · 'Royal commission on marriage and divorce', *Parl. papers* (1955–6), vol. 23, Cmd 9678 · O. R. McGregor, *Divorce in England: a centenary study* (1957) · S. M. Cretney, *Law, law reform and the family* (1998), chaps. 2, 10 · 'Committee on the law of intestate succession', *Parl. papers* (1950–51), 16.637, Cmd 8310 · 'Sixth report', *Parl. papers* (1957–8), 15.729, Cmnd 310 [law reform committee] · Burke, *Peerage* (1967) · private information (1986, 2004) [family]
Likenesses two photographs, c.1910–1942, priv. colls. · W. Stoneman, two photographs, 1938–54, NPG · W. Bird, photograph, 1962, NPG · photograph, Lincoln's Inn, London
Wealth at death £478,582: probate, 20 Sept 1973, *CGPLA Eng. & Wales*

Morton, George Highfield (1826–1900), geologist, was born in Liverpool on 9 July 1826, the son of George Morton, a Liverpool brewer, and his wife, Elizabeth (*née* Bertenshaw). He was educated in Liverpool at the Paddington Academy, the mechanics' institute, and finally the Liverpool Institute, and in 1849 set up business as a paper hanger, based in London Road, Liverpool. On 30 July 1850 he married Sarah Nanny (1829–1898), daughter of Henry Ascroft, ironmonger.

Morton had as a boy acquired an interest in natural history, collecting ammonites as early as 1840, but it was an article he read in *Knight's Store of Knowledge for All Readers* (n.d. [1841]) in the summer of 1845 which ignited his interest in geology. He later wrote of the experience: 'as soon as I began to read the pages on the Geological History of the Earth, a change came over me, for I had found a subject of engrossing interest, something worth living for' (Morton). From about this time he began collecting fossils and minerals, at first around Liverpool, but later from elsewhere in Britain and on overseas trips to France and Belgium. His collection eventually totalled some 7000 specimens which were meticulously catalogued and stored in cabinets built to his own design.

In December 1859 Morton organized the inaugural meeting of what was to become the Liverpool Geological Society, and for almost thirty years served as either secretary or president. He contributed sixty-two papers to its meetings, the majority on aspects of local geology. He was also the author of *The Geology of the Country around Liverpool*, first published in 1863. A second, greatly enlarged, edition appeared in 1891 and this was reprinted in 1897 with an appendix.

In 1864 Morton was appointed as lecturer in geology at Queen's College, Liverpool, the forerunner of Liverpool University. He had become a fellow of the Geological Society of London in 1858, and in 1892 was awarded the Lyell medal in recognition of his work on the geology of the Liverpool area. He died at his home, 209 Edge Lane, Liverpool, following a brief illness, on 30 March 1900, and was buried at Toxteth Park cemetery, Smithdown Road, Liverpool, on 3 April. He was survived by one son and four daughters. A fellow member of the Liverpool Geological Society provided a fitting memorial tribute, calling him 'the father of geology in Liverpool' (*Liverpool Mercury*). Following his death his geological collection was split between the Natural History Museum and University College, Liverpool.

GEOFFREY TRESISE

Sources G. H. Morton, autobiographical note, National Museums and Galleries on Merseyside, Liverpool Geological Society archive · *Liverpool Mercury* (14 Aug 1900) · W. Hewitt, *The Liverpool Geological Society: a retrospect of fifty years' existence and work* (1910) · H. C. Beasley, *Proceedings and Transactions of the Liverpool Biological Society*, 14 (1899–1900), ix–xi · A. S. [A. Straman], *Quarterly Journal of the Geological Society*, 57 (1901), liv–lv · m. cert. · d. cert. [Sarah Nanny Morton] · *CGPLA Eng. & Wales* (1900) · private information (2004) · *Liverpool Daily Post* (3 April 1900)

Archives Liverpool Geological Society, Liverpool, archive · Liverpool Museum, catalogue of mineral and rock collection | U. Lpool L., Boswell archive, special collections, staff papers, D4/15

Likenesses photograph, 1886, Liverpool Geological Society archives, Liverpool · Maull & Fox, photograph, c.1886–1889, Liverpool Geological Society, Liverpool

Wealth at death £5053 8s. 9d.: resworn probate, April 1901, *CGPLA Eng. & Wales* (1900)

Morton, Henry Canova Vollam (1892–1979), travel writer and journalist, was born on 26 July 1892 at 17 Chester Square, Ashton under Lyne, the son of Joseph Thomas Vollam Morton, newspaper editor, and his wife, Margaret Mary Constance Ewart. Educated at King Edward's School, Birmingham, Morton married Dorothy Vaughton (*b.* 1886/7) on 14 September 1915. The marriage failed, and on 4 January 1934 Morton married Violet Mary Muskett, *née* Greig (*b.* 1900/01), herself a divorcée, who was to survive him.

Except for his First World War service in the Warwickshire yeomanry, in which he enlisted as a private in 1914 and rose to the rank of second lieutenant by 1916 and lieutenant in 1918, Morton's entire career was devoted to popular journalism and travel writing. Between 1910 and 1912 he worked for the *Birmingham Gazette and Express*, becoming an assistant editor. In 1913 he moved to London, first editing the *Empire Magazine* and later working briefly for the *Daily Mail*. He returned to London after the war to write for the *Evening Standard*. In 1921 he moved to Lord Beaverbrook's *Daily Express*, where two years later he gained widespread notice reporting the opening of Tutankhamen's tomb.

H. V. Morton, as he styled himself, emerged in the 1920s as one of the *Daily Express*'s most successful columnists. The pivotal moment in his career came in April 1926 when he began to write the series of articles which would be published the following year as *In Search of England*. The book was an immediate success, as it engagingly interwove human interest accounts of a journey around a pastoral England with potted historical and literary vignettes and pronouncements on national identity. Once the approach was set, Morton followed up with similarly titled books on Scotland (1929), Ireland (1930), Wales (1932), South Africa (1948), and London (1951). A prolific writer, who also published accounts of his travels in the Holy Land, Spain, and Italy, and fifteen other works on the British Isles, he had by 1964 sold 2.9 million books, establishing his position as the most popular British travel writer of the twentieth century. Morton was keenly aware of his readers, particularly those in the lower-middle class, insisting that the price of his guides be kept low in order that they might appeal to, and at the same time educate, a large audience in what was the first age of mass democracy in Britain.

Three interrelated themes informed Morton's writings. The first was the claim that the strength of a nation was ultimately determined by the condition of its villages and small towns. Reflecting the ideals of the late Victorian arts and crafts movement and drawing upon the deep love of the countryside he had developed as a youth bicycling through Warwickshire lanes, Morton insisted that only the rural world offered a setting where the occupations, pre-eminently agriculture, which were essential to the physical and emotional well-being, indeed the very survival, of the British people could thrive. The second was the insistence that the industrial and urban revolutions had inflicted fundamental damage on the nation, particularly the rural yeomanry, now subject to ever-increasing foreign competition, and its urban counterparts, the upper-working class and the lower-middle class. Morton developed this line of argument through grim portrayals of city life as well as more humorous accounts of bourgeois American tourists who had achieved material success but who lacked any appreciation of their cultural heritage. The third theme was the hope that through a recognition of the central continuities of British history and national character renewal might be achieved. To Morton the most important element shaping this continuity was Christianity, and it is revealing that he chose to conclude *In Search of England* in a vicar's garden, uniting the pastoral and the spiritual. This approach also carried over into Morton's travel writing on areas other than the United Kingdom, in which he focused only on places and countries, from the Holy Land to Ireland, where faith and life were inextricably linked.

Morton believed that these themes were national in appeal and scope, transcending the narrow confines of any one political party. He espoused them while writing for the *Daily Express*, and equally he espoused them after being lured to its left-wing rival the *Daily Herald*, for which he worked as a special writer between 1931 and 1942. Morton almost welcomed the coming of the Second World War, as he thought it might rescue Britain from the false ideas and malaise which had dominated since the early nineteenth century and reunite the country in a life-and-death struggle to protect its historical and ecological heritage. While Morton did recognize that success in a modern war depended on technology and precision engineering, his wartime writing, which included an account of the 1941 Churchill–Roosevelt meeting which led to the Atlantic charter and a propagandistic novel of what life would be like under a Nazi occupation, emphasized the 'chivalry' of the Royal Air Force and characterized Churchill as an emotional Elizabethan who rose above class to lead a national crusade.

Despite the wide acclaim and wealth which his works had brought Morton, after the Labour Party's 1945 victory he became disenchanted with life in a Britain whose leaders, he argued, were pandering to an increasingly powerful working class and promoting Marxist ideology and state planning over Christian values. To escape these contagions, Morton decided in 1947 to move his family to South Africa, where he believed conditions were not unlike those in England in the 1920s. Morton became a South African citizen, and life at Somerset West, where he settled, brought a measure of contentment. He contemplated writing a memoir to be entitled 'Fair generally', but he abandoned the idea. The last years of Morton's life were increasingly darkened by fears sparked by the decline of British power and the growth of black nationalism, and doubts about the ability of Western governments to survive in a time of crisis that Morton believed was similar to the French Revolutionary era. Morton died on 17/18 June 1979 in South Africa.   C. R. PERRY

Sources Methuen Archives, Rushden, Northamptonshire · CAC Cam., Cecil Roberts MSS · U. Birm., Frances Brett Young MSS · P. Mandler, *The fall and rise of the stately home* (1997) · G. Pawle, 'H. V. Morton: Fleet Street and after', *Blackwood*, 326 (1979), 120–28 · *Quarterly Bulletin of the South African Library*, 34/1 (Sept 1979), 2 · *WWW* · b. cert. · m. cert.
Archives CAC Cam., letters to Cecil Roberts · Methuen Archives, Rushden, Northamptonshire · U. Birm., letters to Francis Brett Young
Likenesses H. Coster, photographs, 1933, NPG

Morton, Sir James (1867–1943), textile and dyestuffs manufacturer, was born on 24 March 1867, at Darvel, Ayrshire, the third of nine children in the family of Alexander Morton (1844–1923) and his wife, Jean, *née* Wiseman (1844/5–1924). Alexander (1844–1923), of hand-loom weaving stock, was the leading entrepreneur in the factory production of lace, mainly for curtains. He had also pioneered direct selling to retailers and diversified into heavier decorative materials, including machine-made carpets. James was educated at Darvel School and Ayr Academy

before joining the firm as an apprentice at the age of sixteen. The firm's success depended on the application of the most modern technology, especially Nottingham lace machinery, and the lowest regional labour costs and unionization in the industry. There was also a strong commitment to stylish designs.

Several of Alexander Morton's sons and relatives were employed by the firm, and by 1895 they were trying to obtain control. James, his brother Gavin, and his cousin Guy became the executive partners, and Alexander assumed the chairmanship, and increasingly turned to hackney horse and pansy breeding and fruit-growing, finally settling in Donegal (1909). By 1895 the firm's annual turnover was £89,000; nearly half this turnover comprised lace and madras, a quarter carpets, and slightly over a quarter tapestry and chenille. Expansion could not be sustained locally because of the scarcity and increasing cost of labour; therefore the firm built a large factory at Carlisle and three carpet factories in Donegal aided by the Irish congested districts board. This expansion was funded by a preference share issue and bank overdrafts.

James Morton's interest in colour and fashion was stimulated by the Arts and Crafts movement associated with William Morris and the Pre-Raphaelites, and was reinforced by his marriage on 21 March 1901 to Beatrice Emily Fagan (1871–1958), an art teacher trained by Charlotte Mason. In 1902 he was disturbed to find that one of his firm's fabrics, which he had coloured, faded badly after only a week in the windows of Liberty's of London, and he spent the next three years trying to improve colour fastness. His work with John Christie of United Turkey Red led to the production of new fast dyes, and in 1905 the first Morton fabrics were sold with guaranteed replacement if they faded. These fabrics, mostly produced at Carlisle, were advertised under the brand name Sundour (dour in Gaelic means water; in Scots, stubborn, hard to move). Within four years Sundour materials accounted for half the firm's annual profits of £16,500, and within seven years three times the profit produced from other output. In 1913 Morton decided to split the firm into two companies: Alexander Morton & Co., which concentrated on lace at Darvel and employed nearly 600 people, and Morton Sundour Fabrics Limited, producing other fabrics at Carlisle. While his father remained chairman of both companies, James Morton became managing director and majority shareholder of Sundour.

Most of the dyes used by Sundour were manufactured in Germany, and when war began in 1914, only five months' supplies were in stock; Morton sought alternative sources, and a chemical plant was built and put into operation to supply his firm's requirements before the German stock was exhausted. By 1918 dyestuffs were being produced to supply other companies; this led to the establishment of Solway Dyes Limited, a subsidiary which also licensed American producers. Morton recognized the demand opportunities, and also the potentiality for further research, and therefore established Scottish Dyes Limited at Grangemouth (1919) with a capital of £300,000, about half of which was raised outside the firm. There followed the discovery of Caledon Jade Green, the fastest dyestuff so far produced; German producers, previously world leaders, had to apply for licences to produce it.

In 1923 Morton sold Scottish Dyes to the British Dyestuffs Corporation, later part of Imperial Chemical Industries. His talents were recognized by ICI, where he served on the dyestuffs division board from 1926 until his death. Morton received a knighthood in 1936 for services to the dye and colour industries.

After selling Scottish Dyes, Morton tried to improve production by seeking to replace the shuttle and loom, and succeeded in combining an innovation in warp-knitting technique with a new method of inserting continuous wefts. By 1935 prototypes (called by Morton 'fly-needle frames') were operational and demonstrated to Samuel Courtauld (1876–1947). A joint company (FNF Limited) was established: Courtaulds took 60 per cent of the shares and provided the working capital and also paid £250,000 for a quarter of the equity in Morton Sundour Fabrics; Morton Sundour took the remaining 40 per cent. FNF did not live up to the expectations of Courtauld and Morton in their lifetimes, but in 1944 an improved device ran at more than three times the speed of the normal warp-knitting machine in a demonstration to the trade. By the 1950s it was being sold worldwide. Morton's association with Courtauld reflected his firm's problems in the depression of the 1930s; profits were slow to recover and research and development were expensive; he lost his chief commercial executive to a rival, and needed time to blood a successor. In the late 1930s he was joined by his elder son, Alastair James Fagan *Morton, who became a great designer, and by his son-in-law, Lieutenant-Commander R. S. E. Hannay, as production manager.

Brought up in a sabbatarian and teetotal home, Morton was a conscientious member of the Church of Scotland, and reared his family of six children according to his beliefs. He was interested throughout his life in art and design, serving during the First World War on a Ministry of Reconstruction committee on adult education, and helping in the formation of the Design and Industries Association. He was an active member of the Royal Society of Arts and of the British Association for the Advancement of Science. In 1923 he became the first recipient of the gold medal awarded to celebrate the Faraday benzene centenary. He died on 22 August 1943 at his home, Dalston Hall, near Carlisle; his wife died on 20 April 1958.

JOHN BUTT

Sources NA Scot., Morton of Darvel muniments, GD326 · J. Morton, *Three generations in a family textile firm* (1971) · W. Morton, *Alexander Morton: pioneer of the lace industry* (Kilmarnock Library, 1960) · *CCI* (1944) · private information (2004) · *Carlisle Journal* (25 April 1958)
Archives NA Scot., Morton of Darvel muniments, corresp. and papers, GD326 · Sci. Mus., business and design papers · V&A NAL, corresp. and papers relating to Morton Sundour Fabrics, diaries, personal corresp., notebooks, and biographical notes
Likenesses G. F. Watts, oils, 1901, priv. coll.; repro. in Morton, *Three generations* · photograph, 1929 (with wife), repro. in Morton, *Three generations* · photograph, 1937, repro. in Morton, *Three generations*
Wealth at death £183,594 13s. 4d.: confirmation, 10 March 1944, CCI

Morton, John (d. 1500), administrator and archbishop of Canterbury, was born in Dorset, at either Bere Regis or Milborne St Andrew, the son of Richard Morton, whose own father had migrated from Nottinghamshire to the south-west. John's uncle served as MP for Shaftesbury in 1437 and his younger brother was sheriff of Somerset and Dorset in 1483. He came, therefore, of a family of middling gentry, prominent in local affairs but with no national profile.

Education and early career to 1471 The first notice of Morton is in 1447, when the pope authorized the bishop of Salisbury to create him notary public. By 1448 he was BCL of Oxford, by 1451 BCn & CL, and in 1452 DCL. During this period his career centred on Oxford; it has been conjectured, but not proved, that he was a member of Balliol College. He practised as a proctor in the chancellor's court from 1448 and was the chancellor's official and commissary in 1451. In 1452 he became principal of the civil-law school and in 1453 of Peckwater Hall, of which he had previously been a fellow. The letters testimonial issued by the university in November 1454 were well deserved, and when forty years later he himself became chancellor of the university (1495–1500)—as also of Cambridge (1499–1500)—it was no empty honour.

In January 1453 Morton obtained his first recorded benefice, the rectory of Shellingford in Berkshire, and it is probable that from this year he was a practising lawyer in the court of arches, of which he was eventually appointed dean in 1474. As Archbishop Thomas Bourchier (d. 1486) was chancellor of England in 1455–6, Morton's translation to royal service was always likely. On 26 September 1456 he became chancellor to Edward, prince of Wales, and continued as such until the Yorkist victory in 1461. In the meantime he began to accumulate lucrative livings. In 1458, for example, he was appointed subdean of Lincoln and a prebendary of Salisbury.

Morton was, almost inevitably, drawn into the developing political crisis in England, and as an eminent lawyer in government service was involved in the drafting of the bill of attainder against Richard, duke of York (d. 1460), in November 1459. Gregory's chronicle relates that on the evening after the second battle of St Albans, fought on 17 February 1461, 'Doctor Morton brought forthe a boke that was fulle of orysons' for a ceremony in which Henry VI blessed the young prince of Wales and dubbed him knight (Gairdner, *Historical Collections*, 214). Such activities, and his close association with Margaret of Anjou and the Lancastrian court, led to Morton's exclusion from the pardon granted by Edward IV on 6 March 1461 after his seizure of the throne. Morton was captured after the battle of Towton while attempting to escape to Scotland, imprisoned in the Tower of London, and included in the bill of attainder of 4 November 1461. He escaped from prison and joined Queen Margaret in France, where he was appointed keeper of the privy seal to Henry VI and

John Morton (d. 1500), tomb effigy

participated in the negotiations leading to the treaty of Tours in June 1462. He subsequently accompanied the queen on both her unsuccessful invasions of Northumberland in 1462 and 1463. Thereafter he remained with the Lancastrian government in exile, and, perhaps despairing of return to England and a meaningful administrative career, in 1469 he matriculated in theology at the University of Louvain. His property in England had been forfeited and his benefices sequestrated in September 1464.

Master of the rolls and conspirator, 1471–1485 When, following the readeption, Lancastrian hopes were finally dashed by the death of Prince Edward at the battle of Tewkesbury (4 May 1471) and by the murder of Henry VI three weeks later, Morton realistically came to terms with the Yorkist regime and on 3 July 1471 received a royal pardon. By Michaelmas he was at work as a master of chancery, and soon he became a valued member of Edward IV's government. On 16 March 1472 he was appointed master of the rolls, in which office he was succeeded in 1479 by his nephew Robert Morton (d. 1497), who in 1486 became bishop of Worcester. During John Morton's tenure of this office under three chancellors the judicial activities of the court of chancery expanded rapidly; the volume of litigation overtook that in the exchequer and approached that of king's bench. The chancery masters were now no longer mere clerks, but were recruited from the ranks of university-trained academic lawyers. That from 2 May 1475 Morton was empowered to fulfil his office by deputy is a reflection of the diplomatic activity in which he was increasingly engaged. Between 1474 and 1482 he was employed as an envoy on several occasions to the courts of France and Burgundy; in 1475 he was involved in the negotiation of the treaty of Picquigny (29 August), and he received a pension of 600 crowns from Louis XI (r. 1461–83). His eminence naturally brought him a plethora of ecclesiastical preferments. Between 1474 and 1478 he acquired at various dates the archdeaconries of Chester, Winchester, Huntingdon, Berkshire, Norfolk, and Leicester, prebends in St Paul's, Wells, York, and Exeter, and the mastership of St Bartholomew's Hospital at Bristol. On 30 October 1478 he was provided by the pope, at royal initiative, to the bishopric of Ely.

An Italian observer remarked how greatly Edward IV relied on Morton's counsel, and indeed the king appointed him an executor of his will. But with the assumption of power by Richard III, Morton's fortunes changed. He was arrested at the council meeting of 13 June 1483 that led to the summary execution of William, Lord Hastings, and by the end of July had been placed in the custody of the duke of Buckingham at Brecon. He was certainly involved in the planning of Buckingham's rebellion, whether or not he instigated it. After the failure of the revolt, having been attainted again in January 1484, he escaped to Flanders, where he actively engaged in the consolidation of an anti-Ricardian coalition, involving both Henry Tudor, whom he had warned of a plot to deliver him from his refuge in Brittany to Richard, and also the kindred of Queen Elizabeth, widow of Edward IV. Although he was pardoned by King Richard in December 1484, in order to win back his loyalty, Morton ignored this and went to Rome, where he arrived before 31 January 1485. His purpose, perhaps, was to secure a dispensation for the marriage of Henry Tudor and Elizabeth of York, and also to prepare the pope for the forthcoming military and political action. If so, he was eminently successful, for after the battle of Bosworth, Pope Innocent VIII (r. 1484–92) gave full support to Henry VII's regime. Morton probably did not mastermind the Tudor rebellion, but he was a vital intermediary who secured papal acquiescence in the enterprise.

Chancellor of England After the Tudor victory Morton returned to England, and assisted at the coronation on 30 October 1485. His attainder was reversed in parliament in November and he was appointed a member of the king's council, and chancellor on 6 March 1487. It is very difficult to evaluate his personal role and influence in the formulation of royal policy, but it is certain that he was among, if not the closest of, Henry VII's advisers; he was present at nearly every council meeting of which record survives, and was responsible for the explanation of the government's intentions to parliament. Under him the original secretarial functions of chancery changed little, but the equitable jurisdiction of its court continued the expansion that had begun while he had been master of the rolls, and statutes gave additional judicial responsibilities to the chancellor himself, so that the drive against disorder came under his general purview. The act of 3 Henry VII c. 1 (commonly known as the Star Chamber Act) set up, under the chancellor's presidency, a single court to replace the various tribunals established over the previous century to deal with abuses of the law resulting from the domination of the regions by great magnates and the maintenance of retinues; in 1495 the chancellor was given responsibility for the investigation of perjury in all the king's courts. These measures were a rationalization of piecemeal developments and gave the chancellor (and the other great officers of state) a new place in the constitution.

Morton was widely blamed for the heavy taxation which characterized the first twelve years of Henry VII's reign, and the Cornish rebels of 1497 singled him out for special hostility. At a higher level of society he had certainly been active in the collection of benevolences in 1491 for the projected French war; but that famous device 'Morton's fork' (by which those who entertained king or chancellor lavishly were told that they could obviously afford to contribute handsomely, while those who, to avoid this fate, were parsimonious, that they must have a great deal stored away from which they could give) was certainly an invention of the early seventeenth-century historian Francis Bacon (d. 1626) rather than of the archbishop. Although the author of the London great chronicle, who came from a group that suffered badly from government financial policy, noted that Morton attracted the hatred of the commons of the land, his own assessment of the chancellor was very complimentary; while the Italian observer Polydore Vergil (d. 1555) was probably very near to the mark when he wrote that it became obvious, after the deaths of Morton and Sir Reginald Bray (d. 1503), that they had been responsible not for initiating harsh policies, but rather for restraining them. Morton's concern for good order and sound government had been tempered by a great commitment to justice, whereas after 1500 the government embarked on a campaign of fiscal terrorism.

Archbishop of Canterbury: church and state By papal bull of 6 October 1486 Morton was translated, at the king's request, from Ely to the vacant archbishopric of Canterbury. Subsequently, and in Henry VII's view belatedly, he was on 20 September 1493 created cardinal-priest of St Anastasia. As the crown's chief minister and primate of all England, Morton faced a delicate task. The level of clerical taxation in Henry VII's first twelve years was high, and, while any attempt to make the church pay a disproportionate amount was resisted, the convocation of Canterbury granted a clerical subsidy whenever parliament made a grant of lay taxation, and in 1489 and 1497 for the first time granted fixed sums rather than a tenth or fifteenth. There was apparently a rationalization of clerical taxation for the benefit of the crown, without an undermining of ecclesiastical liberties. Henceforth the king might not grant to individual corporations exemption from payment or the burden of collection—such decisions were to be made by convocation itself without interference.

Indeed, where there was royal or parliamentary intervention in ecclesiastical affairs it was neither intrusive nor unwelcome to Morton and his episcopal colleagues. Restrictions placed on benefit of clergy served to disadvantage only criminal members of the extended clerical order, and rights of sanctuary were, with papal approval, merely regulated so as to deny this refuge to traitors and to prevent sanctuaries from becoming safe houses for those seeking a base for a continued career of crime and violence. In no way was this the inevitable prelude to the post-Reformation abolition of sanctuary plotted by Thomas Cromwell (d. 1540). Far from condoning the erosion of the rights of the church in favour of the secular government of which he was a leading member, Morton did much to protect the clergy from the hostility of certain powerful elements of lay society, particularly influential lawyers, and it was only after his death in 1500 that ecclesiastics became subject to persistent legal harassment. The archbishop appears to have preserved a balance between strong government and sound finance on the one hand and the maintenance of the liberties of the church on the other.

Morton had probably been instrumental in securing the support of the papacy for the Tudor monarchy, and certainly sought ratification from Rome for the extension of his own authority within the English church. A series of bulls obtained by the archbishop do not represent, as once argued, 'papal aggression', but rather signify Morton's determination to obtain the sanction of the highest universal authority for measures thought necessary for reform in the context of an increasingly nationalist, albeit utterly orthodox, insular church. His strategy was remarkably similar to that of his near contemporaries in Spain and France, Francisco Ximenes and Georges d'Amboise, who sought reform through centralization of power within their own hands as leaders of national members of a universal church.

To this end, Morton fought several battles to undermine the position of religious houses whose exempt status removed them from episcopal and metropolitical control, obtaining a bull empowering him to order reform of abuses and, if this was not effected internally, to conduct visitations. The most famous instance is his attempt between 1487 and 1489 to enforce his jurisdiction over St Albans Abbey; the threat apparently was enough, and there is no evidence of visitation. Neither was the abbot of Waltham Holy Cross, similarly threatened in 1488 because of alleged financial administration, ever troubled by the arrival of the archbishop's commissaries. At the Cluniac house of St Andrew's, Northampton (over which the Burgundian abbey of La Charité-sur-Loire claimed jurisdiction), he intervened in 1488 to obtain the removal of two competing priors—although this took three years. Both the court of arches and the king's council intervened in the affairs of the exempt Cistercian order. In April 1498 the pope authorized Morton, with two other bishops, to visit five unreformed Franciscan houses to effect their transfer to the Observant branch, much favoured by Henry VII. This concern for the reform of the religious life was not motivated solely by a desire to extend the jurisdiction of the church of Canterbury, for there is much evidence of pastoral care for convents in cases where the archbishop had an unchallenged right to act—at Folkestone in his own diocese (1491–4), at Reigate, Surrey (1493), and St Frideswide's, Oxford (1495), during the vacancies of sees.

Defending Canterbury's primacy Morton twice became engaged in litigation at the court of Rome concerning the prerogatives of the church of Canterbury. During the vacancy of the see of Winchester in 1492–3, the archbishop received the revenues of two parish churches normally due to the bishop. His right so to do was disputed by the prior and convent of Winchester, to whom they had been paid in previous vacancies. The case dragged on before papal judges at Rome and in England for five years, until in 1499 a decision, not without ambiguity, was given in the archbishop's favour. In 1494 there erupted the first of two disputes between Morton and Bishop Richard Hill of London, who removed a probably unworthy prior of Holy Trinity, Aldgate, after he had appealed to the archbishop's court. Such contempt of Canterbury's jurisdiction could not be tolerated. Bishop Hill was only absolved from excommunication after the intervention of other bishops and his own complete submission, and only a few months later was the restored prior induced to resign, now that Canterbury's authority was no longer at stake. In the same year, however, Bishop Hill stood as champion of Canterbury's suffragans in his resistance to the archbishop's claim to have the right of granting probate when a testator left 'notable goods' in more than one diocese of the province—the latest round of an ancient dispute which dated back to the late thirteenth century. The ensuing litigation at the papal curia, and its ramifications in England, was particularly acrimonious, and reached no definite conclusion before Bishop Hill's death in February 1496; but in essentials the prerogative testamentary jurisdiction of Canterbury was maintained by Morton, only to be challenged again later by the suffragans of Archbishop William Warham (d. 1532) in concert. They blamed Morton for the extension of Canterbury's claims, while in fact he had merely been defending rights long claimed, and long contested.

Morton, therefore, was profoundly conscious of the rights of his office and of his church of Canterbury, and because of his dominant position in the government of England was able to defend them more successfully than some of his predecessors. Yet, unlike Cardinal Wolsey a generation later, he was working within the traditional structure of the church in England, and there are no contemporary accusations against him of personal aggrandizement. His register contains evidence not only of the defence of Canterbury's rights, but also for an insistence on the collection of every penny due to the archbishop from vacant sees; but these vacancies were also the occasion of the most thorough visitations by Morton's highly competent deputies, and of the correction of faults among monks, clerks, and laity. The record of the *sede*

vacante administration of Norwich diocese in 1499, in particular, is a model of efficient episcopal administration, and reveals the strength of the traditional church in England thirty years before the Reformation. Perhaps the best judgement on Morton's ecclesiastical policy is provided by Master John Harryngton, the proctor of the English Cistercians, who opposed his efforts to undermine their immunity, but obviously admired the archbishop: he had the qualities of a good judge, who wished to expand his jurisdiction; he was a man of learning and wisdom, devoted to the service of God and concerned for the public welfare rather than his own advantage in both ecclesiastical and secular matters; and he did not shrink from the heat and burden of the day.

Cultural interests Morton was certainly one of the great builders of the age. While bishop of Ely he rebuilt the episcopal palace at Hatfield and the castle at Wisbech, and he also had a great dyke cut through the fens from Peterborough to Wisbech, a pioneer effort in drainage. Later he apparently intended to initiate a similar project in Kent, and to construct a new haven at Thanet. At Canterbury it was certainly with his encouragement that the Angel steeple on the cathedral was completed, and fines levied for misconduct in various dioceses were earmarked for the repair of the metropolitical cathedral. In 1493 royal licence was granted for the impressing of stonecutters and bricklayers for a building programme on the manors of the church of Canterbury in Kent, Surrey, and Sussex. The most obvious results were the rebuilding of the palace at Croydon and the great brick gatehouse of Lambeth Palace. The sixteenth-century antiquary John Leland (d. 1552) also credited Morton with works at Maidstone, Allington Park, Charing, and Ford. At Oxford he repaired the canon-law school, and contributed to the rebuilding of St Mary's Church.

The few books whose ownership can be attributed to Morton reveal the range of his interests—not only Roman, canon, and common law, but also Seneca's letters, and works on oratory and rhetoric. The humanist and papal collector Giovanni Gigli (d. 1498) dedicated to him a short tract on the canonization of saints—this was surely connected with aborted plans to petition for the canonization of Archbishop Anselm (d. 1109) and Henry VI. In 1500 Morton financed the printing by Richard Pynson (d. 1530) of the missal according to the use of Sarum. An insight into his character is provided by Sir Thomas More (d. 1535), who as a boy had been in his household, and who was almost certainly provided by the archbishop with the details (if not a Latin text) for his *History of Richard III*. More describes his earliest patron as very learned, honourable in his conduct, and a man of great natural wit, as well as praising his political skills.

Morton's religious preoccupations and personal affections in his last years are reflected in his will. His accumulated estates were distributed to his nephews and to the cathedral church of Canterbury, where he was to be buried under a plain marble slab before Our Lady of the Undercroft. He made provision for masses to be celebrated for thirty years at Canterbury, Ely, and Bere Regis, and for the maintenance for the same period of thirty poor students at the universities, and he left 1000 marks for the needy sick. He also made bequests to Henry VII and to the king's mother, wife, and daughter. He died soon afterwards, at Knole, on 15 September 1500, during an outbreak of plague which also claimed four of his episcopal colleagues.   CHRISTOPHER HARPER-BILL

Sources The register of John Morton, archbishop of Canterbury, 1486–1500, ed. C. Harper-Bill, 1–2, CYS, 75, 78 (1987–91) · W. Campbell, ed., Materials for a history of the reign of Henry VII, 2 vols., Rolls Series, 60 (1873–7) · B. André, Historia regis Henrici septimi, ed. J. Gairdner, Rolls Series, 10 (1858) · Chancery records · St Thomas More, The history of King Richard III, ed. R. S. Sylvester (1963), vol. 2 of The Yale edition of the complete works of St Thomas More · The Anglica historia of Polydore Vergil, AD 1485–1537, ed. and trans. D. Hay, CS, 3rd ser., 74 (1950) · C. Harper-Bill, 'Archbishop John Morton and the province of Canterbury, 1486–1500', Journal of Ecclesiastical History, 29 (1978), 1–21 · C. S. L. Davies, 'Bishop John Morton, the Holy See, and the accession of Henry VII', EngHR, 102 (1987), 2–30 · N. Pronay, 'The chancellor, the chancery and the council at the end of the fifteenth century', British government and administration: studies presented to S. B. Chrimes, ed. H. Hearder and H. R. Loyn (1974), 87–103 · C. Harper-Bill, 'The familia, administrators and patronage of Archbishop John Morton', Journal of Religious History, 10 (1978–9), 236–52 · J. Gairdner, ed., The historical collections of a citizen of London in the fifteenth century, CS, new ser., 17 (1876) [incl. Gregory's Chronicle] · C. Jenkins, 'Cardinal Morton's register', Tudor studies presented to A. F. Pollard, ed. R. W. Seton-Watson (1924), 26–74 · R. J. Knecht, 'The episcopate and the Wars of the Roses', University of Birmingham Historical Journal, 6/2 (1958), 108–81 · Emden, Oxf. · W. F. Hook, Lives of the archbishops of Canterbury, 2nd edn, 12 vols. (1861–84) · C. E. Woodruff, ed., Sede vacante wills, Kent Archaeological Society Records Branch, 3 (1914), 85–93 · muniments of dean and chapter, Canterbury Cathedral, register R, fol. 40

Archives Canterbury Cathedral, archives, muniments of dean and chapter, register R, fol. 40 · LPL, register

Likenesses line engraving (after tomb effigy), NPG · tomb effigy, Canterbury Cathedral [see illus.]

Wealth at death see Woodruff, ed., Wills, Canterbury

Morton, John (1671–1726), naturalist, was the second son of Godly Morton, of Scremby, near Skegness, Lincolnshire. He was admitted to Oundle School, Northamptonshire, on 6 July 1686 at the age of fourteen, and matriculated at Cambridge on 17 December 1688, graduating BA from Emmanuel College in 1691. An ad eundem degree followed at Oxford in 1694, and he proceeded MA in 1695. On 3 June 1694 Morton was ordained deacon (at Peterborough), and was then ordained curate of Great Oxendon, Northamptonshire, where he was rector from about 1707 until 1726. It is also possible that, for a time about 1700, he was vicar of Weston, Lincolnshire.

Morton was a keen local historian and botanist. He was part of a growing group of antiquarians, topographers, naturalists, and collectors, such as Abraham de la Pryme (1672–1704), William Nicolson (1655–1727), and Robert Plot (1640–1696), who were then gathering information about the British countryside. However, although in correspondence with a number of fellow naturalists, Morton carried out his field studies alone and generally restricted his researches to his home county of Northamptonshire. His early influences are revealed in a letter (dated 9 November 1704) to the botanist Richard Richardson (1663–1741) of North Bierley, in which he wrote:

> My acquaintance with Mr. [John] Ray initiated me early in the search and study of plants: from the reading of Dr. [Martin] Lister's books, I became an inquirer after fossil shells; and my correspondence with Dr. [John] Woodward, Dr. [Hans] Sloane, and Mr. [Edward] Lhwyd, has supported my curiosity.   (Extracts from the … Correspondence of Richard Richardson, 85–6)

Morton was elected a fellow of the Royal Society on 30 November 1703. In the society's Philosophical Transactions for 1706 he published a letter:

> to Dr. Hans Sloane, S. R. Secr., containing a Relation of river and other Shells digg'd up, together with various Vegetable Bodies, in a bituminous marshy earth, near Mears-Ashby, in Northamptonshire: with some Reflections thereupon: as also an Account of the Progress he has made in the Natural History of Northamptonshire.

Morton was in correspondence with Sir Hans Sloane from about 1703 until 1716, and in one of his earliest letters (dated 7 February 1703) Morton mentioned his work The Natural History of Northamptonshire, then in progress. For his work on the natural history of Northamptonshire, Morton embarked on a study of all the villages in his home county, using a rigid code of practice for his research and drawing on existing natural history works, such as Lhuyd's Lithophylacii Britannici (1699). He was systematic in his account of the natural history, mineralogy, and geography of Northamptonshire, with a consideration of the local landscape within the wider context of the national geography, and a study of the physical characteristics of his county.

Morton published his work, The natural history of Northamptonshire, with some account of the antiquities; to which is annexed a transcript of Domesday Book, so far as it relates to that county, in 1712. This book dealt largely with 'figured fossils', of which there were several plates (Morton subscribed to the theory of the geologist John Woodward (d. 1728) that, following the Biblical flood, fossils were deposited according to their specific gravities). The botanical section was praised by the botanist Richard Pulteney (1730–1801), but in the History and Antiquities of Northamptonshire (1762–9) by Peter Whalley (1722–1791), the transcript of Domesday was considered inaccurate.

Many of the specimens collected by Morton, and used by him to illustrate The Natural History of Northamptonshire, were given to Sloane for examination; several of them were later recorded in the Sloane collection catalogues. However these represented a small fraction of the specimens given by Morton to Sloane; ultimately nearly 1000 entries in the catalogues of the Sloane collections were assigned Morton's name or bear the initial 'M' beside them. The specimens included not only fossil shells, but also bones, teeth, minerals, rocks, and man-made artefacts. In return, Sloane provided Morton (and other provincial naturalists) with important news, material, and books. Both Morton and Richardson used Lhuyd's work Lithophylacii Britannici for identification purposes in their work. Morton also supplied John Woodward with specimens and exchanged material with Richardson. This interaction enabled the pursuit of in-depth scientific studies and in turn, performed an important social and scientific function. In 1713 Morton wrote to Richardson stating: 'I frequently drank your health with my friend Mr. Buddle, and other of the London botanists', referring to the Revd Adam Buddle (1662–1715).

Morton died on 18 July 1726 at Great Oxendon, and was buried at St Helen's Church, Great Oxendon, where a monument (with an inscription to his memory) was erected at the expense of Sir Hans Sloane. He was survived by his wife, Susanna, daughter of John Courtman, who died on 2 September 1728, at the age of sixty. The couple had at least five sons including John (buried on 19 May 1724 at Stanwick) and Henry who was curate of Oxendon in 1728 and rector of Great Oxendon from 1729 to 1737. Henry Morton married Ann Baggiley of Isham, Northamptonshire, at Great Harrowden in November 1730; they had at least one daughter, Ann. Henry Morton died on 6 September 1737 at the age of thirty-two, and was buried two days later at Great Oxendon.   YOLANDA FOOTE

Sources DNB · BL, Sloane MSS, 4062, 4053, fols. 329–354 · Extracts from the literary and scientific correspondence of Richard Richardson, ed. D. Turner (1835), 85–6 · Nichols, Illustrations, 1.326 · R. Pulteney, Historical and biographical sketches of the progress of botany in England, 1 (1790), 354 · N&Q, 6 (1852), 358 · Venn, Alum. Cant. · J. G. Bartholomew, ed., The survey gazetteer of the British Isles (1904) · Desmond, Botanists, rev. edn · R. Porter, The making of geology: earth science in Britain, 1660–1815 (1977) · E. St. J. Brooks, Sir Hans Sloane: the great collector and his circle (1954) · A. MacGregor, ed., Sir Hans Sloane: collector, scientist, antiquary, founding father of the British Museum (1994) · private information (2004) [T. Roper]
Archives BL, MSS | BL, Sloane MSS, letters to Edward Lhuyd; letters to Sir Hans Sloane

Morton, John (1781–1864), agriculturist, was born on 17 July 1781 at Ceres, Cupar, Fife, the second son of Robert Morton and his wife, Kate (née Pitcairn). He was educated at the parish school in Ceres. His first farm, from 1801, was Wester, near Kilmany, though he spent many 'leisure periods' (as he called them) journeying extensively through Britain, noting changes in farm practice and rural labour conditions (usually based on comparisons with previously published county reports and travel writings).

From 1810 to 1818 Morton farmed one of the earl of Carnarvon's properties at Dulverton in Somerset. He married Jean, daughter of John Chalmers, merchant, and sister of Dr Thomas Chalmers (1780–1847), on 15 January 1812. From 1818 to 1852, he was agent to the Gloucestershire estates of the earl of Ducie, who sanctioned the establishment of Whitfield Example Farm, near Upper Morton, Thornbury. Under Morton, the design and management of the farm aimed to 'reduce the annual expense of culture after the texture of the soil has been changed' to 'a best constituted soil' (Morton). However, while Morton's farm had limestone, clay, and sandstone, mixing soils for most farmers on clay was a forlorn hope; ultimately other measures proved more effective than Morton's ad hoc improvements, although his advocacy of long leases was eventually heeded.

Morton was a man of many parts. He established the Uley agricultural machine factory and invented, among other agricultural appliances, the Uley cultivator, and collaborated with Joshua Trimmer (1795–1857) of Norfolk on An Attempt to Estimate the Effect of Protecting Duties on the Profits of Agriculture (1845) which advocated corn law repeal. However, Morton deserves most credit for his incisive comments on soil classification, partly based on detailed knowledge and observations of earths of transportation, diluvial deposits, and liming procedures, which appeared in his text On the nature and property of soils, their connexion with the geological foundation on which they rest; the best means of increasing their productiveness and the rents and profits of agriculture (1838), which presented the findings of his journeys through Britain. Later editions contained sundry appendices, including the Report on Whitfield (1840). The work earned Morton a fellowship of the Geological Society of London in 1839. He retired to Nailsworth, Gloucestershire, in 1852. He died of 'congestion of the brain' at Morningfield, Avening, near Nailsworth, on 26 July 1864. He left at least two sons, including John Chalmers *Morton.   BRIAN T. BUNTING

Sources B. T. Bunting, 'John Morton, 1781–1864: a neglected pioneer of soil science', GJ, 130 (1964), 116–19 · E. J. Russell, A history of agricultural science in Great Britain, 1620–1954 (1966) · B. T. Bunting, 'The turning of the worm: early nineteenth century concepts of soil in Britain', History of geomorphology: from Hutton to Hack [Binghamton 1988], ed. K. J. Tinkler (1989), 85–108 · G. P. Jones and A. G. Pool, A hundred years of economic development in Great Britain, 1840–1940 (1953) · Allibone, Dict. · J. Morton, On the nature and property of soils (1838) · bap. reg. Scot. · d. cert.
Archives Glos. RO, corresp. and papers
Wealth at death under £3000: probate, 12 Sept 1864, CGPLA Eng. & Wales

Morton, John Cameron Andrieu Bingham Michael [pseud. Beachcomber] (1893–1979), humorous journalist, was born on 7 June 1893 at Park Lodge, Mitcham Road, Tooting, London, the only child of Edward Arthur Morton, journalist and dramatist, and his wife, Rosamond, daughter of Captain Devereux Bingham, of Wartnaby Hall, Leicestershire. His father began his career as a journalist in Paris and later became the drama critic of the Sunday Referee. He wrote the 'book' of the long-running musical San Toy and also adapted the libretto of The Merry Widow for the English stage. John Morton was educated at Park House preparatory school, Southborough, and went to Harrow School in 1907 but made no particular mark there. (It is fair to assume that Harrow inspired his later fictional creation, Narkover.) Morton spent a year at Worcester College, Oxford, but left on account of his father's illness.

Morton was a romantic young man whose first ambition was to be a poet. He was writing revue material for the theatre when the First World War broke out. He enlisted in the Royal Fusiliers and was eventually commissioned in the Suffolk regiment and sent out to the trenches. He was wounded on the Somme, returned to England suffering from shell-shock, and spent the rest of the war in a branch of intelligence known as MI7b. When the war ended Morton published a novel, The Barber of Putney (1919), based on his experiences in the trenches. It was one of the first books of its kind to be published in England.

John Cameron Andrieu Bingham Michael Morton
[Beachcomber] (1893–1979), by Howard Coster, 1933

In 1919 Morton was taken on the staff of the *Sunday Express* as a columnist, inappropriately 'adorning the paper's leader-page with slim verses and stories about fairyland' (Frayn) and was for a short time a reporter on the *Daily Express*, a job at which, he said, he was 'a howling failure'. He took over the 'Beachcomber' column from D. B. Wyndham Lewis in 1924 and wrote it continuously until he was retired in 1975, surviving a number of attempts by Lord Beaverbrook to dismiss him. Over the years he built up a cast of comic characters who became classics of nonsense writing—Mr Justice Cocklecarrot, Dr Smart-Allick, headmaster of Narkover, Captain Foulenough, and the mad scientist Dr Strabismus (Whom God Preserve) of Utrecht. Morton chronicled their activities in short paragraphs parodying the newspaper style. His humour was based on a strong dislike of the twentieth century, which he thought of as godless, noisy, and unpleasant. (Personally he would have no truck with it and refused to use a typewriter or even ride a bicycle.) His column was particularly effective during the Second World War when he jeered at official propagandizing. Radical in some senses, his satires were also filtered through a certain conservatism and xenophobia. His funniest work was pure nonsense which had little or no reference to the real world: for example the saga of the Filthistan Trio, a group of see-sawing Persian acrobats, the 'List of Huntingdonshire cabmen', and the 'Trial of the Seven Red-bearded Dwarves', one of many legal marathons. ('Justice', he once said, 'must not only be done; it must be seen to be believed.') The character Prodnose, a pedantic interrupter, passed into the parlance of newspapers, while others of Morton's sayings—for example, 'Wagner is the Puccini of music'—found their way into the quotation books.

On 29 September 1927 Morton married Mary O'Leary (1897/8–1974), a physician, from Cappoquin, co. Wexford; they had no children. After his marriage Morton virtually disappeared from the social round; he rarely visited London and for a time after the Second World War he lived in Dublin. He returned after two years to settle in Ferring. From there he continued to dispatch his column and also

turned his hand to novels (*Skylighters*, 1934, is notable) and to history. In all he wrote twenty-nine books aside from his journalism and became with *The Bastille Falls* (1936), *Brumaire: the Rise of Bonaparte* (1948) and *Marshal Ney* (1958) a specialist in French history. *St Thérèse de Lisieux: the Making of a Saint* (1954) reflected his strong religious beliefs (he had converted to Catholicism in 1922). His friendship with Hilaire Belloc, who was his greatest influence, and with whom he enjoyed strenuous walking tours, resulted in an affectionate memoir in 1955.

Morton was a stocky, thickset man who wore his hair in a crew-cut like his mentor Hilaire Belloc. In his early days as a journalist he was a familiar figure in the pubs of Fleet Street with his loud laugh, muddy boots, and blackthorn walking stick. He was well known for his practical jokes and once assembled a large and indignant crowd round a pillar box on the pretext that a small boy had been trapped inside. Morton belonged to the circle of Sir John Squire, and there are fictional portraits of him as Mr Huggins in *England their England* by A. G. Macdonell (1933) and as Rowley Meek in *The Innocent Moon* (1961) by Henry Williamson. Morton suggested his own self-portrait in the style of a 'rugged Cornish giant' or as a 'retiring and literary spinster, living in quiet solitude in the depths of Wales' (*The Times*, 23 Nov 1979).

After his wife's death in 1974 Morton was sacked by the *Daily Express* in 1975 and he became severely depressed. He died in a nursing home at 27 St Botolphs Road, Worthing, on 10 May 1979 and was buried at Bagshot. Morton remains one of Britain's foremost modern humorists. Evelyn Waugh said of him that he showed 'the greatest comic fertility of any Englishman'. With D. B. Wyndham Lewis he introduced to the news reading public a taste for anarchy and cutting parody during a period of pomposity in print journalism. Morton's output was colossal and only a fraction of it is reprinted in eighteen Beachcomber volumes (many illustrated by Nicholas Bentley). His comic creations were brought to a wider public as a result of Spike Milligan's *World of Beachcomber* television series in 1968.   RICHARD INGRAMS, rev. CLARE L. TAYLOR

Sources R. Ingrams, introduction, *The bumper Beachcomber*, ed. R. Ingrams (1991) · M. Frayn, introduction, *The best of Beachcomber*, ed. M. Frayn (1991) · *The Times* (28 Nov 1975) · *The Spectator* (19 May 1979) · *The Times* (23 Nov 1979) · b. cert. · m. cert. · d. cert.
Likenesses H. Coster, photographs, 1933, NPG [*see illus.*]

Morton, John Chalmers (1821–1888), writer on agriculture, was born on 1 July 1821, the son of John *Morton (1781–1864), an agricultural agent, and his wife, Jean (*née* Chalmers). He was educated at Merchistoun Castle School, Edinburgh, under his uncle Charles Chalmers. He attended lectures at Edinburgh University, including those of David Low in agriculture; he also took a first prize in mathematics. From 1838 he assisted his father at the Whitfield Example Farm and joined the newly formed English Agricultural Society (later the Royal Agricultural Society). In 1844 he was founding editor of the *Agricultural Gazette*, a position which required his residence in London. In 1854 Low retired from his Edinburgh position; Morton lectured there for some months until John Wilson

(1812–1888) was appointed in Low's place. The following year, on 14 April 1855, Morton married Clarence Cooper Hayward of King's Stanley, Gloucestershire, daughter of the late Drinkwater Scott Hayward.

Morton's abundant writings and editing began with *A Cyclopaedia of Agriculture* (1855), *Morton's New Farmer's Almanac* (1856–70, continuing as an *Almanac for Farmers and Landowners* after 1871), and a *Handbook of Dairy Husbandry* (1860). He also edited the *Prince Consort's Farms* (1863). He was an inspector of the land commission and also served on the royal commission of inquiry into the pollution of rivers (1868–74), to which some of his contribution was on the risks to rural water supply and the problems of abattoir waste after the cattle plague of 1865. An indefatigable editor and compiler, he produced *Handbooks of the Farm* (1881–4), contributing three of seven volumes—on soil, equipment, and 'Diary of the farm'—and revised *The Art of Valuing Rents and Claims of Tenants* in 1876. He was a frequent contributor to the journal of the Royal Agricultural Society and the publications of the Society of Arts. Morton died at his home, Holmleigh, College Road, Harrow, on 3 May 1888. He was survived by his wife.

BRIAN T. BUNTING

Sources E. J. Russell, *A history of agricultural science in Great Britain, 1620–1954* (1966) · G. P. Jones and A. G. Pool, *A hundred years of economic development in Great Britain, 1840–1940* (1953) · A. Briggs, *The age of improvement* (1967) · G. E. Fussell, *More old English farming books, ... 1731–1793* (1950), vol. 2 of *The old English farming books* (1947–91) · J. M. Collinge, *Officials of royal commissions of enquiry, 1815–70* (1984) · *Journal of the Society of Arts*, 1–18 (1850–70) · Allibone, *Dict.* · N. O. Ireland, *Index to scientists of the world from ancient to modern times* (1962) · m. cert. · d. cert. · *CGPLA Eng. & Wales* (1888) · *DNB*

Wealth at death £1742 13s. 3d.: probate, 10 July 1888, *CGPLA Eng. & Wales*

Morton, John Maddison (1811–1891), playwright, was born at Pangbourne-on-Thames on 3 January 1811, the second son of Thomas *Morton (*bap.* 1764, *d.* 1838), himself a noted playwright whose comedies, *The Way to Get Married* (1796) and *Speed the Plough* (1798), continued to be revived in the nineteenth century. Given his middle name after a stockbroker great-uncle, Morton was educated in France and Germany for three years before going to London where, after a brief period at a school in Islington, he attended the Clapham Common school of Charles Richardson, the lexicographer, from 1820 to 1827. Although Lord John Russell gave him a clerkship in Chelsea Hospital (1832–40), Morton's chief interest was the stage. His first staged play was a pantomime in 1833 and his first published farce, *My First Fit of the Gout*, was produced in April 1835 at the Queen's Theatre, Tottenham Street.

Between 1835 and 1885 Morton wrote more than 125 plays, including comedies, comediettas, and a few dramas. His reputation rested, however, on his chief output, his 100 farces: 'neat in construction and humorous in situation', as *The Times* described them (21 Dec 1891). Michael Booth has called Morton 'the great farceur of the people', and his characters are most often drawn from the working or lower middle classes. For instance, *Box and Cox* (Lyceum Theatre, 1 November 1847), his most famous and longest-lasting farce, is subtitled *A Romance of Real Life* and

deals with a journeyman printer and a journeyman hatter. Although, as with most of Morton's farces, the plot comes from two French originals (Labiche and A. Lefranc's *Frisette* and E. F. Prieur and A. Letorzec's *Une chambre à deux lits*), his adaptation was completely and characteristically English. The parody of melodrama, the mirror image dialogue, and the absurd ending in which the absence of a strawberry mark identifies a long-lost brother, were treated with extraordinary adroitness. The farce was widely translated, while *Box and Cox Married and Settled*, *Box and Cox in Caffre Land*, and a Christy minstrel version attest to its influence. In 1866 F. C. Burnand turned some of Morton's dialogue into verse, which Arthur Sullivan set to music as *Cox and Box*, still being played at the end of the twentieth century.

Other Morton farces include *Lend Me Five Shillings* (1846), *Slasher and Crasher* (1848), *Betsey Barker* (1850), *If I had a Thousand a Year* (1867), and *A Most Unwarrantable Intrusion* (1849), revived without much success in 1968.

Farce writing was not well paid in Morton's day, and as the great days of low comedians such as Buckstone, Wright, Harley, and the Keeleys passed, his income fell and he was reduced almost to insolvency. A benefit was held for him in 1880, another in 1889. In the first, W. S. Gilbert played Adolphus Swansdown in Morton's own *Woodcock's Little Game* (1864) and Sullivan conducted *Cox and Box*. In August 1881 Morton was appointed a poor brother of the Charterhouse, where he spent ten years. He died there somewhat unexpectedly on 19 December 1891 after a few days of suffering and was buried in Kensal Green cemetery on 23 December.

JANE W. STEDMAN

Sources *The Athenaeum* (26 Dec 1891), 876 · *The Times* (21 Dec 1891) · *The Times* (24 Dec 1891) · M. R. Booth, ed., *English plays of the nineteenth century*, 4: *Farces* (1973) · C. Scott, 'Introduction', in J. M. Morton, *Plays for home performance* (1889) · A. Nicoll, *Early nineteenth century drama, 1800–1850*, 2nd edn (1955), vol. 4 of *A history of English drama, 1660–1900* (1952–9) · A. Nicoll, *Late nineteenth century drama, 1850–1900*, 2nd edn (1959), vol. 5 of *A history of English drama, 1660–1900* (1952–9; repr. (1959–62) · J. Hollingshead, *My lifetime*, 2 vols. (1895) · *The Era* (18 July 1880) [review of benefit theatrical performance] · 'Morton, Thomas (1764?–1838)', *DNB*

Archives BL, MSS · Morgan L., letters | Theatre Museum, London, Clement Scott MSS, letters relating to his death

Wealth at death £148 13s.: probate, 22 Jan 1892, *CGPLA Eng. & Wales*

Morton, Nicholas (1520/21–1587), papal agent, was born in Bawtry, Yorkshire, the son of Charles Morton (*d. c.*1531), landowner, and his wife, Maud, daughter of William Dallison of Laughton, Lincolnshire, and his wife, Anne. His family was from the gentry and noted for its Catholic piety. He was educated at Cambridge University, graduating BA in 1542–3, MA in 1545, and BTh from Trinity College in 1554. According to a hostile report, he was better known as a sportsman and bon viveur than as an academic. Nevertheless, when Trinity College was founded in 1546 he was one of the original fellows, perhaps through the patronage of Thomas Cranmer, archbishop of Canterbury, who was uncle to his sister's husband.

Morton began a clerical career under Mary I. He was appointed a prebendary at York and one of six preachers at Canterbury Cathedral by Reginald Pole, cardinal and archbishop of Canterbury, in 1556. He was also given two benefices in Kent, at Milton Regis and Pluckley. The accession of Elizabeth I brought an end to Morton's progress in the Church of England and about 1561 he went into exile, unable to accommodate himself to the protestantism of the new regime. He went to Rome, where in 1563 he was made English penitentiary at St Peter's. He was also a member of the English College at Rome, being appointed *camerarius* in 1565, 1567, and 1568. In 1565, he engaged, with others, in a quarrel with Maurice Clenock the *custos* of the college, which was caused by a request to buy some of the college wine. He took his doctorate in Rome, at about this time, although according to one account he was unsuccessful on his first attempt, returning in tears from his examination to the disappointment of his friends who were waiting to celebrate with him over a meal.

From 1565 Morton began to urge Pope Pius IV to take political action against Elizabeth and with the accession of Pius V in January 1566 his pleas were favourably received. Morton hoped to persuade the pope to excommunicate the queen publicly, but it was decided first to send him in February 1569 to England to discover what the religious and political situation of Catholics there was. He told those he visited that Elizabeth was excommunicated already, even if the sentence had not been openly proclaimed. Among others, Morton visited his close relative Richard *Norton in Yorkshire, as well as Henry Percy, eighth earl of Northumberland, and both were to play a prominent part in the rising of northern earls which broke out soon after his departure. Back in Rome, Morton pressed with renewed vigour for the excommunication of the queen to be published. The pope decided to hold a judicial hearing in February 1570 to inquire into her heresy, in part because Philip II was still leaning on the papacy in an effort to avoid an open declaration of excommunication. The witnesses included Morton, who gave evidence that he had been in Lincolnshire at the beginning of Elizabeth's reign when commissioners had administered the oath of supremacy to the clergy. As a result of this trial, Elizabeth was, as Morton had long hoped, finally declared excommunicate on 25 February. In 1571 Morton travelled to the English College at Louvain with 12,000 crowns raised by Pius for the relief of the Catholic refugees there, some of whom had fled England after the defeat of the recent uprising. The English government received reports that Morton returned again to visit England in the 1570s, but he probably did not. About 1575 he was given a benefice in Piacenza by Cardinal Alessandrino Ghislieri, nephew of Pius, which may have been worth 500 crowns a year (*CSP dom.*, 1547–80). He still enjoyed an income of 144 crowns from his office as penitentiary, although he no longer exercised it after about 1580. In 1579 the students at the English College in Rome, who were dissatisfied with its direction, appealed to him for help, and he gave them support in their opposition to his old enemy, Clenock, now rector.

In 1580, having sold all his possessions in Rome, Morton travelled north with Thomas Goldwell, former bishop of St Asaph, to accompany the expedition of Robert Persons, Edmund Campion, and the other seminary priests who were leaving to work as missionaries in England. Morton and Goldwell decided once they had arrived at Paris not to proceed with their plans, because it was felt that their arrival in England would merely infuriate the privy council. The English government continued to monitor Morton's activities. He returned to Rome, and on 27 January 1587 he died, aged sixty-six, and was buried in the chapel of the English College there, where his nephew, Robert, who was executed as a priest in England in 1588, placed a memorial.   PETER HOLMES

Sources DNB · Gillow, *Lit. biog. hist.* · J. Hunter, *South Yorkshire*, repr., 2 vols. (1974), 1.75–7 · J. H. Pollen, *The English Catholics in the reign of Queen Elizabeth* (1920), 143–6, 148, 151, 191, 236, 278, 301, 331, 332, 339 · T. F. Knox and others, eds., *The first and second diaries of the English College, Douay* (1878), 165, 169, 294, 301, 358–9 · N. Sanders, *De visibili monarchia ecclesiae* (Louvain, 1571), 700, 730 · C. W. Field, *The province of Canterbury, the Elizabethan settlement of religion* (1974), 38 · *CSP dom.*, 1547–80, 651, 694; 1581–90, 53 · A. Kenny, 'From hospice to college', *The Venerabile*, 21 (1962), 218–73 [sexcentenary issue: *The English hospice in Rome*]
Archives Bibliotheca Palatina, Parma, Italy, MS 651/n. 2

Morton, Richard (*bap.* 1637, *d.* 1698), ejected minister and physician, was baptized on 30 July 1637 in the parish of Ribbesford, Worcestershire, the son of Robert Morton, the minister from 1635 to 1646 of Bewdley Chapel in that parish and a friend of Richard Baxter. In 1652 he became a batteler at Magdalen Hall, Oxford, matriculating as a commoner on 17 March 1654. He then migrated to New College, where he graduated BA on 30 January 1657, and was soon afterwards appointed chaplain. On 8 July 1659 he proceeded MA, having already become chaplain in the Foley family of Staffordshire; his uncle Thomas Foley was a friend of Richard Baxter and three sons were later influential members of parliament. Through the Foleys, Morton was admitted on 9 February 1659 as curate to the parish of Kinver, where entries in the register are in his distinctive handwriting.

Following his ejection from Kinver in 1662 nothing is certainly known of Morton until 20 December 1670, when on the nomination of Prince William of Orange he was created doctor of medicine at Oxford University. During the intervening years Morton must have studied medicine overseas, probably in the Low Countries; he does not appear to have enrolled at Leiden, despite the evident influence on his work of the research of Sylvius de le Boë, its professor of medicine from 1658 until 1672. During this period Morton had married Sarah, with whom he had three children, Richard [*see below*], Sarah (*b.* 1685), and Marcia (*b.* 1689). After receiving his medical degree he practised as a physician in London, at some point setting up house at Grey Friars Court, Newgate Street, in the parish of Christchurch, Newgate Street. Here, as corporation records and his own will suggest, he remained until his death.

Morton was admitted a candidate of the Royal College of Physicians on 20 March 1676 and a fellow on 23 December 1679. In 1680 he was incorporated as a doctor of medicine at Cambridge. He was one of four fellows of the Royal College of Physicians whose names were omitted in the charter of James II in 1686, perhaps partly because of his earlier sponsorship by William and his standing in the college. He was restored to his position in 1689, was censor in 1690, 1691, and 1697, and was one of the physicians-in-ordinary to the king. Morton is thought not to have actually attended William, but his interest in tuberculosis may have originated from the prince's own continuing respiratory problems. However that may be, his work *Phthisiologia* (1689), dedicated to William III, 'established his reputation at home and abroad for over a century'; 'during the reign of Queen Anne it was one of the text-books advised for reading by the apprentices of the Society of Apothecaries by private tutors in anatomy and pathology' (Trail, 169). In his work on tuberculosis Morton broke with the very widespread prejudice against the use of anatomical dissection as a means of improving medical knowledge. As a result he was 'the first to describe the characteristic enlargement of the thoracic glands, in particular the tracheo-bronchial and broncho-pulmonary groups that were later to be shown to be of great significance in the pathogenesis of the disease' (ibid., 173). Though wrong in attributing its origins to invisible glands in the lungs, Morton was 'the first physician since Galen to envisage a concept of the unity of tuberculosis and the first physician ever to state that tubercles are always present in pulmonary form' (ibid., 166). He also improved diagnosis, distinguishing the dry tubercular cough from the catarrhal one, and his recommendation of fresh air was the best hope for treatment before antibiotics.

Morton seems to have retained a tolerant, dissenting outlook, and corresponded with Joseph Hill, minister of the English church at Rotterdam. He died on 30 August 1698 and was buried in the nave of Christchurch, Newgate Street, on 7 September; he was survived by his wife. Richard Baxter recalled 'a man of great gravity, calmness, sound principles, of no faction, an excellent preacher, of an upright life' (*Reliquiae Baxterianae*, 3.96).

Richard Morton (1668/9–1730), only son of Richard Morton, was admitted to Exeter College, Oxford (as of Enwood, Surrey), on 16 March 1686, and matriculated three days later. After leaving Oxford on 17 October 1688, he migrated to St Catharine's College, Cambridge, where he was admitted as a fellow commoner on 22 November 1688. He proceeded BA in 1691 and doctor of medicine in 1695. He was admitted a candidate of the Royal College of Physicians on 22 December 1695, and fellow on 22 December 1707. He was appointed physician to Greenwich Hospital in April 1716. Morton died at Greenwich on 1 February 1730, and was buried at Plumstead. He contributed verses to the first edition of the second volume of his father's *Pyretologias pars altera, sive exercitatio de febribus inflammatoriis universalibus* (London, 1694).

STEPHEN WRIGHT

Sources Calamy rev. · Munk, *Roll* · R. R. Trail, 'Richard Morton (1637–1698)', *Medical History*, 14 (1970), 166–74 · Wood, *Ath. Oxon.*, new edn, vol. 4 · Wood, *Ath. Oxon.: Fasti* (1820) · M. Burrows, ed., *The register of the visitors of the University of Oxford, from AD 1647 to AD 1658,* CS, new ser., 29 (1881) · HoP, *Commons, 1660–90* · DNB · *Reliquiae Baxterianae, or, Mr Richard Baxter's narrative of the most memorable passages of his life and times*, ed. M. Sylvester, 1 vol. in 3 pts (1696)
Likenesses W. Elder, line engraving, 1692 (after B. Orchard), BM, NPG; repro. in R. Morton, *Puretologia, seu, exercitationes de morbus universalibus acutis*, 2 vols. (1692) · oils, *c.*1692, RCP Lond. · B. Orchard, portrait · R. White, line engraving, BM, NPG; repro. in R. Morton, *Phthisiologia, seu, exercitationes de phthisis tribus libris comprehensa* (1689)
Wealth at death £500 in East India Co.; property in Surrey: will

Morton, Richard (1668/9–1730). *See under* Morton, Richard (*bap.* 1637, *d.* 1698).

Morton, Robert (*c.*1435–1497), bishop of Worcester, was the son of William Morton, MP for Shaftesbury in 1437, and the nephew of Cardinal John Morton (*d.* 1500). He graduated MA from Oxford by 1458, and was licentiate in civil law by 1480, when, as a compliment to his uncle, the university offered to confer a doctorate on him. He was admitted to his first benefice, All Saints', Huntingdon, in 1458; the gap in his recorded career in the nineteen years that followed has led to speculation that he was identical with the composer Robert *Morton, active at the Burgundian court during this period, but this must remain conjectural. It is certain, however, that in 1477 he received a papal dispensation to hold three incompatible benefices, and at the time of his elevation to the episcopate in 1486 he held prebends of St Paul's, Salisbury, York, Beverley, and Wherwell Abbey, and was also archdeacon of both Gloucester and Winchester; he had previously resigned prebends of Lincoln and St George's, Windsor.

On 30 May 1477 Robert Morton was granted by Edward IV reversion of the office of master of the rolls of chancery, should his uncle die or resign. He assumed the office on 9 January 1479, but was deprived of it on 22 September 1483 as a result of his uncle's opposition to Richard III. Having left England, Robert was in Rome with his uncle early in 1485, and his complicity in plots against the king is indicated by the sequestration of his ecclesiastical revenues on 1 April 1485. He was with Henry Tudor's forces at Bosworth on 22 August, and was subsequently one of the commissioners appointed to discharge the office of steward at Henry's coronation on 30 October. He was reappointed to the mastership of the rolls on 13 November 1485, but Master William Elyot was made his coadjutor because of Morton's other employment on the king's business; and indeed, in January 1486 he was one of the signatories to a petition for a dispensation for the king's marriage.

Morton was provided by the pope to the bishopric of Worcester on 16 October 1486, and consecrated on 28 January 1487. Two visitations of his diocese are recorded in 1488 and 1491, and some parts of these he conducted in person. The last English bishop of Worcester before the Reformation (the next four were all Italians), he died in May 1497, having two months earlier obtained from the king a pardon for any offences he might have committed. He was buried, surprisingly, in the nave of St Paul's, London, rather than in his own cathedral church, but among the beneficiaries of his will were Worcester Cathedral priory and All Souls, Oxford, for the performance of his obit.

Robert Morton's career shows no obvious signs of personal distinction or initiative, either in ecclesiastical or political matters. His preferment, throughout his adult life, was almost certainly due to his uncle's eminence. There is no reason, however, to doubt his competence as a lawyer and an administrator, closely involved with chancery at an important stage in its evolution, or that he was a perfectly competent bishop, albeit surrounded by rather more distinguished colleagues.

CHRISTOPHER HARPER-BILL

Sources Emden, *Oxf.* · CPR, 1476–1509 · CEPR letters, vols. 13–16 · *VCH Worcestershire*, 2.38–9 · J. Hutchins, *The history and antiquities of the county of Dorset*, 3rd edn, ed. W. Shipp and J. W. Hodson, 2 (1863), 594–5 · will, PRO, PROB 11/11, sig. 10
Archives Worcs. RO, register, HWRO b 716.093-BA.2648/7 (ii)
Wealth at death see will, PRO, PROB 11/11, sig. 10

Morton, Robert (*fl.* 1457–1479), composer, is identifiable from twelve polyphonic songs, attributed to one Morton. Judging from their style and the dates of their manuscripts, they must have been composed in the years *c.*1460–80, and it seems logical to identify their composer with Robert Morton, singer in the Burgundian ducal chapel from 1457 to 1476. Supporting evidence comes from the anonymous song 'La plus grant chiere de jamais' (Marix, *Les musiciens*), which describes how Morton and Hayne van Ghizeghem (another composer at the Burgundian court) visited Cambrai and astonished the people with their singing and playing. Four of the songs attributed to Morton may be spurious. The remaining eight are typical of the secular products of the Burgundian court, but characterized by exceptional melodic economy. Two of them, 'Le souvenir' and 'N'aray je jamais', are to be numbered among the most successful of their generation.

Evidence that Morton was English comes only in the initial payment to 'Robert Morton, chappellain angloix'. All payments from October 1460 name him Messire Robert Morton, indicating that he had been ordained priest between 1457 and late 1460. From 1 June 1464 to 12 March 1465 and from 1 October 1465 to 30 September 1466 he was seconded to the household of Duke Philip's son, Charles, count of Charolais; and he had a leave of absence from 20 July to 13 August 1470. Otherwise his attendance seems to have been daily until 19 February 1475, after which he appears on the daily payment lists only for 13–14 June; he was replaced on 1 February 1476. In January 1477 a papal document records his paying the annates for a benefice at St Paul, Liège; and on 13 March 1479 he resigned the parish of Goutswaard-Koorndijk. But neither would have required his presence in the Low Countries.

Morton's career after 1457 is puzzling in that within the ranks of the ducal chapel he remained a *clerc* for nearly fifteen years, and became *chappellain* only in 1471–2, though singers were usually promoted within three or four years. Perhaps there was some question as to how long Morton would remain at the court, or perhaps there was some political complication. That is why there seems a possibility

that he can be identified with the Robert *Morton (*c.*1435–1497) who later became bishop of Worcester—none of the documentation for the future bishop bears witness to his having been in England during the years 1457–76, and it is an intriguing coincidence that his uncle John Morton was an envoy to the court of Burgundy from January to June 1474 and again from December 1474 to January 1475, that is, in the last months of Robert Morton's tenure in the choir.

DAVID FALLOWS

Sources *Robert Morton: the collected works*, ed. A. Atlas (1981) · D. Fallows, 'Robert Morton's songs: a study of styles in the mid-fifteenth century', PhD diss., U. Cal., Berkeley, 1978 · J. Marix, *Histoire de la musique et des musiciens de la cour de Bourgogne sous le règne de Philippe le Bon* (1939) · J. Marix, ed., *Les musiciens de la cour de Bourgogne au XVe siècle* (1937) · Emden, *Oxf.*, 2.1320–21 · P. M. Grijpink, *Register op de parochien, altaren … van den officiaal des aartsdiakens van den utrechtschen dom*, ed. C. P. M. Holtkamp (1914–37), 6.108 · A. Roth, *Studien zum früheren Repertoire der päpstlichen Kapelle unter dem Pontifikat Sixtus' IV.* (1991), 452

Morton, Savile (1811–1852), journalist and philanderer, was born on 1 August 1811, the fourth of the five sons who survived infancy of Charles Carr Morton, landed gentleman, of Kilnacrott House, Drumrora, co. Cavan, and his wife, Charlotte (*d.* 1854), second daughter of John Tatlow, of Crover, co. Cavan. He also had three sisters. Morton entered Trinity College, Cambridge, in 1830, as a scholar, and graduated BA and twenty-second wrangler in 1834. An 'Apostle', and close friend of Edward FitzGerald (who called him 'my wild Irishman'), Thackeray, Tennyson, Frederick Tennyson, and Richard Monckton Milnes, he was interested in the classics, literature, architecture, and medicine.

Brilliant but spendthrift, unstable and restless, in the 1830s Morton travelled in Europe, particularly in Italy, with Frederick Tennyson. He was apparently of independent means, but the death of his father revealed that the family estates were deeply in debt. In 1838 he entered the Inner Temple, but was not called to the bar. More and more dependent on concerned but increasingly despairing friends, from 1841 to 1844 he lived in Rome as an artist. Letters to his friends revealed fine descriptive skills and penetrating insights, an ability which enabled him in 1846 to become the foreign correspondent in Constantinople for the *Daily News*, through Thackeray's good offices. He later served in the same capacity in Athens, Madrid, Vienna, Berlin, and Paris, also becoming Paris correspondent of the *Morning Advertiser* in 1852. During his time working as a journalist, Morton travelled in Turkey, Persia, and, with Henry Rawlinson, in Babylonia. His Berlin friends included Varnhagen von Ense, the historian, and Bettina von Arnim, the biographer and reformer. He supported liberal political causes there and in Paris, where he opposed Louis Napoleon's attempts to censor English journalists' reports after the coup of 2 December 1851.

Morton's fair hair, blond beard, genial countenance, and friendly bearing made him attractive to women, and the attraction was mutual. Fickle, heartless, and not quite in touch with reality, he took full advantage of this. From Rome in 1843, his artist friend Augustus Brotherton reported (without malice) that Morton had stolen 'his whore' (F. Tennyson MSS, Lilly Library, University of Indiana, Bloomington), and Edward FitzGerald's letters expressed concern for the misfortunes of the otherwise unidentified 'Poor Elizabeth' whom Morton had seduced and with whom he may have fathered a child, since both Thackeray and FitzGerald later gave her financial assistance (*Letters of Edward FitzGerald*, 1.514, 528, 555; *Letters and Private Papers of … Thackeray*, 2.227; supplement, 1.174). This affair may have been a factor in Thackeray's finding Morton his foreign posting. After Morton fought a duel in Paris in December 1850 Thackeray commented:

> Morton has a genius for scrapes such as no man out of Ireland can ever hope for: and the wonder is that he has lasted up to 40 years of age with a whole skin—Why he is always in some feminine mischief. (*Letters and Private Papers*, 2.726)

He later wrote:

> he is *shocking* about women. Directly I hear of his being fond of one I feel sorry for her. He lusts after her and leaves her … Women think of *reclaiming* a libertine & then, & then all the fat is in the fire. (ibid., 3.24)

By 1851 Morton was involved with the actress Lola Montez (1818–1861), who incited him to fight another duel. Most seriously, in December 1851, he met Harold Elyot Bower (1815–1884), a journalist and Cambridge acquaintance, who was apparently conducting an extra-marital affair. Morton became friendly with Mrs Bower, maintaining that he was helping her to obtain a divorce. In September 1852 she gave birth to her fifth child, claiming Morton as the father. Morton denied it, but Bower became jealous, and fatally stabbed Morton in the neck when he was visiting the Bower household at 2 rue de Sèze on 1 October 1852. Morton died almost immediately.

Thackeray wrote to Milnes that Morton had 'rushed upon his fate. Haven't I often said to you he would come to a violent death?', and he supplemented this, in a letter to Dr John Brown, with:

> He did not care for the woman—at least she was one of a dozen the poor headlong fellow pursued … all the family were crazy, and my poor Savile the maddest wildest and gentlest of creatures—scarce answerable for his actions or his passions. (*Letters and Private Papers of … Thackeray*, supplement, 1.485, 486–7)

Fitzgerald asked 'Didn't he die in character?' and writing to Thackeray reported Frederick Tennyson's comment, 'Morton, he thinks, could only grow a more gigantic Rebel against Good Morals if he grew immortal, and he wishes him Eternal Rest!' (*Letters of Edward FitzGerald*, 2. 71, 75). Morton was buried in Montmartre cemetery, and Bower was acquitted of his murder in December 1852. In 1844 FitzGerald had put together extracts from Morton's letters, hoping publication might provide Morton with some income, but they were rejected by both *Fraser's* and *Blackwood's*. In 1866 he made a fresh selection, 'Fragments of some letters from an ill-starred man of genius', before destroying the originals, but these remain unpublished. Thackeray used the young Morton as his model for Philip Firmin in *The Adventures of Philip* (1861–2) and freely drew on his later life in the Saverne episode in *Denis Duval* (1864). THOMAS BEAN

Sources *The letters and private papers of William Makepeace Thackeray*, ed. G. N. Ray, 4 vols. (1945–6) [with 2 vol. suppl., ed. E. F. Harden (1994)] · *The letters of Edward FitzGerald*, ed. A. M. Terhune and A. B. Terhune, 4 vols. (1980) · J. Pope-Hennessy, *Monckton Milnes: the years of promise* (1949) · *Annual Register* (1852), 402–7 · H. S. Edwards, *Personal recollections* (1900) · Burke, *Gen. GB* · Venn, *Alum. Cant.* · Boase, *Mod. Eng. biog.* · G. N. Ray, *Thackeray*, 2 vols. (1955–8) · Trinity Cam., Houghton MSS

Likenesses G. J. Cayley, drawing, 1850, Trinity Cam., Houghton MSS

Morton, Theodora Matilda (1872–1949), welfare worker, was born on 23 August 1872 at 1 Clifton Villas, Albert Road, South Norwood, London, the daughter of Joseph Morton, master cutler, and his wife, Matilda Morton, *née* Fuessly. She gained experience of social work through working for the Charity Organization Society (COS), which visited the homes of poor families seeking charitable relief. In January 1908 she was employed by the London county council (LCC) as a temporary organizer of its new school care service, which had been set up the year before. Also appointed as a temporary organizer was Douglas Pepler, who had similar experience of working for the COS. The care service comprised a network of care committees attached to elementary schools across London, which provided poor children with school dinners, clothing, and boots, as a way of enabling them to benefit from their attendance at school. Employing Morton and Pepler as temporary organizers reflected the LCC's plan 'of placing the whole work of the Children's Care committees on as uniform and scientific as basis as possible' (Williams, Ivin, and Morse, 44).

After just one year, in 1909, Morton and Pepler were appointed as the first principal organizers of the school care service. Pepler left the service shortly afterwards, but Morton remained in post and proceeded to develop a sound administrative structure for the service, based on a division of London into twelve geographical districts. The care committees were staffed by women volunteers, who selected children for school dinners and provided welfare help; their work was co-ordinated in a systematic manner by professional women employed by the LCC, under Morton's overall supervision. She was a firm defender of the voluntary principle and took the view that welfare help for poor children at school was an educational measure, not a system of poor relief. Like Margaret Frere, the pioneer of the school care service, she believed that it was necessary for care committee workers to establish a strong link between home and school in order to help children effectively; it is possible that her earlier experience of the COS influenced her commitment to visiting families in their homes. Since care committee workers all came from affluent backgrounds, their lives were very different from those of the poor families they visited; they were also unfamiliar with the experience of attending an elementary school, since they and their own children went to private schools. This social divide led initially to suspicion from some children's parents, but many care committee workers managed to persuade them of their genuine concern, especially by acting as their advocate in their dealings with the school.

In 1914, following a massive expansion of health care in schools, the LCC divided the care committees between the education department and the public health department. Those committees under the education department were responsible for welfare issues like school dinners and clothing, while those under the public health department took care of medical inspections and matters of hygiene, such as hair lice. As links between home and school, care committee workers were uniquely placed to help prevent leakage between the stages of medical inspection and treatment and also to act as advocates for the children at clinics and hospitals. Morton was appointed as a half-time principal organizer in each department, with a principal assistant organizer for each department. Although she had resisted this development, believing there was an unbridgeable gulf between the two departments, she used it as an opportunity to extend and to consolidate the role of the school care service. Under her leadership the number of care committees grew rapidly: by 1925 there were nearly 6000 volunteers, which meant that on average there was one voluntary member to 119 children. There were over 900 care committees and only six out of the 1063 elementary schools in London did not have a committee (some committees were shared by more than one school). Her value to the LCC was reflected in her salary, which was £950 per year; this was far higher than the annual salary of women teachers in London, which was usually between £80 and £200.

Miss Morton, who was appointed MBE, retired from the LCC in 1930. She continued to take an interest in the school care service and the COS and she also gave support to the YWCA and King's College, London, which were concerned with the training of social workers. At the time of her death—at St George's Hospital, Westminster, on 14 March 1949—her home was at 55 Queen's Gate, Kensington, London. An obituary in *The Times*, which drew attention to her 'outstanding intellectual power' and 'rare sense of humour', observed that she transformed London's system of children's care through her 'inspiration and administrative ability' (*The Times*, 17 March 1949).

SUSAN WILLIAMS and TENDAYI BLOOM

Sources A. S. Williams, P. Ivin, and C. Morse, *The children of London: attendance and welfare at school, 1870–1990* (2001) • *The Times* (17 March 1949) • b. cert. • d. cert.
Wealth at death £14,523 14s. 8d.: probate, 10 May 1949, CGPLA Eng. & Wales

Morton, Thomas (*bap.* 1564, *d.* 1659), bishop of Durham, was born or more probably baptized in the parish of All Saints Pavement, York, on 20 March 1564, the sixth of nineteen children of Richard Morton, a mercer and alderman of York, and his wife, Elizabeth Leedale. After schooling at York and Halifax he matriculated as a pensioner from St John's College, Cambridge, in Michaelmas 1582 during the mastership of William Whitaker, a powerful Calvinist presence in late-Elizabethan Cambridge, and was admitted as a scholar in 1584. After graduating BA in 1587 and proceeding MA in 1590, he became a fellow of St

Thomas Morton (*bap.* 1564, *d.* 1659), by Simon Luttichuys, 1637

John's in 1592. He was ordained in 1594 and after Whitaker's death took his BD in 1598 and DD in 1606. He was incorporated at Oxford in 1606.

Early career to 1616 Morton was appointed chaplain to Henry Hastings, third earl of Huntingdon, president of the council of the north, shortly before Huntingdon died in December 1595 and, with his fellow chaplain Lancelot Andrewes, soon gained a reputation for skilful disputation with leading Roman Catholics at York. In 1598 his father's influence secured him the rectory of Long Marston in the West Riding, the responsibilities of which he discharged through a deputy. He served as chaplain to Ralph Eure, Lord Eure, formerly sheriff of York and once its MP, on his commercial embassy to the Danes and the Hanse at Bremen in 1602, and took the opportunity to travel widely, broadening his contacts with continental scholars—including Joseph Scaliger at Leiden—and buying books at Frankfurt.

Once back in England in 1603, Morton became chaplain to Roger Manners, fifth earl of Rutland, recently restored to royal favour after the Essex rising. He divided his time between Belvoir and Exeter House and, without parochial responsibilities, began work on the first of his major polemical works. He was diverted by the Gunpowder Plot, publishing *An Exact Discoverie of Romish Doctrine in the Case of Conspiracie and Rebellion* (1605) and *A Full Satisfaction concerning a Double Romish Iniquitie: Hainous Rebellion and more then Heathenish Aequivocation* (1606), which drew him into early, and generally temperate, argument with Richard Broughton, Robert Persons, and the pseudonymous John Brereley; but, as he said in *A Full Satisfaction*, 'we may as well expect grapes from thornes … as loyal subjection from this [Roman Catholic] religion'. In 1606 he completed the publication of his *Apologiae catholicae*, in two parts, the first of which was dedicated to Archbishop Richard Bancroft (1605) and the second to James I (1606). The book was directed against Brereley's *The Apology of the Romane Church* (1604). Like Brereley, Morton employed the new technique of finding support for his own case from the writings of his opponents, while making much of the discrepancies between them, and succeeded in provoking sour Catholic reflections on the way his unusually wide range of textual reference amplified their internal differences and made rebuttal harder. Visiting Oxford in 1606 he met its leading Calvinist divines, among them John King, dean of Christ Church, Henry Airay, president of Queen's, and John Reynolds (*d*. 1607), president of Corpus Christi, as well as the young Daniel Featley of Corpus, who was to become both George Abbot's chaplain and Morton's regular correspondent. Before the year was out Bancroft ensured that James made Morton a royal chaplain.

Morton continued to devote much of his time to publishing polemical works against the authority and pretensions of the Church of Rome until 1610, when his increasing administrative responsibilities coincided with the death that April of his best-known opponent, Robert Persons, shortly followed by that of Bancroft in November. During 1608–9 Bancroft had presided over the most substantial publication with which Morton was to be associated. *A Catholic Appeale to Protestants* (1609) was a co-operative effort by 'a certain number of Divines then at hand', in response to Brereley's renewed attack in *The Protestants Apologie for the Roman Church*, published in St Omer in 1608. The title-page simply stated that it was 'written' by Morton and, as he modestly explained to James in the epistle dedicatory, the task of writing up had fallen to him because he had the time to do it—'my occasions then better sorting'—even though he was the 'weakest and unworthiest of those parties assigned'. John Cosin later noted in his copy of *A Catholic Appeale* that John Overall, the anti-Calvinist dean of St Paul's, whose chaplain he was, had been responsible for its final revision 'and in truth was the chief author of it'; and it is possible that some of its liberal views, such as those on the reservation of the sacrament for delivery to the sick, are not Morton's own (Hunt, 69). Nevertheless, he was closely involved in framing the text. By March 1608 his close friend John Donne, even though not yet in holy orders, had clearly been invited to read and comment on some parts of it; and at some stage Morton wrote to John Howson, the anti-Calvinist Oxford divine, asking him to vet a section of the text. Howson, reading more than he was asked, informed Bancroft and his panel that he had found seventeen errors of substance and, as he later added, 'could have delivered seventeen more'. Bancroft sent him to Morton, who so readily incorporated the amendments that, in Howson's words, they 'parted very good Frends' (Bald, 210; 'John

Howson's Answer', 338). Such editorial care suggests that *A Catholic Appeale* was intended to be a balanced and considered reflection of English protestantism for European consumption as well as a work of high scholarship, one which 'amounted virtually to an official publication of the Church of England' (Milton, *Catholic and Reformed*, 233 n. 26).

With the assistance of Lord Eure, now president of the council of the marches of Wales, Morton was in June 1607 appointed to the deanery of Gloucester, that 'shell without a kernel' as James later described it (*Works of … William Laud*, 3.136). He nevertheless promptly offered the impoverished Donne his Long Marston living, of similar value, in the vain hope that it would provide him with an incentive for taking holy orders. Late in 1609 Morton gained a richer reward, becoming dean of Winchester when George Abbot—already being groomed by Bancroft for the primacy—was translated to the see of Lichfield. Morton may well have owed his nomination to a growing continental reputation, demonstrated by the translation of his work into Dutch. The leading Dutch Calvinist scholar Sibrandus Lubbertus became a frequent correspondent, and Morton himself believed that what persuaded James to favour him over a client of George Home, earl of Dunbar, was Lubbertus's timely dedication to him of his latest work, *Replicatio de papa romano* (Milton, *Catholic and Reformed*, 399).

In May 1610 James I nominated Morton as one of seventeen fellows, none of them bishops, of Chelsea College, a venture proposed by Matthew Sutcliffe and intended, as James later put it, 'for learned divines to be employed in writing, as occasion shall require, for maintaining the religion professed in our Kingdom and confuting the impugners thereof' (Fuller, 3.238); John Overall, Howson, and Robert Abbot were also among the fellows. But the college made a slow start, and never succeeded in establishing itself. Meanwhile Archbishop Toby Matthew of York prompted Bancroft's man of business, Sir Christopher Parkins, by virtue of a grant of next presentation, to nominate Morton in July 1610 as prebendary of Husthwaite in York Minster, a place he retained until his appointment to Durham in 1632.

Morton was happy in the deanery of Winchester. He developed a comfortable relationship with his cathedral chapter and, unlike Abbot, also with the bishop, Thomas Bilson, who was quick to confer the rectory of Alresford on him. He began a lasting friendship with Arthur Lake, a Calvinist moderate, then master of St Cross Hospital as well as Bilson's chaplain, and maintained old ones: his duties allowed him frequent visits to London, where he stayed at times with George Abbot's steward, Sir Robert Hatton or with Dean Overall, in 1614 preaching in St Paul's at the opening of convocation. Morton and Overall were gratified in May 1611 when Theophilus Higgons, whom they had both been counselling at the deanery and with whom Morton had engaged in published debate, recanted from his Roman faith and at Paul's Cross, in the presence of privy councillors and courtiers, returned to the Church of England in a penitential sermon. It was at the deanery that in 1610 Morton first met Isaac Casaubon (d. 1614), an international scholar of uncertain Calvinist allegiance, who made such a lasting impression on him that, as he left for Durham over twenty years later, he erected to his memory in Westminster Abbey a monument by Nicholas Stone at a cost of £60. That Morton was reluctant to allow administrative responsibilities to undermine his scholarly activities is suggested by his attempt to cement his attachment to St John's, Cambridge, by obtaining the mastership of his old college when it fell vacant in May 1612. His rival for the post, Dr Owen Gwynne, one of the senior fellows, owed his swiftly achieved success to the management of another fellow, John Williams. Hacket later supposed that Williams had been prompted by loyalty to his old tutor; but Gwynne and Williams were cousins and, among other considerations, their kinsman, Sir John Wynn of Gwydir, was concerned that the decision on a fellowship for his youngest son, Robin, might well be influenced by the outcome.

Bishop of Chester, 1616–1619 When the opportunity to advance came Morton may not entirely have welcomed it, despite his elevation to the bench of bishops. He never settled at Chester. When Bishop George Lloyd died in August 1615, Morton was not initially considered for a diocese where most of its bishops had had local roots. Dr Gerard Massey, from a wealthy Chester mercantile family, was nominated as Lloyd's successor but died in London in January 1616 before he could be consecrated. Massey had been rector of Wigan, a living currently run down but with an optimum value of roughly £600 a year, its potential worth contrasting sharply with the parlous state of the bishop's revenues. Within days of Massey's death James had bestowed Wigan on John Bridgeman, a promising court preacher as yet short of administrative experience, who was not to be easily detached from his prize. Even before he accompanied James to Scotland in 1617, he had begun restoring his rectorial rights and revenues and, as the Wigan townsmen discovered, enjoyed the king's unqualified support in doing so. It was thus to a bishopric shorn of valuable additional income that Morton was elected on 22 May 1616. He was consecrated at Lambeth on 7 July, but illness meant he did not reach the diocese until October. John Chamberlain thought the reason for his elevation was to 'make roome' at Winchester for John Young, chancellor of Wells and an influential Calvinist insider, whose family had long been close to the king (Chamberlain, 2.2); after the series of west-country Calvinist preferments during 1615–16 involving Robert Abbot, James Montagu, Arthur Lake, Sam Ward, Morton, and Young, Morton alone found himself at a distance from the nexus. He may have given the impression of travelling reluctantly into unfamiliar territory, at a remove from court, to responsibilities with a comparatively limited perspective.

Morton's delayed arrival meant that he missed the beginning of the sabbatarian controversy in Lancashire which led to James I's declaration of sports in 1617, and may not immediately have appreciated its significance. At Trinity assizes, on 8 August 1616, the Lancashire JPs at the sheriff's table had drawn up and agreed 'with the apoyntement of the Judge of Assise [Edward Bromley]' a set of eight orders similar in tone and content to Sir Edward Montagu's sabbatarian bill which had been lost with the premature ending of the 1614 parliament. In particular they provided 'that theare bee no pipinge, dancinge, bowlinge, beare or bull baiting or any other profanacion of the Sabbath Day or any parte of the Day or upon any festivall day in tyme of Devyne service', making no distinction between traditional recreations and physical activities deemed beneficial to the well-being of the nation and idle entertainments which were not. Morton's 1617 visitation articles, in this matter adopting unchanged the wording of Toby Matthews's York set of 1607, equally lacked discrimination and, although more liberal about timing, still left doubts. They asked:

> Whether there are in your … parish or chappellry any rush bearings, bull-baytings, beare-baitings, may-games, moricedances, ailes or any such like prophane pastimes or assemblies on the sabboth to the hinderance of prayers, sermons or other godly exercises. (Fincham, *Visitation Articles*, 1.59)

When James I arrived in Lancashire in August 1617, homeward bound after sensitive and still inconclusive dealings with the Scots over the terms of the articles of Perth, he was soon made aware that all was not well. At Hoghton Tower on Sunday 17 August, after Morton's sermon, he was petitioned by Catholic and moderate Calvinist gentry seeking relaxation in sabbath observance; yet the next day he learned of the disquiet of sterner Calvinists at dancing which had taken place in a neighbouring parish during divine service. Morton cannot have impressed James by his limited grasp of the situation, and it is likely that the king had his doubts about his assurances that the numbers of Catholics in the diocese had recently shown signs of diminishing. James's interest in relaxation extended no further than separating worthy activities from the rest, and permitting their exercise at clearly defined times. Morton's draft provisions, moulded by James into the words of a king rather than those of a bishop, were published on 27 August 1617 at Gerard's Bromley in Staffordshire. They were to form the basis of the nationwide Book of Sports of 1618.

Morton's long and scholarly concentration on the fundamental problems of international Catholicism had not prepared him for the interplay of religious extremes in the local community. In particular his continuing failure within his diocese to bring to conformity an obstinate puritan minority, bound uncompromisingly by conscience, disturbed him. In October 1617—after barely a year at Chester, and possibly with Bridgeman's encouragement—he sought translation to Lincoln, a diocese with similar problems, only to find that his 'remisse course' with his own puritan clergy had 'been prejudiciall to his preferment', his patient dealing with them having been represented to the king as indulgence, according to the recollection of one of them, Thomas Paget (Collinson, 89n.).

For his rehabilitation, Morton turned to his pen. His book, *A defence of the innocencie of the three ceremonies of the church of England … the surplice, the crosse in baptism and kneeling at the receiving of the blessed sacrament* (1618) was his first 'to contend against the Non-conformists' at home after 'many conflicts' on an international plane against the papists, and was dedicated to the marquess of Buckingham 'because the Treatise … was first occasioned by your Lordship'. His attention to some of the problems of protestant conformity raised by the adiaphora was certainly timely, even if his arguments were not in essence new. Both John Buckeridge on Passion Sunday and Lancelot Andrewes on Easter day had already addressed the issue during the 1618 series of Lenten sermons at court, while supporting James's efforts to secure ceremonial obedience in Scotland, arguing that bowing and kneeling were essentially religious duties. Morton's own approach, however, owed more to a view of the relationship between the temporal and spiritual authority of the monarchy with regard to religious conformity put forward, for example, by Bishop Thomas Bilson in his sermon at James's coronation in 1603. Morton argued, like Bilson and others before him, that it was not sufficient to refuse to conform to any of the adiaphora purely for reasons of conscience, as each of the king's subjects also owed obedience to him as supreme governor of the church. That obligation should be recognized by observing the rituals of the Church of England in the practice of divine worship. To do so acknowledged the royal supremacy, spared the scrupulous worshipper's conscience, and contributed to an orderliness in church services by collective participation, as in kneeling for the eucharist, which might persuade doubting Roman Catholics that the Church of England was visibly a united church.

Bishop of Coventry and Lichfield, 1619–1632 As early as 8 August 1618, a month before *A defence of … innocencie* was entered with the Stationers' Company, Chamberlain was reporting that Morton had been translated to Chichester and that Bridgeman had succeeded him at Chester. When he did move, in February 1619, to Coventry and Lichfield in place of Overall, his puritan critic, William Ames, directly linked his translation with the publication of the book. Morton had carefully associated it with Buckingham, but John Barwick later noted that Andrewes had, exceptionally, exercised his influence in a matter of patronage. James I was apparently convinced by such means of Morton's worthiness; even so, a year later he sought assurance from Morton about the corporation of Coventry's current readiness to kneel during divine service before granting a new charter, after finding it remiss when he had passed through in 1617.

At Lichfield, Morton was able to prove himself a conscientious and understanding diocesan, taking pains to improve the quality of his clergy in terms of general education and ability in the pulpit, showing patience in cases of conscience, and improving substantially the values of livings directly in his gift. He and Bridgeman, now indeed bishop of Chester, remained on good terms, serving as each other's proxy in the Lords, and Morton hoped to obtain for his diocese the second of the preachers which Buckingham's secretary John Packer intended to provide from his own pocket, the first having gone to the diocese of Chester. As he was also to do at Durham, he found worthwhile employment for difficult clergy like Anthony Lapthorne in the remoter and less amenable parts of his see, and used his own funds to provide printed copies of the official catechism for children. He attended at least two visitations in person (in 1620 and 1623), and may have done so on other occasions. He proved an amiable overseer, widely welcomed. His visitation articles, based on a set used by Abbot and derived from Bancroft, were comprehensive but restrained and while for example enquiring whether the surplice was worn and the sign of the cross used in baptism, refrained from asking whether this was always so. That he took his preaching seriously is indicated by his use of a fresh text at each of three consecration services for which evidence survives. He had earlier helped Daniel Featley to gain the commission to edit the English translation of Laurence Humphrey's life of a renowned Tudor preaching pastor, John Jewell, and in 1621 was chosen to preach the funeral sermon for his friend John King, bishop of London, from the same Calvinist tradition. In 1624 he was one of two bishops cannily suggested by Lord Keeper Williams to John Packer as suitable deputies for Andrewes if he were unable to preach at the opening of the new parliament. Although Williams thought both were fine scholars, he regarded Valentine Carey, the anti-Calvinist bishop of Exeter, as the superior preacher, while Morton was 'better esteemed by the Lords and other Parliamentary men' (Gardiner, *Fortescue Papers*, 194). The king chose Carey.

Morton first sat in the House of Lords in 1621, and by 1624 had shown himself a ready contributor to debates, close to Archbishop Abbot in his response to shifts of emphasis in foreign policy and within the church, as a consequence of the loss of the Palatinate and the urgency of a suitable match for Prince Charles. Despite Habsburg aggression, James worried many Calvinists by his reluctance to take up arms, preferring to put his trust for as long as he could in diplomacy with Spain. At the end of the session of 1621 it was rumoured that Morton and Abbot had been confined to their homes, possibly for showing undue concern that the attorney-general, Sir Henry Yelverton, should get a fair hearing during proceedings against him for dealings with monopolists, but more probably for hostility to Spain. Morton thought it necessary in September 1623 to remind the secretary of state, Sir Edward Conway, that he was ready to come in person to present a horse and welcome the prince on his return from his ill-judged Spanish mission 'if such be his Majesty's pleasure' (PRO, SP 14/152/88). However, as the parliament of 1624 contemplated the failed match, Morton took advantage of the vengeful line of Prince Charles and Buckingham to make a forceful speech on 18 February in favour of war with Spain, which may not have endeared him to the king. He also had a particular interest in another issue which inflamed Calvinist passions, the parliamentary proceedings in 1624 and 1625 against James's chaplain Richard Mountague and his recent works, *A Gagg for the New Gospell? No: a New Gagg for an Old Goose* (1624) and

Appello Caesarem (1625), which provocatively explored the doctrinal proximity of the Church of England to the Church of Rome. Although both books had been approved by James beforehand, and had since been reported by bishops William Laud, Andrewes, Richard Neile, George Montaigne, and Buckeridge to Buckingham as agreeable to the doctrine of the Church of England, a finding Charles accepted, they still angered Abbot and his Calvinist allies in both houses.

Morton, whose works had been scoured by Mountague and his friends for passages which might be quoted against him, was the senior representative of this aggrieved Calvinist interest at the small conference with Mountague and his defenders, convened by Buckingham at York House in the early days of the new parliament. It met at the urging of Robert Rich, earl of Warwick, and was held over two days, 11 and 17 February 1626, in the presence of several privy councillors and bishops, among them Viscount Saye and the secretary of state John Coke, the sole member of the Commons, as friends of Morton, and James Hay, earl of Carlisle, in Mountague's support. According to the fullest extant account, from John Cosin on Mountague's side, Morton seemed nervous from the outset, precipitately outlining the general charge against Mountague before Buckingham had had a chance to introduce proceedings; and thereafter, if Cosin is to be believed, Morton proved less effective than his partner John Preston. Over a number of heads, taking in articles 11, 12, 17, 19, 21, and 27 as well as the oath of supremacy and the Synod of Dort, he found it difficult to demonstrate that Mountague was seriously in error. He complained in frustration that Mountague 'prevaricates, he says and unsays: but his meaning we know well enough'. There was truth in this; but his struggles to make that meaning plain laid him open to correction on points of doctrine, principally by John Buckeridge, bishop of Rochester and one of Mountague's principals, and to chiding by William Herbert, earl of Pembroke, who like other laymen found him hard to follow, and told him that 'you stretch and wrest a well-meaning man's words too far' (*Works of … John Cosin*, 2.17–81; Tyacke, chap. 7).

The conference ended inconclusively, lacking a final report, and its immediate impact is not easy to assess. For his part, Morton suffered no obvious disadvantage. He was, with Laud and Samuel Harsnett, consulted soon afterwards by the king on church business, which included the need to restore impropriations. Subsequently he was able to publish a conventional rejoinder in *The Grand Imposture of the (now) Church of Rome* (1626), with an unamended second edition (1628), after assuring Charles in the epistle dedicatory that he 'was not writing in any spirit of malignancie to make the Schisme … bigger', but intended simply to remove 'the onely Barre and Partition-wall' between the churches. He took a consistently conciliatory line during the parliament of 1628, in keeping with the closer relationship then developing between the moderate Calvinists and the privy council, and was one of those Calvinist bishops who, at least at first, reacted favourably to the publication in December 1628 of the king's declaration in support of the 'true, usual and literal meaning' of the articles of religion, in which Abbot had after all had a hand, and which was followed in January 1629 by the suppression by royal proclamation of Mountague's *Appello Caesarem*.

Yet tensions remained: dismay at Joseph Hall's careless description in *The Olde Religion* (1628) of Rome as a 'true visible Church', at once rejected by the radical Calvinist Henry Burton, was strongest among his fellow moderate Calvinists, who wanted no association, however unintentional, with Arminian thinking. Hall sought to demonstrate their continuing support in an appendix, *The Reconciler* (1629). Morton, while responding indignantly to the notion that Burton should attack Hall, otherwise restricted himself to a few words of sympathy and encouragement, in marked contrast to Bishop John Davenant of Salisbury who left Hall in no doubt where his error lay and how it should be put right in order to avoid further misunderstanding. An anonymous letter to Laud from the Temple in February 1630, just after Alexander Leighton's arrest, alleged, however, that Laud and Neile had taken unspecified action against the bishops of Salisbury and Coventry who 'do but cross their way by a sermon or book' (PRO, SP 16/161/39). Even so, Morton in 1631, without obvious check, published the first edition of his *Of the Institution of the Sacrament of the Blessed Bodie and Blood of Christ*, which included a liberal view of the place and purpose of 'the table of the Lord'. The second edition in 1635 was vetted, apparently by Laud's chaplain William Bray, but Morton managed to retain his existing comments, with the qualification that 'notwithstanding, you are not to think that wee do hereby oppugne the Appellation of Priest and Altar or yet the now situation thereof in our Church, for use as Convenient and for Order more Decent' (Tyacke, 212–13).

Bishop of Durham, 1632–1641 Morton was translated to Durham in the summer of 1632, succeeding the anti-Calvinist Howson, who had failed to equal Neile's understanding of the diocese. Morton was the first bishop of Durham for almost forty years to have been born in the north of England, and his was to be the last of three Calvinist episcopal promotions between 1625 and 1640. Neither Neile, newly arrived at York, nor Laud was likely to have pressed his case, but Charles may have recognized his suitability for the task, and was not simply removing an elderly old-style Calvinist, unlikely to travel much, still further from the ambit of the court. Morton did not always give satisfaction: his diocesan reports tended to be bland and not entirely regular, causing the king in 1636 to order in a characteristic apostil that he should be 'checked for [his] … slackness' (PRO, SP 16/312/84), and as lord lieutenant he was no more a match than Howson for Neile's enterprise, as the bishops' wars were to show. Yet he proved a sound choice, possessing the broad churchmanship and amiability to repair the damage done by Howson in a diocese and county used to working together in public business despite religious differences.

Morton was helped by the early translation of Augustine Lindsell to the bishopric of Peterborough, the retirement of Marmaduke Blackiston, and the death of Francis Burgoyne—among prominent clergy with Arminian inclinations—enabling him to find successors who were lively but moderate Calvinists. He handled an ungrateful Peter Smart sympathetically when fresh charges were brought against him for nonconformity in king's bench in 1638, and developed an amicable relationship with John Cosin, rector since 1626 of the valuable crown living of Brancepeth, but an absentee since his departure for the mastership of Peterhouse in 1635. In the following year Cosin suffered the embarrassment of presentation by his churchwardens to the Durham consistory court for serious deficiencies in the fabric and furnishings of his church, but Morton handled the matter discreetly, and Cosin saw the bishop's *Antidotum adversus ecclesiae Romanae* through the University Press at Cambridge for him in 1637, in what may well have been an exercise in benign censorship intended to ensure that the work met with the king's satisfaction. By July 1639 Morton was recommending Cosin to Laud for advancement. A presumptuous and aggressive pair of Arminians, Thomas Triplet and Eleazar Duncon, who interpreted any concession to Calvinists as a sign of Morton's weakness and rushed to report it to higher authority, were the only clergy regularly troubling Morton in the later 1630s.

Thomas Wentworth, Viscount Wentworth, who retained his authority as president of the council of the north despite his commitments in Ireland, from the outset found Morton 'peevish' (Pogson, 280) in his attitude to the liberal terms on which recusant compositions were arranged under the northern commission. In the autumn of 1633 Morton wrote to Laud, rather than Neile, complaining that Wentworth's compositions encouraged compounders to 'think themselves free from all command of conference, as concluding they must not be troubled for conscience' (*Works of … William Laud*, 6.334), which had the effect of increasing their numbers while making it almost impossible for Morton to carry on discussions, in which he was long practised, which might lead to conversion. In his view their lives should be made sufficiently uncomfortable to create an incentive for them to wish to become members of the Church of England. Lord Keeper Thomas Coventry, high steward of both York and Hull, was saying as much twice a year to the assize judges, and on the northern circuit Sir George Vernon and Sir Humphrey Davenport were adding to Wentworth's anger by urging the enforcement of the penal laws. Laud forwarded Morton's letter to Wentworth, but was noticeably reluctant to offer advice until he had managed to learn something from the king of his attitude to the new bishop of Durham and to Wentworth's dealings in the business. As he had been forced to do during the royal commission's investigation of Bishop Bridgeman a few months earlier, Laud was having to confront the cost to his principles of an alliance with Wentworth: in this case, Morton's belief that a recusant's religion was a matter of conscience, rather than an opportunity to maximize revenue from

compositions on unduly generous terms, must have weighed with him. His endorsement, after he found the king backed Wentworth rather than Morton, was made at the end of a long letter and has a hollow ring: 'For my own part (and you know it) I did ever think somewhat was wanting there' (ibid., 7.61).

For his part, Wentworth explained that he was not stopping Morton from fulfilling his desire to 'confer with any … which have not compounded, to exercise his talent upon' and win them over to the Church of England. He admitted that Morton was 'a person very learned and honest'; yet asked whether that was 'all what is to be desired of a good Bishop', before declaring 'I have done more towards a Reformation so far as a pecuniary mulct inflicted can effect it than any that went before me' (*Earl of Strafforde's Letters and Dispatches*, 1.171–4). In a letter of 7 March 1634 he expanded on his view of Morton, regarding him as the mouthpiece of those local government officials, such as clerks of assizes and peace, who had lost a useful source of income from recusant fines; innocently:

> he utters the zeale he owes the Church of Christ. But I know the man so well, as that to reforme him is impossible, unlesse a Metropolitan be able to effect it. And therefore to your Lordship I leave him.   (Strafford MSS, 6/30)

At the time Laud did little, and his correspondence remained affable enough to prompt Morton to declare in 1636 that he was 'much beholden to my Lord's Grace of Canterbury for reviveinge me with his letters' (PRO, SP 16/312/40). Wentworth was left to pour out his bitterness to Lord Treasurer Portland, typically complaining in June 1634 that Morton:

> perpetually vexeth them [compounded recusants] for clandestine maryages, christeninges, buryalls and such like, which albeitt they are not exempted from these Ecclesiasticall censures, yet it is not altogether so seasonable to bee persewed thus hotly in the very face of the commission, to hinder the compounders.   (Strafford MSS, 3/98–99)

But when in December 1637 Laud was granted by Charles 'all bonds, fines and arrearages' in the courts of high commission in both provinces to support the costs of building the west end of St Paul's, he realized at first hand not only the inhibiting effect on routine fines from recusants of Wentworth's supplementary exemptions to compounders, but also the scale of the evasion of high commission, which might put northern recusants 'in farr better case than any subjects in England. For besides the Freedome which is granted them, they might have done what they list, criminally allsoe, against all Ecclesiastical Government in the kingdome: a thing of intollerable consequence' (Strafford MSS, 7, fols. 79v–80r, 19 Dec 1637). Even though he assured Wentworth that 'as for the bishop which you mention [Morton] I shall neither rely upon his judgment nor be swayed with his earnestness', Laud had at last adopted a similar position to the bishop of Durham on recusant compositions, although for rather different reasons (*Earl of Strafforde's Letters and Dispatches*, 2.526).

Despite entertaining Charles lavishly at Bishop Auckland and Durham on his way to Scotland in 1633, and having occasional dealings with his old friend John Coke,

Morton had, by the later 1630s, grown out of touch with dispositions at court. Laud's correspondence had evidently revealed nothing of his breach with Windebank; as late as 1636 Morton was looking forward to enjoying Sir Francis's witty conversation at Lambeth. The stirring of the covenanters, however, brought him close to the heart of the action, and made him circumspect. The finished version of a sermon on a text from Romans 13: 1, which he preached briskly—'the shortness of the hour requiring it'—in the king's presence in Durham Cathedral on 5 May 1639 prior to his departure for Newcastle and Scotland, was subjected to royal scrutiny before being passed for printing by the Newcastle and London presses. For publication Morton had added two short passages denying the covenanters' claim that Calvin supported their notion of resistance. Although Charles studied the *Institutes*, he refused to acknowledge that Calvinism was not revolutionary, and ordered the two additions to be left out, thereby driving a wedge between the teachings of Calvin and the preferred doctrines of the Church of England. Morton managed, however, to get *De eucharistia decisio* published in Cambridge in 1640, apparently without delay or amendment, after rumours that, in spite of his sympathetic dealings with John Dury during the 1630s, it first needed to be toned down because of overt anti-Lutheran bias. He was nominated to preach 'first turne' before the king in the chapel at Whitehall on 19 April 1640, early in the Short Parliament, but had urgent business in his diocese. His graphic account of his treatment by the Scots after they had occupied Durham in August 1640 was nevertheless useful to the earl of Manchester—'these things being as lively presented as we could', as he told Charles—in trying to persuade the City of London to lend £200,000 towards the Scottish campaign (PRO, SP 16/469/22).

Final years, 1641–1659 Morton retreated to York and probably never returned to Durham. In 1641 he was present in the House of Lords, that spring busying himself on the subcommittee to the committee considering innovations in religion. At the end of the year, however, his coach was attacked on its way to the house, and he did not attend again. He was one of twelve bishops impeached on 30 December 1641, but his advanced years helped him to escape imprisonment in the Tower. Instead he spent four months in the custody of black rod before being allowed to return to Durham House in the Strand. In April 1645 he was detained for six months by the serjeant-at-arms after refusing to hand over the seal of the county palatine of Durham and using the prayer book rite at a Manners family baptism. After the abolition of episcopacy in 1646 he had difficulty in securing financial support, eventually obtaining a single payment of £1000, but no annuity, from the committee at Goldsmith's Hall. In 1648 he was turned out of Durham House, for a time living with the eighth earl of Rutland at Exeter House, and then with other friends, before unexpectedly meeting Sir Christopher Yelverton, son of the old attorney-general, on the road to London. He returned with him to his home at Easton-Maudit in Northamptonshire where, outliving his host, he died on 20 September 1659, and was buried in the parish church.

A small, sprightly man, Morton had been as generous in his hospitality as he was ascetic in his habits. He had never married, and had already provided for his kinsmen. His will, after bequeathing a chalice to All Saints' parish in York, where he was born, and £10 to the poor of the parish in which he died, consisted of a handful of small bequests to servants and local friends. Its closely written codicil, dated 15 April 1658 in his ninety-fifth year, was however intended for publication by John Barwick, his chaplain, executor, and preacher of his funeral sermon. It comprised his profession of faith, his approbation of the discipline of the church of Christ by bishops who held office by virtue of apostolical succession, and his vindication of his own innocence. He still saw himself as occupying the middle ground as a liberal and moderate Calvinist, dealing with 'opposites on both sides' who sometimes caused the orthodox to contemplate 'wavering to the Right hand and to the Left'. He had 'endeavoured to undeceive' perverse protestants and obstinate Catholics alike by his 'Sermons, Conferences and Writinges', and stressed that 'It was onely their Errors whereat I was offended, and prayed and laboured for the right informeing of their mynds and the Eternal Salvation of their Soules' (PRO, PROB 11/300, fols. 229r–230v).

Morton's approach reflected his late Tudor and early Jacobean origins, when his initial target had been unreformed Catholics at home and abroad whom he had hoped to win over, individually and collectively, to Calvinism. His concern with radical Calvinists was thus, as at Chester, primarily prompted by the effect of their disregard for the Church of England's ceremonial, which discouraged English Catholics from conversion. By the 1620s the increasingly influential anti-Calvinists, however, sought to destabilize moderate Calvinists either by emphasizing the common ground between them or, if rebuffed, by redefining radical Calvinism to include such liberal-minded churchmen as Davenant, Hall, and Morton himself. Not surprisingly, he felt displaced and not entirely trusted. His determined opposition to the extravagant terms of the northern commission's recusant compositions, however, usefully emphasized the embarrassment which Laud himself periodically felt through his association with Wentworth. Morton, standing firmly on principle and shrewdly managing his northern diocese, could justly claim to have vindicated himself in difficult times.

BRIAN QUINTRELL

Sources PRO, SP 14; SP 16 · will, PRO, PROB 11/300, fols. 229r–230v · PRO, LC 5/134 · Strafford papers, Sheff. Arch., Wentworth Woodhouse muniments · J. Barwick, *The life and death of Thomas lord bishop of Duresme* (1660) [inc. Morton's codicil] · R. Baddeley and J. Naylor, *The life and death of Thomas Morton, late bishop of Durham* (1669) · 'John Howson's answer to Archbishop Abbot's accusations at his "trial" before James I', ed. N. W. S. Cranfield and K. Fincham, *Camden miscellany, XXIX*, CS, 4th ser., 34 (1987) · *The works of … John Cosin*, ed. J. Sansom and J. Barrow, 5 vols. (1843–55) · *The correspondence of John Cosin D.D., lord bishop of Durham*, ed. [G. Ornsby], 1, SurtS, 52 (1869) · *The correspondence of John Cosin D.D., lord bishop of Durham*, ed. [G. Ornsby], 2, SurtS, 55 (1872) · *The works of the most reverend* *father in God, William Laud*, ed. J. Bliss and W. Scott, 7 vols. (1847–60) · G. Radcliffe, *The earl of Strafforde's letters and dispatches, with an essay towards his life*, ed. W. Knowler, 2 vols. (1739) · *The letters of John Chamberlain*, ed. N. E. McClure, 2 vols. (1939) · *The manuscripts of the Earl Cowper*, 3 vols., HMC, 23 (1888–9) · K. Fincham, ed., *Visitation articles and injunctions of the early Stuart church*, 2 vols. (1994–8) · *The Fortescue papers*, ed. S. R. Gardiner, CS, new ser., 1 (1871) · E. Axon, ed., *Manchester sessions*, 1: 1616–1622–23, Lancashire and Cheshire RS, 42 (1901) · B. W. Quintrell, ed., *The proceedings of the Lancashire justices of the peace at the sheriff's table during assizes week, 1578–1694*, Lancashire and Cheshire RS, 121 (1981) · [J. Ballinger], ed., *Calendar of Wynn (of Gwydir) papers, 1515–1690*, in the National Library of Wales (1926) · G. T. O. Bridgeman, *The history of the church and manor of Wigan, in the county of Lancaster*, 4 vols., Chetham Society, new ser., 15–18 (1888–90) · *Notes of the debates in the House of Lords, officially taken by Henry Elsing, clerk of the parliaments, AD 1621*, ed. S. R. Gardiner, CS, 103 (1870) · M. Jansson and W. B. Bidwell, eds., *Proceedings in parliament, 1625* (1987) · M. F. Keeler, M. J. Cole, and W. B. Bidwell, eds., *Lords proceedings, 1628* (1983) · A. Milton, *Catholic and Reformed: the Roman and protestant churches in English protestant thought, 1600–1640* (1995) · K. Fincham, *Prelate as pastor: the episcopate of James I* (1990) · N. Tyacke, *Anti-Calvinists: the rise of English Arminianism, c.1590–1640* (1987) · P. Collinson, *The religion of protestants* (1982) · J. Davies, *The Caroline captivity of the church: Charles I and the remoulding of Anglicanism, 1625–1641* (1992) · R. O'Day, *The English clergy: the emergence and consolidation of a profession, 1558–1642* (1979) · F. Pogson, 'Wentworth and the northern recusancy commission', *Recusant History*, 24 (1998–9), 271–87 · M. J. Tillbrook, 'Aspects of the government and society of county Durham, 1558–1642', PhD diss., U. Lpool, 1981 · P. Milward, *Religious controversies of the Jacobean age* (1978) · A. Hunt, 'The Lord's supper in early modern England', *Past and Present*, 161 (1998) · R. C. Bald, *John Donne: a life*, ed. W. Milgate (1970) · M. Greengrass, M. Leslie, and T. Raylor, eds., *Samuel Hartlib and universal reformation: studies in intellectual communication* (1994) · M. Pattison, *Isaac Casaubon, 1559–1614*, ed. [H. Nettleship], 2nd edn (1892) · M. C. Fissel, *The bishops' wars: Charles I's campaigns against Scotland, 1638–1640* (1994) · T. Fuller, *The church history of Britain*, ed. [J. Nichols], 3 vols. (1837)

Archives U. Durham L., letters and legal papers | Durham Cath. CL, Hunter MSS · Lichfield Cathedral Library, letters to Sibrand Lubbert · PRO, SP 14, SP 16 · U. Durham, Mickleton and Spearman MSS, Cosin MSS, letter-books

Likenesses S. Luttichuys, oils, 1637, St John Cam. [*see illus.*] · oils, 1637, St John Cam. · T. Berry, line engraving, pubd 1820 (after unknown artist), BM, NPG · W. Faithorne, line engraving, BM, NPG; repro. in J. Barwick, *Funeral sermon* (1660) · engraving, repro. in J. Barwick, *The life and death of Thomas lord bishop of Duresme* (1660) · portrait, Christ Church Oxf. · portrait, Auckland Castle, Durham

Wealth at death minimal: will, PRO, PROB 11/300, fols. 229r–230v

Morton, Thomas (1580x95–1646/7), colonist in America, was born some time between 1580 and 1595; his birthplace and parents are unknown. A gentleman, and lawyer of Clifford's Inn, he married Alice Miller, a widow of Swallowfield, Berkshire, in 1621 and represented her in legal battles against her son George Miller. He went to New England, most likely in 1624, as a partner in Captain Wollaston's settlement at Passonagessit, later the site of Quincy, Massachusetts. Over the next four years he explored New England, turning his keen eye on the land itself as well as its American Indian and European inhabitants. Early in 1626 Wollaston left for Virginia with some servants. By the summer Morton commanded the settlement and the six or seven men who remained.

On 1 May 1627 Morton's men raised what would be a famous maypole to celebrate the site's new name, Ma-re Mount. The following year the separatist settlers of Plymouth Colony organized with several Massachusetts Bay planters in an effort to stop Morton's trade with the Indians. According to Governor William Bradford they wanted to stop him from trading guns; Morton argued instead that they wanted to eliminate his successful competition in the beaver trade and his practice of Anglicanism. When correspondence with Morton had no effect, Bradford sent Miles Standish to enforce Plymouth's point of view. The pilgrims banished him to the Isles of Shoals for a month, then shipped him to Plymouth, England, where no action was taken against him. In September 1628 John Endicott went to Ma-re Mount and had the maypole chopped down, chastising those of Morton's followers who remained.

To William Bradford's extreme irritation, in 1629 Morton returned, first to Plymouth Colony as scribe to its agent Isaac Allerton and then, after serving Allerton for some weeks, to Ma-re Mount, where he resumed his profitable beaver trade. However, he soon had to deal with the Massachusetts Bay Colony. Late in 1629 John Endicott and Samuel Skelton drew up articles for all the planters to sign, on pain of banishment. The main provision was that they agree to follow the rule of God's word as law in both political and ecclesiastical matters. Morton refused to sign unless a passage was added 'so as nothing be done contrary, or repugnant to the Lawes of the Kingdome of England' (Morton, 159). He rejected the puritans' regulation of the beaver trade and the stock company that was to have one general trade within the colony. For a time, he continued to trade separately from the rest of the colony. In September 1630, however, he was brought before the first session of magistrates and Governor John Winthrop ordered that his goods be confiscated and that he be imprisoned, put in the stocks, and sent as a prisoner to England. His crimes, ironically, were 'his many injuries offered to the Indians, and other misdemeanours'.

This time Morton stayed in England for twelve years, working for Sir Ferdinando Gorges to defeat the Massachusetts Colony, an effort that continued until civil war in England spoiled their plans. Morton's *New English Canaan*, written between 1633 and 1634, told his side of the conflict with the pilgrims and puritans with humour, indignation, and a profound admiration of New England and its native inhabitants.

New English Canaan contains three sections. The first focuses on Indians, 'their manners, and Customes, with their tractable nature and love towards the English'. The second describes the land, flora, and fauna: 'the bewty of the Country with her naturall indowments'. The last describes the colonists, 'what remarkable Accidents have happened there … what Tenents they hould, together with the practice of their Church' (Morton, 11, 59, 103). Morton aimed to encourage English settlement, to teach settlers to learn from the Indians, and to convince those in power in England of the ineptitude of the pilgrims and puritans. These three objectives came together in an elaborate metaphor in which he depicted the land as a woman whose fertility needed to be fulfilled by men. In the poem 'Rise Oedipus' he told the story of the land whose careful and virile husband, the Indians, had died and left her bereft. Her new lover, the pilgrims, was not skilled enough to fulfil her fertility. His poem was attached to the maypole erected at Ma-re Mount and was a part of the challenge he issued to the pilgrims, claiming that he, but not they, had the skill and industry necessary to be a successful husband to the land. Although he celebrated the plague that had decimated the Indians, thereby freeing the land for settlement, he also saw them as the land's former husband and respected their skills. He viewed the pilgrims and puritans as unfit to settle New England because they were not wise enough to copy the Indians and therefore were unable to make full use of the land's bounty.

Morton's story provides an important counterpoint to the better-known puritan version of the settlement of New England. Depictions of Morton in literature and history have ranged from celebration to condemnation. In literature his treatment has reflected changing views on religion, sexuality, and colonization. Among historians he has been seen as a defender of the church by nineteenth-century Anglicans, as a misfit villain by those sympathetic to the puritans, and as a useful corrective to puritan and pilgrim narratives by historians of the late twentieth century, particularly those interested in Native Americans. The latter group has also recognized that Morton's conflict with the pilgrims and puritans disguised deep similarities, since both had the ultimate goal of settling the land.

In summer 1643 Morton returned to Plymouth, New England, and stayed through the winter. Though he was so poor that he had no beer to drink (perhaps not so terrible a fate for the man who said New England had 'waters of most excellent vertues, worthy admiration'; Morton, 92) he was still trying to interest people in new settlements. His 1643 will bequeathed large tracts of New England land, from Rhode Island to Maine, to his cousin and niece. He may have had these tenuously held tracts in mind for the settlements he proposed. On leaving Plymouth, he travelled in Maine, Massachusetts, and Rhode Island, perhaps checking on the land he claimed. In September 1644 he appeared before the court of assistants in Massachusetts, accused of complaining to the English privy council and writing a book against the colonists. He was kept in prison for a year, supposedly awaiting additional evidence from England. No evidence came, and he was fined £100, which he could not pay, and freed. John Winthrop wrote that 'he was a charge to the country, for he had nothing, and we thought not fit to inflict corporal punishment upon him, being old and crazy'. They gave 'him opportunity to go out of the jurisdiction, as he did soon after, and he went to Acomenticus, and living there poor and dispised, he died within two years after' (Winthrop, 2.192). Nevertheless, his legal skills were welcomed in Acomenticus (later York, Maine), and he practised there for a year or two. He died in 1646 or 1647, asserting, according to the colonist Samuel Maverick, that his death was

due to 'his hard usage in prison' ('Clarendon Papers', 40–1). He was buried in Clark's Lane by the Agamenticus River.

EDITH MURPHY

Sources T. Morton, *New English Canaan* (1969) · C. E. Banks, 'Thomas Morton of Merry Mount', *Proceedings of the Massachusetts Historical Society*, 58 (1924–5), 147–92 · D. F. Connors, *Thomas Morton* (1969) · J. Winthrop, *The history of New England from 1630 to 1649*, ed. J. Savage, 2 vols. (1825–6); repr. (1972) · E. Murphy, '"A rich widow, now to be tane up or laide down": solving the riddle of Thomas Morton's "Rise Oedipus"', *William and Mary Quarterly*, 53 (1996), 757–68 · W. Bradford, *Of Plymouth Plantation, 1620–1647*, ed. S. E. Morison (1952); repr. (1967) · C. F. Adams, *Three episodes of Massachusetts history*, rev. edn, 2 vols. (1965) · 'The Clarendon papers', *Collections of the New York Historical Society* (1869) [whole issue], esp. 38–42 [letter from S. Maverick to the earl of Clarendon] · D. F. Connors, 'Thomas Morton of Merry Mount: his first arrival in New England', *American Literature*, 11 (1939), 160–6 · P. R. Sternberg, 'The publication of Thomas Morton's *New English Canaan* reconsidered', *Papers of the Bibliographic Society of America*, 80 (1986), 369–74 · K. O. Kupperman, 'Thomas Morton, historian', *New England Quarterly*, 50 (1977), 660–64 · M. W. Major, 'William Bradford versus Thomas Morton', *Early American Literature*, 5 (1970), 1–13 · C. E. Banks, *History of York, Maine*, 2 vols. (1967), vol. 1 · J. P. McWilliams, 'Fictions of Merry Mount', *American Quarterly*, 29 (1977), 3–30 · PRO, PROB 11/301, sig. 221

Wealth at death poor: Banks, 'Thomas Morton', 159–60, 163–4

Morton, Thomas (*bap.* **1764**, *d.* **1838**), playwright, was baptized on 24 February 1764 at Chester-le-Street, co. Durham, the youngest son of John Morton of Whickham, co. Durham, and his wife, Grace. After the death of his father he was educated at Soho Square School at the charge of his uncle Maddison, a stockbroker. There amateur acting was in vogue, and Morton, who played with Joseph George Holman, acquired a taste for the theatre. He entered at Lincoln's Inn on 2 July 1784, but was not called to the bar.

Morton's first drama, *Columbus, or, A World Discovered* (1792), a historical play in five acts, founded in part upon *Les Incas* of Marmontel, was successfully produced at Covent Garden on 1 December 1792, Holman playing the part of Alonzo. *Children in the Wood*, a two-act musical entertainment, followed at the Haymarket on 1 October 1793, and was more than once revived. Similar fortune attended *Zorinski* (1795), a three-act play founded on the adventures of Stanislaus, re-christened Casimir, king of Poland, staged at the Haymarket on 20 June 1795. In the same year appeared an anonymous pamphlet, *Mr Morton's Zorinski and Brooke's Gustavus Vasa Compared*. *The Way to Get Married* (1796), a comedy in five acts, was produced at Covent Garden on 23 January 1796, acted forty-one times, and became a stock piece, as did *A Cure for the Heart-Ache* (1797), first staged at Covent Garden on 10 January 1797. His other plays for Covent Garden included *Secrets Worth Knowing* (1798), *Speed the Plough* (1798), and *The Blind Girl, or, A Receipt for Beauty* (1801), all of which were moderately successful. A different case, however, was *Beggar my Neighbour, or, A Rogue's a Fool*, a comedy staged at the Haymarket on 10 July 1802, which was assigned to Morton, but unclaimed by him as it was damned on the first night. It was afterwards converted into *How to Tease and Please*, and staged at Covent Garden on 29 March 1810, but again proved a failure, and was not printed under either title. Morton bounced back, however, with the immensely popular *The School of Reform*, or, *How to Rule a Husband* (1805), a five-act comedy featuring the memorable character Tyke and first performed at Covent Garden on 15 January 1805. It was revived many times, including in November 1867 at the St James's Theatre. Morton's star was in ascendancy, and he was paid £1000 in advance for his next comedy, *Town and Country, or, Which is Best* (1807), performed on 10 March 1807, with John Kemble and Charles Kemble in the leading roles. Morton continued to have a long and prolific career as a playwright. Among his other works were: *The Knight of Snowdoun* (1811); *Education* (1813); *The Slave* (1816), in which William Macready played Gambia, the slave; *A Roland for an Olivier* (1819); *Henri Quatre, or, Paris in the Olden Time* (1820), which also featured Macready; *School for Grown Children* (1827); and *The Invincibles* (1828). He also collaborated with his second son, the farce writer John Maddison *Morton (1811–1891), to produce *Writing on the Wall*, and possibly on *All that Glitters is not Gold*.

Morton was a man of reputable life and regular habits, who enjoyed, two years before his death, the rarely accorded honour of being elected (8 May 1837) an honorary member of the Garrick Club; he was, however, frequently ridiculed by William Gifford in the *Baviad*. He was very fond of cricket, and became the senior member of Lord's. For many years he resided at Pangbourne, on the Thames. Morton died on 28 March 1838, leaving a widow and three children.

JOSEPH KNIGHT, *rev.* REBECCA MILLS

Sources D. E. Baker, *Biographia dramatica, or, A companion to the playhouse*, rev. I. Reed, new edn, rev. S. Jones, 1/1 (1812), 526–7 · [J. Watkins and F. Shoberl], *A biographical dictionary of the living authors of Great Britain and Ireland* (1816), 243–4 · [D. Rivers], *Literary memoirs of living authors of Great Britain*, 2 (1798), 66–8 · W. P. Baildon, ed., *The records of the Honorable Society of Lincoln's Inn: admissions*, 1 (1896), 510 · *The thespian dictionary, or, Dramatic biography of the present age*, 2nd edn (1805) · T. Gilliland, *The dramatic mirror, containing the history of the stage from the earliest period, to the present time*, 2 vols. (1808) · Adams, *Drama* · [Clarke], *The Georgian era: memoirs of the most eminent persons*, 3 (1834), 576 · Allibone, *Dict.* · Watt, *Bibl. Brit.*, 2.887 · *Annual Register* (1838) · *GM*, 2nd ser., 9 (1838), 551–2 · *N&Q*, 8th ser., 4 (1893), 229, 292, 432 · *IGI*
Likenesses J. Hopwood, stipple, pubd 1806 (after S. De Wilde), BM · M. A. Shee, oils, exh. 1835, Tate collection · T. W. Hunt, engraving (after M. A. Shee) · W. Ridley, stipple (after W. Naish), BM, NPG; repro. in *Monthly Mirror* (1796) · J. R. Smith, chalk drawing, NPG

Morton, Thomas (1781–1832), shipbuilder and inventor of a ship-building slip, was born at Leith on 8 October 1781, the son of Hugh Morton, wright and builder. He appears to have worked for his father before establishing a ship-building business in Leith, which outlived him as S. and H. Morton & Co. In 1818 he invented his patent slip and built the first one in his own shipyard. A patent for his invention was obtained in Scotland in August 1818 and in the following year for England, Ireland, and the colonies.

Morton himself conceded that the drawing of ships out of the water up an inclined plane was no novelty, but by the provision of a carriage on to which ships were floated at low water, the process was revolutionized. The carriage ran on rails, and when the vessel was secured by means of sliding blocks or shores, the whole was winched clear of

the water without any stress being placed on the vessel itself. The benefits were numerous. Shipbuilders could equip themselves with a patent slip for a fraction of the cost of a dry dock, and effect repairs in a much shorter time and in lighter and more congenial conditions. The apparatus was portable, and more than one vessel could be placed on it at a time. A later estimate of the saving brought by the device was that it reduced the cost of a £170 repair to £3.

For two years after the patent had been granted, no slips were built until one was installed at Bo'ness, Linlithgowshire. More followed, including one at Dumbarton. In 1824 Morton brought a case for infringement of the patent against John Barclay and others. Barclay, whose Stobcross business eventually became the famous shipbuilding firm of Barclay, Curle & Co. Ltd, had installed a patent slip of similar design in 1821. The evidence of the shipbuilder William Denny suggested that the Stobcross device was no more than a clumsy copy of Morton's invention and was based on the slip installed in his own Dumbarton yard by Morton a few months earlier, in February 1821. The case proved to be an overwhelming victory for Morton, a result anticipated by the defenders, who failed even to appear.

The utility of his device did not, however, result in any commensurate reward for Morton and a bill for the extension of his patent was brought to the House of Commons. In 1832, a select committee appointed to consider the question heard that, while at least forty-five slips had been installed, no profit had been made for the first six years of the patent, and that for the entire period of its duration the profit had been only £5737. The committee were sympathetic to Morton, but hostile to the principle of the renewal of patents, and contented themselves with a vague hope that some other measure might lead to more adequate recompense for the inventor. Morton died at Leith on 24 December 1832 and was buried in South Leith parish church.

R. B. PROSSER, *rev.* LIONEL ALEXANDER RITCHIE

Sources T. Morton, *Infringement of a patent: notes of a trial before the jury court at Edinburgh, 15th March 1824* (1824) · 'Select committee on how far it is expedient to extend the patent granted for Morton's slip', *Parl. papers* (1831–2), 5.295, no. 380 · D. Brewster and others, eds., *The Edinburgh encyclopaedia*, 18, vol. 18, pp. 255–6 · H. Clarke, 'A description of the plans adopted at New York for docking ships', *Weale's Quarterly Papers on Engineering*, 4 (1845), 9–11 [section 3, Morton's slip.] · A. Campbell, *History of Leith* (1827), 210–13 · J. C. Irons, *Leith and its antiquities*, 2 [1898], 315 · S. Mowat, *The port of Leith, its history and its people* (1994)

Morton, Thomas (1813–1849), surgeon, was born on 20 March 1813 in the parish of St Andrew, Newcastle upon Tyne, the youngest son of Joseph Morton, a master mariner, and brother of Andrew *Morton (1802–1845), the portrait painter. Thomas was apprenticed to James Church, house surgeon to the Newcastle upon Tyne Infirmary, and, on the completion of his preliminary education there in 1832, he entered University College, London, to finish his medical education. Morton was awarded four prizes: the two gold medals respectively for surgery and midwifery, and two silver medals for anatomy and practical anatomy. Admitted a member of the Royal College of Surgeons on

24 July 1835, he was appointed house surgeon at the North London (later University College) Hospital under Samuel *Cooper (1780–1848), whose only daughter, Mary Ann, he married at Shepperton on 22 November 1841; they had a daughter.

Morton received the unusual honour of being reappointed at the North London when his initial year had ended. In 1836 he was made demonstrator of anatomy jointly with Mr Ellis, a post he held for nine years. In 1842 he became assistant surgeon, becoming the first student of University College to become a member of staff of its newly founded hospital. He was also surgeon to the queen's bench prison in succession to his father-in-law.

The latter years of Morton's time at the hospital were marred by being caught up in the quarrels between the medical staff, and by the frustration of his ambitions. In the period leading up to Samuel Cooper's retirement Morton was delivering a portion of the lectures in surgery and hoped to be appointed in his place. On the selection of the Edinburgh surgeon James Syme as professor of surgery by the governors, Morton felt that he had been shelved and saw no hope of change. Although Syme resigned after only seven months, unhappy with the way he had been received, and Morton was made full surgeon in his place, he was not given the professorship he sought, this office going to James Arnott. Finding his increasing private practice no substitute for the hospital work he desired, Morton's depression continued. This, combined with an obsessive concern about drinking, led to his death by suicide, by taking prussic acid, on 30 October 1849 at his house, 7 Woburn Place, Russell Square, London.

Morton had been one of the ablest of the younger surgeons of his time, and his work had increased the reputation of the medical school attached to University College. His death was a great blow to the prestige of the college, coming as it did so soon after the deaths of John Phillips Potter, Robert Liston, and Samuel Cooper, and the resignation of James Syme. Morton was an excellent teacher of anatomy, and a sound clinical surgeon. He published *Surgical Anatomy of the Perinaeum* (1838), *Surgical Anatomy of the Groin* (1839), *Surgical Anatomy of Inguinal Herniae* (1841), *Anatomical Engravings* (1845), and *Surgical Anatomy, with Introduction by Mr. W. Cadge* (1850). These works are notable for the quality of their illustrations, which were the work of his artist brother, Andrew. Morton was dark-complexioned and sallow, and of a retiring, shy, and sensitive nature, which suggested a melancholy disposition and led him to take too gloomy a view of his prospects in life.

D'A. POWER, rev. PATRICK WALLIS

Sources *The Lancet* (3 Nov 1849) · *GM*, 2nd ser., 32 (1849), 658 · *The Times* (2 Nov 1849) · personal information (1894) · *GM*, 2nd ser., 4 (1835), 75 · *GM*, 2nd ser., 16 (1841), 538 · d. cert.
Likenesses A. Morton, oils, RCSL

Morton, Sir William (*bap.* 1605, *d.* 1672), judge and politician, was baptized at Severn Stoke, Worcestershire, on 5 September 1605, the son of James Morton and his wife, Jane, daughter of William Cookes of Sheltwood, Tardebigge, Worcestershire. His great-grandfather was Sir Rowland Morton of Massington, Hereford, one of Henry VIII's masters of requests. William married Anne (1608–1669), daughter and heir of John Smith of Kidlington, Oxfordshire, on 8 February 1630; they had nine children.

Morton matriculated from Trinity College, Oxford, on 26 October 1621; he graduated BA (1622) and MA (1625) from Sidney Sussex College, Cambridge. He also commenced studies at the Inner Temple on 24 October 1622, and was called to the bar on 28 November 1630. His 1639 mention in Croke's *Reports* indicates that he practised his profession at least until the outbreak of hostilities between the king and parliament. Soon afterward he entered upon a career of vigorous support for the royalist cause, earning a reputation among the local parliamentarians for being 'active and violent … of a high spirit and bold … most obnoxious to the justice of Parliament' (Corbet, 90, 104).

From 1643 to 1644 Morton served the royalist cause as sheriff of Gloucestershire and as a member of Lord Chandos's regiment of horse, during which time 'he had given so frequent testimony of signal courage in several actions, in which he had received many wounds, both by the pistol and the sword, that his mettle was never suspected, and his fidelity as little questioned' (Clarendon, *Hist. rebellion*, 357). Charles rewarded his efforts with a knighthood on 8 September 1643, and in the following spring he was promoted to the rank of lieutenant-colonel and made head of the garrison of Sudeley Castle. On 8 June 1644 Morton was forced to surrender the castle to Sir William Waller after a three-hour bombardment and betrayal by one of his officers who informed Waller of the garrison's lack of provisions. Taken with over 300 of his men, he was escorted to the Tower in London, where he remained imprisoned for an unspecified term. While in prison Morton wrote the unpublished manuscript 'Jus regium, sive, Jus monarchiae Anglicanae', in the hopes of shoring up the monarchy by refuting the co-ordination principle, according to which legislative sovereignty was shared co-ordinately by the king and both houses of parliament. His manuscript attests both to the widespread anti-co-ordination sentiment in royalist circles at this stage of the civil war and to the increasing popularity of the co-ordination principle as it had been developed by the presbyterian clergy following Charles I's *Answer* to parliament's *Nineteen Propositions*. By the summer of 1648 Morton had returned to Gloucestershire, where his actions attracted the attention of parliament, which ordered his arrest and detention for 'carrying on some designs prejudicial to the public' (*CSP dom.*, 1648–9, 228).

After the hostilities concluded Morton returned to the bar, becoming a bencher of the Inner Temple on 24 November 1659, and receiving the degree of serjeant-at-law on 26 October 1660. He stood for Haverfordwest at the 1661 general election but was defeated. The election was declared void in May 1663 and Morton was successful at the subsequent by-election. He was named to twelve committees, 'including those for the better trial and conviction of criminals, the preservation of prize goods, the abolition of damage clere and the five mile bill, all in the Oxford session' (HoP, *Commons, 1660–90*, 3.112). His loyalty and service were again rewarded after the Restoration with rapid preferment. He became recorder of Worcester in 1660, and, with the king's blessing, the commissioners of Gloucestershire made him recorder of Bath in 1662, the same year in which he was also appointed counsel to the dean and chapter of Worcestershire. In July 1663 he was created king's serjeant, and on 23 November 1665 he was appointed judge of the king's bench, serving as third puisne justice under Chief Justice Matthew Hale until his death. He also served as chief justice of the Carmarthen assize circuit from 1660 until this latter appointment. Having avoided censure throughout his tenure, he 'discharged his office with much gravity and learning' (Clarendon, *Hist. rebellion*, 357). Morton was one of the judges who sat at Westminster to hear the appeals of those who had lost their property in the great fire of 1666, and his clients expressed their gratitude by hanging his portrait in the Guildhall. He is most remembered, however, for his severity toward highwaymen and robbers. Morton presided over the trial of Claude Duval, the French page of the duke of Richmond, whose escapades spawned a number of ballads and tales, and whose gallantry and handsomeness had attracted a following among ladies of the upper classes. These women circulated a petition to gain his release, and some observers believed that the king would have granted his pardon if Morton had not threatened to resign. His protest prevailed, and Duval was hanged.

Morton died on 23 September 1672 in his lodgings in Serjeants' Inn, London, and was interred on 1 October in the Temple Church, where a monument to his and his wife's memory is housed in the gallery.

MARY S. REDD MAGNOTTA

Sources HoP, *Commons, 1660–90* · Baker, *Serjeants* · Clarendon, *Hist. rebellion*, vol. 3 · J. Corbet, *An historical relation of the military government of Gloucestershire* (1645) · C. Finger, *Highwaymen: a book of gallant rogues* (1923) · Foss, *Judges*, vol. 7 · E. Foss, *Biographia juridica: a biographical dictionary of the judges of England … 1066–1870* (1870) · DNB · W. Pope, *The memoires of Monsieur du Vall, containing the history of his life and death* (1670) · Sainty, *Judges* · Mrs B. Stapleton, *Three Oxfordshire parishes: a history of Kidlington, Yarnton and Begbroke*, OHS, 24 (1893) · A. R. Warmington, *Civil war, interregnum and Restoration in Gloucestershire, 1640–1672* (1997) · C. Weston and J. Greenberg, *Subjects and sovereigns: the grand controversy over legal sovereignty in Stuart England* (1981) · IGI · funerary monument, Temple Church, London · will, PRO, PROB 11/342, sig. 98
Likenesses attrib. G. Soest, oils, Inner Temple, London · A. Van Dyck, portrait; formerly in possession of Mr Bulkeley Owen · portrait, repro. in E. Dent, *Annals of Winchcombe and Sudeley* (1877)
Wealth at death manor with manor house in Kidlington, Oxfordshire to son James; almshouse in Kidlington established and endowed in memory of deceased wife and children; annuities of £30 to surviving daughters; monetary gifts to grandchildren and daughter-in-law: will, PRO, PROB 11/342, sig. 98

Morville, Hugh de (*d.* 1162), soldier and courtier, was of unknown parentage. He hailed from Morville, near Valognes, in the Manche, and by *c.*1115 had joined the entourage of David, earl of Huntingdon, who became king of Scots in 1124. His earliest known landed base, no doubt the fruits of Earl David's favour, was a sizeable tenancy centred on Bozeat, Northamptonshire, and Whissendine,

Rutland, in the Huntingdon honour. He swiftly established himself as the foremost Anglo-Norman supporter of the Scottish crown after David's enthronement, and witnessed no fewer than 108 of the surviving written acts of royal governance for the period 1124–62. His importance to the 'modernizing' Scottish monarchy was underlined when David I appointed him as his constable and endowed him with the strategic regional fief of Lauderdale, which he developed by building a castle at Lauder, probably his chief Scottish seat, and by founding a Premonstratensian abbey (with canons from Alnwick) at Dryburgh in 1150–52. Although conclusive proof is lacking, it is most likely that King David also granted him another extensive Scottish lordship, Cunningham with Largs, whose main castle was erected at Irvine.

The constableship and the stewardship were the key lay offices to emerge from David I's refashioning of the royal household, the focal agency of government, and Morville's influence appears to have ensured his pre-eminence over the steward as the more senior figure at court and in the conduct of business. In wartime the constable was responsible with the earls for leading royal armies under the king, and Hugh may have been in post by 1138. He participated prominently in King David's invasions of northern England in that year, and was one of the five magnates, including three Scottish earls, compelled to surrender hostages under the Durham treaty of 1139. His first recorded appearance as constable, however, was on 1 November 1140; and, curiously, David's first known constable, Edward son of Siward, remained in office alongside Hugh until *c.*1144. When from 1141 David and his household switched from war enterprise to the political consolidation of the Scoto-Northumbrian realm, there is strong evidence that he entrusted Hugh de Morville with the strategically vital lordship of north Westmorland. Its *caput* was Appleby, where Hugh possibly built the twelfth-century keep. He also seems to have held superiority over Kendal or south Westmorland. He served Malcolm IV from 1153 as assiduously as he had David I, and he remained constable until his death or shortly before it, when he took the canonical habit at Dryburgh.

Hugh de Morville married Beatrice, one of the Beauchamps of Bedford, who figures in a famous anecdote by William of Canterbury. It tells how Beatrice succumbed to an illicit passion for a youth named Lithulf, and how, finding her advances rejected, she revenged herself by persuading Lithulf to come into her husband's presence with his sword drawn, in consequence of which he was condemned to be boiled alive. Little confidence can be placed in the historicity of this story. Hugh and Beatrice had three sons and two daughters. A younger Hugh de *Morville occurs as lord of north Westmorland immediately after the Anglo-Scottish border had reverted to the Tweed–Solway line in 1157, and it seems likely that he replaced his father in that year on the insistence of the English king, Henry II. He rose rapidly in Henry's favour, and has correctly been identified as one of the murderers of Thomas Becket. Richard de *Morville, possibly the second son, inherited the constableship of Scotland, together with his father's Scottish estates and his fees in the Huntingdon honour. Malcolm, the youngest son, killed in a hunting accident in England by 1174, was buried in Leicester Abbey. The two daughters were Ada, who had married Roger Bertram, lord of Mitford, Northumberland, before 1157, and Maud, who married William de Vieuxpont (*d.* in or before 1203) and gave her name to Maulds Meaburn, near Appleby. Hugh and his Morville successors introduced into Scotland numerous fellow Anglo-Normans, several of whom founded notable Scottish dynasties, including the Haigs and the Sinclairs. But the Morville family failed in the male line in 1196, thirty-four years after the death of the elder Hugh, presumably at Dryburgh Abbey, in 1162.

KEITH STRINGER

Sources G. W. S. Barrow, *The Anglo-Norman era in Scottish history* (1980) · K. J. Stringer, 'The early lords of Lauderdale, Dryburgh Abbey and St Andrew's Priory at Northampton', *Essays on the nobility of medieval Scotland*, ed. K. J. Stringer (1985), 44–71 · G. W. S. Barrow, ed., *The charters of King David I: the written acts of David I king of Scots, 1124–53, and of his son Henry earl of Northumberland, 1139–52* (1999) · G. W. S. Barrow, ed., *Regesta regum Scottorum*, 1 (1960) · G. W. S. Barrow, 'Some problems in 12th and 13th century Scottish history: a genealogical approach', *Scottish Genealogist*, 25 (1978), 97–112 · G. W. S. Barrow, *The kingdom of the Scots: government, church and society from the eleventh to the fourteenth century* (1973) · K. J. Stringer, 'State-building in twelfth-century Britain: David I, king of Scots, and northern England', *Government, religion and society in northern England, 1000–1700*, ed. J. C. Appleby and P. Dalton (1997), 40–62 · R. Dahood, 'Hugh de Morville, William of Canterbury, and anecdotal evidence for English language history', *Speculum*, 69 (1994), 40–56 · *Chronica magistri Rogeri de Hovedene*, ed. W. Stubbs, 2, Rolls Series, 51 (1869) · A. O. Anderson and M. O. Anderson, eds., *The chronicle of Melrose* (1936) · W. Fraser, ed., *Liber S. Marie de Dryburgh*, Bannatyne Club, 83 (1847)

Morville, Hugh de (*d.* 1173/4), one of the murderers of Thomas Becket, was the son of an elder Hugh de *Morville (*d.* 1162) and Beatrice de Beauchamp. He was a member of a notable Anglo-Scottish baronial family, and, according to Benedict of Peterborough, was the most eminent of the four knights who played the principal roles in Becket's murder, although at the time of the crime itself, he did not strike a blow. His family prospered in the twelfth century, both in Scotland, where they were given substantial lands by David I, and in England, where Hugh himself came to be particularly highly regarded by Henry II. When Henry recognized the Morville holdings in northern England in 1158, he did so only on the condition that Morville's father handed over his lands there to his son. So he must have been of age by that date, though he may not have attained his majority long before. This would suggest that he was probably just under forty at the time of his death. There seems to be no positive evidence that he married. William of Canterbury, in his life of Becket, attempts to smear the Morville family as a whole by telling a scandalous and possibly authentic story about Morville's mother. From the point of view of Morville's biography the main interest lies in suggesting that his career before the murder offered little scope for slander, so that his relatives needed to be called in to assist.

In spite of a scarcity of evidence, it would appear that Morville enjoyed a successful career under Henry II in the years before 1170. Together with the other murderers he was described by Benedict of Peterborough as a household, indeed, chamber knight of the king. He farmed Knaresborough, Yorkshire, from 1158 to 1173, and is found witnessing royal charters, at Newcastle and (interestingly, in the company of Thomas Becket when chancellor) at Lyons-la-Forêt. These activities probably culminated in 1170, when he almost certainly acted as a royal justice on eyre in company with Robert (III) de Stuteville (*d.* 1183). Amercements from this eyre appear in the pipe rolls under Carlisle and Northumberland, revealing that the justices had been concerned with peacekeeping and castle building in that unquiet region.

Morville was at Henry II's court at Bur-le-Roi, near Bayeux, at Christmas 1170, where Becket's conduct, and above all his excommunication of the bishops who had crowned Henry, the Young King, earlier that year, was angrily discussed. The king's famous outburst, 'What miserable drones and traitors have I nourished and promoted in my household, who let their lord be treated with such shameful contempt by a low-born clerk' (Robertson and Sheppard, 2.429), which later oral tradition renders simply, 'Will no one rid me of this turbulent priest?' (Lyttelton, 4.353), prompted his departure with Reginald *Fitzurse, William de *Tracy, and Richard Brito on their ill-conceived journey to Canterbury. Morville's relatively minor role in the events of 29 December should not be interpreted as an indication of his standing among the four knights. Although Reginald Fitzurse (in whose article the confrontation with Becket is described more fully; [*see* Fitzurse, Reginald]) is represented as their principal spokesman at the initial interview, an exchange between the archbishop and Morville is recorded, in which Becket taunted him with taking an unjustifiably high line. Then, as the knights withdrew, he called Morville back, apparently because of his higher status and more courtly behaviour, and asked him to repeat what he had said. Morville made no reply, but accompanied the other knights to arm, after which they pursued Becket through the palace and into the cathedral. As soon as they had entered, Morville moved away from the others, and stood at the end of the nave, to guard against any attempt to rescue Becket. After the murder itself he rejoined the other knights to loot the archiepiscopal palace, and rode away to Saltwood Castle with them.

In the aftermath of the murder Morville provided shelter for the other knights at Knaresborough Castle, and an anecdote from the collections of Becket's miracles asserts that in at least one instance, another northern figure, Stephen of Galton, was caused great distress by receiving an invitation from the murderer.

Confusion between Hugh de Morville, the murderer, and Hugh de Morville, lord of Burgh by Sands (*d.* 1202), has led to the suggestion that the murderer survived into the thirteenth century. In fact, he was dead certainly by 1174, and probably by the end of 1173, and Roger of Howden is probably correct in asserting that he died while on the pilgrimage to the Holy Land ordered by Pope Alexander

III. His castle of Knaresborough had been committed to the custody of William de Stuteville by Easter 1173, and it has been suggested that this was the result of Morville's own involvement in the northern revolt of 1173–4. However, punishments for this were imposed on two former servants, not himself, and it is more probable that he was in the Holy Land at the time of the revolt. At least part of his lands in Westmorland passed to his sister Maud, since he died without heirs, and through her to the Vieuxpont family. There is, in any case, no indication that he suffered any immediate royal forfeitures for his role in the murder. Like the other murderers he made at least one penitential grant to religion, of 5 marks to the brothers of St Lazarus in Jerusalem.   R. M. FRANKLIN

Sources J. C. Robertson and J. B. Sheppard, eds., *Materials for the history of Thomas Becket, archbishop of Canterbury*, 7 vols., Rolls Series, 67 (1875–85) • E. Magnússon, ed. and trans., *Thómas saga Erkibyskups*, 2 vols., Rolls Series, 65 (1875–83) • G. de Pont-Sainte-Maxence, *La vie de Saint Thomas le martyr*, ed. E. Walberg (Lund, 1922) • R. Howlett, ed., *Chronicles of the reigns of Stephen, Henry II, and Richard I*, 4 vols., Rolls Series, 82 (1884–9) • *Pipe rolls*, Henry II • F. Barlow, *Thomas Becket* (1986) • I. J. Sanders, *English baronies: a study of their origin and descent, 1086–1327* (1960) • private information (2004) • G. W. S. Barrow, *The Anglo-Norman era in Scottish history* (1980) • K. J. Stringer, *Earl David of Huntingdon, 1152–1219: a study in Anglo-Scottish history* (1985) • F. Grainger and W. G. Collingwood, *The register and records of Holm Cultram*, Cumberland and Westmorland Antiquarian and Archaeological Society, Record or Chartulary Series, 7 (1929) • W. Farrer, 'On the tenure of Westmorland *temp.* Henry II, and the date of creation of the baronies of Appleby and Kendal', *Transactions of the Cumberland and Westmorland Antiquarian and Archaeological Society*, new ser., 7 (1906–7), 100–07 • G. Lyttelton, *The history of the life of King Henry the Second*, 6 vols. (1769–73) • N. Vincent, 'The murderers of Thomas Becket', *Bischofsmord im Mittelalter*, ed. N. Fryde and D. Reitz (Göttingen, 2003), 211–72

Likenesses illumination, 1190–1200, BL, Harley MS 5102 • enamelled châsse, 13th cent., S. Antiquaries, Lond. • stained-glass window, c.1206, Chartres Cathedral • reliquary, c.1250, Heidal church, Valdres, Norway • ceiling boss, 14th cent., Exeter Cathedral • ivory plaque, 14th cent., V&A • stained-glass window, c.1350, Christ Church Cathedral, Oxford • alabaster table, 15th cent., BM • painted panel, 1460–99, Canterbury Cathedral • portrait, BL, Cotton MS Claudius B. ii, fol. 341r

Morville, Richard de (d. 1189/90), soldier and courtier, was the first or second son of Hugh de *Morville (d. 1162) and his wife, Beatrice de Beauchamp. He began to attend the Scottish court c.1150, probably accompanied Malcolm IV to Toulouse in 1159, succeeded to the constableship of Scotland in 1162, and held that office until his death. His military responsibilities as constable pressed most heavily during the Anglo-Scottish war of 1173–4. He was with King William the Lion for the siege of Carlisle in 1173, and in July 1174 led a division of the royal army entrusted with harrying Northumberland while William besieged Alnwick. During these operations William was captured, and in December 1174 Richard was one of his sureties in the treaty of Falaise. In all probability he also commanded forces deployed against Galloway in 1175 or 1176, and against Moray and Ross in 1179. But his chief importance was as a prominent courtier who enjoyed the confidence of both Malcolm IV and William the Lion and shared in their counsels in all aspects of royal business. He witnessed 137 of their known written acts of government,

and this is an outstanding record. In 1181 he and other royal intimates were excommunicated by John 'the Scot', bishop of St Andrews, for opposing his free election in 1178 and seeking to foist a royal chaplain on the cathedral chapter.

Contrary to what has often been assumed, Richard de Morville rather than his father seems to have founded the Tironensian abbey of Kilwinning in Cunningham. He established St Leonard's Hospital at Lauder, and made a series of agreements with the Cistercians of Melrose Abbey concerning rights in the royal forest between the Gala and Leader waters. On account of his generosity to Melrose and other good works, he was freed from his vow to found a Cistercian abbey by Pope Urban III (r. 1185–7). His marriage by 1170 to Avice, or Avicia (d. 1191), daughter of William of Lancaster, lord of Kendal, brought him a large estate based on Burton in Lonsdale in the honour of Mowbray. He had a strong castle at Burton, and a manor house and park at Whissendine, Rutland, in the honour of Huntingdon; but his territorial interests, centred on the great provincial fiefs of Lauderdale and Cunningham, remained primarily Scottish. During the war of 1173–4 he forfeited his English estates, but subsequently regained his lands in Lonsdale by redeeming them from William de Stuteville for 300 marks. He and Avice had a son and a daughter: William, who succeeded his father as constable and died childless in 1196 (after 31 July), and Helen, who on William's death transmitted the constableship and the family estates to her husband, *Roland, son of Uhtred, lord of Galloway. The date of Richard's death is given in the chronicle of Melrose as 1189, but its chronology at this point is uncharacteristically suspect, and he may in fact have died in 1190.   KEITH STRINGER

Sources K. J. Stringer, 'The early lords of Lauderdale, Dryburgh Abbey and St Andrew's Priory at Northampton', *Essays on the nobility of medieval Scotland*, ed. K. J. Stringer (1985), 44–71 • G. W. S. Barrow, ed., *Regesta regum Scottorum*, 1–2 (1960–71) • A. C. Lawrie, ed., *Annals of the reigns of Malcolm and William, kings of Scotland* (1910) • G. W. S. Barrow, *The Anglo-Norman era in Scottish history* (1980) • I. B. Cowan and D. E. Easson, *Medieval religious houses: Scotland*, 2nd edn (1976) • [C. Innes], ed., *Liber sancte Marie de Melros*, 2 vols., Bannatyne Club, 56 (1837), vol. 1 • D. D. R. Owen, *William the Lion, 1143–1214: kingship and culture* (1997)

Likenesses seal (showing an armed knight on horseback), NA Scot.

Morvo, John. *See* Kemp, George Meikle (1795–1844).

Morwen, John (b. 1519/20, d. in or after 1583), Roman Catholic priest, was a native of Devon and a kinsman of Robert Morwen, from 1517 perpetual vice-president of Corpus Christi College, Oxford. Recorded as a boy pupil of that college in 1533–4, John Morwen was admitted a scholar on 22 February 1535, aged fifteen years and two months. Having graduated BA in 1538 he was elected a fellow in 1539 and proceeded MA in 1543. In 1552 he supplicated for the degree of BTh. A noted classical scholar, he became his college's Greek reader in 1545; compositions by him in Latin and Greek are preserved in Oxford and London (Bodl. Oxf., MS Bodley 439; BL, Royal MS 13 B.x). In 1538 he showed signs of evangelical sympathies in religion, but perhaps under the influence of the vice-president later took up a firmly conservative position. He studied medicine during the reign of Edward VI, perhaps as a means of avoiding controversy, and in 1551 contributed Greek and Latin epitaphs to the collection lamenting the deaths of Charles and Henry Brandon. Following the accession of Mary, however, he became secretary and chaplain to Bishop Edmund Bonner of London, and in that capacity was involved in the trial of heretics. He also took part in a disputation with Archbishop Cranmer in Oxford in 1555, and preached at Paul's Cross in London on Good Friday 1557.

Morwen was ordained deacon on 21 September 1555 and priest on 28 February 1556, to the title of his Corpus fellowship. But he had already started to accumulate benefices, no doubt the reward of his services to Bonner, being admitted rector of Wickham Bishops, Essex, on 21 July 1554. By 1559 he had acquired three more rectories in London and Essex, including that of St Martin Ludgate, and the prebend of Weldland in St Paul's Cathedral. By March 1560, however, he had been deprived of all his livings, and was imprisoned in the Fleet for upholding the Catholic mass in a sermon delivered in St Martin's. He was released after subscribing the royal supremacy, and may have been briefly protected by William Roper (Sir Thomas More's son-in-law), whose daughter Mary he had tutored. Shortly afterwards, however, he moved to Lancashire, where he soon became a leader of the resistance to the religious settlement of 1559. In 1561 he distributed a broadsheet attacking the new liturgy and denouncing as traitors such Catholic priests as compromised with it, while in 1566 he began to administer an oath binding Catholics to stay away from the services of the Church of England while pledging their loyalty to the pope as head of the church. In 1568 he was one of six recusant priests whose arrest was ordered, but he remained at large, active in Lancashire and Cheshire, until finally captured in 1583. It is not known when he died.

W. A. J. ARCHBOLD, *rev.* ANDREW A. CHIBI

Sources Emden, *Oxf.*, 4.403–4 · J. Strype, *Ecclesiastical memorials*, 3 vols. (1822) · J. Strype, *Memorials of the most reverend father in God Thomas Cranmer*, 2 vols. (1848) · *Miscellaneous writings and letters of Thomas Cranmer*, ed. J. E. Cox, Parker Society, [18] (1846) · Wood, *Ath. Oxon.*, new edn, 1.195–7 · R. W. Dixon, *History of the Church of England*, 6 vols. (1878–1902) · J. G. Nichols, ed., *Narratives of the days of the Reformation*, CS, old ser., 77 (1859) · C. Haigh, *Reformation and resistance in Tudor Lancashire* (1975) · C. Haigh, *English Reformations* (1993) · J. J. Scarisbrick, *The Reformation and the English people* (1984)
Archives BL, Royal MS 221

Morwen, Peter (*d.* 1573?), translator, was born in Lincolnshire. Educated at Oxford University, he graduated BA and was elected to a fellowship at Magdalen College in 1552. In the following summer he supplicated to incept as MA, but his request was rejected because of his strong evangelical leanings. 'A zealous reformer of his time', Morwen was expelled from his fellowship by the college visitor, Bishop Stephen Gardiner, in October 1553 and sought exile in Germany (Wood, *Ath. Oxon.*, 1.454). On the accession of Queen Elizabeth he returned to Oxford, and was ordained deacon by Bishop Edmund Grindal on 25 January 1560. On

16 February 1560 he supplicated once more for the degree of MA, and incepted three days later.

Morwen was appointed rector of Holy Cross Church, Upper Langwith, and rector of St Mary and St Barlock, Norbury, Derbyshire, on 22 July 1561. Three years later he was made rector of St Leonard's, Ryton-on-Dunsmore, Warwickshire, and private chaplain to his old friend Thomas Bentham, the bishop of Lichfield. On 27 October 1567 he was collated to the canonry of Prees in Lichfield Cathedral, where he was succeeded on 6 March 1573. He probably died a few weeks earlier.

Morwen 'became renowned among the academics for his great knowledge in the Latin and Greek tongues' (Wood, *Ath. Oxon.*, 1.454). He translated a pharmaceutical treatise by the German apothecary Conrad Gesner into English, published in 1559 under the title *The treasure of Eūonymus conteyninge the wonderfull hid secrets of nature touching the most apte formes to prepare and destyl medicines*. At the instigation of the London printer Richard Jugge he undertook a translation of Joseph ben Gorion's history of the Jews from Hebrew, published in 1561 as the *Historie of the Latter Times of the Jewes Commune Weale*. Translated to make accessible the history of the Jewish people 'unto our vulgare and familyar communication' (Morwen, *Historie*, sig. A iiv), this popular work went through five editions.

J. ANDREAS LÖWE

Sources Wood, *Ath. Oxon.*, new edn, 1.454 · *Fasti Angl.* (Hardy), 1.617 · Foster, *Alum. Oxon.*, 1500–1714, 3.105

Morwen, Robert (1486?–1558), college head, was born at Harpery near Gloucester. Little is known of his family. He may have had a strong university connection already: one Walter Morewyn was a fellow of Merton College in 1500 and was admitted principal of 'Corner Hall with Urban Hall annexed' on 12 April 1508. Intriguingly, in 1513 John Claymond, the first principal of Corpus Christi College, made payment to him for the land on which the hall was situated, and this came to form part of the site of the new college.

Robert Morwen was admitted BA on 8 February 1507 (from which his probable birth date is derived), incepted MA on 30 June 1511, and proceeded BTh on 28 June 1519. He became a fellow of Magdalen College in 1510 and was bursar in 1511–12, 1514–15, and 1516–17; lecturer in logic in 1513–14 and 1516–17; and junior dean of arts in 1517. He was appointed by Richard Fox, bishop of Winchester, to a position equivalent to that of a fellow (*socii compar*) at Corpus Christi College on its foundation (in order to evade an oath he had taken not to hold another fellowship with his Magdalen one) and perpetual vice-president on 4 July 1517. He was appointed rector of East Knoyle, Wiltshire, in 1523 and of Bishopstone, alias Elsborne, Wiltshire (on the resignation of Claymond), on 18 May 1531. In 1527 he was nominated by Fox to succeed Claymond as president of Corpus when that office should fall vacant and he was sworn in on 26 November 1537 following Claymond's death. During the previous year Morwen had letters patent allowing him non-residency of his parishes in order that he might deputize for Claymond, then disabled by infirmity. He was appointed prebendary of Gloucester on 11 June 1554. On several occasions he unsuccessfully competed for election to the presidency of Magdalen.

In 1551 the government began to put pressure on the religious conservatives at Oxford and Morwen and a number of Corpus fellows were sent to the Fleet prison on 15 June on suspicion of having used ceremonies on Corpus Christi day other than those prescribed in the new Book of Common Prayer. No attempt was made to dismiss him from the presidency and the action, by the standards of the time, can be seen as a subtle warning. Morwen spent a month in the Fleet and a temporary warden was appointed during his detention.

The accession of Mary I provided a much more congenial climate for conservatives like Morwen and he was, indeed, invited to play a small part in Cardinal Reginald Pole's plans for a Counter-Reformation. In 1556 he was appointed to the legatine visitation of the university. Its remit was provided by Pole in a schedule of thirty topics. Apart from general concerns about the observance of statutes, the numbers of students, and the election and performance of officials and fellows, the visitors, more specifically, were to look into whether books had been dispersed 'in the time of schism' or whether heretical books were still retained. Unlike at Cambridge University no record survives of the visitors' progress and the only known outcome of their activities was the exhumation of the body of Catherine Dammartin, the wife of Pietro Martire Vermigli (Peter Martyr), which was thrown on a dunghill, on account of her breaking vows of celibacy in order to marry.

Morwen published no works, no account of his contemporary reputation as a scholar survives, and even the collections of the college library bear no trace of him. However, he was praised by contemporaries as a patron of learning and the college muniments witness his administrative zeal. In 1549 he sold the founders' birthplace at Ropsley, Lincolnshire, and in 1553 acquired Beam Hall (across the street from Corpus), possibly for the purpose of accommodating commoners. He was also a generous benefactor of both Corpus and Magdalen. Morwen left lands in Cowley and Horsepath, both in Oxfordshire, and Duntesbourne Rouse and the advowsons of Duntesbourne, both in Gloucestershire, and Lower Heyford, Oxfordshire, to Corpus. He also left Rewley Meads to provide money for bread to be given to the poor (his cousin Thomas Morwen to administer this bequest should the college be suppressed). He had previously given £80 to Magdalen for the purchase of lands at Standlake which were to be used to endow an annual exhibition for four demis. In December 1557 Morwen donated £5 to Magdalen for the adornment of the high altar.

According to H. E. Salter the obit for Morwen was still observed and:

the members of the College (i.e. the Fellows, Demies and Choir) receive, as in the middle ages, two groats, one groat or half a groat, according to their standing. The Royal Mint supplies the coins from time to time when the supply runs

out. (H. E. Salter, 'A manuscript of Dorchester Abbey', *Oxoniensia*, 2, 1937, 204)

Morwen died on 16 August 1558 and was buried beside his predecessor, Claymond, in Corpus Christi chapel. He was unmarried but had a dog of which he was very fond, in whose praise John Jewel when an undergraduate wrote a new-year ode. His heir was William Morwen, gentleman, his nephew. His exact relationship to Roger Morwent, first scholar and then fellow of Corpus Christi (1528 and 1532) and Robert Morwyn, admitted as a fellow of Magdalen in 1552 is not known. MIHAIL DAFYDD EVANS

Sources T. Fowler, *The history of Corpus Christi College*, OHS, 25 (1893) · J. G. Milne, *The early history of Corpus Christi College, Oxford* (1946) · C. Cross, 'Oxford and the Tudor state', *Hist. U. Oxf.* 3: *Colleg. univ.*, 117–49 · J. McConice, 'Elizabethan Oxford: the collegiate society', *Hist. U. Oxf.* 3: *Colleg. univ.*, 645–732 · J. M. Fletcher and C. A. Upton, 'Destruction, repair and renewal: an Oxford college chapel during the Reformation', *Oxoniensia*, 48 (1983), 119–30 · DNB · Foster, *Alum. Oxon.*

Morys ap Griffith. *See* Griffin, Maurice (*d.* 1558).

Morys [Morris], **Huw** [*called* Eos Ceiriog] (**1622–1709**), Welsh-language poet, was a younger son of Morris ap Siôn ab Ednyfed, a farmer. Some time after 1647 he moved with his family to Pontymeibion, Llansilin, Denbighshire, the farm always associated with his name. His formal education is a matter of conjecture, but he stated in a poem that he served seven years as an apprentice to a barker in Gwaliau, Overton, Flintshire. He seems not to have traded and spent the remainder of his life living at home, firstly with his parents and later with his elder brother's family, possibly helping on the farm, as he refers to his *llaw deilo* ('mucking hand').

Since Morys never married and had few (if any) domestic commitments, he had plenty of time to compose poetry and to indulge in the old tradition of *clera*, that is attending at a patron's house on the occasion of a marriage or burial and at the Tair Gŵyl Arbennig, the three great festivals of the church, Christmas, Easter, and Whitsun, when itinerant poets were expected to present their poems of eulogy or elegy—or both—to their patrons. Morys does not complain about the decline of patronage as frequently or as bitterly as his contemporaries, though this may reflect his own good fortune rather than the general state of patronage at the time. He revelled in visits to his patrons and his favourite families were the Middeltons of Chirk Castle (and especially a cadet branch in Plas Newydd in his own parish of Llansilin), the Mostyns of Gloddaith, Caernarvonshire, and the Owens of Brogyntyn, Shropshire. He was probably the most prolific of all Welsh poets, with over 550 poems attributed to him in the computer index of poems at the National Library of Wales, although some are erroneous attributions. He was also one of the most popular poets among copyists, and consequently the numbers of copies of individual poems can be daunting, making the establishment of reliable texts difficult and time-consuming. A few poems have survived in his own handwriting, particularly in Cwrtmawr MS 224, in the National Library of Wales (pages 1–73) and in a few other fragments, particularly in the Brogyntyn collection in the National Library of Wales.

One of the most notable features of Morys's work is the use of free-metre poetry for the same purpose as his strict-metre poetry—that is to eulogize and to elegize his patrons and to beg for gifts. He was not the first to do this, but it is in his generation that the practice becomes common. The Chirk Castle accounts reveal that poets, harpers, and other musicians were paid for their free-metre poems and carols just as they were for their poems in the more conventional strict metres. Unlike his contemporary, Edward Morris, who experimented within the limitations of the strict metres, Morys was conventional in his use of the traditional metres and confined his experimentation to the free metres. He differed also from his contemporaries in that he addressed his poems to a wider social grouping than the traditional *uchelwyr* (gentry), and mixes the social classes in the same poem. There is a delightful poem addressed to William Salesbury (*d.* 1660), of Rug, Merioneth (a cadet branch of the noted Lleweni family), asking for a viol for Wiliam Probert, an old *cerddor* (musician-poet) who had fallen on hard times, because (according to Morys) he had fallen on his viol and shattered it while he was drunk. A *crwth* (viol) was also sought for Ffowc Rhisiart, a plough for Dafydd Morris from the wardens of Corwen, and an oak to make barrels on behalf of Roger Edwards the cooper, all artisans. These free-metre begging poems follow the convention of their strict-metre predecessors in that a description of the gift sought features prominently, and there is considerable *badinage* at the expense of the supplicant, while the donor is lavishly praised. The traditional begging poems had always included such descriptive elements and this facilitated their transition into free metres.

But there was still a distinction between strict- and free-metre poetry, as may be seen from the three elegies Morys composed on the death of Barbra Miltwn. The formal *cywydd* is the official elegy required to mark the death of this member of two prominent gentry families, by birth the Wynns of Melai and by marriage the Middeltons of Plas Newydd, Llansilin. As the formal expression of the sorrow of the families it includes the traditional elements of genealogies, eulogy, the grief of the neighbourhood on losing a support in time of need, and a comparison with other tragic deaths, in Barbra's case that of Queen Mary, another victim of smallpox. The impact of Barbra's death on the society of north Wales is, by implication, as great as that of the queen, since she was intertwined by her lineage and family ties with the gentry of the whole region; she was *seren naw o siroedd* ('star of nine counties'). The second poem is one of the most celebrated elegies in the Welsh language; it consists of a dialogue between the dead wife and her husband, but since it is an intimate poem, which seeks to reconcile the latter to his loss, Morys could use a free metre. The third poem, which is a *galarnad* (threnody), is one of a pair in the same metre, the other being written on the death of Barbra's widower in 1700. This *galarnad* is the poet's own lament for the death of his young patron, written in the first person and

intensely moving. The dialogue elegy became popular very quickly and was instrumental in making the free metres acceptable for elegies during the eighteenth century. These poems could not be more different and are a testimony to Morys's range as a poet.

Although a lifelong bachelor, Morys was famous for his praise of women's beauty. In these poems his technical virtuosity is displayed at its most intricate, although the complexity of the rhyme schemes and consonantal patterns that he imposed on himself inevitably led to some wordiness and superfluity of adjectives and compound words. This poetry when read silently from a book probably makes less impact than when declaimed, possibly to the accompaniment of harp or *crwth*. The May day and Christmas carols show the same lightness of touch and dazzling word play, but because they use simpler metres they are less wordy, and more appealing.

Several poems that deal with specific historical incidents reveal Morys's attitude towards current events. He was devoted to the Church of England and its supreme governor, the king, and was devastated when the civil war began, destroying the peace and stability of the entire country. His joy at the restoration of Charles II was celebrated in several poems. General Monck was the subject of eulogies, but the Rye House plot was a cause of grave concern for him, provoking laughter in Rome and grief in London at the sight of the children of ancient Britain turning traitor:

Mae chwerthin yn Rhufain a galar yn Llundain
Fynd plant yr hen Frydain yn fradwyr.

He refers specifically to Algernon Sidney (1623–1683), one of the conspirators who planned to assassinate the king and his heir, James, duke of York, as they returned to London from Newmarket ('Cerdd y plot protestannaidd a fu yn Llundain yn 1683'). He was obviously well informed about current events. In 'Carol Haf yn amser rhyfel' ('A summer carol in time of war') which can be dated *c.*1695–6, Morys attempts to raise the spirits of his audience by pointing out the delights of summer and the abundant gifts of God after the dearth of winter. He gives short shrift to those who complain about the high taxes levied to pay for the current wars, and maintains that it would be easier for the king (William III) to defend the realm without cost if all his subjects prayed for grace:

Fe fyddai haws i'r Brenin
Yn ddigost ein hamddiffyn,
Pe ceisiai pawb ar ddeulin,
Blanhigyn, gwreiddyn gras.

Morys's imagination was stirred by reports of the sea battles, and his 'Hanes brwydr rhwng Lloegr a Ffrainc, 1692' ('The tale of the battle between England and France, 1692') was probably based on one of the many ballads published following the sinking of the French *Roi Soleil* by Admiral Russell, since he names both the admiral and the ship. Apart from a few poems such as 'Ar ofyn gostegion yn amser Cromwel' ('On proclaiming marriage banns in Cromwell's time'), which was occasioned by the Marriage Act of 1653, Morys prudently hid his fervent hatred of the puritan cause, often by using the iconography popularized by prophetic poets since the middle ages. Thus the Lion and the young Lions stand for Charles I and his sons, the Lamb is the Church of England, the Sheep are Charles's loyal subjects, and the Shepherds are the priests, but Cromwell is always a Fox or some other predatory animal. It was not until after the Restoration that Morys felt safe enough to give full vent to his feelings, and in 'Drych yr amseroedd cyn 1660' ('A mirror of the times before 1660') he did not spare names, attacking in particular Vavasor Powell, one of the leading puritan preachers in the period before 1653; the poet and prose writer Morgan Llwyd (1619–1659) was castigated also. Morys's contempt for Llwyd's works is a salutary reminder that the modern reverence for Llwydiana was not necessarily shared by his contemporaries.

Morys also wrote two *anterliwtiau* (interludes)—'Y rhyfel cartref' ('The civil war') and a now incomplete 'Y mab afradlon' ('The prodigal son')—both of which reflect his political and religious attitudes as expressed more fluently in his poetry.

Morys was buried on 31 August 1709 in the churchyard of Llansilin where he had served as a churchwarden, and elegies for him were composed by several poets, among them Owen Gruffydd, Llanystumdwy, and Robert Wynne, vicar of Gwyddelwern.   NESTA LLOYD

Sources D. Jenkins, 'Bywyd a gwaith Huw Morys, Pontymeibion, 1622–1709', MA diss., U. Wales, 1948 · G. Thomas, 'Changes in the tradition of Welsh poetry in north Wales in the seventeenth century', DPhil diss., U. Oxf., 1966 · D. Jenkins, 'Carolan haf a nadolig', *Llên Cymru*, 2 (1952–3), 46–55 · T. Parry, *Baledi'r ddeunawfed ganrif*, 2nd edn (1986) · D. Jenkins, 'Rhai o lawysgrifau Huw Morris', *National Library of Wales Journal*, 7 (1951–2), 138–47; but see also E. D. Jones, 'The Brogyntyn Welsh manuscripts', *National Library of Wales Journal*, 7 (1951–2), 165–98, esp. 185–7 · N. Lloyd, 'Cerodi Huw Morys y Barbra Miltwn', ed. J. E. Caerwyn Williams, *Ysgrifau Beirniadol*, 21 (1996), 97–119
Archives Denbighshire RO, manuscript volume of poems · NL Wales, literary MSS
Likenesses figure, Pontymeibion farmhouse · stained-glass window, Llansilin church

Morys, Sir John. See Morice, Sir John (d. 1362).

Moryson, Fynes (1565/6–1630), traveller and writer, was born at Cadeby, Lincolnshire, third son of Thomas Moryson (d. 1591), clerk of the pipe and MP for Great Grimsby in the parliaments between 1572 and 1588–9, and his wife, Elizabeth (d. 1587), daughter of Thomas Moigne and Bridget Hansard of Willingham, Lincolnshire. He matriculated at Peterhouse, Cambridge, on 18 May 1580, graduating BA in 1584 and proceeding MA in 1587. Created a fellow by royal mandate, he began to study civil law and in 1589–90 was bursar of the college; however, having from his 'tender youth … had a great desire to see foreign countries' (Moryson, 1.3.197)—he gave his age in 1589 as twenty-three—he soon sought permission to suspend his fellowship and travel overseas.

By May 1591 Moryson's preparations (which included having his MA incorporated at Oxford) were complete and he left England to spend the next four years travelling and studying in Europe, initially in Germany, Prague, Switzerland (where in 1592 he entered the University of Basel), and the Netherlands. In the spring of 1593 he journeyed by way of Denmark to Danzig, then south through Poland, Moravia, and Austria to Italy, where he enrolled at the University of Padua. Although he enrolled also at Leiden in January 1594, he then went on to explore Naples and Rome, where he completed his visit by having an interview with Cardinal Bellarmine, then hurried back to the relative safety of north Italy, though even there he kept moving constantly during Easter to avoid enquiries into his religion. Early in 1595 he had a brief meeting with Theodore Beza at Geneva, then returned through France (where he was able to catch a glimpse of Henri IV) to Dover, where he landed on 13 May.

Moryson still had 'an itching desire to see Jerusalem … and Constantinople' (Moryson, 1.3.198) and on 8 December 1595 he and his younger brother Henry sailed for Flushing. Passing by sledge, boat, and coach through the Netherlands and Germany they crossed the Alps to Venice, where they took ship for Cyprus and Jerusalem. After spending ten days exploring Jerusalem and its shrines they returned to the coast and soon after both brothers fell ill with what appears to have been dysentery. Henry Moryson died on 4 July 1596 leaving Fynes deeply grieved: he remarks more than once that 'this houre was the first of my old age' (ibid., 1.3.249–50). He made his way to Candia (Crete), however, then on to Constantinople, where he lodged with the English ambassador, Edward Barton. He left Turkey at the end of February 1597 and finally reached London five months later.

In April 1598 Moryson visited Scotland, travelling to Falkland where he saw King James. He had intended to go further but unexpected business—perhaps diplomatic—took him back to England where he then spent 'an ydle yeere' or more putting his journals into order while staying with his sisters, Faith Mussendyne and Jane Allington, who both lived near Healing, Lincolnshire. On the advice of his brother Richard [see below], who was active in the war in Ireland, he left in November for Dublin, where the lord deputy, Sir Charles Blount, Lord Mountjoy, had agreed to employ him to write a journal of Irish affairs. He reached Dundalk on the day that Blount's chief secretary was killed at Carlingford, and was appointed to the vacancy (Moryson, 2.1.84). Early in 1601, while 'still a raw souldier', he was grazed by a bullet (ibid., 2.1.88) and at the end of the year he took part in the siege of the Spanish force which had landed in Kinsale to support Tyrone. Moryson returned to England in 1602 when Blount was appointed lord lieutenant of Ireland and master of the ordnance.

Moryson received a modest pension from Blount, whose death in 1606 allowed him to turn to his own writing. He spent three years compiling a history of the countries he had visited, but found it growing to unmanageable dimensions and abandoned it to begin work on a shorter account of his travels. By 1617 he had completed three parts of this in Latin, and had translated them into English to be published by John Beale as *An itinerary … containing his ten yeeres* travell through the twelve dominions of Germany, Bohmerland, Sweitzerland, Netherland, Denmarke, Poland, Italy, Turky, France, England, Scotland, and Ireland. Divided into three parts' (1617). The three folios of An Itinerary form what are really three distinct works. Part one (of which there is a Latin version, BL, Harleian MS 5133) is a detailed journal of Moryson's travels in Europe and the Near East. Part two centres on a history of the Nine Years' War, using copies of official correspondence and state documents to illustrate the campaign from Blount's perspective; it was reprinted, together with 'of the geographical description of Ireland' (part 3, 3.v) as An History of Ireland from the Year 1599 to 1603 (2 vols., Dublin, 1735), and 'the description of Ireland' is included in Ireland under Elizabeth and James the First (ed. H. Morley, 1890). Part three of An Itinerary consists of essays on the value and difficulties of travel, and on geography and national differences; this part was not fully complete when first published in 1617. A manuscript fourth part (Corpus Christi College, Oxford, MS xciv) was intended by Moryson to complete the printed part three; a large portion of this, with a very extensive biographical introduction, was printed by Charles Hughes under the title of Shakespeare's Europe (1903).

Moryson was well equipped to write his Itinerary. By his own account he was fluent in German, Italian, Dutch, and French, and his linguistic ability served him well in regions where an Englishman might expect to meet hostility: he generally posed as German or Dutch in the more dangerous states in Italy, adopting a second cover as a Frenchman when visiting Cardinal Bellarmine at the Jesuit college in Rome; he dressed as a down-at-heel Bohemian servant to avoid Spanish troops in Friesland; he passed himself off as a Pole when entering France; and he was got up as a German serving-man when a party of disbanded French soldiers robbed him near Châlons. Travelling without substantial funds or official protection, he survived at various times by adopting a deferential posture, avoiding eye contact, attaching himself to other parties of travellers, concealing a reserve of cash, and keeping his religious convictions to himself, as when he used 'honest dissembling' to pass as an English Catholic when lodging with French friars in Jerusalem.

Moryson was a careful and accurate observer, without much literary skill but keenly interested in people and social relationships. If his meticulous accounts of distances and travel expenses in the first part of An Itinerary are at times tedious, in the second part of the work his detailed citation of the documents and correspondence he dealt with as Blount's chief secretary provides a valuable insight into English policy in Ireland; while not insensitive to the horrors of starvation in Ireland, he was an unwavering supporter of Blount and the methods he used to bring Tyrone and his followers to submission.

Moryson's descriptions of inns and their variations in ambience and food are lively and at times humorous, as are his sketches of hard-drinking German artisans and their sober wives, Italian gentlemen and courtesans, Jewish accountants, Irish gamblers, Turkish janissaries, entrepreneurial Dutchwomen and their downtrodden husbands, impoverished Scots, and spendthrift Polish noblemen. He made a valuable attempt to explain the differences in wealth and poverty in the nations of Europe, identifying and analysing the role of market forces, the importance of an adequate supply of currency, the development of labour-saving technology, and the significance of social and economic attitudes. While intensely proud of his own country and its cuisine, he yet tried to bring home to his fashion-mad, free-spending English readers the politico-economic lessons to be learned from Italy, Germany, and the Netherlands.

Little is known of Moryson's later life. He was in London on 26 February 1612, when he attended the funeral of his sister Jane, and in 1613 he revisited Ireland at the invitation of his brother Richard, then vice-president of Munster. Narrowly escaping shipwreck, he landed at Youghal on 9 September and concluded that the apparent tranquillity of Ireland was threatened by further 'combustions from our degenerate English Irish' (Moryson, 2.3.300). He never married. He died on 12 February 1630 in St Botolph's parish, London, not a wealthy man, probably having converted such capital as he had into an annuity which was sufficient for his needs. Under his will of 15 September 1629 he left his pictures, books, and a cabinet to Mr and Mrs Francis Dynn, his best nightcap and handkerchief to his octogenarian brother-in-law, George Allington, his gilded halbert to Mr William Ireland, and all his linen and its trunk to Mrs Susan Ireland, to Sarah Ireland two red chairs with matching stools, to Mr Edward Waterhouse 20s., and to his servant Isaac Pywall all his clothing, beds, and other furniture.

His brother, **Sir Richard Moryson** (c.1571–1628), army officer and politician, was the fifth son of Thomas and Elizabeth Moryson. He matriculated from Peterhouse, Cambridge, in the Lent term of 1585. Between 1591 and 1593 he served as lieutenant and captain under Sir Roger Williams in France and the Low Countries. In the 'Islands' voyage' of 1597 he acted as lieutenant-colonel under Sir Charles Blount and he went as a colonel with Essex's army to Ireland in 1599, where on 5 August he was knighted. Serving as governor at Dundalk and afterwards at Lecale, co. Down, he assisted Blount in the campaign against Tyrone, and became governor of Waterford and Wexford in 1604. In 1607, on the death of Sir Henry Brouncker, president of Munster, Moryson and the earl of Thomond filled the vacant office until Henry, Lord Danvers, was appointed to it. In 1609 Moryson became vice-president of Munster, and he was elected to the Irish parliament in April 1613. He is said to have paid Lord Danvers £3000 to obtain the presidency of Munster, which Danvers was then vacating, but despite Danvers's efforts it was given to Thomond.

A year later Moryson left Ireland and was appointed lieutenant-general of the ordnance in England. He also held from 1616 the office of cessor of composition money for the province of Munster, and in 1618 was granted the reversion of the Munster presidency, which, however, never fell to him. He settled at Tooley Park, Leicestershire, and was elected MP for Leicester in 1621. He died in 1628, survived by his widow, Mary (*d.* 1654), daughter of Sir Henry Harington. His eldest son, Henry, was knighted in October 1627, and his daughter Letitia (Lettice) married Lucius Cary, second Viscount Falkland.

EDWARD H. THOMPSON

Sources F. Moryson, *An itinerary … containing his ten yeeres travell through the twelve dominions*, 3 vols. (1617) · C. Hughes, ed., *Shakespeare's Europe* (1903) · E. H. Thompson, 'Elizabethan economic analysis: Fynes Moryson's account of the economics of Europe', *History of Economic Ideas*, 3/1 (1995), 1–25 · Venn, *Alum. Cant.* · H. Morley, ed., *Ireland under Elizabeth and James the First* (1890) · *The letters and life of Francis Bacon*, ed. J. Spedding, 7 vols. (1861–74), vol. 2 · J. S. Brewer and W. Bullen, eds., *Calendar of the Carew manuscripts*, 1: *1515–1574*, PRO (1867) · *The letters of John Chamberlain*, ed. N. E. McClure, 2 vols. (1939) · *CSP Ire., 1509–1672* · *CSP dom., 1611–18*
Archives BL, itinerary in Ireland, Add. MS 36706 · CCC Oxf., *An itinerary*, pt 4, MS no. xciv
Wealth at death see probate: cited in C. Hughes, ed., 'Introduction', *Shakespeare's Europe* (1903)

Moryson, Sir Richard (*c*.1571–1628). *See under* Moryson, Fynes (1565/6–1630).

Moscheles, Ignaz (1794–1870), pianist and composer, was born in Prague on 23 May 1794, one of five children of a Jewish cloth merchant, Joachim Moscheles (*d.* 24 April 1805). He was given the Jewish name Isack, but used the name Ignaz. His main studies were with the director of the Prague conservatory, Bedřich Diviš Weber. In 1808, partly impelled by what was to be a lifelong admiration for Beethoven, he moved to Vienna, where he studied further with J. A. Streicher, Albrechtsberger, and Salieri. By 1814 he was established as one of the most successful of the city's young piano virtuosos. His tours took him to many European cities, and on 26 May 1821 to England, where for a quarter of a century he was at the centre of British musical life.

Moscheles was first heard in England at a Philharmonic concert in London on 11 June 1821, when he played his popular variations *La marche d'Alexandre* and his second piano concerto (in E♭, op. 56). A brilliant improviser, he based his technique (as his widely used studies show) on the classical precepts of Clementi and others while anticipating the new developments of Chopin and Liszt. The best of his music is to be found in his sonatas rather than in his concertos or virtuoso ephemera. In London he formed friendships with Clementi (whose pianos he favoured), J. B. Cramer, Ries, and Kalkbrenner, and was soon a central figure in London music-making and in the world of other visiting and immigrant musicians. Further appearances followed, and on leaving England in the following year he was given a new passport by Prince Eszterhazy with the title 'Kammervirtuos'. He spent the summer in France, returning to London after the Paris concert season, and making his first reappearance with Cramer in a duet sonata to which he contributed a movement (on this occasion using a Broadwood piano to suit Cramer's style). He was taken up again by fashionable London and played at many soirées but also gave his own concerts; he was elected an honorary member of the London Academy of Music and, by his own account, came to feel increasingly at home in England. After another winter in France he returned in

Ignaz Moscheles (1794–1870), by Maxim Gauci, pubd 1824

January, spending time in Bath and Bristol as well as in London. He gave lessons, played at the oratorio concerts, and, though much of his time was taken up with trivia, worked on compositions including his fourth piano concerto (in E major, op. 64). He left England again at the end of the season, in August.

Further European tours brought Moscheles into contact with many musicians, among them the young Mendelssohn, to whom he gave lessons and who became his closest friend. In Hamburg he met and, on 1 March 1825, married, an amateur pianist, Charlotte Embden (1805–1889); they moved to England on 2 May 1825. Country visits included stays at Stoneham Park, Southampton (where he was a guest with Palmerston), Cheltenham, and Oxford, before they settled at 77 Norton Street, London; here their household belongings included a piano presented by Clementi. In 1830 they moved to 3 Chester Place, Regent's Park. A happy and mutually supportive couple, they were generous hosts, and Moscheles always lived up to his principle that colleagues should play for one another without a fee. He showed great kindness to the dying Carl Maria von Weber, in London in 1826 for the first performance of *Oberon*, then helped Sir George Smart with Weber's funeral arrangements; and Mendelssohn, on his first visit to England, wrote in detail of the couple's careful attention to his wants, adding 'Beide sind die Freundlichkeit selbst' ('They are both kindness itself'; letter to his father, 25 April 1829). Moscheles was often host to Mendelssohn, who stood godfather to his son Felix; they gave a number of concerts together, and shared the conductorship of the Birmingham Festival in 1846. Among many other artists visiting London who benefited from his hospitality were

Paganini, Spohr, and Liszt. He also toured widely, including a visit to Ireland (he found the Irish more musically receptive than the English), and wrote as a consequence his *Souvenirs d'Irlande* (op. 69, 1826). This was followed by *Anklänge aus Schottland* (op. 75, 1826) and a *Fantaisie sur des airs des bardes écossais* (op. 80, 1828). The latter arose partly from a visit to Edinburgh and to Sir Walter Scott. Despite differences over the musical capabilities of the bagpipes, their friendly exchanges included translations of Bürger and Grillparzer which Scott made for Moscheles's album; he later gratefully accepted the dedication of the *Fantaisie*.

The pattern of Moscheles's London life continued in similar fashion for some years, with residence in England sometimes interrupted by summer tours on the continent. Much of his time was taken up with recitals in grand houses and at court. In 1828 he played at Kensington Palace to the duchess of Kent, the young Princess Victoria being sent to bed after his second piece. On many occasions he was irked by the English lack of respect for those performing, as demonstrated at a soirée on 14 April 1832 after the passing of the Reform Bill where the audience included the duke of Wellington and 'the whole Tory party', and at another on 12 December before the king at Brighton Pavilion. He taught the piano at the Royal Academy of Music and developed a circle of talented pupils, including Litolff and Thalberg; he had many aristocratic pupils, but others included a greengrocer's daughter who had been rejected elsewhere. He conducted the Philharmonic Society (1821–46, co-director 1832–41), and, having raised a subscription of £100 from the society to send to the dying Beethoven, continued his services to the composer he admired above all others by conducting the English première of the *Missa solemnis* in 1832 (a private performance on Christmas eve at the house of the amateur musician Alsager in Queen Square). He also translated Anton Schindler's *Biographie von Ludwig Van Beethoven* (1840) into English (1841) (the jealously protective Schindler later wrote a mendacious attack upon him). His concerts included, from 1837, pioneering 'historical soirées' at which, well in advance of his time, he would play Bach and Scarlatti on the harpsichord. Thanks to Sir George Smart, he was enabled to attend Queen Victoria's coronation on 28 June 1838 by singing as a bass in the choir. He began to withdraw from public performance in 1840.

To widely expressed regret, Moscheles and his family left England in 1846 on his acceptance of the post of professor of piano at the Leipzig conservatory (though they made brief return visits). His contribution to English musical life was substantial, at least as much for his encouragement of foreign artists as for his own compositions and concerts. He was very companionable, at ease in English society, and in turn was held in warm regard: he and his wife, who was also very well liked, 'held weekly receptions on a large scale, at which "society", musicians, painters, and literary people of distinction, were wont to foregather' (Kuhe, 76). The diaries and letters copiously quoted in his wife's biography of him, *Aus Moscheles' Leben*

(1872, trans. 1873), give a lively and sympathetic account of English musical life in the twenty-five years between 1821 and 1846. Moscheles died in Leipzig on 10 March 1870.

JOHN WARRACK

Sources *Aus Moscheles' Leben: nach Briefen und Tagebüchern*, ed. [C. Moscheles], 2 vols. (Leipzig, 1872–3) · *New Grove* · F. Blume, ed., *Die Musik in Geschichte und Gegenwart*, 17 vols. (Kassel and Basel, 1949–86) · J. Roche, 'Ignaz Moscheles, 1794–1870', *MT*, 111 (1970), 264–6 · E. Smidak, *Isaak-Ignaz Moscheles* (1988) · F. Moscheles, *Fragments of an autobiography* (1899) · F. Moscheles, ed., *Briefe von F. Mendelssohn-Bartholdy an Ignaz und Charlotte Moscheles* (1888) · J. F. Barnett, *Musical reminiscences and impressions* (1906) · W. Kuhe, *My musical recollections* (1896)
Likenesses M. Gauci, engraving, pubd 1824, NPG [*see illus.*] · C. Baugniet, lithograph, 1846 · engraving, repro. in Moscheles, *Aus Moscheles' Leben*, frontispiece · lithograph, repro. in Roche, 'Ignaz Moscheles' · portrait, repro. in Smidak, *Isaac-Ignaz Moscheles*, jacket

Moseley. *See also* Mosley.

Moseley, Benjamin (1742–1819), physician and opponent of vaccination, was born in Essex. His background is obscure, beyond a claim in Munk's *Roll* that his family came from Lancashire. Moseley received his medical education in London and Paris. On completing his training in 1768 he set up as a surgeon–apothecary in Kingston, Jamaica, where he also held the post of surgeon-general.

Moseley was a man of considerable skill and ability and he was clearly ambitious, cultivating the intellectual style and professional status of an élite and rather old-fashioned physician. His eighteen years of practice in the West Indies served as a platform for his social and professional advancement. While in Jamaica he published a pamphlet on the treatment of dysentery—then a serious problem among military forces in the colony—and a longer work on coffee, one of the island's principal exports. The style of these works was more typical of élite physicians than colonial surgeons: Moseley cited the work of luminaries such as Thomas Sydenham and William Cullen, and discussed the effects of coffee on the various types of bodily constitution.

A sizeable fortune earned from his West Indian practice allowed Moseley to acquire a more distinguished set of qualifications. In 1784 he returned to Britain and obtained, without study, an MD from St Andrews University. In the autumn of 1785 he set out on a tour of the continent, beginning with a visit to Normandy. In 1786 he stopped at Strasbourg, Dijon, Montpellier, and Aix, before moving on to Lausanne, Venice, and Rome in 1787. In the same year he became a licentiate of the Royal College of Physicians, London. By 1788 Moseley had settled down to practise among the London upper classes, and through the patronage of Lord Musgrave obtained the post of physician to the Royal Hospital at Chelsea. He reinforced his new status with further publications. His massive *Treatise on Tropical Diseases* (1787) and shorter *On Hydrophobia* (1808) were unoriginal, consisting of descriptions of various forms of treatment padded out with case histories. His *Treatise on Sugar* (1799) echoed his earlier work on coffee, describing the cultivation and production of sugar, as well as its past medicinal use.

Moseley owes his small place in medical history to his violent objections to vaccination, first expressed in his *Treatise on Sugar* and expanded through a series of ever more intemperate pamphlets and contributions to the anti-vaccination journal the *Medical Observer*. Like other opponents of the new practice, Moseley cast doubt on the relationship between cowpox and smallpox, and thus on whether vaccination with the former could protect against the latter disease. His fear that cowpox might produce other diseases, especially skin complaints, were also shared by a number of practitioners. However, Moseley expressed his objections in a uniquely forceful style. He attacked his medical colleagues for their uncritical adoption of the new procedure, ascribing it to a form of mania. He also identified a far greater and more lurid range of side-effects of vaccination. His *Commentaries on the Lues bovilla* (1806), for example, repeated allegations that vaccination had produced scrofula and whooping cough, but also attributed unique complaints to vaccination—tinea bovilla, elephantiasis bovilla, and lues bovilla—which sprang from the animal origins of cowpox. Moseley was also alone in claiming that vaccination affected patients' intellectual capacities: he reported that children had become idiots and adults had become insane following vaccination. Moseley repeated these allegations before parliamentary inquiries into vaccination in 1802 and 1808. His fears inspired James Gillray's famous cartoon of vaccinated people sprouting cows' heads and tails.

Moseley died on 25 September 1819 at Southend, where he regularly spent the summer, sea-bathing—a favoured form of therapy. He was buried at Chelsea, London.

DEBORAH BRUNTON

Sources *GM*, 1st ser., 89/2 (1819), 374–5 · Munk, *Roll* · *DNB*
Likenesses M.-A. Bourlier, engraving (after R. M. Paye), RCP Lond. · M.-A. Bourlier, stipple (after R. M. Paye), BM, NPG, Wellcome L. · R. M. Paye, portrait, RCP Lond.

Moseley, Edward (1682–1749), public official and planter in America, was born of unnoted parentage, probably in London. There he received a splendid education at Christ's Hospital, a charity school for orphan boys founded in 1552 by Edward VI. Boys customarily finished school at the age of fifteen, and so in December 1697, having studied surveying, Moseley was apprenticed 'in the practice of navigation' to serve on the *Joseph* in trade with Spain through the port of Bilbao. The earliest notice of Moseley in Carolina is that in passing through Charles Town in May 1703 he was engaged to make a catalogue of the library books there. This gave him experience that lasted virtually a lifetime; in 1723, when he turned over seventy-six volumes to Edenton for the use of that North Carolina parish—probably selected from those sent years earlier by the Society for the Propagation of the Gospel—until his death, when his own library had over 400 volumes, he was renowned for possessing a broad range of information. By the end of 1704 he had settled in the Albemarle section of North Carolina and in 1705 he made a good match when he married Ann (b. 1679), daughter of Alexander Lillington and wealthy widow of Governor Henderson Walker.

In the same year, when he was just twenty-three, Moseley made his first appearance in public service, setting a pattern for the remaining forty-four years of his life. As he was often to do in the future he filled several posts in that first year—as justice of the peace, vestryman, and member of the proprietary council. He was sympathetic in his understanding of the rights of others. He acknowledged the desires of Quakers for religious liberty and even supported them in their role in the Cary uprising. Personally, however, he supported the Church of England; from England he ordered copies of the Book of Common Prayer for use in the colony, and about 1723 he gave a silver communion service to St Paul's Church in Edenton that is still in use. He also opposed the use of prerogative authority by the royal and proprietary parties and the impressment of property or labour service.

General concern over multiple office-holding was no deterrent to Moseley and his availability for public service was usually welcomed. He was a member of the colonial assembly for many terms between 1708 and 1734, frequently serving as speaker. He also sat on the council at various times from 1705 until his death, and once was acting governor when the incumbent went to South Carolina. In 1711 he was one of the commissioners appointed to issue paper currency, and some four years later he was appointed public treasurer, in which post he served until 1735; at that time the position was divided and Moseley was made treasurer of the southern district, a service he rendered for the remainder of his life. He was judge of the vice-admiralty court for a time (1724–8) and acted as chief justice in 1744.

A trained surveyor, Moseley acted as surveyor-general of the colony during the years 1706–11 and 1723–31 but, whether officially so designated or not, he served as such on numerous occasions. At other times he performed the common work of preparing plats (large-scale maps showing property boundaries) for land grants. At the other extreme he was one of the surveyors who in 1728 fixed the boundary between Virginia and North Carolina; this report afterwards became well known as William Byrd's history of the dividing line (Byrd relied extensively on Moseley and spoke well of his work). Moseley was also a member of the commission named in 1735 to fix the boundary between the north and south Carolinas, and in 1744 he was engaged in delineating the portion of North Carolina to be retained by the Granville family when the crown purchased their rights in Carolina. Another product of Moseley's knowledge, experience, and skill was his detailed map of the settled eastern portion of North Carolina; dedicated to Governor Gabriel Johnston it was printed in London in 1733 and is an important source of much information not otherwise available.

Need for the revision and printing of the laws of North Carolina was recognized and sometimes discussed from 1736 onward but the want of a printing press stifled action. In 1736, however, Governor Johnston persuaded the assembly to bestir itself and a committee was appointed. Of its four members the most active were Samuel Swann and Moseley. Both were surveyors but Moseley was also skilled in law; the result of their work was *A Collection of All the Public Acts of Assembly; of the Province of North-Carolina* (1751), the first book printed in North Carolina.

From time to time Moseley was referred to as colonel, although there is no evidence that he held such a rank. However, the possibility of an invasion of North Carolina by Spain led the general assembly in 1745 to designate him and other men to erect a fort on the coast; in September 1747, when an invasion did occur, Moseley was among those who rallied in defence of Brunswick Town.

At his death, on 11 July 1749, Moseley owned more than 30,000 acres in plantations in Chowan, Edgecombe, New Hanover, Tyrrell and other counties, as well as town lots in Brunswick and Wilmington. He had over ninety slaves, some of whom were freed by his will. He was survived by six sons and a daughter (John and Edward with his first wife, and Sampson, James, Thomas, William, and Aner (Anna) with his second wife, Ann Hasell), whom he married in 1712 or 1713, after the death of his first wife. He and Ann were probably buried in the cemetery at Moseley Hall, near Rocky Point, New Hanover county, which had been their home since about 1734, when Moseley left Chowan county.   WILLIAM S. POWELL

Sources W. L. Saunders and W. Clark, eds., *The colonial records of North Carolina*, 30 vols. (1886–1907), vols. 1–3 • W. S. Price, 'Moseley, Edward', *Dictionary of North Carolina biography*, ed. W. S. Powell (1979–96) • J. F. Shinn, 'Edward Moseley', *Publications of the Southern History Association*, 3 (1899) • J. Sprunt, *Chronicles of the Cape Fear River*, 2nd edn (1916) • H. T. Lefler, introduction, *A new voyage to Carolina by John Lawson*, ed. H. T. Lefler (1967) • S. B. Weeks, *Libraries and literature in North Carolina in the eighteenth century* (1896) • D. C. McMurtie, *Eighteenth-century North Carolina imprints, 1749–1800* (1938) • K. P. Battle, 'Colonial laymen in the Church of England in North Carolina', *Sketches of the church history of North Carolina* (1892), 91–159 • R. J. Cain, ed., *The Church of England in North Carolina: documents, 1699–1741* (Raleigh, NC, 1999)
Archives North Carolina Division of Archives and History, Raleigh, MSS
Wealth at death more than 30,000 acres in several counties; more than 400 books, extensive silver, houses, furniture, livestock, and other belongings: will

Moseley, Henry (1801–1872), mathematician and writer on mechanics, was born on 9 July 1801, the son of Dr William Willis Moseley, who kept a large private school at Newcastle under Lyme, and his wife, Margaret Jackson. He was educated at the grammar school in Newcastle under Lyme, and when about fifteen years old he attended a school at Abbeville, France. In 1818 he studied at a naval school in Portsmouth; while there he wrote his first paper, on measuring the depth of the cavities seen on the surface of the moon, which was published in the *Philosophical Magazine* of that year. In 1821 he was admitted to St John's College, Cambridge, graduating BA, as seventh wrangler, in 1826, and proceeding MA in 1836.

Moseley was ordained deacon in 1827 and priest in 1828, and became curate at West Monkton, near Taunton. There he devoted himself to mathematics and wrote his first book, *A Treatise on Hydrostatics* (1830). On 20 January 1831 he was appointed professor of natural and experimental philosophy and astronomy at the newly established King's College, London, where he was instrumental in establishing the department of practical science and engineering. He held the post until 12 January 1844, when he was appointed one of the first of her majesty's inspectors of normal schools. He was also chaplain of King's College from 31 October 1831 to 8 November 1833.

On 23 April 1835 Moseley married Harriet, daughter of William Nottidge, of Wandsworth Common, Surrey; they had a son, Henry Nottidge *Moseley. As one of the jurors of the International Exhibition of 1851 he came under the notice of the prince consort, and in 1853 he was presented to a residential canonry in Bristol Cathedral; in 1854 he became vicar of Olveston, Gloucestershire, and he was appointed chaplain in ordinary to Queen Victoria in 1855.

Moseley wrote a number of journal articles, chiefly on statics, as well as the article on definite integrals in the *Encyclopaedia metropolitana* (1837), and a book entitled *The Mechanical Principles of Engineering and Architecture* (1843), which was reprinted in America for the use of the military school at West Point, and was also translated into German. He was elected a fellow of the Royal Society in February 1839. He was also a corresponding member of the Institut de France, a member of the Council of Military Education, and vice-president of the Institution of Naval Architects. He received an honorary DCL from Oxford in 1870. He was active in the promotion of working-class education, and an advocate of the development of commercial or middle schools, to be established on a scientific rather than a literary basis. He died at Olveston on 20 January 1872. He was survived by his wife.   B. B. WOODWARD, rev. R. C. COX

Sources Crockford (1872) • *Transactions of the Institution of Naval Architects*, 13 (1872), 328–30 • Venn, *Alum. Cant.* • C. Knight, ed., *The English cyclopaedia: biography*, 6 vols. (1856–8) [suppl. (1872)] • *CGPLA Eng. & Wales* (1875)
Archives Hove Central Library, Sussex, letters to William Pole • UCL, letters to Society for the Diffusion of Useful Knowledge
Likenesses Maull & Polyblank, sepia photograph, RS
Wealth at death under £25,000: treble probate, 1876, *CGPLA Eng. & Wales* (1872)

Moseley, Henry Gwyn Jeffreys (1887–1915), physicist, the only son of Henry Nottidge *Moseley (1844–1891), Linacre professor of anatomy in the University of Oxford, and his wife, Amabel Nevile Gwyn Jeffreys (d. 1927), was born at Weymouth on 23 November 1887, and educated at Summerfields School, Oxford (1896–1901), then at Eton College, of which he was a king's scholar, and at Trinity College, Oxford, where he was a Millard scholar, graduating with honours in natural science in 1910. On both sides he was descended from families of great scientific ability. His paternal grandfather, Henry Moseley FRS, was professor of natural philosophy at King's College, London, and his maternal grandfather, John Gwyn Jeffreys FRS, was a specialist on molluscs. Moseley soon showed marked originality of mind and interest in science. As an undergraduate he pursued his studies with great determination, with a preference for his own methods; he also rowed every year for the college.

Immediately after graduation he was appointed lecturer in physics in the University of Manchester and began research under the direction of Professor Ernest Rutherford. He soon developed into a rapid and skilful experimenter with unusual powers of continuous work, and showed to a marked degree that combination of practical ability and philosophic insight so necessary for attacking new and difficult problems. Following a number of important investigations in the subject of radioactivity Moseley began, with C. G. Darwin (grandson of Charles Darwin), that work on the X-ray spectra of the elements with which his name is inseparably connected. Following up the demonstration of X-ray diffraction by Max von Laue, W. H. Bragg, and W. L. Bragg had already shown that the wavelength of X-rays could be determined by the crystal method, and had found evidence of bright lines superimposed on the continuous spectrum. Moseley's fellowship having expired, he returned to Oxford to live with his mother and to be on the spot should a position open in the university. He continued his work in the electrical laboratory directed by J. S. Townsend. There he examined systematically the relation between the bright line X-ray spectra given by different elements; he found that all the elements gave similar types of spectra, and that the frequency of vibration of corresponding lines was proportional to the square of a number M which varied by unity in passing from one element to the next. From these observations, he was able to draw conclusions of far-reaching importance in connection with the constitution of atoms.

Shortly before Moseley began his survey of the high frequency spectra of the elements Rutherford had revived the nuclear model of the atom in which the charge Z on the nucleus, rather than the number of electrons orbiting around it, determined the character of the atom. Rutherford's theory of the scattering of alpha particles, on which he had based his atomic model, required that $Z = 2$ for helium and $Z \approx A/2$ for heavy metals, where A is the atomic weight of the metal, counting hydrogen's weight as one. Moseley knew these results, which were obtained during his time at Manchester, and he supposed that his M was related to Rutherford's Z. Since Z for helium had to be two, Z for hydrogen evidently was one. Examining the X-ray spectra from the metals from copper through calcium, Moseley determined that the ordinal number N of their place in the periodic table of the elements differed by one unit from M, making irresistible the inference $M + 1 = N = Z$. On this understanding he called the roll of the elements: if he could not find a specimen that emitted spectra characterized by a given value of M he inferred that the corresponding element had not been discovered and kept a place open for it at $N = M + 1$. After a few erroneous assignments resulting from haste and the difficulty of procuring rare samples and handling their radiations, he deduced that four elements were missing between aluminium ($N = 13$) and gold ($N = 79$), at $N = 43, 61, 72,$ and 75. In this he was almost right; but accepting the opinion of many chemists, he incorrectly identified 72 as a rare earth. Numbers 72 and 75 soon were found in ores of their chemical homologues, zirconium and manganese respectively; the first

and second numbers (43 and 61), which do not exist naturally, were first made in a cyclotron and in a nuclear pile, respectively. Moseley's law that an element's main properties are determined by a whole number defining its nuclear charge ranks in importance with the discoveries of the periodic law of the elements and of spectrum analysis, and is in many respects more fundamental than either.

The difference of one unit between M and $N = Z$ naturally aroused great interest. Moseley explained that the effective nuclear charge acting on the electrons that he held responsible for the production of the line spectra was less than Z owing to screening by electrons closer to the nucleus. He tried to derive a screening of one unit from the quantized version of the nuclear atom that Niels Bohr had proposed during Moseley's last year in Manchester. His ingenious attempt to show that $Z_{eff} = M$, though premature, was later justified when the mechanisms of X-ray emission on the Bohr theory were worked out.

In 1914 Moseley travelled with his mother to Australia to attend the meeting of the British Association. He returned to England in order to enlist at once in the New Army, and he obtained his commission as lieutenant in the Royal Engineers. He took part in the Gallipoli campaign, and was killed in action in the Dardanelles on 10 August 1915 at the age of twenty-seven. He was buried at Gallipoli. He was unmarried and had no girlfriend; he found his satisfaction in intense and continuous work, which allowed him to complete during two years at the outset of his career a set of researches that would surely have brought him a Nobel prize. The premature death of a young man of such brilliant promise and achievement was everywhere recognized as an irreparable loss to science. His friends and scientific admirers in many countries united to erect a memorial tablet in the physical laboratory of the University of Manchester. He bequeathed his property to the Royal Society to aid scientific research, and a studentship bearing his name was instituted.

ERNEST RUTHERFORD, *rev.* J. L. HEILBRON

Sources J. L. Heilbron, *H. G. J. Moseley: the life and letters of an English physicist, 1887–1915* (1974) · J. B. Birks, ed., *Rutherford at Manchester* (1962) · J. L. Heilbron, 'Moseley, Henry Gwyn Jeffreys', *DSB*
Archives MHS Oxf., experimental apparatus · MHS Oxf., papers · NRA, priv. coll., family corresp. | CUL, letters to Lord Rutherford
Likenesses photographs, MHS Oxf.
Wealth at death £1799 6s. 1d.: administration with will, 27 May 1916, *CGPLA Eng. & Wales*

Moseley, Henry Nottidge (1844–1891), naturalist, was born at St Ann's Hill, Wandsworth, Surrey, on 14 November 1844, the son of Henry *Moseley (1801–1872), the mathematician, and Harriet, daughter of William Nottidge of Wandsworth Common. He was educated at Harrow School, where he was an undistinguished student except for his 'experiments on plants, preservation of insects, etc.' (Bourne, vi). In 1864 he entered Exeter College, Oxford. His family hoped that he would take a degree in either mathematics or classics, but these subjects proved so uncongenial to him that he was finally allowed to work with George Rolleston, Linacre professor of human anatomy, physiology, and comparative anatomy. In 1868 Moseley came out with a first class in the natural science schools. Elected to the Radcliffe travelling fellowship in 1869, Moseley, with his close friend, Edwin Ray Lankester, went to Vienna and studied in Rokitanski's laboratory. On returning to England Moseley entered as a medical student at University College, London. In 1871, again with Lankester, who was later to succeed him as Linacre professor, he went to the continent and studied at Leipzig under Professor Carl Ludwig. In 1869 Ludwig had set up his physiological institute at Leipzig, where he was to train an entire generation of physiologists. There Lankester and Moseley, along with the many Britons who followed them, were introduced to the latest experimental techniques which they applied to the study of comparative anatomy. From Leipzig Moseley published his first scientific memoir, 'Ein Verfahren um die Blutgefässe der Coleopteren auszuspritzen' (*Berichte über Die Verhandlungen der Königlich. Sächsische Gesellschaft der Wissenschaften: Mathematische-physische* Classe 1, 1821, 3.276–8).

Moseley had said 'that his favourite reading was Robinson Crusoe, and that he first acquired from Defoe's story the desire to see foreign countries and study their inhabitants and productions' (Bourne, vi). Another childhood influence was Darwin's account of his voyage on the *Beagle*, and, like Darwin, after being invited to join an expedition—that of the *Eclipse* to Ceylon in the autumn of 1871—Moseley never returned to the practice of medicine. During the voyage he made valuable spectroscopic observations in the neighbourhood of Trincomalee and he also formed a miscellaneous collection of natural history objects, including a quantity of land planarians, which he carefully studied on his return to Oxford. The results of this investigation, *On the Anatomy and Histology of the Land Planarians of Ceylon* (1874), were read before the Royal Society.

In 1872 Moseley was appointed one of the naturalists on the scientific staff of the *Challenger*, and accompanied that expedition in its four-year voyage round the world. There being no botanist attached to the expedition, Moseley undertook the collection of plants, and wherever the expedition landed his zeal as a collector led him always to remain on shore until the last moment, trusting his shipmates to retrieve him, and on one occasion the ship had to turn back—he had been left behind at Kerguelen's Land.

Back in England in 1876 Moseley was elected to a fellowship at his old college (Exeter), and spent several years at Oxford working out the results of the expedition and preparing his reports, as well as writing important memoirs on the corals and their allies.

In the summer of 1877 Moseley was commissioned by an English company to report on certain lands in California and Oregon. He took the opportunity to visit Washington Territory, Puget Sound, and Vancouver Island, and to study some of the Indian nations of America. On his return he published a book on *Oregon* (1878), for which he received a formal vote of thanks from the legislative assembly of that state.

In 1879 Moseley was elected a fellow of the Royal Society, and was also appointed assistant registrar to the University of London, a post he held until 1881, when he succeeded his friend and teacher, Rolleston, in the Linacre professorship of human and comparative anatomy at Oxford. (At the same time a new chair of physiology was created.) He became, *ex officio*, a fellow of Merton College.

On 24 February 1881 Moseley married Amabel Nevile Gwyn Jeffreys (*d.* 1927), the daughter of the conchologist John Gwyn *Jeffreys. She travelled with Moseley, assisted him with his work, and shared his enthusiasm for the natural world. She tended Moseley during his long, final illness, and after his early death she was left to raise a son Henry Gwyn Jeffreys *Moseley (1887–1915), and two daughters.

Moseley was a tireless worker. He put enormous effort into his research and teaching. In addition his administrative duties were daunting. Within Oxford he worked tirelessly at the Sisyphian task of reviving the natural science schools, and he secured the Pitt-Rivers anthropological collection for the university, which he then took on the task of housing and organizing.

Outside Oxford, Moseley served twice on the council of the Royal Society, and was on that of the Zoological Society, of which he had become a fellow in 1879, as well as on the council of the Anthropological Institute, which he joined in 1885. He was, besides, a fellow of the Linnean Society from 1880, and of the Royal Geographical Society from 1881. In 1884 he was president of section D of the British Association at Montreal, and received the honorary degree of LLD from McGill University. He was also a founder and member of council of the Marine Biological Association.

Moseley's principal characteristic was an inborn aversion to accept any statement or recorded observation which he had not been able to verify for himself. He was an effective lecturer, very genial outside the classroom, and a staunch friend. Scientifically Moseley, like Lankester and T. H. Huxley, was among the group in Britain who created the new field of biology.

Among Moseley's scientific achievements may be named his discovery of a system of tracheal vessels in *Peripatus* that furnished a new clue to the origin of tracheae, and the memoir on *Peripatus* itself constituted an important contribution towards a knowledge of the phylogeny of arthropods. His investigations on living corals cleared up many doubtful points concerning the relationships between the members of that group, and led to the establishment of the group of hydrocorallin. Moseley also was the discoverer of the eyes on the shells of several species of chiton and his last publication, *On the Presence of Eyes in the Shells of Certain Chitonjdae* (1855), was devoted to its minute structures. It was in recognition of such services to biological science that the Royal Society in 1887 awarded him its royal medal.

Moseley's *Notes by a Naturalist on the Challenger* (1879, 2nd edn 1892) appealed to the widest circle of readers, and approached Darwin's *Journal of the Cruise of the Beagle* in interest and importance. To the official reports of the results of the cruise he contributed a portion of the 'Narrative' and two independent zoological reports: one *On Certain … Corals*, and the other *On the Structure of the Peculiar Organs on the Head of Ipnops*. During his career he also contributed upwards of thirty papers to scientific journals, besides writing the section on zoology for the *Admiralty Manual of Scientific Enquiry* (1886).

Unfortunately the pace of Moseley's life damaged his health. For years before his final illness he suffered from headaches, and depression. In 1887 his health gave way, as a result, it was believed, of overwork. After that date he never again carried out his duties as Linacre chair—he was succeeded by his lifelong friend Lankester—and on 10 November 1891 he succumbed to an attack of bronchitis and died at Firwood, Clevedon, Somerset.

B. B. WOODWARD, *rev.* TERRIE M. ROMANO

Sources G. C. Bourne, 'Memoir', in H. N. Moseley, *Notes by a naturalist* (1892) · *The Times* (13 Nov 1891) · W. J. O'Connor, *Founders of British physiology: a biographical dictionary, 1820–1885* (1988) · Foster, *Alum. Oxon.* · *Nature*, 45 (1891–2), 79–80 · private information, 1894 · b. cert. · m. cert.
Archives NHM, journal of HMS *Challenger* · Oxf. U. Mus. NH, corresp. and MSS · U. Oxf., department of zoology, drawings and photographs | ICL, T. H. Huxley MSS · NL Scot., letters to John Burdon Sanderson · Oxf. U. Mus. NH, letters to Sir E. B. Poulton · UCL, letters to John Burdon Sanderson
Likenesses photograph, repro. in Bourne, 'Memoir', in Moseley, *Notes by a naturalist*, frontispiece · photographs, U. Oxf., department of zoology · photogravure, NPG · wood-engraving, NPG; repro. in *ILN* (28 Nov 1891)
Wealth at death £14,586 12s. 4d.: probate, 13 Jan 1892, *CGPLA Eng. & Wales*

Moseley, Humphrey (*b.* in or before 1603, *d.* 1661), bookseller, son of Thomas Moseley of London, a cook, was bound apprentice to the London bookseller Matthew Lownes on 27 March 1620, and freed by translation from the Cooks' Company into the Stationers' Company on 7 May 1627, by which time he must have reached the age of twenty-four. His father had died before he began his apprenticeship and the name of his mother is not known. Moseley married at an unknown date; he and his wife, Anne (*d.* 1673), had three daughters between 1640 and 1646, of whom only the eldest, Anne, reached adulthood. A fourth child was stillborn in October 1653 and was buried, like their other two daughters Mary and Elizabeth, at the parish church of St Gregory by Paul's, London.

On becoming a freeman Moseley went into business with the bookseller Nicholas Fussell. They carried on a flourishing trade in books at the sign of the Ball in St Paul's Churchyard, and issued a small number of titles under their own imprint between 1629 and 1634, including Donne's *Six Sermons upon Several Occasions*. The partnership was dissolved some time after Moseley had been admitted to the livery of the Stationers' Company on 28 October 1633. He set up his first independent shop at the sign of the Three Kings, against the north-eastern wall of the cathedral, in 1634, but by 1638 he had acquired the premises across the churchyard that he occupied for the rest

of his life at the sign of the Prince's Arms. Between 1638 and the start of the civil war he published three or four books a year, of varying quality, one of which, a hybrid between courtesy book and verse miscellany entitled *The Academy of Compliments* (1640), catered to the taste of middle-class readers and would reach a ninth edition by 1650. From 1645, however, when Moseley reissued Thomas Walkley's edition of Waller's *Poems* and followed up its success with the *Poems* of Milton, he steadily established himself as 'the most prestigious literary publisher of the time' (Potter, 20). Over the next fifteen years the list of poets and dramatists whose works appeared under his imprint included Crashaw, Shirley, Suckling, Beaumont and Fletcher, Cowley, Davenant, Denham, Carew, Cartwright, Stanley, Vaughan, Brome, Middleton, and Massinger. His astute exploitation of the taste for literature associated with the cultural traditions of the Caroline era helped to confirm 'the single-author edition of lyric poetry' as 'a familiar phenomenon in the world of publication' (Marotti, 262) and to establish the individual canons of the dramatists featured in his other major pioneering venture, the 'serial publication of octavo play collections' (Kewes, 'Pocket-books' 8). The same commercial acumen informed his practice of issuing extensive catalogues of his own publications and his 'sensitivity to the untapped market for romance literature', which led him to commission translations of such continental bestsellers as Madeleine de Scudéry's *Ibrahim* (1652) (ibid., 6).

A more ideological commitment is discernible, however, in the prefaces and epistles with which Moseley both introduced new volumes to the public and promoted his own role as 'the preserver of an endangered Royalist or loyalist body of texts' (Marotti, 261). Suckling's plays and poems were recommended in 1646 to 'knowing Gentlemen' who, in 'this Age of Paper prostitutions', were alone capable of looking upon them 'with Civility and Understanding' (Reed, 76). With forty-three pages of commendatory material, the 1647 folio of Beaumont and Fletcher was virtually 'a literary manifesto of Cavalier writers' (Wright, 82); and in his collected edition of Cartwright in 1651 Moseley provided an even greater number of royalist sympathizers with 'a platform' from which they could blame parliament for 'the cultural degeneration' of the present (Potter, 21). When he printed the *Last Remains* of Suckling in 1659, he had the confidence to praise the poet as one who 'liv'd only long enough to see the Sun-set of that Majesty from whose auspicious beams he derived his lustre', and also to congratulate himself as one who had '(now for many years) annually published the Productions of the best Wits of our own, and Forein Nations' (Reed, 101).

Moseley was elected to the governing body of the Stationers' Company in July 1651 and from March 1653 attended meetings relatively regularly. He was elected an upper warden of the company on 7 July 1659, but prolonged illness prevented him from taking an active part in the proceedings of the company during his term. He died on 31 January 1661 and was buried in St Gregory by Paul's on 4 February. Moseley was survived by his wife (who carried on his business until 1664), his eldest daughter, his two brothers, Thomas and Charles, and his two sisters, Frances Hayward and the wife of Richard Frampton.

ROBERT WILCHER

Sources J. C. Reed, 'Humphrey Moseley, publisher', *Oxford Bibliographical Society Proceedings and Papers*, 2 (1930), 55–142 · P. Kewes, '"Give me the sociable pocket-books": Humphrey Moseley's serial publication of octavo play collections', *Publishing History*, 38 (1995), 5–21 · D. F. McKenzie, ed., *Stationers' Company apprentices*, [1]: *1605–1640* (1961) · A. F. Marotti, *Manuscript, print, and the English Renaissance lyric* (Ithaca, 1995), 259–65 · L. Potter, *Secret rites and secret writing: royalist literature, 1641–1660* (1989), 19–22 · L. B. Wright, 'The reading of plays during the puritan revolution', *Huntington Library Bulletin*, 6 (1934), 73–108 · G. B. Evans, '*Comedies, tragi-comedies, with other poems* by Mr William Cartwright (1651): a bibliographical study', *The Library*, 4th ser., 23 (1942–3), 12–22 · P. Kewes, *Authorship and appropriation: writing for the stage in England, 1660–1710* (1998), 183–9 · *STC, 1475–1640* · P. W. M. Blayney, *The bookshops in Paul's Cross churchyard* (1990), 15–16, 67–9 · P. Lindenbaum, 'Humphrey Moseley', *The British literary book trade, 1475–1700*, ed. J. K. Bracken and J. Silver, DLitB, 170 (1996)
Wealth at death various bequests, incl. 20 marks to brother Thomas; 20 shillings to Thomas's wife; £10 to nephew, Thomas; 40 shillings each to nieces; £10 to sister Frances; residue to be divided equally between wife and daughter: will, 30 April 1660, repr. Reed, 'Humphrey Moseley', appx 4, 139–42

Moser, George Michael (1706–1783), chaser and enameller, was born at Schaffhausen, Switzerland, on 17 January 1706, the son of Michael Moser (1683–1739), a highly skilled coppersmith with a knowledge of mechanics and hydraulics. According to Füesslin, Moser moved to Geneva in 1725 and to London in 1726, where he arrived on Easter day, having travelled via Paris and Versailles (Füesslin, 130–32).

In London Moser was first employed by a coppersmith, and then, as a chaser of furniture mounts, by Mr Trotter, a cabinet-maker and upholsterer in Soho. For seven years from about 1730, Moser worked for John Valentine Haidt (1700–1780), a German chaser who joined the Moravian Brethren, became a painter, and died in Bethlehem, Pennsylvania. Moser and Haidt initiated a life class in Haidt's house in Salisbury Court, Fleet Street.

Moser married Mary (1709/10–1782), aged twenty, the daughter of Claude Guynier, an artist from Grenoble, at St Benet Paul's Wharf on 31 January 1730. He paid rates in James Street, Covent Garden, from 1730 to 1732. A son, George Michael, was baptized at St Paul's, Covent Garden, on 15 March 1732, but it seems likely that he died in childhood. In 1737 Moser became the ratepayer on a house (later numbered as 7) in Craven Buildings, off Drury Lane, where he lived until he moved into Old Somerset House in the early 1770s. A daughter, Mary *Moser, the flower painter, was baptized at St Clement Danes on 22 November 1744.

During the 1740s Moser became established as the finest gold-chaser of his generation and an increasingly prominent member of the artistic community. In 1742 Vertue noted that Moser:

> makes great improvements in his Art of Chaseing. who from a low beginning as working in brass-work now by Study & drawing in the [St Martin's Lane] Accadamy &c about this

time has the reputation of the best workman in that way of chaseing Gold smallworks. for watches boxes. Trinkletts etc. (Vertue, *Note books*, 3.107)

He also praised Moser for the gold box chased on the lid with a scene of Mucius Scaevola dated 1741 (Metropolitan Museum of Art, New York). Vertue listed Moser among the members of the Rose and Crown Club, admired his skill in the life class of the St Martin's Lane Academy in 1744–5, and described him as one of the 'principal Directors' of the academy in 1746 (Vertue, *Note books*, 6.171). In 1755 Jean André Rouquet wrote that he knew of only one chaser 'whose abilities really deserve the attention of the curious, and the approbation of his profession: this is Mr. Mosar who has been in possession of both for these many years' (Rouquet, 85).

From the time of his entry into the select group of managers of the St Martin's Lane Academy until his appointment as first keeper of the Royal Academy, Moser was never far from the centre of the artists' attempts to promote instruction and exhibitions. He was among the artists elected on 31 December 1746 as governors of the Foundling Hospital. *The Plan of an Academy*, published in 1755, included chasing among the 'Performances, in which, Art and Genius, Elegance of Fancy, and Accuracy of Workmanship are confessedly united' (p. iv), and listed Moser in the committee chaired by Francis Hayman. Hayman had been Moser's next-door neighbour at 8 Craven Buildings, from about 1743 to 1753.

An indication of Moser's stature in the newly founded Society of Artists is found in *The Combat* (impression in the British Museum, London), an anonymous satirical print of 1762, in which Moser stands prominently at Hayman's shoulder in the ranks of the society which are ranged against William Hogarth mounted as Don Quixote. The caption describes Moser as 'A Swiss Operator who gives a Gusto to the Pallet, rectifys the optick Nerves, and restores Taste to Manufactures' (Paulson, 2.350).

Moser was named a director in the *Charter of Incorporation of the Society of Artists* granted on 26 January 1765. Although he was one of the eight directors who held their seats on 18 October 1768, he resigned with the seven others on 10 November. On 28 November Francis Cotes, Benjamin West, William Chambers, and Moser petitioned the king to patronize a royal academy. Both Moser and his daughter Mary are named in the instrument of foundation dated 10 December 1768. He was elected keeper on 14 December. In Zoffany's *The Academicians of the Royal Academy* (1771–2), he is to be seen adjusting the model.

In 1781 Moser took on the additional task of deputizing for Richard Wilson as librarian, when the latter became ill. Moser's wife, Mary, was buried on 22 August 1782, and he died in New Somerset House on 23 January 1783. At his burial on 30 January at St Paul's, Covent Garden, 'he was followed to his grave in grand funeral pomp by all the capital artists, Sir Josh. Reynolds at their head as chief mourner, Sir Wm. Chambers, &c' (*GM*, 53, 1783, 180). Reynolds's obituary recorded Moser's 'sincere and ardent piety', and paid tribute to his achievements as 'the FATHER of the present race of Artists', because of his teaching in the academies of London for fifty years, and as a gold chaser 'in which art he has always been considered as holding the first rank' (Reynolds, 1.xlvii–xlviii). His extensive collection of works of art was dispersed by Mr Hutchinson in auctions between 17 March and 7 July 1783.

In 1803 George III remembered Moser as a keeper who had had 'zeal as well as ability' (Farington, *Diary*, 6.2199). Zeal was a hallmark of Moser's character, and it sometimes caused friction. He unsuccessfully championed a drawing by Sir Robert Strange in 1765 with a 'warmth and zeal' which staggered his fellow directors of the Incorporated Society of Artists (Strange, 47). In 1775 he clashed with Giovanni Battista Cipriani when the latter was visitor, responsible for the posing of the model in the life school at the Royal Academy. Yet it was the same energy which inspired his teaching, and Reynolds stressed his 'amiable disposition'; 'all that knew him were his friends' (Reynolds, 1.xlvi–xlviii). Lorenz Spengler, the future keeper of the Danish royal *Kunstkammer*, described him in 1743 as 'der freundlichste Herr von der Welt' ('the friendliest man in the world'; Schnetzler, 174).

Moser's career as a gold chaser extended through the rococo into neo-classicism. His signed figure scenes, usually taken from ancient history or mythology, date from the late 1730s to the late 1770s. From the 1750s onwards he also painted in enamel, at first in polychrome, and later *en grisaille* in the style of cameos. His work is particularly associated with watches by Thomas Mudge, George Graham, William Webster, and the firm of Ellicott. In addition to the Mucius Scaevola box, Moser's most ambitious works include a freedom box in the Danish royal collection, a chased and enamelled box in the National Museums of Scotland, boxes in the Gilbert collection, London, and an étui in the Museum zu Allerheiligen, Schaffhausen.

Moser was introduced to the royal family by Lord Bute, and he designed the great seal of George III, in use from 1764 to 1784. The king gave him a 'hatful of guineas' for an enamel (*GM*, 53, 1783, 180), but it is not known if this was the watchcase which he painted for Queen Charlotte with portraits of her two oldest sons (priv. coll.). He was also a medallist, and designed the interior decoration of the rotunda in Vauxhall Gardens. Designs for watchcases and a candlestick by Moser are in the Victoria and Albert Museum, London. RICHARD EDGCUMBE

Sources Vertue, *Note books*, vols. 3, 6 · J. A. Rouquet, *The present state of the arts in England* (1755) · J. C. Füesslin, *Geschichte der besten Künstler in der Schweiz*, 4 (1774), 129–38 · J. Reynolds, *Public Advertiser* (30 Jan 1783); repr. in *The literary works of Sir Joshua Reynolds*, 2nd edn, 1 (1798), xlvi–xlix · *GM*, 1st ser., 53 (1783), 94, 180 · R. Strange, *An enquiry into the rise and establishment of the Royal Academy of Arts* (1775) · E. Edwards, *Anecdotes of painters* (1808); facs. edn (1970) · *The plan of an academy* (1755) · B. Schnetzler, 'Georg Michael Moser', *Schaffhauser Biographien IV: Schaffhauser Beiträge zur Geschichte*, 58 (1981), 173–8 [with bibliography] · R. Paulson, *Hogarth: his life, art and times*, 2 vols. (1971) · Farington, *Diary* · R. Edgcumbe, *The art of the gold chaser in eighteenth-century London* (2000) · V. Nelson, *John Valentine Haidt* (1966) [exhibition catalogue, Abby Aldrich Rockefeller Folk Art Collection, Williamsburg, VA] · B. Allen, 'Carl Marcus Tuscher: a German artist in London', *Apollo*, 122 (1985), 32–5 ·

C. Eimer, *The Pingo family and medal making in eighteenth-century Britain* (1998) · M. Snodin and E. Moncrieff, eds., *Rococo: art and design in Hogarth's England* (1984) [exhibition catalogue, V&A, 16 May – 30 Sept 1984] · I. Bignamini and M. Postle, *The artist's model* (1991) [exhibition catalogue, University Art Gallery, Nottingham, 30 April – 31 May 1991, and Iveagh Bequest, Kenwood, 19 June – 31 Aug 1991] · M. Postle, 'The St Martin's Lane Academy', *Apollo*, 132 [i.e. 134] (1991), 33–8 · minute books, RA · W. H. Hunt, ed., *The registers of St Paul's Church, Covent Garden, London*, 5, Harleian Society, register section, 37 (1909), 131

Archives RA, corresp. and MSS

Likenesses C. M. Tuscher, oils, 1741–3, Geffrye Museum, London · group portrait, oils, *c*.1761 ('An academy by lamplight': the St Martin's Lane Academy), RA · etching, *c*.1762, BM · J. Zoffany, group portrait, oils, 1771–2 (*The Academicians of the Royal Academy*), Royal Collection · R. Earlom, mezzotint, 1773 (after J. Zoffany) · E. Burney, ink and coloured wash drawing, 1779, RA · group portrait, 1780–83 (*The Antique School of the Royal Academy at New Somerset House*), RA · T. Rowlandson, caricature, ink over graphite on paper, *c*.1815, Yale U. CBA, Paul Mellon Collection · G. Dance, drawing, RA · T. Rowlandson, drawing, BM · T. Rowlandson, pen-and-ink caricature, BM · etching, repro. in Füesslin, *Geschichte der besten Künstler in der Schweiz* · watercolour, NPG; repro. in J. Northcote, *The life of Sir Joshua Reynolds*, 2 vols. (1818), vol. 2

Wealth at death He made no will. Administration of his goods granted to Mary Moser, daughter, 10 Feb 1783 (PRO PROB/6/159, fol. 401)

Moser, Joseph (1748–1819), writer and magistrate, was born in Greek Street, Soho, London, in June 1748, the son of Hans Jacob Moser, a Swiss artist, and nephew of the enamellist George Michael Moser (1706–1783). He was instructed in enamel painting by his uncle, and exhibited at the Royal Academy from 1774 to 1782, and again in 1787, but after his marriage in 1780 to a daughter of Peter Liege, an eminent London surgeon, he retired to the country. After three years Moser returned to London, where he wrote for the *European Magazine* and other periodicals, and published many ephemeral political pamphlets, dramas, and works of fiction. Among these was his *Anecdotes of Richard Brothers* (1795), a negative account of the religious enthusiast and his supporter Nathaniel Brassey Halhed.

About 1794 Moser was appointed a deputy lieutenant for Middlesex and a magistrate for Westminster, sitting first at the Queen Square court and subsequently at Worship Street. He held this post until his death at Romney Terrace, Westminster, on 22 May 1819.

F. M. O'DONOGHUE, rev. JOHN D. HAIGH

Sources *GM*, 1st ser., 89/1 (1819), 653 · *European Magazine and London Review*, 44 (1803), 83–5 · D. E. Baker, *Biographia dramatica, or, A companion to the playhouse*, rev. I. Reed, new edn, rev. S. Jones, 1 (1812), 527 · W. T. Lowndes, *The bibliographer's manual of English literature*, ed. H. G. Bohn, [new edn], 6 vols. (1864)

Likenesses W. Ridley, stipple (after S. Drummond), BM, NPG; repro. in *European Magazine* (Aug 1803)

Moser [married name Lloyd], **Mary** (1744–1819), flower painter, was born in London on 27 October 1744, the only surviving child of George Michael *Moser (1706–1783), a gold-chaser and painter in enamels who emigrated to England from Schaffhausen, Switzerland, and Mary (1709/10–1782), the daughter of the painter Claude Guynier of Grenoble. Mary Moser trained with her father, and in 1758 at the age of fourteen she won a prize of £5 in the category of drawings of ornament for girls under eighteen from the

Society for the Encouragement of Art, Manufacture, and Commerce. In the following year she was awarded a silver medal by the same body in the category of polite arts for a painting of flowers. After 1760 Moser exhibited with the Society of Artists until 1768, when she and her father were elected as founding members of the Royal Academy of Art, and George Michael Moser became the first keeper of the academy. Mary Moser and Angelica Kauffman were the only women among the thirty-six founding members. Though considered full academicians they were not expected to attend meetings; however, both participated in votes for annual prizes and the election of new members by sending their ballots to the president. In her later years Moser attended some of the meetings in person.

Moser was one of two founding members designated as flower painters. A tempera painting on paper (1764) of a vase filled with a variety of flowers (V&A) provides evidence of her skill in this genre. She produced botanically accurate studies of individual flowers, such as the seven watercolours of tulips in the Victoria and Albert Museum, in addition to paintings of elaborate arrangements of flowers, some of which were intended to convey symbolic meaning. Six of her pictures in the Fitzwilliam Museum, Cambridge, represent the signs of the zodiac as still lifes of flowers appropriate to the seasons displayed in vases decorated with astrological symbols. According to Joseph Farington, Queen Charlotte employed Moser as drawing mistress for the royal princesses.

In a self-portrait (c.1780; Schaffhausen, Switzerland) Moser represented herself at work on a still-life painting of fruit. She holds her brush poised over the canvas while looking over her shoulder at the viewer. Though Moser gained recognition and the patronage of Queen Charlotte for her flower paintings in oil, watercolour, and gouache, the thirty-six pictures she exhibited at the Royal Academy also included literary and classical subjects, such as *Venus and Cupid* (1776), *Theseus Finding his Father's Sword and Sandals* from Plutarch (1783), and *Cymon and Iphegenia* from Dryden's poem (1789).

Moser's best-known and most elaborate work was the decorative programme made for Queen Charlotte at Frogmore House, Windsor, between 1792 and 1795. According to Joseph Nollekens, Moser received the large sum of £900 for this commission. Designed to simulate a conservatory open to the sky, the room was ornamented with flowers painted in oil directly on the walls as well as large inset canvases (oil) that created the illusion of intricate flower garlands cascading from large stone planters and suspended overhead.

Moser is described as cheerful and intelligent, and her letters reveal an amiable disposition. She had numerous friends, including her fellow artists Benjamin West and Joseph Nollekens and their wives, Richard Cosway, and Maria Hadfield Cosway. In her youth Moser was said to have been infatuated with the artist Henry Fuseli; her letters to him and others contain witty observations about artists, art exhibitions, current fashions, and mutual friends. Moser remained single until 26 October 1793, when she married Captain Hugh Lloyd, a widower. She

continued to paint as Mary Lloyd or Mrs Lloyd until 1802, when increasing near-sightedness made work too difficult. Moser died on 2 May 1819 at her home, 21 Upper Thornhaugh Street, London, and was buried eight days later in Kensington, London, beside her husband, who had predeceased her by many years. Her will (1801) shows that she had considerable wealth and was able to provide for several of her female friends and relatives.

WENDY WASSYNG ROWORTH

Sources J. T. Smith, *Nollekens and his times*, 2nd edn, 2 vols. (1829) · E. C. Clayton, *English female artists*, 2 vols. (1876) · M. Pointon, 'Working, earning, bequeathing: Mary Grace and Mary Moser', *Strategies for showing: women, possession, and representation in English visual culture, 1665–1800* (1997), 131–71 · '…ihr werten Frauenzimmer, auf!', *Malerinnen der Aufklärung* (1993), 91–2 [exhibition catalogue, Roselius-Haus, Bremen, Germany, 1993] · M. Zweig, 'Mary Moser', *The Connoisseur Yearbook* (1956), 104–10 · D. Gaze, ed., *Dictionary of women artists*, 2 vols. (1997) · Graves, *RA exhibitors* · S. C. Hutchison, *The history of the Royal Academy, 1768–1986*, 2nd edn (1986) · W. T. Whitley, *Artists and their friends in England, 1700–1799*, 2 vols. (1928); repr. (1968) · *Women's art show, 1550–1970* (1982), 45 [exhibition catalogue, Nottingham Castle Museum] · *The collected English letters of Henry Fuseli*, ed. D. H. Weinglass (1982)
Archives priv. coll., MSS letters
Likenesses J. Zoffany, group portrait, oils, 1771–2 (*The Academicians of the Royal Academy*), Royal Collection · M. Moser, self-portrait, oils, 1780?, Museum zu Allerheiligen, Sturzenegger-Stiftung, A-1669 Schaffhausen, Switzerland · H. Singleton, group portrait, oils, 1795 (The Royal Academicians in general assembly), RA · G. Bestland, portrait, 1802 (after H. Singleton), BM
Wealth at death unspecified sum in Long Annuities; £7000 as beneficiary of her cousin Joseph Moser's will; bequests in excess of £1200 to friends and family; also bequeathed a silver tea set, jewellery, drawings, prints, and books of prints: will, 1801, PRO, PROB 11/1617, sig. 283, cited in Pointon, 'Working', n. 40; Smith, *Nollekens*

Moses, Elias (1783–1868), clothing retailer and manufacturer, was born on 4 April 1783 in Bungay, Suffolk, the son of Isaac Moses, a Jewish leather merchant from Alsace. His early life remains obscure, but he probably dealt in secondhand clothing in East Anglia before moving to the City of London by the early 1830s. With his wife, Judith (1780–1825), he had six children, including his eldest son, Isaac Moses [**Isaac Moses Marsden** (1809–1884)], with whom he established the firm of E. Moses & Son.

Many of the early retailers of ready-made clothing were Jews and, whether they were based in London or the provinces, often came from a background of dealing in secondhand clothes (slops). By the early 1800s slop dealers were often also textile merchants and, inevitably, making up garments on the side. The retailing of these new garments was typically based in the merchant's warehouse, which doubled as a shop. Indeed, in many of the clothing warehouses tailors might be employed to cut and assemble garments. In the 1820s and 1830s fabric prices fell, and demand for new clothes increased. It was the slop sellers who began to meet the growing demand for cheap standard garments, and clothes retailing became more specialized. In London, in particular, the emergence of high-street stores was obvious, and many of the Jewish former slop sellers moved into the manufacturing and retailing of ready-made clothing.

In 1832 Elias and Isaac Moses established their partnership, first in Ratcliffe Highway in the East End, and soon afterwards in Aldgate, on the edge of the City. There they profited from the increase in demand for emigrant outfits as migration to Australia surged in the early 1840s. In 1846 the original shop's floor space was extended fourfold, and then sevenfold, as the Ready-Made Clothing Emporium at Aldgate became the largest shop in London. By the 1860s E. Moses & Son had several branches throughout Britain and the empire.

Moses operated on what was still a fairly novel concept of low margins on a high turnover. Success depended on being able to keep the prices low and demand growing. Prices were kept low through a combination of cost-cutting in manufacturing and obtaining discounts on fabrics. The application of the techniques of subdivision and specialization in the manufacturing of standard garments was taken to new lengths by manufacturers of ready-made garments in the 1830s and 1840s. Jobs were generally contracted out to small workshops, where conditions of work prompted cries of outrage by the Christian socialists in the early 1840s. It is not known if Moses was one of the worst 'sweaters' of female labour (it was competitor firms which stood accused by Tom Hood and Charles Kingsley), but the vast majority of clothes sold in London shops were put out to East End contractors. In 1851 more than a quarter of all the female tailors in England and Wales lived in the East End.

Manufacturing costs were also kept low through forcing fabric producers to pass on sizeable discounts. Textile firms were happy to do this because of the size of orders Moses was able to put through. Indeed, family alliances through marriage ensured that the second largest retailers were brought into the fold, when Isaac married Rachel, the daughter of Hyam Hyams, another Jewish entrepreneur in the ready-made clothing industry. The Hyams family was already linked to the Leicester-based clothing manufacturers of Hart and Levy, who went on to become one of the largest clothing manufacturers in Britain. Rachel died in 1836 and Isaac married on 25 May 1845 Esther Gomes (1825–1908). In 1865 he adopted the additional surname Marsden.

The real legacy of E. Moses & Son to the world of business was in pioneering new marketing techniques. These important innovations all came in the 1840s. First, the emporium itself was designed to attract custom. It had a high classical portico, tall ground-floor windows, and bright interior lighting, and offered impeccable service to any who wandered in. No building was like it in all of London. Second, little expense was spared in advertising the top-quality clothes, available at such cheap prices and only in the emporium. The advertisements were sometimes placed in magazines but usually they were freely distributed throughout London in the form of little booklets. Many of the latter have survived and show that popular current events were used as the basis for a doggerel (probably composed by Isaac) on the emporium's virtues. Third, clearly displayed fixed prices cut out any haggling and enabled staff to spend their time cultivating the image of a well-to-do West End bespoke tailors by standing in attendance on customers.

The firm founded by Elias Moses was one of the most important retailers of ready-made clothing in the latter half of the nineteenth century. The company claimed that 80 per cent of the British population bought such clothing by 1860, which may have been an exaggeration, but not by much. By that time Britain had the most advanced clothing industry in the world and the most sophisticated retail outlets, supported by marketing techniques pioneered by E. Moses & Son. Elias Moses died on 24 January 1868 at 57 Porchester Terrace, Paddington, London; Isaac Moses Marsden died at his home, 4 Kensington Gardens Terrace, London, on 26 July 1884.   ANDREW GODLEY

Sources S. Chapman, 'The innovating entrepreneurs in the British ready-made clothing industry', *Textile History*, 24 (1993), 5–25 · P. Sharpe, 'Cheapness and economy: manufacturing and retailing ready-made clothing in London and Essex, 1830–1850', *Textile History*, 26 (1995), 203–13 · P. H. Emden, *Jews of Britain: a series of biographies* (1944), 447, 449, 548 · C. Roth, ed., *Encyclopaedia Judaica*, 16 vols. (Jerusalem, 1971–2) · A. Godley, 'The development of the UK clothing industry, 1850–1950: output and productivity growth', *Business History*, 37/4 (1995), 46–63 · private information (2004) · d. cert. · *CGPLA Eng. & Wales* (1868)
Wealth at death under £20,000: probate, 4 March 1868, *CGPLA Eng. & Wales*

Moses, Henry (d. 1870), printmaker, specialized in simple outline etchings of a variety of subjects from the first decades of the nineteenth century. No information has come to light about his birth, early life, or training, and all that is known of him is his work. Thomas Dodd described him as an 'eminent artist distinguished for the neatness and purity of outline' who attained 'the highest proficiency in the decorative and ornamental department of the arts' (Dodd). During his career he turned this skill and accuracy to a variety of subject matter. Additionally, the fact that he worked for patrons as celebrated as James Barry, William Opie, and Benjamin West, then president of the Royal Academy, suggests his reliability and sensitivity.

Henry Moses's skill as well as his diplomacy are evident from the very earliest stages of his career. This is made clear in Joseph Farington's comments on a 'young man of the name of Moses' who, in February 1808, had 'produced some etched outlines of small groupes with which West was much delighted' (Farington, *Diary*, 9.3230). Although it is probable that these particular etchings were intended as independent plates, in 1811 Moses published a volume entitled *The Gallery of Pictures Painted by Benjamin West Esqr.* with a descriptive subtitle 'Engraved in outline by Henry Moses'. As the dedication to this work refers to West's 'liberal permission ... in the free use of his Pictures', a sense of the speculative nature of this venture is evident. Moses's adherence to neo-classical styling and subject matter is also evident in this dedication's rhetorical deference to the amateur furniture designer and patron Thomas Hope.

Throughout his career, Henry Moses's output was marked by his interest in classical genre and design. His Flaxmanesque manner of etching outlines, free from shading or modelling, was not only well suited to the work of Benjamin West but also to a number of plates which depicted classical antiquities. Thomas Dodd's manuscripts record that Moses was one of the engravers attached to the British Museum and assert that he executed more than 170 plates of their 'Etruscan, Grecian, Athenian and … Sicilian' antiquities as well as many in other collections at home and abroad (Dodd). The first of these was a 3s. part-work published as *Select Greek and Roman Antiquities* (1817), which reproduced pieces from the collections at the British Museum. The next was *Selection of Ornamental Sculptures … from the Museum of the Louvre at Paris*, which Moses executed for the publisher W. B. Cooke in 1828. Apart from these plates of antiquities, Moses is known for various series of shipping and a few coastal views. It is not clear how his marine interest developed but he used outline engraving to great effect in capturing maritime life and activities in his *Sketches of Shipping* (1824), where accurately drawn ships are set in suitable port landscapes. Similarly his *Picturesque Views of Ramsgate* (1817) includes busily populated images of ships at harbour with foreground *flâneurs* and distant houses. As a group of drawings in the Victoria and Albert Museum, London, includes a female figure sketching with the aid of a camera lucida, it is possible that Moses was interested in mechanical drawing aids himself. Generally his plates are either signed 'Drawn and Engraved by H. Moses' or they bear his cipher of a superimposed 'H' and 'M'. Henry Moses died, apparently unmarried, at his home, Lincoln Villa, Cowley, Hillingdon, Middlesex, on 28 February 1870.　　　　　　　　　　　　　　　　　LUCY PELTZ

Sources Redgrave, *Artists* · T. Dodd, 'Biographies of British engravers', BL, Add. MS 33403 · Farington, *Diary* · CGPLA Eng. & Wales (1870)

Wealth at death under £600: probate, 23 March 1870, CGPLA Eng. & Wales

Moses, Miriam (1884–1965), local politician, was born on 13 November 1884 at 19 Princes Street, Spitalfields, London, one of nine surviving children of Mark Moses (1855–1921), tailor, and his wife, Hannah (Annie) Ehrenberg (1853/4–1899). Mark Moses had been born in Torun, a port on the Vistula, then part of Germany, and came to Britain as an eight-year-old immigrant child. He established himself as a master tailor in a workshop situated on the lower floors of the tall Georgian house in Princes Street (later Princelet Street) where Miriam was born. Mark Moses became a local councillor, a member of the Whitechapel board of guardians, and a school governor. He was made a JP for the City of London in 1909. An Orthodox Jew, he was also active in Jewish communal life, in several synagogues, on the Board of Deputies of British Jews, and as treasurer of the Federation of Synagogues. Miriam was educated at Old Castle Street elementary school in Whitechapel. Her mother, also an active charity worker, died in 1899 at the age of forty-five when Miriam was only fourteen. Choosing never to marry, she followed in her father's footsteps into public life and Jewish communal service.

On the death of her father in May 1921 Miriam succeeded to his seat on Stepney borough council representing Spitalfields East in the Liberal interest. During the period 1921–31 she was returned five times, always heading the poll by a significant majority. She also held office in the Whitechapel and St George's Liberal Association, of which her father had been chairman for twenty-five years. In 1931 Miriam was elected the first female mayor of Stepney. She stood as an independent, but effectively worked in the Progressive cause, in the face of Labour resentment. In fact, her popularity probably accounted for Labour's failure to take control in Spitalfields East until 1934, when she decided not to stand for re-election.

Miriam Moses combined her political work with practical engagement in social issues. She was particularly concerned to broaden opportunities for youngsters from deprived backgrounds. Among her earliest activities was the role of school manager for the Robert Montefiore and Buxton Street schools, and she was honorary secretary of the Stepney committee of the Children's Country Holiday Fund and chair of the Whitechapel Tuberculosis After-Care Committee. She was a member of the Whitechapel and Stepney board of guardians. About 1922 she became the first woman JP in Whitechapel, and she served on the east London juvenile court that sat at Toynbee Hall.

In 1925, together with Elsie Cohen, who later married Barnett Janner MP, Moses established the Brady Girls' Club at Buxton Street School. It was conceived as the girls' parallel of the Brady Boys' Club that had been founded in 1896. Miriam effectively served as club leader for thirty-three years, living in during the Second World War as warden of the purpose-built Brady Settlement which had been opened in Hanbury Street, in the East End, in 1935. Despite her progressive ideas, the boys' and girls' clubs were kept strictly apart along traditional lines. On retirement in 1958 Miriam appeared on the popular television show *This is your Life*, in which she was brought face to face with many old 'Brady girls' upon whose lives she had exerted such influence.

Miriam saw service on the home front in both world wars: as a Voluntary Aid Detachment nurse at the Bancroft Road Hospital, off London's Mile End Road, in 1914–18, and as chief air raid officer for the neighbourhood in 1939–45. The shelter was located in the basement of the Brady Settlement, and Miriam set up a hostel on the premises for girls made homeless by bombing. She was appointed OBE in 1945, not least in recognition of her outstanding bravery during air raids.

About 1914, the Moses family had moved from the East End to Stamford Hill. Miriam was active on the ladies' guild of the newly built New Synagogue, Egerton Road, not far from the family home in Colberg Place. In 1931, during the same year that she was elected first woman mayor of Stepney, Miriam was the first woman chosen to represent a constituent synagogue of the umbrella United Synagogue on the Board of Deputies of British Jews. She waged a long campaign for the right of women seat-holders to vote in elections for the United Synagogue executive. This right was eventually granted in 1954. She was a founder member and later president of the League of Jewish Women, was on the executive of the Jewish Board of Guardians, and was a vice-president of the Association of Jewish Youth.

As a pioneer woman in public life in the 1930s, Miriam Moses was in favour of the municipal provision of contraception for poor mothers, an issue that she saw as a social question divorced from religion (Marks, 267). Nevertheless, she personally remained attached to traditional Jewish practice and was known for her public observance of the Jewish sabbath and dietary laws. About 1934 Miriam Moses moved from Stamford Hill to West Hampstead. After returning to the East End during the war years, she subsequently retired to north-west London, living in turn in St John's Wood, West Hampstead, and Maida Vale. She died on 24 June 1965, aged eighty, at the Middlesex Hospital, London, and was buried three days later at the Federation Jewish cemetery, Edmonton.

SHARMAN KADISH

Sources The Times (26 June 1965) · Jewish Chronicle (2 July 1965) · East London Advertiser (2 July 1965) · Hackney Gazette (29 June 1965) · Hackney Gazette (6 July 1965) · Tower Hamlets Local History Library, Miriam Moses file [press cuttings mainly from East London Advertiser] · Jewish Year Book (1966) · A. Shapiro, ed., The life and times of Miriam Moses, O.B.E. J.P. 1886–1965: an audio-visual documentary produced by the Springboard Education Trust, 1997 [video film, text of narration, and notes] · M. Lazarus, A club called Brady (1996) · C. Magnus, ed., EMJ: the man and his work (1962) [privately printed memoir of Ernest Joseph, architect of the Brady Clubs, incl. anonymous contribution by Miriam Moses] · L. V. Marks, Model mothers: Jewish mothers and maternity provision in east London, 1870–1939 (1994), 267 · E. R. Smith, 'Jews and politics in the East End of London, 1918–1939', The making of modern Anglo-Jewry, ed. D. Cesarani (1990), 146–7 · b. cert. · CGPLA Eng. & Wales (1965) · Jewish Chronicle (22 Dec 1899) [Hannah Moses] · Jewish Chronicle (27 May 1921) [Mark Moses]
Archives FILM BFI NFTVA, documentary footage | SOUND Springboard Education Trust, London, documentary, 1997
Likenesses double portrait, photographs, 1932 (with Alderman C. Lankester), Hult. Arch.
Wealth at death £7179: probate, 9 Aug 1965, CGPLA Eng. & Wales

Moses, William (bap. 1622, d. 1688), serjeant-at-law, was born in the parish of St Saviour, Southwark, and baptized there on 15 August 1622, the son of John Moses (d. 1625/6), variously recorded as a smith and as a merchant tailor. In 1625 his parents, to escape the plague, took him and his three siblings to Stoke, near Guildford, where his mother's father, John Crow, was rector. In the event both his parents and two of his siblings died there within the year. His grandfather died in 1633, by which time Moses had been for some two years at Christ's Hospital, where he flourished and where his religious views were formed by his reading of Gulielmus Bucanus's Institutions of Christian Religion. He entered Pembroke College, Cambridge, in 1639, where patronage soon acquired him an exhibition, and his forwardness one of Dr Watts's Greek scholarships. He proceeded BA in 1644 and MA in 1647. Pembroke at the time was, according to Moses's biographer, in a depressed state, but Moses soon made a name for himself as a highly successful tutor. After the Cromwellian purges of 1644 he was one of only three Pembroke men to hold a fellowship there. The master, Richard Vines, being frequently absent,

the management of the college devolved largely on Moses. He was one of the Cromwellian visitors appointed for Cambridge in 1654. Vines was ejected for refusing the engagement of 1649 and his successor, Sidrach Simpson, also largely an absentee, died in 1655, whereupon the fellows hastily elected Moses master to prevent another Cromwellian intrusion. As master he continued to display his administrative skills, finally succeeding in realizing for the college the substantial bequest of Sir Robert Hitcham (d. 1636) of Framlingham Castle and land there and elsewhere in Suffolk. With the funds thus available Moses embarked on an ambitious building project, of which the south range of the second court, duly embellished with Hitcham's arms, was completed and much restoration of the existing buildings achieved.

In 1660, when the ejected master, Benjamin Lany, was restored, Moses betook himself to Gray's Inn and soon proved himself an accomplished lawyer, declining an invitation to serve on the presbyterian side at the Savoy conference in 1661. On 17 January 1666 he was chosen solicitor to the East India Company at £20 per annum and served until his death. His value to the company was soon recognized: in 1667 he was sent, with other representatives of the company, to the peace negotiations at Breda, and in the same year he was charged with securing counsel's opinion as to whether the company's charter empowered it to take Fort St George by force of arms; he was then charged with drawing up a petition to the king for a commission under the great seal so to take it. He was also, in this year, deeply involved in defending the company against the charges brought against it by Captain Thomas Skinner in the Lords.

For these dramatic endeavours, and from time to time for others, Moses was rewarded by gratuities from the company amounting to some hundreds of pounds. He also dealt in the company's stock, so acquiring by his death a substantial fortune. His bequests amounted to some £2000, besides real property which yielded some £8000 for exhibitions at both Christ's Hospital and Pembroke College, Cambridge, for boys proceeding from one to the other, a bequest that took so long to settle that the first recorded exhibitioners at Pembroke do not appear until 1720.

Between 26 October and his death in London on 30 October 1688, Moses was created a serjeant-at-law, having been called on 26 June of that year under the sponsorship of Sir Robert Brooke, bt, and Sir John Trevor, master of the rolls. He was buried in November 1688 in Pembroke College chapel, but, despite the wishes of his executors, no monument was erected. A portrayal of him in a window in the chapel is a work of imagination. He did not marry.

ELISABETH LEEDHAM-GREEN

Sources H. Sampson, biography, Pembroke Cam., Archives, MS Cη · account book of Moses's legal and household expenses, Jan 1679–March 1680, BL, Add. MS 26057 · A. L. Attwater, Pembroke College, Cambridge: a short history, ed. S. C. Roberts (1936) · Baker, Serjeants · CSP col., vols. 2–4, 6, 8 [East Indies]; contd as E. B. Sainsbury, A calendar of the court minutes … of the East India Company, ed. W. Foster, 11 vols. (1907–38) · J. Twigg, The University of Cambridge and the English Revolution, 1625–1688 (1990)

Wealth at death bequests of £2000; real property

Moses, William Stainton (1840–1892), spiritualist, was

the eldest son of William Stainton Moses of Dorrington, Lincolnshire. He was educated at Bedford and at Exeter College, Oxford, where he matriculated on 25 May 1858, graduating BA in 1863 and MA in 1865. During his undergraduate years he suffered a nervous breakdown. He took holy orders, and was curate of Maughold in the Isle of Man from 1863 to 1868, and assistant chaplain of St George's, Douglas, from 1868 to 1872, when he became interested in spiritualism and resigned his curacy to become English master at University College School, London. This post he held until 1890, when ill health required his resignation. During his time in London Stainton Moses devoted his leisure almost entirely to the exploration of the mysteries of spiritualism, to which he became a convert. He was the most prominent of the various Church of England clergy who involved themselves in spiritualism. He was a founder of the London Spiritualist Alliance, an active member and one of the vice-presidents of the Society for Psychical Research, a frequent contributor to *Human Nature* and to *Light*, and for some years editor of the latter journal. In 1882 he was a founder of the Ghost Club.

After an intense period of study of spiritualism in 1872, Stainton Moses became a noted medium, especially known for 'automatic writing'; a collection of these writings, *Spirit Teachings* (1883), became one of the most influential texts of British spiritualism. In the 1870s Stainton Moses's inspirational writings appeared widely in the spiritualist press, usually under the pseudonym M. A. Oxon. Specialist books bearing this pseudonym included *Psychography* (1878), *Spirit Identity* (1879), and *Higher Aspects of Spiritualism* (1880). Stainton Moses was in contact with more than eighty spirits, including the prophets Malachi, Elijah, Ezekiel, and Daniel, philosophers such as Plato, Aristotle, and Swedenborg, and public figures such as Napoleon III, President Garfield, and Samuel Wilberforce. Stainton Moses's self-deception, if such it was, has been explained by mental illness and by his growing dissatisfaction with the Church of England (Oppenheim, 78–9). He died at 30 St Peters, Bedford on 5 September 1892, his wife, Mary, surviving him. After his death he continued to play some part in British public life through his contacts with the living.   J. M. RIGG, rev. H. C. G. MATTHEW

Sources *Light*, 12 (1892), 439–40 · J. Oppenheim, *The other world: spiritualism and psychical research in England, 1850–1914* (1985) · A. Lillie, *Modern mystics* (1894) · A. W. Trethewy, *The 'controls' of Stainton Moses* (1923)

Likenesses photograph, repro. in Oppenheim, *The other world*

Wealth at death £242 9s. 7d.: administration, 4 Oct 1892, CGPLA Eng. & Wales

Moshoeshoe (c.1786–1870), paramount chief (morena o

moholo) of the southern Sotho and founder of the BaSotho (Basuto) kingdom, was born, probably about 1786, in the village of Menkhoaneng in the north of modern Lesotho, the son of Mokhachane (d. 1855), a village headman, and of his first wife, Kholu. His parents knew him as Lepoqo, meaning 'dispute', and it was as a teenager, after undergoing initiation, that he acquired a new name, after he had

Moshoeshoe (c.1786–1870), by R. S. Webb, 1860

led his age-mates on a successful cattle raid against a nearby village. 'Moshoeshoe' represented the sound of a razor shearing or shaving; he was 'the shearer' or 'the shaver'.

Moshoeshoe rose to prominence through his ability to retain the loyalty of his followers and to acquire new ones during the violent disruptions (often known as the Difaqane) on the high veld in the early 1820s. In 1824 he based himself on a steep-cliffed, flat-topped mountain known as Thaba Bosiu (the 'mountain of the night'), not far from the Caledon valley. Easily defended, it was never successfully attacked, and remained his capital until his death. From there Moshoeshoe launched many cattle raids, not only on nearby groups but even on the Thembu, south of the Drakensberg. He recruited new followers by lending cattle, as well as by winning a reputation for tolerance and magnanimity towards his enemies. In the years after 1824 his chiefdom incorporated the broken remnants of many others, and gradually a sizeable federal state was created under his authority. By 1836 he ruled an estimated 25,000 people; a decade later that number had more than doubled, as further refugees from conflicts in the region accepted his authority.

In 1843 the British governor at the Cape, Sir George Thomas Napier, agreed to sign an agreement with Moshoeshoe which established a boundary for his territory well west of the Caledon River, though Moshoeshoe himself continued to maintain that his land was anywhere his people lived. In February 1848 Sir Harry Smith, the high commissioner, proclaimed as the Orange River Sovereignty (ORS) the land between the Orange and the Vaal, and in the following year Major Henry Douglas Warden, the British resident in the ORS, drew a new boundary line which Moshoeshoe accepted only with great reluctance and his people disobeyed. When Warden sent a force against the BaSotho to compel compliance, it was defeated by a force commanded by Moshoeshoe's sons at Viervoet, near Thaba Nchu, in June 1851. Moshoeshoe then offered to hand over cattle when Smith's successor, Sir George Cathcart, sought to restore British prestige, but

Cathcart insisted that he would go to Thaba Bosiu itself to collect the cattle he wanted as compensation for the alleged wrongs done by the BaSotho. Again Moshoeshoe's forces inflicted a reverse on the British, this time at the battle of Berea (December 1852). But Moshoeshoe was at once conciliatory, telling the high commissioner that he had 'shown your power … let me be no longer considered an enemy to the Queen'. Peace, he said, 'is like the rain which makes the grass grow, while war is like the wind which dries it up'. Cathcart agreed to withdraw his forces, then called Moshoeshoe 'not only the most enlightened, but the most upright chief in South Africa' (Sanders, *Last of the Queen's Men*, 125).

Though he deplored the way the British denied his people access to firearms and attempted to push them back towards the Caledon valley, Moshoeshoe recognized the power of Britain, and realized that the Boer farmers posed a greater potential threat to his kingdom than distant Britain. After the establishment of the republic of the Orange Free State (OFS) in 1854, Boer encroachment increased, and in 1858 Moshoeshoe fought an inconclusive war (Senekal's War) with the Boer republic. In the wars against the Boers the BaSotho were limited by the inferiority of their firearms and by the prohibition, under the Bloemfontein (1852) and Sand River (1854) conventions, against their importing firearms and ammunition from the British colonies, unlike the Boers. A further conflict in 1865–6 (the War of the Canon's Boom) left the Sotho in a serious plight. When Thaba Bosiu was besieged in August 1865, Moshoeshoe was forced to sue for peace, and to agree to the treaty of Thaba Bosiu (3 April 1866), ceding much territory to the OFS. He had several times asked for 'British protection', but without success. When war broke out again in 1867, he renewed his request, recognizing that he should sacrifice a measure of independence in order that his people might retain their land. This time, in March 1868, his request was granted by High Commissioner Sir Philip Wodehouse, acting on his own initiative and presenting Gladstone's government with a *fait accompli*. Moshoeshoe told him how glad he was that 'my people should have been allowed to rest and to lie under the large folds of the flag of England before I am no more' (Sanders, *Moshoeshoe*, 300). It is clear that Moshoeshoe hoped for the loosest kind of British overlordship, and that his people would be able to regain lost land. But in 1869, when Wodehouse demarcated the boundary between the new British acquisition and the OFS, Moshoeshoe found that his people had lost all the fertile lands west of the Caledon. Though shocked by Wodehouse's concessions to the OFS, Moshoeshoe knew that had the high commissioner not granted protection, the BaSotho would have lost even more land. Moshoeshoe was already old and infirm; but the shock of the boundary demarcation must have helped bring on his death in March 1870.

Moshoeshoe had invited members of the French protestant Paris Evangelical Missionary Society to set up missions in his country in the early 1830s, and he used them to perform quasi-diplomatic functions. In his later years he lost control over his sons and subordinate chiefs, who often acted without reference to him. He long held out against becoming a Christian because most of his people remained committed to traditional beliefs, and because he was not prepared to have only one wife. About 1810 he married his first wife, Mabela ('MaMohato; *d.* 1834), daughter of Seephephe of the Bafokeng. As his wealth and power increased, he acquired more wives until almost the end of his life. Estimates of their number range from twenty to 200. He used his junior wives mainly as domestic servants, and offered them to visitors for the night by way of hospitality. In January 1870, after surrendering his chieftainship to his eldest son Letsie (1811–1891), from his first wife, Mabela, he announced his conversion to Christianity. Though the Catholic missionaries had hoped to secure his conversion, it was to the rival protestants that he turned, and he was about to be baptized by them when he died on 11 March 1870 at Thaba Bosiu, Basutoland, and was buried on the top of Thaba Bosiu. After his death he was venerated and his grave-site became a sacred place for his people.

Moshoeshoe was intelligent, a skilful warrior, and also humane. Unlike Shaka, he ruled by consultation and consent and rarely used capital punishment. He did not drink alcohol or smoke cannabis, stating they would prevent him from making wise decisions. He was a discriminating innovator who—though he never learned to read or write—sometimes wore European clothes, and valued guns, horses, new crops, and Western education. He was known among his people as *monna oa litaba*, 'the man who knows how to handle public affairs'. He created a country, was remarkably skilful in adapting to new circumstances, and showed great shrewdness in his diplomatic dealings with whites. Aware of the realities of power, he realized that in the face of white expansionist pressures, only British protection was likely to enable his people to survive as a nation. His policy of avoiding antagonizing the British paid off in 1868, when he was granted his wish to become 'a child of the Queen' (Sanders, *Moshoeshoe*, 318). His strategy of gaining British protection proved successful: 'he secured the best options that were available' (Thompson, 329). The country he had built up remained intact, if diminished in size. After intrusive Cape rule from 1871 to 1884, Basutoland returned to high commission status—the colonial government continued Moshoeshoe's ban on white land ownership—and eventually become independent Lesotho in October 1966. The unveiling of a statue of Moshoeshoe outside Maseru, the capital of the new country, by his great-great-great-grandson King Moshoeshoe II was a high point in the independence celebrations. CHRISTOPHER SAUNDERS

Sources G. M. Theal, ed., *Basutoland records*, 3 vols. (Cape Town, 1883) · L. Thompson, *Survival in two worlds: Moshoeshoe of Lesotho, 1786–1870* (1975) · P. Sanders, *Moshoeshoe, chief of the Sotho* (1975) · P. Sanders, *The last of the queen's men* (Johannesburg, 2000) · E. A. Eldredge, *A South African kingdom: the pursuit of security in nineteenth century Lesotho* (1993) · J. L. Bosch, 'Moshweshwe', *DSAB* · L. B. Machobane, *Government and change in Lesotho, 1800–1966* (1990) · B. Johannesson and others, *The land the Basotho lost: the dispossession of the Basotho kingdom in the nineteenth century* (Johannesburg, 1992) · T. Keegan, 'The making of the Orange Free State, 1846–54: sub-imperialism, primitive accumulation, and state formation', *Journal of Imperial and Commonwealth History*, 17 (1988–9), 26–54 • G. Haliburton, *Historical dictionary of Lesotho* (1977)

Archives Lesotho Evangelical Church, archives • National Archives of South Africa, Cape Town • National Archives of South Africa, Bloemfontein • Paris Evangelical Missionary Society, archives

Likenesses F. Maeder, drawing, 1845, repro. in Thompson, *Survival* • R. S. Webb, photograph, 1860, repro. in Thompson, *Survival*, frontispiece [*see illus.*] • portrait, repro. in E. Casalis, *Les Bassoutos* (Paris, 1859) • portraits, repro. in G. Y. Lagden, *The Basutos*, 2 vols. (1909) • portraits, National Archives of South Africa, Bloemfontein • statue, Maseru, Lesotho

Mosley, Charles

Mosley, Charles (d. 1756), engraver and printseller, is first mentioned on a print, *The Citadel of Plymouth*, published on 25 July 1737. At the outset of his career he probably executed copies for printsellers: *The Twelve Months*, after Josef Wagner, were probably examples of such work. He continued to engrave frontispieces and illustrations for booksellers, including five after Francis Hayman. He also produced a handful of portraits, notably of theatrical subjects such as *Mrs Clive in the Character of the Fine Lady in Lethe* (1750), and one major plate, *Calais Gate* (1749), with and after William Hogarth. He seems to have been friendly with Hubert Gravelot, for he published several of Gravelot's designs, including *The Celebrated Chimpanzee* (1738). The two men apparently collaborated on *Apelles Britannicus* (1741), a scheme to publish the best art in the royal palaces.

Mosley's own publications were chiefly topical or satirical; many were racily bawdy and some were politically sensitive. His most successful were, perhaps, four prints depicting *The European Race* (1738–40), one of which was also engraved as a fan. In 1749 Mosley ran into trouble. With several other printsellers he was examined before Lord Stanhope over his involvement in *The Cropper* and other satires on the duke of Cumberland's liaison with a Savoyard girl and about a print of 'a Woman almost naked'—probably Mosley's *Iphigenia* (1749), showing the appearance of Elizabeth Chudleigh at a masquerade. Several prints were seized from his shop by king's messengers. In his defence:

> the Examt. pretends that his Business of Print sellings is carried on by his Servt. Maid & that he does not concern himself therein. Being asked whether his Maid Servant buys & sells the obscene prints which were taken out of his Shop or how he came by them, he says that they might be left at his Shop in exchange for other prints for what he knows to the contrary; which is all he chooses to say about them; but says that he is very much ashamed that he has been concerned in such sort of prints & will not do so for the Future, intending to leave off the Business of Printselling. (Atherton, 79)

Mosley did not retire from trade, but he did stop publishing political satire. In late 1750 he moved from Old Round Court in the Strand to a new shop in Maiden Lane, Covent Garden, and in 1752 he took on Robert Sanders as apprentice. Mosley made his will on 6 May 1756, leaving £50 to Elizabeth Pattinson for mourning and his remaining property to his brothers John and William and his sister Jane Collings. He died, unmarried, on 12 May 1756. A total of 123 plates, including the offending *Iphigenia*, were mentioned in the sale of his stock that followed his death. His prints may be found in the British Museum and the National Maritime Museum, London.

TIMOTHY CLAYTON

Sources *A catalogue of the genuine and entire stock in trade of Mr Charles Moseley, printseller* (1756) [sale catalogue, Prestage, London, 14–17 June 1756] • H. Atherton, *Political prints in the age of Hogarth* (1974) • F. G. Stephens and M. D. George, eds., *Catalogue of prints and drawings in the British Museum, division 1: political and personal satires*, 3 (1877); 4 (1883) • *Engraved Brit. ports.* • B. Allen, *Francis Hayman* (1987) • 'Catalogue of prints and drawings', www.nmm.ac.uk, 11 Nov 1988 • *A catalogue of maps, prints, copy-books, &c. from off copperplates, which are printed for, and sold by Henry Overton* (1754), 49 • I. Maxted, ed., *The British book trades, 1710–1777: an index of the masters and their apprentices* (1983) • T. Clayton, *The English print, 1688–1802* (1997), 113, 148–9 • PRO, PROB 11/822, fol. 342

Mosley, Lady Cynthia Blanche

Mosley [*née* Curzon], **Lady Cynthia Blanche** (1898–1933), politician and society figure, was born at The Priory, Reigate, Surrey, on 23 August 1898, the second of three daughters of George Nathaniel *Curzon, later first Marquess Curzon of Kedleston (1859–1925), and his first wife, the American heiress Mary Victoria Leiter [see Curzon, Mary Victoria (1870–1906)]. Her parents considered giving her an Indian name, as Curzon was about to become viceroy of India, but decided that Monyabai or Gyanadai would be too much for a child. Cimmie, as she was known, lived in India until 1905 and later attended school as a boarder at The Links in Eastbourne. During the First World War she worked as a War Office clerk, earning 30s. a week, and as a land girl, where she enjoyed the change of lifestyle. She took courses in social work at the London School of Economics before utilizing her training in the East End of London. She was already something of a rebel against the dictates of her class, and her father's hope that she would marry a peer was dashed when she married the Conservative MP Oswald Ernald *Mosley (1896–1980), from 1928 sixth baronet, whom she had met during Nancy Astor's by-election campaign in 1919. Their wedding took place on 11 May 1920 in the Chapel Royal. They had two sons and a daughter.

Throughout their marriage her husband was chronically unfaithful, but Cynthia Mosley followed him loyally through the vicissitudes of his political career, joining the Labour Party with him in 1924. By any estimation they were unlikely Labour converts—'a pair of magnificent cuckoos in the Labour Party nest'—but their glamour and popular Labour garden parties at Savehay Farm, Denham, made them celebrities within the movement (Brookes, 80). They faced a bitterly hostile Conservative press and she was the likely target of the Conservative play *Lady Monica Waffle's Debut* (1926), about a rich society woman's left-wing pretensions. At party gatherings she stood out in her fur stole and jewellery, but the 'diamond dress' for which newspapers criticized her was in fact decorated with glass baubles. She was tall and attractive with dark hair, prominent teeth, and a square chin, and her father felt she looked the most 'Curzon' of his daughters, though in later years she became heavier owing to illness and stress, and one contemporary remembered her constantly wearing a sad expression.

After campaigning for her husband in 1924 Cynthia Mosley was sought as a candidate by a number of constituencies before being nominated for Stoke-on-Trent. During the general election of 1929 she was mocked for her 'Hyde Park sentiments delivered in a Park Lane accent' (Skidelsky, 159n.) and was falsely accused of neglecting an impoverished brother. (She did, though, irreparably fall out with her father over his share of her considerable American inheritance.) None the less, she won by a 7850-vote majority, the largest swing to Labour of the election and one of the largest majorities of any inter-war woman MP. The Mosleys formed the third husband-and-wife team of MPs, and he presented her with a brooch bearing '7850' set in rubies over a diamond portcullis of Westminster. However, the toll of the campaign was high, as she miscarried shortly afterwards.

Cynthia Mosley did not really understand socialism but had a long-standing sympathy for the underdog. In parliament she spoke on women's unemployment and widows' pensions, and in her memorable maiden speech she reversed the Conservative charge that unemployment insurance would 'demoralize' recipients.

> All my life I have got something for nothing ... Some people might say I showed remarkable intelligence in the choice of my parents but I put it all down to luck ... A great many people on the opposite side of the House are also in that same position ... Are we demoralised? ... I stoutly deny that I am demoralised. (Hansard 5C, 421, 31 Oct 1929)

Throughout their careers Cimmie's warmth and sincerity made her more popular and better trusted than her husband, but after he resigned ostentatiously from the Labour government in May 1930 she soon made the 'heartbreaking' decision to follow him out of the party. Despite the protests of her constituency association, many in the party still liked her and sympathized as she stood stoically by her mercurial and often cruel husband. Begging Trotsky for a visit in September, she told him she thought 'less than nothing' of the Labour government, but 'am a great admirer of yours'. She later swam the Bosphorus from Asia to Europe in 40 minutes ('I thought it so terribly in the Grand Style and Byronic and even rather Mosley' (N. Mosley, 160). She campaigned for her husband's 'New Party', but health considerations and political disillusionment prompted her not to seek re-election. After the party fared poorly in the 1931 election—Oswald came in last place when he stood for Cynthia's Stoke-on-Trent constituency—the New Party became in 1932 the British Union of Fascists (BUF). The violent struggle which he now believed was necessary was abhorrent to her gentle nature, and she threatened to distance herself from the BUF with a newspaper advertisement. But typically she remained publicly loyal, joining him and Mussolini at a fascist parade in Rome and investigating possible designs for a British fascist flag.

Despite the advantages which Cynthia Mosley brought her husband, it is difficult to consider her career as anything but an adjunct to his, and in some ways she was a victim of it. One colleague wrote that she was 'sacrificed to her husband's hurried ambitions' (Hamilton, 181), and she was probably better suited to home and society than to politics. She made little impact in parliament, where her artless speaking style contrasted with her father's, and her own conclusion was that the Commons was futile and a waste of time; among women MPs she is unique if only for subsequently rejecting parliamentarianism. In May 1931 she told readers of the Daily Sketch of her daunting thought that in parliament 'it does not really matter what you say, that it will have no effect on anyone at all, and that you might as well not say it' (N. Mosley, 204). When taunted in parliament that July about her six months' absence, her riposte was to say that 'going round the country ... to rouse people to the incompetence of the Labour Government ... is more important than sitting here' (Hansard 5C, 15 July 1931, col. 674). Her post-political life was increasingly lonely as her husband spent more time on his new cause and with his future wife, Diana Guinness. After an appendix operation she contracted peritonitis and died at 3 Wilbraham Place, London, on 16 May 1933. The leaders of all parties supported the construction of a memorial day-nursery in Kennington, and she was buried the following year in a tomb designed by Lutyens at Savehay Farm.   DUNCAN SUTHERLAND

Sources N. Mosley, *Rules of the game: Sir Oswald and Lady Cynthia Mosley* (1982) • R. Skidelsky, *Oswald Mosley* (1975) • O. Mosley, *My life* (1968) • A. De Courcy, *The viceroy's daughters* (2000) • *Hansard 5C* (1929), 231.421 • *Hansard 5C* (1931), 255.674 • b. cert. • m. cert. • d. cert. • M. A. Hamilton, *Remembering my good friends* (1944) • P. Brookes, *Women at Westminster: an account of women in the British parliament, 1918–1966* (1967) • N. Nicolson, *Mary Curzon* (1977) • L. Manning, *A life for education: an autobiography* (1970) • M. I. Curzon, Baroness Ravensdale, *In many rhythms: an autobiography* (1953) • D. Jarvis, 'British conservatism and class politics in the 1920s', *EngHR*, 111 (1996), 59–84 • *CGPLA Eng. & Wales* (1933)
Archives U. Birm., personal and political MSS
Likenesses J. S. Sargeant, drawing, priv. coll.
Wealth at death £20,951 2s. 1d.: probate, 11 June 1934, *CGPLA Eng. & Wales*

Mosley, Nicholas (*bap.* 1611, *d.* 1672), author and royalist landowner, born at Ancoats Hall, Manchester, and baptized at the collegiate church there on 26 December 1611, was the eldest son of Oswald Mosley (*d.* 1630), merchant clothier, and his wife, Anne (*d.* 1671), daughter of Ralph Lowe of Mile End, Cheshire, and his wife, Margery. After attending school in Manchester, in Michaelmas term 1628 Mosley matriculated as a pensioner from Magdalene College, Cambridge.

On the death of his father on 9 November 1630 Mosley succeeded to the family estate. By 1638 he had married Jane (1617/18–1707), daughter of John Lever, of Alkrington; they had four sons, including Oswald (1639–1726), later sheriff of Staffordshire, and Nicholas (1654–1697), later a member of the Society of Apothecaries, and six daughters.

In July 1642 Mosley attempted to secure Manchester's munitions for the local royalist leader, James Stanley, Lord

Strange. Although subsequently a non-combatant, Mosley was living in royalist quarters in 1643 and was charged with delinquency. His estates, confiscated in 1643, were restored on 18 August 1646 on payment of £120.

In 1653 Mosley published *Psychosophia, or, Natural and divine contemplations of the passions and faculties of the soul of man*, which contained complimentary remarks from future bishops Ralph Brideoake, formerly master of Manchester grammar school, and Samuel Rutter. 'Nicholas Mosley Ancoats Esq' was included on the list of suspected royalists drawn up in 1655 (BL, Add. MSS 34013, fols. 2–55). While his family in general had some presbyterian sympathies, Mosley himself was among several local gentlemen who on 12 January 1658 presented to the local classis a paper questioning aspects of its policy, provoking several months of argument over the validity of the presbyterian system of church government. The gentlemen's case, probably the work of Isaac Allen, rector of Prestwich, was ultimately published as *Excommunicatio excommunicata* (1658), which the classis, led by Richard Heyrick, answered with *Censures of the Church Revived*.

At the Restoration, Mosley, styled 'Captaine of the Auxiliaries raised in the Towne for the defence of his Majesties most Royal Person and prerogative' (Earwaker, *Constables Accounts*, 3.122, n.2), headed an imposing procession to the Manchester collegiate church on the coronation day, 23 August 1661. Borough reeve of Manchester for the year 1661 to 1662 and a feoffee of Chetham's Hospital and Library, he was also a farmer or receiver and chief collector of the Cheshire hearth tax. As a justice of the peace for Lancashire from 1661 until his death, he was energetic in the regulation of alehouses, and suppression of seditious talk and dissenters' meetings. In December 1663, acting with others, he sanctioned the imprisonment of his brother-in-law John *Angier (1605–1677), the prominent presbyterian minister, for preaching contrary to the Act of Uniformity. The notebook kept by Mosley while he was a justice is still extant (Manchester Central Library, MS F 347).

Mosley died at Ancoats on 20 October 1672, and was buried in Manchester collegiate church on 28 October. His widow, Jane, died on 25 June 1707.

MALCOLM GRATTON

Sources E. Axon, ed., 'Mosley family: memoranda of Oswald and Nicholas Mosley of Ancoats', *Chetham miscellanies, I*, Chetham Society, new ser., 47 (1902), 1–63 • *Oliver Heywood's life of John Angier of Denton*, ed. E. Axon, Chetham Society, new ser., 97 (1937) • J. H. Stanning and J. Brownbill, eds., *The royalist composition papers*, 4, ed. J. H. Stanning, Lancashire and Cheshire RS, 36 (1898) • W. Dugdale, *The visitation of the county palatine of Lancaster, made in the year 1664–5*, ed. F. R. Raines, 2, Chetham Society, 85 (1872) • *The registers of the cathedral church of Manchester*, 3 vols. in 4, Lancashire Parish Register Society, 31, 55–6, 89 (1908–49) [introduction by E. Axon] • *The registers of the cathedral church of Manchester*, 2 (1919) [transcription rev. by H. Brierley and others] • will, 12 Dec 1672, Lancs. RO, WCW • G. Ormerod, ed., *Tracts relating to military proceedings in Lancashire during the great civil war*, Chetham Society, 2 (1844) • J. P. Earwaker, ed., *The court leet records of the manor of Manchester*, 4–5 (1887) • J. P. Earwaker, ed., *The constables' accounts of the manor of Manchester*, 3 (1892) • list of royalist suspects, 1655, BL, Add. MS 34013, fols. 2–55 • *DNB* • Venn, *Alum. Cant.* • A. Fletcher, *Reform in the provinces: the government of Stuart England* (1986), 242, 353

Archives Burton upon Trent Archives, Staffordshire, personal account book • Man. CL, notebook, MS F347 • Man. CL, Manchester sessions MSS, memoranda

Wealth at death £841 4s. 9d.—estate; incl. £350 of debt; left one third to wife, one third to be shared equally between six children, the remaining third to the churchwardens of Manchester for use of poor; books, etc., to Oswald his heir: will, 12 Dec 1672, Lancs. RO, WCW

Mosley, Sir Oswald Ernald, sixth baronet (1896–1980), politician and fascist leader, was born at 47 Hill Street, Mayfair, London, on 16 November 1896, the grandson of Sir Oswald Mosley, fourth baronet (1848–1915), of Rolleston-on-Dove, Staffordshire, and the eldest of the three sons of Sir Oswald Mosley (1874–1928), who succeeded to the baronetcy in 1915, and his wife, Katharine Maud (1874–1950), the second child of Captain Justinian Edwards-Heathcote, of Betton Hall, Market Drayton, Shropshire. The Mosleys were an old Staffordshire landed family; until 1846 they were lords of the manor of Manchester. Mosley's paternal grandfather bore a striking resemblance to the popular image of John Bull, and was nicknamed after him.

Early life When Mosley was five Maud Mosley obtained a judicial separation from her husband on account of the latter's infidelities and possibly also to protect Tom, as she called her eldest son, from his father's bullying. Thereafter his childhood was divided between his mother's modest house near her family home in Shropshire and the massive neo-Gothic pile of Rolleston Hall where John Bull presided. In his autobiography, published in 1968, Mosley writes with great affection about country life and country values. He describes a paternalistic enclave, cut off from the industrial midlands, which revolved round farming, horses, and dogs. He downplays the atmosphere of violence which was never far below the orderly surface of rural life. Tom Mosley adored his mother and his paternal grandfather, who in turn worshipped him. To his mother, a pious, fiercely loyal woman, he was a substitute for an absent husband; to his grandfather, a substitute for a ne'er-do-well son. His mother called him her man-child. Later, Mosley would often talk about the need for the adult mind. But in his political life he displayed many characteristics of the spoilt brat who must have what he wanted—now.

In 1905 Tom was sent away to West Down, a small preparatory school for Winchester College. He entered Winchester itself in September 1909, shortly before his thirteenth birthday, his mother's separation from his father breaking the long-standing Mosley connection with Eton. Solitary and somewhat haughty, he had already reached his full height of just over 6 feet by the time he left Winchester at sixteen. He found fulfilment not in the classroom or on the playing field, but in the gym, where he was trained to box and fence by two ex-army NCOs. At fifteen he won the public schools' fencing championship in both foil and sabre. Only an injury to his right leg in the First World War prevented him from being a serious contender

Sir Oswald Ernald Mosley, sixth baronet (1896–1980), by
William Davis, c.1933

for the world championship, though as late as 1937 he represented Britain at the épée. Although he languished scholastically at Winchester, one schoolmaster recalled that he had a 'wonderful imagination and could write a first-class essay' (Skidelsky, 39).

At Sandhurst, which he entered as an officer cadet in January 1914, Tom Mosley first exhibited the aristocratic insolence which later marked his politics. In what he called the 'corinthian tradition', he and a group of high-spirited friends broke out at night, got drunk, and provoked fights with the chuckers-out at London music-halls as well as with fellow cadets. A dispute over some 'misplaced' polo ponies led to a fight in college in which Mosley hit a fellow cadet with a riding crop. A skirmish ensued, in which he fractured his right ankle, and as a result of which he and fifteen other cadets were rusticated. They were soon recalled, however, on the outbreak of war, and Mosley was commissioned in the 16th lancers, a smart cavalry regiment, and sent for training in Ireland.

Mosley's war record was good but did not measure up to his hopes. He volunteered for the Royal Flying Corps, and by Christmas 1914 was flying as an observer in one of their flimsy contraptions over enemy lines. He gained his pilot's certificate, but showing off before his mother at Shoreham in May 1915 he crashed his plane and broke his right ankle for a second time. He was re-posted to his regiment, which needed its officers, in October 1915, before his leg had properly healed. After a few months in the sodden trenches under fire, but battle free, he was sent home for further operations which saved his leg but left him with a permanent limp and, by October 1916, fit only for desk work.

Political formation The experience of war shaped Mosley's political creed. It gave him a double sense of mission—to help build a land fit for heroes and to avoid the disaster of another world war. It also suggested a method for solving social problems, based on wartime organization and class unity. In fascism he would claim to have found an instrument and way of life tempered to the character and ideals of the war generation.

In hospital the twenty-year-old Mosley had started to read for the first time, mainly political biography. Brief spells of work at the Ministry of Munitions and the Foreign Office introduced him to London society. In a capital denuded of eligible young men Tom Mosley, with his dark, aquiline good looks, a slight, but not incapacitating, war wound and an attractively diffident manner, was a social catch. He was invited out by fashionable hostesses at whose London salons or country houses he met the leading politicians of the day. The childhood pattern of mutual seduction was now played out on the larger stage of love and politics. Mosley slept with the hostesses and was taken up by the politicians. This was the period of his apprenticeship, his substitute for a university. As his confidence grew the seduced turned into the seducer. The conqueror of the bedroom became the coquette of the platform.

Encouraged by the Conservative chief whip, Sir George Younger, Mosley stood for parliament as coalition Unionist candidate for the Harrow division of Middlesex and was elected with a handsome majority in the 'coupon' election of December 1918. At twenty-two he was the baby of the house. In May 1920 he married Lady Cynthia (d. 1933) [see Mosley, Lady Cynthia Blanche], the second daughter of the foreign secretary, George Nathaniel, Marquess Curzon of Kedleston, and Mary Leiter, the daughter of Levi Leiter, a Chicago real estate millionaire. Their wedding at the Chapel Royal, St James's Street, was attended by George V and Queen Mary. Their life together started on a high note of mutual passion which was not, however, sustained. Cimmie, as she was always known, was an idealistic, emotional, not very clever woman, who idolized her husband, and wanted to be adored and cherished in return. Mosley's love for her was genuine, and fervently expressed in letters full of baby talk, written in an illegible hand. But he was incapable of fidelity, resented her minding about his love affairs, and he abused her in public for what he saw as her simplicities. Thus was set a pattern of recrimination, remorse, and reconciliation which lasted until her early death from peritonitis in 1933. They were both wealthy. Cimmie inherited a substantial fortune from her Leiter grandfather; Tom got most of the proceeds from the sale of the Rolleston estate in 1919. They bought a town house at 8 Smith Square, Westminster, and (in 1926) a Tudor manor, Savehay Farm, Denham, Buckinghamshire, extended by Sir Edwin Lutyens. They had three children, Vivien, born in 1921, Nicholas (who became a writer) in 1923, and Michael in 1932.

Joins Labour Party Cimmie's charm and good nature proved invaluable assets as Tom Mosley's political career took an increasingly turbulent turn. A natural ambition to shine went together with the themes which he would later develop into clearcut programmes: pacifism abroad, social reform at home, a redivision of politics into those who stood for the pre-war world and the type 'that longs to march forth … like Crusaders, to the winning of a better world' (Skidelsky, 83). Under the influence of Lord Robert Cecil, his first (and only) political mentor, he embraced the League of Nations and took part in Lord Robert's unsuccessful efforts to construct a new centre party made up of moral conservatives, patriotic labour, and fragments of historic liberalism. Twenty months into his first parliament he seized the opportunity to make his mark in a just cause. In a series of probing questions and eloquent, angry speeches, he attacked Lloyd George's use of the Black and Tans to restore order in Ireland through a policy of reprisals. Barracked by his own side he crossed the floor of the house on 3 November 1920, together with Lord Henry Cavendish-Bentinck. T. P. O'Connor, the Irish nationalist leader, wrote to Cimmie: 'I regard him as the man who really began the break-up of the Black and Tan savagery' (ibid., 99). Mosley was now wooed by the Asquithian Liberals, but he preferred to retain his freedom until post-war political alignments became clearer. He held Harrow as an independent in the general elections of 1922 and 1923, though with declining majorities. The second of the elections led to the formation of the first Labour government under Ramsay MacDonald. On 27 March 1924 Mosley applied to join the Labour Party. He was welcomed with open arms by the party leader. For the next seven years the Labour Party was Tom Mosley's political home. He fought Ladywood, Birmingham, in the general election of October 1924, being narrowly defeated by the incumbent, Neville Chamberlain. He was returned to parliament as MP for Smethwick, a neighbouring Birmingham constituency, in a rowdy by-election in December 1926.

Mosley conscientiously trained himself for his new political career. After a tour of the Liverpool slums he remarked: 'This is damnable. The rehousing of the working classes ought in itself to find work for the whole of the unemployed for the next ten years' (Skidelsky, 136). He and Cimmie travelled to India and the United States to study social conditions abroad; in the United States they joined Franklin Roosevelt on a fishing trip. India impressed on Mosley's mind the threat to the Lancashire textile industry of competition from cheap labour; in the United States he thought he saw the answer: mass production for a protected, continental sized home market. In the aftermath of the general strike of May 1926 he spoke in mining villages all over Britain, helped starving miners with lavish donations, and formed a close political alliance with Arthur Cook, the miners' leader, which ensured his election to the national executive of the Labour Party in 1927, 1928, and 1930.

With typical confidence in his own abilities Mosley decided to equip the Labour Party with a modern economic policy. The result was a 24-page pamphlet, *Revolution by Reason* (1925), written with his new Labour Party friend John Strachey. This revealed, for the first time, a political originality of the highest order. Although drawing on the underconsumption theory of J. A. Hobson, it broke with his redistributionary emphasis by proclaiming that the task of socialism was to 'create additional demand to evoke our unused capacity which is at present not commanded either by the rich or by the poor'. At a time when unemployment stood at 10 per cent of the insured workforce Mosley called for an economic council to estimate the gap between actual and potential output, with the budget being unbalanced to any extent necessary to close the gap. 'This was a precise foreshadowing of the Keynesian philosophy of demand management, though minus the theory which justified it'. In its relegation of public ownership it also anticipated Croslandite democratic socialism. Labour's high command was not ready for such innovations, which challenged socialist orthodoxy; it also resented the effrontery of the new recruit. Mosley, wrote Hugh Dalton, was 'very uninstructed' (Skidelsky, 151).

Political style Mosley's political programme attracted much less attention than his political style. By dint of hard practice he had made himself into an effective parliamentary performer. He deepened his voice. He learned to speak without notes by getting someone to read him a leading article from *The Times* and replying to each point '*seriatim* in the order … read' (Skidelsky, 166). From the first, though, Mosley had the knack of provoking his opponents by the use of wounding and contemptuous invective. Although he made himself into a compelling orator—the greatest British platform speaker of the twentieth century—there were two chinks in his oratorical armour. His rhetoric was embarrassing, and he lacked a ready wit to turn away wrath: his repartee was savagely contrived. He aimed to stir his audiences to anger, and that involved demonizing their 'oppressors'. In particular, any attack on his own honour or bona fides would earn a vituperative response.

In the Smethwick by-election the people's oppressors as well as his own tormentors were the capitalists and their subservient newspapers. The Conservative press found it deplorable that an aristocrat, who spent his amply provided private life in beautiful houses, and took his holidays in Venice and the south of France with the beau monde, should be preaching class hatred to the Birmingham mob. Stung by these attacks Mosley hit back savagely; there was some rowdiness at eve-of-poll, when 'Socialist Amazons' manhandled reporters. His tactics, wrote the *Daily Telegraph*, 'have excited in the public bosom a lively feeling of disgust which Mr. Mosley will find it hard to live down' (20 Dec 1926). Throughout the later 1920s he and Cimmie were pilloried as 'rich Socialists'; even his father joined the fray, remarking that his son 'never did a day's work in his life' (Skidelsky, 160). Mosley was never just a demagogue. Much later he remarked that a politician 'must be equally at home at lunch with Keynes or in the evening of an East End pub, at an Oxford high table or at a rowdy street-corner meeting' (ibid., 513–14). In politics as in love he tried to have it both ways.

At the general election of May 1929 Labour won most seats and Ramsay MacDonald formed his second government. Mosley held Smethwick with an increased majority, and Cimmie was also elected Labour MP for Stoke-on-Trent. Mosley may have hoped to be foreign secretary; instead he was made chancellor of the duchy of Lancaster, outside the cabinet. His job was to help the lord privy seal, J. H. Thomas, devise schemes to stimulate employment. Churchill described him as 'a sort of ginger assistant to the Lord Privy Seal and more ginger than assistant I have no doubt' (Skidelsky, 179). Mosley set to work with a high sense of destiny: 'Before we leave this mortal scene, we shall do something to lift the burdens of those who suffer … We of the war generation are marching on' (ibid., 178). In practice, Sir Oswald (as he had become on the death of his father in 1928) marched straight into the wall of Philip Snowden's fiscal orthodoxy at the Treasury. As the world depression deepened that autumn Mosley bombarded ministers with lucid, but unavailing memoranda. Finally he decided to amalgamate them into one big memorandum, which he sent to MacDonald in January 1930. It proposed a small 'war cabinet' serviced by an economic general staff headed by Keynes; protection of the home market; government help for modernizing industry; and a £200 million programme of public works to be financed by borrowing. When it was rejected he resigned. His resignation speech eight days later, on 28 May 1930, was, by universal consent, an outstanding parliamentary performance. Speaking for an hour, without notes and without rhetoric, he marshalled the case for a British new deal. It ended: 'I beg the Government tonight to give the vital forces of this country the chance they await. I beg Parliament to give that lead' (Skidelsky, 216). After this speech he was freely spoken of as a future prime minister.

The New Party Over the next two years Mosley dissipated his hard-won political achievement by a series of catastrophic misjudgements. These were fed by his conviction that an economic catastrophe was unfolding, that the 'old gangs' were incapable of dealing with it, and that only a modern movement of the war generation would have the will and understanding to command the situation. The modern movement, in turn, was defined against the revolutionary challenge of communism. Mosley's last parliamentary manoeuvres can be seen as a deliberate attempt to force his fellow MPs to choose between himself and the old parties. As the choices became starker his support dwindled. Twenty-nine Labour MPs backed his vote of censure at a meeting of the parliamentary party a few days after his resignation speech. In the summer of 1930 he took up the theme of an empire economic bloc to attract tory support. There was interest but no commitment. A 'Mosley manifesto' issued in December 1930, demanding an emergency programme based on the home market and state trading, got seventeen Labour signatures, including

Aneurin Bevan's. Only five Labour MPs and one tory followed him into the New Party, formed on 1 March 1931 with the help of a £50,000 cheque from Sir William Morris, the motor car manufacturer. Mosley hoped that other young Conservatives such as Oliver Stanley, Robert Boothby, and Harold Macmillan might join later.

Mosley himself was expelled from the Labour Party for gross disloyalty. At the moment of launch he had succumbed to a devastating attack of pleurisy and double pneumonia, which kept him out of action for six weeks. It may be fanciful to attribute his physical collapse to psychological causes, but it is undeniable that his illness spared him the worst traumas of an extremely painful break, both with his party in parliament and with his Smethwick constituency association. When he returned to the fray the deed was done. His friends noticed a change in his personality. 'Ever since his illness he has been a different man', John Strachey, who had joined the New Party, told Harold Nicholson, another New Party recruit. 'His faith has left him. He is acquiring a Tory mind. It is a reversion to type' (Skidelsky, 261).

The two main achievements of the New Party were to acquire a private army and lose its parliamentary foothold. The squad of stewards, led by the boxer Kid Lewis, was a response to the breakup of early New Party meetings by Labour loyalists and by communists who saw (and perhaps wanted to expose) the 'cloven hoof of Fascism'. The political identity of the New Party was thus formed not by the national policy which Mosley expounded from the platform, but by battles with the 'reds'. These skirmishes attracted recruits from the militant right by a kind of elective affinity, and led to the exit of John Strachey, Mosley's one first-class intellectual companion. Despite a respectable showing at the Ashton under Lyne by-election in April, the New Party was an irrelevance when the financial crisis broke in August 1931. Mosley had cut himself off from Labour and the Conservatives no longer needed him, having formed a National Government with MacDonald and his leading cabinet ministers. The New Party was wiped out at the general election of October 1931, which returned an enormous 'National' majority to parliament. Mosley came bottom of the poll at Stoke-on-Trent, which he fought in place of Cimmie, who was pregnant with their third child. The recklessness with which Mosley had thrown away his support reminds one of that other brilliant political meteor, Lord Randolph Churchill.

The British Union of Fascists Mosley did not think that his political life was over. He was still only thirty-five. He was convinced that a new crisis was inevitable which would sweep him into power provided he was properly organized. He travelled to Italy to study the modern movement there, meeting Mussolini who shrewdly, but unavailingly, told him not to try the 'military stunt' in England. In the summer of 1932 he worked on his book *The Greater Britain*. The economic programme was the New Party's. Tagged onto it was an unconvincing argument purporting to show why only fascism could carry out the New Party programme. Its appeal to him—and those he hoped to

attract—was more emotional than rational: it was a political evocation of the manly comradeship of the trenches,
and he contrasted its hard, lean modern aesthetic with the
softness and clutter of bourgeois life. There was as yet no
mention of the Jews. The British Union of Fascists (BUF)
was launched on 1 October 1932, with the New Party's
stewards in black shirts, and a defiant message from its
leader: 'Better the great adventure, better defeat, disaster,
better by far the end of that trivial thing called a political
career than … posturing and strutting on the stage of little England amid the scenery of decadence' (O. Mosley,
286).

Although Mosley was heading for political self-
destruction his personal life became more stable after
Cimmie's death in 1933. Mosley was so stricken with grief
and remorse that family and friends feared suicide. But he
was now free to marry his mistress of a year, Diana (1910–
2003), the third, cleverest, and most beautiful of the Mitford sisters, then married to Bryan Guinness (later Lord
Moyne). After Cimmie's death, Diana divorced Bryan
Guinness. She and Mosley (her pet name for him was Kit)
were married in Berlin in October 1936 with Hitler present at the reception. Diana shared Mosley's political
beliefs, but theirs was not a political partnership. She provided an escape from politics. The beautiful homes she
created, and the clever, entertaining people she attracted
to them by her effervescent spirits eased the crash of his
political ambitions. They had two children, Alexander (b.
1938) and Max (b. 1940).

There was to be no escape from the political cage into
which Mosley had trapped himself. The BUF was a projection of his concept of himself as a hero; it had no basis in
political possibility. The economic catastrophe, on which
it was premised, had come and gone and was never to be
repeated. So there was nothing to do but make speeches,
march through towns, and fight the 'reds', while the
National Government presided over a sustained boom.
The dream of a respectable fascism soon faded, victim
both of Mosley's personality and the circumstances. The
tensions generated by his livery and style of campaigning
inevitably meant that he relied heavily on force to secure a
hearing. He was trying to sell a product which aroused
great opposition by methods which demanded complete
identification. The drums, bands, choirs, spotlights,
emblems; the uniformed leader limping down the aisle to
the accompaniment of massed salutes and 'Hail Mosleys';
the stewards grouped in intimidating fashion; Mosley's
rolling eyes and defiant gestures from the platform: all
these symbols of a big Mosley meeting called for surrender or resistance. They worked with audiences which
were wholly or largely sympathetic; they provoked violence from the unconvinced. Similarly uniformed fascist
processions in large towns looked and sounded like the
march of triumphant armies even when heavily shielded
by the police. Reliance on force brutalized and corrupted
Mosley. It made sense only in an atmosphere of incipient
civil war.

Beyond the pale In the first flush of novelty BUF recruitment was brisk, with Lord Rothermere, the *Daily Mail*'s

proprietor, loud in support. But the disastrous mishand-
ling of a giant rally at Olympia, on 7 June 1934, when
blackshirt stewards brutally ejected organized hecklers
before the gaze of a mostly horrified audience of the well
heeled, pricked the bubble of 'respectable' fascism. In the
mid-1930s the British Union, as it was now called, disgraced itself by the cynical exploitation of antisemitism,
particularly in the East End of London. Subsequently Mosley claimed that he attacked 'some Jews' only for exciting
warlike feelings against Nazi Germany. But his anti-war
campaigns had no connection with the British Union's
street corner Jew baiting, which was dictated solely by the
politics of survival. Following the notorious battle of
Cable Street on 4 October 1936 the government passed the
Public Order Act banning political uniforms, and restricting, for the first time, the right of political procession.
With private and municipal proprietors also refusing to
let Mosley their halls for his speeches, his main propaganda outlets dried up.

Mosley was the architect of his own downfall. His fascist
period was not without virtue: his courage shone brightly;
his dedication and loyalty to his unruly movement were
unquestioned; his opposition to another war with Germany was sincere. But these very virtues, in the service of
a misguided cause, were inseparable from brutality, cynicism, and self-deception. They also put him beyond the
pale at a time when a more adroit politician would have
reinvented himself as the non-fascist leader of the peace
movement. In the end, Mosley preferred to be a hero in an
empty room than a serious player in the political game.

When war came, on 3 September 1939, Mosley
instructed his followers to 'do nothing to injure our country, or to help any other Power' (O. Mosley, 400). But he
himself continued his peace campaign. On 23 May 1940 he
and his leading lieutenants were arrested under regulation 18B as security risks. He was interned, first at Brixton,
later with Diana at Holloway, until November 1943, when
a flare-up of phlebitis in his injured leg induced the home
secretary, Herbert Morrison, to sanction his release on
medical grounds. The war ended what remained of his
political reputation. In a life and death struggle he was on
the wrong side, put there not by treachery, but by folly.
Folly in such circumstances becomes a crime for which
there is no forgiveness.

Final decades After the war Mosley started a union movement dedicated to creating a united Europe. But the idea
had little resonance, coming from that tainted source. In
the 1950s he attacked coloured immigration into Britain.
He stood as union movement candidate for North Kensington in the general election of 1959, losing his deposit; a
second intervention at Shoreditch and Finsbury in 1966
fared even worse. His fine autobiography, *My Life*, published in 1968, was a defence of his political career and an
account of his policies for the future. It was followed by a
number of television appearances. In the 'ungovernable'
1970s he was in surreptitious touch with a surprising array
of public figures and intellectuals, more fascinated by

him as a historical survivor than as a contemporary presence. In his last years he suffered from Parkinson's disease. He died peacefully on 3 December 1980 at the beautiful home at Orsay, outside Paris, which Diana had made for him. He was cremated in Paris and his ashes were scattered on the pond at his home at Orsay.

There is always something tragic about the spilling of prodigious gifts. Many attempts have been made to identify Mosley's flaw. To Jo Grimond he epitomizes the aristocratic bully; his son Nicholas sees him as an idealistic hedonist who sought through words to rationalize his crazy belief that he could get away with anything; to Harold Macmillan his flaw was insane impatience. All these interpretations suggest an immaturity, prefigured in his mother's view of him as her man-child. To someone who knew him only in old age the flaw seemed to lie in his mental rigidity: the unrealism of his assumptions led him, by strictly logical processes, to absurd conclusions for action. By the 1970s this mental machinery had become a defensive armour plating, a way of justifying his life. But one fancies it had always been there to some degree. He remained in some ways an extraordinarily intelligent child. This made him both vulnerable and dangerous. He wanted too much, too soon.

Robert Skidelsky

Sources O. Mosley, *My life* (1968) · R. Skidelsky, *Oswald Mosley* (1975) · N. Mosley, *Rules of the game* (1982) · N. Mosley, *Beyond the pale* (1983) · private information (2004) · Burke, *Peerage*
Archives priv. coll. · U. Birm. L., papers | HLRO, corresp. with Lord Beaverbrook · University of Sheffield, corresp. with Robert Saunders, local organizer | FILM BFI NFTVA, *The Frost programme*, Rediffusion, 15 Nov 1967 · BFI NFTVA, documentary footage · BFI NFTVA, record footage | SOUND BL NSA, 'Britain's fascist leader', T3708W BD1 · BL NSA, 'Britain in the 30s: Mosley right or wrong?', NP6953R TR2 · BL NSA, documentary recordings · BL NSA, news recording · BL NSA, oral history interview · BL NSA, performance recording
Likenesses photographs, 1919–66, Hult. Arch. · G. Philpot, oils, 1925, NPG · M. Beerbohm, caricature, drawing, 1931, repro. in *The Spectator* · M. Beerbohm, lithograph caricature, 1931, NPG · W. Stoneman, photograph, 1931, NPG · I. Opffer, chalk drawing, 1932, NPG · W. Davis, photograph, c.1933, Hult. Arch. [*see illus.*] · D. E. Green, pencil drawing, 1968, NPG · D. Low, cartoon, repro. in Skidelsky, *Oswald Mosley*, following p. 256 · B. Thomas, ink drawing, NPG · photographs, NPG

Mosley, Samuel (b. 1641, d. in or before 1680), soldier in America, was born on 14 June 1641 at Mount Wollaston, Braintree, near Quincy, Massachusetts, the son of Henry Mosley (b. 1610/11), who had embarked from England on the *Hopewell* in August 1635. Henry Mosley settled in Braintree and had one other child, a daughter, Sarah, born in 1638. Mosley was a cooper by trade, who at some point before 30 May 1665, when the couple signed a contract, married Ann (b. 1647, d. after 1691), daughter of Isaac Addington (d. 1653) and the sister of Isaac Addington, the future secretary of the colony. They had a son, Samuel, who died young, and two daughters, who survived their father.

In 1668 Mosley was sent to negotiate with the Narragansett Indians. In 1673–4 he was in command of a ship and

on 2 April 1675 he brought some captured pirates into Boston. He was thus on hand in June 1675 when reports came into Boston of an American Indian attack on Swansea. On 26 June 1675 he raised a company of volunteers to supplement the forces being sent to fight the Wampanoag tribe led by King Philip (or Metacom). He spent early July as part of the troops sent into the Narragansett country to negotiate a treaty with that tribe, which proved impossible to enforce. At the end of August 1675 he arrested a group of friendly American Indians at Marlborough for an attack on Lancaster and marched them to Boston to be tried. They were acquitted. He then burnt a village belonging to the peaceful Pennacook tribe. Mosley's volunteers fought in most of the significant actions in the campaign, including the rescue of Lathrop's troops ambushed at Bloody Brook in September, and in the defence of Hatfield in October. Mosley was part of the large force assembled in November to attack the Narragansetts. On 19 December he took part in the 'great swamp fight', an attack on a fortified village of the Narragansett tribe.

Mosley remained suspicious of Christian Indians living near to settler towns, and this led him to intervene in March 1676 at the request of some settlers, fearful of the Indians living under the supervision of John Hoar at Concord. Mosley marched the Indians off to be interned on Deer Island in Boston harbour. By the time the war ended with the death of King Philip in August 1676, Mosley had acquired the reputation as a determined and hard-bitten fighter. Indeed, he was said to be the original of the soldier who took off his wig to fight, hanging it in the branch of a tree, so that he might fight more coolly. Such manipulation of his scalp was said to have instilled fear into his American Indian opponents.

Mosley was included in a warrant of 3 September 1678 authorizing him to take the oath of the governor of Massachusetts relating to the Navigation Acts. He was dead by 26 January 1680, when an inventory was made of his estate. His widow then married Nehemiah Pierce (d. 1691).

Stuart Handley

Sources G. M. Bodge, *Soldiers in King Philip's War* (1896), 59–61, 77–8 · E. S. Moseley, *A genealogical sketch of one branch of the Mosely family* (1878), 14–19 · D. E. Leach, *Flintlock and tomahawk: New England in King Philip's War* (1958) · J. Winsor, *The memorial history of Boston, including Suffolk County, Massachusetts, 1630–1880*, 4 vols. (1880–81), vol. 2 · R. Slotkin and J. K. Folsom, *So dreadfull a judgment: puritan responses to King Philip's War, 1676–1677* (1978), 46–50 · W. Hubbard, *The present state of New-England, being a narrative of the troubles with the Indians* (1677) · J. A. Doyle, *The English in America*, 5 vols. (1887–1907), vol. 2: *The puritan colonies* · CSP col., vols. 9–10 · IGI · D. Gookin, 'An historical account of the doings and sufferings of the Christian Indians in New England in the years 1675, 1676, 1677', *Archaeologia Americana*, 2 (1836), 425–534

Moss, Charles (1711–1802), bishop of St David's and of Bath and Wells, the son of William Moss, a grazier and landowner, and his wife, Sarah, was born at Postwick, Norfolk, and baptized there on 3 January 1712. He was educated at Norwich School and in 1727 entered Gonville and Caius College, Cambridge, as a sizar; two years later, however, the inheritance of a substantial estate from his uncle, Robert Moss, dean of Ely, made him a wealthy youth. He graduated BA in 1731, and in 1735 became MA and a fellow of Caius. He was university moderator in 1737, the year in which he received priests' orders. Moss's reputation as 'good-natured' and 'a promising youth', brought him to the attention of Bishop Thomas Sherlock of Salisbury, who made him his domestic chaplain and from whom he received all his livings. In 1738 he was named to a canonry of Salisbury, and in 1740 he exchanged it for a wealthier one. He was rector of Boscombe, Wiltshire, and Compton Bassett from 1743 to 1750. As Sherlock's chaplain he was active in arranging the bishop's diocesan visitations. In 1744 he also engaged Bishop Sherlock's deist opponents in a pamphlet war over Sherlock's *Trial of the Witnesses* (1729). Moss's contributions, including *The Sequel to the Trial* (1749), proved him to be a powerful Old Testament scholar.

In 1748 Sherlock's appointment to the diocese of London brought further preferment for Moss: in 1749 the archdeaconry of Colchester and in 1750 the rectory of St Andrew Undershaft and the fashionable rectory of St James's, Piccadilly. As archdeacon, Moss arranged his visitations in such a way as to show consideration for the people suffering from smallpox. When Bishop Sherlock became infirm, Moss discharged most episcopal duties as his surrogate. In 1759 Sherlock appointed Moss to the valuable rectory of St George's, Hanover Square, and he was appointed Boyle lecturer for 1759–62; later Archbishop Secker gave him a unique privilege when he extended his tenure as lecturer by one year. Moss's ambitions encouraged him to apply, unsuccessfully, for the vacant deanery of Winchester in 1758; consolation came some weeks later when he was appointed king's chaplain. In spite of rumours that he would marry a cousin of Bishop Sherlock, Moss married the daughter of Sir Stephen Hales in 1760. Moss's daughter was to marry a clergyman, Dr King, for whom the bishop provided livings.

In 1766 Moss was appointed bishop of St David's at the suggestion of the duke of Newcastle and Archbishop Secker. Here he was a reformer, placing the finances of the diocese on a sound footing, and sternly correcting the chapter of St David's, which had fallen prey to non-residence. In spite of his controversial support for the colonists in seeking a bishop for America, he was translated to Bath and Wells in 1773. His support for a bishop for the Americans led to his invitation to be a consecrator of bishops White and Provoost in 1787. However, Moss opposed the Dissenters Relief Bill in 1772 and parliamentary reform later in the century.

At Bath and Wells, Moss was an active and conscientious bishop. He conducted regular visitations into his eighty-sixth year, after which he relied on surrogates, and was a generous almsgiver. He was active in consecrating new churches for the diocese, including a number of chapels in Bath. He supported the evangelical clergy of his diocese and was a staunch friend and supporter of Hannah More in her attempt to establish schools among the poor of Cheddar. He died at his house in Grosvenor Square on 13

April 1802 and was buried in the Grosvenor Chapel, South Audley Street.

Moss's son **Charles Moss** (1763–1811), bishop of Oxford (who should not be confused with his father's nephew, also Charles Moss), was born in London, and entered Christ Church, Oxford, in 1780. He graduated BA in 1783. Charles Moss junior was fortunate in forming a friendship with Lord Grenville at Oxford. His father appointed him to a prebend and the precentorship of Wells as well as the livings of Castle Cary and Wookey in Somerset; but Lord Grenville was instrumental in obtaining for him the chaplaincy to the House of Commons in 1789 and the nomination to the diocese of Oxford in 1807, where in due course he was influential in Grenville's election as chancellor of the university. He died, apparently unmarried, at Oxford on 16 December 1811.   WILLIAM GIBSON

Sources Nichols, *Lit. anecdotes* · Venn, *Alum. Cant.* · S. H. Cassan, *The lives of the bishops of Bath and Wells*, 2 vols. (1829–30) · T. Newton, *Autobiography of Thomas Newton* (1876) · E. Carpenter, *Thomas Sherlock* (1936) · *GM*, 1st ser., 30 (1760), 394 · BL, Add. MSS 37222, 32870, 32877, 39976 · B. Gibson, 'The finances of the diocese of St David's in the eighteenth century: the reforms of Bishop Charles Moss, 1766–73', *Journal of Welsh Ecclesiastical History*, 3 (1986), 49–59 · W. Gibson, 'A Hanoverian reform of the chapter of St David's', *National Library of Wales Journal*, 25 (1987–8), 285–8 · W. Gibson, 'Three Hanoverian prelates', *Somerset Archaeology and Natural History*, 128 (1984), 75–83 · W. Gibson, 'Somerset evangelical clergy', *Somerset Archaeology and Natural History*, 130 (1986), 135–41 · W. Gibson, 'The election of Lord Grenville as chancellor of Oxford in 1809', *Oxoniensia*, 61 (1996), 355–67 · monument inscription, South Audley Street Chapel · Foster, *Alum. Oxon.* · *Fasti Angl.* (Hardy)

Archives BL, Add. MSS 59002, 69045, 69105 | BL, corresp. with duke of Newcastle and others

Likenesses line engraving, pubd 1783, NPG · J. Hoppner, portrait, c.1800, bishop's palace, Wells, Somerset · S. W. Reynolds, mezzotint, pubd 1801 (after J. Hoppner), BM, V&A · G. Romney, oils, bishop's palace, Wells, Somerset

Wealth at death £140,000: will, PRO, probate records

Moss, Charles (1763–1811). *See under* Moss, Charles (1711–1802).

Moss, Harry Neville (1895–1982), draper, was born at 10 The Triangle, Kensington, London, on 25 October 1895, the younger son of George Frederick Moss (1855–1910), master tailor, and his wife, Lucie Phoebe Amy, *née* Campbell. His grandfather, Moses Moss, a bespoke tailor and dealer in secondhand clothes, had opened a shop in Covent Garden, London, in 1860. Moses set up George, the eldest of his five sons, and Alfred (1862–1937) in another shop nearby in 1881, with George responsible for tailoring, and Alfred in overall charge of the business, including the purchase of high-quality secondhand clothing for resale. Both of George's sons joined the business. During the First World War, Harry was commissioned and served at Salonika; the elder brother was killed. His uncle Alfred married late in life.

Before the First World War the firm was winning a reputation as military outfitters, well able to handle the idiosyncratic variations of regimental uniform. A branch was set up in Camberley for Sandhurst officer cadets, and during the war the firm was able to produce high-quality ready-to-wear uniforms at short notice. After the war the firm retained many of its wartime customers and added formal diplomatic and court wear to its range of full-dress military uniforms. In another area the business changed its emphasis from the sale of secondhand and misfit clothing to the hire of morning and evening dress; it continued to make high-quality, hand-finished ready-to-wear suits, which were cheaper than, but hardly distinguishable from, bespoke tailor-made suits.

On 15 June 1920 Moss married Sophia Ida Woolf (d. 1971) at the West London Synagogue in Marylebone. On his return to the firm after the war, Harry Moss gained his uncle's confidence and was made a director in 1921. He gradually brought change into the traditional business, introducing mechanization for routine tailoring processes, while retaining hand-finishing. He rationalized office methods, making card indexes of customers, and—with considerable misgivings—introduced discreet, humorous direct-mail advertising for existing customers. This proved to be a much-appreciated innovation. The premises were largely rebuilt in 1929, but most activities, including tailoring and the care of dress wear for hire, were still carried out under the same roof. In 1934 Moss took over as managing director, a position he was to hold for forty years. At that time around a hundred staff were employed, and turnover was over £220,000 per year.

Following the Second World War, the business changed in several ways. The range of clothing was extended to include women's wear, including wedding and evening dresses, both for sale and hire. New branches were opened; there were thirty-two in 1971, including two in Paris. The firm aimed to attract young customers as well as a more established clientele. It began to advertise extensively, ironically having to emphasize that the firm actually sold clothes as well as hiring them, such had been its reputation for hiring. Annual turnover in 1971 was £3.5 million and the staff numbered 1350. The company, a private limited company since 1914, was converted into a public company in 1947, but the majority of shares still remained under family control. When Harry Moss died in 1982 there were six Mosses in the business.

Moss was committed to ensuring the preservation of his family firm's high reputation, and care for customers and staff alike. He was a respected figure in the menswear trade. Outside his work he devoted much time to the West London Synagogue, and rarely missed the Friday evening service. He enjoyed cricket—he was a redoubtable left-handed opening bat—and golf. He encouraged his firm to sponsor and attend sporting events such as show-jumping, skiing, and golf tournaments. He served as treasurer and governor of an approved school near his home in Surrey, and was president of the Master Tailors' Benevolent Association, and joint president of the Boys' Club Movement. Moss died in Middlesex Hospital, Westminster, on 11 May 1982, survived by a daughter and his son Monty, who had succeeded him as chairman.

FRANCIS GOODALL

Sources W. Tute, *The grey top hat: the story of Moss Bros of Covent Garden* (1961) · *The Times* (17 May 1982) · *Jewish Chronicle* (21 May 1982) · *Drapers' Record* (22 May 1982) · d. cert.

Likenesses photograph, repro. in Tute, *Grey top hat*
Wealth at death £190,477: probate, 29 June 1982, *CGPLA Eng. & Wales*

Moss, Henry Whitehead (1841–1917), headmaster, was born at Lincoln on 23 June 1841, the eldest son of Henry Moss, a draper, and his second wife, Louisa, *née* Bainbridge; there were four sons in all. After early schooling at Lincoln grammar school, Moss went in 1857 to Shrewsbury School (then under the headmastership of Benjamin Hall Kennedy) and thence in 1860 to St John's College, Cambridge. Here he won several university prizes (including the Porson prize three times, as Kennedy had done before him) and was senior classic in 1864. He was elected to a fellowship at St John's, but in 1866, just before his twenty-fifth birthday, and having been ordained earlier in the year, he was chosen, on the nomination of St John's, to succeed Kennedy as headmaster of Shrewsbury School, where he remained for forty-two years.

Under the successive headmasterships of Samuel Butler and Benjamin Kennedy, Shrewsbury had been rescued from being a virtually moribund foundation at the close of the eighteenth century to one which had greatly grown in numbers, while gaining an unparalleled number of university successes in the classics. But the school's location, in a cramped town site, would have been bound to hinder its future, and numbers had been declining in Kennedy's later years as headmaster. Moss's supreme achievement was to persuade the governing body, against much lasting hostility (especially locally, but also among the old boys) that the school had to be moved. Despite his youth, he first made the case for the move soon after his arrival; but it was not until 1875, after much diplomatic manoeuvring over possible sites and a catastrophic error of judgement by Moss himself (involving a birching scandal and arousing national interest) which had the result of ruling out his own choice for the school's new location, that the move to the site at Kingsland was agreed. This was initially of some 27 acres but grew to well over 100 by April 1882. There can be no doubt that this crucial move, virtually a re-foundation, saved the school from relapsing into the status of a local grammar school.

It was during Moss's headmastership that the three term year became the norm. Although no lover of games, he presented the school (on its new site) with a swimming pool. Regarded by the boys as rather distant and unapproachable (perhaps because of the difficulties arising from his appointment at so early an age), he also had the reputation of being a superb raconteur and excellent after-dinner speaker. His industry was prodigious. In politics both Conservative and imperialist, Moss was early convinced of the inevitability of war with Germany, and engaged a master to re-establish the school's cadet corps. With unusual prescience he had already foreseen by 1873 the increasing competition which the study of the classics would meet from other disciplines and which would ultimately lead to their decline in relative importance. He was chairman of the Headmasters' Conference from 1899 to 1902. He probably remained too long as headmaster, and numbers at Shrewsbury were again declining when he retired in 1908, though scholastic successes had been remarkably good.

In 1887 Moss had married Mary Beaufort (d. 1948), the daughter of another Salopian, the Revd William Augustus Beaufort; they had two sons and a daughter, the Egyptologist Rosalind Louisa Beaufort *Moss. From 1887 he had been prebendary of Hereford. In retirement he lived in or near Oxford, latterly at Highfield Park, Headington, and died at 69 Lancaster Gate, London, following a stroke, on 14 January 1917. He was buried in the Shrewsbury cemetery. Such few literary remains as exist consist of some sermons and some Latin verses, preserved (in the case of one sermon and the Latin verses) by the biographical memoir written by his widow.   J. H. C. LEACH

Sources J. H. C. Leach, *A school at Shrewsbury* (1990) · M. Moss, *Moss of Shrewsbury* (1932) · J. B. Oldham, *Headmasters of Shrewsbury School* (1937) · Venn, *Alum. Cant.* · *The Salopian*, 64/1 (1948)
Likenesses P. Baynes, caricature, c.1897, Shrewsbury School · H. Rivière, portrait, 1908, Shrewsbury School
Wealth at death £156,354 13s. 9d.: probate, 18 May 1917, *CGPLA Eng. & Wales*

Moss, Sir Horace Edward (1852–1912), theatre and music-hall manager, was born on 12 April 1852 in Ashton under Lyne, the son of James Moss, a theatre manager. He received some education in Manchester and Glasgow, musical tuition from Andrew Banks, and learned the music-hall business at his father's premises in Greenock. At the age of seventeen he became manager of a travelling company, then proprietor of a diorama of the Franco-Prussian War. In 1877 he leased the Gaiety Music Hall on Chambers Street, Edinburgh, and in 1880 purchased premises in Leith; artistes were booked to appear in both halls, thus establishing the first link in what eventually became a circuit of thirty-nine variety theatres operated by Moss throughout the British Isles. In 1884 Moss added Newcastle upon Tyne to the circuit, and, shortly after, Glasgow. His collaboration in 1890 with Richard Thornton to build the Empire Theatre in Newgate Street, Newcastle, initiated a long and prosperous partnership. 'Empires' became his hallmark, with new premises in Edinburgh (1892, now the Festival Theatre), Sheffield (1895), Glasgow (1897), Leeds (1898), and Nottingham (1898) also bearing the name. The last-named marked the first amalgamation of Moss's interests with Oswald Stoll, whose own circuit was initially launched in Cardiff.

Although the music-hall industry emerged from similar types of enterprises in the major population centres of London, Glasgow, and Manchester in the 1830s and 1840s, with large halls a feature of each city by the 1850s, the lower cash input necessary in the provinces may have enabled Moss and his partners to form wider networks from which to expand than their London-based competitors. They booked the best-known artistes in the business at a time when music-hall was at its most profitable, helping to sanitize music-hall's reputation into the more benignly connotative 'variety', appealing to the middle classes, and being fully acceptable to audiences of both sexes. In December 1899 the multiple public limited liability companies under which Moss, Thornton, and Stoll operated merged into a single corporation, initially capitalized at £1.4 million. Moss Empires Ltd was distinguished by an unusually large percentage of ordinary share capital (about 80 per cent) rather than relying on mortgage debentures and loans. Each new Moss venture floated on the Edinburgh and London stock exchanges in the 1890s, such as the amalgamated syndicate in 1899, was eagerly and fully taken up by a wide range of private investors, signifying great faith in the directors and the future of the industry. While artistes could not become true stars without garnering the praise of Londoners, as entrepreneurs Moss, his partners, and his co-investors profited from touring the London stars in growth economies all over the nation, further streamlining the booking system and reducing the friction of competition in this unified venture.

The Hippodrome (1900) at Charing Cross Road and Cranbourn Street, bordering on Leicester Square, was Moss's first central London property, and he managed it personally for the first five years. It offered large-scale circus, water spectacles, variety, and in the winter months extravagant pantomimes. In 1909 the circus arena was replaced by stalls and the property's distinctiveness was largely forfeited; thereafter it presented variety, opera, and ballet (including the first English performance of *Swan Lake*). While Moss took particular pride in the Hippodrome, the more typical focuses of Moss Empires Ltd immediately after the turn of the century were the expansions into the genteel residential suburbs of London, Manchester, and Birmingham (in contrast to the working-class halls of competitors such as Thomas Barrasford or Frank MacNaghten and the seaside circuit of Walter De Freece) and building replacements for the company's older or incommodious halls in city centres. The syndicate broke up in 1910, partly owing to shareholders' uneasiness with competition and conflicts of interest arising from Stoll's own independent circuit, including the London Coliseum Ltd (1904) in London, which was built up separately from Moss Empires Ltd.

By this time, however, Moss was increasingly withdrawn from business activities, and opted for the life of a country gentleman in Midlothian, where he was both a justice of the peace and deputy lieutenant. He married twice; first, on 19 January 1877, Ellen Alice (d. 1892), the daughter of Leonard Bramwell of Guernsey, and second, in 1902, Florence Nellie, the daughter of J. R. Craig of Peterborough. He had a daughter from his first marriage. He preferred to be a behind-the-scenes organizer, and seems to have been a consummate administrator. Unlike his music-hall contemporaries—such as the gregarious George Edwardes, the personable Stoll, and the politically ambitious De Freece—he did not generate publicity about himself, avoided the limelight, and, despite membership in Greenock and Edinburgh masonic lodges, showed little inclination for professional and fraternal conviviality. Even his choice of clubs was low-key: the Junior Constitutional, Royal Automobile, and Conservative Club (Edinburgh). His name was a virtual endorsement of business integrity, yet he took little part in the more flamboyant aspects of the theatrical and music-hall industries. Nevertheless, he was knighted in 1905, in recognition of his business success and probably also in acknowledgement for arranging several of Edward VII's dinners for the poor. He received the French government's distinction of officer of public instruction in 1912. Days before, on 23 April 1912, he underwent surgery at his home in Regent's Park, and despite an improvement in his health during the summer never resumed public life. He died at his home, Middleton Hall, Gorebridge, Midlothian, on 25 November 1912, and was buried in Portobello cemetery, Edinburgh, on 28 November.   TRACY C. DAVIS

Sources *The Times* (26 Nov 1912), 15c · J. Read, *Empires, hippodromes and palaces* (1985) · A. Crowhurst, 'The music hall, 1885–1922: the emergence of a national entertainment industry in Britain', PhD diss., U. Cam., 1992 · *Who was who in the theatre, 1912–1976*, 3 (1978) · *The Times* (29 Nov 1912), 11b · *The Times* (24 April 1912), 11d · *The Times* (26 April 1912), 11a · J. Parker, ed., *The green room book, or, Who's who on the stage* (1908), 318 · *The Era* (19 Feb 1910), 14, 23 · private information (2004) · Burke, *Peerage* · WWW

Moss, Joseph William (1803–1862), bibliographer, was born at Dudley, Worcestershire. He matriculated at Magdalen Hall, Oxford, on 21 March 1820, and while an undergraduate developed a keen interest in classical bibliography. He graduated BA in 1825, MA in 1827, and MB in 1829, and settled in practice at Dudley.

Moss was elected fellow of the Royal Society on 18 February 1830, but published nothing of a scientific nature. His reputation rests entirely upon his *Manual of Classical Bibliography*, which was published in 1825, in two volumes, containing more than 1250 closely printed pages. It was a remarkable achievement for so young an author. Advertisements declared that the *Manual* combined the advantages of T. F. Dibdin's *Introduction to … Rare and Valuable Editions of the Greek and Latin Classics* (1802), the *Catalogues* of Guillaume De Bure, and J. C. Brunet's *Manuel de librairie* (1810). The author claimed to have consulted more than three thousand volumes, exclusive of innumerable editions and commentaries, and to have produced a more comprehensive and critical work than the similar works by Michael Maittaire, Edward Harwood, and Dibdin. He also described himself as the first to include notices of critical publications connected with each author, together with the literary history of the translations made into the principal languages of Europe.

Despite serious shortcomings, the *Manual* became a standard work of reference. Favourable reviews appeared in 1825 in the *Literary Chronicle*, the *News of Literature*, and the *Gentleman's Magazine*. However, in the same year the *Literary Gazette* severely attacked the book. Moss's detailed reply, which acknowledged his debt to Dibdin and Harwood, met with a rejoinder from the *Literary Magazine*. The *Manual* was reprinted in 1837, with a new title-page, but with no corrections, by Bohn. Three new works by Moss were announced in the reprint, a 'Lexicon Aristotelicum', a 'Catalogue raisonné of the collection of an amateur', and an edition of Lucretius, but, although the first two were said to be in the press, none of these books appeared.

In 1847 Moss moved from Dudley to Longdon, near Lichfield, and in 1848 to the Manor House, Upton Bishop, near Ross, Herefordshire. In 1853 he again moved, to Hill Grove House, Wells, Somerset, where he died on 23 May 1862. Towards the end of his life he was regarded as an eccentric recluse.   E. C. MARCHANT, *rev.* NILANJANA BANERJI

Sources Foster, *Alum. Oxon.* · *GM*, 3rd ser., 13 (1862), 114 · Allibone, *Dict.*

Wealth at death under £6000: probate, 9 Sept 1862, *CGPLA Eng. & Wales*

Moss, Marlow [*formerly* Marjorie Jewel] (1889–1958), artist, was born on 29 May 1889 at 11 Brondesbury Villas, Kilburn, London, the daughter of Lionel Moss, a master hosier and clothier, and his wife, Frannie Jacobs. Moss's decision to make a career in fine art caused a rupture with most members of her family, except her sister Gwen, though she continued to receive a private income. Moss attended the St John's Wood School of Art in 1916–17; she left it for the Slade School of Fine Art, but found both establishments overly traditional and unsatisfactory. A mental breakdown in 1919 was the probable cause of her leaving the Slade to lead a solitary, unproductive life in Cornwall until, stimulated by a biography of Marie Curie, she returned to London in 1923 to study philosophy, literature, architecture, mathematics, and art in the British Museum reading room. She spent 1924–6 in Cornwall, where she studied sculpture at the Penzance Municipal School of Art. In London again, in 1926, she began to paint and took a studio. She changed her forenames from Marjorie Jewel to Marlow, cut her hair very short, and began habitually to wear a cravat and jodhpurs. Max Bill later described her as small and thin, with a narrow face and lively eyes.

In 1927 Moss first visited Paris, then moved there permanently and met her lifelong partner, the Dutch writer Antoinette Nijhoff-Wind (d. 1971). Moss studied with Léger and Ozenfant at the Académie Moderne; she later said of Léger: 'All I understand of the art of painting I owe to his criticism' (*Marlow Moss*, Stedelijk Museum). Most significantly, in 1927 she first saw the work of Mondrian, whom she met two years later and called her 'master'. They remained in close contact until 1938. In 1929 she made her first neo-plastic composition: two black lines crossed in a right angle on a white ground. All her extant and recorded work is abstract, consistent with her much-quoted statement: 'I am no painter, I don't see form, I only see space, movement and light' (ibid.). In 1930 she first used a double line, which Mondrian may have imitated. Working very slowly and applying as many as seven layers of paint, she first drew her image roughly on linen or paper and only painted full-size on canvas after using a ruler to apply mathematical and proportional systems and, perhaps, experimenting with coloured papers. Though Moss's earliest recorded work closely resembled Mondrian's, it diverged after 1932, when she eliminated black lines to make all-white reliefs with wood, rope, and string on linen.

Moss was an active member of the Parisian avant-garde,

a founder member of Abstraction–Création, and exhibited with the Salon des Surindépendants and in international group shows. Yet her reclusive lifestyle contributed to her neglect; though she was an innovative painter, until the 1980s she was dismissed as a minor imitator of Mondrian.

In 1937 Moss bought the Château d'Evreux, at Gauciel in Normandy. It was destroyed by German bombs in 1944, with almost all her pre-war work. She returned to England on 14 May 1940 and rented a bungalow outside Lamorna Cove in Cornwall. In 1941 she returned to the Penzance School of Art to study architecture, which stimulated her to begin to make constructed metal sculptures. A later example, *Balanced Forms in Gun Metal on Cornish Granite* (reinforced metal and granite, 1956–7), was later installed in the Tate Gallery, as was an early post-war painted relief, *White, Black and Yellow* (oil on canvas with wood, 1949). Isolated and desperate to meet fellow abstract artists, Moss contacted Barbara Hepworth and Ben Nicholson and probably met them in 1943. In 1946 she made the first of many regular post-war visits to Paris and exhibited with the Salon des Réalités Nouvelles. A year later she was reunited with Nijhoff. She became a member of the London branch of Group Espace and, in 1953, had her first solo exhibition, at the Hanover Gallery, London, with a second in 1958. Her painting became increasingly colourful, especially after 1956 when she used primary colours without black lines. One of these paintings, *White, Yellow, Blue and Red* (oil on canvas, 1957–8), was later owned by the Stedelijk Museum, Amsterdam. Moss died of cancer on 23 August 1958 in West Cornwall Hospital, Penzance. She was cremated and her ashes were scattered on the sea near Lamorna.　　MARGARET GARLAKE

Sources F. Dijkstra, *Marlow Moss*, trans. A. Wright, rev. edn (1995) • S. Wilson, 'Marlow Moss', *Dictionary of women artists*, ed. D. Gaze (1997) • *Marlow Moss, 1890–1958: Bilder, Konstructionen, Zeichnungen* (Zürich, 1973) [exhibition catalogue, Gimpel and Hanover Gallery, Zürich, 1 Dec 1973 – 19 Jan 1974] • *Marlow Moss* (1962) [exhibition catalogue, Stedelijk Museum, Amsterdam, 30 March – 30 April 1962] • letters to Ben Nicholson, Tate collection, 8717.1.2.3147, 3148, 3149 • P. Dunford, *A biographical dictionary of women artists in Europe and America since 1850* (1990) • R. Rosen, 'Marlow Moss: did she influence Mondrian's work of the thirties?', *Arts Magazine*, 53/8 (1979), 163–5 • d. cert. • b. cert.
Archives Tate collection, letters to Ben Nicholson; corresp. with Paul Vézelay
Wealth at death £8433 14s. 7d.: probate, 26 Nov 1958, CGPLA Eng. & Wales

Moss, Robert (*c*.1666–1729), dean of Ely, was born at Gillingham in Norfolk, the eldest of four sons of Robert Moss of Postwick and his wife, Mary, who held land in Gillingham. He was first educated at Norwich School under John Burton, and went up to Corpus Christi College, Cambridge, on 19 April 1682, under the tutorage of John Corby; he attained his BA in 1686. Moss soon gained the reputation of being an excellent student and disputant, and consequently was given a Norfolk fellowship at Corpus. He was ordained deacon by John Lake, bishop of Chichester, on 26 December 1688 at St Dionis Backchurch, London,

and gained his MA the following year. On 21 September 1690 Moss was ordained priest by Thomas Tenison, bishop of Lincoln, at Buckden and in 1693 was made a preacher for the University of Cambridge. He was put forward for the position of public orator (1695), which he lost by only two or three votes to William Ayloff, and a year later he gained his BD (1696). On 11 July 1698 he was appointed preacher to Gray's Inn and the following year he was given the position of assistant preacher at St James's, Westminster, by the rector, William Wake. He was made chaplain to William III on 30 April 1701, and continued in the position under Queen Anne and George I. On 16 April 1705 Moss was made DD by Queen Anne during her visit to Cambridge University, and in 1708 he was given the Tuesday lectureship at St Lawrence Jewry in the City of London, which he held until 1727.

During 1708 Moss was involved in a controversy with Thomas Greene, master of his old college, concerning the Norfolk fellowship. Greene asked Moss to resign his fellowship as the positions Moss now held gave him a total income of £240. Despite the opinions of two lawyers, who agreed with Greene, Moss refused, and retained his fellowship until 1714. He was installed as dean of Ely on 16 May 1713, and the following year was made rector of Gelston (Gilston), Hertfordshire. The antiquarian John Nichols later claimed that, had it not been for her death in 1714, Queen Anne would have elevated either Robert Moss or George Stanhope to the bishopric of Ely (Nichols, 153).

Moss was an able preacher. Andrew Snape, who edited his sermons and wrote a brief memoir, noted that when Moss preached at Great St Mary's, the church was always full (Moss, x). Moss was a high-churchman and a tory, and was known to frequent the tory October Club. In December 1709 he refused to preach on the thanksgiving day as a protest against the treatment received by Henry Sacheverell, following his inflammatory sermon at St Paul's Cathedral (*Remarks*, 2.320). This support for Sacheverell continued through his trial, when Moss and a number of high-church divines wrote the speech given by Sacheverell to the court on 7 March 1710 (Oldmixon, 435).

During the Bangorian controversy of 1717 Robert Moss was a member of the committee of convocation that condemned Benjamin Hoadly's views. He later published a pamphlet, *The Report Vindicated from Misreports* (1718), in which he defended the conclusions of the committee and the actions of convocation against the bishop. For his involvement against Hoadly, Moss was dismissed as royal chaplain.

At an unknown date Moss married a Mrs Hinton, a widow from Cambridgeshire whom he had met earlier in his career. They seem to have had no children. In later life he increasingly suffered from gout, which had afflicted him since he was young and which finally caused him to lose the use of his limbs. He died on 26 March 1729 and was buried on the north side of the presbytery of Ely Cathedral. In his will he made provision for his widow and a few other relatives. He also left a perpetual annuity of £5 to Gonville and Caius College to establish a sizarship there, in recognition of his long-term friendship with Dr Gooch. However, the majority of his fortune was left to his nephew Charles Moss.   REBECCA LOUISE WARNER

Sources R. Moss, *Sermons and discourses on practical subjects*, ed. A. Snape, 2nd edn, 2 vols. (1736), vol. 1 · J. Bentham, *The history and antiquities of the conventual and cathedral church of Ely* (1771), 238–9 · Nichols, *Lit. anecdotes*, vol. 4 · *Biographia Britannica, or, The lives of the most eminent persons who have flourished in Great Britain and Ireland*, suppl. (1766), 132–4 · Venn, *Alum. Cant.*, 1/3.221 · J. Oldmixon, *The history of England, during the reigns of King William and Queen Mary, Queen Anne, King George I* (1735) · R. Masters, *The history of the College of Corpus Christi and the B. Virgin Mary … in the University of Cambridge* (1753) · *Remarks and collections of Thomas Hearne*, ed. C. E. Doble and others, 2, OHS, 7 (1886) · G. Holmes, *The trial of Dr. Sacheverell* (1973) **Archives** BL, corresp., Add. MS 5831 · BL, letters, papers, poems, Add. MS 10125 **Likenesses** G. Vertue, line engraving, BM, NPG; repro. in Moss, *Sermons* **Wealth at death** provision for widow and other relatives; £5 perpetual annuity to Gonville and Caius College, Cambridge; bulk to nephew: *Biographia Britannica*, suppl., 134

Moss, Rosalind Louisa Beaufort (1890–1990), Egyptologist and bibliographer, was born on 21 September 1890 at Shrewsbury School, Shropshire, second of the six children of the Revd Henry Whitehead *Moss (1841–1917), headmaster of the school, and his wife, Mary, elder daughter of the Revd W. A. Beaufort. Educated at Heathfield School, Ascot, Rosalind Moss enrolled in the Society of Oxford Home Students (later St Anne's College) to read for the recently established diploma in anthropology. She became a pupil of R. R. Marett of Exeter College. He included her in the select company of his anthropological students who participated in the excavation of a prehistoric site in Jersey in 1914 (Marett, 195). In 1917 she was awarded the diploma, and in 1922 the degree of BSc for a thesis which was published in 1925 as *The Life after Death in Oceania and the Malay Archipelago*.

As early as 1917 Rosalind Moss had, to use her own words, 'taken up Egyptology', attending classes by Francis Ll. Griffith, reader in Egyptology in the university. His dismay at having a student to deal with turned to delight at the discovery that she was an ideal potential collaborator in the bibliography of ancient Egyptian monuments which he was supporting. Moreover, she required no payment, having been left a small but adequate settlement by her father. The work was organized from the first by Bertha Porter, a professional bibliographer, who was already elderly. Rosalind Moss would provide the dynamism and organizational skill needed to bring the work to a publishable state, and to adapt its working methods for continuation in the future.

In 1924 Moss made her first visit to Egypt, to verify materials collected for the first volume of *The Topographical Bibliography of Ancient Egyptian Hieroglyphic Texts, Reliefs and Paintings*. Treating the Theban necropolis, it appeared in 1927; volume 2, on Theban temples, was published in 1929; volumes 3–6, covering the rest of Egypt, came out between 1931 and 1939. The seventh volume, on the monuments of Nubia, the oases, and places outside Egypt, brought the original scheme to a triumphant conclusion

in 1951. No other ancient culture was provided with such a comprehensive and useful reference tool.

The work on the *Topographical Bibliography* did not stop with the publication of these volumes. Primary work on new scholarly productions, the rich results of excavations, and the examination of manuscript archives, yielded much new information for inclusion. The system developed by Rosalind Moss in the Griffith Institute in Oxford, newly opened in 1939, nourished by the worldwide scholarly contacts she established, enabled her and her assistants to maintain a powerhouse of reference available for consultation by scholars. Greatly enlarged revisions of volumes 1 and 2 were published between 1960 and 1974; the names of Porter and Moss were now joined by that of Ethel Burney, Moss's close associate. A revised volume 3 was subsequently produced under the editorship of Jaromir Malek, who continued the Moss style and tradition at Oxford.

Until her retirement at the age of eighty Rosalind Moss expended all her energies on the *Bibliography* while she was in Oxford. But foreign travel was her passion, and with Ethel Burney from the early 1930s she visited all European countries except Albania, many parts of Africa and Central America, and the USA and Canada, using travel purposefully to visit scholars, museums, and archives to collect materials for her files. She had a wonderfully persuasive manner, never dreaming that her proper requests could be refused.

Moss's achievement was recognized by her university in 1961 with the granting of the degree of DLitt *honoris causa*. In 1949 she was elected a fellow of the Society of Antiquaries, and in 1967 an honorary fellow of St Anne's College, Oxford. Volume 58 (1972) of the *Journal of Egyptian Archaeology* was dedicated to her. A book of tributes prepared for her one hundredth birthday, *A Dedicated Life*, became in the event a memorial volume. She died, unmarried, at Villa Maria, a nursing home in Springfield Road, Howell Hill, Epsom, Surrey, on 22 April 1990, and was cremated on 3 May at Leatherhead.   T. G. H. JAMES

Sources T. G. H. James and J. Malek, eds., *A dedicated life: tributes offered in memory of Rosalind Moss* (1990) · T. G. H. James, *Journal of Egyptian Archaeology*, 77 (1991), 150–55 · R. Moss, 'Topographical bibliography', *Textes et langages de l'Égypte pharaonique: cent cinquante années de recherches 1822–1972, hommages à Jean-François Champollion*, 3 (1974), 285–8 · *Journal of Egyptian Archaeology*, 47 (1961), 4 · R. R. Marett, *A Jerseyman at Oxford* (1941), 195, 220, 306 · *The Independent* (26 April 1990) · *The Times* (27 April 1990) · personal knowledge (2004) **Archives** Shrewsbury School, Shropshire **Likenesses** photographs, AM Oxf. **Wealth at death** £64,384: probate, 19 June 1990, *CGPLA Eng. & Wales*

Moss, Thomas (*c*.1740–1808), poet, was the only son of Francis Moss, a chandler and soap-boiler of Wolverhampton, Staffordshire. He went to school in Wolverhampton and Rugeley before matriculating in 1757 at Emmanuel College, Cambridge, where he graduated BA in 1761. After taking holy orders he became minister of Trentham, Staffordshire, and he was afterwards for many years minister of Brinley Hill Chapel in Worcestershire, and from 1767 to

1808 he was the perpetual curate of Brierley Hill Chapel in the parish of Kingswinford, Staffordshire.

Moss published anonymously *Poems on Several Occasions* at Wolverhampton in 1769. In an 'advertisement' to this small volume it is stated that most of the poems were written when the author was about twenty. The first piece is the pathetic and popular 'Beggar's Petition', beginning with the line 'Pity the sorrows of a poor old man'. A Latin translation of this poem, 'Mendici supplicatio', was published by William Humphries in 1790, together with a Latin version of Goldsmith's 'Deserted Village'. Moss also published some occasional sermons and *The Imperfection of Human Enjoyments* (1783), a poem in blank verse. He died on 6 December 1808 at Stourbridge, Worcestershire.

THOMPSON COOPER, *rev.* REBECCA MILLS

Sources Venn, *Alum. Cant.*, 2/4.482 · *Poems upon several occasions, by the late Rev. Thomas Moss*, ed. B. Philips (1827), v–vi · H. R. Luard, ed., *Graduati Cantabrigienses*, 6th edn (1873), 332 · J. Chambers, *Biographical illustrations of Worcestershire* (1820), 541 · *GM*, 1st ser., 60 (1790), 971–2 · *GM*, 1st ser., 61 (1791), 352–3 · *GM*, 1st ser., 78 (1808), 1133 · C. H. Cooper, *Memorials of Cambridge*, new edn, 3 vols. (1860–66), vol. 2, p. 379 · W. T. Lowndes, *The bibliographer's manual of English literature*, 2 (1834), 1622 · Watt, *Bibl. Brit.*, 2.687 · Allibone, *Dict.* · will, PRO, PROB 11/1497, sig. 391
Wealth at death fairly well off: will, PRO PROB 11/1497, sig. 391

Mosse, Bartholomew (1712–1759), man-midwife and philanthropist, was born in Wexford, Ireland, one of seven children of the Revd Thomas Mosse (1662?–1731), rector of Maryborough, and his wife, Martha, daughter of the Revd Andrew Nisbet, rector of Timogue. Mosse was apprenticed at approximately age seventeen to John Stone, a prominent Dublin barber–surgeon. In 1733 he completed his apprenticeship and was successful in his examination by the surgeon-general. Mosse married Mary Elizabeth Mallory in 1734 and a son, Michael, was baptized on 12 May 1737. Unfortunately, both mother and baby appear to have died shortly afterwards. In 1738 Mosse was appointed as surgeon in charge of the draft of troops to Minorca. After his sojourn in Minorca, Mosse appears to have travelled through Europe, 'intending to perfect himself in surgery and midwifery' (Wilde, 567). On returning to Dublin, Mosse decided to devote himself to midwifery, becoming a licentiate of midwifery of the King and Queen's College of Physicians in Ireland in 1742. On 6 October the following year Mosse married his cousin Jane Whittingham (*d.* 1764), daughter of the Venerable Charles Whittingham, archdeacon of Dublin, and 'a very agreeable young lady with a large fortune' (*Dublin Newsletter*, 18 Oct 1743). Two children, Charles and Jane, soon followed, in 1745 and 1746 respectively.

The wretchedness of the circumstances of many of the women that Mosse attended moved him deeply and he decided in the early 1740s to establish a charitable lying-in hospital. By 1743 Mosse had begun to raise funds through subscriptions and had secured the patronage of a number of Dublin's most prominent citizens. Once he had sufficient capital, he purchased an old theatre in George's Lane and rapidly converted it into a hospital. The Dublin Lying-In Hospital, the first such institution in the United Kingdom, opened on Friday 15 March 1745. The demand soon

Bartholomew Mosse (1712–1759), by unknown artist, *c.*1745

outstripped the hospital's resources and Mosse looked for new ways to raise funds, soon finding that his real talent was not as a doctor, but rather as an impresario. He staged highly popular theatre and musical productions and lotteries. Despite financial success, the limitations of the original site and the need for a more reliable income led Mosse to conceive of a novel plan. In 1748 he acquired a site on the outskirts of Dublin and built a pleasure garden, as well as a concert room and coffee house. Opened the following year, the New Gardens were a huge success and with the proceeds Mosse began work on a new, purpose-built lying-in hospital designed by Richard Cassells, the prominent architect, on the remainder of the site. Despite taking personal responsibility for this ambitious project, Mosse remained enthusiastic and optimistic, remarking 'to the effect that when the foundation stone was laid he was not worth £500; and although he knew the hospital would cost him above £20,000, yet he never despaired of seeing it finished' (Wilde, 573). Eager to ensure the permanence of the hospital, Mosse petitioned for a royal charter, as well as parliamentary grants. Both were successful, he himself unexpectedly receiving £2000 'as a reward for his great care and diligence' (Kirkpatrick, 38). The Rotunda Hospital was opened on Thursday 8 December 1757 and the old hospital closed. Mosse was appointed the first governor of the hospital, a post he held until his death.

Mosse's schemes, however charitable, were not without censure and he was accused of misappropriating funds, as well as being imprisoned for debt in England (he escaped through a window and hid in the Welsh mountains before returning to Dublin). Despite this, he was a genial and popular man who could often be found with his friends 'at a tavern, which they seldom left before three or four in the morning' (J. T. Gilmour, cited in J. Duffy, *A History of the City of Dublin*, 3, 1861, 315). Seemingly worn out by his exertions, Mosse became ill in the winter of 1758. His condition slowly deteriorated and, on the advice of his physician, he moved to Cullenswood House in Ranelagh, the country house of his friend Alderman Peter Barré. He died there on the 16 February 1759 and was interred at Donnybrook two days later.

L. K. VAUGHAN

Sources A. Browne, 'Bartholomew Mosse, 1712–1759, founder and first master', *Masters, midwives and ladies-in-waiting: the Rotunda Hospital, 1745–1995*, ed. A. Browne (1995), 1–20 · W. Wilde, 'Illustrious physicians and surgeons in Ireland, no. 2: Bartholomew Mosse', *Dublin Quarterly Journal of Medical Science*, 2 (1846), 565–96 · T. P. Kirkpatrick, *The book of the Rotunda Hospital* (1913), 2–145 · J. B. Fleming, 'The mysteries concerning the last illness, death and burial of Bartholomew Mosse', *Irish Journal of Medical Science*, 436 (1962), 147–63 · J. B. Leslie, *Biographical succession list of the clergy of the Leighlin diocese* (1939), 1.61–2 · W. P. Pakenham Walsh, 'Mosse', *Pedigree Register*, 1/3 (1907), 53–7, 73–4 · W. Ball Wright, 'Mosse', *Pedigree Register*, 1/4 (1908), 106–8 · W. P. Pakenham Walsh, 'Mosse', *Pedigree Register*, 1/6 (1908), 170–71
Archives Rotunda Hospital, Dublin, archives, MSS · Royal College of Physicians of Ireland, Dublin, archives, MSS
Likenesses oils, c.1745, Rotunda Hospital, Dublin [*see illus.*] · Van Nost?, marble bust, c.1750, Rotunda Hospital, Dublin
Wealth at death 'The will of Bartholomew Mosse', Kirkpatrick, *Book of the Rotunda Hospital*, 209–15 · had taken sole responsibility for building of Rotunda Hospital, unfinished at death, so substantially indebted; goods auctioned; Jane's £1500 dowry seemingly met, but government granted Mrs Mosse £1000 shortly after subject's death, because family had been damaged by his involvement with hospital; she had to be forcibly evicted from hospital premises the following year: Kirkpatrick, *Book of the Rotunda Hospital*, 47, 52

Mosse [*née* Rouviere], **Henrietta** (d. 1834), novelist, was born in Ireland. Nothing is known of her early life or education. Her first novel, *Lussington Abbey* was published anonymously by the Minerva Press in 1804. On 4 December 1806 at St Marylebone in London she married Isaac Mosse (1766/7–1828), businessman and author of *Enclytica, Being the Outlines of a Course of Instruction on the Principles of Universal Grammar* (1814). She continued to write for Minerva after her marriage, publishing under her own name. Several novels appeared in quick succession, including the well-received *Heirs of Villeroy* (1806); *A Peep at our Ancestors* (1807), a historical novel set in the twelfth century; and *The Old Irish Baronet, or, The Manners of my Country* (1808), modelled on Clara Reeve's successful Gothic novel, *The Old English Baron* (1788). *A Peep at our Ancestors* was allegedly based on 'records and documents', but despite the author's claim to have written a 'correct' sketch of the times, its 'peep' into history is thinly disguised contemporary romance. This novel is graced by a frontispiece engraved portrait of Mosse by H. R. Cook after Ramsey, a dedication to the duke of Leinster, and subscribers list. In 1812 *Arrivals from India, or, Time's a Great Master* was published, with a dedication to Princess Mary. Henrietta

Mosse's reputation was that of the skilled Minerva veteran, writing highly marketable novels of indifferent quality, containing 'nothing to condemn, and certainly nothing very much to commend'. The formulas she deployed differed little from other romance writers, 'with this exception that the fair author keeps in mind the good old moral of virtue rewarded, and vice punished' (*Critical Review*). In 1816 she published *Craigh-Melrose Priory, or, Memoirs of the Mount Linton Family*, translated into French the following year. *A Bride and No Wife* appeared in 1817, with intermittent translation work from French to English.

The 1820s began badly, with Isaac Mosse swindled in business and paralysed by a series of strokes from 1822. Nursing her husband single-handedly, Mosse published at least four novels between 1825 and 1829: *A Father's Love and a Woman's Friendship* (1825), *Gratitude and other Tales* (1826), *Woman's Wit and Man's Wisdom, or, Intrigue* (1827), and *The Blandfords, or, Fate and Fortune* (1829) with assistance from her 'benevolent Patroness', Marchioness Cornwallis. With times bad for all and a deepening sense that 'authorship is become a very doubtful source for existence', Mosse advertised for non-literary work, trying to rally her 'power to exert [herself]' and her innate 'high spirit'. The Royal Literary Fund was relatively generous while Isaac Mosse lived and granted his widow £20 in 1828 after an affecting appeal 'from the side of his coffin'. All previous petitions were based on her husband's single published work, and in 1830 Mosse was obliged to appeal for the first time as author in her own right, staking her claim on past publications and several works in hand: three volumes of 'moral and entertaining tales founded on fact', a work entitled 'The distress of women', and several dramas, 'highly spoken of by the Principals of one or two theatres'. Nevertheless, she despaired of ever seeing them performed, confessing that she felt constrained by lack of 'that energetic principle to urge them forwards' which 'cannot properly belong to the female character' (*Archives of the Royal Literary Fund*, reel 16).

The Royal Literary Fund archive charts a harrowing career up until 1834, when Mosse died 'in a state of great destitution in a miserable attic' at 6 Somers Town Terrace, London. W. Jones of 36 Judd Street, the doctor who tended her in her final illness, appealed to the Royal Literary Fund for aid for a decent burial, but his request was ruled 'inadmissible' (*Archives of the Royal Literary Fund*, reel 16).

DEIRDRE COLEMAN

Sources *Archives of the Royal Literary Fund, 1790–1918*, minutes of general committee, 1984, reels 1a, 2a [microform] · *Archives of the Royal Literary Fund, 1790–1918*, Mosse, Isaac and Henrietta, his widow, 1984, case no. 532, reels 16, 125–6 [microform] · Blain, Clements & Grundy, *Feminist comp.*, 766 · D. Blakey, *The Minerva Press, 1790–1820* (1939) · W. S. Ward, *Literary reviews in British periodicals, 1798–1820: a bibliography*, 2 (1972), 412, 474 · *Critical Review*, 4th ser., 2 (1812), 332 · M. Summers, *The Gothic quest: a history of the Gothic novel* (1938); repr. (1964) · *BL cat.* · *National union catalog*, Library of Congress · *Nineteenth century short title catalogue* (1984–95) · L. Baillie and P. Sieveking, eds., *British biographical archive* (1984) [microfiche] · Allibone, *Dict.* · [J. Watkins and F. Shoberl], *A biographical dictionary of the living authors of Great Britain and Ireland* (1816) · Bénézit, *Dict.* · Thieme & Becker, *Allgemeines Lexikon* · Bryan, *Painters*

Dictionary of painters and engravers [for John Burnet, Ramsey/ Ramsay and for engraver Henry R. Cook (fl. 1800–1845), Thieme-Becker] · *Allgemeines Künstlerlexicon*, 7, 346
Archives Royal Literary Fund, London, archives
Likenesses H. R. Cook, engraving (after Ramsey), BL; repro. in H. Rouviere, *A peep at our ancestors: an historical romance* (1807), frontispiece
Wealth at death in debt; destitute; insufficient funds for decent burial: Royal Literary Fund archives, case no. 532, nos. 35–9

Mosse, Miles (1558–1615), Church of England clergyman, was born in Chevington, Suffolk, the son of Miles Mosse, a yeoman of Chevington. He studied at the grammar school in Bury St Edmunds for six years and was admitted a pensioner of Gonville and Caius College, Cambridge, on 14 April 1575. He proceeded BA in 1578/9 and commenced MA in 1582. He was ordained priest on 7 October 1583 (Lincoln diocese) and was licensed to preach on 8 April 1584. In 1585 he was appointed vicar of St Stephens, Norwich, where he came to know John Erskine, nineteenth earl of Mar, who was for a time 'an Auditor of my Ministery' (Mosse, *Scotlands Welcome*, sig. A2). In 1586 he moved from Norwich to Bury St Edmunds where he served as preacher of the parish of St James, receiving the handsome stipend of £40 per annum. He proceeded to the degree of BTh in 1589 and DTh in 1595. In 1597 he accepted the rectory of Combes, one of the wealthier livings in the archdeaconry of Sudbury, to which he was instituted on 27 May and where he remained until his death in 1615. He was buried in the parish church on 13 September 1615.

Two years before his death Mosse preached at Paul's Cross in London on 'justifying and saving faith distinguished from the faith of the Devils'. The published version of his sermon was dedicated to the lord chief justice, Edward Coke, and was full of praise for Queen Elizabeth's religious policies. Perhaps by 1613 age and Combes had moderated some of Mosse's earlier reforming convictions. He undoubtedly knew John More, the 'apostle of Norwich', from his years in that city, and as one of the so-called 'Cambridge boys'—a sneering allusion by his adversary Thomas Rogers to the select group of Cambridge-trained evangelical ministers who tended to be closet Presbyterians and who exercised control over the famous combination lecture in Bury St Edmunds—his godly connections were impeccable. The Bury lecture was presided over by John Knewstub and included men like Nicholas Bownd, Walter Allen, and Reginald Whitfield. Mosse also appears to have maintained a close connection with such Cambridge puritans as Laurence Chaderton.

Mosse may well have been the organizing force behind the remarkable bestseller entitled *A Garden of Spirituall Flowers*, first published in 1609 and consisting of posthumous treatises of practical divinity from Richard Rogers, Richard Greenham, and William Perkins, with brief contributions from Mosse himself and one George Webbe. He is probably best-known, however, for his lectures on usury published in 1595 under the title, *The Arraignment and Conviction of Usurie* which began life as a series of six sermons delivered at the Monday exercise in Bury between March and July 1594. He quarrelled famously with his neighbour

Thomas Rogers, rector of Horningsheath, who in the context of the Bury exercise had launched a calculated attack on Laurence Chaderton's anonymously published sermon on church government. For his pains Rogers found himself excluded from the exercise. Shortly after these events, Mosse republished the popular catechism by John More and Edward Dering with a short preface dedicated to the bishop of Norwich in which he complained that 'men will speak before they have learned' and that 'manie ministers of the word write much but preach little', statements which the suspicious Rogers interpreted as an attack upon his own efforts as a writer. Rogers responded at length in a bitter attack upon Mosse's preface under the title *Miles Christianus, or, A just apologie of all necessarie writings and writers specialie of them which by their labored writings take paines to build up the church of Christ*, the opening lines of which wished Mosse 'more soundnes of judgement, more substance of learning with more wisdome and discretion in all his actions'. It is doubtful whether the two men were ever reconciled.

Mosse's most lasting achievement was the erection in 1595 of the parish library of St James in Bury St Edmunds, to which he persuaded the neighbouring clergy, gentlemen, and townsmen to donate books. Some of these donations are still recorded in the handwritten bookplates pasted into the volumes. Mosse himself gave a number of books, including commentaries by Aretius, Bullinger's *Decades*, and the works of John of Damascus. By 1599 the library possessed more than 200 volumes, primarily theological works.

JOHN CRAIG

Sources Ri Gree [R. Greenham], Ri Ro [R. Rogers], Wil Per [W. Perkins], M. M. [M. Mosse], and Geo Web [G. Webbe], *A garden of spirituall flowers* (1609) · P. Collinson, 'The beginnings of English sabbatarianism', *Papers read at the first winter and summer meetings of the Ecclesiastical History Society*, ed. C. W. Dugmore and C. Duggan, SCH, 1 (1964), 207–21; repr. in P. Collinson, *Godly people: essays on English protestantism and puritanism* (1983), 429–43 · J. Craig, *Reformation, politics and polemics: the growth of protestantism in East Anglian market towns, 1500–1610* (2001) · J. Craig, 'The "Cambridge Boies": Thomas Rogers and the "brethren" in Bury St Edmunds', *Belief and practice in Reformation England: a tribute to Patrick Collinson from his students*, ed. S. Wabuda and C. Litzenberger (1998), 154–76 · S. H. A. H. [S. H. A. Hervey], *Biographical list of boys educated at King Edward VI Free Grammar School, Bury St Edmunds, from 1550 to 1900* (1908) · N. Jones, *God and the moneylenders* (1989) · M. Mosse, *Justifiying and saving faith distinguished from the faith of the devils in a sermon preached at Paul's Crosse in London, May 9, 1613* (1614) · M. Mosse, *Scotlands welcome: a sermon preached at Needham in the countie of Suffolk on Tuesday, April 5 1603* (1603) · M. Mosse, *The arraignment and conviction of usurie* (1594) · T. Rogers, *Miles Christianus, or, A just apologie of all necessarie writings and writers* (1590) [the copy in the British Library, C 124.c.7, belonged to Thomas Rogers and is interleaved with many notes in Rogers's hand] · Venn, *Alum. Cant.*, 1/3.220 · *The Registrum vagum of Anthony Harison*, ed. T. F. Barton, 2 vols., Norfolk RS, 32–3 (1963–4), pt 2.191, 234, 256

Mosses, Alexander (1793–1837), painter, born in Liverpool, was the son of George Mosses, a plasterer and stucco maker. At an early age he showed a talent for drawing, and was apprenticed from 1 October 1806 to the Liverpool engraver Henry Hole (indenture dated 7 April 1807). He is said to have learned colouring from J. Jenkinson, a Liverpool portrait, landscape, and marine painter. Mosses became a competent draughtsman and colourist. He exhibited at some of the earliest Post Office Place exhibitions. In the exhibition of the Liverpool Academy for 1811 he showed a *View of Birkenhead Priory*, and in the following years landscapes and figural pictures. His only exhibit at the Royal Academy was in 1820: *Dharma Rama and Munhi Rathama, Two Buddhist Priests from the Island of Ceylon*. He became a member of the Liverpool Academy about 1822, was listed as 'master of drawing' in 1827, and professor from 1835. He achieved a reputable position in Liverpool as a portrait painter and teacher. He is said to have discovered and taught William Daniels, a noted Liverpool painter. He was almost certainly the Alexander Mosses whose son, Alexander, was baptized on 19 April 1835 at St Peter's, Liverpool, when the child's mother's name was recorded as Mary Smallwood. (In 1861 George, son of the younger Alexander Mosses, was baptized in the same church.) Mosses painted and exhibited some biblical subjects including, in 1829, *Christ's Agony in the Garden*, and *The Expulsion from Paradise*, and exhibited twice at the Royal Hibernian Association, in 1832 and 1834. He painted the portraits of many eminent men in his locality. In 1831 he exhibited five pictures, the most important of which was the full-length portrait of Thomas Branker, mayor of Liverpool. He also painted a portrait of the Revd John Yates of Liverpool, which was later engraved by F. Engleheart. Other works by Mosses which were engraved included that of a butcher boy, showing the town of Liverpool in the distance, by H. Robinson. Also engraved was the picture of blind Howard, a well-known inmate of the Blind Asylum, and his children, which is in the permanent collection at the Walker Art Gallery, Liverpool, together with a portrait of William Ewart which was presented in 1873 by W. E. Gladstone MP.

Mosses died at his home, 18 Pleasant Street, Clarence Street, Liverpool, on 14 July 1837, leaving a widow and two sons. His brother Thomas Mosses was an engraver in London. ALBERT NICHOLSON, rev. L. R. HOULISTON

Sources *Merseyside painters, people and places: catalogue of oil paintings*, Walker Art Gallery, Liverpool, ed. M. Bennett (1978) [text and pls.] · H. C. Marillier, *The Liverpool school of painters: an account of the Liverpool Academy from 1810 to 1867, with memoirs of the principal artists* (1904) · Bryan, *Painters* · B. Stewart and M. Cutten, *The dictionary of portrait painters in Britain up to 1920* (1997) · E. Morris and E. Roberts, *The Liverpool Academy and other exhibitions of contemporary art in Liverpool, 1774–1867* (1998) · Graves, *RA exhibitors* · Graves, *Artists* · A. M. Stewart and C. de Courcy, *Royal Hibernian Academy of Arts: index of exhibitors and their works, 1826–1979*, 3 vols. (1985–7) · Bénézit, *Dict.* · Thieme & Becker, *Allgemeines Lexikon* · D. T. Mallett, *Mallett's index of artists* (1935) · *Checklist of British artists in the Witt Library*, Courtauld Institute, Witt Library (1991) · *Liverpool Mercury* (21 July 1837) · *Liverpool Lantern* (15 Jan 1881) · IGI
Archives Liverpool Central Library

Mossman, George (*fl.* 1770–1824), physician, practised at Bridge Street, Bradford, Yorkshire, from before 1770 to some time after 1824. On 6 July 1792 he married there a Miss Ramsbotham. A later marriage of a Dr Mossman, physician of Bradford, to Mrs Ramsbottom of Barwick in Elmet, Yorkshire, is also recorded in 1812.

Mossman wrote a number of works on medical subjects,

including *Observations on the Brunonian practice of physic, including a reply to an anonymous publication reprobating the use of stimulants in fevers* (1788) and *An essay to elucidate the nature, origin, and connexion of srophula* [sic] *and glandular consumption, including a brief history of the effects of Ilkley spaw, with observation on the medicinal powers of the digitalis* (1792?). He contributed four papers to Andrew Duncan's *Annals of Medicine* (1797 and 1799, 2.298, 307, 413; 4.432), a paper in the *Medical Repository* (1.577), and numerous papers on the effects of digitalis in consumption to the *Medical and Physical Journal*. GORDON GOODWIN, rev. PATRICK WALLIS

Sources Watt, *Bibl. Brit.* · P. J. Wallis and R. V. Wallis, *Eighteenth century medics*, 2nd edn (1988) · *GM*, 1st ser., 62 (1792), 672 · *GM*, 1st ser., 82/2 (1812), 586
Archives W. Yorks. AS, Bradford, corresp. and papers

Mossman, James (*d.* 1573). *See under* Castilians in Edinburgh (*act.* 1570–1573).

Mossman, Thomas Wimberley (1826–1885), Anglican clergyman, born at Skipton, Yorkshire, and baptized on 5 March 1826 in Doncaster, was the eldest son of Robert Hume Mossman of Skipton and his wife, Maria Louisa Wimberley. He matriculated from St Edmund Hall, Oxford, on 17 December 1845, and while an undergraduate became an adherent of the Oxford Movement. He graduated BA in 1849 and took priest's orders in 1850. He became vicar of Ranby, Lincolnshire, in 1854, and rector of East Torrington and vicar of West Torrington, near Wragby, in the same county, in 1859.

A devoted parish priest, Mossman became more widely known as a leader of the extreme ritualistic party, and was a close associate of Frederick G. Lee. In 1877, having concluded that the Church of England was in schism, Mossman and Lee formed an Order of Corporate Reunion with the aim of establishing an English Orthodox church on Uniate lines. With the encouragement of Ambrose Phillipps De Lisle they set out for Italy in the summer of that year and there received episcopal consecration. Though Mossman maintained a cryptic silence on the exact details, it appears that he was consecrated somewhere in Umbria by the archbishop of Milan, or his suffragan, and henceforth he styled himself bishop of Selby. The order held a 'solemn synod' in London later in the year, but although Lee and Mossman conferred priestly orders on numerous, and sometimes highly unsuitable, candidates it did not long survive as an organized body. During his last illness Mossman was received into the Roman Catholic church by his old friend Cardinal Manning, who travelled to Lincolnshire to receive his submission. He had previously taken steps to resign his rectory, but the legal formalities had not yet been completed when he died at West Torrington rectory on 6 July 1885. He was survived by his wife, Mary, and at least one son, Robert Arthur, a surgeon.

Erudite and austere in his style of living, Mossman was an inveterate supporter of quixotic causes. His scholarly publications included a history of the early church (1873), a translation of Blosius's *Speculum spirituale*, and a translation in five volumes of the gospel commentaries of the Jesuit exegete Cornelius à Lapide (1876–86). In 1881 he received the honorary degree of DD from the University of the South, in the United States.   G. MARTIN MURPHY

Sources H. R. T. Brandreth, *Dr Lee of Lambeth* (1951), 118–45 · *Church Times* (17 July 1885), 555 · *Lincolnshire Chronicle* (10 July 1885), 5 · *The Tablet* (18 July 1885), 103 · d. cert.
Archives Lincs. Arch., family corresp. | BL, letters to W. E. Gladstone, Add. MSS 44438–44461, *passim*
Wealth at death £1005 12s. 6d.: probate, 19 Jan 1886, CGPLA Eng. & Wales

Mossom, Robert (*bap.* 1617, *d.* 1679), Church of Ireland bishop of Derry, son of Raphe Mossome, was baptized at the church of St Michael-on-the-Mount, Lincoln, on 12 January 1617. He was admitted sizar at Magdalene College, Cambridge, on 2 June 1631, but two months later migrated to Peterhouse, which he entered on 9 August. He graduated BA (1635) and MA (1638).

In 1642 Mossom was officiating at York as an army chaplain under Sir Thomas Glemham. About this time he is said to have married Mildred Eland (*fl. c.*1642–1656) of Bedale. Their eldest son, Glemham, was named for Mossom's patron. While at York, Mossom published *Anti-Paraeus, or, A treatise in the defence of the royall right of kings*, a translation from the work of David Owen, and two sermons preached in the cathedral there in 1643, under the title *The king on his throne, or, A discourse maintaining the dignity of a king, the duty of a subject, and the unlawfulnesse of rebellion*. In 1644 he was preacher to the troops under the command of Sir George Wentworth at the siege of Pontefract. After the establishment of the free state, Mossom held fast to the practice and principles of prayer book protestantism, for which he suffered sequestration from a living at Teddington, Middlesex, on 25 July 1650. He then moved to St Peter Paul's Wharf, London, where he continued to use the banned Book of Common Prayer, offering holy communion monthly, 'which brought a great concourse and resort to it' (Bosher, 11). His congregation included members of the nobility and gentry, and was regularly targeted for harassment by the military.

In 1651 Mossom published *Sion's prospect in its first view. Presented in a summary of divine truths, consenting with the faith professed by the Church of England*, a proto-Anglican loyalist text which was still in print in the early eighteenth century. Eventually Mossom fell victim to the wave of repression which followed the abortive royalist risings of 1655, suffering ejection once again. Thenceforth he maintained himself, his wife, and six children by keeping a school. On 24 January 1656 he petitioned the lord protector for permission to continue teaching despite a ban on sequestered ministers. He was able to supply testimonials—one of them from Peter Sterry, chaplain to the lord protector, some of whose children were schooled by Mossom—which stated that Mossom, 'by a strict prohibition and due correction supprest the animositys of his schollers, which have been raised against any of their schools fellows, children of parents engaged on the Commonwealth

behalfe' (*Walker rev.*, 261). Mossom was permitted to continue teaching while further investigation was undertaken. He published *The preachers tripartite, in three books* (1657) and *Variae colloquendi formulae* (1659). Also, an 'R. M., Minister of St. Peter's, Paul's Wharf', delivered a sermon at the funeral of one John G. Holt, esq., at St Martin-in-the-Fields on 19 March 1659, which was published in 1660 under the title *A plant of paradise*.

Mossom actively sought to help shape the manner in which the restoration of church and king was accomplished in 1660. In that year he published *An apology in the behalf of the sequestered clergy*, which appears to have been presented to the Convention Parliament. He was at pains to stress that loyal churchmen had played their part, through 'fasting and prayers and tears', in helping bring about restoration (Spurr, 34). Mossom, who has been accounted one of 'the Laudian party' (Bosher, 160), was an early and frequent beneficiary of royal patronage. By the king's letters mandatory, dated 21 July 1660, he was created DD at Cambridge on 5 September following. Having petitioned for the post of prebendary of Knaresborough-cum-Bickhill in the diocese of York, he was presented by the king on 13 August 1660, installed by proxy on 22 September, collated by the archbishop on 16 February 1663, and installed on 19 February.

By then Mossom had found a comfortable home for himself in the Church of Ireland, having been appointed dean of Christ Church, Dublin, by royal letters patent dated 25 September 1660, and being installed there on 2 February 1661. By patent dated 13 November 1660 he was also presented by the crown to the precentorship of St Patrick's, Dublin, and was installed there on 27 December. He was elected prolocutor of the lower house of convocation at Dublin on 21 May 1661, in which capacity he delivered a congratulatory speech before the duke of Ormond at his arrival to take up the post of lord lieutenant in 1662. After the death of George Wild, bishop of Derry, Mossom was promoted to the vacant see, the richest in Ireland, its income valued at £1800 in the year of his elevation. He preached a sermon at the funeral of his predecessor which was published in 1666. Mossom's patent bears the date 26 March 1666, and he was consecrated by the primate, James Margetson, archbishop of Armagh, assisted by the archbishop of Dublin, Michael Boyle, and the bishops of Kildare and Killala, on 1 April. It has been erroneously stated that he held the deanery of Christ Church *in commendam* with the bishopric. The new bishop's first and most pressing problem was caused by the radical covenanter rebellion that broke out in Galloway, south-west Scotland, in November 1666, in the aftermath of which Ulster was inundated by refugee dissenters. Mossom favoured the hard line, urging the arrest of factious ministers who 'like wild Bores hunted out of a Forrest … throw their fome of seditious doctrine amongst the people' (Greaves, 95). The situation was not helped by the structural failings of the Church of Ireland in Ulster. Reporting on the state of his diocese in 1670, Mossom lamented the ruinous state of the church fabric, owing to which he found that 'the holy offices of God's publick worship were, for the most part, administered either in a dirty cabin or in a common alehouse' (Phillips, 3.146), and complained that twenty-six ministers were serving forty-seven parishes. These shortcomings made it difficult to tackle endemic dissent, and in 1672, when Mossom urged the new lord deputy, the earl of Essex, to take firm action against the presbyterians, he could report that such was their temerity that they had recently erected a large meeting-house within Londonderry itself, a mere two or three doors from the bishop's own mansion. Essex disappointed Mossom's hopes by advising the king to grant the dissenters an indulgence. Tensions rose to such a pitch that in the aftermath of one riot the bishop requested either that he be allowed to retreat to Dublin or England, or that he be sent military support adequate to the task of cowing the tumultuous sectaries. A fragile *modus vivendi* was eventually arrived at, from which both sides could claim some kind of a victory, and some of the heat went out of the situation. In 1678 Mossom permitted the Urney congregants of the Lagan presbytery to build a new meeting-house.

Mossom died at Londonderry on 21 December 1679 and was buried in his cathedral on 1 January 1680. He was succeeded by a son, also Robert, master of chancery at Dublin and father of another Robert, who became dean of Ossory.   SEAN KELSEY

Sources DNB · W. A. Phillips, *History of the Church of Ireland from the earliest times to the present day*, 3 vols. (1933), vol. 3, pp. 145–6 · J. B. Leslie, *Derry clergy and parishes* (1937) · Walker rev. · R. S. Bosher, *The making of the Restoration settlement: the influence of the Laudians, 1649–1662* (1951) · J. Spurr, *The Restoration Church of England, 1646–1689* (1991) · R. Greaves, *God's other children: protestant nonconformists and the emergence of denominational churches in Ireland, 1660–1700* (1997) · IGI

Archives BL

Likenesses portrait; known to be at Mount Eland, co. Kilkenny, Ireland, in 1853

Mossop, Henry (1727/8–1774), actor and theatre manager, was born in co. Galway, the son of the Revd John Mossop (1701/2–1759), Church of Ireland clergyman of the prebend of Kilmeen, Tuam, co. Galway. He was brought up in Dublin by his uncle, a bookseller, and is said to have attended the grammar school in Digges Street. He entered Trinity College, Dublin, in 1745, at the age of seventeen, with the intention of becoming a clergyman. How he became attracted to the theatre is not known. It was evidently his uncle who encouraged him to travel to London about 1748 to try his fortune on the stage. Both David Garrick and John Rich, then London theatre managers, attempted to dissuade Mossop from the acting profession when they first saw him, but a friend, the actor and playwright Francis Gentleman, introduced him to Thomas Sheridan, the manager of Dublin's Smock Alley Theatre. Sheridan obviously discerned some talent in Mossop, who made his acting début at Smock Alley on 30 November 1749 in the demanding part of Zanga in Edward Young's *The Revenge*. It was a role for which he was to remain famous throughout his career. Almost immediately laudatory verses began to appear in the Dublin newspapers, and in the weeks that followed Mossop was applauded in a wide variety of principal roles, including Othello, Iago, and Cassius in *Julius Caesar*. In December 1749 he missed several nights' acting on account of a 'sudden indisposition': his health was never good, and he was frequently ill.

Mossop never conquered his addiction to the fashionable vice of gambling, but he did learn the self-discipline necessary to an actor. From 1749 to 1751 he was seen in increasingly challenging roles, virtually all of which required an actor able to play characters of a mercurial temperament, such as Hotspur in *1 Henry IV*, Bajazet in Nicholas Rowe's *Tamerlane*, and Aboan in Thomas Southerne's *Oroonoko*. However, an argument between Mossop, who could be stern, proud, fiery, and commanding, and Sheridan over a costume seems to have precipitated Mossop's decision to abandon Smock Alley at the end of the 1750–51 season and to travel to London, where he made his début at Garrick's Drury Lane on 26 September 1751, as Richard III. According to contemporaries Mossop was very handsome, of middle stature, well formed, with an expressive face (his eyes were said to indicate a proud and independent mind). But he possessed several stage mannerisms that attracted ridicule. Charles Churchill, in *The Rosciad*, poked fun at his habit of placing his left hand on his hip and extending his right, in a manner redolent of a teapot, and at his mechanical delivery of lines and weighty emphasizing of syllables.

After a shaky start in London, Mossop played to crowded houses in the roles which had proved successful in Dublin. Contemporaries declared that, despite his youth and inexperience, he had the most melodious and clear voice to be heard on the stage in his day. He remained at Drury Lane for three seasons, quickly expanding his repertory. During this time he lived at Newton's Warehouse, Tavistock Square.

At the end of the 1754–5 Drury Lane season Mossop was approached by the interim managers at Smock Alley, Victor and Sowden, who offered him handsome terms to return to Dublin. Mossop accepted, and was again immensely successful, earning £2000 in eighteen nights that season. Despite his popularity in Dublin, Mossop jumped at Garrick's offer to return to Drury Lane for the 1756–7 season, and he remained for three seasons, adding many new roles to his repertory. However, he joined Spranger Barry and Henry Woodward's new Crow Street Theatre in Dublin for the 1759–60 season and never acted on a London stage again. His motives for leaving London are unclear; the most plausible explanation is that his father died in May 1759, leaving him an estate in the city of Dublin worth £200 per annum.

Mossop remained with the Crow Street company for only one season. Both Barry and Mossop were wildly popular favourites, and detailed comparisons of their talents appeared in the press. It must have become clear to Mossop that there was money to be made in exploiting their rivalry, particularly among the wealthy and influential women in the audience. In May 1760 he leased the then dormant Smock Alley and Aungier Street theatres from their owners and set up in management. Barry and

Woodward offered him £1000 per annum and two benefits to remain at Crow Street, but he declined the offer.

Mossop opened the Smock Alley Theatre on 17 November 1760, and the newspapers observed that there was hardly a regular theatregoer who was not an avowed Barryist or Mossopian. For most of the seven years that they were in opposition, Barry's and Mossop's theatres were nearly evenly balanced in virtually every respect. Despite making handsome profits, Mossop's outgoings were larger, not only as a result of the expensive imported actors and the costly mountings he required for his productions, but also because of his heavy losses at the gambling tables. By the end of the 1767–8 season Barry threw in the towel and moved to London. Mossop reigned supreme for the next three years, performing in Crow Street and Smock Alley alternately. The beginning of the end of his career as manager occurred in the autumn of 1771, when the lord mayor of Dublin licensed William Dawson and a few others to open a rival to the Theatre Royal in Capel Street. Although the theatre was relatively small, it attracted enthusiastic audiences, and Mossop's receipts began to slide. His last stage performance took place on 6 March 1771, as Belcour in Richard Cumberland's *The West Indian*. After that night he was taken seriously ill, probably with pneumonia, and was confined to his house. Although pronounced out of danger three weeks later he was forbidden by his doctor to act for another year, and, in fact, never appeared again on the stage. He travelled to London on a recruiting trip in the autumn of 1771 and declined Garrick's offer to perform at Drury Lane. Soon afterwards he was arrested for debt, and his popularity in Dublin is attested by the fact that his erstwhile company organized three benefits on his behalf with the stated aim of releasing him from debtor's prison. He finally declared bankruptcy in January 1772 and was released.

In the summer of 1772 Mossop, at his doctor's instructions, travelled to the south of France to recover his health, but the change of climate had no effect and he returned to London in 1774. He died, in abject poverty, in the Strand, of a 'humoural asthma' on 27 December 1774, and was buried at the expense of his friends in Chelsea churchyard on 1 January 1775. He had never married, although he had lived for a time about 1754 with Sarah Ford, later the wife of the elder George Colman. They had a daughter, Harriet Ann Ford, who became an actress. Mossop was also survived by his sister Elizabeth, who was given a benefit at the Smock Alley Theatre each season for several years after her brother's death.

JOHN C. GREENE

Sources Highfill, Burnim & Langhans, *BDA*, 10.334–44 · J. C. Greene, MS notes to *The Dublin stage, 1745–1820* · *DNB* · W. W. Appleton, *Charles Macklin: an actor's life* (1960) · E. K. Sheldon, *Thomas Sheridan of Smock-Alley: recording his life as actor and theater manager in both Dublin and London* (1967)

Likenesses T. Hickey, chalk drawing, NG Ire.; repro. in *Exshaws Magazine* (Feb 1775) · N. Hone, oils, Garr. Club · J. H. Mortimer, drawing, priv. coll. · W. Ridley, stipple (after drawing by J. H. Mortimer), BM, NPG; repro. in *Monthly Mirror* (Sept 1799) · bust, repro. in *Gentleman's and London Magazine* (Feb 1775) · engraving (as Bajazet

in *Tamerlane*), priv. coll. · engraving (as Osmyn in *The mourning bride*), repro. in *Hibernian Magazine* (Feb 1775) · engraving (as Zanga in *The revenge*), repro. in E. Young, *The revenge* (1777) · oils, NG Ire. · theatrical prints, BM

Mossop [*formerly* Browne], **William** (1751–1805), medallist, was born in Mary's parish, Dublin. His father was one Browne, a Roman Catholic, but his mother remarried a relative of the actor Henry Mossop and changed William's name to Mossop. This allowed him to enter the Blue Coat School in Dublin on 5 February 1762. He left on 26 August 1765 and was apprenticed to James Stone, a seal-cutter of New Street, employed by the linen board. After his apprenticeship he started in business as a die-sinker, announcing in August 1774 that he had moved to no. 4 Bull Lane, near Pill Lane. In 1775 he enrolled as a pupil at the Dublin Society's Drawing School. Stone died around this time, and Mossop continued his former master's business with the linen board until 1781. An advertisement on 20 June 1777 announced that Mossop, described as 'die-sinker, seal and letter-cutter', could now strike medals. His first recorded medal was that of 1782 of the Rt Hon. John Beresford and his wife, which was set on the side of a silver cup. In that year he also married Letitia Parker, who survived him. After a spell living in Bridgefoot Street he left in April 1783 for 13 Essex Quay.

Extant medals produced by Mossop after this date are more common, and following his medal of Lord Pery in 1788 he was described as 'an ingenious artist who has lain long in obscurity' (*Buckinghamshire MSS*, 195). In 1792 he was admitted to the Guild of St Luke, the corporation of painter-stayners and cutlers of Dublin. Between 1792 and 1797 he worked for Carmac, Kyan, and Carmac superintending the issue of the coinage made from the Wicklow copper mines. When this concern failed in 1797 he went back to his former work as a die-sinker. He struck a medal commemorating the destruction of the French fleet in Bantry Bay in 1797, and also a bust of William III for the Orange Association, but the Irish rising of 1798 and union of Ireland and Britain in 1800 saw him find little work. He was even employed by the governors of Simpson Hospital in 1798 in cutting the words over the entrance.

In January 1805 Mossop suffered a paralytic seizure followed by apoplexy, and he died at his home, 68 Mecklenburg Street, on 28 January. He was buried three days later at St Andrew's Church, Dublin. His son William Stephen *Mossop (1788–1827) was also a medallist.

STUART HANDLEY

Sources W. G. Strickland, *A dictionary of Irish artists*, 2 (1913), 132–8 · L. Forrer, *Biographical dictionary of medallists*, 8 vols. (1904–30), vol. 4, pp. 164–9 · *The manuscripts of the earl of Buckinghamshire, the earl of Lindsey ... and James Round*, HMC, 38 (1895), 195

Mossop, William Stephen (1788–1827), medallist, was born in Dublin in 1788, and baptized there on 22 May at St John's Church, the son of William *Mossop (1751–1805), medallist, and Letitia Parker. He was educated at Samuel Whyte's academy, Grafton Street, Dublin, and in 1802 entered the art schools of the Royal Dublin Society under Francis West, the master of the figure school, who also gave him private tuition. His first medal, that of the

Incorporated Society for Charter Schools, was made when he was about seventeen. In 1806 he made a medal for the Farming Society of Ireland, and in 1810 one to commemorate the fiftieth year of George III's reign. In 1813 he received a prize from the Society of Arts for the die of a school medal, and in 1814 gained its prize for a medal bearing the head of Vulcan. He produced the first portrait medal of Daniel O'Connell in 1816, and about 1820 he contemplated a series of forty portrait medals of distinguished Irishmen. Of these he completed one, the medal of Henry Grattan, and nearly finished those of James Ussher, earl of Charlemont, Jonathan Swift, and Richard Brinsley Sheridan. The dies of these were left unhardened, but were afterwards annealed by J. Woodhouse of Dublin, into whose possession they came. His work was usually signed 'Mossop', sometimes 'W. S. Mossop'.

Mossop followed the method adopted by his father in designing the model for his steel dies. He used a preparation of beeswax melted and softened with turpentine, and coloured white or brown. 'He spread this tempered wax upon a piece of glass or slate, adding and working in successive portions until the design was completed' (Frazer, 456). Several of Mossop's steel dies were acquired by the Royal Irish Academy and examples of his wax models and designs cast in plaster also survived in private collections. In addition to his work on medals Mossop prepared the seals of various public bodies, including the Waterford chamber of commerce, the Cork Institution (1807), the County of Sligo Infirmary (1813), the Irish treasury, Londonderry corporation, the Prussian consulate, and Waterford harbour commission. He also made a series of dies for the stamp office, Dublin.

Mossop married in 1813 and he and his wife, Elizabeth Meara, had three sons. He was secretary to the Royal Hibernian Academy from its foundation in 1823 until his death four years later. He wrote a short account of his father and himself, which was printed in Gilbert's *History of Dublin*. Following a gradual mental breakdown Mossop was admitted to the Richmond Lunatic Asylum, Dublin, and died there some months later on 11 August 1827. He was buried in St Andrew's Church on 13 August.

W. W. WROTH, rev. CHRISTOPHER MARSDEN

Sources W. G. Strickland, *A dictionary of Irish artists*, 2 (1913), 138–43 · W. Frazer, 'The medallists of Ireland and their work', *Journal of the Royal Historical and Archaeological Association of Ireland*, 4th ser., 7 (1885–6), 456–66 · L. Forrer, ed., *Biographical dictionary of medallists*, 4 (1909), 169–72 · J. T. Gilbert, *A history of the city of Dublin*, 3 vols., reprint (1972) · L. Brown, *A catalogue of British historical medals, 1760–1960*, 1 (1980)
Likenesses W. Mossop, self-portrait, etching, 1838, NG Ire. · portrait, repro. in Strickland, *Dictionary of Irish artists*, pl. xliii

Mostyn family (*per.* 1540–1642), gentry, were one of the leading gentry families in north Wales. The Mostyn estate was the result of a series of marriages in the fourteenth and fifteenth centuries which brought together what the Welsh poet–genealogists of the sixteenth century described as the Five Courts: Pengwern near Llangollen in Denbighshire, Mostyn in Flintshire, Gloddaith in Caernarvonshire, and Trecastell and Tregarnedd in Anglesey. The first member of the family to inherit them all (in 1540) was Thomas ap Richard ap Hywel or Thomas Mostyn (1490–1558). He and his younger brother, Piers, the ancestor of the Mostyn family of Talacre, were the first to adopt the surname which was the name of his main residence—a change that can be seen in deeds between 1541 and 1547. In 1517 Thomas Mostyn married Jane (1502/3–1572), daughter of Sir William Griffith of Penrhyn, Caernarvonshire. This was a major dynastic alliance between the leading family in north-east Wales and its counterpart in the north-west; the pre-nuptial settlement stipulated that should either party die before the consummation of the marriage another sibling would be provided. The couple had nineteen children, twelve sons and seven daughters. Mostyn also had at least one illegitimate daughter, to whom he left £20 for a marriage portion. He died on 30 August 1558; in his will he left money for prayers for his soul and he was buried at Whitford in Flintshire.

The estate passed to Thomas Mostyn's eldest surviving son, **William Mostyn** (1521–1576), who had already begun to play a part in local affairs. He had some experience of military service under William Herbert, first earl of Pembroke, in suppressing the rebellion of Sir Thomas Wyatt the younger early in 1554 and he was the first member of the family to sit in parliament, representing Flintshire in 1553, 1554, and 1572. Mostyn married Margaret, daughter of Robert ap Hywel of Whittington, Shropshire, by 1542. The couple had three sons and two daughters. Service under Pembroke suggests that the Mostyns moved with the religious changes of the times; unlike their Talacre kinsmen, they certainly conformed after the accession of Elizabeth I and there seem to have been no recusants among them. From 1569 William Mostyn was a JP for Flintshire, being named of the quorum four years later, and sheriff of Flintshire three times and Caernarvonshire once. He began extending the house at Mostyn but died before the work was complete; his heir left it unfinished. His second marriage, to Margaret Goodman (*b.* in or after 1539, *d.* 1594), daughter of Sir William Brereton of Cheshire and his wife, Jane, and widow of a wealthy Cheshire merchant, was part of a double transaction, common among the gentry of north Wales, his new wife's daughter marrying his heir. Mostyn died on 19 September 1576. If his father's will reflected the old faith, his was uncompromisingly protestant. At his death the Mostyn rent roll was just under £300, putting the estate among the most substantial in north Wales at that time.

William Mostyn's eldest son from his first marriage, **Sir Thomas Mostyn** (*c.*1542–1618), was an altogether more significant figure. He represented Flintshire in parliament from 1577 to 1583 and held the usual local offices, being sheriff of Anglesey twice, Flintshire twice, and Caernarvonshire once, JP in the same three counties (he was *custos rotulorum* of Caernarvonshire from 1596), deputy lieutenant of Flintshire and muster master from about 1576, and, from 1602, a member of the queen's council in the marches of Wales. He was the first member of the family to be knighted, the accolade being bestowed when Robert Devereux, second earl of Essex, was entertained at Mostyn on his way to Ireland in April 1599. In the subsidy of 1592 he was assessed at £10; only one Flintshire squire was assessed at a higher figure. According to the family history, it was Sir Thomas Mostyn who began to assemble the famous Mostyn library. Like his father, he married twice. After the death of his first wife, Ursula (*d.* 1578), daughter of William Goodman, with whom he had three sons and two daughters, he married his kinswoman Katherine, daughter of Piers Mostyn of Talacre and his wife, Ellen, and widow of Sir Rhys Griffith of Penrhyn. Katherine Mostyn was the mother of the privateer and spendthrift Piers *Griffith (1568–1628), who, at the same time, married Sir Thomas Mostyn's daughter Margaret. Neither marriage was a success; the activities of Griffith may well have contributed to the failure of them both. Although Sir Thomas Mostyn's allegiance to the Elizabethan settlement seems never to have been in doubt, he was described by a contemporary as 'a man not very rigid against Catholics but one that complied with the times', which made it all the more embarrassing when, about 1582, he came face to face with a seminary priest near his house at Gloddaith and was obliged to arrest him. He died at Mostyn on 21 February 1618 and was buried at Whitford.

Sir Thomas Mostyn was succeeded by his elder surviving son from his first marriage, **Sir Roger Mostyn** (1567/8–1642). Roger Mostyn's relations with his father were particularly bad. There is no explanation of the estrangement but it may have been connected with the son's marriage in 1596 to Mary (1581–1653), daughter of John Wynn of Gwydir, with whom Sir Thomas Mostyn was at odds. Even before Roger Mostyn inherited the estate, he was buying land; he added to the estate itself, and his will shows his determination to provide for his younger sons. His activity in the land market during his father's lifetime may have been financed by the exploitation of the Mostyn coal measures, which he seems to have put on a proper commercial footing; he was certainly independent of his father for many years before he inherited the estate. Mostyn never seems to have been short of ready cash and in 1619, soon after he succeeded, his lands, including the coalmines, were valued at £3275, his annual income being estimated at £1678. He represented Flintshire in parliament from 1621 to 1622, but this was the only occasion on which he did so. There was a convention that the county seat went around the four leading families there in turn, and London seems, in any case, to have had little attraction for Mostyn, although his surviving letters show him to have been well informed about public affairs. When a new parliament was in the offing in 1624 he stated that he did not wish his eldest son, Thomas Mostyn (*d.* 1642), to stand for Flintshire. In the first place it was the turn of another family to represent the county and in the second place he did not wish to see the young man living apart from his wife in the capital, where he might be drawn into bad company. Like his father, Mostyn was sheriff of Flintshire and a JP in that county and in Caernarvonshire, as well as being a deputy lieutenant; in 1617 he was appointed to James I's council in the marches of Wales.

Although Mostyn had no patron in high places, he was on friendly terms with the leading figure from north Wales, John Williams, bishop of Lincoln and keeper of the great seal. His second son, John Mostyn, was in Williams's service. Roger Mostyn was the first of the family to attend university, matriculating at Brasenose College, Oxford, on 8 May 1584 and entering Lincoln's Inn in 1588. He was on friendly terms with his father-in-law; more is known about him than about any of his predecessors because of the voluminous Gwydir correspondence, which reveals that Wynn had a great respect for his judgement. His connection with the Gwydir interest predated his marriage and may possibly have helped to bring it about. From 1593 Mostyn was one of the trustees under the will of Sir John Wynn's uncle, Robert Wynn, the builder of Plas Mawr in Conwy, Caernarvonshire, being the cousin of Robert Wynn's second wife. This trusteeship was to lead to considerable ill feeling and litigation after Robert Wynn's death in 1598, with Mostyn's integrity being called in question. Sir John Wynn may have been instrumental in securing Mostyn's knighthood on 23 May 1606; he also obtained the manor of Mostyn, previously leased by the family, for him. Sir Roger Mostyn died on 18 August 1642 and was buried at Whitford. His eldest son predeceased him some months earlier and the estate was therefore inherited by his grandson Roger Mostyn. He left four other surviving sons, all of whom, together with two daughters, were provided for in his will.

The fact that the Mostyn estate was spread over four counties meant that the family, despite its wealth, never exercised the concentrated local power and influence that some of the leading north Wales families enjoyed. William, Sir Thomas (*d.* 1618), and Sir Roger Mostyn all sat in parliament, but it was local office and the authority that went with it that was important to them, and none of them had any desire to cut a figure at Westminster. However, they were among the leading patrons of the Welsh cultural tradition, the first Thomas Mostyn being the first to enjoy the close relationship with the bardic order that distinguished the family in the sixteenth century. The origins of this relationship are unclear, but William Mostyn was responsible for organizing the eisteddfod at Caerwys, Flintshire, in 1567, which was intended as a public examination of the poets' professional skills. His grandfather Richard ap Hywel was similarly involved in the first Caerwys eisteddfod in 1523.   A. D. CARR

Sources A. D. Carr, 'The Mostyn family and estate, 1200–1642', PhD diss., U. Wales, Bangor, 1976 · L. N. V. L. Mostyn and T. A. Glenn, *History of the family of Mostyn of Mostyn* (1925) · A. D. Carr, 'Gloddaith and the Mostyns', *Transactions of the Caernarvonshire Historical Society*, 41 (1980), 33–57 · A. D. Carr, 'The Mostyns of Mostyn, 1540–1642', *Journal of the Flintshire Historical Society*, 28 (1977–8), 17–37; 30 (1981–2), 125–44 · R. A. Charles, 'Teulu Mostyn fel noddwyr y beirdd', *Llên Cymru*, 9 (1966–7), 74–110 · E. Roberts, 'Eisteddfod Caerwys, 1567', *Transactions of the Denbighshire Historical Society*, 16 (1967), 23–61 · J. G. Jones, *The Welsh gentry, 1536–1640* (1998) · HoP, *Commons, 1509–58*, 2.638–40 · HoP, *Commons, 1558–1603*, 3.107–8 · Venn, *Alum. Cant.* [Sir Roger Mostyn]

Archives Flintshire RO, Hawarden, papers · U. Wales, Bangor, papers | Flintshire RO, Hawarden, Mostyn of Talacre papers, D/MT · NL Wales, Wynn of Gwydir MSS, NLW MSS 465, 466, 9051–9063
Likenesses attrib. D. Mytens, oils, 1634 (Sir Roger Mostyn), Mostyn Hall, Flintshire; repro. in Mostyn and Glenn, *History of the family of Mostyn of Mostyn* · oils (Sir Thomas Mostyn), Mostyn Hall, Flintshire; repro. in Mostyn and Glenn, *History of the family of Mostyn of Mostyn*
Wealth at death £3275 1s. 5d.—Sir Thomas Mostyn: 1618, U. Wales, Bangor, Mostyn 5486

Mostyn, John (1709–1779). *See under* Mostyn, Sir Roger, third baronet (1673–1739).

Mostyn, Sir Roger (1567/8–1642). *See under* Mostyn family (*per.* 1540–1642).

Mostyn, Sir Roger, first baronet (*c.*1624–1690), royalist army officer, was the son of Sir Thomas Mostyn (*c.*1598–1642) of Mostyn Hall, near Holywell, Flintshire, and Elizabeth (1603–1669), daughter of Sir James Whitelocke. In 1637 he was admitted to the Inner Temple. On 22 July 1642, at the parish church of St James, Clerkenwell, Middlesex, he married Prudence (*bap.* 1623, *d.* 1647), daughter of Sir Martin Lumley, bt, of Great Bradfield, Essex, with whom he had four children. His father having died in November 1641, Roger succeeded to the Mostyn estate on the death of his grandfather, Sir Roger, on 18 August 1642. He was quick to side with the king that summer, and was said to have raised 1500 men on the family's interest in the space of twelve hours. When Charles I formally declared war and visited Chester towards the end of September 1642, Mostyn and one Captain Salesbury arrived there with troops of Welshmen, who, after the king's departure, ransacked the houses of supposed parliamentarians. In January 1643 Mostyn, described by this time as colonel, brought a large number of Welshmen into Chester, and once more they gave vent to their loyalty by sacking the townhouse of the parliamentarian MP Sir William Brereton, despite the efforts of city officials to quiet them. Having been appointed governor of Flint Castle, Mostyn repaired it and put it in a state of defence at his own cost, but in the autumn of 1643 after a long siege, during which the garrison was reduced to eating their horses, it was surrendered to Brereton and Sir Thomas Myddleton on honourable terms, as were also both the town and castle of Mostyn. Shortly afterwards, on 18 November, a troop of Irish soldiers landed at Mostyn, and the parliamentarians withdrew hastily from that district. Mostyn also raised some Welsh recruits and, combining with the Irish, captured Hawarden Castle after a fortnight's siege, and probably proceeded towards Chester. Lord Byron, complaining of the defenceless state of Chester in a letter addressed to Lord Digby on 26 April 1645, stated that he was

> left in the towne only with a garryson of citizens, and my owne and Colonell Mostin's regiment, which both together made not up above 600 men, whereof the one halfe being Mostin's men, I was forced soone after to send out of towne

owing to their undisciplined conduct.

Towards the end of 1645 Mostyn went over to Ireland to try to muster recruits for the relief of Chester, and returned the following January with a 'piece of a regiment', some 160 men, and was expected 'to make it up two hundred upon his own credit' in his own county, where he was a commissioner of array and peace (J. R. Phillips, ed., *Memoirs of the Civil War in Wales and the Marches, 1642–1649*, 2, 1874, 290–91). These troops and other royalist forces collected in north Wales under Lord St Paul, were, however, prevented from marching to Chester by Colonel Mytton, who was dispatched by Brereton to intercept them, and caused them to retreat to Denbigh and Conwy, which fell to parliamentarian forces in October and December respectively. On 20 October 1646 the House of Commons ordered that Mostyn, present at Denbigh when it capitulated, ought to be permitted to compound for his estate at a preferential rate, agreeing to treat him as if he had come in within the previous deadline for compounding which had expired in December 1645. But in February 1647 Mostyn applied to compound on the terms granted at the capitulation of Flint in August 1646 instead, and was fined £852, or one-tenth of the value of his estate. Shortly afterwards his sequestration was suspended, he and his father-in-law having given security for payment of his fine. His uncle, Bulstrode Whitelocke, claimed credit for the satisfactory conclusion to Mostyn's business with the committee at Goldsmith's Hall.

Mostyn appears to have lived quietly during the 1650s. His first wife having died in 1647, about 1651 he married Mary (*d.* 1662), daughter of Thomas Bulkeley, Viscount Bulkeley of Cashel, of Baron Hill, Beaumaris. They had eight children in little more than a decade. In the summer of 1655 they entertained Henry Cromwell and his entourage *en route* for Ireland. Although placed in custody briefly in May 1658, Mostyn was shortly restored to liberty at the intercession of Whitelocke, who procured his immediate release 'upon his parole to be at his own house at Mostyn', and to do nothing prejudicial to the existing government (B. Whitelocke, *Memorials of the English Affairs*, 1682, 673). It is not known why he was detained. The following year his mother strenuously denied that Mostyn had any involvement in Sir George Booth's royalist rising. At the Restoration, Mostyn's loyalty during the civil wars was richly rewarded. He was knighted on 5 June 1660, made a gentleman of the privy chamber on 25 June, and created a baronet on 3 August. He was also proposed for membership of the order of the royal oak. But he was no courtier, and passed his public service after the Restoration in local administration. He was made sheriff of Montgomeryshire in 1660. In 1662 his second wife died, but on 24 February 1667 Mostyn married again; his third wife was Lumley Coytmore (1642–1684), of Caernarvonshire. In 1665–6 he was sheriff of Flintshire, and in 1666–7 he was sheriff of Caernarvonshire. In 1674 he was deputy lieutenant in Flint, and again in 1685. Although by family tradition the civil wars had cost Mostyn £60,000, he was evidently able to recoup his losses, notably by exploitation of the coal and lead mines at his disposal, but also by the marriage of his heir, Thomas, to a wealthy Cheshire heiress. In 1684 Mostyn lavishly entertained the duke of

Beaufort and his attendants as they passed through, themselves *en route* for Ireland just as Henry Cromwell had been thirty years earlier. Mostyn died on 4 October 1690 and was buried on 16 October at Whitford, Flintshire. He was succeeded by his third, but eldest surviving, son, Thomas, the first son born to his second wife, Mary.

D. L. Thomas, rev. Sean Kelsey

Sources DWB · *The diary of Bulstrode Whitelocke, 1605–1675*, ed. R. Spalding, British Academy, Records of Social and Economic History, new ser., 13 (1990) · R. Spalding, *Contemporaries of Bulstrode Whitelocke, 1605–1675* (1990) · P. R. Newman, *Royalist officers in England and Wales, 1642–1660: a biographical dictionary* (1981), 266 · GEC, *Peerage* · W. A. Shaw, *The knights of England*, 2 vols. (1906) · A. M. Mimardière and J. P. Ferris, 'Mostyn, Thomas', HoP, *Commons, 1660–90* · IGI
Archives Flintshire RO, Hawarden, Lloyd-Mostyn family papers
Likenesses P. Lely, oils, 1652; at Mostyn Hall, Flintshire, in 1894; copy presented to the corporation of Flint in 1887

Mostyn, Sir Roger, third baronet (1673–1739), politician, was born on 31 July 1673, the eldest son of Sir Thomas Mostyn, second baronet (1651–1692), of Mostyn, Flintshire, and his wife, Bridget, the daughter and heir of Darcy Savage of Leighton, Cheshire. On 10 February 1690 he matriculated from Jesus College, Oxford. He was returned as MP for Flintshire in December 1701, and in the following August for both Cheshire and the Flint boroughs; he elected to sit for the former. In the next four parliaments he sat for Flint boroughs and Flintshire alternately, and retired from the House of Commons in 1734. He also served as constable of Flint Castle (in 1702–5 and 1715–28).

A tory and a supporter of Daniel *Finch, second earl of Nottingham and later seventh earl of Winchilsea, Mostyn strengthened his political ties by marrying, on 20 July 1703, Finch's daughter Lady Essex Finch (d. 23 May 1721); they had six sons and six daughters. He took an active part in parliamentary business from the start, frequently serving as a teller and being appointed to committees. As a high-church supporter he played a prominent role in the promotion of the Occasional Conformity Bill, and he voted for tacking it onto the Land Tax Bill in 1705. In 1711 he was appointed paymaster of the marines, and he was one of the four tellers of the exchequer from 30 December 1714 until 22 June 1716.

After his dismissal in 1716 with Lord Nottingham, Mostyn consistently opposed the government, but does not seem to have become involved in Welsh Jacobite activities. He voted against the Peerage Bill in 1719 and Walpole's excise scheme in 1733, and, having opposed the Septennial Bill in 1716, supported the motion for its repeal in 1734. He was lord lieutenant of Flintshire from 1727 until his death, on 5 May 1739, at Gloddaith, his seat in Caernarvonshire. He was buried at Llan-rhos, Caernarvonshire.

The title passed to Sir Roger's eldest son, Thomas (1704–1758). Of his other sons, Roger (1721–1775) was canon of Windsor, and Savage *Mostyn a vice-admiral. Another son, **John Mostyn** (1709–1779), politician and army officer, was educated at Westminster School (from June 1722) and at Christ Church, Oxford, where he matriculated in 1728. He was made captain-lieutenant in the 2nd

foot guards in 1742. He served as a groom of the bedchamber from 1746 until his death, and in 1747 was elected MP for Malton, Yorkshire, which he represented until 1768. He generally supported the government, even when his patron, Lord Rockingham, had gone into opposition, a course of action which ended his parliamentary career. The second Lord Egmont described him in 1749 as one of the 'most obnoxious men of an inferior degree' in the House of Commons. Whatever his limitations as a politician, however, he enjoyed success in the army. He was promoted colonel in 1754, major-general in 1757, lieutenant-general in 1759, and general in 1772. He became governor and commander-in-chief of Minorca in 1768, and in 1773 was the defendant in an action brought by one Anthony Fabrigas, whom he had banished from the island. He died at his home in Dover Street, London, on 16 February 1779.

G. Le G. Norgate, rev. M. E. Clayton

Sources B. D. Henning, HoP, *Commons* (1983) · HoP, *Commons, 1690–1715* [draft] · P. D. G. Thomas, 'Mostyn, Sir Roger', HoP, *Commons* · J. Brooke, 'Mostyn, John', HoP, *Commons* · T. Wotton, *The baronetage of England*, ed. E. Kimber and R. Johnson, 3 vols. (1771) · *The proceedings at large in a cause on an action brought by Anthony Fabrigas* (1773) · Foster, *Alum. Oxon.* · Venn, *Alum. Cant.*
Archives U. Wales, Bangor, corresp. and papers, incl. as paymaster-general

Mostyn, Savage (c.1713–1757), naval officer, was a younger son of Sir Roger *Mostyn, third baronet (1673–1739), and Lady Essex Finch (d. 1721), daughter of Daniel Finch, seventh earl of Winchilsea. He was educated at Westminster School, which he entered, aged eleven, in June 1725. On 2 March 1734 he was promoted lieutenant of the *Pembroke*. He afterwards served in the *Britannia*, flagship of Sir John Norris, and on 3 July 1739 was promoted commander of the fireship *Duke*, attached to the fleet off Cadiz under Rear-Admiral Nicholas Haddock, by whom, on 17 December 1739, he was posted to the *Seaford*; the rank of captain was confirmed by the Admiralty on 6 March 1740. In April he was appointed to the *Winchelsea*, and towards the end of the year to the *Deptford* (60 guns), one of the fleet which went out to the West Indies with Sir Chaloner Ogle, and, under Vice-Admiral Edward Vernon, took part in the operations against Cartagena in March and April 1741.

In December 1743 Mostyn was appointed to the *Suffolk*, which was, on 24 February 1744, one of the fleet with Sir John Norris off Dungeness. In April he was moved to the *Hampton Court*, one of four ships which, on 6 January 1745, fell in with two French ships of the line off Ushant. Two of the English ships, the *Captain* and the *Sunderland*, parted company. The *Hampton Court* and *Dreadnought* continued the chase; but, although Mostyn's ship came up with the French, it could not engage without the assistance of the *Dreadnought*, and the two Frenchmen got safely into Brest.

In England, Mostyn's conduct evoked unfavourable comment. At his request the Admiralty ordered a court martial which, possibly influenced by his cousin, Daniel Finch, eighth earl of Winchilsea, concluded that Mostyn had done his duty and behaved courageously. However, public opinion was far from accepting the court's decision. He was severely criticized in a pamphlet, *An Enquiry into the Conduct of Captain Mostyn* (1745), attributed to Admiral Vernon. Nearly a year after the verdict of the court martial Mostyn was jeered out of Portsmouth Dockyard by workmen and sailors calling out 'All's well! there's no Frenchman in the way!' (Charnock, 4.431). Nevertheless, during the early months of 1746 Mostyn continued as captain in the *Hampton Court* and commanded a cruising squadron in the Bay of Biscay.

In July 1747 he was returned to parliament as member for Weobley in Herefordshire, a constituency he continued to represent in support of the government until his death. On 22 March 1749, on being explicitly assured of not prejudicing preferment on the military line, he was appointed comptroller of the navy, a post he held for the duration of the peace, during which time he managed the repair and new building of ships in spite of severe retrenchment and reductions in the workforce of the dockyards. On 4 February 1755 he was promoted rear-admiral and during the summer of that year he was second in command of the fleet sent to North America under Vice-Admiral Edward Boscawen; in 1756 he was second in command of the western squadron under, successively, Edward Hawke, Boscawen, and Sir Charles Knowles. Between April and June 1757 he was a junior lord in the short-lived administration of the Admiralty by his cousin, the earl of Winchilsea. Mostyn died, unmarried, on 16 September 1757, leaving £60,000 to his nephew, Roger Mostyn, a politician.

J. K. LAUGHTON, rev. ROGER MORRISS

Sources J. Charnock, ed., *Biographia navalis*, 6 vols. (1794–8) · HoP, *Commons* · *Minutes of the court martial of Mostyn Savage* (1745) · D. A. Baugh, *British naval administration in the age of Walpole* (1965)
Archives U. Wales, Bangor, letters to Sir Roger Mostyn
Likenesses T. Worlidge, etching, BM, NPG
Wealth at death £60,000: HoP, *Commons*

Mostyn, Sir Thomas (c.1542–1618). *See under* Mostyn family (*per.* 1540–1642).

Mostyn, William (1521–1576). *See under* Mostyn family (*per.* 1540–1642).

Motherby, George (bap. 1731, d. 1793), physician, was born in Yorkshire, and was baptized on 7 March 1731 at the Baptist meeting-house, Bridlington, the son of George Motherby and Anne Hotham, described by Nichols as 'a person of rank' (Nichols, *Illustrations*, 8.458), who were married in 1723 in Sculcoates, Yorkshire. He had an elder sister, Anne (Ann; b. 1730), who married George *Robinson (1736–1801), bookseller [*see under* Robinson family], and a brother, Robert. Motherby graduated MD of King's College, Aberdeen, on 17 May 1767. He practised in Königsberg, where he won great renown for his work in vaccination against smallpox, which practice he is said to have brought to the city about 1770. He was said by Nichols to be a physician of eminence at the court of Prussia (Nichols, *Illustrations*, 8.458). He published a well-regarded *New Medical Dictionary* (1775), which had a second edition in 1785. Further editions, which were carefully seen through the

press, in some cases with considerable additions, by George Wallis, appeared in 1791, 1795, and 1801. Motherby died on 19 or 30 July 1793 in Beverley, Yorkshire, being at that time described as 'late of Highgate, Middlesex'.

George Motherby's nephew was **William Motherby** (1776–1847), the son of Robert Motherby and his wife, Charlotte Toussaint, who was French. He was born on 9 December 1776. He studied medicine in Königsberg (1792–3), Berlin (1796), Jena, Vienna, and finally Göttingen (1798), before graduating from the University of Edinburgh in 1799 with a dissertation entitled 'De epilepsia'. The dissertation was dedicated to Immanuel Kant. He practised medicine in Königsberg, where he continued the work of his uncle in vaccinating against smallpox. He was made a *königliche Impfarzt* (doctor with a royal warrant for vaccination), and successfully took responsibility for ensuring that all doctors in the province were supplied with lymph for vaccination. He defended his method of vaccination in two pamphlets published in 1801. From 1803 to 1838 he had a position at the Königsberg Impfinstitut (institute for vaccination). He died there in 1847, having suffered long from the stone. His son Robert Motherby (1808–1860) took over his position at the Königsberg Impfinstitut.

ELIZABETH BAIGENT

Sources W. Ebstein, 'George und William Motherby in ihren Beziehungen zur Variolation und der Kuhpockenimpfung', *Archiv für Geschichte der Medizin*, 4 (1910–11), 31–42 · T. Fischer, *The Scots in Germany* (1902) · *GM*, 1st ser., 63 (1793), 771 · IGI · Nichols, *Illustrations* · P. J. Wallis and R. V. Wallis, *Eighteenth century medics*, 2nd edn (1988)

Motherby, William (1776–1847). *See under* Motherby, George (*bap.* 1731, *d.* 1793).

Motherwell, William (1797–1835), poet and ballad editor, was born in High Street, Glasgow, on 13 October 1797, the second son of William Motherwell (d. 1827), a Glasgow ironmonger descended from an old Stirlingshire family, and his wife, Janet (d. 1811), daughter of William Barnet, a farmer in Auchterarder, Perthshire. Motherwell's father was declared bankrupt in 1801, and the family moved to Edinburgh, where Motherwell attended William Lennie's school from 1805 to 1808, and, briefly, the high school. He was then sent to live with his uncle, a prosperous Paisley ironfounder, and completed his schooling at the local grammar school. At fifteen he was apprenticed as a clerk in the office of the sheriff-clerk at Paisley, and rounded off his formal education by studying classics during the winter term of 1818–19 at Glasgow University. In May 1819 he was appointed sheriff-clerk-depute of Renfrewshire, and held this office until November 1829. As a youth he had entertained radical political views, but unpleasant personal relations with reformers—and particularly an incident in which, while he was carrying out his official duties, a mob nearly threw him into the River Cart—transformed him into a zealous tory. In 1820 he was a sergeant in the Paisley rifle volunteer corps, and later a trooper in the Renfrewshire yeomanry cavalry, which must have appealed to his chivalric disposition. He was keen on exercise, and became a respectable boxer and swordsman.

Motherwell wrote verse from an early age. The song

'Jeanie Morrison' (inspired by a girl at Lennie's school) was begun in his fourteenth year, although not published until May 1832 in *Tait's Edinburgh Magazine*. In 1818 he contributed verse to *The Visitor*, a Greenock miscellany, and in 1820 edited *The Harp of Renfrewshire*, a collection of local poetry and song. In 1824, under the pseudonym Isaac Brown, he published *Renfrewshire Characters and Scenery*, a piece of whimsy in Spenserian stanzas. His *magnum opus* appeared in 1827: *Minstrelsy Ancient and Modern*, a carefully compiled collection of ballads, with a critical introduction surveying previous collections. During its compilation he corresponded with Sir Walter Scott, whose *Minstrelsy of the Scottish Border* he much admired. In 1828 Motherwell founded and edited the *Paisley Magazine*. In the same year he succeeded his friend William Kennedy as editor of the *Paisley Advertiser*, which he ran until 1830, when he was invited to become editor of the tory *Glasgow Courier*. His move to Glasgow coincided with a politically volatile period, and he threw himself into his new work with gusto, campaigning vigorously against reform. In 1832 he contributed to a short-lived Glasgow periodical, *Day*, provided an introduction to the artist Peter Henderson's *Scottish Proverbs*, and issued his own first collection, *Poems, Narrative and Lyrical* (published by David Robertson, for whose *Whistle-Binkie* collections he also supplied material). He collaborated with Hogg to produce an edition of Burns (1835–6), and at his death was said to be preparing a life of Robert Tannahill. His *Poetical Works*, with a memoir by his friend and doctor, James McConechy, appeared in 1847, and in 1849 it was further supplemented and edited by William Kennedy, with a new edition in 1881.

Motherwell was about 5 feet 5 inches in height, well-built, with a large head and kindly face. A restrained conversationalist, even taciturn, he could be eager, sometimes vehement, when deeply moved, but with friends—many of them his political opponents—he was both easy and affable, and was often to be found in one of his two favourite taverns: The Sun, or the Swan with Two Necks. His essentially superstitious temperament led him to write eerie lyrics such as 'Demon Lady', 'The Madman's Love', and the fairy ballad 'Elfinland Wud'. Motherwell's range as a writer was largely confined to the morbidly romantic and sentimental, coloured by his 'taste for the antique' (McConechy, xi). His lyrics of pathos—notably 'Jeanie Morrison' and 'My heid is like to rend, Willie'— were popular throughout the nineteenth century. He was the first after Gray strongly to appreciate and utilize Scandinavian mythology, and his three Norse ballads are energetic yet graceful. In a review of Motherwell's poems, John Wilson (Christopher North) wrote that he had 'fine and strong sensibilities and a powerful intellect' (*Blackwood*, April 1833). He was also admired by Edgar Allan Poe, who presumably saw the 1841 Boston edition of the poems.

However, it is as a ballad collector and editor that Motherwell is now most highly regarded. His editorial principles were remarkably forward-looking: 'tradition being in all matters relative to popular poetry a safe and almost unerring guide' (W. Motherwell, *Minstrelsy Ancient*

and Modern, 1827, iii). He opposed editorial tampering and refining, seeing them as 'pernicious and disingenuous practices' which destroyed authenticity.

Motherwell never married. His income was spent amassing a considerable library, which took twelve days to sell after his death (and included artefacts such as Cromwell's jackboots). One puzzling aspect of his life, given his lack of any appreciable ties with Ireland, was his involvement in Orangeism. Presumably his extreme conservative views caused him to view that movement almost romantically, as a bastion of social order. In any event, he joined the Orange order, in 1833 being appointed district master of the Glasgow lodges. In August 1835 he was summoned to give evidence before a select committee investigating the order's clandestine activities. Under examination he broke down in inarticulate confusion and was sent home. For a time he seemed in good health, but at 4 a.m. on 1 November 1835 at his home, 117 George Street, he was struck with apoplexy. He exclaimed 'My head! My head!', and lapsed into unconsciousness, dying four hours later. He was buried on 5 November in the necropolis, Glasgow, where a memorial and bust by J. Fillans were later erected.   HAMISH WHYTE

Sources J. McConechy, 'Memoir', in *The poetical works of William Motherwell*, new edn (1881) · G. Eyre-Todd, ed., *The Glasgow poets: their lives and poems*, 2nd edn (1906), 233–6 · M. E. Brown, 'The study of folk tradition', *The history of Scottish literature*, ed. C. Craig, 3: *Nineteenth century*, ed. D. Gifford (1988), 404–6 · W. Montgomerie, 'William Motherwell and Robert A. Smith', *Review of English Studies*, new ser., 9 (1958), 152–9 · R. Brown, *Paisley poets: with brief memoirs of them and selections from their poetry*, 2 vols. (1889–90), vol. 1, pp. 299–301 · C. Rogers, *The modern Scottish minstrel, or, The songs of Scotland of the past half-century*, 3 (1856), 230–32 · W. M. Parker, 'William Motherwell: his correspondence with Sir Walter Scott', *Scots Magazine*, 24 (1935–6), 144–50 · J. A. Kilpatrick, *Literary landmarks of Glasgow* (1898), 207, 211–14 · *Whistle-binkie, or, The piper of the party: being a collection of songs for the social circle*, new edn, 1 (1878), 16–23 · *Mr Motherwell's library* (1836) [sale catalogue] · E. R. Wasserman, 'The source of Motherwell's "Melancholye"', *Modern Language Notes*, 55 (1940), 296

Archives NL Scot., notebooks [copies] · U. Glas. L., commonplace book, poems, essays, notes, and corresp. | U. Edin. L., letters to David Laing

Likenesses J. Fillans, wax medallion, 1833, Scot. NPG · A. Edouart, silhouette, Scot. NPG · J. Fillans, bust on monument, necropolis cemetery, Glasgow · J. Fillans, plaster bust, Scot. NPG · A. Henderson, oils, Scot. NPG

Motley (*act.* 1921–*c.*1975), theatre designers, was the trade name of the team of three remarkable women, the sisters **(Audrey) Sophia Harris** [married name Devine] (1900–1966), **Margaret Frances** [Percy] **Harris** (1904–2000), and **Elizabeth Alice Marjorie Montgomery** [married name Wilmot] (1902–1993). Sophia (*b.* 2 July 1900) and Margaret (*b.* 28 May 1904)—known from childhood as Percy—were raised in Hayes, Kent. Their father, William Harris (1867–1924), was a Lloyds' broker, and their mother, Kathleen (1873–1916), an unconventional woman who loved to dress up her children for photographs. Their happy childhood was disturbed, however, by their mother's early death and by the loss of their brother in the First World War. In 1921 they began to study art at the Chelsea Illustrators' School, where they met Elizabeth Montgomery,

Motley (act. 1921–c.1975), by Howard Coster, 1935 [left to right: (Audrey) Sophia Harris, Margaret Frances (Percy) Harris, and Elizabeth Alice Marjorie Montgomery]

whose family had moved to Fulham from Cambridge. Elizabeth's father, William, was born in Liverpool, of Irish-Scottish parentage, and after attending London University joined the Presbyterian church. With his wife, Marta, he moved as curate to Kidlington, Oxfordshire, where Elizabeth was born on 15 February 1902. Subsequently he became a theology lecturer at St John's College, Cambridge, before moving to London in wartime to help to decode German messages.

The three women became friends, united by a passion for the theatre and in particular for the performances at the Old Vic by the rising young actor John Gielgud (1904–2000), who bought some drawings by Elizabeth of him in his Old Vic roles. He took the risk of asking the group to design the costumes for his 1932 Oxford University Drama Society production of Romeo and Juliet, in which professional actors—Peggy Ashcroft and Edith Evans—took the female roles; the undergraduate performers included George *Devine (1910–1966), the future actor and theatre director, who later also became influential in Motley's career.

That Oxford Romeo and Juliet was the first major production to bear the name Motley, taken from As You Like It's 'Motley's the only wear'. Gielgud never liked it ('So anonymous') but it was characteristic of the three women, none of them remotely hungry for personal fame. The production was also marked by the Motley trademarks of simplicity of line and bold clarity of colour.

They were completely united in their approach to their work as organic design rather than decoration, and work was always harmonious between them. Percy, gruffly authoritative in her perennial tweeds and trousers, was the technical genius of the trio—principally responsible for the practical mechanics of the set design, ground plans, and working drawings—while Sophia and Elizabeth, both stylish women and chic dressers (Motley briefly, with Sophia mainly at the helm, entered the world of couture fashion with a London shop, under their joint name, in the 1930s), were unrivalled in their knowledge of period and of modern costume and cutting. Gielgud, the first to appreciate their individual and combined talents, became their lifelong friend and champion.

In the 1930s Gielgud's seasons at the New (later Albery) Theatre and at the Queen's, reintroducing the classics to the commercial stage with a company yoking established stars with emerging talent (who included Ashcroft, Devine, Alec Guinness, and Laurence Olivier), established the nearest thing in London to a permanent ensemble between the Irving–Tree era and the subsidized companies in the 1960s, and Motley was crucial to those seasons. In the course of some sixteen productions for Gielgud in that period their work—innovatory in its insistence on design over decoration and in their use of unconventional (and often cheap) materials such as wool and felt—effected a quiet revolution in British theatre design. Their workshops—originally those of the cabinetmaker Thomas Chippendale—opposite the New Theatre in St Martin's Lane, became a kind of informal club for adventurous young London theatrical talent.

Motley's greatest achievements over that time included Gordon Daviot's chronicle play Richard of Bordeaux (1933), with Gielgud as Richard II against versatile settings of swagged curtains, and Gielgud's 1934 Hamlet, using an impressively flexible multi-level set with Cranach-inspired costumes. They also worked with Michel Saint-Denis, from the Compagnie des Quinze, directing Gielgud in Obey's Noah (1935) and on a dazzling Romeo and Juliet (1935), with Gielgud and Olivier alternating Romeo and Mercutio to Ashcroft's Juliet against a fluid Renaissance setting based on a central rotating tower.

Perhaps the summation of Motley's work with the Gielgud companies was the Queen's Theatre production of Chekhov's Three Sisters (1938), with an extraordinary cast under Saint-Denis that included Gielgud, Ashcroft, Devine, and Michael Redgrave. Motley's designs solved all the technical and logistical problems of the play, which has four settings. Peggy Ashcroft always said that she had never known a production suggest more potently the changing seasons of a play.

In 1939, just before the outbreak of war, Motley designed Gielgud's legendary production of Wilde's The Importance of being Earnest, with Edith Evans as Lady Bracknell to his Worthing. The sets, of subtly heightened naturalism, were much influenced by Gielgud's memories of the William Morris drawing rooms of a Holland Park house that he had visited as a boy.

When war broke out Elizabeth Montgomery and Margaret Harris were in America; Sophia on 27 October 1939 married George Devine and remained in England, where their only child, Harriet, was born. In America they worked on Olivier's New York production of *Romeo and Juliet* (1940), in which he was cast opposite Vivien Leigh. They remained in America throughout the war, their work including Motley's first excursions into ballet, working with Agnes de Mille on productions that included *Tally-Ho* (1944). Among their classical excursions was *The Tempest* (Alvin, New York, 1945), a startling production in a much-praised set of layered crags backed by a vast blue cyclorama.

Elizabeth Montgomery, who married the American writer Patrick Wilmot in 1956, remained in America for the next two decades, working mainly as a highly successful costume designer (still under the Motley name) on a range of productions from Broadway musicals (*South Pacific*, *Paint your Wagon*, and *Can-can*, for example) to opera, including sets and costumes for a stunning *Il trovatore* (Metropolitan Opera, 1959). She also worked in the burgeoning American regional theatre, including a production of *Troilus and Cressida* set during the American Civil War, for the American Shakespeare Festival in Stratford, Connecticut (1961).

Back in England, Percy Harris resumed her career, often with Sophia's collaboration on costumes (Sophia was costume designer on many outstanding British films, including *The Innocents*, 1961, *This Sporting Life*, 1963, and *The Pumpkin Eater*, 1964). She picked up many of her 'family' connections and once more worked with Gielgud and Ashcroft, on *The Heiress* (Haymarket, 1949). Further rewarding ventures with Ashcroft included a Devine production of *Hedda Gabler* (Hammersmith, 1954) against a much lighter setting than was then usual in Ibsen. This was a production of the peripatetic English Stage Company, which in 1956, under Devine, found a London home at the Royal Court Theatre. Its ideals derived from Gielgud's seasons and from the practice of Saint-Denis's ensemble that the author's text governed all production decisions. The designer Jocelyn Herbert (Devine's partner after his divorce from Sophia) defined its ethos as those involved saw it: 'an attitude to life, as well as to theatre' (Mullin, 126). Motley made crucial contributions to the early, pared-down Royal Court aesthetic, and designed productions that included a witty *Country Wife* (1956), using translucent plastic screens painted with line-drawings of period architectural details, and Ibsen's *Rosmersholm* (1959), with Ashcroft, played in bold relief against a back wall of four classical columns with a central double door. The firm also provided the costumes for the first production of John Osborne's *Look Back in Anger* (Royal Court, 1956).

Motley's work at Stratford in the 1950s under Glen Byam-Shaw (another graduate from Gielgud's 1930s seasons) was something of a golden age for the firm. Especially fine were the Ashcroft–Michael Redgrave *Antony and Cleopatra* (1953), using a simple, stepped permanent set with a variously lit backcloth to suggest changes of location, and a buoyant, constantly inventive *Merry Wives of Windsor* (1955). Motley and Byam-Shaw worked often in West End theatre productions too, including Terence Rattigan's *Ross* and another Ibsen—*The Lady from the Sea* (Queen's, 1951)—with shimmering gauzes suggesting the fjord-reflected light. The team also worked at the National Theatre, framing Olivier's Captain in a forbidding fortress setting for *The Dance of Death* (1967). Motley also designed the delicious drollery of Noël Coward's *Hay Fever* in his own production for the National (1965), with Edith Evans and Maggie Smith.

Byam-Shaw was also the key partner in Motley's opera work in England, when Percy was head of design at Sadler's Wells and, later, for English National Opera (ENO) at the Coliseum. Her design work remained constantly fresh and technically adventurous, not least in a later operatic project, the British première of Prokofiev's *War and Peace* (1974) for ENO, an extraordinary achievement using a background of constantly changing projections.

Following Sophia's death at her home, 9 Lower Mall, Hammersmith, on 27 March 1966, and with Elizabeth Montgomery increasingly inactive, Percy Harris—before concentrating exclusively on the London-based design school that later bore the Motley name and continued its legacy—designed a few productions under her own name, including a *Tosca* for ENO and Julian Mitchell's adaptation of Ivy Compton-Burnett's *A Family and a Fortune* (Apollo, 1975), with Alec Guinness—a distillation of the best that Motley stood for. She used her unrivalled knowledge of the period to evoke the ossified world of a late-Edwardian household, with only a few brocaded walls, a trapezoid parquet floor, and rhythmically flown chandeliers. The power of the best theatrical design to suggest rather than naturalistically to reproduce was perfectly illustrated in this production, as it had been in so many others over half a century to bear the credit 'design by Motley'.

Elizabeth Montgomery died at Barnes, Middlesex, on 15 May 1993; Percy Harris died in Northwood, Middlesex, on 10 May 2000.   ALAN STRACHAN

Sources M. Mullin, *Design by Motley* (Newark, DE, 1996) • J. Goodwin, ed., *British theatre design: the modern age* (1989) • J. Croall, *Gielgud: a theatrical life* (2000) • *CGPLA Eng. & Wales* (1966) [Audrey Sophia Devine] • *CGPLA Eng. & Wales* (1993) [Elizabeth Montgomery] • *CGPLA Eng. & Wales* (2000) [Margaret Harris] • m. cert. [Sophia Harris] • d. cert. [Sophia Devine]
Archives University of Illinois, collection | Motley Theatre Design School, Drury Lane, London, history of Motley's teaching, some drawings and set designs
Likenesses H. Coster, photograph, 1935, NPG [*see illus.*]
Wealth at death £79,027—Margaret Frances Harris: probate, 17 June 2000, *CGPLA Eng. & Wales* • under £125,000—Elizabeth Montgomery: probate, 1993, *CGPLA Eng. & Wales* • £8534—Audrey Sophia Devine: probate, 1966, *CGPLA Eng. & Wales*

Mott, Sir Basil, first baronet (1859–1938), civil and mining engineer, was born at Leicester on 16 September 1859, the youngest son of Frederick Thompson Mott, wine merchant, of Birstall Hill near Leicester and his first wife, Elizabeth Ann (daughter of Isaac Dobell), who died in

Sir Basil Mott, first baronet (1859–1938), by Stanhope Alexander Forbes, 1925

1861. The Mott family came from the Weald where, as yeoman farmers, artisans, craftsmen, and later businessmen, they traced their origins to Guillaume de la Motte who came over from Normandy to Hastings in 1524. Mott was educated at Leicester grammar school, at the International College at Isleworth, and at Solothurn in Switzerland. From 1876 to 1879 he was a student at the Royal School of Mines, South Kensington, where he was awarded the Murchison medal and elected to an associateship. After pupillage at Whitwick colliery, Leicestershire, and at Sheffield, Mott spent three years as engineer to the Neston Colliery Company, Cheshire, in charge of all machinery and underground haulage; there he also had his first experience in tunnelling.

James Henry Greathead, an outstanding figure in soft-ground tunnelling and responsible for major developments in the design and application of tunnelling shields, recruited Mott in 1883 to assist in preparing for the construction of the first deep-level 'tube', for the City and Southwark Railway Company, of which his uncle, Charles Grey Mott, was chairman. The line, which was subsequently known as the City and South London Railway, ran between Monument and Stockwell in London. From 1886 Mott served as assistant engineer, pioneering the use of the Greathead shield and employing special techniques, including the use of low pressure compressed air, to overcome local problems of the water-bearing ground. On completion of tunnelling in 1887, Mott, as resident engineer, supervised the equipping and initial operation of the railway, which was originally intended for traction by

means of endless wire ropes, but changed to be one of the first examples of electric traction. In the same year he married Florence Harmar (d. 1923), daughter of William Parker and an accomplished pianist; they had two sons.

Following the death of Greathead in 1896, Mott entered into partnership with Sir Benjamin Baker and shared responsibility for the design and construction of the second deep-level tube, the Central London Railway from Bank Station to Shepherd's Bush, which was opened in 1900. This line first introduced acceleration and deceleration gradients adjacent to stations, with appreciable savings in traction power. After Baker's death in 1907, Mott took into partnership David Hay and David Anderson, serving as senior partner of the firm of consulting engineers until his own death in 1938. In 1932, Mott, Hay, and Anderson were appointed as joint consultants (with Sir Harley Dalrymple-Hay in association with William Halcrow) to the London Passenger Transport Board. Following a visit to the United States, Mott was responsible for the introduction of escalators to Britain, after exhibiting a working escalator which was subsequently built into Earls Court Station. Much work followed for the London underground railways.

Meanwhile, Mott was becoming prominent in bridge design, construction, and reconstruction. In 1906, he was associated with Baker with planning the widening of Blackfriars Bridge in London and subsequently responsible for execution of the work. He was responsible for the new Southwark Bridge, started in 1913 then stopped for the duration of the First World War and completed in 1921. He was also concerned with the widening of Kingston Bridge on the River Thames, the construction of Queensferry Bridge, a lifting bascule bridge, at Chester, the high-level road bridge at Newcastle upon Tyne, Wearmouth Bridge at Sunderland, and the Tees Bridge at Middlesbrough, the first vertical lift bridge in Britain.

After several years of controversy between the relative merits of bridge or tunnel, Mott, a strong advocate for a tunnel, had primary responsibility for the Mersey Tunnel, at the time the largest sub-aqueous tunnel in the world, which was constructed between 1925 and 1934. Extensive pioneering studies of ventilating a tunnel for petrol driven vehicles enlisted the assistance of J. S. Haldane. Mott was consulted by government and reported on many schemes, including the proposed Charing Cross Bridge, road bridges across the rivers Forth and Tay, and the channel tunnel. He was a member of the Severn barrage committee and chairman of the restoration works committee of engineers and architects for the preservation of the fabric of St Paul's Cathedral.

Mott was admitted as a member of the Institution of Civil Engineers in 1895, elected a vice-president in 1920, and president in 1924. In his presidential address he commented that 'it is unfortunate that the existing tube railways [of London] have been constructed in a piecemeal fashion in accordance with ideas of individual promoters and their advisors, without regard to the interests of London as a whole' (*PICE*, 219, 1924–15). He was appointed CB in 1918, created a baronet in 1930, and elected FRS in 1932.

In 1933 he was elected a fellow of Imperial College of Science and Technology.

Mott was a kind, gentle, generous man, a strong character held in awe by his grandchildren. He suffered increasingly in later years from rheumatoid arthritis. He died of cancer at his home, 10 Arkwright Road, Hampstead, on 7 September 1938 and was succeeded as second baronet by his elder son, Adrian Spear (1889–1964).

ALAN MUIR WOOD

Sources E. A. Mott, *Portrait of a family* (1987) · A. Gibb, *Obits. FRS*, 3 (1939–41), 23–38 · private information (2004) · *CGPLA Eng. & Wales* (1938) · d. cert.
Archives ICL, geological notebooks and papers relating to Mersey Tunnel
Likenesses S. A. Forbes, oils, 1925, Inst. CE [*see illus.*] · W. Stoneman, photograph, 1936, NPG
Wealth at death £43,959 3s. 11d.: probate, 4 Nov 1938, *CGPLA Eng. & Wales*

Mott, Charles (*bap.* 1788, *d.* 1851), assistant poor law commissioner, was baptized on 28 August 1788 at Loughton, Essex, the tenth of eleven children of John Mott, keeper of The Crown inn, Loughton, and his wife, Ann Hewes. He was educated at Christ's Hospital, London, after his father secured a nomination. He left the school on 1 October 1803 to be apprenticed, first to Gascoigne, Dawson, and Dixon, sugar brokers, and then to Baring, Mair & Co., commission agents and insurance brokers. He then set up in business on his own in Limehouse. Mott married (the name of his wife has not been discovered), but the relationship was not a success and Mott later lived with Mary Cook, or Stanbury, with whom he had seven or possibly eight children. His private affairs provoked animosity, and after he had attained public prominence an anonymous letter to the poor law commissioners accused him of having previously operated a brothel, of fraudulent conduct, and of having attempted to incarcerate his wife in the asylum he then owned.

Mott's major success during this period was to obtain contracts to manage paupers under the old poor law, first in the parish of Newington, Surrey, and then, after ten years, in the neighbouring parish of Lambeth. He became joint proprietor of the Peckham House Asylum, a private lunatic asylum for 300 mixed private and pauper patients, into which he directed the paupers from the parishes he was managing; he also invested funds in a brewery. These investments were funded by large sums borrowed from family members and acquaintances. Mott claimed that before the introduction of the new poor law system the turnover from his activities amounted to £50,000 per annum; this enabled him to buy a freehold house in Forest Hill, and to keep a carriage and suitable establishment.

The coming of the new poor law ended Mott's contractual earnings but on 4 November 1834 he was appointed an assistant poor law commissioner, for which he received a salary of £700, plus expenses; he was, however, expected to relinquish his commercial interests. Much of his work with the poor law commission was in the north of England; here he proved a more emollient personality than Alfred Power, who had antagonized the poor law unions

in industrial Lancashire and Yorkshire, but he was nevertheless involved in two major controversies. His report on the Bolton union was the target of an attack by John Bowring, Bolton's MP. Further controversy followed when a report which had been covertly compiled by Mott on the activities of the Keighley union was used by the home secretary, Sir James Graham, to attack William Ferrand, MP for Knaresborough and a former chairman of the Keighley Guardians. Although Ferrand subsequently claimed vindication after a parliamentary inquiry he retained an animus against Mott for some considerable time afterwards. Mott ceased to be an assistant commissioner, at the end of 1842, when their numbers were reduced.

The loss of this post, together with financial problems besetting him from the failure of his brewery investment, the demands of his creditors for repayment of their loans, and his high living expenses meant that Mott was now financially hard pressed. First he took on the editorship of the *Poor Law Guide*, which appeared for the first time in March 1843 but folded nine months later; then he persuaded his friend George Coode, one of the assistant secretaries to the poor law commission, to invest in another private lunatic asylum at Haydock Lodge, near Newton-le-Willows in Lancashire, again accepting both private patients and pauper lunatics, who came from Lancashire, north Wales, and other areas. Mott was to be superintendent on a salary of £200, plus a share of the profits; to conceal the involvement of a civil servant with a private speculation the nominal proprietor was Coode's sister Louisa, a resident of Jersey.

As neither Coode nor his sister could readily visit to supervise the venture Mott was given a free rein at Haydock Lodge, which opened for business in February 1844. He entertained lavishly in order to persuade overseers and guardians to send their lunatics to the asylum, and appointed several members of his family to positions within the establishment. Mott himself was frequently absent, having used his influence to secure an elected position as auditor to the local poor law unions for a further £379 per annum.

Haydock Lodge quickly became the focus of a scandal, owing to the persistence of Dr Owen Owen Roberts, a radical Welsh anti-poor law campaigner, who petitioned parliament about the treatment that one of his patients received there. The commissioners in lunacy were forced, with some reluctance, to inquire into the operation of the asylum. In the ensuing furore Coode was required to resign his position with the poor law commission, whereupon he moved to Haydock to find that Mott had expropriated several thousand pounds of fees from the asylum. Dismissed by Coode in May 1846, and pursued through the courts by creditors, Mott fled to the Isle of Man in early October of the same year. He later returned to the mainland to depose evidence for the poor law commissioner, George Cornewall Lewis, in an action against Ferrand arising from the Keighley case, and to continue his work as auditor. It was while on his travels on these duties that Mott was seized by the sheriff's officer and brought before the insolvent debtors court at Lancaster. Released after making an arrangement with his creditors, Mott evidently retained a belief in his own worth as he was soon lobbying Edwin Chadwick to consider him for appointment as an assistant commissioner for the health of towns commission. The appointment, however, did not materialize and Mott ended his working life almost as he began it, working as a commission agent in Manchester. He died of apoplexy on 11 May 1851, at Moor Grove, Rusholme, Manchester. DAVID HIRST

Sources NL Wales, Harpton Court papers · *Hansard 3* · Boase, *Mod. Eng. biog.* · *The Times* (3 Aug 1846), 7a · *The Times* (10 March 1847), 8d · *The Times* (31 Aug 1848), 7c · UCL, Chadwick MSS · 'Return of the number of patients confined ... at Haydock Lodge asylum', *Parl. papers* (1846), 33.459, no. 567 · J. Knott, *Popular opposition to the 1834 poor law* (1986), 204 · W. B. Ferrand, *The great Mott question, or, The mystery unravelled in a letter to Sir J. Graham* (1844) · F. D. Roberts, *Victorian origins of the British welfare state* (1960) · parish register, Loughton, Essex, Society of Genealogists [baptism], 28/8/1788 · d. cert.

Archives NL Wales, Harpton Court MSS · UCL, letters to Edwin Chadwick

Mott, Sir Frederick Walker (1853–1926), neuropathologist, was born in Brighton on 23 October 1853, the only son of Henry Mott, of Brighton, Sussex, who was of Huguenot descent, and his wife, Caroline, daughter of William Fuller, of Pulborough, Sussex. Both parents died when he was a child. He studied medicine at University College, London, where he graduated MB, BSc in 1881 and MD in 1886, and obtained many distinctions. In 1883 he was appointed assistant professor of physiology at Liverpool University, but in the following year returned to London in order to take up the post of lecturer on physiology at Charing Cross Hospital medical school, where he became, in succession, lecturer on pathology, assistant physician, physician, and lecturer on medicine. In 1885 he married Georgina Alexandra, daughter of George Thomas Soley, shipowner, of Liverpool; they had four daughters. He was elected fellow of the Royal College of Physicians in 1892 and fellow of the Royal Society in 1896.

Mott laid the foundation for his subsequent study of the diseases of the nervous system by researches into its normal structure and functions. Most of his earlier work was carried on in Edward Sharpey-Schafer's laboratory at University College, some of it in collaboration with other workers. These investigations included the paths of conduction in the spinal cord, localization in the cerebral cortex (especially relating to movements of the eyes), and the effect of acute anaemia on the brain. These studies were to have great influence on his later work.

In 1895 the London county council decided to appoint a pathologist in charge of the laboratory which it was proposing to establish at Claybury, Essex; all indications pointed to Mott as the most suitable occupant of the post. He stipulated, however, that he wanted to retain his clinical appointment at Charing Cross Hospital, considering it essential that the study of diseased conditions should be combined with clinical observation. The council agreed, and was therefore able to secure Mott's services for a long period of years, during which a vast amount of research work was carried out by him, his pupils, and assistants.

Most of this is published in a series of important volumes as the *Archives of Neurology (and Psychiatry)*.

Subsequently, when the Maudsley Hospital for mental diseases was established at Denmark Hill, Mott's pathological work for the council was transferred to the newer and better-equipped laboratory attached to that institution, and was continued there until his final resignation from the position of pathologist to the London county council asylums in 1923, the age limit having been stretched in order that he might remain in the post as long as possible. But his activities were by no means at an end, as he continued to teach at the Maudsley Hospital, and also accepted the post of lecturer in morbid psychology at the University of Birmingham. He held this position up to the time of his death.

Besides the articles in the *Archives of Neurology*, Mott contributed numerous papers on the nervous system to the *Philosophical Transactions* and *Proceedings* of the Royal Society, to *Brain*, to the *Journal of Physiology*, to the *Proceedings of the Royal Society of Medicine*, and to other scientific and medical periodicals.

Largely owing to Mott's researches it became established that the previously obscure disease of the nervous system known as 'general paralysis of the insane' was, in fact, a manifestation of syphilis, and was associated with the presence of the specific spirochaete. The determination of the association between syphilitic infection and this and other mental disorders is the achievement by which Mott's name will probably be best known. But it was by no means his only important contribution to neuropathology; he further demonstrated the close relation between the nervous system and the sexual organs manifested in dementia praecox, as well as the association of deficient mental condition with degeneration of the thyroid and other endocrine organs.

As the result of these researches Mott firmly and insistently supported the view, which had previously been ignored, that mental disorders are, for the most part, correlated with bodily changes. Indeed, all his work tended to be based on this doctrine. Even in the disorder known as 'asylum dysentery' the cause used to be attributed to a hypothetical nervous affection of the intestine, instead of to an infection associated with micro-organisms, which Mott showed to be its true cause. He wrote a report on his work concerning sleeping sickness, entitled *Histological Observations on Sleeping Sickness and other Trypanosome Infections*, which was published as no. 7 of the Reports of the Sleeping Sickness Commission of the Royal Society in December 1906.

Mott received numerous honours and prizes, as well as appointments to lecturerships, in recognition of his scientific work. He was awarded the Stewart prize of the Medical Association (1903), the Fothergill gold medal and prize of the Medical Society of London (1911), and the Moxon gold medal of the Royal College of Physicians (1919). He was Croonian lecturer (1900), Oliver-Sharpey lecturer (1910), Lettsomian lecturer (1916), and Harveian orator (1925) to the Royal College of Physicians, London, Morrison lecturer to the Royal College of Physicians, Edinburgh

(1921), Huxley lecturer at Charing Cross Hospital (1910), Bowman lecturer to the Ophthalmological Society (1904), and Fullerian lecturer at the Royal Institution. He delivered the Chadwick lecture at the University of Liverpool in 1917 and 1926. At the time of his death he was president of the Royal Medico-Psychological Association.

Mott, an accomplished singer, was devoted to music, especially to vocal music, and published two works. His interest in this was recognized by his election as president of the Society of English Singers in 1923. In 1919 he was created KBE in acknowledgement of his war services as lieutenant-colonel in the Royal Army Medical Corps. His work on shell-shock was especially notable. In the same year he received the honorary degree of LLD from Edinburgh University. He was a good lecturer, always speaking to the point, and an honest investigator. Mott died in Birmingham General Hospital on 8 June 1926 as a result of cerebral haemorrhage, survived by his wife. A memorial volume, *Contributions to Psychiatry, Neurology and Sociology*, edited by J. R. Lord (1929), contains an appreciation of the man and his work by his lifelong friend, W. D. Halliburton, as well as a bibliography of his published writings.

E. A. SHARPEY-SCHAFER, *rev.* RACHEL E. DAVIES

Sources *PRS*, 100B (1926), xxviii-xxx · *Birmingham Medical Review*, 1/6 (1926), 221–32 · *The Lancet* (19 June 1926), 1228 · *BMJ* (19 June 1926), 1063 · personal knowledge (1937) · *CGPLA Eng. & Wales* (1926) · *CGPLA Eng. & Wales* (1927) · J. R. Lord, ed., *Contributions to psychiatry, neurology and sociology* (1929) [incl. list of pubd works]
Archives Wellcome L., certificates and papers
Likenesses W. Stoneman, photograph, 1917, NPG · photograph (after Elliott & Fry), Wellcome L.
Wealth at death £22,241 1s.—save and except settled land: probate, 24 Aug 1926, *CGPLA Eng. & Wales* · £15,387 13s.—limited to settled land: further grant, 17 March 1927, *CGPLA Eng. & Wales*

Mott, Sir Nevill Francis (1905–1996), theoretical physicist, was born on 30 September 1905 in a nursing home at 20 Clarendon Road, Leeds, the elder child of (Charles) Francis Mott, senior science master at Giggleswick School, and his wife, Lilian Mary, *née* Reynolds. A daughter, Joan, was born two years later. Mott's father, who later became director of education for Liverpool, was originally a physicist, and his mother had been the best female mathematician of her year at Cambridge; they had met while working in the Cavendish Laboratory at Cambridge. Mott's early childhood was spent in Giggleswick, and then in Brocton, on the edge of Cannock Chase, being taught at home by his mother until he was ten. He was then sent as a boarder to Baswich House preparatory school where he recalled that the headmaster, G. F. A. Osborne, 'was an excellent teacher, taking me well on in algebra and Latin before I left, and, as far as I can remember, even introducing me to calculus' (Mott, 5). In 1918 Mott won a scholarship to Clifton College, where he spent five unhappy years. Clifton had very good laboratories, but it was a superb mathematics teacher, H. C. Beaven, who made most impression on Mott and turned him towards mathematical physics.

Early research Mott won a major scholarship to St John's College, Cambridge, in December 1923, and began in mathematics in 1924. He compressed the course into two

Sir Nevill Francis Mott (1905–1996), by John Benton-Harris, 1977

years, and obtained first-class honours with a distinction in 1926. He spent his third year struggling to master the new theories of quantum mechanics, with which no one in Cambridge except Paul Dirac, who was too reticent to help much, was familiar. His first significant paper, using Schrodinger's wave mechanics to prove the scattering law that underpinned Rutherford's deduction of the nuclear atom, was published early in 1928, by which time Mott was officially a research student at the Cavendish, working under R. H. Fowler's supervision. Mott never begrudged the intellectual effort spent on learning German in order to follow quantum mechanics, and he later developed strong views about the desirability of scientists learning foreign languages. He became president of the Modern Languages Association in 1954–5.

Mott spent the autumn of 1928 at Niels Bohr's Institute in Copenhagen. There, for the first time, he found a lively and stimulating community of theoreticians and realized 'how [physics] was a social activity and how a teacher should be with students and how beautiful physics could be' (Mott, 25), a realization which had a profound effect on the way that he was to run his own laboratories and the collaboration he promoted between experimentalists and theoreticians. While in Copenhagen he continued to investigate the implications of quantum mechanics for Rutherford's scattering law, applying Dirac's new theory of electron spin to the scattering of electrons by nuclei and deducing that their spins would be polarized in the process. Stimulated by J. R. Oppenheimer's experiments on electron scattering, Mott looked, on his return to Cambridge, at the effect of symmetry in the collisions of two identical Fermi-Dirac particles, such as electrons or alpha particles, predicting anomalous scattering at 45° which was later verified by Chadwick.

> Chadwick took me along to see Rutherford, who said 'if you think of anything else like this, come and tell me.' This certainly made my day. In fact I think it was on this day that I gained complete confidence in my ability to make a career in theoretical physics. (Mott, 30–31)

Mott subsequently spent a term at Göttingen before returning to England to take up a lectureship at Manchester under W. L. Bragg in autumn 1929. His first book, *An Outline of Wave Mechanics* (1930), was based on the lecture course he gave there, and his interest in the properties of materials dates from this time, no doubt stimulated by contact with Bragg and his crystallography group. Mott remained in Manchester for only a year, before returning to Cambridge as a fellow of Gonville and Caius College. He had married Ruth Eleanor Horder (1906–2000), daughter of Gerald Morley Horder, architect's quantity surveyor, on 24 March 1930; she was a classics student at Newnham College to whom he had been engaged for two years, and they bought a house in Sedley Taylor Road. Ruth later taught classics part-time, and gave harpsichord concerts. Through their sixty-six years of marriage, Mott gave Ruth credit for being a 'marvellous understanding wife who creates the conditions in which I can operate' (*Independent*, 12 Aug 1996). Mott was ill at ease with Caius, which he thought over-traditional, but found the Cavendish rather more theory-friendly than previously. At Fowler's suggestion, in collaboration with an experimental physicist, Harrie Massey, he wrote *The Theory of Atomic Collisions* (1933), the first of thirteen authoritative, co-authored books.

Bristol In 1933 Mott succeeded Sir John Lennard-Jones as professor of theoretical physics at Bristol University. He was elected a fellow of the Royal Society in 1936. He went to Bristol determined to build a close collaboration with experimentalists, and found suitable topics in research that Harry Jones, Herbert Skinner, and Clarence Zener were conducting into the structure of metals. Following up Skinner's experiments, they showed in an article published in the *Physical Review* of 1934 that the soft X-ray spectra from light metallic elements demonstrate the existence of a sharp Fermi surface (a theoretical concept introduced by Jones and Zener in 1934 to describe the limit to the energy that metallic electrons can have when the metal is in its ground state). Mott recorded: 'It was a revelation to me that quantum mechanics could penetrate into the business of the metals industry' (Mott, 48). He pursued this insight and, with Jones, published *The Theory of the Properties of Metals and Alloys* in 1936.

Influenced by the work of R. Pohl on colour centres in crystals, Mott next turned his attention to semiconductors, showing, in an article published in the *Proceedings of the Royal Society of London* in 1939, that the process involved

in rectifying junctions between semiconductors and metals was one of thermal excitation, rather than tunnelling, as had previously been believed. In another article, written with R. W. Gurney and published in the *Proceedings of the Royal Society of London* the previous year, he had elucidated the theory of the photographic latent image—how light, absorbed all over a grain of silver bromide in a photographic plate, produces a speck of silver somewhere on the surface—which remains the foundation of photographic theory today. Together with Gurney he published *Electronic Processes in Ionic Crystals* in 1940. Mott and his group opened up the subject of solid-state physics (as it became called) worldwide; the books are notable for their reliance on physical principles and intuitive approximations, and their avoidance of sophisticated mathematics, which horrified some of Mott's continental colleagues; but 'slowly, slowly … the success of their approach became so evident that no-one questioned seriously their value' (R. Smoluchowski, 101).

In Bristol the Motts lived initially in a flat at 4 Caledonia Place, Clifton; they moved in 1939 to 6 Princes Buildings, where they had superb views over the Avon Gorge and the docks. They had two daughters, Elizabeth (Libby) and Alice, born in 1941 and 1943 respectively. Through childhood Libby developed a severe mental handicap and reluctantly they decided in the 1950s that she needed residential care. Alice later married the mathematician Michael Crampin.

During the Second World War, Mott worked first on the propagation of radio waves, and later, from 1943, as superintendent of theory at the armaments research department, where he contributed to the theory of the explosive fragmentation of shell and bomb cases. At the end of the war he was offered professorships at both Oxford and Cambridge. However, he was reluctant to leave Bristol, where he had outstanding support from the university, was assured that he would succeed Arthur Tyndall as head of department, and had just been offered a beautiful Georgian residence, Stuart House, on Royal Fort, right next to the laboratory.

The war stimulated Mott's desire to strengthen physicists' links with industry, and to this end the post-war group he recruited to Bristol had strong interests in the mechanical properties of metals: Charles Frank, Frank Nabarro, J. Mitchell, and Jaques Friedel (who married Ruth Mott's sister, Mary Horder) became world leaders in investigations of dislocations, work-hardening, and fatigue. Mott's own contribution, though impressive, was not as outstanding as his earlier (and later) work on solid-state physics, for he was becoming increasingly involved in university administration. He was also concerned to revive the fortunes of British scientific publishing: '[Since the war] English had become the language of science and the American journals … had cashed in on it. I felt that we should have our share' (Mott, 76). His increasing involvement with the *Philosophical Magazine* dated from this time, as did an interest in science policy. In 1946 he became the first president of the Atomic Scientists' Association, which aimed to investigate proposals for the control of nuclear energy and to put the true facts before the public; he became one of the few British scientists to argue against the UK developing its own atomic bomb, and later, in 1962, he hosted a 'Pugwash' conference on arms control.

Cambridge In 1954 W. L. Bragg resigned the Cavendish professorship at Cambridge, and Mott was elected to succeed him and moved his family to 31 Sedley Taylor Road, Cambridge. In contrast to Bristol he found that 'The Cavendish … was a going concern with little opportunity to start new things; on the research side it took me some time to find a role' (Mott, 102). Among these going concerns was the nuclear research programme, a relic of Rutherford's tenure at the laboratory; one of Mott's first, difficult, decisions was to cancel ambitious plans for a linear accelerator which, he believed, would still not be adequate to rival the American lead in nuclear physics. He continued Bragg's policy of diversification at the Cavendish, and favoured a very open administration, regularly consulting the heads of research groups. He strongly encouraged the molecular biology group, recently successful in their search for the double-helix structure of DNA, in their search for an identity and site independent of the Cavendish, for he foresaw that they would grow out of all proportion to the rest of the laboratory. Into the space thus created he transferred Bowden's group on surface science from the physical chemistry department, providing a nucleus of solid-state physics in the Cavendish. He was able to promote these moves by his membership of the general board, a committee of twelve that made most of the decisions in Cambridge. Despite this position he constantly felt frustrated by the lack of any central policy-making body for the university.

While still seeking a research role Mott threw himself into education policy, at Cambridge and in schools. He argued strenuously for fundamental changes to the Cambridge natural sciences tripos, and also to the scholarship exam which, he thought, encouraged overspecialization in schools. He became chairman of the education committee of the Institute of Physics, and of the Nuffield advisory committee on physical science which was seeking to modernize science teaching in schools; he sat on the government committee on education between the ages of sixteen and eighteen and the Ministry of Education's standing committee on the supply of teachers; and from 1965 to 1975 he served on the education committee of the Royal Society. In 1962 he received a knighthood.

In 1959 Mott was elected master of his college, Gonville and Caius, on the resignation of James Chadwick. The college at the time was very divided between conservative and progressive parties, and Mott was seen as a unifying candidate. He succeeded in his new role, which he enjoyed for several years. Caius gave him an excellent venue for the meetings and conferences he was so fond of organizing, bringing scientists or policy-makers together to stimulate and progress their views. However, the old divisions surfaced again and Mott in turn resigned in 1966.

Semiconductors The origins of Mott's work on amorphous, or glassy, semiconductors, for which he (together with P. W. Anderson and J. H. Van Vleck) received the Nobel prize in 1977, go back to the 1930s, but Mott took the subject up strongly on resigning from the mastership. In a paper published in the *Proceedings of the Physical Society of London* in 1949 he had shown theoretically that certain non-metallic materials would become metals under extreme pressure as the electrons got closer together, and that this 'Mott transition' would be a sharp, rather than gradual one. The required pressure was too high for an experimental test to be practicable, but in 1958 Fritzsche showed experimentally that a comparable effect was seen in the semiconductor germanium as the concentration of impurities (and hence of electrons) increased. In the same year P. W. Anderson suggested that a similar, sharp, metal-insulator transition would occur if solids became disordered (that is, non-crystalline or amorphous), as the randomness localized the electrons, preventing them from moving freely.

These results introduced Mott to the problems of disordered solids, and he introduced new concepts: the 'mobility edge', which separated the localized and unlocalized states in Anderson's theory, the '8-N rule'; and 'minimum metallic conductivity', to describe their behaviour. He gave a comprehensive account of what was by then a vast literature on this subject in *Metal-Insulator Transitions* (1974). In an article published in the *Philosophical Magazine* in 1969 he considered electrical conduction on the insulating side of the transition, formulating the Mott $T^{-1/4}$ law, which strikingly displays his intuitive genius and describes the 'variable range hopping' of electrons between localized states over a distance that is temperature dependent. Mott's collaborator, E. A. Davis, recalled:

> At the time, few groups showed any interest in them. Although the Xerox Corporation in America achieved great success with their first 'dry' photocopying machine, which used amorphous selenium as the photoreceptor, the physics behind the process was not understood. In the Soviet Union, Kolomiets had been working on the properties of glasses; in Germany, Stuke had a small group; and, in the United Kingdom, Spear was studying transport in thin films of germanium and silicon. What Mott did was to bring together these disparate activities using his by now well-tested methods. Pouncing eagerly on new results, he formulated his ideas and communicated them to interested parties. He organized mini-conferences (in the way he had done at Bristol), visited laboratories for personal discussions, suggested PhD topics, and wrote draft papers for wide circulation and comment. Thereby he rapidly became the father figure of a growing community. (Davis, xxii–xxiii)

Mott's understanding that amorphous materials could act as semiconductors ushered in the age of the truly cheap electronic device, for they were much easier to prepare than the crystalline materials used in most previous electronic systems, as they did not need to be anything like as pure. 'These discoveries quite simply ended the notion of the computer as the preserve of aerospace and defence agencies, big industries and scientific research institutes, and added it to the list of household utensils' (*The Times*, 12 Aug 1996).

'Retirement' Mott retired from the Cavendish professorship in 1971, but remained active within the department. Although eighty-one when high-temperature superconductors were discovered in 1986, he plunged into a new area of research, co-authoring two books on the subject with A. S. Alexandrov—*High-Temperature Superconductors and other Superfluids* (1994) and *Polarons and Bipolarons* (1995)—in which they outlined the idea of 'bipolarons', a virtual particle consisting of two electrons and the associated lattice polarization, as the superconducting mechanism. This remained one of a number of competing theories, unresolved at the time of Mott's death in 1996.

Mott had been brought up as an atheist, but Ruth was an Anglican and Mott was attracted by that tradition as evinced in the beauty of church architecture and of traditional services. However, it was not until the 1950s that he began to think deeply about the relationship between science and Christian faith, impelled largely by Mervyn Stockwood, then vicar of Great St Mary's, the Cambridge University church, who persuaded him to talk on 'Science and belief' in 1957. He began to attend his parish church, occasionally preached, and was eventually baptized and confirmed in the mid-1980s, being admitted to the church on a simple statement of his own rather unorthodox beliefs. Mott rejected a substantial fraction of the creed and refused to believe in an omnipotent God who could perform miracles. He did believe, however, that human consciousness could not be explained or understood through the laws of physics and chemistry, but was a God-given gift that allowed man to understand natural beauty. He outlined his beliefs in 1991 when he edited *Can Scientists Believe?*:

> To give meaning to consciousness, a belief in God who is outside us is necessary to me. Without Him life can seem a tale told by an idiot. I believe in God because I wish to do so, to give meaning to human life. (Davis, 323)

In 1980 the Motts left Cambridge to live at Aspley Guise in Bedfordshire, near their daughter Alice and their grandchildren. From there Mott still visited Cambridge for several days a week. Eventually Ruth became too frail to live alone and went to live in a residential home in Cambridge, where Mott would visit her, staying overnight with his sister Joan.

A tall man, Mott was often described as stork-like. He had a wide variety of interests, possessed great charm and friendliness, and loved entertaining. He received many honours, including the Copley, Royal, and Hughes medals of the Royal Society, the French *Chevalier de l'ordre national du mérite*, and numerous honorary degrees. He was made a Companion of Honour in 1995. He died of heart failure in Milton Keynes General Hospital on 8 August 1996, and was survived by his wife, Ruth, and both his daughters.

ISOBEL FALCONER

Sources B. Pippard, *Memoirs FRS*, 44 (1998), 313–28 · E. A. Davis, ed., *Nevill Mott: reminiscences and appreciations* (1998) · N. F. Mott, *A life in science* (1986) · *The Times* (12 Aug 1996) · *The Independent* (12 Aug 1996) · R. Smoluchowski, *The beginnings of solid state physics* (1980) · *WWW* · b. cert. · m. cert. · d. cert. · *Newnham College Cambridge* (2001) [Ruth Mott]

Archives Gon. & Caius Cam., typescript of diary when master of Gonville and Caius | Bodl. Oxf., corresp. with C. A. Coulson · Bodl. Oxf., corresp. with R. E. Peierls · CAC Cam., corresp. with Sir Edward Bullard · CUL, corresp. with Joseph Needham · Duke U., Perkins L., corresp. with F. London · RS, corresp. with Lord Blackett · U. Leeds, Brotherton L., corresp. with E. C. Stoner · U. Sussex, letters to J. G. Crowther · University of Bristol Library, corresp. with Sir Charles Frank · University of Copenhagen, Niels Bohr Institute for Astronomy, Physics, and Geophysics, corresp. with Niels Bohr

Likenesses J. Wood, oils, 1964, Gon. & Caius Cam. · J. Pannett, pastel drawing, 1973, U. Cam., Cavendish Laboratory · J. Benton-Harris, photograph, 1977, NPG [*see illus.*] · A. Newman, photograph, 1978, NPG · D. Dutton, bronze bust, 2000, U. Cam., Cavendish Laboratory · photograph, repro. in *The Times* · photograph, repro. in *The Independent* · photographs, U. Cam., Cavendish Laboratory · photographs, repro. in Mott, *Life in science* · photographs, repro. in Davis, ed., *Nevill Mott*

Wealth at death £960,849: probate, 21 Oct 1996, CGPLA Eng. & Wales

Motte, Andrew (*bap.* 1696, *d.* 1734), engraver and writer on natural philosophy, was baptized at St Botolph, Aldersgate, London, on 16 August 1696, the son of Benjamin *Motte (*d.* 1710) [*see under* Motte, Benjamin (1693–1738)], printer, and his wife, Ann, daughter of the printer Andrew Clarke. Nothing is known of his education, but he was a member of the Spalding Club and, for a brief period, prior to 1727, lecturer in geometry at Gresham College. In that year he published *A treatise of the mechanical powers, wherein the laws of motion and the properties of those powers are explained and demonstrated in an easie and familiar method* (1727; 2nd edn, 1733). The treatise consisted of his geometry lectures which he now offered, as his preface stated, 'to gentlemen, students and industrious and dextrous workmen'.

Two years later Motte published a translation of Isaac Newton's *Principia mathematica* (1687) under the title of *The Mathematical Principles of Natural Philosophy and his System of the World*, to which he added John Machin's *Laws of the Moon's Motion, According to Gravity*. This work ran through several editions, with contemporary introductions, the most recent being in 1968. The original was published by Benjamin Motte and embellished with figures engraved by Andrew Motte. He also engraved the illustrations for two books by Joseph Thurston which his father published. Motte died on 19 February 1734. No will has been traced; it is not known whether he left a wife or children, nor where he was buried.

ANITA McCONNELL

Sources A. Motte, *A treatise of the mechanical powers* (1727), preface · *GM*, 1st ser., 4 (1734), 107 · parish register (baptism), St Botolph, Aldersgate, London, 16 Aug 1696 · H. Hammelmann, *Book illustrators in eighteenth-century England*, ed. T. S. R. Boase (1975), 63 · I. B. Cohen, 'Pemberton's translation of Newton's *Principia*, with notes on Motte's translation', *Isis*, 54 (1963), 319–51

Motte, Benjamin (*d.* 1710). *See under* Motte, Benjamin (1693–1738).

Motte, Benjamin (1693–1738), bookseller and printer, was born in November 1693 in St Botolph, Aldersgate, London, the eldest son of **Benjamin Motte** (*d.* 1710), printer, and his wife, Anne Clarke (1670/71–1737); he was baptized in the parish on 14 November. The family name presumably indicates a French ancestry. Benjamin Motte was the son of a glover from St Albans and was apprenticed to the London printer Eleanor Cotes on 8 July 1668; he was freed on 2 August 1675. He found work as an overseer to the Aldersgate printing house of Mary Clarke, the widow of the printer Andrew Clarke. His business relationship with the Clarke firm was cemented on 5 April 1692, with his marriage to Mary's 21-year-old daughter, Anne, in Westminster Abbey, with whom he had at least three children: Benjamin, Andrew *Motte, and Charles. The family were living in St Botolph, Aldersgate parish, from at least 1693. He apparently began printing under his own name in 1687, but really began printing in earnest only in the 1690s. He was the official printer to the Parish Clerks' Company from 1694 until 1709, printing bills of mortality and *The Parish-Clerk's Guide*. He was also contracted to print many official church documents.

Benjamin (I) Motte's printing house was relatively large and prosperous, and he printed a variety of works, including Samuel Wesley's heroic epic poem *The Life of Christ* (1693), his elegies on Queen Mary and Archbishop Tillotson (1695), and several textbooks. He also produced, often in collaboration with the engraver John Sturt, a number of illustrated books, ranging from grand folios on architecture to more modest emblem books. He was known as the learned printer owing to his command of Latin, and he published a number of classical works; two translations—of Pufendorf and the Lord's prayer—have also been attributed to him. Motte died in December 1710 and was buried in St Botolph's on Christmas eve. His library was sold by auction in 1711. Anne carried on the printing business and even when Benjamin took over the family firm in 1715, she remained active in the trade until at least 1731. She was buried in St Botolph parish on 6 March 1737.

The younger Benjamin Motte was freed by patrimony on 7 February 1715, although his name first appears on an imprint in 1714. He printed only a few titles each year, but he began to function as bookseller from 1719. A long-standing professional connection with the Tooke family of booksellers (which began with Robert Tooke being apprenticed to the elder Motte in 1692) was consolidated when, on the death of Benjamin Tooke, Benjamin was offered a partnership in the Tooke firm in either late 1723 or early 1724; following the death of Samuel Tooke in December 1724, Motte became the only active partner in the firm. On 21 December 1725 he married Elizabeth Brian, the daughter of a minister, Thomas Brian (or Bryan), in the Charterhouse chapel, Finsbury, London; they had two children. The following year Motte became a partner with his brother Charles (*bap.* 1698, *d.* 1731). Between 1731 and 1734 Motte was active on his own, but from 1735 he was again in partnership, this time with his apprentice Charles Bathurst.

Motte's output was large and varied. Alongside many Anglican works, including numerous sermons, he published Restoration literature, instructional manuals, historical studies, scientific treatises, and, following his father's footsteps, classical editions. He also produced a

two-volume abridgement of the Royal Society's *Philosophical Transactions* for 1700–20, in 1721. However, he is most famous for his association with Jonathan Swift, who chose Motte as his publisher following the death of Benjamin Tooke. In October 1726 Motte published the first edition of *Gulliver's Travels*, but his political timidity and caution led him to make a number of changes to the text without Swift's knowledge. An amended second edition restored some of Swift's original text, but it was only with the publication of a Dublin edition by George Faulkner in 1735 that Swift was able to see through the press a text with which he was satisfied.

Gulliver's Travels remained a lucrative work for Motte: it 'hath made a bookseller almost rich enough to be an alderman' (*Correspondence of Jonathan Swift*, 3.198). Despite Swift's misgivings about Motte's handling of the text, he remained loyal to the London bookseller for the rest of the latter's career. In 1732 Swift wrote to Motte promising that he would be the publisher for 'any thing that shall be published with my consent while I am alive or after my death' (ibid., 4.41). Accordingly, Motte published a number of further works by Swift, including the anonymous *An Epistle to a Lady* which led to Motte's arrest in 1734. Motte was also involved in an altercation with Faulkner over the publication of an Irish edition of Swift's works in 1735. However, despite Swift's advocacy, Motte attracted the disapprobation of Pope, following the careless printing of *Miscellanies in Prose and Verse* (1727–32), which included work by Swift, Pope, and others. Pope labelled the publisher 'a common Bookseller' (ibid., 4.65).

Motte died intestate on 12 March 1738, and his estate was administered by his brother-in-law, Thomas Brian. His stock and copyrights were auctioned at a trade sale on 9 December 1740, with a second sale being organized by his former apprentice Bathurst on 15 December 1743.

J. J. CAUDLE

Sources M. Treadwell, 'Benjamin Motte, Jr', *The British literary book trade, 1700–1820*, ed. J. K. Bracken and J. Silver, DLitB, 154 (1995), 198–202 · D. F. McKenzie, ed., *Stationers' Company apprentices*, 3 vols. (1961–78), vols. 2–3 · H. R. Plomer and others, *A dictionary of the printers and booksellers who were at work in England, Scotland, and Ireland from 1668 to 1725* (1922) · T. Belanger, 'Booksellers' sales of copyright: aspects of the London booktrade, 1718–1768', PhD diss., Col. U., 1970 · M. Treadwell, 'Benjamin Motte, Andrew Tooke, and *Gulliver's Travels*', *Proceedings of the first Münster symposium on Jonathan Swift*, ed. H. J. Real and H. J. Vienken (1985), 287–344 · D. Cornu, 'Swift, Motte, and the copyright struggle: two unnoticed documents', *Modern Language Notes*, 54 (Jan 1939), 120–21 · H. Terrink and A. H. Scouten, eds., *A bibliography of the writings of Jonathan Swift*, 2nd edn (1963) · *The correspondence of Jonathan Swift*, ed. H. Williams, 5 vols. (1963–5) · private information (2004) [M. Treadwell, Trent University, Canada]

Motte, Philip de la (*d.* 1805). *See under* Delamotte, William (1775–1863).

Mottershead, Joseph (1688–1771), dissenting minister, son of Joseph Mottershead, yeoman, was born near Stockport, Cheshire, on 17 August 1688. He was educated at Attercliffe Academy under Timothy Jollie, and afterwards studied for a year under Matthew Henry at Chester. He was licensed by Matthew Henry and Samuel Lawrence on

17 March 1710. He preached (1710–12) at Kingsley, Frodsham parish, Cheshire. On 5 August 1712 he was ordained at Knutsford by the Cheshire classis as successor to Samuel Lawrence at Nantwich. Examined on 4 August he defended his thesis 'An angeli et sancti sint adorandi vel invocandi?' in the negative. Matthew Henry visited him in 1713, and died at his house in 1714. In 1717 Mottershead became minister of Cross Street Chapel, Manchester, and held this post until his death. His colleagues were Joshua Jones (d. 1740), John Seddon (1719–1769), and Robert Gore (1748–1779).

While a member of the Manchester classis and a scribe at the Lancashire provincial meeting in 1724, Mottershead remained active in the Cheshire classis, taking part in licensing and ordaining and acting as moderator in 1725, 1737, and 1740. This was not untypical for individual ministers. These voluntary ministerial organizations exchanged ministers across the region, represented the interests of the protestant dissenting ministry, and collaborated with their brethren in adjacent counties. Manchester also had joint responsibility for the provision of preaching at Sale, Cheshire.

When the Young Pretender (Charles Edward Stuart) entered Manchester in November 1745, Mottershead was selected as a hostage for a pecuniary fine, but he had timely warning and avoided the levy, though Jacobite troops were quartered in his house on the night of 27 November. During his protracted ministry at Manchester, Mottershead, whom Halley calls 'a very quiet and peaceable man' (Halley, 2.364 n.), passed from Calvinism to a type of Arianism. Alexander Gordon notes in the *Dictionary of National Biography* that he wavered in his theology, conforming to Socinian doctrine under the influence of Seddon but ending in a 'high type of Arianism'. About 1756 there was a secession from the congregation owing to the Socinian tenets of Seddon, his colleague and son-in-law, leading to the formation of the Independent church at Hunter's Croft.

At Kingsley, Mottershead had married his first wife, Elizabeth, the eldest daughter of Mr Bennett of Hapsford, Cheshire. She died in October 1718, leaving four children. Their only son was educated at Edinburgh as a physician but took Anglican orders, acted as curate in Manchester, and was lost at sea as chaplain of a man-of-war. Their eldest daughter, Elizabeth, married on 9 February 1743 John Seddon, Mottershead's colleague. Their second daughter, Sarah, married John Jones, founder of the banking house Jones, Loyd & Co., whose grandson was Samuel Jones Loyd, first Baron Overstone. Mottershead married, secondly, in January 1721, Margaret Gaskell (*née* Hallows; d. 1740), widow of Nathaniel Gaskell of Manchester; he was her third husband. He married, thirdly, in June 1742, Abigail (d. 1753), daughter of Chewning *Blackmore, the dissenting minister at Worcester [see under Blackmore, William], and Abigail Higgins.

Mottershead published two sermons, a catechism, and some religious discourses, and contributed to Priestley's

Theological Repository under the pseudonym Theophilus. He died on 4 November 1771 and was buried near the pulpit in his meeting-house.

ALEXANDER GORDON, *rev.* JONATHAN H. WESTAWAY

Sources T. Baker, *Memorials of a dissenting chapel* (1884), 27–43, 95–6, 98, 141–3, 159 · J. Toulmin, *Memoirs of the Rev. Samuel Bourn* (1808), 251–7 · J. Hunter, *Familiae minorum gentium*, ed. J. W. Clay, 1, Harleian Society, 37 (1894), 299–300 · will, proved, 20 Jan 1772, Lancs. RO, WCW · W. Urwick, ed., *Historical sketches of nonconformity in the county palatine of Cheshire, by various ministers and laymen* (1864), lxi, 128–30, 414, 452 · B. Nightingale, *Lancashire nonconformity*, 6 vols. [1890–93], vol. 5, pp. 97ff. · *The diary of Richard Kay, 1716–51, of Baldingstone, near Bury, a Lancashire doctor*, ed. W. Brockbank and F. Kenworthy, Chetham Society, 3rd ser., 16 (1968), 5, 22, 38–9, 42, 53, 55, 65, 142 · *The diary of James Clegg of Chapel en le Frith, 1708–1755*, ed. V. S. Doe, 1–2, Derbyshire RS, 2–3 (1978–9) · A. Gordon, ed., *Cheshire classis: minutes, 1691–1745* (1919), 40, 42, 44–7, 52–8, 60–61, 63–77, 79–91, 194 · R. Halley, *Lancashire: its puritanism and nonconformity*, 2 vols. (1869), vol. 2, pp. 364, 447 · J. B. Williams, *Memoirs of the life, character and writings of the Rev. Matthew Henry* (1828), 159, 163, 164 · G. E. Evans, 'Notes on the first register', *Antiquarian Notes*, 1/5 (1899), 36–8 · H. H. Johnson, *Cross Street Chapel, Manchester … 1672–1922* (1922) · H. MacLachlan, *Essays and addresses* (1950), 95 · H. McLachlan, *Warrington Academy: its history and influence*, Chetham Society, 107, new ser. (1943), 20, 109 · J. Orton, *The practical works of the Rev. Job Orton now first collected: consisting of discourses, sacramental meditations, and letters with copious indexes. To which is prefixed a memoir of the author*, 2 vols. (1842), vol. 2, p. 553 · C. Stell, *An inventory of nonconformist chapels and meeting houses in the north of England* (1994) · R. Wade, *The rise of nonconformity in Manchester* (1880), 34sq. · *DNB*

Archives BL, Mottershead genealogy, Add. MS 244 (or 8) 884 · DWL, Blackmore MSS, letters · JRL, Unitarian College collection, letters

Likenesses W. Pether, mezzotint (after portrait by H. Pickering), BM

Wealth at death over £4500: will, proved, 20 Jan 1772, Lancs. RO, WCW

Motteux, Peter Anthony [*formerly* Pierre-Antoine Le Motteux] (**1663–1718**), journalist and translator, was born on 25 February 1663 in the parish of St Étienne-des-Tonneliers, Rouen, France, the eldest of the nine children of Antoine Le Motteux (1637–1679), merchant and haberdasher, and his wife, Isabeau (*née* le Nud). His parents were members of Rouen's beleaguered Huguenot community, and he probably received his schooling (which included an excellent training in Latin) at the Huguenot school at Quevilly. After the revocation of the edict of Nantes on 18 October 1685, Motteux, along with nearly two-thirds of the Rouen Huguenot congregation, sought asylum abroad, abandoning valuable inherited property. He took up residence in London, lodging in the first instance with his relative the merchant Paul Dominique, and was made an English citizen on 5 March 1686. In the same year he was among the petitioners for permission to establish a French protestant church in London. Motteux rapidly Anglicized himself, and soon began to make a living as a miscellaneous writer, supplementing his income first (by 1700) from 'a very genteel place in the General Post-Office, relating to the Foreign Letters' (T. Whincop, *Scanderbeg*, 1747, 263), and later (from c.1705) by trade in East Indian merchandise and works of art. The last activity became the principal occupation of his final decade, and his 'India warehouse' in Leadenhall Street became a well-known social centre for female 'Wits and Beauties' (*The Guardian*, 22 July 1713).

Motteux was twice married. His first wife, Elizabeth (*née* Coborne), whom he married on 15 August 1691, died in December 1694; his second wife, Priscilla, whom he had married by 1699, survived him, and was named sole executor in his will (proved on 24 February 1718). Of his seven known children—Peter, Henrietta, Catherine (*b.* 8 Aug 1699), Isabell Katherine (*bap.* 5 Sept 1700), Jane (*bap.* 19 Sept 1701), Anthony (*bap.* 3 Oct 1705), and Francis (*bap.* 13 April 1710)—three (Catherine, Isabell Katherine, and Jane) are recorded as having died in infancy.

Motteux's English literary début was as the editor of the *Gentleman's Journal* (1692–4), a general magazine modelled on the French *Mercure Gallant*, and an important precursor of *The Tatler* and *The Spectator*. The journal contained poetry, literary and theatrical criticism, songs, enigmas, tales, burlesques, allegories, translations in prose and verse, and essays on the mores, fashions, and scientific discoveries of the time. One of its issues (October 1693) was devoted to 'Pieces written by Persons of the Fair Sex'. Its patrons included such prominent and powerful figures as the duke of Devonshire and the earls of Halifax and Shrewsbury, and its contents displayed Motteux's intimate knowledge of the English cultural scene, and his acquaintance with a wide variety of celebrated literary figures, including Charles Gildon, John Dryden, Matthew Prior, William Congreve, Sir Charles Sedley, Nahum Tate, Tom Brown, Thomas D'Urfey, Thomas Southerne, John Dennis, John Crowne, and John Oldmixon, and musicians, including Henry Purcell, John Blow, and John Eccles.

Motteux's greatest literary successes, in his own time and later, were his translations of the works of Rabelais and of Cervantes' *Don Quixote*. In 1693 he published a revision of Sir Thomas Urquhart's translation of books 1–3 of Rabelais (books 1–2 first published 1653; book 3 previously unpublished), with a new life of Rabelais, preface, and notes. To these he added, in July 1694, a new translation of books 4 and 5, together with a translator's preface. The whole was reissued in 1708. Motteux's understanding of Rabelais's text, his knowledge of the historical context of the French writer's work, and the fluency, vigour, and racy colloquial zest of his English version were immediately recognized, and, though later criticized for verbosity, flippancy, and coarseness, the translation has held its own to this day as the classic English rendering of Rabelais. Volumes 1 and 2 of Motteux's *Don Quixote* (which incorporated contributions from several other writers, including William Wycherley, William Congreve, Sir Samuel Garth, and Tom Brown) appeared in 1700, with volumes 3 and 4 following in 1703. More paraphrastic than some of its later rivals, and more elegantly decorous, and less accurate, than Motteux's Rabelais, the version of *Don Quixote* was nevertheless widely admired throughout the eighteenth and nineteenth centuries for its descriptive lucidity and playful wit, and 'thoroughly deserves the popularity which has kept it in print to the present day' (Arthur Terry, in France, *Oxford Guide*, 418). Motteux's translations from the French also included Malebranche's Platonic dialogue *Christian Conferences* (completed by April 1692; published 1695), Pidou de St Olon's *Present State of the Empire of Morocco* (1695), and Fontenelle's essay 'Of pastorals' (1695). In 1701 he published *A Banquet for Gentlemen and Ladies*, a collection of tales of intrigue, love, and jealousy in the tradition of Boccaccio and Cervantes, four of which had previously appeared in the *Gentleman's Journal*.

Peter Anthony Motteux (**1663–1718**), by Giovanni Antonio Pellegrini [with members of his household]

Motteux was also active in the 1690s and early 1700s as a dramatist and librettist. He produced the comedies *Love's a Jest* (1696) and *Farewell Folly* (acted 1705; published 1707), the mélange *The Novelty* (based on Davenant, 1697), and the tragedy *Beauty in Distress* (1698). The last had a preface—endorsed by a commendatory poem by Motteux's friend John Dryden—defending the play against Jeremy Collier's recent attack on the 'immorality and profaneness' of the English stage. Motteux also supplied texts for various operatic or quasi-operatic entertainments: the masques *The Loves of Venus and Mars* (1696) and *Acis and Galatea* (1701); the operas *The Island Princess* (1699, based on Nahum Tate's adaptation of a play by John Fletcher; the manuscript of Motteux's score is now in the British Library), *Arsinoe* (1705, the first English opera in the Italian style), and *Love's Triumph* (1708); the pastoral *The Temple of Love* (1706); and the interlude *Britain's Happiness* (1704). During this period he also produced a steady stream of occasional and complimentary poems, songs, prologues, and epilogues, including an elegy on the death of Queen Mary; 'Words of a Musical Entertainment ... on the Taking of Namur'; and 'Words for an Entertainment at the Music Feast on St Cecilia's Day' (all 1695). His literary output declined considerably in his later years: only three poems, including *A Poem on Tea* (1712), were published after 1708.

On 19 February 1718 Motteux was 'found dead in a House of very ill Fame, in Star-Court in the Butcher-Row near Temple-Bar ... there being Several Circumstances which ma[d]e it strongly suspected that he was murthered' (*London Gazette*, 22–5 March 1718). He had apparently been conveyed to Star Court the previous evening from White's Chocolate House in St James's, in the company of one Mary Roberts. Several of those present, including Elizabeth Simmerton, the mistress of the establishment, were arrested and charged with having robbed and murdered Motteux, but were acquitted 'to the great Surprize of most People' (Boyer, 15.436). A contemporary account records that Motteux was 'suppos'd to have been strangled by Whores, who forgot to cut the cord They ha[d] ty'd ab^t hi[s] Neck to provok[e] venery' (marginal note in a copy of Gildon's *Lives of the Poets*, BL, 276. f.46, 101). He was buried in the church of St Andrew Undershaft, at the corner of Leadenhall Street and St Mary Axe, on 22 February 1718. His will made provision for a gift of £10 to be distributed by his widow among the deserving poor of the parish of St Andrew, and a further £10 to be distributed among the poor in the place of his death, 'whether it be the same or any Other Parish' (Cunningham, *Peter Anthony Motteux*, 198).

Peter Motteux was clearly a man of immense ability, energy, versatility, and enterprise, who established himself rapidly in a new country, soon securing himself a place at the centre of its literary culture. In his commendatory poem to *Beauty in Distress*, Dryden marvelled at the uniqueness of Motteux's achievement:

But whence art thou inspir'd, and Thou alone
To flourish in an Idiom, not thine own?

It moves our wonder, that a foreign Guest
Shou'd over-match the most, and match the best.
(ll. 48–51)

Pope, less generously, classed Motteux, in *Peri Bathous* (1728), as one of the 'eels', 'obscure authors, that wrap themselves up in their own mud, but are mighty nimble and pert' (*Prose Works*, 2.197), and alluded to Motteux's garrulousness in conversation: 'Talkers, I've learn'd to bear; *Motteux* I knew' ('The fourth satire of Dr John Donne', l. 50). However, though Motteux's plays and most of his occasional poems are now forgotten, the *Gentleman's Journal* marked a significant development in the history of English journalism, and the enduring reputations of the Rabelais and *Don Quixote* have amply justified Dryden's confidence in Motteux's writerly abilities, securing him a permanent place in the literature of his adopted country.

DAVID HOPKINS

Sources R. N. Cunningham, *Peter Anthony Motteux, 1663–1718: a biographical and critical study* (1933) · R. N. Cunningham, 'A bibliography of the writings of Motteux', *Proceedings and Papers of the Oxford Bibliographical Society*, 3 (1933), 317–37 · D. Hopkins, 'The London odes on St Cecilia's day for 1686, 1695 and 1696', *Review of English Studies*, new ser., 45 (1994), 486–95 · A. Boyer, *The political state of Great Britain*, 15 (1718) · *The prose works of Alexander Pope*, 2, ed. R. Cowler (1986) · P. France, ed., *The Oxford guide to literature in English translation* (2000)

Archives BL, letters, Sloane MS 4043, fol. 253; Egerton MS 2623, fol. 68

Likenesses G. A. Pellegrini, group portrait, pen and ink, and wash drawing (with his family), BM [*see illus.*]

Wealth at death bequests: will, Cunningham, *Peter Anthony Motteux*, 197–9

Mottistone. For this title name *see* Seely, John Edward Bernard, first Baron Mottistone (1868–1947).

Mottley, John (1692–1750), writer, was born in London, the son of Dionisia (1659–1731), daughter of John Guise of Abode Court, Gloucestershire, and sister of William Guise, the orientalist of All Souls. The family were firm supporters of the Commonwealth and later of William III. Dionisia Guise had married a Jacobite soldier, Colonel Thomas Mottley, who went into exile with James II, entered the service of Louis XIV, and was killed in 1706 at the battle of Turin. John Mottley was said to have been conceived during a visit to England by his father as a clandestine agent of James's.

Mottley was educated at Archbishop Tenison's Grammar School in St Martin-in-the-Fields, London. With the assistance of the Guise family he obtained a clerkship in the Excise Office in 1708, which, because of an 'unhappy contract', he resigned in the South Sea Bubble year, 1720. Expectations of patronage from Lord Halifax and Sir Robert Walpole were disappointed, and the estate settled upon him by his Guise grandfather had to be sold to cover Mottley's mother's debts. (She died in 1731, estranged from the Guises, living on £30 a year charity from John Percival, who paid £5 for her burial.) Mottley was obliged to enter Grub Street for his living.

By this time Mottley had had some experience in theatre, assisting Susanna Centlivre with *A Bold Stroke for a Wife* (1718), even writing 'one or two entire Scenes of it'

(Mottley, *List*, 191). His own tragedy *The Imperial Captives*, set in ancient Carthage and 'indebted to the French', opened on 29 February 1720 at Lincoln's Inn Fields. It had been puffed in the *Weekly Packet* on 20 February as 'by a gentleman unknown to the town', but, like his ensuing tragedy *Antiochus* (Lincoln's Inn Fields, 13 April 1721), was published under his own name. Thereafter in theatre Mottley concentrated upon comedy. For 'reasons', perhaps a sense of social stigma or fear of the bailiff, nearly all his subsequent writings were published anonymously or pseudonymously. Much of his work was collaborative.

Penelope (Haymarket, 8 May 1728), Mottley's and the classicist Thomas Cooke's ballad-opera burlesque—the first such imitation of *The Beggar's Opera*—recasts Homer's heroine into the landlady of an alehouse and Ulysses into a disbanded regimental soldier from the continental wars. Ulysses' concern about his wife's manner of life in his absence, along with his Jacobite salute to the Royal Oak pub sign, recalls Mottley's father's circumstances. Other comedies followed—*The Craftsman, or, The Weekly Journalist* (Haymarket, 15 October 1728) and *The Widow Bewitched* (Goodman's Fields, 8 June 1730). In 1731 came the stunning success of *The Devil to Pay, or, The Wives Metamorphos'd* (6 August, Drury Lane), which he and Charles Coffey adapted into a ballad opera from Thomas Jevon's old *Devil of a Wife*; when this had in turn been shortened into one act by Theophilus Cibber it became the most popular afterpiece of the century.

In 1734, as Robert Seymour, Mottley (perhaps assisted again by Cooke) re-edited Stow's *Survey of the Cities of London and Westminster*. In 1739, as Elijah Jenkins, he re-edited the contents of several recent jestbooks into the best-selling classic of the genre, *Joe Miller's Jests, or, The Wit's Vade Mecum*. He may also have been the adapter of Thomas Gordon's *Humourist* essays into *A Trip through London* (1728).

At last came the dignified *History of the Life of Peter I, Emperor of Russia* (1739) and *History of the Life and Reign of the Empress Catharine* (1744), openly 'by John Mottley, Esq.'. In his latter years Mottley was almost bedridden from gout. The *Compleat List of All the English Dramatic Poets* of 1747, appended to Thomas Whincop's play *Scanderbeg*, appears to be by Mottley and is therefore his last known work: in the spirit of a reckoning up, he claims his portions of various collaborations and paternity of theretofore unacknowledged works; the entry on himself he made his own memorial. John Mottley died on 30 October 1750.

J. M. RIGG, rev. YVONNE NOBLE

Sources [T. Mottley], 'Susannna Centlivre', 'Charles Coffey', 'Thomas Cooke', 'John Mottley', *A compleat list of all the English dramatic poets*, pubd with T. Whincop, *Scanderbeg* (1747) • E. L. Avery, ed., *The London stage, 1660–1800*, pt 2: *1700–1729* (1960) • A. H. Scouten, ed., *The London stage, 1660–1800*, pt 3: *1729–1747* (1961) • D. E. Baker, *Biographia dramatica, or, A companion to the playhouse*, rev. I. Reed, new edn, 2 vols. (1782) • J. Mottley, dedication, *The widow bewitch'd* (1730) • J. Maclean, 'Elmore and the family of Guise', *Transactions of the Bristol and Gloucestershire Archaeological Society*, 3 (1878–9), 49–78, esp. 69–78 [pedigree of the family of Guise] • J. Percival, *Diary 1730–47*, vol. 1 (1920) • [W. Oldys], 'Diary of William Oldys, esq. Norroy king-at-arms', ed. J. Yeowell, *N&Q*, 2nd ser., 11 (1861), 101–4 • W. Upcott, *A bibliographical account of the principal work relating to English topography*, 3 vols. (1818) • P. B. Anderson, 'Thomas Gordon and John Mottley, *A trip through London*, 1728', *Philological Quarterly*, 19 (1940), 244–60 • E. Esar, 'The legend of Joe Miller', *American Book Collector*, 13/2 (Oct 1962), 11–26

Likenesses engraving, repro. in [T. Whincop], *A compleat list of all the English dramatic poets* [1747]

Mottram, Charles Henry (1807–1876), engraver, was born on 9 April 1807. Of his parents nothing is known. Mottram worked both in line and in mezzotint. Examples of his engraving in the former medium include his reduced-size plate (Thomas Landseer had already produced a larger version) after Sir Edwin Landseer's *The Challenge*, and his large plate after Rosa Bonheur's *Boefs Bretons* (both declared for publication by Henry Graves & Co. in 1862). In the second quarter of the nineteenth century Mottram, like most of his prominent colleagues, eventually turned to the rather speedier technique of mezzotint in response to the urgings of print publishers anxious to meet the increasing demand for prints both in Britain and abroad. He reproduced in this medium Thomas Jones Barker's *The Morning before the Battle* and *The Evening after the Battle* (declared for publication by Graves in, respectively, 1865 and 1866). However, mezzotint could be made even speedier when supplemented by the use of roulettes and other implements for creating textural effects, and Mottram's skill in integrating such effects to achieve a unified whole was unparalleled. Among his most celebrated works using this 'mixed mezzotint' technique are the plates reproducing John Martin's paintings *The Last Judgement*, *The Plains of Heaven*, and *The Great Day of his Wrath*. The three subjects were published in 1225 sets by Thomas McLean in 1854 and their popularity endured at least into the early years of the twentieth century: the publishers and printers Dixon and Ross, of Hampstead Road, London, advertised 'the last grand works of John Martin' in their trade list of 1871 and were still doing so until 1903. Perhaps Mottram's greatest *tour de force* is the very large mixed mezzotint plate after W. Holman Hunt's *Scapegoat*, the engraved image measuring more than 2 feet by 3: over 6 square feet of intricate work. On 29 November 1861 Graves announced the edition, which was to be prefaced by two hundred proofs signed by Hunt and offered for sale at 10 guineas each.

Mottram was a prominent exponent of the ruling machine, a labour-saving device invented by Wilson Lowry (1762–1824) and subsequently developed to a high degree of sophistication. By means of this machine, fine parallel lines could be scribed with a needle, their distance apart controlled by an adjustable ratchet, and delicately bitten into the surface of a metal plate to create a beautifully subtle sky effect, modulating tones being achieved by differing depths of bite. Ernest Gambart, the print publisher, related (in a letter in the archives of the Royal Institution, London) that Mottram was 'the ruler generally employed by all the Engravers for such work [as ruled skies]': an illuminating reference to the collaborative network upon which the engraving trade depended. He was skilled in the use of the steel plates which by the middle of the nineteenth century were to a large extent supplanting the more rapidly wearing copper for reproductive engraving. His expertness in this respect is confirmed by the fact that a steel plate manufactured by John Sellers of Sheffield and shown at the Great Exhibition of 1851 (exhibit 147, class 22) featured a demonstration of a finely ruled sky by Mottram.

Seven of Mottram's reproductive engravings were exhibited at the Royal Academy between 1861 and 1877—a small proportion of his life's work, of which the Printsellers' Association, in its catalogue covering the years 1847 to 1892, listed more than fifty major plates. The engraver died on 30 August 1876 at his home, 92 High Street, Camden Town, London, leaving a widow, Sarah. Examples of his prints are in the British Museum and the Victoria and Albert Museum, London.

ANTHONY DYSON

Sources G. W. Friend, ed., *An alphabetical list of engravings declared at the office of the Printsellers' Association, London*, 2 vols. (1892) • H. Beck, *Victorian engravings* (1973) [exhibition catalogue, V&A] • J. Maas, *Gambart, prince of the Victorian art world* (1975) • E. Gambart, letter, 28 Sept 1848, Royal Institution of Great Britain, London • Graves, *Artists*, new edn • J. H. Slater, *Engravings and their value*, rev. F. W. Maxwell-Barbour, 6th edn (1929); repr. (1978) • *Great Exhibition* (1851), exhibit 147, class 22 [exhibition catalogue, London] • A. Dyson, *Pictures to print: the nineteenth-century engraving trade* (1984) • *DNB* • *CGPLA Eng. & Wales* (1876)
Wealth at death under £800—administration: 25 Sept 1876, *CGPLA Eng. & Wales*

Mottram, Ralph Hale (1883–1971), banker and writer, was born on 30 October 1883 above the eighteenth-century Gurney's Bank in Norwich. He was the eldest son of James Mottram, who like his father and grandfather (James Nasmith Mottram jun. and sen.) was resident chief clerk of the bank, and Mottram's second wife, Fanny Ann Hale. Their position included as perquisite a home in the Bank House, among the ancient streets in the town centre. Both parents were English, but Fanny Mottram, who had been educated in Versailles, insisted that Ralph and his younger brothers, Hugh (who would become an architect and illustrator of Ralph's later books) and Alfred, acquire some French learning. Following his years at the City of Norwich School he spent most of 1899 at M. Rosselet's school in Lausanne, Switzerland, joining the staff of Gurney's Bank in the family tradition on 3 December 1899, just after its merger with what he called 'the great Barclay combine' (Mottram, *Vanities*, 77). His nostalgic *Autobiography with a Difference* (1938) evokes his provincial boyhood in Norfolk, while his novel *Our Mr. Dormer* (1927), written before the war trilogy but publishable only after its success, is a fictionalized family history. Mottram's grandfather was a Unitarian; Mottram continued what he called 'the old-fashioned habit' (ibid., 44) on Sunday mornings at the Norwich meeting-house. Brought up by his father 'in the Liberalism of Gladstone' (ibid., 141), he eschewed party politics even when he held municipal offices in Norwich.

With the exception of the First World War years, Mottram worked at the bank, in what he thought of as servitude, while awakening early to write, hoping to break free into literature. His ambition to be a poet was nurtured by Ada Galsworthy, wife of the novelist, of whose marriage

settlement James Mottram was trustee. John Galsworthy would become a valued friend, and Ralph Mottram would later write a life of Galsworthy (1953) and a memoir of the couple, *For some we Loved* (1956). Of Mottram's sixty books, in nearly every genre, his first two, in 1907 and 1909, were slender volumes of verse published as by J. Marjoram. Nothing followed them into print until the stimulus of war released Mottram's literary imagination.

At the outbreak of war in 1914 Mottram joined a territorial battalion of the Norfolk regiment and soon received a commission, after which he was posted to Flanders. In 1915 he was a company officer in the stagnant yet sanguinary war near Ypres, where the natural cover of the landscape was fast disappearing under mortar and artillery fire, and trenches flooded with liquid mud. He had his fill of combat, recalling his men:

> crouching under a sloppy parapet, while for twenty-four hours great masses of metal were flung over their heads against the objective. Then the 'charge'—the slow and difficult crawl forward to find the enemy trench, that had been so carefully blown to pieces that it could not be identified; the attempt to make some sort of cover, and the inevitable counter-bombardment that wiped out the attackers, until a few famished scarecrows crawled back with the news to their starting-point. (Mottram, *Through the Menin Gate*, 125)

Although battalion officers averaged, Mottram concluded, six weeks of life, he survived several lives before being reassigned into relative safety. Because of his brief French education he proved more valuable in liaison than as an overage subaltern in the line, and was withdrawn to become a roving troubleshooter along the Franco-Belgian border, investigating complaints by landowners and householders about damage allegedly done by British troops. His fictionalization of those years became his first published post-war novel, *The Spanish Farm* (1924). The imagined, centuries-old, Ferme l'Espagnole recalled in its name the Spanish occupation of the Low Countries. Its wartime vicissitudes were reimagined into Mottram's novel, which Galsworthy himself took without success to publishers until Chatto and Windus accepted it on condition that Galsworthy write a preface, without fee.

Understated and compassionate, the novel dealt with war largely in the near distance, for echoes from the stalemated front line could be heard from the oasis-like holdings of sixtyish widower Jerome Vanderlynden and his shrewd young daughter, Madeleine, yet only seen through its effects upon their bourgeois practicality and the British soldiers who ebb and flow through the fictional Flemish backwater. Once it had been awarded the Hawthornden prize, then the premier literary award in England, for 1924, the unpretentious novel became a bestseller.

Mottram then followed it with two popular sequels, *Sixty-Four, Ninety-Four* (1925) and *The Crime at Vanderlynden's* (1926). The first retells the story from the point of view of Lieutenant Geoffrey Skene, an architect in civilian life, who had worried unduly that the war might end without his ever firing a shot. In the final, post-armistice, segment, Captain Stephen Dormer, a bank clerk in civilian life, is given Mottram's actual wartime assignment, and confronts the muddle of peace as Skene had encountered the muddle of war. The novels were less about the carnage of war than about the nearly self-contained civilization, with its administrative hierarchies and arcane social codes, that an enormous army away from home became, seen in the perspective of its impact upon a large farm in Flanders that embodied the continuity of human concerns that survived mere wars.

By the time that Mottram had stitched the three short novels and some related stories into a trilogy as *The Spanish Farm* (1928), the first had been filmed (1927) as *Roses of Picardy*, the cinema sale making it possible for him to retire from the bank, where his brother Alfred also worked, keeping the family's hand in. (The novel would be televised by the BBC in 1968.)

In Mottram's forty-fifth year he became a professional writer, producing, he estimated, 'a yearly average of 200,000 words' (Mottram, *Vanities*, 54), including *Europa's Beast* (1930) and *Come to the Bower* (1949). None of his later works had anything approaching the success of *The Spanish Farm*. Still, Mottram relished his second career. 'I have imported into my production', he wrote late in life, 'the habit of the bank clerk and the discipline of the temporary soldier', writing four days a week from early morning until two, his desk 'a board on my knee' (ibid., 44). He also wrote books on banking history, on Norfolk worthies, on East Anglia, the broads, and Norwich, three autobiographies, and, as late as 1968, further poems. 'Nothing very spectacular', he conceded. 'It is what I wished to do with my life and I have done it' (ibid., 54).

Mottram's first pure memoir, *The Window Seat, or, Life Observed* (1954), described his life from 1883 to the armistice in 1918; the second, *Another Window Seat* (1956), carried his story to the close of his lord mayoralty. *Vanities and Verities* (1958) was a more scrappy memoir, carrying his story only a little further, while filling in interstices in the earlier volumes.

In 1932 Mottram became a fellow of the Royal Society of Literature. Always active, while a writer, in public life, he lectured widely; became a trustee of Manchester College (the Unitarian foundation at Oxford); was a founding member of the Norwich Society, and its secretary for twenty years; and was a member of the Norwich Public Libraries Committee from 1929 to 1963. During the Second World War he was British Council representative to the American 2nd air division, headquartered in Norfolk. He was successively a freeman, magistrate, and, in the coronation year of 1953, lord mayor of Norwich. A promoter of the post-war University of East Anglia, he was made an honorary DLitt by it in 1966.

In 1918 Mottram had married Margaret (Madge) Allan, daughter of a schoolmaster in East Lothian. They had two sons and a daughter. The death of Madge in 1970 after fifty-two years of marriage, when his own health had begun to fail, forced him to leave his home in Eaton, Norwich, and live with his daughter in King's Lynn, where he died on 16 April 1971. Norwich would erect a monument to him on a prominence on Mousehold Heath, overlooking the city he celebrated and loved.

Despite his more than sixty years of literary activity, Mottram's reputation rests only upon the three-year span when he produced the warmly evocative *The Spanish Farm*, which remains one of the pinnacles of English fiction evoked by the experience of the First World War.

STANLEY WEINTRAUB

Sources *The Times* (17 April 1971) · R. H. Mottram, *Vanities and verities* (1958) · R. H. Mottram, *The window seat* (1954) · R. H. Mottram, *Another window seat* (1956) · R. H. Mottram, *A personal record* (1969) · R. H. Mottram, *Through the Menin Gate* (1932) · C. Thayer, 'R. H. Mottram', *British novelists, 1890–1929: modernists*, ed. T. F. Staley, DLitB, 36 (1985), 172–7 · DNB · WWW
Archives Norfolk RO, personal and family papers · Norfolk RO, photocopied MS account of the Mottram family, annotated by him | *Forbes Magazine*, New York, corresp. with John Galsworthy · BL, corresp. with Society of Authors, Add. MS 63307 · Royal Society of Literature, London, letters to the Royal Society of Literature · U. Birm., letters to G. H. Fabes · U. Reading L., letters to George Bell & Sons · U. Reading L., letters to The Bodley Head Ltd
Likenesses H. Coster, photographs, 1930–39, NPG · double photograph (with his brother Alfred), repro. in C. Thayer, 'R. H. Mottram', p. 174 · photograph, repro. in Thayer, 'R. H. Mottram', p. 172
Wealth at death £1427: probate, 6 July 1971, CGPLA Eng. & Wales

Mottram, Vernon Henry (1882–1976), physiologist and nutritionist, was born at Tewkesbury, Gloucestershire, on 14 March 1882, the youngest of three sons of William Mottram, a Congregational minister, and his second wife, Elizabeth Fruen, a schoolmistress. The family also included two sisters and a half-brother. William Mottram's ministry was in Bristol, but in 1887 he was appointed to a chapel in Southwark, and the family moved to London.

Mottram was educated at Caterham School and at St Olave's Grammar School, London. He won a scholarship to Trinity College, Cambridge (1901), where he studied chemistry, botany, physics, and physiology, taking a first in both parts of the natural sciences tripos (1903 and 1905). Among his teachers were Frederick Gowland Hopkins, Hugh Kerr Anderson, and Walter Morley Fletcher. In his second year Mottram won a major scholarship and in 1907 a prize fellowship for a thesis on liver granules and fat infiltration. He then went to Munich for a year to work on fat metabolism under Carl Voigt. Mottram thereafter remained in Cambridge until 1911, continuing his research under Hopkins.

Mottram was first president of the Cambridge Fabian Society and supported a Liberal candidate in the 1906 election. He was interested in education, housing, and public health rather than free trade and home rule. In religion he moved towards agnosticism but later in life he became a member of the Society of Friends. After returning from Munich, Mottram met a new group of Fabians, including John Maynard Keynes, Philip Noel-Baker, and Edgar Douglas Adrian. Mottram practised his hobby of portrait photography upon members of this circle. Many of them professed, but few practised, homosexuality, and Mottram was disturbed to recognize his own leanings in this direction.

In 1911 Mottram became Charles Scott Sherrington's senior demonstrator and lecturer in chemical physiology at Liverpool University. Mottram lived in the university settlement managed by F. Q. Marquis, who later became Lord Woolton, minister of food during the Second World War.

Mottram regarded himself as a pacifist but his pacifism vanished when Germany invaded Belgium. However, he had agreed to go to Canada in September 1914 as a lecturer in physiology at McGill University, Montreal. While in Canada, Mottram developed tuberculosis and spent a year and nine months in sanatoria. In September 1918 he became senior science master at Caterham School and in 1919 took a position involving research on adding 'fat soluble vitamin' to margarine at Lever Brothers in Port Sunlight.

In 1920 Mottram moved to London as professor of physiology at the household and social science department of King's College for Women. This post had become vacant on the departure of Edward Mellanby to a chair at Sheffield. Mottram taught the BSc in household and social science until he retired in 1944. Graduates were employed in teaching, social welfare, and domestic management, and increasingly in the hospital dietetics departments which were opening during the 1920s. Mottram pioneered training courses for dietitians, developing a college diploma (1933) and an academic postgraduate diploma (1936). Six of the eight members of the council of the British Dietetics Association (formed 1935) were graduates of King's. During his early period at King's, Mottram began to see a psychoanalyst and soon formed the view that his apparent sexual orientation was the result of a 'mother fixation'. The analyst suggested that Mottram needed responsibilities and it was after this on 6 July 1921 that he married Elsie Charlotte Bulley (d. 1970), daughter of Harry Samson King, entrepreneur, of St Albans. Mottram had first met Bulley on a young Fabian skiing holiday in 1912. The couple had three sons and lived in Potters Bar.

Mottram was appointed to the Ministry of Health's advisory committee on nutrition in 1931 and drafted the memoranda issued by this committee in the early 1930s. In 1933 he became a member of a committee of the British Medical Association (BMA) which produced a report on the minimum cost of an adequate diet. The BMA used dietary standards which were more generous than those in the ministry's publications. This resulted in public controversy which abated only when representatives of each side were persuaded to meet in conference, and a 'sliding scale of calorie requirements' was agreed. Mottram represented the BMA committee. In 1935, when the ministry's committee was reconstituted, Mottram was not re-appointed. During the later 1930s he became associated with the movement represented by the Committee Against Malnutrition and Children's Minimum Council of which Frederick le Gros Clark and Eleanor Rathbone were leading members.

Mottram was author of many books including *A Manual of Histology* (1923), *Food and the Family* (1925), *The Functions of the Body* (1926), and *Sound Catering for Hard Times* (1932).

With Jessie Lindsay he published *Manual of Modern Cookery* (1927) and with W. M. Clifford, *Properties of Food* (1929). He revised several editions of the classic *Food and the Principles of Dietetics*, first with Robert Hutchison and later with George Graham. Mottram's last book, *Human Nutrition*, appeared in 1948, and was reprinted many times. A revised edition was published by his son R. F. Mottram in 1979. Although Mottram was in agreement with the nutrition movement of the late 1930s, that malnutrition was largely due to poverty, he also clearly regarded nutrition education as important. Such a position was, of course, entirely in keeping with his professional position. All Mottram's books on food and nutrition, whether directed primarily towards students or a general readership, like his many popular articles and broadcasts for the BBC, were distinguished by clear expositions of technical material, and a common-sense approach to practical dietetics. Readers of *Food and the Family*, for example, were advised that if they took a mixed diet containing meat, fish, dairy products, green vegetables, salad, and fruit, it would be as good as any that modern research could suggest.

Mottram's broad interests in science, religion, and mysticism came together in his *The Physical Basis of Personality* (1944). Mottram equated the advance of civilization with the extension of the rights of individuals to develop their personalities; rights which were threatened by Nazism. He gave an account of the mechanisms of inheritance of physical characteristics and their influences upon personality. Mottram drew attention to the effects of environment, but was loath to accept a purely determinist position regardless of whether the emphasis was placed on either nature or nurture. He was equally loath to adopt the position of idealists who rejected science and invoked intellectual abstractions (such as God) in the explanation of phenomena. Mottram argued that widespread occurrence of, and similarity between, accounts of mystical experiences pointed to the existence of an inner 'true self' which interacts with genes and upbringing in determining personality. These notions, he concluded, suggested a possible compromise between the determinist and idealist views. Mottram died on 11 March 1976 at Waterhouse, Monkton Combe, Bath. DAVID F. SMITH

Sources V. H. Mottram, unpubd autobiography, Wellcome L., GC/151/7/1-2 · N. L. Blakestad, 'King's College of Household and Social Science and the origins of dietetics education', *Nutrition in Britain: science, scientists, and politics in the twentieth century*, ed. D. F. Smith (1997), 75-98 · D. F. Smith, 'The social construction of dietary standards: the British Medical Association–Ministry of Health advisory committee on nutrition report of 1934', *Eating agendas: food and nutrition as social problems*, ed. D. Maurer and J. Sobal (1995), 279-304 · *DNB* · *CGPLA Eng. & Wales* (1976)

Archives King's Lond. · Wellcome L., unpublished autobiography | CAC Cam., corresp. with A. V. Hill · PRO, Ministry of Health archives · Wellcome L., British Medical Association nutrition committee papers

Likenesses photograph, BBC WAC · portrait, Wellcome L.

Wealth at death £10,993: probate, 10 Aug 1976, *CGPLA Eng. & Wales*

Mouchel, Louis Gustave [*formerly* Gustave-Louis] (1852–1908), promoter of ferroconcrete, was born on 11 January

1852 at 56 rue Corne de Cerf, Cherbourg, third of the four children of Louis Mouchel, wig maker, and his wife, Félicité Duchemin. He had three sisters. Mouchel attended the college at Cherbourg to train as a naval officer but joined the department of highways, taking an engineering course at the Government School of Mines.

Mouchel spoke English fluently, and in 1875 he moved to Briton Ferry in south Wales, where he initiated a number of business enterprises. He introduced coke making to the area, and formed the Cardiff Washed Coal and Fuel Company, subsequently a client for ferroconcrete. He exported coal and imported ore from mines in Brittany. As French vice-consul, Mouchel was responsible for several south Wales ports and was also a ship broker. He became co-director of various prominent companies, including Eaglesbush colliery, Neath, and the Gwalia Tinplate Company, a modern works 'illuminated with the electric light' (Humphreys, 39). By 1898, when Mouchel became general agent for Hennebique's system of reinforced concrete in the UK, he was a prospering and well-known businessman in south Wales, residing in one of the notable houses in Briton Ferry, a successful entrepreneur with useful contacts.

As Hennebique's agent, Mouchel effectively established the use of reinforced concrete in Britain, particularly for framed buildings. At this time, when reinforced concrete was developed and marketed by rival patentees, Hennebique was expanding his organization rapidly. Mouchel may have been his first client in Britain, for some house property, but the first built project recorded was a provender mill for William Weaver & Co. in Swansea (1897–8), the first multi-storeyed construction in Britain entirely in reinforced concrete. For this project, workmen and even materials, including high quality sand from the Loire, were shipped from France.

It may have been while Hennebique was arranging transport that he and Mouchel first met; as consul, the latter organized French ship movements in Swansea harbour. Mouchel accepted the agency, deciding to make the introduction of Hennebique's material into Britain the 'chief object of his professional life' ('Life and work of Louis Gustave Mouchel', 212). He even coined the term 'ferroconcrete' to describe it. His business organization followed Hennebique's model, employing specially trained engineers and licensed contractors, with nationwide expansion based on regional 'commercial–technical' offices. Mouchel himself underwent training in Hennebique's offices and began to execute working drawings. He also patented designs, especially for underground and marine work, modifying Hennebique's system, and published illustrated books of ferroconcrete works.

Mouchel moved his office to London in 1900, to a new but bare apartment owned by the Great Western Railway Company (itself a client of his). The following year, he moved to his permanent business address, 38 Victoria Street, Westminster, and rapidly established offices throughout the UK. Engineers and draughtsmen from Hennebique's offices in France joined Mouchel. Early clients included the Co-operative Wholesale Society, which had its own building department and obtained a Hennebique licence.

Mouchel possessed enormous energy, organizational skill, and single-mindedness; contemporaries spoke of great personal charm and a magnetic personality which compelled great confidence in himself and in ferroconcrete. His attention to detail ensured an excellent safety record, and his response to a rare failure of a test floor in Manchester in 1902 demonstrated his deep professional commitment. In a twelve-page letter to the client's engineer, presenting a passionate plea for justice in the matter, he wrote:

> if on account of that wretched incomplete test they throw us overboard, I would consider it an iniquity. Because it would be doing us, without justification, the maximum of injury possible and destroying at one stroke … my five years of anxious and arduous work in this country.   (Mouchel to Hunter, 1902, L. G. Mouchel & Partners archives)

Mouchel faced considerable prejudice in Britain. The Institution of Civil Engineers showed little interest in ferroconcrete before 1908, and although the Royal Institute of British Architects investigated it earlier, a speaker questioned the sanity of anyone's using such a heterogeneous combination as concrete and steel. Finally, the use of patent systems, particularly by 'pretentious foreigners' ('The progress of reinforced concrete', *Concrete and Constructional Engineering*, 2, 1907, 11), increasingly came under attack. Nevertheless, Mouchel completed more than 130 framed buildings and numerous other structures.

Mouchel never married and had no hobbies, but 'lived entirely for his work' (*Builders' Journal*). In 1907, suffering from stomach cancer, he formed a company, L. G. Mouchel & Partners Ltd, which was still flourishing almost a century later. Mouchel returned to France and died at 12 rue Vintras, Cherbourg, at his brother-in-law's house on 27 May 1908. He never took British citizenship.

TRICIA CUSACK

Sources 'The life and work of Louis Gustave Mouchel', *Ferro-Concrete*, 3/7 (1912), 211–14 • P. Cusack, 'Agents of change: Hennebique, Mouchel and ferro-concrete in Britain, 1897–1908', *Construction History*, 3 (1987), 61–74 • *Builders' Journal*, 27 (1908), 485 • L. G. Mouchel, letter to W. Henry Hunter, 1902, L. G. Mouchel & Partners archives, West Byfleet, Weybridge, Surrey, 1–12 • E. Humphreys, *Reminiscences of Briton Ferry and Baglan* (1898) • P. Cusack, 'Reinforced concrete in Britain, 1897–1908', PhD diss., U. Edin., 1981 • C. Roch, letter to C. R. J. Wood, 5 June 1958, L. G. Mouchel & Partners archives, West Byfleet, Weybridge, Surrey, 1–18 • P. Cusack, 'Architects and the reinforced concrete specialist in Britain, 1905–1908', *Architectural History*, 29 (1986), 183–96 • P. Cusack, 'François Hennebique: the specialist organisation and the success of ferro-concrete, 1892–1909', *Transactions* [Newcomen Society], 56 (1984–5), 71–8 • *Concrete and Constructional Engineering*, 3/3 (1908), 180 • *Concrete and Constructional Engineering*, 3/4 (1908), 341 • L. G. Mouchel, 'Monolithic constructions in Hennebique's ferro-concrete, and discussion', *RIBA Journal*, 12 (1904–5), 47–61, 84–97 • private information (2004) • b. cert., municipal archives, Cherbourg, France • census returns

Archives L. G. Mouchel & Partners, West Byfleet, Weybridge, Surrey, records and reminiscences | Institut Français d'Architecture, Paris, Hennebique MSS

Likenesses H. Mason, portrait, L. G. Mouchel & Partners Ltd, West Byfleet, Weybridge, Surrey

Wealth at death £79,570 0s. 8d.: probate, 1 July 1908, *CGPLA Eng. & Wales*

Moule, Arthur Evans (1836–1918). *See under* Moule, George Evans (1828–1912).

Moule, George Evans (1828–1912), bishop of mid-China, was born on 28 January 1828 at Gillingham, Dorset, the second of the eight sons of the Revd Henry *Moule (1801–1880), then curate-in-charge at Gillingham and from 1829 to 1880 vicar of Fordington, Dorchester, and his wife, Mary Mullett, *née* Evans (1801–1877). He was the brother of Arthur Evans Moule [*see below*] and of Handley Carr Glyn *Moule. He was educated at home until 1844, in which year he underwent a sudden conversion, the result of a sermon on Acts 28: 24, by Augustus Handley, his father's curate. The effect never passed away: it conditioned his whole subsequent life. In 1844 he was admitted sizar at Corpus Christi College, Cambridge, and in 1850 he graduated with mathematical and classical honours. James Scholefield, the regius professor of Greek, and Frederick Foster Gough helped to turn his thoughts to work abroad. He was ordained deacon at Salisbury in 1851 as curate to his father, and priest in 1852, and he acted as tutor to his father's pupils. From 1855 to 1857 he was also chaplain of the Dorset County Hospital.

In 1857 Moule offered his services to the Church Missionary Society, and in the December of that year he sailed for Shanghai. On the way, at Hong Kong, he married Adelaide Sarah (d. 1909), daughter of Frederick Moule, of Melksham, Wiltshire, and widow of Captain Griffiths; she accompanied him in his missionary travels and the couple had seven children. He was stationed at Ningpo (Ningbo) from 1857 to 1864; in the latter year he began a mission in Hangchow (Hangzhou), in Chekiang (Zhejiang) province, then practically destroyed by the Taiping insurgents. From 1865 to the end of his life the house in Hangchow was his only home. In 1864 he became a member of the Royal Asiatic Society, China branch, and most of his writings were papers in its journal. On the death of Bishop William Armstrong Russell, of north China, he was consecrated (on 28 October 1880 in London) first bishop of the new diocese of mid-China, a post which he held until his resignation in 1906. In 1905 he was elected an honorary fellow by his Cambridge college. He continued to work under the Church Missionary Society until his death, which took place at Auckland Castle, Bishop Auckland, co. Durham, on 3 March 1912, while he was on a visit to England. He was buried in Bow cemetery at Durham.

George Moule was a man of wide interests: music, drawing, woodturning, medicine, swimming, botany (he introduced some hitherto unknown plants to science), and especially literature; all attracted him, and he attained exceptional command of the Chinese language, literary and colloquial. All this, however, was secondary to his missionary work, at which he laboured incessantly by prayer, preaching, teaching, translating, and church administration. During his time in China he had considerable success relative to that of his colleagues: the church membership in Chekiang increased from fewer than 100 to more than

4000. It was a son of one of his early pupils who became the first Chinese bishop—Tsaeseng Sing, assistant bishop in Chekiang. Gentleness, reverence, humour, courage, and diligence were conspicuous in Moule, endearing him to a wide and varied circle of friends.

His brother **Arthur Evans Moule** (1836–1918) was ordained in London in 1861 and went as a missionary to Ningpo in the same year; he served there until 1869, witnessing in 1861 and 1862 the various attempts of the Taipings to capture the city. He returned to Britain in 1869 and from 1871 to 1876 was again at Ningpo. From 1876 to 1879 he was at Hangchow, and from 1882 he was secretary of the mission at Shanghai; he became archdeacon of Shanghai in 1890. Ill health required his return to Britain in April 1894. Moule published widely on Chinese affairs and translated works into Chinese. He took an especial interest in the opium trade, publishing *The Opium Question* (1877) and addressing the church congress at Newcastle on it in 1881. He was married in 1861 to Eliza Agnes Bernau, younger daughter of John Henry Bernau, of Pomerania, also a missionary; three of their children—Walter Stephen Moule, Arthur John Henry Moule, and William Augustus Handley Moule—were missionaries in China. After returning to Britain, Moule was rector of Compton Valence, Dorset, from 1898 to 1902. He was then again in China until 1910. He died on 26 August 1918.

H. W. MOULE, *rev.* H. C. G. MATTHEW

Sources G. E. Moule, *A retrospect of sixty years* (1907) · W. A. H. Moule, *A short memoir of George Evans Moule* (1912) · W. A. H. Moule, *George Evans Moule: a sketch* (1920) · *Journal of the Asiatic Society of China* (1912) [bibliography] · WWW
Archives U. Birm. L., Church Missionary Society, journals and letters to Church Missionary Society
Likenesses photograph, NPG
Wealth at death £873 16s. 2d.: probate, 17 July 1912, *CGPLA Eng. & Wales*

Moule, Handley Carr Glyn (1841–1920), bishop of Durham, was born at Fordington, Dorchester, Dorset, on 23 December 1841. His parents were the classicist and inventor the Revd Henry *Moule (1801–1880) and Mary Mullett Evans (1801–1877); they had a family of eight sons, one of whom died in infancy. The seven brothers, as they were known, were taught at home by their father; one committed suicide, one became a missionary (Arthur Evans *Moule [*see under* Moule, George Evans]), and two became bishops [*see* Moule, George Evans]. Handley, the eighth and youngest son, was named after his godfathers, Augustus Handley and Carr John Glyn. He entered Trinity College, Cambridge, in 1860, and for his first year his tutor was J. B. Lightfoot. Moule had a brilliant university career and became a noted classicist, winning numerous academic prizes. He graduated BA (first class) in 1864 and MA in 1867. He took up a college fellowship and became an assistant master at Marlborough College before he was ordained deacon in 1867 and priest in 1868. Between 1867 and 1872 he was his father's curate, then for five years dean of Trinity College, Cambridge. On his mother's death he returned to Fordington as his father's curate and remained there until Henry Moule died. On 16 August 1881

Moule married Harriot Mary (1844–1915), daughter of the Revd Charles Boileau Elliott; they had two daughters. Though he came from an evangelical home, and was strongly influenced by his mother's faith, Moule did not experience an evangelical conversion until 1866. He later said, 'I am an Evangelical churchman … and of those convictions I am not at all ashamed' (*To my Younger Brethren*, 1892, 254). In 1884 he had another profound religious experience, after which he became thoroughly identified with the Holiness Movement, speaking at the Mildmay conferences and the Keswick Convention, which he considered to be 'the vestibule of heaven' (Harford and Macdonald, 131).

From 1880 Moule was the first principal of Ridley Hall, Cambridge, lecturer at Holy Trinity Church, and an examining chaplain to Bishop J. C. Ryle. As a preacher and teacher Moule exercised an immense influence over undergraduates and theological students and played an important part in making the evangelical party more pietistic and missionary minded. During Moule's principalship more than 500 men were ordained, of whom more than 100 became missionaries and 23 bishops. It was said that Ridley Hall men were pious but not learned. They may have been well taught, but Moule failed to tackle current critical issues. He was an inspiring writer and maintained a steady output of publications, which included devotional writings, biblical expositions, sermons, poems, and tracts. He achieved further academic success in gaining a BD in 1894 (this thesis was expanded and published as *Romans* in the Expositor's Bible series) and a DD in 1895 for his edition of Bishop Ridley's work *A Brief Declaration of the Lord's Supper*. Moule became well known outside Cambridge as a respected evangelical leader, and was in demand as a preacher and speaker. He became a chaplain to Queen Victoria and then to Edward VII. In 1899 Moule was appointed Norrisan professor of divinity at Cambridge, and he continued to have links with Ridley Hall as a council member and later as college visitor.

From 1901 Moule was bishop of Durham. He felt unworthy of following J. B. Lightfoot and B. F. Westcott, and his simple pietism and lack of judgement were severely criticized by his successor, who regarded Moule as a good Christian but a bad bishop. But Hensley Henson was too forthright in his condemnation. It is true that Moule found diocesan business tedious, being too timid in decision making and too ready to accept unsuitable candidates for ordination, but his humility, lack of guile, and godliness won the hearts of his clergy and people. As a bishop his priorities were spiritual and not administrative. He encouraged his clergy to be faithful in their devotions and to be powerful in the pulpit; to preach the good news but not to advocate political causes; to keep the Sabbath; and, like him, to become teetotal. Moule strongly supported mission at home and overseas and urged his clergy to follow his example. While Moule was not as politically astute as Westcott he was not uninformed, and spoke out on political and industrial issues. He believed in a just war, and spoke during the First World War on the 'holiness of patriotism', urging prayer for victory. Though he remained faithful to his evangelical convictions, he was not partisan; tolerant towards Anglo-Catholic practice, he was prepared to sanction the use of incense and the wearing of the alb at communion services.

In 1905 Moule had suffered a severe illness following the death of one of his daughters, and from the autumn of 1915 was away from his episcopal duties for almost a year after an operation and following the death of his devoted wife. He died of pleurisy at 13 Cranmer Road, Cambridge, on 8 May 1920, and was buried next to his wife, daughter, and brother in Bow cemetery, Durham.

A. F. MUNDEN

Sources *Durham Diocesan Gazette*, 15–34 (1902–20) • *The Times* (10 May 1920) • H. C. G. Moule, *Memories of a vicarage* (1913) • J. B. Harford and F. C. Macdonald, *Handley Carr Glyn Moule* (1922) • J. Baird, *The spiritual unfolding of Bishop H. C. G. Moule* (1926) • F. W. B. Bullock, *The history of Ridley Hall, Cambridge*, 2 vols. (1941–53) • A. Smellie, *Evan Henry Hopkins* (1920) • E. S. Woods and F. B. Macnutt, *Theodore, bishop of Winchester* (1933) • *DNB* • *CGPLA Eng. & Wales* (1920)
Archives CUL • Ridley Hall, Cambridge • Tyndale House, Cambridge | Bodl. Oxf., letters to Sir James Marchant • Durham Cath. CL, Lightfoot MSS • LPL, letters to A. J. Mason and J. Mitchinson
Likenesses C. E. Brock, oils, 1897, Ridley Hall, Cambridge • H. G. Riviere, oils, 1914, Auckland Castle, Bishop Auckland, co. Durham
Wealth at death £15,905 11s. 10d.: probate, 11 Aug 1920, *CGPLA Eng. & Wales*

Moule, Henry (1801–1880), Church of England clergyman and inventor of the dry earth closet, was born at Melksham, Wiltshire, on 27 January 1801, the sixth son of George Moule (1768–1830), solicitor and banker, and his wife, Sarah Hayward (1764–1835). He was educated at Marlborough grammar school, and was elected a foundation scholar of St John's College, Cambridge, graduating BA in 1821 and MA in 1826. At Cambridge he fell under the spell of Charles Simeon, the leader of the evangelical party of the Church of England.

Moule was ordained to the curacy of Melksham in 1823, and took sole charge of Gillingham, Dorset, in 1825. He was made vicar of Fordington, Dorset, in 1829, and remained there the remainder of his life. In 1824 he married Mary Mullett Evans (1801–1877), the daughter of a London publisher. Their seven surviving sons, all of whom were educated at Marlborough and Cambridge, included the antiquary, Henry Joseph Moule (1825–1904), the missionary George Evans *Moule (1828–1912), and a bishop of Durham, Handley Carr Glyn *Moule (1841–1920). Another son, Horace Mosley Moule (1832–1873), became a close friend of Thomas Hardy.

Fordington was blighted by appalling housing, sanitation, disease, and immoral behaviour. In 1833 Moule's protests brought to an end the scandalous conduct connected with race meetings at Dorchester. Although he was at first shunned and disliked by most of his parishioners for his puritanism, during the cholera epidemics of 1849 and 1854 his sterling efforts on their behalf won him affection and respect. For some years Moule undertook the duty of chaplain to the troops in Dorchester barracks, for whose use, as well as for a detached district of his own parish, he built in 1846, partly from the proceeds of his published

Henry Moule (1801–1880), by unknown engraver

Barrack Sermons (1845), a church known as Christ Church, West Fordington.

Although untutored in science and engineering, Moule was a noteworthy inventor. Concerned by the unhealthiness of local houses he turned his attention to sanitary science, and invented the dry earth closet. In partnership with James Bannehr of Exeter, he took out a patent for the process. From 1868 onwards he published an extensive series of pamphlets extolling the virtues of the system over water sewerage for dealing with the human refuse of towns and villages. His system was adopted in many private houses, in rural districts, in military camps, in many hospitals, and extensively in India. It remained in use well into the 1930s. In 1855 Moule wrote *Eight Letters to Prince Albert*, urging him as president of the council of the duchy of Cornwall (Fordington's owner) to rehouse parishioners and improve the village sanitary amenities. He also composed letters to *The Times* in 1874 that advocated the extraction of gas from Kimmeridge shale.

An ardent evangelical, Moule's many published sermons and pamphlets were concerned with infant baptism, education, the conversion of the heathen, the heating of churches and greenhouses, and agricultural and horticultural matters. He publicly rebuked Bishop Colenso in 1853 for his disbelief in the literal truth of the Old Testament. Moule died at his home, Fordington vicarage, on 3 February 1880.

G. C. BOASE, rev. W. H. BROCK

Sources *The Times* (5 Feb 1880), 8 · *Dorset County Chronicle* (5 Feb 1880) · H. C. G. Moule, 'Memoir', in [H. C. G. Moule, G. E. Moule, and A. E. Moule], *'Doctrine, manner of life, purpose': sermons preached … on occasion of the death of H. Moule* (1880) · H. C. G. Moule, *Memories of a vicarage* (1913) · R. W. M. Lewis, *The family of Moule* (1938) · T. Ward, *Henry Moule of Fordington* (1983) · R. Gittings, *Young Thomas Hardy* (1975) · L. Wright, *Clean and decent* (1960) · d. cert.

Archives Dorset County Museum, Dorchester · Dorset RO

Likenesses engraving, Dorset County Museum, Dorchester [*see illus.*] · photographs, Dorset county museum, Dorchester · portrait, repro. in Moule, *Memories of a vicarage*

Wealth at death under £1500: probate, 10 March 1880, *CGPLA Eng. & Wales*

Moule, Thomas (1784–1851), antiquary, bibliographer, and topographer, was born on 14 January 1784 in the parish of St Marylebone, Middlesex. He was the eldest of nine children of John Moule (1744–1826) and his wife, Sarah Sophia, *née* Read (1751–1835/6). He was a bookseller in Duke Street, Grosvenor Square, from about 1816 until about 1823 and was subsequently a clerk in the General Post Office, where he was inspector of 'blind' letters, his principal duty being to decipher addresses which were illegible to the ordinary clerks. From about 1822 until his death he held the office of chamber-keeper in the lord chamberlain's department, which gave him an official residence in Stable Yard, St James's Palace. On 16 June 1812 Moule married Mary, daughter of John Carr of Monkwearmouth, co. Durham. A daughter, Sophia Barbara, was born at Pentonville on 4 February 1815; she later 'materially assisted him in his literary pursuits' (*GM*, 211).

Moule's 'first literary task … was the letterpress to accompany Mr J P Neale's *Views of the Seats of Noblemen and Gentlemen*', (11 vols., 1818–27), for which series he either compiled or edited more than 700 articles (*GM*, 210). During the following twenty years Moule contributed the letterpress to a number of illustrated books, including Hewetson's *Views of Noble Mansions in Hampshire* (1825), *Views of Collegiate and Parochial Churches in Great Britain* (1826) by Neale and Le Keux, and Westall's *Great Britain Illustrated* (1830). Moule was a member of the Numismatic Society and contributed to the *Numismatic Chronicle*. 'His study of coins was chiefly directed to those of the medieval period' (ibid., 211).

Moule's first major, but anonymous, work was *A Table of Dates for the Use of Genealogists and Antiquaries* (1820). His writings on heraldry have continued to be of value, in particular *Bibliotheca heraldica Magnae Britanniae* (1822), which, despite a few errors and omissions, remains the only bibliography of British books on heraldry and genealogy published up to 1821; a facsimile edition was published in 1966. The author's copy, interleaved with corrections and additions, is in the British Library, in two volumes, with a third containing further notes. In the preface to the *Bibliotheca heraldica* (p. xv) Moule announced his intention to publish a companion volume on manuscripts, 'Bibliotheca manuscriptorum', which did not, however, materialize. *Heraldry of Fish: Notices of the Principal Families Bearing Fish in their Arms* (1842) was illustrated by woodcuts from drawings made by his daughter. A manuscript of a similar but unpublished work entitled 'Index to trees and birds in heraldry' (*c.*1830) was sold with other items from Sir Thomas Phillipps's collection on 21 June 1893; it is now in the library of the Victoria and Albert Museum (86.RR.53). Moule left other manuscripts, of which the whereabouts are now unknown, and a 'valuable library' (*GM*, 211).

The English Counties Delineated, or, A Topographical Description of England (2 vols., 1837) consisted of maps first published in parts from 1830; the maps are probably Moule's most widely known work. He stated that the chief object of George Virtue, his publisher, was 'to produce a work of obvious utility at a reasonable price, so as to place it within reach of every class' (Moule, *English Counties*, v). The maps, engraved on steel, are distinctive in appearance with borders decorated with elaborate cartouches, coats of arms, vignettes of country scenes and country houses, and other decoration. At a time of great social and economic change they reflected a growing interest in the past. Virtue used the maps in other books he published, sometimes mixing editions indiscriminately. They were incorporated in James Barclay's *Complete and Universal Dictionary* published in various editions between 1842 and 1852; in the 1870s some of the maps were included in the *History of England* by Hume and Smollett. The maps and accompanying text from Barclay's 1842 edition were reprinted in 1990. Moule died in his residence in Stable Yard, St James's Palace, on 14 January 1851; his wife and daughter survived him.　　COLIN LEE

Sources GM, 2nd ser., 36 (1851), 210–11 · BL, Add. MS 45577, fols. 48, 56 · D. Smith, *Victorian maps of the British Isles* (1985), 145–7 · R. Barron, 'Introduction', in T. Moule, *The county maps of old England* (1990), 9–13 · T. Moule, *Bibliotheca heraldica Magnae Britanniae* (privately printed, London, 1822), xv · T. Moule, *The English counties delineated*, 2 vols. (1837), 1.v · BL, Add. MS 22651, fols. 94–7 · Boase, *Mod. Eng. biog.*, 2.1005 · DNB
Archives BL, genealogical collections, Add. MS 45577 · BL, letters on Lancashire topography, Add. MS 22651, fols. 94–7 · V&A NAL, 'Index to trees and birds in heraldry'

Moullin, Edith Ruth Mansell [*née* Edith Ruth Thomas] (1858/9–1941), suffragette and pacifist, was the daughter of Anne (*née* Lloyd) and David Collet Thomas, merchant and shipowner. Her social conscience was evident from her youth onwards: on leaving school she did 'slum work' in Bethnal Green. She helped in a soup kitchen during the dockers' strike and was a founder member of the Anti-Sweating League. She once commented that 'my career has been one long record of a supporter of unpopular causes' (E. R. M. Moullin to Edith How Martyn, 6 Sept 1935, Suffragette Fellowship Collection, 57.116/79). On 20 August 1885 she married Charles William Mansell Moullin (1851–1940), a surgeon at the London Hospital. The couple were firm advocates of women doctors and of women's suffrage. Charles was a vice-president of the Men's League for Women's Suffrage. Edith Mansell Moullin belonged to several suffrage societies: the Women's Freedom League, Women's Social and Political Union until 1913, and the Church League for Women's Suffrage—she had already been honorary treasurer of the Church Socialist League.

Proud of her Welsh parentage, Edith Mansell Moullin organized the Welsh contingent in the suffrage coronation procession of 1911. From this she founded a unique organization based in London dedicated to uniting Welsh people of differing viewpoints to work for women's enfranchisement, the Cymric Suffrage Union. Edith became its vice-president. Small, dark-haired, and passionate in her commitments, she did not draw neat distinctions between her public and personal life. Typically, the family's home in fashionable Wimpole Street was the society's headquarters. There were a few branches in Wales and she went on several speaking tours in north Wales.

The Liberal government's announcement of a manhood suffrage measure which effectively threatened the Conciliation Bill, presaged renewed suffrage militancy in November 1911. Edith sat on the platform with Mrs Pankhurst and Mrs Pethick Lawrence at the Caxton Hall meeting which preceded a demonstration in Parliament Square. She was one of 223 arrested. Charged with trying to break through the police cordon, she denied attempting to disturb the peace, claiming that the police were obstructing her. She spent five days in Holloway. Her suffrage society disbanded and regrouped in October 1912 as the more militant Forward Cymric Suffrage Union (FCSU). Edith was its honorary organizer. It obliged members to put women's suffrage before any other cause, to work for no other political party, and to oppose any government refusing votes for women. Members met regularly at Alan's Tea Rooms, Oxford Circus, and held 'at homes' at Wimpole Street where their hostess carefully cultivated a sense of Welshness via speeches and song. Edith's home also became the centre for a 'Cat and Mouse' committee to aid suffrage prisoners suffering under the Prisoners' Temporary Discharge for Ill Health Act. This act enabled ailing hunger strikers to be released then imprisoned on recovery. Representatives of many suffrage societies attended. Charles Mansell Moullin had already spoken and written against forcible feeding. Edith commented that although she and her husband had lost 'many so-called friends' because of their strong views, she had 'made many more loyal and dear comrades' (E. R. M. Moullin to Edith How Martyn, 6 Sept 1935, Suffragette Fellowship Collection, 57.116/79).

The FCSU continued in wartime. Proceeds from its sales of work relieved distress among Welsh women and children. In October 1914 Edith and Dr Helena Jones launched an appeal to help thirty-six Welsh wives of imprisoned Germans who had been working in Welsh mines. The wives were not receiving relief as they were not considered to be British subjects. By 1916 ill health forced Edith to resign from her FCSU post. She had become a pacifist and well into her seventies would expend her energies in this cause. She was involved with the Society for Cultural Relations with the USSR, which she chaired from 1931. Edith was also a voluntary helper at St Dunstan's, the centre founded by the blind newspaper magnate Sir Arthur Pearson where blindness was treated as a challenge rather than as an affliction. In 1930 she wrote an appreciation of her old friend Emily Wilding Davison. It had been Charles Mansell Moullin who had performed the unsuccessful emergency operation on Davison after she had thrown herself in front of the king's horse at the 1913 Derby.

Charles Mansell Moullin died aged eighty-nine in 1940.

Edith died the following year on 5 March at 2 Cottesmore Court, Stanford Road, Kensington, the London home of their only child, Oswald. She was eighty-two.

ANGELA V. JOHN

Sources Museum of London, Suffragette Fellowship Collection, letters from Edith Mansell Moullin to Edith How Martyn 1930–1935, MSS 57.116/76–79 · A. J. R., ed., *The suffrage annual and women's who's who* (1913) · *Votes for Women* (1910–14) · A. V. John, '"A draft of fresh air": women's suffrage, the Welsh and London', *Transactions of the Honourable Society of Cymmrodorion*, new ser., 1 (1995), 81–93 · A. V. John, '"Run like the blazes": the suffragettes and Welshness', *Llafur: Journal of Welsh Labour History*, 6 (1994), 29–43 · *Ladies Field Supplement* (21 Nov 1914) · A. Morley and L. Stanley, *The life and times of Emily Wilding Davison* (1988) · D'A. Power and W. R. Le Fanu, *Lives of the fellows of the Royal College of Surgeons of England, 1930–1951* (1953) · d. cert. · m. cert.
Archives Museum of London, Suffragette Fellowship collection
Likenesses Lafayette, portrait, repro. in *Ladies Field Supplement* · photograph, Museum of London; repro. in D. Atkinson, *The suffragettes in pictures* (1996) · two photographs, Museum of London
Wealth at death £22,754 4s. 8d.: resworn probate, 7 July 1941, CGPLA Eng. & Wales

Moullin, Eric Balliol (1893–1963), electrical engineer and university teacher, was born at Sandbanks, near Parkstone, Dorset, on 10 August 1893, the only child of Arthur Daniel Moullin, a civil engineer from an old Guernsey family, and his wife, Charlotte Annie Longman. He was delicate in childhood and was educated privately, learning at home the mathematics that won him a scholarship to Downing College, Cambridge. He sat part one of the mathematical tripos in 1913, then embarked on the mechanical sciences tripos. In 1914 ill health forced him to abandon his studies but the following year he returned and in 1916 obtained a first class in the tripos and gained the John Winbolt prize in 1918. Unfit for military service, from 1917 he was a lecturer at the Royal Naval College, Dartmouth. He married, on 2 January 1918, Christobel (b. 1888/9), daughter of Edward Schröder Prior, Slade professor of fine art at Cambridge; they had two daughters.

In 1919 Moullin returned to the Cambridge Engineering Laboratory where he was a very active teacher and research worker for the next ten years. During this time he was attached to King's College as an assistant director of studies. In 1929 he was offered the chair of engineering at Oxford but withdrew with characteristic generosity in favour of R. V. Southwell. He then accepted the newly founded Donald Pollock readership (under Southwell) and two years later became a fellow of Magdalen College. His first marriage having ended in divorce, Moullin married, on 15 December 1934, Joan Evelyn Sinnock (b. 1904/5), daughter of Louis Francis Salzman, a medievalist and sometime editor of the Victoria History of the Counties of England.

On the outbreak of war in 1939 Moullin joined the Admiralty signals establishment at Portsmouth and in 1942 transferred to the Metropolitan-Vickers Electrical Company Ltd of Manchester. At the end of the war he was appointed to the chair of electrical engineering at Cambridge, which had just been founded through the sponsorship of the Institution of Electrical Engineers and the British Electrical and Allied Manufacturers Association.

He was elected to a professorial fellowship at King's in 1946. He retired in 1960. He was awarded the Cambridge ScD in 1939 and was made an honorary LLD of Glasgow University in 1958.

Throughout his career Moullin was an active member of the Institution of Electrical Engineers. He was chairman of the radio section at the outbreak of war, served on council from 1940 to 1949, latterly as vice-president, and was then president for the session 1949–50; in 1963 he was made an honorary member. He was also a governor of the College of Aeronautics until 1949 and a member of the Radio Research Board of the Department of Scientific and Industrial Research, 1934–42.

Throughout his life Moullin was a very original and creative research worker. He was a prolific writer of scientific papers and books. His first book, *The Theory and Practice of Radio Frequency Measurements* (1926), had a considerable influence on the development of radio systems. As a boy he had been a radio amateur helped by his father in a workshop at their home in Swanage and almost to the end of his life he delighted in working in the attic laboratory at his home in Cambridge. Best known of his many inventions was the Moullin valve voltmeter developed during the 1920s, which became a standard laboratory instrument. His second and most important book, *The Principles of Electromagnetism* (1932), formed the basis of his own lectures and had a profound influence by its unique blend of theory and practice. His last book, the *Electromagnetic Principles of the Dynamo*, was mostly written before the end of 1933 but was delayed until 1955 by pressure of other research. His central contribution to the study of electromagnetism was his insistence that the sources of fields are their most important feature and that these sources can be controlled by the engineer to achieve desired effects.

The range of subject matter of these books demonstrated their author's grasp of the whole field of electrical engineering. Although Moullin disliked narrow specialization he was no generalist but had rather a distrust of general statements. He loved detail and delighted in particular cases, on which he focused his powerful mind and which he studied so carefully that they became windows through which one could see a whole landscape. He was an outstanding teacher of engineers, reinforcing his lectures with beautifully designed experiments. He was daily in the laboratory, where he showed a personal interest in individual students and in members of his staff, both academics and technicians. From his research students he called out the best. He did not praise often, but his praise was worth having.

Moullin saw no conflict between academic and industrial engineering, being as much at home in the factory as in the college. He treated colleagues in industry as full partners in a professional enterprise and was an energetic supporter of industrial training schemes. In the university he was a fighter for academic freedom, which he felt was endangered both by central government and by academics in search of power and influence.

He had a keen sense of history and was delighted when

he inherited, in 1947, the Fief des Eperons in Guernsey. On Elizabeth II's visit to the island in 1957 he carried out, as seigneur, his feudal duty of presenting the gilt spurs to the reigning monarch. His scarlet doctor's gown added a splash of colour to the ceremony. He did much work on Guernsey parish registers and wrote several antiquarian papers for La Société Guernsesiaise. In his will he endowed a prize at Downing College for the best student in engineering or history. Moullin died at his home, 21 Sedley Taylor Road, Cambridge, on 18 September 1963. He was survived by his second wife. PERCY HAMMOND

Sources The Times (20 Sept 1963) · Annual Report of the Council [King's College, Cambridge] (1963) · private information (1981) · personal knowledge (2004) · m. certs. · d. cert.
Archives ICL, corresp. with Lord Jackson · Nuffield Oxf., Lindemann MSS
Likenesses photograph, c.1949–1950, Inst. EE
Wealth at death £43,831: probate, 7 Feb 1964, CGPLA Eng. & Wales

Moulson, Sir Thomas (c.1568–1638), merchant and politician, was the second son of Thomas Moulson of Hargrave Stubbs, Cheshire, and his wife, Alice, the daughter of John Aldersey of Spurstow and his wife, Anne. It is reputed that he received an education at Tarvin grammar school. Some time before 1590 he left his native Cheshire for Stade in northern Germany, where he traded for several years as a cloth merchant. During this time, in 1593, he was admitted to the freedom of the London Grocers' Company. After returning to England he married, on 15 December 1600, Anne (d. 1661), the daughter of Anthony Radcliffe, a merchant taylor of London. He settled in the London parish of St Christopher-le-Stocks and continued his business through factors. The couple had two children, but both died in infancy. By 1606 Moulson was the biggest exporter of northern kerseys in London, and as such became a leading member of the Company of Merchant Adventurers; he served as its treasurer in 1616–17 and rose to the governorship by 1624, a position which he held until his death. He was also a founder member of the revived French Company in 1611 and was admitted to the court of assistants of the Grocers' Company in 1613; two years later he served as the company's third warden.

As a successful and therefore wealthy cloth merchant, Moulson was naturally absorbed into the ranks of London's ruling élite. Appointed an assistant of the City's company for the plantation of Ireland in 1615, he was a common councilman by 1617, a member of the prestigious Bridgehouse committee by 1618, and the City's auditor from 1620 to 1622. In 1623, then in his mid-fifties, he was named an alderman and appointed sheriff. Five years later he was elected an MP for London (even though he had not yet achieved knightly status or served as mayor) after London's voters rejected the corporation's own candidates for having supported the forced loan of 1626–7. During his time in parliament he drew attention, among other things, to the threat to England's cloth trade posed by recent Catholic military successes in Germany and spoke of his fear for the safety of protestantism at home.

In 1634 he served as lord mayor and was knighted at Greenwich.

Moulson's religious sympathies were clearly Calvinist—in his will of 1636 he described himself as a member of the elect—and perhaps even puritan, for during the mid-1630s he and his fellow vestrymen of St Christopher-le-Stocks resolved not to hold meetings on the Sabbath and to appoint a lecturer, Mr Hood, to whom Moulson later bequeathed 40s. Shortly thereafter he fell ill. He declined to serve as president of Christ's Hospital in February 1637, and died on 6 December 1638. He was buried in the vault of St Christopher's on 10 January 1639. A generous benefactor of the poor, and of the companies to which he belonged, he also remembered Hargrave, the parish where he was brought up, and its combined school and chapel, which he had built at his own cost in 1627.

ANDREW THRUSH

Sources PRO, PROB 11/178 ff.502v–505 · PRO, PROB 11/306, fol. 203 · PRO, C24/505/15 · W. R. Baumann, The merchant adventurers and the continental cloth trade, 1560s–1620s (1990) · A. Friis, Alderman Cockayne's project and the cloth trade: the commercial policy of England in its main aspects, 1603–1625, trans. [A. Fausboll] (1927) · A. B. Beaven, ed., The aldermen of the City of London, temp. Henry III–[1912], 2 (1913) · R. C. Johnson and others, eds., Proceedings in parliament, 1628, 6 vols. (1977–83) · GL, 4421/1 · GL, MSS 11,592A; 11,588/2; 4423/1; 4425/1; 12806/3; 12806/4 · Bridgehouse Committee materials sold, vol. 1; letter book FF, CLRO, fol. 80v · The obituary of Richard Smyth … being a catalogue of all such persons as he knew in their life, ed. H. Ellis, CS, 44 (1849), 15 · C. T. Carr, ed., Select charters of trading companies, AD 1530–1707, SeldS, 28 (1913), 64 · L. Roberts, The merchants mappe of commerce (1639), 235 · A history of Hargrave and Huxley, ed. J. Whittle (1988) [Hargrave and Huxley Historical Group]

Moulsworth, Martha (1577–1646), poet, was born on 10 November 1577 in or near Oxford (probably at Ewelme), the daughter of Robert Dorsett (d. 1580), a clergyman and a tutor at Christ Church, Oxford, and of his wife, Martha (d. 1580). Moulsworth's father earned a doctorate in divinity from Oxford, where he was a tutor to Sir Philip Sidney while also serving as rector of Ewelme. After he and his wife both died in 1580 the infant Martha was left in the care of her maternal grandmother and step-grandfather, Helena and Ralph Johnson.

Moulsworth penned one of the earliest autobiographical poems in English (certainly one of the first by a female) and therein issued one of the first and most emphatic attacks on educational discrimination against women. This poetic autobiography, The Memorandum of Martha Moulsworth Widdowe (1632), calls for the establishment of a women's university and boasts that educated women might easily excel men in intellectual accomplishments. Moulsworth's complex poem offers a rich overview of the life of an early modern Englishwoman and expresses complicated attitudes toward her roles as daughter, wife, mother, and widow. The poem combines deference and defiance, love and self-assertion, devout submission and spirited self-regard. It ends on a note of great assurance, contentment, and hope.

Most extant information about Moulsworth comes from the Memorandum itself, although many details mentioned there can be authenticated by other documents, such as the wills of both her and her husbands and a sermon preached after her death. Interestingly the main discrepancy between the *Memorandum* and the known facts of Moulsworth's life involves the poem's assertion that her father had taken an active hand in her education, particularly in her learning of Latin. Since her father had died by the time she was two-and-a-half this claim must be understood as either figurative, mistaken, or deliberately false. Perhaps it reflects an educated, opinionated woman's sense of the need for patriarchal sanction.

The bulk of Moulsworth's poem deals with her three marriages and subsequent periods of widowhood. On 18 April 1598, aged twenty, she married Nicholas Prynne, a London goldsmith. In 1602 she bore a son, Richard, and she was pregnant with a daughter, Martha, when Prynne died in late 1603 or early 1604. (Both children were apparently dead by the time she wrote her poem.) On 3 February 1605 the young widow married an older widower (with children), named Thomas Thorowgood, a London draper, who also had a residence in Hoddesdon, 20 miles north of London on the main road to Cambridge. After Thorowgood's death in 1615 Martha probably spent most of her time in Hoddesdon, where she became a prominent citizen and developed an especially close relationship with her stepdaughter Elizabeth Thorowgood. No children resulted from her second marriage.

On 15 June 1619, aged forty-one, Moulsworth married for the third and last time. Her new husband was Bevill Molesworth, a sixty-five-year-old London goldsmith, for whom she seems to have felt great affection and with whom she produced one son, who died while still a boy. When the elder Molesworth died, on 24 February 1631, he was buried in the same grave as his son. The poem his wife wrote less than two years later celebrates Molesworth's excellence as a husband. She claimed still to be weeping for him at the time of writing.

Although the *Memorandum* is the only text (besides her will) written by Moulsworth that is known to survive, a sermon preached after her death at Hoddesdon in the autumn of 1646, following extended sickness, mentions her love of reading, her habit of taking notes, and her interest in such topics as history and theology. During her time in Hoddesdon she took an active, prominent role in local religious affairs. Evidence suggests that her own sympathies may have been Laudian. Although her godson was William Prynne, her most important stepson-in-law, Marmaduke Rawdon, was a committed royalist, who died while serving the king's cause.

Ostensibly written on the author's fifty-fifth birthday *The Memorandum* uses fifty-five couplets to survey Moulsworth's life up to that point. She discusses her birth and baptism, her exemplary father and his alleged role in her early education, her frustration with the marriage market and with the limits on women's formal learning, the rewards of her three marriages, the deaths of her husbands, her confidence in their final resurrection, her thoughts about her relations with them in heaven, and her final resolution not to remarry. Rich in rhetorical balance and sophisticated in design, the poem also features a complex numerological structure and explicit allusions to biblical texts. It is simultaneously witty, humorous, serious, sarcastic, pious, pragmatic, spiritual, worldly, prophetic, and subtle, and the self-portrait it offers seems largely confirmed by the sermon preached after her death by Thomas Hassall, an old friend and confidant. Both the poem and the sermon suggest a thoughtful and lively but ultimately serene and confident person, who enjoyed a happy life despite her varied disappointments. The sermon, though, presents Moulsworth as a more conventional figure than the more daring poem, which lay largely unnoticed in an obscure volume of family manuscripts until it was finally published in 1993.

ROBERT C. EVANS

Sources 'The memorandum of Martha Moulsworth widdowe', Yale U., Beinecke L., Osborn MS, fb 150 · R. C. Evans and A. C. Little, eds., '*The muses females are': Martha Moulsworth and other women writers of the English Renaissance* (1995) · R. C. Evans and B. Wiedemann, eds., '*My name was Martha': a Renaissance woman's autobiographical poem* (1993) · A. Depas-Orange and R. C. Evans, eds., '*The birthday of my self': Martha Moulsworth, Renaissance poet* (1996) · T. Hassall, funeral sermon on Martha Moulsworth, Bodl. Oxf., MS Don. g.9, fols. 31r–55r · PRO, PROB 11/197; 11/159; 11/126; 11/103 [wills of Mouslworth and her 3 husbands]

Archives Yale U., Osborn MS, fb 150

Wealth at death £2293—monetary bequests; plus goods, chattels, jewels, plate, money, debts, lands, fees simple, and copyholds to stepdaughter: PRO, PROB 11/197

Moulton, James Hope (1863–1917), biblical and Zoroastrian scholar, the elder son of the Revd William Fiddian *Moulton (1835–1898), biblical scholar and headmaster of the Leys School, Cambridge, and his wife, Hannah, daughter of the Revd Samuel Hope, was born at the Wesleyan Institution, Richmond, Surrey, on 11 October 1863. His father was one of four brothers, all eminent, the best-known being John Fletcher *Moulton, Lord Moulton, lord justice of appeal. James Moulton was educated at the Leys School from 1875, and then at King's College, Cambridge, of which he was a fellow from 1888 to 1894. Many of his family were Methodist preachers and missionaries; he entered the Wesleyan Methodist ministry in 1886, being appointed assistant to his father at the Leys. In 1890 he married Eliza Keeling Osborn (d. 1915), granddaughter of George Osborn. They had two sons and two daughters; the elder son, Ralph, was killed in action in France in 1916. Moulton left Cambridge in 1902 on his appointment as New Testament tutor at Didsbury College, Manchester. In 1908 he was appointed Greenwood professor of Hellenistic Greek and Indo-European philology in the University of Manchester. His outstanding work here was recognized by the award of doctorates from the universities of Edinburgh, Durham, Berlin, and Gröningen. After his wife's death in 1915, he went to India to lecture to the Parsis on Zoroastrianism, and to qualify himself to write a volume, which was posthumously published (1917) under the title *The Treasure of the Magi*. He left India in March 1917 and joined James Rendel Harris at Port Said. Their ship was torpedoed off Corsica. Moulton 'played a hero's part in the boat', died from exhaustion on 7 April, and was buried at sea, a heroic story which captured the imagination of his generation.

Moulton's interests were wide, but his best work was done on the Greek of the New Testament and on Zoroastrianism. A *Grammar of New Testament Greek*, originally intended to be jointly written by Moulton and his father, was not begun until after his father's death and remained unfinished at the death of the son. The first volume, the *Prolegomena* (1906), was the only one published in his lifetime; but the greater part of the second volume had been written and it was published under the editorship of Wilbert Howard. Moulton's *Grammar of New Testament Greek* was a development of an approach taken by the biblical scholar Adolf Deissmann. In his *Bibelstudien*, Deissmann had published a mass of evidence to show that the vocabulary of the New Testament did not belong to a class by itself, but was to be put in the same category as the ordinary spoken Greek of the time, as preserved in the non-literary papyri. Moulton accepted his demonstration and applied it to the grammar. A well-regarded contemporary, Adolf Harnack, professor of church history in Berlin, spoke of him as 'the foremost expert in New Testament Greek'. Moulton hoped to prepare for English readers an edition of Deissmann's projected lexicon; and he lived long enough to see the publication (1914–15) of two instalments of the *Vocabulary of the Greek Testament*, which he prepared in collaboration with George Milligan. His premature death meant that a projected third volume of his *Grammar*, devoted to the syntax of the New Testament, was never written.

Moulton's study of comparative philology led him to Sanskrit and Iranian; and from the language of the Avesta he naturally passed to the religion. In this field he owed much to the teaching of Edward Byles Cowell, professor of Sanskrit at Cambridge. As well as articles, he published four books on the religion. *Early Religious Poetry of Persia* (1911) was an admirable introduction to the subject, and with it may be coupled *The Teaching of Zarathushtra* (1917), lectures delivered to the Parsis. His most important contribution was made in his Hibbert lectures, *Early Zoroastrianism* (1913). He was inclined to push back the date of Zarathustra several generations before the traditional date of 660–583 BC; and he sought to disengage the true Zoroastrian elements in the Avesta from accretions which he attributed to the magi. The subject is discussed again in the first part of *The Treasure of the Magi*. It is on this work that his posthumous reputation among Zoroastrian and Avestan scholars largely rests. It was the first work in English to argue that the Avesta had its own internal history, and to initiate a line of scholarly investigation (directly continued for at least the next fifty years) which attempted to show how the doctrines of the religion's founder had been modified in the later parts of the Avesta. Moulton was an enthusiast for Zarathustra, and for his teaching, which he regarded as the purest form of non-biblical religion. His scholarship was well regarded by the Parsi community.

Though a scholar of the highest quality and exceptional range Moulton was deeply interested in practical questions. Foreign missions, social reforms at home, and Christian apologetics were always very near his heart. He was eminent for the strength, the loftiness, and beauty of his character, and for the intensity of his religion.

A. S. PEAKE, rev. TIM MACQUIBAN

Sources *Minutes of the Methodist Conference* (1917) · H. K. Moulton, *J. H. Moulton* (1963) · W. F. Moulton, *Memoir* (1919) · personal knowledge (1927)
Archives JRL, corresp. and papers
Wealth at death £4416 8s. 5d.: resworn probate, 9 June 1917, CGPLA Eng. & Wales

Moulton, James Louis (1906–1993), marine officer and military historian, was born on 3 June 1906 at The Terrace, His Majesty's Dockyard, Pembroke Dock, Pembrokeshire, the son of John Davis Moulton (d. 1921), staff captain in the Royal Navy (also JP for Kingston, Jamaica, and later harbour master, Pembroke dockyard), and his wife, Beatrice Nutter, *née* Cox. He was educated at Sutton Valence School before being commissioned into the Royal Marines in 1923. After further education at the Royal Naval College, Greenwich, and initial service in battleships, in 1930 he trained as a pilot and from 1930 to 1935 served in aircraft-carriers. On 19 June 1937 he married Barbara Aline (b. 1915/16), daughter of John Melville Coode, of independent means. They had a son and a daughter.

Prior to the Second World War, Moulton was a student at the army Staff College, Camberley, and then in 1940 served on the staff of the British expeditionary force in France. He was one of the last officers to be evacuated from Dunkirk. After serving with the Royal Marine division in the seizure of Madagascar and with the directorate of combined operations, he assumed command of the newly raised 48 Royal Marines commando in March 1944, and led it during the Normandy landings in June 1944 and later during the combined assault on Walcheren Island in the autumn of that year. At the end of the war he commanded 4 commando brigade. Wounded in action (1944), he was appointed DSO (1944) and mentioned in dispatches (1946, for service with the British army of the Rhine). After the war his career continued to focus on amphibious operations. He was commanding officer of the commando school (1947–9) and of 3 commando brigade (1952–4, serving in the Middle East), and was chief of amphibious warfare from 1957 until his retirement in 1961; he also served as assistant chief of staff to the commandant-general, Royal Marines and as major-general, Royal Marines, Portsmouth (1954–7). He was made OBE in 1950 and CB in 1956.

Moulton was an officer of diverse experiences, including sea duty, flying, and commanding infantry. This perspective proved invaluable in his later career, when he recognized that the amphibious assault was a truly joint and combined endeavour, requiring doctrine, training, and specialized shipping and equipment, such as helicopters and appropriate carriers for ship-to-shore movement. Stated another way, such operations could not be unique to or dominated by any single service, nor planned and executed in an *ad hoc* manner. Although he served as chief of amphibious warfare between 1957 and 1961, a quarter of a century later he was credited with having ensured that Britain had the amphibious shipping necessary to conduct operations in the south Atlantic in 1981, during the Falklands War with Argentina.

After his retirement, Moulton became a military analyst, historian, and editor. For two years (1966–8), he served as defence correspondent for the *Glasgow Herald*. More important, he was first naval editor (1964–9) and then overall editor (1969–73) of *Brassey's Annual*; under his name, he penned ten articles and three editorial forewords in this annual defence publication. He also wrote six books. *Haste to Battle* (1963) told the story of wartime commando operations from the perspective of the commander of 48 Royal Marines commando, while also conveying the spirit of a combat unit. In *A Study of War in Three Dimensions: the Norwegian Campaign of 1940* (1967), he analysed both joint and amphibious operations, candidly noting what the British did wrong in both approach and execution, and what the Germans did right. In *Battle for Antwerp: the Liberation of the City and the Opening of the Scheldt* (1978), he described the joint and combined assault on Walcheren Island and the operations for the vital port of Antwerp, all placed within a larger strategic context. In *Defence in a Changing World* (1964) he addressed the need to assess realistically what is in a nation's interest and to concentrate on the essentials, to have balanced forces, and to retain tradition and overseas commitments only if such are valid. Then, as Britain's role in the world changed and her military power declined, he analysed the NATO alliance, and within it the role and capability of the United Kingdom and the Royal Navy, in *British Maritime Strategy in the 70s* (1969). Moulton also wrote an overview history of his corps, *The Royal Marines* (1972, 2nd edn, 1981). Amid these diverse writings, his analyses remained relevant at the end of the twentieth and beginning of the twenty-first centuries.

Moulton was born while the British empire was still in its ascendancy, was commissioned into the Royal Marines at its greatest height, and commenced his military career in an era still dominated by the big gun battleship. By the end of his military career, the empire was gone, Britain's commitments overseas continued to dwindle, and the naval services were a shadow of their former strength. Throughout all of this he was a consummate professional military officer, an exemplary leader of men in combat and peace, and a realist in assessing international affairs and supporting strategies, in recognizing the possibilities of harnessing technological change to military needs, and in comprehending the need for joint (multiservice) and combined (multinational) operations. He was an excellent example of the experienced, reflective professional which all armed forces need to accomplish effectively the tasks their political leaders assign to them. He represented at its best the dedication and professionalism of the British military officer corps. He died of cancer at St Peter's Hospital, Chertsey, Surrey, on 22 November 1993, and was survived by his wife and two children.

DONALD F. BITTNER

Sources 'Major General J. L. Moulton, CB, DSO, OBE', *Globe and Laurel*, 102/1 (Jan–Feb 1994), 55–6 · *Daily Telegraph* (24 Nov 1993) · *The Times* (27 Nov 1993) · J. L. Moulton, *Haste to battle: a marine commando at war* (1963) · J. D. Ladd, *The royal marines, 1919–1980: an authorised history* (1980) · M. H. H. Evans, *Amphibious operations: the projection of sea power ashore* (1990) · *The Times* (25 May 1957) · *The Times* (27 May 1957) · *The Times* (27 Jan 1960) · *Brassey's Defence Annual* (1962–8), esp. 1964 · *Brassey's Defence Annual* (1970–74) · J. L. Moulton, *Battle for Antwerp: the liberation of the city and the opening of the Scheldt* (1978) · *Navy List* · WWW, 1991–5 · b. cert. · m. cert. · d. cert. · personal knowledge (2004) · private information (2004)
Archives CAC Cam., military and literary papers | King's Lond., Liddell Hart C., corresp. with Sir B. H. Liddell Hart · Royal Marines Museum, Eastney barracks, Southsea, Hampshire, Jerram MSS
Likenesses photograph, repro. in *Daily Telegraph* · photograph, repro. in *The Times* (27 Nov 1993) · photograph, repro. in 'Major General J. L. Moulton', 55
Wealth at death £177,665: probate, 10 Jan 1994, *CGPLA Eng. & Wales*

Moulton, John Fletcher, Baron Moulton (1844–1921), judge and politician, was born on 18 November 1844 at Madeley, Shropshire, the third son of the Revd James Egan Moulton (d. 1866), a Wesleyan minister, formerly headmaster of New Kingswood School, Bath, and his wife, Catherine (d. 1855), daughter of William Fiddian, brassfounder, of Birmingham. Moulton was named after a former vicar of Madeley, John William Fletcher, who had been a friend of John Wesley. He was a younger brother of William Fiddian *Moulton and uncle of James Hope *Moulton.

Moulton received his early education from his father. At the age of eleven he was sent to Kingswood School and was at once placed in the headmaster's class. By thirteen and a half he was head of the school. At sixteen he scored the highest marks in England at the first of the Oxford and Cambridge local examinations. On leaving Kingswood School he was for a short time an assistant master at schools in Biggleswade and Northampton before in 1861 matriculating at London University, winning a studentship of £30. He took his BA degree in mathematics and was alone in the first class both at the intermediate and the final examination (1865). Meanwhile he had been elected to a scholarship at St John's College, Cambridge. His mathematical ability became famous in Cambridge, and he was the only applicant for a mathematics scholarship at London University. Coached by the famous Dr Edward John Routh, he was first Smith's prizeman and senior wrangler in 1868, with the highest marks then known. The same year he won the gold medal for mathematics at London University, and was elected a fellow of Christ's College, Cambridge, few of the St John's fellowships then being open to laymen. Moulton worked both as college tutor and private tutor, and regularly attended the debates of the Union Society, of which he was president in 1868, and then treasurer until he left Cambridge in 1873. The union records show that he was an advocate of votes for women, reform of the university system of education, and Irish conciliation.

In 1873 Moulton read for the bar in London and the following year he was called by the Middle Temple. He read in chambers with William George Harrison, then a busy common-law junior, and soon had general work of his own. In 1875 he married Clara (*d.* 1888), widow of Robert William Thompson, of Edinburgh and Stonehaven. They had at least one child, Hugh Lawrence Fletcher Moulton.

The passing of the Patents, Designs, and Trade Marks Act (1883), which increased the number of patent actions, gave Moulton the opportunity to take on many new cases, and in 1885 he became queen's counsel. His private experiments in electricity meanwhile won him a fellowship of the Royal Society. After Clara's death in 1888 Moulton took the lead in all patent cases of any importance. Scientific facts and problems presented no difficulties to him and he had the gift of easy and lucid speech. He often appeared in parliamentary committee rooms when bills relating to electrical undertakings were being promoted. He was also a favourite advocate in compensation cases and in those concerning trade marks and trade names. In the lengthy litigation over the right of the Kodak Company to register the word 'Solio' as a trade mark, the House of Lords accepted his arguments in spite of the adverse judgments of the two courts below. Moulton appeared in the cases which centred round the Dunlop and Welsbach patents, and he was counsel in the arbitration which settled the price of the London water companies when the Metropolitan Water Board was created. There were not many barristers of his time who earned more than he did.

In November 1885 Moulton was elected to the House of Commons as Liberal member for the Clapham division of Battersea, and began a parliamentary career which received many setbacks. He lost his seat at the general election of 1886, failed to win a seat at the general election of 1892, and had to wait to get back to parliament until 1894 when he was elected member for South Hackney in succession to Lord Russell of Killowen, who, as Sir Charles Russell, had held the seat for eight years. This seat he lost at the general election of 1895. He returned to the House of Commons as member for the Launceston division of Cornwall in August 1898, and continued to sit for that constituency until the general election of 1906.

In 1901 Moulton married his second wife, Mary (*d.* 1909), daughter of Major Henry Davis, of Naples; they had one daughter. At about the same time he also began to take an active part in the House of Commons. He spoke effectively against the Chinese labour ordinances after the Second South African War; made a speech in 1904 which convinced many waverers that the supporters of a 'pure beer' bill were neglecting valuable scientific discoveries, and that beer drinkers had nothing to fear from what was represented as adulteration; and in 1905 he carried through the house a measure which became the Trade Marks Act. Between 1885 and 1905 the Liberals were only in office for about three years, and Moulton had few chances of promotion; but on their return to power in 1906 he was made a lord justice of appeal in succession to Sir James Charles Mathew, knighted, and sworn of the privy council.

During his six years in the Court of Appeal, Moulton cut an impressive figure. His powers of assimilation were his real strength, and he dealt with commercial cases, appeals under the Workmen's Compensation Act, and libel actions as if he had been dealing with them all his career. Notable cases in which his dissenting judgment was upheld by the House of Lords were *Scott* v. *Scott* (1913, the right to order a trial in camera), and *Attorney-General* v. *West Riding of Yorkshire County Council* (1907, the obligation of local education authorities to pay for religious instruction in non-provided schools). In *Cuenod* v. *Leslie* (1909) he showed characteristic independence on the question of a husband's liability for the torts of his wife. From time to time he formed a court with two colleagues—lords justices James Stirling and Robert Romer—each of whom had also been a senior wrangler. In 1912 he succeeded Lord Robson as a lord of appeal in ordinary, and became a life peer with the title of Baron Moulton of Bank in the county of Southampton.

Shortly after the outbreak of the First World War in 1914, Lord Moulton was invited by the government to head a committee to organize the manufacture of high explosives and propellants for British forces. In this capacity, he organized a service which, as the explosives supply department (ESD), became a branch of the War Office. At the armistice in November 1918, ESD was turning out 1000 tons of high explosives a day. Moulton had to overcome great difficulties; there were few factories available and sources of raw materials were limited. Lyddite had been replaced by trinitrotoluene, every 3 tons of which required 2 tons of toluene. It took 600 tons of coal to produce 1 ton of toluene. Moulton suggested mixing ammonium nitrate with trinitrotoluene to produce a new compound explosive, amatol. At a time when shipping facilities were disorganized he had to secure large quantities of nitric acid, sulphuric acid, and glycerine. He had control of the gasworks, coke ovens, and fat and oil supplies of the whole country. After it was decided to use poison gas if the enemy used it first, Moulton undertook its manufacture. During the war his department delivered a total of 612,697 tons of high explosive and 450,487 tons of propellants. For these services in wartime Moulton was created KCB (1915) and GBE (1917). At Christmas 1920 he underwent a slight nasal operation; 8 March 1921 he sat in the House of Lords and seemed to have recovered his usual good health, but in the early hours of 9 March died in his sleep at his London home, 57 Onslow Square, South Kensington. His death, caused by a clot in an artery, was instantaneous. Addressing the lords of appeal two days later, Lord Birkenhead spoke of the intellectual force and dynamic impulse of personality which had enabled a judge to play a supreme part in the war.

THEOBALD MATHEW, rev. HUGH MOONEY

Sources *The Times* (10 March 1921) • *Law Journal* (12 March 1921) • H. F. Moulton, *The life of Lord Moulton* (1922) • *CGPLA Eng. & Wales* (1921)

Archives Sci. Mus., corresp. with Oswald John Silberrad | FILM BFI NFTVA, news footage

Likenesses W. Stoneman, photograph, 1917, NPG • Elliott & Fry, photograph, NPG • T. Haddon, crayon drawing, priv. coll. • Spy [L. Ward], cartoon, lithograph, repro. in *VF* (1900)

Wealth at death £162,506 16s.: probate, 21 June 1921, *CGPLA Eng. & Wales*

Moulton, Robert (*c*.1591–1652), naval officer, was born in Landulph, Cornwall, and probably belonged to a junior seafaring branch of a landed family settled in Devon. His career was bound up with the 'colonial-interloping' nexus of puritan merchants, shipowners, and masters which challenged the established trading companies before the civil war and came into prominence during it. By the late 1620s he was a senior master mariner, commanding the 300 ton *George* in 1629, the year in which he was invited by the Massachusetts Bay Company to establish Matthew Cradock's new shipyard on the Mystic River. He became a freeman in 1631, and three others sharing his surname, possibly his sons, were made freemen in 1638–9. Moulton himself had returned much earlier.

On his return to England, Moulton joined Robert Rich, second earl of Warwick, in a number of privateering ventures, and was a part-owner of a celebrated privateer, the *Constant Warwick*. In 1636 he sailed to the East in the *Dragon* as second in command of the fleet led by John Weddell, which Sir William Courten had sent out by royal commission, and he commanded the *Planter* home from Goa in 1637–8.

On the outbreak of the civil war the navy rallied to parliament, which made Warwick its lord high admiral. Moulton, a firm parliamentarian, became one of its most important commanders. He was captain of the *Swiftsure*, a second-rate, in 1643, and admiral of the forces in the Irish Sea in the summer guards of 1644–6. In this capacity he played a prominent part in strengthening parliament's position in Wales and maintaining its foothold in Ireland. In 1647 he was appointed captain of the *Triumph*, one of the reserve, but he was summoned back to active service in the early summer of 1648 when parliament found itself facing a serious mutiny in the fleet. Rebellion in Kent had spread to the ships stationed in the Downs, and in late May the sailors drove out their admiral and demanded an accommodation with the king. Moulton secured the *Sovereign* and was active in stemming the spread of unrest in the remainder of the fleet, and also did his best to rally support for parliament among shipowners and seafarers in London. The mutineers eventually carried their ships to the Netherlands. In September parliament sent an expeditionary force against them, under Warwick as admiral; Moulton served as his flag captain and showed considerably more resolution than his commander. On one occasion, as the two fleets lay at anchor, Moulton ventured aboard Rupert's flagship to try to win back the allegiance of the sailors; Rupert arrested him, but the Dutch authorities secured his release.

After the fleet's return home in November, Warwick played no further part in naval affairs. Moulton was appointed to command the forces in the Downs, and was the most senior serving officer in the critical weeks that followed, which saw the execution of the king and the establishment of the Commonwealth. His experience and loyalty made him an important figure in the remodelled navy. He served as vice-admiral under the new generals-at-sea in 1649, and sailed with General Robert Blake in March 1650 in the same position in the expedition dispatched to

Portugal against Prince Rupert. As John IV of Portugal had offered protection to Rupert's squadron, no military resolution was possible, and a lengthy stalemate ensued. While the English fleet lay off Lisbon, Moulton was sent ashore to try to negotiate a diplomatic settlement with the king. In October, Rupert at last slipped out and made for the Strait of Gibraltar. Blake and Moulton at once gave chase, and in early November were able to report that the royalist squadron had been almost totally destroyed in Cartagena Bay.

Moulton returned home with Blake in February 1651. A few weeks later, in April, he was nominated navy commissioner and master attendant at Portsmouth, with charge of a dockyard that was rapidly growing in importance. He proved himself an effective administrator, but died in Portsmouth, following a short illness, on 22 September 1652, after little more than a year in office. His wife, Katharine, survived him. He left lands in Suffolk and Kent, and a bequest to the poor of St Mary's, Dover. Their son Robert (*d.* 1668), who was married to the daughter of Commissioner Peter Pett, held several commands in the parliamentary navy in the period 1646–52 and again during the Second Anglo-Dutch War. Another son, James, also served in the parliamentary navy.   BERNARD CAPP

Sources B. Capp, *Cromwell's navy: the fleet and the English revolution, 1648–1660* (1989) · K. R. Andrews, *Ships, money, and politics: seafaring and naval enterprise in the reign of Charles I* (1991) · J. R. Powell, *The navy in the English civil war* (1962) · *CSP dom.*, 1635–6; 1644–52 · *JHC*, 7 (1651–9), 185 · J. R. Powell and E. K. Timings, eds., *Documents relating to the civil war, 1642–1648*, Navy RS, 105 (1963) · *The letters of Robert Blake*, ed. J. R. Powell, Navy RS, 76 (1937) · J. Matthews and G. F. Matthews, eds., *Abstracts of probate acts in the prerogative court of Canterbury* (1911), 340 · PRO, HCA 13/57, 58, 62, 64
Wealth at death lands in Suffolk and Kent: will

Moulton [Muleton, Multon], **Sir Thomas of** (*d.* 1240), landowner and justice, was the son of Thomas of Moulton (*d.* before 1198) and grandson of Lambert of Moulton (*d.* 1166/7) of Spalding Priory and of the honours of Bolingbroke and Richmond, Yorkshire, who held lands in Holland, Lincolnshire. Like his father and grandfather Thomas was active in enlarging his holdings in the fenland of south Lincolnshire. His mother, Eleanor, held property in Boston.

Moulton's career falls into two phases, divided by the baronial rebellion of 1215–17. A knight who fought in Normandy in 1202–3, in Wales in 1211, and in Poitou in 1214, he was, under John, an unlucky speculator, offering fines for offices and other favours that failed to produce expected profits. He owed over £800 when the exchequer reopened after the civil war. In 1205 he purchased the office of sheriff of Lincolnshire, which he held until 1208, but, unable to pay, he was on 21 July 1208 ordered to be imprisoned in Rochester Castle until he had discharged his debt. He regained a measure of royal favour, and on 25 February 1213 was appointed to investigate the extortions of the sheriffs of Yorkshire and Lincolnshire, and in 1214 to inquire into the losses of the church in the bishopric of Lincoln during the interdict. As a northern lord and crown debtor Moulton sided with the barons in 1215, and was one of the rebels who mustered at Stamford in Easter week of that year; in consequence he was one of those excommunicated by the pope in 1216. Before this Moulton had been taken prisoner by the king at Rochester on 30 November 1215, and placed in the custody of Peter de Mauley at Corfe. His lands were entrusted to Ranulf (III), earl of Chester, and, despite the efforts of his sons, he was not restored to liberty until 29 July 1217, when he made his peace with the crown.

Moulton married first, before 1200, Sara, a daughter of Richard of Fleet, a bailiff of the earl of Lincoln. In 1214 he received the custody of the daughters of Richard de Lucy of Egremont (d. c.1213), and by 1218 had married as his second wife Lucy's widow, Ada, the daughter and coheir of Hugh de Morville, baron of Burgh by Sands, Cumberland. For this unauthorized marriage to a widow in royal custody he had to offer a fine of 1000 marks, but obtained in the right of his wife the office of forester of Cumberland.

Under Henry III, Moulton became a major royal agent in the north. In 1218–19 he was one of the itinerant justices for Cumberland, Westmorland, Lancashire, Yorkshire, and Northumberland. After 1224 he sat continually as a justice at Westminster until autumn 1236, and he was an itinerant justice in various counties until August 1234. By the time he left the bench in 1236 he was senior justice of the common pleas. From 1233 to 1236 he was sheriff of Cumberland and also constable of Carlisle Castle. His last administrative activity was in the spring of 1238, as a surveyor of the royal demesne in Cumberland. According to Matthew Paris, Moulton died in 1240, and the chronicler's obituary describes him as having been in his youth a bold soldier, but in his later years a very wealthy man and learned lawyer. Paris implies that Moulton was not always scrupulous about the way he acquired wealth, for he is said to have enlarged his landholdings at the expense of the abbey of Crowland, of which he was a neighbour. He was, however, a benefactor of the Cumberland Cistercian houses of Calder and Holmcultram, and of several Lincolnshire houses, among them the hospital of St John outside Boston, Bourne Abbey, Bullington Priory, and Spalding Priory.

Moulton and his first wife had three sons and a daughter: Alan, who was taken prisoner with his father at Rochester, Lambert, Thomas, a clerk, and Julia, who in 1209 married Robert le Vavasour, a Yorkshire knight. Alan and Lambert married the daughters of Richard de Lucy, Moulton's wards and claimants to the vast northern inheritance of Alice de Rumilly (d. 1187). Alan and his wife received half the honour of Papcastle; their son Thomas took his mother's name, and was ancestor of the Lucys of Cockermouth. Lambert (d. 1246) and his wife, Mabel de Lucy, eventually acquired the barony of Egremont; their grandson Thomas was summoned to parliament from between 1298 and 1299 to 1321 and fought at Caerlaverock in 1300; on the death of Thomas's son, John Moulton, in 1334, the title fell into abeyance. Moulton and his second wife had a son Thomas (d. 1271), who, by his marriage with

Maud, daughter of Hubert (II) de Vaux, acquired the barony of Irthington or Gilsland, Cumberland. Thomas Moulton, third baron of Gilsland, was summoned to parliament from 1297 until his death in 1313. Through his daughter Margaret the barony passed to Ranulf Dacre; from this marriage sprang the titles of Baron Dacre and Baron Dacre of Gilsland.

C. L. KINGSFORD, *rev.* RALPH V. TURNER

Sources R. V. Turner, *Men raised from the dust: administrative service and upward mobility in Angevin England* (1988) · GEC, *Peerage* · D. Crook, *Records of the general eyre*, Public Record Office Handbooks, 20 (1982) · A. Hughes, *List of sheriffs for England and Wales: from the earliest times to AD 1831*, PRO (1898); repr. (New York, 1963) · *Pipe rolls* · *Chancery records* · *Curia regis rolls preserved in the Public Record Office* (1922–) · Chancery Fine Rolls, PRO, C 60 · Exchequer Lord Treasurer's Remembrancer's Pipe Rolls, PRO, E 372 · Paris, *Chron.*, vols. 2, 3, 4.49

Moulton, Thomas (*fl.* 1530?), Dominican friar, called himself 'doctor of divinity of the order of friar preachers'. Little else is known about his life. He was the author of a work dealing partly with medicine, partly with astrology, entitled *This is the myrrour or glasse of helth: necessary & nedeful for every person to loke in, that wyll kepe their body from the syckenesse of the pestilence, & it sheweth howe the planettes do raygne in every houre of the daye and nyghte, with the natures and exposicions of the xii sygnes, devided by the xii monethes of the yere, and shewed the remedies for manye divers infyrmyties and diseases that hurteth the body of manne*. After the prologue and table of contents Moulton gives four reasons for the production of his book: first, the prayers of his own brethren; secondly, the prayers of 'many worthy gentiles'; thirdly, his compassion 'for the pore people that was and is destroyed every daye thereby for default of helpe'; fourthly, the working of pure conscience.

The first edition of Moulton's work was printed and published by Robert Wyer before 1531, and seems to have been popular. At least nine editions were published in London between 1539 and 1565. Moulton's name carried weight as late as 1656, when it appeared on the title-page of a book called the *Compleat Bone-Setter*, which was alleged to have been originally written by him, but contained little of his work. WILLIAM CARR, *rev.* RACHEL E. DAVIES

Sources ESTC · Tanner, *Bibl. Brit.-Hib.* · J. Ames, *Typographical antiquities, being an historical account of printing in England* (1749)

Moulton, William Fiddian (1835–1898), biblical scholar, was born at the minister's house, Leek, Staffordshire, on 14 March 1835, the eldest of the four sons of James Egan Moulton (d. 1866), a Wesleyan Methodist minister, and Catherine (d. 1855), daughter of William Fiddian, a Birmingham brass-founder. His grandfather had been, like his father, a Methodist preacher; and among his ancestors was John Bakewell, Wesley's friend. John Fletcher *Moulton (1844–1921) was his younger brother. William was educated at Miss Egan's Seminary, Worcester, Woodhouse Grove School, near Leeds, from 1846, and Wesley College, Sheffield, from 1850. In 1854, having taught for a year in a private school at Devonport, he went as an assistant master to Queen's College, Taunton, where he remained for

William Fiddian Moulton (1835–1898), by Samuel Alexander Walker, 1874

four years. While at Taunton, in 1854 he gained a BA honours degree in mathematics from London University; two years later, he was awarded an MA from London University, with a gold medal for both mathematics and natural philosophy. Subsequently he also won the university prizes for Hebrew, Greek, and Christian evidences. In 1858 he entered the Wesleyan ministry and was appointed a classical tutor at the Methodist theological establishment, Richmond College, Surrey. He held that position for sixteen years, and spent much of his time on biblical studies. On 14 August 1862 he married Hannah, daughter of the Revd Samuel Hope.

At the suggestion of Dr C. J. Ellicott, bishop of the then united see of Gloucester and Bristol, Moulton published in 1870 a translation of the current standard text, G. B. Winer's *Grammatik des neutestamentlichen Sprachidioms*, which he annotated with his own critical commentary and insights. A new edition appeared in 1876. Moulton later undertook to create a new New Testament grammar, but the project was abandoned on his death.

On the basis of his work on Winer, Moulton was invited to become one of the committee of revisers of the Authorized Version of the New Testament, the edition subsequently known as the Revised Version (1881–5). Here he associated himself closely with the progressive Cambridge school led by F. J. A. Hort, B. F. Westcott, and J. B. Lightfoot. Moulton was specifically responsible for bringing to the attention of the committee those variant readings in pre-Authorized Version editions of the Bible which diverged from the Authorized Version itself; much of the initial research was undertaken by his wife, Hannah. He later acted as secretary to the Cambridge committee for the revision of the Apocrypha, and in collaboration with Hort and Westcott revised the texts of the Wisdom of Solomon and 2 Maccabees.

In 1872 Moulton had been chosen at an unprecedentedly early age to be a member of the legal hundred of the Wesleyan Methodist Connexion. Two years later, in 1874, he was appointed as the first headmaster of the newly founded Leys School, Cambridge, taking up office in February 1875; here he remained for the rest of his life. In 1874 he received the degree of DD from Edinburgh, and in 1877 he was awarded an honorary MA degree at Cambridge. Although a conscientious headmaster who took great interest in the work of teaching, Moulton remained an active scholar. In 1878 he published a *History of the English Bible*, an account in popular form of his historical findings during his revision work. This went through several editions. He produced *The Epistle to the Hebrews* in 1879, as part of Bishop Ellicott's series, and collaborated with William Milligan on *A Popular Commentary on the Gospel of St John* (1880). He wrote in 1879 a preface to E. Rush's *Synthetic Latin delectus*, in 1889 an introduction to *Benjamin Hellier: his Life and Teaching*, and in 1893 a preface to George Pocock's *Methodist New Testament Commentary*. As a result of failing health he was unable to collaborate as fully as he had intended with A. S. Geden on *A Concordance to the Greek New Testament* (1897) and acted only as reviser and editor, leaving most of the actual work to Professor Geden and his own son, the Revd James Hope Moulton.

At the time of his death Moulton had nearly completed the marginal references to the Revised Version of the New Testament, having recently published *The Synoptic Gospels with Marginal References* with F. H. A. Scrivener (1897). In 1890 he was president of the Wesleyan conference and preached the memorial sermon on John Wesley, which was printed in 1891. Alongside his educational and scholarly work, he was for twenty years conference secretary of the examination of ministers on trial, and he also became a justice of the peace in Cambridge.

Moulton died suddenly while walking near Leys School on 5 February 1898. He was buried on 9 February at Histon Road cemetery, Cambridge. As the first headmaster of Leys, he had contributed to the early success of the school. He was a popular and respected figure, not just in nonconformist circles but among Anglican scholars as well. While he was one of the foremost experts of his generation in classical and New Testament Greek, and an accomplished scholar of Hebrew and mathematics, his greatest contribution was to the critical movement within Methodist thought, and to the link he helped to establish between Anglican and nonconformist scholarship.

He and his wife, who survived him, had two sons, the

Revd James Hope *Moulton (1863–1917), whose work later took him to India, and the Revd William Fiddian Moulton (1866–1929), formerly fellow of St John's College, Cambridge. There was also a daughter, who died in infancy.

G. LE G. NORGATE, rev. JOANNA HAWKE

Sources W. F. Moulton, *William F. Moulton: a memoir* (1899) · G. C. Findlay, *William F. Moulton: the Methodist scholar* (1910) · *Methodist Times* (10 Feb 1898) · J. H. Moulton, *Methodist Recorder* (17 Feb 1898) · P. W. Bunting, *Sunday Magazine* (April 1898), 245–50 · G. C. Findlay and T. G. Selby, *British Weekly* (10 Feb 1898) · O. Chadwick, *The Victorian church*, 2 (1970), 46–7, 453 · R. E. Davies, A. R. George, and G. Rupp, *A history of the Methodist church in Great Britain*, 3 (1983) · *CGPLA Eng. & Wales* (1898)
Archives JRL, Methodist Archives and Research Centre, letters received and commonplace book
Likenesses S. A. Walker, photograph, 1874, NPG [*see illus.*] · H. Prater, wood-engraving, NPG; repro. in *ILN* (2 Aug 1890) · bust, City Road Chapel, London · photograph, repro. in Moulton, *William F. Moulton* · photograph, repro. in *Sunday Magazine* · photograph, repro. in *Methodist Recorder* · stipple, NPG
Wealth at death £3072 18s. 0d.: probate, 28 March 1898, *CGPLA Eng. & Wales*

Moultrie, Gerard (1829–1885). *See under* Moultrie, John (1799–1874).

Moultrie, John (1799–1874), Church of England clergyman and poet, was born on 31 December 1799 at Great Portland Street, London (his maternal grandmother's home), the eldest of five sons and two daughters of George Moultrie (1772–1845), rector of Cleobury Mortimer, Shropshire, and his wife, Harriet Fendall (c.1775–1867). Of Scottish descent, the Moultries had emigrated to the American colonies. John Moultrie's grandfather, after whom he was named, was governor of East Florida, and remained a British patriot, while his great-uncle William Moultrie (1730–1805) supported the cause of American independence. Moultrie's childhood was spent in Cleobury Mortimer. His education started at Ramsbury, Wiltshire, and continued at Eton College in 1814.

It was during Moultrie's time at Eton, where he was a contemporary of Winthrop Mackworth *Praed and W. Sidney *Walker (whose *Poetical Remains* he edited in 1852), that Moultrie became known as a poet. Later critics agreed that his precocious talent, with its Byronic influence, was not sustained. However, it is possible that Tennyson's 'Godiva' was indebted to an earlier poem of Moultrie's. Much of Moultrie's best verse was prompted by family bereavement, notably 'My Brother's Grave', written when he was sixteen, and later published in *The Etonian* (1820) under the pseudonym Gerard Montgomery, which he also used in *Knight's Quarterly Magazine*. Moultrie entered Trinity College, Cambridge, in April 1819, was a Bell scholar in 1820, and proceeded BA in 1823 and MA in 1826. In accordance with his father's wishes, he entered the Middle Temple on 24 January 1822, in preparation for a legal career, but he soon acknowledged his unsuitability for the profession. He was subsequently appointed tutor to the three sons of Lord Craven, and remained in Eton for the next six years. In 1825 Lord Craven presented Moultrie to the living of Rugby, where he was to be rector until his

John Moultrie (1799–1874), by unknown photographer

death. In the same year he was ordained deacon and priest, and on 28 July 1825 he married Harriet Margaret (c.1806–1864), the daughter of William *Fergusson (1773–1846), army physician. He moved to Rugby in 1828, the same year that Thomas Arnold took up his appointment as headmaster of Rugby School. A firm friendship developed between them.

> Small hope—perchance small wish—have I
> To leave a poet's name

claimed Moultrie in 'The Three Minstrels' (*Poems*, 1876, 350). He may well be more entitled to the name of poet than many others who professed it. In 1837 Moultrie published *Poems*, which reached a third edition in 1852. This volume focuses on family life, and contains 'Our First Sorrow', a moving record of the loss of a baby son, and 'The Three Sons', prompted by the same event. This poem and 'My Brother's Grave' were the two most often praised and reprinted during Moultrie's lifetime. *The Dream of Life, Lays of the English Church and other Poems* followed in 1843. 'The Dream of Life' acknowledges its debt to Wordsworth in direct quotations used as epigraphs to the four books, 'Childhood', 'Boyhood', 'Youth', and 'Manhood'. It provides glimpses of life at Eton and Cambridge, recording Moultrie's close friendship with Derwent Coleridge, to whom the third book is dedicated, and who wrote the memoir appended to Moultrie's collected poems, published in 1876. In 1845 Moultrie edited Gray's *Poetical Works*. He produced an anti-Catholic poem as a pamphlet publication in 1850, *The Black Fence*. Moultrie's last major collection was *Altars, Hearths and Graves* (1854).

Moultrie was active in promoting the rebuilding of St Andrew's, the parish church at Rugby for which he had earlier edited a hymn collection. He also worked to encourage the building of Trinity, a new parish church for the town's rapidly growing population, and in 1852 published a poem about its construction. He was made an honorary canon of Worcester Cathedral in 1864. A popular figure with his parishioners, he was committed to his pastoral duties up to the time of his death. One of his parishioners allows a glimpse of Moultrie's physique in his comment 'They spoilt a jolly good navvy when they made that old cove a parson' (Coleridge, li). Moultrie caught an infection during a smallpox epidemic, while visiting the sick, and died at the rectory, Rugby, on 26 December 1874. He was buried on 31 December in the family vault outside Trinity Church after a funeral service there. His memorial was to be an aisle added to the new church.

Moultrie's eldest son, **Gerard Moultrie** (1829–1885), Church of England clergyman and poet, was born on 16 September 1829 and followed in his father's footsteps as a clergyman after attending Rugby School and Exeter College, Oxford (BA 1852, MA 1856). He held a teaching post at Shrewsbury School (1852–5), and on 3 July 1855 married Elizabeth, daughter of Charles Alleyne Anstey. They had at least four sons. Moultrie was ordained priest in 1858, and his final appointment was in 1869 as vicar of Southleigh, Witney, Oxfordshire, where he was also warden of St James's College from 1873. He wrote verse almost entirely on devotional subjects, and his publications included *Hymns and Lyrics for the Seasons and Saints' Days of the Church* (1867), *Hymns and Carols for Children* (1869), and *The Espousals of Saint Dorothea and other Poems* (1870). He also translated hymns from Latin, Greek, and German. Moultrie produced an appendix for J. M. Neale's *Essays on Liturgiology and Church History* (1863) and compiled a service book, *Offices for Holy Week and Easter* (1865), with additional meditations and prayers on the Passion. His sister Mary Dunlop Moultrie (1837–1866) contributed several hymns to her brother's *Hymns and Lyrics* (1867). He died in Southleigh on 25 April 1885.   ROSEMARY SCOTT

Sources D. Coleridge, 'Memoir', in *Poems of John Moultrie*, 2 vols. (1876) · J. Blake, *The Times* (30 Dec 1874) · Venn, *Alum. Cant.*, 2/4 · L. C. Sanders, *Celebrities of the century: being a dictionary of men and women of the nineteenth century* (1887) · E. S. Creasy, *Memoirs of eminent Etonians*, new edn (1876) · J. Julian, ed., *A dictionary of hymnology*, rev. edn (1907) · *N&Q*, 9 (8 April 1854) · G. A. Solly, ed., *Rugby School register*, rev. edn, 1: *April 1675 – October 1857* (1933) · H. S. Salt, 'Moultrie's poems', *Macmillan's Magazine*, 57 (1887–8), 123–9 · J. Hutchinson, ed., *A catalogue of notable Middle Templars: with brief biographical notices* (1902) · H. E. C. Stapylton, *The Eton school lists, from 1791 to 1850*, 2nd edn (1864) · *Poems of Tennyson*, ed. C. Ricks, 3 vols., 2nd edn (1987) · *The letters of Alfred Lord Tennyson*, ed. C. Y. Lang and E. F. Shannon, 3 vols. (1982–90) · *IGI* · *Rugby Advertiser* (2 Jan 1875) · m. cert. [Gerard Moultrie] · d. cert. [Gerard Moultrie]
Likenesses photograph, Rugby Library [*see illus.*]

Wealth at death under £1500: probate, 9 Feb 1875, *CGPLA Eng. & Wales* · £22,026 3s. 7d.—Gerard Moultrie: probate, 28 April 1885, *CGPLA Eng. & Wales*

Moultrie, William (1730–1805), revolutionary army officer and politician, in the United States of America, was born on 23 November 1730 in Charles Town, South Carolina, the son of Dr John Moultrie (1702–1771), physician, and Lucretia Cooper (1704–1747). On 10 December 1747 William married Damaris Elizabeth de St Julien; after her death he wed Hannah, *née* Motte (1736–1798?), the widow of Thomas Lynch (1727–1776), on 10 October 1779. Two children of the first marriage survived; the second was childless. By marriage, inheritance, and his own efforts, Moultrie acquired some 200 slaves and at least 10,800 acres, scattered throughout both Carolinas. Nevertheless, he died insolvent. For most of his life he lived at Northampton, a rice plantation in St John parish, Berkeley county, South Carolina.

Moultrie made his name primarily as a military man. Having served as an aide to South Carolina royal governor William Henry Lyttelton during an expedition against the Cherokee Indians in 1759, he became a captain in the local militia on 16 September 1760. He was then part of a combined force of British regulars and provincial troops under Lieutenant-Colonel James Grant that defeated the Cherokee in 1761. Further promotions followed, and by 1774 Moultrie was a South Carolina militia colonel. On 17 June 1775 the revolutionary South Carolina provincial congress accordingly commissioned him colonel of the 2nd South Carolina regiment. Six months later troops from his command killed, captured, and dispersed runaway African slaves on Sullivan's Island near Charles Town. American patriots then fortified this island, from which cannon could cover the entrance to the harbour.

On 28 June 1776 Moultrie commanded the still unfinished fort when a large British naval force under Admiral Sir Peter Parker attacked. Warned that his position was indefensible, Moultrie nevertheless refused to abandon it. In the ensuing battle the Americans suffered fewer than twelve killed; the British lost forty men. The legislature renamed the fort in Moultrie's honour, and the continental congress commissioned him a brigadier-general on 16 September 1776, four days before it made his regiment part of the continental army. Because logistical failures prevented a planned attack on Florida, Moultrie's men initially saw little action.

Beginning in late 1778, however, much fighting occurred in the southern states. On 3 February 1779 Moultrie's forces checked a British advance near Beaufort, South Carolina; in May 1779 his firmness contributed to the patriots' decision not to surrender Charles Town to British troops under Augustine Prevost; and on 20 June 1779 Moultrie took part in an attack on British forces under Lieutenant-Colonel John Maitland near Stono Ferry. But when Sir Henry Clinton, commander-in-chief of the British forces in America, captured the city on 12 May 1780, Moultrie and several thousand Americans became prisoners of war. Released on 9 February 1782, he was promoted major-general on 15 October 1782.

Moultrie's career as a civilian public servant began in 1752 when he was elected to the South Carolina Commons house of assembly. Thereafter he represented St John, Berkeley county, in almost every session of the house until the American War of Independence. Though never among the most active house leaders, he became a member of the first and second South Carolina revolutionary provincial congresses (1775–6), the general assembly (1776–8, 1783–4), the legislative council (1776), the senate (1779–80, 1787–91), and the privy council (1784–7) of the state government. Elected governor of South Carolina on 10 May 1785, he subsequently approved statutes establishing a county court system and in 1790 moving the state capital from Charles Town (now Charleston) to Columbia. In 1788 he sat in the state convention that ratified the United States constitution, which he supported. During his second two-year term as governor (1792–4) the legislature impeached the state attorney-general (William's half-brother, Alexander Moultrie) for misuse of public moneys. Also Citizen Genet, the minister of the revolutionary French government to the United States, landed in Charleston where Moultrie and others welcomed him warmly. No doubt this reception encouraged Genet in the mistaken belief that France could use American bases and manpower for attacks upon British shipping and Spanish territory. However, Moultrie's actions conflicted with President George Washington's policy of neutrality, and United States authorities eventually demanded Genet's recall.

After retiring from public office in 1794, Moultrie continued as president of the South Carolina chapter of the Cincinnati, a national organization of American War of Independence officers which he had helped to found in 1783. He died on 27 September 1805 in Charleston, and was buried at his son's plantation, Windsor Hall, Goose Creek, Berkeley county. His remains were later reinterred at Fort Moultrie, Sullivan's Island, near Charleston. Though sometimes criticized for dilatoriness, Moultrie was a resolute and respected officer who played a significant role in the eventual success of the American War for Independence in the south. ROBERT M. WEIR

Sources W. Moultrie, Memoirs of the American revolution so far as it related to the states of North and South Carolina, and Georgia, 2 vols. (1802); repr. (1968) · R. W. Gibbes, ed., Documentary history of the American revolution, 3 vols. (1853–7); repr. (1972) · S. South, 'The general, the major, and the angel: the discovery of General William Moultrie's grave', Transactions of the Huguenot Society of South Carolina, 82 (1977), 31–49 · H. M. Ward, 'Moultrie, William', ANB · 'The journal of William Moultrie while a commissioner on the North and South Carolina boundary survey, 1772', ed. C. S. Davis, Journal of Southern History, 8 (1942), 549–55 · 'Letters from General Francis Marion and General William Moultrie, 1781–1788', City of Charleston Yearbook (1898), 380–85 · W. G. DeSaussure, On offering the regular toast, on 22d February, 1885, University of South Carolina, Columbia, South Caroliniana Library [to the Cincinnati Society of South Carolina] · South Carolina Gazette · South Carolina and American General Gazette · South Carolina Gazette and Country Journal · W. E. Hemphill and W. A. Wates, eds., Extracts from the journals of the provincial congresses of South Carolina, 1775–1776 (1960) · A. S. Edwards, ed., Journals of the privy council, 1783–1789 (1971) · journals of the South Carolina Commons house of assembly, South Carolina Archives and History Center, Columbia, · journals of the South

Carolina house of representatives, South Carolina Archives and History Center, Columbia, · A. S. Salley, ed., Register of St Philip's parish, Charles Town (Charleston, SC, 1904); repr. (1971) · D. E. Huger Smith and A. S. Salley, eds., Register of St Philip's parish, Charles Town (Charleston, SC, 1927); repr. (1971) · M. K. Hood, ed., Berkeley county, South Carolina, cemetery inscriptions (1995) · A. S. Salley, ed., 'The Moultries', South Carolina Historical and Genealogical Magazine, 5 (1904), 229–60 · W. B. Edgar and N. L. Bailey, eds., Biographical directory of the South Carolina house of representatives, 2 (1977) · R. L. Meriwether, 'Moultrie, William', DAB · M. J. Hutson, 'Early generations of the Motte family', Transactions of the South Carolina Huguenot Society, 56 (1951), 60 · G. C. Rogers, Evolution of a federalist: William Loughton Smith of Charleston, 1758–1812 (1962) · J. J. Nadelhaft, The disorders of war: the revolution in South Carolina (1981) · G. D. Terry, '"Champaign country": a social history of an eighteenth-century lowcountry parish in South Carolina, St Johns, Berkeley county', PhD diss., University of South Carolina, 1981
Archives University of South Carolina, Columbia | L. Cong., N. Greene papers · New York Historical Society, minutes of first meeting of Society of Cincinnati · South Carolina Archives and History Center, Columbia, governors' corresp. and legislative records · South Carolina Historical Society, corresp.; J. Moultrie MSS · South Carolina Historical Society, R. Hutson papers
Likenesses J. Trumbull, oils, 1791?, Yale U. · C. Fraser, portrait?, c.1822, Charleston City Hall, South Carolina · C. W. Peale, oils, Smithsonian Institution, Washington, DC, National Portrait Gallery
Wealth at death nothing; insolvent debtor: South, 'The general, the major, and the angel'; DeSaussure, On offering

Moundeford, Thomas (1550–1630), physician, fourth son of Sir Edmund Moundeford and his wife, Bridget, daughter of Sir John *Spelman (c.1480–1546) of Narborough, Norfolk, was born at Feltwell, Norfolk, where a monument to his father was erected in the parish church. He was educated at Eton College and admitted a scholar of King's College, Cambridge, on 16 August 1568. On 17 August 1571 he was elected a fellow, and graduated BA in 1572 and MA in 1576. On 18 July 1580 he moved to the study of medicine. From 1580 to 1583 he was bursar of King's College and left the college in August 1583. He married, soon after, Mary Hill (1562–1656), daughter of Richard Hill, mercer, of Milk Street, London; she was a very devout and modest woman, well known for her loyalty to Anglican doctrines. The couple continued to live in Cambridge until after he had graduated MD in 1584.

Moundeford then moved to London; on 9 April 1593 he became a licentiate of the College of Physicians, and on 29 January 1594 a fellow. He lived in Milk Street in the city of London. He was seven times a censor of the College of Physicians, was treasurer in 1608, and president 1612, 1613, 1614, 1619, 1621, 1622, and 1623. As a fellow and later president he was active against empirics and other rival medical practitioners. The college's Pharmacopoeia was begun during his period of office.

Moundeford published in 1622 a small book entitled Vir bonus, dedicated to James I, to John, bishop of Lincoln, and to four judges, Sir James Lee, Sir Julius Caesar, Sir Henry Hobart, and Sir Laurence Tanfield. This large legal acquaintance was due to the fact that one of his daughters, Bridget, had, in 1606, married Sir John Bramston (1577–1654), who became, in 1635, chief justice of the king's bench. The book is divided into four parts, 'Temperantia', 'Prudentia', 'Justicia', and 'Fortitudo'. He praises the king, denounces smoking, alludes to the *Basilicon doron*, and shows that he was well read in Cicero, Tertullian, the Greek Testament, and the Latin Bible, and expresses admiration of Beza. The whole is a summary of what experience had taught him of the conduct of life.

Moundeford became blind and had died by December 1630 in Sir John Bramston's house in Philip Lane, London. He was buried in the church of St Mary Magdalen, Milk Street, which was burnt in the great fire. His wife died in her ninety-fourth year, in 1656, in the house in which they had lived together in Milk Street. As well as Bridget he had another daughter, Katherine, who married Christopher Randen of Burton, Lincolnshire, and two sons: Osbert (*d.* 1614), admitted a scholar of King's College, Cambridge, on 25 August 1601, aged sixteen, and Richard (*d.* 1615), admitted a scholar of the same college on 25 August 1603. Both died before their father, and their epitaph, in English verse, is given in Stow's *Survey of London*. It was in the church of St Mary Magdalen.

NORMAN MOORE, *rev.* PATRICK WALLIS

Sources Munk, *Roll* · Venn, *Alum. Cant.* · W. Sterry, ed., *The Eton College register, 1441–1698* (1943) · J. Stow, *A survey of the cities of London and Westminster and the borough of Southwark*, ed. J. Strype, new edn, 2 vols. (1720) · *The autobiography of Sir John Bramston*, ed. [Lord Braybrooke], CS, 32 (1845) · A. J. Orange, *The story of Feltwell* (1970) · G. Clark and A. M. Cooke, *A history of the Royal College of Physicians of London*, 3 vols. (1964–72) · F. Blomefield and C. Parkin, *An essay towards a topographical history of the county of Norfolk*, [2nd edn], 11 vols. (1805–10)

Mounsey, Ann Shepherd. *See* Bartholomew, Ann Shepherd (1811–1891).

Mounsey, Elizabeth (1819–1905). *See under* Bartholomew, Ann Shepherd (1811–1891).

Mounsey, James (1709/10–1773), physician and naturalist, was born at Skipmire, 3 miles west of Lochmaben, Dumfriesshire, the son of the merchant Thomas Mounsey (1658/9–1714) and his second wife, Mary Steel (1683/4–1747), sister of the Lochmaben minister. He studied medicine at Edinburgh University under Charles Alston (1729) and Alexander Monro *primus* (1730) but did not graduate and was apprenticed on 20 March 1731 for three years to the Edinburgh surgeon Thomas Wood, and then signed a three-year contract in July 1736 with the Russian ambassador in London. After working at the St Petersburg Admiralty Hospital he was posted in March 1738, on an outbreak of the plague, to the Russian forces in Ukraine. Accompanying General James Keith, wounded in the Russo-Turkish War, to Paris for medical treatment in November 1738, he graduated MD at Rheims University on 9 November 1739. On his return to Russia he re-enlisted as a doctor to the land militia corps in August 1741, but transferred in 1742 to Keith's army at Åbo, Finland, during the Russo-Swedish War. This was followed by service with the Livonian division, Prince Repin's corps in central Europe (where, as at Kalmar, Sweden, in 1744, he showed great capacity in organizing field hospitals), and, finally, with the 1st Moscow division (1750–56).

In 1747 Henry Baker initiated a correspondence with him, resulting in six publications in the *Philosophical Transactions*, and fellowship of the Royal Society on 8 March 1750. Mounsey's papers included a summary of his very skilful operation at Åbo in 1742 to remove a foetus lodged in a Finnish woman's Fallopian tube for thirteen years (*PTRS*, 45, 1748, 131–7), outlined more comprehensively in the Swedish Academy's *Handlingar* for 1744 (vol. 5, 102–14; in Sweden he had met and corresponded with Linnaeus, narrowly missing election to the academy); one on the 'quab', or 'frog-fish', *Pseudis paradoxa*, a frog from Surinam and the Guianas whose very large tadpoles develop into much smaller froglets (*PTRS*, 45, 1748, 175–6; and see Klaver, 201–2); some excellent descriptions of the Karlsbad thermal springs and salt-mines near Cracow (*PTRS*, 46, 1749, 217–32); and the detailed case history of an English wallpaper stainer whom he treated in Moscow for lead poisoning (*PTRS*, 50, 1758, 19–22; 54, 1764, 15–23). On 1 May 1754 Mounsey married, as his second wife, Joanna Grieve, a relative of James Grieve (1708–1763), Moscow city physician. (He had a son and a daughter by his first marriage.) Two months later he escorted Grand Duke Peter and his wife Catherine to St Petersburg, obtaining microscopes and telescopes made by John Cuff and James Short, the London optical instrument makers. In September 1756 he was sent, on the empress's orders, to treat the former duke of Courland's wife at Yaroslavl, leaving the army, highly commended by the medical chancery, to engage in extremely successful private medical practice at Moscow.

Elected one of the Society of Arts' earliest corresponding members, in April 1755, Mounsey sent it useful information in 1756 and 1760, respectively, about marketing British manufactures abroad and providing winter feed for livestock. Sir John Pringle, in his 'Medical annotations' (5.329 and 7.267–8), and in his November 1776 presidential address to the Royal Society, incorporated Mounsey's findings on the effectiveness of Russian kvass, a drink fermented with malt and rye, and rye bread leavened with malt, in combating scurvy on land, at sea, and in gaols (which Mounsey visited at Moscow and St Petersburg in the early 1750s after reading Pringle's *Observations on the Nature and Cure of Hospital and Jayl Fevers* (1750)). He also mediated the election of Count Kirill Razumovsky, president of the Russian Academy of Sciences, to the Royal Society in 1755, supplying Baker and the society with large numbers of minerals (1749–57) and seeds (1752–5) from Russia, Siberia, Astrakhan, Persia, and Bohemia, and reciprocating with twelve Moscow birds for the twelve prints of birds and a copy of his *Natural History of Uncommon Birds* sent to him in 1757 by George Edwards, to whose *Gleanings of Natural History* he subscribed in 1764. In September 1760 Mounsey became the Empress Elizabeth's personal physician with the title of councillor of state; he tended her at her deathbed in December 1761, and his account of her final illness was printed in the *St Petersburg Journal* on 28 December. Her successor, Peter III, appointed him his chief physician, privy councillor with the rank of lieutenant-general, and archiater, or director, of the medical chancery, responsible for all Russian medical affairs—

civilian, military, and naval. Within four months Mounsey had compiled, and the senate ratified, three significant pieces of medical legislation: a table of ranks, with a supplement, integrating military and civilian posts by rank and function for the first time, an extensive report on medicine in Russia, and a precept for doctors—all evidence of his considerable knowledge, experience, and administrative flair. The tsar was poisoned and strangled on 17 July 1762 and the widowed Empress Catherine dismissed Mounsey, Russia's last archiater, on health grounds and with a pension, five days later.

On arrival at Edinburgh in 1762 Mounsey gave Sir Alexander Dick, president of the Royal College of Physicians, a parcel of medicinal rhubarb seeds (*Rheum palmatum* L.), gathered from a single plant, sown at St Petersburg Apothecaries' Garden in 1754 from seed obtained on the Russo-Chinese border. John Hope, professor of botany, cultivated them at the Royal Botanical Gardens, describing the plant in a letter to Sir John Pringle which appeared in the *Philosophical Transactions* in 1766. For introducing medicinal rhubarb, Mounsey was elected an honorary member of the Royal College of Physicians of Edinburgh in November 1762 and received the Society of Arts' gold medal in 1770. Widely disseminated, the plant was successfully cultivated in Britain for the first time, and specimens grown by John Inglish, another gold medallist, from seed sent by Mounsey to Baker in 1763, produced further seed which Benjamin Franklin propagated in 1770 to John Bartram, the pioneer Philadelphian botanist. Mounsey purchased Killielung Farm near Dumfries and built a mansion in 1763 at Rammerscales, reputedly assassination-proof, on an estate 4 miles south of Lochmaben. He became an Edinburgh city burgess and guild brother in December 1762, and a member of the Philosophical Society of Edinburgh. As shown by his arms matriculated a year later, he was elected master of the Lochmaben masons in 1769 and the burgh's ruling elder to the general assembly in 1768, 1769, and 1772. Thirty-two letters (1747–72) in the Phillimore MSS at the National Library of Wales, Aberystwyth, reveal much about his medical practice, colleagues, and the merchant community in Russia, as well as his continuing interest in natural history. During 1771 he travelled to Latvia to arrange the duke of Courland's election to the Royal Society, whose dining club Mounsey attended on nine occasions between 1771 and 1772. Dying of a bowel infection at Edinburgh on 2 February 1773, before his petition for a baronetcy could be processed, and characterized by James Boswell as 'a very well informed man and communicative', he was commemorated by a 30-foot high monument in Lochmaben's old churchyard.

JOHN H. APPLEBY

Sources J. H. Appleby, '"Rhubarb" Mounsey and the Surinam toad', *Archives of Natural History*, 11 (1982–4), 137–52 · J. H. Appleby, 'British doctors in Russia, 1657–1807: their contribution to Anglo-Russian medical and natural history', PhD diss., University of East Anglia, 1979 · R. W. I. Smith, 'Dr James Mounsey of Rammerscales', *Edinburgh Medical Journal*, 3rd ser., 33 (1926), 274–9 · Henry Baker's correspondence, JRL · C. Klaver, 'The "fish-frog" and the Surinam toad', *Archives of Natural History*, 12 (1985), 201–02 · G. C. G. Thomas, 'Some correspondence of Dr James Mounsey', *Scottish Slavonic Review*, 4 (1985), 11–25 · J. B. Wilson, 'Three Scots in the service of the czars [pt 1]', *The Practitioner*, 210 (1973), 569–74 · J. Pringle, 'Medical annotations', Royal College of Physicians of Edinburgh, vols. 5 and 7 · Mounsey to King of Sweden, 9 Jan 1744, Riksarkivet, Stockholm · W. Pagan, *The birthplace and parentage of William Paterson* (1865) · *The papers of Benjamin Franklin*, 17, ed. W. B. Willcox (1973) · P. J. Wallis and R. V. Wallis, *Eighteenth century medics*, 2nd edn (1988) · private information (2004) · parish reg. (death), Dalton parish, Lochmaben, 1773 · W. Richter, *Geschichte der Medizin in Russland* (1815)

Archives JRL, Henry Baker's corresp. · NL Wales, Phillimore MSS

Likenesses G. F. Schmidt, engraving, 1762, BL · engraving, RS · portrait, repro. in A. Cross, *By the banks of the Neva* (1997)

Wealth at death considerable landed property: will, 29 March 1763, NA Scot. RS (register of sasines) 23/19, fols. 155–6,; fols. 173–4, 180–82, 439–40; RS 23/20, fols. 51–3, 57, 220–21, 375–6, 438–9; RS 23/22, fols. 205–6; SP (Scotland) 5446, no. 36, fols. 96–7, 1772 petition for baronetcy

Mounsteven, John (*bap.* 1644, *d.* 1706), politician, was baptized on 28 April 1644 at St Mabyn, Cornwall, the second surviving son of John Mounsteven (*d.* 1672) of St Mabyn and Elizabeth Tamlyn (*d.* 1664). He was educated at Bodmin School and matriculated from Christ Church, Oxford, on 7 December 1666, obtaining a BA in 1671.

Mounsteven (as he spelt his name—BL, Add. MS 28876, fols. 91, 109) entered government service as undersecretary of state for the northern department under Robert Spencer, second earl of Sunderland, in February 1679, and transferred with Sunderland to the southern department in April 1680, leaving office with Sunderland in February 1681. Upon Sunderland's return to the secretaryship for the north in January 1683, Mounsteven was reappointed under-secretary, again transferring with his master to the southern department in April 1684. There, he remained until October 1688. In the interim he served as provost marshal of Jamaica (1684–9), and was returned to parliament for the Cornish borough of Bossiney in 1685. That same year he purchased Lancarfe, near Bodmin, and became a freeman under that borough's new charter. Although seen as a possible MP for Bodmin by James II's electoral agents in 1688, his position was left 'at six and seven' by Sunderland's fall from office in October 1688 and his subsequent flight to the continent.

Mounsteven was perceived as loyal to Sunderland, however, for when it was rumoured that he would return once again to the secretaryship in August 1693, it was assumed that Mounsteven would regain his old office. However, it was under the auspices of Bishop Trelawny that Mounsteven re-entered parliament for West Looe in 1695. He would seem to have been a moderate tory, signing the association in 1696, but opposing the attainder of Sir John Fenwick later that year. He was also 'blacklisted' in 1701 as opposing preparations for war with France and this may have led to his being dropped by Trelawny at the election at the end of that year. Following the accession of Queen Anne, Mounsteven served for four months as a sub-commissioner of prizes at Plymouth, June–September 1702, and was named in 1703 a commissioner for tin revenue in the duchy of Cornwall. He served in that post until his death gaining 'himself considerable wealth and reputation' (Polsue, 1.79).

Mounsteven was returned for West Looe again at the 1705 election, this time as a supporter of the court. There were rumours that he would serve as under-secretary to Sir Charles Hedges, but nothing came of it. On 19 December 1706 he 'cut his throat from ear to ear' at Brown's Coffee House, King's Street, Westminster. Various reasons were suggested for his suicide including the rejection of a marriage proposal to 'a gentlewoman above his degree', or to his imminent discovery as 'a French pensioner' for the past eighteen years (Polsue, 1.79). A verdict of lunacy was brought in, enabling his brother, William, to inherit Lancarfe. He had never married.　　STUART HANDLEY

Sources HoP, Commons, 1690–1715 [draft] · E. Cruickshanks, 'Mounsteven, John', HoP, Commons, 1660–90 · J. Polsue, A complete parochial history of the county of Cornwall, 1 (1867), 79 · J. Maclean, The parochial and family history of the deanery of Trigg Minor in the county of Cornwall, 1 (1873), 216, 300 · IGI · J. C. Sainty, ed., Officials of the secretaries of state, 1660–1782 (1973), 92

Mount, Richard (bap. 1654, d. 1722), nautical publisher, the only son of three known children of Ralph Mount, yeoman, of Chislet, Kent, and his wife, Mary Court, was baptized on 16 November 1654 at Elmsted, Kent, where his parents had been married in January of that year. In 1670 Mount was apprenticed to William Fisher, bookseller and publisher of Postern Row, Tower Hill, London. Fisher's business, founded by his predecessor William Lugger, was in the heart of maritime London, near the river and Trinity House, and already specialized in mathematical and navigational books. In 1677 Fisher extended this by taking a share in The English Pilot, Mediterranean, part of the first comprehensive English maritime atlas begun by John Seller in 1671, and in 1679 went on to acquire rights, copper plates, and printed sheets for some other parts of The English Pilot and Seller's Atlas maritimus.

Mount married William Fisher's daughter Sarah (bap. 1657?, d. 1717) on 3 October 1682 and from 1684, although he was not formally freed of his apprenticeship until 1693, his name began to appear on publications both jointly with Fisher's and on his own account. When Fisher died in 1692 Mount inherited the business. This inheritance from his father-in-law, which included substantial parts of The English Pilot and copyright in a number of successful maritime books, laid the foundations for the control over English nautical publishing which Mount achieved during the next thirty years.

In his first years as proprietor Mount was in his prime and, as well as continuing to trade as a successful general bookseller and stationer, worked energetically to build on the firm's lead in the maritime field. He published James Atkinson's An Epitome of the Art of Navigation, and acquired sole ownership of popular titles in which Fisher had had a share, such as Andrew Wakeley's The Mariner's Compass Rectified, Nathaniel Colson's The Mariner's New Kalendar, and Richard Norwood's Seaman's Practice. The first three of these remained in the firm's list, with numerous editions, over the next hundred years. In 1693 he became the sole distributor of Grenville Collins's Great Britain's Coasting

Pilot, the first English maritime atlas of the English coast. He tried to publish parts of The English Pilot, which was still incomplete and in complicated multiple ownership, but too many of the plates were still owned by others, principally the chartmaker John Thornton, for his efforts to succeed.

About 1700 Mount took a partner, **Thomas Page** (bap. 1680?, d. 1733), nautical publisher, referred to by Mount in his will as 'brother Page'. Both men came from Kent (where a Thomas Page was baptized in St Nicholas's Church, Rochester, on 12 December 1680, the son of Alexander and Mary Page), and there were connections between their families. Page was not among the half-dozen apprentices formally bound to Mount and when he was made free of the Stationers' Company in 1716 was described as Mount's servant. There is no evidence of the nature of Page's contribution to the partnership, and he does not appear to have had a share in the ownership of many of the firm's books, but his arrival marked the beginning of nearly a century of successful association between the families of the two men. After the death of John Thornton's son, Samuel, in 1715, the firm of Mount and Page acquired Thornton's English Pilot plates and stock, which made them sole owners of all parts of the Pilot. They also acquired the plates of Collins's Great Britain's Coasting Pilot and published a new edition just after Mount's death. With these new acquisitions Richard Mount achieved a near monopoly of English nautical publishing for his firm. Mount regularly brought out new titles and the firm now controlled not only the best selling navigation books but also both the only important English maritime atlases. The firm had its own printing works and printed for several naval departments, including the Navy Office, parts of the Royal Naval Hospital, Greenwich, and the transport board, and for Trinity House, a link which was maintained into the twentieth century by Mount's successors. Outside the maritime world its customers included St Thomas's Hospital and the South Sea Company.

Richard Mount died on 29 June 1722 at his home at Postern Row, Tower Hill, London, after a kick in the leg from a carthorse on London Bridge, and was buried at St Katharine by the Tower. He was a respected sober City figure, and had served twice as master of the Stationers' Company and presented a clock to its court room. He was comfortably off and owned several houses near the Postern Row premises and the right to collect tolls for passing through nearby George Yard. A contemporary commented:

> Mr Mount is not only a moderate, but has a natural antipathy to excess: he hates hoarding either money or goods and being a charitable man, he values nothing but the use of it, and has a tender love for truth.　(J. Dunton, The Life and Errors of John Dunton, 1818, 219)

He requested that his funeral should be private, attended only by his close family and the money saved distributed among his less prosperous relations. He had been fortunate in his inheritance but had turned it to good account.

Mount and his wife had three sons: William, the eldest, who succeeded him in the business, Fisher, and John. He left them advice which extolled moderation and good works, and warned them to 'be very cautious of being decoyed by the specious Pretense of Projectors, or of trusting others too far in the Management of any Part of your Estate; and have a care of adventuring on hazardous Undertakings' (appended to *A Sermon Occasioned by Death of Mr Richard Mount*, 1722).

After the deaths of Richard Mount and Thomas Page, who died in London on 15 March 1733, the firm passed through the hands of three more generations of each family, trading under varying combinations of the Mount and Page names. Page was twice married, first, by 1704, to Elizabeth, of whom no more is known other than that she was the mother of at least four of his children. By 1721 she was dead and at some point after this he married Mary Crompton, who survived him with further children. Richard's son William Mount (1688–1769) led the firm for thirty years, most of them in partnership with Page's son, Thomas Page II (1704–1762). They were followed by William's son, John Mount (1725–1786), and Thomas Page III (1730–1781). They were succeeded by their sons, William Mount II (1753–1815) and Thomas Page IV (1756–1797). The families were linked by marriage no fewer than three times during the century, and both grew prosperous and acquired country houses and land. Richard Mount had left them all the advantages of a virtual monopoly of a specialized market, which was expanding fast as the numbers of English ships increased, but although they were commercially successful for fifty years after his death Mount's descendants perhaps paid too much attention to his urging of caution in their undertakings and too little to his example of vigour. The firm did little or nothing to update or add to their new editions of *The English Pilot* or *Great Britain's Coasting Pilot*, and although many books were reprinted regularly the number of new titles gradually dropped. They failed to meet the higher standards expected as navigational knowledge expanded in the second half of the century or compete with the new businesses attracted into both chart and book publishing by the growing market. They gradually lost their share of the nautical market and by 1800 became purely a stationery business. The name Mount disappeared from the firm's title at the same time, though its successors continued to trade as stationers until 1974, under the name Smith and Ebbs.

SUSANNA FISHER

Sources T. R. Adams, 'Mount and Page: publishers of eighteenth-century maritime books', *A potencie of life: books in society*, ed. N. Barker (1993), 145–77 · W. R. Chaplin, 'A seventeenth-century chart publisher: being an account of the present firm of Smith and Ebbs Ltd', *American Neptune*, 8 (1948), 2–24 · S. Tyacke, *London map-sellers, 1660–1720* (1978), 126 · C. Verner, 'Bibliographical note', in J. Seller and C. Price, *The English pilot: the fifth book*, facs. edn (1973) · C. Verner, 'John Seller and the chart trade in seventeenth-century England', *The compleat plattmaker: essays on chart, map, and globe making in England*, ed. N. J. W. Thrower (1978), 127–57 · D. F. McKenzie, ed., *Stationers' Company apprentices*, 3 vols. (1961–78), vols. 2–3 · parish register, St James the Great, Elmsted, Kent [baptism, parents' marriage] · C. Verner, 'Bibliographical note', in W. Fisher and J. Thornton, *The English pilot: the fourth book*, facs. edn (1967) · T. R. Adams, *The non-cartographical maritime works published by Mount and Page* (1985)

Wealth at death over £6000?; left £2000 to third son; senior partner in thriving publishing business and owner of five houses (four freehold, one leasehold) near Tower Hill: will, PRO, PROB 11/586/143

Mount, William (1544/5–1602), master of the Savoy Hospital, was born at Mortlake, Surrey. Educated at Eton College, he was admitted as a scholar to King's College, Cambridge, on 3 October 1563, aged eighteen. He graduated BA in 1567, and having been admitted to a fellowship on 4 October 1566 he resigned it between 25 December 1569 and 25 March 1570. It is known that he had proceeded DTh by 1594, but no record exists of the degree. He became a chaplain to Lord Burghley and may have held the rectory of Leybourne in Kent between 1582 and 1602. He was the author of manuscripts on the techniques of distilling water (preserved in BL, Lansdowne MSS 65, 68) and was complimented by Matthias de L'Obel, a visitor in 1597, on his skill in this field. On 7 February 1594 he was elected to the mastership of the Savoy Hospital, London, in succession to William Absalom; the appointment was confirmed on 27 February. During his tenure the rules which governed the attendance of the master and chaplain of the hospital were relaxed to enable absence for up to eight weeks at once. He died before 6 December 1602, when Richard Neale was elected his successor. It appears that Mount died in debt to the hospital, and that his books and other moveable possessions were taken in payment.

STEPHEN WRIGHT

Sources R. Somerville, *The Savoy: manor, hospital, chapel* (1960) · Venn, *Alum. Cant.*, 1/3.225 · Cooper, *Ath. Cantab.*, 2.271 · *The letters of John Chamberlain*, ed. N. E. McClure, 2 vols. (1939)
Wealth at death very little: Somerville, *The Savoy*, p. 239

Mountagu, John. *See* Montagu, John (1718/19–1795).

Mountague, Frederick William (1800/01–1841). *See under* Mountague, William (1773–1843).

Mountague, Richard (*bap.* 1575, *d.* 1641), bishop of Norwich and religious controversialist, was baptized on 18 November 1575 at St James-the-Less, Dorney, Buckinghamshire, the son of Lawrence Mountague (*d.* 1580), vicar there, and his wife, Joan Rackley or Radcliff (*d.* 1628), from Wycombe in the same county; his parents were married at Dorney on 30 May 1575. The Mountague family by this time was of prosperous yeoman stock and comparatively affluent, owning lands and tenements in three parishes. Richard had one younger brother, William (1579–1625), but only he was to be 'brought up in learning'. Like his cousin William, Mountague was educated at Eton College (1590–94), from where he was elected to a scholarship at King's College, Cambridge, and admitted on 24 August 1594. Admitted a junior fellow in late summer 1597, he graduated BA in 1598 and proceeded MA early in 1602. Mountague was ordained deacon on 6 May 1604 and priest on 16 May by Thomas Dove, bishop of Peterborough. Shortly after his ordination he resigned his fellowship at King's, but returned to proceed BD in 1609.

Mountague was then employed by the provost of Eton, Henry Savile, as an assistant for his Greek edition of the works of Chrysostom; one of the first books issued from the Eton press was his edition of *Sancti Gregorii Nazianzeni in Julianum invectivae duae* (1610). Mountague's intention to edit the works of Basil the Great was never carried out, probably because of some kind of literary deception by the Jesuits (*Correspondence of John Cosin*, 1.58–9). However, there is some evidence that he was responsible for a Greek text based on 'nonnus' for use at Eton.

Probably in the spring of 1608 Mountague was appointed chaplain to Bishop James Montagu of Bath and Wells and the bishop's patronage also accounts for his first preferment, a prebend at Wells Cathedral which he exchanged two years later for a second stall. About 1610 he married Elizabeth Scull (*d.* 1646); the marriage produced several children—Richard (1612–*c.*1646), Elizabeth, who about 1626 married David Stokes, Maria (1617–1641), probably the 'little Mall' of his letters, Lawrence (*b. c.*1620), and Stephen (*b.* 1627). In May 1610 Mountague received the living of Wootton Courtney, Somerset, from Eton, to which he was elected to a fellowship on 29 April 1613.

In May 1613 Mountague was appointed to a royal living, the rectory of Stanford Rivers, Essex. The bounty of James I also landed him a royal chaplaincy about 1615 and the deanery of Hereford in Michaelmas term 1616. A complicated three-way agreement secured the post for which he had been aiming, a canonry at Windsor: Oliver Lloyd was persuaded to yield the canonry in Mountague's favour (he was admitted on 6 September 1617) and Mountague exchanged his deanery for the archdeaconry of Hereford later the same month. Royal patronage again secured for him the rich living of the rectory of Petworth, Sussex, on 8 April 1623. As a royal chaplain Mountague could have retained all his livings, especially since he held a dispensation from the king, but by early July he had resigned the archdeaconry of Hereford, and within the year David Stokes, his future son-in-law, succeeded him in the Eton fellowship. With this Mountague had achieved his goal: his two cures, Petworth and Stanford Rivers, with Windsor supplying the third corner, formed a convenient triangular circuit for regular annual residence in each place.

Early writings and controversy When Isaac Casaubon, the eminent Greek philologist, died in 1614, he had devoted two years or more to a protestant refutation of the ecclesiastical history compiled by Cardinal Baronius. Mountague had also been quietly at work on a similar attack on Baronius before Casaubon's arrival. However, when Casaubon learned of Mountague's manuscript, he strongly protested, claiming that the latter had plagiarized, though he admitted that even if strikingly similar, the two manuscripts were different—'the same argument but by another treatment' (I. Casaubon, *Epistolae*, 1709, 512–13, 617). Upholding Casaubon's claims Archbishop Abbot intervened, ordering Mountague's work to be suppressed, and it was not published until 1622, when by royal command it appeared as *Analecta ecclesiasticarum excertationum*. In 1615 the king ordered Mountague to take up Casaubon's task of refuting Baronius and five years later named him to an official commission to write the ecclesiastical history of England, a task never completed.

Had Mountague finished his history, Thomas Fuller maintained, 'we had had church-annals to put into the balance with those of Baronius; and which would have swayed with them for learning, and weighed them down for truth'. Mountague's works exhibit a thorough knowledge of patristics and an expertise in Greek and Latin, but his intention, shared with other Caroline and tractarian divines, was to vindicate the historical continuity of the Church of England and to defend it against its enemies on both sides—'to stand in the gapp against Puritanisme and Popery, the Scilla and Charybdis of antient piety' (*Correspondence of John Cosin*, 1.21). The presbyterian divine Robert Baillie lamented in 1641 that there was no one 'to vindicate antiquitie from the hands of Baronius and other Papists', or at least, 'Not in such a longsome, fruitless, humanistick way as Casaubon and Montague hes begun' (R. Baillie, *Letters and Journals*, ed. D. Laing, 1841–2, 1.358).

With the publication of his *Diatribae upon the First Part of the 'Late History of Tithes'* in 1621 Mountague engaged with one of the most popular contemporary controversies. *Diatribae*, dedicated to James I, was one among many challenges to try to beat John Selden using his own weapons of classical and philological learning: 'tithes are not claimed originally by any Custome, or Canon, or Lawe; but by a more sufficient warrant and Character of divine right' (R. Mountague, *Diatribae*, 1621, 43). As Selden's *Historie* helped him to gain national recognition, the *Diatribae* established Mountague's name as a man of letters and a formidable caustic opponent, but his next work, the 'very noyse of which', according to John Heigham, was 'inough to awake the geese in the Capitol', provoked a *cause célèbre* that lasted until his death. About April 1622 Mountague found that certain 'Catholique Limitors' had invaded his parish and were trying to convert his flock. After an invitation to meet them was ignored he drew up three propositions, promising to become a Roman Catholic if any one of them could be disproved. These were: first, that the present Roman church was neither the Catholic church nor a sound branch of the Catholic church; second, that the present English church was not a true member of the Catholic church; third, that none of the points maintained by the Roman church against the English was the perpetual doctrine of the Catholic church. Answered in Heigham's *The Gagge of the New Gospell*, he replied with a cutting rejoinder, *A Gagg for the New Gospell? No: a New Gagg for an Old Goose* (1624), in which, of forty-seven propositions equated with English doctrine, only eight or nine were accepted by Mountague as her true doctrine.

The same year Mountague issued his *Immediate addresse unto God alone … revised and inlarged to a just treatise of invocation of saints* (1624). Three years previously, he explained in the dedicatory epistle, he had preached before the king on Psalm 50, verse 15. Among the auditors was Marco Antonio de Dominis, one-time archbishop of Spalato and dean of Windsor, who accused Mountague of advocating the 'ridiculous Romane Doctrine and Practice of Praying unto Saints and Angels, in time of need'. In response Mountague published the much expanded sermon, but it showed a leniency toward Rome that was highly unpopular and his opinion on the saints was to furnish one of the parliamentary charges against him. In 1625 he carried on the philological warfare with the publication in Frankfurt of *Antidiatribae ad priorem pantem diatribarum J. Caesaris Bulenger*. In the meantime answer after answer to the *New Gagg* poured from the press, and the House of Commons, responding to the complaints of two East Anglian clergy, John Yates and Nathaniel Ward, referred the matter to Archbishop Abbot. The king, however, taking matters into his own hands, summoned Mountague and with his judgement, 'if thou be a Papist, I am a Papist', James gave him permission to answer his detractors and countermanded Abbot's suggestions (Gardiner, 46).

Even the death of the old king did not lay the matter to rest. The bishop of Durham, Richard Neile, whose London house was the centre for the most influential Arminian churchmen in royal circles, proved to be Mountague's most unwavering supporter [see Durham House group]. With his urging and approval Mountague published his most 'dangerous and seditious booke', *Appello Caesarem: a Just Appeale from Two Unjust Informers*, early in 1625. With an imprimatur from Francis White, dean of Carlisle, the book went through two editions that year in spite of Abbot's attempts to stop it. In it Mountague angrily declared that he had been traduced for a papist and an Arminian, but he had 'flatly defied and opposed the One; and God in Heaven knoweth that [he] never so much as yet read word in the other' (R. Mountague, 'Epistle Dedicatory' in *Appello Caesarem*, 1625, a 3). The House of Commons took up the charge at once and accused the author of dishonouring the late king, of disturbing the church and state, and of treating disrespectfully the honour and privilege of parliament. A spirited debate on the matter ended with Mountague's being ordered into the custody of the serjeant-at-arms. He was, however, allowed to return to Windsor on giving a bond of £2000 to the serjeant to appear when parliament reassembled. When a delegation from both houses waited upon the king at Hampton Court on 8 July, Charles informed them that Mountague was his servant and a royal chaplain-in-ordinary, and that he had already taken the cause into his own consideration. On the 11th parliament was prorogued. On 2 August, when the parliament was sitting at Oxford, Mountague was too sick to attend, and after an angry debate involving Sir Edward Coke and the solicitor-general, Robert Heath, the matter was temporarily dropped. With the Commons demanding something more than 'words', the question was far too serious to rest for long.

A conference of five bishops headed by Lancelot Andrewes, held by royal command at Winchester House on 16 January 1626, reported to Buckingham that Mountague 'hath not affirmed anything to be the doctrine of the Church of England, but that which in our opinions is the doctrine of the Church of England, or agreeable thereunto' (W. Laud, *Works*, 6.249). Another conference followed on 11 February, this time held 'at the desire of the

Earl of Warwick' in Buckingham's York House, between Bishop Thomas Morton of Lichfield and John Preston, master of Emmanuel College, Cambridge, representing the opposition to Mountague, and Francis White (soon to be bishop of Carlisle) as his defender, reinforced by Bishop John Buckeridge of Rochester and Mountague's close friend John Cosin, archdeacon of the East Riding. Conflicting reports of victory were circulated by both sides but the outcome is best summed up in the alleged words of the earl of Pembroke, 'none returned Arminians thence, save such who repaired thither with the same opinions' (Fuller, *Church-History*, pt 11, 125).

On 11 March 1626 the committee of religion renewed its attack on the *Appello* and the House of Commons voted a petition to the king that the author might be fitly punished 'according to his Demerits ... and that the books aforesaid may be suppressed and burnt' (J. Rushworth, *Historical Collections*, 1, 1659, 212). Mountague only escaped this punishment in the lower house by the dissolution of parliament on 15 June. The next day Charles issued a proclamation making clear his dislike for any new theological opinion and his intention to prevent the 'least' innovation in church or government.

The period after the proclamation was the lowest point in Mountague's career. He chafed at the apparent abandonment of his cause by all the Arminian bishops except Neile, and redoubled his efforts to secure a bishopric. He had earlier complained that he deserved better of the church—'I beate the bush and other catch the birds' (*Correspondence of John Cosin*, 1.98)—but his episcopal ambitions and solicitations were to be frustrated for almost two years. In the interval his case was reopened when parliament was summoned in mid-March 1628 and his name was now linked with a publication of Cosin's, *A Collection of Private Devotions* (1627)—a book branded as 'Popish trash and trumpery'—and the distribution of Roger Manwaring's unpopular sermons justifying the forced loan. However, any further attempt at censure by the committee of religion was cut short by the prorogation of parliament on 26 June.

Bishop of Chichester and of Norwich In the summer of 1628, however, Mountague finally snagged his 'bird': the patronage of Buckingham and the opportune death of the Calvinist Bishop George Carleton of Chichester, who not long before equitably disputed in print the 'unorthodox' opinions of the *Appello*, secured Mountague's appointment to the vacant see. He was elected on 14 July 1628, received a royal dispensation to hold the rectory of Petworth *in commendam* with the bishopric, and on 22 August was confirmed at Bow church. At his confirmation a disaffected London stationer, William Jones, protested loudly before a large crowd that Mountague was unfit for episcopal office but his objections were dismissed as legally inadmissible by Dr Thomas Ryves. On Sunday 24 August (St Bartholomew's day) Mountague was consecrated in the archbishop's chapel at Croydon, where the guests at dinner following the ceremony were greeted with the depressing news of the assassination of Buckingham at Portsmouth. After the new bishop was installed by proxy on 22 September there remained an important, unfinished transaction, the issue of a royal pardon, which after a great deal of haggling was finally concluded on 16 January 1629. The pardon was also extended to Cosin, Robert Sibthorpe, Manwaring, and Thomas Jackson, president of Corpus Christi College, Oxford. The author of the *Gagg* and *Appello* was forgiven all errors or false doctrine in preaching, writing or printing, but the rumours which circulated that in return Mountague had 'recanted' his Arminian tenets and affirmed the articles of the Synod of Dort were clearly exaggerated.

The episcopal appointment drew sharp fire from puritan opponents who felt Mountague deserved rather 'Fire and faggot than further Preferment' (*An Appeale … Against Richard Mountague*, 25). No other promotion was more deeply offensive nor so effectively widened the gap between Charles and parliament, a point which Peter Heylyn noted as 'an Action in the King [which] seemed more magnanious than safe' (Heylyn, 185). A royal declaration imposing silence was followed on 17 January 1629 by a proclamation suppressing *Appello Caesarem*, but this temporary policy of appeasement was not to be accepted. When parliament assembled in January Mountague claimed his seat as a spiritual lord, but his hopes that a rochet would lend protection against further attacks were soon dashed. An emotional speech by Francis Rous in the Commons on 26 January, expressing the mounting fears and suspicions of an organized movement to subvert the established church, led to an order for a thorough investigation by the committee of religion of the growth of popery and the increase of Arminianism. In the debates that followed, Mountague's name figured prominently as a 'principal disturber of the Church', but in the end all the proposals to proceed against him came to nothing, blocked by the king's mounting exasperation and his order to adjourn on 2 March 1629.

Shortly after the dissolution there appeared a scurrilous puritan pamphlet entitled *Anti-Montacutum: an appeale of the orthodox ministers of the Church of England against Richard Mountague*, (1629, re-issued in 1641), appealing to parliament to censure and degrade the new bishop of Chichester and to burn his books as well. An unflattering description noted 'a sinistrall or gotish looke, promising no good to his Church and Children' (*An Appeale … Against Richard Mountague*, 30). While much of it dealt with his conflict with parliament, an unflattering addition was the portrait of an 'Arminian or meere Mountaguist': he is a 'mungrell Divine' whose religion is 'like a Confection, compounded of many, the least ingredient being Protestantisme' (ibid., 38, misnumbered 36).

Within a fortnight of his installation Mountague had taken up his residence in Chichester and begun his first visitation. He soon discovered that he had no effective control over his own cathedral city, where jurisdiction was exercised by the elderly dean. Sussex congregations may have anticipated an Arminian inquisition, but his first visitation articles were neither lengthy nor excessively inquisitive, although their tenor was decidedly more anti-puritan than anti-papist. Few cases from the diocese were brought before the court of high commission: one concerned an angry squabble over the placement of the altar at St Michael's, Lewes. Mountague's incomplete excommunication book (1631–8) lists only names with no causes attached, but only two clerical deprivations are known to have occurred during his episcopate and one was a case of simony. Mountague seems to have followed a moderate policy towards puritan clergy and his report to Laud in 1634 noted only difficulties in the eastern archdeaconry with puritan justices of the peace, monotonously reporting *omnia bene* despite evidence of a restrained undercurrent of puritanism. Against popish recusants he refused to take harsh measures, a tolerant policy set out in his tract, 'Certaine Considerations touching Recusancy' (CUL, Gg 1/29 98v–103v).

Mountague's considerable patronage followed the principle 'To the Arminians belong the spoils'. The better Sussex preferments were bestowed on clergy loyal to Laudian reform. Chief among them was Mountague's brother-in-law, John Scull, who held in succession two prebends, four vicarages, three rectories, and the chancellorship of the cathedral. While this policy did little to alleviate the long-standing problem of pluralism and non-residence, Mountague had some success in reversing the leasing policy of his predecessors, through raising rents to equitable levels and in refusing to lease properties for three lives. However, his attempts to recover the eight manors out of thirteen appropriated under law (I Eliz. c. 19) by Queen Elizabeth ended in failure. He lost the chief test case relating to Selsey manor which was argued in common pleas in Easter term 1634 and his protracted litigation to regain former episcopal properties in Chancery Lane, London, including Lincoln's Inn, was also unsuccessful.

Despite his constant complaints about the impoverishment of the see, Mountague lived in a comfortable but not imposing style with his family, residing in the rambling palace at Chichester during the winter months and moving to Aldingbourne Manor in the summer. His accounts for 1636–8 show that he spent a good portion of income on restoring Aldingbourne and on maintaining the large town dwelling next to the cathedral. There are also numerous personal items for his wife and children. As he told his close friend, Lord Dorchester, in 1629, he was 'resolved never to make any lease of the Bishopriq to my wife or children … for reasons known to my self' (PRO, state papers domestic, 16/153/73). However, when he was later translated to Norwich the policy was thrown aside: in 1640 he leased the valuable manor of Ludham to his son Richard for a nominal rent. That Mountague seems to have accumulated little or no estate with which to provide for his family is the probable explanation for this reversal of policy.

While Mountague was regarded as Archbishop Laud's confidant, there is little evidence of any close bond of friendship between them: they were simply allies, united in a mutual concern for the church. He was on much closer terms with Laud's onetime ally, Sir Francis Winde-bank, secretary of state, another enthusiastic, if unrealistic, advocate of reunion with the Roman church. Mountague, in spite of criticism based on his writings and recusant contacts that he was a 'Romanizer', held hopes for some sort of a rapprochement with Rome, even an ecumenical conference, and was apparently the first Church of England bishop to hold lengthy conversations with the accredited papal agent, Gregorio Panzani, who was in London between 1634 and 1636. Laud coldly rejected any contacts with papal emissaries and in the end had to take the blame for the clandestine Romanizing. It became clear to Panzani that Mountague was building 'dream castles in the air', particularly after he himself made clear that there could be no concessions from Rome (PRO, 31/9/17). With the arrival of Panzani's successor, George Con, discussions about reunion came to a halt. Mountague was himself aware of the theological differences, but adamantly insisted that the Church of England was an autonomous branch of the Catholic church and his orders valid. However the private dispatches between Rome and London bluntly referred to Mountague only as the 'pseudo-bishop' of Chichester.

Contrary to most public opinion Mountague believed that the pope was an Antichrist but not the Antichrist. Consequently he sent his son Richard to travel abroad with his tutor for three years on a tour that included stops in Rome in 1637. Mountague's dogged belief in the English church's catholicity is evident in his family's religious life. His domestic chaplain, Richard Mileson (who after the bishop's death converted to Rome, becoming a Jesuit in 1643), 'frequently heard the confessions of sixty men and women, among whom was the Bishop's wife' (H. Foley, *Records of the … Society of Jesus*, 8 vols., 1875–83, 7.509). The news of Mountague's activities and opinions were to prove damaging in the hands of William Prynne (*Hidden Workes of Darkness*, 147), but nevertheless, with other Caroline divines, he made a noteworthy contribution to the breakdown of hostility between Roman Catholics and Anglicans and to paving the way to eirenic discussions with Gallican churchmen and with foreign protestants in the eighteenth century. He continued to produce patristical and historical tomes. He was responsible for the second part of *Eusebiou tou Pamphiliou episkopos tes en Palaistine kaisareias apo-deixeos Biblia deka* (Paris, 1628). His *Apparatus ad origines ecclesiasticas* was printed in 1635 with an expanded edition in English (1642) and the first part of his major work *De originibus ecclesiasticis commentationum* was published in 1636 followed by the second in 1640 under the title *Theanthropikon*.

By the end of March 1638 Mountague knew that he was to be translated to the sprawling diocese of Norwich, replacing Matthew Wren, who moved to Ely. The dean and chapter obediently elected him on 4 May and the formalities, completed at St Mary-le-Bow on 12 May, passed by quietly with no repetition of the awkward incident ten years earlier. The size of the diocese of Norwich, the largest in England, had been no obstacle to the determined Wren, an inflexible disciplinarian who had silenced over

fifty clergymen. Mountague's first visitation articles display a radical change in length and content, and he inquired assiduously into every aspect of parish life, including the much-hated practice of receiving at the rail. His attempt to moderate this was strongly opposed by Laud, the king, and Wren. Unlike his predecessor, Mountague was only responsible for five clerical deprivations, including that of the eminent puritan Edmund Calamy. In contrast to Wren he was a model of moderation, described as one who was 'good-indifferent and indulgent in those points [of ceremonies]'. In 1639 his report to Laud emphasized that his diocese was 'as quiet, uniform and conformable, as any in the Kingdom, if not more' (W. Laud, *Works*, 5.364). Within ten months, however, there was increasing disorder and unrest, including pulling down altar rails at Sudbury and Ipswich.

Mountague was beginning to wear out with the infirmities of old age. Gout and stone had taken their toll before he contracted a severe quartan ague in 1632. The duties of a very large diocese added to his worries, so that 'being very weake', he did not appear at the Long Parliament in November 1640. The House of Commons had received a spate of complaints against Wren but Mountague was not attacked until 23 February by a petition from Norwich (*Diurnall Occurrences*, 42). Mountague died at Norwich on 13 April 1641, 'sickness, troublesome times, and then death surprising him' (Fuller, *Worthies*, 44), and was buried on 15 April in the choir before the high altar of the cathedral under a slab bearing the plain inscription 'Depositum Montacutii Episcopi'.

Reputation The stylized portrait of Mountague in the memorial window at Chichester Cathedral bears the legend 'Champion of the English Church'. The artist's representation has little resemblance to the unflattering pen-portrait by a contemporary Anglican divine: 'a meagre face, his chaps as thin as two pieces of parchment, squint-eyed, a black eyebrow; but an eager student' (A. Clark, 'Dr Plume's pocket-book', *Essex Review*, 14, 1905, 23). An added phrase—that Mountague was a 'sharp witt' who 'would be barking at everybody'—is a more exact summary of his disputatious career. As a scholarly and caustic apologist for the Anglican middle path Mountague persisted with a brash defence of the catholicity of the Church of England and a denial that Calvinism could be equated with her doctrine which embroiled him in bitter theological controversy. Briefly he even lent his name to the anti-Calvinist party in England and 'Mountagutian' was used instead of the epithet 'Arminian' (T. Birch, *Court and Times of Charles I*, 1849, 105; *An Appeale … Against Richard Mountague*, 38, misnumbered 36).

Mountague's writings later proved a source for theological ammunition for Oxford Movement luminaries such as Edward Pusey and the lesser known Frederick Oakley. Mountague's erudite, at times cumbrous, scholarship also added lustre to England's growing reputation for patristic studies: he was the first to edit *Photii sanctissimi patriarchae … epistolae*, published a decade after his death in parallel columns of Greek and translated by him into Latin. Fuller's comment that he was 'much skilled in the

Fathers, and Ecclesiastical Antiquity, and in the Latin and Greek Tongues' (L. H. Carlson, 'A history of the Presbyterian party', *Church History*, 11, 1942, 119) was shared by John Selden and Henry Savile. His extensive, if impartial, use of sarcasm was also described by Fuller. Mountague himself excused his vitriolic tongue—'Gall and vinegar are corrosive, but must sometimes be used' (*Appello Caesarem*, 43)—and in spite of it he was one of the most effective propagandists that the Arminian party had, because he had principles backed by courage.

The inheritance which Mountague left his family was largely his scholarly reputation. According to the antiquary Thomas Birch, the bishop died 'very poor … the result of his great Charge in maintaining Scholars beyond of seas to procure him Ms' (BL, Add. MS 4223, fol. 40). Sir Thomas Browne, who practised medicine in Norwich, related that Mountague 'left an excellent Library of bookes, and heapes of paper fayrly writt with his own hand, concerning the ecclesiasticall history. His bookes were sent to London, and as it was sayd, his papers against Baronius & others unto Rome, from whence they never returned' (T. Browne, *Miscellaneous Writings*, ed. G. Keynes, 1946, 154).   JOHN S. MACAULEY

Sources *The correspondence of John Cosin D.D., lord bishop of Durham*, ed. [G. Ornsby], 1, SurtS, 52 (1869) · J. S. Macauley, 'Richard Mountague: Caroline bishop, 1575–1641', PhD diss., U. Cam., 1964 · corresp. of Gregorio Panzani, PRO, 31/9/17 · T. Fuller, *The worthies of England*, ed. J. Freeman, abridged edn (1952) · S. R. Gardiner, ed., *Debates in the House of Commons in 1625*, CS, new ser., 6 (1873) · W. D. Peckham, ed., *The acts of the dean and chapter of the cathedral church of Chichester, 1545–1642*, Sussex RS, 58 (1959) · W. Notestein and F. H. Relf, eds., *Commons debates for 1629* (1921) · W. D. Peckham, 'The acts of Bishop Montague', *Sussex Archaeological Collections*, 86 (1947), 141–54 · F. W. Steer, 'Bishop Montague's personal accounts', *Sussex Archaeological Collections*, 95 (1957), 28–41 · Venn, *Alum. Cant.* · S. Bond, ed., *The chapter acts of the dean and canons of Windsor: 1430, 1523–1672* (1966) · M. Pattison, *Isaac Casaubon, 1559–1614* (1875) · *An appeale of the orthodox ministers of the Church of England against Richard Mountague* (1641) · 'Register of Watson, Andrewes and Mountague', Diocesan RO, Chichester, Ep.I/1/8a · T. Fuller, *The church-history of Britain*, 11 pts in 1 (1655) · P. Heylyn, *Cyprianus Anglicus* (1671) · *Diurnall occurrences … in this great and happy parliament from the third of November, 1640, to the third of November, 1641* (1641) · T. Birch collection, BL, Add. MS 4223, fol. 40 · A. Milton, *Catholic and Reformed: the Roman and protestant churches in English protestant thought, 1600–1640* (1995) · parish register (baptisms), Dorney, Buckinghamshire, 18 Nov 1575 · W. Sterry, ed., *The Eton College register, 1441–1698* (1943) · will, PRO, PROB 11/188, sig. 17 [John Scull] · BL, Harleian MS 7047, fol. 115
Archives Episcopal Library, Durham, Mickleton MSS, letters of Mountague · LPL, Laudian MSS
Likenesses memorial window, Chichester Cathedral
Wealth at death died very poor: T. Birch collection, BL Add. MS 4223, fol. 40; T. Browne, *The miscellaneous writings*, ed. G. Keynes (1946), p. 154

Mountague, William (1773–1843), architect and surveyor, was baptized on 16 May 1773 at St Luke's, Old Street, Finsbury, London, the son of William Mountague (*d.* 1791), City official, and his wife, Sarah. He was a pupil of George Dance the younger, surveyor to the City of London, and worked for him as a clerk for many years. He became district surveyor for the west division of the City in 1808, and surveyor to the City improvement committee in 1812. In

1814 he became Dance's assistant, as assistant clerk of works to the City of London, and was responsible for the completion of Finsbury Circus in 1815. Mountague succeeded Dance as City surveyor in 1816.

As City surveyor, Mountague designed the courts of common pleas and the king's bench at the Guildhall (1823), Farringdon market (1828–9), the City Library (1828), the Gothic panelling under the window at the east end of the Guildhall (1838), and the new ceiling over the ballroom of the Mansion House (1842).

Mountague was elected a fellow of the Institute of British Architects in 1834. He retired in 1839, and died on 12 April 1843. He was buried in the Bunhill Fields burial-ground.

Frederick William Mountague (1800/01–1841), architect and surveyor, was William Mountague's only son and chief assistant. He worked as a surveyor on many improvements in London, and also had a large private practice. He became an associate of the Institute of British Architects in 1835 (retired 1839). While working on a survey on the estate of the duke of Buckingham he was thrown from his gig and died on 2 December 1841.

ANNE PIMLOTT BAKER

Sources Colvin, *Archs.* · D. Strand, *George Dance: architect, 1741–1825* (1971) · *Dir. Brit. archs.* · IGI
Archives RIBA, nomination papers | Hunt. L., letters to Grenville family

Mountain, Armine Simcoe Henry (1797–1854), army officer, fifth son of Dr Jacob *Mountain (1749–1825), of Huguenot descent, first Anglican bishop of Quebec, and his wife, Elizabeth Mildred Wale (*d.* 1836), daughter of John Kentish of Little Bardfield Hall, near Dunmow, Essex, was born at St Louis Street, Quebec, on 4 February 1797. After about three years under a tutor, the Revd T. Monro, rector of Little Easton, Essex, in England, he returned in 1810 to Canada, where he studied under his eldest brother, George Jehoshaphat *Mountain (1789–1863), sometime bishop of Montreal and Quebec, until commissioned ensign in the 96th regiment on 20 July 1815. In November he joined the regiment in Ireland, and there made friends with the bishop of Meath, Thomas Lewis O'Beirne, and with Maria Edgeworth. Edgeworth wrote of him: 'If you were to cut Armine Mountain into a hundred pieces, every one of them would be a gentleman' (Mountain, 8).

In the summer of 1817 Mountain went to Brunswick and studied languages, military drawing, and mathematics at the college there until, on 3 December 1818, he was promoted lieutenant on half pay. The following year he returned to England to see his parents, who were on a visit from Canada. During the next four years he travelled through Germany, France, Switzerland, and Italy with his friend John Angerstein, becoming an accomplished linguist. On his return, through his interest with the duke of York, he was brought into the 52nd light infantry, and after spending a few months in England joined his regiment at Halifax, Nova Scotia, in the autumn of 1823. In 1824 he went on detachment duty to New Brunswick and Prince Edward Island, and in the spring of 1825 was hastily summoned to Quebec to see his father, but the bishop died some days before he arrived. Mountain brought his mother and sister to England in October. He purchased a company in the 76th regiment and was gazetted captain on 26 May 1825. In the spring of 1826 he joined the regiment in Jersey, where he won the friendship of the governor, Sir Colin Halkett, through whose influence and that of Sir Astley Cooper he obtained an unattached majority on 30 December 1826.

For the next two years Mountain was unemployed, and lived with his mother at Hemel Hempstead, Hertfordshire, amusing himself by translating some of Schiller's poems and writing the life of the emperor Adrian for the *Encyclopædia Metropolitana*. In December 1828, through the influence of his friend Lord Dalhousie, he was brought into the 26th (Cameronian) regiment, then stationed at Madras, as regimental major, and in the following May he sailed for India. He arrived at Fort George in September and remained in Madras until autumn 1830, when the regiment marched to Meerut, arriving in March 1831. Mountain visited Dalhousie, then commander-in-chief in India, at Simla in July, and in October marched with him back to Meerut. While visiting Lord William Bentinck, the governor-general, at Delhi, Mountain accepted from his old friend Halkett, who had just been appointed commander-in-chief at Bombay, the appointment on his staff of military secretary, and arrived in Bombay on 21 March 1832. Owing to differences with the governor, Lord Clare, Halkett was recalled towards the end of 1833, and Bentinck, appreciating the discretion with which Mountain had acted, appointed him one of his aides-de-camp. In August 1834 he obtained leave to join a force assembled at Meerut to march to Shekhawati under General Stevenson, and rejoined the governor-general at Calcutta at the end of December, after a journey of nearly 4000 miles. In March 1835 he left for England with Lord William, and spent the next two years at home. In July 1836 he declined the post of military secretary to Sir Samford Whittingham in the West Indies. In February 1838 he rejoined the Cameronians at Fort William, Calcutta.

In 1840 the First Anglo-Chinese War broke out, and Mountain was appointed deputy adjutant-general to the land forces sent from India, first under the command of Colonel Burrell and afterwards under Sir Hugh Gough. He was present at all the chief engagements, including the capture of Tinghai (Dinghai) (5 July), the capture of the Bogue (Humen) forts (26 February 1841), the attack on, and capitulation of, Canton (Guangzhou) (25 May), the capture of Amoy (Xiamen) (26 August), the occupation of Chushan (1 October), the capture of Chinhai (Zhenhai) (10 October), the capture of Ningpo (Ningbo) (13 October), the attack on Chapu (Zhapu) (18 May 1842), the capture of Shanghai (19 June), the capture of Chinkiang (Zhenjiang) (21 July), and the demonstration before Nanking (Nanjing) in August which led to the treaty of peace. At the attack on Chapu, while making a gallant rush into a large building which was being vigorously defended by the enemy, Mountain was struck by three musket balls. He was made a CB.

From China, Mountain returned to India early in 1843, took command of his regiment, and brought it to England, arriving in June. For the next four years he commanded the regiment at various stations in the United Kingdom. He was much concerned with the spiritual and material welfare of his men and their families, establishing a Sunday school and encouraging the use of the regimental reading-room. He also repressed extravagance among the young officers. In June 1845 he received his promotion to colonel in the army on being appointed aide-de-camp to the queen for his services in China. Mountain was twice married—first, in June 1837, to Jane O'Beirne (*d.* 1838), granddaughter of Thomas Lewis O'Beirne, bishop of Meath; they had one daughter who died in 1840. In February 1845 he married Charlotte Anna, eldest daughter of Colonel T. Dundas of Carron Hall, Fingask; she survived him and married Sir John Henry Lefroy.

In August 1847 Lord Dalhousie, then governor-general of India, gave Mountain the appointment of military secretary, and he arrived in India in January 1848, having exchanged into the 29th regiment. After the murder of Anderson and Vans Agnew at Multan, Mountain obtained leave to join his regiment to take part in the Second Anglo-Sikh War under his old chief, Lord Gough. He was made a brigadier-general, and his brigade was composed of his own regiment and the 13th and 30th native infantry. On the death of Colonel Cureton the post of adjutant-general was accepted by Mountain on the condition that he should retain his brigade until the approval of his nomination arrived from home. He took a prominent part in the battle of Chilianwala on 13 January 1849, in which his brigade suffered heavy casualties, and was praised in Gough's dispatch. He also took part in the battle of Gujrat on 21 February, and was afterwards appointed to command the Bengal division of the force under Sir Walter Gilbert to pursue the Sikhs. On the march, near Jhelum, his left hand was seriously injured by a pistol in his holster, which accidentally fired as he was mounting his horse. The accident obliged him to give up his divisional command, and on the arrival of the confirmation of his appointment as adjutant-general he went to Simla in March 1849 to take up his duties.

In the winter of 1849–50 Mountain accompanied Sir Charles Napier, the commander-in-chief, to Peshawar. In November 1850 he met Sir William Gomm, the new commander-in-chief, at Agra, and although Mountain had been ailing since he had recovered from an attack of cholera he was able to go into camp with Gomm. During the summer of 1852 Mountain's health was bad. In November he again went into camp with the commander-in-chief, but at the end of January, after leaving Cawnpore, he became very ill and died of fever at Fatehgarh after a few days' illness, attended by his wife, on 8 February 1854, in a house belonging to Maharaja Duleep Singh, who, with the commander-in-chief, the headquarters' staff, and all the troops, attended the funeral; a monument was placed in the cemetery at Fatehgarh, and a memorial brass tablet in Simla church. R. H. VETCH, *rev.* ROGER T. STEARN

Sources PRO, War Office records · A. S. H. Mountain, *Memoirs and letters of the late Colonel Armine S. H. Mountain*, ed. Mrs A. S. H. Mountain (1857) · dispatches, *LondG* (1840–49) · E. Holt, *The opium wars in China* (1964) · C. Hibbert, *The dragon wakes: China and the West, 1793–1911* (1970) · H. C. B. Cook, *The Sikh wars: the British army in the Punjab, 1845–1849* (1975) · B. Bond, ed., *Victorian military campaigns* (1967) · Boase, *Mod. Eng. biog.* · *GM*, 2nd ser., 41 (1854)
Archives NL Scot., letters to Sir George Brown
Likenesses engraving (after drawing by R. J. Lane), repro. in Mountain, ed., *Memoirs and letters*, frontispiece

Mountain, Sir Edward Mortimer, first baronet (1872–1948), underwriter and insurance company manager, was born on 24 November 1872, the second son of Stanford Henry Mountain, a Southwark hop merchant, and his wife, Louisa, daughter of George Eve. Mountain was educated at Dulwich College, then joined a Lloyd's insurance broker's office. His father died in 1890, leaving an estate of £18,653. In 1897 Mountain married Evelyn Ellen Regina (d. 1950), daughter of August Siegle, a bookseller. Together with others, including his elder brother Henry, Mountain soon established his own broking firm, Hawley Mountain & Co., which in 1902 merged to form Gardner Mountain, specializing in Scandinavian hull risks. In 1904, when the firm took over the marine account of British Dominions to form British Dominions Marine Insurance Company, Mountain became its first managing director. This provided him with the base from which to launch a brilliant career as a manager and underwriter. By 1913 British Dominions had become one of Britain's largest marine insurance companies. Famed for being the one prominent underwriter who had declined the *Titanic*, Mountain also played a leading role in reducing competition in the market. In 1910 he became the first chairman of the Joint-Hull Committee, which brought together Lloyd's and the company underwriters to negotiate marine rates and policy terms. In 1920, when he retired from the committee, he was honoured as the first company underwriter to be elected a member of Lloyd's.

From an early date Mountain diversified, transforming his company into one of Britain's greatest general insurers. Fire and motor underwriting were begun in 1911. The profitability of wartime marine insurance and the rising equity values allowed Mountain to purchase three life-assurance offices—Eagle, Sceptre, and Star—within ten months in 1916–17. The combined company was renamed Eagle, Star and British Dominions. In 1921 the old connection was severed when Mountain sold his interest in Gardner Mountain. Diversification offset the post-war decline in marine insurance, and was also a way of attracting talented managers. In 1916 a new 'all-in' policy was successfully launched, the first to offer householders comprehensive cover against almost all domestic hazards for one premium with the minimum of conditions. This required innovative advertising and extensive marketing, both of which became hallmarks of Eagle Star.

Between the wars Mountain also established connections with several finance houses, notably Philip Hill & Partners, of which he became chairman after the death of Philip Hill in 1944. Several major schemes financed property and industrial companies, including the Odeon cinema chain and the development of the Covent Garden area of London in 1933. Through these associations Mountain also joined the boards of a large number of companies, notably United Drapery Stores and Mosul Oilfields.

Mountain combined the skills of a broker and underwriter with the managerial ability of a company chief executive. At his regular morning meetings, he expected his senior staff to be fully briefed to answer his questions. He was a small man with great authority and exuberance, which extended to a range of outside interests. He appreciated paintings and built up a fine collection of old masters and modern works. He owned properties in Somerset, Perthshire, the Isle of Wight, Surrey, and London, and his country gardens and conservatories produced some of the finest orchid shows in England. From his youth he bred homing pigeons. He owned several yachts, enjoyed golf and shooting, and was a keen angler on stretches of the Tay which he owned near his home at Dunkeld. In his later years, despite being confined by illness to a wheelchair, he continued to go salmon fishing until the day before his death. In 1934 he organized a watch for the Loch Ness monster. He was knighted in 1918 and created a baronet in 1922. He died on 22 June 1948 at Dunkeld House, Perthshire, and was cremated in a private ceremony; his ashes were buried at Stoke Poges in Buckinghamshire. He was survived by his wife and their son, Brian Edward Stanley (1899–1977), who became general manager of Eagle Star in 1947.   ROBIN PEARSON

Sources O. M. Westall, 'Mountain, Sir Edward Mortimer', *DBB* · *The Times* (24 June 1948) · *The Times* (25 June 1948) · *The Times* (28 June 1948) · *Post Magazine and Insurance Monitor* (3 July 1948), 652–3 · *Lloyd's List and Shipping Gazette* (24 June 1948) · *WWW*, 1941–50 · private information (2004) · S. D. Chapman, 'Hogg Robinson: the rise of a Lloyd's broker', *The historian and the business of insurance*, ed. O. M. Westall (1984), 173–89 · *Post Magazine and Insurance Monitor* (1 Jan 1916), 12 · *The Times* (30 June 1948) · *The Times* (11 Aug 1948) · museum brochure, Eagle Star Group Archives, Cheltenham
Archives Eagle Star Group, Cheltenham, related artefacts and MSS | FILM Eagle Star Group Archives, Cheltenham, *The magic scroll* (1930)
Likenesses A. E. Cooper, portrait, 1948, Eagle Star, William Kent House, Arlington Street, London
Wealth at death £582,824 7s. 3d.: probate, 3 Aug 1948, *CGPLA Eng. & Wales*

Mountain [Montaigne], **George** (1569–1628), archbishop of York, was born at Cawood, Yorkshire, the son of Thomas Montaigne or Mountain of Wistow in the same county. He matriculated as a sizar at Queens' College, Cambridge, in Michaelmas term 1586 and graduated BA in 1590. Elected a fellow in 1591, he was admitted in July 1592; he was ordained deacon and priest by Bishop Howland at Peterborough on 28 June 1593 and the same year he proceeded MA.

Mountain first rose to prominence as chaplain to the earl of Essex, with whom he went on the expedition to Cadiz in 1596, when, according to Thomas Fuller, he showed 'such personal valour that out of his gown he

George Mountain [Montaigne] (**1569–1628**), by George Yate,
*c.*1622

While dean of Westminster he officiated at the burials of
Prince Henry and Arabella Stuart and at the reburial of
Mary, queen of Scots, whose body had been escorted from
Peterborough by Richard Neile in 1612. Robert Carr, earl of
Somerset, resided in Mountain's custody for a short spell
between October and November 1615, before moving to
the Tower. It has to be said, however, that Mountain's tenure as dean of Westminster was not terribly auspicious, he
having been described by one historian of the abbey as
'something of a buffoon' (T. Hart in E. Carpenter, ed., *A
House of Kings: the History of Westminster Abbey*, 1966) and
censured by another for getting the famous school into
debt.

Mountain succeeded Richard Neile again, this time as
bishop of Lincoln in 1617, at which point he relinquished
the mastership of the Savoy. His friend Marc Antonio de
Dominis, archbishop of Spalato, assisted in his consecration on 14 December, but five years later Mountain
assisted Neile and John Young, dean of Winchester, in sentencing the archbishop to be banished from the realm.
Mountain's career blossomed as a minor favourite of
James I: he preached regularly at court and in 1619 was
appointed lord high almoner—and entertained the king
at his episcopal manor at Buckden, Huntingdonshire. It
may be from this feast that Mountain earned John Milton's scathing depiction as a 'canary-sucking and swan-
eating prelate' (E. Venables and G. Perry, *Lincoln*, Diocesan
Histories, 1897, 276). Yet everything did not always go
smoothly in his relations with King James, for apparently
he had to curtail one rather long and tedious sermon
given at court at Christmas 1622, possibly the only bishop
ever to have been so interrupted by James I. Mountain's
visitation articles for 1618 survive, as do those for 1621,
1624, and 1627 for London, but he did not publish any of
his sermons.

By 1621, when he was translated to the important bishopric of London, Mountain had clearly thrown in his lot
with the Arminians, a group within the church now rising
to some prominence under the leadership of Lancelot
Andrewes and Richard Neile. On 11 November he presided
over the consecration to the bishopric of Lincoln of John
Williams, dean of Westminster, having sided with Williams and William Laud, then bishop of St David's, against
Archbishop George Abbot, temporarily in disgrace for the
manslaughter of a gamekeeper. As bishop of London,
Mountain used his position as one of the licensers of publications to assist the Arminian cause. Most notably he
was associated with the publication of Richard
Mountague's *Appello Caesarem* early in 1625, John Cosin's
Collection of Private Devotions in 1627, and in the same year,
most controversially, the publication of the sermons of
Robert Sibthorpe and Roger Mainwaring which backed
the forced loan. In London he preached the doctrine of
passive obedience and was commended by Charles I for
permitting the erection and adoration of images in churches, and for suppressing popular lay lectures. There are
hints, however, that Mountain's generally negligent manner permitted some notable nonconformists, such as

would turn his back to no man' (Fuller, *Worthies*, 199).
Returning to Cambridge he was junior proctor of the university in 1600–01. In 1602 he proceeded BD and was
appointed by the crown rector of Great Cressingham, Norfolk, which he served until 1610, enjoying a dispensation
to hold a living so far from Cambridge while still serving
as a college fellow. Mountain first preached at court in
1603, having, on the disgrace of his patron Essex, successfully transferred his allegiance to the earl of Salisbury.
Possibly through the earl's influence he was given the rectory of Aspeden, Hertfordshire, in 1607. That year he proceeded DD and became professor of divinity at Gresham
College, a position he held until 1610. In 1608, probably
through Salisbury again, he was made master of the Savoy
and a chaplain to James I. He subsequently received a living at Cheam, Surrey, in the gift of St John's College,
Oxford, but real promotion came with the deanery of
Westminster in 1610. Three years later he was granted a
coat of arms.

Mountain was disappointed in one desire, namely to
become president of his own college of Queens', to which
he gave some plate in 1614. That June he was made one of
the first governors of the new Charterhouse Hospital.

Thomas Hooker and Thomas Shepard, to preach unrestrained, only to be silenced when Laud succeeded Mountain in London. While bishop of London, Mountain was one of the most active bishops who sat in the court of delegates. He consecrated the new chapel at Lincoln's Inn in 1623, strove with others to draw attention to the plight of St Paul's Cathedral, and was vehement in his defence of the divine right of kings when he preached on the occasion of the burning of the book on resistance by the palatine divine Paraeus at Paul's Cross in 1622. Yet despite his interest in gaining observance of due ceremony in churches, on which matters he issued special orders, Mountain was not one of the Arminian inner circle, and was described by Peter Heylyn as 'a man unactive' and 'one that loved his own ease too well to disturb himself in the concernments of the church' (Heylyn, 174).

Following Neile's translation to Winchester in 1627, Mountain again succeeded him and was elected on 15 February 1628 to Durham, on this occasion not as promotion, but in order to make way for Laud at London. Mountain himself viewed the move as 'the worst kind of banishment, next neighbour to a civil death' (Heylyn, 175). He had scarcely moved from London House in the city to Durham House in the Strand when York fell vacant by the long-awaited death of Toby Matthew in March 1628. According to one story, some witty remarks to the king that he should build upon this 'mountain' were said to have secured him the archbishopric. Yet this does not accord well with Heylyn's résumé, and the appointment may have been made in haste as the Arminians sought a safe candidate for York. Their problems grew worse, for Mountain was elected in July 1628, but died in London on 24 October on the very day that he was enthroned by commission at York. By his own desire he was buried in Cawood church, where his brother Isaac put up a monument to him, with a Latin inscription and verses by the poet Hugh Holland. By his will dated February 1627 Mountain bequeathed the bulk of his property to his brother, £100 to the poor of Cawood, and rings to four young girls.

Mountain was a colourful character who was typical of Jacobean bishops, not only for commonly acknowledged faults, but also for his virtues in his spasmodic efforts to be a preaching bishop, administer his dioceses diligently, and his general concern for education. He founded two scholarships at Queens' College, Cambridge, and his benevolence to the poor was noteworthy. It has to be said, however, that he was definitely one of those who should be classified as a 'court bishop', one who restricted his appearances in his dioceses to the summer months.

ANDREW FOSTER

Sources Venn, *Alum. Cant.* · J. Le Neve, *The lives, characters, … and … benefactions of the protestant bishops* (1790), 1.117 · P. Heylyn, *Cyprianus Anglicus* (1668) · R. Newcourt, *Repertorium ecclesiasticum parochiale Londinense*, 1 (1708), 29–30 · *CSP dom.*, 1603–28 · R. Surtees, *The history and antiquities of the county palatine of Durham*, 1 (1816), xc · PRO, DEL/80/70 · F. B. Williams, *Index of dedications and commendatory verses in English books before 1641* (1962) · K. Fincham, *Prelate as pastor: the episcopate of James I* (1990) · N. Tyacke, *Anti-Calvinists: the rise of English Arminianism, c.1590–1640* (1987) · A. Milton, *Catholic and Reformed: the Roman and protestant churches in English protestant thought, 1600–1640* (1995) · J. Davies, *The Caroline captivity of the church: Charles I and the remoulding of Anglicanism, 1625–1641* (1992) · P. E. McCullough, *Sermons at court: politics and religion in Elizabethan and Jacobean preaching* (1998) [incl. CD-ROM] · J. Sargeaunt, *Annals of Westminster School* (1898) · Fuller, *Worthies* (1662)
Likenesses G. Yate, line engraving, c.1622, BM, NPG [see illus.] · bust on monument, 1628, All Saints' Church, Cawood, North Yorkshire · oils, 19th cent. (after portrait, 1622), Bishopthorpe, York · portrait (after portrait, 1622), bishop's palace, Chichester

Mountain, George Jehoshaphat (1789–1863), bishop of Quebec, second son of Jacob *Mountain (1749–1825) and his wife, Elizabeth Mildred Wale Kentish (d. 1836), was born in Norwich on 27 July 1789, and was brought up in Quebec, whither the family moved in 1793 when Jacob Mountain became first bishop of Quebec. Armine Simcoe Henry *Mountain was his younger brother. George was privately tutored with his brother Jacob by the Revd Matthew Fielde in Canada and, on coming to England in 1805, by the Revd T. Monro. The brothers matriculated from Trinity College, Cambridge, George Mountain graduating BA in 1810 and DD in 1819. He moved again to Canada in 1811, and, becoming secretary to his father, was ordained deacon in 1812 and priest in 1816, at the same time being appointed evening lecturer in Quebec Cathedral. He did sentry duty on the walls of Quebec city during the 1812 war with the United States. He was rector of Fredericton, New Brunswick, from 1814 to 1817, when he returned to Quebec as rector of that parish and bishop's official. In August 1814 he married Mary Hume Thomson of Quebec city. In 1821 he became archdeacon of Lower Canada. Mountain played an important part in educational development, and in establishing a system of free national schools. He was first principal of McGill College and its professor of divinity until 1835.

On 14 February 1836 Mountain was consecrated, at Lambeth, bishop of Montreal, as coadjutor to Dr Charles James Stewart, bishop of Quebec. Dr Stewart shortly afterwards returned to England, and the charge of the entire diocese was under Mountain's care until 1839, when Upper Canada was made a separate see. It was through his earnest exertions that Rupert's Land was also, in 1849, made an episcopal see. He continued to have the sole charge of Lower Canada until 1850, when he secured the constitution of the diocese of Montreal, he himself retaining the diocese of Quebec, by far the poorer and more laborious of the two. During the greater part of his ministerial career he had to perform long, tedious, and often dangerous journeys into the interior of a wild and unsettled country, paying frequent visits to the north-west territory, the eastern townships, the Magdalen Islands, and the shores of Labrador; he also travelled to Rupert's Land, some 3600 miles, in an Indian canoe. His several published visitation journals (1845, 1847) record these journeys, as does, in a different way, his *Songs of the Wilderness* (1846). He devoted much energy to maintaining Anglican rights to the 'clergy reserves' in Canada, and at least deferred their use by other denominations. He was responsible for the establishment in 1845 of the Lower Canadian Church University, Bishop's College, Lennoxville, for the education of clergymen; he eventually obtained a royal charter for it in

1853. In 1853 he travelled to London to chair a convention of colonial bishops on synodical government, which resulted in Mountain being able to hold his first synod session in July 1859. Mountain was a learned theologian, an elegant scholar, and powerful preacher. He died from pneumonia at Bardfield, Quebec, on 6 January 1863; his funeral was held at Quebec Cathedral.

G. C. BOASE, *rev.* H. C. G. MATTHEW

Sources A. W. Mountain, *A memoir of George Jehoshaphat Mountain* (1866) · J. I. Cooper, *The blessed communion: the origins and history of the diocese of Montreal, 1760–1960* (1960) · E. Hawkins, *Annals of the diocese of Quebec* (1849) · W. B. Heeney, *Leaders of the Canadian church* (1920) · C. MacMillan, *McGill and its story, 1821–1921* (1921) · D. C. Masters, *Bishop's University* (1950) · M. Marston, 'Mountain, George Jehoshaphat', *DCB*, vol. 9 · Venn, *Alum. Cant.*

Archives Bishop's University, Lennoxville, Quebec, Quebec diocesan archives

Likenesses portrait, repro. in Mountain, *Memoir* · portrait, repro. in J. G. Wilson and J. Fishe, eds., *Appleton's cyclopaedia of American biography*, 4 (1888), 447–8 · portrait, repro. in F. Taylor, *The last three bishops appointed by the crown for the Anglican church of Canada* (1870), 131–86

Wealth at death under £200—in England: will with a codicil, 25 June 1863, *CGPLA Eng. & Wales*

Mountain, Jacob (1749–1825), bishop of Quebec, was born on 1 December 1749 at Thwaite Hall, Norfolk, son of Jacob Mountain (1710–1752) of Thwaite Hall, and his second wife, Ann Postle (*d.* 1776), formerly of Wymondham, Norfolk. He attended grammar school at Wymondham and Norwich, and, after about two years in a counting house, entered Scarning School, near East Dereham, Norfolk. In 1769 he was admitted to Gonville and Caius College, Cambridge, where he graduated BA, was elected fellow, and ordained deacon, all in 1774. He graduated MA three years later. In 1780 he was ordained Church of England priest, and, on 18 October 1783, married Elizabeth Mildred Wale Kentish (*d.* 1836), daughter of John Kentish of Bardfield Hall, Essex. Of their seven children, who included Armine Simcoe Henry *Mountain, three became clergymen, and one George Jehoshaphat *Mountain, a bishop.

Mountain was first appointed perpetual curate of St Andrew's, Norwich, where he remained for six years. He later became caistor prebendary at Lincoln Cathedral from 1788 to 1790, and examining chaplain from 1790 to 1793 to George Pretyman, bishop of Lincoln, whose acquaintance he had made at Cambridge. He was also rector of Holbeach, Lincolnshire, in 1789–94, and vicar of Buckden, Huntingdonshire, in 1790–94. When the see of Quebec was contemplated in 1793, it was at Pretyman's suggestion to William Pitt that Mountain, a compromise candidate between nominees from the Canadas, be appointed its first bishop. He was nominated to the see by letters patent on 28 June 1793, granted an honorary DD from Cambridge, and consecrated bishop on 7 July in the chapel of Lambeth Palace.

On 1 November, with twelve members of his extended family, Mountain disembarked at Quebec and took charge of a diocese comprising both Lower and Upper Canada. During his thirty-two-year episcopate, the nine clergy he inherited increased to fifty-two, and the seven parishes or missions to forty-nine. He ordained thirty-three deacons

Jacob **Mountain** (1749–1825), by John Downman, 1778

and thirty priests, most of whom were sent from England by the Society for the Propagation of the Gospel in Foreign Parts. He instituted a programme for training clergy on the spot, for which he secured an additional grant from the society. Mountain regarded 'Visitation & Confirmation' as 'the most useful of the Episcopal functions' (J. Mountain to H. Bathurst, 17 Dec 1816, Quebec Diocesan Archives, 123, case T, 3), and made ten tours of his diocese under arduous, often dangerous conditions between 1794 and 1821. In 1804 he consecrated the cathedral of the Holy Trinity at Quebec, built with government funds and provided with a gift of plate from George III. Mountain was a man of presence: a gifted preacher, faithful, energetic, and tenacious in the cause of his church, but out of step with the growing liberalism of the times. An old-fashioned eighteenth-century high-churchman, he failed to adapt his vision of an established church to the needs and conditions of the frontier. In contrast to his rigid public persona, Mountain's family correspondence is warm, intimate, and 'playful' (G. J. Mountain, 6). Besides *Poetical Reveries* (1777) he published several sermons and charges. He died at Marchmont, near Quebec, on 16 June 1825, and was buried on 20 June beneath the chancel of his cathedral. He was survived by his wife who died on 13 April 1836.

MARY ELLEN REISNER

Sources DNB · T. R. Millman, *Jacob Mountain first lord bishop of Quebec* (1947) · T. R. Millman, 'Mountain, Jacob', *DCB*, vol. 6 · [G. J. Mountain], 'Memoir of the late Bishop Mountain', *The Christian Sentinel, and Anglo-Canadian Churchman's Magazine* (Jan–Feb 1827), 5–18 · A. W. Mountain, *A memoir of George Jehoshaphat Mountain* (1866) · J. Strachan, *A sermon, preached at York, Upper Canada, third of July 1825, on the death of the late lord bishop of Quebec* (1826) · A. S. H. Mountain,

Memoirs and letters of the late Colonel Armine S. H. Mountain, ed. Mrs A. S. H. Mountain (1857) • A. R. Kelley, 'Jacob Mountain first lord bishop of Quebec: a summary of his correspondence ... 1793 to 1799', *Rapport de l'Archiviste de la Province de Québec pour 1942–43* (1942–3), 177–259 • A. R. Kelley, 'From Quebec to Niagara in 1794: diary of Bishop Jacob Mountain', *Rapport de l'Archiviste de la Province de Québec pour 1859–60* (1859–60), 121–65 • Quebec Diocesan Archives, J. Mountain, letters, MS 123, case T, 3 • E. Hawkins, *Annals of the diocese of Quebec* (1849) • C. F. Pascoe, *Two hundred years of the SPG*, rev. edn, 2 vols. (1901) • P. Carrington, *The Anglican church in Canada* (1963)

Archives Bishop's University, Lennoxville, Quebec, Quebec diocese archives, MSS, Series C, vols. 1–9 • Bishop's University, Lennoxville, Quebec, Quebec diocesan archives, letters private and personal, unbound MSS, 123, case T, 3 | Archives of the Diocese of Ontario, Kingston, John Stuart MSS, Gr. 11 • Bishop's University, Lennoxville, Quebec, Quebec diocesan archives, Series A, B, and D • Bishop's University, Lennoxville, Quebec, Quebec diocesan archives, Bishopthorpe MSS • Bodl. RH, journals of the Society for the Propagation of the Gospel in Foreign Parts, 26–36 • CUL, SPCK archives, minutes of the Society for Promoting Christian Knowledge, vols. 36–9 • Montreal Anglican diocesan archives, Synod Office, bishops' MSS, RG1.3 • NA Canada, Series G, Q, and S • United Society for the Propagation of the Gospel, London, annual reports, Society for the Propagation of the Gospel in Foreign Parts

Likenesses J. Downman, chalk drawing, 1778, FM Cam. • J. Downman, oils, 1778, NA Canada [*see illus.*] • H. Edridge, oils, 1819, Church House, Anglican Diocese of Quebec, Canada • C. Turner, mezzotint, pubd 1820 (after H. Edridge), BM, NPG • marble bust, Cathedral of the Holy Trinity, Quebec, Canada

Wealth at death son enjoyed private means

Mountain [*née* Wilkinson], **Rosemund** (*c.*1768–1841), singer and actress, was born in London. Her father, whose name was Wilkinson, was a tightrope walker and maker of theatrical wigs and her mother was a minor actress and theatrical dresser. Isabella Wilkinson, a famous rope-dancer and performer on the musical glasses, may have been her aunt. Charles Dibdin taught her singing, and she first appeared at the Haymarket Theatre in unimportant roles in 1782. Her first proper part was Madame Hazard in the burletta *Mount Parnassus* at the Royal Circus (later the Surrey Theatre) on 4 November of that year; the show was highly successful, and ran, as *The Fairy World*, until 1784. She then accompanied her parents to the north of England, where she was engaged by Tate Wilkinson (who was not a relative) for his York circuit. *Lionel and Clarissa* was played for her benefit in December 1784, with Dorothy Jordan as Lionel to her own Clarissa. In the summer of 1786 she performed in Liverpool, and was offered a two-year contract by Thomas Harris of Covent Garden.

Rosemund Wilkinson made her Covent Garden début as Fidelia in *The Foundling* on 4 October 1786; she was to remain at Covent Garden (except for the 1792–3 season, which she spent in Dublin after a quarrel with Harris) until 1798. In Liverpool she had met an Irish violinist, John Mountain. They were married on 5 June 1787, and had one son, baptized in May 1791. John Mountain led the orchestra at Vauxhall Gardens from about 1792 and was leader of the band at Covent Garden from about 1794. Rosemund Mountain was widely praised for her performances, particularly for her singing, and the parts she took were principally musical. They included Lucinda in *Love in a Village*,

Pastoral Nymph in *Comus*, Dorinda in *The Beaux' Stratagem*, Grace in *Poor Vulcan*, Semira in *Artaxerxes*, Mary in *Sprigs of Laurel*, Venus in *Olympia in Uproar*, and Clara in *The Devil of a Lover*. After another quarrel with Harris she finally left Covent Garden in 1798 and toured the provinces and Ireland for two years. While performing in Bristol, she studied with Venanzio Rauzzini in Bath.

In 1800 Mrs Mountain returned to the London stage, initially at the Haymarket, but thereafter at Drury Lane. She sang there for the first time on 6 October 1800, as Polly in *The Beggar's Opera*, 'bursting upon London like a new character'. From then on she was regarded as the best female singer on the English stage, and, on the retirement of Nancy Storace in 1808, took over the latter's roles. In addition to her work in the theatre, Rosemund Mountain sang in oratorios and at Vauxhall Gardens; during the summer seasons she performed in Edinburgh, Dublin, and the provinces. In 1802 she toured with a solo programme of recitations and songs entitled 'The lyric novelist'. Between 1800 and 1809 her parts at Drury Lane included Marianne in *Deaf and Dumb*, Frederika in *The Hero of the North*, Belinda in *The Soldier's Return*, and Rachel in *The Circassian Bride*. She moved with the Covent Garden company to the Lyceum between 1809 and 1811, and returned with them to the new Covent Garden Theatre in 1812 until her retirement in 1815. Her farewell performance was at the King's Theatre on 4 May 1815.

Rosemund Mountain died at her home, 5 Hammersmith Terrace, on 3 July 1841, and was survived by her husband.

L. M. MIDDLETON, rev. ANNE PIMLOTT BAKER

Sources Highfill, Burnim & Langhans, *BDA* • *Oxberry's Dramatic Biography*, 3/48 (1825), 271–9 • R. Fiske, *English theatre music in the eighteenth century*, 2nd edn (1986) • *New Grove* • Grove, *Dict. mus.*

Likenesses T. Cheesman, stipple, pubd 1804 (after A. Buck), BM, NPG • C. Turner, mezzotint, pubd 1804 (after J. Masquerier), BM, NPG • S. G., ivory miniature, 1806, NPG • S. De Wilde, watercolour (as Matilda in *Richard Coeur de Lion*), Garr. Club • S. De Wilde, watercolour, Harvard TC • Eudes, engraving (after T. Cheesman), Harvard TC • K. Mackenzie, stipple (after R. Dighton), BM, NPG • Ridley, engraving, Harvard TC; repro. in *Monthly Mirror* (1797) • Rogers, engraving (as Clara in *The race*; after engraving by C. Turner, 1804, after Masquerier, 1804), repro. in *Oxberry's Dramatic Biography* • G. Romney, oil sketch, Garr. Club; repro. in Highfill, Burnim & Langhans, *BDA*

Mountain, Sarah Ann (1769/70–1842), coach and inn proprietor, married Butler William Mountain (1759–1818) not later than 1790. His father, William Mountain, had been admitted to the Innholders' Company in 1772, his inn being the Swan with Two Necks, Lad Lane, one of London's major coaching inns. Butler William Mountain was admitted to the Innholders' Company in 1808 in respect of the Saracen's Head, Snow Hill, another large coaching inn. Sarah Ann and Butler William Mountain had at least seven children between 1790 and 1812.

When her husband died in February 1818, aged fifty-nine, the business was carried on in Sarah's name. Harris, writing in 1883, described her as 'a very noted and spirited female coach and mail proprietor' (Harris, 156–7). In 1827 her son Peter (baptized in 1803) was managing the business for her, and claimed to have done so since 1818. In

1827 the business employed 200 horses, placing it in the middle rank of London coach enterprises, and in 1836 it had fifteen coaches leaving London every day, mostly from the Saracen's Head, serving most parts of the country. Its best-known coaches were the Rockingham to Leeds and Mountain's Tally-Ho to Birmingham. The business included a coach manufactory at the back of the Saracen's Head.

Upon the arrival of the railways, Sarah Ann Mountain kept her coaches running as long as possible, and was a partner in the last London to Bristol coach. Her will of 1839 stated her residence as the Saracen's Head. She died, aged seventy-two, on 8 February 1842 at Park Lane, Croydon, and was buried on 14 February 1842 at St Sepulchre, Holborn. The business was left to her son Peter.

DORIAN GERHOLD

Sources parish register, Holborn, Sepulchre, GL, MS 7223 · S. Harris, *The coaching age* (1885), 156–7 · 'Commissioners of inquiry into … mail coach contracts', *Parl. papers* (1835), 48.443–4, no. 313 · *IGI* · Innholders' Company, freedom admissions, GL, MS 6651/1 · *Robson's London Directory* (1836) · PRO, PROB 11/1959, 317 · d. cert.

Mountain, Thomas (*c*.1520–1573), religious activist, was, according to his own account, the son of Richard Mountain, 'servant' to Henry VIII and Edward VI. Presumably this was the Richard Mounteyn recorded in 1545 as keeper of the king's garden at St James's. Nothing further is known about his parentage or upbringing. He claimed to have proceeded MA at Cambridge in or before 1545, and to have been ordained priest in 1544, when he should have been at least twenty-four. On 29 October 1545 he was inducted to the rectory of Milton, near Gravesend. At what point he embraced reformed ideas is not clear, but he married in 1548, before it was legal to do so. The name of his wife and the duration of their union are not known. By 1550 he was sufficiently in favour with Archbishop Cranmer to receive the rectory of Tower Royal, a London peculiar belonging to the archbishop. After Edward VI's death on 6 July 1553 he appears to have been an active supporter of the duke of Northumberland. When later accused of having been 'in the field' with the duke he did not deny it. However, he was not arrested until 8 October 1553, apparently for celebrating communion according to the Book of Common Prayer. As this was still legal at that time, it is probable that some other indiscretion was the real cause, although the fact that he seems to have been omitted from the coronation pardon of Northumberland's associates would have been sufficient reason for his arrest.

Mountain was committed to the Marshalsea and remained in prison until August 1555. At some point during this incarceration, as he himself records, he was interrogated by Lord Chancellor Stephen Gardiner, who accused him of being 'one of our new brochyd bretheryn that spekethe ageyenste al good workes' ('The troubles of Thomas Mountayne', 181), a charge which Mountain denied. Good works, he claimed scrupulously, were the fruits of justification, and therefore a duty to all the elect. Because of his imprisonment he was unable to attend the vicar-general's visitation of March 1554, when he was presented as *clericus coniugatus*. Whether he was formally

deprived is not clear, but his rectory disappeared when Whittington College, from which it had been formed, was re-established. Mountain was probably one of those who subscribed to the doctrinal manifesto issued by the imprisoned preachers in May 1554, and like other prisoners managed to obtain copies of forbidden protestant writings. It may have been because of that that he was for a time removed to the Tower, but for reasons which cannot now be recovered Gardiner decided to proceed against him for treason rather than heresy. He was sent down to Cambridge in March 1555, and remained in the castle there until the assizes in August. However, when he was arraigned no evidence was brought against him and he was discharged, four local men standing sureties for him at 3*s*. and 4*d*. each.

Having been released in these extraordinary circumstances, Mountain returned to London and made his way thence to Colchester, from where he took ship to Zeeland. Driven back by bad weather, he then became entangled in the search for George Eagles, alias Trudgeover, a distributor of protestant literature who was operating in that part of Essex. Arrested again on suspicion but without having disclosed his identity, he was brought back to London, but so negligently guarded that he escaped again, and this time succeeded in taking ship from Gravesend to Dunkirk. This escape is not dated, but must have been about the end of 1556. From Dunkirk he made his way to Antwerp, where he found a temporary refuge in the house of the merchant adventurers. For about eighteen months he 'taught school', but then the English council made an effort to suppress heretical activity among the merchant adventurers, and Mountain took refuge in Duisberg, a free city ruled by the duke of Cleves.

That must have been in spring 1558. On Mary's death in November, Mountain returned to London, and in 1559 was rewarded with the rectory of St Pancras in Soper Lane. He resigned this living in 1561, having already been appointed to the nearby benefice of St Faith, where the merchant tailor John Punt stood surety for him. There he remained undisturbed until his death in London in 1573.

DAVID LOADES

Sources 'The troubles of Thomas Mountayne', *Narratives of the days of the Reformation*, ed. J. G. Nichols, CS, old ser., 77 (1859), 177–217 · exchequer, office of first fruits and tenths, composition book, PRO, E334/7 · R. Newcourt, *Repertorium ecclesiasticum parochiale Londinense*, 2 vols. (1708–10) · J. F. Davis, *Heresy and reformation in the south-east of England, 1520–1559*, Royal Historical Society Studies in History, 34 (1983), 139–41 · S. Brigden, *London and the Reformation* (1989) · *LP Henry VIII*, 20/2, no. 1035

Archives BL, Harley MS 425

Mountaine, Didymus. *See* Hill, Thomas (*c*.1528–*c*.1574).

Mount-Alexander. For this title name *see* Montgomery, Hugh, first earl of Mount-Alexander (*b*. in or before 1626, *d*. 1663).

Mountbatten [*née* Ashley], **Dame Edwina Cynthia Annette, Countess Mountbatten of Burma** (1901–1960), director of emergency relief services and vicereine of India, was born at 32 Bruton Street, London, on 28 November 1901, the elder of the two daughters of Wilfrid

Dame Edwina Cynthia Annette Mountbatten, Countess Mountbatten of Burma (1901–1960), by Madame Yevonde, 1940

William *Ashley, Baron Mount Temple of Lee (1867–1939), politician, and his first wife, Amalia Mary Maud (Maudie; 1879–1911), only child of Sir Ernest *Cassel, financier and philanthropist. Edward VII, her grandfather's friend and client, was her godfather, and she was nearly christened Edwardina.

Edwina's childhood was lonely, with an ailing mother, a distracted father, and, from 1914, a determined step-mother whom Edwina and her sister, Mary, found it hard to like. Cassel was Edwina's mainstay; at eighteen, after two years at boarding-school and six months in Italy, she went to live with her grandfather in London at Brook House, his palace in Park Lane. When he died in 1921 Edwina inherited Brook House and the greater part of Cassel's immense fortune. Edwina was now adrift, with nothing to do and, until she was of age, no access to her money. Of all her friends the most sympathetic was Lord Louis (Dickie) *Mountbatten (1900–1979), whose adored father had died in the same week as Sir Ernest. Mountbatten, a lieutenant in the Royal Navy, and younger son of admiral of the fleet the marquess of Milford Haven, formerly Prince Louis of Battenberg, was ambitious, good-looking, and energetic. Despite the misgivings of his mother, Victoria, a granddaughter of Queen Victoria, who thought them both too young and her son too poor, on 18 July 1922 they were married.

Edwina had beauty, wealth, restless energy, and quick intelligence. A woman of extremes, she was jealous of her husband's professional success and of the attention he gave the navy. She consoled herself first with lovers, then with increasingly exotic and testing journeys across the globe, leaving her children, Patricia (b. 1924) and Pamela (b. 1929), in the care of nurses and governesses, Dickie's mother, and Dickie himself.

The war saved the Mountbattens' stormy marriage. At last Edwina's skills and energies were fully tested. Rejected at first by disapproving matrons, she eventually became deputy chairman of the Depot for Knitted Garments for the Navy. Her dedication won respect; that, and her connections, brought her to the Joint War Organization of the Red Cross and the order of St John, where she proved a brilliant administrator, tirelessly visiting bombed cities and shelters across Britain, military camps, and hospitals at home and overseas. Appointed superintendent-in-chief of the St John Ambulance Brigade in 1942, she worked closely with her husband, now chief of combined operations, for the welfare of service-men and their families.

Edwina's greatest contribution came in the aftermath of war. As supreme allied commander south-east Asia, Mountbatten had, in the wake of the Japanese surrender, formidable military and civil responsibility over vast and scattered territory. Edwina assembled teams and equipment to locate and rescue thousands of internees and prisoners of war, venturing at great risk into swamps and jungle. For this and later work she was appointed GCStJ (1945), DCVO (1946), GBE (1947), and CI (1947).

Exhausted, Edwina longed, uncharacteristically, for tranquil family life at Broadlands, the house in Hampshire that had once belonged to Lord Palmerston, which Edwina had inherited from her father in 1939, together with Classiebawn Castle, in co. Sligo. In January 1947, however, Mountbatten was asked to go to India as viceroy to negotiate and achieve the independence of the subcontinent. Impatient with hierarchy and convention, Edwina brought a fresh breeze to the huge enterprise of the viceroy's household, opening it to people of every sort. Her links helped her to inform Mountbatten and his staff as they sought to resolve innumerable difficulties arising from the imminent independence and, inescapably, separation of India and Pakistan. Partition brought bloodshed, as whole populations fled across the country, their meeting places killing grounds. With Edwina at its head, the United Council of Relief and Welfare, co-ordinating all the major voluntary organizations, struggled to help the desperate refugees.

In these demanding times Edwina grew close to Jawaharlal *Nehru, prime minister of India. Six weeks before the Mountbattens' departure in 1948, their task complete, Edwina and Nehru acknowledged the depth of their feelings for each other. For the remaining twelve years of her life they wrote constantly, with rare meetings in England and India. This association, and Edwina's known anti-colonial sympathy, assisted Mountbatten's political opponents. His appointment in 1955 as first sea lord, long sought, was triumphant. Proud of each other's success, loyal, and affectionate, the Mountbattens' partnership at last achieved equilibrium.

Unremitting work as superintendent-in-chief of the St John Ambulance Brigade, with the Save the Children Fund and some hundred other voluntary organizations, wore Edwina out and she died in her sleep at Jesselton, North Borneo, on the night of 20–21 February 1960. As she had wished, she was buried at sea, off Portsmouth, with naval honours, escorted by an Indian warship sent by Nehru.

JANET MORGAN

Sources J. Morgan, *Edwina Mountbatten, a life of her own* (1991) • private information (2004) • *The Times* (22 Feb 1960) • Burke, *Peerage* (1967) • Countess of Brecknock [M. M. J. Pratt], *Edwina Mountbatten: her life in pictures* (1961)
Archives Library of the Order of St John, London • Library of the Red Cross Society, London • priv. coll. • PRO • U. Southampton, archives | FILM BFI NFTVA, documentary footage • BFI NFTVA, news footage • IWM FVA, actuality footage
Likenesses P. A. de Laszlo, oils, 1923, priv. coll. • Mme Yevonde, photograph, 1940, NPG [*see illus.*] • S. Dalí, oils, 1942, priv. coll. • C. Beaton, photograph, 1946, Sothebys, London • E. Halliday, oils, 1948, Rashapati Bhavan, New Delhi • R. Whistler, portrait • photographs, Hult. Arch.
Wealth at death £589,655 5s.: probate, 21 March 1960, CGPLA Eng. & Wales

Mountbatten, George Louis Victor Henry Sergius, second marquess of Milford Haven (1892–1938), naval officer and businessman, was born at Darmstadt on 6 November 1892 as Prince George of Battenberg, third child and elder son of Prince Louis Alexander of Battenberg (1854–1921), later Louis *Mountbatten, first marquess of Milford Haven, admiral of the fleet, and his wife, Princess Victoria Alberta Elizabeth Marie Irene (1863–1950), daughter of Louis IV of Hesse. Prince Louis was brother-in-law of Queen Victoria's daughter Princess Beatrice; his wife was Queen Victoria's granddaughter. Though decidedly a poor relation, Prince George was therefore closely connected with the British royal family and was treated by them with great friendliness. His sister Princess *Alice married Prince Andrew of Greece.

From birth Prince George was destined for a naval career, and he entered the Royal Naval College, Osborne, in 1905, progressed to Dartmouth (1907–9), was promoted to lieutenant in 1914, and served in the battles of Heligoland, Dogger Bank, and Jutland. On 15 November 1916 he married Nadejda (Nada) de Torby (1896–1963), second daughter of the Grand Duke Michael of Russia. In 1918 he joined the gunnery school at Whale Island and qualified as a gunnery lieutenant. In due course he became experimental officer at Whale Island, a post which demanded great technical expertise as well as resourcefulness and powers of organization. These he showed in full measure; he was an outstanding mathematician and renowned as one of the most intelligent and brilliantly inventive of naval officers—though it is fair to say that his inventions were as likely to be directed to the comforts available in his cabin as to the efficiency of the Royal Navy.

In 1922 he qualified at the Royal Naval Staff College and in 1926 was promoted commander. A brilliant career was generally predicted; his younger brother, Louis *Mountbatten, Earl Mountbatten of Burma, always insisted that George was far the most capable member of the family

and would have got to the very top if he had stuck to his career. He lacked Mountbatten's ferocious ambition, however; and when the Royal Navy contracted sharply in the late 1920s he decided not to resist the tide but instead to make some much needed money in business. He had been made a KCVO in 1916 and was promoted to GCVO in 1932.

In 1917, when his father had renounced his German title and was created marquess of Milford Haven, Prince George had become known by courtesy as earl of Medina; in 1921 he succeeded his father in the marquessate. His title and royal connections, coupled with his considerable abilities, eased his passage into civilian life. After a period working in a brokerage house on Wall Street he became chairman and managing director of the British Sperry Gyroscope Company and a director of Electrolux, Marks and Spencer, and various other companies. In November 1937 he was appointed captain on the retired list and would no doubt have returned to active service when war broke out. Early in 1938, however, cancer was diagnosed, and after a painful illness he died on 8 April 1938 at the Empire Nursing Home, Vincent Square, London. He was buried at Bray in Berkshire. 'The sweetest natured, most charming, most able, most brilliant, entirely lovable brother anyone ever had is lost', wrote Mountbatten in his diary.

Though formally less good-looking than his father and brother, Milford Haven possessed outstanding charm, quick intelligence, and an engaging sense of humour. His wife was markedly bohemian in her habits, and Milford Haven was wholly free from pomposity or self-importance; their home, Lynden Manor, near Bray, in Berkshire, provided a pleasant and relaxed atmosphere in which their two children, David and Tatiana, grew up and where their nephew, Prince Philip of Greece, spent much of his school holidays. It was characteristic of Milford Haven that he devoted many hours to laying out an enormously elaborate and technically advanced model railway in the barn at Lynden; then, once it was completed, lost all interest in it and hardly entered the barn again.

PHILIP ZIEGLER

Sources private information (2004) [including duke of Edinburgh, Countess Mountbatten of Burma] • U. Southampton, Hartley Library, Mountbatten MSS • *The Times* (9 April 1938) • *Daily Telegraph* (9 April 1938)
Archives IWM, naval corresp. and papers • U. Southampton, MSS
Likenesses two photographs, c.1914–1922, Hult. Arch.
Wealth at death £72,639 8s. 9d.: probate, 15 June 1938, CGPLA Eng. & Wales

Mountbatten, Louis Alexander, first marquess of Milford Haven [*formerly* Prince Louis of Battenberg] (1854–1921), naval officer, was the eldest son of Prince Alexander of Hesse and his morganatic wife, Countess Julia Theresa von Haucke. He was born Ludwig Alexander at Graz, Austria, on 24 May 1854. The friendship between his mother and Princess Alice, daughter of Queen Victoria and wife of Prince Louis of Hesse (afterwards Grand Duke Louis IV), led to Prince Louis's settling in England as a boy. He was naturalized as a British subject, and entered the

Royal Navy as a cadet in 1868, being promoted to lieutenant in 1876 after accompanying the prince of Wales to India. A brief liaison with the society beauty and actress Lillie *Langtry resulted in the birth of a daughter, Jeanne-Marie Langtry, in March 1881. To avoid scandal, a financial settlement was made, and Prince Louis was appointed to the *Inconstant*, on which he served during the Egyptian war, taking part in the bombardment of Alexandria (11 July 1882). After serving on the royal yacht, he was promoted to commander in 1885.

On 30 April 1884 Prince Louis married his cousin Princess Victoria (1863–1950), eldest daughter of Louis, grand duke of Hesse and by Rhine, at Darmstadt. They had two sons and two daughters: George Louis *Mountbatten (1892–1938), who succeeded in the marquessate; Louis *Mountbatten, later Earl Mountbatten of Burma (1900–1979); *Alice (1885–1969), who married Prince Andrew of Greece; and Louise (1889–1965), who became consort of Gustav Adolf VI of Sweden.

At this period British defence policy was undergoing a gradual readjustment in accordance with the theories of what became known as 'the blue-water school', and Prince Louis was selected by the Admiralty to act as naval adviser to the inspector-general of fortifications, with a view to co-ordinating naval and military ideas. He took up this appointment in 1892, having been promoted captain in the preceding year, and held it until October 1894. In February 1894 he became joint secretary of the naval and military committee on defence, afterwards the committee of imperial defence. During these years he studied the defence problem in its naval and military aspects and was well qualified when, in 1900, he was made assistant director of naval intelligence. He returned to the Admiralty in 1902 as director of naval intelligence, and retained that position until 1905, having been promoted to rear-admiral in 1904.

By this time Prince Louis was regarded throughout the service as an officer who had established his fitness for high command at sea. On leaving the Admiralty in 1905 he hoisted his flag in the *Drake* as rear-admiral commanding the second cruiser squadron. After two years in this post he was selected as second in command of the fleet in the Mediterranean. In the meantime Lord Fisher had become the dominating figure at the Admiralty, and it was no surprise when in 1908 Prince Louis was directed to move to the Atlantic fleet as commander-in-chief. Two years later he was appointed vice-admiral commanding the third and fourth divisions of the newly constituted Home Fleets, and in December 1911 he returned to the Admiralty as second sea lord, becoming first sea lord a year later. This appointment was questionable in view of Prince Louis's German birth, and of the threatening situation which was developing abroad.

In July 1914 a test mobilization of the naval reserves was carried out, and the ships were due to disperse, after carrying out exercises in the English Channel, just as war was becoming increasingly likely. Winston Churchill, first lord of the Admiralty, was absent from his office during the critical weekend (25–7 July) when it had to be decided whether the fleet should be dispersed and the reserve ships demobilized (in accordance with the plans already made), or whether preliminary steps should be taken to place the squadrons at their various war stations. This decision rested with the first sea lord. After consulting Churchill, Prince Louis, as he subsequently explained, 'directed the secretary, as a first step, to send an Admiralty order by telegraph to the commander-in-chief of the Home Fleets at Portland to the effect that no ship was to leave that anchorage until further orders'. War had not then been declared, but the prevision of the first sea lord ensured that when it became inevitable the navy should be ready. By four o'clock on the morning of 3 August naval mobilization had been completed. The prompt initiative which Prince Louis had exhibited in this emergency did not subsequently shield him from attack on account of his 'German origin'. On 29 October 1914, finding his position increasingly untenable, particularly after British losses at sea, he resigned as first sea lord. Distressed at his being made a scapegoat, George V swore him of the privy council. Nevertheless, his family later asserted that his hounding from office was a blow from which he never really recovered.

In July 1917, at the king's request, and in the interests of 'Anglicizing' the royal family, Prince Louis relinquished the style and title of serene highness and prince, assumed for himself and his descendants the surname of Mountbatten, and was raised to the peerage of the United Kingdom as marquess of Milford Haven, earl of Medina, and Viscount Alderney. On 22 August 1921 he was made an admiral of the fleet on the retired list, but his health was failing. He died on 11 September 1921 at 42 Half Moon Street, Piccadilly, London, of heart failure following influenza, and was buried at Whippingham church, on the Isle of Wight.

Prince Louis's connections with other European courts had proved invaluable at times, notably in helping to improve Anglo-Russian relations after the Dogger Bank incident of 1904; and his test mobilization of the British navy in 1914 was vital in preparing the service for the outbreak of war. He was also involved in the invention of various scientific devices, including a cone signalling apparatus, and the introduction of an instrument enabling calculations to be resolved mechanically in naval manoeuvres. His intellectual mind and reserved German manner did not make him popular, but 'what he lacked in imagination was more than balanced by industry and attention to detail' (Hough, 171). Keenly interested in British naval history, he was the first president of the Society of Nautical Research.

ARCHIBALD HURD, rev. JOHN VAN DER KISTE

Sources R. Hough, *Louis and Victoria* (1974) · M. Kerr, *Prince Louis of Battenberg: admiral of the fleet* (1934) · P. Ziegler, *Mountbatten* (1985) · J. van der Kiste, 'My dear Ludwig', *Royalty Digest*, 1 (1991–2), 322–5 · *The Times* (12 Sept 1921)
Archives PRO · U. Southampton L., corresp. and papers | Bodl. Oxf., corresp. with Lord Selborne · IWM, Prince Louis naval papers · NAM, letters to Earl Roberts · NMM, corresp. with Sir J. S. Corbett · CAC Cam., letters to Lord Fisher | FILM BFI NFTVA, 'Lord Mountbatten remembers', BBC1, 28 Oct 1980, 4 Nov 1980; 'Secret

lives', Channel 4, 9 Mar 1995; current affairs footage; documentary footage; news footage

Likenesses Spy [L. Ward], chromolithograph caricature, 1905, NPG; repro. in *VF* (16 Feb 1905) · P. A. de Laszlo, oils, 1914, Broadlands, Hampshire · A. S. Cope, group portrait, oils, 1921 (*Some sea officers of the Great War*), NPG · W. Stoneman, photograph, 1921, NPG

Wealth at death £6533 17s. 1d.: probate, 31 Oct 1921, *CGPLA Eng. & Wales*

Mountbatten, Louis Francis Albert Victor Nicholas, first Earl Mountbatten of Burma (1900–1979),

naval officer and viceroy of India, was born at Frogmore House, Windsor, on 25 June 1900 as Prince Louis of Battenberg, the younger son and the youngest of the four children of Prince Louis Alexander of Battenberg (1854–1921) [*see* Mountbatten, Louis Alexander] and his wife, Princess Victoria (1863–1950) [*see* Mountbatten, Victoria Alberta Elisabeth Mathilde Marie], the daughter of Louis IV of Hesse. Prince Louis Alexander, himself head of a cadet branch of the house of Hesse, was brother-in-law to Queen Victoria's daughter Princess Beatrice; his wife was Victoria's granddaughter. By both father and mother, therefore, Prince Louis was closely connected with the British royal family. One sister, *Alice, married Prince Andrew of Greece, and the other, Louise, married King Gustav VI of Sweden.

Early life Prince Louis, Dickie as he was known from childhood, was educated as befitted the son of a senior naval officer—a conventional upbringing varied by holidays with his German relatives or with his aunt, the tsarina, in Russia. At Locker's Park School in Hertfordshire he was praised for his industry, enthusiasm, sense of humour, and modesty—the first two at least being characteristics conspicuous throughout his life. From there in May 1913 he entered the Royal Naval College, Osborne, as fifteenth out of eighty-three, a respectable if unglamorous position which he more or less maintained during his eighteen months there. Towards the end of his stay his father, now first sea lord, was hounded from office because of his German ancestry. This affected young Prince Louis deeply, though a contemporary recalls him remarking nonchalantly: 'It doesn't really matter very much. Of course I shall take his place' (Ziegler, 36). Certainly his passionate ambition owed something to his desire to avenge his father's disgrace.

In November 1914 Prince Louis moved on to Dartmouth. Although he never shone athletically, or impressed himself markedly on his contemporaries, his last years of education showed increasing confidence and ability, and at Keyham, the Royal Naval College at Devonport where he did his final course, he came first out of seventy-two. In July 1916 he was assigned as a midshipman to the *Lion*, the flagship of Admiral Sir David Beatty. His flag captain, Roger Backhouse, described him as 'a very promising young officer' (Broadlands MSS, O.5. 'naval appointments', 27 Nov 1916), but his immediate superior felt he lacked the brilliance of his elder brother George *Mountbatten—a judgement which Prince Louis himself frequently echoed. The *Lion* saw action in the eight months Prince Louis was aboard but suffered no damage, and by

Louis Francis Albert Victor Nicholas Mountbatten, first Earl Mountbatten of Burma (1900–1979), by Yousuf Karsh, 1943

the time he transferred to the *Queen Elizabeth* in February 1917 the prospects of a major naval battle seemed remote. Prince Louis served briefly aboard the submarine K6—'the happiest month I've ever spent in the service' (Broadlands MSS, Mountbatten to Lady Milford Haven, 22 Jan 1918, vol. 7)—and visited the western front, but his time on the *Queen Elizabeth* was uneventful and he was delighted to be posted in July 1918 as first lieutenant on one of the P-boats, small torpedo boats designed primarily for antisubmarine warfare. It was while he was on the *Queen Elizabeth* that his father, in common with other members of the royal family, abandoned his German title and was created marquess of Milford Haven, with the family name of Mountbatten. His younger son was known henceforth as Lord Louis Mountbatten.

At the end of 1919 Mountbatten was one of a group of naval officers sent to widen their intellectual horizons at Cambridge. During his year at Christ's College (of which he became an honorary fellow in 1946) he acquired a taste for public affairs, regularly attending the union and achieving the distinction, remarkable for someone in his position, of being elected to the committee. Through his close friend Peter Murphy he also opened his mind to radical opinions—'We all thought him rather left-wing' (Broadlands MSS, 'The life and times of Lord Mountbatten', post production scripts, programme 2, reel 3, p. 5), said the then president of the union, Geoffrey Shakespeare.

While still at Cambridge, Mountbatten was invited by his cousin the prince of Wales to attend him on the forthcoming tour of Australasia in the *Renown*. Mountbatten's roles were those of unofficial diarist, dogsbody, and, above all, companion to his sometimes moody and disobliging cousin. These he performed admirably—'you will never know', wrote the prince to Lord Milford Haven, 'what very great friends we have become, what he has meant and been to me on this trip' (Broadlands MSS, prince of Wales to Lord Milford Haven, 19 Sept 1920, vol. 8a). His reward was to be invited to join the next royal tour to India and Japan in the winter of 1921–2, a journey that doubly marked his life in that in India he learned to play polo and became engaged to Edwina Cynthia Annette (1901–1960) [see Mountbatten, Edwina Cynthia Annette], the daughter of Wilfrid William Ashley.

Edwina Ashley was descended from the third Viscount Palmerston and the earls of Shaftesbury, while her maternal grandfather was the immensely rich Sir Ernest Cassel, a friend and financial adviser to Edward VII. At Cassel's death in 1921 his granddaughter inherited some £2.3 million, and eventually also a palace on Park Lane, Classiebawn Castle in Ireland, and the Broadlands estate at Romsey in Hampshire. They were married on 18 July 1922. The union of two powerful and fiercely competitive characters was never wholly harmonious and sometimes caused unhappiness to both partners. On the whole, however, it worked well and they established a formidable partnership at several stages of their lives. They had two daughters.

Naval officer Early in 1923 Mountbatten joined the *Revenge*. For the next fifteen years his popular image was that of a playboy. Fast cars, speedboats, polo, were his delights; above all the last, about which he wrote the classic *Introduction to Polo* (1931) by Marco. Yet nobody who knew his work could doubt his essential seriousness. 'This officer's heart and soul is in the Navy', reported the captain of the *Revenge*, 'No outside interests are ever allowed to interfere with his duties' (Broadlands MSS, O.5. 'naval appointments', 1 Aug 1924). His professionalism was proved beyond doubt when he selected signals as his speciality and passed out top of the course in July 1925. As assistant fleet wireless officer (1927–8) and fleet wireless officer (1931–3) in the Mediterranean, and at the signals school at Portsmouth in between, he won a reputation for energy, efficiency, and inventiveness. He raised the standard of signalling in the Mediterranean Fleet to new heights and was known, respected, and almost always liked by everyone under his command.

In 1932 Mountbatten was promoted commander and in April 1934 took over the *Daring*, a new destroyer of 1375 tons. After only a few months, however, he had to exchange her for an older and markedly inferior destroyer, the *Wishart*. Undiscomfited, he set to work to make his ship the most efficient in the Mediterranean Fleet. He succeeded and *Wishart* was cock of the fleet in the regatta of 1935. It was at this time that he perfected the 'Mountbatten station-keeping gear', an ingenious device which was adopted by the Admiralty for use in destroyers but which never really proved itself in wartime.

Enthusiastically recommended for promotion, Mountbatten returned to the naval air division of the Admiralty. He was prominent in the campaign to recapture the Fleet Air Arm from the Royal Air Force, lobbying Winston Churchill, Sir Samuel Hoare, and A. Duff Cooper with a freedom unusual among junior officers. He vigorously applauded Cooper's resignation over the Munich agreement and maintained a working relationship with Anthony Eden and the fourth marquess of Salisbury in their opposition to appeasement. More practically he was instrumental in drawing the Admiralty's attention to the merits of the Oerlikon gun, the adoption of which he urged vigorously for more than two years. It was during this period that he also succeeded in launching the Royal Naval Film Corporation, an organization designed to secure the latest films for British sailors at sea.

The abdication crisis caused Mountbatten much distress but left him personally unscathed. Some time earlier he had hopefully prepared for the prince of Wales a list of eligible protestant princesses, but by the time of the accession he had little influence left. He had been Edward VIII's personal naval aide-de-camp, and in February 1937 George VI appointed him to the same position, simultaneously appointing him to the GCVO.

Since the autumn of 1938 Mountbatten had been contributing ideas to the construction at Newcastle of a new destroyer, the *Kelly*. In June 1939 he took over as captain and *Kelly* was commissioned by the outbreak of war. On 20 September she was joined by her sister ship *Kingston*, and Mountbatten became captain (D) of the fifth destroyer flotilla.

Mountbatten was not markedly successful as a wartime destroyer captain. In surprisingly few months at sea he almost capsized in a high sea, collided with another destroyer, and was mined once, torpedoed twice, and finally sunk by enemy aircraft. In most of these incidents he could plead circumstances beyond his control, but the consensus of professional opinion is that he lacked 'sea sense', the quality that ensures a ship is doing the right thing in the right place at the right time. Nevertheless he acted with immense panache and courage and displayed such qualities of leadership that, when *Kelly* was recommissioned after several months refitting, an embarrassingly large number of her former crew clamoured to rejoin. When he took his flotilla into Namsos in March 1940 to evacuate Adrian Carton de Wiart and several thousand allied troops, he conducted the operation with cool determination. The return of *Kelly* to port in May, after ninety-one hours in tow under almost constant bombardment and with a 50 foot hole in the port side, was an epic of fortitude and seamanship. It was feats such as this that caught Churchill's imagination and thus altered the course of Mountbatten's career.

In the spring of 1941 the *Kelly* was dispatched to the Mediterranean. Placed in an impossible position, Admiral Sir A. B. Cunningham in May decided to support the army in Crete, even though there was no possibility of air cover. The *Kashmir* and the *Kelly* were attacked by dive-bombers on 23 May and soon sunk. More than half the crew of *Kelly* was lost and Mountbatten escaped only by swimming from under the ship as it turned turtle. The survivors were machine-gunned in the water but were picked up by the

Kipling. The *Kelly* lived on in the film *In which we Serve*, a skilful piece of propaganda by Noël Coward, which was based in detail on the achievements of Mountbatten and his ship. Mountbatten was now appointed to command the aircraft-carrier *Illustrious*, which had been severely damaged and sent for repair to the United States. In October he flew to America to take over his ship and pay a round of visits. He established many useful contacts and made a considerable impression on the American leadership: 'he has been a great help to all of us, and I mean literally ALL', wrote Admiral Stark to Sir A. Dudley Pound (Ziegler, 152). Before the *Illustrious* was ready, however, Mountbatten was called home by Churchill to take charge of combined operations. His predecessor, Sir Roger Keyes, had fallen foul of the chiefs of staff, and Mountbatten was initially appointed only as chief adviser. In April 1942, however, he became chief of combined operations, with the acting rank of vice-admiral, lieutenant-general, and air marshal and with *de facto* membership of the chiefs of staff committee. This phenomenally rapid promotion earned him some unpopularity, but on the whole the chiefs of staff gave him full support.

Combined operations 'You are to give no thought for the defensive. Your whole attention is to be concentrated on the offensive', Churchill told Mountbatten (Ziegler, 156). His duties fell into two main parts: to organize raids against the European coast designed to raise morale, harass the Germans, and achieve limited military objectives; and to prepare for an eventual invasion. The first responsibility, more dramatic though less important, gave rise to a multitude of raids involving only a handful of men and a few more complex operations such as the costly but successful attack on the dry dock at St Nazaire. Combined operations were responsible for planning such forays, but their execution was handed over to the designated force commander, a system which led sometimes to confusion.

The ill results of divided responsibilities were particularly apparent in the Dieppe operation of August 1942. Dieppe taught the allies valuable lessons for the eventual invasion and misled the Germans about their intentions, but the price paid in lives and material was exceedingly, probably disproportionately, high. For this Mountbatten, ultimately in charge of planning the operation, must accept some responsibility. Nevertheless the errors which both British and German analysts subsequently condemned—the adoption of frontal rather than flank assault, the selection of relatively inexperienced Canadian troops for the assault, the abandonment of any previous air bombardment, and the failure to provide the support of capital ships—were all taken against his advice or over his head. Certainly he was not guilty of the blunders which Lord Beaverbrook in particular attributed to him.

Some later commentators have tried to establish that Mountbatten bore almost sole responsibility for the débâcle and that the decision to remount the operation after its initial cancellation was taken on his own authority and without reference to the chiefs of staff. It is true that the minutes of the chiefs of staff committee do not record any decision to relaunch the attack on Dieppe, but this is unsurprising given the extreme secrecy of the project. The minutes equally contain no reference to the race to produce an atom bomb, yet discussion on the subject undoubtedly occurred. All the chiefs, for differing reasons, supported the raid, and Churchill in his memoirs specifically refers to a meeting at which he went through the plans with Mountbatten and Alan Brooke and gave them his full approval.

Where Mountbatten can properly be blamed is over the provision of intelligence. He did not know, and should have known, that between the date of the aborted first raid and 19 August all the channel ports had been reinforced, fortifications strengthened, superior troops brought in, and new gun emplacements built. The targets with which destroyers could possibly have coped in July were impregnable to such attack a month later. The need for the support of a battleship or aerial bombardment, strong even at the earlier date, was irresistible by the time the landings took place. The intelligence service most directly to blame was that of combined operations.

When it came to preparation for invasion, Mountbatten's energy, enthusiasm, and receptivity to new ideas showed to great advantage. His principal contribution was to see clearly what is now obvious but was then not generally recognized, that successful landings on a fortified enemy coast called for an immense range of specialized equipment and skills. To secure an armada of landing craft of different shapes and sizes, and to train the crews to operate them, involved a diversion of resources, both British and American, which was vigorously opposed in many quarters. The genesis of such devices as Mulberry (the floating port) and Pluto (pipeline under the ocean) is often hard to establish, but the zeal with which Mountbatten and his staff supported their development was a major factor in their success. Mountbatten surrounded himself with a team of talented if sometimes maverick advisers—Professor J. D. Bernal, Geoffrey Pyke, Solly Zuckerman—and was ready to listen to anything they suggested. Sometimes this led him into wasteful extravagances—as in his championship of the iceberg/aircraft carrier *Habbakuk*—but there were more good ideas than bad. His contribution to D-day was recognized in the tribute paid him by the allied leaders shortly after the invasion: 'we realize that much of … the success of this venture has its origins in developments effected by you and your staff' (Ziegler, 215).

Mountbatten's contribution to the higher strategy is less easy to establish. He himself always claimed responsibility for the selection of Normandy as the invasion site rather than the Pas-de-Calais. Certainly when operation Sledgehammer, the plan for a limited re-entry into the continent in 1942, was debated by the chiefs of staff, Mountbatten was alone in arguing for the Cherbourg peninsula. His consistent support of Normandy may have contributed to the change of heart when the venue of the invasion proper was decided. In general, however, Alan Brooke and the other chiefs of staff resented Mountbatten's ventures outside the field of his immediate interests and he usually confined himself to matters directly concerned with combined operations.

Mountbatten's headquarters, COHQ, indeed the whole of his command, was sometimes criticized for its lavishness in personnel and encouragement of extravagant ideas. Mountbatten was never economical, and waste there undoubtedly was. Nevertheless he built up at great speed an organization of remarkable complexity and effectiveness. By April 1943 combined operations command included 2600 landing craft and more than 50,000 men. He almost killed himself in the process, for in July 1942 he was told by his doctors that he would die unless he worked less intensely. A man with less imagination who played safe could never have done as much. It was Alan Brooke, initially unenthusiastic about his elevation, who concluded: 'His appointment as Chief of Combined Operations … was excellent, and he played a remarkable part as the driving force and main-spring of this organization. Without his energy and drive it would never have reached the high standard it achieved' (A. Bryant, *The Turn of the Tide*, 1957, 321).

Mountbatten arrived at the Quebec conference in August 1943 as chief of combined operations; he left as acting admiral and supreme commander designate, south-east Asia. 'He is young, enthusiastic and triphibious' (PRO, PREM, 9 Aug 1943), Churchill telegraphed C. R. Attlee, but though the Americans welcomed the appointment enthusiastically, he was selected only after half a dozen candidates had been eliminated for various reasons.

Supreme commander, south-east Asia Mountbatten took over a command where everything had gone wrong. The British and Indian army, ravaged by disease and soundly beaten by the Japanese, had been chased out of Burma. A feeble attempt at counter-attack in the Arakan peninsula had ended in disaster. Morale was low, air support inadequate, communications within India slow and uncertain. There seemed little to oppose the Japanese if they decided to resume their assault. Yet before Mountbatten could concentrate on his official adversaries he had to resolve the anomalies within his own command.

Most conspicuous of these was General Stilwell. As well as being deputy supreme commander, Stilwell was chief of staff to Chiang Kai-shek, and his twin roles inevitably involved conflicts of interest and loyalty. A superb leader of troops in the field but cantankerous, Anglophobe, and narrow-minded, Stilwell would have been a difficult colleague in any circumstances. In south-east Asia, where his preoccupation was to reopen the road through north Burma to China, he proved almost impossible to work with. But Mountbatten also found his relationship difficult with his own, British, commanders-in-chief, in particular the naval commander, Sir James Somerville. Partly, this arose from differences of temperament; more importantly it demonstrated a fundamental difference of opinion about the supreme commander's role. Mountbatten, encouraged by Churchill and members of his own entourage, believed that he should operate on the MacArthur model, with his own planning staff, consulting his

commanders-in-chief but ultimately instructing them on future operations. Somerville, General Sir G. J. Giffard, and Air Marshal Sir R. E. C. Peirse, on the other hand, envisaged him as a chairman of committee, operating like Eisenhower and working through the planning staffs of the commanders-in-chief. The chiefs of staff in London proved reluctant to rule categorically on the issue, but Mountbatten eventually abandoned his central planning staff, and the situation was further eased when Somerville was replaced by Admiral Sir Bruce Fraser.

Mountbatten defined the three principal problems facing him as being those of monsoon, malaria, and morale. His determination that allied troops must fight through the monsoon, though of greater psychological than military significance, undoubtedly assisted the eventual victories of the Fourteenth Army. In 1943, for every casualty evacuated because of wounds, there were 120 sick, and Mountbatten, by his emphasis on hygiene and improved medical techniques, can claim much credit for the vast improvement over the next year. But it was in the transformation of the soldiers' morale that he made his greatest contribution. By publicity, propaganda, and the impact of his personality he restored their pride in themselves and gave them confidence that they could defeat the Japanese.

Deciding what campaign they were to fight proved difficult. Mountbatten, with Churchill's enthusiastic backing, envisaged a bold amphibious strategy which would bypass the Burmese jungles and strike through the Andaman Islands to Rangoon or, more ambitious still, through northern Sumatra towards Singapore. The Americans, however, who would have provided the material resources for such adventures, nicknamed South-East Asia command (SEAC) 'Save England's Asiatic colonies' and were suspicious of any operation which seemed designed to this end. They felt that the solitary justification for the Burma campaign was to restore land communications with China. The ambitious projects with which Mountbatten had left London withered as his few landing craft were withdrawn. A mission he dispatched to London and Washington returned empty-handed. 'You might send out the waxwork which I hear Madame Tussauds has made', wrote Mountbatten bitterly to his friend Charles Lambe, 'it could have my Admiral's uniform and sit at my desk … as well as I could' (Ziegler, 265).

It was the Japanese who saved Mountbatten from so ignoble a role. In spring 1944 they attacked in Arakan and across the Imphal plain into India. The allied capacity to supply troops by air and their new-found determination to stand firm, even when cut off, turned potential disaster into almost total victory. Mountbatten himself played a major role, being personally responsible at a crucial moment for the switch of two divisions by air from Arakan to Imphal and the diversion of the necessary American aircraft from the supply routes to China. Imphal confirmed Mountbatten's faith in the commander of the Fourteenth Army, General W. J. Slim, and led to his final loss of confidence in the commander-in-chief, General Giffard, whom he now dismissed. The battle cost the Japanese 7000 dead; much hard fighting lay ahead, but the Fourteenth Army was on the march that would end at Rangoon.

Mountbatten still hoped to avoid the reconquest of Burma by land. In April 1944 he transferred his headquarters from Delhi to Kandy in Ceylon, reaffirming his faith in a maritime strategy. He himself believed the next move should be a powerful sea and air strike against Rangoon; Churchill still hankered after the more ambitious attack on northern Sumatra; the chiefs of staff felt the British effort should be switched to support the American offensive in the Pacific. In the end shortage of resources dictated the course of events. Mountbatten was able to launch a small seaborne invasion to support the Fourteenth Army's advance, but it was Slim's men who bore the brunt of the fighting and reached Rangoon just before the monsoon broke in April 1945.

Giffard had been replaced as supreme commander by Sir Oliver Leese. Mountbatten's original enthusiasm for Leese did not endure; the latter soon fell out with his supreme commander and proved unpopular with the other commanders-in-chief. A climax came in May 1945 when Leese informed Slim that he was to be relieved from command of the Fourteenth Army because he was tired out and anyway had no experience in maritime operations. Mountbatten's role in this curious transaction remains slightly obscure; Leese definitely went too far, but there may have been some ambiguity about his instructions. In the event Leese's action was disavowed in London and he himself was dismissed and Slim appointed in his place.

The next phase of the campaign—an invasion by sea of the Malay peninsula—should have been the apotheosis of Mountbatten's command. When he went to the Potsdam conference in July 1945, however, he was told of the existence of the atom bomb. He realized at once that this was likely to rob him of his victory and, sure enough, the Japanese surrender reduced operation Zipper to an unopposed landing. This was perhaps just as well; faulty intelligence meant that one of the two landings was made on unsuitable beaches and was quickly bogged down. The invasion would have succeeded but the cost might have been high.

On 12 September 1945 Mountbatten received the formal surrender of the Japanese at Singapore. Not long afterwards he was created a viscount. The honour was deserved. His role had been crucial. 'We did it together' (Ziegler, 295), Slim said to him on his deathbed, and the two men, in many ways so different, had indeed complemented each other admirably and proved the joint architects of victory in south-east Asia.

Mountbatten's work in SEAC did not end with the Japanese surrender; indeed in some ways it grew still more onerous. His command was now extended to include South Vietnam and the Netherlands East Indies: 1.5 million square miles containing 128 million inhabitants, three-quarters of a million armed and potentially truculent Japanese, and 123,000 allied prisoners, many in urgent need of medical attention. Mountbatten had to rescue the prisoners, disarm the Japanese, and restore the various territories to stability so that civil government could resume. This last function proved most difficult, since the Japanese had swept away the old colonial regimes and new nationalist movements had grown up to fill the vacuum. Mountbatten's instincts told him that such movements were inevitable and even desirable. Every effort, he felt, should be made to take account of their justified aspirations. His disposition to sympathize with the radical nationalists sometimes led him into naïvely optimistic assessments of their readiness to compromise with the former colonialist regimes—as proved most notably to be the case with the communist Chinese in Malaya—but the course of subsequent history suggests that he sometimes saw the situation more clearly than the so-called realists who criticized him.

Burma and Malaya Even before the end of the war Mountbatten had had a foretaste of the problems that lay ahead. Aung San, head of the pro-Japanese Burmese national army, defected with all his troops. Mountbatten was anxious to accept his co-operation, overruled Oliver Leese and his civil affairs staff, and cajoled the somewhat reluctant chiefs of staff into agreeing on military grounds that the former rebels should be rearmed. Inevitably this gave Aung San a stronger position than the traditionalists thought desirable when the time came to form Burma's post-war government. Mountbatten felt that, though left wing and fiercely nationalistic, Aung San was honourable, basically reasonable, and ready to accept the concept of an independent Burma within the British Commonwealth; 'with proper treatment', judged Slim, 'Aung San would have proved a Burmese Smuts' (Ziegler, 319). The governor, Sir Reginald Dorman-Smith, conceded Aung San was the most popular man in Burma but considered him a dangerous Marxist revolutionary. When Aung San was accused of war crimes committed during the Japanese occupation, Dorman-Smith wished to arrest and try him. Mountbatten forestalled this move and insisted that Aung San was bound to lead Burma one day and that it would be contrary to British interests to try to frustrate him. Aung San's subsequent electoral victory was hailed by Mountbatten as proof that he had backed the only possible horse; to others it meant that violence and intimidation had been not merely condoned but actively encouraged and rewarded. The murder of Aung San the following year meant that the supreme commander's view of his character was never properly tested.

In Malaya the problem was more immediately one of law and order. Confronted by the threat of a politically motivated general strike, the authorities proposed to arrest all the leaders. 'Naturally I ordered them to cancel these orders', wrote Mountbatten, 'as I could not imagine anything more disastrous than to make martyrs of these men' (Ziegler, 326). Reluctantly he agreed that in certain circumstances Chinese trouble-makers might be deported, but rescinded that approval when it was proposed to deport certain detainees who had not had time to profit by his warnings. His critics maintained that sterner

action in 1945–6 could have prevented, or at least mitigated, the future troubles in Malaya, but Mountbatten was
convinced that the prosperity of Malaya and Singapore
depended on the co-operation of Malay and Chinese, and
was determined to countenance nothing that might divide the two communities. With hindsight it is possible to
see that the largely Chinese guerrillas whom he was disposed to favour were opposed to any sort of foreign influence and would have involved the country in civil war
even earlier than actually happened.

In Vietnam and Indonesia Mountbatten's problem was
to balance nationalist aspirations against the demands of
Britain's allies for support in the recovery of their col-
onies. He was better disposed to the French than the
Dutch, and though he complained when General Douglas
Gracey exceeded his instructions and suppressed the Viet
Minh—'General Gracey has saved French Indo-China'
(Ziegler, 331), Leclerc told him—the reproof was more formal than real. In Indonesia Mountbatten believed that
Dutch intransigence was the principal factor preventing a
peaceful settlement. Misled by Dutch intelligence, he had
no suspicion of the force of nationalist sentiment until
Lady Mountbatten returned from her brave foray to rescue allied prisoners of war. His forces could not avoid conflict with the Indonesian nationalists but Mountbatten
sought to limit their commitment, with the result that
both Dutch and Indonesians believed the British were
favouring the other side. He did, however, contrive to
keep open the possibility of political settlement; only
after the departure of the British forces did full-scale civil
war become inevitable.

Mountbatten left south-east Asia in mid-1946 with the
reputation of a liberal committed to decolonization.
Although he had no thought beyond his return to the
navy, with the now substantive rank of rear-admiral, his
reputation influenced the Labour government when they
were looking for a successor to Viscount Wavell who could
resuscitate the faltering negotiations for Indian independence. On 18 December 1946 he was invited to become
India's last viceroy. That year he had been created Viscount Mountbatten of Burma.

Viceroy Mountbatten longed to go to sea again, but this
was a challenge no man of ambition and public spirit
could reject. His reluctance enabled him to extract favourable terms from the government, and though the plenipotentiary powers to which he was often to refer are not
specifically set out in any document, he enjoyed far
greater freedom of action than his immediate predecessors. His original insistence that he would go only on the
invitation of the Indian leaders was soon abandoned, but
it was on his initiative that a terminal date of June 1948
was fixed, by which time the British would definitely have
left India.

Mountbatten's directive was that he should strive to
implement the recommendations of the cabinet mission
of 1946, led by Sir R. Stafford Cripps, which maintained
the principle of a united India. By the time he arrived,
however, this objective had been tacitly abandoned by
every major politician of the subcontinent with the

important exception of M. K. Gandhi. The viceroy dutifully tried to persuade all concerned of the benefits of
unity, but his efforts foundered on the intransigence of
the Muslim leader Mohamed Ali Jinnah. His problem
thereafter was to find some formula which would reconcile the desire of the Hindus for a central India, from
which a few peripheral and wholly Muslim areas would
secede, with Jinnah's aspiration to secure a greater Pakistan, including all of the Punjab and as much as possible
of Bengal. In this task he was supported by Wavell's staff
from the Indian Civil Service, reinforced by General H. L.
Ismay and Sir Eric Miéville. He himself contributed
immense energy, charm and persuasiveness, negotiating
skills, agility of mind, and endless optimism.

Mountbatten quickly concluded that not only was time
not on his side but that the urgency was desperate. The
run-down of the British military and civil presence,
coupled with swelling inter-communal hatred, was
intensely dangerous. 'The situation is everywhere electric, and I get the feeling that the mine may go up at any
moment' (Ziegler, 372–3), wrote Ismay to his wife on 25
March 1947, the day after Mountbatten was sworn in as
viceroy. This conviction that every moment counted dictated Mountbatten's activities over the next five months.
He threw himself into a hectic series of interviews with
the various political leaders. With Jawaharlal Nehru he
established an immediate and lasting rapport which was
to assume great importance in the future. With V. J. Patel,
in whom he identified a major power in Indian politics,
his initial relationship was less easy, but they soon
enjoyed mutual confidence. Gandhi fascinated and
delighted him, but he shrewdly concluded that he was
likely to be pushed to one side in the forthcoming negotiations. With Jinnah alone did he fail; the full blast of his
charm did not thaw or even moderate the chill intractabil-
ity of the Muslim leader.

Perils of partition Nevertheless negotiations advanced so
rapidly that by 2 May Ismay was taking to London a plan
which Mountbatten believed all the principal parties
would accept. Only when the British cabinet had already
approved the plan did he realize that he had gravely
underestimated Nehru's objections to any proposal that
left room for the 'Balkanization' of India. With extraordinary speed a new draft was produced, which provided
for India's membership of the Commonwealth and put
less emphasis on the right of the individual components
of British India to reject India or Pakistan and opt for independence. After what Mountbatten described as 'the
worst 24 hours of my life' (Ziegler, 387), the plan was
accepted by all parties on 3 June. He was convinced that
any relaxation of the feverish pace would risk destroying
the fragile basis of understanding. Independence, he
announced, was to be granted in only ten weeks, on 15
August 1947.

Before this date the institutions of British India had to
be carved in two. Mountbatten initially hoped to retain a
unified army but quickly realized this would be impossible and concentrated instead on ensuring rough justice
in the division of the assets. To have given satisfaction to

everyone would have been impossible, but at the time few people accused him of partiality. He tackled the problems, wrote Michael Edwardes in a book not generally sympathetic to the last viceroy, 'with a speed and brilliance which it is difficult to believe would have been exercised by any other man' (Edwardes, 178).

The princely states posed a particularly complex problem, since with the end of British rule paramountcy lapsed and there was in theory nothing to stop the princes opting for self-rule. This would have made a geographical nonsense of India and, to a lesser extent, Pakistan, as well as creating a plethora of independent states, many incapable of sustaining such a role. Mountbatten at first attached little importance to the question but, once he was fully aware of it, used every trick to get the rulers to accept accession. Some indeed felt that he was using improper influence on loyal subjects of the crown, but it is hard to see that any other course would in the long run have contributed to their prosperity. Indeed the two states which Mountbatten failed to shepherd into the fold of India or Pakistan—Hyderabad and Kashmir—were those which were subsequently to cause most trouble.

Most provinces, like the princely states, clearly belonged either to India or to Pakistan. In the Punjab and Bengal, however, partition was necessary. This posed horrifying problems, since millions of Hindus and Muslims would find themselves on the wrong side of whatever frontier was established. The Punjab was likely to prove most troublesome, because 14 per cent of its population consisted of Sikhs, who were warlike, fanatically anti-Muslim, and determined that their homelands should remain inviolate. Partition was not Mountbatten's direct responsibility, since Sir Cyril Radcliffe was appointed to divide the two provinces.

Mountbatten always maintained that he had scrupulously held aloof from the process, and Radcliffe himself denied that he had been put under any pressure by the viceroy. Evidence which has subsequently come to light, however, suggests that Mountbatten was further involved than he cared to admit and that he urged on Radcliffe frontier adjustments in favour of the Indians in the Punjab which were to be counterbalanced by concessions to the Muslims in Bengal. The effect, in the Punjab, was that certain important headwaters were awarded to India rather than Pakistan; this made economic and social sense, but the importance of the change was not conceivably great enough to outweigh the damage that would have been done if it had become generally known that the viceroy was interfering in this way. There is no reason to accept, however, the belief still held by many Pakistanis that Mountbatten secured the switch from Pakistan to India of territory in Gurdaspur which gave India easy land access to Kashmir and thus facilitated that state's eventual accession to India. On the contrary, at the time of partition Mountbatten was actively trying to persuade the maharaja of Kashmir that he should accede to Pakistan. At one point he had even managed to convince Nehru that this would be a tolerable conclusion.

Mountbatten had hoped that independence day would see him installed as governor-general of both new dominions, able to act, in Churchill's phrase, as 'moderator' during their inevitable differences. Nehru was ready for such a transmogrification but Jinnah, after some months of apparent indecision, concluded that he himself must be Pakistan's first head of state. Mountbatten was uncertain whether the last viceroy of a united India should now reappear as governor-general of a part of it, but the Indian government pressed him to accept, and in London both Attlee and George VI felt the appointment was desirable. With some misgivings, Mountbatten gave way. Independence day in both Pakistan and India was a triumph, tumultuous millions applauding his progress and demonstrating that, for the moment at least, he enjoyed a place in the pantheon with their national leaders. 'No other living man could have got the thing through', wrote Lord Killearn to Ismay; 'it has been a job supremely well done' (Ziegler, 427).

Communal strife The euphoria quickly faded. Although Bengal remained calm, thanks largely to Gandhi's personal intervention, the Punjab exploded. Vast movements of population across the new frontier exacerbated the already inflamed communal hatred, and massacres on an appalling scale developed. The largely British-officered boundary force was taxed far beyond its powers, and Delhi itself was engulfed in the violence. Mountbatten was called back from holiday to help master the emergency, and brought desperately needed energy and organizational skills to the despondent government. 'I've never been through such a time in my life', he wrote on 28 September, 'The War, the Viceroyalty were jokes, for we have been dealing with life and death in our own city' (Ziegler, 436). Gradually order was restored, and by November 1947 Mountbatten felt the situation was stable enough to permit him to attend the wedding of Princess Elizabeth and his nephew Philip Mountbatten in London. He was created Earl Mountbatten of Burma, with special remainder to his daughter Patricia.

Estimates vary widely, but the best-documented assessments agree that at least 250,000 people lost their lives in the communal riots. Those who criticize Mountbatten's viceroyalty do so most often on the grounds that these massacres could have been averted, or at least mitigated, if partition had not been hurried through. Mountbatten's champions maintain that delay would only have made things worse and allowed the disorders to spread further. It is impossible to state conclusively what might have happened if independence had been postponed by a few months, or even years, but it is noteworthy that the closer people were to the problem, the more they supported Mountbatten's policy. Almost every senior member of the British administration in India and of the Indian government has recorded his conviction that security was deteriorating so fast, and the maintenance of non-communal forces of law and order proving so difficult, that a far greater catastrophe would have ensued if there had been further delay.

Mountbatten as governor-general was a servant of the Indian government and, as Ismay put it, 'it is only natural that they … should regard themselves as having proprietary rights over you' (Ziegler, 465–6). Mountbatten accepted this role and fought doughtily for India's interests. He did not wholly abandon impartiality, however. When in January 1948 the Indian government withheld from Pakistan the 55 million crores of rupees owing after the division of assets, the governor-general argued that such conduct was dishonourable as well as unwise. He recruited Gandhi as his ally, and together they forced a change of policy on the reluctant Indian ministers. It was one of Gandhi's final contributions to Indian history. On 30 January he was assassinated by a Hindu extremist. Mountbatten mourned him sincerely. 'What a remarkable old boy he was', he wrote to a friend, 'I think history will link him with Buddha and Mahomet' (Ziegler, 471).

Mountbatten's stand over the division of assets did the governor-general little good in Pakistan, where he was believed to be an inveterate enemy. When, in October 1947, Pathan tribesmen invaded the Vale of Kashmir, Mountbatten approved and helped to organize military intervention by India. He insisted, however, that the state must first accede and that, as soon as possible, a plebiscite should establish the wishes of the Kashmiri people. When war between India and Pakistan seemed imminent he was instrumental in persuading Nehru that the matter should be referred to the United Nations.

The other problem that bedevilled Mountbatten was that of Hyderabad. He constituted himself, in effect, chief negotiator for the Indian government and almost brought off a deal that would have secured reasonably generous terms for the nizam. Muslim extremists in Hyderabad, however, defeated his efforts, and the dispute grumbled on. Mountbatten protested when he found contingency plans existed for the invasion of Hyderabad, and his presence was undoubtedly a main factor in inhibiting the Indian take-over that quickly followed his departure.

On 21 June 1948 the Mountbattens left India. In his final address, Nehru referred to the vast crowds that had attended their last appearances and wondered 'how it was that an Englishman and Englishwoman could become so popular in India during this brief period' (Ziegler, 478–9). Even his harshest critics could not deny that Mountbatten had won the love and trust of the people and got the relationship between India and her former ruler off to a far better start than had seemed possible fifteen months before.

Return to the navy   At last Mountbatten was free to return to sea. Reverting to his substantive rank of rear-admiral he took command of the 1st cruiser squadron in the Mediterranean. To assume this relatively lowly position after the splendours of supreme command and viceroyalty could not have been easy, but with goodwill all round it was achieved successfully. He was 'as great a subordinate as he is a leader' (Ziegler, 495), reported the commander-in-chief, Admiral Sir Arthur Power. He brought his squadron up to a high level of efficiency, though he did not conceal the fact that he felt obsolescent material and undermanning diminished its real effectiveness. After his previous jobs this command was something of a holiday,

and he revelled in the opportunities to play his beloved polo and take up skin diving. In Malta he stuck to his inconspicuous role, but abroad he was fêted by the rulers of the countries his squadron visited. 'I suppose I oughtn't to get a kick out of being treated like a Viceroy', he confessed after one particularly successful visit, 'but I'd have been less than human if I hadn't been affected by the treatment I received at Trieste' (Ziegler, 490). He was never less, nor more, than human.

Mountbatten was promoted vice-admiral in 1949 and in June 1950 returned to the Admiralty as fourth sea lord. He was at first disappointed, since he had set his heart on being second sea lord, responsible for personnel, and found himself instead concerned with supplies and transport. In fact the post proved excellent for his career. He flung himself into the work with characteristic zeal, cleared up many anomalies and outdated practices, and acquired a range of information which was to stand him in good stead when he became first sea lord. On the whole he confined himself to the duties of his department, but when the Persians nationalized Anglo-Iranian Oil in 1951 he could not resist making his opinions known. He felt that it was futile to oppose strong nationalist movements of this kind and that Britain would do better to work with them. He converted the first lord to his point of view but conspicuously failed to impress the bellicose foreign secretary, Herbert Morrison.

The next step was command of a major fleet; in June 1952 he was appointed to the Mediterranean and the following year he was promoted admiral. St Vincent remarked that naval command in the Mediterranean 'required an officer of splendour' (Ziegler, 508), and this Mountbatten certainly provided. He was not a great operational commander like Andrew Cunningham, but he knew his ships and personnel, maintained the fleet at the highest level of peacetime efficiency, and was immensely popular with the men. When 'Cassandra' of the *Daily Mirror* arrived to report on Mountbatten's position, he kept aloof for four days, then came to the flagship with the news that the commander-in-chief was 'O.K. with the sailors' (Ziegler, 512). But it was on the representational side that Mountbatten excelled. He loved showing the flag and, given half a chance, would act as honorary ambassador into the bargain. Sometimes he overdid it, and in September 1952 the first lord, at the instance of the prime minister, wrote to urge him to take the greatest care to keep out of political discussions.

Mountbatten's diplomatic as well as administrative skills were taxed when in January 1953 he was appointed supreme allied commander of a new NATO Mediterranean command (SACMED). Under him were the Mediterranean fleets of Britain, France, Italy, Greece, and Turkey, but not the most powerful single unit in the area, the American Sixth Fleet. He was required to set up an integrated international naval and air headquarters in Malta and managed this formidable organizational task with great efficiency. The smoothing over of national susceptibilities and the reconciliation of his British with his NATO role proved taxing, but his worst difficulty lay with the other NATO headquarters in the Mediterranean, CINCSOUTH, at Naples under the American admiral R. B. Carney. There were real problems of demarcation but, as had happened with Somerville in south-east Asia, these were made far worse by a clash of personalities. When Carney was replaced in the autumn of 1953, the differences melted away and the two commands began to co-operate.

First sea lord In October 1954, when he became first sea lord, Mountbatten achieved what he had always held to be his ultimate ambition. It did not come easily. A formidable body of senior naval opinion distrusted him and was at first opposed to his appointment, and it was not until the conviction hardened that the navy was losing the Whitehall battle against the other services that opinion rallied behind him. 'The Navy wants badly a man and a leader', wrote Andrew Cunningham, who had formerly been Mountbatten's opponent. 'You have the ability and the drive and it is you that the Navy wants' (Ziegler, 523). Churchill, still unreconciled to Mountbatten's role in India, held out longer, but in the end he too gave way.

Since the war the navy had become the Cinderella of the fighting services, and morale was low. Under Mountbatten's leadership the Admiralty's voice in Whitehall became louder and more articulate. By setting up the Way Ahead committee he initiated an overdue rethinking of the shore establishments, which were absorbing an undue proportion of the navy's resources. He scrapped plans for the construction of a heavy missile-carrying cruiser and instead concentrated on destroyers carrying the Sea Slug missile: 'Once we can obtain Government agreement to the fact that we are the mobile large scale rocket carriers of the future then everything else will fall into place' (Ziegler, 531). The Reserve Fleet was cut severely and expenditure diverted from the already excellent communications system to relatively underdeveloped fields such as radar. Probably his most important single contribution, however, was to establish an excellent relationship with the notoriously prickly Admiral Rickover, which was to lead to Britain's acquiring US technology for its nuclear submarines and, eventually, to the adoption of the Polaris missile as the core of its nuclear deterrent.

In July 1956 Nasser nationalized the Suez Canal. Mountbatten was asked what military steps could be taken to restore the situation. He said that the Mediterranean Fleet with the Royal Marine commandos aboard could be at Port Said within three days and take the port and its hinterland. Eden rejected the proposal since he wished to reoccupy the whole canal zone, and it is unlikely anyway that the other chiefs of staff would have approved a plan that might have left lightly armed British forces exposed to tank attack and with inadequate air cover. As plans for full-scale invasion were prepared, Mountbatten became more and more uneasy about the contemplated action. To the chiefs of staff he consistently said that political implications should be considered and more thought given to the long-term future of the Middle East. His views were

reflected in the chiefs' recommendations to the government, a point that caused considerable irritation to Anthony Eden, who insisted that politics should be left to the politicians. In August Mountbatten drafted a letter of resignation to the prime minister but, without too much difficulty, was dissuaded from sending it by the first lord, Viscount Cilcennin. He was, however, instrumental in substituting the invasion plan of General Sir Charles Keightley for that previously approved by the cabinet, a move that saved the lives of many hundreds of civilians. On 2 November 1956, when the invasion fleet had already sailed, Mountbatten made a written appeal to Eden to accept the United Nations resolution and 'turn back the assault convoy before it is too late' (Ziegler, 545). His appeal was ignored. Mountbatten again offered his resignation to the first lord and again was told that it was his duty to stay on. He was promoted admiral of the fleet in October 1956.

With Harold Macmillan succeeding Eden as prime minister in January 1957, Duncan Sandys was appointed minister of defence with a mandate to rationalize the armed services and impose sweeping economies. There were many embittered battles before Sandys's first defence white paper appeared in the summer of 1957. The thirteenth and final draft contained the ominous words: 'the role of the Navy in Global War is somewhat uncertain' (Ziegler, 552). In the event, however, the navy suffered relatively lightly, losing only one-sixth of its personnel over the next five years, as opposed to the army's 45 per cent and the air force's 35 per cent. The role of the navy east of Suez was enshrined as an accepted dogma of defence policy.

Chief of defence staff In July 1959 Mountbatten took over as chief of defence staff (CDS). He was the second incumbent, Sir William Dickson having been appointed in 1958, with Mountbatten's support but against the fierce opposition of Field Marshal Sir Gerald Templer. Dickson's role was little more than that of permanent chairman of the chiefs of staff committee, but Sandys tried to increase the CDS's powers. He was defeated, and the defence white paper of 1958 made only modest changes to the existing system. Mountbatten made the principal objective of his time as CDS the integration of the three services, not to the extent achieved by the Canadians of one homogenized fighting force, but abolishing the independent ministries and setting up a common list for all senior officers. During his first two years, however, he had to remain content with the creation of a director of defence plans to unify the work of the three planning departments and the acceptance of the principle of unified command in the Far and Middle East. Then, at the end of 1962, Macmillan agreed that another attempt should be made to impose unification on the reluctant services. 'Pray take no notice of any obstructions', he told the minister of defence, 'You should approach this ... with dashing, slashing methods. Anyone who raises any objection can go' (Macmillan, 418).

At Mountbatten's suggestion Lord Ismay and Sir E. Ian

Jacob were asked to report. While not accepting all Mountbatten's recommendations—which involved a sweeping increase in the powers of the CDS—their report went a long way towards realizing the concept of a unified Ministry of Defence. The reforms, which were finally promulgated in 1964, acknowledged the supreme authority of the secretary of state for defence and strengthened the central role of the CDS. To Mountbatten this was an important first step, but only a step. He believed that so long as separate departments survived, with differing interests and loyalties, it would be impossible to use limited resources to the best advantage. Admiralty, War Office, Air Ministry—not to mention Ministry of Aviation—should be abolished. Ministers should be responsible, not for the navy or the air force, but for communications or supplies. 'We cannot, in my opinion, afford to stand pat', he wrote to Harold Wilson when the latter became prime minister in October 1964, 'and must move on to, or at least towards the ultimate aim of a functional, closely knit, smoothly working machine' (Ziegler, 629). 'Functionalization' was the objective which he repeatedly pressed on the new minister of defence, Denis Healey. Healey was well disposed in principle, but felt that other reforms enjoyed higher priority. Although Mountbatten appealed to Wilson he obtained little satisfaction, and the machinery which he left behind him at his retirement was in his eyes only an unsatisfactory partial solution.

Even for this Mountbatten paid a high price in popularity. His ideas were for the most part repugnant to the chiefs of staff, who suspected him of seeking personal aggrandizement and doubted the propriety of his methods. Relations tended to be worst with the chiefs of air staff. The latter believed that Mountbatten, though ostensibly above inter-service rivalries, in fact remained devoted to the interests of the navy. It is hard entirely to slough off a lifetime's loyalties, but Mountbatten tried to be impartial. He did not always succeed. On the long-drawn-out battle over the merits of aircraft-carriers and island bases, he espoused the former. When he urged the first sea lord to work out some compromise which would accommodate both points of view, Sir Caspar John retorted that only a month before Mountbatten had advised him: 'Don't compromise—fight him to the death!' (Broadlands MSS, J172, Sir C. John to Mountbatten, 16 Jan 1963). Similarly, in the conflict between the TSR 2, sponsored by the air force, and the navy's Buccaneer, Mountbatten believed strongly that the former, though potentially the better plane, was too expensive to be practicable and would take too long to develop. He lobbied the minister of defence and urged his right-hand man, Solly Zuckerman, to argue the case against the TSR 2—'You know why I can't help you in Public. It is *not* moral cowardice but fear that my usefulness as Chairman would be seriously impaired' (Ziegler, 587).

The question of the British nuclear deterrent also involved inter-service rivalries. Mountbatten believed that an independent deterrent was essential, arguing to Harold Wilson that it would 'dispel in Russian minds the thought that they will escape scot-free if by any chance the Americans decide to hold back release of a strategic nuclear response to an attack' (Ziegler, 627). He was instrumental in persuading the incoming Labour government not to adopt unilateral nuclear disarmament. In this he had the support of the three chiefs of staff. But there was controversy over what weapon best suited Britain's needs. From long before he became CDS, Mountbatten had privately preferred the submarine-launched Polaris missile to any of the airborne missiles favoured by the air force. Though not himself present at the meeting at Nassau between Macmillan and President John F. Kennedy, at which Polaris was offered and accepted in exchange for the cancelled Skybolt missile, he had already urged this solution and had made plans accordingly.

Although he defended the nuclear deterrent, Mountbatten was wholly opposed to the accumulation of unnecessary stockpiles or the development of new weapons designed to kill more effectively people who would be dead anyway if the existing armouries were employed. At NATO in July 1963 he pleaded that 'it was madness to hold further tests when all men of goodwill were about to try and bring about test-banning' (Broadlands MSS, interviews with Robin Bousfield, transcripts of tapes, vol. 1). He conceded that tactical nuclear weapons added to the efficacy of the deterrent, but argued that their numbers should be limited and their use subject to stringent control. To use any nuclear weapon, however small or 'clean', would, he insisted, lead to general nuclear war. He opposed the 'mixed manned multilateral force' not just as being military nonsense, but because there were more than enough strategic nuclear weapons already. What were needed, he told the NATO commanders in his valedictory address, were more 'highly mobile, well-equipped, self-supporting and balanced "Fire Brigade" forces, with first-class communications, able to converge quickly on the enemy force' (Broadlands MSS, J284, annex A to COS/1918/21/6/65).

Mountbatten's original tenure of office as CDS had been for three years. Macmillan pressed him to lengthen this by a further two years to July 1964. Mountbatten was initially reluctant but changed his mind after the death of his wife in 1960. He later agreed to a further extension, to July 1965, in order to see through the first phase of defence reorganization. Wilson would have happily sanctioned yet another year, but Healey established that there would be considerable resentment at such a move on the part of the other service leaders and felt anyway that he would never be fully master of the Ministry of Defence while this potent relic from the past remained in office. Whether Mountbatten would have stayed on if pressed to do so is in any case doubtful; he was tired and stale, and had a multiplicity of interests to pursue outside.

Mountbatten's last few months as CDS were in fact spent partly abroad, leading a mission on Commonwealth immigration. The main purpose of this exercise was to explain British policy and persuade Commonwealth governments to control illegal immigration at source. The mission was a success; indeed Mountbatten found that he was largely preaching to the converted, since only in

Jamaica did the policy he was expounding meet with serious opposition. He presented the mission's report on 13 June 1965 and the following month took his formal farewell of the Ministry of Defence.

Final years Retirement did not mean inactivity; indeed Mountbatten was still officially enjoying his retirement leave when the prime minister invited him to go to Rhodesia as governor to forestall a declaration of independence by the white settler population. Mountbatten had little hesitation in refusing: 'Nothing could be worse for the cause you have at heart than to think that a tired out widower of 65 could recapture the youth, strength and enthusiasm of twenty years ago' (Ziegler, 648). However, he accepted a later suggestion that he should fly briefly to Rhodesia in November 1965 to invest the governor, Sir Humphrey Gibbs, with a decoration on behalf of the queen and generally to offer moral support. At the last minute the project was deferred and never revived.

The following year the home secretary asked Mountbatten to undertake an inquiry into prison security, in view of a number of recent sensational escapes. Mountbatten agreed, provided it could be a one-man report prepared with the help of three assessors. The report was complete within two months and most of the recommendations were carried out. The two most important, however—the appointment of an inspector-general responsible to the home secretary to head the prison service, and the building of a separate maximum security gaol for prisoners whose escape would be particularly damaging—were never implemented. For the latter proposal Mountbatten was much criticized by liberal reformers who felt the step a retrograde one; this Mountbatten contested, arguing that, isolated within a completely secure outer perimeter, the dangerous criminal could be allowed more freedom than would otherwise be the case.

Mountbatten was associated with 179 organizations, ranging alphabetically from the Admiralty Dramatic Society to the Zoological Society. In some of these his role was formal, in many more it was not. In time and effort the United World Colleges, a network of international schools modelled on the Gordonstoun of Kurt Hahn, received the largest share. Mountbatten worked indefatigably to whip up support and raise funds for the schools, lobbying the leaders of every country he visited. The electronics industry, also, engaged his attention, and he was an active first chairman of the National Electronics Research Council. In 1965 he was installed as governor of the Isle of Wight and conscientiously visited the island seven or eight times a year; in 1974 he became the first lord lieutenant when the island was raised to the status of a shire. A role which gave him still greater pleasure was that of colonel of the Life Guards, to which he was also appointed in 1965. He took his duties at trooping the colour very seriously and for weeks beforehand would ride around the Hampshire lanes near Broadlands in hacking jacket and Life Guards helmet.

Mountbatten's personal life was equally crowded. The years 1966 and 1967 were much occupied with the filming of the thirteen-part television series *The Life and Times of*

Lord Mountbatten, every detail of which absorbed him and whose sale he promoted energetically all over the world. He devoted much time to running the family estates and putting his massive archive in order, and involved himself enthusiastically in the opening of Broadlands to the public, which took place in 1978. He never lost his interest in naval affairs or in high strategy. One of his last major speeches was delivered at Strasbourg in May 1979, when he pleaded eloquently for arms control:

> As a military man who has given half a century of active service I say in all sincerity that the nuclear arms race has no military purpose. Wars cannot be fought with nuclear weapons. Their existence only adds to our perils because of the illusions which they have generated. (Ziegler, 695)

Some of Mountbatten's happiest hours were spent on tour with the royal family in their official yacht *Britannia*. He attached enormous importance to his royal connections and, though his influence was not so significant as he chose to imagine, his voice was often heard and sometimes heeded in Buckingham Palace—too often heard in the view of certain courtiers, who thought him a dangerous busybody. On the whole he spoke for modernization and the pruning of ancient ceremonies; he loved the rituals of state but was realistic enough to see the dangers of treating them as immutable and sacrosanct.

Mountbatten derived particular pleasure from his friendship with the prince of Wales, who treated him as 'honorary grandfather' and attached great value to his counsel. Mountbatten always urged the prince to sow his wild oats and then to marry and stick to a pure girl of good family; the advice was admirable in principle but proved impossible to apply in practice. It is conceivable that, if Mountbatten had lived and retained sufficient vigour, he might have played a father confessor role in the lives of both the prince and princess of Wales and helped to make their marriage less disastrous.

When Princess Anne married, the certificate gave as her surname Mountbatten-Windsor. This was the culmination of a long battle Mountbatten had waged to ensure that his family name, adopted by Prince Philip, should be preserved among his nephew's descendants. He took an intense interest in all the royal houses of Europe and was a source of advice on every subject. Harold Wilson once called him 'the shop-steward of royalty' (private information), and Mountbatten rejoiced in the description.

Death and significance Every summer Mountbatten enjoyed a family holiday at his Irish home in co. Sligo, Classiebawn Castle. Over the years the size of his police escort increased, but the Irish authorities were insistent that the cancellation of his holiday would be a victory for the Irish Republican Army. On 27 August 1979 a family party went out in a fishing boat, to collect lobster pots set the previous day. A bomb exploded when the boat was half a mile from Mullaghmoor harbour. Mountbatten was killed instantly, as were his grandson Nicholas and a local Irish boy. His daughter's mother-in-law, Doreen, Lady Brabourne, died shortly afterwards; his daughter Patricia and son-in-law Lord Brabourne were badly injured but later recovered. Mountbatten's funeral took place in

Westminster Abbey and he was buried in Romsey Abbey on 5 September. He had begun his preparations for the ceremony more than ten years before and was responsible for planning every detail, down to the lunch to be eaten by the mourners on the train from Waterloo to Romsey.

Mountbatten was a giant of a man, and his weaknesses were appropriately gigantic. His vanity was monstrous, his ambition unbridled. The truth, in his hands, was swiftly converted from what it was to what it should have been. But such frailties were far outweighed by his qualities. His energy was prodigious, as was his moral and physical courage. He was endlessly resilient in the face of disaster. No intellectual, he possessed a powerfully analytical intelligence; he could rapidly master a complex brief, spot the essential, and argue it persuasively. His flexibility of mind was extraordinary, as was his tolerance—he accepted all comers for what they were, not measured against some scale of predetermined values. He had style and panache and commanded the loyal devotion of those who served him. To his opponents in Whitehall he was 'tricky Dickie', devious and unscrupulous. To his family and close friends he was a man of wisdom and generosity. He adored his two daughters, Patricia and Pamela, and his ten grandchildren. However pressing his preoccupations he would make time to comfort, encourage, or advise them. Almost always the advice was good.

Among Mountbatten's honours were MVO (1920), KCVO (1922), GCVO (1937), DSO (1941), CB (1943), KCB (1945), KG (1946), privy councillor (1947), GCSI (1947), GCIE (1947), GCB (1955), OM (1965), and FRS (1966). He received an honorary DCL from Oxford (1946) and honorary LLDs from Cambridge (1946), Leeds (1950), Edinburgh (1954), Southampton (1955), London (1960), and Sussex (1963). He was honorary DSc of Delhi and Patna (1948). On Mountbatten's death the title passed to his elder daughter, Patricia Edwina Victoria Knatchbull (b. 1924), who became Countess Mountbatten of Burma.   PHILIP ZIEGLER

Sources P. Ziegler, *Mountbatten: the official biography* (1985) · U. Southampton L., Broadlands archives · R. A. Hough, *Louis and Victoria: the family history of the Mountbattens* (1974) · *History of the combined operations organisation*, HMSO (1956) · *Grand strategy*, 3–6 (HMSO, 1956–64) · *India: the transfer of power, 1942–7*, 9–12 (1980–83) · A. Campbell-Johnson, *Mission with Mountbatten* (1951) · J. Morgan, *Edwina Mountbatten* (1991) · M. Howard, *The central organisation of defence* (1970) · M. Edwardes, *The last years of British India* (1963), 178 · H. Macmillan, *At the end of the day, 1961–1963* (1973) [vol. 6 of autobiography]

Archives Bodl. RH, corresp. and papers relating to visit to Rhodesia · National Archives and Records Administration, Washington, DC · U. Southampton L., corresp. and papers | BL OIOC, corresp. with Sir Hugh Dow, MS Eur. E 372 · BL OIOC, corresp. with R. H. Dorman-Smith, MS Eur. E 215 · BL OIOC, corresp. with Sir Francis Mudie, MS Eur. F 164 · Bodl. Oxf., corresp. with Lord Monckton · Bodl. Oxf., corresp. with third earl of Selborne · CAC Cam., corresp. with D. H. McLachlan and papers relating to Sir Dudley Pound · CAC Cam., corresp. with Sir James Somerville · HLRO, corresp. with Lord Beaverbrook · IWM, letters to Sir Peter Cazalet · JRL, corresp. with Sir C. Auchinleck · NMM, corresp. with Sir Geoffrey Blake · NRA, priv. coll., letters to Admiral Lambe · priv. coll., Broadlands MSS · PRO, PREM series · PRO, corresp. with Lord Ismay, CAB 127/24–5 · SOAS, corresp. with H. V. Hodson · St George's Chapel, Windsor, corresp. with M. F. Bond | FILM BFI

NFTVA, 'Earl Mountbatten of Burma', 23 April 1959 · BFI NFTVA, 'Lord Mountbatten: the last viceroy', ITV, 27 April 1986 · BFI NFTVA, 'How I got my way', BBC 1, 28 Oct 1989 · BFI NFTVA, *Secret lives*, Channel 4, 9 March 1995 · BFI NFTVA, current affairs footage · BFI NFTVA, documentary footage · BFI NFTVA, news footage · BFI NFTVA, record footage · IWM FVA, 'Mountbatten accepts surrender of Japanese forces in South East Asia', 12 Sept 1945, ADM 1231 · IWM FVA, 'Gaumont British news: 1947—the dominions of India and Pakistan', Gaumont British News, 14 Aug 1947, MGH 1394 · IWM FVA, 'Edinburgh honours Lord and Lady Louis', Gaumont British News, 1954, MBY26 · IWM FVA, 'The twentieth century—Mountbatten, man of action', CBS News, 1963, MBY50 · IWM FVA, 'The life and times of Earl Mountbatten of Burma', Rediffusion Television, 1969 · IWM FVA, 'The funeral of Lord Mountbatten', Sept 1979, COI 1153 · IWM FVA, actuality footage · IWM FVA, current affairs footage · IWM FVA, news footage | SOUND BL NSA, 'Lord Louis Mountbatten interviewed by Henry Vincent Hudson', 8 Sept 1965, ICDR 0001106 · BL NSA, 'Lord Mountbatten remembers', xx(1819039.1) [parts 3–5] · BL NSA, 'Mountbatten of Burma', xx(1820368.1) · BL NSA, documentary recording · BL NSA, news recordings · BL NSA, performance recordings · IWM SA, oral history interviews

Likenesses photographs, 1919–77, Hult. Arch. · O. Edis, photographs, 1920, NPG · Yevonde, double portrait, photograph, 1922 (with Edwina Ashley), NPG · P. A. de Laszlo, oils, 1925, Broadland, Hampshire · D. Wilding, photograph, 1930–39, NPG · Yevonde, photograph, 1937, NPG · C. Beaton, photograph, 1940–49, NPG · Y. Karsh, photographs, 1943, NPG [*see illus.*] · H. Coster, photographs, *c*.1944–1945, NPG · B. Hailstone, oils, *c*.1944–1945, IWM · O. Birley, oils, 1946, Royal Naval College, Greenwich · H. Cartier-Bresson, photograph, 1948, NPG · E. I. Halliday, oils, *c*.1949, Government House, New Delhi, India · F. O. Salisbury, oils, 1957, Gov. Art Coll. · J. Ulbricht, oils, 1968, NPG · G. Lonn, oils, 1972, Broadlands, Hampshire · J. Gilroy, oils, 1978, Royal Marines Museum, Eastney barracks, Southsea, Hampshire · A. Newman, photograph, 1978, NPG · C. Sancha, oils, 1978, Trinity House, London · F. Belsky, statue, Foreign Office Green, London · B. Bury, oils, priv. coll. · E. I. Halliday, oils, Former Viceroy's House, New Delhi, India · D. Hill, oils, priv. coll. · P. A. de Laszlo, oils, priv. coll. · W. Stoneman, photographs, NPG · photographs, Broadlands, Hampshire

Wealth at death £2,196,949: probate, 29 Feb 1980, *CGPLA Eng. & Wales*

Mountbatten, Victoria Alberta Elisabeth Mathilde Marie, marchioness of Milford Haven [*formerly* Princess Louis of Battenberg; *née* Princess Victoria of Hesse] (1863–1950), was born on 5 April 1863 at Windsor Castle, the eldest of the seven children of Ludwig IV, grand duke of Hesse and by Rhine KG (1837–1892), and his first wife, Princess *Alice Maud Mary (1843–1878), second daughter of Queen Victoria.

Victoria's early years were spent at her grandparents' house at Bessungen, Germany. In 1866 the family moved into the Neues Palais in Darmstadt, where she shared a bedroom with her sister Ella (later Grand Duchess Serge of Russia) until her marriage. She could remember her father bringing loot back from the war against the French in 1870. Her education, with a governess in Germany, and sometimes at the court of Queen Victoria, was strict. Her mother, whose sense of duty was strong, took all her children to visit the Alice Hospital—her own foundation—to instil in them a duty towards others.

Victoria took the Oxford exams, and emerged from childhood a bright and avid reader. A series of family tragedies brought adult responsibility to her early: in 1873

Victoria Alberta Elisabeth Mathilde Marie Mountbatten, marchioness of Milford Haven (1863–1950), by Hills & Saunders

her brother Fritz fell to his death from a window in Darmstadt, aged two and a half; her youngest sister, Marie, died of diphtheria in 1878, and then her mother, having nursed the family, likewise contracted the illness and died. Thereafter Queen Victoria became a surrogate mother, and Victoria found herself acting as companion to her father and helping to bring up her siblings. A series of letters written to her by Queen Victoria was published in 1975 under the title *Advice to a Grand-Daughter*.

Victoria had known her first cousin, Prince Louis of Battenberg [see Mountbatten, Louis Alexander (1854–1921)], since childhood. He was already serving in the British navy, his career both helped and hindered by his royal connections. In 1883 they became engaged, but Queen Victoria forbade them to marry until the next year; they did so in Darmstadt on 30 April 1884, and from that day on she led the life of a naval officer's wife.

In the ensuing years Louis and Victoria had English homes variously near Chichester, Sussex, at Walton-on-Thames, Surrey, and in London. They spent many summers at Schloss Heiligenberg, Jugenheim (which Louis inherited in 1888), and winters both in Darmstadt and Malta, where Louis held a succession of naval appointments with the Mediterranean Fleet. Victoria continued to spend long periods under the wing of Queen Victoria, and it was at Windsor Castle in February 1885 that she gave birth to her first child, Alice (later Princess Andrew of Greece) [see Alice, Princess]. There were three further additions to the family: Louise (later queen of Sweden) in 1889, George *Mountbatten (later second marquess of Milford Haven) in 1892, and Louis *Mountbatten (later admiral of the fleet the Earl Mountbatten of Burma KG) in 1900.

Louis rose to the top of his profession, serving as first sea lord at the beginning of the First World War. But his German origins brought hostile attacks in the British press and he resigned in 1914, retiring quietly into private life. Victoria accompanied him to Kent House, on the Isle of Wight, where they spent the rest of the war. Further family misfortune came when her sister Alix (tsarina of Russia) was murdered with her entire family in 1918, and again when she learned that Ella, always her favourite sister, had been thrown to her death down a mine-shaft at Alapaievsk, also in 1918. In 1921 Victoria arranged for the transfer of Ella's coffin from Peking (Beijing) to Jerusalem, where it was laid to rest in the Russian Orthodox church of St Mary Magdalene. Victoria was present, accompanied by Louis and her daughter Louise.

Louis had been persuaded by George V to renounce his German title in 1917, adopting instead the surname of Mountbatten. He was created marquess of Milford Haven, earl of Medina, and Viscount Alderney. Victoria volunteered to renounce her German titles at the same time, and from then on was styled the marchioness (and in widowhood dowager marchioness) of Milford Haven.

On 11 September 1921 Louis died, and Victoria lived thereafter in a grace-and-favour apartment at Kensington Palace. She was attentive to her aunts, Princess Louise, duchess of Argyll, and Princess Beatrice. When her daughter Alice was ill during the 1930s Victoria was her only family contact for a time, and, having been a devoted grandmother to Alice's four daughters in the 1920s, she then oversaw the upbringing and schooling of Prince Philip in the 1930s in the absence of his parents. She was proud of her son Lord Louis Mountbatten, and forgiving of his wife, Edwina. After the war Victoria resumed friendly relations with her brother Ernst Ludwig, grand duke of Hesse and by Rhine, and her sister Irène (Princess Henry of Prussia).

Victoria faced further tragedy in her seventy-fifth year, during which her brother Ernst Ludwig died; her granddaughter Cécile and her family were killed in an aeroplane accident; and, shortly afterwards, her son George, second marquess of Milford Haven, died from bone cancer—all within a few months. During the Second World War she spent some time at Windsor Castle with George VI and Queen Elizabeth, having been bombed out of Kensington Palace.

Victoria lived to take pride in the marriage of her grandson Philip to Princess Elizabeth (later Queen Elizabeth II). She remained throughout life a determined, stalwart figure, given to progressive ideas, and with an interest in socialism and philosophy. She was well read and modern in her approach to life, and delivered her views in brisk, forthright manner, brooking no interruption. Highly executive, she once declared: 'I should have been the man of the family' (Vickers, 7).

Victoria wrote an unpublished book of memoirs with help from Baroness Buxhoeveden, the former lady-in-waiting to the tsarina, a copy of which is held in the Mountbatten papers at the Hartley Library, University of Southampton. She died at Kensington Palace on 24 September 1950, and was buried four days later at Whippingham church on the Isle of Wight. HUGO VICKERS

Sources Victoria, marchioness of Milford Haven, unpublished memoirs, U. Southampton, Hartley Library · R. Hough, *Louis and Victoria* (1974) · H. Vickers, *Alice, Princess Andrew of Greece* (2000) · *Burke's guide to the royal family* (1973) · private information (2004) [duke of Edinburgh] · Queen Victoria, *Advice to a grand-daughter*, ed. R. Hough (1975) · *The Times* (Sept 1950)
Archives Royal Arch. | U. Southampton, Hartley Library, Mountbatten papers · Broadlands, Hampshire, Mountbatten papers
Likenesses Hills & Saunders, photograph, NPG [*see illus.*] · P. A. de Laszlo, portrait, Broadlands, Hampshire · photograph, U. Southampton, Hartley Library, Mountbatten papers

Mountcashel. For this title name *see* MacCarthy, Justin, first Viscount Mountcashel (c.1643–1694).

Mount Edgcumbe. For this title name *see* Edgcumbe, George, first earl of Mount Edgcumbe (1720–1795); Edgcumbe, Richard, second earl of Mount Edgcumbe (1764–1839).

Mountevans. For this title name *see* Evans, Edward Ratcliffe Garth Russell, first Baron Mountevans (1880–1957).

Mountford family (*per. c.1370–1495*), gentry, of late medieval Warwickshire, was descended from Sir John Mountford, an illegitimate son of Peter, third Baron Montfort of Beaudesert, Warwickshire, who died c.1369 without any direct legitimate heirs, and Laura Ullenhall. To the four manors his father diverted to him from the legitimate line Sir John was able to add another three by his marriage to Joan, heir of Clinton of Coleshill. This large and valuable north Warwickshire manor became the centre of an estate located primarily in that region. John's son, **Baldwin Mountford** (*d.* 1386), married Margaret, daughter of a neighbour, John, Baron Clinton of Maxstoke. By 1384 he was in the service of John of Gaunt, duke of Lancaster, the lord of Kenilworth in central Warwickshire, and he died in Spain on Gaunt's service. The early death, about 1394, of his elder son, John, meant that his effective heir was his second son, **Sir William Mountford** (*d.* 1452). Both sons were in turn under the guardianship of Richard II's henchman William Bagot but William seems to have avoided his guardian's difficulties in 1399 and by 1407 had made the marriage that took the family into the front rank of the Warwickshire gentry and brought the last of their major land acquisitions. This match, with Margaret, sole heir of Sir John Peche, brought him a further ten Warwickshire manors, mostly in the central and south-eastern parts of the county, and made him its single greatest gentry landowner, worth at least £300 a year in 1417. But even more important in making the family exceptionally influential in Warwickshire was the fact that, unusually, most of its lands were concentrated in this county.

William's early career, however, was marked by a certain amount of unruliness and some difficulties in securing his inheritance. Notably, he became engaged in prolonged litigation for parts of the Montfort of Beaudesert estate, a dispute that came to a head under Henry V. That it was resolved in 1417 by compromise was due largely to the firm national control of Henry V and local control of Richard Beauchamp, earl of Warwick. The Mountfords had already had some more tenuous links with the earls but, after an earlier association with William, Lord Astley, of Astley in north Warwickshire, William Mountford became Beauchamp's close associate. He served in his retinue in France in 1415 and again in 1417–21 (he was knighted during this campaign), 1421–2, 1430–31, and 1437–9. At home he was said to be the earl's 'chief counsellor', receiving the large annuity of 40 marks, and was one of the pivotal figures in the powerful network focused on Beauchamp that knitted Warwickshire together during this period. His links with Beauchamp account for his offices in the county, the first of the family to be consistently among the official élite. He held all the major local offices and was appointed the earl's deputy in his Worcestershire shrievalty. During this period he was able to establish his eldest son, **Sir Baldwin Mountford** (*c.*1412–1474/5), at the Peche manor of Hampton in Arden and marry him to the sister of Sir Richard *Vernon of Haddon, a leading Derbyshire landowner [*see under* Vernon family].

After Warwick's death in 1439 Sir William Mountford was one of several custodians of the Warwick lands during the minority of the earl's son Henry. The others included members of Henry VI's household and, through these, Mountford acquired links to the court. These he proposed to exploit to disinherit his family by his first wife in favour of the sons of his second wife, Joan, daughter of William Alderwyche and widow of William Brokesby. **Sir Edmund Mountford** (*d.* 1494), the eldest son of the second marriage, was in France with his father in 1438, an esquire of the household by 1444, and MP for Warwickshire in 1447. Meanwhile Baldwin, a knight by 1437, received no royal favour and had to wait until 1449 for his first local office. By a series of miscalculations, the new earl of Warwick, Richard Neville, who succeeded Henry's infant daughter in 1449, alienated William and Edmund, with the result that these two looked for protection to Humphrey Stafford, duke of Buckingham (who had bought the Clinton property at Maxstoke in 1438), while Baldwin looked to Warwick. After William's death in 1452 the Mountford dispute became increasingly central to Warwickshire politics, helping to cause the breach between Warwick and the royal court—in which Edmund was now an influential figure—and becoming the focal point of the struggle for control of the county between Warwick and Buckingham. After Queen Margaret's coup in late 1456 Edmund was able to strike and he forced a series of releases from Baldwin and Baldwin's eldest son, **Sir Simon Mountford** (*d.* 1495). However, even with the royal court at Coventry, it seems that Edmund could not establish himself as legitimate heir in the eyes of the War-wickshire gentry, who still preferred Baldwin as an associ-ate. Edmund, who was a knight by mid-1459, remained conspicuously loyal to Henry VI, allegedly sheltering him at Coleshill after the battle of Blore Heath. He was attainted, went into exile with the Lancastrian royal fam-ily after the battle of Towton in 1461, and continued to fight for them until he left permanently for France with Queen Margaret in 1464.

The Yorkist accession gave outright victory to the senior line. Sir Baldwin immediately entered the church, styling himself thereafter 'knight and priest', and took almost no further part in worldly affairs. Simon, who had been knighted by 1461, and had been retained by Warwick in 1456–7, should by rights have succeeded to his grand-father's position in the Warwick affinity. However, although his tenure of local office and links with other members of the affinity in the early 1460s suggested that this was to be the case, he soon contrived to fall out with Warwick. While the earl was mostly away on the king's business, Simon gathered to himself a group of dissidents within the Warwick affinity, some of them in dispute with close servants of the earl. Simon's influence spread south-wards through the county. As it did so, he found the mar-riage alliance made in the 1450s with the daughter of Sir Richard Verney of Compton Verney in south Warwick-shire, himself an adept exploiter of discord among local nobles, especially useful. In 1465 the rising levels of ten-sion climaxed in an affray in which a servant of one of Warwick's closest followers was killed. Warwick, just back from the north with the captive Henry VI, had already removed Simon from the commission of the peace and the earl was soon in Warwickshire as head of an oyer and terminer commission into the affair. But he remained largely ineffectual in Warwickshire and deteri-orating relations with the king soon forced him to come to terms with the Warwickshire dissidents. Even this did not prevent Simon's taking William Hastings's fee in 1469–70 and fighting for Edward IV at Tewkesbury. Indeed, that Edmund still had hopes of returning with the restored Henry VI and recovering the Mountford estates was a strong incentive to Simon to stick with the Yorkists.

Under the duke of Clarence, who succeeded to the War-wick lands in 1471, Simon repeated the 'cuckoo in the nest' pattern but on a grander scale. Emboldened by Clar-ence's failure to establish effective lordship in the mid-lands, Simon began to act as a major local political force. The royal grant of the constableship of Kenilworth Castle in 1475 and further efforts to secure the rest of the Mont-fort lands in 1476 indicate the scope of his ambitions. In 1475 he went to France on Edward IV's expedition and his indenting for sixty-five fighting men reveals the sort of power he had at his disposal. But his attempt on the Mont-fort lands came to nothing and from 1478, once Edward IV had taken over Clarence's lands and local political leader-ship, Simon found his wings severely clipped. He remained a pivotal figure in local society and politics and a consistent local office holder but he no longer dared to try

to create an independent power base. The return and par-don in 1474 of Edmund, who was restored to a single Mountford manor (Remenham, Berkshire), were also incentives to good behaviour. Like most Warwickshire gentry, Simon kept his head well down under Richard III and, despite the reversal of Edmund's attainder after Henry VII's victory in 1485, Simon had no difficulty in being accepted as a loyal subject and local officer and indeed was present at the creation of the future Henry VIII as duke of York in 1494.

As the politics of Warwickshire and the counties to the north became ever more disturbed from 1487, however, Simon found it increasingly difficult to hold his own in local affairs. Unlike several of the other more prominent gentry of north Warwickshire and the north midlands, he was a law-abiding member of the local official establish-ment, most of whom came from the south of the county. Growing tension between the more orderly south War-wickshire gentry, most of them not favoured by the king, and the disorderly north Warwickshire and north-midlands gentry, many of whom were close to the king, led to a confrontation at the sessions of the peace in 1494, in which Simon was actively involved, standing up for the south against the north. These developments may lie behind Simon's implication in the alleged treason plot on behalf of Perkin Warbeck in January 1495 and his execu-tion in February. Although the Henry Mountford who was part of Warbeck's invasion force later that year was prob-ably Simon's son, and Simon may have viewed with fore-boding his own alienation from his immediate neigh-bours and proximity of his half-uncle Edmund to the king, it would have been uncharacteristic of him to have com-mitted treason after such a sure-footed tread through dec-ades of political turmoil. His execution may simply have been the king's exasperated response to the turmoil in the midlands, especially since the worst offenders were people whose importance to him was such that he could not touch them. Simon's confiscated lands were divided among Simon Digby, the earl of Kildare, and Henry VII's close aide, Reynold Bray, who also succeeded to Edmund's manor of Remenham when Edmund died, apparently unmarried, in 1494. Although Simon's heir, Thomas, was partially restored in 1504, Coleshill remained with the Digbys; the family never reattained its former eminence and disposed of its remaining Warwickshire estates in the early seventeenth century. From the time at which they acquired the Peche lands, the Mountfords were an immense presence in the political life of Warwickshire; whether this was used for good or ill depended largely on the ability of the earls of Warwick and, from 1478, of the king, but from the 1460s Simon may be seen as the harbin-ger of that independent gentry power which arguably began to emerge in England during the political crises of the fifteenth century.

The family owned the advowson at Ilmington, one of their Warwickshire manors, and sometimes used it for sons who entered the church, for example Baldwin's full brother, Richard. But their main religious interest was at

Coleshill. William's projected chantry there came to nothing, probably because of the prolonged dispute following his death and because Baldwin's entering the church was thought sufficient for the family souls, but family members may well have been responsible for additions to the church. The surviving evidence suggests that, although careful *rentiers*, the Mountfords tended not to exploit other sources of profit. Indeed their wealth, sufficient to set up cadet branches in nearly every generation, ensured that, even in periods of family feuding, no more than careful management was necessary. The family arms were bend of ten pieces or and azure.

CHRISTINE CARPENTER

Sources C. Carpenter, *Locality and polity* (1992) · *CPR* · *Calendar of the fine rolls*, 22 vols., PRO (1911–62) · *CCIR* · PRO, king's bench records, KB 9, KB 27 · PRO, chancery, court of chancery, early proceedings, C1 · W. Dugdale, *The antiquities of Warwickshire illustrated*, rev. W. Thomas, 2nd edn, 2 vols. (1730) · Birm. CL, Wingfield–Digby collection, esp. MS A473 · HoP, *Commons, 1386–1421* · Shakespeare Birthplace Trust RO, Stratford upon Avon, Archer collection, DR 37, box 73 · PRO, E 179/192/59
Archives Birm. CL, Wingfield-Digby collection
Wealth at death approx. £300 p.a. or more: Birm. CL, Wingfield-Digby MS A 473; Shakespeare Birthplace Trust RO, Stratford upon Avon, Archer coll., DR 37, box 73; PRO, E 179/192/59

Mountford, Baldwin (d. 1386). *See under* Mountford family (*per. c.*1370–1495).

Mountford, Sir Baldwin (*c.*1412–1474/5). *See under* Mountford family (*per. c.*1370–1495).

Mountford, Sir Edmund (d. 1494). *See under* Mountford family (*per. c.*1370–1495).

Mountford, Edward William (1855–1908), architect, was born on 22 September 1855 at Shipston-on-Stour, Worcestershire, the son of Edward Mountford, draper, and his wife, Eliza Devonshire, daughter of William and Mary Richards of Northampton. He was twice married: first, on 28 June 1888, to Jessie Elizabeth, daughter of John Saunders Smith of Northampton, in whose memory he furnished the south chapel of St Anne's Church, St Ann's Hill, London (a building by Sir Robert Smirke); and second, on 11 July 1903, to Dorothy, daughter of A. G. Hounsham of Hampstead Heath. He had a son, who followed him as an architect, from his first marriage, and a daughter from his second.

Mountford grew up in the Cotswolds and was educated privately at Clevedon, Somerset. In 1872 he was articled to Habershon and Pite, architects, and subsequently worked for them as a clerk of works. Lacking the connections that might have secured him patronage, he was employed as assistant to Messrs George Elkington and to Messrs Giles and Gough, before beginning independent practice in 1881. His early works were modest commissions in his native Worcestershire, beginning with a cottage hospital in Shipston-on-Stour. In collaboration with H. D. Appleton (also known as H. D. Searles-Wood) he built a few south London churches in the fourteenth-century Gothic style; and this type of commission formed an occasional part of his employment throughout his career. In his first decade

of practice, however, lack of employment left him free to enter numerous competitions.

Mountford's first real success was in winning the Sheffield town hall competition (1890); and thereafter he was regularly a winner (later still an assessor) of major public competitions. Among the buildings he won in competition (and subsequently built) were: Battersea town hall (1892; now the arts centre); St Olave's Grammar School (1893; now part of the South London College); the Northampton Institute (1896; now City University); and the central criminal court at the Old Bailey (1900–07), which replaced Newgate prison of 1769 and is probably Mountford's most important work. Among his other significant buildings were: Liverpool Technical College (1898); Booth's distillery, Cow Cross Street, Smithfield (1901; dem.); offices and flats at 34 Sloane Square, London (1905); the Northern Insurance Company building, 1 Moorgate, London (1906; with E. A. Grüning); and Lancaster town hall (1906–9), completed by his assistant and partner F. Dare Clapham. He was also among the architects invited to compete for the new Strand Crescent at the Aldwych (1900) and for London county hall (1907).

Mountford was one of the initiators of the 'Wrenaissance' style in the 1890s and one of the most successful practitioners of its developed form of Edwardian baroque, winning a silver medal at the 1900 Paris Exhibition. He was committed to the association of sculpture and painting with architecture, and worked closely with the sculptors Paul Montford, F. W. Pomeroy, and Gilbert Seale, and with the painters Gerald Moira and Sir William Richmond. He also retained an attachment to the vernacular architecture of his childhood and designed his own house at Munstead, near Godalming, Surrey, in 1901, in collaboration with his wife and with the advice of his neighbour Gertrude Jekyll on the garden.

Mountford became an associate of the Royal Institute of British Architects in 1881 and a fellow in 1890; he served on its council and (1907–8) on its prizes and studentships committee. From 1893 to 1895 he was president of the Architectural Association (AA) and acted as an advisory member of the AA school of architecture until his death. He was described as an antiquary (*The Builder*, 94, 15 Feb 1908, 274–5) and travelled in Italy (1880) and later Egypt (for his health). He was also an ardent cricketer and member of the Surrey County Cricket Club. Crippled by arthritis in his mid-forties, he died at his London home, 11 Craven Hill, Lancaster Gate, London, on 7 February 1908.

COLIN CUNNINGHAM

Sources drawings, RIBA BAL, Drawings collection · *DNB* · *Dir. Brit. archs.* · A. S. Gray, *Edwardian architecture: a biographical dictionary* (1985) · C. Cunningham, *Victorian and Edwardian town halls* (1981) · A. Service, *Edwardian architecture and its origins* (1975) · *The Builder*, 94 (1908), 190 · F. D. Clapham, *ArchR*, 23 (1908), 161–62 · *RIBA Journal*, 15 (1907–8), 274–5 · *Building News*, 94 (1908), 244–5 · R. A. Fellows, *Edwardian architecture: style and technology* (1995) · CGPLA Eng. & Wales (1908) · b. cert.
Archives RIBA, nomination papers · RIBA, biography file · RIBA BAL, drawings collection
Likenesses photograph, repro. in *Building News* (11 July 1890) · photograph, repro. in *ArchR*, 161 · portrait, RIBA BAL, Drawings

Collection · portrait, repro. in *Architectural Association Notes*, 8, facing p. 17 · portrait, repro. in W. T. Pike, *Contemporary biographies London*, 272

Wealth at death £23,239 2s. 11d.: probate, 10 March 1908, *CGPLA Eng. & Wales*

Mountford, Sir Simon (d. 1495). *See under* Mountford family (*per. c.*1370–1495).

Mountford, Sir William (d. 1452). *See under* Mountford family (*per. c.*1370–1495).

Mountfort, William (*c.*1664–1692), actor and playwright, was 'the Son of Captain *Mountfort*, a Gentleman of a good Family in *Staffordshire*'. The brief biography prefacing the 1720 edition of Mountfort's plays adds that 'he spent the greatest Part of his Younger Years in that County, without being bred up to any Employment' (pp. iii–iv). Mountfort's modern biographer, Albert Borgman, could not confirm these facts; however, he does point out that several Mountforts lived in Staffordshire during the mid-seventeenth century. The preface further avers that upon Mountfort's 'arriving to Manhood, his Gaiety of Temper and Airy Disposition, which were very conspicuous, could not be easily restrain'd to the solitary Amusements of a Rural Life' (*Six Plays*, iv).

Mountfort first surfaces in theatrical records for the 1678 season, suggesting that by the age of fourteen he had left Staffordshire for London. Employment with the Duke's Company was apparently rapid: on 28 May 1678 he played the Boy in John Leanerd's *The Counterfeits* (Van Lennep, 1.270). His only other known role during this period is that of Jack the barber's boy in *The Revenge, or, A Match in Newgate* (1680). In 1682, when the two companies united, 'Mr. *Monfort* and Mr. *Carlile*', according to the prompter John Downes, 'were grown to the Maturity of good *Actors*' (Downes, 82). None the less, Mountfort continued for three years to play a variety of supporting roles, such as Alphonso Corso in *The Duke of Guise* by Dryden and Lee (1682). He also played smallish parts in several revivals: Metellus Cimber in Shakespeare's *Julius Caesar* (1683?); the roles of Master Tallboy and the Lawyer in Brome's *A Jovial Crew* (1683); and Novel, the 'pert railing Coxcomb' and 'Admirer of Novelties' in Wycherley's *The Plain Dealer* (1682?).

In 1685 came the role that established Mountfort as a major talent in the United Company, that of Sir Courtly Nice in John Crowne's comedy of the same name. John Downes claimed that 'Sir *Courtly* was so nicely Perform'd, that not any succeeding, but Mr *Cyber* has Equall'd him' (Downes, 85). Colley Cibber attributed his subsequent success in the part exclusively to Mountfort's original interpretation:

> If, some Years after the Death of *Monfort*, I my self had any Success … I must pay the Debt, I owe to his Memory, in confessing the Advantages I receiv'd from the just Idea, and strong Impression he had given me, from his acting them. (Cibber, 76)

Acclaim in this and other roles undoubtedly moved Mountfort into the better-paid ranks of 'hireling' actors.

Mountfort's new-found fame as Sir Courtly Nice

brought him to the attention of prominent gentlemen and politicians. Matthew Prior noted in a well-turned couplet how Mountfort's theatrical performances ('That play'd so well Sir Courtly and Jack Daw') rendered him especially '*fit for Politicks and Law*' (Highfill, Burnim & Langhans, *BDA*, 10.355), an observation echoed elsewhere. Sir John Reresby in his memoirs recounts attending a dinner given by Lord Chancellor Jeffreys on 18 January 1686 to which 'my Lord Maior of London was invited and some other gentlemen' (*Memoirs of Sir John Reresby*, 408). After dinner Jeffreys called for Mountfort:

> a gentleman of his that had been a comedian, an excellent mimick, and to divert the company, as he called it, made him give us a caus, that is plead before him in a feigned action, wher he acted all the principal lawyers of the age, in their tone of voice, and action or gesture of body, and thus ridiculed not only the lawyers but the law itselfe. (*Memoirs of Sir John Reresby*, 408)

Some historians think that Mountfort withdrew for a while from the stage and lived as part of the Jeffreys household. There is no evidence to support this conjecture other than some lines from a contemporary lampoon that imagine Mountfort in a *ménage à trois* with Jeffreys and his wife:

> *There's a story of late*
> *That the Chancellor's mate*
> *Has been f----d and been f----d by player*
> *Mountfort;*
> *Which though false, yet's as true,*
> *My Lord gave him his due,*
> *For he had a small tilt at his bum for it.*
> (Highfill, Burnim & Langhans, *BDA*, 10.355)

Whatever the precise nature of his relationship with nobles like Jeffreys, the subsequent shape of Mountfort's career suggests that he did indeed aspire to a gentlemanly persona, both on stage and off. If Cibber's description is accurate, it would appear that nature sufficiently outfitted Mountfort to realize these aspirations:

> Of Person he was tall, well made, fair, and of an agreeable Aspect: His Voice clear, full, and melodious: In Tragedy he was the most affecting Lover within my Memory. … In Comedy, he gave the truest Life to what we call the *Fine Gentleman*; his Spirit shone the brighter for being polish'd with Decency … The *agreeable* was so natural to him, that ev'en in that dissolute Character of the *Rover* he seem'd to wash off the guilt from Vice, and gave it Charms and Merit. (Cibber, 74–5)

Possessed of a 'clear Countertenour' and 'a melodious, warbling Throat', Mountfort occasionally sang in productions (Cibber, 76). In Durfey's *A Fool's Preferment* (1688) and Southerne's *The Wives' Excuse* (1691), he performed songs by Purcell. Late in his career Mountfort showed a talent for musical composition: he wrote 'Great Jove Once Made Love Like a Bull' for Durfey's *The Marriage-Hater Matched* (1692). By the mid-eighties Mountfort played privileged young blades, *roués* who ultimately proved to be honourable, such as Belfond junior in Shadwell's *The Squire of Alsatia* (1688) or loyal, principled young men, such as Don Antonio in Dryden's *Don Sebastian* (1689), 'a young, noble, amorous *Portuguese*, now a Slave'. These were also the roles Mountfort created for himself when he began writing plays in 1688. In his first attempt, *The Injur'd Lovers, or, The Ambitious Father*, Mountfort wrote for himself the part of Dorenalus, a son who is sacrificed to the designs of his ambitious father. Although the production was consecrated by the combined efforts of that thespian trinity, Thomas Betterton, Elizabeth Barry, and Anne Bracegirdle, it proved an indifferent success. Mountfort also tried his hand at a farcical adaptation of Marlowe's *Dr Faustus* entitled *The Life and Death of Doctor Faustus* (1687–8?). Mountfort again shifted genre with his third attempt, *The Successful Straingers* (1690), a tragicomedy based on a story from Paul Scarron's *Le roman comique*. The dedication to Thomas Wharton, comptroller of the royal household, discloses Mountfort's social ambitions, while on stage he once again assumed a courtly persona as 'Silvio, a stranger in Love with *Dorothea*'. The preface, the only essay extant from Mountfort, reveals that his aspirations were not without cost: he alludes to '*a great many Enemies*' (fol. A3r), and he prints by way of retribution some verses that '*were sent me from an unknown hand by the way of Instruction*' (fol. A3v). Although *King Edward the Third* (1691) is included in the 1720 collection of Mountfort's plays—no attribution appears on the original title-page—his authorship remains uncertain.

It was also during this period that Mountfort proved an increasingly competent script doctor. Elkanah Settle, in the epistle dedicatory to *Distress'd Innocence* (1691), acknowledges his indebtedness 'to Mr. *Montfort*, for the Last Scene of my Play which he was so kind to write for me' (fol. A3r). Joseph Harris also praised Mountfort's contributions to his comedy, *The Mistakes* (1691): 'And here's a fresh occasion for my gratitude to *Mr. Monfort*, who in the fith Act has not only corrected the tediousness by cutting out a whole Scene, but to make the Plot more clear, has put in one of his own, which heightens his own Character, and was very pleasing to the Audience' (fol. A2v). In *Greenwich-Park* (1691) the literary ambitions of Mountfort were finally realized. A happy combination of a delightful script and a talented cast—it featured the collective comic talents of Anthony Leigh, James Nokes, and Cave Underhill—the play was an immediate success. Mountfort, as usual, wrote for himself the part of the dashing blade, Young Reveller, while his wife played Florella, his love interest. On 22 July 1686 Mountfort had married the actress Susanna Percival (*bap.* 1666, *d.* 1703), herself the daughter of a minor actor, at St Giles-in-the-Fields, London. The Mountforts had four children, two of whom, a boy and a girl, died in infancy. Their daughter Susanna was born on 27 April 1690 and baptized the following 11 May; she eventually became, according to the 1720 preface, 'an excellent actress' but quit the stage before the age of thirty (p. xi). A second daughter, Mary, was baptized on 27 April 1693, several months after Mountfort's death (Highfill, Burnim & Langhans, *BDA*, 10.356). Mrs Mountfort married another actor after the death of Mountfort, becoming Mrs John Verbruggen for the rest of her career [*see* Verbruggen, Susanna].

Ironically, the very qualities that underwrote Mountfort's romantic persona resulted in his tragic death. Captain Richard Hill, obsessed with the actress Anne Bracegirdle, blamed his amatory failure on Mountfort, convinced that the actor's good looks and chivalrous elegance had captured her heart. On 9 December 1692 Hill and a companion, Charles, Lord Mohun, attempted to abduct Bracegirdle on her way back from a dinner party. Thwarted, the men none the less stood outside Bracegirdle's house, drinking and becoming increasingly raucous. At midnight Mountfort, who customarily passed through the neighbourhood on the way home, was stopped by Hill and Mohun. At this point the details are somewhat confused, especially regarding the extent of Mohun's involvement. Apparently Mohun distracted Mountfort while Hill drew his sword. Before Mountfort had a chance to defend himself, Hill thrust the sword into his right breast, delivering a '*Mortal Wound of the breadth of one Inch, and of the depth of twenty Inches*' (*Tryal*, 8). Hill ran away successfully to the Isle of Wight and then to Scotland; Mohun was captured. Mountfort, after twelve hours of agony, died at Norfolk Street, London, the following day, 10 December 1692. He left his 'Goods & Personall Estate' to his wife (Borgman, 140). Mountfort was buried on 13 December at St Clement Danes; over 1000 people attended. Purcell provided the funeral music.

The transcript of Mohun's trial makes evident the tension at the proceedings—ladies fainted and bystanders jeered—and the external influence. Two key witnesses departed from testimony originally given under oath at Hick's Hall, hinting at pressure from Mohun's family. Bracegirdle's maid, who disappeared conveniently for several days, resurfaced at the trial and complained of threats from Mrs Mountfort and actors in the company. The trial captivated the public: John Evelyn, Narcissus Luttrell, and Charles Hatton mention it, as does Robert Harley: 'This day, the town having clamoured at the delay, gave judgment of not guilty. They have taken a news writer into custody for saying the evidence was strong enough to hang a commoner' (*Portland MSS*, 3.513). The popular press quickly memorialized Mountfort. The celebrated subject of 'A Tragical Song' and 'The Ladies' Lamentation', he also occasioned a lurid romance, *The Player's Tragedy, or, Fatal Love* (1693), which imagines an ill-fated passion between Mountfort and Bracegirdle, paradoxically, the very fiction that precipitated Hill's murderous rage.   DEBORAH PAYNE FISK

Sources Highfill, Burnim & Langhans, *BDA* · W. Van Lennep and others, eds., *The London stage, 1660–1800, pt 1: 1660–1700* (1965) · C. Cibber, *An apology for the life of Colley Cibber*, new edn, ed. B. R. S. Fone (1968) · *Six plays, written by Mr. Mountfort … to which is prefix'd some memoirs of the life of Mr. Mountfort*, 2 vols. (1720) · *The tryal of Charles Lord Mohun, before the house of peers in parliament, for the murder of William Mountford* (1693) · J. Downes, *Roscius Anglicanus*, ed. J. Milhous and R. D. Hume, new edn (1987) · A. S. Borgman, *The life and death of William Mountfort* (1935) · *Memoirs of Sir John Reresby*, ed. A. Browning (1936) · *The manuscripts of his grace the duke of Portland*, 10 vols., HMC, 29 (1891–1931), vol. 3 · G. Langbaine, *An account of the English dramatick poets* (1691); facs. edn with preface by A. Freeman (New York, 1973)

Wealth at death see will, repr. in Borgman, *Life and death*, 141

Mountgarret [Mountgarrett]. For this title name *see* Butler, Richard, first Viscount Mountgarret (*d.* 1571) [*see under* Butler, Piers, first earl of Ossory and eighth earl of Ormond (*b.* in or after 1467, *d.* 1539)]; Butler, Richard, third Viscount Mountgarret (1578–1651).

Mountier, Thomas (*fl.* **1719–1740**), singer, was possibly from Chichester; his name may be of French origin, or a corruption of the English names Mouncher or Mounsher. He was a lay vicar at Chichester Cathedral and according to the chapter books of the cathedral in 1719 was appointed preceptor of the choristers there. An entry in the Chichester Cathedral chapter act book (Cap I/3/2) for 12 May 1732 records that 'Upon reading of Thomas Mountier's letter under his own hand (One of the Lay Vicars of the Cathedral Church aforesaid) his place in the Choir to be void'. An act of 1 August 1733 records that 'Thomas Capell was in August Chapter 1732 admitted … to Teach the Choristers in the room of Thomas Mountier who resigned'.

By mid-1731 Mountier was making a name for himself in London: notices for his benefit concert at the Little Theatre in the Haymarket on 6 May describe him as 'the Chichester Boy, (Who sung at Mr. Smith's Concert [on 2 April], at the Theatre in Lincoln's Inn-Fields' (*Daily Journal*, 29 April 1731). His benefit was held 'At the Request of great Numbers of Gentlemen and Ladies', and Burney says Mountier was the favourite concert singer of that year (Burney, *Hist. mus.*, 2.1001). In March and April 1732 Mountier sang in concerts in Lincoln's Inn Fields and Hickford's rooms, and in November he was announced to sing in Geminiani's weekly series of twenty concerts in Hickford's rooms (*Daily Post*, 15 Nov 1731).

As part of the brief revival of interest in English opera in the early 1730s, Mountier made his first theatrical appearance as Acis in Thomas Arne's production of *Acis and Galatea* at the Haymarket theatre on 17 May 1732, which was also the first time this work had been fully staged, with 'Scenes, Machines, and other Decorations' (*Daily Post*, 6 May 1732). In November he appeared as Phoebus (and subsequently Neptune) in John Frederick Lampe's *Britannia*, and as the King (at the Haymarket) and then Noodle (at Drury Lane) in Lampe's *Opera of Operas* (1733). He continued to sing at Drury Lane in the 1733–4 season, taking parts in *Cephalus and Procris*, the Dryden–Davenant adaptation of *The Tempest*, the pantomime *Cupid and Psyche*, and the masque *Love and Glory*. Otto Deutsch and the *Dictionary of National Biography* suggest Mountier sang Adelberto in Handel's *Ottone* in 1733, but Signor Scalzi was advertised in that role in the November 1733 revival. Mountier makes only one further appearance in London theatre records, singing in a benefit concert for Valentine Snow on 19 March 1740.   SUZANNE ASPDEN

Sources A. H. Scouten, ed., *The London stage, 1660–1800*, pt 3: *1729–1747* (1961) · Highfill, Burnim & Langhans, *BDA*, 10.359–60 · Chichester Cathedral chapter act book, W. Sussex RO, Cap I/3/2 · Burney, *Hist. mus.*, new edn · *Daily Journal* (1 April 1731) · *Daily Journal* (29 April 1731) · *Daily Journal* (10 March 1732) · *Daily Journal* (21 March 1732) · *Daily Journal* (25 March 1732) · *Daily Post* [London] (2 April 1731) · *Daily Post* [London] (15 Nov 1731) · *DNB*

Mountjoy. For this title name *see* Blount, Walter, first Baron Mountjoy (*d.* 1474); Blount, John, third Baron Mountjoy (*d.* 1485) [*see under* Blount, Walter, first Baron Mountjoy (*d.* 1474)]; Blount, William, fourth Baron Mountjoy (*c.*1478–1534); Blount, Charles, fifth Baron Mountjoy (1516–1544); Blount, James, sixth Baron Mountjoy (1532/3–1581) [*see under* Blount, Charles, fifth Baron Mountjoy (1516–1544)]; Blount, Charles, eighth Baron Mountjoy and earl of Devonshire (1563–1606); Stewart, William, first Viscount Mountjoy (*c.*1650–1692); Gardiner, Luke, first Viscount Mountjoy (1745–1798).

Mount-Maurice, Hervey de. *See* Montmorency, Hervey de (*fl. c.*1135–*c.*1189).

Mountmorres. For this title name *see* Morres, Hervey Redmond, second Viscount Mountmorres (1741/2–1797).

Mountney, Richard (1707–1768), judge and classical scholar, was born at Putney, London, where he was baptized on 9 November 1707, the son of Richard Mountney (1671?–1707), an officer of the customs house, and Maria (or Anne), *née* Carey. He had at least one sibling, a sister named Anne who married John Lely, grandson of Sir Peter Lely. He entered Eton College as a king's scholar in 1721, and matriculated as a scholar at King's College, Cambridge, on 1 October 1725. He graduated BA in 1729 and MA in 1735, and was a fellow of King's from 1728 to 1735. At Cambridge he acquired a considerable reputation as a classical scholar, and in 1731 published an edition of Demosthenes' *Orations* that ran to numerous editions and was for many years the standard edition used in the University of Oxford.

Mountney had entered Lincoln's Inn on 16 April 1725 and was called to the English bar on 23 October 1732. In 1735 he married Margaret Jeynton (*d.* 1756) in the joint parish of St Vedast-alias-Foster and St Michael-le-Querne, London; they had no children. Not much is known about his years in practice, save that he was appointed a commissioner of bankrupts in 1739, but his abilities were such that Lord Chancellor Hardwicke apparently held him 'in high regard' (Ball, 134), and the following tribute to his performances at the bar (and also to his literary gifts) was penned by Paul Jodrell, sometime solicitor-general to Frederick, prince of Wales:

> Nature, to you more eminently kind,
> The wide extremes of law and verse have join'd;
> Alike in both you happily succeed,
> Resistless when you sing, as when you plead.
> By the same force of two commanding arts,
> Men gain estates and women lose their hearts.
> Whene'er the venerable coif shall spread
> Its sable honours o'er thy learned head;
> The Muse, expressive of thy other praise,
> Around the silk shall wreathe the sacred bays.
> (*GM*, 51.384)

Hardwicke's opinion of Mountney was clearly very favourable, for in 1741 he was appointed a baron of the Irish court of exchequer, after only nine years of practice and at the very early age of thirty-four. He was one of 'a triad of brilliant men' (Ball, 133) appointed to the

Richard Mountney (1707–1768), by William Hogarth

exchequer court in 1741, the others being John Bowes, who was appointed lord chief baron, and Arthur Dawson.

The triumvirate presided over the Irish exchequer court for fifteen years and together heard the famous ejectment action brought by James Annesley against his uncle Richard Annesley, sixth earl of Anglesey. Annesley claimed from his uncle the barony of Altham, in the Irish peerage, and the Annesley family's Irish estates, saying that he was the legitimate son and heir of Lord Anglesey's elder brother Arthur, fourth Baron Altham. Anglesey, who on his brother's death apparently had had the young James Annesley kidnapped and sold into slavery in America, insisted that he was merely the bastard son of a kitchen maid rejoicing in the name of Juggy Landy.

The action came on for hearing in November 1743. The jury included ten members of the Irish House of Commons, and the parties were represented by almost thirty counsel, including the five law officers—the attorney-general, St George Caulfield; the solicitor-general, Warden Floud; and the three serjeants-at-law—and the recorder of Dublin, Easton Stannard. The trial lasted fifteen days, a fairly modest figure by modern standards but at the time made it the longest trial ever known. Bowes gave an impartial charge to the jury, Mountney's tended to favour the claims of the plaintiff, Dawson's those of the defendant. In the result the jury found for James Annesley, thereby in effect establishing his legitimacy. Because he had little money, however, he was not able to pursue his claims to the Altham peerage, nor the Anglesey earldom and estates in England. Mountney's connection with this remarkable *cause célèbre* did not end with the ejectment action, for he subsequently tried Lord Anglesey and others at Athy assizes on charges of assault on James

Annesley and his colleagues when they were attending the races at the Curragh. A number of the charges were proved, and Anglesey and his co-defendants fined.

In 1748 Mountney published his *Observations on the Probable Issue of the Congress of Aix la Chapelle* and a second edition of Demosthenes' *Orations*, which he dedicated to the late Sir Robert Walpole and to Trinity College, Dublin. In 1754 he declined an offer to become a bencher of Lincoln's Inn, on the ground of his residence in Ireland. Apparently he hoped that he might succeed Bowes as lord chief baron of the exchequer on Bowes's promotion to the woolsack in 1756, although the two had never enjoyed a very friendly relationship. Bowes, however, was replaced by Edward Willes, a cousin of the chief justice of the common pleas in England. Mountney ascribed the rejection of his claims to 'engines of calumny and malice set at work by professed enemies and pretended friends' (Ball, 143), although Ball suggests that his candidacy was more likely damaged by an excessive fondness for liquor; he was known to frequent punch houses and was recorded in a grand-jury book as having been drunk at Westmeath assizes. On 5 October 1759 he married Marie Angélique Madeleine Montgomery (d. 1771), widow of Thomas Montgomery, fifth earl of Mount-Alexander, and daughter of Daniel de la Cherois, of Lisburn. They also had no children.

Mountney's long and satisfactory tenure of his judicial office ended on 7 April 1768, when he died on assize in Belturbet, co. Cavan. He may have been buried at Donnybrook, near Dublin, where a number of family members, including his first wife, Margaret, also were interred.

NATHAN WELLS

Sources F. E. Ball, *The judges in Ireland, 1221–1921*, 2 (New York, 1927) · *N&Q*, 2nd ser., 12 (1861), 170, 254, 526; 3rd ser., 6 (1864), 89, 235 · R. A. Austen-Leigh, ed., *The Eton College register, 1698–1752* (1927) · *GM*, 1st ser., 38 (1768), 198; 51 (1781), 384, 404 · *State trials*, 9.1766 · *Graduati Cantabrigienses (1659–1823)* (1823) · GEC, *Peerage*, new edn, 9.309 · Venn, *Alum. Cant.* · IGI · O. J. Burke, *The history of the lord chancellors of Ireland from AD 1186 to AD 1874* (1879), 124–39

Archives BL, letters to Lord Hardwicke, Add. MSS 35586–35596, *passim*

Likenesses W. Hogarth, portrait; Christies, 22 April 1983, lot 73 [see illus.]

Mountrath. For this title name *see* Coote, Charles, first earl of Mountrath (c.1610–1661).

Mount Stephen. For this title name *see* Stephen, George, Baron Mount Stephen (1829–1921).

Mount Temple. For this title name *see* Ashley, Wilfrid William, Baron Mount Temple (1867–1939).

Mount-Temple. For this title name *see* Temple, William Francis Cowper-, Baron Mount-Temple (1811–1888); Temple, Georgina Cowper-, Lady Mount-Temple (1821?–1901).

Mourant, Arthur Ernest (1904–1994), haematologist and geologist, was born on 11 April 1904 at Fairview Farm, St Saviour, Jersey, the eldest of the three children of Ernest Charles Mourant, farmer, and his wife, Emily Gertrude, *née* Bray. The Mourant family name is found in Jersey records from the early fourteenth century onwards. He started his formal education at the age of five at a small private school where he remained until, taking the preliminary examination of the College of Preceptors at the age of eleven, he achieved such good results that his parents, realizing his academic potential, moved him to the Jersey modern school, a private school for boys. Sitting the junior examination of the College of Preceptors he came third in competition with the whole of the United Kingdom, and one year later he came fourth in the senior examination. Seeing now that an academic career, rather than farming, beckoned, in 1919 he was sent to Victoria College, the local public school for boys, where he distinguished himself academically, although the sporting and military traditions of the establishment did not appeal to him. At this time most Jersey farming families spoke French and English with equal fluency and many also habitually used Jersey Norman French within the home. Mourant's formal education was in English, but the family attended a French-speaking Wesleyan chapel which helped establish the bilingualism which was so useful in his adult life. At school he also studied German and was interested in geography, but the sciences and applied mathematics interested him most. His science master, A. J. Robinson, introduced him to field studies, and Mourant developed a lifelong interest in geology, particularly the geological structure of the island of Jersey. The breadth of his abilities was shown by his winning the king's gold medals for modern languages and mathematics and the King Charles I Channel Islands scholarship to Exeter College, Oxford.

In September 1922 Mourant left his native island for the first time, for Oxford. He found university life exciting and stimulating. He associated with many brilliant contemporaries and attended a wide range of lectures on subjects as diverse as organic chemistry and chemical crystallography, while keeping up his interest in geology. He graduated with a first-class degree in chemistry in 1926, specializing in mineralogy. This led to the award of a King Charles I Channel Islands senior scholarship, and he also won the Burdett-Coutts scholarship in geology, enabling him to work for the degree of DPhil. Taking as his subject the Precambrian volcanic rocks of Jersey, on the advice of Robert Ranulph Marett, a fellow Jerseyman then about to become rector of Exeter College, he travelled in Normandy and Brittany, setting the local rock formations in their wider context.

In the immediate vicinity of the farmhouse where Mourant was born stood a large artificial mound surmounted by two medieval chapels and a tall tower, known as Prince's Tower owing to its association with Philippe D'Auvergne, prince de Bouillon, who directed his Scarlet Pimpernel-like activities from Jersey at the time of the French Revolution. Local antiquarians suspected the mound, alternatively known as La Hougue Bie, of concealing prehistoric remains, and the local antiquarian society, La Société Jersiaise, purchased the property. In 1924 the tower was demolished to permit excavation of the mound, and Mourant, at home for the summer vacation, was present at the discovery of one of the finest neolithic tombs in western Europe. Indeed, being small of stature he slipped in through the partially opened entrance and took the first photograph of the interior.

In 1929, Mourant worked briefly as a demonstrator in geology at the University of Leeds and then obtained a post with the geological survey. He became convinced of the accuracy of the theory of continental drift, later widely accepted as tectonic plate theory, but, finding the priorities of the survey uncongenial, he resigned and returned to Jersey in 1931 where he completed his doctoral thesis. After a brief spell accompanying a wealthy young American on a tour of Italy and Germany he was persuaded by an old schoolfriend, by then a medical practitioner, of the need for a chemical pathology laboratory in Jersey. He therefore established, initially as a private venture, the laboratory which later became the States of Jersey Pathology Laboratory. His interest in the geology and archaeology of the island led to his election to the executive committee of the Société Jersiaise, and he also promoted the work of the League of Nations, becoming honorary secretary of the Jersey branch. He became increasingly conscious of the emotional and intellectual limitations of the life he was living, and, after discussion with friends in the medical profession, decided to train as a doctor.

In January 1939 Mourant moved to London, having been accepted for training by St Bartholomew's Hospital medical college, where he qualified as a medical doctor in 1943. The German occupation of Jersey, in June 1940, brought isolation from his family, and throughout the war years he played a very active role in the Jersey Society in London. He also founded the North London Channel Islands Society, working among Channel Islands refugees. After a period as house physician at Chase Farm Hospital, Luton, and as house surgeon at Friern Hospital, London, he was appointed medical officer at the North London Blood Depot in 1944. This led to his becoming, in 1946, director of the Blood Group Reference Laboratory at the Lister Institute, London, which incorporated, from 1952, the World Health Organization International Blood Group Reference Laboratory. He had found his major life's work.

Mourant refined the existing classification of blood types and researched new, and in some cases obscure, variations. The theory of Robert Russell Race and Sir Ronald Fisher, linking blood groups to three genes producing rhesus factors, which they named C, c, D, d and E, e, intrigued Mourant, and in 1945 he found a serum containing an antibody to factor e. He then developed, with Race and R. R. A. Coombs, the anti-globulin test for blood group antibodies, still in universal use to ensure the compatibility of blood used for transfusion. He applied the study of blood groups to anthropology for the first time, studying the racial distribution of blood types, and in 1954 he published his seminal work, *The Distribution of the Human Blood Groups*. He was a prolific writer, publishing works on such diverse topics as *The Smaller Channel Islands* (1942), *The Blood Groups of the Jews* (1959), *Human Blood Groups and Natural*

Selection (1959), *The Minerals of Jersey* (1961), and *Man and Cattle* (1963). An appendix to his autobiography, *Blood and Stones* (1995), lists 460 known publications and articles in learned journals in both English and French. He was also a popular lecturer in both languages.

Mourant remained as director of the Blood Group Reference Laboratory until 1963, in which year he was appointed director of the Serological Population Genetics Laboratory and senior lecturer in haematology at St Bartholomew's Hospital Medical College, London. His work was recognized by the award of many honours including fellowship of the Royal College of Physicians, London, fellowship of the Royal College of Pathologists, London, and corresponding membership of the Académie des Sciences, Belles-Lettres et Inscriptions de Toulouse. He was elected a fellow of the Royal Society in 1966. He also held several lecturerships and was visiting professor or examiner in a number of universities. He was elected a membre d'honneur of the Société Jersiaise in 1961.

Mourant retired in 1977. On 25 February the following year he married Jean Elizabeth Cameron Shimell (*née* Dickson), who had been his secretary for a long period some years earlier. After returning to Jersey they settled into the dower house of the family farm and Mourant resumed his active interest in local prehistory and geology, producing numerous papers on these subjects, in recognition of which he received the Worth award of the Geological Society of London in 1982. The Arthur Mourant Trust for Archaeology and Geology, set up in his honour, proved a stimulus to the creation of the Jersey Heritage Trust. In 1990 members of the Société Jersiaise subscribed to the commissioning of a bronze portrait bust by the sculptor John Doubleday, which graces the entrance courtyard of its St Helier premises. In retirement he continued to write and, in addition to his scientific works, produced an autobiography which was rounded off by his friend and protégé, Dr G. P. Misson, and published posthumously in 1995. He remained active and in good health until near the time of his death, at St Saviour, Jersey, on 29 August 1994. His funeral was held at Aquila Road Methodist Church, St Helier, and he was buried in the family grave at St Saviour. He was survived by his wife.

F. L. M. CORBET

Sources A. E. Mourant, *Blood and stones: an autobiography*, ed. G. P. Misson (La Haule, Jersey, 1995) · *Jersey Evening Post* (31 Aug 1994) · *The Independent* (6 Sept 1994) · *BMJ* (24 Sept 1994) · *Annual Bulletin* [Société Jersiaise] (1991) · *Annual Bulletin* [Société Jersiaise] (1995) · *WWW*, 1991–5 · personal knowledge (2004) · F. L. M. C. [F. L. M. Corbet], 'Mourant, Arthur Ernest', in F. L. M. Corbet and others, *A biographical dictionary of Jersey*, [2] (1998), 313–6
Archives La Société Jersiaise, St Helier, Jersey, Lord Coutanche Library · Wellcome L., corresp. and papers
Likenesses J. Doubleday, bronze bust, Société Jersiaise, 7 Pier Road, St Helier, Jersey · photograph (with bust), repro. in F. L. M. Corbet and others, *Biographical dictionary of Jersey*, following p. 182

Moutray, John, of Roscobie (1722/3–1785), naval officer, was the younger son of James Moutray (*b*. 1687, *d*. before 1734), laird of Roscobie, Fife, and his wife, Emelia Malcolm (*d*. 1762). On 12 May 1744 Sir Chaloner Ogle made him lieutenant of the *Oxford* in the Caribbean. He held several such posts until appointed on 16 February 1757 to command the hospital ship *Thetis*, in which he was elevated (irregularly) to post rank on 28 December 1758. He commanded a number of ships between 1769 and 1779, but his service was relatively undistinguished. He became laird of Roscobie on his brother's death (18 May 1773).

In March 1779 Moutray was appointed to command the *Ramillies*, and in July 1780 she and the frigates *Thetis* and *Southampton* sailed to escort a large and valuable convoy of merchant ships bound for America and the East and West Indies. Although they were escorted at first by three other warships and, briefly, by the entire Channel Fleet, these had all returned to other duties when, at sunset on 8 August, sails were sighted far to the south. Moutray ignored the report and sailed on until, at midnight, lights were sighted ahead. The merchant ships ignored his belated signal to change course, and the next morning sailed straight into the combined Franco-Spanish fleet, which had been blockading Gibraltar. Virtually all the ships were lost, along with stores much needed by the West Indies fleet, and the loss to the insurers was estimated at £1,500,000. Moutray was tried by a court martial at Jamaica from 13 to 26 January 1781. His lame defence hinged on a claim that the log book had been falsified by the lieutenant and master, whose collusion had a 'sinister [but unspecified] purpose' (*Minutes of the … Court Martial*, 166). Moutray was dismissed his command and, to placate mercantile opinion, the minutes of the case were published, though later historians took the view that the Admiralty was to blame for allocating such an inadequate escort to so valuable a fleet.

The dismissal had no permanent effect on Moutray's career. He was appointed captain of the *Edgar* on 2 March 1782, moved in May to the *Vengeance* (in which he fought his only battle, off Cape Spartel in October), and was appointed commissioner at Antigua in February 1783. Despite the civil nature of this appointment, on 29 December 1784 Admiral Sir Richard Hughes ordered Moutray to hoist a broad pennant and act as the senior officer when Hughes himself was not present. When Nelson brought his command, the *Boreas*, back into English Harbour on 5 February 1785 he immediately objected to Moutray's right to command and to delegate the right to the pennant to a junior captain. Nevertheless he protested his personal friendship for Moutray, arguing only that a commissioner of the navy was not a commissioned sea officer. Nelson referred the case to the Admiralty, thereby bypassing Hughes (for which he was reprimanded), but the issue was academic: Moutray had already been recalled, his health was failing in any case, and he died at Bath on 22 November 1785, aged sixty-two. He was buried at Bath Abbey, where there is a memorial to him, on 26 November. Although his will left his estate to his wife and their children, it also refers to two illegitimate children of him and one Elspet London.

Moutray's wife, **Mary Moutray** [*née* Pemble] (*bap.* 1752, *d*. 1844), friend of Admiral Lord Nelson, was the daughter of Thomas Pemble (*d*. 1785), naval officer, and his wife, Catherine, *née* Selby (*d. c*.1785). She was baptized in Charles parish, York, Virginia, on 15 October 1752; her father was then lieutenant of the *Triton* on the Virginia station. She married John Moutray at Berwick upon Tweed on 2 September 1771, and in 1773 gave birth to twins, Catherine and John. At Antigua, she and John regularly entertained visiting captains at their house, Windsor. Her lively personality captivated the youthful Captain Horatio Nelson, whose letters suggest he was besotted by her, if not by her Caribbean home: 'was it not for Mrs Moutray, who is VERY VERY good to me, I should almost hang myself at this infernal hole', he wrote in September 1784 (*Dispatches and Letters*, 1.110). When her departure was certain, Nelson wrote to his brother:

> My dear, sweet friend is going home … Her equal I never saw in any country or in any situation … What an acquisition to any female to be acquainted with: what an example to take pattern from … What a *treasure* of a woman. God bless her. (ibid., 1.124)

Although Nelson soon began his successful pursuit of Frances Nisbet he extolled Mary's virtues to her with little apparent regard for Frances's sensibilities: 'a more amiable woman can hardly exist', he wrote in August (*Nelson's Letters*, 18), and after the death of Captain Moutray he informed Frances that:

> my amiable Mrs Moutray [is] full of affliction and woe: she is upon the eve of going to France with her family as it was the plan of her late husband. The Duchess of Richmond carried her to court to present her petition for the Commissioner's pension, and both King and Queen were very kind to her and said they had no doubt but she would get the pension, but that hard-hearted Lord Howe in Council opposed the measure as a bad precedent, therefore she has not got it … What has this poor dear soul undergone in one twelve months. Lost father, mother, husband and part of her fortune and left with two children … Indeed my dearest I can't express what I feel for her and your good heart I am sure will sympathise with mine. (ibid., 28)

Not surprisingly several writers have suggested that if Mary Moutray had been widowed in Antigua rather than at Bath then she, and not Frances Nisbet, might have become Mrs Nelson. As it was, Nelson promoted the career of her son John, who became a lieutenant in the navy, and when he died at the siege of Calvi in 1794, Nelson erected a monument to him. Cuthbert Collingwood, too, had been captivated by Mary, and in 1805 wrote her a moving letter informing her of the death of their mutual friend. Collingwood continued to correspond with her, recalling in 1808 his 'frizzling your head for a ball dress at Antigua' (*Private Correspondence*, 258), and even wrote her a poem:

> To you belongs the wond'rous art
> To shed around you pleasure;
> New worth to best of things impart,
> And make of trifles—treasure.
> (Pettigrew, 31–2)

Mary died in co. Meath in 1844; her daughter Catherine ('Kate' to Nelson and Collingwood) had married Thomas de Lacy, archdeacon of Meath, in 1806.   J. D. DAVIES

Sources *DNB* · PRO, Admiralty MSS, esp. ADM 1/5317, fols. 258–328 and ADM 8 [ADM 1/5317, fols. 258–328: court-martial papers] · marquis de Ruvigny and Raineval, *Moutray of Seafield and Roscobie* (1902) · *The dispatches and letters of Vice-Admiral Lord Viscount Nelson*, ed. N. H. Nicolas, 7 vols. (1844–6), vol. 1 · *Nelson's letters to his wife and*

other documents, 1785–1831, ed. G. P. B. Naish, Navy RS, 100 (1958) · *The private correspondence of Admiral Lord Collingwood*, ed. E. Hughes, Navy RS, 98 (1957) · T. Pocock, *Nelson's women* (1999) · PRO, PROB 11/1136, fol. 294 [will of John Moutray] · *The Genealogist*, 7 (1883), 26–7 · *Minutes of the proceedings of a court martial assembled for the trial of Captain John Moutray, of His Majesty's ship the Ramillies* (1782); repr. (1969) · private information (2004) [D. Nicholson, curator of the Historic Dockyard, Antigua] · *IGI* · T. J. Pettigrew, *Memoirs of the life of Vice-Admiral Lord Viscount Nelson*, 2 vols. (1849) · T. Pocock, 'Captain Nelson and Mrs Moutray', *Nelson Dispatch*, 1 (1982), 54–5 · T. Pocock, '"My dear sweet friend": Mrs Moutray and Captain Nelson', *Country Life* (22 Nov 1983), 778–80 · A. J. Jewers, ed., *The registers of the abbey church of SS Peter and Paul, Bath*, 2, Harleian Society, Register Section, 28 (1901), 471

Archives PRO, Admiralty MSS

Likenesses J. Downman, oils (Mary Moutray, née Pemble), repro. in Pocock, *Nelson's women*; priv. coll.

Wealth at death estate at Roscobie and lands in Dunfermline: will, PRO, PROB 11/1136, fol. 294

Moutray, Mary (*bap.* 1752, *d.* 1844). *See under* Moutray, John, of Roscobie (1722/3–1785).

Mowat, Charles Loch (1911–1970). *See under* Mowat, Robert Balmain (1883–1941).

Mowat, Sir Oliver (1820–1903), lawyer and politician in Canada, was born on 22 July 1820 in Kingston, Upper Canada, the eldest of the five children of John Mowat (1791–1860) and Helen Levack (1791–1873), immigrants from Caithness. John Mowat had left the British army after the Anglo-American War of 1812–14 and become a well-to-do merchant in the thriving town of Kingston.

Oliver Mowat was brought up among Scots. He attended St Andrew's Presbyterian Church, where his father was an elder, and the Revd John Cruikshank's private school, followed by Midland district grammar school under headmaster George Baxter. He read law in the Kingston office of John A. Macdonald (1836–40) and with the Toronto equity specialist Robert Easton Burns (1841). When called to the bar in November 1841 he went into partnership with Burns, tying his future to the court of chancery and the rising city of Toronto.

On 19 May 1846 Oliver married Jane Ewart (1824–1893), the attractive daughter of Scots-born John Ewart, a well-known Toronto contractor. They had three sons and four daughters; two of the children died in infancy.

Increasing business in the mid-century presented many cases for equitable settlement, and Mowat, through his dedication and sound legal knowledge, was soon retained in the most important. In 1853 he was employing five clerks and had net earnings of C$14,000. Several of the decisions that he won were upheld by the highest court, the judicial committee of the British privy council. His professional standing was recognized by election in 1853 as a bencher of the Law Society of Upper Canada and appointments in 1856 as queen's counsel and commissioner to consolidate the provincial statutes.

The established lawyer felt the challenge of politics. Elected alderman for 1857 and 1858, Mowat left his imprint on Toronto by his promotion of public parks and reforms in city management. At the same time, though hitherto without party affiliation, he came to the conclusion that it was his 'duty' to oppose the governing Conservatives, who had 'no principle nor patriotism' (Biggar, 77, 79). In the provincial election of December 1857 he ran as a Reformer in the riding of Ontario South, promising to perform his duties as became 'a Christian politician' (ibid., 70).

In the legislature Mowat rose rapidly to a prominent place beside the Reform chief George Brown. Short, near-sighted, and plain-featured, he was not an impressive figure. Nor was he an orator, but he was a convincing speaker because he was lucid, sensible, and tactful. And he was loyal: Brown considered him one of the 'reliables' (letter to Gordon Brown, 11 May 1863, Brown MSS, Public Archives of Canada). He served as provincial secretary in the two-day Brown–A. A. Dorion ministry of 1858, and as postmaster-general in the nine-month Sandfield Macdonald–Dorion administration of 1863. In this post he negotiated improved contracts with the Grand Trunk Railway Company and the Montreal Ocean Steamship Company for carrying mail.

As mounting sectional discord strained the union between Upper and Lower Canada which had been established in 1841, some Reformers proposed dissolution. Mowat, however, supported Brown at the convention of 1859 in endorsing a federal relationship with local governments for local matters and a general government for common concerns. In May 1864, when Brown's motion for a select committee to devise a solution for the deadlock between the Canadas was carried, Mowat was one of the twenty appointees. On 30 June, again as postmaster-general, he was included with Brown in the 'great coalition' to reconstruct the union. At the Quebec conference in October, according to D'Arcy McGee, a fellow delegate, Mowat took a 'constant and honourable share' (*Parliamentary Debates*, 137) in drafting the federal plan that would be embodied in the British North America Act of 1867. On 14 November 1864 his contributions as a father of confederation ended when he accepted the vice-chancellorship of Upper Canada.

In chancery, Mowat rendered about 500 judgments, many of which became Canadian precedents. The work was congenial, and allowed him time for family and the general reading that he enjoyed. But his income was less than as a lawyer, and he was disappointed at being passed over for the chancellorship in 1870. He may have retained some political ambition as well. At any rate, on 24 October 1872 he resigned from the bench and accepted the invitation to head the Liberal government in his native province, which had been renamed Ontario in 1867 and was still adjusting to life in the new dominion of Canada. This unprecedented return of a judge to the political arena was denounced by both the opposition and the legal profession as a 'rude shock' to the independence of the judiciary. Still, the consensus was that, while vice-chancellor, Mowat had shown no 'tendency to fear, favor, or affection' (*Canada Law Journal*, 8, 1872, 264–5; 33, 1897, 748–9).

Mowat, who thus became Ontario premier by appointment, took also the portfolio of attorney-general, and was elected to the legislature in Oxford North. Inexperienced in leading a government and a party, he proved a master of the art. He chose as colleagues men who were of proven ability and integrity like himself, and maintained unity in cabinet and caucus with a firm hand. His government redrew constituency boundaries carefully, but with little evidence of gerrymandering. It utilized patronage, but without scandal, for Mowat personally controlled its volume and required honesty and efficiency in the recipients.

Mowat's Liberals defeated the Conservatives and several third parties in six successive elections, though mostly with small margins in the popular vote, and he remained premier for almost twenty-four years. Contributing to his success, according to one of his ministers, was his 'sagacity' (Ross, 192) in assessing public opinion on divisive questions such as temperance or franchise reform. When Ontarians were ready, his government gradually stiffened restraints on the liquor trade, and widened the electorate until manhood suffrage was reached in 1888. A secret ballot modelled on the English was introduced in 1874. On the other hand, although Mowat sympathized in the 1890s with the suffragettes and, an abstainer himself, with the prohibitionists, he side-stepped both because, in his familiar phrase, 'the time was not ripe' (*The Globe* [Toronto], 11 May 1893).

Issues of religion and race, the most contentious of all, were central in the elections of 1886, 1890, and 1894. Mowat, steadfast in the faith of his fathers, had nevertheless a catholicity of spirit, strengthened by lifelong study of the history of Christianity, which gave him a deep respect for all creeds. He aimed at justice to Ontario's Roman Catholic and French-speaking minorities as well as to the protestant, anglophone majority. Thus, while denying Orangemen a special act of incorporation, which was offensive to Catholicism, he conceded their right to incorporate under a general act; and, while taking steps to improve Roman Catholic separate schools and francophone schools, he refused extension of the separate system, which would have alienated protestants. By his moderation and conciliation he built a party that accommodated disparate elements in the population.

For many years, however, historians remembered not the canny practical politician who presided over the golden age of Ontario Liberalism, but the stubborn defender of provincial rights against the dominion. They claimed that his legal battles with prime minister John A. Macdonald contradicted his own earlier work for confederation and weakened the nation.

Actually, Mowat's federalism was rooted in the Upper Canadian ideology of self-government. Under the British North America Act, he believed, provincial sovereignty was retained, lieutenant-governors possessed the traditional royal prerogatives of escheat, pardon, and appointment of queen's counsel, and provincial legislatures had co-ordinate powers with the federal. In his view it was Macdonald's theory of dominion paramountcy and subordinate provinces that was a false construction. Their jurisdictional clashes were intensified by personal antagonism dating from the 1850s when Mowat joined the Reformers. Political advantage was also at stake. For example, although Macdonald dubbed Mowat a 'little tyrant' (*The Mail* [Toronto], 2 June 1882) for his persistence in their quarrel over the authority to grant liquor licences, the fact was that neither leader wanted to yield control of such a rich source of patronage. Similarly, Mowat resisted dominion disallowance of his Rivers and Streams Act in 1881, 1882, and 1883 because he perceived a threat both to provincial autonomy and to the public interest in Ontario's waterways, which were essential for the lumbering operations that produced considerable revenue for his government.

Mowat's vision for Canada was different from Macdonald's, but he was no less patriotic, as he demonstrated in his 1890s crusade against the advocates of commercial and political union with the United States. His interpretation of the constitution was confirmed by privy council decisions recognizing the provinces within their spheres as 'supreme' (*Hodge*, 1883) and the lieutenant-governors as representatives of the crown in the provinces (*Maritime Bank*, 1892).

Mowat's prolonged boundary struggle with the dominion and province of Manitoba was territorial, not constitutional. Meticulously he gathered evidence to document before the privy council in 1884 and 1888 Ontario's claim from Lake Superior westwards to Lake of the Woods and northwards to the Albany River and James Bay. His victory was complete. Ontario acquired a vast domain with invaluable timber and mineral resources.

Research since the 1960s has turned attention to Mowat's policies for the province's internal development. These were the major part of the 'record' that won repeated favour at the polls. His government stimulated every economic sector, helping Ontario to prosper despite the world depression. Agriculture, still the main occupation, received leadership from a new department of agriculture and a new agricultural college and experimental farm. Business and trade benefited from the political stability, provincial grants to railways criss-crossing the southern peninsula in the 1870s, and numerous public works, including dignified parliament buildings completed in 1893. Opening of the north, to complement the agricultural and industrial south, was aided by immigration propaganda, free land, and colonization railways and roads. Encouragement was given to the infant mining industry while ensuring that it furnish public revenue by a charge on ores. While it was uninterested in reforestation, the government did act to protect the forests from fire, check the extinction of fish and game, and begin three provincial parks for conservation and recreation.

Challenged by the human problems emergent with late nineteenth-century industrialization and urbanization, Mowat departed from the *laissez-faire* of the earlier Reformers and assumed many new responsibilities for the welfare of society, albeit with a wary eye to their cost and political acceptability. His government intervened in employer–employee relations by providing for arbitration of industrial disputes, workmen's compensation,

regulation of working conditions in factories, shops, and mines, and protection, by liens, of mechanics' earnings. Education was brought under a minister, and modernized in so many respects that at the 1893 Chicago Exposition the province was honoured by a special award for 'a system of Public Instruction almost ideal in the perfection of its details' (Ontario Legislative Assembly, *Sessional Papers* 1897, No. 1, Appendix Q). Various measures furnished protection for public health, neglected children, and women's property rights. As *ex officio* bencher, Mowat insisted that the Law Society permit women to study and practise law. As attorney-general, he made the judicial system more efficient by instalments of legislation which culminated in 1881 in fusing, as in England, the old rival common law and equity courts.

Mowat's balanced developmental programmes, hesitant though some appear today, set Ontario on the path towards the economic empire and broad social services of the twentieth century. They reveal the essence of his Liberalism: his consideration for all classes, his adherence to British patterns, his trademark blend of caution and progress. B. B. Osler, one of his supporters, commented: 'He kept the brakes on, but the motive power was always there' (*The Globe* [Toronto], 27 April 1892).

Mowat was created KCMG in 1892 and GCMG in 1897. In 1893 Wilfrid Laurier, the Canadian Liberal leader, nominated him, 'as a veteran in the cause of Reform' (*Official Report of the Liberal Convention*, 1893, 5), to chair the national party convention, and on the eve of the 1896 federal election persuaded him to enter dominion politics. The election won, Mowat resigned the premiership on 13 July, and was appointed a senator and Laurier's minister of justice. His main task was to assist in settling the Manitoba schools controversy.

In Ottawa Mowat found his 'ten-hour days' exhausting (letter to Edward Blake, 1 July 1897, Blake MSS, Archives of Ontario). He returned to Toronto as Ontario's lieutenant-governor on 18 November 1897. But the social and ceremonial functions of this office grew difficult as his strength and eyesight failed. A fall and severe fracture hastened his death, at Government House, on 19 April 1903. He was buried on 22 April in Mount Pleasant cemetery. In his long and diverse public life he had played vital roles in defining the nature of the Canadian federation and transforming Ontario from a small frontier colony to a large, mature province.

A. MARGARET EVANS

Sources C. R. W. Biggar, *Sir Oliver Mowat: a biographical sketch*, 2 vols. (1905) • A. M. Evans, *Sir Oliver Mowat* (1992) [incl. bibliographical notes, pp. 359–415, and notes on sources, pp. 417–21] • D. Swainson, ed., *Oliver Mowat's Ontario* (1972) • E. G. Firth, ed., *Profiles of a province: studies in the history of Ontario* (1967) • J. C. Morrison, 'Oliver Mowat and the development of provincial rights in Ontario', *Three history theses* (Toronto, 1961) • P. Romney, *Mr Attorney: the attorney general for Ontario in court, cabinet and legislature, 1791–1899* (1986) • *Parliamentary debates on the subject of the confederation of the British North American provinces* (1865) • 'Resignation of Vice-Chancellor Mowat', *Canada Law Journal*, 8 (1872), 264–5 • 'Sir Oliver Mowat', *Canada Law Journal*, 33 (1897), 748–9 • G. W. Ross, *Getting into parliament and after* (1913) • R. A. Olmsted, *Decisions relating to the British North America Act, 1867, and the Canadian constitution, 1867–1954*, 1 (1954) • *The Globe* [Toronto] (8 May 1893) • *The Globe* [Toronto]

(11 May 1893) · *The Mail* [Toronto] (2 June 1882) · *The Globe* [Toronto] (27 April 1892) · NA Canada, George Brown MSS · Archives of Ontario, Edward Blake MSS · Ontario Legislative Assembly, *Sessional Papers* (1897) · *Official report of the Liberal Convention* [of Canada] (1893)

Archives Public Archives of Ontario, Toronto | NA Canada, Brown, Laurier, Macdonald, Mackenzie MSS · Public Archives of Ontario, Toronto, Blake, Clarke, Riddell, Whitney MSS · Toronto Archdiocesan Archives, Ontario, Lynch MSS

Likenesses E. J. Palmer, photograph, 1864, Archives of Ontario, Toronto · photograph, 1880–89 (after lithograph), NA Canada · J. C. Forbes, oils, 1890, Oxford County Court House, Woodstock, Ontario · R. Harris, oils, 1892, Government of Ontario Art Collection, Ontario Legislature Building, Toronto · F. J. Rowley, photograph, 1903, NA Canada · W. S. Allward, bronze statue, 1905, Queen's Park, Toronto · D. Patterson, oils, Government House, Toronto

Wealth at death C$105,340.79—incl. notes, mortgages, life insurance, cash, real estate in Ontario and Manitoba: inventory, surrogate court, county of York, Toronto, 1903

Mowat, Robert Balmain (1883–1941), historian, was born on 26 September 1883 at 31 Lutton Place, Edinburgh, the second son of Robert Mowat (1843–1896), bookseller, who became managing director of the firm of Edinburgh publishers W. and R. Chambers, and his wife, Mary-Margaret, *née* Scott. He was educated at George Watson's College, the Merchiston Castle School, Edinburgh University, and Balliol College, Oxford, where he took firsts in *literae humaniores* (1905) and modern history (1906). After a short stint as an assistant master at Eton College (1906–7), Mowat was elected a fellow of Corpus Christi College, Oxford, in 1907. On 28 December 1910 he married Mary George (*b*. 1880/81), only daughter of the social reformer Sir Charles Stewart *Loch. They had five sons and one daughter. During the First World War and its aftermath Mowat served in the naval intelligence department (1915–18), in the war cabinet secretariat (1918–19), and as an aide to General J. C. Smuts of South Africa at the 1919 Paris peace conference. The first of Mowat's major books was *The Wars of the Roses, 1377–1471* (1914), followed by *Henry V* (1919). At this time he also edited two collections of treaties relating to modern Europe (the first appeared in 1916 and the second, co-edited with Sir Augustus Oakes, in 1918).

Mowat remained at Corpus until 1928, holding the positions of assistant tutor in history (from 1907), dean (1914–15), and vice-president (1923), and was later (1937) elected an honorary fellow. He was appointed to a university lectureship in modern history at Oxford in 1925 and in 1925–6 he was visiting professor of modern history at the University of Wisconsin. Although a prolific author, he did not neglect his pupils, and was regarded as a successful college tutor. His magnum opus, a history of European diplomacy, appeared in three volumes: from 1815 to 1914 (1922); between 1914 and 1925 (1927); and from 1451 to 1789 (1928). He also published *The Diplomacy of Napoleon* (1924), *The Diplomatic Relations of Great Britain and the United States* (1925), and in 1929 a biography of Lord Pauncefote, Great Britain's first ambassador to the USA.

From 1928 until his death Mowat was professor of modern history (and sometime dean of the faculty of arts) at the University of Bristol. During the 1930s his focus moved from diplomatic history to more general historical writing on the eighteenth, nineteenth, and twentieth centuries: *The Concert of Europe* (1930), *Contemporary Europe and Overseas, 1898–1920* (1931), *England in the Eighteenth Century* (1932), *The States of Europe, 1815–1871* (1932), *The Age of Reason* (1934), *The Romantic Age* (1937), and *The Victorian Age* (1939). He also wrote a trio of small books dealing with the deteriorating European situation—*Europe in Crisis* (1936), *The Fight for Peace* (1937), and *Peace in Sight?* (1938)—and lives of Edward Gibbon (1936) and Jean-Jacques Rousseau (1938). To books already exceptional in range and fecundity he added six books which constitute collectively a modest contribution to international theory: *The European States System* (1923), *International Relations* (1931), *Problems of the Nations* (1933), *Public and Private Morality* (1933), *Revolution and Recovery* (1934), and *Diplomacy and Peace* (1935).

Mowat's increasing preoccupation with America is reflected in his last four books: *The United States of America* (1938), *The American Entente* (1939), *The American Venture* (1942), and (with Professor Preston Slosson) a *History of the English-Speaking Peoples* (1943). He lectured in the USA on international affairs as a visiting professor for the Carnegie Endowment for International Peace during 1940 and 1941, which involved him in incessant travelling and public engagements to expound the British point of view following the outbreak of war with Germany. He died on 2 September 1941 when the aircraft bringing him back from his American lecture tour crashed at Auchenhone, near Campbeltown, Argyllshire, on the west coast of Scotland.

Although Mowat wrote too much (more than fifty books), and although his preference for exposition over research weakened his work, this must be weighed against his considerable achievements as a university teacher and popular lecturer; his little-recognized contribution to international thought; and his role in creating a presence for history beyond the university. One former student remembered him as 'a man of calibre' (Donnison, 5). A colleague recalled his tolerant, well-balanced, and humane approach in interpreting world events to wider audiences (*The Times*, 6 Sept 1941, 6). The diplomatic theorist Sir Harold Nicolson numbered Mowat's *Public and Private Morality* among 'the bibles of my faith' (Nicolson, 8). Mowat's membership in 1921 and 1925 of Board of Education committees on the historical papers set in secondary schools' scholarship examinations, his authorship of best-selling books for use in schools, and his work in founding the Bristol Record Society (1929) and as general editor of its ambitious publications programme (1929–40) established him as a leading public historian.

Mowat believed that historians could shape the direction of domestic and international politics. Between the wars he advocated a renewed concert of Europe and League of Nations reform to counter threats to European peace. He was also an ardent exponent of a united Christian Europe and of Anglo-American co-operation to ensure long-term international security and economic prosperity. The sources of his beliefs were the ethical and political values of ancient Greece and Rome—he was said to possess 'an austere sense of duty of the old Roman type'

(Livingstone, 77)—and the conviction of the liberal historian and classicist that 'history is a complete ethic' which provides 'an answer to all our moral problems and a solvent for all our spiritual doubts' (R. B. Mowat, 'History as ethics', *Contemporary Review*, 153, 1938, 49).

Mowat's eldest son, **Charles Loch Mowat** (1911–1970), also had a distinguished career as a historian. Born in Oxford on 4 October 1911, he was educated at Marlborough College (1925–30) and St John's College, Oxford (1930–34), where he held a scholarship and took seconds in classical moderations (1932) and modern history (1934). In 1933 he won the university's Gladstone memorial prize for his essay 'How far is British liberty in danger from administrative encroachment?' After graduating he began a long career as a university teacher in the USA, holding posts at Minnesota (1934–6), the University of California at Los Angeles (1936–50), and Chicago (1950–58), becoming professor of British history at Chicago in 1956. In 1958 he returned to Britain to take up the chair of history at the University College of North Wales, Bangor, a post he held until his death.

C. L. Mowat is best remembered for his *Britain between the Wars, 1918–1940*, a work of lasting value which was first published in 1955 and many times reprinted. Although written while Mowat was teaching in the USA, some of the material was gathered on a visit to Britain during 1947–8 when he held a John Simon Guggenheim memorial foundation fellowship. It was a particularly impressive achievement given the inchoate state of contemporary history in Britain at the time of its publication. He subsequently worked to develop that area of study, serving as treasurer to the Association of Contemporary Historians, founded in 1967. His last book, published posthumously, was a review of the sources available to the historian of Britain since 1914. An interest in the work of his grandfather, Charles Stewart Loch, led him to produce *The Charity Organisation Society, 1869–1913* (1961), a pioneering study of private philanthropy before the welfare state. He was on the council of the Historical Association and was elected president shortly before his death. It was a tribute to his skill, tact, and integrity within the profession that he edited the second edition of volume 12 of the New Cambridge Modern History, *The Shifting Balance of World Forces, 1898–1945* (1968) 'without causing the slightest friction or upsetting a single person' among its contributors (Elton, 9–10). His strong personal convictions were reflected by his refusal to take the anti-communist oath required of all academics in California (*History*, 55, 1970, 401). He was married to Ada Wadham of Bristol, with whom he had a son and a daughter. They survived him on his premature death at his home in Llanfairfechan, near Conwy, north Wales, on 23 June 1970.   DEREK DRINKWATER

Sources The Times (3–4 Sept 1941) · The Times (6 Sept 1941) · The Times (16 Sept 1941) · The Times (30 March 1925) · The Times (16 April 1925) · The Times (23 July 1925) · The Times (28 Dec 1926) · The Times (16 April 1928) · The Times (15 July 1929) · The Times (13 May 1932) · The Times (26 May 1932) · The Times (16 Sept 1932) · The Times (15 April 1933) · The Times (5 June 1934) · The Times (31 Aug 1934) · The Times (20 March 1935) · The Times (15 May 1935) · The Times (8 June 1936) · The Times (25 Nov 1936) · The Times (16 March 1938) · The Times (29 Dec 1938) · The Times (21 March 1939) · The Times (12 May 1939) · The Times (16 Sept 1941) · WWW, 1941–50 · P. A. Hunt, Corpus Christi College biographical register, ed. N. A. Flanagan (1988) · R. W. Livingstone, Pelican Record, 25 (1940–42), 76–8 · I. Elliott, ed., The Balliol College register, 1833–1933, 2nd edn (privately printed, Oxford, 1934) · publications, 1930–40, Bristol Record Society · H. Nicolson, Daily Telegraph (8 June 1934) · F. S. V. Donnison, '1919', Corpuscles: a history of Corpus Christi College, Oxford, in the twentieth century, written by its members, ed. B. Harrison (1994) · American Historical Review, 47 (1942), 452–3 · New York Times (3 Sept 1941) · private information, 2004 [R. C. Mowat, son] · F. Eyck, G. P. Gooch: a study in history and politics (1982) · J. D. Fair, Harold Temperley: a scholar and Romantic in the public realm (1992) · b. cert. [Robert Balmain Mowat] · m. cert. [Robert Balmain Mowat] · The Times (27 June 1970) · History, 55 (1970), 401 · G. R. Elton, 'In memoriam', in C. L. Mowat, Great Britain since 1914 (1971), 9–100 · A. Sillery and V. Sillery, eds., St John's College biographical register, 1919–1975 (1978) · Marlborough College register, 1843–1952 (1952) · d. cert. [Charles Loch Mowat]

Likenesses double portrait, clay model (with his wife), priv. coll. · photograph, priv. coll.

Wealth at death £3110.10—Charles Loch Mowat: probate, 2 April 1971, CGPLA Eng. & Wales

Mowatt, Sir Francis (1837–1919), civil servant, was born in New South Wales, Australia, on 27 April 1837, the only son of Francis Mowatt (1803–1891), MP for Falmouth (1847–52) and for Cambridge (1854–7), and his wife, Sarah Sophia, daughter of Captain Barnes of Romford, Essex, of the East India Company's marine service. His sister Jane was married to Vernon *Lushington (1832–1912), permanent secretary to the Admiralty (1849–77).

Mowatt was educated at Harrow School (1851–3) and Winchester College, and went to St John's College, Oxford, in March 1855, but left after a year, having received a nomination to compete for a Treasury clerkship. In one of the first limited competitive examinations conducted by the newly established civil service commission he easily beat the other nominee, but scored only 880 marks out of a possible 1545. His annual salary as a third-class clerk was £100, rising to £250.

On 9 June 1864, at the age of twenty-seven, and with a salary of £430, he married Lucy Sophia (d. 1896), daughter of John Andrew Frerichs of Thirlestaine Hall, Cheltenham, and widow of Count Stenbock of Kolk, Estonia. The couple had three sons and three daughters.

Mowatt spent the whole of his career at the Treasury, reaching the top position of permanent secretary in 1895. He was made CB in 1884, advanced to KCB in 1893, and was created GCB in 1901. Three years after his retirement in 1903 he was sworn of the privy council. In forty-seven years in the department he made steady but unspectacular progress through the ranks, his career and contribution overshadowed by his brilliant older contemporary Reginald Welby, who had joined the Treasury in the same year, and, in his later years, by the younger Edward Hamilton. Unlike either, Mowatt was never chosen to serve as private secretary to Treasury ministers. He spent all of his early and middle career in the divisions, and in those where the opportunities to make a mark or to show potential were far fewer. Where Welby and Hamilton each in turn acquired the reputation of the Treasury's financial expert, Mowatt languished in the dull routine of controlling the expenditure of law courts and the justice system.

He was promoted second-class clerk in 1860, and ten years later first-class clerk in the assistant secretary's division, with a salary of £700 rising to £900. He was promoted principal clerk in charge of that division in 1881, by which time Welby had been promoted over the heads of seven of his seniors to the position of deputy head of the department. That position Mowatt reached in July 1888, at the age of fifty-one, and as assistant secretary and auditor of the civil list, with a salary of £1500. As such he was Welby's deputy, and was appointed permanent secretary on the latter's retirement in 1895. Sir George Murray, a junior colleague who later succeeded him as permanent secretary, remembered 'a keen sense of humour, a genial cynicism, unfailing good temper, and a sagacious appreciation of what was feasible' (*DNB*). There was at that time less obvious friction between the Treasury and the spending ministries, the long-running debate over the nature and effectiveness of its control of expenditure having temporarily subsided after the inquiry of the Ridley commission of 1887.

Mowatt was due to retire in 1902 at the age of sixty-five, but was persuaded to stay on for a further year, partly because of the failing health of Sir Edward Hamilton, who had been groomed for the succession. The post of permanent secretary was divided between them—Mowatt as joint permanent (administrative) secretary, Hamilton as joint permanent (financial) secretary—thus establishing the precedent to be followed until the appointment of Sir Warren Fisher in 1919.

Mowatt's deferred retirement was also owed partly to political expedience. With some relish he became embroiled in that episode for which he is perhaps best remembered. At the end of a long and distinguished career it is perhaps unfortunate that his name became indissolubly linked with the political manoeuvring over free trade which divided Balfour's cabinet. Steeped in the tradition of financial orthodoxy and free trade which characterized the stance of the Treasury and most of its senior officials throughout the second half of the nineteenth century, he was, if anything, more passionately committed to the doctrines of Gladstonian Liberalism than Welby. In his last year of office that commitment led him to compromise his position as the impartial head of the department. The chancellor, Charles Ritchie, was convinced that the corn duty introduced by his predecessor, Hicks Beach, in the budget of 1902 should be withdrawn. The fiscal strategy underlying that budget had been devised largely by Sir Edward Hamilton and his deputy, Robert Chalmers, in a fit of protectionist apostasy which both soon regretted. Ritchie's attempt to repeal the corn duty was defeated in cabinet, and he and his Treasury officials then 'worked hard to pull the mat from under Chamberlain's feet' (Roseveare, 222). Mowatt and other Treasury officials now openly canvassed support for Ritchie among the members of the government. 'In resisting Chamberlain Mowatt was not content, as were his senior colleagues, merely to stiffen the Chancellor Charles Ritchie through the medium of private counsel. ... He remonstrated face-to-face with Chamberlain on the streets' and 'schooled the young Conservative M.P. Winston Churchill in the name of the anti-protectionist cause' (Barberis, 10), something he was to do on several occasions subsequently, to the detriment of Balfour's government (Gilbert, 154). The corn duty was withdrawn in the budget of 1903. Balfour regarded Mowatt's behaviour as 'that of a partisan and consequently subversive of all the loyalty which has characterised the Civil Servants of the Crown, no matter how much the measure is contrary to their individual opinions' (Hamilton, 436–7). The episode served to remind senior officials of the risk of becoming identified publicly with the causes of their political masters.

After retirement Mowatt became an alderman of the London county council, alongside Welby; held directorships of several public companies and appointments connected with the University of London; and served on several royal commissions and official committees. He lived for some years at Patcham, near Brighton, and followed the South Down hunt. Later he returned to London, where, at 41 Sloane Gardens, Chelsea, he died on 20 November 1919, after suffering for some years from arteriosclerosis, attended by his daughter Hilda Russell, whose husband, William Russell, was the executor of his will.

MAURICE WRIGHT

Sources HM Treasury, departmental arrangement books, 1805–1900, PRO, T.197 · H. Roseveare, *The treasury: the evolution of a British institution* (1969) · P. Barberis, *The elite of the elite: permanent secretaries in the British higher civil service* (1996) · *The diary of Sir Edward Walter Hamilton, 1885–1906*, ed. D. W. R. Bahlman (1993) · M. Gilbert, *Churchill: a life* (1991) · *DNB* · *WWBMP* · m. cert. · d. cert.

Archives Bucks. RLSS, corresp. · NRA, priv. coll., corresp. | BL, letters to Sir Henry Campbell-Bannerman and others · Bodl. Oxf., corresp. mainly with Sir William Harcourt · NL Scot., corresp. with Lord Rosebery · Trinity Cam., corresp. with Sir Henry Babington Smith

Likenesses Bassano, photographs, 1898, NPG · C. W. Furse, oils, exh. RA 1904, Gov. Art Coll. · W. Stoneman, photograph, 1918, NPG · portrait, repro. in *Royal Academy pictures* (1904)

Wealth at death £36,030 6s. 2d.: probate, 3 March 1920, *CGPLA Eng. & Wales*

Mowbray, Alfred Richard (1824–1875), church publisher and printer, was born on 28 November 1824 at Leicester, the elder son of William Mowbray (*b.* 1798), lace manufacturer, and his wife, Ann. In early life Mowbray was attracted to the teachings of the Oxford Movement with its object of bringing about a catholic revival in the Church of England. He subsequently trained as a teacher at St Mark's Teacher Training College in Chelsea, where he was noted as a high-churchman. At the age of twenty-one he was appointed headmaster of the church school in Bingham, Nottinghamshire, and in 1848 he married one of the teachers on his staff. This was Susan [**Susan Mowbray** (1829–1911)], youngest child of William Thomas, a Bridgwater innkeeper, and his wife, Hannah. She trained as a teacher at Whitelands College in London from 1843 to 1845. The Mowbrays had seven surviving children, two sons and five daughters.

A stained-glass window in Bingham church, designed by Mowbray and still visible in the late twentieth century, is indicative of his continuing enthusiasm for things ecclesiastical. This moved him, after various other teaching posts, to accept a call to go out to New Zealand to further the work of Bishop Selwyn in creating the new cathedral in Wellington. At this time, however, a visit to Oxford led Mowbray to an encounter with the Revd Thomas Chamberlain, vicar of St Thomas's and an ardent follower of the Oxford Movement in its later ritualist phase. Chamberlain's resolve was to do for the slum poor of his parish what Pusey and Keble had been doing for the intellectual classes, and to teach the truth, as the Oxford Movement saw it, of the Christian faith in simple pictorial but effective ways. He persuaded Mowbray to stay in Oxford and help him in this work.

Mowbray's first involvement was in the social work of the parish, in which he was immensely active. He also formed the Oxford Churchman's Union among undergraduates of the university. But he soon came to see that, if the teaching of the catholic movement were to be more widely spread, there was need for a bookshop to sell tracts and other publications, together with other aids to devotion. For this purpose he opened the first Mowbray bookshop at 2 Cornmarket, Oxford. This prospered so much that he extended his work to church printing and publishing in larger premises at 116 St Aldate Street. Leaflets, tracts, books, and ecclesiastical *objets d'art* of all kinds now poured from this establishment. In his novel *Jude the Obscure* (1895) Thomas Hardy gives a description of what can safely be taken to be Mowbray's shop, since it was unique in Oxford at the time. Jude enters the place and sees that 'it contained Anglican books, stationery, texts and fancy goods; little plaster angels on brackets, gothic framed pictures of saints, ebony crosses which were almost crucifixes, prayer books that were almost missals' (Hardy, pt 2, chap. 2).

A shop was opened in London at 20 Warwick Lane, close to St Paul's Cathedral, and Mowbray's son (Samuel) Edwin was put in charge of it. Some of the firm's publications had immense sales, such as Mowbray's *Plain Tracts*, which ran to over two hundred titles. It also published magazines such as the first *Communicants' Manual*, *The Bread of Life*, and *The Gospeller* (a monthly parish newspaper later succeeded by *The Sign*), which came to have a national distribution.

Mowbray died of heart failure on 17 December 1875 at his home, 116 St Aldate Street, Oxford, aged only fifty-one, and was buried in Holywell cemetery later that month. Edwin Mowbray returned to Oxford after his father's death to run the business as general manager, but was found dead in his bath in October 1897, overcome by escaping gas fumes. Alfred Mowbray's widow, Susan, then took over the business and supervised its transformation into a limited company in May 1903. She died on 25 May 1911 at 26 Winchester Road, Oxford, and was buried in Holywell cemetery beside her husband. Her daughters Marion and Agnes also served as directors, and the latter set up a trust to distribute the income from her shareholding in the firm among surviving family members. This was only terminated in 1988 when the company was taken over by another large bookselling firm.

The bookshop and publishing business founded by A. R. Mowbray was popularly known as Mowbrays. Over many years, and sustained by Susan Mowbray and later generations of the family, through its sale of books, prayer books, church furnishings, and vestments, it made a recognizable mark upon Anglican life, both in Britain and overseas. WILLIAM PURCELL

Sources R. Stanley, 'Susan Mowbray: a woman in a man's world', *Oxfordshire Local History*, 3 (1989), 103–8 • Pusey Oxf., Mowbray papers • T. Hardy, *Jude the obscure* (1895), pt 2, chap. 2 • Boase, *Mod. Eng. biog.* • *CGPLA Eng. & Wales* (1876) • *CGPLA Eng. & Wales* (1911) [Susan Mowbray] • parish register, Leicester, 28 Nov 1824, Leics. RO [birth] • parish register, Bingham, 31 July 1848, Notts. Arch. [marriage] • register (burials), Dec 1875, Holywell cemetery, Oxford
Archives Pusey Oxf., archive
Likenesses photograph, 1870–79 (Susan Mowbray), repro. in Stanley, 'Susan Mowbray' • oils, Dillon's bookshop, 28 Margaret Street, London
Wealth at death under £2000: probate, 4 April 1876, *CGPLA Eng. & Wales* • £38,180 9s. 2d.—Susan Mowbray: probate, 1911, *CGPLA Eng. & Wales*

Mowbray, Elizabeth, duchess of Norfolk (d. **1506/7**). *See under* Mowbray, John (VII), fourth duke of Norfolk (1444–1476).

Mowbray, John (**I**), second Lord Mowbray (**1286–1322**), magnate, was the son of Roger (III) de Mowbray, first Lord Mowbray (d. 1297), and Rose, daughter of Richard de *Clare, sixth earl of Gloucester (d. 1262). Born on 4 September 1286, he was thus a minor when his father died in 1297, and was married the following year in Swansea to Alicia (d. 1331), the daughter and heir of his guardian, William (IV) de Briouze, lord of Bramber, Sussex, and Gower, south Wales, who had agreed to pay 500 marks for the marriage.

On 22 May 1306 John Mowbray was among those knighted with the future Edward II, and on 1 June he received livery of his father's lands while yet under age. On 26 August 1307 he received his first summons to parliament. In 1311 on the death of Roger Lestrange, the second husband of his paternal grandmother, Maud de Beauchamp (d. 1273), Mowbray was entitled to succeed to her share of the lands of her father William (II) de Beauchamp of Bedford in Bedfordshire (including Bedford Castle), in Buckinghamshire, Cambridgeshire, and Kent. This represented the largest accrual of land since the original grants made to the Mowbrays in 1106. It is somewhat curious that, at some time before Lestrange's death, possibly at the time of Mowbray's marriage, William de Briouze had petitioned the king to allow Mowbray to enfeoff his father-in-law with all the estates that Lestrange was holding by courtesy. In 1316 Mowbray secured a licence to grant the Beauchamp manors of Hawnes, Stotfold, and Willington, Bedfordshire, to Briouze for life and in the first collaborative action with Edward II's favourite, Hugh Despenser the younger, Briouze agreed to allow the king to grant the reversion of Mowbray's manors to Hugh. In the same year Briouze secured a licence to settle his Sussex lands upon John and Alicia, expressly excluding the lordship of Gower from the settlement, possibly because he was considering its sale. Although in June 1322 a royal commission of inquiry stated that Briouze had never given Gower to Mowbray, it does appear that by a special grant, of unknown date, Briouze had given the couple the lordship, with reversion to Humphrey (VII) de Bohun, fourth earl of Hereford.

Somewhat precipitately, Mowbray entered Gower in 1320 without royal licence, possibly because he had discovered that his father-in-law was proposing to sell the estates; Bohun indeed had paid a deposit on the lordship. Clearly without scruples, at about the same period Briouze was also bargaining with Roger Mortimer of Chirk, Roger Mortimer of Wigmore, and, most dangerous of all, Hugh Despenser the younger. For the latter, as lord of Glamorgan, acquiring neighbouring Gower was an attractive prospect, so he used Mowbray's entry without a licence to persuade the king to seize the lordship. Mowbray argued that as the lordship was a marcher territory where the king's writ did not run, he had had no need of a licence. In this he was supported by the other marcher lords, ever anxious to maintain marcher immunity and by then fearful of Despenser empire building in south Wales. Mowbray's reaction was violent and briefly successful. He ignored the king's order to him and twenty-nine other lords not to assemble and joined in the ravaging of Glamorgan. It was probably on this account that he was accused of the murder of John Iwayn, although later John Fornaux confessed to Iwayn's decapitation. Edward II was forced to give way; Mowbray attended the parliament that condemned the Despensers in July 1321 and on 20 August received a pardon.

In spite of the acquisition of estates in southern England and Wales, John Mowbray remained essentially a northern lord. He was summoned to all the parliaments from 1307 to 1321, and on 25 February 1308 he attended the coronation of Edward II, but his services to the crown were generally performed in the north. In June 1301 he was summoned to Carlisle to attend the prince of Wales, and in 1306 he served on what proved to be Edward I's last Scottish campaign. In August 1308 and in following years he was again involved in the Scottish wars. On 10 July 1312 he was appointed keeper of the city of York and of the whole county, and on 30 July had an allowance of 500 marks for his expenses. He was acting as keeper again in 1314, 1315, and 1316, when similar allowances were due to him. On 2 August 1313, and again on 9 January 1315, he was made warden of the march towards Carlisle, at the latter date being excused attendance at parliament. On 26 December 1314 he was ordered by the archbishop of York and the bishop of Durham to attend a meeting in York Minster on 3 January following, to devise a plan to resist the Scots in the wake of a failure to secure a truce, and later that year he received 50 marks from the archbishop in recompense for his expenses against the enemy. On 23 March he was made captain and keeper of Newcastle and the county of Northumberland, and was ordered to remain in the north in August for the winter campaign.

Between 1313 and 1316 Mowbray served on a number of commissions of oyer and terminer, his absence from one being noted on the grounds that he was too busy elsewhere. In August and September 1316 he was a commissioner of array in the West Riding, and again in December 1318. On 18 September 1317 he was given the custody of the town and borough of Scarborough, and eight days later of the castle too; these he held until January 1319. About September 1317 he was given the keeping of the castle and manor of Malton, though it required a royal commission empowering the sheriff of Yorkshire to recover the castle with the county posse before he was able to take possession. On 6 February 1319 he was authorized to receive any Scots who wished to surrender, and his debts to the crown were respited on 15 May on account of his war service in Scotland.

Few personal details about Mowbray survive. Although he complained in 1316 that the abbot of Fountains had entered his chase at Nidderdale, hunted and taken deer, he confirmed the monastery's rights to all the lands including Nidderdale that his forebears had granted the abbey, and was admitted to its confraternity in the following spring. He continued to support his ancestors' interests in the monastery at Byland, confirming their charters in 1321, and on 24 May 1319 he made a grant to the chapel of Kirby Bellars, Leicestershire. He appears through this, and through the building of a new house at Melton Mowbray, to have strengthened his family's ties with their estates in the latter county. At Melton he enjoyed a considerable range of rights and privileges, including the levying of fines for various offences and control of a weekly market and two annual fairs. Much new work done at Melton church can be dated to the first decade of the fourteenth century, and may be presumed to be that of Mowbray. A tomb of this date in the south aisle was once held to be that of Mowbray, and though now generally associated with the Bellers family—servants and possibly distant relatives of the Mowbrays—its precise identity remains controversial. According to Dugdale, Mowbray undertook most of the rebuilding of Shustoke church, Warwickshire, where a figure kneeling before St Cuthbert in one of the north windows was presumed to be Mowbray.

How loyal Mowbray was to Edward II before 1320 is unclear. He had attended the Dunstable tournament in 1309, yet on 31 July 1312, as keeper of the county and city of York, he was ordered to arrest Henry Percy for the latter's part in the death of Piers Gaveston, and on 15 August he was commissioned to seize the city for the king in the event of rebellion. It is not known for certain whether he was at the battle of Bannockburn, but on 10 September 1316 he was retained by the king for life in return for 150 marks p.a. In April 1317 he was among those urged by the pope to support Edward II against Thomas of Lancaster, but on 30 November 1317 he was officially appointed by Edward to be keeper of Axholme, his own chief lordship, which he was to guard for the king, and in 1319 he was in the earl of Pembroke's retinue in the campaign against Scotland.

However, Mowbray rebelled when Despenser aggrandizement threatened his newly acquired estates—it was the younger Despenser's challenge to Mowbray over the lordship of Gower that, probably more than any other single factor, provoked the civil war of 1322. Although Mowbray had been pardoned for his activities in Glamorgan, he now joined Thomas of Lancaster, whom he clearly knew well. When his son John (II) *Mowbray was born at Hovingham in 1310, Robert Scot was immediately sent to carry the news to Lancaster, for which he received 20s. Lancaster also witnessed the generous grant of lands, including the Hovingham property, that Mowbray made to young John and his wife, Matilda, possibly in 1319. On 28 June 1321 Mowbray was present at the assembly convened by Lancaster at Sherburn in Elmet, before an attack on the Despensers, and he subsequently ignored a royal prohibition on his assembling with rebels at Doncaster at the end of November, and participated in the siege of Tickhill in January 1322. Having ravaged the surrounding area he marched with Lancaster, who appears to have intended to employ him in negotiations with the Scots. The king ordered the seizure of Mowbray's lands in Axholme on 10 January, and his arrest on 11 March. But five days later Mowbray fought at Boroughbridge, where he was captured alongside Lancaster. Condemned to death, he was drawn and hanged at York on 23 March; his body subsequently remained on display, suspended in chains, for three years, before it was buried in the city's Dominican friary. Although his family's fortunes had reached a new zenith in terms of landed acquisitions during John's lifetime, his political miscalculations now brought the Mowbrays to their nadir. His widow and son were imprisoned, and Alicia was forced to surrender the reversion of the lordship of Bramber to the elder Despenser to obtain her release. She died in 1331, having married, as her second husband, Sir Richard Peshale. The sentence on her first husband was reversed in 1327.

ROWENA E. ARCHER

Sources *Chancery records* · PRO · BL · Berkeley Castle, Gloucestershire, Berkeley Castle MSS · R. E. Archer, 'The Mowbrays, earls of Nottingham and dukes of Norfolk to 1432', DPhil diss., U. Oxf., 1984 · J. R. Maddicott, *Thomas of Lancaster, 1307–1322: a study in the reign of Edward II* (1970) · J. R. S. Phillips, *Aymer de Valence, earl of Pembroke, 1307–1324: baronial politics in the reign of Edward II* (1972) · G. A. Holmes, 'A protest against the despensers, 1326', *Speculum*, 30 (1955), 207–12 · J. C. Davies, 'The Despenser war in Glamorgan', *TRHS*, 3rd ser., 9 (1915), 21–64 · R. R. Davies, *Lordship and society in the march of Wales, 1282–1400* (1978) · *Sir Christopher Hatton's Book of seals*, ed. L. C. Loyd and D. M. Stenton, Northamptonshire RS, 15 (1950) · W. Rees, 'Gower and the march of Wales', *Archaeologia Cambrensis*, 110 (1961), 1–29 · W. Grainge, *The vale of Mowbray* (1859) · G. T. Clark, ed., *Cartae et alia munimenta quae dominium de Glamorgan pertinent*, 4 vols. (1885–93) · G. Williams, ed., *Glamorgan county history*, 3: *The middle ages*, ed. T. B. Pugh (1971) · *Fourth report*, HMC, 3 (1874) · GEC, *Peerage*, new edn, 9.377–80 · N. Fryde, *The tyranny and fall of Edward II, 1321–1326* (1979) · *CIPM*, 7, no. 81
Wealth at death see *CIPM*, vol. 7, no. 81

Mowbray, John (II), third Lord Mowbray (1310–1361), magnate, was the son of John (I) *Mowbray, second Lord Mowbray (1286–1322) of Axholme, Lincolnshire, and Alicia (d. 1331), daughter of William (VII) de Briouze (d. 1326). He was born at Hovingham, Yorkshire, on 29 November 1310 and was baptized in All Saints' Church there. On account of his father's rebellion against Edward II he was imprisoned with his mother in the Tower of London on 22 February 1322.

Mowbray's inheritance was partly dissipated over the ensuing years while the Despensers were in the ascendant. On 9 July 1322 the lordship of Gower and several other estates were granted to Hugh Despenser the younger and Mowbray's mother was forced to grant the latter the reversion of her Sussex lands, including the honour of Bramber. Similarly the reversion of the Mowbray lands in Bedfordshire was granted to Earl Hugh through the co-operation of Alicia's father, who abused his position as a trustee of Mowbray's father in order to assist the Despensers. On the accession of Edward III in January 1327 Mowbray was released from the Tower. His mother's dower was restored to her and she carried this part of Mowbray's inheritance to her second husband, Sir Richard Peshale, who retained Mowbray lands until his death after 1342 in spite of some attempts by Mowbray to recover them by force. Substantial restoration was made to Mowbray on 22 February 1327, though he was still under age, but it excluded the Isle of Axholme, which had been granted to Joan, countess of Surrey, on 3 February.

In spite of the restorations a good deal of Mowbray's life was spent in litigation over his estates. Besides that with Peshale, a dispute between his mother and her cousin Thomas de Briouze concerning his estates in Sussex, which had begun as early as 1338, was still unresolved in 1347 though Mowbray was eventually triumphant. More serious were claims advanced by the Beauchamp earls of Warwick to the lordship of Gower. In 1331 on his mother's death Mowbray paid £300 for her lands including Gower and his visit there in August 1332 may have been to assert control in the region. The sixteenth-century antiquary John Leland believed that he rebuilt the castles at Swansea and Oystermouth. His long absences meant that it was not easy to govern the lordship. It was raided in 1333 and Mowbray's efforts to defend his plundered tenants, which he raised in parliament, only led to unwelcome questions about jurisdiction in the lordship. In the end Mowbray's tenants avenged themselves in 1334, in which year Mowbray was again visiting the lordship. In 1348 he confirmed to his tenants in the Welsh part of the lordship all their laws and customs, freedom from arrest for felony, and pardon for all encroachments. In 1354 Thomas Beauchamp, earl of Warwick, successfully challenged Mowbray's possession of the lordship, a challenge made unsuccessfully by his ancestors in the reign of Edward I, which was based on the argument that it had once belonged to the Newburgh earls of Warwick and that the Briouze title was weak. It was argued that John's right depended upon William de Briouze's gift to John's father and that since the latter had taken it by force his ownership had never been valid. John was apparently unable to prove that the gift had ever been carried out in practice. Edward III had certainly confirmed Alicia de Briouze's right to Gower in 1328, and in 1343, as lord of Gower, John had been ordered to attend the king's son Edward, newly created prince of

Wales. Although there is no evidence that the king interfered in the case, by 1354 Thomas Beauchamp had established himself as one of the leading war captains and at the same time Edward was trying to establish the principle that all marcher lords were subject to the crown, not the principality of Wales. The loss was financially damaging—in 1367 Beauchamp's income from Gower was over £600—and this no doubt contributed to the chronic indebtedness that Mowbray suffered for the whole of his adult life. On numerous occasions he had to be excused for debts to the crown, which nevertheless amounted to 2000 marks at his death, and in 1359 he acknowledged a debt of £10,000 to his brother-in-law, *Henry, duke of Lancaster (d. 1361).

On 28 February 1327 Mowbray's marriage was granted to Henry, earl of Lancaster (d. 1345), and by 4 June he was married to the earl's daughter, Joan. However, from a grant made by his father before 1322, it is apparent that Mowbray was first married while under canonical age, to a woman called Matilda who, in the only surviving reference to their divorce, is named as the daughter of Sir Robert *Holland, principal retainer of Henry of Lancaster's elder brother, Thomas, earl of Lancaster, who had led the antagonism towards Edward II and ultimately paid for it with his life. Although Holland had earned the undying enmity of the Lancastrians by deserting Thomas for the king at a crucial moment in 1322, it is not known for certain if this was the reason for Mowbray's separation from Matilda. However, the grant to Mowbray of a licence to settle two of his manors on Matilda in 1332 suggests that the process of separation was protracted. With Joan he had three children, his heir, John (III) *Mowbray, and two daughters, Eleanor (Alianore), who married Roger de la *Warr, third Lord de la Warr (1326–1370) [see under Warr, de la, family (per. c.1250–1427)], and Blanche. In 1341 he granted her £100 p.a. to support her chamber but she was dead by August 1344 when he was married to one Elizabeth—not the Elizabeth, daughter of John de Vere, earl of Oxford, whom he did eventually marry but who was then still the wife of Hugh Courtenay (d. 1349). In 1353 Mowbray and the earl of Oxford were at odds over de Vere lands that had formed part of Elizabeth's dowry and Mowbray agreed to make an enfeoffment of his own lands, the profits of which were to be used to support Elizabeth and her household.

Throughout his life Mowbray rendered steady and distinguished service to the crown, primarily in the north of England. He was called to every parliament between 1327 and 1360 and was frequently at councils between 1328 and 1359. He was regularly employed by the crown on commissions of array and oyer and terminer. He first served in Scotland in 1327, being summoned in April to bring his men from Wales to Newcastle. Much of his career thereafter was dictated by Edward III's policy of opposition to the claims of the Brus family to the Scottish throne and support for those English lords deprived of their Scottish lands by the Bruces. In July 1333 he assisted in the retaking of Berwick, and after his brief visit to Gower was back guarding the northern border in 1334. He was in Scotland

in 1335, and in 1336 two ships were provided for him to go there. He was ordered back to Scotland at Michaelmas 1339, and on 15 April 1340 was appointed keeper of Berwick for a year and justice in the parts of Scotland occupied by the English king with an allowance of £100 for his equipment. He had with him a force of 468 men as well as '1 maistre engynour and 4 valletz'. In July he was claiming outstanding wages of over £1200 and he reported that 'the whole country is in war up to the gates of the town' (CDS, 3.244, no. 1338). In 1341 he was ordered to send men from Yorkshire to assist John Balliol. By 1344 he was owed over £1800 and in July 1346 was threatening to abandon Berwick if payment was not forthcoming. In spite of this he was present at the battle of Nevilles Cross on 17 October 1346 where he led the 'third battle' with the bishop of Lincoln. He received royal thanks for his services, and the bravery of himself and his men was especially recorded by the Lanercost chronicler. It was no doubt on account of his considerable experience in Scotland that he was summoned to discuss Scottish affairs at the council on 10 December, but he was back in Scotland with a force of 100 men by Easter 1347. From 1351 he was appointed to the peace commissions and in May 1352 was appointed to a commission to defend the Yorkshire coast and, as lord of Gower, to provide 30 Welshmen. In 1355 he was again in Scotland with the king, and on 20 January following witnessed the surrender by Balliol of his claim to the Scottish crown.

The true extent of his service in France is rather uncertain. It was certainly more limited than Froissart's chronicle implies. In 1337 he was ordered to arm his tenants in Gower on the outbreak of war and in 1338 was to provide shipping for the king's journey to France. At the same time he was instructed to reside on his Sussex estates because of fears of a French invasion. Given his service in parliament and in Scotland, however, he cannot have been in Flanders in October 1339. In November 1342 he was ordered to prepare himself and a retinue for war in Brittany. It is uncertain whether he ever went, though Froissart records his presence at the siege of Nantes, for the reinforcements were cancelled on 6 February because of the truce of Malestroit. His participation in the naval engagement off Winchelsea on 29 August 1350 rests on the sole authority of Froissart. It is certainly most improbable, given his known movements, that he was on campaign around Paris in 1360, though he was one of those who took the oath to observe the treaty of Brétigny that year.

Mowbray died of the plague at York on 4 October 1361 and was buried in the Fransciscan church at Bedford. He was survived by his wife, Elizabeth, who died in 1375. His dogged service to the king had earned him surprisingly little reward, his fortunes fluctuating in accordance with royal favour (or its absence). He was commemorated, on account of his grant of rights of waste to his tenants in Axholme, in a stained-glass window in Haxey church; he was portrayed holding a document which was reputedly in recognition of this grant. The window survived until

1626 when it was destroyed in riots that broke out when the rights enshrined in the grant were overturned as a result of the drainage schemes of Cornelius Vermuyden.

ROWENA E. ARCHER

Sources Chancery records · Berkeley Castle, Gloucestershire, Berkeley Castle MSS · R. E. Archer, 'The Mowbrays, earls of Nottingham and dukes of Norfolk to 1432', DPhil diss., U. Oxf., 1984 · J. C. Davies, 'The Despenser war in Glamorgan', TRHS, 3rd ser., 9 (1915), 21–64 · G. Williams, ed., Glamorgan county history, 3: The middle ages, ed. T. B. Pugh (1971) · G. A. Holmes, The estates of the higher nobility in fourteenth-century England (1957) · J. Stevenson, ed., Chronicon de Lanercost, 1201–1346, Bannatyne Club, 65 (1839) · W. B. Stonehouse, The history and topography of the Isle of Axholme (1839) · G. T. Clark, ed., Cartae et alia munimenta quae dominium de Glamorgan pertinent, 4 vols. (1885–93) · CDS, 3.244 · [T. Walsingham], Chronicon Angliae, ab anno Domini 1328 usque ad annum 1388, ed. E. M. Thompson, Rolls Series, 64 (1874) · GEC, Peerage, new edn, 9.383
Likenesses stained-glass window, Haxey church, Lincolnshire; destroyed 1626

Mowbray, John (III), fourth Lord Mowbray (1340–1368),

nobleman, was the son of John (II) *Mowbray, third Lord Mowbray (1310–1361) of Axholme, Lincolnshire, and Joan (d. in or before 1344), daughter of *Henry, earl of Lancaster (d. 1345). Born at the family seat at Epworth on 25 June 1340, he was knighted in July 1355 by the king and the duke of Lancaster along with twenty-six others, including Lionel of Clarence and John of Gaunt, and then crossed to France for the king's meeting with Charles of Navarre. He returned to France the following year to serve in Brittany.

Mowbray received livery of his inheritance on 14 November 1361, and was given robes the following Christmas as a knight-banneret. His inheritance, however, was burdened with the dower settled upon his stepmother Elizabeth de Vere, widow of Hugh Courtenay (d. 1349), who by 1369 had married Sir William Cosynton. Shortly afterwards the couple surrendered to the Fleet prison, having fallen into debt, possibly owing to Mowbray's prosecution of Elizabeth for waste in his estates, for which he was awarded damages of nearly £1000.

As early as 1343 an agreement was made for a double marriage between John (III) Mowbray and Audrey Montagu, the granddaughter of Edward I's fifth son, Thomas of Brotherton, and between John's sister Blanche and Edward, Audrey's brother, to be solemnized the following 24 June. The marriages apparently never took place, but in or about 1349, when Mowbray was still below canonical age, he was married to Elizabeth, the daughter and eventual heir of John, Lord Seagrave (d. 1353), and his wife, Margaret *Brotherton, eldest daughter and eventual heir of *Thomas of Brotherton. Simultaneously a marriage was arranged between Mowbray's sister Blanche and Elizabeth's brother John. At the request of Mowbray's uncle, *Henry, earl of Lancaster, Pope Clement VI granted the necessary dispensations, in order to make peace between the parents and avoid disputes and scandals that might arise on account of their being neighbours. Elizabeth and Mowbray had four children: two daughters, Eleanor and Margaret, and two sons, John (IV) Mowbray, earl of Nottingham (d. 1383), and Thomas (I) *Mowbray, first duke of

Norfolk (d. 1399). Elizabeth predeceased her husband by a few months in 1368. The Seagrave marriage was eventually a major factor in Mowbray fortunes but neither John nor Elizabeth, nor their sons, were to reap the benefit, on account of the enormous jointure of Margaret Brotherton in the Seagrave lands and the latter's own longevity (she lived until 1399) as the sole heir of her father, Thomas. The first beneficiary was John Mowbray's grandson, John (V) *Mowbray, second duke of Norfolk (d. 1432). On Seagrave's death in 1353, however, the king intervened to grant John (III) Mowbray some small parcels of his wife's inheritance, and the first surviving set of reasonably complete estate accounts, those for 1367, show Mowbray's annual income at nearly £800.

There is little evidence of Mowbray's active participation in political or military life. Most of his adult life spanned the years of peace following the treaty of Brétigny, to the observance of which he was bound by oath in 1360, and little is known of him beyond the fact that he was regularly summoned to parliament between 1362 and 1366. On 10 October 1367 he had a licence to nominate attorneys as he was about to go overseas, and these were renominated the following October in view of his remaining abroad for a further year, probably the result of his plans to embark on a crusade. He was killed by Turks in the autumn of 1368 near Constantinople, while making his way to the Holy Land. By 1396 his son Thomas had arranged for his bones to be collected from the East preparatory to burial with his ancestors, the deed recording the endeavour describing him as 'John de Mowbray catholicus'. His will was proved at Lincoln on 17 May 1369.

ROWENA E. ARCHER

Sources Chancery records · Berkeley Castle, Gloucestershire, Berkeley Castle MSS · R. E. Archer, 'The Mowbrays, earls of Nottingham and dukes of Norfolk to 1432', DPhil diss., U. Oxf., 1984 · A. Gibbons, ed., Early Lincoln wills (1888) · exchequer, court of augmentations, ancient deeds, series B, PRO, E326/B9376 · GEC, Peerage, new edn, 9.383–4
Wealth at death income of c.£800 p.a.: accounts of receiver 1367–8 in Berkeley Castle archives

Mowbray, John (V), second duke of Norfolk (1392–1432),

magnate, was the second surviving son of Thomas (I) *Mowbray, first duke of Norfolk (1366–1399), and his second wife, Elizabeth Fitzalan (d. 1425), sister and coheir of Thomas *Fitzalan, earl of Arundel (d. 1415). Born at Calais on 3 August 1392, John succeeded his brother Thomas (II) *Mowbray, who was executed for treason in 1405. In 1407 he became a ward of his great-aunt Joan, countess of Hereford (d. 1419). The allowance of £100 made for his maintenance in 1399 was then increased to £200, and in 1410 reached £300 when he joined the household of Henry IV. That year the king began restoring the Mowbray lands, in spite of John's minority, and in 1411 Ralph *Neville, earl of Westmorland (d. 1425), paid 3000 marks (£2000) for John's custody and marriage. On 12 January 1412 John was married to Katherine *Neville (c.1400–1483), one of the daughters of her father's second marriage, to Joan *Beaufort, on which occasion it seems that the office of marshal, held by Westmorland since 1399, was restored. John is first known to have discharged the office at Henry V's coronation on 9 April 1413, receiving as his fee a silver-gilt alms dish valued at 25 marks. On 4 March 1413 John received full livery of his lands, together with confirmation of the earldom of Nottingham.

On 22 March 1413 John Mowbray received his first summons to parliament, and in the years following he committed himself wholeheartedly to Henry V's French wars. On 29 April 1415 he indented for one year's service with 4 knights, 45 men-at-arms, and 150 archers. As marshal he was appointed on 1 August to inquire into the 'Southampton plot', and was one of those who sentenced the rebels. However, his first experience of war, at the siege of Harfleur, was short-lived, for on 5 October a licence was granted for the earl and fifty-seven of his men to be invalided home. Mowbray was sufficiently recovered from dysentery to go to London in November and greet the victor of Agincourt, before going home to the north, where his son and heir had entered the world two months previously. On 1 May 1416 the earl was one of those who met the emperor Sigismund at Dover, but it is not known whether he attended the king at Calais later that year. On 8 February 1417 he again indented to serve, this time with 100 men-at-arms and 300 archers, and thereafter began five years' unbroken and distinguished service to the king.

Mowbray remained with the army, playing prominent parts in the sieges of Caen (1417), Louviers (1418), and Rouen (1418–19). On 2 and 12 February 1419 he was appointed to the captaincies of Gournay and Neufchâtel respectively, but gave them both up again almost at once, Henry V being apparently unwilling to proceed without his marshal. Thus Mowbray went on to the sieges of Évreux and Vernon (1419). He briefly assisted Gloucester at the siege of Ivry in May, before rejoining the king at Mantes and then Pontoise. Briefly absent to besiege Gisors, he then played a major role in the siege of Melun, and with the earl of March received its surrender in October. He spent the winter with Henry V at Rouen, and in March 1420, with the earl of Huntingdon, successfully took Fresnay-le-Vicomte, and on 16 March routed the dauphin near Le Mans. On Christmas day 1420 John (V) Mowbray indented at Paris to serve as captain of Pontoise with 60 men-at-arms and 180 archers, delaying only to accompany the departing king and his new queen as far as Amiens. This onerous military captaincy thus received priority over both his duties as marshal at Queen Catherine's coronation (performed for him by Richard Beauchamp, earl of Worcester) and his installation as a knight of the Garter (received on his behalf by Rowland Lenthal).

When Henry V returned to France in 1421, he quickly called his marshal to personal service, and it was only the king's death, on 31 August 1422, that allowed Mowbray's return to England. On 9 March following he indented to serve with 115 men-at-arms and 360 archers under the duke of Exeter, and in the company of lords Willoughby and Hungerford. He was not at the battle of Cravant on 31

July, but assisted Jean de Luxembourg, putting his experience of sieges to good use in relieving Bohain, and subsequently besieging, capturing, and firing the fortress of La Folleye in the Laonnais. After 1423 Mowbray's interest in the war waned. It had owed much to his personal service to Henry V and to his office as marshal. His deep military commitment is uniquely documented in his receiver-general's minute account of the expenditure of some £2000 for the Agincourt campaign in order for him to be appropriately equipped, even down to the seat for his own privy, but he had no lands, titles, or offices to give him a vested interest in the survival of English-held Normandy, and until the new king came of age his office of marshal, which carried rights to profits and gave him a special status on campaigns, lay largely dormant. Thus only in 1430, in order to lead the expedition to accompany the young Henry VI to France for his coronation, did he give aid again to the war effort with 120 men-at-arms and 360 archers. Mowbray led 1000 men to assist the duke of Burgundy at the siege of Gournay-sur-Aronde, and was active in the successful assaults on Dammartin, La Chasse, and Mongay in the Île de Paris, but he returned home before the king was crowned.

One curiosity in John (V) Mowbray's military career is his participation in Duke Humphrey of Gloucester's ill-conceived expedition to Hainault in November 1424, which was doubtless the result of the two men's long-standing friendship. The campaign was apparently profitable for the earl, who ravaged the county of Brabant. Since, however, it was a private undertaking, financed by Gloucester rather than the English exchequer, few records of the venture have survived.

Politically, John Mowbray was not a figure of note, his contribution being at best routine, at worst half-hearted. He was so little known at home that in 1422 he was summoned to parliament under the name of Thomas. Though he was present at the council of 5 November which nominated Gloucester to conduct the first parliament of the new reign and was in December appointed to the minority council, his attendance thereafter was largely limited to meetings involving planning for overseas expeditions. Political partisanship can hardly be advanced to explain his involvement in arbitration of the feud between Gloucester and Beaufort in 1426—he was closely linked to both men—or his participation in the appeal to Gloucester to keep within his prescribed powers in October 1427. He did the minimum amount expected, though he did not neglect to perform the office of marshal at Henry VI's London coronation on 6 November 1429.

Beyond Henry V's war John Mowbray's main concerns were twofold. Foremost were his lands. He was the first adult of his line to benefit from the inheritance of the Brotherton and Seagrave estates formerly held by his great-grandmother Margaret *Brotherton, duchess of Norfolk (d. 1399). Following her death, a series of misfortunes—his father's exile, royal confiscation of the estates, and the minority and treason of his brother—had made for a period of administrative upheaval which was compensated for only by the continuous service of his father's officials. Additionally, even at his succession much land was still in the hands of his mother and his sister-in-law, Constance Holland, who was to outlive him. In 1415 he instituted judicial eyres on his lands in south Wales, and imposed severe penalties on his officials there. When his mother died in July 1425 he immediately toured East Anglia where the bulk of her dower estates lay, and he became the first Mowbray to reside at Framlingham.

Further, Mowbray displayed an all-consuming concern with his rights and privileges. He fought against even Henry V to win complete control over the marshalcy. It was perhaps partly because his office concerned itself so often with precedence, that he campaigned to establish the superiority of the earldom of Norfolk over that of Warwick. This was both a personal and a professional quarrel, first aired in parliament in 1414, when he objected to Henry V's granting precedence to Warwick. It was not until 1425 that he pressed the matter most fully, dominating the business in that parliament through his councillor Roger Hunt. When the argument reached stalemate the Commons, fearing a renewal of the Mowbray–Beauchamp quarrels, proposed that Mowbray be restored to his father's dukedom, thus neatly sidestepping the entire issue. On 14 July Mowbray duly paid homage as duke of Norfolk.

Mowbray's last years, apart from the coronation expedition, are obscure. On 1 December 1427 his fee as a royal councillor was increased to 300 marks p.a., but his attendance record did not improve. A debt of £1300 owing for his fees in 1431 was only partly settled before he died. In August 1428 he was involved in a violent quarrel with John Holland, earl of Huntingdon. On 8 November following, Duke John almost drowned when his barge capsized under London Bridge. He made his first will on 12 May 1429, and in it ordered his attorneys to bring his father's bones home from Venice to be buried in the Charterhouse on the Isle of Axholme. Mowbray's second will, dictated at Epworth on the day of his death, 19 October 1432, directed that he too should be buried there, an indication that although East Anglia henceforth would be the Mowbrays' central seat, for John Mowbray the north had always been home. He was succeeded by his son, John (VI) *Mowbray, born in 1415. His widow had three more husbands, Sir Thomas Strangways, John, Viscount Beaumont (d. 1460), and—to the scandal of some contemporaries—Sir John Woodville (d. 1469), and died at a great age in 1483.

ROWENA E. ARCHER

Sources Chancery records · PRO · BL, Additional MSS · Chancery, inquisitions post mortem, C137/63/77 · Arundel Castle archives, West Sussex · Berkeley Castle, Gloucestershire, Berkeley Castle MSS · R. E. Archer, 'The Mowbrays, earls of Nottingham and dukes of Norfolk to 1432', DPhil diss., U. Oxf., 1984 · J. H. Wylie and W. T. Waugh, eds., The reign of Henry the Fifth, 3 vols. (1914–29) · R. A. Newhall, The English conquest of Normandy, 1416–1424: a study in fifteenth-century warfare (1924) · R. A. Griffiths, The reign of King Henry VI: the exercise of royal authority, 1422–1461 (1981) · K. H. Vickers, Humphrey duke of Gloucester: a biography (1907) · R. E. Archer, 'Parliamentary restoration: John Mowbray and the dukedom of Norfolk in 1425', Rulers and ruled in late medieval England: essays presented to Gerald Harriss, ed. R. E. Archer and S. Walker (1995), 99–116 · E. F. Jacob, ed., The register of Henry Chichele, archbishop of Canterbury, 1414–1443, 2,

CYS, 42 (1937) · GEC, Peerage, new edn, 9.605–7 · [J. Raine], ed., Testamenta Eboracensia, 3, SurtS, 45 (1865)
Likenesses stained glass, St Mary's Hall, Coventry
Wealth at death approx. £3000: accounts for 1420–21: Arundel Castle archives MS 1642; various accounts of his mother's dower: Chancery; Phillipps MS in Norfolk RO valor of 1427

Mowbray, John (VI), third duke of Norfolk (1415–1461),

magnate, was the only son of John (V) *Mowbray, second duke of Norfolk (1392–1432), and Katherine *Neville (c.1400–1483).

Youthful employment and eclipse Born on 12 September 1415, John Mowbray was under age at his father's death, when his estates were granted to Humphrey, duke of Gloucester, at a farm of 2000 marks, and his wardship and marriage sold to Anne, countess of Stafford, for £2000. In 1424 he duly married Anne's daughter, Eleanor Bourchier (d. 1474), and in August 1436 accompanied Humphrey on the expedition to relieve Calais, which was being besieged by the duke of Burgundy. This may have been a sensible use of his energies, for there is reason to believe that he was a troublesome young man. Ordinances for his upbringing, probably from 1435, show that he had been leading a disorderly life, with a retinue of equally disorderly followers. Summoned before the council, he was presented with detailed regulations for his daily living, including prescribed hours for his getting up in the morning and going to bed at night. Some of his retainers were dismissed, and new attendants were appointed, who were to endeavour to persuade the young John Mowbray to 'good reule and good governaunce' (Orme, 126).

Whether or not this regimen had the desired effect, Mowbray received livery of his inheritance on 13 September 1436. In 1437–8 he served a year's term as warden of the east march (an appointment for which, perhaps Duke Humphrey was also responsible), in 1438 he was one of the leaders of an expedition to strengthen the defences of Calais and Guînes, under threat once again from the duke of Burgundy, and in 1439 he was one of the English delegation to the peace conference at Oye, near Calais. The embassy of 1439 was the duke's last official trip abroad, possibly, it has been said, because he had little sympathy with the subsequent direction of foreign policy. A similar lack of sympathy with the earl of Suffolk's increasing dominance in domestic affairs also led to the duke's political eclipse during the 1440s in East Anglia, where he and Suffolk had tangled as early as 1434; the duke was imprisoned in 1440 and 1448 as a result of clashes with Suffolk's retainers John Heydon and Sir Robert Wingfield, the latter of whom had defected from Norfolk's affinity. Between 1440 and 1443 he was appointed to inquire into and help defuse disturbances in the city of Norwich, but for the rest of the 1440s had no public duties. In 1449, having in the previous year married his son and heir to the daughter of the earl of Shrewsbury, he may have left England to go on pilgrimage, probably to Rome—licence for this had been granted him in 1446.

Political manoeuvrings In 1450 the followers of Jack Cade named the duke of Norfolk as one of the king's natural counsellors whom Suffolk had excluded from power and who should now be recalled. And indeed, the disgrace and murder of Suffolk in that year opened new opportunities for Norfolk. They were not, however, clear-cut, and in consequence the duke's part in the tangled politics of the 1450s is as difficult to characterize as it is to discern the sort of man he was. He was, it appears, as bitter an opponent of the duke of Somerset as was the duke of York, with whom he was in alliance in 1450, and again in 1453; on 1 December 1450 men from his retinue joined with those from York's in an attack on Somerset at his lodgings in Blackfriars, and in November 1453, after Henry VI became ill, Norfolk was active in the denunciation, arrest, and imprisonment of Somerset. Perhaps, and understandably, the duke was less sure of his ground when it came to the condemnation of the government's conduct at home.

Norfolk supported the government against York in the confrontation at Dartford early in March 1452, and when on 3 April 1454 he was invited to become a councillor under the duke as protector, made a wordy speech promising goodwill but declining to serve on the grounds of ill health. This apparent change of heart may have been due in part to the government's having apparently tried to win Norfolk's support. It was less than energetic in its pursuit of his men charged with disorder in East Anglia, while the duke himself received £200 and a gold cup from the king on 26 May 1452 as a reward for his services. Even so, Norfolk seems just as likely to have been following a calculated policy of caution, even vacillation, one summed up by his either deliberately arriving late or hovering in the vicinity of the first battle of St Albans on 22 May 1455. He did not attend the parliament held shortly after the Yorkist victory, and in the second half of the decade he kept even more in the background. In 1456 he went on pilgrimage to Walsingham on foot, and in 1457–8 may have gone still further afield, to Amiens, Wilsnack (in Brandenburg), Rome, or Jerusalem. He did not take part in the renewed warfare of the autumn of 1459, though he attended the Coventry parliament, and on 11 December took the oath to uphold Henry VI.

It was after the battle of Northampton on 10 July 1460, which he is more likely to have observed from a safe distance than participated in, that Norfolk came to a firmer political decision than any he had made in the past. The death of some of his close relatives and courtier friends at the battle, and the infirm king's capture by the triumphant Yorkist lords no doubt steeled him to change his allegiance from Lancaster to York. Following the Yorkist defeat of the second battle of St Albans on 17 February 1461, he was one of the small group of bishops and barons who on the following 3 March chose Edward, duke of York, to be king of England, and he fought strenuously for the new king at Towton on 29 March 1461; the arrival of his forces during the afternoon may well have decided the battle. He officiated as earl marshal at Edward's coronation on 28 June, and was rewarded in July with a number of lucrative posts; no doubt these would have been only the first of many, had he not died, aged no more than forty-six, on 6 November 1461. He was buried at Thetford Priory. Eleanor, his widow, survived him; she died in 1474

and was also buried at Thetford Priory. An episode reported in May 1451, telling how Norfolk disencumbered himself of nearly all his retinue so that he could turn aside for a private tryst with his wife, suggests that the two were close. Their only child and heir was John (VII) *Mowbray.

Power and responsibility in East Anglia The third duke of Norfolk features a good deal in the Paston letters; at any rate his followers do, especially after the downfall of Suffolk in 1450. Some of them seem to have done much as they pleased in 1452–3, committing one outrage after another; the duke was either unable to control them, or chose not to do so, even though only a year or two earlier he had claimed to have 'nexst the Kynge our soverayn Lord … the princypall rewle and governance throwh all this schir, of whishe we ber our name whyls that we be lyvynge' (*Paston Letters*, 2.259). He was no more able during the 1450s always to get his candidates returned as knights of the shire at parliamentary elections in East Anglia. His power and influence in the region was not unlimited. There are a number of reasons why this was the case. In the first place no nobleman's authority, even under the king's 'good grace and lycence', as the duke expressed it in a proclamation of 1451 or 1452, went unchallenged by other noblemen. In the early 1450s the duke had to contend with the earl of Oxford and Thomas, Lord Scales, as well as with a whole bevy of distinguished, wealthy, and independent East Anglian knights, esquires, and gentlemen.

More specifically, however, there was what has been called the third duke's 'virtually complete exclusion from power at the national level' (Moye, 24). Having little or no access to power and patronage at the centre, he could not expect, save in the heady days immediately after Suffolk's downfall, to exercise provincial patronage and power. At a more local level he faced the additional problem that the Mowbrays were relative newcomers to the East Anglian political scene. The second duke, though a major landowner in the region, had preferred to reside in Lincolnshire when not campaigning in France. Moreover, the essential character of the family's property-holding was that it was dispersed, with nearly 150 properties in 25 counties, Wales, Ireland, and Calais; such dispersal diffused the duke's potential for the effective exercise of authority too widely. Additionally, dispersed estates were difficult to administer, and revenues consequently harder to collect; this was certainly the case with the Mowbray lands, though the third duke went some way towards consolidating the estate and administering it less wastefully. More important still is the fact that the duke's mother, Katherine Neville, outlived him by more than twenty years; while her dower was not excessive, it meant that at no time did the duke enjoy more than two-thirds of his inheritance. As the second duke of Norfolk, too, had been living off a diminished estate and had borrowed heavily, it has been said that his heir was left 'with a hopeless legacy' (Archer, 29).

Was it hopeless in other than a financial sense? The third duke's attempts at a regional dominance in the 1450s have been viewed critically by historians, one of them describing him as 'a disreputable thug by any standards' (Lander, 3). More recently there has been greater charity. Not only was his 'use of ruthless and violent tactics … perhaps no worse than that of his rivals' (Moye, 24), but those tactics were a necessary part of the strategy to 'restore and maintain their [the Mowbrays'] power and prestige following the first duke's banishment in 1398', as well as of 'the struggle to stay afloat financially' (Moye, abstract). While the memory of 1398 goes a long way to explain the 'lukewarmness' of the duke, 'conspicuous and at times inglorious to a degree unusual even in civil war' (Moye, 25), it is less clear why a memory of treason, forfeiture, and disgrace should drive all three fifteenth-century dukes of Norfolk to extravagant expenditure on an affinity that, if it did not quite terrorize three English shires, was none the less cavalier with the rights of others to a safe life and a secure livelihood. Norfolk does appear to have taken chivalry seriously, hence his taking part with the duke of York, equally touchy on chivalric issues, in the pursuit of the duke of Somerset over the loss of Normandy. Yet, not only did he long avoid commitment in the civil war, he also contributed nothing after 1439 towards preventing the loss of either Normandy or Gascony. Possibly that too was a question of memory (and money): it was campaigning for Henry V in France that had led his father into debt.

But ultimately the issue is one of responsibility, in a role that no senior medieval English magnate could avoid, that of politician. As third duke of Norfolk, John Mowbray was a great landowner, the head of what was regarded as a great house, and a provincial potentate. Following his exclusion from politics in the 1440s, he might have been expected to be all the more desirous of being a key player in the tumultuous politics of the 1450s. Instead, and until in 1460 circumstances left him no choice but to declare his loyalties, he sat on the fence. Many medieval aristocrats were irresponsible men. Mowbray's individuality lay in the thoroughness of his irresponsibility.

COLIN RICHMOND

Sources L. E. Moye, 'The estates and finances of the Mowbray family, earls marshal and dukes of Norfolk, 1401–1476', PhD diss., Duke U., 1985 · R. E. Archer, 'Rich old ladies: the problem of late medieval dowagers', Property and politics: essays in later medieval English history, ed. T. Pollard (1984), 15–35 · C. Richmond, The Paston family in the fifteenth century: Fastolf's will (1996) · The Paston letters, AD 1422–1509, ed. J. Gairdner, new edn, 6 vols. (1904) · N. Davis, ed., Paston letters and papers of the fifteenth century, 2 vols. (1971–6) · K. B. McFarlane, The nobility of later medieval England (1973) · K. B. McFarlane, England in the fifteenth century: collected essays (1981) · GEC, Peerage, new edn, 9.605–8 · N. Orme, 'The education of Edward V', BIHR, 57 (1984), 119–30 · J. Watts, Henry VI and the politics of kingship (1996) · R. L. Storey, The end of the house of Lancaster (1966) · J. R. Lander, Government and community: England, 1450–1509 (1980) · H. Castor, 'The duchy of Lancaster and the rule of East Anglia, 1399–1440: a prologue to the Paston letters', Crown, government, and people in the fifteenth century, ed. R. E. Archer (1995), 53–78

Mowbray, John (VII), fourth duke of Norfolk (1444–1476), magnate, was born on 18 October 1444, the only child and heir of John (VI) *Mowbray, third duke of Norfolk (1415–1461), and his wife, Eleanor Bourchier (d. 1474).

Military and political activities The younger John Mowbray was created earl of Surrey and Warenne in tail male on 24 March 1451. This was probably an aspect of the court's policy to detach the third duke from Richard, duke of York, with whom he had been in alliance against the government in 1450; the policy was temporarily successful. The new earl of Surrey was already married, his father having married him to Elizabeth Talbot [see below], daughter of John *Talbot, earl of Shrewsbury (c.1387–1453), and Margaret Beauchamp (d. 1467) [see Talbot, Margaret, under Talbot, John] in October 1448. Much was no doubt expected of an only child who may have been precocious: aged seventeen on the death of his father, he had by then already served on three commissions and for the rest of his minority his services continued to be used by Edward IV. In 1461–2, following the Yorkist victory at Towton, he was stationed in the north, and is recorded as sending victuals from Newcastle upon Tyne to the earl of Warwick, who was besieging Warkworth Castle. Later he was dispatched to Wales, and was active against rebels in the lordship of Denbigh in the spring of 1464. It was probably for such active service that he was allowed to enter his inheritance in March 1465, some months before his twenty-first birthday.

Norfolk's commitment to the Yorkist regime at its outset did not falter during its darkest days in 1469–71; indeed, it was even more clear-cut. He was with Edward at York in March and at Exeter in April 1470 with an impressive retinue in pursuit of rebels, and John (III) Paston wrote to his brother at that time that 'whyll owyr Dwk is thus cherysheid wyth the Kyng ye nor I shall not have a man unbetyn or slayn in thys contré' (Paston Letters, ed. Davis, 1.556). After Edward had been forced into flight from England the following October, Norfolk was among those arrested by the earl of Warwick. Lying low during the readeption of Henry VI, when he was omitted from the commission of the peace in Sussex, he was rearrested when Edward IV's ships appeared off the East Anglian coast in March 1471. Though mysteriously absent from the battle of Barnet on 14 April, Norfolk fought at the battle of Tewkesbury on 4 May, and in the bloody aftermath presided as earl marshal along with the youthful constable of England, Richard, duke of Gloucester, over the proceedings that tried and condemned to death the duke of Somerset and others who had been taken by force from sanctuary in the abbey. Norfolk accompanied Edward both on his triumphal entry into London on 21 May, and on his progress through Kent to take the submission of Thomas Neville (the Bastard of Fauconberg) at Sandwich, and to witness the execution of Nicholas Faunt, the mayor of Canterbury, in that city at the end of the month. In 1475 on the expedition to France he led a contingent of 40 men-at-arms and 300 archers, an exactly similar force to that commanded by John de la Pole, duke of Suffolk. Norfolk died unexpectedly during the night of 16–17 January 1476 at Framlingham, and was buried at Thetford Priory.

Financial difficulties and their causes The character of the fourth duke of Norfolk is not easy to discern. In spite of his admirable loyalty to Edward IV, who was only a little over two years his senior, he has been regarded as 'both obstinate and weak-willed' (McFarlane, *England in the Fifteenth Century*, 253). No doubt it is significant that the king, though willing to rely on the duke for military support, did not make him a councillor, evidently taking a dim view of his political judgement. On one occasion Edward gave it as his opinion that Norfolk was the puppet of Sir William Brandon, one of the duke's own councillors. The experience of the Pastons, on the other hand, was that the duke was immoveable. In the summer of 1469, in an incident made notorious by the Paston letters, he laid siege to Caister Castle, and after five weeks forced its little garrison to surrender. Thereafter no one could persuade him to return the castle to the Pastons—not his councillors, not his wife, not the bishop of Winchester, William Waynflete, not the king's chamberlain, William, Lord Hastings, not the king himself. Such stubbornness is likely to have sprung from the simple fact that Norfolk regarded Caister as his; he had bought it for 500 marks in October 1468 from those who reckoned they had every right to sell it, namely Sir John Fastolf's executors. It was, no doubt, for the same reason that he had launched the siege in 1469: he was taking what was his own. His purchase of Caister was part of the continuing Mowbrays' policy of consolidating their estates: the purchase was made in the same year as the sale to William Herbert, earl of Pembroke, of the family's properties in Gower and Chepstow; a large number of smaller estates distant from East Anglia were sold in the following year; by the 1470s the family's landed resources were concentrated in East Anglia, Sussex, and Surrey. This rationalization made both administrative and above all economic sense. Economic sense was an urgent necessity for the fourth duke, who was in far deeper financial straits than his father.

The reason for Norfolk's problems was straightforward: the longevity of two dowager duchesses. Katherine Neville, the wife of the second duke (d. 1432), survived both her son and grandson. She died in 1483. Eleanor Bourchier, the wife of the third duke, lived until 1474, less than two years before the death of her son. For most of the fourth duke's short life, therefore, two-thirds of the Mowbray estates were held by these two women, leaving him with only a third of his inheritance from which to maintain the ducal family in the fashion to which it had become accustomed and to the standard that society demanded of it. According to a valor made in 1476, the clear annual value of the lands the fourth duke held at his death was £3150; Katherine Neville was in possession at that date of about a third (at most) of the Mowbray inheritance, which, therefore, was in its entirety worth about £4000 a year. Eleanor Bourchier until 1474 had held in jointure, dower, and by generous grant of her son lands worth well over £1000 yearly. Thus, the third of his inheritance upon which the fourth duke had to uphold the ducal status between 1465 and 1474 amounted to a mere £1500 per annum. His immoveability with regard to Caister is, therefore, understandable, and was, indeed, understood, not least by the Pastons, whose patience after 1471

was due in some measure to their recognition of his predicament.

Not that Norfolk was not extravagant. There is no doubt that when compared to his fellow peers the fourth duke spent extravagantly on his affinity. In 1473–4, for example, payments to his affinity came to a little over £300, and in the following year, after he had gained control of his mother's estates, he paid out £850 on fees, wages, annuities, and life tenancies. Hence about a quarter of his available income went to his followers, more than twice as much as historians have come to regard as an average outlay for a peer. Although the fourth duke's practice is unlikely to have been significantly different from that of either his father or grandfather in this respect, he had nothing like their resources, and the motives that prompted his high outlay, at a time when he might have been expected to retrench, are correspondingly mysterious. He may have been insecure as well as obstinate, and therefore felt the need to bind men to him in this fashion—hence the East Anglian gentlemen who conducted the siege of Caister on his behalf. The lists of Mowbray servants, retainers, and followers in the 1460s and 1470s are certainly impressively long, and contain the names of some of the most influential as well as powerful men of the region. In 1469 and afterwards the Pastons faced a formidable opponent.

The dowager duchess The most formidable among the adversaries of the Pastons, although she claimed she was sympathetic to their case for Caister, was the fourth duke's wife Elizabeth Talbot [**Elizabeth Mowbray**, duchess of Norfolk (d. 1506/7)]. The fourth duke was as openhanded to his wife as to his mother. By 1467 her jointure had been expanded to include most of the inheritance, of which in the event of the duke's death she was ensured control. When he died the duchess was pregnant; she either miscarried or the child was stillborn, which left as heir to the Mowbray inheritance a single daughter, Anne, aged three. At once *Edward IV saw the heiress Anne Mowbray as a way of endowing his second son, *Richard, duke of York, aged two. An amicable arrangement was achieved with Elizabeth, a process no doubt made easier by the fact that she was apparently in favour at court, having accompanied the king's sister Margaret to Burgundy for her marriage to Duke Charles in 1468. The duchess was determined on two things, an adequate dower for herself, and the disinheritance of one of Anne Mowbray's two heirs, the opponent of the Talbot family in the fifty-year Lisle–Berkeley dispute, William, Lord Berkeley. Both her conditions were met in a series of settlements arrived at in 1476–7. Elizabeth received property valued at £1309, more than half of the value of her late husband's estates, and Lord Berkeley relinquished all interest in the Mowbray inheritance in return for an agreement by Edward IV to pay the debts he owed to the Talbots. Richard of York, who had been created duke of Norfolk on 7 February 1477, was married to Anne Mowbray in St Stephen's Chapel, Westminster, in January 1478. She was now aged five, he was aged four. Anne died in 1482; Richard died in 1483. Elizabeth Talbot remained an influential figure in East Anglia for over a quarter of a century. In 1492, for instance, she is recorded as intervening to protect the rights of the heir to the manor of Ketteringham, Norfolk. But by the time she died, between 6 November 1506 and 10 May 1507, she may have retired to London. Not only did she direct that she was to be buried in the nun's choir of the Minories in Aldgate, rather than beside her husband at Thetford, but she also left 100 marks to be distributed among the poor of Hackney and Whitechapel.   COLIN RICHMOND

Sources L. E. Moye, 'The estates and finances of the Mowbray family, earls marshal and dukes of Norfolk, 1401–1476', PhD diss., Duke U., 1985 · R. E. Archer, 'Rich old ladies: the problem of late medieval dowagers', *Property and politics: essays in later medieval English history*, ed. A. J. Pollard (1984), 15–35 · C. Richmond, *The Paston family in the fifteenth century: Fastolf's will* (1996) · *The Paston letters, AD 1422–1509*, ed. J. Gairdner, new edn, 6 vols. (1904) · N. Davis, ed., *Paston letters and papers of the fifteenth century*, 2 vols. (1971–6) · K. B. McFarlane, *The nobility of later medieval England* (1973) · K. B. McFarlane, *England in the fifteenth century: collected essays* (1981) · GEC, *Peerage*, new edn, 9.608–9 · C. Ross, *Edward IV* (1974)

Mowbray [*formerly* Cornish], **Sir John Robert, first baronet** (1815–1899), politician, was born at Exeter on 3 June 1815, the only son of Robert Stribling Cornish of that city, and his wife, Marianne, daughter of John Powning of Hill's Court, near Exeter. Admitted at Westminster School on 16 September 1829, he matriculated from Christ Church, Oxford, on 23 May 1833, was elected student in 1835, was president of the union, and graduated BA in 1837 with a second class in *literae humaniores*, and MA in 1839. In 1841 he was called to the bar from the Inner Temple and went on the western circuit. On 19 August 1847 he married Elizabeth Gray (*d.* 16 Feb 1899), only surviving child and heir of George Isaac Mowbray of Bishopwearmouth, co. Durham, and Mortimer, Berkshire; he had already, on 26 July, assumed by royal licence the surname Mowbray, thus recognizing the fortune his wife brought him. They had three sons and two daughters, one of whom, Annie Maud (*d.* 1926), married Charles Thomas *Cruttwell (1847–1911) and was the mother of Charles Robert Mowbray Fraser *Cruttwell (1887–1941).

Mowbray abandoned law for politics, and on 25 June 1853 was elected as a Conservative for Durham City, which he represented until the general election of 1868. He then succeeded Sir William Heathcote as junior member for Oxford University, for which he sat until his death. In 1858 and again in 1866 Lord Derby appointed Mowbray judge-advocate-general. From 1866 to 1868 and from 1871 to 1892 he was church estates commissioner. On 30 November 1868 he was created honorary DCL of Oxford, in 1875 he was elected honorary fellow of Hertford College, and in 1877 honorary student of Christ Church. On 3 May 1880 he was created a baronet and sworn of the privy council. From 1874 to his death Mowbray was chairman of the House of Commons' committee of selection and committee on standing orders, and on the death of Charles Pelham Villiers in 1898 he became 'father of the house'.

Mowbray rarely spoke except on ceremonial occasions and achieved little in national politics save longevity. He was a member of Berkshire county council from 1889. His *Seventy Years at Westminster*, parts of which appeared in

Sir John Robert Mowbray, first baronet (1815–1899), by Bassano, 1898

Blackwood's Magazine, was posthumously published (1900) and contains some instructive and entertaining material for the parliamentary history of the period. He died at his house, 47 Onslow Gardens, London, on 22 April 1899, and was buried at Strathfield Mortimer on the 27th.

A. F. POLLARD, *rev.* H. C. G. MATTHEW

Sources J. Mowbray, *Seventy years at Westminster* (1900) · *The Times* (18 Feb 1899) · *The Times* (24 April 1899) · *The Times* (26 April 1899) · *The Times* (28 April 1899) · Boase, *Mod. Eng. biog.* · W. R. Ward, *Victorian Oxford* (1965) · G. F. R. Barker and A. H. Stenning, eds., *The Westminster School register from 1764 to 1883* (1892) · Foster, *Alum. Oxon.* · J. Foster, *Men-at-the-bar: a biographical hand-list of the members of the various inns of court*, 2nd edn (1885) · Burke, *Peerage* (1999)

Archives LPL, corresp. with A. C. Tait

Likenesses J. Sargent, oils, 1873, repro. in Mowbray, *Seventy years* · after W. W. Ouless, oils, 1886, Oxford and Cambridge University Club, London · Bassano, four negatives, 1898, NPG [*see illus.*] · B. Stone, two photographs, 1898, NPG · C. Dressler, bronze bust, 1900, Palace of Westminster, London · Elliott & Fry, photograph, repro. in *ILN* (29 April 1899), 605 · Maull and Polyblank, carte-de-visite, NPG · Spy [L. Ward], caricature, NPG; repro. in *VF* (8 April 1882)

Wealth at death £188,128 11s.: probate, 16 June 1899, *CGPLA Eng. & Wales*

Mowbray, Robert de, earl of Northumbria (*d.* 1115/1125), magnate, was the son of Roger de Mowbray and nephew of *Geoffrey, bishop of Coutances. According to the early twelfth-century historian Orderic Vitalis, Robert's father, Roger, was from an illustrious Norman family related to the family of Nigel, vicomte of the Cotentin. Roger de

Mowbray attended the Council of Lillebone in 1066. Robert de Mowbray's mother's name is unknown. The family may have had its origins in Montbrai which lies 20 miles to the south-east of Coutances in western Normandy. There was a motte still visible in the 1870s, which may indicate the site of the fortified residence of the lords of Mowbray.

Early life Robert de Mowbray first comes to notice as one of the companions of William the Conqueror's eldest son, Robert Curthose, during the latter's first quarrel with his father in 1078. He accompanied Curthose into exile in 1078, but it is not known when he returned to favour at the Norman court. He also appears confirming the grant to the abbey of St Evroult of the church of Étouvi made by Richard de Coulonces. In Orderic's description of the donation Mowbray is described as 'paramount lord' of this Richard. Although from a wealthy background himself, it is probable that Mowbray benefited greatly from the patronage of his uncle, Bishop Geoffrey. In the plot against William Rufus hatched during Lent 1088 and headed by Odo, bishop of Bayeux, Bishop Geoffrey, and William of St Calais, bishop of Durham (which aimed to reunite the kingdom of England and the duchy of Normandy under Robert Curthose and which broke out into open revolt after Easter), Mowbray joined his uncle in ravaging Bristol, Bath, and all the surrounding area, including the district of Berkeley. The chronicle of John of Worcester calls Mowbray a man skilled in the art of war and he may have been acting as his uncle's military commander during the revolt. The Anglo-Saxon Chronicle does not mention what happened to Mowbray after Odo's defeat, but at the trial of Bishop William of Durham in November 1088, recorded in the contemporary Durham tract *De injusta vexatione Willelmi episcopi*, the bishop asked to be allowed to depart with Robert de Mowbray (called 'Roger' in the text) for Normandy. It is not clear whether Mowbray was sent into forced exile along with the bishop or if he, like his uncle, had become reconciled with William Rufus once Bishop Odo, the leader of the revolt, had submitted in Kent.

The earldom of Northumbria and the slaying of the king of Scots There is some doubt as to when Robert de Mowbray succeeded Aubrey de Coucy as earl of Northumbria. It has been suggested that Aubrey may have resigned his position after the threat of the Danish invasion in 1085. He appears as a tenant in Domesday Book but notices concerning him in the text suggest that he had recently escheated. The sources imply that William I appointed Mowbray, and thus it is usually argued that the beginning of his tenure of the earldom may be dated to 1086–7. If this is the case, then Mowbray did not immediately take up his office as he was in Normandy between the Conqueror's death (9 September 1087) and the rebellion in England which broke out after Easter 1088—the nuns of Holy Trinity, Caen, cited him as one of those who took advantage of the confusion to plunder their lands. It may be doubted that Mowbray's appointment to Northumbria would have been ratified by William Rufus, given Mowbray's earlier

support for Curthose, and perhaps Mowbray's participation in the revolt of 1088 was a result of Rufus refusing to recognize his claim to the earldom. Alternatively, there is evidence to suggest that his uncle, Bishop Geoffrey, exercised comital authority in Northumberland before Robert's appointment. Abbot Stephen's account of the foundation of St Mary's Abbey, York, of 1089, noted that it was Bishop Geoffrey who was exercising authority in Northumbria in the first months of 1088, and it may be the case that it was the bishop who succeeded Aubrey de Coucy and that his nephew acquired the earldom between *c*.1089 and 1091, when William Rufus issued a record of the settlement which he had effected between Mowbray and the bishop of Durham.

In this light it seems that Mowbray's killing of Malcolm III, king of Scots, was one of his first acts as earl; and it proved a successful attempt to remove the greatest threat to the untrammelled exercise of his comital authority between the rivers Tyne and Tweed. In May 1091 Malcolm III had invaded Northumbria with a large army, intending to push on further if he met with success. Rufus and Robert Curthose marched north and restored Bishop William to Durham on 11 September. Malcolm met Rufus in Lothian and Robert Curthose and Edgar Ætheling procured a treaty by which Malcolm would obey Rufus as he had obeyed William I, and Rufus would restore the twelve vills which Malcolm had held in England under the Conqueror and would give him 12 marks of gold each year. But the treaty did not last long. In 1093 Rufus summoned Malcolm III to Gloucester and then refused to see him. Consequently Malcolm returned to Scotland, raised an army, and attacked Northumbria. Robert de Mowbray surprised the Scots king, who was slain by Morael, Mowbray's nephew, sheriff of Northumberland, and also the king's *godsib* or gossip (that is, he had stood together with Malcolm as a baptismal sponsor). The battle took place on St Brice's day, 13 November. Malcolm's son Edward was also killed and his wife, Margaret, died shortly after hearing the news. Gaimar reports that the battle took place at Alnwick and that 3000 men were slain, and he adds that Mowbray killed the king 'whether it was right or wrong' (*L'estoire des Engleis*, lines 6109–10). Orderic Vitalis believed that the Scots were caught unarmed and unawares, possibly because they were travelling under a safe conduct. Rufus and the barons of his court were saddened by the news of Malcolm's death and the whiff of dishonour surrounding the episode may have tarnished Mowbray's reputation at court. The *Historia regum Anglorum* compiled at Durham saw Malcolm's death as divine punishment for his attacks on Northumbria. Two local people placed Malcolm's body on a cart and buried it at Tynemouth, whence it was translated to Dunfermline during the reign of Alexander I (1107–24).

Landed wealth and marriage According to Orderic Vitalis, on the death of Bishop Geoffrey (2 February 1093), Mowbray inherited his 280 manors. Excluding tenements in towns, Domesday Book recorded 265 manors belonging to the bishop, which confirms Orderic's estimate. Bishop Geoffrey has been ranked as the seventh richest baron excluding William I's half-brothers, Odo of Bayeux and Robert de Mortain. The manors were distributed in two main groups, the larger of which was in the west of England and the smaller in the east midlands counties, with one or two estates elsewhere. The inheritance of his uncle's estates, together with the earldom of Northumbria, would have made Robert de Mowbray one of the most powerful barons in William Rufus's kingdom, and may account for the king's harsh treatment of him after the rebellion of 1095. Three months before this rebellion Mowbray married Matilda, daughter of Richer de l'Aigle, whose family had usually supported Duke Robert Curthose against William Rufus in the struggle for the Anglo-Norman realm. Orderic stated that Mowbray's marriage was contracted in order to extend his territories and to forge alliances with the most powerful of his countrymen. Matilda was a niece of Hugh d'Avranches, earl of Chester, and it may be this connection to which Orderic refers.

Northern politics and rebellion Despite his wealth and connections, Mowbray's position in the north was by no means pre-eminent. The *Historia regum Anglorum* attributed to Symeon of Durham records that not long before his death in 1093 Abbot Paul of St Albans had taken possession of the church of St Oswin at Tynemouth with the aid of Mowbray, contrary to the injunctions of the monks of Durham. Paul contracted an illness at Tynemouth and died on the way home, and this was seen as divine retribution for his part in the abstraction of St Cuthbert's property. According to an account of the donation of Tynemouth to St Albans produced at Durham, Mowbray's men, Gumer and Robert Taca, forcibly removed the monk Turchil who was managing the church of St Oswin for the community at Durham. The Durham monks advanced their claim to Tynemouth in a series of spurious documents produced in the twelfth century which claimed that Earl Waltheof, Bishop Walcher of Durham, and Earl Aubrey had granted and confirmed the church of St Oswin to them. The context of Mowbray's action may be a dispute with Bishop William concerning the administration of certain vills in the south of the bishopric over which both claimed jurisdiction. In 1091 Rufus effected a compromise between the two in which, for a payment of £100, Mowbray abandoned his claim to the vills. It thus seems likely that he was also on poor terms with Bishop William and the monks of Durham, and the donation of Tynemouth to the abbey of St Albans may have been an attempt to make redress. The date of this has been debated, but it should perhaps be assigned to the period after the return of Bishop William from exile in 1091 and before the death of Abbot Paul in 1093. It seems that the bishop and the earl were jockeying for a position of authority in the north-east of England: a writ issued on behalf of Rufus ordered Mowbray to restore any land which he had taken from the bishop since the latter's restoration in 1091.

In late 1094 or early 1095 Mowbray plundered four cards (large trading vessels) which had sailed from Norway to Northumbria. The merchants demanded reparations from the king and Rufus ordered Mowbray to appear at his court. The earl refused and Rufus was forced to recompense the merchants from his own treasury. Again Mowbray was summoned to court, and again he refused to appear. It is likely that a third summons was issued, the defiance of which rendered Robert a contumacious vassal. Rufus's attitude towards rebels had hardened considerably as he had grown stronger after the failed revolt of 1088 and he refused to grant the earl hostages or safe passage to his court. Having already sent his younger brother Henry into Northumbria, Rufus gathered an army and marched against Mowbray. At the Tyne he besieged and took the *novum castrum* ('new castle') built by Robert Curthose in 1081 and defended in 1095 by Mowbray's unnamed brother. Some authors believed that Tynemouth is referred to in the sources, but there is no evidence of a castle next to the church there at this date and the inability of Mowbray to defend his position there later in the campaign seems to confirm this. In addition, Rufus issued three charters regarding Tynemouth in favour of the monks of St Albans and, it has been argued, it seems unlikely that he would have issued these while trying to reduce the site. Bypassing Newcastle, Rufus attacked and captured the small castle erected by William de Merlay at Morpeth. Here, according to the sources, Mowbray's best knights were captured. In August the king pushed on to Bamburgh where Mowbray had taken his stand. A charter issued by Edgar, future king of Scots, granting estates in Lothian to the monks of St Cuthbert was issued 'in the year in which King William II built a new castle at Bamburgh against Earl Robert' (Lawrie, 13). Outside the fortification, Rufus erected the siege castle mentioned in Edgar's charter which he called *Malveisin* or *Yfel nehhbur* ('bad neighbour'). During the siege, however, Rufus had to return south in order to make a foray into Wales. In the meantime, Mowbray left Bamburgh, possibly as the result of a trick. According to the chronicle of John of Worcester, Mowbray was offered Newcastle, and so set off with thirty knights. This may have been a ruse to lure him away from Bamburgh, and when he was observed by the garrison of the *Malveisin* they pursued him and warned the custodians of Newcastle. As a result Mowbray was forced to take refuge in Tynemouth, possibly defended only by the ramparts of the settlement. He was able to resist for a time but on the sixth day of the siege he was wounded in the leg and forced to flee to the church of St Oswin. The king's soldiers dragged him from his sanctuary and put him into custody. The historians of the church of St Cuthbert saw this as divine punishment for Mowbray's abstraction of Tynemouth church from the monks of Durham. The earl was paraded before Bamburgh and Rufus threatened to put out his eyes if his wife, Matilda, and his nephew, Sheriff Morael, did not surrender the fortress. They duly handed over Bamburgh to the king.

Imprisonment and death After the rebellion of 1095 Mowbray forfeited his estates and spent the next twenty or thirty years in prison. Initially after his capture he was taken to Windsor and imprisoned in the castle. His nephew Morael purchased his own freedom by disclosing the names of other conspirators, who were subsequently punished. According to Orderic Vitalis, Morael died in exile, an impoverished and reviled figure. Mowbray's wife was granted an annulment of her marriage by Pope Paschal II (r. 1099–1118) and she became the wife of Nigel d'Aubigny, one of Henry I's close associates. According to Orderic, Nigel treated her well until the death of her brother Gilbert de l'Aigle, when he repudiated her, ostensibly on the grounds that she had been his cousin's wife, but more probably because she had failed to bear him any children. Nigel d'Aubigny then married Gundreda, sister of Hugh de Gournai. Mowbray was childless and the estates he had held were broken up, some being used to reward those who had remained loyal to Rufus. The king did not appoint another earl to Northumbria, retaining control of the lands himself, and indeed they must have been a valuable asset in the struggle with his brother for control over Normandy. The Mowbray honour created for Nigel d'Aubigny bore little relation to the conglomeration of lands held by Bishop Geoffrey and his nephew.

Orderic Vitalis painted a thumb-nail sketch of Robert de Mowbray's character. He was distinguished by his great wealth and power, and his audacity and military daring caused him to hold his fellow nobles in contempt and to refuse to obey his superiors. He was heavily built, tall, and strong, had a dark complexion and was covered in hair. He was, by nature, daring and crafty and his features melancholy and harsh. He brooded and scarcely ever smiled when he was speaking. According to a St Albans source, Mowbray became a monk before he died and was buried in the abbey, at the spot where St Symeon's Chapel was later built. The year of his death may be either 1115 or 1125, as the sources variously suggest that he was held prisoner for twenty or thirty years. WILLIAM M. AIRD

Sources Symeon of Durham, *Opera* · John of Worcester, *Chron.* · *ASC*, s.a. 1087, 1093, 1095 · Ordericus Vitalis, *Eccl. hist.* · *Reg. RAN*, vols. 1–2 · R. C. van Caenegem, ed., *English lawsuits from William I to Richard I*, 2 vols., SeldS, 106–7 (1990–91) · *L'estoire des Engleis by Geffrei Gaimar*, ed. A. Bell, Anglo-Norman Texts, 14–16 (1960) · J. Le Patourel, 'Geoffrey of Montbray, bishop of Coutances, 1049–93', *EngHR*, 59 (1944), 129–61 · H. S. Offler, ed., *Durham episcopal charters, 1071–1152*, SurtS, 179 (1968) · F. Barlow, *William Rufus* (1983) · *VCH Northumberland*, vol. 8 · Paris, *Chron.* · A. C. Lawrie, ed., *Early Scottish charters prior to AD 1153* (1905)

Wealth at death est. over £750 p.a.: W. J. Corbett, *Cambridge medieval history*, vol. 5, pp. 510–11

Mowbray, Sir Roger (I) de (d. 1188), magnate, whose surname derived from Montbray in Normandy, was the son of Nigel d'Aubigny (d. 1129) and his second wife, Gundreda de Gournay (d. c.1154), whom he married in 1118. A witness list to one of Mowbray's charters mentions a brother Robert but there are doubts about the authenticity of this list. Mowbray married Alice de Gant (d. c.1181), daughter of the Lincolnshire baron Walter de Gant and widow of the Yorkshire baron Ilbert de Lacy, not long after 1141; with her he had two sons, Nigel and Robert.

Creation of the honour of Mowbray Mowbray's father, Nigel d'Aubigny, had been one of Henry I's most important 'new men', and with his brother William, ancestor of the earls of Arundel, served Henry faithfully. D'Aubigny fought in Henry's armies and acted as an important local official in

northern England, where he probably had custody of a castle in York. He was one of the most frequent attestors to Henry's charters during his lifetime. Henry rewarded d'Aubigny, who was a landless younger son, magnificently. He arranged for him to marry Matilda de l'Aigle, who was divorced by papal dispensation from Robert de Mowbray, the former earl of Northumbria who had been imprisoned since his revolt of 1095, and granted the earl's Norman lands, including Montbray, to d'Aubigny; d'Aubigny retained these lands even after he divorced Matilda (supposedly on the grounds of consanguinity, but probably because the couple had no children) to marry Gundreda. Henry may have granted other Norman lands to d'Aubigny, and Gundreda brought him the Norman castle of Écouché as her marriage portion. Henry I also gave him a huge honour in England, based on lands forfeited by Robert (I) de Stuteville after the battle of Tinchebrai, and comprising the Domesday holdings of Geoffrey de la Guerche and Gospatric, some of the lands held in 1086 by Hugh fitz Baldric and Erneis de Burun, and other estates as well. D'Aubigny also became overlord of the Tison and Arches fees, and at the time of his death in Normandy in 1129 he was one of the most powerful of the Anglo-Norman barons, with a number of castles in England and Normandy.

Military activities and marriage Roger de Mowbray first rose to prominence as one of the leaders at the battle of the Standard in 1138, and indeed the English army set out for the battle from his holding of Thirsk. He may have been fairly young at this time, for Ailred of Rievaulx stated that so great was the fervour against the Scots that he was brought along with the army though still a boy (*puerulus*) and carefully placed among others where he would presumably be safe. The fact that Mowbray had sufficient control over his estates to give land to Byland in the same year and was knighted around the same time seems at first glance to contradict Ailred's statement about his youth, but it is possible that he was rewarded for his participation in battle with an early end to his minority and with a dubbing. Three years later, in 1141, he fought in Stephen's army at the battle of Lincoln and was among those captured by Ranulf (II), earl of Chester and Robert, earl of Gloucester. Probably as part of his settlement with his captors, he granted fourteen knight's fees to Ranulf's follower Eustace fitz John. His marriage to Alice de Gant may be connected with Ranulf's attempts to create a large network of allies and thus may also have resulted from Mowbray's capture at Lincoln. Various charters hint that he and his men were involved in other raiding and fighting during Stephen's reign, and a Durham account describes his stronghold of Thirsk as the base of a raid into Durham, although the raid may have occurred during his minority. Later in Stephen's reign, he probably participated in the campaign of 1149 led by the future Henry II, Ranulf, earl of Chester, and David, king of Scotland. During this period Mowbray seems to have hoped to gain the custody of the castle in York that his father had once held.

Despite or perhaps because of the trouble in England Mowbray chose to accompany Louis VII of France on the second crusade, following in the steps of his maternal grandfather who had participated in the first crusade. The second crusade was a débâcle but Mowbray managed not only to survive but, according to John of Hexham, to gain glory by defeating a Muslim leader in single combat.

In the early part of Henry II's reign, Mowbray's life was quieter. He recovered his Norman estates, lost to Geoffrey of Anjou during Stephen's reign, and some time before 1172 turned them over to his elder son, Nigel, who also seems to have been brought into a prominent role in the governance of his father's estates in England at an early age, frequently witnessing his father's charters and confirming them with his own.

Rebellion against Henry II   In 1174 Mowbray joined the revolt of Henry, the Young King, against Henry II. The reasons for his participation are not certain but he had important grounds for disappointment, unease, and hostility: Henry was clearly trying to raise the size of Mowbray's knights' service; Mowbray had failed to gain custody of the castle in York he desired; and he had been forced to grant to Robert (III) de Stuteville, who was heir to the man who had lost so much land to Nigel d'Aubigny after Tinchebrai and was rising in power as a royal favourite and sheriff of York, the manor of Kirkby Moorside in Yorkshire and a number of knight's fees. On the positive side Mowbray may have hoped to become a royal favourite himself by supporting the young Henry, who was a likely bet to become ruling monarch sooner or later even if the revolt failed. Judging by his treatment of his own heir, moreover, he surely sympathized with the Young King's grievances.

Whatever his motive, Mowbray quickly rebuilt a castle at Kinnard in Axholme, Lincolnshire, and garrisoned his castles at Kirkby Malzeard and Thirsk in Yorkshire. His strongholds provided a potential link between the rebels in the midlands and the king of Scotland, and, if Jordan Fantosme is to be believed, he had widespread support in Yorkshire. However, Henry II's illegitimate son, Geoffrey, the bishop-elect of Lincoln, quickly took action and besieged Kinnard, which was not sufficiently prepared for the attack. Kinnard was soon captured early in May 1174, and at least partially destroyed, and Mowbray's younger son, Robert, constable of the castle, was captured on his way to Leicester, where he had hoped to obtain help from the midland insurgents. Geoffrey then moved into York, where he captured and partially destroyed Kirkby Malzeard and closely invested Thirsk. A castle was built nearby at Topcliffe and placed under the command of William de Stuteville, son of Mowbray's rival, Robert, sheriff of Yorkshire. According to Jordan Fantosme, Mowbray had long since left the area; he left the defence of his castles to his sons, joined William, king of Scotland, shortly after the latter's unsuccessful attack on Wark, and assisted him in subsequent actions. According to William of Newburgh, however, it was only after his setbacks in Lincolnshire and Yorkshire that Mowbray joined King William; he made an alliance and granted his son Nigel as a hostage to the Scottish king. In any case he had joined William before 13 July, when the latter was captured by

royalist forces in a surprise attack outside Alnwick. Mowbray himself barely avoided capture and fled into Scotland. On 31 July he met King Henry at Northampton, surrendered Thirsk to him, and was received into the king's peace. He did not suffer ruin as a result of his rebellion but his castles at Kinnard, Kirkby Malzeard, and Thirsk were destroyed, either at the time of their capture or in early 1176. Moreover, he had forfeited any hope of gaining royal favour; indeed the monks of Kirkstall noted that they lost certain land in 1183–4 because of the hatred the king had for Mowbray.

Religious benefactor   If Mowbray was interested in obtaining royal favour, he was perhaps even more interested in obtaining divine favour and throughout his life he showed himself a notable benefactor to religious houses. He founded Byland Abbey, a member of the Savignac order, which order later merged with the Cistercians. The traditions of the house, although they had become somewhat confused by the time they were written in 1197, show that Mowbray and his mother were not merely donors of land but played an active role in the establishment of the monastery. At some point between 1147 and 1154, probably on his way back from the second crusade, he attended the general council of the Cistercian order. He also founded Newburgh, an Augustinian priory in the North Riding of Yorkshire, and perhaps the nunnery at Villers-Canivet in Normandy. In addition he made grants of property to approximately twenty other religious houses and to many of these he was quite generous; in 1185 the templars drew more than £30 annual rent from the various lands he had given them. Mowbray was also generous to his followers; he created eleven and three-quarters knight's fees before 1166 and several more fractions of fees thereafter, and made other secular grants as well. Some of the new fees derived from grants he was forced to make, but most were to men who were close followers.

The effect of Mowbray's generosity, as well as of the grants he was forced to make due to war and politics, was to shrink the honour's demesne. Much of his vast honour had been subinfeudated by the time he inherited it, for eighty-eight fees had been created before Nigel d'Aubigny's death, but Mowbray gave away still more, including the manor which had been his wife's marriage portion. Moreover, in the immediate aftermath of his participation in the revolt against Henry II, he sold land and rights in the forest of Nidderdale to Fountains Abbey for 620 marks. He sold land on other occasions as well, at one point granting woodland to the abbey at Combe in return for a payment they made to help him settle debts to Jewish moneylenders. Not all transactions represented losses; at one point he and his son Nigel bought the manor of Askham Richard (which he afterwards granted away) from Roger's tenant Juetta de Arches for 220 marks. Overall, however, there was a large net decrease of demesne land and by the end of his life, Roger held little more than the six core demesne manors that would support the family for many years. These estates, however, were very valuable and in some cases, such as Kirkby Malzeard and the

Isle of Axholme, consisted of a number of Domesday vills; as a result they provided a sufficient financial basis for the Mowbray family to remain securely within the baronage until their fortunes began to rise again.

Death on crusade Mowbray, despite his unfortunate propensity for being on the losing side (except at the battle of the Standard), was clearly an eager and able fighter. John of Hexham's praise has been noted above and Jordan Fantosme described him as an experienced fighter and said he and Adam de Port, a fellow rebel in 1174, were 'the best warriors known to men'. Given Mowbray's martial nature and his piety, it is perhaps fitting that he died on crusade. References in his charters suggest that he may have taken part in the crusade led by Philip of Flanders in 1177. He certainly journeyed to Jerusalem in 1186 and stayed on after many other crusaders who had arrived in that year returned home. As a result Mowbray, with his usual bad luck in war, ended up with the army of the kingdom of Jerusalem at the disastrous battle of Hattin on 6/7 July 1187, where he was captured. The templars ransomed him the next year, but he died soon thereafter and was buried in the Holy Land. His estates passed to his son Nigel, who died in the course of the third crusade, and then to his grandson William, who paid relief for them in 1194.

HUGH M. THOMAS

Sources D. E. Greenway, ed., *Charters of the honour of Mowbray, 1107–1191* (1972) · *Chronica magistri Rogeri de Hovedene*, ed. W. Stubbs, 4 vols., Rolls Series, 51 (1868–71) · *Jordan Fantosme's chronicle*, ed. and trans. R. C. Johnston (1981) · R. Howlett, ed., *Chronicles of the reigns of Stephen, Henry II, and Richard I*, 4 vols., Rolls Series, 82 (1884–9) · *Pipe rolls* · Dugdale, *Monasticon*, new edn, vols. 5–6 · *Gir. Camb. opera* · Ordericus Vitalis, *Eccl. hist.* · *Reginaldi monachi Dunelmensis libellus de admirandis beati Cuthberti virtutibus*, ed. [J. Raine], SurtS, 1 (1835) · St Aelred [abbot of Rievaulx], 'Relatio de standardo', *Chronicles of the reigns of Stephen, Henry II, and Richard I*, ed. R. Howlett, 3, Rolls Series, 82 (1886) · Symeon of Durham, *Opera* · E. K. Clark, ed. and trans., 'The foundation of Kirkstall Abbey', *Miscellanea*, Thoresby Society, 4 (1895), 169–208 · P. Dalton, *Conquest, anarchy, and lordship: Yorkshire, 1066–1154*, Cambridge Studies in Medieval Life and Thought, 4th ser., 27 (1994)
Likenesses seal, BL; Birch, *Seals*, 6219

Mowbray, Susan (1829–1911). *See under* Mowbray, Alfred Richard (1824–1875).

Mowbray, Thomas (I), first duke of Norfolk (1366–1399), magnate, was the second son of John (III) *Mowbray, fourth Lord Mowbray (1340–1368), and Elizabeth Seagrave (1338–1364x8), granddaughter of *Thomas of Brotherton, earl of Norfolk. He was born in 1366, although the usually accepted date, 22 March 1366, seems too early, given that his brother John was probably born in August 1365. He was apparently named Thomas as a mark of his mother's devotion to the cult of Thomas Becket. The custody of both John and Thomas was granted in 1372 to Blanche Wake, their great-aunt, and at Richard II's coronation on 16 July 1377, John was created earl of Nottingham. However, he died on 10 February 1383, and two days later Thomas was created earl of Nottingham and, despite his nonage, granted custody of his own inheritance.

The royal favourite, 1382–1386 By this time Mowbray was already on close terms with Richard II, having been

Thomas (I) Mowbray, first duke of Norfolk (1366–1399), illuminated initial [with Richard II]

retained as a king's knight and granted the right to hunt in the royal forests in 1382. The king also purchased for him, for about £1000, the marriage of Elizabeth, (c.1374–1383), daughter of John, Lord Lestrange of Blakemere, and in 1383 made him a knight of the Garter. During the next few years he remained high in the royal favour: he had his own apartments in the royal palaces at Eltham and Kings Langley, and the Westminster chronicler relates that he was one of the group of young *regi familiares* whom John of Gaunt, duke of Lancaster, accused of malignly influencing the king, and who probably plotted Gaunt's assassination in February 1385—for which Gaunt nevertheless forgave them later that year. On 30 June 1385, when about to accompany the king on his expedition to Scotland, Mowbray was granted for life the office of marshal of England (formerly held by his great-grandfather Thomas of Brotherton), and on 12 January 1386 this was converted to a grant in tail male, together with the style of earl marshal. This remained his preferred title until his elevation to a dukedom in 1397, and he was probably responsible for the compilation of a tract outlining the rights and duties of the marshal (BL, Cotton MS Nero D.vi).

By this time, however, there were already signs that Mowbray's relationship with the king was cooling. His first wife, Elizabeth Lestrange, had died on 23 August 1383 after only a few months' marriage, and in July 1384 Mowbray married Elizabeth, daughter of Richard (III) Fitzalan, earl of Arundel. According to the Westminster chronicler, the festivities at Arundel Castle lasted for a week and were attended by the king and queen. It is doubtful, however, whether Richard II approved of the marriage, for he had already clashed acrimoniously with Arundel (and would do so many times again), and may well have been suspicious of the influence that Arundel might now exert on his new son-in-law. Moreover, despite the king's attendance at the festivities, the marriage itself had been contracted without his licence, and he demonstrated his displeasure by ordering Mowbray's lands to be distrained until he had recovered the full value of his marriage. Nor was the king's concern unfounded. During 1386 Mowbray became increasingly resentful of the favour that Richard II was now showing to others—especially Robert de Vere, earl of Oxford—and by the end of the year had grown noticeably closer to the group of lords (led by Arundel and the king's uncle Thomas of Woodstock, duke of Gloucester) who had opposed the king and the court during the Wonderful Parliament of October 1386. In early 1387 Mowbray accompanied Arundel to sea, where on 24 March, off Margate, they successfully attacked a Franco-Flemish wine fleet, capturing 8000 tuns of wine that was then sold in England for 4d. a gallon. However, their victory earned them nothing but envy from the royalists: the St Albans chronicler Thomas Walsingham records that when Mowbray subsequently visited the king expecting gratitude, Richard acted with great coolness towards him, while de Vere simply turned away and refused to speak to either him or Arundel.

The appellant, 1387–1388 Richard's behaviour during the summer and autumn of 1387 merely served to hasten Mowbray's alienation from the court. The commission of government, which had been granted authority in the Wonderful Parliament of 1386 to govern the country for one year, was due to relinquish power in November 1387. However, when Gloucester, Arundel, and their ally Thomas Beauchamp, earl of Warwick, heard of the king's questions to the judges of August 1387, which threatened the lives of those who had opposed him in 1386, they assembled their retinues at Hornsey and appealed of treason five of the king's principal favourites, including de Vere—thus earning the name by which they are known to history, the *lords appellant. By 12 December they had been joined in their appeal by Mowbray and by Henry Bolingbroke, earl of Derby, the son of John of Gaunt. Richard declared that the appeals would be heard in the next parliament, but in the meantime dispatched de Vere to Chester to raise an army. The combined forces of the five appellants met and defeated de Vere's Cheshiremen at Radcot Bridge near Witney on 20 December (although Mowbray apparently arrived too late to take part in the engagement), then returned to London, arrested some fifty of the king's supporters, confronted Richard with linked arms in the Tower of London on 28 December, and probably deposed him for two or three days. Their control of the government was now assured, and when parliament met on 3 February 1388 they secured the conviction and execution of eight of the king's supporters (although not de Vere, who had fled abroad after Radcot Bridge). The Merciless Parliament lasted four months, and resulted in the humiliation of the king and the rout of the courtiers. The appellants' alliance was not an easy one, however, for Mowbray and Bolingbroke were never as committed to the destruction of the court faction as Gloucester, Arundel, and Warwick. The real rift occurred over the question of Sir Simon Burley's fate. Burley, the under-chamberlain of the royal household, was the king's former tutor, and Richard was most anxious to save him. Mowbray and Bolingbroke supported his plea for clemency, as did the king's uncle the duke of York, but Gloucester, Arundel, and Warwick were adamant, and in the end Burley went to his death on 5 May. They were never forgiven for it by the king, whereas the fact that Mowbray and Bolingbroke had argued against it doubtless saved them from the same fate as the three senior appellants when Richard had his revenge in 1397.

The king's servant, 1389–1397 Once the Merciless Parliament had ended on 4 June, the divisions between the appellants soon became even more apparent, with Mowbray in particular rapidly becoming reconciled to the king. Early in 1389 he was granted livery of his lands and formally pardoned his marriage, and at a council meeting on 8 March 1389 it was agreed that he would be granted the wardenship of the east march towards Scotland, to which the custody of Berwick and Roxburgh castles were added in May. He was promised £12,000 a year for this, and agreed to find 400 men-at-arms and 800 archers to serve with him for the months of June and July 1389. However, this appointment infuriated Henry Percy, earl of Northumberland, who thought of the east march as his sphere of influence, and pointedly declined to come to Mowbray's aid when, at the end of June, the Scots invaded the northern counties in force—as a result of which the Scots ravaged the northern counties unopposed. Meanwhile, in May 1389, Richard II had formally resumed power from the council that the Merciless Parliament had appointed to control him, and at a meeting on 15 October 1389 argued strongly for Mowbray's terms as warden of the east march to be improved, but the council held firm and refused to offer him more than the prolongation of his tenure for a further five years. The earl of Northumberland was shortly afterwards appeased with the captaincy of Calais, but in 1391 he and Mowbray exchanged offices, and Mowbray continued to hold the captaincy of Calais until his disgrace in 1398. In 1394 he was also made chief justice of Chester, Flint, and north Wales for life.

During these years Mowbray also enhanced his reputation as a soldier. In March and April 1390 he attended the Anglo-French tournament at St Inglevert, and on 28 May of the same year he was awarded the honours at a tournament at Smithfield after jousting six courses with unrebated lances against the earl of Moray. In 1394–5 he accompanied Richard II to Ireland, where he undertook a number of raids, on one of which he almost captured Art Mac Murchadha, the self-styled king of Leinster. He was subsequently deputed to negotiate with Mac Murchadha, and when he met him near Tullow on 7 January 1395 was able to persuade him to evacuate Leinster; in the following month he received the homage of the Leinster chiefs on the king's behalf, and was shortly afterwards granted the Irish lordship of Carlow. Returning to England with the king in May, he soon found himself appointed, along with the fast-rising Edward, earl of Rutland, and William Scrope, to negotiate a marriage between Richard II and the French princess Isabella (Richard's first wife, Anne of Bohemia, having died the previous year). He, Rutland, and Scrope spent much of the following winter travelling between England and France, until in March 1396 terms for the marriage were successfully concluded. Mowbray also attended the solemnization of the wedding at Calais six months later, where he acted as one of the French king's escort and was deputed by Richard II to negotiate secretly with the dukes of Burgundy and Berri. Richard clearly had considerable faith in Mowbray's diplomatic ability, for in February 1397 he was once more sent abroad (again with Rutland), this time to the imperial diet at Frankfurt which had been called to discuss Anglo-French proposals to end the papal schism and Richard II's ambition to become emperor.

Landed estate and affinity The mid-1390s saw Mowbray at the height of his influence at court, and he used his position to his best advantage, building up both his landed power and his influence. Between 1389 and 1398 he made grants of land, cash or office, amounting in all to some 40 per cent of his income, to more than seventy persons, thereby establishing a retinue of supporters that could rival that of most earls. Most of these recipients came from the areas in which he already held, or stood to inherit, lands. The estates which he had inherited from his brother were concentrated in four main areas: first, in the Isle of Axholme in north Lincolnshire, where his manors were grouped around the traditional *caput honoris* at Epworth Castle; second, a string of manors in northern and central Yorkshire, stretching from Hovingham through Thirsk and Kirkby Malzeard to Nidderdale Chase; third, a group of midland manors based on Melton Mowbray in Leicestershire; and fourth, the honour of Bramber in Sussex, including Horsham, St Leonard's Chase, and Shoreham by Sea, as well as Bramber Castle itself. These properties were probably worth about £1400 a year—a sizeable patrimony, but not one which would have put Mowbray in the first rank of English earls. However, he also had both great expectations and outstanding claims. The former consisted in the properties held by his grandmother Margaret *Brotherton, countess of Norfolk, who held lands in Norfolk and Suffolk worth approximately £2850 a year, which Mowbray stood to inherit at her death. The latter consisted in a claim to the lordship of Gower in south Wales, which had been disputed between the Mowbrays and the Beauchamp earls of Warwick since the early fourteenth century. In 1354 Edward III had awarded Gower to the Beauchamps. Undeterred by the fact that it meant clashing with his former co-appellant, Mowbray brought a writ of error against Warwick, and in June 1397 persuaded Richard II to restore Gower to him—and not merely to restore Gower itself, but also to order Warwick to hand over seventeen of his midland manors in trust to Mowbray for a period of eleven years, so that Mowbray

could recover the £5333 that he reckoned he had lost from the issues of Gower during the previous thirteen years.

Downfall, exile, and death, 1397–1399 Despite the favour that Mowbray now enjoyed, it is unlikely, given his desertion from the king's cause in 1387–8, that Richard fully trusted him, and he was doubtless too well practised in the art of courtly intrigue not to understand this. What seems clear, at any rate, is that it was the misgivings still harboured by each of them about the other that led to his dramatic downfall during the following year. The sequence of events leading to his fall began on 10–11 July 1397 with Richard's sudden arrest of Gloucester, Arundel, and Warwick. The pro-Ricardian French author of the *Traïson et mort de Richart deux roy Dengleterre* claimed that the reason for their arrest was because they, together with Mowbray, Bolingbroke, and others, had conceived a new plot against the king and his supporters, and that Mowbray subsequently betrayed the plot to the king. However, it is now generally accepted that the author of the *Traïson* either fabricated his evidence or misdated a thoroughly garbled account of the events of 1387–8. There is in fact no substantial evidence for a new plot against the king in 1396–7, and Richard's motive in arresting the three senior appellants was most probably a mixture of revenge and a desire fully to assert his authority within the kingdom. Gloucester was arrested at his castle of Pleshey in Essex, promptly dispatched to Calais under Mowbray's care, and never seen in public again. According to the *Eulogium historiarum*, Arundel was only persuaded to come into the king's presence after receiving assurances that he would not be harmed, but having arrived at Westminster he was immediately handed over by the king to Mowbray and taken to Carisbrooke Castle on the Isle of Wight to await his fate (*Eulogium historiarum*, 3.371).

On 5 August, in the great hall at Nottingham Castle, eight of the king's foremost supporters—including Mowbray, but not Bolingbroke—presented a list of charges against Gloucester, Arundel, and Warwick, and formally appealed them of treason. Mowbray was thus the only lord to have acted as an appellant twice during the reign. When parliament met at Westminster on 17 September, the eight lords appeared once again, dressed in a livery of red robes decorated with silken hoops and letters of gold on white silk, and repeated the appeal of treason. Arundel was brought in to stand trial on 21 September and, despite a brave and vigorous defence, convicted and immediately taken away for execution. Thomas Walsingham says that he was accompanied to Tower Hill by Mowbray and the earl of Kent, each of whom he bitterly rebuked, predicting their imminent downfall. On Monday 24 September Mowbray announced in parliament that he was unable to produce Gloucester to answer the charges against him because, 'I held this duke in my custody in the lord king's prison in the town of Calais; and there, in that same prison, he died' (*RotP*, 3.378). Instead, a confession that Gloucester had allegedly dictated was read out, and he was convicted of treason posthumously.

There is no real doubt that Gloucester was murdered, and Mowbray was almost certainly implicated. Two years later, after Richard II's deposition, one of Mowbray's valets called John Hall confessed to his participation in the crime, which probably occurred on the night of 8 September. According to Hall, Mowbray arrived at his lodgings in Calais and told him that he had been ordered by the king and Rutland to put Gloucester to death. Hall begged to be excluded from the affair, but Mowbray told him 'that either he would be there, or he would lose his life, and gave him a great cuff across his head'. Hall and eight others were thus led to a hostel called Princes Inn, where Mowbray left them to their business. Shortly afterwards, Gloucester was brought in, told that he was to die, shriven, and promptly smothered to death with a 'featherbed'. Some time later Mowbray returned to check that his orders had been carried out (RotP, 3.453). Yet, if this account appears to damn Mowbray, Walsingham states that he initially resisted the king's order, and only did the deed at last when the king threatened him with the loss of his own life if he continued to prevaricate ('Annales Ricardi secundi', 221). Mowbray himself claimed that he delayed killing Gloucester for more than three weeks after first being told by Richard to do so, and that he had never been so afraid for his own life as when he first returned from Calais to tell the king that Gloucester was still alive (Great Chronicle of London, 52–3); and, although it might be argued that this is precisely what he would indeed claim, it nevertheless helps to explain why rumours of Gloucester's death were circulating in England several weeks before he actually died. There are, moreover, further indications that Mowbray was far from happy about what was being asked of him in September 1397. A year later, when pronouncing sentence of exile on him, the king declared that one of the reasons for doing so was that at the time of the parliament of 1397 he had gone about arguing 'both privately and publicly' against the annulment of the acts of the parliament of 1388, and that he had even failed to appear 'on the day that the appeal was to be decided' (RotP, 3.383).

Despite his disquiet, in practice Mowbray had little option but to go along with the king's revenge against his former co-appellants, and, having done so, he was duly rewarded. On 29 September, the penultimate day of the parliament, he was elevated to the dukedom of Norfolk, and he and Bolingbroke (who also received a dukedom) were simultaneously pardoned their opposition to the royalist faction in 1387–8, on the grounds that they had restrained the more violent impulses of their co-appellants. Mowbray also received his share of the more tangible spoils, in the form of Arundel's honour and castle of Lewes in Sussex (which bordered his own honour of Bramber), and the seventeen manors in the midlands forfeited by Warwick which had previously been enfeoffed to him for a term of eleven years. Such pleasure as he derived from his gains was to be short-lived, however. By October 1397 rumours were already circulating about his involvement in Gloucester's murder, and he was under no illusions about the value of Richard's pardons, especially in view of what the king can only have viewed as his relapse in September 1397. By December his nerve

had reached breaking point, and, meeting Bolingbroke one day on the road between London and Brentford, he apparently chose to confide in him. According to Bolingbroke's testimony, Mowbray opened the conversation by remarking that the two of them were 'about to be undone' (RotP, 3.360). 'Why?' asked Bolingbroke, affecting ignorance. 'For what was done at Radcot Bridge,' replied Mowbray, going on to explain that had it not been for 'certain people' they would already have been put to death, and that there was a group of conspirators at court who, with the king's connivance, were plotting the downfall of the house of Lancaster and the deaths of several of the leading nobles of the realm, themselves included. Quite what Mowbray expected Bolingbroke to reply to this news is far from clear, but the latter's reaction seems to have caught him unprepared. Bolingbroke promptly told his father about the conversation; Gaunt told the king; and the king summoned both men to his presence. Mowbray now panicked. Parliament was due to meet again at Shrewsbury on 28 January 1398. According to Adam Usk, Mowbray tried to have Gaunt assassinated on his way to Shrewsbury; when this failed, he evidently went into hiding, allowing Bolingbroke a free hand to present his version of the story to parliament on 30 January. Mowbray was immediately stripped of his office of earl marshal and ordered to appear before the king; on 17 February—by which time he appears to have given himself up—the royal escheators were told to seize his goods and certify the king as to their value, and by the end of February he had been incarcerated in Windsor Castle.

Despite his vigorous denial of any knowledge of the conversation reported by Bolingbroke, Mowbray spent the next few months in close confinement—initially at Windsor, but later in the great wardrobe by St Paul's Cathedral—while Bolingbroke was allowed to go free. Richard II made a number of attempts to reconcile the two men, most notably at Windsor on 29 April, but the result of this confrontation was to muddy the waters further, for Bolingbroke now introduced a series of new charges against Mowbray. Specifically, he accused him of misappropriating substantial sums which the king had given to him for the payment of the English garrison at Calais, and of being responsible for Gloucester's death. It was probably the latter charge that finally persuaded Richard to resort to trial by battle, for the last thing that Richard wanted was a public discussion of the circumstances of his uncle's death. Thus it was announced that, since the two men refused to be reconciled, a trial by battle would be held at Coventry on 16 September to determine the truth of the matter, and, when 16 September came, they duly appeared. Both were splendidly arrayed, Mowbray having acquired his armour from Germany, and Bolingbroke his from Milan; the jousting field was surrounded by a moat, and it was clearly one of the great court occasions of the year. Just as the two men were about to join battle, however, Richard II called a halt. Since treason was involved, he announced, and since he did not wish to be responsible for shedding the blood of two men so closely related to him, he had decided to take the matter into his own hands. Thus in order to avoid any future quarrel between the two combatants or their supporters, he declared that Bolingbroke should be exiled for ten years, and Mowbray for the term of his life. Mowbray was also deprived of the additional lands forfeited by the earls of Arundel and Warwick which he had been granted in 1397, and the remainder of his inheritance was seized into the king's hands, with the exception of £1000 a year with which to support himself in exile. This harsher sentence on Mowbray was justified partly by the fact that he had, on 29 April at Windsor, apparently confessed to 'certain civil points' with which Bolingbroke had charged him, partly on account of his relapse in 1397, and partly because the charge against him concerning misappropriation at Calais was evidently regarded as proven. The king also forbade the two men to have any contact with each other during their exile, and ordered them to leave the realm by 20 October. Mowbray was told to spend his exile in Germany, Bohemia, Hungary, or on pilgrimage to the Holy Land, but no geographical limits were set to Bolingbroke's exile (*RotP*, 3.383–4).

Mowbray left England, with a retinue of thirty servants, just after 2 p.m. on 19 October, from the port of Kirkley Road, near Lowestoft in Suffolk, his departure being witnessed by more than a thousand people (including many of Lowestoft's leading citizens and some eighty of the Suffolk gentry), who testified that he was bound for Dordrecht and that, favoured by a good wind, he had already covered 6 leagues by sunset. By 18 February 1399 he had reached Venice, where he persuaded the senate to loan him a galley, and the merchants Antonio Bembo and Giovanni Cane to advance him 750 ducats, so that he could visit the Holy Land—which he evidently did. During his absence, his grandmother Margaret Brotherton, who had been created duchess of Norfolk in 1397, died on 24 March 1399. Before leaving England Mowbray had secured letters patent from the king declaring that if any succession or inheritance should fall to him while in exile, he would be permitted, through his attorneys, to petition for livery of them, but Richard now revoked these letters and seized Margaret's inheritance for himself (as he also did with the similar letters patent that he had granted Bolingbroke, which led to Bolingbroke's return to England and deposition of the king later that year). In this context, Adam Usk's claim that Richard always intended to recall Mowbray looks very unlikely. To what extent Mowbray was aware of all this is not clear, for shortly after (or during) his pilgrimage to the Holy Land he contracted plague, of which he died on 22 September 1399 at Venice, where he was buried in the abbey of St George. The 'Mowbray stone', which is said to have marked his last resting place, was brought back to England in 1839, and is now at Corby Castle, near Carlisle, is more likely to have been associated with Bolingbroke.

Historical significance, character, and family Mowbray has never had an apologist. Walsingham claimed that, because of the revulsion they felt at Gloucester's murder, all those who attended the duel at Coventry were praying for Bolingbroke to win. Later he declared that Mowbray returned from the Holy Land greatly embittered ('in

amaritudine mentis magna') but that he would have been mourned throughout the kingdom, and deservedly so, had he not consented to Gloucester's death ('Annales Ricardi secundi', 226, 321). Recent historians of Richard II's reign have been similarly disinclined to forgiveness, describing him variously as 'proud and presumptious', 'a self-seeking renegade', and 'an intensely ambitious young man with a taste for intrigue'. Yet his ability has also been widely recognized: as a soldier, a diplomat, and a counsellor, he was both experienced and able, and was entrusted with a succession of offices and responsibilities at the highest levels in the realm. That he was also a consummate courtier (in the worst sense of that word) is undeniable, but it may be that the gulf between his landed expectations and his actual income forced him to seek out office and favour in order to maintain his rank. The vicissitudes of his career identify him almost as a weathervane to the changing fortunes of Richard II himself, but also suggest that (until 1397 at least) he had the knack, like Bolingbroke, of being on the winning side. Nor should it be forgotten that it must have taken considerable courage to stand up to the king in the autumn of 1397—far easier simply to be swept along with the tide of royalist reaction, as virtually every other magnate in the kingdom was. The evidence suggests strongly that the crime with which his name has forever been associated, Gloucester's murder, was committed only with extreme reluctance and under threat of his own death—a threat that his own unwillingness to commit the deed did much to stimulate.

If it is possible to say with some confidence that as a politician Mowbray was unscrupulous, acquisitive, and at times impulsive, but also courageous and thoroughly able, it is more difficult to glean any pointers to his private life or character. He evinced a genuine, though not untypical, interest in his predecessors: in February 1384, a year after his brother's death, he organized a procession through London to his burial place at the Whitefriars in Fleet Street, and in 1396 he sent an envoy to Constantinople to retrieve the body of his father, who had been slain by the Saracens in 1368, so that it could be buried alongside that of his brother. His major contribution to religious life in England was his foundation, in 1396, of a Carthusian priory at Epworth. This was one of a number of Carthusian houses that Richard II and his courtiers founded, motivated no doubt by respect for contemplatives. Mowbray himself is said to have had a special devotion to the feast of the Visitation, and the Epworth Charterhouse was called Domus Visitationis Beate Marie Virginis. He was also one of about a score of Englishmen who, in 1396, agreed to join the Militia Passionis Jhesu Christi, a new chivalric order which, it was hoped, would stiffen the drive to expel the Turks from Europe—although none of them in fact accompanied the disastrous Nicopolis crusade later that year.

Mowbray's dukedom was repealed in October 1399, and his widow, Elizabeth Fitzalan, thus demoted to countess of Norfolk. She married Sir Robert Goushill, one of Mowbray's former retainers, in 1401, and, after his death, Sir Gerard Usflete, eventually dying in 1425. She had with

Mowbray at least four children: Thomas (II) *Mowbray, the heir, who was executed in 1405, at the age of nineteen, for rebellion; John (V) *Mowbray, who succeeded his brother and to whom the dukedom of Norfolk was restored in 1425; Margaret, who married Sir Robert Howard; and Isabel, who married first Sir Henry Ferrers, and second James, Lord Berkeley.   C. GIVEN-WILSON

Sources R. E. Archer, 'The Mowbrays, earls of Nottingham and dukes of Norfolk to 1432', DPhil diss., U. Oxf., 1984 • A. Goodman, *The loyal conspiracy: the lords appellant under Richard II* (1971) • A. Tuck, *Richard II and the English nobility* (1973) • GEC, *Peerage*, new edn • *Chancery records* • *Thomae Walsingham, quondam monachi S. Albani, historia Anglicana*, ed. H. T. Riley, 2 vols., pt 1 of *Chronica monasterii S. Albani*, Rolls Series, 28 (1863–4) • L. C. Hector and B. F. Harvey, eds. and trans., *The Westminster chronicle, 1381–1394*, OMT (1982) • F. S. Haydon, ed., *Eulogium historiarum sive temporis*, 3 vols., Rolls Series, 9 (1858) • *The chronicle of Adam Usk, 1377–1421*, ed. and trans. C. Given-Wilson, OMT (1997) • *Knighton's chronicle, 1337–1396*, ed. and trans. G. H. Martin, OMT (1995) [Lat. orig., *Chronica de eventibus Angliae a tempore regis Edgari usque mortem regis Ricardi Secundi*, with parallel Eng. text] • Arundel Castle archives, West Sussex • 'Annales Ricardi secundi et Henrici quarti, regum Angliae', *Johannis de Trokelowe et Henrici de Blaneforde … chronica et annales*, ed. H. T. Riley, pt 3 of *Chronica monasterii S. Albani*, Rolls Series, 28 (1866), 155–240 • A. H. Thomas and I. D. Thornley, eds., *The great chronicle of London* (1938); repr. (1983) • J. H. Wylie, *History of England under Henry the Fourth*, 4 vols. (1884–98) • *RotP*, vol. 3
Archives Arundel Castle, West Sussex, family papers • BL, Cotton MS Nero D.vi
Likenesses illuminated initial, BL, Cotton MS Nero D.vi, fol. 85 [*see illus.*]
Wealth at death approx. £1800 p.a.—incl. lordship of Gower, but excl. lands which should have been inherited from Margaret Marshal: Archer, 'The Mowbrays'

Mowbray, Thomas (II), second earl of Nottingham (1385–1405),

magnate and rebel, was the eldest son of Thomas (I) *Mowbray, first duke of Norfolk (1366–1399), and his second wife, Elizabeth Fitzalan (d. 1425), sister and coheir of Thomas *Fitzalan, fifth earl of Arundel (d. 1415). He was born on 17 September 1385 and was reared in the household of Richard II's second queen, Isabella. He enjoyed a royal annuity and was one of the children who accompanied Richard to Ireland in 1399. The months following his father's death were very unsettled. He was a minor whose lands were in crown hands; his mother was impoverished and without any dower; and the new king's early actions only worsened Mowbray's position. The repeal by Henry IV's first parliament of the acts of that of 1397–8 meant the annulment of the Norfolk dukedom. The office of marshal was granted for life to the earl of Westmorland on 30 October 1399. Over the next two months the king used Mowbray land to reward some of his own followers and to provide for the dowager duchess, the latter process taking over three years to complete. In December 1399 the young Thomas petitioned the council for an increased allowance, and was granted 350 marks p.a., with an additional £58. 6s. 8d. in view of the approach of Christmas. Mowbray requested that the payment be made from his father's lands in south Wales, perhaps in the knowledge that the latter, before going into exile, had requested that provision for his heir be made in this way.

Some time before August 1400 Mowbray married Constance Holland, daughter of John *Holland, duke of Exeter, to whom he had been betrothed in 1391 when the bride was only four. At that time property worth 300 marks p.a. had been enfeoffed by both parents to an eminent body of trustees, including the future Henry IV. It was to Constance, his niece, that Henry IV made the first of his slow, piecemeal restorations of Mowbray property, converting a cash payment of £200 to an equivalent sum in Mowbray estates in East Anglia in 1400. Then in 1402 Henry allowed the transfer of further lands from the hands of Lancastrian custodians into those of long-standing Mowbray followers. The young earl (who was still under age) subsequently made several disbursements in pursuit of the recovery of his property, but it was not until 1 November 1403 that the king granted early livery of the bulk of the inheritance, some weeks later adding the Brotherton lands of Thomas's great-grandmother Margaret *Brotherton, duchess of Norfolk (d. 1399). The grant was not without conditions—first a fine of £1000; and second a requirement to do one year's personal service at Chepstow and on the Welsh march with twenty men-at-arms and sixty archers. Moreover, the king excepted from the restoration the chief Mowbray lordship of Epworth on the Isle of Axholme, Lincolnshire, which was held by Edward, duke of York.

Thomas Mowbray never lived to enjoy full restoration of all his estates. In spring 1405 he joined the Percy–Scrope rebellion in the north of England, a move that is not easily explained. His view of who was to blame for the quarrel between his father and Henry IV, as Henry Bolingbroke, which had led to the former's exile, is unknown. His upbringing in Queen Isabella's household may have inclined him to sympathize with Richard II. But although Henry IV's restorations had been slow and hedged with conditions, given Mowbray's minority the king had not been ungenerous. Mowbray had not finally set off for Chepstow until February or March 1404, and he was back in England in the autumn, having thus done less than a full year's service. The first sign of trouble came in February 1405, when he admitted prior knowledge of the plot to capture the Mortimer heirs at Windsor, but he was pardoned. Then on 1 March came the first outbreak of the dispute between the Mowbrays and the Beauchamps over which of them should have precedence in parliament and council. Being still a minor Mowbray had never received a parliamentary summons, and if he was present at the council, something which remains uncertain, Henry IV may have felt that his youth did not entitle him to challenge the earl of Warwick. There is no evidence that this was the cause of Mowbray's rebellion and Henry was sufficiently confident of the earl's loyalty in April to appoint him to accompany him to Wales with 20 men-at-arms and 120 archers. The only contemporary explanation for Mowbray's disaffection is resentment of the withholding of the marshalcy. His minority is again important, for it would have been exceptional if he had been restored to the office while under age, and Henry's ultimate intentions are perhaps suggested by his permitting Mowbray the style of earl marshal. It is hard to avoid the conclusion that the earl was a headstrong youth with unrealistic expectations.

Thomas Mowbray was an unlikely ally for the earl of Northumberland, Archbishop Scrope, and Lord Bardolf. He had no known personal connections with these conspirators, though he had shown himself willing in February 1405 to become involved in rebellion. As a northern landholder he may have been a welcome addition to the cause, and most of his rebel force seems to have been raised in the north. Certainly no long-standing members of his father's affinity were prepared to follow him into the field. On 28 May Henry IV informed his council from Derby of Mowbray's rebellion, but before he reached the north the earl of Westmorland had confronted Archbishop Scrope and Earl Thomas at Shipton Moor. Westmorland offered to discuss the manifesto that Mowbray and Scrope had issued at York and although Mowbray expressed his reservations, Scrope agreed to their meeting over a cup of wine. As the rebel army dispersed, the two leaders were arrested and imprisoned at Pontefract. On 8 June, Henry IV having reached York, summary sentence of death was passed. No mercy was shown to Mowbray as a minor. The archbishop comforted the fearful earl in his last moments, allowing him to precede him to the scaffold. Mowbray's body was buried in the Greyfriars' Church, York, but his head was set up on Bootham Bar for two months before being rejoined to the corpse.

ROWENA E. ARCHER

Sources Chancery records · PRO · BL, Add. MSS (esp. 16556) · R. E. Archer, 'The Mowbrays, earls of Nottingham and dukes of Norfolk to 1432', DPhil diss., U. Oxf., 1984 · J. H. Wylie, History of England under Henry the Fourth, 4 vols. (1884–98) · J. H. Ramsay, Lancaster and York, 2 vols. (1892) · R. E. Archer, 'Parliamentary restoration: John Mowbray and the dukedom of Norfolk in 1425', Rulers and ruled in late medieval England: essays presented to Gerald Harriss, ed. R. E. Archer and S. Walker (1995), 99–116 · Johannis de Trokelowe et Henrici de Blaneforde … chronica et annales, ed. H. T. Riley, pt 3 of Chronica monasterii S. Albani, Rolls Series, 28 (1866) · GEC, Peerage, new edn, 9.604–5

Wealth at death approx. £1500: inquisition post mortem, PRO; BL, Add. MS 16556

Mowbray, William de (c.1173–c.1224), baron, was the eldest son of Nigel de Mowbray (d. 1191) and Mabel (d. c.1219), probably the daughter of William de Patri, and the grandson of Roger (I) de *Mowbray. He had two or three brothers and a sister. Mowbray was described in the Histoire des ducs de Normandie as being as small as a dwarf but very generous and valiant. He had livery of his lands in 1194 on payment of a relief of £100, and was immediately called upon to pay a sum nearly as large as his share of the scutage levied towards King Richard's ransom, for the payment of which he was one of the hostages. He was a witness to the treaty with Flanders in 1197.

When Richard I died, and John delayed to claim his crown, Mowbray was one of the barons who seized the opportunity to fortify their castles and whose support for John was most in doubt. But, like the rest, he was induced to swear fealty to John by the promises which Archbishop Hubert Walter, the justiciar Geoffrey fitz Peter, and William Marshal made in his name. He apparently served John frequently in military campaigns for he received acquittance from most of the scutages of the reign. When William de Stuteville renewed the old claim of his house to the forfeited family lands in the possession of the Mowbrays, thus ignoring the compromise made by his father with Roger (I) de Mowbray, and Mowbray supported his suit by a present of 2000 marks to the king, John and his great council dictated a new compromise. Stuteville had to accept nine knight's fees and the manor of Brinklow, Warwickshire, in full satisfaction of his claims, and the adversaries were reconciled at a country house of the bishop of Lincoln at Louth on 21 January 1201.

In 1215 Mowbray was prominent among the opponents of John. With other north-country barons he appeared in arms at Stamford in the last days of April. When Magna Carta had been wrung from the king, he was appointed one of the twenty-five executors, and as such was specially named among those excommunicated by Innocent III. During the struggle he pursued family claims to hereditary control of York Castle; the castle was entrusted to his care on 19 June 1215 but in the long run his claims were not satisfied. Mowbray was taken prisoner in the battle of Lincoln in 1217, and had to surrender the manor of Banstead in Surrey, which had formed his mother's marriage portion, to Hubert de Burgh as ransom. His other lands, which had been confiscated, were restored to him in early October 1217 when he made peace with Henry III's government. Three years later, in January 1221, Mowbray was summoned to help capture Skipsea, one of the strongholds of William de Forz, count of Aumale (with Mowbray, one of the twenty-five executors of Magna Carta, who had gone into rebellion once again.

Mowbray is said, in the sixteenth-century recension of the 'Progenies Moubraiorum' (Dugdale, Monasticon), to have married Agnes, a daughter of William d'Aubigny, earl of Arundel, of the elder branch of the d'Aubigny family, but contemporary records mention only a wife named Avice. He had two sons, Nigel and Roger (II). Mowbray founded the chapel of St Nicholas, with a chantry, at Thirsk, and was a benefactor of his grandfather's foundation, Newburgh Priory, where, on his death in Axholme about 1224, he was buried. He was succeeded by his elder son, Nigel, who died childless in 1228, and then by his younger son, Roger (II), who came of age only in 1241 and died c.1266. This Roger's son, Roger (III) (d. 1297), succeeded to the barony and was the father of John (I) de Mowbray.

JAMES TAIT, rev. HUGH M. THOMAS

Sources J. C. Holt, The northerners: a study in the reign of King John, new edn (1992) · Rogeri de Wendover liber qui dicitur flores historiarum, ed. H. G. Hewlett, 3 vols., Rolls Series, [84] (1886–9) · Chronica magistri Rogeri de Hovedene, ed. W. Stubbs, 4 vols., Rolls Series, 51 (1868–71) · D. E. Greenway, ed., Charters of the honour of Mowbray, 1107–1191 (1972) · Dugdale, Monasticon, new edn, vols. 5–6 · Chancery records (RC) · Pipe rolls · F. Michel, ed., Histoire des ducs de Normandie et des rois d'Angleterre (Paris, 1840) · Curia regis rolls preserved in the Public Record Office (1922–), vol. 1 · Rymer, Foedera · C. Roberts, ed., Excerpta è rotulis finium in Turri Londinensi asservatis, Henrico Tertio rege, AD 1216–1272, 1, RC, 32 (1835), 113

Mowlem, John (1788–1868). *See under* Burt family (*per. c.*1830–1964).

Mowll, Howard West Kilvinton (1890–1958), archbishop of Sydney, was born in Dover on 2 February 1890, the eldest son of Henry Martin Mowll (*b.* 1860), solicitor, and his wife and first cousin, Gertrude Emily Worsfold (*d.* 1935). He was educated at the King's School, Canterbury, King's College, Cambridge (BA, 1912; MA, 1915; honorary DD, 1922), and Ridley Hall, Cambridge (1912–13). He served a record five terms, in 1911–12, as president of the evangelical Cambridge Inter-Collegiate Christian Union, following its split with the Student Christian Movement. His leadership here led to his appointment as tutor (1913) and professor (1916–22) at Wycliffe College, Toronto. Before emigrating he was made deacon on 21 September 1913, by Bishop E. A. Knox of Manchester for the bishop of London for the colonies, with a notional title at St James, Dover; he was priested while on leave on 7 June 1914 by Archbishop Randall Davidson of Canterbury.

On the nomination of the Church Missionary Society (CMS) to superintend its missions in western Szechwan (Sichuan), Mowll was consecrated assistant bishop in west China in Westminster Abbey on 24 June 1922. On 23 October 1924 in Mienchu (Mianzhu) he married a vivacious and experienced missionary, Dorothy Anne Martin (1890–1957); to their grief, there were no children. In August 1925 near Mienchu, the Mowlls and other missionaries were kidnapped by red-lamp brigands, mistreated, and eventually ransomed; the incident aroused worldwide attention. Appointed diocesan of west China in 1926, he adopted the CMS policy of devolving authority upon local bishops, including native-born suffragans, as opposed to that of the China Inland Mission, which favoured European missionaries with Chinese subordinates. During a deputational tour to Australia in August 1931 Mowll so impressed leaders of the Anglican Church League, the conservative evangelical strategists of the diocese of Sydney, that in April 1933 the league secured his almost unanimous election as archbishop. He was enthroned on 13 March 1934. Liberal evangelicalism in the diocese was thereafter subjugated.

As archbishop, Mowll worked prodigiously and kept ungodly hours, sometimes summoning his archdeacons at two in the morning. Chaplains rarely stayed the course, but the diocese responded enthusiastically. In November 1935 he appointed the Revd T. C. Hammond, head of the Irish Church Mission, as principal of his theological college, and in May 1936 Canon Charles Venn Pilcher, of Wycliffe College, Toronto, was consecrated as his coadjutor. Pilcher never supplied the archbishop's scholarly shortcomings, but Hammond proved a tenacious defender of conservative evangelicalism. In February 1938 a group of fifty clergy active in the diocese presented him with a memorial claiming that men of one school of thought alone were preferred. Mowll declined to interview the signatories; he replied instead with a questionnaire of Hammond's devising, then sailed for Vancouver. To the public he was known for his sustained protests over the opening of the Sydney Royal Easter (Agricultural) Show on Good Friday, and for organizing an annual procession of witness on that day. During the war both he and Mrs Mowll actively promoted the Church of England National Emergency Fund; for this work, Mrs Mowll was made OBE in 1956. In December 1942 he appointed a special chaplain to youth and valued the employment agency and summer beach camps and youth conferences thus initiated.

In March 1935 Mowll had been narrowly defeated as primate of the Anglican church in Australia. His election to that office, in November 1947, proved the watershed of his episcopate. His perspective widened. Despite opposition from within his diocese he supported both the World Council of Churches, nationally (as president) and internationally, and also the proposed constitution for an autonomous Anglican church in Australia. He visited CMS missions and those of the evangelical Bush Church Aid Society all over the continent. After the expulsion of the CMS from China in 1949 he urged it to establish missions in New Guinea (where he toured in 1951) and south-east Asia, especially Borneo, Sarawak, and Malaya. He encouraged the formation of autonomous provinces in missionary fields worldwide, including east Africa, south Asia, and the Pacific. He and his wife loved to travel. In 1948 they attended the Lambeth conference, the first assembly of the World Council of Churches, in Amsterdam, and the International Missionary Council at Oestgeest. Almost every year thereafter they travelled abroad, for meetings of missionary councils or the World Council of Churches. After 1953 Mowll personally promoted an appeal for missions in south-east Asia. From October 1956 to January 1957 he and his wife, with other Australian bishops, made a visit to China.

Mowll's latter years were marked by a far-reaching postwar expansion of his diocese, though he found himself increasingly isolated because of the death or retirement of faithful retainers. Australian clergy, diocesan-trained, were consecrated as his coadjutors; the death of his wife on 23 December 1957 deprived him of his last confidante. He died unexpectedly in Sydney on 24 October 1958, and his ashes were buried beside the throne of his cathedral on 11 November.

A man of great height and commanding presence, and an unhesitating evangelical who proclaimed a simple gospel, Mowll became one of the most significant figures of the evangelical wing of the Anglican communion. To his many disciples within his diocese (including his biographer), he shone with a 'lustrous' light; to his detractors he was known as Holy Mowlly. His ecumenism and his interest in missions worldwide never diminished his loyalty to the Church of England.   RUTH FRAPPELL

Sources *CGPLA Eng. & Wales* (1959) · R. Frappell and others, eds., *Anglicans in the Antipodes: an indexed calendar of the papers and correspondence of the archbishops of Canterbury, 1788–1961, relating to Australia, New Zealand and the Pacific* (1999) · *The Anglican* (31 Oct 1958) · *Church Times* (31 Oct 1958) · *Australian Church Record* (30 Oct 1958) · *Australian Church Record* (13 Nov 1958) · M. L. Loane, *Archbishop Mowll* (1960) · S. Judd and K. Cable, *Sydney Anglicans: a history of the diocese* (1987) · *Sydney Diocesan Newsletter*, 1/1 (Dec 1958)

Likenesses H. Wrightson, photograph, repro. in Loane, *Archbishop Mowll*, frontispiece

Wealth at death £2389 8s. 1d. in England: Australian probate sealed in England, 7 Aug 1959, *CGPLA Eng. & Wales*

Mowse [Mouse], **William** (*d.* 1588), civil lawyer, was the son of Thomas Mowse, a clothier of Needham Market, Suffolk, and was educated as a civil lawyer at Cambridge, where he obtained the degrees of LLB (1538) and LLD (1552). He was a clerical fellow of Trinity Hall in 1546–7 and was involved in the political vicissitudes which affected Cambridge University during the 1550s. He became master of Trinity Hall in October 1552, but resigned or was removed on Queen Mary's accession the following year, when Bishop Stephen Gardiner (who had been master from 1525 until 1551 or 1552) was reinstated. The following year, Mowse's personal intervention, following a decision of the university, was at least instrumental in ousting Edwin Sandys as vice-chancellor. In 1553 he is reported to have been incorporated at Oxford and to have lectured on civil law, probably as a deputy of the regius professor William Aubrey. On 26 July 1555 he subscribed to the articles of religion; the same year, Gardiner died and the mastership was restored to Mowse (12 November 1555); however, he once again, this time definitively, resigned (or was forced to resign) after the accession of Queen Elizabeth (1558 or 1559). From then on, he seems to have been only intermittently involved in university and college politics, but held ecclesiastical offices, some of which closely related to the specialized areas of civil law practice.

On 7 November 1557 Mowse had been admitted to the College of Advocates. In 1559 the archbishop of Canterbury appointed him vicar-general, official (dean of the arches), judge of the court of audience, and dean of the peculiars; in 1564 his name appears as member of a commission which had to deal with complaints from subjects of the king of Spain who alleged depredations at sea by English sailors. Concurrently, Mowse was appointed to the rectory of Norton (or Green's Norton) in Northamptonshire (12 December 1558), which he held until 18 January 1567; to the prebend of Halloughton in the church of Southwell (2 May 1559), which he held until 1576; to the rectory of East Dereham in Norfolk (1560); and to the prebend of Botevant in the church of York (29 February 1561). The patronage he enjoyed at various stages of his career is only partly documented. In a letter of thanks addressed to Sir William Cecil, he refers to the support he received from Archbishop Cranmer and Sir John Cheke; in 1556, in a commission for his admission as an advocate in the court of Canterbury, he was commended by Archbishop Pole.

Until the end of his life, Mowse kept an interest in his college at Cambridge. In February 1585, shortly after the death of the master, Henry Harvey, his name heads the signatures under a letter addressed by twelve civil lawyers to the lord treasurer, in which the authors unsuccessfully supported Martin Berry, a senior fellow of the college, for designation as the new master. His will, dated 30 May 1586, contained substantial benefactions to Trinity Hall. It provided for a settlement in favour of the college, which

secured a scholarship and a fellowship from 1595 onwards. Perhaps his most lasting bequest was that of his extensive legal library, which constituted (and still constitutes) the nucleus of the collection of sixteenth-century legal imprints at Trinity Hall; it is, on the whole, a fairly conservative collection, focusing mainly on those works of civil and canon law which were most valued at the time in traditional legal education and in legal practice, although it also reflects some interest in legal-humanistic learning and its impact on the fundamental texts of the course of civil law. Some volumes contain marginal annotations, probably Mowse's. After various bequests, among others to Doctors' Commons, the residue, about £1000, was left to Robert Hare for charitable purposes; that sum contributed to the purchase of an estate at Walpole, conveyed to the master and fellows of Trinity Hall for the maintenance of roads around Cambridge. The first milestone on the road to Barkway was adorned with Mowse's arms (or, on a fess between three annulets in chief and as many in base, two and one sable, a cross patée of the field) impaled with the college's arms.

Mowse died, unmarried, in 1588. Assessments by later authors are almost invariably critical of his apparent lack of consistency in religious matters during the years from Edward VI's death until Elizabeth's accession; some authors suggest that he favoured the Catholic religion, and that he contributed to the arguments set forth in defence of the title of Mary, queen of Scots. Mowse's recorded acts may equally be seen to have been primarily inspired by a concern for preserving the interests of his university and his college at a time of political instability, and perhaps also by some sense of self-preservation. His scholarship seems to have been more generally acknowledged. ALAIN WIJFFELS

Sources CUL, MS MM.2.22 · BL, Lansdowne MS 982, fol. 107 · *The sermons of Edwin Sandys*, ed. J. Ayre, Parker Society, 2 (1842) · G. Baker, *The history and antiquities of the county of Northampton*, 2 vols. (1822–41) · J. Barton, 'The faculty of law', *Hist. U. Oxf. 3: Colleg. univ.*, 257–94 · Cooper, *Ath. Cantab.*, vol. 2 · C. Crawley, *Trinity Hall: the history of a Cambridge college, 1350–1975*, new edn (1992) · A. W. W. Dale, ed., *Warren's book* (1911) · J. Lamb, ed., *A collection of letters, statutes and other documents … illustrative of the history of the University of Cambridge during the Reformation* (1838) · *Fasti Angl.* (Hardy) · R. Newcourt, *Repertorium ecclesiasticum parochiale Londinense*, 1 (1708) · H. C. Porter, *Reformation and reaction in Tudor Cambridge* (1958); repr. (1972) · Rymer, *Foedera*, 3rd edn · G. D. Squibb, *Doctors' Commons: a history of the College of Advocates and Doctors of Law* (1977) · J. Strype, *Memorials of the most reverend father in God Thomas Cranmer*, new edn, 2 vols. (1812) · J. Strype, *The life and acts of Matthew Parker*, new edn, 3 vols. (1821) · J. Strype, *Ecclesiastical memorials*, 3 vols. (1822) · J. Strype, *Annals of the Reformation and establishment of religion … during Queen Elizabeth's happy reign*, new edn, 4 vols. (1824) · Venn, *Alum. Cant.* · A. Wijffels, 'From ius commune to common law, and back again: legal books at Trinity Hall: an historical perspective from the Old Library', *Trinity Hall 2000: legal education and learning* (1999), 34–42 · A. Wood, *The history and antiquities of the University of Oxford*, ed. J. Gutch, 1 (1792) · A. Wood, *The history and antiquities of the University of Oxford*, ed. J. Gutch, 2 (1796) · Wood, *Ath. Oxon.*, new edn, vol. 1 · DNB

Wealth at death several bequests; residue of £1000: will

Moxon, Edward (*bap.* 1801, *d.* 1858), publisher and poet, was born at Wakefield and baptized there at All Saints on

12 December 1801, the eldest among the nine children of Michael Moxon, woollen worker, and his wife, Ann. Moxon attended a charity school in Wakefield, the Green Coat School, and at nine was apprenticed to a local bookseller named Smith. He went to London in 1817, continuing his employment as a bookseller, pursuing private studies of literature, and writing verse.

In 1821 Moxon joined Longmans, which published his first book of verse, *The Prospect and other Poems*, in 1826. He had established friendships with writer Charles Lamb and poet Samuel Rogers, both of whom played a role in Moxon's becoming a publisher himself. From Rogers, Moxon borrowed £500 in 1830 and, having left Longmans, established the firm of Edward Moxon at 64 New Bond Street; the firm's first book was Lamb's *Album Verses* (1830).

Moxon ventured into periodical publishing in 1831, launching the *Englishman's Magazine* under the editorship of the Irish poet William Kennedy and the Scottish novelist Leitch Ritchie. The *Englishman's Magazine* ceased publication in October 1832, but its brief run was none the less illustrious, for among its contributors were Alfred Tennyson, Charles Lamb, Leigh Hunt, John Clare, Charles Cowden Clarke, and John Forster, friend and eventual biographer of Charles Dickens. In 1832 Moxon and Forster founded the magazine *The Reflector*, which lasted but three issues and which is not to be confused with the magazine of the same name edited by Leigh and John Hunt two decades earlier. Although *The Reflector* was short-lived, Moxon's firm enjoyed a remarkable book-publishing year in 1832, issuing Tennyson's *Poems*, Barry Cornwall's *English Songs and other Small Poems*, a selected edition of Robert Southey's prose, and Allan Cunningham's *Maid of Elwar*.

Moxon moved the firm to 44 Dover Street in 1833. The new shop was known to be inviting to browsers (not just buyers), to such an extent that Leigh Hunt once observed that Moxon was more a 'secreter' of books than a publisher of them (Merriam, 71). The move from New Bond Street to Dover Street brought no change in Moxon's choice of printers: Bradbury and Evans, the company that printed virtually all the books issued by the firm.

In 1833 Moxon married Charles Lamb's adopted daughter, Emma Isola Lamb (1809–1891), with whom he brought up five children: four daughters and a son, Arthur. The ailing Lamb died in 1834 leaving his private library to his son-in-law. Later Moxon published a selection of Lamb's prose (1836) and one of his poetry and prose (1840).

Probably Lamb was the writer with whom Moxon formed the closest friendship, but arguably his most important publishing relationship was with William Wordsworth, a volume of whose poetry Moxon published in 1831. Wordsworth went on to publish with Moxon a six-volume edition of poems (1836–7), an edition of 415 sonnets (1838), and *The Poems of William Wordsworth* (1845). Stephen Gill has observed that Moxon was 'poet-struck and … determined to build up a publishing house that would be worthy of the Muse. Economics had to be paramount, of course … but his dealings with his authors were never confined to the ledger' (Gill, 388). For instance,

Moxon acceded to Wordsworth's costly request to have his poems published in unbroken stanzas and with wide margins, a layout especially evident in the 1845 volume.

The working relationship with Alfred Tennyson developed solidly as well. Moxon personally oversaw the publication of five more volumes of Tennyson's poetry (in addition to the aforementioned 1830 volume), concluding with *Maud and other Poems* (1855). The firm also published *Idylls of the King* (1859), *Enoch Arden* (1864), and *The Holy Grail and other Poems* (1869), although Moxon did not personally oversee the production of these. J. S. Hagen has detailed how close the friendship between publisher and poet became and how far Moxon offered emotional support to Tennyson, who suffered from depression.

Hagen also notes that Tennyson, with the publication of *In Memoriam* (1850), asked to change his publishing contract with Moxon's firm, giving up some profit from sales in exchange for greater control over design and production. In the case of *In Memoriam* Tennyson insisted on the cautious tactic of ordering a trial run of 1500 copies to gauge reviewers' responses. The responses were generally favourable, but large sales were none the less not expected; however, *In Memoriam* eventually sold so well that Tennyson was able to live comfortably for many years on the proceeds. In any event, Moxon's characteristically flexible, personable approach to publishing was as evident in his dealings with Tennyson as in those with Lamb and Wordsworth.

The relatively sanguine approach to publishing did not exclude Moxon from—and may even have led to his being drawn into—controversy. On 23 June 1841 he was tried for blasphemous libel in connection with his firm's publication of *Queen Mab* in a one-volume edition of Percy Bysshe Shelley's poems (1839). The poem had appeared in a four-volume edition earlier that year, but for that edition Mary Shelley had excised atheistic passages likely to offend some readers. Moxon was charged and tried chiefly because the radical newspaper publisher Henry Hetherington, who had been indicted for libel, sought to derail his own trial by bringing another publisher into the conflict. A certain Thomas Holt was the sole witness for the prosecution. Hetherington had persuaded Holt to buy a copy of Shelley's poetry at Moxon's establishment. The trial of Moxon, therefore, turned out to be something of a test case, one set up not by the government but by another potential defendant.

Thomas Noon Talfourd defended Moxon, arguing in the trial that an entire book should not be condemned because of excerpts taken out of context. He further noted that Shelley himself had expressed doubts about some views suggested in *Queen Mab*, and that such ideas need to be viewed as but one element in the growth of an intellectual's mind. Talfourd also suggested that if Moxon were convicted, the publishers of Henry Fielding, Samuel Richardson, John Milton, Edward Gibbon, Lord Byron, and many other writers would be vulnerable to legal action as well.

In spite of Talfourd's arguments, the jury found Moxon

guilty, but a sentence was not imposed; the prosecution seemed more intent on establishing a precedent than on punishing Moxon, and all parties involved were aware of Hetherington's role with regard to the trial. Edward Moxon editions of Shelley's poems for many years thereafter printed *Queen Mab* without the controversial passages.

Religious issues influenced another controversy into which Moxon was drawn. The publisher John Murray refused in 1848 to publish *Eastern Life Present and Past*, by Harriet Martineau; in a letter to her he referred to it as 'a work of infidel tendency, having the obvious aim of deprecating the authority and invalidating the veracity of the Bible' (Pichanik, 131). Moxon published the book in that year, but reviewers' reactions were similar to Murray's. Martineau subsequently offered *Letters on the Laws of Man's Nature and Development* to Moxon, indicating that she preferred his firm but would not 'urge' the book upon him (ibid., 135). John Chapman published the book in 1851; Moxon's reasons for declining to publish the book remain unknown.

Moxon's way of establishing a personal relationship with authors led to difficulty in at least one case. In 1835 Leigh Hunt borrowed money three times from Moxon's brother William, a solicitor. In 1836, after Hunt had not repaid the loans, William served him with a writ, threatening to arrest him. The resulting legal skirmishes involved Moxon; the publisher Charles Knight; Thomas Noon Talfourd; Lord Holland, a cabinet member; and John Bowring, a member of parliament. In the end Hunt did not go to gaol and did pay the debt. For Moxon the incident was embarrassing and time-consuming.

In the publishing industry at large Moxon served as a go-between, too, as a situation in 1851 revealed. Booksellers had been increasingly distancing themselves from publishers, acting as independent professionals. One result of this development was the practice of 'underselling': selling books at well below the suggested retail price, especially in the United States. Although Moxon did not advocate underselling, he did support booksellers' general right to set the price of books they had purchased from publishers. The controversy led to the Booksellers' Association being dissolved because it had tried to enforce regulations against underselling. Moxon served on a committee that recommended dissolution and helped to draft resolutions supporting free trade. However, one historian of the London book trade observes that 'Moxon apparently avoided making any public statements on behalf of the undersellers, and, all in all, his role in the controversy was negligible' (Barnes, 35).

As early as the 1840s Moxon had begun suffering from lung ailments, but he remained active in his business through 1857, when he was working on the publication of volumes of poetry by Tennyson and Dante Gabriel Rossetti. In April 1858 he prepared a will, and he died at his home, Park Side, Wandsworth, London, on 3 June. He was buried at Wimbledon.

Bradbury and Evans managed Moxon's firm from 1858 to 1864 on behalf of Emma Moxon and her son, Arthur. In 1864 J. Bertrand Payne became manager, but by 1869 Tennyson and Algernon Charles Swinburne had transferred their business to other firms, and that year Payne surrendered his interest in the firm to Emma Moxon for £11,000 (Ostrom, 217). In 1871 Ward, Lock, and Tyler purchased the stock and copyrights from Mrs Moxon and used the name Edward Moxon, Son & Co. until 1877, when the imprint disappeared altogether. Arthur Moxon established his own firm in Paternoster Row in 1878. Emma Moxon died in February 1891.

With regard to scholarly works, Moxon's chief accomplishment was the publication of Richard Monckton Milne's *Life, Letters, and Literary Remains of John Keats* (1848). Scholars have ascertained that Moxon made useful editorial notes to the first edition, which improved the accuracy of reprinted letters in the second edition of 1867 (Wilson).

As a publisher, Moxon was old-fashioned in so far as he cultivated personal relationships with authors, demonstrated an affinity for poetry, and wrote verse himself, but he was progressive in his views of booksellers' changing roles and especially in his publication of one-volume editions of poetry that readers of limited means could afford to purchase. As Gill has observed, Moxon was aware that publishing—'especially publishing of poetry in the age of "Boz"—needed to be innovative and aggressive' (Gill, 415). The roster of authors he published shows him as an important bridge, or 'transition figure' between the literary epochs now known as Romantic and Victorian.

HANS OSTROM

Sources H. G. Merriam, *Edward Moxon: publisher of poets* (1939) • H. Ostrom, 'Edward Moxon (London, 1830–1868); Edward Moxon, Son, and Company (1869–1877)', *British literary publishing houses, 1820–1880*, ed. P. J. Anderson and J. Rose, DLitB, 106 (1991), 213–18 • W. F. Courtney, 'The *Englishman's Magazine*', *British literary magazines*, vol. 3, ed. A. Sullivan (1984), 144–50 • S. Gill, *William Wordsworth: a life* (1989) • J. S. Hagen, *Tennyson and his publishers* (1979) • T. N. Talfourd, 'Speech for the publisher of Shelley', *Monthly Review*, 155 (Aug 1841), 545–52 • M. Moorman, *William Wordsworth: a biography. The later years, 1803–1850* (1965) • J. Welch, 'The Leigh Hunt–William Moxon dispute of 1836', *West Virginia University Philological Papers*, 18 (1971), 30–41 • V. K. Pichanik, *Harriet Martineau: the woman and her work, 1802–76* (1980) • D. Cheney, 'Leigh Hunt sued for debt by a friend', *Books at Iowa*, 27 (1977), 30–56 • E. G. Wilson, 'Moxon and the first two editions of Milne's biography of Keats', *Harvard Library Bulletin*, 5 (1951), 125–9 • N. I. White, 'Literature and the law of libel: Shelley and the radicals of 1840–1842', *Studies in Philology*, 22 (1925), 34–47 • J. J. Barnes, *Free trade in books: a study of the London book trade since 1880* (1964) • T. Lulofs and H. Ostrom, *Leigh Hunt: a reference guide* (1985) • R. McLean, *Victorian publishers' bookbindings in cloth and leather* (1973) • H. Curwen, *A history of booksellers, the old and the new* (1873) • *The letters of Mary Wollstonecraft Shelley*, ed. B. T. Bennett, 2 (1983) • E. Blunden, *Leigh Hunt* (1930) • *DNB* • *ILN* (14 Feb 1891) • d. cert.

Archives BL, letters • Brown University, Providence, Rhode Island, John Hay Library, papers • Cornell University, Ithaca, New York, Olin Library, papers • Hunt. L., papers • Morgan L. • Swarthmore College, Pennsylvania, Friends Historical Library, papers | Lincoln Central Library, Tennyson Research Centre, letters to Lord Tennyson and Lady Tennyson • U. Birm. L., corresp. with Harriet Martineau • Wordsworth Trust, Dove Cottage, Grasmere, corresp.

with William Wordsworth jun.; letters, mostly to William Words-worth

Wealth at death under £16,000: probate, 13 Sept 1858, *CGPLA Eng. & Wales*

Moxon, Elizabeth (*fl.* 1740–1754), writer on cookery, is known chiefly for her sole publication, *English Housewifry, Exemplified in above Four Hundred Receits*, and for her part in the development of publishing in Leeds. Nothing is known of her birth and parentage but she probably spent most of her life in the vicinity of Leeds and Pontefract, Yorkshire.

What is known of Moxon is gleaned from her book, first published in 1741. The *Leeds Mercury* carried an advertise-ment for it in September 1740: 'Ready for the Press, price bound 5s. English Housewifery … by Elizabeth Moxon, Leeds. Printed by James Lister, by whom subscriptions are taken in' (*Leeds Mercury*, 762). Lister was the owner–pub-lisher of the newspaper and a key figure in the expansion of publishing in Leeds. Producing a book like Moxon's, even via subscription, was a gamble. Nevertheless, even at a relatively costly 5s., the book proved highly saleable.

Moxon's modest aims clearly appealed to readers. This was 'A book necessary for Mistresses of Families, higher and lower Women servants, and confined to Things Use-ful, SUBSTANTIAL and SPLENDID, & Calculated for the Preservation of HEALTH, and upon the Measures of FRU-GALITY' (Moxon, title-page). These were conventional sen-timents expressed in contemporary cookery books but Moxon's one-page preface suggests that they were genu-inely felt; she only ventured to write the book with 'thirty Years practice and Experience' (ibid.) behind her and the encouragement of 'ever-honoured Friends' who 'have been long Eye-Witnesses of her Skill and Behaviour in … her Calling' (ibid., preface). Moxon's recipes do not par-ticularly reflect a regional taste. However, with every edi-tion from the second (*c.*1743), distributed in London as well as Leeds and other Yorkshire towns, *English Housewifry* was arguably the first cookery book to travel from the provinces to the capital, rather than vice versa.

On James Lister's death in 1753 the copyright may have been purchased, along with the *Leeds Mercury*, by Griffith Wright; he and his son Thomas continued to print *English Housewifry* in Leeds up to 1785. From the first to the 'fourth' edition (*c.*1749) the book could be bought from 'the Author at her House in Pontefract' (ibid., title-page). Yet by the 1754 edition the 'author' no longer sold her own book. The 1758 ('eighth') edition was not only 'corrected' but also included a separate supplement, 'English Housewifry Improved … by several Gentlewomen in the Neighbour-hood'. Such clues suggest that Moxon possibly ceased to exercise control over her work from about 1753–4; by 1758 she may even have died.

Since there is no indication of marital status in her pub-lications it cannot be confirmed that Moxon is the Eliza-beth Shaw (*b. c.*1701) who on 29 April 1722, in Leeds, mar-ried William Moxon (baptized in Wakefield in 1691 and buried in Wakefield in 1762). If Moxon had been working for 'thirty years' by 1741, however, 1701 is a suspiciously late birth date. Like Hannah Glasse she may have entered

the provincial print market out of financial necessity, as a widow or a single woman without other means of sup-port. Given her lack of authorial pretension it is perhaps ironic that *English Housewifry* places her among the female pioneers of English culinary writing.   S. M. PENNELL

Sources E. Moxon, *English housewifry, exemplified in above four hund-red receits, never before printed* [n.d., *c.*1746]; 4th edn [n.d., *c.*1749]; fur-ther edn (1754); 8th edn (1758) · V. Maclean, *A short-title catalogue of household and cookery books published in the English tongue, 1701–1800* (1981) · L. Hunter, 'Printing in the Pennines', *Traditional food east & west of the Pennines*, ed. C. A. Wilson (1994), 9–37 · *Leeds Mercury* (9–16 Sept 1740) · *Leeds Mercury* (8 Feb 1743) · *Leeds Intelligencer* (6 May 1760) · IGI

Moxon, George (*bap.* 1602, *d.* 1687), clergyman and minis-ter, was baptized at Wakefield, Yorkshire, on 28 April 1602, seventh son of James Moxon, husbandman. He was educated at Wakefield grammar school and Sidney Sussex College, Cambridge, matriculating in 1620 and graduating BA in 1624. Having been ordained in 1626, he became chaplain to Sir William Brereton (1604–1661) of Hand-forth, Cheshire, and then curate of St Helens, Lancashire, where his omission of ceremonies got him into trouble with Bishop John Bridgeman of Chester. Cited for non-conformity in 1637, he sailed for New England.

Moxon and his wife, Ann, of whom nothing is known, joined the Congregationalist church at Dorchester, Massa-chusetts, founded by Richard Mather. However, towards the end of 1637, Moxon was recruited by William Pynchon as minister to the new settlement of Springfield, Massa-chusetts and two of his sons were baptized there, Union in 1641 and Samuel in 1645. By 1646 Moxon was Springfield's fourth largest landowner. His daughters were said to have been bewitched by Hugh Parsons, in an episode that fore-shadowed the Salem witch trials. In May 1652 Parsons was convicted, then acquitted on appeal. Within a few months Moxon took his family to England. Parsons's acquittal helps to explain this decision, but more critical, perhaps, was Moxon's sympathy for Pynchon, who—accused of heresy for his views on the atonement—abandoned New England.

Returning home, Moxon joined John Machin (1624–1664) at Astbury, Cheshire, a sequestered living, and was formally admitted 'one of the publique preachers there', on 26 June 1654, with certificates from Brereton and Wal-ter Cradock among others (Lambeth Palace MS COMM. III/3, lib. 2, fol. 20). Machin was a presbyterian; Moxon gathered a congregationalist church, though no records survive to show whether its existence was formal-ized before the Restoration. Moxon and Machin shared the rectory and preached on alternate Sundays, an unusual, if not unique, arrangement, all the more striking because of their different views on church order. It illus-trates in a distinctive way—in a single parish—the kind of co-operation over public preaching and pastoral care that Richard Baxter (1615–1691) was promoting through the Worcestershire Voluntary Association. Moxon also preached at Rushton-Spencer, Staffordshire, and was an assistant commissioner to the triers for Cheshire.

On 21 February 1661 the former rector of Astbury,

Thomas Hutchinson (*d.* 1675), was reinstated. Moxon continued at Rushton until ejected in August 1662, after which he evaded the Five Mile Act by preaching at a remote farmhouse. In 1667 he settled at Congleton, within Astbury parish, and preached at his house. He was licensed there as a congregationalist teacher on 30 April 1672. Two years later, Moxon's heterodoxy attracted comment when he dissented from the Savoy confession 'in certain points concerning the satisfaction of Christ' (*Calamy rev.*, 359). His church, in which he was assisted by William Marsh, a husbandman, had about seventy members in 1676. After James II's declaration for liberty of conscience, a meeting-house was built, but Moxon did not live to occupy it. Disabled by strokes, he died at Congleton on 15 September 1687. The meeting-house was first used when Eliezer Birch (*d.* 1717), Moxon's assistant from 1678, preached his funeral sermon. The congregation later became unitarian.

Moxon's son, **George Moxon** (*d.* 1684), clergyman and ejected minister, was vicar of Haverhill, Suffolk, in January 1657, and rector of Radwinter, Essex, in 1660. After the reinstatement of the sequestered rector of Radwinter, Richard Drake, Moxon lived with his brother-in-law Samuel Shute at Eaton Constantine, Shropshire. He acted as chaplain when Shute was sheriff of London, 1681. His will, made at Eaton Constantine, on 5 April 1684, which mentions a wife, Martha, and daughter Elizabeth, wife of John Mallart, was proved on 10 June 1684.

ALEXANDER GORDON, rev. SUSAN HARDMAN MOORE

Sources *Calamy rev.*, 359 · S. Innes, *Labor in a new land: economy and society in seventeenth-century Springfield* (1983) · D. D. Hall, ed., *Witch-hunting in seventeenth-century New England: a documentary history, 1638–1692* (1991), 29–60 · register of admissions, committee for the approval of public preachers, LPL, MS COMM III/3, lib. 2, fol. 20 · C. H. Pope, ed., *Records of the first church at Dorchester, Massachusetts* (1891) · W. Urwick, ed., *Historical sketches of nonconformity in the county palatine of Cheshire, by various ministers and laymen* (1864), xxxiv, 155–7
Wealth at death £122 18*s.* 10*d.*—George Moxon: notes of wills, no. 705; will proved 10 June 1684, DWL

Moxon, George (*d.* 1684). *See under* Moxon, George (*bap.* 1602, *d.* 1687).

Moxon, Joseph (1627–1691), printer and globe maker, was born at Wakefield, Yorkshire, on 8 August 1627 and said to have been briefly educated at Queen Elizabeth's Grammar School, Wakefield. His father, James, an extreme puritan, was largely domiciled in London from 1622, migrated to Delft in 1636, and in 1638 moved to Rotterdam to print English Bibles. Joseph accompanied his father and learned the printing trade. Following the parliamentary triumph the family returned to London. With his elder brother James, Joseph Moxon was admitted by patrimony to the Weavers' Company by September 1646, and eighteen years later was elected to the livery. By September 1646 the brothers were established as printers in London, and within three years a dozen books appeared with their imprint, all but one of a puritan nature. The exception, *A Book of Drawing, Limning, Washing or Colouring of Mapps and*

Joseph Moxon.
Born at Wakefeild *August the* 8.th *Anno* 1627.

Joseph Moxon (1627–1691), by Frederick Hendrick van Hove, pubd 1692

Prints (1647), for the map seller Thomas Jenner, presaged Joseph Moxon's future career. From 1650 his brother continued printing on his own.

Joseph Moxon married Susan Marson (*d.* 1659) on 17 February 1648; they had a daughter, Susan, baptized in June 1650, and a son, James. He married secondly, on 8 June 1663, Hannah Cooke, and for a third time in 1668. By 1650 he had begun to study globe and map making and topics in practical mathematics. He visited Amsterdam in the spring of 1652, commissioning an engraver to cut copper globe-printing plates. Later that year, in partnership with John Sugar, he advertised celestial and terrestrial globes of almost 15 inches diameter. At the Sign of Atlas, Moxon built up a business printing maps, charts, globes, and paper mathematical instruments and publishing popular scientific books. His first premises were in Cornhill, and from 1665 to 1686 he was at Ludgate Hill—excepting a six-year enforced move to Russell Street following the great fire of 1666.

Moxon's first independent publication was his translation of William Bleau's *Institutio astronomica*, published in

1654 as *A Tutor to Astronomy and Geography*. Between then and 1684 he published more than thirty popular scientific expositions and technical handbooks. A number, such as *Vignola, or, The Compleat Architect* and *A Tutor to Astronomie …, or, Use of both the Globes* (he was the author of both), ran to several editions in his lifetime. Moxon gained a reputation for printing mathematical texts (John Dansie's *Mathematical Manual*, 1654, and Edward Wright's *Certain Errors in Navigation*, 1657), and particularly of tabulated data (his tables of solar declination, *Primum mobile*, 1656, reprinted in John Newton's *A Help to Calculation*, 1657, together with tables of logarithms); he also set the 230 pages of trigonometrical functions and logarithms in William Oughtred's *Trigonometria* (1657).

Moxon was sufficiently respected by the London mathematical community for thirteen of them to support his petition to Charles II for appointment as hydrographer 'for the making of Globes, Maps and Sea-Platts'—an appointment granted in January 1662. Supporters included three fellows of the Royal Society (Elias Ashmole, Lawrence Rook, and Walter Pope), all known for their royalist sympathies—a counter-weight to James Moxon's reputation as a puritan printer.

As a typefounder, Moxon cut and cast the symbols for John Wilkins's *Essays towards a Real Character and a Philosophical Language* (1668). He designed new roman and italic alphabets, printing a specimen sheet, *Proves of Several Sorts of Letters Cast by Joseph Moxon*, in 1669. It is the first complete English type specimen known. Typographical innovation continued with the special symbols used in John Adams's *Index vilaris* (1680) and the Irish characters commissioned by Robert Boyle for the 1681–5 printing of the Bible in Irish.

Moxon's election to the Royal Society in November 1678 is remarkable for the fact that he was the first tradesman to join the fellowship, a precedent not repeated during the seventeenth century. As hydrographer royal and as a printer and publisher, he had a reputation long known to many fellows. His election is probably linked to the January 1678 publication of the first part of *Mechanick Exercises, or, The Doctrine of Handy Works … of the Smiths Trade*. In a sequence of fourteen parts, Moxon printed illustrated accounts of the trades of the smith, joiner, carpenter, and turner. In July, John Evelyn presented six numbers to the president of the Royal Society. No doubt they created an impression as an exemplar for the languishing programme for a 'history of trades' which the society had begun in the 1660s. Moxon was initially an active member. However, he was one of twenty-three expelled in November 1682 for failure to pay subscriptions.

Moxon speedily added the honorific 'Member of the Royal Society' to 'Hydrographer to the King's Most excellent Majesty' on the title-pages of his books, and retained it despite his expulsion. It appears on his most famous work, *Mechanick Exercises: … Applied to the Art of Printing*, published in twenty-four numbers in 1683–4. Here he details all aspects of printing techniques of his day, capturing for posterity the unrecorded tacit craft skills. The value of the text is not that it explains technical innovation—there is none—but it is the precise record of the printing trade seen through the eyes of a practitioner.

In or shortly after 1686 Moxon ceased to trade, and moved to Warwick Lane to dwell with his son, James, a map engraver. He died in February 1691 and was buried in St Paul's Churchyard on 15 February. James Moxon continued to sell his father's globes and instruments and also republished books from his list. With the mathematical instrument maker Thomas Tuttell, he added a section on mathematical instruments to the third (1700) edition of his father's *Mathematical Dictionary* (1678), the first English-language dictionary devoted to the terminology of mathematics. D. J. BRYDEN

Sources J. Moxon, *Mechanick exercises, or, The doctrine of handy-works*, 2 (1683); repr. as *Mechanick exercises on the whole art of printing* (1683–4), 3rd edn, ed. H. Davis and H. Carter (2003) · S. Tyacke, *London map-sellers, 1660–1720* (1978), 126–7 · G. Jagger, 'Joseph Moxon, FRS, and the Royal Society', *Notes and Records of the Royal Society*, 49 (1995), 193–208 · M. Hunter, *The Royal Society and its fellows, 1660–1700: the morphology of an early scientific institution*, 2nd edn (1994) · D. Bryden, 'The instrument-maker and the printer: paper instruments made in seventeenth century London', *Bulletin of the Scientific Instrument Society*, 55 (1997), 3–15 · D. Bryden, 'Capital in the London publishing trade: James Moxon's stock disposal of 1698, a "Mathematical Lottery"', *The Library*, 6th ser., 19 (1997), 293–350 · D. J. Bryden, 'A 1701 dictionary of mathematical instruments', *Making instruments count*, ed. R. G. W. Anderson, J. A. Bennett, and W. F. Ryan (1993), 365–82
Likenesses engraving, 1686?, repro. in J. Moxon, *A tutor to astronomy, or, The use of both the globes*, 4th edn (1686), frontispiece · F. H. van Hove, engraving, pubd 1692, NPG [see illus.]
Wealth at death £39: Davis and Carter, eds., *Mechanick exercises*

Moxon, Walter (1836–1886), physician, was one of the nine children of William Milson Moxon, an Inland Revenue officer who was distantly related to Edward Jenner (1749–1823); he was born on 27 June 1836, at Midleton, co. Cork, Ireland. After education at a private school he worked as a clerk in a merchant's office in London, and by working in his own time he succeeded in passing the matriculation examination of the University of London. He left the merchant's office and entered Guy's Hospital in 1854. While there he passed the several degree examinations with honours and graduated from London University MB in 1859 and MD in 1864.

Moxon was appointed demonstrator of anatomy before he took his degree, and he held the office until 1866, when he was elected assistant physician to Guy's Hospital, as well as lecturer on comparative anatomy. In 1864 he read at the Linnean Society the paper 'The anatomy of the rotatoria'; in 1866 he published 'Peripheral terminations of motor nerves' in the *Journal of Microscopic Science*, and in 1869 he wrote 'The reproduction of infusoria' for the *Journal of Anatomy and Physiology*. He was elected a fellow of the Royal College of Physicians of London in 1868, and in 1869 he became lecturer on pathology at Guy's Hospital. He contributed many papers to the *Transactions of the Pathological Society*, published *Lectures on Analytical Pathology*, and edited in 1875 the second edition of Samuel Wilks's *Lectures on Pathological Anatomy*. He was then appointed lecturer on materia medica.

Moxon was a skilled and original lecturer, who regularly attracted a large audience. In 1873 he became physician to Guy's Hospital, and in 1882 lecturer on medicine. He wrote for *The Lancet* (30 August 1884) a brief biography of his colleague Hilton Fagge, and contributed many papers to *Guy's Hospital Reports*, the *Medico-Chirurgical Review*, and the *British Medical Journal*. In 1881 Moxon delivered the Croonian lectures at the Royal College of Physicians, 'On the anatomical condition of the cerebral and spinal circulation'. These were published in the *British Medical Journal*. He married in 1861 Selina (b. 1838/9), daughter of Robert Eckett, with whom he had a daughter, and lived in London first at Hornsey and then at Northolme, Broadlands Road, Highgate, having consulting rooms at 6 Finsbury Circus. He was a fluent and emphatic speaker and always commanded attention in the Royal College of Physicians. A contemporary described him as being 'warm-hearted, somewhat impulsive, friendly, hospitable, and generous' (*BMJ*, 235).

Moxon died on 21 July 1886, poisoned by a dose of hydrocyanic acid which he drank in his rooms at Finsbury Circus after visiting his mother's grave at Finchley and while depressed by a delusion that he was developing symptoms of an incurable illness. He was buried in Highgate cemetery, and was survived by his wife. A medal to commemorate his attainments in clinical medicine is awarded triennially by the Royal College of Physicians.

NORMAN MOORE, rev. MICHAEL BEVAN

Sources Munk, *Roll* · *BMJ* (7 Aug 1886), 235 · *The Lancet* (7 Aug 1886), 273–6 · G. D. Pollock, address, *Medico-Chirurgical Transactions*, 70 (1887), 1–34, esp. 20–23 · personal knowledge (1894) · private information (1894) · *CGPLA Eng. & Wales* (1886) · m. cert.
Likenesses portrait (*The past surgeons and physicians of Guy's Hospital*), Wellcome L.
Wealth at death £11,004 16s.: administration with will, 13 Aug 1886, *CGPLA Eng. & Wales*

Moya, (John) Hidalgo [Jacko] (1920–1994), architect, was born in Los Gatos, California, USA, on 5 May 1920, the son of a Mexican-born inventor and craftsman, Hidalgo Moya, and an English mother, Lilian Chataway. He was taken to England by his parents at the age of one and was educated at Oundle School and the Royal West of England College of Art in Bristol. Moya entered the Architectural Association (AA) school of architecture in 1938.

It was at the AA that Jacko Moya, as he was universally known from childhood, met Philip Powell (b. 1921), who entered the school in the autumn of 1939. Moya was already recognized by his tutors as a talented designer and adept draughtsman, but his perceived lack of application was responsible for his relegation to Unit 2, a small group of new students including Powell and (the unrelated) Geoffry Powell, who was later a partner in the firm of Chamberlain, Powell, and Bon. Moya and Philip Powell, who were both judged unfit for war service, became friends and collaborated on student projects.

On graduating from the AA, Powell and, subsequently, Moya went to work for Frederick Gibberd, who had been one of their tutors. In May 1946 their competition entry (designed in collaboration with Powell's elder brother Michael) for a major housing development in Pimlico was placed first out of sixty-four entries. Following the advice of the competition judge, Stanley Ramsey, Westminster council appointed the hastily formed partnership of Powell and Moya to design the first phase of what became Churchill Gardens. Michael Powell quit the firm in 1950 to pursue a distinguished career with the London county council. Constructed in phases between 1947 and 1962, the development was heroic in scale and clearly influenced by inter-war mass housing in Germany and the Netherlands. Environmentally and socially, Churchill Gardens has been widely reckoned one of the most successful of large-scale post-war social housing schemes.

Other housing commissions followed, including the development, combining multi-storey flats and two-storey houses, at Lamble Street, Kentish Town (completed in 1954). Philip Powell and Moya generally collaborated closely on every project, rather than running their own design teams, but the 'vertical feature' designed for the 1951 Festival of Britain was largely the work of Moya, working with the engineer Felix Samuely. The Skylon, destroyed after the South Bank exhibition closed, was an optimistic symbol of renewal. On 23 October 1947 Moya married Janiffer Innes Mary (b. 1922/3), a student of architecture, the daughter of Robert John Hall, an army officer. The marriage, which produced two sons and a daughter, was dissolved in 1985.

Powell and Moya's partnership thrived on the basis of public commissions—mainly housing, hospitals, and educational buildings. During the 1960s it employed more than fifty people, though the natural inclination of both partners was to run a small operation. The Princess Margaret Hospital (as it became) at Swindon was commissioned in 1951, though it was completed only in 1960. Mayfield School, Putney, constructed between 1952 and 1956, was another outstanding design (though it has since been insensitively altered). The 1360-seat Festival Theatre at Chichester, opened in 1962 under the directorship of Laurence Olivier, pioneered the taste for theatre-in-the-round.

Occupying an open site on the edge of the cathedral city, the Festival Theatre remains a dynamic and uncompromising expression of modern architectural and cultural values. Powell and Moya's instincts were radical, but there were contexts in which they had to be tempered. In 1957 the practice was commissioned to design a new residential building for Brasenose College, Oxford—the site was a backyard filled with decomposing lavatories and baths. Completed in 1961, the scheme was a prime example of the 'contextual modernism' which Powell and Moya pioneered. Faced in traditional materials, though with no stylistic concessions to the past, the building made ingenious use of scarce daylight and views out and was the first of a number of the firm's additions to Oxford and Cambridge colleges. (It was also the first Powell and Moya building to be listed, in 1993.) For Christ Church, Oxford, the firm designed Blue Boar quad and the new picture gallery (1965–8), the latter largely buried in the dean's garden. The Cripps building at St John's College, Cambridge, completed in 1967, was the largest (200 rooms) of the Oxbridge schemes and finished to a particularly lavish standard, thanks to the generosity of a benefactor (who later funded Powell and Moya's additions to Queens' College, Cambridge). Moya's erratic habits and sometimes taciturn manner vexed some clients (and colleagues—he was apt to spend several days working on a single detail) but his intensity and powers of imagination struck a chord with many academics.

The award of the royal gold medal for architecture to Powell and Moya in 1974 reflected the high reputation of the practice; Moya was appointed CBE in 1966. The British pavilion which the firm designed for the 1970 Osaka Expo—the scheme was largely Moya's work—hinted at the impending fashion for high tech, though Powell and Moya's work of the seventies and eighties, mostly in the health and education sectors, tended to be pragmatic rather than experimental. The Queen Elizabeth II Conference Centre, opened in 1986, presented a bold face to Westminster Abbey but attracted little comment, even from the prince of Wales, in a year that also saw the completion of Richard Rogers's Lloyd's building. Moya married for a second time on 28 April 1988. His wife was Jean Conder (b. 1922/3), a gilder and restorer, the daughter of Donald Hector Colin Macarthur, an army officer.

Moya retired from practice in 1990 and the partnership with Powell was formally dissolved when the latter retired a year later. In retirement at Rye, Sussex, he pursued an interest in painting—he had always eschewed professional politics and committees. Moya was a deeply private man, whom few colleagues felt they knew well. He died in the Conquest Hospital, St Leonards, Sussex, on 3 August 1994.
KENNETH POWELL

Sources K. Powell, 'Powell & Moya: the first fifty years', *Architects' Journal* (4 July 1996), 27–58 · *Architects' Journal* (11 Aug 1994), 8 · *The Times* (4 Aug 1994) · *The Independent* (11 Aug 1994) · E. Harwood, *England: a guide to post-war listed buildings* (2000) · *WWW* · personal knowledge (2004) · private information (2004) [Sir Philip Powell] · m. certs. · d. cert.
Likenesses double portrait, photograph (with Philip Powell), repro. in *Architects' Journal* · double portrait, photograph (with Philip Powell), repro. in Powell, 'Powell & Moya', 28
Wealth at death £309,673: probate, 16 Jan 1995, *CGPLA Eng. & Wales*

Moyer, Samuel (*c.*1609–1683), republican merchant and financial administrator, was born in Leigh, Essex, the second son of James Moyer, master mariner. Given a merchant's upbringing close to London's dockland, and enrolled as a mercer, he rapidly made his mark among a group of rising 'outsiders', prominent in colonial trades and colonizing ventures, who were challenging the politically conservative oligarchy of mainly Levant and East India Company merchants which dominated the corporation of London before the civil war.

An ardent puritan and uncompromising parliamentarian, Moyer in June 1642 was made a manager of the Sea Adventure, through which the City undertook to find ships and men for the reconquest of Ireland. His talents, his wealth, and the changing times raised him to the court of assistants of the Levant Company from 1644 to 1648, and in 1645 parliament appointed him to the Goldsmiths'

Hall committee, through which royalists redeemed their sequestrated estates by paying compositions. His employment on financial commissions and committees multiplied with the increasing ascendancy of the Independents from 1647, and still more from the establishment of the Commonwealth in 1649. Though not a leveller sympathizer, he sat as a leading London Independent on the committee that drafted the second *Agreement of the People*. The Rump Parliament appointed him to a special commission to overhaul naval and customs administration, to the second high court of justice, to the post of check inwards at the London customs, and to the Hale commission on law reform. He chaired the compounding commission for twenty months in 1650–51. He acquired Pitsea Hall in Essex and nearly £9000 worth of bishops' lands, and in 1653 he was master of the Mercers' Company.

By then, however, Moyer was alienated by the Rump's lukewarm attitude to religious and civil reform, and when Oliver Cromwell expelled it, he was one of the few London aldermen who approved. His unusual combination of financial expertise with millenarian enthusiasm gained him a place on the small council of state that administered the country until the Nominated Assembly (or Barebone's Parliament) took over in July 1653. Both in that body, in which he sat for London, and in its enlarged council of state, he was highly active, and clearly one of the leaders of an emerging radical faction. But he was not re-elected to the council in November, for by then that faction's aims and conduct were offending the moderate majority in the house. When the moderates finally marched out and surrendered their authority to Cromwell, the radical remnant called Moyer to the speaker's chair and sat on until the military evicted them.

Deploring Cromwell's protectorate as a betrayal of the saints' quest for a godly commonwealth, Moyer lost his lucrative customs post and ceased to be publicly employed, except as (nominally) a JP and (from 1655) a master of Trinity House. He did not conspire against the regime, but in February 1659 he and other London republicans presented Richard Cromwell's parliament with the same subversive petition that had led Oliver Cromwell to dissolve his last parliament a year earlier. Moyer spoke in support of it for almost an hour. When the Rump was restored in May, he appeared before it to urge that the government 'may not be too long trusted in any man's hands: that it may not be perpetuated to men'. He returned briefly to the Commonwealth's service, but retired when the Restoration became inevitable and procured a royal pardon. This did not save him from being imprisoned from 1661 to 1667 on suspicion of plotting against Charles II. Thereafter he resumed his City career, serving again on the Levant Company's court of assistants (1669–74, 1677–8, 1679–80), and the committee of the East India Company (1672–82).

Moyer has often been called a Baptist, since he associated closely with such prominent Baptists as William Kiffin and Josiah Berners. He was in fact a Congregationalist, a member of the church of Thomas Goodwin, and John Collins, Goodwin's successor at two removes, was still his 'deare Pastor' when he made his will in 1682; this also named John Owen. Moyer's puritanism was more extreme than Goodwin's or Owen's, but neither fanatical nor over-rigid; for instance, he championed a bill in Barebone's Parliament to abolish lay patronage over ecclesiastical benefices, but he exercised his own right of presentation to the rectory of Pitsea in 1656. He died in July 1683. His will (made on 7 April 1682 and proved on 30 August 1683) attests to considerable wealth and wide commercial interests. His wife, Rebecca, daughter of Thomas Thorold, had evidently predeceased him; the Pitsea estate was entailed on his elder son, Samuel, who was made a baronet in 1671. AUSTIN WOOLRYCH, *rev.*

Sources G. E. Aylmer, *The state's servants: the civil service of the English republic, 1649–1660* (1973) · Greaves & Zaller, *BDBR* · M. Tolmie, *The triumph of the saints: the separate churches of London, 1616–1649* (1977) · A. Woolrych, *Commonwealth to protectorate* (1982) · will, PRO, PROB/11/373, sig, 96 · A. B. Beaven, ed., *The aldermen of the City of London, temp. Henry III–[1912]*, 2 vols. (1908–13)

Wealth at death considerable wealth: will, PRO, PROB 11/373, sig. 96

Moyes [*née* Fraser], **Helen Miller** (1881–1979), women's activist, was born on 14 September 1881 at 1 Grosvenor Crescent, Leeds, one of ten children of James Fraser and his wife, Christiana Sutherland. Her parents were both Scottish. Her father went from Caithness to Edinburgh as a tailor's cutter, then to Leeds, and finally, when Helen was still a child, to Glasgow, where he established a wholesale clothing firm. (According to an account given by Helen in 1908 she took a studio in Glasgow where she painted and did embroidery, but neither in her autobiography nor when interviewed in 1975 did she even hint at such leanings.) Helen grew up in a lively family, with progressive, supportive parents, who strongly believed in improving conditions for workers. As described by her in 1975, her early life was that of a typical middle-class young woman, going to balls and dances, playing tennis, performing in amateur theatricals, collecting for charity, and visiting families in the poorer districts of the city.

Helen Fraser's life was transformed in 1906 when she heard Teresa Billington (subsequently Billington-Greig), one of the early supporters of the Women's Social and Political Union (WSPU), speak about the burning need for women to get the vote. From that day until 1914 Helen's whole life revolved around the women's suffrage movement. She became the first Scottish WSPU organizer and was also among the earliest suffragettes to be imprisoned for attempting to enter the House of Commons. In 1908, however, when the first stones were thrown, she was horrified at the advent of violence and resigned from the WSPU. She was invited to work for the non-militant National Union of Women's Suffrage Societies (NUWSS), under the leadership of Millicent Garrett Fawcett, and in 1910 she was instrumental in setting up the North of Scotland Federation of Women's Suffrage Societies. Much later she recalled that her best audiences were in Aberdeen, as they really appreciated a well-argued, logical speech. Subsequently she worked as an organizer in London and other parts of England and also helped to build up

branches in south Wales. In England she became known as 'the chieftainess because of her fine presence and air of command' (Mitchell, 164).

After war broke out in 1914 Helen Fraser was recruited by the government, in the first instance to organize patrols to watch girls near training camps and subsequently to organize an area in the south-west for the National War Savings Committee. She insisted on being paid the same rate as a man. During that period she was also lent to the Board of Agriculture and Fisheries to make speeches urging women to go and work on the land, and, before rationing, to the Ministry of Food to urge voluntary rationing before it was imposed. In 1917 she was sent on a propaganda tour of America, which was a great success. She 'went to over forty States, spoke 232 times in 228 days' (Moyes, 48). After a brief visit to France, so that she could describe what she had seen at first hand, she went back to the USA for a second tour.

After the war Helen was employed as a commissioner for National Savings, resigning in 1922 to stand as the Liberal candidate for Govan, the first woman to be adopted as an official candidate in Scotland. She was aware that Govan was a safe Labour seat, but she enjoyed electioneering enough to stand a second time, in 1923, for the Hamilton division in Lanarkshire. On that occasion, however, abuse and calumny by the Labour Party candidate made the experience a thoroughly unpleasant one. Her last political invitation was to fight Kelvingrove in Glasgow, but the Conservative candidate was a friend, and she knew that she would poll enough votes to cause him to lose his seat, so she refused and gave up the idea of a career in politics.

Helen then moved to London, earning money from freelance articles on women's issues, and sat on Kensington council for seven years. During that period she was a delegate to all the major international women's conferences.

Helen Fraser called herself a *profound* Christian, believing in mystical, visionary teachings. She was convinced that her not having married was 'meant' because she was free to move into international work. But meanwhile she kept in touch with an old friend named Moyes who had married and gone to Australia, where one of Helen's brothers was also living. Moyes's wife died, and he proposed to her on numerous occasions before she finally agreed and emigrated to Australia in 1938.

As Helen Moyes she wrote an autobiography, published in Australia in 1971, entitled *A Woman in a Man's World*. She continued lecturing on feminist subjects and was one of the surviving suffragettes and suffragists interviewed by Brian Harrison in August and September 1975. She died on 2 December 1979. LEAH LENEMAN

Sources L. Leneman, *A guid cause: the women's suffrage movement in Scotland* (1995) · Brian Harrison taped interview with Helen Fraser Moyes, 19 Aug 1975 and 18 Sept 1975, Women's Library, London · H. Moyes, *A woman in a man's world* (1971) · J. Alberti, *Beyond suffrage: feminists in war and peace, 1914–1928* (1989) · *Votes for Women* (18 June 1908) · *Common Cause* (2 Dec 1909) · *Common Cause* (8 Sept 1910) · H. M. W. Mitchell, *The hard way up: the autobiography of Hannah Mitchell, suffragette and rebel*, ed. G. Mitchell (1968) · letters to Caroline

Phillips in suffrage material donated by Miss R. Watt, Aberdeen Art Gallery and Museum · b. cert.

Archives SOUND NL Aus., recorded interview, 1975 · Women's Library, London, recorded interview, 1975

Likenesses photograph, repro. in Moyes, *Woman in a man's world*, jacket · photograph, repro. in *Common Cause* (2 Dec 1909)

Moyes, Henry (1749/50–1807), lecturer on natural philosophy, was born near Kirkcaldy in Fife, one of three sons and a daughter of Henry Moyes (d. 1774). The latter was tenant at Westmill of Abbotshall, near Kirkcaldy, and a nonconformist. Moyes was left blinded by smallpox in infancy, but he apparently distinguished himself at Kirkcaldy grammar school. In 1793 Dr James Currie described how

> when Dr Adam Smith was writing his profound work on the 'Wealth of Nations' at Kirkaldy [*sic*] in Scotland, he used to wander in the evenings—In these excursions, a blind boy of the village of humble situation, but of great ingenuity, became his constant companion. He became attached to this boy; gave him some instruction himself, and directed his education throughout—In due time he sent him with letters to Hume to the University of Edinburgh. Hume got him what is called a Bursary … and exerted all his characteristic benevolence in his favour. After a few years residence in Edinburgh Smith removed him to Glasgow and furnished him with letters to Dr Reid. He was again equally fortunate, and after many years residence between the two Universities, in due time, the blind man, became a Dr. of physic. This was Moyes.   (Dr James Currie to Thomas Creevey, 24 Feb 1793, Lpool RO, Currie MS 920 CUR)

No record of Moyes's university attendance has been discovered. One account stated that 'in early life he undoubtedly acquired the fundamental principles of mechanics, music, and the languages; and displayed a knowledge of geometry, algebra, optics, astronomy, chemistry, and in short most of the branches of Newtonian philosophy' (Kay, 177). As his blindness precluded Moyes from practising medicine, he became, in Edinburgh, a lecturer on chemistry and natural philosophy, relying on an assistant for the demonstrations.

In 1779 Moyes left for England, and lectured all round the country. A contemporary remarked:

> Dr Henry Moyes, the elegant reader on philosophical chemistry … excelled in the charms of conversation; was happy in his allusions to visual objects; and discoursed on the nature, composition, and beauty of colours, with pertinence and precision. Doctor Moyes was a striking instance of the power, the human soul possesses, of finding resources of satisfaction, even under the most rigorous calamities.   (Bew, 168–71)

In 1783 Joseph Priestley introduced him to Sir Joseph Banks, president of the Royal Society, as:

> an excellent lecturer in philosophy … a phenomenon … being quite blind, and yet superior to most who see. He is a man of most amiable disposition, and tho' he cannot himself make many experiments, he gets them made for him by an assistant, so that none of his hearers ever complain on that account.   (Joseph Priestley to Joseph Banks, 6 Feb 1783, NHM, Dawson Turner MS 3, fol. 17)

Through travel and introductions he joined the network of the men of science. From Manchester he went to Birmingham, where he encountered members of the Lunar Society, but James Watt found him argumentative.

Perhaps Moyes's political radicalism (which may have angered Watt) was the motive behind his visit to the fledgeling United States of America (1784–6). He lectured to rapturous success in Boston, Philadelphia, Baltimore, Princeton, and Charleston, South Carolina, before returning to England. In 1789 he gave two courses of lectures in Dublin. His lectures in Newcastle upon Tyne in 1780 and 1793 proved influential, and he was elected among the first honorary members of the local literary and philosophical society in 1795. Similarly, at Hull in 1792 Moyes appears to have been a prime mover in the formation of a Society for the Purpose of Literary Information, was elected its first president, and had his portrait done by John Russell. During his last decade Moyes travelled extensively, accompanied by his assistant, William Nicol. He spent part of each year recuperating in Fife, where he had acquired Lumbenny, a small property. He never married. He died in Doncaster, where he was holding a lecture course, on 10 December 1807, aged fifty-seven. He was buried in the town on 14 December.

As he never published, Moyes's reputation faded with his memory. More recently, with increasing historical interest in the rise of science in British provincial culture, his role has been reassessed, in particular by Inkster: he was one of a group of itinerant lecturers who helped the ideas of the literary and philosophical movement further permeate the social spectrum, to assist the beginnings of the mechanics' institutes.   A. D. MORRISON-LOW

Sources J. A. Harrison, 'Blind Henry Moyes, "an excellent lecturer in philosophy"', *Annals of Science*, 13 (1957), 109–25 · J. Kay, *A series of original portraits and caricature etchings … with biographical sketches and illustrative anecdotes*, ed. [H. Paton and others], 1 (1837), 177–9 · C. W. Hatfield, *Historical notices of Doncaster*, 3 vols. (1866), 1.386–7 · E. V. Armstrong and C. K. Deischer, 'Dr Henry Moyes, Scotch chemist: his visit to America, 1785–1786', *Journal of Chemical Education*, 24 (1947), 169–74 · A. E. Musson and E. Robinson, 'Science and industry in the late eighteenth century', *Science and technology in the industrial revolution* (1969), 87–189 · G. Bew, 'Observations on blindness and on the employment of the other senses to supply the loss of sight', *Memoirs of the Literary and Philosophical Society of Manchester*, 1 (1785), 159–84, esp. 168–71 · GM, 1st ser., 54 (1784), 325 · I. Inkster, 'Studies in the social history of science in England during the industrial revolution, c.1790–1850', PhD thesis, University of Sheffield, 1977 · C. Frost, *An address delivered to the literary and philosophical society at Kingston-upon-Hull* (1831), 3–6 · W. Hunt, *Hull: the earlier literary associations*, Historical Notices of Hull, 111 (1883) · *Doncaster, Nottingham and Lincoln Gazette* (11 Dec 1807) · *Edinburgh Advertiser* (15 Dec 1807) · services of heirs, NA Scot. · inventory and personal estate and effects of the late Dr Henry Moyes of Lumbenny, NA Scot., CC 8/11/5, fols. 611–14 · testament, Dr Henry Moyes, NA Scot., CC 8/8/137, fol. 379 · Lpool RO, Currie papers · NHM, Dawson Turner MSS

Likenesses J. Russell, pastel drawing, 1792, Hull City Museums and Art Galleries, Ferens Art Gallery · J. Kay, engraving, repro. in Kay, *Series of original portraits*, vol. 1, facing p. 177 · W. Ward, engraving (after portrait by J. Reubens Smith, 1806), BM

Wealth at death £898 10s. ¼d.; plus £1000 invested in 3 per cent consols: NA Scot., CC 8/11/5, fol. 613

Moylan, Francis (1735–1815), Roman Catholic bishop of Cork, was born in that city on 17 September 1735, the second son of John Moylan, merchant in Cork, and his wife, Mary Doran. He was educated at Paris and Montpellier but, having decided to study for the priesthood, transferred to Toulouse, where his Jesuit uncle Father Patrick Doran was a professor at the Irish seminary. There he established a lifelong friendship with Henry Essex Edgeworth, later confessor to Louis XVI. It was during this time too that Moylan developed an animosity towards Voltaire, Rousseau, and the principles of the Enlightenment, which later underpinned his resolute opposition to the United Irishmen. Having completed a doctorate in divinity he was ordained into the priesthood in June 1761 and appointed *curé* of Chatou, where he acted as secretary to Christophe de Beaumont, archbishop of Paris.

In 1764 Moylan returned to his native city, where he remained until his consecration as bishop of Ardfert and Agadhoe in 1775. The years in Killarney represent a formative period in his political development, since it was there that he established a rapport with Lord Kenmare, leader of the Catholic Committee, in which Moylan assumed a prominent role. Under Kenmare's influence Moylan joined the Munster bishops in subscribing to the controversial 'Herveyan' test oath in 1775, and he enthusiastically endorsed their ostentatious declarations of loyalty, delivered during the Whiteboy and Rightboy disturbances, in 1784 and 1786 respectively.

Moylan was translated to the diocese of Cork in 1787 to fill the vacancy created by the scandalous defection to the Church of Ireland of John Butler. During the 1790s he attempted to stem the contagion of the 'French disease' in Ireland. Following the advice of his correspondent and mentor Edmund Burke, he counselled obedience to the crown, gratitude for the recent Relief Acts, and a rejection of 'French fraternity' in all its manifestations. So, while he joined the platform party at the celebrated Catholic Convention of 1792, he is best remembered for his denunciation of the defenders, the United Irishmen, and the rising of 1798. Consequently a favourite of the protestant establishment, he received the freedom of the city of Cork in recognition of his pastoral exhortation to loyalty delivered during the Bantry Bay crisis of 1796. In the following year Lord Lieutenant Camden circulated Moylan's pastoral letter throughout the kingdom, and Chief-Secretary Pelham expressed personal gratitude for his 'seasonable, able and judicious' efforts (England, 188–9). In 1799 he was entertained by the duke of Portland at Bulstrode. Moylan joined his episcopal confrères in acquiescing in the passage of the Act of Union, confident that the measure would bring the Catholic emancipation promised by Pitt and an escape from the tyranny of protestant ascendancy in Ireland. In the event no such relief was forthcoming, and he was forced to spend the later years of his episcopate attempting to undo the royal veto on episcopal nominations conceded during the union debates.

Despite these political preoccupations Moylan's priorities were pastoral, and he attempted to bring the diocese into line with Roman practice following the dislocation of the penal era. He embarked upon an ambitious visitation of the diocese and promoted frequent reception of the sacraments, public devotions, and recitation of the family rosary. Central to this renewal was his attempt to provide

Catholic education. As a curate, in 1771, Moylan had assisted Nano Nagle in the establishment of the Ursulines in Cork; four years later he supported her foundation of the Presentation Sisters. Later, in 1811, he brought Edmund Rice's Presentation (Christian) Brothers to the city. He established a seminary in the diocese and erected a cathedral—that of St Mary and St Ann, Cork—in 1808, in the vaults of which he was interred following his death, in Chapel Lane, Cork, on 10 February 1815.

P. L. NOLAN, *rev.* DÁIRE KEOGH

Sources E. Bolster, *A history of the diocese of Cork; from the penal era to the famine* (Cork, 1989), 133–228 • E. Bolster, ed., 'The Moylan correspondence in Bishop's House, Killarney', *Collectanea Hibernica*, 14 (1971), 82–142; 15 (1972), 56–109 • J. Collins, *A funeral oration of the late Right Reverend Doctor Moylan* (1815) • T. R. England, *Letters from the Abbé Edgeworth to his friends* (1918) • D. Keogh, *The French disease; the Catholic church and radicalism in Ireland* (Dublin, 1993)
Archives Cork and Ross Roman Catholic Diocesan Archive, corresp. and papers as bishop of Cork • Kerry Roman Catholic Diocesan Archive, Killarney, corresp. as bishop of Kerry
Likenesses P. Turnerelli, sculpture on monument?, St Anne's Church, Shandon, Cork • oils, NG Ire.

Moyle, John (1591/2–1661), politician, was the son of Robert Moyle (d. 1604) of Bake in St Germans, Cornwall, and Ann Lock (d. 1604) of Acton, Middlesex. He attended Exeter College, Oxford, matriculating on 10 June 1608 aged sixteen. By a licence of 1 September 1612 he married Admonition (d. 1675), daughter of Sir Edmund Prideaux of Netherton, Devon. Among their children was Walter (1627–1701), sheriff of Cornwall in 1671. The family was well respected in the county, but its fortunes were undoubtedly improved through the offices of Sir John Eliot, the famous parliamentarian, who had matriculated at Exeter College just a few months before Moyle. Their relationship was soured at an early stage when John Moyle complained to Eliot's father of some offensive behaviour on the part of his friend. When the young Eliot visited Moyle to protest, hot words were exchanged, and the enraged Eliot drew his sword, wounding the other man in the side. Later, Eliot wrote a formal apology for this assault and it is said that shame and embarrassment led him to a thorough reform of his behaviour.

Perhaps sensing that the incident left him under a special obligation, Eliot exerted his influence more than once on his victim's behalf. Moyle wrote to him in April and November 1630, during Eliot's imprisonment in the Tower, and Eliot replied in a friendly spirit. It was through the influence of the Eliot family, who controlled the burgess vote in the town, that in November 1640 Moyle's son John was elected member for St Germans Priory in the Long Parliament; although his admission to the house was delayed because of doubts raised about the election he was seated by May 1641. John Moyle senior is probably to be ranked among the puritans of Cornwall, for in 1642 he was reported to favour the exclusion of bishops from the House of Lords, stricter sabbath observance, the abandonment of unscriptural ceremonies, and the removal of insufficient ministers. He was certainly one of the stalwarts of the parliamentarian cause in Cornwall, named under the ordinance of 27 March 1643 as member of its committee for sequestering delinquents' estates. However, the county shortly afterwards fell under royalist control, which lasted until the autumn of 1645.

In March 1646 Moyle was a member of the Cornish county committee, and soon began to involve himself in the expulsion of clergymen, both for royalism and for refusing the covenant. In February 1648 he was elected member of parliament for East Looe. In May 1648 he helped put down the insurrectionary attempts of the royalists, who were strong among the Cornish gentry, and wrote regularly to Francis Buller in London with news of the latest political and military developments; on 31 May he reported from Truro that though the worst was over, very dangerous men had 'not past beyond the seas, but remain in the west lurking in the cliffes and in Tinne pitts; and if we should take them we have no prison to commit them' (Worth, 107). Buller was removed from the commission of the peace after Pride's Purge but Moyle remained active, writing to his former colleague in December 1649 that his reinstatement depended on subscription to the engagement. He continued in parliament and was named to the militia committee of Cornwall under the act passed on 17 March 1653, just before the Rump's dissolution. Moyle was named as one of the commissioners for ejecting scandalous clergy in Cornwall under the ordinance of 28 August 1654 and was named to its militia committee in July 1659 and March 1660. He survived both his eldest son, John, buried at St Germans on 4 February 1658, and his son's only son, Roger, who was only five at his death in December 1660. John Moyle died at Bake on 9 October 1661 and was buried at St Germans on 17 October.

STEPHEN WRIGHT

Sources M. Coate, *Cornwall in the great civil war and interregnum, 1642–1660* (1933) · R. Worth, ed., *The Buller papers* (1896) · Keeler, *Long Parliament* · Foster, *Alum. Oxon.* · J. L. Vivian, ed., *The visitations of Cornwall, comprising the herald's visitations of 1530, 1573, and 1620* (1887) · Boase & Courtney, *Bibl. Corn.* · C. H. Firth and R. S. Rait, eds., *Acts and ordinances of the interregnum, 1642–1660*, 3 vols. (1911) · H. Hulme, *The life of Sir John Eliot* (1957) · A. B. Grossart, ed., *De jure majestatis, or, Political treatise of government* (1628–30) *and the letter book of Sir John Eliot* (1882)

Moyle, John (d. 1714), naval surgeon, having served for many years at sea in merchant ships and ships of war and having been 'in most of the sea fights that we have had with any nation in my time', secured a pension from the crown in 1690. Nothing is known of his early life. In later life, describing himself as 'being grown in years and not capable to hold it longer in that employ' as a surgeon at sea (*Chirurgus marinus*, 1693), Moyle applied himself to writing down his surgical experiences for the benefit of younger surgeons. His published works mention no officer by name, nor any ship on which he served, but there are references to his experiences in the third Dutch War (1672–4) and on anti-piracy patrols off north Africa, as well as service on the Newfoundland banks and in the eastern Mediterranean.

Moyle's short *Abstractum chirurgiae marinae, or, An Abstract of Sea Surgery* (1686) was expanded and republished in 1693 as *Chirurgus marinus, or, The Sea Chirurgion*. This went into at least four editions and continued to be valued as a textbook for more than a century after Moyle's death. Its popularity was due in part to its simplicity and practicality, for it supplied in handbook form instructions on medicines, instruments, and other equipment needed by the ship's surgeon, and also what cases, both medical and surgical, the surgeon at sea might expect to find. Following the success of *Chirurgus marinus*, he produced *The Experienced Chirurgion* (1703) for young surgeons, especially those who practised on land. However, his most interesting book is *Chyrurgic Memoirs* (1708), the frontispiece of which is an engraved portrait of Moyle in full wig. This work contains case histories taken from his journal of sick and wounded men and women treated by him at sea and on land. Included is a description of an above-the-knee amputation carried out in the heat of battle at Tangier.

Moyle was a resident of Westminster for the last years of his life. In his will dated 1 March 1703 and proved on 17 February 1714 he is said to be of the parish of St Martin-in-the-Fields, but he was buried on 20 February 1714 in St Margaret's, Westminster, having lived in the Privy Garden, part of the Whitehall Palace complex. Mary, his wife, survived him, and there were three children: a son, John, and daughters Mary Neret and Susanna Willon, presumably referred to in Moyle's will by their married names. He bequeathed each of his children 1s. only, but to his grandson, James Willon, noted in the will to be 'now beyond the seas', he left £10 provided he claimed it within seven years of Moyle's death and collected it in person.

ANDREW GRIFFIN

Sources J. Moyle, *Chirurgus marinus* (1693) · J. Moyle, *Chyrurgic memoirs* (1708) · J. J. Keevil and others, *Medicine and the navy, 1200–1900*, 2: 1649–1714 (1958) · will, 1 March 1703, Family Records Centre, London, PROB 11/538 sig. 32 (microfilm) · parish register, St Margaret's, City Westm. AC, vol. 9 · *DNB*
Likenesses engraving, repro. in Moyle, *Chyrurgic memoirs*, frontispiece

Moyle, Matthew Paul (1788–1880), surgeon and geologist, born at Chacewater, Cornwall, on 4 October 1788, was the second son of John Moyle and his wife, Julia, daughter of Johnathon Hornblower. He attended lectures in anatomy and surgery at Guy's and St Thomas's hospitals in London, and became a member of the Royal College of Surgeons in 1809. He began practice at Helston, Cornwall, and, in February 1810, married Jane Vivian (d. 1829), daughter of Richard Moyle, surgeon, of Marazion.

Much of Moyle's practice involved attending workers injured in the nearby tin and copper mines, an industry with which his father and elder brother, Samuel (1784–1867), were already connected. As a result Moyle became increasingly interested in geological and mining problems. In 1814 his paper 'Queries respecting the flow of water in the Chacewater mine' appeared in *Annals of Philosophy*; he later communicated papers on geology and mine gases to a number of scientific journals. His studies of gases in mines began after observing deaths from carbon dioxide poisoning in poorly ventilated parts of the mines. Following the death of his first wife Moyle married, in

1830, Frances Elizabeth (*d.* 1849), daughter of William Borlase, surgeon.

Between 1841 and 1879 Moyle kept meteorological records for the Royal Cornwall Polytechnic Society, including observations of barometers and thermometers. He began to study the raised temperatures of mines in 1812, and read a paper on the subject to the Royal Geological Society of Cornwall in 1822. However, unlike Robert Were Fox, who studied the same subject, he could not accept that the increased heat at depth was due to natural causes, but instead attributed it to the activities of miners and chemical reactions in metal ores. He died at Cross Street, Helston, on 7 August 1880.   DENISE CROOK

Sources Boase & Courtney, *Bibl. Corn.* · G. C. Boase, *Collectanea Cornubiensia: a collection of biographical and topographical notes relating to the county of Cornwall* (1890) · M. P. Moyle, 'On the temperature of the Cornish mines', *Transactions of the Royal Geological Society of Cornwall*, 2 (1822), 404–15 · M. P. Moyle, letter, *Royal Cornwall Gazette* (11 May 1822) · A. Pearson, 'A study of the Royal Cornwall Polytechnic Society', MA diss., University of Exeter, 1973 · d. cert.

Wealth at death under £1500: probate, 29 Nov 1880, *CGPLA Eng. & Wales*

Moyle, Robert (1589/90–1638), lawyer and legal official, was descended from the Moyle family of Cornwall and Kent, but his parents' names are unknown. He was admitted to the Inner Temple in 1614 as of Buckwell, in Boughton Aluph, Kent, though he later settled at West Twyford in Middlesex. He pursued the clerical side of the profession and his standing by 1627 was sufficient to qualify him for the appointment of third protonotary of the court of common pleas, an office worth over £1000 a year. The office cost him £4000, of which a quarter was paid in cash and the remainder paid over three years, and it was settled under an agreement between the king and Chief Justice Finch so that it would pass after Moyle's death to trustees for his infant son. Mr Justice Hutton noted at the time of this appointment that Moyle was 'un bon clerk', who 'ad ew bon experience et est fitt pur cest place' (*Diary*, 71); at the time of Moyle's death he wrote that Moyle was 'un ready et bon clerke' (ibid., 111). Moyle was elected an associate of the bench of the Inner Temple upon his appointment in 1627, and he became an ordinary bencher in 1635.

Moyle followed the traditions of his office by collecting precedents of pleading, of which an English translation by John Herne was printed as *An Exact Book of Entries* in 1658. There also survives a manuscript book of Moyle's entries (BL, Add. MS 37321), a manuscript 'book of judgments' (BL, MS Hargrave 364), and some notes by Moyle on the office of protonotary (Lincoln's Inn library, MS misc. 586). He married Margaret (*d.* 1674), daughter of Anthony Oldfield of Spalding, Lincolnshire, and they had four sons and several daughters, including Margaret, who became the wife of Fabian Philipps (1601–1690). Moyle died on 29 August 1638, aged forty-eight, and was buried in West Twyford church, where his children erected a monument in 1657. According to Hutton, Moyle left land worth £500 per annum. His will contained various provisions governing the office of third protonotary, giving his widow the

power to appoint deputies. However, the settlement of the office was held void on his death and Margaret Moyle had to pay £4000 to secure the succession to her brother-in-law George Farmer of Lyon's Inn, on the understanding that he would occupy it until one of her children came of age. In fact Farmer remained in office until 1668, while Margaret married as her second husband someone named Clapham, who was a knight or baronet.   J. H. BAKER

Sources J. H. Baker, *The legal profession and the common law: historical essays* (1986), 252–3, 256 · *The diary of Sir Richard Hutton, 1614–1639*, ed. W. R. Prest, SeldS, suppl. ser., 9 (1991), 71, 111–12 · C. W. Brook, *Pettyfoggers and vipers of the commonwealth* (1986), 127–9 · Rymer, *Foedera*, 1st edn, 20.87–92 · *CSP dom.*, 1635–6, 56; 1637–8, 76 · privy council order book, 1636–7, PRO, fol. 277 · PRO, PROB 11/177, fols. 453–4 [Moyle's will] · PRO, PROB 6/49, admon · monumental inscription, West Twyford, Middlesex · BL, Add. MS 37321 · Lincoln's Inn, London, MS Misc. 586 · BL, MS Hargrave 364

Archives Lincoln's Inn, London, MS Misc. 586

Likenesses bust on monument, *c.*1638, West Twyford church, Middlesex

Moyle, Sir Thomas (*b.* before **1500**, *d.* **1560**), lawyer and speaker of the House of Commons, was probably born at Eastwell, Kent, the fourth of the five sons of John Moyle (*d.* 1500), who sat as MP for Bodmin, and his second wife, Anne, a daughter and heir of Sir Robert Darcy who belonged to a long-established family in Essex, possibly the branch at Tolleshunt Darcy. John Moyle was a substantial landowner in Kent, and also in Cornwall and Devon where his family originated. His feoffees included important people in Kent and he was escheator there, an important factor in explaining Thomas Moyle's later standing in that county. Nevertheless, his father left him property worth only 10 marks yearly, and Moyle had to make his own way in the legal profession. At some point before 1528, he, like his father, married an heiress, Katherine, one of the daughters of Edward Jordeyne (*d.* 1514), a leading goldsmith at Cheapside who was also engaged at the mint in the Tower of London and had a manor at Raynham, Essex.

In 1537 Moyle became a JP for Kent, having apparently acquired the estate at Eastwell once held by his father, and served on numerous commissions in the county thereafter, while in 1557 he was both sheriff of Kent and warden of Rochester Bridge. After the fall of the fourth duke of Buckingham in 1521, one of his chief supporters, George Neville, Lord Bergavenny, came under royal suspicion. A year later Moyle, described as of Gray's Inn, stood surety for him for £100, an episode which shows that Moyle had been accepted in Kentish society. He may have been building up a local practice. During the Christmas season of 1526–7, Moyle acted in the 'disguising' at Gray's Inn by John Rowe to which, famously, Wolsey took exception as an attack upon himself. Moyle was sent to the Fleet prison, and the affair may explain his delayed entry into royal service. He became an ancient of Gray's Inn in 1528 and Lent reader in 1533 and 1539. His readings followed the very recent move to lecture on new, not old statutes. In 1533 he read on 21 Hen. VIII c. 15 on tenancy. The moot cases for his 1539 reading survive in BL, Hargrave MS 253.

In 1537 Moyle was one of four commissioners appointed both to re-establish law and order in Ireland following the Geraldine uprising of 1534–5 and to force through a second stage of reformation legislation which included the dissolution of thirteen lesser monasteries. He may have owed his appointment to his kinsman (and fellow Kentishman) Anthony St Leger, who headed the commission and later became deputy of Ireland. Returning to England in 1538, Moyle was made a general surveyor of crown lands, and also acted as a commissioner for the dissolution of several monasteries, most notoriously at Glastonbury in 1539. Having failed to obtain a voluntary surrender, he and his colleagues found evidence for a charge of treason against the abbot, Richard Whiting, who was subsequently executed.

No doubt as a result of such experience, Moyle became one of the heads of the newly created court of general surveyors of the king's lands in 1542 when that was set up by statute, and when the surveyors' court was absorbed into the second court of augmentations in 1547, he became one of the latter's two assistant directors. He was not involved in the Edwardian plans to reorganize the revenue courts, but he was named in October 1553 to the commission to begin winding up augmentations.

Despite being primarily a fiscal officer, Moyle sometimes prosecuted for the crown, and lost in 1540 against Richard Benger, charged with treason for criticizing the king's taxing of the clergy, but acquitted at the Kent assizes through his own skilful defence. Moyle also gave evidence in 1542 against Lord William Howard, charged with misprision concerning Katherine Howard. Moyle was knighted and chosen speaker of the Commons in January 1542, following his election for an unknown constituency. His was the first customary protestation of unworthiness to be recorded in the Lords' journal. His speakership was also notable for the case of George Ferrers, MP for Plymouth, who was released from imprisonment for debt after the Commons on their own authority claimed the privilege of freedom from arrest in civil actions. Moyle later sat four times for Rochester, a seat often chosen for court nominees, and for King's Lynn in November 1554. His professional usefulness in the Commons is shown by the committal to him of six bills during the session of 1548–9.

Despite Moyle's involvement in monastic dissolutions in England and Ireland, he was a religious conservative. He was one of a group of laymen who took part in the prebendaries' plot of 1543 to overthrow Archbishop Cranmer. The conspirators' aim was to bring to the attention of the council the advance of evangelicalism in Kent. Indeed, they allowed their first victim, Richard Turner, to preach sermons in Moyle's parish church at Westwell in order to expose him as a heretic. Moyle changed course and leaked some of their complaints to Cranmer, but later renewed his attacks on the archbishop. The chronicler John Stow, quoting from an earlier source, alleged that after the notorious murder of Thomas Arden of Faversham in 1551 Moyle and others, 'being Papists', sought to implicate an innocent man, 'hating him for the gospel' (Clark, 84). He was certainly an active supporter of Mary in 1553 and was involved in at least one episode of persecution. There is some doubt about how far Moyle opposed Wyatt's rebellion, but the chronicler John Proctor suggests that he was part of a force at Rochester to take Wyatt in the rear and also names him first on the commission to compound with the rebels.

In November 1554 Moyle quitted parliament without permission and was repeatedly harassed in queen's bench for this offence until Mary's death brought the proceedings to an end. He was ill by 1558 when Sir Henry Jerningham commented that 'Mr Moyle is so diseased that he cannot return' (*CSP dom.*, *1601–3*, 471). But he sued out a general pardon from Elizabeth, and spent 1559 and 1560 dividing up his great estates, mostly acquired while in office.

Moyle's heir was his daughter Katherine, who married Sir Thomas Finch, ancestor of the earls of Winchilsea and Nottingham; another daughter, Amy, who married Sir Thomas Kempe, and had a son, Thomas, predeceased her father. In his will, made on 1 August 1560, Moyle left property at Clerkenwell to his wife, houses in Newgate to his grandchildren, and divided the rest of his estates in Kent, Surrey, Middlesex, Devon, and Somerset between Katherine Finch and Thomas Kempe. He gave land and an endowment to his parish for an almshouse, and left £6 13s. 4d. to Clement Norton, formerly vicar of Faversham and a participant in the prebendaries' plot. Moyle died on 2 October 1560, probably at Eastwell, and was buried there.

PATRICIA HYDE

Sources HoP, *Commons, 1509–58*, 2.642–4 • *Miscellanea Genealogica et Heraldica*, 5th ser., 4 (1920–22), 229–34 • *CIPM, Henry VII*, 2, nos. 246, 422 • D. MacCullough, *Thomas Cranmer* (1996) • W. C. Richardson, *History of the court of augmentations, 1536–1554* (1961) • J. H. Bettey, *Suppression of the monasteries in the west country* (1989) • P. Hyde, *Thomas Arden in Faversham: the man behind the myth* (1996), 124 • H. H. Leonard, 'Ferrers' case: a note', *BIHR*, 42 (1969), 230–34 • J. C. Wedgwood and A. D. Holt, *History of parliament*, 1: *Biographies of the members of the Commons house, 1439–1509* (1936), 616–17 • will, PRO, PROB 11/17, sig. 29 [Edward Jordeyne] • will, PRO, PROB 11/24, sig. 6 [John Moyle] • will, PRO, PROB 11/43, sig. 55 • T. F. Reddaway, *The early history of the Goldsmiths' Company, 1327–1509*, ed. L. E. M. Walker (1975) • *Transactions of the Essex Archaeological Society*, new ser., 21 (1933–4) • M. L. Zell, 'The prebendaries' plot of 1543: a reconsideration', *Journal of Ecclesiastical History*, 27 (1976), 241–53 • W. C. Richardson, *Tudor chamber administration, 1485–1547* (1952) • *Hall's chronicle*, ed. H. Ellis (1809) • P. Clark, *English provincial society from the Reformation to the revolution: religion, politics and society in Kent, 1500–1640* (1977) • J. Proctor, *The history of Wyatt's rebellion* (1554) [repr. E. Arber, *An English garner* (1877–96), vol. 8] • D. M. Loades, *Two Tudor conspiracies* (1965) • *LP Henry VIII*, vols. 4–21 • inquisitions post mortem, second series, PRO, C142/129/26 • BL, Hargrave MS 253 • G. R. Elton, *Policy and police* (1972) • *CSP dom., 1601–3; addenda, 1547–65*

Moyle, Sir Walter (*c*.1405–1479/80), justice, was perhaps the third son of Thomas Moyle of Bodmin. Having been admitted to Gray's Inn, he was a reader there in the autumn term of 1430, in the Lent term of 1437, and in 1443. In 1441 he was common serjeant of London, vacating that office when he became a serjeant, perhaps a king's serjeant, in 1443. Indeed, in a year-book entry for 1452, Moyle declared that where no other arrangements were made, 3s. 4d. was the 'common right' of the serjeant and

1s. 8d. of the attorney. A member of parliament for Bodmin (1429–30 and 1432) and Liskeard (1442), Moyle was summoned to parliaments from 1445 to 1471, being trier of petitions in the parliaments of 1459–61. In the parliament of 1453–4 he was the messenger sent from the Lords to the Commons on 14 February 1454 to declare their decision that Speaker Thorpe's imprisonment by the Yorkists was good and that the Commons had to choose another. In accordance with common practice, Moyle often acted as a feoffee to uses from at least 1446. He was appointed to commissions of inquiry and of oyer and terminer from the 1450s, notably in the west country, and was a commissioner for Kent to raise money for the defence of Calais in 1454, the same year in which he was sent to inquire into troubles in the north. He was also a member of the council of the earls of Stafford and dukes of Buckingham, being retained in 1442/3 (for which, in 1443, he received £2 p.a. from lands at Caliland, Cornwall).

On 9 July 1454 Moyle was appointed a justice of the common pleas (the usage of which court he described, significantly, in a year-book entry of 1459, as 'law'). Reappointed on 8 April 1461, he was knighted in 1465 at the coronation of Edward IV's queen, Elizabeth, and, on the readeption of Henry VI, was again reappointed on 9 October 1470. His patent was renewed by Edward IV in 1471, but although his name had appeared regularly from 1440 onwards, it does not seem to occur in the year-books after Edward's restoration. As justice of the common pleas he held in 1456 that the king was bound by local customary law and, recognizing the creative function of the common-law judges, he explained in 1460 'nous fesons bon rule pur le mischief' (Doe, 36, n. 17). As counsel in the *Prior of Nedeport's case* (1443), and later as judge in *Right's case* (1455), he was involved in contemporary developments concerning the applicability of the action on the case for nuisance. In a case of 1456, when an action of trespass was brought against an infant, Moyle, addressing the plaintiff and lifting up the child in front of the court asked 'Can you find it in your conscience to declare against this infant of such tender age?' (Doe, 149–50).

Moyle married Margaret, daughter of John Lucombe of Stevenstone in Devon. Their son John, who became member of parliament for Bodmin, was father of Thomas Moyle, reader at Gray's Inn. Moyle owned lands in Devon and Somerset though by 1454 he was described as 'of Eastwell, Kent'. He died late in 1479 or in 1480, since his will is dated 11 December 1479 and was proved on 31 July 1480.

NORMAN DOE

Sources Baker, *Serjeants* · S. E. Thorne and J. H. Baker, eds., *Readings and moots at the inns of court in the fifteenth century*, 1, SeldS, 71 (1954) · C. Rawcliffe, *The Staffords, earls of Stafford and dukes of Buckingham, 1394–1521*, Cambridge Studies in Medieval Life and Thought, 3rd ser., 11 (1978) · Sainty, *Judges* · N. Doe, *Fundamental authority in late medieval English law* (1990) · J. C. Wedgwood and A. D. Holt, *History of parliament*, 1: *Biographies of the members of the Commons house, 1439–1509* (1936) · E. Foss, *Biographia juridica: a biographical dictionary of the judges of England … 1066–1870* (1870)

Moyle, Walter (1672–1721), politician and writer, was born at Bake in St Germans, Cornwall, on 3 November 1672 and

Walter Moyle (1672–1721), by George Vertue, pubd 1727

baptized at St Germans on 11 November, the third, but eldest surviving, son of Sir Walter Moyle (1627–1701), MP, and his wife, Thomasine (d. 1683), daughter of Sir William Morice (1602–1682). The Moyles, who had acquired Bake by marriage in the reign of Edward III, were one of the leading parliamentary families in seventeenth-century Cornwall. Walter's grandfather was John *Moyle (1591/2–1661). In his youth Moyle was well grounded in classical learning, probably at Liskeard grammar school. On 18 March 1689 he followed his father and grandfather in matriculating from Exeter College, Oxford. A set of his verses was inserted in the university collection of poems for William and Mary in 1689, but he left Oxford without taking a degree. On 26 January 1691 he was specially admitted at the Middle Temple, where he acquired a firm knowledge of history and the English constitution. However, he found 'there was a drudgery' in 'Law Lucrative' which he could never submit to' (*Whole Works*, 3). Instead, with a growing reputation for 'his good temper and great integrity', 'his wit, learning and judgement' (Polsue, 2.42), he entered London's political and literary society. His principal haunts comprised such coffee houses as Maynwaring's in Fleet Street, the Grecian in Devereux Court, and later Will's, off Covent Garden. Moyle's coterie included such lively and talented 'wits' as William Congreve, John Dennis, Charles Hopkins, John Glanvill, Charles Gildon, Anthony Hammond, Robert Masham, and William Wycherley, men whose common taste in women as well as literature prompted accusations of libertinism. Moyle's early translations of four dialogues by Lucian, written about 1693, were published with John Dryden's commentary and other translations in 1711. Moyle provided appropriate passages from Aristotle and Horace for Dryden's English version of Charles de Fresnoy's *Art of Painting* together with his own explanation of why imitation in art pleases. This won high praise from Dryden, who called him 'a most ingenious young gentleman, conversant in all the studies of humanity much above his years' (*The Works of John Dryden*, ed. W. Scott, 18 vols., 1808, 17.312). Some of Moyle's early observations on Cornish ornithology and botany were reported in the second edition of John Ray's *Synopsis methodica stirpium Britannicarum* (1696).

In 1695 Moyle was elected as MP for Saltash, Cornwall. He later described himself as an 'Old Whig' (*Whole Works*, 241), which placed him alongside 'the king's bitter enemies' (*Fifth Report*, HMC, 376–7) against the 'new whigs' of the Junto. Unsurprisingly, his family's hopes of much-needed court preferment were soon dashed. In pursuit of essentially republican or commonwealth aims that went well beyond the revolution of 1688, Moyle consorted with a wide circle that also attracted independent and tory support. Prominent associates included Lord Ashley, Andrew Fletcher, Robert Molesworth, Charles Montagu, John Toland, and John Trenchard. Thomas Hearne somewhat exaggeratedly described Moyle as the 'Coryphaeus of the Whigs' (T. Hearne, *Reliquiae Hearnianae*, ed. P. Bliss, 3 vols., 1869, 2.265).

Moyle's local fame centred on a speech in the Commons that supported a bill for the encouragement of seamen. However, his name frequently appeared on committee lists on subjects such as outlawries, the disinheritance of protestant heirs by papists, ecclesiastical courts, the regulation of elections, the sale of offices, the embezzlement of naval stores, the relief of debtors, the poor laws, hawkers and pedlars, and the manufacture of lustre. He was particularly active in the matter of the recoinage and was selected to confer with the Lords on the issue. In February 1697 he took the chair of the whole house and reported its findings on the public accounts.

Moyle was also an energetic polemicist. His campaigning reached its climax in response to William III's plans to keep a large standing army after the peace of Ryswick in 1697. Written in conjunction with Trenchard, the highly effective *An argument showing that a standing army is inconsistent with a free government, and absolutely destructive to the constitution of the English monarchy* (1697), won a wide circulation and was reprinted in 1698 and 1703. The pamphlet used abundant classical allusions and references to contemporary continental absolutism to insist that the liberties of Englishmen could only be maintained in peacetime by a citizen army. The court was so outraged that the secretary of state James Vernon ordered the printer before him in an unsuccessful attempt to discover the author's identity.

Moyle was not put forward for Saltash at the general election of 1698, for reasons that are unclear, although his local patron, Colonel Speccott, may simply have acquiesced in the growing practice of dividing the borough between the Buller and Carew families. Moyle still possessed a keen interest in the 'noble sport' of 'ministry hunting' (*Whole Works*, 14–15) and in 1699 he encouraged Hammond's efforts in the parliamentary inquiry into alleged mismanagement and corruption at the Admiralty. However, he shrewdly recognized that while their current tory 'allies' might be 'our protectors in the House of Commons', they were to be avoided as 'our governors in the ministry' (ibid., 19).

Moyle turned increasingly to academic pursuits. In 1698 his translation of Xenophon, *Discourse upon Improving the Revenue of the State of Athens*, appeared alongside Charles Davenant's *Discourse upon the Public Revenues and on the Trade of England* at that author's request. In his *Essay on the Lacedaemonian Government* (1698), he offered a somewhat idealistic portrayal of the provisions made by Lycurgus for the free people of Sparta. He attributed Sparta's stability and harmony to a series of careful constitutional checks and balances and its refusal to be dominated by faction. In 1699 Moyle circulated in manuscript an 'Essay on the constitution of the Roman government'. This erudite work, the most detailed study to date of the causes of the rise and fall of republican Rome, probably stimulated Montesquieu and won the praise of Gibbon. Its attraction for later radicals such as James Burgh and John Thelwall was Moyle's characteristic attempt to relate his historical observations to current circumstances. Imperial degeneration, he maintained, arose from a fatal failure to reinforce the first principles of political equilibrium as the balance of property changed.

On 6 May 1700 Moyle married at Bideford, Devon, Henrietta Maria (*bap.* 1677, *d.* 1762), daughter of John Davie (*d.* 1710), a rich merchant, alderman, and mayor of that town, and his wife, Mary Luscombe (*d.* 1709). In 1701 Moyle succeeded his father at Bake where the couple had two sons and one daughter. Although there is no evidence that he acted as a JP, his 'Charge to the grand jury at Liskeard' in April 1706 admonished the jurors for their religious zealotry and consequent corruption of manners. In the particularly busy year of 1708 he was appointed sub-warden of the stannaries; visited London in connection with a family property matter; and contributed towards erecting new buildings at Exeter College, Oxford. He later deplored the 'Sacheverell madness' (W. Moyle, *Works*, ed. T. Sergeant, 2 vols., 1726, 1.205) of 1709–10; was active in defence measures against the 'unnatural rebellion' (ibid., 1.253) of the Jacobite rising of 1715; and in April 1716 observed the 'uncommon warmth' (Coxe, 2.62–3) generated at the Grecian by the Bill for Septennial Parliaments. Even when originally praising the triennial legislation in 1694 Moyle had feared that 'like a baker's oven, the nation would never be cool' (*Whole Works*, 26) and his belief that bribery had since increased led him to support Stanhope's measure.

Illness increasingly rendered Moyle's life one of 'studious seclusion' (Polsue, 2.53). Construction of his new library at Bake was finished in the autumn of 1713, following which Moyle eagerly stocked it with the best works and editions of classical authors, both Greek and Roman, as well as books on travel and topographical history, ecclesiastical matters, and natural history. Subsequently Moyle copiously annotated many of these items with erudite observations. He also composed often controversial challenges to apparently long-standing misconceptions of classical and ecclesiastical scholarship. For example, his 'Dissertation on the age of Philopatris' cast doubts upon Lucian's authorship, and infuriated Thomas Hearne. Moyle's critique of the alleged 'Miracle of the thundering legion', addressed to 'Mr. K' (possibly Locke's cousin Peter King), drew acrimonious rejoinders from William Whiston and Thomas Woolston, but was defended by the bookseller Edmund Curll in *An Apology for the Writings of Walter Moyle* (1727). Mosheim published a Latin translation at Leipzig in 1733, and it subsequently won Gibbon's praise.

Moyle exchanged visits, gossip on current affairs, notes and antiquities with the Exeter physician and bibliophile, Dr William Musgrave. He also enjoyed exchanging specimens and observations with his near neighbours, the ichthyologist George Jago, vicar of Looe, and the botanist Lewis Stephens, vicar of Menheniot. He corresponded on natural history with William Sherard and Tancred Robinson and shared entomological observations with a Mr Dandridge at Sherard's request. However, his main labour of love was the formation of an ornithological collection, which he hoped would provide additions and improvements to John Ray's earlier work.

In January and May 1720 Dennis wrote affectionately to Moyle in an abortive bid to entice him to visit London again. However, Moyle died at Bake on 10 June 1721, and was buried at St Germans on 13 June. John Fox may well have mistaken cause for effect when he later recorded that Moyle 'lead a very sedentary life by which means he contracted a bad habit and died of polypus in his heart' (Brooking Rowe, 169). The reference in Moyle's monumental inscription in St Germans church to the fame arising from 'his learned tho' posthumous Works' (Polsue, 2.42) bears testimony not only to the many subsequent editions of his writings, but also to Thomas Sergeant's two-volume edition of *The Works of Walter Moyle, none of which were Ever before Published* (1726). Hammond collected those already in print into *The Whole Works of Walter Moyle* (1727) with a prefatory note and some of their mutual correspondence.

None of Moyle's three children married and they all predeceased his widow, who died on 9 December 1762 and was buried at St Germans on 15 December. Bake passed to the descendants of Moyle's younger brother Joseph. In 1808 all of Moyle's beloved books and manuscripts perished when the house was destroyed by fire. A catalogue of his library, listing more than 1500 volumes, has survived in the papers of Francis Gregor (Cornwall RO, PG/1967).

PATRICK WOODLAND

Sources *The whole works of Walter Moyle, esq.; that were published by himself to which is prefixed some account of his life and writings*, ed. A. Hammond, 2 vols. (1727) · C. Robbins, ed., *Two English republican tracts* (1969), 21–39 · C. Robbins, *The eighteenth-century commonwealthman* (1959) · parish registers, Devon and Cornwall Record Society [St Germans, Cornwall; Bideford, Devon; Buckland Brewer, Devon (transcripts)] · will, PRO, PROB 11/582, sig. 206 · J. Polsue, *A complete parochial history of the county of Cornwall*, 2 (1868), 42, 50, 53 · *Fifth report*, HMC, 4 (1876), 370–86 · Boase & Courtney, *Bibl. Corn.*, 1.374–7, 3.1289–90 · G. C. Boase, *Collectanea Cornubiensia: a collection of biographical and topographical notes relating to the county of Cornwall* (1890), 604 · F. A. Turk, 'Natural history studies in Cornwall, 1700–1900', *Journal of the Royal Institution of Cornwall*, new ser., 3 (1957–60), 229–79 · E. H. Rodd, *The birds of Cornwall and the Scilly Islands*, ed. J. Harting (1880) · *William Congreve: letters and documents*, ed. J. C. Hodges (1964) · W. Coxe, *Memoirs of the life and administration of Sir Robert Walpole, earl of Orford*, 1 (1798), 1.62–3 · J. Brooking Rowe, ed., 'Seventh report of the committee on Devonshire records', *Report and Transactions of the Devonshire Association*, 28 (1896), 110–73 · J. Dennis, *Original letters*, 2 vols. (1721), 1.159–62, 211–3 · R. Polwhele, *The history of Cornwall*, 7 vols. (1803–8), vol. 5, p. 113 · Z. Fink, *The classical republican* (1945), 170–74 · Foster, *Alum. Oxon.* · W. H. Rogers, 'Orleigh: an ancient house', *Report and Transactions of the Devonshire Association*, 58 (1926), 185–92, esp. 188–9 · Cornwall RO, Gregor papers, G/1767 · J. L. Vivian, ed., *The visitations of Cornwall, comprising the herald's visitations of 1530, 1573, and 1620* (1887), 334–5 · B. H. Williams, *Ancient West Country families and their armorial bearings* (1916), 150–57 · W. P. Courtney, *The parliamentary representation of Cornwall to 1832* (1889), 153 · L. G. Schwoerer, *No standing armies! The antiarmy ideology in seventeenth-century England* (1974) · J. R. Western, *The English militia in the eighteenth century* (1965) · H. Horwitz, *Parliament, policy and politics in the reign of William III* (1977) · J. P. Kenyon, *Revolution principles: the politics of party, 1689–1720* (1977) · DNB

Archives BL, document of discharge to W. Moyle re manor of Carvarton, Harley MS 2263, art. 224 · St John Cam., corresp. with John Reynolds

Likenesses G. Vertue, line engraving, BM, NPG; repro. in *The whole works of Walter Moyle*, vol. 1 [see illus.]

Wealth at death probably at least several thousand pounds; incl. £1800 left to children; also Bake and other properties: will, PRO, PROB 11/582, sig. 206

Moyne. For this title name *see* Guinness, Walter Edward, first Baron Moyne (1880–1944); Guinness, Bryan Walter, second Baron Moyne (1905–1992).

Moynihan, Berkeley George Andrew, first Baron Moynihan (1865–1936), abdominal surgeon, was born in Malta on 2 October 1865, youngest of three children and the only son of Captain Andrew Moynihan VC (1830–1867), of the 90th regiment, afterwards of the 8th foot (the King's regiment), and Ellen Anne, younger daughter of Thomas Parkin, cabinet-maker, of Hurst near Ashton under Lyne. His father, of Anglo-Irish origin and the third generation of the Moynihan to serve in the army, died of brucellosis (Malta fever) when Moynihan was about eighteen months old; his mother then settled in Leeds with her sister, the wife of Police-Sergeant Alfred Ball. Supported by a small army pension to his mother and a scholarship as an officer's son, and helped by the reputation of his father's decoration for gallantry, Moynihan was educated in London at Christ's Hospital (1875–81) and the Royal Naval School, New Cross (1881–3). He made little intellectual impact but did well at swimming, which remained his favourite recreation. Although he was originally

Berkeley George Andrew Moynihan, first Baron Moynihan (1865–1936), by unknown photographer

intended to follow his forebears into the army, he opted instead to study medicine and entered the Leeds medical school, which was then at the Yorkshire College. He graduated MB, BS (London) in 1887.

Loyal to his home institution Moynihan refused offers of a job elsewhere and was appointed house surgeon to William Mayo-Robson at the General Infirmary at Leeds, a post he held until early in 1889. Some (unrecorded) time in Berlin followed and he was then appointed resident surgical officer at the General Infirmary, a post which gave unrivalled experience of urgent admissions for surgical illnesses and which was generally regarded in the organization of large teaching hospitals as the path to preferment for an appointment to the consultant staff. In this post Moynihan attracted the attention of Thomas Richard Jessop, one of the senior surgeons in the area. Moynihan became Jessop's assistant in 1894 and also began his own private practice, but he was not elected to a vacancy which occurred at the infirmary in the same year, probably owing to (as his biographer notes) his youth and arrogance. However, two years later he became assistant surgeon at the infirmary; was advanced to full surgeon in 1906; and, after serving the then statutory twenty years, was appointed consulting surgeon in 1926. In 1909 he was made professor of clinical surgery in the University of Leeds, an institution which had been founded some years

previously. In later years he had an additional practice in London by commuting from Leeds and employing assistants who profited professionally from the association.

From 1896 the progress of Moynihan's surgical career was rapid, not only locally but also on the national and international stage. In this Moynihan was aided by his manual dexterity, his thoughtfulness about the underlying principles of the rapidly expanding discipline of abdominal surgery, by his undoubted qualities of oratory, and by his craftsmanship in the written word. According to E. W. Hey Groves:

> He took great care of his hands, keeping the skin from getting rough or cracked; while constantly, in idle moments, he practised feats of manual dexterity—for example, knotting and unknotting a piece of string with the fingers of one hand, both left and right.   (Groves, 13 April 1940, 604)

He also had a feel for the apt descriptive phrase: 'making the patient safe for surgery' (referring to the need for pre- and post-operative care), and 'the pathology of the living' (a plea for the study of disease in its early stages), being but two examples. The growth of his clinical practice was rapid and was certainly helped by what his *Dictionary of National Biography* entry called (perhaps a shade unfairly) his 'consummate showmanship'. Nevertheless, his pre-eminence had yet been little recognized in Britain when, in May 1903, he was invited by the American Surgical Association (the senior surgical body in the USA) to read a paper at its meeting. The experience enabled him to form lasting friendships with surgeons who were at the helm of the discipline in the United States, such as the brothers William and Charles Mayo, and George Crile. Publication of a number of texts—now inevitably dated but classics in their time—took place over the years 1903–24 and enhanced his reputation. Virtually nothing that he wrote has stood the scientific test of time, though his interpretation of the cause of duodenal ulcer was justified by the knowledge then available. The analytic approach he adopted was, however, of importance in the development of his clinical method of careful assessment, gentle surgery, and good decision-making, all of which have survived. He was an advocate, though not a practitioner, of the scientific approach to surgery, including the need for surgical research; in particular some of his lectures, including the Hunterian oration in 1927 and the Romanes lecture in Oxford in 1932, endorse this view.

Moynihan is remembered by surgeons chiefly for his surgical artistry but his influence went beyond this. He was part of the surgical establishment: elected to the council of the Royal College of Surgeons in 1912 and its president from 1926 for six years, he fostered its wider influence. He felt that eminent senior practising clinicians such as himself and Lord Dawson of Penn (president of the Royal College of Physicians) should develop and control medical research policy, and he was indeed able to persuade the college of surgeons in 1928 to establish an institute for research relevant to surgery at Buckstone Browne Farm (opened in 1933). However, the influence of the colleges on research was trenchantly opposed by Walter M. Fletcher, then largely responsible for the direction that the Medical Research Council was to take, who espoused the argument that it was not, in Gowland Hopkin's words to Fletcher, '"Distinguished Clinicians" who think the great thoughts which advance medicine'. The view which prevailed after a lengthy and often bitter clash both in public and in private correspondence was not that of Moynihan but of the non-clinical scientists, unfairly dubbed by him as truants from clinical research. Both sides had selective experience to support their views but it can be credibly argued that Moynihan's persistence and rhetoric entrenched an attitude that still persists in medical research in the UK. Moynihan was also unable to gain membership of the Royal Society, which he felt, without objectivity, was his due. He was also, because of his background as a 'provincial' surgeon in Yorkshire, convinced of the need for a more vociferous role for those outside London and campaigned for and founded both the *British Journal of Surgery* in 1913 and the Association of Surgeons of Great Britain and Ireland in 1920. In addition his flamboyance and success resulted in the formation in 1909 of a surgical club—ultimately to be called, when his baronetcy was awarded, the Moynihan Chirurgical Club—which to the end of the century allowed a group of distinguished members of the profession to travel between centres of surgical activity.

Between 1914 and 1915 Moynihan served in France as a consulting surgeon, rising to the rank of major-general. In this role he was influential in setting up the medical services for the British expeditionary force, particularly helped by his good command of both German and French. Later he continued as chairman of the Council of Consultants (1916–19) and as a member of the army medical advisory board. In 1917 he went to the United States as a semi-official delegate of the British government to promote American involvement in the war, a mission he conducted with great success—largely the outcome of his ability to sway an audience. Moynihan was knighted in 1912; appointed CB in 1917 and KCMG in 1918; and made a baronet in 1922. He then, in the same year, became a peer as Baron Moynihan of Leeds. In the Lords he was less successful than would have been predicted from his oratorical experience elsewhere but he had some influence on the affairs of the day in medical fields such as osteopathy. His other honours were numerous and included many honorary doctorates and memberships of societies.

Moynihan was married on 17 April 1895 to Isabella Wellesley Jessop (b. 1872/3), second daughter of his mentor in Leeds, Thomas Jessop. They had a son and two daughters. Lady Moynihan died on 1 September 1936, which seemed to remove Moynihan's will to live; he suffered a fatal stroke six days later at their home, Carr Manor, Meanwood, Leeds. He was buried, in spite of an offer of Westminster Abbey, in the Lawnswood cemetery at Leeds, the city with which he had identified throughout his career.

Moynihan was a complex personality. He had exceptional skills in his chosen field, marked ability for self-promotion, a sense of his own importance, and the possession of the physical and mental ability to achieve. He answered to his own description of the 'ideal' surgeon: 'a handsome man of distinguished presence, a man of wide knowledge and general culture, a man of great technical skill and sound judgment, and a man of compassionate heart'. Whether he fulfilled his own definition is open to some lingering doubt. He stood 6 feet tall and was broad in proportion; until middle life his hair was a fiery red. He was widely read and had an organizational ability that carried him to the front of his profession. Many of his contemporaries thought him over-indulgent of his own skills and the younger generation in the 1920s and 1930s felt that his attitudes should give way to a more truly analytic and scientific approach. However, his was a landmark in the development of British surgical practice and he mixed his individualistic personality with real contributions to surgical care and organization.　　HUGH DUDLEY

Sources D. Bateman, *Berkeley Moynihan, surgeon* (1940) • E. W. H. Groves, 'The life and work of Moynihan [pt 1]', *BMJ* (13 April 1940), 601–6 • E. W. H. Groves, 'The life and work of Moynihan [pt 2]', *BMJ* (20 April 1940), 649–51 • *The Times* (8 Sept 1936) • *Selected writings of Lord Moynihan* (c.1967) • private information (2004) [H. B. Devlin] • *DNB* • *CGPLA Eng. & Wales* (1936) • m. cert.

Archives Association of Surgeons of Great Britain and Ireland, London, MSS • British Journal of Surgery, London, MSS • RCS Eng., MSS • U. Leeds, Brotherton L., notes on visits to clinics in Berlin; papers

Likenesses F. J. Wilcoxon, marble bust, 1926, RCS Eng. • R. Jack, oils, 1927, Leeds General Infirmary; copy, RCS Eng. • W. Stoneman, photograph, 1929, NPG • M. Ayoub, group portrait, oils (*Members of the Council of Royal College of Surgeons, 1926–1927*), RCS Eng. • W. R. Dick, marble bust, Leeds General Infirmary • H. von Herkomer, portrait, priv. coll. • F. J. Wilcoxon, bronze bust, Leeds Medical School • bronze cast of Moynihan's hands, Leeds Medical School • photograph, Wellcome L. [*see illus.*]

Wealth at death £301,834 4s. 10d.: probate, 27 Oct 1936, *CGPLA Eng. & Wales*

Moynihan, (Herbert George) Rodrigo (1910–1990), painter, was born on 17 October 1910 in Santa Cruz de Tenerife, Canary Islands, the elder son and elder child of Herbert James Moynihan, fruit broker, and his Spanish wife, Maria de la Puerta. His childhood and youth were peripatetic and between 1924 and 1927 he attended high school in Madison, New Jersey. In 1927–8 he was once more in Europe and declared his intention to study painting. In 1928 he was enrolled as a student at the Slade School of Fine Art, University of London, where he studied under Professor Henry Tonks. A break in his progress occurred after his first year, when paternal pressure banished him to a broking office in the City; Tonks intervened on his behalf and from then onwards (he graduated in 1931) painting was his life.

An early cosmopolitanism in his outlook and tastes distinguished Moynihan from the run of his fellow students. At the same time there emerged characteristics of both innate conservatism and decided radicalism which were to shape the rest of his career and were marked features of his personality.

Moynihan first came to public notice through the exhibition 'Objective Abstractions' held at Zwemmer's Gallery, London, in March 1934, which he shared with Geoffrey Tibble, Graham Bell, and others. His works, evolved from elements of still life, were thickly encrusted, non-figurative paintings, indebted to the later paintings of J. M. W. Turner and Claude Monet; in this, they ran counter to the prevailing geometric abstraction of, for example, Ben Nicholson or Piet Mondrian. Although the works caused interest, he received little encouragement and, by the late 1930s, he returned to representational painting and gained considerable and increasing success over the following fifteen years. He was associated with, although not a member of, the Euston Road School (1937–9) through his friendship with William Coldstream, Victor Pasmore, Tibble, and Bell. Unlike them, he was not especially drawn to proletarian subject matter and his suave handling of paint and restricted colour range were distinct from, for example, those of Pasmore or Claude Rogers at that time.

In the 1940s Moynihan became a celebrated 'conservative' artist known for his wartime paintings such as *The Medical Inspection* (1943; IWM) and *Private Clarke, ATS* (1943; Tate collection). He was called up in 1940, trained as a gunner, joined the camouflage section, and was invalided out after two years. He was an official war artist (1943–4) and became ARA (1944). After the war he became professor of painting at the Royal College of Art, London (1948–57), and in 1951 he produced his one book, *Goya*. In 1953 he was appointed CBE and in 1954 RA. It seemed he was cast in a mould all too familiar in the history of British art—of brilliant early achievement followed by establishment renown. By the mid-1950s he sensed he was trapped. The renewed possibilities of abstraction, the break-up of his first marriage, and his resignation from the Royal College and the Royal Academy (both 1957) all contributed to remarkable changes in his art and his personal circumstances.

The painterly daring of Moynihan's early objective abstractions was harnessed to boldness of scale and dramatic colour to produce a handful of outstanding works. He was at first encouraged by the example of contemporary French *tachisme* and later by Sam Francis and American abstract expressionism, which he came to know well on several extended visits to New York in the 1960s with his second wife. It was during this period that they jointly edited (with Sonia Orwell and John Ashbery) the influential quarterly *Art and Literature* (1964–8).

Gradually the gestural freedom and liberality of options of this phase became burdensome; a hard-edged abstraction resulted in which areas of discrete colour are enlivened by bands, chevrons, and diamonds of contrasting hues. A 'sense of place' collides with severe geometric organization. At the same time Moynihan continued drawing from nature in the landscape near his homes in France (near Aix-en-Provence) and in Canada (New Brunswick).

In 1971 Moynihan resumed painting from life, chastened yet enriched by his second foray into abstraction. There then began what is perhaps his most notable contribution to painting—a series of still lifes of the quotidian objects on shelf or table top in his studio. They are painted in a light but intense scheme of colour, combining utmost dexterity of handling and subtle, unfussy composition. Such qualities also inform the portraits of the 1970s and 1980s which include penetrating studies of Francis Bacon, Sir William Coldstream, Friedrich von Hayek, and Benedict Nicolson (the last two in the collection of the National Portrait Gallery, as is his *The Rt Hon Margaret Thatcher, PM*, 1984). In 1979 he was re-elected to the Royal Academy, the year after his full-scale retrospective was held there. He had been honoured by a fellowship of University College, London, in 1970.

Moynihan's personality mixed Spanish hauteur, English conservatism, and a mercurial intellectual curiosity. He was well read and well travelled and in conduct was both confidential and secretive, sybaritic yet disciplined. Attractive, attentive, and amorous, he had several love affairs. Early good looks, Mediterranean in cast, continued to give distinction to a face he recorded in a series of perceptive self-portraits. In later years poor health diminished his activities. In painting, his place is assured by the still lifes of his last decades in which visual values alone effect a brooding and magical transformation of the oppressive material of day-to-day life.

On 26 November 1931 Moynihan married the painter Elinor Bellingham Smith [*see below*]. They had one son. They were divorced in 1960 and in the same year he married the painter Anne Diana Wishart (*b.* 1929), divorced wife of Michael Wishart and daughter of Sir James Hamet Dunn, first baronet, industrialist. They also had one son. Moynihan died in London in his South Kensington studio on 6 November 1990.

Moynihan's first wife, **Elinor Bellingham Smith** (1906–1988), painter, was born in December 1906, the daughter of Guy Bellingham Smith, obstetrician and registrar at Guy's Hospital, and a noted collector of drawings and prints. She trained as a ballet dancer, but injury forced her to abandon her career. She then went to the Slade School of Fine Art, where she studied under Henry Tonks and met Rodrigo Moynihan. Following their marriage she found herself at the centre of Moynihan's artistic coterie, latterly at Old Church Street, Chelsea, where she 'dispensed gallons of soup and not a little whisky, and supervised hilarious and crazy get-togethers' (*The Guardian*, 12 Nov 1988). A painter whose style was often compared to Berthe Morisot's, she had seven shows at the Leicester Galleries, London, and was one of the prizewinners in the 'Sixty Paintings for '51', exhibition as part of the Festival of Britain. After the collapse of her marriage she moved to Suffolk, where despite hip trouble and ill health she painted a remarkable series of landscapes, conveying in particular the bleakness and beauty of East Anglia in winter. Her London exhibitions included those at the New Art Centre in 1972, the Fitzroy Gallery in 1980, and the New Grafton Gallery in 1987, and a retrospective at the Royal Academy in 1990. She died on 4 November 1988. Examples of her work are in the Tate Gallery, Aberdeen Municipal Gallery, Wolverhampton Municipal Gallery, Preston Municipal Gallery, and elsewhere.

RICHARD SHONE, *rev.*

Sources R. Shone and J. Ashbury, *Rodrigo Moynihan* (1988) · *The Times* (8 Nov 1990) · *The Independent* (8 Nov 1990) · *The Guardian* (12 Nov 1988) · m. cert. [Elinor Bellingham Smith]
Archives Tate collection, papers | Tate collection, letters to his wife
Likenesses R. Moynihan, self-portrait, oils, NPG

Moysie, David (*fl.* 1577–1614), chronicler and notary public, was probably the son of James Moysie, burgess of Edinburgh, and his wife, Agnes Davidsone (*d. c.*1588). Details of his education are unknown, but he became a writer and notary public in Edinburgh. His name first occurs in an attestation of a lease in 1577. It is also likely that his crown service commenced in this year because he would not have had the necessary information for his *Memoirs of the Affairs of Scotland, 1577–1603* had he not been connected with the court. In 1586 he was a clerk of the privy council, and in the 1590s had moved to the office of the king's secretary, Sir John Lindsay of Kenmuir. On 3 August 1584, he obtained for his 'lawful' son David (indicating that he must have married some time previously) a grant of £32 per annum to assist the young man in his education. When the son died shortly afterwards, the grant was renewed in Moysie's own favour. He appears to have been admitted to the Society of Writers to the Signet some time before 1607 but his membership was suspended on 22 November 1609 until he could obtain proper admission.

Moysie apparently kept a record of events during his years of service, and seems to have collated them into a narrative late in life. In his dedication to King James of the *Memoirs* (Moysie, 1755, iii–iv) he states that he has been in royal service for thirty-seven years, which, if he began that service in 1577, would put the date of writing about 1614. He calls himself 'your Majesty's own old man' and states that he is 'now at the point of death' (Moysie, 1755, iv), which suggests that he died shortly afterwards.

The *Memoirs* were first published by Ruddiman in 1755, using a manuscript in the Advocates' Library (now in the National Library of Scotland) which included an account of the Gowrie conspiracy published by the authority of James VI shortly after that event in 1600. An early review by William Robertson in the year the work appeared found it too biased in the king's favour, owing to Moysie's being a royal servant. A later edition used an earlier manuscript from Wishaw House. ALEXANDER DU TOIT

Sources D. Moysie, *Memoirs of the affairs of Scotland, 1577–1603*, ed. J. Dennistoun, Bannatyne Club, 39 (1830), xi–xxvi · D. Moysie, *Memoirs of the affairs of Scotland* (1755), i–ii, iii–iv · M. Livingstone, D. Hay Fleming, and others, eds., *Registrum secreti sigilli regum Scotorum / The register of the privy seal of Scotland*, 8 (1982), 388 · C. T. McInnes, ed., *Accounts of the treasurer of Scotland*, 13 (1978), 308, 312 · *The Society of Writers to His Majesty's Signet with a list of the members* (1936), 268 · C. B. B. Watson, ed., *Roll of Edinburgh burgesses and guildbrethren, 1406–1700*, Scottish RS, 59 (1929), 363 · F. J. Grant, ed., *The commissariot record of Edinburgh: register of testaments*, 1, Scottish RS, old ser., 1 (1897) · *Edinburgh Review*, 1 (1755), 23–27
Archives NL Scot., Advocates' Library, MS of 'Memoirs'

Mozeen [*née* Edwards], **Mary** [*performing names* Miss Edwards, Mrs Mozeen] (*b.* in or before **1724**?, *d.* **1773**?), singer and actress, was possibly Mary Edwards, daughter of the singer Thomas Edwards (1659?–1730), a member of the king's musick, and his wife, Mary. If so, she would have been born by 18 June 1724, 'when Thomas Edwards drew his will and bequeathed £1000 in trust for the benefit of his children Mary and Thomas' (Highfill, Burnim & Langhans, *BDA*, 10.370).

Miss Edwards first appeared on stage on 19 November 1737 at the Drury Lane Theatre, as a 'country lass' in the pantomime *The Burgomaster Trick'd*, performed by the Lilliputian Company. She then acted Margerina in *The Dragon of Wantley* and Glowworm in the pantomime *Robin Goodfellow* on various occasions during 1738, and quickly established herself as a prominent figure on the London stage. At first associated chiefly with Drury Lane, she played the Page in Thomas Arne's opera *Rosamond* on 8 March 1740. Kitty Clive, who had assisted and possibly taught Edwards during the early stages of her career, took the title role. Edwards sang at Clive's benefit on 17 March 1740 and appeared in *The Tempest* the following May.

Later that year Miss Edwards began to perform at Lincoln's Inn Fields and became associated with Handel. She sang Clomiris in the première of *Imeneo* (22 November) and Achilles in *Deidamia* (10 January 1741) and participated in various revivals. Her performances at Drury Lane during 1741–3 were mainly at benefits for Mrs Clive, although she did appear as Juno in Arne's *The Judgment of Paris* on 12 March 1742. Her association with Handel continued in 1743 at Covent Garden as one of the Philistine and Israelite women in the première of *Samson* (18 February), and in the first London performance of *Messiah* (23 March). The parts written for her by Handel reveal a 'flexible light soprano' (Dean).

Miss Edwards continued to perform at Covent Garden as a singer and actress (she was Jessica in *The Merchant of Venice* on 14 March 1744) and often collaborated with Mrs Clive. In addition there were appearances at the Crown and Anchor tavern in the Strand and at the Haymarket, and in 1745–6 she returned to Drury Lane. Roles included Polly in John Gay's *The Beggar's Opera* and the goddess Hecate in Samuel Howard's *The Amorous Goddess* (25 April 1746), which was her last appearance as Miss Edwards. Shortly afterwards she married the Drury Lane actor Thomas *Mozeen (1720?–1768) and was billed as Mrs Mozeen when playing Miranda in *The Tempest* on 19 May 1746. Following a summer season at Jacob's Wells Theatre in Bristol (2 June–5 September), the Mozeens returned to Drury Lane until May 1748, when Mrs Mozeen made her last London appearance as Peggy in *The King and the Miller of Mansfield* by Robert Dodsley. David Garrick having dispensed with their services, they were engaged by Thomas Sheridan at the Smock Alley Theatre, Dublin. Mrs Mozeen remained in Dublin for two seasons from autumn 1748. It appears that she and her husband separated towards the end of 1749: Thomas Mozeen appeared frequently in London from 1750 onwards, but Mrs Mozeen moved to and performed in Bath (1750–54), followed by Belfast (1754–8) and Edinburgh (1758–65). She was acting in Norwich in 1767 and then returned to Ireland to perform in Belfast, Newry, Kilkenny, and Dublin between 1768 and 1773. Her son was acting in Belfast in September 1768.

Contemporary critical opinion held Mrs Mozeen in higher esteem as a singer than as an actress, in which capacity she was thought to be lacking confidence, conviction, and energy. It was also reported that she 'blushed at the least suggestive joke' (Highfill, Burnim & Langhans, *BDA*), but had 'no very keen scruples' (ibid.) in private, to the extent that Mrs Clive withdrew her support. No details survive after 1773 and it is presumed that Mrs Mozeen died during that year. DAVID J. GOLBY

Sources Highfill, Burnim & Langhans, *BDA*, 10.370–73 · W. Dean, 'Edwards', *New Grove*

Mozeen, Thomas (1720?–1768), actor and writer, was born in England, perhaps in 1720. His parents' names are unknown, but since he was 'of French extraction' (Chetwood, 194) possibly their surname was Mozin. William Chetwood says he was sponsored in some fashion by the radical tory divine Dr Henry Sacheverell: since Sacheverell died in 1724, perhaps it was for naturalization. Mozeen was educated for the law, but, 'probably finding the laboriousness or gravity of that profession unsuitable to his natural disposition, he quitted it for the stage, on which, however, he made no very conspicuous figure' (*Thespian Dictionary*).

Mozeen first acted as Stanley in *Richard III* with Theophilus Cibber in Henry Giffard's company at the old playhouse in Lincoln's Inn Fields (27 December 1742). That season he played a miscellany of supporting parts, such as Albany in *King Lear*, Rossano in Nicholas Rowe's *The Fair Penitent*, and Ratcliff in *Jane Shore* by the same author. For the next season he moved to Covent Garden, then played the first of many summers at Jacob's Wells theatre in Bristol. Mozeen supported Cibber in a short season at the Haymarket in autumn 1744, in such roles as Cassio in *Othello*, Paris in *Romeo and Juliet*, and Pylades in *The Distressed Mother* by Ambrose Philips. He appeared for the rest of the season at Drury Lane, now as Montano in *Othello*, but also as Lothario in *The Fair Penitent* and Valentine in Congreve's *Love for Love*. He returned for the next three seasons in supporting roles.

By 19 May 1746 Mozeen had married another member of the company, a Miss (Mary?) Edwards [see Mozeen, Mary (*b.* in or before 1724?, *d.* 1773?)], who 'sprung up under the Care of that eminent Actress Mrs. Clive' (Chetwood, 194). A year after Garrick assumed the management of the theatre in 1747, the Mozeens went to work instead for Thomas Sheridan in Dublin. While Mrs Mozeen returned to Dublin in 1748–9, her husband is untraced until the autumn of 1750, when he rejoined Garrick at Drury Lane. There he remained until 1764. During those fourteen seasons his acting career was stagnant. He played the same small repertory parts season after season: Sussex in Rowe's *Lady Jane Gray*, Conrad in *Much Ado*, Perez in Congreve's *The Mourning Bride*, Cromwell in *Henry VIII*, the Lieutenant in *Richard III*. By 1763 his name seldom appeared in the bills—only eight times in 1763–4, his last season at Drury Lane. Thereafter he made occasional appearances at Covent Garden, mostly in his old Drury Lane parts: Bardolph in 2 *Henry IV*, Elliot in Otway's *Venice Preserv'd*, and

Blunt in *The London Merchant* by George Lillo. His last appearance was in a new part, Gratiano, in *Othello*, on 5 December 1767.

Mozeen was a little more successful as a writer. His two-act farce *The Heiress, or, The Anti-Gallican* was performed once, at Drury Lane, on 21 May 1759. He wrote a monologue, 'Bucks have at ye All', performed by the celebrated comedian Tom King at Drury Lane on 19 March 1760, and he wrote numerous songs; 'The Subscription', set by Thomas Arne, was sung at Drury Lane on 5 November 1745, and a new song interpolated in *The Fair Quaker of Deal* was performed by the distinguished singer John Beard on 7 October 1755. Many of Mozeen's songs, prologues, and epilogues were written during his summer seasons at Bristol, for performance at Jacob's Wells, and for Sadler's Wells. They were published in *A Collection of Miscellaneous Essays in Verse* (1762), *The Lyrical Pacquet* (1764), and *Fables in Verse*, (2 vols., 1765). His most important work is a short picaresque novel (not a play, as has been supposed) entitled *Young Scarron*, published in Dublin in 1752. The narrator, Bob Loveplay, tells how he and his partner, Will Glitter, assembled a company to play the summer at 'a town in the North'. Allowing both for a romantic subplot and for satire, many of the characters and incidents ring true; it may well reflect Mozeen's experiences during the period in 1749–50 when his movements have not been traced. It is probably quite an accurate picture of theatrical conditions and practices in the smaller provincial towns in the middle of the eighteenth century. Mozeen died on 28 March 1768. His wife continued to perform in the provinces, at least until 1773. A son is known only by a performance in Belfast in 1768. ALAN HUGHES

Sources Highfill, Burnim & Langhans, *BDA* · A. H. Scouten, ed., *The London stage, 1660–1800*, pt 3: *1729–1747* (1961) · G. W. Stone, ed., *The London stage, 1660–1800*, pt 4: *1747–1776* (1962) · B. R. Schneider, *Index to 'The London stage, 1660–1800'* (1979) · *N&Q*, 3rd ser., 5 (1864), 500–04 · W. R. Chetwood, *A general history of the stage, from its origin in Greece to the present time* (1749) · D. E. Baker, *Biographia dramatica, or, A companion to the playhouse*, rev. I. Reed, new edn, rev. S. Jones, 3 vols. in 4 (1812) · *The thespian dictionary, or, Dramatic biography of the present age*, 2nd edn (1805) · T. Wilkinson, *The wandering patentee, or, A history of the Yorkshire theatres from 1770 to the present time*, 4 vols. (1795)

Mozley, Anne (1809–1891), essayist and journal editor, was born on 17 September 1809 in Gainsborough, Lincolnshire, the second daughter and sixth of the twelve children of Henry Mozley (1773–1845) and his wife, Jane Bramble (1783–1867). In 1815 her father moved his inherited printing business to Derby, where he became a leading citizen and supporter of the established church. Anne was educated at home by governesses, who followed the strict schoolroom routine imposed by her mother. This education was supplemented by teaching from local masters with academic connections. Her life remained on the surface that of a woman of intellectual and artistic interests belonging to the commercial élite of a provincial town, her time occupied by her family and her church. She and her sisters visited the poor, taught young women's classes, and undertook ecclesiastical embroidery based on Pugin's illustrations of medieval art. On her mother's death she and her youngest sister moved to Barrow-on-Trent, where they were recorded on census returns as 'annuitants'.

Anne Mozley's family was, however, in transition between the provincial commercial élite and the nation's minor intelligentsia. Although three of her six brothers remained in Derby, two of them expanding their father's printing business into a publishing firm, the others became beneficed clergymen following academic successes at Oxford, and made substantial contributions to serious journalism. The first, Thomas *Mozley (1806–1893), had John Henry Newman as his tutor, and he and one of the publishing brothers married Newman's surviving sisters, thus intertwining the family's personal and publishing interests inextricably with the Oxford Movement. Anne's literary career was made possible by the interests and contacts opened up by her brothers.

Anne Mozley's literary work began when she selected and edited Passages from the Poets (1837), Church Poetry (1843), Days and Seasons (1845), and Poetry, Past and Present (1849) for the high Anglican publisher James Burns. In 1842 Burns established a children's periodical called the Magazine for the Young for which Anne acted as editor, guiding among others the early literary efforts of Charlotte M. Yonge, who later wrote of her 'deft touches of criticism' and 'kind appreciation' (Yonge, 341). In 1846 she published a collection of historical narratives called Tales of Female Heroism, and her only identifiable work of fiction, The Captive Maiden: a Tale of the Third Century.

In 1847, after Newman's conversion to Roman Catholicism, Anne Mozley's brother James Bowling *Mozley (1813–1878) became co-editor of the Christian Remembrancer, an organ of what remained of the Oxford Movement, and his sister contributed long review articles on general topics until it ceased publication in 1868. In 1859 she wrote four articles for the short-lived Bentley's Quarterly Review (one of them the first review to identify the author of Adam Bede as a woman) and in 1861 she began to contribute short essays to the Saturday Review (continuing as a contributor until 1877) and longer ones to Blackwood's Magazine. All this work was unsigned and even the two volumes entitled Essays on Social Subjects: from the 'Saturday Review' (1865) do not identify the author. The bibliographic work done with the records of major Victorian publishers since the 1960s has shown that Anne Mozley averaged two articles a year in Blackwood's between 1865 and 1875, but her contributions to the Saturday Review and the Christian Remembrancer cannot be accurately identified.

Some of Anne Mozley's identifiable journalism dealt with topical religious or political subjects like 'English converts to Romanism' (1866) or 'Mr Mill on the subjection of women' (1869), but the essays she chose to republish were in the tradition stretching from Addison and Steele through Lamb to Thackeray, and discussed the minutiae of social life and the moral problems and obligations it raised, using a conventional man of the world persona and giving no hint of the author's actual sex. Typical pieces reprinted from the Saturday Review dealt with 'Cheerfulness', 'Commonplace people', and 'Social truth',

and from Blackwood's with 'Social hyperbole', 'Temper', and 'Schools of mind and manners'.

On the death of her brother James, Anne Mozley edited his papers, writing biographical introductions to his Letters (1885) and Essays Historical and Theological (1888). In 1884 Newman invited her to edit the letters of his Anglican period. Her nephew Francis Mozley wrote in a 'Memoir' included in her Essays from 'Blackwood' (published posthumously in 1892) that she had accepted the invitation because she felt that 'no one besides was left having such freedom of position and such personal recollection of the events that happened fifty or sixty years before'. Her edition was published in 1891. In 1889 her sight was failing and she returned to Derby to live with her surviving sisters and a niece. Anne Mozley died at St Werburgh, Derby, on 27 June 1891.   ELLEN JORDAN

Sources F. Mozley, 'Memoir', in A. Mozley, Essays from 'Blackwood' (1892) · The letters and diaries of John Henry Newman, ed. C. S. Dessain and others, [31 vols.] (1961–) · Letters of the Rev. J. B. Mozley, ed. A. Mozley (1885) · J. B. Mozley, introduction, in J. B. Mozley, Essays historical and theological, 1 (1878) · T. Mozley, Reminiscences: chiefly of towns, villages and schools, 2 vols. (1885) · C. M. Yonge, 'In memoriam: Anne Mozley', Monthly Packet (Sept 1891), 341 · D. Mozley, Newman family letters (1962) · M. Trevor, Newman, 2 vols. (1962) · P. A. H. Brown, London publishers and printers, c.1800–1870 (1982) · Hodson's booksellers, publishers and stationers directory (1855) · B. Alderson, 'Some notes on James Burns as a publisher of children's books', Bulletin of the John Rylands University Library, 76 (1994), 103–25 · Wellesley index

Archives Birmingham Oratory, Newman archives · NL Scot., corresp. with Blackwoods

Wealth at death £7072 6s. 1d.: probate, 28 July 1891, CGPLA Eng. & Wales

Mozley, James Bowling (1813–1878), theologian and journalist, was born on 15 September 1813 at Gainsborough, Lincolnshire, the eighth of eleven children and fifth son of Henry Mozley (1773–1845), bookseller, printer, and publisher, and his wife, Jane (1783–1867). Among James's elder siblings were Thomas *Mozley and Anne *Mozley. Henry Mozley moved the family and business to Derby in 1815, and in 1822 James followed his elder brother Charles to Grantham grammar school where, precocious and sensitive, he was victimized by its irascible master, the Revd Mr Andrews, and bullied. In June 1827, aged thirteen and guided by Thomas Mozley, he tried for a scholarship at Corpus Christi College, Oxford, failing only because he was too young to take up immediate residence. Anxious to leave Grantham, James was finally withdrawn in 1828. Early in 1829 he was entered for Rugby School, where Thomas Arnold had just become headmaster, but at fifteen was judged too old. After a period of private tuition with the Revd James Dean, Mozley matriculated as a commoner at Oriel College, Oxford, on 1 July 1830, taking up residence in October. Since Thomas Mozley had been an undergraduate at Oriel from 1825 to 1828 and a fellow since 1829, James enjoyed an early introduction to those senior figures soon to be prominent in the Tractarian (or Oxford) movement.

Like his brother Thomas, James belied his reputation as a student of high promise with a third class in literae humaniores in 1834, graduating BA on 4 December 1834 and MA in 1838. He won the chancellor's prize for an English essay in 1835, however, with 'The influence of ancient oracles in public and private life', which John Keble, Oxford's professor of poetry and a leading Tractarian, pronounced 'exceptionally good, and full of promise'. He was unsuccessful in various college fellowship competitions, twice at Oriel due to a reluctance to have two brothers on the foundation, and elsewhere due to his Tractarian affiliations. He remained in Oxford, from late 1837 residing and studying with Edward Bouverie Pusey, the regius professor of Hebrew and a Tractarian, and from the following summer as principal of a house in St Aldates rented by Pusey and John Henry Newman for the support of theological students without college fellowships. Variously dubbed the 'Coenobitium' or 'Monasterio' by Newman, its tenants, including such figures as Mark Pattison and the later converts Charles Seager and Albany Christie, were occupied with work in editing Pusey's Library of the Fathers. While the patristic expertise which Mozley acquired in these years was a foundation of his later scholarship, he also assisted in preparing the extensive Becket material among Richard Hurrell Froude's 'Remains', edited by Keble and Newman and published to controversy in two parts in 1837 and 1839. Ordained deacon on 10 June 1838, Mozley subsequently served as Newman's curate at St Mary's, Oxford, becoming one of his most intimate friends. In July 1840 he finally secured a Lincolnshire fellowship at Magdalen. He later held a succession of college offices, and took his BD in 1846.

Tractarian by conviction and not merely connection, Mozley was a leading contributor to the movement's polemic. He wrote eleven articles on historical and theological subjects for the *British Critic* when it was edited successively by Newman and Thomas Mozley between 1838 and 1843, and a pamphlet defending Newman's Tract 90 in 1845. Moreover, with the movement in paralysis between the suppression of the *Critic* in 1843 and Newman's conversion to Roman Catholicism two years later, he moved to ensure that the high church retained a periodical voice by joining William Scott of Hoxton as joint editor of the relaunched *Christian Remembrancer*, to which he contributed fifteen major articles between 1844 and 1854. He was also active in the foundation of *The Guardian* newspaper, a high-church weekly begun in January 1846.

Mozley, however, never belonged to Tractarianism's extreme wing. The *Remembrancer* was a designedly moderate successor to the *British Critic*, and at Newman's conversion in October 1845 he suffered none of his brother Thomas's spiritual vertigo: 'No one', wrote James the previous May, 'can prophesy the course of his own mind; but I feel at present that I could no more leave the English Church than fly' (*Letters*, 168). His dissociation from Newman was confirmed by critical articles in the *Remembrancer* in January 1846 and 1847, which Newman maintained had exploited confidential conversations between them. But it was Mozley's reaction to the Gorham judgment of 1850 which marked his decisive breach from the movement. The judgment, which provoked further high-church secessions, including those of Henry Manning and Robert and Henry Wilberforce, only reinforced Mozley's orthodoxy. Surrendering his role at the *Christian Remembrancer* in January 1855, he proceeded to issue three works directed to the theological disputes aroused by the case, *A Treatise on the Augustinian Doctrine of Predestination* (1855), *The Primitive Doctrine of Baptismal Regeneration* (1856), and later *A Review of the Baptismal Controversy* (1862). Latitudinarian and eirenic, they sought to demonstrate that the Gorham judgment was consistent with Anglican doctrine and hence to reconcile high-church and evangelical parties. Mozley always retained his high-church sympathies and associations, but decisively withdrew from partisan engagement thereafter.

On 16 April 1856 Mozley accepted the college living of Old Shoreham, Sussex, preparatory to his marriage, in Oxford on 16 July, to Amelia Ogle (*c*.1822–1872), third daughter of James Adey Ogle, Oxford's regius professor of medicine and formerly Newman's mathematical tutor. Amelia's twin sister, Caroline, was married to Mozley's close friend Manuel John Johnson, astronomer and keeper of the Radcliffe Observatory, a Tractarian sympathizer and briefly resident of the St Aldates establishment. The Mozleys had no children.

Mozley remained little known beyond limited theological circles until the appearance of his Bampton lectures of 1865, published as *Eight Lectures on Miracles*, which provoked considerable debate and ran to six editions. The work, which attempted to meet scientific objections to miracles on rationalist grounds, established his wider reputation as a theologian of power and originality. In 1869 Mozley was select preacher at Oxford and, in Gladstone's first act of ecclesiastical preferment, was made a canon of Worcester, partly in return for his active role in Gladstone's election as MP for Oxford University in 1847. After two years at Worcester, Mozley left in 1871 to succeed the ineffectual Robert Payne Smith as regius professor of divinity at Oxford, becoming a canon of Christ Church, and then DD by decree on 11 November. At his appointment, the benefice of Ewelme was separated from the chair so that Mozley could retain his living at Old Shoreham.

Mozley's tenure as regius professor was a troubled one. His wife, Amelia, died from a neuralgic illness on 29 July 1872; thereafter her widowed sister, Caroline Johnson, lived with him at Old Shoreham and assisted in the parish. Three years later, in November 1875, he suffered a stroke from which he only partially recovered. From January 1876 John Wordsworth, later bishop of Salisbury, deputized as regius by delivering Mozley's lectures, and in the spring Mozley spent several months of convalescence at St Leonards, Sussex, preparing his university sermons and Old Testament lectures for publication. He returned to Oxford and presented his professorial lectures directly in Michaelmas term 1876, but the strain again proved too great, and Mozley repaired to Old Shoreham. He suffered a second stroke at the end of December 1877, and died at his vicarage there on 4 January 1878 without regaining consciousness. He was buried a week later in St Sepulchre's cemetery, Oxford, alongside his wife.

Mozley was a notoriously poor lecturer and preacher, but his published work enjoyed the highest reputation. His *Sermons Preached before the University of Oxford and on Various Occasions* (1876), and especially *Ruling Ideas in Early Ages and their Relation to the Old Testament Faith* (1877), his lectures from the 1874–5 academic year, demonstrated the logic and robustness of his mature thought and were widely acclaimed. Mozley's reputation was further enhanced by the posthumous appearance of numerous works edited by his sister Anne. Much of his hitherto anonymous periodical journalism was collected and reprinted with a biographical introduction in two volumes entitled *Essays, Historical and Theological* (1878), while his *Letters* (1885), which constitute a vital source for the Tractarian movement, were similarly edited and introduced. Anne Mozley also edited his *Sermons Parochial and Occasional* and *Sermons Practical and Occasional*, both of 1879, and the repetitive *Lectures and other Theological Papers* (1883). R. W. Church, the Oxford Movement's first chronicler, ultimately judged Mozley, after Newman, 'the most forcible and impressive of the Oxford writers' (*The Oxford Movement*, 1891, 293), while Goldwin Smith, no friend to orthodox religion, considered him 'the greatest theologian … that the Anglican Church possessed' (Middleton, 145).

S. A. SKINNER

Sources *Letters of the Rev. J. B. Mozley*, ed. A. Mozley (1885) · J. B. Mozley, *Essays historical and theological*, 2 vols. (1878) · R. D. Middleton, *Magdalen studies* (1936), 145–74 · *The Times* (5 Jan 1878), 9f · *Church Times* (11 Jan 1878), 15c · *The Times* (8 Nov 1855), 4e–f · *The Times* (5 June 1866), 6b–e · *The Times* (6 June 1866), 6a–d · *The Times* (8 June 1876), 7a–d · *The Times* (27 Dec 1884), 10a · *The Spectator* (3 Feb 1877), 143a–144b · *The Spectator* (5 May 1883) · *The Spectator* (15 Nov 1884), 1515a–1517a · Lord Blachford, 'Mozley's essays, historical and theological', *Nineteenth Century*, 5 (1879), 1013–37 · *The Guardian* (13 June 1883), 884, col. a–885, col. a · *The letters and diaries of John Henry Newman*, ed. C. S. Dessain and others, [31 vols.] (1961–), vols. 2–7, 11–13, 17, 19, 25–8, 30 · H. P. Liddon, *The life of Edward Bouverie Pusey*, ed. J. O. Johnston and others, 4 vols. (1893–7) · T. Mozley, *Reminiscences, chiefly of Oriel College and the Oxford Movement*, 1 (1882), 151–2 · Foster, *Alum. Oxon.* · Boase, *Mod. Eng. biog.*

Archives Birmingham Oratory, Newman corresp., letters to J. H. Newman · BL, corresp. with W. E. Gladstone, Add. MSS 44366–44434, *passim*

Likenesses photograph, repro. in Middleton, *Magdalen studies*, facing p. 145 · wood-engraving (after photograph by C. Rogers), NPG; repro. in *ILN* (2 Feb 1878)

Wealth at death under £12,000: resworn probate, July 1878, *CGPLA Eng. & Wales*

Mozley, John Kenneth (1883–1946), Church of England clergyman, was born on 8 January 1883 at Horsforth, Leeds, the third son of John Rickards Mozley (1840–1931), former fellow of King's College, Cambridge, and an inspector of workhouse schools under the Local Government Board, and his wife, Edith Merivale, daughter of Bonamy Price. Mozley obtained a scholarship at Malvern College (1896–1898), but after a serious illness was moved to Leeds grammar school. He proceeded to Pembroke College, Cambridge, in 1902, where he was a scholar.

Mozley's career in the university was distinguished. He was president of the union, and was placed in the second division of the first class in part one of the classical tripos (1905) and the first class in part two of the theological tripos (1906). He gained the George Williams (1906) and Norrisian (1909) prizes and the Crosse (1906) and Allen (1907) scholarships. He was ordained deacon in 1909 and priest in 1910 and from 1907 until 1919 was a fellow of Pembroke College, Cambridge, of which he became dean in 1909. In 1910 he married Mary Geraldine (d. 1941), daughter of the Revd John William Nutt, fellow of All Souls College, Oxford, and rector of Harpsden, Henley-on-Thames. They had no children.

In 1920 Mozley left Cambridge to take up the office of principal of Leeds Clergy School, where he remained until 1925 when the school was closed for lack of funds. He then moved to a similar post as warden of St Augustine's House, Reading. From 1920 until 1930 he was lecturer of Leeds parish church, a position he regarded highly and to which he returned in the last year of his life.

Mozley was a Liberal in politics, but, on the whole, a conservative in ecclesiastical affairs. He represented an intelligent and well-informed Anglican orthodoxy, but at the same time was deeply influenced by the writings of the Revd Dr Peter Taylor Forsyth, the Congregationalist.

Mozley was seen by some contemporaries as one of the leading figures in the theological world of his generation. He was an important member of the archbishops' commission on Christian doctrine and one of his most learned books, *The Impassibility of God* (1926), was the outcome of research undertaken for that commission. Among his writings his first published work, *Ritschlianism* (1909), was a penetrating account of an influential theological movement. *The Doctrine of the Atonement* (1915) is perhaps the best example of Mozley's power of exposition and the clearest statement of his fundamental convictions. But Mozley's most significant contribution was perhaps his ability to write simply and to interest many among the lay population in theological issues. He wrote a series of popular articles on religious matters for *The Times*. A contemporary said of him that 'though he was a scholarly theologian and churchman he had nothing of the "highbrow" or ecclesiastic about him' (*The Times*, 25 Nov 1946, 7). A good example of his more popular published work is *The Beginnings of Christian Theology* (1931).

The reputation built by Mozley's writings led to his being made a canon of St Paul's in 1930 and chancellor of the cathedral in 1931, playing a role in running the cathedral as well as presenting regular sermons which were both theological and evangelistic in tone. From 1937 to 1944 he was preacher of Lincoln's Inn. In 1941 Mozley felt compelled to resign his canonry because of his poor health, exacerbated by the strain of life in St Paul's during the night bombing of the City, and also the shock of the sudden death of his wife in that year, which was a consequence of the strain of continuous air raids. After his retirement Mozley continued to promote theological study, working particularly with women who were reading for the Lambeth diploma. He died at Merivale, Oak Road, Headingley, Leeds, on 23 November 1946, and was buried at Paddington new cemetery, Mill Hill, London, on 27 November.

W. R. MATTHEWS, *rev.* MARC BRODIE

Sources *The Times* (25 Nov 1946) · *The Times* (26 Nov 1946) · F. W. Roberts, ed., *The Malvern College register: second supplement* (1949) · B. Benham and C. J. Stonebridge, eds., *The book of matriculation and degrees: a catalogue of those who have been matriculated or admitted to any degree in the University of Cambridge from 1901 to 1912* (1915) · Venn, *Alum. Cant.* [John Rickards Mozley] · *WWW* · private information (1959) · *CGPLA Eng. & Wales* (1947)
Wealth at death £26,750 15s. 8d.: probate, 27 March 1947, *CGPLA Eng. & Wales*

Mozley, Thomas (1806–1893), Church of England clergyman and writer, was born on 15 September 1806 at Gainsborough, Lincolnshire, the third son of Henry Mozley (1773–1845), bookseller, printer, and publisher, and his wife, Jane (1783–1867). Anne *Mozley was his younger sister, and James Bowling *Mozley his younger brother. His father moved the family and business to Derby in 1815, and Mozley entered Charterhouse School in June 1820. On 17 February 1825 he matriculated at Oriel College, Oxford, where in April of the following year he became the pupil, and subsequently intimate friend, of John Henry Newman. Despite a promising reputation, Mozley obtained only a third class in *literae humaniores* in 1828, graduating BA in that year and MA in 1831. At Christmas 1828 he became tutor to Viscount Doneraile's son, Hayes St Leger, later the fourth viscount, at Cheltenham, before he and J. F. Christie were elected on 24 April 1829 to the Oriel fellowships vacated by William Churton and E. B. Pusey. Mozley was ordained deacon in December 1831 and priest in the following year.

Early in 1832 Mozley served as temporary curate to the Revd James Round in two parishes, St Runwald's and St Nicholas's, in Colchester, but his health broke down and after a few months he accepted instead the temporary curacy of Buckland, near Oxford. In July of that year he became perpetual curate of the college living of Moreton Pinkney, Northamptonshire. After three years he returned to Oriel to collaborate more closely with Newman, serving as junior treasurer from 1835, though declining the offer of a tutorship. From the inception of the Oxford Movement, Mozley was an ardent supporter, and an enthusiastic distributor of the Tracts for the Times.

On 27 September 1836 Mozley married Newman's sister Harriett Elizabeth (1803–1852), eldest daughter of John Newman (1767–1824), banker and brewer, of London, and his wife, Jemima, *née* Fourdrinier (1772–1836), at St Werburgh's, Derby. (Mozley's elder brother, John (1805–1872), had married Jemima Charlotte (1808–1879), second daughter of the Newmans, in the previous April.) At his marriage he resigned his college fellowship and the living of Moreton Pinkney, and accepted instead the living of Cholderton, Wiltshire, where he directed the rebuilding of the church and improvement of the parsonage. Parochial obstacles to the project, which Mozley recalled late in life as 'a prodigious folly', formed the basis of his only fictional work, *The Church Committee, or, An Incident in the Life of Mr John Wilful*, which appeared anonymously as part of an unfinished series in 1841.

Mozley's first publication of note was a pseudonymous pamphlet of November 1838, *A Dissection of the Queries on the Amount of Religious Instruction and Education*, which was

Thomas Mozley (1806–1893), by Maria Giberne, 1832

addressed to Sir Robert Inglis, MP for Oxford University, and signed 'By a Clergyman of South Wilts'. It denounced the intrusion of the poor law commissioners into the church's management of education, and their survey's susceptibility to exaggerated claims of nonconformist support. The polemical brio of the pamphlet alerted Newman to Mozley's potential as a reviewer for the *British Critic*, a high-church literary and theological quarterly for whose editorial control Newman had successfully manoeuvred earlier that year. Mozley débuted with three articles in the issue of April 1839. Having written sixteen by the time of Newman's retirement as editor in 1841, Mozley was his natural successor. He inaugurated his editorship in July with a notorious attack on the Oxford Margaret professor, Godfrey Faussett, a prominent critic of the Tractarians. The article scandalized even the movement's leaders, confirming Mozley's reputation as one of its *enfants terribles* and reputedly damaging his prospects of preferment. Mozley was at once disinclined and powerless to restrain emerging reviewers such as Frederick Oakeley and W. G. Ward, the immoderate tone of whose articles ultimately precipitated the closure of the *British Critic* in October 1843. In all, Mozley contributed thirty-one articles.

In July and August 1843 Mozley and his wife visited Normandy, where he spent some time in the company of Roman Catholic priests. He returned on the point of conversion and, amid controversy over the Romanizing tone of the *British Critic*, resigned his editorship. Mindful of Mozley's impetuous nature, Newman exhorted him to wait two years before taking any further step. Mozley's undogmatic temperament and theological heterodoxy, reinforced by the anti-Roman sentiments of his wife, swiftly reconciled him to the Church of England, though Harriett Mozley blamed Newman for her husband's attack of 'Roman fever' and thereafter broke off relations with her brother.

In 1844 Mozley began his long association with *The Times*, for which he wrote leading articles almost daily until 1886. A great favourite of John (III) Walter (who was proprietor of the paper from 1847 and had been an undergraduate at Oriel when Mozley was a fellow), he was much the best paid of its leader writers and a stalwart during the long and influential editorship of J. T. Delane. In 1847 he resigned the living of Cholderton, moving to Guilford Street, Russell Square, London. Harriett Mozley, who gained some reputation as the writer of religious tales for children, of which the best known were *The Fairy Bower* (1841) and *The Lost Brooch* (1841), died there on 17 July 1852, whereupon Mozley lived with his sister Elizabeth. He settled at Finchampstead, Berkshire in 1857, and in June 1861 married his second wife, Elizabeth Baker Bradshaw, youngest daughter of George Bradshaw, formerly a captain in the 5th dragoon guards. Mozley's daughter, Grace (1839–1908), his only child, married Dr William Langford, an engineer, on 2 July 1864. They settled in Australia, where she later published two novels.

In 1868 Mozley accepted the Oriel living of Plymtree, Devon, and went on half pay at *The Times*. In the following year he went as the paper's correspondent to Rome to cover the proceedings of the ecumenical council, but after five months his health began to suffer and he returned in the spring of 1870. His two volumes of *Letters from Rome on the Occasion of the Oecumenical Council, 1869–1870* finally appeared in 1891. In 1874 he became rural dean of Plymtree and, in 1876, when the deanery was divided in two, of Ottery St Mary. In 1878 he published *Henry VII, Prince Arthur and Cardinal Morton*, a study of the chancel screen at Plymtree church. His eyesight failing, Mozley resigned the living in 1880 and retired to Cheltenham, where he spent the remainder of his days in literary pursuits. Much the best known of these is his genial and absorbing *Reminiscences, Chiefly of Oriel College and the Oxford Movement* (2 vols., 1882), which, while notorious for its unreliability and anecdotal character, remains indispensable for its picture of first-generation Tractarianism: 'Not even the famous *Apologia*' wrote Mark Pattison, 'will compare with the two volumes … in respect of minute fullness, close personal observation, and characteristic touches' (*The Academy*, 1 July 1882, 1–3). Mozley also published *Reminiscences, Chiefly of Towns, Villages, and Schools* in two volumes in 1885. Three works of theology were hurriedly composed in his later years, *The Word* (1889), *The Son* (1891), and *The Creed, or, A Philosophy* (1893), which included a sketchy autobiographical preface. Speculative in character and discursive in tone, they are notable chiefly for their eccentricity.

Mozley died quietly in his armchair at 7 Lansdowne Terrace, Cheltenham, on 17 June 1893, survived by his second wife. A zealous advocate of the Tractarian movement in his early years, Mozley came to view his youthful radicalism with some nonchalance. His unorthodox views on the Trinity increasingly distinguished him from any church party, while the inaccuracies and indiscretions of the *Reminiscences* drew numerous reproofs. As a Victorian man of letters, however, he has been neglected; the anonymity of his periodical and newspaper journalism, which formed the overwhelming bulk of his writing, has cost Mozley a wider reputation. S. A. SKINNER

Sources T. Mozley, *Reminiscences, chiefly of Oriel College and the Oxford Movement*, 2 vols. (1882) · T. Mozley, *Reminiscences: chiefly of towns, villages and schools*, 2 vols. (1885) · T. Mozley, preface, in T. Mozley, *The creed, or, A philosophy* (1893), v–xix · *The Times* (20 June 1893), 5f · *The Athenaeum* (24 June 1893), 798–9 · *Saturday Review*, 75 (1893), 674 · *Church Times* (23 June 1893), p. 659, col. 4 · *The letters and diaries of John Henry Newman*, ed. C. S. Dessain and others, [31 vols.] (1961–) · *Letters of the Rev. J. B. Mozley*, ed. A. Mozley (1885) · R. L. Arrowsmith, ed., *Charterhouse register, 1769–1872* (1974), 265 · Foster, *Alum. Oxon.* · *GM*, 2nd ser., 6 (1836), 536 · *GM*, 2nd ser., 38 (1852), 324 · *GM*, 2nd ser., 38 (1852), 324 · Crockford (1893) · Boase, *Mod. Eng. biog.* · Allibone, *Dict.* · *Men and women of the time* (1891), 650 · F. W. Newman, *Contributions chiefly to the early history of the late Cardinal Newman* (1891), viii, 72–3, 113–14 · S. J. Kunitz and H. Haycraft, eds., *British authors of the nineteenth century*, another edn (New York, 1955)
Archives Birmingham Oratory, corresp. · News Int. RO | Bodl. Oxf., corresp. with J. H. Newman · LPL, letters to C. P. Golightly
Likenesses M. Giberne, drawing, 1832, priv. coll. [*see illus.*] · photograph (after drawing by M. Giberne, 1832), Oriel College, Oxford · photograph, repro. in G. E. Buckle, S. Morison, I. McDonald, and others, eds., *The tradition established, 1841–1884* (1939), vol. 2 of *The history of The Times*, 126
Wealth at death £2756 17s. 6d.: probate, 9 Sept 1893, *CGPLA Eng. & Wales*

Mubarak ud-Daula (1757/8–1793). *See under* Bengal, nawabs of (*act.* 1756–1793).

Mucklow, William (*bap.* 1630?, *d.* 1713), religious writer, was probably the son of John Mucklo baptized on 31 October 1630 at Northfield in Warwickshire, but nothing else is known of his background and origins. In 1662 he was a prisoner in the London Bridewell with the Quaker Thomas Ellwood and therefore was presumably a Friend before that date. Ellwood recorded in his journal that 'one William Mucklow … having observed that I only was unprovided of lodging, came very courteously to me, and kindly offered me the use of his hammock while I should continue a prisoner' (Ellwood, 137–8). On 14 July 1670 Mucklow married Priscilla Selby (*d.* 1679) at Mortlake in Surrey.

In 1671, Mucklow, along with the Quakers Mary and John Pennyman and Ann and Thomas Mudd, rejected the leadership of George Fox and the increasing organization of the movement at both the central and local level, which had resulted in a more authoritarian structure. Opposition had begun some years before under John Perrot, who among other matters had criticized the Quaker ritual of removing the hat in meetings. This was one of the issues discussed in a tract which has been attributed to Mucklow entitled *The Spirit of the Hat, or, The Government of the Quakers among themselves*, published in 1673 and reprinted in 1700 as *A Bemoaning Letter*. In it he highlighted the tension between the authority of the meeting and that of the individual conscience lamenting that 'those that forbore the custom of their hats in prayer, could not partake of their rights as a member until a renunciation thereof' (p. 23). He went on to declare that refusal to remove the hat did not stem from a 'want of reverence to the Holy, Pure God', but was because Mucklow felt that 'he doth not require this of us, but rather a more spiritual reverence' (pp. 25–6). The pamphlet was also a biting denunciation of Fox's leadership and the growing centralization of the movement in the hands of London Quakers; it was particularly aimed at the newly established central Quaker meeting known as the second day morning meeting, which met each Monday, or as the Quakers termed it, second day, mainly to examine books for publication and also to co-ordinate Quaker ministerial work in London. Mucklow felt that Fox had compromised the original Quaker message of the light as the central guide in religion, and that he was trying to reduce people to 'a formal faith' and 'build up that which they once pulled down' (p. 19). According to Mucklow, 'Foxonian-unity' meant that Quakers had become little better than Catholics, whom he said asked others to 'believe as the church believes'. He went on to add 'so likewise saith G[eorge] Fox; but I say nay, I am not to believe a thing barely because the church believes it, but because it's manifested in me' (pp. 11–12).

A short pamphlet war ensued between Mucklow and leading Quakers, with the publication in 1673 of William Penn's response, entitled *The Spirit of Alexander Copper-Smith … Justly Rebuk'd*, a defence of Quaker organization in which Penn suggested that a lack of the former would result in Ranterism and atheism. Light is thrown on the curious title of this tract from Penn's work *Judas and the Jews* (1673), in which he vindicates the use of authority in the church. Alexander, he says, 'was denied and rejected, notwithstanding that he made profession of Christianity' because he took 'occasion against the apostle's authority, and the power of the Elders in the church' (Penn, *Judas and the Jews*, 12–13). Mucklow was next attributed with having written *Tyranny and Hypocrisy Detected* (1673/4), in similar vein to his previous tract, which was answered in the same year by Penn in *Judas and the Jews*. In the broadside *Liberty of Conscience Asserted Against Impositions* (1673/4) Mucklow denied authorship of *Tyranny and Hypocrisy* and went on to criticize the growing authority of the leading London Quakers when he wrote that 'Christ within us, was then to be head, but now the body without us'. George Whitehead replied to this in *The Apostate Incendiary Rebuked* (1673), describing Mucklow as 'an engine of Satan and member of anti-christ' for 'striking at elders and ancient Friends among us in this city of London', whom he felt had grown in 'that divine understanding, wisdom and power … wherein all the apostates and antichrists in the world can not come near nor touch them' (pp. 3–4). As for the authorship of *Tyranny and Hypocrisy* he insisted that Mucklow had been associated with it in some way. Mucklow

was adamant that he had not been 'one of the cabal' involved in its writing, stating: 'as touching the person that is said to be the author of that book; I declare to you and all the world, that I have not the least acquaintance with him' (Mucklow, *Liberty of Conscience*). This answer did not convince Whitehead who replied, 'he hath appeared in the very same language of the *Spirit of the Hat and Tyranny &c* against us'. He went on to add, however, that Mucklow 'seems to clear himself more from being directly the author of the latter then of the former; for that *Spirit of the Hat* shows forth W. M.'s perverse spirit and language (against the *Body*, and our *Ministry* and Elders) reiterated in this late paper' (G. Whitehead, *Apostate*, p. 24). The question of authorship is indeed an intriguing one; certainly there do seem to be similarities in terms of this group of pamphlets, and Whitehead may well be correct in his point about language-use.

Fox noted in his *Journal* in 1675 that Mucklow and others had 'run out' and become 'open opposers of truth' (*Journal of George Fox*, 2.315), but it would appear that Mucklow gradually became reconciled to the Friends. Early signs of this can be seen in John Pennyman's letters to Mucklow in the early 1690s in which the former regretted the distance which had grown up between them, perhaps because Mucklow no longer wished to continue his attack on the Quaker leadership. Later on 21 July 1704 Whitehead wrote with reference to Mucklow on the title-page of a copy of *The Apostate Incendiary* that the book should not be reprinted for it had 'pleased God to recover him to a better mind; and to be more in charity with Friends than when this was printed, and he hath been kind to Friends for many years last past' (Smith, *Descriptive Catalogue*, 2.190). This is borne out by a revision to Mucklow's will dated 24 December 1712 in which he left a total of £80 to the two men's meetings at the Bull and Mouth and Devonshire House, and to the women's meeting at Aldersgate Street, all in London. Mucklow, who was recorded as a member of Kingston monthly meeting, and was living in Wandsworth, Surrey, at the time he made his will in 1710, died on 18 June 1713 of a 'mortification', aged eighty-two. He was survived by three children: sons John and Selby, and a daughter, Elizabeth, wife of the pamphleteer Thomas Zachary of Beaconsfield. He appears to have been a man of some means for in addition to his bequests he owned properties in Worcestershire and Leicestershire.

CAROLINE L. LEACHMAN

Sources J. Smith, ed., *A descriptive catalogue of Friends' books*, 2 (1867) · J. Smith, ed., *A descriptive catalogue of Friends' books*, suppl. (1893) · *The journal of George Fox*, ed. N. Penney, 2 (1911) · T. Ellwood, *The history of the life of Thomas Ellwood* (1714) · 'Clauses of wills', RS Friends, Lond., London six weeks meeting records, fols. 235-6 · digest registers of births, marriages, and burials, RS Friends, Lond. · *The papers of William Penn*, ed. M. M. Dunn, R. S. Dunn, and others, 1 (1981) · will, PRO, PROB 11/534, sig. 140, fols. 10–11 · *DNB* · *IGI* · J. Pennyman, *A short account of the life of Mr John Pennyman* (1703)
Wealth at death approx. £170; incl. bequest of £80; also houses in Worcester and Leicester: will, PRO, PROB 11/534, sig. 140

Mucnoe (*fl. c.*500). *See under* Connacht, saints of (*act. c.*400–*c.*800).

Mudd, Ann (*b.* 1612/13, *d.* in or after **1693**). *See under* Pennyman, John (1628–1706).

Mudd, John (1555–1631). *See under* Mudd, Thomas (*b.* 1559/60, *d.* in or after 1619).

Mudd, Thomas (*b.* 1559/60, *d.* in or after **1619**), Church of England clergyman and composer, was probably born in London. His father, Henry Mudd, served as organist (1573, 1577) and vicar-choral (July 1574) of St Paul's Cathedral, and until his death (about 1588) as parish clerk at St Dunstan-in-the-West, London, where from 1580 to 1586 he was also the organist. Aged seventeen and following four years at St Paul's School, London, Thomas matriculated at Gonville and Caius College, Cambridge, in 1577. Having apparently been refused his degree on account of his Catholic sympathies, he proceeded BA from Peterhouse (1581) and MA from Pembroke College (1584). While at Cambridge he held an exhibition at Gonville and Caius (1578–87); the manner in which this award was conferred at the request of the dean of St Paul's suggests that Mudd had been closely connected with the cathedral in some way, perhaps as a chorister. However, he took up a fellowship, and discharged the specially created music lecture, at Pembroke College. On 23 February 1582 the vice-chancellor committed him to the Tolbooth for three days because he 'had censured and too saucily reflected on the Mayor of Cambridge' in a lost comedy which he had written (Cooper, *Ath. Cantab.*, 2.99).

On leaving Cambridge in 1592 Mudd was first appointed rector of Cooling, Kent, and then served as vicar of Cobham in the same county (1603–19); he died in or after 1619. He was certainly considered to be one of England's sixteen 'excellent musicians' in 1598, when he was so described in Francis Meeres's *Palladis tamia* (Jeans, 758); nevertheless, so many compositions are attributed simply to 'Mudd' or 'Mr Mudd' that relatively few of them can with certainty be apportioned to a particular individual. It seems likely, however, that this man was responsible for a five-part In nomine, a five-part *In nomine de profundis*, two anthems, two pieces for keyboard, and nine for viols.

Another musical son of Henry was **John Mudd** (1555–1631). Born in London in 1555, John attended St Paul's School and then Gonville and Caius College, Cambridge, between 1573 and 1576. He was appointed master of the choristers at Southwell Minster on 7 July 1582. By Michaelmas 1583 he had become organist at Peterborough Cathedral (where he also served as master of the choristers, 1598/1599–1623) and he was buried there on 16 December 1631, having retired from the post of organist in the previous June. He is usually credited with the composition of two anthems, 'Plead thou my Cause' and 'Sing joyfully'.

A second **Thomas Mudd** (1610x12?–1667), the son of John Mudd, is thought to have been born at Peterborough. On 6 May 1619 he was admitted chorister at the cathedral, probably aged between seven and nine. He succeeded his father as organist on 9 June 1631, but had presumably left before 29 May 1632, when a successor was appointed. Most authorities believe that this man is identical with the Thomas Mudd who occupied a number of similar offices

after the Restoration. At Michaelmas 1631 an isolated payment of 2*s.* 6*d.* was made by the dean and chapter of Ely Cathedral to 'Mr Mudd … for playing one the orgaines' (Payne, 266). This probably relates to either John or Thomas junior; no one called Mudd was ever part of the musical establishment at Ely.

The next reference to a musician named Thomas Mudd occurs in the Exeter Cathedral accounts for 1660–61; in 1662 he was back at Peterborough, where on 15 August he was appointed to a minor canon's place. Having failed to take holy orders, however, he left Peterborough and served briefly as organist of Lincoln Cathedral from late 1662; but here unruly behaviour caused him to be deprived of his office. Matters came to a head on 16 March 1663, when the precentor angrily reported:

> Yesterday Mr Mudd showed the effects of his last week's tip[p]ling, for when Mr Joynes was in the midst of his sermon Mudd fell a-singing aloud, insomuch as Mr Joynes was compelled to stop; all the auditory gazed and wondered what was the matter, and at length some near him, stopping his mouth, silenced him.   (Shaw, 160)

Between March 1664 and March 1665 he was one of the organists of Exeter Cathedral and on 20 August 1666 he was appointed master of the choristers of York Minster, but both were brief appointments, the latter lasting no longer than one month. He was still regarded as York Minster's organist when he was buried at Durham, according to the cathedral register, on 2 August 1667. Of the substantial quantity of church music composed by men identified by this surname—four service settings, a Te Deum, a Magnificat, and fifteen anthems—only a service in D can be confidently attributed to him.   IAN PAYNE

Sources S. Jeans, 'Mudd', *New Grove*, esp. 758–9 · I. Payne, *The provision and practice of sacred music at Cambridge colleges and selected cathedrals, c.1547–c.1646* (1993) · H. W. Shaw, *The succession of organists of the Chapel Royal and the cathedrals of England and Wales from c.1538* (1991) · *DNB* · Cooper, *Ath. Cantab.*, 2.99 · J. Venn and others, eds., *Biographical history of Gonville and Caius College*, 1: 1349–1713 (1897), 73, 90 · M. McDonnell, ed., *The registers of St Paul's School, 1509–1748* (privately printed, London, 1977), 60, 65–6

Mudd, Thomas (1610x12?–1667). *See under* Mudd, Thomas (*b.* 1559/60, *d.* in or after 1619).

Mudd, William (1829–1879), lichenologist, was born in 1829 at Clifton Lodge on or near Clifton Castle estate in Bedale, Yorkshire, and was baptized at Thornton Watlass on 26 April 1829, the third of eight children of Christopher Mudd, steward, and his wife, Mary Purvis. William married Jane Preston (*bap.* 1829), a servant, in Durham on 25 November 1849; their children, four boys, were all born in Great Ayton, North Riding of Yorkshire, between 1852 and 1860.

Mudd's first appointment was to the garden of Joseph Pease at Houndgate, Darlington, where he received his training. His next post was at Great Ayton, where he was in charge of Thomas Richardson's garden, living in Cleveland Cottage. There he came under the influence of George Dixon (1812–1904), superintendent of the North of England Agricultural School, where Mudd probably assisted in practical horticultural instruction. Dixon encouraged him to join a local botanical class and probably instructed him in microscopy, thereby arousing his interest in lichens. Very soon Mudd became an acknowledged expert, corresponding with many of the leading British and foreign lichenologists; his first published paper in 1854 is an account of the remarkable lichens of the Cleveland area. Within a decade Mudd had acquired sufficient expertise in his chosen hobby to write *A Manual of British Lichens*, published in 1861; in this, the first reasonably comprehensive and practical British lichen flora, Mudd followed the example of European lichenologists in recognizing the value of microscopic examination of spores to identify lichens. He also prepared an exsiccata, *Lichenum Britannicorum* (1861), of 301 specimens to accompany his *Manual*. Much of the information used in the compilation of the *Manual* and the majority of the specimens in the exsiccata resulted from his detailed study of Cleveland lichens.

In 1864 Mudd's reputation was such that he was appointed curator of Cambridge Botanic Garden. Unfortunately, this did not prove an entirely happy move; apart from issuing an exsiccata of *British Cladoniae* in 1865, probably assembled before his departure from Great Ayton, his lichenological activities ceased soon after his arrival at Cambridge, where he lived first at 35 Panton Street, later at 4 College Terrace. C. C. Babington, professor of botany at Cambridge, recorded that Mudd 'is quite transforming our Garden. It is so much better already as to be hardly like the same place' (*Memorials*, 6), but there is little other recorded evidence of his activities after this date. In 1868 he was elected an associate fellow of the Linnean Society and in 1877 an associate of the Botanical Society of Edinburgh. In *The Shaping of Cambridge Botany* (1981), Max Walters remarks that Mudd's

> promise seemed to come to nothing in Cambridge. The difficulty may have been partly caused by his state of health, which had apparently been seriously affected by his overwork at microscopy of lichens before he took the Cambridge post; it seems likely, however, that he found the atmosphere of the University and his social position in town and University so alien to his experience that he could make little of it. (Walters, 74)

Mudd added to his annual income of only £100 by instructing pupils studying for the natural sciences tripos and he was a great favourite with the younger members of the university. After Mudd's death it was decided that the next curator should not do private coaching; according to the *Cambridge University Reporter* dated 2 June 1879, the botanical garden syndicate came to the conclusion that the curator ought to devote his whole time and attention to the garden, that it was not desirable that he should take private pupils, and that he would be able to perform his duties with greater efficiency if he lived within the precincts of the garden.

According to the Revd W. Johnson (in *Nature and Naturalists*, 1903), Mudd, when about forty years of age, was 'a tall man well-built and bony, but thin: his complexion was dark, his hair long and black … He was of a nervous, active temperament, with strong religious susceptibilities, and

… subject to melancholy and depression' (Johnson, 156). J. G. Baker, in his obituary of Mudd, wrote

> If any one will look through [his *Manual of British Lichens*], remembering that it is the production of a man who had to educate himself after reaching mature life, and who at the time that he was engaged upon it was working hard with his hands for twelve hours a-day, and keeping a wife and family upon a wage of something like 25s a week, he will see that the book is really a wonderful monument of energy and perseverance … He worked most diligently for many years when placed in circumstances where he had very few advantages, and his friends hoped for great things from him when he transferred to a more favourable position [Cambridge]—a hope that now can never be realized. (Baker, Mudd, 558)

Mudd died at his home after a short illness on 19 April 1879. He was survived by his wife.

Major collections of Mudd's lichens are now housed in the Natural History Museum, London, Oxford University, and the Falconer Museum (Forres). Sadly, few of the lichen epithets bearing his name are currently in use.

MARK SEAWARD

Sources M. R. D. Seaward, 'William Mudd, the celebrated Cleveland lichenologist', *Proceedings of the Cleveland Naturalists' Field Club*, 5/3 (1993), 6–10 · M. R. D. Seaward, '300 years of Yorkshire lichenology', *The Naturalist*, 112 (1987), 37–52 · S. M. Walters, *The shaping of Cambridge botany* (1981) · M. R. D. Seaward, 'British mycologists 20: William Mudd', *Mycologist*, 6 (1992), 176 · W. Johnson, *Nature and naturalists* (1903) · J. G. Baker, *North Yorkshire: studies of its botany, geology, climate and physical geography* (1863) · D. L. Hawksworth and M. R. D. Seaward, *Lichenology in the British Isles, 1568–1975* (1977) · J. G. Baker, 'William Mudd', *Gardeners' Chronicle*, new ser., 11 (1879), 558–9 · *Memorials, journals, and botanical correspondence of Charles Cardale Babington*, ed. A. Babington (1897) · W. Watson, 'Yorkshire associations, lichenological or otherwise', *The Naturalist* (Feb 1941), 29–40 · d. cert. · *CGPLA Eng. & Wales* (1879)

Archives U. Cam., department of plant sciences

Likenesses portrait, repro. in Seaward, '300 years of Yorkshire lichenology'

Wealth at death under £450: probate, 17 May 1879, *CGPLA Eng. & Wales*

Muddiman, Sir Alexander Phillips (1875–1928), administrator in India, was born at Leighton Buzzard on 14 February 1875, the second son of Alexander Phillips Muddiman, bookseller and publisher, and his wife, Anne Griffiths. Muddiman was educated at Wimborne School and University College, London. He passed the Indian Civil Service examination in 1897 and joined the service in Bengal in 1899.

Muddiman's ability attracted attention, but his career did not follow a typical pattern. After three years in the districts he became an under-secretary to the Bengal government, then registrar on the appellate side in the Calcutta high court and, in 1910, deputy secretary in the legislative department of the government of India. He remained quite inconspicuous on the great issues of the day, confining himself largely to legal and technical matters; for example in 1917, amid pleas for increases in executive powers, Muddiman recommended quasi-judicial commissions to deal with those suspected of violent 'sedition'. He played no important part in the making of the Montagu–Chelmsford reforms (1915–19), but was appointed to represent the government of India on Lord Southborough's committee on franchises and other rules of business, touring India and on deputation to London (1918–19). Significant political issues were involved in the details, when the franchise was being extended from a few thousands to several millions of voters, but again Muddiman's role seems to have been chiefly one of drafting, for example of the regulations for the conduct of legislative business. In this narrow sense he was well qualified for his later close involvement with the reformed councils, though there was general surprise when he was appointed president of the council of state, the new central upper house. As chairman he was courteous, imperturbable, and conciliatory.

In March 1924 Muddiman became home member in the government of India. Unlike his notable predecessors, the inventive William Vincent or the influential but inflexible Reginald Craddock, Muddiman did not need to devise new strategies for dealing with nationalist agitation. His term coincided with a largely constitutional phase in the politics of the Indian National Congress, and was remembered chiefly for Muddiman's pledge in March 1925—an early instance of positive discrimination—to reserve places for Muslims in the Indian Civil Service, appointing by nomination to make up any shortfall after the competitive examination. Nor did Muddiman devote great attention to the details of administration. For him the important focus—unintentionally appropriate to the emerging political order—remained the legislature, where he was now the official leader of the assembly (or lower house). Again he showed calm and good humour.

Muddiman was the obvious person, in 1924, to head a committee appointed to report on the workings of the Montagu–Chelmsford reforms, the most exposed and political task of his career. Scarcely had the new legislatures met in 1920 when the Liberal Party, though co-operating in the reforms, called for a constitutional revision to allow at least provincial autonomy. Urgency grew after the election of the Congressite Swaraj Party members in 1924. The Muddiman committee was appointed to resist a constitutional conference demanded of the new British Labour government by the Swaraj Party leader, Motilal Nehru. By this time members of the government of India also expected that full provincial self-government would be conceded, if only to preserve British power at the centre. Muddiman's job was to produce a consensus for further concessions, to forestall more radical revisions. His task was complicated by calls to reverse the 1919 reforms rather than extend them, especially after the formation of a Conservative government in Britain, and the appointment as secretary of state for India of the ignorant and prejudiced Birkenhead, who thought the reforms ill-conceived and 'extremely mischievous' since it was inconceivable that India would ever be fit for dominion government.

The workings of 'dyarchy' (division of the provincial functions of government between civil servants and ministers drawn from the legislatures) had been criticized for a lack of joint deliberations between the two wings of government, for confusions of responsibility, and for excessive financial controls, all matters related to Muddiman's drafting of the rules of business but also inherent in a divided administration. There were more general criticisms of a want of co-operation from British officials and of the lack of real authority vested in the ministers, especially collectively. Though he stuck at the task for eighteen months Muddiman did not succeed in securing a unanimous report from his committee. A minority of four (Sapru, Sivaswamy Aiyer, Jinnah, and Paranjpye) were strongly critical of the system's basic weakness and contradictions, and its operation in Bengal and the Central Provinces. A majority of five concluded that the problems were inevitable and transitional. Their denial of failure was important for resisting pressure to abandon the experiment. Admitted failures, being attributed to diarchy as well as the conditions and spirit of its operation, strengthened the arguments for a further transfer of power to Indians. Such a line was adopted in the report of the Simon commission (1930), but most significantly in practice in the extension of the reforms in 1935.

Muddiman was knighted in 1922 and created KCSI in 1926. In 1928 he was appointed governor of the United Provinces. But he was already a sick man, and on 17 July 1928, after barely six months in office, he died at Naini Tal of heart failure.

As a legal draftsman Muddiman had an elegant and clear style, but he was not a profound or learned lawyer. His good nature and high spirits led him to take a larger part in the British social life of Simla and Delhi than was usual for high officials in colonial India; in particular he was a brilliant bridge player. He was unmarried.

P. G. ROBB

Sources *The Times* (18 June 1928) • *DNB* • 'Report of the reforms enquiry committee', *Parl. papers* (1924–5), vol. 10, Cmd 2360 • D. C. Potter, *India's political administrators, 1919–1983* (1986) • *CGPLA Eng. & Wales* (1928)
Archives Birmingham Oratory, corresp. with J. H. Newman and others • BL OIOC, corresp. with John Simon, MSS Eur F 77 • CUL, corresp. with Lord Hardinge
Wealth at death £10,613 4s. 2d.: probate, 21 July 1928, *CGPLA Eng. & Wales*

Muddiman, Henry (*bap.* 1629, *d.* 1692), journalist, was born in the Strand, London, and was baptized on 5 February 1629, the son of Edward Muddiman, a tailor, originally from Wolfamcote, Warwickshire, and his wife, Alice. He was educated at St Clement Danes school and, from 1647, at St John's College, Cambridge, where he did not graduate, before returning to the Strand to become a schoolmaster. In 1659 he was a member of the Rota club of metropolitan intellectuals. On 26 December 1659 he used the opportunity of the restoration of the Rump Parliament to issue the first of a succession of twice-weekly news-books. It is very likely that he was urged to do so by his neighbour Thomas Clarges, who as brother-in-law and agent of General George Monck (later first duke of Albemarle), was seeking a journalist to publicize the general's actions. Muddiman continued to report the doings of both

Monck and the Rumpers until they quarrelled, whereupon he used his papers to support the former. He was rewarded on 16 April 1660 when the council of state outlawed all news-books except for the pair produced by Muddiman. At the Restoration the privy council confirmed this monopoly, but a former royalist journalist, Sir John Birkenhead, was appointed editorial supervisor of the news-books. Muddiman worked with him until August 1663, when a court intrigue resulted in the removal of the journals from both men in favour of Roger L'Estrange. Muddiman, however, had meanwhile built up a lucrative sideline by sending handwritten news reports to private correspondents, which could include items on parliamentary proceedings that were forbidden in print. He retained this business and the access to the dispatches sent to secretaries of state from which much of his material was drawn and in return he performed clerical work for the secretaries themselves. By 1665 he was wealthy enough to own Coldhern, a country house with 13 acres in Earls Court, west of London.

In 1665 also L'Estrange's ineptitude cost him control of the official news-books; Muddiman regained control because of the regard he had won from both secretaries of state. He launched what became (from February 1666) the London Gazette, which remained the government newspaper until well into the next century. His private newsletters were none the less still fuller and they became celebrated. By 1677 he was sufficiently influential at court to obtain favours there for other people. His monopoly of printed and written news was breached by the Exclusion crisis but was then restored—it was only decisively ended by the revolution of 1688, Muddiman having become too closely associated with the fallen regime. He retired in October 1689, died at Coldhern in March 1692, and was buried on 7 March beside his wife, Mary, who was buried on 26 July 1682, in St Mary Abbots, Church Street, Kensington.

Muddiman's literary style was plain and factual, without witticisms or flourishes, and his character seems similar. He was clearly intelligent, shrewd, and businesslike. Samuel Pepys thought him both learned and mercenary, and both observations appear just. Muddiman must have been charming and amenable to have earned the approval of the secretaries of state. His only personal enthusiasm to feature in the records is a love of horses. His great claim to fame is that he was the first Englishman to build a long and lucrative career out of the dissemination of public news.   RONALD HUTTON, rev.

Sources J. G. Muddiman, *The king's journalist, 1659–1689* (1923) • T. O'Malley, 'Religion and the newspaper press, 1660–85: a study of the *London Gazette*', *The press in English society from the seventeenth to nineteenth centuries*, ed. M. R. A. Harris and A. J. Lee (1986), 25–46 • P. W. Thomas, *Sir John Berkenhead, 1617–1679: a royalist career in politics and polemics* (1969) • parish register, St Martin-in-the-Fields, City Westm. AC • parish register, St Mary Abbots, Kensington, LMA • *CSP dom., 1661–78* • A. Smith, *The newspaper, an international history* (1979), 41–4 • Pepys, *Diary*, vols. 1, 4, 6
Archives BL, newsletters, Sloane MS 3929

Mudford, William (1782–1848), author and journalist, was born on 8 January 1782 at Half Moon Street, Piccadilly,

London. Details of his family background and early schooling are unknown, but in 1800, at the age of eighteen, he came to prominence as an assistant secretary to the duke of Kent. A political career seemed set for him, particularly after he accompanied the duke to Gibraltar on matters of political importance in 1802. He grew disillusioned with this work, however, and shortly thereafter resigned to begin a career in journalism. Combining his knowledge of politics with his interest in reporting, he became parliamentary reporter with the *Morning Chronicle*, a whig party paper that, under the editorship of the strong-minded James Perry between 1789 and 1821, ranked as one of the pre-eminent opposition journals in London. After several years of training under this regime, Mudford took the position of assistant editor at *The Courier*, an evening paper, its tory stance more adequately reflecting his conservative political convictions. In 1817 he took over as editor from T. G. Street, who throughout his tenure had pursued a general campaign against the ruling government, and more specifically against the liberal tory minister George Canning. Under Street's influence Mudford continued this pattern to such an extent that in 1824 Canning publicly charged that Mudford and his paper were undermining British government interests under the influence and pay of the French. Mudford subsequently modified *The Courier*'s stance, and the differences between Mudford and Canning were quickly resolved. In 1827 *The Courier* gave its support to Canning following his accession to the position of prime minister.

Mudford was removed as editor by the proprietors of *The Courier* in 1828, in part because of their opposition to his shift in policy towards Canning, a move they interpreted as a step away from deep-dyed tory principles towards a milder form of whiggism. Mudford also incurred great financial loss at this time due to ill-considered speculations. By then married to Amelia Camp, and with an increasing family, ultimately to number eight sons, including William Heseltine *Mudford, to support, he moved to Canterbury in Kent, where he took up a succession of posts in provincial papers.

To supplement his income Mudford began contributing to literary journals around the country. Between 1829 and 1842 he wrote reviews, commentaries, and fiction for the pages of *Bentley's Monthly Magazine* and *Blackwood's Edinburgh Magazine*. The most notable of these were tales of terror contributed to *Blackwood's* between 1829 and 1830. Such pieces as 'The Iron Shroud', 'Malavolti, a Neapolitan Story', and 'Silent Member', with their emphasis on sensations and their intensely focused, precise narratorial descriptions and renderings of the effects of terror on the individual, were at the core of an influential series of stories published in the pages of *Blackwood's* during this period. In conjunction with other *Blackwood's* writers such as Thomas De Quincey, William Maginn, John Galt, and Samuel Warren, Mudford's work established a distinctive style of sensational fiction which was to have a great influence on succeeding generations of short fiction writers, and in particular on Edgar Allan Poe, who drew on and reworked Mudford's story 'The Iron Shroud' for one of his best-known pieces, 'The Pit and the Pendulum'. Many of Mudford's sketches were later reprinted as *Tales and Trifles from 'Blackwood's' and other Popular Magazines* (1849).

Mudford's literary production included the novels *The Premier* (1831), *Stephen Dugard* (1840), and *Arthur Wilson*, published posthumously in 1872. He also wrote on history and literature, publishing *A Critical Enquiry into the Writings of Samuel Johnson* (1803), *An Historical Account of the Campaign in the Netherlands in 1815* (1817), and *The Contemplatist, or, Essays upon Morals and Literature* (1811). Other work included translations of French texts and edited volumes of essays and biographical texts.

By 1832 Mudford had accumulated enough financial capital to found and edit the *Kentish Observer*. Tory in outlook and priced at 3*d.* a copy, its success encouraged Mudford to produce and edit the *Canterbury Journal*, a smaller, cheaper weekly spin-off priced at a penny and aimed at a more local readership. The *Canterbury Journal* was subsequently merged with other weekly local journals in 1838 to form the *Kentish Herald*. Mudford's son Frederick was to become proprietor and editor of this journal in later years. Another son, William Heseltine Mudford, was to become editor of *The Standard*.

In 1841 Mudford moved back to London to take over from Theodore Hook as editor of *John Bull*. Under his guidance the paper became identified as a voice of the high-church and the tory clergy. He continued as its editor until his death, at his home, 5 Harrington Square, Hampstead Road, London, on 10 March 1848.

DAVID FINKELSTEIN

Sources D. Griffiths, ed., *The encyclopedia of the British press, 1422–1992* (1992) · J. Grant, *The newspaper press: its origin, progress, and present position*, 3 vols. (1871–2) · S. E. Koss, *The rise and fall of the political press in Britain*, 2 vols. (1981–4); repr. (1990) · T. H. S. Escott, *Masters of English journalism* (1911) · R. Morrison and C. Baldick, eds., *Tales of terror from 'Blackwood's Magazine'* (1995) · *GM*, 2nd ser., 29 (1848), 665

Archives NL Scot., corresp. with Blackwoods

Likenesses G. Hayter, group portrait, oils (*The trial of Queen Caroline, 1820*), NPG

Mudford, William Heseltine (1839–1916), journalist and newspaper editor, was born at 45 St George's Street, Canterbury, on 1 March 1839, son of William *Mudford (1782–1848) and his wife, Amelia Camp. He came from a journalistic background: his father was the proprietor of the *Kentish Observer* and the *Canterbury Journal*, and, according to his *Times* obituarist, Mudford's education 'owed nothing to public school or university training'. He went to work for the London *Standard* in the 1860s, becoming a member of the newspaper's parliamentary staff of twelve, and was greatly aided by his mastery of Gurney's shorthand system. *The Standard* was a morning paper, but in 1860 an evening edition was also produced; the paper was owned by James Johnstone (1815–1878), and at the time when Mudford joined it was edited by Thomas Hamber. It was pro-conservative, but always asserted its independence of Conservative Party managers, and was described by the

New Quarterly Review in 1860 as 'with them [the Conservative Party] and not of them' (Koss, 1.137). But by the end of the 1860s *The Standard* was in something of a decline, and Johnstone decided to replace Hamber with Mudford, who was by now an experienced journalist. The date of Mudford's appointment is uncertain, but the most likely conjecture is 1871. James Johnstone later acknowledged Mudford's success by making a codicil in his will which gave Mudford the editorship of the newspaper 'for his lifetime or until such time as he shall voluntarily resign the editorship'. The family beneficiaries of Johnstone's will were excluded from interfering with the running of the paper, and Mudford, who was to have a salary of £5000 a year, was left with effectively absolute power over *The Standard* after Johnstone's death in 1878.

In the same year *The Standard's* new premises in St Bride Street were completed. Mudford had on his staff a highly talented set of journalists and literary men, including G. A. Henty, Charles Norris, Alfred Austin, Byron Curtis, and, later, Sidney Low. The paper had earlier benefited from Conservative Party subsidies in the 1860s, but its rapid rise in circulation in the 1870s and its dramatic increase in the 1880s (between 1874 and the mid-1880s circulation rose from 176,000 to over 250,000), allied to Mudford's safeguarded editorial position, enabled Mudford to assert the paper's independence of Conservative Party control or interference. *The Standard* became one of the most prosperous and influential newspapers of the day, and was second only to *The Times* as a morning paper. Mudford proved himself to be a good manager as well as editor: he used a daily American cable service, and paid £800 for cable dispatches during the Anglo-Afghan War of 1878–80. He replaced old machinery and paid his talented staff well: some 500 in number, they cost the newspaper £1500 a week in salaries alone.

Mudford had access to the leading politicians of the time, but once he achieved absolute control of *The Standard* he deliberately set out to distance himself from direct contact with political society. The story that Mudford rose from the dinner table to receive the card of a 'great statesman' (Lord Carnarvon) with the words 'Tell him I'm out' is probably apocryphal, but it exemplifies his new style. But, while Mudford was anxious to demonstrate his freedom from political entanglements, he was prepared to exploit those of his staff who maintained them. T. H. S. Escott, one of his leader writers, enjoyed close contact with Joseph Chamberlain in the early 1880s. Chamberlain was disappointed by his lack of status in the new Liberal administration; the result was a series of leaks relating to the government's Irish policy in 1880–82, which gave Mudford some exciting exclusives. On 6 April 1881, for instance, *The Standard* received advance information on the terms of the 1881 Irish Land Bill. Even when this source dried up, *The Standard* was still capable of surprising Gladstone. On 17 December 1885 it announced Gladstone's conversion to home rule for Ireland. Gladstone's son Herbert had discussed his father's position on home rule with the editor of the *Leeds Mercury*, Wemyss Reid; *The Standard* obtained the news, possibly through a leak from Reid, who dined with Mudford on 16 December, or through the National Press Association. On 17 December it was published as an exclusive, with a call for a general election as the 'best way of defending the integrity of the Kingdom and the loyalists of Ireland'.

But, although the news was sensational, it was not printed in *The Standard* in a sensational style. There were no brash headlines: Mudford was an old-fashioned editor of a quality newspaper. But this proved a weakness as well as a strength. In the 1890s *The Standard* began to lose its leading position, and its circulation was overtaken by rivals representing the 'new journalism', such as the *Pall Mall Gazette*, *The Star*, and the *Daily Mail*; they invaded *The Standard's* readership, which Mudford described as the 'villa resident order of Englishman'. On 31 December 1899 Mudford relinquished his editorship to Byron Curtis (1843–1907); four years later the paper was sold to Arthur Pearson, and by 1914 it was receiving subsidies from Conservative Party funds. But its influence in foreign affairs survived Mudford's departure.

Mudford's absolute power as editor was reflected in his relationships with his staff, which were cordial, but firm. On 14 October 1891 Byron Curtis refused to accept an article on the leadership of the House of Commons written by Alfred Austin following a discussion with Lord Salisbury, Curtis being unwilling to take the responsibility for it in Mudford's absence. Mudford occasionally admonished Escott for badly composed leaders. Despite his lack of personal contact with his staff, he was considered a good judge of men. His declared policy of 'independence' must be qualified in the light of his use of journalists who had close political contacts, but he never surrendered his editorial veto: although he allowed Austin to send Lord Salisbury his leaders for amendment, he frequently amended the changes. The danger of exercising too much independence is revealed in A. J. Balfour's description of *The Standard* in 1893 as 'of no earthly value to the party in the way of making opinion, as their criticisms are a foregone conclusion' (Koss, 1.337).

Mudford was a cultured and likeable man of a broadly conservative disposition, with an interest in radical toryism. He was described by one of his contemporaries as of medium height, broad-chested, and of strong build. He lived a reclusive retirement at his house, Westcombe Lodge, Wimbledon Common. On 14 October 1916 he slipped and fell into the fireplace; he died at the house from his injuries on 18 October, and was buried at Putney Vale cemetery two days later. Mudford's standing as an editor came from his freedom from proprietorial control, that of his newspaper from his discreet contacts with government sources, a combination which explains J. L. Garvin's description of him as 'the consummate—though almost invisible—editor of the *Standard*' (J. Garvin, *The Life of Joseph Chamberlain*, 1, 1932, 307).　　D. GEORGE BOYCE

Sources S. E. Koss, *The rise and fall of the political press in Britain*, 1 (1981) · L. Brown, *Victorian news and newspapers* (1985) · D. Griffiths, 'The early management of *The Standard*', *Investigating Victorian journalism*, ed. L. Blake, A. Jones, and L. Madden (1990), 120–32 · T. H. S. Escott, *Masters of English journalism* (1911) · J. Hatton, *Journalistic London* (1882) · *The Times* (20 Oct 1916) · b. cert. · d. cert.
Archives BL, letters to T. H. S. Escott, Add. MS 58787
Likenesses engraving (after photograph), repro. in Hatton, *Journalistic London*, 142
Wealth at death £65,288 4s. 4d.: probate, 23 Dec 1916, CGPLA Eng. & Wales

Mudge, Henry (1806–1874), temperance advocate, the son of Thomas Mudge, was born at Tower Hill House, Bodmin, on 29 July 1806. He was educated at St Bartholomew's Hospital, London, and became a licentiate of the Society of Apothecaries in 1828 and a member of the Royal College of Surgeons in the following year. He commenced practice in his native town, where he remained throughout his life.

A member of the local temperance society, Mudge, in 1837, was the first person in Bodmin to sign a pledge of total abstinence. He went on to become an ardent advocate of teetotalism, refusing to administer alcohol as a medicine to his patients, and publicizing the physiological arguments for total abstinence. He contributed articles to several national temperance journals and himself edited the *Western Temperance Luminary* (1838), the *Bodmin Temperance Luminary* (1840–1), and the *Cornwall and Devon Temperance Journal* (1851–8). In 1859 he published a course of lectures entitled *Physiology, health and disease demanding abstinence from alcoholic drinks and prohibition of their common sale*, and in 1863 his alphabetically arranged *Guide to the Treatment of Disease without Alcoholic Liquors* appeared.

Although so stern an advocate of temperance, Mudge did not approve of the Rechabites or the Oddfellows, and attacked their principles in several pamphlets of 1844–6. He addressed the World's Temperance Convention which met in London on 4–7 August 1846, and he was involved in the foundation of the United Kingdom Alliance in 1853.

He was for many years a local preacher and class leader of the Wesleyan Methodist Connexion, and he promoted teetotalism as consistent with biblical principles. He published several sermons on the subject in 1839–40, a period in which teetotalism was unpopular among the Wesleyan leadership and a source of division in many localities. Mudge was also a strong opponent of smoking. He was twice mayor of Bodmin. He died at Fore Street, Bodmin, on 27 June 1874. His only child, a daughter, was the wife of J. S. Pethybridge, a bank manager. His own wife, Susan, had died in 1872.　　MARK CLEMENT

Sources P. T. Winskill, *The temperance movement and its workers*, 4 vols. (1891–2), vols. 2–3 · P. T. Winskill, *Temperance standard bearers of the nineteenth century: a biographical and statistical temperance dictionary*, 2 vols. (1897–8) · B. Harrison, *Dictionary of British temperance biography* (1973) · T. Hudson, *Temperance pioneers of the West: personal and incidental experiences* (1887) · CGPLA Eng. & Wales (1874) · d. cert.
Wealth at death under £4000: probate, 8 Oct 1874, CGPLA Eng. & Wales

Mudge, John (*bap.* 1721, *d.* 1793), surgeon and physician, was baptized at Bideford, Devon, on 6 October 1721, the fourth and youngest son of the Revd Zachariah *Mudge (1694–1769), and his first wife, Mary Fox (*d.* in or before 1762). The horologist Thomas *Mudge was his brother as was the composer the Revd Richard *Mudge. He was educated at Bideford and Plympton grammar schools, and studied medicine at Plymouth Hospital. He soon obtained a large practice, helped by family connections, as well as his skill and charm. In 1777 he published a *Dissertation on the inoculated small pox, or, An attempt towards an investigation of the real causes which render the small pox by inoculation so much more mild and safe than the same disease when produced by the ordinary means of infection*. Mudge was elected a fellow of the Royal Society in 1777, and in the same year was awarded the Copley medal for his *Directions for making the best composition for the metals for reflecting telescopes, together with a description of the process for grinding, polishing, and giving the great speculum the true parabolic curve*, which was printed in *Philosophical Transactions* (PTRS, 67, 1777, 296). *Directions* was also published separately in 1778. Sir John Pringle, the president, remarked: 'Mr Mudge hath truly realised the expectation of Sir Isaac Newton, who, about one hundred years ago, presaged that the public would one day possess a parabolic speculum, not accomplished by mathematical rules, but by mechanical devices'. The manufacture of telescopes continued to occupy much of Mudge's spare time. He made two large ones with a magnifying power of two hundred times. One of these he gave to Count Bruhl, and it eventually passed to the Gotha observatory; the other was left to his son, General William *Mudge (1762–1820).

Despite publishing several successful treatises on medical matters, and frequently being encouraged to move to London, Mudge preferred to remain in Plymouth, where he practised for the remainder of his life, first as surgeon, and, after 1784, when he received the degree of MD from King's College, Aberdeen, as a physician.

The Mudge family had a long-standing friendship with the family of Sir Joshua Reynolds, and when Dr Johnson accompanied Sir Joshua on his visit to Plymouth in 1762, the pair were the guests of Mudge. Boswell recorded that Mudge was 'the celebrated physician, who was not more distinguished for quickness of parts and variety of knowledge than loved and esteemed for his amiable manners'. Johnson became a firm friend of the family, and in 1783 he wrote for Mudge's advice concerning an operation he was considering. 'It is doubtless painful; but', he asked 'is it dangerous? The pain I hope to endure with decency; but I am loth to put life into much hazard'. Other friends and guests of Mudge were John Smeaton, the engineer, James Ferguson, the astronomer, and James Northcote, originally a chemist's assistant, who owed his position in Reynolds's studio to Mudge. Northcote subsequently spoke of Mudge as 'one of the most delightful persons I ever knew. Every one was enchanted with his society. It was not wit that he possessed, but such a perfect cheerfulness and good humour that it was like health coming into the room' (Northcote, 89). A well-known London physician, who was sending a patient to Stonehouse to take the air, told the lady that he was sending her to Dr Mudge and that if his medical skills did not cure her, his conversation would.

Mudge was married three times, and had twenty children. With Mary Bulteel, his first wife, he had eight children. His second wife, Jane, was buried on 3 February 1766 in St Andrew's Church, Plymouth. He then married, on 29 May 1767, Elizabeth Garrett (1735/6–1808). His sons, William and Zachary *Mudge, were the children of his second and third wives respectively. Mudge died on 26 March 1793, and was buried near his father in St Andrew's Church, Plymouth.

THOMAS SECCOMBE, rev. CLAIRE L. NUTT

Sources *GM*, 1st ser., 63 (1793), 376 · S. R. Flint, ed., *Mudge memoirs* (1883), 79–120 · J. Boswell, *The life of Samuel Johnson*, 2 vols. (1791) · Nichols, *Lit. anecdotes*, 9.675–6 · J. Northcote, *The life of Sir Joshua Reynolds*, 2nd edn, 2 vols. (1818), 111 · [Clarke], *The Georgian era: memoirs of the most eminent persons*, 3 (1834), 485 · T. Thomson, *History of the Royal Society from its institution to the end of the eighteenth century* (1812) · W. Hazlitt, *Conversations of James Northcote* (1830), 89 · IGI
Archives BL, letters to Lord Camelford relating to china clay and porcelain, Add. MS 69323
Likenesses J. Reynolds, portrait, c.1752; formerly in possession of Arthur Mudge, Plympton, 1894 · S. W. Reynolds, mezzotint, pubd 1820 (after J. Reynolds), BM, NPG · W. Dickinson, mezzotint (after J. Reynolds), BM · Grozier, engraving (after Reynolds), Wellcome L. · J. Northcote, portrait, repro. in Flint, ed., *Mudge memoirs*

Mudge, Richard (bap. 1718, d. 1763), composer and Church of England clergyman, was baptized at Bideford, Devon, on 26 December 1718, the third of the four sons (there was also a daughter) of Zachariah *Mudge (1694–1769), headmaster and clergyman, and his wife, Mary Fox (d. in or before 1762). His brothers included the watchmaker Thomas *Mudge (1715/16–1794) and the surgeon John *Mudge (bap. 1721, d. 1793). He was educated at Pembroke College, Oxford, from 1735, and graduated BA in 1738 and MA in 1741. He then became curate at Great Packington and Little Packington, Warwickshire, and in 1745 rector at the latter. On 27 March 1747 at St Cross, Oxford, he married Mary Hopkins of St Aldates; they had a daughter, Mary (bap. 1752).

At Packington Hall, seat of Heneage Finch, Lord Guernsey (1715–1777), later third earl of Aylesford, music seems to have flourished, and Mudge was undoubtedly involved. He knew the librettist Charles Jennens, a kinsman of Guernsey, who lived at nearby Gopsall, and he may have been on friendly terms with Handel, copies of whose operas and oratorios exist in Mudge's hand. In 1749 he published the work for which he is known, *Six Concertos in Seven Parts … to which is Added, Non nobis domine*, a competent set that includes both a concerto for trumpet and one for keyboard; the collection ends with an accompanied version of the canon *Non nobis domine* once attributed to William Byrd. The concertos are written along Handelian lines, with Mudge's partiality for chromaticism evident, and they were staples of the provincial music society repertory. His 'Medley' concerto, catalogued at Oxford in 1770, is lost. In 1750, having for some time wanted to leave Packington, Mudge took up the curacy at St Bartholomew's Chapel in Birmingham, and in 1756 he was appointed rector of Bedworth, Warwickshire, where he died on 4 April 1763.

PETER LYNAN

Sources R. Platt, 'New light on Richard Mudge, 1718–63', *Early Music*, 28 (2000), 531–45 · *New Grove* · J. H. Roberts, 'The Aylesford collection', *Handel collections and their history*, ed. T. Best (1993), 47–8 · *IGI*

Mudge, Richard Zachariah (1790–1854), surveyor, was born on 6 September 1790 at Plymouth, the eldest son of William *Mudge (1762–1820), superintendent of the Ordnance Survey, and his wife, traditionally thought to have been Margaret Jane (*d*. 1824), daughter of Major-General George Williamson RA, but probably Katherine Jane, fourth daughter of Colonel John Williamson RA (*c*.1731–1794). They had a daughter and four sons including William *Mudge, naval officer. Richard was educated at Blackheath and at the Royal Military Academy at Woolwich. He was commissioned second lieutenant Royal Engineers on 4 May 1807 and was promoted first lieutenant on 14 July of the same year. In March 1809 he sailed for Lisbon and joined the army under Sir Arthur Wellesley at Abrantes in May. He was present at the battle of Talavera, and in subsequent reconnaissance duties narrowly escaped capture. He accompanied the army in retreat from Talavera to Badajoz and helped to construct the lines at Lisbon, before ill health obliged him to return to England on 20 June 1810.

Mudge was employed under his father on the Ordnance Survey and was for some years in charge of the drawing department at the Tower of London. In 1816 he was appointed to supervise the civilian surveyors to whom the Board of Ordnance had resorted because of the shortage of trained officers. With instruction from his father he hoped to standardize practice among the civilians, but had only modest success. Mudge married on 1 September 1817 Alice Watson, daughter of J. W. Hull of co. Down, with whom he had two daughters, Jane Rosedew (*d*. 1883), who married the Revd William Charles Raffles Flint, and Sophia Elizabeth, who married the Revd John Richard Bogue. Jane was named after Mudge's uncle Richard Rosedew whose property at Beechwood, Devon, Mudge inherited in 1837 on his uncle's death.

In 1819 Mudge went to Dunkirk with his father and Thomas Colby for Anglo-French geodetic observations and in 1821 worked at various places on the north coast of France. He was elected a fellow of the Royal Society by 1823. He remained with the Ordnance Survey, reaching the rank of regimental lieutenant-colonel on 10 January 1837. Thomas Colby's suggestion that Mudge be put in independent command of Ordnance Survey work in England was not adopted and this was probably fortunate since he was not a particularly strong or effective officer.

In 1830 controversy arose over the border between Maine and New Brunswick. The United States claimed highlands running from the heads of the Connecticut River to within 20 miles of the St Lawrence, which, if conceded, would have cut off the direct routes from Quebec to New Brunswick and would have given the United States positions commanding Quebec itself. Britain objected that the claims were incompatible with the treaty of 1783. After a solution proposed by the king of the Netherlands proved unacceptable to the Americans the matter became serious. In 1838 the British government appointed Mudge and George William Featherstonehaugh—a geologist familiar with America—commissioners to examine the physical geography of the disputed territory and report on the American claims. In 1839 the commissioners surveyed the area and the spartan and energetic Featherstonehaugh was left unimpressed by Mudge's preference for ease and comfort. In 1840 they made their report, 'a highly partisan document replete with "natural frontier" arguments based on bogus topographical features' (Stafford, 65). The issue was finally resolved in the Webster–Ashburton treaty of 1842, which, despite Featherstonehaugh's protests, conceded some land in northern Maine to the Americans.

Mudge retired on full pay on 7 September 1850 to live at Beechwood. He died at Teignmouth, Devon, on 24 September 1854 and was buried at Denbury. He published a work advocating a national railway system (1837). His career as a surveyor probably owed more to his father's fame than to his own talents.

ELIZABETH BAIGENT

Sources W. A. Seymour, ed., *A history of the Ordnance Survey* (1980) · R. A. Stafford, *Scientist of empire: Sir Roderick Murchison, scientific exploration and Victorian imperialism* (1989) · *The old series ordnance survey maps of England and Wales*, Ordnance Survey, 8 vols. (1975–92) [introductions to each vol. by J. B. Harley and others] · T. Owen and E. Pilbeam, *Ordnance Survey: map makers to Britain since 1791* (1992) · S. R. Flint, ed., *Mudge memoirs* (1883) · MSS, War office · MSS, Records of the corps of royal engineers · *DNB* · A. McEwen, ed., *In search of the highlands: mapping the Canada-Maine boundary 1839: the journals of Featherstonehaugh and Mudge* (1988)
Likenesses J. Northcote, portrait, 1807; formerly in possession of his daughter, Mrs Bogue, 1894

Mudge, Thomas (1715/16–1794), horologist, second son of Zachariah *Mudge (1694–1769), headmaster and clergyman, and his first wife, Mary Fox (*d*. in or before 1762), was, almost certainly, born at Exeter in late 1715 or early 1716. Soon after his birth his father became master of the grammar school at Bideford, and there Thomas received his early education. On 4 May 1730 his father bound him apprentice to George Graham, successor to Thomas Tompion, the eminent watchmaker of Water Lane, Fleet Street, London. Graham formed a very high estimate of his pupil's ability. On gaining his freedom of the Clockmakers' Company in 1738 Mudge took lodgings and continued to work privately for some years. One of the most famous watchmakers of the time for whom he worked was John Ellicott. When the latter was requested to supply Ferdinand VI of Spain with an equation watch, Mudge was entrusted with the construction of the instrument, although Ellicott's name was attached to it when finished, in accordance with the usual practice. Subsequently, when explaining the action of the watch to some men of science, Ellicott had the misfortune to injure it and, being unable to repair the damage himself, he had to return it to Mudge. This story reached the ears of the Spanish king, who had a passion for mechanical inventions, and he gave Mudge an open commission to construct elaborate and complicated watches. One of these was made to fit the end of a cane. It struck the hours and quarters, repeated the quarters at will, and had an alarm mechanism. The

Thomas Mudge (1715/16–1794), by Nathaniel Dance, in or before 1772

motions of the wheels at the time of striking were revealed by small sliding shutters. The king is reported to have constantly spoken admiringly of the maker.

In 1750 Mudge took premises at 151 Fleet Street and, on 18 November, two days after the death of his former master, George Graham, began to advertise for work. On 27 October 1753 he married Abigail Hopkins of Oxford, who died in 1789. They had two sons. During this period Mudge formed an association with a former fellow apprentice, William Dutton, which led to a partnership by the early 1760s, with both names appearing on their productions. The firm is known to have supplied Dr Johnson's first watch in 1768 and to have constructed a fine watch with temperature compensation for John Smeaton. Mudge also prepared a longitude timekeeper for the young Swiss astronomer Johan Jacob Huber, incorporating Huber's idea of a constant force escapement.

In the late 1760s Mudge became acquainted with Count von Brühl, ambassador-extraordinary from the court of Saxony, who henceforth became a most enthusiastic and supportive patron. This association led, in 1770, to George III's purchase of a gold watch incorporating Mudge's invention of a detached lever escapement; presented to Queen Charlotte and known as 'the queen's watch', it later became part of the Royal Collection. The escapement, which was first applied by Mudge to a clock in the 1750s, remains in use as the best that can be fitted to mechanical watches.

In 1765, Mudge, who was at that time acting as an expert for the board of longitude, published *Thoughts on the Means of Improving Watches, and Particularly those for the Use of the Sea*. In 1771 he quitted active business due to ill health and retired to Plymouth to be with his brother, Dr John *Mudge. (His brother Richard *Mudge, the composer, had died in 1763.) This allowed him to devote all his time and attention to the improvement of chronometers designed to determine, with the aid of the sextant, the longitude at sea. The government, through the agency of the board of longitude, had encouraged the improvement of timekeepers for this purpose, and in 1714 had offered a reward of £20,000 for a method that could determine the longitude within 30 geographical miles; if within 60 geographical miles, half the reward was offered. John Harrison (1693–1776) ultimately obtained the larger reward in 1773 for the performance of his fourth timekeeper. Further rewards were then offered for a more perfect method, and Mudge felt confident that he could attain the degree of exactness required. In 1776 he was appointed watchmaker to the king, and in the same year he completed his first marine chronometer. He submitted it to Dr Hornby, Savilian professor of astronomy at Oxford, who tested it, with satisfactory results. It was then committed to Nevil Maskelyne, astronomer royal, for extended tests at the observatory (1776–7). This chronometer was later housed at the British Museum. The board of longitude in the meantime gave Mudge 500 guineas, and urged him to make another watch in order to qualify for the government's rewards, the terms of which required the construction of two watches of the specified accuracy. Mudge forthwith set about making two more timekeepers, which were so alike that he gave them different coloured shagreen-covered cases, giving rise to their being called 'green' and 'blue'. These were submitted to the same rigorous tests as the first but, like the first, they were described by the astronomer royal as not having satisfied the terms of the reward. In the controversy which followed it was claimed that Maskelyne had not given the timekeepers a fair trial, and that they had gone better in other hands both before and after the period during which they had been under his observation. Mudge's case was strongly urged in a pamphlet issued by his elder son, Thomas *Mudge, entitled *A narrative of facts relating to some timekeepers constructed by Mr. T. Mudge for the discovery of the longitude at sea, together with observations upon the conduct of the astronomer royal respecting them* (1792). Maskelyne retorted in *An answer to a pamphlet entitled A narrative of facts ... wherein ... the conduct of the astronomer royal is vindicated from Mr. Mudge's misrepresentations* (1792), and the controversy closed with the younger Mudge's *Reply to the answer ... to which is added ... some remarks on some passages in Dr. Maskelyne's answer by his excellency the Count de Bruhl* (1792). Mudge was supported throughout by F. X. De Zach, astronomer to the duke of Saxe-Gotha-Altenburg, who had observed the variations of the first of Mudge's chronometers for two years, and by Admiral John Campbell, who carried the chronometer on voyages to Newfoundland in 1785 and 1786 respectively. This chronometer was afterwards stated by the younger Thomas Mudge to vary less than half a second in 24 hours. Harrison had previously entertained similar grievances against Maskelyne and the board of longitude, believing that the astronomer royal favoured a scheme of his own for finding the longitude by lunar tables which disposed him to apply overly rigorous tests to the chronometers.

In June 1791 Mudge's son presented to the board of longitude a memorial, stating that although his father's timekeepers during the time of the public trial had not been adjudged to go within the limits defined for reward, yet as they were superior to any hitherto invented, and were constructed on such principles as would render them permanently useful, the board would be justified in exercising its powers to give him some financial recognition of his labours. The memorial proved unsuccessful, so he carried a petition to the same effect to the House of Commons, and a committee was appointed, consisting of Pitt, Wyndham, Bathurst, and Lord Minto, to consider the value of Mudge's invention. The committee, having been assisted by various eminent watchmakers and men of science, finally voted Mudge the sum of £2500. He died two years after receiving this reward at Thomas's house at Newington Butts, Surrey, on 14 November 1794. He was buried on 21 November at St Dunstan-in-the-West, London. His younger son, John (1763–1847), was on the recommendation of Queen Charlotte, presented to the living of Brampford Speke, near Exeter, by the lord chancellor in 1791.

A fine portrait of Thomas Mudge the elder, later in the possession of the Science Museum, London, was painted for Count Brühl by Nathaniel Dance, and was later engraved by both Charles Townley and L. Schiavonetti. It shows a face which is remarkable for its look of patient intelligence and integrity.

THOMAS SECCOMBE, rev. DAVID PENNEY

Sources T. Mudge, A description, with plates, of the time-keeper invented by the late Thomas Mudge (1799) · Universal Magazine of Knowledge and Pleasure, 97 (1795), 41–7 · S. R. Flint, ed., Mudge memoirs (1883) · 'Report of the select committee of the House of Commons to whom it was referred to consider of the report which was made from the committee to whom the petition of Thomas Mudge, watch-maker, was referred', JHC, 48 (1792–3), 877–920 · R. Good and others, Pioneers of precision timekeeping (1965) · C. Allix, 'Thomas Mudge, clock, watch and chronometer maker', Apollo Miscellany (June 1950), 1–8 · G. Daniels, 'Thomas Mudge, the complete horologist', Antiquarian Horology and the Proceedings of the Antiquarian Horological Society, 13 (1981–2) · T. Mudge jun., A narrative of facts … (1791) · N. Maskelyne, An answer to 'A narrative of facts' … (1792) · T. Mudge jun., A reply to 'An answer …' (1792) · parish registers, St Dunstan-in-the-West and St Mary Magdalene, Fish Street, GL
Archives BM · Mathematisch-Physikalischer Salon, Dresden, Germany · Royal Collection · Time Museum, Rockford, Illinois | NMM · priv. colls.
Likenesses N. Dance, oils, in or before 1772, Sci. Mus. [see illus.] · C. Townley, mezzotint, 1772 (after N. Dance), BM · Baker, engraving, 1795 (after N. Dance), repro. in Universal Magazine, 311 · L. Schiavonetti, engraving, 1799 (after N. Dance), repro. in Mudge, A description with plates, frontispiece · oils (after N. Dance), Guildhall, Clockmakers' Company Museum

Mudge, Thomas (1760–1843), writer on horology, was born on 6 December 1760, the eldest of two sons of Thomas *Mudge (1715/16–1794), watchmaker, of Fleet Street, London, and his wife, Abigail, née Hopkins (d. 1789). Claims that he practised as a barrister in London are undocumented, but he successfully pleaded his aged father's case for a government reward for the excellence

of his chronometers. The younger Mudge began the manufacture of chronometers in Camberwell, employing Robert Pennington, Howells, and other reputable craftsmen to make these to his father's pattern. He himself resided in Newington Place, Surrey, where he set up a transit instrument to regulate the chronometers. His father lived to see the first watch made, and his son secured orders to supply the Admiralty and the Spanish and Danish governments. Finding, however, that it took far longer than estimated to construct each chronometer, and that he was unable to guarantee their satisfactory performance, he sold the business to Pennington.

Around 1786 Mudge married Elizabeth Kingdom (1761–1856), sister of Lady Sophia Brunel. They had eleven children, of whom four died young. After disposing of his business, Mudge moved to St Aubyn's, Jersey, returning in 1830 to reside at Chilcompton, near Bath, Somerset, where he died on 10 November 1843.

ANITA McCONNELL

Sources T. Mudge, A description, with plates, of the time-keeper invented by the late Thomas Mudge (1799) · S. R. Flint, ed., Mudge memoirs (1883) · d. cert.
Archives BL, letters to William Windham, Add. MS 37854
Wealth at death under £2000: will, 1837, London, Bank of England, will abstracts, K2, 12718, 1844

Mudge, William (1762–1820), surveyor, was the ninth of twenty children born to Dr John *Mudge (bap. 1721, d. 1793) of Plymouth. William's mother was John Mudge's second wife and his grandfather was the Revd Zachariah *Mudge. William was born in Plymouth on 1 December 1762 into a notable scientific family: his father was a physician, his uncle Thomas *Mudge (1715/16–1794) a horologist. The family had important artistic connections, notably with Sir Joshua Reynolds and with Dr Johnson, William's godfather. His upbringing led him to appreciate both the scientific and the artistic aspects of map making. His half-brother Zachary *Mudge was a naval officer.

Mudge entered the Royal Military Academy at Woolwich on 17 April 1777 and on 9 July 1779 he was commissioned second lieutenant in the Royal Artillery, and was sent to South Carolina to fight in the American War of Independence. On his return home he was stationed at the Tower of London, and continued his studies under Charles Hutton, professor of mathematics at the Royal Military Academy, amusing himself in his spare time with the construction of clocks. He became an excellent mathematician and, on Hutton's recommendation, was appointed in 1791 to the ordnance trigonometrical survey. He was engaged in geodetic work in the field and in London until 1798, when he became superintendent of the survey on the death of Colonel Edward Williams, widely regarded as a 'dead weight'. Mudge was elected fellow of the Royal Society in the same year and immediately applied to the society for the loan of Jesse Ramsden's 3 foot theodolite which had been lying unused for some time. Once modified and adjusted, it allowed the survey to increase its rate of progress and remained in use until

1853. He also asked Ramsden to complete his zenith sector. Using these instruments he completed the measurement of an arc of meridian from Dunnose, Isle of Wight, to Clifton, Yorkshire, in 1801 to 1802. This achievement, due both to Ramsden's high-quality instruments and to Mudge's skill in directing their use, represented a very considerable advance in the scientific work of the Ordnance Survey and contributed to the international debate over the precise figure of the earth.

As well as developing the Ordnance board's trigonometric survey, Mudge was responsible for the interior or topographic survey, which resulted in the publication of topographical maps at a scale of one inch to a mile, the first being of Kent, published by William Faden in 1801. Finding that such maps were costly to produce, Mudge carried through changes in the organization of the survey, showing a grasp of management and budgeting as well as of the scientific aspects of cartography. He recruited engravers to the drawing office, helping to establish the Ordnance Survey as a map publisher and eventually a map seller. While head of the survey he lived first at the Tower of London and then, from his marriage in 1808 to his death in 1820, at 4 Holles Street, London. His wife was earlier thought to have been Margaret Jane (d. 1824), third daughter of Major-General George Williamson RA, but was probably Katherine Jane, fourth daughter of Colonel John Williamson RA (c.1731–1794). Mudge was apparently a devoted father to his daughter and four sons, who included Richard Zachariah *Mudge, also a noted surveyor, and William *Mudge, naval officer.

In addition to his survey duties Mudge was appointed on 29 July 1809 lieutenant-governor of the Royal Military Academy at Woolwich, and in 1810 public examiner of the new East India Company college at Addiscombe. With three posts he was under extreme pressure, but his management of the cadets was very successful; he took pains to ensure that they were well instructed, notably by Robert Dawson. He also mixed with them socially and spotted the exceptional talents of cadet Thomas Colby whose appointment to the trigonometric survey Mudge secured and who became his personal assistant.

In 1813 it was decided to extend the English arc of meridian into Scotland. Mudge superintended the work and took an active part in the measurement, being described by Wordsworth in his poem 'Black Combe' (1813) as the 'geographical Labourer' whose survey was 'a lonely task, week after week pursued!' The French Bureau des Longitudes applied for permission for Jean-Baptiste Biot to make observations for them on the newly extended meridian. This Anglo-French co-operation was encouraged by the British government, but unfortunately Mudge's ill health meant that the job of accompanying Biot fell to Colby; his and Biot's intense mutual dislike led to the failure of the enterprise, which might have been averted had Mudge been fit to lead the operation. In 1818 Mudge was appointed a commissioner of the new board of longitude. In May 1819 he began the survey of southern Scotland for a one-inch map and in August of that year was

promoted major-general. He died on 17 April 1820, still superintendent of the survey.

Mudge was one of the most important men in the history of the Ordnance Survey since he laid its scientific and organizational foundations and shaped its later development by promoting Colby to succeed him. He published extensively about the Ordnance Survey, notably *A General Survey of England and Wales* (1805) and several *Accounts* (some with Colby and Isaac Dalby) which together give a uniquely detailed history of the survey in its early years.

ELIZABETH BAIGENT

Sources W. A. Seymour, ed., *A history of the Ordnance Survey* (1980) · *The old series ordnance survey maps of England and Wales*, Ordnance Survey, 8 vols. (1975–92) [introductions to each vol. by J. B. Harley and others] · T. Owen and E. Pilbeam, *Ordnance Survey: map makers to Britain since 1791* (1992) · S. R. Flint, ed., *Mudge memoirs* (1883) · private information (2004) · S. Widmalm, *Mellan kartan och verkligheten: geodesi och kartläggning, 1695–1860* (Uppsala, 1990) **Archives** Ordnance Survey, Southampton **Likenesses** J. Northcote, portrait, 1804, Ordnance Survey, Southampton

Mudge, William (1796–1837), naval officer, was the third son of Major-General William *Mudge (1762–1820) and his wife, probably Katherine Jane, fourth daughter of Colonel John Williamson, RA (c.1731–1794). Richard Zachariah *Mudge (1790–1854) was his brother. He was promoted lieutenant in the navy on 19 February 1815. In August 1821 he was appointed first lieutenant of the *Barracouta*, with Captain Cutfield, employed on the survey of the east coast of Africa under Captain W. F. Owen. He was afterwards moved into the *Leven* under the immediate command of Owen. On 4 October 1825 he was promoted commander and appointed to conduct the survey of the coast of Ireland, on which he was employed until his death. He married in 1827 Mary Marinda, the only child of William Rae of Blackheath; they had six surviving children. In addition to *Sailing Directions for Dublin Bay and for the North Coast of Ireland*, which was officially published in 1842, Mudge contributed several papers (mostly hydrographic) to the *Nautical Magazine*, and, in November 1833 to the Society of Antiquaries, an interesting account of a prehistoric village found in a Donegal bog. He died at Howth, near Dublin, on 20 July 1837, survived by his wife, and was buried with military honours in the ground of the cathedral at Howth on 24 July.

J. K. LAUGHTON, rev. ROGER MORRISS

Sources S. R. Flint, ed., *Mudge memoirs* (1883) · J. Marshall, *Royal naval biography*, 4/2 (1835), 175 · *GM*, 2nd ser., 8 (1837), 326 · *Nautical Magazine*, 6 (1837) · L. S. Dawson, *Memoirs of hydrography*, 2 vols. (1885), vol. 1 · K. Ingham, *A history of East Africa* (1962) · R. Oliver and G. Mathew, *History of East Africa*, 1 (1963) · R. Howell, *The Royal Navy and the slave trade* (1987) · G. S. Ritchie, *The Admiralty chart: British naval hydrography in the nineteenth century* (1967)

Mudge, Zachariah (1694–1769), Church of England clergyman, was born at Exeter, of unknown Presbyterian parentage. He went to Exeter grammar school, and then, at the age of sixteen, enrolled in the Presbyterian academy kept at Exeter by Joseph Hallett (1656–1722). Hallett's academy instilled in Mudge a deep love of learning across many fields of enquiry. It was also Mudge's good fortune that in 1711 he was given the pick of the library of the

Zachariah Mudge (1694–1769), by James Watson (after Sir Joshua Reynolds, 1761–2?)

recently deceased George Trosse, a prominent member of the local nonconformist community. Mudge now had, ready to hand, an excellent selection of classical and Hebrew texts.

In 1713 Mudge returned to Exeter grammar school as second master, working under the Revd Samuel Reynolds, father of the painter Sir Joshua. Mudge was to be one of Sir Joshua's lifelong friends. Reynolds reverenced Mudge, telling James Northcote that his friend was 'the wisest man he had ever met with in his life' (Northcote, 1.115). Mudge was also Reynolds's intellectual mentor. The central argument of Reynolds's influential *Discourses*, namely that beauty 'is an idea that subsists only in the mind', is a notion which Reynolds admitted he got from Mudge, who was steeped in Platonic philosophy. Mudge married Mary Fox in 1714. They had a daughter, also called Mary, and four sons.

In the winter of 1717–18 Mudge left his alma mater, and became master of Bideford grammar school. Although successful there, he was spiritually restless. In the early 1720s he entered into a long theological correspondence, now unfortunately lost, with Stephen Weston, bishop of Exeter. Under Weston's influence, Mudge abandoned plans to enter the Presbyterian ministry, and was instead ordained deacon in the Church of England on 21 September 1729. He was priested the next day.

Mudge joined a distinguished company of recent seceders from Presbyterianism, the most prominent being Thomas Secker, later archbishop of Canterbury, who had crossed over in 1721. What split Presbyterianism was a trinitarian debate, which surfaced in the Salters' Hall dispute of 1719. This, in turn, originated from an appeal made by Hallett against the judgement of the Exeter Assembly, a mixed body of Presbyterian and Congregationalist divines, that Hallett was an Arian (Mather, 29). Mudge had experienced the trinitarian debate within Presbyterianism at first hand—from 1710, the year of Mudge's entry, the assistant master at Hallett's academy had been Hallett's son, Joseph (1691?–1744), who corresponded with the Unitarian William Whiston and actively disseminated Whiston's ideas.

Using the propulsive power of Weston's patronage—the bishop had taught Sir Robert Walpole while he was at Eton College, and had the prime minister's ear—Mudge moved ahead very rapidly in his new career. Within three months of ordination he was instituted to the living of Abbotsham near Bideford; in August 1732 he moved on to St Andrew's, Plymouth, one of the richest livings in England; and in 1736 he was made a prebendary of Exeter.

Mudge's meteoric rise was assisted by his first publication. *Liberty: a Sermon* (1731) was a printed version of an address Mudge had given in Exeter Cathedral on 16 September 1731. Mudge's thoughts were powerfully expressed. More importantly, they delighted his new co-religionists almost as much as they angered his former spiritual confrères. Dissenting preachers, Mudge asserted, frequently made up with conceit for what they lacked in experience—'a young man, perhaps, yet of an age in which the law wisely won't trust him with the government of himself, thinks himself qualified to judge decisively upon the administration of God, and the wisdom of ages' (Mudge, 29).

Sermons on Different Subjects came out in 1739. The tone was one of confident dogmatism—'… in things of the greatest importance … it is not only ridiculous, but fatal to be doubtful'; and Mudge also showed himself a strong tory in politics—'there has been ever acknowledged something sacred in the persons of princes, a kind of a Divine cloud hovering round their heads, to which we are naturally prompted to pay a veneration' (*Sermons*, 345, 385).

Sermons gave an inaccurate indication of Mudge's personality. Although dogmatic in public, he was relaxed in private, had a strong pastoral sense, and was especially fond of children. One of his best qualities was a complete lack of any trace of self-importance. He was also renowned for mildly laconic aphorisms. 'If you take too much care of yourself,' he once said, 'nature will cease to take care of you' (Flint, 13).

Mudge's major contribution to scholarship was *An Essay towards a New English Version of the Book of Psalms*, published in 1744. Working from the Hebrew text, Mudge produced a translation of the Psalms which made no concessions to linguistic modernity—it was spiced with 'thees' and 'thys'—was uniformly rhythmic, and at times powerfully poetic. His notes were learned and occasionally witty—a 'party of marauders' (Psalm 18:29) is 'like our modern hussars, sent to scour and plunder a country'. Mudge also spent many years on an English translation of the Hebrew text of the whole Bible but this project, unfortunately, was never completed.

The four sons of Zachariah and Mary Mudge all had interesting careers. Zachariah (1714–1753) was a surgeon, and died on board an Indiaman at Canton; Thomas *Mudge (1715/16–1794) was the renowned watchmaker; Richard *Mudge (*bap.* 1718, *d.* 1763) took holy orders, attaining skill in metaphysics and publishing some concertos; and John *Mudge (*bap.* 1721, *d.* 1793), surgeon and physician, published several medical works and was made FRS. It was at John's house, in 1762, that Mudge met Boswell and Johnson. Mudge made a strong impression on this pair of redoubtable worthies. Boswell was in awe of the eloquence of Mudge's preaching, writing that he was 'idolized in the west' (Flint, 14), and Johnson warmed to Mudge's affable, caring personality, averring that he was 'at once beloved as a companion and reverenced as a pastor' (*London Chronicle*, 2 June 1769). Another friend was the civil engineer John Smeaton, who invited him to attend the completion of the third Eddystone lighthouse in 1759. Smeaton conducted Mudge to the summit of his 'tower of the winds'; and there, in the lantern, the pair sang Psalm 100 'as a thanksgiving for the successful conclusion of this arduous undertaking' (*DNB*).

In 1762, Mary having died, Mudge married Elizabeth Neell (*d.* 1782). This second marriage led to a change in Mudge's routine: he now made an annual pilgrimage to London, and it was on these visits that he met many of the prominent men of his time, including Edmund Burke, David Garrick, and Oliver Goldsmith. He was on his way to London when he suddenly fell ill and died, at Coffleet in Devon, on 2 April 1769. Mudge was buried near the communion table of St Andrew's, Plymouth.

PETER VIRGIN

Sources S. R. Flint, ed., *Mudge memoirs* (1883) · J. Northcote, *The life of Sir Joshua Reynolds*, 2nd edn, 2 vols. (1818) · F. C. Mather, *High church prophet: Bishop Samuel Horsley (1733–1806) and the Caroline tradition in the later Georgian church* (1992) · *DNB* · Boswell, *Life* · *London Chronicle* (2 June 1769) · A. Brockett, *Nonconformity in Exeter, 1650–1875* (1962) · Z. Mudge, *Liberty: a sermon* (1731)
Likenesses J. Reynolds, portraits, 1761–6 · S. W. Reynolds, mezzotint, pubd 1835 (after J. Reynolds), BM, NPG · F. Chantrey, marble bust, St Andrew's, Plymouth · J. Watson, mezzotint (after J. Reynolds, 1761–1762?), BM, NPG [*see illus.*]

Mudge, Zachary (1770–1852), naval officer, a younger son of Dr John *Mudge (*bap.* 1721, *d.* 1793) and his third wife, Elizabeth, *née* Garrett (*c.*1736–1808), and the half-brother of Major-General William *Mudge, was born at Plymouth on 22 January 1770. From November 1780 he was on the books of the *Foudroyant*, with Captain John Jervis, and is said to have been on board her when she captured the *Pégase* on 21 April 1782. During the next seven years he served on the home and North American stations, for some time as midshipman of the *Pégase*, and on 24 May 1789 was promoted lieutenant. In December 1790 he was appointed to the *Discovery*, with Captain George Vancouver, then starting on his celebrated voyage of exploration on the north-west coast of America. In February 1794 Mudge was moved into the *Providence*, with Commander W. R. Broughton, and on 24 November 1797 was promoted commander. In November 1798 he was appointed to the sloop *Fly*, employed on the coast of North America.

On 15 November 1800 he was promoted post captain, and in April 1801 was appointed to the *Constance* (24 guns), in which he was employed convoying merchant ships or cruising with some success against privateers.

In September 1802 Mudge was moved into the frigate *Blanche* (32 guns) in the West Indies. During 1803 and 1804 she captured both enemy merchant ships and privateers. On 19 July 1805, as she was carrying dispatches from Jamaica intended for Lord Nelson at Barbados, she met a small French squadron consisting of the frigate *Topaze* (40 guns), two heavy corvettes, and a brig, which brought her to action about ten in the morning. In a little over an hour she was reduced to a wreck and struck her colours; Mudge and the rest of the officers and crew were taken out of her, and towards evening she sank. Both at the time and afterwards it was questioned whether Mudge had made the best possible defence; the *Topaze* only, it was said, was actively engaged, and her loss was limited to one man killed. On the other hand, the corvettes seriously interfered with the *Blanche*'s manoeuvres, and this was the view taken by the court martial which, on 14 October, acquitted Mudge and complimented him on his able and gallant conduct. On 18 November he was appointed to the *Phœnix* (36 guns), which he commanded for the next five years in the Bay of Biscay and on the coast of Portugal.

Some time before 1814 Mudge married Jane, the daughter of the Revd Edmund Granger, rector of Sowton, Devon; they had several children. In 1814 and 1815 he commanded the *Valiant* (74 guns), but had no further service. He became rear-admiral on 22 July 1830, vice-admiral on 23 November 1841, and admiral on 15 September 1849. He died at his residence, Sydney, near Plympton, Devon, on 26 October 1852, and was buried at Newton Ferrers church; a memorial window was placed in St Andrew's Church, Plymouth. Mudge's eldest son, Zachary, a barrister, died, at the age of fifty-four, on 13 December 1868.

J. K. LAUGHTON, *rev.* ANDREW LAMBERT

Sources B. Anderson, *The life and voyages of Captain George Vancouver* (1960) · G. S. Ritchie, *The Admiralty chart: British naval hydrography in the nineteenth century* (1967) · O'Byrne, *Naval biog. dict.* · S. R. Flint, ed., *Mudge memoirs* (1883) · *GM*, 2nd ser., 38 (1852), 634 · J. Marshall, *Royal naval biography*, 2/1 (1824), 307

Mudie, Charles Edward (1818–1890), founder of a circulating library, was born on 18 October 1818 at Cheyne Walk, Chelsea, London, the youngest son of Thomas Mudie, a Scottish newspaper agent, bookseller, stationer, and lending librarian. Details of Charles Mudie's education are not known, although he is reported as describing it as 'properly cared for' (Curwen, 421), and a friend remarked on the young man's 'studious and thoughtful disposition. … my guess is that his formal education was just short of that required for matriculation' (Espinasse, 27). After several years assisting his father in running his business, in 1840 he opened a shop at 28 Upper King Street, supplying newspapers and stationery as well as loaning books. Within two years the book-lending side of his business had become his main concern. He also dabbled in publishing, producing the first edition in England of James Russell Lowell's *Poems* and Ralph Waldo

Emerson's *Man Thinking: an Oration* in 1844. He married Mary Kingsford Pawling, daughter of the Revd Henry Carpenter Pawling of Lenham, Kent, on 20 April 1847. They had eight children, including Charles Henry Mudie [*see below*], who ran the firm until his death in 1879, and Arthur Oliver Mudie who, on the death of his older brother, assumed control of the business, and eventually became the managing director.

The rise of the three-volume novel as a standard publishing format in the nineteenth century had begun before Mudie's development of his business. But Mudie, in offering unlimited borrowing of fiction and prose works at low subscription rates starting at 1 guinea a year, became a major supplier of reading material for a wide audience unable to afford the cost of new books, including students from the newly opened University of London. By 1852 his business had proved so profitable that new headquarters were found at 510 New Oxford Street, and in the following decades branches were opened in Birmingham, Manchester, and other regional centres. With the purchasing power occasioned by the success of his lending library, which by the mid-century numbered over 25,000 subscribers, he was to play a major part in sustaining the three-volume novel format until the 1890s. Between 1853 and 1862 Mudie is said to have added almost 960,000 volumes to his stock in hand, thus becoming one of the major distributors of fiction in Britain at the time. His business also serviced readers overseas, shipping tin trunks of books to India, Cape Colony, Egypt, and other British colonies. The glee occasioned by the arrival of Mudie's shipments was playfully commented upon by W. S. Gilbert in *Bab Ballads* when he wrote: 'New boxes come from across the sea/ from Mr. Mudie's Libraree'. The reliance of the middle class on Mudie to provide it with reading material was ubiquitous enough to be immortalized in the contemporary doggerel verse:

> As children must have Punch and Judy
> So I can't do without my Mudie.

In 1861 overexpansion, the extravagant costs of renovating his New Oxford Street premises, and competition from other lending libraries brought Mudie to near bankruptcy. He was rescued by a consortium of publishers, who lent him money and supported his business until he returned to solvency in 1864. His business was floated on the stock market as a limited company in the same year, with Mudie retaining half the shares and overall control of the business, while providing his rescuers with a stake in the firm. By the 1870s the firm was once again preeminent in its distribution and supply of literature, so much so that it was frequently attacked by authors and publishers aggrieved at the effect upon book sales of Mudie's censorious selection and exclusion of works for his readers. George Moore's 1885 pamphlet *Literature at Nurse, or, Circulating Morals* was a notable instance of this, attacking censorship in general and Mudie's in particular. The dependence of the three-volume publishing format on Mudie's trade was demonstrated when the firm stopped ordering three-volume novels in 1894. Within two years the format had ceased to exist, and publishers

had begun experimenting with new formats, prices, and outlets for their products, heralding the slow demise of Mudie's Select Library, which closed its doors in 1937.

Mudie was actively involved in civic duties throughout his life, serving as a member of various committees, including a three-year period as a member of the London school board for the Westminster district from 1870 to 1873. In 1879 his favourite and eldest son Charles Henry Mudie died. Mudie never fully recovered from this loss and over the next five years took progressively less interest in his business. By 1884 he had retired from all active duties, relinquishing control of the firm to his son Arthur. He died at his home, 31 Maresfield Gardens, Hampstead, London, on 28 October 1890 and was buried on 1 November.

Charles Henry Mudie (1850–1879), philanthropist and businessman, was born in Adelaide Road, Haverstock Hill, Middlesex, on 26 January 1850. Educated at London University School (1862–4), the Revd N. Jennings's boarding-school in St John's Wood (1864), and under private tutelage (1866), he entered his father's firm in 1871, where he learned all aspects of the business with the understanding that in due course he would succeed his father as head of the firm. On 4 June 1874 he married Rebecca Jane Lermitte of Muswell Hill, Middlesex. His philanthropy centred around education, as he interested himself in working men's clubs and in industrial and reformatory schools (Mudie, 29). A gifted musician and amateur actor, Charles Henry Mudie died tragically young of acute rheumatism and endocarditis on 13 January 1879 in Melford Lodge, Muswell Hill.　　　　　　　　　　　DAVID FINKELSTEIN

Sources G. L. Griest, *Mudie's circulating library and the Victorian novel* (1970) · D. Finkelstein, 'The secret: British publishers and Mudie's struggle for economic survival, 1861–64', *Publishing History*, 34 (1993), 21–50 · J. Sutherland, *The Longman companion to Victorian fiction* (1988) · H. Curwen, *A history of booksellers, the old and the new* (1873) · C. J. Pomponio, 'Charles Edward Mudie', *International Library Review*, 4 (1972) · [M. Mudie], *Charles Henry Mudie: a memorial sketch by one of his sisters* (privately printed, London, 1879) · *The Athenaeum* (1 Nov 1890), 588 · *The Times* (30 Oct 1890) · m. cert. · d. cert. [Charles Henry Mudie] · F. Espinasse, *Literary recollections* (1893), 27 · CGPLA Eng. & Wales (1890) · CGPLA Eng. & Wales (1879)
Archives University of Illinois, Urbana-Champaign, corresp., travel diary, and papers | BL, Bentley MSS · NL Scot., corresp. with Blackwoods
Likenesses R. Taylor, wood-engraving (after photograph by Maull & Polyblank), BM, NPG; repro. in *ILN* (3 Nov 1890) · engravings, repro. in Griest, *Mudie's circulating library* · portrait, repro. in F. Waddy, *Cartoon portraits and biographical sketches of men of the day* (1873), 72–3
Wealth at death £59,347 11s. 1d.: probate, 6 Dec 1890, CGPLA Eng. & Wales · under £3000—Charles Henry Mudie: probate, 10 Feb 1879, CGPLA Eng. & Wales

Mudie, Charles Henry (1850–1879). *See under* Mudie, Charles Edward (1818–1890).

Mudie, Robert (1777–1842), newspaper editor and author, born in Forfarshire on 28 June 1777, was the youngest son of John Mudie, weaver, and his wife, Elizabeth, *née* Bany. After attending the village school he worked as a weaver until he was drafted into the militia. From his boyhood he was an avid reader, an autodidact reared mainly on the

Encyclopaedia Britannica. At the end of his four years of militia service he became master of a village school in the south of Fife. In 1802 he was appointed Gaelic professor and teacher of drawing at Inverness Academy, although he knew little Gaelic. About 1808 he became drawing-master to Dundee high school, but soon also took on the department of arithmetic and English composition. He contributed much to the local newspaper, and ran for some time a monthly periodical. Becoming a member of the Dundee town council, he worked energetically for burgh reform with R. S. Rintoul, editor of the radical *Dundee Advertiser* and later of the London *Spectator*. In politics he was 'an ardent reformer'. He had about this time some acquaintance with Thomas Chalmers, then in St Andrews. Mudie's speeches, attacking corruption on the council, led to the loss of his post as teacher of arithmetic (his drawing post was beyond the council's control). He tried, unsuccessfully, to start a mercantile and mathematical academy and launched two short-lived periodicals, *The Independent* (April–September 1816) and *The Caledonian* (June–October 1821). On the failure of these, in the autumn of 1821 he sold his life appointment as teacher in drawing and moved to London, where he was a reporter on the *Morning Chronicle*, reporting George IV's visit to Edinburgh, which he also described in a volume, *Modern Athens* (1824). He was subsequently editor of the *Sunday Times* and wrote largely in the periodicals of the day.

About 1838 Mudie moved to Winchester, where he was employed by a bookseller named Robbins in writing books, including a *History of Hampshire* (3 vols., 1838) and a stream of other topographical volumes. The enterprise failed, and Mudie returned to London, impoverished and in broken health. He edited the *Surveyor, Engineer and Architect*, a monthly journal; it began publication in February 1840 but was not a financial success. Throughout this unsatisfactory and ultimately wretched career, Mudie maintained a steady flow of publications: at least fifty titles are credited to him. He was an energetic didact, in the Scottish tradition, whose object was 'to combine morality with instruction' (*GM*, 214). 'His quickness of apprehension was great, and his memory extraordinary, so that his knowledge was very various, indeed almost universal' (Duncan, 491). His first works were *The Maid of Griban* (1819) (verses) and *Glenfergus* (3 vols., 1819), a novel. In the 1820s he turned to topography, often writing in a moralizing tone, and produced a long list of volumes, of which two on London, *Babylon the Great* (2 vols., 1825) and *A Second Judgment on Babylon the Great* (2 vols., 1829) are the most striking. For *Things in General* (on London and elsewhere) (1824) he used the pseudonym Laurence Langshank. Mudie became a keen ornithologist and published several volumes, such as *The Feathered Tribes of the British Islands* (2 vols., 1834) and *The Natural History of Birds* (1834); he also wrote on other aspects of biology. He was also the author of books on natural philosophy, mental and moral philosophy, China, India, copyright, and the seasons of the year. Mudie wrote the greater part of the natural history section of the *British Cyclopaedia* (1834), the text to Gilbert's *Modern Atlas of the Earth* (1840), and a topographical account of Selborne prefixed to Gilbert White's *Natural History of Selborne* (new edn, 1850). Mudie died at Pentonville on 29 April 1842, leaving the widow of his second marriage destitute, one son, and four daughters.

GORDON GOODWIN, *rev.* H. C. G. MATTHEW

Sources *GM*, 2nd ser., 18 (1842), 214–15 · Professor Duncan, 'Memoir', in W. Hanna, *Memoirs of the life and writings of Thomas Chalmers*, 1 (1849) · W. Anderson, *The Scottish nation*, 3 vols. (1866–77) · A. L. Strout, 'Robert Mudie', *N&Q*, 172 (1937), 146–9 · W. B. Thomas, *The story of The Spectator, 1828–1928* (1928) · W. Norrie, *Dundee celebrities of the nineteenth century* (1873) · *Surveyor, Engineer, and Architect* (1842), 149 · K. G. Lowe, *The modern Athens: Sir Walter Scott's satire on Edina*, 2 vols. (1935–6) · *DNB*

Mudie, Thomas Molleson (1809–1876), composer, of Scottish descent, was born at Chelsea, London, on 30 November 1809. In 1823 he came third out of thirty-two candidates in the first examination for admission to the Royal Academy of Music, where he studied composition with William Crotch, piano with Cipriani Potter, and clarinet with Thomas Willman, and won several prizes. He was subsequently a professor of the piano there (1832–44). In 1834 he became organist at Gatton, near Reigate, Surrey, the home of Lord Monson, and spent much of his time there until Lord Monson's death in 1840. In 1844, on the death of his friend Alfred Devaux, Mudie went to Edinburgh to succeed him as a teacher of music.

Mudie's successes as a composer were confined mainly to his earlier years. The committee of management of the Royal Academy was so impressed by his song 'Lungi dal caro bene' that it paid for it to be published. Several vocal pieces with orchestral accompaniment and two symphonies, in C and in B♭, were also composed while he was a student. Many of his works were performed at the Society of British Musicians, founded in 1834, and included symphonies, chamber music, songs, and solo piano music. While in Edinburgh he composed a number of piano pieces and songs, and wrote accompaniments for a large proportion of the airs in Wood's collection *Songs of Scotland* (1848). After his return to London in 1863 he published very little, his talents possibly stifled by the drudgery of twenty years of music teaching.

Mudie died in London, unmarried, on 24 July 1876, and was buried in Highgate cemetery.

J. C. HADDEN, *rev.* ANNE PIMLOTT BAKER

Sources Grove, *Dict. mus.* · F. Corder, *A history of the Royal Academy of Music from 1822 to 1922* (1922) · *MT*, 17 (1875–6), 563 [brief mention in Royal Academy of Music news column]

Mueller [*married name* Robertson], **Dame Anne Elisabeth** (1930–2000), civil servant, was born in Bombay on 15 October 1930, the elder child of Herbert Constantin Mueller (1891–1952) and his wife, Phoebe Ann, *née* Beevers (1901–1973). Her parents married while working in India, he a German running an engineering business and she a Yorkshirewoman teaching at Queen Mary's High School in Bombay, the first school Anne attended. Despite their father's German nationality, Anne and her younger brother were registered at the British high commission

Dame Anne Elisabeth Mueller (1930–2000), by Daphne Todd, 1996

and were regarded as British. When war seemed imminent the family moved to Europe. A German with strong anti-Nazi sentiments would have been welcome neither in Germany nor in England. Herbert Mueller bought a vineyard in Slovenia, where Anne's family childhood came to an abrupt end when war broke out. The children and their mother were put on a train for England; Mrs Mueller returned to Slovenia as soon as they had been settled.

Anne briefly boarded at St Helen and St Katharine's School, Abingdon. In 1940 she was moved to Yorkshire, where she and her young brother spent the war years staying with an aunt. This was a most unhappy period for Anne, an intelligent and stubborn child who did not fit easily into the new household. Her mother managed to return to England during the war, but did not make a home for the children. She was initially interned in the Isle of Man and was subsequently permitted to join the ATS. Herbert Mueller also escaped to England, after wartime experiences with the resistance, which are a story in their own right. He took British nationality and relocated his wife and son after the war to a farm in Rhodesia. It was Anne's choice to remain in England and continue her studies.

Anne Mueller attended Wakefield Girls' High School, and during her final year won a three-month scholarship trip to the USA in a national competition. In 1949 she was admitted as an exhibitioner to Somerville College, Oxford, where she read philosophy, politics, and economics. Her failure to achieve a first-class degree in the final honours school in 1952 may reflect some emotional distractions in her final year at Oxford—an unhappy engagement (subsequently terminated) and her father's death just as she was taking her final examinations. She left for Rhodesia immediately after finals to assist her mother.

In 1953 Anne was successful in her second attempt to enter the administrative class of the civil service. Her first post was as an assistant principal in the Ministry of Labour, working on the development of the national employment exchange service. In 1955 she was posted to Paris as a consultant in the manpower division of the Organization for European Economic Co-operation. She spoke good French and loved Paris, which was the perfect setting for a bright and beautiful young woman. In 1956 she suffered extensive injuries in a serious car accident; she endured over twenty operations, and spent about two years in hospitals and rehabilitation centres. Her survival was in doubt, let alone her return to a high-flying Whitehall career. This accident contributed to the disabling arthritis from which she suffered in later life.

In 1958 Anne Mueller was appointed private secretary to Sir Lawrence Helsby, the permanent secretary of the Ministry of Labour, and moved with him to the Treasury. In the same year (23 May) she married James Hugh Robertson (b. 1928), himself a civil servant and the son of a distinguished public servant, Sir James Robertson. They settled in Kensington, a high-flying dual-career couple. Anne was promoted principal in 1960, assistant secretary in 1968, under-secretary in 1972, and deputy secretary in 1977. She served in the Treasury and the Department of Economic Affairs (working on incomes policy), then in the Department of Trade and Industry (DTI), where she was head, first, of the financial and economic appraisal division (dealing with investment incentives) and, on promotion to under-secretary, of the industrial and commercial policy division (seeking to improve industrial performance). As deputy secretary in the DTI from 1977 to 1984 she had a wide-ranging command with responsibility for regional industrial policy and inward investment.

In 1978 the Robertsons' marriage was dissolved. Friendly relations resumed in due course with James Robertson and his second wife, and Anne often visited their home. She herself never married again.

In 1984 Anne Mueller went to the Cabinet Office on promotion to second permanent secretary, thus becoming the most senior woman (at that time) in the civil service. She was put in charge of the new Management and Personnel Office (MPO) created by Margaret Thatcher's administration to replace the former Civil Service Department (CSD) with the aim of updating the training and management skills of civil servants. This was not an easy assignment, partly because of the inevitable demarcation dispute with the Treasury over respective responsibilities for pay. Anne fought her corner with determination and introduced new management methods, flexible working patterns for women 'returners', and performance-related pay. In the MPO, as in the DTI, her reaction was to challenge the conventional wisdom of what could not be done, or had never been done, and to say 'Why not?'. In her MPO post she gave a new impetus to the civil-service commitment to equal opportunities, leaving the civil service a model for other large employers. This period was probably the pinnacle of her civil-service career.

Anne Mueller's final years in the civil service, from 1987 to 1990, were spent as second permanent secretary of HM Treasury, where she was responsible for civil service management and pay. Although hurt to be moved sideways from the MPO post, to which she had been so well suited, she continued to work energetically. It is a pity that she never had the opportunity to show her mettle as permanent secretary in full charge of her own department. She retired on health grounds a few months before her sixtieth birthday. Anne Mueller was a brilliant civil servant, incisive and direct. She had a striking ability to identify the key issues and focus on them without distraction, a characteristic which impressed not only her civil-service colleagues but also those organizations with which she worked in her final decade. She believed passionately in the importance of education, training, and management and took the opportunity, unusual at the time for a civil servant, to acquire a diploma in management studies at Templeton College in 1968.

Anne Mueller was tough. At times she could be intimidating—she did not give or ask for quarter. She could be opinionated, although she was always open to rational argument. She was impatient of those who concentrated on her gender rather than on her work, yet she could not escape being regarded as a role model for other women in worlds where the top ranks were still overwhelmingly a male reserve. Civil servants can rarely claim personal credit for particular policies or achievements. Anne's main professional achievements must be identified with the managerial changes which she initiated in her time at the MPO, which were of limited interest to outsiders. Her reputation in the public service and the wider world hung rather on respect for her abilities, admiration for her personality, and, above all, for her courage.

Despite a diagnosis of Parkinson's disease, Anne's life after retirement was busier than ever. She continued to enjoy travel, shopping, and the cultural activities of London. She would entertain friends at her flat in Kensington and take them to opera at Holland Park and Glyndebourne. At the same time she was actively committed to a string of part-time appointments and directorships. In 1988 she had become a governor of de Montfort University, and in 1991 she was appointed chancellor. In 1992 she became a board member of CARE International, a non-governmental development charity, one of the two British representatives on the international board. She continued her particular interest in training and education, especially women's education, as a member of council of the Institute of Management Studies, the Manchester Business School, Templeton College, Oxford, the London Education Business Partnership, and Queen Mary and Westfield College.

Anne Mueller was appointed CB in 1980 and DCB in 1988, only the second woman to be appointed to this rank in the order. She held honorary degrees from Warwick University, Leicester Polytechnic, Nottingham University, and (of course) de Montfort. She was elected an honorary fellow of her old college, Somerville, in 1984.

Anne Mueller had great elegance, and from girlhood struck those who met her with her charm, chin-up energy, and sense of style. She was a gardener with a strong sense of design. She had an eye for beauty and an interest in accumulating fine objects, clothes, and jewellery. When lameness compelled her to walk with a stick she acquired a wardrobe of particularly elegant canes. After her traumatic accident in Paris, unable to drink from a glass, she took her champagne through a straw. In her last years Anne drove herself on remorselessly, despite increasing physical disability. As chancellor of de Montfort she presided at ceremonies, disregarding the tremors of encroaching Parkinson's and the threat of collapse. As vice-president member of CARE International, she undertook long-distance international flights alone and with her wheelchair in the baggage compartment; she relinquished this role with sorrow only when she suspected that the local support she required was becoming disproportionate. After collapsing in May 2000 she was taken to the Chelsea and Westminster Hospital, where she died on 8 July. Her remains were cremated at Mortlake on 18 July. A packed memorial service in Westminster Abbey on 3 October 2000 showed the respect and affection in which she was held.   ELIZABETH LLEWELLYN-SMITH

Sources personal knowledge (2004) · private information (2004) [Dr Peter Mueller, Mr James Robertson, Ms Colette Bowe, Lord Butler of Brockwell, Sir Peter Carey, Sir John Cassels, Mr Roy Croft, Mr Will Day, Mrs Rosemary James, Sir Richard O'Brien, Sir William Ryrie, Professor Philip Tasker, Mrs Joy Whitby, Sir Richard Wilson] · archives, Somerville College, Oxford · *The Times* (28 July 2000) · *The Guardian* (1 Aug 2000) · *The Observer* (3 June 1984)
Likenesses M. Argles, photograph, 1984, repro. in *The Guardian* · D. Todd, oils, 1996, De Montfort University, Leicester [*see illus.*] · photograph, repro. in *The Times* · photograph, repro. in *Observer* (3 June 1984)

Mueller [Müller], **Sir Ferdinand Jacob Heinrich von** (1825–1896), botanist, was born on 30 June 1825 in Rostock, third of nine children of Christoph Friederich Christian Müller (1794–1835), customs officer, and his wife, Louise (1798–1840), daughter of Johann and Anna Maria Mertens. Only Ferdinand and three sisters survived infancy. After his father died the family moved, in 1836, to Tönning, where his mother contracted to provide a ferry across the Eider and run the associated public house and restaurant. Mueller attended the local school before being apprenticed at Becker's pharmacy in Husum in 1840. At Husum he botanized extensively. When he enrolled at the University of Kiel in 1846 as a pharmacy student he also attended botany classes, and participated in the annual congress of German scientists, among whom he made lasting contacts. Mueller submitted as his thesis a monograph of the flora of south-west Schleswig, but some weeks before the award of the doctoral diploma in August

Sir Ferdinand Jacob Heinrich von Mueller (1825–1896), by Froedel & Co.

1847 he left for South Australia with his two surviving younger sisters, then aged twenty-one and fourteen.

Characteristically, Mueller collected his first Australian specimens, some marine algae, as the vessel in which he was travelling sailed into St Vincent's Gulf. He was quickly absorbed into Adelaide's German community, gained employment in Büttner and Heuzenroeder's Apotheke, and purchased land in the Adelaide hinterland. However, he spent much time in exploration of the botanically little-known colony, penetrating into the interior semi-desert and roaming the wetter areas. He sent specimens, and descriptions, to Otto Sonder, a Hamburg contact made at the Kiel congress, and leading botanists soon provided an important series of descriptions, *Plantae Muellerianae*, in *Linnaea*. He was naturalized on 9 August 1849.

Before Mueller could implement his plan to open a pharmacy on the Victorian goldfields, Lieutenant-Governor Charles La Trobe appointed him government botanist of Victoria on 26 January 1853. Within weeks he began both the first of a series of botanical and geographical explorations of the colony and his forty-three year correspondence with Kew Gardens. He later obtained leave to become the botanist on the 1855–6 north Australian exploring expedition. That journey was botanically very productive, producing more manuscript than William Hooker could process at Kew, and, partly to publish these descriptions, Mueller founded *Fragmenta Phytographie Australiae*, published from 1858 to 1882. Joseph Hooker and George Bentham each revised a paper for him for the Linnean Society, and pressed him to go to London to work up his collections. Indeed, he so

impressed the Hookers with his abilities that they wrote an unsolicited report on his work for the Colonial Office, whose permanent head declined to publish such a 'panegyric' in a parliamentary paper. Already a fellow of the Royal Geographical and Linnean societies, Mueller was elected FRS in 1861, being nominated by W. H. Harvey, Charles Darwin, and both Hookers, among others.

When Mueller resumed his post as government botanist in Melbourne in July 1857, to which was added the directorship of the botanic gardens, he hoped to write the Australian volumes of the colonial floras sponsored by Kew, but, being based in Melbourne, he could not examine the European herbaria holding the early Australian collections. Thus Bentham wrote *Flora Australiensis*, formally acknowledging the 'assistance' of Mueller who loaned his Australian herbarium, group by group, over almost twenty years, usually publishing descriptions first in his *Fragmenta*.

Mueller was a leader in the fledgeling scientific societies of Victoria; he actively promoted exploration and supported acclimatization, importing and exporting through the Melbourne Botanic Gardens potentially useful plants and animals from many parts of the world. From February 1868 Mueller added the prefix von to his name, a right accorded by the king of Württemberg. His enormous number of foreign decorations, including his creation as a hereditary baron by the king of Württemberg in 1871, was one of the weapons used against him in an unscrupulous newspaper campaign in the early 1870s which accused him, among other things, of trading specimens for titles. The government of Victoria removed him from the directorship of the botanic gardens in July 1873, although he remained government botanist until his death. He was created KCMG in 1879. Although engaged twice, to Euphemia Henderson, and later to Rebecca Nordt, a girl many years his junior, von Mueller never married, but financially aided his widowed younger sister, Clara Wehl, and her fourteen surviving children.

The last twenty years of von Mueller's life were financially and administratively difficult, although he remained an important promoter of exploration—of Australia, Papua, and Antarctica—as well as continuing to be taxonomically active, especially in describing new Papuan plants. He strongly supported, and held office in, the Australasian Association for the Advancement of Science, his only trip away from Australia and Tasmania being to New Zealand for its third congress in 1891.

Von Mueller died at his home, 28 Arnold Street, South Yarra, Victoria, from apoplexy, on 10 October 1896. By that time he owned little but his dilapidated house and a few chattels, having for many years employed herbarium assistants at his own expense. His published legacy, however, was extensive, with over 1400 items, including Indian (1880), German (1883), American (1884), and Portuguese (1905, 1929) editions of his *Select Extra-Tropical Plants Readily Eligible for Industrial Culture or Naturalisation* (1876), as well as one complete *Key* (1886, 1888) to the plants of Victoria and important monographs on several Australian plant groups. Although he made no lasting contributions to taxonomic theory, and his scientific arguments against Darwinism in his *Vegetation of the Chatham Islands* (1864) passed unnoticed, his descriptions and geographical distribution data, derived from the encouragement of amateur collectors, provided a firm basis for later Australian botany, which continues to be indebted to his foundation, and assiduous enlargement by purchase and exchange, of the Melbourne Herbarium, a major international collection.

During his lifetime British and American reviewers routinely described von Mueller as 'indefatigable', and his obituaries, appearing in many countries, in newspapers as well as scientific journals, testified to his cosmopolitan reputation, as did the international support of an appeal to erect the memorial on his grave in the St Kilda cemetery in Melbourne, where he was buried on 13 October 1896.

A. M. LUCAS

Sources D. M. Churchill, T. B. Muir, and D. M. Sinkora, 'The published works of Ferdinand J. H. Mueller, 1825–1896', *Muelleria*, 4 (1978), 1–120 · D. M. Churchill, T. B. Muir, and D. M. Sinkora, 'The published works of Ferdinand J. H. Mueller, 1825–1896, Supplement', *Muelleria*, 5 (1984), 229–48 · *Transactions of the Royal Geographical Society of Australasia, Victorian Branch*, 14 (1896), 54–8 · W. B. Hemsley, *Nature*, 54 (1896), 596 · *Gardeners' Chronicle*, 3rd ser., 21 (1897), 110–11 · W. B. Spencer, 'Victorian naturalist', 13 (1896), 87–92 · *Agricultural Journal of the Cape of Good Hope*, 9 (1896), 627–8 · *Leopoldina*, 33 (1897), 142–50 · *Journal of Botany, British and Foreign*, 35 (1897), 272–8 · J. D. H. [J. D. Hooker], *PRS*, 63 (1898), xxxii-xxxvi · *GJ*, 8 (1896), 522–33 · A. M. Lucas, 'Baron von Mueller: protégé turned patron', *Australian science in the making*, ed. R. W. Home (1988), 133–52 · A. Brown-May and S. Maroske, 'Breaking into the quietude: re-reading the personal life of Ferdinand von Mueller', *Public History Review*, 3 (1994), 36–62 · R. W. Home, S. Maroske, and P. J. Lucas, 'Why explore Antarctica?: Australian discussions in the 1880s', *Australian Journal of Politics and History*, 38 (1992), 386–413 · A. M. Lucas, 'Letters, shipwrecks and taxonomic confusion: establishing a reputation from Australia', *Historical Records of Australian Science*, 10 (1994–5), 207–21 · N. Gemmell, 'Some notes on Ferdinand von Mueller and the early settlement of Bugle Ranges', *South Australian Naturalist*, 49 (1975), 51–64 · William Hooker and Joseph Hooker to secretary of state for the colonies, 19 Dec 1857, PRO, CO 201/500, fols. 380–84 · order of probate, Public Records Office, Victoria, Australia, 62/802, Unit 446, VPRS 28/P2 · correspondence, University of Melbourne, Australia, Department of History and Philosophy of Science · birth and baptism register, 1825, Rostock, Marienkirche
Archives RBG Kew, archives, corresp. and papers · Royal Botanic Gardens, Melbourne, Australia · State Library of South Australia, Adelaide, notes | Adelaide botanic gardens, J. G. O. Tepper collection · Auckland Public Library, letters to Sir George Grey · Harvard U., Gray Herbarium · Mitchell L., NSW · Mitchell L., NSW, letters to E. P. Ramsay · Public Record Office, Victoria, Australia, chief secretary's and lands department records · RBG Kew, archives, corresp. and papers · RBG Kew, director's corresp. · RBG Kew, specimens · Royal Botanic Garden, Edinburgh · Royal Botanic Gardens, Melbourne, specimens · Fa. Perthes/Haack, Gotha, Germany, Petermann collection
Likenesses photograph, c.1844, Royal Botanic Gardens, Melbourne · etching, 1861, repro. in S. Maroske and H. M. Cohn, 'Such ingenious birds', *Mulleria*, 7 (1992), 548 · J. W. Lindt, photograph, c.1878, repro. in Churchill, Muir, and Sinkora, 'The published works of Ferdinand J. H. Mueller, 1825–1896', pl. 1 · R. Wendle, lithograph, c.1890 (after photograph), repro. in A. M. Lucas, 'Retrieving biology's past: the Mueller correspondence project', *Biologist*, 36 (1989), 126–8 · J. A. Panton, ink on blotting paper, 1893, Royal Historical Society, Victoria, Australia · Froedel & Co., engraving, RBG Kew [*see illus.*]
Wealth at death £553 14*s*. 6*d*.: probate, 1896, Public Record Office, Victoria, Australia, 62/802, Unit 446, VPRS 28/P2 and associated inventory.

Muggeridge, Edward James. *See* Muybridge, Eadweard James (1830–1904).

Muggeridge, (Thomas) Malcolm (1903–1990), journalist and broadcaster, was born on 24 March 1903 in Croydon, Surrey, the third of five sons, one of whom died in 1922 (there were no daughters), of Henry Thomas Benjamin Muggeridge, Labour politician, and his wife, Annie Booler, from Sheffield. His father, elected MP for Romford in 1929, was a self-educated Fabian with an unwavering dedication to socialism. He was the formative influence on his son's early years and as a small boy Malcolm accompanied him on his street-corner electioneering. After attending Selhurst grammar school, Muggeridge went to Selwyn College, Cambridge, where he studied natural sciences but left with a pass degree (1923). It was here that, under the influence of Alec Vidler (a lifelong friend) and later of Wilfred Knox, his religious instincts were first aroused and he even thought at one stage of following Vidler into the Anglican ministry. However, he opted instead for a teaching post at Union Christian College, Alwaye, near Madras, India, where he remained for two years (1925–7).

But Muggeridge was perpetually restless and, after quarrelling with the college principal, he returned to England and took a job as a supply teacher in Birmingham. Shortly afterwards, in 1927, he married Katherine Rosalind (Kitty; *d.* 1994), daughter of George Cumberland Dobbs (an employee of the famous travel agent Sir Henry Lunn) and his wife, Rosie, the youngest sister of Beatrice *Webb. Kitty thereafter was to be the only permanent fixture in his life.

Muggeridge taught English for a time at Cairo University (1927–30) and while there began to submit reports of the Egyptian political scene to the *Manchester Guardian*. In August 1930 he arrived in Manchester and was recruited on to the staff of the paper as a leader writer, on the recommendation of Arthur Ransome. He would perhaps have risen high on the staff but for the sudden death by drowning of E. T. Scott, who took over the editorship from his famous father C. P. Scott. Muggeridge had developed a strong antipathy to Scott's successor, W. P. Crozier, and was in a mood of disappointment following the formation of the National Government in 1931. In September 1932 he and Kitty decided to go and live in Russia, which they regarded, like many young nonconformists of the time, as the new Jerusalem.

Muggeridge, however, was quickly disillusioned, and after reporting first hand on the Ukraine famine—almost the only western journalist to do so—he went to Switzerland and worked for the League of Nations. In 1934 he took a job in India as assistant editor of the *Calcutta Statesman* and then worked for a short time on the staff of the London *Evening Standard*. Muggeridge always chafed at being a mere journalist and had already written a play and three novels (one of which, *Picture Palace*, a satirical account of

(Thomas) Malcolm Muggeridge (1903–1990), by Snowdon, 1983

his time on the *Manchester Guardian*, had been recalled and suppressed by the publisher). In 1936, encouraged by his great friend Hugh Kingsmill, he abandoned full-time journalism and went to live at Whatlington in Sussex. In 1936 he published a critical biography of Samuel Butler and in 1938 another novel, *In a Valley of this Restless Mind*. He also wrote *The Thirties* (1940), a social survey of the decade, which first revealed his formidable powers as a political satirist and was remarkable for its anarchic wit and skilful use of quotation (a hallmark of Muggeridge's style).

At the outbreak of the Second World War Muggeridge joined the intelligence corps and after a few months was transferred to MI6. He was sent to Delagoa Bay in Mozambique, where he proved an effective agent in the fight to prevent the sinking of allied shipping by German U-boats. He also served in north Africa, Italy, and, at the end of the war, in Paris, where he was instrumental in protecting P. G. Wodehouse, then under suspicion of collaborating with the Germans. He was decorated with the Légion d'honneur and the Croix de Guerre with palm.

Muggeridge always liked to swim against the tide and in 1945 joined the Conservative *Daily Telegraph* as a leader writer. He then became the *Telegraph*'s Washington correspondent (1946–7). He was the paper's deputy editor from 1950 to 1952. Later that year, to universal surprise, he accepted the editorship of *Punch*, the first non-member of staff ever to do so. He proved an effective editor, transforming the staid old periodical with his lively and satirical journalism. But, after an initial rise, the circulation fell again and Muggeridge resigned in 1957. By now he was already involved in television as a presenter of the BBC's *Panorama*, a magazine programme devoted to politics and the arts. Muggeridge had a natural flair for television and with his outspoken views, drawling voice, and long cigarette holder quickly became a household name. Briefly suspended by the BBC in late 1957, after he had published in the USA an article attacking the cult of monarchy, he appeared on a wide variety of programmes throughout the 1960s and 1970s, notably a series of autobiographical documentaries, including *Twilight of Empire* and *Ladies and*

Gentlemen it is my Pleasure—an account of a lecture tour in America. He appeared as himself in the notable Boulting brothers' film *I'm All Right Jack* (1959).

All his life Muggeridge had been restless, dissatisfied, and tormented by strong appetites for women and drink. At about the age of sixty he made a series of renunciations—of drinking, meat-eating, smoking, and casual love affairs. He and Kitty had finally settled at Park Cottage in Robertsbridge, an idyllic setting at the end of a long farm track in the Sussex countryside. Here Muggeridge experienced for the first time a degree of contentment and peace. He developed a routine of early rising, writing, and long walks (in which visitors were expected to join). He rediscovered his faith and became in print and on television a formidable apologist for Christianity. He was the first to introduce Mother Teresa to a worldwide audience with his film *Something Beautiful for God*, later published in book form (1971). Muggeridge was received into the Roman Catholic church in 1982.

Muggeridge was a man of middle height, with bright blue eyes and a bulbous nose. He had an enormous vitality and charm and was blessed with generous instincts which usually won over even his fiercest opponents (of whom there were many). He had no ambition for office of any kind and generally acted on impulse. His enormous success as a television personality came about by chance and may have encouraged a natural vanity. But he never lost the ability to laugh at himself. He was sustained throughout his life by the love of his wife. They had three sons and a daughter. Muggeridge died of bronchopneumonia on 14 November 1990 at Ledsham Court, The Ridge, Hastings, after a long decline and was buried near his father in Whatlington. Kitty Muggeridge died in 1994 in Welland, Ontario, Canada.   RICHARD INGRAMS, *rev.*

Sources M. Muggeridge, *The green stick* (1972), vol. 1 of *Chronicles of wasted time* · M. Muggeridge, *The infernal grove* (1973), vol. 2 of *Chronicles of wasted time* · M. Muggeridge, *Like it was* (1981) · I. Hunter, *Malcolm Muggeridge: a life* (1980) · R. Ingrams, *God's apology, a chronicle of three friends* (1977) · R. Ingrams, *Muggeridge: the biography* (1995) · G. Wolfe, *Malcolm Muggeridge: a biography* (1995) · d. cert.
Archives Stanford University, California, Hoover Institution, diaries | Georgetown University, Washington, DC, letters to Barbara Jackson · JRL, letters to the *Manchester Guardian* · King's Lond., Liddell Hart C., corresp. with Sir B. H. Liddell Hart · U. Sussex, corresp. with *New Statesman* magazine
Likenesses Snowdon, photograph, 1983, priv. coll. [*see illus.*] · photographs, Hult. Arch.

Muggleton, Lodowicke (1609–1698), co-founder of Muggletonianism, was born in July 1609 in Walnut Tree Yard (later New Street), off Bishopsgate Street, London, the youngest of three children of John Muggleton, a farrier, and his first wife, Mary (1576/7–1612), possibly formerly Mary Mayles.

Family background, early life, and marriages Muggleton's family came from Wilbarston, Northamptonshire. His cousin Roger Muggleton was still living there when Lodowicke wrote to him in 1678. Roger would be the only family convert he made, apart from the two daughters of his

Lodowicke Muggleton (1609–1698), by or after William Wood, c.1674

first marriage, and Lodowicke boasted to Roger in his letter that their forefathers were 'all plain men, yet downright honest men' (Reeve and Muggleton, *Spiritual Epistles*, 474).

Muggleton's mother died in June 1612, aged thirty-five. There is poignancy, in *The Acts of the Witnesses*, his memoirs published posthumously in 1699, in his recollecting that 'my Mother loved me', but that when his father remarried 'I was a stranger to my father's house after my mother was dead' (Muggleton, *Witnesses*, 31). He was apprenticed about 1624 to a Walnut Tree Yard tailor, John Quick. A year later he suffered during the plague, but recovered to boast that he had never had an illness in the rest of his life. His recipe for health was to keep away from doctors, and to prefer kitchen broth to bleeding—advice which was passed on in 1941 by one Muggletonian to another, quoting the very words of the master.

In 1630 Muggleton worked under a pawnbroker named Richardson. He passed by the prospect of a good match with that pawnbroker's daughter because of religious scruples about usury, which had been raised by contact with his puritan (later Ranter) cousin William Reeve. In 1631 he went as journeyman tailor to Reeve. There is no evidence at this stage of his life of his later close relationship with Reeve's younger brother, John *Reeve, one which would have such profound consequences for both men.

In 1634 or 1635 Muggleton made the first of his three marriages, to nineteen-year-old Sarah (c.1615–c.1639).

Their oldest daughter, Sarah, he would later describe as one who was 'the most experimental and knowingest Woman, in Spiritual Things of that Sex in London' (Muggleton, *Witnesses*, 37). There was a second daughter who died and the youngest, Elizabeth, survived. After three and a half years of marriage, his wife was dead. In 1641 or 1642 he married another nineteen-year-old, Mary (c.1622–c.1648), and this marriage also produced three children. In a letter to a follower he described the unhappy outcome. The firstborn son had a convulsive fit, when he was merry on his father's lap, and only lived on until the age of three. The second son was ill from the age of three until nine, when he died. The youngest, a daughter, died after three days, along with her mother; all this in only six years of marriage. What is interesting is the moral he drew in his letter of 1674 from this sad tale: not that witchcraft was involved—five years earlier he had written against witchcraft beliefs in *The Witch of Endor* (1669)—but that their children had inherited their mother's 'melancholy and dropsical nature' (Reeve and Muggleton, *Spiritual Epistles*, 413). Muggleton's last and most successful marriage was about 1663, when he married 25-year-old Mary Martin (c.1638–1718), daughter of a wealthy tanner. Not only did she belong to her husband's faith; so did her parents and her younger brother. 'Providence' gave financial security for the rest of his life to Muggleton, 'by my wife', as he acknowledged freely in a letter to an enemy in 1665; otherwise, he wryly pointed out, he might have been badgering some of 'the richer sort of saints' (as in fact his co-founder John Reeve had been earlier reduced to doing) (ibid., 194).

Break with puritanism and encounters with God When civil war broke out Muggleton's fellow puritans mostly sided with parliament. But Muggleton himself deplored the sectarian divisions of the 1640s and withdrew into private contemplation and melancholia until 1650. He then came briefly under the spell of charismatic prophets like Thomas Tany and John Robins. But by April 1651 he had undergone his own profound spiritual awakening. The experience lasted about six hours, and would be repeated for the same duration over the next four nights. Its effects were to drive him back into himself; between then and January 1652 he seems to have attained some sort of equilibrium. *The Acts of the Witnesses* reveals that at this time his cousin John Reeve, also a tailor, was a constant visitor to the Muggleton household, following him from room to room in search of enlightenment from him; the self-advancing element in the account is not hard to detect. Its inevitable effect is to diminish the contribution of Reeve. But he also recognizes that Reeve had that very same spiritual awakening himself in January 1651—that is to say, a month before God spoke to Reeve, and when their religion began. It is interesting that in the incomplete memoirs of a third believer, Thomas Tomkinson, the same claim to a transforming religious experience was made about the same time—in his case, that was ten years or so before he had even heard of God's commission to Reeve (BL, Add. MS 60206, fol. 35).

The commission (in all three cases) therefore post-dated

the experience of conversion, but for all three men what happened in 1652 still made a qualitative difference between their faith and that of all other such faiths, which were grounded only in the personal experiences of believers. In particular, what distinguished their faith from their Quaker rivals was the fact that God had spoken to Reeve's 'external ear' on three successive mornings in February 1652. God had then told Reeve that he and his cousin Lodowicke Muggleton were the two last witnesses in the book of Revelation (chapter 11): Reeve was God's 'ambassador' and Muggleton was Reeve's 'mouth'. They were given the power to bless believers and curse sceptics. Tany and Robins were duly cursed; Muggleton's oldest daughter, Sarah, was the first to be blessed—by Reeve. She was surprised, because she thought that he preferred her younger sister. Between 1652 and 1658 there are a whole series of spectacular London encounters, marked by blessings and curses. In the course of these conflicts the doctrines of the sect were developed. They were an amalgam of many other beliefs of that 'world turned upside down' era. They were communicated under the names of both prophets, but Reeve's is indisputably the voice that counts. In this period there are few letters from Reeve that survive; he preferred oral contact to the written. But there are none at all from Muggleton himself until 1658, and even that one—a blessing on a follower—came after Reeve's death. What was hammered out under their collective names was a set of beliefs which were not, in essence, to be changed by Muggleton after Reeve's death.

They argued that there were two 'seeds' in every person's nature: 'faith' (good) and 'reason' (bad). Retrospectively Muggleton could see that the doomed children of his second marriage were the result of the fact that at the time of their conception the seed of reason had been uppermost in his wife's nature. They believed in three commissions. The first had been the 'age of law'; the text was the Old Testament; the prophet was Moses. The second was the 'age of gospel'; the text was the New Testament; the prophet was Jesus. The third was the 'age of the spirit'; the text was the prophets' writings; the prophets were Reeve and Muggleton. Theirs was a unitarian faith. God was the man Jesus, who came down on earth to participate in humankind's experience, while Moses and Elias looked after things in heaven. The devil was a phantom of men's imagination. Hell was inside oneself. Heaven was 6 miles up in the sky. The soul was mortal, and perished with the body until the resurrection. There would be no thousand-year kingdom of the saints on earth. Witchcraft beliefs were, like dreams, merely the product of men's fears.

Muggleton would later claim that these doctrines offended people more than the commission itself (Muggleton, *Witnesses*, 57). Certainly the claim to instant access to God won the prophets immediate public notoriety: Muggleton described how Reeve was pursued through the churchyards by little gravel-throwing boys shouting, '*There goes the Prophet that damns people*' (ibid., 58). But it was their blasphemous views in denying the Trinity that brought them their six-month prison sentence in Bridewell between September 1653 and April 1654. Four years later Reeve was dead.

Muggleton's leadership and sufferings There was then a power vacuum which one believer, Lawrence Clarkson, attempted to fill. He claimed Reeve's mantle for himself, wrote a number of pamphlets between 1658 and 1660, and seemed intent upon sidelining Muggleton. But Muggleton—hitherto a marginal figure in the story—asserted himself in three ways. He excommunicated Clarkson, although he did not damn him (but he did damn his wife); he revised in 1661 Reeve's earlier 1656 work, which had been put out jointly under both their names, *A Divine Looking Glass*; and he revealed that he had quarrelled with Reeve on the issue of whether God took 'immediate notice' of his subjects. What is fascinating is the peculiar interrelationship of the three actions, whose cumulative effect was to establish his ascendancy. At a personal level, he squashed the challenge of Clarkson (who submitted to his authority). At an ideological level, however, he borrowed from Clarkson the denial of God's 'immediate notice' of his subjects, and wrote it implicitly into his 1661 revision of Reeve's writings. There were good political grounds to delete embarrassing eulogies on Cromwell after 1660. For those later followers who wanted to stick to the 1656 text, which had carried a dedication to the lord protector and described him as God's instrument, that was a sufficient explanation for the changes forced on Muggleton by the Restoration. But others saw it differently: that the revised text went alongside a process (evident in his correspondence with followers) of educating them out of a providential reading of history. This was the view put forward by rebels William Medgate and Walter Buchanan in 1671, who argued for the retention of the 'immediate notice' thesis. This was a much more profound challenge than Clarkson's, and one which Muggleton met ironically with arguments borrowed from Clarkson.

Muggleton claimed to have argued Reeve out of his own 'immediate notice' beliefs before his death. But there is no documentary evidence to support this claim. Medgate and Buchanan would be followed by many others, in the later history of the movement, in claiming the authority of Reeve in urging a return to the old doctrine. The new doctrine, which in denying that God took notice of every human action, located virtuous behaviour in conformity to the law written in one's conscience, was however attuned perfectly to later deist, as well as unitarian, sensibilities, and indeed may well be the most important single reason why Muggletonianism outlasted most of their contemporary products of the era of 'the world turned upside down'.

Confrontations with the enemy did not end with Muggleton's leadership, but they were not sought by the sect. Muggleton's own professed aim was to be 'quiet and still'; he disliked the Quakers for their continuing readiness to challenge authority. He was committed to gaol in Derby in 1663, his books were seized in London in 1670, he was tried for blasphemy at the Old Bailey in 1677. He was found guilty, condemned to the pillory on three separate days, had his books burnt before his face, and was confined to Newgate until 19 July 1677. That date of release (later reckoned as 30 July after the alteration of the calendar) became one of two special anniversaries in the Muggletonian history. The other was the three days when God spoke to Reeve on 3, 4, and 5 February (later reckoned respectively as 14, 15, and 16 February after the alteration of the calendar). These 'holidays' were commemorated by believers well into the twentieth century.

Survival of the sect Muggleton's funeral on 17 March 1698 was attended by 248 believers; he had died at his lodgings in the Postern, London Wall, three days earlier after a fortnight's illness and was buried in Bethlehem new churchyard (opposite the site where Liverpool Street Station now stands). Numbers thereafter went into decline. Muggletonians were not an evangelizing sect: the initiative had to come from the seeker, or, as Muggleton put it, 'God only opens the door to those who knock themselves'. This self-denying ordinance imposed strains which emerge in the correspondence of later Muggletonians. But they were free from the usual sectarian conceit that only believers would be saved. Only believers had the assurance of salvation, but many would be saved (Muggleton thought perhaps half the world) without that assurance. Certainly all children would be saved; equally certainly, no clergymen. That the Muggletonians never expanded as the Quakers did is, in these circumstances, hardly surprising. What is surprising is that they should have lasted for over 300 years.

Only recently have historians discovered how long they really did survive. Although *Chambers's Encyclopaedia* in 1881 had pronounced the sect as extinct, Alexander Gordon, writing in the *Dictionary of National Biography*, spoke of them in the present tense and there were believers around to make the *Encyclopaedia* correct its item in later editions. The archive of the sect was not tracked down until 1974, when it was found to be in the possession of a Kent farmer, Philip Noakes. Before his death in 1979 he gave the eighty-eight volumes of papers to the British Library, where they are now housed.

Reassessment A consequence of the recovery of the manuscripts is an enhancing of Muggleton's reputation. Even through Muggleton's lens, Reeve dominates the earliest years (1652–8). The story is different afterwards. Muggleton exerts a powerful grip on the movement, mainly by letters. He did not travel: he hated the sea, and he was baffled by the motives of migrants. He once forbade his lieutenant Tomkinson to think of emigrating. This was an unusual assertion of leadership. It is true that he had earlier seen off the different challenges from, respectively, Clarkson and Medgate and Buchanan. But he was not one for imposing rules on followers: he preferred those correspondents who sought his advice to make up their own minds. He did not want them, for example, to go to church, but he turned a blind eye on some who did. He thought praying was unnecessary, but condoned the practice if it gave pleasure to his followers. He believed that they were wrong to set so much store on written blessings from him, when oral ones were sufficient, but he still gave them when asked. He was *primus inter pares* certainly. At the 1692 Green Man anniversary dinner, for instance, every person paid 5s.—except the prophet and his wife. Another item read: 'paid for the prophetts coach—3/6'. His ascendancy however manifested itself in his casuist skills, not in claims to infallibility. He is in the same high class as his great Christian contemporary Richard Baxter in this field. Both men were particularly good at dealing with women, above all with melancholic women. In some ways Muggleton was even better equipped to handle his correspondents' anxieties than Baxter was. When women, for instance, wrote to Baxter of their fear of the dark he empathized with them: he had known the same fears. But when they exposed their fear of the Devil, ghosts, witches, and hobgoblins to Baxter, they were writing to one who himself believed in the reality of all these phenomena—made it indeed a litmus test of a Christian's belief in God—and who trembled at the significance of dreams, and who believed in the curative properties of belief in hellfire. Muggleton believed, on the other hand, that witches and ghosts, just like dreams, were produced by fear; hell was inside the self; the Devil was a creation of the imagination; and parents should love their children, but the converse did not follow. He continued with vigour to exercise the power conferred on him since 1652 to bless and to curse; it was not until the eighteenth century that such powers would be called into question by a later generation of believers. The Muggletonian creed which he fashioned had no time for churches, ceremony, and priestcraft. Believers met where they could, often in pubs (at least up until 1869, when they at last acquired a reading-room of their own). There in a pub they would find a side-room to extol the qualities of Muggleton and Reeve to the tune of patriotic ballads of the day. This association with pubs made Macaulay designate the ascetic Muggleton as a 'tippler' (*History of England*, 1.164). He was in truth no more a drunkard than he was a psychotic (A. Jessopp, 'The prophet of Walnut Tree Yard', *Nineteenth Century*, 1884). The recovery of the archive throws into relief the positive qualities of a great and underrated spiritual casuist.

WILLIAM LAMONT

Sources Muggletonian manuscripts, BL, Add. MSS 60168–60256 · J. Reeve and L. Muggleton, *Works*, ed. J. Frost and I. Frost, 3 vols. (1832) · J. Frost and I. Frost, eds., *Sacred remains* (1856) · L. Muggleton, *The acts of the witnesses*, ed. T. L. Underwood (New York, 1999) · C. Hill, B. Reay, and W. Lamont, *The world of the Muggletonians* (1983) · J. Reeve and L. Muggleton, *A volume of spiritual epistles*, ed. A. Delamaine and T. Terry (1820) · J. Reeve and L. Muggleton, *A stream from the tree of life*, ed. J. Peat (1758) · J. Reeve and L. Muggleton, *Supplement to the book of letters*, ed. J. Frost and I. Frost (1831) · IGI

Archives BL, corresp. and papers, Add. MSS 60168–60256 [some copies] | Oxfordshire Record Society, Baskerville collection, E/7/MS/01

Likenesses by or after W. Wood, oils, c.1674, NPG [*see illus.*] · plaster cast of death mask, c.1698, NPG · plaque, 1869, U. Sussex, Meeting House · G. van Cassael, line engraving, BM, NPG · S. Cooper, miniature, repro. in G. C. Williamson, *Lodowick Muggleton* (1919) · W. Wood, portrait, U. Sussex · mezzotint, BM, NPG

Muhammad ʿAbdallah Hasan [Muḥammad ʿAbd Allāh Ḥasan] (1856–1920/21), religious leader, was born north of Buuhoodle, Somaliland, the eldest son of an Ogaden father, Sheikh ʿAbdallah Hasan, and a Dhulbahanta mother, Timiro Seed Magan. Contemporary Britons called him the 'Mad Mullah', but most Somalis referred to him by the Islamic religious titles of *sayyid* or *wadaad*. From 1899 to 1920 Sayyid Muhammad led Somalis in a holy war against Christian foreign rule, and in particular against the British administration of the Somaliland protectorate and its local Somali supporters.

After memorizing the Koran, the young Muhammad had set out on a career of peripatetic Islamic learning which, in the early 1890s, brought him to Mecca. There he joined the Salihiyyah, the reformist Sufi brotherhood founded by the Sudanese Muhammad Salih. On his return to Berbera, by then under British colonial protection (1884–1960), he alienated both the Qadiriyyah brotherhood and the British administration through his reformist theological stances. He puritanically objected to any form of indulgence of the senses during devotional practice and insisted that any Muslim who supported or even tolerated Christian rule in his country deserved to be harassed and killed.

About 1897 Sayyid Muhammad moved inland and founded his own religious settlement in Qoryaweyn. There he began to attract adherents, known as dervishes, who, in joining, submitted to his authority and renounced their clan identity for a religious (Muslim, Salihi) one. Armed hostilities began in 1900. Between 1900 and 1904 the British launched four major expeditions, led by men such as Lieutenant-Colonel E. J. E. Swayne, Brigadier-General W. H. Manning, and Major-General C. Egerton. However, the elusiveness of the enemy and the harsh, dry terrain made supply problems insuperable and doomed any formal, large-scale war effort. The peace agreement of March 1904 gave Sayyid Muhammad an autonomous area near Illig and a sea port. He immediately set out to use these to realize some of his state-building ambitions and to extend his influence. He had surrounded himself with a council of special advisers (*qusuusi*) and a personal bodyguard of low-caste people (*gaarhaye*). He had organized the army into four commands and had created seven administrative divisions, each formally associated with the name of one of his many wives (who included Barni Hirsi, the mother of his eldest son, Mahdi). He sent out and received caravans, and his dhows (flying the dervish flag showing a white turban) plied the seas, exporting hides, skins, and gum in return for firearms, food supplies, and clothing. He conducted an active diplomacy. Apart from writing letters in Arabic, occasionally containing elaborate Islamic theological and jurisprudential arguments about the duty of holy war, he composed a wide range of oral poetry in Somali, from peaceful overture to withering attack.

In 1909, Sayyid Muhammad's Somali opponents, with Italian and British aid, persuaded the leader of the Salihiyyah in Mecca to excommunicate him by letter. Although some Somalis believed that the letter was falsified, it sowed discord in the ranks of his followers. In the following years he moved his headquarters to Talah and institutionalized his power by building more than forty fortresses (where possible surrounded by cultivated fields) in different parts of the country. As war approached in 1914, he intensified his international diplomacy and participated in the international pan-Islamic movement which supported the Ottoman empire against its Christian enemies. It was not until early 1920 that the British were able to move against the sayyid, with aerial bombardments of Talah and other forts. Thus his movement was broken, though he himself escaped. In December 1920 or January 1921, while settled in Imey, the man who had dominated the history of Somaliland for twenty-one years fell sick, probably with influenza, and died near Imey.

Somalis remember Sayyid Muhammad in many ways: as the instigator of ruinous inter-clan warfare as well as the untiring defender of their religion, and as a ruthless local potentate as well as the first fighter for their national independence. Perhaps he was all of this and more. One of his poems contains his own reflections on his career:

> Although I failed to have a flag flown from here to Nairobi, did I not gain religious honour and paradise in victory and defeat? Although I failed to obtain the luscious pastures of the ʿIid and the Nugaal as grazing, did I not successfully ride my steed out to war? Although I failed to get people to show me sympathy and acknowledge their kinship with me, did I not gain God's mercy and [the reward of seeing] the Prophet's countenance? (Jaamac Cumar Ciise, 293)

LIDWIEN KAPTEIJNS

Sources Jaamac Cumar Ciise, *Taariikhdii Daarawiishta iyo Sayid Maxamad Cabdulle Xasan* [The history of the dervishes and Sayyid Muhammad 'Abdallah Hasan] (1976) · A. Sheik-Abdi, *Divine madness: Mohammed Abdulle Hassan, 1856–1920* (1993), 174 · S. S. Samatar, *Oral poetry and Somali nationalism: the case of Sayyid Mahammad Abdille Hasan* (1982) · D. Jardine, *The mad mullah of Somaliland* (1923) · F. Caroselli, *Ferro e fuoco in Somalia* (1911) · Jaamac Cumar Ciise, *Diiwanka Gabayadii Sayid Maxamad Cabdulle Xasan (1895–1921)* [Collection of the poetry of Sayyid Muhammad 'Abdallah Hasan] (1974) · B. G. Martin, *Muslim brotherhoods in nineteenth-century Africa* (1976)
Archives PRO, colonial office file, CO 535, vols. 1–152
Likenesses portrait, repro. in Jardine, *Mad mullah of Somaliland*, frontispiece

Muhammad Ahmad ibn ʿAbdullahi [Muḥammad Aḥmad ibn Abdullāhi; *known as* the Mahdi] (1844–1885), religious leader, was born on 12 August 1844 at Labab island, Dongola province, Sudan. He was one of the five children of ʿAbdullahi Fahl, a boat maker. After studying with several religious teachers he was initiated into the Sammaniyya, a reformist brotherhood brought to the Sudan in 1800 by Sheikh Muhammad al-Sharif Nur al-Daʾim. After years of mystical training and ascetic devotion he received permission (*ijaza*) to initiate students of his own and moved to Aba Island in the White Nile. In March 1881 Muhammad Ahmad manifested himself as 'the Expected Mahdi (or Divinely Guided One)'. The concept of Mahdiship, of a divinely guided leader with special esoteric knowledge who was to appear at the end of times, was part of Islamic tradition and was much debated by African Muslim communities at this period.

The Mahdi called for the re-establishment of the uncorrupted Muslim community of the time of the Prophet. He claimed to be to the Muslims of his own time what Muhammad had been to the first community of believers, and purposefully patterned his actions on those of the Prophet. Thus he called upon his followers to make the *hijra* (migration for the sake of the faith) to join him, as the Prophet had emigrated to Medina; and he called for holy war (*jihad*) against the Egyptian rulers of the Sudan, as the Prophet had led a holy war against Mecca. The Mahdi aimed at establishing a Muslim community characterized by equality and justice, observance of the religious laws, political consultation, and the absence of sensual indulgence and greed. Thus the holy war he called for was also one against each Muslim's own illicit desires; he forbade mixing of the sexes, the consumption of alcohol and tobacco, dancing, slandering or insulting fellow Mahdists, and the desire for wealth. Like the Prophet, the Mahdi selected four *khalifas* (successors or representatives), and declared anyone who did not believe in his Mahdiship a legitimate target for holy war. Thus he criticized 'the evil ʿulamaʾ (religious scholars)', who quoted learned books to deny his claim. Instead he insisted that knowledge of his Mahdiship was not bound to what was predicted in the written texts, but depended on faith and vision: 'None but those saints who are permitted personally to behold their Prophets are permitted to understand fully my reality' (Wingate, 47). It was through visionary colloquy (*hadra*) with the Prophet, the angels, and deceased holy men that the Mahdi legitimized his call: the Prophet Muhammad himself had proclaimed him as Mahdi and given him his sword, and had assigned the prophet Khidr and Azraʾil, the angel of death, to precede his armies.

The Mahdi abolished the title of *sheikh* held by Sufi brotherhood leaders; in 1884 he abolished the Sufi name of 'dervishes' for his followers, renaming them *ansar* (helpers), as the Prophet called his supporters. Nevertheless it was Sufi practice that informed both the legitimation of his Mahdiship and the distinctive symbols of his followers: the patched long shirt (*jubba*), the personal oath of allegiance (*bayʿa*), the Mahdi's prayer book (*ratib*), and the banners which had written on them the confession of faith with the added line: 'Muhammad Ahmad ʿAbdullahi is the Prophet's *khalifa*'. Thus he placed himself in both the tradition of the Prophet and that of the Sufi Islam of the Sudan.

People flocked to the Mahdi's banners. Among the secular causes of his success historians initially emphasized the oppressive and alien character of Egyptian rule in the Sudan, with its heavy taxes, corruption, and increasing employment of Europeans, as well as its interference with the slave trade (which it at first had encouraged). Later historians have emphasized the weakness of Egyptian rule; the deposition of Khedive Ismaʿil (1879) and the outbreak of the ʿUrabist revolution, which was cut short by the British occupation of Egypt in 1882, caused a political vacuum that had its impact on the Sudan. After Mahdist victories in Jebal Qadir (1881), al-ʿUbayd (January 1883), and Shaykan (November 1883) (where Colonel William

Hicks's force was annihilated), the Mahdist armies moved to Khartoum. There, in February 1884, Charles George *Gordon, who only a few years earlier had implemented the Egyptian government's policy of suppressing the Sudanese slave trade, had taken charge as governor-general. Gordon had been sent back by the British government of Egypt with a complex mission, of which one component was withdrawal from the Sudan and the evacuation of Egyptian troops. As he revealed this objective too early, Gordon alienated those pro-Egyptian forces which might have rallied to his support. As the Mahdist troops encircled Khartoum, the Gordon relief expedition, belatedly sanctioned by the British parliament, crept up the Nile from Egypt to Khartoum. It arrived too late—on 25 January 1885 Mahdist troops occupied Khartoum and, apparently against the express orders of the Mahdi, killed Gordon, though his body was never found and there were rumours, both at the time and subsequently, that he was captured.

The Mahdi did not settle in Khartoum but established his residence and capital across the river in Omdurman. There, on 22 June 1885, after a short and violent illness, possibly typhus, he died and was buried the same day; his domed tomb (*qubba*) still stands today. He had perhaps seventy wives whose names are remembered; the first two wives were Fatima bint Ahmad Shardi and, after her death, her sister ʿAisha bint Ahmad Sharfi. He was succeeded as head of state by one of his *khalifas* and earliest adherents, ʿAbdullahi ibn Muhammad, called al-Taʿishi ('of the Taʿisha tribe') after his ethnic, western background. He ruled the independent Mahdist state until it was conquered by the British government of Egypt in 1898.

LIDWIEN KAPTEIJNS

Sources P. M. Holt, *The Mahdist state in the Sudan, 1881–1898: a study of its origins, development and overthrow*, 2nd edn (1979) · M. I. Abu Salim, *Manshurat al-Imam al-Mahdi*, 4 vols. (1963) [Proclamations of the Mahdi] · N. Shuqayr, *Jughrafiyyah wa tarikh al-Sudan* (1972) [Geography and history of the Sudan] · R. S. Kramer, 'Holy city of the Nile: Omdurman, 1885–1898', PhD diss., Northwestern University, 1991 · H. Shaked, 'A historical study of Ismaʾil ʿAbd al-Qadir: Kitab saʾadat al-mustahdi bi sirat al-Mahdi', PhD diss., U. Lond., 1969 · J. S. Trimmingham, *Islam in the Sudan* (1965) · F. R. Wingate, *Mahdism and the Egyptian Sudan*, new edn (1968) · B. Bedri, *The memoirs of Babikr Bedri*, trans. Y. Bedri and G. Scott (1969) · S. El-Fatih, 'The teachings of Muhammed Ahmad, the Sudanese Mahdi', MA diss., U. Lond., 1961 · L. Kapteijns, 'The religious background of the Mahdi and his movement', *African Perspectives*, 2 (1976), 61–81 · *The journals of Major-Gen. C. G. Gordon*, ed. A. E. Hake (1885) · Gladstone, Diaries

Archives National RO, Khartoum, Sudan, Mahdia records and Cairo intelligence papers · U. Durham L., Sudan archive | SOAS, P. M. Holt papers

Likenesses drawing or lithograph, repro. in A. Nutting, *Gordon of Khartoum: martyr and misfit*, following p. 150 · photograph, repro. in R. A. Bermann, *The Mahdi of Allah: the story of the Dervish Mohammed Ahmed* (1932), following p. 20

Muhammad Ali Khan Walahjah (*c*.1717–1795), nawab of Arcot, was born the third of five sons of **Anwar ud-Din Khan** (1674?–1749), whom Asaf Jah, the Mughal *subahdar* of the Deccan and first nizam of Hyderabad, appointed nawab (deputy) of his subordinate *subha* (province) of

Muhammad Ali Khan Walahjah (c.1717–1795), by George Willison, c.1774

Arcot in 1743. But it was not an appointment which Anwar ud-Din or, later, his son ever found easy to hold.

Mughal imperial power had come late to the Deccan and peninsular India, following the conquests by the emperor Aurangzeb of the Bijapur and Golconda sultanates in 1685 and 1687 respectively. It rested uncomfortably on top of the locally constituted authority of a myriad of Hindu kings and chieftains, who continued to resist it. In addition, it faced rivalry from the expansion of the Maratha empire to the west, whose military forces regularly ravaged the region and, in 1689, conquered the Hindu kingdom of Tanjore to the south. A further problem arose after the death of Aurangzeb in 1707, when the Mughal empire went into decline and many provincial governors asserted their autonomy from imperial control. Asaf Jah himself followed this course and attempted to establish Hyderabad as an independent regional state. But so, too, did the family of the original nawabs of Arcot. In 1710 Saadatullah Khan had been appointed nawab, and he subsequently struggled against the Marathas and local chieftains until his death in battle in 1732. Thereafter his extended family repudiated the Hyderabad connection and squabbled among themselves for succession to his office. In 1743 Asaf

Jah marched south with a large army to restore order. He dismissed the various claimants from Saadatullah's line and appointed instead Anwar ud-Din Khan, who had distinguished himself previously in the nizam's service as a soldier and administrator and as nawab of Chicacole.

However, after Asaf Jah and his army returned north, Anwar ud-Din encountered serious difficulties in securing his authority. Saadatullah had been a Dakhni-speaking Muslim, drawn from the local Navaiyat community which had Shiʿi leanings and had long served the courts of Bijapur and Golconda. His relatives continued to hold many key military and civil positions. Anwar ud-Din, by contrast, was an Urdu-speaking Sunni Muslim from north India, whose strong connections among the pan-Indian Mughal élite belied his isolation in the south. Revolt stirred quickly and came to centre on the person of Saadatullah's son-in-law Shams ud-Daula Husain Dost Khan, otherwise known as Chanda Sahib. Widely regarded as the most able general of his times, in 1749 Chanda Sahib put together an army of 40,000 men and laid claim to Arcot. During the resultant battle of Ambur, Chander received the support of the French under the governor of their East India Company at Pondicherry, Joseph-François, marquis de Dupleix. In opposition, the British—albeit somewhat reluctantly—found themselves supporting Anwar ud-Din. For the two contenders to the nawabi, the attraction of a European connection lay in the access which it provided to new military technologies, particularly those of disciplined musketry and rapid-fire field cannon, which initially proved devastating against Indian cavalry formations. Anwar ud-Din himself was killed in the battle on 3 August, leaving his son Muhammad Ali a very doubtful inheritance.

At first it scarcely seemed as if Anwar ud-Din and his lineage had chosen the right side. After their victory at Ambur, Chanda Sahib and the French were in the ascendant. In 1751 Muhammad Ali, who now laid claim to his father's title, was besieged at Trichinopoly and in imminent danger of defeat. However, in a manoeuvre of fateful import, the British then launched a diversionary expedition from Madras under the then little-known captain Robert Clive to attack Chander's capital at Arcot and force him to lift the Trichinopoly siege. Clive further proceeded to hold Arcot against Chander's counter-attack for sufficiently long both to establish his own military reputation and to allow the British time to recruit a broad compact of Indian allies against Chander. From that point the tide of war turned and Chanda Sahib was eventually run to ground and murdered at Trichinopoly in 1752.

So far as rival claimants from Saadatullah's line were concerned, Nawab Muhammad Ali was now secure in his occupation of Arcot. However, this scarcely put an end to his troubles. Two of his four brothers launched their own claims to the succession. More seriously, the authority of his regime continued to be resisted by the numerous petty Hindu chiefs (known to the British as 'poligars') who dominated the interior districts. Progress in bringing them to heel was slow and sometimes produced unforeseen consequences. From 1756 Muhammad Ali's leading general

Yusuf Khan—himself a convert to Islam from a poligar clan—appeared to have gained the upper hand. But in 1760 Yusuf proclaimed himself independent of Arcot and attempted to set up his own kingdom centred on the ancient Hindu capital of Madura. This necessitated the sending of a second nawabi army to defeat Yusuf's first. It was not until after Muhammad Ali's death that the southern poligars were finally subjugated.

Externally, periodic threats continued to come from the Marathas and from Hyderabad. But greater and more persistent dangers were posed by the French and by the expansive claims of a revitalized Mysore state. Although French influence on the Coromandel coast was substantially reduced after the victory of Sir Eyre Coote at Wandiwash in 1760, it remained significant to the west, whence it was felt through the emergence of Mysore as an expansionary power. In 1758 the Hindu Wodeyar dynastic rulers of Mysore were displaced by their principal military commander, Haidar Ali Khan, who proclaimed himself sultan. Haidar and his son and successor Tipu Sultan, with great energy and ability, set about modernizing the Mysore regime and establishing it as a rising force in south India. From the first they looked to the Europeans for help, and initially turned towards the British. But the British company's servants at Madras were by now strongly committed to Muhammad Ali. Having been spurned, Haidar turned to the French. Mysore, with its French connections, now became the deadly rival of Arcot, with its British foundations. In Muhammad Ali's time the two states fought three major wars (1767–9, 1780–83, 1790–92), in the first two of which Arcot came off very much the worse.

In the face of these vicissitudes, Muhammad Ali's simple expedient was to rely ever more heavily on the support of the British for arms and cash. The company supplied him with the bulk of his army, which consisted of British-trained mercenaries, and the company servants advanced him loans. However, these services came at a high price, which bore heavily on his revenues, themselves depleted by the political turmoil. He was also obliged to grant the company and its servants extensive trading privileges. Inevitably he fell into arrears, leading to the company's taking over direct administration of his domains. In 1763 he was obliged to grant the company a *jagir* (revenue assignment) for the Chingleput district surrounding Madras. After the disaster of the Second Anglo-Mysore War the revenues of other and larger stretches of territory were assigned, albeit supposedly on a temporary basis. In effect, the Arcot state became a puppet regime, notionally under the authority of its nawab but *de facto* administered by company officials. This situation lasted throughout the later stages of Muhammad Ali's reign, which ended with his death at Madras on 13 October 1795, and even the reign of his son and successor, Umdat al-Umara (*d.* 1801).

Muhammad Ali's bid to succeed his father as nawab of Arcot concluded in the establishment of the rule of the English East India Company in south India. In consequence he has frequently been portrayed as the victim of European imperialism—which undoubtedly, in many ways, he was. However, a historical status merely as victim

might obscure his own achievements both as a politician and as a practitioner of Indian statecraft. Given his alien origins and the turbulence of the times, it was remarkable that he should have established a state in south India at all, still less one which survived for fifty years and imprinted itself on cultural memory for very much longer. The nawabs of Bengal, who found themselves in a very similar political situation, were consigned to history as early as 1765. And the Walahjah family name continues to convey royal prestige in south Indian society today.

Muhammad Ali's rare survival owed much to his shrewd manipulation of the English company's administration, where he helped to create one of the greatest British political scandals of the later eighteenth century and for a long time to paralyse the ability of the nascent British imperial state to dispose of him. Beginning in the 1750s, in order to finance the heavy demands on him for cash, he took to borrowing money—albeit at exorbitant rates of interest—from the company's own servants in their 'private' trading capacities. This created among company officials a network of interest in his own preservation, if only to ensure that they might get their money back, and revealed a major contradiction in the organization of the company's government between private and public policy.

The network also provided means by which Muhammad Ali was able to influence politics in London. Between 1771 and 1773 his agents among the company's servants in Madras were active in gaining initial support for a conquest of the neighbouring friendly state of Tanjore, simply to lay hand on its revenues and, in 1776, for arresting and imprisoning the Madras governor, Lord Pigot, who was charged by the directors with rescinding the conquest. Later still they entrapped Governor Sir Thomas Rumbold in a web of corruption and rendered the reform policies of Governor Lord Macartney largely ineffective. While the eventual rescinding of the Tanjore conquest perhaps shows the limits of Muhammad Ali's influence, the case also suggested the breadth of his connections. He was said to have had at least six members of parliament, associated with his creditors, firmly in his camp. The scandal of the Arcot debts was finally resolved only in 1805 when a parliamentary inquiry committee knocked down the creditors' claims from £30 million to £2.5 million. The inquiry followed the dynasty's eclipse, which itself reflected a stronger assertion of metropolitan authority in the context of the French revolutionary and Napoleonic wars. But Muhammad Ali was by then dead, having used the pressure of the debts to preserve his patrimony for nearly half a century, and, at his demise, still leaving his creditors largely unpaid. This might be regarded as a considerable triumph, albeit of a curious kind.

Less curious, however, was the way in which Muhammad Ali pursued the strategy of a post-Mughal state builder and fulfilled the aims of every founder of an Indian dynasty to establish the glory and prestige of his family name. Much of the cash, which he gleaned from his creditors, was used not to pay the company's demands, but to invest in cultural projects. At both Arcot and Madras he demonstrated his association with the new power of the Europeans by building magnificent palaces in the European style, drawing especially on the skills of Paul Benfield, who was a military architect and merchant—and also his principal creditor. Muhammad Ali further employed a range of celebrated European artists resident in India, including George Willison. His address to local Muslim and Hindu audiences was more traditional. He distributed a lavish patronage to found mosques and attract Islamic scholars and he resolved the tensions with the Navaiyat community by (possibly in 1747) taking as his principal wife Khadija Begum, a Shi'i from a highly respected Bijapur family. Their son Umdat al-Umara, who also professed Shi'ism, was his anointed heir. With regard to his Hindu subjects, he followed the long-established conventions of south Indian kingship in protecting and endowing Hindu temples. His name became closely associated with the great temples of Tirupati and Rameswaram and with that of Sri Parthasarathi at Madras. In terms of Indian statecraft, he was supremely successful at securing the honour of his dynasty, which continued long after 1801 and even 1855, when, according to the British, the family lost its claim to all government revenues and to a royal title. As late as 1996 his descendants continued to open major religious festivals at the Sri Parthasarathi temple. Far from being merely a victim of European imperialism, Muhammad Ali used his European connections to gain immortality for his family name.

DAVID WASHBROOK

Sources S. M. H. Nainar, ed., *Tuzak-i-Walahjala* (Madras, 1934) • [R. Orme], *A history of the military transactions of the British nation in Indostan*, 4th edn, 3 vols. (1803) • N. S. Ramaswami, *Political history of the Carnatic under the nawabs* (New Delhi, 1984) • H. Dodwell, *Clive and Dupleix* (1920) • J. D. Gurney, 'Fresh light on the character of the nawab of Arcot', *Statesmen, scholars and merchants: essays presented to Dame Lucy Sutherland*, ed. A. Whiteman, J. S. Bromley, and P. G. M. Dickson (1973), 220–41 • L. S. Sutherland, *The English East India Company in eighteenth-century politics* (1952) • S. A. Krishnasvami Aiyangar, *South India and her Muhammadan invaders* (1921) • S. Bayly, *Saints, goddesses and kings: Muslims and Christians in south Indian society, 1700–1900* (1989) • J. Allan and others, eds., *The Cambridge shorter history of India* (1934)
Archives Saeedia Library, Chennai, India, private MSS • Tamil Nadu Archives, Chennai, India, diary; proceedings of the Government of Fort St George
Likenesses G. Willison, portrait, *c.*1774, BL OIOC [*see illus.*] • T. Kettle, portrait, V&A • J. Smart, miniature, V&A

Muhammad Reza Khan (*c.*1717–1791), administrator of Bengal, was probably born at Shiraz in Persia. He was the third of the four sons of Hadi Ali Khan, a physician. When the Khan was about ten years old, his father took his family from Persia to India, where he practised medicine, first at the court of the Mughal emperor in Delhi and then at Murshidabad, the capital of the nawabs of Bengal. Muhammad Reza Khan established himself at the court of the nawabs, marrying the daughter of Rabia Begam, a niece of the nawab, and seeking employment in his government. His service began in the troubled times after the battle of Plassey, when contenders for power in the administration of the province had to seek support from factions among the servants of the British East India Company as well as from the nawabs. Muhammad Reza Khan won his first major success when he became the nawab's *naib* or deputy in the important eastern districts of Dacca. From Dacca he was able in 1765 to win the highest office in the government of Bengal.

The Khan's chance came with the death in February 1765 of Mir Jafar Ali Khan, made nawab of Bengal by the British after Plassey. The new nawab, Najm ud-Daula, was a young boy and so the company's servants were looking for a minister to take control of the government who would be amenable to their influence. They chose the Khan over what they regarded as more dangerous rivals. He reinforced his claims by promising presents to individuals worth more than £50,000. Robert Clive later confirmed the Khan in office under the 1765 settlement with the Mughal emperor which gave the company direct responsibility for the *diwani*, or revenue administration, of Bengal. Muhammad Reza Khan was to be the company's deputy in managing the assessment and collection of revenue under the *diwani* and he was to be the young nawab's deputy in administering what was left to him, mainly the supervision of the criminal courts. The Khan was referred to in British records as 'the minister' or sometimes 'the prime minister' (A. M. Khan, 103).

Muhammad Reza Khan kept his great powers from 1765 until 1772. Clive held him in high esteem, especially in view of the satisfactory revenue yield that he was able to ensure for the company. Clive awarded him a generous salary amounting to some £90,000 a year. In administering for the British the Khan seems to have been inspired by the ideals of Mughal government and by his view of what conditions had been like in pre-Plassey Bengal. 'The Prince is to receive the revenues of the state, to make such laws and regulations only as are consistent with justice; to study the general good of the country and to cherish all his subjects' (A. M. Khan, 15). He was, however, subject to increasing pressures from his British masters, who were beginning to aspire to take a more active role in the administration of Bengal, and who also hoped for a higher return from the province than the Khan was able to produce. In 1770 British company servants were posted into districts to supervise administration. Two years later a new governor, Warren Hastings, took the central administration of the province out of the Khan's hands and transferred it from Murshidabad to the company's own city of Calcutta. In the contemporary phrase, the company was 'standing forth as *diwan*'; there were to be no more Indian 'ministers'.

The removal of Muhammad Reza Khan from office was sudden and brutal. On 27 April 1772 a body of British troops arrested him and carried him off to Calcutta, where he was kept in confinement to answer charges. He had been struck down by a combination of his Indian enemies and the British opponents of his erstwhile friend, Robert Clive. Material against him had been passed to the directors of the East India Company, who ordered his dismissal and trial. The main allegations were that the Khan had been responsible for misappropriating very large sums collected out of the revenues of Bengal, and that he had profiteered from trading in grain during the terrible famine that had devastated parts of Bengal in 1769–70. The investigation dragged on for two years and ended in acquittal. This was the outcome that Warren Hastings, who conducted the prosecution, had intended. He wanted the Khan's power broken but feared that too much probing would reveal that many Europeans had also made illegal profits. The Khan himself had clearly not made a great personal fortune out of his seven years of power. In spite of his high salary, he left office in debt, and he was to remain financially embarrassed for the rest of his life. Others, both British and Indian, no doubt had profited from the collection of revenue under him, but the company's fond hopes that the system could be made to yield much more once supposedly corrupt Indian management had been broken was to be shown to be a delusion.

Political change among the British enabled the Khan to recover some ground. During 1775 and 1776 Hastings lost control of the Bengal council and his opponents patronized Muhammad Reza Khan, restoring him in October 1775 to the office of the nawab of Bengal's deputy for those judicial functions that remained to him. In return the Khan conveyed his ideals of Mughal governance to Hastings's enemy Philip Francis, who was strongly influenced by them in his plans for the future of British government in India. Hastings saw such contacts as hostility and in 1778 took the opportunity of removing Muhammad Reza Khan from office yet again. In 1780 he was restored on orders from Britain; he was to hold his post as deputy to the nawab, with a salary of some £25,000, until shortly before his death.

In the last years of his career Muhammad Reza Khan continued to play an active and respected role. He was recognized to have an unsurpassed knowledge of the Islamic criminal law and supervised its administration conscientiously in appointing judges and presiding over the appeal court. He made a striking impression with his chest 'so broad, his body so erect, his tone of voice so very loud, and his eyes so very full of fire' (Majumdar, 228). He lived in a grand style that, as his critics pointed out, he could not afford, dispensing wisdom 'which he has picked up in ancient times and books, without once minding the ignorance or unadequateness [sic] of his audience' (Ghulam Husain Khan, 3.148–9). To the end of his life he complained that the importunities of his creditors 'made sleep and food tasteless to me' (Majumdar, 282). His second wife, Banni Begam, the widow of his brother, died some time in 1786 or 1787 (Bengal year 1193).

On 1 January 1791 the last governmental responsibilities of the nawab of Bengal, hitherto discharged for him by Muhammad Reza Khan, came to an end. The courts of criminal justice were placed under the direct management of the East India Company. Muhammad Reza Khan duly handed over his records. On 1 October 1791 he died.

The company paid tribute to his 'honourable character, his regard to the English for a long period of time, and the services he had rendered in Bengal' (A. M. Khan, 1).

P. J. MARSHALL

Sources A. M. Khan, *The transition in Bengal, 1756–1775: a study of Saiyid Muhammad Reza Khan* (1969) · N. Majumdar, *Justice and police in Bengal, 1765–1793* (1960) · *Calendar of Persian correspondence: being letters, referring mainly to affairs in Bengal, which passed between some of the company's servants and Indian rulers and notables*, 11 vols. (1911–69) · BL OIOC, Murshidabad MSS, H/594 · G. H. Khan, *A translation of the Sëir mutaqherin, or, View of modern times, being an history of India*, trans. M. Raymond, 3 vols. (1789)
Archives National Archives of India, New Delhi, Persian corresp. [*Calendar of Persian correspondence*]
Wealth at death appears to have had large debts but to have left much property; inheriting family remained important

Muhlenberg, Henry Melchior (1711–1787), Lutheran pastor in America, was born on 6 September 1711 (and baptized the same day, as Heinrich Melchior Mühlenberg) in the Altendorfer Strasse, Einbeck, in Hanover. He was the seventh of the nine children of Nicolaus Melchior Mühlenberg (1665?–1729?), shoemaker and licensed brewer, and his wife, Anna Maria Kleinschmid (1675–1747), daughter of a retired military officer. On 22 April 1745 Muhlenberg married Anna Maria Weiser (1727–1802), with whom he had eleven children.

Little is known about Muhlenberg's physical appearance, except a portrait showing him with gown and wig. By nature somewhat timid and melancholic, Muhlenberg observed the habit of daily consulting biblical lots for divine guidance. Generous and conciliatory in social intercourse, he at times was prone to sarcasm and violent outbursts of temper. Previously blessed with sound health, in his old age Muhlenberg lost much of his hearing and developed rheumatism, asthma, and dropsy, but he kept mentally active to his death.

From 1718 to 1723 Muhlenberg attended the *Ratsschule* in Einbeck, being chiefly occupied in the study of German and Latin. Raised in the Lutheran faith, he was confirmed in 1723. His father's sudden death forced him to leave school and labour for the support of the family. For several years Muhlenberg privately studied arithmetic and organ playing before, in 1732, he returned to the *Ratsschule* for one more year, while taking private lessons in Latin and Greek. In 1733 Muhlenberg found sufficient time, while teaching children in Zellerfeld, in the Harz Mountains, to learn French and Hebrew and to read Latin classics and the New Testament in Greek. With a stipend from the Einbeck council he matriculated at Göttingen University in March 1735. As a student of theology he particularly admired Professor Joachim Oporin, whose homiletic approach and practical-minded piety deeply impressed him. Through Oporin he became acquainted with pietism and, in 1737, ministered to Count Henry XI of Reuss as domestic chaplain.

Muhlenberg left the university in the following year and, upon recommendation of noble benefactors, was introduced to Gotthilf August Francke, director of several charitable establishments in Halle, Prussia, whom he revered as his spiritual mentor. At the Halle orphanage

Muhlenberg gave classes in theology and taught Latin, Greek, and Hebrew. Appointed inspector of the hospital, he acquired considerable medical knowledge. In 1739 he became pastor and inspector of an orphans' home in Grosshennersdorf, upper Lusatia. On Muhlenberg's thirtieth birthday Francke informed him of a call for a pastor extended by three Pennsylvania congregations, which he accepted. Prior to leaving on 8 April 1742, he was acquitted of charges by the Hanover orthodox Lutheran consistory of organizing unlawful pietist conventicles.

During his stopover in London, Muhlenberg made the acquaintance of Friedrich Michael Ziegenhagen, Lutheran court chaplain and influential promoter of Francke's missionary activities in North America. Having embarked at Gravesend on 13 June, Muhlenberg reached Charles Town, South Carolina, on 22 September. After visiting the German Lutherans in Ebenezer, Georgia, he arrived in Philadelphia on 25 November 1742. He was naturalized on 24 September 1754.

In America Muhlenberg was regular pastor in Philadelphia (1742–79), New Hanover (1742–61), Providence (later Trappe; 1742–61), and Germantown (1743–5). Travelling widely, he also served other congregations in Pennsylvania, New York city (1750–51), and New Jersey (1758–9). He was an aggressive evangelist who uncompromisingly opposed orthodox Lutherans, Moravians, self-styled pastors, sectarians, and unbelievers. Neither a rousing preacher nor a great theologian, Muhlenberg proved to be a capable organizer and talented administrator. Advocating a learned ministry and uniform standards for liturgy, ordination, and congregational life, he convened the first Lutheran synod in America in 1748 and mediated in countless controversies over doctrinal issues, participation of laymen, and autocratic tendencies in church councils.

Gifted with diplomatic skills and a strong sense of duty, Muhlenberg decisively contributed to establishing viable Lutheran parishes based on voluntariness and statutory foundations. Maintaining relations with numerous colonial dignitaries, he won recognition as an outstanding leader who prudently steered the German Lutherans through internal crises and political trials. However, Muhlenberg's support of English charity schools for German children, his plan to merge the Lutheran with the Anglican church, and interference with local church affairs drew protest from compatriots who feared for their ethnoreligious identity and congregational autonomy.

During the American War of Independence Muhlenberg agonized over being a native of Hanover. Initially trying to remain loyal to the king, he swore allegiance to the Pennsylvania republic on 27 May 1778. Exactly six years later the University of Pennsylvania honoured him with the degree of doctor of divinity. An attentive chronicler for almost half a century, Muhlenberg published a polemic rejecting orthodox Lutheranism (anonymous, 1741), a report on an executed German chirurgeon (anonymous, 1764), and a sermon praising the repeal of the Stamp Act (1766).

After 1776 Muhlenberg saw his authority dwindle, as younger pastors influenced by the revolutionary spirit assumed the reins of the church. He made his will on 18 June 1782, and added a codicil on 3 February 1787; however, no account or inventory appears to have survived. Muhlenberg died at his home in Providence on 7 October 1787, aged seventy-six, and was buried in the graveyard of Augustus Lutheran Church in Providence three days later.   WOLFGANG SPLITTER

Sources H. M. Mühlenberg, *Selbstbiographie, 1711–1743: aus dem Misssionsarchive der Franckischen Stiftungen zu Halle, mit Zusätzen und Erläuterungen versehen von W. Germann* (1881) · C. H. Glatfelter, *Pastors and congregations* (1980), vol. 1 of C. H. Glatfelter, *Pastors and people: German Lutheran and Reformed churches in the Pennsylvania field, 1717–1793* (1980–81) · T. J. Müller, *Kirche zwischen zwei Welten: die Obrigkeitsproblematik Heinrich Melchior Mühlenbergs und die Kirchengründung der deutschen Lutheraner in Pennsylvania* (1994) · W. M. Splitter, *Pastors, people, politics: German Lutherans in Pennsylvania, 1740–1790* (1998) · *Die Korrespondenz Heinrich Melchior Mühlenbergs: aus der Anfangszeit des deutschen Luthertums in Nordamerika*, ed. K. Aland and others, 4 vols. (Berlin, 1986–93) · *The journals of Henry Melchior Muhlenberg*, ed. T. G. Tappert and J. W. Doberstein, 3 vols. (1942–58) · W. J. Mann, B. M. Schmucker, and W. Germann, eds., *Nachrichten von den vereinigten Deutschen Evangelisch–Lutherischen Gemeinden in Nord-America, absonderlich in Pensylvanien*, 2 vols. (1886–98) · H. T. Lehmann, 'Muhlenberg, Henry Melchior', *ANB*

Archives Archiv der Franckeschen Stiftungen, Halle an der Saale, Germany · Hist. Soc. Penn. · L. Cong. · Lutheran Archives Center, Philadelphia · Pennsylvania Historical and Museum Commission, Harrisburg, Pennsylvania

Likenesses C. W. Peale, oils?, priv. coll.

Muilman, Peter (1705?–1790), antiquary and merchant, was born in Amsterdam, the third of five sons of the merchant Pieter Schout Muilman and his wife, Maria Meulenaer. His own statements and his memorial inscription in Debden church, Essex, give different accounts of his age, and hence of his date of birth, but December 1705 appears the most likely date. In 1722 he joined his elder brother Henry in London, where Henry had started a branch of the family firm. In 1734 Peter married Mary Chiswell (1713–1785), daughter of Richard *Chiswell MP (*bap.* 1672, *d.* 1751) and his wife, Mary Trench (*d.* 1726), of Debden Hall, Debden, Essex, and in 1749 he established himself in that county. With money inherited from his father, Muilman bought Spains Hall and three other estates in Great Yeldham, as well as the manor and other land in Little Yeldham. Spains Hall was his country seat until 1765, when he moved to Kirby Hall, Castle Hedingham.

In Muilman's enthusiasm for making his name in his new county, he became involved in the study of its history. Between 1761 and 1767 he corresponded with Philip Morant, who was then compiling and publishing his *History and Antiquities of Essex*. He supplied Morant with information about Great Yeldham and about the Chiswell family, helped to provide drawings of Castle Hedingham, and gave financial support. He, his only son Richard Muilman Trench *Chiswell (1735–1797), his brother Henry, and two other members of his family, were subscribers to Morant's book, and Morant acknowledged that Muilman had been 'a most generous encourager' of his work

(Morant, 2.301n.). Muilman's name has been more closely associated with *A New and Complete History of Essex by a Gentleman* (1772). That anonymous compilation, issued in parts and usually bound in six volumes, is largely a reworking of Morant's *History*, with the addition of notes on monumental inscriptions—of the omission of which from Morant's book Muilman had complained. Although Muilman claimed in 1773 to have published in six volumes and presented to the king an 'historical description of Essex', clearly a reference to the *History by a Gentleman*, it is unlikely that he was actually the author of that history. The style and spelling of Muilman's autobiographical notes in one copy of the book suggest that his command of English was not adequate to the task. The book's fulsome dedication to Muilman refers to his 'assiduity in assisting the compilation' and Muilman's own correspondence promoting the book refers to 'Mr. Bates' as the author; this was presumably Henry Bate Dudley, later prominent in Essex affairs. Muilman's contribution appears to have been in giving or obtaining plates for illustrations and in collecting, or attempting to collect, information on antiquities.

Muilman was elected fellow of the Society of Antiquaries in 1770, but was expelled in 1775, having falsely claimed to have the support of the society for his plan to compile a history of the whole of Great Britain. He had apparently elicited the support of George III for the scheme, which relied heavily on a questionnaire to be filled in by all the parish clergy in the country, but like so many similar schemes in individual counties, Muilman's came to nothing.

In Muilman's account of his life in the autobiographical notes—which shows that he had a high opinion of himself—he claimed to have been instrumental in lowering the rate of interest from 6 per cent in 1722 to 3 per cent, and to have almost single-handedly prevented a run on the Bank of England during the Jacobite rising of 1745, but the only public office recorded in his obituary in the *Gentleman's Magazine* is that of treasurer of the London Infirmary, to which he was elected in 1748. In Essex he involved himself in local politics, organizing opposition to a road bill in 1767, and campaigning for the opposition whig candidates, Jacob Houblon and Eliab Harvey, against the sitting MPs, Sir William Maynard and John Luther, in 1768.

After the failure of his historical plans in 1775, Muilman seems to have retired from Essex affairs, from historical studies, and from politics. He died on 4 February 1790 at his London house in Marylebone, and was buried at Debden, Essex, the seat of his son, Richard Muilman Trench Chiswell, to whom he left a fortune of £350,000.

JANET COOPER

Sources E. A. Fitch, 'Historians of Essex', *Essex Review*, 5 (1896), 106–20 · E. A. Fitch, 'Historians of Essex', *Essex Review*, 8 (1899), 20–28 · *GM*, 1st ser., 60 (1790), 183 · [H. B. Dudley], *A new and complete history of Essex by a gentleman*, 6 vols., 1772, BL, Royal Library · P. Morant, *The history and antiquities of the county of Essex*, 2 (1768) · Essex RO, D/DPr 569 · Essex RO, T/A 631 · Essex RO, D/DZz 8

Wealth at death approx. £350,000: Fitch 'Historians of Essex', 23

Muir family (*per.* 1849–1992), textile, tea, and general merchants, was brought to prominence by **Sir John Muir**, first baronet (1828–1903), who was born on 8 December 1828 at Hutchesontown, Glasgow, Lanarkshire, the son of James Muir (*c.*1795–1864), a cotton trader, and his wife, Elizabeth Brown (*c.*1809–1874), a descendant of James Finlay (1727–1790), who about 1765 had founded a textile exporting business. John Muir was educated at Glasgow high school, then briefly at Glasgow University, and joined James Finlay & Co. in 1849, at the same time as his first cousin, Hugh Brown Muir (1828–*c.*1908), son of John Muir of Kilmarnock.

The company which James Finlay had founded was expanded by his son Kirkman Finlay (1773–1842), then passed to his grandsons who left its management in other hands. The numerous family partners were uninterested in change and exports were stagnant. John Muir was brought in to revitalize the business. Finlays absorbed Wilson, Kay & Co., another piece-goods exporter, and in 1854 purchased offices in West Nile Street, Glasgow. In 1861 John and Hugh Muir became junior partners, each holding two of the total of forty-five shares, the rest being held by another junior and five senior partners. John Muir married in 1860 Margaret Morrison, eldest daughter of Alexander Kay, one of those seniors, and they raised four sons and six daughters. After his marriage John systematically eliminated the other partners, inducing them to retire or deliberately disagreeing with them, earning himself in Glasgow business circles the covert nickname of the Cuckoo. By 1870 John and Hugh dominated those remaining, namely Alexander Kay and two elderly Finlay relatives, and by 1883 John had become sole proprietor, with two junior non-voting partners. In that year Archibald Buchan, the last of the old Finlay family, tried but failed to obtain a legal injunction to prevent Muir trading under the name of James Finlay & Co.

The outbreak of the American Civil War in 1861 had obliged Finlays to seek alternative sources of cotton. Their two large Scottish mills, at Deanston in Perthshire and Catrine in Ayrshire, each with nearly 1000 hands, came to a standstill. In 1861 Hugh Muir made the first of two visits to India in search of the high-quality raw cotton that had eluded Kirkman Finlay's agents in 1816. At the same time he investigated piece-goods sales in Singapore and Batavia, but finding that Chinese traders operated on extremely small margins, he advised against expanding into those already overstocked markets. In 1865 he re-established a Bombay office and was enthusiastic about the prospects of Indian trade; in 1870 a Calcutta office was reopened, and in 1871 Hugh opened a small London office. There were close links with Samuel Smith MP (1836–1906), a leading cotton broker in Liverpool and also related to the Finlay family.

Existing friction between the cousins came to a head when John, a member of the Free Church of Scotland, dismissed a senior employee for playing chess on the sabbath day, which Hugh, a member of the Kirk of Scotland, considered unjust. In December 1873 Hugh left the partnership and set up Hugh Brown Muir & Co., East India merchants, an independent business in the City of London. He died, probably in London, about 1908.

John Muir made the first of seven visits to Calcutta in 1871, setting up Finlay, Muir & Co. as a private business to act as agent for his own ventures, while the Glasgow firm continued to act as home agent and to export piece-goods, grey-cloth, and yarns to Bombay and Calcutta. The first of these 'rupee companies' registered in India was a jute press, followed in 1873 by a jute mill. Their foundation marked Muir's move into new products. Also in 1873 he moved into the infant tea industry, starting with the Calcutta agency for two small tea estates in northern India, then buying up other estates as they came on to the market. He was one of the first to realize that tea plantations would pay best when consolidated into large centrally administered groups under tight financial control, a management pattern later adopted throughout the industry. Muir floated the private North and South Sylhet Tea companies in 1883, both of which yielded large dividends. In 1896, now endowed with estates throughout the subcontinent, they were amalgamated under Muir as the Glasgow-registered Consolidated Tea and Lands Ltd. In 1894 Muir bought a large tract of high-altitude virgin jungle in the southern Indian state of Travancore and floated the very successful Kanan Devan Hills Produce Company Ltd, which included Darjeeling properties. A branch in Ceylon followed, with tea and rubber estates. Muir exercised a close supervision of the Calcutta office which managed these estates, with weekly reports and instructions passing between Glasgow and Calcutta.

Two other tea companies were registered in Glasgow, their purpose being to bypass the traditional London tea sales and reach directly to new outlets in America, Canada, and Russia—another bold innovation on Muir's part. He set up London warehouses at Orient Dock, established his own tea-brokers and tea-tasters, and owned controlling interests in a tea-packeting and confectionery concern. By the 1890s Muir was the world's major stakeholder in the growing and marketing of tea.

Muir invested heavily in capital developments, especially in southern India and Ceylon, building roads and railways, putting in hydro-electric schemes and telephone systems. He was a harsh employer, both to his Indian labour force and to the young British—mainly Scottish—planters and 'jute-wallahs' whom he recruited, and then had to replace when they fell victim to malaria. Salaries were small and leave infrequent; no wife's passage was paid until 1924, and a planter received a larger allowance for his essential horse than he did for a wife. But 'a berth in Finlays' was sought after, and Finlays always commanded a deep if inexplicable loyalty from employees. At his death Muir had some 90,000 employees on payrolls in Britain and the Indian subcontinent.

Muir's venture into indigo trading in the 1890s, when aniline dyes were already replacing vegetable dyes, was disastrous. Possibly he hoped thereby to acquire valuable land in upper India, but he reaped heavy losses. Another hard-fought battle was more successful. About the time Muir's tea plantations were becoming profitable, Charles Cayzer was attempting to set up a shipping line in Glasgow. Cayzer was introduced to Alexander Stephen of Linthouse, a shipbuilder, and to John Muir as financier. The three men, though they never learned to trust each other, did remarkably successful business together. In 1878 they entered an agreement to build two ships, which became the nucleus of the Clan Line, cargo carriers with some passenger accommodation. Muir stipulated that James Finlay & Co. should hold all the Clan Line agencies east of Suez, and that his tea should be freighted at a favourable rate. By this time a second jute mill was producing a great quantity of gunny (burlap) for export. As the port of Calcutta became overcrowded, Muir advocated the primitive port of Chittagong in East Bengal as an alternative, taking the agency for the Bengal Coal Company, and he forced the Clan Line to serve this port from 1901 by offering huge cargoes of tea and jute. A series of boardroom struggles and deep disagreements marred what was, in fact, a successful partnership. Cayzer resented Muir's bullying tactics and he managed to beat off Muir's attempted take-over, gaining complete control of the Clan Line in 1898. The two men remained, however, mutually necessary to their individual concerns, and they expanded this co-operation into new ventures in South Africa and in the Far East.

All John Muir's children were born at their parents' town house, 6 Park Gardens, Glasgow. The two eldest sons, (Alexander) Kay Muir and James Finlay Muir, attended Glasgow high school and Glasgow University before being sent to Calcutta, where their parents wintered each year. The Muirs took a leading part in Calcutta society, were on friendly terms with the viceroy, and subscribed to local charities. The younger sons, John Buchanan Finlay Muir (*b.* 1876) and Matthew William Muir (1878–1922), were also educated at Glasgow high school and sent out to India. John then went ranching in Wyoming and died young. Matthew, a keen rider, was killed on the hunting field.

With his Indian empire secured, John Muir turned his attention to civic affairs. He was elected a baillie of Glasgow town council in 1886 and three years later became lord provost (1889–92), receiving a baronetcy in 1893. He was largely responsible for the Glasgow International Exhibition of 1888. Its £55,000 surplus was the basis of the Kelvingrove Art Galleries Fund, to which Muir donated £15,000. In 1891 he presided over the passing of the City of Glasgow Act, which by enlarging the municipal boundaries added nearly 10,000 citizens. Gas supplies were extended, and electricity—for which Muir was an early enthusiast—lit the streets. Several notable public buildings were erected during his tenure, and Muir and his wife held glittering public functions in the city chambers. In a popular farewell gesture Lady Muir entertained all the nurses from Glasgow's hospitals. In national politics Muir was a liberal, becoming an active Liberal Unionist after

1886. He was a JP and deputy lieutenant for both Lanark-shire and Ayrshire, and an honorary colonel of the 4th (volunteer battalion) Cameronian Scottish rifles.

When John Finlay, last of Kirkman's sons and a sleeping partner, died in 1873 Muir took over and rebuilt Deanston House, near one of his cotton mills in Perthshire. Lady Muir took a great interest in the welfare of the mill hands at Deanston and was a popular local figure. Muir was an elder of St George's United Presbyterian Church in Glasgow and of the Bridge of Teith Free Presbyterian Church at Deanston. He was a stern parent, trusting his grown-up sons only a little more than his former partners; he wrote to them on 18 October 1898, 'My advice to you both is to fall in *cordially* with *my* views and policy, even when you do not quite understand them' (Finlay archive). His daughters made good marriages into the gentry or the upper mercantile families of Glasgow. Muir undoubtedly sailed close to the wind in some of his financial dealings. He considered shareholders a necessary evil, and the boards of all his public companies were composed of his sons-in-law and other compliant relatives.

Sir John Muir suffered two strokes and died at Deanston House on 6 August 1903. Alexander and James Muir returned from Calcutta on receiving news of their father's first stroke in 1901 and took over direction as trustees, later successive chairmen.

Sir (Alexander) Kay Muir, second baronet (1868–1951), left his mother in possession of Deanston House and bought the large adjoining estate of Blair Drummond. A less domineering man than his father, he nevertheless exercised tight control of James Finlay & Co., modernizing it and converting his father's haphazard collection of companies into a private company, owned by members of the extended Muir family, with the tea and jute companies as wholly owned subsidiaries. In 1919 capital was increased to £2 million and in 1923 it became a public limited liability company. The First World War brought reasonable profits from sales of those staples of warfare—gunny for sandbags, khaki cotton cloth, and tea, though the British staff were depleted by military service and Blair Drummond House became a convalescent hospital. Sir Kay made shrewd private investments. Just before he retired from the chair in 1926, foreseeing possible political instability in the Indian empire, he instigated a new venture, sending planters from southern India and Ceylon to open the first large-scale tea plantations in Kenya, which under his brother's chairmanship quickly began to produce good teas. Sir Kay took a conventional interest in politics as a Liberal Unionist. His main interests were shooting and fishing.

Sir Kay had married in 1910 Grace Frances, daughter of John Adam Richard Newman of Newberry Manor, co. Cork, and widow of Major Henry Charles Windsor Villiers-Stuart of Dromana, co. Waterford; she died in 1920. His second marriage was on 17 March 1924 at Brompton Oratory, Knightsbridge, to the Catholic twenty-year-old Nadejda Constanza Irenea Garilla Euphrosyne, eldest daughter of Dimitri Stancioff, former premier of Bulgaria, then Bulgarian minister in London. The marriage was a very happy one; Lady Nadejda's cosmopolitan background, united to Sir Kay's hospitality and sporting interests, made Blair Drummond the scene of notable house parties at which King Boris of Bulgaria was frequently present. Sir Kay died childless at Blair Drummond House on 4 June 1951; his wife died in 1952. The baronetcy and Blair Drummond estate devolved on his nephew John Harling Muir, the son of his late brother James Finlay Muir.

James Finlay Muir (1870–1948), a man in his father's mould, was an autocrat rather than an innovator. He was ruthless, efficient, and, though much respected, more feared than loved. He married in 1909 Charlotte Escudier (*d.* 1956), daughter of John Harling Turner of Cessnock, Ayrshire. They resided at Braco Castle, Braco, Perthshire, where they raised two sons and a daughter. Charlotte's warmth, hospitality, and practical concern for the enormous Finlay workforce were much appreciated, though labour conditions improved as a result of legislation and the provision of better housing and health services, in which Finlays was slightly ahead of its competitors. Muir took a particular interest in developing the Kenya tea estates. When the slump of 1929–30 severely affected tea and other plantation crops he supported the formation of the international tea quota.

In 1936 James Finlay Muir retired from the chair, which passed in turn to three unrelated chairmen and one grandson of the original Muir, Alexander McGrigor Muir. James Muir was a notable sportsman and enjoyed fine shooting at Braco. He and his wife played their part in local unionist politics and more widely in charitable and social affairs. He died at Braco Castle on 7 September 1948 and was buried privately on his estate. His widow lived on at Braco until her death in 1956.

Sir John Harling Muir, third baronet (1910–1994), son of James Finlay Muir and his wife, Charlotte, was born on 17 November 1910 and educated at Stowe School. He served an apprenticeship on Finlay estates and at Calcutta from 1932 to 1940, followed by war service. He married in 1936 Elizabeth Mary, daughter of Frederick James Dundas of Cawthorne, Yorkshire; they had five sons and two daughters. Under his chairmanship from 1961 to 1975 Finlays divested itself of most of its Indian estates, retaining those in the adjacent subcontinent, and diversified into merchant banking and oil. Muir and his wife maintained the hospitable traditions of Blair Drummond and Braco, in both house and field, before turning over the house and estate to other uses and retiring to a smaller dwelling on the property. He died on 31 May 1994 and was succeeded by his eldest son, Sir Richard James Kay Muir, fourth baronet.

The businesses operated by the Finlays and Muirs were on the whole extremely successful. The first Sir John Muir saw the colonial possibilities of primary crop production and revolutionized the tea industry by his integrated management of the various stages from plant to pot. The Muir family were paternalistic, stern, but respected employers, sustaining Victorian standards of probity and commanding loyalty and hard work from their vast workforce.

Under the second Sir John Muir, Finlays was still an international company, mainly concerned with tea, though cotton textiles had been replaced by interests in North Sea oil; it remained, as it had been in the 1880s, the largest Scottish employer of overseas labour.

MONICA CLOUGH

Sources DSBB · *James Finlay & Co. Limited, manufacturers and East India merchants, 1750–1950* (1951) · *Glasgow Herald* · *Clydeside cameos* (1885) · *Glasgow Herald* (7 Aug 1903) · *The lord provosts of Glasgow, 1833–1902: biographical sketches* (1902) · A. Muir and M. Davies, *A Victorian shipowner: a portrait of Sir Charles Cayzer* (privately printed, London, 1978) · bap. reg. Scot. [Sir John Muir] · d. cert. [Sir John Muir] · *The Times* (18 March 1924), 17c · d. cert. [Sir A. K. Muir] · Walford, *County families* · d. cert. [J. F. Muir] · priv. coll., Muir family papers
Archives James Finlay plc, Glasgow, secretary's department · priv. coll., family papers · U. Glas., Archives and Business Records Centre, Finlay papers · U. Glas., Archives and Business Records Centre, H. B. Muir papers
Likenesses photograph (Sir John Muir), James Finlay plc, Glasgow, board room · photograph (Sir Alexander Kay Muir), James Finlay plc, Glasgow, board room · photograph (James Muir), James Finlay plc, Glasgow, board room · photograph (Sir John Harling Muir), James Finlay plc, Glasgow, board room
Wealth at death £862,802—Sir John Muir: NA Scot., SC 44/43 · £2,345,491 gross—Sir A. K. Muir: NA Scot., SC 44/24/28 · £479,240.40—Sir John Harling Muir: confirmation, Scotland, 1995

Muir, Andrew (1817–1899), merchant, was born on 6 January 1817 at Greenock, Renfrewshire, the youngest of the eight children of James Muir (1771–1834) and his first wife, Jane Pollock (d. 1818). The brothers James and Andrew Muir (1778–1849), born in Paisley, were merchants who became prosperous with the expansion of Greenock in the early nineteenth century. Among their most successful ventures was the straw-hat factory, started in 1808.

Between the ages of nine and thirteen Muir attended Browning's boarding-school at Tillicoultry, Clackmannanshire, but otherwise appears to have been educated privately. After his father's death in 1834 he worked until 1841 with his uncle in the Clyde Pottery Company. From 1842 he led what he later described as an unsettled and wandering bachelor life, pursuing various commercial activities in Canada and America, until 1852, when he was invited by his brother-in-law Archibald Mirrielees to join him in business in Russia.

Archibald Mirrielees (1797–1877), merchant, was born in Aberdeen on 7 September 1797 and went out to St Petersburg from London in 1822. He founded his own importing business there in 1843. His first two wives, Sarah Newbould Spurr (d. 1835) and Mary Cullen (d. 1839), died in Russia. In 1844 he married, as his third wife, Jane Isabella Muir (1810–1875), Andrew's elder sister, with whom he had six children. In St Petersburg he was deeply influenced by the dissenting Scottish minister John Paterson and by the Revd Richard Knill of the London Missionary Society. From 1829 until 1877 he was very active in the British and Foreign Bible Society, and during the Crimean War (1854–6) handled the society's entire business in north Russia. Mirrielees died on 13 February 1877 at Elm Trees, 2 Cleveland Gardens, Castle Hill Park, Ealing, Middlesex, and was buried at Stoke Poges church.

After serving a rigorous five-year apprenticeship, Andrew Muir took over the business in 1857 on his brother-in-law's retirement. Under his direction it expanded considerably and began to operate in Moscow (where Muir became a merchant of the First Guild in 1867) as well as St Petersburg. In the late 1880s his successors converted the Moscow business from wholesale to retail, and Muir and Mirrielees became Russia's first department store. The original building close to the Bolshoi Theatre burnt down in 1900, but a new building on the same site, designed by the Russian architect R. I. Klein, was completed in 1908. As Russia's largest department store, Muir and Mirrielees became celebrated throughout the Russian empire. In 1919, after the revolution, the company was nationalized, but the department store continued to function during the Soviet period, when it became known as Central Universal Stores (TsUM). It was privatized in 1993.

On 16 April 1861 Muir married Alison (Alice) Philip, *née* Bell (1822–1910), the widow of William Philip (1814–1845), a Scottish missionary in South Africa. In 1874 he handed over control of Muir and Mirrielees to his stepson Walter *Philip (1845–1919). After returning with his wife and their five children to London, he purchased 42 Holland Park and founded the London Portland Cement Company.

Muir was a studious and well-informed man. He began reading philosophy and theology at an early age, and never shared the simple evangelical views of other members of his family or Mirrielees. In Russia he supervised the retranslation of the Old Testament into modern Russian for the British and Foreign Bible Society but declined the society's invitation to become an honorary life governor. In London he and his wife became enthusiastic followers of the Revd Stopford Brooke. The family also participated fully in London's cultural life. The three Muir daughters became friendly with Philip and Margaret, the children of Sir Edward Burne-Jones, and in 1904 Anne Evelyn, known as Eva (1864–1946), married Francis Richmond (1868–1933), the son of Sir William Blake Richmond.

Muir's last years were clouded by financial worries. In 1893, while still serving their apprenticeships, his sons Martin and Kenneth were dismissed from Muir and Mirrielees by their stepbrother Walter Philip on the grounds of unsuitability. Muir then committed a large part of his personal fortune to setting them up as owners of a chemical works at Degunino, outside Moscow, but in this venture, too, they were unsuccessful.

Muir died on 12 June 1899 at Bryony Hill, the house that he had built in the village of Hambledon, Surrey, and was buried in Hambledon churchyard.

HARVEY PITCHER

Sources H. Pitcher, *Muir and Mirrielees: the Scottish partnership that became a household name in Russia* (1994) · private information (2004) · CGPLA Eng. & Wales (1877) [Archibald Mirrielees] · d. cert.
Likenesses F. Hollyer, photograph (in his seventies), repro. in Pitcher, *Muir and Mirrielees*, facing p. 111 · photographs, priv. coll.
Wealth at death £35,678 0s. 4d.: probate, 4 Aug 1899, CGPLA Eng. & Wales · under £30,000—Archibald Mirrielees: probate, 12 March 1877, CGPLA Eng. & Wales

Muir, Edwin (1887–1959), poet and literary critic, was born on 15 May 1887 at The Folly, Ayre, on the Orkney mainland, the youngest of six children of James Muir (1833–1902), farmer, and his wife, Elizabeth Cormack (1843–1907). Two years later the family moved to the Bu, a 100 acre farm on the small island of Wyre, where there was a strong sense of community among its few families. Edwin also felt a larger unity—between the human community and the animals and the natural surroundings. In his home the evenings were filled with story-telling and singing. When he was eight the family moved to Garth, another 100 acre—but less good—farm, 4 miles from Kirkwall, on the mainland. He went irregularly to Kirkwall burgh school and began to read voraciously. When he was fourteen the family moved to Glasgow—a sudden transition from a pre-industrial community into the modern world. His father and his second brother, Willie (1877–1902), died within a month of each other. His mother then died three months after his third brother, Johnnie (1879–1906). Muir worked as an office boy in a law office and then in a publishing office; in a beer-bottling firm in Glasgow; and from 1903 to 1914 as a clerk in a bone factory in Greenock. He then returned to Glasgow and worked in a shipbuilding office in Renfrew during the war, having been rejected by the army as physically unfit. As a boy he had experienced two conversions at revivalist meetings but his early religious faith was undermined by what he saw in the slums and by the deaths of his brothers, and was replaced by faith in socialism and later by Nietzscheanism, two philosophies which he desperately tried to reconcile. He was a member of the Clarion scouts, of the Independent Labour Party, and of the guild socialist movement. He contributed to the *New Age*, from 1913, propagandist verses and, later, aphorisms in the manner of Nietzsche, which were collected in *We Moderns* (1918).

Willa *Muir, *née* Wilhelmina Johnston Anderson (1890–1970), remembered Muir at their first meeting in 1918:

> [his] eyes and mouth promised well; his brow was an
> intellectual's, disproportionately wide and high, very
> noticeable above the slight, even meagre body, yet his eyes
> were dreamy looking, sea-blue, with a hint of distance in
> them, and his mouth was well cut, with full, sensitive lips.
> (W. Muir, *Belonging*, 15)

On 7 June 1919 they married: 'My marriage', said Muir, 'was the most fortunate event of my life' (*Autobiography*, 147). He left Glasgow for London, where he became assistant to A. R. Orage on the *New Age* and reviewed for *The Athenaeum* and (drama) for *The Scotsman*. The unhappiness of the Glasgow years had brought him close to nervous breakdown and he underwent a course of psychoanalysis. The analysis, more congenial work, and especially Willa Muir helped him to find inner peace in the years that followed, in Prague, Germany, Italy, and Austria (1921–4). Aged thirty-five he began to write poetry seriously, his *First Poems* (1925) being published by the Hogarth Press.

In Montrose and Buckinghamshire (1924–5), France (1926–7), Surrey (1927–9), Sussex (1929–32), Hampstead (1932–5), and St Andrews (1935–42) Muir made his living by voluminous work as a critic and reviewer; he also wrote

three novels, *The Marionette* (1927), *The Three Brothers* (1931), and—possibly the most successful—the semi-autobiographical *Poor Tom* (1932). Muir shared with Willa a dislike of Calvinism, which was confirmed for him by working on his *John Knox: Portrait of a Calvinist* (1929). He and Willa also had mixed feelings about Scotland, some of which were expressed in his *Scottish Journey* (1935), and even more so in *Scott and Scotland: the Predicament of the Scottish Writer* (1936), where his criticism of Scottish literature and doubts about the viability of Scots as a language for intellectual thought led to the ending of his friendship with C. M. Grieve (Hugh MacDiarmid). His torn feelings about being Scottish and a writer had already been expressed in 1931 to James Whyte, editor of the *Modern Scot* (to which both Muirs contributed): 'we are neither quite Scottish … nor are we quite delivered from our Scottishness … The very words "a Scottish writer" have a slightly unnerving ring to me; what they come down to … is a writer of Scottish birth' (10 Sept 1931, NL Scot., MS 19703.7; *Selected Letters*, 71). He and Willa Muir, a better linguist who did much of the work, produced about forty volumes of translations, mostly from German authors, including Hermann Broch, Lion Feuchtwangler, and Gerhart Hauptmann; they were particularly known for introducing Franz Kafka's works to the English-speaking world.

Muir's criticism is contained in about a thousand reviews, in numerous articles—some collected in *Latitudes* (1924), *Transition: Essays on Contemporary Literature* (1926), and *Essays on Literature and Society* (1949), and posthumously in *Edwin Muir: Uncollected Scottish Criticism* (1982) and *The Truth of Imagination: some Uncollected Reviews and Essays* (1988)—in broadcast talks, and in *The Structure of the Novel* (1928), *The Present Age, from 1914* (1939), and *The Estate of Poetry* (1962), his Charles Eliot Norton lectures at Harvard University. His criticism is marked by scrupulous fairness and independence of judgement; T. S. Eliot thought it 'the best of our time' (*The Times*, 7 Jan 1959). In *An Autobiography* (1954), a longer version of *The Story & the Fable* (1940), an impressionistic narrative as much concerned with dreams and his intellectual development as factual detail, Muir took a more philosophic approach than Willa Muir was to take in *Belonging* (1968). His mature prose reflects his character—quiet, lucid, witty without striving for effect. In 1954 he sent three poems to Janet Adam Smith:

> in doubt and trembling, for I have been writing prose so
> long, finishing my autobiography, that verse is now
> awkward to me: one seems to write prose and poetry with
> different hands, and whether the right or the left is the
> poetic one is hard to say … You mustn't think I am unhappy
> because the poems are; they came from I don't know where.
> (25 Oct 1954, NL Scot., MS 19703.17; *Selected Letters*, 169)

Muir's poetry is generally seen as his great achievement. Coming to the form late ('[initially] I wrote in baffling ignorance, blundering and perpetually making mistakes' (*Autobiography*, 201) he went on maturing to the end, and wrote his best poems when over fifty. He used traditional metres and made no startling innovations in technique, being concerned only to convey his vision clearly and honestly. Beneath the story of his life he saw the fable of man—Eden, the fall, the journey through the labyrinth of time. He made much use of his dreams and of myths, for in them the fable is most clearly seen. In his later poems he was able to relate a widening range of temporal experiences—the Second World War, the communist victory in Prague, fears of atomic war, his marriage—to his perception of an underlying timeless reality. He experienced to the full the doubts and fears characteristic of the twentieth century and came to see the incarnation as the answer to the problems of time and eternity, necessity and freedom; but his poetry embodied vision rather than belief. Immortality was to him a state of being, something immediately experienced. He wrote in 1939 that he had:

> believed for many years in the immortality of the soul; all my poetry springs from that in one form or another; and belief of that kind means belief in God, though my God is not that of the churches, and I can reconcile myself to no church … I look upon myself as an anti-Marx socialist; a man who believes that people are immortal souls and that they should bring about on this earth a society fit for immortal souls. (to Sydney Schiff, 16 Jan 1939, BL, Add. MS 52920, fols. 179–80; *Selected Letters*, 107)

The apparently simple words in his poems carry a great weight of meaning. The poems themselves are mostly short but are not fragments—all are related to his central vision of the mystery of our common humanity. T. S. Eliot was struck by 'the power of his early work' but thought his late work was 'the most remarkable' (Eliot, 10); Willa Muir asked Kathleen Raine, who was to review him in the *New Statesman*, not to 'forget the sweet, lighter poems he wrote. Eliot, in his desire to present Edwin as an orthodox Christian, overdid, I think, the desolations and the saintliness. Edwin's wine could never be contained in any orthodox creed' (7 April 1960, NL Scot., MS 19703, fol. 109). His collected poems, co-edited by Willa Muir, were published in 1960.

From 1942 to 1945 Muir worked for the British Council in Edinburgh, after which he was director of its institutes in Prague (1945–8) and Rome (1949–50), and warden of Newbattle Abbey (1950–55), an adult education college near Edinburgh. After a year as Charles Eliot Norton professor at Harvard (1955–6) he and Willa settled at Swaffham Prior, near Cambridge. He was appointed CBE in 1953 and received honorary degrees from Prague (1947), Edinburgh (1947), Rennes (1949), Leeds (1955), and Cambridge (1958): 'He is now five times a doctor—quite enough' (Willa Muir to Violet Schiff, 1 Nov 1958, BL, Add. MS 52920). He died in Addenbrooke's Hospital, Cambridge, on 3 January 1959 and was buried at Swaffham Prior. He left one son, Gavin (1927–1991), and Willa Muir, who died in 1970.

The Complete Poems of Edwin Muir was published in 1991. Muir was a man of complete integrity; gentle, unassuming, and vulnerable, but with firm tenacity of purpose; sometimes abstracted, but strongly affectionate and quick in sympathy. He spoke in a soft, lilting voice and sang almost in tune.　　　　　　　　AILEEN CHRISTIANSON

Sources E. Muir, *An autobiography*, [rev. edn] (1954); repr. (1993) [1993] • P. H. Butter, *Edwin Muir: man and poet* (1966) • *Selected letters of Edwin Muir*, ed. P. H. Butter (1974) • W. Muir, *Belonging: a memoir* (1968) • BL, E. Muir, Violet and Sydney Schiff collection, Add. MS 52920, fols. 1–181 • W. Muir, notebooks (incl. journals, 9/5), miscellaneous papers and letters, U. St Andr. L., MS dep 9/1–8 • W. Muir, letters and verses, NL Scot., MS 19703 • T. S. Eliot, preface, in *Selected poems of Edwin Muir* (1966) • *The complete poems of Edwin Muir: an annotated edition* (1991) • *Edwin Muir: uncollected Scottish criticism*, ed. A. Noble (1982) • C. J. M. MacLachlan and D. S. Robb, eds., *Edwin Muir centenary assessments* (1990) • M. McCulloch, *Edwin Muir: poet, critic and novelist* (1993) • A. MacLeish, 'Introduction', in E. Muir, *The estate of poetry* (1962) • H. Gardner, *Edwin Muir: the W. D. Thomas memorial lecture* (1961) • H. Gaskill, 'Edwin Muir in Hellerau', *Scottish Literary Journal*, 11/1 (1984), 45–56 • *The letters of Hugh MacDiarmid*, ed. A. Bold (1984) • A. Bold, *MacDiarmid* (1988) • d. cert. • *DNB*

Archives NL Scot., corresp., literary MSS, and papers • NRA, corresp. and papers | BBC WAC, corresp. with BBC • BL, letters to Sydney Schiff and Violet Schiff, Add. MS 52920, fols. 1–181 • LUL, letters to Gerald Duckworth & Co. • NL Scot., letters to William Montgomerie • NL Scot., letters to Kathleen Raine • NL Scot., letters to Janet Smith • NL Scot., letters to William Soutar • Orkney Archives, Kirkwall, corresp. with J. Mary Bosdet • Orkney Archives, Kirkwall, corresp. with E. W. Marwick • Orkney Archives, Kirkwall, letters to Patricia Swale • priv. coll., Ethel Ross and Irene Abenheimer collection • Royal Society of Literature, London, letters to Royal Society of Literature • U. Edin. L., letters to A. C. Aitken, and papers • U. Edin. L., letters to George Mackay Brown • U. Reading L., letters to Hogarth Press • U. St Andr. L., diary, corresp., and Willa Muir's papers

Likenesses photograph, 1917, repro. in Muir, *Belonging*, facing p. 30 • photograph, 1923–4, repro. in Muir, *Belonging*, facing p. 31 • double portrait, photograph, 1928 (with son Gavin), repro. in Muir, *Belonging*, facing p. 31 • B. Niven, double portrait, caricature, 1938 (with Willa Muir), repro. in *The Voice of Scotland*, 1/2, Sept. – Nov. • group portrait, photograph, 1947, repro. in Muir, *Belonging*, facing p. 65 • photograph, 1947, repro. in Muir, *Belonging*, facing p. 65 • M. Gerson, photograph, 1955, NPG • photograph, 1955, repro. in Muir, *Belonging*, facing p. 81 • H. Coster, photographs, NPG • S. Cursiter, group portrait, oils (*Authors in session, 1950*), Art Gallery and Museum, Glasgow • M. Szwarc, bust, Saltire Society, Edinburgh • photograph, Orkney Library Photographic Archive; repro. in McCulloch, *Edwin Muir*, front cover • photograph, NL Scot., leaflet for Edwin Muir Memorial Fund, MS 19670.45

Wealth at death £4874 17s. 8d.: probate, 20 March 1959, CGPLA Eng. & Wales

Muir, Frank Herbert (1920–1998), writer and broadcaster, was born on 5 February 1920 in the Derby Arms hotel, 72 Margate Road, Ramsgate, Kent, the younger son of Charles James Muir (1888–1934), a steam tug engineer from New Zealand, and his wife, Margaret Webber (b. 1891). He was educated at schools in Ramsgate, Broadstairs, and Leyton, east London, before leaving at fourteen to join a firm of carbon paper manufacturers after his father suddenly died of pneumonia. A few years later, after the outbreak of the Second World War, he joined the RAF—because, as he recalled in characteristically droll vein, it seemed to him 'that in the RAF I would get to sit down more' (Muir, 62). In the event he had to sit, stand, and fall, learning parachuting and photography. He was stationed partly in Dorset and partly in allied-occupied Iceland, where he gained his first experience of radio broadcasting and performing comedy sketches to troops in Reykjavík. He said he had had a 'soft war', never firing a shot in anger.

Frank Herbert Muir (1920–1998), by Godfrey Argent, 1970

Muir was demobbed in 1945. Having set his heart on a life in comedy and begun to gravitate to the Windmill Theatre like so many other future stars, he sent material to Ted Kavanagh, the creator of the wartime radio hit *ITMA* who had subsequently founded his own company, Ted Kavanagh Associates, which trained young talent. Kavanagh used him to write for the rising comedian Jimmy Edwards in a comedy series called *Navy Mixture*. The writer for the show's other star, Dick Bentley, was Denis Norden, a Kavanagh employee. Thus the two men first came into contact. They went on to forge, over more than fifteen years, one of the most productive partnerships in British comedy history, considered as synonymous with scriptwriting as Morecambe and Wise were with television.

The first fruit of Muir and Norden's collaboration was a show commissioned by the producer of *Navy Mixture*, Charles Maxwell, *Take It From Here*, which ran on the Light Programme from 1948 to 1960 and broke new ground in its use of sophisticated wordplay and topical jokes and the way in which it acknowledged the literacy of the listener. One example of its wit was the line 'Infamy! Infamy! They've all got it in for me!', often recalled as a line first spoken by Kenneth Williams in a *Carry On* film but actually created by Muir and Norden and first uttered by Dick Bentley, as Caesar, on *Take It From Here*. Similarly, it was Muir and Norden who wrote the parody 'Bal-ham, Gateway to the South', which Peter Sellers made famous. The most famous part of the show, however, was 'The Glums', a lowlife family saga in which Jimmy Edwards was the male chauvinist pig of a father, Dick Bentley his moronic

son Ron, and June Whitfield the perpetually swooning fiancée, Eth.

Muir and Norden had much in common: both were former members of the RAF, both were extremely tall, and both were possessed of extraordinarily fertile minds and an apparently inexhaustible verbal dexterity. Muir was the elder by two years. They worked together in a small top room in the Kavanagh offices in Bruton Street, Mayfair, and developed an effective way of getting a lot of work done. They had only two chairs in their office, 'so that anyone dropping in for idle chatter became tired of standing after a few minutes, and drifted off' (Plomley, 146).

Take It From Here became a huge hit. It made Muir and Norden hot properties. They wrote several radio series for the Canadian funny man Bernard Braden and his wife, Barbara Kelly, and were much in demand on television as it exploded in popularity. They created (in 1956) and wrote *Whack-o!*, with Jimmy Edwards as the conniving, cane-swishing headmaster of Chiselbury School. It ran for four years. They adapted Henry Cecil's *Brothers-in-Law* (1962), giving the young Richard Briers his first leading role. They appeared together as rival panellists in two exceptionally long-running radio panel games, *My Word!* (1956–90), famous for its tortuous puns, and *My Music* (1967–91). They wrote for summer seasons and rewrote for comedy films.

The 1950s, the main period of his partnership with Norden, was a happy decade for Muir. He married on 16 July 1949 Edith Ann Mary (Polly) McIrvine (*b.* 1925), a half-British, half-French former WRNS girl. They had a son, Jamie, and then a daughter, Sally. In 1953 they bought a former farmhouse in 2 acres of rough meadow in Thorpe, near Egham in Surrey, which became the family home and the heart of Muir's emotional security. In 1960 he and Norden appeared together as joint castaways on *Desert Island Discs*. In 1963 he and Polly bought a holiday home on Corsica.

In 1964, when the scriptwriting partnership with Norden was dissolved (though not their friendship), Muir joined the BBC as assistant head of light entertainment. Two notable achievements were his purchase of *All Gas and Gaiters* (1967–71), an affectionate ecclesiastical situation comedy starring William Mervyn, Derek Nimmo, and Robertson Hare, and *The World of Wooster* (1965–7), with Ian Carmichael and Dennis Price (unsurpassable as Jeeves), of which he was executive producer.

After three years at the BBC Muir left to join a new ITV contractor, London Weekend Television. But when in 1969 a boardroom coup ousted its first managing director, Michael Peacock, he and other executives resigned in protest and he 'reverted to being self-unemployed' (*WW*). This was an unnecessarily self-deprecating assessment. Freelancing was what he was best at. He was in demand everywhere. On radio he made more than 100 editions of an anthology show, *Frank Muir Goes into …*, which he co-wrote with Simon Brett and presented with an old RAF comrade, Alfred Marks. On television he became a household name through the BBC2 word game *Call my Bluff*, in which he was a polished team captain for more than twenty years opposite Robert Morley, then Patrick Campbell, and finally Arthur Marshall. Making lucrative television commercials, he donned an Edwardian swimming costume for Hovis and sang 'Everyone's a fruit and nut case ...' to the strains of the *Nutcracker* suite to advertise a Cadbury's chocolate bar.

None of this taxed Muir particularly. Behind the dandified, languid manner, the pink bow tie, and the pipe, was a self-taught, formidably well-read man and gifted writer. His literary output included an anthology entitled *The Frank Muir Book: an Irreverent Companion to Social History* (1976); sixteen *What-a-Mess* books for children about his family's problematical Afghan hound; *The Oxford Book of Humorous Prose* (1990), which ranged from Caxton to Wodehouse; a novel, *The Walpole Orange* (1993); and finally his warm and gentle autobiography, *A Kentish Lad* (1997). He was awarded two honorary degrees, an LLD from St Andrews University, where he was rector (1978), and a DLitt from the University of Kent (1982). Muir and Norden were both appointed CBE in 1980. Muir's scholarship was also recognized when he was invited to become president of the Johnson Society in Lichfield for 1975–6; he argued in his presidential address that Samuel Johnson had a more pronounced sense of humour than either eighteenth-century manners or Boswell's biography allowed him to display. Not for nothing did *The Guardian* call him a 'philosopher of laughter'.

Anners, the house Muir had bought with his wife in the 1950s, was where he spent most of his time in his closing years and where he wrote his funny, modest, bestselling memoirs. He died there of heart failure on the morning of 2 January 1998; his wife and children survived him. He was buried ten days later in the parish church where he worshipped, St Mary's, Thorpe, and with him in the coffin his family placed a copy of the *Sunday Times* review of *A Kentish Lad*, in which the reviewer had paid tribute to Muir's 'enormous fund of curious learning'.

PAUL DONOVAN

Sources F. Muir, *A Kentish lad* (1997) · *The Times* (3 Jan 1998) · R. Plomley, *Desert island discs* (1975) · A. Foster and S. Furst, *Radio comedy, 1938–1968* (1996) · J. Evans, *The Penguin TV companion* (2001) · P. Donovan, *The radio companion* (1991) · b. cert. · m. cert. · d. cert. · *The Guardian* (3 Jan 1998) · *The Independent* (3 Jan 1998) · *WW* (1990)
Archives BBC WAC | SOUND BBC sound archives
Likenesses photographs, *c.*1950–1973, Hult. Arch. · G. Argent, photograph, 1970, NPG [*see illus.*] · group portrait, photograph, repro. in Donovan, *Radio companion*, 187 · portrait, repro. in *The Times* · portraits, BBC Picture Archive, London · portraits, repro. in Muir, *Kentish lad*
Wealth at death £827,770: probate, 20 May 1998, *CGPLA Eng. & Wales*

Muir, James Finlay (1870–1948). *See under* Muir family (*per.* 1849–1992).

Muir [*married name* Leuckert], **Jean Elizabeth** (1928–1995), dress designer, was born on 17 July 1928 at Queen Charlotte's Hospital, London, the daughter of Cyril Vernon Muir, draper's floor superintendent, and his wife, Phyllis Evelyn Coy. Later she preferred to give her birth date as 1933. She attributed her creative pragmatism and what became a legendary self-discipline to Scottish ancestry on

Jean Elizabeth Muir (1928–1995), by Glenys Barton, 1991

her father's side. The understated elegance of a designer famous for her variations on the little black dress derived in part from childhood memories of visits to her great-grandmother, a 'stylish old Scots matriarch', whose imposing drawing room overlooked Regent's Park (Muir, 'Clothes — aesthetics — commerce', 711).

Jean Muir was reticent about the details of her early life. She and her brother, Christopher, seem to have moved from London to Bedford, home of her mother's family, soon after Jean reached school age. Her parents parted when she was still young, and contemporaries at the Bedford Girls' Modern School, which she attended from the age of eleven, were aware of difficult family circumstances. The evidence suggests that she was a fee-assisted pupil at the predominantly fee-paying direct grant school. Her academic achievements were unimpressive, but she showed a precocious talent for needlework, claiming to have been able to sew, knit, and embroider by the age of six, and to have completed her first skirt at eleven. As a teenager she made all her own clothes, being too small to find ready-made garments to fit her. Her intense interests in art and in historical costume were aroused at this early stage.

Muir's first job on leaving school in 1945 was as a clerk in the electoral register office of the shire hall in Bedford. The post appealed to her meticulous cast of mind. But she soon felt the counter-attraction of London and, after a short time in a solicitor's office, found congenial work in Liberty's department store, first in the stockroom, then in scarves and lingerie, graduating to sketching and designing for the model room and the new and glamorous Young Liberty department, an early emanation of the post-war youth cult with which (although Jean Muir would emphatically deny it) her early success was inextricably entwined. She then worked briefly at Jacqmar, where she met the exuberant Danish milliner Aage Tharrup. He introduced her to Jaeger where she spent the next six years as a designer of dresses, sweaters, coats, and suits, liaising with Jaeger's factory and suppliers and learning the complex disciplines of seasonal production. This experience proved invaluable when, in 1962, she established her own label, Jane and Jane, backed by the fashion house of Susan Small. Four years later, after Susan Small had been absorbed by Courtaulds, she and her husband, the German-born Harry Leuckert (b. 1928/9), whom she had married on 16 February 1955, borrowed capital to form their own company, Jean Muir Ltd, setting up their Mayfair headquarters in Bruton Street. Leuckert, the son of Friedrick August Leuckert, dentistry researcher, had trained as an actor at the Royal Academy of Dramatic Art.

Muir's great innovation was what she defined as 'couture ready-to-wear' (Muir, 'Clothes — aesthetics — commerce', 713). She set her mind on evolving clothes that had 'a couture feel', luxurious in materials and beautifully shaped, while eliminating the laborious hand-sewing and elaborate technical and social conventions of the traditional couture house. Muir was always to make clothes for private clients, but ready-to-wear Jean Muir garments were available to the general public, albeit at high prices and through carefully selected stores. These were clothes for newly mobile women, which came to define an era. Muir was a dancer *manquée*. Her own passionate interest in classical ballet gave her a strong sense of anatomical structure. Her favoured fabrics—the famous black jersey, wool, crêpe, cashmere, supple leathers, and suedes—responded to the shifting female body. Her fluency of line made her the natural successor to the great French female couturiers Madeleine Vionnet and Madame Grès. Among her loyal clients were the writer Antonia Fraser, the sculptor Elisabeth Frink, the painter Bridget Riley, and the actress Joanna Lumley, who was at one time a Jean Muir house model. Although the term 'feminism' made Muir shudder, she was designing for the emergent high-profile professional woman of the 1960s and 1970s, the social group from which she drew her friends.

Muir disdainfully rejected the word 'fashion', aiming for gradual stylistic evolution in her clothes rather than 'the flimsy seasonal ins and outs of trends' (Muir, 'Clothes — aesthetics — commerce', 713). There were no shock changes of hemline in her collections. Her colour spectrum was a recurring navy, black, and grey, with only occasional contrasting bursts of colour. She described herself as a dressmaker rather than designer, seeing herself as part of a historic continuity of the craft and trade of clothes. She was a supreme technician, believing that, in making the pattern for a garment, system and accuracy were as important as they were in any engineering process. Her philosophy was rooted in decorum: she saw attention to dress as a sign of self-respect and of regard for the moral order of things. Her influence on the next generation of designers, for instance Jasper Conran, was to be profound.

Muir's attitude to business was always autocratic. In 1986 the company was sold to Coats Paton, owner of Jaeger, but the liaison was unhappy and few people were surprised when Muir and her husband soon regained control.

Of a turnover for Jean Muir Ltd amounting to around £3 million by the early 1990s, £1 million was accounted for by sales to the United States, Muir's second spiritual home, where her understated modern style won many accolades, including the honorary citizenship of New Orleans.

Muir's diminutive figure, clad in navy blue or occasionally black, was a distinctive and, to those who did not know her, an alarming presence on the London scene. Her friend and admirer Sir Roy Strong commented that only she could attend a queen's birthday party dressed like a Neapolitan widow (*The Independent*, 30 May 1995). She was firm in her views, and a mistress of the put-down, delivered with the interrogatory squeak that punctuated her conversation. Only at home in Lorbottle Hall in Northumberland, a fine early nineteenth-century mansion overflowing with her acquisitions of modern art and craft, did she relax a little, wearing tartan trousers, cooking little omelettes, and playing sentimental Scottish ballads on the wind-up gramophone. Her missionary zeal for widespread appreciation of art, craft, and design was formidable. Though not a natural public speaker or committee member, she schooled herself to spread the message that investment in creativity could stem Britain's industrial decline, and she became a heroically active member of the Design Council and a trustee of the Victoria and Albert Museum as well as a royal designer for industry. She was appointed CBE in 1984, and received honorary degrees from Newcastle, Ulster, and Heriot-Watt universities, and an honorary fellowship from Duncan of Jordanstone College of Art, Dundee. It was during her term of office as master of the faculty of royal designers that terminal cancer was diagnosed, a reversal that spurred her on to even more intensive travelling and speech-making during the months left to her. Characteristically, she kept her illness secret even from close friends.

Jean Muir died in a nursing home at 20 Devonshire Place, London, on 28 May 1995 and was survived by her husband, Harry. She was buried on 6 June at the village church of St Bartholomew at Whittingham, Northumberland. A bevy of her London showroom and workshop assistants filed around the coffin dressed in Jean Muir black. The little churchyard was piled high with sprays, wreaths, and nosegays which, perfectionist unto death, she had insisted must be uniformly white.

FIONA MacCARTHY

Sources J. Muir, 'Getting going', *The Designer* (Oct 1979) · J. Muir, 'Clothes — aesthetics — commerce', RDI address, Royal Society of Arts, 17 Nov 1983 [in *Journal of the Royal Society of Arts* (Oct 1984)] · S. Menkes, 'Head mistress with art in her craft', *The Times* (7 Jan 1986) · J. Muir, 'Quick to the cut', *Guardian Weekend* (3 April 1993) · *The Guardian* (29 May 1995) · *The Times* (30 May 1995) · *The Independent* (30 May 1995) · personal knowledge (2004) · *WWW*, 1991–5 · b. cert. · m. cert. · d. cert. · private information (2004)

Archives Jean Muir Ltd, London, archive · RSA, archive | V&A, artefacts, dress collection | FILM BFI NFTVA, 'Very Jean Muir', Channel 4, Aug 1995

Likenesses N. Parkinson, group photograph, 1963 (*London fashion designers*), NPG; repro. in *Life* (18 Oct 1963) · two photographs, 1970–93, repro. in *The Independent* · S. Beljon, photograph, c.1977, NPG · D. Remfry, watercolour, 1981, NPG · G. Barton, ceramic bust, 1991,

priv. coll. [*see illus.*] • A. Green, oils, priv. coll. • three photographs, repro. in *The Times* (30 May 1995)
Wealth at death £4,131,856: probate, 1995, *CGPLA Eng. & Wales*

Muir, John (1810–1882), Sanskritist, was born at Glasgow on 5 February 1810, the eldest son of William Muir (1783–1820), a merchant of Kilmarnock and magistrate of Glasgow, and his wife, Helen Macfie (1784–1866). He was an elder brother of the Indian administrator and principal of Edinburgh University, Sir William *Muir. After receiving his early education at the Irvine Academy, he matriculated in 1823 at Glasgow University, but transferred, without taking a degree, to the East India College at Haileybury, on the nomination of a great-uncle, Sir James Shaw, a former lord mayor of London. In 1829 he was sent to Fort William College, Calcutta, and was subsequently appointed to administrative posts in the North-Western Provinces. A scholar at heart, he readily took up in 1844 the office of principal of the Benares Sanskrit College, which had recently become known also as the Victoria or Queen's College. Although he held the post for only a year he succeeded in developing a scheme, expanded by his successors, notably James Ballantyne, by which instruction in English and in Sanskrit was given concurrently. His views on Brahman education were expressed in speeches and lectures, notably, *Brief lectures on mental philosophy … delivered in Sanskrit to the students of the Benares Sanskrit College* (1845). Although he then returned to district administration, and his conscientiousness was recognized by a CIE in 1878, he was never prominent in the company's service.

Muir retired to Scotland in 1853 to pursue his lifelong interests in higher education and oriental research in Edinburgh. In 1855 he was created DCL at Oxford, and in 1861 LLD at Edinburgh. He remained a frequent contributor to learned journals, such as the *Indian Antiquary* and the *Journal of the Royal Asiatic Society of Great Britain and Ireland.* He was the main originator of a society known as the Association for the Better Endowment of Edinburgh University, and himself furthered its aims by founding in 1862 the regius chair of Sanskrit and comparative philology. With his brother, Sir William Muir, he also founded the Shaw fellowship for moral philosophy, named after their relative and patron, Sir James Shaw. He instituted the Muir lectureship in comparative religion, and offered several prizes, mainly for oriental studies, at both Edinburgh and Cambridge. Although the Sanskrit chair at Edinburgh was disestablished in 1949, the brothers' stimulation of oriental studies in Scotland proved significant.

Muir's earlier works were mainly evangelical addresses to the Hindu élites of India, and as such were chiefly written in Sanskrit. One of the first and most important, the *Mataparīkṣā: a Sketch of the Argument for Christianity and Against Hinduism* (Calcutta, 1839), was answered, also in Sanskrit, by several pandits, notably Nilakanta Goreh. Two heavily revised editions followed (1840; 1852–4). In the following years Muir published both in India and in Britain several other Sanskrit works, dealing with Indian history—particularly the Vedic period, on which he acknowledged his debt to scholars such as H. H. Wilson—

and also with his favourite topics of Christian apologetics and biography. The most noteworthy of his biographies were those of Christ and of St Paul, suggested by the similar works of W. H. Mill. If these writings were mainly derivative, his aim of engaging, usually in versified Sanskrit, with the Brahman élite, was new. However, a work in English, *Original Sanskrit Texts on the Origin and History of the People of India* (5 vols., 1858–70) written 'chiefly for the use of students and others in India', in which he translated many hitherto inaccessible Vedic texts, has proved to be Muir's most long-standing scholarly contribution. It was revised twice in the nineteenth century and reprinted over a hundred years later.

In later years, although Muir remained a Christian, he abandoned his strongly evangelical stance, partly under the influence of Thomas Arnold and mid-nineteenth-century biblical criticism, and partly, it seems, following Brahman responses to his attacks. His religious evolution is evident in a contribution to the biblical 'inspiration' debate of the early 1860s, and in subsequent translations of continental works of biblical criticism, for which he was dubbed a 'heretic' in evangelical circles. While still patronizing towards Sanskrit scholarship, his later publications no longer attacked Hinduism but stressed the value of studying carefully selected Sanskrit literature, such as those translated by him in his *Religious and Moral Sentiments Rendered from Sanskrit Writers* (1875).

Muir was of a reclusive scholarly temperament, which contrasted strongly with the high public profile of his brother Sir William Muir. Although he lacked the originality of some contemporary European orientalists, he was one of the most significant British patrons and scholars of Sanskrit of the mid-nineteenth century. He died unmarried at his home, 10 Merchiston Avenue, Edinburgh, on 7 March 1882, and was buried on 10 March in the Grange cemetery, Edinburgh, after a funeral at the Old Greyfriars Church. AVRIL A. POWELL

Sources R. F. Young, *Resistant Hinduism: Sanskrit sources on anti-Christian apologetics in early nineteenth-century India* (1981) • G. F. L. Marshall, *The Muir Book, compiled … for the descendants of Sir William Muir* (privately printed, 1930) • *Journal of the Royal Asiatic Society of Great Britain and Ireland,* new ser., 14 (1882), ix–xiv • *Edinburgh Courant* (13 March 1882), 5, col. 7 • *The Athenaeum* (18 March 1882), 346–7 • G. Nicholls, *Sketch of the rise and progress of the Benares Patshalla or Sanskrit College* (1907)

Archives BL OIOC | Sanskrit College Library, Benares, India • U. Edin., William Muir MSS

Likenesses J. H. Lorimer, oils, U. Edin. • photograph, repro. in F. E. Pargiter, ed., *Centenary volume of the Royal Asiatic Society of Great Britain and Ireland, 1823–1923* (1923) • portrait, repro. in Young, *Resistant Hinduism* • woodcut engraving, NPG

Wealth at death £24,177 18s. 4d.: confirmation, 29 April 1882, *CCI* • £227 1s. 8d.: additional estate, 25 Oct 1882, *CCI* • £1593 5s. 9d.: further additional estate, 11 Feb 1896, *CCI*

Muir, Sir John, first baronet (1828–1903). *See under* Muir family (*per.* 1849–1992).

Muir, John (1838–1914), naturalist and conservationist, was born in Dunbar, East Lothian, Scotland, on 21 April 1838 to Daniel Muir (1804–1885) and his second wife, Anne Gilrye Muir (1813–1896). John was the third child (of eight)

John Muir (1838–1914), by Orlando Rouland

and first son of this deeply religious, poorly educated shopkeeper and grain dealer of longtime Scottish descent. Daniel Muir, a stern Calvinist and lay preacher, eventually abandoned both the Presbyterian and Episcopalian churches to join the yet more zealous Campbellites (later known as the Disciples, or Churches, of Christ), a denomination of scriptural literalists founded primarily in America by Thomas and Alexander Campbell. Returning to Scotland in the famine-plagued 1840s, the Campbells (father and son) persuaded Muir and other followers to emigrate with them back across the Atlantic, cheap land and religious freedom being the main attractions.

Daniel Muir and his three older children—the others would come later—left Dunbar by rail on 19 February 1849 to sail under abject conditions on an overcrowded boat from Glasgow to New York, a difficult voyage requiring more than six weeks. During it Muir was persuaded to settle in Wisconsin, USA, rather than Ontario (a British colony). From New York, therefore, the Muirs continued up the Hudson River to Albany, through the Erie Canal to Buffalo, and across the Great Lakes to Milwaukee—still very much a frontier town, as Wisconsin had achieved statehood only the year before.

John Muir, then only eleven, grew to adulthood as a tall, wiry manual labourer on farms his father bought near Portage, some 35 miles north of the state capital at Madison. Like Daniel Muir's other children, John was required to memorize Bible verses daily but forbidden to read anything not having practical or religious merit. When he was fifteen two neighbouring boys surreptitiously introduced him to poetry. Quietly defying Daniel and his whip,

John began to read books of all kinds available in their homes. He developed an aptitude for creating mechanical devices and, under his mother's influence, a keen interest in nature.

In 1860, now of age, John took some of his inventions to the state fair at Madison and, despite his relative lack of formal education (he seems to have attended the grammar school in Dunbar and had further schooling in Wisconsin), was admitted to the recently founded University of Wisconsin, which had a faculty of five. During the two years of his studies, beginning in 1861, Muir was introduced to science by Dr Ezra Slocum Carr, formerly of Massachusetts, and to the value-centred views of nature in the writings of William Wordsworth, Ralph Waldo Emerson, and Henry David Thoreau. Carr's wife, Jeanne, became a nurturing adviser and lifelong friend. Muir found no conflict between the geology of Charles Lyell and Louis Agassiz now being taught to him and the indwelling human divinity of the transcendentalists. But he quickly discarded the scriptural literalism and punitive fundamentalism of his father.

After several years in Canada, where he had gone to avoid the American Civil War of 1861–5, Muir found employment in a machine shop at Indianapolis. He lost the use of his right eye due to an accident and was for a time blind in both, but sight in the left gradually returned. During his period of darkness and recovery, Muir experienced a further conversion, abandoning (as he later wrote) all mechanical inventions in favour of the inventions of God.

Attempting in 1867 to emulate Alexander von Humboldt (whose comprehensive writings about natural history had become a major influence), Muir walked 1000 miles through the woods from Indianapolis to the Gulf of Mexico, keeping a journal in the manner of Emerson and Thoreau. He had hoped to go to South America, like Humboldt, but got no closer than Cuba. Instead, Muir crossed Panama and went on by ship to San Francisco, near where the Carrs were now living. He then found employment in the foothills of the Sierra Nevada for a time, working as a shepherd.

From 1869 to 1873 Muir lived in the scenically stunning and recently discovered Yosemite valley, which he explored thoroughly on foot. Finding everywhere traces of the huge but now vanished glaciers that he believed had carved it out of granite, Muir began to communicate his geological views to Mrs Carr by letter and at first hand to the numerous distinguished visitors she sent from the Bay Area to see him. One of these visitors was Therese Yelverton, a former countess escaping from the publicity of her sensational divorce. Her mediocre novel *Zanita: a Tale of the Yo-Semite* (1872) includes a character who is unquestionably based on Muir. Professor Joseph Le Conte of the University of California (where Carr now also taught) was another visitor; after seeing the evidence for himself, he accepted almost all of Muir's ideas. Like Carr, Le Conte had studied geology under Louis Agassiz (Swiss advocate of the Ice Age) at Harvard. Emerson, making his only journey west from Massachusetts, was a further distinguished visitor; he recognized in Muir a kindred spirit. Yet another was Professor John Daniel Runkle, president of the Massachusetts Institute of Technology, who listened to Muir expound on the geological origins of Yosemite valley for five days and was responsible for promulgating his ideas among the east coast establishment. Agassiz himself corresponded with Muir and thought highly of his fieldwork.

Muir's insistence that Yosemite valley was almost entirely the product of slow glacial erosion directly contradicted a previously published theory by the California state geologist and Harvard professor Josiah D. Whitney, who believed that Yosemite had been created suddenly, by a tectonic cataclysm. Muir's unorthodox ideas were presented most fully in the *Overland Monthly*, a San Francisco periodical in which several of his shorter pieces had previously appeared. The extremely dichotomized Muir–Whitney dispute continued to influence geological analyses of Yosemite well into the twentieth century.

Though geology was uniquely important to him, as a protracted record of divine creation, Muir also delighted in botany and pursued it with nearly equal fervour. He knew plants very well, described them accurately, and supplied numerous specimens to professional classifiers; at least three species were named for him. Besides Le Conte, he was closely associated with the noted American botanists Asa Gray and John Torrey, as well as with Charles Darwin's close friend Sir Joseph Hooker, president of the Royal Society of London. Like Emerson, Gray, Torrey, and Hooker all came to California on the recently completed transcontinental railroad and were guided round the Sierra Nevada by Muir. Though numerous plant species attracted him, none aroused Muir's admiration so thoroughly as the giant redwoods, some of them more than 2000 years old, that he did much to preserve.

From 1868 to 1875 Muir was an accomplished mountaineer, probably the best in the United States. Climbing, usually alone, with a minimum of equipment and food, he scaled one Sierra Nevada peak after another, including the highest, Mount Whitney. In 1875 he was trapped for four days atop Mount Shasta by a blizzard and suffered frostbite, permanently damaging his feet. Even so, he made the seventh recorded ascent of Mount Rainier (in Washington state) in 1888 at age fifty, and still climbed occasionally thereafter.

By 1873, however, encouraged by Mrs Carr on the basis of his letters to her, Muir had begun to turn his attention to writing. For seven years he continued to spend his summers in the mountains but wintered regularly in Oakland or San Francisco, where he began to prepare manuscripts based on his summer excursions. A series of short pieces on his adventures, most extolling the beauty and spirituality of nature, appeared in local publications. In several of them he argued that still-pristine landscapes should be preserved for later generations as national parks, as Yellowstone (the only national park at that time) had been. Through his efforts other parks such as Yosemite, Sequoia, Kings Canyon, Mount Rainier, Grand Canyon,

and Petrified Forest eventually came into being, and the idea of national parks spread worldwide.

After marrying Louisa Strentzel (1847–1905) on 14 April 1880, at the age of forty-two, Muir settled down in Martinez, California, east of San Francisco, to manage a large fruit ranch belonging to his wife. The couple had two daughters. He continued his conservationist efforts, travelled widely, and visited Alaska (with its living glaciers) seven times. His major books, all written at Martinez from earlier journals and publications, were autobiographical, adventurous, and full of rhapsodic descriptions. They included *The Mountains of California* (1894), *Our National Parks* (1901), *Stikeen* (1909; an Alaskan dog story), *My First Summer in the Sierra* (1911), *The Yosemite* (1912), and *The Story of my Boyhood and Youth* (1913). *Travels in Alaska* (1915), *A Thousand-Mile Walk to the Gulf* (1916), *The Cruise of the 'Corwin'* (1917; to Alaska), and *Steep Trails* (1918) were posthumous, with further collections since.

In 1892 Muir founded the conservationist Sierra Club, and was its president until his death from pneumonia in Los Angeles on Christmas eve 1914. He left an estate of almost $250,000 and was buried in Martinez at the Strentzel family cemetery. He lived to see the Hetch-Hetchy valley, part of his beloved Yosemite (where he is memorialized), flooded to become a reservoir for the city of San Francisco, despite his efforts to prevent this, but he was spared the agony of world war. In 1903 he had camped out in Yosemite with Theodore Roosevelt, during the latter's presidency of the United States. A well-known photograph shows them together atop Glacier Point. In 1909, still thin, tangle-bearded, and scruffy, Muir served as Yosemite guide to William Howard Taft, also during the latter's presidency. More national parks came into being as a result. Muir received an honorary master's degree from Harvard in 1896 and honorary doctorates from Wisconsin (1897), Yale (1911), and California (1913). During the 1980s Muir was voted the most important person in the history of California; he is commemorated there and in Alaska by dozens of place names. His birthday, 21 April, is a California holiday (with Earth day following). His home at Martinez, 4202 Alhambra Avenue, is now a national historic site. In 1984 a John Muir trust was founded in his home town of Dunbar, Scotland.   DENNIS R. DEAN

Sources autobiographical writings and correspondence by Muir, University of the Pacific, CA · L. M. Wolfe, *Son of the wilderness: the life of John Muir* (1945) · W. F. Badé, ed., *The life and letters of John Muir*, 2 vols. (1923–4) · S. M. Miller, ed., *John Muir: life and work* (1993) · 'John Muir: life and legacy', *Pacific Historian*, 29 (1985), 1–166 · D. R. Dean, 'John Muir and the origin of Yosemite valley', *Annals of Science*, 48 (1991), 453–85 · private information (2004)

Archives University of the Pacific, Stockton, California, Holt-Atherton Library · University of the Pacific, Stockton, California, John Muir Centre for Regional Studies | Muir Historic Site, Martinez, California · Sierra Club, San Francisco, William E. Colby Library · U. Cal., Berkeley, Bancroft Library · Yosemite National Park Research Library, California

Likenesses photograph, *c*.1875, University of the Pacific, Stockton, California, Holt-Atherton Library; repro. in Miller, ed., *John Muir* · statue, after 1991, corner of Alhambra Valley Road and Alhambra Avenue, Martinez, California · M. Muir, oils, Muir National Historic Site, Martinez, California · O. Rouland, portrait,

NPG, Smithsonian Institute [*see illus.*] · photographs, University of the Pacific, Stockton, California, Holt-Atherton Library · portrait, U. Cal., Berkeley, Bancroft Library · portrait, Yosemite National Park Research Library · portrait, Sierra Club, San Francisco, William E. Colby Library

Wealth at death under £250,000: Muir Historic Site, Martinez, California, archives

Muir, Sir John Harling, third baronet (1910–1994). *See under* Muir family (*per.* 1849–1992).

Muir, John William (1879–1931), trade unionist and politician, was born at 202 North Woodside Road, Glasgow, on 15 December 1879, the son of John Muir, a journeyman farrier, and his wife, Annie (*née* Doyle). He became a skilled tradesman at the precision engineering firm of Barr and Stroud, of Anniesland, Glasgow. On 30 October 1918 he married Catherine McMillan Fraser (*b.* 1882/3), daughter of Alexander Fraser, a shipbuilder's clerk; they had two children.

Little is known about Muir's intellectual development before the outbreak of war in 1914, when he was the editor of *The Socialist*, the organ of a small Marxist and syndicalist sect, the Socialist Labour Party. He was drawn at some point into the shop stewards' movement, which expressed the opposition of (especially skilled) workmen on Clydeside to the dilution of labour and to government controls over the munitions workforce. The movement became the Clyde Workers' Committee (CWC), and Barr and Stroud was one of its strongholds. From October 1915 to March 1916 the Clyde Workers' Committee threatened to disrupt munitions production, and Muir, who was regarded as its intellectual leader, presented its case for workplace control of production at famous meetings with Lloyd George as minister of munitions at Christmas 1915. The Clyde Workers' Committee actually disrupted the war effort far less than did more conservative groups of workmen, but in February 1916 the government moved against it. Muir, together with the future communist William Gallacher, was gaoled in April for twelve months for publishing an article entitled 'Should the workers arm?' in the CWC journal *The Worker* (29 January 1916, 73–4); the article said that they should not, and neither Muir nor Gallacher wrote it. The arrests of Muir and Gallacher, and the simultaneous deportation of other leaders of the CWC to Edinburgh, succeeded in breaking up the committee.

Muir's journey away from Marxism may have begun in September 1914, when he resigned his editorship of *The Socialist* because of his support for British participation in the war. It accelerated on his release from prison in 1917, when he came under the influence of John Wheatley, the chief local organizer and ideologue of the Independent Labour Party, which Muir joined. His revolutionary syndicalism had by this time mutated into non-revolutionary guild socialism. Muir subsequently stood unsuccessfully as Labour candidate for the marginal seat of Glasgow (Maryhill) in 1918. He won the seat in 1922, however, and held it until 1924. Muir was one of the ten Glasgow Labour MPs who were sent off to London by a mass meeting at which, appropriately, 'The Red Flag' and Psalm 124 were sung. Like other Clydeside Labour MPs, he spoke passionately in parliament about poverty and unemployment, and was an instinctive supporter of Scottish home rule. During 1923 he persistently attacked the government, especially on pensions and the organized emigration of the children of the unemployed to the dominions, and he delighted in gadfly attacks over alleged scandals. In the 1924 Labour government, he became parliamentary under-secretary at the Ministry of Pensions. His minister was not in the cabinet, however, and the Ministry of Pensions had little influence at a time when Philip Snowden and William Graham (respectively chancellor and financial secretary to the Treasury) insisted on a balanced budget. Muir's role was largely confined to answering parliamentary questions, but he did serve on a committee to examine the draft Pre-War Pensions Bill of the previous government, which the Labour government endorsed. Lack of time, money, new ideas, and a parliamentary majority all prevented the Labour government from making any significant innovations in social policy.

After losing his seat in 1924, Muir was picked by G. D. H. Cole to run the Workers' Education Association, which was deeply split between Marxist and non-Marxist wings. Muir had been firmly in the latter camp since his switch from syndicalism to guild socialism, and he served as a faithful ally to Cole until forced by ill health to retire in 1930. He then returned to Glasgow, where he died in Robroyston Hospital of a spinal tumour on 11 January 1931; he was buried at the western necropolis. In obituaries Muir was described as a 'humble and unassuming man' (*The Scotsman*) and also 'of singularly gentle and lovable disposition' (*Forward*, 10 Jan 1931). He was of slight build, and his friends thought his health had been permanently damaged by his wartime imprisonment. Muir was survived by his wife.

IAIN MCLEAN

Sources I. McLean, *The legend of red Clydeside* (1983) · *Forward* (1914–16) · *Forward* (1922–4) · *Forward* (10 Jan 1931) · D. Kirkwood, *My life of revolt* (1935) · *Hansard 5C* (1922–4) · S. V. Bracher, *The Herald book of labour members* (1923) · W. Knox, ed., *Scottish labour leaders, 1918–39: a biographical dictionary* (1984) · J. P. M. Millar, *The labour college movement* (1979) · 'Glasgow ex-MP's death', *The Scotsman* (12 Jan 1931), 11e · *The Worker* (29 Jan 1916)

Archives Nuffield Oxf., Cole MSS · PRO, cabinet MSS, CAB 23–4 · PRO, ministry of pensions records, PIN 1, PIN 3, PIN 4

Likenesses photograph, repro. in Bracher, *Herald book of labour members*

Wealth at death £137 19s. 9d.: confirmation, 1931, Scotland

Muir, Sir (Alexander) Kay, second baronet (1868–1951). *See under* Muir family (*per.* 1849–1992).

Muir, Kenneth (1912–1950), army officer, was born on 6 March 1912 at Wayside, Lache, near Chester, the only child of Captain (later Colonel) Garnet Wolseley Muir (1876–1954), Argyll and Sutherland Highlanders, and his wife, Mary Williamina Cuninghame. Kenneth Muir came from an army family. His grandparents had named his father Garnet Wolseley after the famous Victorian general. As a boy Muir was accustomed to army life and the domestic upheavals it caused. He was educated as a boarder at Malvern College and was eleven when his father was appointed commanding officer of the Argylls in 1923.

It never occurred to Muir to do otherwise than follow his father into the army and into the Argylls, and he was commissioned in 1932. His early active service was on the north-west frontier of India from 1935 to 1938. There he learnt the golden rules of regimental soldiering: always occupy the hilltops, never let the enemy dominate you from higher ground, and never leave your wounded behind. During the Second World War Muir rose from captain to acting lieutenant-colonel and saw active service, some of it while attached to the military police, in Sudan, north Africa, Italy, France, and Germany. By the end of the war he had earned eight campaign medals and a mention in dispatches.

In early 1950 the short, stocky Major Muir, who had been working in the provost marshal's branch of the War Office, was posted to the Argylls in Hong Kong as the second in command. In August of that year the battalion sailed for Korea with the Middlesex regiment as part of 27 brigade. The brigade were the first British troops to arrive in Korea to reinforce the United Nations forces who had been driven back into a tiny toehold in the south-east corner of the peninsula. They were known as the 'Woolworth brigade' as they relied on the Americans for everything from artillery or aircraft support to rations.

On 23 September 1950, as part of the breakout battle, the Argylls were given the task of taking and holding Hill 282, which was dominated by another higher feature, Hill 388, about 1500 metres to the west. The battalion took the hill, but were heavily counter-attacked by vastly superior numbers of North Koreans from Hill 388. The situation was desperate when Muir went forward with more ammunition. He galvanized the defence by personal example. On the summit, where the fighting was the most desperate, he directed fire, organized ammunition distribution, and collected the wounded into shelter, all the while encouraging those who saw him by his total contempt for the heavy automatic enemy fire hitting the hilltop.

Eventually, with losses mounting and enemy reinforcements continually arriving from Hill 388, Muir called for an American air strike on that hill. Coloured recognition panels were put out on the ground on Hill 282 to indicate the Argylls' position. Despite this, and despite circling round to have a good look, the aircraft attacked Hill 282 with napalm, rockets, and cannon fire. The western part of the hill became an inferno and the Argylls suffered heavily. Nevertheless, despite this Muir organized a successful counter-attack with the twenty or so survivors. For the three hours Muir was on Hill 282 he showed outstanding courage, leadership, and disregard for his own safety. In the end, with only fourteen men unwounded, Muir was shot and killed while personally firing a 2 inch mortar. His last words were: 'Neither the Gooks nor the US Air Force will drive the Argylls off this hill' (Adkin, 35).

The Americans were the first to honour Muir with the posthumous award of their Distinguished Service Cross. He was also awarded the Victoria Cross, which his parents received from King George VI on 14 February 1951. Sadly, crippled by grief and depression, Muir's father took his own life three years later. Major Muir himself was buried in the Commonwealth War Graves cemetery, Korea.

MARK ADKIN

Sources M. Adkin, *The last eleven?* (1991) · C. N. Barclay, *The first commonwealth division* (1954) · T. Carew, *The Korean War* (1988) · E. Linklater, *Our men in Korea* (1954) · G. I. Malcolm, *The Argylls in Korea* (1952) · b. cert. · d. cert. · *CGPLA Eng. & Wales* (1951) · A. Farrar-Hockley, *The British part in the Korean War*, 2 vols. (1990–95) · *The register of the Victoria cross*, 3rd edn (1997)

Wealth at death £760 13*s*. 7*d*.: administration with will, 22 Jan 1951, *CGPLA Eng. & Wales*

Muir, (John) Ramsay Bryce (1872–1941), historian and politician, was born on 30 September 1872 at Otterburn, Northumberland, the oldest of five children of the Revd Alexander Bryce Muir and his wife, Jane, daughter of Thomas Rowatt of Edinburgh. Muir's father, Reformed Presbyterian minister at Otterburn and later Birkenhead, Cheshire, died while Ramsay was a child. After private schooling in Birkenhead, Muir attended University College, Victoria University, Liverpool, from 1889 to 1894, and Balliol College, Oxford, where he held a Brackenbury scholarship and gained first classes in *literae humaniores* (1897) and modern history (1898).

From 1898 to 1899 Muir was assistant lecturer in history, under T. F. Tout, at the University of Manchester. In 1899 he became lecturer in history, and in 1906 professor, at his Liverpool alma mater, where he remained until resigning in 1913. At Liverpool, Muir was active in faculty politics, being influential in promoting student self-government and in securing a university charter in 1903. A visiting lectureship at the University of Punjab in India (1913–14), preceded Muir's assuming the professorship of modern history at the University of Manchester. His tenure at Manchester was interrupted in 1917–19 by service on a commission investigating Calcutta University and Indian post-secondary education. He resigned his professorship in 1921 to begin the political work that monopolized most of the rest of his life.

Muir was a prolific writer of textbooks and popular works on history, international relations, economics, and politics, including the widely used *Short History of the British Commonwealth* (2 vols., 1920–22). He was also co-author (with George Philip and Robert McElroy) of several respected historical atlases. Although Muir projected works of original scholarship, notably a biography of Warren Hastings, his busy life as teacher and subsequently politician precluded them, and his career as a historical writer was 'unfinished' (*DNB*). His only researched study was a *History of Liverpool*, published in 1907.

After the First World War, Muir became interested in the revival of the Liberal Party through a programme of economic and social reform. His book *Liberalism and Industry* (1920), endorsed by the National Liberal Federation, was widely viewed as initiating a Liberal renaissance. He was one of the founders, in 1921, of the Liberal summer school, an annual colloquium on contemporary issues,

(John) Ramsay Bryce Muir (1872–1941), by Elliott & Fry

was followed by the chairmanship (1931–3) and presidency (1933–6) of the NLF. He was a driving spirit behind the party reorganization of 1936, and briefly (in 1936) acted as vice-president of the new Liberal Party Organization (LPO). From 1936 until his death he chaired the education and propaganda committee of the LPO and contributed to party literature. During the early part of the Second World War, Muir was a volunteer writer and lecturer for the Ministry of Information. He died, unmarried, at his home, Roseneath, Elm Park Road, Pinner, Middlesex, on 4 May 1941.

Muir was an articulate if not especially creative political thinker. His ideas in many ways constituted a regression from the radical, social democratic 'new Liberalism' of the early 1900s to a more traditional, individualistic Liberalism. He placed his faith in rational progress and enlightened capitalism, while seeing much room for improvement in the industrial system. He was critical of socialism, which he thought encouraged class conflict, and trade unions, which he believed tyrannized over their members. He viewed defence of private property and personal freedom, and promotion of equal opportunity, as more important obligations of the state than provision of welfare. He maintained that only the industrious and thrifty were worthy of any but minimal social benefits, and that high taxation undermined the motivation needed to create and increase national wealth. Government, he argued, should create a level playing field for free enterprise but resist unnecessary intervention in the economy. He defended free trade, even after it became a political liability in the 1930s.

Muir's ideas paralleled those of David Lloyd George, whose leadership of the Liberal Party in the late 1920s he generally supported although never fully trusted. He was an important contributor to the policy studies sponsored by Lloyd George which in 1928 produced *Britain's Industrial Future*, better known as the yellow book.

Ramsay Muir was impressive and dignified in appearance, and possessed a mellifluous, resonant voice. He was in great demand and much admired as a public speaker, and during his brief parliamentary tenure was respected by colleagues and journalists for his debating skill. He became renowned for his proficiency in digesting and simplifying complex data, in both speech and writing—although he had a weakness for polysyllabic words. He avoided rancour and never belittled opponents. His habitual manner of grave courtesy was relieved by quiet humour and the ability to laugh at his own foibles. Muir's charming eccentricities—as well as his generosity, modesty, sincerity, and idealism—endeared him to many.

D. M. CREGIER

intended to restore interest and confidence in the party as an instrument of change. Under Muir's leadership and inspiration, the school—held in alternate years at Cambridge and Oxford—survived until 1939, although after 1931 it was in decline like the Liberal Party itself. Throughout its existence and beyond, the summer school was a source of ideas for all political parties.

Muir was an assiduous Liberal journalist and propagandist. After sale of *The Nation* in 1922 to a consortium headed by John Maynard Keynes, Muir was considered for the editorship, but he and Keynes were unable to agree on terms. In addition to contributing frequently to *The Nation* from 1923 to 1930, Muir was editor of the *Weekly Westminster*, a subsidiary of the *Westminster Gazette*, from 1923 to 1926. He also edited during the 1930s the *Westminster Newsletter*, a weekly commentary on Liberal Party affairs.

During the 1920s and 1930s Muir was deeply involved in Liberal electoral politics and party organization. A member of the House of Commons for Rochdale for only a few months during the 1923–4 parliament, he unsuccessfully contested this constituency in 1922, 1924, and 1929, as well as other seats in general and by-elections in 1926, 1931, and 1935. He was active in the Liberal and Radical Candidates' Association during the 1920s.

Muir was a prominent figure in the National Liberal Federation (NLF) and the Liberal Central Association, the party's London headquarters. Service as chairman of the party's executive, the organization committee, in 1930–31

Sources *Ramsay Muir: an autobiography and some essays*, ed. S. Hodgson (1943) · *DNB* · *The Times* (5 May 1941), 6e · *The Times* (6 May 1941), 7d [letter] · M. Freeden, *Liberalism divided: a study in British political thought, 1914–1939* (1986) · D. M. Cregier, *Chiefs without Indians* (1982), 149–63 · M. Bentley, *The liberal mind, 1914–1929* (1977) · J. Campbell, *Lloyd George: the goat in the wilderness, 1922–1931* (1977) · T. Wilson, *The downfall of the liberal party, 1914–1935* (1966) · R. J. A. Skidelsky, *The economist as saviour, 1920–1937* (1992), vol. 2 of *John Maynard Keynes* (1983–2000), 22, 136–7 · R. F. Harrod, *The life of John*

Maynard Keynes (1951), 334–6 • D. E. Moggridge, *Maynard Keynes: an economist's biography* (1992), 390–92 • J. Turner, ed., *The larger idea: Lord Lothian and the problem of national sovereignty, 1905–40* (1988), 9–11 • R. Bassett, *Nineteen thirty-one: political crisis* (1958), 296–306 • Liberal Industrial Inquiry, *Britain's industrial future* (1928), 159 n. 1 • S. Maccoby, *English radicalism: the end?* (1961), 473–4, 519 • J. S. Rasmussen, *The liberal party: a study of retrenchment and revival* (1965), 38, 40, 54–5, 62, 288 • K. O. Morgan, *Consensus and disunity: the Lloyd George coalition government, 1918–1922* (1979), 204 • P. Williamson, *National crisis and national government: British politics, the economy and empire, 1926–1932* (1992), 108, 117, 136, 241–2, 449, 513 • B. Wasserstein, *Herbert Samuel: a political life* (1992), 327, 391 • *New York Times* (5 May 1941), 17d • d. cert.

Archives U. Lpool L., Harold Cohen Library • U. Lpool L., Sydney Jones Library, lecture notes | Bodl. Oxf., corresp. with Gilbert Murray • CAC Cam., Thurso MSS • CUL, corresp. with Lord Hardinge • HLRO, letters to David Lloyd George; corresp. with H. Samuel • JRL, *Guardian* archives, letters to the *Manchester Guardian* • King's Cam., Keynes MSS • NA Scot., Lothian MSS • NL Wales, letters to John Glyn Davies; letters to David Lloyd George • priv. coll., Layton MSS • U. Cam., Marshall Library of Economics, corresp. with Lord Keynes • U. Lpool L., corresp. with George Veitch

Likenesses Elliott & Fry, portrait, NPG [*see illus.*] • Times Wide World, photograph, repro. in *New York Times* (5 May 1941), 17d • photograph, repro. in S. Hodgson, ed., *Ramsay Muir*, frontispiece

Wealth at death £20,318 6s. 5d.: probate, 7 July 1942, *CGPLA Eng. & Wales*

Muir, Sir Robert (1864–1959), pathologist, was born at Balfron, Stirlingshire, on 5 July 1864, the second child and only son of the Revd Robert Muir (d. 1882), a Presbyterian minister of saintly character and decidedly liberal outlook, and his wife, Susan Cameron, daughter of William Duncan, a Dundee merchant. Soon after Muir's birth his father became minister of Allans Church, Hawick. One of Muir's four sisters wrote short stories, another was a classical scholar of Edinburgh University, and the youngest, Anne Davidson Muir, acquired fame in Scotland as a painter in watercolours, especially of flowers. In later life Muir, who never married, lived with two of his sisters.

Following a brilliant career at Hawick high school and at Teviot Grove Academy, Muir entered the University of Edinburgh in 1880 with the Sir Walter Scott bursary in classics and mathematics. He graduated MA in 1884 and MB, CM with first-class honours in 1888, after obtaining the Grierson bursary and the much coveted Vans Dunlop research scholarship. He also undertook coaching, for his father's death left him with considerable family responsibilities. Nevertheless he chose the rather precarious career of pathology, largely through the influence of William Smith Greenfield, Edinburgh's unrivalled pathologist and clinician. Muir acquired valuable experience as a clinician, bacteriologist, and what was later called haematologist as assistant to Greenfield (1892–8) and lecturer on pathological bacteriology (1894–8). He examined at the university and at the royal colleges of physicians and surgeons of Edinburgh and fostered closer personal contacts between staff and students, with whom he was a universal favourite. With James Ritchie, lecturer in pathology at Oxford, he wrote the *Manual of Bacteriology* (1897) which went through many editions.

In 1898 Muir was called to the new chair of pathology at St Andrews, held in Dundee, where his reputation as an original researcher and far-seeing administrator led to the offer of the chair of pathology at Glasgow, which he held from 1899 until 1936. There he gained world fame as a teacher, investigator, and writer, for in 1924 his *Textbook of Pathology* became a substantial success and long maintained a place among the leaders. Muir served on the university court at Glasgow, the Medical Research Council (1928–32), the councils of the Imperial Cancer Research Fund and the British Empire Cancer Campaign, and on committees for the investigation of foot and mouth disease. During the First World War he held the rank of lieutenant-colonel and was in charge of the pathological and bacteriological routine of the 3rd and 4th Scottish general hospitals, and also acted as inspector of laboratories in Scotland. Elected FRS in 1911 he served on the council (1926–7) and was awarded a royal medal for his work on immunity in 1929. He was knighted in 1934, and received numerous honorary degrees and fellowships; he was awarded the Lister medal for 1936.

Muir's discoveries fit so well into the mosaic of progress in pathology that it is difficult to realize now how fresh and original they seemed at the time of their announcement. His papers teem with unusual observations and offer many admirable lessons in planning and explaining experiments for the young pathologist. Muir was an unrivalled exponent on diseases of the blood cells, largely because he realized that much of their puzzling behaviour reflects the closely geared relationship between the bone marrow, where the red corpuscles and many of the white corpuscles are formed, and the sites of cell destruction. From these studies came fundamental knowledge about the processes during infection. Red cell destruction was linked up with iron metabolism, since these corpuscles are important iron carriers, and this led him to explain some of the anomalies of anaemia. This brought him to immunology, where he raised the status of the United Kingdom in world immunology. In his latter years he returned to the problems of cancer and in a brilliant series of papers devoted to cancer of the breast he clarified the relationship between the various types. His microscopical study of Paget's disease of the nipple is unsurpassed and has left no doubt about the serious nature of this misleading disease.

Muir was a shy, aloof man who gave praise rarely, never shirked an unpleasant duty, yet seldom made an enemy. Only his most intimate friends knew of the warm heart which was carefully concealed by a deliberately cultivated austerity. He knew instinctively when young people needed help and made it his business to see that it was forthcoming. His habit of absent-mindedly pocketing other people's matches, his fanatical devotion to golf, and his ill-concealed delight in deflating pompous colleagues endeared him to his juniors. Many good stories are told of him, some no doubt invented, for his Olympian reserve was fair game for boisterous Scottish students. They were devoted to the one and only 'Bobby' and he in turn loved them all.

Muir retired in 1936 and spent the remainder of his life

in Edinburgh where he quietly pursued his interest in botany and geology, fished a stream, or played his favourite golf and bridge. He flew to Australia to see his eldest sister when he was close upon ninety; he died peacefully at 25 Belgrave Crescent, Edinburgh, on 30 March 1959.

ROY CAMERON, *rev.* ANITA MCCONNELL

Sources R. Cameron, *Memoirs FRS*, 5 (1959), 149–73 · *Journal of Pathology and Bacteriology*, 81 (1961) · private information (1971) · personal knowledge (1971) · *BMJ* (11 April 1959), 976–7; (18 April 1959), 1050–51 · d. cert.

Archives U. Glas., Archives and Business Records Centre, diaries, corresp., and papers

Likenesses G. F. Watt, oils, 1931, U. Glas. · W. Stoneman, photograph, 1932, NPG · G. H. Paulin, bust, U. Glas., Pathological Institute

Wealth at death £41,684 17s. 8d.: confirmation, 22 May 1959, *CCI*

Muir, Thomas (1765–1799), political reformer, was born in Glasgow on 24 August 1765. He was the only son of James Muir (*c*.1730–1803), a flourishing hop merchant and grocer, and Margaret Smith (*c*.1740–1803), who later bought a small landed property at Huntershill, near Glasgow. Both were devout presbyterians. They sent Thomas to a private school and then to Glasgow University, where he began taking classes as early as 1777, but did not matriculate until 1782. He originally intended to enter the church, but started reading law under John Millar. He withdrew from the university in the autumn of 1785 after getting into trouble because he supported efforts to reform the university. He migrated to Edinburgh and, after completing his legal studies there, was admitted into the Faculty of Advocates on 24 November 1787. He soon built up a successful legal practice in Edinburgh, though he sometimes waived his fee when pleading for poor clients.

An elder of the church at Cadder in Lanarkshire, Muir sat and debated in the general assembly of the Church of Scotland and generally supported the stance taken by the more popular evangelical party against the dominant moderates. He was also friendly with those advocating burgh reform in Scotland and increasingly influenced by the progress of the French Revolution. When Scottish reformers began to found political reform societies, Muir soon played a leading part in their activities. In late 1792 he helped to set up the Association of the Friends of the People in Edinburgh. It was a much less aristocratic society than the London body of that name, and mainly attracted support from the professional and commercial middle classes and the skilled artisans. Muir became the vice-president of the various associated reform societies in Edinburgh, helped establish similar reform societies elsewhere, and made contact with leading United Irishmen. Muir was never as radical as the fearful government and legal authorities came to believe in the heightened political atmosphere of 1792–3. He believed in the need for moderate political reform, rejected all appeals to force, and advocated change by peaceful, constitutional means. He was, however, intoxicated by the heady atmosphere in Britain and France at this time.

At a convention of delegates from various Scottish reform societies, held in Edinburgh on 11–13 December

Thomas Muir (1765–1799), by David Martin

1792 to prepare a united petition for parliamentary reform, Muir read out a printed address from the United Irishmen, which complimented the Scottish nation for its spirit of reform, complained of the existing system of representation, and urged the calling of conventions in all three kingdoms of the British Isles to promote parliamentary reform. There was no suggestion that this convention supported clandestine revolutionary activity, but the alarmed authorities in Edinburgh already suspected Muir of attempting to sow the seeds of sedition.

On 2 January 1793 Muir was arrested on a charge of sedition, but was released on bail. He went to London, where the leaders of the whig opposition entertained him and encouraged him to go to France to remonstrate against the execution of Louis XVI. He arrived in Paris too late to achieve anything, but he enjoyed the company of leading Girondin politicians and the large British community in the French capital. While he was in Paris, France declared war on Britain on 1 February and Muir had no passport to leave the country. Unable to attend his trial, scheduled for 25 February, he was outlawed and struck off the roll of the Faculty of Advocates. Apparently planning to emigrate to the United States, Muir took an American ship bound for Baltimore. When this ship called at Belfast on 17 July, Muir left it and went to Dublin, where he was fêted by the

United Irishmen. On his return to Scotland on 30 July he was promptly arrested and sent as a prisoner to Edinburgh.

On 30 August 1793 Muir was prosecuted in the high court of justiciary by Robert Dundas, the lord advocate, before five judges, who were dominated by Lord Braxfield. He was accused of exciting disaffection by seditious speeches, of advising the purchase and reading of seditious publications, of circulating seditious papers such as Paine's *Rights of Man*, and of publicly reading out such seditious writings as the address of the United Irishmen. His friends urged the employment of an eminent defence lawyer, but Muir unwisely decided to defend himself. Though he did so with spirit, vigour, and dignity, he missed some opportunities that an impartial defence counsel might have exploited more effectively and he was too eager to make political speeches. He did object, in vain, to some of the jurors chosen to hear his case because they belonged to the Goldsmiths' Hall Association, an Edinburgh society of militant loyalists. He called many witnesses to swear that he had often criticized Paine's works and that he had always urged reform by constitutional means, and he made a speech of three hours in his own defence. The case against him was weak and some witnesses, including a scullery maid formerly employed by his family, were possibly bribed and almost certainly coached in their evidence, but his judges made no attempt to be impartial and they made much of his visit to France and his clandestine return.

After a trial that lasted sixteen hours, Muir was unanimously found guilty on 31 August and his judges chose the unusual and unexpected punishment of transportation for fourteen years. The jurors were shocked at the severity of the sentence, but were too intimidated by the political climate among the propertied classes to petition for a lighter sentence. Imprisoned in Edinburgh until November, Muir sailed to the Thames and spent several months in a prison hulk there, where his health was badly affected and where he began to drink very heavily. The legality of his sentence was disputed in parliament, but to no avail, and on 2 May 1794, with three other radicals convicted by the Scottish courts (Thomas Fyshe Palmer, William Skirving, and Maurice Margarot), Muir finally set sail for Botany Bay. During the long voyage these radical convicts fell out among themselves and the disputes continued after their arrival in Australia.

Muir was not compelled to work like most of the convicts and was able to buy a small farm, which he called Huntershill. Early in January 1796 an American trading ship, the *Otter*, put in for supplies and minor repairs. The captain, Ebenezer Dorr, agreed to help Muir to escape and picked him up just off the coast on 11 February. After an amazing series of adventures lasting more than a year, which involved crossing the Pacific to Nootka Sound, taking a Spanish ship down to southern California, crossing Mexico to Vera Cruz, and taking another Spanish ship to Havana, Muir was finally shipped to Cadiz in a Spanish frigate on 25 March 1797. Off Cadiz, on 26 April, this Spanish ship was attacked by two Royal Navy warships. A flying splinter removed Muir's left eye and part of his cheek, leaving him heavily bloodied and severely disfigured. Not recognizing him, the British sent Muir on shore with the rest of the wounded. Though he had fought for Spain, then at war with Britain, the Cadiz authorities detained him as a British prisoner of war, but efforts by the Directory in France eventually secured his release in September.

After a public reception in Bordeaux in late November 1797, Muir reached Paris in December and was welcomed by the Directory. Although his health was poor, Muir exaggerated his own importance, became involved in various futile intrigues, and was forced to plead regularly for funds from the French. He wrote several memoranda to Talleyrand, wrote articles for De Bonneville's *Le Bien Informé*, met Tom Paine and various British radical exiles in Paris, and associated particularly with James Napper Tandy and his group of United Irishmen. He dropped out of sight in September 1797 and may have moved then to Chantilly. His death was registered there by the mayor on 26 January 1799, and reported in *Le Moniteur* on 30 January and in the *Gentleman's Magazine* in February 1799. He was buried at Chantilly, but his grave can no longer be located and, since he predeceased his parents, he left no property. In 1844–5, when reform was again in fashion, the reformers in Scotland finally erected an impressive memorial 90 feet high in Calton cemetery in Edinburgh to commemorate the sacrifice of Muir and the other Scottish political martyrs of 1793.   H. T. DICKINSON

Sources P. Mackenzie, *The life of Thomas Muir* (1831) · G. P. Insh, *Thomas Muir of Huntershill* (1949) · C. Bewley, *Muir of Huntershill* (1981) · J. Wantrup, *The transportation, exile and escape of Thomas Muir* (1990) · M. Donnelly, *Thomas Muir of Huntershill* (1975) · H. W. Meikle, *Scotland and the French Revolution* (1912) · E. W. McFarland, *Ireland and Scotland in the age of revolution* (1994) · *State trials*, vol. 13 · M. Donnelly, 'Muir, Thomas', *BDMBR*, vol. 1 · J. Earnshaw, *Thomas Muir, Scottish martyr* (1959) · F. Clune, *The Scottish martyrs* (1970) · H. W. Meikle, 'The death of Thomas Muir', *SHR*, 27 (1948), 201–2

Likenesses J. Kay, etching, pubd 1793, BM · T. Holloway, line engraving, pubd 1795 (after bust by T. Banks), NPG · T. Banks, bust (made when Muir was in prison) · F. Bonneville, line engraving, NPG · D. Martin, chalk drawing, Scot. NPG [*see illus.*]

Muir, Sir Thomas (1844–1934), mathematician and educationist, was born on 25 August 1844 in Biggar, near Lanark, Scotland, the son of George Muir, railway superintendent, and his wife, Mary Brown. The family moved away from Biggar, and he was sent to Wishaw public school. Afterwards he attended Glasgow University (1863–8), where he was influenced by Lord Kelvin, whom he greatly admired. Muir was the first Greek and first mathematical student of his year, but though Greek was his first love he turned to mathematics.

Muir's first appointment was as mathematical tutor at the University of St Andrews (1868–71), where he made a modest reputation as a mathematician. He continued his mathematical training by spending short periods in Berlin and Göttingen. After St Andrews he became assistant to Hugh Blackburn, professor of mathematics at Glasgow University. Muir remained at the university a short time (1871–4) but in this period discovered his real talent for teaching mathematics. He left to become head of the mathematics and science departments at the high school of Glasgow (1874–92). On 12 October 1876 Muir married Maggie (d. 1919), youngest daughter of Dugald Bell, merchant, of Dunbartonshire, and his wife, Isabella Young. They had two sons and two daughters.

Muir pursued mathematical research in continued fractions and determinants and one of his early contributions drew a published response from the English mathematician Arthur Cayley. Muir won the Keith prize of the Royal Society of Edinburgh in 1884 and again in 1899, and he was one of the founders of the Edinburgh Mathematical Society.

Muir's life took a dramatic turn in 1892 when, seeking a warmer climate for the benefit of his wife's health, he moved to southern Africa. He had considered an application for the vacant chair of mathematics at Stanford University in California but, after a vacancy arose in the Cape Colony to succeed Sir Langham Dale as superintendent-general of education, he applied there instead, and was appointed by Cecil Rhodes, prime minister in the Cape Colony, who was then visiting England. When an official wanted to scrutinize Muir's testimonials, Rhodes is reputed to have exclaimed: 'Damn the testimonials! I have seen the man' (Cape Times, 22 March 1934). He immediately cabled his cabinet to make the appointment.

In his service in the Cape (1892–1915) Muir reorganized the whole public education system from elementary school to university. He abolished the overly academic examinations in the schools, formed an efficient system of training colleges for teachers, and virtually created science teaching. A prime minister of the Cape Colony, J. X. Merriman, said that in Muir's plan educational thought always went ahead of practice and reflected that 'no better day's work had ever been done than when they secured Sir Thomas for South Africa' (Cape Times, 22 March 1934). Some in South Africa even said Muir was 'the man who taught the Cape to read and write'. Reform is never without opposition and literary-minded critics of his plans for education claimed he 'had scotched it but not quite killed it' (Aitken, 'Thomas Muir'). For his part, Muir never regretted his decision to go to Africa, where he found the opportunity fully to employ his wide-ranging skills.

Muir served as vice-chancellor of the University of the Cape in 1897–1901, and was elected FRS in 1900. He was equally a mathematician, educational administrator, teacher, and capable historian of mathematics. He was president of the South African Association for the Advancement of Science in 1910 and represented the Union of South Africa at the Imperial Education Conference in London in 1911. He was knighted in 1915 for his services to science.

Muir's mathematical reputation rests on his work on determinants (a numerical value obtained from an array of numbers). Between 1875 and 1880 he conceived the ambitious project of writing a history of determinants. His first bibliography (forty pages) of writings on determinants appeared in the Quarterly Mathematical Journal of 1881, and a second in 1886. He published his first book, Treatise on the Theory of Determinants, in 1882, and his second in 1890. During the Second South African War (1899–1902) he found determinants offered a welcome distraction from the worries of war and he temporarily revived his previous studies. The 1890 book was the precursor for the volumes which will always be associated with his name, the monumental History of the Theory of Determinants in five volumes, published in 1906–29 (the final volume when he was eighty-six). A projected sixth volume was never finished. The complete work encompasses a catalogue with commentaries of all the known papers on determinants from Leibniz's work in the seventeenth century until 1920. Muir's commentaries varied in length from eighty-four pages devoted to Cauchy's classic paper of 1812 to a few lines for slight contributions. The subject material emphasizes the importance of determinants in nineteenth-century mathematics in contrast to the more fundamental subject of matrices which only developed from a halting start in the 1850s. Muir's work was of great assistance to those who wished to consult the papers of important mathematicians of the eighteenth and nineteenth centuries.

Muir wrote approximately 307 papers, listed in the Royal Society catalogue, mostly on determinants and connected subjects. He was able to return the compliment he received in youth by putting the finishing touches to one of Cayley's own papers. He read widely and enjoyed literature almost as much as mathematics. When Rudyard Kipling visited South Africa as the guest of Rhodes, Muir immediately struck up a friendship with him. He regarded Pauline Smith (who wrote The Little Karoo) as the greatest writer on South Africa, and his refined taste in poetry found expression in his admiration of Roy Campbell's Adamastor. On occasion he was susceptible to the quirky sense of humour often found among mathematicians. Thus, postulating that any book on philosophy will contain a 'hole' in its argument, he went on to conclude that Jan Christian Smuts's Holism and Evolution was especially vulnerable.

Muir was physically active throughout his long life, although after a severe illness he gave up tennis and contented himself with lighter exercise. When he was eighty-nine it was observed that 'his faculties are unimpaired and he still works hard' (Cape Times, 25 Aug 1933, 11). He presented a figure of admiration and curiosity to his neighbours, who watched a gentleman from the Victorian age diligently pursuing mathematics, sitting upright at his desk in winged collar and bow tie, preparing his work. He died at Rondebosch, Cape Town, South Africa, on 21 March 1934 and was buried in the Maitland cemetery near Rondebosch.
A. J. CRILLY

Sources A. C. Aitken, 'Thomas Muir', Journal of the Glasgow Mathematical Association, 1 (1950), 65–76 · H. W. Turnbull, Obits. FRS, 1 (1932–5), 179–84 · A. C. Aitken, Proceedings of the Edinburgh Mathematical Society, 4 (1936), 263–7 · T. Fuller, Cecil John Rhodes (1910) · C. T. Loram, 'The retirement of Sir Thomas Muir', American Mathematical Monthly, 23 (1916), 74–5 · E. H. Neville, Mathematical Gazette, 18 (1934), 257 · W. I. Addison, A roll of graduates of the University of Glasgow from 31st December 1727 to 31st December 1897 (1898) · The

Times (22 March 1934) • *Cape Times* (25 Aug 1933) • *Cape Times* (22 March 1934), p. 10, col. 3 • m. cert.
Archives NL Scot., papers
Likenesses Elliott & Fry, photograph, repro. in Turnbull, *Obits. FRS*

Muir [*née* Anderson], **Wilhelmina Johnston** [Willa; *pseud.* Agnes Neill Scott] (**1890–1970**), novelist and translator, was born on 13 March 1890 at 14 Chapel Place, Montrose, Forfarshire (Angus), the oldest of three surviving children of Peter Anderson (1864/5–1899), draper, and Elizabeth (Betty) Gray, *née* Anderson (1866/7–1930), dressmaker. Her parents were first cousins, originally from Unst, Shetland, and had married on 22 February 1889. Her brothers were Basil Ramsay (1892–1960) and William John (1894–1930).

Early life and education Educated at a small private school (1893–9), Townhead elementary board school (1899–1902), and Montrose Academy (1902–07), she studied classics (1907–10) and English and modern history (1910–11) at St Andrews University, graduating in July 1911 with first-class honours in classics. Awarded the Berry scholarship, she studied English literature from 1911 to 1912. Known as Minnie by her family and during her time at St Andrews University, she took part in the women's debating society, the women's suffrage society, and the students' representative council. She was also on the editing committee of *College Echoes* (the student magazine) from 1910 to 1912. She fell in love with Cecil Wilmot Morrison, a rugby player and medical student with a protracted university career (begun 1903–6, resumed 1910–11, and finally qualified 1916) and they became engaged in the summer of 1911. Two years later Cecil confessed 'his recurrent pecadilloes' and she dramatically threw her engagement ring into the sea from the pier (*Belonging*, 12).

Willa Anderson's first employment was teaching classics at Brancepeth Rectory home school, 4 miles southwest of Durham, from the autumn of 1912 to the summer of 1914, when the beginning of the war led to her becoming an assistant in Latin at St Andrews University classics department (Court minutes, 24 Oct 1914). From 1916 to 1918 she researched an (unfinished) thesis on child educational psychology at Bedford College, London, funded by the Carnegie Trust. She spent a few months in Mansfield House University Settlement, Canning Town, a community in east London, where she taught Bryant and May factory girls (*Belonging*, 17–18), then was vice-principal and lecturer in English, psychology, and education at Gipsy Hill Teacher Training College, from September 1918 to summer 1919, resigning when the principal objected to Edwin Muir's 'atheism' in *We Moderns* (1918).

Marriage to Edwin Muir Willa Anderson met Edwin *Muir (1887–1959) in Glasgow in September 1918. They corresponded and met again in Glasgow and St Andrews, and were married on 7 June 1919 at St Pancras register office, London; in September they set up home in two ground floor rooms in 13 Guilford Street, Bloomsbury. They became Peerie Willa and Peerie Breeks (Edwin Muir's mother's name for him) to each other. Willa Muir worked in a cramming institution in Red Lion Square and then,

Wilhelmina Johnston Muir [Agnes Neill Scott] (**1890–1970**), by Nigel McIsaac, 1944

from January 1920 to 1921, as headmistress at a day continuation school. When Edwin Muir was commissioned to write for *The Freeman* at $60 an article they decided to travel to Prague as 'a good place to start from' ('Mrs Muir's reminiscences'). They left from Leith on 31 August 1921.

The next three years were spent in Prague, Germany, Italy, and Austria, and provided the pattern of the Muirs' marriage, working in teaching and translating with their decisions to change country made almost at random. In 1922 they visited Dresden for the weekend and decided to move there; in due course they met A. S. Neill (an old friend of Muir's from student days) at a bus stop and decided to teach at his school at Hellerau, 6 miles from Dresden (*Belonging*, 71). Their time there included a walking tour, at Easter 1923, with Gerda Krapp (later Liebricht) and others. After the collapse of the German economy in November, they 'fled' to Italy to join Edwin Muir's friend John Holms and his partner, Dorothy Jennings (journal, 20 Aug 1953). On the way, her husband told Muir that Gerda had declared her love for him as he left, and that he ought to return to her. Muir, describing her feelings of emotional pain and insecurity, claims that they never discussed it again once he had decided not to return (*Belonging*, 82–3), but her journals report a painful conversation with him in Newbattle. She could 'still conjure up the emotions of that terrible time' (journal, 20 Aug 1953). What she never knew, apparently, was that he had written from Italy offering to join Gerda, who refused (Gaskill, 49).

About Easter 1924 *The Freeman* suspended publication, ending the Muirs' only regular income. Invited by Ben Huebsch, the New York publisher, to translate three Gerhart Hauptmann plays into English at $100 a play

(*Belonging*, 106), they began the translation work which now provided the basis of their income. Muir had learned Czech and was fluent in German, and later maintained that most of the translation work was hers: 'I am a better translator than he is'; she thought she should have shouted aloud: 'Most of this translation, especially Kafka, has been done by ME. Edwin only helped' (journal, Aug 1953), although she said, during the war, that they divided Kafka in two, translated their own half and then exchanged them for further work (C. Soukup, 24). Their translations between 1925 and 1938 included works by Sholem Asch, Lion Feuchtwangler, Heinrich Mann, and others. Muir also translated Hans Carossa and C. Winsloe as Agnes Neill Scott, and *Five Songs for the Auvergnat ... into Modern Scots* (1931).

Muir as novelist From July 1924 to February 1926 the Muirs lived in Montrose, Penn, Buckinghamshire, and Montrose again (where Muir had a miscarriage in December 1925). They moved to St Tropez, then Menton, between October and May 1927. Muir began her first novel, *Imagined Corners*, in St Tropez. It was not published until 1931, because her work on it had been interrupted by translating and by her son's birth. Muir wrote later that she threw herself into characters, living in them as much as possible: 'they are bound to be versions of myself' (journal, 1948); her relationship with Cecil Morrison formed the model for Elizabeth and Hector's marriage and the starting point for the novel (*Belonging*, 125). When she reread the novel, she thought it had 'no apparent knowledge of social fabric *effects*. Quite pre-Marxian! But a good picture of the world I grew up in' (journal, 1948). Her final judgement was that it contained enough material for two novels (*Belonging*, 163). Despite her reservations, the interlocking stories of the Shand and Murray families in Calderwick make a powerful novel with intense explorations of inner feelings and of the society of the town. The *Glasgow Herald* described it as 'a memorable contribution to the cartography of the soul of Scotland' (2 July 1931).

The Muirs returned to England in May 1927 and settled in the White House, Dormansland, Surrey, where Gavin Anderson Cormack Muir (1927–1991) was born on 29 October. Muir kept the Marmaduke journal, 1927–31, observing his progress from six weeks, including psychological analyses and his reactions to breastfeeding. From March 1929 to October 1932 they were based at Crowborough, Sussex (*Belonging*, 106), then they moved to 7 Downshire Hill, Hampstead. It was here that Edwin Muir had a bare study in the attic and Willa Muir's study was on the ground floor, 'intruded upon at all hours' (ibid., 162). She used to work late into the night, finishing translations and correcting proofs. She finished her second novel, *Mrs Ritchie*, in the press of other work; 'it does not surprise me that I lost control of it in the second half, although the first half is quite good' (ibid., 163). Published in July 1933, it was also set in Calderwick but concentrated on the damage one woman inflicts on her family, herself already damaged by Calvinism and the constriction of possibilities for women. Darker in tone than *Imagined Corners*, it has a

powerful and negative sweep with an overly analytic narrator; 'the result is nearer to science than to art' (*TLS*).

After Gavin was run over and his leg badly broken in July 1933, the Muirs took him to Orkney for a month to recuperate; Gavin and Muir returned for a three-month stay to Isbister House in the summer of 1934, Edwin joining them after driving through mainland Scotland researching his *Scottish Journey*. They moved to St Andrews in August 1935, staying until 1942, because it was cheaper. Muir wrote *Mrs Grundy in Scotland* (1936) for Leslie Mitchell's series The Voice of Scotland. Edwin Muir's *Scott and Scotland* (1936), published in the same series, was more bitter and led to their rift with C. M. Grieve (Hugh MacDiarmid)—known since 1924, he appears to have already disliked Muir, whose 'overpowering presence has always been a nuisance to friends of Edwin's' (*Letters of Hugh MacDiarmid*, 126). Muir collapsed in December 1938 from gynaecological problems caused by Gavin's birth, and had surgery in Dundee conducted by Professor Margaret Fairlie (*Belonging*, 201). In the early years of the war translating work dried up, and Muir taught classics at New Park School, which Gavin attended. She contracted bowel ulcers and, hospitalized in May 1941, experienced, as Edwin Muir held her hand, a 'frozen landscape' without feelings, before recovering her sense of connection (ibid., 207).

In March 1942 Edwin Muir began work for the British Council in Edinburgh and, by August, Muir and Gavin joined him. After the war, Edwin Muir was appointed director of the British Institute in Prague, and Muir took her first flight to join him there in the late summer of 1945. She recorded their stay in her Prague journals, November 1946 to May 1948. The communist coup of February 1948, and subsequent events, led to them leaving Czechoslovakia at the end of July (E. Muir, *Autobiography*, 269). In January 1949 they went to Rome, where Edwin Muir became the director of the British Institute. It closed for financial reasons and they left Rome in July 1950, on the same train as Laurel and Hardy (*Belonging*, 263). Edwin Muir became warden of Newbattle Abbey, Dalkeith—which reopened as an adult education college—a post he held from 1950 to 1955. Muir taught Latin and Greek unofficially but otherwise was the wife of the warden.

Muir's unpublished novel 'Mrs Muttoe and the Top Storey' (finished May 1940) had been closely based on their life in Hampstead. Her second unpublished novel, 'The Usurpers' (written February 1951 to February 1952), was based on her Czechoslovak journals recording the difficult relationship between the British Institute and the British Council, and personal problems between staff. Circulated to Macmillan, Chatto and Windus, and Hamish Hamilton under the pseudonym of Alexander Croy (journal, 14 Oct 1952), it was probably libellous; Muir comforted herself that the rejections were for that reason. But as with the earlier unpublished novel she failed to make the fictional transformation of her autobiographical material that she had so successfully accomplished in *Imagined Corners*.

After their departure for Harvard, in the autumn of 1955

Muir wrote in her journal that 'the whole of Scotland is a locked area for me'. She had loved 'Newbattle and the beech trees' but 'Lowland Scotland infected Newbattle' (journal, 26 Sept 1955). Reflecting on her illness during the war, she thought that she came back to life only to devote herself to Edwin Muir 'and in a lesser way to Gavin' and that she had to kill her 'vanity' and ambition to write:

> My intelligent Unconscious now told me that in killing, or trying to kill, my vanity I had nearly succeeded in killing myself. … All the Willas, the passionate little girl, the ambitious & vital student, the positive, hopeful & happy new wife, came back together & fused.   (journal, 1 Oct, 1955)

Her journals from September to November 1955 record meetings with I. A. Richards, May Sarton, Elena and Edmund Wilson, Robert Lowell, and Karl Miller.

In May 1956 they returned to Britain, Edwin Muir having a grant from the Bollingen Foundation to write on the Ballads. At the start of her 1947-8 journal, Muir had written 'All emigrants are Displaced Persons. My parents were D.P.s in Angus. So I grew up not fitting into Angus tradition and therefore critical, resentful, unsure. Hence my secret desire to *own* a house, to belong somewhere'. Her 'secret desire' was only achieved in this last home together, which they bought at Swaffham Prior, Cambridgeshire. During Edwin Muir's absence as visiting professor at Bristol University, from February to March 1958, Muir's letters about her health, Gavin, and Edwin Muir's absence continued to discuss their relationship and her insecurities:

> My dearest love, our lives are so woven together, with memories & shared experience, that they can't be unwoven, I tell myself; so I have stopped worrying about these having maybe fallen out of love with me. I always was a bit of a Bad Peerie Ting; that is no thing new; so I am just going to leave it at that.   (St Andrews, 9.8.M(i) 14)

Edwin Muir died on 3 January 1959.

Later life Muir paid off the mortgage on the cottage in October 1959, 'so now I can live here till I die' (7 Oct 1959, NL Scot., MS 19703, fol. 103), the money coming partly from the transfer of Edwin Muir's Bollingen grant to her for writing *Living with Ballads*, he having completed only a few notes. She shared ownership with Gavin. However, Muir became peripatetic once more. In August 1963, relieved of financial worries by the continuation of the Bollingen grant until December 1964, she and her cat Popsy moved into Kathleen Raine's basement, 47A Paultons Square, London. *Living with Ballads* was well received on publication in 1965. Forsyth Hardy thought that the early chapters, which referred to her own schooldays at the board school, had a 'very special appeal and character' and Robert Kemp, remembering 'her own excellent writings', welcomed the book as coming out 'with her own stamp' (*Arts Review*, 18 March 1965, St Andrews 9/8). Despite A. S. Neill asking her in 1964 'How are the book plans? Time you cease to be known as Edwin's Frau' (*Arts Review*, 4 Sept 1964, St Andrews 9/8), her last book, apart from *Laconics, Jingles and other Verses* (1969), was to be her memoir of Edwin Muir, *Belonging* (1968). She described it as 'very like a Scotch bun … because it has a bit of everything in it, not classified into layers like a respectable English cake'

(22 March 1968, NL Scot., MS 19703, fol. 61). Much of it is drawn from her journals, but its narrative of her and Edwin Muir's lives, with some passages of feminist and psychological analysis, succeeds in a way that 'The Usurpers' does not.

In February 1969 Muir moved to the British Red Cross Home, Meadowcroft, Cambridge, then, finding the organization too rigid, to a small private nursing home, Church Farm, Over, Cambridgeshire. In the autumn she moved to St Andrews to live with Lillias Chisholm, F. G. Scott's daughter, not understanding the 'transient nature of her impulses' (31 Oct 1969, NL Scot., MS 19703, fol. 196). After nine days, Lillias told her she had made a mistake. She was rescued by Edwin's niece Margaret and nephew Jim with his wife, Ivy, and she moved to Dunoon in October, 'like a stray cat' (10 Dec 1969, NL Scot., MS 19703, fol. 199), not able to face a move back to London. They promised her a home for the rest of her life: 'A short life, I hope' (5 April 1970, NL Scot., MS 19703, fol. 219). Muir died of heart failure on 22 May 1970 at hospital in Dunoon and was cremated at Greenock crematorium on 25 May. Her ashes were scattered on Edwin Muir's grave in Swaffham Prior.

The *Glasgow Herald* obituary (23 May 1970) acknowledged Willa Muir as a 'Scottish woman writer and translator … widow of Edwin Muir and herself a writer of distinction'. Peter Butter, Edwin Muir's biographer, felt able to say in 1990 that her 'greatest work, I think she would gladly agree, was to make possible the production of his poetry' before going on to 'give her credit for what she, in spite of difficulties, achieved as a writer' (Butter, 'Willa Muir', 59). But the reprinting of *Imagined Corners* (1987) and *Mrs Ritchie, Women: an Enquiry* (first published by the Hogarth Press, 1925) and other non-fiction pieces (1996) have enabled an assessment of Willa Muir as a writer in a way that she did not achieve in her lifetime. Passionate, intellectually confident, assertive, emotionally insecure, and, latterly, indomitable in the face of pain from arthritis, with a lifelong feminist awareness apparent in her novels, letters, and journals, she never stopped writing, one of her last letters hoping 'I *might* get a small book done' (5 April 1970, NL Scot., MS 19703, fol. 219).

AILEEN CHRISTIANSON

Sources W. Muir, *Belonging: a memoir* (1968) · St Andrew's University, notebooks (including journals, 9/5), miscellaneous papers (including 'Mrs Muir's reminiscences', 26/2/1963, 9/2) and letters (particularly to Anna Mill, Edwin Muir, A. S. Neill, 9/8), MS deposit, 9/1–8 · letters (esp. to K. Raine, T. Scott) and verses, NL Scot., MS 19703 · P. H. Butter, 'Willa Muir: writer', *Edwin Muir centenary assessments*, ed. C. J. M. MacLachlan and D. S. Robb (1990), 58–74 · P. R. Mudge, 'A quorum of Willas', *Chapman*, 71 (winter 1992–3), 1–7 · C. Soukup, 'Willa in wartime', *Chapman*, 71 (winter 1992–3), 20–24 · K. A. Allen, 'The life and work of Willa Muir, 1890–1955', PhD diss., U. St Andr., 1997 · H. Gaskill, 'Edwin Muir in Hellerau', *Scottish Literary Journal*, 11/1 (1984), 45–56 · *The letters of Hugh MacDiarmid*, ed. A. Bold (1984) · E. Muir, *An autobiography*, [rev. edn] (1954); repr. (1993) · court minutes, 1911, 1912, 1914, U. St Andr. · calendar, 1912–13, U. St Andr. · class slips, 1907–12, U. St Andr. · matriculation register, 1907–8, U. St Andr. · *College Echoes* [U. St Andr.], 22–23 (1908–12) · *Glasgow Herald* (23 May 1970) · reviews, *Glasgow Herald* (2 July 1931) · [A. M. Mackenzie], 'Mrs Ritchie', *TLS* (13 July 1933), 478 [review] · L. Soukup, 'Belonging', *Chapman*, 71 (winter 1992–3), 29–33 · W. Muir, *Living with ballads* (1965) · *Selected letters of Edwin Muir,*

ed. P. H. Butter (1974) · P. H. Butter, *Edwin Muir: man and poet* (1966) · d. cert.
Archives NL Scot., verses, corresp., MSS, notebooks, MS 19670, 19674–19700, 19703 · U. St Andr., corresp., notebooks, papers, MS deposit 9/1–8 | BL, Violet and Sydney Schiff collection · NL Scot., letters to George Mackay Brown · NL Scot., letters to Marian McNeill · NL Scot., letters to William Montgomerie · NL Scot., letters to Kathleen Raine · NL Scot., letters to Tom Scott · NRA, priv. coll., Ethel Ross and Irene Abenheimer collection · Orkney Library, Kirkwall, corresp. with J. Mary Bosdet · Orkney Library, Kirkwall, letters to Patricia Swale · U. St Andr., Sylvia Lehfeldt archive **Likenesses** photograph, 1910, repro. in Muir, *Belonging*, facing p. 30 · N. McIsaac, oils, 1944, Scot. NPG [*see illus.*] · photograph, 1945 (on identity card), repro. in Muir, *Belonging*, facing p. 65 · photograph, 1947, repro. in Muir, *Belonging*, facing p. 65 · photograph, 1960, U. St Andr., Willa Muir MS, 9/8 · photograph, 1967, NL Scot., MS 19703.255 · photograph, 1967, repro. in Muir, *Belonging*, facing p. 81 · B. Niven, caricature, repro. in Bold, ed., *Letters of Hugh MacDiarmid* · group portrait, photograph (with the Student Representative Council), repro. in *College Echoes*, 22 (1910–11) · group portrait, photograph, repro. in *College Echoes*, 22 (1910–11) · group portrait, photograph, repro. in *College Echoes*, 23 (1911–12) · photograph (in old age), repro. in Muir, *Belonging*, inside back cover
Wealth at death £3853 2s.: confirmation, 7 Aug 1970, *CCI*

Muir, William (1787–1869), Church of Scotland minister, was born in Glasgow on 11 October 1787, the third son of William Muir, a merchant. He was educated at the universities of Glasgow and Edinburgh, and the former was later to honour him with the degrees of LLD (1812) and DD (1820). He was licensed to preach by the presbytery of Glasgow in 1810 and was ordained to St George's Church, Glasgow, in August 1812. The following year he married, on 22 June, Hannah, the eldest daughter of James Black, lord provost of Glasgow. They had a daughter and five sons, of whom only two sons survived beyond childhood. Hannah died in 1827, aged thirty-nine. In 1822 he moved to New Greyfriars, Edinburgh, and from there in 1829, on the presentation of the town council, to the newly created parish of St Stephen's, Edinburgh, where he was to remain for the rest of his ministry.

In 1838 Muir was elected moderator of the general assembly of the Church of Scotland, just as the non-intrusion controversy moved into a more acute phase. What had hitherto been a largely pastoral ministry was now diverted by the demands of the times. In the succeeding months he sought to pursue a middle course in church politics but, having failed in his attempts to reconcile the opposing parties, he opted to remain with the established church at the Disruption of 1843. Thereafter he was frequently consulted by the government over the exercise of crown patronage. Indeed, one commentator opined that, 'no Grand Vizier under a passive Sultan ever exercised more influence than he did in such matters' (Douglas, 76). Another churchman, A. K. H. Boyd, picked up on his older colleague's distinguished bearing when he described him as 'the finest-looking human being I ever saw. It was the great Duke of Wellington's face, a thousand times more beautiful. No Archbishop, Cardinal, or Pope, ever looked the High Churchman better than Dr. Muir' (Boyd, 35).

On 3 October 1844 Muir married Anne, the daughter of Lieutenant-General Alexander *Dirom. The following year he was appointed dean of the Order of the Thistle and

chaplain-in-ordinary to Queen Victoria. In 1858 he was appointed a member of the newly created general council of Glasgow University. In 1867 blindness forced his retirement. He died at his home, Ormonde Villa in Edinburgh, on 23 June 1869 and was buried in the Dean cemetery.

LIONEL ALEXANDER RITCHIE

Sources *Fasti Scot.*, new edn, 1.35, 115 · H. Scott, *Fasti ecclesiae Scoticanae*, new edn, 3, 443 · B. W. Crombie and W. S. Douglas, *Modern Athenians: a series of original portraits of memorable citizens of Edinburgh* (1882), 75–7 · *DNB* · *Church of Scotland Home and Foreign Missionary Record* (2 Aug 1869), 448–9 · *Edinburgh Evening Courant* (24 June 1869) · [A. K. H. Boyd], *Twenty-five years of St Andrews*, 4th edn, 1 (1893), 33–9 · Lord Sands, *The story of St Stephen's, Edinburgh, 1828–1928* (1927), 35–50
Archives NA Scot., letters to Lord Dalhousie · U. Edin., New Coll. L., letters to Thomas Chalmers
Likenesses C. Turner, mezzotint, pubd 1822 (after T. Graham), BM, NPG · B. W. Crombie, coloured etching, 1841, repro. in Crombie and Douglas, *Modern Athenians* · bronze profile, Dean cemetery, Edinburgh · caricature, repro. in Crombie and Douglas, *Modern Athenians* · photograph, repro. in Sands, *Story of St Stephen's*
Wealth at death £2933 18s. 8d.: inventory, 10 Aug 1869, NA Scot., SC 70/1/144/524

Muir, William (1805–1888), mechanical engineer, was born on 17 January 1805 at Catrine, Ayrshire, Scotland, the second of the four children (three sons and a daughter) of Andrew Muir, a farmer and businessman. His father was a cousin of William Murdoch, who invented gas lighting. After a local elementary school education and an apprenticeship with Thomas Morton, a carpet loom repairer of Kilmarnock, Muir moved to Glasgow in 1824 to join Girdwood & Co., manufacturers of cotton machinery. In the evening he studied at Glasgow University and also joined the newly founded mechanics' institute.

On leaving Girdwood, Muir worked for a time for the Catrine Company and then for Henry Houldsworth, where he became interested in the lathe. In September 1830 he went to Liverpool for the opening of the Liverpool and Manchester Railway, and then to Manchester, where he heard that his brother Andrew was ill in Truro. After travelling to Cornwall, he obtained employment for a short time at Harvey's foundry in Hayle before moving to London to commence work in April 1831 at Maudslay and Field's large factory in Lambeth, where he met James Nasmyth and Joseph Whitworth. His marriage to Eliza Wellbank Dickinson (1807/8–1882) of Drypool, Hull, took place on 25 August 1832 at St Paul's Church, Covent Garden, London. They had five sons, most of whom became engineers and some of whom worked for the family company.

At Maudslays Muir was promoted to foreman and made responsible for constructing a steam carriage, for which he received a handsome gratuity. In March 1836 he left to join Holtzapffel, toolmakers of Charing Cross and Long Acre, as assistant and representative for a few months, before becoming a foreman at Bramah and Robinson in Pimlico.

In 1840 Muir moved to Manchester and joined Joseph Whitworth, who had established a business there. Muir helped Whitworth to develop his universal screw thread system, which became a British standard, and produced various new tools including the radial drill. He also made drawings for a knitting machine and a road-sweeping machine, together with a working model of the latter.

However, Muir, a strict Sabbatarian, disliked Whitworth's encouragement of Sunday working and, leaving in June 1842, he set up his own business in Berwick Street, Manchester, where he worked on a railway ticket counting machine for Thomas Edmondson. Further work for Edmondson followed, and Muir moved to 59 Oxford Street, Manchester, and subsequently, in 1848, to Miller's Lane, Greengate, Salford, with Edmondson using the upper part of the building as a railway ticket printing office.

In 1852 Muir was asked to supply the Woolwich Royal Arsenal with machinery for making interchangeable rifle sights; and with business increasing, he built the Britannia Works in Sherborne Street, Strangeways, and took on partners. In 1853 he was granted patents on lathes and machines for grinding edge tools and for cutting out garment pieces. These were followed by two further patents on lathes (1856, 1859); two relating to letter-copying presses (1858, 1864); and a patent on planing machines (1867). His cutting machine for making sugar cubes (1863) eventually became widely used, and a labour-saving machine, which could wind cotton balls and bobbins and label them as well, was universally purchased by those in the trade. Muir was a Presbyterian and a supporter of the temperance movement. This resulted in an unusual patent (no. 1 of 1865) for constructing public houses in such a way that prospective drinkers, especially women, would be deterred from entering them.

When Muir retired to Brockley, then on the south-eastern outskirts of London, he maintained his interest in mechanics by writing articles on the subject. He was a member of the Institution of Mechanical Engineers from 1863, and throughout his career was a keen observer and note and sketch taker. His wide experience and diligence made him a most respected, ingenious, and skilful engineer, and one who contributed greatly to industrial progress. By 1887 his company was employing 400 people and had acquired an excellent reputation for the high-quality lathes, tools, and machinery which it supplied worldwide.

Muir was never a robust man, and after an illness of about a month he died at his home, 143 Brockley Road, Brockley, on 15 June 1888 and was buried in Brockley cemetery on 19 June.   CHRISTOPHER F. LINDSEY

Sources R. Smiles, *Brief memoir of the late William Muir, mechanical engineer of London and Manchester* (1888) · 'The engineering and other industries of Manchester and district', *The Ironmonger* (3–10 Sept 1887), 29–30 [repr.] · 'Memoir of William Muir', *Institution of Mechanical Engineers: Proceedings* (1888), 440–42 · *Engineering* (24 Aug 1888), 194 · *Directories, Manchester* · private information (1894) · patents, 1853–65 · d. cert. · *CGPLA Eng. & Wales* (1890)
Archives BL, letters patent · Museum of Science and Industry, Manchester, machine tools · National Museum of Science and Industry, London, model of double grindstones
Wealth at death £1111 5s. 1d.: probate, 8 Jan 1890, *CGPLA Eng. & Wales*

Muir, Sir William (1819–1905), administrator in India and Islamicist, born on 27 April 1819 in Glasgow, was the youngest child of William Muir (1783–1820), a Glasgow merchant, and his wife, Helen Macfie (1784–1866), of Ayrshire. The Sanskrit scholar John *Muir (1810–1882) was his eldest brother. Widowed in 1820, his mother took her four surviving sons and four daughters to Kilmarnock, where William received a sound education at Kilmarnock Academy. He then studied briefly at both Edinburgh and Glasgow universities. Before he was able to graduate he entered East India College, Haileybury, on the nomination of his mother's uncle Sir James Shaw, a former lord mayor of London, who through company contacts obtained nominations as writers or cadets for his indigent nephews. Of the three brothers who had preceded William to Haileybury, two, James and Mungo, died after a short service in India.

After his arrival in India in 1837 Muir was posted to the North-Western Provinces, and remained identified with that region for the next thirty-nine years, notably as its lieutenant-governor in the 1870s. He married, on 7 February 1840, Elizabeth Huntly (d. 1897), daughter of James Wemyss, collector of Cawnpore. A series of junior postings in the revenue and judicial services in Cawnpore, Bundelkhand, and Fatehpur districts, which included responsibility for the settlement report on Hamirpur (1842), was followed by posts in the provincial capital of Agra, first as secretary to the board of revenue in 1848, and then, from 1852, as secretary to Lieutenant-Governor James Thomason, with whose evangelicalism and administrative innovations in the fields of land revenue and education he was very sympathetic. His first twenty years of Indian service proved him sound rather than exceptional.

The sepoy mutiny and subsequent civil uprising of 1857–9 provided Muir with greater scope for initiative. On the death of Lieutenant-Governor John Russell Colvin shortly after rebel advances had necessitated the withdrawal of the European community into the Agra Fort, local responsibility was devolved to three middle-ranking civilians, including Muir. Special responsibility for intelligence made Muir also the nerve-centre for communications within and outside the region of revolt until British recovery began. His intelligence correspondence, an important source for understanding the nature and course of the rising up to January 1858, is deposited in Edinburgh University Library. Muir also wrote a memoir for his children entitled *Agra in the Mutiny* which was published privately nearly forty years later.

While his reliability during the 1857 crisis drew him to the governor-general's attention—Lord Canning appointed him his secretary when the government was transferred to Allahabad in early 1858—Muir's career followed a steady rather than a dramatic course for a further ten years, notably on the provincial board of revenue from 1859 to 1865 and as foreign secretary to the government of India from 1865 to 1868. Although he was made KCSI in 1867, he had been passed over for the lieutenant-governorship of the North-Western Provinces in 1864. If his rather self-effacing character seemed to hold him back, in 1868 his rapport with the viceroy, John Lawrence, finally resulted in the provincial governorship; this appointment was extended until 1874 because of his reputation for maintaining stability. During his final two years in India, Muir was financial member of Lord Northbrook's council in Calcutta. He retired to Britain in late 1876 but continued to play an active role in Indian affairs until 1885, as a member of the Council of India in London. He was then appointed principal of Edinburgh University, his alma mater, retiring in 1903, aged eighty-four, with a reputation for benevolent scholarly patronage rather than for innovation. The Muir Institute, where oriental languages are still taught, commemorates the encouragement given by the Muir brothers, through the endowment of chairs and prizes, to the study of these languages in Edinburgh University.

The entry on Muir in the *Dictionary of National Biography* stressed his contribution to the stabilization of land revenue problems in north-west India after the convulsions of 1857–9. While Muir deserves credit for this, other aspects of his career proved of longer-term significance, notably his Islamic scholarship and his educational endeavours, both in India and in Scotland. On the base provided by his predecessor, Thomason, he attempted to improve the educational provision in the north-west of India, his interests ranging from village vernacular schemes and female education to university provision for the élites of the region. His preoccupation with higher education reflected partly his perception of these élites, particularly the Muslims, as bulwarks of the raj in the north-west, and partly his evangelical conviction that education would be conducive to social reform and hence to 'civilization', and even to his personal goal of the reception of Christian values. The Muir Central College, opened in Allahabad in 1872, marked the fruition of one of his plans when it became, in 1886, the core college for the province's first university. Muir was unsuccessful, however, in efforts to re-establish Persian as a medium of higher education alongside English, although his support for their interests won him the friendship of some influential members of the Muslim élites, notably the 'modernist' Sir Saiyid Ahmad Khan and the nawab of Rampur state. His motives were questioned, however, by those— Saiyid Ahmad Khan among them—who found that his scholarly but evangelical critiques of Islamic civilization and history conflicted with Muslim values.

Muir's publications on Islam were certainly controversial, but because he was the first British scholar to attempt a popular interpretation of Islamic history based on study of the Arabic sources, they were widely regarded as authoritative during the colonial era. While he acknowledged the influence of German Islamicists (notably Gustav Weil), Muir's work, notwithstanding its overt evangelical perspective, is original in many of its linguistic and historical assessments, which reflect sound Arabic learning. His *Life of Mahomet: History of Islam to the Era of the Hegira* (4 vols., 1858–61) was based on his own translation of the Koran and on his study of the Hadith collections and early Arabic biographies of the Prophet. It became the standard English biography, going through several editions in the nineteenth century and provoking retorts from Indian Muslim scholars. Less controversial in his own day, though criticized in the late twentieth century for an 'orientalist' perspective, were his Middle Eastern histories—notably *Annals of the Early Caliphate* (1883) and *The Caliphate: its Rise, Decline and Fall* (1891)—also based on Arabic sources. His scholarship was recognized by election as president of the Royal Asiatic Society in 1884, and by the award of the society's triennial jubilee gold medal in 1903. Other academic honours included the honorary degrees of DCL of Oxford (1882), LLD of Edinburgh and Glasgow, and DPhil of Bologna (1888).

Throughout his career in India, but especially in retirement, Muir used his scholarship to support evangelical efforts to gain influence among Muslims. As a junior officer he had attended missionary debates with Muslims, later assisting the evangelical cause with publications such as *Testimony Borne by the Coran to the Jewish and Christian Scriptures* (1860) and *The Old and New Testaments, Tourat, Zubur and Gospel: Moslems Invited to See and Read them* (1899). The practical help he extended to the tiny Christian convert community in northern India was commemorated at Muirabad, a village established near Allahabad for Christian victims of famine.

Muir died at his home, Dean Park House, Queensferry Road, Edinburgh, on 11 July 1905, and was buried in Dean cemetery. His wife had died in 1897. Their correspondence over half a century reveals a devotedly close marriage. Of fifteen children, all born in India, several sons served in the Indian army, though none reached their father's prominence.

Unusually, there was no biography or memorial publication. Though firmly within the 'paternalist' tradition of late nineteenth-century Indian governors, William Muir presents the paradox of a scholar drawn irresistibly to the Arabic literary heritage and to close friendships with individual Muslims, who nevertheless felt compelled by his religious convictions to denigrate Muslim beliefs and social institutions in both their Arabian and Indian settings. His lieutenant-governorship, at a time of growing tension for Indian Muslims, merits some further study.

AVRIL A. POWELL

Sources W. Muir, *Agra in the mutiny, and the family life of W. and E. H. Muir in the fort, 1857* (1896) · *Kilmarnock Standard, suppl.* (11 Dec 1886) · 'The Sir William Muir number', *Student* (23 Feb 1903) [magazine of the University of Edinburgh] · *The Times* (12 July 1905) · C. J. Lyall, 'Sir William Muir', *Journal of the Royal Asiatic Society of Great Britain and Ireland* (1905), 875–9 · F. F. L. Marshall, *The Muir book* (1930) · m. cert. · Burke, *Peerage* (1901) · *DNB* · *CCI* (1905) · *Glasgow Herald* (18 Dec 1820) · Kilmarnock Midwives Register, 1777–1829
Archives U. Edin. L., corresp. | BL, corresp. with A. Eden, Add. MS 43999 · BL, letters to W. E. Gladstone, Add. MSS 44459–44522, *passim* · Bodl. Oxf., corresp. with Lord Kimberley · CUL, corresp. with Lord Mayo · NRA Scotland, priv. coll., letters to the duke of Argyll

Likenesses G. Simonds, bust, exh. RA 1880, Muir Central College, Allahabad · bust, U. Edin., Old College · crayon; formerly in possession of his eldest son, 1912 · memorial plaque, Dean parish church, Edinburgh · portraits, U. Edin. L.; repro. in 'The Sir William Muir number'

Wealth at death £44,390 3s. 5d.: confirmation, 8 Sept 1905, CCI

Muircheartach. *See* Muirchertach mac Muiredaig (*d.* 534).

Muirchertach [*pseud.* Mac Líacc] (*d.* 1014/1016), poet, cannot be placed in any kindred with confidence. Mac Líacc ('son of stones') would seem to be the pseudonym for a Muirchertach said, in one set of annals, to be the son of Máelchertach, in another the son of Conchertach. Indeed, Roderic O'Flaherty in *Ogygia* (1685) linked Mac Líacc with an Ó Concherta family of Corann in the Sligo–Mayo region. In several annals, Mac Líacc is styled 'ardollam Éirenn', 'leading chief poet of Ireland', and in a seventeenth-century translation of lost annals as the 'arch poet of Ireland and one that was in wonderful favour with king Bryan'. Even the place and date of Mac Líacc's death are uncertain: one text places it at Inis Gaill Duib on the Shannon, while a marginal note in another chronicle records that Mac Líacc was under a (monastic) rule in Ard Oilén ('high island', Galway) when he died. The date of his death is variously recorded in the annals as 1014 and 1016.

Mac Líacc eventually acquired a literary persona. He appears with two other poets, Airard mac Coisse (*d.* 990) and Flann mac Lonáin (*d.* 891x918), in a tale entitled 'Trí hOllamain Chondacht' ('three poets of the Connachta'). While Colm Ó Lochlainn's contention that Mac Líacc was 'a pure invention' (Ó Lochlainn, 42) is refuted by the evidence of the annals, Ó Lochlainn has convincingly argued that the vast majority of the literature attributed to Mac Líacc could not have been written during the tenth and eleventh centuries. Nevertheless, a small corpus of poetry which may be attributable to Mac Líacc with some degree of certainty has survived: 'Dá mac déc Cennéitig cháid', on the twelve sons of Brían Bóruma; 'Findaid in senchas diatá', on the place name Carn Conaill and the Fir Bolg; 'In trá is Foich nó is Beach', on the pedigree of the descendants of Brían mac Echach Mugmedóin, and 'Lorcán lasadh isan áth', on the same subject (both only extant, unedited, in the fourteenth- or fifteenth-century Book of Ballymote); and 'Beannacht, a Bruin, ar Brigit', 'Scíath rígh Gaela, glantar hí', and 'Leasg amleasg sind gu Áth Clíath', all on the privileges of Clann Chellaig. Linguistic analysis of these texts coupled with a close study of their contents and style may one day allow us to verify their attribution to Mac Líacc.   PETER J. SMITH

Sources W. M. Hennessy, ed. and trans., *Chronicum Scotorum: a chronicle of Irish affairs*, Rolls Series, 46 (1866), 256 · *Ann. Ulster* · *AFM*, 2nd edn, vol. 1 · D. Murphy, ed., *The annals of Clonmacnoise*, trans. C. Mageoghagan (1896), 169 · C. Ó Lochlainn, 'Poets on the battle of Clontarf [pt 2]', *Éigse*, 4 (1943–4), 33–47, esp. 42 · R. O'Flaherty, *Ogygia, seu, Rerum Hibernicarum chronologia* (1685), 334 · E. Gwynn, ed. and trans., *The metrical dindshenchas*, 3, Royal Irish Academy: Todd Lecture Series, 10 (1913) · R. Atkinson, ed., *The book of Ballymote: a collection of pieces (prose and verse) in the Irish language*, facs. edn (1887), 89 · K. Meyer, 'Mitteilungen aus irischen Handschriften', *Zeitschrift für Celtische Philologie*, 8 (1910–12), 102–20, 195–232, 119–231

Muirchertach mac Muiredaig [Muirchertach mac Ercae, Mac Ercae] (*d.* 534), high-king of Ireland, is first mentioned in the annals in 482 under the name Muirchertach mac Ercae. The late Middle Irish account of the wives and mothers of Irish kings (*Ban-Shenchus*) gives him an obviously legendary mother, Erc, daughter of Lodarn, king of Alba; his wife is said to have been Duasach, daughter of Daui Tengad Umai (*d.* 502), an early king of the Connachta. From 482 Muirchertach is quite frequently recorded up to 508, when his reign as king of Tara (high-king) is said to have begun. From 508 until 520 he is not mentioned, but from then until his death in 534 there is another cluster of entries. The early sixth-century annals very probably contain some information recorded retrospectively in the late sixth century, when annals began to be written on Iona; such entries, when they can be identified, are in general dependable, although chronological precision cannot be expected. Subsequently, however, these early annals were much expanded, partly in order to incorporate a version of the legend of St Patrick and King Lóegaire, partly to advance particular dynastic interests.

The record of Muirchertach's career has been subject to both these influences. Its length is extremely suspicious, in the first place, and the way it splits into two separate phases does not add credibility. This may all be a consequence of the need felt by the annalists to stretch the careers of the various sons of Níall Noígíallach (Niall of the Nine Hostages) over a period of eighty years, because they were determined to make Patrick's career begin in the year after Palladius was sent to Ireland (431), and they were also determined to make Patrick face Lóegaire mac Néill, ancestor of one of the least successful of the branches of the Uí Néill. Confusion was also aided by the desire of the annalists to obscure the true power of Coirpre mac Néill: thus a victory in 485 ascribed to Coirpre is also attributed to Muirchertach. Finally, there is possible confusion even in his name. Mac Ercae is quite a common first name; the female equivalent, Dar Ercae, was borne by St Mo Ninne of Killevy. Muirchertach is sometimes known as Muirchertach mac Muiredaig, sometimes as Muirchertach mac Ercae (treating mac Ercae as 'son of Erc', simply giving his maternal descent), sometimes as Mac Ercae; both Muirchertach and Mac Ercae are found in Adomnán's life of Columba.

Muirchertach's sons, including *Forggus mac Muirchertaig, lie just within the bounds of reliable annalistic evidence; he himself seems to remain just beyond the limits of reliable knowledge, especially in the legend of his threefold death engineered by a seductress from the other world. The full version of this story, *Aided Muirchertaig meic Ercae*, in which Muirchertach drowns after being pierced by a spear, belongs to the early twelfth century and to the monastery of Dulane in Meath, but it is already foreshadowed in the brief obit in the annals. Even in the most reliable part of his record, in the second phase of entries from 520 until 534, it is evident from the way information is set out that all the annalists had was a tradition of various named battles against opponents in the midlands, in Leinster and in Munster, which they attempted to assign to various years. The surviving impression is of a great war-leader, the founder of the military power undoubtedly possessed by many of his descendants.

T. M. CHARLES-EDWARDS

Sources Adomnán's Life of Columba, ed. and trans. A. O. Anderson and M. O. Anderson, rev. edn, rev. M. O. Anderson, OMT (1991) · Aided Muirchertaig meic Ercae, ed. L. Nic Dhonnchadha (1964) · W. Stokes, ed., 'The annals of Tigernach [8 pts]', Revue Celtique, 16 (1895), 374–419; 17 (1896), 6–33, 119–263, 337–420; 18 (1897), 9–59, 150–97, 267–303, 374–91; pubd sep. (1993) · Ann. Ulster · G. Murphy, 'On the dates of two sources used in Thurneysen's Heldensage': 1. Baile Chuind and the date of Cin Dromma Snechtai', Ériu, 16 (1952), 145–56, esp. 145–51 · M. C. Dobbs, ed. and trans., 'The Banshenchus [3 pts]', Revue Celtique, 47 (1930), 283–339; 48 (1931), 163–234; 49 (1932), 437–89 · W. M. Hennessy, ed. and trans., Chronicum Scotorum: a chronicle of Irish affairs, Rolls Series, 46 (1866) · M. A. O'Brien, ed., Corpus genealogiarum Hiberniae (Dublin, 1962) · K. Meyer, ed., 'The Laud genealogies and tribal histories', Zeitschrift für Celtische Philologie, 8 (1910–12), 291–338 · F. J. Byrne, Irish kings and high-kings (1973)

Muirchertach mac Néill [called Muirchertach of the Leather Cloaks] (d. **943**), king of Ailech, was the son of the high-king *Niall mac Áeda (Niall Glúndub) (d. 919) and Land, the daughter of Eochaid of Dál Riata. Muirchertach was one of the most successful generals of his day and was described as the 'Hector of the Irish'. His expedition round Ireland in 941, to collect hostages for the high-king, was celebrated in the poem 'The Circuit of Ireland'. Despite a distinguished lineage—he was a dynast of Cenél nÉogain—and a military genius admired by his contemporaries, Muirchertach never achieved recognition as high-king as did his father and, later, his son; he was unsuccessful in several attempts to overthrow the reigning high-king, Donnchad mac Flainn.

The earliest notice of Muirchertach is in 921, when a viking army from Dublin under the command of Guthfrith Ua Ímhar raided Armagh on 10 November and then moved northwards. Muirchertach, whose family had many ties to Armagh, intercepted the vikings and defeated them in a battle fought late in the day. Five years later, in 926, Muirchertach attacked a viking fleet at Carlingford Lough and began the first of a series of campaigns against the vikings that would continue to the end of his career. Among the viking casualties was an Albdan, son of Guthfrith; Muirchertach was to be killed by his brother Blacaire seventeen years later. A viking army led by Torulb sailed into Lough Neagh in 930 and plundered the countryside for several years; in 932 Muirchertach defeated that host, and killed Torulb, in a battle fought where the River Main flows into the lough.

Muirchertach had ambitions beyond his resources: he wished to be recognized as high-king. At the time he began his, ultimately unsuccessful, campaigns he was not even the ruler of his hereditary domain, an office held by his cousin Fergal mac Domnaill, the son of his father's paternal half-brother. Nevertheless, in 927 Muirchertach disrupted the fair of Tailtiu, presided over by the high-king, and challenged Donnchad mac Flainn to battle, but they were parted without bloodshed. Two years later Muirchertach again tried to force Donnchad into a battle when he seized the ceremonial site at Tara, compelling

the high-king to lead an army against him; once again battle seems to have been prevented. The weakness of Muirchertach's position was revealed in 933, when he and his brother Conaing were defeated in battle by his cousin Fergal at 'Mag Uatha' (Donegal). Equally revealing was the strength of Cenél nÉogain in relation to their neighbours when Muirchertach's brother Conaing defeated the Ulaid at 'Ruba Conchongalt' in that same year. This led, in turn, to a retaliatory attack by Matudán mac Áeda of Ulaid with the vikings, in which they raided from Slieve Beagh westwards and southwards to Muchnoe (Monaghan), but were intercepted and defeated by Muirchertach.

In 938 Muirchertach ascended to the kingship of Ailech on the death of his kinsman Fergal and resumed his contest with the high-king Donnchad when a battle between them was again prevented. This time there must have been a genuine rapprochement, possibly recognition of Muirchertach as Donnchad's successor, because thereafter the two men worked in harmony. They led a raid on the vikings of Dublin, destroying territory from Dublin to the River Greece (Kildare). In revenge the vikings raided the north in the next year and captured Muirchertach at his fortress at Ailech, but either he was rescued or he escaped. Muirchertach turned his attentions to bringing the provincial kings into submission. In 940 he and Donnchad campaigned in Leinster and Munster, taking hostages as signs of submission. In the same year Muirchertach eliminated a kinsman and possible rival when he slew Niall, the son of the Fergal who had defeated him in 933. The next year, 941, Muirchertach took sole command of the famous 'Circuit of Ireland', an expedition which travelled throughout Ireland taking the submission of all the provincial kings. In the middle of winter he led his army clockwise round Ireland, taking tribute and hostages, who were then turned over to the high-king. His men guarded themselves against the inclement weather with cloaks made of leather, hence the name Muirchertach of the Leather Cloaks. Muirchertach had earlier in the same year led a naval fleet into the Hebrides and collected tribute there. As a descendant of the kings of Dál Riata, being the great-grandson of the Scottish king Cináed mac Alpin, he may have considered that he had hereditary interests in the region. This was to be the last major triumph for Muirchertach. Two years later, on Sunday 26 February 943, he was slain at Ardee (Louth) while fighting an invading viking force. The vikings celebrated their victory by plundering Armagh on the next day.

Muirchertach had two wives: Gormlaith, daughter of Cuilennán mac Máele Brigte, whose son was the future high-king *Domnall ua Néill (d. 980); and Sadb, daughter of Cellach mac Cerbaill (d. 908), of Osraige. Muirchertach's daughter Dúnlaith was the mother of two important kings: the future high-king Máel Sechnaill mac Domnaill (d. 1022) and Glún Iairn, king of Dublin and son of Olaf Cuarán (or Sihtricson; d. 989). Three other sons were Flaithbertach, king of Ailech (d. 949), Murchad, and Flann. Muirchertach may also be the father of the Irish princess Máel Corda, who is named in Landnámabók and Laxdæla saga.

BENJAMIN T. HUDSON

Sources *Ann. Ulster* · Cormcan Eigeas, 'The circuit of Ireland by Muirchertach Mac Néill, prince of Aileach: a poem written in the year 1442', ed. and trans. J. O'Donovan, *Tracts relating to Ireland*, Irish Archaeological Society, 1 (1841), 1–68 · M. C. Dobbs, ed. and trans., 'The Ban-shenchus [3 pts]', *Revue Celtique*, 47 (1930), 283–339; 48 (1931), 163–234; 49 (1932), 437–89 · J. H. Todd, ed. and trans., *Cogadh Gaedhel re Gallaibh / The war of the Gaedhil with the Gaill*, Rolls Series, 48 (1867) · M. A. O'Brien, ed., *Corpus genealogiarum Hiberniae* (Dublin, 1962) · E. Hogan, *Onomasticon Goedelicum* (1910) · W. M. Hennessy, ed. and trans., *Chronicum Scotorum: a chronicle of Irish affairs*, Rolls Series, 46 (1866) · AFM · J. MacNeill, 'Poems by Flann Mainistrech on the dynasties of Ailech, Mide and Brega', *Archivium Hibernicum*, 2 (1913), 37–99 · D. Ó Corráin, *Ireland before the Normans* (1972)

Muirchú [St Muirchú, Muirchú maccu Machthéni] (*fl.* **697**), biographer, is commemorated on 8 June. In his life of St Patrick, Muirchú calls himself Muirchú moccu Machthéni, that is, 'Muirchú descendant of Machthéine'. Although the forms do not correspond exactly, it seems likely that he was a member of the minor kinship group called Tuath Mochthaine which lived on Mag Macha—the plain upon which Armagh lies. The reference by Muirchú to Cogitosus, biographer of St Brigit of Kildare, as *pater* ('father') has been taken by some to indicate a direct genealogical relationship, but since Cogitosus calls himself *nepos hÁedo* ('descendant of Áed'), it is probable that their relationship was of a more spiritual nature. A gloss in one copy of the martyrology of Oengus refers to Muirchú and one Medrán as 'two brothers in *Cell Murchon* among the Uí Ailella' (*Félire Óengusso*, 145): if 'Cell Murchon' is Kilmorgan (in the barony of Corran, co. Sligo), then the Uí Ailella in question were probably those of Tirerrill in modern co. Sligo. Given Muirchú's origin near, and career in, Armagh, it is possible that he retired to Connacht later in life.

Muirchú states that he undertook to write the life of St Patrick on the request of Bishop Áed of Sletty (in what is now Laois), but the exact time at which this request was made is difficult to determine. The so-called *Additamenta* to the Book of Armagh record that Áed visited Armagh during the episcopacy of Ségéne (*r.* 661–88) in order to incorporate Sletty into the Patrician community of Armagh, so it is possible that he met Muirchú and made the suggestion at that point. However, both men also attended the Synod of Birr in 697, at which the law of Adomnán was promulgated, and while the record of this synod entitles Áed 'bishop' it seems he may have retired before 692 when his successor Conchrad is known to have died. If he had retired to Armagh (which is by no means demonstrable) Áed could have made his request any time before his own death in 700.

The life of St Patrick is written in a dramatic and rhetorical style, and as such contrasts with the earlier *Collectanea* of Tírechán. Indeed, Muirchú was one of the earliest Irish hagiographers and stresses himself that only Cogitosus had steered his authorial boat through such uncharted waters. Despite its survival in a number of early manuscripts, most notably the early ninth-century Book of Armagh, reconstruction of Muirchú's original text is hampered by the varying order of the chapters. It is traditionally divided into two parts or 'books', though some have argued that Muirchú was not the author of the second, shorter, book, or that he wrote it after a gap of some years.

The text describes Patrick's evangelizing activities in Ireland, of which the most famous episode is his encounter with the high-king Lóegaire mac Néill and his druids at Tara. Muirchú's sources for the life included the *Confessio* of St Patrick (or at least a text incorporating parts of it), some possible poetical works, and local Armagh legends. In addition, he may have had access to the (now lost) *liber* of St Patrick which Tírechán had summarized, and in fact it is possible that Muirchú's work was commissioned to improve and replace this *liber* in the official Armagh hagiography of Patrick. As such, Muirchú's work is best seen in the context of seventh-century ecclesiastical politics, when Armagh was attempting to appropriate the cult of St Patrick and establish his primacy over Ireland. There are various instances in the life where Muirchú is clearly supporting the claims of Armagh at the expense of other churches, and distorting known facts in so doing. A notable example is the problem over the death and burial place of Patrick. Muirchú explains the evidently accepted location of his death at Saul and burial at Saul or Downpatrick (both in Down) by claiming that, on hearing of his imminent demise, Patrick intended to go to Armagh but was dissuaded by an angel, who stressed however that his 'pre-eminence' would be at Armagh. Furthermore, Muirchú relates that the subsequent dispute over possession of the saint's body was resolved miraculously by what he calls the 'fallacy' of the appearance of two bodies. In such cases, it is often difficult to determine how far Muirchú has manipulated earlier traditions in favour of Armagh, and overall the work is more valuable as a source for the Irish church in the seventh, rather than the fifth, century.

DAVID E. THORNTON

Sources L. Bieler, ed. and trans., *The Patrician texts in the Book of Armagh*, Scriptores Latini Hiberniae, 10 (1979) · *Félire Óengusso Céli Dé / The martyrology of Oengus the Culdee*, ed. and trans. W. Stokes, HBS, 29 (1905) · R. I. Best and H. J. Lawlor, eds., *The martyrology of Tallaght*, HBS, 68 (1931) · *Félire húi Gormáin / The martyrology of Gorman*, ed. and trans. W. Stokes, HBS, 9 (1895) · M. Ní Dhonnchadha, 'The guarantor list of Cáin Adomnáin, 697', *Peritia*, 1 (1982), 178–215 · R. Sharpe, 'St Patrick and the see of Armagh', *Cambridge Medieval Celtic Studies*, 4 (1982), 33–59 · C. Doherty, 'The cult of St Patrick and the politics of Armagh in the seventh century', *Ireland and northern France, AD 600–850*, ed. J.-M. Picard (1991), 53–94 · R. Sharpe, *Medieval Irish saints' lives: an introduction to Vitae sanctorum Hiberniae* (1991)

Muiredach mac Echdach (*fl.* early 6th cent.). *See under* Connacht, saints of (*act.* c.400–c.800).

Muirhead family (*per.* 1877–1976), travel writers, were writers and editors of travel guides for almost a century. The first to become involved in the work was **James Fullarton Muirhead** (1853–1934), the elder son of John James Muirhead JP, goldsmith, and Isabella Fullarton Robertson, of Edinburgh. He was born in Glasgow on 25 December 1853 and educated at Craigmount, a school in Edinburgh, before matriculating in the arts faculty of Edinburgh University in 1870 (MA, 1874). In the summer of 1877 he went to Leipzig to join the staff of the German guidebook publishing house of Karl Baedeker, and was commissioned by them to edit an English-language edition of their guide to London, which was published in 1878. He later compiled Baedeker guides to Great Britain (1887), the United States (1893), and Canada (1894), spending much time in North America to undertake research. In 1894 he married Helen (d. 1947), daughter of Joseph Quincy of Boston, Massachusetts. Muirhead was also the author of *America, the Land of Contrasts* (1898), *American Shrines on English Soil* (1925), and *A Wayfarer in Switzerland* (1926), and translator of several works by the Swiss poet and philosopher Carl Spitteler. Both his sons, Phillips and Langdon, were killed in 1918; in 1923 his only daughter, Mabel, married Gerard Hopkins, who later translated several novels by François Mauriac. James Muirhead died at 18 Bentinck Street, Marylebone, London, on 6 April 1934.

Findlay Muirhead (1860–1935), James Muirhead's younger brother, was born in Glasgow on 9 March 1860. He attended the Royal High School at Edinburgh before going up to Edinburgh University in 1877, from which he graduated MA in 1881, matriculating in the law faculty that latter year. He intended to pursue a career at the Scottish bar, but lack of funds forced him to find other work. After short periods with *The Scotsman* and the *Encyclopaedia Britannica*, in 1887 he joined the staff of Karl Baedeker, by whom his brother had already been employed for ten years. Like his brother he divided his time between Leipzig and London for the next two and a half decades. After a thorough grounding in guide-writing and editing, the two brothers were made responsible for all Baedeker's English editions. Findlay opened a London editorial office at 10 Leighton Crescent, where his staff incorporated additional material likely to interest the cultivated English-speaking tourist. By 1914 they had compiled, edited, and adapted some 200 English editions of twenty-seven titles in the Baedeker series. Findlay had found time also to write *Kings without Crowns* (1887) and to produce *Commercial Geography* (1889), a translation of Zehden's work, and, with his brother, a *Guide to the Public Collections of Classical Antiquities in Rome*, a translation of the work by Wolfgang Helbig, published by Baedeker in 1895. In 1894 he married Mary Blanshard (1859–1926), eldest daughter of Leon M. Clench, barrister, of St Mary's, Ontario. They had one son.

With the outbreak of hostilities in 1914, the Muirheads and their staff in the London Baedeker office found themselves out of a job, but by 1915 the British press were canvassing a British-originated substitute for Baedekers, and with financial backing from Walter Russell Rea (1873–1948), a merchant banker, who had married their sister Evelyn (d. 1930) in 1896, the Muirheads were able to buy from Edward Stanford for £2000 the copyrights of most of the famous Hand-books for Travellers, which had been published previously by John Murray. After setting up Muirhead Guidebooks Ltd (in which James Muirhead had

no active involvement), Findlay made an agreement with Hachette et Cie in Paris whereby Muirhead would translate and adapt Hachette's blue cloth-bound guide to Paris, and Hachette would adapt and publish Muirhead's projected series for the French market.

Distributed by Macmillan, the first Blue Guide launched by the company was Findlay Muirhead's *London and its Environs*, published in London on 31 May 1918. The title the Blue Guides would distinguish them from the ubiquitous red-bound Murrays and Baedekers, while Hachette changed their series title (previously the Guides Joanne, named after their first editor) to Les Guides Bleus. The agreement between the two publishers lapsed in 1933.

Between 1920 and his retirement in 1934 Findlay (who died in London on 15 May 1935) edited some nineteen titles in the series he had originated. Those to parts of France and Italy were written in collaboration with Marcel Monmarché and L. V. Bertarelli respectively.

In 1931 the English series was acquired by Ernest Benn Ltd, with **(Litellus) Russell Muirhead** (1896–1976), Findlay's son, becoming editor in 1934. He was born at 15 Sherriff Road, London, on 3 September 1896, attended University College School, and in 1915–19 served as first lieutenant in the Royal Irish Fusiliers. He completed his formal education at Christ's College, Cambridge, to which he had gained a scholarship just prior to the war. In 1921 he joined his father's firm, and in 1923 married Benedetta (b. 1900), daughter of Didier Lagneau of Paris. They had one son. During his rigorous apprenticeship Russell did much of the groundwork on volumes to which Findlay put his own name as editor, but he was later responsible for extending the series by the compilation of over a dozen new titles to European destinations. He also reviewed books and wrote travel articles irregularly in *The Fortnightly*, edited *Discovery*, a monthly journal of popular scientific news, and gave a number of talks entitled 'Walks in London' for the BBC. Between 1938 and 1949 several Penguin Guides to English counties were published under his editorial aegis.

The contribution of their cultured, self-effacing editor to the growing reputation of the Blue Guides as the most informative, authoritative, and scholarly available in English on the art, architecture, and history of the countries concerned was long unappreciated by their publisher, and it was not until 1951 that Russell Muirhead was invited to join the board of Ernest Benn Ltd. He retired from the board and from active editorship in 1963.

In his later years Russell Muirhead enjoyed the camaraderie of various societies, including the British Archaeological Association, to whose council he was elected in March 1956. He was a fellow of the Society of Antiquaries, and participated in meetings of the Society of Genealogists, the British Record Society, and the London Topographical Society, until progressive lameness caused by a First World War wound made attendance onerous. He died in London on 6 February 1976, and was survived by his wife.

In writing and editing English Baedekers or, after 1918,

by compiling and editing approximately seventy-five editions of some twenty Blue Guide titles, and establishing a name which became as much of a household word as John Murray III's Red Murrays had been during the nineteenth century, James, Findlay, and Russell Muirhead influenced several generations of cultivated English-speaking travellers by the range and quality of guidance they provided. In the 1970s several freelance author–editors were commissioned by Ernest Benn Ltd radically to recompose earlier editions or compile new titles, following the stringent precepts of their predecessors. After 1983, when the company was acquired by A. and C. Black Ltd, the quantity of titles available substantially increased, but with certain exceptions their former indisputable appeal to the educated tourist became less evident.

IAN CAMPBELL ROBERTSON

Sources WWW · *University of Edinburgh Journal*, 6 (1933–4), 307 [obit. James Fullarton]; 7 (1934–5), 293–4 [obit. Findlay] · *The Times* (7 April 1934) · *The Times* (17 May 1935) · *The Times* (10 Feb 1976) · personal knowledge (2004) · private information (2004) · *CGPLA Eng. & Wales* (1934) [James Fullarton Muirhead]

Archives BLPES, letters to Edwin Cannan

Likenesses group portrait, photograph, 1911, priv. coll. · photograph, c.1940 (L. T. Muirhead aged forty-five)

Wealth at death £3814 17s. 11d.—James Fullarton Muirhead: probate, 9 Aug 1934, *CGPLA Eng. & Wales* · £2050 10s. 3d.—Findlay Muirhead: probate, 22 June 1935, *CGPLA Eng. & Wales* · £25,602—(Litellus) Russell Muirhead: probate, 4 May 1976, *CGPLA Eng. & Wales*

Muirhead, Alexander (1848–1920), electrical engineer, was born on 26 May 1848 at Barley Mill, Saltoun, East Lothian, Scotland, the second of the seven children of John Muirhead (1807–1885), farmer, and his wife, Margaret Lauder. He led a solitary childhood after a fall on to his head left him deaf in one ear, and he spent much time making experiments, such as planting a poker among the cabbages to see whether it would grow. By 1857 his father had joined the Electric Telegraph Company in London as a superintendent. Here the family lived in Camden, while always maintaining strong Scottish connections.

Because of his deafness, Alexander was thought to suffer from a learning disability and had a private tutor; but from 1863 he attended University College School and proved instead to be an outstanding pupil, taking many prizes in mathematics and science. At University College, London he graduated BSc with honours in chemistry in 1869, then studied natural sciences in St Bartholomew's Hospital laboratory, obtaining his DSc (in electricity) in 1872. While there he attached wires to a feverish patient's wrist to obtain a record of the patient's heartbeat, probably the first ever electrocardiogram.

Muirhead became scientific adviser to the firm of telegraph engineers founded by his father, with Josiah Latimer Clark and W. M. Warden. His father, elder brother, John, and Alexander himself, all worked on the duplexing of signals in submarine cables (simultaneously receiving and transmitting), but it was Alexander who was to become recognized worldwide for laying the cables, after their system was patented by himself and H. A. Taylor in

1875 (described by him in 'Muirhead's duplex system', *Telegraph Journal*, vol. 7, 1879). The company also made precision measurements of resistance and capacity, and Alexander pioneered the original electrical standards of capacity, which he inaugurated and passed to the National Physical Laboratory. This work was arguably his most significant achievement (explained by him in 'New form of standards of E. M. F.', *Electrician*, vol. 17, 1886).

When his father's firm became Latimer Clark, Muirhead & Co., Alexander and his brother John were made directors, but in 1882 Alexander set up an independent consultancy in Westminster. After his father's death in 1885, the firm continued until 1894. The cable companies then persuaded Alexander to set up his own manufactory which, as Muirhead & Co., moved to Elmers End in Beckenham, Kent, in 1896. On 8 February 1893 Muirhead married Mary Elizabeth (1858–1930), daughter of William Blomfield of Upper Norwood, and they settled at The Lodge, Church Road, Shortlands, Beckenham.

From 1894 Muirhead became involved in the development of wireless after a lecture on Hertzian waves, given by his friend Oliver Lodge (Lodge and Muirhead, 'Syntonic wireless telegraphy,' *Proceedings of the Royal Society*, series A, 82, 1909). The Lodge–Muirhead Wireless Syndicate was formed in 1901; it was later bought out by Marconi in 1911.

Muirhead's many other interests included dynamos, arc lamps, insulating compounds, and the telephone. Always meticulous, his instruments were described by Lodge as 'beautifully designed and constructed' (*Journal of the Institution of Electrical Engineers*, 59, 1921, 782–3). He was elected a member of the Institution of Electrical Engineers in 1877, and FRS in 1904.

Muirhead's health—but not his spirit—had been affected by a serious viral illness in 1891, and deteriorated still further after a slight stroke in 1909. His heart eventually failed on 13 December 1920; he died at his house, The Lodge, Church Road, Shortlands, and was buried three days later in Norwood cemetery, London, by the minister from Bromley Congregational Church. He left substantial bequests, from an estate of £105,806, to the Royal Society and the Established Church of Scotland.

RONALD M. BIRSE, rev. PATRICIA E. KNOWLDEN

Sources M. E. Muirhead, *Alexander Muirhead* (1926) · *Journal of the Institution of Electrical Engineers*, 59 (1921), 782–3 · O. J. L., *PRS*, 100A (1921–2), viii–ix · Muirhead & Co., *Annual report* (1975), 2 · *Norwood News and Croydon Gazette* (13 Feb 1893) [marriage announcement] · *The Post Office London directory* (1879); (1881); (1889); (1891); (1894) · *Register*, Institution of Electrical Engineers · *Patent office printed lists* (1870–87)

Archives Imperial College and Science Museum Library, London, Muirhead & Co. archives · Sci. Mus., telegraphic instruments, etc. (with photographs) · UCL, corresp. with Sir Oliver Lodge

Likenesses Talbotype, 1859–60, repro. in Muirhead, *Alexander Muirhead* · Bourne & Shepherd, Bombay, 1874, repro. in Muirhead, *Alexander Muirhead* · photograph, c.1890, Inst. EE · Lavender, Bromley, c.1892, repro. in Muirhead, *Alexander Muirhead* · photographs, 1902–4, repro. in Muirhead, *Alexander Muirhead* · Elliott & Fry, 1903, repro. in Muirhead, *Alexander Muirhead* · photograph, Sci. Mus.

Wealth at death £105,806 12s. 3d.: probate, 3 March 1921, *CGPLA Eng. & Wales*

Muirhead, Findlay (1860–1935). *See under* Muirhead family (*per.* 1877–1976).

Muirhead, George (*bap.* **1715**, *d.* **1773**), Church of Scotland minister and classical scholar, was born in Dunipace, Stirlingshire, where he was baptized on 24 June 1715, the second son of John Muirhead of Teggetsheugh, of the Muirheads of Lauchop, Lanarkshire, and Margaret Sim. He matriculated at the University of Glasgow in November 1728, and was among the students taught by Francis Hutcheson. After completing the Glasgow arts course he studied divinity at the University of Edinburgh and graduated MA in 1742. Despite some opposition on doctrinal grounds he was licensed to preach by the presbytery of Edinburgh on 28 December 1743. About this time he taught the moral philosophy class at Edinburgh University while the professor, John Pringle, was on leave, and he was one of the seven men whom Hutcheson recommended as Pringle's permanent replacement, but the appointment went to another of Hutcheson's nominees, William Cleghorn.

Muirhead was appointed minister of Monigaff, Wigtownshire, where he was ordained on 4 December 1746, and on 28 January 1748 he was translated to the second charge at the parish of Dysart in the presbytery of Kirkcaldy, Fife. Three years later he was a candidate for the logic chair at the University of Glasgow, but lost to Adam Smith. He tried again the following year, but was also unsuccessful, despite support from David Hume. Finally, on 22 December 1752, he was elected to the Glasgow chair of oriental languages by the professors of the college, with the tacit support of Lord Ilay, third duke of Argyll. As a formality the appointment was subject to a test of competence, which Muirhead provided. Four days after his election he demitted his pastoral charge at Dysart, which was immediately filled by his younger brother Patrick (1718–1807), and on 5 January 1753 he assumed his new position in Glasgow. On 2 December 1754 he moved to the Glasgow chair of humanity (Latin), which he occupied with distinction for the remainder of his life. From 1764 to 1766 he served as dean of faculty, steadfastly supporting the principal, William Leechman, in a series of power struggles within the university. In 1764 he declined to compete for the moral philosophy chair vacated by Adam Smith, and filled by Thomas Reid, even though his seniority might have enabled him to secure it. In early September 1771 he was one of several professors who entertained James Boswell and General Paoli when they visited Glasgow.

From 1753 onwards Muirhead was an active member of the Glasgow Literary Society, which met at the university. As recorded in the society's minutes, the discourses he delivered dealt chiefly with aspects of Greek and Latin literature. Although he is not known to have published anything under his own name Muirhead made a significant contribution to scholarship by editing some of the volumes of the classics that were published by the renowned Glasgow press of Robert and Andrew Foulis, with whom he was closely associated from an early date. The most famous of these works was the 4-volume folio edition of Homer, which Muirhead carefully edited with his colleague, James Moor: two volumes of *The Iliad* in 1756 and two of *The Odyssey* in 1758. He also supervised the Foulises' acclaimed edition of Virgil, which appeared in 1760.

Muirhead never married, but his family connections are of considerable interest in two respects. First, he was closely related to Agnes Muirhead, the mother of James Watt, whom he introduced to other professors at the University of Glasgow, thereby setting the stage for Watt's historic redesign of the Newcomen atmospheric engine after one of the professors asked him to repair a demonstration model. Second, three years after his death, which occurred on 31 August 1773, his older brother, John of Teggetsheugh, and his younger brother, Patrick, donated to the University of Glasgow £100 from George's modest estate to establish in his honour the Muirhead prizes, given annually 'for the promotion of the study of Humanity' (*Deeds*, 204). RICHARD B. SHER

Sources W. I. Addison, ed., *The matriculation albums of the University of Glasgow from 1728 to 1858* (1913) · [A. Carlyle], review of the Foulis edition of *The Iliad*, *Scots Magazine*, 19 (1757), 570 · J. Coutts, *A history of the University of Glasgow* (1909) · *The correspondence of Adam Smith*, ed. E. C. Mossner and I. S. Ross, 2nd edn (1987), vol. 6 of *The Glasgow edition of the works and correspondence of Adam Smith* · [W. Thomson], ed., *Deeds instituting bursaries, scholarships, and other foundations, in the College and University of Glasgow*, Maitland Club, 69 (1850) · P. Gaskell, *A bibliography of the Foulis Press*, 2nd edn (1986) · A. Hook and R. B. Sher, eds., *The Glasgow Enlightenment* (1995) · J. D. Mackie, *The University of Glasgow, 1451–1951: a short history* (1954) · J. Maclehose, *The Glasgow University Press, 1638–1931* (1931) · D. R. Raynor, 'Muirhead, George', *The dictionary of eighteenth-century British philosophers*, ed. J. W. Yolton, J. V. Price, and J. Stephens (1999) · D. Murray, *Robert and Andrew Foulis and the Glasgow press* (1913) · I. S. Ross, *Lord Kames and the Scotland of his day* (1972) · I. S. Ross, *The life of Adam Smith* (1995) · www.origins.net, 26 March 2000 · *Fasti Scot.*, new edn, 2.372, 5.89, 7.405–406 · R. B. Sher, 'Commerce, religion and the Enlightenment in eighteenth-century Glasgow', *Glasgow*, ed. T. M. Devine and G. Jackson, 1: *Beginnings to 1830* (1995), 312–59 · R. B. Sher, 'Professors of virtue: a social history of the chair of moral philosophy at Edinburgh', *Studies in the philosophy of the Scottish Enlightenment*, ed. M. A. Stewart (1990), 87–126 · *A vindication of Mr Hutcheson from the calumnious aspersions of a late pamphlet* (1738) · F. Hutcheson, letter to G. Elliot, 4 July 1744, NL Scot., MS 11004, fol. 57 · W. Rouet, letter [to John Nourse ?], 19 July 1756, U. Edin. L., La.II.511

Archives U. Glas. L., MSS | U. Glas., Archives and Business Records Centre · U. Glas., minutes of the Literary Society in Glasgow College [typescript]

Muirhead, James (1742–1808), songwriter, was born at East Logan Farm, in the parish of Buittle, Kirkcudbrightshire. After elementary training at Dumfries grammar school he studied for the church at Edinburgh University, and was ordained minister of the parish of Urr, Kirkcudbrightshire, on 28 June 1770. Muirhead's one published song is the shrewd and vivid pastoral 'Bess the gawkie' (that is, fool). It first appeared in Herd's *Scottish Songs* (1776). Burns considered it equalled by few Scottish pastorals, pronouncing it 'a beautiful song, and in the genuine Scots taste' (R. H. Cromek, *Reliques of Burns*, 1808). Muirhead married Jean Loudon (*d.* 1826) on 21 August 1777. They had three children: two sons—William and Charles—and a daughter, who married a Captain Skirving.

As a proprietor and freeholder of the county Muirhead was one of the victims of Burns's unsparing satire in *Ballads on Mr. Heron's Election, 1795*, and retaliated in a brochure in which he quoted and liberally translated into verse Martial's *In Vacerram*. He somewhat cleverly made out Vacerras to have been a gauger of very loose principles, implying that Burns was a sycophant who would do anything for whisky; 'no publication in answer to the scurrilities of Burns ever did him so much harm in public opinion, or made Burns himself feel so sore' (Chambers, 4.147). Burns further denounced Muirhead in his election song of 1796, 'Wha will buy my troggin?'.

A scholarly man, Muirhead was known as a mathematician and a naturalist. He furnished particulars of the parish of Urr to Sinclair's *Statistical Account of Scotland* (1790–91). In 1796 he received the degree of DD from Edinburgh University. He died at Spottes Hall, Dumfriesshire, on 16 May 1808.   T. W. BAYNE, *rev.* JAMES HOW

Sources A. Trotter, *East Galloway sketches, or, Biographical, historical and descriptive notices of Kirkcudbrightshire, chiefly in the nineteenth century* (1901) · J. D. Ross, *Who's who in Burns* (1927) · Irving, *Scots.* · C. Rogers, *The modern Scottish minstrel* (1857) · *The life and works of Robert Burns*, ed. R. Chambers, 4 vols. (1891)

Muirhead, James (1830–1889), jurist, was born on 13 November 1830, the eldest of the five sons of Claud Muirhead (1782–1872) of 7 Heriot Row, Edinburgh, and Gogar Park, Midlothian, proprietor of the *Edinburgh Advertiser*, and his wife, Mary Watson. He was a pupil at Edinburgh Academy from 1840 to 1845. He initially embarked on training for a career in commerce and spent time in Lille learning French. He went on to study arts and law at the University of Edinburgh between 1849 and the spring of 1854, and then proceeded to the University of Heidelberg, where he matriculated on 13 May 1854 and studied Roman law under C. A. von Vangerow. He returned to Edinburgh and in the autumn of that year matriculated once more as a law student. A keen member of the Speculative Society, he served as its president between 1858 and 1860. He entered the Inner Temple on 31 October 1854 and was called to the English bar on 6 June 1857, having already been admitted to the Faculty of Advocates on 31 January 1857. Muirhead married at London on 14 April 1857 Jemima Lock Eastlake (*d.* 1891), daughter of George Eastlake of Plymouth, Admiralty law deputy judge-advocate of the fleet. She was the sister of Charles Lock Eastlake (1836–1906), keeper of the National Gallery, London, and the niece of Lady Elizabeth Eastlake (1809–1893), writer on art, and her husband, Sir Charles Lock Eastlake (1793–1865), painter, president of the Royal Academy and director of the National Gallery. A daughter, Helena Elizabeth Mary, was born on 12 March 1863; a son, Claud James, was born on 1 December 1868 but died within the year.

In 1862 Muirhead published *Notes on the marriage laws of England, Scotland, and Ireland, with suggestions for their amendment and assimilation*. In the context of current conflicts between these laws Muirhead set out a plan for a unified law in the United Kingdom. In June 1862 he was elected to the chair of civil law in the University of Edinburgh. This

James Muirhead (1830–1889), by William Hole, *c.*1884

was an appointment of immense importance. The universities were in the midst of major reform after the Universities (Scotland) Act of 1858, and the new degree of LLB had been established. Roman law, to which the civil law chair was essentially devoted, was a central component of the degree and to be taught in the winter and summer sessions. Muirhead brought his German training to the subject and taught the first course in Roman law in the British Isles that took into account the advances in the discipline made on the continent. Initially, after lecturing on the external history of Roman law, he dealt with the substantive law in the framework established by the German pandectists, beginning with general concepts before moving on to property, obligations, family, and succession; from 1876 to 1877, however, he followed the scheme later described in the *Institutes* after dealing with history, and in 1880 he published *The Institutes of Gaius and Rules of Ulpian* (reprinted in 1895) for the use of students, drawing on the best modern scholarship. That he should choose to produce this for his class indicates the trend of his thought on how Roman law should be taught. The work was well received. In 1886 he published *A Historical Introduction to the Law of Rome*. This was a much expanded version of an article written for the ninth edition of the *Encyclopaedia Britannica*. It was a considerable success, reaching a second edition in 1899 (by Henry Goudy), and was translated into Italian and French. It resulted in his election to the Juridical Society of Berlin and the Institute of Roman Law in Rome. Alongside this European renown, Muirhead was recognized at home by the award of the honorary degree of LLD by the University of Glasgow in 1885. A proponent of codification, in 1864 he published his *Codification of Mercantile Law*. Although Muirhead clearly favoured a general codification for all of the United Kingdom, here he argued for that of mercantile law alone. He held up the example of Germany to show the possibilities. He collected a magnificent law library that reflected his interests; it was bought by Owens College, Manchester on his death and was the foundation of the law library of the University of Manchester.

At the same time as he held the chair Muirhead continued a career as an advocate, and in 1874 he was appointed a Conservative advocate-depute. He served in this office until he became sheriff of Chancery in 1880. He held this last office until 1885, when he was appointed sheriff-principal of Stirling, Dumbarton, and Clackmannan. He died at his home at 2 Drumsheugh Gardens, Edinburgh, on 8 November 1889.   JOHN W. CAIRNS

Sources J. Rankine, 'Professor Muirhead', *Juridical Review*, 2 (1890), 27–32 · G. Carle, 'Professor Muirhead', *Juridical Review*, 2 (1890), 32–6 · 'The late Professor Muirhead', *Journal of Jurisprudence*, 33 (1889), 639–41 · *The Student*, 2/4 (1889), 49–50 · W. B. Hole, *Quasi cursores: portraits of the high officers and professors of the University of Edinburgh at its tercentenary festival* (1884), 175–80 · matriculation albums, U. Edin. L., special collections division, university archives · [T. Henderson and P. F. Hamilton-Grierson], eds., *The Edinburgh Academy register* (1914) · *Edinburgh University Calendar* · W. I. Addison, *A roll of graduates of the University of Glasgow from 31st December 1727 to 31st December 1897* (1898) · F. J. Grant, ed., *The Faculty of Advocates in Scotland, 1532–1943*, Scottish RS, 145 (1944) · register of births, parish register, NA Scot. · MS records, Faculty of Advocates · [W. M. Watson], ed., *The history of the Speculative Society, 1764–1904* (1905) · *CGPLA Eng. & Wales* (1890)

Likenesses W. Hole, engraving, *c.*1884 (after drawing), NPG [*see illus.*] · J. Moffat, photograph, repro. in *Juridical Review*, 2 (1890), frontispiece

Wealth at death £7151 8*s.* 7*d.*: confirmation, 3 Jan 1890, *CCI*

Muirhead, James Fullarton (1853–1934). *See under* Muirhead family (*per.* 1877–1976).

Muirhead, James Patrick (1813–1898), biographer, was born on 26 July 1813 at The Grove, Hamilton, Lanarkshire, the son of Lockhart Muirhead and his wife, Anne Campbell. His parents were both Scottish, his father being principal librarian, and from 1808 to 1829 regius professor of natural history, in Glasgow University. His maternal grandmother was the first cousin of James Watt, and left a manuscript which is the earliest surviving account of the engineer's youth. Muirhead was educated first at Glasgow College, where between 1826 and 1832 his name appears frequently in the prize lists (especially for Latin verse). After gaining a Snell exhibition at Balliol College, Oxford, on 3 February 1832, he matriculated there on 6 April 1832. However, he spent his long vacations on alpine expeditions, and in studying German rather than in working for honours, and took only a third class in *literae humaniores*. He graduated BA in 1835 and proceeded MA in 1838. He was admitted advocate at Edinburgh in 1838, and published during the same year a legal treatise. Then, for eight years, he practised law in Edinburgh.

On 27 January 1844 Muirhead married Katharine Elizabeth (*d.* 1890), second daughter of Matthew Robinson Boulton of Tew Park and Soho, Birmingham. His wife shared his classical and literary tastes, but she found the climate of Edinburgh so trying that in 1846 Muirhead gave up a promising career at the Scottish bar, and settled eventually (in 1847) at Haseley Court, Great Haseley, Oxfordshire, which belonged to his wife's family. While still at Oxford he had become acquainted with James Watt jun. of Aston Hall, Birmingham, who later decided to commit the writing of a memoir of his father—the great engineer—to Muirhead.

Muirhead's first endeavour in the field was the translation from French of D. F. J. Arago's *Historical Eloge of James Watt*, which had been read before the Académie des Sciences in 1834: published in 1839, it was the first biography of James Watt, but was brief and adulatory, concentrating essentially on Watt's development of the steam engine. Muirhead then investigated the rival claims of Watt and Henry Cavendish for priority in the discovery of the composition of water. Not only did he have free access to Watt's papers, but he consulted such living authorities as Brewster, Brougham, Davy, and Jeffrey, and visited Paris in 1842 to confer with Arago, Berzelius, and other savants. In 1846 he published what he considered as a clear vindication of Watt's rights in *The correspondence of the late James Watt on his discovery of the theory of the composition of water*, large sections of which were included in his subsequent publications. Watt's claim is not generally accepted today because, while he realized that oxygen was one component of water, he did not determine that the other was hydrogen but thought it some form of phlogiston or heat.

In 1854 Muirhead published his three-volume work *The Origins and Progress of the Mechanical Inventions of James Watt*. Most of the first volume is a detailed biography but often the chronology is confused, leading to wrong conclusions; there are also some important omissions, such as Watt's role as technical adviser on kiln design, glazes, and other similar matters, and as partner from 1768 until his death, in the Delftfield pottery in Glasgow. Selections from Watt's correspondence fill the rest of the first volume and all the second, and are carefully chosen to illustrate Watt's achievements: passages which might be construed as critical or derogatory have been deleted, often without any indication. The third volume contains the full texts and drawings of all Watt's patents and also excerpts from the patent trials of the 1790s. The *Origins* was a work of great magnitude, sifting an enormous mass of material. Muirhead revised it in 1858 for the abbreviated *Life of James Watt with Selections from his Correspondence*. For the modern reader both works suffer through their uncritical, adulatory approach and general failure to place Watt in his contemporary situation. Yet, at the end of the twentieth century, Muirhead's biographies remain the major source for scholars, who generally have not matched his research nor attained the quality of his style.

Muirhead was a keen angler and a good shot. In 1857 he

edited *Winged Words on Chantrey's Woodcocks*, a collection of epigrams by various writers, inspired by Sir Francis Chantrey's feat in killing at one shot and then immortalizing in sculpture two woodcocks flushed at Holkham. In 1875 he published *The Vaux de Vire of Maistre Jean le Houx, advocate, of Vire, edited and translated into English verse, with an introduction*, which won him a delightful letter from the elderly poet Longfellow. Between August 1882 and March 1891 Muirhead contributed to *Blackwood's Magazine* nine original poems and twenty translations from English and Old French poems into Latin or English verse—compositions which, owing to his signature, J. P. M., were occasionally attributed in error to Professor John Pentland Mahaffy. He continued to publish privately similar works until his death at Haseley Court on 15 October 1898. His six children survived him.

B. M. STURT, *rev.* RICHARD L. HILLS

Sources Boase, *Mod. Eng. biog.* · m. cert. · d. cert. · Foster, *Alum. Oxon.* · G. Williamson, *Memorials of the lineage, early life, education, and development of the genius of James Watt* (1856) · S. Smiles, *Lives of the engineers*, new edn, 4 (1878) · Birm. CL, Muirhead collection, Boulton and Watt collection · personal knowledge (1901) · private information (1901)
Archives U. Glas. L., papers | Birm. CL, Muirhead collection, Boulton and Watt archives · NL Scot., corresp. with Blackwoods · U. Edin. L., letters to David Laing · U. Glas. L.
Wealth at death £74,979 4*s.* 2*d.*: resworn probate, Nov 1899, *CGPLA Eng. & Wales* (1898)

Muirhead, John Henry (1855–1940), philosopher, was the third son of John William Muirhead (*d.* 1857), writer to the signet, of Glasgow, and his wife, Mary Burns (*d.* 1891), who claimed a connection with the novelist Susan Ferrier and her nephew the philosopher James Frederick Ferrier. He was born at Glasgow on 28 April 1855. He was educated at the Glasgow Academy (1866–70), and proceeded to Glasgow University, where he was deeply influenced by the Hegelianism of Edward Caird, professor of moral philosophy. He graduated MA in 1875. The same year he won a Snell exhibition at Balliol College, Oxford, to which he went up in Trinity term 1875. His teachers included T. H. Green and R. L. Nettleship. Among his close friends and contemporaries were Henry Jones, J. S. Mackenzie, John MacCunn, D. G. Ritchie, A. C. Bradley, and W. P. Ker. After obtaining a first class in classical moderations (1877) he was, to the surprise of the college, placed in the second class in *literae humaniores* in 1879. He was *proxime accessit* for the Gaisford prize for Greek prose and obtained the chancellor's Latin essay prize in 1881. After failing to obtain a fellowship, he became assistant in Latin to Professor George Gilbert Ramsay at Glasgow University from 1879 to 1885, when he left to study philosophy and theology at Manchester New College in London, and from then on philosophy was the subject to which he devoted himself.

In 1888 Muirhead was appointed lecturer in mental and moral science at the Royal Holloway College; he also lectured for Bedford College and the London Society for the Extension of University Teaching. In the same year he became editor of the Library of Philosophy, a position which he held until his death, and which he used to introduce to English readers many notable works by the prominent leaders of every school of thought, British, continental, and American. In 1886 he helped James Bonar and others to found the Ethical Society, and he also edited the Ethical Library. In 1892 he published his best-known textbook, *The Elements of Ethics*, which found a wide public. In 1897 he was appointed professor of philosophy and political economy in the Mason College at Birmingham. After the conversion of the college into the University of Birmingham (1900), political economy was, to Muirhead's relief, constituted as a separate chair, and he retained the chair of philosophy until his retirement in 1921.

Muirhead's mental and physical vigour continued unimpaired, and in two visits to the United States of America (1921–2 and 1925–8) he lectured extensively. He was elected a fellow of the British Academy in 1931. In retirement he devoted himself to initiating the Contemporary British Philosophy series, editing the Library of Philosophy, acting as chairman of the council of the newly founded British Institute of Philosophy, and maintaining an active interest in the modern developments of philosophy at home, on the continent, and in the United States. He was lecturing and writing to the very end.

Muirhead was far from being simply a stimulating teacher of philosophy. Always a social reformer in many spheres of civic endeavour, at Birmingham he played an important part in converting the Mason College into the first unitary civic university, and for twenty-six years was even more influential in the life of the city than in that of the classroom and senate. His interest in social questions was demonstrated by such publications as *By what Authority?* (1909), a collection of his newspaper articles on the poor-law commission, in which he sought to emphasize the points of agreement between the majority and minority reports. Here, as elsewhere, his simplicity of character, his concern to bring ethical principles to bear in practice, his sympathy with thinkers and systems opposed to his own views, and his determination to find a common denominator underlying apparent antagonisms, earned him respect and affection.

Philosophically, as a young man Muirhead had been deeply influenced by T. H. Green and R. L. Nettleship, as well as by Edward Caird, whose life he wrote in 1921 in collaboration with his friend Sir Henry Jones. Throughout his career he continued to regard Caird's philosophy as 'the true interpretation of the real Hegel' (Robertson and Ross, 382). Consequently, the innovations he sought to make in the more theoretical branches of philosophy were few. He preferred to concentrate, under Green's influence, on the application of idealist thought to moral, social, and political philosophy. Later influences included F. H. Bradley and Bernard Bosanquet, whom he knew well, so that, although his chief interest was ethics—in which his main problem was to state the relations between the end or good and the rule or obligation for achieving it (in 1932 he published *Rule and End in Morals*)—he continued to be throughout his career a prominent representative of the

British school of idealists. This general attitude is maintained particularly in *Coleridge as Philosopher* (1930), which remains the best account of Coleridge's philosophy with emphasis on the Platonic elements in it. This emphasis links it with his *The Platonic Tradition in Anglo-Saxon Philosophy* (1931), which leads from the Platonists of the seventeenth century to Muirhead's own philosophical position, and represents nineteenth-century British idealism as the organic development of a native platonic tradition. It also contains a study of Bradley's metaphysics. Thanks to his wide professional contacts and open and sympathetic attitude towards divergent philosophies, his autobiographical *Reflections by a Journeyman in Philosophy* (1942) and his memorial and other accounts of his contemporaries constitute an informal but reliable history of much of the philosophical thought, including its connections with social thought, in Britain in his day. The open and receptive character of his idealism meant that he was well placed to carry the initial impulse of idealist thought through the currents of later philosophical developments, finding some common ground with pragmatism and the new realism.

Muirhead was twice married: first, on 29 July 1892, to Mary Talbot (*d*. 1922), daughter of the Revd Gilbert Innes Wallas and sister of Graham Wallas; second, in the spring of 1927, to Pauline, daughter of George Bailey, who survived him. There were no children from either marriage. He died at his home, Dyke End, Rotherfield, Sussex, on 24 May 1940, with mental powers unabated.

C. G. ROBERTSON, *rev.* PETER P. NICHOLSON

Sources *John Henry Muirhead: reflections by a journeyman in philosophy on the movements of thought and practice in his time*, ed. J. W. Harvey (1942) [incl. full bibliography and six portraits] · C. G. Robertson and W. D. Ross, 'John Henry Muirhead, 1855–1940', *PBA*, 26 (1940), 381–8 · R. Metz, *A hundred years of British philosophy*, ed. J. H. Muirhead, trans. J. W. Harvey (1938), 305–9 [Ger. orig., *Die philophischen Strömungen der Gegenwart in Grossbritannien* (1935)] · *The Times* (27 May 1940) · private information (1949) · personal knowledge (1949) · *CGPLA Eng. & Wales* (1940)

Archives U. Birm., MSS | Bodl. Oxf., corresp. with Lord Kimberley · JRL, letters to Samuel Alexander · Society of Psychical Research, London, corresp. with Sir Oliver Lodge · U. Edin. L., letters to N. Kemp Smith · U. Newcastle, Robinson L., corresp. with Bernard Bosanquet

Likenesses W. Stoneman, photograph, 1932, NPG

Wealth at death £6870 16s. 7d.: probate, 26 Aug 1940, *CCI*

Muirhead, Roland Eugene (1868–1964), Scottish nationalist and businessman, was born on 24 July 1868 at Lochwinnoch, Renfrewshire, Scotland, the second son of Andrew Muirhead (*d*. 1885), the owner of the Gryffe tannery, and his wife, Isabella Reid. He was educated in Glasgow high school and at the age of fifteen he started a four-year apprenticeship at his father's tannery. When he was nineteen he emigrated to South America and worked as a cattlehand, and eventually moved north to the United States to live in an Owenite colony in Washington state. He subsequently claimed that this experience had shaped his belief in socialism.

Muirhead returned to the United Kingdom in 1891 and after a short period of running a co-operative tannery in London moved north to take over the family business. He was drawn into radical politics both by his own personal experiences and by family influence. His elder sister, Alice Margaret, was an advocate of women's suffrage, and his elder brother, Robert Franklin, was a member of the Socialist Land and Labour League. Through Robert, Roland came into contact with a number of eminent socialists, such as Andreas Schau, R. B. Cunninghame Graham, and Keir Hardie. In 1897 he reorganized the family business to give the workers a share in ownership. His business practice paid dividends and the tannery was successful, which allowed him to channel funds into a wide variety of political and cultural causes.

In 1901 Muirhead joined the Young Scots Society (YSS), a radical Liberal organization which had been formed in response to the wave of jingoism which had swept the country following the Second South African War and the crushing defeat of the Liberal Party at the general election of 1900. Although the YSS had formal ties to the Liberal Party, Muirhead worked hard to turn it into a coalition of progressive political movements in Scotland and consistently argued that the society should back candidates at elections who were the most 'progressive', irrespective of party. In 1906 he provided funding for the socialist weekly, *The Forward*, edited by Thomas Johnston. He also initiated a number of debates between the Fabian Society, the Independent Labour Party, and progressive Liberals in an endeavour to achieve common ground for the progressive cause in Scotland. A wide range of radical campaigns such as railway nationalization, women's suffrage, the Peace Society, and land nationalization received his support. In spite of his endeavours the YSS remained firmly attached to the Liberal camp, and his dissatisfaction with it grew after 1910, when the society failed to back Labour candidates at by-elections.

Muirhead's commitment to radical interventionist policies shaped his support for Scottish home rule. He believed that a Scottish parliament would implement more advanced policies of social reform than could be achieved by Westminster. From 1910 until the outbreak of the First World War he advocated the creation of a Scottish parliament as the top priority for Scottish radicals, as this would be the best way to deliver advanced social and economic policies. At this point in his political career he believed that his political objectives could best be achieved by putting pressure on the Liberal Party, and he questioned the need for a separate socialist party. He viewed nationalists, labourists, socialists, and radical Liberals as belonging to the 'progressive movement' and believed that they could win the Scottish Liberal Party over to their way of thinking. This 'common cause' approach to politics, in which issues and ideals were more important than party, would remain one of his key beliefs.

The onset of war, however, initiated a break with the YSS as the society supported the government, which contradicted Muirhead's pacifist principles. In 1918 he joined the ILP, serving as secretary of the Lochwinnoch branch, and set about re-creating the Scottish Home Rule Association (SHRA), of which he became national secretary. He hoped that the SHRA would be able to emulate some of the qualities that he had tried to instil into the YSS. He wanted to make the organization cross-party in order to maximize support for home rule and retained the pre-war radical faith that ideas of principle could transcend party loyalties. However, such faith was misplaced. He failed to stop the Scottish Trades Union Congress and the Labour Party taking over the association through its use of affiliated membership. When the private member's bill on Scottish home rule, introduced by the Labour MP George Buchanan, failed in 1924 through a lack of parliamentary time, Muirhead and other nationalists within the SHRA wanted to pursue a more vigorous policy—only to find their endeavours blocked by Labour loyalists within the association.

From 1924 to 1928, when increasing calls were made for the formation of an independent nationalist party, Muirhead began to find common cause with other nationalist organizations. In early 1928 he announced that he would stand as an independent home rule candidate, hoping that Labour would turn a blind eye to this. When they did not he called on all like-minded individuals within the SHRA to follow his lead into the National Party of Scotland, which was formed in April 1928, and of which he was the first chairman. He believed that if the party could make a good showing at the polls it would sting the Labour Party into taking the issue of home rule seriously. The National Party, however, failed to make its breakthrough; Muirhead himself was unsuccessful on the three occasions (1929, 1931, and 1935) when he stood as a nationalist parliamentary candidate for Western Renfrewshire. Lack of electoral success led to serious infighting which saw the party take on a more moderate hue, which was not to Muirhead's liking. This dissatisfaction grew with the formation of the Scottish National Party (SNP) in 1934, which was an amalgam of the NPS and the right-wing Scottish Party. Muirhead was elected honorary president of the SNP in 1936, but played little part in policy formulation. He disliked the party's rightward shift, and its 'moderation of principles' led him to fund the publication of the *Scots Independent*, which provided a forum for radical and anti-leadership views. He also endorsed the anti-conscription campaign run by a number of activists following the start of the Second World War. Muirhead lent his support to the radical wing of the SNP, which eventually triumphed in 1942 and ousted the moderates led by John MacCormick, who went on to found the Scottish National Convention, a cross-party organization designed to promote Scottish home rule.

Frustrated with the lack of direction in the nationalist movement during the post-war era, Muirhead founded his own Scottish National Congress in 1950. He continued to provide funding for nationalist pamphlets and literature through the Scottish Secretariat, which he formed in 1926. On 31 October 1945 he married his housekeeper, Flora Ferrier. A tall and austere figure with sharp features, Muirhead retained the common personality characteristics of the early Scottish socialist movement and was

rather dour and serious. He died at Lochwinnoch, Renfrewshire, on 2 August 1964; he was buried there and was survived by his wife.   RICHARD J. FINLAY

Sources R. J. Finlay, *Independent and free: Scottish politics and the origins of the Scottish national party, 1918–1945* (1994) · H. Corr, 'Muirhead, Roland Eugene', *Scottish labour leaders, 1918–39: a biographical dictionary*, ed. W. Knox (1984) · Mitchell L., Glas., Glasgow City Archives, Muirhead MSS
Archives BLPES, papers · Mitchell L., Glas., Glasgow City Archives, corresp. and papers, incl. memoirs · NL Scot., corresp. and papers | NL Scot., corresp. with Sir Patrick Geddes · NL Scot., Gibson MSS · NL Scot., McIntyre MSS
Wealth at death £22,847 15s. 0d.: confirmation, 23 March 1965, NA Scot., SC 58/46/99

Muirhead, (Litellus) Russell (1896–1976). *See under* Muirhead family (*per.* 1877–1976).

Muir Mackenzie. For this title name *see* Mackenzie, Kenneth Augustus Muir, Baron Muir Mackenzie (1845–1930).

Muirshiel. For this title name *see* Maclay, John Scott, Viscount Muirshiel (1905–1992).

Mujibur Rahman, Sheikh (1920–1975), president of Bangladesh, was born in Tungipara, Faridpur district, Bengal, on 17 March 1920, the first of six children of Sheikh Lutfur Rahman, a middle-class landowner, and Sahera Begum. He had one brother and four sisters. Sheikh Mujibur Rahman (usually referred to as Sheikh Mujib or simply Mujib) married a cousin, Begam Fazilat-un-Nisa. They had three sons and two daughters. Their eldest child, Sheikh Hasina Wajed, who was born on 28 September 1947, became the leader of the Awami League, with which her father was associated throughout most of his active political career.

Mujib studied politics and law at the universities of Calcutta and Dacca but did not receive a degree from either. He was heavily involved with student politics and active in the Muslim League in its campaign to gain the partition of India to create a separate homeland for the Muslims. In 1949 he was associated with Husain Shaheed Suhrawardy, a former premier of Bengal and future prime minister of Pakistan, in the founding of the Awami (People's) Muslim League. This party soon changed its name to the Awami League as it decided to admit non-Muslims, who had been barred from membership in the Muslim League. When the Awami League allied with the Krishak Sramik (Farmers' and Workers') Party to defeat the Muslim League in the 1954 East Bengal provincial election, Mujib became minister of commerce, a posting that is generally judged to have been unsuccessful. His principal role, however, had been and would continue to be as a party organizer. When Suhrawardy died in 1963 Mujib became *de facto* leader of the East Pakistan Awami League.

General Muhammad Ayub Khan had taken control of Pakistan in 1958 and banned political parties. When parties were again legalized in 1962, Mujib and his party demanded greater autonomy for East Pakistan. In January 1966 he startled a meeting of opposition leaders in Lahore, West Pakistan, by putting forward his demands in

Sheikh Mujibur Rahman (1920–1975), by Douglas Miller, 1972

the shape of the Six Points. These suggested a parliamentary system of government to replace the presidential system of Ayub, and a number of economic measures that would have given East Pakistan almost complete control over its assets and foreign exchange earnings. Mujib was arrested a number of times, most notably in 1968 when he and others were accused of conspiring with India to gain independence for East Pakistan. The trial was never completed and Mujib was freed to join negotiations between Ayub and the opposition. These failed, and the failure culminated in the resignation of Ayub in March 1969.

Ayub's successor, General Agha Muhammad Yahya Khan, called for elections in December 1970. In East Pakistan Mujib and his Awami League won 160 of the 162 seats, thereby securing a majority of the 300 seats in the national assembly although winning no seats in West Pakistan. The party campaigned on the Six Points, but as negotiations among Mujib, Yahya, and Zulfikar Ali Bhutto, whose People's Party of Pakistan had won a majority of the seats in West Pakistan, failed to establish a common ground on which the national assembly could begin its deliberations on a new constitution, the stance of many of Mujib's party members, and perhaps of Mujib himself, became one of demanding independence rather than autonomy under the umbrella of a united Pakistan. Mujib delivered an important speech on 7 March 1971 during which he came just short of declaring independence, but then and in the next few days declared that Bangladeshis, as they were coming to be known, should no longer pay taxes or obey Pakistani laws. His almost Gandhian approach however failed, and violence broke

out. On 25 March the Pakistan army, hastily reinforced from West Pakistan, cracked down on Bangladeshis, including a particularly forceful attack on Dacca University. Mujib was arrested and transported to prison in West Pakistan. Civil war had begun and would not end until 16 December 1971, when the Pakistan army in Bangladesh surrendered to the combined forces of the Indian army, which had entered the war in early December, and the Mukti Bahini, the liberation army of Bangladesh.

Mujib was to have been tried for treason but the trial was not completed and he was not sentenced. When Bhutto took over the presidency of Pakistan from Yahya Khan in December he declared that he would release Mujib unconditionally, but expressed his hope that the two wings of Pakistan could be reunited. Mujib was released on 7 January 1972 and returned to Dacca (renamed Dhaka) on 10 January after stopping in London and New Delhi. The welcome to the man who would become known as Bangabandhu (Friend of Bengal) was tumultuous. Mujib had been named president of Bangladesh by the government in exile, but chose instead to be prime minister of his proposed parliamentary system of government. A constitution was adopted in 1972 creating a parliamentary form and enshrining the four principles of Mujibbad (Mujibism): secularism, socialism, democracy, and nationalism.

It turned out, however, that leading a country to independence was less difficult than governing a newly independent state, especially one that had been devastated by the civil war. Mujib relied heavily on socialism, only to see both agricultural and industrial production fail to reach pre-independence levels. Corruption was widespread, notably in the distribution of relief supplies that came from many nations. Despite an overwhelming victory for the Awami League in an election in 1973, in which fraud was widely suspected, opposition to Mujib began to grow rapidly. Near famine conditions in 1974 added to the discontent. He also instituted a special military force, the Rakhi Bahini (defence force), which angered many in the regular army.

On 25 January 1975 Mujib pushed through an amendment to the constitution which created a presidential system with himself as president with nearly full powers. He followed this on 6 June 1975 with the establishment of a single-party state. The new party combined the names of the two major parties that had contested as part of the United Front in 1954: Bangladesh Krishak Sramik Awami League. Neither of these steps quelled the growing opposition in the country at large and in the military.

On 15 August 1975 Mujib was assassinated along with his wife, their three sons, and several other members of his family by disgruntled army officers. The assassination of Mujib and his immediate family took place at his residence on Road 32 in the Dhanmondi residential area of Dhaka; he had not moved into the presidential palace. Two daughters who were out of the country survived: Hasina, later, as noted above, the leader of the Awami League and who became prime minister in 1996, and

Rehana, who resided in Brunei. Mujib's residence was converted into a museum, but in the destruction accompanying the assassinations most of the papers and other property of Mujib was destroyed. He was buried in Tungipara.

The memory of Mujib as the liberator of Bangladesh is honoured; his alteration of a democratic system to an authoritarian one is not. This is perhaps best exemplified by the campaign run by the Awami League in the 1991 election, when it campaigned for a return to a parliamentary system as embodied in the unamended 1972 constitution, and avoided reference to the authoritarian actions taken in 1975. The Awami League won the parliamentary election in 1996.

CRAIG BAXTER

Sources M. Ahmed, *Era of Sheikh Mujibur Rahman* (1983) · C. Baxter, *Bangladesh: from a nation to a state* (1997) · M. A. W. Bhuiyan, *Emergence of Bangladesh and role of the Awami League* (1982) · L. Ziring, *Bangladesh from Mujib to Ershad* (1992) · C. P. O'Donnell, *Bangladesh: biography of a Muslim nation* (1984) · *New York Times* · private information (2004)
Archives FILM BFI NFTVA, documentary footage · BFI NFTVA, news footage
Likenesses D. Miller, photograph, 1972, Hult. Arch. [*see illus.*] · photographs, 1972, Hult. Arch.

Mukasa, Ham [Hamu] (*c.*1871–1956), local administrator and chronicler, was born in Buddu district, Buganda, son of a minor chief, Makabugo Sensalire, who later took the baptismal name of Zakaliya, and his wife, Nyakanzana. When Mukasa was twelve, his father was invited to send a son to serve at the court of Kabaka (King) Mutesa I of Buganda, and Mukasa was chosen. When Mutesa was succeeded by Mwanga in 1884, Mukasa came under the influence of Christian pages who began to teach him to read, as part of the preparation for baptism. He thus became endangered during the persecution of Christians in 1886 and was hidden by a senior chief. He was baptized a protestant in 1887, excused by Mwanga for his absence from court, and given a responsible position. In 1888 war broke out between the younger generation at court, who were attracted by what the newly introduced religions, Islam and Christianity, had to offer, and those loyal to traditional beliefs and customs.

In the wars which followed, the Christian faction seized power. Mukasa proved his valour in this conflict, and in 1889 he was rewarded with a minor chieftaincy. He rose rapidly to a position of influence in the native Anglican church, and served on its church council for many years, becoming a renowned preacher. In 1900 his *Gospel of St Matthew with Commentary* was published. About 1898 he married Hannah Wawemuko (*d.* 1919), daughter of a former chief minister (*katikiro*) of Buganda, with whom he had four children.

In 1902 Mukasa was chosen to accompany Apolo Kagwa, katikiro of Buganda, to the coronation of Edward VII, as Kagwa's secretary. Mukasa's account of the visit was edited and translated by the Revd Ernest Millar, the Cambridge missionary who travelled with them, and published as *Uganda's Katikiro in England* (1904), with an introduction by Sir Harry Johnston. In this detailed and lively narrative Mukasa conveys his admiration for Britain and

struggles to find ways of making his experiences comprehensible to Baganda. Regrettably, the Luganda original has never been traced.

In 1905 Mukasa was appointed county chief of Kyagwe, an important position as the area was close to the capital, and a post which he held until 1942. He resided briefly at Ngogwe and then settled at Mukono, building an impressive house nearby which he named Kwata Mpolo, from a Luganda proverb, 'He who goes slowly goes far'. Here, as well as carrying out his administrative duties, he read widely in Swahili and Luganda, collected clocks, measured the rainfall, and indulged his passion for writing, employing several clerks to type his voluminous correspondence, as well as requiring his large household to attend daily prayers, which he led. A man of many parts, he played several instruments, including the Ganda lute and xylophone, and amassed extensive landholdings.

Perhaps most importantly, Mukasa carried out the research for his three-volume *Simuda nyuma* (*Do not Turn back*), a mixture of history, reminiscence, and moral admonition. Volume 1 appeared in 1938 and covered the reign of Kabaka Mutesa during which Christian missionaries arrived in Uganda, and volume 2 followed in 1942, on the reign of Mwanga, who had persecuted the Christians. Mukasa believed that the British, and the missionaries in particular, had brought much that was good to Uganda and he was an apostle of progress, though loyal to his own culture and tradition. This approach had been briefly foreshadowed in a short autobiography, an English translation of which was appended to J. D. Mullins's *Wonderful Story of Uganda* (1900), and can also be noted in 'The rule of the kings of Buganda' which appeared in the *Uganda Journal* in 1946. Mukasa's writings helped to establish Luganda as a literary language.

About a year after the death of his first wife in 1919 Mukasa married again, to Sarah Nabikolo, with whom he had ten more children. She outlived him. He died on 29 March 1956, leaving thirteen children, about forty grandchildren and nearly thirty great-grandchildren. He also left a huge collection of papers, among which was found a carbon copy of the typescript of volume 3 of *Simuda nyuma*. The top copy had allegedly been sent to Britain for publication, but had disappeared. A few of Ham Mukasa's books and papers are now in the archives of Makerere University, Kampala, but most are still at Kwata Mpolo House, a valuable collection which still awaits full examination.

M. LOUISE PIROUET

Sources J. D. Mullins, *The wonderful story of Uganda* (1904) [incl. an autobiography of Ham Mukasa] · J. A. Rowe, 'Myth, memoir and moral admonition: Luganda historical writing, 1893–1969', *Uganda Journal*, 33 (1969), 17–40 · C. Sebuliba, 'The late Ham Mukasa', *Uganda Journal*, 23 (1959), 184–6 · J. V. Taylor, *The growth of the church in Buganda* (1958) · M. Wright, *Buganda in the heroic age* (1971) · M. Twaddle, *Kakungulu and the creation of Uganda, 1868–1928* (1993) · H. B. Hansen, *Mission, church and state in a colonial setting: Uganda, 1890–1925* (1984) · H. Mukasa, *Sir Apolo Kagwa discovers Britain*, ed. Taban lo Liyong, trans. E. Millar (1975); ed. S. Gikandi (1998)
Archives Kwata Mpolo House, near Mukono, Buganda, Uganda · Makerere University, Kampala, Uganda, archives

Likenesses two photographs, repro. in H. Mukasa, *Uganda's Katikiro in England* (1998)

Mulally, Teresa (1728–1803), educationist, was born in October 1728 in Pill Lane, Dublin, and baptized on 17 October, the only child of Daniel Mulally, a provision dealer, and his wife, Elizabeth. The Mulallys' circumstances were apparently comfortable, and Teresa evidently received a good education. When she was seventeen, however, the family suffered a financial and social reverse which forced Teresa to assume responsibility for her own livelihood. About 1748 she moved to Chester at the invitation of an elderly relative, who died a few years later, leaving her a legacy of £70. With this she returned to Dublin, where she set herself up as a milliner. She was astute and industrious, and her considerable savings were augmented by a win of a few hundred pounds in a state lottery. At the same time, she gained a reputation for piety and charitable activities: 'she made ointments and other medicines for the poor, and dressed their sores; and [she] was always, while able, attentive to her sick friends and neighbours, be they rich or poor' (Savage, 56).

By about 1762 Mulally's parents were dead, and she was in a position to retire from business and to devote herself to her philanthropic interests. In an 'Address to the charitable of St Michan's parish' (MS, 1766, St George's Hill archives, Dublin) she indicated the cause to which she intended to address herself:

> There are none whose necessities require more to be considered than the poor children of the female sex … many of them orphans, and the rest, by the helpless condition of their parents, scarce better than orphans. … [These girls] suffer all the hardships of extreme poverty, but … their chief misfortune is to be without any means of instruction, for want of which they grow up in such habits of ignorance, idleness and vice, as render them for ever after not only useless, but highly pernicious to themselves and the public. (Mulally, 'Address')

In 1766 Mulally set up a charity school for girls in an outhouse in Mary's Lane. As the first Roman Catholic institution of its kind in Dublin, the school placed a heavy emphasis on religious instruction. Pupils were also given some academic schooling and were instructed in such skills as dressmaking and housework, 'whereby they may be rendered useful to society and capable of earning honest bread for themselves' (Mulally, 'Address'). In 1771 she established a boarding-school and orphanage which, like the day school, was funded by donations and by the sale of work produced by the pupils.

As a devout Roman Catholic Mulally was anxious to secure the future of her projects by placing them in the hands of a religious congregation. Aware of the similar work on which Nano Nagle was engaged in Cork, Mulally embarked on a correspondence with her and during a number of visits to Cork discussed the possibility of establishing in Dublin a community of Nagle's Presentation Order (then known as the Society of Charitable Instruction). However, shortage of funds and lack of suitable recruits made such an initiative impracticable before Nagle's death in 1784.

By 1787 Mulally had raised enough money to purchase a site at George's Hill, on which she began to build a school and convent. Meanwhile she sought suitable candidates for the proposed Dublin community and, at her urging, a number of postulants entered the novitiate at the mother house of the Presentation Sisters in Cork. In April 1794 the first two sisters were professed for the Dublin convent. In August Mulally travelled to Cork to meet them and accompanied them back to George's Hill, where they established the first house of the Presentation Sisters in Dublin.

With the arrival of the sisters, Mulally handed over the management of the schools and moved from the convent in which she had been living to the orphanage next door. However, although she did not herself take religious vows, she continued to be closely involved in the affairs of the convent and schools. Described by a friend as 'a very keen woman' with 'a cool head, and a masculine understanding which forecasted for ages' (Savage, 181), her shrewdness and knowledge of business helped to establish the foundation on a firm basis during its early years: in 1798, for instance, she successfully applied to the privy council for the relief of the school, as a charitable institution, from parochial taxes.

Mulally's health was never robust, and her correspondence with Nagle mentions a number of illnesses. In late 1802 her health worsened; she died on 9 February 1803 at George's Hill orphanage and was buried in the convent chapel.   ROSEMARY RAUGHTER

Sources R. B. Savage, *A valiant Dublin woman: the story of George's Hill, 1766–1940* (1940) · A. O'Rahilly, 'A letter about Miss Mulally and Nano Nagle', *Irish Ecclesiastical Record*, 5th ser., 40 (1932), 474–81, 619–24 · T. J. Walsh, *Nano Nagle and the Presentation Sisters* (1959) · R. Raughter, 'A discreet benevolence: female philanthropy and the Catholic resurgence in 18th-century Ireland', *Women's History Review*, 6 (1997), 465–84 · parish register, Dublin, St Michan's, 17 Oct 1728

Archives Presentation Convent Archives, George's Hill, Dublin, archives, address to the charitable of St Michan's parish, letters, annals of Presentation Convent, George's Hill · South Presentation Convent archives, Cork

Wealth at death will detailed: Savage, *Valiant Dublin woman*, 185–7

Mulcahy, Richard (1886–1971), Irish revolutionary and politician, was born on 10 June 1886 at 70 Manor Street, Waterford, Ireland, the second child and first son among the eight children of Patrick Mulcahy (*d.* 1923), Post Office clerk, and Elizabeth Slattery. He was educated by the Christian Brothers first at their Mount Sion School in Waterford (to 1897) and latterly at Thurles, co. Tipperary (1898–1902). Subsequently he attended Kevin Street Technical College (1908) and Bolton Street Technical College (to 1914), both in Dublin, and trained as an engineer in the Post Office. On 2 June 1919 he married, at St Andrew, Dublin, Mary Josephine (Min) O'Ryan (1884–1977) of Tomcoole in co. Wexford. They had six children: Padraig, Risteard, Elizabet, Maire, Neilli, and Sean.

As a middle-class Roman Catholic, Mulcahy was radicalized by the circumstances of the drive for independence. He came of age in a time of intellectual ferment and his nationalism was forged in the familiar nationalist organizations—the Wexford and later Keating branches of the

Gaelic League and the Teeling branch of the Irish Republican Brotherhood (IRB), which Mulcahy joined in 1907. He joined the volunteers—the army that led the fight for independence—at their formation on 23 November 1913 at the Rotunda Rink in Dublin. His vision of Irish nationalism was broad and inclusive. His dream was of a free, united, Christian, Irish-speaking Ireland—virtuous and prosperous.

Mulcahy was in Dublin in the Post Office engineering department when the rising of Easter 1916 began. He joined Thomas Ashe of the Fingal Volunteers as his second in command; their engagement at Ashbourne barracks, co. Meath, on 28 April was one of the few successful actions of the 1916 rising. He was afterwards interned in Fron-goch in Wales. After his release in December of that year as part of a general amnesty he became part of the leadership of the volunteers, first as officer commanding the 2nd Dublin battalion and subsequently as officer commanding the Dublin brigade.

In October 1917 Mulcahy was appointed director of training of the volunteer executive and in March 1918 he was appointed chief of staff of the newly formed general headquarters staff of the Irish Volunteers. As such he became one of the architects of the Anglo-Irish war of independence (1919–22), during which there was a price of £10,000 on his head. With Michael Collins he was responsible for forging the volunteers into the army which, by fighting a guerrilla war, forced the British to concede dominion status to the twenty-six counties of the south. Mulcahy was the linchpin of general headquarters—overseeing the struggle, co-ordinating strategy, and developing a professional general headquarters staff. He remained chief of staff during the six months of the truce up until the ratification of the treaty by the Dáil Éireann in January 1922. He supported the treaty and, with Collins, worked arduously to prevent the army from splitting over the terms of the agreement and to conciliate opponents.

Mulcahy was first elected to the Dáil Éireann in the 1918 election and, apart from interludes following defeats at the general elections of 1937 and 1943, remained a TD until 1961. In January 1922 Mulcahy was appointed minister for defence in the post-treaty Dáil government. When civil war broke out he returned to the army as chief of staff and Michael Collins, who was then chairman of the provisional government and virtual leader of the country, returned to the army as commander-in-chief. These two men guided the free state army through the perils of civil war until Collins was killed on 22 August 1922. Mulcahy, who was passed over in favour of W. T. Cosgrave to lead the government, then became commander-in-chief as well as minister for defence, assuming the awesome responsibility of ensuring the survival of the free state. After Collins's death Mulcahy was the figure of strength who steadied the army, guided it to victory, and then set about the equally difficult task of selective demobilization. His absorption with the army, however, did blind him to the growing anti-military sentiment of some of his cabinet colleagues and at times distorted his judgement. An example of this was his encouragement of the revived

IRB in the army ranks—an initiative intended to counteract IRA influence and promote loyalty to the free state government, but interpreted by some as mutinous conduct.

Mulcahy played an important role in setting ethical boundaries to the conflict during both the Anglo-Irish and civil wars with the aim of forestalling a descent into anarchy. His most controversial policy, the summary execution of untried prisoners, was an attempt to restrain and control violence in the army. This injured the reputation of both him and his cabinet colleagues and would be a significant factor for a long time afterwards in excluding Mulcahy from the pantheon of Irish nationalist heroes. After the civil war he continued as minister for defence in the free state cabinet until the army mutiny of March 1924. A number of senior officers, led by General Liam Tobin, demanded the resignation of the army council, which included Mulcahy. The cabinet, in which elements (most notably Kevin O'Higgins) were extremely wary of the power of the army, ordered an inquiry and—effectively over Mulcahy's head—appointed Eoin O'Duffy, the chief of police, to the army command. On 18 March the mutineers gathered in a Dublin pub with the appearance of hostile intent. The adjutant-general, having consulted Mulcahy, ordered their arrest, upon which the cabinet demanded—and got—the resignation of the army council. By resigning on the call of the government—however unjust that might have been—and by refusing to appeal to the army to repudiate the government's decision, Mulcahy and the generals on the army council affirmed that the new state would be ruled by civilian government, and the army de-politicized. The removal of the Irish army from the political process was one of Mulcahy's most significant contributions to the fledgeling state.

After his resignation as minister for defence Mulcahy was briefly cast into the political wilderness. He chaired the Gaeltacht commission in 1925–6—a post to which he was well suited given his love of the Irish language and his belief in the preservation and development of Irish culture. In 1927, under pressure from the rank and file of the pro-treaty Cumann na nGaedheal, President Cosgrave appointed him minister for local government and public health. He was the president's most active lieutenant and assumed the leadership of the party's successor, Fine Gael, when Cosgrave retired in 1944; having lost his Dublin seat at the previous year's general election Mulcahy found a route back to the Dáil via south Tipperary. He travelled the length and breadth of the twenty-six counties trying to revive the lagging fortunes of Fine Gael. As leader he demonstrated the same qualities as he had when he was chief of staff—dedication, loyalty, organization, hard work, and a determination to succeed. In terms of policy initiatives—particularly in the important area of economic policy—he had less to offer. Under his leadership, however, Fine Gael—which at one stage had looked set for oblivion—remained a major opposition party in Irish politics.

Mulcahy was a moving force behind the formation of the inter-party government in 1948. He organized the coalition and, being still dogged by associations dating from the civil war, stood aside for John Costello, a less controversial member of Fine Gael, to become Taoiseach, thus ensuring that Eamon de Valera and Fianna Fáil would be deprived of power. The inter-party government was defeated in 1951, but was re-elected in 1954 for a further three-year period. On both occasions Mulcahy was minister for education.

Mulcahy resigned the leadership of Fine Gael in October 1959 and left the Dáil at the next election. He spent much of his retirement annotating and sorting his extensive collection of papers which spanned his long and distinguished career. He also recorded numerous conversations with contemporaries, family members, and historians about the revolutionary period.

Mulcahy died on 16 December 1971 of cancer at his home in Temple Villas, Dublin. He was remembered as a 'soldier-patriot-politician', 'a man of idealistic principle', and 'a great Christian gentleman' (Valiulis, 243).

MARYANN GIALANELLA VALIULIS

Sources University College, Dublin, Mulcahy MSS · M. Valiulis, *Portrait of a revolutionary: General Richard Mulcahy and the founding of the Irish Free State* (Dublin, 1992) · R. Mulcahy, *Richard Mulcahy (1886–1971): a family memoir* (Dublin, 1999) · M. Valiulis, *Almost a rebellion: the Irish army mutiny of 1924* (Cork, 1985) · J. J. Lee, *Ireland, 1912–1985* (1989) · M. Laffan, *Resurrection of Ireland* (1999) · R. Dunphy, *The making of Fianna Fáil* (1995) · m. cert.
Archives University College, Dublin, corresp. and papers | Military Archives, Dublin, inspection reports, operations reports, gen. staff instruction · NA Ire., minutes of the executive council, government material · University College, Dublin, Ernest Blythe papers, Ernie O'Malley, Cumann na nGaedheal party minute books
Likenesses L. Whelan, group portrait, 1921, repro. in Valiulis, *Portrait*; priv. coll. [on loan to the Irish army] · S. O'Sullivan, charcoal on paper, 1942, NG Ire. · P. Tuohy, oils, repro. in Valiulis, *Portrait*; priv. coll. · P. Tuohy, oils, NG Ire. · photographs, Hult. Arch.

Mulcahy, Samuel [*name in religion* Columban] (1901–1971), abbot of Nunraw, was born on 26 August 1901 at the postmaster's residence in Thurles, co. Tipperary, Ireland, the son of Patrick Mulcahy (*d.* 1923), postmaster, and his wife, Elizabeth Slattery. His grandmother was a convert to Catholicism from an earnest Quaker family. The intensely religious character of his family is evident in the fact that, of eight children, four of his sisters became nuns and he himself aspired to become a missionary in China. He was educated at the Diocesan College, Ennis, Clare (1913–18), and then at the St Columban Major Seminary, Dalgan Park, co. Louth (1918–23).

Towards the end of his theological studies with the Columban fathers Mulcahy was directed to the silent order, the Cistercians. He became a monk in 1923 at Roscrea Abbey, co. Tipperary, where there was talk of a foundation in China. He was ordained priest, taught philosophy, and directed young student monks. In 1944 he was made prior, and in 1947 he was elected first abbot of Nunraw Abbey, Haddington, East Lothian. The community had been founded the previous year and the new abbot was to direct the erection of this first Scottish Cistercian monastery since the Reformation. Construction commenced in 1954 and labour demands were met by manual labour of the monks aided by generous voluntary lay help over a period of twenty years.

Dom Columban was 'a remarkable man; tiny in stature, full of energy, shrewdness, humour and a true sanctity' (Muggeridge, *The Observer*), and he will be remembered in Scotland for the key role he played in the notable events in Christian ecumenism between 1961 and 1966, prompted by John XXIII's call to the churches to be 'open to the signs of the times'. In Scotland there was little likelihood of the official authorities of the Church of Scotland or the Roman Catholic church making the first move towards each other. However, if 'the future belongs to those who see it first' then Dom Columban was at that happy point of a historic junction of man and moment, for in 1961 he invited leading men and women of the Church of Scotland and the Episcopal church to attend the annual meeting of the Roman Catholic Council of Religious Superiors of which he was chairman. In the interest of informality and friendly dialogue the media were excluded. The reaction of the press was to sensationalize this historic encounter between members of the different churches as 'a secret meeting' with innuendoes of a Roman takeover. Presbyterian ministers rushed to distance themselves from the event. There were impassioned letters to the press. As meetings continued the noted biblical scholar William Barclay solemnly asked readers of the *Scottish Daily Express*, 'Are unity moves in danger of going too fast and too far?', and a vigorous correspondence followed (21 and 22 Nov 1965). These voices were but echoes from a past of intolerance. The actual participants remained enthusiastic and soon their initiative gained official approval. The general assembly of the Church of Scotland gave its first tentative acceptance of such inter-church meetings in 1962. In 1966 Leonard Small made the first formal visit of a moderator of the general assembly of the Church of Scotland to Nunraw, thereby setting a precedent for his successors. In the Roman Catholic church the publication by the Scottish Catholic Episcopal Conference on 26 April 1968 of the *Directory Concerning Ecumenical Matters* proved to be a significant milestone. It established the local application, for Catholics in Scotland, of the directives on ecumenism of the Second Vatican Council.

The ensuing years brought unexpected problems to the abbot. A BBC television documentary on Nunraw Abbey in 1967 portrayed a scene which was very different from the thriving optimism of the fifties and early sixties. In the presenter, Malcolm Muggeridge, Dom Columban found a soulmate who shared his concern for the changing attitudes in society, in the church, and in the monastic community. He had the joy of seeing the new abbey ready for occupation in 1969 and felt it was a good time to retire. He continued his monastic life of prayer, spiritual reading, and manual labour; he planted a copse of trees beside the abbey. In June 1971, suffering from high blood pressure, he was taken to St Raphael's Hospital, Edinburgh, and died there on 10 July. He was buried at Nunraw Abbey. 'A man of God', was the conclusion of a BBC tribute by Presbyterian minister Roddie Smith (private information); he had been a good friend and ally from the start in the work for Christian unity.

The building of a monastery on the Lammermuir hills, and the building up of the churches in closer relationship, are the lasting marks of this abbot's remarkable achievements.　　　　　DONALD McGLYNN

Sources personal knowledge (2004) · private information (2004) · Nunraw Abbey, Haddington, East Lothian, Nunraw Abbey files and archives · *Scottish Daily Express* (21 Nov 1965) · *Scottish Daily Express* (22 Nov 1965) · *Scottish Catholic Herald* (26 April 1968) · M. Muggeridge, *The Observer* (20 Aug 1967) · M. Muggeridge, *The Listener* (21 Aug 1967) · M. Muggeridge, *Jesus rediscovered* (1969) **Archives** Nunraw Abbey, Garvald, Haddington, archives and files | FILM BFI NFTVA | SOUND BBC Scotland, Glasgow **Likenesses** G. Sherry, portrait, 1960–69, Nunraw Abbey, Haddington · photographs, Nunraw Abbey, Haddington

Mulcaster, Sir Frederick William (1772–1846), army officer, eldest son of Major-General G. F. Mulcaster, Royal Engineers, was born in St Augustine, Florida, on 25 June 1772. After attending the Royal Military Academy, Woolwich, he received a commission as second lieutenant in the Royal Artillery on 2 June 1792, and in June 1793 he was transferred to the Royal Engineers. He was made first lieutenant in November 1793 before being sent to Portsmouth. In early 1795 he was appointed assistant quartermaster-general in the south-western district. He designed the encampments at Weymouth which were frequently visited by George III and the royal family.

On 1 January 1797 Mulcaster sailed for Portugal and made a military survey of the potential theatre of war there. He then served as military secretary successively to General the Hon. Sir Charles Stuart and Lieutenant-General Fraser. On 11 September 1798 Mulcaster was promoted captain-lieutenant; later that year he was commanding engineer at the siege of Cindadella in Minorca. He was actively employed in Mediterranean operations until 1801, becoming military secretary successively to Sir Charles Stuart, General Fox, and Lord Roslyn. Mulcaster acted as colonial secretary of Minorca after its capture, and as judge of the vice-admiralty court in the Mediterranean. He held the latter appointment for almost two years. Of the 800 prize causes over which he presided only five resulted in appeals to England. His decisions in these were confirmed.

In June 1801 Mulcaster was appointed under-secretary to Lord Chatham, master-general of the ordnance. On 21 September 1802 he was promoted captain, and in December 1803 he was appointed commanding royal engineer and inspector of the royal gunpowder factories at Faversham and Waltham Abbey. On 25 July 1810 he became a brevet major, and on 1 May 1811 a regimental lieutenant-colonel. In January 1812 he was appointed commanding royal engineer of Mauritius and Bourbon and its dependencies. He also acted as surveyor-general and was temporarily the colonial secretary of those colonies. He assumed command of Bourbon at a tense time, the lieutenant-governor having been supplanted, and received the governor's gratitude for restoring peace in the colony through his judicious conduct.

Mulcaster was promoted colonel on 7 February 1817. He returned to England in July of that year, and was placed on half pay in August, when the engineering corps was reduced in size. He was married twice. On 2 September 1804 he married Mary Lucy, youngest daughter of John Montrésor of Belmont, Kent and Portland Place, London, and granddaughter of James Gabriel Montrésor. They had one son, Frederick Montrésor. On 10 September 1822 Mulcaster married Esther, only daughter of William Harris of Petham, Kent. Mulcaster was made a KCH for his services in 1832, and received the reward for distinguished service. He was placed on full pay again on 15 April 1824, and was promoted major-general on 27 May 1825. He served in various capacities on the staff at home, and on 16 July 1834 was appointed inspector-general of fortifications, a post he held until his resignation in July 1845. He was promoted lieutenant-general on 28 June 1838. Mulcaster died at Charlton Park, near Canterbury, Kent, on 28 January 1846.　　　R. H. VETCH, *rev.* S. KINROSS

Sources J. Philippart, ed., *The royal military calendar*, 3rd edn, 5 (1820) · W. Porter, *History of the corps of royal engineers*, 2 vols. (1889) · Chatham, Royal Engineers' Records · PRO, War Office Records · Burke, *Gen. GB* (1893) · J. Haydn, *The book of dignities: containing rolls of the official personages of the British empire* (1851) · A. B. Rodger, *The war of the second coalition: 1798–1801, a strategic commentary* (1964) · R. Muir, *Britain and the defeat of Napoleon, 1807–1815* (1996) · *GM*, 2nd ser., 25 (1846), 425

Mulcaster, Richard (1531/2–1611), schoolmaster and author, was born in or near Carlisle, the son of William Mulcaster, alderman and later MP for that city, and his wife, Margaret. There may have been other children: Robert Mulcaster, possibly a brother, was also returned as MP for Carlisle in 1572, but died after the first session. The family was well established in southern Cumberland. Richard went to Eton College, where he was a king's scholar, and matriculated at King's College, Cambridge, aged sixteen, on 15 August 1548. During his undergraduate years he transferred to Peterhouse, from where he commenced BA in 1554. He did not complete the MA at Cambridge, for in May 1556 he applied for admission to Christ Church, Oxford, and on 17 December he proceeded MA. Perhaps some time during the period 1554–6 he lived in London, for on 4 December 1555 a Richard Mulcaster was to be taken to the Tower and possibly tortured, 'vehemently suspect' of having stolen from his master Dr John Caius, the famous physician and later founder of Gonville and Caius College, who was in London in the 1550s (*APC*, 1554–6, 198). Mulcaster may have completed his degree at Oxford to escape the powerful influence of Caius in Cambridge.

By 1559 Mulcaster had settled in London. In that year he served in Elizabeth's first parliament as one of the two members from Carlisle. He also participated in the pageant welcoming Elizabeth into the city of London, and wrote out its narrative in a book that was then given to the queen; Mulcaster was paid 40s. for it. The book was probably the original of a pamphlet entitled *The Quenes Maiesties Passage*, which appeared in the same year under the imprint of Richard Tottel. Although the printed work is now attributed to Mulcaster by many scholars, he himself describes his *Positions*, published in 1581, as 'my first travell, that ever durst venture upon the print' (Mulcaster, 3).

Mulcaster probably started teaching about the same year as the pageant, and on 13 May 1560 he married Katherine Ashley at the parish church of St Michael Cornhill, London. Nevertheless, the first record of his teaching is his appointment in September 1561 as the first headmaster of Merchant Taylors' School in London, soon to become one of the largest schools in England. He remained there until 1586 when, after a dispute with the merchant taylors over salary, he quit the school. Thomas Fuller (whose son later studied under Mulcaster at St Paul's School) says his parting shot was the bitter 'Fidelis servus perpetuus asinus' ('a faithful servant is ever a beast of burden'; Fuller, 149–50). For the next ten years Mulcaster taught and served as a minister, although there is no record of his ordination. He had a school somewhere outside London and then in the city, on Milk Street, and preached in Lincoln's Inn. Although in 1584 he was given a lease of lands in Middlesex and Devon, he received no living until he was made vicar of Cranbrooke, Kent, on 1 April 1590 and prebendary of Yatesbury, Sarum, on 29 April 1594. In 1598 he was presented with the rectory of Stanford Rivers in Essex. In the record of the visitation of 1606, the parishioners reported 'our parson is not resident' and the church was in disrepair (Essex RO, Chelmsford archdeaconry reg. D/AEV.4, fol. 64v).

In 1596 the Mercers' Company, which governed St Paul's School, turned to Mulcaster for help in a crisis. John Harrison, the high-master, had been asked to leave the school, but refused. Mulcaster taught the boys in a temporary school a short way off and, when the old master was gone, was named as his replacement. He stayed at St Paul's until his retirement twelve years later, a venerable figure, perhaps terrifying to boys—the biographer Thomas Fuller describes him as 'plagosus Orbilius', a reference to Horace's cruel schoolmaster. Although Mulcaster had encouraged his boys at Merchant Taylors' in acting, the revival of the Children of Paul's was the work of Edward Pearce, the choirmaster. In 1608 he left St Paul's on a pension and moved to Stanford Rivers, where there is a brass memorial to his wife, Katherine, who died there on 6 August 1609. Mulcaster died on 15 April 1611 and on the 16th he was buried in the church, next to his wife. He left no will, but the administration of his estate, valued at £89 17s. 7d., was given to his son Peter (there were five other children: Margery, Silvan, Ann, Katherine, and Walter).

From the few accounts available, Mulcaster was a gifted teacher. Along with giving exceptional training in Greek and Latin, he encouraged acting; his boys appeared in performances at court at least five times. Many of his pupils at Merchant Taylors' went on to distinguished careers in the professions, principally in the church. Bishop Lancelot Andrewes especially admired him, and kept a portrait (now lost) of his old master over his study door. Andrewes also supported Mulcaster and his family, and there is a bequest to Peter Mulcaster, Richard's son, in Andrewes's

will. The poet Edmund Spenser was, however, his best-known pupil (it has been ingeniously argued that old 'Master Wrenock' in *The Shepheardes Calender* is an anagram of Mulcaster, 'Mast. Wrenock' being 'Mownckaster').

Mulcaster was a good scholar in Latin and Greek. Hugh Broughton, the Hebraist, described him with a back-handed compliment as 'the best learned in the world in his owne conceit, reasonably in Heathen Greeks in deed' (Broughton, 40). Mulcaster is often said to have been a first-rate Hebraist, but there is no evidence for the claim, for it is certain that Broughton would have mentioned it. On at least one occasion the boys were examined in the Hebrew psalms, so it must have been a school subject. Sir James Whitelock describes having studied Latin, Greek, and Hebrew at Merchant Taylors': he adds that he went to a special tutor for the Hebrew. Certainly Mulcaster kept company for a while with some of the most learned men in England and abroad. There was a letter from Mulcaster to Philip Sidney, dated 3 November 1571. He was especially close to Emmanuel van Meteren, the Dutch merchant and historian who lived in London, having written verses to him in his *album amicorum* (Bodl. Oxf., MS Douce 68). He was a correspondent with Abraham Ortelius, Janus Gruter mentions him in a poem to William Camden of 21 June 1590, and he was known to Carolus Utenhovius and to Janus Dousa. He wrote a Latin quatrain, dated 15 August 1584, in Dousa's *Album amicorum*. Mulcaster also wrote verses for the lord mayor's pageants of 1561 and 1568 and for the queen's reception at Kenilworth. In 1573 he wrote commendatory verses in Latin for J. Baret's polyglot *Alvearie, or, Triple Dictionary*, reprinted in 1580 in the *Alvearie, or, Quadruple Dictionarie*. He also wrote verses in 1575 for the *Sacrae cantiones* of Tallis and Byrd; in 1582 for C. Ocland, *Anglorum praelia*; in 1583 for Claude Holiband (Desainliens), *Campo di fior or else the flourie field of foure languages*; and in 1598 for Richard Hakluyt's *Principal Navigations*. The commendation for the work by V. Strigelius, translated by R. Robinson as *A Third Proceeding in the Harmonie of King Davids Harp* (1595), is in English prose; and in 1578 he wrote a distich in honour of Henry Dowe, one of his former pupils, who died while an undergraduate at Christ Church, Oxford (transcribed by Anthony Wood some time before 1694).

Mulcaster's two books on education, *Positions Concerning the Training up of Children* and *The First Part of the Elementarie* are the first two sections (an introduction and 'first part') of an ambitious and learned, though unfinished, analysis of the education of his time. *Positions*, dedicated to Elizabeth I, set out his basic principles of education, which, following Plato and Aristotle, was to be organized around the needs of the state, and which was to be open to all, rich and poor, male and female (though he did not approve of women continuing in school). Much of *Positions* is given over to an argument in favour of physical education (with medical information borrowed from H. Mercurialis, *De arte gymnastica libri sex*, 1569, but imaginatively reorganized for the English context). Although cautious in its recommendations, the work is remarkably open-minded.

The First Part of the Elementarie, dedicated to the earl of Leicester, takes the reader through some of the grounding principles of the 'elements' (or beginning subjects) and then sets out an elaborate theory of spelling reform. Ben Jonson, who also owned a copy of *Positions*, relied heavily on parts of the book for his *English Grammar*. The 'Peroration' or concluding statement to the *Elementarie* is a defence of the general procedure of argument adopted in both treatises, and is Mulcaster's best sustained piece of writing. It is there that he defends his decision to write his books in English: 'I love *Rome*, but *London* better, I favor *Italie*, but England more, I honor the *Latin*, but I worship the *English*' (sig. Hh 1v). Mulcaster was read and remembered in the next century for his educational writings by Charles Hoole and John Aubrey, among others.

During his years at St Paul's, Mulcaster began writing again. *Poemata*, listed in the Bright sale at Sothebys, March–April 1845, item 4611, as a duodecimo of 1599, is a lost book. The first edition of *Catechismus Paulinus* was perhaps published in 1599 or early 1600 (what may be the first edition, in the St Paul's School Library, lacks a title-page). *Cato Christianus*, an elementary textbook in verse, appeared in 1600. This work has an important preface that recapitulates many of the themes of *Positions*. At the death of Elizabeth, Mulcaster wrote a long poem in Latin entitled *In mortem serenissimae reginae Elizabethae, naenia consolans*, and with it an English version, *The Translation of Certaine Latine Verses*, both published in 1603. It seems appropriate, if his first writing had indeed been for Elizabeth's entry into London in 1559, that his last might be a 'latine Oration' in the entry pageant for James, '*Viva voce* delivered by one of maister *Mulcasters* Schollers, at the dore of the free-schole fownded by the Mercers' (Dekker, sigs. H1v–2v).   WILLIAM BARKER

Sources R. DeMolen, *Richard Mulcaster (c. 1531–1611) and educational reform in the Renaissance* (1991) · Fuller, *Worthies* (1662), under 'Westmerland', 3.149–50 · Wood, *Ath. Oxon.*, new edn, 2.93–5 · A. Wood, *The history and antiquities of the colleges and halls in the University of Oxford*, ed. J. Gutch, 3 vols. in 4 (1786–96), vol. 3, p. 484 · [H. Ellis], 'Biographical anecdotes of Richard Mulcaster', *GM*, 1st ser., 70 (1800), 419–21, 511–12, 603–4 · H. B. Wilson, *The history of Merchant-Taylors' School*, 2 vols. (1814), 85ff. · Venn, *Alum. Cant.*, 1/3.226 · T. A. Walker, *A biographical register of Peterhouse men*, 1 (1927), 181 · Cooper, *Ath. Cantab.*, 3.40–43 · HoP, *Commons, 1558–1603*, 3.108–9 · M. McDonnell, *The annals of St Paul's School* (privately printed, Cambridge, 1959), 164–82 · F. W. M. Draper, *Four centuries of Merchant Taylors' School, 1561–1961* (1962) · W. Barker and J. Chadwick, 'Richard Mulcaster's preface to *Cato Christianus* (1600): a translation and commentary', *Humanistica Lovaniensia*, 42 (1993), 32–67 · R. Mulcaster, *Positions concerning the training up of children*, ed. W. Barker (1994) · C. B. Millican, 'Notes on Mulcaster and Spenser', *ELH: a Journal of English Literary History*, 6 (1939), 211–16 · T. Dekker, *The magnificent entertainment given to King James* (1604) · Essex RO, Chelmsford, Chelmsford archdeaconry reg. D/AEV.4, fol. 64v · H. Broughton, *An explication* (1605) · L. Forster, *Janus Gruter's English years* (1967) · L. Forster, 'The translator of the *Theatre for worldlings*', *English Studies*, 48 (1967), 27–34 · J. A. van Dorsten, *Poets, patrons, and professors* (1962) · J. A. van Dorsten, *The radical arts*, 2nd edn (1973) · C. R. Baskervill, 'Richard Mulcaster', *TLS* (15 Aug 1935), 513 · R. Mulcaster, *The first part of the elementarie which entreateth chefelie of the right writing of our English tung* (1582)
Wealth at death £89 17s. 7d.: DeMolen, *Richard Mulcaster*

Mulgrave. For this title name *see* Sheffield, Edmund, first earl of Mulgrave (1565–1646); Sheffield, Edmund, second earl of Mulgrave (1611–1658); Phipps, Constantine John, second Baron Mulgrave in the peerage of Ireland and Baron Mulgrave in the peerage of Great Britain (1744–1792); Phipps, Henry, first earl of Mulgrave (1755–1831).

Mulhall, Michael George (1836–1900), statistician and journalist, was born on 29 September 1836 at 100 St Stephen's Green, Dublin, the third son of Edward Thomas Mulhall, solicitor. He was educated at the Irish College, Rome, and in 1858 went to South America where his brother, Edward Thomas Mulhall (1832–1899) was working as a sheep farmer. The brothers set up a printing and publishing house in Buenos Aires from which they issued the *Standard and River Plate News*, a four-page weekly newspaper. In 1861 they relaunched it as a daily; Mulhall edited it until he left Argentina in 1878, and maintained his link with it (in 1882 the title was shortened to *The Standard*) until 1884; the paper was, for a century, the doyen of the Argentine press. The brothers also published annually, from 1861 to 1885, the *Handbook of the River Plate*, in English and Spanish. The *Handbook*, replete with description and statistics covering Paraguay and the province which became Uruguay, was intended to encourage immigration from Europe. Although criticized by their fellow Irish for being too favourable towards England, the brothers were highly respected in Buenos Aires.

Some time before 1876 Mulhall married Marion (d. in or after 1911), economist and daughter of E. Macmorrough Murphy, a member of an old Irish family. Their voyage to Buenos Aires was followed by a 2400 mile journey by river steamer through northern Argentina and southern Brazil: Marion Mulhall was the first 'Englishwoman' (as she described herself) to have reached Cuiabá, the capital of Mato Grosso. Both published accounts of this exploit: Mulhall's *Journey to Matto Grosso, September 1876* (1879) was preceded by his wife's *From Europe to Paraguay and Matto Grosso* (1877). She later published *Between the Amazon and Andes, or, Ten years of a lady's travels in the pampas, Gran Chaco, … and Matto Grosso* (1881), for which she received a complimentary diploma from the Royal Italian Geographical Society. The Mulhalls' only child died at Buenos Aires in 1886.

Mulhall's books fall into two categories: travel accounts and statistical compilations. *The cotton fields of Paraguay and Corrientes: being an account of a tour through these countries, preceded by annals of cotton planting in the River Plate territories, from 1862 to 1864* (1864) described his travels in search of supplies of raw cotton to replace those made unavailable by the American Civil War. *The Rio Grande do Sul and its German Colonies* (1873) and *The English in South America* (1878), which described English, Scots, and Irishmen in that continent since the sixteenth century, also carried statistical information.

After his return to Ireland in 1878 Mulhall continued with statistical compilation because he regarded statistics as having great usefulness. His *History of Prices since the Year 1850* (1885) was embellished with coloured diagrams, as

Michael George Mulhall (1836–1900), by Lundstrom, pubd 1900

was the *Balance-Sheet of the World for Ten Years, 1870–1880* (1881). *Industries and Wealth of Nations* (1896) also offered the data in a manner suitable for popular comprehension. His *Dictionary of Statistics* (1884) went through several editions and was last published in 1970. When it first appeared it was the largest single-volume statistical publication in the world, often drawing on foreign official sources, both ancient and modern. Mulhall was unique in his time as an individual compiler, as opposed to government statistical bureaux. He urged the creation of an international statistical bureau and criticized the British government for its indifference to comparative international data.

Mulhall wrote many articles for the *Contemporary Review* after 1880. He was a member of the Royal Society of Arts from 1880; a committee member of the British Association for the Advancement of Science from 1884; a fellow of the Statistical Society; and an honorary corresponding member of the Scottish Geographical Society. In 1896 he travelled in western Europe collecting material for a planned Irish agricultural department. Marion Mulhall was one of the few members of the Roman Arcadia, a society founded in 1690 for the encouragement of science, letters, and arts, elected by virtue of her historical researches, and Mulhall was *cameriere segreto* of the Pope, who sent him a papal blessing *in articulo mortis*. He died at his home, The Peak, Killiney Park, Dublin, on 12 December 1900, and was buried at Glasnevin cemetery.

THOMAS SECCOMBE, *rev.* PHILIP A. HUNT

Sources *The Tablet* (15 Dec 1900), 939 · *The Tablet* (22 Dec 1900), 984 · *The Times* (14 Dec 1900), 10d · *ILN* (15 Dec 1900), 929 · Boase, *Mod. Eng. biog.* · H. Boylan, *A dictionary of Irish biography* (1978) · J. S. Crone, *A concise dictionary of Irish biography*, rev. edn (1937) · Allibone, *Dict.* · *Men and women of the time* (1899) · *WWW, 1897–1915* · J. J. Delaney and J. E. Tobin, *Dictionary of Catholic biography* (Garden City, NY, 1961), 832 · A. G. Youll, *The forgotten colony* (1981)

Likenesses Lundstrom, engraving, NPG; repro. in *ILN* [*see illus.*] · M. M. Mulhall, engraving, repro. in M. M. Mulhall, *Explorers in the New World before and after Columbus* (1909), frontispiece

Mulholland, Andrew (1791–1866), cotton and linen manufacturer, born on 2 February 1791 at Belfast, came of an old Ulster family. He married in 1817 Elizabeth, daughter of Thomas McDonnell of Belfast. His father, Thomas, was in 1819 head of Thomas Mulholland & Co., a firm of cotton manufacturers of Union Street, Belfast. Andrew was employed in this firm, which, on the death of his father, was carried on by himself and a brother, Thomas, under the title of T. and A. Mulholland. On 10 June 1828 their cotton mill in York Street was burned down. No machinery capable of spinning high-quality yarn had yet been introduced into the manufacture of linen at Belfast, but Andrew had observed that the supply of yarns made by hand was quite insufficient to meet the demands of the Belfast spinners, and that quantities of flax were shipped across to Manchester to be spun and reimported as yarn. He accordingly decided in 1828 to install the newly invented wet flax-spinning machinery in a small mill in St James's Street, and subsequently equipped the rebuilt mill in York Street with the same machinery. The first bundle of flax yarns produced by machinery in Belfast was thrown off in 1830 from the York Street mill; the firm of Murland, however, disputed priority with the Mulhollands in the introduction of wet-spinning, but the Mulhollands factory was the first to use steam power. A decade later Mulhollands was one of thirty-five flax-spinning mills in Ulster, and one of the largest, employing 900 workers and containing 15,000 spindles. Power was generated by three steam engines supplying a total of 115 hp. The firm remained a major employer in Belfast until well into the twentieth century.

After his brother Thomas's death Andrew carried on the business single-handed. On the grant of a corporation to Belfast in 1842 Andrew became a member of it, was mayor in 1845, and presented the town with the organ in Ulster Hall at a cost of £3000. In 1846 he retired to Springvale, Ballywalter, co. Down, and subsequently became justice of the peace, deputy lieutenant, and served as high sheriff for co. Down and Antrim. He died on 24 August 1866 at Springvale. His son, John *Mulholland (1819–1895), assisted Cobden in his negotiation of a commercial treaty with Napoleon III in 1860, entered parliament as member for co. Down in 1874, sat for Downpatrick, 1880–85, and was in 1892 raised to the peerage of the United Kingdom under the title of Baron Dunleath of Ballywalter.

A. F. POLLARD, *rev.* L. A. CLARKSON

Sources P. Ollerenshaw, 'Industry, 1820–1914', *An economic history of Ulster, 1820–1940*, ed. L. Kennedy and P. Ollerenshaw (1987), 69–71 · E. R. R. Green, *The Lagan valley, 1800–50: a local history of the industrial revolution* (1949), 112–15 · W. A. McCutcheon, *The industrial archaeology of Northern Ireland* (1980), 296–7 · A. Takei, 'The first Irish linen mills, 1800–1824', *Irish Economic and Social History*, 21 (1994), 28–38 · *CGPLA NIre.* (1866)

Archives PRO NIre., letters to James Emerson Tennent

Wealth at death under £70,000 in Great Britain and Ireland: probate, 6 Nov 1866, *CGPLA Ire.*

Mulholland, John, first Baron Dunleath (1819–1895), textile manufacturer, was born at Belfast on 16 December 1819, the only son of Andrew *Mulholland (1791–1866) and his wife, Elizabeth, *née* MacDonnell. In 1840, following education at Belfast Royal Academy, John Mulholland went into partnership with his father. The elder Mulholland remains one of the most famous figures in the history of the Ulster linen industry who, together with his brother, Thomas, introduced the wet-spinning of flax into Belfast in 1828, using steam-powered machinery. When John Mulholland joined the firm twelve years later, the Mulholland mill was one of the largest of thirty-five flax-spinning enterprises in Ulster, employing 900 workers and containing 15,000 spindles. John Mulholland became the sole proprietor in 1846, when his father withdrew to the rural pleasures of Ballywalter Park, later known as Springvale, purchased from the Matthews family, who had owned it from early in the century.

In 1851 Mulholland married Frances Louise, daughter of Hugh Lyle of Knockintarn, co. Londonderry. They had three sons. Mulholland took as his managing partner his sister's husband, Nicholas de la Cherois Crommelin, and together they created an integrated spinning and weaving business, reorganized in 1851 as the York Street Flax Spinning Company. Crommelin retired in 1860 and was replaced by Ogilvy Blair Graham. The company prospered during the cotton famine of the 1860s and adopted limited liability in 1865—one of the first businesses in Ireland to do so—with a nominal share value of £500,000. It survived the depression that followed the American Civil War by careful attention to overseas marketing and further integration. Branches were opened in Paris (1870), New York (1871), Berlin (1872), London (1874), and Melbourne (1892). In 1883 it purchased a bleach works at Muckamore in co. Antrim. By the time John Mulholland died, the York Street Flax Spinning Company was the largest integrated flax-spinning and -weaving business in the world.

Although Mulholland remained nominally in control, his connection with the business became increasingly tenuous, and he left the day-to-day supervision to the board of directors, including R. R. Reade and Sir William Crawford. When the firm adopted limited liability, he sold a substantial portion of his personal shares for £164,250 and with the proceeds of the sale purchased the Southwell estate, property of the former lord of the manor in Downpatrick, co. Down, as well as land in co. Tyrone—adopting, as his father had done, the lifestyle of a country gentleman. Mulholland also became well known, in Britain, if not in Ireland, as an enthusiastic yachtsman, the owner of the *Egeria*. When he died, the *Northern Whig* (13 December 1895) commented, a little tartly, that 'he has for the past quarter of a century been seen very little in Belfast'. The *News Letter* (13 December 1895) was more charitable, declaring that he 'never lost his interest in Belfast and its people'.

These conflicting assessments of Mulholland's later life stemmed in part from the different political perspectives of the two newspapers, for Mulholland had political ambitions in the Conservative and Unionist cause. At the 1868 general election the Belfast Conservative Association nominated Sir Charles Lanyon, architect and former lord mayor, together with Mulholland as candidates. Mulholland was unpopular among working men, which may indicate his reputation as an employer, and they ran a small-time Orange landowner against him. Mulholland lost. However, in 1874 he was elected for the tiny constituency of Downpatrick (dismissed contemptuously by the *Northern Whig* as a pocket borough), and remained an MP until the seat was abolished in 1885.

As a political figure Mulholland's achievements were modest. In 1860 he was 'one of those chosen to consider and report on the negotiations for a commercial treaty with France'. In 1868 he served on a royal commission appointed to consider the advantages of the state buying the Irish railways. He was high sheriff for co. Down in 1868 and for co. Tyrone in 1873. He was a JP for co. Antrim and co. Down, and deputy lieutenant for co. Antrim. He received an honorary LLD from Trinity College, Dublin in 1881. In 1892 he was raised to the peerage as Baron Dunleath of Ballywalter, co. Down.

Mulholland's other principal interest was the Church of Ireland. He assisted in the financial settlement following disestablishment in 1869, and was a member of the general synod, and the synods of the dioceses of Down and Connor, and Dromore. He was a generous supporter of the Church of Ireland Young Men's Society. He died at his London home, 7 Eaton Square, on 11 December 1895 after a long illness, and was buried on 17 December at the family home, Springvale, in the parish of Ballywalter. His wife survived him and his eldest son, Herbert Lyle Mulholland (1854–1931), succeeded to the title.

L. A. CLARKSON

Sources *Northern Whig* (13 Dec 1895) · *Belfast News-Letter* (13 Dec 1895) · E. Boyle, 'Mulholland, John', *DBB* · I. Budge and C. O'Leary, *Belfast: approach to crisis. A study of Belfast politics, 1613–1970* (1973) · d. cert.
Wealth at death £583,266 17s. 3d.: probate, 1 Feb 1896, *CGPLA Ire.*

Mulira, Eridadi Medadi Kasirye (1909–1995), politician and publisher in Uganda, was born on 28 February 1909 in Kamese, a remote part of Koki, once an independent territory in the south-west of the Buganda kingdom, the central heartland of the Uganda protectorate under British rule. He was one among the sixteen children of Nathaniel Ndaula Mulira, a Koki prince, chief, teacher, and evangelist, brought up by one of the pioneer Anglican missionaries and his wife, Esteri. Mulira attended Uganda's leading school, King's College Budo, before completing his education at Makerere College, Kampala, and at the Prince of Wales Teacher Training College, Achimota, Gold Coast. On 7 January 1939 he married Rebecca Mukasa Allen (c.1920–2001), daughter of chief Ham Mukasa. Rebecca was active in church work, public service, and women's movements until her death in 2001. They had seven children, two daughters and five sons.

Trained as a secondary schoolteacher, Mulira served on numerous educational and cultural committees and wrote several books, poems, and plays, contributing to *A Luganda Grammar* (1954), considered one of the best Bantu grammars published at the time. In 1947 he was granted a colonial scholarship to study linguistics in London and for a year acted as assistant lecturer at the School of Oriental and African Studies. He edited several newspapers and from 1953 to 1961 was the proprietor of *Uganda Empya*, one of the first independent papers in the country. A committed Anglican, Mulira also undertook a number of church responsibilities and in 1948 attended the first meeting of the World Council of Churches in Amsterdam.

Mulira was best known for his political activities. He was particularly concerned about the implications of genuinely representative and democratic government for Uganda. In 1950 the Fabian Colonial Bureau published his *Troubled Uganda*, an analysis of contemporary politics still quoted by historians today. On 28 November 1953 Mulira was elected to the Buganda *lukiko* (local parliament) only two days before the *kabaka*, Mutesa II, was exiled to Britain for refusing to co-operate with British constitutional plans. Mulira played a key role in the negotiations for the *kabaka*'s return, acting as a member of a *lukiko* delegation and of a committee chaired by Sir (William) Keith Hancock to discuss constitutional reform.

Hancock warmly acknowledged Mulira's contribution, describing him as a man who 'served God in both Church and State' (Hancock, 108). Mulira's Christianity informed his politics. In January 1955 he founded the Progressive Party, a grouping of mainly Buganda protestant intellectuals which was tacitly supported by the Anglican church, and he was its president until 1959. Mulira's party was critical of Buganda's chiefs, opposing plans to grant them extra *mailo* land and calling for an end to corruption in the Buganda government. Unsurprisingly, Mulira rapidly lost official favour and in July 1956 was expelled from the *lukiko* on a tendentious charge of insulting the *kabaka*, though the ruling was later overturned by a protectorate court.

The place of Buganda in the post-colonial state was a particularly thorny issue in the run-up to decolonization in Uganda. In such a highly charged political context, Mulira's moderate Progressives were unable to attract popular support. Attempting to regain the initiative, in 1959 Mulira joined the more radical, pro-Buganda National Movement which organized the 1959 trade boycott of Asian traders. Owing to the accompanying violence, the movement was proscribed and on the governor's orders Mulira was temporarily deported to northern Uganda. A highly principled, if ambitious, politician, Mulira described his actions as a change only of tactics, insisting that he remained 'a Christian nationalist' (Mulira to H. M. Grace, *c*.September 1959, 02 Bp 211/26, Namirembe archives, Uganda). The bishop of Uganda, Leslie Brown, still looked on him 'with pride and affection to give a really Christian lead' in Ugandan politics (ibid., L. Brown to Mulira, 22 June 1960).

Yet Mulira was never able to find a mass following for his 'Christian nationalism'. After his return from exile, he joined Kabaka Yekka, the 'King Alone' movement (becoming its publicity secretary in 1963) and in February 1962 was re-elected, as a Kabaka Yekka candidate, to the *lukiko*. From there he was selected to represent Buganda in the national assembly, and he was a member of parliament when Uganda became independent in October 1962. In the turbulence of independent Uganda, Mulira was one of

only four MPs prepared to vote against the Obote constitution of April 1966. Thereafter he took a less prominent political role, focusing instead on church, publishing, and business activities. After the overthrow of the Idi Amin (1979) and second Obote governments (1985), in the more stable years before his death under President Museveni, Mulira again became active in local government. He died in Uganda on 24 March 1995.   CAROLINE HOWELL

Sources *New Vision* [Uganda] (11 April 1995) · *Who's who in East Africa, 1967–1968* (1968) · M. L. Pirouet, *Historical dictionary of Uganda* (1995) · D. E. Apter, *The political kingdom in Uganda: a study in bureaucratic nationalism*, rev. 3rd edn (1997) · D. A. Low, 'Political parties in Uganda', *Buganda in modern history* (1971), 167–226 · *Uganda Argus* (25 April 1958) · *Uganda Argus* (21 Oct 1958) · *Uganda Argus* (26 Feb 1959) · *Uganda Argus* (8 July 1959) · *Uganda Argus* (24 Feb 1962) · *Uganda Argus* (27 April 1962) · 'E. M. K. Mulira', [n.d., *c*.1949], Bodl. RH, Fabian Colonial Bureau 33/3, MS Brit. Emp.s.365 · 'Brief biographical notes on members of the Hancock committee', 22 June 1954, PRO, CO 822/894 · W. K. Hancock, 'Thinking and doing: Buganda', *Professing History* (1976), 90–109 · 'Notes of talk given by E. M. K. Mulira', 21 Dec 1948, U. Birm. L., special collections department, Church Missionary Society archive, AF 35/49 G3 A7/1–3

Archives Bodl. RH, Fabian Colonial Bureau, MSS Brit. Emp. s.365 · Church of Uganda, Namirembe archives, especially file 02 Bp 211/26 · LPL, Fisher papers · PRO, CO 822/1354 · SOAS, Conference of British Missionary Societies, Box 281 · U. Birm., Church Missionary Society archives, AF G3 A7 series · U. Lond., Institute of Commonwealth Studies, W. K. Hancock, Buganda papers

Likenesses double portrait, photograph (with Kwame Nkrumah), repro. in *New Vision* [Uganda] · group portrait, photograph, repro. in *The Times* (15 Dec 1953)

Mullard, Stanley Robert (1883–1979), radio engineer and industrialist, was born in Bermondsey, London, on 1 November 1883, the third of five children of Robert Mullard and his wife, Ann, *née* Ludford. He left school at the age of fourteen, joining Mackey's Electric Lamp Company Ltd, where his father was works manager, in 1899. He joined the Institution of Electrical Engineers as a student in 1903, becoming a full member in 1910 and a fellow in 1928. By the early age of twenty-three he was a director of the Mackey company. Two years later, in 1908, he married Emmie Gladys Winifred, daughter of George Walter Hole, an estate agent.

The Mackey company failed in 1909, and Mullard went to the lamp factory of Société Anonyme des Usines Pintsch in Paris. He returned to England in 1910 to take charge of Ediswan's research laboratory at Ponders End, Middlesex. Ediswan was then experimenting with silica (fused quartz) instead of conventional glass envelopes for filament lamps; silica has a low coefficient of thermal expansion, and so was subject to lower stresses as the lamps warmed up. Mullard put this experience to good use when commissioned in the Royal Naval Volunteer Reserve in 1916. He was posted to the wireless telegraphy establishment in HMS *Vernon* to assist in developing silica radio valves for high-powered wireless transmitters. The first successful silica valve, produced in September 1920, had an output of 10 kilowatts on test—sixty times the maximum power from contemporary valves with glass envelopes.

After demobilization in 1919, Mullard was appointed managing director of the 'Z' Electric Lamp Manufacturing

Company and also continued his research for the Royal Navy. On 17 September 1920 he set up the Mullard Radio Valve Company, which at first used part of the 'Z' Company's works at Southfields, Wimbledon, and then moved to its own premises in Claybrook Road, Hammersmith in 1921. Mullard's company was financed largely by the Radio Communication Company (RCC), on the strength of an order for 250 silica valves (at £66 each) from the Admiralty. Mullard's new business did not depend on producing transmitting valves alone. The broadcasting boom of the 1920s created a market for small receiver valves as well. In 1923 the company moved to new premises in Nightingale Lane, Balham, increasing its manufacturing capacity to meet the demand. Mullard's experience of all aspects of electric lamp production was invaluable. His company established a reputation for efficiency; he was soon selling valves at about half the prices of other manufacturers. But success brought unwelcome attention from powerful rivals. In 1922 the Marconi group brought a suit against Mullards, alleging infringement of their patents. Mullard fought the case as far as the House of Lords, with judgment given in his favour at every stage. However, it is unlikely that his small company could have survived this action on its own resources. It depended on the support of RCC and of the Admiralty; both would have been liable for substantial royalties had Marconis won the case.

But the company lacked the capacity to develop its own techniques. In 1925 Mullard therefore agreed to sell 50 per cent of Mullards stock to N. V. Philips' Gloeilampenfabrieken of the Netherlands, in order to benefit from Philips's research and patents. In return, the Dutch firm gained entry to the heavily protected British valve market. But, despite Mullard's personal reassurance, the powerful new shareholder exerted an increasing influence on the company's activities. The strength of the existing shareholders was reduced at about the same time by Marconi's acquisition of RCC. Philips was then able to purchase the remaining equity (in Mullard's name), the company becoming a fully owned subsidiary of Philips in January 1927. Mullard apparently misunderstood the full implications of this takeover. He was an experienced engineer and administrator, a competent organizer and team leader. From 1920 to 1925 he had been personally responsible for his company's policies. Appointed managing director by the Philips board in 1927, he appears to have expected this state of affairs to continue. The new owners, understandably, insisted on deciding important matters for themselves. After considerable friction, Mullard resigned in 1930, ostensibly on medical advice. He remained a director until 1970, but his duties were purely nominal.

Described by a friend as 'grim, saturnine, take-it-or-leave-it, a good business man' (*Daily Telegraph*), Mullard had an aversion to publicity. The Philips takeover left him with a sense of grievance, exacerbating his reticence about business affairs. He withdrew entirely from the radio industry after 1930, devoting his time to horticulture. In later years he said that he had made more money from growing carnations than he received for his contributions to electronics. Mullard died at Brooklands Nursing Home, Paddockhall Road, Haywards Heath, Sussex (where he was then resident), on 1 September 1979. He was survived by a son and three daughters.

ROWLAND F. POCOCK

Sources *Daily Telegraph* (3 Sept 1979) · G. R. M. Garratt and I. Nicholson, 'Mullard, Stanley Robert', *DBB* · K. Geddes and G. Bussey, *The setmakers: a history of the radio and television industry* (1991) · S. G. Sturmey, *The economic development of radio* (1958)
Archives Philips Electronics UK Ltd, Croydon, archives
Likenesses photographs, Philips Electronics UK Ltd
Wealth at death £48,994: probate, 5 Dec 1979, *CGPLA Eng. & Wales*

Mullen, Barbara Eleanor (1914–1979), actress, was born on 9 June 1914 in Boston, Massachusetts, USA, the eldest of the three children of Patrick Mullen (1883–1972), a writer and actor, and his wife, Bridget McDonough (1879–1948). Her mother, who had four children from a previous marriage, was variously occupied as a boarding-house keeper, a bootlegger, and a speakeasy proprietor.

Barbara Mullen was brought up as a Roman Catholic, surrounded by the strong Irish traditions and culture of parents who were first-generation immigrants from the Aran Islands and Connemara. She was educated at Sts Peter and Paul School in Boston. At three she was entering Irish dance competitions and on one notorious occasion, when returning home with her father after a competition, she was left in the rain outside a bar; the resulting pneumonia led to lifelong asthma. She recovered sufficiently to become the Irish dance champion of America, embarking on many successful tours in variety until 1934 when a boating accident and a chance meeting ended her dancing career.

Virtually abandoning the family in 1923, Pat Mullen had returned to the Aran Islands. Barbara Mullen re-established contact with him in the early 1930s. On an extended visit she met the composer Gerald Finzi, who encouraged her to enrol at the London Webber Douglas School of Dramatic Art in 1934; there her classmates included Michael Dennison, Dulcie Gray, and Stewart Granger.

On graduation, her stage career began inauspiciously when she appeared as Alice in *Dick Whittington* at the Players' Theatre, London, in 1939. But in April 1949, when *Jeannie* by Aimée Stuart opened at Wyndham's Theatre, Barbara Mullen came into her own. Despite the press attention focused on her father—who had acted in Robert Flaherty's acclaimed documentary film *Man of Aran*—Barbara Mullen's performance in *Jeannie* opposite Eric Portman earned her high praise in her own right. She was soon established as a leading player on the West End stage. Her many appearances in London and on tour included Mrs de Winter in *Rebecca*, the stage play of Daphne Du Maurier's novel (1941); the title role in J. M. Barrie's *Peter Pan* at the Adelphi in 1941, opposite Alastair Sim's Hook and Joan Greenwood's Wendy; Maggie Wylie in *What Every Woman Knows* (1948, also by Barrie); and the first stage Miss Marple in Agatha Christie's *Murder at the Vicarage* (1949). In 1940–

Barbara Eleanor Mullen (1914–1979), by Gordon Anthony

41 she made a brief foray into the recording world with two records of folk-songs; the second one, accompanied by Gerald Moore, was described as 'not to be missed' (*Gramophone*, April 1941). On 28 May 1941 Barbara Mullen married the maker of documentary films John Elston Taylor (1914–1992). Their first daughter, Brigid, was born in 1943 and the second, Susannah, in 1948.

Meanwhile in 1942, recreating the title role in the film version of *Jeannie*, Barbara Mullen began a successful screen career, mainly as a character actress in supporting roles. Her polished performances won her valued professional respect. Included in her credits were Ellen Kirby in *Thunder Rock* by Robert Ardrey (1942); Mrs Smedhurst in *A Place of One's Own* (1944); Veronica in *Corridor of Mirrors* (1948); Molly Fagan in *The Gentle Gunman* (1952); Mrs Fulton in *The Siege of Pinchgut* (1959); and Dr Shaw in *The Very Edge* (1962).

It was not until 1962 that Barbara Mullen achieved the high profile commonly accorded by television, when she played Janet, Dr Cameron's Scottish housekeeper in the BBC's production, *Dr Finlay's Casebook*. Originally intended as a six-episode series, *Finlay* was an instant critical and popular success. It ran until 1971 and was then broadcast as radio drama. Janet, Dr Cameron (Andrew Cruickshank), and Dr Finlay (Bill Simpson), the residents of Arden House at Tannochbrae, became household names and the series attracted a devoted audience. Now a nationally recognized figure, Barbara Mullen was sought by the advertising media in the role of the reliable housekeeper whose dependability bestowed assurance on products ranging from television sets to tomato soup. She was twice invited

on the radio programme *Desert Island Discs*; her appearance on the television show *This is Your Life* in 1964 earned top viewing ratings.

From 1971 to 1975 television continued to offer roles in plays, including *Juno and the Paycock* by Sean O'Casey, and also brought guest appearances in the series *Dixon of Dock Green* and *The Saint*. Very much 'the personality', Barbara Mullen was invited onto the American television shows *I Spy*, *Douglas Fairbanks Presents*, and *The Danny Thomas Show*. Barbara Mullen returned to the West End stage in 1975 to play Miss Marple in *Murder at the Vicarage*, twenty-six years after she had created the role, and in 1977 she appeared in *Arsenic and Old Lace* by Joseph Kesselring.

Less publicized was Barbara Mullen's dedication to the Save the Children Fund, for which she became a goodwill ambassador. She was a director of Pilot Films Ltd and of Falcon Productions Ltd, and when contracts permitted she involved herself in her husband's documentary film work. Esteemed a fine actress and regarded affectionately by colleagues, she was essentially a family woman with a strong will, a dry sense of humour, and a propensity for argument. Among her recreations she listed fishing, writing, and darts. She published a volume of memoirs, *Life is My Adventure* (1937), and wrote short stories and plays. Barbara Mullen died of a heart attack on 9 March 1979 at Hammersmith Hospital, London. She was cremated at Mortlake crematorium that month and her ashes were buried in Teeranea in Connemara.   P. S. BARLOW

Sources private information (2004) · B. Mullen, *Life is my adventure* (1937) · F. Stephens, ed., *Theatre World Journal*, 1 (1950) · L. Halliwell, ed., *The filmgoer's companion* (1973) · I. Herbert, ed., *Who's who in the theatre*, 16th edn (1977) · allmovie.com, 12 Sept 2000 · A. Young, 'The first lady of Tannochbrae', *Glasgow Herald* (10 March 1979) · *Daily Telegraph* (10 March 1979) · *Glasgow Herald* (10 March 1979) · *The Times* (Nov 1979)

Archives FILM BFI NFTVA, *This is your life*, BBC 1, 5 March 1964 · BFI NFTVA, performance footage | SOUND BL NSA, performance recordings

Likenesses photographs, 1940–79, Hult. Arch. · G. Anthony, photograph, NPG [*see illus.*]

Mullen, Madeleine ffrench- (1880–1944), medical officer and hospital administrator, was born in Malta in 1880, the eldest of three children, one son and two daughters, of fleet surgeon St Laurence ffrench-Mullen RN and his wife. Her mother suffered ill health for a number of years after her birth and Madeleine was placed in the care of her maternal grandmother in Ireland. When her father retired the family returned to Ireland. Madeleine's father was an ardent Parnellite and local elections were run from the family home at Dundrum in co. Dublin. After his death in the 1890s the family travelled on the continent, living in Germany and Belgium. ffrench-Mullen, who had been living in Brussels at the outbreak of the First World War, returned to Dublin in 1914.

In Dublin ffrench-Mullen looked after Belgian refugees and became active in the Irish nationalist movement. She became acquainted with Dr Kathleen *Lynn and the two women soon became firm friends. In 1915 ffrench-Mullen went to live with Lynn at her home in Rathmines in Dublin. She remained there until her death. Lynn and ffrench-

Mullen were introduced by the writer, actress, and nationalist, Helena Molony, to the Irish Citizen Army which had been formed by the socialist and trade unionist James Connolly during the 1913 lock-out in Dublin. Both women became active in the army. ffrench-Mullen became a sergeant and Lynn was appointed its chief medical officer. In the 1916 rising ffrench-Mullen was in the St Stephen's Green garrison where she was in command of the first aid station. She was arrested after the rising and spent a number of weeks in Arbour Hill and Kilmainham gaols and then in Mountjoy prison. On her release from prison she helped to establish the Connolly Co-operative Society in Liberty Hall, Dublin. Its purpose was to give employment to workers whose livelihoods had been lost in consequence of their role in the rising. In 1919 she was returned as a Sinn Féin candidate to the Rathmines urban district council. She was also active in Cumann na dTeachtaire (League of Women Delegates), a group interested in political affairs and the health issues of women and children.

During the influenza epidemic she, along with others, organized an emergency hospital in Charlemont Street, Dublin. In 1919 she also helped to establish St Ultan's Hospital in the city. Originally it was proposed that a hospital be established to treat children who suffered from venereal diseases, the fear being that venereal disease would become rife on the return of soldiers from the front. The committee of the hospital was part of a group known as Slainte na nGaedeal (Irish Health) which was concerned with the health of the nation. However, the hospital was organized as a general one for children, although it was also concerned with the health of mothers, who were encouraged to attend lectures at the hospital. ffrench-Mullen acted as secretary to the hospital for twenty-five years before her death. She drew up its annual reports, planned its housing schemes, and visited the United States on fund-raising trips. She was secretary to the Ultan Utility Society, which built homes for the people whose tenement lodgings were demolished for the enlargement of the hospital.

ffrench-Mullen died suddenly in a Dublin nursing home, on 26 May 1944, and was buried in Glasnevin cemetery in the city four days later.   MARIA LUDDY

Sources *Annual Report* [St Ultan's Hospital] (1944) · *Irish Press* (27 May 1944) · *Sunday Express* (28 Sept 1952) [report on St Ultan's Hospital] · 'M. ffrench-Mullen's statement to the Military History Bureau', c.1916, Allen Library, Dublin [in fact transcript from ffrench-Mullen's diary.]
Archives Allen Library, Richmond Street, Dublin, typescript document relating her experiences during the 1916 Easter rising and corresp.
Likenesses photographs, repro. in *Annual Report*
Wealth at death £2051 1s. 6d.: probate, 18 Dec 1944, CGPLA *Éire*

Mullens, Joseph (1820–1879), missionary, was born in London on 2 September 1820, the son of Richard Mullens. He entered Coward College (the Congregationalist institution affiliated to London University) in 1837, and graduated BA in 1841. In June 1842 he offered himself for service in India to the London Missionary Society (LMS) and after a session at Edinburgh studying philosophy was ordained as a Congregationalist minister at Barbican Chapel on 5 September 1843. Shortly afterwards he sailed for India in the company of the Revd Alphonse Lacroix, a Swiss missionary returning to Calcutta after furlough. Mullens settled at Lacroix's mission at Bhawanipur, just outside Calcutta, and on 19 June 1845 he married one of his daughters, Hannah Catherine (1826–1861), a fluent Bengali speaker who was committed to evangelical work among local women. In 1846 he succeeded to the pastorate of the native church at Bhawanipur, where he remained for another twelve years.

Mullens had a gift for publicizing the achievements of missionaries in India and not just the members of his own society. In 1851 he initiated a series of decennial statistics on protestant missions in India and Ceylon which was to become of major assistance for societies trying to raise funds at home. He studied Hinduism in some depth to be able to refute hecklers he met while street preaching, and he published several works to enable other missionaries to do the same, including *Vedantism, Brahmism and Christianity Examined and Compared* (1852) and *The Religious Aspects of Hindu Philosophy* (1860). He took a prominent part in all the protestant missionary conferences in India, beginning with the first in 1855, and, having returned to Britain on furlough in 1858, he was a secretary to the protestant mission conference at Liverpool in 1860. Here he pleaded with missionaries to abandon their doctrinal differences in the field and not to inflict European squabbles on their converts.

While on furlough Mullens and his wife prepared for the press *Brief Memorials of the Revd A. F. Lacroix* (1862), and they had not long returned to India when Hannah died, on 21 November 1861. In 1865 Mullens became joint (and in 1868 sole) foreign secretary of the LMS, a post far better suited to his talents for generating publicity and raising funds than that of missionary. In 1865–6 he toured the LMS mission stations in India and China, and in 1870 he made a promotional tour of the United States and Canada. He was awarded honorary DD degrees by William College, Massachusetts (1861), and Edinburgh University (1867).

In 1873 Mullens visited the LMS missionaries at Madagascar and he wrote up his tour in *Twelve Months in Madagascar* (1875). In April 1879, following the death of Dr Thomson of the mission on Lake Tanganyika, he travelled with two inexperienced missionaries to east Africa, planning to help them settle into Dr Thomson's mission. In early July, however, he caught a severe cold, and he died on 10 July 1879 at Chakombe in central Africa. He was buried at the nearby Church Missionary Society mission of Mpwapwa on 12 July. Mullens's death was lamented in the evangelical world; many societies looked upon him as a spokesman not just for the Congregationalists, but for missionary endeavour in general.   KATHERINE PRIOR

Sources DNB · *The Missionary Herald* (1 Oct 1879) · *Conference on missions held in 1860 at Liverpool*, ed. Secretaries of the conference [1860] · ecclesiastical records, BL OIOC, N/1/67, fol. 204 · B. H. Badley, *Indian missionary directory and memorial volume*, 3rd edn (1886) · A. G. Roussac, *New Calcutta directory* (1862) · E. Stock, *The history of the Church Missionary Society: its environment, its men and its work*, 2 (1899)
Archives DWL, letters and papers · SOAS, letters

Likenesses stipple, NPG

Müller, Ernest Bruce John Iwan- (1853–1910), journalist, born at 8 Hereford Square, South Kensington, London, on 26 March 1853, was the only son of Sévère Félicité Iwan-Müller (1821–1856), and Anne (1825–1910), daughter of John Moule of Elmsley Lovett, Worcestershire. One sister, Gertrude Elizabeth, survived him, his other sister, Anne, having died young. His paternal grandfather, a Russian named Trubetskoy, was exiled from his native country for political reasons and for some years led a nomadic life under the assumed name of Iwan-Müller. He finally settled in Paris and married Harriet, the daughter of Charles Wilkin, artist and engraver. After his death the family moved to London where Sévère became a banker. After his marriage Sévère returned to France, apparently to act as financial agent to a French nobleman. He died there and his young widow returned to her family in Droitwich, where Ernest Iwan-Müller spent his childhood.

After four years (1863–7) at a preparatory school at Thurmaston in Leicestershire, Iwan-Müller was sent to King's College School, London, where he remained until 1871. In May 1873 he matriculated as an unattached student at Oxford, entering New College the following October. He graduated BA (with a first class in *literae humaniores*) in December 1876, and proceeded MA in 1880. As an undergraduate he was a prominent speaker at the Oxford Union and a frequent contributor to the *Shotover Papers*, a humorous journal, modelled on the Cambridge *Light Green*, which enjoyed great popularity in the university. In this he was the driving force. The sometimes sharp, personal satire offended some undergraduates and prompted Douglas Sladen, then still a schoolboy, to take legal action. But Iwan-Müller's witty parody of Swinburne was long remembered.

After graduating, Iwan-Müller was senior classics master at Brackenbury's School, Wimbledon; in 1879 he returned to Oxford, remaining there until 1884 as a private tutor and coach.

During these years he was an active member of the Canning Club, revived by Lord Curzon as a debating club for budding Conservative politicians. Curzon respected his abilities and, hearing from A. J. Balfour that an editor was needed for the *Manchester Courier*, he recommended Iwan-Müller. In May 1884 Iwan-Müller left Oxford to take up this post, which he held until June 1893, and in which he did much to promote a great revival of Conservatism in Lancashire. He also worked closely with Balfour on press presentation of political issues, an occupation that was enlarged and extended as Balfour came to prominence in the Conservative Party.

In June 1893 Iwan-Müller went to London as assistant editor of the *Pall Mall Gazette*, under Harry Cust. In February 1896 Iwan-Müller and Cust were both dismissed by Astor, the paper's proprietor, who disliked their anti-American stance. A few months later Iwan-Müller joined the *Daily Telegraph*, on which he remained until his death. Besides his regular work as a leader writer, he undertook several special missions for that journal, including a long visit to South Africa during the Second South African War, a visit to Ireland in 1907, and another to Paris during the crisis caused by the Austrian annexation of Bosnia and Herzegovina in the autumn of 1908. While in South Africa Iwan-Müller kept a journal in the form of frank letters addressed to his sister and two woman friends. It clearly presents the role he enjoyed playing. He helped his old friend, Alfred Milner, the high commissioner, keeping him briefed on events in the Cape parliament at a time when martial law legislation was being debated, and watching Rhodes on his behalf when he was away in Pretoria. He also wrote articles for the Cape and the London press aimed at discrediting those favouring a conciliatory settlement with the Boers. These were based on information provided by and, in one case, carefully drafted by Milner or his staff. He remained in close contact with Milner thereafter and acted as an intermediary between Milner and Balfour during the cabinet crisis following Chamberlain's resignation in 1903, when it was hoped that Milner would accept office. While living in London he also contributed many articles on political subjects to the *Quarterly Review*, the *Fortnightly Review*, and other leading magazines. His published works are *Lord Milner in South Africa* (1902) and *Ireland To-Day and To-Morrow*, (1907); he left an unfinished biography of Sir Robert Morier, later completed by Morier's daughter.

Iwan-Müller was conspicuous among the journalists of his time for the range of his knowledge, especially in the field of foreign politics. He enjoyed the confidence of some of the leading public figures of the day, notably Balfour and Lord Salisbury, and perhaps no journalist was ever better acquainted with the inner history of important public events. His discretion was unfailing, and he was trusted and consulted by the leaders of his party to an exceptional extent. A 'genial giant' of exuberant vitality, he was a welcome guest, while his generosity, especially to the less successful members of his own profession, was unbounded. He died, unmarried, at his home, 16 Chelsea Court, Chelsea, on 14 May 1910, and was buried at Brookwood cemetery.

ALFRED MILNER, *rev.* JACQUELINE BEAUMONT

Sources U. Oxf., archives · family MSS, priv. coll. [in possession of Captain Sarell, Sir Roderick Sarell] · personal knowledge (1960) · *The Times* (16 May 1910) · *Daily Telegraph* (16 May 1910) · D. Sladen, *Twenty years of my life* (1915)
Archives BL, corresp., Add. MSS 51316, 52914 | BL, Balfour MSS · Bodl. Oxf., Milner MSS · Bodl. Oxf., Sanders MSS
Likenesses portrait (after H. Glazebrook), copy, priv. coll. · taunt photograph, Bodl. Oxf., GA OXON fol. 8 584 [editors of Shotover MSS 1874–1875]
Wealth at death £1237 0s. 11d.: probate, 20 June 1910, *CGPLA Eng. & Wales*

Müller, Friedrich Max (1823–1900), Sanskritist and philologist, was born on 6 December 1823 in Dessau, the capital of the small duchy of Anhalt-Dessau in Germany, the only son of the popular lyric poet Willhelm Müller (1794–1827), and his wife, Adelheid (1799?–1883), elder daughter of Präsident von Basedow, the prime minister of the duchy.

Friedrich Max Müller (1823–1900), by George Frederic Watts, 1894–5

Early life and education Müller was named after his mother's elder brother Friedrich, and after Max, the leading character in C. M. von Weber's opera *Der Freischütz*, Weber being his godfather and a close friend of his parents. In later life, after his final settlement in England, he adopted Max as part of his surname, Müller alone 'being as distinctive a name as Smith without a prefix' (G. Max Müller, 1.2).

His father died suddenly in October 1827, when Müller was not yet four years old. Müller was devoted to his mother, and her grief cast a gloom over his childhood. In his *Autobiography* he describes how day after day his mother would take him and his sister to their father's grave, where she would stand for hours, sobbing and crying. Nevertheless, the 'depressing atmosphere' at his home failed to have a lasting effect on Müller, who remained 'brimful of fun and mischief'.

At the age of six Müller entered the *Gymnasium* or high school in Dessau, where he was remembered as a lively boy, popular among his schoolfellows. At Easter 1839, following the death of his maternal grandfather, he was sent to the Nicolai School in Leipzig, where he received a sound grounding in the study of the classical authors. He stayed in the household of a family friend, Dr Carus, and there continued a musical education which had begun before he was six, when a neighbouring musician had secretly taught him to play the pianoforte as a surprise for his mother. Müller joined in the Carus family's musical soirées, and saw much of Felix Mendelssohn, who was at that time conductor of the Gewandhaus concerts in Leipzig.

In order to qualify for a small scholarship from the Anhalt government, Müller found that he had to pass his examination for admission to the University of Leipzig not at Leipzig but at Zerbst in Anhalt. The schools in Anhalt laid a greater stress on mathematics, the sciences, and modern languages than Müller's school in Leipzig, so it was necessary for him to become proficient in these subjects in a very short time. However, he passed the examination with a first class, and obtained the scholarship, worth about £6 per year, without which he would have been unable to attend the university.

On entering the University of Leipzig in the summer term of 1841 Müller decided to concentrate on Greek and Latin. However, he began to find study of the classical languages insufficiently challenging, since he could read Greek and Latin at sight, and could even speak the latter with ease, Latin being still a language of instruction in German schools and universities at that time. He attended lecture courses on a wide variety of topics, which, besides the classical languages, covered such subjects as Hebrew, Arabic, aesthetics, anthropology, and psychology. Attracted by the 'charm of the unknown', he began to attend the lectures of Professor Hermann Brockhaus who had come to Leipzig in the winter of 1841 as the university's first professor of Sanskrit. In the winter term of 1843–4 he heard Brockhaus lecture on the *Rig Veda*, the study of which was to be Müller's life work. In September 1843, at the age of nineteen, he passed the examination for the degree of doctor of philosophy. Too poor to buy the dress coat necessary for the occasion, he wore a borrowed one. While at Leipzig, he began to work on what was to be his first book, a German translation of the Sanskrit collection of didactic fables, the *Hitopadeśa*, which was published in March 1844 and dedicated to Brockhaus. Naturally gregarious, Müller found time to participate fully in the student life of Leipzig, even to the extent of fighting three duels.

Berlin and Paris Müller went to Berlin in March 1844, having decided to spend a year at the university studying comparative philosophy with Franz Bopp and, more especially, philosophy with Friedrich Schelling, the idealist philosopher. He also wished to examine the Chambers collection of Sanskrit manuscripts which had recently been acquired by the king of Prussia. Bopp's lectures he found a disappointment, the great pioneer of the science of comparative philology then being prematurely infirm, but Schelling received him kindly, and Müller continued to attend his lectures, even though their expense was a burden to him. Müller eked out his small stipend by translating and copying Sanskrit manuscripts. At that time he wrote in his diary, 'I *cannot* give up Sanskrit, though it holds out no prospect for me' (Chaudhuri, 43). Short of funds, he nevertheless mingled in Berlin society, and was a welcome guest at several musical and artistic households.

In December 1844 Baron Hagedorn, a boyhood friend, invited Müller to stay at his expense in his apartment in Paris. Müller had long felt that a stay in Paris was indispensable for the continuance of his Sanskrit studies, so he accepted the offer, arriving in that city in March 1845. During the fifteen months he stayed in Hagedorn's rooms, his host never once appeared. This caused much hardship to Müller, who was consequently forced to live at his own expense, supporting himself by copying manuscripts and assisting other scholars. Müller's chief object in visiting Paris was to meet and study with the eminent French Sanskritist Eugène Burnouf. The two rapidly became close friends. At the time of their first meeting, Müller's interest lay mainly in the philosophy of the *Upanisads*, but Burnouf encouraged him to undertake instead what was to be his *magnum opus*, the preparation of the first printed edition of the *Rig Veda*. Müller began copying and collating manuscripts of the text of the work, which consists of some 1028 hymns. At Burnouf's prompting, he decided to publish it with the commentary of the fourteenth-century Vedic scholar Sayana, itself a voluminous work, filling about four thousand pages of folio manuscript.

Among Müller's fellow students at Paris were the Sanskrit scholars Rudolf Roth and Theodore Goldstücker. He was on friendly terms with the latter, but between Roth and Müller there was a coolness dating from an occasion when Roth helped himself too freely to a dish of oysters which the two were sharing. This incident was trivial enough in itself, but it was not to be entirely unconnected with some of the academic controversies of Müller's later life. Roth was to become co-author with Otto von Böhtlingk of the great Sanskrit lexicon the *Sanskrit-Wörterbuch*, and in late 1845 Müller received an offer from Böhtlingk to go to St Petersburg, where Böhtlingk was a member of the Imperial Russian Academy, and there print his edition of the *Rig Veda*, in collaboration with Böhtlingk and at the expense of the academy. Müller, dissatisfied by guarantees given by the academy, rejected the offer. Böhtlingk and his associates, displeased by Müller's eventual success in finding a publisher for the *Rig Veda* in England, were to become hostile critics of Müller and his works.

Early years in Oxford While working in Paris, Müller felt the need to consult certain manuscripts which were held in London at the library of the East India Company, and by June 1846 he had saved enough money for a short visit to England. He had intended to stay in England for three weeks but the country was to be his home for the rest of his life. On the voyage from Boulogne he met the famous correspondent of *The Times*, William Howard Russell. The two became lifelong friends. 'So simple, so straight, and so learned; kindly and grave, but with a keen sense of humour, and a most bright and joyous disposition' (G. Max Müller, 1.51): such were Russell's later recollections of Müller. Another lifelong friendship begun at that time was with the Prussian minister in London, Baron von Bunsen. Bunsen, a diplomat and a man of the world, was able to provide his younger friend with patronage and an entrée into London society. It was at the persuasion of Bunsen and of Horace Hayman Wilson, Boden professor of Sanskrit at the University of Oxford and librarian of the East India Company, that the board of directors of the East India Company agreed to underwrite the considerable expense of printing and publishing Müller's edition of the *Rig Veda*. Bunsen provided the invitation that resulted in Müller's first visit to Oxford, where in 1847 he lectured to the British Association on 'the relationship of Bengali to the Aryan and aboriginal languages of India'. The few days he spent in Oxford delighted him, and he felt 'a silent love' for the city which was to be his home.

In February 1848 Müller was visiting Paris, collating manuscripts in the Bibliothèque Royale, when the revolution broke out. Bullets came through the windows of his lodgings. Managing somehow to safeguard his manuscripts, he hurried back to London, where he was the first to report to Bunsen at the Prussian legation the news of Louis Philippe's flight from Paris. Bunsen immediately took him to see Palmerston, to whom Müller related the events he had witnessed in Paris, illustrating his account with one of the bullets that he had retrieved from his room.

Müller's edition of *Rig Veda* was being printed in Oxford at the university press, and in May 1848 he decided to settle there in order to give closer attention to the project. The kindness and hospitality he met with in Oxford did much to assuage his homesickness. In late 1849 the first volume was published, after four laborious years spent in what were often very trying conditions. The chief difficulty was in collating and understanding the manuscripts of Sayana's commentary, which had been made by scribes who did not fully understand its meaning, and were consequently full of errors which had to be emended by Max Müller as he was thenceforward known. Furthermore, Sayana's commentary abounds in quotations taken without reference from many other works, most of which had not then been edited or published; all these quotations had to be checked and explained. It was a gigantic undertaking. For the subsequent volumes, which appeared at regular intervals, Max Müller was able to pay assistants who helped with the more mechanical aspects of the work. The sixth and final volume was published in 1874, Max Müller having presented the last sheet of the last volume to the first international congress of orientalists held in London in September of that year.

Max Müller's lively personality soon made him a popular figure in Oxford society, particularly in the more musical households, where his skill as a pianist made him a very welcome guest. His future in Oxford was secured in early 1851 when he was appointed deputy Taylorian professor of modern European languages, in place of Francis Henry Trithen, the incapacitated holder of the chair. On Trithen's death in 1854 Max Müller succeeded to the full professorship. The first course of lectures he gave was on the history and origin of modern languages, the second on the *Nibelungen*. The lectures were a great success and attracted large audiences, since he had the gift of interesting a non-specialist audience. He prepared a textbook consisting of extracts from German literature, which was published as *German Classics* in 1858. As Taylorian professor, the main focus of his teaching was on the development of the modern European languages; his lecturing on

Sanskrit was mostly confined to the illustration of comparative philology. Nevertheless, his *History of Ancient Sanskrit Literature* published in 1859 showed that he was still able to find time for active research into Vedic literature. For the later dramas and lyric poems of Sanskrit's classical period, he had little appreciation, regarding them as mere 'pretty ditties'. As teaching aids for the language, in 1866 he published a *Sanskrit Grammar* and an annotated edition of the *Hitopadeśa*.

In 1851 Max Müller had been made an honorary MA of the university and a member of Christ Church through the sponsorship of his friend and patron Dean Gaisford, and in 1854 he became a full MA by decree of convocation. In 1855 he became a naturalized British citizen. He was appointed a curator of the Bodleian Library in 1856, resigning in 1863. He held the post once again between 1881 and 1894. In 1858 he accepted the offer of a fellowship of All Souls.

On 3 August 1859 Max Müller married Georgina Adelaide, the elder daughter of Riversdale William *Grenfell, a copper smelter, and his wife, Charlotte. Their marriage was happy, and four children were born: Ada in 1860, Mary in 1862, Beatrice in 1864, and John in 1867. Both parents were devastated by the death of Ada at the age of fifteen in 1876. Mary also predeceased her parents, dying in 1886, having married F. C. *Conybeare in 1883.

In May 1860 Wilson, the professor of Sanskrit at Oxford, died suddenly. Max Müller was the best-qualified candidate to fill the vacant chair, but Monier Williams, who had been professor of Sanskrit at the East India College at Haileybury until its closure in 1858, stood as an opposing candidate. At that time the holders of many Oxford chairs were elected by the entire body of Oxford MAs, of whom most were country clergymen. Elections to chairs resembled parliamentary elections, far more regard being paid to the political and religious views of the candidates than to their academic qualifications. The burning question in mid-nineteenth-century Oxford was whether the university should be a religious or a secular institution. Max Müller's Christianity was grounded in a liberal Lutheranism, and he had no empathy for the theological and ecclesiastical struggles of contemporary Oxford, which he regarded with detached amusement. Williams, who was the candidate of the evangelical party, was no more than a competent scholar, unable to rival Max Müller in terms of ability or achievement. Williams's supporters waged a press campaign against Max Müller, in which they urged that his religious views and German birth rendered him unworthy of the chair. These considerations weighed heavily with the country clergy, who at best had a minimal understanding of the nature of Sanskrit, and who flocked to Oxford in large numbers for the election, which was held in December 1860. Williams was elected with 833 votes, against 610 for Max Müller, whose bitter disappointment at this defeat rankled for many years.

Later life After 1860 the focus of Max Müller's career changed. He continued his work on the *Rig Veda*, but most of his energy was devoted to the preparation of popular books and lectures, mostly in the fields of comparative philology and comparative mythology. The need to compensate for his rebuff at Oxford, where he remained Taylorian professor, led him to seek acclaim among a wider audience. His lectures on the science of language, given at the Royal Institution, London, in 1861 and 1863, were a great public success. The published lectures were reprinted fifteen times between 1861 and 1899. Max Müller became one of the leading figures of Victorian public life, engaging in public debates on topical questions, chiefly through the medium of letters to *The Times*.

Despite some opposition, in 1865 Max Müller was elected oriental sub-librarian of the Bodleian Library, but his health broke down under the strain of holding this post together with the Taylorian chair, and he resigned the sub-librarianship in 1867. In the following year the university abolished the Taylorian chair and in its place created a new chair of comparative philology, specifically for him. This relieved him from the necessity of lecturing on modern languages and added to his salary. Max Müller was thus the first occupant of a chair founded by the university itself, all previous chairs having been established by royal or private benefactions. In December 1875, the final volume of the *Rig Veda* having been published in the previous year, he decided to resign this chair and to return to Germany. His ostensible reason for resigning was to make himself free to concentrate on Sanskrit studies, but pique at the university's decision to make Monier Williams an honorary doctor of civil laws appears to have been the underlying motive. However, he was prevailed upon to change his mind; the university allowed him to retain the title and salary of professor of comparative philology while a deputy was appointed to do the work. He held the chair until his death.

The last thirty years of Max Müller's life were chiefly devoted to writing and lecturing on comparative religion. His *Introduction to the Science of Religion* was published in 1873. Lectures on this topic were given at the Royal Institution in 1870, in 1873 at Westminster Abbey, where in 1878 he inaugurated the annual Hibbert lectures on the science of religion, and at the University of Glasgow, where he was Gifford lecturer from 1888 to 1892. The most important project of these years was his founding and editing of a series of English translations of Indian, Arabic, Chinese, and Iranian religious texts. The Sacred Books of the East were intended for a general readership, and were translated by various scholars, Max Müller himself contributing translations of selections from the hymns of the *Rig Veda*, the *Upanisads*, and the *Dhammapada*, a Buddhist text. The volumes were published by Oxford University Press. The university and the government of India underwrote the cost of their production. Of the forty-nine volumes of translation in the series, only one remained to be published at the time of Max Müller's death. In 1887 the maharaja of Vijayanagara offered to underwrite the cost of a second, corrected edition of the *Rig Veda*, and to pay the salary of an assistant. The new edition, published in 1892, was largely the work of Max Müller's assistant, Maurice Winternitz, who corrected the text and checked the proof sheets. In 1897 Max Müller published a large work, *Contributions to the Science of Mythology*.

Despite poor health in the last two years of his life, Max Müller continued to write, publishing in 1899 *The Six Systems of Hindu Philosophy*, as well as producing essays and material for his autobiography. He died at his home, Parks End, 7 Norham Gardens, Oxford, on 28 October 1900, and was buried in the Holywell cemetery, Oxford, on 1 November 1900. His wife survived him.

Significance and reputation　Max Müller was a pioneer in the fields of Vedic studies, comparative philology, comparative mythology, and comparative religion, which he was chiefly responsible for introducing and popularizing in Britain. However, owing to the rapid advance of knowledge in these fields in the latter half of the nineteenth century, many of his ideas and a large part of his methodology had become obsolete long before his death. His work in comparative mythology and comparative religion was largely based on philological identifications which were later demonstrated to be untenable, and his philological methodology was replaced by the nascent science of anthropology. His strange theory that mythology is a 'disease of language' is taken from Sayana. Initially, he believed that languages were linked to race, being the expression of the thought of the races who spoke them, and he freely wrote of 'the Aryan race' and the 'Semitic race'. He modified his views in the 1880s, but he continued to write of an 'Aryan blessing' and a 'spiritual succession which began with the first apostles of that noble speech'. Such romanticism informed his support for German nationalism and Prussian expansion, and he engaged in a public controversy with Gladstone in which he championed the German cause in the Franco-Prussian war.

In India, Max Müller was regarded as a great and learned pandit. In 1862 an assembly of Brahmans met near Poona to correct their manuscripts of the *Rig Veda* by the first three published volumes of his edition. He never visited India, and his view of the country was idealized. His writings on India were an important element in the formation of western ideas about Indian religion and also in India's opinion of itself, particularly in their dissemination of the myth of India's spirituality.

Max Müller was largely responsible for the revival of Buddhist scholarship in Japan, through his encouragement of young Japanese scholars with whom he came into contact from the 1870s. After his death, his library was acquired by Tokyo University.

Max Müller was a gifted literary stylist, producing a large number of articles and books on a variety of topics. His 1881 translation of Kant's *Critique of Pure Reason* demonstrates his mastery of English and German prose. Though philosophers have tended to prefer Norman Kemp Smith's 1929 translation, Max Müller's stylish version of the *Critique* has continued to be well regarded. He even wrote a romance, *Deutsche Liebe* (1857), which went through thirteen editions and was translated into English, French, Italian, and Russian. Collections of his articles and reminiscences were published as *Chips from a German* *Workshop* (1867–75) and *Auld Lang Syne* (1898–9). He was dictating his *Autobiography* (1901) to his son at the time of his death. However, the sheer volume of his literary production was not compatible with the production of original research, of which he did little in the latter part of his life.

Naturally gregarious, Max Müller enjoyed great social acclaim, mixing with many of the royal families and leading figures of Europe. Dapper in appearance, he took a childlike pleasure in the many awards that he received: he was a privy councillor, he held Prussian and Italian knighthoods, the northern star of Sweden, the French Légion d'honneur, the Bavarian Maximilian, the German Albert the Bear, and the Turkish Mejidiye. He held several honorary doctorates, and was honoured by many learned societies.

His social acclaim, the honours he received, and the fact that he did little original research in his later years, led other, more austere scholars, such as Roth and the American Sanskritist W. D. Whitney, to attack Max Müller. There may have been some justification in their assessment of his later career, but their attacks should not detract from the importance of his pioneering achievements, especially in the fields of Vedic studies and comparative philology.

R. C. C. FYNES

Sources　G. Max Müller, *The life and times of the Right Honourable Friedrich Max Müller* (1902) · F. Max Müller, *My autobiography: a fragment* (1901) · F. Max Müller, *Chips from a German workshop* (1880) · F. Max Müller, *Auld lang syne* (1898–9) · N. C. Chaudhuri, *Scholar extraordinary: the life of Professor the Rt. Hon. Friedrich Max Müller PC* (1974) · D. M. Schreuder, 'The Gladstone–Max Müller debate on nationality and German unification: examining a Victorian controversy', *Historical Studies: Australia and New Zealand*, 18 (1978–9), 561–81 · J. Leopold, 'Britische Andnerdungen der Arishcen Rassen Theorie auf Indien, 1850–1870', *Saeculum*, 25 (1974), 386–411 · J. Leopold, 'The Arian theory of race in India, 1870–1920', *Indian Economic and Social History Review*, 7 (1970), 271–97 · Gladstone, *Diaries* · d. cert.

Archives　Bodl. Oxf., corresp., personal and family papers · U. Oxf., Taylor Institution, lectures and notes | All Souls Oxf., letters to Sir William Anson · Balliol Oxf., letters to Sir Robert Morier · BL, corresp. with W. E. Gladstone, Add. MS 44251 · BL OIOC, letters to Sir Mountstuart Grant Duff, MSS Eur. F 234 · BL OIOC, letters to H. H. Wilson, MSS Eur. E 301 · Bodl. Oxf., letters to H. W. Acland · CUL, corresp. with Charles Darwin · JRL, corresp. with E. A. Freeman · King's AC Cam., letters to Oscar Browning · NL Scot., letters to J. S. Blackie · Pembroke College, Oxford, letters to Sir Peter Renouf · University of Oregon, letters to Moncure Conway

Likenesses　B. Joy, bust, 1873 (now lost) · B. Joy, medallion, 1873, repro. in G. Max Müller, *Life and letters*, facing p. 453 · R. Lehmann, crayon drawing, 1894, BM · G. F. Watts, oils, 1894–5, NPG [*see illus.*] · H. von Herkomer, watercolours, 1895, All Souls Oxf. · W. L. Colls, photograph, 1898, repro. in Max Müller, *Life and letters*, vol. 2, frontispiece · Barraud, photograph, NPG; repro. in *Men and Women of the Day*, 3 (1890) · C. L. Dodgson, photograph, NPG · W. & D. Downey, woodburytype photograph, NPG; repro. in W. Downey and D. Downey, *The cabinet portrait gallery*, 4 (1893) · Hill & Saunders, two cartes-de-visite, NPG · Lock & Whitfield, woodburytype photograph, NPG; repro. in T. Cooper, *Men of mark: a gallery of contemporary portraits* (1878) · W. Rothenstein, BM · Walker & Cockerell, photograph (aged thirty), repro. in Max Müller, *My autobiography*, facing p. 262 · H. J. Whitlock, carte-de-viste, NPG · three photogravures, NPG

Wealth at death £18,998 4*s.* 8*d.*: resworn probate, Nov 1901, *CGPLA Eng. & Wales*

Müller, George Friedrich (1805–1898), preacher and philanthropist, was born at Kroppenstaedt, Prussia, on 27 September 1805, the son of John Frederick Müller (*d.* 1840). When he was four years old his father received an appointment as excise collector at Heimersleben. At the age of ten he entered the Cathedral classical school at Halberstadt as preparation for university. His mother died when he was fourteen. During the next year he left school to live with his father and to study with a tutor, and in late 1821 he spent several weeks in prison as a result of dissolute living—at the age of only sixteen. After two and a half years at the *Gymnasium* at Nordhausen he joined the University of Halle. Though intended for the ministry, Müller displayed little evidence of Christian piety until an evangelical conversion experience in late 1825 altered the course of his life. From this point onwards he devoted himself exclusively to religious and charitable activities.

Müller briefly gave instruction in German to three American professors, including Charles Hodge of Princeton, but in June 1828 he was offered an appointment by the London Society for Promoting Christianity among the Jews. He arrived in London in March 1829 to study Hebrew and Chaldee and prepare for missionary service. But in 1830, finding that he could not accept some of the conditions of appointment of the society, he left and became pastor of Ebenezer Chapel, Teignmouth, at a salary of £55 a year. On 7 October of the same year he married Mary Groves (*c.*1797–1870), the sister of an Exeter dentist, Anthony Norris Groves, who had given up his practice to devote himself to mission work in Persia. Towards the end of the same year Müller adopted the principles that trust in God and sincere prayer were sufficient for all purposes in material as well as in spiritual things. He accordingly abolished pew rents, refused to take a fixed salary or to appeal for contributions towards his support—simply placing a box at the door of the church for freewill offerings—and resolved never to incur debt either for personal expenses or in religious work, and never to save money for the future.

After about two years in Teignmouth, Müller went to Bristol, which became his home for the rest of his life. There he and others, including his friend Henry Craik, carried on congregational work, schools, the Scriptural Knowledge Institution, and other organizations. But it was as founder of the Ashley Down Orphanage that Müller was chiefly known. Inspired by orphanages at Halle erected by August Francke in 1720, which he had visited earlier, Müller established homes at Bristol on a similar plan. The project began with the care of just a few orphans, but gradually grew to immense proportions: eventually some two thousand orphan children were being cared for in five enormous houses erected on Ashley Down. The substantial funds associated with building and maintaining the enterprise were voluntarily contributed without even direct appeal, often as a result of the wide circulation of Müller's autobiography, *A Narrative of some of the Lord's Dealings with GM* (1837, 1841; 3rd edn, 1845).

George Friedrich Müller (1805–1898), by Frank Holmes, in or before 1895

Ironically, Müller's primary motive for launching the ambitious project stemmed not from his concern for orphan children (although that was acute), but from a desire to provide an example of Christian faith in action for others to emulate. Visitors to the site included the novelist Charles Dickens, whose concerns about the standards of the operation were apparently removed.

By the time he had become established at Bristol, Müller had adopted the principles of church practice and theory which were being enunciated at that time by members of the Brethren movement. He remained affiliated with the less strident branch of the Brethren for the remainder of his life. Like others in this following, he believed strongly in separation from nominal and establishment Christianity.

Müller became a naturalized British subject on 18 December 1861. His wife, Mary, died in February 1870, and on 30 November of the following year he married Susannah Grace (*c.*1823–1895), the daughter of Benjamin Sangar. When Müller was over seventy they set out on a worldwide mission, which, with brief intervals at home, took seventeen years and covered much of Britain and the continent. They also made several journeys to the United States and Canada, and visited India, Australia, and China to preach the gospel. By 1892 they had travelled some 200,000 miles in their missionary travels.

From 1872 Müller was assisted in his work at Bristol by James Wright, who had married Müller's only surviving child, Lydia (*d.* 1890), in the previous year. (A son, Elijah, had died in 1835 when only fifteen months old.) Wright carried on with the supervision of the project after Müller's death, which occurred at the orphanage in Bristol on 10 March 1898. He was buried on 14 March in Arnos Vale cemetery following services at both the orphanage and Bethesda Chapel.

In the course of his life Müller received funds totalling approximately £1,500,000. He was responsible for the education of thousands of pupils, he circulated vast quantities of Bibles in different languages, as well as smaller portions of scripture and tracts, and he was a great supporter of missionaries. In addition, he employed as many as 112 assistants at one time. A man of great energy and vision, he was one of the most remarkable religious figures of the Victorian era. His legacy included an outstanding example of Christian civility and charity, together with the work of the Scriptural Knowledge Institution and the orphanage project (the latter continued as the Müller Homes for Children.) Though the original houses were sold (eventually becoming the site of the Bristol College of Technology), the enterprise endured as a series of modern group homes with house parents. Müller's vision remained intact.

T. B. JOHNSTONE, rev. D. ANDREW PENNY

Sources G. Müller, *Autobiography of George Müller*, ed. G. F. Bergin, 4th edn (1929) · A. T. Pierson, *George Müller of Bristol* [1899] · H. H. Rowden, *The origins of the Brethren, 1825–1850* (1967) · F. R. Coad, *A history of the Brethren movement* (1968) · N. Garton, *George Müller and his orphans* (1963) · W. H. Harding, *The life of George Müller: a record of faith triumphant* (1914) · F. G. Warne, *George Müller: the modern apostle of faith, and his successors*, 7th edn (1911) · R. Steer, *George Müller: delighted in God* (1981)
Likenesses F. Holmes, photograph, in or before 1895, NPG [*see illus.*] · oils (after portrait, priv. coll.), repro. in Harding, *Life of George Müller*, facing title page · three photographs, repro. in Bergin, ed., *Autobiography*, frontispiece, facing p. 336, facing p. 671
Wealth at death £223 19s. 4d.: probate, 9 May 1898, *CGPLA Eng. & Wales*

Müller, (Frances) Henrietta (1845/6–1906), women's rights activist and theosophist, was born in Valparaiso, Chile, daughter of William Müller, a German emigré businessman and JP for Hertfordshire, and his wife, Maria Henrietta Müller. She grew up in Chile with little formal schooling but was evidently well-educated; she spoke six languages and travelled widely in Europe and America. In 1873 she entered Girton College, Cambridge, taking a third in the moral science tripos in 1877.

Inspired by recent efforts by feminists, including Girton's founder mistress, Emily Davies, to enable women to enter public life, Müller devoted herself to social and political causes concerned with the advancement of women. While still at Cambridge she became involved with Emma Paterson's efforts to set up trade unions among women and helped to found the Women's Printing Society. Upon leaving Cambridge in 1878, a woman of independent means with no need to earn her living, she stood for the Lambeth division for election to the London school board; an investment of £12,000 and the efforts of many female assistants ensured that she was returned top of the poll. She remained a member until 1885, independent of political party and renowned for her close relations with teachers, which enabled her to carry out small but significant practical reforms. On discovering, for example, that the girls had to sew a number of stitches to the inch which exceeded that of the finest work sold in London shops she had the number reduced to save their eyesight.

In 1882 Müller presided at the meeting which planned the first hall of residence for women in Bloomsbury. In 1883 she succeeded in getting the London school board to employ women clerks, cannily pointing out that this would save money since women were paid less than men.

In fact she was in favour of equal pay for the sexes and shortly afterwards proposed that female junior teachers, who earned two-thirds the wage of men in equivalent jobs, should be paid the same. She lost, equal pay for teachers not being fully implemented until 1961.

A poor-law guardian herself, Müller founded the Society for Promoting the Return of Women as Poor Law Guardians about 1883 and was its first secretary. In 'The work of women as poor law guardians' in the *Westminster Review* of April 1885 she argued that such work was eminently suited to women because their sphere was the home, and poor-law work was simply 'domestic economy on a larger scale'. Similar reasoning—women's suitability for work with the young—underlay her article about the work of the London school board in the *Westminster Review* of January 1888. 'The future of single women' (*Westminster Review*, 65, Jan 1884) suggested that spinsters, possessing women's superior qualities of insight and self-control yet free from men's demands in marriage, should undertake the task of protecting the rights of women and children. 'What woman is fitted for' (*Westminster Review*, 71, Jan 1887) was an attack on contemporary marriage which, Müller claimed, stunted women's humanity.

During the 1880s Müller was a member of the executive of the National Vigilance Association (NVA) which, in campaigning against the sexual exploitation of women and girls, supported government moves to close down brothels. Müller, however, was concerned that this could leave prostitutes open to harassment and destitution, a view shared by the Personal Rights Association, to which she also belonged. In 1888 Müller resigned from the NVA over this point and because the NVA attempted to prosecute birth-control pamphlets as 'vicious literature'. Müller herself favoured contraception to free women from continual child bearing until men learned self-control. Recognizing that contraception might give men even freer access to women's bodies, she argued that women must control its use.

At a time when the criminal justice system was entirely in men's hands, Müller campaigned for women police, magistrates, and jurors. On one occasion she resisted an order for all women to leave the court during an incest case, observing that the young victim needed 'one or two of her own sex in court to give her their moral support' (Jeffreys, 62). She supported the temperance movement because she perceived a connection between men's drinking and domestic violence and impoverishment. She was on the executive of the National Society for Women's Suffrage and a tax resister.

In 1885 Müller joined the Men and Women's Club, a London circle of freethinkers founded by Karl Pearson. Unusually for a mixed gathering, the group discussed such issues as prostitution, (hetero)sexuality, marriage, birth control, and women's emancipation. Müller contributed to several debates but resigned in 1888. She accused the men of laying down the moral parameters of the debate and refusing to examine their own motives and behaviours, particularly with respect to sexual licence. In the same year she founded the *Women's Penny Paper*, adopting the editorial pen-name Helena B. Temple. Claimed to be the only paper in the world conducted, printed, and published entirely by women, the *Women's Penny Paper* covered a range of issues of interest to women. It has been described by David Doughan and Denise Sanchez as exhibiting an 'uncompromising feminism', unequalled by any other journal of the period (Burton, 303).

Throughout the 1880s Müller's heart was in the 'woman's movement'. Around 1890, however, she 'gradually withdrew from civic efforts' and embarked upon a spiritual quest. She joined the Theosophical Society about 1891, drawn by its ideas of universal brotherhood and complementary male and female aspects to the spirit. In 1892 she travelled to India on a lecture tour on behalf of the Theosophists. The original plan was that she would accompany Annie Besant, but Besant cancelled at the last minute, so Müller went alone. Both Besant and Müller attended the Parliament on Religions in Chicago in September 1893, where Müller addressed the Theosophical Congress. Touring Ceylon and India in November 1893, this time with Besant, Müller's lectures drew crowds of Indian women, mostly in purdah, who had come to see 'the renowned woman-suffragist' (Nethercot, *Last Four Lives*, 17). For the first time, the Indian section of the Theosophical Society allowed Indian women to attend its convention, where Müller was also present. Many articles on Indian women appeared in the *Women's Penny Paper* before it ceased publication in 1893.

At the Parliament of Religions in 1893 Müller met Swami Vivekananda, who in 1897 founded the Ramakrishna mission. This combined India's traditional spiritual disciplines with western-style philanthropy, and it is to this mission that Müller transferred her energies. She edited *The Yoga of Christ, or, The Science of the Soul* (1894) and Vivekananda's *From Columba to Almora* (1897). M. S. Kilgour writes in her obituary in the *Girton Review* (Lent term, 1906) that 'She spent many years in India, during part of this time living as a native among the natives in the hills. Wherever she went she sought to study not only the religion of the people, but the position held by women … and in some of the most secluded parts of India she had a measure of encouragement among the natives, and was able to secure in some degree better treatment for the women.' In 1895 she adopted a young Bengali man, hoping he would study law and become a politician dedicated to reform.

Müller subsequently lived in China and America, maintaining a permanent address at the Westminster Palace Hotel in London. She died on 4 January 1906 in Washington, DC. Her will of 1897 left personal effects worth £12,750 to her sister Eva *McLaren; there was no mention of the adopted son. In 1912 Eva McLaren gave £500 in memory of her sister to Girton College, to which Müller had in her lifetime given furniture and drawings by John Varley.

As a feminist, Müller's writings reveal a characteristic mixture of Victorian sexual essentialism and hard-hitting analysis of male power. This approach fed tactically into dominant ideologies but brought Müller up against fierce opposition: she was accused of being a 'man-hater'. Her campaigns, ideas, and subsequent withdrawal into spirituality have many parallels among later feminists, and her disappearance from historical record is typical for a woman whose life contained hard lessons for the men and women of her own and later generations.

ROSEMARY AUCHMUTY

Sources M. S. Kilgour, *Girton Review*, Lent term (1906), 13 • *The Times* (17 Jan 1906), 6 • K. T. Butler and H. I. McMorran, eds., *Girton College register, 1869–1946* (1948) • L. Bland, *Banishing the beast: English feminism and sexual morality, 1885–1914* (1995) • A. Turnbull, '"So extremely like parliament": the work of the women members of the London school board, 1870–1904', *The sexual dynamics of history*, ed. London Feminist History Group (1983), 134–48 • P. Hollis, *Ladies elect: women in English local government, 1865–1914* (1987) • J. R. Walkowitz, *City of dreadful delight: narratives of sexual danger in late-Victorian London* (1992) • A. M. Burton, 'The white woman's burden: British feminists and the Indian woman, 1865–1915', *Women's Studies International Forum*, 13 (1990), 295–308 • B. Stephen, *Girton College, 1869–1932* (1933) • C. Dyhouse, *Feminism and the family in England, 1880–1939* (1989) • S. Jeffreys, *The spinster and her enemies* (1985) • C. A. Moore, *The Indian mind: essentials of Indian philosophy and culture* (1967) • A. H. Nethercot, *The first five lives of Annie Besant* (1961) • A. H. Nethercot, *The last four lives of Annie Besant* (1963) • A. Taylor, *Annie Besant: a biography* (1992) • census returns, 1881
Archives UCL, Pearson MSS
Wealth at death £12,750 15s. 7d.: administration, 5 Feb 1906, *CGPLA Eng. & Wales*

Müller, Hugo Heinrich Wilhelm (1833–1915), chemist, was born on 31 July 1833 at Tirschenreuth, Bavaria, the son of a spinning-mill owner. The family later moved to Weiden, in the Oberfalz, Bavaria. He received his early education at Nuremburg, and in 1850 entered the University of Leipzig, where he attended lectures on chemistry, physics, mineralogy, and geology. In 1852 he moved to Göttingen to study under Friedrich Wöhler (1800–1882), and in the same year he published his first mineralogical notice. In 1853 he obtained his doctorate, and in the spring he joined Liebig as assistant in Munich.

In the spring of 1854 Müller moved to London, at the suggestion of A. W. Hofmann, to take up the post of private assistant to Warren De la Rue at the De la Rue printing company, based at Bunhill Row. Müller's first assignment was the investigation of Burmese naphtha (Rangoon tar). He mixed with a circle of talented chemists, including Friedrich August Kekulé and, later, Peter Griess, Carl Alexander Martius, and William Henry Perkin. De la Rue and Müller published a number of chemical papers together during 1856–62. Müller studied coal-tar derivatives, including phenol, which he converted into rosolic acid. The results were published in 1859, in which year he joined the Chemical Society of London. Of major academic interest was his work during the early 1860s on the chlorination of benzene, which, he demonstrated, was enhanced by the presence of small amounts of iodine. This was later applied to other organic compounds. The German chemist Heinrich Caro, employed by Roberts, Dale & Co. of Manchester, supplied Müller with mineral pigments and lakes made from the aniline dye mauve, used at De la Rue for printing postage stamps from 1864.

Müller specialized in the colours, varnishes, and fugitive inks which made the firm's reputation as a leading security printer.

In 1866, Müller became a fellow of the Royal Society. He assisted De la Rue with the latter's pioneering work on celestial photography. In 1868, they devised a non-polarizable silver chloride voltaic element of constant electromotive force, and combined 11,000 cells each containing this element, to generate an electromotive force that was not previously considered possible. They carried out a major study of electrical discharges in gases using exhausted tubes, the results of which were published during 1868–83. In 1869, Müller acted as an intermediary between the Perkin firm of chemical dyestuffs manufacturers and the German company BASF, both of which had filed similar British patents for the manufacture of synthetic alizarin. Müller's contribution to the success of De la Rue led to contracts from the colonies and foreign governments, for which he was rewarded with a directorship. He became an expert in the field of paper making, which led him to the study of compounds present in leaves of various plants (1873–1912). Later, he turned to the species of the genus *Primula*, and was the first to discover naturally occurring flavone.

Müller married Elisabeth Rusel Crosby in 1878, whereupon he assumed British nationality. They took up residence at Park Square East, Regent's Park, London, and in 1885 purchased an estate at Camberley, Surrey, where Müller created an outstanding garden. Apart from Müller's responsibilities at De la Rue, he acted as foreign secretary of the Chemical Society during 1869–85, and was its president during 1885–7. He was also a member of the convivial B Club of the Chemical Society, and of the chemical section of the British Association. From 1889 to 1915 he was closely connected with the Lawes Agricultural Trust. Müller retired from De la Rue in 1902, from which time he worked at the Davy–Faraday Laboratory, attached to the Royal Institution. He was president of the Mineralogical and Crystallographic Society of Great Britain from November 1901 to November 1904. Following the outbreak of war in 1914, he resigned his positions; according to Henry E. Armstrong, this was because of sympathies with Germany. Müller died at his home at Crosby Hill, Camberley, on 23 May 1915. His widow and daughter donated £1000 to the Chemical Society research fund and for the triannual Hugo Müller lecture.

ANTHONY S. TRAVIS

Sources JCS, 111 (1917), 572–88 · Berichte der deutschen chemischen Gesellschaft, 48 (1915), 1023–6 · L. Houseman, *The house that Thomas built: the story of De la Rue* (1968) · T. S. Moore and J. C. Philip, *The Chemical Society, 1841–1941* (1947) · C. Reinhardt and A. S. Travis, 'The introduction of aniline dyes to paper printing and Queen Victoria's postage stamps', *Ambix*, 44 (1997), 11–18
Archives Oxf. U. Mus. NH, corresp. relating to mineralogy · RS | Deutsches Museum, Munich, Caro MSS
Wealth at death £495,306 9s. 8d.: resworn probate, 29 July 1915, CGPLA Eng. & Wales

Muller, John (1699–1784), mathematician and engineer, was born in Germany in 1699. Nothing is known of his family. His first book, *A Mathematical Treatise Containing a*

System of Conic-Sections, with the Doctrine of Fluxions and Fluents*, was published in London in 1736. It is dated from the Tower of London, where Muller was a mathematical instructor in the drawing office, and was dedicated to the master-general of the ordnance, the duke of Argyll and Greenwich. In 1741 Muller was appointed deputy head-master of the new Royal Military Academy, Woolwich, at a salary of £200 a year, by the master-general. In 1754 Muller officially became first master of the academy upon Martin Folkes's death, although he had performed all Folkes's teaching and administrative duties since 1741. At first the academy was a mere school, where the masters, Muller and Thomas Simpson, resented military interference, and the boys defied the masters at will. Subsequently matters improved, the cadet company was formed, the academy was enlarged, and Muller was appointed professor of fortification and artillery, a post he held until he was superannuated and pensioned in September 1766.

Muller's works were standard textbooks at the academy into the nineteenth century. They included *The Attack and Defence of Fortified Places* (1747), *A Treatise Containing the Elementary Part of Fortification* (1746), which criticized French fortification practices of the day, *A Treatise Containing the Practical Part of Fortification* (1755), which covered fortifications, bridges, and other civil engineering projects, and *A Treatise of Artillery* (1757) which had been used at the academy in manuscript as early as 1750. It was later reissued with a supplement in 1768. Muller's other writings included numerous editions of his *Elements of Mathematics* (1748, also titled *A System of Mathematics*) and *A New System of Mathematics* (1769), as well as *The Field Engineer* (1759), from the French of the Chevalier de Clairac.

In 1759 Muller sided with Robert Mylne in his winning design for Blackfriars Bridge, which used elliptical arches (a topic Muller had covered in *Practical Fortification*) rather than the semicircular ones championed by Thomas Simpson and Samuel Johnson. Muller married, on 29 December 1774, at St Martin-in-the-Fields, Westminster, Mary Horn, who survived him. 'The scholastic father of all the great engineers which this country employed for forty years' (Boswell, *Life*, 1.351), Muller died in April 1784 at the age of eighty-five. His library was sold the following year.

H. M. CHICHESTER, rev. STEVEN A. WALTON

Sources O. F. G. Hogg, *The Royal Arsenal: its background, origin, and subsequent history*, 2 vols. (1963) · E. G. R. Taylor, *The mathematical practitioners of Hanoverian England, 1714–1840* (1966) · W. D. Jones, *Records of the Royal Military Academy (1741–1840)* (1851) · Boswell, *Life* · Nichols, *Lit. anecdotes* · PRO, PROB 11/1119 sig 399 · GM, 1st ser., 54 (1784), 475 · parish register (marriage), 29 Dec 1774, London, St Martin-in-the-Fields
Likenesses T. Major, engraving (after J. Hay, 1774)

Müller, Sir William (d. 1846), writer on military and engineering science, described himself as an officer of the electoral Hanoverian cavalry, who, at about the end of the eighteenth century, became the first-appointed public instructor in military science in the University of Göttingen, which conferred upon him the degrees of doctor of philosophy and master of arts (Müller, *Military Operations*, preface; Müller, *Handbuch*). He claimed that during the ten years he held that post he made many experiments in artillery, and travelled in France, Prussia, the Netherlands, Bohemia, and Austria to inspect battlefields and ordnance. He also claimed to have under his instruction many distinguished officers, including German and Russian princes, who served in both the German and the French armies during Napoleon's subsequent campaigns (Müller, *Science of War*, 1, preface).

After the French seized Hanover a second time in 1807, Müller went to England, and on 24 April 1809 was appointed a second lieutenant of engineers in the King's German Legion, in British pay, becoming first lieutenant on 20 May 1809 and second captain on 13 December 1812. He was employed in the home district. He published several works in English, in 1810 patented an improvement in pumps, and in 1813 was employed on an extensive survey of the coast around the mouths of the River Elbe, which work was after the peace continued as far as Boulogne. The German legion being disbanded, Müller, with other Hanoverian officers was placed on half pay from 24 February 1816, when he was appointed a captain of engineers in the newly reformed Hanoverian army, and was again engaged on survey work. In 1828 he patented in England an instrument he called a cosmosphere, consisting of mounted terrestrial and celestial globes 'for the solution of problems in navigation, spherics, and other sciences'. He published extensively on artillery, war, and other subjects. His works included *Elements of the Science of War* (3 vols., 1811). Müller, who was appointed KH, died at Stade, in Hanover, where he had long resided, on 2 September 1846.   H. M. CHICHESTER, rev. JAMES FALKNER

Sources *Army List* · *Staats-Kalendar, Hanover* · *Neuer Nekrolog der Deutschen*, 24 (1846) · N. L. Beamish, *History of the king's German legion*, 2 vols. (1832–7) · W. Müller, *A relation of the military operations of the Austrian and French armies in the campaign of 1809* (1810) · W. Müller, *Handbuch der Verfertigung des groben Geschützes* (1807) · W. Müller, *Elements of the science of war, containing the modern principles of the theory and practice of the military sciences*, 3 vols. (1811)

Müller [Miller, Muller], **William James** (1812–1845), landscape painter, was born on 28 June 1812 at 13 Hillsbridge Place, Bristol, the second of the three sons of Johann Samuel *Miller (formerly Müller) (1779–1830), geologist, naturalist, and first curator of the Bristol Institution, and his wife, Margaret James (d. 1836) of Bristol. The sons reverted to the German form of their surname in adulthood. He was educated at home by his mother. By the age of twelve his drawing of a mummy-case had excited much admiration from the committee of the Bristol Institution and in 1825 the pioneer anthropologist J. C. Pritchard presented him with a paintbox for a drawing done to illustrate one of Pritchard's lectures. In the same year he illustrated W. D. Conybeare's lectures on the exciting fossil-finds at Lyme Regis in Dorset, many recently collected by Müller's father.

Müller was apprenticed to the Bristol artist James Baker Pyne in 1827, an arrangement amicably terminated after two years. The friendship of the curate of St Mary Redcliffe, James Bulwer, was perhaps of greater importance. They sketched together in and around Bristol, particularly in 1831 and 1832. Müller was lastingly influenced by Bulwer's collection of over a hundred drawings by John Sell Cotman and especially by the freedom of Cotman's technique, his warm colouring, and his decidedly emotional response to architecture. It was doubtless at Bulwer's instigation that Müller visited Norfolk and Suffolk early in 1830. In October 1831 he witnessed the Bristol riots, the bloodiest disturbances in England in the nineteenth century. His bold oil and watercolour sketches of the havoc and destruction (now in the City of Bristol Museum and Art Gallery) form one of the most impressive of all visual records of a national disaster before the advent of the camera.

In 1833 Müller first exhibited at the Royal Academy and, in the same year, he twice visited Wales, the second time on a long walking tour with Samuel Jackson and John Skinner Prout. A year later, in July, he and George Arthur Fripp set out on a seven-month sketching tour, visiting Belgium, travelling up the Rhine to Switzerland and across the Splügen Pass to the Italian lakes. They spent two months in Venice and were briefly in Florence, Rome, and Tivoli, before returning to Bristol in February 1835. Müller exhibited at the Royal Academy in 1836 but not again until 1840, perhaps partly because of pressure of work and the demands of dealers and patrons, to whose requests he all too easily acquiesced with immaculately composed oils which could be both bland and repetitive.

In September 1838 Müller left for Greece and Egypt. Many of his expressive watercolours of the acropolis, executed during his six-week stay in Athens, linked the Parthenon with the surrounding countryside and embued the ruins with a grandeur which matched the proud ideals of the new Greek state. In November he arrived in Alexandria, six weeks after David Roberts, the first significant British artist to visit Egypt. Müller then travelled to Cairo, where he was fascinated by the costumes, the bazaars, and the slave market, before sailing slowly up the Nile as far as Thebes and the temples at Luxor and Karnac and the Valley of the Kings. A surprising number of the oil paintings he was to paint on his return to England were Egyptian genre subjects, whose novel and exotic subject matter disguised the artist's self-confessed inexperience as a figure painter. Some of his landscapes, however, do convey his awe and the sense of history and solitude, so brilliantly suggested in many of the watercolour sketches.

In the autumn of 1839 Müller moved to London, settling the following year at 22 Charlotte Street in Bloomsbury, where he joined a society of artists known as the Clipstone Street Academy. In June 1840 he travelled to France, following a commission to make drawings for a book of plates which was published in August 1841 by Henry Graves & Co. as *Müller's Sketches of the Age of Francis 1st*. Although the period figures were probably drawn by Louis Haghe, the lithographer, the book demonstrates Müller's exceptional competence as an architectural draughtsman. He made two further visits to north Wales, for three weeks in the winter of 1841–2 and for six weeks in the autumn of 1842, staying at Rowen and sketching unremittingly in extremes of weather.

In the spring of 1843 the archaeologist Charles Fellows invited Müller to accompany his fourth expedition to Turkey. In September Müller left England for eight months, travelling independently with his pupil, Harry Johnson. They were delayed at Smyrna (İzmir) for three weeks before joining the expedition on 1 November at Xanthus, the ancient capital of Lycia, where Müller camped for three months and made excursions to Tlos and Pinara and, on the return journey, to Telmessus (Fethiye). He was not the expedition's official artist and was therefore free to draw the austere rainswept Turkish landscape, its ruins, and its people. Often in a sombre range of colours—a reflection of the dreadful weather he suffered—his watercolours of half-imperial size were completed in the field with remarkable speed, sometimes within two hours. Four of the five ensuing oil paintings which he submitted to the Royal Academy in 1845 were to be very badly placed. He had already been seriously ill the previous year and now, exhausted from overwork and profoundly dejected, his health deteriorated sharply. In May 1845 he returned to Bristol, where he died at the age of thirty-three on 8 September at 1 Park Row, the home of his brother Edmund Gustavus Müller. He was buried on 12 September in Lewin's Mead burial-ground in Brunswick Square, Bristol.

Müller's obituarist in the *Art Union* (October 1845, 318–19) wrote that he had died with 'fortune in his grasp as surely as fame'. Prices soon rose dramatically and forgeries abounded: in 1869 the *Western Daily Press* (23 December 1869) could state that 'a Bristol gentleman without "a Müller" is without his credentials to critical status'. N. Neal Solly's excellent biography of Müller was published in 1875, and his work was the focus of the largest exhibition yet devoted to a single artist, held in Birmingham at the City Art Gallery in 1896. Thereafter it was Müller's own extraordinary facility in the studio, and his fluent essays in the manner of Jacob van Ruisdael, Nicolaes Berchem, Poussin, and Constable, which were to undermine his reputation until it was restored by the more selective approach of the exhibitions at the City of Bristol Museum and Art Gallery in 1962 and 1991 and at the Tate Gallery in London in 1984. These galleries—as do the Victoria and Albert Museum and British Museum in London and the City of Birmingham Museum and Art Gallery—have good collections of his works.

FRANCIS GREENACRE

Sources N. Neal Solly, *Memoir of the life of William James Müller* (1875) · F. Greenacre and S. Stoddard, *W. J. Müller, 1812–1845* (1991) [exhibition catalogue, City of Bristol Museum and Art Gallery] · *Art Union*, 7 (1845), 318–19 · J. Beavington Atkinson, 'William Müller', *The Portfolio*, 6 (1875), 164–8, 185–92 · W. J. Müller, 'An artist's tour in Egypt', *Art Union*, 1 (1839), 131–2 · W. J. Müller, 'Letter from Xanthus', *Art Union*, 6 (1844), 41–2 · W. J. Müller, 'The artist in Xanthus: days and nights in Tlos', *Art Union*, 6 (1844), 209–11 · W. J. Müller, 'Letters from Xanthus', *Art Union*, 6 (1844), 356–8 · W. J. Müller, 'Visit to the crocodile caves', *Art Union*, 8 (1846), 79–81 · C. G. E. Bunt, *The life and work of William James Müller of Bristol* (1948) · [H. Jelly], 'Biographical sketch. J. S. Miller, esq. A. L. S.', *Bath and Bristol Magazine, or, Western Miscellany*, 2 (1833), 112–20 · B. Llewellyn and R. Hamlyn, *William Müller, 1812–1845* (1984) [Tate Gallery, London, exhibition handlist]

Archives County Reference Library, Bristol, letters to patrons · priv. coll., MS notes

Likenesses N. Branwhite?, miniature, *c.*1829, NPG · N. Branwhite, wash, *c.*1835, Bristol Savages, Red Lodge, Park Row, Bristol · W. J. Müller, pencil, *c.*1836, Bristol Museum and Art Gallery · N. Branwhite, miniature, *c.*1844, Tate collection · daguerreotype, *c.*1844, Bristol Museum and Art Gallery · N. Branwhite, plaster bust, *c.*1846, Bristol Museum and Art Gallery; marble version is in Bristol Cathedral · C. K. Childs, woodcut (after bust by N. Branwhite), BM, NPG; repro. in *Art Journal* (1850) · W. J. Müller, self-portrait, miniature, NPG

Mulley, Frederick William, Baron Mulley (1918–1995), politician, was born in Leamington Spa on 3 July 1918, the elder son of William John Mulley, general labourer, and his wife, Mary, *née* Boiles. His father came originally from Wisbech but met his wife, a domestic servant, of Whitnash, near Leamington Spa, when serving in Leamington Spa during the First World War. Mulley was educated at Bath Place Church of England school before winning a scholarship to Warwick School, which he left at the age of eighteen with the higher school certificate. He was unable to go to university because his father was unemployed. Between 1936 and 1939 he was an accounts clerk under the national health insurance scheme. He joined the Worcestershire regiment as a lance-sergeant in 1939, but was taken prisoner at Dunkirk. While a prisoner of war in Germany, 1940–45, he obtained a BSc in economics and qualified as a chartered secretary. After the war he was admitted as an adult scholar to Christ Church, Oxford, on the basis of an essay on the economics of a prisoner of war camp, which explained how cigarettes became currency. He gained first-class honours in philosophy, politics, and economics in 1947. Subsequently he was a research student at Nuffield College, Oxford, and also a research fellow in economics at St Catharine's College, Cambridge, 1948–50. In 1948 he married Joan Doreen, daughter of Alexander Morris Philips, of London. There were two daughters, Deirdre (*b.* 1951) and Corinne (*b.* 1953). Mulley had joined the Labour Party and the National Association of Clerks in 1936. In 1945 he contested the safe Conservative seat of Sutton Coldfield, but in 1950 he became member of parliament for the Park division of Sheffield, a seat that he held for over thirty years. He was called to the bar at the Inner Temple in 1954.

In 1962 Mulley published *The Politics of Western Defence*. In October 1964 he became deputy to Denis Healey, secretary of state for defence. His ministerial career then extended throughout the Labour governments of 1964–70 and 1974–9. From December 1965 he was minister of aviation. From January 1967 he was a minister of state at the Foreign Office. He was then minister of transport, from October 1969 until June 1970. In March 1974 he returned as minister of transport under the secretary of state for the environment, Anthony Crosland, before joining the cabinet as secretary of state for education and science in June 1975. His final appointment, in September 1976, was as secretary of state for defence.

Mulley was one of the few people of working-class origin who both achieved cabinet status in Labour governments and survived the course. Unlike George Brown and

James Callaghan, he had won a university education. Unlike George Brown, he was of a disposition that enabled him to work with colleagues. But unlike Brown and Callaghan, his manner and personality were curiously retiring for a politician, let alone a cabinet minister, and his influence was mainly exercised in the background of Labour politics. In that role he showed tolerance of those who differed from him, combined with a determination to preserve the unity of the Labour Party. Thus, though of the Labour right, he opposed Gaitskell's demand in early 1955 that Aneurin Bevan should lose the whip. It fell to him to preside, as chairman of the Labour Party, over the special party conference on Europe called on 26 April 1975, shortly before the referendum on British membership. Himself a committed 'European', the emphasis of Mulley's own contribution was on the importance of party unity.

In their diaries Richard Crossman and Barbara Castle were patronizingly dismissive of Mulley. For example, Crossman wrote of 'poor old Fred' (*Diaries of a Cabinet Minister*, 2.526). Castle complained that at one cabinet meeting which was discussing Mulley's education budget, 'Fred Mulley put up a doleful dirge … Poor Fred has such a whining voice and is so humourless that he merely succeeds in sounding comical' (*Castle Diaries, 1974–76*, 596). But these were criticisms from the middle-class left of a determined working-class right-winger of annoyingly stable temperament who knew how to fight his corner without extravagant language. Even Crossman admitted that Mulley could be effective in argument

> Tony Crosland is fifteen times the man Fred Mulley is but dim little Mulley boring away at his departmental brief gets the Department's way even though he's a bore, whereas despite his brilliance Tony doesn't even succeed in helping his Department.   (*Diaries of a Cabinet Minister*, 2.724)

The ministerial appointments held by Mulley demonstrated the extent to which he was trusted by prime ministers Harold Wilson and James Callaghan. This was not due to any expectation that he would prove an innovator in the departments for which he was responsible. Rather, Wilson and Callaghan could feel confident that he would not cause them anxiety owing to ambition or lack of loyalty. It was a bonus to have in senior office a minister whose working-class credentials were unassailable, whose intellectual calibre and personal integrity were undoubted, and who yet appeared willing to serve relatively uncomplainingly. From the point of view of his prime ministers, the only problem was that Mulley's loyalty to the trade union movement sometimes took priority over the loyalty he owed to the government. He was a lifelong member of the Clerical and Administrative Workers' Union and its various incarnations, and it was natural that his union should promote him as a candidate for the trade union section of the national executive committee (NEC) of the Labour Party. He served on the committee, with brief intervals, for twenty-five years, a record that would have been impossible for an uncharismatic minister of right-wing views if he had had to fight for a place in its constituency section.

For Wilson and Callaghan, Mulley's membership of the NEC brought both benefits and problems. The Wilson and Callaghan governments found themselves increasingly at odds with the NEC. It was a benefit that Mulley, as a member both of the government and the NEC, could help to rebut the criticisms to which government policies were subjected. Mulley's role became increasingly important as the number of ministers who were also members of the NEC declined in the second half of the 1970s. By April 1976 there were only five ministers among the thirty-one members of the NEC, and not all the five could be trusted to respect the collective responsibility of government. Generally, Mulley was a loyal exponent in the NEC of often unpopular arguments, sometimes to the point of self-denial. For example, as secretary of state for education, he was critical of the public expenditure cuts proposed by Chancellor Healey in December 1975. Cutting expenditure on education was not, in Mulley's view, the sort of thing that a Labour government should be doing. Benn quoted him as saying in cabinet, 'If this is the way it's got to be, let the Treasury and the Think Tank run the country' (Benn, *Against the Tide*, 476). Nevertheless, when similar criticisms were raised in the NEC, Mulley gave no support.

The problems of Mulley's strategic position coupling government and NEC became acute whenever Labour found itself at odds with the trade unions. Mulley could never forget his base in the trade union movement and that his annual election to the NEC depended on the confidence of his electorate, the trade union leadership. In 1959–60 Mulley, normally a loyal Gaitskellite, opposed his leader when Gaitskell, against widespread union opposition, announced his proposal to rewrite clause 4 of the Labour Party constitution. Then, on 26 March 1969, Mulley, in the NEC, opposed the trade union reforms embodied in Castle's white paper *In Place of Strife*. In this he was following the then home secretary, James Callaghan, also a dissident from government policy. Both would live to regret their actions during the winter of discontent in 1979, when Mulley, now secretary of state for defence, had to consider the use of troops to keep essential supplies moving. When, in July 1975, Healey, as chancellor of the exchequer, was negotiating an incomes policy with trade union leaders, it was Mulley, in cabinet, who, fearful of a breach between the government and the trade unions, proposed the compromise that avoided the immediate enactment of statutory powers of enforcement which was opposed by the unions. Legislation granting such powers was to be kept in reserve rather than brought forward at once. In the summer of 1977 Mulley, together with some other members of the government generally regarded as being on the right wing of the Labour Party, joined the picket line in the Grunwick strike over trade union recognition. The strike was strongly supported by the trade union movement, but the violence to which it gave rise widened the alienation of the public from the trade unions and, hence, from the government.

In 1982, when the Labour Party had moved violently to

the left, Mulley was deselected as parliamentary candidate by his constituency party, a harsh judgment for so loyal a representative. After the general election of 1983 he was elevated to the Lords and passed the remainder of his life in the comfortable obscurity that, despite his considerable ability, he appeared to cherish. He died in Sheffield on 15 March 1995; he was survived by his wife and two daughters.

EDMUND DELL

Sources H. Wilson, *Final term: the labour government, 1974–1976* (1979) · H. Wilson, *The labour government, 1964–1970: a personal record* (1971) · R. H. S. Crossman, *The diaries of a cabinet minister*, 3 vols. (1975–7) · *The Castle diaries, 1964–1970* (1984) · *The Castle diaries, 1974–1976* (1980) · A. Benn, *Office without power: diaries, 1968–72* (1988) · T. Benn, *Against the tide: diaries, 1973–1976* (1989) · T. Benn, *Conflicts of interest: diaries, 1977–1980*, ed. R. Winstone (1990) · *The backbench diaries of Richard Crossman*, ed. J. Morgan (1981) · K. O. Morgan, *Callaghan: a life* (1997) · J. Callaghan, *Time and chance* (1987) · *The political diary of Hugh Dalton, 1918–1940, 1945–1960*, ed. B. Pimlott (1986) · P. M. Williams, *Hugh Gaitskell: a political biography* (1979) · B. Donoughue, *Prime minister: the conduct of policy under Harold Wilson and James Callaghan* (1987) · private information (2004) · personal knowledge (2004) · *The Times* (16 March 1995) · *The Independent* (16 March 1995) · WWW · *Debrett's Peerage*
Archives priv. coll., MSS | King's Lond., Liddell Hart C., corresp. with Sir B. H. Liddell Hart
Likenesses two photographs, 1964–77, repro. in *The Independent* · photograph, 1976, Hult. Arch. · photograph, 1977, repro. in *The Times*
Wealth at death £178,536: probate, 17 June 1995, CGPLA Eng. & Wales

Mullin, Allen (1653/4–1690), surgeon and anatomist, the son of Patrick Mullin of Ballicoulter, Ireland, entered Trinity College, Dublin, as a sizar at the age of eighteen on 27 February 1672. He graduated BA in 1676, MB in 1679, and MD in 1684, when he was elected a fellow of the King and Queen's College of Physicians in Ireland.

Mullin built a thriving practice and became a respected anatomist. Perhaps his most unusual subject was an elephant that had died in a fire in Essex Street, Dublin, on 17 July 1681. Eventually, after an argument with local butchers, who claimed the right to dismember the creature, and a free-for-all between the butchers and the carpenters (who were building a shed around the animal), Mullin was able to begin his dissection. He later sent a letter detailing his findings to the Royal Society via Sir William Petty. This, together with another communication (via Robert Boyle) to the society concerning Mullin's work on the eye, was published as *An Anatomical Account of the Elephant Accidentally Burnt in Dublin … Together with a Relation of New Anatomical Observations in the Eyes of Animals* (1682). Mullin was elected FRS in 1683. In the same year he became one of the founders of the Dublin Philosophical Society. During the following year he designed a laboratory for the society to be situated above an apothecary's shop at Crow's Nest, off Dame Street. Mullin read a number of papers before the society on topics including deformities in animals, consumption, and ovarian disease. He also wrote of his experiments to determine the quantity of blood in humans, done by draining blood from a number of animals and calculating its weight in relation to the total weight of the animal.

In 1686 Mullin left Dublin and went to London, 'on account of a scandalous love intrigue, of which he was ashamed' (Kirkpatrick, 58). In London he became a regular visitor to Jonathan's Coffee House in Exchange Alley, which was popular with members of the Royal Society. Mullin, who had been impressed by Hans Sloane's work on the natural history of the Caribbean, then accepted the chance to travel to Jamaica with William O'Brien, Lord Inchiquin, who was interested in investigating some local mines. They set out in 1690 but stopped on the way at Barbados, where Mullin 'met with some friends who made him drink hard, which threw him into a calenture [fever] of which he died' (Kirkpatrick, 58).

IAN LYLE

Sources D. Coakley, *Irish masters of medicine* (1992) · T. P. C. Kirkpatrick, *History of the medical teaching in Trinity College, Dublin, and of the School of Physic in Ireland* (1912) · C. A. Cameron, *History of the Royal College of Surgeons in Ireland*, 2nd edn (1916) · 'Early Dublin philosophers: dead elephant', *Irish Times* (17 May 1941)

Mulliner, Thomas (*fl.* 1545–1575), music copyist, is of obscure origins. The statement that he was master of St Paul's School cannot be verified, and is derived solely from an annotation in his manuscript of keyboard music (BL, Add. MS 30513) by John Stafford Smith, an eighteenth-century owner of the book. A Mulliner or Mullyner was employed as a clerk in the choir of Magdalen College, Oxford, during 1557–8, while a Thomas Mulliner held a similar position at Corpus Christi College, Oxford, during 1563–4, having been appointed as 'organorum modulator' on 3 March 1563. It is very likely that the latter musician (if the two were not in fact identical) was also the owner and copyist of Add. MS 30513. Nothing further is known of his life.

Mulliner's one surviving manuscript is his chief claim to notice and was copied, as far as can be determined, between about 1545 and 1575. His ownership is testified by an inscription:

> Sum liber thomae mullineri
> johanne heywoode teste
> ('I am the book of Thomas Mulliner, witness John Heywood')

That he was the copyist is a valid inference from the handwriting. The John Heywood recorded in the inscription could have been the vicar-choral of St Paul's (*c.*1490–1574), John Heywood the court dramatist and entertainer (*c.*1497–1578), or someone else of that name. A protracted period of copying is entirely likely, though the main contents could easily have been finished by 1560 or even earlier; however, some virginalistic music added at the beginning of the manuscript and some pieces for cittern and gittern at the end seem to be somewhat later. The book is a major source of organ music by John Redford and John Blitheman and the primary source of a number of vocal and instrumental works in short score. It also contains a brief partsong and a cittern piece by Mulliner himself.

JOHN CALDWELL

Sources D. Stevens, *The Mulliner Book: a commentary* (1952) · D. Stevens, ed., *The Mulliner book*, Musica Britannica, 1 (1951) · T. Fowler, *The history of Corpus Christi College*, OHS, 25 (1893) · F. Knights, 'Thomas Mulliner's Oxford career', *The Organ*, 75 (1996), 132–5

Archives BL, holograph: anthology of music by various composers, Add. MS 30513

Mullins, Claud William (1887–1968), lawyer and writer, was born on 6 September 1887 at 17 Southampton Street, London, the eldest of the four children (three sons and a daughter) of Edwin Roscoe *Mullins (1848–1907), sculptor, and his wife, Alice (1856–*c*.1936), daughter of John Pelton JP, a successful Croydon grocer. His father's illness precipitated the young Mullins's withdrawal from Mill Hill School and, after a period travelling in Europe, he became a London county council clerk in 1907.

Dissatisfied with the limited intellectual stimulus afforded by his administrative duties, Mullins read for the bar and, having been awarded a certificate of honour in the bar finals, was called by Gray's Inn in 1913. His career was interrupted by war service, and thereafter he did not find it easy to build up a practice. He used his enforced leisure to express in books (notably *In Quest of Justice*, 1931) and articles a dissatisfaction, in part founded on his studies of foreign systems, with English law and procedure.

Mullins made no secret of his readiness to accept judicial office and was appointed a Metropolitan Police magistrate on 29 June 1931. He quickly formed strong views about the fact that disputes between husbands and wives under the Summary Jurisdiction (Separation and Maintenance) Act of 1925 were treated in the same way as prosecutions, heard before crowds of prurient onlookers, and fully reported in the local press. Mullins thought it wrong to regard matrimonial disputes solely as matters of law, and he believed magistrates ought to be trained in the causes of marital disharmony and thus enabled to dispense social help to those who came before them.

In an attempt to promote the radical changes he thought necessary, Mullins drafted the Summary Jurisdiction (Domestic Procedure) Bill which was introduced into the House of Lords in 1934 by the young Lord Listowel. Although the bill's more radical provisions (for example, giving magistrates' courts powers to hear 'conciliation summonses' and to advise the spouses on matters detrimental to their happiness) were unacceptable to lawyers and administrators, the bill generated sufficient support to persuade the government that the magistrates' domestic jurisdiction ought to be investigated by the committee on social services in magistrates' courts (chaired by S. W. Harris). The resulting Summary Procedure (Domestic Proceedings) Act of 1937 gave effect to recommendations intended to humanize magistrates' domestic hearings, not least by separating them from the processing of criminal prosecutions.

Mullins was also largely instrumental in drawing public attention to the excessive use of imprisonment for debt and thus in influencing the decision to appoint the (Fischer Williams) departmental committee on imprisonment by courts of summary jurisdiction (1934). That committee's recommendations formed the basis of the Money Payments (Justices' Procedure) Act of 1935. This provided that those failing to pay fines, affiliation orders, or rates should not be sent to prison without inquiry into the reasons for failure to pay.

Mullins was justifiably proud of his part in bringing about these reforms, but his success was only partial. Indeed, the Harris committee specifically rejected his fundamental belief that 'conciliation' in family disputes was a matter for the courts themselves. The clear distinction between adjudication on the one hand and social work on the other, drawn by the committee and subsequently consistently followed by orthodox opinion, was the antithesis of Mullins's beliefs. Mullins's attempts to secure for the magistrates an enhanced role in the reformed divorce law brought about by A. P. Herbert's Matrimonial Causes Act of 1937 were also unsuccessful.

From the outset Mullins's relationship with his magisterial brethren was uneasy and in 1936 the metropolitan magistrates, evidently vexed by what they believed to be Mullins' proclivity for self-advertisement, unanimously censured his conduct. The Home Office concluded that Mullins had done nothing prejudicial to the impartial administration of justice, but complaints (about ill-considered remarks about birth control, among other things) were made not only in private correspondence but on the floor of the House of Commons. In 1942 Herbert Morrison, less tolerant of Mullins's eccentricities than his predecessor, Sir John Simon, publicly rebuked Mullins.

In 1947 Mullins retired from the bench on grounds of ill health, and devoted the rest of his life to writing, lecturing, and voluntary work.

Mullins had married (Elizabeth) Gwendolen (1904–1997), a craftswoman, younger daughter of Augustus Philip Brandt, banker, on 28 May 1925. They had one son (Edwin Brandt Mullins, a writer on artistic and other subjects) and two daughters (Ann Dally, psychiatrist and medical historian, and Barbara Mullins, craftswoman). Mullins died, aged eighty-one, on 23 October 1968 at the Royal West Sussex Hospital, Chichester, Sussex. He was cremated and, after a funeral service at Graffham church, his ashes were scattered in the woods where he used to walk.

Mullins deserves to be remembered for his pioneering role in seeking to civilize the legal consequences of family breakdown and in helping to create a climate of opinion favourable to conciliation as a preferred alternative to litigation in such matters. As Sir Alexander Maxwell, the permanent under-secretary at the Home Office, put it to the home secretary on Mullins's retirement, 'with his egoism and assertiveness, [Mullins] has combined a very genuine zeal for improving the work of the Courts and for helping the numerous classes of unfortunate people with whom the Summary courts come into contact' (Maxwell to Chuter Ede, 3 Feb 1947, Home Office MSS, PRO, HO45/21034).   S. M. Cretney

Sources C. Mullins, *Fifteen years hard labour* (1948) · C. Mullins, *One man's furrow* (1963) · *WWW* · S. M. Cretney, 'Marriage saving and the early days of conciliation: the role of Claud Mullins', *Law, law reform and the family* (1998), chap. 5 · private information (2004) · 'Mullins, Edwin Roscoe', *DNB* · G. Behlmer, 'Summary justice and working-class marriage in England, 1870–1940', *Law and History Review*, 12 (1994), 229–75 · G. K. Behlmer, 'Summary justice and working-class marriage', *Friends of the family, the English home and its guardians, 1850–1940* (1998), 181–229 · *The Times* (24 Oct 1968) · Home Office MSS, PRO · b. cert. · d. cert. · *CGPLA Eng. & Wales* (1969)

Archives NRA, priv. coll., private papers, diaries
Likenesses photographs, priv. coll.
Wealth at death £73,155: probate, 1 April 1969, *CGPLA Eng. & Wales*

Mullins, Edwin Roscoe (1848–1907), sculptor, born at 1 Great James Street, Bedford Row, Holborn, London, on 22 August 1848, was a younger son and sixth child in a family of five sons and three daughters of Edward Mullins (*d.* in or before 1884) of Box, Wiltshire, solicitor, and his wife, Elizabeth Baker. After being educated at Louth grammar school and Marlborough College (1863–5), Mullins was trained in the art schools of Lambeth and the Royal Academy, and in the workshop of John Birnie Philip. Between 1866 and 1874 he studied under Professor Wagmüller at Munich, where he shared a studio with Edward Onslow Ford. He gained a silver medal at Munich and a bronze medal at Vienna for a group entitled *Sympathy* exhibited in 1872. He was a regular exhibitor at the Royal Academy, the Grosvenor Gallery, and the New Gallery from 1874 onwards. He was best known for his ideal works. These were criticized by Walter Armstrong for their 'coldness' (Armstrong, 142) but admired by other contemporary critics for their simplicity and restraint. There are two examples in the Art Gallery and Museum, Glasgow: *Morn Waked by the Circling of the Hours* (marble; dated 1887) and *Isaac and Esau: Bless Me, Even Me Also, O My Father* (marble; dated 1904).

Mullins executed many portraits including busts of Dr Martineau (1878); W. G. Grace (1887); the Rt Hon. C. T. Ritchie (1889), and Sir Evelyn Wood (1896), among others, which he exhibited at the Royal Academy. He executed statuettes of W. E. Gladstone (1878); Val Prinsep ARA (exh. RA, 1880); Sir Rowland Hill, and Edmund Yates (1878). His public statues include those of General Barrow (marble; 1882) for the senate house of Lucknow; Henry VII (stone; 1883) for King's College, Cambridge; and William Barnes, the Dorset poet (1887), for Dorchester. His most unusual work was the circus horse in Brighton cemetery, executed in 1893 as a memorial to Mr Ginnett, a well-known circus owner. Mullins married on 4 June 1884 Alice (1856–*c*.1936), daughter of John Pelton JP, of Croydon. They had one daughter and three sons, the eldest of whom was Claud William *Mullins.

Mullins was particularly interested in architectural sculpture. He told the Royal Institute of British Architects:

> We may note the tendency of sculpture when separated from architecture, in the popular form it takes at exhibition, to develop into a species of bric-a-brac. ... Too often the work, when done, is only suitable to become part of a rich man's collection of treasures, that only the few can possess, rather than fitted to the nation as a whole as it could do if it were executed for public buildings. (Beattie, 46)

The most important surviving examples of his architectural decoration are the pediment of the Harris Museum and Art Gallery, Preston, Lancashire, and five decorative relief panels for Braithwaite Hall, Croydon Municipal Buildings (1896).

He published a practical guide to sculpture techniques entitled *A Primer of Sculpture* in 1890 and was appointed

teacher of modelling, with special reference to architectural decoration, at the new Central School of Arts and Crafts in 1896. Mullins died at Shirley, Walberswick, Suffolk, on 9 January 1907, aged fifty-eight. His remains after cremation at Golders Green were buried at Hendon Park.

S. E. FRYER, *rev.* EMMA HARDY

Sources M. H. Spielmann, *British sculpture and sculptors of to-day* (1901) · W. Armstrong, 'E. Roscoe Mullins', *The Portfolio*, 20 (1889), 141–3 · *Art Journal*, new ser., 27 (1907), 92 · *The Times* (14 Jan 1907) · S. Beattie, *The New Sculpture* (1983) · B. Read, *Victorian sculpture* (1982) · 'Figures from the pediment, Harris Free Library, Preston', *The Builder*, 54 (1888), 45, pl. 2 · photographs, Courtauld Inst., Conway Library · b. cert. · m. cert. · d. cert. · *CGPLA Eng. & Wales* (1907)
Archives Courtauld Inst., Conway Library, MSS
Wealth at death £13,194 8*s.* 4*d.*: resworn probate, 9 March 1907, *CGPLA Eng. & Wales*

Mullins, George (*d.* 1775), landscape painter, about whose parents and early life nothing is known, about 1756 studied in the Dublin Society Schools under James Mannin, winning a premium for landscape in 1763 and another for a history piece in 1768. His first job was painting in Thomas Wyse's manufactory in Waterford, lacquering and decorating tin trays and snuff boxes similar to those made in Birmingham. While in Waterford he taught Thomas Roberts. By 1765 he was back in Dublin, where he married the owner of the Horseshoe and Magpie, an alehouse in Temple Bar. From there he exhibited at the Society of Artists in Ireland landscapes and a few subject pictures. He exhibited for the last time in 1769 giving as his address Shaw's Court, Dame Street, where the Dublin Society Schools were established. In 1768 he painted a series of four Italianate landscapes for the earl of Charlemont (board of works, Dublin). In 1770 he went to London, where he lived with Robert Carver, the Irish landscape and theatrical designer, and exhibited landscapes at the Royal Academy, of which the *Fishing Party* (1772; Ashmolean Museum, Oxford) was almost certainly one. Horace Walpole observed correctly that his work was in the manner of Cornelis van Poelenburgh and purchased an example. Mullins made at least two views of Llangollen, one of which seems to show Wynnstay, the seat of Sir Watkin Williams Wynn, in the background. Edward Croft Murray attributed a ceiling in Chirk Castle, Denbighshire, to Mullins but this is by no means a certain work. He died in London in 1775.

L. H. CUST, *rev.* ANNE CROOKSHANK

Sources A. Pasquin [J. Williams], *An authentic history of the professors of painting, sculpture, and architecture who have practiced in Ireland ... to which are added, Memoirs of the royal academicians* [1796]; facs. edn as *An authentic history of painting in Ireland* with introduction by R. W. Lightbown (1970), 7 · W. G. Strickland, *A dictionary of Irish artists*, 2 vols. (1913) · A. Crookshank and the Knight of Glin [D. Fitzgerald], *The painters of Ireland, c.1660–1920* (1978) · E. Croft-Murray, *Decorative painting in England, 1537–1837*, 2 (1970), 248 · G. Breeze, *Society of Artists in Ireland: index of exhibits, 1765–80* (1985) · private information (2004)

Mullins [Molyns], **John** (*d.* 1591), Church of England clergyman, was a native of Somerset. He graduated BA from Magdalen College, Oxford, in 1542, becoming a fellow that year, and proceeded MA in 1545. A member of the evangelical circle surrounding John Foxe, Laurence Humphrey, and Thomas Bentham, he was appointed college lecturer in moral philosophy (1547), then in natural philosophy (1549). In 1550 he signed a petition against President Owen Oglethorpe's preference for the 'unlearned and papists' (Bloxam, 2.309–11). Mullins contributed (in Greek) to the universities' tribute to the two boy dukes of Suffolk, *Epigrammata varia … in morte*[m] *duorum fratrum Henrici et Caroli Brandoni* (1552). He was ordained deacon according to the protestant ordinal on 29 March 1551, proceeded BTh the following year, and was appointed Magdalen's dean of divinity in 1553, but that October, three months after Mary's accession, was deprived of his fellowship by Stephen Gardiner and thereafter went into exile. In 1554 he arrived in Zürich with Humphrey and Bentham among others. There he defended the Edwardian prayer book against the liturgical innovations introduced in Frankfurt by John Knox's party. Once the Knoxians had departed for Geneva, however, he acted as Greek reader at Frankfurt until 1559.

Mullins returned after Elizabeth's accession, and was appointed prebendary of Kentish Town in St Paul's on 24 July 1559, and then archdeacon of London on 28 November, in both cases by letters patent *sede vacante*. In 1561 he was one of several candidates for the provostship of Eton but was allegedly rejected (in favour of William Day) because he was married, and he came second to Humphrey (with seventeen votes against twenty-five) in the election for the presidency of Magdalen. The same year he was instituted rector of Theydon Garnon, Essex, holding it until death. In the convocation of 1563, with other leading reformers, he tried to introduce, in seven articles, a radical programme of liturgical reform, then abstained from voting on a more moderate set of six articles. In 1565 he signed the petition against enforcement of the canonical vestments that Humphrey, Thomas Sampson, and Miles Coverdale submitted to the ecclesiastical commissioners.

According to Anthony Wood, Mullins was 'reverenced for his great learning and frequent preaching' (Wood, *Ath. Oxon.*, 1.581). Henry Machyn, no advanced protestant, noted a sermon of his in 1560 as 'goodly' (*Diary of Henry Machyn*, 234), yet none survives except as notes taken by an anonymous auditor (LPL, MS 739). Despite his reputation and the fact that he was chaplain to the queen and to Edmund Grindal, he was apparently not granted the degree of DTh for which he supplicated in 1566; but he was made a fellow of Manchester College in 1578, and was nominated in 1581 to dispute with the Jesuit Edmund Campion. In 1577 Archbishop Grindal collated Mullins to the rectory of Bocking, Essex, and appointed him and John Still (rector of Hadleigh, Suffolk) joint commissaries for his peculiars in Essex and Suffolk, an office that carried the title dean of Bocking—a commission renewed by John Whitgift upon his elevation to Canterbury in 1583.

Like many churchmen of his generation, Mullins found himself in a more conservative position as time passed. In 1572 he was unwillingly put in charge of John Field, under arrest over the recently published *Admonition to the Parliament*, advocating a Genevan pattern of discipline. The collection of documents published in 1573 as *A Brief Discourse of the Troubles Begun at Frankfort* was professedly a response to a sermon given by Mullins at Paul's Cross on this issue. In 1576, when Elizabeth was demanding their suppression, he reported that no prophesyings (clerical exercises) took place within his archdeaconry. Instead he himself supervised meetings of the clergy for study and if he found their answers unsatisfactory 'then do I myselfe open the meani[n]g' of the set scriptural passages (LPL, MS 2003, fol. 23r). In 1581 he and others 'withdrew themselves' from Aylmer's proceedings against Robert Wright for nonconformity (Strype, *Aylmer*, 60), but he examined the separatist Henry Barrow in 1587.

The identity of Mullins's wife is unknown, but she appears to have predeceased him, for in his will of 1588 he appointed his daughter Mary (wife of Walter Chetwynd) as his executor and bequeathed £200 to found two scholarships at Magdalen. He died, according to Wood, on 22 May 1591 and was buried in the north aisle of St Paul's Cathedral. Mary was granted probate on 9 June.

JULIAN LOCK

Sources Emden, *Oxf.*, 4.408 · J. R. Bloxam, *A register of the presidents, fellows … of Saint Mary Magdalen College*, 8 vols. (1853–85), vol. 2, pp. lxx, 308, 311; vol. 4, pp. 61–8, 113–14 · W. D. Macray, *A register of the members of St Mary Magdalen College, Oxford*, 8 vols. (1894–1915), vol. 2 · Wood, *Ath. Oxon.*, new edn, 1.581 · R. Churton, *The life of Alexander Nowell, dean of St Paul's* (1809) · [W. Whittingham?], *A brieff discours off the troubles begonne at Franckford* (1575); repr. with introduction by [J. Petherham] as *A brief discourse of the troubles begun at Frankfort* (1846) · J. Strype, *Annals of the Reformation and establishment of religion … during Queen Elizabeth's happy reign*, new edn, 4 vols. (1824) · J. Strype, *Historical collections of the life and acts of … John Aylmer*, new edn (1821) · J. Strype, *The life and acts of Matthew Parker*, new edn, 3 vols. (1821) · J. Strype, *The history of the life and acts of the most reverend father in God Edmund Grindal*, new edn (1821) · C. M. Dent, *Protestant reformers in Elizabethan Oxford* (1983) · C. H. Garrett, *The Marian exiles: a study in the origins of Elizabethan puritanism* (1938), 234–5 · W. P. Haugaard, *Elizabeth and the English Reformation: the struggle for a stable settlement of religion* (1968) · will, PRO, PROB 11/77, sig. 48 · diocese of London visitation records, GL, MSS 9537/2–8 · London episcopal register, GL, MS 9531 · P. Collinson, 'John Field and Elizabethan puritanism', *Elizabethan government and society: essays presented to Sir John Neale*, ed. S. T. Bindoff, J. Hurstfield, and C. H. Williams (1961), 127–62; repr. in P. Collinson, *Godly people: essays on English protestantism and puritanism* (1983), 335–70, esp. 347 · *The writings of Henry Barrow, 1587–1590*, ed. L. H. Carlson (1962) · A. D. Bell, 'Some early records of All Saints, Theydon Gernons', *Essex Review*, 35 (1926), 190–203 · A. Hoffmann, *Bocking deanery: the story of an Essex peculiar* (1976) · *The diary of Henry Machyn, citizen and merchant-taylor of London, from AD 1550 to AD 1563*, ed. J. G. Nichols, CS, 42 (1848) · IGI · Faculty Office register, LPL, F1/B, fol. 63v · register of Archbishop Whitgift, LPL

Archives LPL, letter, MS 2003, fol. 23r

Wealth at death over £228 6s. 8d. in specific bequests; Bocking £35 10s. p.a.; archdeaconry £23 13s. 4d.; Theydon Garnon £17: will, PRO, PROB 11/77, sig. 48; *Valor ecclesiasticus*

Mullock, Richard (1851–1920), sports administrator, was born on 31 May 1851 in Newport, Monmouthshire, the eldest of the four children of Henry Mullock (1826–1914), a local commercial printer, and his wife, Henrietta (1819–1896). The Mullock family played a prominent role in the municipal, commercial, philanthropic, and artistic life of nineteenth-century Newport. Richard Mullock, who entered into partnership with his father in 1877, invested his own energies outside the daily routine of the family printing business in the organization of local and national sport.

Mullock helped bring the Newport athletic club into existence in 1874, when he handed over a £100 profit from an athletics meeting he had arranged to the secretary of the town cricket club, Edward Bellerby. The two men occupied the joint secretaryship until 1883. Mullock's administrative skills were also in evidence as secretary of the Newport Infirmary from 1877 to 1884, but it was as an energetic promoter of the emerging game of rugby football that he became most widely known. He arranged the first erratically flickering 'electric light' match seen in Wales, when Newport played against Cardiff at Rodney Parade on 16 October 1878, and then pulled off another coup by inviting the crack English side Blackheath to play their first ever fixture in Wales, against Newport on 20 November 1879. The subsequent drubbing by the 'heathens' of the leading Welsh side of the time convinced Mullock that rugby in Wales would improve only if it were taken out of the unambitious hands of its Neath-based organizing body, the South Wales Football Union. On his own initiative he met with other Welsh club representatives at Swansea in March 1880 and then proceeded to open independent negotiations with the Rugby Football Union in London, who on 30 November 1880 considered 'a letter from Mr. R. Mullock of Newport, Monmouthshire, proposing a match with Wales'. Drawing on a wide range of personal, club, and college contacts Mullock hurried to assemble a side that played the full English fifteen at Blackheath on 19 February 1881.

Although Mullock's scratch team was heavily defeated, the momentum generated by his bold move proved unstoppable. With characteristic bravado, and to the chagrin of official Welsh rugby circles, he summoned representatives of eleven clubs to the Castle Hotel, Neath, on 12 March 1881, and the Welsh Rugby Union (WRU) came into existence. Mullock, who had precipitated its birth, was elected both secretary and treasurer, and the retrospective award of caps to the fifteen who had played at Blackheath gave official recognition to Wales's first international team. For the next decade the purposeful Mullock, portly in appearance and brusque in manner, ran the fledgeling union's affairs until his perceived high-handedness and casual approach to financial matters provoked his downfall. Having narrowly survived a bid to unseat him at the WRU's annual meeting in 1886, he obtained a stay of execution in 1887, when he was able to report the union's first credit balance, and for the next two years he was one of Wales's three nominees on the International Rugby Board (founded in 1886). But whereas in the WRU's early years Mullock had met some of its expenses from his own pocket, by 1890 he was rumoured to be guilty of financial impropriety, and the following year he was forced to relinquish the treasurership. He

remained as honorary secretary, but only for one more year: at the WRU's annual general meeting on 10 September 1892 he was awarded a testimonial of 100 guineas and the decision was taken to appoint a paid secretary.

Had Mullock enjoyed the annual stipend of £50 voted to his successor, W. H. Gwynn of Swansea, by the WRU he might have been saved from his subsequent financial difficulties. In April 1893 he was declared a bankrupt, although he continued in the family firm, which in 1897 bound the testimonial book for A. J. Gould, illuminated by Mullock himself. His considerable artistic talent won him high praise as curator of the fine art section of the Royal National Eisteddfod held in Newport in 1897, and he was renowned as a skilled copyist of engravings. When in 1902 he was sued in court for £3 of goods he pleaded that the £1 a month he earned from selling drawings was insufficient to support his wife, Emily (née Phillips), whom he had married in March 1874, and their six children. He left the Newport area and disappeared from public view. The family's artistic streak was inherited by his daughter Dorothy Mullock, whose stylish illustrations for two plays by Clifford Bax, *The Rose and the Cross* (1918) and *Prelude and Fugue* (1923), indicate her currency in fashionable London circles of the time.

Richard Mullock died in St Thomas's Hospital, London, on 8 July 1920, after an operation for throat cancer. By then he was living and working as a printer's clerk in Chiswick, in an elusive obscurity far removed from the publicity that had surrounded him as the founding father of the Welsh Rugby Union.   GARETH WILLIAMS

Sources D. Smith and G. Williams, *Fields of praise: the official history of the Welsh Rugby Union, 1881–1981* · J. Wilson and R. Cucksey, *Art and society in Newport: James Flewitt Mullock and the Victorian achievement* (1993) · J. Billot, *History of Welsh international rugby* (1970) · W. J. T. Collins, ed., *Newport athletic club: the record of half a century* (1925) · *South Wales Argus* (16 July 1920) · *Western Mail* [Cardiff] (17 July 1920) · minute books, 1892–3, Welsh Rugby Union · minute books, 1880–81, Rugby Football Union
Likenesses photograph, repro. in J. B. G. Thomas, *The illustrated history of Welsh rugby* (1980), 22 · photograph, repro. in A. Richards, *A touch of glory: 100 years of Welsh rugby* (1980), 49

Mulock, Dinah Maria. *See* Craik, Dinah Maria (1826–1887).

Mulready, William (1786–1863), painter, was born on 1 April 1786 at Ennis, co. Clare, Ireland. His grandfather, James Mulready, died before 1792 and his father, Michael Mulready (a leather breeches maker), had at least two brothers: William, who died without issue in 1822, and James, who died in 1797. Nothing is known of Mulready's mother except that she was still alive in 1811 when she modelled for a painting by John Linnell (*A Woman at a Table Drinking*). Michael Mulready is believed to have served as model for John Linnell's *Removing Timber* (1808), Wilkie's *Duncan Gray* (1814), and for several works by Mulready including *The Village Buffoon* (1815–16; RA diploma gallery). Although there is anecdotal evidence of siblings, none seems to have reached maturity.

William Mulready
(1786–1863), self-
portrait, c.1835

Early years About 1788 the family moved to Dublin and thence, about 1791, to London. Mulready never left England again. By 1792 the Mulreadys were settled in the Bayswater area of London. They were Roman Catholics and some of their son's early education was probably with priests but as an adult Mulready demonstrated no religious affiliation. Mulready attended various small private schools and acquired some Latin but, by his own account, the bookstalls of St Paul's Churchyard provided an important resource and encouraged his taste for classics in translation and canonical authors like Shakespeare, Cervantes, and Goldsmith, all of whom he later drew upon for subject matter. As an adult he tried to acquire Greek and German. In 1796 or early 1797 Mulready encountered the painter and art teacher John Graham (1754–1817), who used him as a model, lent him prints to copy, and encouraged his parents to foster their son's talent. Mulready was a precocious youth and made rapid progress. He entered the Royal Academy Schools in 1800 at the age of fourteen following tuition and sponsorship from Thomas Banks (1735–1805); he was awarded the great silver palette by the Society of Arts in 1801 for a drawing (now lost); he was exhibiting at the Royal Academy by 1803, and in 1806 he was awarded the Royal Academy's silver medal for draughtsmanship. During 1805 he assisted Robert Ker Porter (1777–1842) on his panorama *The Battle of Agincourt* for which he was never paid. After a hiatus (during which two paintings characteristic of this early period, *The Mall, Kensington Gravel Pits*, 1811–12, and *Near the Mall, Kensington Gravel Pits*, 1812–13, both now in the Victoria and Albert Museum as part of the Sheepshanks bequest, failed to satisfy patrons), Mulready's name went forward for election to associate membership of the academy in 1813. He received no votes and was not elected until November 1815, with elevation to academician in February 1816.

Mulready himself expressed the fear that irregularities in his personal life had jeopardized his professional opportunities and he remained, for much of his life, reticent about his domestic affairs. The protective attitudes of his friends and biographers reinforced an image of the artist as a figure of reclusiveness, moral rectitude, and civic responsibility which prevailed for over a century. A string of awards and honours underscored his reputation: member of the Athenaeum (1824), honorary member of Leeds Academy of Art (1853), the Royal Academy of Amsterdam (1856), the Royal Hibernian Academy (1860), and chevalier in the Légion d'honneur following his contribution of nine paintings to the 1855 Universal Exhibition in Paris.

Marriage and domestic life While attending the Royal Academy Schools Mulready met John Varley (1778–1842), who, together with John Linnell (1792–1882), became a close lifelong friend. Through studying with Varley, and acting as his resident assistant, Mulready perfected his watercolour technique; he also made the acquaintance of the artist's sister, Elizabeth Robinson Varley (1784–1864), herself a landscape artist who exhibited at the Royal Academy, the British Institution, and the Society of Painters in Water Colours between 1811 and 1828. In 1803 William, then aged seventeen, and Elizabeth married. Four sons were born: Paul Augustus (1804–1864), William (1805–1878), Michael (1807–1889), and John (1809–1893). All became artists and Paul was the father of A. E. (Augustus Edwin) Mulready (1855–1938). Michael was known to have collaborated with his father and confusion, which prevails in salerooms today despite the technical superiority of works in Mulready's hand, also occurred during his lifetime, with instances of owners asking him to sign or authenticate works long after their date of origin. William and Elizabeth Mulready were formally separated in 1810 though they parted earlier; financial strains on the household were considerable (Mulready frequently borrowed from Linnell in these years), despite clear evidence of rigorous attempts to control expenditure, and overcrowding and professional competition did not make matters easier. The declared cause of marital strife was, however, sexual infidelity (probably on both sides). Elizabeth confesses to having sought a bed at the house of an unmarried man but claims, admittedly some years after the alleged events, that her love for her husband had been rewarded with blows and insults and that he had not only a number of other women in his life but had also taken a 'low boy' to his bed. Despite attempts to gain access to her children, Elizabeth was obliged to cede their upbringing to her estranged husband, for whom a house full of boys was inspirational for his art but a challenge in parenting that he failed to meet. The Mulready boys were regarded as unruly and both Linnell and Sheepshanks were called in to help deal with the eldest, who was especially problematic. Mulready made provision for his wife in his will, and Elizabeth enjoyed not only financial security but also contact with her grandchildren in later life.

William and Elizabeth Mulready lived at a succession of London addresses; they appear first to have lived with John Varley at Broad Street, Golden Square. By 1808 they had moved to share a house with Linnell at 30 Francis Street, Bedford Square, where they occupied the two first-floor rooms with Linnell on the top floor. The couple's youngest son was born in Holland Street on 27 June 1809 but Mulready was at this date still using the Francis Street address, so the couple may, by this date, have separated. By 1811 Mulready had moved out of the West End back to the area where his parents, with whom Linnell had lodged, were still resident. On the rural fringes of London and characterized by gravel pits, small-scale farming, dilapidated cottages, brick-kilns, and the parklands surrounding Kensington Palace, Holland Park, and Campden House, the area enjoyed good light and was popular with artists: A. W. Callcott, William Collins, and David Wilkie lived in the vicinity. Mulready never returned to central London. At first he occupied a cottage (probably his parents' home) in Robinson's Row, just off Kensington gravel pits (now Notting Hill Gate). By 1826 he was living at Moscow Cottages, Bayswater (behind Moscow Road), and two years later, on 25 March 1828, he signed a lease on the first of the substantial villas constructed in Linden Grove (now Linden Gardens) on the Ladbroke estate just off Notting Hill Gate by Thomas Allason which was to be his home for the remainder of his life. While drawings suggest he harboured ambitions for the interior and for the gardens of this villa, and his friends and patrons George Loddiges (1784–1846) and his brother Conrad, the Hackney horticulturalists, were to supply plants, the evidence of his frequent visitors suggests that little progress was made.

Among the women in Elizabeth Mulready's testimony are cited 'Harriet' and 'Mrs. Lekie'. It seems almost certain that the former was the artist Harriet Gouldsmith (1787–1863), who had been one of Mulready's pupils and who was also amorously associated with Linnell. The latter was Elizabeth Forbes Leckie, who may have been a widow and who became Mulready's lifelong companion after the separation. The painting *Father and Child* (priv. coll.) is based on a sketch labelled 'James Leckie and little Mary' and shows a small child learning to read on the knee of a youth. While nothing is known about James (he may have been a son of Elizabeth Leckie), Mary was most probably Mary Mulready Leckie, daughter of Mulready's companion. Elizabeth Leckie retained her own residence but was evidently well known to Mulready's friends (she is mentioned in Henry Cole's diary). Mary was Mulready's ward and an artist in her own right, exhibiting under her maiden name at the Royal Academy from 1840 to 1844 and, after her marriage to John Jeffries Stone in 1843, in her married name (1845–6). She named her first child Edward Mulready Stone and William Mulready acted as godfather. The close ties of affection between Mulready and his ward (he wrote to her regularly and lovingly) and between Mary and the Mulready boys, as well as the circumstantial evidence outlined above, justifies the inference that Mary was Mulready's natural daughter.

Book illustrations Mulready was introduced early into the society of cultivated men. Among the publications of William Godwin's Juvenile Library was *The Looking Glass: a True History of the Early Years of an Artist* (1805), based upon conversations between Godwin and Mulready. Between 1805 and 1806 Mulready, often in company with George Dawe

(1781–1829) and John Linnell, was a frequent visitor to Godwin's home at 41 Skinner Street. By 1807 Mulready had become the Juvenile Library's chief (and possibly only) illustrator, claiming later to have executed 307 designs in two years at 7s. 6d. each. Some of these were engraved by William Blake. Here, alongside George Cruikshank (1792–1878), who worked in Godwin's children's bookshop, Mulready developed a narrative style that exploited the traditions of Thomas Bewick (1733–1828) and his brother, John, and which, when refined into the compositional devices of paintings like *The Wolf and the Lamb* (1820; Royal Collection) and *First Love* (1838–9; V&A) drew eulogies from critics like Hippolyte Taine and W. M. Thackeray. He never abandoned his interest in book illustration; in 1843 he designed all the illustrations for John Van Voorst's edition of Goldsmith's *The Vicar of Wakefield*, the popularity of which led to commissions for several oil paintings based upon the designs: *The Whistonian Controversy* (1843), for Thomas Baring (priv. coll.); *Choosing the Wedding Gown* (1845), for John Sheepshanks (V&A); and *Haymaking: Burchell and Sophia* (1847; priv. coll.). He also contributed to Edward Moxon's edition of Tennyson's *Poems* (1857).

Patrons Mulready's meeting with his most loyal patron, John Sheepshanks (1784–1863), is said to have occurred when the artist defended Sheepshanks from an assailant by deploying the pugilistic skills for which he was renowned (it is alleged he trained with Daniel Mendoza), and which he practised with his sons and with fellow artists. His portrait of Sheepshanks seated in his Bond Street apartment receiving tea and the morning mail from his maid while portfolios of drawings lie by his side (1832–4; V&A) is a landmark in the evolution of the detailed, small-scale portrayal of collectors in intimate domestic settings. In 1852 Mulready completed a highly worked view from the window of Sheepshanks's house at Blackheath (V&A). Another patron, Sir John Swinburne, whom he met through his self-effacing work for the Artists' Benevolent Fund (to which he donated the copyright of *The Wolf and the Lamb*), shared his enthusiasm for boxing; in 1823–4, when the boxing promoter John Thurtell (1784–1824) was on trial for murder, Mulready attended the proceedings, drew and made notes on the deportment of the prisoner in the dock, and dispatched an account to Sir John. He taught the Swinburne children, painted their portraits, and was a regular visitor to their Northumberland home, Capheaton, where he sketched in the open air. He enjoyed a similar relationship with William Walter Legge, fifth earl of Dartmouth, whose wife and child he portrayed (priv. coll.) and whose children he taught. Mulready met Henry Cole (who remained an intimate friend until Mulready's death) in 1839, when Cole was deputed to invite Mulready to design the first pre-paid postage envelope. The artist supported Felix Summerly (Cole) by contributing to his Art Manufactures (book illustrations and a design for a milk-jug based on *Haymaking*) but the envelope, with its image of Britannia supervising deliveries of letters to the four corners of the globe, released in 1840, and widely ridiculed, generated large numbers of caricatures, and was quickly withdrawn, causing the artist much chagrin. Other patrons included the politician Sir Robert Peel (1750–1830), who purchased *A Boy Firing a Cannon*, exhibited at the Royal Academy in 1827; John Gibbons, the Bristol iron-founder, who purchased *A Sailing Match*; and Robert Vernon (1774–1849), who purchased *The Last In* (1835; Tate collection). That Mulready's work was sought after, at least after the early 1820s, by the aristocrat as well as by the newly wealthy manufacturer, and that patrons were prepared to pay high prices, is not in doubt. He took many months to prepare and complete each subject and desirous purchasers were sometimes disappointed. Henry McConnel, the Lancashire cotton manufacturer, offered Mulready 100 guineas for a drawing of a street preacher and 1000 guineas for a painting of the same subject. No painting was ever executed though some preparatory drawings exist (V&A). Thirty-eight years later (in 1860) McConnel was still trying to purchase a painting by the artist.

Paintings Mulready's most distinguished paintings—often bearing titles which allude with studied ambiguity to contemporary social concerns while imaging bucolic past times, timeless classical poses, and nostalgic glimpses of rustic domesticity—were produced between 1820 and 1850 often on commission for patrons who paid in advance instalments. *The Careless Messenger Detected* (1821; priv. coll.) for the second earl of Durham, *Open your Mouth and Shut your Eyes* (1835–8; V&A) for Sheepshanks, and *Train up a Child in the Way he Should Go* (1841; Forbes Collection, Battersea, London) for Thomas Baring use a child or children as central players in a moral drama that inflects concerns with social education, violence, sexual desire, and racial marginalization. In many cases, the titles were appended only at exhibition stage, with working titles (such as 'Lascars' for *Train up a Child*) indicating in the artist's account book the development of the theme. What was explicit in some early paintings—*The Widow* (1823; priv. coll.), based on lines from the *Satyricon* of Petronius, was described by Ruskin as a subject unfit for representation and remained unsold until 1841—was treated with subtle obliqueness and framed in utopian visual language in his later work. Mulready's technical proficiency has ensured that works like these have survived in outstanding condition; his working methods (several stages of drawing and note-taking followed by a charcoal chiaroscuro sketch and an oil study, and careful financial record-keeping) permit a detailed understanding of the thought processes and professional practices undergone in Mulready's quest for perfection.

Mulready was admired for his diligence, his application, and his commitment to learning: he attended Michael Faraday's lectures at the Royal Institution in 1829, was interested in chromatology, and was a regular and (unusually) conscientious visitor in the life class at the Royal Academy, drawing alongside the students he was supervising. One of his best-known remarks was made to the royal commissioners enquiring into the effectiveness of the Royal Academy: 'I have from the moment I became a visitor in the life school drawn there as if I were drawing for a prize' ('Royal commission … Royal Academy').

Shortly after giving evidence before the commissioners, Mulready died at his home, 1 Linden Grove, Kensington gravel pits, London, on 7 July 1863. He was tall, manly in form, and was regarded by his contemporaries as exceptionally handsome. Portraits of him exist by John Linnell (NPG) and by Frederick Bacon Barwell (design for a commemorative mosaic at V&A), as well as several minor self-portraits. His modest private funeral on 13 July 1863, arranged by his son Michael, was according to Anglican rites and attended by only three Royal Academicians and a small number of friends including Richard Redgrave (1804–1888) and Henry Cole (1806–1882). He was buried at Kensal Green cemetery, London, where a grand tomb, featuring a full-length effigy and relief scenes of his most celebrated paintings, by Godfrey Sykes (1825–1866), was built to mark his grave.

Reputation and output Mulready's claim to fame rests first on a (relatively small) body of exquisitely produced oil paintings, sometimes on panel like the Dutch masters whose work he emulated and sometimes on canvas with thin washes and stippling of brilliant clashing pigments laid over a white ground—described in 1840 by Thackeray as 'gaudy' and 'prismatic' ('Picture gossip', *Fraser's Magazine*, 21, 1840, 726). The subjects of the early years are chiefly landscapes and picturesque cottage subjects including views of Hampstead Heath, Middlesex, painted on small panels of millboard, depictions of gravel pits, and cottages in or near St Albans which, while owing much to John Crome (1768–1821), share with Linnell's work of this period a *plein-air* freshness of vision. In the middle and later years he painted elaborately structured narrative scenes involving children and adolescents. His technique inspired the Pre-Raphaelites, who nominated him to the Hogarth Club, and the high prices fetched by paintings in his studio sale (Christies, 28–30 April 1864) were still remembered in 1877. Second, there is a large corpus of drawings in varied media from chalk, through pencil, to pen and ink (Whitworth Art Gallery, University of Manchester; V&A) ranging from thumb-nail compositional sketches to analytical studies after nature and large-scale, highly finished life drawings within which discipline he continued working until his death, producing images of great technical mastery much admired by Queen Victoria, who acquired one (Royal Collection), but disliked by John Ruskin, who thought them bestial and degraded. Third, Mulready interacted socially and intellectually with some of the most influential artists, writers, and arts administrators of his era.

MARCIA POINTON

Sources K. M. Heleniak, *William Mulready* (1980) · M. Pointon, *Mulready* (1986) [exhibition catalogue, V&A] · A. Rorimer, *Drawings by William Mulready* (1972) · J. Dafforne, *Pictures by William Mulready, RA* (1872) · F. G. Stephens, *Memorials of William Mulready, RA* (1890) · *Catalogue of the whole of the remaining drawings … of William Mulready* (1864) [sale catalogue, Christies, 28–30 April 1864] · W. Godwin [T. Marcliffe], *The looking glass: a true history of the early years of an artist* (1805) · 'Royal commission to inquire into … the Royal Academy', *Parl. papers* (1863), vol. 27, nos. 3205, 3205-I; repr. in *Education: Fine Arts*, 5 (1968) · A. T. Story, *The life of John Linnell*, 2 vols. (1892) · J. Pye, *Patronage of British art: an historical sketch* (1845) · M. Pointon,

'The benefits of patronage', *Gazette des Beaux-Arts*, 6th ser., 96 (1980), 75–84 · M. Pointon, 'Painters and pugilism', *Gazette des Beaux-Arts*, 6th ser., 92 (1978), 131–40 · *CGPLA Eng. & Wales* (1863) · H. Cole, diary, V&A NAL · RA

Archives priv. coll., MSS · Tate collection, letters, papers, and sketches · V&A NAL, account book, notebook, and corresp. | FM Cam., Linnell diary and corresp. · Northumbd RO, Swinburne MSS

Likenesses D. Wilkie, group portrait, oils, 1814 (*The refusal*), V&A · J. Linnell, oils, 1833, NPG; unfinished version, NG Ire. · W. Mulready, self-portrait, oils, *c*.1835, NPG [*see illus.*] · T. Bridgford, pencil drawing, *c*.1842, NG Ire. · T. Bridgford, black and red chalk drawing, 1844, NG Ire. · C. Martin, pencil drawing, 1844, BM · C. H. Lear, chalk drawing, 1846, NPG · Cundall & Downes & Co., carte-de-visite, *c*.1860, V&A · F. B. Barwell, oils, *c*.1862, V&A · C. W. Cope, etching, 1863, NG Ire. · H. Weekes, marble bust, 1866, Tate collection · G. G. Adams, medal, 1877, NPG · J. King, oil on panel (after photograph by P. H. D., 1885), NG Ire. · photograph, NPG

Wealth at death under £12,000: probate, 17 Aug 1863, *CGPLA Eng. & Wales*

Mulroney the Great. *See* O'Carroll, Mulroney (*c*.1470–1532).

Mulso family (*per. c.***1350–1460**), gentry, of Northamptonshire, must have originated in Mulsoe, Buckinghamshire, but a branch was already established at Newton by Geddington, Northamptonshire, in 1346. **Henry** [i] **Mulso** (*fl.* 1359–1380) 'of Geddington' appears in records over a period of about twenty years as a merchant and shopowner in Thames Street, London, and as a middle-ranking member of the Northamptonshire gentry. His relationship to the next owner of Newton, **John** [i] **Mulso** (*d.* in or before 1410) is uncertain, and likewise to his more prominent contemporary **William** [i] **Mulso** (*d.* 1376) king's clerk and successor to William Wykeham as surveyor of the works at Windsor in 1361. A canon of St George's Chapel, Windsor, and (again in succession to Wykeham) dean of St Martin's-le-Grand from 1364, William became a chamberlain of the exchequer of receipt in 1365 and ten years later keeper of the king's wardrobe. His close association with the court enabled him to build up a moderately sized estate in Buckinghamshire, adding Chesham and Stoke Poges to his lordship of Mulsoe, which he finally alienated in mortmain before his death in 1376.

The last quarter of the fourteenth century saw the Newton branch of the family achieve some prominence in the person of John [i] Mulso, who was a lawyer with a clientele among the nobility and courtiers of Richard II. As a committed supporter of the king he was entrusted with local offices: JP in 1384, escheator in 1385 and 1391–2, MP in the parliaments of September 1388 and 1397–8, and sheriff in 1393–4, 1395–6, and 1397–9. In August 1397 he—or possibly his namesake (and perhaps his brother), **John** [ii] **Mulso** (*fl.* 1367–1422), who was a burgess of Calais and household retainer of Thomas (I) Mowbray, earl of Nottingham—was ordered to bring the chief justice, William Rickhill, secretly to Calais to record a forced confession of treason by the duke of Gloucester, held there in Nottingham's custody. In July 1399 he raised men in Northamptonshire to resist the invasion of Henry Bolingbroke, but

by 1410 he was dead. After the death of his first wife, Margaret, he married Joan, with whom he is commemorated in a small but beautiful brass in Newton church. He had acquired the manor of Pilton from the executors of his friend Sir William Thorpe in 1391 and had raised the family into the office-holding élite of the shire.

John [i] Mulso had three sons: **Thomas** [i] **Mulso** (*d.* 1446) with his first wife, **Henry** [ii] **Mulso** (*d.* 1425) and **John** [iii] **Mulso** (*d.* in or before 1416) with his second. John [iii] made the least mark. In 1401 he married Alice, widow of William Spernore, and two years later they acquired the important manor of Finedon, Northamptonshire, which was devised to their two sons, John [iv] and Thomas [ii], both of whom served in France between 1417 and 1431. John [iii] held no shire office and had died by 1416. By contrast his brother Henry [ii] served as escheator (1395–7) and aulnager (1398–9) in Northamptonshire and used the family's connection with the house of York to become the duke's lieutenant in Jersey and constable of the Tower of London. He served on the duke of Clarence's expedition to Aquitaine in 1412 and at Harfleur in 1415 where, by 1421, he had become lieutenant to Lord Cromwell. He subsequently returned to England to be elected to parliament for Northamptonshire in 1422. By then he was already in the service of Humphrey, duke of Gloucester, and was treasurer of his household by 1423. In November 1424 he was preparing to accompany the duke to Hainault, but by April 1425 he had returned. He made his will on 1 June and died shortly afterward. His marriage to Joan had produced two sons to whom he left his armour, and two unmarried daughters; he asked to be buried in the north aisle of Geddington church, but no monument remains.

It was Thomas [i] Mulso, the eldest and longest-surviving son of John [i], who was to sustain the family's role in the shire in the first quarter of the fifteenth century, serving as sheriff (1409–10) and escheator (1419–20) and being elected to parliament in 1417. He held the Mulso inheritance in Newton, Pilton, and Finedon, and acquired further lands at Little Ocle and at Kettleborough in Suffolk. In 1412 his landed income was assessed at not less than £54 p.a. placing him among the middling gentry. He too probably had some legal competence and was a frequent feoffee and witness for the local gentry and nobility. But after 1422 he held no further offices, occupying himself with his estates, though he did not die until 1446. His will, made in 1439, provided lands for his two younger sons, **William** [ii] **Mulso** (*d.* after 1461) and **Sir Edmund Mulso** (*d.* 1458), and money for the marriage of their sister Margaret, thereby reducing the full inheritance of **Thomas** [ii] **Mulso** (*d.* 1460), the eldest.

By 1445 this next generation had already undertaken service in France—Thomas [ii] from 1436, under a sequence of professional captains, and Edmund accompanying Richard, duke of York, to Normandy in 1441. There he held captaincies at Lisieux, Neuburg, Pont-Audemer, and Pont-de-l'Arche, received knighthood, and won a place among the select band of ducal counsellors, alongside Sir William Oldhall and Sir Andrew Ogard. After York's return in 1446 Sir Edmund became constable of

Fotheringhay Castle and joint steward of Rayleigh, while Thomas [ii], temporarily relinquishing his English lands, became his brother's lieutenant at Pont-de-l'Arche and Elbeuf and York's captain in Bernay. In June 1449 Edmund accompanied the duke to Ireland where he was made seneschal of Meath; when the political crisis of 1450 brought York back from Ireland, all three brothers gave him open support. Edmund and others of the duke's bodyguard were targeted by the court; William [ii] became the duke's retainer with a large fee; and Thomas [ii] returned from France to sit in the parliament of November 1450 alongside Edmund as York's nominees. When in 1451–2 York found himself excluded from the court and forced into armed confrontation, Edmund and Thomas [ii] raised men in Northamptonshire for his march to Dartford where they were probably present.

Although the brothers avoided reprisals like those taken against Oldhall, they remained under a cloud until York's fortunes improved with his first protectorate in 1454. Then, and again in November 1455, Edmund was engaged on diplomatic missions and Thomas [ii] was rewarded with an advantageous lease of the royal manor of Geddington in November 1454. Edmund joined Warwick's garrison at Calais in March 1456 but did not live to face the ultimate test of civil war. He made his will on 1 May 1458, asking to be buried in St Michael Paternoster Royal where he endowed prayers for Richard of York. As his executors he named his brother William [ii] and William Oldhall, who two years later was buried nearby. Though well rewarded for his loyalty to Richard of York, Edmund remained a professional soldier–counsellor and never established himself as a significant landowner.

Thomas's later years were spent managing the Mulso lands in Northamptonshire and Suffolk, cultivating an obscurity which was suddenly terminated by his death on 25 July 1460, two weeks after the battle of Northampton and perhaps as a consequence of it. He left three daughters, one by his first wife, Anne, two by his second, Katherine. His heir, Alice, was already married to Henry Tresham (younger brother of the ardent Lancastrian Sir Thomas *Tresham) to whom all the Mulso estates now passed. When Tresham was killed at the battle of Tewkesbury in 1471 the Mulso lands, by a kind of political justice, escheated to York's son, Edward IV.

In their brief span the Mulsos were never among the leading gentry of Northamptonshire; their modest estates, acquired through local legal practice, were not significantly augmented either by a fortunate marriage of the heir or by service in war which the younger sons had to undertake.   G. L. HARRISS

Sources HoP, *Commons, 1386–1421*, vol. 3 · HoP, *Commons, 1422–1504* [draft] · J. S. Roskell, *The Commons in the parliament of 1422* [1954] · J. C. Wedgwood and A. D. Holt, *History of parliament, 1: Biographies of the members of the Commons house, 1439–1509* (1936) · *Chancery records* · E. F. Jacob, ed., *The register of Henry Chichele, archbishop of Canterbury, 1414–1443*, 2, CYS, 42 (1937) · P. A. Johnson, *Duke Richard of York, 1411–1460* (1988) · A. Marshal, 'The role of English war captains in England and Normandy, 1436–61', MA diss., U. Wales, Swansea, 1975 · private information (2004) [A. Curry, database of Englishmen serving in France] · R. A. Griffiths, *The reign of King Henry VI: the exercise of royal authority, 1422–1461* (1981) · Reg. Stafford, LPL, fol. 131 · inquisition post mortem, PRO, C139/181/66 · will, PRO, PROB 11/4, sig. 24 [Sir Edmund Mulso] · J. Stevenson, ed., *Letters and papers illustrative of the wars of the English in France during the reign of Henry VI, king of England*, 2/2, Rolls Series, 22 (1864) · J. Stow, *A survey of London*, rev. edn (1603); repr. with introduction by C. L. Kingsford as *A survey of London*, 2 vols. (1908); repr. with addns (1971), vol. 1 · J. Bridges, *History of Northamptonshire*, 2.349 · *Calendar of the fine rolls*, 22 vols., PRO (1911–62) · *CClR* · *CPR* · *Inquisitions and assessments relating to feudal aids*, 4, PRO (1906), 31, 44, 118; 6, PRO (1921), 496

Likenesses double portrait, brass sculpture (John Mulso his second wife), Newton church, Northamptonshire

Wealth at death £54 p.a. for lands in Northamptonshire, Rutland, and Suffolk; Thomas [i] Mulso: *Feudal aids*, 4.31, 44, 118; 6.496

Mulso, Sir Edmund (d. 1458). *See under* Mulso family (*per. c.*1350–1460).

Mulso, Henry (fl. 1359–1380). *See under* Mulso family (*per. c.*1350–1460).

Mulso, Henry (d. 1425). *See under* Mulso family (*per. c.*1350–1460).

Mulso, Hester. *See* Chapone, Hester (1727–1801).

Mulso, John (d. in or before 1410). *See under* Mulso family (*per. c.*1350–1460).

Mulso, John (d. in or before 1416). *See under* Mulso family (*per. c.*1350–1460).

Mulso, John (fl. 1367–1422). *See under* Mulso family (*per. c.*1350–1460).

Mulso, Thomas (d. 1446). *See under* Mulso family (*per. c.*1350–1460).

Mulso, Thomas (d. 1460). *See under* Mulso family (*per. c.*1350–1460).

Mulso, William (d. 1376). *See under* Mulso family (*per. c.*1350–1460).

Mulso, William (d. after 1461). *See under* Mulso family (*per. c.*1350–1460).

Multon, Thomas de. *See* Moulton, Sir Thomas of (d. 1240).

Mulvany, Charles Pelham (1835–1885), writer and Church of England clergyman, was born in Dublin on 20 May 1835, the son of Henry William Mulvany, barrister, and grandson of a captain in the Royal Navy who took part in the battle of Bunker Hill (17 June 1775) during the American War of Independence. He entered Trinity College, Dublin, in 1850, became a scholar in 1854, and graduated BA at Dublin University as first-honour man in classics in June 1856. Before this date he had written verse in *The Nation* using the signature C. P. M. Sch.; he was editor of the *College Magazine* during 1856 and 1857, and also wrote for the *Irish Metropolitan Magazine* in 1857 and 1858.

Although Mulvany later claimed to have served as a surgeon with the British navy, he was more likely to have been a surgical assistant—he certainly never practised medicine privately. He emigrated to Canada in 1859, and in 1866 joined the 2nd battalion of the Queen's Own Rifles in response to the Fenian rising. He then moved to Lennoxville, Lower Canada, and enlisted in the militia at Sherbrooke, rising to the rank of lieutenant. He also joined the faculty of Bishop's College at Lennoxville as a lecturer in classics and in 1867 helped to establish a literary periodical there, the *Students' Monthly*. In that year he left the college to take up the post of principal at the Niagara high school in Ontario.

Mulvany retired from teaching in 1868 to become an Anglican minister. He was ordained by John Travers Lewis, the bishop of Ontario, becoming a deacon in 1868 and a priest in 1872. He was a licenced curate to All Saints' Church in Kingston, Ontario, in 1868, and later to various parishes in Lanark, Prince Edward, and Northumberland counties in Ontario.

After ten years of rural parish service Mulvany retired from active clerical work and moved to Toronto. He became a constant contributor to Canadian newspapers and magazines, devoting the greater part of his later life to literary work. He kept up his connection with Trinity College by his brilliant contributions to the first three volumes of *Kottabos*, issued respectively in 1874, 1877, and 1881. His collection *Lyrics of History and Life* appeared in 1880. He also published histories of the county of Peterborough (1884) and of Toronto (1884); the latter, *Toronto Past and Present*, is still useful to historians for its depiction of the city in the late nineteenth century. His *History of the North-West Rebellion of 1885*, however, is marked by a conservatism characteristic of the white English-speaking Canadian population of the time. At the time of his death he was preparing a history of the Liberal Party in Canada. His last-published verses, entitled 'Our boys in the north-west away', appeared in *The Globe*, Toronto's daily newspaper, as late as 25 May 1885. He died at 69 Augusta Terrace, Toronto, on 31 May 1885. It is possible that an Elizabeth Mulvany, who died in childbirth in Toronto in July 1880, was his wife.

THOMAS SECCOMBE, *rev.* MEGAN A. STEPHAN

Sources G. Killen, 'Mulvany, Charles Pelham', *DCB*, vol. 11 · H. J. Morgan, ed., *The Dominion Annual Register and Review for 1885* (1886), 273–4 · D. J. O'Donoghue, *The poets of Ireland: a biographical and bibliographical dictionary* (1912), 324 · J. G. Wilson and J. Fiske, eds., *Appletons' cyclopedia of American biography*, 4 (1888), 458 · *The Globe* [Toronto] (1 June 1885)

Mulvany, George Francis (1809–1869). *See under* Mulvany, Thomas James (1779–1845).

Mulvany, Thomas James (1779–1845), painter and art administrator, was born in Dublin, and was a pupil of Francis West at the Dublin Society school. He began his career as a miniature painter, and sent eight miniatures to an exhibition in the Parliament House in 1802, but he later painted mainly figures and landscapes, which he exhibited between 1810 and 1814 at the rooms of the Dublin Society in Hawkins Street. When the Dublin Society sold the rooms, depriving the artists of an exhibition venue, Mulvany and his brother John George Mulvany were among those who pressed for the foundation of a national academy for Irish artists on the lines of the Royal Academy in London. When a charter was granted, in 1823, and the

Royal Hibernian Academy founded, with Francis Johnston as the first president, the Mulvanys were among fourteen original academicians. Thomas Mulvany was appointed the first keeper in 1826, and showed pictures continuously at Royal Hibernian Academy exhibitions until his retirement in 1844. His paintings include *A Blind Beggar* (1826) and *View at Dieppe* (1826); two of his engravings, *Armagh Castle* and *Ruins of St Andrew's Church*, illustrate T. Bell's *Essays on the Origin and Progress of Gothic Architecture in Ireland* (1829).

Mulvany was also a writer, and contributed a series of articles on Irish artists to *The Citizen*. His planned biography of Irish artists never appeared, but he did edit *The Life of James Gandon* (published in 1846). He died on 27 February 1845 at his home, Dirker Lodge, Cross Avenue, Booterstown, and was buried at Mount Jerome cemetery, Dublin, where there is an inscription to his memory.

George Francis Mulvany (1809–1869), art administrator and painter, one of Mulvany's three sons, was born in Dublin and studied at the Royal Hibernian Academy school and in Italy. A prolific painter of mediocre portraits and subject paintings, he exhibited at the academy from 1827 until his death. He became an associate in 1830 and a full member in 1835, and succeeded his father as keeper in 1845. He was an enthusiastic promoter of art institutions and was one of the foremost advocates for the foundation of the National Gallery of Ireland, of which he was appointed director in 1862. He died after a short illness at his home at 18 Herbert Place, Dublin, on 6 February 1869, and was buried four days later in Mount Jerome cemetery, Dublin. L. H. CUST, *rev.* ANNE PIMLOTT BAKER

Sources W. G. Strickland, *A dictionary of Irish artists*, 2 vols. (1913); repr. with introduction by T. J. Snoddy (1989) · A. M. Stewart and C. de Courcy, *Royal Hibernian Academy of Arts: index of exhibitors and their works, 1826–1979*, 3 vols. (1985–7) · Boase, *Mod. Eng. biog.* · IGI
Likenesses G. F. Mulvany, portrait (of his father), repro. in Strickland, *Dictionary of Irish artists* (1913), vol. 2, facing 156
Wealth at death £400—George Francis Mulvany: administration, 26 Feb 1870, *CGPLA Ire.*

Mumford, James (c.1606–1666), Jesuit, was born in Norfolk or Suffolk. The names of his parents and place of birth and baptism are unknown. In 1626 he entered the Jesuit noviciate at Watten in Flanders and about 1635 was ordained priest at Liège, where he made his final profession in 1641. An able theologian, he filled both academic and pastoral offices in the Jesuit colleges at St Omer, Watten, and Liège, where he was elected rector in 1648. In 1641 his *The Remembrance for the Living to Pray for the Dead* was published at St Omer. This achieved great and lasting popularity, being reprinted and reissued in five editions and translated into Latin, German, Italian, and French, the last edition, printed as part of St Joseph's Ascetical Library, appearing in 1871. Together with an anonymous commentary on the doctrine of purgatory, *A Vindication of St Gregorie his Dialogues*, ascribed by his contemporaries to Mumford, his theologically conservative stance provoked a critical response from the secular priest Thomas White, alias Blacklow, entitled *Devotion and reason, wherein modern* *devotion for the dead is brought to solid principles and made rational.* The annual letters of the college at Liège for 1650 noted that *The Remembrance* was nearly sold out and that a printer in Cologne had undertaken to reprint 300 copies free of charge in thanksgiving for the recovery from serious illness of his wife and child. The equally popular *Catholick scripturist, or, The plea of the Roman Catholics, shewing the scriptures to hold the Roman faith in above forty of the chief controversies now under debate* and *The question of questions, which rightly solved resolveth all our questions in religion. The question is, who ought to be our judge in all these our differences? This book answereth this question and hence sheweth a most easy, and yet most safe way, how among so many religions, the most unlearned and learned may find the true religion* by Optatus Ductor (James Mumford) were published in Ghent in 1658. Again, these works were reprinted in several editions, including a revised edition by W. Gordon (Glasgow 1841), and another published under the auspices of the Catholic Institute in 1863.

These scholarly activities were put to one side when, in 1650, Mumford was sent to England. He was stationed at Norwich as a member of the Jesuit College of the Holy Apostles, a district comprising Norfolk, Suffolk, and Essex. He had already visited the Jesuits' London House of Probation of St Ignatius in 1638 but this posting to Norfolk was to last for the remainder of his life. The annual catalogue of the English province for 1655 names him among the Norwich Jesuits and comments upon his poor health. It is possible that at some time in the mid-1650s he was elected rector of the Holy Apostles as his contemporary biographer, when recording his rectorship at Liège, added that he was also rector at another college in England (Southwell, 380).

Mumford was active in Norwich and in 1657 or 1658 was arrested, paraded round the city in his vestments, with the altar vessels dangling from the soldiers' spears, and then imprisoned in the common gaol. After a few days he was sentenced to be taken in custody by sea to Yarmouth. However, once there he was returned to Norwich, following a dispute over jurisdictions. In Norwich he was more humanely treated, being allotted his own cell where Catholics were permitted to visit and to bring him books, notably his breviary. It was reported that he occupied his imprisonment in writing *The Catholick Scripturist*. After some months he was released on bail and bound over to appear at the assizes. These appearances were achieved with some inconvenience as he had moved his base some distance from the city. After several appearances the only witness to his being a priest failed to appear at the assizes. Mumford was discharged and was able to resume his work at the college. He died on 9 March 1666 but his burial place is not known.   JOY ROWE

Sources T. M. McCoog, *English and Welsh Jesuits, 1555–1650*, 2, Catholic RS, 75 (1995), 248 · [N. Southwell], *Bibliotheca scriptorum Societatis Jesu* (1676), 380 · G. Oliver, *Collections towards illustrating the biographies of the Scotch, English and Irish members of the Society of Jesus*, 2nd edn (1845), 46 · T. Jones, ed., *A catalogue of the collection of tracts for and against popery*, 2, Chetham Society, 64 (1865), 306, 406 · H. Foley, ed., *Records of the English province of the Society of Jesus*, 2 (1875), 457–9, esp. 457; 7 (1882), 532 · Gillow, *Lit. biog. hist.*, 5.142 · T. H. Clancy, *English Catholic books, 1641–1700: a bibliography*, rev. edn (1996), 116–17, 178, 695–704, 1071 · G. Anstruther, *The seminary priests*, 2 (1975), 349–54 · DNB

Archives Archives of the British Province of the Society of Jesus, London, Catalogi varii Prov. Angl. Soc. Jesu, 1642–1771, vol. 1411/3

Mummery, Albert Frederick (1855–1895), political economist and mountaineer, was born on 10 September 1855 at 4 Laureston Place, Dover, the son of William Rigden Mummery, a tanner, and his wife, Esther Ann Gange. The family had moved from Deal to Dover around 1850, on acquiring the tannery at nearby Stembrook. They lived at Maison Dieu, a Jacobean mansion adjoining the town hall in Dover, where Mummery's father was mayor from 1865 to 1867. After his father's death in 1868 he and his elder brother William Gange Mummery took over the family tanning business at Dover and Canterbury, which provided him with the means to devote his leisure to mountaineering and economics.

Mummery first visited Switzerland with his family in 1871 and during subsequent visits to the Alps in the 1870s he developed a passion for climbing. He completed a series of innovative climbs with Alexander Burgener, his guide, between 1879 and 1881. These included first ascents of the Zmutt Ridge of the Matterhorn, the Aiguille Verte from the Charpoua glacier, and the Aiguilles des Charmoz and Grépon. In 1880, however, his election to the Alpine Club was blocked by a snobbish coterie for reasons which remain unclear, possibly out of jealousy at his climbing record, but more probably because he was 'in trade'. In the mid-1880s he appears to have climbed in the maritime Alps and Algeria.

During the 1880s Mummery also developed an interest in political economy. On 7 March 1883 he married Mary Petherick (1859–1946), daughter of John William Petherick, solicitor of Exeter, at the Congregational church, Southernhay, Exeter. They had one daughter, Hilda. Through mutual friends Mummery met the economist J. A. Hobson, who was then teaching at Exeter. According to Hobson, over the course of several years Mummery 'entangled me in a controversy about excessive saving, which he regarded as responsible for the underemployment of capital and labour in periods of bad trade' (Hobson, 30).

Mummery and Hobson collaborated on *The Physiology of Industry* (1889). They argued that over-saving 'impoverishes the Community, throws labourers out of work, drives down wages, and spreads that gloom and prostration through the commercial world which is known as Depression in Trade' (p. iv). Their under-consumptionist arguments constituted a systematic alternative to orthodox equilibrium economics. They also contributed to contemporary debates on marginal productivity and monetary policy, and *The Physiology of Industry* was severely criticized by classical economists for its heretical implications. For Mummery and Hobson, saving and thrift were not virtues and there was necessarily a conflict between the interests of individuals and those of the community. Structural flaws in the economy also required intervention to attain equilibrium. John Maynard Keynes thought the book marked 'in a sense, an epoch in economic thought' ('General theory', *Collected Writings*, 7.365). Its central themes were developed by Hobson in later works.

After the late 1880s Mummery became one of the best-known mountaineers of his generation. In 1888 he completed the first ascent of Dych Tau in the Caucasus, after which he was elected to the Alpine Club. He remained, however, an outsider at the club, which was at that time dominated by gentlemen educated at public schools and the universities. He occasionally climbed with his wife or her friend Lily Bristow. In the 1890s he completed a series of difficult, guideless ascents in the Alps with J. Norman Collie, Geoffrey Hastings, and William Cecil Slingsby, including first guideless ascents of Dent du Requin, Aiguille du Plan, and the Brenva face of Mont Blanc. He contributed a chapter on chalk cliff climbing to W. P. Haskett-Smith's *Climbing in the British Isles* (1894), but apart from such climbing near Dover Mummery rarely climbed in Britain. He was tall, thin, ungainly, and had back trouble from birth, and he wore wire-rimmed glasses to correct his short-sightedness. He disliked his appearance and was rarely photographed.

Mummery described his ascents in *My Climbs in the Alps and Caucasus* (1895), which included a chapter by his wife. He regarded mountain climbing 'as unmixed play', and he had no interest in combining it with scientific pursuits: 'the essence of the sport lies, not in ascending a peak, but in struggling with and overcoming difficulties'. He defended climbing via new routes and countered accusations that he was a 'mere gymnast'. In his chapter on climbing the Grépon with guides, without guides, and then with a woman, he simplified and popularized Leslie Stephen's earlier remark that all mountains pass through the stages 'an inaccessible peak—the most difficult ascent in the Alps—an easy day for a lady' (pp. viii, 111, 136–7, 160). Mummery's advocacy of guideless climbing and his high tolerance for risk distinguished him from his mid-Victorian predecessors, but his philosophy of climbing remained popular among later generations of mountaineers.

In 1895 Mummery planned to retire from the family business to devote himself to economics after climbing in the Himalayas. He attempted Nanga Parbat, near Astor, Kashmir, India, in a small party with Collie and Hastings, supported by Lieutenant C. G. Bruce. They ascended Diamirai peak, and Mummery reached 21,000 feet on Nanga Parbat, but then he and two Gurkhas, Rangobir Thapa and Goman Singh, disappeared crossing a high pass. They were last seen on 24 August 1895 and were presumed killed in an avalanche.

Mummery's later works on political economy have also vanished: his papers relating to the subject were given to J. A. Hobson after his death but subsequently disappeared. The rest of his family papers were destroyed in a bombing raid on Exeter in 1942.   PETER H. HANSEN

Sources T. S. Blakeney, 'Some notes on A. F. Mummery', *Alpine Journal*, 60 (1955), 118–31 • W. Unsworth, *Tiger in the snows: the life and adventures of A. F. Mummery* (1967) • A. L. Mumm, *The Alpine Club register*, 3 (1928) • *Alpine Journal*, 17 (1895), 566–8 • J. Phelby, ed., *J. A. Hobson after fifty years* (1994) • M. Freeden, ed., *Reappraising J. A. Hobson* (1990) • C. Mill, *Norman Collie: a life in two worlds* (1987) • J. N. Collie, *Climbing in the Himalaya and other mountain ranges* (1902) • C. G. Bruce, 'The passing of Mummery', *Himalayan Journal*, 3 (1931), 1–12 • J. A. Hobson, *Confessions of an economic heretic* (1938) • P. H. Hansen, 'Vertical boundaries, national identities: British mountaineering on the frontiers of Europe and the empire, 1868–1914', *Journal of Imperial and Commonwealth History*, 24 (1996), 48–71
Archives Alpine Club, London, G. W. Young MSS • BL, T. S. Blakeney MSS, Add. MS 63124 • BL OIOC, Lord Elgin MSS, MS Eur. F 84 • Zentralbibliothek, Zürich, W. A. B. Coolidge MSS
Likenesses photograph, *c*.1888 (with his daughter), Alpine Club, London • photograph, *c*.1892 (with his wife), BL, Add. MS 63124, fol. 56 • L. Bristow, photograph, 1893, Alpine Club, London • photograph (in his twenties), Alpine Club, London
Wealth at death £12,325: probate, 16 May 1896, *CGPLA Eng. & Wales*

Mun, Thomas (*bap.* 1571, *d.* 1641), merchant and writer on economics, was baptized at St Andrew Hubbard, London, on 17 June 1571, the third son of John Mun (*d.* 1573), merchant of London and Hackney, and Margaret Barwick. Of Essex ancestry, John Mun established himself as a figure of some repute with London, probably gaining the office of provost of moneyers in the royal mint, and taking arms in August 1562. His trading connections with the Mediterranean and northern Europe were a more direct catalyst for the advance of his offspring into overseas commerce, although his death left the family facing an uncertain future. Stability came in the form of his associate Thomas Cordell, who married John's widow. Cordell was one of the founding members of the new Levant Company, and both Thomas and his elder brother John (1564–1615) entered this trade. Although ultimately to achieve great success as a merchant, Thomas experienced the vicissitudes of trade at first hand during his apprenticeship overseas. In his later writings he reported that he had 'lived long in Italy', and gained sufficient credit with Ferdinand I, grand duke of Tuscany, to receive an interest-free loan of 40,000 crowns for trade with Turkey (T. Mun, *England's Treasure*, 1664, 44–5, 126). However, in the course of his Mediterranean business he was seized by Spanish warships near Corfu in 1596, and faced the prospect of a life of slavery in the galleys. In a letter to a Levant Company member he lamented how he and his crew were 'dead of hunger and cold, [with] no money nor friends to help us', and, while they were awaiting sentence in Naples, rumours circulated that they might be burnt as heretics (*Salisbury MSS*, 6.397–8). Evidently mercantile colleagues came to Mun's rescue, but it is unclear whether this experience seriously affected his early progress. In 1600 a list of Levant Company members still recorded him as a 'servant' of William Garraway, thus suggesting that he had yet to become a full member (ibid., 10.214). On a more promising note, the first certain evidence of his return to England concerns a loan made to Lionel Cranfield, which was repaid by the latter in December 1611, and on 29 December 1612 he married Ursula (*d.* 1655), daughter of

John Malcott esquire of Bedfordshire. They settled in the City parish of St Helen, Bishopsgate, and subsequently had at least one son, John (d. 1670), and two daughters.

Mun rose to prominence by diversifying his investments, and by revealing a particular talent as an economic polemicist. In 1615 he was elected to the committee directing the affairs of the East India Company, and he served with distinction over the ensuing quarter of a century. His Mediterranean experience and contacts appear to have been most useful for the company, and he was a hardworking servant to its interests, being frequently entrusted with tasks vital to its future. His skill on paper was perhaps his most valuable contribution to the corporate cause, and in 1621 he penned *A discourse of trade, from England unto the East Indies, answering to diverse objections which are usually made against the same, by T.M.*, which enjoyed a second edition in that same year. The main objective of this work was to defend the company against the charge of draining the country of bullion, considerable amounts of which had to be exported to India in the absence of English goods suitable for the oriental market. Mun argued that coin was merely a medium of exchange, and that the volume of traffic, and more particularly the balance of trade, were more important considerations in determining national prosperity. He did not advocate tight controls over the flow of international trade, however, and simply urged his countrymen to be less attached to foreign luxuries, declaring particular distaste for 'our common excesses of food and raiment, which is grown to such a height in most degrees of people' (p. 57). These arguments dominated his economic outlook for the rest of his life, and, although the significance of the balance of trade had been aired by earlier writers, Mun's assertion of its importance profoundly influenced English economic thought for the ensuing 150 years. More immediately, his sturdy defence of the East India Company was echoed by its apologists throughout the seventeenth century, including Henry Robinson, Josiah Child, and Charles Davenant.

Thoughts of enduring fame were clearly not Mun's priority, and his immediate objectives were much more practical. The ideas of his first pamphlet were distilled for government scrutiny into a synopsis entitled 'Reasons to prove that the trade from England unto the East Indies doth not consume, but rather increase the treasure of this kingdom'. The country's continuing economic difficulties embroiled him in a bitter controversy with Gerard Malynes, who argued that the root cause of the nation's economic ills was a failure to regulate currency exchange rates rather than the balance of trade. Mun found significant support from Edward Misselden, who was also linked to the East India Company. As well as backing his views on the balance of trade, Misselden extolled Mun's professional abilities, enthusing that 'his diligence at home, his experience abroad, have adorned him with such endowments, as are rather to be wisht in all, then easie to be found in many merchants of these times' (E. Misselden, *The Circle of Commerce*, 1623, 36–7). The immediate impact of Mun's writings can be measured by his appointment in April 1622 to the committee of twelve ordered by the privy council to investigate the causes of the general decay of trade. Their subsequent report bore the heavy imprint of Mun himself, with great emphasis on the current deficit in England's balance of trade with other countries, and a sturdy defence of the East India Company's export of bullion. In common with the rest of the committee, he sat on its successor, the standing commission of trade, and in a series of reports submitted in 1623 continued to refute the arguments of Malynes as 'mere fallacies and froth' (BL, Add. MS 34324, fols. 169–70).

These commercial controversies ensured Mun a much higher public profile, and he found his services ever more in demand, with an embattled East India Company proving particularly insistent. In November 1621 he had obstinately refused to travel to India to put the company's operations in better order, despite impassioned pleas by the company's leaders to rescue their situation overseas. Mun felt that his constitution was not up to the rigours of the task, and argued that 'he hath matter for his charity to work upon at home, and doth cast his eye upon his family with as much and perhaps more tenderness than another' (*CSP col.*, 3.487). It was only with great reluctance that he could be importuned to serve as deputy governor of the company in 1624–5, but such reticence could not mask a very real commitment to his duties on the committee. In particular, he played a leading role in lobbying the crown to seek redress from the Dutch after the notorious massacre of company servants at Amboyna, and was singled out by the company for garnering wider support, being entrusted with the handling of 'the number of books to be printed and compounding with the press' (ibid., *1622–4*, 424). He also maintained his interest in the bullion controversy, and in March 1624 informed the company's court that 'he doubted not to satisfy the Parliament that the strength, the stock, the trade, and the treasure of the kingdom are all greatly augmented by the East India trade' (ibid., 256–7). He still feared for the future of the trade, and warned his fellow committeemen in May 1627 that 'unless his Majesty do not effectually curb the insolence of the Dutch, the company can promise to themselves nothing but loss and destruction of their estates' (ibid., *1625–9*, 352–3). The following year he had further opportunity to remind national leaders of their stake in the trade when directed by the company to draft a remonstrance to the House of Commons in its defence.

Mun's prominence as a guardian of the East India trade ensured him respect within governing circles, but his enduring fame stems from a work that appeared only twenty-three years after his death: *England's treasure by forraign trade, or, The balance of our forraign trade is the rule of our treasure*. Its exact date of compilation is uncertain, although most experts concur that its genesis lies with the great economic controversies of the 1620s and his campaign to justify the privileges of the East India Company. In common with other writers of the age, he encompassed a range of economic concerns in this work, most notably the decline of the fisheries, but the passages dealing with the balance of trade remained its chief attraction for seventeenth and eighteenth-century audiences. Many of its arguments were anticipated by his earlier writings, especially its anti-Dutch bias and its critique of Malynes, but its lasting influence was secured by Mun's brilliance in asserting the significance of the balance of trade in a systematic and coherent manner, which made it accessible to a very wide audience. Even though Mun warned against attempts to influence the flow of trade between countries, the tract has been widely seen as the bible of 'mercantilist thought', its arguments encouraging successive generations of politicians to introduce protectionist measures to ensure that the nation maintained a favourable balance of trade with other countries. In his professional capacity Mun had worked hard to educate ministers concerning the importance of foreign trade, but he was only too aware of the detrimental effects of international rivalry on overseas commerce.

During his remaining years Mun proved himself a loyal servant of the East India Company, spurred on by the perceived threat of the Portuguese and the Dutch. His colleagues continued to avail themselves of his literary skills, asking him to draft a response to an attack from domestic rivals in 1633. His petition of 1628 was actually reprinted in 1641, when the company deemed it to be 'of great advantage' for a renewed request for parliamentary aid (Sainsbury, 2.143). He died later that year, and although the exact date of his demise is uncertain, the company re-elected him to the committee on 2 July, and his body was interred in the chancel of St Helen, Bishopsgate, on 21 July. His 'well-loved' wife, Ursula, was buried next to him on 11 September 1655 (will, PRO, PROB 11/186, sig. 92). It was left to his son John to publish his most famous work in 1664, who, without undue exaggeration, described his father as 'in his time famous among merchants, and well known to most men of business, for his general experience in affairs, and notable insight into trade' (*England's Treasure*, dedication). The subsequent success of *England's Treasure* paid testament to his abilities, with further editions in 1669, 1698, 1700, 1713, and 1755. Its continuing topicality was ensured by the country's emergence as a major imperial power, and even though many critics highlighted the difficulties of ascertaining the balance of trade with other countries, few challenged the importance of an advantageous balance for national strength. Both this tract and the *Discourse of Trade* of 1621 have been reprinted several times in the nineteenth and twentieth centuries, reflecting Mun's perceived status as one of the key economic writers of the Stuart age.

Before his death Mun had begun to plough his commercial gains into landed investment. He bought an estate at Otteridge, in Bearsted, Kent, and, with two of his offspring marrying into the gentry of that county, his family's influence within the City predictably waned. His eldest son, John, married Elizabeth, daughter of Walter Harlackenden of Woodchurch and Hollingbourne, Kent, and continued the purchase of estates in the Bearsted area. This

match produced Thomas (c.1645–1692), who gained election to parliament for Hastings in 1681 and 1689, and, in his capacity as a baron of the Cinque Ports, attended the coronations of James II and William and Mary.

PERRY GAUCI

Sources F. C. Cass, *East Barnet*, 2 vols. (1885–92), 217–19 · *CSP col.*, 3.431–2, 484, 487–8; 4.134, 256–7, 261–2, 297, 299, 424, 449; 6.248, 352–3, 489, 491; 8.316, 319–20, 382, 579 · B. E. Supple, *Commercial crisis and change in England, 1600–1642* (1959), 185–8, 268–70 · J. O. Appleby, *Economic thought and ideology in seventeenth-century England* (1978), 37–41 · BL, Add. MS 34324, fols. 155–78 · G. J. Armytage, ed., *Middlesex pedigrees*, Harleian Society, 65 (1914), 143–4 · *Calendar of the manuscripts of the most hon. the marquis of Salisbury*, 6, HMC, 9 (1895), 397–8; 10 (1904), 214 · will, PRO, PROB 11/186, sig. 92 · C. Wilson, *England's apprenticeship, 1603–1763*, 2nd edn (1984), 59–60 · W. B. Bannerman, ed., *The registers of St Helen's, Bishopsgate, London*, Harleian Society, register section, 31 (1904), 17–19, 135, 294, 302 · R. Ashton, *The city and the court, 1603–1643* (1979), 120 · E. B. Sainsbury, ed., *A calendar of the court minutes … of the East India Company*, [1–2]: 1635–43 (1907–9)

Archives BL, MS reports, Add. MS 34324

Wealth at death unknown, but clearly wealthy; incl. properties in London, Kent, and Dorset; also £3000 of new lands to be purchased in trust: will, PRO, PROB 11/186, sig. 92

Munby, Alan Noel Latimer (1913–1974), bibliographical historian and book collector, was born in Hampstead, London, on 25 December 1913, the elder child and only son of Alan Edward Munby, architect, and his wife, Ethel Annie Greenhill. He was educated at Clifton College and King's College, Cambridge, where he obtained second classes in part 1 of both the classical (1934) and English (1935) triposes. His keen interest in old books, first aroused by schoolboy visits to the dozen or so booksellers in Bristol, blossomed under the stimulus of Cambridge. There he formed his earliest, and remarkably ambitious, collection, of eighteenth-century English verse, largely through purchases at Gustave David's shop. On leaving Cambridge in 1935 he obtained a post, through the good offices of his parents' friend Mrs Quaritch Wrentmore, as a cataloguer in the antiquarian bookshop of Bernard Quaritch. Two years later he moved to Sothebys, again as a book cataloguer.

In 1936 Munby had joined the Territorial Army as an officer in Queen Victoria's Rifles and at the outbreak of war he was posted to the 1st battalion in Kent. On 22 May 1940 they landed at Calais as part of a small and hastily assembled garrison to defend the town against three Panzer divisions. They had to surrender and five years in German prisoner-of-war camps followed, at Laufen, Warburg, and Eichstätt. Munby consoled himself by producing a camp guide in the style of Baedeker, by lecturing on the English novelists, and by writing Betjemanesque verse and ghost stories in the style of M. R. James. He even managed to have a limited and signed edition of one story printed on the private press of the bishop of Eichstätt. When the war ended he was posted to London and after demobilization returned to Sothebys.

In 1947 Munby was invited to return to King's as librarian and a year later was elected to a fellowship. The college had already received the bequest of the library of Lord Keynes and Munby was outstandingly successful in attracting other gifts and deposits: an early tenth-century Juvenal given by J. W. Hely-Hutchinson, the T. S. Eliot collection of John Hayward, and the papers of Rupert Brooke, E. M. Forster, John Maynard Keynes, Roger Fry, Clive and Vanessa Bell, and many others. He did not confine his enthusiasm for bibliographical pursuits to King's. One of his earliest initiatives after returning to Cambridge was to organize a weekend for visiting bibliophiles, marked by exhibitions in colleges and at the Fitzwilliam Museum. He was president of a society of undergraduate book collectors which met in his rooms, co-founder (in 1949) of the Cambridge Bibliographical Society, and author of a valuable short guide, *Cambridge College Libraries* (1960).

Before returning to Cambridge, Munby had already collaborated with Desmond Flower in writing *English Poetical Autographs* (1938). Some of his wartime verse was issued in a rigorously limited edition (*Lyra catenata*, 1948) and his ghost stories appeared under the title *The Alabaster Hand* (1949). Meanwhile, in 1946, he had been invited to write the life of Sir Thomas Phillipps. It was a subject which gave full range to Munby's scholarly gifts and wide bibliographical knowledge, and to his feeling for human eccentricity and sense of the absurd. *Phillipps Studies*, published in five volumes between 1951 and 1960, provided the first comprehensive account of the bibliophiles and bookdealers of the nineteenth century, besides evoking so vivid a portrait of the baronet himself that Phillipps has since become of interest to collectors in his own right. The book was written with a rare sense of style, somewhat influenced by Macaulay, of whose works Munby formed the pre-eminent collection.

Munby served his college as praelector from 1951 to 1960 and as domus bursar from 1964 to 1967, when his duties involved supervising a major programme of building. He was a learned and witty lecturer with a felicitous sense of timing, much in demand in both Britain and America. His appointments included the Lyell readership in bibliography at Oxford in 1962–3 and the Sandars readership at Cambridge in 1969–70; the latter lectures were published under the title of *Connoisseurs and Medieval Miniatures, 1750–1850* (1972). *The Cult of the Autograph Letter in England* (1962) was based on lectures given at King's College, London. Munby was made LittD (Cambridge) in 1962, honorary fellow of the Pierpont Morgan Library, trustee of the British Museum in 1969 and a member of the British Library board in 1973, and was serving as president of the Bibliographical Society at the time of his death.

Besides illuminating the most spectacular age of English book collecting, Munby's writings broke new ground in drawing attention to the importance of booksellers' and auction catalogues as historical sources. He was general editor of the series of reprints Sale Catalogues of Libraries of Eminent Persons, and joint author, with Lenore Coral, of the posthumously published *British Book Sale Catalogues, 1676–1800* (1977). His own collection consisted of 7000 to 8000 volumes of early bibliography, sale catalogues, and material relating to libraries, the book trade, and connoisseurship, and included many notable rarities. Part was acquired after his death by Cambridge University Library, the remainder forming two sales at Sothebys. The Macaulay collection had been given during his lifetime to Trinity College, Cambridge.

Munby (always known as Tim from the second syllable of his third name) was married twice. His first wife, Joan Edelsten (*b.* 1912/13), whom he married on 9 September 1939, was the daughter of Hubert McDonald Edelsten, a shipping merchant. She died before his return from captivity. On 27 October 1945 he married Sheila Rachel (*b.* 1920/21), a nurse and daughter of Vivian Francis Crowther-Smith, solicitor, of London. They had one son. Munby died in Cambridge on 26 December 1974. A Munby fellowship in the university library was established in his memory with money subscribed by his friends.

Generosity was the outstanding trait of Munby's character, expressed in gifts, in help and advice to friends and acquaintances, and in hospitality liberally offered by his wife and himself at their successive Cambridge homes. Although a dedicated collector, he could hardly be prevented from giving his books away to those he considered better qualified to own them, and he was never happier than when discovering volumes bearing on the history of their collections to present to his fellow members of the Roxburghe Club. He took particular pleasure in matching a friend's qualifications to an appropriate appointment. His sense of fun added a special delight to time spent in his company. He was a keen shot, often combining a day's shooting with a visit to his host's library, and a skilful carpenter. ANTHONY HOBSON, *rev.*

Sources A. Neave, *The flames of Calcus* (1972) · *TLS* (11 May 1973) · P. Wilkinson, *Alan Noel Latimer Munby* (1975) · *The Times* (27 Dec 1974) · *Book Collector*, 24 (1975), 191–201 · *Modern literary manuscripts from King's College, Cambridge* (1976) · A. N. L. Munby, *Essays and papers*, ed. N. Barber (1977) · private information (1986) · personal knowledge (1986) · CGPLA Eng. & Wales (1975) · m. certs.
Archives Bodl. Oxf., corresp. and papers relating to Sir Thomas Phillipps and his collection · CUL, corresp. and literary papers · King's AC Cam., corresp. and papers · Trinity Cam., notes and papers made and collected by him relating to Dawson Turner | BL, corresp. with Sir Sydney Cockerell, Add. MS 52741 · Bodl. Oxf., corresp. with J. W. Hely-Hutchinson · King's AC Cam., corresp. with J. W. Carter · U. Reading L., letters to The Bodley Head Ltd · University of Kent, Canterbury, letters to Cecil Clarabat
Wealth at death £97,148: probate, 9 June 1975, CGPLA Eng. & Wales

Munby, Arthur Joseph (1828–1910), diarist and civil servant, was born in York on 19 August 1828, the eldest of the six sons and one daughter of Joseph Munby (1804–1875), a solicitor, and his wife, Caroline Eleanor, *née* Forth. He was educated at St Peter's School, York, and then at Trinity College, Cambridge (1848–51). His first, unsuccessful, career was as a barrister (being called to the bar in 1855). In 1860 he accepted employment with the ecclesiastical commission, but aspired to a literary career. Some initial successes here (his first book of poems was published in 1852 and he was a runner-up in the 1859 Burns centenary poetry competition) were followed by disappointments, particularly in 1861 when he was rejected for the librarianship of the Middle Temple. He worked for the commission until his

Arthur Joseph Munby (1828–1910), by unknown photographer, 1873 [with Ellen Grounds, a pit girl]

retirement in 1888. He died of pneumonia at his home, Wheeler's Farm, Pyrford, near Guildford, Surrey, on 29 January 1910 and was buried on 3 February at Pyrford parish church. Publication of his will caused a minor scandal in July 1910 by disclosing that in 1873 he had married a working-class woman, Hannah *Cullwick (1833–1909), following a long clandestine relationship, but had insisted that this remain secret from his family and friends because she continued working as a servant and refused to 'become a lady'.

Early assessments of Munby's career (including his obituary in *The Times*, 5 February 1910, and his *Dictionary of National Biography* entry, written by his friend Austin Dobson) focused on his literary activities and offered a generous assessment of his poetry, his main publications being *Benoni* (1852), *Verses Old and New* (1865), *Dorothy* (1880), *Vestigia retrorsum* (1891), *Poems Chiefly Lyric and Elegiac* (1901), and *Relicta* (1909). However, this assessment has not withstood the passing of time and the poetry is now little read. His greater and lasting accomplishment is seen as his diary, partly published by Derek Hudson in 1972, which is extensive and covers a fascinatingly wide range of people and activities. Its dominant themes include his daily life over a period of enormous social, economic, and political change, his record of topical events, the relationship with Hannah Cullwick, close literary friendships, involvement

in Christian socialism through the Working Men's College, his forays into *haute bourgeois* (although still 'serious') London society, and the collections he made of representations of different kinds of working women.

Over the period of the diary—from 1859 to 1898—many changes impacted upon Munby's life, including the opening of the 'underground railway', expansions to women's employment and accompanying struggles to achieve women's rights, moves to extend working-class educational opportunities, and attempts to reform the Church of England, including through the work of the ecclesiastical commission. As well as these his diaries often record public events with posterity most definitely in mind, including the July 1860 British Association meeting in Oxford when the bishop of Oxford spoke against, and Thomas Huxley lectured on, the theological as well as scientific consequences of Charles Darwin's *The Origin of Species*. The entry for 10 January 1863 records the opening of the first underground railway in London, on which Munby travelled from Paddington to Farringdon Street, while entries for April and May 1864 first record the noises of workmen heard from his quarters in Fig Tree Court in the Temple as building of the Embankment was started. The growing volunteer movement and the formation of hundreds of rifle corps in 1859, and especially during 1860 within the Working Men's College, were recorded with much approval, although Munby himself did not join, feeling 'shrinking' at the thought of 'acting with so many other men' (Munby, diary). His admiration, and then solemn mourning, for the 'manly' prince consort is also recorded, with some interesting passages (December 1861 and January 1862) about the public reverberations of Prince Albert's death. Glimpses and impressions of the prince of Wales (later Edward VII), the Tooley Street fire (the most serious since the Great Fire of London), and exhibitions, concerts, and other events at the Crystal Palace were all recorded. So were the demonstrations of silent appreciative working-class support for Garibaldi on the part of many thousands of people during an appearance at the Crystal Palace in April 1864 and, in June 1864, his own thoughts on the thousands of people living and sleeping rough in London streets. In the autumn of 1888 he recorded the moral panic surrounding the Jack the Ripper murders, which led to his being surrounded and harangued by collier men.

On this latter occasion Munby was staying with Hannah Cullwick in Hadley, Shropshire. Cullwick and Munby had met by chance in a London street in 1854. Against the odds, considering how many such encounters Munby had, they kept in contact, and in 1854, on a visit to her family in Shifnal, Shropshire, Cullwick began keeping her own diary, which she sent at regular intervals to Munby. The relationship was the result of her conviction that it was better to love at one remove a 'gentleman' than to be cowed and subjugated in marriage with a working-class man, and of his already-existing 'interest' in rough working women. Cullwick's diary was kept from 1854 to 1873 and is of almost unique importance in providing detailed information about the life, family circumstances, and working routines of those involved in that most typical employment for working women in Victorian England, domestic service. The relationship went through various vicissitudes, including Munby's attachments to a number of other women. They eventually married on 14 January 1873. He apparently expected that she would gradually come to live and behave more like 'a lady'; however, the reverse happened, and she became increasingly angry both at the transformations of dress, demeanour, and behaviour required, and at her husband's insistence that their relationship be kept secret. Following a major disagreement, she returned to Shropshire in 1877 and continued to work in a variety of domestic service roles.

Some of Munby's most important friendships—with Robert Borland, William Ralston, Vernon and Godfrey Lushington, and Richard Litchfield—began at Cambridge. Litchfield, one of the founders of the Working Men's College, also gave him his entrée into Christian socialist circles. It was thus that Munby attended inaugural meetings in 1854 of the Working Men's College, where he taught from 1857 until the 1880s, and was later a council member and always an admirer of F. D. Maurice, no matter what criticisms were made of Maurice's conservatism on matters of class and of college governance by more radical and agnostic members such as F. J. Furnivall. Through the college he also became acquainted with Dante Gabriel Rossetti, John Ruskin, and council members J. M. Ludlow, John Westlake, Thomas Hughes, and Charles Kingsley. He also retained close and affectionate links with two other friends, Richard Blackmore and Whitley Stokes, both met when reading for the bar in the chambers of Hugh Cairns. Two literary circles formed pivotal points in his social life: the 'tabacco parliaments' of the publisher and Christian socialist Alexander Macmillan from 1859, and the meetings from 1866 to 1874 of the Pen and Pencil Club at Aubrey House, founded by Clementia Taylor, feminist wife of radical MP Peter Taylor. It was through the Taylors' gatherings that Munby approvingly met Barbara Bodichon, Lydia Becker, Elizabeth Blackwell, and other well-known feminists of the day, including Elizabeth Malleson, the key figure in founding the Working Women's College in 1864, which Hannah Cullwick briefly attended (in 1874) and Munby fervently supported.

Munby's friendship with Whitley Stokes acted as the bridge between these literary and reforming circles and those of the *haute bourgeoisie* that Munby sought out during the 1860s and 1870s. Munby much admired the former classical actress Helen Faucit, a friend of Stokes's who was married to the prince consort's biographer Theodore Martin. At the Martins' 'at homes' he fell in silent love with the portraitist Mary Severn (later Newton), and admired the 'good and the great' who he met or saw in such gatherings, including Robert Browning and William Makepeace Thackeray.

From early adulthood Munby had a fascination with the stark contrasts between delicate white-handed gentlemen, who employed a class of others to do the manual work (dressing, shopping, cooking, cleaning) that daily life requires, and the brawny, dirt-begrimed women servants who typically performed this. His fascination extended to other 'unbecoming women', including the large numbers who performed manual work in Victorian society (for example, delivering milk, working on the coal 'pit brow', moving into or out of prostitution, collecting refuse, gutting and skinning slaughtered animals, performing as trapeze artists and 'human cannon balls' or 'blacking up' to sing in the so-called 'nigger troupes' that performed in London streets). He was also interested in those who broke the law and appeared in court and those disfigured by accident or disease. However, his greatest fascination was with representations of these in his diary (Hudson) and extensive photograph collection (Hiley): he was a collector *par excellence*, although his collections were made to satisfy specifically private interests.

Controversy still continues as to the nature of Munby's interest in working women and their 'dirt'. Some commentators see this and his collections of representations thereof as perversion and therefore necessarily sexual in nature. Others resist the imposition of post-Freudian categories on a pre-Freudian figure, and relatedly also reject reading all obsession as a priori sexual. However, regardless of the merits of either argument, Munby's diary does act as an important source for those interested in literary, artistic, reforming, and Christian socialist circles between 1859 and 1898.   LIZ STANLEY

Sources D. Hudson, *Munby, man of two worlds: the life and diaries of Arthur J. Munby, 1828–1910* (1972) • M. Hiley, *Victorian working women: portraits from life* (1979) • *The diaries of Hannah Cullwick*, ed. L. Stanley (1984) • L. Davidoff, 'Class and gender in Victorian England: the diaries of Arthur J. Munby and Hannah Cullwick', *Feminist Studies*, 5 (1979), 87–141 • L. Stanley, 'Biography as a microscope or kaleidoscope? The case of "power" in Hannah Cullwick's relationship with Arthur Munby', *Women's Studies International Forum*, 10 (1987), 19–31 • A. Munby, diary, Trinity Cam., Munby collection
Archives Trinity Cam., diaries, literary MSS, and notebooks • York City Archives, genealogical notebook and papers | Bodl. Oxf., letters to Bertram Dobell • University of Chicago Library, letters from William Bell Scott
Likenesses photograph, 1873, Trinity, Cam. [*see illus.*] • portraits, Trinity Cam., Munby collection
Wealth at death £25,867 12s.: probate, 18 June 1910, CGPLA Eng. & Wales

Munby, Giles (1813–1876), botanist, was born in York, the youngest of three sons of Joseph Munby, (*d.* 1816), lawyer and under-sheriff of the county, and Jane Pearson, but lost both his parents when very young. On leaving school he was apprenticed to a surgeon in York, named Brown, and tended the poor during the cholera epidemic of 1832. He entered the medical school of the University of Edinburgh, where he attended the botanical lectures and excursions held by Professor Graham, gaining the professor's gold medal for the best herbarium. Munby then 'walked the hospitals' in London and, in 1835, in Paris, where he began a lifelong friendship with John Percy, the metallurgist. Together they studied under Adrien de Jussieu and his assistants, Guillemin and Decaisne, and Munby passed the examinations for the degree of MD at Montpellier, though he never took up the diploma. The friends visited Dijon and, after returning to Edinburgh, started out once more, in 1836, for the south of France.

Munby's first publications were notes on the botany and entomology of these trips, contributed to Loudon's and Charlesworth's *Magazine of Natural History* in 1836. Soon afterwards he took up residence at St Bertrand de Comminges, in the department of Haute-Garonne, acting as curator of the museum of a M. Boubée and giving lessons in botany, but in 1839 he accepted the offer of a free passage from Marseilles to Constantinople. Unfavourable winds landed him at Algiers, where he resolved to stay and investigate the flora. With occasional visits to England, he lived in Algiers from 1839 to 1844, collecting plants, cultivating oranges, shooting, and practising medicine among the Arabs and French soldiers. He was skilled in treating ophthalmia, a common condition; he himself was extremely short-sighted.

In 1844 Munby married Jane Welsford, daughter of the consul at Oran, and settled at La Senia, a small estate near Oran. In 1859 his wife's health caused them to move to Montpellier, where she died in February 1860, leaving two sons and three daughters (not eight children as J. D. Hooker has it in the *Gardeners' Chronicle*). While in Oran he acted as vice-consul after his father-in-law's death. Following his wife's death, Munby returned to England, settling at Wood Green, Middlesex. In 1862 he married Eliza Mary Ann Buckeridge, who survived him. In 1867 the couple moved to Alice Holt, near Farnham, Surrey, where Munby devoted himself to the cultivation of Algerian plants and bulbs. He died of inflammation of the lungs on 12 April 1876, and was buried at Rowledge, Hampshire.

Munby was a skilful vegetable anatomist, as well as a most industrious collector and an acute discriminator of living plants. He distributed several sets of herbarium specimens to botanical contemporaries and at his death his own herbarium was presented to Kew. Munby was an original member of the Botanical Society of Edinburgh, and in his later years he joined the Royal Horticultural Society, becoming a member of the scientific committee. From time to time he exhibited rare plants from his own collection. His principal work was the *Flore de l'Algérie* (1847) which contains 1800 species arranged on the Linnaean system, with six plates from drawings by his sister. A great number of the species and genera he described were then unknown to science: 200 species had been missed by the only other list, Desfontaines's *Flora Atlantica* (1804). Munby's book was corrected and rearranged in the natural system, and translated into Latin, as *Catalogus plantarum in Algeriâ … nascentium* (1859). This contained 2600 species, of which 800 were new, and the second edition (1866) contained 364 more. For this work he received formal thanks from the French government and a bequest of books. Much of his success can be attributed to his speaking French, Arabic, and Spanish. His medical ability led him to be looked on as a hakim by the Arabs. At the time of his death he was engaged upon a *Guide du botaniste en Algérie*. The name *Munbya* was first given to a genus of herbs by Boissier and then to two other genera of plants,

both now obsolete. Munby's older brother Joseph (1804–1875), a solicitor in York, was the father of A. J. Munby, the poet and diarist. G. S. BOULGER, *rev.* JANET BROWNE

Sources H. J. Wilkinson, *Annual Report* [Yorkshire Philosophical Society] (1907), 70–71 · J. D. Hooker, 'The late Giles Munby', *Gardeners' Chronicle*, new ser., 6 (1876), 260–62 · *Transactions of the Botanical Society* [Edinburgh], 13 (1879), 12–14 · *Journal of Botany, British and Foreign*, 14 (1876), 160 · A. J. Munby, *A memorial of Joseph Munby of Clifton Holme near York* (1875) · *CGPLA Eng. & Wales* (1876) · D. Hudson, *Munby, man of two worlds: the life and diaries of Arthur J. Munby, 1828–1910* (1972), 7

Archives RBG Kew | RBG Kew, plants and drawings · York Museum, plants and drawings

Likenesses portrait, RBG Kew; repro. in Hooker, 'The late Giles Munby', 261

Wealth at death under £2000: probate, 18 May 1876, *CGPLA Eng. & Wales*

Muncaster. For this title name *see* Pennington, John, first Baron Muncaster (*bap.* 1741, *d.* 1813); Pennington, Lowther, second Baron Muncaster (1745–1818) [*see under* Pennington, John, first Baron Muncaster (*bap.* 1741, *d.* 1813)].

Muncaster, Claude Grahame [*formerly* (Oliver) Grahame Hall] (1903–1974), landscape and marine painter, was born on 4 July 1903 in Gay Street, West Chiltington, near Pulborough, Sussex, the second of the three children of the painter Oliver Hall (1869–1957) and Sarah Stephenson (1875/6–1946), daughter of Willie Stephenson of Oxen Park in the Lake District, near Coniston, Lancashire, and his wife, whose maiden name was Muncaster. His early years and most of his adult life were spent in Sussex, where the landscape was to provide lifelong inspiration. As a child he was also excited by ships and the sea encountered on trips to the Sussex coast, and his first ambition was to be a sailor. He began to paint and draw during the latter part of his time at Queen Elizabeth's School, Cranbrook, Kent (1914–19). Gray (as he was known) had no formal art training but learned by copying works by the English landscape painters under the direction of his father, and with the encouragement of his father's fellow artists. He was inevitably influenced by his father and his almost spiritual response to nature, but a teaching relationship between them failed. As Grahame Hall he first exhibited pictures at the Royal Academy in 1921 and 1922, landscapes and coastal views remaining his preferred choice of subject until the end of his working life. For the sake of his own independence and to avoid insinuations that his father was helping him with his pictures he adopted the name Claude Muncaster in 1922, using the family name of his Cumbrian maternal grandmother and the first name Claude after the seventeenth-century French landscape painter Claude Lorrain whom he admired. It was not until 1945 that he formally changed his name by deed poll.

Despite lack of formal training Muncaster developed into a painter with a sound academic technique, and was suspicious of artistic developments on the continent and in Britain. He refused to become modern and his ideal was 'to carry on the best traditions of English painting' (Muncaster, 14). His best period was during the mid-1920s and his work has much in common with that of the British etchers of the first decades of the twentieth century with whom he shared an emphasis on draughtsmanship and an interest in landscape and industrial and travel subjects, as exemplified by his critic at times, Sir Henry Rushbury. He worked first in watercolour, but also in oils, and produced a small group of at least thirty etched plates in which the 'assured etched line is fine, crisp and sensuous … the shipping compositions are the most satisfying' (Guichard, 52). His interest in the sea was profound and lasting and he made several voyages, notably that in the four-masted barque *Olivebank* from Melbourne to Cardiff, the subject of his first book, *Rolling Round the Horn* (1933), which was illustrated with his drawings and photographs. His shipboard compositions are perhaps his most original. He was a founder member of the Society of Marine Artists (1939), which became the Royal Society of Marine Artists during his presidency (1958–74).

Muncaster's first one-man exhibition at the Fine Art Society in 1926 was followed by others in London, other British towns and cities, and abroad. He was elected an associate of the Royal Society of Painters in Water Colours in 1931, becoming a full member in 1936 and its president from 1951 to 1960; he also became a member of the Royal Society of British Artists in 1946 and a member of the Royal Institute of Oil Painters in 1948. In 1933 he married Primrose Keighley Balfour (*b.* 1913), daughter of the industrialist Sir Arthur Balfour (later Lord Riverdale of Sheffield). They had two sons: the elder, Martin Muncaster, became a radio and television broadcaster and wrote a biography of his father, *The Wind in the Oak* (1978).

Muncaster's interest in teaching resulted in two books: *The Student's Book of Water-Colour Painting* (1938) and *Landscape and Marine Painting in Oil and Water-Colour* (1958). He also illustrated John Masefield's poem 'Bird of Dawning' and produced illustrations for *The Sphere* and the *Illustrated London News*. During the Second World War he was a lieutenant-commander in the Royal Naval Volunteer Reserve (1940–44) working as an adviser to the Admiralty on the camouflage of ships at sea, which provided opportunities for travel. In 1946 the Royal Academy (Edward Stott Fund) purchased his oil painting *Shipyard at Palma, Majorca*. In 1946–7 Queen Elizabeth commissioned watercolours of Windsor, Sandringham, and Balmoral, and a large panoramic oil painting, *Balmoral from Lochnagar*. He subsequently undertook commissions for panoramic views of industrial subjects: these include *London from the Shell Building* (1962, priv. coll.), *Aerial View of Bradford, with St John's Works* (priv. coll.), *The Demolition of London Bridge* (priv. coll.), and *'Southampton Castle' Entering Durban* (Union Castle Mail Steamship Co. Ltd).

Throughout the 1960s Muncaster continued to travel, to carry out commissions, and to have exhibitions, but he was increasingly suffering from ill health, including serious eye problems, and he painted his last picture in 1969. Even when extremely ill he was able to express his art and philosophy through a series of broadcasts, *Thoughts for the Day*, for BBC radio, in collaboration with his son Martin. He died of cancer of the liver on 30 November 1974 at his home, Whitelocks, Sutton, near Pulborough, Sussex, a house he had lived in since 1960, and also as a child from 1914. He was buried in Sutton churchyard. His work is represented in the Tate collection, in public collections throughout the United Kingdom, in Cape Town, South Africa, and in Australia and New Zealand.

ROGER QUARM

Sources M. Muncaster, *The wind in the oak: a biography of Claude Muncaster* (1978) · private information (2004) · E. H. H. Archibald, *Dictionary of sea painters* (1980) · A. Wilson, *A dictionary of British marine painters* (1967) · F. Spalding, *20th century painters and sculptors* (1990), vol. 6 of *Dictionary of British art* · *A celebration of marine art: fifty years of the Royal Society of Marine Artists* (1996) · D. Brooke-Hart, *20th century British marine painting* (1981) · K. M. Guichard, *British etchers, 1850–1940* (1977) · Graves, *RA exhibitors* · *WWW* · *Who's who in art* (1974) · artist's file, archive material, Courtauld Inst., Witt Library · *CGPLA Eng. & Wales* (1975) · *Debrett's Peerage*

Archives NRA, priv. coll., diaries · NRA, priv. coll., MSS autobiographical recollections (illustrated)

Likenesses J. Pannett, drawing, priv. coll. · photographs (some early), priv. coll.

Wealth at death £19,575: probate, 14 March 1975, *CGPLA Eng. & Wales*

Munchensi, Warin de (*c*.1195–1255), landholder and soldier, was born probably in the mid-1190s, the second son of William de Munchensi and Aveline, daughter of Roger de Clare, earl of Hertford. His father's death in 1204 followed by that of his brother (perhaps in 1208) left him a minor in the custody of his uncle William d'*Aubigny, earl of Arundel. He was ill-treated by King John, who on 23 December 1213 demanded 2000 marks in relief and quittance of his father's Jewish debts; he was to pay quickly, guaranteeing his good behaviour by pledging his lands. This doubtless drove him into rebellion; he remained a rebel until 1217, when he was captured by royalists in the battle of Lincoln on 20 May. However, he was swiftly reconciled with Henry III and restored to his lands. Thereafter he loyally served the crown on almost all the military campaigns of the next four decades.

Munchensi was married twice: first, between 1219 and 1222, to Joan, the youngest daughter of William *Marshal, earl of Pembroke; and second, and more modestly, shortly after November 1234, to Denise, widow of Walter Langton and daughter and heir of Nicholas of Anstey of Hertfordshire. Their son was the baronial leader William de *Munchensi. In 1251 Munchensi was cited before the bishop of Lincoln, apparently falsely, for misconduct towards Denise. The benefits of his first marriage matured only in December 1245 when his heirs became, in turn, heirs to one fifth of the Marshal estate (£700 p.a.); this inheritance easily doubled the Munchensi lands, which extended across five counties (Norfolk, Essex, Kent, Gloucestershire, and Northamptonshire). However, his son of that marriage, John, died about June 1247, leaving the Marshal property to the daughter, Joan, and on 13 August Henry III engineered her marriage to his newly arrived Poitevin half-brother, William de *Valence. After that Munchensi came into favour, and received frequent gifts from the king. He died on about 20 July 1255.

It is difficult to see why Matthew Paris described Munchensi in his famous obituary as one of the wisest and most noble barons, 'zealous for the peace and liberty of the realm' (Paris, 5.504): he may have had in mind his opposition to King John, or his distinguished military career, or even some contributions to parliamentary debate now lost. But flattery to a benefactor of St Albans Abbey seems more likely, since Paris also praised his 'huge and noble will' (Paris, 5.534). The Augustinian priory at Dunstable, which also noted Munchensi's death, was another probable beneficiary. Paris's figure of 200,000 marks for the will is an exaggeration, since Munchensi's estates were worth some £500 p.a., but Munchensi bequeathed 300 marks to Gravesend Hospital, and in 1258 William de Valence (probably with the connivance of Joan) still kept 900 marks of the inheritance at Waltham Abbey, doubtless one of the many causes of later friction between the two families. Denise de Munchensi, having bought her freedom to marry for 200 marks from the Poitevin Guy de Rochford, in 1257, was married for a few years to a Robert Butyller and, apparently, lived on until 1304. She founded Waterbeach Abbey, Cambridgeshire, in 1293, and may have been the dedicatee of the well-known thirteenth-century French phrase book composed by Walter of Bibbesworth.   H. W. RIDGEWAY

Sources Chancery records (RC) · C. Roberts, ed., Excerpta è rotulis finium in Turri Londinensi asservatis, Henrico Tertio rege, AD 1216–1272, 1, RC, 32 (1835), 268 · J. C. Holt, Magna Carta (1965), 107–8 · G. W. Watson, 'Fitz Piers and De Say', The Genealogist, new ser., 34 (1917–18), 181–9 [introduction and pedigree table] · The historical works of Gervase of Canterbury, ed. W. Stubbs, 2: The minor works comprising the Gesta regum with its continuation, the Actus pontificum and the Mappa mundi, Rolls Series, 73 (1880), 111 · Paris, Chron., 4.213; 5.504, 534 · Ann. mon., 3.172, 196 · J. S. Brewer, ed., Monumenta Franciscana, 1, Rolls Series, 4 (1858), 112 · Dugdale, Monasticon, new edn, 6.1554 · GEC, Peerage
Wealth at death £500 p.a. from estates; bequeathed 300 marks to Gravesend Hospital

Munchensi, William de (c.1235–1287), baronial leader, was the son of Warin de *Munchensi (c.1195–1255) and his second wife, Denise (d. 1304?). He was a minor at his father's death, and for fifteen months his lands were in the wardship of his brother-in-law, William de *Valence, in consideration of a grant of £500 from the king. He succeeded on 20 October 1256. Like many other wards of the king's favourites Munchensi rebelled over the following years. Even in July 1260 he was consorting (according to the close rolls) with Henry Hastings, Nicholas of Segrave, and Geoffrey de Lucy, all former royal wards. In December 1261 these barons lay at the core of the unsuccessful resistance to the king's overthrow of the provisions of Oxford. In May 1263 they again defied the king; following this rebellion Munchensi was one of those who swore to abide by the decision of Louis IX in December 1263. On 14 May 1264 he fought at Lewes in the division under Gilbert de Clare, earl of Gloucester, perhaps being knighted before the battle. He supported Montfort, but was not really prominent in his regime. He witnessed the peace of Canterbury establishing the new government and was summoned to Montfort's Model Parliament held in January 1265. In February, when relations between Montfort and Gilbert de Clare soured, he was one of the four arbiters appointed to negotiate between them. He was with the younger Simon de Montfort at Kenilworth, and was taken

prisoner there by Edward on 2 August. He was released on bail to his mother in June 1266, but may have again taken up arms as one of the disinherited in 1266, as his lands were granted outright to William de Valence. He was pardoned in February 1267 and submitted to the dictum of Kenilworth, but a little later he supported Gilbert de Clare's occupation of London. There is no doubt that Valence's harshness provoked his rebellion. It was not until December 1267 that Munchensi was able to redeem his lands from him for 2000 marks, which he paid within two years. In 1269, despite a penalty bond for 1000 marks, he refused to go on crusade with Valence, preferring to remain in Gilbert de Clare's retinue for several years. Munchensi was not fully pardoned until 1275.

Munchensi married Amicia (parentage unknown) before sunrise on 24 August 1279, at the door of the parish church of Hill Croome, Worcestershire—an irregular ceremony, the validity of which was unsuccessfully challenged in 1283. They had an only daughter, Denise, who married between 1294 and 1297 Hugh de Vere, son of Robert de Vere, earl of Oxford; in 1287 and 1290 William de Valence attempted, unsuccessfully, to have her declared illegitimate. At her death without children in 1313 Munchensi's lands passed to Aymer de Valence, earl of Pembroke, his sister's son.

Munchensi served in Wales in 1277, 1282, 1283, and finally in August 1287 under Edmund, earl of Cornwall, when he was killed at the siege of Dryslwyn Castle by the fall of a wall which had been undermined. He was described by Bartholomew Cotton (p. 168) as 'a valiant knight and wary in war'. He bequeathed 1000 marks 'in aid of the Holy Land' (CClR, 1313–18, 195). There is ample room for confusion between this William and a senior branch of the Munchensi family, often in royal service, the heads of which during the thirteenth century were also called William; they were settled at Edwardstone, Suffolk.   H. W. RIDGEWAY

Sources Close rolls of the reign of Henry III, 11, PRO (1932), 79 · CClR, 1313–18, 195 · Calendar of inquisitions miscellaneous (chancery), PRO, 1 (1916), 349, 679, 718, 758 · Calendar of the fine rolls, PRO, 1 (1911), 240 · RotP, 1.16–17 · Ann. mon., 4.133–4, 310 · Bartholomaei de Cotton … Historia Anglicana, ed. H. R. Luard, Rolls Series, 16 (1859), 168 · [W. Rishanger], The chronicle of William de Rishanger, of the barons' wars, ed. J. O. Halliwell, CS, 15 (1840) · J. Williams ab Ithel, ed., Annales Cambriae, Rolls Series, 20 (1860), 109 · J. W. W. Bund, ed., Register of Bishop Godfrey Giffard, September 23rd, 1268, to August 15th, 1301, 2, Worcestershire Historical Society, 15 (1902), 2.314, 358–61, 364 · J. E. Morris, The Welsh wars of Edward I (1901), 212–13
Wealth at death bequeathed 1000 marks in aid of the Holy Land

Munda, Constantia (fl. 1617), author, wrote The worming of a mad dogge, or, A soppe for Cerberus the jaylor of hell: no confutation but a sharpe redargution of the bayter of women (1617), the third and last response to Joseph Swetnam's The araignment of lewde, idle, froward, and unconstant women, or, The vanitie of them choose you whether (1615).

It is impossible to determine the gender of the writer behind The Worming. In Mortalities Memorandum (1621) Rachel Speght refers to Constantia as a woman, but the knowledge of Greek, Latin, and Italian texts and of legal language demonstrated in *The Worming* makes this doubtful. The ranting use of language ('your turbulent mind is defecated'; Munda, sig. C1r) also makes one question Munda's alleged female gender. Constantia does, however, dedicate *The Worming* to 'The Right Worshipful Lady her most deare Mother, the Lady Prudentia Munda' and offers 'her writing hand' that penned this pamphlet 'in recompense' for the 'pangs of sorrow you sustain'd / In child-birth' (ibid., sig. A3r). Constantia establishes her persona as the daughter of a lady; if her social status is aristocratic, this could account for her learned references.

Although Constantia includes some of the traditional arguments for the worth of women, such as that women are 'the meanes / Of all mens being', *The Worming* is more of a satirical attack on Swetnam and on his desire 'to please / The giddy-headed vulgar' than a defence of women. Constantia attacks the popular press, which has 'become the receptacle of every dissolute Pamphlet' (Munda, sig. B2r) and the public theatre, where 'every fantasticke Poetaster ... will strive to represent unseemely figments imputed to our sex' (ibid., sig. B3r). Calling Swetnam an 'ill-favoured hunks' (ibid., sig. E1v), Constantia accuses him of plagiarism, repeatedly corrects his inaccurate allusions, and charges him with 'Nero-like ... ripping up the bowels of thine own mother' when he says that all women are evil (ibid., sig. D2r). She speculates that Swetnam knows so much about brothels because he has spent so much time in them (ibid., sig. C3r).

The Worming was printed for Laurence Hayes by G. Purslowe, the same printer who produced the second edition of Swetnam's *Araignment*; it appears to be a rushed job to take advantage of the profits accruing to Swetnam's bookseller. Hayes entered *The Worming* in the Stationers' register on 29 April 1617, without indicating an author, which has led to speculation as to whether the author of the pamphlet was in his employ.

SUSAN GUSHEE O'MALLEY

Sources C. Munda, *The worming of a mad dogge, or, A soppe for Cerberus the jaylor of hell: no confutation but a sharpe redargution of the bayter of women* (1617) · L. Woodbridge, *Women and the English Renaissance: literature and the nature of womenkind, 1540–1620* (1984) · S. O'Malley, 'Introduction', *Defences of women: Jane Anger, Rachel Speght, Ester Sowernam and Constantia Munda*, ed. S. O'Malley, *The early modern Englishwoman: a facsimile library of essential works by women*, pt 1, vol. 4 (1996) · E. V. Beilin, *Redeeming Eve: women writers of the English Renaissance* (1987) · A. R. Jones, 'Counterattacks on the bayter of women: three pamphleteers of the early seventeenth century', *The Renaissance Englishwoman in print* (1990) · S. Shepherd, introduction, *The women's sharp revenge: five women's pamphlets from the Renaissance*, ed. S. Shepherd (1985) · B. Travitsky, '"The lady doth protest": protest in the popular writings of Renaissance Englishwomen', *English Literary Renaissance*, 14 (1984), 255–83

Munday, Anthony (*bap.* 1560, *d.* 1633), playwright and translator, was baptized on 13 October 1560 in St Gregory by Paul's, London, the son (and possibly only child) of Christopher and Jane Munday, both of whom died when Anthony was a child, some time before January 1571.

Early life and education In January 1581 Munday received the portion from his mother's estate. Additional evidence about his birth comes from an examination taken on 22 May 1598 in the consistory court of London. Here he testified that he was thirty-eight years old, that he had been born in St Gregory's parish, and that for the past twenty years he had lived in the parish of St Giles Cripplegate (Eccles, 100). This testimony concerned the will of Francis Roberts, a minor canon, who on his deathbed had summoned Anthony Munday to write the will, even though Munday had never written a will before. Additional witnesses confirmed Munday's testimony, one reporting that Roberts willed Munday to set down that his wife should have all his goods, 'And then & ther mr Anthony Monday taking pen & ynck did write this will word for word as is here written' (Eccles, 101).

There is no evidence about Munday's education, other than his apparent study with Claudius Hollyband, a London Huguenot, in the 1570s. Hollyband taught Latin, French, and Italian, all of which Munday certainly knew. In the preface to the *Mirrour of Mutabilitie* Munday refers to his parents' spending liberally on his education, which may have been with Hollyband. Christopher Munday had been a member of the Drapers' Company but practised his trade as a stationer, a not uncommon pattern for Drapers. Following his father's example, Anthony Munday became an apprentice to the printer John Allde in 1576, binding himself for a term of eight years. On 21 June 1585 he received freedom of the Drapers' Company by patrimony. The Drapers' freedom list describes him as 'a Poet by Cripplegate', indicating the principal place of his London residence. Regularly in his later printed texts he signs himself as 'Citizen and Draper'. Evidence from December 1615 suggests that Munday also enjoyed the freedom of the Merchant Taylors' Company (Forker, 30–31).

In the autumn of 1578 Munday abandoned his apprenticeship and with Thomas Nowell travelled to Europe, principally France and Italy. The details of his stay in the English College in Rome, beginning in February 1579, Munday provides in his *The English Roman Life* (1582, 1590). He had returned to London by July 1579. Some evidence suggests that he may have later travelled to the Low Countries in 1595–6 (Schrickx, 484–5).

By the early 1580s Munday apparently was an actor. This information derives in part from the Catholic *True Report of the Death of M. Campion Jesuit* (early 1582), itself an answer to Munday's *Discovery of Edmund Campion* (1582). The writer claims: 'Munday, who was first a stage player (no doubt a calling of some credit), after an apprentice which time he well served with deceiving of his master' (Ayres, xviii). The latter claim Allde himself disputed. The *True Report* continues in its account of Munday as actor: 'I omit to declare how this scholar new come out of Italy did play extempore, those gentlemen and others which were present can best give witness of his dexterity, who being weary of his folly, hissed him from his stage.'

Marriage and family By 1582 Munday had married Elizabeth (*d.* 1621). From this marriage came five children, as recorded in the register of St Giles Cripplegate: Elizabeth, baptized on 28 June 1584; Roase, baptized on 17 October 1585 and buried the following January; Priscilla, baptized on 9 January 1587; Richard, baptized on 27 January 1588;

and Anne, baptized on 5 September 1589. Priscilla married Edward Pearson at St Mary Magdalen, Bermondsey, in 1622. Elizabeth, their mother, was buried at St Giles Cripplegate on 7 October 1621. Anthony Munday then married Gillian, who survived him.

Richard Munday received the freedom of the Drapers' Company on 13 January 1613, but he functioned professionally as a painter–stainer. In February 1609 Anthony Munday along with George Herne gave bonds of £20 in behalf of Richard, who had been accused of fathering a bastard child. The case was dismissed. On 10 July 1612 at St Mary-le-Strand, Richard married Joan Lacy, who survived his death in 1640. Starting in 1613 and continuing for twenty-five years, Richard Munday painted banners and other objects for lord mayor's shows, including the pageant of 1618, *Sidero-Thriambos*, written by his father, Anthony.

Religion Why Munday abandoned his apprenticeship with Allde and travelled to Europe, spending most of his time in Rome, remains intriguing. He says in *English Roman Life* that he went to absorb the culture and learn languages. Some scholars have found this explanation too facile and have sought elsewhere for answers. Celeste Wright concludes that Munday went to Rome as a Catholic convert, not as a spy. This theory rests on Munday's involvement with the Catholic-leaning printers Allde and John Charlewood and with his Catholic patron, Edward de Vere, earl of Oxford, to whom Munday dedicated his early works *The Mirrour of Mutabilitie* (1579) and *Zelauto* (1580). Some scholars detect a Catholic sympathy in Munday's writings.

But after his return to London in 1579 Munday launched a series of tracts that can only be categorized as virulently anti-Catholic, such as *A Breefe Discourse of the Taking of Edmund Campion* (1581), *A Discoverie of Edmund Campion and his Confederates* (1582), and *A Breefe Aunswer Made unto Two Seditious Pamphlets* (1582). Campion and Robert Persons had arrived in England in June 1580 on the first Jesuit mission, and they brought a number of priests from the English College in Rome. Munday testified in November 1581 against priests whom he had met in Rome and even against Campion, whom he did not know. Campion and several other priests were executed in December 1581.

Munday's *English Roman Life* (1582) has, as a historical document, according to Ayres:

> two distinct claims to importance. It offers historians of English Catholicism a unique and detailed record of daily life in the English College in Rome at that time, and a participant's account of a crucial episode in the College's development, the successful rebellion early in 1579 of the English students against their Welsh rector Maurice Clenocke

and the institution of Jesuit control (Ayres, xix–xx). The general reliability of the account has been verified by other sources. Munday shrewdly dedicates his text to Thomas Bromley, lord chancellor; William, Lord Burghley; and Robert, earl of Leicester, thinking, Munday writes, 'myself in as safe security under your honourable

favour as Ulysses supposed himself under the buckler of Ajax'.

Munday begins with an account of the European travels before he and Nowell reached Rome, through Paris, Bologna, Florence, and Siena. The vivid description that he gives of daily life in the English College moves regularly between attraction and repulsion. Clearly, some of the features in the seminary life appealed to him. Flagellation, however, was not one of these. Munday writes: 'The Jesuits have, some of them, to whip themselves, whips with cords of wire, wherewith they will beat themselves till with too much effuse of blood they be ready to give up the ghost' (*English Roman Life*, 39). One of the Jesuits compelled Munday into his chamber to watch such flagellation; but Munday went away, 'lamenting to see a spectacle of so great folly'. Routinely after supper the priests would sit around a great fire and see who could say the most outrageous things about Queen Elizabeth and her court. Munday takes a dim view of the religious relics that he saw in various churches in Rome. He is both horrified by and attracted to the bacchanalian activities of Carnival. As a participant in the open rebellion of the English students he gained an audience with Pope Gregory XIII, which he records in vivid detail. Munday left the seminary some time after Easter 1579, but Nowell stayed on until he was later dismissed as being unfit to be a priest.

Not only did Munday write these various anti-Catholic tracts, he also became actively involved in tracking down priests and other recusants. He worked as an intelligencer for Richard Topcliffe during the 1580s, and for Sir Thomas Heneage, treasurer of the chamber, who paid messengers until his death in 1595. From 1588 to 1596 Munday signed his publications 'Anthony Munday, Messenger of Her Majesties Chamber'. Queen Elizabeth on 19 July 1587 granted to Munday for his good services leases in reversion of crown property in Cambridgeshire, Cumberland, Merioneth, Norfolk, Northamptonshire, Nottinghamshire, and Suffolk, and a reversion, to begin in 1611, of the fishery part of the Water of Tamar in Cornwall (patent roll, 29 Eliz., part 16, C66/1301). However zealous Munday was in tracking down recusants, he clearly benefited from the activity. After the Gunpowder Plot the bishop of London employed Munday for this work. Even as late as 1612 the poet Hugh Holland was indicted for recusancy 'ex testimonio *Anthonij Munday*' (Eccles, 103). Munday exhibited equal zeal in hunting down puritans. He became involved in the Martin Marprelate controversy in the late 1580s at the request of the archbishop of Canterbury, John Whitgift. His first duty was to seek out a clergyman named Giles Wigginton, whom Munday delivered to the archbishop after tricking him into revealing his puritan leanings and knowledge of the Marprelate tracts. Wigginton later complained: 'I was treated like a Turk or Dog … This Mundy … seemeth to favour the Pope and to be a great dissembler' (Turner, 84). The Marprelate tract *The Just Censure and Reproof of Martin Junior* (1589) singles out Munday for attack. Never succeeding in actually capturing 'Martin Marprelate', the bishops finally gave up, and Munday turned his attention elsewhere.

Early literary writing Having returned from Rome in 1579, Munday launched his literary career, which became as busy and productive as it was diverse. Two works of his from 1577 are lost; his first surviving publication was *The Mirrour of Mutabilitie, or, Principall Part of the Mirrour for Magistrates* (1579), printed by his former master John Allde. The dedication and most of the prefatory material focuses on the earl of Oxford. In the dedication Munday discusses his recent foreign travels. The work responds to a medieval tradition and specifically to the mid-sixteenth-century *Mirrour for Magistrates*. Munday divides his *Mirrour* according to the structure of the seven deadly sins and writes each 'tragedy' in a different stanzaic form. He uses Old Testament figures who represent certain qualities, usually vices. For example, Nebuchadnezzar represents pride; Solomon, uxoriousness; Ahab, idolatry. Each figure 'speaks' and then the author responds. The *Mirrour of Mutabilitie*, Turner writes, 'hammers home its moral in every instance, sometimes at the expense of the narratives' (Turner, 28). Munday refers to the examples as 'excellent Historyes, bothe pleasant and profitable', which would be the goal of such a publication.

In 1580 Munday published the paradoxical *The Paine of Pleasure*. Here he examines in verse some twenty-three 'pleasures', such as beauty, love, honour, music, study, that all have a countering 'pain' that vitiates the pleasure. This conundrum resolves in the twenty-third pleasure, Divinity, which leads Munday to urge that we:

> love our God, which is our onely friend,
> That saves our soules, and bodies from annoy.

Munday appends to this text 'The Authors Dream', which begins with an idyllic state of things—no crime, no need for money, lawyers getting rid of their books. But then the dream turns in a dire direction where envy, hatred, and destruction reign. He concludes soberly:

> Come not a fire to plague the world, with an infernall paine.
> From which God shield both man and childe, and grant us of
>   his grace.

Munday moves to a lighter, although important, subject in *A Courtly Controversie between Love and Learning* (1581); and certainly this poetic fantasy offers a respite from the anti-Catholic tracts so regularly flowing from his pen at this point. In the poem a lady, named Caliphia, from Padua, debates with a scholar from Siena named Palunor. She argues for the power of love; and he, for learning. Perhaps beginning to feel a bit desperate, Palunor offers awful examples of the distortion of love: for instance, Nero and Sporus, and an Egyptian father who forces his daughter into prostitution. The lady rightly calls these examples 'detestable, yea or rather divelish discourses'. She instead cites loyal wives and expands her definition of love to include patriotism. The lady triumphs, but the scholar concedes little: 'And thus the Ladie and the Scholar departed: the Scholler to his Lodging, and the Ladie to her home.' Turner insists that nothing can 'blow from the *Courtly Controversie* a certain dismal damp and malodorous mustiness' (Turner, 50). In this judgement alliteration wins against accepting the playful tone of the poetic exercise.

A Banquet of Daintie Conceits (1588) includes twenty-two poems that may be sung to music, although Munday in an address to the reader acknowledges 'I have no jote of knowledge in Musique'. But, curiously, the collection contains two final songs, one that 'maybe sung to *A. Munday his Galliard*', and the other 'may be sung to *A. Mundy his Toy*'. Although at the end he promises 'the second service of this Banquet', very soon to be published, no such publication appears. This book has the odd distinction of being the only literary work dedicated to Richard Topcliffe, Munday's mentor in papist-hunting.

Munday's lengthy prose romance *Zelauto: the Fountaine of Fame* appeared in 1580 and survives in only one copy. On the title-page Munday refers to himself as a 'Servant to the Right Honourable the Earle of Oxenford'; and in the dedicatory epistle he wishes the earl 'all happines in this Honorable estate, and after death eternall life'. Having 'sufficiently seene the rare vertues of your noble minde, the heroycall quallities of your prudent person', Munday places *Zelauto* among all the books that have been dedicated to Oxford. He reveals that the work remains unfinished but promises more in the future. Munday signs the dedication: 'Your Honours moste dutifull servant at all assayes'. In the dedication 'To the well disposed Reader', the author links his romance to John Lyly's *Euphues* (1578) as he seeks the readers' 'courteous consentes'.

The duke of Venice, Gonzalo Guicciardo, has a son, Zelauto, who desires to travel. His father grants the request for a term not to exceed six years. This basic situation informs the sprawling chivalric romance that follows. Munday writes in the 'Argument': 'Zelauto accompanied with his knight, departed from the Court of his famous Father, and tooke shipping to goe unto Naples, from thence, he travailled unto Valentia in Spayne' (*Anthony Munday's 'Zelauto'*, 11–12). There he meets English merchants who sing the glories of England, feeding Zelauto's desire to visit the country, which he does, spending some time in Queen Elizabeth's glorious court. Only the press of additional travel sends him away, this time to Persia and eventually Sicily in the sixth year of his travels. In Sicily he encounters a Christian knight named Astraepho, who lives in a cave. These two engage in lengthy conversations, which is where *Zelauto* begins.

Jack Stillinger astutely observes: 'Living as long as he did (1560–1633), Munday could have written a string of books reflecting all the trends in the course of Elizabethan fiction. As it is, he managed to embody most of them in his one novel' (*Anthony Munday's 'Zelauto'*, ix). Part 1 includes Zelauto's description of his travels from the beginning up to the point of his departure from England and ends when the two men retire to supper. In part 2 Zelauto narrates his adventures in Persia and the book ends as Astraepho excuses himself to prepare dinner. He gives Zelauto something to read, and that forms the whole of part 3, which abruptly breaks off. Stillinger notes the several connections between Zelauto's journeys and Munday's recent European travels (ibid., xiv–xv). Three types of literature inform *Zelauto*: courtly love romance, the jest book, and the Italian novella. This disjointed work, while offering some improvement over earlier English prose fictions, seems, according to Stillinger, to have had almost no influence on later fiction (ibid., xxvii). However, in the context of Munday's other early writings, the work represents a significant achievement and demonstrates his wide-ranging literary experimentation.

Translations *Zelauto* may have inspired Munday to translate numerous French, Italian, and Spanish texts, especially romances. In the late 1580s and 1590s particularly, he functioned single-handedly as a major translation factory, churning out continental prose romances. His work as translator continued through most of his literary career. The earl of Oxford and his family were the dedicatees of some of the translations. For example, in the 1619 edition of the three books of *Primaleon of Greece*, Munday dedicates the books to Henry Vere, the earl's son, successor to his father. He writes: 'Sir, having sometime served that most noble Earle your Father, of famous and desertfull memory; and translating divers Honourable Histories into *English*, out of *French*, *Italian*, and other Languages, which he graciously pleased to countenance with his Noble acceptance' (sig. A3, bk 1). Therefore, whether to respond to specific requests or to curry favour, Munday set on a course of translation.

Palmerin d'Oliva, emperor of Constantinople, his sons, Palmendos and Primaleon, and grandson, Palmerin of England, dominate a huge sweep of romance history, all of which Munday captures in translation. The stories emanated from Spain in the sixteenth century and passed through France, and Munday's translations created a market for them in England that remained vibrant well into the seventeenth century, to judge by published editions. His edition of *Palmerin d'Oliva*, dedicated to the earl of Oxford, was published in 1588 in two separate parts for purely commercial reasons, as he himself confesses. In this translation Munday promises more of the history, and *Palmerin* was followed by *Palmendos* (1589), dedicated to Sir Francis Drake; *Palladine* (1588), dedicated to the earl of Essex; and *Primaleon* (1595). Munday translated Francisco de Moraes's version of the history in *The First and Second Parts, of the No Lesse Rare, Historie of Palmerin of England* (1596), and the third part in 1602. Many of these texts were reissued in new editions in Munday's lifetime.

Primaleon, Prince of Greece, written by an anonymous Spanish author and translated by Munday from the French, had a chequered publishing history in translation and may serve as a possible source for Shakespeare's *The Tempest* in the analogies between Prospero and the Knight of the Enclosed Isle. The translation of book 1 appeared in 1595, book 2 in 1596, and all three books in 1619, a quarto volume of 726 pages. There had been some ten editions of the Spanish version between 1512 and 1588; thus Munday taps into a well-established and popular romance tradition. The Knight of the Enclosed Isle appears briefly in disguise at the end of book 2, but his principal actions occur in book 3, wherein 'old wounds are healed, friendships reaffirmed, marriages arranged', as in *The Tempest*, and there is a 'central and benevolent mage-*cum*-master of ceremonies; a central action devoted to the manipulation

of groups of isolated mariners; and a story line that is ebulliently harmonizing and keenly attentive to patrimonial issues' (Schmidgall, 430).

In *Palmendos* (1589), Munday promises *Amadis of Gaule*, which he translated from Nicholas de Herberay's French translation of the original Spanish and published probably in 1590 (it had been licensed in 1589). Books 3 and 4 appeared in 1618, dedicated to the earl of Montgomery. Munday also published a work by José Teixeira, translated as *The strangest adventure that ever happened: containing a discourse of the king of Portugal Dom Sebastian* (1601). This king of Portugal, lost in Africa at the battle of Alcazar, had not been heard of since 1578; but in 1598 a man appeared in Italy claiming to be Dom Sebastian. Teixeira's book contains letters, divine oracles, and testimonials of witnesses, all purporting to prove the legitimacy of this claimant. Eventually he was dismissed as an impostor. These translations, along with others, document Munday's continuing interest in romance.

Plays In 1598 Francis Meres in *Palladis tamia* named Munday in a distinguished list of playwrights (including Shakespeare) as being among the best for comedy and added after Munday's name: 'our best plotter'. Whatever Meres may precisely have had in mind, this evaluation offers Munday extraordinary recognition in the midst of a flourishing theatrical world. Munday had had some experience as an actor, but by the 1590s he clearly formed part of Philip Henslowe's stable of playwrights, writing for performances at the Rose Theatre. Evidence of Munday's connection with the Henslowe group comes from Henslowe's invaluable *Diary* that records his day-to-day transactions. Overwhelmingly Munday in writing plays collaborated with other dramatists, such as Michael Drayton, Thomas Dekker, Henry Chettle, Thomas Middleton, Thomas Heywood, and John Webster. His greatest theatrical productivity came in the 1590s; indeed, after 1602 he seems to have abandoned the regular theatre.

The first play attributed to Munday, *Fedele and Fortunio* (1585), was a translation and adaptation of an Italian play by Luigi Pasqualigo. Of Munday's plays this one has the distinction of having been performed at Queen Elizabeth's court; in fact, the text includes a prologue and epilogue explicitly written for this performance. Munday freely changed many of the elements of the original Italian play, for example transferring the pranks of the Italian pedant to Captain Crackstone, one of Pasqualigo's minor characters. The basic story centres on Victoria and her favoured suitor Fortunio, Fedele her cast-off lover, and Virginia who desires Fedele. The young ladies seek help from the enchantress Medusa. Eventually Fedele forces Fortunio to believe that Victoria has been compromised and thus wins her for himself. Virginia readily transfers her love to Fortunio. The liveliness of Munday's play contrasts sharply with an earlier Latin version by Abraham Fraunce, dedicated to Philip Sidney.

Keen to exploit the popularity of Robert Greene's *Friar Bacon and Friar Bungay*, Munday wrote his own version of two characters who have magical powers: 'John a Kent and John a Cumber' (*c*.1590). The text of this play, not printed until the nineteenth century, exists in Munday's own hand, complete with his signature and the date 1590 (Hunt., HM 500). Some version of this play may have received production at the Rose Theatre in 1594. Derived from English folklore, John a Kent does battle with the Scottish wizard John a Cumber through magic and disguises. Indeed, at one point Cumber disguises himself as Kent, and later Kent disguises himself as Cumber. The battle rages over the young princesses Sidanen and Marian, who love the Welsh princes Griffin and Powesse, respectively. But their fathers want them to marry Morton and Pembroke. With the help of the puckish Shrimp, and after a series of magical contests, John a Kent triumphs and returns the young ladies to their true loves.

Like 'John a Kent and John a Cumber', 'The Book of Sir Thomas More' (c.1593) exists only in manuscript, in the British Library (BL, Harleian MS 7368). It was never published in Munday's lifetime, although it was possibly performed. This collaborative effort by Munday and several others generates considerable interest because the alleged Hand D in the manuscript has been identified as that of Shakespeare. The manuscript mainly exists in Munday's own hand:

> The most reasonable conclusion is that the authorship of the original *Book* should be attributed to Anthony Munday in the same measure as that of the three parts of *Henry VI* is acknowledged Shakespeare's … at all events his [Munday's] was the task of giving final shape to the work of his collaborators, and this is more than sufficient title to authorship.   (Gabrieli and Melchiori, 14)

Chettle, Dekker, Shakespeare, and Heywood have all been assigned parts of the revision of the play. Hand C in the manuscript was that of the company bookkeeper who began to copy some of the new material while revisions were still under way.

The play manuscript stirs attention also because of the evidence of censorship by Edmund Tilney, master of the revels, who deletes whole scenes and rids the play of references to foreigners, replacing the references with the word 'Lombards'. Curiously, Tilney's comments appear only in the part of the play clearly in Munday's hand. The censorship comes in part because of political circumstances. There was strong feeling against foreigners among London citizens at the time, and the play's sympathetic portrayal of anti-alien 'rebels' of 1517 might have seemed inflammatory. McMillin argues that the play was written for performance by Lord Strange's Men between the summer of 1592 and the summer of 1593 'and that the representation of the Ill May-Day uprising was intended to reflect the crisis over aliens that was troubling the City during those months' (McMillin, 72).

The play itself effectively traces Sir Thomas More's development from sheriff to knight, to privy councillor, to lord chancellor, and then his precipitous decline. His fame advances because of his involvement in and response to the Ill May Day events of 1517. The playwrights also include an appearance by More's friend Erasmus. The final part, More's decline and fall, did not undergo revision. The play includes effective scenes between More and

his family, especially when he resides in the Tower. The hangman leads More to the block as the play closes. More says:

> We go to sigh, that o'er, to sleep in rest.
> … No eye salute my trunk with a sad tear;
> Our birth to heaven should be thus: void of fear.
> (v. iv.114–18)

Henslowe's *Diary* records a payment of 4s. to Munday and Drayton on 22 December 1597 for a play, 'Mother Redcap' (now lost), presumably performed at the Rose Theatre in that season. In early January 1598 Munday and Drayton received a final payment of 15s. for the play. Just a few weeks later, in February, Munday received a payment of £5 'for a play boocke called the firste parte of Robyne Hoode'. On 22 and 28 February 1598 Henslowe records two more payments to Munday, this time for 'his seconde parte of the downefall of earlle huntyngton surnamed Roben Hoode'. Henry Chettle also received a payment for the second part, becoming Munday's collaborator (*Henslowe's Diary*, 85–7). These two plays, *The Downfall of Robert, Earl of Huntington* and *The Death of Robert, Earl of Huntington*, did not receive publication until 1601, although one or both were performed at court in the 1598 season.

Munday incorporates folk tradition and historical resources, such as Grafton's *Chronicle* and Holinshed's *Chronicles*, for his rich material. Although Munday seems to have planned a single play to cover the entire history, perhaps because of popularity Henslowe convinced Munday and Chettle to provide a sequel. In the plays Munday offers some of the familiar events of the Robin Hood legend: his banishment, his merry life in Sherwood Forest with his yeomen and Maid Marian (also called Matilda), his service to the poor and his dedication to justice, his support of Richard I against the usurpation of Prince John, and finally his tragic death at the hands of his wicked uncle the prior of York. Munday gives Maid Marian (called Matilda) a courtly history as daughter of Lord Lacy and betrothed of the earl; she is also the object of Prince John's amorous attention. After Robin Hood's death, Matilda fights on. For the broad outlines of her story Munday closely followed Drayton's *Matilda*.

Several payments in Henslowe's *Diary* for June 1598 reveal Munday's involvement with Chettle, Drayton, and Robert Wilson in writing a sequel to the Robin Hood plays, called 'Richard Coeur de Lion's Funeral' (lost), apparent testimony to the success of the earlier plays. Munday, Dekker, Drayton, and Richard Hathway collaborated on 'Valentine and Orson' (lost), according to Henslowe's payments in 1600. Henslowe disbursed 40s. to Robert Shaw, Chettle, Drayton, and Munday in October 1601 for the writing of 'The Rising of Cardinal Wolsey' (lost). Munday received full payment of £3 from Henslowe in December 1602 for 'The Set at Tennis' (lost), to be performed at the Fortune Theatre; this was apparently Munday's last play.

In October 1599 Munday, Drayton, Wilson, and Hathway received £10 for writing the first part of *The True and Honorable History of Sir John Oldcastle* (published 1600), to be performed at the Rose. This play functions as an 'answer' to Shakespeare's characterization of Oldcastle in his history plays in the character renamed as Falstaff. The prologue says:

It is no pamperd glutton we present
Nor aged Councellor to youthfull sinne,
But one, whose vertue shone above the rest,
A valiant Martyr, and a vertuous peere.

Of course Munday and his collaborators succeed no more than Shakespeare in presenting an accurate historical portrait, because the chronicles had presented Oldcastle as a heretic and cowardly traitor. The play explores his close relationship with Henry V and his persecution at the hands of the bishop of Rochester.

Civic pageants Munday continued this involvement with drama by writing civic pageants, principally lord mayor's shows: street drama presented by the guild to which the new mayor belonged on the occasion of the mayor's inauguration on 29 October. After the mayor took the oath of office he processed through London's streets and encountered there various dramatic scenes, drawn from allegory, history, and mythology. Several major dramatists of the period, excepting Shakespeare, wrote the lord mayor's shows, though none matched Munday's output. At least eight of his pageant texts survive, and he participated in the production of several others from 1602 to 1623. Indeed, he turned his interest from the regular public theatre to this form of street drama. Guild records help document his extensive connection to these civic pageants and the usual pattern of the negotiations between the guild and the playwright as the guild made its choice of a dramatist and worked out the costs and payments. In addition, Munday prepared the civic entertainment in 1610 for the festivities surrounding the investiture of Prince Henry as prince of Wales.

According to guild records Munday was responsible for the mayoral show of 1602, but no text survives. The ravages of the plague prevented a pageant in 1603. But in October 1604 Ben Jonson and Munday collaborated in producing the mayor's pageant. Records of the Haberdashers show a payment of £2 'to Antony Mundey for his paines' and £12 'to Benjamyn Johnson for his device, and speech for the Children' (Robertson and Gordon, 63). Although the guild spent £1 10s. for 'printing the bookes of the device', none has survived. The records do not indicate what 'paines' Munday expended, but clearly participation in a pageant could be financially worthwhile. Typically the dramatist incurred responsibility for seeing to the printing of the text, usually 300–500 copies. Collaboration of various kinds defines the procedure in these pageants. Even though Jonson had poked fun at Munday in *The Case is Altered* (1599), he did not refuse to work with him.

With *The Triumphes of Re-United Britania* (1605), the first extant lord mayor's show of the Jacobean era, Munday made his mark. He single-handedly created a text unlike the much simpler pageant texts of the Elizabethan era. His work bristles with arcane historical discussion, with vivid description of the pageant devices, with learned marginal notes, and with poetic verses spoken by the fictional characters. He even experiments with the verse by using the Chaucerian rhyme royal stanzaic pattern.

According to the Merchant Taylors' account book, the total cost for this pageant exceeded £710, partly because bad weather forced a second performance a few days later. Munday furnished various things, ranging from apparel for the children, breakfast for the child actors, cloth, and 'printing the books of the speeches in the pageant and the other shows'. For these expenditures Munday received reimbursement from the Merchant Taylors.

In this pageant Munday explores the Brutus–Trojan myth of British history, what he refers to in the text as 'the antiquitie of *Brytaine*' (*Pageants and Entertainments*, 3). He remains the only pageant writer to focus on this myth, and he consciously makes it work to honour the relatively new King James I. Several reasons may have governed Munday's choice: his antiquarian interest in ancient British history, his recognition of a good story, and his desire to earn some royal favour by sounding the theme of union and honouring James. In the pageant text Munday sums up the function of Brutus and the link to James, whom Munday calls 'our second Brute … by whose happye comming to the Crowne, *England*, *Wales*, and *Scotland*, by the first *Brute* severed and divided, is in our second *Brute* re-united, and made one happy *Britania* again' (*Pageants and Entertainments*, 7). Brutus and his three sons, Locrine, Camber, and Albanact, appear and speak, celebrating the kingdom's joy of unity, made possible by James.

After the pageant of 1609, *Camp-Bell, or, The Ironmongers Faire Feild*, of which only a fragmentary text survives, Munday turned his attention in 1610 to the investiture festivities for Prince Henry, and quickly put together a pageant (31 May) at the City's request. Corporation of London records prove his authorship, although his name does not appear on the title-page. Munday wrote two brief speeches: one performed by Corinea riding on a whale as the prince landed at Chelsea; and the other, Amphion on a dolphin, as Henry arrived at Whitehall. Records show payments to two well-known actors of the King's Men who represented Corinea and Amphion: John Rice and Richard Burbage.

Munday and the Goldsmiths' guild enlisted the services of John Lowen, also a member of the King's Men, to perform the role of Leofstane, by whom Munday means to suggest the first mayor of London, in the 1611 show, *Chruso-thriambos: the Triumphes of Golde*. Lowen, himself a goldsmith, agreed: 'he hathe promysed verye diligentlie and carefully to effect upon conference with Mr Mundy the poet, at which tyme he came and agreed that himselfe should provide a horse and furniture' (Robertson and Gordon, 81). Leofstane and Time go to the 'tomb' of Nicholas Faringdon, four times mayor in the fourteenth century; and, according to the stage directions, '*Time striketh on the Tomb with his silver wand, and then Faringdon ariseth*' (*Pageants and Entertainments*, 56). These former goldsmiths join in the celebration of the new mayor.

In 1614 and 1615 Munday wrote pageants honouring his own guild, the Drapers' Company: *Himatia-Poleos* (1614) and *Metropolis coronata* (1615). In both, Munday expends considerable space in recounting the glorious history of the Drapers. Unexpectedly, Robin Hood and his men appear in the 1615 pageant, 'fitted with Bowes and Arrowes' (*Pageants and Entertainments*, 91). Robin Hood and Friar Tuck address the new mayor at night; and the pageant closes with a charming song by them:

> What life is there like to *Robin Hood*?
> It is so pleasant a thing a:
> In merry *Shirwood* he spends his dayes,
> As pleasantly as a King a.
> (ibid., 95)

Munday wrote the river pageant *The Triumphs of the Golden Fleece* (1623), a small and rather disappointing part of Thomas Middleton's *The Triumphs of Integrity*, which also honoured the Drapers' Company. Munday represents Jason and the Argonauts, appropriate emblems for the Drapers.

Relying on history, allegory, and iconographical tradition, Munday created a successful pageant, *Chrysanaleia*, for the installation of the Fishmonger mayor in 1616. On one device he depicts a pelican 'with all her tender brood' located near a lemon tree. Munday suggests that the pelican, who nourishes her young from the blood of her own breast and within a year dies, functions as an 'excellent type of government in a Magistrate, who, at his meere entrance into his yeares Office, becommeth a nursing father of the Family' (*Pageants and Entertainments*, 107). The main dramatic action occurs at an arbour where lies Sir William Walworth, lord mayor in the late fourteenth century, on a tomb. With the sounding of trumpets, London's Genius 'strikes on him with his wand, whereat he begins to stir, and coming off the Tombe, looks strangely about him' (*Pageants and Entertainments*, 112). In Walworth, Munday celebrates the guild's history when Walworth as mayor rescued King Richard II in 1381 during the Jack Straw–Wat Tyler uprising. A final chariot includes a representation of King Richard and various allegorical qualities that support a kingdom. In speeches Walworth offers an interpretation of the whole pageant. The Fishmongers' records reveal something of the guild's dealings with Munday, including his appearance before the group in December when he asked for an additional £10 because he had 200 more books than he had requested and because some of the costumes had been damaged. The company agreed to give him £5, 'which he is content thankfully to accept in full satisfaction of all his demaundes' (Robertson and Gordon, 91).

Munday fared somewhat better in 1618 with his pageant *Sidero-thriambos* when he appeared before the Ironmongers on 2 November, as noted in the guild records:

> In Consideracion of Anthony Mundyes good performance of his business undertaken and of the spoyling of his Pageant apparaile by the foule weather it was agreed to give him three powndes as a free guift of the Companie besides and above the Contract.   (Robertson and Gordon, 96)

Richard Munday helped with the preparations by making two 'kettle drumme Banners'. John Grinkin, who had worked earlier with Munday, assisted, as did Gerard Christmas, who began a long career of serving as artificer for mayoral pageants.

History In the midst of pageant writing that regularly intersected with London's historical life, Munday turned formally to writing history, his first publication being *A Briefe Chronicle of the Success of Times, from the Creation* (1611). This tome attempted nothing less than a recounting of the world's history from creation to the present moment. At the same time Munday busied himself with revising and adding material to John Stow's *Survey of London*. His friend Stow had died in 1605 and bequeathed to Munday the task of carrying on the work of the *Survey*. Interestingly, in the pageant text *Himatia-Poleos* (1614) Munday refers explicitly to Stow as having misled him about the guild to which the first mayor of London belonged. This error he had made in the 1611 pageant text, *Chrusothriambos*. Munday's own personal research has ferreted out the mistake. But he defends Stow:

> In whose behalf I dare yet boldly maintaine, that no such error escaped from him wilfully or willingly, his care and endeavour was so great, but mis-information, or incapacitie of reading, may ... wrong better men then any that are concerned in this case.   (*Pageants and Entertainments*, 74)

With great tact Munday thus exposes the historical problem.

Finally, in 1618, Munday finished and published the new edition of the *Survey*. In the dedication to the mayor Sir George Bolles, he recollects Stow: 'Much of his good mind he had formerly imparted to me, prevailing with mee so farre, by his importunate perswasions, to correct what I found amisse, and to proceed in the perfecting of a Worke so worthy.' Munday claims to have appeared before the council in the Guildhall where he 'received encouragement and command from the whole Court, to proceed in the perfecting of this worthy Worke'. He also reveals that he had worked on the *Survey* for twelve years. Although he contributed many new details, Munday did not alter the organization or approach of the book. He continued working on another revision that eventually appeared in 1633, the year of his death. The City of London in December 1623 recognized his historical contribution in his *Briefe Chronicle* and in the *Survey* by decreeing that 'in consideration of his age and present wants' he should have 'granted unto him yearly, during his natural life, the nomination and benefit of one person to be made free of this Cittie by redemption' (Turner, 169). This arrangement brought him a comfortable pension, a just reward for a writer who had lived by his pen since 1579.

Death During an illness in March 1629 Munday made his will in which he names his wife, Gillian, as his executor and reveals that he possibly had deceived her about his financial standing when he married her. For example, when he names his surviving children, Richard, Elizabeth, and Priscilla, he says that they 'being all married, haveing had their severall portions already in bountyfull manner, and not knoweinge in what poore condition I married with this my present wife ... their expectation from me can be nothinge' (Turner, 171). Munday does leave the children 12d. each, 'which they maye take as a love token rather then in any respect of need they have'. The impress of the seal affixed to the will was 'the pelican in her piety' (Hotson, 4), perhaps recalling the pageant of 1616. Death came in August 1633, and Munday was buried in St Stephen, Coleman Street, on 9 August. An epitaph in the church survives, appropriately enough, only in the 1633 edition of Stow's *Survey*, which refers to Munday as 'ancient Servant to the City, with his Pen, in divers imployments, especially the *Survay of London*' (p. 869):

He that hath many an ancient Tombstone read,
… that survaid
Obstruse Antiquities, and on them laid
Such vive and beauteous colours with his Pen
(ibid.)

now rests under the marble tomb. In his writings:

He has a Monument, more faire, more rich,
Than polisht Stones could make him, where he lies
Though dead, still living, and in that, nere dyes.
(ibid.)

The appraised value of his moveables, entered in probate of his will on 14 August 1633, amounted to the considerable sum of £135 7s. 10d. (Hotson, 4). In recognition of Munday's major contribution to the literary and historical life of the City of London, officials granted his wife a continuation of his pension and a gift of £10 'in consideration of his *Survey*' (Turner, 171).

The epitaph's assurance that Munday 'Though dead, still living' remains at best an optimistic hope. Certainly in the areas of translations, civic pageants, and historical writing Munday made significant contributions. And he had a more diverse, richer professional literary career than most of his better-known contemporaries. But he has mainly been ignored. Meres's claim that Munday was among the best in comedy and 'our best plotter' has left more recent readers slightly puzzled. In light of the dazzling literary accomplishments of the sixteenth and seventeenth centuries, Munday has remained on the margins of attention. DAVID M. BERGERON

Sources C. Turner, *Anthony Mundy: an Elizabethan man of letters* (1928) · C. Turner Wright, 'Young Anthony Mundy again', *Sudies in Philology*, 56 (1959), 50–68 · M. Eccles, 'Anthony Munday', *Studies in the English Renaissance drama*, ed. J. W. Bennett, O. Cargill, and V. Hall (1959), 95–105 · *Pageants and entertainments of Anthony Munday: a critical edition*, ed. D. M. Bergeron (1985) · G. R. Hayes, 'Anthony Munday's romances of chivalry', *Library*, 6 (1925), 57–81 · J. Robertson and D. J. Gordon, eds., 'A calendar of dramatic records in the books of the livery companies of London, 1485–1640', *Malone Society Collections*, 3 (1954) · *Anthony Munday's 'Zelauto: the fountaine of fame'*, ed. J. Stillinger (1963) · D. M. Bergeron, *English civic pageantry, 1558–1642* (1971) · L. Hotson, 'Anthony Mundy's birth-date', *N&Q*, 204 (1959), 2–4 · *Henslowe's diary*, ed. R. A. Foakes and R. T. Rickert (1968) · A. Munday, *The English Roman life*, ed. P. Ayres (1980) · A. Munday and others, *Sir Thomas More*, ed. V. Gabrieli and G. Melchiori (1990) · I. A. Shapiro, 'Munday's birthdate', *N&Q*, 201 (1956), 2–3 · J. C. Meagher, 'Hackwriting and the Huntingdon plays', *Elizabethan theatre*, ed. J. Russell Brown and B. Harris (1966), 196–219 · S. McMillin, *The Elizabethan theatre and 'The book of Sir Thomas More'* (1987) · G. Schmidgall, 'The Tempest and Primaleon: a new source', *Shakespeare Quarterly*, 37 (1986), 423–39 · C. Forker, 'Two notes on John Webster and Anthony Munday', *English Language Notes*, 6 (1968), 26–34 · R. Prior, 'Anthony Munday as father and grandfather', *N&Q*, 218 (1973), 453–4 · W. Schrickx, 'Anthony Munday in the Netherlands in October 1595', *N&Q*, 242 (1997), 484–5 · T. Merriam, 'Chettle, Munday, Shakespeare, and *Sir Thomas More*', *N&Q*, 237 (1992), 336–41 · M. St Clare Byrne, 'Anthony

Munday and his books', *Library*, 1 (1921), 225–56 · A. Kenny, 'Anthony Munday in Rome', *Recusant History*, 6 (1962), 158–62 · Commissary Court, London, acts bk 18, p. 203 · parish register, London, St Gregory by Paul's, 13 Oct 1560 [baptism] · parish register, London, St Giles Cripplegate, 7 Oct 1621, GL [burial: Elizabeth Munday, wife] · parish register, St Stephen, Coleman Street, 9 Aug 1633 [burial] · Arber, *Regs. Stationers*

Wealth at death £135 7s. 10d.: Commissary Court, London, acts bk 18, p. 203

Munday, Eliza. *See* Salmon, Eliza (1787–1849).

Munday, Henry (*bap.* **1623**, *d.* **1682**), schoolmaster and physician, was the son of Henry Munday of Henley-on-Thames, Oxfordshire, and was baptized there on 21 September 1623. He matriculated at Corpus Christi College, Oxford, on 20 May 1642, and afterwards became a postmaster or portionist of Merton College; he graduated BA on 2 April 1647.

After enjoying, according to Wood, 'some petit employment' (Wood, *Ath. Oxon.*) during the civil wars and the Commonwealth, Munday was elected headmaster of the free grammar school at Henley-on-Thames in 1656. He appears to have written only one work, *Biochrēstologia, seu, Commentarii de aere vitali* (1680), which was republished on a number of occasions in several different countries. To his work as a teacher he added the practice of medicine, and the school suffered in consequence. His death saved him from likely dismissal. He died from a fall from his horse as he was returning home from a visit to John, third Baron Lovelace, at Hurley, Berkshire, on 28 June 1682, and was buried in the north chancel of Henley church. His estate was administered for 'Alicia and Marie Mundy, minors'. BERTHA PORTER, *rev.* PATRICK WALLIS

Sources Foster, *Alum. Oxon.* · parish register (baptism), 21 Sept 1623, Henley-on-Thames · Wood, *Ath. Oxon.* · administration, July 1682, PRO, PROB 6/57, fol. 98v

Mundeford, Osbert [Osbern] (*d.* **1460**), soldier and military administrator, was the son of Osbert Mundeford (1381–1456), a Norfolk landowner who fought in France in 1415, and Margaret Barrett. Between 1431 (or possibly 1427) and 1438 Osbert junior served in Sir John Fastolf's garrison of Fresnay, being marshal of the garrison from 1433. He was present at the recovery of Le Mans in 1428 and at various field actions in the 1430s. By 1444 he was captain of Beaumont-sur-Sarthe, and by the following year *bailli* and captain of Le Mans under the command of Edmund Beaufort, earl of Dorset (*d.* 1455), as governor of Maine and Anjou. Once Beaufort was installed as lieutenant-general of Normandy further offices and rewards came Mundeford's way. On 18 April 1448 he was granted a crown annuity of £40 p.a. for good service in France and Normandy. From June 1448 he assisted John Stanlowe, *trésorier général* of Normandy, and at the latter's death in September 1448 took up this office himself, attempting a thorough overhaul of tax collection in the duchy over the next year. As *bailli* and captain of Le Mans he was reluctant to implement the royal decision of December 1445 that Maine should be surrendered to the French, and raised continual objections until the *comté* was handed over in March 1448.

When hostilities formally reopened in July 1449, Munde-ford, who had been involved in various embassies to the French, was operating between Vernon and Mantes to collect revenues and foodstuffs for the English army. By this time he was also captain of Pont-l'Évêque and of Fresnay. Taken prisoner on 12 August 1449 at Pont-Audemer, and imprisoned in the castle of Châteaudon, he was therefore absent from his garrison of Fresnay when it fell in March 1450, but its composition for surrender involved Munde-ford's own release from French captivity.

The exact date of Mundeford's return to England is not known, but in August 1451 he took out a protection to cross to Calais in a reinforcing army, and was afterwards marshal of Calais under Edmund Beaufort. But he was back in England by 10 September 1458, when he was appointed to investigate the defence of the Isle of Wight. Following the failure of Henry Beaufort, duke of Somerset (d. 1464), to capture Calais from the Yorkists in April 1460, Mundeford was commissioned to gather troops at Sandwich to reinforce the Lancastrians at Guînes, but in June a Yorkist force from Calais fell upon Sandwich, and defeated Mundeford in a short, sharp fight. Taken across the channel, he was summarily executed on the sands below the Tour de Rysbank.

Mundeford had married (after 1441) Elizabeth, widow of Thomas Berney and probably the daughter of John Clipsby or Clippesby. She had links with the Pastons, and the only child of her marriage to Mundeford, Mary, may have been brought up in the Paston household. Under age at her father's death, Mary married Sir William Tindale, to whom Mundeford's principal estates passed. Mundeford had inherited the north-west Norfolk manors of Mundford, Hockwold-cum-Wilton, and part of the manor of East Lexham. By 1460 he had also acquired property in Feltwell. Elizabeth Mundeford's dower from her first marriage was the manor of Braydeston, Norfolk, but the Mundefords had to fight hard to gain and hold it against the machinations of the notoriously aggressive and avaricious Thomas Daniel, one of Henry VI's squires of the body. Elizabeth Mundeford also experienced considerable difficulty in securing her jointure in the manor of East Lexham in the early 1460s.   ANNE CURRY

Sources N. Davis, ed., *Paston letters and papers of the fifteenth century*, 2 vols. (1971–6) · C. Richmond, *The Paston family in the fifteenth century: the first phase* (1990) · *Chronique de Mathieu d'Escouchy*, ed. G. Du Fresne de Beaucourt, new edn, 3 vols. (Paris, 1863–4), vol. 3 · J. Stevenson, ed., *Letters and papers illustrative of the wars of the English in France during the reign of Henry VI, king of England*, 2 vols. in 3 pts, Rolls Series, 22 (1861–4) · J. Stevenson, ed., *Narratives of the expulsion of the English from Normandy, 1444–1450*, Rolls Series, 32 (1863) · Bibliothèque Nationale, Paris, MSS français · BL, Add. charters · BL, Add. MSS · accounts various, PRO, E101 · inquisitions post mortem, PRO, C139 · PRO, French rolls, C76 · *Chancery records* · Rymer, *Foedera* · Archives Communales de Mantes · R. A. Griffiths, *The reign of King Henry VI: the exercise of royal authority, 1422–1461* (1981) · F. Blomefield and C. Parkin, *An essay towards a topographical history of the county of Norfolk*, [2nd edn], 11 vols. (1805–10)

Archives Bibliothèque Nationale, Paris, MS français 4054, fol. 47

Mundella, Anthony John (1825–1897), hosiery manufacturer and politician, was born at Leicester on 28 March 1825. His father, Antonio Mundella, a political refugee

Anthony John Mundella (1825–1897), by London Stereoscopic Co., *c*.1883

from Como in Italy, emigrated to England about 1820 and was naturalized at Bradford where he first settled. Shortly thereafter he moved to Leicester where he taught foreign languages and where he married Mundella's mother, Rebecca. She was the daughter of Thomas Allsop, who was of Welsh descent; she was then employed as a frame-work knitter and lace embroiderer in the local industry.

Early life Although his father was a Roman Catholic, Mundella's early education was provided by St Nicholas national school, set up under voluntary contributions to provide an Anglican education for the poorer classes. Leicester was and remained a centre of popular radical agitation, and it was at school that Mundella had his first taste of political controversy. In August 1832 he attended a public procession through the town in support of the Reform Bill, one of 2000 local boys who marched at the front wearing special caps and medals. Mundella was also carrying a banner, the prominence of which brought him to the attention of the school authorities who promptly expelled him.

Although he was later readmitted on payment of a small fine his formal education was soon after brought to an abrupt and premature close. The loss of family earnings caused by his mother's failing eyesight, brought on by incessant work, necessitated his employment as a printer's devil for a local firm. In 1836, now aged eleven, he was apprenticed as a stockinger with the Leicester firm of William Kempson. During this period, as he later related, he enjoyed a formative experience of the morally improving kind beloved of popular Victorian biography. It was his duty to sleep on the premises and one night he was witness to a burglary, showing sufficient coolness to remain hidden, raise the alarm, and secure the thieves' apprehension. As the chief witness for the prosecution at the trial Mundella was singled out for praise by Chief Justice Denman, the trial judge. As Mundella later related, 'his eulogium was ever before me, and from that moment I was stimulated to prove myself through life worthy of the praises bestowed upon me' (*The Times*, 29 July 1897, 10b).

Chartist and hosier During the 1830s and 1840s the Leicester hosiery trade was in a poor condition and provided a harsh school for the apprentice stockinger. Mundella saw at first hand the shocking condition of the frame-work knitters, ravaged by low wages, chronic unemployment, and hunger. The knitters turned to Chartism and so too the young Mundella, inspired to political action by the local Chartist preacher and teacher Thomas Cooper. At the height of the Chartist agitation in 1842, Mundella attended Cooper's lectures and readings at the Shakespeare Room in Humberstone Gate and, at the age of fifteen, made his first political speech in support of the Charter. Economic salvation for the frame-work knitters was to come from technical innovation, with the application of steam power and factory production techniques to the hosiery trade—a process in which Mundella was to play an important role in the coming years. Mundella's own employer, Kempson, had taken out a patent in 1842 to improve techniques and a rival, Collins, introduced the first steam-powered rotary frame in 1845. In the same year, at the age of nineteen, Mundella took a decisive step, leaving Kempson's to become an overseer of one of the large warehouses owned by the Leicester hosiers, Harris and Hamel. Mundella's new employers had themselves taken out two new patents to improve the manufacture of fancy hosiery, prospering to such an extent that employees' wages increased dramatically, and Mundella, now enjoying a salary of £200 per annum plus commission, joined the ranks of the middle classes. Rising prosperity was accompanied by domestic happiness and increased social standing. On 12 March 1844 he married Mary (*d.* 1890), daughter of William Smith, a warehouseman of Kibworth Beauchamp, Leicestershire; Mundella was then aged nineteen and his bride was 'of full age'. By all accounts it was a happy and successful marriage which was to last some forty-four years. At this time he also became superintendent of a large poor Sunday school at which he taught—the beginning of a long association with the cause of popular education.

Mundella's Chartist sympathies were shared by his employer William Harris. Both men were involved in attempts at political accommodation between middle-class radicals and Chartist leaders in the town—reflecting the tension between Mundella's early political allegiance

and his rising social status. With the revival of the Chartist agitation in 1848 Mundella emerged briefly as a local leader, signing the Leicester declaration as secretary of the local association. Yet in his speech before a mass audience at the Amphitheatre on 17 April Mundella's theme was a call for joint action by the middle and working classes to reform an aristocratic parliament by means of a large extension of the franchise. A week later Mundella appeared on a platform to support Joseph Hume's more limited resolution on franchise reform. The final collapse of the Chartist agitation spurred on a growing alliance between local Chartists, radicals, and whigs, which resulted in their common support for both Harris and another radical candidate, Ellis, at fresh polls later in 1848. Both were duly elected and Mundella's evolution from Chartism to advanced Liberalism was now complete.

At this juncture Mundella left Leicester and, at the age of twenty-three, accepted a partnership in the Nottingham hosiery firm of Jonathan Hine & Sons, then in the process of building a new steam-powered factory, a model of its kind completed in 1851. Over the next twenty years Hine and Mundella were at the forefront of technological advance in the hosiery trade. Mundella made his fortune, becoming a captain of his industry. His particular genius was in searching out new inventions and realizing their commercial success. A series of joint patents with local inventors taken out in the 1850s and 1860s allowed the production of fully fashioned machine-produced hosiery at lower prices and increased output, supplying an ever increasing domestic and European market. By 1857 his firm employed some 4000 workers, 10 per cent in the factory and the rest home-based frame-work knitters. Mundella was one of the most progressive factory employers of the day, paying high wages and providing clean and well-lit working conditions for a wholly adult workforce, who were employed for less than nine hours a day.

During the 1850s Mundella was part of a rising manufacturing élite who were replacing the old political order in Nottingham. In 1853 he was elected sheriff and in 1857 alderman on the town council. He was also vice-chairman of the local Liberal Party where he gained a reputation as an effective wire-puller. It was local tories in Nottingham who initiated a xenophobic and antisemitic campaign against him based on his physical appearance, foreign parentage, and commercial interests. Such campaigns were to be a feature of his political career.

Mundella's enthusiasm for education remained—he was appointed to the board of the Nottingham People's College, an institute of adult education which was the forerunner of University College, Nottingham. In 1859 he was active in the local volunteer movement—he was one of the first five volunteers to be enrolled in the Robin Hood rifle corps, rising to captain of the 1st company (1860–66). By now he had also established himself as a spokesman for the hosiery trade. He was appointed chairman of the Nottingham chamber of commerce at its foundation in 1860 and accompanied Richard Cobden's delegation to Paris to negotiate a treaty of commerce, securing new markets for English stockings. Cobden's influence on

Mundella, as with many mid-Victorian manufacturers, was profound, and he remained a convinced free-trader all his life. In the same year Mundella emerged as a successful proponent of industrial arbitration. A series of local frame-work knitters' strikes, arising from disparities in pay with their factory counterparts, led to the setting up of a board of arbitration under his chairmanship, with equal numbers of representatives from both sides of the industry. The board, which was the first of its kind and served as a model for several other trades, proved an effective mechanism and secured the abolition of the local truck system, the reduction of frame rents, and the consolidation of piece-rates for domestic frame-work knitters. Under Mundella's stewardship industrial relations in the hosiery trade improved as wages were increased, under the benign trading conditions of the mid-Victorian era.

Into parliament: education reform and the battle for trade union recognition Thus by the early 1860s Mundella had established himself as a prominent and popular figure. This was not without personal cost. In 1863 he suffered a nervous breakdown and travelled to Italy to recuperate. During his extended absence his firm was converted to a limited company in 1864, growing from strength to strength with business interests in Nottingham, Saxony, and New England. By the spring of 1865 he had fully recovered. His views on social harmony and industrial peace, in particular his early recognition of the positive role which trade unions could play in this process, brought him a wider audience, most crucially the national leadership of the new model craft unions in London, with whom he was to build a close political alliance. This culminated in his election in 1868 as MP for Sheffield, which he represented (from 1885 the Brightside division of that city) until his death, nearly thirty years later.

Mundella's main concerns on entering parliament were education and trade union reform. In the mid-1860s he had established his credentials as an education reformer with the call, then in advance of other reformers, that elementary education be made compulsory; furthermore, that a system of technical schools be established to improve the skills of the British workforce—views informed by his experience of continental standards and practice. He was a staunch supporter of the 1870 Education Act, working closely with W. E. Forster to secure its passage against the opposition of the National Education League. On the question of religious instruction he opposed the secularists, arguing for a conscience clause and broad non-denominational teaching. Again, his efforts were focused on compulsory attendance, which drew from Forster a compromise—school boards were empowered to enforce attendance but the act did not make this obligatory. Following the decision in *Hornby* v. *Close* regarding trade union funds and the backlash which followed the 'Sheffield outrages', Mundella was a natural ally of the London-based craft union leaders George Odger, Robert Applegarth, and George Howard in their attempts to fashion a respectable trade unionism based on arbitration and legal sanction. At Sheffield Mundella

had defeated Joseph Roebuck, the arch-critic of trade unionism, and in the Commons he emerged, together with Thomas Hughes, as the main representative of trade union demands for reform.

In response to Mundella's private member's bill in 1869 the government passed a temporary bill securing trade union funds from embezzlement and in 1871 the home secretary, H. A. Bruce, introduced a Trade Union Act which established the legality of trade unions as corporate bodies and gave protection to their funds via a system of legal registration. Owing to pressure from Mundella the contentious third clause dealing with intimidation and molestation was separated from the bill and passed as the Criminal Law Amendment Act. This became the subject of a long-running trade union agitation to secure repeal on the grounds that strike action and picketing should be governed by the general criminal law, not specific legislation aimed at one social class.

Arbitration, the Factory Acts, and labour laws Mundella's efforts in the fields of education and trade union reform were complemented by a continued interest in arbitration. In September 1871 he brokered a deal which ended the Newcastle engineers' strike, and in 1872 he introduced the Arbitration Act, which extended the provisions of 1867 by making voluntary agreements mutually binding. In 1872 he played a role in the passage of the Mines Regulation Bill, in particular the clauses restricting the hours of work of women and children. Within the confines of Victorian political economy and the accepted role of state intervention, Mundella pressed a coherent programme of social legislation aimed at the amelioration of the conditions of the working population. In the parliament of 1868–74 he established a reputation as a hard-working back-bench MP with expertise on social questions and was an important link between official front-bench Liberalism and the constituent elements of popular Liberalism in the country, notably the trade unions. However, it was following the Liberal defeat in 1874 that Mundella was to achieve his most memorable legislative victories, albeit indirectly, with the assistance of the incoming Conservative administration.

The first of these was the Factory Act of 1874. Mundella was already the parliamentary champion of the campaign to secure a further reduction in the hours of work permitted for women and children, but his attempt to pass a nine hours bill in 1872 and 1873 had been frustrated: the Liberal administration, nearing its end, was tired, divided, and increasingly fearful of the reaction of manufacturers, whose opposition was now effectively organized by a Federation of Employers. By contrast, Disraeli's incoming Conservative government, in the guise of its Liberal–Conservative home secretary, R. A. Cross, offered a more sympathetic hearing. Thus Mundella's reintroduction of the bill was received with a promise of government legislation which met his aspirations more than half way. His role thereafter, one in which he was successful, was to defend the bill from attempts by manufacturers to weaken its provisions and from the criticisms of more doctrinaire radicals such as Henry Fawcett, who opposed government regulation and viewed the restrictions on adult female labour as sexual discrimination. Cross's attempt to seize the political initiative on this question for the Conservatives was ignored by the delegates of the textiles districts who expressed their thanks to Mundella on the final passage of the bill. Ten years later, in August 1884, at a gathering in Manchester, Mundella's wife Mary was presented with a fine bust of him by Sir Edgar Boehm, the gift of 80,000 factory operatives in recognition of his services. On 3 July 1874 Mundella was elected to the Political Economy Club, filling the vacancy created by the death of John Stuart Mill.

Mundella's second great personal achievement as a back-bench MP was the labour law reforms of 1875. After the 1871 act he mounted a campaign against the parallel regulation, the Criminal Law Amendment Act, on the grounds that it imposed excessive restrictions on picketing. Following the legal decision in the gas stokers' case in December 1872, which was interpreted as undermining the legality of trade unions that was supposed to have been established in 1871, this campaign was widened to include reform of the Masters and Servants Acts and specific immunity for trade unions from prosecution under the law of conspiracy. Although his initial attempts at reform were unsuccessful, it is now clear that the new home secretary, Robert Lowe, had by the autumn of 1873 conceded in private what became the basis of the settlement of 1875.

Again, following the 1874 general election, R. A. Cross looked to take the initiative. However, in its final form the legislation of 1875 was a truly cross-bench measure, being the subject of significant amendment by the Liberal opposition. In this Mundella played a key role, both as an unofficial whip and in the arguments he deployed during the debates. The Employers and Workmen Bill which replaced the old Masters and Servants Acts limited penalties for breach of contract to civil damages. Yet a vestige of penal servitude remained in the form of imprisonment for non-compliance with the courts' orders. During the committee stage Mundella first secured a reduction in the term of imprisonment and then its replacement with a system of sureties to be repaid in the event of non-compliance. A Conspiracy and Protection of Property Bill was brought in to reaffirm the legality of trade unions and amend the law of conspiracy which would only apply to criminal actions arising out of trade disputes. Under pressure from Mundella and Lowe this bill was recast, repealing the contentious Criminal Law Amendment Act and defining coercion and intimidation in more general terms, thereby removing a whole class of penalties specifically aimed at workmen. These changes secured a final political settlement of the question, fully acceptable to the trade union leadership. Again it was Mundella who was the chief recipient of their thanks. In the settlement of the labour question he had played a central role, and served as a vital bridge between the trade unions and the Liberal leadership, which underscored the support which late Victorian trade unionism gave to the Gladstonian Liberal Party. Mundella was the original 'Lib-Lab'.

Liberal front-bencher, 1880–1895 Between 1874 and 1880, the years of opposition, Mundella established a prominent position on the advanced wing of the Liberal Party. His expertise on social questions, in particular education, was widely recognized and on the return of the Liberals to power in 1880 he entered Gladstone's second ministry as vice-president of the council and was sworn a privy councillor. He was *de facto* head of the education department, as his titular head, Lord Spencer, allowed him a free hand. His first action was to bring in a bill to complete the system of compulsory attendance at elementary schools, allowed for in 1870 and extended in 1876. He also set about a series of inquiries and reorganizations covering the whole sphere of educational activity—some of which he saw bear fruit, and others which paved the way for subsequent action. The scientific schools at South Kensington were consolidated into a single body comprising two divisions, the Royal School of Mines and the Normal School of Science. A committee was established whose report laid the foundations for higher education in Wales. During Mundella's term of office the two university colleges of Cardiff and Bangor were established and funded by central government grant. A bill which proposed the expansion of intermediate schools throughout Wales, part rate-, part state-aided under committees on a county basis, fell with the defeat of the ministry in 1885. A royal commission to inquire into foreign technical schools produced recommendations on curriculum reform which were widely adopted by provincial school boards. More significantly, in 1882 Mundella introduced a revised education code which began the move away from the rigid system of payment by exam results. Henceforth grant assessments for infant schools would recognize manual employments and organized play. In higher schools a 'merit grant' was introduced to reward non-examination based achievement and the teaching of a wider class of subjects was encouraged by making them eligible for grants, including elementary science. Curriculum reform was accompanied by reorganization of the schools inspectorate and improvements in teacher training. This built on and consolidated the work started by W. E. Forster in 1870. On 9 March 1882 Mundella was elected a fellow of the Royal Society. In 1884 he proposed the creation of a separate education department with a minister of cabinet rank, but was frustrated by Lord Carlingford, Spencer's successor as lord president of the council. Mundella's attempts to control and improve the system of pupil-teachers and to establish a system of intermediate schools in Wales was seen by the voluntary and endowed sectors as a direct challenge to their existence and he came under increasing attack from their mouthpiece Cardinal Manning. At the same time the issue of 'free schools' was pushed forward in Joseph Chamberlain's 'unauthorised programme' of 1885. At first Mundella was wary of such a commitment, fearing the breakdown of the delicate compromise of 1870. Having left office with Gladstone's government in June 1885, he was freed from the restrictions of collective responsibility and in the autumn of that year he declared himself in favour of free attendance, paid for by government grants but administered locally through elected county authorities. But a Mundella–Chamberlain link-up was not to be.

Loyal to Gladstone and an enthusiastic home-ruler, Mundella was elevated to the cabinet as president of the Board of Trade when Gladstone returned for the brief third ministry of 1886. In his short period of office he introduced a series of administrative changes. The system of consular trade reports was overhauled to improve the dissemination of commercial intelligence. A fisheries department was established which drew together separate responsibilities from a number of departments and formed the nucleus of the future Ministry of Agriculture and Fisheries. In addition he established a small bureau to collect and disseminate labour statistics and appointed Mr Burnett, secretary of the Amalgamated Engineers' Trade Society, as its labour correspondent.

The biggest problem Mundella faced and where he came unstuck was that of railway freight rates. The system of preferential rates had long been the subject of criticism by domestic freight users. His Railways and Canal Traffic Bill, which was introduced in March 1886, proposed a dramatic extension of the Board of Trade's powers via the mechanism of special courts which would enforce 'reassessments', that is, reductions in freight charges. Such compulsion was violently resisted by the railway companies who were able to marshal shareholder opinion against the measure. Mundella's bill, justified on the grounds of state regulation of a vital monopoly, provided a golden opportunity for Liberal and Conservative critics of home rule to attack and weaken the government. In the vital division on home rule, which spelt the end for the ministry, some twenty-six Liberal opponents had railway interests. The bill was shelved, although in 1888 a similar measure was passed by Lord Salisbury's Conservative ministry. Back in opposition between 1886 and 1892, Mundella remained on the Liberal front bench where his political energies returned to education. In 1887 he was elected a vice-president of the National Association for the Promotion of Technical Education, which in 1889 saw the passage of the Technical Instruction Act—vesting the newly created county councils with powers to supply or aid supply of technical and manual instruction. In November 1888 he became president of another newly created pressure group, the National Education Association, set up to oppose the proposals of the Cross commission on the Elementary Schools Acts. The war between the 'voluntaryists' and the supporters of the board schools was now at its hottest.

Mundella also turned again to the issue of child labour and during late 1888 and early 1889 sponsored a bill for the prevention of cruelty to children. The NSPCC was set up in the same year to press a public campaign. Mundella's act of 1889 prohibited the employment of children under ten and made it a misdemeanour punishable by imprisonment to neglect or ill-treat them. Following a struggle in the Commons an exception was made for children employed in theatres although this was reversed in the Lords, which allowed children of seven upwards to be so employed, providing they had a magistrate's ticket. Mundella regarded the measure as one of his greatest successes.

After a short illness his wife, Mary, died at their London home on 14 December 1890 and was buried on 20 December in the family grave at Church cemetery in Nottingham. Despite his great loss, or perhaps because of it, Mundella remained a full-time politician. In 1890 he was appointed chairman of the trade and treaties committee, where he used his position to oppose the rising demand to promote tariff preferences with the empire. Between 1891 and 1892 he was a member of the royal commission on labour and as chairman of the section dealing with chemical, building, textile, clothing, and miscellaneous trades, took the innovative step of appointing four women inspectors to investigate the position of women in industry.

With the election of a minority Liberal administration in 1892, Mundella returned to the cabinet as president for the Board of Trade for the second time. The most pressing issue upon his return was that of railway freight charges. The mechanism for rate revisions under the 1888 act had broken down and pressure for reductions from traders and farmers was once again growing. This time, however, Mundella was wary of a frontal assault on the railway interest and instead in 1893 appointed a parliamentary committee to inquire into the powers conferred on the railway companies to fix maximum charges. At the same time he pushed through legislation to reduce the hours of work of railway employees. Progress was made in the sphere of administrative reform. The small statistical bureau set up in 1886 was, in January 1893, expanded and established as a separate labour department with a headquarters staff and thirty correspondents in the provincial towns to report on local conditions. The labour department published a regular *Labour Gazette* to disseminate labour information to the working classes. Its second task was to undertake special inquiries into the conditions of labour. Mundella also looked to extend the role of the Board of Trade in the settlement of trades disputes. A bill empowering the board to take the initiative in the establishment of local boards of arbitration was introduced in July 1893, but not finally enacted until 1896 by the Conservatives—with his support. During the summer and autumn of 1893 Mundella was heavily engaged in behind the scenes moves to end the midland coal strike. This was not achieved until November when both parties met at the behest of Lord Rosebery and agreed to a conciliation board. With the Railway Servants Act, a North Sea Fisheries Act—which ratified the convention prohibiting floating grog shops—and the creation of a labour department, the 1893 session was considered a success for Mundella.

However, in 1894 Mundella's ministerial career was brought to a sudden and abrupt close through his resignation following the collapse of the New Zealand Loan and Mercantile Agency. He had been a director of the company from 1870 until 1892 when he resigned under newly established rules, on joining the cabinet. The company, which provided loans to colonialists to produce and sell sheep meat for consumption in the UK domestic market, went into liquidation in 1893 and was the subject of a Board of Trade inquiry. Mundella's post as president of the board made his position untenable since he was a party to the inquiry being carried out by his own department. The perceived conflict of interest led to growing pressure to resign, which he did with effect from 12 May 1894.

Final years and his legacy At the general election of 1895, which was disastrous for the Liberal Party as a whole, Mundella was returned unopposed for his Sheffield constituency for the last time. In the House of Commons he rejoined the Liberal front bench and took a prominent role in opposing the education bills of 1896 and 1897, which were seen as an attack on the board schools by setting up a system of separate payments to voluntary schools, via the county councils. Mundella fought the measure line by line, but such parliamentary battles were taking their toll; during the night of the 13 July he was struck down by paralysis and did not regain consciousness. He died on 21 July 1897 at his London home, 16 Elvaston Place, South Kensington. Following a service in London at St Margaret's, Westminster, on 26 July, his body was taken by rail to Nottingham where a further service was held at St Mary's Church before interment in the family grave at Church cemetery on 27 July. The route of the funeral cortège through Nottingham was lined with a large crowd of sympathetic spectators. Such was the press of onlookers at the entrance to the cemetery that a third service was held at the graveside.

Mundella was survived by his two daughters, Maria Theresa, who remained unmarried and lived at Elvaston Place, and Polly, who had married Roby Thorpe of Nottingham. Polly's daughter Dorothea Mary Roby (d. 1942) married Godfrey Rathbone Benson, first Baron Charnwood (1864–1945). In the field of education reform Mundella stands out as one of the architects of the system created in 1870, a consistent and effective campaigner in the fields of child labour and adult and technical education. Throughout his life he worked tirelessly to bring about the reconciliation of capital and labour and was an originator of industrial arbitration. A pragmatic social reformer, he was the archetypal progressive Liberal manufacturer, a political class of men who were the backbone of the parliamentary Liberal Party after 1868. Moreover, in his support for greater government intervention on social questions his political career provides a link with the 'new Liberalism' of the 1890s and reflected the growing tendency of the age to look to the state for solutions to problems previously the domain of voluntary effort.

JONATHAN SPAIN

Sources W. H. G. Armytage, *A. J. Mundella 1825–1897: the liberal background to the labour movement* (1951) · J. Spain, 'Trade unionists, Gladstonian liberals and the Labour law reforms of 1875', *Currents of radicalism: popular radicalism, organised labour, and party politics in Britain, 1850–1914*, ed. E. F. Biagini and A. J. Reid (1991), 109–34 ·

Boase, *Mod. Eng. biog.*, vol. 6 · J. F. C. Harrison, 'Chartism in Leicester', *Chartist studies*, ed. A. Briggs (1959), 99–146; repr. (1962) · A. Temple Patterson, *Radical Leicester: a history of Leicester, 1780–1850* (1954) · G. R. Searson, *A quarter of a century's liberalism in Leicester, 1826–1850* [n.d., c.1880] · R. J. Conklin, *Thomas Cooper the chartist, 1805–92* (1935) · R. A. Church, *Economic and social change in a midland town: Victorian Nottingham, 1815–1900* (1966) · I. G. Sharp, *Industrial conciliation and arbitration in Great Britain* (1950) · *The Times* (22 July 1897), 6a · J. Beckett and others, eds., *A centenary history of Nottingham* (1997) · H. W. McCready, 'Britain's labour lobby 1867–75', *Canadian Journal of Economics*, 22 (1956), 141–60 · m. cert.

Archives University of Sheffield, corresp. and MSS | Bishopsgate Institute, London, corresp. with George Howell · BL, corresp. with W. E. Gladstone, Add. MS 44258 · Bodl. Oxf., corresp. with Sir William Harcourt; letters to J. E. Thorold Rogers · Sheff. Arch., corresp. with Sheffield chamber of commerce · Sheff. Arch., corresp. with H. J. Wilson · U. Birm. L., corresp. with Joseph Chamberlain · U. Nott. L., MSS relating to National Education Association · University of Sheffield, letters to Henry Joseph Wilson

Likenesses London Stereoscopic Co., carte-de-visite, c.1883, NPG [*see illus.*] · A. S. Cope, oils, exh. RA 1894, Sheffield town hall · B. Stone, photograph, 1897, Birmingham Reference Library · J. E. Boehm, plaster bust, Mapping Art Gallery, Sheffield · caricature, chromolithograph, NPG; repro. in *VF* (9 Dec 1871) · woodcut, NPG

Wealth at death £42,619 1s. 3d.: probate, 29 Nov 1897, CGPLA Eng. & Wales

Munden, Sir John (c.1645–1719), naval officer, was a younger brother of Sir Richard *Munden, and served under him as lieutenant of the *Saint David* in the Mediterranean from 1677 to 1680. Between 1681 and 1688 he was lieutenant of the *Constant Warwick*, the *Mary Rose*, and the *Charles Galley*, gaining a captain's commission for the *Half Moon* fireship on 23 July 1688. He moved to the *Edgar* on 14 December 1688 and briefly commanded the *Dover* in the spring of 1689. During that year's campaign he was flag captain to John, Lord Berkeley, rear-admiral of the red, aboard the *Hampton Court*, and held the same post under Berkeley's successor, Ralph Delaval, aboard the *Coronation* in 1690, fighting in her at the battle of Beachy Head. Munden commanded the *Lennox* from 1691 until 1693, and was part of Delaval's squadron at the battle of Barfleur (19 May 1692). He commanded the *Saint Michael* from 1693 to 1696, going in her to the Mediterranean in 1695 as part of Admiral Russell's fleet, and served as captain of the *London* in 1696–7 and, briefly, of the *Ranelagh* in 1699. In May 1699 he took command of the *Winchester*, and was responsible in 1700 for arranging a treaty with Algiers which led to the release of English slaves. He returned to England in November 1700 and was promoted to rear-admiral on 14 April 1701. On 1 July, as his squadron was escorting the king to Holland, William III knighted Munden aboard the *William and Mary* yacht.

In January 1702 Munden took command of a squadron intended to intercept a powerful French force expected to sail from Rochelle to Corunna, then on to the West Indies. Sailing in May, he cruised off Corunna, but the French slipped past him in the night and on the following morning, 28 May, they entered port safely. He considered the harbour too well defended and narrow to contemplate an attack, and, after cruising for some days, returned to Portsmouth. He was court-martialled for negligence on 13

July but acquitted, and returned to his command. However, public opinion had been highly critical of him for not pursuing the French into Corunna harbour, and the privy council was dissatisfied with his acquittal. Even one of Munden's friends found his attempts to justify his failure to attack unconvincing: 'I did not find out that his judgment and his hearing were so alike, thick and unready, till then' (*Portland MSS*, 8.109). The queen and the government yielded to the public pressure and dismissed him. He retired to Chelsea, where he was described in his old age as 'a very plain man in his conversation and dress, of a fair complexion' (*Memoirs of the Secret Services*, 109–10). He died on 13 March 1719. Munden never married. By his will, dated 20 September 1717, he made bequests to three nephews, including a Brigadier Richard Munden, and to five nieces.   J. K. LAUGHTON, *rev.* J. D. DAVIES

Sources PRO, Admiralty MSS · NMM, Sergison MSS, SER/136 · PRO, PROB 11/568, fols. 23–4 · *CSP dom.*, 1700–03 · *The manuscripts of his grace the duke of Portland*, 10 vols., HMC, 29 (1891–1931), vol. 8, p. 109 · *Memoirs of the secret services of John Macky*, ed. J. M. Grey, Roxburghe Club (1895), 109–10 · *Le Neve's Pedigrees of the knights*, ed. G. W. Marshall, Harleian Society, 8 (1873), 370–71 · N. Luttrell, *A brief historical relation of state affairs from September 1678 to April 1714*, 5 (1857) · W. A. Shaw, *The knights of England*, 2 vols. (1906)

Likenesses M. Dahl, oils, 1705, NMM

Wealth at death left a house and other land in Chelsea, a tenement in Fulham, exchequer annuities, and South Sea Company stock: will, PRO, PROB 11/568, fols. 23–4

Munden, Joseph Shepherd (*bap.* 1758, *d.* 1832), actor, was baptized on 19 May 1758 at St Andrew's, Holborn, London, the son of Joseph Munden, a poulterer in Brook's Market, Leather Lane, Holborn, and his wife, Alice. For a short time, at the age of twelve, he was apprenticed to an apothecary, but his fine handwriting obtained him a situation with Mr Druce, a law stationer in Chancery Lane. Within a few years he left for Liverpool, probably to try his luck as an actor, but instead ended up in the town clerk's office for about two years. Stories of his early life are unreliable, but he seems to have visted Rochdale, Chester, Whitchurch, Birmingham, and Woodstock, and also to have attempted to join a number of strolling companies. After returning to London he certainly appeared during 1779 and 1780 in private performances at the Haymarket Theatre, where Hurst, the manager of the theatre in Canterbury, saw his promise and engaged him in November 1780. Hurst persuaded him to take on the first line in low comedy, in which he proved very successful. He later appeared at Brighton. On the death of the low comedian in Austin and Whitlock's circuit, he successfully applied to replace him, and appeared in Chester, Whitehaven, Newcastle upon Tyne, Manchester, Preston, and Liverpool. He eventually became a shareholder in the circuit of theatres that included both Newcastle and Chester, but sold his shares in 1790 when he was invited to Covent Garden to replace the recently deceased comedian John Edwin. While associated with the Newcastle circuit, Munden introduced an actress, Mary Ann Jones, as his wife. In 1789 she eloped with another actor, Hodgkinson, who subsequently left her. She died shortly afterwards, but Munden took care of her children. On 20 October 1789

Joseph Shepherd Munden (*bap.* 1758, *d.* 1832), by John Opie, *c.*1801

he married Frances Butler (*d.* 1837), a young actress in the company. They had two sons, one of whom died in infancy.

For his Covent Garden début, on 2 December 1790, Munden successfully appeared as Sir Francis Gripe in Susannah Centlivre's *The Busybody* and Jemmy Jumps in John O'Keeffe's *The Farmer*. He was soon playing original parts, including his celebrated Old Dornton in Thomas Holcroft's *The Road to Ruin* (18 February 1792), in which he demonstrated that a low comedian could 'display the greatest power over the tragedy of domestic life' (Munden, 44). Among other successful new roles were Old Rapid (in Thomas Morton's *A Cure for the Heartache*, 1796), Crack (in *The Turnpike Gate*, by Thomas Knight, 1799), Sir Robert Bramble (in *The Poor Gentleman*, by George Colman the younger, 1801), and the British Seaman (in Thomas Dibdin's *The Cabinet*, 1802). Dibdin and O'Keeffe wrote parts especially for him, and by 1798 he had also taken over roles earlier associated with Richard Wilson and John Quick. From the early 1800s Munden made regular, highly lucrative visits to the provinces during the summer recesses. In 1806, however, he had an attack of gout which temporarily stopped performances of Colman's new play *We Fly by Night*. In 1811 he quit Covent Garden: difficulties had been simmering since 1800, after a disagreement between Thomas Harris and the principal actors at Covent Garden over increases in benefit payments and the fine levied in the event of sickness, and also through an altercation with Harris over Munden's refusal to play in Colman's *John Bull* in 1803. The new dispute was over Covent Garden's refusal to pay his full salary during a prolonged absence through gout. He threatened to resign, an offer the management accepted with alacrity.

Munden was engaged in the summer of 1811 at the Haymarket Theatre (where he had acted in the 1797–8 season), and appeared on 13 July as Old Dornton and then in Colman's burlesque *The Quadrupeds of Quedlinbergh*, as well as playing prominent roles in established comedies. From now on he began to undertake more provincial engagements and to invest his earnings regularly. After reappearing at the Haymarket in 1812 he made his début at Drury Lane on 4 October 1813, as Sir Abel Handy in Thomas Morton's *Speed the Plough*. He largely played old favourites there; his last original role was an old sailor, Dozey, in Dibdin's *Past Ten O'Clock and a Rainy Night* (1815). Another successful role, although not original, was Kit Sly in Charles Johnson's *The Cobbler of Preston*. By 1822–3 his appearances had become infrequent, and he now declined new parts on account of gout. His farewell benefit took place on 31 May 1824, when he played Sir Robert Bramble and Old Dozey. In the tavern scene he toasted the health of 'old Joe Munden's friends' and was greatly applauded. At the end of the farce (overcome not only by the occasion but possibly by drink) he came forward and, in Charles Lamb's view, unwisely read his farewell speech: 'He stammered and he pressed his heart—and put on his spectacles,—and blustered his written gratitudes,—and wiped his eyes, and bowed—and stood,—and at last staggered away for ever!' (Lamb, 'Munden's farewell').

'Mr Munden was by far the greatest comedian we ever saw', wrote Sir Thomas Talfourd (Munden, 294), while John Bannister described him 'as one of the best comic actors that ever trod the stage' (Adolphus, 2.327). The most reported aspect of Munden's acting was the use of his face, with its luminous blue eyes, capable of conveying passion without language, its thick eyebrows, and its odd, rather ugly mouth. Talfourd felt his facial expression resembled a series of Greek comedy masks; to Leigh Hunt, his features were like the reflections of a man's face in a ruffled stream: 'they undergo a perpetual undulation of grin' (*Critical Essays*, 32). Lamb considered that Munden's collection of faces was infinite: 'He is not one, but legion; not so much a comedian, as a company' ('On the acting of Munden'). Hazlitt reckoned there was no one on the stage who could draw up his eyebrows, thrust out his tongue, or drop his underjaw so astonishingly. Munden's skill in using his face, said Lamb, was accompanied by an ability to throw 'a preternatural interest over the commonest daily life objects'. Lamb, who also describes how 'a tub of butter, contemplated by him, amounts to a Platonic idea' (ibid.), considered this quality was due to the power of Munden's imagination:

> he could impress upon an audience an *idea*—the low one perhaps of a leg of mutton and turnips; but such was the grandeur and the singularity of his expressions that that simple expression would convey to all his auditory a notion of all the pleasures they had received from all the legs of mutton and turnips they had ever eaten in their lives. (Lamb, letter, *The Athenaeum*)

Leigh Hunt also tells how Munden could make something

out of nothing by a certain intensity of contemplation. He apparently used almost as much colouring in his make-up as Joseph Grimaldi did and dressed his characters carefully, always providing his own costume and sometimes spending large sums for outfits and wigs that he fancied. Henry Fuseli, the painter, is said to have much admired Munden when he saw him dressed as one of the witches in *Macbeth*. His voice was equally effective: 'If he laid an emphasis on the word *Holborn* or *butter*, he did it in such a manner that you thought there was more in *Holborn* or *butter*, than it ever before entered into your head to conceive' (Leigh Hunt, *Autobiography*, 1.239). William Robson recalled 'his comic stage-speaking, short, sharp and breaking into falsetto' (Robson, 179–80), while Hazlitt reported that 'he trolls his voice about with his tongue in the most extraordinary manner' (*London Magazine*, January 1820). In repose Munden's face looked sedate; in general appearance he was a short, stout, well-formed man, who walked with a shuffling sort of gait.

Munden achieved his effects by playing at rather a slow pace and was not the most accommodating of actors: 'It was very difficult to confine him; he came up close to the lamps and, sideways, edged himself from one end of them to the other ... and made his first and last appeal to the Gods' (Boaden, *Life of Mrs Jordan*, 1.179). The comedian and memoirist Joe Cowell believed that Munden 'endeavoured to alter his pure and natural style to suit the declining taste of his auditors, and compete with the caricaturists by whom he was surrounded' (Cowell, 1.21). When Cowell objected to some business of Munden's as unnatural, while performing at Drury Lane, Munden's response was, 'Nature be d—; make the people laugh' (ibid.). Yet the *Mirror of the Stage* (13 January 1823) suggested that his facial expressions were attributable to nature rather than to grimace and that, in so far as a stage persona was 'a *concave* mirror to nature', it was necessary for him to heighten the colouring of the portrayal he presented and that he had the right to use his discretion in doing so. Munden certainly 'studied' his parts with discrimination, imagination, and observation. Cowell, who thought him the best comedian he had ever seen, claims he 'identified himself with a character, and never lost sight of it—his pathos went to the heart at once, and his humour was irresistible' (Cowell, 1.21). The *Theatrical Inquisitor* of July 1813 was impressed by the fact that Munden's characters were so well developed that their effect lasted long after the performance. Leigh Hunt reckoned Munden a genuine comedian, since he possessed insight into character as well as the ability to depict surface. Talfourd felt he 'shared largely in that pathos which belongs in a greater or lesser degree to all true comedians' (Munden, 296), adding that Munden had reasons for everything he did on stage. W. Robson praised the actor for the tears he made him shed as Old Dornton.

Munden's range was limited, but within that range he was versatile. Even if he played three drunken parts on the same night, he would be fresh in each. He was able to portray serious old men, such as Old Dornton, and comic ones, such as Sir Francis Gripe. Moreover, he could appear kind-hearted or testy; not surprisingly, Sir Anthony Absolute was another frequent role. Thomas Gilliland praised his portrayals of sailors and cunning rustics. Shakespearian roles included Launce, Autolycus, Menenius, Dogberry, and Polonius (to the Hamlets of both John Philip Kemble and Kean). According to his son he played Polonius as a venerable and dignified old man, drawing humour only from those lines in which he 'acquiesced in Hamlet's vagaries' (Munden, 48), although Robson felt 'it was all comedy with him' (Robson, 179). 'Lady Macbeth', observed Lord Byron, 'died with Mrs Siddons; Polonius will with Munden' (Munden, 48).

Munden was fond of convivial society and had a large circle of acquaintances; he was secretary of the Beefsteak Club. However, after his retirement he lived in a state of poverty caused by a pathological refusal to spend any money. His gout often confined him to his bedroom for months on end. He died at his home, 2 Bernard Street, Russell Square, London, on 6 February 1832 and was buried at St George's, Bloomsbury.   JIM DAVIS

Sources T. S. Munden, *Memoirs of Joseph Shepherd Munden, comedian* (1844) · C. Lamb, 'The old actors', *London Magazine*, 6 (1822), 349–51 · C. Lamb, 'Munden's farewell', *London Magazine* (July 1825) · C. Lamb, letter, *The Athenaeum* (11 Feb 1832) · *Oxberry's Dramatic Biography*, 2/21 (1825) · T. Gilliland, *The dramatic mirror, containing the history of the stage from the earliest period, to the present time*, 2 vols. (1808) · L. Hunt, *The autobiography of Leigh Hunt, with reminiscences of friends and contemporaries*, 3 vols. (1850) · L. Hunt, *Critical essays on the performers of the London theatres* (1807) · J. Leigh Hunt, *Dramatic essays*, ed. L. H. Houtchens and C. W. Houtchens (1950) · *The complete works of William Hazlitt*, ed. P. P. Howe, 21 vols. (1930–34) · W. Robson, *The old play-goer* (1846) · J. Boaden, *Memoirs of the life of John Philip Kemble*, 2 vols. (1825) · J. Boaden, *The life of Mrs Jordan*, 2 vols. (1831) · J. Cowell, *Thirty years passed among the players in England and America*, 2 pts (1845) · J. Roach, *Roach's authentic memoirs of the green room* (1796) · *Mirror of the Stage* (13 Jan 1823) · J. B. Matthews and L. Hutton, eds., *Actors and actresses of Great Britain and the United States from the days of David Garrick to the present time*, 5 vols. (1886), 2.4, 5 · Genest, *Eng. stage* · T. Dibdin, *The reminiscences of Thomas Dibdin*, 2 vols. (1827) · *GM*, 1st ser., 102/1 (1832), 279–80 · J. Adolphus, *Memoirs of John Bannister, comedian*, 2 vols. (1838) · *IGI*

Archives Harvard TC, corresp., MSS

Likenesses W. Loftis, watercolour, 1793 · S. De Wilde, two oil paintings, 1795–9, Garr. Club · J. Opie, oils, *c*.1801, Garr. Club [*see illus.*] · S. De Wilde, pencil and watercolour drawing, 1808, Garr. Club · J. Zoffany, oils, 1811, Garr. Club · G. Clint, oils, 1821, Garr. Club · J. Knight, oils, 1827, Garr. Club · G. Clint, oils, NPG · G. Dance, pencil drawing, NPG · S. De Wilde, pencil and watercolour drawing, Garr. Club · S. De Wilde, watercolour, Harvard TC · S. Drummond, oils, Garr. Club · J. Lonsdale, charcoal and sanguine drawing, Garr. Club · W. Ridley, engraving (after miniature), repro. in *Monthly Mirror* (Feb 1799) · M. A. Shee, oils, Garr. Club · R. Smirke, portrait, priv. coll. · J. Turmeau, black chalk with pencil and watercolour, Garr. Club · W. Wood, miniature · Wray and Thornthwaite, engravings (after S. De Wilde), repro. in *Bell's British Library* (1791) · prints, BM, NPG

Wealth at death under £20,000: will, *GM*, 280

Munden, Sir Richard (1639/40?–1680), naval officer, was described by Le Neve as the son of 'Munden the ferryman at Chelsea' (Marshall, 370–71), and his father's occupation is confirmed in other sources. Although Le Neve named Munden's parents as Richard (1602–1672) and Elizabeth (1608–1694), another possible candidate for his father might be John Munden, waterman of Chelsea, who made

his will in 1673. Sir John *Munden was his younger brother. Sir Richard's monument at Bromley church implies that he served in merchant ships prior to the Second Anglo-Dutch War. His first known naval post was as captain of the *Swallow Ketch*, to which he was commissioned on 17 August 1666. She was employed primarily on convoy duty in the English Channel. After leaving her in July 1667 he commanded the *Portsmouth Sloop* from January to September 1668, and was acting master attendant at Deptford Dockyard in 1670. He commanded the *Princess* in the 1672 campaign, serving in the admiral of the Blue squadron division at the battle of Solebay. On 7 January 1673 he took command of the *Assistance*, which, with three hired vessels and two fireships, was to escort the outward bound East Indies fleet as far as St Helena, where it was to rendezvous with the homeward bound fleet and escort it to England. Unknown to Munden, the Dutch had captured St Helena in December 1672, so when the English squadron arrived off the island on 4 May it was to find it in enemy hands. The Dutch garrison put up a determined but brief resistance, and Munden's victory seemed to be complete when, four weeks later, he was able to surprise and capture three homeward bound Dutch East India vessels. Munden returned to England in August 1673 and was knighted by the king on 6 December, also receiving £2500 of royal bounty for his services. Despite his success there was some criticism of Munden's tactics and behaviour in this campaign—in 1683 Pepys's clerk Richard Gibson wrote a damning indictment of the St Helena operation, accusing Munden of being a poor navigator, incompetent at paperwork, and of having provided too loose a cover for the English East India ships, all of which charges seem somewhat irrelevant given the actual outcome of Munden's operations. More convincing is the opinion of another of Pepys's correspondents, made when Munden had just returned from St Helena, that he was 'a young man of no common merit' (James Hayes to Pepys, 22 Aug 1673, MS Rawl. A191, fol. 50). He remained in command of the *Assistance* until November 1674, returning to sea again in April 1677 as captain of the *St David*, engaged in convoy work in the Mediterranean. He arrived at Plymouth with the homeward trade on 12 May 1680, but died in June. He was buried in Bromley church, where his monument states that 'having been (what upon public duty, and what upon merchants' accounts) successfully engaged in fourteen sea-fights … he died in the prime of his youth and strength, in the 40th year of his age'.

Munden married Susanna Gore; they had five daughters and a son, Richard, born posthumously. The post-mortem inventory of his house in Bromley revealed an estate worth almost £6000, including shares in four merchant ships, chairs and carpets from Turkey, other materials from India, and a 'Japan cabinet' (PRO, PROB 4/14421).   J. D. DAVIES

Sources *Le Neve's Pedigrees of the knights*, ed. G. W. Marshall, Harleian Society, 8 (1873), 370–71 · inventory, 1682, PRO, PROB 4/14421 · Bodl. Oxf., MS Rawl. A. 191, fol. 50 · PRO, ADM 106/20, fols. 57 and 211 · J. MacKenzie, 'The retaking of St Helena, 1673: "we haveing noo other business too doo … "', *Les flottes des Compagnies* *des Indes, 1600–1857* [Lorient 1994], ed. P. Haudrère (Vincennes, 1996), 183–93 · W. D. Christie, ed., *Letters addressed from London to Sir Joseph Williamson*, 1, CS, new ser., 8 (1874), 187 · memorial at Bromley church, Middlesex · PRO, Admiralty MSS · W. A. Shaw, *The knights of England*, 2 vols. (1906)

Wealth at death £5936 18s. 1d.: inventory, PRO, PROB 4/14421

Mundy, Sir George Rodney (1805–1884), naval officer, the son of General Godfrey Basil Mundy (d. 14 March 1848) and his wife, Sarah Bridges (d. 17 July 1871), the youngest daughter of George Bridges *Rodney, first Lord Rodney, was born in London on 19 April 1805. In February 1818 he entered the Royal Naval College at Portsmouth, where he met his lifelong friend Thomas Sabine Pasley. In December 1819, having gained the medal of his class, giving him two years sea time, he was appointed to the frigate *Phaeton* on the North American station. He afterwards served on the Mediterranean and South American stations, and on 4 February 1826 was confirmed in the rank of lieutenant and appointed to the *Eclair*, which arrived back in England in September 1827. For the next twelve months he was on the coast of Portugal, in the *Challenger* with Captain Adolphus FitzClarence, and in the *Pyramus* with Captain G. R. Sartorius. On 25 August 1828 he was promoted commander. In 1832 he was on board the *Donegal* as confidential agent under Sir Pulteney Malcolm on the coast of the Netherlands, and in 1833 was employed by the first lord of the Admiralty on a special mission to the Netherlands and Belgium. In August 1833 he was appointed to the *Favourite* for service in the Mediterranean. He paid her off in the early months of 1837, having been already advanced to post rank on 10 January 1837.

In October 1842 Mundy was appointed to the frigate *Iris*, which was employed during the early part of 1843 on the west coast of Africa. As the ship was very sickly she was sent home and paid off. She was then refitted at Portsmouth, and again commissioned by Mundy, for service in India and China. She arrived at Singapore in July 1844. Following routine service, in 1846 she was taken by the commander-in-chief, Sir Thomas John Cochrane, to Borneo, where, in co-operation with 'Raja' James Brooke, Mundy was engaged for the next six months in a brilliant series of operations against the Borneo pirate tribes, on which he published *Narrative of events in Borneo and Celebes down to the occupation of Labuan … together with a narrative of the operations of HMS Iris* (2 vols., 1848). His share in this service ended with his formally taking possession of Labuan on 24 December 1846, after which he returned to Singapore, and early in April 1847 sailed for England, where he arrived on 26 July.

In July 1854 Mundy was appointed to the *Nile*, a screw battleship of 91 guns, then in the Baltic. She was again in the Baltic in 1855. During September and October Mundy commanded a detached force in Biorko Sound, which he secured against strong Russian forces. This position had a major role in plans for an assault on Kronstadt the following year. In 1856, after the end of the war, the *Nile* was ordered to the West Indies. On 30 July 1857 Mundy was promoted rear-admiral and on 23 June 1859 was nominated a CB. In 1859 and 1860, with his flag in the *Hannibal*, as

second in command in the Mediterranean, he had the delicate task of protecting British interests at Palermo and at Naples during the revolutionary civil war, and, as far as possible, of mitigating its horrors. In 1861, at the time of the departure of the French army of occupation, he commanded the detached squadron on the coast of Syria. Towards the end of that year his health broke down, and he returned to England. His arduous services and tact during a difficult time were rewarded by a KCB (10 November 1862), an honour solicited for him by his cousin Henry Pelham Clinton, fifth duke of Newcastle, who had always supported his career. He afterwards published *HMS Hannibal at Palermo and Naples during the Italian revolution, with notices of Garibaldi, Francis II, and Victor Emmanuel* (1863).

On 15 December 1863 Mundy was promoted vice-admiral, and from 1867 to 1869 he was commander-in-chief in the West Indies; on 26 May 1869 he was promoted admiral. His last appointment was as commander-in-chief at Portsmouth (1872–5). On 2 June 1877 he was nominated a GCB, and on 27 December 1877 he was promoted admiral of the fleet on the retired list.

Mundy was known in the navy for his strict observance of old-fashioned etiquette and for a certain pomposity, which sprang partly from the high value he placed on his rank and partly from pride at being the grandson of Lord Rodney. Although somewhat eccentric and the subject of many contemporary stories, he was courteous and considerate to subordinates. An able and effective officer at all levels of command, he benefited from his family connections with both the duke of Newcastle and his famous ancestor. He was not married. He died at his London residence, 12 Chesterfield Street, Mayfair, on 23 December 1884.   J. K. LAUGHTON, *rev.* ANDREW LAMBERT

Sources L. M. S. Pasley, *Life of Sir T. S. Pasley* (1900) · J. W. D. Dundas and C. Napier, *Russian war, 1854, Baltic and Black Sea: official correspondence*, ed. D. Bonner-Smith and A. C. Dewar, Navy RS, 83 (1943) · R. S. Dundas, *Russian war, 1855, Baltic: official correspondence*, ed. D. Bonner-Smith, Navy RS, 84 (1944) · A. D. Lambert, *The Crimean War: British grand strategy, 1853–56* (1990) · V. Stuart, *The beloved little admiral* (1967) · Boase, *Mod. Eng. biog.* · Walford, *County families* · Burke, *Peerage*

Archives Harrowby Manuscript Trust, Sandon Hall, Staffordshire, letters to Sir Alfred Ryder · NL Scot., corresp. with Sir Thomas Cochrane · NL Scot., corresp. with Charles Graham

Likenesses G. F. Clarke, oils, Admiralty, Portsmouth

Wealth at death £29,775 15s. 10d.: probate, 30 Jan 1885, CGPLA Eng. & Wales

Mundy, John (c.1555–1630), organist and composer, was born probably in London, the elder son of the composer William *Mundy (c.1529–1591?), vicar-choral of St Paul's Cathedral and gentleman of the Chapel Royal and his wife, Mary Alcock. He graduated BMus at Oxford on 9 July 1586 and proceeded DMus on 2 July 1624. By June 1585 he was living in the cloisters at Windsor, and he was clerk and organist at St George's Chapel, in succession to John Merbecke, presumably from then or earlier—and at any rate from 1586/7, when he is mentioned in the accounts—until his death. During his time at St George's, Nathaniel Giles was organist and choirmaster, and Mundy was succeeded by William Child.

Mundy's principal work is *Songs and Psalmes* (1594), a collection of secular and sacred pieces for three, four, and five voices dedicated to Robert Devereux, second earl of Essex, who was probably Mundy's patron. The model for the set was probably the *Psalmes, Sonets and Songs* (1588) of William Byrd. The contents show Mundy to be among those composers such as Orlando Gibbons who are associated more with the older partsong tradition than with the late sixteenth-century madrigal. The idiom is mostly polyphonic and conservative, though there is some up-to-date madrigalian word-painting in the songs and hints of it even in the psalms.

Mundy's other vocal music consists largely of Latin and English sacred works. The former include motets and a setting of the Lamentations of Jeremiah, but it is not clear for what purpose the Latin music was written. It is unlikely to have been used liturgically, given Mundy's dates and career, and it is possible that some of the pieces, such as the Kyrie in the Gyffard partbooks and the six-voice respond *Dum transisset sabbatum*, were pedagogical exercises. The English works consist of both verse and full anthems, and Mundy was one of the pre-Commonwealth composers whose church music was revived in the early years of the Restoration, for the text of 'O Lord our governor' appears in James Clifford's collection *The Divine Services and Anthems* (1663). Perhaps the best of his anthems is 'Sing joyfully', for bass soloist and instrumental consort. The modern view of Mundy's vocal music is that it is generally rather mundane and certainly the work of a minor musician. But up to the eighteenth century at least Mundy's reputation fared better: according to John Hawkins, Mundy was an 'excellent musician … and, as far as can be judged by the words he has chosen to exercise his talent on, a religious and modest man, resembling in this respect Bird' (Hawkins, 2.499). More anthems and much English service music, as well as some sacred Latin pieces and instrumental works, are of doubtful authorship and are compositions of either John or his father.

The instrumental pieces of certain attribution include four In nomines for string consort in five and six parts. Among Mundy's compositions for keyboard are a set of variations on 'Goe from my window' and a meteorological fantasia, the sections of which contrast representations of fair weather, lightning, thunder, and a clear day. Though amateurish in its construction, it is nevertheless an attractive exercise in programmatic writing unusual for the period. These two pieces and other keyboard works by Mundy are contained in the Fitzwilliam virginal book, one of the most important sources of keyboard music of the period. Mundy died in Windsor on 29 June 1630 and was buried there in the chapel cloisters.　　PETER LYNAN

Sources H. W. Shaw, *The succession of organists of the Chapel Royal and the cathedrals of England and Wales from c.1538* (1991), 343 · J. Hawkins, *A general history of the science and practice of music*, new edn, 3 vols. (1853); repr. in 2 vols. (1963), vol. 2, pp. 499, 571 · *New Grove*, 2nd edn · P. Le Huray, *Music and the Reformation in England, 1549–1660* (1967) · D. Mateer, 'The "Gyffard" partbooks: composers, owners, date and provenance', *Royal Musical Association Research Chronicle*, 28 (1995), 21–50

Mundy, Peter (*b. c.*1596, *d.* in or after 1667), traveller and diarist, the son of Richard Mundy (*d.* before 1635), a pilchard merchant, came from Penryn in Cornwall. Mundy probably received his early education at the free school in Penryn and in 1609 he was sent by his father to Bayonne in Gascony to learn French. In 1611 he served as a cabin boy to Captain John Davis, sailing between the English factories scattered throughout the Mediterranean, and then spent four years in Spain as a factor and another four in Constantinople. During his overland progression home through the early summer of 1620, he began to make notes of his travels and observations, a habit which he would continue for the rest of his life.

In 1622 Mundy was contracted for a term of five years to the merchant Richard Wyche, working as an agent and accountant. In October 1627 he successfully petitioned the directors of the East India Company for employment and so set out for Surat on the *Expedition*, engaged for £25 per annum for five years. In Surat he was initially employed as a writer in the company's offices before travelling as an under-factor to the court of the Mughal emperor in Agra, where he witnessed the initial phases of the construction of the Taj Mahal. After a short spell in England at the end of his contract he again sought out employment in the East, sailing on the *Royall Mary* in April 1636 and trading through the South China Sea before returning home in December 1638. From 1639 until 1647 he travelled around the Baltic. When he returned to England in October 1647 he concluded that between 1611 and 1647 he had travelled more than 100,833⅝ miles and had been subject to 1000 dangers.

Sporadically over the next seven years Mundy collated the notes of his trips and assembled them into a chronological manuscript, supplementing the work with his own illustrations; though perhaps originally intended for publication, the work was not printed until the early twentieth century. During this hiatus from travel he must have married, for the registers of St Gluvias Church, Penryn, contain an entry under 1 March 1651 of the baptism of Peter, described as the son of Peter and Ann Mundy. From 1655 to 1656 Mundy travelled again to India, before retiring to London in 1658 to write an appendix to his manuscript in which he detailed contemporary events. In 1663 he moved back to Penryn, where he continued his chronicle up to the proclamation of the treaty of Breda, which was read in Penryn on 11 September 1667. He probably died shortly afterwards.

RICHARD RAISWELL

Sources *The travels of Peter Mundy in Europe and Asia, 1608–1667*, ed. R. C. Temple and L. M. Anstey, 5 vols. in 6, Hakluyt Society, 2nd ser., 17, 35, 45–6, 55, 78 (1907–36) · *The travels of Peter Mundy*, ed. J. Keast (1984) · *CSP col.*, vols. 6, 8 · parish register, St Gluvias, Penryn, Cornwall, 1 Mar 1651 [baptism of Peter Mundy, son]
Archives Bodl. Oxf., travels in Europe and Asia | BL, Harley MS 2286

Mundy, Sir Robert Miller (1813–1892), colonial governor, was the youngest son of Edward Miller Mundy MP(1750–1822) of Shipley Hall, Derbyshire, and his third wife, Catherine, the daughter of Nathaniel Coffin and the widow of

Richard Barwell. He entered as a cadet at the Royal Military Academy, Woolwich, in February 1828, and became a lieutenant in the Royal Artillery in June 1833. In March 1841 he joined the horse artillery. He became a second captain in April 1844 and major by brevet on selling out in October 1846. In 1841 he married Isabella, the daughter of General Leyborne Popham of Littlecote, Wiltshire. After enjoying country life in Hampshire for a time, he volunteered for service in the Turkish army on the outbreak of the Crimean War, and was a lieutenant-colonel in the Osmanli horse artillery until August 1856. He received the medal of the third class of Mejidiye.

In September 1863 Mundy was appointed lieutenant-governor of Grenada, West Indies, and embarked on a colonial career. He acted temporarily as governor of the Windward Islands in 1865, of British Guiana from May 1866 to September 1867, again of the Windwards in 1868–9, and of the Leeward Islands in 1871. From Grenada he was transferred in February 1874 to the permanent appointment of lieutenant-governor of British Honduras. He retired on pension in 1877 and settled in Hampshire.

Mundy was created CMG in 1874 and KCMG in 1877. He died at his home, Hollybank, Emsworth, Hampshire, on 22 March 1892, survived by his wife.

C. A. HARRIS, rev. LYNN MILNE

Sources Colonial Office List (1889) · Burke, Peerage (1889) · Walford, County families (1898) · HoP, Commons
Archives Derby Central Library, colonial and family papers | Bodl. Oxf., Wodehouse MSS, corresp. with Lord Kimberley
Wealth at death £2864 10s. 8d.: probate, 27 April 1892, CGPLA Eng. & Wales

Mundy, William (c.1529–1591?), composer, was probably born in London. He had two sons with his wife, Mary Alcock: John *Mundy (c.1555–1630), who was also a composer; and Stephen (c.1556–1640), who was a gentleman of the royal household during the reigns of James I and Charles I. The first record of William Mundy's life occurs in 1543 when his name appears at the top of a list of the choristers of Westminster Abbey, where he was presumably head boy. His voice must have broken about 1544, and he is next listed in 1547 as a singing man at the parish church of St Martin Ludgate. Between 1548 and 1558 he held the post of parish clerk at St Mary-at-Hill, the church where Thomas Mundy, probably a kinsman, had been sexton since 1527; the parish clerk was one of the singing men of the choir of this musically very active church. By 1559 Mundy had taken up an appointment as a lay vicar of St Paul's Cathedral, where he is recorded as having sworn loyalty that year to Elizabeth's Acts of Supremacy and Uniformity. The final step in Mundy's career was made on 21 February 1564 when he was admitted as a gentleman of the Chapel Royal, apparently as a bass. He evidently died in 1591, since the Chapel Royal cheque book records the appointment of his successor in October of that year.

Mundy was the youngest of a group of composers whose compositional careers spanned the Reformation. Like his elder colleagues, Thomas Tallis and John Sheppard, he wrote music to both Latin and English texts: for liturgical use in the pre-Reformation rite and the vernacular Book of Common Prayer, and for domestic devotional use. Although not always as colourful as Sheppard's, Mundy's compositions display the careful craftsmanship to be found in the music of his great inspiration, Thomas Tallis. Mundy engages less closely with the challenges of text setting than Tallis or Byrd; nevertheless, the outstanding quality of much of Mundy's output ensures his place in the top echelon of Tudor composers. He was clearly much esteemed by his contemporaries. In A Plaine and Easie Introduction to Practicall Musicke (1597) Thomas Morley included him in a group of seven eminent Tudor composers whom he considered to be 'nothing inferior' to the greatest continental composers of the day. In a Latin pun the anthologist Robert Dow compared him with William Byrd, stating that Mundy was as the moon to Byrd's sun.

Mundy's earliest surviving works are contained in the Gyffard partbooks of c.1558, and include two mass settings, a Kyrie and a Magnificat. The difficulties in editing and realizing some of the music in this unusual collection have led some writers to dismiss Mundy's contributions as being the least effective of his output. Recent editorial work and performance, however, have produced a more favourable impression. Two large-scale votive antiphons, Vox patris caelestis and Maria virgo sanctissima were probably composed during the reign of Mary I, but stylistically hark back to before the Reformation. Vox patris is particularly fine and may have been written for the celebrations surrounding Mary's wedding in 1554. Mundy's devotional music, extending to eight psalm settings and three motets, is among his finest. Of the psalms, Adhaesit pavimento and Adolescentulus sum ego are outstanding, the latter existing also as a contrafactum 'Bow down thine ear'. A further psalm setting, Miserere mei, survives in an incomplete but restorable state.

It is difficult accurately to assign all the surviving ten English service settings, since six are attributed to Mundy rather than William Mundy, and could therefore equally be by his son John. The evening service 'to Mr Parsons' completes one of Robert Parsons's sets of morning canticles which he may have left unfinished owing to his untimely death in 1572. The service in medio chori is a setting of the evening canticles on a grand scale for a split five-voice choir and a group of soloists. Of the three anthems for full choir, 'O Lord the maker of all things' and 'O Lord, I bow the knees' are among the finest of their type. Two pieces in verse style, 'Ah, helpless wretch' and 'The Secret Sins', are early examples of the genre that Gibbons was to make famous in the next century. A limited amount of consort music for viols survives, including an In nomine and a piece apparently adapted from a vocal original, O admirabile, dulcior melle. ALISTAIR DIXON

Sources R. G. Reeve, 'The life and works of William Mundy', PhD diss., U. Lond., 1980 · D. Mateer, 'The "Gyffard" partbooks: composers, owners, date and provenance', Royal Musical Association Research Chronicle, 28 (1995), 21–50 · BL, Harley MS 5800 [pedigree] · E. F. Rimbault, ed., The old cheque-book, or book of remembrance, of the Chapel Royal, from 1561 to 1744, CS, new ser., 3 (1872) · E. Pine, The Westminster Abbey singers (1953), 260 · PRO, E 301/88 [chantry certificates, 1547] · T. Morley, A plaine and easie introduction to practicall *musicke* (1597) · J. Baldwin, partbooks, Christ Church Oxf., MSS 979–983

Munis (*fl.* **5th cent.?**). *See under* Meath, saints of (*act. c.*400–*c.*900).

Munk, William (1816–1898), physician and biographer, eldest son of William Munk, an ironmonger, and his wife, Jane Kenward, was born on 24 September 1816 at Battle, Sussex. After education at University College, London, he graduated MD at Leiden in 1837.

Munk began practice in London in September 1837. His first appointment was as demonstrator of morbid anatomy at St Thomas's Hospital. He was later given honorary appointments at the Eastern, Tower Hamlets, and Queen Adelaide dispensaries, and at the Royal Infirmary for Asthma, Consumption and Diseases of the Chest, and at the Royal Hospital for Incurables. In 1844 he became a licentiate of the Royal College of Physicians; he was elected a fellow in 1854 and the Harveian librarian of the college in 1857, an office he held until his death. In that year he published *Memoirs of the Life and Writings of J. A. Paris, MD*, concerning a former president of the Royal College of Physicians, and the first of several such memoirs and biographical works.

In 1861 the work for which Munk is most remembered was published in two volumes. This was *The Roll of the Royal College of Physicians of London*. A second edition of this work appeared in 1878 in three volumes, extending the study to 1825. Volume eight appeared in 1988. It is the best general work of reference on the physicians of England, exact in its references to the manuscript records of the Royal College of Physicians, and containing much valuable information from other sources, the origin of which is not always indicated. The *Roll* was not originally intended for publication, and, as a result, its bibliography is imperfect; yet, despite the occasional inaccuracy, almost every subsequent writer on subjects relating to the history of English physicians owes a great deal to Munk. In 1884 Munk edited a further very successful historical work, *The Gold-Headed Cane* [of William MacMichael], the history of a cane passed through a line of famous physicians, including Radcliffe, Mead, and the Pitcairns, and now in the possession of the Royal College of Physicians. In 1887 he published *Euthanasia, or, Medical Treatment in Aid of an Easy Natural Death*, a plea for the recognition of the physician's duty not to end life but to render its passing in hopeless cases more easy. This, together with several essays on medical subjects in *The Lancet*, was his only writing on explicitly medical topics.

Munk was elected physician to the Smallpox Hospital in February 1853, and he held office there for forty years. It was as a leading authority on the treatment of smallpox that Munk was best-known as a physician. He attracted much attention for his arguments in favour of increased use of narcotics and analgesics for the relief of pain. When Prince Arthur (afterwards duke of Connaught) had smallpox at Greenwich in October 1867, Munk was called in consultation.

William Munk (1816–1898), by John Collier, 1898

Munk lived for a long time at 40 Finsbury Square, London, and enjoyed a considerable practice. He became a Roman Catholic in 1842, and from 1857 to 1865 was the medical adviser of Cardinal Wiseman. Munk was generous in passing on information to other scholars. He admired the Royal College of Physicians, but late in life was inclined to think that in it, and in the world at large, past times were the best. He was for many years an active member of the committee of the London Library. He married on 30 April 1849 Emma, eighteenth child of John Luke, of Exeter. He died on 20 December 1898 at his house, leaving two sons and three daughters.

NORMAN MOORE, *rev.* PATRICK WALLIS

Sources Munk, *Roll* · *BMJ* (24 Dec 1898), 1914 · *The Lancet* (31 Dec 1898) · R. W. Innes Smith, *English-speaking students of medicine at the University of Leyden* (1932) · personal knowledge (1901) · private information (1901)
Archives Exeter Central Library, West Country Studies Library, collections towards a history of the medical worthies of Devon · RCP Lond., papers on medical biography, incl. original MS of Munk's *Roll*
Likenesses J. Collier, oils, 1898, RCP Lond. [*see illus.*]
Wealth at death £9056 18s. 3d.: resworn probate, Oct 1899, CGPLA Eng. & Wales (1898)

Munn, Paul Sandby (1773–1845), watercolour painter, was born on 8 February 1773 in Thornton Row, Greenwich, Kent, one of at least two sons of James Munn, carriage decorator and landscape painter, and his wife, Charlotte Mills. James Munn, who was an occasional exhibitor at the Society of Artists and Free Society of Artists exhibitions between 1764 and 1774, named his son after the artist Paul Sandby who became the boy's godfather and introduced him to watercolour painting. Munn was an early visitor to Dr Thomas Monro's 'academy' in London and by 1799 he had joined the sketching society founded by Thomas Girtin, known as Girtin's Sketching Club. After Girtin's death the society was guided by John Sell Cotman and Munn became its secretary in 1803. The members of these societies met in the evenings at the house of each member in turn and drew a subject set by the host, usually a literary or historical theme with a landscape setting. In 1808 Munn's pupil Francis Stevens formed a further club which lasted until 1851.

Munn exhibited landscapes in watercolour at the Royal Academy from 1799 to 1805 and at the Old Watercolour Society from 1806 to 1815, having been elected an associate of the society in 1805. Many of his softly tinted drawings are pedestrian in character, but on occasion he produced atmospheric and even dramatic watercolours such as *Rocky Chasm, Gordale Scar* (1803, Leeds City Art Gallery) and *Bedlam Furnace, Madeley Dale, Shropshire* of the same year (Tate collection). These and a number of his other best works derive from studies made in the company of Cotman on tours of Wales in 1802 and northern England in 1803. Between 1802 and 1804 Cotman lodged at 107 New Bond Street, the London home and business premises which Munn shared with his brother, William Munn. The brothers sold stationery and prints and Munn produced watercolours for sale as copy material for amateur artists. His involvement in printselling may have prompted his interest in the new process of lithography and in 1807 he contributed *An Old Watermill* to one of the earliest published sets of lithographs produced in London by G. J. Vollweiler. He also contributed to the illustrations for John Britton's *Beauties of England and Wales* (1801–18).

In 1811 Munn was in Hastings and he may have settled there in that year, though he subscribed to fifteen copies of Cotman's *Miscellaneous Etchings* of 1810–11 for the Bond Street shop. His later life seems to have been spent as a teacher of drawing and music in Hastings. Little is known of his personality, but Mrs Cholmeley of Brandsby, Yorkshire, found him 'rough peculiar mannered' in contrast with Cotman who was 'more mannered and gentleman-like' (Clarke, 98). He was married to Cecilia, daughter of Captain Timothy Essex, and died from the effects of diabetes, childless, at Margate, Kent, on 11 February 1845. The Victoria and Albert Museum and the British Museum in London and the Ashmolean Museum in Oxford are among the public collections which have examples of his works.

SUSAN SLOMAN

Sources S. D. Kitson, *The life of John Sell Cotman* (1937) · DNB · J. Hamilton, *The Sketching Society, 1799–1851* (1971) [exhibition catalogue, V&A] · M. Clarke, *The tempting prospect: a social history of English watercolours* (1981) · Mallalieu, *Watercolour artists* · M. Rajnai and M. Allthorpe-Guyton, *John Sell Cotman, 1782–1842: early drawings (1798–1812) in Norwich Castle Museum* (1979) · I. O. Williams, *Early English watercolours and some cognate drawings by artists born not later than 1785* (1952) · Graves, *RA exhibitors*, vol. 5 · O. Meslay, A. Serullaz, and B. Jobert, *D'Outre-Manche: l'art britannique dans les collections publiques françaises* (1994) · C. White, *English landscape, 1630–1850* (1977) [exhibition catalogue, Yale U. CBA] · R. T. Godfrey, *Printmaking in Britain* (1978) · *The art of Paul Sandby* (1985) [exhibition catalogue, Yale U. CBA, 10 April – 23 June 1985] · d. cert.

Munni Begam (1723?–1813), consort of Mir Jafar Ali Khan, nawab of Bengal, was probably born in 1723, reputedly the daughter of 'a poor widow' from the village of Balkonda, near Sikandra in northern India (Torrington, 9.76). The widow gave her to a slave woman who took her to Delhi where she trained her to dance. The troupe of dancers came to Murshidabad to perform at the wedding of one of the grandsons of the nawab of Bengal. There Munni stayed and was given to *Mir Jafar Ali Khan (c.1691–1765) [see under Bengal, nawabs of], a general in the nawab's army. They had two sons, who were eventually to become nawabs of Bengal. On the birth of her first child she lost the status of a slave.

Mir Jafar, who had conspired with the British, became nawab of Bengal after the battle of Plassey in 1757. At the end of his life Munni Begam apparently managed Mir Jafar's household. On his death in February 1765, the eldest of Munni Begam's children, Najm ud-Daula, succeeded and reigned for just over a year. She was given charge of his household too. She continued to manage the household of her second son, the nawab Saif ud-Daula, who reigned from 1766 until 1770, when he was succeeded by the son of another of Mir Jafar's begams, Munni Begam's lifelong rival, Babbu Begam. Munni Begam was at first demoted from the management, but took the chance of reasserting herself when a new governor, Warren Hastings, arrived in Bengal in 1772.

Munni Begam was to be a loyal supporter of Hastings, who regarded her as a valuable ally at the court at Murshidabad, both for the East India Company and for himself personally. He appointed her as guardian to the young nawab, *Mubarak ud-Daula [see under Bengal, nawabs of], with a handsome salary. In her turn Munni Begam authorized the payment of more than £15,000 to Hastings as allowances for his 'entertainment' when he visited Murshidabad in 1772. Later she presented his wife with a set of ivory furniture. Hastings's allies were, however, in danger when a majority hostile to him took control of the company's council in 1774. In May 1775 they dismissed Munni Begam, accusing her of misapplying large sums of the nawab's money. An inquiry proved inconclusive, but she was to be pilloried many years later by Edmund Burke in his accusations at Hastings's trial as 'This woman [who] had been sold as a slave; her profession a dancer, her occupation a prostitute' (*Correspondence of Edmund Burke*, 7.264). When Hastings regained power, so did Munni Begam. In 1778 she had a salary restored to her at a reduced rate and was able again to assert her influence over the nawab's affairs. She continued to dominate the court of Mubarak ud-Daula and of his successors until her death on 10 January 1813, an event marked by the East India Company by the firing of ninety guns for her supposed age. She was buried at Jafarganj in Murshidabad.

After the death of Mir Jafar, Munni Begam lived in a small house at Murshidabad. She never went out and she observed strict purdah, but she asserted a powerful influence through her eunuchs, by copious letters, and by cultivating important Europeans; 'all the English Gentlemen', she once wrote, 'had regarded her as their Mother' (Munni Begam to Cornwallis, received 18 March 1793, BL OIOC, H/594, fol. 393). The historian Ghulam Husain Khan suavely commented that 'she is a woman of infinite merit; and her good sense as well as her steadiness of temper are never so remarkable as when she has any scheme to carry forward' (Khan, *Translation*, 3.41). Hastings paid tribute to 'the Elegance, no less than the correctness of her Manners' (Hastings to J. Macpherson, 6 Feb 1785, BL, Add. MS 29116, fol. 148). A European woman who saw her, however, reported 'that she is very short and fat, with vulgar, large, harsh features and altogether one of the ugliest women she ever beheld' (Abdul Ali, 153). Although she complained of the inadequacy of her allowances for the expenses of the household, she left a fortune of the equivalent of more than £150,000. She endowed a large mosque at Murshidabad. P. J. MARSHALL

Sources *Calendar of Persian correspondence: being letters, referring mainly to affairs in Bengal, which passed between some of the company's servants and Indian rulers and notables*, 11 vols. (1911–69) · G. H. Khan, *A translation of the Sëir mutaqherin, or, View of modern times, being an history of India*, trans. M. Raymond, 3 vols. (1789) · A. F. M. Abdul Ali, 'Munni Begam, the "Mother of the Company"', *Bengal Past and Present*, 29 (1925), 148–54 · B. Banerji, 'The mother of the company', *Bengal Past and Present*, 32 (1926), 37–48 · BL OIOC, Murshidabad MSS, H/594 · N. Majumdar, *Justice and police in Bengal, 1765–1793* (1960) · Warren Hastings's memoranda to his successor, BL, Add. MS 29116 · F. W. Torrington, ed., *Trial of Warren Hastings: minutes of the evidence*, 10 vols. (Dobb's Ferry, NY, 1974) · *The works of Edmund Burke*, 8 vols. (1854–89) · A. M. Khan, *The transition in Bengal, 1756–1775: a study of Saiyid Muhammad Reza Khan* (1969) · K. M. Mohsin, *A Bengal district in transition: Murshidabad, 1765–1793* (1973)
Archives National Archives of India, New Delhi, Persian corresp.
Wealth at death Rs15,000,000 [over £150,000]—value of wealth in treasure, jewels, cash, cloth, etc.: Banerji, 'The mother of the company'

Munnings, Sir Alfred James (1878–1959), artist, was born on 8 October 1878 at Mill House, on the River Waveney, Mendham, Suffolk, the second of the four sons of the miller John Munnings (1839–1914), who was the tenth child of a successful farmer, and his wife, Emily, *née* Ringer (1850–1945), one of nine children of a local farmer.

Childhood His mother suffered frequent bouts of melancholia, a tendency which Munnings inherited together with her love of music, poetry, and nature. His boisterous and extrovert father gave public and family readings from the classics and nurtured his children on poetry and literature. Munnings inherited from him his rumbustious social nature, a love of words, a sense of showmanship, and an artistic talent. Living beside the river he was fascinated with the movement and colour of water which became a constant theme in his pictures and writings. But horses were his lifelong obsession. Great teams of shires brought corn to the mill and he learned the feel and scent of horses from an early age when he was put up in front of his father to ride. As he drove with his family through the countryside the movement of the grey mare drawing the

Sir Alfred James Munnings (1878–1959), by unknown photographer, *c*.1912

trap held his attention far more than did the passing scenery. At the age of four his favourite toy was a wooden horse called Merrylegs, which his father taught him to draw. Because of his mother's illness he went to a dame's boarding-school for a few months when he was four. Afterwards he had a governess for three years until he went to the village school and then to Redenhall Commercial School, followed by four unhappy terms at Framlingham College. He was always drawing horses—from memory or from his imagination—and he demonstrated a remarkable talent which led his parents to send him to the local vicar's daughter for drawing lessons from the age of eight. At fourteen and a half Munnings was apprenticed for six years to Page Brothers, the Norwich lithographers, and for nine hours a day he created imaginative posters and advertisements. In the evenings he studied for two hours at the Norwich School of Art where his favourite model was the cast of a horse's head from the Parthenon. Early mentors were his headmaster, Walter Scott, who encouraged him to pursue art; James Reeve, curator of the Norwich Museum, who bought one of his early pictures for £85; and Shaw Tomkins, manager of Caley's chocolate factory and one of Page Brothers' most important customers, who commissioned him to design posters and boxes and took him on business trips to Europe when he introduced him to fine art galleries and a lively social life. Tomkins also gave him his first commission—a portrait of his father, Daniel Tomkins, sitting on a garden bench with his dog beside him.

Early works Alongside his escalating commercial work for many firms Munnings painted intensively and in ten years sold 110 pictures for up to £100 each through the Norwich art circle. Often he paid a landlord with a small picture as part of his bill. In 1899 two of his small paintings, *Stranded* and *Pike-Fishing in January*, were accepted for the summer exhibition of the Royal Academy; he also showed a landscape at the Royal Institute of Painters in Water Colours. Some months later his career was interrupted when he was blinded in his right eye after it was accidentally pierced by a thorn. After weeks in a nursing home with both eyes bandaged he began a long struggle to overcome his lack of binocular vision. It was a permanent handicap which he rarely mentioned but, together with his recurrent gout, doubtless contributed to his explosive temper.

Handsome and gregarious, Munnings invariably became the life and soul of many parties in East Anglian public houses, and his lively travels with the Gypsies resulted in some of his finest paintings. He often stayed with friends in London, revelling in a hectic social life, and at twenty-four spent the first of several periods of study at the Académie Julian in Paris. East Anglia remained his favourite place to paint, and for several summers he travelled there with a caravan of his own horses managed by a scruffy young handler called Shrimp, who became a frequent model. They parted when Munnings joined the group of painters at Newlyn in Cornwall and became the focus of a social group including Dame Laura Knight, her husband Harold Knight, (S. J.) Lamorna Birch, and Stanhope Forbes. There he met Florence Carter Wood (1888–1914), a brilliant young horsewoman and painter ten years his junior who came from a wealthy family. He probably fell in love with her when he saw her riding side-saddle, her habit flowing over the horse's back giving the centaur-like impression that horse and rider were one. (It was a potent image which he used to portray his wife.) Despite opposition from her parents they married on 19 January 1912; she attempted suicide on their honeymoon and succeeded two and a half years later. Her death apparently had little effect on Munnings's work, whose subjects then included the hop-pickers in Hampshire, horses and Gypsies, country-race meetings, hunting scenes, and a tender romantic portrait of a young girl which formed the basis of an academy painting entitled *Evelyn*. He was a fast painter and averaged thirty to forty medium-sized or large canvases a year in addition to the many watercolour sketches and small canvases invariably produced as preliminaries to his large works.

In 1914 Munnings volunteered for the army but was rejected three times because of the lack of sight in his eye. In desperation he became a scrapper in 1917, scratching the necks of Canadian soldiers' horses to look for mange, until in 1918 he was appointed civilian official war artist to the Canadian cavalry in France. His dramatic paintings of troops in action and lumberjacks working in the forests, and a fine equestrian portrait of General J. E. B. Seely (later Lord Mottistone), were exhibited at the Royal Academy.

The portrait elicited a stream of lucrative and prestigious commissions from sitters, including the amateur steeplechase jockey Lord Mildmay on Davy Jones; the prince of Wales; Lord Harewood; the princess royal; and Lord Birkenhead, lord chancellor of England, which Munnings rated as about his best portrait of a man on horseback.

In 1918 he was elected an associate of the Royal Academy and, from his first London studio in Glebe Place, pursued an exciting social life. He felt financially secure when James Connell & Sons of Old Bond Street bought his three academy pictures and all his Cornish Gypsy and horse paintings at his own price. 'I was a millionaire … I'd care for nobody', he boasted in defiance of his early insecurity and failed marriage. The Chelsea Arts Club became his second home until his foul language, in which he could curse for ten minutes without repeating himself, resulted in his temporary suspension. He joined the Arts Club, the Royal Academy Dining Club, and the Garrick Club, where he revelled in reciting his sixty-verse 'Ballad of Anthony Bell' and John Masefield's 'Reynard the Fox' which the poet had asked him to illustrate. He similarly entertained at the Café Royal and at the many great houses in which he stayed between the wars to portray the owners and their horses and hounds. In the evenings he would play the piano and compose poems about the assembled company.

Sculpture Munnings's first attempt at sculpture (for which he received no formal training), made at the instigation of a young sculptor friend, Whitney-Smith, had been a small statuette of his mare Augereau. In Newlyn an artist friend, Charles Simpson, later commented that his painting represented the furthest limits to which a picture could go in approaching the art of the sculptor. This aspect of his paintings was the outcome of a protracted study of anatomy partly based on George Stubbs's *Anatomy of the Horse* (1766) and also on visits to the stables of a local veterinary surgeon. His horse studies always reflected, over that of other equestrian painters, his unparalleled love and understanding of the animals' characters. His sculpting ability was recognized in 1919 when his friend Sir Edwin Lutyens, who considered that his horse paintings showed a sculptor's grasp of essential form, invited him to sculpt a bronze statuette of a young cavalry officer on horseback, Edward Horner, who was killed in the war, for a memorial in Mells church, Somerset, commissioned by his parents, Sir John and Lady Horner. This led twelve years later to a commission for a sculpture of the famous racehorse Brown Jack, a bronze statuette of which was placed in the royal enclosure at Ascot.

Major commissions In 1919 Munnings bought the house of his dreams—as he called Castle House, Dedham, Essex—an elegant Georgian house with 40 acres of grounds on which he built a studio and kept horses to ride, hunt, and paint. A year later he married a young divorcee, Violet McBride (b. 1885), who was a fine horsewoman and the daughter of a London riding master, Frank Golby Haines. As with Florence, he had been completely captivated by seeing her riding side-saddle on a magnificent horse, looking as if horse and rider were one. Seven years his junior, she took over all their domestic and financial affairs, leaving him free to paint. She encouraged him, often against his will, to accept many commissions from wealthy society figures rather than leaving him free to paint the country scenes he loved and which came to be seen as his best works. 'He was never such a good artist after he married me', she admitted. 'It meant painting for money.' But the commissions enabled him to keep his thirty-four horses. Munnings wrote to her daily when he was away from home; she never curtailed his club life nor complained about his solitary painting expeditions. It was a childless marriage in which she surrounded herself with dogs. He gave her power of attorney so he need never enter a bank again, asked her for money when he needed it, and maintained an illusion of independence by hiding pound notes between the pages of books in his library. She was a favourite equestrian model of his.

Munnings travelled abroad: to paint Robert de Rothschild's family at Chantilly; to judge an international art exhibition at Pittsburgh, where he was exhausted by painting too many millionaires; to Spain, where he was revolted by the use of horses in the bullring; and to Ireland, from where his study of *Kilkenny Horse Fair* was accepted as his diploma work when he was elected Royal Academician in 1925.

Severe gout made Munnings increasingly irritable and he had frequent mood swings. He gradually abandoned painting in watercolour because he felt its immediacy interrupted his work on large oils such as *The Ascot Procession Crossing Windsor Park*, painted at the invitation of Queen Mary. Bought for the Royal Collection, it hung in the royal box for several Ascot meetings. He much preferred Epsom, with its Gypsies, to Ascot, and he enjoyed the smaller intimate meetings at Sandown and Hurst Park, and at Newmarket, which he thought was the most beautiful course in the world. There the Jockey Club loaned him an old horse-box on the course to use as a studio, and it was in this that he painted some of his best racing pictures. He bought the old grammar school schoolroom at Dedham to convert into a large studio. He loved the views of the countryside from the building and, like his writer friend Adrian Bell, grew very concerned about the loss of old country values and the desecration of the land by mechanization.

During the Second World War Munnings retired to his cottage on Exmoor, where, despite gout in his right wrist, he painted landscapes, Dartmoor ponies, and hunting scenes, and, feeling more at peace with himself than he had since the early Newlyn days, wrote gentle reflective poetry rather than the long ballads and obscene verses in which he once indulged. His peace was shattered, however, when he reluctantly agreed to stand as president of the Royal Academy in succession to Sir Edwin Lutyens, who had defeated him for office in 1938. On 14 March 1944 he beat Augustus John by twenty-four votes to seventeen and in June received a knighthood in the king's birthday honours.

President of the Royal Academy Munnings was the Royal Academy's most controversial president. He ignored protocol at council meetings, was frustrated when duty stopped him from painting, and counteracted the boredom of selecting pictures for the summer exhibition by writing letters and articles to the press. His notoriously short temper was aggravated by sleepless nights caused by heavy air raids and increasing gout. He was temporarily appeased by his successful exhibition at the Leicester Galleries, by receiving the freedom of Norwich, and by hosting splendid dinners at the academy. At one of these he made Sir Winston Churchill the first Royal Academician extraordinary, after persuading him to submit six paintings anonymously to the summer exhibition when all were accepted. At Churchill's suggestion, in 1949 he revived the academy's men-only annual banquet after a lapse of ten years. His uninhibited sixteen minute after-dinner speech at it made academy history: he berated the academy, the Arts Council, the Tate Gallery, and Anthony Blunt (surveyor of the king's pictures), and ranted against modern art, including 'those foolish daubers' Cézanne, Matisse, and Picasso, whose influence, he said, had defiled British tradition. While sackfuls of letters showed that, in general, the public agreed with him, the BBC received forty objections to his use of the word 'damned'. He was privately rebuked by Churchill, not for the tenor of his speech but for publicizing a private joke. Churchill had said to him 'Alfred, if you met Picasso coming down the street would you join with me in kicking his something, something …?' and he had replied 'Yes Sir, I would.'

Despite its public appeal, the after-dinner speech ostracized Munnings from the art world. He resigned the presidency of the academy at the end of the year to make 'a joyous return to painting', which he interrupted by an unsuccessful attempt to have one of his reviled moderns, Stanley Spencer, prosecuted for obscene painting. He lectured against modern art and what he perceived as the subversive activities of the Arts Council; and also against mechanized farming, promoting instead the need for more ecological methods. He also wrote a highly acclaimed, copiously illustrated three-volume autobiography. Persistent gout, increasing physical disability, and a rarely voiced fear of diminishing eyesight aggravated his irritability. He became too ill to attend his retrospective exhibition of 200 paintings at the Royal Academy in 1956; by April 1959, with both hands bandaged, he could not even write.

Munnings died in his sleep at Castle House on 17 July 1959. After a private cremation at Colchester, Essex, his ashes were interred in the crypt of St Paul's Cathedral, London, where his memorial plaque was placed next to that of John Constable. A memorial service was held a week later in St James's, Piccadilly. His estate and possessions were left to his wife. In fulfilment of his wish that his estate and the paintings in his possession should be left to the nation, his widow worked to establish, through trusts, an art museum at their Dedham home where a large collection of his work is hung (now the Sir Alfred Munnings

Art Museum). Together with many other paintings in private and public collections, including the Castle Museum in Norwich, the Canadian War Museum in Ottawa, the Royal Academy, and the Tate collection, the Sir Alfred Munnings Art Museum helps to endorse the artist's belief that he would be remembered best as a painter of the English landscape rather than primarily as a horse painter.

JEAN GOODMAN

Sources J. Goodman, *AJ: the life of Alfred Munnings, 1878–1959*, new edn (2000) [incl. comprehensive bibliography] · R. Pound, *The Englishman* (1962) · A. Munnings, *An artist's life* (1950) · A. Munnings, *The second burst* (1951) · A. Munnings, *The finish* (1952) · S. Booth, *Sir Alfred Munnings, 1878–1959, a centenary tribute: an appreciation of the artist and a selection of his paintings* (1978) · *Alfred Munnings, 1878–1959* (1978) [exhibition catalogue, Man. City Gall.] · L. Knight, *Oil paint and grease paint* (1936) · L. Knight, *The magic of a line* (1965)
Archives Munnings Trust, Castle House, Dedham · Norfolk RO, sketches and humorous verses, MC 742/1–4 · Norwich Castle Museum · RA, corresp. and MSS | BL, corresp. with Sir Sydney Cockerell, Add. MS 52741 · JRL, letters to the *Manchester Guardian* · Norfolk RO, corresp., sketches, and letters to John Moody, MC 1235, 1248/2, 1263 · Tate collection, corresp. with Lord Clark · TCD, corresp. with Thomas Bodkin · U. Leeds, letters to Henry Seymour, seventh Earl Bathurst | FILM BFI NFTVA | SOUND BL NSA
Likenesses photograph, *c*.1912, Norwich Castle Museum and Art Gallery [*see illus.*] · A. C. Cooper, photographs, 1945, NPG · F. Kovacs, plaster medallion, *c*.1949, NPG · J. Gilroy, drawing, Garr. Club · F. Kovacs, bronze cast, NPG · P. Laib, photograph, NPG · A. J. Munnings, self-portrait, ink drawing, NPG · A. J. Munnings, self-portrait, oils, NPG · A. J. Munnings, self-portrait, oils (with his wife), NPG · A. J. Munnings, self-portrait, pen-and-ink drawing, V&A · A. R. Thomson, ink drawing, Athenaeum, London · carved profile on memorial tablet, St Paul's Cathedral, London · photograph, repro. in Goodman, *Life of Alfred Munnings*, jacket
Wealth at death £71,626 19s. 4d.: probate, 27 May 1960, *CGPLA Eng. & Wales*

Munro. *See also* Monro.

Munro, Alexander (1825–1871), sculptor, was born on 26 October 1825 and baptized on 12 November 1825 in Inverness, the son of John Munro (*c*.1800–1879), dyer, and Isabella Macbean (*c*.1801–1888). His talent for carving thick slate pencils as heads and figures attracted the interest of Peter Scott, rector of Inverness Academy, and of several local notables, who combined to further his education. In 1844 Harriet, duchess of Sutherland, arranged with Charles Barry for him to work on the new Houses of Parliament.

In London Munro worked under John Thomas and frequented the studio of Patric Park. His first application to join the Royal Academy Schools was rejected, but gave rise to an invitation to train in the studio of E. H. Baily which maintained a strong connection with Flaxman whose pupil Baily was. Munro eventually enrolled in the Royal Academy Schools in 1847 and soon became a devoted friend of D. G. Rossetti and thus a member of the Pre-Raphaelite circle. It was through circulating *The Germ* that he met Arthur Hughes. Munro's early portraits included those of W. M. Rossetti and Millais (low-relief: cast, *c*.1854; Ashmolean Museum, Oxford; marble, priv. coll.). Munro is often accused, rightly or wrongly, of unleashing the fury of the press against the PRB by revealing the meaning of its initials (Pre-Raphaelite Brotherhood) to his journalist

Alexander Munro (1825–1871), by Arthur Hughes, *c*.1870

friend Angus Reach. He is also remembered as having incurred the scorn of the art critic and anthologist F. T. Palgrave (in contrast to the latter's lavish praise of Thomas Woolner) in the handbook to the fine art collections of the London International Exhibition in 1862. Woolner (the only Pre-Raphaelite Brotherhood sculptor) and Munro certainly followed divergent strands of Pre-Raphaelitism: Woolner emphasized in his sculpture truth to nature (like William Holman Hunt), Munro (like Rossetti), poetic imagination.

In 1849 Munro completed a chimney-piece (des.) for the Sutherlands at Dunrobin Castle and had two busts accepted at the Royal Academy; from then onwards he exhibited there every year. At the Great Exhibition of 1851 he showed a plaster cast of *Paolo and Francesca*. He owed his enthusiasm for Dante to Rossetti, who also made drawings on this theme from Dante's *Inferno*. Munro's smoothly modelled interpretation conveys the tenderness and the intensity of the moment before the fatal kiss. The work made a deep impression on W. E. Gladstone, who commissioned a marble copy of it (1852; Birmingham Museum and Art Gallery).

In 1852 Munro settled in a house in Pimlico, which he shared until 1858 with Arthur Hughes. In 1855 his teaching at the Working Men's College in Great Ormond Street brought him into the orbit of F. D. Maurice and Ruskin. His house became a focus for an ever-widening circle of friends, including artists, writers, publishers, and journalists. He enjoyed 'rambles' to different parts of the British Isles, and these became increasingly connected with commissions. He explored Normandy and, with Rossetti, Paris; he visited Italy three times. On 30 September 1861 Munro married Mary (1834–1872), fourth daughter of Robert Carruthers; they had two sons. From 1865 he fought a long battle with cancer and spent the winter months in Cannes, where in 1869 he built a house, the Villa de la Tourelle. He died in Cannes on 1 January 1871 and was buried in the protestant cemetery there.

Little remains of Munro's architectural sculpture. Examples include a frieze at Cliveden, Buckinghamshire, and a stone tympanum relief, *King Arthur and the Knights of the Round Table* (1857–8, after a design by Rossetti), over the entrance to the Oxford Union Society building. The latter, however, is a fine example of Pre-Rahaelite sculpture in complete harmony with its architectural setting. The final medium of Munro's work is generally marble or Caen stone; some is cast in bronze, and in 1863 he exhibited an early example of a group in aluminium. Some maquettes and plaster casts inscribed with his monogram have survived. His work consisted mainly of portrait busts and especially medallion portraits, a choice of form which owes much to his architectural training. These medallions are oval or circular, about 16 inches to 24 inches in height or diameter, and consist of low-relief profiles or high-reliefs typically with the head almost in the round. Several have subsequently been permanently attached to a wall or monument, for example, those of Pauline Trevelyan (Wallington, Northumberland), Honora Glynne (Hawarden church, Flintshire), and Prosper Mérimée (the protestant cemetery, Cannes, France). The relief of David Scott, which Munro modelled 'showing prodigious celerity and certainty of hand', was made for his monument in the Old Dean cemetery, Edinburgh (W. B. Scott, letter to W. C. Trevelyan, 15 Nov 1859, Robinson Library, University of Newcastle upon Tyne).

Munro made some conventional busts, among them those of William Henry Hunt (1861; Royal Watercolour Society, Bankside, London) and Victor Cousin (1867; Institut de France, Chantilly); but his talent lay in portraying a more private mood in his sitters, as in the pensive *Benjamin Woodward* (1861/2; Oxford University Museum of Natural History). This work typifies the aspect of Munro's style described by W. M. Rossetti as 'early' (diary, 22 May 1849, in Fredeman, 5), and is characteristic of 'a formal purism' related to early Italian art (Read, 180). Munro disliked ceremony and delighted in catching a spontaneous likeness, for example that of George MacDonald returning with windswept hair from a seaside walk (*c*.1857/9; bronze medallions, Scottish National Portrait Gallery, Edinburgh, and King's College, Aberdeen). One of his busts of Josephine Butler shows her hair in intricate coils (Walker Art Gallery, Liverpool); in another, her hair is flowing down her back (Girton College, Cambridge). In his relief of Agnes Gladstone, aged eleven, her hair ripples round her shoulders (1853/4; priv. coll.) and in a relief of 1867 a nimbus of hair fans out round the head of Pauline Geneviève, duchess of Vallombrosa (priv. coll.). Munro often introduced flowers and foliage into his medallions

and these, or a lock of hair, or the wing of a dove, tend to stray across the rim. This free decorative style is typical of his work.

Munro carved a number of ideal works with literary themes: *Undine* (various versions, 1856–69; marble, Cragside, Northumberland); *Sabrina* (exh. RA, 1861; Ackland Art Museum, University of North Carolina at Chapel Hill); *Young Romilly* (exh. RA, 1863; National Gallery of Scotland, Edinburgh). He also made three fountain sculptures: a *Boy and Dolphin* (Hyde Park, London) and two nymphs, one at Boston, Lincolnshire, the other in Berkeley Square, London. Historical portraiture gave him scope for imaginative interpretation of his subjects based on earlier likenesses including, where possible, historically accurate detail. One of his last works was *Queen Mary II* (1869; Old Bailey, London); but his most important series of commissions was the creation of six statues for the new Oxford University Museum (1856–63): *Hippocrates*, *Galileo*, *Newton*, *Leibniz*, *James Watt*, and *Humphrey Davy*. Preserved indoors, the carving remains crisp. A second *James Watt* (now in Chamberlain Square) has been exposed to the traffic pollution of central Birmingham since 1869. Munro's statues and groups of children including *Measurement by Foxglove* (Edith and Emily Gathorne Hardy; exh. RA, 1859), *The Sound of the Shell* (Kenneth and Mary Matheson; exh. RA, 1861; priv. coll.) *The Baffled Hawk* (Ronald Ferguson; exh. RA, 1863; priv. coll.) combine likeness and imaginative interpretation.　KATHARINE MACDONALD

Sources *The exhibition of the Royal Academy* (1849–70) [exhibition catalogues] · B. Read and J. Barnes, eds., *Pre-Raphaelite sculpture* (1991), esp. 46–65, 94, 110–30 · B. Read, *Victorian sculpture* (1982) · W. E. Fredeman, ed., *The P.R.B. journal* (1975) · *The Pre-Raphaelites*, Tate Gallery · U. Newcastle, Robinson L., Trevelyan MSS · letters from, to, and concerning Alexander Munro, priv. coll. · St Deiniol's Library, Hawarden, Gladstone Archive · register, 1847, RA, Royal Academy Schools · *Inverness Courier* (14 Jan 1871)

Archives BL, letters · Bodl. Oxf., letters · St Deiniol's Library, Hawarden, letters to Sir Thomas Gladstone · U. Newcastle, letters to Sir Walter Trevelyan and Lady Trevelyan

Likenesses A. Hughes, 1852–4 · J. E. Millais, pencil drawing, 1853, William Morris Gallery, Walthamstow · C. L. Dodgson, photograph, *c*.1858–1859, Princeton University, New Jersey · J. Brett, pencil drawing, 1861, priv. coll. · C. L. Dodgson, caricature, *c*.1861, Princeton University, New Jersey · C. L. Dodgson, double portrait, photograph, 1863 (with Mary Munro), Princeton University, New Jersey · A. Hughes, chalk drawing, *c*.1870, priv. coll. [see illus.] · A. Hughes, drawing, 1871, Scot. NPG · two portraits, 1871 (after A. Hughes, *c*.1870), Scot. NPG · engraving (after photograph by O. G. Rejlander), repro. in *ILN* (28 Jan 1871)

Wealth at death under £5000: probate, 10 Oct 1871, *CGPLA Eng. & Wales*

Munro [*married name* Munro-Ashman], **Anna Gillies Macdonald** (1881–1962), campaigner for women's suffrage and magistrate, was born at 32 Gladstone Street, Glasgow, on 4 October 1881, the elder daughter of Evan Macdonald Munro (*c*.1854–1913), schoolmaster of Edinburgh, and his wife, Margaret Ann MacVean (1858–1892) of Glengilp, Knapdale, Argyll. The family lived in Edinburgh until the death of Anna's mother in 1892, when Anna, with her sister, Eva, was taken to live at Venturefair House, Townhill,

Anna Gillies Macdonald Munro (1881–1962), by unknown photographer

Dunfermline, the home of Revd Jacob Primmer, a Church of Scotland minister whose wife was Evan Munro's sister.

As a young woman Anna Munro became involved in social work among the working classes in London through the Wesleyan Methodist Sisters of the People, which she joined because she admired their socialist ideals rather than out of religious conviction. It is ironic that when she later became president of this movement her duties included conducting services of worship, as she had all but abandoned any church connection on moving south. It was while working in London's East End that she became aware of the activities of the women's suffrage movement. She joined the Women's Social and Political Union and founded its Dunfermline branch in 1906. She later followed her friend Teresa Billington-Greig into the Women's Freedom League (WFL), becoming her private secretary in 1907. In January 1908 she was imprisoned in Holloway for six weeks for her part in demonstrations outside the home of the cabinet minister Richard Haldane. From 1908 to 1912 she served as organizing secretary for the Women's Freedom League Scottish council. She helped organize an annual holiday campaign, aimed at reaching the Glasgow workers as they enjoyed their summer holidays on the Clyde coast. Setting up summer headquarters of the WFL in Rothesay on the island of Bute,

they then held meetings at Dunoon, Kirn, and Largs. She also helped organize the 1911 census protest, whereby members of the WFL encouraged women to refuse to participate in the census—on the principle of 'no taxation without representation'. In 1912 Anna Munro was one of four members of the WFL who marched the entire route of the Women's Freedom League Edinburgh–London march. She addressed the rallies in Edinburgh and London at both ends of the route.

In addition to her Scottish campaigning, Anna Munro also travelled in rural areas of England in a horse-drawn caravan, conducting open-air meetings from the tailboard. She apparently displayed great eloquence, speaking entirely without notes, and addressing large gatherings. She was a tall, elegant, attractive woman, and was apparently admired by many of the men who attended the meetings, although she made it her policy not to reply to any letters she received from men. However, following one of her meetings at Thatcham, near Reading, she received a letter from Sidney Ashman, who had been present at the meeting with his sisters. She agreed to meet, mistakenly thinking that 'Sidney' was one of the sisters whom she had spoken to at the meeting. Romance blossomed, and the couple were married on 4 April 1913 at Wandsworth register office, London. They set up home in the Reading area, where Sidney was beginning to build up a business in road haulage. Shortly after their marriage Anna Munro was imprisoned for her part in holding an illegal suffrage meeting in Hyde Park. Their two children, a son and a daughter, were born while they were living in their first home at Park Farm, Thatcham. They lived at Aldermaston, from 1923 until 1929 when they bought their own home, Venturefair, at Padworth, near Reading. Throughout her married life Anna Munro continued to campaign for women's rights, remaining active in the WFL right up until its disbanding in 1961. Although she and her husband had adopted the surname Munro-Ashman on their marriage, Anna continued to be known as Anna Munro in all her WFL activities. This was a conscious choice, made so as not to jeopardize her husband's growing business. She also chose not to stand for parliament on the grounds that it might interfere with her husband's business, and because it would mean her being away from her children too much. Although she was a dedicated socialist, she seems to have had the ability to hold her socialist views comfortably alongside her upper-middle-class standing. She was not on visiting terms with the local 'gentry', and was much more comfortable in the company of the working-class people of Beenham, a mining village near Reading, among whom she campaigned during elections, taking them to the polls in her Daimler motor car. One of her greatest rivals was J. H. Benyan of Englefield Manor, a leading local landowner, who publicly opposed her being made a magistrate. He is reported to have said that this would happen only 'over his dead body', and she was not in fact appointed a magistrate until after his death in 1935. She served as a magistrate until the late 1950s, retiring from the bench only when she was forced to do so because of hearing difficulties.

Anna Munro was a supporter of the temperance movement and president of the National British Total Abstinence Movement, and her parties were noted for the non-alcoholic cocktails which she very expertly created. In later life she served on various local committees, and as both chairman and president of the local Labour Party. She also campaigned against compulsory vaccination. Her own children had not been vaccinated because she was opposed, not to vaccination itself, but to compulsion in any form. She encouraged her own children in their chosen careers, her son as a doctor and her daughter as an almoner at the local hospital. On 11 September 1962 Anna Munro suffered a heart attack and died that day at her home at Venturefair, Padworth. Having left instructions in her will, she was cremated at Reading crematorium. She was survived by her husband.   VIRGINIA RUSSELL

Sources interviews on British women's history in the 20th century, about Anna Munro-Ashman, Brian Harrison with Dr Donald Munro-Ashman, son of Anna Munro-Ashman, Women's Library, London, 303.420 922 INT, tape 15/1 · L. Leneman, *A guid cause: the women's suffrage movement in Scotland* (1991) · E. King, *The Scottish women's suffrage movement* (1978) · b. cert. · m. cert. · d. cert. · census returns for Scotland, 1881, 1891 · postal directories, Dunfermline · M. Lovejoy, 'Miss Anna Munro', unpublished essay, May 1982, Women's Library, London · *CGPLA Eng. & Wales* (1962)
Likenesses photograph (in front of banner of the Women's Freedom League Scottish campaign), Glasgow Museum, suffragettes photographic collection, 1280 [*see illus.*] · photograph, Glasgow Museum, suffragettes photographic collection, 1280, ref. 81.1; repro. in Leneman, *Guid cause* · photograph (in prison dress), Glasgow Museum, suffragettes photographic collection, 1280, ref. 81.2
Wealth at death £4511 11s. 0d.: administration, 1962

Munro, Sir Hector (1725/6–1805/6), army officer, was the son of Hugh Munro, merchant, of Clayside, Sutherland, and his wife, Isobel Gordon (1706/7–1799), a granddaughter of Sir Robert Gordon, second baronet, of Embo. Munro's career in the army and politics spanned the second half of the eighteenth century, and he became well known through his military exploits in India between 1764 and 1782. He appears to have gone into combat before acquiring his first formal commission, fighting against the Jacobites in 1745–6; he was rumoured to have been captured and to have escaped. On 28 May 1747 he was appointed ensign in Loudoun's highlanders, an unnumbered regiment, where his company commander was Sir Harry Munro of Foulis, a distant relative. The regiment embarked shortly afterwards for the Low Countries, and saw distinguished service at Bergen-op-Zoom (July to September 1747) at the tail end of the War of Austrian Succession. Loudoun's highlanders were disbanded in June 1748, but Munro secured a reappointment to the peacetime army as an ensign in the 48th foot (Lord H. Beauclerk's), on 4 February 1749; he was promoted lieutenant in the 31st foot, in Ireland (5 January 1754), and in August 1756 captain of his own company in the newly raised 2nd battalion 31st foot, which in April 1758 became the 70th foot.

At the height of the Seven Years' War, in 1759, Munro was appointed junior major in the 89th (Highland) regiment, newly raised on the estates of the duke of Gordon

Sir Hector Munro (1725/6–1805/6), by unknown artist, 1785

by Major Staats Long Morris, who had married into the Gordon family. Munro owed his promotion to the recommendation of the dowager duchess of Gordon. The regiment, with Munro in command, was sent to Bombay at the end of 1759, but part, under Munro, was diverted to Madras, where a campaign in the Carnatic was being waged against the French by Colonel Eyre Coote. Munro arrived on 2 September 1760 and joined Coote in the blockade of Pondicherry, where the French had their headquarters. After the fall of Pondicherry in January 1761 he resumed his journey to Bombay, capturing minor French posts on the south-west (Malabar) coast on the way.

The 89th was recalled to Britain at the end of the war (1763), but Munro was left in charge of a remnant of the regiment (ninety-seven men), and was asked in 1764 to take them to Bengal where, in a lull in the war being fought against Indian powers in the Ganges valley, the East India Company's forces were mutinying. He took over command of the Bengal army at Patna, from Major John Carnac, on 12 August 1764, and was confronted by severe unrest in the sepoy battalions, who had received a far smaller share of the 'donation' made to the army by the grateful puppet nawab of Bengal, Mir Jafar, than the European troops. Munro believed that 'regular discipline and strict obedience to orders is the only superiority Europeans possess in this country over the natives' (Mason, 106) so, despite the justice of the sepoys' claims, he ruthlessly brought them back into line by court-martialling and executing twenty-four of the ringleaders (by blowing them away from guns), and disbanding the most rebellious battalion in ignominy.

With discipline restored, Munro marched the army to the frontier between Bihar and Oudh (400 miles northwest of Calcutta) where the nawab wazir, Shuja ud-Daula of Oudh, the wandering Mughal emperor, Shah Alam II, and the deposed former nawab of Bengal, Mir Kasim, were threatening invasion. Along the way, Munro drilled his troops in more sophisticated tactical forms and rehearsed them in the battle plan he hoped to adopt when he encountered the wazir and his allies. The forces met at Buxar on 22 October 1764.

The forces of the wazir lay in a carefully prepared, entrenched position, but the following day, confident in his numerical superiority (40,000 to 7000 by British reckoning), and probably also because he had large numbers of cavalry while the British had few, Shuja ud-Daula chose to challenge Munro out in the open field. In the ensuing battle Munro showed skill, resolution, and tactical insight. The opening, recklessly pressed attacks by the Mughal cavalry at one point threatened to surround and engulf Munro's smaller force, but they were eventually repelled with heavy losses by the disciplined firepower of the company's Indian and European infantry and their field guns. Munro then ordered a resolute assault at bayonet point on the enemy's left flank positions, and Shuja's whole army collapsed into an undisciplined rout. Munro was thus rewarded for the work he had put into disciplining and training his forces before the battle. Company casualties were 847 killed and wounded; by British estimates, Shuja lost 2000 killed, and 133 of his guns.

The battle of Buxar marked the pinnacle of Munro's military career. More importantly, it was one of the decisive battles in the establishment of the British raj. It converted the nawab wazir of Oudh, ruling a pivotal province for the control of northern India, into a supplicant for British support, and it led, within a year, to the Mughal emperor officially clothing the nakedness of the East India Company's military power by appointing it *diwan* (revenue collector) of Bengal and Bihar, effectively making the British the rulers of the richest provinces of India.

Munro resigned his command on 6 January 1765, and returned to Britain a lieutenant-colonel and greatly enriched by prize money. He probably never envisaged returning to India, and settled down to improve his estate at Novar. He used his new-found wealth to campaign for election to parliament as member for Inverness burghs, a seat he held from 1768 to 1802, generally supporting the government. He lost heavily in the Ayr Bank failure of 1772 (but did not abate his electoral expenditure), which possibly caused him to exploit his company and parliamentary contacts and his military record to secure appointment in 1777 as commander-in-chief at Madras, with a local royal commission as major-general and a seat on the Madras council.

The Carnatic had been relatively peaceful since the company's army had been worsted in a brief war (1767–8) with Haidar Ali, the ambitious and skilful ruler of Mysore, a state lying to the west of Madras, over the Eastern Ghats. Unlike Bengal, where the East India Company was effectively the master, the political situation in the Carnatic was more ambiguous. The administration of the interior was still in the hands of the local Mughal authority, represented by the nawab of Arcot, Muhammad Ali Khan, who maintained his power by borrowing large sums of money at exorbitant rates of interest from company servants, thus giving them a stake in maintaining, even expanding, his power to keep their investments safe. The company was none the less regarded as the paramount military power in the Carnatic: the nawab's ill-paid, ill-disciplined forces would count for little in a war with a neighbouring state, and his corrupt, ramshackle government's inability to organize supplies was to contribute to Munro's disastrous campaign against Haidar in 1780. It was fortunate for the company that the Carnatic was at peace in the years following its defeat by Haidar in 1768, because there was prolonged internecine strife on the corrupt Madras council (which did not abate after Munro's arrival in 1778 and in which he became embroiled). The trouble was stirred up by the nawab and his British allies, and related to the titanic struggle back in London between Lord Clive and the leading director of the East India Company, Laurence Sulivan (a friend of Munro's), for control of the company.

The company's luck ran out in 1778 when Britain became involved in a war with France over the issue of American independence, and later (1781) with the Dutch. All three had settlements on the Coromandel coast. When news of the war reached Madras, Munro efficiently mobilized the army and quickly attacked Pondicherry, taking it, after a six-week siege, on 17 October 1778, with 781 casualties. On his urging, the French settlements on the Malabar coast were also captured. But this stirred up Haidar Ali's wrath, because he claimed these settlements were under his protection. Menacing noises came from Seringapatam as early as March 1779; they were ignored by Munro and the governor, but other councillors took them seriously, urging that the army be concentrated at Madras. Haidar Ali, with 90,000 men, was moving from the Ghats onto the Carnatic plain in June 1780 before Munro and the governor agreed to order two major outlying detachments, one 60 miles to the south at Pondicherry, the other 200 miles to the north under Colonel Baillie, to rejoin the main army out in the field. Inexplicably, except that he disdained Haidar's power and skill, and against the advice of his second in command, Lord Macleod, Munro ordered the rendezvous to be at Conjeeveram, an open town 40 miles inland in lightly held enemy country (his aim was to relieve Arcot, the capital of the Carnatic, a further 40 miles to the west), rather than under the guns of Madras. Haidar's scouting cavalry gave him a full strategic appreciation of the disposition and movements of the British, so while his main force pinned down Munro's army of 5200 men (which was in any case nearly immobilized for lack of supplies), he sent his son, Tipu Sultan, with 6000 horse, 5000 infantry, and a 400-strong detachment of French artillery, to intercept Colonel Baillie and his 2800 infantry and guns coming down from the north. Baillie's force was destroyed: Munro had heard cannon fire and received an appeal for help from Baillie, but sent only a detachment to his relief, which shared in the débâcle. Munro and his army, now totally demoralized and running out of supplies, fled back in disorder to Madras, leaving Haidar the virtual run of the Carnatic.

It was the worst defeat suffered by British arms in the Carnatic in the eighteenth century. One Madras civil servant wrote to another that Munro's 'conduct is condemned by the Army universally' (R. Sulivan to J. Sulivan, 18 Oct 1780, Bodl. Oxf., MS Eng. hist. b.190, fols. 44–6), and Munro challenged another councillor to a duel for his derogatory remarks. Warren Hastings, the governor-general at Calcutta, reacted by dismissing the governor, Sir Thomas Rumbold, and sending General Sir Eyre Coote to supersede Munro. Munro served loyally under Coote as his second in command the following year, when he beat Haidar twice in field actions (at Porto Novo on 1 July, and at Polillur on 27 August 1781), and then retired sick to Madras. He had one last chance to win back some of his tattered reputation when in November 1781 he commanded a successful expedition to take the Dutch base down the coast at Negapatam. Munro could also console himself, on the voyage home the following year (he resigned on 27 September 1782), with the knighthood granted for the capture of Pondicherry and the prize money he had received. The news awaiting him in London, that he had been dismissed their service by the East India Company for the Baillie disaster, was tempered by a royal commission as major-general on the British establishment.

Back in Scotland, Munro attended to his Novar estates, building an oriental folly, the Gates of Negapatam, and spending some £120,000 on general improvements. He was a vigorous pioneer of the introduction of sheep into the highlands, ultimately provoking widespread resistance by tenants on his estates. Troops had to be called in to restore order after protests in July and August 1792 against rent increases, the loss of arable, and the enclosure of common grazing. Munro resumed his parliamentary duties (he had never relinquished his seat), consistently supporting the government, and had his portrait painted by Reynolds. His active military career had ended, but his promotions continued: he became colonel of the Black Watch on 1 June 1787, a lieutenant-general in 1793, and general on 1 January 1798.

Munro had carried through valuable reforms in the Madras and Bengal armies, had been bold and victorious at Buxar, had taken several forts elsewhere, and had made a fortune in India. But Baillie's defeat lay heavily upon his reputation and probably upon his heart. He was a robust and handsome man, apparently unmarried, with two sons and a daughter, Jean, who married the army officer and politician Sir Ronald Craufurd Ferguson. He died at Novar on either 27 December 1805 (according to his tombstone) or 6 January 1806 (according to the *Scots Magazine*,

1806, 79), and was buried there. He was succeeded in his estates by his brother, Sir Alexander Munro, who had a career in the diplomatic and revenue services.

G. J. BRYANT

Sources V. C. P. Hodson, *List of officers of the Bengal army, 1758–1834*, 4 vols. (1927–47) · Fortescue, *Brit. army*, 2nd edn, vols. 2–3 · M. Wilks, *Historical sketches of the south of India, in an attempt to trace the history of Mysoor*, 3 vols. (1810–17) · *DNB* · H. D. Love, *Vestiges of old Madras, 1640–1800*, 4 vols. (1913) · HoP, *Commons, 1754–90* · J. M. Holtzman, *The nabobs in England, 1760–1765* (1926) · M. M. Stuart, 'The Scottish nabobs', NL Scot., accession no. 9620 · Bengal secret consultations, 1764, BL OIOC, range A, vol. 5 · Madras select committee proceedings, BL OIOC, range 251, vols. 87–9 · Madras select committee proceedings, BL OIOC, range C, vols. 63–9 · Madras select committee proceedings, BL OIOC, range D, vols. 1–3 · Munro's order book, 1764, BL, Add. MS 6049, fols. 154–200 · Munro's order book, 1764, BL, Add. MS 6050, fols. 1–15 · journal of Sir Hector Munro's campaign, 26 Aug–14 Sept 1780, BL, Add. MS 29215, fols. 9–22 · P. Mason, *A matter of honour: an account of the Indian army, its officers and men* (1974) · A. Mackillop, 'The highlands and the returning nabob: Sir Hector Munro of Novar, 1760–1807', *Emigrant homecomings: the return movement of emigrants, c.1600–c.2000* (2003)

Archives BL OIOC, home misc. series, corresp. relating to India · NRA Scotland, priv. coll., papers · University of Minnesota, Minneapolis, Ames Library of South Asia, letterbooks

Likenesses oils, 1785, NPG [*see illus.*] · plaster replica, 1796 (after medallion by J. Tassie), Scot. NPG; cast from a medallion in possession of R. W. Cochran Patrick, 1893 · J. Reynolds, portrait

Munro, Hector Hugh [*pseud.* Saki] (1870–1916), short-story writer, was born on 18 December 1870 in Akyab, Burma, the youngest of the three children of Colonel Charles Augustus Munro (1844–1907), inspector-general of police in Burma, and Mary Frances Mercer (d. 1872). He was proud to belong to the ancient clan Munro. Owing to the death of his mother and his father's absence abroad he was brought up with his brother and sister by two aunts in the village of Pilton, near Barnstaple, Devon. The aunts' stern, unsympathetic methods and the children's resentment are reflected in some of Munro's most memorable stories, in which dictatorial aunts are worsted by their charges. He was educated at a preparatory school in Exmouth and for four terms at Bedford grammar school (later known as Bedford School), until in 1887 Colonel Munro returned from Burma and took the children on extensive continental travels. In 1893 Munro joined the Burma police, but malaria brought him home fifteen months later. After recuperating in Devon he decided to earn his living as a writer in London.

Munro's first book, *The Rise of the Russian Empire* (1900), cost him much labour but it was a false start, although Russia always fascinated him. When Francis Carruthers Gould introduced him to the *Westminster Gazette* in 1900 Munro began contributing brief political satires, signing himself Saki, the name of the 'cypress-slender Minister of Wine' in the *Rubáiyát of Omar Khayyám*. In 1901 the *Westminster* published the first of his short stories about an exquisite young man named Reginald; these were later published in book form as *Reginald* (1904).

Munro went to the Balkans as special correspondent for the *Morning Post* in 1902, then to Warsaw, St Petersburg (where he witnessed the 1905 massacre), and Paris. His dispatches show his right-wing convictions, criticizing inefficiency and unnecessary repression, but respecting strong government. He returned to London in 1908, taking a flat at 97 Mortimer Street, Cavendish Square. Handsome and impeccably dressed, with a slightly crooked smile that rarely became a laugh, he seems to have moved on the fringes of polite society with few, if any, intimate friends. Some people knew he was homosexual, with many young contacts, but that side of his life had to be secret.

By 1909 Munro had begun writing the short stories which were to make his reputation. Originally published in the *Westminster* and from 1911 in the *Morning Post* and elsewhere in the tory press, the stories were collected as *The Chronicles of Clovis* (1911), *Beasts and Super-Beasts* (1914), *The Toys of Peace* (1919), and *The Square Egg* (1924). Original though his best work is, its line of descent is clear: his epigrammatic style and witty, amoral young men such as Clovis Sangrail derive from Oscar Wilde, his fantastical humour owes much to Lewis Carroll, and some of his grimmer stories, like his politics, put him close to Kipling. In his turn he influenced comic writers of the next generation such as A. A. Milne, Noël Coward, and P. G. Wodehouse.

His methods were simple but ingenious. Characters are defined with a bizarre name and a deft phrase or two, the wit depends on perfect wording and unexpected turns, and the action is often some kind of practical joke, aimed at deflating pretension or exposing cowardice. Many of the stories bring animals into formerly placid households: a leopard in the bedroom, a wolf at a dinner party, a boar in the orchard. Occasionally the forces of wild nature are embodied in what Munro may have thought of as their truest image, a naked boy, beautiful and cruel.

In some ways Munro remained a boy himself, delighting in practical jokes and exotic animals, and scornful of the regulated adult world. Religion struck him as absurd. With his knowledge of less orderly places, he saw respectable English life as fragile and anaemic. The compression demanded by a newspaper column exactly suited the ruthless precision of his satire and the limitations of his talent. In his few long works the lack of mature human sympathy which runs throughout his writing is revealed as a real deficiency, wonderfully funny though its effects can be when confined to a few pages. He wrote two novels, *The Unbearable Bassington* (1912), the story of a wayward young man whose eventual exile may be the author's comment on his own isolation, and *When William Came* (1913), a portrait of England shamefully giving way to a German invasion (William being the Kaiser).

Munro enlisted in the ranks in August 1914 despite his age, first joining King Edward's Horse but soon transferring to the 22nd Royal Fusiliers. The contempt for pacifists and shirkers expressed in his wartime articles has been seen, inaccurately, as a betrayal of his earlier self, as though he had turned against drones such as Clovis, but Clovis would surely have enlisted too, enjoying patrolling in no man's land just as his creator did, imagining himself to be a wolf hunting fat farmers' wives. Like many others

Munro welcomed the war as the return of honour to a society which had become hypocritical and weak-willed. He refused a commission, preferring to serve as corporal and eventually lance sergeant, faultlessly courageous and efficient. His malaria recurred in November 1916, but he discharged himself from hospital on the 11th when he heard an offensive was due. The battle of the Ancre began on the 13th. Munro was killed by a sniper's bullet the next day during the final assault on Beaumont Hamel. He is listed on the Thiepval memorial as one of the many soldiers whose bodies were never found.

DOMINIC HIBBERD

Sources A. J. Langguth, *Saki: a life of Hector Hugh Munro* (1981) · E. Munro, 'Biography of Saki', in Saki, *The square egg and other sketches* (1924) · DNB · Commonwealth War Graves Commission, Maidenhead

Archives U. Reading L., corresp. and papers | BL, corresp. with League of Dramatists, Add. MSS 63417–63419 · Ransom HRC, corresp. with John Lane

Likenesses photographs, repro. in Langguth, *Saki*

Wealth at death £963 11s. 4d.: probate, 23 Dec 1916, *CGPLA Eng. & Wales*

Munro, Hugh Andrew Johnstone, of Novar (1797–1864), art collector, was born in London on 13 February 1797, the only son (there was also a daughter) of Sir Alexander Munro (d. 1809), at one time consul-general in Madrid, and his wife, Margaret Penelope Johnstone. His uncle was General Sir Hector Munro. On the death of his father in 1809 he became head of the Munros of Novar and succeeded to large estates, including that of Novar House, Ross-shire, thus becoming one of the chief landed proprietors in the counties of Ross, Cromarty, and Moray. From 1814 to 1817 he was a gentleman commoner at Christ Church, Oxford, but appears to have left without taking a degree. In 1816 he was admitted to Lincoln's Inn but there is no record of his ever being called to the bar. His London house was at 6 Hamilton Place.

Munro was an amateur artist and a distinguished collector, becoming, like Elhanan Bicknell, one of the chief patrons of J. M. W. Turner. He was of a shy, diffident, and even morbid temperament, a characteristic which enabled him to mix on more intimate terms than other collectors with the somewhat shy but more forceful and eccentric Turner. They became close friends, travelling together through France to Italy in 1836 and sketching alongside each other. Turner is said to have suggested the tour to help alleviate Munro's depression. He had financed Turner's journey to Venice in 1833 and in 1844 he became one of the four trustees of Turner's charity for the relief of decayed and indigent artists. He was also one of Turner's executors.

Unlike Bicknell, Munro formed a large collection of old masters in addition to the work of Turner and other contemporary British artists, such as Richard Bonington, John Constable, and Sir David Wilkie. This included Raphael's *Madonna dei candelabri* (Walters Arts Gallery, Baltimore), Veronese's *Vision of St Helena* (National Gallery, London), and Rembrandt's *Lucretia* (National Gallery, Washington). His collection of Turners was of greater and paramount importance. He owned some dozen oils, twenty or so large drawings, and fifty-five vignettes, all of which fetched high prices at sales from the collection during his lifetime and after his death. Among the more important Turner oils were *Venus and Adonis* (c.1803; priv. coll.), *Venice from the Porch of Madonna della Salute* (1837; commissioned by Munro but not liked by him, later sold, and now in New York, at the Metropolitan Museum), *Snow-Storm, Avalanche and Inundation* (1837; Art Institute, Chicago), *Modern Italy, the Pifferari* (Glasgow Art Gallery), and *Ancient Italy* (1838; priv. coll.). At his death the whole collection, old and modern masters, numbered some 2500. Seven sales by Christies between 1860 and 1878 aroused great public interest.

Munro never married. He had several illegitimate children, his son by Penelope Forbes being the distinguished classical scholar, also called Hugh Andrew Johnstone *Munro. Munro died at Novar House on 22 November 1864.   KENNETH GARLICK, *rev.*

Sources W. Thornbury, *The life of J. M. W. Turner*, 2 vols. (1862) · G. Redford, *Art sales: a history of sales of pictures and other works of art*, 2 vols. (1888) · M. Butlin and E. Joll, *The paintings of J. M. W. Turner*, 2 vols. (1977) · J. Holloway, 'H. A. J. Munro of Novar', *Review of Scottish Culture* (autumn 1991) · Foster, *Alum. Oxon.* · d. cert. · S. Whittingham, 'Munro [Munro of Novar], H(ugh) A(ndrew) J(ohnstone)', *The dictionary of art*, ed. J. Turner (1996)

Munro, Hugh Andrew Johnstone (1819–1885), classical scholar, born at Elgin, Moray, on 19 October 1819, was the illegitimate son of Penelope Forbes and Hugh Andrew Johnstone *Munro (1797–1864) of Novar, Ross-shire, the owner of a famous collection of pictures. His early youth was spent at Elgin. He was sent to Shrewsbury School in August 1833, and did well there. In 1836 Dr Benjamin Hall Kennedy (later of *Latin Primer* fame) became headmaster; Munro himself put on record (in his memoir of Edward Meredith Cope prefixed to the latter's posthumous edition of Aristotle's *Rhetoric*) the powerful influence of his enthusiasm and scholarship on the sixth form. In October 1838 Munro entered Trinity College, Cambridge, as a pensioner, was elected scholar in 1840, and university Craven scholar in 1841. In 1842 he graduated second classic (MA, 1845), and gained the first chancellor's medal. He was elected fellow of Trinity in 1843, and after staying in Paris, Florence, and Berlin, took holy orders and lectured on classical subjects at Trinity. From then until his death Trinity College was his home, though he made many visits to the continent, and usually spent part of the summer in Scotland.

Munro first attracted attention in Cambridge by his lectures on Aristotle; his first publication was a paper, read to the Philosophical Society on 11 February 1850, in which he reviewed with exceptional power and frankness Whewell's interpretation of Aristotle's account of inductive reasoning. Five years later, in the *Journal of Sacred and Classical Philology*, he published an important paper on Aristotle in which he maintained the Eudemian authorship of the fifth, sixth, and seventh books of the *Nicomachean Ethics*. The theory was adopted by Grant in his edition, and most British scholars agreed that Munro proved his point. But the main work of his life was in other fields.

Munro early turned his attention to Lucretius's poem *De rerum natura*; between 1849 and 1851 he collated all the Lucretian manuscripts in the Vatican and Laurentian libraries, and examined those at Leiden. When the *Journal of Sacred and Classical Philology* began to appear in 1854, he contributed several papers, chiefly on Lucretius. In 1860 he edited a text with a critical introduction; and in 1864 he published a revision of his text, with introductions, a prose translation, and a full commentary. The book was considered the most valuable contribution to Latin scholarship by a British scholar that century. In the three subsequent editions he tended more and more to defend the traditional text in passages where he had originally followed Lachmann in emendation.

In 1867 Munro published a text of the Latin poem known as *Aetna*, following the accidental discovery in the university library of a much better manuscript than any previously known. In 1868 he published a text of Horace, with a remarkable introduction, Horace's text being one of the most difficult problems of philology.

In 1869 a professorship of Latin was founded at Cambridge in honour of Dr Kennedy, and Munro was elected without competition. Shilleto expressed the general feeling when he wrote: 'Esto professor carus editor Cari, Carus Sabrinae, carior suae Grantae.' This position he resigned in 1872. His lectures did not attract undergraduates. He had no flow of language, spoke with a measured deliberation, and was sometimes absent-minded and digressed from his topic. He was made a LittD in 1884, received honorary degrees from Oxford (1873), Edinburgh (1872), and Dublin (1882), and in 1882 was president of the Philological Society.

Munro's publications included, besides classical texts and commentaries, articles in the *Transactions of the Cambridge Philosophical Society*, the *Journal of Sacred and Classical Philology*, and the *Journal of Philology*. *Criticisms and Elucidations of Catullus*—Munro's last book—appeared in 1878. Much of it had already been printed as articles in the *Journal of Philology*, to which he was a constant contributor from its first publication in 1864. This book contains the strongest evidence of his knowledge and appreciation of literature, both ancient and modern.

Throughout his life Munro enjoyed composing Greek and especially Latin verse, and many specimens may be seen in the *Sabrinae Corolla* and *Arundines Cami*. Though all his published Latin verses are translations, he often expressed his own thoughts in this form in private letters or in books given to friends. His verses have been attacked as not Ovidian. Against this Munro defended himself with characteristic vigour in his 'Modern Latin verse' in *Macmillan's Magazine* (February 1875). The charge is, perhaps, true; but if his verses are not Ovidian, they are certainly Latin. Just before his death he had privately printed a collection of these translations, and gave copies to his friends.

Munro had a high position among British scholars, with an unusual soundness of judgement and a love of great literature, in several languages. He considered Dante the greatest poet.

Munro's character, like his intellect, was strong. Generally reserved, and sometimes absent-minded, he united dignity and courteousness with a marked simplicity, and a strong antipathy for the false or mean. He had few intimate friends: to them his attachment was extraordinarily strong. He was of middle height and strongly built. His forehead was broad and massive, with thick nut-brown hair growing close to the head. The lines round the mouth were strongly marked and the lips tightly compressed. The general expression of his face was of strength and benignity.

Munro's strong constitution and temperate habits gave every promise of a long life; but in the spring of 1885 he suffered from insomnia and, going abroad for change and rest, he was attacked at Rome by an inflammation of the mucous membrane, and, when this was abating, a malignant abscess, which proved fatal, appeared on the neck. He died at the Hotel Quirinal, via Nazionale, Rome, on 30 March 1885. He was buried in the protestant cemetery at Rome, where his college erected a marble cross. Memorial brasses were also placed in Trinity College chapel and at Elgin Academy.   J. D. Duff, *rev.* Roger T. Stearn

Sources *The Athenaeum* (4 April 1885), 440–41 · personal knowledge (1894) · private information (1894) · Venn, *Alum. Cant.* · Boase, *Mod. Eng. biog.* · Foster, *Alum. Oxon.* · *CGPLA Eng. & Wales* (1885)

Likenesses F. Tuttle, oils, 1865, Trinity Cam. · T. Woolner, marble bust, 1886, Trinity Cam. · marble bust, FM Cam. · photograph, BM

Wealth at death £21,873 8s. 10d.: resworn probate, June 1885, *CGPLA Eng. & Wales*

Munro, Sir **Hugh Thomas**, of Lindertis, fourth baronet (1856–1919), mountaineer and landowner, was born on 16 October 1856 at 27 Eaton Place, London, the eldest of the nine children of Sir Campbell Munro of Lindertis, third baronet (1823–1913), and his wife, Henrietta Maria (*d.* 1912), daughter of John Drummond. Munro enjoyed a privileged childhood at the family residence in London and at their Scottish country estate near Kirriemuir, Forfarshire. The climbing career for which he gained posthumous fame began at the age of seventeen when, having travelled to Stuttgart to learn German, he first holidayed in the Alps. This trip also marked the beginning of a lifetime punctuated by foreign travel and interwoven with the martial and diplomatic networks of the British empire. As a young man Munro's training for a career in business was placed on hold after he found in military service a more obvious means to satisfy this wanderlust. Having spent several years abroad serving as an aide-de-camp, he travelled to the Cape of Good Hope in 1880. While this trip was initially restorative following an attack of pleurisy, an opportunist streak helped him secure a post as private secretary to Sir George Pomeroy Pomeroy-Colley, the governor of Natal. With the outbreak of hostilities in the Basuto War, Munro volunteered for active service and was given a posting as a courier in Landrey's Horse, an irregular cavalry corps. Much later in life his appointment as a king's messenger of foreign dispatches would revive

these field skills, although in the rather more luxurious circumstances which international diplomacy afforded.

Following his return to Britain from southern Africa, Munro's attention turned north to the ancestral seat in Forfarshire. First as estate manager and heir apparent, then, following his father's death in 1913, as laird and fourth baronet, Lindertis was the focus for family life and a base for local activism on behalf of the Conservative Party. A member of the central council of the Conservative Party in Scotland, he stood unsuccessfully as a parliamentary candidate for Kirkaldy district of burghs at the general election of 1885, but was subsequently elected a member of Forfarshire county council. He married Selina Dorothea, the daughter of Major-General Thomas Edmond Byrne, on 29 August 1892; the couple had a son and three daughters before the premature death of Selina in May 1902. Although he had a predictable enthusiasm for field sports and highland dress, family memories also reveal a less conventional dimension to Munro's establishment image. An idiosyncratic vein of natural mysticism was evidenced by a belief in the supernatural, his abilities as a water diviner, and the existence of heavenly music. That he had experienced the last of these atmospheric phenomena in the Scottish mountains is entirely appropriate. It was here, scaling the heights, that Munro was in his element.

Permanently bearded, compact, and wiry of stature, Munro was renowned among the membership of the Scottish Mountaineering Club for powers of endurance and resourcefulness, and for his redoubtable character on even the most demanding expeditions. Despite this muscular image, combined with a pair of feet small and nimble enough to secure his reputation as a skilled highland dancer, Munro was no mountain gymnast. He would happily skirt precipitous rock faces in favour of the simplest route leading to any mountain peak. Such an approach aligned him with the 'salvationist' tendency of the Scottish Mountaineering Club, as opposed to the rope-bound 'ultramontane' with whom they enjoyed a jocular, very masculine rivalry. A near permanent fixture at early outings and social gatherings, Munro's 'clubbable' nature led to his election as honorary president in 1894. He was equally comfortable walking alone. Equipped with compass, aneroid barometer, maps, thermometer, and measuring poles, he navigated his way across entire hill ranges, covering prodigious daily distances. The many published accounts of these arduous solo expeditions are functional and factual in character rather than effusive. However, they do attest to an enduring fascination with topographical survey techniques, and an obvious frustration with the still flawed 1-inch maps being produced by the Ordnance Survey. Thus his progress on any route was punctuated by regular stops to take aneroid readings, measure distances between prominent landscape features, fix summit heights, and scribble detailed notes on visible montane panoramas. It is tempting to see this enthusiasm for recorded fact and classificatory order as an extension of a boyhood yen for natural history, indulged in collections of butterflies, birds' eggs, shells, and fossils.

While measuring Scotland's 'mountains' was at first Munro's private passion, this pedestrian odyssey was to be afforded official sanction by the Scottish Mountaineering Club in 1889. His commission, to assemble an accurate list of all summits rising to heights of 3000 feet or above, clearly reflected the club's constitutional objective of furthering scientific study in the mountains. The completion of the project consumed Munro for three years. With a tenacity verging on fanaticism he even undertook some of the necessary field expeditions under cover of darkness in winter conditions. These clandestine operations were deemed the most effective means to respect the claims to privacy made by fellow sporting landowners. The results of these labours originally appeared in the club's journal of 1891. 'Munro's tables', as they would soon become known, listed some 283 mountains by name, height, grid reference number, and according to seventeen geographical areas. This did not mark an end to his efforts. Munro remained committed to the continual revision and refinement of the tables for the remainder of his life. Indeed, when he succumbed to pneumonia on 19 March 1919 at the Red Cross canteen which he had helped establish in Tarascon, southern France, a second edition of his treasured tables was very close to completion.

Steeped in the traditions of Victorian field science and imperial exploration, Hugh Munro's schema for mountain classification has since become a key influence on the popular understanding and experience of Scotland's geography. Thousands of 'Munro-baggers' devote their weekends to collecting the country's summits, with the long-term objective of 'compleating'. Ironically Munro, having failed to climb three peaks, was not the first to accomplish this feat. For active 'Munroists', and those now confined to the armchair, this discovery is emblematic of a contested and intriguing legacy. Munro's specific criteria for the award of mountain status were far from transparent. Although he relied heavily on repeatable scientific practice, this was combined with value judgements on the relative merits of different landscapes. Thus while certain shapely peaks were considered deserving of inclusion in the tables, less distinctive points of the required height were assigned the more lowly status of a 'top'. Although revised metric maps produced by the Ordnance Survey, depicting the 3000 feet contour with greater accuracy, have led to the discovery and deletion of Munros, other amendments have been made by the Scottish Mountaineering Club on less obviously objective grounds. That ultimate sanction for these decisions still lies with just one organization means that the whole question of promotion to, and deletion from, the tables remains highly contentious among the climbing community. The debates show few signs of subsiding.

Munro was buried near Lindertis on 2 April 1919. From his graveside several 'mountains' are in view.

HAYDEN LORIMER

Sources R. Campbell, ed., *The Munroist's companion* (1999) • T. Weir, 'Munro and his mountains', *Scotland* (1980), 61–8 • R. Campbell, 'Munro and the salvationist tendency', *Scottish Mountaineering Club Journal*, 34 (1989), 219–27 • W. Douglas, 'Obituary of Munro', *Scottish Mountaineering Club Journal*, 15 (1919), 214–19 • *Kirriemuir Observer* (4 April 1919) • R. Campbell, 'Munro's tables, 1891–1991', *Scottish Mountaineering Club Journal*, 35 (1991), 21–7 • Burke, *Peerage* (1999) [Munro of Lindertis] • WWW

Archives NL Scot., Scottish Mountaineering Club holdings

Likenesses photograph, repro. in Campbell, ed., *Munroist's companion*, p. 43

Wealth at death £151,063 6s. 8d. in UK: inventory, 14 July 1919, CCI

Munro, Ian Arthur Hoyle (1923–1997), medical journalist, was born on 5 November 1923, in Bradford, Yorkshire, the only son of Gordon Alexander Munro (1889–1934), chartered accountant, and his wife, Muriel Rebecca, *née* Hoyle (d. 1938). He was educated at Huddersfield College, Yorkshire; Paston School, North Walsham, Norfolk; Royal Liberty School, Romford, Essex; and Guy's Hospital medical school, London, where he graduated in 1946. After service with the Royal Army Medical Corps and a short period of training in radiology he joined the editorial staff of *The Lancet* in 1951. Thus almost the whole of his working life was spent on this weekly medical journal. He was appointed deputy editor in 1964 and was editor from July 1976 until his retirement in November 1988. In 1948 he married Olive Isabel (b. 1926), the only daughter of Ernest and Isabella Jackson, and herself a doctor. In 1959 they settled at Oakwood, Bayley's Hill, Sevenoaks, Kent. They had three sons and two daughters.

Not all medical editors are journalists, but working for a weekly journal in medicine demands that both hats be available and, sometimes, worn at the same time. Munro was happier in the campaigning journalist role but he knew that uncomfortable facts should be made available even if they ran counter to things he believed in, such as women's choice in the abortion law reform debate and family planning. If studies on oral contraceptive safety pointed to the need for caution he did not hesitate to publish. Towards the end of his editorship the journal switched from selective to routine outside refereeing of biomedical research, so he was the last of a line prepared occasionally, even with difficult decisions, to go by his gut feeling for a paper's validity and usefulness to readers.

Throughout Munro's time the journal's editorial staff wrote anonymously; his true bibliography would be prodigious, with countless editorials, news notes, book reviews and so on. *The Lancet* in 1951 was still in essence a British journal. By the time Munro retired it was far more international and thus less able to cover in detail British medico-political affairs. Munro was a staunch supporter of the idea and the ideals of the National Health Service (NHS), and he believed that this model of health care delivery deserved worldwide attention. Any government or medical body seeming to lose sight of those ideals would soon feel his editorial wrath; he once called upon a secretary of state to resign, though he mellowed years later to concede that that might have been 'a bit over the top'. Perhaps because of his interest in radiology and also because of the era in which he studied medicine, the danger of nuclear war was a professional concern too. In *The Lancet* Munro supported the activities of International Physicians for the Prevention of Nuclear War, and later he became the first president of Physicians for Human Rights, UK. To him nuclear weapons and the testing of them were medical matters.

A major outside interest was sport; Munro's passion for cricket was lifelong and his performance of it nearly so, for he played the game, in the dogged style of another Yorkshireman, Geoffrey Boycott, far longer than his contemporaries. This was a world apart: newcomers to *The Lancet* were sometimes bemused to see Munro's large-framed, bespectacled figure proceeding around the office with curious movements of the limbs—until told that this was the editor practising for the weekend. For too long a sort of cold war persisted between *The Lancet* and the British Medical Association's organ, the *BMJ*, stemming from the 1940s when the two weeklies stood on opposite sides (*The Lancet* for, the *BMJ* against) in the furore over the birth of the NHS. Munro built bridges, choosing a sporting arena to do this. Even then, while other staff enjoyed the croquet, the two journals' editors were seen engaged in serious debate about the rules; no sport, to Munro, was a matter for levity. When retirement beckoned the *BMJ* generously dedicated a dinner to him; a hatchet, already blunted, was finally buried. There was a celebratory collection of essays, too, referring to Ian Munro's steadfastness ('swerving neither to the right nor the left'). But he was a man of the left in politics, medical and other, and that was where he firmly stayed.

In retirement Munro's medical interests remained, and beautifully honed letters of the type that had got him into journalism in the first place were still being composed in the month before his death, which took place at the Kent and Sussex Hospital, Tunbridge Wells, on 22 January 1997. He was buried at St George's Church, Sevenoaks Weald, Kent, on 31 January; he was survived by his wife and five children.   DAVID SHARP

Sources *The Times* (7 Feb 1997) · *Medical Register* · *Medical Directory* · *WWW* · personal knowledge (2004) · private information (2004) [Olive Munro] · d. cert.
Likenesses photograph, Office of *The Lancet* · photograph, repro. in *The Times*
Wealth at death £277,688: probate, 20 Aug 1997, *CGPLA Eng. & Wales*

Munro, Innes (d. 1827), army officer and writer, was related to Sir Hector Munro of Novar. He was appointed on 29 December 1777 to a lieutenancy in the 73rd, afterwards 71st, highlanders, then raised by Lord Macleod. As lieutenant and captain in the 1st battalion of that regiment he took part in the campaigns of 1780–84 against Haidar Ali, which he afterwards described, and at the close was placed on half pay as a captain of the disbanded 2nd battalion of the regiment. On 8 July 1793 he was brought on full pay as captain in the Scottish brigade (disbanded as the 94th foot in 1818). He belonged to that regiment until 1808, when he left the army as major and brevet lieutenant-colonel. He had served for many years as paymaster of a recruiting district.

Munro, who had married Ann, daughter of George Gordon, minister of Clyne, died at his seat, at Poyntzfield, Cromarty, in 1827. He published *A narrative of the military operations on the Coromandel coast against the combined forces of the French, Dutch and Hyder Ally Cawn, from the year 1780 to the peace in 1784* (1789), and *A Guide to Farm Book-Keeping Based on Actual Practice* (1821). John Donaldson wrote that the latter was 'the most complex idea that has ever been published. It may amuse the gentleman, but would never suit the farmer' (Donaldson, 113).

H. M. CHICHESTER, rev. JAMES LUNT

Sources I. Munro, *A narrative of the military operations on the Coromandel coast* (1789) · *Army List* · J. Donaldson, *Agricultural biography* (1854)

Munro, James (1832–1908), politician and temperance advocate in Australia, was born on 7 January 1832 at Glen Dubh in the parish of Eddrachillis, Sutherland, the second son of Donald Munro, a tenant farmer, and his wife, Georgina, *née* Mackey. He left Armadale village school in 1848 to be apprenticed to Constable's printing works in Edinburgh. Here he soon joined the total abstinence movement. On 28 November 1853 he married Jane, the daughter of Donald Macdonald, a fellow printer, and in 1858 they migrated to Victoria with their three children.

After working as a printer, from the mid-1860s Munro emerged in the three main areas of his public life—property investments, the abstinence movement, and politics. In 1865 he established the Victorian Permanent Property Investment and Building Society, of which he was secretary for seventeen years. He acquired interests in the Melbourne Woollen Mill Company and the Victoria Permanent Fire Insurance Company. In 1882 he established the Federal Banking Company and the associated Federal Building Society, which became his main means to extensive land dealing, speculation, and manipulation during the Melbourne land boom.

Munro won respect for his puritanical Presbyterianism and charitable activities. He was on the board of management of the Toorak Presbyterian Church (1878–92), a board member of the Alfred Hospital (1876–85), and a vice-president of the Caledonian Society of Melbourne. Sabbatarian and total abstinence advocacy preoccupied him, and he was prominent in the order of Rechabites, the Melbourne Total Abstinence Society (president, 1878–92), the Permissive Bill Association, and its successor, the Victorian Alliance for the Suppression of Liquor Traffic (president, 1881–92). He was also president of the two international temperance conferences held in Melbourne. He was a major shareholder in the grandiose temperance coffee palaces in Melbourne (Federal, Grand, and Victoria) and in Geelong and Broken Hill, which all soon ran into financial difficulties.

Having entered local politics, in 1872–3 Munro was shire president of Gardiner shire. He stood unsuccessfully for parliament in 1869 but held various seats over twelve years between 1874 and 1890. As a supporter of protective tariffs, railway building, land reform, and votes for women (which be hoped would help the temperance campaign), he was associated with various shades of liberals, though he was in cabinet for only three months. One of his main parliamentary achievements was pressing for the 1880 International Exhibition.

In the late 1880s Munro reached the brief peak of his public life. He was one of the principal land boomers and acquired large leaseholds throughout the north of Australia. Having borrowed heavily to finance his investments, he appeared as a man of great wealth, living in a mansion in suburban Armadale. In 1887 he established the Real Estate Mortgage and Deposit Bank, and in 1890 he visited Britain to raise more capital for his speculations. His criticism of the Gillies–Deakin coalition government's financial management led to his leadership of the more liberal parliamentary opposition. In October 1890 Munro carried a no-confidence motion and on 5 November he formed his own government, though he was hardly the man to implement financial reform.

The fragility of the boom, government finances, and his own financial empire now began to fracture. Munro struggled through 1891 to salvage his fortune and the government, but on 16 February 1892 he resigned and took refuge as Victorian agent-general in London. His escape was short-lived and he returned to witness the collapse of the Federal Bank in January 1893 and to file for bankruptcy in the following month, his failures contrasting with his moral pretensions.

After living on the charity of his family, Munro started a small suburban estate agency and auction room, and twice more stood unsuccessfully for parliament. He was widowed in 1904 and died at his daughter's residence in Caulfield, Melbourne, on 25 February 1908, survived by four of his five sons and his three daughters. He was buried at St Kilda on 27 February.   DON GARDEN

Sources AusDB · M. Cannon, *The land boomers* (1966) · G. Serle, *The golden age: a history of the colony of Victoria, 1851–1861* (1963) · G. Serle, *The rush to be rich* (1971) · T. W. H. Leavitt, ed., *Australian representative men* (1887) · A. Sutherland, *Victoria and its metropolis* (1888) · *Table Talk* (9 Oct 1891) · *Table Talk* (6 Oct 1893) · *The Argus* [Melbourne] (26 Feb 1908) · parish register (banns and marriages), 1853, Edinburgh

Munro, Neil [*pseud.* Hugh Foulis] (**1863–1930**), novelist and journalist, was born on 3 June 1863 (and not 1864 as often stated) in Crombie's Land, Inveraray, Argyll. His mother was Ann Munro, a kitchen maid, perhaps at Inveraray Castle. His death certificate names John Thompson Munro, farmer, as his father, but despite the lack of any concrete evidence, it has been rumoured that his father was of the house of Argyll. Soon after his birth Neil and his mother moved to his grandmother Ann McArthur Munro's home in McVicar's Land, and in this Gaelic-speaking household he lived for most of his childhood. In 1875 his mother married Malcolm Thomson, prison governor.

Munro's formal education at Inveraray parish school under the scholarly Henry Dunn Smith was supplemented by his voracious appetite for reading. About 1877 he left school and became a clerk to William Douglas, a local lawyer, but found the work tedious and even then seems to have been preparing himself for a career in journalism. Like many young Gaels, however, he found no other satisfactory employment in the highlands and on 1 June 1881 he moved to Glasgow. There he soon became a reporter, working successively on the *Greenock Advertiser*,

Neil Munro [Hugh Foulis] (1863–1930), by William Strang, 1903

the *Glasgow News*, the *Falkirk Herald*, and, finally, the paper he was to remain with for the rest of his working life, the *Glasgow Evening News*, where he was made chief reporter under the editor James Murray Smith at the age of only twenty-three. In the meantime he had married Jessie Ewing Adam, daughter of Hugh and Euphemia Adam, on 23 July 1885.

Although a gifted journalist Munro believed this to be the inferior side of the writer's craft and sought to become a novelist, making his first mark on the literary scene in 1896 with his innovative collection of short stories *The Lost Pibroch and other Sheiling Stories*. In these powerful and somewhat bitter highland pieces he seeks to counteract—perhaps too extremely—the sentimentality of contemporary Scottish kailyard and 'Celtic twilight' writing, and to portray the highlander accurately in a language which captures Gaelic idiom.

In 1897 Munro reduced his journalistic commitment to two anonymous weekly columns, 'The Looker on' and 'Views and reviews', to allow himself to concentrate on his literary work, and in 1898 his well-judged romantic historical novel *John Splendid* appeared. Told from the Campbell point of view, it deals with the sack of Inveraray by Montrose and his subsequent victory over the Campbells at Inverlochy in 1645. Like most of Munro's novels it is set in a period of major social change, and analyses its effects on the highlands.

In 1899 the partly autobiographical novel *Gilian the Dreamer* was published. It deals with a young boy whose undisciplined poetic gifts manifest themselves in excessive sensibility and impede his maturity and his ability to act effectively. He has affinities with Tommy Sandys in J. M. Barrie's *Sentimental Tommy* (1896) and his failure to grow up properly makes him a kind of highland Peter Pan. This was followed by three tales, *Doom Castle* (1901), *The Shoes of Fortune* (1901), and *Children of Tempest* (1903), all loosely connected with the aftermath of the Jacobite rising of 1745.

Munro published a vast number of highly amusing sketches in his column 'The Looker on'. For their publication in book form he used the pen name Hugh Foulis. These included stories about the waiter Erchie MacPherson and the commercial traveller Jimmy Swan, but most famous of all were his tales of the eccentric captain Para Handy and the crew of the puffer *The Vital Spark*. The first of these appeared in 1905, and he continued to produce them for most of his working life. Ironically, it is for these he was best remembered.

After *Children of Tempest* Munro felt that he had carried the theme of highland historical romance far enough and turned with *The Daft Days* (1907) and later *Fancy Farm* (1910) to the contemporary scene, but with far less success. In 1908 he was honoured with an LLD from Glasgow University, and in 1909 with the freedom of Inveraray. Not surprisingly, then, he returned to historical romance and in 1914 produced his finest novel, *The New Road*. Ostensibly this is the story of the hero's quest for information about his Jacobite father's mysterious death, but at a deeper level it examines the forces which shape individual destinies. Like Scott's *Waverley* (1814) it shows the hero's gradual disillusionment with the superficial glamour of the highlands as he begins to recognize many of the chiefs for the scoundrels that they are. Eventually he comes to believe that only by trade will the highlands ultimately be civilized, and that the instrument to achieve this will be the new road that Wade is building between Stirling and Inverness. This road becomes a symbol of a more civilized and prosperous way of life for Gaeldom but, at the same time, it will destroy the old Gaelic way of life for ever.

With the outbreak of the First World War Munro returned to full-time journalism. In 1915 his son Hugh was killed in France, near Albert. This trauma, coupled with the pressure of work on the *Glasgow Evening News*—he became editor in 1918—seemed to inhibit further large-scale literary production. From this time, apart from the short story collection 'Jaunty Jock and other Stories' (1918), only the typescript of the first ten chapters of a novel entitled *The Search*, a sequel to *The New Road*, survives.

In 1927, in failing health, Munro reluctantly retired from the newspaper, where he was loved for his kindness and affability. In retirement he wrote a *History of the Royal Bank of Scotland* (1928) and articles for the *Daily Record and Mail*. In October 1930 he was honoured with a second LLD,

this time from Edinburgh University. Munro died a few months later on 22 December, as the result of cerebral thrombosis at his home, Cromalt, in Craigendoran, Helensburgh, and was survived by his wife, one son, and four daughters. He was buried at Kilmalieu cemetery, Inveraray. In 1935, at the dedication of the monument erected to his memory in Glen Aray, R. B. Cunninghame Graham praised him as the 'apostolic successor of Sir Walter Scott'.

Munro's high literary reputation declined after 1925 when he became the object of adverse criticism by C. M. Grieve (Hugh MacDiarmid) who accused him of escapism and not dealing with the great national and highland issues of the day. Late twentieth-century scholarship, however, has shown that Munro's critique of highland life was much more penetrating than MacDiarmid had perceived.   RONALD W. RENTON

Sources L. Bratton, unpublished biography [by Neil Munro's granddaughter] · b. cert. · d. cert. · H. Völkel, *Das literarische Werk Neil Munros* (1996) · R. W. Renton, 'The major fiction of Neil Munro', MPhil. diss., U. Glas., 1997
Archives NL Scot., corresp. and papers | Horner Art Gallery and Reference Library, letters to Thomas Fraser · Inveraray primary school, Neil Munro Society archive · NL Scot., letters to William Blackwood and Sons, and J. P. MacGillivray · NL Scot., letters to John Macleay · U. Glas. L., special collections department, letters to R. G. Smith
Likenesses W. Strang, pastel drawing, 1903, Scot. NPG [*see illus.*] · S. Dean, oils, Scot. NPG · pencil drawing, repro. in *The Bailey* (24 July 1907) · photographs, priv. coll.
Wealth at death £7529 3s. 3d.: 1930, CCI

Munro, Robert (*c.*1645–1704), Roman Catholic priest, was born in Ross-shire, the son of George Munro. After conversion to Roman Catholicism he entered the Scots College, Douai, on 17 May 1663, was at the Scots College, Paris, from February 1666 until February 1668, took the missionary oath at the Scots College, Rome, on 6 June 1668, and left Rome as a missionary priest in 1671.

Munro's priestly work was mainly in Strathglass and Glengarry, but missionary journeys took him to Moidart (1678), to the isles (1679), and to Knoydart (1688). His success at winning converts earned him criticism from the presbyteries of Dingwall and Inverness. In 1678 he accompanied Alexander Leslie on a visitation of the highlands and islands ordered in Rome by the Congregatio de Propaganda Fide. In the following year, against the wishes of Alexander Dunbar, prefect apostolic for Scotland, Munro joined the army of Lord MacDonnell of Glengarry against the earl of Argyll, who had been ordered to disarm papists, especially in the highlands. In 1688 Munro joined the Jacobite army as chaplain and was present at the battle of the Boyne. In 1696 he was arrested, imprisoned, and banished.

On his arrival on the continent Munro was imprisoned again, in Ghent, but was released through the efforts of Louis Innes and the Jesuits, and stayed for a short time at the Scots College, Paris. On his return to Scotland he was captured at sea, imprisoned at Plymouth and London, and banished again. Nevertheless he was soon back at his priestly labours in the Scottish highlands. In 1702 he subscribed to a letter of appeal against the Jesuits who had been accusing secular priests of Jansenism. In 1704 he was arrested, thrown across a horse as he was too ill to ride, and taken to Glengarry Castle where, left unattended for two days, he died on 17 January 1704, regarded as a martyr.   BRIAN M. HALLORAN

Sources W. Clapperton, 'Memoirs of Scotch missionary priests', 1901, Scottish Catholic Archives, Columba House, Edinburgh, 149–60 · J. Ritchie, *Robert Munro, highland priest* [n.d.] · W. Forbes-Leith, ed., *Memoirs of Scottish Catholics*, 2 vols. (1909), vol 2, pp. 218, 403 · itinerary of Alexander Leslie, visitor of the Scots mission, U. Aberdeen, King's College, 2260 box R · J. F. S. Gordon, *Ecclesiastical chronicle for Scotland*, 4: *Journal and appendix to Scotichronicon and Monasticon* (1875), 584–5 · P. J. Anderson, ed., *Records of the Scots colleges at Douai, Rome, Madrid, Valladolid and Ratisbon*, New Spalding Club, 30 (1906), 45, 118 · Bishop Geddes's memoirs and letters, John Thomson's missionary memoirs 1688–1787, Scottish Catholic Archives, Columba House, Edinburgh, Blairs collection (BL) · M. Dilworth, 'Munro, Robert', *DSCHT* · B. M. Halloran, *The Scots College, Paris, 1603–1792* (1997), 52, 67, 81, 105, 209
Archives Scottish Catholic Archives, Edinburgh, BL collection, letters

Munro [Monro], **Sir Robert, of Foulis, sixth baronet** (1684–1746), army officer and politician, was born on 24 August 1684, probably at Foulis, Ross-shire, the eldest son of Sir Robert Munro, fifth baronet (*d.* 1729), and his wife, Jean, daughter of Duncan *Forbes of Culloden (1643–1704). He was the great-nephew of the royalist general Sir George Monro. He may have attended Edinburgh University before joining the army. He served in Flanders, being commissioned a captain of the 1st foot in 1710. He entered parliament for Tain burghs in 1710 and voted with the whigs. He married, probably in 1713, Mary (*d.* 1732), daughter of Henry Seymour MP, of Woodlands, Dorset. They had three sons and a daughter.

In December 1714 Munro wrote from London about the slow allocation of places in Scotland but opined that 'our Scots great men' will 'all agree in opposing the Tories' (*More Culloden Papers*, 2.50–51). Munro himself was appointed lieutenant-colonel and captain of an independent company later that month. He was active in the Jacobite rising of 1715 in assisting John Sutherland, sixteenth earl of Sutherland, in detaining William Mackenzie, fifth earl of Seaforth, and a Jacobite force of three thousand in Caithness which prevented them from reinforcing the main Jacobite army under John Erskine, twenty-second earl of Mar, and this enabled Mar's march south to be checked. The price was somewhat heavy, however, as Seaforth's men ravaged the Munro estates. Upon taking Inverness in November 1715 Munro was appointed governor until he was succeeded by Simon Fraser, twelfth Lord Lovat, the following year. In April 1716 General William Cadogan sent Munro to London to report on the situation in Scotland, adding an encomium to his messenger as 'the first man in this kingdom who took arms for his majesty … the preservation of Inverness is very much owing to his vigilance and resolution … and not less useful in Parliament than in the field' (BL, Add. MS 61161, fol. 228). As a reward for his loyalty, in 1716 Munro was appointed a commissioner of forfeited estates, which post he

continued to hold until the commission was wound up in 1725. As a supporter of the whig government he was credited with £6000 fictitious stock by the South Sea Company in March 1721 which he sold back to the company at a profit a month later.

Munro succeeded his father on 11 September 1729 and continued to sit for Tain burghs at Westminster, dividing his time between Foulis and London. He was also active as an elder in the Church of Scotland, representing Dingwall in the general assembly, and forming a notable acquaintance with the nonconformist minister Dr Philip Doddridge, who educated his eldest son at an academy in Northamptonshire. Munro seems to have had surplus capital which he lent to his neighbours, for in September 1735 he was unable to lend money because he himself was owed £70,000 Scots 'interest and principal' (BL, Add. MS 39189, fol. 143). In 1739 he was named lieutenant-colonel of a new highland regiment known as the Black Watch. Munro undertook the regiment's training in Scotland. At the 1741 general election Munro lost his seat in the Commons to Charles Areskine, the lord advocate, who was a protégé of Archibald Campbell, earl of Ilay, the government's chief manager in Scotland. Munro petitioned against Areskine's return and the election was declared void. In the resultant by-election Munro lost out again, this time to the new lord advocate, Robert Craigie, backed by the new Scottish secretary, John Hay, fourth marquess of Tweeddale. Munro's regiment was marched to London in April 1743, whereupon it suffered some desertions following rumours that it was destined for the West Indies. In fact they were sent to Flanders, where they fought at Fontenoy on 11 May 1745, using the peculiar tactic of falling to the ground when the French fired, and then rushing in on the enemy before they had chance to reload and discharging their own volley. The only man in the regiment not to fall to the ground was Munro—'the fat knight' (*More Culloden Papers*, 3.89)—who, owing to age and corpulence, preferred to remain upright. The regiment then covered Cumberland's retreat from the battle. In June 1745 Munro was promoted colonel of the 37th foot.

The outbreak of the Jacobite rising of 1745 saw Munro and his new regiment ordered to Scotland, where it fought at the battle of Falkirk on 17 January 1746. The Jacobite clans overran his position, but Munro held firm and was killed, along with his brother Dr Robert Munro. Other reports had Munro killed after the battle while his brother was tending his wounds. He was buried the following day in Falkirk churchyard. He was succeeded by his son Harry, who was able to regain the parliamentary seat of Tain burghs in the general election of 1747.

STUART HANDLEY

Sources R. R. Sedgwick, 'Munro, Robert', HoP, *Commons, 1715–54* · GEC, *Baronetage* · A. Mackenzie, *History of the Munros of Fowlis* (1898), 96–138 · Walpole, *Corr.*, 19.204 · B. Lenman, *The Jacobite clans of the Great Glen* (1984), 86–7, 120, 133, 138 · BL, Add. MSS 39189–39190 · BL, Add. MS 61161, fol. 228 · D. Warrand, ed., *More Culloden papers*, 5 vols. (1923–30), vols. 2–4 · *Commons Journals*, 19.569, 571, 578 · *Descriptive list of secretaries of state: state papers Scotland, series 2, 1688–1782* (1996)

Archives BL, letters to Mackenzie of Siddie, Add. MSS 39189–39190 · NL Scot., letters to Forbes family

Munro, Sir Thomas, first baronet (1761–1827), army officer in the East India Company and administrator in India, was born on 27 May 1761 at Glasgow, the second of the seven children of Alexander Munro (*d.* 1809), a Glasgow merchant trading with Virginia, and his wife, Margaret, *née* Stark (*d.* 1807).

Education and early career The Munros, members of the Scottish Episcopal church, were minor members of Glasgow's merchant community who lived comfortably but unostentatiously on the booming tobacco trade with America. The family valued education and Thomas, who attended Glasgow grammar school and, from the age of thirteen to sixteen, Glasgow University, where mathematics and chemistry were favourite subjects, supplemented a good formal education with voracious reading. He was expected to become a merchant and from 1777 to 1779 was apprenticed in the accounting office of Sommerville and Gordon, a large Glasgow company trading with the West Indies. But the effects of the American War of Independence (1775–83) bankrupted his father, and in 1779 a cadetship in the East India Company's army was obtained for him instead. Alexander Munro struggled to re-establish his financial position but, from this time, Thomas's parents, his two sisters, Erskine and Margaret, and his two youngest brothers, James and William, were dependent on the funds the three eldest boys, Daniel, Thomas, and Alexander, sent home from India.

Thomas Munro, who was 6 feet tall and of lean and athletic build, was eighteen years old when he saw his first military service in the often ineptly conducted Second Anglo-Mysore War (1780–84). The war increased concerns in Britain over the company's arbitrary, insolvent, and inefficient rule and, in 1784, the India Act was passed to provide a more satisfactory government structure for British India. Perceptive statesmen, including Munro, recognized the value of Indian resources and the prestige of ruling India to Britain's position as a world power. But India was valuable also to able, ambitious men with inadequate access to patronage: careers could be built there to advance their status at home. Pitfalls for the most determined careerist, however, existed in the jealousy between the crown and company armies, between the company's civil and military services, and between the judicial and revenue branches of the civil service; in increasing tension between the company and the British government over control of Indian policy; and in factional rivalries within the company. In addition, in the intellectual climate generated by the French Revolution and the impeachment of Warren Hastings, interest in Britain in forms of government—their morality as well as their practical expediency—made it imperative for administrative recommendations for India to be justified on both grounds. Munro's rise to prominence took place within this setting. A strong-minded, intelligent, and articulate man, who was also generous and good-humoured—

Sir Thomas Munro, first baronet (1761–1827), by Ramsay Richard Reinagle

although his humour could be bitingly sarcastic when directed at his critics—Munro made enemies as well as loyal friends and worked hard for success.

Reforming Indian land tenure Promotion, determined by seniority in the company service, was slow, and Munro was further handicapped by having no influential connections and by partial deafness. In 1781 he was told that the latter, the result of measles, disqualified him from a coveted appointment as adjutant—an incident that suggests his deafness may sometimes have limited the appointments for which he was considered suitable. Interested in the science as well as the practice of warfare, Munro wrote perceptive accounts of military affairs during the 1780s and 1790s, which his father abstracted and sent to influential people, hoping they would be impressed and promote his son's career. But it was through his own efforts, during tedious years of garrison duty, to learn Indian languages and study the political and military systems of Mysore and the Marathas (states that threatened British interests) that Munro obtained advancement. In 1788 he joined the intelligence department under Captain Alexander Read, with whom he served until 1799. During Lord Cornwallis's prosecution of the Third Anglo-Mysore War (1790–92) they worked in intelligence and supply, but when the war concluded with the cession of territory to Madras presidency by Mysore's ruler, Tipu Sultan, Cornwallis, recognizing the importance of language skills, appointed Read to organize the revenue system of one of the ceded districts, the Baramahal, and Munro became his assistant. The appointment of military officers to important civilian posts angered Madras civilians, but the assignment proved to be a turning point in Munro's career.

Read and Munro took a different approach to land tenure and revenue collection from Cornwallis, who favoured large landed proprietors as agents of agricultural improvement, an English-type judiciary, and Europeans, not Indians, in all important positions. In Bengal Cornwallis adapted the local *zamindari* system to achieve these ends. *Zamindars*, large landholders who had also acted as tax collectors and magistrates, gained ownership of the lands they had administered and permanently fixed revenue assessments, but lost their judicial powers. Read and Munro took over a land tenure and revenue system known as ryotwar (ryot means peasant), customary in parts of south India, and adapted it to their ends. Munro wanted to create a society of numerous small but independent landowners rather than a few great ones, on the ground that the widest possible distribution of agricultural wealth benefited both individuals and the state. He expected inevitable differences in applications of skill and industry by individual cultivators to create a substantial, middling rank of yeoman farmers who would recognize that their prosperity depended on law and order, and would support the company government that provided it. Munro disliked both *zamindari* and *mahalwari* (coparcenary tenure, a third alternative system) on the ground that neither large landowners with numerous tenants nor communal landholders had much incentive to work hard to increase production. The ryotwari system regarded the state as supreme landlord but made individual peasants into small landowners. A detailed survey placed a value on each field—a fixed percentage of what it might, considering the nature of its soil, be expected to produce—and each cultivator then paid rent directly to a state collector for the land he wished to cultivate, receiving an annual receipt in return that gave him title to the land. As incentives for improved production, Munro, ideally, wanted low and fixed rents. The ryotwari system rarely operated in practice as Read and Munro intended; quiet compromises with local peasant élite interests were often necessary. But it provided the basis for Munro's future administrative work and, owing partly to his ability as a writer to promote it in terms that paid attention to both practical and moral considerations, and partly to increasing dissatisfaction with the *zamindari* system, ryotwar attracted interest.

The outbreak of the Fourth Anglo-Mysore War (1799) brought Munro back to army supply, but the death of Tipu Sultan in May ended it, and Munro and his friend John Malcolm were appointed secretaries to the commission established by the governor-general, Lord Wellesley, to arrange the settlement of Mysore. Munro forged a lasting friendship with one of the commissioners: the governor-general's brother, Arthur Wellesley, later duke of Wellington.

With the commission concluded Munro was appointed collector of the newly acquired district of Kanara, 8300 square miles of difficult terrain, scattered landholdings, and potentially unruly people. Munro remained in Kanara only from July 1799 to October 1800, but his success under difficult circumstances established his reputation as a skilled administrator. He restored order, partly by gaining support for company rule from the region's most militant landholders by granting them low revenue assessments; he kept Arthur Wellesley's army efficiently supplied as it hunted down a predatory Maratha adventurer; and he wrote two reports that impressed the authorities. In addition to providing a detailed analysis of the condition of the region, he claimed to have found evidence, in the form of village records, suggesting the land tenure system he favoured: numerous small, privately owned agricultural holdings with moderate, fixed revenue assessments, was the traditional form in Kanara. Later research has failed to discover these records and possibly Munro exaggerated the evidence to promote his own system. His authoritative reports, however, convinced Lord Wellesley that he should be given an even more challenging task: the settlement of the disordered region the nizam of Hyderabad was ceding to the company under the terms of a new alliance.

Munro spent seven years in the Ceded Districts, an arid region half the size of England, perpetually threatened by famine and home to numerous militant *poligars* (local warrior chiefs). Wellesley hoped Munro would transform the *poligars* into responsible *zamindari* landlords, thus achieving his dual objectives of pacification and the introduction of the Bengal revenue and judicial system. But Munro suppressed the *poligars* and introduced the ryotwari revenue system which, he claimed, promoted law, order, prosperity, and the 'attachment' of the people, because when everyone was the proprietor of their own land, everyone had an interest in the stability the company government provided. Munro was criticized for his repression of the *poligars*. His revenue policies met with opposition and, as a soldier holding civilian office, he was resented by Madras civilians. But his tough stance on the *poligars* brought order, few Madras civilians had the language skills required for his job, and his logistical skills were highly valued by Arthur Wellesley during the Second Anglo-Maratha War (1803–5). In October 1806 even the civilians of the Madras board of revenue conceded that the satisfactory state of the Ceded Districts was due to 'the superior merits of … Lieutenant-Colonel Munro' (Gleig, 2.238).

In August 1807, on the eve of his departure for Britain on leave, Munro wrote two minutes which represent his mature thought on the administration of British India. One compared the relative merits of the ryotwari and *zamindari* systems; the second, 'Trial by panchayat' (*panchayat* means jury or court of arbitration), contained Munro's recommendations on judicial matters. Munro was tired of administration but anxious he would find nothing to do in Britain. These minutes helped him obtain his next important post.

In Britain, and return to India as judicial commissioner For the three years of his official leave Munro was restless and frustrated, and often wished he had never left India. But in 1811, after obtaining an extension to his leave, he became involved in Indian affairs as an informal adviser to the London authorities who were preparing the 'fifth report' on the state of the Indian government prior to the company's charter renewal application (1813). Munro was consulted on army reform and on trade and missionary issues, but it was on his revenue and judicial recommendations, for which support was growing, that his opinion was most keenly sought. His most dedicated disciple, James Cumming, a member of the permanent staff of the government Board of Control for India and author of the Madras section of the 'fifth report', incorporated many of Munro's reports in its appendix. By 1814 it was decided, although not unanimously, to abandon the policy of introducing the *zamindari* system throughout British India and to use Munro's ryotwari revenue and judicial system instead in those districts of the Madras and Bombay presidencies not yet settled.

On 30 March 1814 Munro married the much younger Jane (d. 21 Sept 1850), daughter of Richard Campbell of Craigie, Ayrshire. She was the cultivated woman with a mind 'above the common' and pleasant disposition he had hoped to find (MS Eur. F/151/144) and their marriage was happy. They had two sons, Thomas (1819–1901), and Campbell (b. 1823). Munro also had an illegitimate daughter, Jessie Thompson. It is not known whether her mother was Indian or European, but she was raised by an army family in Shropshire and, in his will, Munro left her £100 per annum, specifying that it should remain under her control, not her husband's, if she married.

Munro returned to Madras in September 1814 with his new wife and a well-paid, prestigious appointment as judicial commissioner. He opposed the introduction of the English judicial system to India on the ground that, evolving out of English historical experience—the struggle to ensure that civil liberties were protected by the law—it was unsuitable for a state ruled by foreign conquerors where the people were not 'free' in either a political or legal sense. In India, Munro believed, government must protect the people, and his judicial recommendations had three main objectives: the use of traditional Indian forms that the people understood, protection of the cultivator from corrupt officials and oppressive social superiors— partly to ensure his revenue system could work effectively—and the employment of Indians in judicial administration because they understood local attitudes and would benefit, morally, from participating in public service. In giving magistrates' powers to revenue collectors, using Indian judges and juries for minor crimes and civil trials, and using Indians to supervise the police, Munro aroused the antagonism of British judicial officials, and it took two

years and pressure from London to induce the Madras government to enact the required legislation. The antagonism, inevitably, persisted, and when Munro was appointed to command a reserve division of the army during the Third Anglo-Maratha War (1817–18), the Madras authorities were uncooperative. This did not, however, prevent him from conducting a brilliant, if unorthodox, campaign.

Unable to join his division owing to the presence of enemy troops, Munro took control over the resources of 3000 square miles of the peshwa of Poona's territory and created a broad corridor of company-controlled territory between the Madras presidency and Poona, with only a few companies of sepoys, some irregular infantry, and the help of local inhabitants who resented Maratha rule. John Malcolm described Munro's strategy as

> successful in a degree, that a mind like his alone could have anticipated. The country comes into his hands by the most legitimate of all modes, the zealous and spirited efforts of the natives, to place themselves under his rule.   (Gleig, 1.503)

Munro worked closely with his friend Mountstuart Elphinstone, former resident at the peshwa's court, in bringing the latter to sue for terms of surrender. In recognition of his services Munro was made CB in 1818 and promoted major-general in 1819. The names of Munro, Malcolm, and Elphinstone are often linked as the protagonists of an important school of thought on Indian governance.

Governor of Madras, and death Suffering, temporarily, from ill health and eyesight problems, Munro resigned his civil and military commissions in 1819 and sailed for Britain with no intention of returning to India. But he was almost immediately offered the governorship of Madras, an honour as governorships usually went to British politicians, not company officials, and in June 1820 he and Lady Munro returned to Madras. He had been made KCB on accepting the governorship.

To win renown as a governor was difficult because the overriding authority of the governor-general and the checks imposed by presidency councils, boards of revenue, and judiciaries seriously inhibited a governor's freedom of action. But the directorate, to ensure Munro's system would be given a full trial, appointed to the council and board of revenue men who not only supported Munro's policies but who were also on good terms with him personally. His governorship was remarkable for its lack of discord. He made several tours of the presidency to examine conditions and make himself accessible to the people, and he analysed and documented his findings in an impressive series of minutes that provided the basis for his policy directives, writings that continued to command respect as statements of sound administrative principles throughout the period of British rule.

Munro submitted his resignation as governor in September 1823, but the First Anglo-Burmese War (1824–6) began before differences between the company and the British government over his successor were resolved, and he offered to remain for the duration of the war. In 1825 there was a movement to have the governor-general, Lord

Amherst, recalled, ostensibly for his unsatisfactory conduct of the war but probably for political reasons. Munro was named as one of two likely replacements but, owing largely to Wellington's support, Amherst remained. Munro also supported Amherst, and provided the inexperienced governor-general with much help with the organizational problems of the war, for which Munro was made a baronet on 6 August 1825.

With the war over, there were differences and delay again over who should succeed Munro. Lady Munro returned to Britain in 1826 because their second son was ill, and surviving letters to his wife from the usually reserved Munro indicate, poignantly, the personal toll of public life. He had first come to India forty-seven years earlier and, as he put it, only excellent health and 'great temperance' had allowed him to endure the rigours of Indian service so long (Gleig, 2.176–7). While waiting for his successor Munro made a farewell tour of the Ceded Districts. He died of cholera in his tent at Puttecondah on 6 July 1827. He was buried next day at nearby Gooty but his body was later re-interred in St Mary's Church, Madras. In a tribute to Munro, one of his closest associates in the Madras government, Chief Secretary David Hill, stated that 'His, without question, was the greatest mind which ever applied itself to the practical study of Indian affairs … I hope that his writings will be collected, as an inestimable treasury of wisdom and experience to Indian statesmen' (NL Scot., MS 6370). He was succeeded as baronet by his son Thomas.

One of the most respected of East India Company officials, Munro rose to high office by ability rather than patronage, through his contribution to the military expansion of the company's territories and, more importantly, as the chief architect of the ryotwari land tenure, revenue, and judicial system, later known as 'the Munro system', which provided the administrative framework for much of southern and western India throughout the period of British rule. At the end of the twentieth century few statues of British pro-consuls remained on display in India, but a fine bronze representation of Sir Thomas Munro on horseback still dominated Mount Road (Anna Salai), near Fort St George at Madras.

MARTHA MCLAREN

Sources BL OIOC, Munro MSS, MS Eur. F 151 · G. R. Gleig, *Life of Major-General Sir Thomas Munro*, 3 vols. (1830) · A. J. Arbuthnot, ed., *Major-General Sir Thomas Munro … selections from his minutes and other writings*, 2 vols. (1881) · B. Stein, *Thomas Munro: the origins of the colonial state and his vision of empire* (1989) · T. H. Beaglehold, *Thomas Munro and the development of administrative policy in Madras, 1792–1818: origins of 'The Munro System'* (1966) · N. Mukherjee, *The ryotwari system in Madras, 1792–1827* (1962) · M. McLaren, 'Writing and making history: Thomas Munro, John Malcolm and Mountstuart Elphinstone: three Scotsmen in the history and historiography of British India', PhD diss., Simon Fraser University, Canada, 1992 · R. E. Frykenberg, 'The silent settlement in South India, 1793–1853', in R. E. Frykenberg, *Land tenure and peasant in south Asia* (1977) · M. McLaren, 'From analysis to prescription: Scottish concepts of Asian despotism in early nineteenth-century British India', *International History Review*, 15/3 (1993), 469–501 · B. Stein, 'Idiom and ideology in early ninteenth century south India', *Rural India: land,* *power and society under British rule*, ed. P. Robb (1983) · Burke, *Peerage* (1967) · letters, NL Scot., MS 6370

Archives BL, letter-book, Add. MS 50137 · BL, minutes as governor of Madras, Add. MS · BL, papers, Add. MSS 22071–22081 · BL OIOC, corresp. and papers; corresp. and papers, MS Eur. F 151 · BL OIOC, corresp. and papers, home misc. series · JRL, corresp. and papers, mainly relating to India · NL Scot., letters and memorandum | BL, corresp. with Arthur Wellesley, Add. MSS 29238–29239 · BL OIOC, letters to Lord Amherst, MS Eur. F 140 · BL OIOC, letter-book and copies of letters to Mountstuart Elphinstone, MSS Eur. D 466, E 225 · BL OIOC, letter-book to Mountstuart Elphinstone, MSS Eur. F 87–89 · BL OIOC, Mountstuart Elphinstone MSS, letters in collections of EIC officials, MS Eur. F 88 · BL OIOC, William Fullerton Elphinstone MSS, letters in collections of EIC officials, MS Eur. F 89 · Mount Stuart Trust archive, Rothesay, letters to Lord Hastings · U. Southampton L., corresp. with Arthur Wellesley

Likenesses F. Chantrey, bronze statue, *c.*1828, Mount Road, Madras, India · F. Chantrey, bust, *c.*1840, AM Oxf. · H. Raeburn, oils; in possession of Munro family, 1894 · R. R. Reinagle, oils, Oriental Club, London [*see illus.*] · M. A. Shee, oils, NPG · bas-relief profile, St Mary's Church, Madras, India

Wealth at death £164,398—incl. investments in India, England, and Scotland: BL OIOC, Munro collection, MS Eur. F 151/203

Munro, William (1818–1880), army officer and botanist, was born at Druids Stoke, Gloucestershire, the eldest son of William Munro. He entered the army as an ensign in the 39th Dorsetshire regiment of foot on 20 January 1834. His subsequent steps in the regiment, all by purchase, were to lieutenant in April 1836, captain on 2 July 1844, major on 7 May 1852, and lieutenant-colonel on 11 November 1853. He served with the regiment for many years in India, and as adjutant was severely wounded at the battle of Maharajpur on 29 December 1843, where the regiment suffered heavy losses. He commanded the regiment at the siege of Sevastopol and commanded the supports of the 3rd division in the attack on the Redan on 18 June 1855. He was made companion of the Bath (military division) in 1857 and a member of the Légion d'honneur and the order of the Mejidiye, and was awarded English and Turkish Crimean medals. He commanded the 39th during its subsequent service in Canada and at Bermuda, retiring on halfpay in 1865.

Munro was a keen botanist, particularly as a collector, and corresponded with some of the best-known botanists of his day, including J. D. Hooker. He began collecting in the Indian state of Coorg in 1834, and subsequently managed to combine with his military duties 'so close a study of the characters, nomenclature, affinities, and classification of grasses as to have been for many years the most trustworthy referee on that difficult order' (*Gardeners' Chronicle*). A 'Monograph on the bamboos' in the *Transactions of the Linnean Society* (26, 1868, 1–157), was his most important paper. He also established gardens at various military stations in India, Canada, and the West Indies. After he retired from active service he established himself at Taunton, Somerset, and commenced a general monograph of the whole order of Gramineae (grasses), in continuation of the *Prodromus* of A. and C. de Candolle. This monograph was not completed. He was author of some nine papers between 1842 and 1868 on subjects as diverse as fossil plants, snakebite, timber trees, and grasses. He also published *Hortus Agrensis, or, Catalogue of All Plants … in the Neighbourhood of Agra* (1844).

Munro was married; his wife's name was Sarah Hannah. He became a major-general on 6 March 1868 and commanded the troops in the West Indies in 1870–6, when he served as acting governor of Bermuda. He was made a lieutenant-general on 10 February 1876, was appointed honorary colonel, 93rd Sutherland Highlanders, on 11 October the same year, and became a full general on 25 June 1878. He died at his home, Monty's Court, Norton Fitzwarren, near Taunton, on 29 January 1880. His wife survived him.

H. M. Chichester, rev. Andrew Grout

Sources *Gardeners' Chronicle*, new ser., 13 (1880), 169 · F. A. Stafleu and R. S. Cowan, *Taxonomic literature: a selective guide*, 2nd edn, 3, Regnum Vegetabile, 105 (1981), 660–61 · *Transactions of the Botanical Society* [Edinburgh], 14 (1883), 158–9 · *Journal of Botany, British and Foreign*, 18 (1880), 96 · *Hart's Army List* · A. W. Kinglake, *The invasion of the Crimea*, 8 vols. (1863–87) · Desmond, *Botanists*, rev. edn · *CGPLA Eng. & Wales* (1880)
Archives RBG Kew, corresp. and papers | BM, Greek relics collected from the Crimea · Harvard U., Arnold Arboretum, letters to Asa Gray · RBG Kew, herbarium
Likenesses portrait, Hunt Institute for Botanical Documentation, Pittsburgh, Hunt Botanical Library
Wealth at death under £16,000: probate, 20 Feb 1880, *CGPLA Eng. & Wales*

Munrow, David John (1942–1976), early woodwind instrumentalist, was born in Birmingham on 12 August 1942, the only child of Albert David Munrow, director of physical education in Birmingham University, and his wife, Hilda Ivy Norman. He was educated at King Edward VI School, Birmingham, where he became proficient on the bassoon and recorder, and after a period of teaching and travelling in South America (which laid the foundations of his considerable collection of exotic and folk instruments) he read English at Pembroke College, Cambridge (1961–4), obtaining a second class in both parts of the tripos (1963 and 1964).

Munrow's enthusiasm and organizational energy quickly brought him to the forefront of university musical life (he was elected president of the university music club in 1964), and a partiality for early music (especially Purcell and the English baroque) was encouraged by Thurston Dart and bore fruit in a recorder consort, several chamber ensembles, and many large-scale concerts, including the first modern performance of William Boyce's Cambridge ode. His lecture-recitals demonstrating many species of woodwind instrument (given first with Christopher Hogwood and later with his wife, Gillian Reid) marked the start of a career of evangelistic communication with all levels of music-lover. His marriage to Gillian Veronica, daughter of William Robert Reid, principal officer in the ministry of home affairs in Northern Ireland, took place in 1966. There were no children.

In 1964 Munrow enrolled at Birmingham University for an MA on a study of D'Urfey's *Pills to Purge Melancholy*, and from 1966 to 1968 he was a member of the wind band of the Royal Shakespeare Company, providing incidental music in Stratford and London, during which time he founded the ensemble with which he was associated for the remainder of his life, the Early Music Consort of London. This made its début in Louvain in 1967 and first appeared in London in 1968. With a variety of well-constructed and strikingly presented programmes this ensemble (James Bowman, Oliver Brookes, Christopher Hogwood, and, later, James Tyler) conveyed his enthusiastic and colourful ideas on music ranging from early medieval to late baroque to a worldwide audience, with frequent international tours (the Middle East in 1973, Italy in 1973 and 1975, Australia in 1974, the USA in 1974 and 1976), an annual series of London concerts, and regular recordings for Decca (Argo) and later EMI, which attracted major awards, such as the Grammy award in 1975 and the Edison award in 1976. He became honorary associate of the Royal Academy of Music in 1970.

Between 1967 and 1974 Munrow was a part-time lecturer in the music department of Leicester University, and in 1968 he became professor of recorder at the Royal Academy of Music, London, a post he held until 1975. During this period he was in demand as a virtuoso exponent of the repertory for the baroque recorder (he recorded Bach's 'Brandenburg' concertos several times under conductors including Sir Adrian Boult and Neville Marriner) and made several recordings which displayed and documented the full range of the recorder family (particularly *The Art of the Recorder*, EMI, 1975).

Munrow was constantly willing to experiment; in addition to the wide range of little-known repertory which he researched for the consort's programmes and recordings (Dufay, Mouton, Landini, Binchois, Josquin), he co-operated with folk musicians such as Dolly Collins and the Young Tradition in studio recordings, and arranged (occasionally composed) music for television and cinema where he felt it could increase the public awareness of early instruments and their repertory (*The Six Wives of Henry VIII*, *Elizabeth R.*, *A Man for All Seasons*, *The Devils*—with Peter Maxwell Davies—*Zardoz*, *La course en tête*, and so on). First performances given by the consort and Munrow include *Translations* (1971) and *Recorder Music for Recorder Player and Tape* (1973) by Peter Dickenson, and Elisabeth Lutyens's *The Tears of Night* (1972). Almost all his published writings were associated with recordings, in particular *Instruments of the Middle Ages and Renaissance* (1976), a popular and well-illustrated book that incorporated and assessed current thinking on organology, combining musicological tenacity with a player's insight. Such a venture he held to be meaningless without the accompaniment of a series of recordings to bring the instrumental sounds to life.

Munrow devised and presented radio and television programmes with vitality and wit, the most influential being a BBC Radio 3 series, *Pied Piper*, which ran from 1971 to 1976 with four programmes a week and attracted an audience far wider than the younger listeners for whom it was designed. The same impetuous enthusiasm, restrained by a very conscious self-discipline, informed all his music-making; he abhorred the idea of remoteness, and as a keen (though diminutive) athlete and sailor (once an Outward Bound instructor), a lover of literature and paintings, an informed historian, a good linguist, and an animated mimic and raconteur he was the antithesis of an academic specialist. At the start of his public career showmanship sometimes got the better of discretion and a certain brashness was criticized in his performances. Later, however, he developed a strong feeling for the liturgical repertory of the late middle ages and Renaissance; shortly before he died he was planning a reformed consort to explore this territory. His last recordings (*Music of the Gothic Era*) reflect this maturity. Munrow died by his own hand at Chesham Bois, Buckinghamshire, on 15 May 1976. CHRISTOPHER HOGWOOD, *rev.*

Sources D. Scott, 'Munrow, David (John)', *New Grove* • *Early Music*, 4/3 (1976), 376–80 • *The Times* (17–18 May 1976) • *MT*, 117 (1976), 596 • personal knowledge (1986) • *CGPLA Eng. & Wales* (1976)
Archives FILM BFI NFTVA, documentary footage | SOUND BL NSA, performance recordings • BL NSA, *Talking about music*, 312, 1LP0152846 S2 BD1 BBC TRANSC
Wealth at death £40,125: probate, 7 July 1976, *CGPLA Eng. & Wales*

Munshi Isma'il (*fl.* **1771–1773**). *See under* Indian visitors (*act. c.*1720–*c.*1810).

Munster. For this title name *see* Schulenburg, (Ehrengard) Melusine von der, *suo jure* duchess of Kendal and *suo jure* duchess of Munster (1667–1743); FitzClarence, George Augustus Frederick, first earl of Munster (1794–1842).

Munster, saints of (*act. c.***450**–*c.***700**), were holy figures whose cults centred on the medieval province of Munster (modern counties Clare, Limerick, Tipperary, Waterford, Cork, and Kerry), including Osraige (Ossory, modern co. Kilkenny). While having an overall provincial kingship, Munster was divided into several geographical-political regions. This is reflected in the cults of its saints.

The main dynastic power in Munster up to the end of the tenth century was that of the Eóganachta. The east of the province was dominated by Eóganacht Chaisil while the west formed the distinctive region of Iarmumu (west Munster) under the rival Eóganacht Locha Léin. With the rise of the Dál Cais (from east Clare) in the tenth century this was overshadowed by the division of a northern Tuadmumu (Thomond) from a southern Desmumu (Desmond). Such divisions were superimposed on older patterns. Munster was inhabited by many ancient and scattered population groupings. The profusion of peoples is reflected in a profusion of minor saints and churches. This was undoubtedly encouraged by the lack of strong central authority from the Eóganacht kings. The result is a bewildering confusion of separate traditions. Finally, the eastern boundaries of the province were controlled by the powerful and semi-autonomous kingdom of Osraige. This kingdom was alienated to the Uí Néill in the second half of the ninth century but subsequently gravitated towards the adjacent province of Leinster. Unsurprisingly, its saints look towards both Munster and Leinster. Saints were drawn into this world of shifting alliances long after their deaths. They generally flourished in the sixth and

seventh centuries, but their cults continued to be elaborated throughout the middle ages. After the thirteenth century there is a lacuna in the sources and the modern use of ancient cult sites, in some cases, cannot be traced back beyond the seventeenth and eighteenth centuries.

The most important of the widespread but disparate sources are hagiographical lives, either in Irish or Latin, or both, which are extant for many Munster saints. The Latin lives, in general, are found in the three great thirteenth- and fourteenth-century collections known as the Codex Salmanticensis, Codex Insulensis, and Codex Kilkenniensis. None of them is directly dependent on the others but they often used common sources, and some of the individual lives are significantly earlier than the date of their inclusion in the collections. Furthermore, it has been argued that a group of lives in the collections, mainly emanating from north Munster and adjacent kingdoms in Leinster and Mide (Meath), can be dated to the eighth century. Certainly, some of these lives betray convincing signs of an early origin. Several Irish language lives are preserved in later medieval manuscripts such as the fifteenth-century Book of Lismore. But many of the texts are known only because they were transcribed by the Franciscan Mícheál Ó Cléirigh (Michael O'Clery) in the 1620s and 1630s. Fortunately, Ó Cléirigh was an accurate copyist. Nevertheless, many of the lives he transcribed date at the earliest from the thirteenth century. Even demonstrably later lives contain early strata, however.

Some saints are mentioned only in the martyrologies and their notes. These texts are calendars, which list saints, Irish and foreign, against their appropriate feast day—that is, the traditional day of the saint's death. The most important of the martyrologies are the martyrology of Tallaght from the first half of the ninth century and *Félire Óengusso* from later in the same century. The latter was heavily annotated and the *scholia* (notes) dating from the ninth through to the twelfth century contain very important material. Another significant source is the martyrology of Gorman, composed between 1166 and 1174 by Máel Muire *Ua Gormáin (Marianus Gorman). This martyrology is heavily dependent on the martyrology of Tallaght and helps to fill the gap in the latter between 1 November and 16 December. The most important later martyrology is the martyrology of Donegal, compiled by Mícheál Ó Cléirigh about 1630. Ó Cléirigh's information is not to be dismissed lightly, since he had access to many early sources, some of which are no longer extant.

One of the most interesting early sources for the origins of several Munster cults is the text of the so-called west Munster synod, preserved among the Laud genealogies. It may have been written during the reign of the Eóganacht Locha Léin king, Máel Dúin (*d.* 786), who is mentioned in the text, though it purports to describe events in the second half of the sixth century. It names several saints who attend a synod called by the king of Ciarraige Luachra (north Kerry). The text's enumeration of the regions where each saint wields jurisdiction is a useful pointer to the geographical distribution of the cults.

The difficulty with source material spills over into a difficulty regarding chronology. The chronology of this shadowy period, the age of saints, is not always certain, especially as this age was, in part, a retrospective construct. The hagiography is a monument to this work, in which saints of different centuries are brought into contact with each other in the name of contemporary monastic politics. In particular, this served to justify large monastic federations known as *paruchiae*. A saint could be associated with several churches but, in general, his burial place was at the leading church in the *paruchia*.

Most important saints are recorded in the monastic annals. While the annals of Ulster are contemporary from the second half of the sixth century, they have a distinct northern bias and are not always helpful for Munster saints. The first part of the Munster annals of Inisfallen was compiled about 1092, probably from documents emanating from the great monastery of Emly. Despite the relative lateness of compilation this set of annals does much to counter the northern emphasis of the annals of Ulster. Other important chronicles include *Chronicum Scotorum*, the annals of Tigernach, the annals of Clonmacnoise, and the annals of the four masters. The latter was compiled in the seventeenth century under the guidance of Mícheál Ó Cléirigh. Like the martyrology of Donegal it contains early material, despite the late date of its compilation.

Finally, one of the identifying characteristics of Irish hagiography is the importance of genealogy. Through genealogy a saint was often linked with powerful dynasties. Indeed, Irish saints were rarely of non-aristocratic origin. The Irish genealogies were being compiled from the seventh century, and perhaps earlier. Changes in a saintly genealogy usually represent changes in patronage and the rise and fall of dynasties. There is often some confusion over the names of the mothers of the saints; most can be taken from the tract 'On the mothers of the saints', preserved in the twelfth-century Book of Leinster and later manuscripts.

The pre-Patrician Munster saints Ireland was Christianized mainly in the fifth century. Many were involved but the cult of St Patrick swallowed up the work of others. The hagiography of the Munster saints Ailbe, the elder Ciarán, Déclán, and Ibar, however, centres on the important trope of pre-Patrician Christianity. All four are imagined as bishops. According to traditions elaborated in Latin lives, these saints were themselves Christian before the coming of Patrick during the fifth century (the precise date of his arrival is uncertain) and preceded him in his missionary activity in Munster. The annals, on the other hand, place these saints as either contemporary with or later than Patrick. Furthermore, pre-Patrician claims did not significantly impinge on Munster politics: the primacy of the see founded by Patrick at Armagh was accepted in Munster by the seventh century.

Ailbe [Albeus] (*d.* 534?), a bishop and church founder, was the most significant of these saints. His feast day was celebrated on 12 September, according to the martyrology of Tallaght and *Félire Óengusso*. He was a member of the Dál

Cairpri Arad, a relatively minor Munster people. Ailbe's most important church and burial site was Emly (Imlech Ibair), the chief church in Munster for several centuries. The abbot of Emly is mentioned as an authority on the paschal question in Cummian's seventh-century letter to Ségéne, the abbot of Iona. Undoubtedly, Emly was bolstered by the support of the Eóganachta. The annals record abbots drawn from Eóganacht Áine, Eóganacht Locha Léin, Eóganacht Airthir Chliach, and Eóganacht Chaisil.

The hagiographical material associated with Ailbe is quite extensive. The Latin life in Codex Salmanticensis is the earliest recension, the other lives derivative. The Irish life is an abbreviated version of the Latin original. The Salmanticensis life seems to be the innovator in regard to Ailbe's pre-Patrician status and his independence from Patrick, something downplayed in the other two recensions and directly contradicted by the date of his death given in the annals of Ulster. It has been argued that the original life was a relatively early production, perhaps as early as the eighth century; one commentator has suggested that it was composed about the time of the first promulgation of the Law of Ailbe in 784. This life consciously models Ailbe on Patrick, whom he at times surpasses. The picture is rather different from Tírechán's seventh-century *Collectanea*, in which Patrick ordains Ailbe. In Ailbe's life the founder of Emly is consecrated a bishop in Rome, is visited by Patrick's angel, Victor, and is acknowledged by the bishops Déclán and Ibar. Patrick himself, contrary to most versions of his legend, especially that in the early tenth-century *Vita tripartita*, leaves the Munster king, Óengus mac Nad Fraích, in Ailbe's care. Emly's ambitions are fairly clear. Although the pre-Patrician motif is dominant, the saint is also associated with other traditions. Ailbe's father is named Olchú (or Olcán, or Olcnais; literally 'great hound'), his mother Sant or Sanclit. Ailbe, the son of the 'great hound' is abandoned as the offspring of illicit sex and raised by wolves, much like Romulus and Remus. In the later stratum of the Irish life of Mac Creiche, Ailbe is referred to as the warhound of 'Slíab Crot' (Slieve Grud, co. Tipperary). Ailbe is also mentioned in the context of an other-world voyage in a late eighth-century litany of pilgrim saints. It has been suggested that this was written at Lismore and is good evidence for the widespread nature of Ailbe's cult. Moreover, Ailbe's community, enjoying everlasting life on an other-world island, is encountered in the late eighth-century *Navigatio sancti Brendani*.

Emly itself maintained its importance right through the early middle ages. It was a literary centre and produced, for example, the late ninth-century *Riagol Ailbi Imlecha*, a monastic rule, authored retrospectively on Ailbe. The text of the west Munster synod suggests that the abbot of Emly has authority over all of Munster. Another sign of Emly's influence is the number of its abbots recorded in the annals. Flann mac Fairchellaig (*d.* 825?) was undoubtedly the most famous. He was also abbot of Cork and Lismore. The church suffered an eclipse following the tenth- and eleventh-century rise of the Dál Cais. Marcán (*d.* 1010),

Brian Bóruma's brother, became abbot of Emly and several other churches. The creation of a church at nearby Cashel was a further blow, but Emly recovered sufficiently in the twelfth century to become an episcopal see.

Ciarán mac Luaigne [Kyaranus; Piran] (*fl.* 450–500), bishop and patron of Ossory, was also imagined as flourishing in the fifth century. His main foundation was the great monastic church of Saigir (Seir Kieran). He is commemorated on 5 March in *Félire Óengusso* and he is often referred to as 'sen', old, Ciarán to differentiate him from his namesake, *Ciarán of Clonmacnoise, the founder of Clonmacnoise [*see under* Meath, saints of]. The hagiographical tradition devoted to Ciarán is complex. There are two Latin and two Irish lives. The fuller of the Latin texts is that preserved in Codex Kilkenniensis, in comparison with which the life in the Salamanca collection is abbreviated. Both are difficult to date. Of the Irish lives, one is a translation of the longer of the Latin lives, while the second Irish life, as it stands, is a post-Reformation production. Nevertheless, the latter contains the oldest materials, particularly in its pro-Munster treatment of Osraige politics. In these lives Ciarán is portrayed as a wild man, dressed in skins. His first monks are forest animals. Otherwise, his pre-Patrician career follows that of Ailbe. Unlike the latter, however, Ciarán is always subordinate to Patrick, whom he first meets in Italy. Indeed, his lives make little mention of Ailbe, Déclán, and Ibar. They are more interested in extending the rights of Saigir.

Yet, there is an even older stratum to Ciarán's cult which hints at pre-seventh-century conditions. The genealogies and martyrologies point to an ancient tradition in which his father Lugna was of the Osraige while his mother Liadán was from the Corco Loígde. The latter claimed to be the first people in Ireland to receive Christianity. Despite his paternity he is raised among the Corco Loígde, a possible sign of his original affiliation. Furthermore, there is strong evidence for Corco Loígde suzerainty over Osraige in the early historic period. Indeed, Ciarán's life brings the saint and Conchraid mac Duach, one of the Corco Loígde kings of Osraige, together as allies. Another old tradition, contained in the late eighth-century litany of pilgrim saints, is that Ciarán went on a voyage to the other world. Whatever the saint's guise, however, his hagiographers do not hide the wealth and importance of Saigir. It was the burial place of the Osraige kings. The church ruins still contain some early grave slabs and the base of a high cross. Ciarán has been mistakenly identified with the Cornish saint *Piran.

Déclán mac Eircc [Declanus] (*fl.* late 5th cent.) was the founder of the important monastery of Ardmore (Ard Mór) and patron of the Dési (modern co. Waterford). The monastery, where the saint died and was buried, was situated on the south-east coast in the kingdom of Dési Muman. Déclán is commemorated on 24 July in the martyrologies. The founder saint and bishop was a member of the Dési royal dynasty through his father, Ercc (Ercbran). His mother, Dethiden, is not given a genealogical affiliation. The close links between church and aristocracy indicated by the position of the saint's father are highlighted by the hagiographers. The main source for Déclán's life and cult is a roughly twelfth-century Latin life preserved only in Codex Kilkenniensis, but possibly containing earlier materials. The Irish life, transcribed by Ó Cléirigh, is dependent on the Latin. The earlier text is very much influenced by the Salamanca life of Ailbe. It describes Déclán's journey to Rome, where he makes the acquaintance of Ailbe. Later, on his way back to Ireland, he meets Patrick. Throughout, Déclán is shown as subordinate to these two saints. It is Patrick who tells him where to settle. Déclán eventually converts the Dési with Patrick's blessing. Much of the stress in the life on Déclán's episcopal status fits the twelfth-century period of church reform, during which Ireland was re-organized into a full diocesan system. In the event, Ardmore ultimately failed to win the status of an episcopal see, which was given to Lismore. An impressive round tower marks the site of the medieval monastery.

Ibar mac Lugna [Ibhar, Ybarus] (*d.* 500/01), bishop, is the most shadowy of the four Munster pre-Patrician saints. His feast day is placed on 23 April in the martyrologies and he is reputed to have died in 500 or 501. He is remembered as the founder of a monastery at Beggerin Island (Becc Ériu, Inis Fáil) in Wexford harbour, which survived despite being plundered by the vikings in 813; in 1182 it was granted to St Nicholas's Monastery in Exeter. Ibar makes many appearances in the lives of other saints, particularly in the lives of Déclán and Ailbe, the late seventh-century life of Mo Ninne (Dar Erca, Monenna) and the roughly thirteenth-century Latin life of Abbán. A brief text, concerning Ibar, in the twelfth-century Book of Leinster adds little. In the life of Ailbe, Ibar acknowledges Ailbe's precedence, a prudent claim since Emly was called Imlech Ibair ('Emly of Ibar'), suggesting the primacy of Ibar. In the life of Déclán, Ibar is a companion of the other pre-Patrician bishops.

While these lives give Ibar indelibly Munster associations, he was also a national figure. He is portrayed as the adviser of the Ulster saint Mo Ninne and the maternal uncle of the Leinster saint Abbán moccu Corbmaic. According to the genealogies of the Loígse, Ibar baptized the sons of their early historic king, Barr. Ibar's father, Lugna, was of the Ulster Uí Echach Ulad (from modern co. Down), while his mother, named Bassar in 'On the mothers of the saints', was a member of the Dési Breg in the midlands. According to this text, Bassar was the mother of four saints including Ibar, a common but significant genealogical fiction. Clearly, Ibar was an important saint, the records of whose deeds may have been lost. Among these may have been a voyage text, for Ibar's quest is mentioned in the litany of pilgrim saints.

The traditions of west and north-west Munster Geographically and politically Iarmumu formed a discrete region within the province. Its kings were the Eóganacht Locha Léin, whose power-base was centred around modern Killarney. While the hagiographers implicitly recognized the separate entity of Iarmumu, they were explicitly concerned with linking west Munster both with the rest of the province and with Connacht to the north. Furthermore, the Eóganacht Locha Léin had influence over the old kingdoms of Corco Duibne (Dingle peninsula) and Ciarraige Luachra. The latter, in particular, valued its independence, both from the nearby, and therefore more threatening, power of Iarmumu and from Eóganacht Chaisil. The text of the west Munster synod, which emanates from Ciarraige and may have been composed at Ardfert, details the relationship between the Ciarraige and Eóganacht. These details are mediated through saints.

Caimín [Caimmíne, Mo Chammóc] (d. 644?), one of the claimed founders of the monastery of Inis Celtra (Holy Island) on Lough Derg, is commemorated in the martyrologies on 25 March. The saints' genealogies are unsure of the identity of his father, who is named both Colmán and Dímmae. His maternal genealogy is more important, however. Under the year 662 in the annals of the four masters, Caimín is described as the uterine brother of Guaire Aidne (d. 633), an Uí Fhiachrach king of Connacht, and a central figure in a series of tales from the region. The kingdom of Uí Fhiachrach Aidne (south-west Galway) bordered on Munster. Moreover, Guaire was linked through blood and friendship with a number of west Munster figures, so much so that one critic has detected the remains of a literary cycle surrounding Guaire, which described political events in the seventh and eighth centuries and was written no later than the ninth. Caimín's cult suffered through possible confusion with *Cumméne Fota (d. 662), abbot of Clonfert [see under Connacht, saints of], and through the dominance of Colum mac Crimthainn, the patron of Inis Celtra. One unpublished Irish metrical life celebrates the saint. His main claim to prominence, however, was his conflict with Guaire Aidne in the eleventh-century saga Cath Cairn Chonaill. In the battle of Carn Conaill (649), Diarmait, son of Áed Sláine, joint king of Tara with his brother Bláthmac, defeated Guaire. In the saga account, however, Guaire's defeat is the direct result of Caimín's curse, for the king had outraged the saint. Guaire is saved through repentance, and reconciliation with the church. The church of Inis Celtra itself flourished despite viking incursions up the Shannon. It formed part of the paruchia of Terryglass. Impressive remains, including earthworks from the early monastic settlement, several churches, a round tower, and two high crosses, can still be seen on Holy Island.

Guaire is also associated with Cumméne Fota and the latter's frequent companion, the Dési holy fool and saint, **Comgán mac Dá Cherda** [Mac na Cerda, Comgán moccu Cerda] (d. 645). While Mac Dá Cherda is very much a figure of saga, he has been tentatively identified with Comgán, the abbot of Emly, mentioned in the west Munster synod. Mac Dá Cherda, through his mother Rím, was supposedly the brother of both Guaire and Cumméne. Although he is generally affiliated to a minor branch of the Dési, the Uí Rossa, one Irish anecdote transfers him to the main branch of the Dési and relates that, having been struck with madness by God, he found holiness through his friendship with Cumméne. In another anecdote, relations between Guaire, Cumméne, and Mac Dá Cherda help to link Clonfert and Ardfert, the two principal churches of the familia of St Brendan of Clonfert.

Cult dedications are particularly rich in Corco Duibne. One of the most impressive churches on the Dingle peninsula is Kilmalkedar (Cell Máele Cétair). The church is Romanesque and an ogham stone, alphabet stone, and early cross-pillar are among the remains still in situ. The church is dedicated to **Máel Cétair mac Rónáin** (fl. 6th–7th cent.?). Unfortunately, there is very little extant information about this saint. He is not recorded in the annals and his floruit can only be a guess. His name literally means 'the servant of the cedar', in other words the servant of the cross, which indicates a cult of the cross at Kilmalkedar. Otherwise, the only substantial information concerning Máel Cétair is contained in the late twelfth-century martyrology of Gorman, which gives his feast day as 14 May; later notes appended to it state that Máel Cétair was descended from the royal family of the Ulaid. Kilmalkedar's significance, however, was local to Corco Duibne, for the church does not make an appearance in the annals of monastic rivalry.

The Clare coast north of the Shannon estuary was dominated by two ancient Munster peoples: the Corco Baiscinn and the more northerly Corco Mruad. From the tenth century they were subsumed into the Ó Briain region of Tuadmumu. One of the major saints of Corco Mruad was **Mac Creiche** [Mac Cride] **mac Pessláin** (fl. late 6th cent.) of Kilmacreehy (Cell Mac Creiche) and Killoran (Cell Máele Odrain). His feast day was celebrated on 11 August according to the martyrology of Donegal. In recent times, however, it has been celebrated on the first Sunday of August, known as Garland Sunday (Domnach Chrom Dubh), particularly around the west Clare town of Liscannor. Mac Creiche's Irish life was transcribed by Mícheál Ó Cléirigh from a copy made by Melaghlin O'Callanan, the coarb of the saint, at Killoran in 1528. Contrary to the opinions of earlier scholars, it has been shown to contain valuable information and two historical strata. The earlier refers to west Munster events in the seventh century and may well have been written towards the end of that century or in the eighth. Here, Mac Creiche is affiliated through his father, Pesslán, to the Corco Mruad, and through his mother to the Ciarraige. The saint shows particular attachment to his maternal kindred, being referred to as their garmac or dutiful son. Furthermore, he gains the confidence and support of two Eóganacht Locha Léin kings, Crimthainn and his son, the important Áed Bennán (d. 619). Unlike other tales emanating from Iarmumu in this period, the text shows considerable hostility towards Connacht. Mac Creiche is opposed to Connacht before finally winning the submission of the early Uí Briúin king, Áed mac Echach (d. 577). Throughout the life, Mac Creiche, as bishop, acknowledges the superior status of Ailbe as archbishop of Munster. This is consistent with the portrayal of Mac Creiche as Ailbe's foster child in the eighth-century life of the latter saint. The second section of Mac Creiche's life may date from the early tenth century, and makes Ailbe the father of Mac Creiche. Mac Creiche is identified as a saint of Cenél Fermaic, a more minor people who lived near Corco Mruad. Undoubtedly, this reflects a local aspect of his cult. This section of the composite life does not know of the saint's maternal genealogy. He gains the submission of Ciarraige Luachra through St Brendan, rather than through his mother's kindred.

Mac Creiche is a saint of widespread attachments but no major monastery. In the notes of the martyrology of Donegal he is tutored by Mochta of Lugbad (Louth). According to the eighth- or ninth-century Latin life of Colum mac Crimthainn, Mac Creiche was the original incumbent of Inis Celtra, which at the request of an angel he handed over to Colum. His cult stretched from Corco Mruad to Araid Tíre and Múscraige Tíre. He survived as a saint on a popular, as opposed to a monastic, level.

The greatest saint of Corco Baiscinn was **Senán mac Geirrcinn** [Mo Shenóc, Senanus] (*fl.* 6th cent.) of Inis Cathaig (Scattery Island, Iniscathy). In hagiography he is often linked with the sixth-century patron of Wales, David. So in *Félire Óengusso* his feast day, like David's, is on 1 March. The Welsh link may reflect ancient connections between Munster and Wales, particularly Dyfed. Senán's most famous hagiographical deed was his defeat of the mythical river monster, called the Cathach, who gave his name to Inis Cathaig. The event is commemorated on 8 March in *Félire Óengusso* and is celebrated in detail in his tenth- or eleventh-century Irish life preserved in the Book of Lismore. There is also a metrical Latin life of the saint, but it is much later, and hardly predates the thirteenth century. In the earlier *Vita tripartita*, Patrick foretells Senán's sanctity. According to the Irish life he was the son of Gerrcenn who, unusually in terms of Irish convention, was a Corco Baiscinn peasant rather than a nobleman. His mother is named Coímgell. According to his life, Senán became a monk with the Osraige saint, Notail. Eventually, he defeated the Cathach to found a monastery on Scattery. The island had never before been inhabited and so, according to the hagiographers, was free of the stain of original sin.

Inis Cathaig was a wealthy and successful monastery. Senán was the patron of both Corco Baiscinn and the powerful Uí Fhidgeinte (modern co. Limerick). Much of his life concerns itself with relations with the latter. The monastery reached its height before the tenth century. One of its abbots, the Uí Fhidgeinte Ólchobur mac Flainn (*d.* 796), became king of Munster. Moreover, it has been argued that the Old Irish poem praising Senán, *Amra Senáin*, was composed towards the end of the ninth century by the bishop-king of Munster, Cormac mac Cuillennáin (*d.* 908). Despite a decline, owing as much to the rise of Dál Cais as to viking depredations, the monastery remained important within the Shannon region. It was recognized as an episcopal see, representing Corco Baiscinn and Uí Fhidgeinte, at the Synod of Kells-Mellifont in 1152. This status was short-lived but Inis Cathaig retained rights over churches on both banks of the Shannon estuary. A fourteenth-century text, *Morbuile Senáin*, provides a valuable and rare insight into the development

of a cult during this era. The text is a list of Senán's miraculous interventions in contemporary affairs. As might be expected during this period, the Ó Briain lords of Thomond are prominent beneficiaries of the saint. Moreover, the text lists several churches in Clare owing allegiance to Inis Cathaig. A poem, following the prose account, brings Senán into contact with most major Irish saints. The medieval remains on Scattery Island are impressive, including the highest round tower in Ireland. The cult of Senán outlived Inis Cathaig, and is still of considerable importance in co. Clare.

Inis Cathaig was also a famous burial-ground. Senán was not the only saint supposedly buried there. Another was **Canir** [Cannera] (*fl.* 6th cent.). She was a saint of the Benntraige in the south of Munster, and is known mainly through an episode which occurs towards the end of the Irish life of Senán but was probably originally independent. Canir, it is said, journeyed to Inis Cathaig, where she wished to die and be buried. Senán at first refused to allow this because she was a woman. Eventually, he relented, moved by Canir's stubbornness, rather than by her impassioned plea for equality.

The most westerly of the great Munster monastic sites was the church and burial site of **Énda mac Conaill** [Endeus] (*fl.* 6th cent.?) on Inismore (Inis Mór), the largest of the Aran Islands. These islands in Galway Bay were ruled by the Eóganacht Ninussa, a minor branch of the great Munster dynastic federation. The islands contain a large number of neolithic and early Christian sites. Many of the latter are associated with Énda, particularly Killeany (Cill Éinne), the site of the ancient monastery. Énda is commemorated on 21 March in the martyrologies. He is not mentioned in the annals but probably flourished in the sixth century. Most sources make him the son of Conall mac Daimíne (*d.* 609), a member of a royal dynasty of Airgialla (of mid-Ulster), and Aebfind, the daughter of Ainmire, king of Fir Arda Ciannachta (modern co. Louth). Yet, according to the Latin life of the saint, which is twelfth- or thirteenth-century in its present form but contains far earlier material, the Aran Islands were granted to Énda by the fifth-century Munster king Óengus mac Nad Fraích, despite the fact that the saint flourished a century later than the legendary king. One of the earliest references to Énda is contained in the *Navigatio sancti Brendani*. In the text Brendan visits Énda and receives his blessing before embarking on his voyage. In his life Énda is celebrated as the teacher of Brendan, or Columba (Colum Cille) and of Ciarán of Clonmacnoise, with whom he made a pact, signalling good relations between Aran and Clonmacnoise.

In Irish tradition Énda is known as an *athláech*, a former layman. His life claims that he was converted from warfare to religious life through his saintly sister Fáenche. According to the Middle Irish notes to *Félire Óengusso*, another of his sisters, Caírech, founded the church of Cluain Bairenn (Clonburren) in Uí Maine (south-east Galway). Énda's religious education is not completely entrusted to a woman, however. His life also brings him into contact with a teacher of saints, *Mo Nennus (Maucennus, Mugint, Mo-Nennius), at 'Rosnat', a British monastery identified, often though uncertainly, with Whithorn.

Énda's successor at Aran, and companion in the life, was Pupu (Pupeus, Pubeus). According to the notes in *Félire Óengusso* and a poem in the genealogies of the saints, Pupu was identical with Nem moccu Birn (d. 655), a supposed brother of Ciarán of Saigir, commemorated in Tallaght on 14 June. His name may preserve the memory that Aran had been under Corco Loígde control at some early stage, as had Osraige, Ciarán's land.

The monastic settlement suffered a decline. The exposed position of the Aran Islands on the Atlantic made them and their religious communities an easy prey for vikings. During post-Norman times they were caught between the rival Uí Briain and Uí Flaithbertaig, and Aran's monasteries and churches fell into ruin.

The saints of Uí Fhidgeinte and Dál Cais Mid-Munster was dominated by the Uí Fhidgeinte in present-day co. Limerick, the Eóganacht Áine, Eóganacht Airthir Chliach, and Eóganacht Chaisil. Eóganacht traditions tended to be centred on the pre-Patrician saint Ailbe. The Uí Fhidgeinte, however, also claimed to be Eóganacht, although their artificial grafting onto the main Eóganacht stem is an obvious enough fiction. The Uí Fhidgeinte were broken into two major branches, the Uí Chonaill Gabra in west Limerick and the Uí Chairpri in east Limerick. To the north of Uí Fhidgeinte, Tuadmumu was subject to the rising power of Dál Cais. Close neighbours, the Uí Fhidgeinte were the more powerful of the two until the dramatic surge in Dál Cais power towards the end of the tenth century.

Íte ingen Chinn Fhalad [M' Íte; Deirdre; Ita] (d. 570/577) of Killeedy (Cluain Credail, Cell Íte) was far and away the most important of the Uí Fhidgeinte saints. She is commemorated on 15 January in *Félire Óengusso*, where she is called 'grian bán ban Muman', 'the white sun of Munster's women'; the annals of Ulster record her death in either 570 or 577. She was regarded as the patron of Munster and had an unusually high standing for a female saint. This is reflected in her hagiographical dossier which includes two major revisions of a probably eleventh-century Latin life that is no longer extant. The notes of *Félire Óengusso* preserve a late ninth-century Old Irish poem, *Ísucán*, put into her mouth. According to the genealogies and the life preserved in Codex Kilkenniensis, Íte was a member of the Dési. Her father is named Cenn Fáelad in the genealogies of the saints. The life follows the example of Brigit in describing the opposition Íte meets in pursuit of her vocation. It is no surprise when the hagiographer explicitly calls Íte a second Brigit. The genealogies of the saints even make Íte's mother, Necht, a daughter of Dallbrónach, and thus a sister of Brigit's mother. Her life says that Íte eventually founded the church of Killeedy in Uí Fhidgeinte, where she was buried, with the co-operation of the royal family of the Uí Chonaill Gabra.

Despite this apparently straightforward link between saint and dynasty, there is strong evidence that Íte was originally the patron of the Corco Óche, the weaker neighbours of the Uí Chonaill. Killeedy was situated at the foot of Slíab Luachra, which formed the natural southern boundary of Uí Chonaill, an area inhabited by the Corco Óche. The annals of Ulster under the year 552 record the battle of Cuilen won by the Uí Chonaill Gabra over the Corco Óche through the prayers of Íte. Yet, in a probably eighth-century account of a battle (probably the same although it is called the battle of Méinde) the Corco Óche are the victors over the Uí Chonaill, through the intercession of Íte. The difference between the two accounts represents the displacement of the Corco Óche by the Uí Chonaill, and the latter's absorption of the saint's cult. This is completed in the life's version of the battle, in which the Uí Chonaill are the foster people of Íte and she their fosterer. Her support for them in battle, at this stage represented as a struggle against the hosts of Iarmumu, is an extension of this role. Íte's status as foster mother gained her national recognition. She was imagined as the fosterer of the saints Brendan, Cumméne Fota, and Mo Chóemóc. Her maternal characteristics are best celebrated in the Old Irish poem *Ísucán*. The image of Íte, suckling the infant Jesus, fits in particularly well with the personality ascribed to her by the hagiographers.

One of the odder aspects of Íte's cult is that while she founded a religious house for women, it seems to have passed at a fairly early date into male hands. Several of the abbots are recorded in the annals of the four masters. Íte may have been a second Brigit, but the women of her church did not emulate the success of the abbesses of Kildare. The monastery flourished, but was plundered several times by the vikings. It went into decline following the heavy Norman settlement of Limerick. A Romanesque church can still be seen on the site of the medieval monastery.

The church of **Mainchín mac Setnai** (fl. late 6th cent.) of Luimnech (at the head of the Shannon estuary, later Limerick) was caught up in the rivalries of Dál Cais, Uí Fhidgeinte and vikings. There are several saints of this name, but the most likely candidate is mentioned in the martyrology of Donegal on 29 December. This Mainchín is attached to the genealogical stem of the Dál Cais through his father, Sétna, and seems to be identical with the Mainchín who appears as Mac Creiche's disciple in the life of that saint. The church was subsumed in the growth of the viking city of Limerick in the tenth century, Mainchín becoming the patron of the city. The saint is also associated with Bruree (Brug Ríg) further south, where his feast is celebrated on 2 January, perhaps through confusion with St Manchéne, commemorated on that day in *Félire Óengusso*. Both Bruree and Luimnech were, from early times, contested by Dál Cais and Uí Fhidgeinte. Mainchín's cult as a Dál Cais saint reflects this.

Nessán [Mo Nessóc] (d. 556), the deacon and founder of Mungret (Mungairit), was one of the most important of the Uí Fhidgeinte saints. His feast day is 25 July in *Félire Óengusso*. Mungret, situated not far from present-day Limerick, was wealthy and powerful. Several of its abbots are recorded in the annals. Cummian's seventh-century letter to Ségéne refers to Nessán as a father of the Irish church, and to his successor, the abbot of Mungret, as an authority of note. Furthermore, the saint is given jurisdiction over Corco Duibne in the West Munster synod. This reflects a genealogical link with Corco Duibne and, perhaps, the extent of Mungret's influence. Moreover, the saint's cult is well attested in the early tenth-century *Vita tripartita*. Here, Nessán shows Patrick the respect he deserves, even though Patrick has been insulted by the Uí Fhidgeinte king, Lonn. Nessán is rewarded with a religious vocation and founds Mungret, where he is eventually buried. Considering the importance of Mungret, it is disappointing to find no extant life of the founder saint. Nessán does make stray appearances in the lives of other saints, notably in that of the Eóganacht patron, Ailbe, but the strength of the saint's cult is best attested by the wealth of Mungret. The monastery survived the raiding of the Norse and the close proximity of their city, Limerick. In the twelfth century it adopted the rules of the canons regular and claimed episcopal status at the Synod of Kells-Mellifont in 1152. Although its claims were derailed by the powerful see of Limerick, Mungret continued to flourish. Several buildings dating from the twelfth to the fifteenth century can still be seen on the site.

The heyday of Uí Fhidgeinte passed with the tenth century, when their Dál Cais neighbours rose to be the dominant power in Munster. The Dál Cais leader Brian Bóruma became king not only of the province, but of the country. The chief church of Dál Cais was Killaloe (Cell Dá Lua). Little is known of its founder Mo Lua (Da Lua); there is an isolated anecdote in the eighth-century life of Cainnech. More important was **Flannán mac Toirrdelbaig** [Flannanus] (*fl.* 7th cent.), Killaloe's patron, whose cult was largely the creation of the Ó Briain kings, descendants of Brian Bóruma. Flannán was not prominent enough to be mentioned in the early martyrologies and his feast day, 18 December, is recorded only in the martyrology of Donegal. His father, the king Toirrdelbach, was the ancestor of the Ó Briain rulers, the main branch of the Dál Cais royal dynasty. The development of Flannán's cult took place during the eleventh and twelfth centuries. The large hagiographical dossier built up on him at this time is the last example of the conscious cult building which had dominated Irish religious life since the seventh century. The twelfth-century Latin life of Flannán, of which there are two main recensions, was probably composed between 1163 and 1167 in Killaloe by an Irish cleric who was trained on the continent. He also seems to have been the author of the Latin life of Mo Chuille (Mochulleus) whose church of Tulla lay not far from Killaloe.

Killaloe rose at the expense of the rival Eóganacht monastery of Emly. That monastery and Ailbe, its patron, are denigrated in the life of Flannán. Ailbe is described as a demon rather than a saint. Killaloe was dominated by members of the Dál Cais royal dynasty. The first abbot to be mentioned in the annals, Scandlán mac Taidc (*d.* 991), was succeeded by Brian Bóruma's brother, Marcán. The latter took over the abbacy at Inis Celtra, Emly, and Terryglass, a clear sign of Ó Briain ambitions. Killaloe became the see of the Ó Briain diocese of the same name in the twelfth century. Flannán is an instructive example of the type of political motivations that could underlie a saint's cult, motivations which are often obscure in the earlier and more fragmentary material.

South Munster The south coast of Munster was dominated by the Corco Loígde (west Cork), Eóganacht Raithlind (south Cork), Uí Liatháin (east Cork), and Dési Muman. The Corco Loígde were among the most ancient inhabitants of the province, and seem to have preserved some of the oldest hagiographical traditions. Coastal trade was important in the region. This was extended by the growth of viking Cork as the most significant maritime focus in south Munster. The lands of Múscraige Mittine (mid-Cork) and Fir Maige Féne (mid-Cork, around Fermoy) lay further inland. The Múscraige seem to have originated as allies of the Eóganacht in early historic times. Fir Maige Féne, on the contrary, had many anti-Eóganacht associations.

The Corco Loígde successfully maintained an honoured status *vis-à-vis* their powerful Eóganacht neighbours during the early medieval period. Their major church was the foundation of **Fachtna mac Mongaig** (*fl.* 6th cent.), bishop, at Ros Ailithir (Ross Carbery). According to *Félire Óengusso* Fachtna's feast day was celebrated on 14 August. Little is known of the saint's background. His father is named Mongach, and is attached to the genealogical stem of Corco Loígde. According to the notes to *Félire Óengusso* Fachtna was abbot of Dair-Inis. The latter was a church founded from Lismore by its abbot Máel Anfaid. The same source has Ciarán of Saigir, a saint with strong Corco Loígde links, foretell Fachtna's coming. Prominent and successful, Ros Ailithir had a noted school. The annals of Inisfallen record that its lector was captured by the vikings but ransomed by Brian Bóruma in 990. At the Synod of Kells-Mellifont in 1152 Ros Ailithir became the episcopal see of the tiny diocese of Ross, a diocese that encompassed the territory of Corco Loígde.

One of the largest monasteries in the region, Cork (Corcach), lay east of Ros Ailithir and in the centre of Eóganacht Raithlind power. Its patron, bishop, and founder was **Findbarr mac Amairgin** [Finnbar; Báirre] (*fl.* 6th cent.?), who is commemorated on 25 September in the martyrologies. Findbarr is celebrated in several lives, both Latin and Irish. The two major Latin lives are independent of each other, but derive from a common source that has been dated to the end of the twelfth century and the beginning of the thirteenth. The Irish life was probably composed between 1215 and 1230 and draws on the ultimate common exemplar of the Latin lives. It also contains some other, earlier material. In particular, it depicts the saint as being conceived out of wedlock, a detail glossed over in the Latin lives. In the Irish life the saint's mother is a slavewoman belonging to the king of Eóganacht Raithlind, while his father, Amairgen, is a Connachtman. In all the lives the king plans to kill the couple, but is dissuaded by Findbarr, speaking from the womb. This signals the beginning of the relationship between the Eóganacht kings and the monastery.

The monastery flourished during the early medieval period, and claimed a large *paruchia* under its hereditary Uí Shelbaig abbots. In Findbarr's Latin life Cork claims jurisdiction over Ros Ailithir, through the simple device of portraying Findbarr as Fachtna's teacher. Furthermore, the saint dies in neighbouring Cloyne, where he is clearly treated as having jurisdiction, but his body is brought back to be buried in Cork.

The monastery flourished even after the creation of the viking town of Cork. Following the rise of Dál Cais and decline of Emly it became one of the principal churches of the Eóganacht. An attempted Dál Cais take-over was signalled by the intrusion of three Dál Cais abbots into the monastery in the second half of the eleventh century and first half of the twelfth. Cork, however, recovered and was recognized as an independent see in the synods of the twelfth century.

Móin Mór (Bairnech, Baile Mhuirne, Ballyvourney), the church and nunnery of **Gobnait** [Mo Gobnat] (*fl.* 6th cent.?) lay west of the monastery of Cork on the borders of Múscraige Mittine and Eóganacht Locha Léin. Its patron, Gobnait, is commemorated on 11 February in *Félire Óengusso* and was affiliated to the Múscraige. Her church never had more than local importance and Gobnait is not the subject of a life. She does appear in the life of Abbán, where she is very much the junior partner of the male saint. Furthermore, Findbarr's life lays claim to the church by asserting that it was founded not by Gobnait, but by a disciple of Findbarr. Her cult flourished there, however, and the remains of the medieval church can still be seen. Locally, the saint's day is still celebrated.

The great monastery of Cloyne (Cluain Uama) was located in the kingdom of Uí Liatháin. Its patron and founder was **Colmán mac Lénine** (530–606), whose feast day is recorded as 24 November in *Félire Óengusso* and the martyrology of Donegal. The genealogies make him a descendant of Ailill Aulomm through his father, Lénín, and thus a member of the Eóganachta. He is often associated with Íte and with Brendan, who is credited with converting Colmán to the religious life. Believed to have been formerly a professional poet, Colmán has been generally accepted as the author of *Luin oc laib*, a poem which praises Domnall mac Muirchertaig (*d.* 566?), the king of Tara. There are also fragments of a poem on the death of the Uí Néill king Áed Sláine (*d.* 604). It has been argued that Colmán founded Cloyne upon receiving it as a grant from the Eóganacht king Cairpre Crom (*d.* 580?). The monastery pursued a tradition of learning in keeping with its patron, being praised as a centre of legal studies in the Triads of Ireland. Like other wealthy churches Cloyne survived early viking aggression, and in the twelfth century became the see of the diocese of the same name. Little survives of the medieval monastery, however, except for a round tower.

The Fir Maige Féne were a prominent south Munster people. The most important church in their kingdom was Brí Gobann (Brigown parish in Mitchelstown). This was founded by **Findchú mac Finnloga** [Finnchú] (*d.* 655/665), son of Finnlug of the Connacht Uí Briúin. His mother, Idnait, was of the Ciannachta. Findchú is celebrated on 25 November in the martyrologies. Most of what is known about the saint comes from his eleventh- or twelfth-century Irish life preserved in the Book of Lismore, but originally copied from the lost Book of Monasterboice. According to the life Findchú was baptized by Ailbe, studied with *Comgall [see under Ulster, saints of], and succeeded the latter as abbot of Bangor, before eventually founding his own monastery in Fir Maige. The life celebrates Findchú's dealings with all of the Irish provinces, rather than the local doings of Fir Maige. The saint fosters the son of a Leinster king, defeats the Uí Chennselaig, enables a Dési king to go to heaven, and saves Munster from both an Ulster and an Uí Néill invasion. He anachronistically defeats foreigners, characters inspired by the vikings, in Connacht. Findchú is represented as having dealings with several Eóganacht kings, but most especially with Cairpre Crom. Findchú's amazing austerities form another leitmotif of the text. The life, however, seems incomplete and contains no account of the saint's death. There are at least two conflicting traditions. The annals of Inisfallen simply record his death in 655, while the annals of the four masters include him among the many clerics who died from the great plague, the *buide Conaill* in 665. Of the church of Brí Gobann little remains. Its round tower was destroyed in 1720.

Another important saint of the region was **Mo Laga mac Duib Dligid** [Lóichín; Lóchéne] (*fl.* late 6th cent.?), son of Dub Dliged of Tulach Mín Mo Laga (Labbamolaga, Templemolaga). He belonged to the Uí Chúscraid branch of the Fir Maige and his church lay on their lands. His mother, Minchollait, came from the Caenraige, a minor people. Mo Laga is commemorated on 20 January in *Félire Óengusso*. The Irish life of the saint, a production heavily influenced by saga, brings him into contact with Cumméne Fota and Mac Dá Cherda, as well as the seventh-century king of Munster Cú Cen Máthair (*d.* 665). Throughout the life he is represented as the special patron of Fir Maige, yet his cult seems to have spread beyond them. The patron of Singland (Saingil) near Limerick is identically named but affiliated to the Dál Cais. This affiliation, however, represents Dál Cais dominance in this area and their appropriation of the cult.

Cranat ingen Buicín (*fl.* 6th cent.) was a fairly significant local Fir Maige saint. She may possibly be identifiable with the Craebnat commemorated on 17 July in the martyrology of Donegal. Her Irish life is more of an anecdote than a full-blown hagiographical production. The saint's refusal of marriage to the king of Munster, Cairpre Crom, and her gouging out of her own eyes—eyes that are miraculously restored—to avoid this fate are clearly modelled on the example of the more famous Brigit. Cairpre, however, dies as a result of his temerity towards the saint. In this anecdote she is represented as the uterine sister of the king of Fir Maige, and the daughter of Buicín. Her two churches were Kilcranatan (Cell Cranatan) and Hermitage (Dísert Cranatan), both in Fir Maige Féne.

The real ecclesiastical tensions that are often subsumed into the glories of the age of saints are apparent in the career of **Mo Chutu mac Fínaill** [Carthach, Carthagus; Carthach the younger] (*d.* 637), abbot of Rahan (Rathan) and abbot–founder of Lismore (Les Mór Mo Chutu). His feast day is celebrated on 14 May in the martyrologies. He was of the Ciarraige Luachra through his father Fínall (Fíngein). His mother Finmed came from Corco Duibne. According to the notes to *Félire Óengusso* he was fostered by another Carthach, **Carthach mac Fianáin** [Carthach the elder] (*fl.* late 6th cent.), whose feast day is 5 March. The latter was identified as the son of the king of Munster and the sexually straying pupil of Ciarán of Saigir. Mo Chutu became abbot of Rahan in the lands of the southern Uí Néill. The annals of Ulster record his expulsion from Rahan in 637 during Easter, which may refer to an episode in the Easter controversy that raged in the Irish churches during the seventh century. As a Munster cleric Mo Chutu would have taken a pro-Roman approach which could have led to his expulsion. Following this, Mo Chutu travelled to Dési where he founded the great monastery of Lismore. In the several recensions of his life, both Irish and Latin, which go back to an eleventh- or twelfth-century Latin original, the Easter question is a non-issue. Instead, Mo Chutu stands against the tyrannical actions of the Uí Néill kings and is welcomed by the Dési. He appears as an equally heroic figure in the saga *Indarba Mo Chutu a r-Raithin* ('The expulsion of Mo Chutu from Rahan'). It must have been a matter of satisfaction to the hagiographers that Lismore surpassed Rahan in importance, becoming one of the great monasteries of the province and easily surviving the vikings. It was patronized by the kings of Munster, particularly the Mac Carthaig of Desmond, and was prominent in the church reform movement. Its influence was such that it surpassed Ardmore, the rival Dési church, and became the see of the diocese of Lismore.

Saints of the borderlands: Múscraige Tíre, Éle, and Osraige
Munster's northern and eastern boundaries were to prove fluid throughout the early medieval period. Múscraige Tíre (north Tipperary), Éle (Tipperary), and Osraige bordered on Leinster, and Osraige was successfully to claim Leinster status in the ninth century. The lands of this region were dotted with monastic foundations large and small. The contested nature of Osraige politics, in particular, seems to have stimulated much intellectual activity. It is no surprise, then, that the lives of these major saints should look, Janus-like, two ways. The saints inhabited a borderland between the conflicting claims of Munster and Leinster.

The monastery of Terryglass (Tír Dá Glass), which lay very close to the border of Munster in Múscraige Tíre, was one of the wealthiest churches in the midlands. Its founder, **Colum mac Crimthainn** [Columba] (*d.* 549), was of the Leinster Uí Chremthannáin. His father is named as Crimthann mac Nainnida and his mother as Minchloth. Colum is commemorated on 13 December in *Félire Óengusso*. He died in the great plague of 549 along with several other important ecclesiastics. His Latin life

dates from either the ninth or tenth century. During this period the annals record a number of abbots of Terryglass who were also abbots of Clonenagh (Cluain Ednech). The life is clearly dependent on the earlier life of Fintan, the patron of Clonenagh. Throughout Colum's life, Fintan is portrayed as his disciple, reflecting the dominance of Terryglass over Clonenagh. The life relates that Colum's main foundation is Inis Celtra, which had previously been inhabited by Mac Creiche; that a disciple, Mo Cheme, is associated with Terryglass; and that Colum's body was translated from Inis Celtra to Terryglass by his successor Nad Cáem. It also links Colum with the so-called teacher of the Irish saints, Finnian of Clonard, and with Nessán, and Colum Cille.

Colum's cult was promoted by the subsequent success of Terryglass. The monastery controlled a large *paruchia*, including Clonenagh and Inis Celtra. It had good relations with Tallaght and the Céli Dé reform movement in the ninth century. It also enjoyed similar relations with Lorrha, and Kildare, the chief church in Leinster. During the eleventh century it came under the influence of Dál Cais. Brian Bóruma's brother Marcán became abbot of Terryglass and Clonenagh. Terryglass was noted for its literary production, the most notable achievement of which was the great twelfth-century codex known as the Book of Leinster. Despite its illustrious history, the monastery suffered a precipitous decline in the latter half of the twelfth century and effectively vanished from the clerical scene. Its jurisdiction was passed to Lorrha.

The large monastery of Lorrha (Lothra) lay only a few miles north of Terryglass in Múscraige Tíre. Its founder was **Ruadán mac Fergusa Birn** [Ruadanus] (*d.* 584). He was counted, along with Colum, Brendan, and Cainnech, as one of the twelve apostles of Ireland and, like them, was supposedly taught by Finnian of Clonard. According to the genealogies of the saints his father was Fergus mac Echdach (or Fergus Birn) of the Eóganacht, while his mother may be the otherwise unknown Cáel, mentioned in the tract 'On the mothers of the saints'. Although Ruadán is mentioned in only one collection of annals, his feast day is commemorated on 15 April in the martyrologies. Of his life, three Latin recensions are extant, and a lost version formed the basis for the Irish life: none is later than the twelfth century. Genealogically Ruadán was of the Eóganacht Chaisil, and his monastery remained strongly pro-Munster in its politics. A tenth-century Munster poem portrays him as an advocate of the province's rights.

Ruadán's most famous association, however, was with the cursing of Tara during the reign of the Uí Néill king, Diarmait mac Cerbaill (*d.* 565). This legend makes its appearance in saga and hagiography, although none of the accounts are later than the eleventh century. In these, Diarmait outrages Ruadán by violating Lorrha's right of sanctuary. In retaliation Ruadán, with a band of fellow saints, fasts against Diarmait and curses Tara before gaining satisfaction. Since this same king was so admired by Adomnán, it has been suggested that the story arose as

Munster propaganda against the Uí Néill. This interpretation appears in the Book of Rights, which probably dates from the reign of Muirchertach Ua Briain (*d.* 1119), the most powerful monarch of his day. Ruadán's reputation became fixed: an eleventh- or twelfth-century poem on the saints of Ireland notes that he loved cursing. The church at Lorrha flourished throughout the early middle ages. In the twelfth century it adopted the rule of the canons regular. The bases of two high crosses survive on the site of the ancient monastery, the crosses themselves having been destroyed during the Cromwellian invasion.

Crónán moccu Éile [Mo Chua; Cronanus] (*d.* 665) was the founder of Roscrea (Ros Cré), the largest monastery in the kingdom of Éle. The saint's feast day is commemorated on 28 April in *Félire Óengusso*. According to the genealogies his father, Odrán, was of Éle while his mother, Cóemri, belonged to Corco Baiscinn. There are two extant recensions of his Latin life, the earlier and more complete of which, preserved in Codex Kilkenniensis, is unlikely to predate the twelfth century. The life brings Crónán into contact with Clonmacnoise, and Mo Chóemóc. One of its major set pieces is Crónán's deliverance of Éle from the aggressive Osraige. It also celebrates the composition of the illuminated Book of Dimma; this manuscript was the prized possession of Roscrea for centuries. Roscrea flourished, partly, because it was situated on the Slige Dála, one of the five royal routes of Ireland. The Céli Dé reformers did not find this conducive to ascetic life and set up their reformed church on the more isolated island in nearby Lough Cré. Despite the relative importance of Roscrea, Crónán does not figure prominently in the hagiography of other saints. The remains of a Romanesque church, a round tower, and a twelfth-century high cross mark the site of the monastery. The Céli Dé house is no longer so isolated, for Lough Cré has been drained.

Mo Chóemóc mac Béoáin [Cóemán; Pulcherius] (*d.* 656), founder of Leamakevoge (Liath Mo Chóemóc, Liath Mór, Leigh), was the other major saint of Éle. His feast day is recorded as 13 March in *Félire Óengusso*. Unlike Crónán, Mo Chóemóc was not related by birth to the Éli. According to the genealogies his father, Béoán, belonged to the Conmaicne of Connacht, while his mother, Ness, of the Dési, was Íte's sister. According to the twelfth- or thirteenth-century Latin life of the saint, his father owed his life to Íte's intervention and Mo Chóemóc's birth came about through her prophecy. He was raised in Uí Chonaill Gabra and fostered by Íte. Like many other saints in the lives, he was tutored by Comgall of Bangor, before eventually founding his own monastery. It seems likely that Mo Chóemóc's cult, like Íte's, owed much to the Corco Óche who were displaced by the Uí Chonaill. Mo Chóemóc is frequently linked with Mo Lua from Corco Óche. Overall, though, Mo Chóemóc's life is firmly concerned with the monastic politics of Éle and its neighbours. Several structures, dating from the eleventh to the fifteenth centuries, can still be seen at Leamakevoge.

Mo Lua moccu Óche [Lugaid, Lugidus] (554–609), the founder and abbot of Clonfertmulloe (Cluain Ferta Mo Lua) in Osraige and of Druim Snechta (Drumsnat) in the Ulster kingdom of Fernmag was a saint of national significance. He is commemorated on 4 August in the martyrology of Tallaght. The genealogies name his father as Carthach of the Corco Óche, and his mother as Sochla from Osraige. This pattern, of an Osraige saint affiliated with an ancient Munster people, is familiar from the hagiography of Ciarán of Saigir. Mo Lua's affiliation is also highlighted in the West Munster synod where he is given authority over Corco Óche. The tradition preserved in the notes of *Félire Óengusso* that his father was Carthach the Elder, Ciarán of Saigir's pupil and Mo Chutu's fosterer, is clearly late.

There are several recensions of Mo Lua's life. The oldest, contained in Codex Salmanticensis, may date from as early as the eighth century. Even at this early stage the Corco Óche element of the cult is played down. The Corco Óche lose their independent character, being identified as part of Uí Fhidgeinte, on the advice of whose king Mo Lua is said to have founded his monastery. Otherwise, his career follows the normal route of pupillage under Comgall of Bangor and, for good measure, Finnian of Clonard, after which he follows in his contemporaries' footsteps by going to Rome. There is a notable Leinster element in the life. Besides Crónán of Roscrea, most of Mo Lua's associates are from Leinster, including the great St Máedóc. This reflects the border nature of Clonfertmulloe which lay almost exactly between Osraige, Éle, and the Leinster kingdom of Loígsi. It was sited near the Slieve Bloom mountains on one of the main passes into Munster, and was supposedly founded on land donated by the king of Loígsi. The conflict between Munster and Leinster is highlighted after Mo Lua's death at the unidentified 'Tuaim Domnich'. Drawing on the familiar example of Muirchú's life of Patrick, the hagiographer relates that the people of Munster and Leinster contended for the saint's body, which, however, made its way miraculously to Clonfertmulloe, where it was buried. Even in death he mediated between the two provinces. Indeed, Clonfertmulloe thrived on its strategic position. Cumméne's seventh-century letter to Ségéne refers to the abbot of Clonfertmulloe as an authority. The change in secular and ecclesiastical politics in the twelfth century and the upheaval of the Norman invasion weakened the monastery, and little now remains of it.

Cainnech moccu Dálann [Cannicus] (521/527–599/600) was the abbot and founder of Aghaboe (Achad Bó Chainnig) and Kilkenny (Cell Chainnig) in Osraige. He is commemorated on 11 October in the martyrology of Tallaght and the annals of Ulster record his birth in either 521 or 527 and his death in either 599 or 600. His cult spread widely, and there are several Scottish dedications to the saint, including St Andrews (Cill Rigmónaig). He was also imagined to be the pupil of the Welsh saint, Cadog of Llancarfan. Cainnech's father, Luigthech (Lugaid), was of the Corco Dálann, who lived near Derry. His mother is named as Mella. Cainnech's northern pedigree is matched by connections with northern saints. He appears as Comgall's companion both in the life of that saint and in the recensions of his own life, the oldest of which is eighth- or early ninth-century. Additionally, the lives often place him in the company of Columba (Colum Cille), drawing some of their passages from Adomnán's seventh-century life of that saint.

Cainnech's earliest hagiographer is intent on making his saint as well travelled and illustrious as possible. Cainnech journeys in Britain and in Italy as well as throughout Ireland. Surprisingly little of the life takes place in Cainnech's chief foundation of Aghaboe, where he was buried, and rather more on the island in Lough Cré, near Roscrea, a place of supernatural manifestations. Aghaboe became the most important church in Osraige, eclipsing even Saigir. It declined in the twelfth century, however, and its place as head of Cainnech's *paruchia* was taken by Kilkenny. During the twelfth century Kilkenny became an episcopal see and eventually the stronghold of the Norman lords of Ormond.

Lachtín mac Tarbín [Lachtnaín; Mo Lachtóc] (*d.* 622/627) was abbot of Achad Úr (Freshford) and Belach Febrat (Ballyhoura Hills), the former one of the more important churches in southern Osraige. It produced the impressive early twelfth-century arm shrine, known as St Lachtín's Arm. Unfortunately, however, there is no extant life of the founder saint. He is commemorated on 19 March in *Félire Óengusso* and the annals record his death in 622 and in 627. The west Munster synod assigns him, and his successors, authority over the Múscraige. This is related to his paternal affiliation: his father, Tarbín, was of the Múscraige. The Latin life of Mo Chóemóc makes Lachtín a disciple of Comgall of Bangor. Like many saints, Lachtín has left little more evidence of his cult than a date in a calendar and a church site.

Conclusion The Norman invasion stands as a caesura across the history of medieval Munster. The later medieval collections of lives were the work of a different type of scholar from those who animated the age of saints. The decline of the political dynasties that had underpinned the saints' cults resulted in literary stagnation. The saints survived, outside the monasteries, in popular traditions and folklore. With the final defeat of Gaelic Ireland in the seventeenth century holy wells replaced literary lives and great monasteries as the focus for the saints.

ELVA JOHNSTON

Sources *Ann. Ulster* · S. Mac Airt, ed. and trans., *The annals of Inisfallen* (1951) · *AFM* · W. M. Hennessy, ed. and trans., *Chronicum Scotorum: a chronicle of Irish affairs*, Rolls Series, 46 (1866) · D. Murphy, ed., *The annals of Clonmacnoise*, trans. C. Mageoghagan (1896); facs. edn (1993) · W. Stokes, ed., 'The annals of Tigernach [8 pts]', *Revue Celtique*, 16 (1895), 374–419; 17 (1896), 6–33, 119–263, 337–420; 18 (1897), 9–59, 150–97, 267–303, 374–91; pubd sep. (1993) · R. I. Best and H. J. Lawlor, eds., *The martyrology of Tallaght*, HBS, 68 (1931) · *Félire Óengusso Céli Dé / The martyrology of Oengus the Culdee*, ed. and trans. W. Stokes, HBS, 29 (1905) · W. Stokes, ed., *The martyrology of Gormán*, HBS, 9 (1895) · M. O'Clery, *The martyrology of Donegal: a calendar of the saints of Ireland*, ed. J. H. Todd and W. Reeves, trans. J. O'Donovan (1864) · K. Meyer, ed., 'The Laud (610) genealogies and tribal histories', *Zeitschrift für Celtische Philologie*, 8 (1911), 291–338, 418–19 · M. A. O'Brien, ed., *Corpus genealogiarum Hiberniae* (Dublin, 1962) · P. Ó Riain, ed., *Corpus genealogiarum sanctorum Hiberniae* (Dublin, 1985) · W. W. Heist, ed., *Vitae sanctorum Hiberniae ex codice Salmanticensi nunc Bruxellensi* (Brussels, 1965) · C. Plummer, ed., *Vitae sanctorum Hiberniae* (1910) · C. Plummer, ed. and trans., *Bethada náem nÉrenn / Lives of Irish saints*, 2 vols. (1922) · W. Stokes, ed., *Lives of the saints from the Book of Lismore*, 2 vols. (1890) · F. J. Byrne, *Irish kings and high-kings* (1973) · A. Gwynn and R. N. Hadcock, *Medieval religious houses: Ireland* (1988) · E. Hogan, ed., *Onomasticon Goedelicum, locorum et tribuum Hiberniae et Scotiae* (1910) · J. F. Kenney, *The sources for the early history of Ireland* (1929); repr. (1979) · Lord Killanin and M. V. Duignan, *Shell guide to Ireland* (1962) · T. W. Moody and others, eds., *A new history of Ireland*, 9: *Maps, genealogies, lists* (1984) · C. Plummer, 'A tentative catalogue of Irish hagiography', *Miscellanea Hagiographica Hibernica* (1925) · R. Sharpe, *Medieval Irish saints' lives: an introduction to the 'Vitae sanctorum Hiberniae'* (1991)

Munthe, Axel Martin Fredrik (1857–1949), physician and author, was born on 31 October 1857 at Oskarshamn, Sweden, youngest of the three children of Martin Fredrik Munthe (1816–1877), apothecary, and his second wife, Aurora Louisa Uparsky (*d.* 1889). His forebears were wealthy landowners from Munte, near Ghent, but when the family joined the Lutheran church in the sixteenth century they were forced to flee to Scandinavia. Munthe was a delicate child with weak eyesight. He later wrote of a grim upbringing under a tyrannical father, but this was softened by a love of nature and music, and family letters suggest that he was a happy child. At sixteen he entered Uppsala University to read medicine, but after two years signs of consumption made him fear for his life and he travelled to southern Europe, and had his first glimpse of Capri. At Menton he met Professor Courty, a teacher of gynaecology, who found him a place under his tuition at the medical school at Montpellier. From there he went to Paris to complete his MD degree in 1880, the youngest student ever to do so, with a controversial thesis on haemorrhage after pregnancy.

In the same year Munthe returned to Stockholm to marry a medical student he had met in Paris, Ultima (1861–1895), daughter of Karl Johan Hendrik Hornberg, a Stockholm apothecary. They spent nearly a year in Capri, where Munthe had to deal with a typhus epidemic and the effects of an earthquake in Ischia, earning the lasting gratitude of the local population. Back in Paris in 1881, and influenced by the renowned neurologist Jean-Martin Charcot (1825–1893), Munthe became a general practitioner specializing in nervous diseases; he was soon in demand by Parisian and expatriate English high society, while treating his impecunious artist friends, and the poor, free of charge. In 1884 he read in *The Times* of a cholera epidemic in Naples, and hurried there to help. In order to raise money he sent dispatches to the Stockholm daily press. These were later collected in his first book, *Från Napoli* (1885), which was translated into English as *Letters from a Mourning City* (1887) and published by his lifelong friend John Murray. On his return from Naples he acted as correspondent for the Swedish *Aftonbladet*.

Around this time Munthe's health broke down, his marriage ended in divorce, and he departed, penniless, to Anacapri. Early in 1890 the Italian government invited him to Rome, where he set up practice in a house formerly occupied by John Keats at piazza di Spagna 26. He soon began

Axel Martin Fredrik Munthe (1857–1949), by Howard Coster, 1937

to make enough money to embark on the building of San Michele, on the site of Tiberius's villa in Anacapri, a project which occupied some twenty years and which brought him into conflict with archaeologists who disapproved of his incorporation of material from historical sites. He was appointed physician to Crown Princess Victoria of Sweden in 1893, and in 1909 he became principal court physician, despite the objections of her doctors, who criticized his methods of treatment.

On 16 May 1907 Munthe married Hilda Pennington (1877/8–1967), daughter of John Pennington Mellor, descendant of an ancient aristocratic family. There were two sons of this marriage, Viking ('Peter') and Malcolm, though Munthe and his wife seldom lived together. Munthe obtained British citizenship in 1914 in order to take part in military action, and in spite of being fifty-seven and blind in the right eye he served with the Red Cross in France. He wrote 'in pain and anger' an anonymous account of the conflict, Red Cross and Iron Cross (1916), which deeply offended the Germans.

After the war Munthe travelled widely with the Swedish court, from 1926 residing with the queen. He spent holidays at Southside, the seventeenth-century home of his wife's family at Wimbledon, Surrey, as well as in their houses abroad. Later, in order to avoid the bright light and the crowds of visitors to San Michele, he moved to a nearby medieval tower at Materita. There, reclusive and almost blind, he wrote The Story of San Michele (1929), which Henry James had suggested might help his chronic insomnia. Purporting to be his autobiography from childhood, it was an admitted mix of fact and fantasy, displaying his

powerful imagination, a gift for telling stories, and an ability to portray characters in the round, while revealing little of the author's inner life. It was an immediate best-seller, and by the time of Munthe's death had sold nearly a million copies in Britain and had been translated into thirty-seven languages. The Second World War in Europe forced Munthe to leave Capri, having accepted the offer of temporary accommodation in Stockholm, in the palace of his old friend Gustav V of Sweden.

Munthe was a tall, fair, commanding figure, with deep blue eyes when young. He possessed physical and mental courage, was nonconformist, ascetic, and humble in spite of a certain haughtiness. Brought up in the Lutheran faith, he was agnostic in later life. He was a sentimental lover of animals and had an artistic temperament, with an eye for pictures in spite of his poor sight; he was a competent pianist, and an avid collector. His success as a doctor was due to an autocratic attitude to patients, a flair for diagnosis, and a deep compassion for people from all walks of life; yet despite his many qualities he aroused the antagonism of many doctors, naturalists, and archaeologists.

Failing health and repeated attacks of asthma frustrated Munthe's hopes of returning to southern Europe, and he died of old age in Stockholm on 11 February 1949. His funeral took place on 17 February in the Chapel of the Holy Cross, where he was buried. Munthe could have been wealthy but he gave away most of his money anonymously to deserving individuals and causes; at his death he had 'little more than was needed to cover the many legacies he had willed to animals and friends' (Munthe and Uexküll, 186).

ALEX PATON

Sources G. Munthe and G. Uexküll, The story of Axel Munthe (1953) • A. Munthe, The story of San Michele, 1st illustrated edn (1936) • T. Burnett, 'introduction', in A. Munthe, The story of San Michele (1991) • The Times (12 Feb 1949) • F. R. Nye, 'Axel Munthe', New Zealand Medical Journal, 102 (1989), 290–92 • A. Paton, 'The mysterious Dr Munthe', Journal of Medical Biography, 1 (1993), 31–4 • D. P. B., A short history of Southside House, from 1687 to the present [n.d.] • M. Munthe, Hellens: a Herefordshire manor (1957) • private information (2004) [M. Munthe] • G. Karlsson, 'Munthe, Martin Axel Frederik', Svenskt biografiskt lexikon, ed. G. Nilzén, 26 (1987–9), 48–55
Archives Pennington-Mellor-Munthe Trust, Southside House, Wimbledon Common, London, collection • San Michele Foundation, Stockholm, Sweden, collection • School Teachers Cultural Foundation, Castello di Lunghezza, Rome, collection • Villa San Michele, Anacapri, Italy, collection | BL, corresp. with Society of Authors, Add. MS 63307 • Cumbria AS, Carlisle, letters to Lord Howard of Penrith • John Murray, London • Keats House, 26 Piazza di Spagna, Rome • NL Scot., letters to R. B. Cunninghame Graham • U. Birm. L., letters to F. Brett Young and J. Brett Young
Likenesses portraits, c.1881–c.1938, repro. in Munthe and Uexküll, Story of Axel Munthe • H. Coster, photograph, 1937, NPG [see illus.] • memorial plaque, protestant cemetery, via Ciao Cestio 6, Rome
Wealth at death £1412 8s. 4d.: administration with will, 27 Nov 1951, CGPLA Eng. & Wales

Muntz, George Frederick (1794–1857), political reformer and industrialist, eldest son of Philip Frederick Muntz (d. 1811) and his wife, Catherine, née Purden, was born in Great Charles Street, Birmingham, on 26 November 1794. His ancestors were Poles, whom persecution drove to

France. Muntz's grandfather, born in a country château near Soulz sur la Forêt, was a landowner of very aristocratic position. During the French Revolution the family was broken up, and Philip Frederick Muntz, the father, travelled extensively, and after spending some time as a merchant at Amsterdam moved to England, and finally to Birmingham. There, partly owing to the advice of Matthew Boulton, he bought a share for £500 in the firm of Mynors and Robert Purden, merchants. The firm was afterwards widely known as Muntz and Purden. He married Catherine, Purden's daughter, on 6 March 1793, and resided at Selly Hall, Worcestershire.

George Frederick was educated at home until his twelfth year, when he was sent to Dr Currie's school at Small Heath, Birmingham, and after a year joined the family business. He spoke French and German well. On the death of his father on 31 July 1811 he managed the metalworks which the elder Muntz had established in Water Street, Birmingham. Muntz made a large fortune by the manufacture and extended application of what became known as 'Muntz metal'. The invention closely resembled that of James Keir, who patented in 1779 'a compound metal, capable of being forged when red hot or when cold, more fit for the making of bolts, nails, and sheathing for ships than any metals heretofore used or applied for those purposes'. The similarity of the Keir to the Muntz metal was first noticed in 1866 in the *Birmingham and Midland Hardware District* volume of reports, and in the discussions that followed it was shown that in the autumn of 1779 Matthew Boulton had brought the invention to the notice of the Admiralty. Whether Muntz knew of Keir's efforts is uncertain, but he first introduced the metal into universal use. In 1837 he became a partner with the copper smelters Pascoe, Grenfell & Sons of London and Swansea, but his principal metalworks were at French Walls, near Birmingham. In 1832 he took out two patents (nos. 6325 and 6347), one for 'Muntz's metal', and one for 'ships' bolts of Muntz's metal', and in 1846 a patent for an 'alloy for sheathing ships' (R. B. Prosser, *Birmingham Inventors and Inventions*, privately printed, 1881).

On 5 October 1818 Muntz married Eliza, daughter of the Revd John Pryce and his wife, Mary Devereux. They had seven sons and two daughters. From his youth Muntz had been fascinated by politics, especially the 'currency question'. As a follower of Thomas Attwood's high tory radical currency reformers he wrote a famous series of letters in 1829 to the duke of Wellington, urging a change of policy. He was associated with Attwood again in helping to repeal the Test and Corporation Acts, and in advocating Catholic emancipation and reform of parliament. In 1829, in conjunction with Attwood and Joshua Scholefield, he founded the Birmingham Political Union for the Protection of Public Rights, believing political reform to be a necessary prelude to currency reform. This and a genuine humanitarian concern led him to sign on 5 January 1830 a memorial to the high bailiff of Birmingham (William Chance), asking him to call a meeting to consider the 'general distress', and 'to form a general political union between the lower and the middle classes of the people',

for the 'further redress of public wrongs and grievances' by 'an effectual reform in the Commons House of Parliament'. The high bailiff refused, but a meeting of fifteen thousand people was held, chaired by Muntz, and numerous meetings followed on 'Newhall Hill' until the Reform Bill was passed.

Muntz's unpolished oratory and his thorough contempt for all convention made him a favourite with the population, and an acceptable speaker at meetings of the working class. In a famous incident at the height of Wellington's unpopularity, Muntz coined the phrase, popularized by Francis Place: 'To stop the duke, go for gold'. Dangerous runs on the banks followed and contributed to Wellington's failure to form a government in May 1832. Warrants for the arrest of Attwood, Scholefield, and Muntz were found in the Home Office, completed but unsigned.

On 24 May 1840 Muntz was elected MP for Birmingham, replacing Attwood, and he retained the seat, despite serious opposition, until his death. Muntz's brand of tory radicalism fitted no accepted mould and his fierce political independence infuriated potential allies. Although opposed to universal suffrage, he voted for the Charter and was elected an honorary Chartist deputy for Birmingham. Hostile to sanitation standards and environmental controls, he nevertheless supported factory reform. He was a free-trader who yet often spoke up for protection. As a parliamentary speaker he was often obscure and epigrammatic. His legislative achievements included only an Act for the Prevention of Explosions on Steamers, but he induced a reluctant minister to adopt the system of perforated postage stamps, and to give a substantial sum to the inventor.

In local politics Muntz vigorously opposed church rates. At one of the Easter vestry meetings in St Martin's Church, Birmingham, he demanded to see the books and was refused access to them. He proposed that the rector should be removed from the chair, and a riot ensued. An application was made to the court of queen's bench against him and three others, and the case was tried at Warwick on 30 March 1838 before Mr Justice Parke for 'unlawful and riotous assembly'. After three days' trial they were virtually acquitted, but Muntz was found guilty of 'an affray' and acquitted on twelve other counts. Muntz appealed and the court decided that 'the proceedings were illegal, and that the prosecution should never have been instituted'. 'The costs were £2500, but Muntz refused any aid in paying them'.

Early in May 1857 signs of ill health were evident and were exacerbated by the recent death of a daughter. Muntz's mother, who survived him, had a premonition that he would die on the same day as his father, 31 July, and he believed this too. Indeed he 'died within a few hours of that day', on 30 July 1857, at Umberslade Hall, Warwickshire, where he latterly resided. Muntz was physically very imposing: muscular, heavy, and possessing an enormous black beard. He also had an aggressive self-confidence which resulted in frequent physical confrontations with commercial and political opponents throughout his life. His younger son Philip Albert Muntz

(1839–1908), was Conservative MP for Warwickshire (Tamworth division) from 1884 until his death, and was created a baronet in 1902. He ran the family business with the eldest son, George Frederick junior, following their father's death.   SAMUEL TIMMINS, *rev.* MATTHEW LEE

Sources Aris's *Birmingham Gazette* (1857) · *Birmingham Journal* (1857) · Boase, *Mod. Eng. biog.* · E. Edwards, *Personal recollections of Birmingham and Birmingham men* (1877), 79–88 · C. Flick, 'Muntz metal and ship's bottoms: the industrial career of G. F. Muntz', *Transactions of the Birmingham and Warwickshire Archaeological Society*, 87 (1975), 69–88 · [J. Grant], *Portraits of public characters*, 2 vols. (1841) · R. K. Dent, *Old and new Birmingham: a history of the town and its people*, 3 vols. (1879–80) · D. Fraser, *Urban politics in Victorian England* (1976) · Burke, *Peerage* (1924)
Archives BL, corresp. with Sir Robert Peel
Likenesses caricature, 1842, repro. in Flick, 'Muntz metal and ship's bottoms', facing p. 73 · caricature, 1879–80, repro. in Flick, 'Muntz metal and ship's bottoms', facing p. 73 · J. Doyle, satirical drawings, BM · portrait, repro. in *ILN*, 1 (1842), 92 · portrait, repro. in *ILN*, 14 (1849), 196

Müntz, Johann Heinrich [John Henry] (1727–1798), painter and architect, was born on 28 September 1727 in the town of Mulhouse, the second of three children of Martin Müntz, a schoolmaster, and his wife, Judith, *née* Dolfuss (Dollfus; 1697–1763). In 1748, while a captain of a Swiss regiment in the French army, Müntz recorded Gothic monuments in Spain. Accepted as a painter by Mulhouse's Tribu des Maréchaux, a guild whose members included painters, masons, and glaziers, in September 1751, he travelled to Rome, where he copied ancient vases until 1753. The following year, on Jersey in the Channel Islands, he met the artist and dramatist Richard Bentley (1708–1782), who introduced him (by letter) to Horace Walpole. Engaged by Walpole to paint at Strawberry Hill, Müntz created a fine series of topographical drawings, copied old masters, and began to experiment with encaustic painting processes. Unfortunately, relations were broken off following a quarrel in late 1759 during which Walpole questioned his veracity. In 1760 Müntz published *Encaustic, or, Count Caylus's Method of Painting in the Manner of the Ancients* dedicated to Lord Richard Edgcumbe, a friend of Walpole's. Other patrons to whom he was introduced during his time at Strawberry Hill included the connoisseur John Chute, for whom he copied old masters and drew views of his home, The Vyne, Hampshire, and the collector Richard Bateman, for whom he designed the Gothic dining room in his house at Old Windsor, Berkshire. During the same period he created a 'Gothic cathedral' (1759) for William Chambers at Kew, Surrey and wrote a proposal for a treatise on Gothic architecture. At the 1762 Society of Artists he exhibited his designs for Lord Charlemont's Gothic vase room at Marino, co. Dublin.

Abandoning England for the continent, Müntz recorded landscapes in Jerusalem and Greece in 1763 and 1764, then painted arcadian landscapes in Holland until 1777, concurrently working as a metallurgist and writing treatises on smelting and the oval in ancient vases. His metallurgical experience led to an appointment with the treasury of Poland in 1778, which in turn led to a position as Prince

Stanislaw Poniatowski's companion, recording and illustrating the latter's travels, during which time Müntz was appointed major in the Polish army and joined a masonic lodge. Following a move to Kassel, Germany, in 1786, he produced paintings of Wilhelmshöhe gardens, landscapes, and two further treatises on etching and painting. Müntz became a member of the Kassel Royal Art Academy and the Academy of Artists and Architects in 1793. After his death in Kassel in May 1798, Müntz was buried at Oberneustadt Deutsche Gemeinde, Kassel, and a monument in his honour was erected in Riede Park.

TERESA SOPHIA WATTS

Sources Walpole, *Corr.*, vols. 9–10, 13–14, 21, 35, 40 · Mulhouse Archives, Taufbuch der Stadt Mulhouse, 476 · M. Dollfus, *Histoire et généalogie de la famille Dollfus de Mulhouse, 1450–1908* (1909) · J. H. Müntz, 'Proposals for publishing … a course of Gothic architecture', 1760, BL, Add. MSS 6/71, P.S.3/9168 · J. H. Müntz, 'Voyages pittoresques par Müntz, 1763–1786', State Historical Museum, Moscow, fond 446, nos. 3219, 3220, 3222 · J. H. Müntz, 'Vorstellung und ausführliche Beschreibung von dem Silber und Kupfer Schmeltz-werck', 1772, Krakow National Museum, B. Czart. Rep., no. 816 · E. Edwards, *Anecdotes of painters* (1808); facs. edn (1970) · H. Knackfuss, *Geschichte der Königlichen Kunstakademie zu Kassel* (1908) · T. S. Watts, 'The life and work of Johann Heinrich Müntz (1727–1798)', PhD diss., University of Toronto, 1986 · *Casselische Polizey- und Commerzien Zeitung* (21 May 1798), burials · J. Hoffmeister, *Gesammelte Nachrichten über Künstler und Kunsthandwerker in Hessen seit etwa 300 Jahren* (Hannover, 1885) · Graves, *Soc. Artists* · Thieme & Becker, *Allgemeines Lexikon* · E. Meininger, *Les anciens artistes-peintres et décorateurs mulhousiens jusqu'au XIXe siècle* (Mulhouse, 1908)
Archives BM · Graphische Sammlung Albertina, Vienna · Koninklijk Huisarchief, The Hague · Krakow National Museum · Kunstinstitut Marburg, prints and drawings room · Landesmuseum Oldenburg Gemäldegalerie · Musée Teyler à Haarlem · Musées Royaux des Beaux-Arts de Belgique, Brussels, De Grez collection · Museum Boymans-van Beuningen, Rotterdam · RIBA · Rijksprentenkabinet, Amsterdam · Städelsches Kunstinstitut, Frankfurt am Main · Staatliche Kunstsammlungen, Schloss Wilhelmshöhe, Kassel · State Historical Museum, Moscow · The Vyne, near Basingstoke, Hampshire · University of Warsaw, prints and drawings room · V&A NAL · Verwaltung der Staatlichen Schlösser und Gärten Hessen, Bad Homburg · Yale U., Farmington, Lewis Walpole Library · Yale U. CBA
Likenesses miniature (in uniform)
Wealth at death died in poverty, according to Caroline Condrad: Caroline Conredi to Landgrave Wilhelm IX, Nov 1758, Marburg Staatarchiv

Mura. *See* Muru mac Feradaig (*fl.* c.600–c.650) *under* Ulster, saints of (*act.* c.400–c.650).

Murch, Jerom (1807–1895), Unitarian minister and municipal activist, was born on 29 October 1807 in Honiton, Devon, the fourth of the seven children of William Murch (1767–1853), tinsmith and ironmonger, and his second wife, Ann, *née* Burnard (1775–1856), of Colyton. He had five other siblings from his father's first marriage.

In 1827 Murch attended the General Baptist Academy in London, and in 1828–9 London University. He became pastor at the Unitarian chapel, Diss, Norfolk, in 1829, where he met his future wife, Anne Meadows Taylor (1800–1893), the daughter of wealthy Unitarians. They married on 1 June 1830 and had two sons: Charles Jerom (1833–1891) and Arthur (1836–1885).

Between 1833 and his retirement from ill health in 1846 Murch was pastor at Trim Street Chapel, Bath. He published sermons and open letters in defence of his denomination and *A History of the Presbyterian and General Baptist Churches in the West of England* (1835), which provided evidence of Unitarian property rights. Politicized by these endeavours he became leader of the local whig/radical group and later president of the United Liberal Association.

Murch played leading roles in Bath's major philanthropic, cultural, and educational initiatives, acting on occasion as president of the Mechanics' Institute (later the Athenaeum); the Bath Literary Club; the Mineral Water Hospital; and the boards of governors of Bath high school and King Edward's School and of the Bath Royal Literary and Scientific Institution. He was vice-president of the Bath and West of England Society; magistrate for Somerset from 1857 and deputy lieutenant in 1867; president of the Somerset Archaeological and Natural History Society in 1876; and president of the British and Foreign Unitarian Association in 1866.

By the late 1850s Murch was Bath's leading citizen, and before his election to council in 1862 he was invited to officiate at the Bath meeting of the British Association for the Advancement of Science in 1864. By the end of his life he had completed seven mayoralties: 1863–4; 1864–5; 1876–7; 1877–8; 1886–7; 1890–91; 1892–3. However, at a by-election on 7 May 1873 he failed to be elected as one of the city's MPs because of his support for Gladstonian Liberalism and secular education.

In 1864 Murch planned a comprehensive reform programme for Bath, which included the building of a modern municipal hotel with hot-water treatment baths, extension of the water supply, a solution for drainage and river pollution problems, and the removal of privileges from the freemen. Although the improvement bill failed because of the speculative nature of the hotel scheme, by 1869 he chaired the private company running the Grand Pump Room Hotel, which operated with a civic suite of baths. The Bath Act 1870 and subsequent provisional orders improved the water supply and the Bath Act 1879 extinguished freemen's rights.

Although Murch had extended the concept of civic service his successes were marred: management problems dogged the hotel; in 1879 the West of England and South Wales Bank failed during his chairmanship; and he did not complete his plan for the city as flooding and drainage problems remained. However, from 1878 he championed the campaign to uncover the Roman baths in the city, and during his last two mayoralties achieved the construction of new civic buildings, the foundation-stone of which he laid in 1893. He was knighted on 21 May 1894. Jerom Murch died on 13 May 1895 at his Bath home, Cranwells, Weston Park, and was buried on 17 May at the Unitarian cemetery, Lyncombe Vale, Bath.   ALEX KOLACZKOWSKI

Sources A. E. Kolaczkowski, 'The politics of civic improvement: Bath, 1835–79', PhD diss., University of Bath, 1995 · A. E. Kolaczkowski, 'Jerom Murch and Unitarianism in Bath, 1833–45', *Transactions of the Unitarian Historical Society*, 21 (1995–6), 15–29 · *Unitarian Herald* (18 May 1895) · *The Inquirer* (18 May 1895) · *The Times* (14 May 1895) · *Bath Chronicle* (16 May 1895) · *Bath Herald* (18 May 1895) · *Bath Journal* (18 May 1895) · J. Murch, 'Bath celebrities with fragments of local history', 1893 · Murch MSS, Bath Library · Trim Street Chapel MSS, Bath RO · Bath city council minutes, 1833–80, Bath RO · J. Murch, 'A short memoir of the Murch family', 1854, priv. coll. · 'The British Association for the Advancement of Science: Bath Meeting', *Bath Chronicle* (1864) · Burke, *Gen. GB* · d. cert. [Ann Murch] · d. cert. · *Bath Directory* (1850–95)

Archives Bath and North East Somerset RO, Bath, corresp. · Bath Reference Library, letters, pamphlets, and scrapbooks | Bath and North East Somerset RO, Bath, Trim Street Chapel archive · Bath and North East Somerset RO, Bath, Bath city council archive · NL Scot., corresp. with Lord Rosebery

Likenesses T. Brock, marble bust, 1878, Bath Royal Literary and Scientific Institution, Bath · Berryman, photograph, 1892, Bath Library · S. J. Solomon, two oil paintings, 1894, Victoria Art Gallery, Bath; damaged · T. Brock, bronze bust, 1895, Victoria Art Gallery, Bath · photograph, 1934 (after S. J. Solomon, 1894), Victoria Art Gallery, Bath · photograph, Bath RO

Wealth at death £2543 16s. 9d.: probate, 5 Sept 1895, *CGPLA Eng. & Wales*

Murchison, Charles (1830–1879), physician, was born on 26 July 1830 at Vere, Jamaica, the younger son of Alexander Murchison, physician and cousin to the geologist Sir Roderick Impey *Murchison. On his father's retirement in 1833 the family returned to Scotland and settled in Elgin, near their ancestral home. In 1845 Murchison enrolled at the University of Aberdeen as an arts student; in 1847 he went on to Edinburgh University as a medical student, graduating MD there in 1851 with a thesis entitled 'The structure of tumours'. At Aberdeen he won the prize for Greek; at Edinburgh he won prizes in botany, surgery, and midwifery, and a gold medal for the best thesis of his year. Initially Murchison was headed for surgery. He passed the examination of the College of Surgeons in Edinburgh in 1850 and became house surgeon to James Syme. Murchison was also an ardent botanist, interested in plant anatomy and physiology. After graduation Murchison spent a year as physician to the British embassy at Turin. After a short period as resident clinical physician at the Edinburgh Infirmary in 1852, he trained in midwifery at the Rotunda Hospital in Dublin, studied briefly in Paris, and was then appointed assistant surgeon to the East India Company in January 1853. In Calcutta Murchison was appointed professor of chemistry at the Bengal Medical College. In 1854 he served on the medical staff in the Burmese campaign. Returning to London in the autumn of 1855, he quickly passed the membership examination of the Royal College of Physicians and obtained posts as physician to the Westminster General Dispensary, and as anatomical demonstrator and later lecturer on botany at St Mary's Hospital. In 1856 Murchison added the posts of assistant physician at the London Fever Hospital (full physician, 1861–70) and at the King's College Hospital, resigning the latter post in 1860 in protest at administrative policies. He then served as assistant physician at the Middlesex Hospital (full physician after 1860), before moving to St Thomas's Hospital to become physician and lecturer in medicine in 1871. In the autumn of 1873 he traced the origin of an epidemic of typhoid fever to a polluted milk supply; the grateful residents in west London presented him with a testimonial. In July 1859 Murchison married Clara Elizabeth, daughter of Robert Bickersteth, a Liverpool surgeon; they had nine children. During the same year Murchison was elected fellow of the Royal College of Physicians, and in 1866 fellow of the Royal Society. He was also a member of the Epidemiological and Pathological societies, the Linnean Society, and the Botanical Society of Edinburgh. Shortly before his death he was appointed physician to the duke and duchess of Connaught.

On his return to London Murchison began a prolific publishing career, at first drawing on his background in botany and experience in India and Burma, turning later to fever and to a remarkable range of aspects of pathology. Murchison published over 300 papers, mainly in the *Edinburgh Medical and Surgical Journal*, the *British and Foreign Medico-Chirurgical Review*, and the *Transactions of the Pathological Society*. It was with the Pathological Society that he was most closely associated, publishing 143 papers in its *Transactions*, serving as honorary secretary from 1865 to 1869, as treasurer from 1869 to 1877, and as president from 1877 to his death. He served the *British Medical Journal* as editor of a section reviewing the contents of foreign medical journals and, occasionally, as a leader writer.

As a medical author Murchison was known for his exhaustive works on liver diseases and on continued fever. On the former subject he published in 1860–61 *A Clinical Treatise on the Diseases of the Liver*, a translation from the German by Friedrich Frerich, following this in 1868 with his own *Clinical Lectures on the Diseases of the Liver, Jaundice and Abdominal Dropsy*, to which were added in the second (1877) and third (1885) editions his 1873 Croonian lectures entitled 'Functional derangements of the liver'. Murchison's work on the liver reflected the perspective of a society physician seeking to comprehend ill-defined digestive complaints. Though able reviews of the clinical literature, his works did not fully integrate the research of physiologists or the new discipline of the biochemists, who disproved several of his main hypotheses in the last quarter of the century.

Murchison's *Treatise on the Continued Fevers of Great Britain* (1862) was ground-breaking, being the first major work on the subject in English for over twenty years, at the same time a compendium of centuries of medical literature and a lucid treatment of what had been one of the most confused areas of medicine. The first edition was controversial in asserting the still contested distinctiveness of typhus, relapsing, and typhoid (or as Murchison called it 'pythogenic') fever, a matter on which he departed from the views of his predecessors at the London Fever Hospital. Murchison presented these distinctions as an application of the numerical method of Pierre Louis, and used them to reinterpret past epidemics and to help to assess the efficacy of rival therapies. The second edition was controversial for Murchison's refusal to accept William Budd's claim that typhoid was communicated by a living germ, excreted by sufferers and ingested by new victims in contaminated water or food. Drawing on the experiments of Karl Thiersch and the ideas of Justus Liebig, Murchison viewed the typhoid poison as a state of fermentation of excreta, usually, though not necessarily, the excreta of a typhoid sufferer. These issues were not fully resolved until early in the next century with the recognition of non-symptomatic carriers of the typhoid bacillus. It is a mark of Murchison's abilities as a medical scholar that the liver and fever books—both thorough, clear, and scrupulously cautious—were translated into French, German, and Dutch during a period when most biomedical translation was in the other direction. A German translation of *Continued Fevers* appeared in 1867 by W. Zuelzer, French translations in 1878 (by Lutaud) and 1896 (by Thoinot and du Biot). A Dutch translation of *Clinical Lectures* was published in 1870 by Noever de Brauw and a French translation in 1878 by J. Cyr. There were posthumous English third editions of the *Clinical Lectures* (by T. Lauder Brunton in 1885) and of the *Treatise* (by W. Cayley in 1884).

Throughout his adult life Murchison was a field naturalist, interested in geology as well as botany. In the early 1870s he edited the geological manuscripts of his longtime friend Hugh Falconer. Murchison died suddenly on 23 April 1879 in his consulting rooms as a result of a longstanding heart condition, and was buried at Norwood cemetery on 26 April. He was survived by his wife, two sons, and four daughters. Both at St Thomas's, and in Edinburgh, which had awarded him an LLD in 1870 and where he maintained many close friendships among the medical and surgical faculties, there were meetings to organize a memorial. These led to the commissioning of a bust, placed in St Thomas's Hospital, and to a Murchison scholarship in medicine.

In many ways Murchison epitomized the mid-Victorian ideal of a gentlemanly scientist-physician. He was at once a superb scholar, an accomplished pathologist, an excellent clinician, a stimulating and well-organized teacher, and a popular society practitioner. Though a 'keen controversialist' (Munk, *Roll*), Murchison engaged his critics with a dignity and civility that were often lacking in contemporary medical disputation.   CHRISTOPHER HAMLIN

Sources *BMJ* (26 April–21 June 1879), 648–953 *passim* · M. Pelling, *Cholera, fever and English medicine, 1825–1865* (1978) · *The Lancet* (3 May 1879), 645–6 · *The Lancet* (17 May–28 June 1879), 717, 753, 787, 863–4, 900, 933 · C. E. A. Winslow, *The conquest of epidemic disease: a chapter in the history of ideas* (1943) · Munk, *Roll* · 'Charles Murchison (1830–1879)', *Journal of the American Medical Association*, 213 (1970), 1028–9 · *PRS*, 29 (1879), xxiii–xxv · J. Britten and G. S. Boulger, eds., *A biographical index of deceased British and Irish botanists*, 2nd edn, ed. A. B. Rendle (1931), 224 · F. Garrison, *An introduction to the history of medicine* (1913) · T. Chen and P. Chen, *Understanding the liver: a history* (1984) · *DNB*

Archives Guy's and St Thomas's hospitals, London, casebooks · RCP Lond., papers relating to milk epidemic and to proposed fever hospital at Hempstead · Wellcome L.

Likenesses E. Roscoe Mullins, marble bust, exh. 1881, St Thomas's Hospital, London · H. J. Fradelle, chalk and wash drawing, RCP Lond. · portrait, repro. in J. D. Cromie, *History of Scottish medicine*, 2 (1932), 722 · portrait (*Buildings and famous alumni of St Thomas's Hospital, London*), Wellcome L.

Wealth at death under £50,000: probate, 15 May 1879, *CGPLA Eng. & Wales*

Murchison [*née* Hugonin], **Charlotte**, **Lady Murchison** (**1788–1869**), geologist, was born, according to the inscription on her tombstone, on 18 April 1788, probably in the family's home, Nursted House, near Petersfield, Hampshire, one of at least three children of General Francis Hugonin (*d*. 1836) and his wife, Charlotte (*d*. 1838), daughter of Mileson and Elizabeth Edgar. Nothing is known of her childhood or youth.

In early summer 1815 Charlotte Hugonin met Roderick Impey *Murchison (1792–1871); she married him on 29 August 1815 in the church of Buriton in Hampshire. They had no children, but a daughter of Roderick's brother lived with them for some years. From 1816 to 1818 the Murchisons toured the continent. It is likely the tour was Charlotte's idea, an attempt to curb her husband's spending and to interest him in intellectual pursuits. They travelled through Italy, visiting Genoa, Naples, and Rome, where they became acquainted with Mary Somerville (1780–1872), the scientific writer, who became a lifelong friend. It was also in Rome that Charlotte caught a malarian fever that nearly caused her death, and whose symptoms returned at intervals all through her life. After returning to England in 1818 the Murchisons lived at Barnard Castle, co. Durham, at the house of Charlotte's late grandfather. In 1820 or 1821 they moved to Melton Mowbray where Roderick Murchison dedicated himself to foxhunting. Charlotte constantly tried to interest him in more intellectual pursuits, and finally succeeded in 1824, aided by Humphry Davy (1778–1829) and by financial problems. The couple moved to London, and Roderick Murchison began to attend lectures on geology and chemistry.

In the summer of 1825 the Murchisons undertook geological fieldwork along the south coast of England, with Charlotte collecting fossils and sketching the outcrops along the coast. In Lyme Regis she went fossil-hunting with the palaeontologist Mary Anning (1799–1847); the two women became good friends and soon established a frequent correspondence. The following year the Murchisons undertook fieldwork in Yorkshire and the Hebrides. Charlotte carried out the actual fossil-hunting, and collected many specimens which Sowerby (1788–1871) later described in the *Mineral Conchology of Great Britain* (1812–34). She also made many sketches of outcrops and fossils. Sowerby named one of the cephalopods *Ammonites murchisonae* 'as a just tribute for the ardour with which [Mrs Murchison] has pursued the study of fossil conchology, the pleasing effects of which those who are so happy as to be acquainted with her know how to appreciate' (Sowerby, 6.96). Other palaeontologists including William Buckland (1784–1856) used Charlotte's collection of fossils for their work. In 1828 Charlotte accompanied her husband and Charles Lyell (1797–1875) to the Auvergne region of France and to northern Italy. Again she participated actively in the expedition, and Lyell esteemed her as 'an invaluable assistant' (*Life, Letters, and Journals*, 184). Two years later the Murchisons were exploring Germany and the Alps. From the early 1830s until 1838, Roderick Murchison worked on greywacke deposits in Wales, and again Charlotte was frequently at his side. A number of her sketches are reproduced in her husband's *The Silurian System* (1839).

On her mother's death in 1838 Charlotte Murchison inherited a fortune, and this enabled the couple to move in 1840 to fashionable Belgrave Square. Their soirées there became an important meeting place for scientists and politicians, and their success was mainly due to Charlotte's social abilities. However, as the years passed, her health became steadily worse. She was unable to accompany her husband to Russia, although in 1847 they both travelled in the Alps and Italy, combining science and the therapeutic benefits of a better climate. In time Charlotte was confined to her home, although it appears she still participated mentally in her husband's work and advised him in his scientific activities, and was probably able to visit people in the locality. After a prolonged phase of feeble health, Charlotte Murchison died from bronchitis at her home, 16 Belgrave Square, on 9 February 1869; she was buried at Brompton cemetery, London, on 13 February.

Whereas contemporaries knew and cherished her influence and abilities, she later became considered a mere appendage to her husband. However, without her Roderick Murchison would have never been a geologist. As Mary Somerville said:

> Mrs Murchison was an amiable accomplished woman, drew prettily and what was rare at the time she had studied science, especially geology and it was chiefly owing to her example that her husband turned his mind to those pursuits in which he afterwards obtained such distinction. (Patterson, 29)

It was she who introduced him into the geological world, and it was her money and social position which helped him achieve such extraordinary prominence within it (he was knighted in 1846 and made baronet in 1866). She took an active part in the scientific pursuits which she had initiated, and her views are intimately connected with Roderick Murchison's work. Charlotte Murchison also played a role in making higher education accessible to women: in 1831 it was her wish to attend Lyell's geological lectures at King's College that caused them to be opened to both sexes.   M. KÖLBL-EBERT

Sources A. Geikie, *Life of Sir Roderick I. Murchison*, 2 vols. (1875) · M. Kölbl-Ebert, 'Charlotte Murchison *née* Hugonin, 1788–1869', *Earth Science History*, 16 (1997), 39–43 · F. Buckland, 'Souvenirs of the life of Lady Murchison', *Land and Water* (13 Feb 1869) [copy in British Geological Survey Archive, 1/748] · J. Sowerby, *The mineral conchology of Great Britain*, 6 (1827) · *Life, letters, and journals of Sir Charles Lyell*, ed. Mrs Lyell, 2 vols. (1881) · E. C. Patterson, *Mary Somerville and the cultivation of science, 1815–1840* (1983) · M. Somerville, *Personal recollections, from early life to old age, of Mary Somerville* (1873) · L. G. Wilson, *Charles Lyell, the years to 1841: the revolution in geology* (1972) · J. A. Secord, *Controversy in Victorian geology: the Cambrian–Silurian dispute* (1986) · C. L. Fenton and M. A. Fenton, *Giants of geology* (1952) · P. R. Crowther, 'Murchison and *The Quorn at Quenby* in 1823 by John Ferneley', *Transactions of the Leicester Literary and Philosophical Society*, 76 (1985), 64–70 · H. S. Torrens, 'Mary Anning (1799–1847) of Lyme: "the greatest fossilist the world ever knew"', *British Journal for the History of Science*, 28 (1995), 257–84 · W. D. Lang, 'Three letters by Mary Anning, "fossilist", of Lyme', *Proceedings of the Dorset Natural History and Archaeological Society*, 66 (1945), 169–73 · *GM*, 2nd ser., 5 (1836) [obit. of Francis Hugonin] · Burke, *Gen. GB*

Archives U. Edin. L., family papers | Bodl. Oxf., Somerville collection · GS Lond., Roderick I. Murchison MSS · NHM, letters to J. de C. Sowerby
Likenesses drawing, repro. in H. Faul and C. Faul, *It began with a stone: a history of geology from the stone age to the age of plate tectonics* (1983), fig. 8.1 · oils (of Murchison?), Tarredale(?) House, Easter Ross
Wealth at death under £100: probate, 3 June 1869, *CGPLA Eng. & Wales*

Murchison, Sir **Roderick Impey**, baronet (1792–1871), geologist and geographer, born on 19 February 1792 at Tarradale in Easter Ross, was the elder son of Kenneth Murchison and his wife, Barbara, the daughter of Roderick Mackenzie of Fairburn. The Murchisons were a highland clan who lost their ancestral lands for participating in the rebellions of 1715 and 1745. Kenneth Murchison was educated for the medical profession, went out to India in 1769, and amassed a fortune as a surgeon in the service of the East India Company. After seventeen years he returned to Scotland, purchased Tarradale, and married in 1791. After Roderick's birth in 1792 and Kenneth's in 1794, their father's health began to fail and he died at Bath in 1796. His widow settled in Edinburgh with her two boys, and before long married Colonel Robert Macgregor Murray, a friend of her late husband.

Education and military career In 1799 Roderick was placed at the grammar school, Durham, where he led in mischief more often than in his class. In 1805 he entered the military college at Great Marlow in Buckinghamshire, where he kept up his Durham reputation, but developed an interest in the practical aspects of his studies, especially topographical appraisal. In 1807 he was gazetted ensign in the 36th infantry regiment, but did not join until the following winter. The regiment was then quartered at Cork, but during the summer it landed in Portugal, where it fought with distinction at Vimeiro, and afterwards shared in Sir John Moore's Spanish campaign and disastrous retreat to Corunna. The regiment embarked for England in January 1809, where it remained, but in the autumn Murchison went to Sicily as aide-de-camp to his uncle, General Sir Alexander Mackenzie, returning in 1811. Mackenzie was then appointed to a command in Armagh, and took Murchison with him. Missing the Peninsula campaign, Murchison purchased a captaincy, but the peace of 1814 placed him on half pay. He was in Paris when the news of Napoleon's landing arrived. Fleeing to England, Murchison exchanged to a cavalry regiment in hope of seeing active service, but his troop remained at home. As a consolation he met Charlotte [*see* Murchison, Charlotte], daughter of General and Mrs Hugonin, whom he married on 29 August 1815, and shortly afterwards retired from the army.

Murchison's early career in science This was the turning-point of Murchison's life, for he came under the influence of a thoughtful, cultivated, and affectionate woman, but it was still some years before he settled down to scientific work. He thought briefly of being ordained, but gave up the idea and started with his wife in 1816 for a tour on the continent. The excursion had two objectives: weaning

Sir Roderick Impey Murchison, baronet (1792–1871), by Camille Silvy, 1860

Murchison of his idle habits and reducing their expenditure. They remained abroad until 1818, chiefly at Rome and Naples, where Murchison plunged enthusiastically into the study of art and antiquities. On his return to England he sold Tarradale for £27,000 and settled down at Barnard Castle, co. Durham, devoting himself to field sports. He continued to live beyond his means, moving to Leicestershire in 1822, borrowing from his father-in-law, and speculating in shaky foreign funds. In 1823, when drastic change had become inevitable, he met Sir Humphry Davy, and determined to move to London to pursue science instead of the fox. In the autumn of 1824 he began to attend lectures diligently at the Royal Institution. He was admitted on 7 January 1825 a fellow of the Geological Society, and that science quickly kindled his enthusiasm. The following summer was devoted to fieldwork around Nursted, Kent (where his father-in-law lived), and to a tour to Cornwall. Murchison's first paper, a 'Geological sketch of the north-western extremity of Sussex, and the adjoining parts of Hants and Surrey', was read to the Geological Society at the end of 1825. In 1826 he was elected FRS, and spent the summer examining the Jurassic rocks of Yorkshire and on the east and west coasts of Scotland. His monograph proving that the Brora coalfield of Scotland was the same age as Jurassic formations in England was the first of several papers that quickly made him one of the most prominent members of the Geological Society. From the start of his geological career, Murchison focused his efforts on stratigraphy, following the principles of superposition and palaeontological dating. In 1827 he travelled with Adam Sedgwick in the highlands; in 1828, accompanied by his wife, with Charles Lyell in the volcanic district of the Auvergne and in northern Italy. At this time Murchison leaned towards Lyell's gradualist views on geological change, but from 1829, when he and the catastrophist Sedgwick worked in the Alps, he increasingly emphasized drastic disturbance in the history of the earth's crust.

The Silurian System After five years of service as secretary of the Geological Society Murchison was elected president in 1831, and turned his attention to the older Palaeozoic rocks underlying the Carboniferous or the Old Red Sandstone, known as the 'transition', or 'greywacke'. These formations, outcropping conspicuously in Wales and the west of Britain, were, geologically speaking, an almost unknown land. The highly contorted ancient strata were known to contain fossils, however, so that a downward extension of the stratigraphical column—and therefore the history of life—was at least a possibility. In the summer of 1831 Sedgwick worked on the northern part of Wales, Murchison on the more southern district. At one time a joint tour had been suggested, but the intention was never realized. Murchison, having discovered a conformable, fossiliferous sequence from the Old Red Sandstone down into the transition strata, devoted the next two summers to similar work. In 1834 the two friends were together in Wales, endeavouring to mesh their separate work, but they parted without discovering that the lower part of Murchison's system of strata (to which with typical patriotism he assigned in 1835 the name Silurian to honour the indigenous British tribe) was equivalent to the upper part of that called Cambrian by Sedgwick. The preparation of Murchison's book took a long time, but fieldwork went on, and in 1836 he made the first of three journeys to Devon to unravel another greywacke district. At last, at the end of 1839, *The Silurian System* was published, embodying the results obtained by Murchison himself, or supplied to him by others. It was an important milestone in geology, for it established the oldest fossil-bearing classification then known. Murchison took great pride in his system as an important period in the history of life and as a geographical entity whose expansive potential provided ample scope for his overweening ambitions. His Silurian territoriality came to a head in the celebrated and protracted dispute with Sedgwick over the Cambrian–Silurian boundary. Each man wanted to prove that his own system contained the fossil evidence for the origin of life. Murchison annexed new fossil discoveries to his system, encroaching on Sedgwick's until their friendship was ruined, the British geological community had taken sides, and Murchison won the contest (for the day) by wearing down his opponent through superior advocacy and public relations. The dispute was settled only after several decades of controversy with the adoption of

Charles Lapworth's 1879 proposal that an 'Ordovician system' define the debatable ground.

The researches of Sedgwick and Murchison in the west of England were followed by papers in which they proposed the establishment of a Devonian system intermediate between the Carboniferous and Silurian, and so equivalent to the Old Red Sandstone. In 1839 they visited Germany and the Boulonnais to confirm their views. As with the Silurian system the birth of the Devonian occasioned much controversy, for Sir Henry De la Beche, director-general of the Geological Survey of Great Britain, and others opposed Murchison and Sedgwick, arguing that the Devonian rocks could not be classified exclusively by fossils and were, on structural evidence, older, perhaps Silurian strata. This apparently serious anomaly threatened Murchison's belief that the Silurian predated the establishment of terrestrial vegetation and thus could serve as a reliable indicator to avoid pointless exploration for coal. Characteristically, Murchison overcame the dissenters and built a consensus favouring his own view by a campaign of patient fieldwork, manoeuvring, and intimidation.

In the same year Murchison's social influence was increased by his wife's inheritance, which enabled him to move to a grand mansion at 16 Belgrave Square, which became a famous intellectual salon. He also planned a visit to Russia, where the comparatively undisturbed Palaeozoic rocks presented fewer difficulties than in Britain. Accompanied by the French palaeontologist Edouard de Verneuil, and aided by the officials and savants of Russia, Murchison travelled to the shores of the White Sea, and thence to Nizhniy Novgorod, Moscow, and back to St Petersburg. In the following summer the two travellers returned to Moscow, and, after examining the Carboniferous rocks in the neighbourhood, made for the Ural mountains, followed them southwards to Orsk, thence westward to the Sea of Azov and the Donets coalfield before returning to Moscow. After a third visit to St Petersburg by way of Scandinavia and Finland, *The Geology of Russia and the Ural Mountains* by Murchison, von Keyserling, and de Verneuil was published in April 1845. The book established a third Palaeozoic system—the Permian—separating the Carboniferous rocks from secondary (Mesozoic) strata and confirmed the succession of Europe's ancient rocks as far east as the Urals.

Honours other than scientific now began to come in. From the emperor of Russia Murchison had already received the orders of St Anne and of Stanislaus, and in 1846 he was knighted by Peel after prolonged entreaty. In 1843 he was elected president of the Royal Geographical Society which he had helped found in 1830, but geology remained his focus until the 1850s. In 1847–8, Sir Roderick and Lady Murchison were on the continent, revisiting Rome, Naples, and the eastern Alps. This journey resulted in an important paper on the geological structure of the Alps, Apennines, and Carpathians (*Quarterly Journal of the Geological Society*, 5.157). Murchison for some time had been occupied in recasting *The Silurian System* into a more compact and updated form, and the new book, entitled *Siluria*, appeared in 1854. It synthesized new Palaeozoic research around the world and set forth criteria for the occurrence of coal and gold.

Murchison and the Royal Geographical Society The following year brought an important change in Murchison's life, for on the death of De la Beche he was appointed director-general of the Geological Survey. Coupled with a revived interest in the Royal Geographical Society, the new post enabled Murchison to shape much of Britain's overseas research effort, both in the official empire and beyond. He appointed many colonial geological surveyors, as well as organizing and writing the scientific instructions for every major expedition to leave Britain during the spate of exploration between 1850 and 1870. This new imperial field of endeavour not only combined geology and geography, which Murchison considered sister sciences, in a three-dimensional taxonomic enterprise of global scale, but provided boundless scope for his ambitions and patriotism. In the mutually beneficial bargain largely struck by Murchison, science helped take an inventory of, develop, and justify the empire, while the empire offered science access to invaluable overseas data. Murchison therefore played a critical part in forging enduring links between science and government. His 'close connections' with politicians of every stripe heightened his ability to extend government patronage to geologists in nearly every colony and to arrange sponsorship for explorers in every continent. Through his popular annual addresses to the Royal Geographical Society, he also preached a consistent gospel of imperial expansion; on occasion, though unsuccessfully, he urged specific annexations on ministerial friends such as Clarendon.

1856 also witnessed the beginning of a new piece of geological work, the attempt to unravel the complicated structure of the Scottish highlands. A journey undertaken in 1858 with Charles Peach made clear that the Torridon sandstone of the north-western highlands was much less ancient than a great series of coarse gneissose rocks, to which Murchison gave the name of 'fundamental gneiss', afterwards identifying it with the Laurentian gneiss of North America, first identified by Sir William Logan. The Torridon sandstone contained no fossils, but it was followed by quartzites and limestones which Murchison inferred from their fossils to be of lower Silurian age, although they were later classed as Cambrian and Ordovician. Above these, in apparent sequence, came crystalline (Moine) schists which made up much of the central highlands and the southern part of the north-western highlands, and which Murchison regarded as Silurian strata altered by metamorphism. Professor J. Nicol, who had been at first associated with Murchison, disagreed, maintaining these schists to be part of the fundamental gneiss, brought up by faulting. Murchison accordingly revisited the highlands in 1859 with Professor Andrew Ramsay, and in 1860 with Alexander Geikie, returning convinced of the accuracy of his view, which he maintained in a joint paper with Geikie read to the Geological Society in 1861. But Nicol, as the work of Lapworth and others has shown, was nearer a correct understanding.

This highland tour closed the more active part of Murchison's life. Although he continued to visit places of geological interest, much of his time was occupied by official duties at the Geological Survey, and by other duties arising from his position in scientific affairs. After 1864 he wrote few more papers, but continued president of the Royal Geographical Society until 1871. Early in 1869 Lady Murchison died, and in November 1870 Sir Roderick suffered a stroke. From this he partially recovered, but he died of bronchitis on 22 October 1871 at his home, 16 Belgrave Square. Four days afterwards he was laid in Brompton cemetery by his wife's side. They had no children and his patronage of young geologists, notably Alexander Geikie, was an attempt to leave intellectual sons.

Murchison received more honours than any contemporary scientist. Besides the distinctions mentioned above, he was made a KCB in 1863 and a baronet in 1866—characteristically, after prolonged lobbying. He received honorary degrees from Oxford, Cambridge, and Dublin, and was an honorary member of numerous foreign societies, including the academies of sciences in France and Russia. He was president of the geographical and the geological sections of the British Association ten times altogether, and of the association itself (which he helped to found) in 1846. He was for sixteen years president of the Royal Geographical Society, for which services he earned the founder's medal in 1871. He was also twice president of the Geological Society, receiving its Wollaston medal, and was awarded the Copley medal of the Royal Society.

In person Murchison was tall, wiry, muscular, of a commanding presence and dignified manner. He was fortunate not only in the society of a wife who saved him from becoming a mere idler, but also in the possession of means which from the first placed him above want, and in later life were very ample, due to a series of timely inheritances that more than made up for his financial mismanagement. His will was proved at less than £300,000 in 1873. He was well aware of the advantages of aristocratic friends and royal favour. His social influence was exercised for the benefit of science and its workers, as well as for his own advancement. One of his last acts was to contribute half the endowment to a chair of geology at Edinburgh, which he ensured went to his protégé Geikie. He was a hospitable host, a firm and generous friend—especially to fellow Scots like the explorer David Livingstone—though, particularly in his later years, too self-appreciative and intolerant of opposition. He was energetic and industrious, enjoyed good health, and was methodical and punctual in his habits. His contributions to scientific literature totalled more than 180 papers, in addition to the books already mentioned.

Murchison's legacy Murchison's stratigraphic work was largely sound, although, as his mistakes regarding the Welsh and Scottish highland successions and his extreme disputatiousness attest, his concern to enlarge his scientific dominions and vanquish those who threatened his realm sometimes led him to defend untenable positions. His motto was 'labour conquers all': it might have been 'never give an inch'. Geologically, his greatest weakness was the superficiality of his fieldwork—ironically, the reverse of his greatest strength, which was a keen eye for country that rapidly apprehended the dominant geological features of a district. His knowledge of palaeontology was limited, but he was able to turn to others for help; of petrology he knew even less, and his opposition to new techniques being developed in Germany delayed their acceptance in Britain, especially by the Geological Survey. Similarly, his catastrophist views on mountain building, glaciation, and erosion helped perpetuate out-of-date theories on these geological processes, though he championed the careers of scientists like Ramsay and Geikie, who espoused more progressive views. His famous claim to have predicted the Australian gold rush was nothing more than an educated guess; with his slightly more scientific prognostication of Africa's structure, he was proved right for the wrong reasons. Although no ardent religious believer, Murchison also resolutely opposed Darwin's evolutionary theory.

In geography, Murchison's fame rests on his promotion of overseas exploration, for without his unremitting labour Britain's mid-Victorian record of discovery would undoubtedly be the poorer. The more than twenty geographical features around the world named in his honour remain as a monument to his steadfast pursuit of geographical knowledge. He lacked theoretical powers, but gained fame as a keen and astute observer. The earth sciences in Britain have never had a more dedicated and effective promoter—one who deliberately tied the interests of science to those of the nation in pursuit of cultural, economic, and imperial hegemony.

T. G. BONNEY, rev. ROBERT A. STAFFORD

Sources A. Geikie, *Life of Sir Roderick I. Murchison*, 2 vols. (1875) · M. J. S. Rudwick, *The great Devonian controversy: the shaping of scientific knowledge among gentlemanly specialists* (1985) · J. A. Secord, *Controversy in Victorian geology: the Cambrian–Silurian dispute* (1986) · R. A. Stafford, *Scientist of empire: Sir Roderick Murchison, scientific exploration and Victorian imperialism* (1989) · D. R. Oldroyd, *The highlands controversy: constructing geological knowledge through fieldwork in nineteenth-century Britain* (1990) · J. C. Thackray, 'Essential source material of Roderick Murchison', *Journal of the Society of the Bibliography of Natural History*, 6 (1971–4), 162–70

Archives American Philosophical Society, Philadelphia, corresp. and papers · BGS, corresp. and papers · BL, corresp., Add. MSS 46125–46128 · GS Lond., corresp. and papers · NL Scot., corresp. · NRA, priv. coll., accounts, letters to his wife, and notebooks · RGS · RS · Sci. Mus., corresp. · U. Cam., Sedgwick Museum of Earth Sciences, notebook · U. Edin. L., corresp. and papers · UCL, maps and sections of Scottish rocks · Wellcome L., corresp. | Auckland Public Library, letters to Sir George Gray · BGS, letters to Charles Peach · BGS, letters to Trenham Reeks · BL, corresp. with Lord Aberdeen, Add. MSS 43248–43253 · BL, letters to Charles Babbage, Add. MSS 37184–37201 · BL, letters to W. E. Gladstone, Add. MSS 44389–44783 · BL, letters to Sir Austen Layard, Add. MSS 38996, 39166–39118 · BL, letters to A. Panizzi, Add. MSS 36717–36723 · BL, corresp. with Sir Robert Peel, Add. MSS 40419–40584, *passim* · Bodl. Oxf., British Association MSS · Bodl. Oxf., Clarendon MSS · Bucks. RLSS, corresp. with Lord Cottesloe · CUL, letters to G. Featherstonhaugh · CUL, letters to R. Harkness · CUL, corresp. with Lord Mayo · Devon RO, letters to William Buckland · Elgin Museum, letters to George Gordon · Hergest Croft, Kingston, Hergest Trust archives, corresp. with R. W. Banks · ICL, corresp. with Thomas Huxley · National Archives of Zimbabwe, Harare, corresp. with David Livingstone · NHM, letters to Sir Richard Owen and William Clift · NHM, letters to members of Sowerby family · NL NZ, Turnbull L., letters to Gideon Algernon Mantell · NL Scot., letters to J. A. Grant · NL Scot., corresp. relating to David Livingstone · NMG Wales, letters to Sir Henry de la Beche · NRA, priv. coll., letters from David Livingstone · Oxf. U. Mus. NH, letters from John Phillips · RGS, Livingstone MSS · RGS, council minute books · RGS, colonial office, foreign office, and general corresp. · RS, corresp. with Sir John Herschel · Sci. Mus., letters, mainly to Mrs Ford · Scott Polar RI, corresp. with Jane Franklin · St Deiniol's Library, Hawarden, letters to Sir John Gladstone · Trinity Cam., corresp. with William Whewell · U. Edin., Geikie MSS · U. St Andr. L., corresp. with James Forbes · W. Sussex RO, letters to duke of Richmond

Likenesses W. Drummond, lithograph, 1836, BM · R. Westmacott, plaster bust, 1848, Scot. NPG · T. H. Maguire, lithograph, 1849, BM, NPG · S. Pearce, oils, 1850–60, NPG · J. Brown, engraving, 1851 (after W. H. Pickersgill, 1849), RS · P. Merimée, cartoon, 1860, NL Scot., Muchison MSS · C. Silvy, carte-de-visite, 1860, NPG [*see illus.*] · photograph, 1864 (with David Livingstone), Geology Museum, Bath · Spy [L. Ward], pencil and wash, 1868, NPG · H. Weekes, bust, 1871, Geological Museum, London · Ape [C. Pellegrini], caricature, chromolithograph, NPG; repro. in *VF* (1870) · H. W. Pickersgill, oils, U. Edin. · Spy [L. Ward], cartoon, repro. in *VF* (26 Nov 1870) · bust, GS Lond. · bust, Institute of Geological Sciences, London · photograph, repro. in *ILN*, 58 (1868), 413 · photograph, repro. in *ILN*, 48 (1866), 237 · photographs, Institute of Geological Sciences · photographs, NPG · portrait, National Gallery, London

Wealth at death under £300,000: resworn probate, April 1873, CGPLA Eng. & Wales (1871)

Murcot, John (1624/5–1654), Independent minister, was born at Warwick, the son of Job Murcot, a lawyer, and his wife, Joan Townshend. He was taught by Thomas Dugard at the King's School, Warwick, and in 1642 matriculated from Merton College, Oxford, aged seventeen, where he studied under the supervision of the puritan Ralph Button. Murcot left Oxford when it was garrisoned by the king, and went to stay with John Ley, presbyterian minister of Budworth in Cheshire. On returning to Oxford after the war he graduated BA on 30 March 1647 but soon returned to Cheshire. In January 1648 Murcot produced for the Manchester classis evidence of 'his good conversation and sufficient abilities, and of his call to the church of Astbury in Cheshire', and he was ordained at Manchester on 9 February (Shaw, 1.69). Soon afterwards he left Astbury for Eastham, in the Wirral, and there, 'being resolved to change his condition and, discoursing with a friend about it, there was proposed unto him Hester … whom he afterward took to be the companion of his life' ('Moses', 6). Before the wedding, but after the death of the bride's father, Ralph Marsden, rector of West Kirby, the godly parishioners of that village invited Murcot to be their new minister. Before 30 June 1648 he was succeeded at Eastham by Richard Banner. Presented to the rectory of West Kirby by the committee for plundered ministers, he signed from there on 6th of that month the Cheshire ministers' *Attestation*.

Murcot was not a complaisant pastor: 'An Irish lord quartering at West Kirby being bound for Ireland was observed to be a prodigious swearer, belching out most horrid oaths in great abundance'. On hearing of this, Murcot:

Here stand, and live in thy immortall page
Thou Golden Preacher in an Iron Age
Ireland laments thy losse, whose powerfull word
Wrought on her greater conquests then the Sword;
Their bodies were Subdu'd by Armes and Arts
But thou (blest conquerour) didst win their Hearts.

John Murcot (1624/5–1654), by William Faithorne the elder, pubd 1657

rides the same night six miles to a magistrate, procures a warrant; the trembling constables at first are astonished to think of approaching in such a way to guilty greatness, but being animated by Mr Murcot they served their warrant, which provoked a new rage to the multiplying of fresh oaths even without number to the great amazement of the standers by. Notwithstanding the boisterous menaces, and outrage of this great man, his horses were seized on and kept, till he paid £20 which was employed as a stock for the poor.

For Murcot's biographer, 'This exemplary act of justice procured and prosecuted by Mr Murcot's active zeal, so daunted and overawed his lordship that during his abode there he held his tongue and mouth as it were with bit and bridle' ('Moses', 7–8). Murcot was no less hard on more ordinary offenders. When he arrived to suppress an alehouse, one man:

> having a brow of brass, thinks to outface both sacred and civil officers, and saith, 'Shall I fear Murcot?' calls for more beer, and in a bravado drinks to him, who pledged him with stern silence and frowning aspect. The names of the ringleaders are returned to the justices and they constrained to pay their fines.

Neither did the toast maker escape. Although the sickness which had afflicted the area had abated, 'yet this man is very shortly after visited, and by that signal stroke from the hand of the Lord, hurried out of the land of the living'. The next Sunday Murcot chose a text to illustrate 'the dreadfulness of wrath deserved; and so severe and cutting

were his rebukes' that 'the guilty shrink down into their seats, like affrighted birds into their hollow trees' ('Moses', 9).

Murcot was active elsewhere, notably against John Knowles, 'a formidable and blazing comet at Chester', who was spreading Socinian doctrines there. Together with Samuel Eaton, a former pastor at West Kirby, Murcot laboured 'to pluck up the stinking weed which has begun to spread and fasten its contagious roots', and they succeeded in having Knowles removed from his position in the city. Not all radical puritans were convinced of the need to repress such heresies. A newly covenanted congregation at Chester 'expressed their desires of enjoying Mr Murcot who is sent unto and requested to preach among them by way of trial' but was 'entreated not to intermeddle with the present controversy or engage against Mr Knowles' ('Moses', 11). Murcot refused: 'I cannot live without ordinances at West Kirby, nor like a salamander in the fire at Chester' ('Moses', 12). It seems that his uncompromising approach had already led to tensions at the former place, where the pastor, after 'several meetings with the people … plainly told them, that he could not live without the ordinances, nor administer them as formerly: to which some (unwilling to be new moulded) replied, that he might then take his liberty and be gone'; despite the regrets of the godly, 'an amicable accord cannot be accomplished, and therefore he resolves to weigh anchor, and spread his sails to the leading gale of providence' ('Moses', 9).

Following an invitation from the parliamentary commissioners the gale of providence blew his ship to Dublin. There Murcot disembarked in summer 1651, to be entertained by Sir Robert King in his own house. He was offered a position at Belfast, but declined it. In October a rota of ministers was drawn up to attend the commissioners at Cork House, Dublin, each morning at 8.30, to seek God's guidance, and Murcot was nominated for the Wednesday duty. He was also appointed to serve as one of several lecturers at Christ Church, Dublin, and by November 1651 he had taken up a position as the preacher of St Michan's Within, also in Dublin. In April 1652 he was granted £20 for accommodation during the commissioners' visit to Munster, and at Cork the Independents sought to persuade him to serve as their pastor. Murcot considered the invitation seriously, but one factor which helped persuade him against acceptance was the fact that at Cork religion was less tightly regulated than in the capital. Back in Dublin, in December 1652, he was one of seven ministers selected to plan the campaign for the propagation of the gospel in Ireland, and to nominate English and Irish preachers. It seems that about February 1653, after several weeks' thought, Murcot accepted the pastorate of the Independent congregation at Dublin in succession to John Rogers, who had returned to England the previous year.

Meanwhile, however, the Independents at Cork petitioned that Murcot and Joseph Eyres should be sent to them, and in April 1653 the commissioners ordered Murcot to Munster. It seems possible that this had to do with his attitude to rebaptized members who remained among the Dublin Independents. There was no escape from the issue at Cork. Just before his arrival a controversy had arisen between the influential Edward Worth and Dr John Harding over infant baptism. Never one to hold back on matters of principle Murcot entered the lists on the side of Worth; a stream of sermons and position papers followed, generating much acrimony but little light. On leaving Cork in June 1653 Murcot regretted the experience: 'The Lord pardon me that ever I yielded to that wrangling dispute' ('Moses', 22). He returned to Dublin and took up the pastorate of the gathered congregation, combining it with public preaching at St Audoens. On 5 July 1654 he was one of five men commissioned to investigate whether Irish citizens of Athy exempted from transplantation because of their conversion had in fact 'upon any conscientious grounds deserted popery, or for any feigned consideration or by-ends pretended the embracing of Protestantism' (Dunlop, 2.434).

Later that month Murcot travelled to England armed with a letter of recommendation from the commissioners to Oliver Cromwell designed to ensure the speedy completion of the family business which had brought him. He arrived back in Dublin in mid-October to find his family stricken with fever, and on 11 November 1654 there occurred the death of his second youngest child, Job. By this time Murcot himself had fallen ill, and on 3 December he died, at the age of twenty-nine. Murcot's biographer knew the cause of his premature end:

> he served his God, and his generation, with all his might. He ran faster than the others, and was therefore sooner out of breath. He screwed up the pegs so high, that the strings of his several faculties crack, and can hold out no longer. He did with so much vehemency and contention of spirit, continually stir up himself to take hold on God, and followed so hard after him, that he sunk under the burden of his own endeavours. ('Moses', 39)

Murcot was buried in Christ Church Cathedral. The funeral procession was led by Lord Deputy Charles Fleetwood, followed by his council, the mayor and aldermen, and many citizens; the sermon was preached by Dr Samuel Winter. Murcot's widow, Hester, was granted the very large annual sum of £100 during the protector's pleasure, though in 1656 this was withdrawn and property to the value of £25 p.a. at Kilmackeoge, co. Dublin, was granted to her and her children. In 1657 *The Several Works of Mr John Murcot*, dedicated to Fleetwood and Henry Cromwell, was issued by Samuel Winter, Richard Chambers, Samuel Eaton, Joseph Carryl, and Thomas Manton. It contains prefaces by each of them, a portrait of John Murcot engraved by Faithorne, and the remarkable biography on which so much knowledge of him rests.

STEPHEN WRIGHT

Sources *The several works of Mr John Murcot* (1657) • 'Moses in the Mount … being a narrative of the life and death of Mr John Murcot', *The several works of Mr John Murcot* (1657) ['written by a friend' with a preface of its own signed J. G. from Dublin, Oct 1655] • St J. D. Seymour, *The puritans in Ireland, 1647–1660*, Oxford Historical and Literary Studies, 12 (1921) • W. Urwick, ed., *Historical sketches of nonconformity in the county palatine of Cheshire, by various ministers and laymen* (1864) • *Walker rev.* • R. Dunlop, *Ireland under the Commonwealth*, University of Manchester Publications, Historical Series, 17–18 (1913) • T. Barnard, *Cromwellian Ireland* (1975) • W. A. Shaw, ed., *Minutes of the Manchester presbyterian classis*, 1, Chetham Society, 20 (1890) • *Foster, Alum. Oxon.* • F. L. Colvile, *The worthies of Warwickshire who lived between 1500 and 1800* [1870]

Likenesses W. Faithorne the elder, line engraving, BM, NPG; repro. in *Several works* [see illus.] • pen-and-ink drawing, NPG

Murdac, Henry (d. 1153), abbot of Fountains and archbishop of York, was a native of the north of England. John of Hexham described him as a man of excellent character and noble birth who before his entry into the monastic life had served in the household of Archbishop Thurstan of York, both in the church and in the diocese of York. He was evidently a man of learning, and attained the title of *magister*. He was the recipient of a letter written by St Bernard of Clairvaux, in which he exhorted Murdac to abandon the world of learning in order to enter the monastic life: 'Believe me who have experience', he wrote, 'you will find much more labouring amongst the woods than you ever will amongst books' (*Letters*, 156). The letter closed with a reference to two of Murdac's pupils, William and Ivo, who had evidently become monks at Clairvaux.

Henry Murdac entered the monastic life as a Cistercian monk at Bernard's own monastery of Clairvaux where he joined a fellow Yorkshireman, William, who was Bernard's secretary and later first abbot of Rievaulx. In 1134 Bernard sent Murdac as founder abbot of Clairvaux's new colony at Vauclair in the diocese of Laon, where Murdac remained for nine years. In 1143 Richard, second abbot of the Yorkshire abbey of Fountains, which since 1133 had been a daughter house of Clairvaux, died at Clairvaux and Bernard decided to send Henry Murdac to Fountains. It was a critical moment in the diocese of York, for the Cistercians had become recognized leaders of the opposition to the archbishop-elect, William Fitzherbert (d. 1154) [see William of York]; and the death of Abbot Richard robbed the reform party of one of its most influential voices. Bernard wrote to the prior and monks of Fountains, commending Henry Murdac to them, and ordering them to take his advice and that of the abbot of Rievaulx in the election of a new abbot. Bernard wrote to Murdac himself giving him full authority to correct the abbey in any way he might find necessary, and ordering him to abide by the decision of the monks should they elect him as their abbot.

As St Bernard had hoped, Murdac was elected as abbot of Fountains, either late in 1143 or early in 1144, and became leader of the movement to oust the now suspended archbishop. Indeed, so closely identified was Murdac with the opposition to William Fitzherbert that in 1146 a band of the archbishop's supporters raided Fountains Abbey and destroyed some of the newly constructed buildings. Murdac himself, lying in prayer before the altar, escaped harm. The severity of the fire, vividly described in the *Narratio de fundatione* of the abbey, has been corroborated by archaeological investigation at Fountains. The following year saw the deposition of William Fitzherbert by the Cistercian pope, Eugenius III, at the Council of Rheims which Murdac attended, and the issue of a papal mandate to hold a fresh election. When the electors met at Richmond on 24 July 1147 a number, including Robert de Gant, dean of York, and Hugh de Puiset, treasurer, supported Master Hilary (later bishop of Chichester) while others, notably the bishops of Durham and Carlisle, and the precentor and archdeacons of York, settled on Henry Murdac as their candidate. The matter was referred to the pope who decided in favour of Henry Murdac; Murdac received confirmation and consecration at the hands of the pope at Trier on 7 December 1147, and received the pallium from him.

On his return to the north of England Murdac declined to resign the abbacy of Fountains, and instead ruled that house through suffragan abbots, Maurice (during 1148) and Thorald (from 1148 to 1150), both monks of Rievaulx, and Richard (in or after 1150 to 1153) who moved to take up office from the abbacy of Murdac's former house of Vauclair. As abbot of Fountains, Murdac presided over a period of reform and expansion during which daughter houses were established at Woburn (1145), Lysa, Norway (1146), Barnoldswick (later Kirkstall) and Vaudey (1147), and Meaux (1151); three third-generation houses were also founded through the line of Newminster. Murdac was a champion of the Yorkshire Cistercians: for instance he upheld the actions of the monks of Barnoldswick in destroying the parish church of the vill in which they had settled because it interfered with their worship.

As archbishop, Murdac did not succeed in gaining universal recognition. The king refused to accept him in preference to his own candidate. The chapter of York was divided. The citizens of York remained loyal to Fitzherbert and refused to allow Murdac to enter the city when he attempted to do so in 1148. In retaliation Murdac excommunicated his fiercest opponents, Hugh de Puiset and William le Gros, count of Aumale and earl of York, and placed York under an interdict. He took up residence first at Beverley and then in the archiepiscopal manor of Ripon only a few miles from his abbey of Fountains. He was recognized as archbishop by the bishops of Durham and Carlisle, who had supported his election. However, of more political significance were his contacts with David I of Scotland whom he met, with Henry of Anjou, son of the Empress Matilda, at Carlisle. Doubtless it was on this occasion that King David and Henry Murdac discussed the projected Scottish invasion of York in 1149 which may have had as one of its aims the establishment of Murdac in his archiepiscopal see.

Henry Murdac was reconciled with King Stephen in early 1151, an action which was forced on the king because of the weakness of royal authority in Yorkshire and the danger of a damaging alliance between a consecrated archbishop of York and the Scottish king. Murdac's restoration to royal favour enabled him to enter York, where he was enthroned on 25 January 1151. He marked his return by restoring on the high altar the written ancient privileges which, it was recorded by John of Hexham, had been pledged by Fitzherbert in order to raise money to pursue his case in Rome. Murdac also granted relics to the cathedral church and rights in Patrington to the canons. He evidently came to terms with his former enemy, William le Gros, count of Aumale: Aumale established a Cistercian abbey at Meaux as a daughter house of Fountains (1151) and Murdac confirmed the foundation and granted to it, for the soul of Archbishop Thurstan, two carucates in Wawne and a ferry. Shortly after his reconciliation with the king the archbishop acted on a diplomatic mission to Rome on the king's behalf in order to seek papal permission for the coronation of Stephen's son, Eustace.

As archbishop, Murdac was an energetic reformer. He introduced new statutes into the church of Hexham, and converted the church of St Oswald, Gloucester, to the use of regular canons, drawing the first colony under Prior Humphrey from the priory of Lanthony. He aspired to introduce a similar change at Beverley on the death of its provost, Thurstan, but he died before he was able to implement it. He intervened in the affairs of the Benedictine abbeys of Whitby and Selby to depose their abbots. His *acta* show him to have issued routine charters of confirmation for the religious houses of his diocese, and his own house of Fountains received three such charters. He also ratified the Gilbertine foundation at Watton, a double house established about 1150, and there he himself placed as a child oblate the young girl who later achieved notoriety as the 'nun of Watton'. After Murdac's reconciliation with King Stephen, King David did not hinder the archbishop in performing episcopal functions in north Yorkshire, and he heard, at Carlisle, Murdac's complaints about the damage done to his forest there by the mining activities of the king's men. In the last few months of his life Henry Murdac opposed the election to the see of Durham of Hugh de Puiset, treasurer of York, and one of his leading opponents in 1147 and after. He excommunicated the prior and archdeacons of Durham, and refused their request, made personally to him in York on Ash Wednesday 1153, for recognition of the validity of the election and withdrawal of the sentence. His actions brought on him once again the animosity of the people of York and he was forced to withdraw to Beverley, where he refused all entreaties to reconsider.

It was at Beverley that Henry Murdac died on 14 October 1153, and he was buried among the tombs of the archbishops in York Minster. His death came within a few months of those of two other Cistercians whose intervention had prolonged the York election dispute, St Bernard of Clairvaux and Eugenius III. Murdac's death left the way open for the brief restoration of William Fitzherbert, and its dramatic climax. Murdac was a fierce and outspoken advocate of reform and proponent of Cistercian monasticism, and within his own order, at least, he appears to have retained a reputation for sanctity after his death. He was the first archbishop in England since the Norman conquest to have been elected and consecrated without the consent of the king, and his election was thus a landmark in relations between church and state in twelfth-century England.

JANET BURTON

Sources J. R. Walbran, ed., *Memorials of the abbey of St Mary of Fountains*, 1, SurtS, 42 (1863) · *The letters of St Bernard of Clairvaux*, trans. B. S. James (1953) · John of Hexham, 'Historia regum continuata',

Symeon of Durham, *Opera*, vol. 2 • R. Howlett, ed., *Chronicles of the reigns of Stephen, Henry II, and Richard I*, 1, Rolls Series, 82 (1884) • J. E. Burton, ed., *York, 1070–1154*, English Episcopal Acta, 5 (1988) • J. Raine, ed., *The priory of Hexham*, 1, SurtS, 44 (1864) • *The historical works of Gervase of Canterbury*, ed. W. Stubbs, 2 vols., Rolls Series, 73 (1879–80) • D. Knowles, 'The case of Saint William of York', *Cambridge Historical Journal*, 5 (1935–7), 162–77, 212–14 • D. Nicholl, *Thurstan: archbishop of York, 1114–1140* (1964) • D. Knowles, *The monastic order in England*, 2nd edn (1963)

Murdoch, George

Murdoch, George (1715–1795), merchant and civic leader, was born in January 1715 in Glasgow, where he was baptized on 23 January, the son of James Murdoch, a city merchant, and Elizabeth, *née* Wingate. He obtained his Glasgow burgess ticket through his father in 1737. About three years later he married Margaret Leitch (*d*. before 1757), whose brother, Andrew Cochrane, would later serve as lord provost of Glasgow. Murdoch became Cochrane's partner in Cochrane, Murdoch & Co., bankers and shareholders in several ventures. The firm became the managing partners of the Glasgow Arms Bank, which was founded in November 1750 by a partnership of more than two dozen prominent merchants. It was the first bank founded on an extended co-partnery basis, and 87 per cent of the partners had tobacco interests. Friction with the Royal Bank of Scotland in Edinburgh came to a head when one of its agents sued Cochrane, Murdoch & Co. in their capacity as managers of the Arms Bank, but the agent lost his case and the Arms Bank prospered. In 1763 Cochrane, Murdoch & Co. sold out to Spiers, Murdoch & Co., which included Murdoch's nephew Peter Murdoch as a partner. The bank failed in the crisis of 1793, but all creditors were paid.

In 1749 Murdoch built a fine mansion in Argyll Street, which later became the Buck's Head inn, and during the 1750s he built another mansion at Frisky Hall in Dunbartonshire. He had eight or nine children with his first wife, and following her death he married about 1757 her sister-in-law, Janet Bogle, the widow of Glasgow merchant George Leitch. Neither that marriage nor a third one, with Amelia Campbell (1737/8–1798), produced any offspring.

Murdoch was one of the most successful of the second generation of Glasgow tobacco merchants who diversified into other fields. In 1768 he and his brother John, along with William Cunninghame, already partners in a Virginia company, set up the Dalnottar Iron Company in order to supply bar, plate, and red iron, and to manufacture tools, rails, and other kinds of ironware. The initial capital was £6000, but that amount doubled within twenty years. As the company prospered the partners, with other tobacco merchants, extended into the Muirkirk Iron Company in 1781 in an effort to safeguard basic supplies of pig iron. Murdoch also invested in the Glasgow Ropeworks and in the Glasgow Bottleworks Company, a logical development from his nephew Peter's investment in the Anderston Brewery, in which he too had a share. The brewery had just begun brewing porter, and that enterprise required green glass bottles which the bottleworks was able to supply.

Murdoch was active in civic affairs and was lord provost of Glasgow for a record four terms: 1754–5, 1755–6, 1766–7, and 1767–8. During his first term the Arms Bank lent £1000 to the town council 'for road works', but the money was swallowed up in 'general purposes'; thereafter the bank frequently lent money to the council. As provost, Murdoch laid out a great many trees and walks on Glasgow Green and enacted harsh legislation against those who vandalized civic property. In 1755 he attempted to enforce order on the fleshers by building a town herb market for oatmeal and greens and a fleshers' market for authorized slaughtering, though the fleshers resisted such efforts at centralizing their activities. He also approved the demolition of the old medieval ruins of Little St Mungo's Chapel for the building of a handsome coaching inn, the Saracen's Head, and he established Glasgow's famous north-west burial-grounds. The crowning achievement of his civic career was the erection over the River Clyde of Jamaica Bridge, built by John Adam, with its seven arches designed by William Mylne. Murdoch laid the foundation-stone in 1767, though the bridge did not open until 1772. He ended his public career as controller of customs at Greenock and Port Glasgow from 1771 to 1784, an important post with authority over all harbours from Ayr to Stornoway during a period of great expansion. He died at Frisky Hall on 19 September 1795 and was buried in Blackfriars churchyard, Glasgow. He was survived by his wife Amelia, who died in November 1798, aged sixty.

MONICA CLOUGH

Sources J. R. Anderson, ed., *The provosts of Glasgow from 1609 to 1832* (1942) • T. M. Devine, *The tobacco lords: a study of the tobacco merchants of Glasgow and their trading activities, c.1740–1790* (1975) • D. R. [D. Robertson], rev., *Glasgow, past and present: illustrated in dean of guild court reports and in the reminiscences and communications of Senex, Aliquis, J.B., &c*, 3 vols. (1884) • J. O. Mitchell, *Old Glasgow essays* (1905) • C. W. Munn, *The Scottish provincial banking companies* (1981) • J. Gibson, *The history of Glasgow* (1778)

Murdoch, Dame (Jean) Iris

Murdoch, Dame (Jean) Iris (1919–1999), novelist and philosopher, was born on 15 July 1919 at 59 Blessington Street, Dublin, the only child of Irene Alice Cooper Richardson (1899–1985) and (Wills John) Hughes Murdoch (1890–1958). Since her birth occurred seven months after her parents married on 7 December 1918, the marriage was probably hasty. Her father was a quiet, unambitious civil servant, who in 1950 retired from a 'personal grade' of assistant registrar-general, working at Somerset House on census returns; her mother, on marriage, gave up a promising career as a professional singer. Her father's family had farmed in a small way in Ballymullan, co. Down, probably for eight generations. Yeoman farmers and merchants, and mainly Presbyterian, they had Quaker connections, while her Belfast cousins, with whom she spent many summer holidays before the Second World War, were brought up within what in Ulster are called Brethren (elsewhere Plymouth Brethren). On her mother's side she was proudly descended from Alexander Richardson, of Crayhallock (now known as Drum Manor) in co. Tyrone, 'planted in Ireland in 1616 to control the wild Irish' (Conradi, *Life*, 16); a Grayhallock house occurs in her novel *An Unofficial Rose*. The Richardson family motto *Virtuti paret robur*, which Murdoch quoted in *The Green*

Dame (Jean) Iris Murdoch (1919–1999), by Tom Phillips, 1984–6

Knight, means 'strength obeys virtue'. The Richardsons, a highly interrelated family, mainly Church of Ireland, though also with Quaker connections, began as major landowners in the seventeenth century, continuing as minor gentry in the eighteenth. Murdoch's great-great-aunt Frances Elizabeth Fisher published volumes of verse such as *Love or Hatred* and *The Secret of Two Houses*; a better-known female cousin, the Australian Ethel Florence Lindesay *Richardson (1870–1946) wrote, under the pen-name Henry Handel Richardson, *The Fortunes of Richard Mahony*, and *Myself when Young*, which refers to mutual Irish cousins. Thereafter the family's status steeply declined. Iris Murdoch's maternal grandfather worked in a solicitor's office, probably as a clerk, while her maternal uncle was a car mechanic.

Murdoch clung to a deep identification with Ireland throughout her life. Irish protestantism even in its non-Ulster mode is a social and cultural identity as much as a religious one. Some of its elements—the cult of a lost house, a preoccupation with good manners together with a love of drama and occasional flamboyant emotionalism, a superstitious bent towards occultism and magic, an inability to grow up, an obsession with the hauntings of history, and a disturbed love–hate relation towards Ireland itself—found in Elizabeth Bowen and W. B. Yeats, were also present in Iris Murdoch. Murdoch's protestant Irishness made of her, like Bowen, a 'naturally separated person' (Foster, 108). And like Yeats she later elevated herself socially 'by a sort of moral effort and a historical sleight-of-hand' (ibid., 214), and conquered Clandeboye,

one of the Guinnesses' ancestral homes, and Bowens Court.

Early life and education The family, whose compactness and intimacy were remarkable, soon moved from Blessington Street in Dublin, which Murdoch remembered as 'wide, sad, dirty … full of idling dogs and open doorways' (Murdoch, *The Red and the Green*, 144), to Brook Green, Hammersmith, London. About 1926 Hughes Murdoch bought a small, semi-detached house at 4 Eastbourne Road in Chiswick. In the year before Iris Murdoch entered the progressive Froebel Demonstration School at Colet Gardens and was introduced to the strange glories of 'knights and ladies'. At least once a term the children would assemble at the 'king's court', with the so-called dames and squires in two lines, their households lined up behind them in order of age. The headmistress, Miss Bain, would enter, walking down the aisle in a velvet cloak and cardboard crown, the boys bowing and girls curtseying. There was also jousting. In 1932 Iris Murdoch won a scholarship to Badminton School in Bristol, run by the equally eccentric, formidable, idealistic Beatrice May Baker (BMB), later an influential friend.

In 1938 Murdoch won a scholarship to Somerville College, Oxford, to read 'greats'. Contemporaries were struck by her remarkable assurance, her blonde hair, attractiveness, and spiritual grace, and recalled her amateur acting skills. She moved in different worlds while belonging essentially to herself. The classicist Eduard Fraenkel, whose long-running seminar on Aeschylus's *Agamemnon* she attended, and her philosophy tutor, the theologian-philosopher Donald MacKinnon, were lifelong influences. She soon joined the Communist Party, converting Frank Thompson, elder brother of E. P. Thompson, to the cause in her second term. He noted that, although 'her figure was too thick to be good' (Conradi, *Life*, 90), she gave a pleasing impression of harmony. Of her many admirers, Thompson was the most remarkable, and his murder in 1944, with the Special Operations Executive in Bulgaria, a major blow. Friendships with philosophers began in Oxford, above all with Philippa Foot, with whom Murdoch lived for eighteen months during the war. Having decided to tell each other of the men who had asked to marry them, Foot's list was soon done. As Murdoch's list went on and on, Foot asked crossly whether it might not save time if Iris listed the men who had *not* yet asked her to marry them.

War work and post-war philosophy Ten days after winning an outstanding first in 1942 Murdoch became assistant principal in the Treasury, where she stayed for two years, spending evenings with the writers and artists of bohemian Fitzrovia, and writing, sometimes through the night. In 1944—the year when T. S. Eliot at Faber turned down her second novel—she joined the United Nations Relief and Rehabilitation Administration (UNRRA), designed to address the unprecedented problems of housing, clothing, feeding, and, with luck, rehabilitating more than 8 million refugees. Murdoch worked for fifteen months at headquarters on Portland Place, London, then briefly in Brussels, where she met Jean-Paul Sartre, before moving to four camps in Austria. Her novels are full of displaced persons: the refugee, 'the person who is literally an exile' (Murdoch, 1957 BBC interview), seemed an appropriate symbol for contemporary man. In Innsbruck she met Raymond Queneau, whose work she greatly admired, and whose *Pierrot mon ami* she translated into English.

Murdoch returned to London in 1946, winning a place at Vassar College and a Commonwealth scholarship. But because the puritanical and literal-minded Murdoch had declared herself a member of the Communist Party on her application for an American visa she was prevented by the McCarran Act from entering America and denied a visa. For the rest of her life she required a separate waiver to visit. At this difficult time she became Anglo-Catholic, going to mass, and taking retreats at the Anglican Benedictine convent of Malling. Christian belief had failed her by 1953. Thereafter she could not believe in a personal god demonic enough to have created the world whose sufferings were clear to her, yet she wanted religion to survive, too. She wanted Buddhism to educate Christianity, to create a non-supernatural religion. God and the afterlife were essentially anti-religious bribes.

From 1947 to 1948 Murdoch studied philosophy at Newnham College, Cambridge, and briefly met Wittgenstein, whose work deeply interested her. In 1948 she won a philosophy tutorship at St Anne's, Oxford, where she stayed until 1963, after which she lectured at the Royal College of Art for four years. Teaching absorbed her, and she was dedicated, generally liked, and admired by her students. Yet Murdoch's quarrel with the constrictions of the exam-led curriculum—as with Oxford philosophy itself—made her want to range more freely: in 1949 she asked some students to read Lenin's *State and Revolution*. Students from other colleges and disciplines, especially mature postgraduates, profited most, while those most needful of coaching for 'schools' sometimes expressed frustration. She blamed herself if her students did badly.

First books In 1953 Murdoch's first book, *Sartre: Romantic Rationalist*, was published by Bowes and Bowes in their series Studies in Modern European Thought. If Murdoch had, as a thinker, two modes, one lapidary and compressed, the other discursive and rambling, this belongs to the first category. It is a brilliant work, revealing a novelist's capacity to sink and merge her personality within the mind of another, and criticizes Sartre's ideas and novels accessibly. In that year her first novel, *Under the Net*, was accepted for publication. It came out in May 1954 and contained two self-representations, one of Murdoch as the narrator Jake Donaghue, an Irish Londoner with 'shattered nerves', once in the Young Communist League and now disaffected, translating a French novelist (just as Iris had translated Queneau) and, like Murdoch, about to turn into a novelist in his own right. Anna Quentin, whom Jake believes that he loves, is a persona Murdoch wished to shed. Anna has a 'taste for tragedy', and is emotionally promiscuous. The *Times Literary Supplement* hailed a 'brilliant talent' (7 November 1958) that, despite a lack of 'fit' between characters and plot, promised great things.

Kingsley Amis in *The Spectator* (7 November 1958) admired her complete control of her material. London is a real presence, almost another character in this novel, as in many of her novels.

Murdoch might have married Franz Baermann Steiner, a Prague-born anthropologist and poet, had he not died in November 1952. Steiner introduced Murdoch to the Bulgarian-born German-speaking writer Elias Canetti, with whom Murdoch was closely associated from January 1953 until late 1955. Although she denied putting friends into her novels, Canetti is the original for the enchanter Mischa Fox of her second novel, *The Flight from the Enchanter* (1956), as well as its dedicatee. Iris Murdoch wrote, in all, twenty-six novels, and in many of the best the influence of Canetti can be felt. He probably inspired the manipulative, erotic puppet-master Julius King in *A Fairly Honourable Defeat* (1970) as well as the jealous, rapacious, tyrannical Charles Arrowby, narrator of *The Sea, the Sea* (1978). Murdoch remarked that her early work concerned freedom, and her later work, love. In fact her best work also explores power, and knowing Canetti helped that exploration. Murdoch spoke in interviews of having witnessed the effects of an 'alien god' figure entering into situations. The author of one misogynistic, black novel, *Auto-da-Fe*, and of the idiosyncratic *Crowds and Power*, Canetti attracted apostles or 'creatures'.

Marriage and critical acclaim Murdoch escaped from Canetti—and won some respite from a complex set of involvements with both sexes—into marriage with the pre-eminent literary critic John Oliver Bayley (b. 1925) on 14 August 1956. He was willing to live in the country, and they bought Cedar Lodge at Steeple Aston, where they stayed for thirty years, famous for their happiness and domestic squalor. Stuart Hampshire remarked of their appearances together that they reminded him of Hansel and Gretel. And although Murdoch conducted a wide range of compartmentalized friendships, conversation with Bayley about books was ceaseless. When Bayley celebrated Henry James's *The Golden Bowl* in his influential *The Characters of Love*, her novels—*A Severed Head* (1961), *An Unofficial Rose* (1962)—became Jamesian. When he wrote a brilliant study of Tolstoy, his ideas about Tolstoy found their way into *The Nice and the Good* (1968). When he praised Dostoyevsky's *Notes from Underground* (1974), her novels *The Black Prince* (1973) and *A Word-Child* (1974) took on the form of that fable. They together constituted a neo-liberal criticism, both believing against fashion that a high pleasure in literature came from the creation of character; Shakespeare and Tolstoy accomplished that creation best.

The Bell (1958), which some thought Murdoch's best novel, explores the hunger for the spiritual in a post-theistic age. Michael Meade, first of many muddled gay male 'seekers', is animated wonderfully from within. Murdoch's own search for peace of mind at Malling lay behind the troubled quests of her leading characters, and *The Bell* is her first novel to be fuelled by Platonism, in which Good substitutes for God, and any authentic spiritual tradition, including appreciation of the visual arts, provides a means of ascent. *The Bell* brought fame and commercial success, and Chatto printed 30,000 hardback copies within ten weeks. She was praised as 'the foremost novelist of her generation', her book a 'joy ... running over with purpose and intelligence', while the *Times Literary Supplement* praised in it the rare conjunction of a 'brilliant imagination and a passionate concern for conveying ... moral concepts' (*New Statesman*, 15 Nov 1958; *The Times*, 6 Nov 1958; *TLS*, 7 Nov 1958).

William Golding praised Murdoch for achieving what he found hard: locating her work believably in the twentieth century. She achieved this best in the 1970s but a formula of psychological myth-versus-modernity recurs throughout. The social range of the early novels was unremarkable: bohemians and refugees in *Under the Net* and *The Flight from the Enchanter*, schoolmasters in *The Sandcastle* (1957), motley seekers in *The Bell*. With *A Severed Head* (1961) there is a marked shift upwards, into what Angus Wilson irritably termed 'expenses-sheet pseudo-elegance'. Yet the point of the 'high' social world in *A Severed Head* was precisely to contrast the 'primal' appetites and impulses (violence and incest) that get unmasked within it. The triumphant, uproariously successful adaptation for the stage, with J. B. Priestley, at the Criterion Theatre, London, in June 1963 was strongly cast. It was by far the best of the three stage adaptations of her novels, and brought her in nearly £18,000 in its first two years.

Although Murdoch's two Irish novels—the allegorical and atmospheric Gothic romance *The Unicorn* (1963) concerning her theme that life might be a spiritual quest or pilgrimage, and *The Red and the Green* (1965), a study of the Easter rising—offered much that was of interest, the 1960s did not produce her best work. She was perhaps repeating herself, and writing too fast. Soon the adjective 'Murdochian' entered the language to describe a world of baroque coincidence and erotic imbroglio which could lend itself to parody. A new novel gestated for between nine months and one year, a time she would describe as tormented, with a terrifying, dizzying sense of myriad possibilities and of floating unrelated fragments, after whose resolution she would announce triumphantly to John Bayley: 'I've finished it!' At this point she had blocked out an elaborate scene-by-scene plan detailing each successive conversation and piece of action. All that then remained was the pleasurable part, the mere writing of the novel itself, always longhand with a Mont Blanc fountain pen.

Murdoch gave the Leslie Stephen lecture in November 1967, entitled 'The sovereignty of good over other concepts'. It formed the third essay in a 100-page monograph commissioned by D. Z. Phillips. *The Sovereignty of Good* was never conceived of as a book, and its coherence is fortunate, not designed. It is none the less Murdoch's best-known work of philosophy, whose influence has grown since publication. It was fiercely original. To 'come out' then as a Platonist in morals during the proliferation of post-structuralism seemed bizarre. It was a passionately argued attack on both Anglo-Saxon and French orthodoxies, the fruit of a thorough professional involvement with the school of thought to which it was opposed. It also lucidly proposed a powerful and interesting 'rival soul-picture'. It was said to have returned moral philosophy 'to the people', those 'not corrupted' (Conradi, *Life*, 493) by academic philosophy: lay readers gained illumination from it, as well as philosophers. It located value, perhaps unusually for so passionate a Platonist, within attention to good things in *this* life, as well as in the spiritual quest itself. In 1976 she gave the Romanes lecture, published as *The Fire and the Sun: why Plato Banished the Artists*. Her contemporary David Pears noted that she was at war with the desiccation and detailed casuistry of contemporary philosophy, seeking what the American philosopher William James called a tender-minded approach; one in which, as in the Renaissance, the sense of wonder at nature was not at odds with the desire to understand it.

Iris Murdoch introduced a new moral seriousness to the English novel, and her philosophical works established her as one of the leading thinkers of her day. Yet her novels are not programmatic, but test her own high-minded ideas. *A Fairly Honourable Defeat* came out in the same year as *The Sovereignty of Good*, and Rupert, its Platonist, has his work physically torn up, ending drowned in his swimming-pool—dead, his adversary comments, of vanity. Similarly Marcus, the Platonist of *The Time of the Angels* (1966), loses his nerve and abandons his monograph. Gerard, the Platonist of *The Book and the Brotherhood* (1987), is vain and effete. In landmark essays such as 'Against dryness' (1961) she pleaded for a return to the difficult naturalistic idea of 'character'. She wanted to create memorable, free characters but felt that her plots got in the way. In three novels of the 1970s she best succeeded. All show the inspiration of Shakespeare, by whose genius she longed to be touched. *A Fairly Honourable Defeat* (1970), which rewrites *Much Ado about Nothing* in South Kensington, inaugurates her artistic maturity. *The Black Prince* (1973) plays with *Hamlet*, has a Dostoevskian aspect, and is her most intimate and difficult work. *The Sea, the Sea* (1978), which won the Booker prize, reworks *The Tempest*.

In *Metaphysics as a Guide to Morals* (1992), which wrote up the Gifford lectures she had given in 1982, Murdoch spoke of positive icons like objects of prayer: objects, persons, events whose contemplation bought an access of good spiritual energy. It was received with a certain baffled respect. Its rhetoric gets into *The Good Apprentice* (1985), one of two marvellous late novels (the other is *The Green Knight*, 1993). These are saved from the shapelessness that hurts much of her later work by cannibalizing and reworking earlier myths. *The Good Apprentice* recycles the parable of the prodigal son, *The Green Knight* the legend of Sir Gawain.

Last years Murdoch's collection *Existentialists and Mystics: Writings on Literature and Philosophy* was well received in 1997. After three years of increasing confusion and forgetfulness, she was in that year diagnosed as suffering from Alzheimer's disease. Few artists can have declined under such a glare of publicity. She attended the launch party, in Blackwell's, Oxford, of *Iris: a Memoir*, the first of John Bayley's three memoirs of her, each of which described her condition. In 2001 Kate Winslet and Dame Judi Dench acted her in a film based on these memoirs. She died in The Vale in Oxford, a home for Alzheimer's patients, on 8 February 1999, and was cremated at Oxford crematorium.

Iris Murdoch deserves chiefly to be remembered for her astonishing productivity and achievement. She played a major role in English life and letters for nearly half a century, and became an icon to a generation; she won many honours and was appointed DBE in 1987. She was sometimes portrayed as a bourgeois grandee living an unworldly, detached intellectual life, inventing a fantastical alternative world for compensation. 'Real life is so much odder than any book', she wrote to a friend. Her novels are not just stylized comedies of manners with artificial complications, but reflect lived experience, albeit wonderfully transmuted. She made out of a mixture of love-romance and spiritual adventure story a vehicle capable of commenting on modern society, and was not the heir—as she early and wrongly imagined—to George Eliot, but to Dostoyevsky with his fantastic realism, his hectically compressed time schemes, his obsessions with sado-masochism and with incipient moral anarchy. Her best novels combine Dostoyevsky with Shakespearian romance and love-comedy.   PETER J. CONRADI

Sources personal knowledge (2004) · private information (2004) · P. J. Conradi, *Iris Murdoch: a life* (2001) · R. F. Foster, *Paddy and Mr Punch: connections in Irish and English history* (1993) · J. Bayley, *Tolstoi and the novel* (1966) · J. Bayley, *Iris: a memoir of Iris Murdoch* (1999) · J. Bayley, *Iris and the friends* (2000) · J. Bayley, *Widower's house* (2001) · J. Bayley, 'Character and consciousness', *New Literary History*, 5 (1974), 225–35 · P. J. Conradi, 'Iris Murdoch and Dostoevsky', *Dostoevskii and Britain*, ed. W. J. Leatherbarrow (1995), 277–91 · I. Murdoch, interview, 4 Feb 1957, BBC European productions, *Meeting writers*, no 5, ref. 4222 · I. Murdoch, *The red and the green* (1965) · m. cert.
Archives Bodl. Oxf., MS draft of Romanes lecture · Bodl. Oxf., papers concerning service with the United Nations · NRA, corresp. and literary MSS · U. Reading, Iris Murdoch Chatto & Windus archives · University of Bristol, corresp. and statement relating to trial of *Lady Chatterley's lover* · University of Iowa Libraries, Iowa City, corresp. and literary MSS | BLPES, letters to M. J. Oakeshott · Bodl. Oxf., letters to David Hicks · U. Leeds, letters to Norah Smallwood · Viking, New York, corresp. with Viking
Likenesses photographs, 1939–66, Hult. Arch. · G. Freund, bromide print, 1959, NPG · A. Newman, bromide print, 1978, NPG · T. Phillips, two oil paintings, 1984–5, NPG · T. Phillips, oils, 1984–6, NPG [*see illus.*] · T. Phillips, pencil drawing, 1985, NPG · T. Phillips, portrait, 1986?, NPG · T. Phillips, three drawings, 1986, NPG · D. Moore, colour print, 1992, NPG
Wealth at death £1,803,491: daily papers, March 1999

Murdoch, John (1747–1824), teacher and writer, was born at Ayr on 25 March 1747, the son of John Murdoch and Margaret Robison. He attended schools in Ayr and completed his studies at Edinburgh University. After working as an assistant at a private academy, he became a schoolmaster at Ayr Academy, where Burns was one of his pupils. Murdoch described Burns as 'very apt', although his 'ear' was 'remarkably dull', and his voice 'untuneable' (*DNB*).

Murdoch had to leave Ayr upon a complaint lodged against him by the Revd Dr William Dalrymple on 14 February 1776, that he had spoken of the minister in a derogatory manner. Seeking to broaden his horizons, Murdoch left for London, from where he exchanged several letters with Burns. After a short stay there, he went on to Paris, where he formed a lifelong friendship with the secretary to the British embassy, Colonel Fullarton. On returning to London, Murdoch taught French and English at his home in Staple Inn, and in the homes of pupils; among his students was Talleyrand. In London he saw Burns's younger brother, William, just before that brother's death. Murdoch assisted with the funeral preparations, and sent an account of them to Burns, this letter being his last communication with the poet.

Murdoch married in 1780. Among his publications were *Essays on the Revolutions of Literature* (1771), translated from Carlo Denina, *A Radical Vocabulary of the French Language* (1782), a collection of essays and fiction entitled *Pictures of the Heart* (1783), *Orthography of the French Language* (1788), and a work on spelling and pronunciation entitled *The Dictionary of Distinctions* (1811).

In old age, Murdoch fell into distress, and was forced to appeal for public support. He died on 20 April 1824, survived by his wife.   DOUGLAS BROWN

Sources [J. Watkins and F. Shoberl], *A biographical dictionary of the living authors of Great Britain and Ireland* (1816) · R. Inglis, *The dramatic writers of Scotland* (1868) · *The life and works of Robert Burns*, ed. R. Chambers, rev. W. Wallace, [new edn], 4 vols. (1896) · *European Magazine and London Review*, 3 (1783), 130–31 · *N&Q*, 2nd ser., 12 (1861), 419 · *GM*, 1st ser., 94/2 (1824), 186–7 · M. Lindsay, *The Burns encyclopedia*, 2nd edn (1970) · *The letters of Robert Burns*, ed. J. de Lancey Ferguson, 2nd edn, ed. G. Ross Roy, 2 vols. (1985), vol. 1 · *The letters of Robert Burns*, ed. J. de Lancey Ferguson, 2nd edn, ed. G. Ross Roy, 2 vols. (1985), vol. 2 · bap. reg. Scot. · *DNB*

Murdoch, John (1818–1903), journalist and customs and excise official, was born on 15 January 1818 at Lynemore Farm, Ardclach, Nairnshire, Scotland, the second child and eldest son of the nine children of John Murdoch, farm manager, and Mary McPherson, daughter of an Invernessshire landowner. The family moved to Athol in Perthshire in 1821, then a strongly Gaelic-speaking district. Murdoch had no formal education, but educated himself in science and chemistry.

Murdoch's commitments to highland issues began with the family's move to Islay in 1827. Traditional customs were still extant on the island. This, together with the later abrupt clearance of the estate and the potato famine, deeply impressed Murdoch and prompted his *Descriptive and Historical Sketches of Islay* (1850). Highland land reform and politics remained his main concerns, and the modern crofting community owes its existence to Murdoch perhaps more than anyone else. He joined the excise service in 1838, beginning a career that lasted thirty-five years. His first posting was to Kilsyth. His pacifist and religious beliefs—including total abstinence from alcohol and tobacco—were formed there, partly through first-hand involvement in the 1839 'Kilsyth revival', a local evangelical 'rising'. A career of much mobility took him to Armagh, Lancashire (where he heard Richard Cobden and John Bright but was shocked by the drinking habits of lower-class Englishmen), Islay, Dublin, Waterford, Guildford, London, Shetland, and Inverness.

Murdoch's transfer to Dublin in 1853 stimulated a life-long interest in Irish affairs, principally on agricultural and political issues but also embracing language and literature. Murdoch helped to establish the Dublin Chemical Society and the *Agricultural Review*. He also met A. M. Sullivan (1829–1884), editor and later owner of *The Nation*, and Irish nationalist MP. Sullivan supported Murdoch's career as a campaigning journalist. Murdoch had first advocated the principle of 'the land for the people' in newspaper articles in 1851–2; these included pieces on highland destitution in the *Argyleshire Herald*, which he helped to found in 1851. He wrote numerous articles on Celtic issues for *The Nation*, making connections between the Irish and highland land questions. He was also involved in improving salaries for excise staff via the *Civil Service Gazette*. On 4 April 1856 he married Eliza Jane Tickell, whom Murdoch called in his autobiography his first and last sweetheart; they had six children. Several short-term postings ended with an appointment to Shetland in 1864 before Murdoch moved to Inverness in 1866.

It was in Inverness that Murdoch first proposed a highland newspaper to express and direct the gathering sentiments of highland political agitation. These were being channelled through the Gaelic Society of Inverness, of which Murdoch was elected honorary secretary in 1871, and through the writings of people such as Charles Fraser Macintosh and John Stuart Blackie. *The Highlander* became a major forum for political opinion on highland affairs. In his first editorial, on 16 May 1873, Murdoch wrote, 'We this day place in the hands of Highlanders a journal which they can call their own.' However, Murdoch was no Celtic romantic. He and *The Highlander* campaigned for what would today be seen as the human rights of the Gaelic-speaking peoples. Murdoch visited the USA and Canada in late 1879, to raise money, and he spoke at a meeting in Philadelphia with Charles Stewart Parnell and John Dillon. He was a physically powerful man and a stimulating orator, and he had great presence in his highland dress.

Despite support from overseas and native highlanders, *The Highlander* ceased publication in 1881, and Murdoch moved to Glasgow in that year. Secretary of the Scottish Land Restoration League from 1884, and the parliamentary candidate for Partick in the general election of 1885, he was also chairman of the founding meeting of the Scottish Labour Party in Glasgow in May 1888. Later articles on highland politics, influenced by the writings of the American land-reformer, Henry George, appeared chiefly in the *Paisley and Renfrewshire Gazette*. Even though he later became blind, Murdoch continued to speak on highland politics until 1901. He died at Hampden, Caledonian Road, Saltcoats, on 29 January 1903, as a result of influenza and pneumonia.   CHARLES W. J. WITHERS

Sources J. Murdoch, autobiography, 1889–98, Mitchell L., Glas. · *The Highlander* (1873–81) · *The Highlander* (16 May 1873) · J. Hunter, ed., *For the people's cause: from the writings of John Murdoch, highland* and Irish land reformer (1986) · *The Nation* (1842–91) · *The Nation* (1896–1903) · *Argyleshire Herald* (1851–1903) · *Campbeltown Journal* (1851–5) · *Paisley and Renfrewshire Gazette* (1864–1903) · *Civil Service Gazette* (1864–73) · J. Murdoch, *Descriptive and historical sketches of Islay* (1850) · d. cert.

Archives Mitchell L., Glas. | NL Scot.

Likenesses photograph, priv. coll.; repro. in Hunter, ed., *For the people's cause*

Murdoch, John (1819–1904), missionary and book agent, was born in Glasgow on 22 July 1819, the third, but eldest surviving, child in the family of ten sons and two daughters of John Murdoch and his wife, Margaret Smith. The family were members of the Wellington United Presbyterian Church, and in that environment John, a devout Christian, participated in home mission work. At Glasgow high school he excelled in classics and drawing: for a time he trained in the Netherlands to be a painter, but he returned to Scotland in 1838 determined to be a teacher. He enrolled in the Normal Seminary in Glasgow, the first school in Britain devoted entirely to the training of teachers, and one steeped in the principles of moral training then also taking shape in many other parts of Europe. In 1842 he obtained an appointment as headmaster of a government central and normal (teacher training) school in Kandy, Ceylon.

For his work in Kandy, Murdoch received the approval of his superiors in the educational department, and he was appointed for a time to a seat in the legislative council. Despite this success he was disturbed about the propriety of teaching the Bible in government schools which were supported by taxes imposed on Buddhists and Hindus. On his own initiative he began to give religious instruction out of school hours only to those who wished to attend. Under difficult financial conditions in 1848 the government determined to raise school fees, a move which Murdoch thought would ruin the schools, and in August 1849 he resigned from government service and began to formulate what was to become his missionary vocation as a promoter and disseminator of Christian literature. He founded the Ceylon Tract Society in Colombo and became concerned for the Tamil workers being shipped in to work on the coffee plantations of Ceylon. He wrote an appeal on their behalf which led to the founding of the Tamil Cooly Mission of the Church Missionary Society in 1855. In this work he was supported by an annual grant from his home church in Scotland.

After visiting the Tinnevelly region of south India, Murdoch became aware of the need for instructional materials in the schools there, and he conceived the idea of a Christian book society for India which would publish and disseminate Christian school books and tracts. He secured support from the Anglican bishops of Colombo and Madras, and became the sole agent of the South India School Book Society. Murdoch visited the United Kingdom in 1855 and secured the approval of the United Presbyterian synod for his scheme; he was also accepted as a missionary of the United Presbyterian synod with his project as his mission.

Murdoch was in the south of India during the mutiny and rebellion of 1857. Following that upheaval, several missionary societies joined forces in founding the Christian Vernacular Education Society (CVES), which pursued its aim of promoting the spread of vernacular elementary schooling among the masses in India by establishing normal schools to train Christian teachers and by publishing vernacular textbooks. John Murdoch was made CVES agent in India. However, the society failed to appeal successfully to British Christian philanthropy and experienced the difficulties common among ecumenical organizations. Only three co-operative training institutions were founded—one at Amritsar in the Punjab, one at Dindigul near Madura in south India, and one at Ahmednagar in the Bombay presidency—and for the most part, missionary societies maintained normal schools for students of their own denominations. After these first attempts at establishing training schools, the CVES became almost exclusively a book-publishing agency, with Murdoch at its head for the rest of the century. In 1891 it changed its name to the Christian Literature Society for India.

Murdoch's work for the CVES led him to travel to all parts of India and to engage extensively in the affairs of educational missionary work. In 1864 he wrote *The Indian Missionary Manual*, which went through four editions and became a standard work of advice for newcomers to the mission field. He was engaged on behalf of Indian missions generally in petitioning the government for more generous financial support for missionary and other private schools, and he was a strong critic of the policy of the government which forbade religious instruction in its schools. Through extensive publications, including *Hints on Education in India: with Special Reference to Vernacular Schools* (1860), *National Education in India* (1863), and *Education in India: a Letter to the Marquis of Ripon* (1881), Murdoch made himself a ubiquitous presence in discussions of Indian educational policy. In 1873 he was a member of a committee examining school books used in the government schools in Madras, and, typically, he published his own dissenting views (defending an earlier pamphlet of 1872 entitled *The Idolatrous and Immoral Teachings of some Government and University Text-Books in India*). The committee's recommendations were not, however, markedly different from his own. At the end of the century Murdoch joined with many others in interpreting the emerging nationalist agitation in India as a consequence of the failure of the educational system to foster ethical, moral, and religious training. On this point he wrote numerous pamphlets of advice to both students and the government.

Murdoch made an annual circuit of India; in later years he also made two visits to the United States, one to Australia to visit his brother's family, and two to China, where on the second visit in 1891 he was instrumental in the formation of the Christian Literature Society for China. Murdoch was awarded an honorary LLD by the University of Glasgow in 1871. In 1889 the Bible Society made him a life governor, and in 1904 he was awarded the kaisar-i-Hind medal by the Indian government. Murdoch died, unmarried, in his home in Madras on 10 August 1904, while working on a book which was published posthumously that year, as *A Patriot's Duty to his Country*. He was buried locally.

DAVID W. SAVAGE

Sources H. Morris, *The life of John Murdoch, the literary evangelist of India* (1906) · D. W. Savage, 'Evangelical educational policy in Britain and India, 1857–60', *Journal of Imperial and Commonwealth History*, 22 (1994), 432–61 · A. W. McClymont, *The travelling bookman, John Murdoch of Madras* (1947)
Archives U. Glas. L., diary | SOAS, United Society for Christian Literature archives · U. Birm. L., Church Missionary Society archives

Murdoch, John Burn- (1852–1909), army officer, was born at Edinburgh on 17 June 1852, the eldest son of William Burn-Murdoch (1822–1878), MD Edinburgh, second son of John Burn-Murdoch (1793–1862) of Garlincaber, Perthshire. His mother was Jessie Cecilia, daughter of William Mack. The father's younger brother, James M'Gibbon Burn-Murdoch, was father of Colonel John Francis Burn-Murdoch, a distinguished cavalry officer. Educated at the Edinburgh Academy, at Nice for a year, and at the Royal Military Academy, Woolwich, Burn-Murdoch entered the Royal Engineers on 2 May 1872. He served in the Anglo-Afghan War of 1878–80, and was at the engagement of Charasia on 6 October 1879 and the operations round Kabul in December 1879, including the storming of the Asmai heights, when he was severely wounded while employed in blowing up one of the Afghan forts. He was mentioned in dispatches.

Burn-Murdoch took part in the 1882 Egyptian campaign with the contingent from India under Major-General Herbert Taylor Macpherson. The engineers were commanded by Sir James Browne, known as Buster Browne (1839–1896), and Burn-Murdoch and William Gustavus Nicholson were the two field engineers. On reaching Bombay with his companions on 6 August, Burn-Murdoch aided Browne in preparing all the requisite material, and arrived at Suez, where they repaired the roads, local canals, and railways. From Isma'iliyyah they reached Qassasin on 11 September, and were present at the battle of Tell al-Kebir on the 13th. Immediately afterwards Burn-Murdoch, with the Indian force, pushed on for some 30 miles to Zaqaziq, and took a foremost part in seizing the railway there; General Browne sent a captured train back under Burn-Murdoch to help bring in the 72nd regiment, 6 miles off. The brilliant seizure of Zaqaziq, in which Burn-Murdoch did useful service, deprived the rebels of command of the railway and facilitated the capture of Cairo. He was mentioned in dispatches and received the Mejidiye (fifth class).

Burn-Murdoch was promoted captain on 2 May 1884, major on 6 August 1891, and lieutenant-colonel on 1 March 1900. Meanwhile he served in India in the state railways, and in 1893 became commanding engineer of state railways and subsequently was chief engineer of the Southern Mahratta Railway. He married in August 1889 Maud (d. 1893), widow of William Forster; they had no children (his wife already had three sons and a daughter). Burn-

Murdoch retired on an Indian pension on 28 May 1900 and died at Bridge of Leith Cottage, Doune, Perthshire, on 30 January 1909. He was buried in Old Kilmadoch burial-ground.   H. M. VIBART, *rev.* JAMES LUNT

Sources Burke, *Gen. GB* · *Hart's Army List* · *Army List* · W. Porter, *History of the corps of royal engineers*, 2 (1889) · J. J. McLeod, *Life and times of General Sir James Browne* (1905) · J. F. Maurice, *Military history of the campaign of 1882 in Egypt*, rev. edn (1908) · Lord Roberts [F. S. Roberts], *Forty-one years in India*, 2 vols. (1897) · H. B. Hanna, *The Second Afghan War*, 1 (1899) · B. Robson, *The road to Kabul: the Second Afghan War, 1878–1881* (1986)
Wealth at death £7470 3*s.*: confirmation, 20 April 1909, *CCI*

Murdoch, Sir **Keith Arthur** (1885–1952), journalist and newspaper proprietor, was born on 12 August 1885 at a'Beckett Street, Melbourne, the third of seven children of Patrick John Murdoch (1850–1940), Presbyterian minister, and his wife, Annie (1856–1945), daughter of the Revd George Brown and his wife, May. Patrick and Annie had emigrated from Aberdeenshire, Scotland, a year earlier. Murdoch grew up in semi-rural Camberwell, where his father was minister. Extremely shy and afflicted with a humiliating stammer, he attended several schools before emerging from Camberwell grammar school as dux in 1903. When Keith elected not to go into the church or to university, Patrick Murdoch introduced him to his friend David Syme, the Scottish-born proprietor of the Melbourne *Age*. Keith, who had learned shorthand and professed an insatiable appetite for newspapers, was employed at 1½*d.* a line as correspondent for the outlying district of Malvern.

After four years of long hours and assiduous saving, Murdoch went to London in April 1908 to seek treatment for his stammer, attend the London School of Economics, and 'become a moving force' in journalism (Murdoch papers). While visiting speech experts, he read widely and attended lectures and parliamentary debates. But he was desperately lonely and, despite impressive references, struggled to secure journalistic assignments. Late in 1909, after his speech collapsed at an interview with the *Pall Mall Gazette*, Murdoch sailed for Melbourne. He returned to the *Age* as a staff reporter and then commonwealth parliamentary reporter, and constant exercising brought his stammer under reasonable control. He became close to the prime minister, Andrew Fisher, a friend of his father, and other ministers in the Labor government, including George Pearce and W. M. Hughes, whom he entertained at an aunt's guest house. In 1912 Murdoch became Melbourne representative of the Sydney *Sun*. In July 1914 he provisionally accepted the editorship of a Labour afternoon newspaper, but the launch of the *World* was postponed by war.

In September 1914 Murdoch came second to C. E. W. Bean in the Australian Journalists' Association ballot to appoint an official Australian war correspondent. In July 1915 he left for London to take up the managing editorship of the United Cable Service, which serviced the *Sun* and the Melbourne *Herald* and operated out of the London *Times* office. Fisher and Pearce, the defence minister, commissioned him to investigate *en route* mail services and other matters affecting the Australian Imperial Force. Murdoch obtained permission from General Sir Ian Hamilton briefly to visit the 'sacred shores' of Anzac (Zwar, 24), where he cabled emotional dispatches back to Australia. The British war correspondent Ellis Ashmead-Bartlett, appalled by the conduct of the Gallipoli campaign, gave Murdoch a sealed letter to carry to the prime minister, H. H. Asquith. This letter was intercepted by the British army. However, on 23 September Murdoch sent Fisher his own letter condemning the 'deplorable' bungling of the British army and lauding the 'magnificent manhood' of Australian troops (Zwar, 33; Carlyon, 497).

Murdoch shared his impressions with Geoffrey Dawson and Lord Northcliffe, respectively editor and proprietor of *The Times*. Murdoch was introduced to cabinet ministers and persuaded to send Asquith a copy of his sensational letter. It provided ammunition to the anti-Dardanelles faction and contributed to Hamilton's recall and the evacuation of troops. At the 1916 Dardanelles commission and later, Murdoch vigorously defended his actions, denying that he had made exaggerated claims and broken a pledge of censorship.

When the Australian prime minister, W. M. Hughes, visited Britain in 1916 and 1918 Murdoch acted as his publicist and assistant speech-writer and hosted dinner parties for him with guests such as David Lloyd George, Andrew Bonar Law, and General William Robertson. Murdoch was assigned to persuade overseas troops to support the Hughes Nationalist government's unsuccessful conscription referendums. Murdoch visited France and Belgium as an unofficial war correspondent and extended the United Cable Service to India and South Africa. Increasingly styling himself as a military and political strategist, he fell out with Hughes during the latter's pugnacious performance at the Paris peace conference in 1919.

When Murdoch covered for *The Times* the visit of the prince of Wales to Australasia in 1920, the *Australasian Journalist* reported that Murdoch's rise to fame had been 'meteoric' (23 June 1920, 126). He had developed an almost filial relationship with Northcliffe, interrogating him about newspaper techniques, barging into his office, and holidaying at his Riviera villa. But while Murdoch revered Northcliffe as the 'Chief of All Journalists (of all ages)', he knew he could not be his employee and 'puppet' (Zwar, 61). In 1921 Murdoch, anxious not to loosen his grip on 'Australian affairs and sentiment' (Murdoch papers), was appointed editor of Melbourne's only afternoon newspaper, *The Herald*.

Murdoch had Northcliffe send him critical commentaries on the stodgy *Herald*. With the encouragement of Theodore Fink, chairman of the Herald and Weekly Times Ltd, Murdoch overhauled the newspaper, painstakingly critiquing each section and recruiting bright young journalists and artists at attractive salaries. He was installed as managing editor in 1922 and the board began to fracture. The rejuvenated *Herald*, featuring more pictures and human interest stories and tighter sub-editing, was soon targeted by a Sydney-based company, which launched afternoon and morning newspapers in Melbourne. In 1925 the interloper retreated to Sydney: the *Evening Sun* was discontinued and the *Sun News-Pictorial* acquired by the Herald and Weekly Times. Other challenges to *The Herald*'s afternoon monopoly were also to fail. While Murdoch became a director in 1926 and managing director in 1928, he continued to prepare daily 'managing editor's notes' on *The Herald*.

Tall and solidly built, with dark wavy hair and piercing eyes, Murdoch was an eligible man about town who lived alone with his servants, acquiring antiques and *objets d'art*. On 6 June 1928 at Scots Church, Melbourne, he married with Presbyterian rites nineteen-year-old Elisabeth Joy Greene (*b.* 1909). They had three daughters and a son. The close and affectionate family divided their time between a mansion in Toorak and Cruden Farm at Langwarrin, south of Melbourne. While he found it difficult to relax, Murdoch enjoyed collecting gadgets, playing chess, horse-riding, and fishing.

As *The Herald* and *Sun-News Pictorial* thrived, 'Lord Southcliffe' established Australia's first national media chain. In 1931 he became chairman of Advertiser Newspapers Ltd, publisher of Adelaide's morning *Advertiser*. The Herald and Weekly Times then obtained a controlling interest in Adelaide's afternoon newspaper *The News* and Murdoch joined the board of News Ltd thus giving the *Herald* group monopoly newspaper control in Adelaide. In 1933 Murdoch helped create the Brisbane *Courier-Mail* and Queensland Newspapers Ltd, and he and the Herald and Weekly Times also had interests in Perth and several radio stations.

Although Murdoch travelled between states often, *The Herald* remained his favourite newspaper. Energetic and insatiably curious, 'KM' had a phenomenal memory and was rather strait-laced. He liked journalists to have a good education, dress well, and travel. Some of his 'Young Men' were trained and tested at luncheons in the Herald and Weekly Times directors' dining-room, where politicians, businessmen, and art figures gathered. By early 1931 Murdoch had decided to throw all his resources behind Joseph Lyons, who withdrew support from James Scullin's troubled Labor government in disagreement over its handling of the depression crisis. When Lyons founded the United Australia Party (UAP) and formed government, Murdoch began to think of himself as a kingmaker, although he was never really a 'party man'.

In 1933, the year he was knighted, Murdoch joined the board of trustees of the public library, which included the National Gallery of Victoria. He confronted the conservative Melbourne art establishment, displaying a moderately advanced and broadly tolerant artistic appreciation. In 1939 he became chairman of trustees and commissioned the *Herald*'s art critic Basil Burdett to curate a travelling exhibition of French and British modern art, the likes of which had never been seen in Australia. Murdoch became founding chairman of the newly autonomous National Gallery in 1945 and relentlessly lobbied for a site for a new building. He belonged to the Oriental Ceramic Society of London and had *The Herald* endow a chair of fine arts at the University of Melbourne.

A consummate organizer, Murdoch in 1935 oversaw the amalgamation of existing cable services into Australian Associated Press, later to form a partnership with Reuters. He was also the driving force behind the establishment of Australian Newsprint Mills Pty Ltd, which started producing the country's first newsprint in Tasmania in 1941. In June 1940 R. G. Menzies' UAP government appointed Murdoch director-general of information. However, Murdoch alienated fellow proprietors when he clumsily issued a regulation compelling newspapers to correct misstatements; the regulation was withdrawn and he resigned in December. In 1942 Murdoch became chairman of the Herald and Weekly Times and head of the Australian section of the Empire Press Union.

Persuasive at the conference table and pungent in all he wrote, Murdoch was a little awkward in interviews and speeches, a relic of his early stammer. During the war he resumed writing articles for the *Herald* chain, advocating an all-party national government and pontificating on military strategy. He flayed the war policies and leadership of John Curtin and his Labor government; it has been suggested that in 1943 a minister unsuccessfully attempted to entice Murdoch away from his vociferous newspapers with a posting overseas. Murdoch travelled abroad regularly and was a leading founder of the Australian-American Association. After the war he sought to dispense with the services of 'Coms and their fellow travellers' (Dumas papers) on his staff, opposed bank nationalization, and supported the Liberal Party.

Diagnosed with heart strain in the early 1930s, Murdoch had operations for prostate and bowel cancer in the late 1940s. He made bad investments in pastoral properties and worried incessantly about providing for his family's security and for a base for his son, Rupert, who he predicted would be 'a good newspaper man' (Dumas papers). Shortly before retiring from most directorships in 1949, he persuaded the *Herald*'s board to sell him its shares in the Adelaide *News*. He retained the chairmanship but preserved few shares in the Herald and Weekly Times; instead he took out a large overdraft to invest heavily in News Ltd and Queensland Newspapers Ltd. In 1950 Murdoch secretly considered leaving *The Herald* and buying into the Melbourne morning *Argus* with the London *Daily Mirror* group, but the deal fell through. He died in his sleep at Cruden Farm, Langwarrin, Victoria, on the night of 4–5 October 1952 and was cremated on 7 October at a funeral at Toorak Presbyterian Church. He was survived by his wife, Elisabeth, and their four children.

BRIDGET GRIFFEN-FOLEY

Sources Sir Keith Murdoch papers, NL Aus., MS 2823 · Sir Lloyd Dumas papers, NL Aus., MS 4849 · C. E. Sayers, papers, State Library of Victoria, Melbourne, La Trobe manuscript collection, MS 10601 · D. Zwar, *In search of Keith Murdoch* (1980) · 'Keith Murdoch, journalist' (Herald and Weekly Times, Melbourne, 1952) · L. Carlyon, *Gallipoli* (2001) · J. Hetherington, *Australians* (1960) · J. Monks, *Elisabeth Murdoch: two lives* (1994) · D. Garden, *Theodore Fink: a talent for ubiquity* (1998) · L. B. Cox, *The National Gallery of Victoria, 1861 to 1968* (c.1970) · *Australian Journalist* (23 June 1920), 126 ·

G. Serle, 'Murdoch, Sir Keith Arthur', *AusDB*, vol. 10 · private information (2004) [Dame Elisabeth Murdoch]
Archives NL Aus., MSS | BL, corresp. with Lord Northcliffe, Add. MS 62179 · NL Aus., Dumas MSS, corresp. and papers · State Library of Victoria, Melbourne, La Trobe manuscript collection, Sayers MSS, corresp. and papers
Likenesses G. Lambert, drawing, priv. coll.
Wealth at death £358,852: *Sydney Morning Herald* (12 Dec 1952), 4

Murdoch, Patrick (*d.* 1774), Church of England clergyman and writer, was born in Dumfries; details of his parents are unknown. He was educated at the University of Edinburgh, where he distinguished himself in mathematics, and was the pupil and friend of Colin Maclaurin, from whom he probably acquired his interest in Newtonian philosophy and science. In 1729 he was appointed tutor to John Forbes, only son of Lord President Duncan Forbes of Culloden, and accompanied him on the grand tour, visiting Paris, Orléans, Montauban, Rome, and other continental cities. Forbes later paid frequent visits to Murdoch, and placed his eldest son, Duncan, under his tuition. Murdoch was also travelling tutor to the younger sons of James Vernon, ambassador to the court of Denmark. Previously ordained in the Scottish Episcopal church, he was presented by Vernon to the rectory of Stradishall in Suffolk in 1738. It was at this time that his friend the poet James Thomson wrote the poem 'To the Rev Mr Murdoch, Rector of Stradishall in Suffolk, 1738'. On 20 March 1745 Murdoch was elected a fellow of the Royal Society; he published eight papers in the society's *Transactions* during his life. In 1748 he was admitted MA at Cambridge *per literas regias*. William Leman gave him the rectory of Kettlebaston, Suffolk, in 1749, which he resigned in 1760 on being presented by Edward Vernon to the vicarage of Great Thurlow; but he still continued to live at Stradishall. In 1756 he accompanied his friend the diplomat Andrew Mitchell to Berlin, where he remained until 1757, conducting part of the official correspondence, while Mitchell was with the army. He received the degree of DD from the University of Edinburgh on 4 September 1763.

According to John Hill Burton, Murdoch was the 'little round fat oily man of God' described by James Thomson in the sixty-ninth stanza of his *Seasons*, canto 1. This was considered unlikely by Andrew Bisset because the hostility of the stanza was incompatible with Thomson's friendship with Murdoch. Murdoch's memoir of the poet was attached to almost all editions of Thomson's works after 1762.

Murdoch prefixed a life of Colin Maclaurin to that author's *Account of Sir Isaac Newton's Philosophical Discoveries*, published in London in 1748, which he saw through the press for the benefit of Maclaurin's children. Murdoch also edited the illustrations of perspective from conic sections, *Neutoni genesis curvarum per umbras* (1746). He contemplated a complete edition of Newton's works, and by 1766 had found a publisher in Andrew Millar, but increasing infirmities obliged him to abandon the undertaking. In addition to several Royal Society papers published in 1758, Murdoch also wrote *Mercator's Sailing, Applied to the True Figure of the Earth* (1741) and published in London in

1762, under the title *A New System of Geography*, a translation of a portion of the work by Anton Friedrich Buesching, relating to the European states, to which he prefixed three explanatory essays. A letter written by Murdoch to Andrew Mitchell on 27 March 1742 states that he had found a prospective wife, a considerable heiress whose relatives approved of him as a possible match. However, nothing came of this, and Murdoch was a bachelor when he died in the parish of St Clement Danes, London, in October 1774.

GORDON GOODWIN, rev. ALEXANDER DU TOIT

Sources *The Suffolk garland* (1818), 24–6 · [H. R. Duff], ed., *Culloden papers* (1815), 127–8, 177–8, 278–9, 306–12 · A. Bisset, *Memoirs and papers of Sir Andrew Mitchell, K. B.*, 2 vols. (1850), 1.37–42 · D. Laing, ed., *A catalogue of the graduates ... of the University of Edinburgh*, Bannatyne Club, 106 (1858), 243 · Nichols, *Lit. anecdotes*, 3.656; 8.465 · T. Thomson, *History of the Royal Society from its institution to the end of the eighteenth century* (1812), appx 4, p. xliv · *The works of James Thomson*, ed. P. Murdoch, 1 (1762), 457 · J. H. Burton, *Lives of Simon, Lord Lovat, and Duncan Forbes of Culloden* (1847)
Archives NL Scot., letters, MS 3278 | BL, Birch collections · BL, Egerton MSS · NL Scot., Culloden MSS · NL Scot., corresp. with Forbes family
Wealth at death see will, NL Scot., M8 8494

Murdoch, Richard Bernard (1907–1990), actor and comedian, was born on 6 April 1907 at the family home in Keston, Kent, the only son of Bernard Murdoch, tea merchant, and his wife, Amy Florence, daughter of Avison Terry Scott, archdeacon of Tonbridge. He was educated at Charterhouse School and at Pembroke College, Cambridge, which he left without gaining a degree, his appetite for a career in show business being whetted by success with the Cambridge Footlights.

Murdoch's professional stage career began in 1927 at the King's Theatre, Southsea, in the chorus of the musical play *The Blue Train*. He then worked in the chorus and played small parts in various musical comedies and revues including *That's a Good Girl* (1928), *Oh Letty!* (1929), *Cochran's 1930 Revue*, and *Stand up and Sing* (1931). This was followed in the 1930s by André Charlot's West End revues and the musical comedy *Over she Goes* (1936). By the mid-1930s his reputation as a first-class light comedian was growing. In 1932 he married Peggy, daughter of William Rawlings, solicitor. They had one son and two daughters.

In 1938 the BBC teamed Murdoch with Arthur Askey in the radio series *Band Waggon*, in which they were alleged to live in a flat in Broadcasting House, and many sketches were based on this notion. Their humour was a forerunner of much radio comedy to come, for although their comic interludes took up only ten minutes of the weekly one-hour programme, the fantasy of their living in Broadcasting House, and the creation of such mythical characters as Mrs Bagwash the charlady and her daughter Nausea and their pet animals, a goat called Lewis, and two pigeons Basil and Lucy, preceded *ITMA* and *Hancock's Half Hour* and was a strong influence on many nascent comedy scriptwriters.

In 1938, after two series, the stage rights to *Band Waggon* were acquired by the impresario Jack Hylton, and Murdoch with Askey and a supporting cast toured the provincial music-halls and finished with a run at the London Palladium in 1939. The debonair, sophisticated West End style of Murdoch blended neatly with the more down-to-earth humour of Liverpudlian Arthur Askey, whose reputation was based on his successes in seaside concert parties. It was Askey who gave Murdoch the nickname Stinker. Together they were enormously successful.

In 1941 Murdoch joined the Royal Air Force as a pilot officer working in the intelligence sector of Bomber Command. Later he was posted to the Air Ministry in London, where he was promoted to squadron-leader in the directorate of administrative plans, under the command of Wing Commander Kenneth *Horne. The two quickly became friends and as both were regular broadcasters it was only a matter of time (1944) before they dreamed up the mythical RAF station *Much Binding in the Marsh*. This became the RAF segment of a services series *Merry Go Round*, alternating with the Royal Navy show *HMS Waterlogged*, written by and starring Eric Barker, and the army contribution *Stand Easy*, with Charlie Chester.

Murdoch and Horne wrote the scripts of the *Much Binding* shows and when peace came in 1945 they duly transferred it to a civilian milieu, where it thrived until 1954. From then on Richard Murdoch's career was varied and interesting and included a tour of South Africa, a season in Canada playing William the waiter in G. B. Shaw's *You Never can Tell*, and a round-the-world trip for the Australian Broadcasting Corporation in a series of programmes called *Much Murdoch*.

His next major success was the BBC radio series *The Men from the Ministry* (1961–77), in which he co-starred first with Wilfrid Hyde-White and later with Deryck Guyler. Towards the end of his life Richard Murdoch appeared in several episodes of the television series *Rumpole of the Bailey*, playing the aged barrister Uncle Tom.

Murdoch was 6 feet 1 inch tall and good looking. He was always polished and well mannered and was, to quote James Green, the show business columnist, 'a subtle and charming comic actor'. Murdoch died on 9 October 1990. As a keen golfer he could not have wished for a better end, for he died while playing golf at Walton Heath, Surrey.

BARRY TOOK, rev.

Sources N. Hackforth, *Solo for Horne* (1976) · B. Took, *Laughter in the air: an informal history of British radio comedy* (1976) · *The Times* (10 Oct 1990) · *CGPLA Eng. & Wales* (1991)
Likenesses photographs, Hult. Arch.
Wealth at death £190,212: probate, 15 June 1991, *CGPLA Eng. & Wales*

Murdoch, Sir Thomas William Clinton (1809–1891), civil servant, born on 22 March 1809 in London, was the son of Thomas Murdoch FRS of Portland Place and his wife, Charlotte, daughter of John Leacock of Madeira. He was educated at Charterhouse School, and entered the Colonial Office as a junior clerk in 1826. He married in 1836 Isabella Anne, daughter of Robert Lukin, an official in the War Office.

In September 1839 Murdoch went out under Sir George Arthur to Canada to act as chief secretary, and, after acting also during part of 1841 as provincial secretary for Lower Canada, returned to the Colonial Office in September 1842. He became a senior clerk there in May 1846.

In November 1847 Murdoch was appointed to the important position of chairman of the colonial land and emigration commissioners in succession to Thomas Frederick Elliot (1808–1880). The commission had been set up in 1840 to assist emigration to the colonies, but by the 1850s, as the Australian colonies gained responsible self-government, assisted emigration was in decline. As a result, the work of the office became limited to the enforcement of the Passenger Acts (which regulated conditions on emigrant ships) and collecting colonial statistics. Murdoch was an influential opponent of the unsuccessful parliamentary bills promoted by the National Emigration League in the early 1870s to provide government subsidies for emigration as a means of relieving poverty in Britain. He argued that state support would merely reduce the flow of voluntary emigration, and published statistics to show the steady growth of the latter. His administrative ability and judgement were highly regarded, and he was knighted KCMG in January 1870. Later that year he was sent by the government on a diplomatic mission to Canada in connection with the Red River rebellion and then to the USA to discuss the international convention on the regulation of emigration.

Murdoch retired on pension in December 1876; the commission was wound up in March 1878, when its functions were transferred to other departments. He was a great reader, and spent his later years chiefly among his books. Murdoch died on 30 November 1891 at his home, 88 St George's Square, London. His eldest son, Charles Stewart Murdoch (1838–1908), became an assistant undersecretary at the Home Office.

C. A. HARRIS, rev. M. C. CURTHOYS

Sources private information (1894) · *Colonial Office List* · Walford, *County families* · Boase, *Mod. Eng. biog.* · F. H. Hitchins, *The colonial land and emigration commission* (1931) · H. L. Malchow, *Population pressures: emigration and government in late nineteenth-century Britain* (1979) · W. P. Morrell, *British colonial policy in the age of Peel and Russell* (1930) · W. P. Morrell, *British colonial policy in the mid-Victorian age* (1969)
Wealth at death £9498 0s. 3d.: probate, 30 Dec 1891, *CGPLA Eng. & Wales*

Murdoch, William (c.1539–1616), Jesuit, was probably a native of Dunkeld, Scotland, where he attended the grammar school. In 1559 he was part of the household of Robert Crichton, bishop of Dunkeld, where he was supplied with hose, shoes, and sword. His next appearance is his entry into the Society of Jesus at Rome on 29 August 1563, having matriculated in January of that year as a poor student at Louvain. By 1567 he was recorded as a student of the Roman college. In 1568 he was sent to the college at Paris, then directed by the Scottish Jesuit Edmund Hay, and was still there in 1571. He was ordained priest in 1572. In 1584 he is found at the college at Pont-à-Mousson in Lorraine. By 1588 he was ripe for the Scottish mission, where he stayed two years or so. A reference in 1593 to William Murdoch, writing master in Edinburgh, though plausible because of his fine italic hand, must be to a kinsman, one William Murdoch who graduated from St Salvator's College, St Andrews, in 1575. In 1593 Murdoch was in Pont-à-Mousson again. By 16 July 1594, however, he was once more in Scotland, and appointed superior there in November 1599; he is found on Speyside and elsewhere in the north-east.

King James VI was not far out in claiming that Murdoch spent twenty years in Scotland. The 1594 visit began at Aberdeen, where with Huntly's Jesuit brother, James Gordon, he arrived under cover of night having sailed to Scotland from Calais. The boat on which he arrived was searched for papal gold; it was seized, but the occupants had gone forward to Huntly. In October of that year the Catholic earls of Erroll and Huntly won the battle of Glenlivat against the royal forces sent north to counter them, although they were prevented from enjoying the fruits of victory, thanks to the sending of additional troops. Murdoch visited the earls of Caithness and Sutherland, remaining in the latter's household after Sutherland's death teaching letters and manners, and celebrating a requiem mass for Lady Auchindown. He traversed the north-east, baptizing children, celebrating mass, and acting as a physician. There were odd visits to Edinburgh, under false names such as Gilbert Mackie (sometimes mistakenly given as William) and Andrew 'Stinsonius' (Steinston). One of his companions was David Law, Catholic brother of the protestant bishop, James Law.

Murdoch saw Father Abercrombie off to Poland from Dundee in 1606. On his capture by the authorities in July 1607, Murdoch was thoroughly interrogated and his possessions seized. His confession scarcely told his captors anything new, but papers taken on his person were revelatory as to other missionaries. On the king's orders, he was exiled in September after ritual humiliation at the Edinburgh Mercat Cross, and returned to Pont-à-Mousson to act as confessor until his death on 22 August 1616. The source for his activities, in addition to his confession, is a long letter of 10 October 1608 to the Jesuit general, Acquaviva. Apart from the north-east, Murdoch visited many Perthshire families; but when the northern earls gave up their campaign to restore Catholicism, his company must have become more restricted, and by the time he reached his sixties, his own campaign was at an end, since to return to Scotland would have meant death.

JOHN DURKAN

Sources J. Durkan, 'William Murdoch and the early Jesuit mission in Scotland', *Innes Review*, 35 (1984), 3–11 · R. Pitcairn, ed., *Ancient criminal trials in Scotland*, 2, Bannatyne Club, 42 (1833), 530–31 · R. K. Hannay, ed. and trans., *Rentale Dunkeldense*, Scottish History Society, 2nd ser., 10 (1915), 358–9, 361–2 · Justiciary records, 1604–11, NA Scot., JC 2/4, unfoliated, RH9/2/180 · Archivum Romanum Societatis Iesu, Rome, Anglia 31/II, fols. 147–50 · *Reg. PCS*, 1st ser., 7.355 · *Reg. PCS*, 1st ser., 14.478–80, 487–90 · J. F. K. Johnstone, *The alba amicorum of George Strachan, George Craig, Thomas Cumming*, Aberdeen University Studies, 95 (1924) · J. Stuart, ed., *The miscellany of the Spalding Club*, 5, Spalding Club, 24 (1852), 116 · J. Stuart, ed., *Extracts from the council register of the burgh of Aberdeen*, 2: *1570–1625*, Spalding Club, 19 (1848), 85 · L. Carrez, ed., *Catalogi sociorum et officiorum Provinciae Campaniae Societatis Jesu*, 10 vols (1897), vol. 1, pp. 34, 47, 79–100; vol. 2, p. 202 · *Matricule de l'Université de Louvain*, 4, ed. A. Schillings (1961), 648 · *Original letters relating to the ecclesiastical affairs of Scotland: chiefly written by … King James the Sixth*, ed. D. Laing, 2 vols., Bannatyne Club, 92 (1851), vol. 1, pp. 377–8 · Archivum Romanum Societatis Iesu, Rome, Flandro-Belg. 80, fol. 4; Rom. 70, fol. 64; Rom. 78b, fols. 32, 49, 56; Franc 22, fol. 8v

Archives Archivum Romanum Societatis Iesu, Rome, autobiographical letter of 10 Oct 1608

Murdoch, William. *See* Murdock, William (1754–1839).

Murdoch, William Lloyd (1854–1911), cricketer, was born at Sandhurst near Bendigo, Victoria, Australia, on 18 October 1854. He was the son of Gilbert William Lloyd Murdoch (1826–1854), at one time a corporal in the United States army, and his wife, Edith Susan Hogg. His father, of Scottish ancestry, had emigrated from Maryland to Australia in 1849. After being educated at Dr Bromley's school in Ballarat and at Bonwick School, Melbourne, Murdoch moved to Sydney, New South Wales, where he was articled to a solicitor and subsequently practised until 1891.

Murdoch made his début as a cricketer for New South Wales in 1875 and made nineteen appearances for the state until 1884. Against Victoria at Sydney in 1882 he made 321. He was selected for Australia in what was retrospectively seen as the second test match to be played against England, at Melbourne in 1877. In the following year he toured England as a wicket-keeper and batsman. In 1880 he made the first of four tours to England as the Australian captain, heading the batting averages on each occasion and doing much to sustain the reputation he had acquired in Australia in the 1880s as the 'W. G. Grace of Australia'. In the first test played in England, at the Oval in 1880, he carried his bat for 153 not out in Australia's second innings. Australia had followed on 271 runs behind and Murdoch's contribution reduced the margin of defeat to five wickets. His outstanding innings on the 1882 tour was 286 not out against Sussex. On his third tour as captain, in 1884—again against England—he made 211 at the Oval, the first double-century in a test match.

In 1879 the family firm for which he worked was dissolved and Murdoch was declared bankrupt with debts of £775. He had, nevertheless, been able to embark on his cricket tours to England, and his marriage (on 8 December 1884) to Jemima Watson (d. 1917), daughter of a wealthy goldmine owner from Bendigo, gave him financial security. In 1888–9 he paid an extended visit to England and, on his return, was the choice of the players—but not the press—to captain Australia for a fourth time. The 1890 tour was a 'failure' but 'it would be wrong to say that he (himself) failed', reported *Wisden*.

Immediately after returning home Murdoch took the decision to move permanently to England with his family. Thanks to his wife he enjoyed financial independence. He knew the country well and was encouraged by his friend W. G. Grace. He disliked the vicious attacks being made on players—and especially on himself for being past his best—by an increasingly savage Australian press. Finally, he simply wanted to play cricket at first-class level for a few more years. While awaiting qualification for Sussex, he toured South Africa in the winter of 1891–2 and his appearance for England at Cape Town in March 1892 gave him the distinction (again retrospectively)—of playing test cricket for two countries. The match represented his only performance at test match level as a wicket-keeper, since that position had been filled in the Australian team during his career by J. McC. Blackham.

Murdoch captained Sussex from 1893 to 1899, and under his leadership the county's fortunes revived. His best scores during this period were 226 against Cambridge University at Hove (1895) and 172 against Hampshire at Southampton (1894). But with increasing years and weight his batting deteriorated. He subsequently played first-class cricket (1901–4) for the London County Cricket Club founded by W. G. Grace at the Crystal Palace, making several good scores against first-class counties, including 155 against Lancashire at Old Trafford in 1903. His last important score was 140 at the Oval in 1904, when he played as substitute for the Gentlemen against the Players. His being invited to join the side on the second day, after a player had dropped out through injury, was held by the MCC to be contrary to the laws but no action was taken by the authorities. Of fine physique, Murdoch was an orthodox and correct batsman who played with a straight bat. He had a wide range of strokes, especially the off-drive and the cut. As a batsman he was excelled only by W. G. Grace on hard, true pitches, and by few in defence on soft, treacherous wickets. As a captain he was a resourceful tactician. His second 'career', from 1893 onwards, enabled him to compile nearly 17,000 runs besides securing 243 dismissals as a wicket-keeper. In his London county days he usually opened the batting with Grace, the two great veterans of nineteenth-century cricket in Australia and England playing out their last years together.

Murdoch was a genial, good-tempered man whom C. B. Fry called 'genuinely and unaffectedly amusing' (*Oxford Companion to Australian Sport*, 1992, 732). Contemporaries recognized his relaxed and easy manner. He died on 18 February 1911, during a test match between Australia and South Africa at Melbourne. During the lunch interval that day he suffered a stroke, from which he died without recovering consciousness. His body was returned to England, and was interred at Kensal Green cemetery, London, on 18 May 1911; his wife and five children survived him.

GERALD M. D. HOWAT

Sources   *The Times* (20 Feb 1911) • *The Times* (19 May 1911) • *Cricket* (18 Sept 1882) • *Cricket* (24 April 1890) • *Cricket* (23 Feb 1911) • *Wisden* (1912) • A. Haygarth, *Arthur Haygarth's cricket scores and biographies*, 14 (1895) • J. Pollard, ed., *Australian cricket* (1982) • *AusDB*
Likenesses   London Stereoscopic Co., photograph, *c.*1882, repro. in *Cricket* (24 April 1890) • E. Hawkins, photograph, *c.*1890, Lord's, London, Marylebone Cricket Club • photograph, *c.*1890 (with W. G. Grace), Albert Gregory Collection, Australia; repro. in J. Pollard, ed., *Pictorial history of Australian cricket* (1983)

Murdock [*formerly* Murdoch], **William** (1754–1839), engineer and inventor, was born on 21 August 1754 at Bellow Mill, Old Cumnock, Ayrshire, the second son and third child of seven, of John Murdoch, miller and millwright,

and his wife, Anne, sister of the agent for the Boswell estates, which the mill served. His father and grandfather had been gunners in the Royal Artillery. William Murdoch is thought by some to have changed his name to Murdock on arriving in England, but it seems more likely that this alteration was gradual and accidental over the course of several years.

Murdock was brought up in his father's trade, and his family connection with James Boswell, who visited Boulton and Watt's celebrated Soho works in Birmingham in March 1776, probably inspired and secured Murdock's employment there in August 1777. Murdock had little, though good, formal education, but a practical turn of mind and a passion for solving mechanical problems in simple but original ways, together with his commanding physique—he was broad and over 6 feet tall—commended him to Boulton. He became within a few months Boulton and Watt's principal pattern maker and an assistant engine erector. By March 1779 he was erecting an engine, only Boulton and Watt's fourth, on his own at Wanlockhead. Here he began a series of improvements on Watt's basic design, seldom with Watt's prior permission and often to his irritation at Murdock's 'disposition to amend' (Griffiths, 137), but usually with his eventual approval. Murdock continued these improvements during his twenty years of service in Cornwall, where he was sent in the autumn of 1779 as Boulton and Watt's technical supervisor.

Gradually, if often reluctantly, Boulton and Watt came to realize that in Cornwall they not only had 'the most active man and best engine erector I ever saw' (Griffiths, 102), but an inventor of rare talent. The problem was that although many of his inventions—from wooden valve seats and economical wooden pipe-boring machinery to compressed-air water pumps and iron cement— improved the efficiency and thus the earning potential of the engines, it was their installation and uninterrupted running that made the real money. Watt's testy letter of 12 September 1786 to Boulton about Murdock's experiments with a steam carriage typifies their usual attitude: 'I wish William could be brought to do as we do, to mind the business in hand, and let such as Symington and Sadler throw away their time and money, hunting shadows' (ibid., 132).

In four major areas—steam-engine design, self-propelled vehicles, machine tools, and gas lighting—Murdock made significant contributions to the advance of technology. Such rotary motion as there was for machinery at the outset of the industrial revolution was provided by windmills, horses, or water-wheels. Boulton had the vision to realize as early as November 1776 that if the up-and-down movement of the steam pumping engine could be directly translated to rotary motion, industrial production would be transformed and Boulton and Watt would make a great deal of money. Murdock's pragmatic approach turned that vision to reality when, in the summer of 1781, he invented the 'sun and planet' gear. In this device a fixed cogwheel, the 'planet', at the end of the pump rod of a reciprocating engine, revolved about a second and usually larger rotating shaft, the 'sun', on the driveshaft of the machinery to be turned. This device was added to Watt's own impractical solutions in his patent of October 1781 at the very last minute and it was successfully applied straight away to a small engine at Soho and on the small winding engines at Wheal Maid. Correspondence and drawings in the Boulton and Watt archives, as well as a wealth of contemporary testimony, establish that Murdock was the actual inventor. The 'sun and planet' gear remained an essential mechanical device during the early years of the industrial revolution; it was superseded only when the unexploited crank patent of Wasborough and Pickard expired in 1794 and their design became freely applicable.

Murdock's two other major steam-engine inventions were less dramatic in their immediate effect but far longer-lived. The D-slide valve was patented in September 1799; Watt in old age confessed that at first 'he set his face against it (but) now am satisfied it is an improvement after all as … it has rendered the engine much simpler and there are so fewer parts to go wrong' (Griffiths, 216); it was to be the principal valve mechanism on steam engines and locomotives for almost a hundred years.

Murdock's oscillating cylinder, which dispensed with the beam and tilted the whole cylinder through ninety degrees, overcame the disadvantages of the excessive weight and high centre of gravity of conventional steam engines and became the basis for marine engine design for the first thirty years of the nineteenth century. Although it was not exploited by Boulton and Watt, Murdock had the pleasure in old age of seeing Joshua Field's much enlarged version of it power the *Great Western* on the first steam crossing of the Atlantic in 1838.

Murdock spent some time on the design and construction of a steam carriage which actually worked—or rather a series of four increasingly large and powerful working models, the first some time between 1783 and early 1784. The second model, slightly larger and built in 1785, occasioned Murdock's only bid to break away from Boulton and Watt to file a patent of his own. But although his formal contract with that business had ended in August 1782, Boulton, who saw 'his carriage … travel a mile or two in River's great room in a circle making it carry the fire shovel, poker, and tongs' (Griffiths, 161), persuaded Murdock to return to Cornwall. Boulton, encouraged by a jealous Watt, gradually stifled the steam carriage idea and it was left to Murdock's neighbour in Redruth, Richard Trevithick, to develop and expand the invention.

About 1792, while residing at Redruth, Murdock began a series of experiments on the illuminating properties of gases produced by distilling coal, wood, peat, and suchlike. Initially he appears to have heated coal in a kettle with a thimble over the spout, and ignited the gas so produced. But by 1794 a much larger retort in his back yard allowed him to light his living room, as Francis Trevithick later wrote: 'Those still live who saw the gas-pipes conveying gas from the retort in the little yard to near the ceiling of the room, just over the table. A hole for the pipe was made in the window-frame' (Trevithick, 64).

In 1798–9 Murdock, fed up with Cornwall and not a little apprehensive for his life, so often in jeopardy from the uncertain temper of the Cornish miners, returned to the Soho works in Birmingham, where he continued his experiments. Towards the end of 1800 these were seen by the Manchester textile manufacturer George Lee, who was inspired first to light his own home by gas in 1804, 'not without occasional offence to the [nasal?] engines of the gentleman and lady and their visitors' (Griffiths, 259). Lee's enthusiasm was to lead to the real birth of the gas industry when, on 1 January 1806, the first fifty lights (of what was quickly to become a 904-light installation) were lit at the mill of Phillips and Lee in Manchester. Murdock reported on his discovery in February 1808, in a paper to the Royal Society, written for him by Watt junior and given by Sir Joseph Banks. This was intended to secure priority for Boulton and Watt in the right to manufacture gaslighting plant. However, although his work earned Murdock the society's Rumford medal it earned him little else, as the younger Boulton and Watt soon abandoned the gaslight market.

As far as Boulton and Watt were concerned, the principal purpose of Murdock's return to Birmingham had been to supervise the new foundry, as well as to install and invent the many new machine tools required for its successful operation. These were greatly admired by James Nasmyth in 1830, who described Murdock in his autobiography as an incomparable mechanic. The use of compressed air—long a favoured motive force with Murdock—and the concept of a single central source of power to drive large numbers of independently controlled machines made the Soho works the most advanced of their day and a prototype for the mass production engineering works of the nineteenth century.

When Murdock contracted malaria in June 1783 he was nursed by Anne Paynter, daughter of the mine captain at Chacewater and Polgooth, where he was then installing an engine. Anne became pregnant and, not without pressure from both Boulton and Anne's father, Murdock married her by special licence on 27 December 1785. Twins were born between 26 July and 4 August 1786 but, to Murdock's great grief, they died in 1788. A son, William, followed in July 1788; a second son, John, was born in May 1790, but Anne Murdock died a few days afterwards. Murdock built himself in 1817 a grand gentleman's residence, Sycamore House, at Handsworth, in which intrigued visitors such as Walter Scott and Joshua Field could observe piped gaslight, compressed-air doorbells, and a convection-operated meat-spit. By the time he was forcibly retired by Boulton jun. and Watt jun. in 1830, Murdock was earning 'the sum paid annually exceeding our own emoluments' (Griffiths, 332): £1000 a year in salary. Having sensibly declined a partnership in 1810, he was comfortably off and when he died was worth between £30,000 and £40,000.

Although never reaching again the creativity of the years 1780 to 1805 Murdock was, almost until his death, inventing and speculating on possible inventions such as harnessing pedestrian power and using tidal forces for the production of power. For sixty years he was the linchpin of Boulton and Watt, loyally serving the fathers and later guiding the sons but never sacrificing his independence of character. He was stubborn, short-tempered, and difficult, but generous with his time and ideas. Murdock died at Sycamore House, Handsworth, on 15 November 1839.

JOHN C. GRIFFITHS

Sources J. Griffiths, *The third man* (1992) · H. W. Dickinson and R. Jenkins, *James Watt and the steam engine* (1927) · D. Chandler and A. D. Lacey, *Rise of the gas industry in Britain* (1949) · A. Murdoch, *Light without a wick* (1892) · S. Smiles, *Men of invention and industry* (1884) · *James Nasmyth, engineer: an autobiography*, ed. S. Smiles (1883), chap. 9 · F. Trevithick, *Life of Richard Trevithick, with an account of his inventions*, 2 vols. (1872)
Archives Birm. CA, corresp. and drawings | priv. coll., Gibson-Watt family MSS
Likenesses W. Bloye, group portrait, bronze, Birmingham · F. Chantrey, marble bust, Handsworth church · F. Chantrey, pencil drawing, NPG · J. G. Gilbert, oils (in middle age), Birmingham Museums and Art gallery · J. G. Gilbert, portrait (in old age), Royal Edinburgh Society · J. F. Skill, J. Gilbert, W. and E. Walker, group portrait, pencil and wash (*Men of science living in 1807–08*), NPG · plaster bust (after F. Chantrey), Scot. NPG · portraits, repro. in Griffiths, *Third man*
Wealth at death £30,000–£40,000?

Mure, David, Lord Mure (1810–1891), judge and politician, was born on 21 November 1810, the fourth of the ten children of Colonel William Mure of Caldwell, vice-lieutenant of Renfrewshire and rector of Glasgow University, and his wife, Anne, daughter of Sir James Hunter *Blair, baronet, of Dunskey in Wigtownshire. He had two brothers and seven sisters of whom the most prominent besides himself was his eldest brother, William *Mure (1799–1860), historian and Peelite MP. Mure was educated at Westminster School and then at the University of Edinburgh, where he was a member and president of the Speculative Society, and was called to the Scottish bar in 1831. He specialized in conveyancing and succession law in a modest practice which benefited from his brother's west of Scotland connections. In 1841 he married Helen Tod (*d.* 1849); they had one son and three daughters.

Like his eldest brother, Mure was a conservative, but he cannot be counted as a Peelite. From 1843 to 1846, during Peel's second administration, he was one of the junior counsels for the crown in Scotland and was appointed to the same office under the Derby administration in 1852, thus showing his allegiance to the rump of the Conservative Party in the years after the split over corn-law repeal. From 1853 to 1858, however, Mure was sheriff of Perthshire, an appointment made under the Aberdeen coalition indicating that despite taking office under Derby he remained at least part-way acceptable to the Peelites and their whig allies in Scotland. He again accepted office in Derby's second administration, first as solicitor-general for Scotland from the summer of 1858, and then in the spring of 1859 as lord advocate for Scotland in succession to Charles Baillie, who became a court of session judge as Lord Jerviswoode. Mure's career is often compared with Baillie's: both came from well-established Conservative families; both became sheriffs in 1853; both were lord advocate for a short period in 1858–9; and both eventually served as court of session judges.

Mure succeeded in narrowly winning Buteshire—thanks largely to the exercise of the duke of Hamilton's influence on the Isle of Arran—at the general election of 1859, and thus for the first time had a parliamentary seat to go with his new office. This, however, marked the high point of his political career. The fall of the Derby ministry in June of that year meant that he left political office for the last time after only a few weeks as lord advocate. In 1865 he accepted the office of lord ordinary in the outer house of the court of session from the whig lord advocate, James Moncreiff, with the courtesy title of Lord Mure. He thus again showed his cross-party acceptability. As a judge of 'first instance' he was apparently successful (few of his judgments were reversed), and popular. In 1874 he was made a lord of justiciary. In the inner house of the court of session he made his mark in the period following the failure of the City of Glasgow Bank in the 1880s. He resigned from the bench in 1889.

Mure was a strong supporter of the established Church of Scotland, defending its control over educational provision, and was for many years an elder at St Stephen's Church in Edinburgh. He died at Bournemouth on 11 April 1891, and was buried at the Dean cemetery in Edinburgh.

GORDON F. MILLAR

Sources *The Scotsman* (13 April 1891) · *Glasgow Herald* (13 April 1891) · *The Times* (13 April 1891) · *Parliamentary Pocket Companion* (1864) · G. W. T. Omond, *The lord advocates of Scotland, second series, 1834–1880* (1914) · Irving, *Scots.*
Archives NL Scot., family corresp.
Wealth at death £112,454 4*s.* 9*d.*: confirmation, 30 May 1891, *CCI*

Mure, Sir William, of Rowallan, baronet (1594–1657), writer and politician, was the son of Sir William Mure, baronet, of Rowallan (*d.* 1639), from whom he inherited the title and the estate of Rowallan, Ayrshire, and Elizabeth Montgomerie, the sister of the pre-eminent Scottish Jacobean poet Alexander *Montgomerie. Mure's poetry later articulated the desire to continue this literary genealogy. It is probable that Mure attended Glasgow University, and returned to pursue a prolific writing career at Rowallan and, according to the testimony of his incomplete *Historie and Descent of the House of Rowallan*, 'delyted much in building and planting … & reformed the whole house exceidingly' (*Works*, 2.256). Mure's first marriage, to Anna Dundas, daughter of Dundas of Newliston, produced six children. After Anna's death he married Jane Hamilton, Lady Duntreath; they had four children.

Mure's range as a writer is varied. With the exception of 'The Kings Majestie Came to Hamilton on Monday the xxviii July [1617]', published in *The Muses Welcome* (1618), his earliest extant writing survives in manuscript. Prominent among this material is a collection of secular love lyrics, entitled 'Livre des amours', whose stanzaic variety probably denotes their potential for musical setting. The evidence of Mure's lute books (containing only musical transcriptions) suggests that these lyrics were intended for musical recitation or performance within the intimate social setting of the large private house, and embody the wider cultural movement in post-1603 Scotland away from a court-based literary culture. Mure's short sonnet sequence 'to Margareit' combines Neoplatonism and witty eroticism. These lyrics are ostensibly linked to a series of religious poems by a 'trinity' of sonnets entitled 'Fancies Farewell', which proclaims the evolution of his writing, tuned to 'a higher key' (*Works*, 1.195), from *eros* to *agape*. Mure's sonnets of spiritual crisis fuse manneristic conceits, reflecting English devotional metaphysical poetry, with an arresting spareness.

Mure's exploration of spiritual penitence and the self's relationship with God is magnified in his unpublished but extensive psalm translations, which may have been created for private devotion. Mure's later, published, religious writing is exemplified by *A Spirituall Hymne, or, The Sacrifice of a Sinner* (1628), a translation of Robert Boyd's Latin *Hecatombe Christiana* (1627), which dramatizes the Last Judgment and personal salvation through an apocalyptic rhetoric infused with Christian Neoplatonism. Its companion poem, *Doomesday Containing Hells Horrour and Heavens Happinesse*, fuses a similarly agonistic vision of the apocalypse with the sensual mysticism of divine adoration. *The True Crucifixe for True Catholickes* (1629) is a long polemic in couplets with extensive marginal annotations from scripture against idolatry, asserting the devotional way to discover the purity of 'Christ's true pourtrait' (*Works*, 1.213).

In the 1640s, after the death of his father, Mure became politically and militarily active, an engagement reflected in his poetry. *A Counter-Buff to Lysimachus Nicanor, a Pretended Jesuite*, a poetic defence of the covenant, 'A band of truth and power' (*Works*, 2.3), was published anonymously in response to the *Epistle* of John Maxwell, bishop of Killala in 1640. *Caledons Complainte Against Infamous Libells* is a fierce anti-monarchical allegory of the 'suffering [Scottish] nation' (ibid., 2.25), probably published in 1641.

In 1643 Mure is recorded as being a member of the parliament in Edinburgh. He acted as a military commander for a covenanting regiment drawn from Ayrshire at Duns Law. In 1644 Mure was wounded at Marston Moor, 'a sore blow at the battle upon my back with the butt of a musket', he wrote to his son (*Works*, 1.xvii), but later temporarily led a regiment at Newcastle. He apparently withdrew from active political conflict thereafter, though his son William became a prominent covenanter. Mure's political radicalism is continued in his last major work, *The Cry of Blood and of a Broken Covenant* (1650); addressed to Charles II, the poem mourns the execution of his predecessor and appeals for military insurrection on behalf of 'the Lord's … Battell' (ibid., 2.35). A manuscript translation of books 1 and 4 of Virgil's *Aeneid*, 'Dido and Aeneas', also survives. Mure died in 1657. He was succeeded by his son, on whose death in 1700 the baronetcy ceased.   S. M. DUNNIGAN

Sources U. Edin. L., MS La.III.453 · U. Edin. L., MS La.III.454 · U. Edin. L., MS La.III.487 · *The works of William Mure of Rowallan*, ed. W. Tough, 2 vols., STS, 40–41 (1898) · W. Mure, *Historie and descent of the house of Rowallane*, ed. [W. Muir] (1825) · R. D. S. Jack, 'Scottish sonneteer and Welsh metaphysical: a study of the religious poetry of Sir William Mure and Henry Vaughan', *Studies in Scottish Literature*, 3 (1965–6), 240–47 · H. M. Shire, *Song, dance and poetry at the court of Scotland under King James VI*, ed. K. Elliott (1969) · M. Spiller, 'Poetry after the Union', *The history of Scottish literature*, ed. C. Craig, 1: *Origins to 1660*, ed. R. D. S. Jack (1987), 141–62
Archives NRA Scotland, priv. coll., MSS

Mure, William, of Caldwell (1718–1776), politician and author, was born in December 1718, the eldest son of William Mure of Caldwell (d. 1722), whose estate near Beith straddled the boundary of Renfrewshire and Ayrshire, and his wife, Anne (d. 1747), daughter of Sir James *Stewart of Goodtrees (1635–1713), lord advocate, and widow of James Maxwell of Blawarthill (d. 1706), heir of Pollok, who died childless. The Mure family was typical of those dominating public life in the west of Scotland: strongly presbyterian but attracted to enlightenment and improvement in the framework of a conservative social order.

After the death of his father Mure was brought up by his mother and a tutor, the Revd William Leechman, later professor of divinity at Glasgow University, of which, through Mure's influence, eventually he was principal. Mure studied law at Edinburgh and Leiden, completed his studies in 1740, then made a tour into France. Having returned to Scotland in 1742 he was chosen MP for Renfrewshire, a seat he held unopposed until 1761. He was initially an opponent of Archibald Campbell, third duke of Argyll, and of the ministry of Henry Pelham but was won over by 1753. On 25 February 1752 he married Katherine (1734–1820), daughter of the judge James Graham, Lord Easdale (1696–1750), and his wife, Katherine Hepburn. They had two sons and four daughters.

Mure never distinguished himself at Westminster, preferring to stay at home and improve his lands, which included the reconstruction of Caldwell House by Robert Adam. He also advised neighbours on similar projects. His consequent friendship with John Stuart, third earl of Bute, proved the true key to his political career. Bute formed his own connection in London as tutor to the future George III and gathered the nucleus of a parliamentary faction of his own from among Scots MPs, including Mure, who had become disenchanted with the Argathelian–Pelhamite regime. In Scotland this connection tempered the duke of Argyll's power even before a new reign. Reward followed on the deaths of George II in 1760 and Argyll in 1761; the one propelled Bute to the head of British affairs while the other created a Scottish vacuum into which his friends moved. In 1761 Mure became baron of the Scots exchequer, being henceforth known as Baron Mure. He dealt with most Scottish official business, especially if it had some fiscal element. Bute's fall in 1763 stopped Mure from cementing his political control but he made a mark with it nevertheless. For distribution of patronage—particularly academic patronage—he insisted that merit, not connections, must be decisive. Both doubtless came into play when, against opposition from an evangelical presbytery, he appointed Leechman principal of Glasgow University, where he himself was rector (1764–5). His hand was seen more surely at work in choosing as principal of Edinburgh University in 1763 William Robertson, whom Bute had commended 'to promote our great undertaking' (Mure, 2.146), presumably the ensuing sequence of histories. This heralded the university's golden age.

Mure had been an earnest youth but grew convivial through his other great friendship, with David Hume, and later through the sociability of a beautiful but wayward wife. By the time that the correspondence of Mure and Hume began, in 1742, they already stood on intimate terms, as is clear from their uninhibited letters preserved in the Caldwell papers published by the Maitland Club in 1854. To them we owe many insights into the delightful character of 'le bon David' and a record of his outspoken comments on politics. It was in one of these letters that he gave his view on the gathering crisis between Britain and her colonies: 'I am an American in my principles, and wish we would let them alone, to govern or misgovern themselves as they think proper' (Mure, 3.259). When in Edinburgh Mure and Hume frequented their respective homes at Abbeyhill and St David's Street. They died within five months of each other, Mure of a gastric malady at Caldwell House, Ayrshire, on 25 March 1776. Hume wrote: 'Baron was the oldest and best friend I had in the world. I should be inconsolable, did I not see an event approaching which reduces all things to a level' (ibid., 1.35). Mure's widow attended Hume's deathbed, urging him to 'burn a' his wee bookies' (ibid.), a proposition that rendered him speechless.   MICHAEL FRY

Sources [W. Mure], ed., *Selections from the family papers preserved at Caldwell*, 3 vols., Maitland Club, 71 (1854) · A. Murdoch, 'Lord Bute, James Stuart Mackenzie and the government of Scotland', *Lord Bute: essays in re-interpretation*, ed. K. Schweitzer (1988), 117–46 · R. L. Emerson, 'Lord Bute and the Scottish universities', *Lord Bute: essays in re-interpretation*, ed. K. Schweitzer (1988), 147–79 · E. Haden-Guest, 'Mure, William', HoP, *Commons, 1715–54* · E. Haden-Guest, 'Mure, William', HoP, *Commons, 1754–90*
Archives NL Scot., corresp. and papers | Mount Stuart Trust Archive, Isle of Bute, letters to Lord Bute and Lady Bute
Likenesses engraving, repro. in Mure, ed., *Selections*, vol. 2

Mure, William (1799–1860), classical scholar, was born at Caldwell, Ayrshire, on 9 July 1799, the eldest son of William Mure of Caldwell, colonel of the Renfrew militia, and lord rector of Glasgow University (1793–4), and his wife, Anne, eldest daughter of Sir James Hunter *Blair, baronet, of Dunskey, Wigtownshire, and was thus grandson of William *Mure (1718–1776), baron of exchequer, and a descendant of the Mures of Rowallan. The MP and judge Lord Mure [see Mure, David] was his younger brother. He was educated at Westminster School, at the University of Edinburgh, and afterwards in Germany at the University of Bonn. On 7 February 1825 he married Laura, second daughter of William Markham of Becca Hall, Yorkshire. They had three sons and three daughters.

When he was about twenty-two Mure contributed an article on Spanish literature to the *Edinburgh Review* (possibly vol. 38, February 1823); he subsequently contributed articles on classical subjects to both the *Edinburgh Review* and the *Quarterly Review*. His first independent publication was *Brief Remarks on the Chronology of the Egyptian Dynasties* (against Champollion), issued in 1829. It was followed in 1832 by *A Dissertation on the Calendar and Zodiac of Ancient*

Egypt. In 1838 Mure began a tour in Greece, leaving Ancona for Corfu on 17 February. He studied the topography of Ithaca, and visited Acarnania, Delphi, Boeotia, Attica, and the Peloponnese. He published a *Journal of a Tour in Greece and the Ionian Islands* in 1842. His principal work, *A Critical History of the Language and Literature of Ancient Greece*, was issued in five volumes between 1850 and 1857. It deals with only a part of the subject, namely the early history of writing, Homer, Hesiod, the early lyric poets and historians Herodotus, Thucydides, and Xenophon; it contains no account of the dramatists, orators, or any literature after 380 BC.

Mure succeeded to the Caldwell estates on his father's death on 9 February 1831. He was, like his father, for many years colonel of the Renfrewshire militia, and was lord rector of Glasgow University in 1847–8. He was Conservative MP for Renfrewshire from 1846 to 1855 but seldom spoke in the house. He was created DCL by Oxford University on 9 June 1833. He was a man of commanding presence, winning manners, and kindly disposition. He died at his home, 55 Rutland Gardens, Kensington Road, London, on 1 April 1860, aged sixty.

W. W. WROTH, *rev.* RICHARD SMAIL

Sources GM, 3rd ser., 8 (1860), 634 · Boase, *Mod. Eng. biog.* · Allibone, *Dict.* · Irving, *Scots.* · *Wellesley index*
Archives NL Scot., accounts, journals, and papers | NL Scot., letters to John Lee · U. Edin. L., letters to David Laing

Muredach (d. 771). *See under* Dál Riata, kings of (act. c.500–c.850).

Murford, Nicholas (d. 1641), salt maker, whose origins are unknown, is thought to have been a rope maker of Aldeburgh before moving to Great Yarmouth, where in 1626 he petitioned for land to erect a ropery. His first application was turned down but permission was granted in May 1628. He prospered in this trade and in February the following year was admitted a free burgess of the port. A later petition for an eight-year lease, to extend his premises, was rejected although he was allowed to remain on the site.

At this time there was much concern in the district that supplies of salt, vital to the herring-curing industry and normally obtained from France and Spain, were unreliable. This led several speculators, Murford among them, to consider setting up a local salt works. In 1632 Murford, claiming that he had been experimenting for some years, obtained a patent. He had, however, to contend with the king's decision to grant a monopoly to another group of speculators who already held a monopoly for salt in Ireland and who, by 1631, were seeking to extend their licence to England. By this time Murford and his partner had received £600 from William Sandys for their work. In petitioning the king, Murford and his associate Hanworth claimed to have spent £5000 in setting up their manufactory. Murford painted an extremely rosy picture of the huge quantity of salt that he would ultimately produce, and the consequently large revenues that would flow to the king. The competitors, who were based at North Shields and South Shields, made similar claims; they were granted the patent but Murford was allowed to continue production for the time being.

As time passed, Murford's operations apparently prospered more than those of the northern group. Possibly he was favoured by good weather which enabled him to concentrate the brine by natural evaporation, thus reducing the quantity of coal needed to dry the brine to salt; in any case, he was producing this salt where it was needed. A royal surveyor came to inspect his works and a charter of incorporation was prepared in May 1636. In 1637 the king intervened personally to increase Murford's production, by seeking to expropriate stretches of salt marsh owned by great landlords who immediately resisted this attempt. Murford himself expanded over 24 acres on the nearby island of Cobholm, claiming to have expended £10,000–£11,000 on boiling pans, engines, and other equipment. He brought in about a hundred people to work for him, whose obvious poverty on arrival convinced the officials that they would cause a nuisance and become a charge upon the town. Murford's ships were also contravening local loading restrictions.

At the peak of his success, Murford thus saw his position weakening and, with the help of courtiers with shares in his company, he sought to obtain an import monopoly, promising to pay the king £10,000 annually for ten years. Before these negotiations could bear fruit, however, another merchant, Thomas Horth, secured the monopoly with a more attractive proposal. Murford fought on: in February 1638 he was heard in the Star Chamber and in July at the Greenwich court. His claim that his process, relying on natural evaporation, was more reliable than that of the northern producers, who evaporated their brine over coal fires, was rejected. By 1639 his career as a salt maker had ended. He could not raise the dues which he had promised and his works were closed down, having produced, it would appear, salt worth a mere £300. Murford was imprisoned, for 'animating others with their refractory obstinacy' ('At the court of Oatelands …', 1640), and later claimed that his health had been undermined by the worries of litigation, and that his family and friends, among whom he presumably included those courtiers who had supplied capital, would suffer in the event of his death.

During this brief episode, Murford had risen from a rope maker to an entrepreneur with courtiers eager to share his enterprise, which had looked likely to monopolize salt imports along the east and south-east coasts of England. Murford died in April 1641. He left two sons, Nicholas and Ephraim, and two daughters, Elizabeth and Judith, who petitioned unsuccessfully for relief in respect of their father's losses.

The younger **Nicholas Murford** (*fl.* 1638–1652)—whom the *Dictionary of National Biography* conflates with his father—is said to have been a puritan merchant at Lynn (Beloe, viii). In 1647 one Francis Todd petitioned the committee of the navy for admission to the office for keeping purser's accounts, formerly held by Nicholas Murford. Murford wrote sycophantic verses in praise of various Cromwellian worthies, from which it emerged that

before 1650 and again in 1652 he was held in the Fleet prison. Appealing for restitution of his father's outlay in the salt business, he wrote from prison in February 1652 that he had been 'Out of Westminster hurried to Newgate … illegally' (BL, Add. MS 28602, fol. 12). Lord Ireton, he insisted, had promised to try to help him to recover the £13,000 expended by his father in 1632 for the good of the commonwealth.

Nicholas Murford married Amye Longstreath on 23 August 1646 at Lynn. Their daughter Amy, born in 1647, died in 1650; a son, John, was born and died in 1651. The fate of a second John, born in 1652, is unknown. The date of Murford's own death is unknown.

ANITA MCCONNELL

Sources J. K. Gruenfelder, 'Nicholas Murford, Yarmouth salt-producer', *Norfolk Archaeology*, 41 (1990–93), 162–70 · Privy council register (1638) · Privy council register (1639) · BL, Add. MS 28602, fol. 12 · *CSP dom.*, 1639; 1647; 1655 · E. M. Beloe, introduction, in N. Murford, *Fragmenta poetica*, ed. E. M. Beloe (1914) · 'A most humble declaration … concerning the making of salt here in England', All Souls Oxf., MS 276 no. 101, 7ff. · Petitions and remonstrances collection of tracts, 1638–75, BL, fol. 221 ['At the court of Oatelands'] · W. H. Price, *The English patents of monopoly* (1906), 112–18

Murford, Nicholas (*fl.* 1638–1652). *See under* Murford, Nicholas (*d.* 1641).

Murgatrod [Murgatroid], **Michael** (1551–1608), ecclesiastical administrator, was a Yorkshireman, the son of William Murgatrod and his wife, Frances Hippon of Newhall. Through his mother he was related to the Gascoignes of Lazingcroft, and it was at Richard Gascoigne's expense that he studied at Cambridge. He matriculated at Jesus College in 1573 and graduated in 1577. He became a fellow in the same year, a position he retained until 1600, and proceeded MA in 1580. Greek reader of his college, he delivered addresses to the students which survive (BL, Harley MS 4159). He also had practical abilities that brought him to the attention of Archbishop John Whitgift. On 25 June 1593 he was granted the registrarship of the court of arches, having probably been long employed by Whitgift, for on 8 July 1595 he was appointed proctor in the court of arches, in acknowledgement of many years' service as the archbishop's household servant and secretary. Later he was promoted to become comptroller and then steward to Whitgift, who on 14 February 1597 rewarded him with the reversion of the office of commissary of faculties, the position Murgatrod occupied when he died. He also acted as an attorney to the archbishop, was present on 9 July 1599 at the dedication of the latter's foundation of Croydon hospital and school, and financed the glazing of one of the hospital chapel's windows.

Murgatrod remembered his benefactors, and when he took out a grant of arms in 1598 its principal elements came from the arms of Whitgift and Gascoigne. He died, aged fifty-six, probably at Croydon, on 10 April 1608 and was buried two days later in the south aisle of Croydon parish church, below a black and white marble monument which showed him kneeling at a desk. This monument does not survive, having probably been destroyed in the fire that ravaged Croydon church in 1867. In his will, drawn up the day before he died, Murgatrod requested burial 'where the late Archebyshop lieth buried'. His principal legatee was 'my beloved wief Anne' (née Bickerstaffe, the widow of a Mr Yeomans), whom he left with child. References to his brother-in-law John Mitton suggest that she was his second wife. Murgatrod left cash legacies totalling over £3300; their beneficiaries included an unmarried daughter, and a son-in-law for whom he had previously built a house in Waddon. He himself had a house in Croydon and leased a farm at Waddon and property in London's Fleet Street.

Murgatrod was the compiler of Lambeth Palace Library manuscript 178, whose contents are listed as 'memoirs of affairs in church and state in Archbp Whitgift's time'. The volume does not contain memoirs in a literary sense, but is a collection of papers in Murgatrod's hand of mostly unattributed papers dealing with a wide range of religious and secular issues. Covering the perceived threat from both presbyterianism and Catholicism, it provides evidence for the close collaboration between Whitgift, his chaplain Richard Bancroft, and the chancellor, Sir Christopher Hatton, in the late 1580s. The account of Hatton's becoming chancellor of Oxford University in 1588, presented 'by waie of a letter to Mr Murgetrode' (fol. 46), was certainly written by Bancroft. Murgatrod is, however, named as the author of arguments opposing a parliamentary bill against pluralism contained in Lambeth Palace Library manuscript 2004.   HENRY SUMMERSON

Sources LPL, MSS 178; 2004; TB1; CM1/21 · will, PRO, PROB 11/111, sig. 44 · BL, Harley MS 4159 · J. Foster, ed., *The visitation of Yorkshire made in the years 1584/5 … to which is added the subsequent visitation made in 1612* (privately printed, London, 1875) · J. Strype, *The life and acts of John Whitgift*, new edn, 3 vols. (1822), vol. 2 · Cooper, *Ath. Cantab.*, 2.480–81 · J. Aubrey, *The natural history and antiquities of the county of Surrey*, 2 (1718), 20 · Venn, *Alum. Cant.*, 1/3.228 · M. H. Ousley, 'Notes on the right arms of John Whitgift, lord archbishop of Canterbury, 1583–1604', *Surrey Archaeological Collections*, 63 (1966), 95–129 · S. W. Kershaw, 'Whitgift's Hospital, Croydon', *Surrey Archaeological Collections*, 9 (1888), 353–64 · P. Collinson, *The Elizabethan puritan movement* (1967) · DNB

Wealth at death £3300 in cash bequests: PRO, PROB 11/111, sig. 44

Murimuth, Adam (1274/5–1347), historian and diplomat, was born between Michaelmas 1274 and Michaelmas 1275. Nothing is known for certain of his family. He possibly came from Fifield, Oxfordshire, where John Muremuth held the manor in 1316. Other possible members of the family include: Richard Murimuth, royal clerk in 1328–9, royal chaplain in 1332, rector of Achecote, Lincolnshire, in 1333, dean of Wimborne in 1338, prebendary of Oxgate, at St Paul's, 1339–54, and Banbury, Lincoln, in 1342; John Murimuth, Adam's attorney during his absences abroad in 1314 and 1323; Thomas Murimuth, also a king's clerk, presented to the prebend of Holleye at Westbury on Adam's resignation in 1337; and Adam Murimuth junior, who probably held the prebend of Harleston, St Paul's, was rector of Thurgarton, Norfolk, 1327–8, and was also a prebendary of Exeter, dying in 1370.

Murimuth was educated at Oxford, where he had graduated as doctor of civil law by 1308, at which date he was advocate of the court of arches, and was granted a pension of 40s. by Bishop Walter Stapledon of Exeter (d. 1326), until he received a benefice. He was ordained subdeacon on 20 May 1312, and received letters dismissory from Archbishop Walter Reynolds (d. 1327) permitting him to receive deacon's or priest's orders on 15 May 1314. His career frequently took him abroad on ecclesiastical and royal business, mainly to Avignon, but also to Sicily and the French court. For this he received considerable ecclesiastical preferment. He held the rectories of Hayes, Middlesex (1312–14), Lyminge, Kent (1315–16/17), Wotton under Edge, Gloucestershire (1316), Lyminge again (1318), Cliffe, Kent (from 1318 until at least 1327), and Wraysbury, Buckinghamshire (from 1337 until his death). He was canon and prebendary of Glasney, Cornwall (1314–18), Hereford (1316–27), where he held the prebend of Bullinghope (1320–21), Wells (from 1317), where he held Holcombe, Crediton (1318), Exeter (from 1318 until his death), and St Paul's (from 1325 until his death), where he held the prebend of Ealdstreet (1325–8), and of Neasden (1328–38), and was canon of Westbury-on-Trym and prebendary of Holleye (1331–7). He was confirmed precentor of Exeter for life in 1329, an office that he exchanged for Wraysbury in 1337. His closest associations were possibly with Exeter and London, since he alluded to his use of the libraries of Exeter and Westminster in his chronicle.

In 1312 Murimuth undertook the first of his many missions abroad: he was appointed one of the proctors of Oxford University at the court of Rome in a complaint against the black friars. About the same time he was appointed by Archbishop Robert Winchelsey (d. 1313) to represent him at Avignon in his cause against Walter Langton (d. 1321). In 1313 he was apparently acting at Avignon, as agent for the chapter of Canterbury, in the latter's unsuccessful bid to secure the confirmation of Thomas Cobham (d. 1327) in the archbishopric. In 1314 he was employed at Avignon by the king to secure the preferment of John Sandale (d. 1319) to the deanery of St Paul's. Murimuth was still acting at Avignon for the king, for the chapter of Canterbury, for the bishop of Hereford, and perhaps for the University of Oxford in 1317 and 1318. In August 1318 he received a pension of 60s. from the chapter of Canterbury for his faithful counsel. After 1318 Murimuth spent more time in England. In May 1319 he was proctor for the chapter of Canterbury in the parliament held at York and in a letter dated 28 May 1319 William Melton (d. 1340) alludes to information with which Murimuth had furnished him. Later in 1319 he was again sent to Avignon by the king to obtain the pope's assent to a grant from the clergy. During 1321 and 1322 he was official and vicar-general for Stephen Gravesend, bishop of London. In August 1323 he was sent by the king to King Robert of Sicily concerning Edward II's claims to lands in Provence, and was also employed on the king's behalf at Avignon against the Scots and to represent Edward's complaints against his late envoy, John Stratford (d. 1348).

In 1325 Murimuth was vicar-general for Archbishop Reynolds, and on 21 August had letters of protection as intending to go with the king to France. In 1327 he was one of the deputation from the chapter of Exeter Cathedral to the king on the death of Bishop James Berkeley. He had a dispute with the chapter of Canterbury as to his pension, in 1334, but continued to act as official for the diocese, and in 1335 appears as commissary for the archbishop. In 1337 he appears to have served for the last time as a diplomatic adviser, when he was asked to examine the articles of accusation brought against Edward III at the French court, and to suggest the best way for Edward to respond. He is mentioned on 5 June 1338 as receiving a lease of the manor of Barnes from the chapter of St Paul's; in 1339 he was an official of the court of Canterbury, and vicar-general of Archbishop Stratford; and in 1340 was executor of the bishop of London. In 1345 he exercised his right as canon of London to present his own clerk to a London living. He had probably died (at the age of seventy-two) before 26 June 1347, when his successor at Wraysbury was instituted. Murimuth's rewards for his skilled and trusted diplomacy may have left him disappointed. In 1334 Bishop John Grandison (d. 1369) reproved him for his overambition and frequent absence from Exeter, and it is possible to read disappointment in his chronicle, in his frequently sharp criticism of papal provision and of individuals appointed to bishoprics.

Murimuth was the author of a work which he styles *Continuatio chronicarum*, and which covers the period from 1303 to 1347. According to his own account in his preface, he found that the chronicles at Exeter did not proceed beyond 1302, nor those at Westminster beyond 1305. He therefore used the Westminster chronicles to 1305, and after this, when he was of an age to judge for himself, and write in his own manner *ex libro dierum meorum* ('from the book of my days'), he based his history on what he had himself heard and seen. Since Murimuth describes himself in his preface as canon of London, he clearly wrote after 1325, and possibly not until 1338. In its first form the history was brought down to 1337, a second edition, marked by Murimuth's beginning to record his age annually, carried it on to 1341, and possibly a third to 1343; in its final form the work ends with the year of the author's death, 1347. The history to c.1337 is meagre and disappointing, given his career. It was 'probably made up from scanty notes and from personal recollection' (*Adae Murimuth continuatio chronicarum*, xv). The notices of English history are slight, especially in the middle years of Edward II's reign when Murimuth was abroad, but his comments on Edward's death are of value, as is the record of England's relations with the court of Rome.

For its last nine years the chronicle is much fuller, and is of particular value for the campaigns and negotiations in the early years of the Hundred Years' War, and for parliamentary activity against papal provisions. Murimuth was an ardent supporter of Edward III's claim to France, but disapproved of the way the war was run. His strong views on this, as on papal matters, have the added interest of being those of a seasoned diplomat familiar with the worlds he was criticizing. For this portion Murimuth's position at St Paul's gave him access to documents and private information. The *Continuatio chronicarum* is somewhat confused by Murimuth's perverse adoption of Michaelmas as the beginning of the year (six months later than most contemporaries). The chronicle survives in nine main manuscripts and was first edited by Anthony Hall (Oxford, 1722), an edition that presents the true chronicle to 1337 from Oxford, Queen's College, MS 304, with a continuation to 1380, which is not Murimuth's work. In an edition for the English Historical Society in 1846 Thomas Hog published the true text to 1346, with the continuation to 1380. The full text down to 1347 (based on BL, Harley MS 3836) was edited for the Rolls Series by Edward Maunde Thompson in 1889, where an account of the extant manuscripts will be found on pages xvii–xxii.

There is no strong evidence for other works by Murimuth. Murimuth's reference to the *Liber dierum meorum* may be nothing more than a rhetorical expression and at most a private journal. Henry Wharton, in the late seventeenth century ascribed to him the authorship of the continuation of the *Flores historiarum*, which has been published under the title of *Annales Paulini* in *Chronicles of Edward I and Edward II* in the Rolls Series, but this is unlikely to be correct. The annals undoubtedly show some connection with Murimuth's work, but differences in dating and interest argue against Murimuth's authorship. It has recently been considered more likely that Murimuth borrowed from the *Annales Paulini* than vice versa. In the *Flores historiarum*, Murimuth is said to have written a history from 1313 (*sic*) to 1347; and the brief narrative of 1325 and 1328 printed in the Rolls Series edition of the *Flores* is in the main extracted from his chronicle.

C. L. KINGSFORD, *rev.* WENDY R. CHILDS

Sources *Adae Murimuth continuatio chronicarum. Robertus de Avesbury de gestis mirabilibus regis Edwardi tertii*, ed. E. M. Thompson, Rolls Series, 93 (1889) · W. Stubbs, ed., *Chronicles of the reigns of Edward I and Edward II*, 2 vols., Rolls Series, 76 (1882–3) · Emden, *Oxf.*, 2.1329–30 · A. Gransden, *Historical writing in England*, 2 (1982) · *CEPR letters*, vols. 2–3 · *Chancery records* · Rymer, *Foedera*, new edn · J. B. Sheppard, ed., *Literae Cantuarienses: the letter books of the monastery of Christ Church, Canterbury*, 3 vols., Rolls Series, 85 (1887–9) · H. R. Luard, ed., *Flores historiarum*, 3 vols., Rolls Series, 95 (1890) · N. Triveti: *Annalium continuatio, ut et Adami Murimuthensis chronicon cum ejusdem continuatione*, ed. A. Hall (1722) · *Adami Murimuthensis chronica*, ed. T. Hog, EHS, 8 (1846)

Archives BL, Chronicon, Add. MS 32167 · BL, Harley MS 3836 · Queen's College, Oxford, MS 304

Murison, Alexander Falconer (1847–1934), jurist and author, was born at Walhowe, in the parish of Deer, Aberdeenshire, on 3 March 1847, the eldest of the four sons of Alexander Murison, a crofter of Walhowe, and his wife, Elspeth, daughter of William Murison, a crofter of Bridgefoot, near Fraserburgh, Aberdeenshire. He was proud to recall that he had once acted as a herd-boy on his native hills. In his autobiography, written at the age of eighty-six, he vividly described the struggles involved in securing a better education than that afforded by the local village schools. Having won a bursary at Aberdeen grammar school, he showed his gift for languages, winning school prizes for Latin and Greek and gaining the first bursary at Aberdeen University, where he graduated with first-class honours in classics.

On leaving university, Murison returned to his old school as head English master (1869–77), and soon proved to be an inspiring teacher. In 1870 he married Elizabeth (d. 1924), the elder daughter of William Logan, shopkeeper, of Fetterangus, Aberdeenshire; they had two sons, the younger of whom, (James) William Murison (d. 1945), became a chief justice of Zanzibar and of the Straits Settlements.

Murison then decided to go to London, where he entered the Middle Temple on 16 November 1876 and was called to the bar on 29 June 1881. During this period Murison supported himself by teaching and by journalism, practising before the privy council and the Chancery Division. On 1 October 1883 he succeeded W. A. Hunter, to whom he owed much, as professor of Roman law at University College, London. In 1901 he was appointed professor of jurisprudence there and in 1913 he became deputy professor of Roman-Dutch law. He held these posts concurrently until he retired in 1925, having been in the service of the college as professor for forty-two years, during which he was also dean of the faculty of laws (1912–24), and a member of the senate of the University of London (1921–4). In 1915 he was appointed deputy reader in Roman law at Oxford, and in 1916 deputy professor to Henry Goudy, the regius professor of civil law. That Murison did not succeed Goudy to the chair on the latter's retirement was attributed by his contemporaries to his advancing years. In 1924 he was appointed KC by Lord Chancellor Haldane.

During the forty-two years in which he held office in London, Murison set himself the stupendous task of collating the codices of the text of Justinian's *Institutes*. Pursuit of this aim led him to all the great law libraries of Europe, always travelling third class (and on one occasion in a cattle-truck) because of the meagreness of his pay and the paucity of his private means. But his immense erudition, his mastery of practically every European language except Turkish, his accomplishment as a Latin, Greek, and Hebrew scholar, combined with his engaging modesty and charm, made him friends everywhere among foreign jurists, and won him an international reputation for scholarship. Unfortunately the colossal undertaking was never completed, and the results remain in manuscript in voluminous notebooks. Almost the only published contribution in English made by Murison on the civil law is a historical introduction entitled 'The external history of Roman law' prefixed to the second edition (1885) of W. A. Hunter's *Roman Law*. As his poverty diverted him from pursuing the success that might have been his at the bar, by enticing him into the production of educational textbooks and journalism (he joined the staff of the *Daily Chronicle* in early days and from 1902 to 1912 was editor of the *Educational Times*), so also the versatility of his mind led him to play truant to the cause of jurisprudence, for he translated the whole of Horace (1931) and of Pindar (1933) into verse, Virgil's *Bucolics and Georgics* (1932), and the first twelve books of the *Iliad* (1933) into English hexameters, and Schiller's *Wallenstein* (1931) into English verse with the

original metres. A translation of books xiii to xix of the *Iliad* remained in manuscript. In Italy, where his scholarship was highly esteemed among his contemporaries, he published a characteristic treatise, *Il diritto nei poeti Latini* (1935), which was read at the International Congress of Roman Law held in Rome in 1933. His intellectual vigour remained unimpaired to the last.

The honorary degree of LLD was conferred on Murison in 1893 by the University of Aberdeen, for the lord rectorship of which he stood against Lord Huntly in 1896 and was but narrowly beaten. In politics an ardent Liberal, he unsuccessfully contested, at four general elections, in 1900, 1906, and 1910, three Conservative strongholds, the Bridgeton division of Glasgow, the universities of Glasgow and Aberdeen, and, twice, the Central division of Glasgow.

Murison died at his home, 26 Victoria Road, Clapham Common, London, on 8 June 1934.

J. H. MORGAN, *rev.* ERIC METCALFE

Sources J. Foster, *Men-at-the-bar: a biographical hand-list of the members of the various inns of court*, 2nd edn (1885), 332 · A. F. Murison, *Memoirs of 88 years, 1847–1934*, ed. A. L. Murison and J. W. Murison (1935) · *CGPLA Eng. & Wales* (1934)

Archives CUL, Royal Commonwealth Society collection, letters and papers · UCL, notes, translations, etc.

Likenesses portrait, repro. in Murison, *Memoirs of 88 years*

Wealth at death £6322 10s. 6d.: probate, 23 July 1934, *CGPLA Eng. & Wales*

Murison, David Donald (1913–1997), lexicographer, was born at 2 King Edward Street, Fraserburgh, Aberdeenshire, on 28 April 1913, the only child of Alexander Murison, journeyman joiner, and his wife, Isabella Magdalene Bathia Donald. The family moved to Aberdeen when he was seven, and he was educated at Aberdeen grammar school and Aberdeen University, from which he graduated in 1933 with first-class honours in classics. He then went to Cambridge, and graduated in 1936 with a first in the classical tripos. He also studied comparative philology and Old English, Celtic, and Norse. After Cambridge he returned to Scotland, which he left only once during the rest of his life. He spent two years as assistant to the professor of Greek in Aberdeen, together with the poet Douglas Young, who became a lifelong friend. During the Second World War he worked as a forester, probably near Aberdeen, and as a market gardener near Stirling. On 8 November 1940 he married Hilda Mary Angus (b. 1907/8), electricity showroom assistant, and daughter of John Angus, window cleaner. There were no children of the marriage.

In 1946 Murison was invited to become deputy editor of the *Scottish National Dictionary* (SND), and later in the year, on the death of its first editor, William Grant, he became editor. SND deals with one of the languages of lowland Scotland—the variety of English brought to Scotland in the seventh century and still spoken by the majority of the people of Scotland but not accorded full status in any Scottish institutions since the fifteenth century. SND covers the history of this language in the later modern

David Donald Murison (1913–1997), by unknown photographer

period, from approximately 1700 until the twentieth century. It belongs to the series of dictionaries of individual periods and varieties of the English language which were envisaged by the editors of the *Oxford English Dictionary* as being a necessary follow-up to their seminal work. *SND* was published in ten weighty four-part volumes between 1931 and 1976, and Murison was the editor of eight of those volumes.

Murison put his own imprint as a historical linguist upon *SND*, altering the methodology and vastly increasing the thoroughness with which up-to-date information on Scots usage of the second half of the twentieth century was gathered; he greatly widened and deepened the coverage of written Scots on which the main dictionary text was based; and he changed the layout of the text, so that it both conveyed its information much more clearly, and corresponded more closely with the other great historical dictionaries. Thus *SND* became, under his editorship, more than one of the period dictionaries of English; it was also an astonishing record of the persistence of the Scots language in both standard and dialectal forms through all kinds of vicissitudes, persecution, neglect, denigration, and disregard. Though unknown to most Scottish people, Murison was extremely important in helping to form the cultural identity of twentieth-century Scotland: he helped give respectability to the modern Scots language in the eyes of the Scottish authorities as well as of the Scottish people. Even in the 1960s children would still be given the strap in Scottish schools for speaking Scots, and the idea of writing Scots in an educational context was unthinkable. By the end of the century Scots was recognized as a powerful medium of expression, acceptable in many real-life situations, school contexts, and literary genres, including the debates of the new Scottish parliament or the works of a Booker prizewinner. Murison's principal shortcomings were arguably his distrust of the use of computers in lexicography, and his lack of enthusiasm for urban as compared with rural dialects.

In physical stature Murison was compact. In manner he was extremely genial, favouring a slightly ironic tone. His listeners could not always be sure whether he was in earnest or not; and he enjoyed their uncertainty. An enthusiastic supporter of the cause of Scotland as a nation, he was nevertheless suspicious of institutionalized politics and indeed of all politicians. He could also be obstinate and dour, especially where he felt that his principles or integrity might be compromised, or that the Scots dictionaries were not being sufficiently supported or valued by academic or political supremos. He was a man of many contradictions: extremely unassuming and shunning self-advertisement, to the extent of refusing all public or academic honours for himself, he was nevertheless tireless in promoting the *SND* and its aims, and was an extremely effective fund-raiser on its behalf. He was an enthusiastic lecturer on Scots language at Aberdeen, Edinburgh, and Glasgow universities, and indeed contributed greatly to the development of Scots as an academic discipline. He also supervised research by many scholars, and encouraged and supported many more, giving his time unstintingly both by correspondence and in person, either in the dictionary office or at his home. In addition to his monumental work on *SND*, he published many articles and reviews, and, after his retirement, several popular books on Scots language and related topics. In his determination 'to get to Z' he refused to take holidays for most of his time as editor. He hated big parties and formal celebrations, and refused to attend them (including the party to celebrate the conclusion of the *SND*); but, supported by his wife, Hilda, was extremely hospitable to friends, colleagues, and visitors, and was always a most entertaining companion and public speaker. He was a friend and mentor of many of the literati of the first twentieth-century Scottish literary renaissance, from the 1930s onwards. Many of them also used (perhaps a better word would be ransacked) *SND* in their commitment to the revival of Scots as a literary language, including the most famous of them all, a good friend of Murison's, Christopher Grieve (Hugh McDiarmid).

Murison enjoyed robust health for most of his life, but in his later years suffered from Parkinson's disease. He died at his home, 14 Dennyduff Road, Fraserburgh, on 17 February 1997. His final instructions were characteristic of him—there was to be no public announcement of his death, and no ceremonial at his burial. He was survived by his wife, Hilda. MAIRI ROBINSON

Sources A. J. Aitken, 'Foreword', *Scotland and the lowland tongue*, ed. J. D. McClure (1983), vii–xiv · *The Guardian* (5 March 1997) · *The Scotsman* (22 Feb 1997) · *The Times* (4 March 1997) · *The Independent* (27 Feb 1997) · NL Scot., Scottish National Dictionary Association MSS · roll of graduates, U. Aberdeen · *Fasti*, U. Cam. · b. cert. · m. cert. · d. cert.

Archives NL Scot., Scottish National Dictionary Association MSS

Likenesses photograph, repro. in *The Scotsman* · photograph, News International Syndication, London [*see illus.*]

Wealth at death £197,573.66: confirmation, 29 April 1997, NA Scot., SC/CO 1000/40

Murless, Sir (**Charles Francis**) **Noel** (1910–1987), race-horse trainer, was born on 24 March 1910 at Duckington Grange, Malpas, Cheshire, the elder son (there were no daughters) of Charles Herbert Murless, farmer, and his wife, Mary Constance, daughter of Frank Lloyd, auctioneer, of Wrexham, north Wales. Having ridden and hunted from early boyhood, Noel Murless was inspired to make a career in racing by seeing Poethlyn, owned by his parents' neighbour, Mrs Hugh Peel, win the Grand National in 1919.

For a short time Noel Murless, while performing the duties of a stable lad, rode in steeplechases and hurdle races with limited success, as an amateur and then as a professional, for Frank Hartigan, a trainer in Weyhill, Hampshire. On leaving Weyhill in 1930, Murless began a period of five years as assistant to Hartigan's brother Hubert, first at the Curragh, and then at Penrith in Cumberland. In July 1935 he commenced training at Hambleton Lodge, near Thirsk in the North Riding of Yorkshire, with five horses belonging to Lady Maureen Stanley, Dick Taylor, J. T. Rogers, and Andrew Johnstone. On 2 September 1935 he obtained his first success with J. T. Rogers's Rubin Wood in the Lee plate at Lanark. He had only one winner again in 1936, but in 1939 he won ten races.

During the Second World War Murless conducted a small stable at Middleham in Yorkshire, having been rejected by the forces because of injuries to his feet sustained in 1930. On 28 November 1940 he married Gwendolen Mary Lindsay, daughter of William Lindsay Carlow, coal exporter, of Craigend, Troon, Ayrshire; they had one daughter, Julia. After the war Murless came further to the fore, and in 1946 he was leading northern trainer with thirty-four races worth £15,337 to his credit. He was leading northern trainer again in 1947, obtaining his first important success with Closeburn in the Stewards' Cup at Goodwood. Following the retirement of Fred Darling at the end of 1947, Murless was invited to succeed him in the powerful Beckhampton stable, near Calne in Wiltshire, on the recommendation of the stable jockey Gordon Richards, who had been greatly impressed by his always carrying his own saddle and other evidence of personal attention to detail. Patrons of the stable included George VI, J. A. Dewar, the whisky millionaire, Sir Percy Loraine, Major and Mrs Macdonald-Buchanan, and Colonel Giles Loder. In his first season at Beckhampton, Murless almost brought off the Newmarket classic double. The Cobbler was only beaten by a head in the Two Thousand Guineas, and Queenpot won the One Thousand Guineas. At the end of that season of 1948, Murless was champion trainer, having won sixty-three races worth £66,542. In 1949 Major Macdonald-Buchanan's Abernant was beaten by a short head in the Two Thousand Guineas, but G. R. H. Smith's Ridgewood won the St Leger. The grey Abernant became an excellent sprinter, twice winning both the July Cup at Newmarket and the Nunthorpe stakes at York (1949 and 1950).

Having moved to the palatial Warren Place stable at Newmarket towards the end of 1952, Murless performed a remarkable feat by winning the Two Thousand Guineas

Sir (Charles Francis) Noel Murless (1910–1987), by unknown photographer, 1972

and Derby of 1957 with Sir Victor Sassoon's Crepello, a heavy-topped colt with far from the best legs. In 1957 he also won the Oaks with Carrozza, leased by the queen from the National Stud, and thus became that year's champion trainer, having won races worth £116,898. He was the first to amass a six-figure sum in a season. In 1959 he broke his own record by winning £145,727, when Ali Khan's grey filly, Petite Étoile, won the One Thousand Guineas, Oaks, Sussex stakes, Yorkshire Oaks, and Champion stakes.

During 1960 Murless won the Derby and St Leger with Sir Victor Sassoon's St Paddy. Although another St Leger was won with Vera Lilley's ill-tempered Aurelius in 1961, and Murless was champion trainer for the third consecutive time, the season was marred by Sir Victor's Pinturischio being so badly nobbled while favourite for the Derby that he could never run again. A third record was broken in 1967, when Murless won sixty races worth £256,899, including the Two Thousand Guineas and Derby with H. J. Joel's Royal Palace, and One Thousand Guineas with R. C. Boucher's Fleet. The King George VI and Queen Elizabeth stakes and the Eclipse stakes were won by Stanhope Joel's Busted, who had improved greatly since joining Murless from Ireland. When champion trainer again in 1968, Murless won the One Thousand Guineas with Caergwrle, bred and owned by his wife. Murless was champion trainer for the ninth and final time in 1973, obtaining the last of his nineteen classic successes with G. Pope's Mysterious in the Oaks. He retired at the end of 1976, and sold Warren Place to his son-in-law, Henry Cecil.

A tall, handsome man, with rather aquiline features and large brown eyes in a weather-beaten face, Murless had brown hair, which was silver in late middle age, brushed straight back from his forehead. He was impatient with people who sought information about horses with a view to making money, something to which he himself was almost indifferent. On the other hand, he would go to a great deal of trouble, not least with younger people, to help those anxious to increase their knowledge of the thoroughbred. Although he had no liking for the limelight, he had many close friends, mainly among owners and breeders, who found him a generous and amusing host. He was knighted in the silver jubilee honours in June 1977, and elected to the Jockey Club the following month. To a great extent his success was due to his inexhaustible patience and natural empathy with his horses, whose hallmark was a muscular robustness. To conserve nervous energy, he always kept them absolutely relaxed. On taking over Beckhampton, he gave orders that the horses' heads should be held by one rack chain, instead of three, while being dressed over, so that they could cope with irritation by flies.

Murless died on 9 May 1987 of emphysema and chronic bronchitis at his home, The Bungalow, Woodditton, Newmarket. His daughter Julia married Henry Cecil, the racehorse trainer, in 1966. RICHARD ONSLOW, rev.

Sources T. Fitzgeorge-Parker, *The guv'nor* (1980) · *Sporting Life* (11 May 1987) · *The Times* (11 May 1987) · *The Independent* (11 May 1987) · private information (1996) · personal knowledge (1996) · d. cert.
Likenesses photograph, 1972, Empics Sports Photo Agency, Nottingham [*see illus.*] · photograph, 1977, Hult. Arch.
Wealth at death £220,880: probate, 21 Oct 1987, *CGPLA Eng. & Wales*

Murlin, John (1722–1799), Methodist preacher, was born at St Stephen, Brenwell, Cornwall, in the early part of August 1722, the second son of Richard and Elizabeth Murlin or Morlen. His father, who died in 1735, was a farmer in that parish, and until his death he was assisted by his son. At Michaelmas 1735 the boy was apprenticed as a carpenter for seven years, and then served for several years in that trade. In April 1749 he was converted to Methodism, soon became a local preacher, and at John Wesley's invitation travelled in west Cornwall as an itinerant preacher from 12 October 1754 to August 1755. On 11 February 1762 he married in London Elizabeth Berrisford (1710–1786), second daughter of John Walker, a London tradesman, and the widow of John Berrisford, a cashier in the Bank of England. He later served in many parts of England and Ireland, his stay in any town being usually limited to a few weeks. He was stationed in London in 1755, 1766, 1768, 1770, 1776, 1779, and 1782; he was at Bristol during several years, and in 1784 was resident at Manchester.

Murlin was a Methodist of the primitive stamp, but of

great independence. In 1760 he and two other preachers at Norwich began, 'without Wesley's permission, or consulting any of their coadjutors', to administer the sacrament, to Charles Wesley's intense annoyance (Tyerman, 2.381). Murlin published a defence of his position in a *Letter to Rev. Joseph Benson on the administration of the sacraments in Methodist chapels by unordained ministers* (1794). Through his marriage he came into considerable property, and in 1770 Wesley wrote with much bitterness that many of his preachers would go where they liked. 'Mr. Murlin *says* he must be in London. 'Tis certain he has a mind to be there. Therefore, so it must be: for you know a man of fortune is master of his own motions' (*Letters*, 5.196). When 'an angel blowing a trumpet was placed on the sounding-board over the pulpit' at Halifax in 1779, Murlin refused to preach under it, and when a majority of one voted for its removal he 'hewed it in pieces' (*Works of John Wesley*, 23.124–5). Murlin himself states that the dispute was settled by John Wesley, who 'gave judgment against the angel; and … Mr Joseph Bradford made a burnt sacrifice of it on the altar of peace' (Murlin, 1.137). In the pulpit he was always in tears and was known, like James Nalton, the seventeenth-century minister, as the Weeping Prophet. He was a loyal and devoted Methodist itinerant, if at times inclined to sit light to the discipline of the conference.

Murlin's wife died at Bristol on 18 January 1786, being buried at Temple Church, London. Her funeral sermon was preached by Jeremiah Brettell on 24 January, and a memoir by her husband appeared in the *Arminian Magazine* (9, 1786). In 1787 ill health compelled Murlin's retirement to High Wycombe, Buckinghamshire, but he preached in Great Queen Street Chapel, London, in the winter of 1798–9. He died of a paralytic stroke at High Wycombe on 7 July 1799, and was buried in the same vault with John Wesley in the City Road Chapel, London.

W. P. COURTNEY, rev. JOHN A. NEWTON

Sources J. Murlin, 'The life of Mr John Murlin', *The lives of early Methodist preachers, chiefly written by themselves*, ed. T. Jackson, 3rd edn, 3 (1866) · *The works of John Wesley*, [another edn], 23, ed. F. Baker and others (1995) · *Arminian Magazine*, 2 (1779), 530–36 · *Arminian Magazine*, 9 (1786), 422–8 · C. Atmore, *The Methodist memorial* (1801) · G. Osborn, *Outlines of Wesleyan bibliography* (1869) · J. Murlin, 'The experience of Mr John Murlin', *The experience of some … Methodist preachers*, 2 vols. (1782–3), 1.91–140 · L. Tyerman, *The life and times of the Rev. John Wesley*, 2nd edn, 3 vols. (1872) · *The letters of the Rev. John Wesley*, ed. J. Telford, 8 vols. (1931)
Archives JRL, Methodist Archives and Research Centre, sermon notes
Likenesses Ridley, stipple (aged fifty-six), NPG; repro. in *Arminian Magazine*, 2 (1779), facing p. 530 · Ridley, stipple (aged seventy-five), repro. in *Methodist Magazine* (April 1798), facing p. 157

Murnaghan, Sheelagh Mary (1924–1993), politician and barrister, was born in Dublin city on 26 May 1924, the eldest of six children. Her family background was Catholic and strongly nationalist; her grandfather George Murnaghan had been a nationalist MP until 1910. Murnaghan was educated by the Catholic Loreto sisters in Omagh, co. Tyrone, where her family resided. Murnaghan began an arts degree at the Queen's University of Belfast in 1942 but the following year changed to a law degree. She became president of the University Literary and Scientific Debating Society in 1947. She was awarded an LLB in 1947, and afterwards read for the bar. She was one of the first women barristers in the north of Ireland. She was also a keen sportswoman and played for the Irish international women's hockey team, touring with the team (which she captained in 1955–6 and 1957–8) in South Africa in 1950 and the United States in 1954. Her international hockey career ended in 1959.

Murnaghan became a member of the Ulster Liberal Association in 1959. Shortly after joining the party she was selected as a Liberal candidate in her home constituency of South Belfast. However, she did not win a seat. In 1961 she was selected as a candidate for a Queen's University by-election. Her election campaign focused on the deficiencies of the Unionist government, and she won the seat, owing primarily to a large Unionist abstention and an increase in the non-Unionist vote. On taking her seat at Stormont in December 1961 she gained a reputation as a radical and active member of parliament. She retained the seat in the 1962 Northern Ireland general election, and was returned unopposed in 1965. Murnaghan was the only Liberal MP to sit in the Northern Ireland parliament in its lifetime, 1921–72. During her eight-year parliamentary career Murnaghan spoke on a diverse range of subjects and pushed for the introduction of Liberal policies through Stormont. There were three issues that were of particular concern and interest to her: the plight of travelling people, criminal law reform, and human rights. She raised issues about the provision of properly equipped campsites for travelling families, their harassment by local authorities, and their national insurance entitlements. Such concerns found few supporters. Her first private member's bill, the Homicide and Criminal Responsibility Bill, was introduced in 1963 and focused on making provision for homicides not then covered by the law, and also sought to abolish capital punishment. The bill was narrowly defeated (by twenty-three votes to nineteen) and the government introduced its own Criminal Justice Bill in 1963, the major difference from Murnaghan's bill being the retention of the death penalty.

Murnaghan made four attempts to have a human rights bill enacted, intended to counter racial, religious, and sexual discrimination. The first bill was introduced in June 1964. She believed that 'one cannot legislate unjust discrimination out of existence. One can, however, give a lead by making it perfectly clear to every citizen what he may or may not do' (Hansard 5C, 56.1989). The bill was defeated on a second reading in the commons by twenty-three votes to seventeen on 16 June 1964. Her second human rights bill was also defeated on a second reading in February 1966. Arguing for support for this second bill Murnaghan stated 'It is utterly incredible that in a predominantly Christian community a man's religion should be weighed against him in the balance in his daily life' (Hansard 5C, 62.685). A third attempt to have a human rights bill enacted was made in February 1967; this again failed, as did another attempt in December 1967. Opposition to the bills was based on the belief that adequate legislative provision against discrimination existed under the Government of Ireland Act (1920).

Attempts to introduce the bill for the fifth time failed with the abolition of the Queen's University seat. Murnaghan failed to win a seat for North Down in the 1969 general election. Events in Northern Ireland overtook her parliamentary attempts to legislate for reform. The civil rights marches and demands, and the outbreak of violence, were to alter the face of parliamentary politics in Northern Ireland. The introduction of direct rule in 1972 ended her political opportunities. Murnaghan was a member of the Community Relations Commission and supported many of the demands of the civil rights movement. She was chosen by the secretary of state for Northern Ireland, William Whitelaw, to be a member of his special advisory committee in 1972. Jeremy Thorpe was later to recall that one of the first remarks made to him by Murnaghan was 'In Northern Irish politics I don't know which is the greatest obstacle, to be a woman, a Catholic or a Liberal. I am all three' (The Times, 22 Sept 1993). Sheelagh Murnaghan died, unmarried, on 14 September 1993 from lung cancer at Beaconsfield Marie Curie Centre, Kensington Road, Belfast. She was cremated at Roselawn crematorium in Belfast two days later.

MARIA LUDDY

Sources The Times (18 Sept 1993) · Belfast News-Letter (30 May 1972) · Belfast News-Letter (3 Jan 1969) · Belfast News-Letter (17 Feb 1969) · Irish News and Belfast Morning News (9 Feb 1970) · d. cert. · Northern Ireland House of Commons debates, Hansard 5C, 62 (1966), 685–94 · Northern Ireland House of Commons debates, Hansard 5C, 56 (1964), 16 June 1964, 1989 · G. Gillespie, 'The Ulster liberal party, 1956–1973', MSSc diss., Queen's University of Belfast, 1984 · CGPLA NIre. (1993)

Likenesses photograph, repro. in Belfast News-Letter (17 Feb 1969) · photograph, repro. in Belfast News-Letter (3 Jan 1969)

Wealth at death £15,000: probate, 26 Nov 1993, CGPLA NIre.

Murphy, Alfred John (1901–1980), metallurgist and academic administrator, was born on 26 February 1901 at Deansgate Lane, Timperley, Altrincham, Cheshire, the son of William Murphy, journeyman iron turner and his wife, Martha Ann Goodier. He attended Altrincham high school to 1917 before graduating from Manchester University with first-class honours in chemistry in 1920. Throughout his career he was faced by a series of challenges of increasing severity and it is a measure of his wisdom, patience, determination, and diplomacy that he overcame all with conspicuous success. From Manchester, Murphy moved to University College, Swansea, to undertake metallurgical research before joining the National Physical Laboratory in 1923. There he was concerned with the characteristics of silver–tin–mercury amalgams, an investigation requiring the development of novel low temperature techniques. In 1927 he married a colleague at the laboratory, Helen Eulalie Blanche (d. 1974), daughter of Herbert Findlay Millar of Ulster Spring, Jamaica. There were two sons of the marriage.

Murphy joined J. Stone & Co. Ltd as chief metallurgist in 1931, subsequently becoming technical director of J. Stone & Co. Light Metal Forgings Ltd and chairman of Stone-Fry Magnesium Ltd. The demands of the Second

World War resulted in the development of new light alloys based on magnesium, their quality control, and widespread novel applications. He was attracted back to academic life in 1950 to take up the newly created chair of industrial metallurgy at Birmingham University, where he overcame the difficult task of consolidating all metallurgical activities by becoming overall director in 1953. He was a founder member of the Institute of Metallurgists, president of the Institute of Metals (1951), and chairman of the Inter-Sciences Metallurgical Council (1949–55).

By 1955 the fledgeling College of Aeronautics at Cranfield had been in existence for nine years. Although the quality of the exclusively postgraduate teaching and research had become accepted within the aeronautical fraternity, there had been growing pains and the position of principal was vacant. The board of governors turned to Murphy who, having accepted the appointment, quickly realized the potential of the college. The cutbacks and rationalization of the aircraft industry in the succeeding five years threatened the existence of Cranfield, but Murphy introduced the concept of diversification whereby the various departments expanded their activities into related scientific and engineering disciplines. A further challenge arose in 1963 when the report of the committee on higher education chaired by Lord Robbins recognized the excellence of Cranfield's work but left its future undecided. While there were those both inside and outside Cranfield who considered that the only future lay in amalgamation with a larger institution, Murphy, with the strong backing of the board of governors chaired by Lord Kings Norton, proposed a path of expansion and independence. An academic advisory committee was established and by 1965 a proposal was made to the secretary of state for education and science seeking independent degree awarding status for Cranfield. There followed four years of persistent and hard negotiations which came to fruition in 1969 when a royal charter established the Cranfield Institute of Technology (later Cranfield University). Justifiably Murphy became the first vice-chancellor, a position he held briefly before his retirement in 1970. His wise policies and convictions laid the foundations for his successors to build upon and without them it is questionable if Cranfield would have survived.

Outside Cranfield, Murphy was chairman of the British Cast Iron Association (1968–70), an independent member of the Aeronautical Research Council (1961–4), and a fellow of the Royal Aeronautical Society. Besides a number of significant papers he edited an authoritative volume on *Non-Ferrous Foundry Metallurgy* (1954). He retained a strong interest in metallurgy and associated research throughout his life. He was made an honorary DSc of Cranfield in 1970 and received the platinum medal of the Institute of Metals in 1971. Although he was appointed CBE in 1964, the lack of wider recognition of his contributions to higher education in the United Kingdom is possibly due to his own dislike of being in the public eye. As a man he was respected by his colleagues, a person with whom it was pleasant to work not least because of his sense of humour.

He was generous and encouraging to his colleagues. Murphy retired to Bedford where he continued his involvement with local technical bodies until his death at home, 4 Riverside Towers, from a stroke, on 26 September 1980.

HENRY CHILVER, *rev.* DENIS HOWE

Sources *The Times* (1 Oct 1980) · *Journal of the Institute of Metals*, 79 (1951), 117–28 · *Metals and Materials*, 5 (1971), 121 · *Journal of the Institute of Metals*, 35 (1926), 107–29 · *Metals and Materials*, 15 (1981), 22 · personal knowledge (1986, 2004) · b. cert. · d. cert.
Wealth at death £99,745: probate, 1 Dec 1980, *CGPLA Eng. & Wales*

Murphy, Arthur (1727–1805), playwright and actor, was born on 27 December 1727 at Clooniquin, co. Roscommon, Ireland, the son of Richard Murphy (d. 1729), a merchant, and his wife, Jane French (*c*.1701–1761). Along with his mother and his brother James [*see below*], Murphy moved to London in 1735 before sailing the next year to France where he lived with Mrs Arthur Plunket, his mother's sister, in Boulogne. In 1738 under the name Arthur French, he entered the English College at St Omer, near Boulogne, where he stayed for six years.

Murphy spent from 1747 until 1749 in Cork, where his uncle Jeffrey French MP had obtained a clerkship for him. He then worked in the banking house of Ironside and Belchier in Lombard Street, London, until the end of 1751. In 1752–4 Murphy served on the staff of the *Covent-Garden Journal* and published the *Gray's Inn Journal*. He became acquainted with Samuel Johnson in 1754, in which year also, being some £300 in debt, he took to the stage, making his acting début, at Covent Garden as Othello. Murphy acted until 1756, when he began *The Test*, an anonymous political weekly opposing Pitt and supporting Henry Fox. In 1757 he contributed to both the *London Chronicle* and the *Literary Magazine*, and was admitted to Lincoln's Inn. He was eventually called to the bar in 1762. He also contributed dramatic criticism to the *London Chronicle* from 1758.

On 2 January 1756 Murphy's farce *The Apprentice* was performed at Drury Lane. This was followed by *The Spouter, or, The Triple Revenge*, published anonymously in the same year. His *The Englishman from Paris* received its only performance at Covent Garden on 3 April 1756. At the end of the season Murphy had earned enough to pay off his debts and be £100 to the good. His first tragedy, *The Orphan of China* (1759), was first performed at Drury Lane on 21 April 1759. This was followed the next year by *The Desert Island* and a comedy, *The Way to Keep Him*. A number of his plays are now lost; however, the majority of them are now printed in Schwartz's (1979) edition.

In 1761 three events occurred which were important in Murphy's life: the death of his mother, which affected him deeply; his taking the actress Ann *Elliot (1743–1769) as his mistress; and his renting of Drury Lane, with Samuel Foote, for the summer season. At this time he also conducted a pamphlet war with Charles Churchill. In the following year he published *The Works of Henry Fielding, Esq; with the Life of the Author* and began *The Auditor*, another political periodical opposing Pitt, this time supporting Bute.

In 1765 Murphy introduced Johnson to Henry and Hester Thrale; it is noteworthy that he was one of the few members of Johnson's circle to support Hester Thrale in her later decision to marry her daughters' music instructor, Piozzi. From 1765 until 1778 Murphy was one of the commissioners of bankruptcy.

In 1779 Murphy sat for Reynolds and was also made recorder for the borough of Sudbury, a post he held until 1789. He was active in opposing the actions of the mob during the Gordon riots of 1780. In 1786 he began writing reviews for the *Monthly Review*, and saw the publication of his collected works in seven volumes. He followed this in 1792 with his *Essay on the Life and Genius of Samuel Johnson*. Murphy published a translation of Tacitus in 1793, but suffered that year with a severe urinary disorder.

In 1795 Murphy received a legacy of £2000 from Mrs Ford, a relative, to which was added a legacy of £1000 from Mrs James Plunkett in 1798. He again became commissioner of bankrupts in 1796, and resigned that post in 1805. Murphy published a *Life of David Garrick* (1801), was made one of the benchers of Lincoln's Inn (1802), and received a royal pension at the instigation of Henry Addington, chancellor of the exchequer, at £200 per annum. Despite this Murphy remained in debt and was forced to sell his residence, 'the westernmost house in Hammersmith Terrace' (*DNB*), and part of his library. He later lived in Brompton, but was in the habit, when writing, of staying in a hotel at Richmond.

While Murphy was a significant acquaintance of Johnson, it is important to consider him as more than a Johnsonian satellite. He was, for example, an able classicist, from his student days at St Omer to his 1793 translation of Tacitus. He had a memory of Johnsonian proportion and stood a public examination at St Omer at which he demonstrated that he had committed the *Aeneid* to memory.

As a lawyer Murphy earned a total for his services of some £11,000, then a significant sum. His clients included Edmund Burke and Henry Thrale. While the stage remained his primary love it did not occupy the whole of his attention. As editor, poet, essayist, biographer, autobiographer, critic, translator, and political writer, as well as dramatist, he may be compared with Oliver Goldsmith for the breadth and polish of his work.

Murphy's plays were often quite successful. During a period when £300 might be received for a popular play and £500 for a great success, Murphy earned over £600 for *Know your Own Mind*, approximately £600 for his most successful tragedy, *The Grecian Daughter* (1772), and some £800 for *The Way to Keep Him*. A number of his plays—*The Citizen* (1763), *Know your Own Mind* (1778), *Three Weeks after Marriage* (originally *What We Must all Come To*, 1764), and *The Old Maid* (1761)—were all performed well into the nineteenth century, and *The Way to Keep Him* was performed as late as 1925–6. While he is commonly charged with too liberal borrowing from earlier continental and British sources, Murphy freely acknowledged his debts. The use of such materials was common among practising dramatists.

At the same time Murphy should not be considered a forgotten genius. Johnson's comment on Pope that while he seldom surpasses expectation he seldom falls below it could be applied, fairly, to Murphy.

Murphy was fairly well built and narrow-shouldered, had an oval face with a fair complexion and full light eyes, and was marked with smallpox. He died on 18 June 1805 at his residence, 14 Queen's Row, Knightsbridge. He was buried at St Paul's, Hammersmith, in the grave he had previously bought for his mother. An epitaph was placed there by his executor and biographer, Jessé Foot.

Murphy's elder brother, **James Murphy** [*known as* James Murphy French] (1725–1759), is a shadowy figure. Born at St George's Quay, Dublin, in September 1725, he was educated at Westminster School. Like Arthur he later studied law (though at the Middle Temple) and was called to the bar. Like Arthur he also wrote occasionally for the *Gray's Inn Journal*, and he attempted two dramatic works, a comedy entitled 'The Brothers' and a farce entitled 'The Conjuror, or, The Enchanted Garden'. Neither of these works was either printed or performed. He used his mother's maiden name and was known as James Murphy French. James was a friend of the actor West Digges, one of Boswell's early idols, and introduced his brother Arthur to the world of the London theatre, most importantly to Samuel Foote, the actor and playwright, and Arthur's eventual collaborator. The brothers' uncle Jeffery French MP owned property in Jamaica, and James moved there in hopes of practising law, but died on 5 January 1759, soon after his arrival, from an intense fever.

RICHARD B. SCHWARTZ

Sources *The plays of Arthur Murphy*, ed. R. B. Schwartz, 4 vols. (New York, 1979) • J. P. Emery, *Arthur Murphy: an eminent English dramatist of the eighteenth century* (Philadelphia, 1946) • H. H. Dunbar, *The dramatic career of Arthur Murphy* (New York, 1946) • *New essays by Arthur Murphy*, ed. A. Sherbo (East Lansing, Michigan, 1963) • J. Foot, *The life of Arthur Murphy, esq.* (1811) • *DNB*

Archives JRL, MSS letters | JRL, letters to Hester Lynch Thrale • V&A NAL, corresp. with David Garrick

Likenesses N. Dance, oils, 1777, NPG • W. Ridley, stipple, 1798 (after S. Drummond), BM, NPG; repro. in *Monthly Mirror* (1798) • E. Scriven, stipple, pubd 1807 (after P. Turnerelli), BM, NPG • P. Condé, stipple (aged seventy-two; after T. R. Poole), BM, NPG • N. Dance, oils, NG Ire. • engraving, Folger; repro. in Emery, *Arthur Murphy*

Wealth at death negligible: Emery, *Arthur Murphy*, 169

Murphy, Denis (1833–1896), Jesuit and historian, was born in Scarteen near Newmarket, co. Cork, on 12 January 1833, the son of Timothy Murphy and his wife, Joanna O'Connell. He was educated in the Jesuit college at Clongowes Wood, co. Kildare, and was admitted to the society as a novice in his sixteenth year. During his religious and theological training, he studied in France, Spain, and Germany. He soon began to devote himself to teaching and historical research. He was professor of history and literature at the Jesuit colleges of Clongowes Wood; Limerick; and Milltown Park, Dublin; and finally at University College, Dublin.

Murphy's best-known work, published at Dublin in 1883, was *Cromwell in Ireland*, a work of over 450 pages, the first modern account of the 1649–51 military campaign, previously (as was only to be expected) a topic for party invective rather than history. In his preface, Murphy proclaimed his intention of being balanced, and in this he was remarkably successful. A new edition appeared in 1885 and another, posthumously, in 1897. Another important historical work was his edition of L. O'Clery's *Life of Hugh Roe O'Donnell, Prince of Tirconnell, 1586–1602* (1893), which he was the first to translate into English. The parallel bilingual text is preceded by a historical introduction. Murphy also published *The Annals of Clonmacnoise* (1896) and *Triumphalia chronologica Monasterii Sanctae Crucis in Hibernia* (1895). He edited for many years the *Journal of the County Kildare Archaeological Society*, to which he contributed several papers, and was connected with similar publications in Cork, Waterford, and Belfast. His last published work was *A School History of Ireland* (in T. A. Finlay's School and College series), issued in 1894, which was remarkable for containing a eulogy of Charles Stewart Parnell. At the suggestion of the Irish bishops, he compiled an account of those put to death for the Roman Catholic religion in Ireland during the sixteenth and seventeenth centuries. He had finished correcting the proofs of this work (*Our Martyrs*) the day before his unexpected death.

Murphy received the honorary degree of LLD from the Royal University of Ireland in recognition of his historical writings. He was vice-president of the Royal Irish Academy and a member of the council of the Royal Society of Antiquaries in Ireland. He was found dead in his bed, on the morning of 18 May 1896, in his rooms at University College, St Stephen's Green, Dublin, and was buried at Glasnevin cemetery on 20 May.

G. LE G. NORGATE, *rev.* PATRICK J. CORISH

Sources M. R. [M. Ronan], 'Sketch of the author', in D. Murphy, *Cromwell in Ireland: a history of Cromwell's Irish campaign*, new edn (1897) [posthumous edn] · *Irish Catholic Directory* (1897), 356–7 · *Irish Catholic* (23 May 1896) · *The Tablet* (23 May 1896) · *The Times* (25 May 1896)
Archives Archives of the Irish Province of the Society of Jesus, Dublin

Murphy, Denis Brownell (d. 1842), miniature painter, was born in Dublin. He was educated at the Dublin Society's drawing schools, where he was taught by John Robert West and received a prize for drawing in 1763. He exhibited miniatures at the Society of Artists in Ireland exhibitions in 1765 and 1768. He advertised his miniature portrait practice in several Dublin newspapers and it appears that he was employed by jewellers to supply miniature portraits.

Murphy was a patriot and strong sympathizer with the cause of United Ireland in 1798, but in that year moved for professional reasons to Whitehaven, Cumberland, with his English wife, Minnie (d. 1854), and family. In 1802 they moved to Newcastle upon Tyne, and then in 1803 to London, settling first at Hanwell, Middlesex. Murphy had considerable practice as a miniature painter and was in that capacity attached to the household of Princess Charlotte, being in 1810 appointed miniature painter-in-ordinary to her royal highness. He copied one or two of Lely's famous 'Beauties', then at Windsor Castle (later at Hampton

Court), and by command of the princess completed a series of miniature copies of these, adding some from pictures not at Windsor. Murphy had apartments assigned him at Windsor during the progress of this series, which was from time to time inspected and approved by the royal family. The set was not completed at the time of the princess's death in 1817, which put an end to the work and to Murphy's connection with the court. The paintings were sent to her husband, Prince Leopold, with a claim for payment, but to the painter's great disappointment were declined and returned. The set of twenty-one miniatures were, however, purchased by a friend, Sir Gerard Noel, and it was suggested that use should be made of them by having them engraved as a series, with illustrative text by Murphy's daughter, the writer on art Mrs Anna Brownell *Jameson. This work was successfully completed and published in 1833 under the title of *The Beauties of the Court of King Charles the Second*.

Murphy occasionally exhibited miniatures in enamel or on ivory at the Royal Academy from 1800 to 1827, but his work did not attain any great distinction. His sitters included the engraver and illustrator Thomas Bewick (National History Society of Northumbria collection, Hancock Museum, Newcastle upon Tyne), the landscape painter John Crome (National Portrait Gallery, London), and William Wordsworth (in the collection of the earl of Mayo in 1913). Murphy died in London in March 1842 and was survived by his wife and five daughters.

L. H. CUST, *rev.* PAUL CAFFREY

Sources W. G. Strickland, *A dictionary of Irish artists*, 2 (1913), 157–9 · B. S. Long, *British miniaturists* (1923), 306 · D. Foskett, *Miniatures: dictionary and guide* (1987), 604 · H. Blättel, *International dictionary miniature painters / Internationales Lexikon Miniatur-Maler* (1992), 660–61 · P. Caffrey, 'Irish portrait miniatures, c.1700–1830', PhD diss., Southampton Institute, 1995 · A. Crookshank and the Knight of Glin [D. Fitzgerald], eds., *Irish portraits, 1660–1860* (1969) [exhibition catalogue, Dublin, London, and Belfast, 14 Aug 1969 – 9 March 1970] · G. Breeze, *Society of Artists in Ireland: index of exhibits, 1765–80* (1985), 30 · A. B. Murphy Jameson, *The beauties of the court of King Charles the Second* (1833), 5 · Graves, *RA exhibitors*, 4.153 · A. Le Harivel, ed., *National Gallery of Ireland: illustrated summary catalogue of drawings, watercolours and miniatures* (1983), 564 · private information (1894)

Murphy [Morphy], **Edward** (1650/51–1728), Roman Catholic archbishop of Dublin, was born in Balrothery, north of Lusk, co. Dublin. The names of his parents are unknown. After studies at the Irish College in Salamanca, he was ordained at Madrid in 1677, and in 1685 acted as secretary to a provincial synod in Dublin. In 1687 he became, by papal provision, parish priest of St Audoen's in Dublin. He was a member of the chapter from 1688 and vicar-general of Dublin under two archbishops from at least as early as 1697 until his promotion to the diocese of Kildare and Leighlin on 11 September 1715. He was consecrated on 18 December by Edmund Byrne, archbishop of Dublin. Although he seems to have continued to live in Dublin for the sake of safety, as bishop of Kildare he was much appreciated by his clergy, who in 1722, when rejecting a proposal that Leighlin should be constituted a separate diocese, asserted that under Murphy's rule they had 'enjoyed concord, fraternal charity and regular discipline'.

On the death in December 1723 of Edmund Byrne, divisions within the chapter made it advisable to appoint another archbishop who would not occupy the see for long. Murphy, in poor health and about seventy-four years of age, was accordingly translated to the metropolitan see by a papal brief dated September 1724. He had no mensal parish but lived in Cook Street close to his old parish chapel of St Audoen's. From c.1726 Bernard Dunne, now bishop of Kildare, served as his assistant.

At Dublin, Murphy restored peace among the clergy, although the regular clergy found him severe. The famine of 1727, which left the starving poor of Dublin to wander the streets, added greatly to the claims on his purse and pastoral concern. By October 1725 he was actively seeking a coadjutor, but without reference to the Stuart court in exile. Eventually, in November 1728, he asked Rome to appoint as his coadjutor with right of succession the chancellor of the diocese, Joseph Walsh. Since Walsh was over seventy, disputes in the chapter broke out again, so that Murphy left to his successor a legacy of discord worse even than that he had himself inherited in 1724. In December 1728 he died of an incurable sickness at the age of seventy-seven in Cook Street, Dublin, and was buried, it is supposed, in St James's churchyard. His will was that of a relatively poor man with neither a house nor even a library to bequeath. The closest relatives among his beneficiaries were two nephews, Michael and Richard Morphy, the latter from Leixlip, near Dublin.

Murphy's chief contribution was not as archbishop of Dublin, a post he filled for only four years in his old age, but in his undocumented work as vicar-general in Dublin and bishop of Kildare and Leighlin at the very height of the penal laws. At Dublin it fell to him to rule the diocese until the appointment of an archbishop in 1707; in Kildare his episcopal rank left him constantly exposed for ten years to the danger of discovery and transportation.

HUGH FENNING

Sources *DNB* · W. M. O'Riordan, 'A list of 17th-century Dublin priests', *Reportorium Novum*, 3 (1962), 138 · N. Donnelly, *A short history of some Dublin parishes*, 17 pts? (1905–11), 6.48–9; 8.174; 11.52–3; 16.104–7 · P. Fagan, *Dublin's turbulent priest: Cornelius Nary (1658–1738)* (1991) · W. Carrigan, 'Catholic episcopal wills … province of Dublin', *Archivium Hibernicum*, 4 (1915), 69–71 · W. M. O'Riordan, 'The tombs, monuments and epitaphs of the … archbishops of Dublin', *Irish Ecclesiastical Record*, 5th ser., 72 (1949), 144–65 · C. Giblin, ed., 'Catalogue of material of Irish interest in the collection *Nunziatura di Fiandra*, Vatican archives [pt 4]', *Collectanea Hibernica*, 5 (1962), 7–130, esp. 105, 114–16 · C. Giblin, ed., 'Catalogue of material of Irish interest in the collection *Nunziatura di Fiandra*, Vatican archives [pt 5]', *Collectanea Hibernica*, 9 (1966), 7–70, esp. 9–11 · P. Fagan, ed., *Ireland in the Stuart papers*, 1: 1719–42 (1995), 63–4 · The Vatican, Vatican City, archives of Propaganda Fide, CP 34B, fol. 17, 214–15; SOCG 589, fols. 277–78; SC Irlanda 7, fols. 498; SC Irlanda 9, fol. 45 · D. J. O'Doherty, 'Students of the Irish College, Salamanca (1595–1619) [pt 2]', *Archivium Hibernicum*, 3 (1914), 87–112, esp. 111
Wealth at death approx. £50; also books and furniture: will

Murphy, Francis (1795–1858), Roman Catholic bishop of Adelaide, was born at Navan, co. Meath, on 20 May 1795, the eldest son of Arthur Murphy and his wife, Bridget. He was educated at St Finian's College, Navan, and in 1815 entered St Patrick's College, Maynooth. In 1825 he was ordained priest by Dr Daniel Murray, archbishop of Dublin. After serving as missioner at Bradford in Yorkshire for three years, he in 1829 took charge of St Anne's, Toxteth Park, Liverpool. In 1838 he went out to New South Wales with Dr W. Ullathorne, and on the latter's recall to England became vicar-general of Australia that year. On 8 September 1844 he was consecrated in St Mary's Cathedral, Sydney, bishop of the newly established suffragan see of Adelaide, being the first bishop consecrated in Australia. His diocese at this period contained only 1500 Roman Catholics, and he came to it with only £150 which had been subscribed in Sydney. He held services in a store in Pirie Street, Adelaide, until his sole assistant, Michael Ryan, obtained a site and built a church in West Terrace. The discovery of gold in 1851 caused the dispersal of a large portion of his congregations, and his churches were kept open only by Ryan visiting the goldfields, and there collecting money from the Adelaide diggers. When the excitement had somewhat subsided, he began building a cathedral in Victoria Street, designed by Charles Hansom, but did not live to see it finished. He, however, succeeded in establishing twenty-one churches, served by thirteen priests, and in the management of his diocese won general esteem. A tall, sandy-haired man, Murphy was an attractive and ecumenical preacher. His enthusiasm for temperance shamed protestants into reviving their own temperance societies. Murphy died of consumption at West Terrace, Adelaide, on 26 April 1858, and was buried within the precincts of his unfinished cathedral.

G. C. BOASE, *rev.* H. C. G. MATTHEW

Sources *South Australian Register* (27 April 1858) · *The Tablet* (24 July 1858) · F. Byrne, *History of the Catholic church in South Australia* (1896) · M. Beever, 'Murphy, Francis', *AusDB*, vol. 2
Archives Downside Abbey, near Bath · Sacra Congregazione di Propaganda Fide, Rome

Murphy, Sir Francis (1809–1891), politician in Australia, the son of Francis Down Murphy, head of the Cork convict transportation department, was born in Cork, Ireland. Educated privately at first, he later studied medicine in Dublin and London (MRCS, 1835). After migrating to Sydney in 1836, he was appointed a colonial surgeon in 1837. In 1839 he married Agnes, the daughter of Dr David Reid RN, and retired from medicine to devote himself to farming and pastoralism.

Murphy then moved to the Port Phillip district, and about 1846 acquired Tarawingee station on the Ovens River. He was elected a member of the legislative council of Victoria in 1851 and was appointed chairman of committees. In 1853 he sold Tarawingee and lived in Melbourne, where he became president of the central roads board. He supported measures to preserve the national school system, and in the constitutional debate of 1854 opposed universal suffrage for the assembly and proposed that the council be elected from a nominated electoral body.

Murphy was elected to the legislative assembly in 1856, and won the speakership with the promise that he would not take part in debates. In an assembly with unstable ministries, ignorant members, and divisions over constitutional reform, land ownership, secular education, and protection, Murphy was notable for his dignity, courtesy, and impartiality. Although conservative by temperament, he worked with reforming ministries of the day and is reputed to have twice given vital support to them. In 1861 he supported the election of a radical ministry which planned to throw open crown land for small farmers. In 1865 he ruled that linking tariff charges to an appropriation bill did not constitute a tack, thus frustrating attempts by conservatives and free traders to separate the two matters. It ensured that the McCulloch ministry was able to introduce the first stages of protection.

Opposed in the 1866 election, Murphy was elected for Grenville with ministerial help, and remained speaker until his defeat in 1871. He was then elected to the legislative council, on which he sat from 1872 to 1876. He also sat on the royal commissions on the Burke and Wills expedition (1861) and intercolonial legislation (1870), chaired the Industrial Exhibition committee (1866) and the anti-transportation committee (1863), was a member of the committee to choose the site for New Zealand's capital, and represented Victoria at the Delhi imperial celebrations in 1877.

Murphy held squatting leases in partnership with Sir James Palmer, president of the legislative council, between 1860 and 1869, and owned substantial real estate. He lived in Collingwood long after it became 'a noxious industrial suburb' of Melbourne, supporting local improvements and serving in the East Collingwood volunteer rifles. He was knighted in 1860 and was president of the Melbourne Club in 1862. A director of the National Bank from 1863, he resigned as chairman in 1870 after shareholders criticized board decisions.

Murphy belonged to that small band of pre-gold gentlemen pioneers who negotiated the 1850s in comfortable circumstances and entered public life. Survived by his wife and nine children (who made good marriages), he died at his home, Edgecumbe, St Kilda Road, Melbourne, on 30 March 1891, and was buried in Christ Church, South Yarra on 1 April. A grandson, H. D. Murphy, was the model for the central character in Patrick White's *The Twyborn Affair*.   PAUL DE SERVILLE

Sources The Argus [Melbourne] (31 March 1891) • The Argus [Melbourne] (1 April 1891) • AusDB • J. H. Heaton, Australian dictionary of dates and men of the time (1879) • K. Thomson and G. Serle, A biographical register of the Victorian legislature, 1851–1900 (1972) • G. Serle, The golden age: a history of the colony of Victoria, 1851–1861 (1963) • G. Blainey and G. Hutton, Gold & paper (1963) • R. Spreadborough and H. Anderson, eds., Victorian squatters (Melbourne, 1983) • P. de Serville, Port Phillip gentlemen and good society in Melbourne before the gold rushes (1980) • P. de Serville, Pounds and pedigrees: the upper class in Victoria, 1850–80 (1991) • Index to marriages, New South Wales, Australia [old records], vol. 23, no. 400
Likenesses C. Summers, marble bust, State Library of Victoria, Australia

Murphy, Francis Stack (1807–1860), serjeant-at-law, was born in Cork, the son of Jeremiah Murphy, a wealthy merchant, whose brother John was the Catholic bishop of Cork from 1815 to 1847. He was educated at Clongowes Wood College, co. Kildare, and was one of the pupils of Francis Sylvester Mahony, a frequent contributor and one-time editor of *Fraser's Magazine*. Proceeding to Trinity College, Dublin, where he matriculated on 7 November 1825, he graduated BA in 1829 and MA in 1832. He studied law in London, and in 1833 was called to the English bar. In 1834 he became associated with *Fraser's Magazine* as an occasional contributor, assisting 'Father Prout' (the pseudonym of Francis Mahoney) in his popular 'Reliques'. He was a noted classical scholar, and was responsible for some of Mahony's Greek and Latin verses. Mahony introduced him in his 'Prout Papers' as 'Frank Cresswell of Furnival's Inn'. In 1837 Murphy became Liberal MP for co. Cork, and retained the seat for sixteen years. He was a late supporter of free trade, in favour of national education in Ireland, and opposed to the Tenant League. On 25 February 1842 he was made serjeant-at-law. He resigned his parliamentary seat in September 1853, following an appointment as a commissioner of bankruptcy in Dublin. He died on 17 June 1860 at his home, 1 Earl's Court Gardens, Old Brompton, London. Murphy was a clever lawyer, and was noted for his wit; many of his remarks were recorded in C. G. Duffy's *League of North and South* (1886) and in B. C. Robinson's *Bench and Bar* (1891).

A first cousin, **Jeremiah Daniel Murphy** (1806–1824), born in Cork, developed as a boy a rare talent for languages, mastering Greek, Latin, French, Portuguese, Spanish, German, and Irish. He contributed to *Blackwood's Magazine* some Latin verse: 'Adventus regis' (December 1821), and an English poem, 'The Rising of the North' (November 1822). He died of heart disease on 5 January 1824. His precocity was commemorated in English and Latin verse in *Blackwood's* the following month.

D. J. O'DONOGHUE, rev. ERIC METCALFE

Sources Boase, Mod. Eng. biog. • Burtchaell & Sadleir, Alum. Dubl. • WWBMP • Wellesley index • W. Bates, The Maclise portrait-gallery of 'illustrious literary characters' (1883) • Annual Register (1860), 464 • GM, 3rd ser., 9 (1860), 212 • CGPLA Eng. & Wales (1861)
Likenesses D. Maclise, group portrait, lithograph, 1835 (The Fraserians), BM • portrait, repro. in Bates, Maclise portrait-gallery, 464–7 • portrait, repro. in ILN, 4 (1884), 107
Wealth at death under £1500: administration, 3 Jan 1861, CGPLA Eng. & Wales

Murphy, Frank (1889–1955), radio manufacturer, was born on 16 June 1889 at Penwith Villa, 25 Wrottesley Road, West Plumstead, Woolwich, London, the youngest son of the seven surviving children of John James Murphy (1853–1917), schoolmaster, and his wife, Annie, née Leggo (1855–1924). Following John Murphy's appointment as headmaster of Holmes Road School, Kentish Town, in north London, the family moved to Upper Holloway in 1890, but returned to Plumstead shortly afterwards, where Frank and his younger sister Ethel were enrolled in the local board school.

From an early age, Frank Murphy displayed a precocious

talent for mathematics. He won a scholarship to the East London Technical College, graduating in 1908 with honours in electrical engineering, but lack of funds prevented him from taking up the offer of a mathematics exhibition at St John's College, Oxford. Although not apparent at the time, the frustration and resentment at this checked potential was to mark much of his private life and business career. Murphy was an essentially serious young man, regularly attending the Highgate Road Baptist Chapel where he met, then married on 22 June 1912, his first wife, Hilda Constance (1889–1980), the only child of Charles and Edith Howe of Tufnell Park. The following year the first of three children was born. At the time, Murphy was working as a Post Office engineer, a step up from his first job on the assembly line at the Western Electric Company at Woolwich, where the tedium was relieved by postgraduate evening classes on the development of the cathode ray tube.

In 1916, when the Post Office released him for military service, Murphy was sent to France as a squadron wireless operator, to be recalled just eight months later to set up an officers' wireless training school at Farnborough, returning to France some weeks later to take charge of the ground-to-air communications operating between Folkestone and Cologne. By the time of his demobilization in 1919, Murphy's future career was still an issue, but after a chance meeting with (Charles) Rupert Casson, a budding copywriter, the two men formed the Engineering Publicity Service (EPS), an advertising company with clients in the engineering field. By 1924 EPS had changed its name to Murphy Casson Ltd, and over the next four years rising profits provided the Murphy family with a comfortable standard of living. Yet material security offered scant compensation for unexplored talents and in 1928 Murphy announced his intended withdrawal from the partnership in order to start his own radio manufacturing company.

Murphy Radio Ltd, located in the new Welwyn Garden City, was registered on 9 September 1929 with a nominal capital of £6000 and a staff of seven. By 1936 the company was acknowledged as one of the leaders in the field, with 600 staff at Welwyn and sales at an all-time high. With the help of his erstwhile business partner, Murphy set about establishing two fundamental principles—reliability and value for money. Full-page advertisements ran in the *Radio Times* featuring Murphy himself, promoting the notion of 'a square deal' rather than the technical wizardry favoured by his competitors. The image of the homely and dependable managing director, 'the man with the pipe', had particular resonance during the uncertainty of the depression. With only approved Murphy dealers supplying and servicing his sets, costs could be pared to the bone and the risks of buying through 'contacts in the trade' were eliminated. *Murphy News*, the in-house magazine begun in 1933, encouraged all employees to share the same level of business integrity vaunted by Murphy.

In January 1937 Murphy chose to announce his resignation from the board to start a new venture producing and selling good-quality furniture for the mass market. For many years his personal philosophy, that of applied knowledge, had been in conflict with the need to generate profits for shareholders. Murphy fervently believed that industry should be governed by a constitution enshrining workers' rights and obligations. The time between his resignation and the registration of Frank Murphy Ltd in 1938 was taken up with the preparation of a prospectus entitled *A New Conception for Business*. Murphy set out six basic principles based on the acceptance of applying knowledge with integrity in the service of society. Not surprisingly, these rather esoteric views found few takers and within two years the liabilities of the company were too great for it to continue in business. The long process of winding up was begun and Murphy again found himself subject to the same pattern of high promise and dashed hopes.

The pressure on his marriage from failed business ventures, combined with the unexpected death of his elder son in 1942, led Murphy to spend increasing time with his widowed daughter-in-law, Audrey, *née* Phillips (*b.* 1912), and her two children. The endless gossip generated by this liaison finally broke his marriage and in 1947 he emigrated to Canada with Audrey in a last effort to get his ideas accepted. Their short-lived marriage (annulled in 1949) underscored the forlorn task Murphy had set himself. The one time 'face of radio', a man of unquestionable intellectual capacity, found no ready market in Canada and instead was reduced to taking on odd jobs and driving taxis. Shortly before his death in Toronto on 26 January 1955, Murphy secured the post of mathematics teacher at a Toronto high school, completing a life of elusive promise. BARBARA TROMPETER

Sources [J. Long], *A first class job! The story of Frank Murphy, radio pioneer, furniture designer and industrial idealist* (1985) · PRO, records of Murphy Radio Ltd, BT/31/36954/242218 · PRO, records of Frank Murphy Ltd, BT/31/35839/339555 · b. cert. · m. cert. · d. cert., Ontario, Canada

Likenesses photographs, 1908–35, repro. in Long, *First class job!*
Wealth at death £1373 3s. 5d.: administration, 1 Nov 1955, *CGPLA Eng. & Wales* · C$343; a gold watch: Long, *First class job!*

Murphy, James (1725–1759). *See under* Murphy, Arthur (1727–1805).

Murphy, James Cavanah (1760–1814), architect and antiquary, was born at Blackrock, near Cork. He worked as a bricklayer, but after showing a talent for drawing he went to Dublin to study. His name appears in a list of the pupils of the drawing school of the Dublin Society about 1775, as working in miniature, chalk, and crayons. Afterwards Murphy practised in Dublin, and in 1786 was one of seven architects who were consulted about the additions to the House of Commons. He was one of two architects commissioned to carry out James Gandon's design for these. At the end of 1788 he went to Portugal, commissioned by William Burton Conyngham to make drawings of the Dominican church and monastery of Batalha. In 1795 he published *Plans, elevations, sections, and views of the church of Batalha … to which is prefixed an introductory discourse on the principles of Gothic architecture*, a German translation of which appeared in 1828. In the catalogue of the RIBA drawings collection John Harris noted that 'this great book with its carefully measured drawings may well have had an influence on the Gothic Revival in England comparable with that which [James] Stuart and [Nicholas] Revett's *Antiquities of Athens* had on the neo-Greek Revival' (*Catalogue of the drawings collection*, 98).

Murphy was back in Dublin in 1790, and was in England at the end of the year. From 1802 to 1809 he lived in Cadiz, where he held a diplomatic post, and devoted most of his time to the study of Moorish architecture.

Murphy returned to England in 1809 and, apart from taking out a patent for a method of preserving timber and other substances from decay in 1813, he spent the last few years of his life preparing for publication his notes on Arabian architecture. He died, (unmarried), on 12 September 1814 in Edward Street, Cavendish Square, London, with only part of his book published. *The Arabian Antiquities of Spain* (1813–16), including 110 plates with drawings by Murphy, was reprinted in 1815 with historical and antiquarian descriptions by Thomas Hartwell Horne. The majority of Murphy's drawings are of architectural details and ornaments, but in the British Museum there is a view of Tynemouth, in the style of Joseph Farington. Other examples of his work are in the British Museum and the RIBA collection.

BERTHA PORTER, *rev.* ANNE PIMLOTT BAKER

Sources T. C. Croker, *Researches in the south of Ireland* (1824), 204 · J. Gandon and T. J. Mulvany, eds., *The life of James Gandon* (1846) · J. Lever, ed., *Catalogue of the drawings collection of the Royal Institute of British Architects: L–N* (1973) · Mallalieu, *Watercolour artists* · Redgrave, *Artists*
Archives RIBA BAL, diary; sketchbook with architectural notes and drawings · S. Antiquaries, Lond., drawings and papers relating to the Batalha Monastery | BM, department of prints and drawings, design for completing monument to King Emmanuel (drawing) for *Plans, elevations, sections*, 1795 · S. Antiquaries, Lond., volume of studies and copies of Murphy's letters
Likenesses W. C. Newton, line engraving (after M. A. Shee), NPG · portrait (after M. A. Shee), repro. in J. C. Murphy, *Travels in Portugal* (1795)
Wealth at death £5000: administration, 1814

Murphy, Jeremiah Daniel (1806–1824). *See under* Murphy, Francis Stack (1807–1860).

Murphy, John (1753–1798), Roman Catholic priest and insurgent leader, was the youngest of four sons and one daughter born to Thomas Murphy and Johanna Whitty of Tincurry, near Ballycarney, co. Wexford. The family were tenant farmers and used their 70 acres of good land to produce grain and cured bacon for the thriving Dublin market. Murphy reputedly learned Greek and Latin from a local schoolmaster and under the influence of the Jesuit parish priest, Dr Andrew Cassin, was ordained by Bishop Nicholas Sweetman of Ferns in late 1779. Advanced clerical training had to be undertaken overseas as various 'penal law' statutes prohibited the operation of Catholic seminaries in Ireland prior to 1795. From June 1780 Murphy attended the austere Dominican College of St Thomas in Seville, Spain, where he graduated in March 1785.

Upon returning to co. Wexford, Murphy was appointed curate of Kilcormick (also known as Boolavogue) in the parish of Monageer. His tenure was unremarkable and seemingly unaffected by the advent of social and political upheaval as the impact of the French Revolution began to reverberate in Wexford in 1791–3. Whatever his personal sympathies and associations, there was nothing in his known actions to suggest involvement in the radical Society of United Irishmen which attracted numerous adherents in Wexford from the spring of 1797. This apparent detachment gave way to pragmatic decision making in November 1797 when a bid by Wexford magistrates to have martial law proclaimed was opposed by the liberal landlord Lord Mountnorris. Murphy's assistance in preparing a declaration of loyalty from his parishioners was only belatedly obtained by Mountnorris and his reticence came to the attention of Bishop James Caulfield. The bishop regarded Murphy as an unimpressive and impressionable cleric whom, significantly, he had failed to promote to a parish of his own. Amends were made on 18 April 1798 when another loyal petition from Boolavogue was presented to the government. This was a last-ditch attempt to avoid the often brutal programme of counter-insurgency in operation elsewhere. The gesture came too late to stem the tide of popular disaffection or to establish Murphy's credentials as a priest of good standing with conservatives. In the last week of April, Wexford was exposed to the frequently indiscriminate ravages of state terror which partially disarmed and disrupted the United Irishmen at the cost of rendering them more desperate and militant.

The rising commenced in the eastern province of Leinster on 23–4 May 1798 and had spread to Wexford by the 26th amid well-founded rumours that captured rebels and their dependants had been massacred. Threats issued to Boolavogue men who handed in illegal weapons at Ferns convinced Murphy that his parishioners stood to gain more by joining the insurrection than by exposing themselves to the increasing threat posed by state forces. He was evidently in command that evening when rebels skirmished with loyalist yeomen at the Harrow and then led the insurgents to Camolin Park and Rockspring to recover previously surrendered arms. Murphy rose to prominence at the battle of Oulart Hill on the 27th when a company of the North Cork militia were annihilated, a victory which accelerated the build-up of popular forces and resulted in their capture of Enniscorthy. While Murphy's status in Wexford's insurgent army has been consistently overstated in nineteenth-century historiography and by P. F. Kavanagh in particular, there is little doubt but that he was the premier clerical insurgent commander of the rising. He was present in Three Rocks camp on 30 May when rebels under Thomas Cloney defeated a military relief force *en route* to the county town. This presaged the abandonment of Wexford's administrative centre and yielded the bulk of its hinterland to rebel control. After a conference of United Irish officers at Windmill Hill on the 31st, Murphy joined a sizeable column sent to the north of the county to prepare for an advance through Wicklow to Dublin. It was jointly commanded by Edward Fitzgerald of Newpark, Edward Roche of Garrylough, Anthony Perry of

Inch, Father Michael Murphy of Ballycanew, and others known to John Murphy from the pre-rising period. Having failed to exploit a victory at Tubberneering on 4 June, owing in part to his insistence that Carnew should be reconnoitred before they moved on Dublin, the rebel assault on the strategic coastal town of Arklow faltered on the 9th. Contrary to many accounts, John Murphy was not present at Arklow and had remained at Castletown in consequence of tactical disagreements.

Murphy's authority was re-established by 19 June when the rebels encamped at Kilcavan Hill followed him to Vinegar Hill in response to a majority decision of the leadership to concentrate all forces on the high ground overlooking Enniscorthy. Many loyalist prisoners were subjected to kangaroo court proceedings at the camp, although it does not appear that Murphy was directly implicated in the atrocities which ensued. The battle of Vinegar Hill went very badly for the outgunned insurgents on 21 June and claimed the life of Murphy's brother Patrick. The rebels nevertheless managed to retreat in reasonable order and a substantial element under Murphy separated from the Fitzgerald/Perry column before passing through Ferrycarrig to Three Rocks camp. When it was discovered that their comrades in Wexford town were negotiating surrender on the 22nd, Murphy's men commenced a gruelling march to the Blackstairs Mountains with a view to sparking or reviving the rising in the midland counties. The exhausted insurgents fought with mixed success at Killedmond, Goresbridge, and Castlecomer over the following days as it became increasingly apparent that the mood of the Kilkenny and Queen's county people was strongly against joining the rebel effort. On retracing their steps through difficult terrain towards Wexford, Murphy's column left Kilcumney Hill on the 25th and sustained heavy losses when attacked by state forces around Scullogue Gap.

Murphy lost contact with his men during their march from Kilcumney and took shelter on the evening of the 26th at Killoughternane with his bodyguard, John Gallagher. The fugitives sought the protection of the Murphy family at Rathgeeran until the 29th when they returned to Killoughternane for a short stay. On moving towards Tullow, co. Carlow, on 1 July they were trapped by two yeomen the following morning in their Castlemore farmyard billet. A perfunctory court martial sentenced Murphy and Gallagher to death on 2 July for the crime of rebellion, although the defendants remained unidentified by name if not by occupation. They were hanged after severe public flogging in the market square. Unusually, Murphy's dead body was not only decollated but had its torso burned in a barrel of pitch. This maltreatment was evidently carried out to intimidate local rebel sympathizers and, perhaps, in consequence of loyalist hostility towards Catholic priests. His charred remains were interred later in July in the old Mullawn graveyard, Tullow, and were reunited with the decayed skull once it was removed from the spike on the Sessions House.

Murphy's exalted position in the rising's folklore and balladry and a variety of political and religious circumstances in the late 1800s ensured that he was Wexford's premier hero figure of 1798 and a household name in Ireland throughout the twentieth century. This process was greatly boosted by P. F. Kavanagh whose *Popular History of the Insurrection of 1798* (1898) advanced the unfounded thesis that Wexford was unreceptive to revolutionary politics until brutalized into action by the counter-insurgency of state forces in April 1798. Kavanagh was motivated by Catholic church hostility towards the Irish Republican Brotherhood (Fenians) in the 1870s and deliberately over-emphasized Murphy's role in the rising to imply that the people should look to Catholic clergy rather than pluralist subversive leaders in times of crisis. The best-selling book set the tone for the celebrations of the centenary of 1798 in the south-east of Ireland and, along with P. J. McCall's internationally popular song 'Boolavogue', copper-fastened Murphy's exalted status. He is commemorated by a substantial Oliver Sheppard bronze memorial in Enniscorthy. RUÁN O'DONNELL

Sources N. Furlong, *Fr. John Murphy of Boolavogue, 1753–1798* (Dublin, 1991) · N. Furlong, 'The church and Fr. John Murphy of Boolavogue, 1753–1798', *Protestant, Catholic and dissenter: the clergy and 1798*, ed. L. Swords (Dublin, 1997), 186–218 · *Memoirs of Miles Byrne*, 3 vols. (Paris, 1863) · K. Whelan, 'The role of the Catholic priest in the 1798 rebellion in county Wexford', *Wexford: history and society*, ed. K. Whelan (Dublin, 1987), 296–315 · *DNB*
Archives Dublin Roman Catholic archdiocese · NA Ire., Rebellion papers
Likenesses J. Murray?, oils, 1830–70 (after sketch by unknown artist), priv. coll.
Wealth at death modest, curate of parish; home burned

Murphy, John (*fl.* 1778–*c.*1817), printmaker, was born in Ireland. Successive authorities have dated his birth to about 1748, but nothing is known about him until 1778, when his career in London commenced. From then until 1788 he lived in the house at 4 Air Street, Piccadilly, of the bookseller Patrick Keating and his son George Keating, a printmaker and later an important publisher of Roman Catholic books. Both Murphy and George Keating published prints from this house, and in 1784 collaborated on a portrait of the Catholic divine Arthur O'Leary, which was drawn by Murphy and scraped in mezzotint by Keating. In 1789 Murphy appears to have moved with the Keatings to 18 Warwick Street, Golden Square, but by 1791 he had moved out and soon established himself on the north side of Paddington Green.

Murphy engraved a few portraits in mezzotint but specialized in history, especially scripture history, having engraved plates at the outset of his career for the Houghton Gallery, a series of engravings published by John Boydell between 1774 and 1778. He scraped about a dozen mezzotints for Boydell and was employed by a number of other printsellers, including James Birchall and John Jeffryes, although he published a proportion of his plates himself. He worked after an unusually wide variety of painters, both ancient and modern, and interpreted historical paintings by Beschey, Caravaggio, da Cortona, Eckhout, Luca Giordano, Guercino, Rembrandt, Rosa, Snyders, and Titian as well as modern subject pieces by

Dagoty, Kauffmann, Livesay, Morland, Northcote, Ramberg, Reinagle, Singleton, Stothard, Stubbs, West, and Wheatley. Among his most striking pieces were large mezzotints of animals after Northcote, Snyders, and Stubbs.

In 1785 Murphy took James Daniell as his pupil, and at the close of his apprenticeship in 1792 he published Daniell's *A Lion*, after John Graham. He also published stipples by James Godby, which may be the reason for the time-honoured assertion (apparently false) that Murphy was also a stipple engraver. Murphy had some talent as a designer and was probably the artist who drew a series of views for *A Tour on the Lakes of Westmoreland*, published by Ackermann in 1800. In 1805 he published a mezzotint of *The Settling Family Attacked by Savages* by Keating, after Henry Singleton, but his active career as an engraver and publisher ended at about that date. A private plate of Viscount Courtenay is dated 1809 but may have been engraved earlier. According to a list of living artists published in 1820 in *Annals of the Fine Arts*, ed. J. Elmes (5 vols., 1817–20), Murphy was then residing in Howland Street. A selection of his prints can be seen in the department of prints and drawings at the British Museum.

TIMOTHY CLAYTON

Sources W. G. Strickland, *A dictionary of Irish artists*, 2 vols. (1913) · *Neue Bibliothek der schönen Wissenschaften und der freyen Künste*, 25.187; 28.167, 169; 31.319; 43.329; 48.157; 53.116; 54.374 · C. Le Blanc, *Manuel de l'amateur d'estampes*, 4 vols. (Paris, 1854–89) · J. C. Smith, *British mezzotinto portraits*, 4 vols. in 5 (1878–84) · private information (2004) · D. Alexander, 'Chronological checklist of singly issued English prints after Angelica Kauffman', *Angelica Kauffman: a continental artist in Georgian England*, ed. W. W. Roworth (1992), 179–89 · J. Charringtons, 'Catalogue of prints after Rembrandt', rev. D. Alexander, in C. White, D. Alexander, and E. D'Oench, *Rembrandt in eighteenth century England* (1983), 119–49 [exhibition catalogue, Yale U. CBA] · J. Simon, ed., 'The account book of James Northcote', *Walpole Society*, 58 (1995–6), 21–125, esp. 57–9, 70 · C. Lennox-Boyd, R. Dixon, and T. Clayton, *George Stubbs: the complete engraved works* (1989), 271 · H. von Erffa and A. Staley, *The paintings of Benjamin West* (1986) · M. Webster, *Francis Wheatley* (1970) · *Annals of the Fine Arts*, 4 (1820), 655 · J. R. Abbey, *Scenery of Great Britain and Ireland in aquatint and lithography, 1770–1860* (1952) · D. Snelgrove, *British sporting and animal prints, 1658–1874* (1981)

Murphy, John Thomas (1888–1965), political activist, was born at 235 Gorton Lane, Gorton, Manchester, on 9 December 1888, the son of John Murphy, a blacksmith's striker in an iron foundry, and Sarah Pratt. His father was an Irish Catholic and his mother an English Baptist; Murphy himself was a Primitive Methodist in his teens. He left Wincobank council school, Sheffield, at the age of thirteen to take up an apprenticeship at Vickers' Brightside engineering works in Sheffield, where he became a lathe turner. His studious capabilities were turned away from trying to enter the civil service towards reading revolutionary literature, and he became a militant shop steward highly influenced by syndicalist ideas. During the First World War, after leading a remarkably successful illegal strike by 12,000 Sheffield workers, Murphy encouraged the co-ordination of stewards' organization across the city's munitions factories into a Sheffield Workers' Committee. By 1917 he had become a recognized leader of the national Shop Stewards' and Workers' Committee movement, which had sprung up within the engineering industry.

J. T. Murphy was a prolific writer in *Solidarity*, the paper of the wartime stewards' movement, and his pamphlet *The Workers' Committee* (1917), became the chief theoretical statement to emerge from the movement. The pamphlet, which developed and expounded the novel theory of independent rank-and-file organization capable of fighting independently of the union leadership wherever necessary, represented an important development on the strategy of pre-war syndicalism. After the war Murphy, profoundly influenced by the impact of the Bolshevik Revolution in Russia, helped to draw out the full revolutionary implications of the stewards' militant wartime activities, and conceived the workers' committees as embryonic soviets, the institutional form through which the working class could take control of society.

Murphy subsequently made a significant contribution to the formation and early development of British communism. After joining the syndicalist-inclined Socialist Labour Party (SLP) in 1917, he stood as an SLP parliamentary candidate in the general election of 1918, and then helped forge negotiations for the merger of the various small Marxist groups into a united British Communist Party. In 1920 he went as a shop stewards' delegate to the Second Congress of the Communist International in Moscow, where he completely embraced the Bolshevik notion of a revolutionary party capable of leading the working class to power. His abilities were soon recognized by the Russian leaders and, after helping to launch the Red International of Labour Unions, he became a member of the presidium of the executive committee of the Communist International based in Moscow between 1926 and 1928 (during which he was given the 'honour' of moving Trotsky's expulsion from the Comintern). On 18 January 1921 he married Ethel (Molly) Morris (1890–1964), who was a full-time organizer of the Women's Social and Political Union in Sheffield and later a nurse for the wounded Spanish republican soldiers on the civil war battlefront around Madrid. They had one son.

During the 1920s and early 1930s Murphy also served as a leading full-time central committee member of the British Communist Party, with responsibility for the party's industrial activities, and as editor of *Communist Review*. One of the most gifted of his generation of self-educated intellectuals within the leadership of British communism, Murphy made a distinctive theoretical contribution to a number of controversial trade union and political debates in a series of articles for various journals. However, his loyal and unquestioning attachment to the defence of the USSR and the rising Stalinist bureaucracy was to affect profoundly his independent political judgement and distort his revolutionary socialist politics. It led him to support every twist and turn of Stalinist policy inside Britain, including in the late 1920s the adoption of an ultra-left stance, denouncing the Labour Party as 'social fascist'. Ironically, in 1932 Murphy was expelled (after his resignation was ruled 'impermissible') from the Communist Party over his support for a campaign for trade credits to be granted to the USSR, and he became a strong critic of the organization he had helped to construct. After a spell as the general secretary of the Socialist League, a left-wing ginger group inside the Labour Party, he went on to campaign for a 'people's front' alliance against the threat posed by Nazi Germany and in support of the allied effort during the Second World War.

J. T. Murphy died at his home, 4 Broughton Gardens, Highgate, London, of a cerebral haemorrhage on 13 May 1965. His reflections on the crucial period in the history of the British working-class movement in which he played such a prominent role were recorded in *Preparing for Power* (1934) and in his autobiography, *New Horizons* (1941).

RALPH DARLINGTON

Sources R. Darlington, *The political trajectory of J. T. Murphy* (1998) · J. T. Murphy, *New horizons* (1941) · J. Hinton, *The first shop steward movement* (1973) · J. Hinton, 'Introduction', in J. T. Murphy, *Preparing for power* (1972), 11–16 · J. Hinton, 'Introduction', in J. T. Murphy, *The Workers' Committee* (1972), 3–9 · W. Kendall, *The revolutionary movement in Britain, 1900–21* (1969) · L. J. Macfarlane, *The British communist party: its origin and development until 1929* (1966) · People's History Museum, Manchester, J. T. Murphy and Communist Party archives · Russian Centre for the Preservation and Study of Documents of Recent History, Moscow, Comintern archives · M. Murphy, *Suffragette and socialist* (1998) · b. cert. · d. cert. · m. cert.

Archives People's History Museum, Manchester, MSS | People's History Museum, Manchester, Communist Party MSS · Russian Centre for the Preservation and Study of Documents of Recent History, Moscow, Comintern archives

Wealth at death £1536: probate, 17 Aug 1965, *CGPLA Eng. & Wales*

Murphy, Marie-Louise (1737–1814), royal mistress and artist's model, was born in Rouen, France, on 21 October 1737. Of Irish descent, she was the fifth daughter of Daniel Murphy de Boisfailly (*d.* 1753), a shoemaker who had served in the French army, and his wife, Margaret Hickey. The family moved to Paris, where her father died in June 1753 and where her mother traded in second-hand clothes, which implies their poverty. Giovanni Casanova visited two of the Murphy sisters in their filthy lodgings, naming the younger Hélène—who appears in fact to have been Marie-Louise. Her beauty and that of her older sister Victoire captivated the Académie Royale de Peinture. Victoire became the academy's official model and Marie-Louise was expected to succeed her. In 1752 Boucher immortalized Marie-Louise by painting her lying naked on a couch, a work which exposed her to Madame de Pompadour, *maîtresse en titre* of Louis XV (1710–1774). Pompadour feared being replaced, as she may not have had sexual relations with the king for some years. She therefore planned to have Louis introduced to women who would satisfy him sexually, but who would pose no threat to her role as royal confidante. J. L. Soulavie claimed that Pompadour arranged for Boucher to pose Murphy in a painting depicting the holy family, which would hang in the oratory of Marie Leczinska, Louis's pious queen. The roving royal eye thus settled on Marie-Louise, who was spirited off to Versailles in March 1753.

Marie-Louise was the first of several unofficial royal mistresses to be lodged in the Parc-aux-Cerfs, a small house where Louis could visit her discreetly. Though removed from court, 'la petite Morfi' became a focus for intrigue. The marquis d'Argenson, dismissed as foreign minister in 1747, detested Pompadour for her influence and gleefully noted that her disgrace was imminent, because the king was smitten with his younger mistress. Yet Louis never presented Murphy at court and never dismissed Pompadour. On 21 May 1754 Marie-Louise gave birth to his child, who would have been taken away and brought up under an assumed name. During the pregnancy the king took another young woman as his unofficial mistress, possibly Murphy's sister Marie-Brigitte. Marie-Louise was given a dowry, banished from Versailles, and married to Jacques de Beaufranchet d'Ayat (1731–1757) in Paris on 25 November 1755. He was a captain in the Beauvoisis regiment and owned a poor estate at Ayat in the Auvergne, from which he drew a scanty income and where Marie-Louise now lived. One of the witnesses at their wedding was the prince de Soubise, who was Beaufranchet's commander-in-chief when, two years later, on 5 November 1757, he was killed at Rossbach. This brief marriage produced a son, Louis-Charles-Antoine de Beaufranchet, who served as a royal page in 1771 before becoming an infantry officer in 1774. He was later a republican brigadier-general in the Vendée, but was suspended because of his aristocratic background in July 1793. He was granted a pension in 1798 and in 1803 was appointed member of the *corps législatif* for the Puy-de-Dôme. He died in Paris in July 1812.

Shortly after her first husband's death Marie-Louise married François-Nicolas Le Normand (*d.* 1783), a revenue official at Riom. He was later appointed receiver-general for the *vingtième* in Paris, and then treasurer of the *marc d'or*, a tax levied on new appointments and titles. When he died in 1783 she was granted a royal pension of 12,000 livres. At some point during the revolution she lived at Le Havre with her grandchildren, but during the terror she was arrested in Paris as a suspect and held at the Ste Pélagie and then at the English Benedictine convent. On her release she married Louis-Philippe Dumont (1765–1853), deputy for the Calvados in the Convention and, until May 1798, in the Conseil des Cinq-Cents. He was then appointed treasury paymaster in the Calvados, but divorced her in January 1799. Marie-Louise died in Paris on 11 December 1814.

MICHAEL RAPPORT

Sources *Journal et mémoires du marquis d'Argenson*, ed. E. J. B. Rathery, 7–9 (Paris, 1865–7) · E. de Goncourt and J. de Goncourt, *Madame de Pompadour* (1982) · E. Welvert, 'Étude critique de quelques textes relatifs à la vie secrète de Louis XV', *Revue Historique*, 35 (1887), 292–303 · J. G. Alger, *Englishmen in the French Revolution* (1889) · E. de Goncourt and J. de Goncourt, *French XVIII century painters: Watteau, Boucher, Chardin, La Tour, Greuze, Fragonard* (1948) · J. L. Soulavie, *Mémoires historiques et anecdotes de la cour de France, pendant la faveur de la marquise de Pompadour* (1802) · *Mémoires de Jacques Casanova de Seingalt, écrites par lui-même*, 2 (1876), chap. 14 · J. Madival and others, eds., *Archives parlementaires de 1787 à 1860*, 1st ser., 13 (Paris, 1882), 350 · J. Mavidal and others, eds., *Archives parlementaires de 1787 à 1860*, 2nd ser., 5 (Paris, 1865), 189–90 · *Gazette Nationale, ou, Le Moniteur Universel* (7 Aug 1803) · François Boucher,

1703–1770 (1986) [exhibition catalogue, Metropolitan Museum of Art, New York] · *DNB*

Likenesses F. Boucher, oils, 1752 (*La Rêveuse* or *La jeune fille couchée*, also known as *Girl on a couch*, or *The blonde odalisque*), Aeltere Pinakothek, Munich, Germany · F. Boucher, pencil study (for *La Rêveuse*), Heseltine coll., London

Murphy, Michael (*c*.1767–1798), Roman Catholic priest and Irish nationalist, was born in Ballinoulart in co. Wexford, where he received informal education prior to his ordination in 1785. Legally barred from pursuing further Catholic religious studies in Ireland, he attended the Irish College in Bordeaux and from 1792 ministered Ballycanew parish in the diocese of Ferns. In keeping with the instructions of Archbishop John Troy, he voiced opposition to the spread of the seditious United Irishmen in the spring of 1798 and urged his parishioners to surrender their arms and swear the oath of allegiance. Such efforts were clearly insincere given that he and many of his relatives and close associates were prominent members of the organization. James Caulfield, bishop of Ferns, attributed Murphy's militancy during the 1798 rising to 'incapacity and riotous temper' (Furlong, 27) and it may be that poor career prospects strengthened an interest in radical politics gained in France. Murphy went into hiding in early May 1798 and re-emerged as a rebel leader when fighting commenced in northern Wexford on 26 May.

Murphy appeared that day at the rebel/refugee camp on Kilthomas Hill and became one of a few Catholic priests to join the popular cause. He was present when Kilthomas was attacked by the military but rallied the survivors ahead of the rebel capture of Enniscorthy on the 28th. He was then an acknowledged leader, having joined forces with the insurgent army attached to Father John Murphy of Boolavogue (who was not related to him) and Edward Roche of Garrylough. On 1 June he and Anthony Perry commanded a sizeable detachment that was heavily defeated by cavalry on Ballyminaun Hill. Arklow was Murphy's final battle. On 9 June about 15,000 insurgents moved from Gorey to assault the strategic Wicklow port. Command dissension was the probable reason why Murphy remained in Coolgreany during the early stages of the battle, but on learning of a planned withdrawal he went forward to lead the third and final pike charge on the positions of the Durham and Dunbartonshire fencibles. His appearance galvanized the demoralized rebel forces, who were reputedly impressed by his bizarre claim, supported by the display of spent musket balls, that they were invulnerable to the vastly superior British firepower. Murphy was soon felled by grapeshot while carrying a banner proclaiming 'liberty or death' and a general retreat began.

Murphy's fate sparked a minor controversy in the early 1800s arising from allegations that Welsh cavalrymen had eaten his heart and greased their boots with his fat. Such stories were probably inspired by the orders of Lord Mountnorris that Murphy's arm be severed from his partially burnt corpse. The loyalist historian Sir Richard Musgrave added to this confusion in 1801 by publishing an unposted letter said to have been recovered from the priest's body. It claimed that 100,000 rebels would converge on Dublin in the event of victory at Arklow and made sinister reference to revolutionary tribunals. Murphy is commemorated by a substantial memorial unveiled in Arklow in 1903.   RUÁN O'DONNELL

Sources D. Gahan, *The people's rising: Wexford, 1798* (1995) · E. Hay, *History of the insurrection of Wexford* (1803) · R. O'Donnell, *The rebellion in Wicklow, 1798* (1998) · N. Furlong, *Fr. John Murphy of Boolavogue, 1753–1798* (1991) · K. Whelan, 'The Wexford priests in 1798', *Protestant, Catholic and dissenter: the clergy and 1798*, ed. L. Swords (1997) · *DNB*

Murphy, Patrick (1782–1847), predictor of the weather, was probably of Irish Roman Catholic descent. He first came to notice while briefly resident in Rome in 1823–4, when he proposed a scheme to clear the Roman Campagna of miasmata, the supposed source of fever. He presented this scheme to the marquess of Hastings and to various Vatican officials, without more than polite acknowledgement. Murphy crossed the Alps in early 1824 on his way back to London. There he offered a three-part disquisition on meteorology and the cause and the elimination of miasmata by techniques of cultivation to a bookseller, who passed the three sections to individual readers and, receiving favourable reports from two of these, agreed to bear the cost of publication. The third reader then returned the section dealing with the atmosphere, where Murphy had denied the existence of electricity, with a bad report, whereupon the relationship between publisher and author cooled markedly. The paucity of surviving copies of *An Inquiry into the Nature and Causes of Miasmata* (1825) hints at low sales.

Murphy left England in the spring of 1826, possibly to live in Paris, and was next in the public light when he published *Rudiments of the primary forces of gravity, magnetism and electricity in their agency on the heavenly bodies* (1830). Electricity was reinstated, but Murphy's grasp of physics remained tenuous, and was not helped by his dislike of Isaac Newton, whom he relentlessly denigrated, suggesting that most advances in physics and astronomy had occurred either before or after Newton's day. His first edition of *Astronomical Aphorisms* was presented to the Astronomical Society in 1829, who apparently declined to keep it. His later works on the theme of atmosphere and astronomy show the same muddled thinking, not enlivened by their lengthy extracts from popular scientific journals in English and French.

In 1838 Murphy came to prominence with his *Weather Almanac on Scientific Principles*, forecasting the weather day by day through the year. His prediction for 20 January was 'fair, probably lowest degree of winter temperature'. The day turned out to be considerably colder than normal for the time of year. This circumstance raised his celebrity and the shop of his publisher, Whittaker & Co., was besieged with customers. The almanac ran to forty-five editions and the 'prophet' cleared £3000, which he almost immediately lost in an unsuccessful speculation in corn. His success was limited, the predictions for the year being partly right on 168 days and decidedly wrong on 197 days.

Fraser's Magazine of 1838 lambasted 'Murphy, the meteorological quack':

> Mr Murphy knows quite well, that his *Almanac* is another attempt to turn John Bull's love of quackery to a profitable and promising account ... While claiming to have demonstrated the principal laws of movement and temperature by proofs never even supposed by Newton to exist, he nevertheless reveals abysmal understanding of such basic facts as the essential sameness of electricity and magnetism. He stands accused of meteorological Jesuitry, Delphic ambiguity, and equivocation. (*Fraser's Magazine*, 1838, 378)

A harsh judgement, but justified.

Despite his signal lack of success in weather prediction Murphy persevered with his almanacs, and was in the process of bringing out an almanac for 1848 when he died at his lodgings, 108 Dorset Street, off Fleet Street, London, on 1 December 1847. He was buried on 6 December in the upper ground at St Bride's, Fleet Street, the cause of death being recorded as bronchitis. A note in *The Times*, quoting *The Globe*, described him as a disciple of Father Matthew. No will or administration has been found and it is presumed that he died penniless.

G. C. BOASE, rev. ANITA MCCONNELL

Sources GM, 2nd ser., 30 (1848), 443 · N&Q, 7th ser., 1 (1886), 70, 117 · ILN (11 Dec 1847), 383 · Fraser's Magazine, 17 (1838), 378–84 · R. Chambers, ed., *The book of days: a miscellany of popular antiquities in connection with the calendar*, 1 (1863), 137 · The Times (7 Dec 1847), 8a · parish register, London, St Bride's, Fleet Street, 6 Dec 1847, GL, MS 5551/3 [burial] · d. cert.

Murphy, Robert (*bap.* 1807, *d.* 1843), mathematician, was born in Beecher Street, Mallow, in the north of co. Cork, and baptized on 8 March 1807 into the Church of Ireland, in Mallow, the sixth child of seven boys and two girls of John Murphy (*d.* 1814), shoemaker and parish clerk in Mallow, and his wife, Margaret (*d.* 1832). He showed little interest in his father's craft but preferred reading. In 1817 the eleven-year-old was run over by a cart outside his home and he spent eighteen months recuperating from a fractured thigh bone. During convalescence he occupied himself with solving 'cuts' from a Cork almanac where the originality of his submitted solutions caught the attention of Mulcahy, a well-known tutor, who hastened to Mallow to meet the anonymous problem-solver. Amazed to find a boy on crutches, Mulcahy delivered his verdict: 'you have a second Sir Isaac Newton in Mallow: pray look after him' (De Morgan, 337). Murphy was saved from the cobbler's trade and between 1819 and 1823 received a classical education in Mr Hopley's school in Mallow, free of charge.

In 1824 Murphy published a pamphlet refuting John Mackey's published claim that a method for 'duplicating the cube' had been found (a deceptively deep mathematical problem of constructing a cube of twice the volume of a given cube using only the methods of Euclidean geometry). Without sufficient grounding in the classics, Murphy failed to gain entry to Trinity College, Dublin, but Robert Woodhouse, who had dismissed a recommendation that Murphy be accepted at Cambridge, reversed his decision on closer study of Murphy's pamphlet. Murphy was

admitted on 7 July 1825 at Gonville and Caius College; his backers in Mallow had provided money for the first year but subsequently Murphy accepted college loans. In January 1829 he graduated BA as third wrangler in the mathematical tripos, proceeding MA in 1832.

In May 1829 Murphy was elected to a Perse fellowship of Caius; on 4 June 1831 he was ordained deacon in the Church of England (Chichester) and in 1831–3 was junior dean responsible for student discipline. He conducted original research and his Cambridge career seemed assured. However, he soon found himself in financial difficulty, his inability to handle what little money he had being compounded by his natural generosity. One of his first acts on gaining his fellowship was to reimburse Hopley's widow for the education he received in Mallow. Moreover, he acquired 'dissipative habits' which included an appreciation of the college wine cellar, and gambling. Murphy supplemented his meagre income with such unlikely college appointments as Hebrew lecturer (1830–35) and Greek lecturer (1832). On surer ground he was a university examiner in mathematics (1833).

Murphy was a widely respected mathematician. He was a member of the Cambridge Philosophical Society (1830–35) and served on its council (1832, 1835). His early scientific work lay in integral transforms and their application to electrostatics. On a suggestion of William Whewell, Murphy wrote *Elementary Principles of the Theories of Electricity, Heat, and Molecular Actions* (1833), designed for Cambridge students. It contained new material and cited the work of Poisson and Ampère. Murphy recognized the importance of George Green's celebrated '1828 Essay' which was eventually published in *Crelles Journal*. Few writers gave the mathematical theory of electricity so thoroughly and clearly as Murphy, and forty years on William Thomson remarked that Murphy's account still satisfied him.

On 5 June 1834 Murphy was elected to the Royal Society. In the same year he was promoted to a Frankland junior fellowship with an income of £25 per half-year. In July 1835 he hoped to be a candidate for the prestigious Cambridge Plumian chair made vacant by George Biddell Airy's appointment as astronomer royal, but James Challis was elected and Murphy, perhaps seeing his ambition blocked, returned to Ireland in the new year.

Murphy was drawn back to England in October 1836 when he heard that G. J. Pelly White, professor of mathematics at University College, London, had drowned off Sark. He did not know Augustus De Morgan had been appointed to the chair (for the second time). Murphy was reduced to living in cheap lodging houses, earning a scanty living by writing and taking private pupils. De Morgan made arrangements for him to write for the Society for the Diffusion of Useful Knowledge and supply popular articles for Charles Knight's *Penny Cyclopaedia*. In these surroundings, Murphy published two papers in the *Philosophical Transactions of the Royal Society*. In the second he set out the theory of differential operators and delineated the principal ideas in the calculus of operations, including non-commutative ones, a calculus which fuelled Boole's and Cayley's work in invariant theory.

Desperate for money and abandoned by his pupils, Murphy wrote *A Treatise on the Theory of Algebraical Equations* (1839, repr. 1847). It was more than a textbook and after Murphy's death De Morgan inscribed his copy: 'He kept body and soul together while writing it—and, I think, did the same for the subject' (Smith, 4). Murphy maintained his connection with Gonville and Caius and in 1838 was promoted to another junior fellowship (£95 per half-year). He believed his luck had changed when he was appointed as examiner in mathematics and natural philosophy in London University (£200 for sixteen days of examining) in October but his hopes of a senior fellowship at Caius remained illusive.

Murphy is a tragic figure in the history of mathematics. His twenty-two publications on electricity and pure mathematics received attention from contemporaries, and had he led a stable life, and not suffered from his 'illness' (possibly alcoholism), he would surely have taken a leading place in a Cambridge school of mathematics. He died of consumption on 12 March 1843 at 21 East Street, Holborn.

A. J. CRILLY

Sources G. D. Smith, 'Robert Murphy', *History of Mathematics, Monash University*, 31 (July 1984) · L. Creedon, 'The life and work of Robert Murphy', MSc diss., University College, Cork, 1992 · [A. De Morgan], 'Robert Murphy', *Supplement to the Penny Cyclopaedia of the Society for the Diffusion of Useful Knowledge*, 2 (1846), 337–8 · D. M. Cannell, *George Green: mathematician and physicist, 1793–1841* (1993) · J. J. Cross, *Integral theorems in Cambridge mathematical physics, 1830–1855*, ed. P. M. Harman (1985), 112–48 · E. Koppelman, 'The calculus of operations and the rise of abstract algebra', *Archive for History of Exact Sciences*, 8 (1971–2), 155–242 · *Mallow Field Club Journal*, 7 (1989) · Venn, *Alum. Cant.* · J. Venn and others, eds., *Biographical history of Gonville and Caius College*, 2: 1713–1897 (1898) · *Catalogue of scientific papers*, Royal Society, 4 (1870), 554 · R. Murphy, *Refutation of a pamphlet written by the Rev. John Mackey* (1824) · R. Murphy, *A treatise on the theory of algebraical equations* (1839) · D. Barry, 'Robert Murphy: mathematician of true genius', *Mallow Field Club Journal*, 4 (1986)

Archives BL, letters to Charles Babbage, Add. MSS 37186–37201 · UCL, letters to the Society for the Diffusion of Useful Knowledge

Likenesses J. Woodhouse, portrait, repro. in *Gonville and Caius College, Cambridge painted* (c.1828)

Murphy, William (1834–1872), public lecturer, was born at Castletown-Conyers, co. Limerick, Ireland, on 1 August 1834, the eldest son of Michael Murphy, master of the national school at Castletown-Conyers. His family was originally Roman Catholic, but converted to the Church of Ireland during William's boyhood. When this perceived apostasy became public knowledge the family fled to Slangan, near Westport, in co. Mayo, but allegedly continued to be persecuted by Roman Catholics. Murphy was educated at a school in Westport and subsequently trained as a scripture reader at a college in Ballinasloe, co. Galway. During the 1850s he first worked for two years as a scripture reader for the Irish Society and then for seven years for the Irish Church Missions to Roman Catholics, successively in Dublin and in Bandon, co. Cork.

In 1859 Murphy married his wife, Margaret, and in 1860, following her wishes, left the Irish Church Missions to run a boot and shoe shop in Dublin. The business, however, was not a success, and in 1862 he decided to abandon it and move to England to resume his former career as a protestant evangelist. Initially he operated on a freelance basis in Bristol, Cardiff, and Bath, but in 1864 was taken up by the fledgeling Protestant Evangelical Mission and Electoral Union, which supported his work for the remainder of his life.

Between 1864 and 1871 Murphy travelled extensively throughout England, delivering anti-Roman Catholic lectures. His activities extended from Northumberland to Devon, but were concentrated in Lancashire, the west midlands, and the London area. Normally he gave a series of addresses in each district he visited, culminating in an exposé of the confessional, at which he sold copies of *The Confessional Unmasked*, a tract originating in the 1830s and reprinting salacious extracts from Roman Catholic works of moral theology. Murphy was driven by his personal sense of the spiritually and materially oppressive character of Roman Catholicism, and his rhetoric combined crude polemic with evangelical calls to repentance and faith.

Murphy's progress around the country was frequently associated with disturbances, usually initiated by groups of Irish Catholics who sought to silence him. Protestants then retaliated. On a number of occasions, most notably at Birmingham in June 1867—when Park Street was largely demolished— at Ashton under Lyne in May 1868, and also at Stalybridge and Rochdale, full-scale riots resulted. Murphy himself, however, denied that he ever incited others to violence, and pointed out that those who might be offended by what he said need only stay away. Both central and local government agonized over the conflicting demands of free speech and public order, and in April 1869 the Liberal home secretary, Henry Austin Bruce, controversially invoked obsolescent legislation to prevent him from lecturing in Tynemouth. An outraged Murphy demanded a personal interview with the home secretary so 'that I may know on what possible grounds I have been denied liberty and protection' (PRO, HO45/7991, fol. 209). Bruce refused to meet Murphy, and the latter continued publicly to represent himself as a crusader for free speech exposed to the tyranny of mob rule connived at by the authorities. Murphy's supporters erected a large wooden structure in Carr's Lane, Birmingham.

On 20 April 1871, at Whitehaven in Cumberland, Murphy was ambushed before his lecture by a large gang of Irish miners, who severely beat him up and left him for dead. He made a partial recovery, and attempted to resume lecturing in December 1871, but his injuries triggered the chronic pneumonia that led to his death at his home at Providence Place, Lady Pool Lane, Aston, Birmingham, on 12 March 1872. He was survived by his wife. In the eyes of his supporters, who turned out in their thousands for his funeral and interment in the old cemetery, Birmingham, on 18 March, he was a martyr to protestantism and free speech. Others dismissed him as a mere troublesome rabble-rouser, but it was undeniable that his brief and turbulent career starkly and intriguingly exposed the dilemmas raised for the liberal British state by Murphy's repeated claim to have the constitutional right to unrestrained public utterance of sentiments which others found highly offensive.   JOHN WOLFFE

Sources Monthly Record of the Protestant Evangelical Mission and Electoral Union (1871–8) • PRO, HO45/7991 • W. L. Arnstein, Protestant versus Catholic in mid-Victorian England (1982) • D. C. Richter, Riotous Victorians (1981) • J. Wolffe, The protestant crusade in Great Britain, 1829–1860 (1991) • Boase, Mod. Eng. biog. • DNB • The Standard (14 March 1872) • CGPLA Eng. & Wales (1872)
Archives PRO, letters and MSS, HO45/7991
Wealth at death under £600: probate, 2 July 1872, CGPLA Eng. & Wales

Murrant, Sir Ernest Henry (1889–1974), shipping company executive, was born on 15 July 1889 at Brixton, London, the only son of Henry John Murrant (1857–1943), in his later life a self-employed builder, and Minna Augusta Schultz (1852/3–1931). He experienced only a rudimentary education in south London before leaving school at the age of thirteen. On 1 August 1914 he married May (1884–1973), the youngest daughter of John Archer, a tailor, of Belfast. The couple had two children, one of whom, a daughter, died in infancy.

Apart from spells during the two world wars when Ernest Murrant was seconded to government service, he spent his whole working life with the shipping company Furness Withy. He joined the firm in 1902 as an office boy following an introduction secured by his father. His outstanding shorthand skills brought him to the notice of his superiors, and Murrant was soon appointed secretary to Sir Frederick Lewis, who became chairman of Furness Withy in 1919, when the company was reorganized to buy out the Furness family interest. Murrant worked closely with Lewis, not just as his personal secretary, but with executive responsibility for seeing through the chairman's ideas. Murrant was elected a director of Furness Withy in 1924, and deputy chairman in 1935, by which time the firm was an integrated, multinational company, which operated on its own account and controlled a diversified portfolio of assets. Upon the death of Lewis (then Lord Essendon) in 1945, Murrant was appointed chairman.

Murrant's chairmanship was conservative and uncontroversial, as he grappled with the problems facing British shipowners after the Second World War. Furness Withy accumulated substantial reserves, but under Murrant's guiding hand the firm doubled its fleet tonnage by 1959, and opened new routes to replace those lost to foreign competition. His style of leadership was probably that of strong central control, epitomized by Lord Essendon, rather than the decentralized managerial system that became more common in the 1960s. With hindsight it is clear that Murrant may have overlooked crucial business opportunities, though many of the lost chances of British shipping occurred after his retirement, from ill health, in 1959.

Murrant's public career started at the outbreak of the First World War in 1914, when he joined the Board of Trade as a member of the shipping control committee, advising upon the collection and distribution of neutral and captured enemy tonnage to allied owners, for which work he was appointed MBE in 1918. During the Second World War Murrant was appointed by the minister of war transport as special representative in the Near East, responsible for co-ordinating allied tonnage, liaising with friendly governments, and advising the Middle East Supply Centre, services recognized by his appointment as KCMG in 1944. The remainder of Sir Ernest's public career was entirely conventional. He enjoyed many directorships in shipping and the financial services sectors, and was a member of a number of City livery companies. He retained a keen interest in the training and welfare of seamen throughout his life, assuming a number of important voluntary responsibilities for these areas. He was also president of the chamber of shipping (1947–8), and he served on official inquiries into Britain's shipping industry.

To business colleagues Murrant may have appeared somewhat cold, with a ferocious capacity for hard work. To his family he was a devoted husband and kindly father, who in his last years preferred the quiet of home to the bustle of society. His wife's death in 1973 seemed to sap his own will to live, and, after increasing ill health, he died on 29 March 1974, at his home, Browning's Manor, Blackboys, near Uckfield, Sussex. He was cremated at Framfield, near Uckfield. His son, Geoffrey, subsequently became deputy chairman of Furness Withy.

ROBERT G. GREENHILL

Sources R. G. Greenhill, 'Murrant, Sir Ernest Henry', DBB • The Times (30 March 1974) • WWW • CGPLA Eng. & Wales (1974) • The Log [house magazine of Furness Withy] (May–June 1959), 5–11 • private information (2004) [Geoffrey Murrant, son]
Likenesses portrait, Seaman's Hospital, Greenwich, London, Furness Withy group • portrait, Chamber of Shipping, London
Wealth at death £325,278: probate, 23 April 1974, CGPLA Eng. & Wales

Murray family (per. 1768–1967), publishers, was an important book trade dynasty famous for publishing the works of Byron, the Quarterly Review, and Darwin's Origin of Species.

The house of Murray was established in the late eighteenth century by **John Murray** [formerly McMurray; John [i] Murray] (1737–1793), bookseller and publisher, who was born at Edinburgh on 1 January 1737, the only surviving son of Robert McMurray (1698–1768), lawyer, and Jean (bap. 1703, d. 1742), daughter of James Ross of Dundee and Elizabeth Philips. There were three elder daughters, Elizabeth, Janet, and Robina. In 1768 when Murray established himself in business at London he dropped the prefix 'Mc' from his name. He matriculated at Edinburgh University for one term in 1752. In the following year he began a career in the marines that led to a commission in July 1762. Little is known of his service during the Seven Years' War, after which he retired on half pay. On 3 March 1763 he married, at Chatham, Nancy (bap. 1745, d. 1776), daughter of Captain William Weemss and Ann Weber of Brompton, near Chatham. There were no children from the marriage.

Murray's search for gainful employment separated him from his wife and brought him to the north of Scotland to work on the Gordonstoun estate and afterwards to Edinburgh, where job opportunities eluded him. He occupied himself in writing a short novel, 'The History of Sir Launcelot Edgevile', published in the *Court Miscellany*, and a pamphlet on the Edinburgh theatre, but realized that he lacked the talent to pursue a literary career with any chance of success. In the spring of 1766 he returned to England and reluctantly was reinstated in the marines at Chatham.

In October 1768 Murray learned that the well-established London bookselling business of William Sandby at 32 Fleet Street could be bought for £1000. With £700, the sum of his wife's dowry, and the additional funds borrowed from friends, he ventured upon a career about which he knew little or nothing. To the poet William Falconer, who declined to be a partner, he remarked: 'Many blockheads in the trade are making fortunes' (Murray letter-book, 16 Oct 1768). Murray's first publication was the fifth edition of Lyttelton's *Dialogues of the Dead*, a title Sandby had first published in 1760. From his bookshop Murray also sold stationery, and at different times dealt in medicines, lottery tickets, Irish linen, Tassie's gems, beer, wine, and game birds.

The House of Lords decision of 1774 on literary property enabled Murray to exploit the market for reprinting. He produced inexpensive editions of the poems of Thomas Gray in 1776 and James Thomson in 1778, both enhanced with illustrations and critical assessments. He also bought into such large-scale ventures as the *Works of the English Poets*, edited by Samuel Johnson. A legal dispute in 1777 with the Revd William Mason over the copyright in three short poems in the Gray edition led Murray to defend himself in public with *A Letter to W. Mason Concerning ... the Practices of Booksellers*, but in the court of chancery he lost the case.

In 1775 an inheritance of more than £2000, his share of the proceeds from the sale of an Irish estate belonging to his maternal uncle, enabled Murray to expand his business. He had published a dozen titles in 1772, a figure which rose to over forty by 1778 and continued to increase. Murray published about 1000 titles during a twenty-five-year career. More than one-third contain his name alone in the imprint. The others reflect deals he made with traders either in London or in cities such as Edinburgh and Dublin.

Murray published in many fields, but medical and scientific titles account for one-quarter of his output. The names of William Cullen, Gilbert Blane, C. B. Tyre, and James Wood were foremost in his lists. He also published translations of important continental books, such as those by Karl Scheele and Torbern Bergman. The *Medical Commentaries*, a quarterly publication edited by Andrew Duncan, was established by Murray in 1773 and achieved a wide circulation for many years. One of Murray's most ambitious and successful undertakings was his edition of Lavater's *Essays on Physiognomy*, published in forty-one parts and sold by subscription over a period of ten years beginning in 1788. It was a lavish production with hundreds of engravings by the leading artists of the day, including Gillray and Blake.

The real money Murray made from fiction, poetry, and drama came from buying shares with other booksellers and reprinting the works of such writers as Shakespeare, Milton, Defoe, Fielding, Sterne, and Smollett. In the historical line he published several Scottish writers including John Millar, Gilbert Stuart, and Sir David Dalrymple, but it was his regret that a history as popular as those written by Hume, Robertson, or Gibbon eluded him.

As a means of promoting his own publications, and as investments in their own right, Murray involved himself in several periodical publications. The most successful of these was the *English Review*. Edited by Murray himself, it was established in January 1783 and continued monthly until 1797, when it merged with Joseph Johnson's *Analytical Review*. Although essentially a literary journal, Murray included a political article each month that was a cogent summary of national and international affairs. William Godwin wrote this article until Murray dismissed him, and in other departments of the *English Review* Murray employed such men as Thomas Holcroft and Thomas Beddoes.

Whenever an issue arose about which Murray felt strongly, his instinct was to write about it, either in a letter to a newspaper or magazine or in a separate pamphlet. Disputes with authors and other traders occupied his pen, but on other occasions he felt moved to write on such topics as the Hume–Rousseau controversy and the affairs of the East India Company. As well as the *Letter to W. Mason* (2nd edn, 1788), he wrote three separate publications: *A Letter ... Occasioned by the late Theatrical Disturbances* (1766); *An Author's Conduct to the Public, Stated in the Behaviour of Dr. William Cullen* (1784); and the *Defence of Innes Munro* (1790).

During his marriage to Nancy Weemss, Murray fathered a child with another woman. He supported this boy, named Archibald, and later established him in a career at sea. Murray's wife died of consumption in September 1776, and on 23 February 1778 he married her younger sister Hester Weemss (*bap.* 1746, *d.* 1815), who had lived with the Murrays in London at different times. With Hester he had seven children, three of whom survived to maturity. The first, John [ii] [*see below*], who carried on the business, arrived just nine months after their marriage. A daughter, Jane, followed in 1780 and another girl, Mary Anne, was born in 1787. In May 1782 Murray suffered a life-threatening stroke. Since his days in the marines, evenings of sometimes excessive drinking in such London establishments as the Peacock Tavern in Gray's Inn Lane and at Munday's Coffee House had taken a physical toll. However, he regained his health and by heeding this warning lived ten further years.

Murray died on 6 November 1793 after an illness of several months. He was buried across the street from his shop at St Dunstan-in-the-West. Under the name of his widow, Hester, the business was run by Murray's long-serving shop assistant, Samuel Highley. Hester Murray is listed in several imprints in 1794 and 1795, but she published little of consequence. At his death Murray's estate was valued at more than £12,000, but a legal dispute with his partners in Lavater's *Essays on Physiognomy* reduced this figure by nearly £4000. His correspondence and other papers are preserved in the firm's archive.

John Samuel Murray [John [ii] Murray] (1778–1843), publisher, was born on 27 November 1778 at 32 Fleet Street, London, the eldest and only surviving legitimate son of John [i] Murray and his second wife, Hester. He was educated at private schools in Cobham, Uxbridge, Edinburgh, Margate, Gosport, and finally in Kennington, London. While at Gosport Murray lost the sight in his right eye when it was accidentally pierced by his writing master's penknife. During visits home he was put to work in the bookshop.

When his father died in November 1793 Murray, who was not quite fifteen, was apprenticed to Samuel Highley, his father's assistant, and an agreement was drawn up by which Murray, when he came of age in 1799, would become a full partner of Highley. Under this arrangement the business continued along much the same lines as under its founder, focusing primarily on medical works. Murray became free of the Stationers' Company on 2 December 1800, and was immediately cloathed in the livery. By this time the firm of Murray and Highley had amassed over £2300 in capital stock, shares, and copyrights. However, the two partners 'disagreed on too many important matters to work together effectively or live happily in the same house' (Zachs, 248). On 24 March 1803, following arbitration, they formally separated, Highley establishing himself as a medical publisher a few doors down at 24 Fleet Street.

Murray's first publication of importance after the dissolution of the partnership was *The Revolutionary Plutarch*, which was warmly received. In 1805 an old family friend, Mrs Maria Eliza Rundell, offered him a collection of recipes which he published as *A New System of Domestic Cookery*. It was an immediate success. Although Mrs Rundell originally had regarded the work as a 'free gift' to Murray (Smiles, 2.121), its copyright became a bone of contention unresolved until 1823, when Murray paid her £2000.

In 1803 Murray began a correspondence with the Edinburgh publisher Archibald Constable. Soon afterwards a close working relationship developed, and Murray took over from Longmans the London agency of Constable's publications, including the *Edinburgh Review*. When Constable offered Walter Scott £1000 for the copyright of *Marmion*, a quarter share was offered to William Miller of 50 Albemarle Street (to where Murray moved in 1812) and the other quarter to Murray, which he took up. However, the business relationship between Murray and Constable began to sour over financial matters and finally broke off in 1813.

In February 1809 Murray launched the *Quarterly Review*, a tory counterblast to Constable's *Edinburgh Review*, with William Gifford as its first editor and Walter Scott as an adviser and supporter. Because Gifford was an unbusinesslike editor, and the publication of the *Quarterly* was often delayed, it was several years before it succeeded. One of the most influential journals of the age, it did not cease publication until 1967. Among the important early contributors were John Wilson Croker, John Barrow, and Robert Southey. Gifford resigned in 1824 and was succeeded briefly by John Taylor Coleridge. J. G. Lockhart, Scott's son-in-law, then took up the editorship. Murray's attempt at a daily newspaper in 1825, *The Representative*, was a costly failure. Young Benjamin Disraeli, the editor, persuaded him to take a half share, but competition was too great, and debts forced Murray to sell his recently acquired house in Whitehall Place. The coolness that this caused in Murray's long-standing family friendship with Isaac D'Israeli was soon repaired.

During visits to Edinburgh, Murray courted Anne (1782–1845), daughter of the late Charles Elliot, the Scottish bookseller with whom his father had done much business. They were married in Edinburgh on 6 March 1807, and their son John [iii] [*see below*] was born in London on 16 April 1808, the first of five children.

Murray's move to 50 Albemarle Street in June 1812 placed him at the centre of London literary life. He purchased the early eighteenth-century house from William Miller for just under £4000, pledging his copyright in Rundell's *Domestic Cookery* and Scott's *Marmion* until the purchase was paid off in 1821. The elegant drawing room became a meeting place for many of the chief literary and political figures of the day, among them Thomas Moore, George Crabbe, Robert Southey, Madame de Staël, George Canning, and Benjamin Disraeli. It was there on 7 April 1815 that Lord Byron and Walter Scott first met.

No author is more closely associated with the house of Murray than Byron. On his return to England in July 1811 the poet gave the first two cantos of *Childe Harold's Pilgrimage* to Robert Charles Dallas, who was duly impressed and offered them without success to the publisher William Miller. He then took the manuscript to Murray, who paid Dallas £500 for the copyright and published the poem in March 1812. In the wake of *Childe Harold*'s success, a warm relationship developed between poet and publisher. Byron's best-known works appeared under the firm's imprint, and Murray, who paid out more than £15,000 for Byron's copyrights, prospered from the sale of his works. In July 1819 he published with some trepidation the first two cantos of *Don Juan*, and with considerably more, cantos 3–5 in August 1821. Thereafter Murray refused to have anything further to do with the poem. With the breakdown of Byron's marriage in 1816 and his (self-) exile in Italy, their friendship was sustained in a correspondence that is one of the most lively and revealing of the period (*Byron's Letters and Journals*, ed. L. Marchand, 1973–94). However, this friendship collapsed in 1822 over Murray's editing (on the advice of Gifford and Croker) of Byron's poetry and his careless handling of the text. Nor were matters helped by Byron's increasing outspokenness, Murray's concern with his own rising reputation, and the difficulty in resolving differences at a distance.

In 1820 Moore was offered 2000 guineas by Murray for Byron's memoir, which the poet had given him on the condition that it was not published in his lifetime. Gifford advised the publisher that some of it was unfit for publication, and after Byron's death a meeting was held on 17 May 1824 at Albemarle Street at which, after heated discussion, it was reluctantly agreed to burn the manuscript. Those present were Murray, his son John, Moore, John Cam Hobhouse, and representatives of Lady Byron and Augusta Leigh.

Murray's range of publications was very wide. His judgement, supported by the recommendations of his distinguished literary advisers, was usually good. In addition to the *Quarterly Review*, Murray issued the *Journal of Arts* for the Royal Institution, and from 1813 the *Navy List*, describing himself as 'Bookseller to the Admiralty'. Murray's Family Library, published between 1829 and 1834, was a venture in producing cheaper books for a wider reading public. This series of almost fifty volumes, priced at 5s. each, largely contained new works rather than reprints.

Among the better-known poets and playwrights in Murray's lists were Crabbe (to whom he was very generous), Coleridge, Gally Knight, Fanny Kemble, and Felicia Hemans. Among scientists he published Humphry Davy, Michael Faraday, Charles Babbage, Roderick Murchison, Mary Somerville, and Charles Lyell, whose *Principles of Geology* (1830) was in print for most of the century and who introduced Charles Darwin to Murray. Among political economists Murray published Thomas Malthus, David Ricardo, and John Austin, whose brilliant wife, Sarah, translated many works from the German for Murray.

Another popular speciality of the firm was travel literature. Murray published books on Africa by Mungo Park, John Lewis Burckhardt, and Dixon Denham and Hugh Clapperton. In the field of polar exploration Sir John Barrow and Sir John Franklin were Murray authors. He also published Sir Gardner Wilkinson on ancient Egypt, William Martin Leake on Morea, T. Stamford Raffles on Java, and Elizabeth Rigby (Lady Eastlake) on Russia. Mariana Starke's *Travels on the Continent*, first published in 1820, was a precursor to the popular Murray Handbook series later developed by John [iii] Murray. Murray also published the travel writings of Mrs Maria Graham (Lady Callcott), better known for her enduring *Little Arthur's History of England*.

In 1814 Murray published Jane Austen's *Emma* and the second edition of *Mansfield Park* for the author, charging her his commission of 10 per cent. On the same terms he issued *Northanger Abbey* and *Persuasion* posthumously. He brought out Madame de Staël's *De l'Allemagne* at great speed in 1813, commissioning at least seven printers for the English and French three-volume sets. The novels of the indomitable Frances Trollope were also published by Murray, and it was with his influence that her son Anthony obtained employment with the Post Office.

Murray issued several part-publications, in which illustrations were an important element. For these he engaged such well-known artists as J. M. W. Turner, A. W. Callcott, Charles Barry, and the engravers William and Edward

Finden on several projects. A number of these illustrated books—notably beginning in 1819 with James Hakewill's *Picturesque Tour of Italy*, and continuing with the popular *Landscape Illustrations* of Byron and of the Bible—were issued in parts in very large numbers.

The extensive record Murray left of his career as a publisher—correspondence, ledgers, daybooks, subscription books, records of trade dinners—shows him businesslike and systematic in his dealings with authors, employees, and other traders. Such was his success 'that he is sometimes mistakenly credited with having established the house' (Zachs, 1). Murray was a founder member of the Athenaeum Club. He died on 27 June 1843, leaving all his property, including his profitable share in the Stationers' Company English stock, to his wife, Anne, who died two years later. He was buried in Kensal Green cemetery, London.

John Murray [John [iii] Murray] (1808–1892), publisher, was born on 16 April 1808 at 32 Fleet Street, London, the eldest of the five children of John [ii] Murray and his wife, Anne. From 1819 to 1826 he was educated at Charterhouse School. In 1827 he spent a year at Edinburgh University, where his chief study was of geology and mineralogy. He also explored much of Scotland, making careful notes of features of interest and setting a pattern for future travels.

In the following year Murray embarked on his career in the family publishing house at 50 Albemarle Street, London. Visits to the continent from 1829 prepared the way for his first major publishing initiative. Struck by the difficulty of obtaining the kind of information he wanted, he filled notebooks with history, architecture, geology, and practical details. On his return he arranged his material along routes and compiled general accounts of the countries concerned, leading to the highly successful series of Murray 'handbooks'. Before the project outgrew the capacities of one man, he prepared three handbooks himself, dealing with the Netherlands, Belgium, Germany, and Switzerland; another, on France, followed later. The series was launched in 1836, at an auspicious time when railways were beginning to open up new possibilities for travel. Within fifteen years these red handbooks covered nearly the whole of the continent. Karl Baedeker, in producing his own guides, acknowledged his debt to the Murray model.

The handbooks fitted well with the publishing policy that developed during Murray's early years with the firm. His father, chastened by memories of financial setbacks in the 1820s, cast an increasingly jaundiced eye on verse and fiction and chose to opt out of that volatile if expanding market. This disposition was shared by the son: he had met Byron, Scott, and Goethe, but cared little for novels (other than Scott's) or poetry. Physically, too, his field of vision had long been constricted, and Lord Ernle described him as having 'the most strained and tired-looking eyes' he had ever seen (Paston, xiii). This did not prevent him grappling diligently with manuscripts and small print. He was a less adventurous man of business than his father had been in his heyday, but more methodical. Though initially kept in the background, he conducted most of the office correspondence and played a leading role as his father's health failed. On becoming head of the firm in June 1843 he found that his father's will left all property to his mother, putting him in the position of having to buy the business back from her and pay annual interest in the mean time. He felt obliged to postpone thoughts of marriage, and only after his mother's death did he propose to Marion Smith (1815–1893), an Edinburgh banker's daughter whom he had known for many years. They married on 6 July 1847; 50 Albemarle Street remained his home. Two daughters and two sons survived to maturity. In due course the sons, John [iv] [*see below*] and Hallam, joined their father and his cousin Robert Cooke as partners in the firm. In 1851, out of profits from the handbooks, Murray bought 4 acres at Wimbledon on which he built a house. He named it Newstead after Byron's Newstead Abbey, and endowed it with a fine library. From then on the family spent the summer months there. Both at Albemarle Street and in Wimbledon the Murrays entertained frequently, bringing together well-known people from a variety of backgrounds, regardless of whether they had any business connection with the firm.

What Murray did inherit from his father was high standing in the publishing world, a select back list, and a considerable number of distinguished friends and authors who were staunch supporters, such as Henry Hallam, Dean Milman, Sir Charles Lyell, Sir John Barrow, and Lord Mahon (later Earl Stanhope), while J. G. Lockhart and John Wilson Croker continued to act as pillars of the *Quarterly Review*. Murray's accession brought no major policy changes. Travel, history, biography, and memoirs remained the staple of the business. Nor did the *Quarterly*'s politics change, although its tone became less partisan after Croker's retirement. When Gladstone complained in 1868 about some rough handling in its pages, Murray reminded his friend that it was not the *Quarterly* that had changed over the decades, for it 'continues doggedly to its old Conservative principles' (Paston, 208). One project did offer an immediate opportunity to signalize the change of management in 1843. This was the idea, discussed in only general terms before his father's death, of a cheap series aimed in part but not wholly at colonial customers, to take advantage of the 1842 Copyright Act's provisions against foreign piracy of British copyright works. Three months after Murray's accession, his Colonial and Home Library made a scrambled début with a new edition of George Borrow's *The Bible in Spain* as its flagship title. Colonial sales failed to live up to expectations, but home demand was sufficient to ensure that the series survived for some sixty years, although in an attenuated form.

The solid Murray reputation attracted a continuing flow of manuscripts. Much of the routine of assessing and retouching new material fell to one or other of Murray's readers or literary advisers. Since 1841 Frances Trollope's brother Henry Milton had acted in that capacity; he was succeeded in 1850 by his son John (later Sir John Milton).

The firm's concentration on non-fiction meant that certain types of manuscript were shut out almost automatically. The survivors had to circumvent a number of other pitfalls. Murray was a loyal, old-fashioned churchman, and would have nothing to do with irreligion or anything that appeared offensive to morals or good taste. He refused Kinglake's *Eothen* because of its 'wicked spirit of jesting at everything' (CUL, Add. 7633.4, 1844) and Harriet Martineau's *Eastern Life: Present and Past* because it was 'a work of infidel tendency' (Murray letter-book, 29 Feb 1848). When published elsewhere, both succeeded, and stirred no outcry. Murray was also a stickler for authenticity. Herman Melville, whose *Typee* and *Omoo* he published, was one travel writer who was pressed for evidence that he had actually experienced all he described, and was dropped after he appeared to stray into the world of romance. On the other hand, Murray, once convinced, was quick to spring to the defence of an author such as Paul Du Chaillu, whose stories of gorillas in his *Explorations in Central Africa* were initially scoffed at by disbelievers.

The 1840s had seen an infusion of new attitudes into British publishing, but Murray was conservative in business. He won only hollow victories from litigation against those who ignored his claim to copyright in certain American authors, an area shrouded in legal confusion. He was a strong upholder of retail price maintenance, until that was overthrown in 1852 by an arbitration decision (none the sweeter for coming from three Murray authors led by Lord Campbell). His response to new developments sometimes seemed improvised, as with Murray's Railway Reading, consisting mostly of reprinted works issued irregularly from 1851 and varying in size, price, and binding.

None the less, Murray achieved considerable success in the firm's chosen niche, aided by his authors' recognition of fair dealing. Among those he enlisted were George Melville, Charles Darwin, Lord Campbell, A. H. Layard, Robert Curzon, John Motley, Samuel Smiles, David Livingstone, George Grote, Isabella Bird, Paul Belloni Du Chaillu, Dean Arthur Stanley, and Heinrich Schliemann—a spread of names typical of the areas in which Murray's commercial and personal interests lay. In November 1859 he managed to put two best-sellers on sale on the same day, one being Darwin's *Origin of Species*, perhaps the most momentous book of the century, and the other Samuel Smiles's *Self-Help*, synonymous with the Victorian social ethic. A number of these authors, alongside other notable writers, also appeared in the pages of the *Quarterly Review*, edited by Lockhart until Whitwell Elwin took over in 1853. Another stalwart of Albemarle Street, William Smith, combined editing the *Quarterly* from 1867 to 1893 with maintaining his remarkable array of dictionaries, in which Murray invested much capital.

Publishing an author like Darwin was scarcely undertaken in a crusading spirit. The manuscript of *The Origin of Species* left Murray perplexed and sceptical, but he prudently suppressed his doubts and forged a relationship with Darwin that was profitable to both. Lyell's *Principles of Geology*, published by his father in Murray's early days with the firm, and popular ever since, had laid some of the foundations on which Darwin built. Geology was Murray's favourite hobby, but it was also one of the most strife-ridden sciences of his day. Concerned to leave geological room for an act of creation, he wrote his *Scepticism in Geology* to counteract Lyell's concept of a world slowly and constantly changing, and issued it under a pseudonym (Verifier) in 1877.

Apart from the *Quarterly Review*, which long outlived him, Murray's experience with periodicals was disappointing. In 1869 he provided the capital for a new literary monthly, *The Academy*, but could not persuade its editor, Charles Appleton, to lighten its severely scholarly tone. Murray withdrew from the venture within a year, but did not abandon the idea of having his own monthly. When *Murray's Magazine* appeared in January 1887, he made sure it was pitched at a more accessible level; and, as serialization had become a standard part of the magazine formula, the house ban on fiction was suddenly breached. In 1887 Murray took over, from Blackwoods, Emily Lawless's Irish novel *Hurrish*, and used her next novel, *Major Lawrence, F.L.S.*, as the opening serial in the new magazine. Five more followed from other authors, but before the fifth had run its course the magazine closed in December 1891.

Throughout his life one of Murray's chief pleasures was foreign travel, and one of his great restoratives was walking. He was elected a member of the Alpine Club in 1858. A man of robust constitution, he never formally retired from active publishing, but when he was eighty-three his health began seriously to decline. He died at 50 Albemarle Street on 2 April 1892 and was buried on 6 April at St Mary's Church, Wimbledon. He lacked the panache of his father in his glory days, but Elizabeth Rigby's assessment at the time of his father's death proved accurate: 'in all that concerns the stability of the great publishing-house, his son is quite fitted to take his place' (Paston, 38).

Sir John Murray [John [iv] Murray] (1851–1928), publisher, was born at 50 Albemarle Street, London, on 18 December 1851, the eldest son of the five children of John [iii] Murray and his wife, Marion. His childhood was spent largely at the family home, Newstead.

Murray was sent to Eton College, and in 1870 he entered Magdalen College, Oxford. His father, anxious that his son should lose no time in joining the firm, allowed him only two years at university. He prized the lifelong friendships he had made at Oxford and always maintained that his presidency of the Magdalen junior common room taught him to run a business. For the next twenty years he learned the trade, initially as his father's assistant and then spending time in each department. During his training he helped to edit the *Quarterly Review* and worked on revisions of the handbooks to London and Scotland. He became a partner in 1878.

On 4 March 1878 Murray married Katherine Evelyn (Evie) (*d.* 1938) of Warthill, Aberdeenshire, fourth daughter of William Leslie, sometime MP for Aberdeenshire, and his wife, Matilda. This prompted the comment that the Murrays always returned to Scotland for their wives.

They had one son, John [v] [*see below*], and two daughters, Amy Marion and Dorothy Evelyn. Mrs Murray was often ill with a depressive nervous condition.

Murray's younger brother, Alexander Henry Hallam Murray (1854–1934), known as Hallam, joined the firm in 1876 and became a partner in 1884. He was educated at Eton College, at Gonville and Caius College, Cambridge, and afterwards at the Slade School of Fine Art. A very accomplished landscape and architectural watercolour painter, and an admirer of Ruskin, he exhibited at the Royal Academy in 1884 and thereafter. In 1885 he married Alicia Maria Du Cane (1861–1947) and settled at Sandling, Hythe, in Kent.

Upon the death of John [iii] Murray in April 1892, John [iv] Murray inherited five-eighths of the business and the Albemarle Street property, while the remaining three-eighths, together with Newstead, went to Hallam. As a publisher Hallam's strengths lay largely in the decisions relating to typography, paper, printing, illustration, and binding. He became responsible for the production of the Handbooks for Travellers, and he himself travelled extensively in Europe, often to Fiesole, where he had a large circle of friends. He also ventured to India, Australia, and north Africa. Hallam is seen at his best in writing, illustrating, and publishing *The High Road of Empire* (1905) and in illustrating H. W. Nevinson's *Sketches on the Old Road through France to Florence* (1904).

John [iv] Murray's chief personal service to literature was to edit the six original manuscript versions of the historian Edward Gibbon's *Autobiography* (1896). He was a founder of the Publishers' Association, becoming president in 1899, and in that year played a leading part in setting up the net book agreement. The Copyright Act of 1911 was drafted largely at 50 Albemarle Street. Following family tradition, Murray was a staunch Anglican and tory. He was a member of the board of the Great Ormond Street Hospital for Sick Children for forty-two years and on the committee of the Athenaeum Club, where it was said that if his boots were left outside his door they would walk on their own to the club and then up the stairs to the billiard room. He was also a member of the Roxburghe Club.

In 1898 Murray published the first of a six-volume edition of Byron's letters and journals, edited by the poet's grandson Lord Lovelace. By this time the Murrays, who had been collecting manuscript material since Byron's death, had come to regard the poet as their own property. Lovelace withdrew from the editorship part way through publication having refused permission to print controversial letters relating to the causes of Byron's marital troubles. The Murrays had a right to publish but continued the series without the contentious correspondence. Lovelace published a defence of his grandmother in a book entitled *Astarte* (1905) and the Murrays replied with *Lord Byron and his Detractors* (1906).

In 1900 the firm resumed publishing fiction. One of the first titles, Laurence Housman's *An English-woman's Love Letters*, became one of the most popular novels of the time, backed by an uncharacteristically aggressive advertising campaign. The Handbooks for Travellers were sold to Stanfords in 1901 (save for India and Japan), the preparation of such guidebooks having become too specialized for a general publisher. Stanfords immediately regretted their bargain but were held to the contract. The *Monthly Review*, under the editorship of Sir Henry Newbolt, restarted in 1900 and was of good literary quality, but was abandoned in 1907. A more successful venture was the Wisdom of the East series, which began in 1905, having been initiated the year before by the Orient Press. Edited by Cranmer Byng (both father and son), it ran to 122 booklets at 5s. each and continued until the 1950s.

In the early 1900s the firm was becoming well known as publishers to the establishment, and that reputation was confirmed by the eagerly awaited appearance of the *Letters of Queen Victoria* (1907–32). Murray was more proud of this title than any other, as no private correspondence of a sovereign had been published in modern times. However, in 1906 *The Times* attacked the Murrays for declining to make the first series of the correspondence available cheaply to the Times Book Club (which would have been in breach of the net book agreement). John and Hallam sued, and in May 1908 the jury awarded them a substantial £7500 in damages.

Late in 1908 there was a serious dispute between the brothers, and Hallam resigned from the partnership. The cause was kept secret even in the family, and files for this period were destroyed. The probable cause for the rift was Murray's proposed introduction of his 24-year-old son, John, into a full partnership. Long-standing difficulties with Hallam's wife, Alicia, who believed her husband to be undervalued, exacerbated the situation. An undisclosed financial settlement was reached, and Hallam left the firm, taking with him in addition some Byron manuscripts, literary portraits, and books. Hallam lived for another twenty-six years at Hythe in Kent, friendly but no longer intimate with his brother.

The only significant event of the war years was the daring acquisition for £18,000 of the house of Smith Elder after the death of Reginald Smith in December 1916. There were long-established family and business ties between the Smiths and Murrays. Indeed, the original Smith started his career at Albemarle Street in 1814. Murray knew that the copyrights of Smith's prominent writers would provide the next generation with financial security. It turned out to be an acquisition of singular importance.

In 1919 John [iv] Murray wrote a dutiful but rather dull biography of his father. The sixth and final volume of Byron's *Letters and Journals* appeared in 1922, and the centenary of the poet's death in 1924 brought Murray both an honorary degree from the University of Athens and the order of the Redeemer (of Greece). His knighthood (KCVO) came in 1926 during the publication of the second series of the *Letters of Queen Victoria*. Murray's last, rather surprising, publishing venture was in progress when he died, *The Story of San Michele* (1929) by Alex Munthe, a Murray author since 1887. No one could have foretold that this curious book would sell over a million copies in Britain alone. It was translated into thirty-seven languages and remained

in the firm's catalogue for nearly fifty years. On 30 November 1928 Sir John [iv] Murray died at 7 Wilbury Road, Hove, Sussex, of blood poisoning. He was buried at Wargrave, Berkshire, the home of his daughter Dorothy.

Sir John Murray [John [v] Murray] (1884–1967), publisher, was born on 12 June 1884, the only son of Sir John [iv] Murray and his wife, Katherine Evelyn. Known as Jack, he had two younger sisters. Like his father, he was educated at Eton College and Magdalen College, Oxford, where he gained a degree in modern history in 1905. In the following year he went on a world tour before entering the family business, becoming a partner in 1909. He was the last editor of the long-established *Quarterly Review*.

At the beginning of the 1914–18 war Murray, then serving as high sheriff of the county of London, joined his regiment, the Scottish horse. He rose to the rank of lieutenant colonel, serving in Egypt, at Gallipoli, and in France. His regiment was subsumed into the Black Watch, but he later transferred to the Royal Scots, and commanded their 12th battalion. In 1918 he was made DSO for personal bravery and awarded a Croix de Guerre (Belgium). On 16 August 1916 he married Lady Helen de Vere (1892–1971), the fifth and youngest daughter of the first Earl Brassey. There were no children of the marriage.

At the end of the war Murray, despite relatively little knowledge of the trade, was confirmed in an equal partnership with his father. His abilities were first harnessed to the tasks of integrating the newly acquired Smith Elder business, editing the *Cornhill Magazine*, and publishing the third series of the *Letters of Queen Victoria*. Upon the publication of the ninth and final volume of this correspondence in 1932—four years after his father's death—Murray was created KCVO. An administrator by nature, he worked from dawn to dusk, but discovered few if any best-selling authors for the firm during the 1930s and 1940s. Moderate profits were achieved by publishing past successes in cheaper editions, the well established schoolbook list, new books from authors inherited from both his father and Smith Elder, dull memoirs of politicians, military men, and aristocrats, travel books, and works on nineteenth-century history, a field in which Murray had a detailed knowledge.

Murray could write a review at short notice and correct an index with fastidious accuracy. He took pride in knowing the pedigree of every important British family. Like his father, he was a member of the Church of England and a staunch tory, serving for a time on the Westminster city council. He was also a long-standing member of the Roxburghe Club and a life member of the Athenaeum Club. He was a trustee of the Westminster Hospital and treasurer of the Friends of Great Ormond Street Hospital, where there was a John Murray ward. In later years he was chairman of the Deafened Ex-servicemen's Fund and suffered himself from increasing deafness, a handicap 'which was so cruelly in conflict with his natural gaity and wit' (speech of John [vi] Murray at the firm's 200th anniversary dinner in 1968, Murray archive). Murray would tell anyone he thought verbose to 'come back when you have less time' (private information). Throughout his life he refused to own a car.

Murray's nephew, John Grey Murray (John [vi]), known as Jock [*see below*], entered the firm in 1931. When he returned from service after the war his Uncle Jack is said to have greeted him with the reassuring words: 'It's all right, Jock, I haven't taken on any new manuscripts in your absence' (private information). For nearly thirty years the two very different men directed affairs from Albemarle Street, but it was Jock Murray who brought in the many best-selling books published after the war. There were times when the traditions of the past clashed with the need to modernize. In 1951, with great reluctance, John [v] accepted that it was necessary for the business to change from being a partnership, and it became a limited company.

Sir John [v] Murray died at his home, Flat 5, 49 Lowndes Square, London, on 6 October 1967 after one day's illness. At this time the firm employed about eighty people and published a similar number of books annually.

John Arnaud Robin Grey [Jock] **Murray** [John [vi] Murray] (1909–1993), publisher, was born on 22 September 1909 at Woodside, Wargrave, Berkshire, the eldest son of Thomas Robinson Grey (1861–1945), a barrister who was later employed in the accounts department at the firm, and Dorothy Evelyn (1881–1958), the daughter of Sir John [iv] Murray. He had an elder sister, Evelyn Marion. By deed poll in 1930 he added 'Murray' to his name. In the words of his son, John [vii] Murray: 'The Grey line brought to the house flair and a new natural instinct for publishing'.

John [vi] was also educated at Eton College and at Magdalen College, Oxford, where in 1928 he met John Betjeman and Osbert Lancaster, who became lifelong friends as well as his authors. From an early age he was groomed to enter the firm and succeed his uncle. He was fond of recalling a youthful encounter with Conan Doyle on the stairs at Albemarle Street: 'If this is an author', he said to himself, 'what fun to be a publisher' (private information). His boyhood stammer was cured by Lionel Logue, who subsequently helped George VI.

Murray entered the firm in 1931 and became a salaried partner in 1933. It was from Leonard Huxley that he first learned the art of dealing with authors. 'A contributor to the *Cornhill* told me that he preferred a letter of rejection from Dr. Huxley to one of acceptance from any other editor' (*A Poet and his Publisher*). Jock Murray himself later told an author: 'Like a diamond your work will sparkle if cut' (private information). In the early 1930s he assisted with the editing of the *Quarterly Review* and the *Cornhill Magazine*. After the war the *Cornhill* was relaunched by Peter Quennell and continued under Murray's editorship until 1975, when it ceased publication.

Murray married Diana Mary Ramsden James (*b*. 1911) on 29 March 1939. They had four children, including a son, John Richmond Murray (John [vii]) born in 1941. During the Second World War Murray served for five years in the Royal Artillery, attaining the rank of major. For his role in organizing air transport for Arnhem he was made MBE in 1945. During the war Noel Carrington took Murray's place as a literary adviser.

A group of leading authors was not only published by Murray but also became his closest friends: Freya Stark, Osbert Lancaster, and John Piper were godparents to his children. To Murray a close friendship with his authors was an essential part of publishing and won him loyalty that became the envy of other publishers with the arrival of 'chequebook' publishing in the 1970s. The steady flow of popular authors to the Murray list only increased with the publication of John Betjeman's *Continual Dew* in 1937, a group collaboration involving Piper and Lancaster, with a jacket by McKnight-Kauffer. Thereafter Murray published most of Betjeman's work.

Kenneth Clark's association with the firm began in 1949 with the publication of *Landscape into Art*. It continued with *The Nude* in 1956, a reprint of *The Gothic Revival* six years later, and was capped with Clark's best-selling *Civilisation*, published jointly with the BBC to complement the 1969 television series. 'Clark's gift for connecting vivid narrative with visual explanation owes much to Jock's ability to fit text and pictures together seamlessly' (Barker, preface). For Freya Stark, author of the *Valley of the Assassins* and *Baghdad Sketches*, Murray would go to extraordinary lengths to supply whatever she needed, wherever she was. One of the more unusual items was a hip-bath sent to Stark in Yemen. Other notable authors published by Murray included C. Northcote Parkinson, Sir Arthur Grimble, Walter Starkie, Iris Origo, Patrick Leigh Fermor, Dervla Murphy, Leslie Marchand, Doris Langley Moore, and Ruth Prawer Jhabvala.

The typography, illustration, and production of books from the 1950s, 1960s, and 1970s gave the firm's imprint a distinctive look that was largely the vision of Jock Murray. Artists such as John Piper and Reynolds Stone were important contributors and advisers. Special editions of publications were often produced, typically bound in half buckram with Cockerell marbled paper.

Less glamorous but of increasing importance during Jock Murray's tenure was the development of the long-standing educational list, which became the financial backbone of the house. D. G. McKean's O level *Introduction to Biology*, with its large format and clarity of illustration, was a landmark in publishing, selling 5 million copies in eight languages. The Success Studybooks helped satisfy the fast-expanding need for self-teaching texts. Under the direction of Kenneth Pinnock the turnover of the Murray education department increased by over 100 per cent in the 1970s and 1980s, by which time more than half the firm's business was in educational and scientific titles.

Murray himself made an important personal contribution to Byron scholarship. He traced this passion not only to the modernity of the poet's words but to the need to expiate the guilt he felt for his ancestor (John [ii] Murray) burning the poet's memoirs. Initially he assisted Peter Quennell with *Byron: a Self-portrait* (1950), and for nearly ten years he collaborated with Leslie Marchand to produce the much-praised edition of Byron's *Letters and Journals* (1973–94). He also worked closely with Doris Langley

Moore, author of *The late Lord Byron* (1961), *Lord Byron Accounts Rendered* (1974), and *Ada Countess of Lovelace* (1977). Such was his obsession for Byron that there was nowhere, however distant, he would not travel in search of an unpublished letter. His Byron knowledge was prodigious, he knew all the great Byron scholars, and had worked closely with many of them including, as a young man in the 1930s, T. J. Wise, the great bibliophile and forger, helping him compile his Ashley Library catalogue.

In 1975 Murray was created CBE for services to literature. He was an engaging raconteur and humorous public speaker. Middling in height, thin, and energetic, with longish hair, he sported a characteristic bow-tie and a colourful set of braces. An expressive pair of raised eyebrows and the signature exclamation 'Extraooordinary' endeared him to friends, authors, and employees alike. He had a genuine gift for friendship, an equable temperament which sometimes belied a darker, depressive side to his nature. For many years Murray kept a commonplace book in which he recorded humorous anecdotes, notable quotations from books, *bons mots*, proverbs, and the like. *A Gentleman Publisher's Commonplace Book* (1996), edited by his son John R. Murray, is a posthumous tribute to a man who reinvigorated a business that could claim to be the oldest independent family-run publishing house in the world. Jock Murray died at the Royal Free Hospital, Hampstead, London, on 22 July 1993.

During the course of his career, and particularly towards its end, at a time when the publishing industry was changing dramatically, John [vi] Murray continued to be a strong proponent of the net book agreement, which his ancestor (John [iv] Murray) had played a part in establishing. He served on the councils of the Royal Geographical Society and the Publishers' Association and was a member of the Literary Society, the Society of Dilettanti, and the Roxburghe Club. An accomplished tree surgeon, he once remarked, 'Publishers naturally take to forestry because they can cut and chop to their heart's content without authors complaining' (speech to the Society of Bookmen, 6 Dec 1979). The house of Murray remained in family hands until May 2002 when it was sold to Hodder Headline, who promised to retain the John Murray imprint.

WILLIAM ZACHS, PETER ISAAC, ANGUS FRASER, and WILLIAM LISTER

Sources W. Zachs, *The first John Murray and the late eighteenth-century London book trade* (1998) • parish register, St Dunstan-in-the-West, GL [burial: John [i] Murray] • S. Smiles, *A publisher and his friends: memoir and correspondence of the late John Murray*, 2 vols. (1891) • John Murray, London, archives • T. Moore, *The life of Lord Byron* (1844) • D. F. McKenzie, ed., *Stationers' Company apprentices*, [3]: *1701–1800* (1978) • beadle's book, Stationers' Company, Stationers' Hall, London, pp. 386 and 633 • S. Bennett, 'John Murray's Family Library', *Studies in Bibliography*, 29 (1976), 139–66 • G. Paston [E. M. Symonds], *At John Murray's, 1843–1892* (1932) • J. Murray, *John Murray III, 1808–1892* (1919) • A. Fraser, 'A publishing house and its readers, 1841–1880: the Murrays and the Miltons', *Papers of the Bibliographical Society of America*, 90 (1996), 5–47 • A. Fraser, 'John Murray's Colonial and Home Library', *Papers of the Bibliographical Society of America*, 91 (1997), 339–408 • W. B. C. Lister, *A bibliography of Murray's Handbooks for Travellers* (1993–4) • *Wellesley index*, vol. 1 • J. Murray to H. Martineau, 29 Feb 1848, John Murray, London, archives, letter-book • J. Murray, letter to A. W. Kinglake, 1844, CUL, Add. MS 7633.4 • *The Times* (1 Dec 1928) • *Yorkshire Post* (1 Dec 1928) • *Manchester Guardian* (1 Dec 1928) • *Publishers Circular* (8 Dec 1928) • A. C. Ainger, *Memories of Eton 60 years ago* (1917) • Burke, *Gen. GB* • L. Huxley, *The house of Smith Elder* (1923) • A. Sullivan, ed., *British literary magazines*, 3–4 (1984–6) • Lord Ernle [R. Prothero], *Whippingham to Westminster* (1938) • '*The Times*' and the publishers, Publishers' Association (privately printed, 1906) • F. Macmillan, *The net book agreements and the book war, 1906–1908* (1924) • introduction, A. Munthe, *The story of San Michele* (1991) [Folio Society edition] • introduction, E. Gibbon, *Memoirs of my life* (1984) [Folio Society edition] • *The Times* (7 Oct 1967) • *The Bookseller* (14 Oct 1967) • bishop of Bath and Wells, memorial service address, 7 Nov 1967 [John [v] Murray; notes] • *WWW* • P. Quennell, *The wanton chase* (1980) • P. Quennell, *The marble foot* (1976) • Lord Gorrell, *One man … many parts* (1956) • *The Independent* (24 July 1993) • J. Murray, *A poet and his publisher* (1976) [English Association presidential address] • J. R. Murray, ed., *A gentleman publisher's commonplace book* (1996) • N. Attallah, interview, *The Oldie* • N. Barker, preface, *From the bookshelves of Jock Murray* (1977) [sale catalogue, G. Heywood Hill Ltd] • J. Murray, unpublished speech to the Society of Bookmen, 6 Dec 1979 • private information (2004)

Archives Bodl. Oxf., corresp. [John [ii] Murray] • Hunt. L., letters [John [ii] Murray] • John Murray, London, archives • John Murray, London, archives, letter-books of John Murray Ltd [John [iv] Murray; John [v] Murray] • John Murray, London, archives, long autobiographical MS written by John [iv] Murray, c.1925 • NL Scot., corresp. [John [v] Murray] • University of Iowa Libraries, Iowa City, corresp. [John [ii] Murray] | BL, letters to J. C. Hobhouse, Add. MSS 36456–36469, *passim* [John [ii] Murray] • BL, letters to Charles Babbage, Add. MSS 37186–37201 [John [iii] Murray] • BL, letters to J. W. Croker, Add. MSS 41125–41127 [John [iii] Murray] • BL, business corresp. with W. E. Gladstone, Add. MSS 44259–44260 [John [iii] Murray] • BL, corresp. with Sir A. H. Layard, Add. MSS 38942–39107, *passim* [John [iii] Murray] • BL, corresp. with Samuel Butler, Add. MSS 44033–44038 [John [iv] Murray] • BL, letters to J. P. Gilson, Add. MS 47687 [John [iv] Murray] • BL, corresp. with W. E. Gladstone, Add. MSS 44259–44260 [John [iv] Murray] • BL, letters to Sir E. W. Hamilton, Add. MS 48619 [John [iv] Murray] • BL, letters to Sir Austen Layard, Add. MSS 39036–39100 [John [iv] Murray] • BL, corresp. with G. M. Tuckwell, Add. MS 43967 [John [iv] Murray] • BL, corresp. with Sydney Cockerell, Add. MS 52741 [John [v] Murray] • BLPES, corresp. with V. R. Markham [John [v] Murray] • Bodl. Oxf., letters to Lord Lovelace [John [iii] Murray] • Bodl. Oxf., letters to Sir William Napier [John [iii] Murray] • Bodl. Oxf., letters to Mary Somerville and William Somerville [John [iii] Murray] • Bodl. Oxf., corresp. with Lord Lovelace and Lady Lovelace [John [iv] Murray] • CAC Cam., corresp. with Lord Esher [John [iv] Murray] • CAC Cam., corresp. with Monty Belgion [John [v] Murray] • Derbys. RO, letters to P. Turnbull [John [iv] Murray] • Herts. ALS, letters to Lord Lytton [John [iii] Murray] • NL Scot., corresp. with Blackwoods [John [ii] Murray] • NL Scot., letters to Sir Walter Scott [John [ii] Murray] • NL Scot., letters to J. S. Blackie [John [iii] Murray] • NL Scot., corresp. with Blackwoods [John [iii] Murray] • NL Scot., corresp. with J. G. Lockhart [John [iii] Murray] • NL Scot., corresp. with Blackwoods [John [iv] Murray] • NL Scot., corresp. with Lord Rosebery [John [iv] Murray] • NRA, priv. coll., letters to D. Livingstone [John [iii] Murray] • PRO, letters to Sir J. C. Ross, BJ2 [John [iii] Murray] • Queen's University, archives, corresp. with Ralph Disraeli [John [iii] Murray] • Royal Anthropological Institute of Great Britain and Ireland, London, corresp. with W. Crooke [John [iv] Murray] • U. Edin. L., letters to T. J. Torrie [John [iii] Murray] • U. Nott. L., letters to J. E. Denison [John [iii] Murray] • U. Nott. L., letters to Louisa Denison [John [iii] Murray] • U. St Andr. L., corresp. with J. D. Forbes [John [iii] Murray] • University of Victoria, British Columbia, Betjeman archive [John [vi] Murray] | FILM Central Television, 'Your obedient servant', John [vi] Murray on Byron, 1988 [John [vi] Murray]

| SOUND Wordsworth Trust, 'An experience of authors', Lakeland Audio cassette [John [vi] Murray]

Likenesses D. Allan, oils, 1777 (John [i] Murray), John Murray, London, archives · oils, c.1785 (John [i] Murray), John Murray, London, archives · J. Tassie, glass medallion, 1791 (John [i] Murray), John Murray, London, archives · watercolour miniature, c.1791 (John [i] Murray), John Murray, London, archives · W. Brockeden, pencil and chalk drawing, 1837 (John [ii] Murray), NPG · T. Lupton, mezzotint, pubd 1840 (John [ii] Murray; after J. W. Gordon), BM, NPG · D. O. Hill & Robert Adamson, photograph, 1843–8 (John [iii] Murray), NPG · D. O. Hill, photograph, c.1845 (John [iii] Murray), National Museum of Photography, Film and Television, Bradford, Royal Photographic Society collection · J. Gibbon, pastels, 1864 (John [iii] Murray), John Murray, London, archives · Maull & Fox, photograph, c.1880 (John [iii] Murray), John Murray, London, archives · G. Reid, oils, 1881 (John [iii] Murray), John Murray, London, archives · C. W. Furse, oils, c.1891 (John [iii] Murray), NPG · W. Stoneman, photograph, 1932 (John [v] Murray), NPG · F. Stark, charcoal, 1969 (John [vi] Murray), John Murray, London, archives · D. Hill, oils, 1977 (John [vi] Murray), John Murray, London, archives · J. Bratby, oils, c.1980 (John [vi] Murray), priv. coll. · J. Springs, pen and ink, 1989 (John [vi] Murray), John Murray, London, archives · E. Finden, stipple (John [ii] Murray; after H. Pickersgill), repro. in E. Finden, *Illustrations on life and works of Byron* (1833) · D. Maclise, pencil drawing (John [ii] Murray), National Gallery, London; on loan to V&A · H. W. Pickersgill, oils (John [ii] Murray), John Murray, London, archives · R. T. & G., wood-engraving (John [iii] Murray), NPG; repro. in *ILN* (9 April 1892) · engraving (John [ii] Murray; after Pickersgill), repro. in Smiles, *A publisher and his friends*, vol. 2, frontispiece · mezzotint (John [ii] Murray; after unknown artist), NPG · portraits (John [iv] Murray), John Murray, London, archives · portraits (John [v] Murray), John Murray, London, archives · woodcut (John [iii] Murray; after photograph by Maull & Fox), NPG

Wealth at death over £12,000—John [i] Murray: John Murray, London, archives · £33,415 15s. 8½d.—John [ii] Murray: will, PRO, PROB 11/1982, fol. 395v; valuation of estate in John Murray, London, archives · £75,858 16s. 11d.—John [iii] Murray: resworn probate, May 1895, *CGPLA Eng. & Wales* · £148,528 11s. 6d.—John [iv] Murray: resworn probate, 1929, *CGPLA Eng. & Wales* · £126,640 3s. od.—John [v] Murray: probate, 1967, *CGPLA Eng. & Wales* · £186,047—John Arnaud Robin Grey Murray: probate, 1993, *CGPLA Eng. & Wales*

Murray, Adam (d. 1706), Williamite army officer, is supposed by tradition to have been brought up at Ling, outside Claudy, co. Londonderry, where his father, Gideon Murray (d. 1690), said to have been a native of Philiphaugh, Selkirkshire, is thought to have settled and farmed from 1648. His mother is said to have been a 'Miss Macky (a Scotch lady)' (Graham, 350). Before the outbreak of the Jacobite conflict Murray's only military experience was that of a tory-hunter.

In early 1689 Murray raised a troop of horse and was given a captaincy in Colonel Stewart's regiment. When King James's army marched on Londonderry in April 1689, Murray was sent by the governor, Robert Lundy, on 15 April, with thirty dragoons to support the infantry and prevent the Irish crossing the Finn at Clady, co. Tyrone. Murray's men held the ford until their ammunition was spent, and retreated to Culmore, where on the next day he took command of a further 400 horsemen. Fearing that Lundy and his council would treat with the Irish, on 18 April Murray fought his way back to Londonderry, where 'the multitude, having eagerly desired and expected his coming, followed him through the streets with great

expressions of their respect and affection' (Mackenzie, 28–9). He urged all those who were against surrender to wear white armbands and went with 'a strong guard of soldiers and officers' (*Murray's Case*) to Lundy and told him that he was 'either a fool or a knave' (Mackenzie, 29). The violence threatened by Murray and his men against Lundy prevented the council from meeting again. His opposition to Lundy 'both in the council and especially by his influence on the multitude was the only thing that prevented the surrender of the city to King James' (Mackenzie, 29–30). He discharged his men from any treaty that Lundy might make and that night seized the keys to the city gates and stores and appointed his own guards. Henry Baker and George Walker succeeded as the new governors and Lundy fled the city. Murray was elected the colonel of horse. On the following day Lord Strabane came to the walls to persuade the city to surrender and offered Murray a colonel's commission in the Irish army and £1000 from King James.

Murray commanded the horse in the successful sally to Pennyburn mill on 21 April. According to three local authorities, he personally killed the French general, the marquis de Maumont, although the French reports describe Maumont as having been shot in the head by a musketeer. Murray led a second sally to Pennyburn on 25 April, in which Maumont's successor, Pusignan, received a fatal wound. He was much celebrated during the siege. According to Aickin, 'The name of Murray grew so terrible that he alone was thought invincible: where'er he came, the Irish fled away' (Hempton, 72). In mid-May General Richard Hamilton resorted to sending Murray's octogenarian father to the city to persuade his son to surrender. The mission proved futile, not least because the old man counselled resistance rather than surrender.

Murray was active throughout the siege in leading small patrols to attack the enemy's lines. On 18 June, while commanding a boat on a hazardous trip upstream to drop off messengers, he was wounded in the head. His last action was an attack on the enemy's trenches on 17 July. He was shot through both thighs and did not fully recover until the end of October.

After the siege was raised on 1 August, Major-General Percy Kirke amalgamated the remnants of Murray's regiment with those of Colonel Baker's, but nearly all Murray's men 'refused, and went off into the country with their carbines and pistols, and the major-general seized the saddles, as he did also Colonel Murray's horse, which he had preserved with great care during all the siege' (Mackenzie, 47). In 1691 Murray commanded the militia in Ulster, and after the war, in 1694, he was given the colonelcy of Lord Charlemont's regiment of foot, but was placed on half pay in 1697. He never received his pay for his wartime service and 'having no estate is brought into considerable debts and his family brought to ruin and misery' (*Murray's Case*). He petitioned the House of Commons for relief, pointing out that 'I commanded the first regiment of horse that served their majesties in Ireland, and the first that we hear of that eat their horses' (*Murray's Case*).

Murray died in 1706. His descendants are said to be from his marriage to Isabella Shaw who, it seems, predeceased him, as a petition from his widow in 1706 is signed by a Mary Murray. His religious allegiance, whether episcopalian or presbyterian, was to be a subject of debate among historians. He was buried in Glendermot churchyard and John Mitchelburne, military governor of Londonderry during the latter part of the siege, was buried alongside him in 1721. In 1837 the Irish Society erected a monument over his grave; his sword is in the possession of the Derry Cathedral chapter house.   PIERS WAUCHOPE

Sources G. Walker, *A true account of the siege of London-Derry* (1689) · J. MacKenzie, *A narrative of the siege of London-Derry* (1690) · *The state of Colonel Adam Murray's case to the honourable House of Commons assembled in parliament* (1698?) · J. Aickin, *Londerias, or, A narrative of the siege of Londonderry* (1699) · J. Michelburne, *Ireland preserv'd, or, The siege of London-Derry*, 2 pts (privately printed, London, 1708) · T. Ash, *A circumstantial journal of the siege of Londonderry* (1792) · J. Hempton, ed., *The siege and history of Londonderry* (1861) · T. Witherow, *Derry and Enniskillen in the year 1689* (1879) · *Négociations de M. le Comte d'Avaux en Irlande, 1689–90*, ed. J. Hogan, 1, IMC (1934), 117 · C. D. Milligan, *The Murray Club centenary* (1947) · C. D. Milligan, *History of the siege of Londonderry, 1689* (1951) · P. Macrory, *The siege of Derry* (1980) · *Calendar of the manuscripts of the marquess of Ormonde*, new ser., 8 vols., HMC, 36 (1902–20), vol. 8 · J. Redington, ed., *Calendar of Treasury papers*, 3, PRO (1874) · J. Graham, *Ireland preserved, or, The siege of Londonderry and battle of Aughrim* (1841)

Murray, Alexander, of Elibank, **Jacobite earl of Westminster** (1712–1778), Jacobite agent, was born on 9 December 1712, the sixth son of Alexander Murray, fourth Lord Elibank (1677–1736), and his wife, Elizabeth (*d.* 1756), daughter of the Edinburgh surgeon and politician George Stirling. He was commissioned into the 26th regiment of foot (the Cameronians) on 11 August 1737, but never advanced beyond the rank of lieutenant. Like his brother Patrick *Murray, fifth Lord Elibank, Murray was attracted to Prince Charles Edward, but neither joined the prince when he arrived in Scotland in 1745. Horace Walpole wrote that 'both were such active Jacobites that if the Pretender had succeeded they would have produced many witnesses to testify their great zeal for him'. Yet both were 'so cautious that no witnesses of actual treason could be produced by the Government against them' (Walpole, 1.17).

Although he came of an old and distinguished border family, Murray was without means until he contracted a marriage of convenience, details of which are unknown, which brought him an income of £3000 a year. He lent Prince Charles a few hundred pounds at a high rate of interest at a time when the Stuart heir was in dire financial straits, and this gave him access to the prince's innermost circle. In autumn 1750, when Prince Charles's prospects improved sufficiently for him to pay a brief secret visit to London and be received into the Church of England, Murray became embroiled in a political disturbance. During a hotly disputed Westminster election he supported the anti-government candidate, Sir George Vandeput, and on 20 January 1751 a complaint was laid that he had exhorted a mob to violence by shouting, 'Will no one have courage enough to knock the dog down?' (*Scots peerage*, 3.514).

Alexander Murray of Elibank, Jacobite earl of Westminster (1712–1778), by Allan Ramsay, 1742

Murray was summoned before the House of Commons on 1 February and was committed to Newgate prison. When brought before the house again and ordered to kneel to receive sentence, he refused, telling the speaker, 'Sir, I beg to be excused; I never kneel but to God' (Walpole, 1.29). He was recommitted to Newgate for contempt, and held for a further two months before being again brought before the house. When release was refused he attempted unsuccessfully to obtain a writ of habeas corpus, but was freed on 25 June when parliament was prorogued. He drove to his brother's house in Henrietta Street surrounded by a great crowd carrying a banner proclaiming, 'Murray and Liberty'. Such displays incensed the authorities. Publication of a pamphlet pleading his case led to the imprisonment of the suspected author, and on 25 November a motion was carried in the Commons recommitting Murray to prison. By then, however, he had fled to France.

While pursuing his quarrel with the House of Commons, or very soon after, Murray became embroiled in an attempt to seize the Hanoverian royal family and set the Stuarts back on the throne. There is no evidence that Prince Charles himself instigated this coup during his visit to London, but Murray became so deeply enmeshed in the affair that it became known as the Elibank plot. Many leading Jacobites became involved, including Sir John Graeme, Henry Goring, Lady Primrose, Jeremy Dawkins, MacDonald of Lochgarry, and Earl Marischal, then Frederick of Prussia's envoy in Paris.

The plan was to seize St James's Palace and the Tower of London, kidnap George II and members of his family, and take them to France. Murray later proposed that the king should be assassinated, but Prince Charles, to his credit, refused to sanction this. In its final shape the plan was simply to seize the king and his family on 10 November 1752, at which point Charles would sail to England. However, when Murray landed secretly in October to lead the attack on the royal palace and the Tower, he found that none of the expected troops had materialized and the English Jacobites were in a high state of alarm, with good reason. Their suspicion that the plan had been leaked to London was confirmed the following spring when Archibald Cameron was arrested and executed. Clementine Walkinshaw, whom Charles had just brought to Ghent as his mistress, was blamed, but the real betrayer of the plot was Alasdair Ruadh MacDonnell, alias Pickle the Spy.

Murray remained in exile for the next two decades, still within the prince's innermost circle, criticizing Charles for his drinking, trying to persuade him to send Walkinshaw away, and acting as go-between to the prince's other mistresses. James Edward Stuart created him earl of Westminster in 1759. Outside the Jacobite movement he corresponded with David Hume and meddled in the affairs of others—in a quarrel between his friend Captain Forbes and John Wilkes, as well as in the bitterly disputed lawsuit over who should succeed to the dukedom of Douglas. According to Lord Elcho, Murray tried to abduct Elcho's mother to steal her money (Lord Elcho, *Short Account of the Affairs of Scotland in the Years 1745-6*, 1907, 164-5). He was permitted to return from exile in April 1771. He died at Taplow, Buckinghamshire, on 27 February 1778, and was buried there on 7 March.   HUGH DOUGLAS

Sources DNB · *Scots peerage*, vol. 3 · C. Petrie, 'The Elibank plot, 1752-53', TRHS, 4th ser., 14 (1931), 175-96 · F. McLynn, *Charles Edward Stuart: a tragedy in many acts* (1988) · GEC, *Peerage* · H. Walpole, *Memoirs of King George II*, ed. J. Brooke, 3 vols. (1985)
Archives U. Edin. L., corresp.
Likenesses A. Ramsay, oils, 1742, National Museum of Scotland; on loan to Scot. NPG [*see illus.*] · J. Faber junior, mezzotint (after A. Ramsay), Scot. NPG

Murray, Alexander, Lord Henderland (1736-1795), judge, born in Edinburgh, was the son of Archibald Murray of Murrayfield, near Edinburgh, advocate. He was called to the Scottish bar on 7 March 1758, the year in which his *Disputatio juridica ... de divortiis et repudiis* was published. He succeeded his father as sheriff-depute of the shire of Peebles in 1761, and as one of the commissaries of Edinburgh in 1765. He married, on 15 March 1773, Katherine (1737-1828), daughter of Sir Alexander Lindsay, bt, of Evelick, Perthshire. Their eldest son, William, practised at the English bar; the younger was Sir John Archibald *Murray, Lord Murray (1778?-1859). A daughter, Amelia Jane, died unmarried in 1798.

On 24 May 1775 Murray was appointed solicitor-general for Scotland, and at the general election in September 1780 was returned to the House of Commons for Peeblesshire. The only speech he is recorded to have made in parliament was in opposition to Sir George Savile's motion relating to the petition of the delegated counties for a redress of grievances. He succeeded Henry Home, Lord Kames, as an ordinary lord of session and a commissioner

of the court of justiciary, and took his seat on the bench with the title Lord Henderland, from his estate in Peeblesshire, on 6 March 1783. Henderland was joint clerk of the pipe in the court of exchequer, an office which, through the influence of Lord Melville, was subsequently conferred on his two sons. He took part in the trials for sedition at Edinburgh in 1793. He died of cholera at Murrayfield on 16 March 1795.

G. F. R. BARKER, *rev.* ANITA McCONNELL

Sources J. Foster, *Members of parliament, Scotland ... 1357-1882*, 2nd edn (privately printed, London, 1882), 262 · J. Kay, *A series of original portraits and caricature etchings ... with biographical sketches and illustrative anecdotes*, ed. [H. Paton and others], new edn [3rd edn], 1 (1877), 243-4, 302, 307, 418; 2 (1877), 96, 346 · G. Brunton and D. Haig, *An historical account of the senators of the college of justice, from its institution in MDXXXII* (1832), 537 · J. Grant, *Cassell's old and new Edinburgh*, 3 vols. [1880-83], vol. 2, pp. 81, 255, 270; vol. 3, pp. 103-4 · *Scots Magazine*, 23 (1761), 224 · *Scots Magazine*, 27 (1765), 448 · *Scots Magazine*, 35 (1773), 222 · *Scots Magazine*, 57 (1795), 206 · Burke, *Gen. GB*
Archives NL Scot., journal notes on legal cases | NL Scot., letters to sixth marquess of Tweeddale
Likenesses J. Kay, caricature, etching, 1842, BM, NPG

Murray, Alexander (1775-1813), linguist, was born on 22 October 1775 at the farm of Dunkitterick, Kirkcudbrightshire, son of Robert Murray (1706-1797), a shepherd, and his second wife, Mary Cochrane (b. 1739). In the autumn of 1781 Robert, somewhat reluctantly, taught his precocious son the alphabet, and later Alexander gained access to a Bible and psalm book. From eight to seventeen he had some sixty weeks of broken education at village schools. Largely self-taught, he was encouraged by a succession of clergymen. In this way he mastered English and the rudiments of Latin, Greek, and Hebrew, knew something of French and German, and began the study of Abyssinian. In the intervals he worked partly as a shepherd (hindered by his near-sightedness) and partly as a tutor to children remote from school like himself, and the small income from these sources helped him to obtain books.

From 1793 to 1794 Murray translated Arnold Drackenburg's German lectures on Roman authors, and when he visited Dumfries with his version in June 1794, after unsuccessfully offering it to two separate publishers, he met Burns, who advised him not to publish before going to college (Moncrieff). The father of Robert Heron (1764-1807) lent him useful books, and James M'Harg, a merchant of contraband tea, with literary contacts in Edinburgh, proposed that Murray should visit the university authorities. His parish minister, J. G. Maitland of Minnigaff, gave him an introductory letter to Principal G. H. Baird, which led to an oral examination, in which Murray agreeably surprised his examiners by his knowledge of Homer, Horace, the Hebrew psalms, and French. Admitted to Edinburgh University in November 1793 as a deserving student, he won his way by scholastic distinctions and the help of private teaching. Lord Cockburn remembered him as a fellow student, 'a little shivering creature, gentle, studious, timid, and reserved' (*Memorials ... by Henry Cockburn*, 276). He continued his brilliant career

Alexander Murray (1775–1813), by Andrew Geddes, 1812

by a course of studies at Divinity Hall (1797–1802), and became a licentiate of the Church of Scotland.

Murray in 1794 formed the acquaintance of John Leyden, a linguist of his own age, and with a similar history (*Poetical Remains of … Leyden*, xvii), and among his friends were Dr Anderson, editor of *The British Poets*, Henry Brougham, Francis Jeffrey, Thomas Brown, Thomas Campbell, and others. Through Leyden he became a contributor to the *Scots Magazine*, and he edited the seven numbers of that periodical from February 1802, inserting verses of his own under one of the signatures B, X, or Z. He was meanwhile diligently studying languages. From the spoken tongues of Europe he moved on to those of western Asia and north-east Africa, especially the dialects of Abyssinia. These studies led him to contribute to three successive numbers of the *Scots Magazine* a biography of Bruce, the Abyssinian traveller, which he afterwards expanded into a volume (1808). Constable the publisher, struck with his abilities, engaged him in September 1802 to prepare a new edition of Bruce's *Travels* (7 vols., 1805; new edn, 1813). His ten-month residence with the traveller's son, James Bruce, proved a painful ordeal, owing to James's jealous and obstructive tactics, but he successfully completed the edition, which sold well (Constable, 1.222–43). At the same time (1802–5) Murray worked for the *Edinburgh Review*, and his letters to Constable mark a writer with an easy, humorous, incisive style, keenly alive to the importance of literary excellence and a wide and generous culture. Almost from the outset, as De Quincey says, he had before him 'a theory, and distinct purposes' (*Collected Writings*, 10.34).

In 1806 Murray was appointed assistant to Dr James

Muirhead (1742–1808), parish minister of Urr, Kirkcudbrightshire, whom he fully succeeded at his death in 1808. On 9 December 1808 Murray married Henrietta (*d. c.*1825), daughter of a parishioner, James Affleck. He soon became popular both as a man and a preacher. Among his own literary projects in 1808 were an edition of the classics, suggested by Constable, and a history of Galloway, which he seriously contemplated, and about which he had some correspondence with Scott (Constable, 1.267). In 1811 he translated, with approbation, an Ethiopic letter from the governor of Tygrè for George III, brought home by Salt, the Abyssinian envoy, whose familiarity with the revised edition of Bruce's *Travels* prompted his suggestion of Murray to Marquess Wellesley as the only capable translator 'in the British dominions'. Murray's chief interest, however, was comparative philology, and on 13 August 1811 he wrote to Constable that he had mastered the Sami language, that he saw 'light through the extent of Europe in every direction', and that he trusted to unite the histories of Europe and Asia by aid of their respective languages (Constable, 304–6).

In July 1812, after a keen contest involving some acrimony, Murray was appointed professor of oriental languages in Edinburgh University. His interests were greatly helped by the advocacy of Dr Baird and Salt, and the active help of Constable (*Scots Magazine*; Constable, 1.320–36). He received from the university on 17 July the degree of doctor of divinity. He entered on his work at the end of October, and published at the same date *Outlines of Oriental Philology* (1812) for the use of his students. He lectured through the winter, despite some physical weakness, attracting both students and literary men to his room. His health completely gave way in the spring, and he died of consumption at Edinburgh on 15 April 1813, leaving his widow and a son and daughter. He was buried in Greyfriars churchyard. Mrs Murray survived about twelve years, supported by a government pension of £80, which was granted to her in return for Murray's translation of the Abyssinian letter. The daughter died of consumption in 1821, and the son, who was practically adopted by Archibald Constable, qualified for a ship's surgeon, and was drowned on his first voyage (Constable, 1.336). A monument to Murray, a granite obelisk, 70 feet high, was erected near his birthplace in 1834, and it received a suitable inscription in 1877, in which year a monument was also erected in Greyfriars churchyard.

Murray's promising scholarly career was cut short. But he proved himself an ideal editor and biographer, and his impulse, method, and style had a permanent influence. His *Letters to Charles Stuart, M.D.* appeared in 1813. His great and pioneering work, the *History of the European languages, or, Researches into the affinities of the Teutonic, Greek, Celtic, Slavonic, and Indian nations*, was edited by Dr Scott and published, with a life by Sir H. W. Moncreiff, in two volumes in 1823.   T. W. BAYNE, rev. JOHN D. HAIGH

Sources T. Murray, *The literary history of Galloway* (1822), 282–325 · H. W. Moncreiff, 'Life of Alexander Murray', in A. Murray, *History of the European languages* (1823), xxix–cxix · T. Constable, *Archibald Constable and his literary correspondents*, 1 (1873), 213–336 · J. Reith,

The life and writings of Rev. Alex. Murray (1903) · *The poetical remains of the late Dr John Leyden: with memoirs of his life by the Rev. James Morton*, ed. J. Morton, ed. J. Morton (1819) · *Memorials of his time, by Henry Cockburn* (1856), 276 · *The collected writings of Thomas De Quincey*, ed. D. Masson, new edn, 10 (1890), 34 · *Scots Magazine and Edinburgh Literary Miscellany* (Aug 1812) · bap. reg. Scot.
Archives NRA Scotland, priv. coll., corresp. and papers · Yale U., notebooks | NL Scot., corresp. with Archibald Constable
Likenesses A. Geddes, pencil drawing, 1812, Scot. NPG [*see illus.*]

Murray, Alexander Stuart (1841–1904), museum curator, was born at Arbirlot, near Arbroath in Forfarshire, on 8 January 1841, the eldest son in a family of four sons and four daughters of George Murray (*b.* 1814), a tradesman, and his wife, Helen Margaret Sayles (*b.* 1819). His younger brother George Robert Milne *Murray (1858–1911) was keeper of the department of botany at the British Museum from 1895 to 1905. After being educated at the Royal High School, Edinburgh, Murray attended Edinburgh University in 1863–4, but did not graduate. He also attended Berlin University in 1865, where he studied philology and archaeology under August Böckh, Emil Hübner, and August Wilhelm Zumpt; Henry Nettleship (1839–1893) was a fellow student.

On 14 February 1867 Murray was appointed assistant in the department of Greek and Roman antiquities at the British Museum, under Charles T. Newton, then keeper. The Blacas and Castellani collections had just been purchased, and John Turtle Wood's excavations were in progress at Ephesus. Between 1867 and 1886 Murray worked energetically under Newton's direction, acquiring a close knowledge of the whole collection of Greek and Roman antiquities. In the first five years alone he entered in the museum's register over 5000 items from the Blacas and other collections and catalogued over 2000 bronzes. He was highly regarded by Newton (a notoriously strict judge of his subordinates), and contributed through his fluency in German to Newton's grasp of new archaeological research published in that language.

On 13 February 1886 Murray succeeded Newton as keeper of the department of Greek and Roman antiquities. The recent removal of the natural history collections to South Kensington, the completion of the new building known as the 'White wing' at Bloomsbury, and other alterations had greatly increased the available space for the exhibition of antiquities. An additional gallery was allocated to the Elgin marbles, and a further reorganization of the galleries devoted to Greek and Roman antiquities became for many years Murray's main preoccupation. The objects were set out with greater consideration than before for effect and space, and at the same time all the fittings and labels were improved. Murray was always helpful to visitors to his department, and patiently answered the enquiries of correspondents.

For many years Murray made it a practice to visit the continent, especially Greece, Italy, Sicily, or Spain, gaining familiarity with important classical sites and foreign collections and with foreign archaeologists. The only occasions on which he took part in work in the field were in 1870, when he visited the site of Priene with Newton to copy Greek inscriptions, and in 1896, when he was temporarily in charge of the excavations at Enkomi (Salamis) in Cyprus. He subsequently wrote most of the Enkomi section of *The British Museum: Excavations in Cyprus* (1900).

Although Murray did not see through the press a departmental catalogue of his own, he was a careful reader and critic of all the publications of his assistants, and contributed introductions to several volumes by them. His text for *Terracotta Sarcophagi, Greek and Etruscan, in the British Museum* (1898) was vitiated by the later discovery that the 'Etruscan' sarcophagus was a fake. Murray wrote widely on classical archaeology independently of his official work, and published among other works *A History of Greek Sculpture* (2 vols., 1880; 2nd edn, 1890), *The Sculptures of the Parthenon* (1903), based on lectures to the Royal Academy, and three other books on mythology and antiquities. He also contributed an excursus on the pottery of Cyprus to Luigi Palma di Cesnola's *Cyprus* (1877), and articles on a wide variety of topics to learned journals, to the *Contemporary Review* and *Quarterly Review*, and to the ninth edition of the *Encyclopaedia Britannica*. His writings showed the breadth of his knowledge, and were full of observations on points of detail; but his contemporaries found his style difficult, and a century later his works were little read, apart from the Enkomi excavation report, which was reprinted in 1970. From 1879 all his work on early Greece was coloured by his reluctance to accept the early date for Mycenaean culture, which was gradually being established beyond controversy.

Murray was made LLD of Glasgow University in 1887. He was corresponding member of the Royal Prussian Academy and of the Académie des Inscriptions et Belles-Lettres of the French Institute, a member of the German Archaeological Institute, a fellow of both the Society of Antiquaries (1889) and the British Academy (1903), an honorary associate of the Royal Institute of British Archaeologists (1890) and a vice-president of the Society for the Promotion of Hellenic Studies (1891).

Murray maintained through life his Scottish accent and his adherence to the presbyterian Church of Scotland. He was small in stature and somewhat quick-tempered—on occasion outspoken to the point of offence—but his underlying courtesy and warmth ensured his popularity. He was twice married: first on 21 December 1872 to Sarah Jane (Jenny) Handcock (*c.*1839–1874), daughter of William Hill, a farmer, and second, on 5 April 1881, to Anne Murray Welsh (1836–1922), youngest daughter of David and Jean Welsh, of Tillytoghills Farm, Fettercairn, Kincardineshire. There were no children by either marriage. Murray died of pneumonia at his official residence in the museum on 5 March 1904 and was buried at Kensal Green cemetery on 9 March 1904.
ARTHUR HUGHES, *rev.* B. F. COOK

Sources A. H. Smith, 'Alexander Stuart Murray', *Biographisches Jahrbuch für die Altertumswissenschaft*, 20 (1907), 100–103 · E. Maunde Thompson, 'Alexander Stuart Murray', *PBA*, [1] (1903–4), 321–3 · *Man*, 4 (1904), 56 · *Journal of the Royal Institute of British Archaeologists* (19 March 1904), 274 · personal knowledge (1912) · private information (1912) · staff applications, BM · *Original Papers*, 2nd ser.,

18/2679 (4 March 1872) [held at BM] · matriculation records, U. Edin. L., special collections division, university archives · graduation album, U. Glas., Archives and Business Records Centre · General Register Office for England · *CGPLA Eng. & Wales* (1904) · m. cert. · minutes of the standing committee of trustees, 11 Feb 1893, BM, vol. 46, p. 19, no. 142

Archives BM, department of Greek and Roman antiquities
Likenesses Elliott & Fry, photograph, repro. in *Man*
Wealth at death £1801 10s. 5d.: resworn probate, 20 April 1904, *CGPLA Eng. & Wales*

Murray, Alexander William Charles Oliphant, Baron Murray of Elibank (1870–1920), politician and businessman, was born at 2 Albion Villas, Folkestone, Kent, on 12 April 1870, the eldest son in the family of four sons and five daughters of Commander Montolieu Fox Oliphant Murray RN (1840–1927), later tenth Baron Elibank in the peerage of Scotland, who in 1911 became the first Viscount Elibank in the peerage of the UK, and his wife, Blanche Alice (1844–1936), daughter of Edward John Scott of Southsea, Hampshire. As heir apparent to the peerage Murray was known as the master of Elibank, and his nickname in politics was the Master. He was educated at Cheltenham College (1882–8). As a young man he found ungainful but instructive employment as assistant private secretary at the Colonial Office (1892–5). On 1 August 1894 he married Hilda Louisa Janey Wolfe (1872–1929), daughter of James Wolfe Murray of Cringletie, Peeblesshire.

In October 1900 Murray was elected Liberal MP for W. E. Gladstone's old seat of Midlothian, which he held until 1906. From 1906 to 1910 he represented Peebles and Selkirk, and from 1910 to 1912 again Midlothian. When the Liberals returned to power he held office, first as comptroller to the household (1905–9), then as under-secretary of state for India (1909–10), and finally as parliamentary (patronage) secretary to the Treasury and Liberal chief whip (1910–12). The post of chief whip was exceptionally demanding at this time because of the constitutional crisis following the Lords' rejection of the 1909 budget, and the Liberals' dependence on the Irish party.

In these difficult circumstances Murray was a highly effective operator, with a gift for backstage negotiation and intrigue much assisted by his natural bonhomie. He was liked by politicians of all parties and factions; in particular, he was just as close to the Asquith family as to David Lloyd George. He also had the confidence of the new king, George V, and of his two private secretaries, Francis, first Viscount Knollys, and Sir Arthur Bigge (later Baron Stamfordham), who disagreed with each other on the constitutional issue. He was sworn of the privy council in 1911.

On 7 August 1912 Murray resigned, ostensibly in order to rehabilitate the Elibank estates which his father had made over to him. At the invitation of the Liberal industrialist Weetman Pearson (later first Viscount Cowdray), he became a director of S. Pearson & Son. On 13 August 1912 he was raised to the peerage as Baron Murray of Elibank.

There was, perhaps, another reason for Murray's withdrawal from politics. In 1911 he had acquired, with Lloyd

Alexander William Charles Oliphant Murray, Baron Murray of Elibank (1870–1920), by unknown artist

George and the attorney-general, Sir Rufus Isaacs (later first marquess of Reading), a personal shareholding in the American Marconi Company, soon after the British Marconi Company had entered into a large contract with the British government. He had also bought 3000 American Marconi shares for Liberal Party funds. News of these transactions gradually leaked out and the matter was investigated by a parliamentary select committee, which reported on party lines. Murray was summoned to appear before it in the spring of 1913, but by then he was in South America acting for Lord Cowdray. His replies pleading inability to attend were sent from Bogota, and 'Bogota' became at the time a favourite tory catcall at political meetings. In November 1915 he returned briefly to public service as director-general of recruiting in Lloyd George's Ministry of Munitions, but by then his health was already beginning to fail.

Murray's appearance and character are well described by J. A. Spender: 'His ample figure and full-moon face, with its fringe of curls, were always a pleasant vision, and he had a persuasive manner that was hard to resist ... his chronic good humour soothed many savage breasts' (Spender, 1.235).

Murray died on 13 September 1920, at his home on the Tweed, Elibank, Walkerburn, Selkirkshire, and was buried on 17 September at Darnhall, Eddleston, Peeblesshire. His wife survived him. They had no children, and the barony conferred on him became extinct.

JOHN GRIGG, *rev.*

Sources A. C. Murray, *Master and brother: Murrays of Elibank* (1945) • J. A. Spender, *Life, journalism and politics*, 2 vols. (1927) • Burke, *Peerage* • GEC, *Peerage* • E. S. Skirving, ed., *Cheltenham College register, 1841–1927* (1928) • *CCI* (1921)
Likenesses watercolour, Scot. NPG [*see illus.*]
Wealth at death £37,859 1s. 3d.: confirmation, 14 Jan 1921, *CCI*

Murray, Alma (1854–1945), actress, was born on 21 November 1854 in London, the daughter of Leigh Murray (1825–1895), actor, and his wife, Sarah Mannering (1830–1872). She was educated privately. On 8 January 1870 she made her first appearance on the stage at the Olympic Theatre, London, in *The Princess* by W. S. Gilbert. For the next nine years she was fairly regularly employed, sometimes in London, sometimes touring in the provinces. On 30 September 1876 she married Alfred William *Forman (1840–1925), the first translator into English of Wagner's *Der Ring des Nibelungen*. They had one child, Elsa (1878–1966). In 1879 she joined Henry Irving's company at the Lyceum, playing in *The Iron Chest* (by George Colman the younger), *The Merchant of Venice* (in which she played Jessica), *The Corsican Brothers* (by Dion Boucicault), and a one-act curtain-raiser, called *Bygones*, by A. W. Pinero, who was, at the age of twenty-four, a minor actor in the Irving company. Clement Scott, the senior theatre critic of the day, in his review of *The Merchant of Venice*, referred to 'the silvery voice and intelligent utterance of Miss Alma Murray' (Scott, 169).

During the 1880s Alma Murray began to establish a widespread reputation as a particularly fine speaker of verse plays, sometimes in London theatre productions but often in single performances in assembly halls in and around London. Thus in 1884 she appeared at Prince's Hall in Robert Browning's play *The Balcony* and in 1885 at St George's Hall in Browning's *Colombe's Birthday* (playing the title role). And in 1886 she 'secured a triumph'—to quote the entry which she herself wrote for *Who's Who in the Theatre*—as Beatrice in a single performance of Shelley's *The Cenci*, a performance so much admired by George Bernard Shaw that he tried very hard, in collaboration with the Shelley Society, to create a suitable circumstance for a repetition of it, an effort in which he was finally foiled by the ridiculous censorship regulations under which the British theatre suffered at that time. (Shelley's play is about an incestuous rape and Lord Lathom, the reader of plays in the lord chamberlain's office, refused to grant it a performance licence.) In 1888 she played one more Browning play: *A Blot in the Scutcheon*, at the Olympic Theatre. Somewhat later, in July 1911 she once again deserted the 'popular' theatre to appear in a 'poetic' play: she was the Queen Geneviève in M. Maeterlinck's *Pelléas et Mélisande* (played in English) at the Lyceum. (The play had been written in 1892, translated into English by Lawrence Alma-Tadema in 1895, and made into an opera by Debussy in 1902.)

On the strength of her enhanced reputation after playing Beatrice in *The Cenci*, Shaw invited Alma Murray in 1894 to play Raina in the first production of *Arms and the Man* which ran for fifty performances at the Avenue Theatre in London. The original plan had been for this part to be played by Florence Farr, the producer and the lessee of the theatre. Shaw had the tricky task of talking her out of the leading role and persuading her to play Louka, the self-willed servant girl. His guile succeeded and Alma Murray played Raina for the whole run. 'Miss Alma Murray lent her seriousness and charm (invaluable qualities both, as it happened) to the part of Raina; Miss Florence Farr made a memorable figure of the enigmatic Louka', said William Archer in *The World* on 25 April 1894.

Long before *Arms and the Man*—indeed, before Shaw had written any plays at all—he had said in a letter to Alma Murray (24 February 1888), in which he praised her acting though he disliked the play she was in: 'I wish I could write you a real play myself, but unfortunately I have not the faculty' (*Collected Letters*, 188). But he never did, even when he had discovered that he *had* 'the faculty'. Though she lobbied him energetically for parts from time to time she played only once more in a Shaw play: she was the Mrs Eynesford-Hill in the first production of *Pygmalion* in 1914. However, she became one of that seemingly endless procession of pretty women to whom Shaw paid court, at least in writing. He wrote to her on 1 June 1894:

> whenever any woman gives me the pleasure your playing [in *Arms and the Man*] tonight did, I cannot help falling violently in love with her; and I can no longer support the spectacle of Forman's [her husband] domestic happiness. He is a most intolerable usurper and monopolist; and the advantage he has taken of the mere accident of his knowing you before I did appears to me altogether unjustifiable. (ibid., 437–8)

And as late as December 1904, when she was fifty, Shaw—writing to tell her why he felt it would be inadvisable to try to revive *Arms and the Man* and why he had not cast her as Nora in *John Bull's other Island* at the Court Theatre, and why he was not going to cast her as Mrs Clandon in *You Never can Tell*—said, 'I can never think of you as middle-aged' (*Collected Plays*, 473).

Much earlier, in 1891, Alma Murray had made an attempt to challenge the supremacy (and near-monopoly) of Janet Achurch and Elizabeth Robins in the playing of those strange and powerful young women in the early productions in England of Ibsen's plays. She tentatively mooted a plan to present the first English production of *Rosmersholm* with herself as Rebecca; but it was, again, Shaw, who stepped in to tell her, in a letter dated 25 November 1890, that he had already persuaded Florence Farr to undertake such a production. (It played briefly at the Vaudeville Theatre in February 1891.)

Alma Murray appeared less and less frequently from 1915 onwards, and she retired completely from the stage shortly after the end of the First World War. She outlived her husband by twenty years and died in London on 3 July 1945 at the age of ninety.   ERIC SALMON

Sources I. Herbert, ed., *Who's who in the theatre*, 17th edn, 2 vols. (1981) • A. C. Ward, *Specimens of English dramatic criticism* (1945) • C. W. Scott, *From 'The bells' to 'King Arthur': a critical record of the first-night productions at the Lyceum Theatre from 1871 to 1895* (1896) • *Collected letters: Bernard Shaw*, ed. D. H. Laurence, 4 vols. (1965–88), vols. 1–2 • *The Bodley Head Bernard Shaw: collected plays with their prefaces*, 1

(1970) · *The Oxford Ibsen*, ed. J. W. McFarlane, 6 (1960) · *Letters from George Bernard Shaw to Miss Alma Murray* (privately printed, Edinburgh, 1927) · *The World* (25 April 1894)

Likenesses photograph, repro. in D. H. Laurence, ed., *Collected letters: Bernard Shaw*

Murray, Amelia Matilda (1795–1884), writer and courtier, the fourth daughter of Lord George *Murray (1761–1803), bishop of St David's, and Anne Charlotte (1765–1844), second daughter of Lieutenant-General Francis Ludovic Grant, was born on 30 April 1795 at Hunton, Kent. An elder brother, George *Murray, became bishop of Rochester. From girlhood she was associated with the court, her mother being lady in waiting to the princesses Elizabeth and Augusta. One of her most intimate friends was Lady Byron, with whom she shared a deep interest in the education of destitute and delinquent children. With her mother she was a founder member of the Children's Friend Society, and on 3 August 1836 she showed the young Princess Victoria around the Royal Victoria Asylum at Chiswick, 'a most interesting and delightful establishment' (Esher, 1.162), which took in destitute children and trained them for domestic service before dispatching them to the colonies. Influenced by her reading of Cesare Beccaria on *Crimes and Punishment*, she was particularly interested in the establishment of a system of juvenile reformatories, and it was with a view to furthering this cause that she sought a place at court. Despite her age, she was appointed maid of honour to Victoria in 1837. Her attempts to interest the queen in the education and reform of the young were regularly undermined by Lord Melbourne, who thought such ideas dangerous nonsense: '"All that intermeddling *produces* crime," he said. We … then had a great deal of fun with Miss Murray about Education', the queen remarked (ibid., 2.148). The Infant Felons Act of 1840 was partly due to her efforts, although it was never implemented. In 1847 she published a small volume, *Remarks on Education*, dedicated to the queen.

In 1854–5 Murray travelled in the United States, Cuba, and Canada, where she examined the institutions of slavery. On her return to England, she published her letters to Lady Byron and others as *Letters from the United States, Cuba and Canada* (1856). The volume, which included a defence of slavery based on her observations of the institution during her travels in the South, was not well received. Moreover, discussion of politics being deemed incompatible with court office, she resigned as woman of the bedchamber, which post she had held since 1853. She published two further works, *Recollections from 1803 to 1837, with a Conclusion in 1868* (1868), and *Pictorial and Descriptive Sketches of the Odenwald* (1869). She died, unmarried, on 7 June 1884 at her home at Glenberrow, Castlemorton, Worcestershire.

K. D. REYNOLDS

Sources W. A. Lindsay, *The royal household* (1898) · R. Davenport-Hill and F. Davenport-Hill, *The recorder of Birmingham* (1878) · Allibone, *Dict.* · Boase, *Mod. Eng. biog.* · Viscount Esher, *The girlhood of Queen Victoria*, 2 vols. (1912)

Wealth at death £3689 17*s.* 0*d.*: probate, 31 July 1884, *CGPLA Eng. & Wales*

Murray, Andrew (*d.* 1297), patriot and soldier, came of a family, originally Flemish, which had settled in the province of Moray about the middle of the twelfth century. His father, Andrew Murray, was the lord of Petty, near Inverness, and of Avoch, in the Black Isle. In the war of 1296 between John, king of Scots, and Edward I of England, Murray fought from the outset on the Scottish side, and was captured with his father and his uncle, Sir William Murray le Riche, lord of Bothwell, at the battle of Dunbar on 27 April. He escaped from imprisonment in Chester in the following winter, however, and returned to Moray. The government which Edward imposed on Scotland after the defeat and forced abdication of King John had proved repressive and there was already growing opposition to it throughout the country. Although his father was still an English prisoner, in early 1297 Murray assumed leadership of what had by now become open rebellion in the north of Scotland. His campaign against the English opened inauspiciously with an abortive attempt on Castle Urquhart in May 1297, but over the next two months he enjoyed greater success, and his tactic of harassing and isolating garrisons gradually loosened the English grip on Moray. He was aided by the incompetence of the administration under John de Warenne, earl of Surrey (*d.* 1304), Edward's lieutenant, and Hugh of Cressingham, the treasurer, and by the equivocal attitude to the rebellion of Scottish magnates ostensibly loyal to Edward, and by August the principal castles in the region, including Elgin, Banff, and Inverness, had fallen to him.

Murray's achievements in the north had been matched by those of William Wallace to the south and, probably in late August, they merged their forces to meet the threat of an English army led by Warenne and Cressingham. At Stirling, on 11 September, the highly disciplined Scottish infantry under the joint command of Murray and Wallace inflicted a signal defeat on the English, whose losses in cavalry and infantry, with Cressingham among the dead, were high. But Murray himself received wounds which were ultimately fatal, and it is uncertain exactly what part he played, with Wallace, in the events which followed the battle. He and Wallace are named as 'commanders of the army of the kingdom of Scotland' in a letter of 11 October to the mayors and communes of Lübeck and Hamburg, and a similar style is employed in a letter of protection to Hexham Priory on 7 November. There is, however, no evidence that Murray actually participated in the invasion of northern England by then in progress and it is Wallace alone who is thereafter named as being in command of the Scots, suggesting that Murray died at some time during the month of November. His posthumous son, another Andrew *Murray, who was born at Whitsun 1298, later married Christian, sister of Robert I, and was guardian of Scotland during the minority of David II.

ANDREW FISHER

Sources *CDS*, vols. 1–2 · Rymer, *Foedera*, new edn · *Johannis de Fordun Scotichronicon, cum supplementis … Walteri Boweri*, ed. W. Goodall, 2 vols. (1759) · *The chronicle of Walter of Guisborough*, ed. H. Rothwell, CS, 3rd ser., 89 (1957) · H. Maxwell, ed. and trans., *The chronicle of Lanercost, 1272–1346* (1913) · F. Palgrave, ed., *Documents* *and records illustrating the history of Scotland* (1837) • J. Stevenson, ed., *Documents illustrative of the history of Scotland*, 2 vols. (1870) • E. M. Barron, *The Scottish war of independence*, 2nd edn (1934) • G. W. S. Barrow, *Robert Bruce and the community of the realm of Scotland*, 2nd edn (1976) • R. Nicholson, *Scotland: the later middle ages* (1974), vol. 2 of *The Edinburgh history of Scotland*, ed. G. Donaldson (1965–75) • E. L. G. Stones, ed. and trans., *Anglo-Scottish relations, 1174–1328: some selected documents*, OMT (1965) • A. Fisher, *William Wallace* (1986)

Murray [Moray], **Sir Andrew**, **of Bothwell** (1298–1338), soldier and administrator, was the posthumous son of Andrew *Murray, who died of wounds received at Stirling Bridge in 1297; his grandfather was then still alive. Nothing is known of his youth, save that in November 1300 he was thought to be living in Moray among the English king's enemies. He may well have been taken south in 1304 or 1306–7, because a prisoner Andrew Murray was released with others by Edward II in the aftermath of Bannockburn. Otherwise he first appears, as witness to a royal charter, on 1 April 1320, five days before the date of the declaration of Arbroath. The draft of that document includes among the senders a 'panetar' of Scotland (the 'panetar', or pantler, was the officer responsible for the royal household's bread supply); this was a family honour which Murray had probably inherited from his great-uncle (d. 1300), and its presence here suggests that his name preceded these words and had been deleted—as were the same words in the final version. He was knighted by 1320. In July 1326, when he was already father of two sons and a widower, Murray married the king's sister Christian *Bruce, widow of Sir Christopher Seton, and was given the Garioch as the dowry. But he was a rare witness to royal acts thereafter, and there is no evidence that he participated in the Weardale campaign of 1327.

At the invasion of the 'disinherited' in 1332 the Scottish community looked to the extended Bruce family for leadership, and after the death of Donald, earl of Mar, at Dupplin Moor they chose Murray, who may have been keeper of Berwick at the time, to be guardian of the kingdom. With Sir Archibald Douglas he tracked Edward Balliol from Perth to Galloway and then to Roxburgh, where, during an attempt to break the bridge at Kelso, Murray risked his person to save a follower. He was taken prisoner and sent to Edward III, still officially at peace with David II.

By the time Murray was allowed to ransom himself, in the summer of 1334, Berwick was in English hands and the purpose of Edward III to annex the southern counties of Scotland was clear. David II was in France, Scotland had been briefly subdued by the two Edwards, but was once more in active 'rebellion', and Murray hastened north to besiege Sir Henry de Beaumont in Dundarg Castle on the north coast of Buchan. Although Edward III hoped to relieve it, after bombardment by a siege engine it capitulated on 23 December 1334.

Scotland was falling rapidly into disorder when John Randolph, earl of Moray and now guardian, held a parliament, attended by Murray, at Dairsie, near Cupar, Fife, in April 1335, for while the patriotic party was not strong enough to expel Edward III, Edward was unable to control

Scotland. David Strathbogie, titular earl of Atholl, had deserted to the patriotic cause, but was scarcely popular at the parliament, which could resolve only on a policy of scorched earth. By August 1335 Edward III was installed in Perth with a large army, the guardian, Moray, was a prisoner in England, and Strathbogie had negotiated a submission which included many patriotic magnates. None the less enough remained faithful to meet at Dumbarton in September 1335 and once more choose Murray as guardian.

Despite the usual view that he was a stout patriot, Murray employed the next two months in short truces frequently extended, negotiating with Edward III for a settlement which would make some provision for David Bruce. During these talks he learned that his wife, Christian Bruce, was besieged in Kildrummy Castle by Strathbogie, acting as lieutenant for Edward Balliol. With a force of about 1000, and apparently with the agreement of the English negotiators, Murray marched north to the relief of his wife. Strathbogie broke off the siege and came south to the Dee near Ballater. There, at Culblean Hill on 30 November 1335, Murray, Sir William Douglas, and their forces came upon Strathbogie's men from the rear; Douglas's men broke their charge and Murray took them from the flank. They turned and fled, save Strathbogie and his retinue, who fought on to the death. The forces were small, but the importance of the victory great, for it gave Murray the heart to refuse the compromise terms negotiated; from that time, the chroniclers noted, the war turned in favour of the Scots.

During the winter of 1335–6 Murray unsuccessfully besieged Cupar Castle, Fife, and held a council at Dunfermline at which he was confirmed as guardian, before marching north to besiege Strathbogie's widow in Lochindorb Castle. Edward III once more came to Perth, and set out with a small force to rescue the lady and if possible destroy Murray. He saved the lady and ravaged much of the country of Moray, but Murray eluded him and, in Edward's absence—the English king returned to spend the end of 1336 in Bothwell—took and destroyed the castles of Dunnottar, Kinneff, Lauriston, and Kinclaven. Cupar again held out in February 1337, but St Andrews Castle fell before a siege engine called Buster. Edward III had gone home, so Murray took his engine to Bothwell and battered down the castle (which was his own heritage) in March 1337. In August, as though the days of Robert I had returned, he was raiding Cumberland, in September Northumberland, taking much loot. Lothian remained nominally in English control, but in fact both sides destroyed its economy, as happened when Murray failed to take Edinburgh at the end of 1337. He had adopted scorched earth tactics and rendered untenable the castles which he took. In short, at a high cost to Scotland, he made it too expensive, too chancy, too time-consuming, for Edward III to hold, and in 1338 Edward turned his attention to France. Murray retired to his castle at Avoch on the Black Isle, where he died that year at an unknown date in Lent (25 February to 12 April). He was buried nearby at Rosemarkie, but his remains were afterwards removed to Dunfermline Abbey.

The nickname the Rich, sometimes attributed to Murray, is not well attested, though he did pay off a very large ransom. His second wife, Christian Bruce, lived on until 1356. He and his first wife, whose identity is unknown, had two sons, John and Thomas, who succeeded to the estates in turn. The second son, **Sir Thomas Murray** [Moray] **of Bothwell** (d. 1361), panetar of Scotland, entered England about September 1351 as a hostage for David II, then on ticket-of-leave in Scotland, soon after succeeding his deceased brother, John. He would return home in 1352, and was apparently knighted by 1353; he participated in the negotiations for the release of David II in 1354 and was party to the treaty of Berwick of 5 October 1357. While he was not named as hostage for payment of David's ransom, he was among the eight prominent magnates from whom three special hostages were to be sent if David failed to keep up payment. Late in 1358 he delivered himself to Edward III as a prisoner, but was given leave to go home; if he went, he was back by July 1359 and remained thereafter in London, where he died, probably of plague, in 1361. He was certainly not held as a special hostage, and must have gone in place of one of the ordinary hostages named in the treaty. He and his wife, Joanna Murray (d. after 1401), daughter of Maurice Murray, earl of Strathearn, had no surviving children, and it is not clear how Bothwell and other lands passed to her second husband, Archibald, third earl of Douglas.   A. A. M. DUNCAN

Sources R. Nicholson, *Edward III and the Scots: the formative years of a military career, 1327–1335* (1965) · *RotS*, vol. 1 · G. Burnett and others, eds., *The exchequer rolls of Scotland*, 23 vols. (1878–1908) · G. W. S. Barrow, *Robert Bruce and the community of the realm of Scotland*, 3rd edn (1988) · *Scots peerage* · R. Nicholson, *Scotland: the later middle ages* (1974), vol. 2 of *The Edinburgh history of Scotland*, ed. G. Donaldson (1965–75) · *The 'Original chronicle' of Andrew of Wyntoun*, ed. F. J. Amours, 6, STS, 1st ser., 57 (1908) · F. J. H. Skene, ed., *Liber pluscardensis*, 1 (1877), 267

Murray, Andrew, first Lord Balvaird (c.1597–1644), Church of Scotland minister, was the second son of David Murray (d. in or before 1627) of Balgonie and Binn, and Agnes, daughter of Sir William Moncreiffe of Moncreiffe. He graduated MA from St Andrews University in 1618, and on 1 October 1622 was admitted as parish minister of Abdie in Fife, having been presented by his grandfather, the first Lord Stormont. By a contract of 30 April 1628 he married Elizabeth, daughter of David, Lord Carnegie, later first earl of Southesk, and having inherited estates on the death of his grandfather in 1631 he was, on 15 June 1633, 'after dinner' (*Historical Works of Balfour*, 4.367) dubbed a knight by Charles I at Seton. Whether the king was aware that in bestowing a knighthood on a minister of the Church of Scotland he was doing something unprecedented is unknown. Quite possibly Murray was simply presented to him as a well-connected country gentleman, and there is no evidence of controversy on the matter.

The allegation that in February 1638 Sir Andrew was the second man to sign the national covenant, which aimed at uniting the country against the king's religious policies, is implausible. The covenanters, having carefully arranged that the earl of Sutherland, as senior noble present, sign first, are unlikely to have let an obscure gentleman-minister slip in immediately after him. As to the claim that later in the year Murray (in his capacity as a gentleman) gave support to a libel (accusation) against the bishops, he told James Gordon that he had 'never concurred' in it, his name and those of others having been inserted without their knowledge (Gordon, 1.127). Murray was later said to have tried to help the king's representative, the marquess of Hamilton, reach a compromise with the covenanters at the November to December 1638 general assembly, but this is unlikely because in March 1639 his royalist father-in-law was accused of trying 'to divert yow [Murray] from the course you were ingadgit in' (*Laing MSS*, 1.203). This makes it clear that Murray, for a time at least, supported the covenanters.

When the king went to Scotland in 1641 and was forced into a settlement with the covenanters which amounted almost to a surrender he created Murray Lord Balvaird. It was said that this was to reward the support the latter had given in 1638, but it more probably reflects the fact that Murray was by this time a rich country gentleman with aristocratic connections and the likelihood of further lands coming to him by inheritance—which they did in 1642 when he inherited the lands (but not the title) of Stormont. In 1641 as in 1633 there is no sign that it was thought incongruous that such promotion in the civil hierarchy of society should be awarded to a parish minister.

However, in June 1643, when the convention of estates met, Balvaird sought to take his seat as a noble, and though his name does not appear in the roll of members present he evidently voted, and this drew attention to his dual status. In August the general assembly of the church passed an act 'for Master Andrew Murray … his exercise his calling of the Ministrie, and for rejecting honours, etc. Incompatible with that calling' (A. Peterkin, ed., *Records of the Kirk of Scotland*, 1843, 361), though Robert Baillie's interpretation of the act as stipulating that Balvaird should 'give over voicing [voting] in parliament, under pain of deposition and other censure' (*Letters and Journals of Robert Baillie*, 2.91) suggests that it was exercising his privileges as a noble rather than mere use of titles which was forbidden, since according to presbyterian principles it was an unacceptable mixing of church and state for a minister to sit in parliament. Balvaird's death on 24 September 1644, when he was said to have been aged about forty-seven, prevented further controversy.

Balvaird's appointment as minister of Abdie had been a matter of family patronage rather than spiritual vocation, a way of providing for a younger son (the parish had been left vacant for ten years before his appointment). By 1634 another gentleman (who eventually inherited a baronetcy) had joined him in Abdie as assistant or colleague, to share the income. Balvaird was a wealthy but obscure gentleman, and only the anomalies of his status rescue him from complete oblivion.   DAVID STEVENSON

Sources *DNB* · *GEC, Peerage* · *Scots peerage* · *Fasti Scot.*, new edn · J. Gordon, *History of Scots affairs from 1637–1641*, ed. J. Robertson and

G. Grub, 3 vols., Spalding Club, 1, 3, 5 (1841) · *The letters and journals of Robert Baillie*, ed. D. Laing, 3 vols. (1841–2) · *The memoirs of Henry Guthry, late bishop*, ed. G. Crawford, 2nd edn (1748) · *The historical works of Sir James Balfour*, ed. J. Haig, 4 vols. (1824–5) · *Report of the Laing manuscripts*, 1, HMC, 72 (1914)
Likenesses attrib. G. Scougal, oils, Scone Palace, Perth

Murray, Andrew Dickson (1812–1878), naturalist, was born on 19 February 1812 in Edinburgh, the eldest son of William Murray (1793–1848) of Conland, Perthshire, and his wife, Mary Thomson (d. 1871). Following in his father's footsteps, he trained for a legal career, and became a writer to the signet on 15 June 1837. After serving an apprenticeship with his father, he joined the firm of Murray and Rhind, and initially practised law in Edinburgh.

Publishing his first scientific paper at forty, Murray quickly established himself as a prolific author. Focusing on entomological and botanical subjects, he published approximately eighty papers between 1852 and 1878. The event which spurred him was, undoubtedly, his involvement with the Oregon Association, which sought to amass a collection of seeds of the conifers of the western coast of North America. Appointed a joint secretary of the committee responsible for organizing the resultant expedition of John Jeffrey in 1850, Murray oversaw the distribution of the beetles and cones of conifers as they arrived in England.

Murray perceived nature as law-bound. Earlier, as part of his call for humanitarian reforms of the penal system, his *Letter to the secretary of state for the Home department on the proper treatment of criminals with a proposal for a substitute for the ticket of leave system* (1856) argued that statesmen had not accorded proper attention to the 'laws of Nature'. However, having attended university lectures on natural history and medicine, he turned his back on a legal career and held a one-session interim appointment as professor of natural science at New College, Edinburgh, following the death of John Fleming in 1857. In the same year, he was elected a fellow of the Royal Society of Edinburgh.

Murray constructed his career in natural history around a specialist's knowledge of conifers (Coniferae) and beetles (Coleoptera). Although his first monograph, *Catalogue of the Coleoptera of Scotland* (1853), had a rather parochial focus, many of his publications were a testament to 'network research': he relied on family, friends, and colleagues to provide specimens and information from the Americas, Africa, and Asia. Among this network were three members of the Botanical Society of Edinburgh (part of the United Presbyterian mission at Old Calabar), who provided Murray with materials to publish a series of articles in the *Annals and Magazine of Natural History* between 1857 and 1871, which metamorphosed into his *List of Coleoptera from Old Calabar* (1878). Similarly, Robert Fortune and John Veitch supplied him with the specimens and information from Japan which led to pieces in the *Proceedings of the Royal Horticultural Society* (republished as *The Pines and Firs of Japan* in 1863). Material from his brother in North America was used for articles including the 'Notes on conifers' published in the *Gardeners' Chronicle* between 1866 and 1876.

In his general approach to natural history and his later interest in biogeography, Murray seemed to follow the injunctions of John Fleming (1785–1857). Although primarily a zoologist, Murray accepted the presidencies of both the Royal Physical Society and the Botanical Society of Edinburgh in 1858–9, so that he could properly address questions of philosophical moment.

In his presidential address to the Botanical Society, Murray critically examined Charles Darwin's and Alfred Russel Wallace's Linnean Society papers of 1858. This marked the beginning of his opposition to Darwin's theory of evolution by natural selection. He published articles in the *Proceedings of the Royal Society of Edinburgh* and in the *Edinburgh New Philosophical Journal*, and began a minor correspondence with Darwin. He argued that modification, hybridization, reversion to type, and attraction were all elements of inviolable laws that had been set in motion by the creator. His main argument was a variant on one that stressed the absence of intermediary evolutionary forms of organisms. Eyeless insects of the same genera, he observed, existed in caves separated by vast geographical barriers. Because examples of the respective genera were not found outside the caves, they must have been created for their specific, local, physical conditions; they were not descendants of a common ancestor.

At the request of his relative John Murray, lord high advocate, Andrew Murray produced *The Skip-Jack or Wireworm and the Slug* for parish schools in 1858—a move which marked the beginning of his commitment to economic entomology. On 4 September of the same year, he married Jane Rogers (d. 6 Oct 1885) in London. He moved to London in January 1861, and became assistant secretary of the Royal Horticultural Society (RHS), a member of the Entomological Society of London, and a fellow of the Linnean Society. But his strongest links remained with the RHS. Described by *The Times* as 'complete as possible, and florid as the gardens and the shows with which it is connected' (4 Dec 1863, 5, col. c–d), his *Book of the Royal Horticultural Society, 1862–1863* (1863) provided a history of the RHS and a description of the garden at South Kensington. In 1865 he was elected a member of council. By this time, contemporaries knew him as:

> somewhat uncouth in figure, and with a countenance that rarely relaxed into a smile, he yet had a kindness of manner that made him respected by all, and a fund of dry humour that told irresistibly upon his hearers, although uttered with what almost amounted to an appearance of unconsciousness on his part. (*Entomologist's Monthly Magazine*, 14, 1878, 216)

Murray continued with his own research in zoology by publishing, in 1864, his most respected piece of taxonomic work, 'Monograph of the family of *Nitidulariae*' in the *Transactions of the Linnean Society of London*. He also made an early contribution to biogeography with his *Geographical Distribution of Animals* (1866). Like others, he now claimed to accept evolution, but shorn of the mechanism of natural selection. Proclaiming himself an adherent of the 'law' of inertia, he denied any automatic, Malthusian tendency for population expansion. He also supported the belief that Australia was the last preserve of Mesozoic life forms. In a bid to create a forum for his research interests, he established the *Journal of Travel and Natural History* (1868, one volume).

On the creation of the scientific committee of the RHS in 1868, Murray became a leading member, and investigated horticultural pests. Under the auspices of the RHS he began to amass a collection of insects beneficial and baneful to agriculture and horticulture. As the collection grew, it was transferred to the Bethnal Green branch museum, where Murray continued to oversee its organization. He produced a descriptive *List of the Contents of the Collection of Economic Entomology* in 1877. His *Economic Entomology: Aptera* (1877) was the first, and only, of eight projected manuals that were meant to accompany the collection.

In 1869 Murray accompanied J. D. Hooker, Robert Hogg, and others as a British delegate to the Botanical Congress at St Petersburg. He also supervised some of the arrangements for the British contributions to the Moscow International Exhibition in 1872. As an expert on economic entomology, he petitioned the government to take action to eradicate insect pests, when the British public feared an imminent invasion of the Colorado potato beetle in 1877. Although unsuccessful with his plea, he assisted the government with identification of Colorado beetles.

As a consultant to a mining venture, Murray travelled to North America in 1873–4. Visiting California, Utah, and Ontario, he found opportunities to engage in his natural history pursuits. When the RHS council resigned *en masse* in 1874, Murray followed suit from San Francisco. He contracted an illness in Utah and, although he seemed to rally, he suffered a gradual decline over the next four years. Nevertheless, he remained active until the end. Two months before his death, he assumed the position of scientific director of the RHS. On 10 January 1878, however, he succumbed to his illness at his home at 67 Bedford Gardens, Kensington, London. He was buried at Kensal Green cemetery two days later.   J. F. M. Clark

Sources *Gardeners' Chronicle*, new ser., 9 (1878), 50 · *Gardeners' Chronicle*, new ser., 9 (1878), 86–7 · *Journal of the Royal Horticultural Society of London*, 5 (1879) · *The Times* (15 Jan 1878) · *Canadian Entomologist*, 10 (1878) · *Entomologist's Monthly Magazine*, 14 (1878–9), 44–5 · *The Society of Writers to His Majesty's Signet with a list of the members* (1936) · H. R. Fletcher, *The story of the Royal Horticultural Society, 1804–1968* (1969) · J. T. Johnstone, 'John Jeffrey and the Oregon expedition', *Notes from the Royal Botanic Garden Edinburgh*, 20 (1939), 2–53 · *The correspondence of Charles Darwin*, ed. F. Burkhardt and S. Smith, 8 (1993) · *The correspondence of Charles Darwin*, ed. F. Burkhardt and S. Smith, 9 (1994) · S. A. Neave, *The centenary history of the Entomological Society of London, 1833–1933* (1933) · *Gardeners' Chronicle* (22 Aug 1868), 893 · [J. D. Hooker], review, *Gardeners' Chronicle* (22 Sept 1866), 902 · P. J. Bowler, *Life's splendid drama: evolutionary biology and the reconstruction of life's ancestry, 1860–1940* (1996) · J. F. Clark, 'Beetle mania: the Colorado beetle scare of 1877', *History Today*, 42/12 (1992), 5–7 · M. L. Blaisdell, *Darwinism and its data: the adaptive coloration of animals* (1992) · P. F. Rehbock, *The philosophical naturalists: themes in early nineteenth-century British biology* (1983) · bap. reg. Scot.
Archives Royal Botanic Garden, Edinburgh, minute book | BL, Charles Babbage corresp. · BL, Sherborn autographs · BL, Alfred Russel Wallace MSS · Oxf. U. Mus. NH, Hope Library · Provincial Archives of Manitoba, Winnipeg, Hudson's Bay Company archives · U. Cam., Darwin corresp.

Murray, Andrew Graham, first Viscount Dunedin (1849–1942), judge, was born on 21 November 1849 at Edinburgh, the only child of Thomas Graham Murray (1816–1891), of Stenton near Dunkeld, Perthshire, writer to the signet and crown agent for Scotland, and his wife, Caroline Jane (*d.* 1906), daughter of John Tod, writer to the signet, of Kirkhill, Midlothian. On both sides Murray came from a legal background. His paternal grandfather, Alexander Murray of Murrayshall, had been an advocate. John Tod was one of the founders of the leading Edinburgh solicitors' firm of Tod, Murray, and Jamieson, in which Murray's father was a partner.

Education and early legal and political career Murray was educated at a private school in Tunbridge Wells and was a Spencer scholar at Harrow School. From there he proceeded with a scholarship to Trinity College, Cambridge, where he graduated with a second class in classics in 1872. The effort he put in at school appears to have been diverted more into sports at Cambridge. Murray, together with a college friend, made a pioneering eight-hole golf course on Midsummer Common. He also further developed the skills at rackets he had shown signs of at school. His education thus far had also given Murray an English veneer which never wholly rubbed off, even in later life.

From Cambridge, Murray went to Edinburgh University where he passed through the ordinary law classes. He then spent, according to the usual practice, a year in his father's practice before being admitted to the Scottish bar in July 1874. It is worth noting that in choosing the bar he had given up his claim to 'probably the richest prize in the legal profession in Scotland' of a partnership in this firm for the somewhat less certain career of an advocate (*Glasgow Herald*, 22 Aug 1942). Murray was an early friend of R. L. Stevenson, who was admitted to the bar on the same day in the following year and who was said to have consulted Murray when writing *Weir of Hermiston*. Both were members of the Speculative Society at the university, in which Murray held the offices of librarian and president. On 1 October 1874 Murray married Mary Clementina (1857–1922), seventh of the eight daughters of Admiral Sir William Edmonstone MP of Duntreath, Stirlingshire, fourth baronet. They had one son and three daughters. Murray's first wife was very active in the support of charitable and patriotic causes in Edinburgh.

Tradition had it that Murray spent the year at Tod, Murray, and Jamieson, studying Italian rather than law. Doubts were expressed about his ability to concentrate and at the start of his career as an advocate he 'enjoyed himself in every lawful manner' (*Scotsman*, 22 Aug 1942). Golf, dancing ('hard and late'), and shooting and fishing (though he lacked the patience for the latter and preferred games to both) helped to fill up the time left by the practice he had. In his physical prime Murray was tall, slender, and athletic, with a well-knit frame, muscular and energetic. Some of his energy was, nevertheless, obviously taken up by extensive legal reading. It was at this time that

Andrew Graham Murray, first Viscount Dunedin (1849–1942), by Sir James Guthrie, 1910

he read the work on feudal law by George Ross (his uncle by marriage). He later referred to this as having given him the grounding in the area in which he was to enjoy a leading reputation. Murray also brought together a number of advantages which ensured that by the mid-1880s he had a large and lucrative practice, specializing in conveyancing and patent cases. These included an ability to switch rapidly from one occupation to another and the gift of clear-headed, logical, and lucid exposition. Though he was not an orator, he excelled in arguing a case with imperfect preparation, not only because he was acute, but also due to his absence of nervousness. To these personal skills Murray at the outset added the backing of his father's firm and family legal connections.

In 1888 Murray was appointed advocate-depute in the crown office, and in 1890 he was considered for the vacant post of solicitor-general for Scotland. Passed over on this occasion in view of the stronger claims of Sir Charles Pearson, he was made sheriff of Perthshire, but he became

solicitor–general in 1891 when Pearson succeeded James Robertson as lord advocate. At this time he also became a queen's counsel. In October 1891 Murray was elected to parliament as a Conservative member for Bute, the seat Robertson had vacated on his elevation to the bench. This was the seat that Murray's uncle David Mure had represented some thirty years before. Murray had previously and unsuccessfully contested East Perthshire, also as a Conservative, at the 1885 general election. He represented Bute until he became a judge more than thirteen years later, and he was also lord lieutenant from 1901 to 1905. Murray was not, however, a natural constituency politician. In addition to not being an orator, he displayed either an absent-mindedness or a too-obvious exertion to make himself agreeable in this field of activity.

Out of office from 1892, Murray again became solicitor-general when the Conservatives returned to power in 1895. In the following year he succeeded Sir Charles Pearson, who had become a judge, as lord advocate, and he also became a privy councillor. Murray's friend and ally, Scott Dickson, became solicitor-general in his place. As lord advocate Murray earned a reputation as an excellent administrator, open to those he worked with and conciliatory in his approach to business. He was not, however, counted a great success as a parliamentary debater.

In 1903 Lord Balfour of Burleigh resigned over tariff reform, and as a consequence Murray succeeded him as secretary for Scotland with a seat in the cabinet. He accepted this appointment with some reluctance as it involved a cut in his official salary from £5000 to £2000, but he was reportedly mollified by the assurance that he would retain any claims to a judicial appointment that would have been his as lord advocate. In his short tenure of office Murray was involved in the negotiations which preceded the introduction of the Churches (Scotland) Bill. He was also brought into closer official contact with Edward VII and was credited with being a mentor to the king in Scottish matters for the remainder of the reign.

Member of the Court of Session In early 1905 Murray was appointed to succeed Lord Kinross, who had died, as lord president of the Court of Session and lord justice-general. His mother was present to see him take his seat. Just before taking up this position he was raised to the peerage as Baron Dunedin of Stenton in Perthshire. His friend Hugh Pattison Macmillan, later his biographer and colleague as a House of Lords' appeals judge, believed that this period in the chair of the first division of the Court of Session was the summit of Dunedin's career. Of his immediate predecessors, Robertson had been more interested in politics and Kinross had been prevented by ill health from exercising vigorous leadership. Dunedin, by contrast, was really interested in legal problems and believed strongly in the integrity of the law of Scotland. He was also able to 'breathe fresh life into his colleagues' (*Scotsman*, 22 Aug 1942) in a relationship helped by his accessibility to argument and a lack of vanity which allowed him to admit that his first view might be wrong. In his relations with the bar Dunedin did not continue to be an advocate when he became a judge and apparently enjoyed listening to a well-arranged presentation, interrupting only to clear away obscurities. As an example of Dunedin's courage in the pursuit of justice and readiness to brush aside technicalities, Macmillan cites the case of his willingness to arrange payment so that an appellant from the Court of Session who had run out of funds could take a case on to the House of Lords (*Scottish Law Review*, 151). Dunedin had been in the majority in the case in question and the outcome saw this judgment overturned. In his opinions Dunedin tried to seek out the principle involved in a case and welcomed the opportunity to restate appropriate legal rules, which gave his judgments the authoritative reputation of being a storehouse of legal opinion. As a result, however, they were not always restricted to a statement of what was strictly necessary for a decision and were marked by occasional colloquialisms and circumlocutions.

Lord of appeal-in-ordinary In 1913 Dunedin was chosen to fill one of the two new positions as a lord of appeal-in-ordinary created to strengthen the supreme appeals court. Accepting this position removed him from a leadership role to one of playing his part in a team. He appears to have made the adjustment well and was thereafter involved in many of the landmark judgments handed down in his nineteen-year tenure. Commentators have seen a contrast between his work during this period and that of the other Scottish law lord at the time, Lord Shaw of Dunfermline. In the case *R. v. Halliday* in 1917 over the internment of a British citizen in wartime, Shaw, in the minority, emotionally invoked the liberty of the subject, while Dunedin, with the majority, was in favour of upholding the regulations regarding the defence of the realm. This approach to the law, 'pure and simple, touched, if at all by common sense' (*Law Journal*, 3 Oct 1942, 317), was also evident in Dunedin's agreement with the majority in *Bowman v. The Secular Society*, also in 1917, that a bequest to a rationalist society was legal. In this he was opposed by Lord Chancellor Finlay who appears to have thought that Christianity was in some danger. Dunedin presided in 1920 at the hearing of the *Attorney-General v. De Keyser's Royal Hotel*, probably the best-known of the wartime cases he was called upon to judge. He delivered the leading judgment that the company concerned was entitled to full compensation under the Defence Act 1842 for the requisition of property for defence purposes. This judgment was to be superseded in 1939 by the more restricted provisions of the Compensation (Defence) Act. Other cases worth mentioning with which Dunedin was concerned and which reached the House of Lords included *Sinclair v. Brougham* (1914), in which he dealt at length with the problem of 'unjust enrichment' and argued that English equity should be able to deal as well as other systems with the problem of equitable restitution. In *Lord Advocate v. Marquess of Zetland* (1920), one of the last cases to deal with the intricacies of Scottish feudal law, Dunedin, on ground he knew so well, was able to assist his colleagues in dealing with the abstruseness of the points at issue. Finally, *Cantiare San Rocco v. Clyde Shipbuilding and Engineering* (1924) allowed Dunedin to display his preference for the Scottish law of restitution as against the English law as it then stood.

Comparisons between the English and Scottish legal systems were a theme also in Dunedin's published writings. His letter to *The Times* of 20 April 1927 discussed the rights of crown and subject under Scottish law and contained a comment characteristic of his terse, pungent, witty style: 'in England you have to find the remedy in order to discover the right, whereas in Scotland you have to find the right in order to discover the remedy'. His 'Fifty years: the bench and the bar', published in the same newspaper on 18 February 1932, was a valuable reflective piece on legal developments in both countries which traced the replacement of feudal cases in Scotland by those generated by companies and workmen's compensation legislation; it also pointed out that a new class of scientific lawyer, concerned with patent cases, had left judges struggling to keep pace in this area. In all these developments Dunedin makes clear his firsthand experience or direct shaping involvement. He recounts, for instance, his ticking off by Joseph Chamberlain for inserting a clause in the Scottish version of workmen's compensation legislation which allowed the use of paid lawyers in such proceedings. Chamberlain had in the end to give way, having been brought to see that companies would simply use specially trained non-lawyers to the disadvantage of inexperienced employee litigants. Similarly, Dunedin's expression of regret at the passing of judges of high individuality and purely Scottish education such as Lord Deas echoes the belief at the Scottish bar that one reason for Dunedin's early success had been his courageous and tactful handling of the person whose outspokenness from the bench he had so much enjoyed.

Other activities Though more active in writing to the press in later life, and a source of information and guidance—often, owing to his judicial position, not available for publication—to the *Law Journal*, Dunedin was otherwise not a prolific writer. *A Digest of Registration Cases*, which first appeared in 1877, and the historical pamphlet *A short account of the principality of Scotland and the title of prince and steward of Scotland* (1892), are titles which can be mentioned.

In 1900 Dunedin became the keeper of the great seal of the principality of Scotland, an office he held until 1936. Many other honours were also bestowed on him in this later period in his life. He was awarded the GCVO in 1923 and created Viscount Dunedin of Stenton in 1926. Honorary LLD degrees were bestowed by the universities of Edinburgh, Glasgow, Aberdeen, Toronto, Chicago, and Columbia, and that of DCL by Oxford. He was elected an honorary bencher of the Middle Temple, London, in 1910. In addition to being lord lieutenant of Bute, he was also a deputy lieutenant of the county of the city of Edinburgh.

In December 1922 Dunedin's first wife died and in July 1923 he married Jean (1885–1944) [*see* Murray, Jane Elmslie Henderson], daughter of George Findlay, merchant, of Aberdeen. The second Lady Dunedin was probably best-known as the first director of Scottish War Savings from

1916 to 1923. She was created CBE in 1920 for her work in this position. Lady Dunedin had been assistant editor at Everyman from 1914 to 1916 and was to be editor in 1933–4. She published works of her own also, such as *Three Aspects of the Russian Revolution* (1918).

Dunedin was reportedly very proud of his wife's achievements, and it is a matter for speculation how far his second marriage encouraged him in the discovery of new activities aside from the law and in his greater participation in current affairs through letters to the press. This is not to say that his early pace of social activity had abated before this time. Profuse hospitality, friendships in high social circles, and a lasting preference for dancing over more sedentary evening pleasures, all showed Dunedin's taste for the good life. Golf continued to be an interest. Dunedin was captain of the Royal and Ancient Golf Club in 1892 and of the Honourable Company of Edinburgh Golfers in 1893–4. He was also a good tennis and billiards player and had some experience of coaching as a sport. Mechanical and technical things were another interest. Dunedin was a pioneer motorist, and he was also said to have been one of the first MPs to ride into Palace Yard on a bicycle. He was responsible for the design of his house, 7 Rothesay Terrace, Edinburgh. As he had been no orator in politics, so he was no raconteur on the after-dinner circuit, but he told a good story and reportedly gave after-dinner speeches in languages other than English. In addition to a good knowledge of French, which he spoke with a marked British accent, Dunedin took up the study of Romanian and German in middle age and enjoyed showing off his linguistic proficiency. To all these social qualities and activities must be added his wit. On Hugh Macmillan's appointment to be his House of Lords' colleague in 1930, for instance, Dunedin telegraphed 'heartiest congratulations to *myself*' (*Scottish Law Review*, 151), most probably a reference to the inspiration Macmillan said he had derived from the older man's example.

Dunedin retired as an appeals judge in March 1932, having confided to Macmillan that his memory was failing. This was still not matched, however, by any comparable loss of interest in pursuing an active life. Dunedin became a keen amateur film-maker, and in 1935 he was appointed the first honorary fellow of the Cinema Institute, of which he was a founder patron. He also exhibited a marked wanderlust, travelling widely in different parts of the world.

Viscount Dunedin died in an Edinburgh nursing home on 21 August 1942, having been ill for some time previously, and he was buried three days later at Caputh churchyard in Perthshire. He was survived by his widow, who died in March 1944, and by two of his daughters from his first marriage.

Assessment Dunedin held a sequence of high offices, both political and judicial, on his way to becoming a law lord, and was the recipient of a range of honours. A unionist, his career was a product of the union from his education to his easy movement between the Scottish and English legal systems in later life, and beyond that his contact as an appeals judge with colonial cases. His place in history, however, is not that of a well-known public figure. Rather

it is of the kind that fades more quickly from the public mind, namely that of a great lawyer of his generation. Hugh Macmillan ranks him with Inglis and Watson as the best that the Parliament House, Edinburgh, produced in the half century that Dunedin himself looked back on in his *Times* article of 1932. His judgments were seen as standing in the Scottish tradition of substance rather than form, and of principle rather than precedent. His varied and highly active life outside his profession, and his apparent wish to be counted a man of the world rather than as a legal scholar, should not detract from his obvious interest in the law as an intellectual exercise. In addition Dunedin was concerned above all with the sound and rational administration of the law. His rejection, after trying it out as a junior, of the parliamentary bar as too turbulent, and his preference for feudal and patent cases, are indicative of this; so too are the references to his contribution to legal development, especially with respect to workmen's compensation legislation, from his friend Lord Macmillan.   GORDON F. MILLAR

Sources *The Scotsman* (22 Aug 1942) · *The Times* (24 Aug 1942) · *Glasgow Herald* (22 Aug 1942) · *WWW*, 1941–50 · *Law Journal* (29 Aug 1942), 273 · *Law Journal* (3 Oct 1942), 317–18 · *Scottish Law Review*, 58 (1942), 149–52, 158 · *DNB* · A. G. Murray, 'Fifty years: the bench and the bar', *The Times* (18 Feb 1932) · A. G. Murray, 'The crown as litigant: procedure in Scots law—rights of the subject', *The Times* (20 April 1927) · *The Times* (26 Aug 1942) [the Lord Chancellor, Viscount Simon's tribute] · *The Times* (9 Sept 1942) [report of the Lord Chancellor, Viscount Simon's tribute in parliament] · *The Scotsman* (22 Aug 1942) [death notice] · *The Scotsman* (24 Aug 1942) · *The Scotsman* (25 Aug 1942) [funeral report] · *WWBMP*, 2.262 · *WWW*, 1941–50 [Viscountess Dunedin] · *WWW*, 1981–90 [Baron Macmillan of Aberfeldy] · *The Society of Writers to His Majesty's Signet: with a list of the members* (1936), 272 [entry for Thomas Graham Murray] · S. P. Walker, *The Faculty of Advocates, 1800–1986* (1987), 135–6 · F. J. Grant, ed., *The Faculty of Advocates in Scotland, 1532–1943*, Scottish RS, 145 (1944), 63 · A. Eddington, *Edinburgh and the Lothians at the opening of the twentieth century: contemporary biographies* (1904); facs. edn pubd as *A dictionary of Edwardian biography: Edinburgh and the Lothians* (1983), 165 · *The Times* (22 March 1944) [second Lady Dunedin] · *The Scotsman* (23 March 1944) [second Lady Dunedin] · *The Scotsman* (4–5 Dec 1922) [first Lady Dunedin] · [W. M. Watson], ed., *The history of the Speculative Society, 1764–1904* (1905), 42, 160

Archives PRO, papers as chairman of Irish Free State Compensation Committee, CO 905/17–18 | Bodl. Oxf., letters to H. H. Asquith · U. Leeds, Brotherton L., letters to Sir Edmund Gosse

Likenesses J. Guthrie, oils, 1910, Parliament House, Edinburgh, Faculty of Advocates [*see illus.*] · W. Stoneman, photograph, 1926, NPG · W. Stoneman, photograph, 1936, NPG · R. Guthrie, pen-and-ink drawing, 1937, NPG · Spy [L. Ward], caricature, chromolithograph, BM; repro. in *VF* (22 Oct 1896) · photograph, repro. in *The Scotsman* (22 Aug 1942) · photograph, repro. in *The Times* · photograph, repro. in *Glasgow Herald*

Murray, Sir Andrew Hunter Arbuthnot (1903–1977), politician and businessman, was born on 19 December 1903 in Edinburgh, the city with which he was associated throughout his life. His parents were Alfred Alexander Arbuthnot Murray, writer to the signet and fellow of the Royal Society of Edinburgh, and his wife, Mary, *née* Moir. He was educated in Edinburgh at Daniel Stewart's College and George Heriot's School, where he was sports champion in 1922. He then entered business as an insurance broker.

Murray was elected to Edinburgh town council for the North Leith ward in 1928. He served on the council until 1951, being latterly elected for the Liberton ward, albeit with one year's absence in 1934. Leith suffered as much as any other industrial town from the depression of the 1930s and Murray's record of social work was a distinguishing feature of his career. He quickly rose to prominence on the council, serving as the city's honorary treasurer between 1943 and 1946 and as lord provost from 1947 to 1951.

Murray was widely respected as lord provost, being described by contemporaries as a 'tireless and devoted personality' (*The Scotsman*, 22 March 1977, 4). He exercised a central influence over the post-war redevelopment of the city of Edinburgh. Slum properties in the Old Town were cleared, and replaced by estates in the suburbs, while the Old Town's historical character was preserved. He also championed the city's artistic scene. Having, during the Second World War, revived the Leith pageant, he was instrumental in the foundation of the Edinburgh festival in 1947. He argued that the festival could engender a 'better spirit of understanding between men and women, through an appreciation of the arts' (*The Times*, 24 Aug 1948, 4f) and towards that end he travelled to Belgrade to bring the Yugoslav National Ballet to Edinburgh. He was awarded the freedom of the city of Athens in 1950, in recognition of his efforts to promote the city of Edinburgh abroad. As lord provost he received a knighthood in 1949 and an honorary doctorate in laws from Edinburgh University in 1950. After his period of office ended he was commissioned, in 1953, as a deputy lieutenant of the county of Edinburgh.

Known as a supporter of the National Liberal Party, Murray was adopted as Unionist candidate for the marginal Labour seat of Central Edinburgh following the 1950 general election, but resigned before the 1951 election took place. He was adopted by Leith Liberal Association in 1954 to contest the town's parliamentary seat as an independent but finished a distant third to the Labour MP, James Hoy, in the 1955 election. Seeing no future for the National Liberal cause, he persuaded the Leith Liberals to rejoin the Scottish Liberal Party, of which he became a vice-president in 1957. He fought Leith as a Liberal candidate in 1959, but saw his vote drop and he again finished third. It was to be his last parliamentary contest. Murray was elected president of the Liberal Party in 1960, serving for twelve months, and was a treasurer of the party for three years from 1962. He was not universally popular within the party, given his previous connections with the National Liberals; nevertheless, the Liberals benefited from association with such a senior figure in lowland Scottish politics as well as from his assistance during a period of considerable financial strain.

Murray was as prominent in Scottish business as in politics, sitting on the boards of the stores group Hide & Co. and the Scottish Motor Traction Company. He was also, briefly, chairman of the Equitable Industrial Company of Scotland. His involvement with the latter two firms ended with litigation in which he played a prominent part in the defence of small shareholders' rights in the face of hostile takeover bids.

Murray was appointed OBE in 1945 for his involvement with the fire service before and during the Second World War. He was elected commandant of the Edinburgh Auxiliary Fire Service in 1938 and was responsible for its being one of the few to be close to its full authorized strength on the outbreak of the conflict. He was made fire inspector of the headquarters of the fire brigades division of the Scottish home department in 1942. He was closely allied with the order of St John of Jerusalem throughout his life, becoming a companion of the order in 1949, a knight of the order five years later, and a chancellor of the order in 1963. At his death he was preceptor of the ancient Knights Templar institution at Torphichen, West Lothian, and held the title of chancellor of the priory of Scotland.

In his later years Murray remained committed to several of the causes he had first espoused in his youth. He was a governor of George Heriot's School and chaired the governors of Carberry Tower, a Church of Scotland youth centre opened in 1962. He died on 21 March 1977, at his home, 1 Randolph Place, in the New Town of Edinburgh. His obituary in *The Scotsman* (22 March 1977) recalled the occasion when, as captain of the orange colours, an archaic council post which entitled the holder to the use of a white stallion in an official capacity, Murray had acquired such an animal and ridden it through Edinburgh. A subsequent lord provost, Sir Herbert Brechin, summed him up as 'a great figure' who 'commanded attention wherever he went' (*Evening News*, 22 March 1977, 9). He was unmarried.   ROBERT INGHAM

Sources *Evening News* [Edinburgh] (22 March 1977), 9 · *The Scotsman* (22 March 1977), 4 · private information (2004) · *The Times* (24 Aug 1948), 4f · *The Times* (25 March 1950), 3d · *The Times* (11 Jan 1951), 5c · *The Times* (23 Jan 1951), 6g · *The Times* (21 Jan 1953), 10c · *The Times* (21 May 1956), 6g · *The Times* (27 June 1956), 7a · *The Times* (30 Sept 1960), 6f · *The Times* (23 March 1961), 8d · *The Times* (1 Feb 1966), 15e · *The Times* (2 Feb 1966), 15e · P. Abercrombie and D. Plumstead, *A civic survey and plan for the City and Royal Burgh of Edinburgh* (1949) · S. Mullay, *The Edinburgh encyclopedia* (1996), 18, 196–201, 218–19 · d. cert. · J. Thorpe, *In my own time* (1999) · *The Times* (23 Sept 1961), 8
Archives FILM British Pathé, London, archival footage · Reuters, London, Reuters Archives, archival footage
Likenesses photograph, repro. in *The Scotsman* · photograph, repro. in *Edinburgh Evening News* · photograph, repro. in *Edinburgh Evening News* (3 April 1951), 5 · photograph, repro. in *The Times* (23 Aug 1950), 8
Wealth at death £872.17: confirmation, 28 July 1977, *CCI*

Murray [*née* Home Drummond], **Anne**, duchess of Atholl (1814–1897), courtier, was born in Edinburgh on 17 June 1814, the only daughter and second of the three children of Henry Home Drummond, MP (1783–1867), of Blair Drummond, Perthshire, and Christian Stirling (1779–1864), elder daughter of Charles Moray of Abercairny. She was rejected, sight unseen, as the potential bride of an unspecified duke before marrying, on 29 October 1839, George Augustus Frederick John Murray (1814–1864), Baron Glenlyon and heir presumptive to the dukedom of Atholl. The marriage was successful, Anne Glenlyon observing to her father in its early days, that 'my ticket in

Anne Murray, duchess of Atholl (1814–1897), by Sir Francis Grant

the marriage lottery is a prize' (Abercairny MSS). They had an only child, a son, born in 1840, later seventh duke.

Connections with the court were initially formed in 1842, when Victoria and Albert visited the Glenlyons at Dunkeld, in Perthshire, during their first visit to Scotland; this visit was also the occasion of Victoria's first attendance at a Church of Scotland service, in Blair Atholl. In 1844 the royal couple again visited the Glenlyons, taking over Blair Castle during September. These connections were made the more important by financial difficulties: the Atholl estates were held in trust during the lifetime of the fifth duke who was insane, and the Glenlyons actively sought positions at court to enhance their incomes. In 1846 Glenlyon obtained the position of lord in waiting from Peel, whom he supported in parliament, but changes in the administration removed him from the court after six months. On 14 September 1846, Glenlyon succeeded as sixth duke of Atholl (which he and his wife consistently spelt Athole).

In March 1852 Anne Atholl was invited to serve at the head of the female household as mistress of the robes under the Derby administration, which position she filled until the following January. In May 1854 she was invited to become a lady of the bedchamber, a position of lower rank than that which she had previously held, but which involved closer contact with the queen through regular residence at court. Their relationship was always friendly, in part because the duchess understood how to manage the queen, 'the complete folly of opposition if started at once, without any care, and the ease with which advice may be given and well received, if you don't begin in

antagonism' (Ponsonby, 63). The death of the duke in 1864 from cancer of the neck after a lengthy illness, drew the duchess closer to the queen, who took comfort from the presence of another mourning widow, describing her as 'so wise, so excellent and so pleasant and so truly Scotch' (Fulford, 26).

After the death of the duke, Anne Atholl lived at Dunkeld House with her cousin Emily Murray MacGregor as a companion, and here the queen stayed with her on a number of occasions. She took an active interest in the local community, particularly in the school for girls which she had opened in Dunkeld in 1856. She continued to hold her position at court, and served as acting mistress of the robes with the dowager duchesses of Bedford and Roxburghe during Gladstone's final ministry when no duchess could be persuaded to accept the office. She denied having party political opinions, although her husband and father had been Peelites and her son, who succeeded as seventh duke in 1864, was a Conservative; Miss Murray MacGregor, by contrast, was a convinced Gladstonian.

Anne Atholl died at Dunkeld House on 18 May 1897 at the age of eighty-two and was buried four days later with her husband in the ruined Old Kirk at Blair Atholl.

K. D. REYNOLDS

Sources Blair Castle, Perthshire, Atholl MSS · NA Scot., Abercairny MSS · K. D. Reynolds, *Aristocratic women and political society in Victorian Britain* (1998) · GEC, *Peerage* · W. A. Lindsay, *The royal household* (1898) · Burke, *Gen. GB* (1914) · *Your dear letter: private correspondence of Queen Victoria and the crown princess of Prussia, 1865–1871*, ed. R. Fulford (1971), 26 · M. Ponsonby, ed., *Mary Ponsonby* [1927], 63 · *The letters of Queen Victoria*, ed. G. E. Buckle, 3 vols., 3rd ser. (1930–32), vol. 3, p. 163 · Queen Victoria, *More leaves from the journal of a life in the highlands, from 1862 to 1882* (1884) · d. cert.
Archives Blair Castle, Perthshire, corresp. and papers, incl. royal corresp. | NA Scot., Abercairny MSS
Likenesses S. Watson, portrait, 1849, Blair Castle, Blair Atholl, Perthshire · Graves, portrait, 1895 (after F. Grant), Blair Castle, Blair Atholl, Perthshire · G. K. Terrell, portrait, 1897, Blair Castle, Blair Atholl, Perthshire · F. Grant, portrait, Blair Drummond, Perthshire [*see illus.*]
Wealth at death £9316 18s. 9d.: confirmation, 24 July 1897, *CCI*

Murray, Sir Archibald James (1860–1945), army officer, was born on 21 April 1860 at Woodhouse, near Kingsclere, Hampshire, the third child of Charles Murray, landed proprietor, and his wife, Anne, daughter of Captain John Baker Graves, of the 19th regiment, and later judge at Kurunegala, Ceylon. Educated at Cheltenham College, Murray entered the army through the Royal Military College, Sandhurst, and in 1879 was gazetted to the 27th regiment which, two years later, became the Royal Inniskilling Fusiliers. His early service was abroad, at Hong Kong, Singapore, and the Cape, where in 1888, as a captain, he took part in the suppression of a Zulu rising. In 1890 he married Caroline Helen (d. 1910), daughter of Lieutenant-Colonel Henry Baker Sweet of Hillersdon, Tiverton. They had a son.

In 1897 Murray gained entrance to the Staff College, Camberley; among his fellow students were the future field marshals W. R. Robertson, D. Haig, and E. H. H.

Sir Archibald James Murray (1860–1945), by Walter Stoneman, 1919

Allenby. Thoughtful and reserved in manner, Murray seemed old for his years, and was generally spoken of at the college as 'Old Archie'.

At the end of the two-year course Murray rejoined his battalion, but on the outbreak of the Second South African War he was appointed intelligence officer on the staff of Sir William Penn Symons, commanding in Natal, and was with him when he was mortally wounded, and his senior staff officer killed, in the opening frontier fight at Talana. The next-in-command was ill, and Murray, appointed chief of staff by him, managed skilfully to extricate the British force from its advanced position and bring it back to Ladysmith. His reputation as a field soldier was deservedly high and he was promoted lieutenant-colonel in 1900. Henceforward generals competed for his services. He was on the staff of Sir George White during the siege of Ladysmith; and during 1900 was senior staff officer to Sir Archibald Hunter of the 10th division. In October 1901 Murray was promoted to command the 2nd battalion of his regiment in India, soon to be warned for service in South Africa, where it arrived in February 1902. In leading his men in an attack in the northern Transvaal, for which he was appointed to the DSO, he was dangerously wounded in the abdomen.

Between the Second South African War and the First World War Murray held a series of important staff appointments: senior general staff officer of the 1st division (Aldershot); director of military training, general staff, at the War Office, 1907–12 (Haig being one of the other two directors); and inspector of infantry (1912–14). He was promoted major-general in 1910, the year in which his first wife died. In 1912 Murray married Mildred Georgina, daughter of his former Colonel, William Toke Dooner, of Maidstone.

Murray had held the command of the 2nd division for six months when war was declared in 1914, but he was appointed chief of the general staff of the British expeditionary force (BEF) at the express wish of Sir John French, under whose command he was serving at Aldershot. The early days of the campaign—the battles of Mons and Le Cateau, the retreat on Paris, the advance to the Marne and the Aisne, the transfer of the BEF to Flanders, and the first battle of Ypres—were more than strenuous, and according to French's reminiscences, *1914*, at the end of the year Murray had fallen sick. He was obliged in January 1915 to go to England for rest, and Robertson (who was then quartermaster-general) took his place. In February 1915 Lord Kitchener appointed Murray deputy chief of the Imperial General Staff for the special purpose of superintending the training of the New Army, and in September he was promoted chief of the Imperial General Staff (CIGS). In December, however, French resigned and was replaced by Haig, and Robertson became CIGS.

Murray was appointed to a command in Egypt, where he arrived in January 1916, with instructions to secure the safety of the Suez Canal, administer martial law in Egypt, and reorganize the troops evacuated from Gallipoli. That his forces were to be regarded as the 'imperial strategic reserve' made the task Murray confronted in Egypt all the more challenging and he was widely considered an excellent choice for the job. He tackled his large and complex workload with determination and enthusiasm.

In August, after an invading enemy force had been defeated at Romani (20 miles from the canal) it was decided that the Egyptian expeditionary force (EEF) would advance across the Sinai peninsula. By December, in spite of opposition and physical difficulties, this had been successfully achieved with the laying of a railway line and a 12 inch water main across the desert. As Allenby would note in his dispatches: 'Murray's brilliant campaign in Sinai had removed the danger to Egypt, and had forced the enemy back across his own frontier'. Early in 1917 Murray was instructed to advance into Palestine. Frustration with the attritional war on the western front, combined with religious attachments to the land of Palestine, led Prime Minister Lloyd George to urge for an ambitious offensive in the east. On 26 March an attempt was made to capture Gaza: though the objectives were initially secured, poor communications in the command structure resulted in troops being pulled out at the last minute. Murray none the less sent home a positive report of the battle and was then directed to renew operations and occupy Jerusalem. Although Murray protested that the operations required more forces than were at his disposal, he obeyed his instructions and attacked Gaza again. However, the Turkish troops fought notoriously well on the defensive and inflicted upon Murray a serious defeat, the scale of which had an immediate effect on the troops.

A change in command was deemed necessary and Murray was superseded by Allenby, who took over on 29 June. With additional forces the EEF under Allenby's command made dramatic advances in the autumn of 1917 (including the highly publicized capture of Jerusalem in December). While the view that Murray's departure marked a new beginning for the EEF gained wide currency in the light of Allenby's significant achievements, Murray's preparations for the Palestine campaign are also widely acknowledged. Allenby himself, in his final dispatch, noted his indebtedness to his predecessor 'who, by his bridging of the desert between Egypt and Palestine, laid the foundations for the subsequent advances of the Egyptian Expeditionary Force'. Murray by his foresight and strategic imagination 'brought the waters of the Nile to the borders of Palestine, planned the skilful military operations by which the Turks were driven from strong positions in the desert over the frontier of Egypt, stood all tests and formed the cornerstone of my success'.

On his return to England, Murray became general officer commanding at Aldershot in August 1919. In 1920 he published the full text of his dispatches. He retired from the army in 1922 and died at his home, Makepeace, Park Lane, Reigate, on 23 January 1945. He was appointed KC (1911), KCMG (1915), GCMG (1917), and GCB (1928). Murray was a grand officer of the Légion d'honneur and a member of a number of other European orders.

J. E. EDMONDS, *rev.* MARTIN BUNTON

Sources *Sir Archibald Murray's despatches, June 1916–June 1917* (1920) · *The Times* (25 Jan 1945) · *The royal Inniskilling fusiliers, December 1688 to July 1914* (1934) · J. F. Maurice and M. H. Grant, eds., *History of the war in South Africa, 1899–1902*, 4 vols. (1906–10) · J. E. Edmonds, ed., *Military operations, France and Belgium, 1914*, 2 vols., History of the Great War (1922) · J. E. Edmonds, ed., *Military operations, France and Belgium, 1915*, 2 vols., History of the Great War (1927–8) · G. MacMunn and C. Falls, *Military operations: Egypt and Palestine*, 3 vols., History of the Great War (1928–30) · private knowledge (1959) · private information (1959) · M. Hughes, *Allenby and British strategy in the Middle East, 1917–1919* (1999) · J. Newell, 'British military policy in Egypt and Palestine, August 1914 to June 1917', PhD thesis, U. Lond., 1990 · J. Newell, 'Allenby and the Palestine Campaign', *The First World War and British military history*, ed. B. Bond (1991) · J. Newell, 'Learning the hard way: Allenby in Egypt and Palestine, 1917–1919', *Journal of Strategic Studies*, 14/3 (Sept 1991), 363–87 · *CGPLA Eng. & Wales* (1945)

Archives IWM, diaries, corresp., and papers · PRO, papers, W079/62–65 | CAC Cam., corresp. with Sir E. L. Spears

Likenesses W. Stoneman, photograph, 1919, NPG [*see illus.*] · A. Fuller, portrait; in possession of family, in 1989

Wealth at death £28,193 1s. 2d.: probate, 19 June 1945, *CGPLA Eng. & Wales*

Murray [*née* Herbert], **Catherine, countess of Dunmore** (1814–1886), promoter of the Harris tweed industry, was born on 31 October 1814 at Arlington Street, St James's, London, daughter of George Augustus *Herbert, eleventh earl of Pembroke (1759–1827), and his second wife, Catherine, only daughter of Semyon Romanovich, Count Vorontsov, Russian ambassador to the court of St James's. Her father was English, and her mother was of Russian descent.

Catherine Herbert married Alexander Edward Murray, sixth earl of Dunmore, on 27 September 1836, at Frankfurt-am-Main. They had four children: Susan Catherine Mary (*b.* 7 July 1837), Constance Euphemia Woronzow (*b.* 28 Dec 1838), Charles Adolphus *Murray (*b.* 24 March 1841), and Alexandrina Victoria (*b.* 19 July 1845). Catherine was sometime lady-in-waiting to Queen Victoria. Following the death of her husband in 1845, she inherited the Dunmore estate of some 150,000 acres, on the Hebridean isle of Harris.

Lady Dunmore took an active interest in the Harris estate. The potato famine of 1846–7 brought great hardships to the Scottish highlands and islands, and Catherine offered financial assistance to those of her tenants wishing to emigrate. This took the form of free passage, together with an allowance to maintain the emigrés until they could support themselves.

Although her offer was not accepted by any of the people on her estate, Lady Dunmore was commended for these 'relief' operations. More importantly, at a time of such severe economic difficulty, Lady Dunmore was instrumental in the promotion and development of Harris tweed, a sustainable and much-needed local industry. She recognized the quality of the tweeds made by the women of Harris, and perceived the sales potential of the fabric. The Murray family tartan had been copied in tweed by Harris weavers, and proved a great success. The first full-length cloth was made into suiting for the Dunmore estate keepers and ghillies. Lady Dunmore then introduced her friends to the advantages of Harris tweed for outdoor wear, and endeavoured to widen the market. This she achieved through establishing a scheme to improve the quality by removing irregularities in the cloth, and so bring it in line with machine-made cloth. Dyeing, spinning, and weaving for Harris tweed were all carried out by hand, which often resulted in uneven quality. Lady Dunmore organized and financed training in Alloa for a number of Harris women to learn how to weave more intricate patterns. She also aimed to devise new blends of natural, more subtle dyes in contrast to the traditional pronounced checks.

By the late 1840s the London market was established. Improvements in Harris tweed encouraged by Lady Dunmore, together with her promotional skills, led to a significant increase in sales of tweed. So too did the increasing popularity of sporting activities in the highlands.

Indeed, the fabric was particularly suited to the demands of outdoor pursuits, being warm, relatively light, and shower resistant. Hand-made tweed produced in the Outer Hebrides, and elsewhere, became known as Harris tweed. Legal action was taken against sellers of cloth using this trade name for cloth woven outside the Hebrides, and the term is now commonly applied only to that produced on Lewis and Harris.

Catherine, countess dowager of Dunmore, died, aged seventy-one, on 12 February 1886, at Carberry Tower,

Inveresk, Musselburgh, and was buried at Dunmore, Stirlingshire. The Harris tweed industry owes its development and subsequent success substantially to her action and inspiration.   CHRISTINE LODGE

Sources *Scots peerage*, vol. 3 · W. R. Scott, *Report to the board of agriculture for Scotland on home industries in the highlands and islands* (1914), Cd 7564 xxxii · Notes on the historical development of the Harris tweed industry and the part played by the Harris Tweed Association Ltd, 1961, Highland Region Archive, D190 · J. McNeill, *Report to the board of supervision on the western highlands and islands* (1851) · F. Thompson, *Harris tweed: story of a Hebridean industry* (1969) · *The Scotsman* (13 Feb 1886) · d. cert.
Wealth at death £1748 10s. 7d.: confirmation, 13 July 1886, *CCI*

Murray, Catherine (1870/71–*c*.1882). *See under* Knock, visionaries of (*act.* 1879).

Murray, Charles, first earl of Dunmore (1661–1710), army officer and politician, the second son among the twelve children of John *Murray, first marquess of Atholl (1631–1703), and his wife, Lady Amelia Sophia Stanley (1633–1703), daughter of James *Stanley, seventh earl of Derby, was born on 28 February 1661 at Knowsley, Lancashire. Charles was the most Anglicized son of the family, and the one closest to his mother's relations. After seeking a commission from William of Orange in 1680, he was appointed on 25 November 1681 as lieutenant-colonel of the new Scots Greys dragoons, a much coveted post. Having attended the 1684 French siege of Luxembourg and served in western Scotland during Argyll's rebellion, he became the Scots Greys' colonel on 6 November 1685. On 6 December 1682 he married in London (a love match) Catherine (*d.* 1710), daughter of Richard Watts of Great Munden, Hertfordshire, and granddaughter of the courtier Major-General Robert Worden. On 28 July 1683 James, duke of York, appointed Murray master of the horse to Princess Anne (already his friend), and on 18 January 1685 master of the horse to the duchess, reappointing him soon after she became queen. In the 1685 English parliament he was MP for Wigan (through the Derby influence), and court candidate there in 1688. Encouraged by James, the marquess in 1684 resolved to transfer the inheritance of his main highland estate in Atholl from his eldest son, John, Lord *Murray (later first duke of Atholl), whom they considered insufficiently loyal, to Lord Charles. This plan, revived, provided the territorial basis when James created him (Scottish) earl of Dunmore on 6 August 1686; but he renounced his claim in a 1689–90 family settlement.

In 1688 Dunmore led the Scots Greys in the campaign against William. At the revolution he lost the regiment and his court post; he offered to follow Mary of Modena to France. On his return to Edinburgh on 20 March 1689 Dunmore strongly influenced his wavering father towards Jacobitism during the Convention Parliament, and encouraged the Scots Greys' plotting. Suspected of fomenting highland revolt, he was imprisoned in Edinburgh Castle from June 1689 until January 1690. Bailed, he retreated to England for a decade, despite knowing of the developing Montgomery plot. In June 1691 he introduced his disaffected father among London plotters, but, while corresponding with James II via his vehemently Jacobite

Charles Murray, first earl of Dunmore (1661–1710), by Sir Godfrey Kneller, 1683

wife, declared that he was waiting on events (Blancard to Dykveldt, 19 June 1691, *Seventh Report*, HMC, 199, mistaking him for his brother 'Moray'). However, during the 1692 invasion attempt he was one of a London group including Charles, second earl of Middleton, who planned a rising in support. They were captured together in hiding on 16 May and committed to the Tower, but were bailed on 16 August. Middleton became James's chief minister in France in 1693, but, though a significant Jacobite code (Bodl. Oxf., MS Carte 256, fol. 25*v*) bracketed them then as 'Moses' and 'Aaron', no further Jacobite activity by Dunmore is known. Suffering increasingly from the stone, he retreated among his Stanley kin. He was arrested at Lathom House in March 1696 and detained at Liverpool until July. He then settled at Chester.

James II's death transformed Dunmore's loyalties. He had, besides, nine children surviving (out of ten), and, to support them, little but his £500–600 a year in England and (from the Stanleys' Orange ancestors) in the Netherlands, apart from large, but unpaid, family bonds. He returned to Scotland. While his brother Atholl held office, he rationally hoped for a Treasury or Ordnance place. He was sworn of the privy council on 4 February 1703, and finally took his seat in the new Scottish parliament on 21 May 1703. He was one of the semi-Jacobite cavalier party, but, after Lord Commissioner Queensberry broke with them, joined the court side. He defended his brother Atholl in the council against Queensberry's false 'Scotch plot' allegations, but thereafter followed the court line, like the earl of Balcarres. George Lockhart of Carnwath denounced both as worthless and self-interested, 'so no party was much a gainer or loser by having or wanting such a couple', and as living largely for drink (true of Dunmore, probably partly as an analgesic). Lockhart claimed that he had 'sold his honour for a present which the queen had yearly given his lady since the late revolution' (*Lockhart Papers*, 1.64–5).

In 1704 Dunmore was appointed to a committee of parliament for examining the public accounts. His £200 recompense, for which no funds were available, was paid him from the notorious £20,000 sent from England for the final parliamentary session. He attempted to bribe Atholl to stay away from the union debates with a promise of his arrears: Atholl, though paid £1000, attended, and Dunmore apparently received part of the sum, due on a bond. He voted consistently for the union and the court's related policies. In 1707 he was appointed governor of Blackness Castle. The Dunmores' first three sons had entered the army; the eldest died on service in 1704. The parents solicited the Marlboroughs (whom Lady Dunmore had openly denounced in 1689 for betraying James) for the others' advancement. Dunmore died, in recently bestowed apartments at Holyrood Palace, on 19 April 1710, and was buried five days later in Holyrood Abbey. His bereaved widow died in England a few months later, about December 1710 or early January 1711; administration was issued on 22 January. Queen Anne granted £300 a year to bring up the youngest children. The two sons who succeeded him symbolized Dunmore's divided legacy. John *Murray, second earl, fought at the battles of Blenheim and Dettingen and died a full general (other sons became a lieutenant-general and a brigadier-general). Dunmore's fifth son, William, joined the rising of 1745 and was convicted of treason; he succeeded as third earl and died while under town arrest at Lincoln.

PAUL HOPKINS

Sources J. J. H. H. Stewart-Murray, seventh duke of Atholl, *Chronicles of the Atholl and Tullibardine families*, 5 vols. (privately printed, Edinburgh, 1908), vols. 1, 2, 5 · Blair Castle, Perthshire, Atholl MSS · NA Scot., Dunmore MSS, box 1, RH4/195/1 [microfilm] · *Scots peerage* · *Seventh report*, HMC, 6 (1879) · *Report on the manuscripts of Allan George Finch*, 5 vols., HMC, 71 (1913–2003), vol. 4 · *The manuscripts of Lord Kenyon*, HMC, 35 (1894) · *The manuscripts of his grace the duke of Buccleuch and Queensberry … preserved at Drumlanrig Castle*, 2 vols., HMC, 44 (1897–1903) · C. Dalton, ed., *The Scots army, 1661–1688* (1909) · *The Lockhart Papers*, ed. A. Aufrere, 2 vols. (1817) · I. Cassidy, 'Murray, Charles', HoP, *Commons, 1660–90* · letters from Lord and Lady Dunmore to duke and duchess of Marlborough, 1708–10, and the duchess's endorsements, BL, Add. MS 61474, fols. 175, 189–91; Add. MS 61475, fols. 16–20; Add. MS 61692, fols. 95–6 · GEC, *Peerage*, new edn · *APS*, 1702–7 · C. Lindsay [earl of Balcarres], *Memoirs touching the revolution in Scotland*, ed. A. W. C. Lindsay [earl of Crawford and Balcarres], Bannatyne Club (1841) · W. A. Shaw, ed., *Calendar of treasury books*, 25–8, PRO (1954–5) · J. Creichton and J. Swift, 'Memoirs of Captain John Creichton', in J. Swift, *Miscellaneous and autobiographical pieces*, ed. H. Davis (1962) · codenames, [1693], Bodl. Oxf., MS Carte 256, fol. 25v

Archives NA Scot., Dunmore MSS, box 1 [microfilm] | Blair Castle, Perthshire, Atholl MSS

Likenesses G. Kneller, oils, 1683, Scot. NPG [*see illus.*]

Murray, Lord Charles (1691–1720), Jacobite army officer, was born at Falkland on 24 September 1691, the fourth son of John *Murray, first duke of Atholl (1660–1724), and his

first wife, Katherine, Lady Hamilton (*bap.* 1662, *d.* 1707), daughter of William Douglas of Selkirk and Anne, duchess of Hamilton. Like his elder brothers William *Murray, styled second duke of Atholl, and Lord George *Murray, he received an army commission and served as a cornet in the 5th dragoons in Flanders from 1712 to 1713, where he ran up considerable debts. Influenced by his brothers he developed Jacobite sympathies on his return and signalled them by leaving the family's traditional Presbyterian worship for the Scottish Episcopal church, much to the chagrin of his father. *En route* for a military posting in Ireland he left the army and joined the 1715 Jacobite rising, leading a regiment of Athollmen across the Forth and into England. Charles was well liked as a commander, and frequently dismounted to walk with his men at the head of the regiment wearing highland dress. With great courage he defended a barrier at the battle of Preston in Lancashire (12 November 1715), but was taken prisoner when the Jacobites surrendered. Court-martialled and found guilty of mutiny because he still held an army commission as a half-pay officer, through his father's influence he alone escaped execution but remained in prison until the 1717 Act of Grace afforded him an official pardon. His health broken by imprisonment, Charles was reconciled to his father by his stepmother, Mary Ross, but spent the remainder of his life outside Scotland, living on an allowance in a series of rented lodgings. Failing to win permission to court the daughter of Sir Henry Bunbury of Chester, he settled in London, where he died unmarried in August 1720, aged twenty-eight.

MARGARET D. SANKEY

Sources DNB · J. J. H. H. Stewart-Murray, seventh duke of Atholl, *Chronicles of the Atholl and Tullibardine families*, 5 vols. (privately printed, Edinburgh, 1908), vol. 2 · *Scots peerage* · R. Patten, *The history of the late rebellion*, [another edn] (1718)

Archives NA Scot.

Wealth at death disinherited; lived on allowance from family; no estate

Murray, Charles (1754–1821), actor, was born at Cheshunt, Hertfordshire, the first of the six children of Sir John *Murray, bt (1714/15?–1777), of Broughton, Peebles, and his Quaker second wife, whose maiden name was Webb. He had three half-brothers. His father, notorious as Murray of Broughton, was secretary to the Young Pretender, and saved his skin by turning king's evidence after the failure of the Jacobite rising of 1745. Charles received a classical education, and travelled in France. After acquiring 'a competent knowledge of pharmacy and surgery' he served as surgeon's mate in the navy. When posted to Guinea he resigned 'from a presentiment that he should not survive the fatal influence of the climate' (Gilliland, 872).

A success on the amateur stage led Murray to York, where Tate Wilkinson engaged him to play Carlos in Colley Cibber's *The Fop's Fortune, or, Love Makes a Man* on 21 April 1773. He was billed 'for family reasons' as 'Mr. Raymur' (Wilkinson, 1.173). By 1775 he was playing leading roles such as Lothario in Nicholas Rowe's *The Fair Penitent*, Young Bevil in Richard Steele's *The Conscious Lovers*,

Bassanio in *The Merchant of Venice*, and Young Marlow in Oliver Goldsmith's *She Stoops to Conquer* at York and in Wilkinson's circuit of northern theatres. While playing at Wakefield on 15 September 1776, he was insulted as a player by 'a gentleman in liquor' (Wilkinson, 1.233). At the theatre an apology was demanded for his response, which Murray refused, resenting, as a gentleman, the insult to his profession. A boycott obliged the manager to dismiss him. 'In losing Murray in consequence of the riot', Wilkinson wrote, 'I lost an excellent actor' (Wilkinson, 1.240).

After briefly returning to sea, Murray found employment at Norwich, where the theatre committee instructed the manager: 'If Mr. Murray wants an Engagement for Mrs. Murray, Mr. Griffith is desired not to exceed one Pound Sixteen Shillings p week for both' (Eshleman, 31 Oct 1777). This was a reference to Murray's first wife, whose name is unknown; she was twenty-one when she died on 21 January 1780. Murray soon formed another alliance. Anne Payne (*née* Acres) was a member of the Norwich company. Her husband, Jonathan Payne, did not die until 1784, but the playbills were calling her Mrs Murray by 1782. Their children, Maria, Harriet (1783–1844), later Mrs Henry Siddons [*see under* Siddons, Henry], and William Henry *Murray (1790–1852), went on the stage. Murray's eldest son, Charles (*b.* 1780), was probably the child of his first marriage. Murray may have been the author of a tragedy, *The New Maid of the Oaks* (1778), and he certainly wrote *The Experiment* (performed 10 May 1779), a farce, both published in Norwich.

After eight seasons in Norwich the Murrays moved to Bath, where he opened on 8 October 1785 as Overreach in Philip Massinger's *A New Way to Pay Old Debts*, and continued in leading parts such as Pierre in Otway's *Venice Preserv'd*, Macbeth, and Iago. He remained at Bath for eleven seasons, and became known as 'a great actor—void of conceit & ostentation' (Penley, 68). Later roles included old men, such as Adam in *As You Like It* and Old Dornton in Thomas Holcroft's *The Road to Ruin*; for his farewell in Bristol he played Polixenes to the Perdita of his daughter Harriet in *Florizel and Perdita*.

Murray's chance to act in London had arrived: he played Shylock at Covent Garden on 30 September 1796. It was customary to test provincial 'stars' in leading business for a night or two. Rarely, one succeeded; most limped home. Murray stayed, but principally in supporting roles. The *Monthly Mirror* found him weak in the Tubal scene because 'his powers sunk under the weight of passion'; he was best in the trial 'because it required no great exertion of voice; … Indeed the whole of this scene merits the denomination of GREAT ACTING' (*Monthly Mirror*, 2, 1796, 365). In his early seasons at Covent Garden, Murray's occasional leading parts, such as Iago, met with less approbation than his sympathetic old men. Old Norval in John Home's *Douglas* 'gave us exquisite delight', said the *Monthly Mirror* (ibid., 439), and as Strictland in Benjamin Hoadley's *The Suspicious Husband* he was 'in manner, in look, and in delivery, the very character which the author designed' (Dutton, vol. 1, no. 2, 54). Of Stockwell in Richard Cumberland's *The West Indian*, Dutton exclaimed, 'Indeed it is a

work of supererogation to enlarge on the merits of this excellent performer' (Dutton, vol. 1, no. 5, 183). In later seasons Murray settled into a repertory of 'interesting old men' (*Thespian Dictionary*) and other parts that called for the gentler passions, such as Hamlet's Ghost, the original Hermit in Cumberland's *Joanna*, and Morrington in Morton's *Speed the Plough*. There are two portraits of him as the first Baron Wildenheim in Elizabeth Inchbald's Kotzebue adaptation *Lover's Vows* (11 October 1798). He made his farewell at Covent Garden as Brabantio in *Othello* on 17 July 1817.

Murray soon moved to Edinburgh to be near his children Harriet and William, who had succeeded to the management of the city's theatre when Henry Siddons died in 1815. He died there on 8 November 1821. Murray was a provincial actor who fell short of attaining the first rank in London, partly because the attempt was delayed too long, but also through deficiency of passion: 'Mr. Murray will always interest, though he may never astonish an audience' (Waldron and Dibdin, 133). The youthful fire he exhibited at Wakefield was no longer to be seen in London, either on or off the stage: 'as a private gentleman, he is said to be very respectable, and his conversation elegant and entertaining' (Gilliland, 2.873).   ALAN HUGHES

Sources Highfill, Burnim & Langhans, *BDA* · C. B. Hogan, ed., *The London stage, 1660–1800*, pt 5: *1776–1800* (1968) · B. R. Schneider, *Index to 'The London stage, 1660–1800'* (1979) · L. Fitzsimmons and A. W. McDonald, *The Yorkshire stage, 1766–1803* (1989) · T. Gilliland, *The dramatic mirror, containing the history of the stage from the earliest period, to the present time*, 2 vols. (1808) · T. Wilkinson, *The wandering patentee, or, A history of the Yorkshire theatres from 1770 to the present time*, 4 vols. (1795) · T. Dutton, *The dramatic censor, or, Weekly theatrical report*, 4 vols. (1800–01) · *The thespian dictionary, or, Dramatic biography of the present age*, 2nd edn (1805) · F. G. Waldron and C. Dibdin, *A compendious history of the English stage, from the earliest period to the present time* (1800) · *N&Q*, 8th ser., 2 (1892), 391 · *The Monthly Mirror: Reflecting Men and Manners, with Strictures on their Epitome, the Stage*, 2 (1796), 365, 439 · D. H. Eshleman, ed., *The committee books of the Theatre Royal, Norwich, 1768–1825* (1970) · H. Bryant, A. Hare, and K. Barker, eds., *Theatre Royal, Bath: a calendar of performances at the Orchard Street Theatre, 1750–1805* (1977) · J. C. Dibdin, *The annals of the Edinburgh stage* (1888) · B. S. Penley, *The Bath stage: a history of dramatic representations in Bath* (1892)

Likenesses J. Chapman, engraving, repro. in *Thespian dictionary* · G. Dupont, oils (as Baron Wildenheim in *Lovers' Vows*), Garr. Club · J. W. Gordon, oils (as Baron Wildenheim in *Lovers' Vows*; after G. Dupont), Garr. Club · W. Leney, engraving (as Demetrius in *The Brothers*), repro. in J. Bell, *Bell's British theatre* (1797) · Maddocks, engraving (as Heartley in *The Guardian*; after De Wilde), repro. in *Minor British theatre* (1805) · watercolour (as Tobias in *The Stranger*; after De Wilde), Garr. Club

Murray, Charles (1864–1941), poet and civil engineer, was born on 28 September 1864 in the village of Alford, Strathdon, Aberdeenshire, the second of three children of Peter Murray (1833–1926), carpenter and land steward, and his wife, Margaret Robbie (1838–1868). Peter Murray had a passion for reading, a reputation for composing pointed rhymes in the vernacular, and a fine collection of geological specimens; his son—surveyor, civil engineer, and poet—combined his father's artistic and practical interests. Charles Murray completed his elementary education at the local Gallowhill School. Later he looked back with gratitude on his schooldays:

> I was raised upon Ramsay, Fergusson and Burns, and the old Scots, and all my life as a boy I was taught to look for quaint phrases, out of the way expressions and to study and delight in the original characters of the countryside. (Murray, *Dinner*)

In his teens he began to write Scots verse. Like Thomas Hardy, the young Murray was in touch with a rich folk music tradition, playing with a 'strong bow-han' for dancing in Alford (Murray, letter to Alexander Mackie). Just after the turn of the century he corresponded with Gavin Greig, supplying information and material for what was to become the great Greig–Duncan folk song collection.

After being apprenticed at Walker and Beattie, Aberdeen, surveyors and civil engineers, from 1881 to 1887, Murray left for South Africa in 1888, working first in an architecture and engineering practice. In 1895 he married Cape Town-born Edith Emma Rogers (1871–1946). After a period managing goldmines, Murray served in the Second South African War. Entry to public service followed, and his advancement was rapid: deputy inspector of mines for the Transvaal in 1901, by 1910 he was secretary for public works, Union of South Africa.

Murray's poems began to appear in print only after his departure for South Africa; significantly he first published in W. E. Henley's *Scots Observer*, a periodical which reflected the progressive literary tastes, imperialist sympathies, and Scottish cultural interests of its editor and his associates. These included Stevenson and James Logie Robertson (Hugh Haliburton), important figures in the revival of the vernacular poetic tradition. Like Kipling, Henley's most celebrated contributor, the vernacularists reinvigorated a stale poetic diction by drawing on the energies of the colloquial and the demotic. Apart from the twelve copies of *A Handful of Heather* printed for friends in 1893, Murray's poems first appeared in book form in the 1900 *Hamewith* (Wyllie, Aberdeen). Despite its success, Murray had difficulty finding a larger publisher willing to undertake a revised and enlarged edition. Ironically, the expanded *Hamewith* (Constable & Co., Edinburgh and London, 1909) was an immediate success. It consisted of forty-five poems, all but two in a Scots based on the dialect of his native north-east. Murray was convinced that he had exhausted his creative powers, but the First World War provided fresh stimulus, and *A Sough o' War* (1917) contains some of his best work. The only other collection published in his lifetime was *In the Country Places* (1920). A collected edition, *Hamewith and other Poems*, followed in 1927; *Hamewith: the Complete Poems* (1979) included the uncollected work published as *Last Poems* (1969). Fresh impressions of *Hamewith* appeared throughout the 1930s and 1940s. Murray was awarded an honorary LLD by the University of Aberdeen in 1920 for his services to the vernacular.

For young writers between the wars the future seemed to lie with the experimental, the metropolitan, and with a radical new political order of left or right: Murray, a best-seller, an 'amateur', an imperialist, and a north-east Scot, came to symbolize all that was reactionary. The modernism of C. M. Grieve (Hugh MacDiarmid) and his allies now seems more a cul-de-sac than a high road to the future, and in a Europe of the regions, Murray's regional affiliations seem contemporary again—for his poetry communicates above all a vivid sense of the distinctive life and character of north-east Scotland. His work is not merely descriptive, however, and its significance is by no means confined to his native region. Several poems, including 'The Whistle'—long his best known—show the impact of the forces of cultural standardization on local speech and traditional ways. Rural life is not depicted nostalgically, however: in 'The Antiquary' the past is associated with superstition and cruelty, while in 'The Packman' social change is celebrated in the pedlar's rise to prosperity. Despite their patriotic sentiments, several of Murray's war poems convey the traditional peasant sense that war is an irrelevance, while the bleakly poignant 'When will the war be by' offers none of the conventional consolations for a girl's loss of her soldier-lover. 'Gin i was God' is a powerfully succinct and sardonic expression of post-war disillusionment.

Murray was created CMG in 1922 for services to the Union of South Africa, and retired in 1924. He spent his last years in the north-east at his home, The Lythe, Banchory, Kincardineshire, dying there on 12 April 1941. Three days later his remains were cremated in Aberdeen. He was survived by his wife, son, and two daughters.

Murray's poetry demonstrated that the vernacular was still vigorous, and inspired other writers to explore the literary potentialities of contemporary spoken Scots. The continuing availability of Scots as a medium for serious poetry owes much to Murray's efforts. Despite attacks from the late 1920s onwards by Hugh MacDiarmid and his Scottish Renaissance allies, who identified Murray with the outdated tendencies he had helped to defeat, his work continued to be popular, especially in the north-east, until after the Second World War. Though closely related to the Doric of the north-east, Murray's Scots is an artful literary construct; and, far from being the naïve amateur of letters depicted in some literary histories, Murray was a dedicated craftsman who constantly revised and polished his work. His *Complete Poems*, edited by Nan Stepherd, appeared in 1979.

COLIN MILTON

Sources J. F. Tocher, 'Charles Murray', *Aberdeen University Review*, 28 (1940–41), 210–16 · *Press and Journal* [Aberdeen] (14 April 1941) · *The Scotsman* (14 April 1941) · *The Times* (14 April 1941) · C. Milton, 'From Charles Murray to Hugh MacDiarmid', *Literature of the north*, ed. D. Hewitt and M. Spiller (1983), 82–108 · C. Milton, 'Modern poetry in Scots before MacDiarmid', *The history of Scottish literature*, 4: *Twentieth century*, ed. C. Craig (1987), 11–36 · A. Mackie, ed., *Dinner in honour of Charles Murray (Hamewith)*, Palace Hotel, Aberdeen, Monday December 2 1912 [1913] [incl. account of proceedings and text of speeches] · C. Murray, letter to Alexander Mackie, 13 May 1914, U. Aberdeen, MS U595

Archives NL Scot., corresp. and MSS · NRA, corresp. and literary papers | NL Scot., letters to William Will · U. Aberdeen, corresp. relating to *Aberdeen University Review*; letters to Alexander Keith

Likenesses H. S. Gamley, bust, 1925, Aberdeen Art Gallery · J. F. Watt, portrait, 1925, Aberdeen Art Gallery · photograph, repro. in Mackie, ed., *Dinner in honour of Charles Murray*

Wealth at death £5849 0s. 7d.: confirmation, 12 Aug 1941, *CCI*

Murray, Charles Adolphus, seventh earl of Dunmore (1841–1907), traveller, born in Grafton Street, London, on 24 March 1841, was the only son of Alexander Edward Murray, sixth earl of Dunmore (1804–1845), and his wife, Lady Catherine (1814–1886), fourth daughter of George Augustus *Herbert, eleventh earl of Pembroke. He succeeded his father as seventh earl on 15 July 1845. Educated at Eton College, he served with the Scots Fusilier Guards from 1860 to 1864. He married on 5 April 1866 Lady Gertrude (1847–1943), third daughter of Thomas William *Coke, second earl of Leicester. Their only son, Alexander Edward, succeeded as eighth earl of Dunmore. They also had five daughters. A Conservative, he was lord-in-waiting to Queen Victoria from 1874 until 1880 (his mother had been a lady of the bedchamber in 1841–5). He was also lord lieutenant of Stirlingshire from 1874 to 1885, and honorary colonel of the 1st volunteer battalion of the Cameron Highlanders from 1896 to 1907.

A strong and active man, Dunmore travelled in many parts of the world, including Africa and the Arctic, but his principal journey was made in 1892 through Kashmir, western Tibet, Chinese Tartary, and Russian central Asia. He started from Rawalpindi in April 1892, reached Kashgar in Chinese Turkestan in December 1892, and continued west through Ferghana and Transcaspia, reaching Samarkand in January 1893. He had ridden and walked 2500 miles, traversing forty-one mountain passes and sixty-nine rivers. His account of the journey, *The Pamirs* (1893), was a pleasant travel book, but of no great scientific or geographical value, and was not flatteringly reviewed in the professional press. His novel *Ormisdale* was also published in 1893.

A few years before Dunmore's death he and other members of his family became Christian Scientists, and in 1907 he claimed that his daughter had cured him of rupture by the methods of Christian Science. He died suddenly of heart failure on 27 August 1907 at Manor House, Frimley, near Camberley, and was buried at Dunmore, near Falkirk, Stirlingshire.

S. E. Fryer, rev. Elizabeth Baigent

Sources *The Times* (28 Aug 1907) · *WW* · Burke, *Peerage* (1939) · Burke, *Peerage* (1958) · GEC, *Peerage* · *Proceedings* [Royal Geographical Society], 3 (1858–9), 2, 10, 145, 291

Likenesses Spy [L. Ward], caricature, chromolithograph, NPG; repro. in *VF* (14 Dec 1878)

Wealth at death £14,318 8s. 10d.: probate, 4 Nov 1907, *CGPLA Eng. & Wales*

Murray, Sir Charles Augustus (1806–1895), diplomatist and author, second son of George Murray, fifth earl of Dunmore (1762–1836), and his wife, Lady Susan Hamilton (d. 1846), daughter of Archibald, ninth duke of Hamilton, was born on 22 November 1806. He was educated at Eton College and at Oriel College, Oxford, where he matriculated on 21 May 1824, and graduated BA and was elected to a fellowship of All Souls in 1827; he proceeded MA in 1832. While an undergraduate Murray had John Henry Newman as his tutor. 'He never inspired me', wrote Murray, 'or my fellow-undergraduates with any interest, much less respect; on the contrary, we disliked, or rather distrusted, him. He walked with his head bent, abstracted, but every now and then looking out of the corners of his eyes quickly, as though suspicious. He had no influence then; it was only when he became vicar of St Mary's that the long dormant power asserted itself' (Maxwell, 56).

Murray's chief undergraduate friend was Sidney Herbert (later Baron Herbert of Lea), but it was in company with Lord Edward Thynne, son of the second marquess of Bath, that Murray, who was a great athlete, performed his most famous feat of endurance. Having been 'gated' for a minor offence, Murray made a bet that he would ride to London, 60 miles, and back in one day. Having left Oxford shortly after 8 a.m., he and Thynne rode to London, changed their clothes, mounted two hacks and rode in the park, dined at a club, saw the first act of a play, and were back at the gate of Oriel three minutes before midnight. They had relays of horses at Henley and Maidenhead.

After taking his degree Murray was admitted student of Lincoln's Inn in 1827 and read for the bar with Nassau Senior. His mother's house was a favourite rendezvous of literary and political characters, and Murray, a very handsome and charming young man with a strong interest in literature, and an excellent classical scholar, formed many friendships with people distinguished in both fields. He became a frequent guest at Samuel Rogers's breakfast table, and left numerous notes of scenes and incidents which he witnessed there. When travelling in Germany in 1830 he met Goethe, at that time minister of the grand duchy of Weimar.

In 1834 Murray visited the United States and in 1835 he joined a group of wandering Pawnees: his three months in the wilds, with many exciting adventures and narrow escapes, were afterwards described, together with his visit to Cuba, in his *Travels in North America* (1839). During his stay in America, Murray fell in love with Elise, daughter of James Wadsworth, a wealthy gentleman living near Niagara, who disapproved of their betrothal, and forbade all communication between them. Their only contact between 1835 and 1849 was through the indirect means of a novel written by Murray, *The Prairie Bird* (1844), in which he managed to convey the assurance of his unalterable constancy. In 1849, however, the father died, and the couple were able to marry in 1850. Elise died a year later in childbirth; the son, Charles James, later became MP for Coventry.

In 1838 Murray was appointed groom-in-waiting at the court of Queen Victoria, and a few months later he became master of the household, an office which he held until 1844, when he was eased out in Prince Albert's reform of the household. He then entered the diplomatic service as secretary of legation at Naples. In 1846 he became consul-general in Egypt during the viceroyalty of Mehmet Ali (of whom he wrote a memoir, published in 1898). He remained there until 1853, when he was appointed to Bern as minister to the Swiss confederation. Murray's official connection with Egypt was memorable for his success in securing, in 1849, for the Zoological Society the first hippopotamus ever to be imported into Britain. The animal was safely lodged in the gardens in May 1850, and lived there until its death in 1878.

In 1854 Lord Clarendon selected Murray to go as envoy and minister-plenipotentiary to the court of Persia, which turned out an unfortunate mission for him. The shah was entirely under the control of his grand vizier, Sadr-i A'zam, who, suspecting Murray of interference with his ascendancy, made allegations against the British envoy, and threatened to ally with Russia in the Crimean War, with the aim of expanding Persian influence and perhaps gaining territory in Afghanistan. When Murray tried to employ Mirza Hashim Khan as a newswriter in the British mission, the shah captured Khan's wife. Murray issued an ultimatum and on 19 November 1855 struck his flag and withdrew from Tehran to Baghdad. Once there, he was sidelined by the Foreign Office, which dealt with Persia through Stratford Canning at Constantinople. When Persia intervened at Herat on the Afghanistan frontier in July 1886, an ultimatum was issued and war followed in December, in which the Persian army was fairly quickly defeated. Murray was much blamed in the Commons and in *The Times* for this course of events, but he was defended by Clarendon, the foreign secretary, and by Palmerston. The peace treaty negotiated with Persia in 1857 was based on a commercial treaty which Murray had drawn up in 1856; Murray exchanged the ratified treaty on 2 May 1857 and returned to Tehran in July 1857, being ceremonially received and the quarrel of 1855 set aside. Murray himself attributed the disfavour he incurred from the shah's government to a novel policy initiated by the British cabinet, under which the custom of giving presents, an immemorial part of oriental diplomacy, was strictly prohibited, and the queen's representative had to go empty-handed before the shah and the sadr, while the French and Russian ministers came with their hands full of gifts.

In 1859 the Persian mission was transferred to the India Office, and Murray, preferring to serve under the Foreign Office, was appointed minister at the court of Saxony. On 1 November 1862 he married the Hon. Edythe Susan Esther Fitzpatrick (d. 1906), daughter of the first Baron Castletown. They had one son, Cecil, who died tragically on the anniversary of his father's death. In 1866 Murray was appointed KCB, having been a companion of the Bath since 1848, and was appointed minister at Copenhagen. The climate of Denmark proved too severe for his wife, however, and he applied for and obtained the British legation at Lisbon, which he kept until his final retirement from the service in 1874. He was sworn of the privy council on 13 May 1875.

Murray's remaining years were spent in cultivated leisure. His charming manner, immense and varied store of reminiscences, and strikingly handsome appearance combined to make him a very well-known figure in society. An excellent linguist, he devoted much study to oriental languages and philology, on which (along with theology), he left numerous notes and fragmentary treatises. He read and spoke fifteen languages.

Murray lived during his later years at the Grange, Old Windsor, Berkshire, spending the winter months in the south of France. He died in Paris on 3 June 1895. His intellectual gifts and singular versatility deserved a greater eminence than he attained; no doubt he would have achieved this, had less affluent circumstances compelled him to concentrate his energy on a single object.

H. E. MAXWELL, rev. H. C. G. MATTHEW

Sources H. Maxwell, *The Honourable Sir Charles Augustus Murray, K.C.B.* (1898) · J. B. Kelly, *Britain and the Persian Gulf, 1795–1880* (1968) · private information (1901)

Archives LPL, letters relating to Anglican chaplaincy at Dresden · NA Scot., corresp., journals, literary MSS, and papers · NRA, priv. coll., corresp. | BL, corresp. with James Brant, Add. MS 42566 · BL, letters to Sir Austen Layard, Add. MSS 38997–39002, *passim* · BL, letters to Lord Palmerston, Add. MS 48555 · BL, corresp. with Sir Robert Peel, Add. MSS 40438–40559 · Bodl. Oxf., Aberdeen MSS; Brant MSS; Layard MSS · Bodl. Oxf., corresp. with Lady Byron · Bodl. Oxf., letters to Lord Clarendon · Hants. RO, letters to Lord Malmesbury · King's AC Cam., letters to Oscar Browning · Lpool RO, letters to Lord Derby · Lpool RO, letters to Lord Stanley · PRO, letters to Lord Ampthill, FO 918/56/29–60 · PRO, corresp. with Stratford Canning, FO 352 · PRO, corresp. with Lord John Russell, PRO 30/22 · PRO, letters to Lord Odo Russell, FO 918 · U. Southampton L., corresp. with Lord Palmerston · W. Yorks. AS, Leeds, letters to Lord Canning

Likenesses G. Zobel, mezzotint, pubd 1853 (after W. Maddox), BM, NPG · W. Maddox, portrait · carte-de-visite, All Souls Oxf.

Wealth at death £308,461 6s. 4d.: probate, 29 Jan 1896, CGPLA Eng. & Wales

Murray, Charles Fairfax (1849–1919), artist and art connoisseur, was born on 13 September 1849 at 14 High Street, Bow, in London, the son of James Dalton Murray (1808–1876), a draper, and Elizabeth Scott (1816–1853). About 1862 he was working in an engineering drawing office, but he entered Edward Burne-Jones's studio about 1866–7, as an assistant. Murray exhibited a painting, *Children in the Woods* (exh. RA, 1867), and began work for William Morris. His tasks included transferring designs to stained glass (including the windows of the Castle Howard chapel), doing miniature illustrations for Morris's poems (including *A Book of Verses*, 1870, *Virgil*, 1875, and the *Ruba'yat*, 1872, painting panels on furniture, and transferring Burne-Jones's designs to the South Kensington Museum panels. In 1869–70 he worked in Rossetti's workshop as assistant, factotum, and proof-reader of Rossetti's poems, and in October 1870 he travelled with Morris to Bruges. Touring Italy in 1871–2 he executed copies of the Camposanto frescoes in Pisa: Burne-Jones showed John Ruskin these copies and Ruskin hired Murray as a copyist, sending him to Italy where he copied for Ruskin until 1883. Murray began living in Florence after 1878, periodically returning to London from about 1884–5. He took a studio in Holland Park on 19 November 1886, and leased Burne-Jones's home, The Grange, from 1898. His paintings are in a late Pre-Raphaelite style, while his copies encompass both Renaissance and Pre-Raphaelite art, including copies of several of Rossetti's paintings.

Murray's major contributions were as collector, art dealer, connoisseur, and buyer, for public museums as well as for private collectors. His own collections included Italian and English art, especially Pre-Raphaelite art, rare and illuminated books, incunabula of different origins, and a complete series of the Kelmscott editions, forming one of the finest European book collections. Ruskin praised Murray's knowledge of Italian art in *Ariadne Florentina* in 1872, and in 1877 Murray acquired Verrocchio's *Madonna and Child* for him for £100. During the late 1870s he was a consultant for Charles Moore of the Fog Art Museum at Harvard University. During the 1890s he was a consultant for several directors of the Fitzwilliam Museum—J. H. Middleton, M. R. James, and Sydney Cockerell—and was a generous benefactor of that museum, donating Titian's *Tarquin and Lucretia* in 1918. He worked for two directors of the National Gallery, Frederick Burton and Edward Poynter, obtaining works by several early Italian painters, including Duccio, Matteo di Giovanni, Nicolò di Buonaccorso, Andrea del Castagno, Giovanni Bellini, and Barna da Siena, and donating a Pietro Lorenzetti painting in 1882. He worked for the South Kensington Museum under Thomas Armstrong for whom he purchased Orcagna's mosaic from the west front of Orvieto Cathedral about 1890—and for his successor, J. H. Middleton. He also advised Edward Hooper of the Boston Museum of Fine Arts in 1897. His publications include several volumes on the rare books in his collections, a catalogue of the duke of Portland's collection (1894), and catalogues of his drawing collections. He was an agent for the art dealership Agnew's and for the dealer Martin Colnaghi. In 1903–6 he sold his Pre-Raphaelite collection to the Birmingham City Museum; between 1907 and 1910 he sold his Renaissance drawings to Pierpont Morgan for £40,000 (Pierpont Morgan Library, New York). He gave paintings to the Dulwich Gallery in 1911, and three years later sold some of his collection at Georges Petit, Paris, for 1,668,800 Fr. After his death, his library was sold in England; his son John's collection was sold in 1929; the remaining collection was sold in 1961.

Murray was a typical Victorian connoisseur, who valued sensibility above science. He looked for 'quality', holding that the identity of the artist should not affect appreciation of a work of art on its own merits; although happy to give attributions, he wisely recognized that these were merely opinions open to revision as art historical studies advanced. Murray advised the budding connoisseur to train the eye by the study of one school at a time, holding that connoisseurship was 'just a question of memory and practice'. This workmanlike attitude to his profession was underpinned by a shrewd eye to the financial value of art: when asked if his reattributions had devalued one client's collection, Murray replied that 'it is worth … about two-and-a-half times as much as it was before' (Benson, 216–18).

On 10 April 1875 Murray married Angelica Albina Isolina Collevicchi (*d. c.*1927), a seventeen-year-old, originally from Volterra; they lived in Siena and after 1878 in Florence. They had six surviving children, three daughters and three sons, all born in Florence and holding dual nationalities. One other daughter died very young. In February 1888 Murray met Blanche Richmond (*d.* 1952), with whom he had a family in London of six children. Murray died at his home, 77 Barrowgate Road, Chiswick, Middlesex, on 25 January 1919. His drawings are held by his family and in the Victoria and Albert Museum and the Dulwich Picture Gallery in London, the Ashmolean Museum in Oxford, the Birmingham Art Gallery, the Walker Art Gallery in Liverpool, the Whitworth Gallery in Manchester, the Pierpont Morgan Library in New York, and the Delaware Art Museum, and in the universities of Yale, Princeton, and Stanford.   JULIE F. CODELL

Sources A. C. Benson, *Memories and friends* (1924), 205–21 · W. S. Spanton, *An art student and his teachers in the sixties with other rigmaroles* (1927), 63–116 · S. Beresford, 'Preraffaellismo ed estetismo a Firenze negli ultimi decenni del XIX secolo', *L'idea di Firenze: atti del convegno, Firenze* [Florence 1986], ed. M. Bossi and L. Tonini (Florence, 1989), 191–210 · J. Codell, 'Charles Fairfax Murray and the Pre-Raphaelite "Academy": writing and forging the artistic field', *Collecting the Pre-Raphaelites: the Anglo-American enchantment*, ed. M. F. Watson (1997), 35–49 · J. Clegg and P. Tucker, *Ruskin and Tuscany* (1993) · D. S. MacColl, *Burlington Magazine*, 34 (1919), 122 · *The Times* (28 Jan 1919) · C. Cable, 'Charles Fairfax Murray, assistant to Dante Gabriel Rossetti', *Library Chronicle of the University of Texas at Austin*, new ser., 10 (1979), 81–9 · R. Elzea, 'The correspondence between Samuel Bancroft, Jr. and Charles Fairfax Murray, 1892–1916', *Delaware Art Museum Occasional Paper*, 2 (Feb 1980) [entire issue] · priv. coll. · b. cert. · *CGPLA Eng. & Wales* (1919) · P. Tucker, 'Responsible outsider – Charles Fairfax Murray and the South Kensington Museum', *Journal of the History of Collections*, 14 (2002), 115–37
Archives Hunt. L., collections · JRL, collection · Morgan L., collection · NRA, priv. coll., family MSS · Ransom HRC, letters | Bodl. Oxf., letters to F. G. Stephens · Delaware Art Museum, Wilmington, Bancroft collection · U. Lpool, letters to John Sampson · University of British Columbia, Angeli-Dennis collection
Likenesses C. F. Murray, *c.*1870–1875, Delaware Art Museum, Wilmington, Bancroft collection · C. F. Murray, pencil drawing, *c.*1880–1884, FM Cam.
Wealth at death £11,553 11*s.* 10*d.*: probate, 25 July 1919, *CGPLA Eng. & Wales*

Murray, Charles Thomas McKinnon [Chic] (1919–1985), comedian and actor, was born on 6 November 1919 at 26 Duncan Street, Greenock, the only surviving child of William Irvine Murray (1879–1933), railway goods checker, and his wife, Isabella Forrest McKinnon (1882–1958). He left school at Greenock in 1934 when he was fifteen and obtained an apprenticeship at Kincaid's marine engineering works. A few years later he formed a musical act with workmates and friends which had a fair amount of local success especially during the war years.

Murray married Maidie Dickson (*b.* 1922), daughter of Hugh Beaton Dickson, maintenance engineer, and Anne Sinclair, on 28 April 1945. She was an established Scottish variety performer and persuaded Chic to leave his job as a marine engineer to form a comedy/musical double act. On stage Chic at 6 feet 2 inches towered over his partner's petite 5 feet nothing. From the beginning he was determined not to be just another Scottish comic. He was a storyteller, something many audiences were slow to appreciate. Describing in detail apparently mundane activities like going downstairs and leaving the house, he made them seem extraordinary. Standing almost stationary centre stage he spoke to the audience in quiet, deadpan tones without any gestures that might deflect attention from the words. Journalist Jack House described him as 'a complete original, who turned familiar words and phrases into something out of this world' (House, 81).

Signed by the Bernard Delfont agency in 1955 the duo climbed steadily to top billing at the major variety theatres in Britain and on television but Chic was left to go solo when Maidie retired in the early 1960s. Unlike other top comics he failed to secure a regular television series as variety theatres closed and, although still busy, he allowed his career to drift. His links to the Delfont agency loosened and he was looking after his own affairs. Self-management was not his strong point and both his career and his health suffered from lack of proper attention. In 1972 he and his wife divorced.

Chic Murray played cameo roles in a number of films beginning with the spoof James Bond film *Casino Royale* (1967). He gained particular praise and welcome favourable publicity as the headmaster in *Gregory's Girl* (1981) and the bank manager in the television film drama *Saigon—Year of the Cat* (1983). His economical style suited the camera and from a low point his career seemed to be taking off in a new direction. Somehow, perhaps due to ill health as well as ill luck, it never happened. There was one final acting success when in 1984 he played the former Liverpool Football Club manager Bill Shankly in the musical play *You'll Never Walk Alone* at the Everyman Theatre, Liverpool. He died on 29 January 1985 at 7 Bruntsfield Crescent, Edinburgh, from a perforated duodenal ulcer. His funeral service was on 1 February at Mortonhall crematorium in the city.

Chic Murray was successful in variety, television, cabaret, film, and on radio and was one of the most impersonated performers in show business, in itself a tribute to his unique talent. He was a major influence on younger comedians such as Billy Connolly who declared him 'the funniest man on earth', the artist who set the standard to which he aspired (Yule, 269). ARCHIE L. FOLEY

Sources A. Yule, *The best way to walk: the Chic Murray story* (1989) · *The Scotsman* (30 Jan 1985) · *The Times* (30 Jan 1985) · personal knowledge (2004) · private information (2004) · J. House, *Music hall memories* (1986) · b. cert. · m. cert. · d. cert.

Archives U. Glas. L., Scottish Theatre archive, contracts and theatre programmes [copies] | FILM BFI NFTVA, performance footage | SOUND BL NSA, 'Chic Murray: the comic's comic', BBC Radio 2, 9 Dec 1997, H9516/1 · BL NSA, performance recording

Wealth at death £31,082.28: confirmation, 25 June 1985, *CCI*

Murray, Daniel (1768–1852), Roman Catholic archbishop of Dublin, was born on 18 April 1768 at Sheepwalk, near Arklow, co. Wicklow, the son of Thomas Murray, a farmer, and his wife, Judith. He was taught locally and by Dr Betagh SJ in Dublin. At the age of sixteen he was sent to study in Salamanca. A doctor of theology, he was ordained priest in 1792 and was appointed a curate in Arklow. In 1798, while the Wexford insurgents advanced on the town, he was warned that he was to be shot on sight by the yeomanry. His parish priest was murdered and his

Daniel Murray (1768–1852), by unknown engraver

thatched church was burnt; he escaped to Dublin where he served as a curate and acquired a reputation as a preacher. During this period he became acquainted with two women who later, with his encouragement, founded religious communities, Frances Ball and Mary Aikenhead. Ball's sister Anna Maria O'Brien became his lifelong friend, and indeed had introduced him to Aikenhead.

In 1808 John Thomas Troy, archbishop of Dublin, petitioned the pope to have Murray as coadjutor; Murray was appointed titular archbishop of Hierapolis *in partibus infidelium* with the right of succession to Troy. He was consecrated by Troy on 30 November 1809. As coadjutor he carried out the more laborious episcopal duties such as confirming children and conducting the parochial visitations in rural areas. He was, moreover, responsible for carrying out the duties of an ordinary parish priest in his mensal parish. He was also closely involved by Troy in all matters of importance to the diocese and the church in Ireland.

Advantage was taken of the open toleration of the Catholic church in Ireland to introduce a greater display of religion. In Dublin there were sufficient wealthy Catholics to allow the construction of fine churches. Bells were publicly tolled for worship, nuns in religious habits appeared in the streets, confraternities and charitable societies were established, and, not least important, the Catholic archbishop could call openly on the lord lieutenant in Dublin Castle. Archbishop Murray was anxious to have nuns serving outside their convents, and devoted much time and energy to training Mary Aikenhead and to the foundation of her order.

In 1804 the Catholic Lay Committee had been reconvened to work for Roman Catholic emancipation, in conjunction with some members of parliament. Various schemes were proposed which involved the concession of a measure of control over the clergy to the government. In 1813 George Canning introduced an Emancipation Bill which included a right for the government to veto appointments of Catholic bishops. The Catholic Board, as it then was, split into 'vetoists' and 'anti-vetoists'; Murray took the latter position. On 16 February 1814 Monsignor Quarantotti, who was managing the church from Rome during the exile of Pope Pius VII, conceded the veto to the government in the 'Quarantotti rescript'. The Irish bishops sent Murray to Rome to protest, and the rescript was revoked. He also dealt with the property of the Irish church which had been seized by the French, and promoted Mary Aikenhead's order. As the pope confirmed the veto in his 'Genoese letter', Murray was again sent to Rome in 1815: on Good Friday 1816, he compared the supporters of the veto to those who bound Jesus to the cross. It was next proposed that as an alternative safeguard, the ancient right of the clergy to elect their own bishop should be restored. To this the bishops were opposed, and Murray was denounced in unmeasured terms by Daniel O'Connell, himself now the leading anti-vetoist.

Troy dead, Murray succeeded as archbishop of Dublin on 11 May 1823. With the other bishops he dealt with questions of ecclesiastical discipline and decided questions on which they wished to have a common policy. After the passing of the Emancipation Act in 1829, the bishops issued a statement that all priests were to withdraw from political activity, though each bishop had discretion in his own diocese. The issue was to become a burning one, but Murray always opposed political activity by his clergy. Within his own province he organized, along with James Doyle, bishop of Kildare and Leighlin, a synod in 1831 that brought the discipline in the province into conformity with post-penal conditions.

Murray also took a prominent position in the debates on education. In 1812 the report of the inquiry by the commissioners of education had recommended that all Irish children be educated together, with a common core of religious education. The government channelled state aid through the Kildare Place Society, established for this purpose. At first the Catholic bishops acquiesced, but following allegations of proselytism, they tried unsuccessfully to establish a Catholic Education Society. The lord lieutenant, Lord Wellesley, was well disposed towards Catholics, so they approached him, Murray negotiating with him over a period of several years. In 1826 the Catholic bishops published their recommendations for a system of state-aided education. Dr John MacHale, then coadjutor bishop of Killala, regarded these requirements as unalterable; Murray did not. In 1831 an act establishing a board of national education was passed, and Murray was appointed one of the commissioners on the board. The bishops, excepting MacHale, concurred with Murray. The board took over the work of the Kildare Place Society in training teachers, paying their salaries and providing school books and equipment at moderate prices. Its success was largely due to the harmonious relationship between Murray and the protestant archbishop of Dublin, Richard Whately, who was also on the board. Murray, unlike MacHale, took a tolerant view when Whately smuggled some of his own views into the textbooks he prepared for the schools.

In 1836 Murray set about completing his cathedral, commenced in 1815. He was active until extreme old age: at eighty-four he confirmed 1500 children in a ceremony lasting four hours. He took an interest in foreign missions, and assisted in the formation of a college for missionary priests. His advice was sought on many matters by the government and he declined the offer of a privy councillorship. During the famine he devoted all his efforts to the relief of the poor, and, unlike some bishops, he was appreciative of the efforts of the government to provide relief.

From 1836 onwards Murray suffered much opposition from MacHale and the group of bishops which he headed, and also from many of his own clergy and people. The chief issue was whether the government education system was compatible with the Catholic faith. The issue was complicated when O'Connell gained the support of many of the clergy for the repeal of the Act of Union. Murray refused to involve himself in secular politics, or to condemn reasonable acts of the government. Feelings against him ran high: he was accused of being a 'Castle bishop', of co-operating too closely with the government. MacHale's faction made two attempts to get his views on education condemned by the Holy See.

Murray was the most attractive figure among the Irish bishops of his day, and arguably the greatest. He had a gentle, sly humour. He was a clear-sighted man who distinguished between the desirable and the attainable. Although known as a mild man, he could be firm on matters of principle and he spoke his mind openly even to Rome. Two volumes of his sermons were published in Dublin in 1859, but they are not to modern taste.

On 23 February 1852 Murray presided at the requiem mass for Richard Lalor Sheil. The following morning he suffered a stroke, and he died at his residence in Mountjoy Square, Dublin, on 26 February without recovering consciousness. He was interred in his cathedral.

DESMOND KEENAN

Sources Dublin Diocesan Archives, Murray papers, MSS 24/5, 30/7, 32/5, 32/6, 34/5, 35/4 • F. P. Carey, *Archbishop Murray of Dublin, 1768–1852* (1951) • W. Meagher, *Notices of the life and character of Most Reverend Daniel Murray* (1853) • *Dublin Evening Post* (1809–52) • *Saunders' Newsletter* [Dublin] (1809–52) • S. A. [S. Atkinson], *Mary Aikenhead: her life, her work and her friends*, 2nd edn (1882) • R. R. Madden, *The United Irishmen: their lives and times*, 2nd edn, 4th ser. (1860) • M. Ronan, *An apostle of Catholic Dublin* (1944) • *Scritture riferite nei congressi Irelanda*, Propaganda archives • J. F. Broderick, *The Holy See and the Irish movement for the repeal of the union with England, 1829–1847* (1951) • S. Cannon, *Irish episcopal meetings, 1788–1882* (1979) • D. H. Akenson, *The Irish education experiment: the national system of education in the nineteenth century* (1970)
Archives Dublin Roman Catholic diocesan archives, Dublin, corresp. and papers as archbishop | TCD, corresp. with Lord Donoughmore
Likenesses J. Hogan, marble bust, 1844 (after plaster bust), NG Ire. • T. Farrell, statue, 1855, Marlborough Street church, Dublin •

N. J. Crowley, oils, NG Ire. • attrib. Crowley, oils, St Vincent's Hospital, Dublin • Pistrucci, lithograph (after bust by P. Turnerelli), NPG • engraving, NPG [see illus.] • portrait (after painting by Crowley), repro. in D. Murray, Sermons, 2 vols. (1859), frontispiece

Murray, Sir David, of Gorthy (1567–1629), poet and courtier, was the second son of Robert Moray of Abercairney and Catherine, daughter of William Murray of Tullibardine. Little can be established about his early life until 1599, when he appears as gentleman of the prince's bedchamber, an appointment in Henry's household which he retained on the removal of the royal court to London in 1603. He received a knighthood on 26 May 1605.

The nature of Murray's personal and political life is defined by the seemingly loyal and intimate relationship which he sustained with Prince Henry. In 1610 the enlargement of the prince's household ensured the appointment of Murray to groom of the stole. A letter from Lord William Roos to Murray in 1612 portrays Murray, being 'so great a Puritan', as the prince's cautious, protective confidant in the question of the potential Medici marriage (Birch, 320). A contemporary account of the prince's death bears witness to the significance that Murray had assumed: Prince Henry 'would many times call upon Sir David Murray, Knight, (the onely man in whom he had put choise trust,) by his name, David! David! David!' (Nichols, 482–3). In the account of Sir Charles Cornwallis, Murray himself 'in this one death suffered many' (Nichols, 483).

As a member of the royal household Murray is recorded as the recipient of several gifts (in the accounts for 1615–16 he received £5200 to pay unspecified debts). After the death of Henry it appears that Murray's political and social influence at the Jacobean court declined, and he turned to business ventures. He received a charter from Charles I which granted him the estate of Gorthy.

Murray's first and most substantial publication was The Tragicall Death of Sophonisba (1611), modelled on Italian tragedy. Largely a dramatic monologue delivered by Sophonisba before her death, the lament of this female martyr to love is also a meditation on fate, reputation, and death. A short sonnet sequence, Caelia, was published in 1611 with Sophonisba; the sequence, influenced by Neoplatonism, is occasionally recondite in its mythological and political metaphors. While often classified as conventional and imitatively English, both the sonnet sequence and Sophonisba reflect developments in Scottish poetry post-1603 as well as European literary influences that shaped the literature of the earlier Scottish Jacobean court. In 1615 Murray published a Paraphrase of the CIV Psalme on the subject of divine creation, and an amatory pastoral, The Complaint of the Shepherd Harpalus, was published separately in 1625.

Murray was not only the writer but the subject of a number of poetic dedications: in Patrick Gordon's Neptunus Britannicus Corydonis (1613), and as Henry's faithful subject praised in John Owen's Epigrammatum (1622). The commendatory poem which Michael Drayton produced for Sophonisba (1611) suggests a personal friendship, while the possibility of collaboration between Drayton and Murray

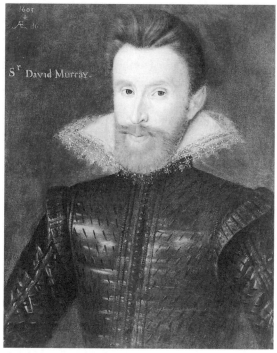

Sir David Murray of Gorthy (1567–1629), by unknown artist, 1603

in the writing of Sophonisba has been suggested (Newdigate, 197). Murray died in 1629, unmarried and with no heir.

S. M. DUNNIGAN

Sources Poems of Sir David Murray of Gorthy, ed. T. Kinnear, Bannatyne Club, 2 (1823) • R. D. S. Jack, The Italian influence on Scottish literature (1972) • J. Nichols, The progresses, processions, and magnificent festivities of King James I, his royal consort, family and court, 4 vols. (1828) • T. Birch, ed., The life of Henry, prince of Wales (1760) • H. M. Klein, ed., English and Scottish sonnet sequences of the Renaissance, 2 vols. (1984) • M. Spiller, 'Poetry after the Union', The history of Scottish literature, ed. C. Craig, 1: Origins to 1660, ed. R. D. S. Jack (1987), 141–62 • D. Irving, The history of Scottish poetry, ed. J. A. Carlyle (1861) • C. Cornwallis, A discourse of the most illustrious prince, Henry, late prince of Wales (1641) • B. H. Newdigate, Michael Drayton and his circle (1941) • R. Douglas and others, The baronage of Scotland (1798)

Likenesses oils, 1603, Scot. NPG [see illus.] • line engraving, repro. in D. L. [D. Laing], Specimen of a proposed catalogue of a portion of the library at Britwell House (1852) • oils, Abercairney, Perth and Kinross

Murray, David, first viscount of Stormont (d. 1631), politician, was probably born some time before 1560, the second son of Sir Andrew Murray of Balvaird (d. 1572×3) and his second wife, Jonet Graham (fl. 1542), fourth daughter of William, second earl of Montrose. He entered royal service as the king's cupbearer and, in 1584, was appointed as a master stabler in the royal household. These are the only details concerning his education and formative years. By 1585 he held lands in Kinross-shire, and in 1586 he was granted Auchtermuchty in Fife. The first of a number of dramatic incidents in which he was involved occurred in 1588 in connection with the latter. On 5 November he went to Auchtermuchty accompanied by twenty-four others to take formal possession of the property which he had recently been granted by the king. On their approach, however, twenty-three tenants rang the town's common bell, calling out more than 100 people who pursued him and his company. One James Maxwell caught up with Murray, wrestled him to the ground, and, in the struggle, Murray lost a finger from his right hand and, 'undoubtedly he had perished there, if the Laird of Balwearie had not intervened' (Scot, 114). The case was brought before the privy council and a number of those involved were warded or put to the horn.

With the death of his elder brother, Sir Andrew of Balvaird (otherwise 'of Arngask'), on 13 November 1590, David Murray was styled 'tutor of Balvaird', as guardian of his nephew Andrew. He obtained further property in Fife in December 1593 when he received lands at Falkland. As his time in royal service wore on he gathered strength and influence. In 1596 he was noted by Calderwood in his *History* to have been one of the 'cubicular courteours' sidelined by the new financial commission known as the Octavians (Calderwood, 5.510–11). In November and December of that year these cubiculars, who also included Sir George Hume, later earl of Dunbar, allegedly tried to turn the kirk against the Octavians. They told certain ministers that the Octavians were behind the ostensibly unauthorized return of the exiled Catholic earls of Huntly and Erroll in the previous summer and that four of them were actually Catholics. They also told the Octavians that the ministers were making these very accusations to turn the people against them and that they were at risk from zealous lay protestants in Edinburgh. If true, this points to a certain unscrupulousness in Murray.

Murray was knighted late in 1598 or early in 1599. In April of the latter year he was admitted to the privy council and made comptroller, replacing Sir George Home of Wedderburn. He first attended the council in July and in September 1599 he was first styled 'of Gospertie', when he was commissioned by the privy council to accept certain offers from MacDonald of 'Knockinsay' for establishing order in Kintyre and Islay (*Reg. PCS*, 1st ser., 6.24). In the following December he attended a convention of estates at the royal palace of Holyrood.

In 1600 Murray became firmly established as a trusted royal servant as a result of his support of the king in the aftermath of the so-called Gowrie conspiracy of 5 August. Along with his brother Alexander, John Ruthven, second earl of Gowrie, son of the executed leader of the Ruthven raiders of 1582, lured the king to his house in Perth. There, according to James, an attempt was made on the king's life and the brothers were killed by those coming to the king's aid. Murray was on the privy council which issued the official version of events in Edinburgh on the following day and, on 7 August, he was on the council at Falkland which seized the property of the Ruthvens, ordered the bailies of Perth not to bury the bodies, and banned anyone called Ruthven from a 10 mile radius of the king and queen. On 9 and 20 August he sat on a panel of officers of state to examine the 'witnesses' in the investigation of the 'conspiracy'. He was rewarded with a substantial amount of the former Ruthven properties, notably the barony of

Ruthven and the estates of the former Augustinian abbey of Scone, where he added a second courtyard to complete a palace begun there by the Ruthvens in the 1580s. By November 1601 he had also supplanted Ruthven influence over Perth by becoming its provost and he continued in this office 'almost everie yeere' apparently 'by his private moyen' until February 1628 when the privy council annulled his election because an act of parliament had restricted the magistracy to indwellers of burghs. His right to be provost had been annulled by the privy council before, in November 1619 and, because of repeated disobedience, he was ordered to enter ward in Edinburgh Castle, although he was later absolved owing to ill health.

In May 1601 Murray was named as one of the officers of state to consult with ministers appointed by the general assembly to discuss the establishment of a 'constant platt' for provision of stipends. The hope was that a uniform system of financing the kirk could be devised to replace the unwieldy one which had prevailed since 1560. In July 1601 he was named as one of the componitors to the treasurer and, in November, he was appointed to a commission of six, including the chancellor, the king's advocate, and the collector, to draw up an agreement between foreign clothmakers and the bailies of Edinburgh. It was hoped that they would settle in the capital and promote improvements in the Scottish textile industry.

In 1603 Murray accompanied James VI south to take up the throne of England. Moreover, he personally advanced money to pay the fees of the officers of the royal household to enable the royal journey to take place. In the following August he obtained money and a royal commission to raise a guard of forty horsemen to act as a flying police force, to ensure the execution of the orders of the privy council and the apprehension of criminals and outlaws. In his capacity as captain of the guard he was sent to Kintyre in the summer of 1605 to receive the obedience of 'the principallis of the Clannis' of the southern Hebrides and to collect crown dues there. This mission was beset by delays and in August of that year he was given a lieutenancy and made justice and commissioner for the privy council in those islands, perhaps to encourage his departure by augmenting his authority (*Reg. PCS*, 1st ser., 7.59, 115–16).

Murray attended the parliament at Perth in 1604, where he was elected one of the lords of the articles, the committee which drafted legislation and received petitions. At that parliament he was also appointed as a commissioner to negotiate closer union with England and was first recorded as 'David Lord Scone'. In February of the same year he married Elizabeth Beaton or Bethune (*d.* 1658), daughter of James Beaton, laird of Creich; they had no children. From March 1605 he appears in privy council sederunts as Lord Scone, and the barony of Ruthven and the lands of Scone Abbey were formally erected into the lordship of Scone on 1 April. He first sat in parliament as Lord Scone in July 1606. In that year his uneasy association with the kirk began to develop. In January he had been on the packed jury for the trial for treason of six of the ministers who, in July 1605, had held a general assembly at Aberdeen in defiance of a royal command. In the aftermath of their trial the king submitted to the kirk articles emphasizing royal supremacy and episcopal power. Scone was the bearer of these to the synod of Fife. In 1607 his most dramatic confrontation with the kirk occurred. In December 1606 the king convened a meeting of hand-picked ministers which was declared to have been a general assembly after it rose. It agreed that presbyteries should have permanent moderators and its records were altered to make it seem that it had also agreed to permanent moderation of regional synods by bishops or their nominees. Scone was ordered to ensure that the synod of Perth and Stirling accepted its constant moderator at Perth on 7 April 1607. In defiance, the synod elected its own moderator and he threatened to discharge the meeting. The synod countered with a demand for freedom of action. Again Scone threatened dissolution and the synod claimed the authority of Jesus, provoking his intemperate response, 'Thair is no Jesus heir!' (*Autobiography and Diary of … Melvill*, 704). Chaos resulted as Scone lunged into the moderator's chair to prevent him from taking office and ordered the removal of the stools; the synod continued, standing up. The bailies of Perth refused to eject the ministers in spite of their provost's command and, when Scone locked the ministers out after a recess, they met outside, made a formal protest and left. Later in the year he was a commissioner from the privy council to the presbyteries of Perth and Dunkeld to ensure their acceptance of constant moderators.

In November 1607 Scone was charged by the privy council with neglecting his duty as captain of the guard because he had failed to apprehend the earl of Crawford and the laird of Edzell. His devoted royal service continued, however, when he sat on the assize at the trial of Lord Balmerino in 1608 and as a royal commissioner at a conference with clergy at Falkland in May 1609 which attempted to remove controversies over royal ecclesiastical policy. He resigned as comptroller in 1609 after revelations that he had been involved in some financial dishonesty over the granting of a tack of the customs. He attended parliament again in that year and was again elected to the lords of the articles. In January 1610 he was named as one of the new, streamlined privy council of thirty-five and in February was appointed as a lay member of the court of high commission under the archbishop of St Andrews. Later in that year he became justice of the peace for Fife and Kinross; in 1613 this was extended to Perthshire, Strathearn, and Menteith, and he was reappointed justice for Fife and Kinross in 1614. In 1610 he was also appointed as an assessor to the earl of Dunbar in his capacity as treasurer. In July 1611 he was reappointed as captain of the guard but was replaced soon after by Sir Robert Ker of Ancrum.

Scone attended the parliament of 1617 when he was again elected to the committee of the articles. In 1618 he was a royal commissioner to the general assembly at Perth which enacted the five articles of Perth, reforming worship in the kirk to bring it more into line with English practices. In the following year, as in 1609, he was a royal commissioner to a conference between bishops and ministers designed to try to quell opposition to the imposition of the five articles. At this conference it became clear that enforcement was impossible and the bishops agreed with Scone that they would tell the king that he had successfully carried out his commission if he would give the king a sanitized report of the level of nonconformity. He was again chosen as one of the lords of the articles at the parliament of 1621 at which the five articles were ratified and he then hastened to London to inform the king of this success. On 16 August 1621, as a reward for his services to the crown, particularly in the ecclesiastical sphere, he was created viscount of Stormont. After this he retreated from the forefront of politics, perhaps devoting his time to his estates, for a gateway on the north drive of Scone Palace bearing his arms is thought to date from 1624. He was, however, appointed to a number of crown commissions and attended conventions of estates in October 1625 and July 1630. He was named as a member of Charles I's privy council in March 1626 but his attendance fell away during the 1620s, and by 1628 he was excusing his absence through ill health. In spite of this, he was appointed once more to the reconstituted privy council on 30 March 1631, only five months before his death at Scone on 27 August. On 23 December he was buried in the Old Kirk there, part of which survives as the Stormont mausoleum, where his fine baroque memorial remains. It consists of the tomb itself and three further levels. The first has Stormont himself kneeling in prayer at a lectern, supported by armed knights, the second consists of angels and an inscription, and the whole is surmounted by his arms. Murray had no children, and his estates and titles passed to his nephew Mungo (or Kentigern) Murray, a son of the earl of Tullibardine. Sir John Scot of Scotstarvet wrote of Stormont that 'albeit an ignorant man, yet he was bold and got great business effectuated; for he was the king's commissioner when the five articles … were brought in' (Scot, 114).

ALAN R. MACDONALD

Sources *Scots peerage* [see also 8.196] · *Reg. PCS*, 1st ser. · *Reg. PCS*, 2nd ser. · J. Scot, *The staggering state of Scottish statesmen from 1550 to 1650*, ed. C. Rogers (1872) · *APS* · J. M. Thomson and others, eds., *Registrum magni sigilli regum Scotorum / The register of the great seal of Scotland*, 11 vols. (1882–1914) · M. Livingstone, D. Hay Fleming, and others, eds., *Registrum secreti sigilli regum Scotorum / The register of the privy seal of Scotland*, 8 (1982) · K. M. Brown, *Bloodfeud in Scotland, 1573–1625* (1986) · Royal Commission on the Ancient and Historical Monuments of Scotland, National monuments record of Scotland · D. Calderwood, *The history of the Kirk of Scotland*, ed. T. Thomson and D. Laing, 8 vols., Wodrow Society, 7 (1842–9) · *The autobiography and diary of Mr James Melvill*, ed. R. Pitcairn, Wodrow Society (1842) · P. Corser and others, *South east Perth: an archaeological landscape* (1994) · GEC, *Peerage*

Archives Scone Palace, Perthshire, corresp. and MSS

Likenesses M. Gheeraerts junior, oils, 1614, Scot. NPG · baroque tomb, Stormont Mausoleum, Scone Palace

Murray, David, seventh Viscount Stormont and second earl of Mansfield (1727–1796), diplomatist and politician, was born on 9 October 1727, the eldest son of David, sixth

Viscount Stormont (c.1689–1748), and Anne (d. 1735), only surviving child of John Stewart of Invernytie in Perthshire. He was the nephew and ultimately the heir of the great lawyer William *Murray, first earl of Mansfield. Murray and his uncle rose higher in and integrated more fully into the British political establishment than any other Scotsmen since the second duke of Argyll and his brother the earl of Ilay during the ministry of Sir Robert Walpole. For most Scotsmen a career in the British army or service as a colonial administrator was the chosen route, but for Murray it was the diplomatic service. His ascent was the more remarkable because he came from a family with strong Jacobite sympathies. His father had been fined and imprisoned after the 1715 rising; two other Murrays were also prosecuted, while another relative, James Murray, went into exile and eventually became the Pretender's secretary of state. William Murray, during the early phase of his career, had struggled to throw off the taunts that he was sympathetic to the cause of the Stuarts.

Murray's success was the result of a deliberate family strategy of integration into the emerging British state together with his uncle's crucial influence: as Mansfield rose in importance, so Murray secured appointments to match. Mansfield's lack of a direct male heir ensured that he took a paternal interest in his young relative's career: one well-placed contemporary noted in 1756 that Stormont was 'not only his nephew but looked upon by him as his son' (Lord Holdernesse to Andrew Mitchell, 17 Sept 1756, BL, Add. MS 6832, fol. 90).

Education and early career In pursuit of this family strategy, and treading exactly in the footsteps of his uncle, the young David Murray was educated with future members of the British establishment, first at Westminster School and then at Christ Church, Oxford, where he matriculated in 1744 and graduated BA in 1748, the same year that he became Viscount Stormont upon his father's death (23 July). While a student he first exhibited the outstanding intellectual abilities and strong interest in classical scholarship that he retained throughout his life. These would lead no less an authority than Winckelmann to describe him as 'the most learned person of his rank whom I have yet known' and to praise particularly his accomplishments in Greek. After leaving Oxford, Stormont, like most young aristocrats, set out on the fashionable grand tour, which was to occupy him for the next five years. Having left England late in 1748, he travelled at a very leisurely pace through France (serving briefly as an unpaid attaché at the Paris embassy in 1751) and on to Italy, up through Germany, and then, by way of the Low Countries, back to Paris, which he reached late in 1752. He returned to England the next year and resumed the social life of a young aristocrat.

Although his ambitions were considerable, his prospects were rather clouded. The mid-eighteenth century was the heyday of anti-Scottish prejudice in England, and the likelihood of a young Scottish peer's securing a post in London was not very great. Stormont himself recognized this: he subsequently wrote that he knew that 'with the dead weight of a Scotch title it would not be possible for me to make my way at home' (Hastings MSS, 3.138). He therefore looked towards diplomacy, in which—in company with many of his fellow countrymen—he was to make his career for the next two decades. Characteristically he prepared conscientiously, by intensive study of recent political events and by writing a manuscript history of the development of the European states system since the peace of Westphalia in 1648.

At the very end of 1755 Stormont secured his first post when Mansfield's influence—his uncle was by now attorney-general and a close political ally of the duke of Newcastle—was sufficient to obtain for him the position of envoy-extraordinary to Saxony-Poland, then ruled by Augustus III. This was an appointment of considerable stature, if not outstanding importance, especially for a twenty-eight-year-old diplomatic novice. He took up residence in Dresden in June 1756, and moved with the rest of Augustus III's court to Warsaw in that autumn, after the Prussian invasion of Saxony that launched the continental Seven Years' War. Shortly after Frederick the Great's invasion of the electorate in late August 1756 the diplomatic débutant made an ill-advised and equally ill-fated attempt to mediate, unofficially and without instructions, between the Prussian king and Augustus III, for which he was roundly and justifiably censured by the government at home. Stormont's years in Warsaw also saw his marriage in August 1759 to a young widow, Henrietta Frederica de Berargaard (1736/7–1766), daughter of Graf Heinrich von Bünau, an experienced diplomat and one of the Saxon ministers. This was an unusual marriage for a British diplomat to contract, particularly for a nobleman whose career had been so carefully planned, and it rested upon romantic affection rather than family calculation.

During these years Stormont was a competent, if rather uninspired, diplomat, apparently well suited to the life of a second-rank European court with which Britain's relations were rather distant. His own ambition, together with Mansfield's steadily increasing influence—the earl had become lord chief justice in November 1756—ensured that his career did not stagnate. Having entered the diplomatic service, Stormont was determined to rise as high as he could, and already he viewed service abroad as a route to an eventual office at home. In the spring of 1761, through the intermediacy of his political colleague the duke of Newcastle and of his fellow Scot the earl of Bute, Mansfield was able to secure the nomination of Stormont as ambassador-extraordinary and one of three British plenipotentiaries to the proposed peace congress at Augsburg, which was intended to bring the Seven Years' War to an end. The congress never actually met, but Stormont's nomination highlighted his growing stature. Two years later he secured the prestigious embassy of Vienna, with the rank of ambassador. His increasing importance and his links with the ministry were also evident in his selection in July 1763 as one of the sixteen representative peers of Scotland. These men were in practice a government list and could vote by proxy in the House of Lords. Stormont was reappointed in 1768, 1774, 1780, 1784, and

1790, though he only became an active member of the House of Lords when he returned from France in 1778.

Ambassador in Vienna The decade that Stormont spent at the Habsburg court (he arrived in November 1763 and finally left in December 1772) consolidated his reputation as a diplomat. With the ending of the Seven Years' War Britain believed it was an opportune moment to renew the traditional links with the Habsburgs, which had been severed by the Franco-Austrian treaty of May 1756, the centrepiece of the famous diplomatic revolution of that year. These hopes were exaggerated and quickly proved to be illusory, as Stormont found at the very end of 1763 when he broached the question of a renewed alliance with the Habsburg state chancellor Wenzel Anton von Kaunitz. The latter, the architect of the diplomatic revolution, intended to uphold the French treaty that he had concluded in 1756, though he wished for good relations with Britain, which were soon established.

Stormont's personal contribution was considerable: his embassy restored a remarkable degree of harmony to Anglo-Austrian diplomacy. His wife's role in this was significant. Links between Vienna and the court in Dresden were traditionally close, and her own standing as a Saxon aristocrat helped her husband when he first arrived in the Habsburg capital. Lady Stormont was a woman of enormous charm and liveliness, and this made up for the rather reserved, serious, and dour manner of her husband. She was especially important in securing Stormont's admission to the private society of the imperial family and also of Kaunitz, which was important for the success of his embassy. Her own health was never especially good, and the notoriously unhealthy climate of the Austrian capital soon took its toll: she died on 16 March 1766 at the age of twenty-nine. Her death had a traumatic impact upon Stormont, himself an extremely sensitive man: he suffered something approaching a nervous breakdown and was given an extended leave of absence. He went on a leisurely progress round Italy and into southern France, and returned to Vienna only in July 1768.

The outbreak of war between Russia and the Ottoman empire in that autumn (this would continue until 1774) gave Vienna a central position in British diplomacy, and Stormont was closely involved in the unsuccessful attempts to mediate in the conflict. Increasingly, however, Britain ceased to play any political role in eastern Europe, and was forced to watch as Poland's three powerful neighbours, Austria, Prussia, and Russia, moved towards a partition, which was finalized in 1772. The official British reaction to this was muted: by now events in the eastern half of the continent were of little interest to ministers in London. Stormont, however, was outraged by the cynicism of the transaction, and during his final months in Vienna became involved in some shadowy private diplomacy in a futile attempt to avert the planned partition.

The origins of this are complex and go back to Stormont's period in Warsaw during the Seven Years' War. His friendship with members of two of the leading noble families, the Czartoryski and the Poniatowski, and especially with the young aristocrat Stanisław Poniatowski, made him very sympathetic to the Polish cause. His links with Polish noblemen continued when he left Warsaw for Vienna. There, during the 1760s, he corresponded with King Stanisław August (as Poniatowski became after his election to the Polish throne in 1764) and continued to work unofficially for Poland's interests. Stormont was drawn into some secret pro-Polish diplomacy centring on the Sardinian diplomat Gerolamo Luigi Malabaila, conte di Canale, whose own marriage into the Habsburg aristocracy had facilitated the privileged access he enjoyed to the court in Vienna.

In the early 1770s, as the partitioning powers' objectives became apparent, this secret network tried unavailingly to prevent Austrian involvement in the seizure of Polish territory and in this way wreck the whole scheme. Once partition was formally announced, with the signature of the treaties in August 1772, Stormont protested loudly and publicly in Vienna for several weeks, though his action was quite unofficial and unknown to his superiors in London. It is indicative of the special place that he had secured at the Habsburg court—and also of the empress Maria Theresa's own ambivalence about the partition— that no representations were made to London about these protests, though this would have been perfectly justifiable. Stormont's emotional commitment to Poland and to Poniatowski was sufficient for him to imperil a carefully planned career. He and his uncle Mansfield also actively encouraged the Polonophile and pamphleteer John Lind, whose *Letters Concerning the Present State of Poland* (1773) offered a hostile account of the first partition and were an extension of King Stanisław August's campaign against it.

Ambassador in Paris and secretary of state Stormont left Vienna in December 1772. Mansfield, by now an important adviser to ministers and a political confidant of George III, had secured his appointment as ambassador to France. This embassy was the apex of the British diplomatic service, in stature the equivalent of a cabinet post. Stormont was one of the few professional diplomats to fill it during the eighteenth century, and also one of the few Scotsmen to do so. He was now clearly the leading British diplomat of his generation: that status and his uncle's immense influence were sufficient to secure his nomination. The Paris embassy, however, was less successful than its predecessor. This was largely a result of the evident deterioration of relations with France, which moved after the outbreak of the American colonial revolt in spring 1775 to assist the rebels at first unofficially and then openly. Stormont's main task was to preside over the diplomacy that ultimately led to war in 1778 and to delay the rupture as long as he could. With the signature of Franco-American treaties of friendship and alliance in January of that year, relations were broken off and he left the French capital in March; formal declarations of war followed in the summer.

During the period Stormont spent at the French court he married on 5 May 1776 his second wife, Louisa Cathcart

(1758?–1843), the third daughter of his fellow Scottish diplomat and nobleman Charles Schaw *Cathcart, ninth Lord Cathcart, who had been ambassador in Russia. To the two daughters of his first marriage this second added three daughters and a son, David William Murray, third earl of Mansfield (1777–1840), who was born in Paris in March 1777. In October 1778 Stormont was appointed to the post of lord justice general for Scotland, a sinecure that he continued to hold until 1794.

Relations with France were central to the next phase of Stormont's public career. The two and a half years that he spent as secretary of state for the northern department (October 1779–March 1782) were dominated by the diplomacy of the American War of Independence after the intervention of France and Spain. His fellow secretary the earl of Hillsborough was a nonentity, handling only some minor and routine aspects of Britain's diplomacy. Stormont, though formally responsible only for the conduct of relations with those powers that lay within the northern department, acted as *de facto* foreign secretary, anticipating the geographically unified direction of Britain's diplomacy that would be created by the establishment of the Foreign Office in 1782. One of a handful of career diplomats to be appointed to a secretaryship of state during the eighteenth century, he brought into office an unparalleled knowledge of Europe. But the extended period he spent at Dresden, Warsaw, Vienna, and Paris was not without its drawbacks. He also brought to his post two decades of exposure to ideas about British foreign policy: ideas that were always orthodox, often outdated, and at times dangerously rigid. As northern secretary he was to demonstrate a degree of inflexibility and occasionally dogmatism: he never fully made the transition from diplomat to statesman. Yet his professionalism and conscientiousness, particularly in corresponding with diplomats abroad (which had been neglected by his predecessor), were important during the second half of the war in America, with Britain either at war or in dispute over commercial clashes with most of Europe, which came to a climax with the formation of the armed neutrality in 1780. Stormont's handling of British foreign policy was always competent, though seldom more than that.

Final years Stormont left office when the North administration fell in March 1782. Briefly lord president of the council in 1783 (April–December), during the following decade he was an important critic of government policy and a stalwart of the opposition in the House of Lords, speaking often and usually well. He resumed his support of the younger Pitt's ministry after the outbreak of the war with revolutionary France in 1793, and in the following year returned to office as lord president of the council, a post he continued to hold until his death. On 20 March 1793 he succeeded to the earldom of Mansfield on the death of his uncle, through a special remainder established in the previous year. The scholarly interests that were a feature of his whole life continued to the end. In July 1793 he was awarded the degree of DCL by the University of Oxford, and in the same year he became chancellor of Marischal College, Aberdeen. He died at Brighton on 1

September 1796, and was buried at the side of his uncle in the north cross, Westminster Abbey, London, on 9 September. Their shared resting place symbolized how the two men, whose careers intersected at so many points, had together travelled the long and difficult road from their family's Jacobite past to the very heart of the eighteenth-century Hanoverian state. H. M. SCOTT

Sources *Scots peerage* · *GM*, 1st ser., 66 (1796), 795–6 · H. M. Scott, 'Anglo-Austrian relations after the Seven Years' War: Lord Stormont in Vienna, 1763–1772', PhD diss., U. Lond., 1977 · H. M. Scott, *British foreign policy in the age of the American revolution* (1990) · D. B. Horn, *British public opinion and the first partition of Poland* (1945) · R. Butterwick, *Poland's last king and English culture* (1998) · *Report on the manuscripts of the late Reginald Rawdon Hastings*, 4 vols., HMC, 78 (1928–47), vol. 3, pp. 67–111 [Stormont's correspondence with Francis, tenth earl of Huntingdon, 1748–1756] · BL, Add. MS 6832, fol. 90

Archives Kenwood House, London, corresp. and bills · NRA Scotland, priv. coll., corresp. and papers · Scone Palace, Perthshire, Stormont MSS · U. Edin. L., notes on Greek language | BL, letters to Lord Grantham, Add. MSS 24157–24165 · BL, letters to R. Gunning and W. Eden, Egerton MSS 2701–2703; Add. MSS 34413–34415 · BL, corresp. with Lord Hardwicke, etc., Add. MSS 35480–35661 · BL, corresp. with Lord Holderness, etc., Add. MSS 6804–6829 · BL, corresp. with Lord Newcastle, Add. MSS 32729–32950, 33100 · BL, corresp. with Lord Sandwich and R. Phelps, Stowe MSS 257–261 · Hunt. L., letters to Lord Huntingdon · NL Scot., letters to Hugh Elliot · NMM, letters to Lord Sandwich · Northumbd RO, Newcastle upon Tyne, letters to Horace St Paul · priv. coll., letters to Lord Cathcart · PRO, state papers · U. Nott. L., letters to Lord Portland

Likenesses P. Batoni, oils, 1768, Scone Palace, Tayside region · G. Romney, oils, 1783, Christ Church Oxf. · M. Buccarelli, oils, Scone Palace, Tayside region · attrib. M. Buccarelli, oils, Scone Palace, Tayside region · S. Harding, watercolour drawing, BM · attrib. D. Martin, oils, Scone Palace, Tayside region

Murray, David (1842–1928), lawyer and antiquary, was born at Glasgow on 15 April 1842, the eldest son of David Murray, a writer to the signet in Glasgow, and Ann Hunter Guthrie. He attended Merchiston Castle School in Edinburgh, and the University of Glasgow from 1857. He graduated MA in 1863 and was apprenticed in a solicitor's office. When he qualified in 1863 he went into partnership with his father's surviving partner George Smith. Four years later he formed a new partnership with David T. Maclay and John A. Spens to form the firm of Maclay, Murray, and Spens—known to generations of Glaswegians as 'Delay, Worry and Expense'. The new firm specialized in commercial and property work. In 1872 Murray married Frances Porter (d. 1919), of Broadfield, Renfrewshire, daughter of Arthur Francis Stoddard, a carpet maker. They had a son and three daughters, the youngest of whom was the suffragist and author Eunice Guthrie *Murray.

Murray acted as solicitor to Lewis *Potter (1807–1881), a prominent director of the City of Glasgow Bank. After the bank's collapse in 1878 he prepared Potter's defence against charges of fraud. This involved meticulous research in the bank's archives and the preparation of volumes of exhibits, work much to Murray's taste. The trial early in 1879 was widely reported and Potter was sent to prison for eighteen months. In the wake of the trial Murray, as solicitor to the company, became involved in the immensely complicated task of winding up the bank's affairs and the sequestration of Lewis Potter's own estate. His chief task was to help to reconstruct the New Zealand and Australian Land Co. Ltd Reduced, managed by Potter, and of which the City of Glasgow Bank held a large number of shares as collateral. The company, founded in 1866, was merged with the Canterbury and Otago Association Ltd to form a new New Zealand and Australian Land Company, controlling some 2 million acres in New Zealand and in Australia. The new firm immediately started selling land, disposing of nearly 1 million acres over the next ten years. Murray, as solicitor to the company, was responsible for the Scottish end of all the transactions, along with the management of the remaining properties. This strategy did not solve the company's financial problems and in 1888 Murray had to prepare a massive petition to the High Court in London to reduce the capital further.

This expertise in company law won Murray many company clients, including the Paisley thread manufacturers J. and P. Coats, Sir William Arrol & Co. Ltd, the Dowanhill Estate Company (which became the longest liquidation case in Scottish history), and Wylie and Lochhead, the Glasgow cabinet-makers. As lawyer to J. and P. Coats he was engaged in the registration of patents and trademarks throughout the world, and their protection in the courts. He was the legal adviser when Coats amalgamated with its rival, Clarks of Paisley, in 1896. This commercial work also brought him many private clients, including members of the Coats family, Sir James T. Whitelaw (a Glasgow wine and spirit merchant), Frank Dubs, the Glasgow locomotive builder, and Sir William Arrol, the engineer. He was regularly called on to defend the property interests of his corporate and private clients against proposed legislation, for example the Glasgow and Suburban Railway Bill in 1887 and the Glasgow Building Regulations Bill in 1892.

Murray was an expert on Scottish property and building contract law, writing two books on the subject and acting for the Glasgow and South Western Railway in an important contract case between 1908 and 1917 that went to the House of Lords three times. He served as dean of the faculty of procurators in Glasgow from 1895 to 1898. He wrote books on the history of his own profession in the west of Scotland and of accountancy more generally. He was also deeply interested in Scottish history, writing widely in the field and acting as president of the Glasgow Archaeological Society (1895–6 and 1904–7) and vice-president of the Society of Antiquaries in Scotland from 1900 to 1902. A committed member of the Church of Scotland, he served on many committees, particularly those concerned with the reform of church law. He started collecting books when he was eight, and by the end of his life had accumulated a huge library, largely relating to Glasgow and the west of Scotland, and law, mostly bequeathed to the University of Glasgow. He served on the university court from 1896 to 1899 and from 1903 to 1928, where his views were often cautious. He was made an honorary LLD by the university in 1888. In 1927 Murray published his *Memories of the Old College of Glasgow*, describing the institution before it abandoned its original site in the High

Street. His son, Anthony Stoddard Murray, was killed in March 1918, and his wife died the following year. David Murray died at his home, Moore Park, Cardross, on 2 October 1928, and was buried at Cardross.

MICHAEL S. MOSS

Sources Lecture on the life of David Murray by Professor David Walker, 1992, U. Glas. · U. Glas. L., special collections department, David Murray MSS · McLay, Murray and Spens, Glasgow, MSS · D. Murray, *Law relating to the property of married persons* (1891) · obits., especially report of general council of the University of Glasgow, 1929
Archives NRA Scotland · NRA, priv. coll., letter-books, antiquarian and archaeological notebooks, papers · U. Glas. L., MS collection · U. Glas. L., ledgers of family trusts, notebooks
Likenesses portrait, U. Glas. L.
Wealth at death £101,905 13s. 10d.: confirmation, 1929

Murray, David Christie (1847–1907), novelist and journalist, born on 13 April 1847 in High Street, West Bromwich, Staffordshire, was one of the six sons and five daughters of William Murray, printer and stationer of West Bromwich, and his wife, Mary Withers. He attended private schools at West Bromwich and Spon Lane, Staffordshire, but at the age of twelve was set to work in his father's printing office.

Murray began his career in journalism at an early age by writing leaders for the *Wednesbury Advertiser*. He soon became part of the staff of the *Birmingham Morning News* working under George Dawson, reporting police court cases at 25s. a week and rapidly winning the approval of his employer as an admirable descriptive writer, notably in his descriptions of colliery disasters which brought him more than a local reputation. In January 1865—without friends, funds, or prospects—he went to London, where he found casual employment at Messrs Unwin Brothers' printing works. In May he enlisted as a private in the 4th Royal Irish dragoon guards, and accompanied his regiment to Ireland, but after a year a great-aunt purchased his discharge. From that time his profession was journalism or foreign correspondence, varied by novel-writing. When in London he passed his time in bohemian society. In 1871 he became parliamentary reporter for the *Daily News* and on 5 September of that year married Sophia Harris (b. 1847/8) of Rowley Regis, near Birmingham, daughter of William Harris, a farmer. They had one daughter, who died young. After his wife's death he married, on 17 November 1880, Alice Lydia Mary West (b. 1856/7), daughter of William West, a warehouseman; they had one son, Archibald. He also had four illegitimate children.

Murray travelled a great deal and wrote extensively on foreign affairs. He represented *The Times* and *The Scotsman* during the Russo-Turkish War of 1877–8. He described a tour through England in the disguise of a tramp in a series of articles for *Mayfair*. From 1881 to 1886 he lived mainly in Belgium and France, and from 1889 to 1891 he was based in Nice. Subsequently he resided for a time in north Wales. He made lecture tours through Australia and New Zealand in 1889–91, and through the United States and Canada in 1894–5. Australia was described by him in articles in the *Contemporary Review* in 1891. In *The Cockney Columbus* (1898) he collected letters on the United States from the *New York Herald*. In 1892 he was editor of *The Morning*, a short-lived Conservative daily London paper. A few years later he contributed ethical, literary, and political articles to *The Referee*, which were collected as *Guesses at Truth* (1908). From 1898 he devoted much energy to writing and lecturing to support Emile Zola's plea on behalf of Captain Alfred Dreyfus, a French officer, who had been wrongfully condemned for espionage.

In 1879 Murray had contributed his first novel, *A Life's Atonement*, periodically to *Chambers's Journal of Popular Literature, Science and Arts*. From then until his death in 1907 scarcely a year passed without the publication of one or at times two novels. Between 1887 and 1907 he occasionally collaborated with Henry Herman or Alfred Egmont Hake. His novels *Joseph's Coat* (1881) and *Val Strange* (1882) achieved a notable success. *By the Gate of the Sea* (1883) and *Rainbow Gold* (1885), which first appeared in serial form in the *Cornhill Magazine* under the editorship of James Payn, assured his reputation. *Aunt Rachel* (1886) was critically acclaimed. Murray's fiction abounds in vigour. The loosely constructed plots contain incidents drawn freely from his journalistic experiences. His style gives evidence of his profession as a journalist, but he is effective in describing the neighbourhood and inhabitants of Cannock Chase, the area in Staffordshire which served as a setting for most of his novels. He also wrote several volumes of rambling autobiography, including *A Novelist's Notebook* (1887), *The Making of a Novelist: an Experiment in Autobiography* (1894), and *Recollections*, the last published posthumously in 1908.

Murray died at his home, 4 Lancaster Road, Belsize Park, London, on 1 August 1907 after a long illness caused by abdominal problems, during which he endured much discomfort. He was buried at Hampstead. A memorial tablet in copper with a pewter medallion was unveiled at West Bromwich Public Library in December 1908.

ELIZABETH LEE, *rev.* SAYONI BASU

Sources *The Times* (2 Aug 1907) · *Men and women of the time* (1899) · H. Murray, *A stepson of fortune* (1909) · D. C. Murray, *Recollections* (1908) · D. C. Murray, *A novelist's notebook* (1887) · D. C. Murray, *The making of a novelist: an experiment in autobiography* (1894) · Allibone, *Dict.* · WW · m. certs. · d. cert. · CGPLA Eng. & Wales (1908)
Archives NRA, corresp. and literary papers · Sandwell Community History and Archive Service, Smethwick, genealogical notes | JRL, letters to M. H. Spielmann · U. Leeds, Brotherton L., letters to Clement Shorter
Likenesses W. H. Bartlett, group portrait, oils (*Saturday night at the Savage Club*), Savage Club, London · photogravure, repro. in Murray, *Recollections* · woodcut (after photograph by J. Ganz of Brussels), NPG; repro. in *Harper's Magazine* (June 1888)
Wealth at death £50: administration with will, 20 July 1908, CGPLA Eng. & Wales

Murray, David Leslie (1888–1962), writer and newspaper editor, was born on 5 February 1888 in London, the son of Charles Murray, a stockbroker. His father had gone as a youth to southern Africa and prospered there before returning to England. Murray was educated at Harrow School, where he was awarded an entrance scholarship in classics and history, and at Balliol College, Oxford, where he was a Brackenbury history scholar. He was awarded a first in *literae humaniores* in 1910 and was John Locke scholar in 1912. Although he did not pursue an academic career, he was throughout his life interested in theological and philosophical questions, and his first book, published in 1912, was *Pragmatism*. On going down from Oxford he acted for a while with various touring companies, but short-sightedness made it difficult to continue in that career. He wore thick glasses which quickly steamed up, and this also prevented him from going into the armed forces in 1914, but he worked in the intelligence department of the War Office from 1916 to 1919.

In 1920 Murray joined *The Times*, where two-thirds of his salary was paid by the *Literary Supplement*, and one-third by the main paper. Here he became a popular figure, with his generous and helpful ways, and with a hearty laugh that shook his whole substantial frame. He was able to pursue his pleasure in the theatre by writing drama reviews for the paper, and going to plays and the music-hall with two friends, the *Daily Mail* theatre critic Maurice Willson Disher and the theatrical historian W. MacQueen-Pope (with whom in 1953 he wrote a book, *Fortune's Favourite*, about Franz Lehár). He wrote numerous book reviews for the *Literary Supplement*, at first mainly on philosophy and ballet, another of his interests, and as time passed he became effectively the assistant editor of the paper under Bruce Richmond, the editor. In 1923 he published a theological study, *Reservation: its Purposes and Methods*; in 1926 a collection of his longer *Literary Supplement* reviews (which had of course been anonymous in the paper), *Scenes and Silhouettes*; and in 1927 an impressionistic biography of Disraeli.

In 1928 Murray started writing novels, and in the same year married (Margaret) Leonora *Eyles (1889–1960), daughter of Thomas Andrew Tennant Pitcairn, a china manufacturer. His wife became a well-known novelist—and herself was a reviewer for the *Literary Supplement*. Murray eventually published fourteen novels, most of them historical adventures and romances. He had a sense of period and an exuberance of style that made him for a time a very popular writer; an advertisement once appeared in the *Literary Supplement* that said 'Cure your blues with light-hearted D. L. Murray' and showed him jumping over a hedge on a horse. The first of these novels, set in nineteenth-century Italy, was *The Bride Adorned* (1929), while his first great success was *Regency* (1936), which told the story of four generations of women in Brighton (where he lived), the first of them a mistress of the prince regent. At home he kept an army of toy soldiers which he would move about on the carpet to simulate the battles that he was writing about in his books.

In the 1930s, wanting to concentrate on his novels, Murray worked mainly at home for the *Literary Supplement*, writing reviews, and came into Printing House Square only on Mondays and Tuesdays to read and pass the pages. He was offered the editorship when Bruce Richmond retired at the end of 1937, and accepted the post with some hesitation, getting the management's agreement that he should come in on only three days a week.

Murray became editor at a time when it was thought the *Literary Supplement* should be lightened and made more popular in character, and at the instance of Stanley Morison, the typographer and *éminence grise* at *The Times*, he faithfully set about making some changes in this direction, including lists of recommended books, light leaders, and so on. He conducted the supplement successfully through the greater part of the Second World War, which also saw the paper's political tone change, along with that of *The Times* itself, towards a greater acceptance of socialist ideas. Murray wrote fewer reviews as editor but occasionally contributed powerful articles, such as one in which he attacked the pacifist ideas of the formerly prolific contributor John Middleton Murry, and another in which he compared Bernard Shaw's style of argument to that of Goebbels.

However, the circulation did not go up with the changes, and Morison decided that the policy should be reversed. Murray learned by chance at the end of 1944 that Charles Morgan had been sounded out as a possible editor of the paper, and he resigned, mortified, although he had always declared he would leave at the end of the war. Stanley Morison himself became editor in February 1945, with the avowed intention of 'making the *Lit. Supp.* hard to read again' (private information).

Murray continued to write novels, but after the war he had less success with them. His wife died in 1960, and on 29 August 1962 he committed suicide by taking poison. He died at New End Hospital, Hampstead, London.

DERWENT MAY

Sources *The Times* (31 Aug 1962) · I. McDonald, *The history of The Times*, 5 (1984) · N. Barker, *Stanley Morison* (1972) · News Int. RO · private information (2004) [A. Crook] · S. Jameson, *Journey from the north*, 2 vols. (1969–70) · *CGPLA Eng. & Wales* (1962) · m. cert. · d. cert. · I. Elliott, ed., *The Balliol College register, 1833–1933*, 2nd edn (privately printed, Oxford, 1934)
Wealth at death £—18,394 18s.: probate, 21 Nov 1962, *CGPLA Eng. & Wales*

Murray, David Stark [*pseud.* Irwin Brown] (**1900–1977**), pathologist and medical politician, was born on 14 July 1900 at 244 Main Street, Barrhead, near Glasgow, the only son of the four children of Robert Murray (1869–1950), journalist and Labour politician, and his wife, Margaret Brown McKinlay (*d.* 1944). Murray studied medicine at the University of Glasgow. He graduated MB in 1925 and decided early in his career to specialize in pathology. He became pathologist to the Lambeth Hospital, London, in 1927. On 22 March that year he married Jean Aitken Stirling (*b.* 1901/2), a mercantile clerk, daughter of James Stirling, an engineers' machinist, and his wife, Catherine Cherry; they had one daughter.

Murray worked in the London area until his retirement in 1965. From 1948 he was group pathologist at the Kingston Hospital, and his most important professional achievements were accomplished in his role in the setting up of laboratories at the Royal Richmond and Kingston hospitals, and in organizing the central sterile supplies department, also at Kingston. Following the creation of the National Health Service he served on a number of official bodies, notably as chairman of the blood transfusion service of the south-west metropolitan region.

In addition to his professional responsibilities, Murray was a prolific writer, being the author of more than twenty books, pamphlets, and chapters, as well as of innumerable articles in the professional, political, secularist, and lay press. His written work dealt with a wide range of issues but was underpinned by a fundamental commitment to socialism and to the idea that the discoveries and method of science could provide models for social reorganization. In one work he explained how the distribution of blood in the human body provided a perfect example of distribution, transport, and co-ordination, in contrast to what he perceived as the anarchy of the capitalist system. Similarly, Murray, a lifelong anti-racist, argued that Nazism was based on a racial theory which was blatantly unscientific, and therefore demonstrably wrong.

Science and medicine were, for Murray, deeply integrated with the wider society. A number of his works, such as *Science Fights Death* (1936), argued that advances in medical science were increasingly bringing disease and ill health under control, and that under the proper conditions this could be expected to continue. But he was clear that these proper conditions depended on the achievement of a socialist society. He strongly believed that environmental surroundings and the general standard of living were crucial determinants of individual and national health. He was equally convinced that the socialization of the welfare system had a key role to play in the transformation to a socialist society. It was this which led him to his lifelong agitation for what he considered a truly socialist health service.

Consequently in 1930 Murray and other left-wing doctors such as Somerville Hastings founded the Socialist Medical Association, an organization which Murray would repeatedly claim to have been instrumental in the creation of the National Health Service. The association was affiliated to the Labour Party in 1931. It campaigned for a free, comprehensive, and universal state medical service, democratically controlled and with doctors as salaried employees; and until 1945 it played an important role in formulating Labour's health policy. Murray was a key member of the association. He was elected to its executive committee in 1931, and in 1951 became its president, a post he retained until 1970. His family had been an extremely important influence on him, especially his socialist, journalist father. It was therefore no surprise that one of his main roles in the association was as editor of its periodicals, respectively *Socialist Doctor*, *Medicine Today and Tomorrow*, and *Socialism and Health*. Not only did Murray edit these, he was also a major contributor, sometimes under pseudonyms such as Irwin Brown. His literary style was direct and pugnacious, a reflection of his more general character. Clearly liked and admired by a wide circle of friends and colleagues, Murray could none the less be abrasive in both writing and speech, something which did not always endear him to the wider labour movement.

The advent of the National Health Service in 1948 brought much that Murray and his Socialist Medical Association colleagues had campaigned for. However, while defending the service's general principles, activists such as Murray became more and more concerned about what they saw as its inherent weaknesses, especially its concessions to the medical profession, its undemocratic administrative structures, and its failure to introduce health centres. In part this reflected the increasingly strained relationship over both strategy and tactics between the Labour health minister Aneurin Bevan and the association.

Consequently, Murray devoted considerable energy from the late 1940s to producing critiques of the National Health Service, culminating in his last major book, *Blueprint for Health*, published in 1973. This was a wide-ranging work in which he attacked the continuing existence of private practice, for example. In its place Murray argued for medical teamwork, for such was the complexity of modern medicine that no one doctor could fully comprehend it. This was an argument Murray had been using since the 1930s, and it is important in further understanding his political and medical philosophy. It was on the basis of teamwork that he consistently argued for the introduction of health centres, for instance: there doctors and other medical and health-care professionals could work together towards the single end of patient care. Even more fundamentally, such a method of working was in itself socialistic. Murray always held that at its most altruistic medicine could provide a model for broader social organization and thus that socialism was inherent in medical practice as well as in nature itself.

Murray's was an engaged and committed life. While remembered in particular for his advocacy of socialized medicine, he also devoted considerable energy to causes such as secularism, and to the writing of popular works on science and medicine. He died from renal failure on 16 September 1977 at the Downs branch of the Royal Marsden Hospital, in Sutton, London, and was survived by his wife.   JOHN STEWART

Sources D. S. Murray, *Why a national health service?* (1971) · *The Lancet* (1 Oct 1977) · J. Stewart, *The battle for health: a political history of the Socialist Medical Association, 1930–51* (1999) · J. Stewart, 'The "backroom boys of state medicine": David Stark Murray and Bevan's national health service', *Journal of Medical Biography*, 4 (1996), 229–35 · F. Honigsbaum, *The division in British medicine* (1979) · b. cert. · m. cert. · d. cert.
Archives U. Hull, Socialist Medical Association archives
Likenesses B. McKim, photograph, repro. in *The Lancet*
Wealth at death £5348: probate, 15 Dec 1977, *CGPLA Eng. & Wales*

Murray, (Katharine Maud) Elisabeth (1909–1998), educationist, was born on 3 December 1909 at Seatoller, 3 Hills Road, Trumpington, near Cambridge, the third child of Harold James Ruthven Murray (1868–1955), HM inspector of schools and writer of a comprehensive *History of Chess* (1913), and his wife, Kate Maitland, *née* Crosthwaite (1873–1951), amateur violinist, participant in the women's suffrage movement, and daughter of the headmaster of

Carlisle grammar school, the Revd Samuel M. Crosthwaite. James *Murray (1837–1915), the lexicographer, was her grandfather. From her parents Elisabeth Murray inherited a keen social conscience, together with an abhorrence of cant and mere social convention. She was also strongly influenced by her brothers, Donald (1899–1941), an intensely practical man, and Kenneth (1902–1972), the first surveyor of antiquities in Nigeria.

After a childhood in which she delighted to challenge the superiority of her siblings, and after schooling at Birmingham (Edgbaston), London (St Paul's Girls' School), and Colchester (county high school—where she first became interested in archaeology), Murray gained entry in 1928 to Somerville College, Oxford, to read modern history, specializing in the medieval period. In 1931 she graduated with second-class honours and was elected to a Rosa Hovey research scholarship to read for the BLitt. The work for which she was awarded the latter degree (in 1933), on the constitutional history of the Cinque Ports, was a substantial contribution to scholarship, and was published in 1935. Much as she delighted in life at Oxford, she knew the need to seek employment and thought about a future as a factory inspector; but the lure of academia proved strong and after a season excavating in Samaria (at Ahab's palace) and several years tutoring on the Mary Worthington wing, Ashburne Hall, University of Manchester, she accepted appointment in 1938 as assistant tutor and registrar at Girton College, Cambridge. The onset of the Second World War led to rapid promotion—domestic bursar and fellow (1942) and, as well as acting director of studies in both architecture and music, junior bursar (1944). The demands taxed her to the full, but her great physical energy, administrative efficiency, and effectiveness in getting things done carried her through and prepared her for her major professional appointment, as principal at Bishop Otter College, an Anglican college in Chichester, Sussex, for young women training to teach in primary schools.

At the time of taking up her post (May 1948), the college exuded the clutter and bric-a-brac of a site that, after extensive use by the services during the war, was 'making do'. But the climate of purpose changed radically with Murray's arrival and, with an eye to a new style and in keeping with the optimism of the post-war period, she instigated a master-plan that was to provide new teaching rooms and student residences, a new dining-room and assembly hall, and, on the site of the old kitchen garden, a new chapel. Taking a close interest in proceedings, Murray showed herself to be an architect's client, and ensured that the development of the fabric served the needs and purpose of the users. She knew that buildings—and she gave as meticulous attention to the internal arrangements as to the outer, choosing colour schemes, furniture, and textiles—communicated a view of life; and for students the college became a site for discovery, a microcosm of the post-war world, drenched with optimism and hope. With assistance from her head of art, Sheila McCririck, contemporary art, including work by Hitchens, Sutherland, Spencer, and Heron, was collected, national figures were invited to speak to students and staff, the governing body was enlarged, procedures for self-appraisal were instituted, and co-education was established. By the time of her retirement in 1970 numbers had more than doubled, and Murray was acknowledged as an innovative figure in mid-century education.

Retirement to the family home, Upper Cranmore, in Heyshott, near Midhurst, brought new challenges and a continuing commitment to service through scholarship and public office. With access to the papers of her grandfather, Murray prepared a biography of James Murray, *Caught in the Web of Words* (1977), that was acclaimed in both Britain and the United States, by scholars and by the general reader. Published by Yale University Press (Oxford University Press initially found the text too provocative, but later bought the paperback rights), the volume threw new light on the trauma involved in the construction of a great national artefact, and celebrated the achievement of those, such as James Murray, who were largely self-educated. Murray also sat for fifteen years as an independent on Chichester district council, played a crucial role in excavations at Fishbourne Roman palace and in the establishment of Pallant House Gallery, and contributed her energy and standing to the work of many local societies and organizations.

Throughout her life Murray fought against ignorance. Her personal enthusiasms and her knowledge were deployed to ensure that all in her charge never slipped below the point to which culture had brought them. She died of bronchopneumonia on 6 February 1998; at Pendean, a nursing home in West Lavington, near Midhurst; her funeral took place at Heyshott, Sussex, on 12 February and, after cremation at Chichester, her ashes were subsequently interred at Heyshott on 8 October the same year. In her will, after personal and familial bequests, she donated from her estate gifts to the Sussex Historic Churches Trust, to her local church at Heyshott, to the Murray Downland Trust (which she had founded for conservation work on the South Downs), to Somerville College, to Pallant House, and to Christian Aid. At a thanksgiving service in Chichester Cathedral on 15 May 1998 she was lauded for her tenacity, for her vitality, and for a keen sense of fun; she lived a life of service, not just for her own generation but for those that followed also. She was unmarried.

PAUL FOSTER

Sources W. Sussex RO, Murray papers, ACC. 9601 · P. Foster, ed., *Flints, ports, otters and threads: a tribute to K. M. Elisabeth Murray* (1998) · P. Foster, *The Bishop Otter art collection* (1989) · G. P. McGregor, *Bishop Otter College and policy for teacher education, 1939–1980* (1981) · P. Ruthven-Murray, *The Murrays of Rulewater: a genealogical history of a border family* (1986) · personal knowledge (2004) · private information (2004) · *WWW* [forthcoming] · b. cert. · d. cert. · *The Times* (17 Feb 1998) · will · Somerville College records
Archives W. Sussex RO | University College, Chichester, Bishop Otter archives
Likenesses A. Gaskin, pencil and watercolour, 1927, repro. in Foster, ed., *Flints*; priv. coll. · photograph, *c.*1975, W. Sussex RO; repro. in Foster, ed., *Flints* · P. Hodgkinson, modernist abstract sculpture, 1993 (*The Murray Relief*), University College Chichester, Bishop Otter Campus, Paradise Court

Wealth at death £261,136: probate, 10 July 1998, *CGPLA Eng. & Wales*

Murray [*married names* Tollemache, Maitland], **Elizabeth**, **duchess of Lauderdale** and *suo jure* **countess of Dysart** (*bap.* **1626**, *d.* **1698**), noblewoman, baptized on 28 September 1626 at St Martin-in-the-Fields, London, was the eldest of the five daughters of William *Murray, first earl of Dysart (*d.* 1655), and his wife, Catherine (*d.* in or after 1651), daughter of Colonel Norman Bruce. At about this time her parents moved to Ham House, near Richmond. Realizing that she was highly intelligent, her father made sure that she received an intellectual education, and she was taught philosophy, history, divinity, and mathematics as well as the more conventional domestic skills. Well-shaped and pretty, with a long, oval face and unfashionable red-gold hair, she always attracted attention and revelled in showing off her learning.

At the outbreak of the civil war in England in 1642 Lord Dysart was sent to Scotland to liaise with the royalists there, while his redoubtable wife remained at Ham to repel parliament's repeated attempts at sequestrating the property. These preoccupations prevented them from arranging marriages for their daughters, and it was not until Lady Elizabeth was in her early twenties that they finally addressed the question of her future. Her father had thoughts of marrying her to the learned but impoverished Sir Robert Moray, later one of the founders of the Royal Society, but in the end she was engaged to Sir Lionel Tollemache, bt (1624–1669), the unexceptional but extremely rich owner of estates in Suffolk and the midlands.

After the wedding in 1648 Lady Elizabeth was expected to settle down to domesticity. She did produce eleven children, including Lionel Tollemache (1649–1727), born on 30 January 1649, and Thomas *Tollemache (*c.*1651–1694), both later members of parliament, but a quiet life in the country was not for her. The advice which her husband later gave to their eldest son was a vivid reflection of his own experience. Wives, he said:

> are but too apt to take advantage of the fondness of theire husband, and upon it growe insolent and imperious, and inclined to pervert the laws of nature by indeavouringe a superiority over the husband and if shee getts the reignes in her own hands, away shee will runn with it, you scarce ever will stopp her in the whole course of her life. (Tollemache, 63)

Dominating, energetic, sexually attractive, and ambitious, Elizabeth much preferred the role of 'the Lady of Ham House', where she held court after her mother's death in 1649; among her regular guests was Oliver Cromwell. She also claimed to have been in correspondence at this period with John *Maitland, second earl of Lauderdale (1616–1682), a presbyterian Scot with an arrogant manner, a fierce intellect, and a quick humour. According to Gilbert Burnet, who knew her later in Scotland, when Lauderdale was a prisoner after the battle of Worcester in 1651 'she made him believe he was in great danger of his life, and that she saved it by her intrigues with Cromwell',

Elizabeth Murray, duchess of Lauderdale and *suo jure* countess of Dysart (*bap.* 1626, *d.* 1698), by Sir Peter Lely, *c.*1648

but there is no contemporary evidence for this, and Lauderdale was in no such predicament.

Lady Elizabeth's friendship with Cromwell was useful in providing a cover for her own royalist activities. In 1653 she became an active member of the secret organization known as the Sealed Knot, carrying on a coded correspondence with exiled supporters of Charles II, travelling on the continent on mysterious missions and even visiting the king himself. She inherited her father's titles on his death in 1655, becoming countess of Dysart in her own right, but she still did not halt her espionage activities. Her worried husband, who took no part in politics, asked her to give up her continental trips, but she paid no heed and in 1659 their house at Helmingham seems to have become a rallying point for royalists, who were by now rejoicing at the death of Cromwell and the visible disintegration of his son's government. In 1660 Charles II was restored, and the following year he rewarded Elizabeth with a pension of £800 a year.

Sir Lionel had never been robust. He went to France for treatment in 1668, but died in Paris in January 1669 at the age of forty-four. One of the first people to go to Ham to offer his sympathy was the earl of Lauderdale, now Charles II's powerful secretary of state for Scotland. His own wife was ill, his visits to Ham grew ever more frequent, and it was generally believed that Countess Elizabeth became his mistress at this time. Lauderdale and his wife separated, and she travelled to Paris, where he rented a house for her and paid her a large allowance on condition that she never return to Britain. Elizabeth complained to the countess of Tweeddale that people defamed

'the best of men, our good friend [Lauderdale]' and made him 'guilty of all his ladyes faults', while pitying his wife's 'tryales under his tirany'. Afraid that Countess Anna might return to Britain, she suspected 'the old mialling lady will be invited to settle at Brunstin [one of Lauderdale's Scottish properties] which I only suspect as I often do wheer my friend is concerned' (Cripps, 89–90). Countess Anna died in Paris on 6 November 1671, sending her husband a last message to say that she retained nothing but tender memories of him despite 'the unhappy truth' that his love for her 'had suffered an interruption' (NL Scot., MS 14414, fol. 3). Less than four months later, on 17 February 1672, Elizabeth scandalized even the relaxed court of Charles II by marrying the recently bereaved widower. On 1 May that year, Lauderdale became a duke.

In her element as the consort of a powerful man with a character as strong as her own, Elizabeth used all her influence to further his career and wherever they were—at Ham, in Edinburgh, or at Thirlestane Castle, his new Scottish residence—they lived in extravagant style. Together they set in hand an elaborate programme of improvements at Ham House, installing stuccowork ceilings, carved panelling, and rich furnishings, and they employed craftsmen from England and the Low Countries to decorate Thirlestane Castle and their other Scottish properties. As time passed there were increasing complaints about Elizabeth's greed and the corruption of Lauderdale's regime in Scotland. Finally, he fell from power after suffering a stroke in March 1680. He died at Tunbridge Wells on 24 August 1682. Genuinely griefstricken, Elizabeth none the less plunged immediately into a long and bitter legal dispute with her brother-in-law over the payment of her husband's debts and his funeral expenses. Elderly and arthritic, she seldom left Ham in her later years, and died there on 5 June 1698. She was buried in Petersham church on 16 June.

ROSALIND K. MARSHALL

Sources D. Cripps, *Elizabeth of the Sealed Knot* (1975) · W. C. Mackenzie, *The life and times of John Maitland, duke of Lauderdale, 1616–1682* (1923) · *Bishop Burnet's History of his own time*, new edn, ed. G. Burnet, T. Burnet, and others, 4 vols. (1809) · W. H. Harland, *Ham common and the Dysarts* (1894) · *Scots peerage* · M. Tomlin, *Ham House* (1986) · E. D. H. Tollemache, *The Tollemaches of Helmingham and Ham* (1949) · P. Watson and B. D. Henning, 'Tollemache, Lionel', HoP, *Commons, 1660–90*, 3.575–6 · B. D. Henning, 'Tollemache, Hon. Thomas', HoP, *Commons, 1660–90*, 3.576 · BL, Add. MS 23 · Leics. RO, Tollemache papers · Ham House inventories, V&A, department of furniture and woodwork · NL Scot., MS 14414, fol. 3
Archives Darnaway Castle, Moray MSS · Leics. RO, Tollemache MSS
Likenesses attrib. J. Carlile, group portrait, oils, *c.*1648, Ham House, London · P. Lely, oils, *c.*1648, Ham House, London [*see illus.*] · P. Lely, oils, 1650–54, Ham House, London · P. Lely, double portrait, oils, *c.*1672, Ham House, London · J. Carlile, oils, Thirlestane Castle, Berwickshire · attrib. P. Lely, oils, Buccleuch Estates, Selkirk · oils, Ham House, London · pastel, Holyroodhouse, Edinburgh
Wealth at death considerable wealth, incl. Ham House; duke of Lauderdale had left her all his personal possessions, as well as property in Scotland

Murray, Elizabeth Leigh (1815–1892). *See under* Murray, Henry Leigh (1820–1870).

Murray, Eunice Guthrie (1878–1960), suffragist and author, was born on 21 January 1878 at Moore Park, Cardross, Dunbartonshire, the third and youngest daughter of David *Murray (1842–1928), a lawyer, and his wife, Frances Porter Stoddard (d. 1919). Frances Murray, whose parents on both sides were American with strong links to the abolitionist movement, shared with her husband an interest in all aspects of the women's movement. Eunice Murray was educated at St Leonard's School, St Andrews. Her two older sisters, Dorothy and Sylvia, graduated MA at Glasgow University and BA at Girton College, Cambridge, respectively.

In the late nineteenth century Eunice Murray became involved in philanthropic activities. She was active in the local branch of the League of Pity, volunteered regularly at a local settlement, and was an advocate for temperance. On 9 November 1896 she recorded reading about the formation of the National Union of Women's Suffrage Societies, commenting: 'I should like to join such a society for the question of the emancipation of my sex is a stirring one and leads to vital matters' (Murray, journals).

After the militant movement reached Scotland Murray, her mother, and sister Sylvia joined the Women's Freedom League (WFL). The WFL had a strong presence in Scotland, and from 1909 onwards Murray was the secretary for 'scattered members'—all those who did not live in Edinburgh, Glasgow, or Dundee. She was one of the three Scottish members on the WFL's national executive committee and in 1913 was described as president for Scotland of the WFL.

In June 1908 Teresa Billington-Greig asked Murray to ascertain the views of her neighbours toward women's suffrage. She received such a discouraging response that she concluded: 'If Cardross is an example 'twill be our great great great grandchildren that will vote' (Murray, journals). Nevertheless, she threw herself wholeheartedly into the campaign. She was articulate and persuasive both in print and in person, and her letters appeared regularly in the press. She went on to write suffrage pamphlets, including *The Illogical Sex*, *Prejudices Old and New*, and her most popular one, *Liberal Cant*, all published by the Scottish council of the WFL.

A telling response to Murray's oratory comes from a letter published in the *Glasgow Herald* on 17 July 1913 from a John Hunter in Rothesay, who had been disappointed when he learned that Murray would be appearing instead of the usual WFL speaker: 'but once I heard her convincing, eloquent and logical speech I was quite delighted, and feel persuaded if people had the opportunity of hearing her, and if Cabinet Ministers had that privilege, the vote would be won without delay'.

In 1913 Murray attended the International Woman Suffrage Alliance conference in Budapest. After her return, on 17 November, she was arrested for obstruction after attempting to address a meeting near Downing Street. Although she could not have contemplated taking part in the arson and destruction campaign of the Women's Social and Political Union—'my type of mind could never do the things they do'—she was aware that those tactics brought awareness of the issues to everyone, and she laid no blame on the women—'No—I blame the Government' (Murray, journals).

At the beginning of the war in August 1914 many women were thrown out of work, and their plight was a major concern of the WFL. A Women's Suffrage National Aid Corps was formed, with branches in Edinburgh and Glasgow, and Murray was on the executive committee. The WFL continued to campaign for the vote during the war years. In speeches and articles Murray stressed the dangers women would face in the labour market when the war ended, and also spoke about the changes brought about by the war in the attitudes of women previously in domestic service and other subservient positions. She also wrote a suffrage pamphlet, published by the WFL, about all the praise women were getting for their efforts during the war, entitled *Woman: the New Discovery*.

Murray had works published in a number of genres, including novels, local histories, and a memoir of her mother. In 1930, when most Scottish historians were interested only in political history, she published *Scottish Women of Bygone Days*, in which she broke with the traditional approach and discussed social and domestic life, including witchcraft, education, and sports. The book was dedicated *To the Women of All Ages who Defied Convention and Held Aloft the Banner of Progress*. In 1935 she turned to an older model and produced biographies in *A Gallery of Scottish Women*. An interest in social history developed later in Scotland than in many other countries, but again Eunice Murray was a pioneer. *Scottish Homespun* (1947) was a fascinating account of Scottish traditional costumes, and was illustrated by photographs of dolls (many of whose clothes were made by Murray herself). In the conclusion to this work Murray wrote that: 'Women have a two-fold calling, for not only are we as wives and mothers the guardians of the future, but we are also the custodians of the past' (*Scottish Homespun*, 105).

In 1918 Murray had the distinction of being the first woman to stand in a parliamentary election in Scotland—as an independent candidate at Glasgow (Bridgeton)—but she was unsuccessful. In 1923 she was elected on to Dunbartonshire county council, and in the same year she became the first president of the local Scottish Women's Rural Institute. But she did not restrict herself to campaigning on local issues, for she was involved with the National Trust for Scotland soon after its inception, serving on its council and executive committee from 1931, and donating generously to many of its appeals. Murray, who never married, was appointed MBE in 1945. She died on 26 March 1960 of cardio-vascular degeneration and cerebral thrombosis at her family home, Moore Park, Cardross, Dunbartonshire.

LEAH LENEMAN

Sources L. Leneman, *A guid cause: the women's suffrage movement in Scotland* (1995) • E. Crawford, *The women's suffrage movement: a reference guide, 1866–1928* (1999) • unpublished journals of Eunice Murray, priv. coll. [held privately by Mrs Patricia H. Cowan, widow of Eunice Murray's nephew, Alan Cowan] • L. E. N. Mayhall, 'The making of a suffragette: the uses of reading and the legacy of radicalism, 1890–1918', *Singular continuities: tradition, nostalgia and identity in modern British culture*, ed. G. Behlmer and F. Leventhal (2000), 75–

88 · E. Ewan, 'A realm of one's own: the place of medieval and early modern women in Scottish history', *Gendering Scottish history: an international approach*, ed. D. Simonton, T. Brotherstone, and O. Walsh (1999), 19–36 · S. Livingstone, *Bonnie fechters: women in Scotland, 1900–1950* (1994) · private information (2004) [archivist, National Trust for Scotland] · b. cert. · d. cert. · *CGPLA Eng. & Wales* (1966) · *Glasgow Herald* (17 July 1913) · E. King, *The hidden history of Glasgow's women: the new factor* (1993)

Archives priv. coll., journals
Likenesses photograph, repro. in King, *Hidden history of Glasgow's women*
Wealth at death £122,367 3s. 1d.: confirmation, 27 April 1960, *CCI*

Murray, Sir (George) Evelyn Pemberton (1880–1947), civil servant, was born at 7 Eaton Square, London, on 25 July 1880, the only son of Sir George Herbert *Murray (1849–1936), civil servant, and his wife, Helen Mary (d. 1932), daughter of John *Mulholland, later first Baron Dunleath. His father was successively chairman of the Board of Inland Revenue, secretary of the Post Office, and sole permanent secretary of the Treasury until his retirement in 1911. His son—who was always known as Evelyn—followed in the steps of his father. He was educated at Eton College and at Christ Church, Oxford, from where he was awarded an *aegrotat* in the final examination in *literae humaniores* in 1903. In that year he joined the civil service as a junior examiner in the Board of Education, which made appointments by patronage, and from 1905 to 1909 he was private secretary to three successive presidents of the Board of Education. On 10 January 1906 he married Muriel Mildred Elizabeth (1884/5–1961), daughter of Philip Beresford Hope of Bedgebury Park, Kent.

Murray was promoted rapidly to commissioner of customs and excise in 1912 and to his father's old office as secretary of the Post Office in 1914. He was the youngest secretary of the Post Office, and also the longest serving. He remained at St Martin's-le-Grand until 1934, when he returned to his former position at customs and excise until his retirement in 1940.

In 1914 the Post Office was the single largest employer in the country, with a staff of 250,000 and a revenue of £32.6 million. Its business extended beyond the mail services with the addition of financial services and the successive nationalization of telegraphs in 1870 and telephones in 1912. There were major problems concerning labour relations, negotiation with transport companies for the carriage of mail within Britain and across the seas, the adoption of new technology, and relations with foreign administrations. Murray arrived at the Post Office at the end of a period of rapid growth and development, and spent the next twenty years preserving the *status quo* to the best of his ability. The outbreak of the First World War meant that his task was not easy. Staff shortages, the dislocation of transport, mounting costs, and the need to cut services, dominated his first five years at the Post Office. After the war, he faced conflicting pressures. The public demanded the restoration of pre-war levels of service and charges. Unions were seeking higher wages, which had serious consequences in a labour-intensive service. The Treasury pressed for a speedy return to surplus. Murray thus faced severe problems of wartime dislocation and post-war reconstruction. The Post Office did well to avoid a breakdown of services during the war, and to recover from a deficit of £6.7 million in 1920–21 to a surplus of £12.3 million in 1933–4. His success in coping with the disruptions of the war was marked by his knighthood in 1919.

Murray was a conservative, aloof, and patrician figure, and consequently his administrative style had serious weaknesses. D. O. Lumley, who was Murray's personal secretary from 1922 to 1927, provided an insight into his working methods. He arrived at St Martin's-le-Grand a little before noon and remained until 8 p.m., which allowed him to minimize contact with his colleagues. Lumley remarked that Murray 'said very little as a rule, his instructions were laconic and he disliked going into explanations or answering any but the most essential questions' (Lumley, 'The last secretary to the Post Office'). He was punctilious about acquiring facts and would summon officials to provide information. What he would not do was discuss the issue with his officials, or allow them to take part in meetings with the Treasury and the postmaster-general, which he kept in his own hands. The one area in which he did delegate responsibility was labour relations. His emphasis was on orderly transaction of administration, which gave him a horror of anything so vulgar as commercial business practices. He opposed delegation of executive power to the regions although his father had observed before the First World War that the highly centralized system was breaking down. Murray did nothing to produce a workable scheme of reform.

After the war, the select committee on telephones suggested the creation of two distinct organizations for post and telecommunications, which was implemented in a limited form in 1922 with the creation of two new offices of director of postal services and director of telegraphs and telephones, below the secretary. But centralization of power in the hands of the secretary's office remained a problem, and in 1932 a committee of inquiry under the chairmanship of Lord Bridgeman recommended a regional structure to execute policy, with the central office in London concentrating on policy. The committee also recommended the abolition of the autocratic position of the secretary, and the appointment of a functional board with a director-general as the *primus inter pares*. Murray was vehemently opposed to the changes, which were 'based on incomplete knowledge and a misconception of the position'. In his view, the existing system had proved its worth and 'it would be safer to mend it rather than to scrap it', although he did have enough self-awareness to realize that 'my own inclination by temperament has been to the conservative side' (Post Office archives, Post 33/5529, M8566/1940). His departure from the Post Office coincided with the implementation of the reforms in 1934, and it is significant that his career did not progress. Lumley's assessment of his time at the Post Office is a fair one, that 'chinks in the palpably top heavy structure of the Post Office did not show themselves earlier, solely because of the immense administrative ability and experience which Murray brought to its management' (Lumley,

'The last secretary to the Post Office'). He had the abilities to keep an existing structure in reasonable working order but he had little inclination to reform or change.

Both Murray and his father were at some time heirs presumptive to the dukedom of Atholl; his grandson George Iain became the tenth duke in 1957. Murray's only child, George Anthony (*b.* 1907) was killed in command of an artillery regiment in Italy in 1945. Murray died of cancer at his London home, 23 Fursecroft, George Street, Bryanston Square, on 30 March 1947.   MARTIN DAUNTON

Sources M. J. Daunton, 'Murray, Sir George Evelyn Pemberton', *DBB* · M. J. Daunton, *Royal Mail: the Post Office since 1840* (1985) · *WWW* · Burke, *Peerage* (1967) · b. cert. · m. cert. · d. cert. · *CGPLA Eng. & Wales* (1947) · D. O. Lumley, 'The last secretary to the Post Office', Post Office archives, Post 33/5529, M8566/1940
Archives Bodl. Oxf., letters to H. H. Asquith · Post Office Archive
Likenesses W. Stoneman, photograph, 1930, NPG · photograph, repro. in Daunton, 'Murray, George Evelyn Pemberton'
Wealth at death £40,414 19s. 3d.: administration with will, 25 Aug 1947, *CGPLA Eng. & Wales*

Murray, Lady Evelyn Stewart- (1868–1940), Gaelic folklorist and needlewoman, was born on 17 March 1868 at Blair Castle, Perthshire. She was the third daughter of John James Hugh Henry Stewart-Murray, seventh duke of Atholl (1840–1917) and his wife, Louisa (1844–1902), eldest daughter of Sir Thomas Moncreiffe, seventh baronet, of Moncreiffe, Perthshire. Like her three sisters and two surviving brothers, Lady Evelyn had a conventional upbringing, being educated by governesses at Blair Castle. She was presented at court in 1887. After teenage illnesses in 1881 and 1887, she took up the study of Gaelic. Initially encouraged by her father, her enthusiasm burgeoned, and between February and November 1891 she collected 240 Gaelic stories from a wide area of the family estate and west Perthshire, walking many miles, ignoring meals, and working late into the night. Her family considered her activities inappropriate and her enthusiasm disproportionate, and she came into frequent conflict with her parents, especially her mother who was dismayed and infuriated by Evelyn's refusal to participate in the normal social activities of her class. At the end of 1891, Lady Evelyn was sent to Switzerland on what was intended to be a short visit, but she then refused to return to Scotland. In 1895 she settled in Belgium, where she lived on a small allowance from her parents. She never married, but generally had a servant or companion with her. She maintained contact with her siblings through letters and occasional visits, but never saw her parents again, and in 1907 made arrangements so that she need not even correspond with her father. Her interest turned to needlework, and she became both a collector and a highly skilled practitioner, her own work culminating in a piece depicting the British arms, which has been regarded as being perfect of its kind.

During the First World War Lady Evelyn remained in Belgium, which was suffering terribly under German occupation; her family tried to relieve her privations by sending food and clothing, but her passbook photograph of this period (the only surviving adult likeness) shows the image of a frail, aged lady, although she was only forty-six.

After the war, her greatest work completed and her parents dead, she lived on quietly in Belgium, absorbed in her garden, music, and books. To escape the outbreak of the Second World War and in deteriorating health, she returned to Britain, where on 30 July 1940 she died at the house of her brother James at Easter Moncreiffe, Perthshire. She was buried beside her sister Helen at Tirinie on the Atholl family's Perthshire estates.

Lady Evelyn Stewart-Murray's needlework collection was placed on display at Blair Castle, and her Gaelic stories went to the School of Scottish Studies at the University of Edinburgh. Although one scholar has assessed Lady Evelyn's life as one of 'tragedy and wasted potential' (Jalland, 279), the importance of her work as both needlewoman and collector of folk stories was beginning to be recognized some sixty years after her death.

JANE ANDERSON

Sources J. J. H. Stewart-Murray, seventh duke of Atholl, *Chronicles of the Atholl and Tullibardine families*, 5 vols. (privately printed, Edinburgh, 1908) · Blair Castle archive, Atholl MSS · P. Jalland, *Women, marriage and politics, 1860–1914* (1986) · M. Dick-Digges, et al., *Lady Evelyn's needlework collection* (1988) · S. Robertson and P. Young, *Daughter of Atholl: Lady Evelyn Stewart-Murray, 1868–1940* (1996) · *CCI* (1941)
Archives Blair Castle, Perthshire, letters and notes · U. Edin., notebooks
Likenesses photographs, 1868–91, Blair Castle, Perthshire · photograph, 1914, Blair Castle, Perthshire · O. Leyde, portrait (as a child), Blair Castle, Perthshire
Wealth at death £354 13s. 1d.: confirmation, 9 Jan 1941, *CCI*

Murray [*née* Rudman], **Frances** [Fanny] (1729–1778), courtesan, was, according to her *Memoirs* born as Frances Rudman at Bath, the only surviving triplet of Thomas Rudman (*d.* 1741), a musician. Hinde and others dispute this version of her birth and believe she came from London. Fanny, as she was called, was such a beautiful woman, with her 'perfect oval' face and 'coral lips and chestnut hair', that the rake Richard Rigby challenged Horace Walpole's poem *The Beauties* (1746), which listed the most beautiful women in England, because it did not include her (*Memoirs*, 6–7). Two popular prints of her were produced; in addition Lord Chancellor Hardwicke is said to have seen a portrait of her naked with another courtesan, Kitty Fisher, in the collection of the earl of Sandwich's brother, William Montague.

All sources agree that as a twelve-year-old flower-seller Fanny was seduced by Jack Spencer (1708–1746), grandson of the first duke of Marlborough, either on the steps of Covent Garden Theatre or in the abbey churchyard at Bath. Deserted by Spencer in Bath, Fanny soon came to the attention of the city's elderly master of ceremonies, Richard (Beau) Nash (1674–1761) and she went to live with him as his mistress in his mansion in St John's Court. The liaison was short-lived and within a couple of years Fanny had left him, assumed the name of Murray, and moved to Covent Garden, London.

While the *Memoirs* contains much that is spurious it gives a vivid account of Fanny's early, miserable career in London, where 'a variety of lovers succeeded each other'. She was soon pox-infected and destitute, with 'her small stock exhausted in chirurgical fees' (*Memoirs*, 89). She was always in debt: when she worked for the procurer Madam Maddox, from whose establishment in the Old Bailey she 'dressed up in dabs for the patrole of Fleet Street and the Strand', she kept only 6*d.* of her weekly earnings of £5 10*s.* 6*d.*, the rest being taken up in board, lodgings, and clothing (ibid., 92).

About 1747 Fanny's fortunes began to improve: Jack Harris, the celebrated 'negociator in women', included her as a new face in his *List of Covent Garden Ladies*, even though she had been on the town for four years, and this meant that she could increase her price to 2 guineas. Harris described her as one that 'may be put off for a virgin any time these twelve months' (*Memoirs*, 101). Her most important clients included John Montague, fourth earl of Sandwich, and Sir Richard Atkins of Clapham, who supplied most of her income until his sudden death in 1756. There is an anecdote recorded in *Notes and Queries*, but dismissed in the *Memoirs* (p. 149), that when Sir Richard gave her money because she complained of penury she 'clapped' his 'twenty-pound note between two pieces of bread and butter and ate it, saying to the donor "D— your twenty pound!—what does it signify"' (*N&Q*, 6th ser., 2, 1880, 486; *Memoirs*, 149).

Following Atkins's death Fanny sought support from the family of the man who had first seduced her. Jack Spencer had died in 1746 but his son John Spencer, first Earl Spencer, was determined to make amends for what his father had done. It is said that he offered the popular actor David *Ross (1728–1790) an allowance of £200 per annum if he would marry Fanny, and this he did, probably in the 1750s. Fanny settled into a life of married respectability until her past caught up with her in 1763. In that year the earl of Sandwich tried to expose his parliamentary adversary John Wilkes as the author of *Essay on Women*—an indecent parody of Pope's *Essay on Man*—which contained a dedication to Fanny, widely thought to be Fanny Murray, but possibly Frances Fielding. Fanny Murray died on 1 April 1778, probably in London. Her husband survived her.   BARBARA WHITE

Sources *Memoirs of the celebrated Miss Fanny Murray*, 2nd edn (1759) · H. Bleackley, *Ladies fair and frail: sketches of the demi-monde during the eighteenth century* (1909) · E. J. Burford, *Wits, wenchers and wantons: London's low life, Covent Garden in the eighteenth century* (1986) · *N&Q*, 6th ser., 2 (1880), 486 · *N&Q*, 7th ser., 12 (1891), 307, 470 · *N&Q*, 10th ser., 9 (1908) · *N&Q*, 2nd ser., 81 (1857) · T. Hinde, *Taken from the pump room: nine hundred years of Bath, the place, its people and its gossip* (1988), 40 · Highfill, Burnim & Langhans, *BDA*
Likenesses Johnson, engraving (*The celebrated Miss Murray*; after Page) · J. Macardell, engraving (after H. Morland, 1756), BM

Murray, Gaston (1826–1889). *See under* Murray, Henry Leigh (1820–1870).

Murray, Lord George (1694–1760), Jacobite army officer, born on 4 October 1694 at Huntingtower near Perth, was the sixth son of John *Murray, first duke of Atholl (1660–1724), and Lady Katherine Douglas, later Hamilton (*bap.* 1662, *d.* 1707), eldest daughter of Anne *Hamilton, duchess of Hamilton in her own right, and William Douglas, earl of Selkirk and third duke of Hamilton [*see* Hamilton,

Lord George Murray (1694–1760), by Sir Robert Strange

William (1634–1694)]. As a younger son of the duke of Atholl he bore the courtesy title Lord George Murray. On 3 June 1728 he married Amelia (1710–1766), only daughter of James Murray of Glencarse, Mugdrum, and (through his wife) Strowan. They had three sons and two daughters, of whom John *Murray became third duke of Atholl, James a major-general, and George *Murray vice-admiral of the white; Amelia married the master of Sinclair and, second, Farquharson of Invercauld, while Charlotte died unmarried.

Jacobite rising (1715) and exile Lord George was educated at Perth grammar school, whence he ran away on at least one occasion. On 16 March 1710 he complained to his father that he had been denied the Candlemas privilege of protecting a boy who was whipped, 'and strongly urged that on account of the "affront" he might be permitted to leave school' (*DNB*). In December 1710 he went up to Glasgow University, but left in 1711 to go 'to Flanders as ensign of the 1st regiment, the Royals' (ibid.). Sick at Dunkirk, he gambled and got into debt. On leave in 1715, Lord George was with his father in Atholl. After the earl of Mar raised King James's standard, Lord George, together with two of his brothers, William *Murray, then marquess of Tullibardine and later titular second duke of Atholl, and Lord Charles *Murray (who, accompanying William Mackintosh of Borlum's brigade south, was taken at Preston), held commands in the Atholl brigade. Tullibardine was the general officer commanding, being promoted major-general in the course of the campaign; the two other Murrays were battalion commanders in a force originally of three and eventually of six battalions. At the time of the battle of Sheriffmuir Lord George was raising cess in Fife, and so was not with the Atholmen on the defeated left wing. Afterwards both Tullibardine and Lord George attempted unsuccessfully to negotiate an indemnity via their father in exchange for their submission to government. This came to nothing, and they escaped to the continent in 1716, sailing from South Uist aboard the *Marie Therese*. In June that year Lord George was at Avignon, suffering, like many of the exiles, from illness. In 1718 he was living in poverty at Bordeaux, and in the same year 'a bill for treason was found against him at a court of oyer and terminer held at Cupar' (ibid.).

In 1719, Lord George served as brigadier (possibly major-general) at Glenshiel under the Earl Marischal and marquess of Tullibardine, and was wounded in the fighting. While on the run with his Bible in the mountains following the battle, he may have experienced a kind of spiritual conversion. On 19 April 1720 he sailed from Methil in Fife and landed at Rotterdam, going on to France. There James III (James Francis Edward Stuart) (James Stuart, Stuart claimant to the throne) paid for him to go to the Paris Academy. He fought a duel with Campbell of Glendaruel and made unsuccessful visits to Venice and Turin to try to gain a Venetian or Sardinian commission. He secretly returned to Scotland on 17 August 1724 to visit his dying father while negotiations for a pardon, instigated by his father and permitted by King James, were in progress. Although the duke died in November, in 1725 Lord George's pardon 'passed the Great Seal' (*DNB*).

Following his marriage in 1728 Lord George lived the life of a country gentleman on a lease of the lands 'on disadvantageous terms' (Tomasson, 3) round Tullibardine Castle from his elder brother James *Murray, now second duke of Atholl and supporter of the Hanoverian regime. In the 1730s he declined an offer from Tullibardine to send his 'eldest son to France' to be raised a Jacobite (ibid., 12) and in 1739, possibly to help his family's ambitions, he took the oaths of abjuration. In 1743 he visited London, and is very likely to have kissed George II's hand there. In 1745 James, second duke of Atholl, appointed Lord George sheriff depute in order to support the authorities in general and General Cope in particular against the Jacobites. Lord George agreed to his eldest son receiving a commission in the government forces.

The Jacobite rising of 1745 About this time the Jacobite duke of Perth asked Lord George what he would do in the event of a rising, and Lord George answered that he would lead out his men for the government and then take them over to the prince (Charles Edward Stuart, the Young Pretender)—indeed, such Atholmen as joined Cope largely deserted. After the duke left Blair, Lord George prepared to abandon his role as an 'ally and informant of Cope' (Lang, 121) and to join the prince. He acceded to the prince's forces north of Perth on 3 September, writing a pessimistic letter of self-justification to James, second duke of Atholl, the same day. His wife, who called him her 'Don Quixote' (Tomasson, 19) now fell ill: in early 1746 she gave birth to a child, who died shortly afterwards. On the 9th Lord George wrote a letter to his eldest son, who was a pupil at Eton College, further justifying his conduct. His whig friends were surprised, and so were some Jacobites. It appears that from the first Murray of Broughton, Prince Charles's secretary, was suspicious of him, and the suspicions allayed by Lord George's gallantry were raised repeatedly by his domineering arrogance and lack of respect for the prince, whom he 'saw as a reckless adventurer' (McLynn, *Jacobite Army*, 46). It is certainly possible that he was deeply suspected from the first. None the less, he was, together with the duke of Perth and his brother William, now styled duke of Atholl, appointed lieutenant-general. In total, the army they commanded never exceeded 11,000–14,000 men, and fewer than half of these made the historic march into England.

At Prestonpans on 21 September, where Lord George commanded the left wing, he took the responsibility of recommending Robert Anderson of Whitburgh's path through the morass which protected the government forces to the prince, so enabling the surprise attack which led to the destruction of Cope's army. On the other hand, he threw down his gun in rage before the battle when he learned that the prince had deployed the Atholl brigade without his consent, while his own battle plans were made without consultation. On the field, his clemency showed itself in his saving the life of a party of government troops by persuading them to surrender. On 24 September, he requested Tullibardine to raise three battalions to raise the cess in the counties of Fife, Perth, and Forfarshire. Probably at Edinburgh, Lord George designed 'a simple method of drill which could be easily taught and understood' in order to train the large numbers of irregulars coming in to the army (Carswell, 36). He also took good care of provisions throughout the whole campaign in England: as a result 'losses through sickness during the campaign were negligible' (McLynn, *Jacobite Army*, 29). On the prince's council, he first of all made himself unpopular by suggesting (for propaganda reasons) that no Catholics should serve on it, and then apparently opposed the proposed march into England—though he appears to have changed his mind on this issue: on 11 October, he wrote to Tullibardine imploring troops so that the army could 'march imediatly' on England (Burton and Laing, 80). Yet by reports of his conduct on council he considered a full-scale French invasion on the south coast unlikely, and feared a repeat of the débâcle of 1715, being also pessimistic about the likelihood of desertion from the British army. Indeed, the evidence is that Lord George was pessimistic about the whole enterprise: he was certainly aware of the danger of delay, repeatedly importuning Tullibardine (who was at this time general officer commanding north of the River Forth) to bring up the Perthshire recruits to Edinburgh. Lord George was also a man with more interest in Britain, the British state, and Britishness than most other Jacobites, and he made himself no more popular by opposing Charles's proposed abolition of the 1707 Act of Union. After the decision had been taken to march into England, it was Lord George who again contravened the prince's wish to attack Wade at Newcastle by instead suggesting bypassing him via Cumberland, or at the least dragging him across England for a battle by making a feint to Newcastle while marching to Carlisle. His arguments in favour of this won the support of most of the Jacobite commanders, and the prince was obliged to accede, although Lord George's wise support for a system of espionage was blocked by Charles Edward. A gulf began to open between Charles and his commander, which was exacerbated when Lord George marched south with the lowland regiments, while Charles accompanied the clansmen.

At Carlisle Lord George first declined to command the siege, and then resigned his commission in a pet because Charles suggested that Perth, a Catholic, should take the surrender. Eventually he resumed it, with Perth, who abnegated himself for the sake of the Stuarts, volunteering to take over responsibility for the baggage (this voluntary humiliation also prevented the current baggage commander, Ogilvy, resigning his commission). On resuming his command, Lord George continued to press for a return to Scotland, and was swayed by the prince's assurance that he had letters from English supporters promising 'to join him at Preston' (McLynn, *Jacobite Army*, 51). Some did, but no heavyweights were among them: the prince none the less gave further details of assurances he had received, as Lord George prepared a route which would enable progress to London while giving the appearance of leaning towards north Wales. At Manchester, Lord George suggested a compromise solution of marching 'the length of Derbyshire' (ibid., 99) before deciding on a retreat to Scotland. On 2 December, Lord George's feint towards Wales drew the British commander, the duke of Cumberland, out of position, and the way lay open towards London. On 4 December, the Jacobite army entered Derby.

At the council of war which followed, Lord George's determination to secure a retreat from Derby was, in the last resort, an inextricable mixture of affronted pride and prudent generalship. If he felt misled by Charles's repeated assurances of French support, his own sanguine expectations of the Lancashire Jacobites had been equally disappointed. The failure of the prince's prediction at Preston a week earlier that Sir Watkin Williams Wynn and his horse would join between Macclesfield and Derby may have been the final straw for Lord George and other senior officers. Certainly he found a ready audience: with the detachment even of Tullibardine (at times at least) and the captain of Clanranald, only Colonel O'Sullivan and the duke of Perth supported the prince, some of whose strongest supporters were not on the council. What if they had marched on? It is almost certain that the Jacobite army would have reached London first, where their seventeen battalions, two regiments of horse, and artillery would have surely outfaced four battalions' worth of regulars and the trained bands. What would have happened then has long been a matter for speculation. For a quarter of a millennium, the retreat from Derby has retained its status as one of the great controversial decisions, a classic 'what if?' of history. On the one hand, some authorities continue to view Lord George as resolving to pursue the only course of action which could sensibly be said to be open to him; on the other, he and his allies are accused of throwing away 'the best chance there had been of a restoration of the Stuarts ... when they held most of the trump cards' (Cruickshanks, 100). Poor intelligence hampered him: most importantly, no Jacobite commander knew the real, and to some extent genuine, state of French preparedness. Whatever that may be, Lord George's consummate extrication of the Jacobite army from England with only one minor engagement and few casualties was an outstanding success. At Clifton on 17 December 1745 his courageous rearguard action protected the strung-out Jacobite army from being overtaken by Cumberland.

Once back in Scotland, Lord George again demanded of an unwell and petulant prince that he 'relinquish power' to his military commanders as 'an emergency measure' (Hook and Ross, 88): this may have been precipitated by the prince's refusal to grant him reinforcements at Clifton. On 17 January, after receiving reinforcements from the northern Jacobite army, Lord George advised Charles to gain the height of Falkirk Muir: again 'his movements were cleverly disguised by a feint' (Lang, 243). On the high ground, Murray's astute use of Jacobite firepower at close quarters broke Lieutenant-General Henry Hawley's dragoons and delivered victory. Lord George's decision to press for a retreat from Stirling at the end of January—'a mutiny in all but name' (Hook and Ross, 92)—was based on an exaggeration of the rate of desertion, possibly born out of a rising panic on the subject clear in the Atholl correspondence of that January. On the 21st he wrote to Tullibardine that 'you should let every Taxman [tacksman] in Atholl know that if they do not come out at your order, their Tacts are broke, besides distroying all they have' (Burton and Laing, 150); on the 27th he wrote asking his brother to make an example of deserters. His concerns appear to have been overstated, and they further fed Charles's resentment. The retreat which ensued was a shambles and, despite Lord George's offer to make a stand in Atholl, both he and the prince were at angry loggerheads at the last council of war at Crieff on 2 February, from which the army retreated further in three columns, Lord George taking the east coast route to Aberdeen. Although the Jacobites had some success on their home ground in February and March, Lord George was by this time involved in tentative peace negotiations with the prince of Hesse, while being unable to dislodge government forces from Atholl. He was in fact surprised by Sir Andrew Agnew's Blair garrison, and, as at Moy, only noise and concealment prevented the exiguous numbers of Lord George's advance party being detected. Before he could press home the siege which followed, he was recalled to Inverness to face the duke of Cumberland (31 March).

The battle of Culloden (1746) and its aftermath To his credit, Lord George strongly advised against the 'improper ground' of flat and boggy Culloden Moor as the site of the battle (Hook and Ross, 105), but the prince was unwilling to accept his general's alternative site on the other side of Strathnairn because he feared both that with food so low the army would disintegrate and that Cumberland would outflank them, take Inverness, and leave his men without an urban base of any kind. Even if the Jacobites sought to defend Inverness in a siege, the final encounter would only be postponed. Lord George's role in calling off the abortive night attack in the early hours of the 16th only deepened the prince's distrust of him. In the end, Lord George commanded the right wing, but even before the battle his view was clear: 'We are putting an end to a bad affair', he told Lord Elcho (Tomasson and Buist, 155). On the battlefield, his positioning of the Atholl brigade helped to place the Jacobite front line at a slant which hindered their effectiveness. None the less, Murray took them through the government front line and captured two cannon before being thrown from his horse. He retired to bring up more men to press home the attack, but the firepower of the British army was already turning the day.

The duke of Cumberland subsequently claimed that Lord George's battle orders contained a command to give no quarter. This was out of keeping with Lord George's conduct at Prestonpans and that of the Jacobite army throughout the campaign, and there is no evidence of it in the surviving copies of Murray's orders: though in fairness it should be noted that Murray had earlier implied that Dutch troops under British command should receive no quarter (Burton and Laing, 31–2). None the less it was an insult, used as a cloak for government brutality; senior Jacobite officers such as Lord Balmerino denied it from the scaffold. Having conducted the remnants of the Jacobite right and centre from the field, the day after the battle (17 April) Lord George, in resigning his command, wrote a letter of reproach to the prince from Ruthven, where the remnants of the army gathered, stating his concern that there had been no guaranteed aid from France and that the site chosen for Culloden had been so disastrous. Lord George had lost many men and had met his weak and ill brother Tullibardine by Loch Moy: he was at a peak of fury, and this letter, often cited, does not represent his balanced assessment. Subsequently he regretted his thrawn and oppositional stance towards Charles. The prince received this letter about ten days later, by which time the rising, leaving aside isolated pockets of resistance, was in a state of collapse. Lord George himself went into hiding, probably in Glenartney in Atholl.

After eight months on the run, Lord George sailed on 16 December and landed in the Netherlands on Christmas day. He was, of course, attainted, and the influence of his family in securing his rehabilitation with government was now at an end. From the end of 1746 to August 1748 he travelled in Venice, Bologna, Germany, Poland, the Netherlands, and Rome, where he was on 27 March 1747. James, the Old Chevalier, who had long befriended Lord George, introduced him to the pope and proposed a pension for him of 400 livres, also seeking support for him from the French court. In April, Charles wrote to ask his father that Lord George should be imprisoned. Unsurprisingly, therefore, an attempted reconciliation with the prince in Paris in July 1747 came to nothing when Charles would not see Murray.

Lord George's family were turned out of Tullibardine Castle by James, second duke of Atholl, in 1746. Towards the end of the 1740s, Lady Murray joined her husband; on occasion at least one of the children came visiting. Despite the prince's treatment of him, Lord George remained a Jacobite. In 1755, in an interesting letter, he opined that if France had supplied 'a proper force' in 1745 'his R.[oyal] H.[ighness] could not have failed of success' because 'many, very many' wished the Stuarts well and 'would have turned to the side that had success' (Clark, 132). Indeed, it seems likely that at this stage Lord George was still prepared to take up arms. In 1759, Lord George's name was put forward by Lord Blantyre as that of a likely senior figure in the proposed Jacobite rising of that year, among whose aims would be to 'restore the Privy Council and Parliament of Scotland, and to re-establish the old laws, customs and privileges of that kingdom' (Nordmann, 204). But by this time he and the prince were permanently estranged. Lord George lived for some years at Cleves and Emmerich, before moving to Medemblik in the Netherlands at the end of 1759. He died there on 11 October 1760 and was buried in the town. He was survived by his wife, who died on 29 March 1766.

Reputation Although he could still offer a balanced assessment of Lord George while on the run after Culloden, Charles quickly came to regard Murray as little better than a traitor, and treated him accordingly. He was not alone in this (misjudged) view, which probably had its roots in the perceived paradox of arrogance and defeatism in Lord George's style of command. In his poem 'Latha Chuil-Lodair' ('Culloden day') John Roy Stewart, colonel of the Edinburgh regiment, excoriated his commanding officer thus: 'My curses upon Lord George Murray … The flatterer of merciless guile' (Campbell, 173).

Such opinions only confirm that Lord George Murray's reputation rests on the assessment of his conduct and capabilities in 1745, which in turn depend on three other appraisals: the decision at Derby, the quality of the prince's generalship, and the military ability of the Irish staff officers, particularly Colonel O'Sullivan, who have tended to receive a bad press from the memoirs of the Scottish Jacobites who distrusted them. For a long time, scholars have tended to downplay the views of the anti-Murray faction. In particular, Chevalier de Johnstone's high opinion of Lord George, epitomized in his oft-quoted view that if the prince had slept through the campaign he would have had the crown on his head when he awoke, has often been cited without any note being taken of the fact that Johnstone was the general's aide-de-camp. Lord George, among others, was jealous of the Irish officers: not only did they enjoy the prince's favour, they also risked little if they were captured as they were in the French or Spanish service, and would thus be prisoners of war rather than 'traitors'. Again, many Jacobite scholars have tended to follow this line. There may be something in Lord George's loyal pessimism which appeals to the post-Jacobite historian: but if we do not take temperament for achievement, it may be more fairly said that Lord George Murray was a brave, petulant, and gifted—though conservative—field commander. An 'epicure' (Tomasson, 24) and a family man, he was unlike many Jacobites in not being much of a Scottish nationalist: his interest was rather 'that the prestige of Great Britain should be upheld among the nations of the world' (ibid., 11). In the 1740s he was steadily conforming to the new ways of the British aristocracy (the schooling of his son at Eton rather than Perth grammar school being evidence of this). It is likely that his differing political outlook in this area, much more in keeping with that of his whig contemporaries, affected his relationships with the passionate Scottish nationalists of the Jacobite army, who liked to keep alive the speech of court Scots and the culture of the Stuart Renaissance. In the field, his undoubted qualities as a general were compromised in an inherently risky campaign by a disinclination to take risks: Murray did not consistently see the need to advance into England, did not want to fight Wade and win the crucial battle on English soil, did not want to advance from Derby, and retreated after Falkirk rather than following up the advantage of his victory. Brave and successful as he was in battle, he was no Napoleon, Alexander, or Hannibal, but would have filled (as in a lesser key, his children filled) the place of a gifted general officer in an established army with good resources and a chain of command not vitiated by the jealousy he was prone to incite and the arrogance he was prone to show.

MURRAY G. H. PITTOCK

Sources DNB · K. Tomasson, *The Jacobite general* (1958) · *Scots peerage* · J. H. Burton and D. Laing, eds., *Jacobite correspondence of the Atholl family* (1840) · K. Tomasson and F. Buist, *Battles of the '45* (1962) · A. Lang, *Prince Charles Edward Stuart* (1903) · M. Hook and W. Ross, *The 'Forty-Five* (1995) · C. Nordmann, 'Choiseul and the last Jacobite attempt of 1759', *Ideology and conspiracy: aspects of Jacobitism, 1689–1759*, ed. E. Cruickshanks (1982), 201–17 · A. L. Carswell, 'The most despicable enemy that are', *1745*, ed. R. Woosnam-Savage (1995), 29–40 · E. Cruickshanks, *Political untouchables: the tories and the '45* (1979) · M. G. H. Pittock, *Jacobitism* (1998) · J. C. D. Clark, *English society, 1688–1832: ideology, social structure and political practice during the ancien régime* (1985) · J. L. Campbell, *Highland songs of the 'Forty-Five* (1933) · D. Dobson, *Jacobites of the '45* (1993) · F. J. McLynn, *The Jacobite army in England, 1745: the final campaign* (1983) · F. J. McLynn, *Charles Edward Stuart: a tragedy in many acts* (1988) · F. McLynn, *The Jacobites* (1985) · A. M. Smith, *Jacobite estates of the Forty-Five* (1982) · NL Scot., MS 874 · J. Baynes, *The Jacobite rising of 1715* (1970) · B. G. Seton and J. G. Arnot, eds., *The prisoners of the '45*, Scottish History Society, 3rd ser., 13–15 (1928–9) · GEC, *Peerage*, new edn · R. Douglas, *The peerage of Scotland*, 2nd edn, ed. J. P. Wood, 2 vols. (1813)

Archives NL Scot., letters · Stirling Council Archive Services, papers | Blair Castle, Perthshire, Atholl MSS · Blair Castle, Perthshire, corresp., journals, and papers relating to Jacobite rising · Worcester College, Oxford, letters to A. Lumsden

Likenesses R. Strange, drawing, Scot. NPG [*see illus.*] · portrait, repro. in Hook and Ross, *The 'Forty-Five*, 40; priv. coll.

Murray, George (1741–1797), naval officer, was born on 22 August 1741 at Tullibardine, Perthshire, the fourth son and fifth of the seven children of Lord George *Murray (1694–1760), Jacobite army officer, and Amelia, *née* Murray (1710–1766). His paternal grandfather was John Murray, first duke of Atholl, and his maternal grandfather was James Murray of Glencarse and Strowan. His father and

his father's older brother, the marquess of Tullibardine, supported the Jacobite risings in 1715, 1719, and 1745–6. Lord George Murray, who served as a lieutenant-general under Prince Charles Edward Stuart, the Young Pretender, fled to the continent after the Jacobite defeat at Culloden. Young George Murray remained in Scotland and never saw his father after 1746. From 1755 to 1756 he attended the school of William Rose at Kew, and then he entered the Royal Naval Academy at Portsmouth where he remained until 1758.

Murray began his naval career in 1758 as a midshipman on the ship of the line *Newark* (80 guns), flagship of Vice-Admiral Francis Holburne, a fellow Scot. After a cruise in the channel, he went in 1759 to India in the *Falmouth* (50 guns). He returned to England in 1762 in the frigate *Terpsichore*, passed his lieutenant's examination, and was appointed to the sloop *Swift*. In 1763 he was moved to the frigate *Tartar* which the next year joined the squadron at Jamaica where he was promoted commander of the sloop *Ferret* in 1765. While serving on the Jamaica station he surveyed Mobile harbour in British West Florida and collected for his brother, the third duke of Atholl, specimens of flora and fauna and Native American artefacts from that region to form a valuable collection at Blair Castle in Scotland. Posted as captain of the frigate *Renown* in 1768, he transferred to another frigate, the *Adventure*, and returned to England in 1769. From 1770 to 1775 he was on half pay and then he was appointed to the frigate *Levant* in the Mediterranean where he served until 1779. Having next been appointed to the frigate *Cleopatra* in 1780, he served in the downs, the channel, and the North Sea where he participated in the battle of Dogger Bank on 5 August 1781. In December 1782 he was appointed to his first ship of the line command, the *Irresistible* (74 guns), which was paid off at the end of the American War of Independence.

While on half pay (1783–90) Murray retired to Perthshire. On 13 May 1784 he married Wilhelmina King (c.1738–1795), daughter of Thomas, fifth Baron King of Ockham, and established his residence at Stanley House, Strathord. They had no children. In 1790 Murray purchased the estate of Pitkeathly near Bridge of Earn in Perthshire. At the general election of 1790 Murray, with the approval of Henry Dundas, political manager in Scotland for William Pitt, was elected member of parliament for the Perth burghs on the interest of his nephew, the fourth duke of Atholl. In parliament he gave silent support to the Pitt government and willingly vacated his seat in March 1796 for a friend of Dundas.

Murray resumed his naval career in August 1790 at the time of the Nootka crisis with Spain when he was appointed to the *Defence* (74 guns). The dispute, however, was soon resolved, and the *Defence* was paid off in November. In September 1792 Murray was appointed to the *Vengeance* (74 guns) and made commander-in-chief in the Medway at Chatham with the temporary rank of commodore. On outbreak of war with France in February 1793, Murray was given command of the *Duke* (98 guns) and made a colonel of the Royal Marines. In March he sailed for the West Indies in the fleet of Admiral Alan Gardner. While off Martinique in June the *Duke* was severely damaged by lightning, and Murray returned to England with a convoy in October. He was then transferred at Plymouth to another ship of the line, the *Glory* (98 guns).

Murray was made commander-in-chief of the North American squadron based on Halifax, Nova Scotia, in March 1794, and was promoted rear-admiral in April and vice-admiral the next year. Murray's squadron—consisting of his flagship, the *Resolution* (74 guns), two other ships of the line, four frigates, and a sloop—sailed from England in May and reached Halifax in August after touching at the Delaware and Sandy Hook. Although the North American station was not a major theatre, important British interests, such as the colonies in North America, trade, and the fisheries required naval protection. With a cruising area extending from the Gulf of St Lawrence and the Bay of Fundy southwards to the Bahamas and eastwards from the coast of the United States to Bermuda, Murray's inadequate force, always short of seamen and including small vessels, operated under adverse conditions. An additional burden were the frequent confrontations with the United States over neutral rights and obligations.

For more than two years Murray, a seasoned and experienced officer, conducted his command with vigilance, restraint, and tact. His squadron almost completely cleared North American waters of French men-of-war and privateers. He won the praise of the mercantile and shipping interests of British North America for providing adequate and timely convoys, especially for the critical cargoes of masts and naval stores bound for England. Seeing the need for an auxiliary operating base farther south than Halifax in order to expedite cruising during the winter months and to lessen the need to use the territorial waters of the United States, Murray persuaded the Admiralty to add Bermuda to his command. He authorized the survey of the anchorage at Bermuda, which would later be known as Murray's anchorage, and ordered the building of storehouses and water tanks for supplying the squadron and the establishment of a naval hospital. When Murray became aware of the availability of cedar timber and shipbuilders in the islands he initiated the building at Bermuda of sloops and smaller vessels that were critically needed by his squadron and the British navy elsewhere.

At the beginning of Murray's third year in the North American command, Earl Spencer, first lord of the Admiralty, recommended that he should remain on the station and not be recalled when his three-year tour of overseas duty ended. Spencer emphasized that Murray, well known and liked in America, was familiar with the peculiar difficulties of the station where he had served with distinction. Murray, however, suffered a stroke in May 1796; this was followed by a more severe attack in October which forced him to relinquish the command. His departure from America elicited warm expressions of appreciation, public and private, especially in Bermuda and Nova Scotia, for his defence of the colonies and the protection

of trade. He also received testimonials of affection and professional commendation from his subordinates in the squadron. After returning to England Murray died on 17 October 1797 at the home of his nephew, Lord George Murray, at Hunton in Kent. He was buried at Ockham in Surrey near his wife, who had died on 28 December 1795. A memorial tablet to his memory was erected in the parish church of All Saints at Ockham.

Although he was held in high esteem by his superiors, both civilian and naval, and by his fellow officers and subordinates, Murray has not received the recognition he deserves. Despite his success as commander-in-chief in North America Murray's career as a flag officer was comparatively brief and entirely confined to an overseas station far distant from the scenes of major actions. Moreover his career has been sometimes confused with that of a younger admiral of the same name, Sir George Murray (1755–1819).   MALCOLM LESTER

Sources PRO, Admiralty papers, ADM 1/492, 493, 494 · Blair Castle archive, Blair Castle, Blair Atholl, Perthshire · J. J. H. H. Stewart-Murray, seventh duke of Atholl, *Chronicles of the Atholl and Tullibardine families*, 5 vols. (privately printed, Edinburgh, 1908) · D. R. Fisher, 'Murray, George', HoP, *Commons* · D. Syrett and R. L. DiNardo, *The commissioned sea officers of the Royal Navy, 1660–1815*, rev. edn, Occasional Publications of the Navy RS, 1 (1994) · J. J. Colledge, *Ships of the Royal Navy*, rev edn, 2 vols. (1987–9) · *Private papers of George, second Earl Spencer*, ed. J. S. Corbett and H. W. Richmond, 4 vols., Navy RS, 46, 48, 58–9 (1913–24) · BL, department of manuscripts, Althorp MSS · *GM*, 1st ser., 67 (1797), 900 · J. Penrose, *Lives of Vice-Admiral Sir Charles Vinicombe Penrose KCB and Captain James Trevenen* (1850) · C. Petrie, *The Jacobite movement*, 2 vols. (1948–50) · W. Duke, *Lord George Murray and the forty-five* (1927) · K. Tomasson, *The Jacobite general* (1958) · E. W. Brayley, J. Britton, and E. W. Brayley, jun., *A topographical history of Surrey*, 5 vols. (1841–8)

Archives Blair Castle, Perthshire, MSS | BL, Althorp MSS · PRO, Admiralty papers, ADM 1/492, 493, 494

Wealth at death £50,000: *GM*, 979

Murray, Sir George (1759–1819), naval officer, was born at Chichester and baptized at St Peter the Great Church in the town on 16 April 1759, the second son of Gideon Murray (1721–1772), magistrate and alderman, and his wife, Anne Stringer. In 1770, when eleven years old, he joined the frigate *Niger* (Captain Francis Banks), and he later transferred with Banks to the *Pembroke* (60 guns), serving mostly in the Mediterranean. Two years after this he joined the *Panther* (60 guns), flagship of Commodore Molyneux Shuldham on the Newfoundland station, and he spent most of the next six years off North America. After joining the *Romney* (50 guns), flagship of Rear-Admiral Montagu, Murray was lent to the schooner *Placentia* and was shipwrecked off Cape Race in 1775. In the *Bristol* (50 guns; Sir Peter Parker's flagship) he was at the bloody but unsuccessful attack on Charles Town, South Carolina, on 28 June 1776; and he was also in the *Chatham* (50 guns) with Parker at the occupation of Rhode Island. In January 1778 he moved to the *Eagle* (64 guns), Lord Howe's flagship, before taking part in the summer operations against D'Estaing.

On his return home Murray was promoted lieutenant on 31 December 1778 and appointed to the frigate *Arethusa* (Captain Charles Everitt). On 19 March 1779 she was wrecked near Ushant when chasing a French frigate, and Murray was taken prisoner. He occupied his time studying French and the organization of the French navy, and was released on parole a year later—on the instigation it is said of Sartine, the French minister of marine, who admired his spirited conduct in chastising an American privateers-man who appeared in public wearing British naval uniform and the royal cockade.

After nine months in the *Marlborough* (74 guns) Murray joined the *Monmouth* (64 guns) commanded by James Alms, his fellow townsman, before sailing in April 1781 to the East Indies. On passage she took part in Commodore George Johnstone's inept action off the Cape Verde Islands against Suffren. In the East Indies Murray fought in all five actions between Sir Edward Hughes and Suffren, moving after the second to Hughes's flagship *Superb* (74 guns), where Thomas Troubridge was a fellow lieutenant. In the action on 3 September 1782 Murray was wounded; he was promoted by Hughes to captain on 12 October for his gallantry, and given command of the frigate *San Carlos*. After the fifth action he moved to the *Inflexible* (64 guns), before returning to England in June 1784 to pay her off.

Murray is believed to have devoted the next six years to study, including two years in France to improve his knowledge of French language and literature. In June 1790 he commissioned the frigate *Triton* and in the following April he was sent to survey the Great Belt and the approaches to Copenhagen, an experience which proved invaluable ten years later. He sailed to Halifax in September 1791 and became senior naval officer, Jamaica, in the following May. He returned home in June 1793, transferred to the frigate *Nymphe* in December, and was present at Lord Bridport's action against the French off Lorient on 23 June 1795. On leaving the *Nymphe* he married, in St John the Evangelist, Westminster, on 15 September 1795, Ann (1763–1859), daughter of Colonel Christopher Teesdale; two weeks later he was back at sea.

After a year in the *Formidable* (90 guns) Murray commanded the *Colossus* (74 guns) off Cape St Vincent on 14 February 1797, but damage to her foreyards put her out of action early in the battle. In May 1798 Lord St Vincent sent the *Colossus* to join Rear-Admiral Horatio Nelson in the Mediterranean as 'Murray is too good a fellow to be left there [Lisbon] when so much is to be done' (*Dispatches and Letters*, 3.15). The ship's condition, however, was such that in December she had to return home to refit, but on the way she was wrecked on the Scillies in a gale. One man was killed and many of Sir William Hamilton's less valuable treasures which she was bringing home were lost. Murray was 'fully acquitted' at the subsequent court martial, blame being attributed to the 'badness of the weather and the rotten state of the best bower cabel though it had never been used' (PRO, ADM 1/5348).

After two years in the *Achille* (84 guns) in the channel, Murray moved in March 1801 to the *Edgar* (74 guns). Because of Murray's knowledge of the difficult navigation the *Edgar* led the fleet into action at Copenhagen on 2 April, receiving heavy fire from four Danish ships before anchoring opposite the *Jylland*, whom she engaged for four hours until the truce. The *Edgar*'s 'running rigging was entirely shot to pieces, the masts and yards very much wounded, the sails shot through in various places and rendered unserviceable'; 31 men were killed and 104 wounded (PRO, ADM 51/1371, *Edgar*'s log, 2 April). Murray 'set a noble example of intrepidity', wrote Nelson to Sir Hyde Parker on 3 April (*Dispatches and Letters*, 4.315). He continued in the Baltic in command of a squadron watching the Swedish fleet at Karlskrona until August 1801 when he transferred to the *London* (90 guns) and paid her off at the peace.

On the renewal of war Nelson selected Murray as his first captain (or chief of staff) in the *Victory*, a testing post which he held during the long watch off Toulon (1803–5) and the chase to the West Indies in 1805. Murray hesitated to accept the appointment, one which sometimes led to disagreements between admiral and first captain, who both feared that professional confrontations would damage their friendship. Nelson, however, assured him 'that even should everything go contrary to his wishes, he would waive the rank of *Admiral*, and explain or expostulate with him as his *friend* Murray' (*Naval Chronicle*, 1807, 189).

Murray was promoted rear-admiral on 23 April 1804 but the death of his father-in-law, to whom he was executor, prevented his accompanying Nelson on his last voyage and he remained ashore until 1806. That November he was appointed commander-in-chief of the naval operations against Buenos Aires: 'George Murray is the flag officer, of all others, I wish should succeed Rear-Admiral Stirling', wrote St Vincent to Admiral John Markham on 26 June 1806 (*Selections from the Correspondence of … Markham*, 56). He arrived only to witness the failure of General John Whitelocke's assault on Buenos Aires in July 1807, the navy's task being limited to convoying and landing the troops in June and embarking them again from Buenos Aires and Montevideo after the repulse. Murray returned home in January 1808.

Though not again employed, Murray was promoted vice-admiral on 25 October 1809 and created KCB on 2 January 1815. He was an alderman of Chichester for many years and mayor in 1815; he died suddenly on 28 February 1819, aged fifty-nine, at North Street, Chichester, and was buried on 8 March in the precincts of Chichester Cathedral. His memorial there depicts the *Edgar* leading the fleet at Copenhagen. His eldest son was born on the second anniversary of that battle: 'if one of his names is not *Baltic*', wrote Nelson, 'I shall be very angry with you indeed—he can be called nothing else'. Murray went better and baptized him George Saint Vincent Thomas Nelson (Thomas for Troubridge; NMM, MS 84/174/20, 13 April 1803). Murray was much liked in the navy; St Vincent, for example, in a letter to the second Earl Spencer, 12 November 1798, called him 'a most valuable officer and amiable man' (*Private Papers of George, second Earl Spencer*, 486). His widow died in Boulogne in 1859, aged ninety-five.

                                                                C. H. H. OWEN

Sources DNB · admiralty documents, PRO, ADM 1/5348; 51/1371 [*Edgar*'s log, 2 April 1801] · admiralty documents, PRO, ADM 34,

ADM 36, ADM 107/7 · 'Biographical memoir' of Murray, *Naval Chronicle*, 18 (1807), 176–91 · NMM, Murray MSS, MS 84/174 and HSR/ C/2–4 · *The dispatches and letters of Vice-Admiral Lord Viscount Nelson*, ed. N. H. Nicolas, 7 vols. (1844–6) · BL, Murray MSS, Egerton MS 3265 · J. H. Owen, Notes for an unwritten biography of Admiral Murray, 1963, W. Sussex RO, MP873 · *Selections from the correspondence of Admiral John Markham*, ed. C. Markham, Navy RS, 28 (1904) · J. D. Grainger, ed., *The Royal Navy in the River Plate, 1806–1807*, Navy RS, 135 (1996) · *Private papers of George, second Earl Spencer*, ed. J. S. Corbett and H. W. Richmond, 4 vols., Navy RS, 46, 48, 58–9 (1913–24) · monumental inscription, Chichester Cathedral

Archives BL, letter-book, Egerton MS 3265 · BL, orders, Add. MS 34970 · NMM, MSS, MS 84/174 and HSR/C/2–4

Likenesses H. R. Cook, stipple, pubd 1807, NPG · W. Say, mezzotint, pubd 1819 (after C. Woolcott), BM · C. Woolcott, oils, 1819, repro. in C. Beresford, *Nelson and his times* (1897) · J. Parker, engraving (after R. Smirke), repro. in *Commemoration of four great naval victories* (1803)

Wealth at death £20,000: PRO, death duty registers, IR 26/791/573, 14 July 1819

Murray, Lord George (1761–1803), inventor of a shutter telegraph system and bishop of St David's, was born at Dunkeld House, Dunkeld, Perthshire, on 30 January 1761, the second surviving son of John *Murray, third duke of Atholl (1729–1774), and his wife, Charlotte Murray, Baroness Strange (1731–1805). He matriculated at New College, Oxford, on 28 June 1779 and graduated BA in 1782. On 18 December 1780, at Farnborough, Hampshire, he married Anne Charlotte Grant (1765–1844), the daughter of Lieutenant-General Francis Grant (1717–1781). In 1787 Murray became archdeacon of Man and rector of Hunton, Kent. However, the sea seems to have been his true love. He corresponded regularly with an uncle and namesake, George *Murray (1741–1797), who rose to vice-admiral. He sent his eldest son into the navy, and in 1790 invented a form of rudimentary paddle wheel. On 17 October 1794 he wrote to the Admiralty to propose a shutter telegraph system for communicating between the dockyards and London, especially in the event of an invasion. His system had two columns mounting six shutters in a vertical frame 20 feet high, and could handle sixty-three changes. Tested in the summer of 1795, Murray's telegraph proved superior to that invented almost simultaneously by a fellow clergyman, John Gamble, who was understandably aggrieved at the outcome. In December 1795 the Admiralty signed a contract for lines to Deal and Sheerness, and on the 18th Murray was introduced to George III. The Deal line was finished in January 1796, and in March Murray was given direction of the entire Admiralty telegraph system. However, the proposed lines to Plymouth, Torbay, and Falmouth were cancelled in June, and rather than the £16,500 he had expected to receive for them, Murray had to be content with an order in council for £2000, granted on 8 August 1796. Thereafter, Murray abandoned any direct involvement with the telegraph system, but in 1798 his obsession with invasion came to the fore again when he organized a volunteer defence force in his part of Kent.

On 22 October 1800 George III wrote to Pitt requesting Murray's promotion to the newly vacant see of St David's. He was officially nominated on 19 November, admitted DD on 27 November, elected on 6 December, confirmed

the following day, and consecrated on 8 February 1801. One of his main concerns was to improve the finances of the bishopric, both for its own sake and for his own: it was the third poorest in England and Wales, and Murray's own financial management had been chaotic (in 1797 he had an income of £750 and debts totalling £6000). Murray visited the outlying parts of his diocese, something no bishop had done for many years, and began to reform the uneconomic system of leases. His own financial position was made more secure in 1802 when he became additionally dean of Bocking, Essex. During that year Murray observed at first hand the controversial election for the Carmarthenshire county seat, in which the two candidates spent (by his estimate) some £30,000:

> the rancour of the people towards each other is very disgraceful to them and continues from generation to generation. As neutrals we have heard all the stories of both parties, and were we to believe half of them should be led to conclude that there is not one honest man in the Principality. (Lincs. Arch., Hawley MS 6/3/41)

Murray died in Cavendish Square, London, on 3 June 1803, after:

> coming down on a damp, cold night, in a state of perspiration, from a committee in the house of lords, and waiting some time at the door for his carriage, he felt an immediate chill, which brought on a violent fever in a few hours, that carried him off in three days. (*GM*)

He was buried at the Grosvenor Chapel, Audley Street, London, on 22 June 1803. He bequeathed debts totalling £13,000 to his widow and nine surviving children. To give her some means of support, his widow was in 1809 made a lady-in-waiting to the princesses Amelia and Elizabeth. Murray's eldest son, John (b. 1782), an acting commander in the Royal Navy, died at Jamaica on 8 December 1803; his second son, George *Murray (1784–1860), became bishop of Sodor and Man, and later of Rochester. His fourth daughter was the courtier and humanitarian writer Amelia Matilda *Murray. Lord George Murray achieved an unlikely posthumous fame in the 1990s when his shutter telegraph system became regarded as one of the vital early inventions that ultimately led to the development of the internet. Moreover, his and his wife's prolific breeding saved the dukedom of Atholl: after the direct line died out in 1957, the tenth and subsequent dukes were direct descendants of Lord George Murray.   J. D. DAVIES

Sources J. D. Davies, '"We like this country extremely": Lord George Murray, bishop of St David's and progenitor of the internet', *Carmarthenshire Antiquary* [forthcoming] · letters to Sir Henry Hawley, Lincs. Arch., Hawley MS 6/3/36–44 · NA Scot. · Blair Castle, Perthshire, Atholl MSS · PRO, ADM 106/2220-21 · J. J. H. H. Stewart-Murray, seventh duke of Atholl, *Chronicles of the Atholl and Tullibardine families*, 5 vols. (privately printed, Edinburgh, 1908), vols. 3–4 · G. Wilson, *The old telegraphs* (1976) · T. W. Holmes, *The semaphore: the story of the admiralty-to-Portsmouth telegraph and semaphore lines, 1796 to 1847* (1983) · *Fasti Angl.* (Hardy), 1.307 · *Scots peerage* · E. Murray, F. Drummond, and E. F. Oakeley, eds., *The cousin book* (1935), 2–3 · [G. Murray], *A sermon preached on the 16th of December 1792, at a country church in the county of Kent* (1793?) · private information (2004) [J. Anderson] · *GM*, 1st ser., 73 (1803), 601

Archives Blair Castle, Perthshire, Atholl MSS · Lincs. Arch., letters to Sir Henry Hawley · PRO, ADM 206
Likenesses J. Zoffany, oils (as a young boy), Blair Castle, Perthshire · miniature (in his teens or early twenties), Blair Castle, Perthshire
Wealth at death debts totalling £13,000: Davies, '"We like this country extremely"'

Murray, Sir George (1772–1846), army officer and politician, was born in the old house of Ochtertyre, Crieff, Perthshire, on 6 February 1772, the younger son of Sir William Murray of Ochtertyre, fifth baronet (1746–1800), and Lady Augusta Mackenzie (1746–1809), youngest daughter of George, third earl of Cromarty. He was well educated by tutors, at Edinburgh high school from 1781 to 1785 under Dr Alexander Adam, and at Edinburgh University, before being sent to Geneva to learn French. In March 1789 he was commissioned ensign in the 71st foot, and in June 1790 transferred to the 3rd foot guards (later Scots guards). As a subaltern in the 3rd (Scots) guards he served throughout the campaigns in the Low Countries from 1793 to 1795, except for a few months in 1794 after promotion as lieutenant and captain on 16 January 1794. On returning home his Perthshire neighbour, Major-General Alexander Campbell of Monzie, invited him to act as aide-de-camp, but he only saw service in Newcastle upon Tyne, in Perthshire, and in Belfast during the Irish rising. However, two firm friendships he had formed, that with Colonel Robert Anstruther, and with Colonel the Hon. Alexander Hope, whose sister had married Murray's brother, drew him towards service in the quartermaster-general's branch of the staff. Both had served with Austrian armies, in which the quartermaster-generals had been intensively trained to act as expert operational consultants to their commanders, and both, among others, were anxious to see a similar arrangement in the British army, which notoriously lacked any such officer. Thus in 1799, within a month of Murray's promotion as captain-lieutenant and lieutenant-colonel in August 1799, Robert Anstruther, as quartermaster-general of the Helder expeditionary force, took him on as senior assistant quartermaster-general; and although Murray was wounded on the first day, Anstruther requisitioned him again in 1800, when, as Major-General Abercromby's quartermaster-general, he was sent from Gibraltar to the Levant to make preparations for the landing in Egypt. Murray shared in all the actions of the victorious campaign. Returned home, he gladly seized the opportunity to become, as it was said, a 'Scientifick' by entering the Royal Military College at High Wycombe, recently established for the instruction of the quartermaster-general's officers. But after only five happy months (March to July 1802) he was requested by General William Grinfield to act as adjutant-general in the West Indies.

On the renewal of the war in 1803 Murray was recalled to the Horse Guards by General Robert Brownrigg, the quartermaster-general of the forces, who in November 1804 sent him to Dublin to remodel the department in Ireland on the new lines as deputy quartermaster-general, an appointment he held until 1812. In 1805 he acted as deputy in the luckless expedition to Hanover. In 1807 he acted as chief of the quartermaster-general's department in the army commanded by Lord Cathcart, which was sent to the Baltic to prevent the Danish fleet from falling into Napoleon's hands, and the plan adopted by Cathcart was largely his. In April 1808 Castlereagh sent him as quartermaster-general to Stockholm ahead of a force under Sir John Moore to offer assistance to Gustavus Adolphus, the king of Sweden, whose terms, however, proved to be unacceptable. He was at once ordered on to Portugal as quartermaster-general to the troops to be commanded by Sir Harry Burrard and Sir Hew Dalrymple as reinforcements to the army of Arthur Wellesley (the duke of Wellington). He landed on 21 August just as the battle of Vimeiro was beginning and was involved in the series of negotiations leading to the notorious convention of Cintra, and on the recall of the generals he acted as quartermaster-general to Sir John Moore's army, which, after entering Spain, was obliged to retreat and re-embark at Corunna in January 1809. Here he suffered the loss not only of Sir John Moore but also of his old friend and mentor Robert Anstruther.

Promoted colonel on 9 March 1809, Murray was most gratified to be appointed quartermaster-general in the Peninsula under Wellesley, whom, since working with him in Denmark, he had regarded as his ideal of a commander. He held this appointment, with a year's interval in 1812, until the end of the war in 1814. His punctual, businesslike methods, tactful handling of the officers in his department, extraordinary topographical memory, and imperturbability in moments of crisis, enabled him, almost intuitively, to interpret Wellington's wishes, to reduce them to unambiguous operation orders, and then, as he said, to watch, 'day and night even, their just execution'. Until the arrival in 1812 of his replacement, Colonel J. W. Gordon, the true value of such assistance was not perhaps fully appreciated by Wellington, who was soon expressing his dissatisfaction and his anxiety for Murray's return. Murray needed little prompting and was back at headquarters on 17 March 1813, in time to plan the great advance into Spain. He had been promoted brigadier-general in 1811, major-general in 1812 and, on 11 September 1813, after the victory of Vitoria, was made KB. In December 1814 he accepted a lieutenant-general's command in Canada. There news of the renewal of war in Europe did not reach him until 30 May 1815, too late for him to take any part in the fighting, much to Wellington's disappointment. But on the organization of the army of occupation he was appointed chief of staff of the allied army of 150,000 men and quartermaster-general of the British contingent. He received several foreign honours. On 14 June 1820 he was made a DCL at Oxford and in January 1824 was elected a fellow of the Royal Society.

Murray was governor of the Royal Military College, Sandhurst, from 1819 to 1824. From 1824 to 1830 he was MP for Perth County in the Dundas interest. He succeeded Viscount Beresford as lieutenant-general of the ordnance in

1824 and from 1825 he held the command-in-chief in Ireland until 26 May 1828, when, on William Huskisson's resignation as secretary of state for the colonies, Wellington offered him the vacant post. Murray had by this time married, on 28 April 1825, Lady Louisa Erskine (1777–1842), sister of the first marquess of Anglesey and estranged wife of Lieutenant-General Sir James Erskine, bt, who had died during the divorce proceedings. From 1828 they and their daughter, born in Erskine's lifetime and the 'Miss Murray' of Thomas Lawrence's famous portrait now at Kenwood House, London, lived in style at 5 Belgrave Square, London, then newly built.

As colonial secretary Murray was a conscientious administrator though an uninspiring speaker in the house, and he supported Catholic emancipation. He left office on the fall of the Wellington government in November 1830. He opposed parliamentary reform and was defeated in the 1832 general election, but was re-elected for Perthshire in a by-election in 1834. He stood unsuccessfully for Westminster in 1837, and for Manchester in 1839. He was master-general of the ordnance in Peel's brief ministry of 1834–5 and again, but without a seat in cabinet, in Peel's ministry of 1841 to June 1846. He was successively colonel of the 72nd foot from 1817, of the 42nd from 1823, and of the Royal Scots from 1843 after receiving promotion as general in November 1841. His constant employment in state office prevented him from realizing his cherished ambition of writing a history of the Peninsular War. He did on the other hand contribute critical reviews of William Napier's *History of the War in the Peninsula* to the *Quarterly Review* in 1836 (so earning the 'Jacobin Colonel's' undying hostility and many officers' sincere gratitude) and, more to his liking, he prepared an edition of his operation orders to accompany an elaborate *Atlas* of the war (1841). He later edited Marlborough's dispatches in five volumes (1845).

Murray was described as tall and thin, with a very winning countenance and manners entirely devoid of affectation. Lady Murray had died on 23 January 1842 and, following a long illness, Murray died in his home in Belgrave Square, London, on 28 July 1846. He was buried on 5 August beside his wife in Kensal Green cemetery, Middlesex; Wellington attended the interment. Murray was after Wellington the most respected soldier of his time in Britain, whose opinion carried immense weight both at home and abroad and not only on military matters.

S. G. P. WARD

Sources NL Scot., Murray MSS, Adv. MSS 1–207 (47.1.1–46.6.8) · NL Scot., Murray MSS Acc. 6026/28–35 · PRO, W. O. 80 · Scottish Register House, Hope of Luffness MSS, G. D. 364 · Royal Military Academy, Sandhurst, Le Marchant MSS · Sir W. Clinton, MS diary, JRL · Hopetoun House, Linlithgow MSS · *The dispatches of … the duke of Wellington … from 1799 to 1818*, ed. J. Gurwood, 2nd edn, enl., 8 vols. (1844–7) · *Supplementary despatches (correspondence) and memoranda of Field Marshal Arthur, duke of Wellington*, ed. A. R. Wellesley, second duke of Wellington, 15 vols. (1858–72) · *GM*, 2nd ser., 26 (1846), 424–6 · Burke, *Peerage* (1967) · S. G. P. Ward, *Wellington's headquarters: a study of the administrative problems in the Peninsula, 1809–14* (1957) · S. G. P. Ward, 'General Sir George Murray', *Journal of the Society for Army Historical Research*, 58 (1980), 191–208 · N. Gash, *Mr Secretary Peel: the life of Sir Robert Peel to 1830* (1961) · N. Gash, *Sir Robert Peel: the life of Sir Robert Peel after 1830* (1972) · *DNB* · W. Steven, *The history of the high school of Edinburgh* (1849) · LPL, Erskine v. Erskine case MSS · parish register, parish of Sunninghill, 1813–37, Berks. RO [marriage] · grave, Kensal Green cemetery, London · *Gazettes*

Archives NL Scot., corresp. and papers; family corresp. · PRO, corresp. and papers, WO80 | BL, corresp. with Lord Aberdeen, Add. MS 43238 · BL, corresp. with Sir Rowland Hill, Add. MSS 35059–35060 · BL, letters to Sir John Moore, Add. MS 57543 · BL, letters to Macvey Napier, Add. MSS 34619–34620 · BL, corresp. with Sir Robert Peel, Add. MSS 40367–40588 *passim* · Lpool RO, letters to Lord Stanley · NA Scot., corresp. with Lord Dalhousie · NA Scot., corresp. with G. W. Hope · NAM, letters to Sir Benjamin D'Urban, 7805/46 · NL Scot., letters to Sir Robert Kennedy · NL Scot., corresp. with Lord Lynedoch · NL Scot., corresp. with eighth marquess of Tweeddale · NRA Scotland, priv. coll., letters to Lord Hopetoun · priv. coll., letters to Lord Seaton · PRO NIre., corresp. with Lord Anglesey, D619 · PRO NIre., corresp., with Lord Belmore, D3007 · U. Southampton L., letters to first duke of Wellington · W. Sussex RO, letters to duke of Richmond · Woburn Abbey, letters to George William Russell

Likenesses T. Heaphy, pencil and watercolour drawing, 1814, NPG · T. Lawrence, oils, 1829, priv. coll. · J. Linnell, crayon, 1832, Scot. NPG · H. W. Pickersgill, oils, 1832, Perth Art Gallery · J. Linnell, chalk drawing, 1836, NPG · J. Linnell, chalk drawing, 1836, Scot. NPG · J. P. Knight, oils, exh. RA 1843, Wellington Museum, London · H. Meyer, stipple (after portrait by T. Lawrence, 1812), BM, NPG; repro. in W. Jerdan, *National portrait gallery of illustrious and eminent personages*, 5 vols. (1830–34), vol. 2 · H. W. Pickersgill, oils, Scot. NPG

Wealth at death approx. £9700: will; PRO, solicitors' accounts, 1845–9, W.O. 80/6

Murray, George (1784–1860), bishop of Rochester, the second son of Lord George *Murray (1761–1803), bishop of St David's, and his wife, Anne Charlotte Grant (1765–1844), and great-grandson of Lord George Murray, the Jacobite general, was born at Farnham, Surrey, on 12 January 1784. One of his sisters was the writer and courtier Amelia Matilda *Murray. He matriculated at Christ Church, Oxford, in 1801, graduating BA in 1806 and MA in 1810. He married on 5 May 1811 Lady Sarah Hay Drummond, second daughter of Robert, ninth earl of Kinnoull. They had five sons and six daughters.

In 1808, like his father before him, Murray became archdeacon of Man, and on 22 May 1813 he was nominated bishop of Sodor and Man by his kinsman the duke of Atholl. Following his consecration on 6 March 1814, he was created DD by diploma at Oxford. As bishop, he attempted to improve the social and intellectual status of the Manx clergy by the judicious exercise of his episcopal patronage.

Murray was translated to Rochester in 1827, and from 1828 to 1845 held this see with the deanery of Worcester *in commendam*. Although personally untroubled by the implications of Roman Catholic emancipation in 1829, and critical in 1834 of the harsher aspects of the Poor Law Amendment Bill, Murray was on most matters an inflexible conservative, and delivered a long and important speech against the Reform Bill on its second reading on 13 April 1832. He consistently opposed measures proposed by the ecclesiastical commission for the reform of the church in England and Ireland during the 1830s, objected to the threatened suppression of the diocese of Sodor and Man in 1836, deplored the weakening of church control over

George Murray (1784–1860), by Samuel Lane, exh. RA 1849

the appointment of schools inspectors in 1840, and voted and protested against the repeal of the corn laws in 1846. While reluctant to become involved in the notorious dispute of 1848–53 between the dean and chapter of Rochester and the Revd Robert Whiston, his eventual judgement, as visitor, provided an equitable basis for the resolution of this seemingly intractable argument. Although he assisted at the consecration of Michael Solomon Alexander as bishop for Jerusalem in 1841, he also played a leading part in the Bishops' Remonstrance against the appointment of the supposedly heterodox Renn Dickson Hampden to the see of Hereford in December 1847. However, he took care on this occasion to dissociate himself from Hampden's other critics, of the Tractarian school, whose extremism and taste for innovation he had already deplored in his episcopal charges of 1840 and 1843.

Murray continued to make occasional contributions to debates in the House of Lords until 1857, and was said to have been the last English bishop to wear his wig out of doors. He died at his town house in Chester Square, London, on 16 February 1860, and was buried in the family vault at Kensal Green cemetery. At the time of his death he was the oldest member of the episcopal bench.

RICHARD SHARP

Sources *The Times* (17 Feb 1860) · *The Times* (23 Feb 1860) · Boase, *Mod. Eng. biog.* · [H. T. Ryall], *Portraits of eminent conservatives and statesmen*, 2 [1846], no. 17 · C. K. Francis Brown, *A history of the English clergy, 1800–1900* (1953), 216 · R. A. Soloway, *Prelates and people: ecclesiastical social thought in England, 1783–1852* (1969) · P. Virgin, *The church in an age of negligence: ecclesiastical structure and problems of church reform, 1700–1840* (1989) · R. Arnold, *The Whiston matter* (1961)

Likenesses B. R. Faulkner, oils, exh. RA 1829, Christ Church Oxf. · J. Learmouth, bust, 1836 · S. Lane, oils, exh. RA 1849, NPG [*see illus.*] · W. and F. Holl, engraving (after B. R. Faulkner) · F. C. Lewis, stipple (after J. Slater), BM, NPG · T. H. Maguire, lithograph · oils, Blair Castle

Murray, Sir George Herbert (1849–1936), civil servant, was born on 27 September 1849 at Southfleet, Kent, the elder son of George Edward Murray (1818–1854), fellow of All Souls College, Oxford, and rector of Southfleet, and his wife, Penelope Frances Elizabeth Pemberton Austin (*d.* 1910), youngest daughter of Brigadier-General John Austin. The great-grandson of Lord George *Murray, bishop of St David's, second son of John *Murray, third duke of Atholl, he was heir presumptive to the dukedom from 1865 to 1871 and second heir presumptive at the time of his death.

Educated at Harrow School and Christ Church, Oxford, Murray took third-class honours in the school of *literae humaniores* in 1872. He entered the Foreign Office in the following year under the system of limited competition after nomination by the secretary of state, and was transferred to the Treasury in 1880, with a post as second-class clerk in the department of the auditor of the civil list. Murray married on 23 September 1879 Helen Mary (*d.* 1932), eldest daughter of John Mulholland, later first Baron Dunleath. He was appointed secretary to successive royal commissions on the depression of trade (1886), on gold and silver (1887), and on conditions in the western highlands and islands of Scotland (1889). He was private secretary to the first lord of the Treasury throughout Gladstone's last ministry (August 1892 to March 1894), a post he retained under Lord Rosebery. In 1897 he was appointed chairman of the Board of Inland Revenue, and in 1899 transferred to the Post Office as secretary. In 1903, on the retirement of Sir Francis Mowatt, he became joint permanent secretary of the Treasury, in conjunction with Sir Edward Hamilton, who handled financial matters, while Murray dealt with administration. When Hamilton retired in October 1907 Murray became sole permanent secretary, and in 1909, additionally, auditor of the civil list. He retired from the civil service on 23 July 1911.

Although described by Hamilton as a 'born administrator' (MSS Asquith, vol. 19, 25 Sept 1907), there is evidence to suggest that Murray was somewhat lacking in imagination. In 1906–7 he chaired the government factories and workshops committee, which had been set up to inquire into 'the economy of production (of munitions) in time of peace and the power of expansion in time of war'. Unfortunately Murray seems to have showed much more interest in economy than in expansion, and it has been claimed that the committee's recommendations contributed to the 'shell shortage' of 1915 (Trebilcock, 152–4). He was a civil servant of the old school, who worked best by written minutes, and who, when Lloyd George became chancellor in 1908, refused to adapt to the latter's habit of ignoring paperwork and relying on oral briefings. As a result, Lloyd George bypassed Murray and looked to Robert Chalmers, the chairman of the Board of Inland Revenue, for advice on more than revenue matters, as well as to John Bradbury, the principal clerk in charge of the Treasury's finance division. Having been brought up in Gladstonian principles of public finance, Murray's personal political inclination was towards this school of Liberalism, and he was opposed to many of the ideas introduced in Lloyd George's budget of 1909, particularly the supertax and allowances for taxpayers with children.

Murray had a dry sense of humour: he once opposed a proposal to spend money on a subway under Whitehall for the secret disposal of army's archives in the event of an invasion on the grounds that 'the last objective of any intelligent invader … would be the War Office' (Asquith, 1.256). He was very fond of gossip and enjoyed the good things in life, being a connoisseur of food, wine, and cigars. He regularly attended dinners at Grillons, The Club, and the Society of Dilettanti, and was a familiar figure at Brooks's.

Murray was appointed KCB in 1899, GCB in 1908, and GCVO in 1920, and was sworn of the privy council in 1910. He was elected an honorary student of Christ Church in 1913. He continued to be a public servant in his retirement: on the outbreak of war in 1914 he took a leading part in the management of the Prince of Wales's Fund and in 1915 he became chairman of the committee on the employment of soldiers and sailors disabled in the war. He was a member of the Haldane committee which reported on the machinery of government in 1918. He also held directorships in a number of companies, including the Westminster Bank and the Southern Railway.

Murray was predeceased by his wife, who was honoured with a CBE in 1914 and died on 19 February 1932. He died at his home, 39 Bryanston Court, London, on 4 April 1936. He was survived by a son, Sir George Evelyn Pemberton *Murray (1880–1947) KCB, who was successively secretary to the Post Office and chairman of the board of customs and excise, and a daughter, Irene Helen.   G. C. PEDEN

Sources DNB · The Times (6 April 1936) · B. K. Murray, The people's budget, 1909/10: Lloyd George and liberal politics (1980), 78–80, 122–3, 164–6 · H. Roseveare, The treasury: the evolution of a British institution (1969), 178, 228–31, 244 · Bodl. Oxf., MSS Asquith · H. H. Asquith, Memories and reflections, 1852–1927, ed. A. Mackintosh, 2 vols. (1928), vol. 1, pp. 254–6 · C. Trebilcock, 'War and the failure of industrial mobilisation, 1899–1914', War and economic development: essays in memory of David Joslin, ed. J. M. Winter (1975), 139–64 · PRO, Treasury records · Foster, Alum. Oxon. · Burke, Peerage (1879) · Burke, Peerage (1931) · Burke, Peerage (1959)
Archives BL, corresp., Add. MSS 49458 passim · Blair Castle, Perthshire, corresp. and papers · NRA Scotland, priv. coll., corresp. and MSS | BL, letters to Herbert, Viscount Gladstone, Add. MSS 46055–46072 · BL, corresp. with W. E. Gladstone, Add. MSS 44335, 44516–44520, 44522, 44524–44525, 44648 · Bodl. Oxf., corresp. with H. H. Asquith · Bodl. Oxf., corresp. with Sir William Harcourt and Lewis Harcourt · CUL, letters to Lord Acton · NL Scot., corresp. with Lord Rosebery · NL Scot., corresp. mainly with Lord Rosebery · PRO NIre., letters to Lady Londonderry · Tyne and Wear Archives service, letters to Lord Rendel
Wealth at death £27,991 11s.: probate, 29 May 1936, CGPLA Eng. & Wales

Murray, George Raymond Beasley- (1916–2000),

Baptist minister and biblical scholar, was born on 10 October 1916 at 34 Horton Road, Hackney, London, the son of Alfred George Beasley (1890–1917), grocer's assistant, and his wife, Kathleen Lydia Brady (1895/6–1950). His father served with the anti-aircraft section of the Royal Garrison Artillery and was killed in a road accident on 13 December 1917. His mother subsequently married, in 1919, George Murray, a fitter, and George thereafter took his stepfather's name in addition to his own. He had an uneasy childhood in Leicester. Performing at public concerts before the age of seventeen, his career seemed set as a concert pianist. This was interrupted by an encounter with a couple of students from Spurgeon's College, London, which led to his conversion, and a commitment to serve in the Baptist ministry. For this, following secondary education at the City of Leicester Boys' School, he undertook study at Spurgeon's College and King's College in the University of London. Amid the London blitz he began his first pastorate at Ilford (1941–8), then for two years at Cambridge, he combined the pastorate with further studies at Jesus College. This provided him with just the right combination of pastoral experience and scholarly study for becoming a tutor at Spurgeon's in 1950. In 1956 he was called to the international Baptist seminary at Rüschlikon, near Zürich. In 1958 he was called back to become the principal of Spurgeon's College, in which position he served for fifteen years. He was so committed to this work that he declined the offer of the prestigious Rylands chair of biblical criticism in the University of Manchester. In 1973, however, he accepted the senior post of professor in New Testament interpretation at Southern Baptist Theological Seminary in Louisville, Kentucky, which gave him greater opportunity to develop his mature theological thought. In 1980 he returned to Britain to a very active retirement. He married Ruth Weston (b. 1922) on 4 April 1942, a marriage that lasted for fifty-eight years and produced one daughter and three sons, one of whom also served as principal of Spurgeon's College from 1986 to 1992.

Beasley-Murray believed that evangelical faith must rest upon sound theological scholarship, and this objective he served superbly well. His first major work was Jesus and the Future (1954), a study based on Mark, chapter 13, to which he returned in one of his last substantial works, Jesus and the Last Days (1993). His Baptism in the New Testament (1962), the standard twentieth-century treatment of the subject, for which he was awarded the London DD, remained in print for almost forty years. Again this was a recurring theme of his work. A third seminal work was his Jesus and the Kingdom of God (1986), which secured him a Cambridge DD. Many other writings included significant commentaries on Matthew (1984), John (1987), and the Book of Revelation (1974). Never blinkered in his evangelicalism, he led the team that translated Rudolf Bultmann's commentary on John (1971) and himself translated Baptism in the Thought of St Paul (1950), by the distinguished Roman Catholic scholar Rudolf Schnackenburg. He received honorary doctorates from McMaster University, Hamilton, Canada, and the council for national academic awards in Britain.

Although never narrowly sectarian, Beasley-Murray served his denomination well not only in preparing men and women for ministry but also in serving, for example, on the editorial committee that produced the new hymnbook of 1962. For ten years he chaired the denomination's advisory committee for church relations, and in this capacity in 1967 he presented to the assembly the important report *Baptists and Unity*, urging a maintenance of ecumenical relations. He acted upon his own precepts by working for the British Council of Churches and serving as secretary of the European section of the faith and order commission of the world council. A wholly convinced Baptist, he demonstrated a generous spirit towards other traditions that was unique among those of his own faith and order. Thus in a Festschrift to a former colleague at Rüschlikon, the acknowledged authority on baptism in the New Testament, he reached the conclusion that infant baptism could in certain circumstances be considered as 'a valid accommodation of the norm', and made a remarkable appeal:

> Churches which practise believer's baptism should consider acknowledging the legitimacy of infant baptism, and allow members of Paedobaptist churches the right to interpret it according to their consciences. This would carry with it the practical consequences of believer-baptist churches refraining from baptising on confession of faith those who have been baptised in infancy. ('The problem of infant baptism: an exercise in possibilities', *Festschrift for Günter Wagner*, Faculty of the Baptist Theological Seminary, 1994, 13)

The call to 'demythologize' the gospels became newsworthy in the controversy surrounding the publication of Bishop John Robinson's *Honest to God*, and Beasley-Murray became ever more conscious of the need for devoted scholarship to assemble a coherent text of the New Testament from the many manuscripts and fragments which lie behind the text, and then to interpret and apply the message that the text exhibited. Controversy came to his own denomination in 1971, when the Baptist Union Assembly debated the question 'how much of a man was Jesus Christ?' Believing that the historic faith was under threat, Beasley-Murray, who in 1968 had been president of the union, vacated the chair of the union's council so that he could participate in the debate. More important than the debate was the scrupulous quality and impartiality of the scholarship he devoted to exploring and defending basic New Testament themes. He thereby showed that dedicated scholarship could fulfil an evangelistic purpose. George Beasley-Murray died in the Royal Sussex County Hospital, Brighton, on 23 February 2000, survived by his wife.   J. H. Y. BRIGGS

Sources P. Beasley-Murray, *Fearless for truth* (2002) · *The Times* (15 March 2000) · *The Independent* (18 March 2000) · *WWW* · private information (2004) · personal knowledge (2004) · b. cert. · m. cert. · m. cert. [mother's remarriage] · d. cert. · Commonwealth War Graves Commission, www.cwgc.org [debt of honour register]

Likenesses photograph, repro. in *The Times* · photograph, repro. in *The Independent*

Murray, George Redmayne (1865–1939), physician, was born at Newcastle upon Tyne on 20 June 1865, the eldest son of William Murray (1839–1920), a physician, and his wife, Frances Mary (*d*. in or before 1885), daughter of Giles Redmayne. Murray was educated at Eton College and, from 1883, at Trinity College, Cambridge, where he graduated in 1886 with first-class honours in part one of the natural sciences tripos. He then joined a group of Cambridge medical students who had been attracted to University College Hospital, London, by the teaching of Sydney Ringer and Victor Horsley. He won the Fellowes junior clinical silver and the senior clinical gold medals, and passed his final examinations in 1888. He graduated MB in 1889, and obtained the MD in 1896. He envisaged a career in experimental medicine, and between 1889 and 1890 he visited medical clinics in Berlin and Paris, carrying letters of introduction from Horsley. He returned to Newcastle in 1891, and worked there as pathologist to the Hospital for Sick Children, and was lecturer in bacteriology and comparative pathology in the University of Durham College of Medicine. While in that post, and at the early age of twenty-six, Murray made the discovery that brought him fame.

Murray devised an effective treatment for myxoedema, which is due to deficiency of thyroid hormone, by the injection of an extract of sheep thyroid. This was the first example of successful hormone replacement therapy, and reduced the scepticism towards organotherapy in Great Britain. Horsley was a member of the committee set up by the London Clinical Society in 1882 to investigate myxoedema and other diseases in which defective thyroid function was suspected. It reported in 1888. In February 1890 Horsley suggested animal thyroid grafts for the treatment of myxoedema. Murray and Horsley corresponded about treatment, and in December 1890 Horsley noted that injection of thyroid extract could do no harm. Murray said that his idea of injecting thyroid extracts came from hearing about successful therapy of a human with a sheep thyroid graft, and the suggestion that the rapid improvement following the graft was due to simple absorption of the juice of the sheep's thyroid gland by the tissues of the patient. Murray's writings give no indication that he was aware of the attempts of C.-E. Brown-Sequard in Paris to rejuvenate old men by the injection of testicular extracts, or the *British Medical Journal*'s sceptical note in 1889 on 'the pentacle of rejuvenescence'.

In February 1891 Murray showed a patient with myxoedema at a meeting of the Northumberland and Durham Medical Society in Newcastle, and suggested that 'it would be worthwhile to try the hypodermic injection of an emulsion or extract of the thyroid gland of the sheep'. He obtained permission from the patient, and at the October meeting he showed her greatly improved after six months' treatment. These findings were published in the *British Medical Journal* in 1891 as were further cases in 1892. The effectiveness of the treatment was rapidly confirmed. Hector W. G. Mackenzie and E. L. Fox separately introduced oral treatment in 1892, and Murray's first patient was then treated with oral thyroid extracts for many years. The minute book of the British Medical Association notes a grant of £15 for the year 1893–4 for studying thyroidectomy in animals.

Murray married, in 1892, Annie Katharine, daughter of Edward Robert Bickersteth, a well-known Liverpool surgeon, a cousin of Edward Bickersteth (1814–1892), dean of Lichfield, and of Robert Bickersteth, bishop of Ripon (1816–1884). They had three sons, two of whom were killed in the First World War, and a daughter.

With his reputation established, Murray was appointed Heath professor of comparative pathology at Durham in 1893, and physician to the Royal Victoria Infirmary at Newcastle in 1898. In 1908 he was appointed professor of systematic medicine at Manchester University, which carried with it the post of physician to the Manchester Royal Infirmary. The choice of Murray for the vacant post raised a storm of local opposition, which his friendliness and competence overcame. However, he did not return to experimental medicine, but occupied himself in teaching, medical practice, and university administration. He retired in 1925.

Murray received many honours. He was Goulstonian (1899) and Bradshaw (1905) lecturer to the Royal College of Physicians, and on the council (1914–17), member of the Medical Research Committee (1916–18), which later became the Medical Research Council, and president of the Association of Physicians in 1936. Honorary degrees were conferred upon him by Durham and Dublin universities. Two of his most practical achievements were work as a member of several departmental committees of the Home Office on dust diseases in card-room workers, and his service as a consulting physician to the British forces in Italy, 1918–19. He retired from active work, because of increasing angina, a few years before his death. He died at his home, the Manor House, Mobberley, Cheshire, on 21 September 1939. He was survived by his wife.

GEOFFREY L. ASHERSON

Sources *BMJ* (30 Sept 1939), 707–8 · *The Lancet* (30 Sept 1939), 767 · C. N. Armstrong, 'George Redmayne Murray, 1865–1939: the first use of thyroid extract for the treatment of myxoedema', *Medicine in Northumbria: essays on the history of medicine in the north-east of England*, ed. D. Gardner-Medwin, A. Hargreaves, and E. Lazenby (1993), 310–15 · M. Borell, 'Organotherapy, British physiology, and the discovery of the internal secretions', *Journal of the History of Biology*, 9 (1976), 235–68 · G. R. Murray, 'Note on the treatment of myxoedema by hypodermic injections of an extract of the thyroid gland of a sheep', *BMJ* (10 Oct 1891), 796–7 · G. R. Murray, 'The life-history of the first case of myxoedema treated by thyroid extract', *BMJ* (13 March 1920), 359–60 · *DNB* · *CGPLA Eng. & Wales* (1939) · personal knowledge (1949) [*DNB*] · *WWW* · Venn, *Alum. Cant.*
Likenesses photograph, repro. in *The Lancet*, 766
Wealth at death £29,167 14s. 2d.: probate, 6 Dec 1939, *CGPLA Eng. & Wales*

Murray, George Robert Milne (1858–1911), botanist and algologist, was born at Arbroath, Forfarshire, on 11 November 1858, one of the eight children of George Murray (*b.* 1814), a tradesman, and his wife, Helen Margaret Sayles (*b.* 1819). Alexander Stuart *Murray (1841–1904), keeper of Greek and Roman antiquities at the British Museum, was an older brother. Murray was educated at

Arbroath high school, and in 1875 studied under Anton de Bary at Strasbourg. In 1876 he became an assistant in the botanical department of the British Museum. Initially responsible for the cryptogamic collections, in 1895 he became keeper of the department. He was lecturer on botany at St George's Hospital medical school from 1882 to 1886, and to the Royal Veterinary College from 1890 to 1895. In 1884 he married Helen (*d.* 1902), daughter of William Welsh of Walker's Barns and Boggieshallow, Brechin, Forfarshire; the couple later had a son and a daughter.

In 1886 Murray acted as naturalist to the solar eclipse expedition to the West Indies, an area to which he returned on a dredging expedition the following year. Two years later he chartered a tug for a dredging expedition 300 miles west of Ireland, on which he was accompanied by a party of naturalists. In 1901 he became director of the civilian scientific staff of the national Antarctic expedition in HMS *Discovery*, under Captain R. F. Scott, although he accompanied the expedition only as far as Cape Town. For some years he devoted much of his vacations to the collection of phytoplankton in the Scottish lochs from the fishery board's yacht *Garland*. Murray was elected a fellow of the Linnean Society in 1878, apparently in contravention of the by-laws, as he was then under age, and became its vice-president in 1899. He was elected a fellow of the Royal Society in 1897.

Murray's main contribution to botany is his work on marine algae. He wrote a number of papers on the subject, including 'The distribution of marine alga in space and time' (*Journal of the Linnean Society*, 1883) and 'A comparison of the marine floras of the warm Atlantic, the Cape of Good Hope and the Indian Ocean' (*Phycological Memoirs*, 1892). He also reported on the discovery of at least one new species of phytoplankton. Apart from his work on marine algae, Murray also wrote the section on fungi in Henfrey's *Elementary Course of Botany* (3rd edn, 1878), contributed the articles on fungi and vegetable parasitism to the ninth edition of the *Encyclopaedia Britannica* (1879 and 1885), and published a *Handbook of Cryptogamic Botany*, together with Alfred William Bennett. Between 1882 and 1885 he published three reports on his investigations of the salmon disease, undertaken at the instance of Professor Huxley. From 1892 to 1895 he edited *Phycological Memoirs, being Researches Made in the Botanical Department of the British Museum*, of which three parts appeared, each containing papers by him, and in 1895 he published *Introduction to the Study of Seaweeds*. He also edited *The Antarctic Manual* for the expedition of 1901, arranging the contents and securing contributors, but only writing some four pages of instructions on plant collecting. He retired from his position at the British Museum in 1905, on the grounds of ill health. He died at Stonehaven, Kincardineshire on 16 December 1911.   G. S. BOULGER, *rev.* PETER OSBORNE

Sources *The Times* (19 Dec 1911) · *The Times* (21 Dec 1911) · *Gardeners' Chronicle*, 3rd ser., 50 (1911), 466 · *Journal of Botany, British and Foreign*, 50 (1912), 73 · Desmond, *Botanists*, rev. edn · *WWW* · *Men and women of the time* (1899)

Archives Scott Polar RI, journal | NL Scot., corresp. with Sir Patrick Gedders · Scott Polar RI, letters to H. R. Mill
Likenesses photograph, repro. in *Journal of Botany*, 73
Wealth at death £560 18*s*.: confirmation, 11 Jan 1912, *CCI*

Murray, Sir Gideon, of Elibank, Lord Elibank (*c.*1560–1621), politician and judge, was the third son of Sir Andrew Murray of Blackbarony (*c.*1500–1572), Peeblesshire, and Grisel Bethune or Beaton (*d.* 1579), daughter of Sir John Bethune of Criech in Fife and widow of William Scott of Buccleuch.

Murray is first recorded in a charter of 18 July 1565 by which he received the lands of Glenpole in Ettrick Forest. He attended the University of Glasgow, from which he graduated with the degree of MA in 1581. Soon afterwards (1582), he entered the ministry as minister of the parish of Auchterless in the presbytery of Turriff in Aberdeenshire. Being the holder of this charge, the revenues of which had been appropriated to the cathedral church of St Machar at Aberdeen before the Reformation, also meant that he was styled 'Chantor of Aberdeen', being first recorded as such in the *Register of the Privy Council* in April 1583 (*Reg. PCS*, 3.563–4). His career in the kirk was, however, dramatically cut short by his murder of a man named Atchison in 1585, for which crime he was imprisoned in Edinburgh Castle. The countess of Arran, wife of James Stewart, earl of Arran, who effectively governed Scotland from 1583 to 1585, intervened on his behalf. As a result he was released on the orders of the young James VI on 20 May 1585 and entered the service of his nephew (the son of his half-brother) Walter Scott of Buccleuch as chamberlain of his estates. In June 1587 Murray entered into an irregular marriage with Margaret, daughter of Dionysius Pentland, an Edinburgh miller. Margaret later took a case on behalf of herself and her children before the commissary court of Edinburgh as a result of which Murray was forced into having their marriage regularized by that court on 6 June 1601 and thus their three children, Patrick, William, and Agnes, were legitimated (NA Scot., lords and barons of Elibank, GD32/1/5).

During his time in the service of the laird of Buccleuch, Murray travelled to the continent as far as Italy. When he returned to Scotland he became involved in a border feud. Murray's master, Scott of Buccleuch, as the laird of Johnstone's uncle, was drawn into the long-running feud between the Maxwells and Johnstones. This culminated, on 7 December 1593, with Murray leading 500 Scotts against the Johnstones at the battle of Dryfe Sands at which Lord Maxwell was killed.

Murray was first recorded in crown service in July 1592 when he was given a commission by the privy council to demolish certain houses belonging to Walter Scott of Harden. Scott of Harden had been involved with 'the lait tressonable fact perpetrat aganis his Hienes awne persone at Falkland' when Francis Stewart, earl of Bothwell, made one of his characteristically unorthodox attempts to gain an audience with the king by forcing an entry into the royal palace in Fife. In March 1595 Murray was granted the lands of Elibank in Selkirkshire, which were erected into a barony in September 1601 thus giving him his designation as laird of Elibank. In October 1602 he was one of the border landlords who subscribed the king's 'general band' against thieves, murderers, and oppressors in the borders. This was part of the crown's strategy to bring order to the marches with England by persuading landlords to undertake responsibility for the conduct of their tenants. After the succession of James VI to the throne of England in 1603 Murray was appointed a border commissioner. He was knighted for his services on 4 March 1605 and in August 1607 was appointed to a new border commission under the earls of Dunbar and Cumberland, for which he received payment of £800. He was also appointed to the next border commission in 1611. In 1610 he was admitted to the refashioned privy council, appointed a commissioner for the exchequer, and received further money from the crown, through the offices of the earl of Dunbar, in the form of an annual pension of £1200. This was confirmed by parliament in October 1612 where Murray sat for the first time as a shire commissioner for Selkirkshire. At this meeting of the estates he was also elected as one of the lords of the articles, the business committee for receiving petitions and drafting legislation.

In November 1613 Murray became an ordinary lord of session, taking the title Lord Elibank. In December 1614 he was involved in examining the arrested Jesuit missionary John Ogilvie, who was subsequently executed for treason and canonized in 1976. His involvement in religious matters continued in 1615 when he was appointed a member of the unified court of high commission, the supreme court in all matters of ecclesiastical discipline throughout Scotland, under John Spottiswoode, archbishop of St Andrews. As a lord of session he was also appointed to a commission of justiciary for the north in 1616. As a result of taking on this wide array of duties for the crown his annual pension was augmented to £2400 and he was granted, for the duration of his life and that of his sons, the right to import 30 tuns of wine duty free.

Having been appointed one of the 'New Octavians' in April 1611 to manage the royal finances in Scotland, in November 1612 Elibank was given the offices of treasurer-depute, comptroller, and collector-depute of the new ecclesiastical lands with an annual salary of £1500. The lord high treasurer in Scotland was his cousin Robert Ker of Ferniehirst, earl of Somerset, who treated his office as an honorary one and, as a result, Elibank appears to have acted as *de facto* royal treasurer in Scotland. In this capacity he was instrumental in seeing to the repairing and enhancing of a number of royal properties in Scotland—notably in the reconstruction after its collapse of the north range at Linlithgow Palace in 1617 in the new Scottish Renaissance style. In the summer of the same year he also successfully oversaw the financing of James VI's only visit to Scotland subsequent to the regal union.

King James was so pleased with his good services to the crown that he became very fond of Elibank. On a visit by him to court, James is said to have bent down to pick up a glove which the treasurer-depute had dropped, saying that 'My predecessor, Queen Elizabeth, thought she did a favour to any man who was speaking with her when she let her glove fall, that he might take it up and give it her again; but, sir, you may say a king lifted up your glove' (Scot, 66). Elibank was suddenly to fall from favour in 1621, however, when 'calumnies' were spread about him at court by Sir James Stewart, who alleged that he had been involved in financial mismanagement. Mortally offended by this, he was sent back to Scotland and a day set for his trial. He took to his bed and refused to take either food or drink, 'imagining that he had no money either to get meat or drink to himself, and that way he died after a fortnight's sickness, of abstinence', in Edinburgh on 29 June 1621 (Scot, 66). His wife, three sons (Patrick, who was later raised to the peerage as Lord Elibank, William, and Walter, who was presumably born after June 1601), and one daughter (Agnes, who married Sir William Scott of Harden) all survived him. He left them assets to the value of £34,630 Scots after all debts were paid.

ALAN R. MACDONALD

Sources Scots peerage · Fasti Scot., new edn · J. Scot, The staggering state of Scottish statesmen from 1550 to 1650, ed. C. Rogers (1872) · Reg. PCS, 1st ser. · viscounts and barons of Elibank, NA Scot., GD32 · commissariot of Edinburgh, register of testaments, NA Scot., CC8/8/51, fols. 121–6
Archives NA Scot., viscounts and barons of Elibank, letters, writs, and copies of accounts as treasurer depute, etc., GD32 | NA Scot., letters to earl of Mar
Wealth at death £34,630 12s. 6d. Scots: commissariot of Edinburgh, register of testaments, NA Scot., CC8/8/51, fols. 121–6

Murray, (George) Gilbert Aimé (1866–1957), classical scholar and internationalist, was born in Sydney, Australia, on 2 January 1866, the second son of Sir Terence Aubrey *Murray (1810–1873) and his second wife, Agnes Ann, née Edwards (c.1835–1891). Murray's father, a prosperous stock farmer, had been since 1862 president of the legislative council of New South Wales; his elder brother Sir (John) Hubert Plunkett *Murray (1861–1940) later became governor of Papua. The family thus belonged to a colonial élite, though Murray's paternal ancestors had been expropriated from their Irish estates by the English in the seventeenth century and the Murrays thus tended to be 'agin the government'. W. S. Gilbert, after whom Murray was named, was his mother's cousin. In his childhood and youth Murray was known as George; he became Gilbert on his marriage in 1889. In 1875 he was sent to Southey's, a boarding-school 80 miles from Sydney. The bullying of pupils and mistreatment of animals he witnessed there prompted a lifelong detestation of cruelty in any form.

Education and marriage As Sir Terence's fortunes declined, the Murrays moved into progressively smaller houses. Four years after his father's death in 1873 George was taken to England by his mother to complete his education. This began with a year at a dame-school in Brighton and continued at Merchant Taylors' School, one of the nine leading (Clarendon) public schools, then still in London. Here Murray did well in rugby and won several prizes for his work as well as learning a little Hebrew. Francis Storr, head of the modern (non-classical) side of the school and an intelligent Liberal, became a strong influence and

(George) Gilbert Aimé Murray (1866–1957), by Elliott & Fry

a friend. Murray now began to read Spencer and Comte, and especially J. S. Mill, a lifelong influence, whose philosophical radicalism was reinforced for Murray by the idealism of Shelley. In 1884 he went on to St John's College, Oxford, to which the school was linked, with scholarships which eased a financial burden his mother could hardly have borne.

Already an accomplished composer in Latin and (especially) Greek, Murray was coached before he went up to Oxford by the well-known classical tutor J. Y. Sargent, who had examined at Merchant Taylors'. In his first year he won two university classical prizes, the Hertford and the Ireland—the former open to first- and second-year students, the latter to all years—as well as scoring forty runs in the freshmen's cricket match. He proceeded to gain first classes in both classical moderations (1885) and literae humaniores (1888), and to gain three more prizes for composition and the Craven scholarship (1886). His precocious gifts led to friendship with several Oxford scholars, including three eccentrics: Thomas Snow (his college tutor), Robinson Ellis, and David Margoliouth. He was also befriended by Arthur Sidgwick of Corpus Christi College, whose liberalism and instinctive feeling for Greek resonated with Murray's talents and assumptions.

By the end of his student career Murray had already

become involved in political debate, and had spoken several times at the Oxford Union. His support of home rule for Ireland was predictable but placed him in a small minority. His allegiance to Mill was tested, but not broken, by the idealist critiques developed in Oxford. Religion, too, was explored, and the agnostic Murray formed a friendship with the Anglican Charles Gore, then head of Pusey House. Several colleges offered him fellowships, and in 1888 he chose New College (taking an examination which the college had offered to waive). By this time he had finished his first work, the utopian adventure *Gobi or Shamo*; after several rejections, with support from Andrew Lang it was published by Longmans in 1889.

In 1887 Murray met Rosalind Howard, later countess of Carlisle, and with other promising young men was invited to the family home, Castle Howard. Here he met, and promptly fell in love with, his hostess's beautiful eldest daughter Lady Mary Henrietta (*d.* 1956). At first rejected, he paid court for two years, powerfully supported by Mary's mother, who when her daughter attempted to make conditions, overruled them. The engagement was finally announced in October 1889. By this time Murray was in a position to support a wife, since he had in July been elected to the chair of Greek at Glasgow and could expect an income of £1350 a year. His youth—he was twenty-three—and a lack of evidence of his social standing caused concern among the electors, but were swept aside by glowing academic testimonials and the support of Mary's father (the ninth earl of Carlisle) and James Bryce. The couple were married on 2 December 1889 at Castle Howard by Benjamin Jowett. The arrangements were made by the countess of Carlisle and Murray's mother was in effect excluded from the occasion, which remained a source of bitterness until her death in 1891.

Professor of Greek at Glasgow At Glasgow Murray entered a teaching environment very different from that of Oxford. He faced large classes (100 was not uncommon) of beginning students, some of them older than their new professor; most of them had never previously encountered Greek, which was compulsory for the general degree. Murray was obliged to collect and bank the student fees which formed part of his professorial income, and to mark large quantities of scripts, though in this he was helped by two assistants. Luckily he discovered a natural authority as a teacher and became a successful lecturer, though he intensely disliked the disciplinary aspects of the role. The contrast was noticed between Murray's unforced eloquence and the plainer style of his predecessor Richard Claverhouse Jebb. In his inaugural lecture Murray followed Jebb in taking a wide view of his subject, declaring that 'Greece, not Greek, is the real subject of our study. There is more in Hellenism than a language, although that language may be the liveliest and richest ever spoken by man.'

On his appointment Murray became a member of a local élite. He and Lady Mary played their part in social functions, and he made some firm friends, including A. C. Bradley; but their determined liberalism alienated some of his colleagues. In 1889 Murray became a director of the local workers' co-operative, and he and his wife shopped at the local Co-op. In politics he held to a Gladstonian Liberalism, and remained loyal to the teaching of Mill and of his follower John Morley. His public criticism of official policy in the First South African War placed him in a somewhat beleaguered radical Liberal minority. He also campaigned consistently for teetotalism, a speech to the university's Total Abstinence Society being printed as *Claims of Total Abstinence* (1894). The Glasgow teaching year ran from November to April, and thus left ample time for writing, though Murray suffered from a series of illnesses, which led in 1892 to his securing a year's leave on medical grounds. Much of this period was spent on what was to be his only return to Australia. In 1893 he circulated other scholars with a proposal for a series of classical texts. This came to nothing, as did a plan to compile an index to Euripides; but his ideas may have influenced D. B. Monro, Ingram Bywater, and Charles Cannan, who were planning what became the Oxford Classical Text series. In 1896 Murray accepted an invitation to contribute a text of Euripides. On all these projects he received much-appreciated advice from the great German Hellenist Ulrich von Wilamowitz-Moellendorff (1848–1931), to whom he wrote (in Greek) in 1894 after reading the latter's celebrated edition of Euripides' *Heracles*. Murray sent some of his most promising pupils to Wilamowitz's seminar, the first being Dorothy Murray (no relation) in 1901. The coincidence of name perhaps led to the supposition by his pupil Maurice Bowra and a later regius professor, Hugh Lloyd-Jones, that Murray himself studied under Wilamowitz. The encounter with Wilamowitz, whom he did not in fact meet until the latter's visit to England in 1908, was the most important of Murray's scholarly life: he was exhilarated by Wilamowitz's breadth of scholarship and his concern to bring ancient Greek literature to life, his commitment to the staging of his own translations of Greek drama, and his love (which Murray shared) of the plays of Ibsen. As Murray said in his presidential address to the Classical Association in 1918, 'The Scholar … must so understand as to relive'.

The other major product of Murray's time in Glasgow was his *History of Ancient Greek Literature* (1897), based on his student lectures. The book is eloquent, but though enthusiastically reviewed by his friend Verrall, had a mixed reception among classical scholars. In his preface Murray wrote that 'to read and re-read the scanty remains now left to us of ancient Greek literature is a pleasant and not a laborious task'; the Cambridge Greek scholar Henry Jackson wrote in his copy, 'Insolent puppy'. The major weakness of the book was that it fell between two stools, the short inspirational essay and the longer, more comprehensive account. Nevertheless it was several times reprinted.

In 1897 Murray was urged by his doctor to resign his chair on the ground of ill health, and in 1899 finally did so. One of his medical advisers encouraged him to apply for a pension under a contractual clause relating to permanent incapacity; but he later became reluctant to sign a certificate, and Murray withdrew his application. The Murrays, with their children Rosalind (*b.* 1890), Denis (*b.* 1892), and Agnes (*b.* 1894), moved to Churt in Surrey, to a house bought for them by Lady Carlisle. It was on her financial support that Murray now relied until 1905. The nature of his illness is unclear, but it is likely that both physical and psychosomatic illness played a part. An additional factor was the health of their daughter Rosalind: she had had diphtheria and pneumonia and was, Murray claimed, 'absolutely forbidden to live in Glasgow or anywhere near' (letter to David Murray, 31 March 1899, U. Glas., Archives and Business Records Centre, Mu.22–f.7 [10]). Rosalind was eventually dispatched abroad in the care of companions, and did not emerge into ordinary society until she was eighteen. In these early years the Murrays' marriage was not always harmonious. As well as concerns about their own and their children's health, they had clashes of temperament to deal with, and serious quarrels can be detected in their correspondence, even where it was later weeded by their daughter Rosalind and by Murray's secretary Jean Smith to remove evidence of disagreement.

While at Churt Murray began working on Euripides for the Oxford Classical Text series; his text appeared in three volumes in 1902, 1904, and 1909. For the first volume he relied heavily on material sent by Wilamowitz, but in 1901 he travelled to Paris, and in 1903 to Florence and Rome, to inspect manuscripts of the plays. The volumes were several times reprinted and enjoyed a long life, being replaced only by the text of James Diggle (1981, 1984, 1994). In his preface the new editor praised Murray's sober judgement, though he was less impressed by his care in collating manuscripts. Murray himself wrote to Bertrand Russell on 7 May 1901 that 'It is like laboriously cleaning a very beautiful statue' (Bodl. Oxf., MS G. Murray 165.13); in 1908, in the final stages of the project, he called it a 'disgusting task' (West, 118). This may explain why in 1906 Murray refused an invitation from Oxford University Press to produce an Oxford Classical Text edition of Sophocles; a task which he unsuccessfully urged on Wilamowitz in the following year. But it was in any case not Sophocles but Euripides, with his psychological insight, rationalism, and scepticism—not least towards established religion—who attracted Murray.

The other major task Murray worked on at Churt was a series of translations of Euripides and Aristophanes. Published from 1902 onwards, they were widely performed on stage, and made Murray's name in theatrical circles. They were also taken up by amateurs, including working-class groups. Murray gave readings from them in schools, universities, and elsewhere, impressing his audiences with his beautiful voice. Even in his late eighties his voice retained much of its beauty: in a review of Wilson's *Murray* Peter Levi described it as 'preposterously golden' (*The Independent*, 28 Jan 1988). It later became fashionable (a fashion led by T. S. Eliot) to decry the style of the translations as a too-faithful echo of Swinburne and Morris. Their original auditors, however, must have found in them a clarity and eloquence missing from the stilted language of many contemporary translations from Greek literature. Murray's reading of the *Hippolytus* at Cambridge in 1902

brought praise from Bertrand Russell, a cousin of Lady Mary's, to whom he became very close. He also met Rudyard Kipling, but while admiring his work he was repelled by him.

Murray's involvement with the theatre went well beyond these translations. During his recuperative sea journey in 1892–3 he had begun a play, *Carlyon Sahib*, a rather grim utopian tale set in India. Its production in 1899 was not a success, but by this time Murray had come into contact with leading members of the theatrical world, notably the critic William Archer, the actor–manager Harley Granville Barker, and the playwright and critic George Bernard Shaw. Of these the first became a firm friend, the second produced plays for Murray, and the last caricatured him, his wife, and his mother-in-law in *Major Barbara* (1905): Murray's character Adolphus Cusins was played by Barker. Archer advised Murray on his second play, *Andromache*, an attempt to write a tragedy for modern times. It was produced in 1901 but failed, though it impressed some severe critics, including Shaw and A. E. Housman. The philosopher Henry Sidgwick found it 'very spirited and excellent reading: but it seemed to me that between deliberate erudite barbarism and spontaneous natural modernity what we used to call the "Hellenic spirit" has somehow slipped through' (Sidgwick to H. G. Dakyns, 7 May 1900, Schultz collection, Newnham College, Cambridge). Murray's venture into theatrical life brought him into contact with several leading ladies, and led to quarrels with Lady Mary. In 1908 he admitted to her that 'I do become charmed by a certain kind of beauty … these rather emotional friendships do come drifting across my heart' (Wilson, 144), but reaffirmed his love for her, while insisting on the right to act according to his own judgement.

Murray also made academic friends in this period, including the Cambridge classical scholars Arthur Verrall and his friend Jane Harrison. In both cases their styles of work resonated powerfully but only partially with his own. Verrall, whom he had met in Switzerland in 1894, was an eloquent re-creator of Euripidean drama with a strong theatrical sense, but his interpretations were vitiated by rationalist fantasy. Some of the emendations he offered of Euripides' text Murray described as 'subtle and attractive', but treated with caution. Harrison was the moving spirit of what has been called Cambridge ritualism: the reinterpretation of Greek tragedy as a product of ritual practices. She, Murray, and her protégé Francis Cornford exchanged ideas about the new potential of anthropology for the analysis of Greek literature and religion, and (unusually for the time) contributed to each other's books. Thus Harrison's *Themis: a Study of the Social Origins of Greek Religion* (1912), which was dedicated to Murray, included his 'Excursus on the ritual forms preserved in Greek tragedy'. Murray, however, always remained unwilling to abandon his vision of a liberal and progressive Hellenism for Harrison's focus on primitive origins and chthonic religion. He recognized that each generation had constructed its own picture of Greece—the 'serene classical Greek' of Winckelmann was a phantom—but, while acknowledging that 'there is more flesh and blood in the Greek of the anthropologist', insisted that 'he is … a Hellene … without the spiritual life, without the Hellenism' (Murray, *A History of Greek Literature*, 1897, xv).

Professor of Greek at Oxford In 1905 the family moved to Oxford, after Murray accepted an offer of a fellowship at New College. At Oxford he found several talented undergraduates, including J. D. Denniston and Arnold Joseph Toynbee, later to become his son-in-law. In 1908 Murray was appointed regius professor of Greek in succession to Ingram Bywater; he had been dubious of his fitness for the post, and was ready to work with another candidate, the Scottish Hellenist John Burnet. In the same year Wilamowitz visited Oxford, giving two addresses in translations made by Murray; and in his inaugural lecture at Oxford Murray quoted Wilamowitz's declaration that 'ghosts will not speak till they have drunk blood; and we must give them the blood of our hearts', pleading for a revivifying of Greek studies. To this end he urged a reconstruction of the Oxford classical course to make it more integrated, wider in scope, and less mechanical in its training. For much of his time there, until he retired in 1936, Murray worked to broaden what he saw as an unduly limited and unintegrated Greats curriculum of history and philosophy: literature hardly figured, being largely confined to the first half of the preliminary (moderations) course, and the subjects which did were rarely placed within a wider context. To remedy this he organized a series of lectures prefatory to the course; these came to be known as the 'Seven against Greats' (a reference to Aeschylus's *Seven Against Thebes*, in which a band of heroes attacks the seven-gated city). The metaphor was apt for a challenge mounted from without to a system of teaching dominated not by professors, but by college tutors. Murray himself was never a 'college man', though he proved a staunch supporter of Somerville College until his death.

The most contentious issue Murray faced on taking up his chair, however, was that of compulsory Greek—a requirement made by Oxford (and Cambridge) of all students. The debate on whether it should be maintained, which had begun in 1870, had flared up recently, and Murray, with some heart-searching, adhered to his commitment to 'Greece, not Greek'. He became a leading spokesman for the abolition of the requirement by the university, making a number of enemies in the process. In 1909–10 he pressed a compromise position which was rejected. The issue was raised again after the First World War, and compulsory Greek was finally abolished in March 1920. By this time Murray was an influential member of the prime minister's committee on the position of classics in the educational system, appointed in 1919. In its report, published in 1921 and in part written by Murray, the committee concluded that while the position of Latin was fairly secure, Greek was in a precarious position, being taught to under 5 per cent of secondary school pupils.

At Glasgow Murray had considered a political career, but after his resignation resolved to devote himself to Greek literature, and refused several invitations to stand for parliament. Nevertheless he continued to speak in public about causes dear to his heart, including women's suffrage (he supported the suffragists but not the suffragettes). An important educational initiative in which Murray was involved for the rest of his life began when he agreed to act as general editor of the Home University Library in 1911. This series of short books, written by experts in an accessible style and aimed at the intelligent reading public, proved very popular; by the end of 1913 over a million had been sold. Murray's own contribution was *Euripides and his Age* (1913). In it he presented the poet as a radical and freethinker; the book belonged to a contemporary revaluation of a dramatist whom the Victorians had regarded as inferior to Aeschylus and, especially, Sophocles. If this was his best-known book, perhaps his best was *The Rise of the Greek Epic* (1907), based on a series of lectures at Harvard. In it Murray attempted to mediate between unitarian (single-author) and analytical (multipe-author or disintegrationist) views of the Homeric poems by seeing them as the products of a coherent tradition which moved steadily towards the expurgation of cruder elements in favour of a higher humanity. (In an appendix he discussed the possibility that some passages in the version handed down had been affected by bowdlerization.)

Another American lecture series, at Columbia in 1912, produced Murray's *Four Stages of Greek Religion* (1912). Here he again argued for a progressive Hellenism, highlighting the virtues of fifth-century Athens and reacting against the primitivist emphases of Jane Harrison. The book revealed its author to be a reverently agnostic rationalist with a maturing scepticism about religion.

International relations and Liberalism After the outbreak of war in 1914 Murray became increasingly involved in government activities, his initial doubts about Britain's declaration of war having been overcome by Sir Edward Grey's speech to the House of Commons on 3 August 1914. He wrote several pamphlets for the bureau of information, including *The Foreign Policy of Sir Edward Grey* (1915), and made lecture tours of Sweden and the USA. In 1917, despite the rise to power of Lloyd George, whose policies he detested, Murray became a civil servant and worked part-time for the Board of Education, whose president was his friend H. A. L. Fisher. He used his position to help those imprisoned as conscientious objectors, notably Bertrand Russell. Throughout the war Murray was involved in discussions about international peace, some of them within the League of Nations Society (1915), whose vice-president he became in 1916. In 1919 he was persuaded to stand as a Liberal parliamentary candidate for Oxford University; he did not campaign and barely saved his deposit.

By this time Murray was working for the League of Nations Union (1918), and on the foundation of the League of Nations itself in 1920 he began a long association which lasted until the Second World War, working with his friend Robert Cecil. In 1921 he attended the league's assembly by arrangement with his friend Jan Smuts, to whom he remarked on the 'rather large proportion of small dark Latin nations' (Murray to Smuts, 8 Oct 1921;

Murray, 185). He joined the league's committee of intellectual co-operation on its foundation in 1922 and succeeded Cecil as its chairman in 1928. Between the wars Murray was tireless in chairing international meetings, mediating, conciliating, and smoothing over differences. A proposal by George V to offer him membership of the Order of Merit in 1921 was blocked by Lloyd George; he was eventually appointed in 1941. (He had refused offers of knighthood in 1912 and 1917.) His name had also been on the list of the peerages that the Liberal government was contemplating creating if a forced creation became necessary in 1910 to get its budget through the House of Lords.

All this outside activity inevitably curtailed the time Murray spent on his university duties, and in 1923 the vice-chancellor, Lewis Farnell, asked Murray if his League of Nations Union duties were compatible with retaining his chair; Murray responded by offering up to half his salary to fund a readership in Greek. This was subsequently filled by Edgar Lobel. It was for Murray's efforts in the field of international relations that he became best-known, and he was a powerful inter-war Liberal presence; his stature was such that in 1929 Ramsay MacDonald's government considered asking him to become ambassador in Washington. Yet he was never an ordinary Liberal: his mind has been described as 'freakishly individual', and some found him 'oppressively virtuous and intellectual' (Bentley, 171). After his defeat in 1918 he stood unsuccessfully as candidate for the Oxford University parliamentary seat on five further occasions (1919, 1922, 1923, 1924, 1929). His political choices had in some ways led him into the wilderness. Like other Liberals, he had been sidelined by the growth of the Labour Party, and in Oxford his commitment to Asquith had distanced him politically from Herbert Fisher, who supported Lloyd George. Murray's drift away from party politics led him in the 1930s to a dead-end destination: the well-intentioned but bloodless Next Five Years Group, whose manifesto he signed in 1935.

The Murrays had moved in 1919 to their final home, Yatscombe on Boars Hill outside Oxford; after 1921 their finances were bolstered by inheritances from the earl and countess of Carlisle. They had difficulties with their two youngest children, Basil (b. 1902) and Stephen (b. 1908), and the health of the eldest son, Denis, had never recovered from his internment during the war. Denis died prematurely in 1930, Basil in 1937. The most serious blow, however, was the death of their daughter Agnes from peritonitis in 1922. This may have deepened Murray's involvement in the Society for Psychical Research, of which he had been president in 1916. He had taken part in psychic séances since the turn of the century and was regarded as having strong telepathic powers. Changes in relations within the family were manifested in part in religious commitments. In 1925 Lady Mary joined the Quakers, for whom she worked devotedly. Rosalind converted to Catholicism in 1933, and in 1939 published *The Good Pagan's Failure*, an anti-rationalist manifesto containing thinly veiled criticism of both her parents.

In the 1930s Murray played a major part in efforts to relocate and employ German refugee scholars. His collaboration with William Beveridge of the London School of Economics led to the foundation in 1934 of the Society for the Protection of Science and Learning, in which he worked with the Aristotelian scholar David Ross and with Walter Adams. One of the most notable refugee scholars brought to Oxford was Eduard Fraenkel, who was in 1935 elected to the Corpus chair of Latin. Fraenkel played a large part in advising Murray on the Oxford Classical Text edition of Aeschylus, to the point where Murray became tired of his somewhat peremptory admonitions. Advice was also forthcoming from Ludwig Radermacher of Vienna and from Denys Page. The resulting text, which appeared in 1937, was not well received, and has indeed been described as perverse and eccentric (Lloyd-Jones, 209). It is perhaps significant that in the lengthy discussion of his predecessors in his massive edition of the *Agamemnon* (1950), Fraenkel makes no mention of Murray. Murray in turn found Fraenkel's edition Germanic, lacking in taste despite all its learning: a judgment which echoed the contrast he had made during the First World War between English sensitivity to style and Teutonic systematic learning ('German scholarship', *Quarterly Review*, 223, 1915, 330–39). A later revision (1955), accomplished with the help of Eric Dodds, Edgar Lobel, and Paul Maas, suffered from a failure to take adequate account of the work of the Polish scholar Aleksander Turyn on the manuscript tradition of Aeschylus. It was sharply criticized after Murray's death by a combative young Cambridge scholar, who quoted the remark of the car designer Alec Issigonis that a camel was a horse designed by a committee (R. D. Dawe, *The Collation and Investigation of Manuscripts of Aeschylus*, 1964, 9–10). The replacement Oxford Classical Text, edited by Denys Page (1972), makes no mention of Murray's text—another significant silence. A general book on Aristophanes (*Aristophanes*, 1933) also received little critical acclaim. It was not a major work of scholarship, and the preface opens with the statement: 'There is little or no research in this book'; but it includes a notable discussion of the poet's skill as a parodist.

Murray's retirement from his chair in 1936 was marked by two collaborative volumes reflecting the breadth of his work: *Greek Poetry*, a set of academic essays, and *Essays in Honour of Gilbert Murray*, a wide-ranging tribute by eighteen friends. The appointment to the regius chair was in practice made by the prime minister, and Murray approached Stanley Baldwin with suggestions. The Oxford candidates were the learned but dry John Denniston and Maurice Bowra, whose scholarship Murray thought lacking in 'quality, precision and reality' (Murray to Baldwin, 2 June 1936 Bodl. Oxf., MSS G. Murray 77.138–40). His preferred candidate was Eric Dodds—also admired by Fraenkel—who was duly appointed to succeed him. Murray's intervention was unwise, breaking as it did the convention that one should not influence the appointment of a successor, and caused some scandal in Oxford; but in the event Dodds proved a worthy holder of the chair.

The League of Nations remained a major preoccupation

for Murray after his retirement, but its fortunes declined after its failure to prevent or end the Ethiopian war of 1935–6. Murray later declared that he and his colleagues had overestimated the reasoning powers of the masses and underestimated the strength of nationalism; nor had they realized that the league could not function properly unless the USA joined it. His continuing commitment to the league's ideals was reflected in his being elected president of the United Nations Association three times after the Second World War. Yet he became in this period increasingly conservative in his views. In 1950 he voted Conservative; in 1955 he was pleased with the Conservative election victory, and remarked that 'nearly all the educated people I meet are Liberal, but vote Conservative' (Wilson, 391). In 1956, to the surprise and alarm of some fellow Liberals, he supported the Anglo-French military action in Suez, regarding Nasser's nationalization of the canal as a barbaric encroachment on the civilized world. Within the United Nations Murray felt that 'We lie at the mercy of a mass of little barbarous nations, intoxicated with their own nationality who constitute a great majority of the Assembly' (ibid., 392).

Death and reputation From 1952 onwards Lady Mary was unable to cope with ordinary social life. Her death in September 1956 was a heavy blow for Murray, who became noticeably more frail. He himself died at Yatscombe on 20 May 1957 and was, according to his wishes, cremated. His final days gave rise to a controversy which was magnified by the religious divisions between his children. Shortly before his death he was visited by a Roman Catholic priest, but it remains unclear whether any rites were administered or, if so, whether Murray was capable of requesting or understanding them. A newspaper interview given by his (Catholic) daughter Rosalind led to a bitter argument within the family, and to public protests against his interment in Westminster Abbey, which nevertheless took place there, at the request of the United Nations Association, on 5 July 1957.

Murray's reputation as a scholar has suffered posthumously. Like his friend and fellow Hellenist J. W. Mackail, as a young man he abandoned plans to go to Germany to learn the methods of systematic research which were so highly developed there. Though his mastery of Greek gave him great insight into ancient texts, examining the minutiae of their transmission was not his forte, and in this area he remained a gentleman amateur. It is remarkable by modern standards that though regius professor of Greek for twenty-eight years, Murray published only a handful of articles in classical journals: indeed he once expressed a 'physical abhorrence for writing in periodicals' (West, 119). Nor did he produce commentaries on ancient texts, like his predecessor and successor in the Oxford chair. His interest was not in research, but in bringing Greece ('Greece not Greek') alive for those he taught: both undergraduates and the public at large. The decline in his posthumous reputation has been due largely to the passing of the generational styles and assumptions which underlay the success of his attempts to make the ancient world live for his contemporaries.

Where other scholars saw classical Greece as an eternal exemplar, Murray sought to reconstruct Hellenism as a progress toward perfection: a progress which involved constant struggle against opposing forces. More than anyone else he embodied a lifelong commitment to this ideal, in which for him Greece, liberalism, and international peace were equally involved. Yet his unremitting concern for others was based on an essentially aristocratic liberalism, and this, as his son-in-law Arnold Toynbee observed, came into increasing conflict after 1914 with the determination of the oppressed to improve their own lot (Murray, 214–16).

Gilbert Murray was seen even in his lifetime as a kind of secular saint; his friend Salvador de Madariaga called him a 'civic monk'. He was never a pacifist, and many were surprised at his sense of the thrill in war and his buoyancy at its outbreak in 1939. The extremism of others only strengthened his resolve to act fairly toward them; a serenity founded on inner strength persisted through marital problems, personal tragedies (notably the premature deaths of three of his five children), and the apparent collapse of the causes he believed in. His high principles, austere lifestyle, and teetotalism might suggest a humourless prig; as might Virginia Woolf's account of him in her diary:

> The cleanliness of Gilbert was remarkable; a great nurse must rub him smooth with pumice stone every morning; he is so discreet, so sensitive, so low in tone and immaculate in taste that you hardly understand how he has the boldness to beget children. (*Diary*, 1, 1977, 210, Oct 1918)

Yet a sense of humour and of the absurd both animated his conversation and enlivens his letters. His party tricks ranged from accomplished mimicry to taking his socks off without removing his shoes. Until old age he was physically fearless, whether in walking up ladders with his hands free (a favourite entertainment) or in attempting difficult routes through snow and ice. A man of many friends, he was nevertheless remarkably self-sufficient: as J. A. K. Thomson, who knew him better than most, commented after his death, 'while he was one of the friendliest, he was one of the remotest of men' (Thomson, 254). Eric Dodds's conclusion was that 'Whether he is to be ranked with the greatest of scholars depends on one's conception of scholarship; but that he was a truly great man no one who knew him could doubt' (Murray, 19).

CHRISTOPHER STRAY

Sources G. Murray, *An unfinished autobiography: with contributions by his friends*, ed. Jean Smith and A. Toynbee (1960) · D. Wilson, *Gilbert Murray OM* (1987) · F. J. West, *Gilbert Murray: a life* (1984) · R. L. Fowler, 'Gilbert Murray', *Classical scholarship: a biographical encyclopedia*, ed. W. W. Briggs and W. M. Calder (New York, 1990), 321–34 · J. A. K. Thomson, 'Gilbert Murray, 1866–1957', *PBA*, 43 (1957), 245–70 · DNB · *Essays in honour of Gilbert Murray* (1936) · S. Arlen, *The Cambridge ritualists: an annotated bibliography of the works by and about Jane Ellen Harrison, Gilbert Murray, Francis M. Cornford, and Arthur Bernard Cook* (1990) · H. Lloyd-Jones, *Blood for the ghosts: classical influences in the nineteenth and twentieth centuries* (1982), 195–214 · J. A. Thompson, 'Murray, Gilbert', *Biographical dictionary of internationalists*, ed. W. F. Kuehl (Westport, Connecticut, 1983) · P. E. Easterling, 'Gilbert Murray's reading of Euripides', *Colby Quarterly*, 33 (1997), 113–27 · A. D. Harvey, 'Gilbert Murray in the Public Record Office', *Oxford*

Magazine (1999), 12–13 [4th week, Michaelmas Term, 1999] • W. M. Calder and E. C. Kopff, 'The student–teacher topos in biographical fiction: Gilbert Murray and Ulrich von Wilamowitz-Moellendorff', *Classical Philology*, 72 (1977), 53–4 • U. Glas., Archives and Business Records Centre • C. Collard, 'Gilbert Murray on Rudyard Kipling: an unpublished letter', *N&Q*, 238 (1993), 63–4 • M. Bentley, *The liberal mind, 1914–1929* (1977) • D. J. Whittaker, 'Gilbert Murray: monk and missionary', 1985, Bodl. Oxf. [unpubd paper for Gilbert Murray Trust] • J. E. Rose, *The intellectual life of the British working class* (2001)

Archives Bodl. Oxf., corresp. and papers • NRA, corresp. and literary papers | BL, corresp. with Lord Cecil, Add. MSS 51132–51135 • BL, corresp. with Sir Sydney Cockerell, Add. MS 52741 • BL, corresp. with F. C. Cornford and F. M. Cornford, Add. MSS 58418, 58427 • BL, letters to George Bernard Shaw, Add. MS 50542 • BL, corresp. with the Society of Authors, Add. MS 56761 • Bodl. Oxf., letters to R. W. Chapman • Bodl. Oxf., corresp. with L. G. Curtis • Bodl. Oxf., corresp. with H. A. L. Fisher • Bodl. Oxf., letters to J. L. L. B. Hammond and Barbara Hammond • Bodl. Oxf., corresp. with J. L. Myres • Bodl. Oxf., corresp. relating to Society for Protection of Science and Learning • Bodl. Oxf., letters to E. J. Thompson • Bodl. Oxf., letters to Sir Alfred Zimmern • Bodl. RH, corresp. with Lord Lugard • Castle Howard, North Yorkshire, family letters to the ninth earl and countess of Carlisle • CUL, letters to Stanley Baldwin • HLRO, corresp. with Herbert Samuel • HLRO, corresp. with David Soskice • JRL, letters to *Manchester Guardian* • King's AC Cam., letters to Sir John Sheppard • King's AC Cam., letters to Sir John Sheppard • King's Lond., Liddell Hart C., corresp. with Sir B. H. Liddell Hart • McMaster University, Hamilton, Ontario, corresp., mainly with Bertrand Russell • NA Scot., corresp. with Lord Lothian • NL Scot., letters to Rachel Annand Taylor • NL Wales, corresp. mainly with Clement Davies • NL Wales, letters mainly to Gwilym Davies • Royal Society of Literature, London, letters to the Royal Society of Literature • Trinity Cam., letters to R. C. Trevelyan • U. Birm. L., corresp. with Sir Anthony Eden • Women's Library, London, letters to Dame Kathleen Courtney | SOUND BBC WAC

Likenesses Lord Carlisle, drawing, c.1890, probably Castle Howard, North Yorkshire; repro. in Wilson, *Gilbert Murray*, 34–5 • photograph, 1891, repro. in Wilson, *Gilbert Murray*, 34–5 • G. C. Beresford, photographs, 1913–16, NPG • W. Stoneman, photograph, 1917, NPG • F. A. Newbery, oils, c.1924, U. Glas.; [on loan] • E. Kapp, drawing, 1928, Barber Institute of Fine Arts, Birmingham • photogravure, 1934, NPG • F. Dodd, charcoal drawing, 1937, St John's College, Oxford • L. L. Toynbee, oils, 1950, NPG • L. L. Toynbee, oils, 1954, Library of the Prime Minister's Office, Canberra, Australia • Y. Karsh, photograph, 1955, NPG • Baron Studios, photograph, 1956, repro. in West, *Gilbert Murray*, frontispiece • A. John, chalk drawing, 1957, NPG • O. Edis, two photographs, NPG • Elliott & Fry, photograph, NPG [*see illus.*] • Melnikoff, bronze head, National Liberal Club, London • W. Rothenstein, lithograph, NPG • W. Rothenstein, pencil sketch, NPG • photographs, NPG

Wealth at death £37,525: probate, 17 Sept 1957, *CGPLA Eng. & Wales*

Murray, (William Ewart) Gladstone (1893–1970), publicist and television company executive, was born at Maple Ridge, British Columbia, on 8 April 1893, the son of Paul Murray and Hannah Mackay. He owed his forenames to the Grand Old Man of British Liberalism who had become prime minister for the fourth time the previous year. He was educated at King Edward's High School, Vancouver, and McGill College of British Columbia. After graduating from McGill University in Montreal he worked for a year as a journalist in North and South America; he then went as a Rhodes scholar to New College, Oxford. Between 1914 and 1918 Murray served in the Royal Flying Corps. He logged 2000 hours of combat flying and was several times

wounded; he was awarded the DFC, MC, and Croix de Guerre and was also decorated by the Italian government. After the war, he was for two years the aeronautical correspondent of the *Daily Express*. He subsequently worked briefly as publicity director for the League of Nations Union and as publicity manager of the Radio Communications Company. Murray married in 1923 Eleanor, daughter of John Powell JP, of Wrexham. They had a son and a daughter.

Murray's managing director at the Radio Communications Company, Major Basil Binyon, became one of the founding directors of the British Broadcasting Company. It was partly on Binyon's recommendation, in 1924, that he was taken on by John Reith to be the fledgeling company's director of publicity. Murray was also on friendly terms with Peter Eckersley, the BBC's chief engineer; another who spoke highly of him to Reith was Lord Beaverbrook, his employer at the *Express*. As was customary in those post-war years, he styled himself Major Gladstone Murray. Asa Briggs, in his *History of Broadcasting in the United Kingdom*, describes him as 'colourful' and 'convivial' and gives him credit for the skill and energy with which he watched over BBC interests in those early years. It was at his suggestion, during the 1926 general strike, that the BBC broadcast 'editorials' giving nightly appreciations of the strike situation, and Murray shared the writing of these with Reith.

Murray remained at the BBC for eleven years. He was acting controller (programmes) for three months in 1934–5, an appointment that occasioned serious conflict with the then controller (administration), Admiral Carpendale. Later in 1935, following a major reorganization, Murray became one of two assistant controllers in the programme division. He was popular with his subordinates. One of them, Maurice Gorham, wrote later that they felt better off under him than under any other chief in the BBC: 'Throughout my time at Savoy Hill he remained the most talked-about of BBC personalities, rumoured simultaneously to be about to replace Reith and to be about to leave' (Gorham, 38–9).

Such rumours were not calculated to improve Murray's relations with a director-general always jealously watchful of his own position and profoundly mistrustful of the whole breed of journalists. 'The Beaverbrook press have resumed their filthy personal articles', Reith noted in his diary in March 1934, adding, 'I am more than disgusted with Murray's complete ineffectiveness' (Reith diaries, 23 March 1934). And a year later, more ominously:

> I have had Dawnay get out of Murray an exposé of his so-called 'intelligence' work, with respect to the press. It is a most damning document and confirms all the suspicions and uneasiness which I have felt with respect to him for all these years.   (ibid., 3 April 1935)

In March 1936 Reith persuaded the board to require Murray's resignation. The ground had been well prepared by the classic BBC device of character assassination by annual report. 'He is a bad case', Reith wrote in his diary, 'and it is monstrous, and not my fault, that he has been tolerated for so long' (Reith diaries, 1 April 1936)—a curious observation for a famously autocratic chief executive. Murray appealed, was granted grace leave, and before his dismissal took effect was appointed general manager of the newly formed Canadian Broadcasting Corporation (CBC). (Three years previously he had been seconded to the commission set up to advise the Canadian government on the development of broadcasting.)

Murray did the job for six years, and did it well. In 1942, however, the CBC came under the scrutiny of the committee on broadcasting of the Canadian House of Commons. Although they praised Murray's work, they also reported that the CBC board had felt some lack of confidence in his ability in financial matters. He was replaced as general manager and appointed director-general of broadcasting, Canada. It was a grandiloquent title for a non-job; he sensibly resigned from it the following year. At the age of fifty, Murray's career in public service was effectively over.

Murray then founded the Responsible Enterprise Movement. He lectured for several years on its behalf, and contributed frequently to reviews and magazines in North America on a range of topics. There was a strong emphasis on free market economics and industrial relations, but he also addressed himself to more nebulous subjects, under such headings as 'Will freedom survive?' and 'Canada's place in civilization'.

Murray was a life associate of the Royal Society of St George and he had an honorary LLD from Florida Southern College. In his youth he was a notable track athlete; he also played squash, tennis, and golf. His health in later years was indifferent. He died in hospital in Toronto on 28 February 1970, aged seventy-six.   IAN McINTYRE

Sources J. C. W. Reith, diaries, BBC WAC · A. Briggs, *The history of broadcasting in the United Kingdom*, rev. edn, 5 vols. (1995) · P. Scannell and D. Cardiff, *A social history of British broadcasting*, [1] (1991) · M. Gorham, *Sound and fury: twenty-one years in the BBC* (1948) · broadcasting files, BBC WAC
Archives BBC WAC | SOUND BL NSA, performance recording

Murray [*née* Norman; *other married name* Bennet], **Grace** (1715–1803), follower of Methodism, daughter of Robert and Grace Norman, was born in Newcastle upon Tyne on 23 January 1715 into a Church of England family. At twenty-one she married Alexander Murray (*d.* 1742), a sea captain, from a respectable Scottish family which had lost fortune and position through loyalty to the Stuart cause. The young couple engaged in worldly pursuits, but while her husband was at sea Grace heard John Wesley and George Whitefield preach. She was converted in 1739 and received by Charles Wesley into the London Wesleyan Methodist Society, where her name is included on the Foundery class lists of 1742. John Wesley made her one of the Foundery band leaders. When her husband was lost at sea in 1742 Grace returned to Newcastle, where she became a class leader and was appointed housekeeper when the Orphan House in Newcastle opened in 1745. Wesley encouraged her to travel around that area, where she showed particular skill in leading women's classes. He took Grace as one of his travelling companions on his third visit to Ireland (April–July 1749). On their return Grace travelled on her own through south-east England before going back to Newcastle. Although she never attempted to preach, her work was highly regarded and done 'by Mr. Wesley's direction' (Bennet, 19).

John Wesley contemplated marrying Grace and she was probably the nearest he came to having a true love, but the affair became very complicated. John *Bennet (1715–1759), one of Wesley's most trusted and successful preachers, had fallen in love with Grace while being nursed by her at the Orphan House in 1746. They corresponded for the next two years. In August 1748 Wesley too was nursed by Grace, proposed to her, and they entered into what Wesley believed to be a formal contract of marriage on the basis of his promise to marry her. In September John Bennet also proposed and she accepted, telling him she was not committed to Wesley. For almost a year she swung between the two and in July 1749 pressed Wesley into a contract *de praesenti*, effectively a private marriage ceremony. However, it seems that Wesley's indecision, coupled with Charles Wesley's fears about the marriage, prevented Wesley from fulfilling his intentions. Charles acted swiftly and on 3 October 1749 in St Andrew's Church, Newcastle upon Tyne, Grace married Bennet in his presence. For a while it seemed there would be a serious rift between John, Charles, John Bennet, and Grace, but George Whitefield acted as reconciler. Wesley's distress at losing Grace was evident in the poem he wrote just after the event.

In 1752 John Bennet, who had already been moving towards Calvinism, seceded from the Wesleyan Methodist Connexion and finally settled down as an Independent minister at Warburton, near Warrington. He died there in 1759 aged forty-five. After several years Grace rejoined the Wesleyan Methodists, meeting Wesley for the last time in 1788 in London. She died on 23 February 1803 and was buried in the Independent burial-ground at Chinley, Derbyshire.   E. DOROTHY GRAHAM

Sources W. Bennet, *Memoirs of Mrs Grace Bennet* (1803) · *The works of John Wesley*, [another edn], 20, ed. F. Baker and others (1991) · H. D. Rack, *Reasonable enthusiast: John Wesley and the rise of Methodism* (1989) · R. P. Heitzenrater, *The elusive Mr Wesley*, 2 vols. (1984) · *The works of John Wesley*, [another edn], 26, ed. F. Baker and others (1982) · J. C. Bowmer, 'John Wesley's first marriage', *Proceedings of the Wesley Historical Society*, 36 (1967–8), 110–11 · A. Mountfield and H. J. F., 'John Bennet', *Proceedings of the Wesley Historical Society*, 7 (1910), 116–18 · P. J. Lineham, 'Bennet, John', *The Blackwell dictionary of evangelical biography, 1730–1860*, ed. D. M. Lewis (1995) · *IGI*
Archives BL, J. Wesley MSS · JRL, Methodist Archives and Research Centre, Colman collection of Wesleyana
Likenesses portrait (aged over eighty), Wesley's Chapel, City Road, London, Museum of Methodism

Murray, (Eustace Clare) Grenville (1824–1881), journalist and diplomatist, was the illegitimate son of Richard Grenville, second duke of Buckingham and Chandos (1797–1861); his mother's details are not known. He matriculated at Magdalen Hall, Oxford, in 1848, and was entered as a student of the Inner Temple in 1850, although he does not seem to have been called to the bar.

Lord Palmerston, the foreign secretary, recruited Murray for the diplomatic service, and he was sent as an attaché to the British embassy at Vienna on 14 July 1851.

He simultaneously arranged with the *Morning Post* to serve as their Vienna correspondent. Such a contravention of the conventions of the Foreign Office was brought to the notice of the British ambassador, Lord Westmorland. Though protected from dismissal by the interest of Palmerston, Murray was subsequently ostracized from the British chancery. On 7 April 1852 he was temporarily transferred to Hanover, and on 19 October 1852 he was appointed to the undesirable post of fifth paid attaché at Constantinople, where his relations with Lord Stratford de Redclyffe (then Sir Stratford Canning) were the reverse of cordial and led to his banishment as vice-consul to Mitylene on the island of Lesbos. In 1854 he published *Roving Englishman*, a series of chapters on travel, in which the Turkish ambassador was satirized as Sir Hector Stubble. From Foreign Office records it appears that he returned to England in 1854, staying there until 1857, when he was sent briefly to Tehran and then, in July 1858, made consul-general at Odessa. In 1868 he returned to England, after nearly eleven years of perpetual discord with the British residents in Odessa, and in 1869 was finally dismissed from the Foreign Office after a long and acrimonious inquiry (from which 306 pages of 'parliamentary papers relative to the complaints against Mr Grenville-Murray as her Majesty's Consul-General at Odessa' were issued). Complaints included the alleged forging of birth and marriage certificates, the levying of excessive consular fees, and the 'ill treatment of Miss Owen'. After leaving the Foreign Office Murray began to contribute to the first numbers of *Vanity Fair*, and in the following year started the *Queen's Messenger*, a weekly journal which served as a prototype of the later *Society Papers*.

After insulting Robert John, second Lord Carrington, in a newspaper article Murray was publicly horsewhipped by Carrington's son, Lord Carrington, outside the Conservative Club in St James's Street, London, on 22 June 1869. He sued Carrington (who was found guilty at the Middlesex sessions on the same day) for the assault, but was generally felt to have been in the wrong. His reputation was not enhanced by the charge of perjury that had been made against him only a few days earlier (17 July) for having denied authorship of the article which had purportedly slandered Carrington. Although remanded by the Bow Street magistrates until 29 July, he jumped bail and went to Paris, effectively exiling himself from England. In France he became known as the Count de Rethel d'Aragon, having taken the title of the Spanish lady whom he had married. He produced several novels, but was at his best in short satirical pieces, and he wrote numerous caustic essays and humorous sketches for the English and American press. He acted as Paris correspondent of the *Daily News* and the *Pall Mall Gazette*, and was an early contributor to *Cornhill Magazine* and *The World*, of which he was for a short time joint proprietor. He also published character sketches in the *Illustrated London News*, and 'Queer Stories' in *Truth*. One of the most irreverent and witty journalists of his day, Murray helped to introduce candour into discussion of public affairs, but was also instrumental in paving the way for respectable journalists

to rely frankly on gossip in order to acquire readers and to boost newspaper sales. He died at Passy on 20 December 1881 and was buried in Paris on 24 December.

THOMAS SECCOMBE, *rev.* JOSEPH COOHILL

Sources *The Times* (24 Dec 1881) · private information (2004) · T. H. S. Escott, *Masters of English journalism* (1911); repr. (1970), 263–5 · *Truth* (29 Dec 1881) · GEC, *Peerage*, new edn
Archives Hunt. L., letters to Grenville family · Lpool RO, letters to Lord Stanley · Northants. RO, letters to Fane family

Murray, Henry Leigh [*real name* Henry Leigh Wilson] (1820–1870), actor, was born in Sloane Street, London, on 19 October 1820. While a clerk in a merchant's office he joined some amateurs in a small theatre in Catherine Street, Strand, and made his first appearance about 1838 as Buckingham in *King Richard III*. Parts as Cassio, Macduff, Faulconbridge, and Iago followed, and on 2 December 1839, under Hooper, the manager of the York circuit, he made at Hull his début as a professional actor, playing Ludovico in *Othello*. In September 1840, under the name Leigh, perhaps to avoid confusion with his manager, he appeared at the Adelphi Theatre, Edinburgh, under William Henry Murray, as Lieutenant Morton in *The Middy Ashore*. While occasionally visiting Dundee, Perth, and other towns, he remained in Edinburgh, at the Theatre Royal or the Adelphi, until the spring of 1845. In 1841 he married Elizabeth Lee [*see below*], a member of the company. Their daughter Alma Murray also went on the stage. Among the characters he played were Jan Dousterswyvel in *The Lost Ship*, Hotspur, and Mark Antony, in which character he took his farewell of the Edinburgh stage. His salary in Edinburgh in 1842 was £1 10*s*. weekly; his wife received £2 15*s*.

Murray's first appearance in London took place at the Princess's under Maddox on 19 April 1845, as Sir Thomas Clifford in Sheridan Knowles's *The Hunchback*, with Lester Wallack, by whom he had been brought from Edinburgh, as the Hunchback. He played Icilius to W. C. Macready's Virginius, De Mauprat to his Richelieu, and went with him in the autumn of 1846 to the Surrey, where he played secondary characters in Shakespeare and Loveless in Vanbrugh's *The Relapse*. On the recommendation of Charles Dickens he was chosen to play at the Lyceum Alfred Heathfield in Albert Smith's adaptation of *The Battle of Life*. Murray remained at the Lyceum under the Keeley and the Mathews managements. His Marquis de Volange in J. R. Planché's *The Pride of the Market* won special recognition. In Dublin in 1848 he supported Helen Faucit, playing Romeo, Jaffier, Biron, Leonatus, Beverley, Claude Melnotte, Charles Surface, and other parts. After quitting the Lyceum for the Olympic he became stage-manager under Stocqueler, and afterwards under Spicer and Davidson. Here he played character parts in pieces then in vogue, such as *Time Tries All* and *His First Champagne*. In the representations given during 1848 and 1849 at Windsor Castle he played Lorenzo in *The Merchant of Venice*, Laertes in *Hamlet*, and Octavius in *Julius Caesar*. He accompanied William Farren, whose stage-manager he became, to the Strand and back to the Olympic, and then accompanied Benjamin Webster to the Adelphi, where in April 1853 he played

Henry Leigh Murray (1820–1870), by Herbert Watkins, late 1850s

in Mark Lemon's farce *Mr Webster at the Adelphi*, and the following October made a high mark in Webster's *Discarded Son*, the first of many adaptations of *Un fils de famille*. In September 1854 he left the Adelphi, and in the next year was at Sadler's Wells. In March 1858 he was, at Drury Lane, the first M. Bernard in Stirling Coyne's *The Love Knot*, and in November he enacted at the St James's the original Harrington in James Kenney's *London Pride, or, Living for Appearances*. A benefit was given him at Drury Lane in June 1865, with a view to aiding him in a trip to the south to improve his failing health; representations were given by various London actors. Murray died on 17 January 1870 and was buried on 22 January in Brompton cemetery.

Murray played a large range of characters, and was in his time unequalled as Harry Dornton, Sir Charles Pomander in *Masks and Faces*, and Birchall in *The Vicar of Wakefield*. He was also well regarded as Captain Absolute and Charles Surface.

His wife, **Elizabeth Leigh Murray** (1815–1892), was the second daughter of the playwright Henry *Lee (1765–1836), who was manager of the Taunton circuit for fifty years. She appeared at the age of five in *Little Pickle*, and played a round of characters in her father's theatres, as well as in York, Leeds, and Hull. She appeared in London at the Olympic under Madame Vestris, playing Cupid in an extravaganza of that name, and accompanied her manager to Covent Garden, where on 30 September 1839 she took part in the opening performance of *Love's Labour's*

Lost. She then went to Sadler's Wells, and after playing in various provincial towns reached Edinburgh, where she first appeared, under the name of Miss E. Lee, as Lady Staunton in *The Whistler of the Glen, or, The Fate of the Lily of St Leonards*, an adaptation of *The Heart of Midlothian*, and again in 1841 as Mrs Leigh. After returning to London she played numerous original parts, in many of which she supported her husband. She was seen as Apollo in Frank Talfourd's *Diogenes and his Lantern* (Strand, February 1850), Lady Lavender in *The Love Knot* (Drury Lane, March 1858), Patty in *The Chimney Corner* (Olympic, February 1861), Lady Lundie in Wilkie Collins's *Man and Wife* (Prince of Wales's, February 1873), and in a variety of other roles at the Lyceum, Opera Comique, and Court theatres. She died on 25 May 1892.

Murray's younger brother, **Gaston Murray** (1826–1889), whose real name was Garstin Parker Wilson, was born in London and first appeared on stage at the Lyceum on 2 March 1855 as Tom Saville in Boucicault's *Used up*. In 1857 he took part in the Windsor Castle theatricals, and in 1859 was engaged at the Theatre Royal, Manchester, playing Laertes in *Hamlet*, Faust in the English *Faust and Marguerite*, and Orlando in *As You Like It*. In 1863, at the St James's Theatre, he played Sir Benjamin Backbite in *The School for Scandal* and Sir George Touchwood in *The Belle's Stratagem*. He also performed at the Strand, Queen's, Haymarket, Covent Garden, and Olympic theatres. He was appointed treasurer of the Covent Garden theatre during the run of *Babil and Bijon*, and was elected director and secretary of the General Theatrical Fund. At the time of his death he was described as a collector of rents for the corporation of London. He died on 8 August 1889 at 19 Loughborough Road, Lambeth. His wife, **Mary Frances Murray** (d. 1891), known as Mrs Gaston Murray, the daughter of Henry Hughes, of the Adelphi Theatre, was born near Frankfurt in Germany, and first appeared on stage in 1851 at the Guildford theatre as Sophia in *The Rendezvous*. She made her début on the London stage in 1853, at the Lyceum, as Emma Thornton in Pelham Hardwicke's *A Bachelor of Arts*. She was a capable actress and played intelligently many parts at the Globe, the Court, the Olympic, and the St James's, including Mrs Penguin in J. Palgrave Simpson's *A Scrap of Paper*. Her Mrs Primrose in *The Vicar of Wakefield* at the Lyceum was excellent. In May 1889, at the opening of the Garrick Theatre, she was the original Mrs Stonehay in Pinero's *The Profligate*. She died on 15 January 1891.

JOSEPH KNIGHT, rev. NILANJANA BANERJI

Sources *The Era* (23 Jan 1870) · *The life and reminiscences of E. L. Blanchard, with notes from the diary of Wm. Blanchard*, ed. C. W. Scott and C. Howard, 2 vols. (1891) · *Era Almanack and Annual* (1871) · *Era Almanack and Annual* (1872) · *Era Almanack and Annual* (1890) · *Era Almanack and Annual* (1892) · *Era Almanack and Annual* (1893) · C. E. Pascoe, ed., *The dramatic list*, 2nd edn (1880) · E. Reid and H. Compton, eds., *The dramatic peerage* [1891]; rev. edn [1892] · J. C. Dibdin, *The annals of the Edinburgh stage* (1888) · Hall, *Dramatic ports.* · J. W. Marston, *Our recent actors*, 2 vols. (1888) · [S. Bancroft and M. E. Bancroft], *Mr and Mrs Bancroft on and off the stage: written by themselves*, 2 vols. (1888) · [S. Bancroft and M. E. Bancroft], *Mr and Mrs Bancroft on and off the stage: written by themselves*, 6th edn (1889) · [S. Bancroft and M. E. Bancroft], *Mr and Mrs Bancroft on and off the stage: written by themselves*, 8th edn (1891)

Likenesses S. Pearce, chalk drawing, 1851, Garr. Club · H. Watkins, photograph, 1857–9, NPG [*see illus.*] · J. H. Baker, stipple (after S. Pearce), BM · portrait, repro. in *Tallis's Dramatic Magazine* · prints, Harvard TC · two stipple and line engravings (after daguerreotypes), BM, NPG
Wealth at death £233 13s. 11d.—Mary Frances Murray: probate, 11 March 1891, CGPLA Eng. & Wales · £865 10s. 3d.—Elizabeth Leigh Murray: probate, 21 June 1892, CGPLA Eng. & Wales · £1264 9s. 3d.—Gaston Murray: probate, 1889, CGPLA Eng. & Wales

Murray, Hilda Mary Emily Ada Ruthven (1875–1951), philologist and university teacher, was born on 17 November 1875 at Hammer's Lane, Mill Hill, London, the fifth child and eldest daughter of the lexicographer Sir James *Murray (1837–1915) and his second wife, Ada Agnes, née Ruthven (1845–1936). She moved with other members of the Murray family to 78 Banbury Road, Oxford, in 1885, and was educated at the Oxford High School for Girls. From there she gained an exhibition as a home student at the University of Oxford. She graduated in modern languages (French and German) in 1896, and obtained first-class honours in English language and literature in 1899. From 1899 until 1915 she was a lecturer in Germanic philology at Royal Holloway College in the University of London. In 1915 she became director of studies and lecturer at Girton College, Cambridge, first in medieval and modern languages and from 1917 in English and in historical and comparative philology. She was appointed vice-mistress of Girton in 1924, and held this post until she retired in 1936. On retirement she lived with her mother and younger sister Rosfrith at Sunnyside, Kingsley Green, Sussex. She was unmarried.

In her early years in Oxford, like her brothers and sisters, Hilda Murray assisted her father with the sorting and alphabetizing of illustrative examples submitted by outside readers for possible inclusion in the *Oxford English Dictionary*. She also undertook to collect statistical details of various kinds—the number of main words and subsidiary words, as well as the number of current, obsolete, and alien words, and so on—for inclusion in the fascicles of the dictionary as they appeared. She also revised her father's article on the English language for the eleventh edition of the *Encyclopaedia Britannica* (1910).

Hilda Murray's edition of the Middle English poem *Erthe upon Erthe* was published in 1911 as a volume in the series of early English works issued by the Early English Text Society. It was dedicated to her distinguished father, 'quem quamvis longissimo intervallo sequi tamen conor' ('whom though far behind I yet strive to follow'). The poem survives in more than twenty Middle English manuscripts of the fourteenth and fifteenth centuries, which adds to the complications of producing an edition. Its grim message is a reminder of man's mortality, with a play on two meanings of the word 'erthe', the substance of which God made the body of Adam and other creatures, and the earth to which all creatures return: 'Memento homo quod cinis es et in cinerem reverte re'. This was a favourite theme for commonplace books, and its popularity is emphasized by the fact that versions of it were still being inserted on walls and tombstones up to the beginning of the nineteenth century, and also on the spare leaves at the beginning and end of numerous manuscripts.

Hilda Murray's edition of selected works of the Scottish poet Robert Henryson (d. c.1490) was published in 1930. This small book contains five Aesopian fables ('The Twa Mys', 'The Fox and the Cock', 'The Fox and the Wolf', 'The Sheep and the Dog', and 'The Fox, the Wolf, and the Cadger'). It also contains 'The Testament of Cressaid', a work of just over 600 lines in the seven-lined Chaucerian stanza, and a moralizing pastoral lyric called 'Robene and Makyne', a 'disputoison' (debate) on the model of the French *pastourelle* between a shepherd (Robene) and an unattractive woman (Makyne, a diminutive of Matilda) about the nature of love.

As a tutor at Girton, Hilda Murray was formidable. One of her pupils, Muriel Bradbrook (who succeeded her as a teaching fellow at Girton in 1936), remembers that 'her knowledge was daunting' and the comments pencilled on her pupils' weekly essays were caustic: '"Have you any manuscript authority for that variant?" she once asked when I made a slip in translating Chaucer' (Bradbrook, 45). But she had a warm and kindly side too, and when Miss Bradbrook's father died at the end of her first year, leaving a young family, Miss Murray 'was tenderness itself' (ibid.). She died in hospital at 9 College Lane, Chichester, Sussex, on 23 August 1951, and was buried in the cemetery at Fernhurst, Sussex, on 27 August.

R. W. BURCHFIELD

Sources K. M. E. Murray, *Caught in the web of words: James A. H. Murray and the 'Oxford English dictionary'* (1977) · P. Ruthven-Murray, *The Murrays of Rulewater: a genealogical history of a border family* (1986) · H. M. R. Murray, ed., *Erthe upon erthe*, EETS (1911) · *Henryson: selected fables*, ed. H. M. R. Murray (1930) · M. Bradbrook, essay, *My Cambridge*, ed. R. Hayman (1977), 40–52 · CGPLA Eng. & Wales (1951) · private information (2004) [Fernhurst parish council office; Oxford high school; St Anne's College, Oxford]
Archives Royal Holloway College, Egham, Surrey, papers | SOUND Girton Cam., reminiscences by students of Girton College, Cambridge
Likenesses portraits, repro. in Murray, *Caught in the web of words* · portraits, repro. in Ruthven-Murray, *Murrays of Rulewater*
Wealth at death £1490 17s. 8d.: probate, 24 Oct 1951, CGPLA Eng. & Wales

Murray, Sir (John) Hubert Plunkett (1861–1940), colonial governor and judge, was born on 29 December 1861, in Manly, Sydney, New South Wales, the elder son of Dublin-born Sir Terence Aubrey *Murray (1810–1873) and his second wife, Agnes Ann (c.1835–1891), third daughter of Welsh-born John Edwards of Hammersmith, London, governess to her husband's two daughters and son from his first marriage. He was the elder brother of the classical scholar (George) Gilbert Aimé *Murray (1866–1957).

Early years and education Hubert's father lost his lands and his money through drought, sheep disease, and over-liberality in 1865. Hubert and his elder stepbrother were in the fine house near Lake George when bailiffs and creditors stripped its contents, before being driven over 200 miles of rough road in the middle of a storm to Sydney. There their mother maintained a close family circle in a succession of smaller and smaller urban households in

Sir (John) Hubert Plunkett Murray (1861–1940), by E. C. Freedwell, 1920s

support of her husband's continuing political career as president of the legislative council of New South Wales; he was knighted in 1869. It was also an educated household with a good library, for Sir Terence had been taught classics in Dublin, and his wife, a cousin of W. S. Gilbert, was a lively conversationalist and fluent linguist who, after her husband's death in 1873, ran a successful school for the young ladies of Sydney to support her family. Although Sir Terence was Roman Catholic, his religious views were liberal to the point of eccentricity, and he left their spiritual fortunes to his Anglican wife. Hubert was baptized into the Church of England as an infant, and only reluctantly did his father agree, in the face of outside pressure, to his Catholic baptism in 1869, a ceremony his father did not attend and which was not followed by regular religious practice by Hubert.

After preparatory school in Melbourne, Hubert was sent in 1872 to the Sydney Church of England grammar school, where he had a brilliant scholastic and athletic record, becoming captain of school. In 1878 he joined his mother, who had sold her school at a profit, and Gilbert in England, where he went to Brighton College. Having had a sound classical education in Sydney, Hubert gained a demyship of Magdalen College, Oxford, but he was expelled from Brighton for striking a master who had called him a wild Irishman. The intervening year, before he could go up to Oxford, he spent at a German academy at Sinzig Remagen. After he arrived in Oxford in 1881, he took firsts in classical moderations and Greats, graduating

in 1886, but his associates in Oxford were not scholars but athletes and 'hearties', for he rowed and boxed and in 1885 was a member of the university athletics team. He ate his dinners at the Inner Temple and was called to the bar in 1886, the year in which, under the auspices of the West London Boxing Club, and possessing a massive physique (standing 6 feet 3 inches and turning the scales at over 14 stone), he became amateur heavyweight champion of England under the Queensberry rules.

Legal career, 1886–1904 With this impressive record Murray returned to Sydney in 1886. Admitted to the New South Wales bar, he then failed in private practice, attributing this to his Oxford education which repelled clients. His mother and others, however, described his aloof manner, his arrogant-seeming saunter, and an air of superiority, enhanced by his sense of a distinguished fighting Irish gentlemanly ancestry. Although in 1889 he married, in an Anglican church, Sybil Maud (d. 1929), fifth daughter of Richard Lewis Jenkins MD of Nepean Towers, a rich family friend, his income from the bar in that year was £35 'and rapidly approaching vanishing point' (*Selected Letters*, 8). With the birth of a son, Terence, in 1891 and a daughter, Mary, in 1893, he was driven to accept a post as a parliamentary draftsman at £700 p.a., work which 'will drive me into a lunatic asylum' (ibid., 9). His position, given his brilliant promise, seemed to him ridiculous, his 'living death' only relieved by some crown prosecution work on circuit which, however, separated him from his family. When Gilbert visited Sydney in 1893, he detected in his brother signs of heavy drinking and of Roman Catholicism, with Sybil, although loving and patient, no real companion.

Murray tried to relieve his monotony by becoming a practising Catholic in 1896, and by joining a volunteer militia unit, the New South Wales Irish rifles, of which he became commanding officer in 1898. He was bitterly opposed to the Second South African War, but, thinking it his duty to his regiment, he sailed for Cape Town in command of troops aboard ship in January 1900. At first frustrated by command of a rear railway depot, he finally found some fighting, swimming the Modder River under fire, and then taking part in a dashing mounted infantry ride into Pretoria. He hated his subsequent duty of burning Boer farms, while, as part of a force vainly pursuing the Boer general De Wet, he formed a contempt for British officers, although he was himself commissioned into the imperial force as a major, and held the rank of lieutenant-colonel in the Australian force. His younger son, Patrick, was born in England while he was in South Africa. Returning to Australia in 1901, his legal career was scarcely more successful, although he occasionally acted as a district court judge. The family separation had affected his wife, and he forswore alcohol. In 1904, in the hope that his wife could live with him for half the year, he applied for the post of chief judicial officer of British New Guinea, about to become the Australian Territory of Papua. But Port Moresby, the capital, then with fewer than fifty inhabitants, was too tropical, malarial, and primitive for his family, and he spent most of the rest of his life alone, except for periods of leave and occasional family visits to Port

Moresby. His salary, however, enabled him to maintain his wife in Australia, and to educate his elder son in England and his daughter and younger son in Australia.

Judge and legal adviser, 1904–1908 As the only judge, sitting without jury or counsel, Murray had to administer a slightly adapted Queensland code. He inherited the view that in small stateless, chiefless, indigenous societies speaking some two hundred different languages there was no body of custom which could be codified, yet he became immediately aware that the motives for what were crimes under European law were Papuan ones. 'At present I do little or nothing but sentence people to death for murder' Murray wrote to Lady Mary Murray on 24 October 1904 (*Selected Letters*, 33), but Papuan custom he held to be a sufficient mitigating factor as to allow him to commute such sentences to a relatively short term of imprisonment. His intention was to educate in European ways prisoners who, in committing murder, had fulfilled Papuan social obligations. His judicial work led Murray to a fascinated interest in Papuan customs, an interest stimulated both by his own classical knowledge and by his acquaintance in Port Moresby with the anthropologist C. G. Seligman.

Murray was not only a judge. As legal adviser he was a member of the executive government. As such, he was drawn into the factions which divided the administration of Captain F. R. Barton during the interregnum between Britain's formal relinquishment of authority in March 1901 and the proclamation of the Australian Papua Act in September 1906. With division between a Colonial Office party and an Australian one in British New Guinea, Murray found his position difficult, especially when invited by Alfred Deakin, the Australian prime minister, privately and confidentially to offer his views on present and future policy and administration. When the Australian government decided on a royal commission to recommend policy, Murray by permission repeated in evidence what he had written to Deakin: Papuans were certainly protected, but development of a potentially rich possession was discouraged. In his opinion, the interests of Papuans and Europeans were not incompatible but the former must learn habits of industry, while the latter must be actively encouraged by government. The Australian government also took this view. Murray was appointed acting administrator in 1907 and then lieutenant-governor, the title adopted for the head of administration, in 1908. He retained the position of chief judicial officer, combining judicial circuit with inspections and some exploration of difficult country.

Enlightened policies Murray had drafted the native land and labour ordinances in 1906 in order to carry out Australian policy. The former provided that only the government could buy land from Papuans, and then make it available to Europeans for plantations, chiefly rubber and coconuts for copra, on thirty-year leases. Such land would be purchased only if Papuans were willing to sell and if it was surplus to their present and future needs. The latter allowed licensed private recruiters to bring labourers before a government officer to ensure that they were willing to engage under indenture, and that the numbers recruited were not so great as to cause the disintegration of their social group. Murray was satisfied that enough land was available to Europeans, and that there was sufficient labour to work it, without damaging the interests of the Papuans. By 1912 he believed that Papua could rely on the skill of the settlers—over 140 plantations—soon to dispense with the annual Australian subsidy of £30,000, and to become self-supporting. Between 1906 and 1912, he reported, revenue had increased by 152 per cent, trade by 109 per cent, and shipping by 162 per cent.

Confident by 1911 that development by Europeans was well under way, Murray put forward a scheme to pacify the whole of still largely unexplored Papua, with an indigenous population estimated at 300,000. 'My scheme is to pacify the whole Territory first, and then tax the natives, the proceeds of the taxation being used to provide schools for them—especially technical schools' (*Selected Letters*, 71). He embarked on peaceful penetration, with new stations and more field staff to patrol, establishing government influence and then control, under strict orders never to fire unless their own or their native police escort's lives were at actual risk. 'When you are dead, you may shoot', was the Papuan service parody. The influence gained was maintained by the appointment of village constables, first introduced by Sir William MacGregor in the 1890s. When Murray wrote his book *Papua or British New Guinea* in 1912, his optimism about both development and native policy permeated it. He was appointed CMG in 1914.

Before the First World War Murray hoped for transfer to the imperial colonial service, with its chances of promotion to larger colonies, but he was disappointed. His optimism about Papua faded. The First World War reduced both his field staff and Papuan trade. After the war, the application of the Australian Navigation Act to Papuan shipping prevented recovery; when it was lifted, the great depression halted further development, despite unfulfilled hopes of oil and gold strikes. Murray was further disappointed when the former German colony of New Guinea was not combined with Papua under his governorship. In 1920, complaining that the Papuan government discriminated against Europeans, an unofficial meeting of residents of Port Moresby led to an ineffectual telegram to the king asking for Murray's removal from office.

Nevertheless, throughout the 1920s and 1930s, Murray's reputation as an enlightened colonial governor grew, as he published his second book, *Papua of Today*, in 1925, and a dozen articles and addresses on native administration. The balance of Papuan and European interests that he proclaimed, although now inclined to stress Papuan protection, especially against European demands for labour, were not dissimilar to Lord Lugard's dual mandate nor to the League of Nations' 'sacred trust'. As early as 1919 he had begun to look for a social anthropologist to assist his government's understanding of indigenous society. He claimed that in Papua he was true to the spirit of indirect rule, even if there was no chiefly system. It was in these years that the 'Murray policy' was so named by his admirers, although later critics described it as benevolent paternalism. His achievement was recognized by advancement to KCMG in 1925, and by an address in 1937 from the unofficial residents of Papua, including former opponents.

Apart from the peaceful penetration of new country and some limited encouragement of indigenous development, however, primary education Murray left to missionary schools which were subsidized by the government. There was no development of village councils and local government, Papua being still a 'stone age' country, not comparable with contemporary Africa or Asia. In any case, with revenue limited by the relative failure of development, with a small Australian subsidy, his resources were not adequate for education and training programmes.

Death in office Despite public reputation, Murray in his sixties privately despaired. His first wife died in 1929; his second marriage in 1930 to Mildred Blanche Bloomfield, daughter of Henry Bloomfield Trench and widow of George Arthur Pomeroy Vernon, who also was unable to live in Port Moresby, ended in judicial separation in 1936. From May 1934 he suffered heart trouble, but was determined not to resign until he could be sure of a successor who would continue his policy. War, in 1939, filled him with horror and disgust. In February 1940 he set off on tour of south-east Papua in the government yacht in a mood 'to curse God and die' (*Selected Letters*, 241). Taken ill, he died in his sleep in the hospital at Samarai of lymphatic leukaemia on 27 February, his body taken for burial in the old cemetery at Port Moresby. After forty days of mourning, and watch fires burning on the hills, the Papuan ceremony concluded with the words: 'He promised us all "I will not leave you. I will die in Papua." His words were the words of a true man, for his body lies in our ground' (West, 262).

Murray's colonial governorship of thirty-three years was unique. He successfully established law and order in Papua and early colonial development. Well-educated and intelligent, he reflected and wrote about the initial problems of colonial rule, bearing comparison, although he worked in a smaller sphere, to colonial governors such as Sir Donald Cameron, Sir Arthur Gordon, and Lord Lugard, and to the highest standards of his own day.

F. J. WEST

Sources NL Aus., Murray family MSS · records of the Papuan (previously British New Guinea) Administration, Commonwealth Archives Office, Canberra · Bodl. Oxf., MSS Gilbert Murray · Mitchell L., NSW, Murray MSS · NL Aus., Atlee Hunt MSS · F. J. West, *Hubert Murray: the Australian pro-consul* (1968) · *Selected letters of Hubert Murray*, ed. F. J. West (1970) · *Annual Report* [Territory of Papua] (1906–40) · private information (2004) [family, colleagues] · b. cert.

Archives Mitchell L., NSW · NL Aus., corresp. and papers | Bodl. Oxf., Gilbert Murray MSS · NL Aus., Deakin MSS; Atlee Hunt MSS · NL Aus., corresp. with Viscount Novar

Likenesses E. C. Freedwell, photograph, 1920–29, NL Aus. [*see illus.*] · photographs, repro. in West, *Hubert Murray*

Murray, Hugh (1779–1846), geographer, born at North Berwick, Haddingtonshire, Scotland, was the younger son of Matthew Murray (1735–1791), and grandson of George Murray (*d.* 1757). These two and Hugh's elder brother, George (1772–1822), were ministers of North Berwick. His mother was daughter of John Hill, minister of St Andrews, and sister of Henry David Hill, professor at St Andrews. At an early age Hugh entered the Edinburgh excise office as a clerk, but finding the work gave him ample leisure, he turned to writing. After trying his hand at fiction and philosophy he began to concentrate on geography. His first geographical work was an enlargement and completion of J. Leyden's *Historical Account of Discoveries and Travels in Africa* (1817). Similar works by him on Asia (3 vols., 1820) and North America (1829) followed.

Murray's *magnum opus* was the *Encyclopaedia of Geography* (1834), of which the geographical part was written by himself, while W. J. Hooker, R. Jameson, W. Wallace, and W. Swainson contributed other sections. A supplement was published in 1843. The work contained eighty-two maps and over a thousand woodcuts. It was well received, and an American edition (1843) in three volumes, edited by Thos. G. Bradford, had a large sale. Murray also wrote prolifically for the press, and produced, wholly or in part, fifteen volumes for the Edinburgh Cabinet Library, including the *Southern Seas* (1826), the *Polar Seas* (1830), *British India* (1832), *China* (1836), *British America* (1839), *Africa* (1830), and *The United States* (1844). His co-authors were often respected natural historians.

On 22 January 1816 Murray was elected fellow of the Society of Edinburgh, to whose *Transactions* he contributed. He was for a time editor of the *Scots Magazine*, and was a respected fellow of the Royal Geographical Society of London. He died of inflammation of the lungs after a short illness, while on a visit to London, at 3 Wardrobe Place, Doctors' Commons, on 4 March 1846.

Without ever apparently having left Britain, Murray wrote prolifically on the geography of many lands. His works were compilations in an encyclopaedic style which, although regarded at the time as models of scientific geography, rested largely on factual comprehensiveness, rather than on understanding of process.

G. LE G. NORGATE, *rev.* ELIZABETH BAIGENT

Sources *Journal of the Royal Geographical Society*, 16 (1846), xl · *Fasti Scot.* · S. Maunder, *The biographical treasury*, new edn, rev. W. L. R. Cates (1870) · Ward, *Men of the reign* · *Literary Gazette* (7 March 1846) · *Literary Gazette* (11 April 1846) · d. cert.

Likenesses A. Geddes, pencil with chalk, 1813?, Scot. NPG

Murray, Sir James. See Pulteney, Sir James Murray-, seventh baronet (*c.*1755–1811).

Murray, James, of Pardewis (*d.* 1592), courtier and administrator, was the third son of Sir William Murray of Tullibardine (*d.* 1563) and his wife, Katherine (*d.* in or after 1576), daughter of Sir Duncan Campbell of Glenorchy. First recorded in 1542, Murray came to prominence in 1564, when on 24 August Queen Mary obtained a passport for him to travel through England, his ultimate mission being to the earl of Bothwell, then exiled in France. On 30 May 1565 he obtained another passport to pass through

England to France, again to bear messages to and from the earl.

Murray seems to have had inside knowledge of the circumstances of Darnley's murder on 10 February 1567. Convinced of Bothwell's responsibility, he was one of the anonymous 'calumniators' who posted placards at the Edinburgh tollbooth naming Bothwell and others as the killers of the queen's husband. A rival propagandist responded with placards accusing four of Mary's French servants. By 14 March Murray had publicly revealed his authorship, causing the privy council to issue orders for his arrest, which he evaded. On 29 March Bothwell reportedly asked the minister of Dunfermline whether Murray had been known to speak evil of himself, to which the minister replied 'that he had never heard him say well of him' (*CSP for.*, 1566–8, 198). Following the earl's rigged acquittal (on 12 April), Murray fixed more placards to the tollbooth, offering to accept Bothwell's challenge to his accusers to single combat. In May he posted further placards, now offering with five others to fight six followers of Bothwell whom he named as the killers. At Carberry on 15 June he was the first to accept Bothwell's renewed challenge to single combat, but the earl declined on the grounds of rank, whereupon the challenge was taken up by the challenger's elder brother, Sir William *Murray of Tullibardine, who received the same response.

Following the civil war Murray obtained various lands and revenues in Fife from Dunfermline Abbey, including Pardewis. His sister Euphemia had married Robert Pitcairn, royal secretary and the abbey's commendator. Murray himself was married about 28 July 1572 to Marion, daughter of Sir Simon Preston of Craigmillar, provost of Edinburgh. She died some time before 17 April 1582, by which date he had married Agnes Lindsay (*d.* after 1611), with whom he was granted lands in Tunygask, Fife. There were three children of his second marriage: John (*d.* 1606), Patrick, and Jean, who married Alexander Lindsay of Canterland. In 1579 the crown rewarded Murray's services with a pension from the thirds of the Methven provostry, exchanged in 1582 for a life pension of £50 from Coupar Angus Abbey.

In 1579 Murray undertook a diplomatic mission to England on border matters, and from then until May 1583 he was master of the king's wardrobe. He supported the Ruthven raid of 23 August 1582, when James VI was seized by a pro-English and strongly protestant faction. In this he may have been moved by religious sympathies, since his father had supported the reforming cause in 1559–60. After the king's escape he was forfeited (along with many others) by the earl of Arran's regime on 22 August 1584, but was restored when the raiders' faction regained power in 1585. Murray died in September 1592.

J. R. M. SIZER

Sources *Scots peerage*, 462–4 · *CSP for.*, 1564–8 · *Reg. PCS*, 1st ser., vols. 1–2 · *CSP Scot.*, 1563–9 · D. Calderwood, *The history of the Kirk of Scotland*, ed. T. Thomson and D. Laing, 8 vols., Wodrow Society, 7 (1842–9), vols. 4–5 · G. Buchanan, *History of Scotland*, 18 (1690) · J. M. Thomson and others, eds., *Registrum magni sigilli regum Scotorum / The register of the great seal of Scotland*, 11 vols. (1882–1914), 1513–1608 · G. Donaldson, ed., *Registrum secreti sigilli* (1963–82), 1567–84 · C. T. McInnes, ed., *Accounts of the treasurer of Scotland*, 12 (1970) · H. Drummond, *The queen's man: Mary queen of Scots and the fourth earl of Bothwell—lovers or villains?* (1975) · J. Wormald, *Mary queen of Scots: a study in failure* (1988) · NA Scot., CC8/8/26, fols. 349v–350v · M. D. Young, ed., *The parliaments of Scotland: burgh and shire commissioners*, 2 vols. (1992–3)

Wealth at death £522 11s. 8d., incl. debts owed to him: NA Scot., CC 8/8/26 fol. 350r

Murray, Sir James, Lord Philiphaugh (1655–1708), politician and judge, was born on 11 July 1655 at Eddleston, Peeblesshire, the eldest son of Sir John Murray of Philiphaugh (*d.* 1675) and Anne, daughter of Sir Archibald Douglas of Cavers. His father was parliamentary commissioner for Selkirkshire in 1661–3, a commissioner for supply in 1661 and 1667, and commissioner for the borders in 1665. He was educated at Edinburgh University, graduating in 1674. He succeeded his father in August 1675 and soon continued the family link with parliament. Like his father he was a member for Selkirkshire, and he sat in the convention of estates that assembled in Edinburgh in June 1678, and was elected member for the same county in 1681. His career in parliament and the estates was lengthy and he was a commissioner for supply in 1678, 1685, 1690, and 1704.

Murray's early career stumbled on account of his apparent shortcomings as sheriff of Selkirk, in which post he had also succeeded his father. A dispute between him and Urquhart of Meldrum, a commander of the king's troops, began his temporary eclipse. The case came before the privy council in November 1680 and the issue seemed to be a clash of jurisdiction between Urquhart as justice of the peace and Murray as sheriff. However, the main concern of Urquhart—and of the privy council as it happened—was that Murray had 'malversed and been remiss in punishing conventicles' (*Historical Notices*, 277). Thus when the privy council ruled on the case in October 1681 Murray found himself deprived of his right as sheriff of Selkirk. Lauder of Fountainhall suggests that he was a minor victim of the collapse in patronage of Elizabeth, duchess of Lauderdale, her influence having 'dried up' (ibid., 331).

This was not, however, the end of Murray's difficulties. He was arrested and committed to prison in 1684, following the discovery of the 1683 Rye House plot to assassinate Charles II. In September 1684 he was brought before the privy council and, on being threatened with torture, made his confession and threw himself on the mercy of the first duke of Queensberry. He was released on bond of caution, and eventually received royal pardon, but on condition that he testified against his so-called accomplices. Indeed, it was his testimony which led to the controversial double trial and execution of Robert Baillie of Jerviswood, and which was used in cases against Walter Scott, earl of Tarras, Patrick Hume, earl of Marchmont, George Pringle of Torwoodlie, and others, many of whom were forfeited in their absence. As a contemporary observed a few years later, Murray 'had a chief hand in ruining many families' (Melville, 77).

In spite of unpopularity with some, after the revolution of 1688 Murray's fortunes began to recover. He was

Sir James Murray, Lord Philiphaugh (1655–1708), by unknown artist

appointed an ordinary lord of session in November 1689 with the title Lord Philiphaugh, and in 1701 parliament ratified the barony of Philiphaugh in his name and that of his heirs. Yet, his post-revolution career was to depend on his role as a close personal adviser to James Douglas, second duke of Queensberry, the most important political manager in Scotland from 1700 to 1707. Though it did take a few years for Queensberry to make his mark at court—he was only twenty-six years old at the revolution—in May 1696 Philiphaugh joined the privy council and became a lord of exchequer. In 1698 Queensberry tried unsuccessfully to press on King William the appointment of Philiphaugh as lord justice clerk. Lively party politics, but especially the factions clustered around Queensberry and the tenth earl and first duke of Argyll, made consensus over appointments quite impossible. Queensberry's elevation in 1700 to king's commissioner to parliament actually reduced the scope for agreement. Thus, while in 1701 there was general agreement to replace the earl of Selkirk as clerk register, Queensberry's nomination of Philiphaugh was countered by the candidatures of Sir William Hamilton of Whitelaw and Adam Cockburn of Ormiston. Nevertheless, after the succession of Queen Anne, Philiphaugh was appointed clerk register in November 1702. He held this position until July 1708 apart from a period from June 1704 to 7 April 1705. The so-called 'Queensberry' or 'Scotch plot', a futile attempt by the duke to incriminate political rivals, led to Philiphaugh being temporarily replaced by James Johnston and the brief removal from office of the duke himself.

When in power, Queensberry was provided with effective political advice by Philiphaugh. In 1700 the latter encouraged necessary concessions to be made to parliament over resentments at the failure of the Darien scheme. Although in 1703 the passing of the Act of Security and the Act anent Peace and War were set-backs for both men, after returning to power in 1705 Philiphaugh assisted Queensberry in successfully steering the treaty of Union through a divided Scottish parliament.

In his memoirs John Macky describes Murray as of 'fair complexion, fat, middle sized' but 'clever', and he certainly had the wit to rekindle an effective political career after early false starts. Murray married first, on 24 April 1678, Anne, daughter of Patrick Hepburne of Blackcastle, and second (c.1681), Margaret, daughter of Sir Alexander Don of Newton. He had no children by his first marriage, but three sons and five daughters by the second. He was succeeded by his eldest son, John (b. 1682). His will and testament have not survived yet he was clearly a man of means, with lands at Kershope in Roxburghshire as well as at Philiphaugh in Selkirkshire, an estate which had been in the family since the 1520s. Murray died at Inch in Wigtownshire on 1 July 1708.   A. J. MANN

Sources *Historical notices of Scotish affairs, selected from the manuscripts of Sir John Lauder of Fountainhall*, ed. D. Laing, 1, Bannatyne Club, 87 (1848), 227, 331, 556 · R. Douglas and others, *The baronage of Scotland* (1798), 106 · M. D. Young, ed., *The parliaments of Scotland: burgh and shire commissioners*, 2 (1993), 529–30 · *Memoirs of the secret services of John Macky*, ed. A. R. (1733) · register of the great seal, NA Scot. [numerous commissions, vols. 14–15; property, vols. 73, 79] · D. Laing, ed., *A catalogue of the graduates … of the University of Edinburgh*, Bannatyne Club, 106 (1858), 105 · G. Brunton and D. Haig, *An historical account of the senators of the college of justice, from its institution in MDXXXII* (1832), 436 · P. W. J. Riley, *King William and the Scottish politicians* (1979), 7, 6, 34, 123–57 · privy council registers, decreta, NA Scot., PC.2.26, fol. 188v · privy council registers, acta from 9/1696, NA Scot., PC.1.51 · NA Scot., earls of Stair MSS, GD 135, 1219, 1220, 1230, 1861 · W. H. L. Melville, ed., *Leven and Melville papers: letters and state papers chiefly addressed to George, earl of Melville … 1689–1691*, Bannatyne Club, 77 (1843) · NA Scot., Leven and Melville MSS, GD 26 · *State papers and letters addressed to William Carstares*, ed. J. M'Cormick (1774) · Register House old parish registers, Edinburgh and Peebleshire, NA Scot., OPR. 760.CH2; OPR. 685.1/44 [marriage, birth]
Likenesses oils, Scot. NPG [*see illus.*]

Murray, James, second duke of Atholl (1690–1764), politician, was born at Edinburgh on 28 September 1690, the third son of John *Murray, first duke of Atholl (1660–1724), politician and landowner, and Lady Katherine Hamilton (*bap.* 1662, *d.* 1707). His brothers included William *Murray, styled second duke of Atholl, and Lord George *Murray. He was made captain and lieutenant-colonel of a grenadier company of the 1st foot guards (King's company) on 1 January 1712, and captain and lieutenant-colonel of the Royal Scots infantry regiment on 14 June 1714.

Murray first entered politics in 1715 as MP for Perthshire, and was re-elected in 1722. On the attainder in February 1716 of his elder brother William for his part in the previous year's Jacobite rising, an act of parliament vested the family honours and estates in James as the next heir (he had joined the duke of Argyll at Perth in January–February 1716 on the Hanoverian side, marching with him in pursuit of the Jacobites to Aberdeen). After the rising he moved to London, and succeeded to the peerage on the death of his father in 1724 (at which point Jacobite supporters also identified William as second duke). On 28 April 1726 James married Jane Frederick (c.1693–1748), widow of James Lannoy of Hammersmith and granddaughter of Sir John Frederick, alderman of London. An act of 1733 extended the 1716 act, providing that the attainder of Tullibardine should not extend to prevent descent of honour and estate to James, second duke of Atholl and his heirs, or to any male heirs of John, first duke, other than William and his heirs.

In June 1733 Atholl replaced the earl of Ilay as lord privy seal, and on 21 September was chosen as a Scottish representative peer; he was reselected in 1734, when he was also invested with the Order of the Thistle. As maternal great-grandson of James Stanley, seventh earl of Derby, he succeeded in 1736, on the death of James, tenth earl, to the ancient barony of Strange of Knockyn, Wotton, Mohun, Burnel, Basset, and Lacy, and to the sovereignty of the Isle of Man. From 1737 to the general election of 1741 he sat in parliament both as an English baron and as a Scottish representative peer.

On the approach of the highland army after the landing of the Young Pretender in 1745, Atholl fled southwards. Tullibardine, his attainted elder brother, seized Blair Castle, the family seat. Atholl joined the duke of Cumberland in England, and, having arrived with him in Edinburgh on 30 January 1746, went northwards. On 9 February he summoned his vassals to muster at Dunkeld and Kirkmichael to join the Hanoverian side.

After the death of his wife in 1748 Atholl married Jean Drummond (d. 1795), daughter of John Drummond of Megginch, Perthshire, on 7 May 1749; they had no children. Jean, a very attractive woman, had jilted one Dr Austin for the duke, inspiring his song 'For lack of gold she left me, oh!'.

In 1754 Atholl was passed over as a member of the forfeited estates commission on General Bland's opinion that he was 'too much a highlander', who would keep up the distinctions between highlands and lowlands. The previous year one of his daughters from his first marriage, Lady Charlotte, married her cousin John *Murray, third duke of Atholl (1729–1774), the eldest son of Atholl's Jacobite brother George. Atholl had brought John up in his father's absence, and in 1760 Atholl caused anxiety by proposing John as a candidate for his old seat, Perthshire. In the by-election of 1762 he was still opposing the ministry's candidate. Despite this, in 1763 he was promoted to keeper of the great seal, resigning the privy seal to the duke of Queensberry, and to lord justice general, in place of Ilay.

Atholl took seriously ill in December that year, and died at Dunkeld on 8 January 1764; he was buried at Dunkeld Cathedral. He was survived by his second wife, who afterwards married General Lord Adam Gordon (d. 1801) and who died on 22 February 1795. Of his two daughters from his first marriage, Jean married John, earl of Crawford,

and Charlotte survived her sister to inherit the barony of Strange and sovereignty of the Isle of Man in 1764; her husband succeeded as third duke.

MAIRIANNA BIRKELAND

Sources GEC, *Peerage* · A. Murdoch, 'The people above': politics and administration in mid-eighteenth-century Scotland (1980) · A. M. Smith, Jacobite estates of the Forty-Five (1982) · J. M. Simpson, 'Murray, Lord James', HoP, *Commons* · DNB · Blair Castle archives · private information (2004)
Archives NL Scot., corresp., incl. legal corresp. · U. Edin. L., corresp.
Likenesses J. Davidson, oils, c.1738, Blair Castle, Perthshire · A. Ramsay, oils, 1743, Scot. NPG · J. Cheere, gilded bust, 1748, Blair Castle, Perthshire · J. Faber junior, mezzotint (after J. Davidson), BM, NPG
Wealth at death annual estates rental £9200: Blair Castle archives

Murray, James (1702–1758), Church of Scotland minister, was born at Dunkeld, Perthshire, and appears to have been related to the dukes of Atholl. He was educated at Marischal College, Aberdeen, where he was awarded the degree of MA. After completing his studies he was licensed as a probationer in the ministry but declined invitations to settle in Scotland. Instead he moved to London, where he became assistant preacher to the congregation at Swallow Street, Piccadilly. He may have been the James Murray ordained at Nightingale Lane in October 1737. Although an excellent classical scholar he was unpopular as a preacher and his 'sentiments are said to have given disgust to his hearers' (Wilson, 4.48). He resigned and returned to Scotland, residing for a time in the household of James Murray, second duke of Atholl. There he wrote his only known publication, *Aletheia, or, A System of Moral Truths* (2 vols., 1747). He died in London in 1758, aged fifty-five.

J. M. RIGG, rev. M. J. MERCER

Sources W. Wilson, *The history and antiquities of the dissenting churches and meeting houses in London, Westminster and Southwark*, 4 vols. (1808–14), vol. 4, p. 48 · *Transactions of the Congregational Historical Society*, 17 (1952–5), 65 · A. Chalmers, ed., *The general biographical dictionary*, new edn, 22 (1812–17), 527–8

Murray, James (1722–1794), army officer and colonial governor, was born on 21 January 1722, at Ballencrieff, Haddingtonshire, Scotland, the fifth son of Alexander Murray, fourth Lord Elibank (1677–1736), and his wife, Elizabeth (1684–1756), the daughter of George Stirling, a surgeon and the MP for Edinburgh City. Murray's father had lost heavily in the South Sea Bubble the year before his birth, and he was brought up in a setting of pride, frugality, and self-reliance. He was educated privately at Haddington, and later at William Dyce's academy in Selkirk. In 1736 he became a cadet in the 3rd Scots regiment in the Dutch service, and in 1740 he returned to England and received a commission in the 4th (Wynyard's) marines. Henry Murray, his elder brother, was lieutenant-colonel of that regiment.

Wynyard's marines formed part of the force under Lord Cathcart which embarked on the disastrous Cartagena expedition in 1740. In November 1741, while still on the expedition, Murray transferred as a captain to the 15th

James Murray (1722–1794), by unknown artist, *c.*1767

foot, with which he remained until 1759. The 15th foot suffered severely during the campaign, and returned to England only in December 1742.

The regiment was involved in the defence of Ostend in 1745 by a mixed force of British and Austrians (during which Murray was seriously wounded), and in the Lorient expedition of 1748. At Lorient, Murray was captain of the grenadier company of the 15th which attacked the French with great gallantry, the only creditable event in an incompetent military episode. On 17 December of that year, after the peace of Aix-la-Chapelle, when his regiment was posted to the south coast of England on garrison duty, Murray married Cordelia (1722–1779), the eldest daughter of John Collier of Hastings. Murray became a major in the 15th the following year and in January 1751 purchased the lieutenant-colonelcy, when the regiment was in Ireland.

Military service in Quebec In the early years of the Seven Years' War Murray commanded the regiment on the Rochfort expedition of 1757 and was a witness for the defence at the ensuing trial of Sir John Mordaunt. He took the regiment out to North America in 1757 and commanded a brigade at the siege and capture of Louisburg, Cape Breton, in 1758, earning General Wolfe's commendation for his services. Wolfe subsequently chose him as the junior brigadier at the siege of Quebec—Townshend and Monckton being the other two. Murray commanded the left wing of the army in the battle on the Plains of Abraham on 13 September 1759, when Wolfe fell. Murray, described as 'a man of the most ardent and intrepid courage, passionately desirous of glory, and emulous of the reputation Wolfe had acquired' (*Annual Register*, 1760, 7), later felt that

his contribution to the victory had been inadequately acknowledged.

Quebec surrendered on 18 September and Murray was left in command of the occupation with 4000 troops, while the rest of the army sailed away with the fleet before winter closed the St Lawrence River. He spent the winter of 1759–60 under appalling conditions, preparing for an expected siege by the regrouping French forces. He was almost without funds; food and fuel supplies were inadequate; drunkenness and thieving were rife among the soldiers and had to be met with savage discipline; and sickness was prevalent. During the first nine months of the occupation 1000 men died, and there was a daily average of an equal number sick, chiefly of scurvy.

On 26 April 1760 the French landed in the vicinity with a superior force and threatened the outposts at Lorette and St Foy. On 28 April Murray marched out with 2000 men and twenty guns and attacked the French at St Foy with great vigour, inflicting heavy losses. The audacity of the attack with a force so inferior surprised the French, but the British were outnumbered three to one, and after losing one-third of their number were driven back into the city, which was forthwith besieged by an army of 15,000 men. Murray's dispatches reporting this reverse reached London to create an inaccurate but lingering impression that he had almost lost Quebec through his impetuosity.

By 15 May de Levis, the French commander, disheartened by the arrival in the St Lawrence of a naval squadron under Lord Colville, raised the siege and retired to Montreal, where he joined the remaining French forces under De Vaudreil.

Murray's troops thereafter moved upriver, to form part of the force converging under General Amherst which brought about the capitulation of the French in Montreal on 13 September. Control of Canada passed to the victors.

Governor of Canada Following the capitulation of Montreal, Canada was subjected to a military regime. The colony was divided into three separately administered districts—Quebec, Trois Rivières, and Montreal—which were placed under Murray, Ralph Burton, and Thomas Gage respectively, each being responsible in turn to Amherst, the commander-in-chief, in New York. Murray's primary concern throughout the military regime of 1760–63 was security, for neither the return of the French nor a revolt by the Canadians could be ruled out.

On the establishment of civil government, proclaimed in Britain in November 1763 and inaugurated in Canada in August 1764, the districts were united into the province of Quebec, and Murray was appointed as the first governor, a position he held until 1766. Provision was made for him, as governor, to be assisted by two lieutenant-governors, but these positions were discontinued after both Gage and Burton declined to fill them. Murray had meanwhile been made colonel commandant of a battalion of the 60th Royal Americans in October 1759, and was promoted major-general in July 1762.

On Murray's proclamation as governor, the civil and

military governments were separated. This caused eventual friction with Burton, who in 1764 was given command of all the troops in the province. Murray maintained that, in Quebec, which was not only a conquered colony but one where the governor had always been the military chief, authority could not be shared. In September of the same year he suppressed, without resorting to extreme measures, a dangerous mutiny of the troops at Quebec, who, in consequence of a stoppage of supplies, threatened to march to New York and lay down their arms to General Amherst.

Murray faced great problems during the period of his administration in attempting to create a viable system of government for Canada which could reconcile the conflicting pressures he had inherited. The forms of government and the laws to be observed in the new colony were promulgated, but his efforts to alleviate the discontent of the conquered population, and to strike a balance between the religion and traditions of his Canadian subjects and the Anglicization pressed on him from the London government and the growing British community of merchants and traders, met with only partial success.

Representatives of the people were summoned to Quebec by the government in 1765; but the attempt to form a representative assembly failed, principally because the Catholics objected to the test oath imposed by statute. Murray's efforts to conciliate the French Canadians incensed the British settlers, who accused him of sacrificing their interests to French prejudices. Murray's position was not made easier by the belief among the British trading community that he lacked any business sense and, as an aristocrat and soldier, despised their attitudes and activities. His reluctance to provide some form of representative government provided them with ammunition progressively to undermine his authority with their powerful contacts in London, and his blunt independence and irascible nature had in any case already done little to endear him in ministerial circles.

A minor outbreak of civil disorder in Montreal in 1764 gave Murray's adversaries sufficient grievances to prompt the London government in April 1766 to recall him to account for the disorders in Montreal and, in general, his administration of Quebec. He left Canada, never to return, in June. An inquiry in the House of Lords after his return home, on a series of alleged malpractices, fully absolved Murray from these charges, which were dismissed as groundless and scandalous. These events left him, a man of great integrity, with an abiding resentment that he had been pilloried unnecessarily, and he made no contribution to the eventual framing of the Quebec Act of 1774 which laid down the future pattern of administration. Perhaps the most significant, if unforeseen, legacy of Murray's administration was in setting the precedent of conciliar rather than representative government, which was to become a pattern for crown colony government throughout the British empire over the next century.

Governor of Minorca After his retirement from Canada in 1766, Murray was for a time on the Irish staff, and then an inspecting general of the southern district. In December 1767 he exchanged his colonelcy in the 60th foot for that of the 13th foot. He became a lieutenant-general on 25 May 1772, and in 1774 was appointed lieutenant-governor of Minorca. In April 1779 he was appointed governor of the island, following the death of the non-resident governor, General Mostyn. As the likelihood of war with Spain became apparent, Murray's wife Cordelia returned to England, where she died, childless, on 26 June, soon after her arrival.

Shortly after war broke out with Spain in June 1779 a new lieutenant-governor took post in the person of Sir William Draper, with whom Murray's relations were initially cordial but deteriorated progressively. In 1781 Minorca was threatened with a siege. Murray sent off his young second wife, Anne (whom he had married on 14 March 1780), the daughter of Abraham Whitham, consul-general of Majorca, and their infant daughter, to Leghorn. He then prepared for a vigorous defence of Fort St Philip, which dominated Minorca's great natural harbour. On 20 August he was blockaded by 16,000 French and Spanish troops under the duc de Crillon, a French commander of repute who had been taken into the Spanish service. Murray's garrison consisted of only just over 2000 regular troops, 400 of whom were invalids, and all more or less unhealthy, as well as 200 seamen from a sloop scuttled earlier. Murray was thus faced, at the age of sixty, with a rerun of the siege of Quebec. His meritorious conduct during the siege earned him the nickname Old Minorca from his troops.

Despairing of reducing the place, which had formidable fortifications, de Crillon secretly offered Murray a bribe of £1 million sterling to surrender. Murray spurned the insult. On 16 October 1781 he wrote back to de Crillon, in French:

> when your brave ancestor was desired by his sovereign to assassinate the Duc de Guise he returned the answer that you should have done when the King of Spain charged you to assassinate the character of a man whose birth is as illustrious as your own or that of the Duc de Guise. I can have no further communication with you except in arms.

De Crillon replied: 'Your letter restores each of us to our place; it confirms the high opinion I always had of you' (Mahon, 400–03).

During the last four months of the siege relations between Murray and Sir William Draper deteriorated over arguments as to the limits of their operational authority, to the point that Sir William was relieved of his command in January 1782. On 5 February Murray's garrison was so reduced by the ravages of scurvy that only 600 men remained partially fit for duty. A capitulation was arranged and the remnants of the garrison marched out between two lines of French and Spanish troops, and laid down their arms declaring 'they had surrendered them to God alone as the victors could not plume themselves in taking a hospital' (*Annual Register*, 1782, 242).

Court martial On returning to England Draper preferred twenty-nine miscellaneous charges against Murray, who was tried by a general court martial presided over by Sir

George Howard, which sat between November 1782 and January 1783.

The court fully and honourably acquitted Murray of all the charges levelled against him except two—the issue of an order 'derogatory to his lieutenant-governor' (the trigger for the final rupture between himself and Sir William) and some interference with auction dues on the island—for which it sentenced him to be reprimanded. On the proceedings being submitted to the king:

> in consideration of the zeal, courage and firmness with which General Murray appears to the court to have conducted himself in the defence of Fort St Philip, as well as his former long and approved services, His Majesty has been pleased to dispense with any other reprimand.   (Mahon, 430–31)

Immediately afterwards, a Mr Sutherland brought an action against Murray for illegal suspension from the office of judge of the vice-admiralty court of Minorca. The matter had been referred home and the king had approved Murray's action, but a jury, the king's approval notwithstanding, gave damages against him to the amount of £6000. On 6 May 1785, on a division by 57 to 22, the House of Commons, acknowledging Murray's long career of service, decided that the damages, and Murray's costs, should be paid out of the public funds.

Murray, who was made a full general in February 1783 and colonel of the 21st fusiliers in June 1789, and was governor of Hull, retired to his residence at Beauport House, near Battle, Sussex, and died there on 18 June 1794. He was buried in the parish church of Ore, near Hastings. He was survived by his wife, three daughters, and a son, James Patrick Murray, who became a major-general and MP.

JAMES DREAPER

Sources R. H. Mahon, *Life of Lt-Gen. the Hon. James Murray* (1921) • *DCB*, vol. 3 • A. C. Murray, *The five sons of 'Bare Betty'* (1936) • BL, Add. MS 21628, fol. 302 • PRO, WO 71/100 • PRO, CO 174/12–14 • W. Draper, *Observations on Lt Gen Murray's defence* (1783) • *Sentence of court martial for trial of Hon. Lt-Gen James Murray* (1783) • *Journal of siege of Quebec, 1759–60*, Quebec Literary and Historical Society, Historical Document (1871) • Walpole, *Corr.* • *Annual Register* (1759) • *Annual Register* (1760) • *Annual Register* (1763) • *Annual Register* (1782) • *CSP dom.*, 1760–69

Archives E. Sussex RO, family corresp. • NA Canada, corresp. and journals • NA Scot., corresp. • NL Scot., journal • NRA, priv. coll., corresp. and letterbooks relating to Quebec and Minorca | BL, corresp. with Sir Frederick Haldimand, Add. MSS 21666, 21668, 21683, 21697 • BL, corresp. with Lord Liverpool, Add. MSS 38211–38217, 38306–38308 • Bodl. Oxf., corresp. with Lord Guilford • CKS, corresp. with Lord Amherst • NRA Scotland, priv. coll., letters to Allan Macpherson • NRA, priv. coll., letters to J. Oswald • PRO, corresp. with Lord Amherst, WO34 • U. Mich., Clements L., corresp. with Thomas Gage

Likenesses oils, c.1767, NPG [*see illus.*] • Gillray, cartoon, 1782

Murray, James (1732–1782), Independent minister, was born at Fans, near Earlston, in Berwickshire. He was raised in a 'reputable and religious family' (Hone, vi). He entered the university at Edinburgh at a time when it was undergoing a radical change in both its teaching methods and curriculum—events which had brought about a 'quickening of the spirit of intellectual enquiry' (R. G. Cant, 'Origins of the Enlightenment: the universities', *The Origins and Nature of the Scottish Enlightenment*, ed. R. H. Campbell

and A. S. Skinner, 1982, 47). He studied divinity with Professor Hamilton and seems to have completed his course probably in 1760, when he received a certificate from Dr Hamilton on 28 April. He appears to have been influenced by the Enlightenment movement within Scotland, maintaining throughout his life that 'no man could be a real Christian, who was not a warm and zealous friend to civil and religious liberty' (Hone, iv). His friends viewed him as a minister who was willing to promote views that were 'new and liberal' (ibid., v).

The established Church of Scotland had experienced various divisions over the previous thirty years, and Murray left Edinburgh to become the assistant to John Sayers, minister of the Broadgate meeting-house at Alnwick. A disagreement with the minister led to Murray's dismissal by the church, although a large number of the congregation separated and built a chapel in Baliffgate Square, ordaining Murray as their first minister. Murray moved to Newcastle upon Tyne in 1764, where he remained for the rest of his life as minister of High Bridge Chapel. He published several works on religious subjects during the late 1760s and early 1770s, including *The History of Religion* (1764), and *A History of the Churches of England and Scotland* (1771–2).

Murray was a severe critic of the evangelical awakening, associated with John Wesley and George Whitefield, and wrote against them in his famous *Sermons to Asses* (1768); the text is dedicated to them and to two others, as most 'worthy of a dedication of a work of this kind'. Although contemporaries within Scotland saw the revival movement associated with Whitefield as 'one of the most remarkable effusions of the Spirit on some corners of the land … since the Reformation' (T. Gillespie, 'Dunfermline sermons for 1746', Dunfermline Public Library, fol. 80r), Murray did not associate himself with such an enthusiastic form of religion. His commitment to protestantism led him in 1778 to oppose Sir George Saville's bill to remove certain Catholic disabilities, and he published *News from the Pope to the Devil* and *Popery not Christianity* in 1781 as well as using his pulpit and various other public meetings to 'petition against the Catholic claims' (Hone, viii).

During the American War of Independence, Murray opposed the policy of Lord North, first lord of the Treasury and leader of the House of Commons, who introduced various bills in parliament which led to the outbreak of the war. His attitudes contrasted with those of the moderate party in the Church of Scotland who had influenced his early thinking, and who had no sympathy with the American 'rebels' because they threatened social and political law and order. Strangely enough, Murray followed the lead of evangelicals within Scotland who opposed fighting those who were members of the church and who supported the Americans' struggle for political rights. He published *The Finishing Stroke to Mr Wesley's Calm Address to the People of England* (1778), and *An Impartial History of the Present War in America*, in two volumes in the same year (this was reprinted a number of times in the next few years in both England and America). The American crisis brought Murray's liberal and sometimes radical views to the attention of the government. He was a powerful orator and drew crowded congregations to his public lectures, speaking on current events of political and social significance. He did not hesitate in using his pulpit to speak against government policy which impeded the rights of citizens to enjoy political and religious freedom. He is said to have been one of the principal editors of the *Freemen's Magazine, or, The Constitutional Repository* (1774), a political journal supporting John Wilkes, and complaining about the loss of liberty under the current government. His contemporary Thomas Bewick spoke of him as a 'cheerful ... sensible, pleasant man—a most agreeable companion, full of anecdote and information'. Murray married Sarah Weddell of Mouson, Northumberland (*d.* 1798), and they had several children. He died at Newcastle on 28 January 1782. KENNETH B. E. ROXBURGH

Sources W. Hone, 'Biographical sketch', in J. Murray, *Sermons to asses* (1819) [preface] · *ESTC* · *DNB* · E. Mackenzie, *A descriptive and historical account of the town and county of Newcastle upon Tyne*, 2 vols. (1827)

Likenesses Pollard, line engraving (after Van Cook), NPG · engraving, repro. in J. Murray, *Travels of the imagination*, new edn (1828) · portrait, repro. in J. Murray, *An impartial history of the present war in America*, 2 vols. (1778) · portrait, repro. in J. Murray, *Sermons to Asses*, ed. [W. Hone], new edn (1817) · stipple, NPG

Murray, Sir James (1788–1871), physician, was born in co. Londonderry, the son of Edward Murray and his wife, Belinda, daughter of John Powell. He was admitted as a licentiate of the Edinburgh College of Surgeons and as a licentiate in midwifery in 1807, and as licentiate of the Royal College of Surgeons in Ireland (army) of the Dublin college in 1808. After hearing lectures given at Edinburgh by John Dalton, Murray determined to establish the 'exact proportions of heat, or electricity, naturally belonging to ... living atoms, in a state of health' (Murray, *Electricity*, 6). In 1809 he married Mary, daughter of George Sharrock, with whom he had several children.

After qualifying Murray was appointed resident medical officer in a Belfast hospital and dispensary, where he experimented with electrical apparatus. His career prospered under the patronage of the marquess of Donegal, who owned Belfast Castle. About 1809 Murray developed a fluid magnesia, which he widely publicized. Epsom salts had long been known as a purgative; Murray's Fluid Magnesia, specially prepared and marketed by the firm of Sir James Murray & Son, was an aqueous solution of magnesium carbonate recommended as a palatable laxative and as a remedy for acidities, indigestion, heartburn, and gout. Murray developed a lemon syrup to mix with fluid magnesia to form a pleasant effervescing aperient for women and child patients. He also marketed Sir James Murray's Pure Fluid Camphor, a tonic for weak nerves, low fever, and diarrhoea. Some colleagues deprecated his descent into commerce; on several occasions he was forced to protect his business by litigation after his rights were infringed.

Murray graduated MD at Edinburgh University in 1829, and was appointed in 1831 as resident physician to the lord lieutenant of Ireland, the marquess of Anglesey, by whom

he was knighted in 1833. He received an honorary degree of MD from Dublin University in 1832 and was appointed inspector of anatomical schools in Ireland (which post he held until a few months before his death). He was also a member of the central board of health. He travelled abroad with Anglesey in 1834–5, remitting rapturous letters about the architectural, artistic, and historic glories of Florence and Rome. At this time, and on a further visit to Italy in 1844, he studied malaria, developing a theory that the fever was caused by electro-galvanic currents and accumulations. He was passionately responsive to the natural beauties of Italy and relished the social brilliance of his connection with the viceroy. It was both a personal pleasure and a professional success to be confirmed as resident physician to Anglesey's successors as lords lieutenant of Ireland, the marquess of Normanby (1835) and Viscount Ebrington (1839). It cannot have been convenient that Murray's eldest child, John Fisher *Murray, in 1841 published a novel, *The Viceroy*, satirizing 'the worms and sycophants of Irish lord lieutenancy' (*Athenaeum*, 9 Jan 1841, 35). When Earl De Grey was appointed viceroy in 1841, Murray's appointment at Dublin Castle was not renewed. In 1848 Murray married again; he and his second wife, Mary, daughter of Samuel Allen, had one daughter.

For some years Murray was physician to the Netterville Dispensary and to the Anglesey Lying-In Hospital, Dublin. He was the first physician to recommend inhalation of iodine in water vapour for respiratory diseases, and in 1829 he published his *Dissertation on the influence of heat and humidity, with practical observations on the inhalation of iodine* (reissued in 1837, with additions on his technique of tracheotomy, as *Medical Essays*). His *Dissertation* examined body temperatures in numerous diseases, and the effects of heat and fluidity on medicinal substances; it suggested that dilution aided the effects of most medicines. Electrotherapeutics, however, commanded Murray's greatest interest. In *Electricity as a cause of cholera or other epidemics, and the relation of galvanism to the action of remedies* (1849), he collected his 'views of Voltaic agency on the laws of life' (p. 4). He argued that epidemics were caused by disturbances of natural electricity; either depletion or excess of electricity in the nervous system could derange the vital organs; '*nervous energy* and *electric power* seemed to be *identical*, or, at least, ... they appeared to stand in the relation of *cause* and *effect*' (ibid., 9). During the cholera epidemic of 1832 he made strenuous efforts to save patients by removing atmospheric pressure from the external surface of their bodies using an air pump of his own devising. Murray advocated the medical use of atmospheric pressure in air-baths. He reported his many experiments in numerous publications.

Murray resented the credit of his discoveries being stolen by others, and the 'intrigues of supercilious ignorance, and jealous mediocrity' (Murray, *Medical Essays*, v). He remained of Herculean frame and strength until shortly before dying on 8 December 1871 at his home, 19 Upper Temple Street, Dublin. He was buried at Glasnevin cemetery, Dublin. RICHARD DAVENPORT-HINES

Sources *ILN* (23 Dec 1871) · *ILN* (6 Jan 1872) · *The Lancet* (16 Dec 1871) · Marquess of Anglesey [G. C. H. V. Paget], *One-leg: the life and letters of Henry William Paget, first marquess of Anglesey* (1961), 280–81 · M. Pelling, *Cholera, fever and English medicine, 1825–1865* (1978) · J. Murray, *Electricity as a cause of cholera or other epidemics* (1849) · J. Murray, *Medical essays* (1837)
Archives Plas Newydd, Anglesey, Anglesey MSS
Likenesses engraving (after photograph by T. Cranfield), repro. in *ILN* (6 Jan 1872), 16
Wealth at death under £1500: probate, 19 March 1872, *CGPLA Ire.*

Murray, James (1831–1863), architect, was born in Armagh, northern Ireland, on 9 December 1831. He was articled to the architect Walter Scott of Liverpool in 1845, and afterwards practised there in partnership with Thomas Denville Barry. He moved to Coventry, and subsequently settled in London, where he executed several works in connection with E. Welby Pugin between 1857 and 1859, including a group of almshouses at Albury, Surrey (1857). At the dissolution of this partnership he returned permanently to Coventry. His works were principally schools, shops, villas, and churches in Coventry and the midlands. His most important work included the Justice Rooms, Coventry, and the corn exchanges at Coventry (1856), Banbury (1857), and St Albans (1853). He also built churches at Warwick, Bolton, Grange-over-Sands, Sunderland, Stratford upon Avon, Coventry, and Birmingham. He designed the school of science and art, Stoke-on-Trent, in 1858–60 (later the public health department), and Coventry School of Art in 1863 (converted). He was elected FRIBA in 1860. He published *Modern architecture, ecclesiastic, civil, and domestic: Gothic and classic buildings erected since 1850*, pt 1 (1862), which includes illustrations of his own work. Murray died on 24 October 1863 at Warwick Green South, Coventry, leaving a widow, Maria Jane. He was succeeded in his practice by Thomas E. Murray and H. E. Thomas of Liverpool.

A printed *List of the Works of James Murray (1831–63)* is filed with Murray's drawings in the RIBA collection; his entry in the catalogue notes that 'his style, with its strong geometrical shapes and polychromatic details, has similarities with the work of [William] Butterfield. He was reckoned to have had considerable ability but he died very young' (Lever, 100).

ALBERT NICHOLSON, *rev.* VALERIE SCOTT

Sources *A compendium of Pevsner's Buildings of England*, ed. M. Good (1995) [CD-ROM] · *The Builder*, 21 (1863), 780, 807–8 · J. Lever, ed., *Catalogue of the drawings collection of the Royal Institute of British Architects: L–N* (1973), 100 · *Dir. Brit. archs.* · *CGPLA Eng. & Wales* (1864)
Archives RIBA BAL, biographical file; RIBA nomination papers; drawings collection
Wealth at death under £1000: probate, 4 Aug 1864, *CGPLA Eng. & Wales*

Murray, Sir James Augustus Henry (1837–1915), lexicographer, was born in the village of Denholm, near Hawick, Roxburghshire, on 7 February 1837, the eldest of the four sons and one daughter of Thomas Murray (1811–1873), a village tailor, of Hawick, and his wife, Mary (1803–1888), the sixth child of Charles Scott, a linen manufacturer of Denholm.

Formative years in Scotland Thomas Murray was highly regarded in Denholm. He was an elder of the Congregational church and a promoter of the Total Abstinence and Horticultural societies, of the Reading Room Club, and of other institutions contributing to the welfare of the village. His formal education was limited, however, and there was certainly no tradition of academic scholarship in the ancestral families of the Murrays or the Scotts that would account for the emergence of the lexicographical prodigy that his son proved to be. James Murray is reputed to have known the letters of the alphabet by the time he was eighteen months old and to have acquired a knowledge of the written forms of Greek letters before he was seven. He is also known to have copied out on scraps of paper some lists and passages in Hebrew and Chinese written in copies of the Bible that happened to come into his parents' possession.

Murray was educated first at Cavers School, the parish school of his native village. It was a 3 mile walk from Denholm, and his lifelong interest in botany may well have begun among the many wild flowers that grew beside the footpaths that took him to and from this school. In 1845 he moved to Denholm School, which took pupils from infancy until they were old enough to go out to work. He was soon recognized to be a pupil of unusual ability: he took in his stride the names of the parts of speech, the elements of geography and mathematics, and, as the only boy taking the subject, an outline knowledge of Latin. In his out-of-school hours he became interested in astronomy and in identifying the Latin names of plants, as well as the names of rock formations and other features of geology, and the classification of the names and varieties of animals.

An outbreak of cholera in Denholm in 1849 closed the school and led to an arrangement for Murray to spend six months as a cowherd on a friend's farm near by, where he remembered 'hammering away at [his] Latin grammar and *Lectiones Selectae*' in his spare time. The family returned to Denholm at the end of summer 1849, but Murray did not return to his old school. He went instead to Minto School, a mile and a half from Denholm, where he fell under the influence of an inspiring new schoolmaster, John Rankin Hamilton, and a new syllabus. He began work on four new languages: French, German, Italian, and classical Greek.

Murray left school at fourteen and a half, and helped the family budget by taking temporary employment of various kinds. He learned how to bind books and declared on the flyleaf of the first issue of John Cassell's serial publication *Popular Educator* (1852) 'Knowledge is power' and 'Nihil est melius quam vita diligentissima'. In 1854 he left home and was accepted first as a junior assistant master at the grammar school in Hawick, and then, in 1857, he became headmaster of a private school called the Hawick Academy. His extra-curricular activities continued in the same vein as before: he acquired an outline knowledge of the written form of up to twenty-five foreign languages (his own figure), including Russian and Tongan, and also made a close study of the local border dialect. In addition to his language work, he explored the geological structure of the Teviotdale district, and its flora and fauna.

In August 1856 a public meeting was called in Hawick at which it was agreed to form an archaeological society, with James Murray as its secretary. By 1858 Murray's interests had widened to include philology. In Edinburgh in 1857 he had attended a vacation course on elocution by Alexander Melville Bell, the inventor of a phonetic system called 'Visible Speech', a set of symbols designed to record the pronunciation of every sound used in human speech. Melville Bell's son Alexander Graham Bell, the inventor of the telephone, later became Murray's friend; when he moved to London Melville Bell was one of those who introduced him to the Philological Society. Reflecting a more general movement in Europe, the Hawick Archaeological Society turned its attention in 1859 to philology, and in particular to the history and nature of the variety of English used in the Hawick area. As a typical example of the new thinking, Prince Louis-Lucien Bonaparte, nephew of Napoleon, persuaded Henry Scott Riddell, the president of the society, to translate parts of the Bible into lowland Scots.

James Murray, by now alerted to the need for someone to investigate the nature and history of varieties of English extant in the British Isles, learned Gaelic, began his research into the dialects of Scotland's southern counties, and planned a phonetic key to Jamieson's *Etymological Dictionary of the Scottish Language* (1808). He also began studying the language of the Anglo-Saxon period, especially that used in the surviving works of King Alfred. Members of the Hawick Archaeological Society placed many books at his disposal. He absorbed them all, including the language of the Bible as translated into Gothic (also formerly called Moeso-Gothic) AD *c*.350 by Bishop Ulfilas (or Wulfila), preserved in a manuscript of the fifth or sixth century entitled the Codex Argenteus.

Migration to London At this stage of his life Murray was in many respects a recluse—interested, it would seem, only in the pursuit of a scholarly *vita diligentissima*. He was also a 'tall, strong, healthy, good-looking boy' who wore his hair to shoulder length in the fashion of his time. At the time of his appointment to Hawick grammar school 'he was encouraging the growth of the red beard, which turning to snow white in later years, was to contribute to his striking and patriarchal appearance' (K. M. E. Murray, 26).

On 12 August 1862 Murray married Margaret (Maggie) Scott (1834–1865) an infant-school mistress, the daughter of a Hawick clerk. She had taught for three or four years in a primary school near Manchester, but at the time of her marriage was living in Belfast. She and Murray were married in the Fisherwick Presbyterian Church, Belfast, after which they lived in Hawick, with Murray returning to teach at the Hawick Academy. In January 1864 Maggie gave birth to a daughter, but both mother and daughter were 'weak and ailing', and the baby died in August of that year. Their doctor recommended that for the sake of Maggie's health—she was suffering from consumption in an advanced stage—they should migrate to a place in a more equitable climate. The place turned out to be London. Murray found rented accommodation in Nunhead Lane, near Dulwich, and accepted a post as a bank clerk in the Chartered Bank of India, Australia, and China in

Sir James Augustus Henry Murray (1837–1915), by S. S. McClure

Threadneedle Street. The couple attended the Congregational church at Camberwell. Murray was soon invited to preach, and to take part in the educational work of the church. But Maggie's health did not improve, and she died in September 1865.

Before Maggie's death the Murrays had become friendly with the Ruthven family, who were near neighbours in Camberwell, and on 17 August 1867 James Murray married the eldest daughter, Ada Agnes Ruthven (1845–1936). Alexander Graham Bell was his best man. The marriage proved remarkably happy—where Murray was 'naive in dealing with money matters', Ada was by contrast exceptionally businesslike.

Murray obtained a reader's ticket at the British Museum, and revived his earlier interest in comparative philology and in the study of the border dialects. Through Melville Bell he met Alexander John Ellis, who was writing an important history of English pronunciation. Ellis in turn introduced Murray to Henry Sweet, who was also to make signal contributions to the study of the English language. It was not long before Murray met other philologists: these included Richard Morris, who, along with A. J. Ellis, Walter Skeat, and Melville Bell, introduced him to the activities of the Philological Society and the publications of the Early English Text Society. Murray made progress with the project close to his heart: the preparation of his book *The Dialect of the Southern Counties of Scotland* (finally issued by the Philological Society in 1873). He was invited to deliver papers at meetings of the society, and duly gave three papers between 1868 and 1869. He had entered new territory in the systematic study of dialects of the English language as found in Scotland, referring to them as 'Scotch dialects', as was customary at the time. He also joined the English Dialect Society.

Perhaps Murray's most important scholarly connection, however, was with Frederick J. Furnivall, a mercurial scholar, who had deservedly established a reputation as an energetic founder of organizations designed to promote the study of English language and literature. Murray produced several editions for Furnivall's Early English Text Society: *The Minor Poems of Sir David Lindesay* (1871), *The Complaynt of Scotlande* (1872, 1873), and *Romance and Prophecies of Thomas of Erceldoune* (1875). This editorial work, apart from its value to Middle English scholarship, formed an ideal background to the stern lexicographical task that lay ahead.

Mill Hill School Murray's work as a bank clerk came to an end in 1870 when he became a schoolmaster at Mill Hill School, which had been established in 1807 as the 'Protestant dissenters' Grammar School'. Mill Hill was then a village just north-west of London. A particular attraction of the post was that he was offered a rented house, with a garden, only five minutes' walk from the school. His years there were among the happiest of his life, his 'Arcadian Years' as he called them. He founded a Natural History Society, and encouraged his pupils to explore the countryside and learn how to classify the local flora and fauna, for example by listing all the quadrupeds to be found locally—mice, voles, weasels, and so on. He had a real talent for

teaching, dating from his early childhood when he had done his best to pass on his knowledge and enthusiasms to his younger brothers. His school lessons were interesting and entertaining—it was said that 'a nominal geography class might easily develop into a lecture on Icelandic roots'. Another tradition has it that in teaching German he composed doggerel verses and stories to illustrate the declension of German nouns. He often preached in the school chapel, and his sermons had two dominant themes—the doctrine of work and his belief in divine guidance.

Elisabeth Murray neatly summarizes the pressures on her grandfather as he worked away on a wide range of activities:

> In the years 1870 to 1875 it must be remembered that besides his school duties he was also working on dialects with [A. J.] Ellis … He was helping Ellis, [Henry] Nicol and [Frederick] Elworthy with their proofs: he was writing papers for the Philological Society: he was working on numerous texts for the Early English Text Society in addition to the three he actually published, … and he was also reviewing books for the *Academy* and the *Athenæum*. (K. M. E. Murray, 116–17)

In addition to all this he was now studying for an external London BA degree, which he completed in 1873. In 1874 he was awarded the honorary degree of LLD by the University of Edinburgh. He was now entitled to wear a 'full-dress gown of extra Saxony light scarlet cloth, faced with rich blue silk' (a revival of the old ceremonial dress worn at the university before the Reformation) and a cap of a pattern worn by his hero John Knox. Murray wore the cap to work in for the rest of his life. In 1878 he was elected to the office of president of the Philological Society.

Between 1868 and 1888 the Murrays had eleven children, and all were brought up in an intellectual atmosphere. They were discouraged from the reading of novels, and encouraged to write their own stories and poems. They produced a series of magazines. Their father helped them to form the Sunnyside Amateur Debating Society, Sunnyside being the name of the house at Mill Hill and later of the family's home in Oxford. Family holidays in Hastings, the Isle of Wight, the Lake District, Wales, and elsewhere were characterized by Murray's insistence that the children should pursue his own boyhood hobbies—history, archaeology, botany, geology, and so on. All the Murray children were given first names drawn from Anglo-Saxon literature and history, with second and other names honouring relations from their father's or mother's families.

The early years of the 'New English dictionary' In 1857, at the suggestion of the dean of Westminster, Richard Chenevix Trench, the Philological Society resolved to prepare a large dictionary of the English language, intending to include as comprehensive a collection as possible of English words and meanings that had survived the Norman conquest or been introduced into the language after the conquest. The hope was that the final product, 'by the completeness of its vocabulary, and by the application of the historical method to the life and use of words, might be worthy of the English language and of English scholarship' (preface to vol. 1 of the *Oxford English Dictionary*).

The project was motivated by the need for a more up-to-date dictionary than the latest editions of the three standard dictionaries of the time, those of Charles Richardson, Noah Webster, and Joseph Worcester. These were three very respectable dictionaries, but the difference was that the proposed new one was to be based on historical principles: that is, each word and meaning was to be supported by evidence drawn from works of every kind—those of famous authors, such as Chaucer, Malory, Shakespeare, Milton, Pope, Wordsworth, and Dickens, but also those of 'minor' authors, private letters, glossaries and early dictionaries, technical handbooks, newspapers, learned journals, and so on.

Herbert Coleridge was appointed editor, and as a first step he established an ambitious reading programme in which quotational evidence was to be systematically gathered. Several hundred readers were drawn into the scheme, including F. J. Furnivall, the novelist Charlotte Yonge, and the etymologist Professor W. W. Skeat. One of the odder incidents in the history of the dictionary was that a particularly prolific contributor of illustrative quotations, Dr W. C. Minor, was later discovered to have been confined in the Broadmoor Asylum for the Criminally Insane during the time of his contributions—he had shot and killed a man some years before in an apparently motiveless attack. Minor provided an invaluable service to the dictionary with his painstaking lexicographical research.

The importance of these readers to the larger project cannot be overemphasized. One reader (Thomas Austin) had produced 165,000 supporting quotations by the time that the first volume (A–B) was published in 1888. Furnivall had produced 30,000 in the same period, and Minor came up with between 5000 and 8000 quotations. Ultimately, the dictionary was very much a collaborative effort. Other assistants, including members of Murray's own family, helped with sorting and filing the material as it arrived. About fifty names, including those of Charlotte Yonge and W. W. Skeat, are listed in the preface to volume 1 as having sub-edited, or prepared for sub-editing, the quotational evidence submitted to the editor.

However successful the reading of sources was to become, in the early years of the project it proved inadequate. What Dean Trench had grandly described in 1857 as 'this drawing as with a sweep-net over the whole extent of English literature' had by 1860 garnered only about one-tenth of the quotations that were ultimately needed. In 1861 Herbert Coleridge died. Furnivall was persuaded to take on the editorship, but his methods of work were erratic and in the end unsuccessful. As a first step he proposed the compilation of a concise dictionary, and forecast that such a book could be produced in three years. Both ideas came to nothing. Negotiations with Macmillan as possible publisher of the society's dictionary also proved to be unfruitful, and the dictionary's future was uncertain.

The Oxford University Press   In March 1879, after a series of prolonged discussions, the Philological Society came to an agreement with the Oxford University Press concerning the editing and publication of what was now to be known as *The Oxford English Dictionary* (*OED*). After consulting several scholars, among them Frederick Furnivall, Henry Sweet, and the comparative philologist Max Müller, the delegates of the press offered the task of editing the dictionary to James Murray. He was invited to edit the material for publication in parts. It was proposed that he would be able to compile the successive fascicles with help from a small editorial staff while he was still teaching at Mill Hill School. Murray, estimating that the dictionary could be finished in ten years in an estimated 7000 pages, accepted. In fact the first fascicle, consisting of words in the range A–Ant, was not published until 1884, and the last one in 1928, forty-four years later. (Volume publication, collating the fascicles, also took place over this span of time). In its final form the dictionary consisted of more than 16,000 pages.

Murray arranged for a workroom to be built in the small front garden of his house in which to store all the accumulated piles of illustrative quotations that had arrived over the years; it was also to serve as a suitable place for editing the dictionary itself. He jokingly called this building his scriptorium. Elisabeth Murray describes the initial chaos in graphic terms:

> Many of the sub-editors had clearly found difficulty in packing up hundredweights of [dictionary] slips. Some were sent in sacks in which they had long been stored, and when opened a dead rat was found in one and a live mouse and her family in another ... Many of the bundles had stood for so many years in unsuitable places that the slips were crumbling with damp and the writing had faded.   (K. M. E. Murray, 174)

It was clear that much additional work needed to be done before the editing could begin.

Nor did it take long for Murray to discover that much of the reading of sources already conducted was inadequate. Moreover, many early English texts previously existing only in manuscript form or in inadequate editions were being issued while work on the dictionary continued. These new editions, many published by the Early English Text Society, needed to be taken into account by the voluntary readers. One other set-back was that the excerpting of eighteenth-century works having been allocated to a group of American readers, the organization of their work had proved to be unsystematic.

In 1885 the second part (Ant–Batten) of the dictionary was published. Murray left Mill Hill and moved with his family to Oxford, where he could devote his whole time to the dictionary. He worked, with a small group of modestly paid assistants, in a new scriptorium built for the purpose in the garden of his house at 78 Banbury Road. The Mill Hill scriptorium, which had been planned from the beginning as a portable building, was presented to Mill Hill School, the costs of its removal being met by money raised from an appeal to old boys. Murray's idea was that it would be a quiet place for the boys to read in, especially on Sundays. It was burnt down by accident in 1902, but was replaced, and there is still a 'Murray scriptorium' used as a reading-room at the school.

Three more editors Before the editing of words in the letter B had been completed it became obvious that another editor should be appointed, to work for a year under Murray's supervision, and then, with a small team of assistants, to produce some later sections of the dictionary. Henry Bradley was this second independent editor, beginning in 1889. He and his assistants had a separate office in Broad Street, Oxford. At the end of the nineteenth century, by which time less than half the dictionary had been completed, a third co-editor was needed. The person appointed, in 1901, was W. A. Craigie, who had joined the staff of the dictionary in 1897. His work as an independent editor began with the letter Q, and by 1928, when the dictionary was completed, he had edited nearly a fifth of the *OED*. In the same period he was appointed professor of Anglo-Saxon in the University of Oxford, and also played a leading role in two other lexicographical projects. A fourth editor, C. T. Onions, who had been an editorial assistant on the staff of the dictionary, first in 1895 in Murray's team and later in Bradley's, became responsible from 1914 to 1928 for fascicles in the range Sub–Sz, parts of the letter W, and the whole of the letters X, Y, and Z.

The thirty years from 1885 to 1915 that Murray spent in Oxford were almost wholly devoted to his work on the dictionary. Except for brief holidays in Britain and an absence of some months in 1905 on a visit to the Cape Colony, during which he received an honorary LittD degree from the University of Cape Town, he worked unceasingly on the dictionary with a small staff of assistants including some of his children.

Throughout the preparation of the dictionary he had to endure what his biographer called 'The Triple Nightmare: Space, Time, and Money'. The project was plagued by a lack of adequate office space in which to accommodate the editorial staff and their essential books, as well as the pigeon-holes for the quotation slips. There was also mounting pressure from the delegates of the University Press, who feared that the return on their investment was increasingly at risk because the dictionary was taking much longer to prepare than had seemed likely when the contract was signed in 1879. Murray felt persecuted by what he saw as harassment to accelerate the rate of completion of the fascicles.

Murray gave occasional lectures on the project, the best-known of which was the Romanes lecture, 'The evolution of English lexicography', which he delivered on 22 June 1900 in the Sheldonian Theatre, Oxford. It gave an outline account of the emergence of interlinear glosses (some Latin/Latin, others Latin/English) in England in the pre-conquest period, and the later transformation of individual glosses into classified and alphabetized lists of 'hard words', then into dictionaries of 'hard words', and finally into dictionaries of 'the whole' language, including ordinary words such as the definite and indefinite articles, adverbs, prepositions, phrasal verbs, and so on—arguably

the most difficult entries to compile in any modern dictionary. The scale of the *OED* was astonishing by comparison with that of any English dictionary published before the end of the nineteenth century. Murray had revolutionized the whole process by which the English language was mapped.

Murray had the satisfaction of receiving honorary degrees from nine universities, Cambridge and Oxford among them in 1913 and 1914 respectively. The *OED* was dedicated to Queen Victoria in 1897. Murray was knighted in 1908. He died at his home in Oxford on 26 July 1915 from heart failure, following a year of ill health which culminated in a bout of pleurisy, one of many such illnesses caused by working in his cold, damp scriptorium. Sheer determination had earlier that month driven this ill, old man of seventy-eight to complete a double section of the dictionary, covering entries in the range 'Trink' to 'Turndown', on schedule. He was buried on 30 July in the Wolvercote cemetery on the northern outskirts of Oxford, and was survived by his wife and children.

Continuations and parallels The *OED* was completed in 1928, the editing of the fascicles after Murray's death having been entrusted to his colleagues Henry Bradley, W. A. Craigie, and C. T. Onions. Some other dictionaries on historical principles have been produced or are in hand in Germany, Sweden, France, and the Netherlands, each of them presenting its material in a manner broadly similar to that of the *OED*. Several dictionaries of varieties of English with the entries presented historically—in Scotland, the USA, Canada, the Caribbean, Australia, South Africa, and New Zealand—were published in the twentieth century. All owe a great deal to the methodology of Murray's pioneering work.

A one-volume supplement to the twelve-volume *OED*, edited by W. A. Craigie and C. T. Onions, was published in 1933, and a four-volume supplement, edited by R. W. Burchfield, was published between 1972 and 1986. The contents of these four volumes, together with some additional material, were absorbed in the second edition of the *OED* in 1989. The twelve volumes of the *OED* had become twenty volumes by 1989. It is expected that the third edition will be double that size.

Later editions of the dictionary have departed from Murray's basic principles in only two important ways. He had not given sufficient attention to the English used outside the British Isles, whereas since the 1972–86 supplement the *OED* has attempted to cover the language as it is written and spoken throughout the world. And, as was to be expected of a Victorian lexicographer, Murray drew a veil over all coarse words: none of the ancient 'four-letter' words was included in his dictionary.

At the time of Murray's death in 1915 the portions of the *OED* for which he was personally responsible amounted to about half of the whole. Henry Bradley's tribute to Murray in the *Proceedings of the British Academy* is just:

> When the remaining part of the last volume is finished, the Oxford English Dictionary will stand unrivalled in its completeness as a record of the history of the vocabulary of

a living language, and it is to Murray far more than to any other man that the honour of this great achievement will belong.

R. W. BURCHFIELD

Sources K. M. E. Murray, *Caught in the web of words* (1977) · J. A. H. Murray, *The evolution of English lexicography* (1900) [Romanes lecture]; repr. with introduction by R. W. Burchfield, *International Journal of Lexicography*, 6/2 (1993), 89–122 · H. Frowde, ed., *Frederick James Furnivall: a volume of personal record* (1911) · *The Periodical* [Oxford University Press], 5/83 (15 Sept 1915) · 'Sir James Murray: in memoriam', *A new Oxford dictionary on historical principles* [a note, 1 Oct 1915, prefixed to the section of vol. 9, containing 'Standard'–'Stead'] · H. Bradley, 'Sir James Murray, 1837–1915', *PBA*, [8] (1917–18) · *DNB* · *Sir James A. H. Murray: a self-portrait*, ed. G. F. Timpson [n.d., c.1957] · M. K. C. MacMahon, 'James Murray and the phonetic notation in the *New English dictionary*', *Transactions of the Philological Society* (1985), 72–112 · D. R. Raymond, ed., *Dispatches from the front: the prefaces to the Oxford English dictionary* (1987) · R. W. Burchfield, 'The *Oxford English dictionary* and the state of the language ', *Scholarly Publishing* (May 1988), 168–78 · 'The history of the *Oxford English dictionary*', *Oxford English dictionary*, ed. J. A. Simpson and E. S. C. Weiner, 2nd edn (1989), vii–xxiii · S. Winchester, *The surgeon of Crowthorne* (1998)

Archives Bodl. Oxf., corresp. relating to *Oxford English Dictionary* | Bodl. Oxf., letters to A. S. Napier · ICL, letters to S. P. Thompson · NL Scot., corresp. · U. Birm., corresp. with Edward Arber · U. Edin. L., letters to Sir Archibald Geikie

Likenesses photograph, c.1885, repro. in Murray, *Caught in the web of words*, frontispiece · S. S. McClure, photograph, NPG [*see illus.*] · W. Rothenstein, lithograph, BM

Wealth at death £3836 17s. 9d.: probate, 22 Sept 1915, *CGPLA Eng. & Wales*

Murray, Sir James Wolfe (1853–1919), army officer, was born on 13 March 1853, the eldest son of James Wolfe Murray (1814–1890) of Cringletie, near Peebles, Peeblesshire and his first wife, Elizabeth Charlotte (*d.* 4 Oct 1857), daughter of John Whyte-Melville. The addition of Wolfe to the family name derived from Murray's grandfather being a godson of General James Wolfe of Quebec fame. Murray was educated at Glenalmond College then Harrow School (1867–9). After attending the Royal Military Academy, Woolwich, he was commissioned lieutenant, Royal Artillery, on 12 September 1872. He was promoted captain on 1 November 1881 and, after passing Staff College, began a period of almost continued staff service for the remainder of his military career, much of it on intelligence duties. He was deputy assistant adjutant and quartermaster-general of the north British district from January to August 1884 before entering the War Office's intelligence branch in a similar capacity. He advanced to deputy assistant adjutant-general in the intelligence branch in June 1887, becoming head of section D with responsibility for Russia, central and south Asia, and the Far East. He was promoted major in January 1889 and, after a brief spell of regimental service from July 1890 to March 1892, returned to the War Office as a special service officer from April 1892 to January 1894. From the War Office he moved to Aldershot as deputy assistant adjutant-general for instruction, and remained in post until February 1897. However this was interrupted by special service on the lines of communication for the Asante expedition between November 1895 and February 1896, for which he was rewarded with a brevet lieutenant-colonelcy on 25 March 1896. He went to India as assistant adjutant-general in January 1898 and was serving as assistant quartermaster-general for intelligence at army headquarters when the Second South African War broke out in October 1899.

Murray was sent to South Africa to act on the lines of communication with the Natal field force under Sir Redvers Buller, being progressively colonel on the staff and then both brigadier-general and major-general commanding lines of communication between September 1899 and November 1900. These were local ranks and Murray, who had received his substantive colonelcy in March 1899, was created KCB for his services. He returned to India to command a brigade in May 1901, being promoted to major-general on 1 January 1903 and appointed quartermaster-general in India in May 1903. On 12 February 1904 he became master-general of the ordnance and fourth military member of the new army council, established as a result of the War Office reconstitution committee chaired by Reginald Brett, Lord Esher. However, in something of a precursor of his future ineffectualness at the highest level, Murray found it difficult to comprehend his precise responsibilities in the new system and he was also bitterly opposed to the army reform scheme advocated by the secretary of state for war, H. O. Arnold-Forster. In particular, Murray opposed the attempt to institute both long- and short-service recruiting simultaneously, but he also objected to the creation of a 'blue ribbon' general staff, which would become the only route for promotion to high rank. Indeed, Murray offered and then withdrew his resignation on three occasions in his first six months of office. The temperamental Arnold-Forster concluded at an early stage, 'If ever there was a wholly useless member of a Board, it is this tiresome, but no doubt well-meaning Scotsman' (Arnold-Forster, diary, 12 July 1904, BL, Add. MS 50339). Arnold-Forster was hard put to understand how Murray had gained his apparently high reputation, commenting on another occasion, 'He really sometimes gives the impression of being only half-witted' (Arnold-Forster, diary, 10 Nov 1905, BL, Add. MS 50352). In the event Arnold-Forster's scheme was swept away by the Balfour government's resignation in December 1905, but it was already apparent that it could not prevail against the entrenched military opposition. Murray himself took up the divisional command at Secunderabad in March 1907 and was promoted lieutenant-general on 1 April 1909. After his tour in India in February 1911 he was general officer commanding (GOC) in Scotland then South Africa.

On the outbreak of the First World War in August 1914 most of the general staff departed for Flanders with the expeditionary force, while Field Marshal Lord Kitchener became secretary of state for war. On 25 October 1914 Sir Charles Douglas, who had acted as chief of the Imperial General Staff since March, died of overwork and Murray was hastily recalled from South Africa to replace him. It was said that Murray was a master of detail but lacked breadth of view, but in any case the War Office was utterly dominated by Kitchener, whose autocratic and secretive methods were ill-suited to the proper functioning of the staff system. Murray was certainly not the man to challenge Kitchener's authority and he was noted for his total silence in meetings of the war council, hence the nickname of Sheep bestowed on him by Churchill. This was especially true of the planning for the Gallipoli expedition in 1915, Murray's only response to a direct question on strategy addressed to him in February 1915 being that 'he had no suggestions to make' (minutes of war council, 16 Feb 1915 PRO, CAB 42/3). Examined before the Dardanelles commission in 1917, Murray remarked of his relationship with Kitchener that 'it did not appear to me that he, having so to speak, taken the whole thing in hand and working on it almost entirely himself, to be necessary or desirable that I should interfere' (Dardanelles commission: minutes of evidence, Q.2605, PRO, CAB 19/33). He also professed to leaving meetings with 'a very indistinct idea of any decision having been arrived at all' (ibid., Q.2648). Murray neither saw the plans for the expedition nor even suggested that he should. Following Bulgaria's entry to the war in September 1915 the cabinet finally acted to reconstitute the general staff, and on 25 September 1915 Murray was replaced by Sir Archibald Murray.

Following his departure from the War Office Murray was employed on a special mission to Russia before becoming GOC at eastern command in 1916. Appointed colonel-commandant of the Royal Artillery on 9 April 1917, he retired on 5 May 1918. Murray was twice married: first, on 14 May 1875, to Arabella (d. 1909), daughter of W. Bray, with whom he had two sons and three daughters; and, secondly, in 1913 to Fanny, daughter of James Scott Robson and widow of Sir Donald Horne Macfarlane (d. 1904). Murray died suddenly of heart failure at Cringletie, Peeblesshire, on 17 October 1919.   IAN F. W. BECKETT

Sources J. Gooch, *The plans of war: the general staff and British military strategy, c.1900–1916* (1974) · I. Beckett, 'Arnold-Forster and the Volunteers', *Politicians and defence: studies in the formulation of British defence policy, 1845–1970*, ed. I. Beckett and J. Gooch (1981) · G. Cassar, *Kitchener: architect of victory* (1977) · B. Bond, *The Victorian army and the Staff College, 1854–1914* (1972) · T. G. Fergusson, *British military intelligence, 1870–1914* (1984) · R. Williams, *Defending the empire: the conservative party and British defence policy, 1899–1915* (1991) · J. Bertie, 'H. O. Arnold-Forster at the war office, 1903–1905', PhD diss., U. Lpool, 1974 · *Army List* · Minutes of evidence of the Dardanelles commission, PRO, CAB 19/33 · Burke, *Peerage* (1907) · *WWW, 1916–28* · H. O. Arnold-Forster, diary, BL, Arnold-Forster MSS, Add. MSS 50335–50353 · *DNB*

Archives UCL, school of Slavonic and east European studies, papers relating to Russia | BL, Arnold-Forster MSS, Add. MSS 50335–50353

Likenesses W. Stoneman, photograph, 1917, NPG · Spy [L. Ward], caricature, chromolithograph, NPG; repro. in *VF* (4 May 1905)

Wealth at death £43,116 17s. 4d.: confirmation, 26 Jan 1920, CCI

Murray [née Findlay], **Jane Elmslie Henderson** [Jean], Viscountess Dunedin (1885–1944), journalist, was born on 25 December 1885 at 50 Victoria Street, Aberdeen, the daughter of George Findlay, hat merchant, and his wife, Jane Elmslie Henderson. Both her parents were recorded as deceased on 11 January 1886, when her birth was registered, and nothing is known of her early life.

Jean Findlay first came to public notice as a contributor and translator associated with the journal *Everyman* in 1914. This began in 1912 as a literary review, and was being edited at the outbreak of the First World War by Dr Charles Sarolea, the Belgian consul in Edinburgh. At that time it concerned itself with fund-raising and publicity on behalf of Belgium, and Jean Findlay contributed to this. She acted as a war correspondent, reporting from Flanders, and for example, in 1916, on Belgian children as refugees in Switzerland. In 1915 she made a fund-raising lecture tour to Canada. Her translation *The Barbarians in Belgium* (1915), from the work by Pierre Nothomb, appeared in support of the cause. She also helped to start a YMCA for the Belgian army and was an honorary member of the Belgian government committee of propaganda. In recognition of the large sums that she helped to raise for Belgium and other services she was made a member of the order of Queen Elizabeth of Belgium.

From late 1916 until early 1917 Jean Findlay was acting editor of *Everyman*. After giving up this position she continued writing and in 1918 she published *Three Aspects of the Russian Revolution*, from the work by Émile Vandervelde. In late 1916, at the suggestion of Baron Strathclyde, she became involved with the work of the savings movement in Scotland. Serving as the director of Scottish Savings from 1916 until 1923, she was a leading figure in various savings campaigns, which included wartime visits to British troops in France and public meetings throughout Scotland. Her abilities as a platform speaker were of great use in helping to build up this largely voluntary movement; in 1920 she was made a CBE in recognition of her efforts.

On 12 July 1923 Jean Findlay married Andrew Graham *Murray (1849–1942), first Baron Dunedin, lord of appeal-in-ordinary, at a ceremony in the private chapel of Lambeth Palace. They had no children. As the second Lady Dunedin she reportedly encouraged her husband to broaden his interests beyond the law and his existing recreations. Her striking good looks attracted comment until the end of her life (*The Times*, 22 March 1944). In 1926, on her husband's elevation, she became the first Viscountess Dunedin.

Between December 1933 and September 1934 Viscountess Dunedin renewed her association with *Everyman*, this time as its editor. By her own account she returned as a result of a request to guide the paper back to stability and revive its coverage of varied interests. Her network of contacts was useful in providing a range of distinguished contributors who suited the readership.

In addition to those honours already mentioned Viscountess Dunedin was a lady of grace of St John of Jerusalem; she was also the first honorary secretary of the Scottish League of Nations Union. Her husband died in an Edinburgh nursing home in August 1942, after a long illness. She survived him by almost two years, dying of cancer at her home, 42 Lower Sloane Street, London, on 20 March 1944.   GORDON F. MILLAR

Sources *The Times* (22 March 1944) · *The Scotsman* (23 March 1944) · *WWW, 1941–50*, 1941–50, 4.337 · *Hutcheson's womans who's who, 1934–*

1935, 166 · *Scottish Thrift*, 41–42 (Sept–Oct 1923) · *Everyman* (Oct 1912–March 1917) · *Everyman* (Dec 1933–Sept 1934) · b. cert. · m. cert. · d. cert. · *The Times* (13 July 1923) · *The Times* (15 Dec 1933) · *The Times* (24 Aug 1944) · *The Scotsman* (13 July 1923) · *The Scotsman* (25 Aug 1942) · *Glasgow Herald* (22 Aug 1942) · 'Murray, Andrew Graham, first Viscount Dunedin', *DNB*

Wealth at death £37,678 gross: *The Times*

Murray [*née* Clarke], **Joan Elisabeth Lowther** (1917–1996), cryptanalyst and numismatist, was born at 45 Idmiston Road, West Norwood, London, on 24 June 1917, the youngest child (there were three sons, and another daughter) of William Kemp Lowther Clarke, a Church of England clergyman, and his wife, Dorothy Elizabeth Fulford. She was educated at Dulwich high school and at Newnham College, Cambridge, where she obtained a double first in mathematics and was a wrangler. While still an undergraduate, she was recruited by Gordon Welchman for the Government Code and Cypher School (GCCS) at Bletchley Park, the British code-breaking centre during the Second World War. When she joined GCCS in June 1940, she was assigned to Hut 8, which was responsible for the solution of naval Enigma ciphers. These were among the most difficult GCCS had to attack, partly because the naval Enigma machine, M3, was issued with eight rotors, compared with five for army and air force Enigma. She worked in a small inner room as a cryptanalyst with Alan Turing, Peter Twinn, and Tony Kendrick. Her initial task was to use the first British bombe (a high-speed key-finding aid invented by Alan Turing), which had entered service on 18 March 1940, against documents captured from the patrol boat *Schiff 26*. These enabled her and her co-workers to break about six days of April traffic over a period of three months.

Clarke helped to test Banburismus, a highly ingenious procedure invented by Turing, which used Bayesian probability theory to reduce the number of M3 rotor combinations to be tested by the bombes from 336 to between 6 and 126. She became very adept at Banburismus, which she greatly enjoyed. Without it, the solving of naval Enigma would have been much slower, since bombes were in very short supply until mid-1943.

Hut 8 could not make further progress until Enigma keys and indicator books were captured in February and May 1941. Its cryptanalysts therefore sometimes worked on other Enigma ciphers. When the outstandingly versatile Colonel John Tiltman recovered the plain text of signals enciphered on railway Enigma (a rewired version, code-named Rocket by GCCS, of commercial Enigma) in July 1940, Clarke helped to recover the wiring of its rotors, and to solve Rocket traffic in early 1941. She returned to naval Enigma in March 1941, when GCCS received Enigma key lists taken from an armed trawler, *Krebs*. She worked on material recovered from a patrol boat, *München*, which, with other captures, led to the speedy breaking of the main naval Enigma key, Heimisch (known to GCCS as Dolphin) from August 1941 onwards; keys were captured for June and July. One of her important contributions accelerated the solution of naval *Offizier* signals, which were

extremely difficult to break, since they were re-enciphered with a second set of plugboard settings (which interchanged ten pairs of letters), adding 150,000,000,000,000 further possible settings to a key.

Clarke became engaged to Turing in the spring of 1941, although the engagement was kept secret, and she did not wear her ring in Hut 8. The engagement was broken off by mutual consent in the late summer because of Turing's homosexuality. She remained friends with Turing for the rest of his life.

In mid-December 1942, after a blackout of almost 11 months, Hut 8 broke into the critically important four-rotor Enigma key, Triton (code-named Shark by GCCS), which was used by the Atlantic U-boats. However, in early March GCCS had to warn the Admiralty that Shark and its vital intelligence might again be lost, possibly for months. Clarke helped to ensure that naval intelligence's worst fear was not realized. Hut 8 was forced to use extremely short extracts (sometimes of only four letters) from short 'sighting' signals from the U-boats to program the three-rotor bombes until four-rotor bombes entered service in June 1943.

At the end of 1943 US Navy code-breakers in OP-20-G were allotted responsibility for breaking Shark, because US Navy four-rotor bombes were much more reliable and plentiful than the British model. Clarke remained in Hut 8 as a highly capable member of a small team which initially concentrated on M3 ciphers, such as Dolphin, although it continued to break some Shark keys until early 1945.

After the war Clarke worked in GCHQ, as GCCS became, until her marriage in 1952. Her husband was Lieutenant-Colonel John Kenneth Ronald (Jock) Murray, a retired army officer in India, who also worked at GCHQ. They had no children. She rejoined GCHQ in 1962 and retired in 1977. After her retirement she helped Sir Harry Hinsley on appendix 30 to volume 3/2 of *British Intelligence in the Second World War*, which was a substantially revised assessment of the Polish, French, and British work in breaking Enigma.

Murray was a gifted numismatist whose research was recognized by the award of the prestigious Sanford Saltus medal in 1987; this was for a 'magisterial paper' which established 'the sequence of the gold unicorns and heavy groats of James III and James IV [of Scotland], an extremely complex series which had caused great difficulty for previous students' (*Numismatic Circular*, 405).

Joan Murray was unique as the only female cryptanalyst to work in Hut 8. She was also its longest-serving member. Her acute intelligence enabled her fully to hold her own with her co-workers in Hut 8, and to make a significant contribution to its work in helping the allies to win the battle of the Atlantic, among other successes. She was also known as one of the really good cryptanalysts in GCHQ. Although very shy and retiring, she was an enthusiastic and encouraging colleague, and was much liked and admired by all who worked with her at GCCS and GCHQ. She was appointed MBE in 1947.

Murray died on 4 September 1996 at her home, 7 Lark-fields, Headington, Oxford. She was predeceased by her husband. RALPH ERSKINE

Sources R. E. [R. Erskine], 'In memoriam: Joan E. L. Murray, MBE', *Intelligence and National Security*, 13/2 (1998), 213–14 · R. Erskine, I. J. Good, and E. Weiss, 'Joan Elizabeth Lowther Clarke Murray, MBE', *IEEE Annals of the History of Computing*, 23 (2001), 67–72 · J. Murray, 'Hut 8 and naval Enigma, part I', *Codebreakers: the inside story of Bletchley Park*, ed. F. H. Hinsley and A. Stripp (1993), 119–22 · R. Erskine, 'Kriegsmarine short signal systems—and how Bletchley Park exploited them', *Cryptologia*, 23/1 (1999), 65–92 · F. H. Hinsley and others, *British intelligence in the Second World War*, 1–3 (1979–88) · d. cert. · b. cert. · CGPLA Eng. & Wales (1996) · 'The history of Hut Eight', PRO, HW 25/2 · *Der Schlüssel M—Verfahren M Offizier M und Stab*, Bundesarchiv-Militärchiv, Freiburg, Germany, M. Dv. Nr. 32/2 · *Numismatic Circular* (Nov 1996), 405 · private information (2004) [R. Noskwith, S. Wylie]
Wealth at death £756,694: probate, 20 Dec 1996, CGPLA Eng. & Wales

Murray, John, of Falahill (d. 1510), landowner and supposed outlaw, was the eldest son and heir of Sir Patrick Murray (d. before 27 Feb 1493), laird of Falahill in Peeblesshire, eldest son of the John Murray (d. c.1477), laird of Falahill, who was herdsman for James III's queen, Margaret of Denmark, in Ettrick Forest and keeper of Newark Castle near Selkirk. The younger John Murray is not to be confused with others of the same name, including his cousin, who was ancestor of the Murrays of Philiphaugh and Elibank, and his own son and heir. He was included in his father's lease of Falahill, Hangandschaw, and Lewinshop in 1484 and became seventh laird of Falahill on his father's death.

Murray is supposedly the outlaw of an early sixteenth-century border ballad, which describes how a man called Murray occupied Ettrick Forest in Selkirkshire and swore to defend it against all comers, until on the approach of James IV he agreed to do homage to the king on condition that he was made hereditary sheriff of the forest. The ballad contains internal evidence to suggest that if there was an outlaw Murray, he is more likely to have been the seventh laird's grandfather, mentioned above. But it may also reflect developments in the reign of James IV, who made several effective justice ayres in southern Scotland, gave Ettrick Forest as part of Margaret Tudor's marriage jointure in 1503, and had dealings with John Murray, the seventh laird, on a number of occasions. In 1489 Murray received 20 angels from James IV to buy himself a horse; the king granted him the Peeblesshire lands of Grevistoun on 9 February 1490 and on 5 November 1497 gave to John Murray of Falahill, as his 'familiari armigero', the Lothian lands of Cranstoun Riddel. In 1501 Murray was deputy to Thomas, second Lord Erskine, sheriff of Peebles, and regularly supplied sheep and horses to James IV. But, most significantly, Murray assigned to Queen Margaret a sasine of dowry of Ettrick Forest in 1503, and between 29 January 1508 and 30 November 1509 he was made sheriff of Selkirk.

Murray married, before 1501, Janet Forrester, widow of Sir John Schaw of Knockhill, and they had four children: John (d. 1513), laird of Falahill, who married Margaret, daughter of Patrick Hepburn, earl of Bothwell (d. 1508); James, who succeeded his brother John; William, ancestor of the Murrays of Romano; and Patrick, laird of Broadmeadows. John Murray was dead by 31 July 1510. He was killed in feud by Andrew Ker of Gateschaw and Thomas, brother of Philip Scott of Aidschaw (not by a Scott of Buccleuch, as the ballad states). MICHAEL A. PENMAN

Sources J. M. Thomson and others, eds., *Registrum magni sigilli regum Scotorum / The register of the great seal of Scotland*, 11 vols. (1882–1914), vol. 2 · G. Burnett and others, eds., *The exchequer rolls of Scotland*, 9–12 (1886–9) · *APS*, 1424–1567 · T. Dickson and J. B. Paul, eds., *Compota thesaurariorum regum Scotorum / Accounts of the lord high treasurer of Scotland*, 1–4 (1877–1902) · [T. Thomson] and others, eds., *The acts of the lords of council in civil causes*, 1478–1503, 3 vols. (1839–1993) · [T. Thomson], ed., *The acts of the lords auditors of causes and complaints, AD 1466–AD 1494*, RC, 40 (1839) · K. W. Murray, 'The outlaw Murray', *The Genealogist*, new ser., 12 (1895–6), 217–21 · *Scots peerage* · N. Macdougall, *James III: a political study* (1982) · N. Macdougall, *James IV* (1989) · *Sir Walter Scott's Minstrelsy of the Scottish border*, ed. T. F. Henderson, 1 (1902), 302–26 · R. Pitcairn, ed., *Ancient criminal trials in Scotland*, 1, Bannatyne Club, 42 (1833), pt 1 · M. Keen, *The outlaws of medieval legend*, 2nd edn (1977)
Archives NA Scot., Elibank MSS, GD 32

Murray [Moray], **John** (1575–1632), Church of Scotland minister, was the fourth son of Robert Moray of Abercairney, Perthshire, and Catherine, daughter of William *Murray (d. 1583) of Tullibardine, and younger brother of Sir David *Murray (1567–1629) of Gorthy. He was educated at the University of Edinburgh, graduating MA on 10 August 1595. Murray was minister of Borthwick in the presbytery of Dalkeith in 1597, and was appointed to the parish of Leith, Edinburgh, in 1603. Before December 1604, when David, the elder of their two children, was born, he had married Margaret Leslie, eldest daughter of James Leslie, master of Rothes (d. 1607), and granddaughter of Andrew Leslie, fifth earl of Rothes (d. 1611). Margaret's sister Grizel was the second wife of Alexander Seton, first earl of Dunfermline (1556–1622) and chancellor of Scotland from 1605 to 1622, while her brother, John Leslie (1600–1641), became sixth earl of Rothes in 1611.

A convinced presbyterian, Murray was soon at odds with royal policy regarding the church. Preaching at Leith in 1607 the minister compared the institution of bishops to the 'creeping in of the antechristeane yoke' upon the kirk of Scotland, and 'most falslie and erroniouslie' criticized the 'rites and ceremoneyis' of the Church of England (*Reg. PCS*, 8.493). Copies of the speech were widely circulated by presbyterian activists (including, notably, David Hume of Godscroft), and it was printed at London as *A Godly and Fruitefull Sermon Preached at Lieth in Scotland* (1607). As a consequence of his 'impertinent sermon', the minister was hauled before the privy council on 25 February 1608. The examination was conducted by the chancellor, Dunfermline, who—refusing to condemn his brother-in-law—'favourablie dismissed [Murray], and sent him home' (Calderwood, 6.701). This judgment infuriated the king, and, following a 'sharpe letter' of rebuke to the council in May (ibid.; *Reg. PCS*, 8.492–3), Murray was deprived of his charge and imprisoned in the castle of Edinburgh.

Following his release from prison in 1609 Murray was ordered to confine himself within the town of New Abbey, Kirkcudbrightshire. In defiance of the terms of his parole he preached at Dumfries and Traquair, and lived for six months at Dysart, Fife. In 1612 he was living at Prestonpans, where he acted as assistant to his lifelong friend and fellow nonconformist minister, John Ker, and preached every Sunday without challenge from the authorities. He was restored to the ministry at Dunfermline in 1614 (probably as a result of the patronage of the chancellor), but continued in his opposition to the bishops. During this period Murray penned *A dialogue betwixt Cosmophilus and Theophilus anent the urging of new ceremonials upon the Church of Scotland* (1620), a work which was heavily critical of the five articles of Perth and was published anonymously in Amsterdam. Somewhat fortuitously authorship of the pamphlet was ascribed to the exiled minister David Calderwood, whose connections (since both men used the same printer in the Netherlands) were no doubt responsible for the production and circulation of the piece, and Murray was never questioned over its production. Nevertheless, on 12 December 1621 he was summoned before the high commission on charges of failing to observe the aforementioned articles, and—on 3 January 1622—was deprived of his ministry for a second time.

Murray suffered much for his presbyterian principles, and contemporary allegations that his difficulties were compounded by the 'malice of the bishops' are not entirely without foundation (Calderwood, 6.699). Despite his restoration to the ministry in 1614 Murray was denied a stipend on account of his continuing refusal to recognize the episcopal authorities. Neither was the minister a stranger to personal tragedy. During his confinement at New Abbey, Murray lost both of his children to a fatal illness, and, on 22 June 1620, his wife, Margaret, died. He ministered at Dunfermline without remuneration for some months afterward, but, on being deprived in 1622, was forced to take up lodgings at the house of his brother Sir David Murray of Gorthy, at Fowlis Wester, Strathern. It was probably during this period that Murray married his second wife, Mary Melville; they had a daughter, Jean. He continued to preach, and on 24 June 1624 was ordered by the privy council to confine himself more strictly within the bounds of Fowlis. On Sir David's death in 1629 the estate of Gorthy passed to another brother, Sir William, and Murray was obliged to remove a second time to Prestonpans. He died at the home of his old friend in January 1632. At the time of his death the minister's finances were in a perilous state. He possessed no ready cash, and his net estate (excluding his library, valued at £200) was estimated at a mere £96 Scots.   VAUGHAN T. WELLS

Sources D. Calderwood, *The history of the Kirk of Scotland*, ed. T. Thomson and D. Laing, 8 vols., Wodrow Society, 7 (1842–9), vol. 6 · *Reg. PCS*, 1st ser., vol. 8 · *Fasti Scot.*, new edn, vols. 1–2 · Edinburgh testaments, NA Scot., CC8/8/55, fols. 242r and 242v · J. Livingstone, *Memorable characters … of the most eminent divines* (1759) · *Scots peerage*, vol. 7 · J. Row, *The history of the Kirk of Scotland, from the year 1558 to August 1637*, ed. D. Laing, Wodrow Society, 4 (1842) · *STC, 1475–1640*, no. 1503.5 · *DNB*
Wealth at death £296 Scots: will, NA Scot., CC8/8/55, fols. 242r and 242v

Murray, John, first earl of **Annandale** (d. 1640), politician and courtier, was the seventh of eleven (or youngest of nine) sons of Sir Charles Murray of Cockpool (1528–1605) and his wife, Margaret Somerville, daughter of Hugh *Somerville, Lord Somerville. By 1636 he was the last surviving son, and inherited the family estates in succession to his brothers James and Richard. Introduced to the court as a young man, probably by one of the Maxwell earls of Morton, Murray succeeded his brothers as a gentleman of the king's bedchamber and master of the king's horse. He attained to a position of some favour with James VI, receiving lands in Fife and Lothian and, after 1603, in Surrey and co. Donegal. His Scottish landholdings consisted of the lands of Lochmaben in Dumfriesshire, which Robert I, the Bruce, had brought to the crown in 1306. He also held Dundrennan in Galloway, being commendator of the former Cistercian abbey there and he was provost of Lincluden collegiate kirk near Dumfries and steward of Annandale.

Murray travelled south to remain at court after the accession of James VI to the English throne in 1603. Once there he became closely involved in the royal decision-making processes relating to Scottish affairs and by 1609 was a groom of the king's bedchamber. He corresponded with Alexander Seton, first earl of Dunfermline, chancellor of Scotland, and Thomas Hamilton, first earl of Melrose, lord advocate and Scottish secretary. They became increasingly prominent in the government of Scotland after the death in 1611 of George Hume, earl of Dunbar, and John Murray benefited through his connections with them. He was married, in or before 1611, to one of Queen Anne's servitors, Elizabeth Shaw, daughter of Sir John Shaw of Broich; they had three daughters, one before they married, and one son, James, who succeeded to his father's titles as well as those of the second Viscount Stormont.

In 1617 the lands of the abbey of Holywood near Dumfries were erected into a barony for John Murray and on 28 June 1622, by which time he was keeper of the privy purse, he was made Viscount Annan and Lord Murray of Lochmaben. In March 1625 he became earl of Annandale and Lord Murray of Tynningham, under which title he sat in a convention of estates in the following year, after having attended the funeral of James VI and I at Westminster in May. Under that monarch he had been one of the commissioners of the middle shires, the Anglo-Scottish border counties, and in 1625 he was reappointed to this commission by Charles I.

In 1634 Annandale was appointed to the new ecclesiastical court of high commission in Scotland, which had its origins in the reign of James VI. He seems, however, to have remained involved with the affairs of secular government, and between 1636 and 1639 he frequently travelled back and forth between London and Edinburgh on the king's business, occasionally appearing at meetings of the privy council in Edinburgh. He appears not to have been prominently involved in the controversies surrounding the covenanting revolution, perhaps because of his advancing years, although he did take part in the opening ceremony or 'riding' of parliament in 1639. He died at London on 22 September 1640, having suffered from 'the stone', and was buried at Hoddom in Dumfriesshire on 13 October 'without aney funerall ceremoney' (*Historical Works of Balfour*, 2.428).   ALAN R. MACDONALD

Sources *Scots peerage*, vol. 1 · W. Fraser, ed., *The book of Carlaverock: memoirs of the Maxwells, earls of Nithsdale*, 2 vols. (1873) · W. Fraser, ed., *The Douglas book*, 4 vols. (1885) · *The historical works of Sir James Balfour*, ed. J. Haig, 4 vols. (1824–5) · J. Gordon, *History of Scots affairs from 1637–1641*, ed. J. Robertson and G. Grub, 1, Spalding Club, 1 (1841) · *Reg. PCS*, 2nd ser. · GEC, *Peerage* · *Reg. PCS*, 1st ser., vols. 6–14
Archives NRA, priv. coll., estate and legal papers, some corresp. with earls of Annandale and Hartfell, Scot. Survey no. 2171

Murray, John, first marquess of Atholl (1631–1703), nobleman, was born on 2 May 1631, the eldest son of John Murray, first earl of Atholl (*d.* 1642), and Jean, daughter of Sir Duncan Campbell of Glenorchy. He succeeded his father as second earl of Atholl in June 1642. In November 1644 it was proposed to send him to university with his 'codisciples' but he avoided this by pleading 'the necessitie of my owne caise, and the hard conditione of the tyme' (Murray, 1.131–2), his estates having been ravaged during the civil wars between the royalist marquess of Montrose and the covenanters.

Royalism and retirement, 1648–1659 In May 1648, Atholl, aged seventeen, was appointed a colonel in the army of the engagement, which joined royalists and covenanters in seeking to rescue Charles I from his English captors. When the kirk party seized power in Scotland on the defeat of the engagers, Atholl's castle of Blair was garrisoned. The church urged in March 1649 that he should be 'constantly bred in this town [Edinburgh]', he being the son of a Roman Catholic and therefore suspect (Mitchell and Christie, 2.227), but resolved otherwise to deal with him leniently as he was a minor.

In October 1650 Atholl and other royalist nobles plotted to free Charles II from the control of the kirk party in the incident that became known as the 'start'. Charles was to leave Perth on 3 October, ostensibly to go hunting, while Atholl and his colleagues seized the town with forces from the highlands. The plan was ruined by the king's indecision, and by 5 October he was back in the control of the covenanters. It was said that Atholl had gathered over 1000 men in arms, and when the king sent him orders to disband (6 October) he refused unless guaranteed indemnity for his actions. Agreement on this was reached, but then in late October he signed the northern band to stand together in arms with other royalists. The church, desperate to avoid civil war in time of English invasion, was still inclined to leniency to Atholl, promising on 24 October to be 'verie tender of your Lordship in respect of your age' (Mitchell and Christie, 3.92). In early November he and the other northern royalists finally disbanded.

One of the royalists' main grievances was that they were not being allowed to join with the Scottish army in resisting the English invasion of the country led by Oliver Cromwell, and in December the regime bowed to their pressure, Atholl being one of those appointed a colonel. He was allowed to regain custody of Blair Castle. Further pressure led to the appointment of Atholl (after he had at

John Murray, first marquess of Atholl (1631–1703), by Jacob de Wet [in allegorical costume]

last declared repentance for joining the engagement) and others to a committee for managing the affairs of the army, in March 1651. In June he was admitted to the ruling committee of estates, but the regime was fast collapsing under English pressure, and by November he had capitulated to the English.

On the outbreak of a royalist rising in the highlands against the English in 1653 Atholl was in a difficult position, for his Perthshire estates were vulnerable to both highland and English attack, and his tenants favoured continued submission to the English. However, after a short hesitation he joined the royalists and took an active part in their disunited and ultimately unsuccessful venture. On 24 August 1655 he signed a new capitulation with the English, being promised the return of his estates, which had been confiscated, and in the weeks that followed the remaining royalist nobles submitted. On 5 May 1659 Atholl married Lady Amelia Sophia (1633–1703), daughter of James *Stanley, seventh earl of Derby, and he seems to have lived mainly in England during the next few years—both Blair Castle and his house in Dunkeld had been destroyed by the English.

Political and military service, 1660–1678 The restoration of monarchy in 1660 brought Atholl reward for his loyalty; entry to the Scottish privy council (February 1661, though he did not take his seat until November 1662), the sheriffship of Perthshire, and the office of justice general (16 August 1661). Inclination to a military life brought him command of a troop of horse in 1666, and he took part in dispersing presbyterian rebels at the battle of Rullion Green on 28 November. Appointments as captain of the highland watch in 1667–9, colonel of a militia regiment in 1668, and to captaincy of the king's Scottish life guards in 1670 (a post Charles II had promised him several years earlier) followed. In the same year Atholl became fifth earl of Tullibardine, in succession to his cousin. In 1672 he became lord privy seal, and in January 1673 was made an extraordinary lord of session, though he resigned office as justice general in 1675 (as he had promised to do when appointed to the privy seal). He proved active in suppressing conventicles (illegal gatherings of presbyterian dissidents), and it was alleged that through arbitrary fines 'Lord Athol made of this in one week £1900 sterling' (*Bishop Burnet's History*, 1.662). Such services brought him promotion to marquess of Atholl on 7 February 1676. Late in 1677 the regime in Scotland, dominated by the duke of Lauderdale, feared that rebellion by the conventiclers concentrated in the western lowlands was imminent, and highland landlords were ordered to gather forces ready to march south to resist, Atholl being commissioned on 26 December to raise most of the Perthshire forces. This 'highland host' gathered in Stirling in January 1678, Atholl's contingent being by far the largest (about 2300 men out of a total force of 6700), its size being designed 'to shew his greatness' (*Bishop Burnet's History*, 2.137), and he acted as president of the committee which commanded the force. The host marched to Glasgow and spent several weeks quartered in the shires of Ayr, Lanark, and Renfrew, but late in February orders were given for most of it to withdraw, it being hoped that it had overawed the populace sufficiently to prevent rebellion.

Disaffection and return to loyalty, 1678–1685 Many landowners were becoming disillusioned by Lauderdale's policies for dealing with the dissidents, seeing them as unnecessarily harsh, ineffectual, and economically damaging. Atholl joined the duke of Hamilton, the spokesman of this viewpoint on the privy council, in travelling to London (without royal permission) in March 1678 to try to influence Charles II on the matter. Since Atholl had been until shortly before a leader of support for Lauderdale in council, captain of the guard, and the main figure in the highland host, he had been 'as deep as any other both in advising and executing' official policies (*Lauderdale Papers*, ed. O. Airy, 3 vols., 1884–5, 1.136), so his sudden move to opposition caused surprise. Once in London and faced with royal displeasure he hastily backtracked, explaining 'that he was made to believe that there was necessity for their going [to London], but he now found no such thing'. He had come, he explained, because Lauderdale had 'taken up a spleen against him' for some reason and had 'threatened to take his places [offices] away from him' (Murray, 1.178). Once this climb-down had brought him kind words from the king he withdrew to Scotland and announced that he was ill, and would take his physicians

and travel to France. However, the crisis having passed, so did his need for a health cure, though his brief defiance of Lauderdale led to his being deprived of the command of the Scottish life guards.

After Atholl returned to Scotland he showed some sympathy with the plight of the conventiclers, leading the bishop of Galloway to complain of 'the great and insolent field conventicles in Perthshire, it being as much influenced by the marquis of Athole's example, as directed by his authority' (R. Wodrow, *History of the Sufferings of the Church of Scotland*, 4 vols., 1828–30, 2.50). However, when rebellion broke out in 1679 he took part in defeating the dissidents, being present at the battle at Bothwell Bridge on 22 June. With the fall of Lauderdale from power, royal favour was restored. Atholl became vice-admiral of Scotland in 1680, and presided in the Scottish parliament in 1681, the chancellor having died. His hopes of himself becoming chancellor were dashed in 1682, 'a great disappointment, for he thought himselfe secure in the office' (J. Lauder, *Historical Observes*, 1840, 89). He was appointed king's lieutenant of Argyll and Tarbat on 5 August 1684, the earl of Argyll having been condemned for treason and fled abroad. He led 1000 troops into Argyll to disarm the population and arrest leading members of the clan Campbell, and in May 1685 was sent back into Argyll as the earl had landed in Kintyre to lead a rebellion. He gathered 'about 4000 men' by his own account (Murray, 1.250), and within a few weeks had scattered Argyll's disorganized supporters and captured the earl himself, who was executed. Summary executions marked the suppression of the rebellion, but there is no evidence to support stories that Atholl had to be restrained by orders from the council from greater severity.

Jacobitism and compromise, 1687–1689 Atholl's services and social status were rewarded in June 1687 when he was one of the six nobles who were appointed the first members of the Order of the Thistle, newly created by James VII and II. During the 1688 crisis when William of Orange invaded England, Atholl remained firmly committed to the Stuart cause he had served since youth. The success of William and the flight of James led many Scottish politicians to hasten to London to declare their loyalty to the new regime, but Atholl sought to maintain James's government, presiding in the privy council, which on 14 December commissioned him to act as commander-in-chief in Scotland. But he had few men to preside over, and almost none to command. By early January 1689 Atholl had decided that collapse was unavoidable and the time had come to put self-preservation before principle, as so many others had already done. At last he travelled south to pay court to William in London, explaining that he had felt it necessary to remain in Scotland to maintain order there in William's interests, though his wife complained (3 January) this public-spiritedness had been misunderstood: 'I have bin allmost tempted to wish he had gon from me with the crowd, which consider'd their own interest and safety, which *he* did not' (Murray, 1.271). However, his explanations were too late to be convincing, and his advances were coldly received by William. The only hope, therefore, of protecting his interests seemed to be to return hastily to his Jacobite allegiance.

By the time the convention of estates met in Edinburgh on 14 March 1689 Atholl was regarded as one of the Jacobite leaders, and when it became clear that the Williamites had a majority, he agreed to the secret proposal of John Graham, Viscount Dundee, that the Jacobites should withdraw and hold a rival convention in Stirling. However, he was irresolute, and at the last minute insisted that the plan to withdraw be delayed for a day. This Dundee refused to accept, and in the event some Jacobites withdrew with him and others remained in Edinburgh. According to the earl of Balcarres, Atholl's call for delay 'broke all our measures' (Lindsay, 29), fatally dividing King James's supporters. He continued to attend the convention but (with the duke of Queensberry) withdrew from it when the vote was taken which deposed King James and declared the throne vacant. However, as soon as the crucial issue had been decided they returned and stated that they accepted the validity of the decision, and that William was best suited to fill the vacancy. Doubting that a Jacobite rising could succeed, Atholl thus again accepted the new regime, and on 13 April he wrote to William expressing his loyalty.

Dundee's campaign and its aftermath The marquess had made his decision, but whether the men of Atholl would accept it was doubtful, for Jacobite sympathies were strong among them, and his own sons were divided in their loyalties. The Atholl estates were likely to be of crucial importance in the combining civil war, both in terms of manpower and geography. If their several thousand fighting men had been put in the Jacobite balance, it would have given Dundee's rising a credibility it otherwise lacked. Moreover in seeking to recruit an army Dundee was likely to retire through Atholl, and then advance south through it when he had one. Thus Atholl's commitment to William's cause was seen as being of crucial importance, and he was expected to rally his men to the new king's cause. Atholl himself, however, simply wanted to escape involvement. He probably had no wish to see his men fight against King James, even if he had abandoned hope for his cause. Perhaps more crucially, given the mood of the men of Atholl, he must have doubted whether they would obey his orders. His solution was evasion. He sent orders that his men should support William, and ordered the arrest of Dundee if he passed through Atholl, but then he made himself scarce, so he could not be blamed if the orders were not obeyed.

Dundee was not arrested, and on 10 March was able to advance through Atholl unhindered and occupy Dunkeld. Atholl hurried away to take the waters at Bath. 'Athol is gone to England, who did not know what to do', commented Dundee scornfully (Macaulay, 4.1624n). From Bath he innocently expressed his shock and 'gret surprise to heare that the Atholl menne' had refused to declare for William. He confided his demoralization to his son: 'what I desire is to live retired and not medel with the world for I have served it for long and now it is mor then tyme to live

with God and myselfe' (Murray, 1.282–3). His abandonment of his Scottish responsibilities at so crucial a time naturally aroused the suspicions of William's regime, but he explained that he and his wife had been urged by physicians 'to go to the baths for our health, being troubled with violent paines' (Melville, 22). A letter from his wife to their son on 13 July indicates that he was indeed ill: 'Since my Lord pumped his head there is falln so sad a defluxion in one eye that … he has not bin able to looke up, eat, drink or sleep', being in perpetual torment (Murray, 1.285). However, his behaviour bore obvious similarities to his reaction to involvement in political crisis in 1678: indecision culminating in a sudden need to be elsewhere for the sake of health. Possibly his illnesses were psychosomatic: genuine, but brought on by stress he found intolerable.

Dundee's victory at Killiecrankie on 27 July 1689 led to Atholl being arrested and taken to London, arriving on 7 August, but it was soon accepted that though some of his men had fought for Dundee he was no threat to the regime. After the collapse of the Jacobite rising he was released. Back in Scotland he took part in negotiations to persuade highland Jacobites who remained in arms to submit, though in 1690–91 he had contacts with Jacobite plotters. None the less his expressed wish to retire from public life was genuine. He lost his seat on the council and the keepership of the privy seal; and though he remained vice-admiral, that gave him no more than a few perks (including, rather appropriately, the right to stranded whales). In December 1692 his wife fondly recorded that he 'is at curling, a divirtisement I am very glad he takes some delight in, for this many years he has had noe diversion att all' (Murray, 1.334). Financial problems were aggravated by a ruling in 1689 that the forfeiture of the earl of Argyll was null and void. The new earl pursued Atholl in court for losses caused by the latter's expeditions in 1684 and 1685, and in 1699 Atholl was ordered to pay over £4200 sterling compensation. A compromise of about £2600 was agreed, but Atholl had to borrow most of the money needed to pay the debt.

Death and reputation In 1701 the marchioness reported that she and her husband were 'a very cresy old couple, growing weaker' (Murray, 1.485), and Atholl died on 6 May 1703, three months after his wife. Both were buried in Dunkeld Cathedral, Atholl being buried there on 17 May. Shortly before his death Queen Anne had decided to honour Atholl's family (largely because of his son's services to the regime), and issued a patent creating him a duke. But she ordered her commissioner, the duke of Queensberry 'not to deliver the patents of honour with which he was instructed till after the [end of the session of the Scottish] Parliament' (Laing MSS, 2.22). On Atholl's death the patent was therefore suppressed and a new one issued to his son, John *Murray.

Atholl's life was that of a grandee, owing his prominence to his position as great landowner and highland chief rather than to ability or ambition. As a soldier, in organizing the 'host' of 1678 and in his Argyll campaigns in 1684 and 1685, he proved efficient, but he never had to face an organized enemy, and his reactions to political events in 1653, 1678, and 1689 do not suggest that he would have been a decisive commander. To Jacobites he became a scapegoat, whose weakness and hesitancy had ruined any hope of success for Dundee's rising. Macaulay raised him to heights of infamy by denouncing him as having been 'the falsest, the most fickle, the most pusillanimous, of mankind', 'his abilities were mean, his temper false … and cruel' (Macaulay, 2.828; 4.1556). In his defence, it can be pointed out that Atholl had not sought leadership in the Jacobite cause, but had it briefly thrust upon him in the form of presidency of the council and appointment as commander-in-chief in December 1688, merely because he was one of the few who had not yet deserted the sinking ship. He remained loyal for longer than most. But once his resolution broke his conduct became spectacularly disreputable—approaching William, veering back to Jacobitism, then back to William, then abdicating responsibility by his flight to Bath. In being false he was not a coldly calculating politician, but a panic-stricken ditherer.

DAVID STEVENSON

Sources DNB · GEC, *Peerage* · *Scots peerage* · J. J. H. H. Stewart-Murray, seventh duke of Atholl, *Chronicles of the Atholl and Tullibardine families*, 5 vols. (privately printed, Edinburgh, 1908) · *Reg. PCS*, 2nd ser. · *Reg. PCS*, 3rd ser. · *Manuscripts of the duke of Atholl … and of the earl of Home*, HMC, 26 (1891) · *Bishop Burnet's History* · *Historical notices of Scotish affairs, selected from the manuscripts of Sir John Lauder of Fountainhall*, ed. D. Laing, 2 vols., Bannatyne Club, 87 (1848) · W. H. L. Melville, ed., *Leven and Melville papers: letters and state papers chiefly addressed to George, earl of Melville … 1689–1691*, Bannatyne Club, 77 (1843) · C. Lindsay [earl of Balcarres], *Memoirs touching the revolution in Scotland*, ed. A. W. C. Lindsay [earl of Crawford and Balcarres], Bannatyne Club (1841) · H. Mackay, *Memoirs of the war carried on in Scotland and Ireland*, ed. J. M. Hog and others, Bannatyne Club, 45 (1833), 12 · A. F. Mitchell and J. Christie, eds., *The records of the commissions of the general assemblies of the Church of Scotland*, 3 vols., Scottish History Society, 11, 25, 58 (1892–1909) · J. R. Elder, *The highland host of 1678* (1914) · D. Stevenson, *Revolution and counter-revolution in Scotland, 1644–1651*, Royal Historical Society Studies in History, 4 (1977) · F. D. Dow, *Cromwellian Scotland, 1651–1660* (1979) · T. B. Macaulay, *The history of England from the accession of James II*, new edn, ed. C. H. Firth, 6 vols. (1913–15) · *Report on the Laing manuscripts*, 2, HMC, 72 (1925)
Archives Blair Castle, Perthshire, corresp. and papers · NL Scot., legal corresp. · U. Edin., MSS relating to dispute with brother | BL, letters to Lord Godolphin, Add. MS 28055 · BL, letters to duke of Lauderdale and Charles II, Add. MSS 23115–23138, 23245–23247, *passim* · Buckminster Park, Grantham, corresp. with duke of Lauderdale · College of William and Mary, Williamsburg, Virginia, corresp. with earl of Dunmore · NA Scot., corresp. with Lord Leven · NA Scot., corresp. with earl of Mar · priv. coll., letters to duchess of Hamilton
Likenesses R. Cooper, stipple (after P. Lely), NPG · L. Schuneman, oils, Dunvegan Castle, Isle of Skye · J. de Wet, oils, Blair Castle, Perthshire [*see illus.*]

Murray, John, first duke of Atholl (1660–1724), army officer and politician, was the eldest son of John *Murray, first marquess of Atholl (1631–1703), and Lady Amelia Sophia Stanley (1633–1703), fourth daughter of James *Stanley, seventh earl of Derby. He was born at Knowsley, Lancashire, on 24 February 1660. On 24 May 1683 he married his first wife, Lady Katherine Hamilton (*bap.* 1662, *d.*

John Murray, first duke of Atholl (1660–1724), by Thomas Murray, 1705

1707), eldest daughter of William Douglas (later Hamilton), third duke of Hamilton; they had six sons and one daughter who survived childhood. Katherine died on 17 January 1707, and three years later Murray married (on 26 June 1710) Lady Mary Ross (1687–1767), second daughter of William, twelfth Lord Ross. This marriage produced three sons who survived childhood, including Lord John *Murray.

Early military career, 1678–1690 Lord John Murray, as he was first known, was born into an Episcopalian family, but he had professed Presbyterianism by the mid-1690s. George Lockhart of Carnwath, the contemporary Jacobite commentator, observed that by the early eighteenth century Murray 'courted, and preserved his interest with, the Presbyterian ministers, professing always to be firm to their Kirk government, hearing them in the churches, and patronizing them much more than those of the episcopal perswasion' (*Scotland's Ruine*, 41). Lockhart also observed that Murray 'made no great figure in the first part of his life. And the first mention I find of him was his conveening as many of his friends, followers and vassals as he could to oppose my Lord Dundee [1689]' (ibid., 40). However, as early as 1678 Murray had accompanied his father and the notorious 'highland host' as part of the suppression of covenanting activities in south-west Scotland.

In 1682 he was a captain of both the infantry and horse militia in Perthshire. As the son-in-law of William, third duke of Hamilton, the man who had defeated Murray's father for the presidency of the 1689 convention, John is reputed to have influenced his father in acknowledging William of Orange. The house of Atholl was notoriously (and perhaps pragmatically) divided over the revolution, but Murray has been described as 'the Williamite arm of the Atholl interest' (Riley, *King William*, 108).

His father's departure for Bath before the meeting of the 1689 parliament left Murray in charge of the Atholl estate and men, whom he was anxious to prevent joining the rising of John Graham of Claverhouse, Viscount Dundee. Dundee wrote to Murray urging him to hold Blair Castle for King James, but when no reply was received, Dundee instructed Stewart of Ballechin, Atholl's bailie, to seize the castle. Murray assembled 1500 of the clan, with a view to blockading the castle and forcing Ballechin out. However, many of Murray's followers withdrew to protect their livestock against Dundee's advancing army. Others withdrew when they learned that Murray was determined to support William of Orange. Murray attempted to dissuade General Hugh Mackay from marching into Atholl, but his request was rejected. In a dispatch from Dunkeld on 26 July (prior to the battle of Killiecrankie on the following day), Mackay declared that if Blair Castle was not in Murray's hands by the time he arrived, then he would hang Ballechin over the highest wall, and that if Murray supported Ballechin's actions he would burn Blair Castle from end to end. In a second dispatch of 26 July, Mackay instructed Murray to post himself at the entry of the pass on the side of Blair Castle. Murray obeyed this order, but he was unable to muster more than 200 men. Fifty Atholl men are reputed to have fought with Viscount Dundee at Killiecrankie, while large numbers of the clan afterwards joined the Jacobite rebels under the command of Murray's brother Lord James of Dowally. Atholl men also joined in the pursuit of the routed government forces in the aftermath of Killiecrankie. Murray received scathing criticism from General Mackay on account of the clan's behaviour, for which he held Murray responsible. However, Murray was opposed to his brother's stand, and appears to have been embarrassed by such conduct. On 7 June 1690 he was appointed as a commissioner of supply for both Perthshire and Fife.

Politics, 1691–1704 Murray was one of the commissioners appointed to inquire into the Glencoe massacre. He was active in securing evidence to bring the perpetrators to justice, affirming that it concerned 'the whole nation to have that barbarous action … laied on to the true author and contriver of it' (*Atholl MSS*, 45). On 12 February 1694 Murray was given the command of a regiment to be raised in Scotland, and on 17 December of the following year he was made sheriff of Perthshire for life. As a result of changes in William III's ministry, on 14 January 1696 he was appointed as one of the secretaries of state, along with Sir James Ogilvy, the future earl of Seafield. He was

created earl of Tullibardine, Viscount Glenalmond, and Lord Murray on 27 July 1696, without prejudice to his succession to the titles of his father. As earl of Tullibardine he was the high commissioner to the parliamentary session which met from 8 September to 12 October 1696, his ennoblement coming about because custom dictated that only a peer could represent the king in parliament. Tullibardine's appointment as high commissioner had the direct approval of William III, who wrote from Loo on 28 August that 'the knowledge we have of his capacity, as well as his zealous affection and firm fidelity to our person and government will certainly render him acceptable' (*Scots peerage*, 1.479). However, he resigned the secretaryship in 1698 having faced intense political and factional pressure from the Queensberry and Argyll interests in Scottish politics, and having failed to secure the presidency of the court of session for Sir William Hamilton of Whitelaw (despite royal assurance), the post going instead to Sir Hugh Dalrymple of Stair, indicating Queensberry's triumph. His replacement during the parliamentary session of 1698 (19 July – 1 September), which Tullibardine attended, was Patrick Hume, first earl of Marchmont. The patent creating him earl of Tullibardine was recorded on 19 July, and on the same day he took the oath of allegiance and subscribed the assurance and association in favour of William III. He also attended the parliamentary sessions of 21–30 May 1700 and 29 October 1700–1 February 1701, when the Darien crisis was the leading political issue. He was a strong supporter of the project, and his anger at its perceived sabotage was reflected in his voting, albeit in a minority, in favour of a full parliamentary act, as opposed to an address, to the king, outlining the house's outrage. On 28 January he was one of seventy-eight members who voted against the continuation of the armed forces until December 1702; on 31 January he also voted against a resolve for the continuation of 1100 men for four months over and above the quota of 3000 men already decided upon. He did not attend the final session of the Williamite parliament which sat from 9 to 30 June 1702.

On the accession of Queen Anne, Tullibardine was made a privy councillor and then lord privy seal in April 1703. On the death of his father, he was created marquess of Tullibardine and first duke of Atholl; in February 1704 he was also made a knight of the Thistle. During the 1703 parliament Lockhart of Carnwath argued that Atholl 'trimmed betwixt Court and Cavaliers' and that he would probably have continued to do so, 'had not been the Duke of Queensberry trumped up the plot upon him' (*Scotland's Ruine*, 41). The proposed Jacobite plot in which Queensberry, on the evidence of Simon Fraser (later Lord Lovat), implicated Atholl did 'so exasperate him [Atholl] against the Court' that he 'joyned entirely with the Cavaliers'. Atholl's revolution principles were dropped and 'he became all of a sudden a violent Jacobite, and took all methods to gain the favour and confidence of the Cavaliers' (ibid.). Lockhart stated that this was 'in some measure obtained', particularly in Fife, Forfarshire, Perth, and other northern areas. Thus, Atholl 'affected extreamly to be the head of that party and outrival the Duke of Hamilton' (ibid.).

Opposing the Act of Union It was as lord privy seal that Atholl attended the 1704 parliamentary session (6 July–28 August). On 17 July he proposed that the Queensberry plot should be examined by parliament, though this never came to fruition. On 5 August he was appointed as a commissioner of supply for the separate areas of Perthshire, Fife, and Forfarshire. His prominent opposition stance during the 1705 parliamentary session (28 June–21 September) prompted his proposal on 1 September to add a clause to the draft act for a treaty of union with England, stating that negotiating commissioners were not to leave Scotland or enter into any treaty negotiations until the English parliament had repealed the Alien Act. His request was defeated, but prior to voting on the clause he declined a formal protestation concerning this issue adhered to by an additional seventy-nine members. Parliament then proceeded to consider the means to nominate the Scottish commissioners to negotiate a treaty. This resulted in the volte-face of James Douglas, fourth duke of Hamilton, who proposed that the commissioners should be chosen by the queen and not parliament. Hamilton's motion was carried late in the day, with many members absent. Prior to voting on the act for a treaty (with the right of nomination invested in the queen), Atholl submitted another formal protestation, adhered to by seventy-three members, against the act. In July 1706 Atholl was offered payment of arrears of salary if he would absent himself from the forthcoming parliamentary session to vote on the treaty negotiated during the summer. An indirect approach was also made through Atholl's brother Charles *Murray, first earl of Dunmore, now aligned to Queensberry, but the offer was rejected by Atholl's wife on her husband's instructions.

Atholl was a leading opponent of the treaty of Union when its articles were debated and voted on in the final session of the Scottish parliament (3 October 1706–25 March 1707). Prior to the vote on article 1 of the treaty (4 November), Atholl handed in a protestation, adhered to by sixty-five members, against an incorporating union. He thereafter voted against this article and consistently against the majority, but not all, of the treaty provisions. He also adhered to others' protestations, including that on 12 November 1706 from Lord Belhaven which claimed that the future of the Church of Scotland would not be secure in an incorporating union. And prior to voting against article 2 (Hanoverian succession), he supported the Earl Marischal, who stated that the future succession should not be determined until 'there be such Conditions of Government settled and enacted as may secure the Honour and Sovereignty of this Crown & Kingdom, the freedom, frequency and power of Parliament, the Religion, liberty and trade of the Nation from English or any foreign influence' (*APS*, 11.325). On 18 November he voted with Lord Annandale against article 3 of the treaty (that the united kingdom of Great Britain be represented by one and the same parliament entitled the parliament of Great Britain). On 7 January 1707 Atholl also handed in a

protestation against article 22 of the treaty and the future Scottish representation of forty-five members in the House of Commons and sixteen peers in the House of Lords. For Atholl such representation was an attack and slur on the rights of the Scottish peers and the rights of the shires and burghs. It was, he stated, 'plain and evident that this from a Soveraign Independent Monarchie shall dissolve it's Constitution and be at the disposal of England whose Constitution is not in the least to be altered by this Treaty' (ibid., 387). However, Atholl also extended the scope of his protestation to deal with wider issues relating to the treaty. He referred to the anti-union addresses and petitions being handed in to parliament as indicating that 'there is a generall dislike and aversion to the incorporating Union as contained in these articles' (ibid.). Accordingly, Atholl stated that the queen should be informed of the 'Inclinations of her People' and that a new parliament should be called by the queen, if she thought fit. Such a parliament, in Atholl's view, could 'satisfie the minds of the people, and creat a good understanding betwixt the two Kingdoms by an Union upon honourable, just and equall terms which may Unite them in affection and interest the surest foundation of peace and tranquillity' (ibid.).

Atholl is not recorded in the voting rolls for article 4 of the treaty, concerning the issue of freedom of trade. Therefore, he either abstained from the vote or was absent from parliament. According to official parliamentary voting records he was not present in parliament on 16 January 1707, when the complete treaty was ratified, an absence which might be explained by the death of his first wife on the 17th. Interestingly, and despite his stand against the court, Atholl received a payment of £1000 sterling (£12,000 Scots) out of the £20,000 sterling sent north for the payment of arrears of salary by the court. Atholl had recorded arrears of £1500 sterling (£18,000 Scots), but he was in debt to his brother Lord Dunmore. According to P. W. J. Riley, Atholl 'offered to transfer his arrears to him leaving him to make the best bargain with the court' (Riley, *Union of England and Scotland*, 259). Dunmore received a court payment of £200 sterling (£2400 Scots), though he had no recorded arrears, and, according to Riley, may have received Atholl's payment of £1000 sterling. Dunmore himself voted in favour of the Union, which means that Atholl 'could have benefited indirectly from it, whilst himself opposing the court though abstaining or absent on the ratification vote' (ibid.).

Atholl's public objection to union was not restricted to the political sphere. According to Gilbert Burnet, Atholl was 'believed to be in foreign correspondence and was strongly set on violent methods' to oppose the treaty (*Bishop Burnet's History*, ed. Burnet and Burnet, 800). It was a view confirmed by Lockhart of Carnwath, who claimed to know that:

> he was very frank and chearful to enter into any, though the most desperate, measures in the years 1706 and 1707, to obstruct the Hanoverian succession, and especially the Union, because, perhaps, he had but a small estate and could not expect to make so great an appearance after the Union as

if the kingdom of Scotland remained. But be the reasons what they will, certain it is he would have gone to the field rather than it should have passed, and had others been as forward as himself. (*Scotland's Ruine*, 41)

On 27 December 1706 Atholl voted against a proclamation discharging 'Unwarrantable and seditious Convocations and Meetings' (*APS*, 11.371–2), which was issued in the context of continued public disorder and fears over a possible armed uprising. Cameronian–Jacobite negotiations were conducted through John Ker of Kersland to attempt to secure pragmatic co-operation between Jacobites and Cameronians to resist the Union by force. Atholl's highlanders were to secure the pass of Stirling, and Lockhart states that Atholl 'frankly undertook what was demanded and seemed very keen to have the project executed' (*Scotland's Ruine*, 182). According to his own account, Ker was persuaded by Queensberry's arguments to dissuade the Cameronians from proceeding any further (J. Ker of Kersland, *The Memoirs of John Ker*, 3 vols., 1726 [repr. 1727], 30–34).

Later political career, 1708 onwards In the aftermath of the Union, Atholl was suspected by the privy council of being involved in the projected Jacobite invasion of 1708. Yet in his dealings with Scottish Jacobites, Nathaniel Hooke (1664–1738), found Atholl an elusive character who gave no definite commitment to support a Jacobite rising. Following the expedition's failure Atholl was summoned to appear before the privy council at Edinburgh, but a physician was sent instead to confirm that Atholl was too ill to attend. In response dragoons were ordered to seize Blair Castle, though the order was later countermanded upon 'just certificate of his dangerous illness' (N. Luttrell, *A Brief Historical Relation of State Affairs from September 1678 to April 1714*, 6 vols., 1857, 6.298). Accordingly, no further action was taken against Atholl. In 1710 he was chosen as one of the sixteen Scottish representative peers in the election, at which the tories were returned to power. Having been appointed an extraordinary lord of session on 7 November 1712, he was again chosen as a representative peer in 1713. Atholl acted as lord high commissioner to the general assembly of the Church of Scotland in 1712, 1713, and 1714. He was reappointed as lord privy seal in 1713, but this was superseded in 1714. Atholl obtained letters under the great seal in 1713 continuing the office of sheriff of Perthshire to him for life, and, on his death, to his eldest surviving son, Lord William.

Following the death of Queen Anne in August 1714, Atholl proclaimed George I king, at Perth. None the less, he was thereafter deprived of the office of lord privy seal, though he was appointed lord lieutenant of Perthshire in August 1715. As at the aftermath of the revolution of 1688, the house of Atholl was divided over the Jacobite rising of 1715. Atholl and his son James *Murray, later second duke (1690–1764), sided with the Hanoverian cause, but his sons William *Murray, marquess of Tullibardine, Lord George *Murray, and Lord Charles *Murray all followed James Francis Edward Stuart, the Pretender. In 1715 Atholl obtained an act of parliament for vesting his honours in his second surviving son, James, as a result of the participation of his eldest son, William, in the Jacobite rising. Atholl himself was involved in supporting the government against Jacobite activities. On 27 July 1715 he wrote to the provost of Perth offering to supply two or three hundred men to guard the burgh. On 7 September he sent information to John Campbell, second duke of Argyll, informing him of the movements of John Erskine, earl of Mar. Atholl informed Argyll that he would prevent Mar from passing through his territory, and that he would guard the fords and boats on the River Tay between Dunkeld and Loch Tay. On 9 October Atholl wrote to the earl of Sutherland seeking the latter's presence in Atholl with military aid. Atholl assured Sutherland that the north side of the River Forth could be recovered if Sutherland came with a force of between two and three thousand men. Despite this approach Atholl received no reply from Sutherland. In the wake of the battle of Sheriffmuir, he stated his intention of marching to Perth to recover the town from the Jacobite rebels, though this intention was not fulfilled. After the retreat and dispersal of the rebels, Atholl was particularly active in collecting weapons from those involved in the uprising. He further ingratiated himself with the government by his capture of the highland folk hero Rob Roy MacGregor on 3 June 1717, despite his friendship with MacGregor over several years.

Atholl died at Huntingtower, Perthshire, on 14 November 1724, and was buried at Dunkeld on 26 November. Lockhart of Carnwath offered an ambivalent assessment of the abilities of a politician who was 'endowed with good natural parts, though by reason of his proud, imperious, haughty, passionate temper he was no ways capable to be the leading man of a party which he aimed at' (*Scotland's Ruine*, 42). He was, Lockhart added:

> selfish to a great degree, and his vanity and ambition extended so far that he could not suffer an equal ... He was reputed very brave, but hot and headstrong, and, though no scholar nor orator, yet expressed his mind very handsomely on publick occasions. (ibid.)

This was a view endorsed by Macky, who believed Atholl was 'of a very proud, fiery, partial disposition; [he] does not want sense, but cloaks himself with passion, which he is easily wound up to when he speaks in public assemblies' (*Memoirs of the Secret Services*, 184). On his death the dukedom passed to his second son, James, while his eldest son, William, was styled second duke by Jacobite sympathizers.

JOHN R. YOUNG

Sources DNB · APS, 1689–1707 · *Scotland's ruine: Lockhart of Carnwath's memoirs of the Union*, ed. D. Szechi (1995) · *Scots peerage* · J. J. H. Stewart-Murray, seventh duke of Atholl, *Chronicles of the Atholl and Tullibardine families*, 5 vols. (privately printed, Edinburgh, 1908) · P. W. J. Riley, *King William and the Scottish politicians* (1979) · P. W. J. Riley, *The Union of England and Scotland* (1978) · B. Lenman, *The Jacobite risings in Britain, 1689–1746* (1984) · W. Ferguson, *Scotland's relations with England* (1977) · J. Elder, *The highland host of 1678* (1914) · P. Hopkins, *Glencoe and the end of the highland war* (1998) · *Manuscripts of the duke of Atholl ... and of the earl of Home*, HMC, 26 (1891) · *Bishop Burnet's History of his own time*, ed. G. Burnet and T. Burnet, 2 vols. (1724–34) · *Memoirs of the secret services of John Macky*, ed. A. R. (1733)

Archives Blair Castle, Perthshire, corresp. and papers · NL Scot., legal corresp. · NRA, priv. coll., corresp. and papers | BL, letters to Lord Godolphin, Add. MS 28055 · College of William and Mary, Williamsburg, Virginia, corresp. with earl of Dunmore · NA Scot., corresp. with Lord Leven · NA Scot., corresp. with earl of Mar · NA Scot., letters to duke of Montrose · NL Scot., corresp. with first and second marquesses of Tweeddale · NRA, priv. coll., letters to duchess of Hamilton · U. Edin. L., MSS relating to family dispute with his brother

Likenesses T. Murray, oils, 1705, Blair Castle, Tayside [*see illus.*] · T. Murray, oils, Blair Castle, Tayside

Murray, John (1670/71–1748), library agent and book collector, of Sacombe in Hertfordshire, was born in London probably on 24 January, in either 1670 or 1671. Little is known about his personal and family life except that he appears to have had a lower middle-class background. His father was a pawnbroker in Houndsditch, London, and his uncle a merchant in Edinburgh. There is no evidence for Murray's education and he did not attend any university. He lived and worked in the area of Shoreditch in London and regularly travelled around England. He may also have worked as a bookseller for some time. In 1721 he bought a house in Sacombe, Hertfordshire.

Murray moved in a wide circle of antiquaries, book collectors, and booksellers in London and Oxford. Among them were antiquarian collectors such as Thomas Rawlinson, Thomas Granger, James West, and Walter Clavell, the bookseller Christopher Bateman, and the engraver George Vertue. Important friends were the antiquary and library agent John Bagford, the collector Edward Harley, and the antiquaries William Stukeley and Thomas Hearne. According to Vertue, Murray was called the Philosopher. Most of the information about Murray derives from his correspondence with Hearne, and Hearne's comments on his friend in his diaries and publications. Hearne always respected Murray as a collector and bookdealer even though the collectors Thomas and Richard Rawlinson were less appreciative and referred to him as the Houndsditch Pawnbroker in contempt of both Murray's and his father's professions. Murray shared his intense interest in early printed books with John Bagford, whom he joined on trips to the Dutch town of Haarlem in search of books and manuscripts. Murray himself owned a valuable collection of early printed books, which he kept at Sacombe. A list of his Caxtons is in De Ricci's *Census of Caxtons* (1909).

Some of Murray's antiquarian materials were published by Hearne, with whom he shared an interest in Reformation historians, particularly Sir Thomas More. Thus he procured for Hearne a manuscript copy of William Roper's biography of More together with an engraved portrait of More for Hearne's edition of Roper's work (1716). Murray owned the famous manuscript 'The Play of Sir Thomas More' (BL, Harleian MS 7368), which is thought to bear Shakespeare's autograph on three pages. He lent it to Hearne who discussed the manuscript in *Liber niger scaccarii* (1728). Hearne regularly consulted Murray on a variety of scholarly and antiquarian issues and urged him to find early editions of English chronicles, for example by John Hardyng, John Rastell, and John Stow. According to

Hearne, Murray owned a considerable number of manuscript works of the poet laureate John Skelton.

Murray thought of retiring from his 'book running' business from about 1729. He told Hearne more than once that he wanted to stop buying books and thought of selling most of his collections. Hearne regretted that his friend had never produced a catalogue of his possessions. Murray had hunted for books especially for Edward Harley and during a period of illness in 1735 he sent Harley a hamper of books and papers 'which has bin the product of my whole Life and am Gladd att going out of ye world they will be so well reposited' (*Diary of Humfrey Wanley*, lxxvi). Murray died in 1748, the cause of his death and the place of his burial unknown. His library was sold on 8 May 1749. Parts of the collections were bought by Richard Rawlinson and are today in the Bodleian Library, Oxford.

THEODOR HARMSEN

Sources Bodl. Oxf., MSS Rawl. letters 27c, 112 · *Remarks and collections of Thomas Hearne*, ed. C. E. Doble and others, 11 vols., OHS, 2, 7, 13, 34, 42–3, 48, 50, 65, 67, 72 (1885–1921) · T. F. Dibdin, *Bibliomania, or, Book madness: a bibliographical romance*, 2nd edn, [2 vols.] (1811), 437–8 · *The diary of Humfrey Wanley, 1715–1726*, ed. C. E. Wright and R. C. Wright, 2 vols. (1966), vol. 1, pp. lxxv–lxxvi; vol. 2, p. 457 · C. E. Wright, *Fontes Harleiani: a study of the sources of the Harleian collection of manuscripts* (1972), xxvii, 247–8 · T. H. B. M. Harmsen, *Antiquarianism in the Augustan age: Thomas Hearne, 1678–1735* (2000) · W. D. Macray, *Catalogus codicum … Ricardi Rawlinson*, 5 vols. (1862–1900) · S. De Ricci, *A census of Caxtons* (1909), 174 · C. E. Wright, 'Portrait of a bibliophile VIII: Edward Harley, 2nd earl of Oxford, 1689–1741', *Book Collector*, 11 (1962), 158–74, esp. 169 · W. Y. Fletcher, *English book collectors* (1902), 159 · T. F. Dibdin, *The bibliographical decameron*, 3 (1817), 283 · *A catalogue of an entire library … belonging to a gentleman lately deceas'd* (1749) [Murray's library; sale catalogue, London, 8 May 1749] · T. Hearne, ed., *Liber niger Scaccarii*, 2 (1728), 745–9 · J. Bagford, 'An essay on the invention of printing, by Mr. John Bagford, with an account of his collections for the same by Mr. Humfrey Wanley, FRS, communicated in two letters to Dr. Hans Sloane', *PTRS*, 25 (1706–7), 2397–410 · B. J. Enright, 'Richard Rawlinson: collector, antiquary, and topographer', DPhil diss., U. Oxf., 1956, appx B

Archives Bodl. Oxf., corresp., MSS Hearne, diaries; MSS Rawl., letters

Likenesses portrait, 1752, BL, Add. MS 323551, fol. 1 · G. Vertue, engraving

Murray, John, second earl of Dunmore (1685–1752), army officer and politician, the son of Lord Charles *Murray (1661–1710), who was created earl of Dunmore in the Scottish peerage by James VII in 1686, and his wife, Catherine (d. 1710), daughter of Richard Watts of Great Munden, Hertfordshire, was born on 31 October 1685 at Whitehall, Westminster, London. He was styled Viscount Fincastle from his elder brother's death in 1704 until he succeeded his father in 1710 as earl of Dunmore. Pursuing a military career, he was commissioned an ensign in the 3rd foot guards in 1704 and fought at Blenheim the same year. Promotion was steady and at times rapid: Dunmore became colonel of his regiment in 1712 (a position he held until his death), brigadier-general in 1719, major-general in 1735, lieutenant-general in 1739, and general in 1745. In the same year he was made governor of Plymouth. His active service took place largely on the continent, where he served under a variety of commanders and gained the reputation of being a reliable subordinate. He was part of Lord Cobham's Vigo expedition in 1719, and in 1743 fought under George II at Dettingen, where he was one of sixteen British generals made knights-banneret on the field by the king. He later served under the earl of Stair and the duke of Cumberland in the Low Countries. His lone major command came in 1745 when Cumberland and almost all British troops in the Low Countries were withdrawn to meet the Jacobite threat in Britain, leaving Dunmore in command of remaining allied forces. Greatly outnumbered, he was unable to prevent the capture of Antwerp by the French or their overall dominance in the Austrian Netherlands.

When Dunmore was not on active service his life focused on the court and parliament. A firm supporter of the Union of 1707, he served as a representative peer in 1713–14 and 1727–52. In 1720 he purchased the manor of Stanwell, Middlesex, and appears thereafter to have spent little time in Scotland. Despite the Jacobite leanings of some of his relatives, he remained staunchly Hanoverian in his sympathies and opposed the Jacobite risings of 1715 and 1745. He exerted himself to save his brother and heir, William Murray of Taymount, who had joined the Forty-Five. Having obtained statements from loyal peers that his brother had helped to save the lives and property of Hanoverian supporters, he successfully interceded with the ministry for a pardon. In politics Dunmore allied himself with Archibald Campbell, earl of Ilay and subsequently third duke of Argyll. He supported Sir Robert Walpole during the excise crisis of 1733 when the fourteen representative peers present divided equally, though in general he did not figure prominently in the upper house's proceedings. He was a lord of the bedchamber to George II from 1732 until his death; on one occasion, according to Lord Hervey, he provoked the king by being overly inquisitive about his health. Dunmore never married, though, according to Lady Mary Wortley Montagu, he lived for a number of years with Mary, Lady Lansdown (d. 1735). He died on 18 April 1752 in London, and was buried at Stanwell on 24 April. He was succeeded by his brother William.   WILLIAM C. LOWE

Sources College of William and Mary, Williamsburg, Virginia, USA, Dunmore MSS · Fortescue, *Brit. army*, vol. 2 · John, Lord Hervey, *Some materials towards memoirs of the reign of King George II*, ed. R. Sedgwick, new edn, 3 vols. (1952) · P. C. Yorke, *The life and correspondence of Philip Yorke, earl of Hardwicke*, 1 (1913) · *The complete letters of Lady Mary Wortley Montagu*, ed. R. Halsband, 2 (1966) · *Scots peerage*, vol. 3 · E. Timberland, *The history and proceedings of the House of Lords*, 7 vols. (1742), vols. 4–7 · J. Black, *Culloden and the '45* (1990) · GEC, *Peerage*, new edn, vol. 4 · J. S. Shaw, *The management of Scottish society, 1707–1764: power, nobles, lawyers, Edinburgh agents and English influences* (1983) · J. Hayes, 'Scottish officers in the British army, 1714–1763', *SHR*, 37 (1958), 23–33

Archives College of William and Mary, Williamsburg, Virginia, family MSS and corresp. · priv. coll., papers [photocopies]

Murray, Lord John (1711–1787), army officer, born on 14 April 1711, was the eldest son of John *Murray, second marquess and first duke of Atholl (1660–1724), and his second wife, Mary (1687–1767), daughter of William Ross, twelfth Lord Ross of Halkhead, and was half-brother of the Jacobite leaders William *Murray, marquess of Tullibardine (1689–1746), and Lord George *Murray (1694–1760). A godson of Queen Anne, he was educated at a private school in Chelsea, possibly at St Andrews University, and at Leiden University. He was appointed ensign in the 3rd foot guards on 7 October 1727, on the recommendation of General Wade, and lieutenant and captain in the 3rd foot guards (Scots guards) in 1733, in which he became captain-lieutenant in 1737, and captain and lieutenant-colonel in 1738. In 1743 he served in Germany as aide-decamp to George II.

Murray was brought up a whig and owed his advancement to his half-brother James (1692–1764) who, displacing the attainted Jacobite heir William, in 1724 became second duke of Atholl. From his coming of age in 1734 to 1761 Murray was MP for Perthshire, where Atholl had the predominant interest. Murray supported Walpole until his fall in 1742, then attached himself to Henry Pelham and the duke of Newcastle. He unsuccessfully applied to Newcastle for transfer to a dragoon regiment or the government of Kinsale in 1753. He was not popular with the Perthshire freeholders, who thought he neglected their interests by staying in Scotland in November 1759, instead of presenting their case to parliament on the Distilling Bill. Moreover his relations with Atholl deteriorated. He believed that since Lord George was attainted he should have the succession to the dukedom, and he resented Atholl's marrying his daughter to Lord George's son John Murray (1729–1774), and Atholl's reconciliation with Lady George. In 1760 Atholl nominated his son-in-law as candidate for Perthshire. Insufficiently supported, Lord John withdrew the day before the election. Disappointed of his hope of gaining, through Newcastle, a command at home or overseas, he tried to win court favour through the earl of Bute. On 8 January 1764 Atholl died, and Murray unsuccessfully opposed the succession of John Murray to the dukedom. At the 1764 Perthshire by-election, as his own candidature was unacceptable, Murray supported the government candidate Colonel David Graeme against the Atholl interest. In 1768 and 1769 he attempted to gain election in Elgin burghs, and in 1773 again attempted Perthshire, but had no support and withdrew. After this he sold most of his Scottish estates and did not again attempt to enter parliament.

On 25 April 1745 Murray was appointed to the colonelcy of the 43rd (from 1749 the 42nd, and from 1758 Royal) Highlanders, the Black Watch, which he held until May 1787. He served with them in Flanders in 1745, although he was absent from Fontenoy (30 April 1745), and in the unsuccessful attack, commanded by Lieutenant-General James St Clair, on the French Atlantic naval base, L'Orient (September 1746). In 1747 he was at the attempted relief of Hulst and the defence of Fort Sandberg (May), and commanded the British troops in the retreat to Welshorden, as well as at the defence of Bergen-op-Zoom, but he did not go with the 42nd to North America in 1756. He was devoted to his regiment, did much to foster its national character, tried to obtain good officers from Scotland, and promoted the welfare of its former soldiers. In London in

1758 he marched in full highland uniform at the head of the many highlanders disabled at the disastrous attack on Ticonderoga (July 1758) to plead their claims before the Chelsea board, with the result that every man received a pension. He offered every man a cottage and garden on his estate rent-free. He became major-general in 1755, lieutenant-general in 1758, and general in 1770. He wanted a command in the American War of Independence but was disappointed. In 1779–80 he raised at his own expense a second battalion to the 42nd, which in 1786 became the 73rd foot and in July 1881 was re-linked to the 42nd as 2nd battalion.

Murray married at Sheffield, on 13 September 1758, a Yorkshire lady of property, Miss Mary Dalton of Bannercross, daughter of Richard Dalton, a Sheffield merchant, and they had one daughter, Mary. Murray retired to Bannercross in 1773 following the collapse of his political ambitions. He died in Paris on 26 May 1787, the senior general in the army. His daughter married Captain (afterwards Lieutenant-General) William Foxlowe, who took the name of Murray in 1782.

H. M. CHICHESTER, *rev.* ROGER T. STEARN

Sources E. Haden-Guest, 'Murray, Lord John', HoP, *Commons, 1754–90* · E. Haden-Guest, 'Murray, Lord John', HoP, *Commons, 1715–54* · Burke, *Peerage* (1967) · GEC, *Peerage* · GM, 1st ser., 57 (1787), 548 · R. Cannon, ed., *Historical record of the forty-second, or the royal highland regiment of foot* (1845) · P. Groves, *History of the 42nd royal highlanders: 'the black watch'* (1893) · N. McMicking, *Officers of the black watch, 1725 to 1937* (1937) · P. Howard, *The black watch (royal highland regiment) (the 42nd regiment of foot)* (1968) · J. Black, *Britain as a military power, 1688–1815* (1999)

Archives JRL, military and personal corresp. and papers · NL Scot., legal corresp. | BL, corresp. with earl of Liverpool, Add. MSS 38210–38217, 38306–38309, *passim* · U. Edin. L., letters to second duke of Atholl

Murray, Sir John, of Broughton, baronet [*called* Secretary Murray, Mr Evidence Murray] (1714/15?–1777), Jacobite

agent and alleged traitor, the younger son of Sir David Murray, baronet, and Margaret, widow of Thomas Scott of Whitside and daughter of Sir John Scott of Ancrum, was born into a loyalist family of the barony of Broughton in Peeblesshire. Unlike the *Dictionary of National Biography*, which gave his birth date as 1718, Robert Fitzroy Bell argued in support of Murray's own matriculation statement for the University of Leiden which, in 1735, maintained that he was twenty, an age which accords with his subsequent Masonic initiation and allows for his previous education at Edinburgh University from March 1732. After two years at Leiden Murray went to Rome. His enrolment (20 August 1737) into the Roman lodge was witnessed by, among others, the painter Allan Ramsay; Murray's affiliation, on his return to Edinburgh in 1738, to Masonic lodge Canongate Kilwinning no. 2 is commemorated by the retrospective excision of his name from their transactions. Also in 1738 he seems to have met Prince Charles Edward Stuart, who apparently made a profound impression on his near contemporary; they met again in Paris in 1744. By that date Murray had been identified by James Edgar, secretary to James III (James Francis Edward Stuart), as a successor to a declining Colonel Urquart as the

Jacobites' official correspondent between Rome and Scotland, in which unsalaried position he was ratified by the duke of Hamilton. About 1739 Murray married Margaret, daughter of Colonel Robert Ferguson of Nithsdale, and at the same time purchased the ancestral home of Broughton. He had also visited France on the death (in 1743) of Cardinal Fleury and thereafter liaised with those French, Scots, and exiled Jacobites contemplating the exploitation of the War of the Austrian Succession to their various ends.

From then until the Jacobite rising of 1745 there is every evidence that Murray discouraged the idea of an unsupported landing in Scotland, and erred only by relying on the earl of Traquair to convey a letter (framed by Murray) from concerned parties in Scotland to Charles Edward in time to prevent the prince's coming. In the vacuum before this dreaded arrival Murray none the less oversaw the printing in Edinburgh of two boxes of royal proclamations and manifestos, plus the gathering of some arms, and although he aspired, via the younger Glengarry, to a nomination as an aide-de-camp, he seems from the first to have assumed the duties of a secretary, or general administrator, for which an essentially non-military education fitted him. (A commission in Rothes's Irish regiment from February 1743, signed by d'Argenson, minister of war, would later be invoked in an unsuccessful attempt to give him immunity as a French prisoner of war.)

Murray's quotidian involvement in the Jacobites' march south to Derby and back beyond the Forth can be recovered from a range of contemporary accounts. Unlike his successor, Hay of Restalrig, no complaint was made of his contribution other than that of undue influence with the prince. Seriously ill from March 1746 he escaped Culloden and was among those who initially aspired to defy this disaster by a short-term guerrilla war in the highlands until French help, or the lack of it, could be confirmed; this was at a time when the safety and movements of Charles Edward himself were initially unknown. Murray was involved—again, honourably as far as can be ascertained—in the secretion of those divisive French funds, wrested from the teeth of a patrolling Royal Navy, better known as the Loch Arkaig treasure. At this point, with Donald Cameron of Lochiel, he watched the rump of the Jacobite leadership embark to France; with Lochiel he aimed subsequently for the Netherlands via Leith, and it is worth noting that he endeavoured to secure Lochiel's passage during his own initial captivity. Murray was captured on 27 June 1746 at his sister's house, Polmood, Peeblesshire, and was transported to London. He was examined on 13, 22, and 27 August, again in November, and once more in the context of the trial of Simon, Lord Lovat, in February, and in March 1747 when he was alleged to have betrayed former Jacobite associates. Released from the Tower after Lovat's execution, but not officially pardoned until 7 June 1748, of his subsequent life few details are known aside from his inheritance of the baronetcy on the death, without children, of his nephew, Sir David, in 1770.

None the less Murray remained a prominent figure

among Jacobites who, attempting to explain the failure of the 'Forty-Five, cast him as a convenient villain and, against stiff opposition, 'the most deeply stained and opprobriated name in the papers of Scottish history' (Duke, 60). There is, for example, the chilling rejoinder of Sir John Douglas of Kelhead before the privy council to the question 'Do you know this witness?': 'Not I; once I knew a person who bore the designation of Murray of Broughton, but that was a gentleman and a man of honour, and one that could hold up his head' (J. G. Lockhart, *Memoirs of the Life of Sir Walter Scott, bart.*, 1842, 49). Walter Scott's father is said to have broken a teacup disingenuously proffered to a shrouded Murray during a business visit about 1764 with the words: 'I may admit to my house, on a piece of business, persons wholly unworthy to be treated as guests by my wife. Neither lip of me or mine come after Murray of Broughton' (ibid.). An earlier poem 'For S.M. on his turning evidence *quantum mutatis ab illis*' Aberdeen University Library, MS 2222, published in revised form in London in 1747), condemns its subject to retire from all human society and rot, while gloating that solitude itself would be no safe retreat from the reproaches of conscience; like Marley's ghost, Murray 'may drag [his] Heavy chains along'. His irredeemability is further affirmed elsewhere in a 10-line comparison with Judas Iscariot (Pittock, 59–61).

What had Murray done to deserve such criticism? The case against him, then and in subsequent academic studies, claims that he was of a minority who gave the sanguine prince false encouragement to attempt a revolution via a landing in Scotland, regardless of French backing (see, for example, Pittock, 'New Jacobite songs', 61). Moreover, in his capacity as royal secretary he was allegedly one of the prince's entourage who frustrated the access and counsel of those Scots who were chiefly engaged during the campaign. According to the memoirs of Maxwell of Kirkconnel and Lord Elcho he was guilty of further poisoning the always prickly relations between Charles Edward and Lord George Murray. Writing in 1927, for example, Winifred Duke implies that it was Murray's corrosive effect on this relationship, and less his turning king's evidence after his capture—the traditional source of his opprobrium—which proved his more destructive contribution to the 'Forty-Five.

Yet such condemnations need revision in the light of a better understanding of the nuances of the Jacobite rising. Traquair rather than Murray must bear the greater responsibility for the cross-communications of 1745. How far Murray undermined his namesake Lord George cannot be reconstructed, other than by surmise, from either of their memoirs; sources for this, Kirkconnel (Murray's 'implacable foe') and Elcho, have their own agendas and prejudices. Of his 'Judas' testimony before the Hanoverian authorities, it had (if Murray himself is excluded) only one victim—Lord Lovat—for whom it was both fitting and overdue; that it prejudiced the safety of Traquair and those English Jacobites who had chosen the better part of valour hints at the possible motivation—namely, the

embittered disillusionment felt by Murray when witnessing the rapid English and Scottish rewriting of history in the wake of Culloden. Certainly the retrospective vilification of Murray's part in the origins and conduct of the campaign is suggestive of a collective denial on the part of the survivors of the post-Derby *sauve qui peut*. In Murray's own words, if 'virtue [may be] admird and Esteemed even by those who have not the fortitude to pursue it [,] the Coward is said in his heart to hate his fellow Coward' (Bell, 252). Equally, Murray's contribution to the logistic and military successes of the 'Forty-Five and its aftermath have long been overlooked; even the author of 'For S.M.' credits him with initial idealism and integrity. His 'everlasting Infamy' is not his only claim on posterity.

Not surprisingly a number of unsubstantiated rumours continued to circulate concerning Murray's actions after his formal pardon in 1748. The story that in later life, on losing his reason, he was confined to a semi-private asylum at Broughton, where 'the meanest mechanics of different denominations … gratify their curiosity and boast of interviews with mad Secretary Murray' (Bell, xxx) seems almost too Hogarthian, though as Bell notes it would account for the incomplete state of his (dictated?) *Memorials*, drafted from about 1757, and would be understandable given the shadow under which he lived. The *Memorials* deny another slur, on the marital fidelity of his first wife, a figure later addressed sympathetically by John Buchan in *A Lost Lady of Old Years* (1899), but who disappears from the historical record after 1749. The legality of his second marriage to a Miss Webb cannot be proved, but it resulted in a further six children, the eldest being Charles *Murray, the comic actor. Sir James Murray died at Cheshunt, Hertfordshire, on 6 December 1777.

EIRWEN E. C. NICHOLSON

Sources DNB · *Memorials of John Murray of Broughton*, ed. R. F. Bell, Scottish History Society, 27 (1898) · W. B. Blaikie, ed., *Origins of the 'Forty-Five and other papers relating to that rising*, Scottish History Society, 2nd ser., 2 (1916); facs. repr. (1975) · W. Duke, *Lord George Murray and the '45* (1927) · M. G. H. Pittock, 'New Jacobite songs of the Forty Five', *Studies on Voltaire and the Eighteenth Century*, 267 (1989)
Archives NL Scot., letters

Murray, John (*c.*1714–1775), diplomat, was believed to have been born on the Isle of Man. In 1748 he married Bridget Wentworth, *née* Milbanke (*d.* 1774), the widow of Sir Butler Cavendish Wentworth (*d.* 1741), and the daughter of Sir Ralph Milbanke, fourth baronet, and his first wife, Elizabeth D'Arcy. Murray entered the diplomatic stage in 1754, when he was appointed British resident at Venice. He arrived in Venice on 9 October 1754 accompanied by his wife, who kept her former name, Lady Wentworth, and his sister Elizabeth, who later married Consul Joseph Smith (1673/4–1770), a leading art collector.

Murray's appointment appears to have been based largely on nepotistic grounds. There was little coincidence in the fact that he attained the post of resident shortly after a cousin of his wife, Robert D'Arcy, fourth earl of Holdernesse, became secretary of state for the north, in March 1754. Murray makes this clear in a letter to Holdernesse, in which he wrote that his wife 'grows fat, my sister the same' and 'in short my lord, you have put us into so good a pasture that if we don't change the soil we shall all burst' (*Complete Letters of Lady Mary Wortley Montagu*, 127). Murray, who was certainly of 'great weight' (Ingamells, 691), indulged in many of the pleasures afforded by Venice. He and Casanova devoted themselves to pursuing, seducing, and swapping women across the city. Casanova, who described his fellow rake as a 'handsome Bacchus painted by Rubens' (ibid.), notoriously recorded how he witnessed Murray making love to his long-standing and syphilis-ridden mistress, 'Ancilla', only a few minutes before she died.

Murray's sexual reputation earned the enmity of Lady Mary Wortley Montagu, who found him a 'scandalous fellow in every sense of that word' and wrote: 'he is not to be trusted to change a sequin, despis'd by this government for smuggling, which was his original profession, and always surrounded by pimps, and brokers, who are his Privy Counsellors' (*Complete Letters*, 127). Her disapproval was heightened by their political differences; as Lady Wortley Montagu commented: 'Our great minister, the Resident, affects to treat me as one in the opposition. I am inclin'd to laugh rather than be displeased at his political airs' (ibid., 137).

During his residency Murray amassed an important collection of paintings that included several by Titian, many by other Venetian painters, and a Dürer. His wife patronized the young Angelica Kauffman when she came to Venice in 1765 and arranged her visit to London in 1766. Murray's love of his residency at Venice met with an unpleasant shock when he was promoted to the position of ambassador at Constantinople. He left Venice on 11 May 1766 and arrived in Constantinople on 2 June. The following year he made clear his displeasure at his move: 'I came here much against my inclination, having refused the embassy in repeated letters' (Murray to Preston, 29 Sept 1767, PRO, SP 110/87). Lady Wentworth did not accompany him but travelled back with Kauffman to England, where she landed on 22 June 1766. Murray was ambassador at Constantinople during the Russo-Turkish War of 1768–74. Much of his time was concerned with attempts to secure a mediatory role for Britain, which had abandoned its former indifference to the politics of the region. However, like his European counterparts, Murray was unable to obtain a position as mediator in the peace talks between Russia and the Ottoman empire. A diplomat of 'mediocre abilities' (Anderson, 41), he did manage to maintain cordial relations with the Ottoman empire but was unable to stem the downward spiral of the Levant Company's fortunes during this period. As ambassador, he seemingly gave precedence to the virtue of honesty in diplomacy, stating early in his ambassadorship: 'I am determined to put an end to this horrid scene of corruption or quit my embassy' (Murray to Turner, 10 Sept 1767, PRO, SP 110/87).

Towards the end of 1774 Murray required leave to go home to England in order to attend to affairs after the death of his wife. Granted such leave, he departed Constantinople on 25 May 1775 and, with the intention of returning, chose Consul Hayes to act as chargé d'affaires in the interim. However, Murray was never to return to Constantinople, nor did he make it to England, for he died en route, at the Lazzaretto in Venice, on 9 August 1775. He was buried in the protestant cemetery in the Lido.

ZOË HOLMES

Sources PRO, SP 97/43–51, SP 99/70, SP 110/86–87 · J. Ingamells, ed., *A dictionary of British and Irish travellers in Italy, 1701–1800* (1997) · *The complete letters of Lady Mary Wortley Montagu*, ed. R. Halsband, 3 (1967) · D. B. Horn, ed., *British diplomatic representatives, 1689–1789*, CS, 3rd ser., 46 (1932) · M. S. Anderson, 'Great Britain and the Russo-Turkish war of 1768–74', *EngHR*, 69 (1954), 39–58 · Walpole, *Corr.*, vols. 21–3 · H. M. Scott, *British foreign policy in the age of the American Revolution* (1989) · GEC, *Baronetage* · I. Grundy, *Lady Mary Wortley Montagu* (1999)

Archives PRO, corresp. whilst ambassador at Constantinople, SP 97/43–51, SP 99/70, SP 105/317, SP 110/86–87 | BL, letters to R. Gunning, Egerton MSS 2698–2703, *passim* · BL, corresp. with Sir Robert Keith, Add. MSS 35504–35509; 35572–35573, *passim* · NRA, priv. coll., letters to Lord Cathcart

Murray, John, third duke of Atholl (1729–1774), politician, was born on 25 April 1729, the eldest son of Lord George *Murray (1694–1760), Jacobite army officer, and his wife, Amelia Murray (*d.* 1766), only surviving child and heir of James Murray of Glencarse and Strowan. His father being in exile, Murray was brought up by his uncle James *Murray, second duke of Atholl (1690–1764). He was educated at Eton College between 1742 and 1745. While there he was appointed, though he never served, as a captain in Loudoun's new infantry regiment on the outbreak of the Jacobite rising of 1745. After Eton he attended the Soho Academy, London (1746–7), and was then sent by his uncle to the University of Göttingen (1751–3) in an attempt to distance him from his father and from allegations of his being a Jacobite sympathizer.

On his return Murray married, on 23 October 1753, his cousin Lady Charlotte Murray (1731–1805), daughter and heir of his uncle James; they had eleven children, seven sons and four daughters. The duke, intending his title to pass to Murray, now began to involve him in the management of the family estate. In 1761 Murray was elected MP for Perthshire: his father had died in the previous year, so he was able to support the Bute and then the Grenville administrations free from accusations of Jacobitism.

On the death of his uncle on 8 January 1764 Murray became third duke of Atholl, the appointment being confirmed by the House of Lords on 7 February. The second

John Murray, third duke of Atholl (1729–1774), by John Kirk, 1774

duke's death also provided Murray's wife with the English barony of Strange and the sovereignty of the Isle of Man. This latter title was sold in 1765 to the British government in return for £70,000, the retention of landed property (on payment of an annual sum), and the continued patronage of the bishopric and fishing and mineral resources. On 21 August 1764 and again in 1768 he was chosen as a representative peer, and in 1767 was invested with the Order of the Thistle.

Increasingly disaffected with politics from the mid-1760s, Atholl retired to his estate to study and practise forestry. On 5 November 1774 he drowned in the River Tay at Dunkeld, where he was buried. He was survived by his wife, who died on 13 October 1805, and by their remaining children, including John, fourth duke of Atholl (1755–1830), created Earl Strange and Baron Murray of Stanley in 1786; Lord James Murray; Lord George *Murray, bishop of St David's; Lord Charles Murray, dean of Bocking, Essex; and Lady Amelia Murray, who was married first to Thomas Ivie Cooke, army officer, and later to Sir Richard Gamon.

T. F. HENDERSON, rev. ROBERT CLYDE

Sources DNB · E. Haden-Guest, 'Murray, John', HoP, Commons · A. Murdoch, 'The people above': politics and administration in mid-eighteenth-century Scotland (1980) · B. Lenman, Integration and enlightenment: Scotland, 1746–1832 (1992) · R. Souter, Patronage and politics in Scotland, 1707–1832 (1986) · GEC, Peerage, new edn
Archives Blair Castle, Perthshire, Atholl MSS · NA Scot. · NL Scot., legal corresp. and papers | NL Scot., Mackenzie of Delvine MSS
Likenesses J. Zoffany, group portrait, oils, 1765–7, Blair Castle, Perthshire · J. Kirk, silver medal, 1774, Scot. NPG [see illus.] · etching, BM

Murray, John, fourth earl of Dunmore (1730/31–1809), colonial governor, was the eldest son of William Murray, third earl of Dunmore (1696–1756), and Catherine Nairne, daughter of William *Nairne (formerly Murray), the second Lord Nairne, and Margaret Nairne, daughter of the first Lord Nairne. Despite the third earl's support of the Young Pretender (Charles Edward Stuart), the family retained the title to which John succeeded in 1756. On 21 February 1759 he married Charlotte Stewart (d. 1818), daughter of Alexander Stewart, sixth earl of Galloway, and Catherine Cochrane, daughter of the fourth earl of Dundonald. They had nine children. In 1761 Dunmore became a representative peer of Scotland, a post he filled until 1790 except for 1774–6.

Dunmore supported Lord North's ministry, and became governor of New York in 1770 and of Virginia a year later. In both colonies he obtained sizeable land grants and allied with speculators such as Sir William Johnson and George Washington. To the delight of the Virginia élite, Lady Dunmore and their children joined him in February 1774. Dunmore dissolved the Virginia assembly in May 1774 to halt criticism of the Coercive Acts punishing Boston for its 'Tea Party', but a successful expedition against western Indians distracted him from imperial affairs for the rest of the year. The acclaim for his victory may have blinded him to the strength of Virginian opposition to imperial taxes. His removal of public munitions from the

John Murray, fourth earl of Dunmore (1730/31–1809), by Sir Joshua Reynolds, 1765

Williamsburg magazine on 21 April 1775 brought widespread condemnation, and in June he fled from Williamsburg to Norfolk.

Having sent his family to Britain, Dunmore raised a loyalist force and commenced military operations in Hampton Roads. Several local victories persuaded him to issue an emancipation proclamation in November, offering freedom to slaves and indentured servants 'appertaining to Rebels' who enlisted with him (R. L. Scribner and B. Tartar, eds., Revolutionary Virginia: the Road to Independence, 1978, 4.334). The proclamation sealed his reputation among most Virginians. Despite the arrival of reinforcements from the 14th regiment, on 9 December Dunmore was unable to hold the land approach to Norfolk at Great Bridge against Virginia troops, and he withdrew with a number of loyalists, mainly Scottish merchants, to boats in the harbour. On 1 January 1776 British vessels began cannonading the city and dispatched landing parties, whom Virginia and North Carolina troops quickly beat back. For three days the American forces raged out of control and burned the bulk of the town, though Dunmore bore the blame until the twentieth century. With the proclamation and the burning, Virginia opinion rapidly turned to independence. Dunmore lingered offshore until May, when naval reinforcements helped him move to Gwinn's Island. The Virginians again drove him off in July, and in August he abandoned the Chesapeake.

Dunmore resumed his former post as representative peer, and became a principal lobbyist for compensation to loyalists. With General Cornwallis's march through the American south in 1780–81, the ministry ordered Dunmore to Charles Town, South Carolina, preparatory to resuming power upon Cornwallis's anticipated victory. After the defeat at Yorktown, Dunmore advocated expanding the empire on the Gulf coast and into the Mississippi valley. In 1786 he became governor of the Bahamas, a key site for loyalist exiles seeking to trade with Spanish Florida. Dunmore strengthened the islands' defences and opened free ports to expedite British inroads into the Caribbean trade. Opposition grew because of costs, buccaneering expeditions he sanctioned into Florida, and his challenge to the dominance of the pre-eminent American Indian trader in that region, Alexander McGillivray. The resulting legislative battles were reminiscent of those in Virginia, though the factions were more evenly balanced on the islands. In 1794 Lady Dunmore's brother-in-law and the governor's chief patron, the marquess of Stafford, resigned from the ministry, and Dunmore additionally lost favour at court because his daughter Augusta secretly married a son of George III, in violation of the Royal Marriages Act. Dunmore was dismissed in July 1796, and with Lady Dunmore retired to Ramsgate, Kent, where he died on 25 February 1809, aged seventy-eight. He and Lady Dunmore, who died in 1818, are buried on the Isle of Thanet, Kent.   JOHN E. SELBY

Sources DNB · J. E. Selby, *Dunmore* (1977) · P. B. Catey, 'Dunmore: colonial governor of New York and Virginia, 1770–1782', diss., University of Pittsburgh, 1939 · J. L. Wright, 'Lord Dunmore's loyalist asylum in the Floridas', *Florida Historical Quarterly*, 49 (1970–71), 370–79 · B. Quarkes, 'Lord Dunmore as liberator', *William and Mary Quarterly*, 15 (1958), 494–507 · GEC, *Peerage*
Archives College of William and Mary, Williamsburg, Virginia, corresp.
Likenesses J. Reynolds, oils, 1765, Scot. NPG [*see illus.*] · J. Scott, mezzotint (after J. Reynolds), NPG · portrait, NG Scot.

Murray, John (1737–1793). *See under* Murray family (*per.* 1768–1967).

Murray, Sir John, eighth baronet (1768?–1827), army officer, was the eldest son of Sir Robert Murray, sixth baronet (*d.* 1771), and his second wife, Susan, daughter of John Renton of Lamberton. He was half-brother of Sir James Murray-*Pulteney. Educated at Westminster, he was appointed ensign, 3rd foot guards (Scots guards) on 24 October 1788, and became lieutenant and captain in that regiment on 25 April 1793. He served in Flanders in 1793–4, as aide-de-camp first to the Hanoverian field marshal Freytag, and afterwards to the duke of York; and he was present at St Amand, Famars, the sieges of Valenciennes and Dunkirk, at Tournai, and in the winter retreat through Holland to Bremen.

On 15 November 1794 Murray was appointed lieutenant-colonel, 2nd battalion, 84th foot. He commanded the 84th

at the capture of the Cape of Good Hope in 1796, and took it on to India. In 1798 he was sent into the Red Sea with a small force, which, at the urgent request of the Ottoman government to the sultan of San'a', then sovereign of Aden, was allowed to remain there for a time. In 1799 Murray was appointed British commissioner in the Red Sea, and was sent with 300 men to occupy Perim in the straits of Bab al-Mandab, the aim being to intercept communication with India through the Red Sea. The troops landed on 3 May 1799, and remained until 1 September. Finding that the island yielded no fresh water, and that the shore batteries could not command the straits, Murray withdrew his detachment to Aden, where they were hospitably entertained, and remained until March 1800. Early in the following year Murray was appointed quartermaster-general of the Indian army proceeding to Egypt under Major-General David Baird; after many delays in the Red Sea this force arrived at Quseir in June 1801, crossed the desert to Cairo, and descended the Nile.

Murray returned to India with Baird's troops, and commanded the Bombay division, which joined the force of Major-General Arthur Wellesley (later Viscount Wellington) at Poona in May 1803; he also commanded in Gujarat during the subsequent operations against the Marathas, who were led by their chieftain, Jeswant Rao Holkar. From Gujarat he moved into Malwa, and on 24 August 1804 occupied Holkar's capital. Murray lacked self-confidence and was inefficient and unenterprising. Wellesley disapproved of many of his proceedings, and in September 1804 recommended he be relieved of his command in Malwa. In January 1805 Murray advanced to Kota, endangering his line of communications and placing his force in a vulnerable position. On notification of his promotion to major-general from 1 January 1805 he returned home. He commanded a brigade in the eastern counties in 1806–7, and the troops of the King's German Legion with Sir John Moore in the expedition to Sweden in 1808, and afterwards in Portugal. He joined Sir Arthur Wellesley's army in Portugal in 1809, and acted ineffectively, failing to seize his opportunity at the passage of the Douro in May 1809. When Beresford was made a local lieutenant-general, Murray, who was his senior, was unwilling to serve under him, and returned home aggrieved.

Murray had little time for a parliamentary career but, by paying the local electoral manipulator, John Kibblewhite, was MP for the scot and lot borough of Wootton Bassett, Wiltshire, from 1807 to 1811. In April 1811 Murray succeeded his elder half-brother, Sir James Murray Pulteney (*d.* 26 April 1811), in the baronetcy, receiving a fortune of over £500,000; he succeeded him also as MP for the freeholder boroughs of Weymouth and Melcombe Regis, Dorset, and thereafter generally supported the government. In 1812 he had to pay £7000 to avert a poll. Following his political intrigues and conflict with the electorally influential Johnstone trustees, he was defeated in the general election of June 1818. Murray appears to have applied for employment in the Peninsular army. But in a letter in February 1811 Wellington recommended that his application be rejected: 'He is a very able officer, but when he was here before he was disposed not to avoid questions of precedence, but to bring them unnecessarily to discussion and decision' (*Dispatches*, 4.588). Murray became lieutenant-general on 1 January 1812, and later was appointed to the army in Sicily under the command of Lord William Bentinck.

On 26 February 1813 Murray arrived at Alicante, and took command of a motley force of British, Sicilians and others there, of whom Major-General John Mackenzie had been in command since the retirement of General Frederick Maitland during the previous November. Wellington suggested the recapture of Tarragona, 'which with the means at your command should not be a difficult operation' (ibid., 6.389, letter dated 29 March 1813). Murray delayed indecisively. The French under Louis Suchet attacked Murray in the strong position to which he had advanced, at Castalla, and were defeated by his force on 13 April 1813: Murray failed to take advantage of the victory. On 31 May 1813 Murray sailed north from Alicante on the east coast of Spain, and on 3 June he disembarked before reaching Tarragona. At his disposal, including Spaniards, was a force of 12,000 men, of whom only 4500 were British and Germans. On the approach of Suchet to raise the siege, Murray, whose movements had been marked by nervous indecision, hastily re-embarked his troops on 12 June, leaving some guns and stores behind. Instead of obeying his instructions to proceed to Valencia to support the Spaniards there in case of withdrawal from Tarragona, Murray landed some of his troops at the Col de Balaguer, where Lord William Bentinck arrived and assumed command four days later.

Wellington condemned Murray's disregard of his instructions and his ready sacrifice of his guns and stores, which Murray defended on principle as having been resorted to successfully by French strategists. 'I have a very high opinion of ... talents', Wellington wrote in a passage which, though anonymous in his published dispatches, apparently applies to Murray, 'but he always appeared to me to want what is better than abilities, viz. sound sense' (ibid., 6.665–7).

Admiral Benjamin Hallowell, who commanded the naval force at Tarragona, complained of Murray's conduct, and Wellington recommended he be court martialled; there was public indignation, and the government ordered a court martial. After a long delay Murray was arraigned at Winchester on 16 January 1815, before a general court martial, of which Sir Alured Clarke was president, and General George Harris, Sir Samuel Auchmuty, Sir George Beckwith, Sir Edward Paget, and other distinguished officers were members. The three charges were very verbose: the first alleged unmilitary conduct; the second neglect of duty and disobedience to Wellington's written instructions; and the third, neglect of proper preparations and arrangements for re-embarking his troops, 'to the prejudice of the service and the detriment of the British military character'. The prosecution was unskilled and used almost no Spanish evidence and, according to Sir John Fortescue, Murray 'displayed an audacity of falsehood which appears to have paralysed his accusers' (Fortescue, *Brit. army*, 9.71). He lied and unjustly blamed General Copons, the Spanish commander he had deserted. After sitting for fifteen days the court acquitted Murray on all charges except so much of the first part of the third charge (abandoning the guns and stores) as amounted to an error in judgement, for which they sentenced him to be admonished. The prince regent dispensed with the admonition and in 1816 awarded Murray a GCH. Possibly, as Fortescue suggested, 'Murray had from the beginning been under the protection of the Court' (Fortescue, *Brit. army*, 9.72). He demanded a medal for Castalla, and a red riband 'to cancel former injuries' (ibid.). In 1818 he was transferred from the colonelcy of the 3rd West India regiment to that of 56th foot. He became a full general in 1825. He had the orders of the Red Eagle of Prussia, and St Januarius of Naples. Murray married, on 25 August 1807, Anne Elizabeth Cholmondeley Phipps, only daughter and heir of Constantine John *Phipps, second Baron Mulgrave. She died on 10 April 1848; they had no children.

Murray was a liberal patron of art, and collected some good pictures. His portrait appears in the first of a set of four pictures of patrons and lovers of art, commissioned by him about 1826, painted by Pieter Christoph Wonder and now in the National Portrait Gallery. He died at Frankfurt am Main, Germany, on 15 October 1827.

Historians have confirmed the verdict of contemporary critics of Murray. Sir John Fortescue wrote, 'He must be pilloried by history without mercy as a cowardly and dishonourable man, unworthy to hold his Sovereign's commission, or to wear the red coat of a British soldier' (Fortescue, 9.73).   H. M. CHICHESTER, rev. ROGER T. STEARN

Sources J. Philippart, ed., *The royal military calendar*, 3rd edn, 2 (1820) · G. P. Badger, letter, *The Times* (31 May 1858) · J. Mill, *History of India*, 6 (1818) · W. F. P. Napier, *History of the war in the Peninsula and in the south of France*, new edn, 6 vols. (1886) · *The dispatches of ... the duke of Wellington ... from 1799 to 1818*, ed. J. Gurwood, new edn, 1–4 (1837) · *GM*, 1st ser., 97/2 (1827) · shorthand notes on trial of Sir John Murray, 1815 · Burke, *Peerage* (1959) · R. G. Thorne, 'Murray, John', HoP, *Commons* · Fortescue, *Brit. army*, vols. 5, 7, 9 · P. Moon, *The British conquest and dominion of India* (1989)
Archives BL, corresp. and papers, Add. MSS 12267, 19502–19505 · NL Scot., corresp. and papers | BL, letters to Sir Joseph Banks, Add. MSS 33978–33980 · BL, corresp. with Major Shawe, Add. MS 13782 · BL OIOC, corresp. with Sir Richard Jones, MS Eur. C 234 · NA Scot., corresp. with Henry Dundas · U. Nott. L., corresp. with Lord William Bentinck
Likenesses P. C. Wonder, oils, 1826, NPG

Murray, John (1778–1820), chemist and public lecturer, was educated in Edinburgh, where he rose rapidly to eminence as a popular freelance lecturer on chemistry, materia medica, mineralogy, and geology, and as the prolific author of celebrated textbooks on chemistry and materia medica, most of which went through several editions in Britain and the USA. The best-known were *Elements of Chemistry* (1801; 6th edn, 1828), *Elements of Materia medica and Pharmacy* (1804), *A System of Chemistry*, (1806–7; 4th edn, 1819) and *A System of Materia medica and Pharmacy* (1810; 6th edn, 1832).

Murray was often cautious in his chemical views but

took a wide view of chemistry and coined a few new terms. Highly regarded as an ingenious chemist by Humphry Davy, he did not seek to discredit French chemistry during the Napoleonic wars. As a follower of Berthollet he offered the most sustained challenge to Davy's view that chlorine was an element, suspected Proust's claim about the constant composition of chemical compounds, and denied Dalton's theory of mixed gases. As a philosophical chemist he published anonymously in 1802 a comprehensive and judicious *Comparative view of the Huttonian and Neptunian systems of geology in answer to the illustrations of the Huttonian theory of the earth by Professor Playfair.*

As a practical chemist Murray devised stoves for Edinburgh churches and by 1815 had used his knowledge of the relative densities of the dreaded firedamp and air to invent a safety lamp, but this did not attain the popularity of the devices of Davy and George Stephenson. He should not be confused with John Murray (1786–1851), who was also a scientific lecturer. He was elected an honorary fellow of the Geological Society of London in 1807, and a fellow of the Royal Society of Edinburgh in 1812 and of the Royal College of Physicians of Edinburgh in 1815. He became MD gratis of St Andrews in 1814. He died suddenly on 22 June 1820 at home in Nicholson Street, Edinburgh, and he was buried at Edinburgh on 29 June.

His son **John Murray** (1798–1873), surgeon, was born on 19 April 1798. He edited the later editions of his father's works, and followed him as an extramural lecturer on chemistry in Edinburgh. He became a fellow of the Royal College of Surgeons, Edinburgh, in November 1826, having previously been apprenticed to John Aitkin, a surgeon in Edinburgh. He afterwards emigrated to Melbourne, where he died on 4 June 1873.   JACK MORRELL

Sources *Edinburgh Evening Courant* (29 June 1820); repr. in *The Scotsman* (1 July 1820) • N. Campbell and R. M. S. Smellie, *The Royal Society of Edinburgh, 1783–1983* (1983) • J. Golinski, *Science as public culture: chemistry and enlightenment in Britain, 1760–1820* (1992) • T. Thomson, *The history of chemistry*, 2 vols. (1830–31) • J. R. Partington, *A history of chemistry*, 3–4 (1962–4) • D. R. Dean, *James Hutton and the history of geology* (1992) • *Edinburgh Evening Courant* (1798–1820) • private information (1995) • *Encyclopaedia Britannica*, 9th edn (1875–89), vol. 17, pp. 62–3

Murray, John (1785/6–1851), writer on science and public lecturer, was born in Stranraer, Scotland, the son of James Murray (1748/9–1788), sea captain, and his wife, Grace (1749/50–1827). Early in his life he seems to have developed scientific interests and in 1815 he published *Elements of Chemical Science as Applied to Arts and Manufactures*, describing himself as a lecturer on the philosophy of physics and of chemistry. In 1816 he published a volume entitled *Minor Poems* which was dedicated to Capell Lofft (1751–1824). In the same year he lectured at the Surrey Institution, established in the early part of the nineteenth century in Blackfriars Road, London, on the model of the Royal Institution. He gave an annual course there for many years, and became well known as a lecturer at mechanics' institutes in various parts of the country. He was involved with the Society for the Diffusion of Useful Knowledge, and its

founder, Lord Brougham, in an address to the Leeds Philosophical Society, described him as one of the best lecturers in the world. He was industrious and wrote with facility and clearness, but the wide range of subjects to which he gave attention prevented him from attaining eminence in any.

Murray was much interested in the miners' safety lamp, and took part in the discussion which arose about 1816 after the publication of Sir Humphry Davy's papers in the *Philosophical Transactions*. In that year Murray published papers in the *Philosophical Magazine* in which he showed that a sieve of hair or whalebone, or a sheet of perforated cardboard, formed an effectual barrier to the passage of flame. He also exhibited at his lectures an experimental safety lamp, the body of which consisted of muslin rendered incombustible by steeping it in a solution of phosphate of ammonia, and which was quite effective. From these experiments Murray derived a theory of the efficiency of the safety lamp which was opposed to that propounded by Davy. A summary of his researches on this subject is given in his *Observations on Flame and Safety Lamps* (1833). In 1835 he gave evidence on the safety lamp and ventilation before the select committee of the House of Commons on accidents in mines. Among his opponents was John Murray (1778–1820), with whom he has been frequently confused.

Murray was a fellow of the Society of Antiquaries (1822) and of the Geological (1823), Linnean (1819), and Horticultural (1824) societies, and he is also described on his tombstone as 'PhD' and 'MA'. He is sometimes referred to by contemporary writers as Dr Murray, or Professor Murray. In a letter in the *Mining Journal* of 10 May 1851 he claimed to have written twenty-eight separate works; upwards of twenty are mentioned in the British Library catalogue. They cover a great variety of topics. His contributions to scientific journals relate to chemistry, physics, medicine, geology, natural history, and manufactures. The *Royal Society's Catalogue of Scientific Papers* lists about sixty, but there is confusion arising from there being more than one John Murray. Murray wrote much in the *Mechanics' Magazine* from 1831 to 1844, and also in the *Mining Journal*, of which he was a steady correspondent for about the last ten years of his life. In the 1830s he was prominent in the scriptural geology debate, and two of his books, *The Truth of Revelation* (1831, 1840) and *A Portrait of Geology* (1838), were devoted to reconciling the geological record and the account of creation in Genesis, and to related matters.

Murray lived in Hull for many years, certainly in the 1840s but possibly from as early as 1824; at the end of 1850 he moved to Broadstone House, near Stranraer, where he died on 28 June 1851, aged sixty-five, his death having been accelerated by financial worries. He was buried in the old Inch churchyard, where there is a tombstone commemorating several members of his family.

R. B. PROSSER, *rev.* JOHN SHORTER

Sources *Galloway Advertiser and Wigtownshire Free Press* (3 July 1851) • private information (1894) • private information (2004) • T. J. Mortenson, 'British scriptural geologists in the first half of the nineteenth century', PhD diss., Coventry University, 1996, 275–

314 • W. Leng, 'J. Murray's apparatus for saving life at sea', *Annual Report of the Whitby Literary and Philosophical Society* (1999), 23–6 **Archives** U. Edin. L., corresp. | U. Edin., New Coll. L., letters to Thomas Chalmers • UCL, letters to Society for the Diffusion of Useful Knowledge

Murray, John (1798–1873). *See under* Murray, John (1778–1820).

Murray, John (1808–1892). *See under* Murray family (*per.* 1768–1967).

Murray, Sir John (1841–1914), marine scientist and oceanographer, was born at Cobourg, Ontario on 3 March 1841, the second son of Robert Murray, an accountant from Scotland who had settled in Upper Canada about 1834, and his wife, Elizabeth Macfarlane. He attended public school in London, Ontario, and later studied at Victoria College, Cobourg. At the age of seventeen he went to Scotland to complete his education under the care of his maternal grandfather, John Macfarlane, of Coney Hill, Stirlingshire. Murray attended the high school at Stirling and afterwards studied at the University of Edinburgh. His name appears on the university rolls for two periods, 1864–5 and 1868–72. He began his studies as a medical student but attended classes in the subjects which appealed to him; he never took examinations and did not graduate. In 1868, Murray shipped as surgeon on the whaler *Jan Mayen*. During seven months' voyage in northern seas he reached a latitude of 81° N, explored part of Spitsbergen, and landed on Jan Mayen Island. He returned with a collection of marine organisms and also records of observations on currents, on the temperature of the air and of the sea, and on the distribution of sea ice.

On his return to Edinburgh Murray found congenial conditions in the physics laboratory and studied there until 1872, under Peter Guthrie Tait, doing experimental work on thermal conductivity and on the construction of an electrical deep-sea thermometer. In 1872 he took a considerable share in the preparation of the scientific apparatus for the *Challenger* expedition, intended scientifically to explore the world oceans under the direction of Charles Wyville Thomson (1830–1882), professor of natural history in the University of Edinburgh. When a vacancy on the expedition's staff unexpectedly arose he was appointed, almost at the last moment, one of the naturalists, and this led to the great work of his life.

During the *Challenger's* voyage—which lasted nearly three and a half years—the physics, chemistry, geology and biology of the great ocean basins were investigated, especially those of the deep sea, about which little was known. Murray devoted himself particularly to near-surface plankton organisms, especially the foraminifera and radiolaria, and to the study of ocean floor sediments. He demonstrated the part played by near-surface foraminifera in forming deep-sea globigerina ooze. He also worked on improvements in sediment samplers, the sounding apparatus, and deep-sea thermometers. Thomson put Murray in charge of the collections—unrivalled in range and importance—made during the expedition. Shortly after their return, the 'Challenger' office' was

Sir John Murray (1841–1914), by unknown photographer

opened at 32 Queen Street, Edinburgh, to deal with the collections, and for nearly twenty years this was the place to which marine scientists from all over the world went to work and to discuss the results of the expedition. Murray was appointed chief assistant in the office and, owing to Thomson's failing health, became responsible for organizing the study of the collections.

In 1882, after Thomson's death, Murray became director of the office and editor of the *Report on the Scientific Results of the Voyage of HMS Challenger* (1880–95). In fifty volumes, this was the work of experts from many countries, their labours co-ordinated and encouraged by Murray. During the later years of this period Murray's task was made difficult by an unsympathetic Treasury, particularly when the completion of the report was long overdue, and he spent a large amount of his own money in completing the publication.

During much of this time Murray and his friend Professor A. F. Renard, of Ghent, studied the marine sediments. In 1891 their report, *Deep Sea Deposits*, was published, establishing the general classification of deep-sea sediments that was still being used, over one hundred years later. As a result of this work, samples of sediments obtained by surveying ships and by various expeditions after *Challenger* were sent to Murray, creating a unique collection. Another result of Murray's observations during the expedition was his well-known paper 'The structure and origin of coral reefs and islands' (*Proceedings of the Royal Society of Edinburgh*, 10, 1880), in which he disagreed with Darwin's view that the form of atolls was due to subsidence of the land forming the foundation of the reef. Murray put forward the view that coral reefs formed where sediments accumulated on banks and submarine peaks. He held that as coral colonies approached the surface of the sea they assumed the atoll form owing to the more abundant supply of food and more vigorous growth on the outer margin, and to the removal of dead coral from the interior by currents and by dissolution of calcium carbonate. Murray's work stimulated several decades of research on coral reefs and the formation of atoll lagoons, but had to give ground to Charles Darwin's explanation that reefs formed on subsiding pedestals. Murray was joint author of the *Narrative of the Cruise of HMS Challenger* (1885), and he drew up the last two volumes of the *Report* (1895), which form an impressive summary of the results of the expedition, and in which he reviewed comprehensively the history of oceanography.

In 1880 and 1882 Murray and Captain T. H. Tizard explored the Faeroe Channel in the government surveying ships *Knight Errant* and *Triton*. They demonstrated the existence of the Wyville Thomson Ridge, between Scotland and the Faeroe Islands, which accounted for differences in bottom temperatures and faunas first noted in 1868 by Wyville Thomson and W. B. Carpenter. He established small marine laboratories at Granton and at Millport (1885); the latter developed into the laboratory of the Scottish Marine Biological Association. Murray's steam yacht, *Medusa*, built and equipped for marine biological work, enabled him with the help of several younger colleagues to carry out marine research along the west coast of Scotland between 1883 and 1894. The results were published in 1918 by his former secretary, James Chumley, with the title *The Fauna of the Clyde Sea Area*.

Two years after the *Challenger* reports were finished Murray undertook a bathymetrical survey of the freshwater lochs of Scotland with a capable young collaborator, Frederick Pullar. Several important papers on the results had appeared when in 1901 Pullar was drowned while attempting to save the lives of others. His father—Laurence Pullar, Murray's oldest friend—was determined that the survey should be continued, and provided funds for a staff of assistants; they began work in 1902 and carried on the investigations until 1909. Some 60,000 soundings were made in 562 lochs, and the records of these and of other scientific results, forming the most extensive limnological survey anywhere to that date, were published in six volumes by Murray and Pullar in 1910.

When the *Challenger* office was closed (in 1895) Murray bought a house, Villa Medusa, near his residence Challenger Lodge, in Wardie, near Granton, to serve as a library and laboratory. This housed Murray's samples of oceanic sediments, *Challenger* samples and records until 1921, when the collections and the greater part of his library were moved to the British Museum (Natural History); it was also the headquarters of the lochs survey. Like the

Challenger office previously, Murray's home and laboratory attracted a stream of scientific visitors and collaborators.

As the result of his detection of calcium phosphate in rock specimens brought in 1887 from Christmas Island in the Indian Ocean, Murray urged the annexation of the island, which took place the next year. In 1891 Murray and G. Clunies Ross, of the Cocos Islands, obtained a lease of Christmas Island, and in 1897 they formed a company to develop its mineral resources. Murray also paid the expenses of two scientific expeditions to the island in 1897–8 and 1908. Following the first expedition, Murray married, in 1889, Isabel, only daughter of Thomas Henderson, shipowner, of Glasgow; they had two sons and three daughters.

As a result of the first expedition Dr C. W. Andrews of the British Museum (Natural History), brought home extensive collections. *A Monograph of Christmas Island* (1900), which gives the results of the first expedition, is important as a record of the indigenous fauna and flora of an isolated tropical island before human contact. Murray himself made two exploring visits (1900, 1908) to the island. He claimed that the Treasury had received from the island in the form of rents, royalties, and taxes a sum exceeding the cost of the *Challenger* expedition and the publication of its results. This was an exaggeration in his time, but true by the 1920s.

In 1909 Murray visited Copenhagen and urged upon the International Council for the Exploration of the Sea the need for an oceanographic expedition to the north Atlantic. Shortly thereafter, he offered to pay the operating expenses of a four-month expedition on condition that the Norwegian government lent the research vessel *Michael Sars* and her scientific staff for the purpose. The offer was accepted, and in April 1910 the vessel left Plymouth with Murray on board and with the Norwegian marine biologist Dr Johan Hjort as leader of the scientific staff. The immediate results of this expedition—including important physical and biological observations at all depths between Europe and North America—were published in *The Depths of the Ocean* by Murray and Hjort in 1912; this volume summarized the oceanography of its era and served as a text for many years.

A description of 1426 samples of deposits from the floor of the Atlantic Ocean, gathered during thirty-five cruising expeditions between 1857 and 1911, was being prepared under Murray's supervision at the time of his death. The work was completed by James Chumley, who added a discussion of the results, and the monograph was published (1924) in the *Transactions of the Royal Society of Edinburgh*.

Murray received honorary degrees from several universities, was elected FRS in 1896, and created KCB in 1898. From 1896 to 1898 he was scientific member of the fishery board for Scotland, and he filled various offices in the scientific societies of Edinburgh. His recreations were yachting—during which he carried on soundings, dredging, and other observations—golf, and motoring. He was killed in a motor accident at Kirkliston, near Edinburgh, on 16 March 1914.

The exploration of the deep sea during the late nineteenth century is due largely to Wyville Thomson and John Murray. Murray left an enduring mark on the science of oceanography through his research, his influence on others, and through his estate, which funded the John Murray expedition to the Indian Ocean in 1933 and the John Murray travelling studentships which began in 1948. He was an original, suggestive, broad-minded thinker and did not hesitate to attack established views if they did not coincide with his conclusions. A strong and forceful personality, he was confident of his own opinion and somewhat brusque, occasionally domineering, in manner, but full of good humour, and most helpful and friendly to his assistants and to other investigators who sought his aid. To a large degree it was his influence that transformed oceanography from a patchwork of unrelated disciplines into a coherent science.

J. H. ASHWORTH, *rev.* ERIC L. MILLS

Sources A. E. S. [A. E. Shipley], *PRS*, 89B (1915–17), vi–xv • J. G. Kerr, *Proceedings of the Royal Society of Edinburgh*, 35 (1914–15), 305–17 • W. A. Herdman, 'An address upon Sir John Murray, KCB, FRS, the pioneer of modern oceanography', *Proceedings and Transactions of the Liverpool Biological Society*, 32 (1918), 30–60 • M. Deacon, *Scientists and the sea: a study of marine science* (1971) • H. L. Burstyn, 'Science pays off: Sir John Murray and the Christmas Island phosphate industry, 1886–1914', *Social Studies of Science*, 5 (1975), 5–34 • W. N. Boog Watson, 'Sir John Murray—a chronic student', *University of Edinburgh Journal*, 23 (1967–8), 123–38 • W. S. Bruce, 'Sir John Murray, KCB, FRS, "Pour le Mérite": an appreciation', *Internationale Revue der Gesamten Hydrobiologie*, 7 (1914), 84–101 • *CCI* (1914)
Archives NHM, diary of HMS *Challenger*; notebook of HMS *Challenger*; HMS *Challenger* records • RBG Kew, corresp. and papers relating to HMS *Challenger* • Royal Museum, Edinburgh | Elgin Museum, letters to George Gordon • Harvard U., Museum of Comparative Zoology, Alexander Agassiz letters • NHM, letters to Albert Gunther and R. W. T. Gunther • Oxf. U. Mus. NH, letters to Sir E. B. Poulton • Scott Polar RI, letters to Hugh Mill • U. Edin. L., Alexander Agassiz letters
Likenesses D. Macnee, portrait, 1876 • G. Reid, oils, 1913, Scot. NPG • Spy [L. Ward], watercolour, NPG • photograph, repro. in W. A. Herdman, *Founders of oceanography* (1923), facing p. 94 • photograph, NPG [*see illus.*] • photographs, U. Oxf., department of zoology, H. N. Moseley albums
Wealth at death £67,519 13*s.* 4*d.*: confirmation, 25 March 1914, *CCI* • £30,491 12*s.* 2*d.*: eik additional estate, 9 June 1914, *CCI*

Murray, Sir John (1851–1928). *See under* Murray family (*per.* 1768–1967).

Murray, John (1879–1964), educationist and politician, was born on 28 February 1879 at Fraserburgh, Aberdeenshire, the eldest son of Francis Robert Murray, fish curer, and his wife, Isabella Watt. He was educated at Robert Gordon's College, Aberdeen. In 1896 he entered the University of Aberdeen as first bursar, graduating in 1900 with honours in Greek and Latin, having won the Simpson Greek prize and the Seafield Latin medal. In 1901 he went up as an exhibitioner to Christ Church, Oxford, on a Fullerton scholarship. He took first-class honours in classical moderations in 1903 and in *literae humaniores* in 1905. In the same year he was elected prize fellow of Merton College, and in 1908 student and tutor of his old college, Christ Church, where in 1910 he became censor. Murray published nothing except the occasional political piece in the

John Murray (1879–1964), by Reginald Grenville Eves, 1939

Oxford Magazine (which he edited from 1911 to 1914) during his years as a don, but the Oxford system of education had made a lasting impression.

In 1915 Murray left Oxford to join the labour department of the newly created Ministry of Munitions. By the end of the war he had reached the fairly senior rank of assistant commissioner in the labour adviser's department. In the general election of December 1918 he stood as a Coalition Liberal in Leeds West, and was elected with a large majority. He was soon given minor administrative work to do as officer in charge of a section of the Board of Education concerned with university awards to former servicemen. In 1920–21 he was chairman of the central committee on trusts, a body set up under the Profiteering Acts, 1919–20. The committee had powers to investigate and report on price increases, and during Murray's chairmanship published a large number of brief reports, on which little or no action was taken.

In 1921 Murray married Ellen, widow of George Harwood (1845–1912), Liberal MP for Bolton, and daughter of Sir Alfred *Hopkinson (1851–1939). In 1922 he stood as a national (Lloyd George) Liberal in Leeds West and retained his seat by a narrow majority in a straight fight against Labour, but in 1923, when the Conservatives fielded a candidate, Murray came third, at the bottom of the poll. In 1924 he retreated to Kirkcaldy, but succeeded only in reducing the Labour majority. He fought a by-election in the safe Conservative seat of Ripon in 1925, his last attempt to re-enter parliament. Murray was never a leading member of the Liberal Party, but during his brief parliamentary career he spoke lucidly and with originality; in happier days for Liberals he would undoubtedly have achieved office. His speeches in the house showed a certain radicalism: he favoured sympathetic treatment of the unemployed and was an early (and lifelong) advocate of family allowances. In later years he described himself as an individualist and associated with Sir Ernest Benn in the Society of Individualists. Already in the by-election at Ripon in 1925 he had openly disagreed with Lloyd George's plans for nationalization of land and the coal industry, and privately expressed his dislike of what he called 'promise-politics'.

In 1926, after nearly three years in the political wilderness, Murray was appointed principal of the University College of the South West, Exeter, in succession to W. H. Moberly. Although Murray at first hoped to return to politics one day, he was to spend the rest of his working life in the service of the University College, declining in 1929 the vice-chancellorship of the University of Sheffield. He inherited a college with cramped buildings and few endowments, partly engaged in training teachers for elementary schools, but mostly preparing students for external degrees of the University of London. The college had two assets: recognition by the University Grants Committee as a grant-receiving institution; and a magnificent and almost empty site of 150 acres on the north-western outskirts of Exeter. It was Murray's object to develop these assets until the college became a full university. The first need was money. Murray plunged happily into the business of fund-raising, which he likened to 'a perpetual by-election'. While he was principal the substantial sum of £250,000 was raised for buildings, scholarships, and chairs. He was not the man to suffer a fool gladly—unless a prospective benefactor: the largest benefaction ever received by the college was owing to Murray's tact, firmness, and inexhaustible patience exercised over a period of fourteen years in the face of considerable provocation. Murray sought to combine in Exeter the merits of Oxford and Aberdeen: he promoted the Oxford system of residence and of tutorial teaching and he envisaged Exeter as providing for poor English boys and girls the educational ladder that Aberdeen offered to aspiring Scotsmen like himself. In addition he strove to provide an international dimension to the college by attracting students from Europe, the United States, Africa, and the Middle East. In all this he had considerable success, but the final prize—a university charter—eluded him. He retired, unwillingly, in 1951. Murray received three honorary doctorates: LLD from Aberdeen (1930), LittD from Columbia, New York (1939), and, fittingly, DLitt from Exeter (1956), conferred at the first degree congregation held by the new university that he had done much to foster. In 1963 the University of Exeter named a new hall of residence Murray House in his honour, though with accommodation for 150 students it was built on a larger scale than he would have thought desirable.

Murray was eloquent, formidable, autocratic, and in his later years careless of administrative forms. He gave time and money generously to help students and staff. He wrote occasionally for the *Hibbert Journal* and the *Contemporary Review* and circulated privately a humorous fantasy *Shinid* (1938) in celebration of English hospitality in an Irish setting. He was a staunch Christian and as a member of the De La Warr committee on higher education in east Africa in 1936–7 wrote a minority report opposing secular education there; in his view the mission schools should have continued to monopolize popular education even in territories three-quarters non-Christian—'an educated pagan is a pagan still'. Murray died in London on 28 December 1964. B. W. CLAPP

Sources MSS, University of Exeter · *The Times* (30 Dec 1964) · *The Times* (2 Jan 1965) · B. W. Clapp, *The University of Exeter: a history* (1982) · private information (1981) · *CGPLA Eng. & Wales* (1965) · b. cert.

Archives BL, letters to Albert Mansbridge · University of Exeter, Northcote House, University of Exeter MSS

Likenesses R. G. Eves, oils, 1939, University of Exeter, Murray House [*see illus.*] · photographs, University of Exeter

Wealth at death £26,208: probate, 16 Feb 1965, *CGPLA Eng. & Wales*

Murray, Sir John (1884–1967). *See under* Murray family (*per.* 1768–1967).

Murray, Sir John Archibald, Lord Murray (1778?–1859), politician and judge, was born in Edinburghshire, the second son of Alexander *Murray, Lord Henderland (1736–1795), lord of session, and Katherine (1737–1828), daughter of Sir Alexander Lindsay, of Evelick, Perthshire, and a niece of the first Lord Mansfield. He was educated at Edinburgh high school, at Westminster School, and at the University of Edinburgh.

Murray was a member of a circle of young reforming whigs in early nineteenth-century Edinburgh, many of whom later came to national prominence. At university he was a member of the Juvenile Literary Society, of which Henry Brougham and Francis Horner were the leading spirits, and of the Speculative Society, of which he became president. His correspondence with Horner, until the latter's early death in 1817, forms part of the *Memoirs of Francis Horner* published in 1843. On the establishment of the *Edinburgh Review* in 1802, Sydney Smith, Francis Jeffrey, Horner, and Murray, among others, met for a time as joint editors in Jeffrey's house, and Murray was himself an occasional early contributor. The *Edinburgh Review* was then a focal point for the whigs' urging of reform as the best way to avoid the status quo collapsing into revolution in Britain, as had happened in France.

In 1800 Murray was called to the Scottish bar. His early career as an advocate was distinguished, but since he was wealthy he did not pursue his early efforts. In 1826 he married Mary (d. 1862), eldest daughter of William Rigby of Oldfield Hall, Cheshire. Their only child died young.

Together with Francis Jeffrey and Henry Cockburn, Murray was consulted in 1830 about how the Scottish positions should be filled in the incoming whig ministry. He took a prominent part in the agitation which led to the passing of the Scottish Reform Bill and was heavily involved in whig electioneering in Scotland for the 1832 election. In December of that year he was himself

Sir John Archibald Murray, Lord Murray (1778?–1859), by Sir John Watson-Gordon, 1856

returned unopposed for the newly created Leith burghs constituency. His position as clerk of the pipe, a sinecure, left him open to attacks during this election as a whig place-hunter. Caricatured as 'The Piper', he gave up the office soon after. On the elevation of Jeffrey to the bench in 1834, Murray succeeded him as lord advocate. Apart from the short interruption of Peel's first ministry (from December 1834 to April 1835), he held this office until April 1839. He introduced a large number of bills into the House of Commons, including measures for university reform and for giving elected officials to small towns. However, Murray's failure to concentrate his efforts—in a parliamentary situation in which Scottish business was anyway marginalized—meant that he succeeded in carrying only a few minor reforms.

A high point in Murray's parliamentary career came in 1839 when he and the other Scottish law officers were attacked by the friend of his youth, Lord Brougham, for their conduct in the case of five Glasgow cotton-spinners, who formed the executive of the cotton-spinners' association and who were tried on charges including murder and conspiracy which arose from a wage dispute. Brougham, presenting petitions against the sentence of transportation for the few lesser charges against the accused, held Murray, who was responsible as lord advocate, to have bungled the management of the prosecution. Murray answered the accusation by portraying the judgment as one in the interests of working people's freedom in the face of trade combination pressure. He successfully defended the Scottish legal system as fair to the interests of the accused in such a way as to win strong Commons'

backing for his position and to bring Brougham explicitly to exempt Murray from accusations of incompetence in later attempts at petitioning in the matter.

In 1839 Murray left parliament for the court of session. He was knighted and took his seat on the bench as Lord Murray. The position he had won among the whigs in his youth, his contribution to the *Edinburgh Review*, his part in the movement in 1830–32 to get the Scottish Reform Bill passed, and his campaigning efforts in the subsequent 1832 election, all mark a career which was successful until that time. Thereafter, however, his record as lord advocate, in part because of an absence of single-mindedness, lacked substantial achievement, a failure which was critical at a time of growing radical political and ecclesiastical pressure on the Scottish whigs. It was compensated for in the eyes of some of his contemporaries by a generous patronage of the arts and various charities and by his famously profuse hospitality. As a result he enjoyed a special position in Edinburgh and London society. Sir Walter Scott in his *Journal* records enjoyable evenings spent in the company of political opponents at Murray's house in Edinburgh, and Harriet Martineau celebrates his and Lady Murray's tea parties at Westminster when he was lord advocate.

Murray died at Great Stuart Street, Edinburgh, on 7 March 1859, still in office as a judge; he was buried on 11 March at the West Church burial-ground, Edinburgh. His wife died in 1862.   GORDON F. MILLAR

Sources *The Scotsman* (8 March 1859) [death notice] · *The Scotsman* (12 March 1859) [funeral report] · *The Scotsman* (14 March 1859) · G. W. T. Omond, *The lord advocates of Scotland, second series, 1834–1880* (1914), 1–46 · H. Martineau, *Biographical sketches, 1852–1868*, 2nd edn (1869), 71–7 · *Journal of Henry Cockburn: being a continuation of the 'Memorials of his time', 1831–1854*, 2 vols. (1874) · *The journal of Sir Walter Scott*, 2 vols. (1890–91) · *Memoirs and correspondence of Francis Horner, MP*, ed. L. Horner, 2 vols. (1843) · H. Cockburn, *Circuit journeys*, 2nd edn (1889) · Irving, *Scots.*, 376 · F. J. Grant, ed., *The Faculty of Advocates in Scotland, 1532–1943*, Scottish RS, 145 (1944) · *Hansard 3* (1838), 40.931–7, 1073–83, 1124–6; (1839), 46.791–2; (1839), 47.1028–9 · *DNB*

Archives NL Scot., corresp. and papers | BL, corresp. with first and second barons Brougham and Vaux, Add. MS 40687 · BL, corresp. with Lord Holland, Add. MS 51644 · Glos. RO, letters to Daniel Ellis · NA Scot., corresp. with Andrew Leith Hay · NL Scot., corresp. with John Burton, Amelia Campbell, and Henry Cockburn; corresp. with John Lee and Andrew Rutherford; letters to second earl of Minto · U. Edin. L., corresp. with David Laing · U. Edin., New Coll. L., letters to Thomas Chalmers · UCL, corresp. with James Brougham

Likenesses W. Walker, mezzotint, pubd 1835 (after H. Raeburn), BM · J. Watson-Gordon, oils, 1856, Scot. NPG [*see illus.*] · G. Hayter, group portrait, oils (*The House of Commons, 1833*), NPG · drawing, repro. in B. W. Crombie, *Modern Athenians: a series of original portraits of memorable citizens of Edinburgh, 1837–47* (1882)

Wealth at death £60,751 2s. 9d.: confirmation, 29 April 1859, NA Scot., SC 70/1/100/749–769

Murray, John Arnaud Robin Grey (1909–1993). *See under* Murray family (*per.* 1768–1967).

Murray, John Fisher [*pseud.* Maire] (1811–1865), poet and humorist, eldest son of Sir James *Murray (1788–1871), a doctor, and his wife, Mary Sharrock, was born in Belfast on

11 February 1811 and after a local education studied medicine at Trinity College, Dublin, where he graduated BA in 1830 and MA in 1832.

After graduation Murray began to contribute light sketches of London fashionable life to *Blackwood's Magazine*, and worked closely with William Maginn and Sir Samuel Ferguson. He became a Young Irelander, and in 1834 his *Repeal No Remedy, or, The Union in Ireland Completed* appeared in London, 'addressed at this crisis to every Englishman'. In 1838, *Father Tom and the Pope* was serialized in *Blackwood's Magazine*. It was a burlesque on Irish Catholicism, caricaturing a popular Irish contemporary preacher as a drinking crony of the pope, and for professional reasons it appeared anonymously. A year later *Father Tom* was published in book form and became a best-seller in England and America, a new edition appearing in New York as late as 1920. The book was attributed to Samuel Ferguson, but it is now understood to be a collaboration between Ferguson, Maginn, and Murray.

In 1839 Murray published *Lady Flora Hastings, or, The Court-Doctor Dissected*, a bitter attack on Dr James Clark, who had falsely accused Lady Flora Hastings of pregnancy resultant upon a secret marriage, when in fact she was severely ill. The pamphlet ran to four editions within a year. The following year a series of papers called *The Irish Oyster Eater* appeared in *Blackwood's Magazine*, later collected as a book, and later that year Murray published a pamphlet *The Chinese and the Ministry*. He started contributing to various Conservative, Unionist periodicals such as the *Belfast Vindicator* in the belief that 'if you make an impression on the North, then Ireland is free' (Duffy, 2.15). In 1841 his novel *The Viceroy* was serialized in *Blackwood's Magazine*. It was a satiric portrait of fashionable Dublin society which was later published in three volumes.

When *The Nation* was founded in 1842, Murray became a regular contributor, dividing his time between journalism and the production of several London guidebooks. *Environs of London: Western Division* (1842) was followed by the more successful *World of London*, published in 1843 and revised in 1845. *A Picturesque Tour of the Thames* appeared later that year to favourable reviews, and was reissued in 1849 and 1853. His work for *The Nation* was represented by an essay in *The Voice of the Nation*, a collection of articles from the paper published in 1844. Murray spent his later years in retirement, contributing poems to *The Nation* under the pseudonyms JFM or Maire. Some were reprinted in Edward Hayes's extremely popular anthology, *Ballads of Ireland*, published in 1855 with many subsequent editions.

Murray died at his home, 70 Capel Street, Dublin, on 20 October 1865, and was buried in Glasnevin cemetery. He was survived by his wife, Hannah.

KATHERINE MULLIN

Sources E. Hayes, *The ballads of Ireland*, 2 vols. (1855) · Boase, *Mod. Eng. biog.* · D. J. O'Donoghue, *The poets of Ireland: a biographical dictionary with bibliographical particulars*, 1 vol. in 3 pts (1892–3) · 'Ferguson, Sir Samuel', *DNB* · 'Murray, Sir James (1788–1871)', *DNB* · 'Hastings, Lady Flora Elizabeth', *DNB* · Allibone, *Dict.* · C. G. Duffy, *Four years of Irish history, 1845–1849: a sequel to 'Young Ireland'* (1883), 15 · *Northern Whig* (27 Oct 1875) · *CGPLA Ire.* (1865)

Archives BL, accounts with and letters to Richard Bentley, Add. MSS 46614, 46650–46651 · NL Scot., letters to Blackwoods
Wealth at death under £800: probate, 8 Nov 1865, *CGPLA Ire.*

Murray, John George Stewart-, eighth duke of Atholl (1871–1942), army officer and landowner, was born on 15 December 1871 at Blair Castle, Perthshire. He was the fifth child and eldest surviving son of John James Stewart-Murray, seventh duke of Atholl (1840–1917), and his wife, Louisa (1844–1902), eldest daughter of Sir Thomas Moncreiffe. Throughout his life he was known by family and friends as Bardie from his original courtesy title, marquess of Tullibardine. Bardie was brought up by Gaelic-speaking nurses at Blair Castle with his three older sisters and two younger brothers before being sent to Farnborough School in 1882. He then followed into his father's house, Mr Evans's, at Eton College, between 1885 and 1890. After travel abroad he sat army exams and entered the Royal Horse Guards in 1892. In 1898 he joined the Egyptian campaign as staff officer to Lieutenant-Colonel Broadwood, served to the end of the campaign, and was awarded the DSO.

Before leaving for Egypt, Lord Tullibardine had met Katharine Ramsay [see Murray, Katharine Marjory Stewart- (1874–1960)], daughter of Sir James Ramsay of Bamff, Alyth, and after his return they married on 20 July 1899. Shortly afterwards he left to serve in South Africa, seeing action in various battles before being the first regular soldier to enter Ladysmith. In 1900 he raised and commanded the Scottish Horse regiment first from colonials then, with the assistance of his father, from his fellow countrymen. At the conclusion of the war he was made MVO. He then settled back on the family estate before standing for parliament; having stood unsuccessfully for East Perthshire in 1906, he was elected as a Unionist for West Perthshire in 1910, taking a keen interest in land issues.

On the outbreak of war, Tullibardine mobilized with the Scottish Horse, and after training saw action at Gallipoli before the regiment was amalgamated with other units and he returned to Scotland. This proved fortuitous, as his father died in January 1917 and he was able to take up running the estate, turning the castle into a Red Cross hospital, assisted by the duchess. Once he was duke of Atholl public and business affairs grew to dominate the coming years; he was appointed lord high commissioner to the general assembly of the Church of Scotland in 1918, 1919, and 1920. He became a knight of the Thistle in 1918 and a privy councillor and lord chamberlain in 1921, being responsible for organizing Princess Mary's wedding. In 1921 he and the duchess entertained the crown prince of Japan at Blair. In 1919 he initiated the Scottish national war memorial in Edinburgh Castle and chaired the committee which saw the project to completion in 1927. Through his royal connections he collaborated with Queen Mary on the redecoration of Holyrood Palace from 1921 to 1929. Through the 1920s, in order to increase family income, he became director of the Jamaica Sugar Corporation, the Anglo-Argentine Tramway Company, Atholl Steel Houses, the London Clinic, and other companies.

However, most of these became loss-making ventures, adding to the problem of estate finances. With the loss of sporting rental after the Wall Street crash disaster seemed inevitable, but in 1932 the estate was formed into a company with a large injection of capital from Lady Cowdray, whose granddaughter, Angela Pearson, had married the heir to the dukedom, Antony Murray. Strict economies were initiated, including land sales throughout the 1930s, and in 1936 the duke and duchess were instrumental in opening Blair Castle to the public. Throughout these years the duke had been very supportive of his wife, who had been elected MP for Kinross and West Perthshire in 1923 and became minister of education. However, her warnings against the rise of fascism had put her at odds with her party, and in 1938 she resigned and fought a by-election which she narrowly lost.

The duke became involved in preparations for war but his increasing ill health in 1939–40 limited his activities, and it was the duchess and Tony Murray's wife, Angela, who oversaw the arrival of evacuees at the castle and lodges. After a further period of illness Atholl died at his home, Eastwood House, Dunkeld, on 15 March 1942 and was buried three days later in the private graveyard at Old Blair.

Although succeeded by his brother, Lord James, who died unmarried in 1957, Atholl's longer-term plans for the succession were disrupted when Antony Murray was killed in Italy in the last days of the war, leaving a widow and young son of thirteen. However, Angela Murray took on the running of the estate, turning it into a viable business, thus fulfilling the eighth duke's object of keeping the estate intact to face the future.   JANE ANDERSON

Sources J. J. H. H. Stewart-Murray, seventh duke of Atholl, *Chronicles of the Atholl and Tullibardine families*, 5 vols. (privately printed, Edinburgh, 1908) · letters, Blair Castle, Perthshire, archives · K. M. Stewart-Murray, duchess of Atholl, *Working partnership, being the lives of John George, eighth duke of Atholl, and of his wife Katharine Marjory Ramsay* (1958) · GEC, *Peerage*
Archives Blair Castle, Perthshire, letters and MSS · NL Scot., corresp. relating to Scottish War Memorial | NL Scot., corresp. with Lord Haldane
Likenesses J. Guthrie, oils, 1904, Blair Castle, Perthshire · F. Watt, portrait, 1921, Blair Castle, Perthshire · photographs, Blair Castle, Perthshire
Wealth at death £27,306 4s. 2d.: confirmation, 20 Jan 1943, CCI

Murray, John Samuel (1778–1843). *See under* Murray family (*per.* 1768–1967).

Murray, Katharine Marjory Stewart- [*née* Katharine Marjory Ramsay], **duchess of Atholl** (1874–1960), public servant and politician, was born in Edinburgh on 6 November 1874, the eldest of the five children of Sir James Henry *Ramsay, tenth baronet (1832–1925), of Bamff, east Perthshire, lawyer, landowner, and historian, and his second wife, Charlotte Fanning Stewart (*d.* 1904). Agnata Frances *Butler was her half-sister. Katharine was educated at Wimbledon high school and the Royal College of Music, where she studied composition under Sir Hubert Parry and relinquished the proceeds of a scholarship to her contemporary Samuel Coleridge-Taylor. Her mother, a singer,

was also musical, and Katharine hoped initially for a career as a pianist or composer, but terminated her studies before their completion and returned home. Music remained a hobby throughout her life, but after marrying John George Stewart-*Murray, marquess of Tullibardine (1871–1942), son of the seventh duke of Atholl, on 20 July 1899 she embarked on a life of public service. She became marchioness of Tullibardine on her marriage, and duchess of Atholl on her husband's succession to the title of the eighth duke of Atholl in January 1917.

Katharine Stewart-Murray's public work began with organizing district nursing associations in Perthshire from 1902 onwards. She shared her husband's interest in military matters (he served in the Nile expedition, the Second South African War, and the First World War), and she edited and contributed to a *Military History of Perthshire* (2 vols., 1908). Through her husband's campaigns for parliament she was introduced to politics: as the marquess of Tullibardine he stood unsuccessfully as Conservative candidate for Perthshire Eastern in 1906, but won Perthshire Western in January 1910, holding the seat until his succession to the peerage in 1917. From 1908 to 1918 she was president of the Perthshire Women's Unionist Association. In some ways the couple's roles were to be the reversal of those of a traditional political couple; he was more skilled as a host and homemaker, while she eventually proved to be a more successful politician. Katharine remained devoted to Bardie, as he was known, but her natural aloofness made it difficult for her to demonstrate affection towards him or close friends. He was unfaithful for much of their childless marriage, but this freed her to turn from her domestic life towards other matters. She directed her energies towards numerous official committees: she was a member of the departmental committee on medical and nursing services in the highlands and islands of Scotland (1912) and on Scottish tinkers (1917–18), and of the central agricultural wages committee for Scotland (1918–20). She was a prominent figure in Perthshire local government and voluntary associations, presiding over the Perthshire branch of the British Red Cross Society from 1909, serving as a member of the Perthshire education authority and the Association of Education Authorities in Scotland (1919–24), and chairing the Scottish board of health's Consultative Council for the Highlands and Islands (1920–24). During the First World War she organized welfare for the troops. In 1918 she was created one of the first dames of the British empire.

Despite the duchess of Atholl's Conservative affiliation, it was the Liberal prime minister, David Lloyd George, who first suggested that she stand for parliament. George V warned that politics would distract her from domestic responsibilities, but she felt safe leaving such duties to her husband, who encouraged her and helped her to practise public speaking and replying to hecklers. Although as a former anti-suffragist she was an unusual choice as Scotland's first woman MP, she felt that by standing she would help acclimatize Conservative men to women in politics, and that anything in that direction should be encouraged.

In 1923 she was narrowly elected member for Kinross and West Perthshire, her husband's former constituency.

When the Conservatives returned to power in 1924 it was felt that they needed to follow the example set by Labour in 1923 and appoint a woman minister. Temperamentally Atholl was better suited to ministerial office than the more senior Nancy Astor, and her experience in Scottish education led prime minister Stanley Baldwin to appoint her parliamentary secretary to the Board of Education. She did not get on with her pompous and autocratic chief, Lord Eustace Percy, who sent her away for much of the time to school prize-givings and international conferences. She did exercise some influence over policy, tempering Percy's enthusiasm for economizing; however, she opposed raising the school-leaving age on the grounds that 'the little hands of children' were still needed in industry. She failed to dissuade Percy from his plan to include educational funding in block grants to local authorities, and was forced on this occasion to appeal directly to Baldwin, with whom she enjoyed a long friendship. Eventually her objections once again prevailed. In June 1926 she was awarded an honorary DCL by Oxford, making her the first woman so honoured; in all, she received seven honorary doctorates from British and overseas universities.

Atholl's front-bench career ended with the Conservatives' defeat in 1929, and when they returned to power as part of the National Government in 1931 she was not reappointed to office. Nancy Astor warned the party leadership against appointing her on the grounds that she was not a feminist. Atholl never renounced her opposition to feminism; like many women of her privileged class she could not appreciate the need for women to have the vote. In parliament she angered feminists by opposing an equal franchise bill, enfranchising women at twenty-one rather than thirty, on the grounds that this would give female voters a numerical advantage because of the war's depletion of the male population. She also voted against a bill for equal pay in the civil service (she was a member of the royal commission on the civil service, 1929–31), and denied that women voters had a special claim on her, even though they had 'a charming habit' of thinking that women MPs were responsible only to them. None the less she supported the ordination of women in the Presbyterian church and published *Women and Politics* (1931), a book intended to provide 'the facts' that women needed to exercise properly their duties as citizens. It had an unapologetic Conservative slant, extolling the virtues of private property, capital, traditional marriage, and the empire, in which she hoped women would take an increased interest.

Atholl's own interest in the empire led her in 1929 to join left-wing independent MP Eleanor Rathbone in establishing a committee to investigate the brutal practice of 'female circumcision' in Muslim colonies such as Kenya. She admitted that the task was difficult, and no doubt the subject's unpleasantness and the derision of many male colleagues made it especially so, but eventually a report on the matter was commissioned. With this and subsequent issues she made good her pledge to co-operate with women MPs of any party on worthy causes, though she opposed the creation of a women's party. Her other political contribution to the status of women was a successful private member's bill in 1929 granting unwed mothers in Scotland the same financial assistance available to those in England and Wales.

Atholl's efforts on behalf of colonial women provided an early demonstration of the courage which characterized the latter years of her political career, as well as the single-mindedness with which she typically pursued each of her interests to the exclusion of other causes and issues. As she explained in *Women and Politics*, she felt that an MP's role was to uncover the facts and make them known, though she was not always effective in doing so. Although she had been known as a useful campaigner against women's suffrage, she was not a stimulating speaker in the House of Commons, and one contemporary noted that she focused on the substance of her speeches and did not court the ear of her audience, speaking in a hurried style. During her five years on the front bench, at least, her speaking style partly resulted from Eustace Percy's undermining her confidence. Her manner of dress was also plain, and throughout her adult life she wore a long tweed or tartan skirt with a long wool jacket and single string of pearls. Combined with her humourlessness and slight, upright appearance she looked rather like a schoolmistress; during her last campaign she perhaps solidified this image by incorporating a large map of Europe and pointer into her speeches. Yet those who saw her simply as a staid, even reactionary, figure were to be surprised as the sensitivity to cruelty which she demonstrated over Africa was further drawn out by world events and overrode considerations of both her party and her own career.

The duchess first clashed with her government over its proposals, introduced in 1934, for a new Indian constitution. Feeling that India was not ready for greater self-rule, she taxed MPs' patience with her endless but thoroughly researched speeches against the India Bill, being consequently dubbed the Begum of Blair. After supporting the candidature of Randolph Churchill, who stood as an opponent of the government's plans against an official Conservative candidate in the Wavertree by-election in February 1935, she was threatened with the loss of the party whip, but along with five others voluntarily resigned the Conservative whip in protest. After the Italian invasion of Abyssinia in October 1935 she returned to the fold, but the Spanish Civil War brought her again into conflict with her own government. Initially her interest was humanitarian, as she established and led an all-party national joint committee which brought refugee children to England. But she came to criticize the government's refusal to enforce a non-intervention pact, which Germany and Italy were violating by supporting Franco against the legitimately elected government. Determined as always to research and publicize the facts, she visited Spain with Rathbone and the Labour MP Ellen Wilkinson, and presented her findings in *Searchlight on Spain* (1938), which sold 300,000 copies in Britain and was translated into Spanish, French, and German. Despite the book's success, she alienated Conservatives who welcomed Franco as a bulwark against communism, as well as the many pro-Franco Catholics in her constituency and those with financial interests in Spain. This latest rebellion and her fraternization with left-wing elements was more damaging than her defiance over India, which could be forgiven as die-hard adherence to true Conservative principles. Her continued protests to prime minister Neville Chamberlain resulted in the loss of the party whip in April 1938, after which she sat as an independent.

Along with Rathbone, Atholl also studied first hand the situation in eastern Europe, and wrote an account of labour conditions in Soviet Russia, *The Conscription of a People* (1931). She was one of the first British politicians to understand fully the Nazi menace by reading an unexpurgated translation of Hitler's *Mein Kampf*. Finally her opposition to the government's policy of appeasement, and her resultant conflict with her constituency association, prompted her in November 1938 to resign from parliament and force a by-election on the issue. At the 1935 election her constituency Conservative association had agreed to respect her independence in foreign affairs, but her refusal to compromise and meet their concerns strained their tolerance to breaking point. She had refused to believe that their support for appeasement reflected popular opinion, and many voters also felt that she had been neglecting local problems through her preoccupation with overseas matters. She stood as an independent, rather than as an independent Conservative, which with hindsight she admitted to have been a mistake. Her campaign, however, commanded the support of numerous political and literary figures, primarily from the Labour and Liberal parties. Despite the support of fellow Conservative anti-appeasers Winston Churchill and Robert Boothby, neither felt secure enough to risk antagonizing their own local parties by campaigning for her. Having already lost a recent by-election fought largely on the issue of appeasement, the government took her challenge seriously. Fifty Conservative MPs travelled north to warn that a vote for the duchess was a vote for war, and in a more sinister twist local landowners were alleged to have offered their tenants bonuses—or threats—on the understanding that they vote against her. These various factors contributed to her narrow defeat by a Conservative opponent in a two-way contest. Subsequent events in Europe vindicated her position, and would have saved her political career had she remained in parliament a few months longer, but after Churchill assumed the Conservative leadership in 1940 she abandoned plans to return as an independent MP for the Scottish Universities.

Instead of making a political comeback she devoted herself to war work, serving as honorary secretary of the Scottish invasion committee, which prepared for an attempted German invasion, and the Perthshire Red Cross. After her husband's death in 1942 she succeeded him as colonel-in-chief of the Scottish Horse. From 1945

she was the founding chair of the British League for European Freedom, a response to Soviet oppression in eastern Europe: having crusaded against the excesses of Nazi Germany and Fascist Spain in the 1930s she now found herself denounced from the left as a 'fascist beast'. In 1958 she published a disappointing autobiography, *Working Partnership*. An increasingly lonely figure in the political world, she served the league until her death in Edinburgh on 21 October 1960. She was buried in the grounds of Blair Castle.   DUNCAN SUTHERLAND

Sources S. Hetherington, *Katharine Atholl, 1874–1960: against the tide* (1989) · *DNB* · K. M. Stewart-Murray, duchess of Atholl, *Working partnership, being the lives of John George, eighth duke of Atholl, and of his wife Katharine Marjory Ramsay* (1958) · K. Atholl, *Women and politics* (1930) · C. Rigg, 'The failure of an anti-appeaser: the case of the duchess of Atholl and the West Perth and Kinross by-election of 1938', *History Teaching Review* (1984), 34–8 · B. Harrison, 'Women in a men's house: the women MPs, 1919–45', *HJ*, 29 (1986), 623–54 · S. Ball, 'The politics of appeasement: the fall of the duchess of Atholl and the Kinross and West Perth by-election, December 1938', *SHR*, 69 (1990), 49–83 · A. S. Williams, *Ladies of influence: women of the elite in interwar Britain* (2000) · GEC, *Baronetage* · private information (2004) [archivist, Blair Castle] · Burke, *Peerage*
Archives Blair Castle, Perthshire, papers · NRA, priv. coll., corresp. and political papers | BL, corresp. with Lord Cecil, Add. MS 51142 · BL OIOC, corresp. relating to Indian self-government proposals, MS Eur. D. 903 · CAC Cam., Churchill papers · CAC Cam., corresp. with Sir E. L. Spears · King's Lond., Liddell Hart C., corresp. with Sir B. H. Liddell Hart · NL Scot., corresp. and papers relating to Scottish National War Memorial · U. Reading, corresp. with Nancy Astor | FILM BFI NFTVA · British Pathé, London
Likenesses G. Henry, portrait, 1903, Blair Castle, Perthshire · J. Guthrie, portrait, 1924, Blair Castle, Perthshire · S. Yourievitch, bronze bust, 1924, Blair Castle, Perthshire · W. Stoneman, photograph, 1925, NPG · H. Coster, photograph, 1930–39, NPG
Wealth at death £65,967 8s. 9d.: confirmation, 11 Jan 1961, NA Scot., SC 70/1/1462 pp. 441–52 · £335 14s. 6d.: additional inventory, 18 May 1961, NA Scot., SC 70/1/1473 pp. 595–8

Murray, Keith Anderson Hope, Baron Murray of Newhaven (1903–1993), agricultural economist and university administrator, was born at 62 Great King Street, Edinburgh, on 28 July 1903, the third of five sons (there were no daughters) of Lord Charles David Murray (1866–1936), judge of the court of session, and his wife, Ann Florence (Annie), fifth daughter of David Nicolson, of Parsons Green, Edinburgh. He followed his father through Edinburgh Academy and Edinburgh University, taking a degree in agriculture with the intention of becoming a farmer. After a year with the board of agriculture, however, he was awarded a Commonwealth Fund fellowship for study in the United States at Cornell University, returning in 1929 with a PhD and a budding international reputation as an agricultural economist. After further postgraduate study at Oxford (collecting a BLitt), he joined the University Agricultural Economics Research Institute at that university, which was at that time contributing much to the development of Oxford economics. His first book, *Land and Life* (1932), was immediately followed by another, *The Planning of Agriculture* (1933), and he was on the road to a significant academic career. His work in agricultural economics culminated in the publication in 1955 of the *Agriculture* volume in the official *History of the Second World War*.

In 1937 however he took a step into administration which he came to regard as the turning point of his career. He was appointed fellow and bursar of Lincoln College, which was going through a very difficult time financially. Only thirty-four, he injected new life into the college, transforming its economy and earning high praise from its junior members for his accessibility.

On the outbreak of the Second World War, Murray was drafted into the Ministry of Food, but subsequently worked as a radar controller in the RAF for two years before being appointed director of food and agriculture in the Middle East Supply Centre, with the responsibility of ensuring food supplies not only for the allied forces in the region, but also for the civilian population. Meanwhile, in 1944 the fellows of Lincoln College elected him in his absence as their new rector. With characteristic energy he also remained as bursar, and in the immediate post-war years he transformed the college intellectually, socially, financially, and in sport. His achievements were noted widely outside Oxford, and he is said to have declined many offers of high positions in order to consolidate his work in the college.

In 1952 however Murray yielded to heavy pressure from friends and colleagues within the university world, and accepted the chairmanship of the University Grants Committee at what was to be a critical period in the history of British universities. He served two full terms, retiring in 1963. During that decade were laid the foundations of the expansion and transformation of the university system. Murray himself was from the outset an expansionist—not at that time a particularly fashionable view in academic circles. His decade in office saw annual capital expenditure on universities increase fifteenfold, and seven new universities planned and designated. In this period however the number of students had still not kept pace with the increase in the relevant age group, still less with the number of those qualified by their earlier education. Murray himself saw his job as providing the universities with the tools and physical structure they needed for what he perceived to be the unavoidable task of long-term expansion. He was also convinced that the universities would not tackle this satisfactorily unless they could be assured of autonomy in doing so. This implied control by the universities of the use of the resources allocated to them, as well as control over admissions, appointments, promotions, discipline, and above all over the content of teaching and research. With the financial, physical and organizational foundations in place Murray encouraged the government in the early 1960s to appoint what was to become the Robbins committee to map out the future expansion. Though he was not himself a member his influence was said (by the secretary of the committee) to have rivalled that of Lord Robbins himself, and almost every aspect of the committee's report affecting universities was developed from the foundations laid down by Murray's work at the University Grants Committee over the previous decade.

Throughout his career Murray was always ready to add extra jobs to his already busy load. He was indeed a leading member of the 'great and the good', an 'all-purpose public man'. While still at Oxford he served as a city councillor, on the county education committee, and as a magistrate. On the international scene he was in the late 1940s a member of the committee of inquiry into disturbances in the Gold Coast, which led to a new constitution which was the first step to the independence of Ghana. While at the University Grants Committee he accepted an invitation from the government of Australia to chair a commission which led directly to the remarkable development and expansion of Australian universities in the 1960s. After his 'retirement' he spent eight years as director of the Leverhulme Trust (1964–72), and combined this with trusteeship of the other great private foundation concerned with research and education in the UK, the Wellcome Trust (1965–73). He also served on the boards of the Metal Box and British Aero companies, though the private sector never really engaged his enthusiasm.

Murray was a large man in every sense: tall, genial, and energetic. He moved easily and confidently in government circles, both Westminster and Whitehall. In one sense he could be said to have presided over the last golden years of a University Grants Committee system, in which relations between British governments and universities were characterized by personal trust and mutual respect. He was, he admitted, fortunate in that all the key stages of his career—Lincoln College, the University Grants Committee, and Leverhulme—involved the management of growth and expansion rather than curtailment and retrenchment.

Murray was honoured both by the government and by universities at home and abroad. He was knighted in 1955, appointed KCB in 1963, and created a life peer in 1964. Chancellor of the University of Southampton from 1964 to 1974, he received honorary degrees from Oxford, Cambridge, Bristol, Liverpool, Leicester, Edinburgh, Southampton, and Hull, as well as from California and Western Australia. He was a devout Presbyterian, with a firm commitment to his values, but in no way censorious of others. With a wide circle of affectionate friends, he did not marry, and spent the last decade of his life quietly in his small flat in Westminster. He died in London on 10 October 1993.

GEOFFREY CASTON

Sources *The Independent* (16 Oct 1993) · *The Times* (12 Oct 1993) · *WWW, 1991–5* · J. P. Carswell, *Government and the universities* (1985) · V. Green, *The commonwealth of Lincoln College, 1427–1977* (1979) · *Hist. U. Oxf.* 8: 20th cent. · 'Report', *Parl. papers* (1962–3), 9.639, Cmnd 2154 [on higher education] · Burke, *Peerage* · *CGPLA Eng. & Wales* (1993)
Archives Lincoln College, Oxford, MSS
Likenesses A. C. Davidson-Houston, oils, 1954, Lincoln College, Oxford · photograph, repro. in *The Times*
Wealth at death £1,173,780: probate, 24 Nov 1993, *CGPLA Eng. & Wales*

Murray, Keith Day Pearce (1892–1981), architect and industrial designer, was born on 5 July 1892 in Stokes Road, Mt Eden, Auckland, New Zealand, the son of Charles Henry Murray, a stationer, and his wife, Lilian Day, *née* George. His father was from Peterhead, Scotland, and his mother was from Nelson, New Zealand. Murray's principal career was as an architect, though it is for his industrial design of the 1930s that he has become renowned.

Murray was first educated at King's College, Remuera, Auckland. In 1906 he emigrated to Britain with his parents, and from 1906 to 1907 attended Mill Hill School, London. He served with distinction with the Royal Air Force and Royal Flying Corps during the First World War, earning the Military Cross in 1917, and the Croix de Guerre Belge. Following the war, Murray attended the Architectural Association School in London. He completed his studies in 1921, and that year was elected an associate of the Royal Institute of British Architects.

From 1921 Murray worked in the office of Maxwell Ayrton. However, his career as an architect reached a hiatus following the economic crash of 1929. Forced to seek other employment, he made in 1931 a number of sketches of glassware with the intention of finding a British manufacturer to produce them. Murray already had a keen interest in glass having been introduced to the subject by a collector friend. He had himself acquired a number of pieces of pre-1850 English glass, and at the 1925 Exposition Internationale des Arts Décoratifs et Industriels Modernes in Paris was profoundly influenced by the contemporary Swedish, Finnish, Austrian, and Czech glass that he saw. Murray later described how this experience had caused him to analyse what he found unsatisfactory in post-1850 English glass, and concluded that this was largely due to excessive cutting which obscured the clarity of the glass; this decoration often being poorly designed and applied to indifferent shapes. Inspired by the modern continental glass he had seen, he was convinced 'that there was no reason why the qualities of old English glass should not be given modern expression' (Murray, 'The designer and his problem', 53).

In 1931 Murray was introduced to Marriot Powell of Whitefriars glassworks by Harry Trethowan of Heal & Sons. Powell had samples of Murray's designs made up, but these were unsuccessful, as the designs were unsuited to Whitefriars' production methods. Trethowan then introduced Murray to Hubert Williams-Thomas, managing director of Stevens and Williams. Williams-Thomas wanted to develop a modern line to compete with Swedish imports, and employed Murray on a freelance basis for about two months each year from 1932 to 1939. Murray designed glass exclusively for the firm, and following a thorough study of the production processes in use at the factory, made about 150 new designs each year. For Murray, form and function were the essential elements of design. The glass, which was either free-blown or mould-blown and most often decorated with shallow cutting or engraving, was sold through selected retailers in the midlands and south-east of England.

Murray sought similar work with other industrial manufacturers, and following an introduction to Felton Wreford, the manager of Wedgwood's London showrooms, was invited to visit their factory in Stoke-on-Trent in 1932. This visit proved successful, and Josiah Wedgwood invited him to design on a freelance basis, and to

study the various production processes at the factory. Murray was employed on a similar basis to that at Stevens and Williams, and rapidly developed a range of functional tableware and vessels. His designs combined modernism with the neo-classicism of eighteenth-century Wedgwood pottery, and, as with his designs for glass, were based on clear and uncomplicated shapes. Many of his designs were produced using the new range of matt glazes developed by Norman Wilson. One hundred and twenty-four shapes were shown in the 'Exhibition of new Wedgwood shapes designed by Keith Murray' at John Lewis, Oxford Street, London, at the end of 1933. Murray's designs proved popular, and many items remained in production well into the 1950s. His last design work for Wedgwood was undertaken during the period 1946 to 1948, when he assisted in the design of elements of the Commonwealth service, a new table service for large-scale production and export. In addition to pottery and glass, Murray also produced a number of designs for silver for Mappin and Webb in 1934.

From the outset, Murray received substantial recognition for his industrial design. He was awarded a gold medal at the 5th Triennale, Milan, 1933. His work was also shown at the exhibition 'British industrial art in relation to the home', Dorland Hall, London, 1933, the Royal Academy exhibition 'British art in industry', Burlington House, London, 1935, and at the Universal Exhibition, Paris, 1937. In 1936 he became one of the first ten royal designers for industry, and was from 1945 to 1947 master of the Faculty of Royal Designers for Industry. His designs were closer to the international modern movement than those of any other British designer, and were celebrated by the modernist critics of the day. Herbert Read for example described his Wedgwood mugs as 'better than anything else in modern British ceramics' (Tyler and others, 21).

In 1936 Murray returned to his original career, commencing his architectural practice with partner Charles White. Appropriately, their first major commission was the design of the new Wedgwood factory at Barlaston, near Stoke-on-Trent. The foundation stone was laid in September 1938, and, despite set-backs due to the onset of the Second World War, production began at the factory in 1940. Murray's plans for a modernist white ceramic façade had to be dropped due to wartime restrictions, but the factory layout was clear and logical, based on the various stages of pottery manufacture. In 1939 Murray was made a fellow of the Royal Institute of British Architects. From 1939 to 1941 he again served with the RAF. Following the war, his practice, which later became Murray, Ward & Partners, designed numerous industrial and office buildings, including the Hong Kong air terminal and the British European Airways engineering base in London airport.

In 1948 Murray married Mary Beatrice de Cartaret Hayes, the daughter of Lieutenant-Colonel R. Malet. The couple had one daughter, and lived at Stephouse, Tarrant Gunville, Blandford, Dorset. Though no longer really connected with the firm, Murray was presented with a retirement gift from Wedgwood in 1967. He died on 16 May 1981.

Examples of his industrial design can be found in numerous public collections, notably the Victoria and Albert Museum, London, which organized a travelling exhibition of his work in 1976. Murray, however, remained at all times modest about his design achievements, seeming surprised by the interest shown in what he considered a sideline to his career as architect. ALUN R. GRAVES

Sources L. Tyler, D. Lloyd-Jenkins, and M. Findlay, *Keith Murray in context* (1996) · [J. Hawkins], *Keith Murray: a travelling exhibition arranged by the circulation department of the Victoria and Albert Museum* (1976) · K. Murray, 'The designer and his problem II: the design of table glass', *Design For Today*, 1 (1933), 53–6 · D. Taylor, 'Keith Murray F.R.I.B.A., R.D.I. (1892–1981)', *British glass between the wars*, ed. R. Dodsworth (1987), 31–5 · M. Batkin, 'Keith Murray', *Wedgwood ceramics, 1846–1959: a new appraisal* (1982), 204–11 · *The Times* (21 May 1981) · *WW* (1978), 1773 · J. Hawkins and K. Murray, interview, 18 Feb 1977, V&A, ceramics and glass department · K. Murray, 'Some views of a designer', *Journal of the Society of Glass Technology*, 19 (1935) · *CGPLA Eng. & Wales* (1981)

Archives Wedgwood Museum, Stoke-on-Trent

Likenesses photographs, *c*.1946–1948, Wedgwood Museum, Stoke-on-Trent

Murray, Lindley (1745–1826), grammarian and lawyer, was born at Swatara, near Lancaster, Pennsylvania, on 22 April 1745, the eldest of the twelve children of Robert Murray (1721–1786) and his wife, Mary, *née* Lindley (*d*. 1780). Murray's father had emigrated from Ireland to America in 1732, and became one of the leading New York merchants of the time. (The name Murray Hill in that city still testifies to the Murray family's former prominence there.) His mother was the daughter of a Quaker politician, and upon their marriage Robert Murray converted to Quakerism.

Murray spent his first school years at an academy in Philadelphia (the home of many of his Quaker relatives) which had recently been founded by Benjamin Franklin, and at a school in New York. As the eldest son he was destined for the merchant business, and he was placed in his father's 'counting house' at the age of eleven. Murray himself had different ambitions, and after an apprenticeship with a Quaker merchant in Philadelphia he ran off—'taking my books and all my property with me', as he later wrote in his *Memoirs of the Life and Writings of Lindley Murray* (1826)—to Burlington in New Jersey in order to learn French. His father subsequently relented and allowed Murray to train as a lawyer instead, a not uncommon profession for the son of a merchant.

Murray's legal career started in 1767, the same year in which he married Hannah Dobson (1748–1834), daughter of another prominent Quaker family. Foreseeing the American economic depression, Murray's father set up business in London, where after a few years he was joined by his family, including the newly married couple. His father returned to New York in 1768, while Murray and his wife stayed on in London until 1771. In New York, the effects of the oncoming revolution were beginning to be felt by the Murrays: the various non-importation agreements threatened to hit this family of merchants hard. An attempt to evade current regulations and its subsequent cover-up—known as the *Beulah* affair, after the name of

the ship which carried the forbidden goods—eventually led to Murray's definitive move to England, not for reasons of ill health as he claimed in his *Memoirs*, but by way of banishment. Owing to the Murrays' political position as loyalists, their New York property would have been confiscated if it had not apparently been for the intercession of the New York mayor James Duane: in exchange for the banishment of one of the members of the family, past misbehaviour would be forgiven and possessions allowed to be kept.

Murray and his wife went to England in 1784, where they settled in Holdgate, near York, where there was a large Quaker community. None of the events leading to the Murrays' forced exile are referred to in the *Memoirs*, which had been completed by 1809 but were published by Murray's assistant Elizabeth Frank after his death. Possibly the *Memoirs* originally served a different purpose, namely to provide Murray's American agent with biographical information of the author whose books he was trying to market. At Holdgate, Murray engaged in literary activities, and in 1787 he published *The Power of Religion on the Mind*, which was later followed by the textbooks that earned him the title 'father of English grammar'. His chief claim to fame rests on the publication of what would now be called a complete teaching method for English: a grammar, a book of exercises, a reader, and a 'spelling book' (or, more appropriately, an elementary reader). His *English Grammar* was published in 1795, a book he had been asked to write by a couple of teachers at a Quaker school for girls in York.

As there were many grammars available at the time, Murray felt that he had nothing substantially new to offer; consequently, he viewed his grammar as a mere 'compilation'—but, because he refrained from mentioning his sources, this caused him to be accused of plagiarism. Immediately upon this accusation, Murray supplied his sources in the introduction to the fourth edition, published in 1798: Harris, Johnson, Lowth, Priestley, Beattie, Sheridan, Walker, and Coote. The grammar proved immediately popular: a sixty-fifth edition has been recorded as published in London in 1871. Other editions and reprints appeared in the United States (many of them unauthorized), where the grammar proved a successful rival to Webster's *Grammatical Institute of the English Language*, part 2 (1784). It was also published in Ireland, India, Canada, Germany, France, and Portugal, and it was translated into many languages: French, German, Dutch, Swedish, Spanish, and Russian. The Dutch translation of the grammar was in turn translated into Japanese. This worldwide popularity of the work marks the beginning of the development of English as a world language. For native speakers of English the *Grammar* likewise proved an excellent tool, both for teaching in the classroom and for individual study. In their clarity and succinctness the rules set out by Murray are eminently learnable (echoes of Murray are found in diverse nineteenth-century novels, such as those by George Eliot, Dickens, Thackeray, and Melville), and the material is presented in gradable form, with the basic rules in the main text and further expansions in footnotes.

An *Abridgement* of the grammar appeared in 1797, which proved equally if not more popular, given the number of editions and reprints recorded. It was also printed in a special edition for blind readers, with embossed characters (Boston, 1835), and translated into Marathi (Bombay, 1837). There was even a board game, called *A Journey to Lindley Murray's*, which was published a few years later. Also in 1797 Murray's *English Exercises* were published, with a separate *Key to the Exercises* (1797). His *English Reader* came out in 1799, followed by *A Sequel to the English Reader* in 1800 and an *Introduction to the English Reader* in the year after that. While in Britain Murray was best known for his *Grammar*, in the United States his *Reader* was the most popular of his textbooks (259 editions and reprints were published there between 1815 and 1836 only), very likely because of the Enlightenment interest reflected in the texts selected. Murray's *English Spelling-Book* was published in 1804 and reprinted more than fifty times within the next fifty years. Outside Britain and America, the book was also published in India (Calcutta, 1836) and Spain (Cadiz, 1841). Other schoolbooks published by Murray were his *Lecteur françois* (1802) and his *Introduction au lecteur françois* (1807). For the benefit of mothers teaching their children, he published *A First Book for Children* (1804).

Murray dominated the field for schoolbooks for a long time, both in England and in America. The *Grammar* continued to be printed down to the 1870s, and the last American edition of the *Reader* came out in 1856. Even in the 1920s his name must still have been well known, for one of the chapters in James Joyce's *Ulysses* is a parody of the style advocated by Murray in his *Grammar*. Murray's books did not go uncriticized: in 1868 the American G. Washington Moon published *The Bad English of Lindley Murray and other Writers on the English Language*, and some thirty years earlier a parody of the *Grammar* had appeared in Britain, called *The Comic English Grammar*, by Percival Leigh (1840); the book was published in Dutch in 1865 by Jacob van Lennep, under the title *Vermakelijke Spraakkunst*. These publications suggest that by then the popularity of Murray and his books was on the decline, even though they continued to be printed for much longer. A facsimile edition, entitled *Educational Works*, was published in 1996.

Other books written by Murray include *A Selection from Bishop Horne's Commentary on the Psalms* (1812), *A Biographical Sketch of H. Tuke* (1815), *A Compendium of Religious Truth and Practice* (1815), and *The Duty and Benefit of a Daily Perusal of the Holy Scriptures in Families* (1816).

The ill health Murray used as an excuse for deciding to move to England indeed appears to have been a fact after his arrival there, but not before; it is possible that he suffered from a form of arthritis which caused him to be confined to a wheelchair and later to the house altogether. Despite his illness he was active in the Quaker community in York, where he was a minister of the 'monthly meeting' between 1791 and 1802, when he resigned.

Murray died at Holdgate on 16 February 1826, following what was probably a stroke he had suffered about a month earlier; he was buried at Bishophill, York. His wife, who died on 25 September 1834, survived him by eight years. The couple had no children. Murray sold the copyright of his books to his publishers, and the proceeds he applied 'not to my own private use, but to charitable purposes, and for the benefit of others' (*Memoirs*). One beneficiary was Trinity Lane School (later the Mount School, York), the school for which he had originally written his *English Grammar*. In his will Murray provided for his wife, and after her death the sum of $30,500 was invested in a New York fund, the proceeds of which were to be spent in educating former black slaves and Indians.

INGRID TIEKEN-BOON VAN OSTADE

Sources C. Monaghan, *The Murrays of Murray Hill* (1998) • I. Tieken-Boon van Ostade, ed., *Two hundred years of Lindley Murray* (1996) • S. Allott, *Lindley Murray, 1745–1826: Quaker grammarian of New York and old York* (1991) • R. C. Alston, *A bibliography of the English language from the invention of printing to the year 1800*, 1 (1965) • 'In commemoration of the 200th anniversary of the publication of Lindley Murray's *English grammar*', *Asterisk: a Monthly Journal for Historical Studies* [Japan], 4/12 (1995) • D. A. Reibel, ed., *Lindley Murray (1745–1826): the educational works* (1996) • I. Michael, 'More than enough English grammars', *English traditional grammars*, ed. G. Leitner (1991), 11–26 • 'Dictionary of Quaker biography', RS Friends, Lond. [card index]

Archives NL Wales, letters | RS Friends, Lond., letters to Joseph Cockfield

Likenesses T. A. Dean, stipple (after E. Westoby), BM, NPG; repro. in E. Frank, ed., *Memoirs of the life and writings of Lindley Murray* (1826) • caricature, engraving, repro. in P. Leigh, *The comic English grammar* (1840) • engraving, William Sessions Limited Archives • engraving, Haverford College Library, Pennsylvania • portrait, probably Haverford College, Pennsylvania, Charles Roberts autograph collection • portrait, probably Haverford College, Haverford, Pennsylvania, Quaker collection • portrait, repro. in J. J. Smith, *Recollections of John Jay Smith*, 189? • portrait, repro. in W. M. Oland Bourne, *History of the Public School Society of the City of New York* (1870) • silhouette, RS Friends, Lond.

Wealth at death $30,500: Monaghan, *The Murrays*, 128–9; Allott, *Lindley Murray*, 44

Murray, Louisa (1818–1894), writer, was born at Carisbrooke, Isle of Wight, on 23 May 1818, the eldest of the nine children of Lieutenant Edward Murray (*c*.1783–1863), 100th regiment, and Louisa Rose (*c*.1797–*c*.1878), daughter of Major Charles Lyons, 7th fusiliers. She grew up in co. Wicklow, Ireland (a frequent setting in her fiction), but emigrated with her family in 1844 to Canada, where she became a schoolteacher on Wolfe Island, near Kingston, Ontario.

In 1851, on Susanna Moodie's recommendation, Murray's novel *Fauna* was serialized in the *Literary Garland* (Montreal). Contemporaries praised her dialogue and delighted descriptions of primitive nature, but this early (if over-romanticized) treatment of the Canadian ethnic mosaic includes a strong plea for female autonomy and recognition of the damage caused by imposing European culture on native Indians. It was reprinted several times, in New York and Belfast. *Settlers of Long Arrow* (1861, serialized in *Once a Week*) adds the French-Canadian element, while the more technically sophisticated *Cited Curate* (1863, *British-American Magazine*, Toronto) shifts to Catholic–protestant violence and class barriers in Ireland.

Here and in another Irish tale, *Little Dorinn* (1873), her allusive style effectively places the colonial experience against literary and historical tradition.

In Murray's last twenty years, prolific and versatile, she 'gave character' (Fidelis, 1064) to emerging periodicals, including the *Canadian Monthly*, *The Nation*, and *The Week*; none of her criticism, essays, or poetry, however, was published in book form. Intelligent, well read, and sensitive, she could also be 'formidable … exacting and quick to take offence' (family memoir, Louisa Murray MSS), and wrote feelingly on suppressed literary talent in women. She died of dysentery at her home, Glen-Farm in Stamford, near Niagara, on 28 July 1894.

MARY S. MILLAR

Sources B. Godard, 'Murray, Louisa Annie', *DCB*, vol. 12 · J. Zelmanovits, 'Louisa Murray, writing woman', *Canadian Woman Studies*, 7 (1986), 339–42 · H. J. Morgan, *Types of Canadian women*, 1 (1903) · Fidelis [A. M. Machar], 'A loss to Canadian literature', *The Week*, 11, 45 (5 Oct 1894), 1063–4 · A. E. Wetherald, 'Some Canadian literary women: III. Louisa Murray', *The Week*, 5, 21 (19 April 1888), 335–6 · Ontario census returns for Wolfe Island, 1851, 1861, 1871; for Stamford, 1881, 1891 · Queen's University, Kingston, Ontario, Agnes Etherington Centre, corresp. of Daniel Fowler to Louisa Murray, 1864–94 · *Weekly British Whig* (30 Sept 1863) [obit. of Edward Murray] · *Susanna Moodie: letters of a lifetime*, ed. C. Ballstadt and others (1985) · M. L. Murray, family memoir, 1923 · Ontario registry of deaths
Archives priv. coll.
Likenesses daguerreotype, repro. in Morgan, *Types*, 250

Margaret Alice Murray (1863–1963), by Lafayette, 1928

Murray, Margaret Alice (1863–1963), Egyptologist and folklorist, was born in Calcutta on 13 July 1863, the younger daughter of James Charles Murray (d. 1891) and his wife, Margaret Carr (d. 1913?). James Murray, whose family had been in India for several generations, was managing partner of a firm of Manchester merchants; his wife was from a Northumbrian family, and had gone to India as a missionary and social worker among Indian women. Margaret Murray's early life was spent partly in India and partly in England, with a period (1873–5) in Bonn, Germany. She was educated mainly by her mother, but when she was in England without her parents she normally stayed with her uncle John Murray, vicar of Lambourn, Berkshire, and later rector of Rugby. From him she acquired an interest in ancient monuments. Nevertheless she first decided on a nursing career, and trained for three months—the most her father would permit—in Calcutta General Hospital in 1883 as the first 'lady probationer' in India; she acted briefly as sister-in-charge during an epidemic. She returned to England in 1886 but had to give up her hopes of a nursing career because she was too small (only 4 feet 10 inches) to qualify. She next tried a career in social work, first in Rugby and then in Bushey Heath, Hertfordshire, where her parents settled in 1887, but found it uncongenial.

Murray's main career did not begin until her sister, Mary, who had been impressed by the work of the famous Egyptologist W. Flinders Petrie, prevailed on her to study under him. In January 1894 she entered his department at University College, London, where she made rapid progress under the tuition of J. H. Walker and F. Ll. Griffith.

Petrie, recognizing her abilities, started her on research and encouraged her to publish the result, as 'The descent of property in the early periods of Egyptian history' (*Proceedings of the Society of Biblical Archaeology*, 17 (1895), 240–45). She remained Petrie's devoted disciple for the rest of her life; it was even rumoured that she had wanted to marry him.

In 1898, after Griffith's departure from London, Murray took over the teaching of the beginners' language classes. Despite her lack of formal qualifications she was appointed a junior college lecturer the following year, and was later promoted assistant (1909), lecturer (1921), senior lecturer and fellow (1922), and assistant professor (1924); in 1931 she gained the degree of DLitt. After Walker's death in 1914 she effectively ran the Egyptology department, since Petrie was absent for much of the year on excavations, and she was largely responsible for organizing the teaching into a formal training course (1910) leading to a certificate in Egyptian archaeology. This involved her in a wide range of subjects: besides Egyptian language, history, art, and religion, there were drawing, photography, surveying, mineralogy, and dating of objects, as well as anthropology and ethnology. Her salary was not high, and in order to bring her income up to £200 per annum she undertook much outside teaching, mostly evening classes but also extension lectures at Oxford (1910) and London (1911), and proved a conscientious cataloguer, first of the Egyptian collection of the Society of Antiquaries of Scotland, to which she belonged from 1900, and later of the Egyptian antiquities in the National Museum of Ireland, the Royal Scottish Museum, Manchester University Museum, and the Ashmolean Museum, Oxford.

Murray's first experience of fieldwork came when she assisted Petrie in his excavations at Abydos in 1902–3 and she also worked in Saqqara in 1903–4, but later her teaching duties prevented her from digging except in the summer, when work in Egypt is virtually impossible; but she took such opportunities as were available, excavating in Malta (1920–23) and Minorca (1930–31). After she retired from University College in 1935—the normal retirement rules having been suspended for seven years, for she was then seventy-two—she went on a lecture tour of Norway, Sweden, Finland, and Estonia. She then spent time with Petrie in Palestine (where he had retired in 1933); she was involved especially in his work at Petra (1937) and Tell Ajjul (Gaza; 1938).

Murray was highly industrious, and published more than a hundred books and articles (see her bibliography in *Folklore*, 72, 1961, 560–66), including several valuable excavation reports, such as *The Osireion at Abydos* (1904), *Saqqara mastabas* (2 vols., 1905–37; perhaps her best work), and *Seven Memphite Tomb Chapels* (1952, with Hilda Flinders Petrie). Of the works she intended for a wider audience, such as *Egyptian Temples* (1931), the best-known is *The Splendour that was Egypt* (1949), unfortunately not one of her best, since it was marred by her uncritical acceptance of Petrie's superseded chronology and of the theory that inheritance in Egypt was matrilineal and led to frequent sibling marriages. In general her scholarship showed breadth of interest rather than profundity; she was not an expert philologist, and was occasionally guilty of making unsubstantiated statements. Perhaps the main criticism that might be levelled is that she tended to take a myopic view of Egyptian civilization; lack of perspective is particularly evident in her failure to appreciate the important outside influences which were manifest in the Proto-Dynastic period. Nevertheless, her knowledge of the language was of the greatest help to Petrie. At heart she was a true archaeologist who enjoyed concentrating on the material remains. Her main legacy to the study of the ancient world was probably her fieldwork, together with her influence on the large number of Egyptologists who were her pupils.

Murray was remembered as a forceful character, with bright blue eyes that could flash in indignation; her strength of character was shown in her success in the hitherto entirely male world of professional Egyptologists. Like her mother, she was determined to do whatever she could to improve the conditions of women. This had been her motive for attempting a career in social work, and was shown in her time at University College by her undemonstrative but unfailing support for her female colleagues and pupils. Furthermore she ventured into territory not then considered suitable for women by her involvement in anthropology. This began as part of her Egyptology, but became a second academic legacy after, in two ground-breaking books, *The Witch-Cult in Western Europe* (1921) and *The God of the Witches* (1933; 2nd edn, 1952), she explained medieval European witchcraft as a survival

of the pre-Christian nature cult of the horned god (Cernunnos). This theory was controversial but proved popular and widely influential. She became a recognized authority on the subject, a fellow of the Royal Anthropological Institute from 1926 and a member of the Folk-Lore Society from 1927 (its president for 1953–5). However, her later, characteristically independent-minded, 'attempt to attribute the death of certain English monarchs to the survival of the killing of the divine king in a Frazerian context'—in *The Divine King in England* (1954)—'can hardly be regarded as among her more convincing anthropological contributions' (*Folklore*, 74, 1963, 569). Another idiosyncrasy was her occasional practice of the arts she studied; more than once she was reported by friends to have cast spells in a saucepan to try to reverse academic appointments of which she disapproved (Janssen, 56). Such activities may not have been entirely serious, for she was practical and quite unsuperstitious, and her sense of humour was well developed, as is shown by her remark to Leonard Cottrell in a BBC broadcast she made at the age of ninety-six: 'I've been an archaeologist most of my life and now I'm a piece of archaeology myself' (*Folklore*, 72, 1961, 437).

Murray remained relatively active in her old age and in her hundredth year published not only her last academic work, *The Genesis of Religion* (1963), but also her fascinating autobiography, *My First Hundred Years*. Two days after her hundredth birthday she was still able to attend a celebration held in her honour by University College, but she died a few months later, on 13 November 1963, at the Queen Victoria Memorial Hospital, Welwyn, Hertfordshire. She never married. Her funeral was held and her body cremated on 20 November at Golders Green crematorium, Middlesex.   MAX MALLOWAN, rev. R. S. SIMPSON

Sources M. A. Murray, *My first hundred years* (1963) · *The Times* (15 Nov 1963), 21a · *The Times* (19 Nov 1963), 15a · personal knowledge (1981) · R. M. Janssen, *The first hundred years: Egyptology at University College London, 1892–1992* (1992) · M. S. Drower, *Flinders Petrie: a life in archaeology* (1985) · M. Williams, 'Ninety-eight years young', *Folklore*, 72 (1961), 433–7 · W. R. Dawson and E. P. Uphill, *Who was who in Egyptology*, 3rd edn, rev. M. L. Bierbrier (1995), 303 · *The Times* (21 Nov 1963), 16e · *Folklore*, 74 (1963), 568–9 · d. cert.

Archives Folklore Society, London, corresp. and papers relating to folklore · UCL, autograph collection · UCL, lecture notes | BLPES, letters to C. G. Seligman

Likenesses two photographs, 1908–13, repro. in Murray, *My first hundred years* · photograph, 1910?, repro. in *Folklore* (1961) · W. Brunton, portrait, 1917, UCL · Lafayette, photograph, 1928, NPG [see illus.] · Lafayette, 1931?, repro. in Janssen, *First hundred years* · photograph, 1940–1949?, repro. in M. S. Drower, *Flinders Petrie* · double portrait, photograph, 1953 (with Hilda Petrie), repro. in *Picture Post* (24 Sept 1953) · S. Rickard, bronze head, exh. RA 1961 · A. Chappelow, photograph, 1963, repro. in Murray, *My first hundred years* · P. Lichfield, photograph, 1963, repro. in Murray, *My first hundred years* · two photographs, 1963, repro. in Janssen, *First hundred years* · S. Rickard, bronze bust, c.1965, UCL · photograph (aged ninety-eight?), repro. in *Folklore* (1961) · photographs, UCL

Wealth at death £13,174: probate, 29 Jan 1964, CGPLA Eng. & Wales

Murray, Mary Frances (d. 1891). *See under* Murray, Henry Leigh (1820–1870).

Murray, Matthew (1765–1826), mechanical engineer, was probably born in Gateshead. Little is known of his early life, before his marriage at Gateshead on 25 September 1785 to Mary Thompson, while still an apprentice whitesmith. He found work as a journeyman in a mechanic's shop in Stockton-on-Tees in 1787, before being recruited by John Marshall of Leeds in 1789 to make flax-spinning experiments. Marshall was working to improve a machine patented by Kendrew and Porthouse of Darlington, from whom he had bought a licence in 1788, and where he probably met Murray.

From 1790 Murray worked to equip Marshall's new factory in Holbeck, Leeds, with flax-spinning machinery. His first patent for 'spinning flax, cotton, silk etc.' was taken out in 1790; a second followed in 1793 for 'instruments and machines for spinning fibrous materials'. Murray's system of sponge weights and wet spinning of flax revolutionized the industry. Samuel Smiles thought that Murray's greatest achievements were in improving machinery for heckling and spinning flax, and the Society of Arts recognized this in 1809 by awarding him their gold medal for his heckling machine.

In 1793 Marshall bought a Boulton and Watt steam engine, of which Murray had charge, and to which he introduced some improvements. Murray left Marshall's employment in 1795, to set up in partnership with David Wood (1761–1820), whose background was similar to his own. The partners received some assistance from Marshall, built their factory next to his, and continued to supply most or all of his machinery. A fire destroyed Marshall's mill in 1796, and the subsequent rebuilding and re-equipping boosted their new enterprise. While Wood ran the flax-spinning machinery business, Murray was increasingly diverted into steam engines and other innovative work. He was renowned for the quality of his greensand casting technique. In 1797 he was already making steam engines, and his patent of 1799 listed several improvements, including the horizontal cylinder and self-acting damper. By then James Fenton (1754–1834) had joined the firm, investing further capital and acting as business manager.

As Murray continued to patent steam engine innovations, there developed a bitter rivalry with Boulton and Watt. Murray's patent of 1801, for improved air pumps and other innovations, and of 1802, for a self-contained compact engine with a new type of slide valve, were contested and overturned by the Birmingham firm. Murray had included too many improvements in each patent, losing all because some were not entirely original. He was forced to defend his reputation through press advertisements denying that all his ideas had come from Boulton and Watt. After this experience Murray rarely used patents.

Murray's famous Round Foundry, actually a fitting shop, was built in 1802. It was 81 feet in diameter and four storeys high, and was equipped with a 20 horsepower beam engine. A copy of this engine supplied to the Russian government earned Murray a gold medal. In the same year, Murray built for himself Steam Hall, an early centrally heated house. Fenton, Murray, and Wood then employed about 160 men in their works, although attempts to expand were frustrated by Boulton and Watt's agent buying up surrounding land.

Besides his skills as a mechanic and draughtsman, Murray was a talented organizer, successfully operating one of the first integrated engineering factories in the world. His firm began to export in 1804, notably to Sweden, and at the same time brought in William Lister (d. 1811), a sleeping partner, who invested considerable capital. Stimulated by Murray's inventiveness, the firm branched into millwork and machine tool manufacture, producing the first boring machine with a screw feed, and the first metal planer; the latter was apparently kept secret and was employed to produce flat surfaces for his slide valves.

Murray continued to design and construct beam engines, and by 1811 was working with Trevithick on a high-pressure engine subsequently fitted to a boat and successfully used on passenger service, an early application of steam to passenger traffic. In 1812 Murray built for the Middleton Railway in Leeds the first commercially successful steam locomotives, and achieved the first sustained demonstration of the utility of steam locomotion. His 4 horsepower engines ran on Blenkinsop's patent rack-rail, and remained in service until the 1830s. Murray also supplied an engine for a steam tug in Mississippi in 1815 or 1816. In his later years, Murray continued to work on machine tools, textile machinery and dyehouse plant, also patenting in 1814 a hydraulic press for packing cloth. He developed interests in marsh drainage, and gas- and waterworks, and worked as consulting engineer to factories, mines, and other industrial installations.

Murray died on 20 February 1826, and was buried at St Matthew's Church, Holbeck, his grave marked by a cast-iron obelisk. His personal estate, valued at £8000, was divided among three daughters and a son, with significant items, such as his mechanical books and drawings, control of his share of the business, and a diamond ring given by the empress of Russia, bequeathed to the family of his eldest child, Margaret Jackson. His only son died in obscurity in Russia, and the firm did not survive long under Murray's son-in-law, Richard Jackson, closing in 1842.

Murray was said to have been frank and open, with a genial temperament, and always accessible to his workmen. His enduring legacies were innovations in every branch of contemporary mechanical engineering, a pioneering role in developing the engineering factory, and the training of almost an entire generation of leading engineers in Leeds.

GILLIAN COOKSON

Sources T. Turner, 'History of Fenton, Murray and Wood', MScTech diss., University of Manchester, 1966 · E. K. Scott, ed., *Matthew Murray, pioneer engineer* (1928) · G. Cookson, 'Early textile engineers in Leeds, 1780–1850', *Publications of the Thoresby Society*, 2nd ser., 4 (1994), 40–61 · S. Smiles, *Industrial biography: iron-workers and tool-makers* (1863), 260–64 · W. G. Rimmer, *Marshalls of Leeds, flax-spinners, 1788–1886* (1960) · *DNB* · D. Cardwell, *The Fontana history of technology* (1994), 211, 219 · parish register (marriages), St Mary's Church, Gateshead

Archives U. Leeds, Brotherton L., E. K. Scott MSS

Likenesses watercolour drawing, repro. in Scott, ed., *Matthew Murray*, frontispiece; priv. coll.
Wealth at death £8000 personal estate: will, 1826, Borth. Inst., University of York, Ainsty

Murray, Maurice, earl of Strathearn (*d.* 1346), magnate, was probably the eldest son of Sir John Murray (*d. c.*1333) of Drumsargard in Lanarkshire, who supported Robert Bruce's seizure of the Scottish kingship as early as 1306. Maurice's mother is unknown, but by about 1320 Mary, daughter of Malise, seventh earl of Strathearn, was probably his stepmother, and her father at that time gave Maurice's father minor Tayside lands. Although he was a relatively unimportant noble, the second phase of Scotland's wars of independence gave Maurice the opportunity to enhance his local and national position by service to the Bruce cause. He may have been old enough to fight for the infant David II against Edward Balliol's English-backed invasion at Dupplin (1332) and Halidon Hill (1333). But he first appears on record, of age and in his father's lands, after David had taken refuge in France in May 1334, serving as sheriff of Lanark by October 1334 and supporting Andrew Murray (guardian for David II from 1335 to 1338) in his rejection of English peace terms at Berwick in August 1335. The Lanercost chronicler alleges that in 1335 Maurice killed Sir Godfrey Ros, the pro-Balliol sheriff of Ayr and Lanark, in revenge for Ros's murder of Maurice's (unnamed) brother. In fact Ros appears to have been alive in 1336, though Murray's ability to lead an armed following from Lanarkshire for the Bruce cause undoubtedly gave him standing there, so that the fifteenth-century chronicler Walter Bower styled him 'Lord of Clydesdale'.

In 1339 Murray led a division at the successful siege of Perth organized by Robert the Steward (guardian in 1338–41). But it was after David II's return from France in June 1341 that Murray's career took off and he became a royal favourite, useful both in recovering ground lost to English occupation and in acting as a restraint on the king's ostensible supporters who had increased their regional power in the king's absence, in particular Robert the Steward. In November 1341 Maurice helped his kinsman Sir William Murray of Tullibardine recover his lands from Sir William More of Abercorn, a kinsman of the Steward's wife. Among several royal grants to Maurice between 1341 and 1346 was custody of Stirling Castle in July 1342, shortly after its recovery in a siege whose success the chroniclers attribute to the Steward's leadership. In the same year David also gave Maurice the large baronies of Strathaven in Lanarkshire and Sprouston and Hawick in Roxburghshire. David no doubt looked to Murray to act as a counterweight to the regional influence of the Steward in Clydesdale and of William Douglas in Liddesdale and the border marches—the relations of both these men with the crown had rapidly deteriorated after 1341.

On 31 October 1343 David granted Murray and his male heirs the vacant earldom of Strathearn. Murray may have sought confirmation of his claim to this title in the right of his wife. Yet the grant surely prompted a challenge by the Steward (long-time lord of Methven and, by 1342, earl of neighbouring Atholl) and other lords with ambitions in central Scotland. In a tense parliament at Scone in June 1344 David had to direct a reassertion of the crown's effective forfeiture of Malise, eighth earl of Strathearn (who was represented there by his son-in-law William, earl of Ross); the Steward as guardian had originally seen Malise cleared of treason at a parliament at Perth in 1339, despite his surrender of his earldom to Edward Balliol. Strathearn was reconfirmed to Murray; in the same parliament he was named among the cautioners (securities) for the followers of the murdered Alexander Ramsay in their feud with Douglas of Liddesdale, whose cautioners included the Steward.

Murray was a regular royal charter witness and itinerant household retainer between 1341 and 1346. Towards the end of that period he was created a justiciar, perhaps north of the Forth, and he would undoubtedly have become a key figure in David II's regime had he not been killed, along with many of the king's closest supporters, in the battle of Nevilles Cross, outside Durham, on 17 October 1346; with David captured, the Steward fled the field and had secured Strathearn for himself by 1357.

Murray had a papal dispensation dated 10 July 1339 to marry Joanna Menteith (*d.* after 1364), widow successively of (remarkably) Malise, seventh earl of Strathearn (*d. c.*1325), for a time Murray's step-grandfather, and John Campbell, earl of Atholl (*d.* 1333), with whom Murray was related within the third degree. Murray is not recorded as having had legitimate issue, although he may have had a bastard, Maurice, to whom David granted lands near Edinburgh in 1358. His widow married William, earl of Sutherland (another royal favourite), in 1347. Their daughter, Joanna, married first Thomas Murray of Bothwell (*d.* 1361) and second, about 1362, Archibald Douglas, later lord of Bothwell and Galloway and third earl of Douglas; his possession of Drumsargard (but not of Hawick, Sprouston, Strathaven, and other lands) was briefly challenged by Maurice Murray's younger brother, Alexander.

MICHAEL A. PENMAN

Sources G. W. S. Barrow and others, eds., *Regesta regum Scottorum*, 6, ed. B. Webster (1982) · G. Burnett and others, eds., *The exchequer rolls of Scotland*, 1 (1878) · W. Bower, *Scotichronicon*, ed. D. E. R. Watt and others, new edn, 9 vols. (1987–98), vol. 7 · *Scots peerage*, vol. 8 · J. M. Thomson and others, eds., *Registrum magni sigilli regum Scotorum / The register of the great seal of Scotland*, 11 vols. (1882–1914), vol. 1 · J. M. Thomson, 'A roll of the Scottish parliament, 1344', *SHR*, 9 (1911–12), 235–40 · S. I. Boardman, *The early Stewart kings: Robert II and Robert III, 1371–1406* (1996) · J. Stevenson, ed., *Chronicon de Lanercost, 1201–1346*, Bannatyne Club, 65 (1839) · W. Fraser, ed., *The Red Book of Menteith*, 2 vols. (1880) · *The new statistical account of Scotland*, 6 (1845) · A. Theiner, *Vetera monumenta Hibernorum et Scotorum historiam illustrantia* (Rome, 1864) · J. A. Wilson, *A history of Cambuslang* (1929)

Murray, Mungo (*bap.* 1705, *d.* 1770), writer on shipbuilding, was born in Fowlis Wester, near Crieff, Perth, where he was baptized on 18 March 1705, the son of James Murray. Little is known of his early years. On 3 August 1733, also at Fowlis Wester, he married Margaret Gory. In 1738 he entered the naval dockyard at Deptford as a shipwright, having completed the customary seven-year apprenticeship at an unknown shipyard. It was in 1754 that his first book, *Treatise on Shipbuilding and Navigation*, was published. On the title page he describes himself as 'Shipwright in his Majesty's yard, Deptford' and in an advertisement it is stated that in the evenings, from six to eight, except Wednesdays and Saturdays, he taught 'the several branches of mathematics treated of in the book' and sold mathematical instruments (Murray, *Treatise*).

In May 1758 Murray was appointed to Lord Howe's ship, the *Magnanime*, then at Portsmouth. Ostensibly a midshipman, Murray was employed, it would seem, as a teacher of mathematics and navigation, and on 9 January 1760 he received a warrant as schoolmaster. In June 1762 he moved, with Howe, to the *Princess Amelia*, which was paid off at the peace. During his service in the *Magnanime*, which embraced the battle of Quiberon Bay, he published *The rudiments of navigation ... compiled for the use of young gentlemen on board the Magnanime* (1760). The dedication of this book is to Henry, earl of Gainsborough, the author having instructed him in 'the Principles of navigation'.

In 1764 Murray wrote a short note on an eclipse of the sun, which was printed in the *Philosophical Transactions* (vol. 54, 171). In the following year he issued a new and enlarged edition of his *Treatise on Shipbuilding*, and at some later date *Four prints (with references and explanations), exhibiting the different views of a sixty-gun ship*. On the title page Murray describes himself as carpenter of the *Weymouth*; another of his publications was *Forty Plates of Elevations, Sections, and Plans of Different Vessels* (1760?). He died on 19 October 1770. When in the *Magnanime* his wages were paid to Christian Murray, presumably his mother or daughter.

J. K. LAUGHTON, *rev.* PHILIP MACDOUGALL

Sources M. Murray, *Treatise on shipbuilding and navigation* (1754) · M. Murray, *The rudiments of navigation ... compiled for the use of young gentlemen on board the Magnanime* (1760) · Deptford royal dockyard description book, Sept 1748, PRO, ADM 106/2976 · muster book of HMS *Magnanime*, 1758, PRO, ADM 36/6107 · bap. reg. Scot. · m. reg. Scot.

Murray, Sir Oswyn Alexander Ruthven (1873–1936), Admiralty official, was born at Mill Hill, near London, on 17 August 1873, the fourth son and the fourth of the eleven children of Sir James Augustus Henry *Murray (1837–1915), then a schoolmaster and later first editor of the *Oxford English Dictionary*, and his second wife, Ada Agnes (1845–1936), daughter of George Ruthven, of Kendal. The family moved to Oxford in 1885, where Oswyn was educated at the Oxford high school as a day boy and from 1891 at Exeter College, Oxford, where he held a classical scholarship and was placed in the first class in classical moderations (1893), *literae humaniores* (1895), and jurisprudence (1896). In 1897 after the higher civil service competitive examination he was appointed to the Admiralty secretariat. Later in the year he won the Vinerian (law) scholarship but declined the offer of a resident fellowship in law at St John's College. As resident clerk at the Admiralty from 1898 until 1901 he became close to G. J. Goschen, then first lord, who made him his assistant private secretary; from 1901 to 1904 he served as private secretary to H. O. Arnold-

Forster and E. G. Pretyman, when they were parliamentary and financial secretaries. He became assistant principal clerk in 1904. On 1 August 1900 he married Mildred Octavia, who survived him, fourth daughter of the Revd Septimus March. They had a son and a daughter.

Murray's exceptional ability was recognized early and in October 1904 he was selected for the post of assistant director of victualling and clothing, and in 1905 became director. His obituary in *The Times* commented that from Murray's years in this department 'the lower deck will remember him with gratitude as the man who entirely reformed the feeding of the Navy' (*The Times*, 11 July 1936, 16). The standard ration was thoroughly overhauled, the savings system (of money taken in lieu of portions of the ration) abolished, a messing allowance introduced, the contract canteen arrangement placed on a sound footing, and a school of cookery established in the home ports— 'more progress than had been seen since Trafalgar' (ibid.). Murray's wife later wrote that in his reform of conditions Murray regarded the sailors 'as his big family' (Murray, 64).

Murray was brought back to the secretariat in 1911 as the assistant (or deputy) secretary of the Admiralty, and was actively concerned with the preparations for war as its likelihood increased, and then with the difficulties of administration during the conflict. In 1917 Sir Eric Geddes was made first lord of the Admiralty, with a brief to reform its management. He appointed Murray as permanent secretary on 7 August 1917, in place of Sir Graham Greene who was transferred to the Ministry of Munitions. Murray ultimately became 'probably the ablest secretary of the Admiralty in modern times' (Marder, 4.216). Extremely talented in administration and in dealing with the intricate budgetary and other manoeuvring necessary with bureaucracy, Murray managed both to preserve much of the resources of the navy at a time of severe government cost-cutting and to make many needed reforms. Admiral Sir William Fisher referred to him as the 'great man who did more for the navy in his time than, perhaps, anyone else' (Murray, v). Negotiating the navy estimates occupied much of Murray's time during each year, but he was so successful in this that the navy was in a much more powerful position when war broke out again in 1939 than it might have been had the position not been 'held by a man of such high ability as Murray' (Roskill, 1.209).

A reserved man, but one with an almost 'boyish simplicity ... [which] gave him a directness and certainty in dealing with complicated problems' (*The Times*, 11 July 1936, 16), Murray's main outside interest was research in Devon family history, in which he became a recognized authority. He was appointed CB in 1910, KCB in 1917, and GCB in 1931, and was elected an honorary fellow of Exeter College in 1919. He died at his home, Annery, Akehurst Street, Roehampton, London, on 10 July 1936, and was cremated at Golders Green, Middlesex, on 14 July.

V. W. BADDELEY, *rev.* MARC BRODIE

Sources M. O. Murray, *The making of a civil servant* (1940) · *The Times* (11 July 1936) · A. J. Marder, *From the Dreadnought to Scapa Flow: the Royal Navy in the Fisher era, 1904–1919*, 5 vols. (1961–70) · N. A. M.

Rodger, *The admiralty* (1979) · S. W. Roskill, *Naval policy between the wars*, 2 vols. (1968–76) · J. Foster, *Oxford men, 1880–1892: with a record of their schools, honours, and degrees* (1893) · K. M. E. Murray, *Caught in the web of words: James A. H. Murray and the 'Oxford English dictionary'* (1977) · *CGPLA Eng. & Wales* (1936) · personal knowledge (1949)

Archives Exeter Central Library, west country studies library, corresp. relating to Devon genealogy | PRO, letters to Sir Vincent Baddeley, ADM 225

Likenesses W. Stoneman, photographs, 1920, NPG · photograph, repro. in Rodger, *Admiralty*, following p. 148 · photographs, repro. in Murray, *Making of a civil servant*

Wealth at death £7887 14*s*.: probate, 12 Aug 1936, *CGPLA Eng. & Wales*

Murray, Patrick, fifth Lord Elibank (1703–1778), literary patron, was born on 27 February 1703, the son of Alexander Murray, fourth Lord Elibank (1677–1736), and his wife, Elizabeth (*d.* 1756), daughter of George Stirling of Keir. Admitted to the Faculty of Advocates in 1722, Murray opted for a military career. He rose to the rank of lieutenant-colonel and participated in the siege of Carthagena in 1740. He retired from the army on 10 March 1742.

In 1735 Murray married Maria Margaretta (1693?–1762), daughter of Cornelius de Jonge d'Ellemeet of Holland, and the wealthy widow of William, Lord North and Grey. Elibank had no legitimate issue, but did father at least five natural sons. He succeeded his father as Lord Elibank in 1736.

A tory in politics, Elibank was at times suspected of Jacobitism. He avoided overt participation in the Jacobite rising of 1745 and in later life regarded with approval those who showed a conciliatory attitude toward former rebels. (A brother, Alexander *Murray of Elibank, lent his name to the 'Elibank plot' of 1750–52 and was created earl of Westminster by the Pretender in 1759.)

In the 1750s Elibank became a significant figure in Scottish cultural life. A member of the Select Society, he was intimately associated with the Edinburgh literati though publishing only four pamphlets himself. John Ramsay of Ochtertyre noted that while Elibank was 'too lazy to be an author, few men were better qualified to co-operate with them' and that Elibank, Lord Kames, and David Hume constituted 'a literary triumvirate, from whose judgment … there was no appeal' (*Scotland and Scotsmen*, 1.318–19). He was an early patron of William Robertson and John Home, both of whom were at one time ministers of country parishes near his seat at Ballencrieff in Haddingtonshire.

Elibank's contemporary reputation derived largely from the impact of personal contact. Boswell described him as 'a man of great genius, great knowledge, and much whim' (*London Journal*, 50–51) and Samuel Johnson, who visited Elibank on his 1773 trip to Scotland, wrote: 'I never met [Elibank] without going away a wiser man' (Chapman, 278). He delighted in arguing unconventional viewpoints and paradoxes, and possessed a broad range of intellectual interests.

Often taking up causes that promoted Scottish national pride and equality within the union, Elibank was deeply involved during the Seven Years' War in the unsuccessful campaign to establish a Scottish militia. He was also among those who encouraged James Macpherson in his Ossian 'translations'. Both efforts reflected a vision of Scots as a warrior race with a heritage as worthy as that of the English. He pursued a variety of economic interests, subscribing to the Firth and Clyde Canal and holding a partnership in a Dumfries bank. He was also an East India Company proprietor and recipient of a West Florida grant of 20,000 acres from his nephew, Governor George Johnstone.

Elibank added his voice to those who objected to ministerial interference in peers' elections. His own hope of winning a seat in the upper house was damaged in 1763 by publication of a purported letter from the Pretender in Wilkes's *North Briton* extolling Elibank's contributions to the Jacobite cause. When in 1771 the government proposed Lord Dysart, an Englishman with a Scottish title, to fill a vacancy, Elibank joined several Scottish peers in protesting against his candidacy, writing a pamphlet in favour of free elections of representative peers. The ministry dropped Dysart's candidacy, though sustaining little long-term damage to its dominance of peers' elections.

Elibank died at Ballencrieff on 3 August 1778. Ultimately Elibank left a stronger impression on his contemporaries than on the course of events, perhaps meriting John Ramsay's lament: 'What a pity that so much genius and knowledge should have evaporated chiefly in talk' (*Scotland and Scotsmen*, 1.320).   WILLIAM C. LOWE

Sources *Scotland and Scotsmen in the eighteenth century: from the MSS of John Ramsay, esq., of Ochtertyre*, ed. A. Allardyce, 2 vols. (1888) · *Autobiography of the Rev. Dr. Alexander Carlyle … containing memorials of the men and events of his time*, ed. J. H. Burton (1860); repr. as *Anecdotes and characters of the times*, ed. J. Kinsley (1973) · R. B. Sher, *Church and university in the Scottish Enlightenment: the moderate literati of Edinburgh* (1985) · J. Robertson, *The Scottish Enlightenment and the militia issue* (1985) · *Johnson's Journey to the western islands of Scotland*, ed. R. W. Chapman (1924) · *Boswell's London journal, 1762–63*, ed. F. A. Pottle (1950), vol. 1 of *The Yale editions of the private papers of James Boswell*, trade edn (1950–89) · *Scots peerage*, vol. 3 · J. Boswell, *The life of Samuel Johnson*, 2 vols. (1791) · R. F. A. Fabel, *Bombast and broadsides: the lives of George Johnstone* (1987) · R. L. Emerson, 'The social composition of Enlightened Edinburgh: the Select Society of Edinburgh, 1754–1764', *Studies on Voltaire and the Eighteenth Century*, 114 (1973), 291–329 · [P. Murray and Lord Elibank], *Considerations on the present state of the peerage of Scotland; addressed to his grace, the Duke of Buccleugh, by a peer of Scotland* (1771) · *DNB* · A. C. Murray, *The five sons of 'Bare Betty'* (1936)

Archives NA Scot., corresp. and papers | Hunt. L., letters to Sir William Pulteney

Likenesses portrait, repro. in A. C. Murray, *Five sons of 'Bare Betty'*, facing p. 26

Wealth at death estates in Berwickshire and East Lothian, assessed for land tax at £4053 19*s*. 7*d*. (Scots), based on 1650s valuations; apparently fifteenth largest assessment in East Lothian (£2567): L. R. Timperly, ed., *A directory of landownership in Scotland c.1770* (1976), 85, 120, 122

Murray, Patrick Aloysius (1811–1882), theologian, was born at Clones, co. Monaghan, on 18 November 1811. He entered the Roman Catholic seminary at Maynooth on 25 August 1829 and, having been ordained for the diocese of Clogher in 1837, returned to the college in 1838 as professor of English and French literature. In 1841 he was appointed to the chair of theology, and held the post for forty-one years. Nearly two thousand future priests passed through his classes. His weighty *Tractatus de ecclesia Christi* (3 vols., 1860–66) became, in its compendium edition, a standard seminary manual. Other works included *Sponsa mater et Christi* (1858), a poem, and Murray was also a frequent contributor to the *Dublin Review*, for which he wrote articles on subjects ranging from Thomas Hood's poetry to the First Vatican Council.

Murray was a formidable figure. On Thomas Carlyle, visiting Dublin in 1849, he left the impression of 'a big, burly mass of Catholic Irishism … head cropped like stubble, red-skinned face, hard grey Irish eyes; full of fiery Irish zeal, too, and rage—a man of considerable strength, not to be loved by any manner of means' (Carlyle, 53). A less prejudiced observer, his pupil Walter MacDonald, remembered him as 'more ultramontane than the Pope, … a bigot, if ever there was one … but a holy man' (MacDonald, 55–6). He died at St Patrick's College, Maynooth, on 15 November 1882, and was buried within its precincts. His diary of 1863–82, preserved at the college, throws some light on the confrontation between its teaching staff and Cardinal Cullen.   G. MARTIN MURPHY

Sources DNB · *Freeman's Journal* [Dublin] (17 Nov 1882) · P. J. Corish, *Maynooth College, 1795–1995* (1995) · W. MacDonald, *Reminiscences of a Maynooth professor* (1926), 55–6, 81–2 · T. Carlyle, *Reminiscences of my Irish journey in 1849* (1882), 53 · P. J. Corish, 'Gallicanism at Maynooth: Archbishop Cullen and the royal visitation of 1853', *Studies in Irish history presented to R. Dudley Edwards*, ed. A. Cosgrove and D. McCartney (1979), 176–89 · W. J. Fitzpatrick, *Memories of Father Healy of Little Bray* (1904), 11, 26–8 · *Wellesley index*
Archives NRA, priv. coll., diaries · St Patrick's College, Maynooth, diary
Wealth at death £777 4s. 6d.: administration, 14 June 1883, CGPLA Ire.

Murray, Sir (Francis) Ralph Hay (1908–1983), radio broadcaster and diplomatist, was born at the rectory in Partney, Lincolnshire, on 3 March 1908, the elder son and second of three surviving children of the Revd Charles Hay Murray (1869–1923), a high-church Anglican clergyman, and his wife, Mabel (1869–1953), eldest daughter of Samuel Charles Umfreville, of Ingress Abbey, Greenhithe. Through his father he was descended from John Murray, third duke of Atholl. He was educated at Brentwood School, Essex (1922–7), where he was head boy, before studying modern languages at St Edmund Hall, Oxford, with an open exhibition in French. After graduating with a second-class degree in 1930, he held a Laming fellowship—connected to Queen's College, Oxford—which enabled him to continue his language learning in Berlin, Madrid, Budapest, and Vienna. While in Vienna he met Countess Mauricette Vladimira Marie von Küenburg (1906–1996), only child of Count Bernhard von Küenburg (d. 1918), secretary to Emperor Franz Josef's cabinet. They married in Payerbach, Austria, on 10 April 1935, and had four children, Ingram (b. 1937), Nicholas (b. 1939), Georgina (b. 1942), and Simon (b. 1948).

In 1933 Murray passed the consular service exam but he turned down an appointment in Peking owing to the uncertain health of his mother. A short stint writing for a Bristol newspaper followed, before he joined the BBC's news section in 1934. The BBC was then undergoing a transformation in its news methods. Instead of relying upon agency wire sources, it was branching out into its own news-gathering. Murray was one of the young turks who led the way, initially as a sub-editor and from 1935 as a reporter in the news talks department. Commentary-style features—previously the preserve of newspapers—became the norm. Murray gave one of the BBC's earliest outside broadcasts, reporting on the Crystal Palace fire in 1936. Towards the end of the year he was appointed BBC foreign correspondent at the League of Nations and his lucid descriptions of the Geneva scene were fed directly into news bulletins. He also provided eyewitness reports of Germany's *Anschluss* with Austria in March 1938 and was one of the first journalists to travel through the Sudetenland after the Munich agreement of September 1938.

Early in 1939 Murray was earmarked for a position in Electra House, a covert propaganda organization established by Campbell Stuart in April that year. It was named after its London Embankment address, the headquarters of Cable & Wireless. Murray became a full-time member at the outbreak of the Second World War when it relocated to Woburn Abbey in Bedfordshire. His official accreditation, however, was with the Foreign Office. He was responsible for running the studio at Wavendon, near Woburn, which prepared 'black' propaganda for transmission from the nearby MI6 station at Whaddon Hall. The broadcasts included material by German refugees that emphasized the corrupt and unstable nature of the Nazi regime: dirty jokes and scandalous stories were interspersed between popular dance tunes. Before June 1940 the target audience was the German public but after the fall of France this shifted to resistance movements in occupied countries. In July 1940 Electra House became the propaganda arm of the Special Operations Executive (SOE) and over the next year Murray worked closely with Ivone Kirkpatrick of the Foreign Office and Hugh Carleton Greene, the controller of German broadcasts at the BBC, preparing 'black' radio shows.

From July 1941 SOE's tactics shifted to sabotage and dirty tricks, prompting its propaganda specialists to be subsumed within the Foreign Office's political warfare department, renamed the political warfare executive (PWE) in March 1942. Murray consequently moved to Bush House in London where he pushed for the construction of a powerful radio transmitter, Aspidistra, in Ashdown Forest (necessary to overcome German jamming), which became operational from October 1942. His next assignment—which he had taken up by the beginning of 1943—was as the PWE representative to the Greek government in exile, based in Cairo. One aspect of his role was advising on the best methods for offsetting the influence of communist partisans. In July he joined the allied invasion force in Sicily as part of its political warfare division and stayed on for the Italian mainland campaign. As the war drew to a close in Italy, he raced ahead to Vienna and helped establish a British presence for the allies.

On 1 May 1945, a day after Hitler's suicide, Murray was

appointed assistant secretary in the Allied Control Commission for Germany and Austria. The position kept him in Vienna in a public relations capacity—at the cutting edge of the developing cold war with the Soviet Union. He was transferred in April 1946 to a similar publicity role at the office of the special commissioner in south-east Asia, based at Singapore. His remit was to gain the support of the different populations, and particularly their fractious authorities, so that recovery programmes could be instigated.

By July 1947 Murray's politico-media expertise was required back in London. Soviet propaganda was criticizing Britain's international policies, while also undermining the cohesiveness of the Labour government. At the behest of Ernest Bevin a new department within the Foreign Office was established to provide material for counter-attacks. Murray helped set it up and he also gave it a suitably discreet name, the information research department (IRD), becoming its first head on 25 February 1948. By August the staff had risen from three to fifteen, but it was still too small to do the work required, especially after the start of the Berlin blockade in June. Additional specialists were therefore appointed and, at Murray's instigation, the mounting costs of the department were shifted to the secret vote. He was promoted to counsellor in November 1948. His immediate priorities in 1948–9 were to counter communist electoral successes in Italy and France but the IRD's efforts spread far and wide. The central task was to prepare briefs and articles for planting in news media in countries vulnerable to Soviet subversion. Prominent intellectuals were commissioned to write pieces, among them Stephen Spender, George Orwell, Bertrand Russell, and Malcolm Muggeridge. Two complementary themes were deployed: the first emphasized the positive features of British and Western life, while the second highlighted the ruthless aspects of Soviet dictatorship. Murray was made a CMG in 1950.

Experience in dealing with dictators was Murray's main qualification for his first diplomatic posting overseas—as counsellor at the Madrid embassy from May 1951 to April 1954. Franco's Spain was just emerging from international isolation, having been barred from joining the United Nations until 1950 on account of its wartime neutrality and fascistic political system. However, the country was now being viewed as an important cold war ally. A Gibraltar crisis temporarily upset what was otherwise a smooth transition for Spain's rehabilitation, with Murray acting as chargé d'affaires in 1952 and 1953.

In April 1954 Murray was appointed minister at the Cairo embassy. That summer an agreement was concluded with Nasser's military regime which brought about a phased British withdrawal from the Suez base by June 1956. However, London's hopes that friendlier relations might ensue proved unwarranted, and by March 1956 Anthony Eden was intent on removing Nasser from power. Murray played a pivotal role in the covert operation aimed at doing this (which was code-named Omega and also involved the CIA). 'Black' radio broadcasts sought to isolate Nasser in Egypt and across the Middle East. But before Omega had a chance to work, Nasser nationalized the Suez Canal Company in July, after which Eden preferred a quick military solution. Murray's responsibilities shifted as a consequence. He had been helping to co-ordinate Omega from London when the crisis broke and he remained there to help with the invasion preparations. As the senior Foreign Office representative on the interdepartmental Egypt official committee, he oversaw the search for an alternative government in Egypt. He worked closely with MI6 as it contacted prominent Egyptian figures with the aim of creating a multi-party alternative government. One such person was General Muhammad Neguib, the figurehead of the junta at the time of the *coup d'état* in 1952, who had since fallen out with Nasser. From August onwards Britain's 'black' broadcasts to Egypt called upon the Egyptian people to return 'honest General Neguib' to public life.

Murray's insightful work resulted in his appointment (on 19 September 1956) as political adviser to the allied commander-in-chief, General Keightley, to take effect at the start of the invasion. With the onset of the Suez War at the end of October, he accompanied Britain's senior military officers in the landings at Port Said. Eden's premature cease-fire on 5 November frustrated him, not least because the Anglo-French forces were on the verge of capturing the canal. His attitude was that, having gone in, Britain should not have stopped. By nature a very discreet man, this was one of the few incidents about which he spoke frankly with his family. In 1957 he was made a CB, a decoration not usually awarded to foreign service officers, for his work on the Suez operation.

The post-Suez break in Anglo-Egyptian relations meant that Murray required a new posting, and in May 1957 he was appointed assistant under-secretary of state in the Foreign Office. His remit was to oversee policy towards the Soviet Union and he accompanied Harold Macmillan on his visit to Khrushchov in February 1959. Another Foreign Office promotion followed in 1961, when he became deputy under-secretary of state with a responsibility for 'information work'. He was made a KCMG in 1962 before being appointed ambassador to Greece in February that year. He remained there until July 1967, having had to deal with the colonels' *coup* of April that year.

After retiring from the foreign service Murray served as director of several companies connected with shipping, political consultancy, and oil exploration, as well as being a BBC governor between 1967 and 1973. He was translating a history of modern Greece by former Greek prime minister Spyridon Markezinis, a friend from his time in Athens, when he died on 11 September 1983 at his home, 3 Whaddon Hall Mews, Whaddon, Buckinghamshire. He was buried in Stoke Hammond churchyard, and was survived by his wife and their four children.

Murray was a public servant at a time when the British state was responding to the age of mass communications. As a BBC correspondent in the 1930s, his precise accounts and patrician accent helped define the tone of broadcasting, while his reports from Europe demonstrated the value of journalism for propaganda purposes. During the

Second World War he was co-opted into the secret areas of the state, where he developed an expertise in psychological warfare. After 1945 the cold war led Murray to help shape Britain's policies in the global struggle for hearts and minds. His natural reserve and downcast demeanour—dominated by sad-looking eyes surrounded by dark circles—made him well suited to this clandestine world.

MICHAEL T. THORNHILL

Sources A. Briggs, *The history of broadcasting in the United Kingdom*, rev. edn, 2 (1995) · M. Balfour, *Propaganda in war, 1939–45* (1979) · D. Garnett, *The secret history of PWE, 1939–46* (2002) · E. Howe, *The black game* (1982) · D. Lerner, *Psychological warfare against Nazi Germany* (1971) · 'IRD origins and the establishment of the foreign office information research department, 1946–48', *History notes, Foreign and commonwealth office general services command* (1995) · M. T. Thornhill, 'Alternatives to Nasser', *Contemporary British History*, 13/2 (summer 1999), 11–28 · D. Wright, *Old Brentwoodian Society Chronicle* (April 1984) · D. Wright, 'OB headed anti-Soviet campaign', *Old Brentwoodian Society Chronicle* (Oct 1995) · *WWW* · Burke, *Peerage* · FO List (1960) · will · *CGPLA Eng. & Wales* (1984) · private information (2004) [Ingram Murray, eldest son]
Archives BBC WAC, papers · PRO, FO 1110/1–165; FO 371 | SOUND BBC NSA, documentary recordings, news reports
Likenesses photograph, 1945, Gov. Art Coll. · photograph, 1954, repro. in E. Shuckburgh, *Descent to Suez* (1986)
Wealth at death £70,689: probate, 11 Sept 1984, *CGPLA Eng. & Wales*

Murray, Sir Robert. See Moray, Sir Robert (1608/9?–1673).

Murray, Robert (*bap.* 1633, *d.* 1725?), financier and writer on trade, was born in the Strand, London, and baptized on 12 December 1633, the son of Robert Murray, a Scot, a citizen and tailor of London, and his English wife. Entered as an apprentice in the books of the Clothworkers' Company on 29 January 1650, he took up his freedom on 6 March 1661. In 1676 he published a proposal for a lumbard, a bank which extended credit on the security of goods deposited in warehouses. Aubrey suggests that Murray did indeed establish a 'banke of credit' at Devonshire House in Bishopsgate, London, but little else is known of its operation (*Brief Lives*, 2.91). Israel Tonge's methods for teaching children to write by writing in black ink over engravings of letters in red ink was continued after his death in 1680 by Murray who engraved 'severall plates printed-off in red letters, by which meanes boyes learne (to admiration)' (ibid., 2.262).

On 27 March 1680 Murray and William Dockwra opened the offices of the penny post, established, according to an early advertisement in *Smith's Current Intelligence*, 'for Conveying letters to any part of the City, or Suburbs, for a penny a letter' (Todd, 18). Hugh Chamberlen and probably Henry Neville Payne were also involved in the undertaking in its early stages. Whether Murray should be given sole credit for inventing the post was debated by contemporaries and the debate has continued among historians. The partnership with Dockwra probably ended when the privy council issued a warrant for Murray's arrest on 25 May 1680 and he was accused of having induced a hawker to sell seditious materials, including an appeal supporting Monmouth's claim to the throne. By September of the following year Murray was working as an agent for Lord Shaftesbury and went to France on his account. It is not known what happened to Murray when Shaftesbury went into hiding and fled a year later.

Dockwra claimed that he 'often bayl'd him [Murray] to keep him out of prison'; ironically Murray advertised a debt-collecting agency in 1682 (Todd, 26). Also in that year Murray, in association with Chamberlen, proposed a number of revenue-raising schemes to the corporation of London and in an agreement dated 29 August the projectors were promised a third of the profits arising from their proposals. The most significant of these was for a bank of credit, which accepted both subscriptions of money and deposits of goods. Arrangements were made for subscriptions from the mayor and common councilmen to establish the office, and although some members of the corporation were persuaded to subscribe to the bank, the scheme foundered. Aubrey's suggestion that Murray was 'clarke to the generall company for the revenue of Ireland, and afterwards clark to the committee of the grand excise of England' (*Brief Lives*, 2.91) has been questioned. Robert Murray may have been the Murray who was the register of hackney coaches in November 1687 against whom many objections were made.

In 1690 Murray, again with Chamberlen, petitioned for exclusive rights to establish a penny post in the provinces. During the 1690s he proposed a number of other trade and financial schemes, some of which were published, including proposals for an exchequer credit, a national land bank, modelled on the bank of Amsterdam, and a scheme to secure wool against exportation. In order to raise more money for the war against France he suggested transferring the excise duty on malt drinks to malt. In August 1697 William Lowndes at the Treasury was approached to compensate Murray for his proposals to parliament; Murray had been 'in custody in a sponging house for a month' (Redington, *Calendar of Treasury Papers, 1697–1701–2*, 80). Murray offered the lord high treasurer a 'scheme for tin' in January 1704 (Redington, *Calendar of Treasury Papers, 1702–1707*, 226). A Robert Murray was paymaster of the lottery in July 1720 (the lottery itself had been suspended in 1714, but the post remained), and was involved in the proposal to discharge the unsubscribed orders into the capital stock of the South Sea Company. Aubrey gives his death date as probably 1725, and by 1726 he was being referred to as the late Robert Murray, esquire. There is, however, some doubt about whether this is the same Robert Murray who established the penny post (Todd, 27). His will has not been traced.

NATASHA GLAISYER

Sources T. Todd, *William Dockwra and the rest of the undertakers* (1952) · J. K. Horsefield, *British monetary experiments, 1650–1710* (1960) · R. D. Richards, 'Early English banking schemes', *Journal of Economic and Business History*, 1 (1928), 36–76 · J. R. Kellett, 'Some late seventeenth-century schemes for the improvement of the corporation of London's revenue', *Guildhall Miscellany*, 1/9 (1958), 27–34 · *Brief lives, chiefly of contemporaries, set down by John Aubrey, between the years 1669 and 1696*, ed. A. Clark, 2 (1898) · private information (2004) [D. E. Wickham, Clothworkers' Company] · W. R. Scott, *The constitution and finance of English, Scottish and Irish joint-stock companies to 1720*, 3 (1911) · J. Redington, ed., *Calendar of Treasury papers*, 2, PRO (1871) · J. Redington, ed., *Calendar of Treasury papers*, 3, PRO (1874) ·

J. Redington, ed., *Calendar of Treasury papers*, 6, PRO (1889) · W. A. Shaw, ed., *Calendar of treasury books*, 10/2, PRO (1935)

Murray, Ruby Florence Campbell (1935–1996), singer, was born on 29 March 1935 at 84 Moltke Street, Donegal Road, Belfast, the youngest of four children of Daniel Murray (*d.* 1969?), a labourer, originally from Scotland, and Wilhelmina (Winifred) Murray, *née* Connolly (*d.* 1989). She was named after a 20-stone local comedienne and chip shop assistant but in her pomp became as much part of the mythology of Belfast as George Best and Harland and Wolff. Furthermore she has achieved immortality in British folklore, as 'a Ruby Murray' has evolved as rhyming slang for 'a curry'.

Murray left school in Fane Street aged fourteen and worked in several teenage deadbeat jobs. Her ambition to be a singer, however, was fired at the age of four when she was taken to see G. H. Elliott, the music-hall entertainer known as the 'chocolate coloured coon'. Against a background of strict laws regarding child performers, she began singing solo aged ten on various stages—large, small, and makeshift—throughout Ireland and Britain. Four years after her professional début at the age of twelve, she joined the cast of a touring revue, *Yankee Doodle Blarney*. Playing at the Metropolitan Theatre in London's Edgware Road she was spotted again by producer Richard Afton, who had been responsible for her pre-teen Irish television appearances. He signed her to succeed Joan Regan as resident singer in the television series *Quite Contrary* and two days later she made a record—'Getwell Soon'—for conductor Ray Martin's Columbia Records, but it made little impression. Her second release at the beginning of 1955 was 'Heartbeat', the success of which led her to take the pop world by storm, her massive popularity making her one of the most successful stars in the history of British popular music. In November of that year she was voted favourite female vocalist by readers of *New Musical Express*, receiving 1000 more votes than Alma Cogan and twelve times as many as Petula Clark.

With an immediately recognizable voice, intimately husky, gentle, and soothing, Ruby Murray's simple style disguised skilful phrasing coupled with a freshness and an appearance of vulnerability and innocence. Once she had five records simultaneously in the top twenty, the accolade list of the 1950s, and her total of eighty weeks in the music charts was surpassed by no other female artist until Madonna in 1985. She earned the sobriquet 'Heartbeat Girl' after her first hit, but perhaps her indelible signature tune was 'Softly, Softly', a wistful love ballad sung with an Irish lilt and trademark involuntary catch in the throat. During a hectic period in the mid-1950s she starred with Norman Wisdom in *Painting the Town* at the London Palladium, had her own television show and, proving she could dance as well as sing, topped the bill in variety and pantomime, performing also overseas wherever British troops were based. She had a mixed reception in the United States, sometimes mobbed by hysterical crowds and warmly commended by Frank Sinatra, but booed in a Chicago club for refusing to sing Irish rebel songs. She sang the theme song to a rather limp comic film *It's Great to be Young* (1956) but in the same year gave a refreshing and totally natural performance as a singing chambermaid in the film *A Touch of the Sun*, starring Frankie Howerd.

On 23 August 1957 Ruby Murray married Bernard Burgess (*b.* 1929?), a member of the Jones Boys harmony group. They had a son and a daughter. She enjoyed further modest hits in the UK in 1959 and 1970, and continued to tour at home and abroad—notably in Africa—but never recaptured the success that she had enjoyed in the mid-1950s. Her increasing dependence on alcohol and valium put both her career and her marriage under strain; the latter was further undermined by her infatuation with the comedian Frank Carson, which made her rendition of 'I'll Walk the Rest of the Way'—a song about an extramarital affair—seem bleakly autobiographical. She and Burgess were eventually divorced in 1977; thereafter she lived with Ray Lamar, a theatrical impresario, and they married in 1993.

Always fondly remembered by many, Ruby Murray was greeted with a standing ovation when she appeared with a host of other stars in the *Forty Years of Peace* concert programme (1985). Yet four years earlier she had been fined for drunk and disorderly conduct in Torquay and her final London appearance in March 1993 revealed a frail and uncertain performer. She died of bronchial pneumonia and liver cancer in Torbay Hospital on 17 December 1996. Her obituary in the *Irish News* (18 Dec 1996) stressed that 'her memory will remain a potent force in the lives of many, particularly in Northern Ireland' but her background had left her ill-equipped to cope with the pressures of stardom and with increasing adversity. A bittersweet tale of triumph and transformation is told in the play *Ruby* by Marie Jones, performed in April 2000, recalling 1950s Belfast when, for a time, she had held the world in her hands.   GORDON PHILLIPS

Sources J. Moules, *Softly, softly: the tears behind the triumphs of Ruby Murray* (1995) · C. Larkin, *The Virgin encyclopedia of fifties music* (1998) · *Daily Telegraph* (18 Dec 1996) · *The Independent* (18 Dec 1996) · *The Times* (18 Dec 1996) · *Modern Irish lives: dictionary of 20th century biography* (1996) · *Encyclopedia of popular music* (1989–98) · *Guinness book of British hit singles* (1998) · *Irish News* (18 Dec 1996) · *Irish Times* (18 Dec 1996) · www.rubymurray.org, Nov 2001 · b. cert.
Likenesses F. Wood, oils, *c.*1955, priv. coll. · photographs, 1955–8, Hult. Arch. · portraits, priv. coll.

Murray [*née* Maese; *other married name* Aust], **Sarah** (1744–1811), travel writer, is of unknown parentage. It has been suggested that she may have been the Sarah Maese who ran a girls' school in Beaufort Square, Bath, in the 1760s and published *The School: being a Series of Letters, between a Young Lady and her Mother* in 1766 but there is no conclusive evidence and no record of the school has survived. A letter exists which may link Sarah Maese to the bluestocking Elizabeth Montagu (Montagu letters) but this link remains unproven. She married her first husband, the Hon. William Murray (1734–1786), a naval officer, brother of the earl of Dunmore, by special licence on 11 August 1783. From 1782 to 1793 she lived at 23 Kensington Square, Kensington, London. She then moved to 19 Kensington Square and while living there, in 1802, she married again. George

Aust (*d.* 1829), her second husband, served as under-secretary of state for foreign affairs from 1790 until 1796 and as secretary and registrar of Chelsea Royal Hospital. She remained at 19 Kensington Square until 1806, when she and George Aust moved to Noel House on the site of Palace Gate; there George had built a new house for which Sarah laid out the grounds.

In May 1796 Sarah Murray began a five-month tour of Scotland with the specific aim of writing a guidebook. Travelling by carriage with a maid and manservant, Murray set out to 'see every thing worth seeing' (Murray, 43). *A companion, and useful guide to the beauties of Scotland, to the lakes of Westmoreland, Cumberland, and Lancashire* was published in 1799. As well as giving a full description of Murray's own travels, the book provided specific information about inns, horses, road conditions, prices, equipment, and mileages. Reviews of the book appeared in the *British Critic* (October 1799) and the *Monthly Review* (April 1800). It was well received by the critics, who considered its detailed practical information to be of particular interest. They also expressed their admiration for Murray's intrepidness, although the *Monthly Review* commented 'that she rather over-rates the difficulties and dangers which it was necessary to encounter, before a perfect view of the country could be obtained' (p. 404).

Until the 1790s no guidebooks were available to guide the English tourist in his or her own travels around the highlands. Earlier travellers had relied on human guides, often Gaelic-speaking, together with descriptions by those few who had gone before, such as Martin Martin and Thomas Pennant. Murray's *Companion, and Useful Guide to the Beauties of Scotland*, although not the first guidebook, was certainly one of the earliest to be published.

Murray depicted herself as a model for 'adventurers, who may follow my steps' (Murray, vii), and her frequent inclusion of advice aimed specifically at women made it evident that she expected both women and men to read and follow her. She demanded considerable physical courage and fitness from her followers sending them up mountains, into boats, and across rickety foot-bridges, and advising them to 'creep' to the foot of waterfalls, 'skip' from rock to rock in fast-moving rivers, and 'scramble' up and down difficult ascents and descents. They were also expected to tolerate the discomfort of bad inns, all for the sake of beauty.

Murray frequently claimed to be a true 'lover of nature' (Murray, 111) whose enthusiasm for the landscape made her oblivious of hazards. The book is replete with descriptions of Murray, a widow of fifty-two at the time of the trip, engaged in adventurous and physically demanding travel.

A second series of journeys resulted in the 1803 publication of *A companion and useful guide to the beauties in the western highlands of Scotland, and in the Hebrides. To which is added, a description of part of the main land of Scotland, and of the Isles of Mull, Ulva, Staffa, I-Columbkill, Tirii, Coll, Eigg, Skye, Raza, and Scalpa*. During one of these journeys, in 1801, she became the first woman to ascend one of the Cairngorms, a feat she carried out on horseback. This new volume was

reviewed in the *Annual Review* (1803), *Monthly Review* (February 1804), and *British Critic* (June 1804). Although the reviews were a little less favourable than the previous set, a second edition of both volumes was published in 1805. In 1810 Murray published a combined and updated edition of the two guidebooks under the name 'The Hon. Mrs. Murray Aust'.

Sarah Aust died childless on 5 November 1811 at Noel House and was buried on 11 November 1811 with William Murray, her first husband, in St Mary Abbots Church, Kensington. A marble tablet to her memory was erected within the church by George Aust, her second husband.

ELIZABETH HAGGLUND

Sources T. Faulkner, *History and antiquities of Kensington* (1820) · H. Hobhouse, ed., *Southern Kensington: Kensington Square to Earl's Court*, Survey of London, 42 (1986) · *The museums area of South Kensington and Westminster*, Survey of London, 38 (1975) · parish register, Kensington, St Mary Abbots · *Scots peerage*, vol. 2 · *DNB* · *GM*, 1st ser., 57 (1787), 90 · *GM*, 1st ser., 81/2 (1811), 586 · E. Hagglund, 'Tourists and travellers: women's nonfictional writing about Scotland, 1770–1830', PhD diss., U. Birm., 2000 · Elizabeth Montagu to Sarah Scott, Hunt. L., Montagu letters, MO5821 · A. Ponsonby, *Records of Kensington Square* (1986) · I. Mitchell, *Scotland's mountains before the mountaineers* (1988) · J. M. Collinge, ed., *Office-holders in modern Britain, 8: Foreign office officials, 1782–1870* (1979) · D. Lysons, *The environs of London*, 3 (1795) · D. Lysons, *Supplement to the first edition of 'The environs of London'* (1811) · E. Jones-Parry, 'Under-secretaries of state for foreign affairs, 1782–1855', *EngHR*, 49 (1934), 308–20 · J. D. G. Scott, *Story of St Mary Abbots Kensington* (1942) · W. J. Loftie, *Kensington picturesque and historical* (1888) · Watt, *Bibl. Brit.*, vol. 1 · *An historical and descriptive account of the Royal Hospital, and Royal Military Asylum: at Chelsea* (1805) · J. Glendening, *The high road: romantic tourism, Scotland, and literature, 1720–1820* (1997) · S. Murray, *A companion, and useful guide to the beauties of Scotland* (1799)

Murray, Sir Terence Aubrey (1810–1873), pastoralist and politician in Australia, was born at Balliston, co. Limerick, Ireland, the third child of Captain Terence Murray (*d.* 1835), paymaster of the 48th foot, and his wife, Ellen, *née* Fitzgerald. Brought up as a Roman Catholic by his paternal grandmother, Murray learned classics and mathematics at Revd William White's school in Dublin. In April 1827 he reached New South Wales in the *Elizabeth* with his father and sister, and spent four years running his father's sheep station at Lake George, north-east of the site where Canberra was later built; he received an adjoining grant in 1832. Tall and strong, with a fiery temper and dark penetrating eyes, he walked with a swagger that appeared arrogant. He became a 'bold and skilful horseman and four-in-hand whip' (*Sydney Daily Telegraph*, 22 July 1887), enjoyed angling and hunting kangaroos, and, in his solitary existence, found solace in books.

In April 1833 Murray was gazetted a magistrate. He built a substantial house on Winderradeen, his combined grants and inherited lands at Lake George, in 1837. That year he (and Thomas Walker) purchased Yarralumla on the Limestone plains, which became his principal residence (the house later became the home of the governor-general of Australia in Canberra). The severe drought of the late 1830s caused Murray to establish out-stations in the Snowy Mountains for his starving stock. In the depressed 1840s he boiled down his sheep for tallow. At St

James's Church of England Church, Sydney, on 27 May 1843, he married Mary (Minnie; 1820–1858), the daughter of Lieutenant-Colonel J. G. N. Gibbes, collector of customs. Fearing bankruptcy, he settled Yarralumla on her.

Murray represented the counties of Murray, King, and Georgina (1843–51) and Southern Boroughs (1851–6) in the partially elected legislative council. In Sydney, he lived at the Australian Club. Liberal in outlook, he opposed capital punishment, the high price of land, denominational education, and, despite the chronic shortage of labour, renewed transportation. In 1852–3 he sat on the select committee that drew up the new constitution. After responsible government was granted to the colony in 1856, Murray represented Southern Boroughs (1856–9) and Argyle (1859–62) in the legislative assembly. He served under Charles Cowper as secretary for lands and works (26 August to 2 October 1856) and acting auditor-general for three weeks. He was again secretary for lands and works under Cowper from 7 September 1857, but resigned on 12 January 1858 following criticism for his prolonged absences. Minnie died at Winderradeen on 2 January 1858, survived by two of their five daughters and an infant son.

After his resignation, Murray sat in the legislative assembly with the opposition. He was known for his honesty of purpose and 'often carried away his opponents by his earnestness and impetuosity, even when they might … doubt his judgment' (*Sydney Morning Herald* 24 June 1873). One of few landowners to oppose the squatting system, in 1859 he introduced bills to abolish capital punishment and primogeniture. He was elected speaker of the legislative assembly on 31 January 1860. He wrote next year to Henry Parkes, 'I have scarcely any trouble in the maintenance of order—but, nevertheless its a weary thing to sit all through a long debate' (Parkes correspondence, 55.276, letter of 18 Sept 1861). He was nominated for life to the legislative council on 13 October 1862 and appointed its president the next day at a salary of £1200.

At Winderradeen, on 4 August 1860, Murray married Agnes Anne (*c*.1835–1891), the third daughter of John Edwards of Hammersmith, London, his daughters' governess and a cousin of W. S. Gilbert, in both Church of England and Roman Catholic ceremonies. His financial difficulties worsened: Yarralumla was now controlled by his first wife's family; he lost 20,000 sheep through footrot in 1860–61; and he entertained extravagantly. Owing some £25,000, he was unable to pay his creditors, and Winderradeen was stripped of furniture in September 1865. His friends rallied generously and he avoided bankruptcy, but had to sell his library.

Henceforward Murray lived in rented houses in Sydney, occupying a distinguished social position, and devoted to literature and 'all objects of scientific investigation' (Revd W. B. Clarke, cited in Wilson, 222). He was executive commissioner for the Paris Universal Exhibition (1866–7) and was knighted in 1869. He died of cancer in office on 22 June 1873, at Richmond House, Darlinghurst, Sydney, and was buried with Church of England rites in St Jude's churchyard, Randwick, on the 24th. His widow opened a school to support her stepchildren and sons, John Hubert *Murray (1861–1940), who became a colonial administrator, and George Gilbert Aimé *Murray (1866–1957), later regius professor of Greek at Oxford.

MARTHA RUTLEDGE

Sources NL Aus., Murray family papers · S. M. Mowle, *Reminiscences, 1822–1851*, Mitchell L., NSW [compiled 1899] · G. Wilson, *Murray of Yarralumla* (1968) · C. D. Coulthard-Clark, ed., *Gables, ghosts and Government House* (1988), 1–26 · *Sydney Morning Herald* (24 June 1873), 5 · *Sydney Morning Herald* (26 June 1873), 4 · *Sydney Morning Herald* (23 Feb 1891), 1 · M, 'The late Sir Terence Aubrey Murray', *Daily Telegraph* [Sydney] (22 July 1887), 3 [letter to the editor] · Parkes correspondence, Mitchell L., NSW · M. S., 'Lady Terence Aubrey Murray', *Town and Country Journal* [Sydney] (4 Nov 1908), 39 · F. West, *Hubert Murray* (1968) · d. cert., Registrar general's office, Sydney, Australia

Archives Bodl. Oxf., corresp. and papers [microfilm] · NL Aus. | Mitchell L., NSW, Parkes MSS

Likenesses daguerreotype, NL Aus. · photograph (in robes of the president of legislative council), NL Aus.

Wealth at death A$1400: probate, New South Wales

Murray, Sir Thomas, of Bothwell (d. 1361). *See under* Murray, Sir Andrew, of Bothwell (1298–1338).

Murray, Thomas (1564–1623), royal tutor and college head, was the son of Murray of Woodend. He attached himself to the Scottish court and followed James VI to London in 1603, by which year he had married Jane Drummond (d. 1647). By 26 June 1605, when he was granted a pension of 200 marks, he had been appointed tutor to Charles, duke of York, the future Charles I. Over the next few years Murray was presented by the king for an advowson to the mastership of Christ's Hospital at Sherburn, near Durham, and received several additional awards. He helped to oversee the administration of Charles's lands in the north of England and was authorized in January 1612, along with Sir Robert Carey and Sir James Fullerton, to suppress disorders in his household.

In February 1613 Isaac Wake reported that Murray was 'much courted' because close to Charles, who had recently become heir to the throne, but that 'his honesty makes him well esteemed'. A staunch supporter of protestant causes, he corresponded with like-minded diplomats such as Wake, Thomas Edmonds, and Dudley Carleton, passing information they provided along to the prince. He acted as an intermediary with Carleton during the latter's service in the Netherlands, in arranging the purchase of models of 'warlike engines' for Charles's use. In 1617 he became secretary to Charles, now prince of Wales, and obtained a promise from the king that he would succeed the incumbent, Sir Henry Savile, as provost of Eton. Over the next few years, however, he found himself at odds with the increasingly pro-Spanish orientation of the king. In 1615 Archbishop Gladstanes of St Andrews had attempted to have him removed from his post as tutor, being 'ill-affected to the estate of the kirk'. In 1618 Murray wrote to Sir Albert Morton that harmony could be restored between James and his people only by stricter treatment of recusants. In August 1621 he was placed under house arrest for failing to prevent a chaplain to the prince from presenting him with a tract opposing his marriage to the Spanish infanta. Within little more than a month he had been replaced as Charles's secretary by a former ambassador to Spain, Francis Cottington.

When Savile died on 19 February 1622 many observers thought that Murray's recent fall from favour would prevent him from becoming provost of Eton, but although several rivals, including Savile's son-in-law, Carleton, presented themselves, James quickly issued a letter to the vice-provost and fellows directing that Murray be selected. Almost exactly a year later (20 February 1623) Murray fell dangerously ill. He died at Eton on 9 April after a botched operation to remove a kidney stone and was buried in the college chapel. He was survived by his wife, who received a pension of £500 in recognition of his past services, and by five sons and two daughters, among them Anne (Anna), later Anne *Halkett. Several of Murray's poems appeared posthumously in an anthology of Scottish Latin verse published in 1637.

R. MALCOLM SMUTS

Sources *DNB* · *CSP dom.*, *1603–23* · BL, Add. MS 18639, fols. 127–8 · A. Johnston, *Delitiae poetarum Scotorum* (1637)
Archives LPL, corresp.

Murray, Sir Thomas, of Glendoick, baronet, Lord Glendoick (*c.*1633–1684/5), lawyer and judge, was the second son of Thomas Murray of Cassochie and Woodend (*d.* 1666), advocate, and Jean, daughter of Anthony Murray, parson of Utricholm (perhaps Ulcombe) in Kent. The father was made sheriff-depute of Perthshire in 1649, commissary of Caithness in 1650 and 1661, and died in 1666. The son, having adopted the law as his profession, was admitted to the Faculty of Advocates on 14 December 1661.

Murray's career in government was to depend on the patronage of his second cousin Lady Elizabeth Murray, countess of Dysart, but anonymity in the 1660s was only broken by her marriage to the secretary of state, the duke of Lauderdale, in 1672. Thereafter, office and preferment quickly came Murray's way. On 4 June 1674 he was made a senator of the college of justice with the title Lord Glendoick from an estate in the Carse of Gowrie which he had purchased and which was ratified to him by parliament on 3 February 1672. On 2 July 1676 he was created a baronet of Nova Scotia. Most important of all, in November 1677 he was appointed lord clerk register in succession to Sir Archibald Primrose, whose resignation had been engineered after various intrigues by the countess of Dysart. However, Murray's rise to office depended too much on Lauderdale and after the duke was overthrown in 1680 Murray was soon removed. In October 1681 the office of clerk register was given to Sir George Mackenzie of Tarbet, a firm opponent of Lauderdale.

Murray's renown, particularly for Scots law, rests on his well-known edition of the acts of parliament of Scotland. In accordance with Scottish tradition he was, as clerk register, responsible for the printing of the acts, and this was confirmed in 1679 by a royal licence granting him, for the now usual term of nineteen years, the copyright for printing 'the whole acts, laws, constitutions, and ordinances of the parliament of the kingdom of Scotland, both old and new' (*Reg. PCS*, 5.481–2). The gift was ratified by parliament in 1681 and in May of that year Murray commissioned the printers David Lindsay and John Cairnes of Edinburgh, who were licensed in turn for nineteen years, to 'print, sell and distribute' the acts (privy seal registers, PS.3.3. 300–01). In November 1682 this licence became the subject of a dispute between the king's printer, Agnes Campbell, who claimed the right to print statutes and boldly printed her own edition, and Lindsay and his partners Cairnes and George Wedderburn, but the privy council confirmed the clerk register's right to choose whichever printer he wished and Campbell was forced to burn her stock. Murray's right to the acts was personal and outlived his tenure as clerk register. As for the text of his edition, very little editing took place and it was copied directly, including typographical errors, from Sir John Skene's edition of 1597, updated to 1681 from sessional publications. Murray's edition, printed in both folio and duodecimo in 1681, was none the less a bible of the Scottish legal profession into the nineteenth century.

Murray was obviously well educated and may be the Thomas Murray who graduated from Edinburgh University in 1654. His refusal to take the test oath in 1681 contributed to his fall but also testifies to religious principle. Murray's testamentary inventory indicates the produce and livestock of an active estate farm. He married Barbara (*bap.* 1638), daughter of Thomas Hepburn of Blackcastle, minister of Oldhamstocks, on 10 October 1667. They had perhaps five sons and three daughters, Thomas, John, William, Anthony, Emilia, and Elizabeth surviving their father's death, two infants being buried at Greyfriars in Edinburgh (1674–5). Both Thomas (*d.* 1701) and John (*d.* 1714) succeeded to the baronetcy. At the time of his death Murray had net debts of over £15,000 Scots in spite of his inventory of livestock and being a creditor for outstanding rentals and other sums. He died between 10 December 1684, the date of his will, and 12 March 1685, when his testament was proved. His wife survived him.

A. J. MANN

Sources *Reg. PCS*, 3rd ser., 5.481–2; vol. 6; 7.257, 708 · *APS*, *1670–86* · *Historical notices of Scotish affairs, selected from the manuscripts of Sir John Lauder of Fountainhall*, ed. D. Laing, 1, Bannatyne Club, 87 (1848), 311, 393 · J. Lauder, ed., *The decisions of the lords of council and session*, 1 (1759), 205 · privy seal registers, NA Scot., PS.3.3. 300–1 · register of testaments (Edinburgh), NA Scot., CC8/8/75 · register of testaments (Dunblane), NA Scot., CC.6/5/19, 12 March 1685 · Register House old parish registers, Dysart and Oldhamstocks, NA Scot. [parents' marriage, marriage] · G. Brunton and D. Haig, *An historical account of the senators of the college of justice, from its institution in MDXXXII* (1832), 403 · M. D. Young, ed., *The parliaments of Scotland: burgh and shire commissioners*, 2 (1993), 527 · D. Laing, ed., *A catalogue of the graduates … of the University of Edinburgh*, Bannatyne Club, 106 (1858), 75 · GEC, *Peerage* · H. Paton, ed., *Register of interments in the Greyfriars burying-ground, Edinburgh, 1658–1700*, Scottish RS, 26 (1902)
Archives BL, letters to duke of Lauderdale and Charles II, Add. MSS 23137–23138, 23243–23247 · Buckminster Park, Grantham, corresp., mainly with duchess of Lauderdale
Wealth at death £15,000 Scots in debt of full estate: register of testaments (Dunblane), NA Scot., CC 6/5/19, 12 March 1685

Murray [Murrey], **Thomas** (1663–1735), portrait painter, was of Scottish origin and received his first lessons in art from one of the De Critz family. Subsequently he became a pupil of the eminent portrait painter John Riley, taking over his practice when Riley died in 1691. In 1703 he painted Queen Anne for the Society of the Middle Temple in London, showing her crowned and in royal robes. His many full-length oil paintings include a portrait of John, first duke of Atholl, in Garter robes, with Dunkeld House in the background (1705, Blair Castle collection). For this he charged the duke, possibly his kinsman, 30 guineas sterling. Other examples of his work are in the collections of the National Portrait Gallery, the Royal Society, and the Royal College of Physicians, London.

Murray's self-portrait (Galleria degli Uffizi, Florence) shows a handsome man, and he is reputed to have been hard-working and popular with his clients because of his courteous, diplomatic manner. Although he complained of poverty, he left £40,000 made, it was said, by usury and investment as much as by painting. When he died, a childless widower, on 1 June 1735, his address in the *Gentleman's Magazine* was Southampton Row and his forename erroneously given as John (*GM*, 332). He bequeathed his fortune to a nephew, requesting that a monument to him, complete with marble bust, be erected in Westminster Abbey, provided it was not too expensive. The nephew, sharing his parsimonious ways, prudently had him buried at much less cost in St Paul's, Covent Garden, instead.

ROSALIND K. MARSHALL

Sources Vertue, *Note books*, vols. 1, 3–5 · F. Moücke, *Museum Florentinum* (1762), ix · Redgrave, *Artists*, 2nd edn · J. J. H. H. Stewart-Murray, seventh duke of Atholl, *Chronicles of the Atholl and Tullibardine families*, 5 vols. (privately printed, Edinburgh, 1908), vol. 2 · private information (1894) [G. Scharf] · Waterhouse, *18c painters* · R. Jeffree, 'Murray, Thomas', *The dictionary of art*, ed. J. Turner (1996) · *GM*, 1st ser., 5 (1735), 332 · *DNB*
Likenesses A. Bannerman, engraving (after self-portrait by T. Murray), repro. in H. Walpole, *Anecdotes of painting in England* (1762) · T. Murray, self-portrait, oils, Uffizi Gallery, Florence, Italy · J. Smith, mezzotint (after self-portrait by T. Murray), BM, Scot. NPG · mezzotint (after self-portrait by T. Murray), BM, NPG; repro. in C. Lasinio, *Ritratti originali dei pittori esistenti nella Reale Galleria di Firenze*, 5 vols. (1791–6)
Wealth at death £40,000: Vertue, *Note books*, vol. 3, p. 75

Murray, Thomas (1792–1872), printer and author, was born on 16 February 1792 in the parish of Girthon, Kirkcudbrightshire, fourth child and the second son of the six children of William Murray and Margaret Grierson. He was educated at the parish school, and at Edinburgh University, which he entered in 1810. At this time he was friendly with Thomas Carlyle and the oriental scholar Alexander Murray; they are said to have walked together from Galloway to Edinburgh each session during their college career.

Murray was destined for the ministry of the Church of Scotland, but after obtaining licence and preaching for some time, he took to literary pursuits. He became connected with Sir David Brewster and the staff of writers on *Brewster's Cyclopædia*, forming acquaintances with Leonard Horner and John Ramsay McCulloch, who imbued him with his free-trade principles and a taste for political economy. In 1843 he was one of the founders of the Edinburgh

Galloway Association, the prototype of numerous county associations which flourished in Edinburgh, acting as secretary until his death in 1872. In 1846 he was one of the founders and original members of the Edinburgh Philosophical Institution (of which Thomas Carlyle was president until his death), and acted for about thirty years as secretary of the Edinburgh School of Arts (1844–72). For six years (1854–60) he was a member of the Edinburgh town council, where he was associated with the whig or moderate liberal party.

In 1841 Murray established at 21 George Street, Edinburgh, the printing business of Murray and Gibb, which later became her majesty's printers for Scotland and proved to be a highly successful business. He married Janet, daughter of Alexander Murray of Wigton, with whom he had two daughters. He had a reputation for wisdom and kindliness, and was a patient, if not profound, scholar. He wrote *The Literary History of Galloway* (1822), and several biographical works, including *The Life of John Wycliffe* (1829). He produced an edition of *The Letters of David Hume* in 1841. He died at Elm Bank, near Lasswade, on 15 April 1872, survived by his wife.

GEORGE STRONACH, rev. DOUGLAS BROWN

Sources *The Scotsman* (16 April 1872) · bap. reg. Scot. · private information (1894) [Lady Hunter]
Archives NL Scot., autobiographical notes | NL Scot., letters to Thomas Carlyle
Wealth at death £7847 6s. 9d.: confirmation, 1874, NA Scot., SC 70/1/167, 418–23

Murray, Thomas Cornelius (1873–1959), playwright, was born on 17 January 1873 at his parents' bar and grocery store in Pound Lane, Macroom, co. Cork, the seventh of the eleven children of Cornelius Murray and his wife, Honora, *née* Kelleher. After being educated at the national school in Macroom, as well as at the Latin School there, in 1891 he was awarded a queen's scholarship to train for two years at St Patrick's Training College, Drumcondra. He then taught in several schools near Cork city, including St Mary's, Carrigtwohill, where he met his future wife, Christina Moylan (d. 1944), the daughter of the principal. In 1900 he was appointed principal of the national school at Rathduff, near Blarney, where he earned a local reputation for being exacting and sarcastic. Murray and Christina married on 31 July 1903 at Holy Trinity, Cork, and subsequently had one son and four daughters. The performance and publication of his third play, *Maurice Harte* (1912), with its theme of a seminarian who loses his faith, caused Murray to fall foul of Father Laurence Murphy, his parish priest and school manager in Rathduff. A period of strained relations ensued; it was with some relief that Murray accepted appointment as the headmaster of the Inchicore Model Schools in Dublin in 1915, where he remained until his retirement in 1932, living first in Kilmainham and, after 1931, in Ballsbridge.

Murray's literary career, which he sustained alongside his professional duties as a teacher, began with essays on educational issues which he published in Father Tom Finlay's *New Ireland Review* and with poems and stories for the

Cork Examiner, the *Irish Weekly*, *The Leader*, and *Shan Van Vocht*. It was not until 1909 that he attempted a play, *The Wheel of Fortune*, at the request of his friend the novelist, playwright, and critic Daniel Corkery, who had recently founded the Cork Little Theatre with Terence MacSwiney and Tom O'Gorman. Its modest success led him to a further attempt, *Birthright*, which was staged by the Abbey Theatre (27 October 1910), a play that remained a staple of the company's repertoire over the next two decades and won Murray an international reputation when it was taken on tour in 1911 to America, where it was seen and admired by Eugene O'Neill. *Birthright* established what were to be the consistent strengths of Murray's drama: a tightly constructed narrative which moves with an implacable force towards a tragic outcome that is the product of character not of chance; a serious engagement with the hardships of peasant life (Murray's father had moved to Macroom to avoid a life in impoverished tenant farming); an ability to create a believable verisimilitude by showing how country lives are affected by slow, quiet, daily routines and the larger pattern of demands occasioned by seasonal change; a refusal to sit in judgment on the characters he constructs; and a remarkable skill in interweaving the archetypal (here the story of Cain and Abel) into the seemingly mundane. Most impressive is Murray's way with dialogue, which binds these other qualities into an organic whole: at its best this is remarkable for the careful pacing, as if the characters dimly apprehend some imminent catastrophe that is about to overtake them but are searching for the right words to elicit certain confirmation of their intuitions of disaster or to deflect its impact. There is therefore a restless tension surging and building behind a seemingly placid surface to the conversation and the eventual eruption is the more profound for the preceding suppression. Murray by this means invests a confident, spare realism with a degree of poetry.

Maurice Harte, which was staged by the Abbey company in 1910, confirmed a further excellence: Murray's skill in writing what were consummately ensemble plays where the dramatic interest was shared between a range of subtly differentiated characters (here a mother of intransigent determination, a son torn between honouring her ambitions for him and his own integrity, a kindly father confused by the resulting emotional upheaval and fearful of intruding, a younger son on whom falls the demand to find a wealthy wife whose dowry must offset the debts incurred in securing his brother's education, and a parish priest whose own faith is challenged by his inability to offer more than platitudes and meaningless pity). Murray, on whom an early influence was a reading of Racine's *Athalie*, was rare among his contemporaries in writing about the place of Catholicism in his characters' experience and in doing so without resorting to mawkish piety or rhetorical insistence.

Three one-act plays followed: *Sovereign Love* (1913) was a redrafting of *The Wheel of Fortune*, sharpening its satirical and farcical attack on arranged marriages; *The Briery Gap* (1917), a fierce if miniature tragedy, remained unperformed because of its compassionate treatment of the theme of illegitimate pregnancy; and *Spring* (1918) explores the penny-pinching tensions and petty cruelties involved in caring for the elderly in an indigent household. All were perfectly structured dramas catering for a long-standing Abbey tradition of triple bills of plays by different writers. *The Serf* (1920) and *Aftermath* (1922) were considered sound, even if they did not appreciably advance Murray's creativity; but *Autumn Fire* (1924) was immediately judged a masterpiece for the manner in which within a credible peasant situation Murray deftly investigated a tragic situation that parallels the myth of Theseus, Phaedra, and Hippolytus, though those classical and archetypal roots are never openly admitted. (If Racine's *Phèdre* was an influence, it was wholly subsumed in Murray's invention.) By a significant coincidence O'Neill staged that same year *Desire under the Elms*, which explores precisely the same emotional and mythical territory. Murray's triumph with *Autumn Fire* marked a watershed in his career: while two plays, the one-act *The Pipe in the Fields* (1927) and *Michaelmas Eve* (1932), stay in the genre of peasant drama, they noticeably lack the depth of implication that enriches his earlier work and the latter seems unsure of its direction both in terms of plot and theme (several possible endings are extant). *The Blind Wolf* (1928) showed Murray attempting to move away from his usual subject matter by dramatizing a Hungarian tale about greed and murder but the result was considered rightly as overly melodramatic and sensational. With *A Flutter of Wings* (1930) Murray embarked on a series of plays of middle-class life, sometimes rural, sometimes urban: *A Stag at Bay* (1934), *A Spot in the Sun* (1938), *Illumination* (1939), and *The Green Branch* (1943). None was successful. What a reviewer for the *Evening Mail* (11 Nov 1930) observed of one of them is true of all the last plays, except for *The Pipe in the Fields* where realism extends into the visionary and transcendent: Murray 'does not seem to be quite sure of himself, quite sure of what his characters are to say, and the whole point of the play is by no means clear'. Once his characters become educated and articulate, the dialogue seems conventionally theatrical—stilted, thin, and brittle—rather than natural, flowing, and idiomatic.

Murray tends to be classified in histories of the Irish theatre as one of the 'Cork realists', but his early plays survived beyond their initial productions, which the work of Padraic Colum or R. J. Ray, with whom he is regularly grouped, did not; and, unlike theirs, his drama survived to influence a later generation of Abbey dramatists (George Shiels and Brinsley McNamara). One Cork connection proved an enduring benefit: Lennox Robinson, whose *The Lesson of his Life* shared the bill with *The Wheel of Fortune* in 1909. Robinson directed his own play and Murray observed him in rehearsal with astonishment and admiration. Subsequently Robinson directed all Murray's plays at the Abbey until 1928, their shared Cork background ensuring that they were properly responsive to the nuances in each other's artistry.

Honours came late to Murray: *Birthright* won the bronze medal for drama at the Olympic Festival in Paris (1924); in 1949 the National University awarded him an honorary DLitt. In retirement he began a projected work of autobiographical fiction but only the first volume, *Spring Horizon* (1937), was finished; interestingly it demonstrated how much a childhood spent within the family store furnished him with the material (plots and dialogue) for his early plays. Murray at this time took on a number of official roles to further the interests of writers: he was a member for some years of the film censorship appeal board, vice-president of the Irish Academy of Letters, treasurer and later president of the Irish Playwrights' Association, and director of the Authors' Guild of Ireland. His major plays were translated into German, Spanish, Welsh, Breton, Irish, Japanese, and Korean and continued to be revived by amateur groups or in radio broadcasts into his final years. After the death of his wife in 1944, Murray became increasingly reclusive; he admitted to a depressive mind-set that deepened after the death of his son, Niall, from cancer in 1951 and the departure for Australia a year later of his daughter Pauline, a cloistered nun, to establish a convent for the Poor Clares in Sydney. Murray died at his home, 11 Sandymount Avenue, Ballsbridge, Dublin, aged eighty-six, of viral pneumonia on 7 March 1959 and was buried at the Star of the Sea Church, Sandymount.

RICHARD ALLEN CAVE

Sources A. J. DeGiacomo, '"The people I knew": T. C. Murray—a biocritical introduction to the plays', PhD diss., Boston College, USA · *Selected plays of T. C. Murray*, ed. R. A. Cave, Irish Drama Selections, 10 (1998), vii–xxiii · R. Hogan and M. J. O'Neill, eds., *Joseph Holloway's Abbey Theatre* (1967) · M. OlAodha, 'T. C. Murray: dramatist', *Plays and places* (1961) · A. E. Malone, *The Irish drama* (1929) · R. Welch, ed., *The Oxford companion to Irish literature* (1996)
Archives NL Ire., papers | NL Ire., letters to Joseph Holloway · NL Ire., letters to Frank Hugh O'Donnell
Likenesses S. O'Sullivan, red chalk and charcoal on paper, 1929, NG Ire. · photographs, priv. coll.

Murray, Sir William, of Tullibardine (*d.* **1583**), administrator, was the eldest son of Sir William Murray of Tullibardine (*d.* 1563) and his wife, Katherine (*fl.* 1513–76), daughter of Sir Duncan Campbell of Glenorchy. He had a long pedigree and extensive lands in lowland Perthshire. His date of birth is unknown, but details of William and two younger brothers date back to November 1542, and he contracted to marry Agnes Graham, daughter of William, second earl of Montrose, on 15 April 1547. The couple's eldest grandchild was born in 1574. Murray's father had a long pro-English record and was a member of the lords of the congregation who opposed the queen regent in 1559–60, though he was not beyond obtaining from her a grant of the Tullibardine lands to his son, reserving his liferent, during the last days of her regency, on 24 May 1560. The younger Murray made his most important connection in 1557, when his sister Annabella married John, sixth Lord Erskine, later first earl of Mar; Murray often acted in concert with Erskine. He was also often associated with the fourth earl of Atholl, a more distant blood relation.

Murray succeeded his father on 30 January 1563. He visited France at an unknown date, and returned to Scotland via England in February 1565. He brought a supplication for restoration from the exiled fourth earl of Bothwell—but also alleged that Bothwell had spoken dishonourably against Mary and threatened the earl of Moray and William Maitland of Lethington. A hostile memorandum at this time described him as a 'young hede' who would support the earl of Lennox, Darnley's father, in his bid for power at Moray and Maitland's expense (*CSP Scot.,* 1563–9, 119). He received his first reward for this support on 15 May 1565, when he was knighted at the creation of Darnley as earl of Ross.

On Mary's marriage to Darnley on 29 July, Moray, the Hamiltons, and the fifth earl of Argyll rose in rebellion. The Campbells raided Murray's lands, and Murray himself blamed Colin Campbell of Glenorchy, his cousin and neighbour. He had the council summon Campbell and send 300 hagbutters to Perth to threaten him, which successfully detached the latter from his clan chief, Argyll, and forced his neutrality.

The queen appointed Murray as comptroller on 27 August 1565; he replaced Sir John Wishart of Pittarrow, who had joined the rebels. Murray also became a privy councillor on 21 September, though he took the councillor's oath only on 5 November. The post of comptroller involved supervision of the collection of revenues from the crown lands and the customs, with responsibility for supplying the financial needs of the royal household. Until 1574 Murray also held the related post of collector-general of thirds of benefices. His immediate task, to find money for troops to suppress the rebellion, he accomplished by diverting money from ministers' stipends. The period was so unsettled that his first accounts as comptroller were not rendered until 1569. He modernized the accounts, changing from parchment rolls to paper books and from Latin to Scots.

Murray was suspected of plots against Mary at the time of the parliament of March 1566, being ordered into ward the previous day, 6 March; he did not obey this order, though he did not attend the parliament either. He was not actively involved in the murder of Riccio on 9 March, and was one of those ejected from Holyrood on the night of the murder, along with Atholl, Maitland, and Sir James Balfour, but whether they were 'in some feir of ther lyves' (Melville, 149) is doubtful. On 29 July he was appointed foud (chief magistrate) of Shetland, though there is no evidence that he appointed a deputy to carry out the duties of the post; when he went to Shetland later, it was for a different purpose. At an unknown later date he sold the office to Robert Stewart, later earl of Orkney.

On 11 February 1567, the day after the murder of Darnley, Murray was one of those who interrogated witnesses. He argued for a speedy prosecution of the most likely suspects, but finding no support he left the court. His brother James *Murray posted placards in Edinburgh denouncing Bothwell and his adherents as the murderers. After Bothwell's abduction of Mary on 24 April, Sir William on 7

May became an early and prominent adherent to the confederacy formed at Stirling to liberate her, and reportedly brought Mar in to join it. He had to be reconciled to Argyll when the latter also joined.

On 7 June Mary attempted to appoint a new comptroller, James Cockburn of Skirling, but his tenure of office was never effective and the privy council (of which Mary had lost control) dismissed him on 5 July. Murray and his followers were among those who occupied Edinburgh for the confederates on 11 June. He seconded his brother in offering to accept Bothwell's challenge to single combat at Carberry on 15 June; Bothwell declined to fight James as he was not a peer, though Murray claimed to be 'his better in estate, and in antiquity of house many degrees above him' (*Knox's History*, 2.211).

On Mary's imprisonment in Lochleven Castle, Murray was one of the few permitted access to her. There on 16 July he obtained the queen's signature to a remarkable deed recognizing that he had advanced her £8000 and was also superexpended in the comptrollership by £15,000. It noted 'the estait of the present tyme, quhairin his comptis apperandlie are nocht to be haistilie herd', and authorized him to repay himself by collecting for his own use all oustanding revenues for 1565 and 1566 without rendering accounts (*Exchequer Rolls*, 19.353–5). He was reluctant to countenance Mary's deposition, but urged her to sign the abdication deeds to save her life, which she did on 24 July. By Mary's own account he 'reminded her of a certain password, which had been agreed upon between her majesty and himself' (Nau, 59); another account mentions 'ane ryng in spetiell tokne' (*CSP Scot.*, *1569–71*, 111). On 29 July he attended the coronation of James VI.

Murray may have been encouraged in his loyalty to the new regime by hostility to its opponents, the Hamiltons. He told the English ambassador on 6 August that their professions of support for Mary were hypocritical. They stood in succession to the crown and in fact sought Mary's death—'For she beinge taken awaye, theye accompt but the lytle kinge betwixte them and home, which maye dye' (*CSP Scot.*, *1563–9*, 374). On 19 August Murray and Sir William Kirkcaldy of Grange set sail in pursuit of Bothwell, with four ships and 400 hagbutters. They captured one of Bothwell's ships and some of his followers in Shetland, but Bothwell himself escaped to Norway. They returned in mid-September.

Murray retained the comptrollership, though Wishart, his predecessor, was closer to Regent Moray. A satirical anti-Moray tract represented Wishart as advising the regent that Murray was one of the 'men that hes over grit power in this cuntrie' (Bannatyne, 10). There seems to be no truth in Calderwood's circumstantial account of Murray's support for Mary at the battle of Langside, on 13 May 1568; Murray did not sign the Marian bond, and a contemporary account names him as having fought for the regent. The report that he plotted with the Hamiltons to assassinate the regent shortly afterwards also seems unfounded. However, at the convention of estates of 30 July 1569 he joined the minority who voted to seek a divorce between Mary and Bothwell, seen as a prelude to

her restoration. By March 1570 he was supporting the bid by the Hamiltons and Maitland for Mary's restoration. He was absent from the convention of estates that elected Lennox regent on 17 July. He may then have tried to be neutral. He was at any rate preoccupied by a major local issue: the feud between his brother, Alexander Murray of Drumfin, and the Reidheugh family, which burst out in the summer of 1571.

Murray reappeared as a supporter of the king in July 1572, negotiating with the remaining Marians. Regent Mar, before his death in Stirling on 17 October 1572, left the keeping of Stirling Castle and the young king jointly to his brother and to Murray. However, Mar's successor as regent, Morton, reportedly made Murray relinquish this office as the price for retention of the comptrollership. In 1573 the end of the civil war saw an improvement in the comptrollery finances, though Murray's superexpenses rose again during the late 1570s.

During this period Murray gave his allegiance to the second earl of Mar, not to his former associate Atholl who engineered Morton's resignation as regent on 12 March 1578. In the convention of estates of May, Murray supported Morton's successful return to power (backed by Mar) as head of the council. However, once again Calderwood's circumstantial account of how Morton bribed Murray to gain access to Mar and the king in Stirling seems to be unfounded. Murray was still allied to Morton in the spring of 1580. Their enemies alleged misappropriation of funds, and schemed to charge Murray and the collector of thirds with 'sudden reckonings', whereupon 'the sacrifice of their bodies should have acquitted their accounts in their own persons' (*CSP Scot.*, *1574–81*, 418). There is no evidence that Morton tampered with the comptroller's accounts, though he did with the treasurer's.

Murray recognized, sooner than Morton, the importance of relations with the young king. His brother James began a court career in 1579, and on 10 June 1580 two of his younger sons, William and Alexander, were appointed gentlemen of the king's chamber; their letters of appointment commended the education which their father had arranged for them in France. However, on the more formal establishment of the chamber on 24 September, they lost their places, probably because of the growing influence of the earl (later duke) of Lennox, who became chamberlain on that date.

On 26 August 1580 substitutes were appointed to act for Murray: his eldest son, John (later first earl of Tullibardine), and John Fenton, comptroller clerk since 1562. Murray was now 'subject to infirmitie and seiknes, speciallie the gut, sa inconstant and suddane of itself that quhen he is maist willing to gif attendance on his majesteis service than maist suddanlie will he be charged with the said seiknes'; his wife too was grievously ill (*Register of the Privy Seal*, *1575–80*, no. 2470). The English ambassador regarded the substitution as a manoeuvre to protect him from his enemies. It was rumoured in February 1581 that Murray had been replaced by Captain James Stewart, but this did not happen, and he was named to serve on several parliamentary commissions in November. In July 1582 Lennox was said to be about to accuse him of treason; Murray supported the Ruthven raid of 23 August which overthrew Lennox. He demitted the comptrollership on 26 November, being succeeded by Fenton. His last surviving account (to 31 October 1580) shows him superexpended by £5277 Scots. Murray died at Gask on 16 March 1583. His testament (registered in 1599) shows that James VI owed him 5000 merks, and in 1611 the king was still worrying about how to repay the debt to his son.   JULIAN GOODARE

Sources CSP Scot., 1547–83 · G. Burnett and others, eds., *The exchequer rolls of Scotland*, 23 vols. (1878–1908), vols. 19–21 · *Reg. PCS*, 1st ser., vols. 1–3 · J. Dawson, ed., *Clan Campbell letters, 1559–1583*, Scottish History Society, 5th ser., 10 (1997) · G. Donaldson, ed., *Accounts of the collectors of thirds of benefices, 1561–1572*, Scottish History Society, 3rd ser., 42 (1949) · J. Goodare, 'Queen Mary's Catholic interlude', *Innes Review*, 38 (1987), 154–70 · G. R. Hewitt, *Scotland under Morton, 1572–1580* (1982) · A. L. Juhala, 'The household and court of King James VI of Scotland, 1567–1603', PhD diss., U. Edin., 2000 · C. Nau, *The history of Mary Stewart*, ed. J. Stevenson (1883) · *Memoirs of his own life by Sir James Melville of Halhill*, ed. T. Thomson, Bannatyne Club, 18 (1827) · *John Knox's History of the Reformation in Scotland*, ed. W. C. Dickinson, 2 vols. (1949) · D. Calderwood, *The history of the Kirk of Scotland*, ed. T. Thomson and D. Laing, 8 vols., Wodrow Society, 7 (1842–9) · R. Bannatyne, *Memoriales of transactions in Scotland, 1569–1573*, ed. [R. Pitcairn], Bannatyne Club, 51 (1836) · NA Scot., Edinburgh testaments, CC8/8/33 · M. Livingstone, D. Hay Fleming, and others, eds., *Registrum secreti sigilli regum Scotorum / The register of the privy seal of Scotland*, 7 (1966) · C. Innes, ed., *The black book of Taymouth*, Bannatyne Club, 100 (1855)
Wealth at death £8705 Scots—and land: NA Scot., Edinburgh testaments, 28 May 1599, CC8/8/33

Murray, William, first earl of Dysart (d. 1655), courtier, was the son of William Murray, minister of Dysart, Fife, and his wife, Margaret. In 1603 his uncle Thomas *Murray, tutor to the future Charles I, took him to London and had him appointed as the prince's whipping boy. William was about Charles's age and soon became his close companion. He accompanied the prince to Spain in 1623 and was named a groom in his bedchamber, with a pension of £500, in May 1625, shortly after Charles's accession. He thereafter continued to receive rewards, including another £400 pension in 1626, beneficial leases on crown lands, a share of the imposts on Rhenish wines, and a commission to investigate ship captains for withholding the tenth share of prize goods due to the crown, which entitled him to keep a portion of any money he recovered. His rigorous efforts to exploit this last grant, by summoning merchants from provincial cities to interrogations in London, provoked several bitter complaints. In or before 1636 he married Catherine (d. in or after 1651), daughter of Colonel Norman Bruce; they had five daughters.

Murray obtained Ham House from the crown in 1626, built the brick wall around its grounds in 1633, and embarked on extensive renovations of the interior between 1637 and 1639. Much of this work survives as perhaps the best-preserved example of the domestic architecture of the Caroline court still in existence. It incorporates tapestry cartoons employed by the architect Francis Cleyn, the director of the Mortlake factory, to simulate

the effect of frescoes, and plaster statues of Mars and Minerva flanking the hall fireplaces that are thought to be portraits of Murray and his wife. Ham House also still houses Murray's collection of paintings, many of which may still be hanging in their original positions. These include copies of masterpieces owned by Charles I, a royal portrait given to Murray by the king, original works by Flemish and Italian masters, and an important collection of miniatures by John Hoskins. Murray obviously shared the artistic interests of the king's circle. It is probably significant that he procured a warrant in February 1637 directing that Van Dyck be paid £1200 for pictures for Charles and Henrietta Maria—the largest single payment to the artist during his residence in England—and another in April 1640 directing that Hoskins be appointed limner to the king.

In 1632 Charles sent Murray to the Spanish Netherlands as a personal emissary to his mother-in-law, Marie de' Medici, when it was rumoured that she was about to take her exiled court to England. Marie reassured Murray that she intended to stay in Flanders, but in 1639 she did finally arrive in England and Charles felt morally obliged to pay her court's expenses, at the rate of £30,000 a year, until she could be persuaded to leave. The following spring she agreed to move to Cologne but the rulers of the Spanish Netherlands denied her request to travel through their territories. Murray was thereupon dispatched to The Hague, to ask the prince of Orange to gain permission for her to pass through the northern Netherlands. Charles also entrusted him with a message to his sister, the exiled queen of Bohemia, assuring her that he had settled a misunderstanding with her son, the elector palatine.

Murray made a suitable personal representative because, as a man of low birth without political office, he lacked the standing to represent the British state. Yet his capacity to circumvent formal institutional channels, through private negotiations conducted largely behind the scenes, was obviously a potential source of significant political influence. It is uncertain how far he actually involved himself in affairs of state in the 1630s because his activities might well have left few documentary traces. The fact that he was rarely mentioned as a significant participant in factional struggles by observers of the court suggests, however, that his role was probably limited. He certainly acted as a broker of minor patronage, as a number of privy seal warrants he procured granting lesser offices and other benefits to numerous individuals demonstrate. He corresponded with Henry Vane the elder during the latter's diplomatic missions to the Netherlands and Germany between 1629 and 1632, warning him on one occasion that he was being maligned as too 'German and puritan'. But no evidence has come to light indicating that he ever tried to form political alliances with members of the council or to meddle in policy debates before the emergence of the covenanting movement in the late 1630s.

Thereafter Murray's involvement increased, no doubt partly because he was related to several leading covenanters, and thus an obvious person to open private channels of communication between Charles and his opponents. In

June 1639 he went to the Scottish army with the king's permission, dining with the covenanter general, Lesley, and other rebel leaders. He accompanied the king to the north in 1640, but was sent back to London in September with a copy of the Scots' most recent petition for the queen, which she received before the council had been informed of its contents. He again followed Charles to Scotland in 1641 and toward the beginning of October became centrally involved in a plot to arrest or possibly assassinate the earls of Hamilton and Argyll, known as the 'incident'. Murray may simply have acted as the king's obedient instrument, although some contemporaries thought otherwise. Clarendon states that Charles later told him that when he first received incriminating information about Argyll and Hamilton he decided not to act on it, fearing that charges against them could not be proved and that a failed prosecution would only further poison the political atmosphere. 'But being with great confidence assured by Will Murray of his bedchamber, whom he singularly trusted, that the proofs would be sufficient' and that the majority of the Scottish nobility were ready to turn against Hamilton and Argyll, he decided to allow a prosecution to go forward (Clarendon, *Hist. rebellion*, 1.389n.). The incriminating information came chiefly from Montrose—a covenanter general but a bitter rival of Argyll—who sent three progressively stronger written accusations through Murray to the king. Murray also seems to have initiated a plot involving the earls of Crawford and Almond, lords Ogilvie and Gray, and several other Scottish officers, to lure Hamilton and Argyll into a trap in the withdrawing room at Holyroodhouse in Edinburgh, where they would either be killed or arrested and taken to a royal ship, to place them beyond the possibility of a rescue. This was foiled when one officer told of the plot informed General Lesley, who in turn warned the intended victims, causing them to flee Edinburgh.

Although it further damaged Charles's credibility in both England and Scotland, the 'incident' appears to have strengthened Murray's position. Rumours were soon circulating in England that he was to be promoted to a gentleman of the bedchamber, while some Scots believed, toward the end of 1641, that he and the duke of Lennox were able 'to guide all the court much at their pleasure' (Baillie, 1.332). More surprisingly, his plotting did not destroy his credibility among the covenanters. Instead of seeking revenge, Hamilton enlisted him as a go-between to patch up a face-saving accommodation with the king. Murray continued to correspond with Hamilton over several months, warning him in April 1642 that they were both being maligned at court for wanting a compromise. In May he returned to the Netherlands on a secretive mission to Henrietta Maria, while in the summer he again went to Scotland to attempt to persuade the covenanters to remain neutral in the English civil war. It is possible, although not certain, that he may even have sought their active assistance against parliament. In light of these activities it is not surprising that in February 1642 the Long Parliament voted Murray a person unfit to attend

upon the king. Some English royalists also evidently mistrusted him, since Clarendon states that he was widely blamed for having divulged Charles's intention to arrest the five members in January 1642 to Lord Digby, who in turn informed the parliamentary leaders, and that he was also suspected of secretly encouraging Sir John Hotham to refuse the king entry into Hull later in the year.

During the civil wars Murray continued to act intermittently as an emissary between Charles, Henrietta Maria, and Scottish politicians. He was with Henrietta Maria in Paris when the first civil war ended but returned to England after the king surrendered to the Scots, in an effort to act once more as an intermediary. The English arrested him as a spy in Canterbury in February 1646 and held him for several months in the Tower, but eventually released him after he posted a £5000 bond and promised to attempt nothing against the state. On 7 July Charles wrote to the queen: 'I am freshly and fiercely assaulted from Scotland for yielding to the London propositions; likewise Will Murray is let loose upon me from London for the same purpose' (Bruce, 63). Somewhat to the king's surprise Murray did not press him to capitulate to the Scots' demands but instead tried to broker a compromise by exploring 'how best to accommodate it [a treaty] without going directly against my conscience' (ibid., 65). Charles no longer entirely trusted Murray but continued to negotiate through him until November. He also involved him in contingency plans for an escape to the continent. According to Gilbert Burnet it was in this period that Murray was created earl of Dysart, although he prevailed upon the king to antedate the patent to 3 August 1643, to give him precedence over rivals he disliked. Burnet also states, probably correctly, that Murray failed to have the patent pass the seals until after the regicide. Circumstantial evidence indicates that he assumed his title only in 1651. The title passed to his eldest daughter, Elizabeth *Murray.

After the Scots surrendered Charles to the English, Murray was forbidden his presence and he soon returned to the continent. In 1648 he undertook another mission to Scotland, negotiating with Hamilton over the engagement. He remained involved in attempts to restore Charles II to the throne in the aftermath of the regicide, acting once more as an emissary to the Scots in 1650. He died in Edinburgh on 6 December 1655, leaving behind a shadowy and somewhat sinister reputation, at least in England. Burnet characterized him as a man:

> well turned for a court, very insinuating, but very false; and
> of so revengeful a temper that rather than any of the
> counsels given by his enemies should succeed, he would
> have revealed them, and betrayed both the king and them.
> (*Bishop Burnet's History*, 1.447)

Yet it is doubtful that anyone could have preserved a reputation for honesty among Englishmen while engaging in repeated secretive negotiations between Charles I, Henrietta Maria, and major Scottish politicians as different as Montrose and Argyll. The fact that Murray retained enough credibility to remain a useful intermediary in negotiations between the royal family and presbyterian politicians throughout more than a decade of bitter political infighting and civil war indicates that he must have been more than a mendacious and spiteful minor courtier. His career is perhaps the single most striking proof that a courtly 'politics of intimacy', based entirely on personal relationships with leading political figures, rather than office or public action, remained important even during the upheavals that momentarily destroyed the court itself.

R. MALCOLM SMUTS

Sources CSP dom., 1625–49 • Fourth report, HMC, 3 (1874), 162–8 • DNB • Charles I in 1646: letters of King Charles the first to Queen Henrietta Maria, ed. J. Bruce, CS, 63 (1856) • Bishop Burnet's History • C. Russell, The fall of the British monarchies, 1637–1642 (1991) • Clarendon, Hist. rebellion • [R. Baillie], Letters and journals, ed. R. Aiken, 2 vols. (1775) • PRO, SO 3/9–11 • P. Donald, An uncounselled king: Charles I and the Scottish troubles, 1637–1641 (1990) • Ham House (1999) [National Trust guidebook] • K. Brown, 'Courtiers and cavaliers: service, Anglicisation and loyalty among the royalist nobility', The Scottish national covenant in its British context, ed. J. Morrill (1990), 155–94 • GEC, Peerage • PRO, SP 77/22

Archives Buckminster Park, Grantham, Lincolnshire, Tollemache papers | PRO, SP 16; SO 3/9–12

Likenesses C. Johnson, oils, Ham House, London • D. Patton, engraving, Ham House, London • plaster statue (of Mars; possibly portrait of Murray?), Ham House, London

Murray, William. See Nairne, William, styled second Lord Nairne and Jacobite first earl of Nairne (1664–1726).

Murray, William, styled second duke of Atholl and marquess of Tullibardine (1689–1746), Jacobite leader and army officer, was born on 14 April 1689 at Edinburgh, second and eldest surviving son of John *Murray, first duke of Atholl (1660–1724), and his first wife, Lady Katharine Douglas, later Hamilton (bap. 1662, d. 1707), eldest daughter of the third duke and duchess of Hamilton. He was educated briefly at the University of St Andrews, where his father was chancellor, and won the silver arrow there for archery. In 1707 or early 1708 he entered the navy. In a letter dated at Spithead on 29 August 1708, he gives his father an account of an unsuccessful landing on the coast of France in which he was involved: subsequently he visited Genoa, Venice, and Minorca with the service. Lord William Murray, as he at first was, became marquess of Tullibardine on the death of his elder brother, John, at Malplaquet on 31 August 1709; he was always known to the British government by that title. By 1712 he had left the navy and went to live in London for the next two years, where he ran into debt, a problem which was to be lifelong. By 1714 at the latest he was receiving moneys from the Stuart court. In the Jacobite rising of 1715 he commanded three battalions raised by his family from Atholl, being promoted major-general: he was described at this time as a 'modest, good-natured young gentleman' (Terry, 64). His force fought on the defeated left wing at Sheriffmuir. When James embarked from Montrose he was unable to take Tullibardine with him, as he was still at Brechin, though he subsequently escaped to France in 1716, sailing from South Uist with his brother, Lord George *Murray (1694–1760), aboard the Marie Therese. In early 1717 he was created Jacobite duke of Rannoch, marquess of Blair, earl of Glentilt, Viscount Glenshee, and Lord

Strathbran, titles which he never used. In Britain he had been attainted (17 February 1716), and the titles and estates of the family had been conferred on a younger brother, Lord James *Murray (1690–1764).

Tullibardine was appointed commander-in-chief in Scotland for the 1717 invasion plan proposed with Swedish assistance, and retained this title in sharing the command with the Earl Marischal in the 1719 rising: disputes over precedence contributed to the defeat of the Jacobites at Glenshiel on 10 June. Despite a reward of £2000 for his capture, Tullibardine again succeeded in making his escape, sailing from Harris for the Loire on 1 March 1720. On the death of his father in November 1724 he was recognized as duke of Atholl by the Jacobites. However, he had by this time retired to private life, as being in his own view 'unfit … for meddling with the deep concerns of state' (Thomson, 2.100). He resided close to Paris, where he got into repeated financial difficulties, even though his brother the duke added an allowance to the support granted him by the Jacobite leadership. In 1736 he was imprisoned for debt in Paris, but successfully appealed to the parlement to be set free on the grounds of his rank. In the late 1730s he was placed in retreat with the Abbé Dunne, later bishop of Ossory, some 30 miles from Fontainebleau, in order to keep him out of the hands of cheats in Paris. At this time (1737) Tullibardine took the alias of William Kateson. After leaving Dunne in 1739 he was again at risk of going to prison for debt. There is a clear implication that at this time Tullibardine was childish and vulnerable to the extent of being on the verge of mental illness, as well as being in physical ill health.

In July 1745 Tullibardine was one of the 'seven men of Moidart' who landed with Prince Charles (Charles Edward Stuart) in Scotland. Despite a gout problem which rendered him unable to walk on the day of the landing and other signs of premature ageing (he was thought by one observer to be seventy, though in fact only fifty-six), he played an active part in the rising that followed. At Glenfinnan on 19 August he unfurled the royal standard and read James VIII's manifesto proclaiming a regency in favour of Prince Charles. He marched south into Atholl, where his brother fled from Blair Castle, where Tullibardine entertained the prince, who ate his first pineapple there. When the prince left for Perth at the beginning of September, where he was joined by Lord George Murray, Tullibardine remained at Blair, where his presence greatly facilitated recruitment from the Atholl estates, many there regarding him as the legitimate duke. From 22 September until the march of the army south from Edinburgh, Tullibardine, who was one of three lieutenant-generals, acted as 'Commander-in-Chief of His Majestie's Forces benorth the River of Forth' (Burton and Laing, 26); he was also president of the privy council. The prince was clearly heavily reliant on him to provide additional recruitment from the several thousand Athollmen who could theoretically be raised, the Jacobite Correspondence of the Atholl Family implying that the march south was in part delayed by the difficulty of raising the Perthshire men quickly enough. Lord George wrote on 14 October asking for Tullibardine to come on pain of 'the uter ruine of the Cause', but twelve days later he was still exasperatedly replying to one of the prince's aides-de-camp that 'were it to gain the Universe, it is impossible to make more dispatch than I do' (ibid., 91, 134). None the less, Tullibardine was crucial to the war effort, sustaining recruiting as far away as Deeside before joining Prince Charles with about 600 men at Dalkeith. On the return from England a second, even more desperate, phase of recruiting began, amid threats and complaints. On 7 February Tullibardine sent out the 'general Crosstarie' (the fiery cross, used to raise men in the countryside) throughout Glenalmond (ibid., 191). When Lord George proposed to besiege Blair in March, Tullibardine was clearly fearful for family treasures, writing on 26th that, 'Our great-great-grandfather, grandfather, and father's pictures, will be an irreparable loss in blowing up the house' (ibid., 215). At the battle of Culloden, the Atholl brigade's three battalions stood at the heart of the front line. Tullibardine fled south after the battle: when his horse tired, he was unable to proceed on foot and sought refuge at Archibald Buchanan's house on Loch Lomond. Buchanan's son William was married to Tullibardine's cousin, but none the less betrayed him to the garrison at Dumbarton Castle, whence the marquess was sent by way of Edinburgh to the Tower of London, where he died, childless, on 9 July 1746, worn out by years of exile and privation. He was buried in the chapel there. Those who betrayed him were held in contempt, and indignation at the event led to the penning of a Jacobite one-act drama based on it, which exists in various copies.

Tullibardine was in no way a remarkable figure: a Jacobite to the core, he was nevertheless a man of limited talents as a soldier, statesman, or ideologue, although in this latter capacity his presbyterian upbringing made him rather an unusual supporter of the Stuarts. He was a man dedicated more than most of his, or any other, class to a single task: the restoration of his royal master to the thrones of England, Scotland, and Ireland. For this he died an early death, without which the scaffold would have claimed him. MURRAY G. H. PITTOCK

Sources DNB · J. H. Burton and D. Laing, eds., *Jacobite correspondence of the Atholl family* (1840) · D. Szechi, *Jacobitism and tory politics, 1710–14* (1984) · A. Lang, *Prince Charles Edward Stuart*, new edn (1903) · H. Tayler, ed., *The Jacobite court at Rome in 1719*, Scottish History Society, 3rd ser., 31 (1938) · 'List made at Perth 5 November 1715', NL Scot., MS 1498 · J. Sinclair, *Memoirs of the insurrection in Scotland in 1715*, ed. W. Scott (1858) · U. Aberdeen, MS 2222 · GEC, *Peerage* · M. Hook and W. Ross, *The 'Forty-Five* (1995) · K. Thomson, *Memoirs of the Jacobites of 1715 and 1745*, 3 vols. (1845–6) · C. S. Terry, ed., *The Jacobites and the union* (1922) · H. Tayler, ed., *Jacobite epilogue* (1941)

Archives Blair Castle, Perthshire, journals and corresp., MSS · NA Scot., Dalhousie muniments, letters from France · NL Scot., corresp. · Royal Arch., corresp. and related material | NL Scot., corresp. with marquess of Tweeddale · NRA Scotland, priv. coll., Cameron MSS, letters to John Cameron of Lochiel · priv. coll., Stewart-Murray MSS

Likenesses portrait (as a young man), priv. coll.; repro. in Tayler, ed., *Jacobite epilogue*

Murray, William, first earl of Mansfield (1705–1793), judge and politician, was born on 2 March 1705 at his

William Murray, first earl of Mansfield (1705–1793), by John Singleton Copley, 1782–3

ancestral home, Scone Abbey, later to be known as Scone Palace, near Perth, the fourth son among the fourteen children (six brothers and eight sisters) of David Murray, fifth Viscount Stormont (d. 1731), and Margery (d. 1746), only child of David Scott of Scotstarvet. Except in the case of his brothers David, later sixth Viscount Stormont (c.1688–1748), and James (c.1690–1770), little is known about Murray's numerous siblings. The family environment was strongly Jacobite; Murray's father openly supported James Stuart, the Old Pretender, and was sentenced to a year's imprisonment and a fine of £500 after he refused to appear in Edinburgh to answer suspicions about his participation in the uprising of 1715. After a short period as a member of parliament in London (1711–15) William's brother James tied his career to the Old Pretender, eventually becoming secretary of the court in exile in France and Italy and earl of Dunbar in the Jacobite peerage. One of James's and William's sisters, Marjorie, was also—with her husband, John *Hay of Cromlix, Jacobite duke of Inverness—enmeshed in the Stuart court.

The Murray siblings who left Scotland evidently corresponded with the family infrequently, if at all; at least, very few letters have been discovered. James wrote while living in France in 1763, 'I hear my brother has been made Lord Chancellor of England, but as I have not had a letter from home for thirty years, I know not if it be true or not'

(Tayler, 140). Not a single letter from William to his parents survives at Scone Palace or elsewhere.

Education After attending Perth grammar school William Murray at the age of fourteen travelled in 1719 by horseback from Scotland to London, never to return, ultimately giving rise to Samuel Johnson's remark, 'Much can be made of a Scot, if caught young.' Following the advice of his brother James, he entered Westminster School, and was in that year elected king's scholar. Initially it seemed that studying law in England would be too costly for family resources, and William reluctantly directed himself towards the church. This restriction was said to be erased by the generous intervention of Thomas Foley, first Baron Foley, whose son Thomas was a friend of Murray's at Westminster School and later at Christ Church.

Murray excelled at Westminster. He developed a life-long association with several of his fellow king's scholars, including Thomas Clarke (made master of the rolls in 1754), Robert Henley (made lord keeper in 1757 and lord chancellor in 1761), and three others in particular: Andrew Stone, later secretary to Thomas Pelham-Holles, duke of Newcastle; Thomas Newton, afterwards bishop of Bristol; and James Johnson, afterwards bishop of Worcester. Much later, John Scott, the future Lord Chancellor Eldon, shifted his practice from king's bench to chancery because of what he perceived to be a preference in Mansfield 'for young lawyers who had been bred at Westminster School and Christ Church' (Twiss, 1.70).

As Scott related, Murray proceeded to Christ Church, Oxford, where he matriculated on 18 June 1723. In the long vacation of 1725 Murray visited his brother James in Paris, and wrote to his brother-in-law John Hay, Jacobite duke of Inverness and secretary of state to the Pretender, asking pardon for 'the ambition of a young man' and desiring Lord Inverness 'to make a tender of my duty and loyalty to the King—a very small present but all I have to offer' (Tayler, 230). This episode may have been prompted more by family loyalty than Jacobite convictions, but accusations of Jacobitism haunted Murray's career in later life.

Otherwise, Murray's university career was characterized by a devotion to classical studies expected from the Oxford undergraduates of the period, although he did better than some others at the routine exercises he performed. In 1727 he won the university's prize for a Latin verse composition on the death of George I, earning the enmity of his defeated contemporary William Pitt. Murray's poem was called 'a very wretched production' by Campbell, who observed that 'the art of grinding Latin verses must have been extremely low at Oxford' (Campbell, *Chief Justices*, 2.325).

In April 1724 Murray was entered at Lincoln's Inn. After graduating BA from Oxford in 1727 he went into residence at Lincoln's Inn, proceeded MA from Christ Church in June 1730, and was called to the bar in November 1730. Murray took his time at Oxford and at Lincoln's Inn seriously, exhibiting two characteristics that served him all his life: a readiness to perform the long hours of drudgery and apprenticeship necessary to develop a thorough grounding in a subject or a skill; and an irrepressible intellectual curiosity. Later, when a newcomer to the judicial bench, he wrote to his fellow judge Sir John Eardley Wilmot about a pending case: 'While the Company is at cards I ply my Rubbers at this Work not the pleasantest in the World but what must be done, I love to do, & have it over' (Oldham, *Mansfield Manuscripts*, 1.11). While at Oxford he 'attended lectures on the Pandects of Justinian, which gave him a permanent taste for that noble system of jurisprudence' (Campbell, *Chief Justices*, 2.327). He also studied oratory while a student at Lincoln's Inn, practising the art to the point of speaking in front of a mirror while being coached by a friend, the poet Alexander Pope. It is not known how Murray and Pope met, but they remained close until Pope's death in 1744. In the early part of his career Murray seems to have been identified with Pope's literary and tory circle, company that accorded with his family's Jacobitism, but he maintained his friendships with his more whiggish friends from Westminster, and the pragmatic seems always to have dominated the romantic in his character.

The young barrister After spending the long vacation of 1730 on the continent, William was called to the bar on 23 November and took up chambers at 5 King's Bench Walk in the Inner Temple. His earliest business of consequence appears to have come from Scottish sources. He appeared as junior counsel in a number of Scottish appeals in the House of Lords in 1733 and 1734. The journal of the commissioners for trade and plantations (the 'Board of Trade') reveals appearances by Murray in the prolonged dispute from 1734 to 1737 between the Penns and Lord Baltimore over the boundaries of Maryland, and in 1734–5 as counsel for the agent of New Hampshire in a boundary dispute with Massachusetts Bay. He represented the trustees of a Georgia company in 1736 in a dispute with South Carolina over laws regulating the India trade, and in 1737–8 he acted for a Rhode Island agent in a boundary dispute with Massachusetts Bay. During the 1730s Murray appeared before the bar of the House of Commons and its committees. He spoke on the Quakers' Tithe Bill in 1735 in a rare display of opposition to religious toleration. Thereafter, Murray flirted with the idea of entering politics, and was offered the whig candidacy for the Oxford University by-election in 1737, but, as he later recalled, 'the great business that I was then coming into at the Bar of the House of Commons made it imprudent for me to think of coming into Parliament' (speech before the cabinet council, 23 Feb 1753, BL, Add. MS 33050). Eclipsing in importance any previous case with which Murray had been involved was the debate over the terms of the retributory bill brought into parliament in April 1737 to punish the city of Edinburgh for failing to prevent the lynching of Captain John Porteous. Porteous had been sentenced to death in Edinburgh after he had ordered the city guard to fire on an unruly crowd at an execution, but had been reprieved by Queen Caroline, acting as regent during the absence of George II in Hanover. Murray acted as counsel for the lord provost of Edinburgh. Ultimately the city was given only nominal punishment, and Murray's role as counsel was widely praised.

In December 1737 Murray served with great skill as junior counsel for William Sloper, accused by Theophilus Cibber of criminal conversation (adultery) with his wife, the actress Susannah Maria Cibber. Murray showed that Theophilus Cibber had arranged his wife's affair; by Murray's own account, 'business poured in upon me on all sides' (Holliday, 36) from then on. Murray may have overemphasized the importance of the case for his career, but nevertheless by 1738 his practice was strongly launched. He does not appear to have had a moment of self-doubt.

On 20 September 1738, at Raby Castle, co. Durham, Murray married Lady Elizabeth (Betty; *bap.* 1704, *d.* 1784), daughter of Daniel *Finch, seventh earl of Winchilsea and second earl of Nottingham. Elizabeth's grandfather (who died before she was born) was Heneage Finch, first earl of Nottingham, the great seventeenth-century lord chancellor. Elizabeth was an intelligent, sociable woman, and she and Murray shared an evidently happy, if childless, marriage of forty-six years until her death in 1784.

From about the time of his marriage Murray enjoyed an increasing flow of business in the court of chancery, appearing in dozens of cases before Philip Yorke, baron and later first earl of Hardwicke, lord chancellor. He became a strong admirer and friend of Hardwicke, and may have been inspired by him to apply equitable notions in his king's bench decisions.

High politics In addition to his growing chancery practice, Murray's involvement with Scottish appeals, colonial disputes, and the bar of the House of Commons continued into the early 1740s. During this time he was also drawn into the duke of Newcastle's circle. Murray's friend Andrew Stone was Newcastle's secretary; Hardwicke had been a Newcastle confidant from about 1735; and in 1738 Murray and Newcastle had become near neighbours, both residing in Lincoln's Inn Fields. In 1742 Newcastle contrived Sir John Strange's resignation as solicitor-general in order to make room for Murray, who took office on 27 November 1742; two days later Murray was returned to the Commons as MP for Boroughbridge, a seat in Newcastle's gift. The next year his status was recognized when he became a bencher of Lincoln's Inn.

In the House of Commons, Murray quickly became a force of consequence, often clashing with an old rival from Oxford, William Pitt. Murray's style of cool cerebration was likened to Cicero; Pitt's fiery oratory, to Demosthenes. Pitt was judged the superior orator in the Commons; to most observers Murray's manner was more appropriate to the House of Lords. Murray's appointment was favoured by Newcastle's friends, but some in the ministry questioned the preferment of someone with personal ties to so many members of the opposition, including tories such as Sir William Wyndham and Henry St John, Viscount Bolingbroke, as well as the various Jacobite Murrays. Any residual Jacobite loyalty that Murray had was tested when in 1746 and 1747 he and the attorney-general, Sir Dudley Ryder, prosecuted the leaders of the rising of 1745. Campbell observed that 'It must have been

a painful task for Murray to take an active part in these prosecutions, for the prisoners were connected with his family by blood or alliance; but he did his duty with firmness and moderation' (Campbell, *Chief Justices*, 2.359). Murray was indeed scrupulous to avoid any hint of favouritism or leniency, as is evident from the accounts of the trials in Ryder's diaries.

As solicitor-general Murray was required to develop a close working relationship with Ryder, who had held his post since 1737. The ministry (principally Newcastle as secretary of state, and Hardwicke as lord chancellor) relied on them for services including legal opinions on questions of domestic and international law, decisions about initiating and handling litigation, and the drafting of proposed bills for consideration in parliament. Murray did the initial drafting, submitting each document to Ryder for annotation. One such case arose in 1752 after 'the King of Prussia ... had sought to remodel the law of nations in a way that would have rendered naval superiority in time of war of little avail' (Campbell, *Chief Justices*, 2.376). A memorial was prepared by the Prussian minister spelling out details of the Prussian position, such as its denial of the validity 'of all the proceedings in the courts of Admiralty of England for a condemnation of neutral ships or goods by reason of an alleged violation of the duties of neutrality' (ibid., 2.347). To this, a 'masterly answer' was returned, one so thorough and forceful that the Prussians submitted. According to his early biographer John Holliday, Murray frequently declared to his friends that it 'was entirely his own composition, although it bears the signature of two distinguished civilians, and of his colleague in office, as well as his own' (Holliday, 424), but Ryder's diary shows Ryder's active participation in the final draft (Oldham, *Mansfield Manuscripts*, 1.18).

The close of Murray's period as solicitor-general was shadowed by an accusation that could have ended his career. In 1753 the recorder of Newcastle upon Tyne, Christopher Fawcett, sponsored by Henry Liddell, Baron Ravensworth, made public accusations that Murray and two others—Murray's friend Andrew Stone and another classmate from Westminster School—had some twenty years earlier, in Fawcett's presence, toasted the health of the Old Pretender. Not only was Murray a senior law officer, but Stone was sub-governor to the young prince of Wales, afterwards George III. The matter was formally investigated by the cabinet, before whom Murray appeared to deny the accusation. His speech (preserved at BL, Add. MS 33050, fols. 200–68) satisfied its hearers of his innocence, but Murray was infuriated by the business. He found the method of investigation taken by the cabinet 'too much like inquisition', and he 'talked with great warmth against Lord R. but more against F. whom he called villain' (Ryder, diary, 20 February 1753, Oldham, *Mansfield Manuscripts*, 1.19).

Subsequently, John Russell, fourth duke of Bedford, a former secretary of state then in opposition, but friendly to Murray, moved in the House of Lords that the examination by the cabinet be laid before the house, arguing that the examination had been conducted by an improper court resembling the seventeenth-century Star Chamber, and that the character of the three accused would be better vindicated by a full inquiry by the Lords. The sentiment among the Lords was almost universally opposed to the motion, but in the debate, nearly all of the cabinet members present spoke to explain their interpretation of the evidence that they had heard. Murray stated that 'the whole House, Strangers as well as members, appeared fully convinced of the injustice and absurdity of the motion as well as of the innocence of the accused', and that the motion 'justified the persons accused more than anything could have done' (Ryder, diary, 23 and 28 March 1753, Oldham, *Mansfield Manuscripts*, 1.20).

On 2 May 1754 Ryder became chief justice of the court of king's bench, and Murray was elevated to attorney-general. This arrangement lasted for little more than two years, as Ryder died on 25 May 1756. Murray was Ryder's natural successor, both by tradition (as the incumbent attorney-general) and by ability. Newcastle tried unsuccessfully to induce him to remain in the House of Commons, even if for a short time. Murray insisted that the appointment be accompanied by a peerage, eventually overcoming the resistance of George II. On 8 November 1756 he was called to the degree of serjeant-at-law, sworn in as chief justice of the court of king's bench, and created Lord Mansfield, baron of Mansfield. He had no connections with the town, but probably chose the title to emphasize his close relationship with Newcastle; Viscount Mansfield had been a subsidiary title of the Cavendish dukes of Newcastle in the seventeenth century.

Home and property For the first fifteen years of their married life, William and Elizabeth Murray lived exclusively in London, initially at Lincoln's Inn Fields, later at Bloomsbury Square. In 1754 Murray purchased Kenwood House, a country home on the northern edge of Hampstead Heath, from John Stuart, third earl of Bute. Expanded and improved under the architectural supervision of the Adam brothers, adorned by impeccably landscaped grounds, and supplied by its own dairy, Kenwood became the epitome of genteel country living. There Mansfield could entertain political colleagues, and show his generosity by opening his kitchen and dairy to the local needy. Lady Mansfield wrote to her nephew in May 1757, 'Kenwood is now in great beauty. Your Uncle is passionately fond of it. We go thither every Saturday and return on Mondays but I live in hopes we shall now soon go thither to fix for the Summer' (Oldham, *Mansfield Manuscripts*, 1.25). Two of Mansfield's great-nieces, Elizabeth and Anne Murray, took up permanent residence at Kenwood about 1763, as did Dido Elizabeth *Belle, a mulatto daughter of his nephew the naval officer John *Lindsay. Mansfield doted on all three young ladies.

Of Mansfield's deportment at his Sunday levees, James Boswell wrote, 'He himself sat with his tye wig, his coat buttoned, his legs pushed much before him, and his heels off the ground, and knocking frequently but not hard against each other, and he talked neatly and with vivacity' (*Papers of Boswell*, 9.48). Another observer recalled the 'happy and engaging art, which [Lord Mansfield] possessed, of putting the company present in good humour with themselves: I am convinced they naturally liked him the more for his seeming to like them so well' (Cumberland, 2.344).

Throughout his life Mansfield was financially astute. In his late twenties he was entrusted with family money to invest in government securities. His early propensity to become a moneylender is revealed in a promissory note from Andrew Stone among surviving papers at Scone Palace, dated 10 May 1737 and in amount of £45, on which Murray wrote on 15 August 1750, 'This has not been paid' (Oldham, *Mansfield Manuscripts*, 1.28). Among many financial accounts that survive at Scone Palace is a summary of Mansfield's assets as of January 1789, revealing a total value of over half a million pounds, the largest component being mortgages. According to the *London Chronicle* for 9 July 1783:

> The wisdom of Lord Mansfield, and the other best judges, who lay out their money on landed securities, in preference to the funded property of the country, now becomes more and more apparent [in view of] the present melancholy state of the Stocks.

Mansfield's income from investments was additional to the sums he accrued from his offices. His salary as chief justice of the court of king's bench was £4000, but it was more than doubled by income from the office of chief clerk and other offices, all of which generated additional payments according to the caseload. Occasional extra assignments generated further income, for example Mansfield's services as deputy speaker of the House of Lords (for which he received £500 per annum) and as the house's speaker in 1770 and again in 1783–4, by which he received fees for the introduction of private bills. Mansfield ended his judicial career a fabulously wealthy man. This he accomplished without inheriting wealth, instead building upon and wisely investing the earnings from his successful law practice before going on the bench.

Lord chief justice and political controversy Murray's political career had been characterized both by caution and a willingness to seize opportunities for his own advancement, qualities noted by Ryder in his diary. He had occasionally been directly consulted by George II on political questions, and these conferences increased after Mansfield became chief justice. Barely six months after taking office, Mansfield wrote to Hardwicke:

> I am just come from Kensington, where I was by order to deliver the [exchequer] Seal, & Mr. Fox was there to receive it. Upon my going into the Closet, the King did me the Honour to talk to me of the present melancholy Situation, & bid me tell Him what I thought. I did so very sincerely & made a great Impression. The result was that I have brought the Seal back, & am to speak to the Duke of Newcastle & your Lordship.   (11 June 1757, BL, Add. MS 35595)

Mansfield was appointed a privy councillor on 19 November 1756, soon after the formation of the Devonshire administration, and he continued to attend until he distanced himself from government when Pitt, as earl of Chatham, formed a ministry in 1766. He acted twice as chancellor of the exchequer, the custom being that the lord chief justice filled that post when it was otherwise vacant, in 1757 and again in 1767. Later, in 1770 and again in 1783, he acted as speaker of the House of Lords while the great seal was in commission pending the designation of a new lord chancellor. Through most of his thirty active years in the House of Lords, Mansfield was a leading voice in debate, closely attended by his colleagues. Horace Walpole, upon listening to Mansfield's speech in 1758 opposing a proposed bill for expansion of habeas corpus, observed:

> He spoke for two hours and a half: his voice and manner, composed of harmonious solemnity, were the least graces of his speech. I ... own that I never heard so much argument, so much sense, so much oratory united ... Perhaps it was the only speech which, in my time at least, had real effect: that is, convinced many persons. (Walpole, 3.120)

The political issue with which Mansfield was most entwined as lord chief justice was the publication of *North Briton* no. 45 by John Wilkes in 1763. The affair thrust Mansfield's attitudes to two points of controversy into focus: the competence of juries to decide the substance of charges of seditious libel, and the validity of general warrants. Mansfield recommended that Wilkes's parliamentary privilege should be no bar to his prosecution for seditious libel, but the chief justice of the common pleas, Charles Pratt, had pronounced otherwise, and it was believed by the attorney-general, Charles Yorke, that Mansfield would want parliament to decide on the question first, which both houses did by the end of November. A second case involved the validity of the general warrant used to seize Wilkes's papers; on 6 December Pratt ruled in the court of common pleas that general warrants were contrary to the constitution. Mansfield appears to have disapproved of the way Pratt handled the case, but in opinions given on 18 June 1765 in the case of *Money* v. *Leach*, Mansfield and his fellow king's bench judges all agreed that general warrants were void (PRO/TS 11/923/3237). Wilkes absconded to France before he could be tried. Meanwhile the trial of Wilkes in the court of king's bench proceeded on 21 February 1764. The jury found Wilkes guilty of the fact of publication, as directed by Mansfield. Mansfield approved a doctrine shaped early in the eighteenth century by Sir John Holt that gave judges complete control over the matter of what was or was not seditious, leaving to the jury only the basic questions of whether a defendant in fact wrote or published or sold a writing and what any blanks or innuendo in the publication meant. The jury would be instructed to return a guilty verdict if the defendant was responsible for the publication, even if the jury considered it harmless. Mansfield thus retained control of the question of whether *North Briton* no. 45 was seditious, and was responsible for sentencing Wilkes to outlawry on 1 November after he repeatedly failed to present himself before the court. Mansfield was thus confirmed in the enmity of radical opinion and of the mob.

Wilkes returned early in 1768, and surrendered himself for trial; Mansfield ruled him free to leave the court as he had not been formally arrested. The reversal of Wilkes's outlawry by the court of king's bench on the basis of a trivial error in the pleadings won Mansfield a temporary popularity and the congratulations of Newcastle for his 'most able and judicious conduct' (Thomas, 248), embarrassing a ministry formally led by Chatham and other political enemies of Newcastle and Mansfield.

During Mansfield's tenure, the most significant challenge to judicial control of seditious libel occurred in 1770 in prosecutions of publishers and sellers of Junius's 'Letter to the king'. In the first trial on 2 June 1770 John Almon was convicted, but one juror, who had raised a question during the trial, filed a post-trial affidavit claiming to have been misled by Mansfield's response. Then when the printer of the *Public Advertiser*, Henry Sampson Woodfall, was tried on 13 June 1770 for reprinting the letter, the jury found Woodfall guilty of printing and publishing only, and on 13 July the printer of the *London Evening-Post*, John Miller, was acquitted. Both juries thus rejected Mansfield's direction. Junius's letter of 14 November 1770 abused Mansfield as a Scot and a lapsed Jacobite who had corrupted English law by introducing ideas from Roman law and the civil law of other nations. It also accused him of exercising secret influence over the government while refusing to take the public position of minister. Mansfield rejected the advice of the attorney-general, William De Grey, that the government should prosecute the printers of the newspapers who had published Junius's letter of 14 November 1770, and kept his resolve following the further letters of 5 October 1771 and 21 January 1772. As with Wilkes, he did not want to give Junius publicity or to use his position to fight what would be construed as a personal battle. As a result, he was accused of political timidity, but Mansfield always distinguished between his position as a judge and that of a minister. His allegiance was always to the crown. In 1782 he spoke in opposition to a bill restraining revenue officers from voting for members of parliament, describing the measure as 'tending to the dangerous depression of regal power ... in all mixed monarchies, the crown must have its equal share of power' (*Morning Chronicle*, 4 June 1782). He noted that he was not blind to the popular torrent then running in favour of lessening the influence of the crown, but thought that this was a part of the natural prejudice that ran against the government, and that it must be kept in check.

Junius had accused Mansfield of covertly advising George III, but it is questionable whether he really was as close to the king in the early part of his reign as has been believed. Mansfield was an old ally of Newcastle; his wife was the aunt of Newcastle's political heir Charles Watson-Wentworth, second marquess of Rockingham, and so Mansfield was associated with a faction that the king mistrusted. As a judge, however, he considered himself placed at the king's service. He remained involved in the drafting of parliamentary bills as lord chief justice, and seems to have been largely responsible for the Royal Marriages Act of 1772, introduced at the desire of George III following the marriages of the king's younger brothers to controversial commoners; according to the *London Evening-Post* of 22 February 1772, this bill 'is the work of

Lord Mansfield. It is his suggestion, his contrivance, and in every other respect peculiarly his own'. As the issue of the American colonies came to dominate political debate he found that his position aligned him with George III and Lord North. He began to attend meetings of the privy council once more early in North's premiership. Those in the opposition who believed that government was conducted by secret influence imagined Mansfield as an intriguer: Edmund Burke wrote to Rockingham on 5 January 1775 that an investigation into Bute's former secretary and prominent 'king's friend' Charles Jenkinson 'would be to discover my Lord Bute, and my Lord Mansfield' (*The Correspondence of Edmund Burke*, ed. T. W. Copeland and others, 10 vols., 1958–78, 3.90). Burke was mistaken in assuming that Bute and Mansfield were allies, but his interpretation of Mansfield's role in the government was widely accepted among opponents of the ministry. Burke's opinion of Mansfield was close to that expressed by Junius; Horace Walpole also suspected Mansfield's activities. All three contributed towards the establishment of Mansfield's historical reputation as one of an ultra-conservative in politics who encouraged George III to assert the royal prerogative, an interpretation that neglected Mansfield's whig history and dedication to the principles of law over political considerations. Contemporary printmakers depicted him as a co-conspirator with the king against America. Mansfield's conviction that the demands of the colonists were incompatible with the maintenance of the British constitution provided the North ministry and George III with an adviser of great authority who enhanced the inclinations of king and minister against an innovative reinterpretation of the relations between Britain and her colonies. However, his early willingness to speak on the subject in the House of Lords receded, because 'everything said in Parliament was immediately wafted to America, and converted to the purpose of counteracting the measures to which it related' (*Lloyd's Evening Post*, 20 March 1776).

Mansfield was rewarded for his service to George III when on 31 October 1776 he was created earl of Mansfield, with a special remainder to Louisa (*née* Cathcart), Viscountess Stormont, wife of his nephew David *Murray, seventh Viscount Stormont; Mansfield named his nephew's wife as his successor 'owing to a notion then prevalent that no British peerage granted even in remainder to a Scottish peer would enable such peer to sit in Parliament' (GEC, *Peerage*, 8.388). He remained sympathetic to North's ministry, although in 1778 and 1779 he supported the proposed reconstruction of the administration in order to accommodate Chatham. His personal dislike of Chatham was overcome by his conviction that only this measure would avert the collapse of government. His withdrawal from privy council meetings from 1779 was interpreted as a sign that the ministry lost his confidence.

As a legislator, Mansfield was especially interested in social issues. He was involved in the regulation of private insane asylums; in 1777 he was reported to be working on a bill to protect young women from seduction. His other legislative initiatives included the preparation of a measure that could be used against fraudulent claimants in insolvency cases in 1781, and in 1786 he convened a meeting of judges at his house in Lincoln's Inn Fields to seek a solution to the vexing repetition of perjury in court proceedings, although no legislation was forthcoming.

In his later years Mansfield, in political philosophy, became suspicious and untrusting, viewing world affairs with a melancholy eye. He believed avidly in the importance of strong, principled leadership, and in a letter to Warren Hastings reflected that 'the Fate of Empires has often, & generally does, depend upon One Man. We lost the West Indies for want of such a Man & had it not been for you, We should have lost the East' (27 Sept 1783, BL, Add. MSS 29160). That year, he voted with the Fox–North coalition on the India Bill, but changed sides following the king's message indicating his opposition to the measure. Nathaniel Wraxall thought that he supported the opposition to the ministry of William Pitt the younger in 1784, although age probably curtailed his political activity from then on.

Mansfield on the bench Vigorously disciplined in his own work habits, Mansfield hated circuitousness and inefficiency in the law courts. He read newspapers during prolix legal arguments to discourage long-winded barristers; he kept court in session for long hours, even on holidays, to get through heavy caseloads, and he cut through procedural red tape whenever he could. He always ensured that the court sat until even the most junior counsel had been heard. He gained a reputation in the nineteenth century for having sought to dominate his fellow judges, but the evidence suggests that he in fact placed a great reliance on the skills of his colleagues, particularly in the first few years of his period as chief justice. For the most part, Mansfield's relationships with his junior judges, and with barristers appearing before him, were cordial and respectful; decisions reached by the court reflected a remarkable degree of unanimity. He also strove, though a common-law judge, to reach equitable solutions in cases that he tried, as long as he could do so without upsetting established legal principles or without offence to a higher value. This inclination anticipated the eventual merger of law and equity, but it provoked outcries from those like Junius and Charles Pratt who felt that Mansfield was undermining the basis of English common law by introducing ideas from other legal traditions.

Yet in the realm of commerce Mansfield understood the need for stability and predictability. He stated in a 1779 insurance case (*Milles* v. *Fletcher*) that 'The great object in every branch of the law, but especially in mercantile law, is certainty'. He gained a reputation, in the words of his protégé Francis Buller, as 'the founder of the commercial law of this country' (*Lickbarrow* v. *Mason*), which was justified especially in cases dealing with insurance and negotiable instruments. The sheer volume of marine insurance litigation that arose—accelerating as the years went by because of Mansfield's evident aptitude for and interest in the subject—facilitated the articulation of principles of indemnity and the perception of relationships between insurance rules that had never before been accomplished. This, in turn, encouraged the development of rules for life and fire insurance. Mansfield also modernized the law of negotiable instruments to accommodate an aggressive mercantile economy, at times adapting and incorporating into the common law principles that had been long established on the continent.

Mansfield is sometimes said to have been an early contributor to women's rights, owing to his decisions dealing with contracts between merchants and married women. Mansfield's true objective was to protect the merchants from women who presented themselves as feme sole, later taking shelter behind their married state. In these cases, nevertheless, Mansfield demonstrated his appreciation of the adaptability of the common law to change. He remarked on the case of *Ringstead* v. *Lady Lanesborough* in 1783:

> In process of Time, through the Succession of Ages, New Manners arise, New Modes of Acting diversify the Subject & beget Cases within the letter but not within the Reason of the general Rule. Inconvenience, Injustice and many Absurditys must follow if the letter of a general Rule was to govern Cases not within the Reason, & therefore Exceptions are implied from Time to Time, as the Cases fit to be excepted arise, and the Exceptions form a System of Law together with the Rule.   (Scone Palace MSS, 1st ser., box 68; Oldham, *Mansfield Manuscripts*, 1.199)

In a letter to the *Morning Post* of 10 February 1778, an admirer observed that Mansfield 'knows that law originates in common sense and his audiences are surprised when they hear that all its intricacies … when fairly developed, coincide entirely with it'. Mansfield was not always successful, however, in keeping common sense and legal principles aligned. Two famous attempts that failed were in the law of contracts and real property. In the 1765 case *Pillans and Rose* v. *Van Mierop* he declared that 'the ancient notion about the want of consideration was for the sake of evidence only', so that proof of consideration was not necessary if the contractual transaction could be shown by other evidentiary means. This notion was overruled by the House of Lords in *Rann* v. *Hughes* (1778). In 1770, in *Perrin* v. *Blake*, Mansfield tried to implement what he viewed as the clear intent of a testator, disregarding a venerable rule that had been established in *Shelley's Case* in the reign of Elizabeth and followed faithfully since. His decision was reversed by the exchequer chamber, where the prime mover was Justice William Blackstone, a repulse so decisive that it 'involved retreat upon the whole front of real property' (Fifoot, 181).

Mansfield was a committed free trader, even to the point of endorsing trading with the enemy. He thought that statutory restrictions on market practices such as forestalling and engrossing, dating from the reign of Edward VI, were regressive, and he welcomed their repeal in 1772. He opposed combinations of labour to raise wages because, in addition to disrupting the public peace, they threatened to raise wages above 'what the trade would bear, thus driving capital away' (Daniels, 51). In intellectual property cases, Mansfield encouraged juries to give strong common-law protection to trademark ideas. He upheld authors' common-law property rights in their writings in 1769 in the landmark copyright decision in *Millar* v. *Taylor* (overturned by the House of Lords in 1774 in *Donaldson* v. *Beckett*). Mansfield believed that patent rights were advantageous to the economy, but he saw and met the need to adapt patent law to more sophisticated technological times, something that he accomplished by subtle changes in legal principles and by careful jury guidance on damage awards.

Despite his dramatic support for authors' rights in *Millar* v. *Taylor*, Mansfield's conduct over the prosecutions of Wilkes and the printers of Junius showed that he was not a friend to freedom of the press. The controversy culminated during his tenure as chief justice in *R.* v. *Shipley*, tried at Shrewsbury in 1784 before Francis Buller, in which a harmless dialogue written by Sir William Jones and published by his brother-in-law William Davies Shipley, dean of St Asaph, was held libellous, though on a motion in arrest of judgment Shipley was released on a technicality. Mansfield did not create the doctrine that withheld from the jury the question whether a publication was seditious, but perhaps his loyalty to the crown led him to cling tenaciously to an awkward procedure that was out of joint with the times. Shortly before his death the procedure was overturned by Fox's Libel Act of 1792.

Where the interests of the government or the crown, or the needs of the mercantile economy, were not central, Mansfield was a guardian against injustice. He is famous for the Somerset case of 1772, in which a former slave was brought before the court by a writ of habeas corpus obtained by the abolitionist Granville Sharp. James Somerset had been clapped in irons by his former master and was being shipped out to be sold in Jamaica. Mansfield believed that freeing the slaves would have a harshly negative impact on the British economy, and so was reluctant to issue a formal decision and tried hard to get the parties to settle, which the parties had resolved not to do. When the decision issued, the actual holding went only so far as to say that a master could not by force dispatch a slave out of the country. Nevertheless it proved to be a forceful contribution to the abolitionist cause, and Mansfield is justifiably credited for his declaration that 'Slavery is of such a nature as not to be introduced by inference from principles either natural or political', that 'it must be from positive law', and that it 'is so odious that it must be construed strictly' (Oldham, *Mansfield Manuscripts*, 2.1230).

Mansfield was a strong believer in religious toleration; as he once stated, 'My desire to disturb no man for conscience' sake is pretty well known, and, I hope, will be had in remembrance' (Campbell, *Chief Justices*, 2.529). One of his important rulings in this regard, in 1767, was that the City of London's practice of raising money by electing dissenters to the position of sheriff, and then fining them £400 if they refused to serve, violated the Corporation and Toleration Acts. His beliefs caused him to interpret statutes restricting religious freedom so narrowly that he virtually invited juries to render the statutes impotent, an invitation that the jurors cheerfully accepted. An unfortunate result of this behaviour was that Mansfield became a target of the anti-Catholic mob that pillaged London in the Gordon riots of 1780. Mansfield's house in Bloomsbury Square, including his splendid library, was sacked and burnt, and he and Lady Mansfield barely escaped with their lives.

Much of Mansfield's judicial energy throughout his thirty active years on the bench was devoted to the conduct of jury trials. Given the choice, he might have dispensed with juries—he cautioned against extending the practice to Scotland—but, notwithstanding, his relationship with his juries was customarily cordial and efficacious. He told James Boswell that juries always took his direction, 'except in political causes where they do not at all keep themselves to right and wrong' (*Papers of Boswell*, 6.109). Extraordinarily effective was Mansfield's teamwork with special juries. He did not invent either the special jury or its frequent composition, especially in London, of merchants, but he perceived how the special jury might be used instrumentally to establish legal principles by identifying mercantile practices and folding those practices into the common law.

Final years Accused occasionally of political timidity, criticized at times for his tenacious allegiance to the crown and his resistance to freedom of the press, Mansfield nevertheless gained the reputation by the 1780s of having become one of England's greatest judges. Even John Wilkes became an admirer, remarking (perhaps unfairly) that to hear the puisne judges deliver their judgments after their chief had concluded, 'was like a draught of hog's-wash after a bottle of champagne' (Polson, 1.318). Throughout his life Mansfield's habits were temperate and his physical health unusually good, save for an occasional bout with rheumatism. On 11 December 1785, aged eighty, he wrote to the duke of Rutland, 'I go down hill with a gentle decay, and I thank God, without gout or stone' (*Rutland MSS*, 3.268). On 1 November the *London Chronicle* had reported that Lord Mansfield 'has been obliged to give up the pleasure of riding on horseback owing to a weakness in his wrists'. He had survived his wife, who died at Kenwood on 10 April 1784.

Mansfield continued to perform the duties of chief justice until spring 1786, when it became physically difficult for him to exercise the functions of the role. He clung to office despite incapacity, supposedly in order to overcome the resistance of George III to Mansfield's preference that his protégé and fellow judge Francis Buller become his successor as chief justice of king's bench. He did, however, tender a letter of resignation to Lord Chancellor Thurlow in November 1786 which, though expressing the hope that Buller would be designated, was not conditional on that event (Oldham, *Mansfield Manuscripts*, 1.43). Thurlow evidently did not communicate Mansfield's resignation request to the king, and nearly two more years passed until the resignation took place and Lloyd Kenyon was named chief justice. After his resignation, Mansfield lived in retirement at Kenwood. He continued to improve the grounds and entertained visitors, including parties of barristers. On 1 August 1792 the prohibition against Scottish peers sitting in the House of Lords by right of their British

peerages having been lifted in 1782, he was given a second earldom of Mansfield, located in Middlesex to distinguish it from the earlier (Nottinghamshire) earldom, with remainder to his nephew Viscount Stormont. He died at Kenwood House on 20 March 1793, and was buried in the north cross, Westminster Abbey, on 28 March.

JAMES OLDHAM

Sources G. Adams, 'Dido Elizabeth Belle, a black girl at Kenwood', *Camden History Review*, 12 (1984), 10–14 · J. H. Baker, *An introduction to English legal history*, 3rd edn (1990) · J. H. Baker, *The legal profession and the common law: historical essays* (1986) · W. Blackstone, *Commentaries on the laws of England*, 4 vols. (1765–9); 13th edn (Dublin, 1796) · H. Brougham, *Historical sketches of statesmen who flourished in the time of George III*, 2nd edn (1889) · J. Buchan, *Some eighteenth century byways and other essays* (1908) · John, Lord Campbell, *The lives of the chief justices of England*, 3 vols. (1849–57) · J. Campbell, *Lives of the lord chancellors*, 4th edn, 10 vols. (1856–7) · J. Cradock, *Literary and miscellaneous memoirs*, 2 vols. (1826) · R. Cumberland, *Memoirs of Richard Cumberland written by himself*, 2 vols. (1806–7) · G. W. Daniels, *The early English cotton industry* (1920) · D. B. Davis, *The problem of slavery in the age of revolution, 1770–1823* (Ithaca, N.Y., 1975) · J. P. De Castro, *The Gordon riots* (1926) · D. Duman, *The judicial bench in England, 1727–1875* (1982) · *The works of Alexander Pope*, ed. W. Elwin and W. J. Courthope, 10 vols. (1871–89) · W. D. Evans, *A general view of the decisions of Lord Mansfield in civil causes*, 2 vols. (1803) · C. Fearne, *An essay on the learning of contingent remainders and executory devises* (1772) · E. Fiddes, 'Lord Mansfield and the Somerset case', *Law Quarterly Review*, 50 (1934), 499–511 · C. H. S. Fifoot, *Lord Mansfield* (1936) · Foss, *Judges* · E. Foss, *Memories of Westminster Hall*, 2 vols. (Boston, MA, 1874) · M. D. George, 'The combination laws reconsidered', *Economic Journal (Suppl.), Economic History Series*, 1/2 (1927), 214–28 · R. Gore-Browne, *Chancellor Thurlow: the life and times of an eighteenth century lawyer* (1953) · H. G. Graham, *The social life of Scotland in the eighteenth century*, 4th edn (1950) · P. Hamburger, 'The development of the law of seditious libel and the control of the press', *Stanford Law Review*, 37 (1985), 661–765 · A. Hamilton, *The infamous 'Essay on woman', or, John Wilkes seated between vice and virtue* (1972) · D. Ryder, diary, MS transcriptions by K. L. Perrin, Harrowby Manuscript Trust · E. Heward, *Lord Mansfield* (1979) · P. Hoare, *Memoirs of Granville Sharpe, esq.* (1820) · Holdsworth, *Eng. law* · J. Holliday, *The life of William late earl of Mansfield* (1797) · *The diary and letters of His Excellency Thomas Hutchinson*, ed. P. O. Hutchinson, 2 vols. (1883–6) · *Journal of the commissioners for trade and plantations [1704–82]*, 14 vols (1920–38) · *Letters of the celebrated Junius*, new edn, 2 vols. (1797) · *Lord Eldon's anecdote book*, ed. A. L. J. Lincoln and R. L. McEwen (1960) · *The manuscripts of his grace the duke of Rutland*, 4 vols., HMC, 24 (1888–1905) · A. Murphy, *The life of David Garrick, esq.* (1801) · J. Nicholls, *Recollections and reflections, personal and political, as connected with public affairs during the reign of George III*, 2 vols. (1822) · J. Oldham, *The Mansfield manuscripts and the growth of English law in the eighteenth century*, 2 vols. (1992) · J. Oldham, 'The work of Ryder and Murray as law officers of the crown', *Legal record and historical reality*, ed. T. G. Watkin (1989), chap. 9, 157–73 · H. Phillips, *Mid-Georgian London: a topographical and social survey of central and western London about 1750* (1964) · A. Polson, *Law and lawyers, or, Sketches and illustrations of legal history and biography*, 2 vols. (1840) · H. Roscoe, *Westminster Hall, or, Professional relics and anecdotes of the bar, bench, and woolsack*, 3 vols. (1825) · [W. Murray], trial notebooks, miscellaneous king's bench papers, correspondence, accounts, related documents, Scone Palace, Perth, Scotland · *Private papers of James Boswell from Malahide Castle*, ed. G. Scott and F. A. Pottle, 18 vols. (privately printed, Mount Vernon, NY, 1928) · R. R. Sedgwick, 'Murray, Hon. William', HoP, *Commons, 1715–54* · W. Seward, *Anecdotes of distinguished persons, chiefly of the last and two preceding centuries*, 5th edn, 4 vols. (1804) · F. O. Shyllon, *Black slaves in Britain* (1974) · R. Stevens, *Law and politics: the House of Lords as a judicial body, 1800–1976* (1978) · H. A. H. Tayler, *The Jacobite court at Rome in 1719* (1938) · Cobbett, *Parl. hist.* · H. Twiss, *The public and private life of Lord Chancellor*

Eldon, 2 vols. (Philadelphia, 1844) • H. Walpole, *Memoirs of the reign of King George the Second*, ed. Lord Holland, 2nd edn, 3 vols. (1847) • E. Washburn, 'Somerset's case and the extension of villeinage and slavery in England', *Proceedings of the Massachusetts Historical Society*, 7 (1864), 308–26 • W. Wiecek, 'Somerset: Lord Mansfield and the legitimacy of slavery in the Anglo-American world', *University of Chicago Law Review*, 42 (1974), 86–146 • J. E. Wilmot, *Memoirs of the life of the Right Honourable Sir John Eardley Wilmot, knt.* (1802) • P. C. Yorke, *The life and correspondence of Philip Yorke, earl of Hardwicke*, 3 vols. (1913) • P. D. G. Thomas, *John Wilkes: a friend to liberty* (1996) • A. Valentine, *Lord North*, 2 vols. (1967) • J. J. Sack, *From Jacobite to conservative: reaction and orthodoxy in Britain, c.1760–1832* (1993) • PRO, TS 11/923/3237 • GEC, *Peerage*

Archives NRA, priv. coll., judge's notebooks, corresp., and papers | BL, letters to Lord Hardwicke, Add. MSS 35590–35596, *passim* • BL, corresp. with Lord Holderness, Egerton MSS 3437–3457 • BL, corresp. with Lord Liverpool, Add. MSS 38205–38578 • BL, corresp. with duke of Newcastle, etc., Add. MSS 32697–33072, *passim* • Sheff. Arch., letters to Lord Rockingham • U. Nott. L., letters to duke of Newcastle, etc. • U. Nott. L., corresp. with duke of Portland

Likenesses J. B. van Loo, oils, *c.*1732, Scone Palace, Perthshire; version, NPG • J. B. van Loo, oils, *c.*1737, Scone Palace, Perthshire • J. B. van Loo, oils, *c.*1738, RCP Lond. • J. M. Rysbrack, marble bust, 1743, Scone Palace, Perthshire • D. Martin, oils, *c.*1757, priv. coll. • J. Zoffany, group portrait, oils, 1767–8 (Charles Macklin as Shylock), Tate collection • D. Martin, oils, 1770, Christ Church Oxf.; versions, Scone Palace, Perthshire, Scot. NPG • J. Reynolds, oils, *c.*1776, Scone Palace, Perthshire • D. Martin, oils, 1777, Scot. NPG • oils, 1777 (after D. Martin, 1770), Scot. NPG • J. Nollekens, marble bust, 1779, Kenwood House, London • J. Tassie, Wedgwood medallion, 1779, BM; version, Scot. NPG • paste medallion, 1779 (after J. Tassie), Scot. NPG • J. S. Copley, oils, 1782–3, NPG [*see illus.*] • F. Bartolozzi, chalk drawing, *c.*1783, Metropolitan Museum of Art, New York • J. S. Copley, group portrait, oils, 1783 (*The collapse of the earl of Chatham in the House of Lords, 7 July 1778*), Tate collection; on loan to NPG • J. Reynolds, oils, 1785, Scone Palace, Perthshire • J. Reynolds, oils, 1785, Lincoln's Inn, London • Z. Bartolozzi, stipple and line engraving, pubd 1786 (after J. Reynolds) • J. Nollekens, marble bust, 1790, Belvoir Castle, Leicestershire • J. Jones, stipple, pubd 1791 (after W. Grimaldi), BM • J. Flaxman, marble effigy, 1795–1801, Westminster Abbey • E. H. Baily, marble statue, 1855, Palace of Westminster, London • Mason, oils, 1866 (after J. Reynolds), Scot. NPG • J. Collyer, engraving (after J. Reynolds), repro. in Blackstone, *Commentaries* • J. S. Copley, chalk study for portrait of 1783, BM • J. S. Copley, sketch, Boston Athenaeum • D. Martin, oils, Faculty of Advocates, Parliament House, Edinburgh • D. Martin, red chalk drawing, Scot. NPG • J. Nollekens, bust, Trinity Hall, Cambridge

Murray, William Henry (1790–1852), actor and theatre manager, was the son of the actor and playwright Charles *Murray (1754–1821) from his liaison with the married actress Anne Payne, and younger brother to the actress Harriet *Siddons [*see under* Siddons, Henry]. He was born at Bath, where as a child he appeared as Puck, probably on 11 March 1794, when, for his father's benefit, *A Midsummer Night's Dream* was played, with his sister Maria as Titania. Maria later married Joseph Leathley Cowell, and became the mother of Samuel Houghton Cowell. William accompanied his father to London, and from the season of 1803–4 played various small parts at Covent Garden under the Kemble management. He later said that he owed his training in stage-management and the manipulation of theatrical spectacle to Charles Farley, the stage-manager at Covent Garden. On 20 November 1809 he made his first

William Henry Murray (1790–1852), by Sir John Watson-Gordon, exh. Institute for Encouragement of Fine Arts in Scotland 1825

appearance in Edinburgh, with which city he remained associated for forty-two years. His brother-in-law Henry *Siddons had secured the royal letters patent, and on leaving the theatre in Shakspere Square had fitted up as a playhouse the Circus in Leith Walk. Until 1811 Murray filled many small parts there, at first, according to his own confession, with very little success. In January 1810, as stage-manager, he produced *The Tempest*.

Murray moved with the company to the theatre in Shakspere Square. On 12 April 1815 Henry Siddons died, and Murray, on behalf of his sister Harriet and her children, entered on the management, which was then heavily in debt. From the first he displayed much energy, and a summer engagement of Eliza O'Neill was a great success. On the opening of the season of 1815–16 Harriet Siddons, who had retired, reappeared. In January 1816 Murray played Sebastian to his sister's Viola in *Twelfth Night*. Engagements of Charles Kemble and Charles Mathews followed, and were succeeded by the appearance of Edmund Kean. Murray's own parts were subordinate. He played Ross to Kemble's Macbeth on the last night of the latter's appearance in Edinburgh, and, for his own benefit in April 1817, Tony Lumpkin in *She Stoops to Conquer*. Despite taking his company to Glasgow, and engaging Frederick Yates and many good actors, the fortunes of the house continued to decline until February 1819, when *Rob Roy Macgregor, or, Auld Lang Syne* was produced. This was probably the greatest and most enduring theatrical success which had then been known in Scotland. Murray was Captain Thornton. He was then seen as Flutter in *The Belle's Stratagem*, Horatio in *Hamlet*, one of the Dromios in *The Comedy of Errors*, and other parts. He also directed the pantomime, and showed some ability as a pantomimist.

Between 1820 and 1825 a number of adaptations of Sir Walter Scott's novels enjoyed a huge success. In *The Heart of Midlothian* Murray was Black Frank and his wife Effie Deans. On the visit of George IV to the Edinburgh Theatre (27 August 1822) he resumed his part of Captain Thornton. He went on to play Wamba in a version of *Ivanhoe* compiled by himself, the Laird of Balmawhapple in a version of *Waverley*, and Joshua Geddes in a version of *Redgauntlet* attributed to himself. Sir Kenneth of Scotland in *The Talisman* and Roland in *Mary Stuart*, his own adaptation of *The Abbot*, were two of his other successful roles. In the season of 1825–6 he made a great hit as Paul Pry. His farce *No*, produced in February 1827, had much success, and was followed in June by his drama *Gilderoy*. In 1829, in Planché's *Charles XII*, he played the part of Adam Brock. A piece of sharp practice in obtaining a manuscript copy of this piece is commented on by Planché in his *Recollections and Reflections* (1872), and led to the passing of the first Dramatic Authors' Act. In 1830, on the expiration of Henry Siddons's patent, the theatre became the property of Harriet Siddons, who had paid the purchase money.

Having refused an offer to act at Covent Garden, Murray remained at Edinburgh, and secured the lease not only of the Theatre Royal, but also, in conjunction with Yates, of the playhouse in Leith Walk, which had been known during the previous ten years as the Pantheon and latterly as the Caledonian, but under Murray was renamed the Adelphi. His management of both theatres proved an unbroken success (the partnership with Yates lasted only one year). The Theatre Royal opened for the first time under Murray's direct management in November 1830, with John Tobin's *The Honeymoon*, in which Murray played Jaques. Among other parts in which Murray was seen in the next ten years were Sir Benjamin Backbite, Bob Acres, Caliban, Falstaff, Figaro, and Dick Luckless in *The Highland Widow*, taken from Scott's *Chronicles of the Canongate*. Newman Noggs in *Nicholas Nickleby* and Bumble in *Oliver Twist* also belong to this period. For his benefit in May 1843 he played Shylock.

In 1848, through age, Murray resigned the position of stage-manager. He made his last appearance on the Edinburgh stage for his benefit on 22 October 1851 at the Adelphi, as Sir Anthony Absolute. He was said to be in bad health, and so tired of his profession that he destroyed his diary and all books connected with his stage life, and gave away his stage wardrobe. He acted more than once afterwards, however, in Aberdeen and Dundee. He retired with a competency to live in St Andrews. On returning from a party at Professor Playfair's on 5 May 1852 he was taken ill, and died at St Andrews later on the same day. Murray was twice married. His first wife was a Miss Dyke, the sister-in-law of the poet Thomas Moore (1779–1852); the second was a Miss Gray, a member of his company. She survived until 1888. He had several children: more than one daughter played occasionally at the Theatre Royal, and a son, Henry Murray, became an actor in middle life.

A talented actor in juvenile parts where no deep emotion or pathos had to be displayed, Murray was good also in comedy, and in what are known as 'character' parts he excelled. He wrote many dramas intended to serve a temporary purpose, and without literary aim. *Diamond Cut Diamond*, an interlude, from *How to Die for Love*, a translation from Kotzebue; *Cramond Brig*, assigned by error to Lockhart, and depreciated by Scott; *Mary Stuart*; *Gilderoy*; and a burlesque of *Romeo and Juliet* were among his successes. His management was judicious and resolute, but did not escape the charge of being penurious; his relations with playwrights were not always satisfactory, or even creditable; and he suffered in later years from depression, uncertain temper, and an unreasonable fear of bankruptcy. About 1819 he helped to found the Edinburgh Theatrical Fund, and became one of its directors. A special feature in his management consisted of the addresses he spoke at the beginning and close of a season and on other occasions. These were in both verse and prose, well written, effective, and humorous. A collection of them was published in 1851. Murray was staid, formal, and a little pedantic. Scott often makes friendly reference to him, and records how on an occasion in 1827 Murray, answering the question 'Who wrote Shakespeare?' after one had answered Ben Jonson and another Finis, said, 'No, it is Sir Walter Scott; he confessed it at a public meeting the other day.'

JOSEPH KNIGHT, *rev.* NILANJANA BANERJI

Sources J. C. Dibdin, *The annals of the Edinburgh stage* (1888) · Hall, *Dramatic ports.* · Genest, *Eng. stage* · W. H. Murray, *The farewell and occasional addresses delivered by W. H. Murray, Esq.* (1851) · *The Theatre*, 1 (1851–2) · *Theatrical Inquisitor, and Monthly Mirror*, 4 (1814), 186–90 · J. G. Lockhart, *The life of Sir Walter Scott*, [new edn] (1893) · A. Mathews, *Memoirs of Charles Mathews*, 4 vols. (1838–9) · *The journal of Sir Walter Scott*, 2 vols. (1890–91) · J. Tallis, *Dramatic Magazine* (1850–51) **Archives** NL Scot., genealogical papers **Likenesses** J. Watson-Gordon, oils, exh. Institute for Encouragement of Fine Arts in Scotland 1825, Garr. Club [*see illus.*] · W. Allan, oils, Scot. NPG · B. W. Crombie, pencil drawing, Scot. NPG · likeness, repro. in B. W. Crombie and W. S. Douglas, *Modern Athenians* (1882), no. 44 · oils, Garr. Club · portrait, repro. in *The national drama* (1825)

Murray, William Staite (1881–1962), potter and teacher of pottery, was born on 9 September 1881 at 103 High Street, Deptford, London, the third son of the six children of James Murray, merchant, and his wife, Arabella, daughter of Abel Staite, cheesemonger, of London. From an early age he showed an aptitude for drawing, and after short periods at Haberdashers' Aske's School in New Cross and possibly at nearby Colfe's School, he was sent around the age of twelve to cousins who were professional artists. This stay lasted for two years until his father, a strict Calvinist of Scottish descent, decided that the life of an artist held little prospects, and in 1895 he arranged employment witBlokkers, a firm of bulb and seed merchants at Akersloot in North Holland. Although far removed from the life of an artist, Murray gained a useful knowledge of botany, made a small collection of Delft and Nankin pottery, then a fashionable interest, and travelled widely, visiting Belgium, Germany, and France, where he studied painting.

In the Netherlands, Murray was introduced to theosophy, a religious movement based on Buddhist and Hindu mysticism founded by Helena Petrovna Blavatsky in the United States some twenty years earlier. Very different from his own religious background, the sect offered Murray a meaningful structure for his own ideas. Later he was to become a committed Buddhist. About 1900 Murray was sent to the USA and Canada, probably to further his knowledge of horticulture, though nothing is known of his experiences there.

Back in London, Murray's father made him manager of Blokker and Murray, bulb and seed merchants in New Cross, though the business was not a success. Through family connections he became friendly with Kathleen Harriet (d. 1952), daughter of Richard Medhurst, a ship and chandlery business owner, who shared his love of painting. They married on 6 June 1905, setting up home at 111 Tyrwhitt Road, Lewisham, Kent. Keen to develop his artistic interests Murray attended evening pottery classes at Camberwell School of Arts and Crafts where its principal, William Dalton, himself an enthusiastic potter, had initiated a course. Murray also continued to paint and even tried bronze casting. Perhaps inspired by the 1910 exhibition of Song and Yuan dynasty Chinese pottery and porcelain at the Burlington Fine Arts Club in Savile Row, Murray was inspired to develop further his potting skills. In sharp contrast to the accepted court porcelains of the Ming dynasty the Song pots highlighted integration of form with glaze and decoration. The exhibition stimulated other artist potters, notably Reginald Wells and George Cox.

For a time Murray became closely associated with the painter Cuthbert Hamilton, who was a friend of Wyndham Lewis, founder of the Vorticists, and he became part of a loose-knit group of radical painters, sculptors, and poets. Potting took up more and more of Murray's time, and a street directory of 1916 lists him as 'artist potter'. At this time he had a pottery at 18 Yeoman's Row, off Brompton Road, shared with Cuthbert Hamilton, where they made earthenware with painted decoration. Many of his designs carried out on shallow bowls espoused abstract Vorticist principles, often in asymmetrical compositions. The First World War curtailed production when from 1915 to 1918 Murray served in the machine-gun corps at Grantham.

Following the end of the war Murray found a new direction in his work by setting up his own workshop in 1919 at his brothers' foundry in Rotherhithe, building a high-temperature gas-fired kiln with the aim of producing high-fired stoneware inspired by Song dynasty wares. A fascinating link with the work of the pioneering Martin brothers, makers of individual salt-glaze wares, took place when Murray visited Robert Wallace Martin, the last surviving brother. This was possibly to seek advice on high-temperature firing, as little technical information was generally available.

Murray was also encouraged by the work of Bernard Leach, who in 1920 returned from Japan with the potter Hamada Shoji and set up a workshop in St Ives producing among other wares high-fired stonewares, and unlike Murray had the advantage of having spent time in Japan and China. Murray and Leach met in 1921 at an exhibition of the latter's work in London. A friendship was struck, and Murray visited St Ives, learned to throw on a Japanese wheel that was pushed round with a stick, and from Hamada learned much about high-temperature glazes and oriental brushwork. To improve the firing Murray experimented with a two-chamber oil-fired kiln, claiming in a letter to *The Times* to 'have successfully used crude oil for burning pottery since 1923', a system which allowed a great measure of control (22 Sept 1926). The design was patented in 1926.

From this time Murray worked only in stoneware, producing wheel-thrown bowls and magnificent bottles,

William Staite Murray (1881–1962), by unknown photographer, *c*.1930

many with brush decoration. In 1920 he moved to Wickham Road, Brockley, near Lewisham, where he worked with his only assistant, whom he named Molly as he did not like her forename. By 1924 Murray had made sufficient technical advances to produce convincing pieces in a Song-like style, and had begun to develop an individual style, with full-bodied forms often covered with such classic glazes as 'temmoku', 'hare's fur', and 'chun'. Patronage from such important collectors as George Eumorfopoulos and later Eric Milner-White, dean of York, helped to establish his reputation. His pots were shown at typical craft events such as the Red Rose Guild annual exhibition in Manchester, as well as in galleries usually devoted to fine art. In 1929 he moved to Court Cottage, Bray, Berkshire, taking Molly with him.

In 1925 Murray was appointed head of pottery at the Royal College of Art, London, in preference to Bernard Leach, a position he held until 1939. He was tall and thin, and an influential teacher, though by his own and his students' accounts he did little actual instructing, preferring instead to 'create an atmosphere' in which students could develop. Notable students include R. W. Washington, Sam Haile, and Henry Hammond, who later became head of the ceramics department at Farnham School of Art. As a member of the radical Seven and Five Society and with artists including Barbara Hepworth and Ben and Winifred Nicholson, Murray showed his pots alongside paintings and sculpture, and could and did place substantial sums on his pieces. Some were left with little decoration, the thrown vessels relying on the strong form and rich glaze for their impact. Others were highly decorated with painted and incised decoration that often covered the whole piece. The finest were given titles such as *Persian Garden* and to emphasize the abstract quality of the work *Serenity*, *Cadence*, and *Aulos*.

In 1939 Murray and his wife went to Rhodesia to visit relatives, and frustrated in their attempts to return by the Second World War they eventually settled at Odzi, near Umtali, Rhodesia. Although intending to return to England, news of rationing and austerity kept them in Rhodesia and Murray never made another pot. Kathleen died on 25 July 1952, the same day on which Murray received a letter of greeting from the International Conference of Potters and Weavers at Dartington Hall, Devon. Much of his time was devoted to forming a Buddhist Society in Umtali. Diagnosis of cancer encouraged him to make a brief visit to England where he took the opportunity to burn virtually all his papers and hold a farewell exhibition in November 1958 at the Leicester Galleries, London. He returned to Rhodesia in December, where he died of cancer at the general hospital, Umtali, on 7 February 1962.

With Bernard Leach, William Staite Murray was one of the towering figures of the art and craft world in the 1920s and 1930s. As a near contemporary of Leach (Murray was six years older) they had a great deal in common in a shared interest in oriental aesthetics, in Far Eastern religions, and in high-fired stoneware ceramics, but after an initial friendship fundamental differences in approach to the role of craft in the modern world kept them apart. Murray regarded himself as an artist making art objects with no use other than to be beautiful, and did not share Leach's interest in the Arts and Crafts movement or his belief that craft could play a social role. Following a decline in his reputation as a major twentieth-century artist potter, a major retrospective in 1984 firmly established his strength as both potter and artist. His insistence that his work be seen as art is a debate that continues to engage artist–makers. Examples of his work are in the Victoria and Albert Museum, London, the Milner-White Collection at York City Art Gallery and Southampton Art Gallery, and the Crafts Study Centre at the West Surrey School of Art, Farnham.   EMMANUEL COOPER

Sources M. Haslam, *William Staite Murray* (1984) [exhibition catalogue, Cleveland Gallery and V&A, 1984] · J. Webber, *Crafts*, 14 (1975), 25–33 · H. Hammond, 'A magnetic teacher', *Crafts*, 14 (1975), 33–4 · R. Hyne, 'William Staite Murray: potter and artist', *Ceramic Review*, 92 (March–April 1985) · *CGPLA Eng. & Wales* (1962)
Archives Holburne Museum of Art, Bath, papers
Likenesses photograph, *c*.1930, unknown collection; copyprint, NPG [*see illus.*]
Wealth at death £59,985 14*s*. (in England): probate, 3 Sept 1962, *CGPLA Eng. & Wales*

PICTURE CREDITS

Morant, Harry Harbord [the Breaker] (1864?–1902)—Australian War Memorial negative number A05311

Morant, Sir Robert Laurie (1863–1920)—© National Portrait Gallery, London

Mordaunt, Charles, third earl of Peterborough and first earl of Monmouth (1658?–1735)—© National Portrait Gallery, London

Mordaunt, John, second Baron Mordaunt (1508–1571)—Principal and Fellows of Brasenose College, Oxford

Mordaunt, John, first Viscount Mordaunt of Avalon (1626–1675)—© Copyright The British Museum

Morden, Sir John, baronet (bap. 1623, d. 1708)—courtesy of the Trustees of Morden College

More, Alexander (1616–1670)—© National Portrait Gallery, London

More, Sir George (1553–1632)—private collection. Photograph: Photographic Survey, Courtauld Institute of Art, London

More, Hannah (1745–1833)—© National Portrait Gallery, London

More, Henry (1614–1687)—© National Portrait Gallery, London

More, Jacob (1740–1793)—Galleria degli Uffizi, Florence, Italy / Bridgeman Art Library

More, Sir John (c.1451–1530)—The Royal Collection © 2004 HM Queen Elizabeth II

More, Kenneth Gilbert (1914–1982)—© reserved; collection National Portrait Gallery, London

More, Sir Thomas (1478–1535)—© The Frick Collection, New York

Morecambe, Eric (1926–1984)—Arnold Newman / Getty Images; collection National Portrait Gallery, London

Morell, Thomas (1703–1784)—© National Portrait Gallery, London

Mores, Edward Rowe (1730–1778)—© National Portrait Gallery, London

Moresby, John (1830–1922)—© National Portrait Gallery, London

Morfill, William Richard (1834–1909)—© Estate of Sir William Rothenstein / National Portrait Gallery, London

Morgan, Augustus De (1806–1871)—© National Portrait Gallery, London

Morgan, Charles Langbridge (1894–1958)—© courtesy the Artist's Estate / Bridgeman Art Library; collection National Portrait Gallery, London

Morgan, Daniel (1735?–1802)—Independence National Historical Park

Morgan, Sir George Osborne, first baronet (1826–1897)—© National Portrait Gallery, London

Morgan, Sir Henry (c.1635–1688)—© National Portrait Gallery, London

Morgan, Sydney, Lady Morgan (bap. 1783, d. 1859)—National Gallery of Ireland

Morgan, William (1750–1833)—© National Portrait Gallery, London

Morgan, William Frend De (1839–1917)—© National Portrait Gallery, London

Morier, James Justinian (1782–1849)—© National Portrait Gallery, London

Morier, Sir Robert Burnet David (1826–1893)—© National Portrait Gallery, London

Morin, Nea Everilda (1905–1986)—Alpine Club Photo Library, London

Morison, Sir Alexander (1779–1866)—Scottish National Portrait Gallery

Morison, James (1770–1840)—© National Portrait Gallery, London

Morison, Robert (1620–1683)—© National Portrait Gallery, London

Morison, Stanley Arthur (1889–1967)—by permission of the Syndics of Cambridge University Library

Morland, George (1763–1804)—© National Portrait Gallery, London

Morland, Sir Samuel, first baronet (1625–1695)—Ashmolean Museum, Oxford

Morley, Eric Douglas (1918–2000)—© News International Newspapers Ltd

Morley, George (1598?–1684)—Christ Church, Oxford

Morley, Henry (1822–1894)—© National Portrait Gallery, London

Morley, John (1656–1732)—© National Portrait Gallery, London

Morley, John, Viscount Morley of Blackburn (1838–1923)—The British Library

Morley, Robert Adolph Wilton (1908–1992)—Rank (courtesy Kobal)

Morley, Samuel (1809–1886)—© National Portrait Gallery, London

Morrell, Lady Ottoline Violet Anne (1873–1938)—© courtesy the Artist's Estate / Bridgeman Art Library; collection National Portrait Gallery, London

Morris, Edward Patrick, first Baron Morris (1859–1935)—Scottish National Portrait Gallery

Morris, Gouverneur (1752–1816)—courtesy of the Historical Society of Pennsylvania Collection, Atwater Kent Museum of Philadelphia

Morris, Henry (1889–1961)—Archives Dept., University Library UEA, Norwich

Morris [Burden], Jane (1839–1914)—St Bride Printing Library

Morris, John Humphrey Carlile (1910–1984)—The President and Fellows of Magdalen College Oxford

Morris, Lewis (1671–1746)—Brooklyn Museum of Art, Dick S. Ramsay Fund and John Hill Morgan, 43.196

Morris, Lewis (1701–1765)—© National Museums and Galleries of Wales

Morris, Sir Lewis (1833–1907)—© National Portrait Gallery, London

Morris, Margaret Eleanor (1891–1980)—© Estate of Frederick William Daniels; collection National Portrait Gallery, London

Morris, Mary [May] (1862–1938)—© National Portrait Gallery, London

Morris, Michael, first Baron Killanin (1827–1901)—© National Portrait Gallery, London

Morris, Mowbray (1819–1874)—© reserved; News International Syndication; photograph National Portrait Gallery, London

Morris, Sir Philip Robert (1901–1979)—© National Portrait Gallery, London

Morris, Robert (1735–1806)—New Orleans Museum of Art: Museum Purchase, the General Acquisition Fund

Morris, Thomas [Old Tom Morris] (1821–1908)—reproduced by kind permission of the Royal and Ancient Golf Club of St Andrews

Morris, William (1834–1896)—© National Portrait Gallery, London

Morris, William Richard, Viscount Nuffield (1877–1963)—© National Portrait Gallery, London

Morrison, Arthur George (1863–1945)—© National Portrait Gallery, London

Morrison, Herbert Stanley, Baron Morrison of Lambeth (1888–1965)—© National Portrait Gallery, London

Morrison, John Sinclair (1913–2000)—© National Portrait Gallery, London

Morrison, Robert (1782–1834)—© National Portrait Gallery, London

Mort, Thomas Sutcliffe (1816–1878)—Government Printing Office collection, State Library of New South Wales

Mortensen, Stanley Harding (1921–1991)—Getty Images – Michael Lawn

Mortimer, Harry (1902–1992)—© News International Newspapers Ltd

Mortimer, John Hamilton (1740–1779)—Towner Art Gallery, Eastbourne

Mortimer, Penelope Ruth (1918–1999)—© David Bennett; collection National Portrait Gallery, London

Mortimer, (Charles) Raymond Bell (1895–1980)—© Cecil Beaton Archive, Sotheby's; collection National Portrait Gallery, London

Morton, Charles (1819–1904)—© National Portrait Gallery, London

Morton, Sir Desmond John Falkiner (1891–1971)—© National Portrait Gallery, London

Morton, (Henry) Digby (1906/7–1983)—© reserved; collection National Portrait Gallery, London

Morton, John (d. 1500)—by kind permission of the Dean and Chapter of Canterbury; photographer: Mrs Mary Tucker

Morton, John Cameron Andrieu Bingham Michael [Beachcomber] (1893–1979)—© National Portrait Gallery, London

Morton, Thomas (bap. 1564, d. 1659)—by permission of the Master and Fellows of St John's College, Cambridge

Moscheles, Ignaz (1794–1870)—© National Portrait Gallery, London

Moshoeshoe (c.1786–1870)—© reserved / Oxford University Press

Mosley, Sir Oswald Ernald, sixth baronet (1896–1980)—Getty Images – William Davis

Mosse, Bartholomew (1712–1759)—Rotunda Hospital, Dublin; photograph National Portrait Gallery, London

Motley (act. 1921–c.1975)—© National Portrait Gallery, London

Mott, Sir Basil, first baronet (1859–1938)—courtesy of the Institution of Civil Engineers Archives

Mott, Sir Nevill Francis (1905–1996)—© John Benton-Harris

Motteux, Peter Anthony (1663–1718)—© Copyright The British Museum

Moule, Henry (1801–1880)—courtesy of the Dorset County Museum

Moulton, William Fiddian (1835–1898)—© National Portrait Gallery, London

Moultrie, John (1799–1874)—courtesy of the Collection in Rugby Library

Mountain [Montaigne], George (1569–1628)—© National Portrait Gallery, London

Mountain, Jacob (1749–1825)—Downman / National Archives of Canada / C-100660

Mountbatten, Dame Edwina Cynthia Annette, Countess Mountbatten of Burma (1901–1960)—© Yevonde Portrait Archive; collection National Portrait Gallery, London

Mountbatten, Louis Francis Albert Victor Nicholas, first Earl Mountbatten of Burma (1900–1979)—© Karsh / Camera Press; collection National Portrait Gallery, London

Mountbatten, Victoria Alberta Elisabeth Mathilde Marie, marchioness of Milford Haven (1863–1950)—© National Portrait Gallery, London

Mountney, Richard (1707–1768)—Christie's Images Ltd. (2004)

Mowbray, Sir John Robert, first baronet (1815–1899)—© National Portrait Gallery, London

Mowbray, Thomas (I), first duke of Norfolk (1366–1399)—The British Library

Moxon, Joseph (1627–1691)—© National Portrait Gallery, London

Moyle, Walter (1672–1721)—© National Portrait Gallery, London

Moynihan, Berkeley George Andrew, first Baron Moynihan (1865–1936)—Wellcome Library, London

Mozley, Thomas (1806–1893)—private collection

Mudge, Thomas (1715/16–1794)—Science Museum / Science & Society Picture Library

Mudge, Zachariah (1694–1769)—© National Portrait Gallery, London

Mueller, Dame Anne Elisabeth (1930–2000)—by Daphne Todd O.B.E., P.P.R.P., N.E.A.C. / Collection: De Montfort University